CineBooks
MOVIE
List

CineBooks
Evanston, IL 1989

Editorial and Sales Offices
CINEBOOKS
990 Grove Street
Evanston, IL 60201

Copyright © 1989, CINEBOOKS

ISBN: 0-933997-26-4

CINEBOOKS
A division of News America Publishing Incorporated

Printed in the United States

INTRODUCTION

The CINEBOOKS MOVIE LIST offers essential information on all the sound films included in the first nine volumes of THE MOTION PICTURE GUIDE (TM) (an encyclopedia covering films from the silent era to 1984) and its Annuals (covering the years 1985-1988). As such, it is a quick reference guide to more than 28,000 films, virtually all of the sound theatrical movies ever released in the US (documentaries, X-rated, and made-for-tv films are not included).

The MOVIE LIST is divided into five sections, the first offering an alphabetical listing of the films, with year of US release, Star Rating, and Parental Recommendation. At the bottom of each right-hand page are explanations of the ratings and directions for locating the film reviews in CineBooks' volumes. Cross references are included in the list for films known by more than one title.

The MOVIE LIST also includes listings of the films by Star Rating, Parental Recommendation, and Genre, along with a listing of CineBooks' selections of the best films from each of the genres.

Throughout this guide, films available on videocassette are displayed in **BOLD**. Since video availability changes on almost a daily basis, this represents only what was available at the time the lists were compiled.

As publisher of THE MOTION PICTURE GUIDE, CineBooks is dedicated to providing the most comprehensive motion picture information to libraries, educational institutions, video retailers, film professionals and buffs, and movie fans.

TABLE OF CONTENTS

CINEBOOKS MASTERLIST

The following is an alphabetical listing of all films included in THE MOTION PICTURE GUIDE and its Annuals, covering more than 28,000 US theatrical releases from 1927 to 1988.

Each entry includes the title, year of US release, Star Ratings, and Parental Recommendations for the films. An explanation of the ratings, and directions for locating the film reviews in CineBooks' volumes, is displayed at the bottom of each right-hand page. Cross references are included for films known by more than one title.

Bold indicates films available on videocassette.

A NOS AMOURS **½ (1984, Fr.) PR:O
A NOUS LA LIBERTE ***** (1931, Fr.) PR:A
AARON LOVES ANGELA ** (1975) PR:O
AARON SLICK FROM PUNKIN CRICK **
(1952) PR:AA
ABANDON SHIP *** (1957, Brit.) PR:C-O
ABANDONED *** (1949) PR:C
ABBOTT AND COSTELLO GO TO MARS *
(1953) PR:A
ABBOTT AND COSTELLO IN HOLLYWOOD *
(1945) PR:AA**
ABBOTT AND COSTELLO IN THE FOREIGN LEGION
** (1950) PR:A
ABBOTT AND COSTELLO IN THE NAVY
(SEE:IN THE NAVY)
ABBOTT AND COSTELLO LOST IN ALASKA
(SEE:LOST IN ALASKA)
**ABBOTT AND COSTELLO MEET CAPTAIN KIDD **
(1952) PR:A**
**ABBOTT AND COSTELLO MEET DR. JEKYLL AND
MR. HYDE *½ (1954) PR:A**
**ABBOTT AND COSTELLO MEET FRANKENSTEIN
**** (1948) PR:A**
ABBOTT AND COSTELLO MEET THE INVISIBLE
MAN **½ (1951) PR:A
ABBOTT AND COSTELLO MEET THE KEYSTONE
KOPS ** (1955) PR:A
**ABBOTT AND COSTELLO MEET THE KILLER,
BORIS KARLOFF ** (1949) PR:A**
ABBOTT AND COSTELLO MEET THE MUMMY **
(1955) PR:A
ABBY ** (1974) PR:O
ABDICATION, THE ** (1974, Brit.) PR:C-O
ABDUCTION * (1975) PR:O
ABDUCTORS, THE ** (1957) PR:A
ABDUL THE DAMNED * (1935, Brit.) PR:C
ABDULLAH'S HAREM *½ (1956, Brit./Egypt.) PR:O
ABE LINCOLN IN ILLINOIS * (1940) PR:AA**
ABIE'S IRISH ROSE ** (1928) PR:A
ABIE'S IRISH ROSE * (1946) PR:C
ABILENE TOWN * (1946) PR:A**
ABILENE TRAIL ** (1951) PR:A
ABOMINABLE DR. PHIBES, THE *
(1971, Brit.) PR:O
ABOMINABLE SNOWMAN OF THE HIMALAYAS,
THE ** (1957, Brit.) PR:A
ABOUT FACE ** (1952) PR:A
ABOUT LAST NIGHT ** (1986) PR:O
ABOUT MRS. LESLIE ** (1954) PR:A
ABOVE AND BEYOND *** (1953) PR:A
ABOVE SUSPICION *** (1943) PR:A
ABOVE THE CLOUDS ** (1934) PR:A
ABOVE THE LAW **½ (1988) PR:O
ABOVE US THE WAVES *** (1956, Brit.) PR:A
ABRAHAM LINCOLN ***½ (1930) PR:A
ABROAD WITH TWO YANKS ** (1944) PR:A
ABSENCE OF MALICE **½ (1981) PR:O
ABSENT-MINDED PROFESSOR, THE *
(1961) PR:AA**
ABSOLUTE BEGINNERS *** (1986, Brit.) PR:C**
ABSOLUTE QUIET *** (1936) PR:C
ABSOLUTION * (1981, Brit.) PR:O
ABUSED CONFIDENCE **½ (1938, Fr.) PR:C-O
ACAPULCO GOLD zero (1978) PR:O

ACCATTONE! ** (1961, It.) PR:O
ACCENT ON LOVE *½ (1941) PR:A
ACCENT ON YOUTH **½ (1935) PR:A
ACCEPTABLE LEVELS **½ (1983, Brit.) PR:C
ACCIDENT ** (1967, Brit.) PR:O
ACCIDENTAL DEATH ** (1963, Brit.) PR:C
ACCIDENTAL TOURIST, THE * (1988) PR:C-O**
ACCIDENTS WILL HAPPEN ** (1938) PR:A
ACCOMPLICE *½ (1946) PR:A
ACCORDING TO MRS. HOYLE *½ (1951) PR:A
ACCOUNT RENDERED ** (1957, Brit.) PR:A
ACCURSED, THE ** (1958, Brit.) PR:A
ACCUSED, THE **½ (1988) PR:O
ACCUSED **½ (1936, Brit.) PR:A
ACCUSED, THE *** (1949) PR:C
ACCUSED
(SEE:MARK OF THE HAWK)
ACCUSED OF MURDER **½ (1956) PR:A
ACCUSED—STAND UP ** (1930, Fr.) PR:A
ACCUSING FINGER, THE **½ (1936) PR:A
ACE, THE
(SEE:GREAT SANTINI, THE)
ACE ELI AND RODGER OF THE SKIES **
(1973) PR:A
ACE HIGH ** (1969, It.) PR:O
ACE IN THE HOLE
(SEE:BIG CARNIVAL, THE)
ACE OF ACES *** (1933) PR:C
ACE OF ACES ** (1982, Fr./Ger.) PR:O
ACE OF SPADES, THE ** (1935, Brit.) PR:A
ACES AND EIGHTS ** (1936) PR:A
ACES HIGH *** (1977, Brit.) PR:C
ACES WILD * (1937) PR:A
ACQUA E SAPONE ** (1985, It.) PR:C
ACQUITTED * (1929) PR:C
ACROSS 110TH STREET ** (1972) PR:O
ACROSS THE BADLANDS ** (1950) PR:A
ACROSS THE BRIDGE *** (1957, Brit.) PR:C
ACROSS THE GREAT DIVIDE * (1976) PR:AA**
ACROSS THE PACIFIC ***½ (1942) PR:A
ACROSS THE PLAINS *½ (1939) PR:A
ACROSS THE RIO GRANDE ** (1949) PR:A
ACROSS THE RIVER * (1965) PR:C
ACROSS THE SIERRAS ** (1941) PR:A
ACROSS THE WIDE MISSOURI *** (1951) PR:A
ACT, THE ** (1984) PR:O
ACT OF LOVE **½ (1953) PR:C
ACT OF MURDER, AN ***½ (1948) PR:C
ACT OF MURDER ** (1965, Brit.) PR:C
ACT OF THE HEART * (1970, Can.) PR:C
ACT OF VENGEANCE * (1974) PR:O
ACT OF VIOLENCE *** (1949) PR:C
ACT ONE **½ (1964) PR:A
ACTION FOR SLANDER **½ (1937, Brit.) PR:A
ACTION IN ARABIA ** (1944) PR:A
ACTION IN THE NORTH ATLANTIC ****
(1943) PR:A
ACTION JACKSON *½ (1988) PR:O
ACTION OF THE TIGER ** (1957) PR:A
ACTION STATIONS * (1959, Brit.) PR:A-C
ACTORS AND SIN *** (1952) PR:C
ACTOR'S REVENGE, AN *½ (1963, Jap.) PR:O
ACTRESS, THE **½ (1953) PR:A
ADA * (1961) PR:C
ADALEN 31 *** (1969, Swed.) PR:C
ADAM AND EVE zero (1958, Mex.) PR:O
ADAM AND EVELYNE ** (1950, Brit.) PR:A
ADAM AT 6 A.M. * (1970) PR:O
ADAM HAD FOUR SONS * (1941) PR:A**
ADAM'S RIB ***½ (1949) PR:A

ADAM'S WOMAN **½ (1972, Aus.) PR:C
ADDING MACHINE, THE *** (1969) PR:C
ADDRESS UNKNOWN ** (1944) PR:A
ADELE HASN'T HAD HER SUPPER YET zero
(1978, Czech.) PR:C
ADERYN PAPUR **½ (1984, Brit.) PR:A-C
ADIEU PHILLIPINE * (1962, Fr./It.) PR:C
ADIOS AMIGO ** (1975) PR:C
ADIOS GRINGO *½ (1967, It./Fr./Sp.) PR:A
ADIOS SABATA * (1971, It./Sp.) PR:A
ADMIRABLE CRICHTON, THE **½
(1957, Brit.) PR:A
ADMIRAL NAKHIMOV ** (1948, USSR) PR:C
ADMIRAL WAS A LADY, THE ** (1950) PR:A
ADMIRALS ALL ** (1935, Brit.) PR:A
ADMIRAL'S SECRET, THE * (1934, Brit.) PR:A
ADOLESCENT, THE ** (1978, Fr./W.Ger.) PR:C
ADOLESCENTS, THE ** (1967, Can.) PR:C
ADOLF HITLER—MY PART IN HIS DOWNFALL *
(1973, Brit.) PR:A
ADOPTION, THE * (1978, Fr.) PR:O
ADORABLE **½ (1933) PR:A
ADORABLE CREATURES *½ (1956, Fr.) PR:O
ADORABLE JULIA ** (1964, Fr./Aust.) PR:C
ADORABLE LIAR *½ (1962, Fr.) PR:C
ADRIFT *½ (1971, Czech.) PR:O
ADUEFUE ** (1988, Fr./Ivory Coast) PR:C
ADULT EDUCATION
(SEE:HIDING OUT)
ADULTERESS, THE ** (1959, Fr.) PR:O
ADULTEROUS AFFAIR zero (1966) PR:A
ADVANCE TO THE REAR **½ (1964) PR:A
ADVENTURE *** (1945) PR:A
ADVENTURE FOR TWO * (1945, Brit.) PR:A**
ADVENTURE IN BALTIMORE **½ (1949) PR:AA
ADVENTURE IN BLACKMAIL ** (1943, Brit.) PR:A
ADVENTURE IN DIAMONDS **½ (1940) PR:A
ADVENTURE IN MANHATTAN ** (1936) PR:A
ADVENTURE IN ODESSA ** (1954, USSR) PR:C
ADVENTURE IN SAHARA ** (1938) PR:A
ADVENTURE IN THE HOPFIELDS **½
(1954, Brit.) PR:AA
ADVENTURE IN WASHINGTON ** (1941) PR:C
ADVENTURE ISLAND *½ (1947) PR:A
ADVENTURE LIMITED * (1934, Brit.) PR:A
ADVENTURE OF SALVATOR ROSA, AN **½
(1940, It.) PR:A
**ADVENTURE OF SHERLOCK HOLMES' SMARTER
BROTHER, THE **** (1975, Brit.) PR:AA**
ADVENTURERS, THE **½ (1951, Brit.) PR:C
ADVENTURERS, THE zero (1970) PR:O
ADVENTURES AT RUGBY
(SEE:TOM BROWN'S SCHOOL DAYS)
ADVENTURE'S END *½ (1937) PR:A
ADVENTURES IN BABYSITTING **½ (1987) PR:C
ADVENTURES IN IRAQ *½ (1943) PR:A
ADVENTURES IN SILVERADO ** (1948) PR:A
ADVENTURES OF A ROOKIE ** (1943) PR:A
ADVENTURES OF A YOUNG MAN *** (1962) PR:A
ADVENTURES OF ARSENE LUPIN **½
(1956, Fr./It.) PR:A
ADVENTURES OF BARRY McKENZIE *
(1972, Aus.) PR:C-O
**ADVENTURES OF BUCKAROO BANZAI: ACROSS
THE 8TH DIMENSION, THE *** (1984) PR:C-O**
ADVENTURES OF BULLWHIP GRIFFIN, THE *
(1967) PR:AA**
**ADVENTURES OF CAPTAIN FABIAN **
(1951) PR:A**
ADVENTURES OF CASANOVA ** (1948) PR:A

Finding entries in **THE MOTION PICTURE GUIDE** ™		**STAR RATINGS**	**PARENTAL RECOMMENDATION (PR:)**
Years 1929-83	Volumes I-IX	★★★★★ Masterpiece	AA　Good for Children
1984	Volume IX	★★★★ Excellent	A　Acceptable for Children
1985	1986 ANNUAL	★★★ Good	C　Cautionary, some objectionable scenes
1986	1987 ANNUAL	★★ Fair	O　Objectionable for Children
1987	1988 ANNUAL	★ Poor	
1988	1989 ANNUAL	zero Without Merit	**BOLD:** Films on Videocassette

ADVENTURES OF DON COYOTE ** (1947) PR:A
ADVENTURES OF DON JUAN ** (1949) PR:A**
ADVENTURES OF FRONTIER FREMONT, THE * (1976) PR:AA**
ADVENTURES OF GALLANT BESS **½ (1948) PR:AA
ADVENTURES OF GERARD, THE ** (1970, Brit.) PR:A
ADVENTURES OF HAJJI BABA ** (1954) PR:C
ADVENTURES OF HAL 5, THE * (1958, Brit.) PR:A
ADVENTURES OF HERCULES (SEE:HERCULES II)
ADVENTURES OF HUCKLEBERRY FINN (SEE:HUCKLEBERRY FINN)
ADVENTURES OF HUCKLEBERRY FINN, THE **½ (1960) PR:AA
ADVENTURES OF ICHABOD AND MR. TOAD ** (1949) PR:AA**
ADVENTURES OF JACK LONDON (SEE:JACK LONDON)
ADVENTURES OF JANE, THE *½ (1949, Brit.) PR:A
ADVENTURES OF JANE ARDEN ** (1939) PR:A
ADVENTURES OF KITTY O'DAY **½ (1944) PR:A
ADVENTURES OF MARCO POLO, THE *** (1938) PR:A
ADVENTURES OF MARK TWAIN, THE * (1985) PR:AA**
ADVENTURES OF MARK TWAIN, THE **** (1944) PR:AA
ADVENTURES OF MARTIN EDEN, THE ***½ (1942) PR:A
ADVENTURES OF MICHAEL STROGOFF (SEE:SOLDIER AND THE LADY)
ADVENTURES OF PC 49, THE ** (1949, Brit.) PR:A
ADVENTURES OF PICASSO, THE * (1980, Swed.) PR:O
ADVENTURES OF QUENTIN DURWARD, THE (SEE:QUENTIN DURWARD)
ADVENTURES OF RABBI JACOB, THE ** (1973, Fr.) PR:C
ADVENTURES OF ROBIN HOOD, THE *** (1938) PR:AA**
ADVENTURES OF ROBINSON CRUSOE, THE ***½ (1954) PR:AA
ADVENTURES OF RUSTY ** (1945) PR:A
ADVENTURES OF SADIE, THE ** (1955, Brit.) PR:A
ADVENTURES OF SCARAMOUCHE, THE ** (1964, Fr.) PR:C
ADVENTURES OF SHERLOCK HOLMES, THE ** (1939) PR:A**
ADVENTURES OF TARTU, THE * (1943, Brit.) PR:A**
ADVENTURES OF THE AMERICAN RABBIT, THE ** (1986) PR:AA
ADVENTURES OF THE WILDERNESS FAMILY, THE * (1975) PR:AA**
ADVENTURES OF TOM SAWYER, THE ***½ (1938) PR:AA
ADVENTURESS, THE **** (1946, Brit.) PR:A
ADVENTUROUS BLONDE **½ (1937) PR:A
ADVERSARY, THE **½ (1973, India) PR:A
ADVICE TO THE LOVELORN * (1933) PR:A**
ADVISE AND CONSENT ** (1962) PR:C**
AERIAL GUNNER **½ (1943) PR:A
AFFAIR AT AKITSU ** (1980, Jap.) PR:O
AFFAIR BLUM, THE ** (1949, Ger.) PR:C
AFFAIR IN HAVANA * (1957) PR:O
AFFAIR IN MONTE CARLO ** (1953, Brit.) PR:A
AFFAIR IN RENO ** (1957) PR:A
AFFAIR IN TRINIDAD ** (1952) PR:C
AFFAIR LAFONT, THE **½ (1939, Fr.) PR:O
AFFAIR OF SUSAN * (1935) PR:A
AFFAIR OF THE SKIN, AN * (1964) PR:O
AFFAIR TO REMEMBER, AN *** (1957) PR:A
AFFAIR WITH A STRANGER ** (1953) PR:A
AFFAIRS IN VERSAILLES (SEE:ROYAL AFFAIRS IN VERSAILLES)
AFFAIRS OF A GENTLEMAN ** (1934) PR:A
AFFAIRS OF A MODEL ** (1952, Swed.) PR:O
AFFAIRS OF A ROGUE, THE ** (1949, Brit.) PR:A
AFFAIRS OF ADELAIDE ** (1949, US/Brit.) PR:C
AFFAIRS OF ANNABEL * (1938) PR:A**
AFFAIRS OF CAPPY RICKS * (1937) PR:A
AFFAIRS OF CELLINI, THE *** (1934) PR:C
AFFAIRS OF DOBIE GILLIS, THE ** (1953) PR:A
AFFAIRS OF DR. HOLL ** (1954, Ger.) PR:A
AFFAIRS OF GERALDINE ** (1946) PR:A
AFFAIRS OF JIMMY VALENTINE (SEE:UNFORGOTTEN CRIME)
AFFAIRS OF JULIE, THE * (1958, Ger.) PR:C
AFFAIRS OF MARTHA, THE **½ (1942) PR:A
AFFAIRS OF MAUPASSANT *** (1938, Aust.) PR:A
AFFAIRS OF MESSALINA, THE zero (1954, It.) PR:O
AFFAIRS OF SUSAN *** (1945) PR:A
AFFECTIONATELY YOURS **½ (1941) PR:A
AFRAID TO TALK ** (1932) PR:C
AFRICA SCREAMS * (1949) PR:AA**
AFRICA—TEXAS STYLE! * (1967, US/Brit.) PR:AA**
AFRICAN FURY (SEE:CRY THE BELOVED COUNTRY)
AFRICAN MANHUNT zero (1955) PR:A
AFRICAN QUEEN, THE *** (1951, US/Brit.) PR:AA**
AFRICAN TREASURE * (1952) PR:A
AFRICAN, THE ** (1983, Fr.) PR:C
AFTER HOURS ** (1985) PR:O**
AFTER MIDNIGHT WITH BOSTON BLACKIE ** (1943) PR:A
AFTER OFFICE HOURS *½ (1932, Brit.) PR:A
AFTER OFFICE HOURS ** (1935) PR:A
AFTER THE BALL ** (1932, Brit.) PR:C
AFTER THE BALL **½ (1957, Brit.) PR:A
AFTER THE DANCE ** (1935) PR:A
AFTER THE FALL OF NEW YORK * (1984, It./Fr.) PR:O
AFTER THE FOG * (1930) PR:C
AFTER THE FOX * (1966, US/Brit./It.) PR:A**
AFTER THE REHEARSAL ** (1984, Swed.) PR:C-O
AFTER THE THIN MAN ***½ (1936) PR:A
AFTER TOMORROW ** (1932) PR:A
AFTER TONIGHT *½ (1933) PR:A
AFTER YOU, COMRADE ** (1967, South Africa) PR:A
AGAINST A CROOKED SKY ** (1975) PR:C
AGAINST ALL FLAGS **½ (1952) PR:A
AGAINST ALL ODDS * (1984) PR:C-O
AGAINST THE LAW ** (1934) PR:C
AGAINST THE TIDE * (1937, Brit.) PR:A
AGAINST THE WIND **½ (1948, Brit.) PR:A
AGATHA * (1979, Brit.) PR:C
AGATHA CHRISTIE'S ENDLESS NIGHT (SEE:ENDLESS NIGHT)
AGE FOR LOVE, THE * (1931) PR:A
AGE OF CONSENT ** (1932) PR:C
AGE OF CONSENT ** (1969, Aus.) PR:O
AGE OF ILLUSIONS ** (1967, Hung.) PR:O
AGE OF INDISCRETION ** (1935) PR:C
AGE OF INFIDELITY ** (1958, Sp.) PR:O
AGE OF INNOCENCE ** (1934) PR:C
AGE OF INNOCENCE *½ (1977, Can.) PR:A
AGE OF THE MEDICI, THE * (1979, It.) PR:C
AGENCY * (1981, Can.) PR:O
AGENT 8 3/4 ** (1963, Brit.) PR:C
AGENT FOR H.A.R.M. ** (1966) PR:C
AGENT ON ICE * (1986) PR:O
AGGIE APPLEBY, MAKER OF MEN * (1933) PR:A
AGITATOR, THE * (1949) PR:A
AGNES OF GOD * (1985) PR:C**
AGONY AND THE ECSTASY, THE * (1965) PR:A**
AGOSTINO ** (1962, It.) PR:C
AGUIRRE, THE WRATH OF GOD * (1977, Ger.) PR:O**
AH, WILDERNESS! **** (1935) PR:AA
AH YING *** (1984, Hong Kong) PR:A
A-HAUNTING WE WILL GO **½ (1942) PR:AA
AIDA ** (1954, It.) PR:A
AIMEZ-VOUS BRAHMS (SEE:GOODBYE, AGAIN)
AIN'T MISBEHAVIN' **½ (1955) PR:A
AIR CADET ** (1951) PR:A
AIR CIRCUS, THE ** (1928) PR:A
AIR DEVILS * (1938) PR:A
AIR EAGLES * (1932) PR:C
AIR FORCE ** (1943) PR:A**
AIR HAWKS **½ (1935) PR:A
AIR HOSTESS * (1933) PR:A
AIR HOSTESS ** (1949) PR:A
AIR MAIL *** (1932) PR:A
AIR PATROL * (1962) PR:C
AIR POLICE * (1931) PR:A
AIR RAID WARDENS **½ (1943) PR:AA
AIR STRIKE * (1955) PR:A
AIRBORNE ** (1962) PR:A
AIRPLANE! **½ (1980) PR:C
AIRPLANE II: THE SEQUEL ** (1982) PR:C
AIRPORT ** (1970) PR:A
AIRPORT 1975 ** (1974) PR:C
AIRPORT '77 ** (1977) PR:C
AIRPORT '79 (SEE:CONCORDE, THE—AIRPORT '79)
AKE AND HIS WORLD **½ (1985, Swed.) PR:O
AL CAPONE ** (1959) PR:C-O**
AL JENNINGS OF OKLAHOMA ** (1951) PR:A
ALADDIN zero (1987, It.) PR:A
ALADDIN AND HIS LAMP ** (1952) PR:AA
ALAKAZAM THE GREAT! **½ (1961, Jap.) PR:AA
ALAMBRISTA! *** (1977) PR:C
ALAMO, THE ** (1960) PR:AA**
ALAMO BAY ***½ (1985) PR:O
ALASKA * (1944) PR:A
ALASKA HIGHWAY * (1943) PR:A
ALASKA PASSAGE * (1959) PR:A
ALASKA PATROL ** (1949) PR:A
ALASKA SEAS *½ (1954) PR:A
ALBERT, R.N. ** (1953, Brit.) PR:A
ALBUQUERQUE ** (1948) PR:A
ALCATRAZ ISLAND *½ (1937) PR:A
ALERT IN THE SOUTH ** (1954, Fr.) PR:A
ALEX AND THE GYPSY *½ (1976) PR:C
ALEX IN WONDERLAND ** (1970) PR:C
ALEXANDER GRAHAM BELL (SEE:STORY OF ALEXANDER GRAHAM BELL, THE)
ALEXANDER HAMILTON **½ (1931) PR:A
ALEXANDER NEVSKY ** (1939) PR:C**
ALEXANDER THE GREAT * (1956) PR:A**
ALEXANDER'S RAGTIME BAND ***½ (1938) PR:AA
ALF 'N' FAMILY **½ (1968, Brit.) PR:C
ALFIE * (1966, Brit.) PR:O**
ALFIE DARLING * (1975, Brit.) PR:O
ALFRED THE GREAT ** (1969, Brit.) PR:C
ALFREDO, ALFREDO * (1973, It.) PR:O
ALF'S BABY * (1953, Brit.) PR:A
ALF'S BUTTON *½ (1930, Brit.) PR:AA
ALF'S BUTTON AFLOAT *½ (1938, Brit.) PR:A
ALF'S CARPET * (1929, Brit.) PR:A
ALGIERS *** (1938) PR:C**
ALI BABA * (1954, Fr.) PR:A
ALI BABA AND THE FORTY THIEVES ***½ (1944) PR:AA
ALI BABA GOES TO TOWN **½ (1937) PR:AA
ALIAS A GENTLEMAN ** (1948) PR:A
ALIAS BIG SHOT **½ (1962, Arg.) PR:C
ALIAS BILLY THE KID *½ (1946) PR:AA
ALIAS BOSTON BLACKIE ** (1942) PR:A
ALIAS BULLDOG DRUMMOND ** (1935, Brit.) PR:A
ALIAS FRENCH GERTIE *½ (1930) PR:A
ALIAS JESSE JAMES **½ (1959) PR:A
ALIAS JIMMY VALENTINE *½ (1928) PR:A
ALIAS JOHN LAW * (1935) PR:A
ALIAS JOHN PRESTON *½ (1956) PR:A
ALIAS MARY DOW ** (1935) PR:A
ALIAS MARY SMITH * (1932) PR:A
ALIAS NICK BEAL *** (1949) PR:A
ALIAS THE BAD MAN *½ (1931) PR:A
ALIAS THE CHAMP * (1949) PR:A
ALIAS THE DEACON ** (1940) PR:A
ALIAS THE DOCTOR *½ (1932) PR:A
ALIBI ** (1929) PR:C
ALIBI * (1931, Brit.) PR:A
ALIBI, THE ** (1939, Fr.) PR:C
ALIBI, THE **½ (1943, Brit.) PR:C
ALIBI FOR MURDER * (1936) PR:A
ALIBI IKE ** (1935) PR:AA
ALIBI INN * (1935, Brit.) PR:A
ALICE ***½ (1988, Switz./Brit./W. Ger.) PR:O
ALICE ADAMS * (1935) PR:A**
ALICE DOESN'T LIVE HERE ANYMORE **½ (1975) PR:O
ALICE IN THE CITIES * (1974, W./Ger.) PR:A**
ALICE IN WONDERLAND * (1933) PR:AA**
ALICE IN WONDERLAND * (1951) PR:AA**
ALICE IN WONDERLAND **½ (1951, Fr.) PR:A
ALICE, OR THE LAST ESCAPADE **½ (1977, Fr.) PR:C
ALICE, SWEET ALICE ** (1978) PR:O
ALICE'S ADVENTURES IN WONDERLAND * (1972, Brit.) PR:A
ALICE'S RESTAURANT ** (1969) PR:O
ALIEN * (1979) PR:O**
ALIEN CONTAMINATION zero (1982, It.) PR:O
ALIEN FACTOR, THE ** (1984) PR:C
ALIEN NATION ** (1988) PR:O
ALIEN PREDATOR * (1987) PR:O
ALIEN THUNDER ** (1975, US/Can.) PR:C
ALIENS ** (1986) PR:O**
ALIMONY * (1949) PR:C
ALIMONY MADNESS zero (1933) PR:C
ALIVE AND KICKING *** (1962, Brit.) PR:AA
ALIVE ON SATURDAY *½ (1957, Brit.) PR:A
ALL ABOUT EVE *** (1950) PR:A**
ALL-AMERICAN, THE ** (1932) PR:A
ALL-AMERICAN, THE ** (1953) PR:A
ALL-AMERICAN BOY, THE * (1973) PR:O
ALL-AMERICAN CHUMP * (1936) PR:A
ALL-AMERICAN CO-ED *½ (1941) PR:A
ALL-AMERICAN SWEETHEART * (1937) PR:A
ALL-AROUND REDUCED PERSONALITY—OUTTAKES, THE ** (1978, Ger.) PR:A
ALL ASHORE ** (1953) PR:AA
ALL AT SEA *½ (1935, Brit.) PR:A
ALL AT SEA *½ (1939, Brit.) PR:A
ALL AT SEA *** (1958, Brit.) PR:A
ALL AT SEA *½ (1970, Brit.) PR:A
ALL BY MYSELF ** (1943) PR:A
ALL CREATURES GREAT AND SMALL * (1975, Brit.) PR:AA**
ALL FALL DOWN **½ (1962) PR:C
ALL FOR MARY ** (1956, Brit.) PR:A
ALL HANDS ON DECK * (1961) PR:A

ALL I DESIRE **½ (1953) PR:A
ALL IN ** (1936, Brit.) PR:A
ALL IN A NIGHT'S WORK **½ (1961) PR:C
ALL MEN ARE ENEMIES * (1934) PR:A
ALL MINE TO GIVE ** (1957) PR:AA
ALL MY SONS **** (1948) PR:C
ALL NEAT IN BLACK STOCKINGS **
    (1969, Brit.) PR:C
ALL NIGHT LONG ** (1961, Brit.) PR:C
ALL NIGHT LONG **½ (1981) PR:C
ALL NUDITY SHALL BE PUNISHED **
    (1974, Braz.) PR:O
ALL OF ME **½ (1934) PR:C
ALL OF ME * (1984) PR:A-C**
ALL OVER THE TOWN ** (1949, Brit.) PR:AA
ALL OVER TOWN * (1937) PR:A
ALL QUIET ON THE WESTERN FRONT ***
    (1930) PR:C**
ALL RIGHT, MY FRIEND *½ (1983, Jap.) PR:A
ALL SCREWED UP ** (1976, It.) PR:O
ALL THAT GLITTERS *½ (1936, Brit.) PR:A
ALL THAT HEAVEN ALLOWS **** (1955) PR:A
ALL THAT JAZZ **½ (1979) PR:O
ALL THAT MONEY CAN BUY
    (SEE:DEVIL AND DANIEL WEBSTER, THE)
ALL THE BROTHERS WERE VALIANT ***
    (1953) PR:A
ALL THE FINE YOUNG CANNIBALS * (1960) PR:C
ALL THE KING'S HORSES * (1935) PR:A
ALL THE KING'S MEN *** (1949) PR:C**
...ALL THE MARBLES ** (1981) PR:C
ALL THE OTHER GIRLS DO! ** (1967, It.) PR:C
ALL THE PRESIDENT'S MEN ***½ (1976) PR:C
ALL THE RIGHT MOVES ** (1983) PR:C
ALL THE RIGHT NOISES ** (1973, Brit.) PR:O
ALL THE WAY, BOYS * (1973, It.) PR:C
ALL THE WAY HOME *** (1963) PR:A
ALL THE WAY UP ** (1970, Brit.) PR:A
ALL THE YOUNG MEN **½ (1960) PR:A
ALL THESE WOMEN ** (1964, Swed.) PR:O
ALL THINGS BRIGHT AND BEAUTIFUL ***
    (1979, Brit.) PR:AA
ALL THIS AND HEAVEN TOO *** (1940) PR:A
ALL THROUGH THE NIGHT **** (1942) PR:A
ALL WOMAN zero (1967) PR:O
ALL WOMEN HAVE SECRETS * (1939) PR:A
**ALLAN QUATERMAIN AND THE LOST CITY OF
    GOLD * (1987) PR:A-C**
ALLEGHENY UPRISING ** (1939) PR:A
ALLEGRO NON TROPPO * (1977, It.) PR:A**
ALLERGIC TO LOVE ** (1943) PR:A
ALLEY CAT *½ (1984) PR:O
ALLIGATOR * (1980) PR:O**
ALLIGATOR NAMED DAISY, AN ***
    (1957, Brit.) PR:A
ALLIGATOR PEOPLE, THE ** (1959) PR:C
ALLNIGHTER, THE zero (1987) PR:C-O
ALLONSANFAN *½ (1985, It.) PR:O
ALLOTMENT WIVES, INC. *½ (1945) PR:A
ALLURING GOAL, THE * (1930, Ger.) PR:A
ALMOST A BRIDE
    (SEE:KISS FOR CORLISS, A)
ALMOST A DIVORCE * (1931, Brit.) PR:A
ALMOST A GENTLEMAN *½ (1938, Brit.) PR:A
ALMOST A GENTLEMAN zero (1939) PR:A
ALMOST A HONEYMOON * (1930, Brit.) PR:A
ALMOST A HONEYMOON * (1938, Brit.) PR:A
ALMOST ANGELS ** (1962) PR:AA
ALMOST HUMAN zero (1974, It.) PR:O
ALMOST MARRIED ** (1932) PR:C
ALMOST MARRIED ** (1942) PR:A
ALMOST PERFECT AFFAIR, AN * (1979) PR:C
ALMOST SUMMER *½ (1978) PR:A
ALMOST TRANSPARENT BLUE **½
    (1980, Jap.) PR:O
ALMOST YOU **½ (1984) PR:C
ALOHA zero (1931) PR:A
ALOHA, BOBBY AND ROSE ** (1975) PR:C
ALOHA SUMMER **½ (1988) PR:C
ALOMA OF THE SOUTH SEAS *** (1941) PR:A
ALONE AGAINST ROME * (1963, It.) PR:C
ALONE IN THE DARK ** (1982) PR:O
ALONE IN THE STREETS ** (1956, It.) PR:C
ALONE ON THE PACIFIC *** (1964, Jap.) PR:AA
ALONG CAME JONES * (1945) PR:A**
ALONG CAME LOVE * (1937) PR:A
ALONG CAME SALLY * (1934, Brit.) PR:A

ALONG CAME YOUTH * (1931) PR:A
ALONG THE GREAT DIVIDE **½ (1951) PR:C
ALONG THE NAVAJO TRAIL ** (1945) PR:A
ALONG THE OREGON TRAIL * (1947) PR:A
ALONG THE RIO GRANDE * (1941) PR:A
ALPHA BETA ** (1973, Brit.) PR:C
ALPHABET CITY * (1984) PR:O
ALPHABET MURDERS, THE *½ (1966) PR:A
**ALPHAVILLE, A STRANGE CASE OF LEMMY
    CAUTION *** (1965, Fr.) PR:A**
ALRAUNE ** (1952, Ger.) PR:O
**ALSINO AND THE CONDOR **½
    (1983, Nicaragua) PR:C**
ALTERED STATES ** (1980) PR:O
ALVAREZ KELLY **½ (1966) PR:A
ALVIN PURPLE **½ (1974, Aus.) PR:C
ALVIN RIDES AGAIN ** (1974, Aus.) PR:O
ALWAYS * (1985) PR:O
ALWAYS A BRIDE * (1940) PR:A
ALWAYS A BRIDE ** (1954, Brit.) PR:A
ALWAYS A BRIDESMAID *½ (1943) PR:A
ALWAYS ANOTHER DAWN * (1948, Aus.) PR:A
ALWAYS GOODBYE * (1931) PR:A
ALWAYS GOODBYE ** (1938) PR:A
ALWAYS IN MY HEART ** (1942) PR:AA
ALWAYS IN TROUBLE ** (1938) PR:AA
ALWAYS LEAVE THEM LAUGHING ** (1949) PR:A
ALWAYS TOGETHER **½ (1947) PR:A
ALWAYS VICTORIOUS ** (1960, It.) PR:A
AM I GUILTY? ** (1940) PR:A
AMADEUS *** (1984) PR:C**
AMANTI
    (SEE:PLACE FOR LOVERS, A)
AMARCORD * (1974, It.) PR:O**
AMATEUR, THE ** (1982) PR:C
AMATEUR CROOK zero (1937) PR:A
AMATEUR DADDY * (1932) PR:A
AMATEUR GENTLEMAN *** (1936, Brit.) PR:A
AMAZING ADVENTURE, THE
    (SEE:ROMANCE AND RICHES)
AMAZING COLOSSAL MAN, THE ** (1957) PR:A
AMAZING DOBERMANS, THE *½ (1976) PR:AA
AMAZING DR. CLITTERHOUSE, THE ***
    (1938) PR:C
AMAZING GRACE * (1974) PR:A
AMAZING GRACE AND CHUCK ** (1987) PR:A-C
AMAZING MR. BEECHAM, THE * (1949, Brit.) PR:A
**AMAZING MR. BLUNDEN, THE **
    (1973, Brit.) PR:C**
AMAZING MR. FORREST, THE * (1943, Brit.) PR:A
AMAZING MR. WILLIAMS **½ (1939) PR:A
AMAZING MR. X, THE
    (SEE:SPIRITUALIST, THE)
AMAZING MONSIEUR FABRE, THE **½
    (1952, Fr.) PR:A
AMAZING MRS. HOLLIDAY *** (1943) PR:AA
AMAZING QUEST OF ERNEST BLISS, THE
    (SEE:ROMANCE AND RICHES)
**AMAZING TRANSPARENT MAN, THE zero
    (1960) PR:C**
AMAZON QUEST * (1949) PR:A
AMAZON WOMEN ON THE MOON ** (1987) PR:O
AMAZONIA—THE CATHERINE MILES STORY
    (SEE:WHITE SLAVE)
AMAZONS * (1987) PR:O
AMBASSADOR, THE ** (1984) PR:C
AMBASSADOR BILL ** (1931) PR:A
AMBASSADOR'S DAUGHTER, THE ** (1956) PR:A
AMBUSH * (1939) PR:A
AMBUSH ** (1950) PR:A
AMBUSH AT CIMARRON PASS ** (1958) PR:A
AMBUSH AT TOMAHAWK GAP ** (1953) PR:C
AMBUSH BAY *** (1966) PR:C
AMBUSH IN LEOPARD STREET ** (1962, Brit.) PR:C
AMBUSH TRAIL * (1946) PR:A
AMBUSH VALLEY * (1936) PR:A
AMBUSHERS, THE ** (1967) PR:A
AMELIE OR THE TIME TO LOVE **½
    (1961, Fr.) PR:A
AMERICA, AMERICA ** (1963) PR:A
AMERICA 3000 * (1986) PR:C
AMERICAN ANTHEM *½ (1986) PR:C
AMERICAN COMMANDOS * (1986) PR:O
AMERICAN DREAM, AN * (1966) PR:O
AMERICAN DREAMER ** (1984) PR:A-C
AMERICAN EMPIRE * (1942) PR:A**
AMERICAN FLYERS ** (1985) PR:C

AMERICAN FRIEND, THE * (1977, Ger.) PR:C**
AMERICAN GIGOLO zero (1980) PR:O
AMERICAN GOTHIC ** (1988, Brit./Can.) PR:O
AMERICAN GRAFFITI ** (1973) PR:C**
AMERICAN GUERRILLA IN THE PHILIPPINES, AN
    *** (1950) PR:A
AMERICAN HOT WAX * (1978) PR:A**
AMERICAN IN PARIS, AN *** (1951) PR:AA**
AMERICAN JUSTICE ** (1986) PR:O
AMERICAN LOVE *½ (1932, Fr.) PR:A
AMERICAN MADNESS * (1932) PR:A**
AMERICAN NIGHTMARE zero (1984) PR:O
AMERICAN NINJA ** (1985) PR:O
**AMERICAN NINJA 2: THE CONFRONTATION **½
    (1987) PR:C-O**
AMERICAN POP * (1981) PR:O
AMERICAN PRISONER, THE ** (1929, Brit.) PR:A
AMERICAN ROMANCE, AN *** (1944) PR:A
AMERICAN SOLDIER, THE *** (1970, Ger.) PR:C
AMERICAN SUCCESS COMPANY, THE ***
    (1980) PR:C
AMERICAN TABOO ** (1984) PR:O
AMERICAN TAIL, AN ** (1986) PR:AA
AMERICAN TRAGEDY, AN * (1931) PR:C
AMERICAN WAY, THE
    (SEE:RIDERS OF THE STORM)
**AMERICAN WEREWOLF IN LONDON, AN **½
    (1981) PR:O**
AMERICAN WIFE, AN ** (1965, It.) PR:O
AMERICANA * (1981) PR:C**
AMERICANIZATION OF EMILY, THE **
    (1964) PR:C
AMERICANO, THE ** (1955) PR:A
AMERICATHON * (1979) PR:C
AMIGOS ** (1986) PR:C
**AMIN—THE RISE AND FALL zero
    (1982, Kenya) PR:O**
AMITYVILLE HORROR, THE ** (1979) PR:O
AMITYVILLE 3-D * (1983) PR:O
AMITYVILLE II: THE POSSESSION * (1982) PR:O
AMONG HUMAN WOLVES ** (1940, Brit.) PR:A
**AMONG THE CINDERS **½
    (1985, New Zealand/Ger.) PR:O**
AMONG THE LIVING *** (1941) PR:C
AMONG THE MISSING * (1934) PR:A
AMONG VULTURES *
    (1964, Ger./It./Fr./Yugo.) PR:A
AMOROUS ADVENTURES OF MOLL FLANDERS,
    THE **½ (1965) PR:C
AMOROUS MR. PRAWN, THE ** (1965, Brit.) PR:C
AMOS 'N' ANDY *½ (1930) PR:A
AMOUR, AMOUR * (1937, Fr.) PR:A
AMPHIBIOUS MAN, THE ** (1961, USSR) PR:AA
AMPHYTRYON ** (1937, Ger.) PR:A
AMSTERDAM AFFAIR, THE **½ (1968, Brit.) PR:C
**AMSTERDAM KILL, THE **
    (1978, Hong Kong) PR:O**
AMY **½ (1981) PR:AA
ANA *** (1985, Portugal) PR:C
ANASTASIA ** (1956) PR:A**
ANATAHAN * (1953, Jap.) PR:C
ANATOMIST, THE *½ (1961, Brit.) PR:C
ANATOMY OF A MARRIAGE (MY DAYS WITH
    JEAN-MARC AND MY NIGHTS WITH FRANCOISE)
    **½ (1964, Fr.) PR:O
ANATOMY OF A MURDER ** (1959) PR:C**
ANATOMY OF A PSYCHO * (1961) PR:C
ANATOMY OF A SYNDICATE
    (SEE:BIG OPERATOR, THE)
ANATOMY OF LOVE * (1959, It.) PR:C
ANCHORS AWEIGH ** (1945) PR:AA**
AND BABY MAKES THREE ** (1949) PR:A
AND GOD CREATED WOMAN ** (1957, Fr.) PR:O
AND GOD CREATED WOMAN zero (1988) PR:O
AND HOPE TO DIE * (1972, Fr/US) PR:C**
...AND JUSTICE FOR ALL ** (1979) PR:O
AND MILLIONS WILL DIE * (1973) PR:O
**AND NOW FOR SOMETHING COMPLETELY
    DIFFERENT ** (1972, Brit.) PR:O**
AND NOW MIGUEL ** (1966) PR:AA
AND NOW MY LOVE * (1975, Fr.) PR:C**
**AND NOW THE SCREAMING STARTS **
    (1973, Brit.) PR:O**
AND NOW TOMORROW **½ (1944) PR:A
AND ONE WAS BEAUTIFUL *½ (1940) PR:A
...AND PIGS MIGHT FLY
    (SEE:ADERYN PAPUR)

AND QUIET FLOWS THE DON **½
(1960, USSR) PR:A
AND SO THEY WERE MARRIED *** (1936) PR:AA
AND SO THEY WERE MARRIED
(SEE:JOHNNY DOESN'T LIVE HERE ANYMORE)
AND SO TO BED *½ (1965, Ger.) PR:O
AND SOON THE DARKNESS * (1970, Brit.) PR:O
AND SUDDEN DEATH * (1936) PR:A
AND SUDDENLY IT'S MURDER! **½
(1964, It.) PR:C
AND THE ANGELS SING *** (1944) PR:A
AND THE SAME TO YOU * (1960, Brit.) PR:A
AND THE SHIP SAILS ON * (1983, It./Fr.) PR:A**
AND THE WILD, WILD WOMEN *½
(1961, It.) PR:C-O
AND THEN THERE WERE NONE ** (1945) PR:A**
AND THEN THERE WERE NONE
(SEE:TEN LITTLE INDIANS)
AND THEN THERE WERE NONE
(SEE:TEN LITTLE INDIANS)
AND THERE CAME A MAN ** (1968, It.) PR:AA
AND WOMEN SHALL WEEP *½ (1960, Brit.) PR:C
ANDERSON TAPES, THE **½ (1971) PR:C-O
ANDREI ROUBLOV *** (1973, USSR) PR:A
ANDREW'S RAIDERS
(SEE:GREAT LOCOMOTIVE CHASE, THE)
ANDROCLES AND THE LION ** (1952) PR:A
ANDROID * (1982) PR:O**
ANDROMEDA STRAIN, THE **½ (1971) PR:A
ANDY **½ (1965) PR:A
ANDY HARDY COMES HOME ** (1958) PR:AA
ANDY HARDY GETS SPRING FEVER ***
(1939) PR:AA
ANDY HARDY MEETS DEBUTANTE **½
(1940) PR:AA
ANDY HARDY'S BLONDE TROUBLE ***
(1944) PR:AA
ANDY HARDY'S DOUBLE LIFE **½ (1942) PR:AA
ANDY HARDY'S PRIVATE SECRETARY **
(1941) PR:AA
ANDY WARHOL'S DRACULA *
(1974, Fr./It.) PR:O**
**ANDY WARHOL'S FRANKENSTEIN **½
(1974, Fr./It.) PR:O**
ANGEL **½ (1937) PR:C
ANGEL *** (1982, Ireland) PR:C
ANGEL ** (1984) PR:O
ANGEL AND SINNER *** (1947, Fr.) PR:C
ANGEL AND THE BADMAN ***½ (1947) PR:A
ANGEL, ANGEL, DOWN WE GO zero (1969) PR:O
ANGEL BABY ** (1961) PR:C
ANGEL COMES TO BROOKLYN, AN **
(1945) PR:AA
ANGEL FACE *** (1953) PR:C
ANGEL FROM TEXAS, AN ** (1940) PR:A
ANGEL HEART **½ (1987) PR:O
ANGEL IN EXILE ** (1948) PR:A
ANGEL IN MY POCKET ** (1969) PR:AA
ANGEL LEVINE, THE ** (1970) PR:A
ANGEL OF VIOLENCE
(SEE:MS. 45)
ANGEL ON MY SHOULDER ***½ (1946) PR:A
ANGEL ON THE AMAZON ** (1948) PR:A
ANGEL PASSED OVER BROOKLYN, AN
(SEE:MAN WHO WAGGED HIS TAIL, THE)
ANGEL RIVER ** (1986, US/Mex.) PR:O
ANGEL STREET
(SEE:GASLIGHT)
ANGEL 3: THE FINAL CHAPTER * (1988) PR:O
ANGEL UNCHAINED * (1970) PR:C
ANGEL WHO PAWNED HER HARP, THE **
(1956, Brit.) PR:A
ANGEL WITH THE TRUMPET, THE **
(1950, Brit.) PR:C
ANGEL WORE RED, THE ** (1960) PR:A
ANGELA ** (1955, It.) PR:A
ANGELA zero (1977, Can.) PR:O
ANGELE ** (1934, Fr.) PR:C
ANGELIKA
(SEE:AFFAIRS OF DR. HOLL)
ANGELINA ** (1948, It.) PR:C
ANGELO ** (1951, It.) PR:C
ANGELO IN THE CROWD ** (1952, It.) PR:A
ANGELO MY LOVE ** (1983) PR:O
ANGELS ALLEY *½ (1948) PR:A
ANGELS BRIGADE * (1980) PR:O
ANGELS DIE HARD * (1970) PR:O
ANGELS FROM HELL * (1968) PR:O
ANGELS HARD AS THEY COME * (1971) PR:O
ANGEL'S HOLIDAY ** (1937) PR:A
ANGELS IN DISGUISE *½ (1949) PR:A
ANGELS IN THE OUTFIELD ***½ (1951) PR:AA
ANGELS OF DARKNESS * (1956, It.) PR:O
ANGELS OF THE STREETS ** (1950, Fr.) PR:C
ANGELS ONE FIVE ** (1954, Brit.) PR:A
ANGELS OVER BROADWAY ** (1940) PR:A**
ANGELS WASH THEIR FACES **½ (1939) PR:A
ANGELS WITH BROKEN WINGS ** (1941) PR:A
ANGELS WITH DIRTY FACES *** (1938) PR:C**
ANGI VERA *** (1980, Hung.) PR:C
**ANGKOR-CAMBODIA EXPRESS *
(1986, Thai./It.) PR:O**
ANGRY BREED, THE * (1969) PR:O
ANGRY HILLS, THE ** (1959, Brit.) PR:A
ANGRY ISLAND **½ (1960, Jap.) PR:A
ANGRY MAN, THE ** (1979, Fr./Can.) PR:C
ANGRY RED PLANET, THE * (1959) PR:A
ANGRY SILENCE, THE **½ (1960, Brit.) PR:C
ANGUISH ***½ (1988, Sp.) PR:O
ANIMAL CRACKERS * (1930) PR:AA**
ANIMAL FARM ** (1955, Brit.) PR:A
ANIMAL HOUSE
(SEE:NATIONAL LAMPOON'S ANIMAL HOUSE)
ANIMAL KINGDOM, THE *** (1932) PR:A
ANIMALS, THE *½ (1971) PR:O
ANITA—DANCES OF VICE ***½ (1987, Ger.) PR:O
ANITA GARIBALDI ** (1954, It.) PR:C
ANN CARVER'S PROFESSION * (1933) PR:A
ANN VICKERS *½ (1933) PR:A
ANNA **½ (1951, It.) PR:C-O
ANNA **½ (1981, Fr./Hung.) PR:A
ANNA AND THE KING OF SIAM **** (1946) PR:A
ANNA CHRISTIE ***½ (1930) PR:C
ANNA CROSS, THE ** (1954, USSR) PR:A
ANNA KARENINA ** (1935) PR:A**
ANNA KARENINA *** (1948, Brit.) PR:A
ANNA LUCASTA ** (1949) PR:C
ANNA LUCASTA **½ (1958) PR:C
ANNA OF BROOKLYN ** (1958, It.) PR:C
ANNA OF RHODES ** (1950, Gr.) PR:A
ANNABEL TAKES A TOUR ** (1938) PR:A
ANNABELLE'S AFFAIRS ** (1931) PR:A
ANNAPOLIS FAREWELL ** (1935) PR:A
ANNAPOLIS SALUTE * (1937) PR:A
ANNAPOLIS STORY, AN ** (1955) PR:A
ANNE DEVLIN ** (1984, Ireland) PR:C
ANNE-MARIE * (1936, Fr.) PR:A
ANNE OF GREEN GABLES ** (1934) PR:A
ANNE OF THE INDIES ** (1951) PR:A
ANNE OF THE THOUSAND DAYS **
(1969, Brit.) PR:C-O**
ANNE OF WINDY POPLARS *½ (1940) PR:A
ANNE ONE HUNDRED ** (1933, Brit.) PR:A
ANNE TRISTER *** (1986, Can.) PR:O
ANNIE * (1982) PR:AA**
ANNIE GET YOUR GUN ***½ (1950) PR:AA
ANNIE HALL ** (1977) PR:C-O**
ANNIE LAURIE ** (1936, Brit.) PR:A
ANNIE, LEAVE THE ROOM *½ (1935, Brit.) PR:A
ANNIE OAKLEY * (1935) PR:AA**
ANNIE'S COMING OUT *** (1985, Aus.) PR:C
ANNIHILATORS, THE ** (1985) PR:O
ANNIVERSARY, THE * (1968, Brit.) PR:O**
ANONYMOUS VENETIAN, THE zero (1971) PR:C
ANOTHER CHANCE
(SEE:TWILIGHT WOMEN)
ANOTHER COUNTRY ** (1984, Brit.) PR:C
ANOTHER DAWN ** (1937) PR:A
ANOTHER FACE **½ (1935) PR:A
ANOTHER LANGUAGE ***½ (1933) PR:A
ANOTHER LOVE STORY **½ (1986, Arg.) PR:O
ANOTHER MAN, ANOTHER CHANCE *
(1977, Fr./US) PR:C-O**
ANOTHER MAN'S POISON *** (1952, Brit.) PR:C
ANOTHER PART OF THE FOREST *** (1948) PR:C
ANOTHER SHORE * (1948, Brit.) PR:A
ANOTHER SKY * (1960, Brit.) PR:A
ANOTHER THIN MAN * (1939) PR:A**
ANOTHER TIME, ANOTHER PLACE ** (1958) PR:A
**ANOTHER TIME, ANOTHER PLACE *½
(1984, Brit.) PR:O**
ANOTHER WOMAN ** (1988) PR:C**
ANTARCTICA * (1984, Jap.) PR:A**
ANTHONY ADVERSE * (1936) PR:A**
ANTHONY OF PADUA zero (1952, It.) PR:O
ANTI-CLOCK zero (1980) PR:C-O
ANTIGONE *** (1962, Gr.) PR:A
ANTOINE ET ANTOINETTE ** (1947, Fr.) PR:A
ANTONIO DAS MORTES *** (1970, Braz.) PR:C-O
ANTONY AND CLEOPATRA ** (1973, Brit.) PR:A
ANTS IN HIS PANTS * (1940, Aus.) PR:AA
ANY GUN CAN PLAY ** (1968, It./Sp.) PR:C
ANY MAN'S WIFE * (1936) PR:A
ANY NUMBER CAN PLAY **½ (1949) PR:A
ANY NUMBER CAN WIN *** (1963, Fr.) PR:A
ANY WEDNESDAY ** (1966) PR:C-O
ANY WHICH WAY YOU CAN **½ (1980) PR:C
ANYBODY'S BLONDE * (1931) PR:A
ANYBODY'S WOMAN ** (1930) PR:A
ANYBODY'S WAR zero (1930) PR:A
ANYONE CAN PLAY ** (1968, It.) PR:O
ANYONE FOR VENICE?
(SEE:THE HONEYPOT)
ANYTHING CAN HAPPEN ** (1952) PR:A
ANYTHING FOR A SONG * (1947, It.) PR:A
ANYTHING FOR A THRILL * (1937) PR:A
ANYTHING FOR LOVE
(SEE:11 HARROWHOUSE)
ANYTHING GOES *** (1936) PR:A
ANYTHING GOES **½ (1956) PR:A
ANYTHING MIGHT HAPPEN ** (1935, Brit.) PR:A
ANYTHING TO DECLARE? *½ (1939, Brit.) PR:A
ANZIO ** (1968, It.) PR:A
APACHE * (1954) PR:A**
APACHE AMBUSH ** (1955) PR:A
APACHE CHIEF * (1949) PR:A
APACHE COUNTRY * (1952) PR:A
APACHE DRUMS *** (1951) PR:A
APACHE GOLD ** (1965, Ger.) PR:A
APACHE KID, THE * (1941) PR:A
APACHE RIFLES ** (1964) PR:A
APACHE ROSE * (1947) PR:A
APACHE TERRITORY ** (1958) PR:A
APACHE TRAIL ** (1942) PR:A
APACHE UPRISING ** (1966) PR:A
APACHE WAR SMOKE ** (1952) PR:A
APACHE WARRIOR **½ (1957) PR:A
APACHE WOMAN ** (1955) PR:A
APARAJITO * (1959, India) PR:A**
APARTMENT, THE ** (1960) PR:C-O**
APARTMENT FOR PEGGY *** (1948) PR:A
APE, THE * (1940) PR:C
APE MAN, THE * (1943) PR:C
APE WOMAN, THE ** (1964, It.) PR:C
APOCALYPSE NOW ***½ (1979) PR:O
APOLLO GOES ON HOLIDAY **
(1968, Ger./Swed.) PR:A
APOLOGY FOR MURDER * (1945) PR:A
APPALOOSA, THE ** (1966) PR:C
APPASSIONATA *½ (1946, Swed.) PR:A
APPLAUSE *** (1929) PR:A
APPLE, THE * (1980, US/Ger.) PR:C-O
APPLE DUMPLING GANG, THE ** (1975) PR:AA
**APPLE DUMPLING GANG RIDES AGAIN, THE *½
(1979) PR:AA**
APPOINTMENT, THE * (1969) PR:O
APPOINTMENT FOR LOVE *** (1941) PR:A
APPOINTMENT FOR MURDER * (1954, It.) PR:C
APPOINTMENT IN BERLIN ** (1943) PR:A
APPOINTMENT IN HONDURAS ** (1953) PR:A
APPOINTMENT IN LONDON ** (1953, Brit.) PR:A
APPOINTMENT WITH A SHADOW *½ (1958) PR:A
APPOINTMENT WITH CRIME **½
(1945, Brit.) PR:A
APPOINTMENT WITH DANGER *** (1951) PR:C
APPOINTMENT WITH DEATH * (1988) PR:A-C**
APPOINTMENT WITH FEAR * (1985) PR:O
APPOINTMENT WITH MURDER *½ (1948) PR:A
APPOINTMENT WITH VENUS
(SEE:ISLAND RESCUE)
APPRENTICE TO MURDER * (1988) PR:C
APPRENTICESHIP OF DUDDY KRAVITZ, THE *
(1974, Can.) PR:A**
APRES L'AMOUR *** (1948, Fr.) PR:O
APRIL BLOSSOMS ** (1937, Brit.) PR:A
APRIL FOOLS, THE **½ (1969) PR:C
APRIL FOOL'S DAY ** (1986) PR:O
APRIL IN PARIS ** (1953) PR:A
APRIL LOVE ** (1957) PR:AA
APRIL 1, 2000 * (1953, Aust.) PR:A
APRIL ROMANCE
(SEE:APRIL BLOSSOMS)
APRIL SHOWERS **½ (1948) PR:A
ARABELLA ** (1969, US/It.) PR:A
ARABESQUE * (1966) PR:C**
ARABIAN ADVENTURE *½ (1979, Brit.) PR:AA
ARABIAN NIGHTS *** (1942) PR:AA
ARABIAN NIGHTS **½ (1980, It./Fr.) PR:O
ARCH OF TRIUMPH * (1948) PR:C**
ARCTIC FLIGHT *½ (1952) PR:A
ARCTIC FURY * (1949) PR:AA
ARCTIC HEAT
(SEE:BORN AMERICAN)
ARCTIC MANHUNT * (1949) PR:A
ARE HUSBANDS NECESSARY? **½ (1942) PR:A
ARE THESE OUR CHILDREN? * (1931) PR:A
ARE THESE OUR PARENTS? * (1944) PR:A
ARE WE CIVILIZED? * (1934) PR:A
ARE YOU A MASON? *½ (1934, Brit.) PR:A
ARE YOU LISTENING? * (1932) PR:A
ARE YOU THERE? zero (1930) PR:AA
ARE YOU WITH IT? **½ (1948) PR:AA
ARENA ** (1953) PR:A
ARENA, THE zero (1973) PR:O
AREN'T MEN BEASTS? ** (1937, Brit.) PR:A
AREN'T WE ALL? ** (1932, Brit.) PR:A
AREN'T WE WONDERFUL? **½ (1959, Ger.) PR:A
ARGENTINE NIGHTS *½ (1940) PR:AA
ARGYLE CASE, THE ** (1929) PR:A
ARGYLE SECRETS, THE *½ (1948) PR:A
ARIA ** (1988, US/Brit.) PR:O
ARIANE ** (1931, Ger.) PR:A
ARIANE, RUSSIAN MAID * (1932, Fr.) PR:A
ARISE, MY LOVE *** (1940) PR:A

ARISTOCATS, THE *** (1970) PR:AA
ARIZONA
(SEE:MEN ARE LIKE THAT)
ARIZONA *** (1940) PR:A
ARIZONA BADMAN * (1935) PR:A
ARIZONA BOUND ** (1941) PR:A
ARIZONA BUSHWHACKERS ** (1968) PR:A
ARIZONA COLT * (1965, It./Fr./Sp.) PR:C
ARIZONA COWBOY, THE ** (1950) PR:A
ARIZONA CYCLONE * (1934) PR:A
ARIZONA CYCLONE ** (1941) PR:A
ARIZONA DAYS *½ (1937) PR:A
ARIZONA FRONTIER *½ (1940) PR:A
ARIZONA GANGBUSTERS * (1940) PR:A
ARIZONA GUNFIGHTER * (1937) PR:A
ARIZONA KID, THE *½ (1930) PR:A
ARIZONA KID, THE ** (1939) PR:A
ARIZONA LEGION ** (1939) PR:A
ARIZONA MAHONEY * (1936) PR:A
ARIZONA MANHUNT *½ (1951) PR:A
ARIZONA MISSION
(SEE:GUN THE MAN DOWN)
ARIZONA NIGHTS * (1934) PR:A
ARIZONA RAIDERS **½ (1965) PR:A
ARIZONA RAIDERS, THE ** (1936) PR:A
ARIZONA RANGER, THE **½ (1948) PR:A
ARIZONA ROUNDUP * (1942) PR:A
ARIZONA STAGECOACH *½ (1942) PR:A
ARIZONA TERRITORY *½ (1950) PR:A
ARIZONA TERROR * (1931) PR:A
ARIZONA TERRORS ** (1942) PR:A
ARIZONA TO BROADWAY **½ (1933) PR:A
ARIZONA TRAIL ** (1943) PR:A
ARIZONA TRAILS * (1935) PR:A
ARIZONA WHIRLWIND * (1944) PR:A
ARIZONA WILDCAT ** (1938) PR:AA
ARIZONIAN, THE ** (1935) PR:A
ARKANSAS JUDGE *½ (1941) PR:A
ARKANSAS TRAVELER, THE *½ (1938) PR:A
ARM OF THE LAW * (1932) PR:A
ARMCHAIR DETECTIVE, THE *½ (1952, Brit.) PR:A
ARMED AND DANGEROUS *½ (1977, USSR) PR:A
ARMED AND DANGEROUS *½ (1986) PR:C
ARMED RESPONSE *½ (1986) PR:O
ARMORED ATTACK
(SEE:NORTH STAR)
ARMORED CAR **½ (1937) PR:A
ARMORED CAR ROBBERY * (1950) PR:A**
ARMORED COMMAND **½ (1961) PR:C
ARMS AND THE GIRL
(SEE:RED SALUTE)
ARMS AND THE MAN ** (1932, Brit.) PR:A
ARMS AND THE MAN ** (1962, Ger.) PR:A
ARMY BOUND * (1952) PR:A
ARMY GAME, THE ** (1963, Fr.) PR:C-O
ARMY GIRL ** (1938) PR:A
ARMY SURGEON * (1942) PR:A
ARMY WIVES * (1944) PR:A
ARNELO AFFAIR, THE *** (1947) PR:A
ARNOLD * (1973) PR:C
AROUND THE TOWN * (1938, Brit.) PR:A
AROUND THE WORLD **½ (1943) PR:A
AROUND THE WORLD IN 80 DAYS **
(1956) PR:AA**
AROUND THE WORLD IN EIGHTY WAYS **
(1987, Aus.) PR:A-C**
**AROUND THE WORLD UNDER THE SEA **
(1966) PR:A**
AROUSERS, THE * (1973) PR:O
ARRANGEMENT, THE * (1969) PR:O
**ARREST BULLDOG DRUMMOND **
(1939, Brit.) PR:A**
ARRIVEDERCI, BABY! * (1966, Brit.) PR:C-O
ARROW IN THE DUST ** (1954) PR:A
ARROWHEAD **½ (1953) PR:C
ARROWSMITH ** (1931) PR:A**
**ARSENAL STADIUM MYSTERY, THE *
(1939, Brit.) PR:A**
ARSENE LUPIN *** (1932) PR:A
ARSENE LUPIN RETURNS **½ (1938) PR:A
ARSENIC AND OLD LACE ** (1944) PR:A**
ARSON FOR HIRE * (1959) PR:A
ARSON GANG BUSTERS *½ (1938) PR:A
ARSON, INC. ** (1949) PR:A
ARSON SQUAD *½ (1945) PR:A
ART OF LOVE, THE **½ (1965) PR:A
ARTHUR *½ (1931, Fr.) PR:C
ARTHUR ***½ (1981) PR:C
ARTHUR TAKES OVER ** (1948) PR:A
ARTHUR 2 ON THE ROCKS * (1988) PR:C
**ARTHUR'S HALLOWED GROUND **½
(1986, Brit.) PR:C**
ARTISTS AND MODELS ***½ (1937) PR:AA
ARTISTS AND MODELS **½ (1955) PR:A
ARTISTS AND MODELS ABROAD **½ (1938) PR:A
ARTURO'S ISLAND *½ (1963, It.) PR:C
AS GOOD AS MARRIED ** (1937) PR:A
AS HUSBANDS GO **½ (1934) PR:A
AS LONG AS THEY'RE HAPPY *** (1957, Brit.) PR:A
AS LONG AS YOU'RE NEAR ME **
(1956, Ger.) PR:A
AS THE DEVIL COMMANDS * (1933) PR:A
AS THE EARTH TURNS ** (1934) PR:A
AS THE SEA RAGES * (1960, Ger.) PR:A
AS YOU DESIRE ME *** (1932) PR:A
AS YOU LIKE IT * (1936, Brit.) PR:A**
AS YOU WERE * (1951) PR:A
AS YOUNG AS WE ARE *½ (1958) PR:C
AS YOUNG AS YOU FEEL *** (1951) PR:A
ASCENDANCY ** (1983, Brit.) PR:C
ASCENT TO HEAVEN
(SEE:MEXICAN BUS RIDE)
ASH WEDNESDAY * (1973) PR:C
ASHANTI **½ (1979) PR:O
ASHES AND DIAMONDS * (1961, Pol.) PR:C**
ASK A POLICEMAN ** (1939, Brit.) PR:A
ASK ANY GIRL *** (1959) PR:A
ASK BECCLES * (1933, Brit.) PR:A
ASKING FOR TROUBLE *½ (1942, Brit.) PR:A
ASPHALT JUNGLE, THE *** (1950) PR:C**
ASPHYX, THE ** (1972, Brit.) PR:C
ASSA ***½ (1988, USSR) PR:C
ASSAM GARDEN, THE *½ (1985, Brit.) PR:A-C
ASSASSIN * (1973, Brit.) PR:C
ASSASSIN, THE * (1953, Brit.) PR:A
ASSASSIN, THE * (1965, It./Fr.) PR:O
ASSASSIN FOR HIRE ** (1951, Brit.) PR:C
ASSASSINATION *½ (1987) PR:A-C
ASSASSINATION BUREAU, THE ***
(1969, Brit.) PR:O
**ASSASSINATION OF TROTSKY, THE **
(1972, Fr./It.) PR:O**
ASSAULT, THE ** (1986, Neth.) PR:C**
ASSAULT *½ (1971, Brit.) PR:O
ASSAULT OF THE KILLER BIMBOS ** (1988) PR:O
ASSAULT OF THE REBEL GIRLS zero (1960) PR:A
ASSAULT ON A QUEEN ** (1966) PR:A
ASSAULT ON AGATHON * (1976, Brit./Gr.) PR:O
ASSAULT ON PRECINCT 13 * (1976) PR:O**
ASSIGNED TO DANGER *½ (1948) PR:A
ASSIGNMENT IN BRITTANY ** (1943) PR:A
ASSIGNMENT K * (1968, Brit.) PR:A
ASSIGNMENT: KILL CASTRO
(SEE:CUBA CROSSING)
ASSIGNMENT OUTER SPACE zero (1960, It.) PR:C
ASSIGNMENT—PARIS *** (1952) PR:A
ASSIGNMENT REDHEAD
(SEE:MILLION DOLLAR MANHUNT)
ASSIGNMENT TERROR zero
(1970, Ger./Sp./It.) PR:C-O
ASSIGNMENT TO KILL * (1968) PR:C
ASSISI UNDERGROUND, THE * (1985) PR:C**
ASSISTANT, THE ** (1982, Czech.) PR:C
ASSOCIATE, THE * (1982, Fr./Ger.) PR:A**
ASTERO * (1960, Gr.) PR:A
ASTONISHED HEART, THE *** (1950, Brit.) PR:C
ASTOUNDING SHE-MONSTER, THE zero
(1958) PR:C
ASTRO-ZOMBIES, THE zero (1969) PR:C
ASYA'S HAPPINESS ***** (1988, USSR) PR:A-C
ASYLUM * (1972, Brit.) PR:O**
AT
(SEE:HORSE, THE)
AT CLOSE RANGE ***½ (1986) PR:O
AT DAWN WE DIE * (1943, Brit.) PR:A
AT GUNPOINT **½ (1955) PR:A
AT LONG LAST LOVE ** (1975) PR:A
AT MIDDLE AGE ** (1985, Chi.) PR:C
AT SWORD'S POINT **½ (1951) PR:A
AT THE CIRCUS * (1939) PR:AA**
AT THE EARTH'S CORE * (1976, Brit.) PR:C
AT THE RIDGE ** (1931) PR:A
AT THE STROKE OF NINE ** (1957, Brit.) PR:A
AT WAR WITH THE ARMY **½ (1950) PR:A
ATALIA ** (1985, Israel) PR:C
ATHENA **½ (1954) PR:A
ATLANTIC ** (1929, Brit.) PR:A
ATLANTIC ADVENTURE *½ (1935) PR:A
ATLANTIC CITY *½ (1944) PR:A
ATLANTIC CITY ** (1981, US/Can.) PR:C-O**
ATLANTIC CONVOY ** (1942) PR:A
ATLANTIC FERRY * (1941, Brit.) PR:A
ATLANTIC FLIGHT * (1937) PR:A
ATLANTIS, THE LOST CONTINENT *½ (1961) PR:A
ATLAS * (1960) PR:C-O
ATLAS AGAINST THE CYCLOPS * (1963, It.) PR:A
ATLAS AGAINST THE CZAR zero (1964, It.) PR:A
ATOLL K
(SEE:UTOPIA)
ATOM AGE VAMPIRE * (1961, It.) PR:C
ATOMIC BRAIN, THE * (1964) PR:O
ATOMIC CITY, THE ** (1952) PR:A
ATOMIC KID, THE * (1954) PR:A
ATOMIC MAN, THE * (1955, Brit.) PR:A
ATOMIC SUBMARINE, THE ** (1960) PR:A
ATRAGON **½ (1965, Jap.) PR:A
ATTACK! *** (1956) PR:O
ATTACK AND RETREAT
(SEE:ITALIANO BRAVA GENTE)
**ATTACK OF THE CRAB MONSTERS *½
(1957) PR:A**
ATTACK OF THE 50 FOOT WOMAN * (1958) PR:A
ATTACK OF THE GIANT LEECHES zero
(1959) PR:C-O
**ATTACK OF THE KILLER TOMATOES *
(1978) PR:C**
ATTACK OF THE MAYAN MUMMY zero
(1963, US/Mex.) PR:C
ATTACK OF THE MUSHROOM PEOPLE *
(1964, Jap.) PR:A
ATTACK OF THE PUPPET PEOPLE *½ (1958) PR:A
ATTACK OF THE ROBOTS * (1967, Fr./Sp.) PR:C
ATTACK ON THE IRON COAST **
(1968, US/Brit.) PR:A
ATTEMPT TO KILL ** (1961, Brit.) PR:A
ATTENTION, THE KIDS ARE WATCHING **
(1978, Fr.) PR:C
ATTIC, THE ** (1979) PR:C-O
ATTILA * (1958, It.) PR:C
ATTORNEY FOR THE DEFENSE * (1932) PR:A
AU HASARD, BALTHAZAR ***** (1970, Fr.) PR:C-O
AU REVOIR LES ENFANTS **½ (1988, Fr.) PR:A-C
AUDREY ROSE ** (1977) PR:C
AUGUST WEEK-END * (1936, Brit.) PR:A
AUGUSTINE OF HIPPO ** (1973, It.) PR:A
AULD LANG SYNE *½ (1929, Brit.) PR:A
AULD LANG SYNE *½ (1937, Brit.) PR:A
AUNT CLARA **½ (1954, Brit.) PR:A
AUNT FROM CHICAGO **½ (1960, Gr.) PR:C
AUNTIE MAME ** (1958) PR:A**
AURORA ENCOUNTER, THE ** (1985) PR:C
AUSTERLITZ **½ (1960, Fr./It./Yugo.) PR:A
AUTHOR! AUTHOR! ** (1982) PR:A
AUTUMN **½ (1988, USSR) PR:C
AUTUMN CROCUS * (1934, Brit.) PR:A
AUTUMN LEAVES * (1956) PR:C**
AUTUMN MARATHON ** (1982, USSR) PR:A
AUTUMN SONATA zero (1978, Swed.) PR:O
AVALANCHE *½ (1946) PR:A
AVALANCHE * (1978) PR:O
AVALANCHE EXPRESS *½ (1979) PR:C
AVANTI! ** (1972) PR:C
AVE MARIA ** (1984, Fr.) PR:O
AVENGER, THE * (1931) PR:A
AVENGER, THE * (1933) PR:A
AVENGER, THE * (1964, Fr./It.) PR:C
AVENGER, THE * (1966, It.) PR:C
AVENGERS, THE *** (1942, Brit.) PR:A
AVENGERS, THE * (1950) PR:A
AVENGING ANGEL *½ (1985) PR:O
AVENGING FORCE **½ (1986) PR:O
AVENGING HAND, THE ** (1936, Brit.) PR:A
AVENGING RIDER, THE * (1943) PR:A
AVENGING WATERS * (1936) PR:A
AVIATOR, THE * (1929) PR:A
AVIATOR, THE *½ (1985) PR:A-C
AVIATOR'S WIFE, THE ** (1981, Fr.) PR:O
AWAKENING, THE * (1938, Brit.) PR:A
AWAKENING, THE ** (1958, It.) PR:AA
AWAKENING, THE *½ (1980) PR:O
AWAKENING OF JIM BURKE *½ (1935) PR:A

Finding entries in **THE MOTION PICTURE GUIDE ™**

Years	Volumes
1929-83	Volumes I-IX
1984	Volume IX
1985	1986 ANNUAL
1986	1987 ANNUAL
1987	1988 ANNUAL
1988	1989 ANNUAL

STAR RATINGS

★★★★★	Masterpiece
★★★★	Excellent
★★★	Good
★★	Fair
★	Poor
zero	Without Merit

PARENTAL RECOMMENDATION (PR:)

AA	Good for Children
A	Acceptable for Children
C	Cautionary, some objectionable scenes
O	Objectionable for Children

BOLD: Films on Videocassette

AWAY ALL BOATS ** (1956) PR:A
AWFUL DR. ORLOFF, THE zero (1964, Sp./Fr.) PR:O
AWFUL TRUTH, THE ***** (1937) PR:A
AWFUL TRUTH, THE **½ (1929) PR:A
AZAIS * (1931, Fr.) PR:A
AZTEC MUMMY, THE zero (1957, Mex.) PR:O
AZURE EXPRESS ** (1938, Hung.) PR:A

B

B. F.'S DAUGHTER **** (1948) PR:A
B.S. I LOVE YOU *½ (1971) PR:O
BABBITT ** (1934) PR:A
BABE RUTH STORY, THE *** (1948) PR:AA
BABES IN ARMS ***½ (1939) PR:AA
BABES IN BAGDAD *½ (1952) PR:A
BABES IN TOYLAND *** (1934) PR:AA
BABES IN TOYLAND ** (1961) PR:AA
BABES ON BROADWAY ***½ (1941) PR:AA
BABES ON SWING STREET * (1944) PR:A
BABETTE GOES TO WAR ** (1960, Fr.) PR:C
BABETTE'S FEAST *** (1988, Den.) PR:A
BABIES FOR SALE ** (1940) PR:C
BABY, THE zero (1973) PR:C-O
BABY AND THE BATTLESHIP, THE ***
   (1957, Brit.) PR:A
BABY BLUE MARINE **½ (1976) PR:C
BABY BOOM *** (1987) PR:A
BABY DOLL ** (1956) PR:O
BABY FACE ** (1933) PR:O
BABY FACE HARRINGTON ** (1935) PR:A
BABY FACE MORGAN ** (1942) PR:A
BABY FACE NELSON ** (1957) PR:O
BABY, IT'S YOU ** (1983) PR:C-O
BABY LOVE zero (1969, Brit.) PR:O
BABY MAKER, THE **½ (1970) PR:O
BABY: SECRET OF A LOST LEGEND **½
   (1985) PR:C
BABY, TAKE A BOW ** (1934) PR:AA
BABY, THE RAIN MUST FALL ** (1965) PR:C
BABYLON *** (1980, Brit.) PR:O
BACCHANTES, THE *½ (1963, Fr./It.) PR:A
BACHELOR AND THE BOBBY-SOXER, THE ****
   (1947) PR:AA
BACHELOR APARTMENT * (1931) PR:C
BACHELOR BAIT * (1934) PR:A
BACHELOR DADDY ** (1941) PR:A
BACHELOR FATHER ** (1931) PR:A
BACHELOR FLAT ** (1962) PR:A
BACHELOR GIRL, THE * (1929) PR:A
BACHELOR IN PARADISE ** (1961) PR:A
BACHELOR IN PARIS ** (1953, Brit.) PR:A
BACHELOR MOTHER ** (1933) PR:C
BACHELOR MOTHER **** (1939) PR:A
BACHELOR OF ARTS * (1935) PR:A
BACHELOR OF HEARTS *½ (1958, Brit.) PR:A
BACHELOR PARTY zero (1984) PR:O
BACHELOR PARTY, THE ***½ (1957) PR:C
BACHELOR'S AFFAIRS ** (1932) PR:A
BACHELOR'S BABY * (1932, Brit.) PR:A
BACHELOR'S DAUGHTERS, THE **½ (1946) PR:A
BACHELOR'S FOLLY
   (SEE:CALENDAR, THE)
BACK AT THE FRONT **½ (1952) PR:A
BACK DOOR TO HEAVEN ** (1939) PR:A
BACK DOOR TO HELL * (1964) PR:A
BACK FROM ETERNITY *½ (1956) PR:C
BACK FROM THE DEAD * (1957) PR:C-O
BACK IN CIRCULATION ** (1937) PR:A
BACK IN THE SADDLE * (1941) PR:A
BACK PAY * (1930) PR:A
BACK ROADS ** (1981) PR:O
BACK ROOM BOY *½ (1942, Brit.) PR:A
BACK STREET **½ (1932) PR:A
BACK STREET **** (1941) PR:A
BACK STREET ** (1961) PR:A
BACK STREETS OF PARIS **½ (1962, Fr.) PR:C-O
BACK TO BATAAN **** (1945) PR:A
BACK TO GOD'S COUNTRY * (1953) PR:A
BACK TO NATURE * (1936) PR:A
BACK TO SCHOOL ***½ (1986) PR:C
BACK TO THE BEACH **½ (1987) PR:C
BACK TO THE FUTURE ***½ (1985) PR:C
BACK TO THE WALL *½ (1959, Fr.) PR:O
BACK TRAIL * (1948) PR:A
BACKFIRE **½ (1950) PR:A
BACKFIRE! *½ (1961, Brit.) PR:A
BACKFIRE *** (1965, Fr.) PR:C
BACKGROUND * (1953, Brit.) PR:C
BACKGROUND TO DANGER *** (1943) PR:A
BACKLASH * (1947) PR:A
BACKLASH ** (1956) PR:A
BACKLASH *** (1986, Aus.) PR:O

BACKSTAGE * (1937, Brit.) PR:A
BACKTRACK ** (1969) PR:A
BAD AND THE BEAUTIFUL, THE ***** (1952)   PR:C
BAD BASCOMB **½ (1946) PR:AA
BAD BLONDE *½ (1953, Brit.) PR:C
BAD BLOOD **** (1987, Fr.) PR:A-C
BAD BOY * (1935) PR:A
BAD BOY *½ (1938, Brit.) PR:A
BAD BOY * (1939) PR:A
BAD BOY *½ (1949) PR:A
BAD BOYS *** (1983) PR:O
BAD CHARLESTON CHARLIE zero (1973) PR:A
BAD COMPANY * (1931) PR:A
BAD COMPANY *** (1972) PR:A
BAD COMPANY *** (1986, Arg.) PR:O
BAD DAY AT BLACK ROCK ***** (1955)   PR:A
BAD DREAMS ** (1988) PR:O
BAD FOR EACH OTHER * (1954) PR:A
BAD GIRL * (1931) PR:C
BAD GIRL
   (SEE:TEENAGE BAD GIRL)
BAD GUY *½ (1937) PR:A
BAD GUYS zero (1986) PR:C-O
BAD LANDS **½ (1939) PR:A
BAD LITTLE ANGEL ** (1939) PR:AA
BAD LORD BYRON, THE ** (1949, Brit.) PR:A
BAD MAN, THE *½ (1930) PR:A
BAD MAN, THE **½ (1941) PR:A
BAD MAN FROM RED BUTTE *½ (1940) PR:A
BAD MAN OF BRIMSTONE *** (1938) PR:A
BAD MAN OF DEADWOOD * (1941)   PR:A
BAD MANNERS *½ (1984) PR:C
BAD MAN'S RIVER * (1972, Sp.) PR:A
BAD MEDICINE ** (1985) PR:C
BAD MEN OF MISSOURI **½ (1941) PR:A
BAD MEN OF THE BORDER *½ (1945) PR:A
BAD MEN OF THE HILLS * (1942) PR:A
BAD MEN OF THUNDER GAP * (1943) PR:A
BAD MEN OF TOMBSTONE **½ (1949) PR:C
BAD NEWS BEARS, THE ***½ (1976) PR:C
BAD NEWS BEARS GO TO JAPAN, THE *½
   (1978) PR:C
BAD NEWS BEARS IN BREAKING TRAINING, THE
   * (1977) PR:C
BAD ONE, THE * (1930) PR:C
BAD SEED, THE *** (1956) PR:C
BAD SISTER *½ (1931) PR:A
BAD SISTER * (1947, Brit.) PR:A
BADGE OF HONOR * (1934) PR:A
BADGE OF MARSHAL BRENNAN, THE *
   (1957) PR:A
BADGE 373 * (1973) PR:O
BADGER'S GREEN *½ (1934, Brit.) PR:A
BADGER'S GREEN ** (1949, Brit.) PR:A
BADLANDERS, THE *** (1958) PR:A
BADLANDS * (1974) PR:O
BADLANDS OF DAKOTA **½ (1941) PR:A
BADLANDS OF MONTANA ** (1957) PR:A
BADMAN'S COUNTRY **½ (1958) PR:A
BADMAN'S GOLD *½ (1951) PR:A
BADMAN'S TERRITORY ** (1946) PR:A
BAGDAD ** (1949) PR:A
BAGDAD CAFE ***½ (1988, W. Ger.) PR:C-O
BAHAMA PASSAGE * (1941) PR:A
BAILOUT AT 43,000 * (1957) PR:A
BAIT *½ (1950, Brit.) PR:A
BAIT ** (1954) PR:C
BAKER'S HAWK *** (1976) PR:A
BAKER'S WIFE, THE **** (1940, Fr.) PR:C
BAL TABARIN * (1952) PR:A
BALACLAVA
   (SEE:JAWS OF HELL)
BALALAIKA **½ (1939) PR:A
BALBOA * (1986) PR:O
BALCONY, THE *** (1963) PR:O
BALL AT SAVOY * (1936, Brit.) PR:A
BALL AT THE CASTLE * (1939, It.) PR:A
BALL OF FIRE *** (1941) PR:A
BALLAD IN BLUE
   (SEE:BLUES FOR LOVERS)
BALLAD OF A GUNFIGHTER *½ (1964) PR:A
BALLAD OF A HUSSAR ** (1963, Fr.) PR:A
BALLAD OF A SOLDIER **** (1960, USSR) PR:A
BALLAD OF CABLE HOGUE, THE ***½
   (1970) PR:C
BALLAD OF COSSACK GLOOTA **
   (1938, USSR) PR:A
BALLAD OF GREGORIO CORTEZ, THE ***
   (1983) PR:C-O
BALLAD OF JOSIE **½ (1968) PR:A
BALLAD OF NARAYAMA ** (1961, Jap.) PR:C
BALLAD OF NARAYAMA, THE ****
   (1984, Jap.) PR:C
BALLERINA * (1950, Fr.) PR:A
BALLOON GOES UP, THE * (1942, Brit.) PR:A
BALTHAZAR
   (SEE:AU HASARD BALTHAZAR)
BALTIC DEPUTY *½ (1937, USSR) PR:A

BALTIMORE BULLET, THE **½ (1980) PR:C
BAMBI **** (1942) PR:AA
BAMBOLE! ** (1965, It.) PR:C
BAMBOO BLONDE, THE **½ (1946) PR:A
BAMBOO PRISON, THE ** (1955) PR:A
BAMBOO SAUCER, THE * (1968) PR:A
BANANA MONSTER, THE
   (SEE:SCHLOCK)
BANANA PEEL **½ (1965, Fr.) PR:C
BANANA RIDGE *½ (1941, Brit.) PR:A
BANANAS *** (1971) PR:C
BAND OF ANGELS **** (1957) PR:A
BAND OF ASSASSINS ** (1971, Jap.) PR:C
BAND OF OUTSIDERS ** (1966, Fr.) PR:C-O
BAND OF THE HAND ** (1986) PR:O
BAND OF THIEVES ** (1962, Brit.) PR:A
BAND PLAYS ON, THE * (1934) PR:A
BAND WAGGON ** (1940, Brit.) PR:A
BAND WAGON, THE **** (1953) PR:A
BANDE A PART
   (SEE:BAND OF OUTSIDERS)
BANDIDO ** (1956) PR:A
BANDIDOS * (1967, It.) PR:A
BANDIT, THE ** (1949, It.) PR:A
BANDIT KING OF TEXAS ** (1949) PR:A
BANDIT OF SHERWOOD FOREST, THE **
   (1946) PR:AA
BANDIT OF ZHOBE, THE * (1959) PR:A
BANDIT QUEEN * (1950) PR:A
BANDIT RANGER * (1942) PR:A
BANDIT TRAIL, THE *½ (1941) PR:A
BANDITS ** (1988, Fr.) PR:C
BANDITS OF CORSICA, THE ** (1953) PR:A
BANDITS OF DARK CANYON * (1947) PR:A
BANDITS OF EL DORADO * (1951) PR:A
BANDITS OF ORGOSOLO *** (1964, It.) PR:A
BANDITS OF THE BADLANDS *½ (1945) PR:A
BANDITS OF THE WEST * (1953) PR:A
BANDITS ON THE WIND ** (1964, Jap.) PR:A
BANDOLERO! *½ (1968) PR:A
BANG BANG KID, THE *½ (1968, US/Sp./It.) PR:A
BANG, BANG, YOU'RE DEAD *½ (1966) PR:A
BANG THE DRUM SLOWLY *** (1973) PR:A
BANG! YOU'RE DEAD **½ (1954, Brit.) PR:C
BANISHED ** (1978, Jap.) PR:C
BANJO * (1947) PR:AA
BANJO ON MY KNEE *** (1936) PR:A
BANK ALARM * (1937) PR:A
BANK DICK, THE **** (1940) PR:A
BANK HOLIDAY * (1938, Brit.) PR:C
BANK MESSENGER MYSTERY, THE *
   (1936, Brit.) PR:A
BANK RAIDERS, THE *½ (1958, Brit.) PR:A
BANK SHOT ** (1974) PR:A
BANNERLINE ** (1951) PR:A
BANNING * (1967) PR:C
BANZAI * (1983, Fr.) PR:C-O
BANZAI RUNNER * (1987) PR:C
BAR ESPERANZA ** (1985, Braz.) PR:O
BAR 51—SISTER OF LOVE *½ (1986, Israel) PR:O
BAR L RANCH * (1930) PR:A
BAR SINISTER, THE **½ (1955) PR:A
BAR 20 * (1943) PR:A
BAR 20 JUSTICE * (1938) PR:A
BAR 20 RIDES AGAIN * (1936) PR:A
BAR Z BAD MEN * (1937) PR:A
BARABBAS *** (1962, It.) PR:C
BARBADOS QUEST
   (SEE:MURDER ON APPROVAL)
BARBARELLA * (1968, Fr./It.) PR:O
BARBARIAN, THE ** (1933) PR:C
BARBARIAN AND THE GEISHA, THE **
   (1958) PR:A
BARBARIAN QUEEN ** (1985) PR:O
BARBARIANS, THE * (1987, US/It.) PR:O
BARBAROSA *** (1982) PR:C
BARBARY COAST *** (1935) PR:A
BARBARY COAST GENT ** (1944) PR:A
BARBARY PIRATE * (1949) PR:A
BARBED WIRE ** (1952) PR:A
BARBER OF SEVILLE, THE * (1947, It.) PR:A
BARBER OF SEVILLE * (1949, Fr.) PR:A
BARBER OF SEVILLE, THE ***
   (1973, Ger./Fr.) PR:A
BARBER OF STAMFORD HILL, THE *½
   (1963, Brit.) PR:A
BARBERINA *½ (1932, Ger.) PR:A
BARCAROLE *½ (1935, Ger.) PR:A
BARE KNUCKLES zero (1978) PR:O
BAREFOOT BATTALION, THE ** (1954, Gr.) PR:A
BAREFOOT BOY * (1938) PR:A
BAREFOOT CONTESSA, THE ***½ (1954) PR:A
BAREFOOT EXECUTIVE, THE *** (1971) PR:AA
BAREFOOT IN THE PARK *** (1967) PR:A
BAREFOOT MAILMAN, THE *½ (1951) PR:A
BAREFOOT SAVAGE
   (SEE:SENSUALITA)
BARFLY **** (1987) PR:O

BARGAIN, THE * (1931) PR:A
BARGEE, THE ** (1964, Brit.) PR:C
BARKER, THE * (1928) PR:A
__BARKLEYS OF BROADWAY, THE *** (1949) PR:A__
BARN OF THE NAKED DEAD zero (1976) PR:O
BARNACLE BILL ** (1935, Brit.) PR:A
BARNACLE BILL ** (1941) PR:A
BARNACLE BILL (SEE:ALL AT SEA)
BARNUM WAS RIGHT * (1929) PR:A
BARNYARD FOLLIES *½ (1940) PR:A
BAROCCO *½ (1976, Fr.) PR:O
__BARON BLOOD *½ (1972, It.) PR:C__
BARON MUNCHAUSEN * (1962, Czech.) PR:A
BARON OF ARIZONA, THE *** (1950) PR:A
BARONESS AND THE BUTLER, THE ** (1938) PR:A
BARQUERO *** (1970) PR:O
__BARRACUDA * (1978) PR:C__
BARRANCO * (1932, Fr.) PR:A
BARRETTS OF WIMPOLE STREET, THE **** (1934) PR:A
BARRETTS OF WIMPOLE STREET, THE **** (1957) PR:A
BARRICADE ** (1939) PR:A
BARRICADE *½ (1950) PR:A
BARRIER, THE * (1937) PR:A
BARRIER ** (1966, Pol.) PR:A
__BARRY LYNDON *** (1975, Brit.) PR:C-O__
__BARRY MC KENZIE HOLDS HIS OWN *½ (1975, Aus.) PR:C__
BARS OF HATE * (1936) PR:A
BARTLEBY *½ (1970, Brit.) PR:A
BARTON MYSTERY, THE * (1932, Brit.) PR:A
BASHFUL BACHELOR, THE *½ (1942) PR:A
BASHFUL ELEPHANT, THE *½ (1962, Aust.) PR:A
__BASIC TRAINING zero (1985) PR:O__
__BASILEUS QUARTET *** (1984, It.) PR:O__
__BASKET CASE * (1982) PR:O__
__BASKETBALL FIX, THE *** (1951) PR:A__
BASTILLE *** (1985, Neth.) PR:C-O
BAT, THE ** (1959) PR:C
__BAT PEOPLE, THE ** (1974) PR:C__
__BAT 21 *** (1988) PR:O__
BAT WHISPERS, THE *** (1930) PR:A
__BATAAN **** (1943) PR:C__
BATHING BEAUTY **½ (1944) PR:A
__BATMAN **½ (1966) PR:AA__
__BATTERIES NOT INCLUDED ** (1987) PR:AA__
BATTLE, THE **½ (1934, Fr.) PR:A
BATTLE AT APACHE PASS, THE ** (1952) PR:A
BATTLE AT BLOODY BEACH *½ (1961) PR:A
__BATTLE BENEATH THE EARTH * (1968, Brit.) PR:A__
__BATTLE BEYOND THE STARS ** (1980) PR:C__
BATTLE BEYOND THE SUN zero (1963) PR:O
BATTLE CIRCUS ** (1953) PR:A
__BATTLE CRY **½ (1955) PR:A__
BATTLE CRY **½ (1959) PR:A
BATTLE FLAME **½ (1959) PR:A
BATTLE FOR MUSIC *** (1943, Brit.) PR:A
__BATTLE FOR THE PLANET OF THE APES ** (1973) PR:A__
__BATTLE HELL ** (1957, Brit.) PR:A__
BATTLE HYMN ** (1957) PR:A
BATTLE IN OUTER SPACE *½ (1960) PR:A
__BATTLE OF ALGIERS, THE *** (1967, It./Algeria) PR:C__
BATTLE OF AUSTERLITZ (SEE:AUSTERLITZ)
BATTLE OF BLOOD ISLAND * (1960) PR:A
__BATTLE OF BRITAIN, THE **** (1969, Brit.) PR:A__
BATTLE OF BROADWAY ** (1938) PR:A
BATTLE OF GALLIPOLI ** (1931, Brit.) PR:A
BATTLE OF GREED * (1934) PR:A
BATTLE OF LOVE'S RETURN, THE * (1971) PR:A
__BATTLE OF NERETVA *** (1969, Yugo./It./Ger.) PR:A__
BATTLE OF PARIS, THE * (1929) PR:A
BATTLE OF ROGUE RIVER *½ (1954) PR:A
BATTLE OF THE AMAZONS * (1973, It./Sp.) PR:A
__BATTLE OF THE BULGE ***½ (1965) PR:A__
BATTLE OF THE CORAL SEA ** (1959) PR:A
BATTLE OF THE RAILS **½ (1949, Fr.) PR:A
BATTLE OF THE RIVER PLATE, THE (SEE:PURSUIT OF THE GRAF SPEE)
__BATTLE OF THE SEXES, THE *** (1960, Brit.) PR:A__
BATTLE OF THE VILLA FIORITA, THE * (1965, Brit.) PR:A
BATTLE OF THE V1 (SEE:MISSILES FROM HELL)
__BATTLE OF THE WORLDS ** (1961, It.) PR:A__
BATTLE STATIONS * (1956) PR:A
BATTLE STRIPE (SEE:MEN, THE)
__BATTLE TAXI * (1955) PR:A__
BATTLE ZONE ** (1952) PR:A
BATTLEAXE, THE ** (1962, Brit.) PR:A
BATTLEGROUND **** (1949) PR:A
BATTLES OF CHIEF PONTIAC * (1952) PR:A
__BATTLESTAR GALACTICA * (1979) PR:A__
__BATTLETRUCK **½ (1982) PR:C__
BATTLING BELLHOP, THE (SEE:KID GALAHAD)
BATTLING BUCKAROO * (1932) PR:A
__BATTLING MARSHAL * (1950) PR:A__
__BAWDY ADVENTURES OF TOM JONES, THE **½ (1976, Brit.) PR:O__
BAXTER ** (1973, Brit.) PR:C
__BAY BOY **½ (1984, Can.) PR:C__
BAY OF ANGELS **½ (1964, Fr.) PR:C
BAY OF SAINT MICHEL, THE ** (1963, Brit.) PR:A
BAYAN KO ***½ (1985, Phil./Fr.) PR:O
BAYOU *½ (1957) PR:A
BE MINE TONIGHT ** (1933, Brit.) PR:A
BE MY GUEST *½ (1965, Brit.) PR:A
BE MY VALENTINE, OR ELSE... (SEE:HOSPITAL MASSACRE)
BE YOURSELF ** (1930) PR:A
BEACH BALL **½ (1965) PR:A
__BEACH BLANKET BINGO *** (1965) PR:A__
__BEACH GIRLS ** (1982) PR:C-O__
BEACH GIRLS AND THE MONSTER, THE * (1965) PR:C
BEACH HOUSE PARTY (SEE:WILD ON THE BEACH)
__BEACH PARTY ** (1963) PR:A__
BEACH RED ** (1967) PR:A
__BEACHCOMBER *** (1938, Brit.) PR:A__
BEACHCOMBER **½ (1955, Brit.) PR:A
BEACHES * (1988) PR:C
BEACHHEAD *** (1954) PR:C
BEADS OF ONE ROSARY, THE ** (1982, Pol.) PR:A
BEAR, THE ** (1963, Fr.) PR:AA
__BEAR, THE **½ (1984) PR:C__
__BEAR ISLAND *½ (1980, Brit./Can.) PR:C__
__BEARS AND I, THE ** (1974) PR:C__
__BEAST, THE ** (1975, Fr.) PR:O__
__BEAST, THE ***½ (1988) PR:O__
BEAST FROM THE HAUNTED CAVE *½ (1960) PR:C
__BEAST FROM 20,000 FATHOMS, THE ** (1953) PR:C__
__BEAST IN THE CELLAR, THE *½ (1971, Brit.) PR:C__
__BEAST MUST DIE, THE * (1974, Brit.) PR:A__
BEAST OF BABYLON AGAINST THE SON OF HERCULES (SEE:HERO OF BABYLON)
BEAST OF BLOOD *½ (1970, US/Phil.) PR:C-O
BEAST OF BUDAPEST, THE *½ (1958) PR:C
BEAST OF HOLLOW MOUNTAIN, THE ** (1956) PR:A
BEAST OF MOROCCO (SEE:HAND OF NIGHT, THE)
BEAST OF THE CITY, THE *** (1932) PR:C-O
BEAST OF THE DEAD (SEE:BEAST OF BLOOD)
BEAST OF YUCCA FLATS, THE *½ (1961) PR:C
__BEAST WITH A MILLION EYES, THE zero (1956) PR:A__
__BEAST WITH FIVE FINGERS, THE *** (1946) PR:C__
__BEAST WITHIN, THE * (1982) PR:O__
__BEASTMASTER, THE *½ (1982) PR:C__
BEASTS OF BERLIN *½ (1939) PR:C
BEASTS OF MARSEILLES, THE ** (1959, Brit.) PR:C
__BEAT, THE *½ (1988) PR:C-O__
BEAT GENERATION, THE * (1959) PR:C
"BEAT" GIRL (SEE:WILD FOR KICKS, Brit.)
__BEAT STREET **½ (1984) PR:A-C__
BEAT THE BAND * (1947) PR:A
__BEAT THE DEVIL **** (1953) PR:A__
BEATNIKS, THE * (1960) PR:O
__BEATRICE *** (1988, Fr./It.) PR:O__
BEAU BANDIT * (1930) PR:A
BEAU BRUMMELL *** (1954) PR:A
__BEAU GESTE ***** (1939) PR:A__
__BEAU GESTE *** (1966) PR:A__
BEAU IDEAL *½ (1931) PR:A
BEAU JAMES **½ (1957) PR:A
__BEAU PERE * (1981, Fr.) PR:O__
BEAUTIFUL ADVENTURE * (1932, Ger.) PR:A
__BEAUTIFUL BLONDE FROM BASHFUL BEND, THE *** (1949) PR:A__
BEAUTIFUL BUT BROKE *½ (1944) PR:A
BEAUTIFUL BUT DEADLY (SEE:DON IS DEAD, THE)
BEAUTIFUL CHEAT, THE *½ (1946) PR:A
BEAUTIFUL PRISONER, THE * (1983, Fr.) PR:C
BEAUTIFUL STRANGER ** (1954, Brit.) PR:C
BEAUTIFUL SWINDLERS, THE ** (1967, Fr./It./Jap./Neth.) PR:O
BEAUTY AND THE BANDIT * (1946) PR:A
BEAUTY AND THE BARGE *½ (1937, Brit.) PR:A
__BEAUTY AND THE BEAST ***** (1947, Fr.) PR:A__
__BEAUTY AND THE BEAST zero (1963) PR:C__
BEAUTY AND THE BOSS * (1932) PR:A
BEAUTY AND THE DEVIL **½ (1952, Fr./It.) PR:A
BEAUTY FOR SALE *½ (1933) PR:A
BEAUTY FOR THE ASKING * (1939) PR:A
BEAUTY JUNGLE, THE ** (1966, Brit.) PR:C
BEAUTY ON PARADE *½ (1950) PR:A
BEAUTY PARLOR * (1932) PR:A
BEBO'S GIRL **½ (1964, It.) PR:A
BECAUSE I LOVED YOU * (1930, Ger.) PR:C
BECAUSE OF EVE *½ (1948) PR:C-O
BECAUSE OF HIM **½ (1946) PR:A
BECAUSE OF YOU *½ (1952) PR:A
BECAUSE YOU'RE MINE *½ (1952) PR:AA
__BECKET **** (1964, Brit.) PR:C__
__BECKY SHARP ** (1935) PR:C__
BECAUSE THEY'RE YOUNG ** (1960) PR:C
BED AND BOARD ** (1971, Fr.) PR:C
BED AND BREAKFAST * (1930, Brit.) PR:A
BED AND BREAKFAST * (1936, Brit.) PR:A
BED OF ROSES *½ (1933) PR:A
BED SITTING ROOM, THE ***½ (1969, Brit.) PR:C
__BEDAZZLED ***½ (1967, Brit.) PR:C__
BEDELIA ** (1946, Brit.) PR:A
BEDEVILLED ** (1955) PR:C
__BEDFORD INCIDENT, THE ***½ (1965, Brit.) PR:C__
__BEDKNOBS AND BROOMSTICKS ***½ (1971) PR:AA__
__BEDLAM *** (1946) PR:C__
__BEDROOM EYES *½ (1984, Can.) PR:O__
__BEDROOM WINDOW, THE *** (1987) PR:O__
BEDSIDE * (1934) PR:A
BEDSIDE MANNER ** (1945) PR:A
__BEDTIME FOR BONZO **½ (1951) PR:AA__
BEDTIME STORY, A ** (1933) PR:AA
BEDTIME STORY *** (1942) PR:A
BEDTIME STORY **½ (1964) PR:C
BEDTIME STORY * (1938, Brit.) PR:AA
BEEN DOWN SO LONG IT LOOKS LIKE UP TO ME * (1977) PR:A
__BEER *½ (1986) PR:O__
__BEES, THE * (1978) PR:C__
BEES IN PARADISE ** (1944, Brit.) PR:A
__BEETLEJUICE ***½ (1988) PR:C__
BEFORE AND AFTER zero (1985) PR:C
__BEFORE DAWN **½ (1933) PR:A__
BEFORE HIM ALL ROME TREMBLED *½ (1947, It.) PR:A
__BEFORE I HANG ** (1940) PR:A__
BEFORE I WAKE (SEE:SHADOW OF FEAR)
BEFORE MIDNIGHT * (1934) PR:A
BEFORE MORNING * (1933) PR:A
BEFORE THE REVOLUTION *½ (1964, It.) PR:C
BEFORE WINTER COMES ** (1969, Brit.) PR:C
BEG, BORROW OR STEAL * (1937) PR:A
BEGGAR STUDENT, THE * (1931, Brit.) PR:A
BEGGAR STUDENT, THE * (1958, Ger.) PR:A
BEGGARS IN ERMINE ** (1934) PR:A
BEGGARS OF LIFE **** (1928) PR:A-C
BEGGAR'S OPERA, THE *** (1953) PR:C
__BEGINNER'S LUCK ** (1986) PR:O__
BEGINNING OF THE END *½ (1957) PR:C
BEGINNING OR THE END, THE *** (1947) PR:A
__BEGUILED, THE ** (1971) PR:O__
__BEHAVE YOURSELF **½ (1951) PR:C__

Finding entries in **THE MOTION PICTURE GUIDE ™**

Years 1929-83	Volumes I-IX
1984	Volume IX
1985	1986 ANNUAL
1986	1987 ANNUAL
1987	1988 ANNUAL
1988	1989 ANNUAL

STAR RATINGS

★★★★★	Masterpiece
★★★★	Excellent
★★★	Good
★★	Fair
★	Poor
zero	Without Merit

PARENTAL RECOMMENDATION (PR:)

AA	Good for Children
A	Acceptable for Children
C	Cautionary, some objectionable scenes
O	Objectionable for Children

BOLD: Films on Videocassette

BEHEMOTH, THE SEA MONSTER *
  (1959, Brit.) PR:A
BEHIND CITY LIGHTS ** (1945) PR:A
BEHIND CLOSED SHUTTERS ** (1952, It.) PR:O
BEHIND GREEN LIGHTS ** (1935) PR:A
BEHIND GREEN LIGHTS ** (1946) PR:A
BEHIND JURY DOORS * (1933, Brit.) PR:A
BEHIND LOCKED DOORS ** (1948) PR:A
BEHIND LOCKED DOORS zero
  (1976, South Africa) PR:O
BEHIND OFFICE DOORS ** (1931) PR:A
BEHIND PRISON GATES ** (1939) PR:A
BEHIND PRISON WALLS ** (1943) PR:A
BEHIND STONE WALLS * (1932) PR:A
BEHIND THAT CURTAIN *** (1929) PR:C
BEHIND THE DOOR
  (SEE:MAN WITH NINE LIVES, THE)
BEHIND THE EIGHT BALL **½ (1942) PR:A
BEHIND THE EVIDENCE * (1935) PR:A
BEHIND THE HEADLINES ** (1937) PR:A
BEHIND THE HEADLINES *½ (1956, Brit.) PR:A
BEHIND THE HIGH WALL *½ (1956) PR:C
BEHIND THE IRON CURTAIN
  (SEE:IRON CURTAIN, THE)
BEHIND THE IRON MASK *½ (1977) PR:C
BEHIND THE MAKEUP ** (1930) PR:C
BEHIND THE MASK ** (1932) PR:C
BEHIND THE MASK * (1946) PR:A
BEHIND THE MASK **½ (1958, Brit.) PR:C
BEHIND THE MIKE *½ (1937) PR:A
BEHIND THE NEWS * (1941) PR:A
BEHIND THE RISING SUN *** (1943) PR:C
BEHIND YOUR BACK ** (1937, Brit.) PR:A
BEHOLD A PALE HORSE ***½ (1964) PR:C
BEHOLD MY WIFE * (1935) PR:C
BEING, THE *½ (1983) PR:C
BEING THERE ***** (1979) PR:C
BELA LUGOSI MEETS A BROOKLYN GORILLA *
  (1952) PR:A
BELIEVE IN ME *** (1971) PR:O
BELIEVERS, THE zero (1987) PR:O
BELIZAIRE THE CAJUN *** (1986) PR:C
BELL' ANTONIO ** (1962, It.) PR:C-O
BELL, BOOK AND CANDLE *** (1958) PR:A
BELL-BOTTOM GEORGE *½ (1943, Brit.) PR:A
BELL DIAMOND *** (1987) PR:C
BELL FOR ADANO, A ***½ (1945) PR:A
BELL JAR, THE *½ (1979) PR:O
BELLA DONNA *½ (1934, Brit.) PR:A
BELLA DONNA * (1983, Ger.) PR:C
BELLAMY TRIAL, THE ** (1929) PR:C
BELLBOY, THE ** (1960) PR:AA
BELLE DE JOUR ***½ (1968, Fr.) PR:O
BELLE LE GRAND *½ (1951) PR:A
BELLE OF NEW YORK, THE ** (1952) PR:A
BELLE OF OLD MEXICO * (1950) PR:A
BELLE OF THE NINETIES **½ (1934) PR:A
BELLE OF THE YUKON *½ (1944) PR:A
BELLE STARR *** (1941) PR:A
BELLE STARR'S DAUGHTER * (1947) PR:A
BELLES OF ST. CLEMENTS, THE **
  (1936, Brit.) PR:A
BELLES OF ST. TRINIAN'S, THE ***
  (1954, Brit.) PR:AA
BELLES ON THEIR TOES **½ (1952) PR:AA
BELLISSIMA *** (1952, It.) PR:C
BELLMAN, THE **½ (1947, Fr.) PR:C
BELLS, THE ** (1931, Brit.) PR:C
BELLS ARE RINGING ***½ (1960) PR:AA
BELLS zero (1981, Can.) PR:O
BELLS GO DOWN, THE **½ (1943, Brit.) PR:A
BELLS OF CAPISTRANO *½ (1942) PR:A
BELLS OF CORONADO ** (1950) PR:AA
BELLS OF ROSARITA *** (1945) PR:AA
BELLS OF ST. MARY'S, THE **** (1945) PR:AA
BELLS OF SAN ANGELO *** (1947) PR:A
BELLS OF SAN FERNANDO * (1947) PR:A
BELLY OF AN ARCHITECT, THE ***
  (1987, Brit./It.) PR:O
BELOVED ** (1934) PR:A
BELOVED BACHELOR, THE ** (1931) PR:A
BELOVED BRAT ** (1938) PR:A
BELOVED ENEMY *** (1936) PR:C
BELOVED IMPOSTER * (1936, Brit.) PR:A
BELOVED INFIDEL * (1959) PR:A
BELOVED VAGABOND, THE *½ (1936, Brit.) PR:A
BELOW THE BELT **½ (1980) PR:C
BELOW THE BORDER ** (1942) PR:A
BELOW THE DEADLINE *½ (1936) PR:A
BELOW THE DEADLINE ** (1946) PR:A
BELOW THE SEA ** (1933) PR:A
BELSTONE FOX, THE *** (1976, Brit.) PR:AA
BEN **½ (1972) PR:A
BEN HUR ***** (1959) PR:A
BEND OF THE RIVER ** (1952) PR:C
BENEATH THE PLANET OF THE APES **
  (1970) PR:AA
BENEATH THE 12-MILE REEF ** (1953) PR:A

BENEATH WESTERN SKIES * (1944) PR:A
BENGAL BRIGADE * (1954) PR:A
BENGAL TIGER ** (1936) PR:A
BENGAZI ** (1955) PR:A-C
BENJAMIN ^**½ (1968, Fr.) PR:O
BENJAMIN *** (1973, Ger.) PR:AA
BENJI ***½ (1974) PR:AA
BENJI THE HUNTED *** (1987) PR:AA
BENNY GOODMAN STORY, THE **½ (1956) PR:AA
BENSON MURDER CASE, THE ** (1930) PR:A
BENVENUTA ** (1983, Fr.) PR:C
BEQUEST TO THE NATION
  (SEE:NELSON AFFAIR, THE)
BERKELEY SQUARE *** (1933) PR:A
BERLIN AFFAIR, THE ** (1985, Ger./It.) PR:O
BERLIN ALEXANDERPLATZ * (1933, Ger.) PR:A
BERLIN CORRESPONDENT **½ (1942) PR:A
BERLIN EXPRESS **½ (1948) PR:C
BERMONDSEY KID, THE *½ (1933, Brit.) PR:A
BERMUDA AFFAIR * (1956, Brit.) PR:A
BERMUDA MYSTERY * (1944) PR:A
BERNADETTE OF LOURDES **½ (1962, Fr.) PR:A
BERNARDINE *½ (1957) PR:AA
BERSERK ** (1967) PR:O
BERSERKER zero (1988) PR:O
BEST DEFENSE zero (1984) PR:O
BEST FOOT FORWARD *** (1943) PR:A
BEST FRIENDS ** (1982) PR:A
BEST FRIENDS zero (1975) PR:O
BEST HOUSE IN LONDON, THE **½
  (1969, Brit.) PR:A
BEST LITTLE WHOREHOUSE IN TEXAS, THE *
  (1982) PR:O
BEST MAN, THE ***½ (1964) PR:C
BEST MAN WINS ** (1948) PR:AA
BEST OF ENEMIES * (1933) PR:A
BEST OF ENEMIES, THE *** (1962) PR:A
BEST OF EVERYTHING, THE * (1959) PR:C-O
BEST OF THE BADMEN *** (1951) PR:A
BEST OF TIMES, THE *½ (1986) PR:O
BEST SELLER ***½ (1987) PR:C
BEST THINGS IN LIFE ARE FREE, THE ***½
  (1956) PR:AA
BEST WAY, THE ** (1978, Fr.) PR:C
BEST YEARS OF OUR LIVES, THE *****
  (1946) PR:A
BETRAYAL *½ (1932, Brit.) PR:A
BETRAYAL **½ (1939, Fr.) PR:A
BETRAYAL, THE * (1948) PR:A
BETRAYAL, THE *½ (1958, Brit.) PR:A
BETRAYAL ***½ (1983, Brit.) PR:O
BETRAYAL, THE
  (SEE:KAMILLA)
BETRAYAL FROM THE EAST ** (1945) PR:AA
BETRAYAL: THE STORY OF KAMILLA
  (SEE:KAMILLA)
BETRAYED *** (1954) PR:C
BETRAYED **½ (1988) PR:O
BETRAYED WOMEN *½ (1955) PR:C
BETSY, THE * (1978) PR:O
BETTER A WIDOW * (1969, It.) PR:O
BETTER LATE THAN NEVER ** (1983) PR:C
BETTER OFF DEAD **½ (1985) PR:C
BETTER TOMORROW, A ***½
  (1987, Hong Kong) PR:O
BETTY BLUE **** (1986, Fr.) PR:O
BETTY CO-ED * (1946) PR:A
BETWEEN FIGHTING MEN * (1932) PR:A
BETWEEN HEAVEN AND HELL **½ (1956) PR:A
BETWEEN MEN ** (1935) PR:A
BETWEEN MIDNIGHT AND DAWN ** (1950) PR:C
BETWEEN THE LINES *** (1977) PR:C
BETWEEN TIME AND ETERNITY *½
  (1960, Ger.) PR:A
BETWEEN TWO WOMEN * (1937) PR:C
BETWEEN TWO WOMEN ** (1944) PR:A
BETWEEN TWO WORLDS **½ (1944) PR:A
BETWEEN US GIRLS * (1942) PR:C
BEVERLY HILLS COP *** (1984) PR:O
BEVERLY HILLS COP II * (1987) PR:O
BEWARE * (1946) PR:A
BEWARE, MY LOVELY *½ (1952) PR:C
BEWARE OF BLONDIE ** (1950) PR:AA
BEWARE OF CHILDREN * (1961, Brit.) PR:A
BEWARE OF LADIES ** (1937) PR:A
BEWARE OF PITY *** (1946, Brit.) PR:A
BEWARE SPOOKS ** (1939) PR:A
BEWARE! THE BLOB ** (1972) PR:A
BEWITCHED *** (1945) PR:C
BEYOND A REASONABLE DOUBT ** (1956) PR:C
BEYOND AND BACK * (1978) PR:A
BEYOND ATLANTIS zero (1973, Phil.) PR:O
BEYOND EVIL *½ (1980) PR:A
BEYOND FEAR *½ (1977, Fr.) PR:C
BEYOND GLORY **½ (1948) PR:A
BEYOND GOOD AND EVIL *
  (1984, It./Fr./Ger.) PR:O
BEYOND MOMBASA ** (1957) PR:A-C

BEYOND REASONABLE DOUBT **
  (1980, New Zealand) PR:C
BEYOND THE BLUE HORIZON ** (1942) PR:A
BEYOND THE CITIES * (1930, Brit.) PR:A
BEYOND THE CURTAIN *½ (1960, Brit.) PR:A
BEYOND THE DOOR zero (1975, It./US) PR:O
BEYOND THE DOOR II zero (1979, It.) PR:O
BEYOND THE FOG zero (1981, Brit.) PR:O
BEYOND THE FOREST * (1949) PR:C
BEYOND THE LAST FRONTIER ** (1943) PR:A
BEYOND THE LAW ** (1934) PR:A
BEYOND THE LAW *½ (1967, It.) PR:C
BEYOND THE LAW ** (1968) PR:C
BEYOND THE LIMIT *½ (1983) PR:C
BEYOND THE LIVING
  (SEE:NURSE SHERRI)
BEYOND THE PECOS ** (1945) PR:A
BEYOND THE POSEIDON ADVENTURE *
  (1979) PR:A-C
BEYOND THE PURPLE HILLS *½ (1950) PR:A
BEYOND THE REEF zero (1981) PR:C
BEYOND THE RIO GRANDE * (1930) PR:A
BEYOND THE ROCKIES *** (1932) PR:A
BEYOND THE SACRAMENTO *** (1941) PR:A
BEYOND THE TIME BARRIER * (1960) PR:C
BEYOND THE WALLS ***½ (1985, Israel) PR:O
BEYOND THERAPY * (1987) PR:O
BEYOND THIS PLACE
  (SEE:WEB OF EVIDENCE)
BEYOND TOMORROW ** (1940) PR:A
BEYOND VICTORY ** (1931) PR:C
BHOWANI JUNCTION ** (1956) PR:C
BIBLE...IN THE BEGINNING, THE ***
  (1966) PR:AA
BICYCLE THIEF, THE ***** (1949, It.) PR:A-C
BIDDY * (1983, Brit.) PR:A
BIG ***½ (1988) PR:A-C
BIG AND THE BAD, THE ** (1971, It./Fr./Sp.) PR:C
BIG BAD MAMA zero (1974) PR:O
BIG BEAT, THE ** (1958) PR:A
BIG BIRD CAGE, THE zero (1972) PR:O
BIG BLOCKADE, THE *½ (1942, Brit.) PR:A
BIG BLUE, THE *½ (1988, Fr.) PR:A
BIG BLUFF, THE * (1933) PR:A
BIG BLUFF, THE *½ (1955) PR:C
BIG BONANZA, THE ** (1944) PR:A
BIG BOODLE, THE ** (1957) PR:C
BIG BOSS, THE *** (1941) PR:A
BIG BOUNCE, THE zero (1969) PR:O
BIG BOY ** (1930) PR:A
BIG BRAIN, THE ** (1933) PR:A
BIG BRAWL, THE **½ (1980) PR:C
BIG BROADCAST, THE ** (1932) PR:AA
BIG BROADCAST OF 1936, THE **½ (1935) PR:AA
BIG BROADCAST OF 1937, THE ** (1936) PR:AA
BIG BROADCAST OF 1938, THE *** (1937) PR:AA
BIG BROWN EYES **½ (1936) PR:A
BIG BUS, THE **½ (1976) PR:A
BIG BUSINESS * (1930, Brit.) PR:A
BIG BUSINESS * (1934, Brit.) PR:A
BIG BUSINESS * (1937) PR:A
BIG BUSINESS ** (1988) PR:C
BIG BUSINESS GIRL *½ (1931) PR:A
BIG CAGE, THE ** (1933) PR:A
BIG CAPER, THE *½ (1957) PR:C
BIG CARNIVAL, THE ***½ (1951) PR:O
BIG CAT, THE *½ (1949) PR:C
BIG CATCH, THE * (1968, Brit.) PR:A
BIG CHANCE, THE * (1933) PR:A
BIG CHANCE, THE * (1957, Brit.) PR:A
BIG CHASE, THE ** (1954) PR:A
BIG CHIEF, THE **½ (1960, Fr.) PR:A-A
BIG CHILL, THE *** (1983) PR:C
BIG CIRCUS, THE **½ (1959) PR:A
BIG CITY **½ (1937) PR:A
BIG CITY **½ (1948) PR:AA
BIG CITY BLUES *** (1932) PR:C
BIG CITY, THE ** (1963, India) PR:A
BIG CLOCK, THE **** (1948) PR:C
BIG COMBO, THE *** (1955) PR:O
BIG COUNTRY, THE ***½ (1958) PR:A
BIG CUBE, THE ** (1969) PR:O
BIG DADDY * (1969) PR:O
BIG DAY, THE ** (1960, Brit.) PR:A
BIG DEAL ON MADONNA STREET, THE ***
  (1960) PR:A
BIG DOLL HOUSE, THE * (1971) PR:O
BIG EASY, THE *** (1987) PR:O
BIG EXECUTIVE ** (1933) PR:A
BIG FELLA ** (1937, Brit.) PR:A
BIG FISHERMAN, THE ** (1959) PR:A-C
BIG FIX, THE **½ (1978) PR:C
BIG FIX, THE *½ (1947) PR:A
BIG FOOT * (1973) PR:O
BIG FRAME, THE * (1953, Brit.) PR:A
BIG GAMBLE, THE * (1931) PR:A
BIG GAMBLE, THE ** (1961) PR:A
BIG GAME, THE ** (1936) PR:A

BIG GAME, THE
(SEE:FLESH AND THE WOMAN)
BIG GAME, THE * (1972) PR:C
BIG GUNDOWN, THE ** (1968, It.) PR:A
BIG GUNS
(SEE:NO WAY OUT)
BIG GUSHER, THE *½ (1951) PR:A
BIG GUY, THE *** (1939) PR:A
BIG HAND FOR THE LITTLE LADY, A ***
(1966) PR:A
BIG HANGOVER, THE ** (1950) PR:A-C
BIG HEART, THE
(SEE:MIRACLE ON 34TH STREET)
BIG HEARTED HERBERT *** (1934) PR:A
BIG HEAT, THE ** (1953) PR:C**
BIG HOUSE, THE ***½ (1930) PR:C
BIG HOUSE, U.S.A. *** (1955) PR:O
BIG JACK *½ (1949) PR:C
BIG JAKE ** (1971) PR:O
BIG JIM McLAIN ** (1952) PR:C
BIG JOB, THE *** (1965, Brit.) PR:A
BIG KNIFE, THE **** (1955) PR:O
BIG LAND, THE ** (1957) PR:A
BIG LEAGUER *½ (1953) PR:A
BIG LIFT, THE * (1950) PR:A-C**
BIG MEAT EATER **½ (1984, Can.) PR:O
BIG MONEY ** (1930) PR:A
BIG MONEY, THE ** (1962, Brit.) PR:A
BIG MOUTH, THE ** (1967) PR:AA
BIG NEWS ** (1929) PR:A
BIG NIGHT, THE * (1951) PR:C
BIG NIGHT, THE ** (1960) PR:C
BIG NOISE, THE ** (1936) PR:A
BIG NOISE, THE * (1936, Brit.) PR:A
BIG NOISE, THE **½ (1944) PR:AA
BIG OPERATOR, THE **½ (1959) PR:O
BIG PARADE, THE *** (1987, Chi.) PR:A-C
BIG PARTY, THE ** (1930) PR:A
BIG PAYOFF, THE ** (1933) PR:A
BIG POND, THE **½ (1930) PR:A
BIG PUNCH, THE ** (1948) PR:A
BIG RACE, THE ** (1934) PR:AA
BIG RED *½ (1962) PR:AA
BIG RED ONE, THE * (1980) PR:C**
BIG SCORE, THE * (1983) PR:C
BIG SEARCH, THE
(SEE:EAST OF KILIMANJARO)
BIG SHAKEDOWN, THE *½ (1934) PR:A
BIG SHOT, THE * (1931) PR:A
BIG SHOT, THE ** (1937) PR:A
BIG SHOT, THE **½ (1942) PR:A
BIG SHOTS * (1987) PR:C**
BIG SHOW, THE * (1937) PR:A**
BIG SHOW, THE *½ (1961) PR:A
BIG SHOW-OFF, THE ** (1945) PR:C
BIG SKY, THE ***½ (1952) PR:A
BIG SLEEP, THE *** (1946) PR:C**
BIG SLEEP, THE *½ (1978, Brit.) PR:C
BIG SOMBRERO, THE *½ (1949) PR:A
BIG SPLASH, THE * (1935, Brit.) PR:A
BIG STAMPEDE, THE ** (1932) PR:A
BIG STEAL, THE * (1949) PR:C**
BIG STORE, THE **½ (1941) PR:AA
BIG STREET, THE **½ (1942) PR:A
BIG SWITCH, THE * (1950, Brit.) PR:O
BIG TIMBER *½ (1950) PR:A-C
BIG TIME ** (1929) PR:A
BIG TIME OR BUST ** (1934) PR:A
BIG TIP OFF, THE *½ (1955) PR:C
BIG TOP PEE-WEE **½ (1988) PR:A
BIG TOWN ** (1932) PR:C
BIG TOWN * (1947) PR:AA
BIG TOWN, THE ** (1987) PR:O
BIG TOWN AFTER DARK ** (1947) PR:AA
BIG TOWN CZAR * (1939) PR:C
BIG TOWN GIRL **½ (1937) PR:A
BIG TOWN SCANDAL ** (1948) PR:AA
BIG TRAIL, THE * (1930) PR:A**
BIG TREES, THE * (1952) PR:A-C
BIG TROUBLE **½ (1986) PR:C
BIG TROUBLE IN LITTLE CHINA ***
(1986) PR:C-O
BIG WEDNESDAY *½ (1978) PR:A-C
BIG WHEEL, THE ** (1949) PR:A-C
BIGAMIST, THE * (1953) PR:C
BIGGER SPLASH, A ** (1984) PR:O
BIGGER THAN LIFE ** (1956) PR:C
BIGGEST BUNDLE OF THEM ALL, THE **
(1968) PR:A
BIKINI BEACH ** (1964) PR:A
BIKINI SHOP, THE
(SEE:MALIBU BIKINI SHOP)
BILL AND COO ** (1947) PR:AA
BILL CRACKS DOWN * (1937) PR:A
BILL OF DIVORCEMENT, A **** (1932) PR:A-C
BILL OF DIVORCEMENT **½ (1940) PR:C
BILLIE ** (1965) PR:A
BILLION DOLLAR BRAIN * (1967, Brit.) PR:C
BILLION DOLLAR HOBO, THE * (1977) PR:A
BILLION DOLLAR SCANDAL * (1932) PR:A
BILL'S LEGACY *½ (1931, Brit.) PR:A
BILLY BUDD **½ (1962) PR:C
BILLY IN THE LOWLANDS * (1979) PR:A-C
BILLY JACK * (1971) PR:O
BILLY JACK GOES TO WASHINGTON **
(1977) PR:C
BILLY LIAR ***½ (1963, Brit.) PR:A-C
BILLY ROSE'S DIAMOND HORSESHOE
(SEE:DIAMOND HORSESHOE)
BILLY ROSE'S JUMBO
(SEE:JUMBO)
BILLY THE KID ** (1930) PR:A
BILLY THE KID **½ (1941) PR:A
BILLY THE KID IN SANTA FE * (1941) PR:A
BILLY THE KID RETURNS * (1938) PR:A**
BILLY THE KID TRAPPED ** (1942) PR:A
BILLY THE KID VS. DRACULA ** (1966) PR:A
BILLY THE KID WANTED ** (1941) PR:A
BILLY THE KID'S FIGHTING PALS * (1941) PR:A
BILLY THE KID'S RANGE WAR * (1941) PR:A
BILLY THE KID'S ROUNDUP ** (1941) PR:A
BILLY TWO HATS **½ (1973, Brit.) PR:O
BILOXI BLUES ***½ (1988) PR:C-O
BIMBO THE GREAT * (1961, Ger.) PR:A
BINGO BONGO **½ (1983, It.) PR:AA
BINGO LONG TRAVELING ALL-STARS AND MOTOR
KINGS, THE **½ (1976) PR:A-C
BIOGRAPHY OF A BACHELOR GIRL **½
(1935) PR:A
BIONIC BOY, THE * (1977, Hong Kong/Phil.) PR:O
BIQUEFARRE ** (1983, Fr.) PR:A
BIRCH INTERVAL * (1976) PR:A**
BIRD ** (1988) PR:C-O**
BIRD OF PARADISE **½ (1932) PR:C
BIRD OF PARADISE *½ (1951) PR:C
BIRD WATCH, THE *½ (1983, Fr.) PR:C
BIRD WITH THE CRYSTAL PLUMAGE, THE ****
(1970, It./Ger.) PR:C
BIRDMAN OF ALCATRAZ ** (1962) PR:C**
BIRDS, THE * (1963) PR:C**
BIRDS AND THE BEES, THE **½ (1965) PR:A
BIRDS COME TO DIE IN PERU ** (1968, Fr.) PR:C
BIRDS DO IT * (1966) PR:A
BIRDS OF A FEATHER * (1931, Brit.) PR:AA
BIRDS OF A FEATHER ** (1935, Brit.) PR:A
BIRDS OF PREY
(SEE:PERFECT ALIBI, THE)
BIRDS OF PREY * (1987, Can.) PR:C-O
BIRDS OF PREY ** (1988, Phil.) PR:C
BIRDS, THE BEES AND THE ITALIANS, THE **
(1967) PR:O
BIRDY ** (1984) PR:O**
BIRTH OF A BABY ** (1938) PR:C
BIRTH OF THE BLUES *** (1941) PR:A
BIRTHDAY PARTY, THE ** (1968, Brit.) PR:C
BIRTHDAY PRESENT, THE ** (1957, Brit.) PR:C
BISCUIT EATER, THE ** (1940) PR:AA
BISCUIT EATER, THE **½ (1972) PR:AA
BISHOP MISBEHAVES, THE ** (1933) PR:AA
BISHOP MURDER CASE, THE *** (1930) PR:A
BISHOP'S WIFE, THE * (1947) PR:A**
BITE THE BULLET * (1975) PR:C**
BITTER CREEK ** (1954) PR:A
BITTER HARVEST ** (1963, Brit.) PR:C
BITTER RICE *** (1950, It.) PR:O
BITTER SPRINGS ** (1950, Aus.) PR:A
BITTER SWEET **½ (1933, Brit.) PR:A
BITTER SWEET * (1940) PR:A**
BITTER TEA OF GENERAL YEN, THE ***
(1933) PR:C
BITTER TEARS OF PETRA VON KANT, THE **½
(1972, Ger.) PR:O
BITTER VICTORY **½ (1958, Fr.) PR:C
BITTERSWEET LOVE ** (1976) PR:C
BIZARRE BIZARRE ** (1939, Fr.) PR:A
BIZET'S CARMEN ** (1984, Fr./It.) PR:A-C**
BLACK ABBOT, THE * (1934, Brit.) PR:A
BLACK ACES ** (1937) PR:A
BLACK AND WHITE ** (1986, Fr.) PR:O
BLACK AND WHITE IN COLOR ***
(1976, Fr.) PR:C
BLACK ANGEL *** (1946) PR:A
BLACK ANGELS, THE zero (1970) PR:O
BLACK ARROW * (1948) PR:A**
BLACK BANDIT ** (1938) PR:A
BLACK BART **½ (1948) PR:C
BLACK BEAUTY ** (1933) PR:AA
BLACK BEAUTY **½ (1946) PR:AA
BLACK BEAUTY ** (1971, Brit./Ger./Sp.) PR:AA
BLACK BELLY OF THE TARANTULA, THE *
(1972, It.) PR:O
BLACK BELT JONES ** (1974) PR:O
BLACK BIRD, THE * (1975) PR:A-C**
BLACK BOOK, THE *½ (1949) PR:A
BLACK CAESAR **½ (1973) PR:O
BLACK CAMEL, THE **½ (1931) PR:A
BLACK CASTLE, THE ** (1952) PR:C
BLACK CAT, THE ***½ (1934) PR:C
BLACK CAT, THE ** (1941) PR:A
BLACK CAT, THE *½ (1966) PR:O
BLACK CAT, THE *½ (1984, It./Brit.) PR:O
BLACK CAULDRON, THE ***½ (1985) PR:A-C
BLACK CHRISTMAS * (1974, Can.) PR:O
BLACK COFFEE *½ (1931, Brit.) PR:A
BLACK DAKOTAS, THE ** (1954) PR:A-C
BLACK DEVILS OF KALI, THE
(SEE:MYSTERY OF THE BLACK JUNGLE)
BLACK DIAMONDS * (1932, Brit.) PR:A
BLACK DIAMONDS ** (1940) PR:A
BLACK DOLL, THE *½ (1938) PR:A
BLACK DRAGONS ** (1942) PR:A
BLACK EAGLE ** (1948) PR:A
BLACK EYE *½ (1974) PR:O
BLACK EYES ** (1939, Brit.) PR:A
BLACK FRIDAY ** (1940) PR:A
BLACK FURY ***½ (1935) PR:C
BLACK GESTAPO, THE * (1975) PR:O
BLACK GIRL ** (1972) PR:A
BLACK GLOVE * (1954, Brit.) PR:A
BLACK GOLD ** (1947) PR:A
BLACK GOLD *½ (1963) PR:A-C
BLACK GUNN * (1972) PR:O
BLACK HAND, THE * (1950) PR:C**
BLACK HAND GANG, THE * (1930, Brit.) PR:A
BLACK HILLS * (1948) PR:A
BLACK HILLS AMBUSH *½ (1952) PR:A-C
BLACK HILLS EXPRESS ** (1943) PR:A
BLACK HOLE, THE * (1979) PR:A-C**
BLACK HORSE CANYON ** (1954) PR:A
BLACK ICE, THE * (1957, Brit.) PR:A
BLACK JACK
(SEE:CAPTAIN BLACK JACK)
BLACK JACK * (1973) PR:C
BLACK JACK **½ (1979, Brit.) PR:AA
BLACK JOY **½ (1977, Brit.) PR:O
BLACK JOY **½ (1986, Brit.) PR:O
BLACK KING *½ (1932) PR:A
BLACK KLANSMAN, THE * (1966) PR:O
BLACK KNIGHT, THE **½ (1954) PR:A-C
BLACK LASH, THE *½ (1952) PR:A
BLACK LEGION, THE * (1937) PR:C**
BLACK LIKE ME ** (1964) PR:C
BLACK LIMELIGHT *½ (1938, Brit.) PR:A
BLACK MAGIC ** (1949) PR:C
BLACK MAMA, WHITE MAMA zero (1973) PR:O
BLACK MARBLE, THE **½ (1980) PR:C-O
BLACK MARKET BABIES *½ (1946) PR:A
BLACK MARKET RUSTLERS * (1943) PR:A
BLACK MASK * (1935, Brit.) PR:A
BLACK MEMORY * (1947, Brit.) PR:A
BLACK MIDNIGHT *½ (1949) PR:AA
BLACK MOON *½ (1934) PR:C
BLACK MOON **½ (1975, Fr.) PR:C
BLACK MOON RISING **½ (1986) PR:O
BLACK NARCISSUS * (1947, Brit.) PR:A-C**
BLACK OAK CONSPIRACY *½ (1977) PR:C
BLACK ORCHID *** (1959) PR:C
BLACK ORPHEUS * (1959, Fr./It./Braz.) PR:C**
BLACK PANTHER, THE *½ (1977, Brit.) PR:O
BLACK PARACHUTE, THE ** (1944) PR:A
BLACK PATCH * (1957) PR:C

Finding entries in **THE MOTION PICTURE GUIDE ™**

Years	Volume
1929-83	Volumes I-IX
1984	Volume IX
1985	1986 ANNUAL
1986	1987 ANNUAL
1987	1988 ANNUAL
1988	1989 ANNUAL

STAR RATINGS

★★★★★	Masterpiece
★★★★	Excellent
★★★	Good
★★	Fair
★	Poor
zero	Without Merit

PARENTAL RECOMMENDATION (PR:)

AA	Good for Children
A	Acceptable for Children
C	Cautionary, some objectionable scenes
O	Objectionable for Children

BOLD: Films on Videocassette

BLACK PIRATES, THE * (1954, Mex.) PR:C
BLACK PIT OF DOCTOR M * (1958, Mex.) PR:O
BLACK RAVEN, THE *½ (1943) PR:A
BLACK RIDER, THE * (1954, Brit.) PR:A
BLACK RODEO ** (1972) PR:C
BLACK ROOM, THE * (1935) PR:C**
BLACK ROOM, THE zero (1984) PR:O
BLACK ROSE, THE ** (1950) PR:A**
BLACK ROSES *½ (1936, Ger.) PR:A
BLACK SABBATH * (1963, It.) PR:O**
BLACK SAMSON ** (1974) PR:O
BLACK SCORPION, THE *½ (1957) PR:C
BLACK SHAMPOO zero (1976) PR:O
BLACK SHEEP ** (1935) PR:A
BLACK SHEEP OF WHITEHALL, THE *½ (1941, Brit.) PR:A
BLACK SHIELD OF FALWORTH, THE **½ (1954) PR:A-C
BLACK SIX, THE * (1974) PR:C
BLACK SLEEP, THE *½ (1956) PR:C
BLACK SPIDER, THE *½ (1983, Switz.) PR:O
BLACK SPURS ** (1965) PR:A
BLACK STALLION, THE ** (1979) PR:AA**
BLACK STALLION RETURNS, THE *½ (1983) PR:A-C
BLACK SUN, THE *½ (1979, Czech.) PR:A
BLACK SUNDAY *½ (1961, It.) PR:O
BLACK SUNDAY ***½ (1977) PR:C
BLACK SWAN, THE **** (1942) PR:A
BLACK TENT, THE ** (1956, Brit.) PR:A
BLACK 13 ** (1954, Brit.) PR:A
BLACK TIGHTS ** (1962, Fr.) PR:A**
BLACK TORMENT, THE ** (1965, Brit.) PR:A
BLACK TUESDAY ** (1955) PR:C
BLACK TULIP, THE *½ (1937, Brit.) PR:A
BLACK VEIL FOR LISA, A *½ (1969, It./Ger.) PR:C
BLACK WATCH, THE *** (1929) PR:C
BLACK WATERS ** (1929) PR:A
BLACK WHIP, THE ** (1956) PR:A
BLACK WIDOW *½ (1951, Brit.) PR:A
BLACK WIDOW *** (1954) PR:C
BLACK WIDOW **½ (1987) PR:O
BLACK WINDMILL, THE **½ (1974, Brit.) PR:C
BLACK ZOO *½ (1963) PR:C
BLACKBEARD THE PIRATE **½ (1952) PR:A-C
BLACKBEARD'S GHOST * (1968) PR:AA**
BLACKBOARD JUNGLE, THE **** (1955) PR:C
BLACKENSTEIN * (1973) PR:O
BLACKJACK KETCHUM, DESPERADO ** (1956) PR:A
BLACKMAIL * (1929, Brit.) PR:A**
BLACKMAIL **½ (1939) PR:A
BLACKMAIL *½ (1947) PR:A
BLACKMAILED *½ (1951, Brit.) PR:A
BLACKMAILER *½ (1936) PR:A
BLACKOUT **½ (1940, Brit.) PR:A
BLACKOUT *½ (1950, Brit.) PR:A
BLACKOUT *½ (1954, Brit.) PR:A-C
BLACKOUT ** (1978, Fr./Can.) PR:A-C
BLACKOUT * (1988) PR:O
BLACKWELL'S ISLAND **½ (1939) PR:A
BLACULA * (1972) PR:O**
BLADE ** (1973) PR:O
BLADE IN THE DARK, A *½ (1986, It.) PR:O
BLADE RUNNER ** (1982) PR:O**
BLADES OF THE MUSKETEERS *½ (1953) PR:A
BLAME IT ON RIO zero (1984) PR:O
BLAME IT ON THE NIGHT * (1984) PR:C
BLAME THE WOMAN *½ (1932, Brit.) PR:A
BLANCHE ** (1971, Fr.) PR:C
BLANCHE FURY **½ (1948, Brit.) PR:A-C
BLARNEY KISS *½ (1933, Brit.) PR:A
BLAST OF SILENCE **½ (1961) PR:C
BLAST-OFF
(SEE:THOSE FANTASTIC FLYING FOOLS)
BLASTFIGHTER *½ (1985, It.) PR:O
BLAZE O' GLORY **½ (1930) PR:A
BLAZE OF GLORY * (1963, Brit.) PR:A
BLAZE OF NOON ** (1947) PR:A-C
BLAZING BARRIERS * (1937) PR:A
BLAZING FOREST, THE ** (1952) PR:A-C
BLAZING FRONTIER *½ (1944) PR:A
BLAZING GUNS *½ (1943) PR:A
BLAZING SADDLES * (1974) PR:C-O**
BLAZING SIX SHOOTERS ** (1940) PR:A
BLAZING SIXES * (1937) PR:A
BLAZING SUN, THE ** (1950) PR:A
BLAZING TRAIL, THE *½ (1949) PR:A
BLEAK MOMENTS ** (1972, Brit.) PR:C
BLESS 'EM ALL * (1949, Brit.) PR:A
BLESS 'EM ALL
(SEE:ACT, THE)
BLESS THE BEASTS AND CHILDREN * (1971) PR:A-C**
BLESS THEIR LITTLE HEARTS *** (1984) PR:O
BLESSED EVENT ***½ (1932) PR:A-C
BLIND ADVENTURE * (1933) PR:A
BLIND ALIBI ** (1938) PR:A

BLIND ALLEY ***½ (1939) PR:C
BLIND ALLEY
(SEE:PERFECT STRANGERS)
BLIND CHANCE ***½ (1987, Pol.) PR:O
BLIND CORNER
(SEE:MAN IN THE DARK)
BLIND DATE * (1934) PR:A
BLIND DATE
(SEE:CHANCE MEETING)
BLIND DATE * (1984) PR:O
BLIND DATE ** (1987) PR:C
BLIND DEAD, THE ** (1972, Sp.) PR:O
BLIND DESIRE *½ (1948, Fr.) PR:A
BLIND DIRECTOR, THE *½ (1986, Ger.) PR:O
BLIND FOLLY * (1939, Brit.) PR:A
BLIND GODDESS, THE ** (1948, Brit.) PR:A
BLIND JUSTICE ** (1934, Brit.) PR:A
BLIND MAN'S BLUFF ** (1936, Brit.) PR:AA
BLIND MAN'S BLUFF * (1952, Brit.) PR:A
BLIND MAN'S BLUFF
(SEE:CAULDRON OF BLOOD)
BLIND SPOT * (1932, Brit.) PR:A
BLIND SPOT *½ (1958, Brit.) PR:A
BLIND TERROR
(SEE:SEE NO EVIL)
BLINDFOLD *½ (1966) PR:A
BLINDMAN * (1972, It.) PR:O
BLISS *½ (1985, Aus.) PR:O
BLISS OF MRS. BLOSSOM, THE ***½ (1968, Brit.) PR:C
BLITHE SPIRIT ***** (1945, Brit.) PR:A
BLOB, THE *½ (1958) PR:A-C
BLOB, THE * (1988) PR:O**
BLOCK BUSTERS zero (1944) PR:A
BLOCK NOTES-DIE UN REGISTA-APPUNTI
(SEE:INTERVISTA)
BLOCKADE ** (1928, Brit.) PR:A
BLOCKADE zero (1929) PR:A
BLOCKADE *** (1938) PR:A
BLOCKHEADS ***½ (1938) PR:AA
BLOCKHOUSE, THE ** (1974, Brit.) PR:A
BLOND CHEAT * (1938) PR:A
BLONDE ALIBI * (1946) PR:A
BLONDE BAIT * (1956, US/Brit.) PR:A
BLONDE BANDIT, THE *½ (1950) PR:A-C
BLONDE BLACKMAILER * (1955, Brit.) PR:A
BLONDE BOMBSHELL
(SEE:BOMBSHELL)
BLONDE COMET * (1941) PR:A
BLONDE CRAZY *** (1931) PR:A
BLONDE DYNAMITE *½ (1950) PR:A
BLONDE FEVER ** (1944) PR:A
BLONDE FOR A DAY * (1946) PR:A
BLONDE FROM BROOKLYN ** (1945) PR:A
BLONDE FROM PEKING, THE *½ (1968, Fr.) PR:A
BLONDE FROM SINGAPORE, THE *½ (1941) PR:A
BLONDE ICE * (1949) PR:C
BLONDE IN A WHITE CAR
(SEE:NUDE IN A WHITE CAR)
BLONDE INSPIRATION *½ (1941) PR:A
BLONDE NIGHTINGALE *½ (1931, Ger.) PR:A
BLONDE PICKUP *½ (1955) PR:A
BLONDE RANSOM ** (1945) PR:A
BLONDE SAVAGE * (1947) PR:A
BLONDE SINNER * (1956, Brit.) PR:C
BLONDE TROUBLE ** (1937) PR:A
BLONDE VENUS ** (1932) PR:C-O**
BLONDES AT WORK * (1938) PR:A
BLONDES FOR DANGER ** (1938, Brit.) PR:A
BLONDIE **½ (1938) PR:AA
BLONDIE BRINGS UP BABY *½ (1939) PR:AA
BLONDIE FOR VICTORY *½ (1942) PR:A
BLONDIE GOES LATIN ** (1941) PR:AA
BLONDIE GOES TO COLLEGE *½ (1942) PR:AA
BLONDIE HAS SERVANT TROUBLE *½ (1940) PR:AA
BLONDIE HITS THE JACKPOT *½ (1949) PR:AA
BLONDIE IN SOCIETY *½ (1941) PR:AA
BLONDIE IN THE DOUGH * (1947) PR:AA
BLONDIE JOHNSON *½ (1933) PR:A
BLONDIE KNOWS BEST *½ (1946) PR:AA
BLONDIE MEETS THE BOSS *½ (1939) PR:AA
BLONDIE OF THE FOLLIES **½ (1932) PR:A-C
BLONDIE ON A BUDGET *½ (1940) PR:AA
BLONDIE PLAYS CUPID ** (1940) PR:AA
BLONDIE TAKES A VACATION ** (1939) PR:AA
BLONDIE'S ANNIVERSARY ** (1947) PR:AA
BLONDIE'S BIG DEAL ** (1949) PR:AA
BLONDIE'S BIG MOMENT ** (1947) PR:AA
BLONDIE'S BLESSED EVENT ** (1942) PR:AA
BLONDIE'S HOLIDAY *½ (1947) PR:AA
BLONDIE'S HERO ** (1950) PR:AA
BLONDIE'S LUCKY DAY *½ (1946) PR:AA
BLONDIE'S REWARD *½ (1948) PR:AA
BLONDIE'S SECRET * (1948) PR:AA
BLOOD * (1974, Brit.) PR:C
BLOOD ALLEY *½ (1955) PR:A-C
BLOOD AND BLACK LACE ** (1965, It.) PR:O

BLOOD AND GUTS **½ (1978, Can.) PR:O
BLOOD AND LACE ** (1971) PR:O
BLOOD AND ROSES * (1961, Fr./It.) PR:C-O
BLOOD AND SAND ** (1941) PR:C**
BLOOD AND STEEL ** (1959) PR:A
BLOOD ARROW *½ (1958) PR:A-C
BLOOD BATH * (1966) PR:C
BLOOD BATH * (1976) PR:O
BLOOD BEACH *½ (1981) PR:C
BLOOD BEAST FROM OUTER SPACE **½ (1965, Brit.) PR:C
BLOOD BEAST TERROR, THE * (1967, Brit.) PR:C
BLOOD CREATURE
(SEE:TERROR IS A MAN)
BLOOD DEMON ** (1967, Ger.) PR:O
BLOOD DINER * (1987) PR:O
BLOOD DRINKERS, THE *½ (1966, US/Phil.) PR:O
BLOOD FEAST zero (1963) PR:O
BLOOD FEAST zero (1976, It.) PR:O
BLOOD FEUD * (1979, It.) PR:O
BLOOD FROM THE MUMMY'S TOMB ** (1972, Brit.) PR:O
BLOOD IN THE STREETS ** (1975, It./Fr.) PR:C
BLOOD LEGACY
(SEE:LEGACY OF BLOOD)
BLOOD MANIA zero (1971) PR:O
BLOOD MONEY ***½ (1933) PR:C
BLOOD MONEY zero (1974, US/Hong Kong/It./Sp.) PR:O
BLOOD OF A POET, THE * (1930, Fr.) PR:C**
BLOOD OF DRACULA *½ (1957) PR:O
BLOOD OF DRACULA'S CASTLE zero (1967) PR:O
BLOOD OF FRANKENSTEIN ** (1970) PR:O
BLOOD OF FU MANCHU, THE * (1968, Brit.) PR:O
BLOOD OF GHASTLY HORROR
(SEE:PSYCHO-A-GO-GO)
BLOOD OF THE VAMPIRE *½ (1958, Brit.) PR:O
BLOOD ON MY HANDS
(SEE:KISS THE BLOOD OFF MY HANDS)
BLOOD ON SATAN'S CLAW, THE ** (1970, Brit.) PR:O
BLOOD ON THE ARROW ** (1964) PR:C
BLOOD ON THE MOON
(SEE:COP)
BLOOD ON THE MOON * (1948) PR:A**
BLOOD ON THE SUN ***½ (1945) PR:O
BLOOD ORANGE * (1953, Brit.) PR:A
BLOOD ORGY OF THE SHE-DEVILS * (1973) PR:O
BLOOD RELATIVES * (1978, Fr./Can.) PR:O
BLOOD ROSE, THE ** (1970, Fr.) PR:O
BLOOD SIMPLE ** (1984) PR:O
BLOOD SISTERS zero (1987) PR:O
BLOOD SPATTERED BRIDE, THE * (1974, Sp.) PR:O
BLOOD SUCKERS
(SEE:DR. TERROR'S GALLERY OF HORRORS)
BLOOD, SWEAT AND FEAR * (1975, It.) PR:C-O
BLOOD TIDE * (1982) PR:O
BLOOD WATERS OF DOCTOR Z * (1982) PR:O
BLOOD WEDDING * (1981, Sp.) PR:A**
BLOODBATH AT THE HOUSE OF DEATH zero (1984, Brit.) PR:C-O
BLOODBROTHERS **½ (1978) PR:O
BLOODEATERS * (1980) PR:C
BLOODHOUNDS OF BROADWAY *** (1952) PR:A
BLOODLINE ** (1979) PR:O
BLOODLUST * (1959) PR:O
BLOODSPORT ** (1988) PR:O
BLOODSUCKERS
(SEE:INCENSE FOR THE DAMNED)
BLOODSUCKERS FROM OUTER SPACE * (1987) PR:O
BLOODSUCKING FREAKS zero (1982) PR:O
BLOODTHIRSTY BUTCHERS *½ (1970) PR:O
BLOODY BIRTHDAY * (1986) PR:O
BLOODY BROOD, THE zero (1959, Can.) PR:O
BLOODY KIDS *½ (1983, Brit.) PR:O
BLOODY MAMA zero (1970) PR:O
BLOODY PIT OF HORROR, THE zero (1965, It.) PR:O
BLOOMFIELD *½ (1971, Brit./Israel) PR:C
BLOSSOM TIME
(SEE:APRIL BLOSSOMS)
BLOSSOMS IN THE DUST **½ (1941) PR:A
BLOSSOMS ON BROADWAY ** (1937) PR:A
BLOW OUT zero (1981) PR:O
BLOW TO THE HEART ** (1983, It.) PR:O
BLOW-UP * (1966, Brit.) PR:O
BLOW YOUR OWN TRUMPET * (1958, Brit.) PR:A
BLOWING WILD ** (1953) PR:C
BLUE *½ (1968) PR:C
BLUE ANGEL, THE *** (1930, Ger.) PR:O**
BLUE ANGEL, THE **½ (1959) PR:O
BLUE BIRD, THE *½ (1976) PR:AA
BLUE BIRD, THE ** (1940) PR:AA
BLUE BLOOD *½ (1951) PR:AA
BLUE BLOOD * (1973, Brit.) PR:C
BLUE CANADIAN ROCKIES * (1952) PR:A

BLUE CITY *½ (1986) PR:O
BLUE COLLAR * (1978) PR:O**
BLUE COUNTRY, THE ** (1977, Fr.) PR:C-O
BLUE DAHLIA, THE **** (1946) PR:C
BLUE DANUBE * (1932, Brit.) PR:A
BLUE DEMON VERSUS THE INFERNAL BRAINS * (1967, Mex.) PR:O
BLUE DENIM *** (1959) PR:C-O
BLUE FIN **½ (1978, Aus.) PR:A
BLUE GARDENIA, THE *** (1953) PR:C
BLUE GRASS OF KENTUCKY **½ (1950) PR:AA
BLUE HAWAII ** (1961) PR:A
BLUE HEAVEN ** (1985) PR:O
BLUE IDOL, THE * (1931, Hung.) PR:A
BLUE IGUANA, THE * (1988) PR:O
BLUE JEAN COP
(SEE:SHAKEDOWN)
BLUE LAGOON, THE **½ (1949, Brit.) PR:A-C
BLUE LAGOON, THE * (1980) PR:O
BLUE LAMP, THE ***½ (1950, Brit.) PR:C
BLUE LIGHT, THE *½ (1932, Ger.) PR:A
BLUE MAX, THE * (1966) PR:C**
BLUE MONTANA SKIES *½ (1939) PR:AA
BLUE MURDER AT ST. TRINIAN'S **½ (1958, Brit.) PR:AA
BLUE PARROT, THE * (1953, Brit.) PR:A
BLUE PETER, THE
(SEE:NAVY HEROES)
BLUE SCAR * (1949, Brit.) PR:A
BLUE SIERRA ** (1946) PR:AA
BLUE SKIES **** (1946) PR:AA
BLUE SKIES AGAIN ** (1983) PR:A
BLUE SMOKE * (1935, Brit.) PR:A
BLUE SQUADRON, THE * (1934, Brit.) PR:A
BLUE STEEL *½ (1934) PR:A
BLUE SUNSHINE **½ (1978) PR:A
BLUE THUNDER * (1983) PR:C**
BLUE VEIL, THE ** (1947, Fr.) PR:A
BLUE VEIL, THE **½ (1951) PR:A
BLUE VELVET ** (1986) PR:O**
BLUE, WHITE, AND PERFECT **½ (1941) PR:A
BLUEBEARD **½ (1944) PR:A
BLUEBEARD
(SEE:LANDRU)
BLUEBEARD *½ (1972) PR:O
BLUEBEARD'S EIGHTH WIFE *½ (1938) PR:A-C
BLUEBEARD'S TEN HONEYMOONS *½ (1960, Brit.) PR:A-C
BLUEPRINT FOR MURDER, A ***½ (1953) PR:A-C
BLUEPRINT FOR ROBBERY *½ (1961) PR:A
BLUES BROTHERS, THE *½ (1980) PR:C-O
BLUES BUSTERS ** (1950) PR:A
BLUES FOR LOVERS ** (1966, Brit.) PR:A
BLUES IN THE NIGHT *** (1941) PR:A
BLUME IN LOVE ***½ (1973) PR:O
BMX BANDITS **½ (1983) PR:AA
BOARDWALK **½ (1979) PR:C-O
BOAT, THE ** (1982) PR:C-O**
BOAT FROM SHANGHAI * (1931, Brit.) PR:A
BOAT, THE
(SEE:DAS BOOT)
BOATNIKS, THE **½ (1970) PR:AA
BOB AND CAROL AND TED AND ALICE ***½ (1969) PR:O
BOB MATHIAS STORY, THE **½ (1954) PR:AA
BOB, SON OF BATTLE
(SEE:THUNDER IN THE VALLEY)
BOBBIE JO AND THE OUTLAW zero (1976) PR:C-O
BOBBIKINS ** (1959, Brit.) PR:A
BOBBY DEERFIELD ** (1977) PR:C
BOBBY WARE IS MISSING * (1955) PR:A
BOBO, THE ** (1967, Brit.) PR:A-C
BOB'S YOUR UNCLE * (1941, Brit.) PR:A
BOCCACCIO ** (1936, Ger.) PR:A
BOCCACCIO '70 * (1962, Fr./It.) PR:O
BODY AND SOUL *** (1931) PR:A
BODY AND SOUL *** (1947) PR:C**
BODY AND SOUL zero (1981) PR:C
BODY DISAPPEARS, THE **½ (1941) PR:A
BODY DOUBLE zero (1984) PR:O
BODY HEAT ** (1981) PR:C**
BODY ROCK *½ (1984) PR:C
BODY SAID NO!, THE * (1950, Brit.) PR:AA
BODY SNATCHER, THE * (1945) PR:A**
BODY STEALERS, THE *½ (1969) PR:A
BODYGUARD **½ (1948) PR:A
BODYHOLD *½ (1950) PR:A
BOEFJE * (1939, Ger.) PR:AA
BOEING BOEING *** (1965) PR:C
BOFORS GUN, THE ***½ (1968, Brit.) PR:A-C
BOGGY CREEK II *½ (1985) PR:C
BOHEMIAN GIRL, THE *½ (1936) PR:A
BOHEMIAN RAPTURE * (1948, Czech.) PR:A
BOILING POINT, THE *½ (1932) PR:A
BOLD AND THE BRAVE, THE ** (1956) PR:A
BOLD CABALLERO **½ (1936) PR:A
BOLD FRONTIERSMAN, THE ** (1948) PR:A
BOLDEST JOB IN THE WEST, THE * (1971, It.) PR:A-C
BOLERO **½ (1934) PR:A-C
BOLERO * (1982, Fr.) PR:A
BOLERO zero (1984) PR:O
BOMB IN THE HIGH STREET *½ (1961, Brit.) PR:A
BOMBA AND THE ELEPHANT STAMPEDE
(SEE:ELEPHANT STAMPEDE)
BOMBA AND THE HIDDEN CITY * (1950) PR:A
BOMBA AND THE JUNGLE GIRL *½ (1952) PR:A
BOMBA ON PANTHER ISLAND * (1949) PR:A
BOMBA THE JUNGLE BOY *½ (1949) PR:A
BOMBARDIER * (1943) PR:A**
BOMBARDMENT OF MONTE CARLO, THE ** (1931, Ger.) PR:A
BOMBAY CLIPPER ** (1942) PR:A
BOMBAY MAIL ** (1934) PR:A
BOMBAY TALKIE * (1970, India) PR:C
BOMBERS B-52 ** (1957) PR:A
BOMBER'S MOON ** (1943) PR:A
BOMBS OVER BURMA * (1942) PR:A
BOMBS OVER LONDON *½ (1937, Brit.) PR:A
BOMBSHELL ***½ (1933) PR:A-C
BOMBSIGHT STOLEN *½ (1941, Brit.) PR:A
BON VOYAGE *½ (1962) PR:AA
BON VOYAGE, CHARLIE BROWN (AND DON'T COME BACK) * (1980) PR:AA**
BONA ***½ (1984, Phil.) PR:O
BONANZA TOWN * (1951) PR:A
BOND OF FEAR * (1956, Brit.) PR:A
BOND STREET **½ (1948, Brit.) PR:A
BONDAGE *½ (1933) PR:C
BONJOUR TRISTESSE * (1958) PR:C-O**
BONNE CHANCE **½ (1935, Fr.) PR:A
BONNIE AND CLYDE ** (1967) PR:O**
BONNIE PARKER STORY, THE **½ (1958) PR:O
BONNIE PRINCE CHARLIE *** (1948, Brit.) PR:A
BONNIE SCOTLAND ** (1935) PR:AA
BONZO GOES TO COLLEGE ** (1952) PR:AA
BOOBY TRAP * (1957, Brit.) PR:A
BOOGENS, THE * (1982) PR:A
BOOGEY MAN, THE zero (1980) PR:O
BOOGEYMAN II *½ (1983) PR:O
BOOGIE MAN WILL GET YOU, THE *** (1942) PR:C
BOOK OF NUMBERS **½ (1973) PR:O
BOOLOO *½ (1938) PR:A
BOOM! * (1968) PR:O
BOOM TOWN **** (1940) PR:A
BOOMERANG * (1934, Brit.) PR:A
BOOMERANG ** (1947) PR:C**
BOOMERANG ** (1960, Ger.) PR:A-C
BOOST, THE *½ (1988) PR:O
BOOT HILL * (1969, It.) PR:A
BOOTHILL BRIGADE **½ (1937) PR:A
BOOTLEGGERS *½ (1974) PR:A-C
BOOTS AND SADDLES * (1937) PR:A
BOOTS! BOOTS! * (1934, Brit.) PR:A
BOOTS MALONE ***½ (1952) PR:A
BOOTS OF DESTINY * (1937) PR:A
BOP GIRL GOES CALYPSO ** (1957) PR:A
BORDER BADMEN * (1945) PR:A
BORDER BANDITS * (1946) PR:A
BORDER BRIGANDS *½ (1935) PR:A
BORDER BUCKAROOS * (1943) PR:A
BORDER CABALLERO *½ (1936) PR:A
BORDER CAFE *½ (1937) PR:A
BORDER DEVILS ** (1932) PR:A
BORDER FEUD * (1947) PR:A
BORDER FLIGHT ** (1936) PR:A
BORDER G-MAN *½ (1938) PR:A
BORDER HEAT **½ (1988) PR:O
BORDER INCIDENT *** (1949) PR:C
BORDER LAW **½ (1931) PR:A
BORDER LEGION, THE *½ (1930) PR:A
BORDER LEGION, THE *½ (1940) PR:A
BORDER OUTLAWS *½ (1950) PR:A
BORDER PATROL *½ (1943) PR:A
BORDER PATROLMAN, THE ** (1936) PR:A
BORDER PHANTOM **½ (1937) PR:A
BORDER RANGERS *½ (1950) PR:A
BORDER RIVER **½ (1954) PR:A
BORDER ROMANCE * (1930) PR:A
BORDER SADDLEMATES zero (1952) PR:A
BORDER STREET * (1950, Pol.) PR:A**
BORDER TREASURE * (1950) PR:A
BORDER VIGILANTES ** (1941) PR:A
BORDER WOLVES * (1938) PR:A
BORDER, THE **½ (1982) PR:O
BORDERLAND *½ (1937) PR:A
BORDERLINE **½ (1950) PR:A
BORDERLINE ***½ (1980) PR:C
BORDERTOWN *** (1935) PR:C
BORDERTOWN GUNFIGHTERS *½ (1943) PR:A
BORIS GODUNOV ***** (1959, USSR) PR:A
BORN AGAIN **½ (1978) PR:A
BORN AMERICAN * (1986, US/Fin.) PR:O
BORN FOR GLORY **½ (1935, Brit.) PR:A
BORN FREE * (1966) PR:AA**
BORN IN EAST L.A. **½ (1987) PR:O
BORN IN FLAMES **½ (1983) PR:O
BORN LOSERS ** (1967) PR:O
BORN LUCKY * (1932, Brit.) PR:A
BORN OF FIRE zero (1987, Brit.) PR:O
BORN RECKLESS **½ (1930) PR:C
BORN RECKLESS ** (1937) PR:A
BORN RECKLESS * (1959) PR:A
BORN THAT WAY * (1937, Brit.) PR:A
BORN TO BE BAD * (1934) PR:A
BORN TO BE BAD ***½ (1950) PR:A
BORN TO BE LOVED ** (1959) PR:A
BORN TO BE WILD ** (1938) PR:A
BORN TO DANCE *** (1936) PR:A
BORN TO FIGHT *½ (1938) PR:A
BORN TO GAMBLE zero (1935) PR:A
BORN TO KILL ** (1947) PR:A
BORN TO KILL ** (1975) PR:O
BORN TO LOVE *½ (1931) PR:A
BORN TO SING * (1942) PR:A
BORN TO SPEED *½ (1947) PR:A
BORN TO THE SADDLE *½ (1953) PR:A
BORN TO THE WEST **½ (1937) PR:A
BORN TO WIN **½ (1971) PR:C
BORN WILD * (1968) PR:C
BORN YESTERDAY *** (1951) PR:A**
BORROW A MILLION * (1934, Brit.) PR:A
BORROWED CLOTHES * (1934, Brit.) PR:A
BORROWED HERO *½ (1941) PR:A
BORROWED TROUBLE *½ (1948) PR:A
BORROWED WIVES * (1930) PR:A
BORROWING TROUBLE * (1937) PR:A
BORSALINO *** (1970, Fr.) PR:O
BORSALINO AND CO. **½ (1974, Fr.) PR:O
BOSS, THE *** (1956) PR:A
BOSS NIGGER *½ (1974) PR:C
BOSS OF BIG TOWN ** (1943) PR:A
BOSS OF BULLION CITY *½ (1941) PR:A
BOSS OF HANGTOWN MESA *½ (1942) PR:A
BOSS OF LONELY VALLEY * (1937) PR:A
BOSS OF THE RAWHIDE *½ (1944) PR:A
BOSS RIDER OF GUN CREEK * (1936) PR:A
BOSS' WIFE, THE * (1986) PR:C-O
BOSS'S SON, THE **½ (1978) PR:A
BOSTON BLACKIE AND THE LAW **½ (1946) PR:A
BOSTON BLACKIE BOOKED ON SUSPICION ** (1945) PR:A
BOSTON BLACKIE GOES HOLLYWOOD ** (1942) PR:A
BOSTON BLACKIE'S CHINESE VENTURE ** (1949) PR:A
BOSTON BLACKIE'S RENDEZVOUS **½ (1945) PR:A
BOSTON STRANGLER, THE * (1968) PR:O**
BOSTONIANS, THE ** (1984) PR:A-C
BOTANY BAY **½ (1953) PR:C
BOTH ENDS OF THE CANDLE
(SEE:HELEN MORGAN STORY, THE)
BOTH SIDES OF THE LAW * (1953, Brit.) PR:A
BOTTOM OF THE BOTTLE, THE *** (1956) PR:A
BOTTOMS UP *** (1934) PR:A
BOTTOMS UP * (1960, Brit.) PR:A
BOUDOIR DIPLOMAT * (1930) PR:C
BOUDU SAVED FROM DROWNING ***½ (1967, Fr.) PR:C
BOUGHT *½ (1931) PR:A-C

Finding entries in **THE MOTION PICTURE GUIDE ™**

Years	Volumes
1929-83	Volumes I-IX
1984	Volume IX
1985	1986 ANNUAL
1986	1987 ANNUAL
1987	1988 ANNUAL
1988	1989 ANNUAL

STAR RATINGS

★★★★★	Masterpiece
★★★★	Excellent
★★★	Good
★★	Fair
★	Poor
zero	Without Merit

PARENTAL RECOMMENDATION (PR:)

AA	Good for Children
A	Acceptable for Children
C	Cautionary, some objectionable scenes
O	Objectionable for Children

BOLD: Films on Videocassette

BOULDER DAM ** (1936) PR:A
BOULEVARD NIGHTS **½ (1979) PR:O
BOUND FOR GLORY ***½ (1976) PR:A-C
BOUNTIFUL SUMMER ** (1951, USSR) PR:A
BOUNTY, THE *** (1984) PR:O
BOUNTY HUNTER, THE **½ (1954) PR:A
BOUNTY HUNTERS, THE ** (1970, It.) PR:A-C
BOUNTY KILLER, THE *** (1965) PR:A-C
BOWERY, THE **** (1933) PR:A
BOWERY AT MIDNIGHT *½ (1942) PR:A
BOWERY BATTALION * (1951) PR:A
BOWERY BLITZKRIEG * (1941) PR:A
BOWERY BOMBSHELL zero (1946) PR:A
BOWERY BOY * (1940) PR:A
BOWERY BOYS MEET THE MONSTERS, THE * (1954) PR:A
BOWERY BUCKAROOS *½ (1947) PR:A
BOWERY CHAMPS *½ (1944) PR:A
BOWERY TO BAGDAD ** (1955) PR:A
BOWERY TO BROADWAY *** (1944) PR:A
BOXCAR BERTHA **½ (1972) PR:O
BOXER ** (1971, Pol.) PR:A
BOXER, THE (SEE:RIPPED OFF)
BOXOFFICE *½ (1982) PR:C-O
BOY. . .A GIRL, A zero (1969) PR:O
BOY, A GIRL AND A BIKE, A * (1949, Brit.) PR:A
BOY, A GIRL, AND A DOG, A * (1946) PR:A
BOY AND HIS DOG, A zero (1975) PR:O
BOY AND THE BRIDGE, THE ** (1959, Brit.) PR:A
BOY AND THE PIRATES, THE **½ (1960) PR:AA
BOY CRIED MURDER, THE * (1966, Ger./Brit./Yugo.) PR:C-O
BOY, DID I GET A WRONG NUMBER! **½ (1966) PR:AA
BOY FRIEND *½ (1939) PR:A
BOY FRIEND, THE ***½ (1971, Brit.) PR:A
BOY FROM INDIANA *½ (1950) PR:A
BOY FROM OKLAHOMA, THE **½ (1954) PR:A
BOY IN BLUE, THE *½ (1986, Can.) PR:C-O
BOY MEETS GIRL ***½ (1938) PR:A
BOY MEETS GIRL *** (1985, Fr.) PR:O
BOY NAMED CHARLIE BROWN, A **½ (1969) PR:AA
BOY OF THE STREETS ** (1937) PR:A
BOY ON A DOLPHIN *** (1957) PR:C
BOY RENTS GIRL (SEE:CAN'T BUY ME LOVE)
BOY SLAVES *½ (1938) PR:A
BOY SOLDIER ***½ (1987, Wales) PR:C-O
BOY TEN FEET TALL, A *** (1965, Brit.) PR:AA
BOY TROUBLE *½ (1939) PR:A
BOY! WHAT A GIRL *½ (1947) PR:A
BOY WHO CAUGHT A CROOK *½ (1961) PR:AA
BOY WHO COULD FLY, THE **** (1986) PR:A
BOY WHO CRIED WEREWOLF, THE ** (1973) PR:A-C
BOY WHO STOLE A MILLION, THE *** (1960, Brit.) PR:AA
BOY WHO TURNED YELLOW, THE * (1972, Brit.) PR:AA
BOY WITH THE GREEN HAIR, THE *** (1949) PR:AA
BOYD'S SHOP ** (1960, Brit.) PR:A
BOYFRIENDS AND GIRLFRIENDS ***** (1988, Fr.) PR:A
BOYS, THE ** (1962, Brit.) PR:C
BOYS FROM BRAZIL, THE ***½ (1978) PR:C-O
BOYS FROM BROOKLYN, THE (SEE:BELA LUGOSI MEETS A BROOKLYN GORILLA)
BOYS FROM SYRACUSE *** (1940) PR:A
BOYS IN BROWN *½ (1949, Brit.) PR:AA
BOYS IN COMPANY C, THE *** (1978, US/Hong Kong) PR:O
BOYS IN THE BAND, THE *** (1970) PR:O
BOYS NEXT DOOR, THE *** (1985) PR:O
BOYS OF PAUL STREET, THE ** (1969, Hung./US) PR:A
BOYS OF THE CITY *½ (1940) PR:A
BOYS' RANCH *½ (1946) PR:A
BOY'S REFORMATORY * (1939) PR:A
BOYS TOWN ***** (1938) PR:AA
BOYS WILL BE BOYS * (1936, Brit.) PR:A
BOYS WILL BE GIRLS * (1937, Brit.) PR:AA
BOYS' NIGHT OUT *** (1962) PR:C
BRACELETS * (1931, Brit.) PR:A
BRADDOCK: MISSING IN ACTION III * (1988) PR:O
BRADY'S ESCAPE **½ (1984, US/Hung.) PR:C
BRAIN, THE * (1965, Ger./Brit.) PR:A
BRAIN DAMAGE **½ (1988) PR:O
BRAIN EATERS, THE *½ (1958) PR:C
BRAIN FROM THE PLANET AROUS, THE *½ (1958) PR:C
BRAIN MACHINE, THE ** (1955, Brit.) PR:A
BRAIN OF BLOOD *½ (1971, Phil.) PR:C
BRAIN THAT WOULDN'T DIE, THE ** (1959) PR:O
BRAIN, THE **½ (1969, Fr./US) PR:A
BRAINSTORM *** (1965) PR:C
BRAINSTORM *** (1983) PR:C-O
BRAINWASHED **½ (1961, Ger.) PR:A-C
BRAINWAVES **½ (1983) PR:O
BRAMBLE BUSH, THE ** (1960) PR:O
BRAND OF FEAR * (1949) PR:A
BRAND OF THE DEVIL *½ (1944) PR:A
BRANDED * (1931) PR:A
BRANDED *** (1951) PR:A
BRANDED A COWARD ** (1935) PR:A
BRANDED MEN ** (1931) PR:A
BRANDY FOR THE PARSON ** (1952, Brit.) PR:A
BRANNIGAN **½ (1975, Brit.) PR:A-C
BRASHER DOUBLOON, THE *** (1947) PR:A
BRASIL ANNO 2,000 * (1968, Braz.) PR:A
BRASS BOTTLE, THE ** (1964) PR:A
BRASS LEGEND, THE ** (1956) PR:A
BRASS MONKEY (SEE:LUCKY MASCOT, THE)
BRASS TARGET ** (1978) PR:A-C
BRAT, THE * (1930, Brit.) PR:A
BRAT, THE ** (1931) PR:A
BRAVADOS, THE *** (1958) PR:C
BRAVE BULLS, THE **** (1951) PR:A
BRAVE DON'T CRY, THE ** (1952, Brit.) PR:A
BRAVE ONE, THE ** (1956) PR:AA
BRAVE WARRIOR ** (1952) PR:A
BRAZIL ** (1944) PR:A
BRAZIL ***½ (1985, Brit.) PR:O
BREAD AND CHOCOLATE **½ (1978, It.) PR:A
BREAD, LOVE AND DREAMS **½ (1953, It.) PR:O
BREAD OF LOVE, THE *** (1954, Swed.) PR:A
BREAK IN THE CIRCLE, THE *½ (1957, Brit.) PR:A
BREAK OF DAY *** (1977, Aus.) PR:A
BREAK OF HEARTS **½ (1935) PR:A
BREAK THE NEWS **** (1938, Brit.) PR:A
BREAK TO FREEDOM (SEE:ALBERT, R.N)
BREAK, THE *½ (1962, Brit.) PR:A
BREAKAWAY * (1956, Brit.) PR:A
BREAKDOWN *½ (1953) PR:A
BREAKER! BREAKER! *½ (1977) PR:C
BREAKER MORANT **** (1980, Aus.) PR:A-C
BREAKERS AHEAD * (1935, Brit.) PR:A
BREAKERS AHEAD * (1938, Brit.) PR:A
BREAKFAST AT TIFFANY'S **** (1961) PR:A
BREAKFAST CLUB, THE **½ (1985) PR:O
BREAKFAST FOR TWO **½ (1937) PR:A
BREAKFAST IN BED ** (1978) PR:C
BREAKFAST IN HOLLYWOOD ** (1946) PR:A
BREAKHEART PASS *** (1976) PR:C
BREAKIN'2: ELECTRIC BOOGALOO ***½ (1984) PR:A-C
BREAKIN' **½ (1984) PR:A-C
BREAKING ALL THE RULES ** (1985, Can.) PR:O
BREAKING AWAY **½ (1979) PR:C-O
BREAKING GLASS **½ (1980, Brit.) PR:C-O
BREAKING POINT, THE *** (1950) PR:A
BREAKING POINT ** (1976) PR:C-O
BREAKING POINT, THE * (1961, Brit.) PR:A
BREAKING THE ICE ** (1938) PR:A
BREAKING THE SOUND BARRIER *** (1952) PR:A
BREAKOUT *** (1960, Brit.) PR:A
BREAKOUT *½ (1975) PR:C
BREAKTHROUGH **½ (1950) PR:A
BREAKTHROUGH **½ (1978, Ger.) PR:C
BREATH OF LIFE * (1962, Brit.) PR:A
BREATH OF SCANDAL, A *½ (1960) PR:A
BREATHLESS **** (1959, Fr.) PR:O
BREATHLESS ** (1983) PR:O
BREED APART, A *½ (1984) PR:A-C
BREED OF THE BORDER * (1933) PR:A
BREEDERS zero (1986) PR:O
BREEZING HOME ** (1937) PR:A
BREEZY *** (1973) PR:O
BREWSTER McCLOUD **½ (1970) PR:C
BREWSTER'S MILLIONS ***½ (1935, Brit.) PR:A
BREWSTER'S MILLIONS **** (1945) PR:A
BREWSTER'S MILLIONS ** (1985) PR:O
BRIBE, THE *** (1949) PR:C
BRIDAL PATH, THE **½ (1959, Brit.) PR:A
BRIDAL SUITE ** (1939) PR:A
BRIDE, THE **½ (1985) PR:C
BRIDE AND THE BEAST, THE * (1958) PR:C
BRIDE BY MISTAKE * (1944) PR:A
BRIDE CAME C.O.D., THE *** (1941) PR:A
BRIDE COMES HOME ***½ (1936) PR:A
BRIDE COMES TO YELLOW SKY, THE (SEE:FACE TO FACE)
BRIDE FOR HENRY, A * (1937) PR:A
BRIDE FOR SALE **** (1949) PR:A
BRIDE IS MUCH TOO BEAUTIFUL, THE ** (1958, Fr.) PR:O
BRIDE OF FRANKENSTEIN, THE ***** (1935) PR:C
BRIDE OF THE DESERT *½ (1929) PR:A
BRIDE OF THE GORILLA * (1951) PR:A
BRIDE OF THE LAKE **½ (1934, Brit.) PR:A
BRIDE OF THE MONSTER * (1955) PR:A
BRIDE OF THE REGIMENT **½ (1930) PR:A
BRIDE OF VENGEANCE **½ (1949) PR:A
BRIDE WALKS OUT, THE **½ (1936) PR:A
BRIDE WITH A DOWRY ** (1954, USSR) PR:A
BRIDE WORE BLACK, THE ** (1968, Fr./It.) PR:C
BRIDE WORE BOOTS, THE *** (1946) PR:A
BRIDE WORE CRUTCHES, THE * (1940) PR:A
BRIDE WORE RED, THE *** (1937) PR:A
BRIDE, THE ** (1973) PR:C-O
BRIDEGROOM FOR TWO * (1932, Brit.) PR:A
BRIDES ARE LIKE THAT **½ (1936) PR:A
BRIDES OF BLOOD zero (1968, US/Phil.) PR:O
BRIDES OF DRACULA, THE **½ (1960, Brit.) PR:O
BRIDES OF FU MANCHU, THE ** (1966, Brit.) PR:A
BRIDES TO BE * (1934, Brit.) PR:A
BRIDGE AT REMAGEN, THE **** (1969) PR:C
BRIDGE OF SAN LUIS REY, THE **** (1929) PR:A
BRIDGE OF SAN LUIS REY, THE ***½ (1944) PR:A
BRIDGE OF SIGHS *½ (1936) PR:A
BRIDGE ON THE RIVER KWAI, THE ***** (1957) PR:C
BRIDGE TO THE SUN **½ (1961) PR:A
BRIDGE TOO FAR, A *** (1977, Brit.) PR:C
BRIDGE, THE *** (1961, Ger.) PR:A
BRIDGES AT TOKO-RI, THE **** (1954) PR:A
BRIEF ECSTASY * (1937, Brit.) PR:A
BRIEF ENCOUNTER ***** (1945, Brit.) PR:A
BRIEF MOMENT **½ (1933) PR:A
BRIEF RAPTURE *½ (1952, It.) PR:C
BRIEF VACATION, A ***½ (1975, It.) PR:C
BRIGADOON *** (1954) PR:A
BRIGAND OF KANDAHAR, THE ** (1965, Brit.) PR:A
BRIGAND, THE *** (1952) PR:A
BRIGGS FAMILY, THE *½ (1940, Brit.) PR:A
BRIGHAM YOUNG—FRONTIERSMAN *** (1940) PR:A
BRIGHT EYES *** (1934) PR:AA
BRIGHT LEAF *** (1950) PR:A
BRIGHT LIGHTS * (1931) PR:A
BRIGHT LIGHTS **½ (1935) PR:A
BRIGHT LIGHTS, BIG CITY **½ (1988) PR:O
BRIGHT ROAD *** (1953) PR:A
BRIGHT VICTORY **** (1951) PR:A
BRIGHTNESS **** (1988, Mali) PR:O
BRIGHTON BEACH MEMOIRS ***½ (1986) PR:C
BRIGHTON ROCK *** (1947, Brit.) PR:C
BRIGHTON STRANGLER, THE **½ (1945) PR:AA
BRIGHTY OF THE GRAND CANYON ** (1967) PR:A
BRILLIANT MARRIAGE * (1936) PR:A
BRIMSTONE *** (1949) PR:A
BRIMSTONE AND TREACLE *** (1982, Brit.) PR:C
BRING ME THE HEAD OF ALFREDO GARCIA **** (1974) PR:O
BRING ON THE GIRLS *** (1945) PR:A
BRING YOUR SMILE ALONG *** (1955) PR:A
BRINGING UP BABY ***** (1938) PR:A
BRINGING UP FATHER *½ (1946) PR:A
BRINK OF LIFE ** (1960, Swed.) PR:C-O
BRINK'S JOB, THE **½ (1978) PR:A-C
BRITANNIA MEWS (SEE:AFFAIRS OF ADELAIDE)
BRITANNIA OF BILLINGSGATE *½ (1933, Brit.) PR:A
BRITISH AGENT ***½ (1934) PR:A
BRITISH INTELLIGENCE ** (1940) PR:A
BRITTANIA HOSPITAL *** (1982, Brit.) PR:C
BROADCAST NEWS **** (1987) PR:C-O
BROADMINDED ** (1931) PR:A
BROADWAY *** (1929) PR:A
BROADWAY *** (1942) PR:A
BROADWAY BABIES ** (1929) PR:A
BROADWAY BAD **½ (1933) PR:A
BROADWAY BIG SHOT ** (1942) PR:A
BROADWAY BILL ***½ (1934) PR:A
BROADWAY DANNY ROSE **** (1984) PR:A-C
BROADWAY GONDOLIER **½ (1935) PR:A
BROADWAY HOOFER, THE ** (1929) PR:A
BROADWAY HOSTESS ** (1935) PR:A
BROADWAY LIMITED ** (1941) PR:A
BROADWAY MELODY OF 1936 ***½ (1935) PR:A
BROADWAY MELODY OF 1940 *** (1940) PR:A
BROADWAY MELODY OF '38 *** (1937) PR:A
BROADWAY MELODY, THE *** (1929) PR:A
BROADWAY MUSKETEERS **½ (1938) PR:A
BROADWAY RHYTHM ** (1944) PR:A
BROADWAY SCANDALS ** (1929) PR:A
BROADWAY SERENADE **½ (1939) PR:A
BROADWAY THROUGH A KEYHOLE **½ (1933) PR:A
BROADWAY TO CHEYENNE ** (1932) PR:A
BROADWAY TO HOLLYWOOD **½ (1933) PR:A
BROKEN ARROW ***½ (1950) PR:A
BROKEN BLOSSOMS *½ (1936, Brit.) PR:A
BROKEN DREAMS ** (1933) PR:A
BROKEN ENGLISH *½ (1981) PR:O
BROKEN HORSESHOE, THE * (1953, Brit.) PR:A

BROKEN JOURNEY *** (1948, Brit.) PR:A
BROKEN LANCE ***½ (1954) PR:A
BROKEN LAND, THE ** (1962) PR:A
BROKEN LOVE ** (1946, It.) PR:A
BROKEN LULLABY *** (1932) PR:A
BROKEN MELODY *½ (1938, Aus.) PR:A
BROKEN MELODY, THE *½ (1934, Brit.) PR:A
BROKEN MIRRORS **½ (1985, Neth.) PR:O
BROKEN ROSARY, THE * (1934, Brit.) PR:A
BROKEN STAR, THE ** (1956) PR:A
BROKEN WING, THE * (1932) PR:A
BRONCO BILLY * (1980) PR:C**
BRONCO BULLFROG * (1972, Brit.) PR:A
BRONCO BUSTER **½ (1952) PR:A
BRONTE SISTERS, THE ** (1979, Fr.) PR:A
BRONX WARRIORS
(SEE:1990: THE BRONX WARRIORS)
BRONZE BUCKAROO, THE ** (1939) PR:A
BROOD, THE *½ (1979, Can.) PR:C
BROOKLYN ORCHID * (1942) PR:A
BROTH OF A BOY *½ (1959, Brit.) PR:A
BROTHER ALFRED * (1932, Brit.) PR:A
BROTHER FROM ANOTHER PLANET, THE **½ (1984) PR:O
BROTHER JOHN ** (1971) PR:A
BROTHER ORCHID ***½ (1940) PR:A
BROTHER RAT ***½ (1938) PR:A
BROTHER RAT AND A BABY **½ (1940) PR:A
BROTHER SUN, SISTER MOON * (1973, Brit./It.) PR:A**
BROTHERHOOD OF SATAN, THE * (1971) PR:C-O
BROTHERHOOD OF THE YAKUZA
(SEE:YAKUZA, THE)
BROTHERHOOD, THE ***½ (1968) PR:C-O
BROTHERLY LOVE **½ (1970, Brit.) PR:O
BROTHERS ** (1930) PR:A
BROTHERS ** (1977) PR:C
BROTHERS ** (1984, Aus.) PR:O
BROTHERS AND SISTERS ** (1980, Brit.) PR:A
BROTHERS IN LAW **½ (1957, Brit.) PR:A
BROTHERS IN THE SADDLE ** (1949) PR:A
BROTHERS KARAMAZOV, THE ***½ (1958) PR:C-O
BROTHERS OF THE WEST * (1938) PR:A
BROTHERS O'TOOLE, THE * (1973) PR:A
BROTHERS RICO, THE **½ (1957) PR:C
BROTHERS, THE ** (1948, Brit.) PR:A
BROWN ON RESOLUTION
(SEE:BORN FOR GLORY)
BROWN SUGAR * (1931, Brit.) PR:A
BROWN WALLET, THE ** (1936, Brit.) PR:A
BROWNING VERSION, THE *** (1951, Brit.) PR:A**
BRUBAKER ***½ (1980) PR:C-O
BRUCE LEE AND I zero (1976, Chi.) PR:C-O
BRUCE LEE—TRUE STORY *½ (1976, Chi.) PR:C-O
BRUSHFIRE * (1962) PR:A
BRUTE, THE ** (1952, Mex.) PR:A-C
BRUTE AND THE BEAST, THE * (1968, It.) PR:C
BRUTE FORCE ** (1947) PR:C**
BRUTE MAN, THE ** (1946) PR:A
BUBBLE, THE ** (1967) PR:A
BUCCANEER, THE ** (1958) PR:A
BUCCANEER, THE *** (1938) PR:A
BUCCANEER'S GIRL ** (1950) PR:A
BUCHANAN RIDES ALONE ** (1958) PR:A
BUCK AND THE PREACHER * (1972) PR:C
BUCK BENNY RIDES AGAIN ** (1940) PR:A
BUCK PRIVATES **½ (1941) PR:AA
BUCK PRIVATES COME HOME **½ (1947) PR:AA
BUCK ROGERS
(SEE:DESTINATION SATURN)
BUCK ROGERS IN THE 25TH CENTURY * (1979) PR:A-C
BUCKAROO BANZAI
(SEE:ADVENTURES OF BUCAKAROO BANZAI: ACROSS THE 8TH DIMENSION, THE)
BUCKAROO FROM POWDER RIVER ** (1948) PR:A
BUCKAROO SHERIFF OF TEXAS * (1951) PR:A
BUCKET OF BLOOD ** (1934, Brit.) PR:O
BUCKET OF BLOOD, A ** (1959) PR:A
BUCKSKIN ** (1968) PR:A
BUCKSKIN FRONTIER ** (1943) PR:A
BUCKSKIN LADY, THE *½ (1957) PR:A
BUCKTOWN zero (1975) PR:C
BUDDHA ** (1965, Jap.) PR:C
BUDDIES **½ (1983, Aus.) PR:A
BUDDIES **½ (1985) PR:O
BUDDY BUDDY ** (1981) PR:C
BUDDY HOLLY STORY, THE ***½ (1978) PR:A-C
BUDDY SYSTEM, THE * (1984) PR:A-C**
BUFFALO BILL ***½ (1944) PR:AA
BUFFALO BILL AND THE INDIANS, OR SITTING BULL'S HISTORY LESSON zero (1976) PR:C
BUFFALO BILL, HERO OF THE FAR WEST ** (1962, It.) PR:A
BUFFALO BILL IN TOMAHAWK TERRITORY ** (1952) PR:A
BUFFALO BILL RIDES AGAIN * (1947) PR:A
BUFFALO GUN * (1961) PR:A
BUG * (1975) PR:A-C
BUGLE SOUNDS, THE ** (1941) PR:A
BUGLES IN THE AFTERNOON ** (1952) PR:A
BUGS BUNNY, SUPERSTAR * (1975) PR:AA**
BUGS BUNNY/ROAD-RUNNER MOVIE, THE
(SEE:GREAT AMERICAN BUGS BUNNY-ROAD RUNNER CHASE)
BUGS BUNNY'S THIRD MOVIE—1001 RABBIT TALES ** (1982) PR:AA
BUGSY MALONE ***½ (1976, Brit.) PR:AA
BUILD MY GALLOWS HIGH
(SEE:OUT OF THE PAST)
BULL DURHAM ***½ (1988) PR:O
BULLDOG BREED, THE *½ (1960, Brit.) PR:A
BULLDOG DRUMMOND * (1929) PR:A**
BULLDOG DRUMMOND AT BAY * (1937, Brit.) PR:A
BULLDOG DRUMMOND COMES BACK *½ (1937) PR:A
BULLDOG DRUMMOND ESCAPES ** (1937) PR:A
BULLDOG DRUMMOND IN AFRICA ** (1938) PR:A
BULLDOG DRUMMOND STRIKES BACK **** (1934) PR:A
BULLDOG DRUMMOND'S BRIDE *½ (1939) PR:A
BULLDOG DRUMMOND'S PERIL * (1938) PR:A**
BULLDOG DRUMMOND'S REVENGE *½ (1937) PR:A
BULLDOG DRUMMOND'S SECRET POLICE *½ (1939) PR:A
BULLDOG EDITION ** (1936) PR:A
BULLDOG JACK
(SEE:ALIAS BULLDOG DRUMMOND)
BULLDOG SEES IT THROUGH * (1940, Brit.) PR:A
BULLET CODE **½ (1940) PR:A
BULLET FOR A BADMAN **½ (1964) PR:A
BULLET FOR JOEY, A **½ (1955) PR:A
BULLET FOR PRETTY BOY, A * (1970) PR:C
BULLET FOR SANDOVAL, A ** (1970, It./Sp.) PR:C
BULLET FOR STEFANO *½ (1950, It.) PR:A
BULLET FOR THE GENERAL, A **½ (1967, It.) PR:C
BULLET IS WAITING, A *½ (1954) PR:A
BULLET SCARS * (1942) PR:A
BULLETPROOF zero (1988) PR:O
BULLETS FOR O'HARA * (1941) PR:A
BULLETS FOR RUSTLERS * (1940) PR:A
BULLETS OR BALLOTS ***½ (1936) PR:A
BULLFIGHTER AND THE LADY * (1951) PR:A**
BULLFIGHTERS, THE ** (1945) PR:A
BULLIES * (1986, Can.) PR:O
BULLITT ** (1968) PR:C**
BULLSHOT **½ (1983) PR:A-C
BULLWHIP ** (1958) PR:A
BUNCO SQUAD *½ (1950) PR:A
BUNDLE OF JOY ** (1956) PR:A
BUNGALOW 13 * (1948) PR:A
BUNKER BEAN ** (1936) PR:A
BUNNY LAKE IS MISSING ***½ (1965) PR:C
BUNNY O'HARE ** (1971) PR:C
BUONA SERA, MRS. CAMPBELL ** (1968, It.) PR:C
BUREAU OF MISSING PERSONS * (1933) PR:A**
BURG THEATRE *½ (1936, Ger.) PR:A
BURGLAR zero (1987) PR:O
BURGLAR, THE ** (1956) PR:A
BURGLARS, THE ** (1972, Fr./It.) PR:C
BURIED ALIVE * (1939) PR:A
BURIED ALIVE * (1951, It.) PR:C
BURIED ALIVE zero (1984, It.) PR:O
BURKE AND HARE * (1972, Brit.) PR:O
BURKE & WILLS * (1985, Aus.) PR:A-C**
BURMA CONVOY ** (1941) PR:A
BURMESE HARP, THE *** (1985, Jap.) PR:O
BURN * (1970, Fr./It.) PR:O**
BURN 'EM UP O'CONNER ** (1939) PR:A
BURN WITCH BURN ** (1962) PR:O
BURNING AN ILLUSION **½ (1982, Brit.) PR:C
BURNING CROSS, THE *½ (1947) PR:C
BURNING GOLD * (1936) PR:A
BURNING HILLS, THE ** (1956) PR:A
BURNING QUESTION, THE
(SEE:REEFER MADNESS)
BURNING UP * (1930) PR:A
BURNING YEARS, THE ** (1979, It.) PR:O
BURNING, THE zero (1981) PR:O
BURNT EVIDENCE ** (1954, Brit.) PR:O
BURNT OFFERINGS * (1976) PR:C-O
BURY ME AN ANGEL zero (1972) PR:O
BURY ME DEAD *** (1947) PR:C
BURY ME NOT ON THE LONE PRAIRIE ** (1941) PR:A
BUS IS COMING, THE ** (1971) PR:C-O
BUS RILEY'S BACK IN TOWN **½ (1965) PR:A
BUS STOP ***½ (1956) PR:A
BUSH CHRISTMAS **½ (1947, Aus.) PR:AA
BUSH CHRISTMAS ** (1983, Aus.) PR:AA
BUSHBABY, THE **½ (1970) PR:AA
BUSHIDO BLADE, THE ** (1982, Brit./US) PR:O
BUSHWHACKERS, THE *** (1952) PR:A
BUSINESS AND PLEASURE ** (1932) PR:A
BUSMAN'S HOLIDAY * (1936, Brit.) PR:A
BUSMAN'S HONEYMOON **½ (1940, Brit.) PR:A
BUSSES ROAR **½ (1942) PR:A
BUSTED UP * (1986, Can.) PR:O
BUSTER **½ (1988, Brit.) PR:C-O
BUSTER KEATON STORY, THE *½ (1957) PR:A
BUSTIN' LOOSE ** (1981) PR:O
BUSTING * (1974) PR:C**
BUSYBODY, THE **½ (1967) PR:A
BUT NOT FOR ME **½ (1959) PR:A
BUT NOT IN VAIN * (1948, Brit.) PR:A
BUT THE FLESH IS WEAK * (1932) PR:A
BUTCH AND SUNDANCE: THE EARLY DAYS * (1979) PR:C
BUTCH CASSIDY AND THE SUNDANCE KID *** (1969) PR:A**
BUTCH MINDS THE BABY **½ (1942) PR:A
BUTCHER BAKER (NIGHTMARE MAKER) * (1982) PR:O
BUTCHER, THE
(SEE:LE BOUCHER)
BUTLER'S DILEMMA, THE ** (1943, Brit.) PR:A
BUTLEY * (1974, Brit.) PR:O
BUTTERCUP CHAIN, THE * (1971, Brit.) PR:O
BUTTERFIELD 8 * (1960) PR:O**
BUTTERFLIES ARE FREE **½ (1972) PR:A
BUTTERFLY ** (1982) PR:O
BUTTERFLY ON THE SHOULDER, A ** (1978, Fr.) PR:C-O
BUY ME THAT TOWN **½ (1941) PR:A
BWANA DEVIL ** (1953) PR:A
BY APPOINTMENT ONLY *½ (1933) PR:A
BY CANDLELIGHT **½ (1934) PR:A
BY DESIGN ** (1982) PR:O
BY HOOK OR BY CROOK
(SEE:I DOOD IT)
BY LOVE POSSESSED ** (1961) PR:O
BY THE LIGHT OF THE SILVERY MOON *** (1953) PR:A
BY WHOSE HAND? *** (1932) PR:A
BY WHOSE HAND? *** (1932) PR:A
BY YOUR LEAVE *** (1935) PR:A
BYE BYE BARBARA ** (1969, Fr.) PR:A
BYE BYE BIRDIE * (1963) PR:A**
BYE BYE BRAVERMAN *½ (1968) PR:A
BYE-BYE BRAZIL * (1980, Braz.) PR:C-O**
BYE BYE MONKEY ** (1978, It./Fr.) PR:O
BYGONES *** (1988, Neth.) PR:C
BYPASS TO HAPPINESS * (1934, Brit.) PR:A

C

C.H.O.M.P.S. ** (1979) PR:AA
C.H.U.D. ** (1984) PR:O
C-MAN **½ (1949) PR:A
C.O.D. * (1932, Brit.) PR:A
C. C. AND COMPANY * (1971) PR:O

CABARET *** (1972) PR:C**
CABIN IN THE COTTON *** (1932) PR:A-C
CABIN IN THE SKY ***½ (1943) PR:AA
CABINET OF CALIGARI, THE ** (1962) PR:A
CABIRIA
(SEE:NIGHTS OF CABIRIA)
CABOBLANCO ** (1981) PR:C
CACCIA TRAGICA
(SEE:TRAGIC PURSUIT, THE)
CACTUS **½ (1986, Aus.) PR:C
CACTUS FLOWER ** (1969) PR:C
CACTUS IN THE SNOW *½ (1972) PR:A
CADDIE **½ (1976, Aus.) PR:C
CADDY, THE ** (1953) PR:A
CADDYSHACK ***½ (1980) PR:C-O
CADDYSHACK II * (1988) PR:C
CADET GIRL *½ (1941) PR:A
CADET-ROUSSELLE ** (1954, Fr.) PR:A
CAESAR AND CLEOPATRA **** (1946, Brit.) PR:A
CAESAR THE CONQUEROR *½ (1963, It.) PR:C
CAFE COLETTE *½ (1937, Brit.) PR:A
CAFE DE PARIS ** (1938, Fr.) PR:A
CAFE EXPRESS **½ (1980, It.) PR:C
CAFE HOSTESS *½ (1940) PR:A
CAFE MASCOT *½ (1936, Brit.) PR:A
CAFE METROPOLE *** (1937) PR:A-C
CAFE SOCIETY ** (1939) PR:A
CAFFE ITALIA *** (1985, Can.) PR:C-O
CAGE OF EVIL ** (1960) PR:A-C
CAGE OF GOLD ** (1950, Brit.) PR:A
CAGE OF NIGHTINGALES, A *** (1947, Fr.) PR:A
CAGED *** (1950) PR:O
CAGED FURY ** (1948) PR:A
CAGED FURY * (1984, Phil.) PR:O
CAGED HEAT
(SEE:RENEGADE GIRLS)
CAGED WOMEN * (1984, It./Fr.) PR:O
CAGLIOSTRO ** (1975, It.) PR:C
CAHILL, UNITED STATES MARSHAL **
(1973) PR:C
CAIN AND MABEL ** (1936) PR:A
CAINE MUTINY, THE ** (1954) PR:A**
CAIN'S WAY * (1969) PR:O
CAIRO **½ (1942) PR:A
CAIRO ** (1963) PR:A
CAIRO ROAD ** (1950, Brit.) PR:A
CAL * (1984, Ireland) PR:O**
CALABUCH **½ (1956, Span./It.) PR:A
CALAMITY JANE **½ (1953) PR:AA
CALAMITY JANE AND SAM BASS ** (1949) PR:A
CALAMITY THE COW *½ (1967, Brit.) PR:AA
CALCULATED RISK *½ (1963, Brit.) PR:A
CALCUTTA *** (1947) PR:A
CALENDAR, THE * (1931, Brit.) PR:A
CALENDAR, THE * (1948, Brit.) PR:A
CALENDAR GIRL *½ (1947) PR:A
CALIFORNIA ** (1946) PR:A
CALIFORNIA * (1963) PR:A
CALIFORNIA CONQUEST ** (1952) PR:A
CALIFORNIA DOLLS
(SEE:ALL THE MARBLES)
CALIFORNIA DREAMING ** (1979) PR:C
CALIFORNIA FIREBRAND *½ (1948) PR:A
CALIFORNIA FRONTIER ** (1938) PR:A
CALIFORNIA GIRLS * (1984) PR:O
CALIFORNIA JOE * (1944) PR:A
CALIFORNIA MAIL, THE * (1937) PR:A
CALIFORNIA PASSAGE ** (1950) PR:A
CALIFORNIA SPLIT ** (1974) PR:C
CALIFORNIA STRAIGHT AHEAD *½ (1937) PR:A
CALIFORNIA SUITE ***½ (1978) PR:A-C
CALIFORNIA TRAIL, THE * (1933) PR:A
CALIFORNIAN, THE *½ (1937) PR:A
CALL, THE * (1938, Fr.) PR:A
CALL A MESSENGER *½ (1939) PR:A
CALL HER SAVAGE ** (1932) PR:A
CALL HIM MR. SHATTER *
(1976, Hong Kong) PR:O
CALL IT A DAY *½ (1937) PR:A
CALL IT LUCK * (1934) PR:A
CALL ME ** (1988) PR:O
CALL ME BWANA ** (1963, Brit.) PR:A
CALL ME GENIUS **½ (1961, Brit.) PR:A
CALL ME MADAM *** (1953) PR:A
CALL ME MAME *½ (1933, Brit.) PR:A
CALL ME MISTER *** (1951) PR:A
CALL NORTHSIDE 777 **** (1948) PR:A
CALL OF THE BLOOD * (1948, Brit.) PR:A
CALL OF THE CANYON ** (1942) PR:A
CALL OF THE CIRCUS *½ (1930) PR:A
CALL OF THE FLESH ** (1930) PR:A
CALL OF THE JUNGLE * (1944) PR:A
CALL OF THE KLONDIKE *½ (1950) PR:A
CALL OF THE PRAIRIE * (1936) PR:A
CALL OF THE ROCKIES * (1938) PR:A
CALL OF THE SEA, THE *½ (1930, Brit.) PR:A
CALL OF THE SOUTH SEAS *½ (1944) PR:A
CALL OF THE WILD ***½ (1935) PR:AA
CALL OF THE WILD *½
(1972, Ger./Span./It./Fr.) PR:A
CALL OF THE YUKON * (1938) PR:A
CALL OUT THE MARINES ** (1942) PR:A
CALL THE MESQUITEERS *½ (1938) PR:A
CALLAN **½ (1975, Brit.) PR:C
CALLAWAY WENT THATAWAY ***½ (1951) PR:AA
CALLBOX MYSTERY, THE * (1932, Brit.) PR:A
CALLED BACK *½ (1933, Brit.) PR:A
CALLING, THE
(SEE:BELLS)
CALLING ALL CROOKS *½ (1938, Brit.) PR:A
CALLING ALL HUSBANDS * (1940) PR:A
CALLING ALL MARINES *½ (1939) PR:A
CALLING BULLDOG DRUMMOND **
(1951, Brit.) PR:A-C
CALLING DR. DEATH ** (1943) PR:A
CALLING DR. GILLESPIE ** (1942) PR:A
CALLING DR. KILDARE ** (1939) PR:A
CALLING HOMICIDE ** (1956) PR:A-C
CALLING PAUL TEMPLE *½ (1948, Brit.) PR:A
CALLING PHILO VANCE *½ (1940) PR:A
CALLING THE TUNE * (1936, Brit.) PR:A
CALLING WILD BILL ELLIOTT ** (1943) PR:A
CALM YOURSELF zero (1935) PR:A
CALTIKI, THE IMMORTAL MONSTER **½
(1959, It.) PR:C
CALYPSO ** (1959, Fr./It.) PR:A-C
CALYPSO HEAT WAVE ** (1957) PR:A
CALYPSO JOE *½ (1957) PR:A
CAME A HOT FRIDAY **½
(1985, New Zealand) PR:C
CAMEL BOY, THE * (1984, Aus.) PR:AA**
CAMELOT * (1967) PR:A-C**
CAMELS ARE COMING, THE ** (1934, Brit.) PR:A
CAMEO KIRBY * (1930) PR:A
CAMERA BUFF *** (1983, Pol.) PR:A
CAMILA **½ (1985, Arg./Sp.) PR:O
CAMILLE *** (1937) PR:A-C**
CAMILLE 2000 zero (1969) PR:O
CAMMINA CAMMINA ** (1983, It.) PR:AA
CAMORRA **½ (1986, It.) PR:O
CAMP ON BLOOD ISLAND, THE **½
(1958, Brit.) PR:O
CAMPBELL'S KINGDOM **½ (1957, Brit.) PR:A
CAMPUS CONFESSIONS ** (1938) PR:A
CAMPUS HONEYMOON *½ (1948) PR:A
CAMPUS MAN **½ (1987) PR:C
CAMPUS RHYTHM *½ (1943) PR:A
CAMPUS SLEUTH * (1948) PR:A
CAN-CAN ** (1960) PR:A-C
CAN SHE BAKE A CHERRY PIE? ** (1983) PR:C
CAN THIS BE DIXIE? *½ (1936) PR:A
CAN YOU HEAR ME MOTHER? ** (1935, Brit.) PR:A
CAN'T BUY ME LOVE ** (1987) PR:C
CAN'T STOP THE MUSIC zero (1980) PR:C
CANADIAN MOUNTIES VS, ATOMIC INVADERS
(SEE:MISSILE BASE AT TANIAK)
CANADIAN PACIFIC ** (1949) PR:A
CANADIANS, THE ** (1961, Brit.) PR:A
CANAL ZONE zero (1942) PR:A
CANARIES SOMETIMES SING * (1930, Brit.) PR:A
CANARIS *** (1955, Ger.) PR:C
CANARY MURDER CASE, THE **½ (1929) PR:A
CANCEL MY RESERVATION * (1972) PR:A
CANDIDATE, THE ***½ (1972) PR:A-C
CANDIDATE, THE zero (1964) PR:C
CANDIDATE FOR MURDER ** (1966, Brit.) PR:A
CANDIDE *½ (1962, Fr.) PR:A
CANDLELIGHT IN ALGERIA **½ (1944, Brit.) PR:A
CANDLES AT NINE *½ (1944, Brit.) PR:A
CANDLESHOE **½ (1978) PR:AA
CANDY * (1968, It./Fr.) PR:O
CANDY MAN, THE zero (1969) PR:O
CANDY MOUNTAIN ****
(1988, Switz./Can./Fr.) PR:C
CANICULE
(SEE:DOG DAY)
CANNABIS *½ (1970, Fr.) PR:O
CANNERY ROW * (1982) PR:C-O**
CANNIBAL ATTACK * (1954) PR:A
CANNIBAL GIRLS *½ (1973) PR:C
CANNIBALISTIC HUMANOID UNDERGROUND
DWELLERS
(SEE:C.H.U.D.)
CANNIBALS, THE *½ (1970, It.) PR:C-O
CANNIBALS IN THE STREETS * (1982, It./Sp.) PR:O
CANNON AND THE NIGHTINGALE, THE **½
(1969, Gr.) PR:A
CANNON FOR CORDOBA ** (1970) PR:C-O
CANNONBALL ** (1976, US/Hong Kong) PR:C
CANNONBALL EXPRESS * (1932) PR:A
CANNONBALL RUN II zero (1984) PR:O
CANNONBALL RUN, THE zero (1981) PR:A
CANON CITY **½ (1948) PR:A
CAN'T HELP SINGING **½ (1944) PR:A
CANTERBURY TALE, A **½ (1944, Brit.) PR:A
CANTERVILLE GHOST, THE *** (1944) PR:AA
CANTOR'S SON, THE *½ (1937) PR:A
CANYON AMBUSH * (1952) PR:A
CANYON CITY * (1943) PR:A
CANYON CROSSROADS **½ (1955) PR:A
CANYON HAWKS * (1930) PR:A
CANYON OF MISSING MEN, THE * (1930) PR:A
CANYON PASSAGE *** (1946) PR:A
CANYON RAIDERS *½ (1951) PR:A
CANYON RIVER ** (1956) PR:A
CAPE CANAVERAL MONSTERS * (1960) PR:A
CAPE FEAR ***½ (1962) PR:O
CAPE FORLORN
(SEE:LOVE STORM)
CAPER OF THE GOLDEN BULLS, THE *½
(1967) PR:A
CAPETOWN AFFAIR *½
(1967, US/South Africa/Afr.) PR:C
CAPONE zero (1975) PR:O
CAPPY RICKS RETURNS * (1935) PR:A
CAPRICE * (1967) PR:A
CAPRICIOUS SUMMER *** (1968, Czech.) PR:C
CAPRICORN ONE * (1978) PR:C**
CAPTAIN APACHE * (1971, Brit.) PR:C
CAPTAIN APPLEJACK *½ (1931) PR:A
CAPTAIN BILL * (1935, Brit.) PR:A
CAPTAIN BLACK JACK * (1952, US/Fr.) PR:A
CAPTAIN BLOOD ** (1935) PR:A**
CAPTAIN BOYCOTT *½ (1947, Brit.) PR:A
CAPTAIN CALAMITY * (1936) PR:A
CAPTAIN CAREY, U.S.A **½ (1950) PR:A
CAPTAIN CAUTION *½ (1940) PR:A
CAPTAIN CHINA ** (1949) PR:A
CAPTAIN CLEGG
(SEE:NIGHT CREATURES)
CAPTAIN EDDIE **½ (1945) PR:AA
CAPTAIN FROM CASTILE **** (1947) PR:C-O
CAPTAIN FROM KOEPENICK *** (1933, Ger.) PR:A
CAPTAIN FROM KOEPENICK, THE ***
(1956, Ger.) PR:A
CAPTAIN FURY *** (1939) PR:A
CAPTAIN GRANT'S CHILDREN zero
(1939, USSR) PR:AA
CAPTAIN HATES THE SEA, THE *** (1934) PR:A
CAPTAIN HORATIO HORNBLOWER ***½
(1951, Brit.) PR:A
CAPTAIN HURRICANE zero (1935) PR:A
CAPTAIN IS A LADY, THE *½ (1940) PR:A
CAPTAIN JANUARY * (1935) PR:AA**
CAPTAIN JOHN SMITH AND POCAHONTAS **
(1953) PR:A
CAPTAIN KIDD **½ (1945) PR:A
CAPTAIN KIDD AND THE SLAVE GIRL *½
(1954) PR:A
CAPTAIN KRONOS: VAMPIRE HUNTER ***
(1974, Brit.) PR:O
CAPTAIN LIGHTFOOT ** (1955) PR:A
CAPTAIN MIDNIGHT
(SEE:ON THE AIR LIVE WITH CAPTAIN
MIDNIGHT)
CAPTAIN MILKSHAKE *½ (1971) PR:O
CAPTAIN MOONLIGHT * (1940, Brit.) PR:A
CAPTAIN NEMO AND THE UNDERWATER CITY
**½ (1969, Brit.) PR:A
CAPTAIN NEWMAN, M.D. **½ (1963) PR:C
CAPTAIN OF THE GUARD ** (1930) PR:A
CAPTAIN PIRATE **½ (1952) PR:A
CAPTAIN SCARLETT *½ (1953) PR:A
CAPTAIN SINDBAD *** (1963) PR:A
CAPTAIN SIROCCO
(SEE:PIRATES OF CAPRI)
CAPTAIN THUNDER zero (1931) PR:A
CAPTAIN TUGBOAT ANNIE ** (1945) PR:A
CAPTAINS COURAGEOUS *** (1937) PR:AA**
CAPTAIN'S KID, THE ** (1937) PR:A
CAPTAINS OF THE CLOUDS **½ (1942) PR:A-C
CAPTAIN'S ORDERS *½ (1937, Brit.) PR:A
CAPTAIN'S PARADISE, THE ** (1953, Brit.) PR:A**
CAPTAIN'S TABLE, THE * (1936, Brit.) PR:A
CAPTAIN'S TABLE, THE **½ (1960, Brit.) PR:A
CAPTIVATION zero (1931, Brit.) PR:A
CAPTIVE CITY *** (1952) PR:A
CAPTIVE CITY, THE *½ (1963, It.) PR:C
CAPTIVE GIRL *½ (1950) PR:A
CAPTIVE HEART, THE *** (1948, Brit.) PR:C
CAPTIVE HEARTS ** (1988) PR:C
CAPTIVE OF BILLY THE KID **½ (1952) PR:A
CAPTIVE WILD WOMAN *** (1943) PR:A
CAPTIVE WOMEN *½ (1952) PR:A
CAPTURE, THE *** (1950) PR:A
CAPTURE THAT CAPSULE zero (1961) PR:C
CAPTURED ** (1933) PR:A
CAR, THE * (1977) PR:C
CAR 99 **½ (1935) PR:A
CAR OF DREAMS ** (1935, Brit.) PR:A
CAR WASH * (1976) PR:C**
CARAVAGGIO **½ (1986, Brit.) PR:O
CARAVAN ** (1934) PR:A
CARAVAN ***½ (1946, Brit.) PR:A

__CARAVAN TO VACCARES ** (1974, Brit./Fr.) PR:C__
CARAVAN TRAIL, THE *½ (1946) PR:A
CARAVANS ** (1978, US/Iranian) PR:C
__CARBINE WILLIAMS *** (1952) PR:A__
__CARBON COPY **½ (1981) PR:C__
CARD, THE
(SEE:PROMOTER, THE)
CARDBOARD CAVALIER, THE ** (1949, Brit.) PR:A
__CARDIAC ARREST zero (1980) PR:O__
__CARDINAL, THE *** (1963) PR:C__
CARDINAL, THE zero (1936, Brit.) PR:A
CARDINAL RICHELIEU **½ (1935) PR:A
__CARE BEARS ADVENTURE IN WONDERLAND, THE * (1987, Can.) PR:AA__
__CARE BEARS MOVIE II: A NEW GENERATION ** (1986) PR:AA__
__CARE BEARS MOVIE, THE **½ (1985, Can.) PR:AA__
CAREER *½ (1939) PR:A
CAREER **½ (1959) PR:C
CAREER GIRL *½ (1944) PR:A
CAREER GIRL zero (1960) PR:C
CAREER WOMAN ** (1936) PR:A
CAREERS *½ (1929) PR:A
__CAREFREE *** (1938) PR:A__
__CAREFUL, HE MIGHT HEAR YOU **½ (1984, Aus.) PR:A-C__
CAREFUL, SOFT SHOULDERS *½ (1942) PR:A
CARELESS AGE * (1929) PR:A
CARELESS LADY * (1932) PR:A
CARELESS YEARS, THE **½ (1957) PR:A
CARETAKER, THE
(SEE:GUEST, THE)
CARETAKERS, THE **½ (1963) PR:C
CARETAKERS DAUGHTER, THE * (1952, Brit.) PR:A
CAREY TREATMENT, THE ** (1972) PR:C
CARGO TO CAPETOWN **½ (1950) PR:A
CARIBBEAN ** (1952) PR:A
CARIBBEAN MYSTERY, THE **½ (1945) PR:A
CARIBOO TRAIL, THE *** (1950) PR:A
CARLTON-BROWNE OF THE F.O.
(SEE:MAN IN THE COCKED HAT)
CARMELA ** (1949, It.) PR:A
CARMEN *½ (1931, Brit.) PR:A
CARMEN **½ (1946, It.) PR:A
CARMEN ** (1949, Sp.) PR:A
__CARMEN ***½ (1983, Sp.) PR:C__
CARMEN
(SEE:BIZET'S CARMEN)
CARMEN, BABY * (1967, Yugo./Ger.) PR:O
__CARMEN JONES *** (1954) PR:C__
CARNABY, M.D. * (1967, Brit.) PR:C
__CARNAGE zero (1986) PR:C__
__CARNAL KNOWLEDGE * (1971) PR:O__
CARNATION KID ** (1929) PR:A
CARNEGIE HALL **½ (1947) PR:A
CARNIVAL *½ (1931, Brit.) PR:A
CARNIVAL ** (1935) PR:A
CARNIVAL * (1946, Brit.) PR:A
CARNIVAL **½ (1953, Fr.) PR:A
CARNIVAL BOAT *½ (1932) PR:A
CARNIVAL IN COSTA RICA ** (1947) PR:A
__CARNIVAL IN FLANDERS *** (1936, Fr.) PR:A__
CARNIVAL LADY * (1933) PR:A
__CARNIVAL OF BLOOD zero (1976) PR:C__
CARNIVAL OF SINNERS *** (1947, Fr.) PR:A
__CARNIVAL OF SOULS *** (1962) PR:C__
CARNIVAL QUEEN *½ (1937) PR:A
__CARNIVAL ROCK ** (1957) PR:A__
__CARNIVAL STORY **½ (1954) PR:A__
__CARNY *** (1980) PR:O__
CAROLINA *½ (1934) PR:A
CAROLINA BLUES ** (1944) PR:A
CAROLINA CANNONBALL * (1955) PR:A
CAROLINA MOON * (1940) PR:A
CAROLINE CHERIE ** (1968, Fr.) PR:C
CAROLLIE CHERIE **½ (1951, Fr.) PR:A
CAROUSEL **** (1956) PR:A
__CARPETBAGGERS, THE ** (1964) PR:C__
CARRIE *** (1952) PR:C
__CARRIE **½ (1976) PR:O__
CARRINGTON V.C.
(SEE:COURT MARTIAL)
CARRY ON ADMIRAL **½ (1957, Brit.) PR:A
CARRY ON AGAIN, DOCTOR ** (1969, Brit.) PR:C
CARRY ON CABBIE **½ (1963, Brit.) PR:C
CARRY ON CAMPING **½ (1969, Brit.) PR:C
__CARRY ON CLEO *½ (1964, Brit.) PR:C__
CARRY ON CONSTABLE **½ (1960, Brit.) PR:C
__CARRY ON COWBOY ** (1966, Brit.) PR:A__
__CARRY ON CRUISING ** (1962, Brit.) PR:C__
__CARRY ON DOCTOR ** (1968, Brit.) PR:C__
__CARRY ON EMANUELLE * (1978, Brit.) PR:O__
CARRY ON ENGLAND * (1976, Brit.) PR:A
CARRY ON HENRY VIII ** (1970, Brit.) PR:O
CARRY ON JACK ** (1963, Brit.) PR:A
CARRY ON LOVING *½ (1970, Brit.) PR:C-O
__CARRY ON NURSE **½ (1959, Brit.) PR:A__
CARRY ON REGARDLESS ** (1961, Brit.) PR:C
CARRY ON SCREAMING ** (1966, Brit.) PR:A
CARRY ON SERGEANT **½ (1959, Brit.) PR:A
CARRY ON SPYING **½ (1964, Brit.) PR:A
CARRY ON TEACHER ** (1962, Brit.) PR:A
CARRY ON TV
(SEE:GET ON WITH IT)
CARRY ON UP THE JUNGLE ** (1970, Brit.) PR:A
CARRY ON, UP THE KHYBER **½ (1968, Brit.) PR:A
CARRY ON VENUS
(SEE:CARRY ON JACK)
__CARS THAT ATE PARIS, THE ***½ (1974, Aus.) PR:O__
CARSON CITY **½ (1952) PR:A
CARSON CITY CYCLONE ** (1943) PR:A
CARSON CITY KID *½ (1940) PR:AA
CARSON CITY RAIDERS ** (1948) PR:A
CARTER CASE, THE * (1947) PR:A
__CARTHAGE IN FLAMES *½ (1961, Fr./It.) PR:C-O__
CARTOUCHE * (1957, It./US) PR:A
CARTOUCHE *** (1962, Fr./It.) PR:A
CARVE HER NAME WITH PRIDE *** (1958, Brit.) PR:A
CARYL OF THE MOUNTAINS * (1936) PR:AA
CASA MANANA zero (1951) PR:A
CASA RICORDI
(SEE:HOUSE OF RICORDI)
__CASABLANCA ***** (1942) PR:A__
CASANOVA ** (1976, It.) PR:O
CASANOVA AND COMPANY
(SEE:SOME LIKE IT COOL)
CASANOVA BROWN ***½ (1944) PR:A
CASANOVA IN BURLESQUE **½ (1944) PR:A
CASANOVA '70 *** (1965, It.) PR:O
__CASANOVA'S BIG NIGHT ** (1954) PR:A__
CASBAH ***½ (1948) PR:C
CASE AGAINST BROOKLYN, THE **½ (1958) PR:A
CASE AGAINST FERRO, THE ** (1980, Fr.) PR:C
CASE AGAINST MRS. AMES, THE *½ (1936) PR:A
CASE FOR PC 49, A *½ (1951, Brit.) PR:A
CASE FOR THE CROWN, THE * (1934, Brit.) PR:A
CASE OF CHARLES PEACE, THE *½ (1949, Brit.) PR:A
CASE OF CLARA DEANE, THE * (1932) PR:A
CASE OF DR. LAURENT **½ (1958, Fr.) PR:C
CASE OF GABRIEL PERRY, THE * (1935, Brit.) PR:A
CASE OF MRS. LORING
(SEE:QUESTION OF ADULTERY, A)
CASE OF PATTY SMITH, THE *½ (1962) PR:C-O
CASE OF SERGEANT GRISCHA, THE * (1930) PR:A
CASE OF THE BLACK CAT, THE *** (1936) PR:A
CASE OF THE BLACK PARROT, THE ** (1941) PR:A
CASE OF THE CURIOUS BRIDE, THE ** (1935) PR:A
CASE OF THE 44'S, THE * (1964, Brit./Den.) PR:C
CASE OF THE FRIGHTENED LADY, THE * (1940., Brit.) PR:C
CASE OF THE HOWLING DOG, THE ** (1934) PR:A
CASE OF THE LUCKY LEGS, THE **½ (1935) PR:A
CASE OF THE MISSING MAN, THE * (1935) PR:A
CASE OF THE RED MONKEY *½ (1955, Brit.) PR:A
CASE OF THE STUTTERING BISHOP, THE *½ (1937) PR:A
CASE OF THE VELVET CLAWS, THE ** (1936) PR:A
CASE VAN GELDERN ** (1932, Ger.) PR:C
__CASEY'S SHADOW *** (1978) PR:A__
CASH McCALL *** (1960) PR:C
CASH ON DELIVERY **½ (1956, Brit.) PR:A
CASH ON DEMAND ** (1962, Brit.) PR:C
CASINO DE PARIS ** (1957, Fr./Ger.) PR:C
CASINO MURDER CASE, THE *½ (1935) PR:A
__CASINO ROYALE ** (1967, Brit.) PR:A__
CASQUE D'OR **** (1956, Fr.) PR:C
CASS TIMBERLANE *** (1947) PR:C
__CASSANDRA CROSSING, THE ** (1977, Brit.) PR:C__
CASSIDY OF BAR 20 ** (1938) PR:A
CAST A DARK SHADOW *** (1958, Brit.) PR:A
__CAST A GIANT SHADOW ***½ (1966) PR:A-C__
CAST A LONG SHADOW *½ (1959) PR:C
__CASTAWAY COWBOY, THE ** (1974) PR:AA__
CASTE * (1930, Brit.) PR:A
CASTILIAN, THE ** (1963, Sp./US) PR:C
__CASTLE, THE *** (1969, Ger.) PR:C__
CASTLE IN THE AIR * (1952, Brit.) PR:A
__CASTLE IN THE DESERT *½ (1942) PR:A__
CASTLE KEEP *** (1969) PR:C
CASTLE OF BLOOD **½ (1964, Fr./It.) PR:O
CASTLE OF CRIMES *½ (1940, Brit.) PR:A
__CASTLE OF EVIL * (1967) PR:C__
CASTLE OF FU MANCHU, THE * (1968, Ger./Sp./It./Brit.) PR:C
CASTLE OF PURITY *** (1974, Mex.) PR:C-O
CASTLE OF TERROR
(SEE:CASTLE OF BLOOD)
CASTLE OF THE LIVING DEAD ** (1964, It./Fr.) PR:C
CASTLE OF THE MONSTERS *½ (1958, Mex.) PR:C
CASTLE ON THE HUDSON **½ (1940) PR:C
CASTLE SINISTER zero (1932, Brit.) PR:C
__CASUAL SEX? **½ (1988) PR:O__
CAT, THE ** (1959, Fr.) PR:C
CAT AND MOUSE *½ (1958, Brit.) PR:C
CAT AND MOUSE
(SEE:MOUSEY)
__CAT AND MOUSE ** (1975, Fr.) PR:A-C__
CAT AND THE CANARY, THE *** (1939) PR:A
__CAT AND THE CANARY, THE ** (1979, Brit.) PR:A__
CAT AND THE FIDDLE *** (1934) PR:A
CAT ATE THE PARAKEET, THE zero (1972) PR:A
__CAT, THE *½ (1966) PR:AA__
__CAT BALLOU **** (1965) PR:A-C__
CAT BURGLAR, THE *½ (1961) PR:C
__CAT, THE **½ (1975, Fr.) PR:C__
CAT CREEPS, THE *** (1930) PR:AA
CAT CREEPS, THE ** (1946) PR:AA
__CAT FROM OUTER SPACE, THE *** (1978) PR:AA__
CAT GANG, THE *½ (1959, Brit.) PR:AA
CAT GIRL ** (1957) PR:C
CAT IN THE SACK, THE * (1967, Can.) PR:C
CAT MURKIL AND THE SILKS zero (1976) PR:O
__CAT ON A HOT TIN ROOF **** (1958) PR:C__
CAT O'NINE TAILS * (1971, It./Ger./Fr.) PR:O
__CAT PEOPLE *** (1942) PR:C__
__CAT PEOPLE **½ (1982) PR:O__
__CAT WOMEN OF THE MOON * (1953) PR:A__
CATACOMBS
(SEE:WOMAN WHO WOULDN'T DIE, THE)
CATALINA CAPER, THE * (1967) PR:A
__CATAMOUNT KILLING, THE ** (1975, Ger.) PR:C__
CATCH AS CATCH CAN ** (1937, Brit.) PR:A
__CATCH AS CATCH CAN ** (1968, It.) PR:C__
__CATCH ME A SPY **½ (1971, Brit./Fr.) PR:A-C__
CATCH MY SOUL **½ (1974) PR:C
__CATCH THE HEAT * (1987) PR:C__
__CATCH-22 *** (1970) PR:O__
CATCH US IF YOU CAN
(SEE:HAVING A WILD WEEKEND)
CATERED AFFAIR, THE **** (1956) PR:A
CATHERINE & CO. ** (1976, Fr.) PR:O
__CATHERINE THE GREAT *** (1934, Brit.) PR:C__
CATHY'S CHILD **½ (1979, Aus.) PR:C
__CATHY'S CURSE * (1977, Can.) PR:O__
CATLOW ** (1971, Sp.) PR:C
CATMAN OF PARIS, THE **½ (1946) PR:A
__CAT'S EYE ** (1985) PR:C__
CAT'S PAW, THE *** (1934) PR:A
CATSKILL HONEYMOON zero (1950) PR:A
__CATTLE ANNIE AND LITTLE BRITCHES **½ (1981) PR:C__
CATTLE DRIVE *** (1951) PR:AA
CATTLE EMPIRE **½ (1958) PR:A
CATTLE KING **½ (1963) PR:A
CATTLE QUEEN * (1951) PR:A
__CATTLE QUEEN OF MONTANA ** (1954) PR:A__
CATTLE RAIDERS *½ (1938) PR:A
CATTLE STAMPEDE * (1943) PR:A
CATTLE THIEF, THE *½ (1936) PR:A
CATTLE TOWN ** (1952) PR:A
CAUGHT zero (1931) PR:A
__CAUGHT ** (1949) PR:C__
CAUGHT CHEATING * (1931) PR:A
CAUGHT IN THE ACT zero (1941) PR:A
CAUGHT IN THE DRAFT *** (1941) PR:AA
CAUGHT IN THE FOG * (1928) PR:A

CAUGHT IN THE NET *½ (1960, Brit.) PR:AA
CAUGHT PLASTERED * (1931) PR:A
CAUGHT SHORT ** (1930) PR:A
CAULDRON OF BLOOD ** (1971, Sp.) PR:C
CAULDRON OF DEATH, THE * (1979, It.) PR:O
CAUSE FOR ALARM * (1951) PR:C**
CAVALCADE *** (1933) PR:A
CAVALCADE OF THE WEST * (1936) PR:A
CAVALIER, THE * (1928) PR:A
CAVALIER OF THE STREETS, THE *½ (1937, Brit.) PR:A
CAVALIER OF THE WEST ** (1931) PR:A
CAVALLERIA RUSTICANA (SEE:FATAL DESIRE)
CAVALRY * (1936) PR:A
CAVALRY COMMAND ** (1963, US/Phil.) PR:A
CAVALRY SCOUT ** (1951) PR:A
CAVE GIRL zero (1985) PR:O
CAVE OF OUTLAWS ** (1951) PR:A
CAVE OF THE LIVING DEAD * (1966, Yugo./Ger.) PR:A
CAVEMAN ** (1981) PR:C
CAVERN, THE **½ (1965, It./Ger.) PR:A
CAYMAN TRIANGLE, THE * (1977) PR:C-O
CEASE FIRE **½ (1985) PR:O
CEDDO ** (1978, Nigeria) PR:C
CEILNG ZERO ***½ (1935) PR:A
CELESTE **½ (1982, Ger.) PR:A
CELIA *½ (1949, Brit.) PR:A
CELINE AND JULIE GO BOATING *** (1974, Fr.) PR:C
CELL 2455, DEATH ROW ** (1955) PR:C
CELLAR DWELLER *½ (1988) PR:O
CEMENTERIO DEL TERROR ** (1985, Mex.) PR:O
CENSUS TAKER, THE ** (1984) PR:O
CENTENNIAL SUMMER **½ (1946) PR:AA
CENTO ANNI D'AMORE ** (1954, It.) PR:C
CENTRAL AIRPORT ** (1933) PR:A
CENTRAL PARK ** (1932) PR:A
CENTURION, THE * (1962, Fr./It.) PR:A
CEREBROS DIABOLICOS * (1966, Mex.) PR:A
CEREBROS INFERNAL (SEE:BLUE DEMON VERSUS THE INFERNAL BRAINS)
CEREMONY, THE ** (1963, US/Sp.) PR:C
CERTAIN FURY zero (1985) PR:O
CERTAIN SMILE, A ** (1958) PR:C-O
CERTAIN, VERY CERTAIN, AS A MATTER OF FACT... PROBABLE ** (1970, It.) PR:O
CERVANTES (SEE:YOUNG REBELS)
CESAR ***½ (1936, Fr.) PR:A
CESAR AND ROSALIE * (1972, Fr./It./Ger.) PR:C**
CHA-CHA-CHA BOOM * (1956) PR:A
CHAD HANNA *** (1940) PR:A-C
CHAFED ELBOWS ** (1967) PR:C-O
CHAIN, THE ***½ (1985, Brit.) PR:C
CHAIN GANG *½ (1950) PR:C
CHAIN GANG * (1985) PR:O
CHAIN LETTERS **½ (1985) PR:O
CHAIN LIGHTNING *** (1950) PR:A
CHAIN OF CIRCUMSTANCE * (1951) PR:A
CHAIN OF EVENTS *½ (1958, Brit.) PR:A-C
CHAIN OF EVIDENCE *½ (1957) PR:A
CHAIN REACTION * (1980, Aus.) PR:C**
CHAINED **½ (1934) PR:C
CHAINED FOR LIFE *½ (1950) PR:C
CHAINED HEAT zero (1983, US/Ger.) PR:O
CHAINSAW HOOKERS (SEE:HOLLYWOOD CHAINSAW HOOKERS)
CHAIRMAN, THE * (1969) PR:A-C**
CHALK GARDEN, THE **½ (1964, Brit.) PR:A
CHALLENGE, THE **½ (1939, Brit.) PR:A
CHALLENGE, THE ** (1948) PR:A
CHALLENGE zero (1974) PR:O
CHALLENGE, THE ** (1982) PR:C
CHALLENGE FOR ROBIN HOOD, A *½ (1968, Brit.) PR:A
CHALLENGE OF THE RANGE ** (1949) PR:A
CHALLENGE THE WILD * (1954) PR:AA
CHALLENGE TO BE FREE ** (1976) PR:A
CHALLENGE TO LASSIE **½ (1949) PR:AA
CHALLENGE, THE (SEE:IT TAKES A THIEF)
CHAMBER OF HORRORS ** (1941, Brit.) PR:A
CHAMBER OF HORRORS * (1966) PR:O
CHAMELEON zero (1978) PR:C
CHAMP ***½ (1931) PR:AA
CHAMP, THE **½ (1979) PR:AA
CHAMP FOR A DAY **½ (1953) PR:A
CHAMPAGNE CHARLIE ** (1936) PR:A
CHAMPAGNE CHARLIE **½ (1944, Brit.) PR:A
CHAMPAGNE FOR BREAKFAST * (1935) PR:A
CHAMPAGNE FOR CAESAR *** (1950) PR:AA**
CHAMPAGNE MURDERS, THE ** (1968, Fr.) PR:C
CHAMPAGNE WALTZ **½ (1937) PR:A
CHAMPION *** (1949) PR:C**
CHAMPIONS * (1984) PR:C**
CHAN IS MISSING *** (1982) PR:C
CHANCE AT HEAVEN ** (1933) PR:A
CHANCE MEETING *** (1954, Brit.) PR:A
CHANCE MEETING **½ (1960, Brit.) PR:C
CHANCE OF A LIFETIME, THE **½ (1943) PR:A
CHANCE OF A LIFETIME zero (1950, Brit.) PR:A
CHANCE OF A NIGHT-TIME, THE * (1931, Brit.) PR:A
CHANCES *** (1931) PR:A
CHANDLER *½ (1971) PR:A
CHANDU THE MAGICIAN **½ (1932) PR:A
CHANEL SOLITAIRE *½ (1981) PR:C
CHANGE FOR A SOVEREIGN *½ (1937, Brit.) PR:A
CHANGE OF HABIT *½ (1969) PR:C-O
CHANGE OF HEART ** (1934) PR:A
CHANGE OF HEART ** (1938) PR:A
CHANGE OF HEART (SEE:HIT PARADE OF 1943)
CHANGE OF HEART, A (SEE:TWO AND TWO MAKE SIX)
CHANGE OF MIND *½ (1969) PR:C
CHANGE OF SEASONS, A * (1980) PR:C-O
CHANGE PARTNERS *½ (1965, Brit.) PR:C
CHANGELING, THE * (1980, Can.) PR:O**
CHANGES *½ (1969) PR:O
CHANNEL CROSSING ** (1934, Brit.) PR:A
CHANT OF JIMMIE BLACKSMITH, THE * (1980, Aus.) PR:O
CHAPMAN REPORT, THE zero (1962) PR:O
CHAPPAQUA * (1967) PR:O
CHAPTER TWO * (1979) PR:C**
CHARADE ** (1953) PR:A
CHARADE ** (1963) PR:A-C**
CHARGE AT FEATHER RIVER, THE **½ (1953) PR:C
CHARGE OF THE LANCERS ** (1953) PR:A
CHARGE OF THE LIGHT BRIGADE, THE *** (1936) PR:A**
CHARGE OF THE LIGHT BRIGADE, THE *** (1968, Brit.) PR:C
CHARGE OF THE MODEL-T'S * (1979) PR:AA
CHARING CROSS ROAD *** (1935, Brit.) PR:A
CHARIOTS OF FIRE ** (1981, Brit.) PR:AA**
CHARLATAN, THE * (1929) PR:A
CHARLES AND LUCIE **½ (1982, Fr.) PR:A
CHARLES, DEAD OR ALIVE **½ (1972, Switz.) PR:C
CHARLESTON zero (1978, It.) PR:A
CHARLEY AND THE ANGEL **½ (1973) PR:AA
CHARLEY MOON *½ (1956, Brit.) PR:A
CHARLEY-ONE-EYE *½ (1973, Brit.) PR:C
CHARLEY VARRICK ***½ (1973) PR:C
CHARLEY'S AUNT *½ (1930) PR:A
CHARLEY'S AUNT ***½ (1941) PR:AA
CHARLEY'S (BIG-HEARTED) AUNT *½ (1940, Brit.) PR:A
CHARLIE BUBBLES **½ (1968, Brit.) PR:C
CHARLIE CHAN AND THE CURSE OF THE DRAGON QUEEN zero (1981) PR:A
CHARLIE CHAN AT MONTE CARLO ** (1937) PR:A
CHARLIE CHAN AT THE CIRCUS **½ (1936) PR:A
CHARLIE CHAN AT THE OLYMPICS **½ (1937) PR:A
CHARLIE CHAN AT THE OPERA ***½ (1936) PR:A
CHARLIE CHAN AT THE RACE TRACK *** (1936) PR:A
CHARLIE CHAN AT THE WAX MUSEUM *½ (1940) PR:A
CHARLIE CHAN AT TREASURE ISLAND ** (1939) PR:A
CHARLIE CHAN CARRIES ON *** (1931) PR:A
CHARLIE CHAN IN BLACK MAGIC *½ (1944) PR:A
CHARLIE CHAN IN EGYPT *** (1935) PR:A
CHARLIE CHAN IN HONOLULU **½ (1938) PR:A
CHARLIE CHAN IN LONDON **½ (1934) PR:A
CHARLIE CHAN IN PANAMA **½ (1940) PR:A
CHARLIE CHAN IN PARIS ** (1935) PR:A
CHARLIE CHAN IN RENO **½ (1939) PR:A
CHARLIE CHAN IN RIO * (1941) PR:A
CHARLIE CHAN IN SHANGHAI ** (1935) PR:A
CHARLIE CHAN IN THE CITY OF DARKNESS * (1939) PR:A
CHARLIE CHAN IN THE SECRET SERVICE * (1944) PR:A
CHARLIE CHAN ON BROADWAY **½ (1937) PR:A
CHARLIE CHAN'S CHANCE ** (1932) PR:A
CHARLIE CHAN'S COURAGE *½ (1934) PR:A
CHARLIE CHAN'S GREATEST CASE **½ (1933) PR:A
CHARLIE CHAN'S MURDER CRUISE ** (1940) PR:A
CHARLIE CHAN'S SECRET * (1936) PR:A**
CHARLIE MC CARTHY, DETECTIVE ** (1939) PR:AA
CHARLIE, THE LONESOME COUGAR **½ (1967) PR:AA
CHARLOTTE'S WEB ***½ (1973) PR:AA
CHARLTON-BROWN OF THE F.O. (SEE:MAN IN A COCKED HAT)
CHARLY * (1968) PR:A-C**
CHARMING DECEIVER, THE zero (1933, Brit.) PR:A
CHARMING SINNERS *½ (1929) PR:A
CHARRO * (1969) PR:A
CHARTER PILOT ** (1940) PR:A
CHARTROOSE CABOOSE *½ (1960) PR:A
CHASE, THE *** (1946) PR:A
CHASE, THE * (1966) PR:O
CHASE A CROOKED SHADOW ***½ (1958, Brit.) PR:A
CHASE FOR THE GOLDEN NEEDLES (SEE:GOLDEN NEEDLES)
CHASER, THE **½ (1938) PR:A
CHASERS, THE (SEE:GIRL HUNTERS, THE)
CHASING DANGER ** (1939) PR:A
CHASING RAINBOWS ** (1930) PR:A
CHASING TROUBLE zero (1940) PR:A
CHASING YESTERDAY *½ (1935) PR:A
CHASTITY ** (1969) PR:C
CHASTITY BELT, THE * (1968, It.) PR:C
CHATO'S LAND ** (1972) PR:O
CHATTANOOGA CHOO CHOO * (1984) PR:A-C
CHATTERBOX **½ (1936) PR:A
CHATTERBOX * (1943) PR:A
CHE! * (1969) PR:C
CHE? ** (1973, It./Fr./Ger.) PR:O
CHEAP DETECTIVE, THE * (1978) PR:C**
CHEAPER BY THE DOZEN ***½ (1950) PR:AA
CHEAPER TO KEEP HER zero (1980) PR:O
CHEAT, THE ** (1931) PR:C-O
CHEAT, THE ** (1950, Fr.) PR:C-O
CHEATERS ** (1934) PR:A
CHEATERS, THE ***½ (1945) PR:A
CHEATERS, THE **½ (1961, Fr.) PR:O
CHEATERS AT PLAY ** (1932) PR:A
CHEATING BLONDES **½ (1933) PR:A
CHEATING CHEATERS ** (1934) PR:A
CHECK AND DOUBLE CHECK (SEE:AMOS 'N' ANDY)
CHECK IS IN THE MAIL, THE ** (1986) PR:C-O
CHECK YOUR GUNS ** (1948) PR:A
CHECKERBOARD *½ (1969, Fr.) PR:O
CHECKERED COAT, THE ** (1948) PR:A
CHECKERED FLAG, THE * (1963) PR:C
CHECKERED FLAG OR CRASH *½ (1978) PR:C
CHECKERS **½ (1937) PR:A
CHECKMATE * (1935, Brit.) PR:A
CHECKMATE zero (1973) PR:O
CHECKPOINT **½ (1957, Brit.) PR:A
CHEECH AND CHONG'S NEXT MOVIE zero (1980) PR:O
CHEECH AND CHONG'S NICE DREAMS zero (1981) PR:O
CHEECH AND CHONG'S THE CORSICAN BROTHERS zero (1984) PR:O
CHEER BOYS CHEER ** (1939, Brit.) PR:A
CHEER THE BRAVE * (1951, Brit.) PR:A
CHEER UP! *½ (1936, Brit.) PR:A
CHEER UP AND SMILE *½ (1930) PR:A
CHEERS FOR MISS BISHOP **½ (1941) PR:A
CHEERS OF THE CROWD zero (1936) PR:A
CHELSEA GIRLS, THE ** (1967) PR:O
CHELSEA LIFE * (1933, Brit.) PR:A
CHELSEA STORY *½ (1951, Brit.) PR:A
CHEREZ TERNII K SVEZDAM **½ (1981, USSR) PR:A
CHEROKEE FLASH, THE ** (1945) PR:A
CHEROKEE STRIP *½ (1937) PR:A
CHEROKEE STRIP ** (1940) PR:A
CHEROKEE UPRISING ** (1950) PR:A
CHESS PLAYERS, THE ** (1978, India) PR:C
CHESTY ANDERSON, U.S. NAVY * (1976) PR:O
CHETNIKS *½ (1943) PR:A
CHEYENNE **½ (1947) PR:A
CHEYENNE AUTUMN ** (1964) PR:A**
CHEYENNE CYCLONE, THE * (1932) PR:A
CHEYENNE KID, THE * (1930) PR:A
CHEYENNE KID, THE *½ (1933) PR:A
CHEYENNE KID, THE * (1940) PR:A
CHEYENNE RIDES AGAIN *½ (1937) PR:A
CHEYENNE ROUNDUP *½ (1943) PR:A
CHEYENNE SOCIAL CLUB, THE * (1970) PR:C**
CHEYENNE TAKES OVER *½ (1947) PR:A
CHEYENNE TORNADO * (1935) PR:A
CHEYENNE WILDCAT ** (1944) PR:A
CHICAGO CALLING *½ (1951) PR:A
CHICAGO CONFIDENTIAL **½ (1957) PR:A
CHICAGO DEADLINE *** (1949) PR:A
CHICAGO KID, THE ** (1945) PR:A
CHICAGO KID, THE (SEE:FABULOUS BASTARD FROM CHICAGO, THE)
CHICAGO 70 ** (1970) PR:C
CHICAGO SYNDICATE ** (1955) PR:A
CHICK *½ (1936, Brit.) PR:A
CHICKEN CHRONICLES, THE * (1977) PR:C
CHICKEN EVERY SUNDAY **½ (1948) PR:A
CHICKEN WAGON FAMILY * (1939) PR:A
CHIDAMBARAM ** (1986, India) PR:O

CHIEF, THE * (1933) PR:A
CHIEF CRAZY HORSE **½ (1955) PR:A
CHILD, THE * (1977) PR:O
CHILD AND THE KILLER, THE * (1959, Brit.) PR:C
CHILD IN THE HOUSE **½ (1956, Brit.) PR:A
CHILD IS A WILD THING, A ** (1976) PR:O
CHILD IS BORN, A ** (1940) PR:A
CHILD IS WAITING, A * (1963) PR:A**
CHILD OF DIVORCE **½ (1946) PR:A
CHILD OF MANHATTAN * (1933) PR:C
CHILD UNDER A LEAF ** (1975, Can.) PR:O
CHILDHOOD OF MAXIM GORKY * (1938, USSR) PR:A
CHILDISH THINGS zero (1969) PR:O
CHILDREN, THE **½ (1949, Swed.) PR:AA
CHILDREN, THE zero (1980) PR:O
CHILDREN GALORE * (1954, Brit.) PR:A
CHILDREN OF A LESSER GOD ** (1986) PR:C-O**
CHILDREN OF BABYLON zero (1980, Jamaica) PR:O
CHILDREN OF CHANCE * (1930, Brit.) PR:A
CHILDREN OF CHANCE * (1949, Brit.) PR:A
CHILDREN OF CHANCE ** (1950, It.) PR:A
CHILDREN OF CHAOS ** (1950, Fr.) PR:C
CHILDREN OF DREAMS zero (1931) PR:A
CHILDREN OF GOD'S EARTH ** (1983, Norway) PR:C
CHILDREN OF HIROSHIMA **½ (1952, Jap.) PR:C-O
CHILDREN OF PARADISE *** (1945, Fr.) PR:C**
CHILDREN OF PLEASURE * (1930) PR:A
CHILDREN OF RAGE * (1975, Brit./Israeli) PR:O
CHILDREN OF SANCHEZ, THE * (1978, US/Mex.) PR:O
CHILDREN OF THE CORN *½ (1984) PR:C-O
CHILDREN OF THE DAMNED ** (1963, Brit.) PR:O
CHILDREN OF THE FOG * (1935, Brit.) PR:A
CHILDREN SHOULDN'T PLAY WITH DEAD THINGS **½ (1972) PR:O
CHILDRENS GAMES * (1969) PR:C-O
CHILDREN'S HOUR, THE ***½ (1961) PR:C
CHILD'S PLAY ** (1954, Brit.) PR:A
CHILD'S PLAY ** (1972) PR:A-C
CHILD'S PLAY **½ (1988) PR:O
CHILLY SCENES OF WINTER **½ (1982) PR:C
CHILTERN HUNDREDS, THE (SEE:AMAZING MR. BEECHAM, THE)
CHIMES AT MIDNIGHT ***½ (1967, Sp./Switz.) PR:C
CHINA *** (1943) PR:C
CHINA CLIPPER ** (1936) PR:A
CHINA CORSAIR * (1951) PR:C
CHINA DOLL **½ (1958) PR:C
CHINA GATE ** (1957) PR:C
CHINA GIRL *** (1942) PR:A
CHINA GIRL **½ (1987) PR:O
CHINA IS NEAR **½ (1968, It.) PR:C-O
CHINA 9, LIBERTY 37 **½ (1978, It.) PR:O
CHINA PASSAGE ** (1937) PR:A
CHINA SEAS ***½ (1935) PR:A
CHINA SKY **½ (1945) PR:C
CHINA SYNDROME, THE ** (1979) PR:A**
CHINA VENTURE ** (1953) PR:C
CHINA'S LITTLE DEVILS *½ (1945) PR:C
CHINATOWN *** (1974) PR:O**
CHINATOWN AFTER DARK zero (1931) PR:A
CHINATOWN AT MIDNIGHT ** (1949) PR:C
CHINATOWN NIGHTS ** (1929) PR:A
CHINATOWN NIGHTS *½ (1938, Brit.) PR:A
CHINATOWN SQUAD ** (1935) PR:A
CHINCERO (SEE:LAST MOVIE, THE)
CHINESE BOXES * (1984, Ger./Brit.) PR:O**
CHINESE BUNGALOW, THE * (1930, Brit.) PR:A
CHINESE CAT, THE * (1944) PR:A
CHINESE DEN, THE ** (1940, Brit.) PR:A
CHINESE PUZZLE, THE *½ (1932, Brit.) PR:A
CHINESE RING, THE * (1947) PR:A
CHINESE ROULETTE *** (1977, Ger.) PR:O
CHINO ** (1976, Ital.,/Span.,/Fr.) PR:A-C
CHIP OF THE FLYING U ** (1940) PR:A
CHIP OFF THE OLD BLOCK *** (1944) PR:A
CHIPMUNK ADVENTURE, THE **½ (1987) PR:AA
CHIPS ** (1938., Brit.) PR:A
CHIQUTTO PERO PICOSO *½ (1967, Mex.) PR:A
CHISUM * (1970) PR:A**
CHITTY CHITTY BANG BANG **½ (1968, Brit.) PR:AA

CHIVATO * (1961) PR:A-C
CHLOE IN THE AFTERNOON * (1972, Fr.) PR:O**
CHOCOLATE SOLDIER, THE * (1941) PR:A**
CHOCOLATE WAR, THE * (1988) PR:C**
CHOICE OF ARMS ** (1983, Fr.) PR:C
CHOIRBOYS, THE **½ (1977) PR:O
CHOKE CANYON ** (1986) PR:A
CHOOSE ME * (1984) PR:O**
CHOPPERS, THE * (1961) PR:C-O
CHOPPING MALL ** (1986) PR:O
CHORUS LINE, A * (1985) PR:C**
CHOSEN, THE *½ (1978, Brit./It.) PR:O
CHOSEN, THE * (1982) PR:A**
CHOSEN SURVIVORS *½ (1974, US/Mex.) PR:C
CHRIST STOPPED AT EBOLI (SEE:EBOLI)
CHRISTIAN LICORICE STORE, THE *½ (1971) PR:C
CHRISTIAN THE LION ** (1976, Brit.) PR:AA
CHRISTINA * (1929) PR:A
CHRISTINA ** (1974, Can.) PR:C
CHRISTINE * (1959, Fr.) PR:C
CHRISTINE * (1983) PR:C-O
CHRISTINE JORGENSEN STORY, THE * (1970) PR:O
CHRISTINE KEELER AFFAIR, THE *½ (1964, Brit.) PR:O
CHRISTMAS CAROL, A ***½ (1938) PR:AA
CHRISTMAS CAROL, A ** (1951, Brit.) PR:AA
CHRISTMAS EVE **½ (1947) PR:A
CHRISTMAS HOLIDAY *** (1944) PR:A
CHRISTMAS IN CONNECTICUT ***½ (1945) PR:AA
CHRISTMAS IN JULY ***½ (1940) PR:A
CHRISTMAS KID, THE **½ (1968, US/Sp.) PR:C
CHRISTMAS STORY, A ** (1983) PR:A**
CHRISTMAS THAT ALMOST WASN'T, THE * (1966, It.) PR:A
CHRISTMAS TREE, THE ** (1966, Brit.) PR:AA
CHRISTMAS TREE, THE ** (1969, Fr.) PR:A
CHRISTOPHER BEAN * (1933) PR:A
CHRISTOPHER COLUMBUS **½ (1949, Brit.) PR:A
CHRISTOPHER STRONG * (1933) PR:C**
CHROME AND HOT LEATHER ** (1971) PR:O
CHRONICLE OF ANNA MAGDALENA BACH **½ (1968, It./Ger.) PR:A-C
CHRONOPOLIS ***½ (1982, Fr.) PR:A-C
CHU CHIN CHOW ** (1934, Brit.) PR:A
CHU CHU AND THE PHILLY FLASH ** (1981) PR:A
CHUBASCO *½ (1968) PR:A
CHUKA ** (1967) PR:C
CHUMP AT OXFORD, A **½ (1940) PR:A
CHURCH MOUSE, THE ** (1934, Brit.) PR:A
CHUSHINGURA ***½ (1963, Jap.) PR:C
CIAO MANHATTAN zero (1973) PR:O
CIGARETTE GIRL ** (1947) PR:A
CIMARRON ** (1931) PR:A**
CIMARRON ** (1960) PR:A
CIMARRON KID, THE *½ (1951) PR:A
CINCINNATI KID, THE ** (1965) PR:A-C**
CINDERELLA * (1937, Fr.) PR:A
CINDERELLA ** (1950) PR:AA**
CINDERELLA JONES ** (1946) PR:AA
CINDERELLA LIBERTY ** (1973) PR:C-O
CINDERELLA SWINGS IT * (1942) PR:A
CINDERFELLA ** (1960) PR:A
CIPHER BUREAU *½ (1938) PR:A
CIRCLE, THE **½ (1959, Brit.) PR:C
CIRCLE CANYON * (1934) PR:A
CIRCLE OF DANGER ** (1951, Brit.) PR:C
CIRCLE OF DEATH *½ (1935) PR:A
CIRCLE OF DECEIT ** (1982, Fr./Ger.) PR:O**
CIRCLE OF DECEPTON ** (1961, Brit.) PR:C
CIRCLE OF IRON *½ (1979, Brit.) PR:O
CIRCLE OF LOVE * (1965, Fr.) PR:C-O
CIRCLE OF POWER (SEE:MYSTIQUE)
CIRCLE OF TWO ** (1980, Can.) PR:O
CIRCUMSTANTIAL EVIDENCE ** (1935) PR:A
CIRCUMSTANTIAL EVIDENCE *½ (1945) PR:C
CIRCUMSTANTIAL EVIDENCE * (1954, Brit.) PR:C
CIRCUS (SEE:INVITATION TO THE DANCE)
CIRCUS BOY ** (1947, Brit.) PR:AA
CIRCUS CLOWN ** (1934) PR:A
CIRCUS FRIENDS ** (1962, Brit.) PR:AA
CIRCUS GIRL *½ (1937) PR:A

CIRCUS KID, THE ** (1928) PR:A
CIRCUS OF FEAR (SEE:PSYCHO-CIRCUS)
CIRCUS OF HORRORS * (1960, Brit.) PR:O
CIRCUS OF LOVE ** (1958, Ger.) PR:C
CIRCUS QUEEN MURDER, THE **½ (1933) PR:C
CIRCUS WORLD * (1964) PR:A**
CISCO KID * (1931) PR:AA
CISCO KID AND THE LADY, THE **½ (1939) PR:A
CISCO KID RETURNS, THE *½ (1945) PR:A
CISCO PIKE ** (1971) PR:O
CITADEL, THE ** (1938) PR:A**
CITADEL OF CRIME * (1941) PR:C
CITIZEN KANE *** (1941) PR:A**
CITIZEN SAINT ** (1947) PR:AA
CITIZENS BAND * (1977) PR:C**
CITY ACROSS THE RIVER **½ (1949) PR:C
CITY AFTER MIDNIGHT ** (1957, Brit.) PR:C
CITY AND THE DOGS, THE ***½ (1987, Peru) PR:O
CITY BENEATH THE SEA ** (1953) PR:C
CITY, FOR CONQUEST ***½ (1941) PR:A
CITY GIRL *½ (1930) PR:A
CITY GIRL *½ (1938) PR:C
CITY GIRL, THE **½ (1984) PR:O
CITY HEAT *½ (1984) PR:O
CITY IN DARKNESS (SEE:CHARLIE CHAN IN THE CITY OF DARKNESS)
CITY LIMITS *½ (1934) PR:A
CITY LIMITS **½ (1985) PR:C
CITY LOVERS zero (1982, South Africa) PR:C
CITY NEWS **½ (1983) PR:C
CITY OF BAD MEN ** (1953) PR:A
CITY OF BEAUTIFUL NONSENSE, THE ** (1935, Brit.) PR:A
CITY OF BLOOD * (1988, South Africa) PR:O**
CITY OF CHANCE *½ (1940) PR:C
CITY OF FEAR **½ (1959) PR:C
CITY OF FEAR *½ (1965, Brit.) PR:C
CITY OF MISSING GIRLS * (1941) PR:Aa
CITY OF PAIN ** (1951, It.) PR:C
CITY OF PLAY *½ (1929, Brit.) PR:A
CITY OF SECRETS **½ (1963, Ger.) PR:O
CITY OF SHADOWS * (1955) PR:A
CITY OF SILENT MEN * (1942) PR:C
CITY OF SONG (SEE:FAREWELL TO LOVE)
CITY OF SONGS (SEE:VIENNA, CITY OF SONGS)
CITY OF THE DEAD (SEE:HORROR HOTEL)
CITY OF THE WALKING DEAD * (1983, Sp./It.) PR:O
CITY OF TORMENT *** (1950, Ger.) PR:C
CITY OF WOMEN *** (1980, It./Fr.) PR:O
CITY OF YOUTH **½ (1938, USSR) PR:C
CITY ON A HUNT (SEE:NO ESCAPE)
CITY ON FIRE * (1979, Can.) PR:O
CITY PARK *½ (1934) PR:A
CITY SENTINEL (SEE:BEAST OF THE CITY)
CITY STORY * (1954) PR:C
CITY STREETS ***½ (1931) PR:A
CITY STREETS *½ (1938) PR:A
CITY THAT NEVER SLEEPS * (1953) PR:A**
CITY UNDER THE SEA *½ (1965, Brit.) PR:A
CITY WITHOUT MEN * (1943) PR:A
CLAIR DE FEMME * (1980, Fr.) PR:O
CLAIRE'S KNEE ***½ (1971, Fr.) PR:C-O
CLAIRVOYANT, THE * (1935, Brit.) PR:A**
CLAMBAKE ** (1967) PR:AA
CLAN OF THE CAVE BEAR, THE *½ (1986) PR:O
CLANCY IN WALL STREET * (1930) PR:A
CLANCY STREET BOYS ** (1943) PR:A
CLANDESTINE *½ (1948, Fr.) PR:C
CLARA'S HEART *½ (1988) PR:C
CLARENCE * (1937) PR:A
CLARENCE AND ANGEL **½ (1981) PR:C
CLARENCE, THE CROSS-EYED LION *** (1965) PR:AA
CLARETTA AND BEN **½ (1983, It./Fr.) PR:O
CLASH BY NIGHT ** (1952) PR:C**
CLASH OF THE TITANS **½ (1981) PR:AA
CLASS * (1983) PR:O
CLASS ENEMY ** (1984, Ger.) PR:O
CLASS OF '44 ** (1973) PR:C

Finding entries in **THE MOTION PICTURE GUIDE ™**

Years	
Years 1929-83	Volumes I-IX
1984	Volume IX
1985	1986 ANNUAL
1986	1987 ANNUAL
1987	1988 ANNUAL
1988	1989 ANNUAL

STAR RATINGS

★★★★★	Masterpiece
★★★★	Excellent
★★★	Good
★★	Fair
★	Poor
zero	Without Merit

PARENTAL RECOMMENDATION (PR:)

AA	Good for Children
A	Acceptable for Children
C	Cautionary, some objectionable scenes
O	Objectionable for Children

BOLD: Films on Videocassette

CLASS OF MISS MAC MICHAEL, THE *½ (1978, Brit./US) PR:O
CLASS OF 1984 zero (1982, Can.) PR:O
CLASS OF NUKE 'EM HIGH * (1986) PR:O
CLASS RELATIONS **½ (1986, Ger.) PR:A-C
CLAUDELLE INGLISH *½ (1961) PR:C-O
CLAUDIA ***½ (1943) PR:A
CLAUDIA AND DAVID ***½ (1946) PR:AA
CLAUDINE * (1974) PR:A**
CLAY ** (1964, Aus.) PR:C-O
CLAY PIGEON, THE **½ (1949) PR:A
CLAY PIGEON *½ (1971) PR:O
CLAYDON TREASURE MYSTERY, THE ** (1938, Brit.) PR:A
CLEAN AND SOBER * (1988) PR:O**
CLEANING UP ** (1933, Brit.) PR:A
CLEAR ALL WIRES *½ (1933) PR:A
CLEAR SKIES *** (1963, USSR) PR:A-C
CLEAR THE DECKS ** (1929) PR:A
CLEARING THE RANGE * (1931) PR:A
CLEGG ** (1969, Brit.) PR:O
CLEO FROM 5 TO 7 ** (1961, Fr.) PR:C
CLEOPATRA ***½ (1934) PR:C
CLEOPATRA ***½ (1963) PR:A-C
CLEOPATRA JONES * (1973) PR:O
CLEOPATRA JONES AND THE CASINO OF GOLD * (1975, U./S./Hong Kong) PR:O
CLEOPATRA'S DAUGHTER ** (1963, Fr./It.) PR:C
CLIMAX, THE * (1930) PR:A
CLIMAX, THE **½ (1944) PR:A
CLIMAX, THE **½ (1967, Fr./It.) PR:C-O
CLIMBING HIGH **½ (1938, Brit.) PR:A
CLINIC, THE ** (1983, Aus.) PR:O
CLIPPED WINGS * (1938) PR:A
CLIPPED WINGS *½ (1953) PR:A
CLIVE OF INDIA *** (1935) PR:A
CLOAK AND DAGGER * (1946) PR:A**
CLOAK AND DAGGER * (1984) PR:C**
CLOAK WITHOUT DAGGER (SEE:OPERATION CONSPIRACY)
CLOCK, THE ***½ (1945) PR:A
CLOCKMAKER, THE * (1976, Fr.) PR:O**
CLOCKWISE * (1986, Brit.) PR:A**
CLOCKWORK ORANGE, A * (1971, Brit.) PR:O
CLONES, THE *½ (1973) PR:A
CLONUS HORROR, THE ** (1979) PR:O
CLOPORTES *** (1966, Fr./It.) PR:C-O
CLOSE CALL FOR BOSTON BLACKIE, A **½ (1946) PR:A
CLOSE CALL FOR ELLERY QUEEN, A ** (1942) PR:A
CLOSE ENCOUNTERS OF THE THIRD KIND ** (1977) PR:A**
CLOSE HARMONY **½ (1929) PR:A
CLOSE TO MY HEART **½ (1951) PR:A
CLOSE-UP ** (1948) PR:A
CLOSELY WATCHED TRAINS ***½ (1967, Czech.) PR:C
CLOTHES AND THE WOMAN ** (1937, Brit.) PR:A
CLOUD DANCER ** (1980) PR:A
CLOUDBURST **½ (1952, Brit.) PR:A
CLOUDED CRYSTAL, THE ** (1948, Brit.) PR:A
CLOUDED YELLOW, THE *** (1950, Brit.) PR:A
CLOUDS OVER EUROPE * (1939, Brit.) PR:A**
CLOUDS OVER ISRAEL **½ (1966, Israel) PR:C-O
CLOWN, THE * (1953) PR:A**
CLOWN AND THE KID, THE * (1961) PR:A
CLOWN AND THE KIDS, THE *½ (1968, US/Bulgaria) PR:AA
CLOWN MURDERS, THE ** (1976, Can.) PR:C
CLOWN MUST LAUGH, A *½ (1936, Brit.) PR:A
CLUB, THE **½ (1980, Aus.) PR:C
CLUB EARTH (SEE:GALACTIC GIGOLO)
CLUB HAVANA * (1946) PR:A
CLUB LIFE ** (1987) PR:O
CLUB PARADISE ** (1986) PR:C
CLUE *½ (1985) PR:O
CLUE OF THE MISSING APE, THE ** (1953, Brit.) PR:AA
CLUE OF THE NEW PIN, THE ** (1929, Brit.) PR:A
CLUE OF THE NEW PIN, THE **½ (1961, Brit.) PR:A-C
CLUE OF THE SILVER KEY, THE **½ (1961, Brit.) PR:A-C
CLUE OF THE TWISTED CANDLE ** (1968, Brit.) PR:A
CLUNY BROWN ** (1946) PR:A**
C'MON, LET'S LIVE A LITTLE *½ (1967) PR:A
COACH *½ (1978) PR:C-O
COAL MINER'S DAUGHTER ** (1980) PR:A-C**
COAST GUARD ** (1939) PR:A
COAST OF SKELETONS ** (1965, Brit.) PR:A
COAST TO COAST *½ (1980) PR:A
COBRA zero (1986) PR:O
COBRA, THE * (1968) PR:A
COBRA STRIKES, THE * (1948) PR:A
COBRA WOMAN ** (1944) PR:A
COBWEB, THE **½ (1955) PR:A
COCA-COLA KID, THE ***½ (1985, Aus.) PR:O
COCAINE COWBOYS * (1979) PR:O
COCAINE WARS *½ (1986) PR:O
COCK-EYED WORLD, THE ** (1929) PR:C
COCK O' THE NORTH *½ (1935, Brit.) PR:A
COCK O' THE WALK **½ (1930) PR:A
COCK OF THE AIR ** (1932) PR:A
COCKEYED CAVALIERS ** (1934) PR:A
COCKEYED COWBOYS OF CALICO COUNTY, THE ** (1970) PR:AA
COCKEYED MIRACLE, THE **½ (1946) PR:AA
COCKFIGHTER (SEE:BORN TO KILL)
COCKLESHELL HEROES, THE * (1955, Brit.) PR:A**
COCKTAIL * (1988) PR:O
COCKTAIL HOUR *½ (1933) PR:C
COCKTAIL MOLOTOV *** (1980, Fr.) PR:A
COCOANUT GROVE **½ (1938) PR:AA
COCOANUTS, THE ** (1929) PR:A**
COCOON * (1985) PR:C**
COCOON: THE RETURN **½ (1988) PR:A
CODE NAME: EMERALD **½ (1985) PR:C
CODE NAME, RED ROSES (SEE:RED ROSES FOR THE FUEHRER)
CODE NAME TRIXIE (SEE:THE CRAZIES)
CODE OF HONOR * (1930) PR:A
CODE OF SCOTLAND YARD **½ (1948) PR:C-O
CODE OF SILENCE ** (1960) PR:C
CODE OF SILENCE * (1985) PR:O**
CODE OF THE CACTUS * (1939) PR:A
CODE OF THE FEARLESS * (1939) PR:A
CODE OF THE LAWLESS *½ (1945) PR:A
CODE OF THE MOUNTED * (1935) PR:A
CODE OF THE OUTLAW *½ (1942) PR:A
CODE OF THE PRAIRIE ** (1944) PR:A
CODE OF THE RANGE *½ (1937) PR:A
CODE OF THE RANGERS *½ (1938) PR:A
CODE OF THE SADDLE *½ (1947) PR:A
CODE OF THE SECRET SERVICE *½ (1939) PR:A
CODE OF THE SILVER SAGE *½ (1950) PR:A
CODE OF THE STREETS *½ (1939) PR:A
CODE OF THE WEST ** (1947) PR:A
CODE 7, VICTIM 5 *½ (1964, Brit.) PR:A
CODE TWO **½ (1953) PR:A
COFFY * (1973) PR:O
COGNASSE ** (1932, Fr.) PR:A
COHENS AND KELLYS IN AFRICA, THE *½ (1930) PR:A
COHENS AND KELLYS IN ATLANTIC CITY, THE ** (1929) PR:A
COHENS AND KELLYS IN HOLLYWOOD, THE ** (1932) PR:A
COHENS AND KELLYS IN SCOTLAND, THE **½ (1930) PR:A
COHENS AND KELLYS IN TROUBLE, THE ** (1933) PR:A
COLD FEET * (1984) PR:C**
COLD JOURNEY *½ (1975, Can.) PR:C
COLD RIVER *½ (1982) PR:A
COLD SWEAT ** (1974, It./Fr.) PR:O
COLD TURKEY *** (1971) PR:A
COLD WIND IN AUGUST *** (1961) PR:O
COLDITZ STORY, THE * (1955, Brit.) PR:A**
COLE YOUNGER, GUNFIGHTER ** (1958) PR:A
COLLECTOR, THE ** (1965) PR:C
COLLEEN *** (1936) PR:A
COLLEGE COACH ** (1933) PR:A
COLLEGE CONFIDENTIAL ** (1960) PR:C
COLLEGE COQUETTE, THE zero (1929) PR:A
COLLEGE HOLIDAY **½ (1936) PR:A
COLLEGE HUMOR ** (1933) PR:A
COLLEGE LOVE *½ (1929) PR:A
COLLEGE LOVERS *½ (1930) PR:A
COLLEGE RHYTHM ** (1934) PR:A
COLLEGE SCANDAL ** (1935) PR:A
COLLEGE SWEETHEARTS * (1942) PR:A
COLLEGE SWING * (1938) PR:A
COLLEGIATE * (1936) PR:A
COLLISION * (1932, Brit.) PR:A
COLLISION COURSE (SEE:BAMBOO SAUCER, THE)
COLONEL BLIMP (SEE:LIFE AND DEATH OF COLONEL BLIMP, THE)
COLONEL BLOOD ** (1934, Brit.) PR:A
COLONEL BOGEY ** (1948, Brit.) PR:A
COLONEL CHABERT *½ (1947, Fr.) PR:A
COLONEL EFFINGHAM'S RAID ** (1945) PR:A
COLONEL MARCH INVESTIGATES ** (1952, Brit.) PR:A
COLONEL REDL * (1985, Hung./Aust./Ger.) PR:O**
COLOR ME BLOOD RED zero (1965) PR:O
COLOR ME DEAD *½ (1969, Aus.) PR:C
COLOR OF DESTINY, THE ***½ (1988, Braz.) PR:C-O
COLOR OF MONEY, THE ***½ (1986) PR:C-O
COLOR OF POMEGRANATES, THE *** (1980, USSR) PR:C-O
COLOR PURPLE, THE ** (1985) PR:A-C
COLORADO *½ (1940) PR:A
COLORADO AMBUSH *½ (1951) PR:A
COLORADO KID zero (1938) PR:A
COLORADO PIONEERS ** (1945) PR:A
COLORADO RANGER * (1950) PR:A
COLORADO SERENADE ** (1946) PR:A
COLORADO SUNDOWN ** (1952) PR:A
COLORADO SUNSET **½ (1939) PR:A
COLORADO TERRITORY *** (1949) PR:A
COLORADO TRAIL ** (1938) PR:A
COLORS * (1988) PR:O**
COLOSSUS OF NEW YORK, THE *½ (1958) PR:A
COLOSSUS OF RHODES, THE ** (1961, It./Fr./Sp.) PR:A
COLOSSUS: THE FORBIN PROJECT ***½ (1969) PR:A
COLT COMRADES * (1943) PR:A
COLT .45 **½ (1950) PR:A
COLUMN SOUTH ** (1953) PR:A
COMA ** (1978) PR:A
COMANCHE **½ (1956) PR:A
COMANCHE STATION **** (1960) PR:A
COMANCHE TERRITORY ** (1950) PR:A
COMANCHEROS, THE **½ (1961) PR:A
COMBAT SHOCK zero (1986) PR:O
COMBAT SQUAD *½ (1953) PR:A
COME ACROSS * (1929) PR:A
COME AND GET IT * (1936) PR:A**
COME AND SEE ***½ (1986, USSR) PR:O
COME BACK BABY zero (1968) PR:O
COME BACK CHARLESTON BLUE ** (1972) PR:O
COME BACK LITTLE SHEBA **** (1952) PR:A-C
COME BACK PETER * (1952, Brit.) PR:A
COME BACK PETER * (1971, Brit.) PR:C
COME BACK TO THE 5 & DIME, JIMMY DEAN, JIMMY DEAN **½ (1982) PR:O
COME BLOW YOUR HORN *** (1963) PR:A-C
COME CLOSER, FOLKS * (1936) PR:A
COME DANCE WITH ME ** (1950, Brit.) PR:A
COME DANCE WITH ME! *½ (1960, Fr.) PR:C-O
COME FILL THE CUP ***½ (1951) PR:C
COME FLY WITH ME ** (1963) PR:A
COME LIVE WITH ME ***½ (1941) PR:A
COME 'N' GET IT (SEE:LUNCH WAGON)
COME NEXT SPRING **½ (1956) PR:AA
COME ON, THE **½ (1956) PR:A
COME ON, COWBOYS *½ (1937) PR:A
COME ON DANGER! **½ (1932) PR:A
COME ON DANGER * (1942) PR:A
COME ON GEORGE ** (1939, Brit.) PR:A
COME ON, LEATHERNECKS *½ (1938) PR:A
COME ON, MARINES *½ (1934) PR:A
COME ON RANGERS ** (1939) PR:A
COME ON TARZAN ** (1933) PR:A
COME OUT FIGHTING ** (1945) PR:A
COME OUT OF THE PANTRY **½ (1935, Brit.) PR:AA
COME SEPTEMBER **½ (1961) PR:A
COME SPY WITH ME * (1967) PR:A
COME TO THE STABLE ***½ (1949) PR:AA
COMEBACK, THE ** (1982, Brit.) PR:C
COMEBACK TRAIL, THE *½ (1982) PR:O
COMEDIANS, THE **½ (1967) PR:C
COMEDY! *** (1987, Fr.) PR:C-O
COMEDY MAN, THE **½ (1964) PR:A
COMEDY OF HORRORS, THE ** (1964) PR:A
COMES A HORSEMAN *½ (1978) PR:A-C
COMET OVER BROADWAY ** (1938) PR:A
COMETOGETHER zero (1971) PR:O
COMFORT AND JOY * (1984, Brit.) PR:A-C**
COMIC, THE * (1969) PR:A
COMIC MAGAZINE ***½ (1986, Jap.) PR:O
COMIN' AT YA! * (1981) PR:O
COMIN' ROUND THE MOUNTAIN ** (1951) PR:AA
COMIN' ROUND THE MOUNTAIN ** (1936) PR:AA
COMIN' ROUND THE MOUNTAIN * (1940) PR:AA
COMIN' THRU' THE RYE * (1947, Brit.) PR:A
COMING ATTRACTIONS (SEE:LOOSE SHOES)
COMING HOME ** (1978) PR:C-O**
COMING OF AGE ** (1938, Brit.) PR:A
COMING OUT PARTY * (1934) PR:A
COMING-OUT PARTY, A **½ (1962, Brit.) PR:A-C
COMING TO AMERICA **½ (1988) PR:O
COMING UP ROSES ***½ (1986, Brit.) PR:A
COMMAND, THE *** (1954) PR:A
COMMAND DECISION ***½ (1948) PR:A
COMMAND PERFORMANCE ** (1931) PR:A
COMMAND PERFORMANCE *½ (1937, Brit.) PR:A
COMMANDO **½ (1962, It./Sp./Bel./Ger.) PR:C
COMMANDO **½ (1985) PR:O
COMMANDO SQUAD ** (1987) PR:C
COMMANDOS STRIKE AT DAWN, THE ***½ (1942) PR:A

COMMISSIONAIRE *½ (1933, Brit.) PR:A
COMMITMENT, THE * (1976) PR:C
COMMITTEE, THE ** (1968, Brit.) PR:C
COMMON CLAY *½ (1930) PR:A
COMMON LAW, THE *½ (1931) PR:C
COMMON LAW WIFE * (1963) PR:O
COMMON TOUCH, THE **½ (1941, Brit.) PR:A
COMMUNION
   (SEE:ALICE, SWEET ALICE)
COMPANEROS ** (1970, It./Sp./Ger.) PR:C
COMPANIONS IN CRIME *½ (1954, Brit.) PR:A
COMPANY OF COWARDS
   (SEE:ADVANCE TO THE REAR)
COMPANY OF KILLERS ** (1970) PR:A
COMPANY OF WOLVES, THE ***½
   (1985, Brit.) PR:O
COMPANY SHE KEEPS, THE **½ (1950) PR:C
COMPELLED ** (1960, Brit.) PR:A-C
COMPETITION, THE *½ (1980) PR:C
COMPLIMENTS OF MR. FLOW **½ (1941, Fr.) PR:A
COMPROMISED *½ (1931) PR:A
COMPROMISED! zero (1931, Brit.) PR:A
COMPROMISED DAPHNE
   (SEE:COMPROMISED!)
COMPROMISING POSITIONS * (1985) PR:C-O**
COMPULSION **** (1959) PR:C-O
COMPULSORY HUSBAND, THE ** (1930, Brit.) PR:A
COMPULSORY WIFE, THE ** (1937, Brit.) PR:A
COMPUTER FREE-FOR-ALL ** (1969, Jap.) PR:O
COMPUTER WORE TENNIS SHOES, THE **
   (1970) PR:AA
COMRADE X *** (1940) PR:A
COMRADES *** (1987, Brit.) PR:C
CON ARTISTS, THE * (1981, It.) PR:O
CON MEN, THE * (1973, It./Sp.) PR:O
CONAN THE BARBARIAN ** (1982) PR:C-O
CONAN THE DESTROYER * (1984) PR:C**
CONCENTRATIN' KID, THE *½ (1930) PR:A
CONCENTRATION CAMP *** (1939, USSR) PR:A
CONCERNING MR. MARTIN **½ (1937, Brit.) PR:A
CONCORDE, THE—AIRPORT '79 ** (1979) PR:A-C
CONCRETE ANGELS *½ (1987, Can.) PR:C-O
CONCRETE JUNGLE, THE * (1962, Brit.) PR:C**
CONCRETE JUNGLE, THE ** (1982) PR:O
CONDEMNED **½ (1929) PR:C
CONDEMNED OF ALTONA, THE ** (1963) PR:O
CONDEMNED TO DEATH ** (1932, Brit.) PR:A
CONDEMNED TO LIFE
   (SEE:WALK IN THE SHADOW)
CONDEMNED TO LIVE ** (1935) PR:A
CONDEMNED WOMEN * (1938) PR:A
CONDORMAN **½ (1981) PR:AA
CONDUCT UNBECOMING * (1975, Brit.) PR:A-C**
CONDUCTOR, THE *** (1981, Pol.) PR:A-C
CONE OF SILENCE
   (SEE:TROUBLE IN THE SKY)
CONEY ISLAND ***½ (1943) PR:A
CONFESS DR. CORDA **½ (1960, Ger.) PR:C
CONFESSION **½ (1937) PR:A
CONFESSION
   (SEE:THE DEADLIEST SIN)
CONFESSION, THE **** (1970, Fr.) PR:C
CONFESSIONAL, THE zero (1977, Brit.) PR:O
CONFESSIONS FROM A HOLIDAY CAMP *
   (1977, Brit.) PR:A
CONFESSIONS OF A CO-ED ** (1931) PR:A
CONFESSIONS OF A NAZI SPY **** (1939) PR:C
CONFESSIONS OF A NEWLYWED **½
   (1941, Fr.) PR:A
CONFESSIONS OF A POLICE CAPTAIN *
   (1971, It.) PR:A**
CONFESSIONS OF A POP PERFORMER *
   (1975, Brit.) PR:O
CONFESSIONS OF A ROGUE *** (1948, Fr.) PR:A
CONFESSIONS OF A WINDOW CLEANER *
   (1974, Brit.) PR:O
CONFESSIONS OF AMANS, THE *** (1977) PR:C-O
CONFESSIONS OF AN OPIUM EATER **
   (1962) PR:C
CONFESSIONS OF BOSTON BLACKIE ***
   (1941) PR:A
CONFESSIONS OF FELIX KRULL, THE **½
   (1957, Ger.) PR:C-O
CONFESSOR **½ (1973) PR:A
CONFIDENCE **½ (1980, Hung.) PR:C-O
CONFIDENCE GIRL *½ (1952) PR:A
CONFIDENTIAL ** (1935) PR:A

CONFIDENTIAL AGENT **½ (1945) PR:C
CONFIDENTIAL LADY ** (1939, Brit.) PR:A
CONFIDENTIAL REPORT
   (SEE:MR. ARKADIN)
CONFIDENTIALLY CONNIE **½ (1953) PR:A
**CONFIDENTIALLY YOURS! ***½
   (1983, Fr.) PR:A-C**
CONFIRM OR DENY ** (1941) PR:C
CONFLAGRATION
   (SEE:ENJO)
CONFLICT *½ (1937) PR:A
CONFLICT **½ (1939, Fr.) PR:O
CONFLICT ***½ (1945) PR:A
CONFLICT OVER WINGS
   (SEE:FUSS OVER FEATHERS)
CONFORMIST, THE * (1971, It./Fr.) PR:C**
CONGO CROSSING ** (1956) PR:A
CONGO MAISIE *½ (1940) PR:A
CONGO SWING
   (SEE:BLONDIE GOES LATIN)
CONGRESS DANCES **½ (1932, Ger.) PR:A
CONGRESS DANCES ** (1957, Ger.) PR:A
CONJUGAL BED, THE **½ (1963, It.) PR:A
CONNECTICUT YANKEE, A ** (1931) PR:AA**
CONNECTICUT YANKEE IN KING ARTHUR'S
   COURT, A ** (1949) PR:AA**
CONNECTING ROOMS ** (1971, Brit.) PR:A
CONNECTION, THE **½ (1962) PR:O
CONQUERED CITY **½ (1966, It.) PR:C
CONQUERING HORDE, THE **½ (1931) PR:A
CONQUEROR, THE *½ (1956) PR:C-A
CONQUEROR OF CORINTH
   (SEE:CENTURION, THE)
CONQUEROR WORM, THE * (1968, Brit.) PR:O**
CONQUERORS, THE ** (1932) PR:A
CONQUEST * (1929) PR:C
CONQUEST *** (1937) PR:C
CONQUEST * (1984, It./Sp./Mex.) PR:O
CONQUEST OF CHEYENNE ** (1946) PR:A
CONQUEST OF COCHISE *½ (1953) PR:A
CONQUEST OF MYCENE *½ (1965, It./Fr.) PR:A-C
CONQUEST OF SPACE *½ (1955) PR:A
CONQUEST OF THE AIR *½ (1940) PR:A
CONQUEST OF THE EARTH *½ (1980) PR:A
**CONQUEST OF THE PLANET OF THE APES **½
   (1972) PR:A**
CONRACK ***½ (1974) PR:A
CONSCIENCE BAY *½ (1960, Brit.) PR:C
CONSEIL DE FAMILLE
   (SEE:FAMILY BUSINESS)
CONSOLATION MARRIAGE **½ (1931) PR:A
CONSPIRACY zero (1930) PR:A
CONSPIRACY ** (1939) PR:A
CONSPIRACY IN TEHERAN * (1948, Brit.) PR:A
CONSPIRACY OF HEARTS **½ (1960, Brit.) PR:AA
CONSPIRATOR ** (1949, Brit.) PR:A-C
CONSPIRATORS, THE **½ (1944) PR:A
CONSTANCE *** (1984, New Zealand) PR:O
CONSTANT FACTOR, THE **½ (1980, Pol.) PR:C-O
CONSTANT HUSBAND, THE ***½ (1955, Brit.) PR:C
CONSTANT NYMPH, THE *** (1943) PR:A
CONSTANT NYMPH, THE **½ (1933, Brit.) PR:A
CONSTANTINE AND THE CROSS **½
   (1962, It.) PR:C-O
CONSUELO, AN ILLUSION **½
   (1988, Chile/Swed.) PR:C
CONSUMING PASSIONS ** (1988, US/Brit.) PR:O
CONTACT MAN, THE
   (SEE:ALIAS NICK BEAL)
CONTACTO CHICANO zero (1986, Mex.) PR:O
CONTAR HASTA TEN ** (1986, Arg.) PR:O
CONTEMPT ** (1963, Fr./It.) PR:C-O**
CONTENDER, THE ** (1944) PR:A
CONTEST GIRL
   (SEE:BEAUTY JUNGLE, THE)
CONTINENTAL DIVIDE ** (1981) PR:A-C
CONTINENTAL EXPRESS ** (1939, Brit.) PR:A
CONTINENTAL TWIST
   (SEE:TWIST ALL NIGHT)
CONTRABAND
   (SEE:BLACKOUT)
CONTRABAND LOVE *½ (1931, Brit.) PR:A
CONTRABAND SPAIN ** (1955, Brit.) PR:A
CONTRACT, THE *** (1982, Pol.) PR:A
CONVENTION CITY *** (1933) PR:A
CONVENTION GIRL * (1935) PR:A
CONVERSATION, THE ** (1974) PR:A-C**

CONVERSATION PIECE ** (1976, Ital.,/Fr.) PR:C
CONVICT 99 **½ (1938, Brit.) PR:A
CONVICT STAGE *½ (1965) PR:A
CONVICTED **½ (1931) PR:A
CONVICTED *½ (1938) PR:A
CONVICTED *** (1950) PR:A
CONVICTED WOMAN ** (1940) PR:A
CONVICT'S CODE *½ (1930) PR:A
CONVICT'S CODE * (1939) PR:A
CONVICTS FOUR * (1962) PR:A**
CONVOY **½ (1940) PR:A
CONVOY * (1978) PR:C
COOGAN'S BLUFF ***½ (1968) PR:C-O
COOL AND THE CRAZY, THE ** (1958) PR:C-O
COOL HAND LUKE ** (1967) PR:C**
COOL IT, CAROL! *½ (1970, Brit.) PR:O
COOL MIKADO, THE ** (1963, Brit.) PR:A
COOL ONES, THE * (1967) PR:A
COOL WORLD, THE **½ (1963) PR:C-O
COOLEY HIGH * (1975) PR:C**
COONSKIN **½ (1975) PR:O
COP, A ** (1973, Fr.) PR:O
COP ***½ (1988) PR:O
COP HATER *** (1958) PR:C
COP-OUT ** (1967, Brit.) PR:C-O
COPACABANA ** (1947) PR:A
COPPER, THE ** (1930, Brit.) PR:A
COPPER CANYON *** (1950) PR:A
COPPER SKY * (1957) PR:A
COPS AND ROBBERS **½ (1973) PR:A
CORDELIA **½ (1980, France/Can.) PR:C-O
CORN IS GREEN, THE ***½ (1945) PR:A
CORNBREAD, EARL AND ME **½ (1975) PR:C
CORNERED *½ (1932) PR:A
CORNERED ***½ (1945) PR:C
CORONADO ** (1935) PR:A
CORONER CREEK *** (1948) PR:C
CORPSE CAME C.O.D., THE **½ (1947) PR:A
CORPSE GRINDERS, THE zero (1972) PR:O
CORPSE OF BEVERLY HILLS, THE **
   (1965, Ger.) PR:O
CORPSE VANISHES, THE *½ (1942) PR:C
CORPUS CHRISTI BANDITS ** (1945) PR:A
CORREGIDOR ** (1943) PR:C
CORRIDOR OF MIRRORS **½ (1948, Brit.) PR:A
CORRIDORS OF BLOOD * (1962, Brit.) PR:C-O**
CORRUPT ** (1984, It.) PR:O
CORRUPTION * (1933) PR:A
CORRUPTION ** (1968, Brit.) PR:O
CORRUPTION OF CHRIS MILLER, THE **
   (1979, Sp.) PR:O
CORSAIR ** (1931) PR:C
CORSICAN BROTHERS, THE ** (1941) PR:A**
CORVETTE K-225 **** (1943) PR:A
CORVETTE SUMMER * (1978) PR:C-O**
COSH BOY
   (SEE:SLASHER, THE)
COSMIC EYE, THE * (1986) PR:AA**
COSMIC MAN, THE **½ (1959) PR:A
COSMIC MONSTERS *½ (1958, Brit.) PR:A
COSSACKS, THE *½ (1960, It.) PR:A
COSSACKS IN EXILE * (1939, USSR) PR:A
COSSACKS OF THE DON zero (1932, USSR) PR:A
COSTELLO CASE, THE * (1930) PR:A
COTTAGE ON DARTMOOR
   (SEE:ESCAPED FROM DARTMOOR)
COTTAGE TO LET
   (SEE:BOMBSIGHT STOLEN)
COTTON CLUB, THE ***½ (1984) PR:O
COTTON COMES TO HARLEM * (1970) PR:O**
COTTON QUEEN *½ (1937, Brit.) PR:A
COTTONPICKIN' CHICKENPICKERS zero
   (1967) PR:C
COUCH, THE * (1962) PR:O
COUCH TRIP, THE **½ (1988) PR:O
COUNSEL FOR CRIME ** (1937) PR:A
COUNSEL FOR ROMANCE ** (1938, Fr.) PR:A
COUNSELLOR-AT-LAW **** (1933) PR:A
COUNSEL'S OPINION ** (1933, Brit.) PR:A
**COUNT DRACULA **
   (1971, Sp./It./Ger./Brit.) PR:C-O**

Finding entries in **THE MOTION PICTURE GUIDE** ™		**STAR RATINGS**		**PARENTAL RECOMMENDATION (PR:)**	
Years 1929-83	Volumes I-IX	★★★★★	Masterpiece	AA	Good for Children
1984	Volume IX	★★★★	Excellent	A	Acceptable for Children
1985	1986 ANNUAL	★★★	Good	C	Cautionary, some objectionable scenes
1986	1987 ANNUAL	★★	Fair	O	Objectionable for Children
1987	1988 ANNUAL	★	Poor		
1988	1989 ANNUAL	zero	Without Merit	**BOLD:** Films on Videocassette	

COUNT DRACULA AND HIS VAMPIRE BRIDE ** (1978, Brit.) PR:C-O
COUNT FIVE AND DIE **½ (1958, Brit.) PR:A
COUNT OF BRAGELONNE, THE (SEE:LAST MUSKETEER, THE)
COUNT OF MONTE CRISTO, THE ** (1934) PR:AA**
COUNT OF MONTE-CRISTO ** (1955, Fr./It.) PR:A
COUNT OF MONTE CRISTO * (1976, Brit.) PR:A**
COUNT OF THE MONK'S BRIDGE, THE ** (1934, Swed.) PR:A
COUNT OF TWELVE * (1955, Brit.) PR:A
COUNT THE HOURS ** (1953) PR:A
COUNT THREE AND PRAY **½ (1955) PR:A
COUNT YORGA, VAMPIRE ** (1970) PR:O
COUNT YOUR BLESSINGS * (1959) PR:A-C
COUNT YOUR BULLETS *** (1972) PR:O
COUNTDOWN ***½ (1968) PR:A
COUNTDOWN AT KUSINI **½ (1976, Nigeria) PR:C
COUNTDOWN * (1985, Hung.) PR:C**
COUNTDOWN TO DANGER *½ (1967, Brit.) PR:AA
COUNTER-ATTACK *** (1945) PR:A
COUNTER BLAST ** (1948, Brit.) PR:A
COUNTER-ESPIONAGE ** (1942) PR:A
COUNTER TENORS, THE (SEE:WHITE VOICES, THE)
COUNTERFEIT ** (1936) PR:A
COUNTERFEIT COMMANDOS ** (1981, It.) PR:O
COUNTERFEIT CONSTABLE, THE *½ (1966, Fr.) PR:A-C
COUNTERFEIT KILLER, THE ** (1968) PR:A
COUNTERFEIT LADY *½ (1937) PR:A
COUNTERFEIT PLAN, THE **½ (1957, Brit.) PR:A
COUNTERFEIT TRAITOR, THE ***½ (1962) PR:A-C
COUNTERFEITERS, THE ** (1948) PR:A
COUNTERFEITERS, THE *½ (1953, It.) PR:A
COUNTERFEITERS OF PARIS, THE **½ (1962, Fr./It.) PR:C
COUNTERPLOT * (1959) PR:A
COUNTERPOINT **½ (1967) PR:A-C
COUNTERSPY MEETS SCOTLAND YARD ** (1950) PR:A
COUNTESS DRACULA *** (1972, Brit.) PR:O
COUNTESS FROM HONG KONG, A * (1967, Brit.) PR:C
COUNTESS OF MONTE CRISTO, THE ** (1934) PR:A
COUNTESS OF MONTE CRISTO, THE * (1948) PR:A
COUNTRY ** (1984) PR:C**
COUNTRY BEYOND, THE * (1936) PR:A
COUNTRY BOY zero (1966) PR:A
COUNTRY BRIDE zero (1938, USSR) PR:A
COUNTRY DANCE (SEE:BROTHERLY LOVE)
COUNTRY DOCTOR, THE **½ (1936) PR:A
COUNTRY DOCTOR, THE zero (1963, Portugal) PR:A
COUNTRY FAIR *½ (1941) PR:A
COUNTRY GENTLEMEN ** (1937) PR:A
COUNTRY GIRL, THE ** (1954) PR:A-C**
COUNTRY MUSIC HOLIDAY * (1958) PR:A
COUNTRYMAN * (1982, Jamaica) PR:C**
COUNTY CHAIRMAN, THE *** (1935) PR:A
COUNTY FAIR, THE * (1932) PR:A
COUNTY FAIR **½ (1933, Brit.) PR:A
COUNTY FAIR *½ (1937) PR:A
COUNTY FAIR *½ (1950) PR:A
COUP DE FOUDRE (SEE:ENTRE NOUS)
COUP DE GRACE **½ (1978, Ger./Fr.) PR:C
COUP DE TETE (SEE:HOTHEAD)
COUP DE TORCHON * (1981, Fr.) PR:O**
COURAGE ** (1930) PR:A
COURAGE (SEE:RAW COURAGE)
COURAGE OF BLACK BEAUTY ** (1957) PR:AA
COURAGE OF LASSIE *** (1946) PR:AA
COURAGE OF THE WEST **½ (1937) PR:A
COURAGEOUS AVENGER, THE * (1935) PR:A
COURAGEOUS DR. CHRISTIAN, THE *½ (1940) PR:A
COURAGEOUS MR. PENN, THE *½ (1941, Brit.) PR:A
COURIER OF LYONS ** (1938, Fr.) PR:A
COURRIER SUD ** (1937, Fr.) PR:A
COURT CONCERT, THE *** (1936, Ger.) PR:A
COURT JESTER, THE ***½ (1956) PR:AA
COURT MARTIAL ***½ (1954, Brit.) PR:A
COURT MARTIAL ** (1962, Ger.) PR:A-C
COURT-MARTIAL OF BILLY MITCHELL, THE ** (1955) PR:A**
COURT MARTIAL OF MAJOR KELLER, THE **½ (1961, Brit.) PR:A-C
COURT OF THE PHARAOH, THE **½ (1985, Sp.) PR:C
COURTIN' TROUBLE *½ (1948) PR:A
COURTIN' WILDCATS *½ (1929) PR:A
COURTNEY AFFAIR, THE **½ (1947, Brit.) PR:A
COURTSHIP OF ANDY HARDY, THE **½ (1942) PR:A
COURTSHIP OF EDDY'S FATHER, THE ***½ (1963) PR:AA
COUSIN, COUSINE * (1976, Fr.) PR:O**
COUSINS, THE * (1959, Fr.) PR:C-O**
COUSINS IN LOVE * (1982) PR:O
COVENANT WITH DEATH, A ** (1966) PR:C
COVER GIRL **** (1944) PR:AA
COVER GIRL KILLER **½ (1960, Brit.) PR:C-O
COVER ME BABE zero (1970) PR:O
COVER-UP ** (1949) PR:A
COVERED TRAILER, THE *½ (1939) PR:AA
COVERED WAGON DAYS *½ (1940) PR:A
COVERED WAGON RAID *½ (1950) PR:A
COVERED WAGON TRAILS * (1930) PR:A
COVERED WAGON TRAILS * (1940) PR:A
COVERGIRL * (1984, Can.) PR:O
COVERT ACTION * (1980, It.) PR:O
COW AND I, THE *** (1961, Fr./It./Ger.) PR:A
COW COUNTRY *½ (1953) PR:A
COW TOWN *½ (1950) PR:A
COWARDS zero (1970) PR:C-O
COWBOY ***½ (1958) PR:A
COWBOY AND THE BANDIT, THE * (1935) PR:A
COWBOY AND THE BLONDE, THE ** (1941) PR:A
COWBOY AND THE INDIANS, THE ** (1949) PR:A
COWBOY AND THE KID, THE * (1936) PR:A
COWBOY AND THE LADY, THE *** (1938) PR:A
COWBOY AND THE PRIZEFIGHTER ** (1950) PR:A
COWBOY AND THE SENORITA ** (1944) PR:A
COWBOY BLUES * (1946) PR:A
COWBOY CANTEEN **½ (1944) PR:A
COWBOY CAVALIER * (1948) PR:A
COWBOY COMMANDOS *½ (1943) PR:A
COWBOY COUNSELOR ** (1933) PR:A
COWBOY FROM BROOKLYN **½ (1938) PR:A
COWBOY FROM LONESOME RIVER *½ (1944) PR:A
COWBOY FROM SUNDOWN * (1940) PR:A
COWBOY HOLIDAY *½ (1934) PR:A
COWBOY IN AFRICA (SEE:AFRICA—TEXAS STYLE!)
COWBOY IN MANHATTAN *½ (1943) PR:A
COWBOY IN THE CLOUDS ** (1943) PR:A
COWBOY MILLIONAIRE ** (1935) PR:A
COWBOY QUARTERBACK *½ (1939) PR:A
COWBOY SERENADE ** (1942) PR:A
COWBOY STAR, THE ** (1936) PR:A
COWBOYS, THE * (1972) PR:A-C**
COWBOYS FROM TEXAS * (1939) PR:A
COYOTE TRAILS * (1935) PR:A
CRACK IN THE MIRROR *** (1960) PR:C
CRACK IN THE WORLD *½ (1965) PR:A
CRACK-UP, THE *** (1937) PR:A
CRACK-UP ***½ (1946) PR:A
CRACKED NUTS *½ (1931) PR:AA
CRACKED NUTS * (1941) PR:A
CRACKERJACK (SEE:MAN WITH 100 FACES)
CRACKERS zero (1984) PR:A-C
CRACKING UP * (1977) PR:O
CRACKING UP (SEE:SMORGASBORD)
CRACKSMAN, THE ** (1963, Brit.) PR:A
CRADLE SONG * (1933) PR:A
CRAIG'S WIFE ** (1936) PR:A-C**
CRANES ARE FLYING, THE *** (1960, USSR) PR:A**
CRASH, THE * (1932) PR:A
CRASH * (1977) PR:C-O
CRASH DIVE **** (1943) PR:A
CRASH DONOVAN ** (1936) PR:A
CRASH DRIVE * (1959, Brit.) PR:A-C
CRASH LANDING * (1958) PR:A
CRASH OF SILENCE **½ (1952, Brit.) PR:A
CRASHIN' THRU DANGER * (1938) PR:A
CRASHING BROADWAY * (1933) PR:A
CRASHING HOLLYWOOD **½ (1937) PR:A
CRASHING LAS VEGAS *½ (1956) PR:A
CRASHING THRU * (1939) PR:A
CRASHING THRU * (1949) PR:A
CRASHOUT ** (1955) PR:C
CRATER LAKE MONSTER, THE * (1977) PR:A
CRAWLING EYE, THE * (1958, Brit.) PR:C
CRAWLING HAND, THE * (1963) PR:A
CRAWLING MONSTER, THE (SEE:CREEPING TERROR, THE)
CRAWLSPACE * (1986) PR:O
CRAZE zero (1974, Brit.) PR:C
CRAZIES, THE * (1973) PR:O**
CRAZY BOYS **½ (1987, Ger.) PR:O
CRAZY DESIRE **½ (1964, It.) PR:C
CRAZY FAMILY, THE *** (1986, Jap.) PR:O
CRAZY FOR LOVE * (1960, Fr.) PR:C-O
CRAZY HOUSE ** (1943) PR:A
CRAZY HOUSE (SEE:NIGHT OF THE LAUGHING DEAD)
CRAZY JACK AND THE BOY (SEE:SILENCE)
CRAZY JOE ** (1974) PR:O
CRAZY KNIGHTS * (1944) PR:A
CRAZY LOVE (SEE:LOVE IS A DOG FROM HELL)
CRAZY MAMA zero (1975) PR:O
CRAZY OVER HORSES ** (1951) PR:A
CRAZY PARADISE * (1965, Den.) PR:O
CRAZY PEOPLE ** (1934, Brit.) PR:A
CRAZY QUILT, THE ** (1966) PR:A
CRAZY THAT WAY *** (1930) PR:A
CRAZY WORLD OF JULIUS VROODER, THE * (1974) PR:C-O
CRAZYLEGS, ALL AMERICAN **½ (1953) PR:AA
CREATION OF THE HUMANOIDS * (1962) PR:C
CREATOR * (1985) PR:O**
CREATURE ** (1985) PR:O
CREATURE CALLED MAN, THE * (1970, Jap.) PR:C
CREATURE FROM BLACK LAKE, THE *½ (1976) PR:C
CREATURE FROM THE BLACK LAGOON * (1954) PR:A**
CREATURE FROM THE HAUNTED SEA **½ (1961) PR:C
CREATURE OF THE WALKING DEAD *½ (1960, Mex.) PR:C
CREATURE WALKS AMONG US, THE * (1956) PR:A
CREATURE WASN'T NICE, THE * (1981) PR:A
CREATURE WITH THE ATOM BRAIN * (1955) PR:O
CREATURE WITH THE BLUE HAND ** (1971, Ger.) PR:O
CREATURES (SEE:FROM BEYOND THE GRAVE)
CREATURES OF THE PREHISTORIC PLANET (SEE:HORROR OF THE BLOOD MONSTERS)
CREATURE'S REVENGE, THE (SEE:BRAIN OF BLOOD)
CREATURES THE WORLD FORGOT *½ (1971, Brit.) PR:O
CREEPER, THE ** (1948) PR:O
CREEPER, THE * (1980, Can.) PR:O
CREEPERS ** (1985, It.) PR:O
CREEPING FLESH, THE ** (1973, Brit.) PR:O
CREEPING TERROR, THE * (1964) PR:C
CREEPING UNKNOWN, THE ** (1956, Brit.) PR:C
CREEPS (SEE:SHIVERS)
CREEPSHOW * (1982) PR:O**
CREEPSHOW 2 * (1987) PR:C-O
CREMATOR, THE *** (1973, Czech.) PR:O
CREMATORS, THE **½ (1972) PR:C
CRESCENDO * (1972, Brit.) PR:A
CREST OF THE WAVE **½ (1954, Brit.) PR:A
CRIES AND WHISPERS ** (1972, Swed.) PR:C**
CRIES IN THE NIGHT (SEE:AWFUL DR. ORLOFF, THE)
CRIES IN THE NIGHT (SEE:FUNERAL HOME)
CRIME AFLOAT * (1937) PR:A
CRIME AGAINST JOE **½ (1956) PR:C
CRIME AND PASSION *½ (1976, U.S.,/Ger.) PR:C-O
CRIME AND PUNISHMENT ***½ (1935, Fr.) PR:A
CRIME AND PUNISHMENT ***½ (1935) PR:C
CRIME AND PUNISHMENT * (1948, Swed.) PR:A
CRIME AND PUNISHMENT ** (1975, USSR) PR:A
CRIME AND PUNISHMENT, U.S.A. **½ (1959) PR:A
CRIME AT BLOSSOMS, THE ** (1933, Brit.) PR:A
CRIME AT PORTA ROMANA ** (1980, It.) PR:O
CRIME BOSS *½ (1976, It.) PR:C
CRIME BY NIGHT ** (1944) PR:A
CRIME DOCTOR, THE ** (1934) PR:A
CRIME DOCTOR **½ (1943) PR:A
CRIME DOCTOR'S COURAGE, THE *½ (1945) PR:A
CRIME DOCTOR'S DIARY, THE ** (1949) PR:A
CRIME DOCTOR'S GAMBLE ** (1947) PR:A
CRIME DOCTOR'S STRANGEST CASE *½ (1943) PR:A
CRIME DOCTOR'S WARNING ** (1945) PR:A
CRIME DOCTOR'S MAN HUNT *½ (1946) PR:A
CRIME DOES NOT PAY **½ (1962, Fr.) PR:C-O
CRIME IN THE STREETS **½ (1956) PR:C-O
CRIME, INC. * (1945) PR:A
CRIME NOBODY SAW, THE * (1937) PR:A
CRIME OF DR. CRESPI, THE ** (1936) PR:C
CRIME OF DR. FORBES **½ (1936) PR:A
CRIME OF DR. HALLET ** (1938) PR:A
CRIME OF HELEN STANLEY * (1934) PR:A
CRIME OF HONOR * (1987) PR:O
CRIME OF MONSIEUR LANGE, THE ** (1936, Fr.) PR:C-O**
CRIME OF PASSION *** (1957) PR:C
CRIME OF PETER FRAME, THE ** (1938, Brit.) PR:A
CRIME OF THE CENTURY, THE ** (1933) PR:A

CRIME OF THE CENTURY * (1946) PR:A
CRIME ON THE HILL ** (1933, Brit.) PR:A
CRIME OVER LONDON ** (1936, Brit.) PR:A
CRIME PATROL, THE * (1936) PR:A
CRIME RING * (1938) PR:A
CRIME SCHOOL ** (1938) PR:AA
CRIME TAKES A HOLIDAY ** (1938) PR:A
CRIME UNLIMITED * (1935, Brit.) PR:A
CRIME WAVE **½ (1954) PR:A-C
CRIME WITHOUT PASSION **** (1934) PR:A
CRIMES AT THE DARK HOUSE **½
(1940, Brit.) PR:A-C
CRIMES OF PASSION zero (1984) PR:O
CRIMES OF STEPHEN HAWKE, THE **
(1936, Brit.) PR:A-C
CRIMES OF THE FUTURE *½ (1969, Can.) PR:O
CRIMES OF THE HEART *½ (1986) PR:C-O
CRIMEWAVE ** (1985) PR:C
CRIMINAL, THE
  (SEE:CONCRETE JUNGLE, THE)
CRIMINAL AT LARGE * (1932, Brit.) PR:A
CRIMINAL CODE ** (1931) PR:A
CRIMINAL CONVERSATION **½
  (1980, Ireland) PR:C
CRIMINAL COURT * (1946) PR:A**
CRIMINAL LAWYER ** (1937) PR:A
CRIMINAL LAWYER **½ (1951) PR:A
CRIMINAL LIFE OF ARCHIBALDO DE LA CRUZ,
THE ***½ (1962, Mex.) PR:O
CRIMINALS OF THE AIR ** (1937) PR:A
CRIMINALS WITHIN zero (1941) PR:A
CRIMSON ALTAR, THE
  (SEE:CRIMSON CULT, THE)
CRIMSON BLADE, THE ** (1964, Brit.) PR:A
CRIMSON CANARY *** (1945) PR:A
CRIMSON CANDLE, THE *½ (1934, Brit.) PR:A-C
CRIMSON CIRCLE, THE * (1930, Brit.) PR:A
CRIMSON CIRCLE, THE ** (1936, Brit.) PR:A
CRIMSON CULT, THE zero (1970, Brit.) PR:O
CRIMSON EXECUTIONER, THE
  (SEE:BLOODY PIT OF HORROR, THE)
CRIMSON GHOST, THE
  (SEE:CYCLOTRODE X)
CRIMSON KEY, THE **½ (1947) PR:A
CRIMSON KIMONO, THE *** (1959) PR:A-C
CRIMSON PIRATE, THE ** (1952) PR:A**
CRIMSON ROMANCE * (1934) PR:C**
CRIMSON TRAIL, THE **½ (1935) PR:AA
CRIPPLE CREEK **½ (1952) PR:A
CRISIS *** (1950) PR:A
CRISS CROSS ****½ (1949) PR:C
CRITICAL CONDITION *½ (1987) PR:C
CRITIC'S CHOICE ** (1963) PR:A
CRITTERS **½ (1986) PR:C-O
CRITTERS II: THE MAIN COURSE ** (1988) PR:C
CROCODILE zero (1979, Thai./Hong Kong) PR:O
"CROCODILE" DUNDEE ***½ (1986, Aus.) PR:A-C
"CROCODILE" DUNDEE II ** (1988) PR:C
CROISIERES SIDERALES * (1941, Fr.) PR:A
CROMWELL ** (1970, Brit.) PR:A
CRONACA DI UNA MORTE ANNUNCIIATA
  (SEE:CHRONICLE OF A DEATH FORETOLD)
CROOK, THE *** (1971, Fr.) PR:A
CROOKED BILLET, THE * (1930, Brit.) PR:A
CROOKED CIRCLE *½ (1932) PR:A
CROOKED CIRCLE, THE ** (1958) PR:A-C
CROOKED LADY, THE ** (1932, Brit.) PR:A
CROOKED RIVER * (1950) PR:A
CROOKED ROAD, THE *½ (1940) PR:A
CROOKED ROAD, THE ** (1965, Brit./Yugo.) PR:C
CROOKED SKY, THE ** (1957, Brit.) PR:A
CROOKED TRAIL, THE * (1936) PR:A
CROOKED WAY, THE ** (1949) PR:A-C
CROOKED WEB, THE ** (1955) PR:A
CROOKS AND CORONETS
  (SEE:SOPHIE'S PLACE)
CROOKS ANONYMOUS **½ (1963, Brit.) PR:A-C
CROOKS IN CLOISTERS ** (1964, Brit.) PR:A
CROOKS TOUR * (1940, Brit.) PR:A
CROONER *** (1932) PR:A
CROSBY CASE, THE * (1934) PR:A
CROSS AND THE SWITCHBLADE, THE **
(1970) PR:A
CROSS CHANNEL *½ (1955, Brit.) PR:A-C
CROSS COUNTRY **½ (1983, Can.) PR:O
CROSS COUNTRY CRUISE * (1934) PR:A-C
CROSS COUNTRY ROMANCE *** (1940) PR:A

CROSS CREEK ** (1983) PR:C
CROSS CURRENTS ** (1935, Brit.) PR:A
CROSS-EXAMINATION * (1932) PR:A
CROSS MY HEART ** (1937, Brit.) PR:A
CROSS MY HEART ** (1946) PR:A
CROSS MY HEART **½ (1987) PR:O
CROSS OF IRON *** (1977, Brit./Ger.) PR:O
CROSS OF LORRAINE, THE *** (1943) PR:C-O
CROSS OF THE LIVING *½ (1963, Fr.) PR:C-O
CROSS ROADS *½ (1930, Brit.) PR:A
CROSS STREETS * (1934) PR:A
CROSS-UP *½ (1958) PR:A
CROSSED SWORDS ** (1954) PR:A
CROSSED SWORDS **½ (1978) PR:A
CROSSED TRAILS *** (1948) PR:A
CROSSFIRE ** (1933) PR:A
CROSSFIRE ** (1947) PR:A**
CROSSING DELANCEY * (1988) PR:C**
CROSSOVER DREAMS * (1985) PR:C-O**
CROSSPLOT ** (1969, Brit.) PR:A
CROSSROADS ***½ (1938, Fr.) PR:A
CROSSROADS ***½ (1942) PR:A
CROSSROADS * (1986) PR:C-O**
CROSSROADS OF PASSION **½ (1951, Fr.) PR:A
CROSSROADS TO CRIME ** (1960, Brit.) PR:C
CROSSTALK **½ (1982, Aus.) PR:A
CROSSTRAP *½ (1962, Brit.) PR:C
CROSSWINDS **½ (1951) PR:A
CROUCHING BEAST, THE * (1936, US/Brit.) PR:A
CROW HOLLOW ** (1952, Brit.) PR:A-C
CROWD INSIDE, THE * (1971, Can.) PR:C
CROWD ROARS, THE ***½ (1932) PR:A-C
CROWD ROARS, THE * (1938) PR:A**
CROWDED DAY, THE **½ (1954, Brit.) PR:A
CROWDED PARADISE **½ (1956) PR:C
CROWDED SKY, THE **½ (1960) PR:A
CROWN VS STEVENS ** (1936) PR:A
CROWNING EXPERIENCE, THE ** (1960) PR:A
CROWNING GIFT, THE *½ (1967, Brit.) PR:A
CROWNING TOUCH, THE ** (1959, Brit.) PR:A
CRUCIBLE OF HORROR *½ (1971, Brit.) PR:C
CRUCIBLE OF TERROR * (1971, Brit.) PR:O
CRUCIFIX, THE **½ (1934, Brit.) PR:A
CRUEL SEA, THE ** (1953, Brit.) PR:A**
CRUEL SWAMP
  (SEE:SWAMP WOMEN)
CRUEL TOWER, THE *** (1956) PR:A
CRUISER EMDEN *** (1932, Ger.) PR:A
CRUISIN' DOWN THE RIVER **½ (1953) PR:A
CRUISING zero (1980) PR:O
CRUSADE AGAINST RACKETS **½ (1937) PR:A
CRUSADER, THE * (1932) PR:A
CRUSADES, THE ***½ (1935) PR:A
CRY BABY KILLER, THE *** (1958) PR:C
CRY BLOOD, APACHE **½ (1970) PR:O
CRY DANGER *** (1951) PR:A
CRY DR. CHICAGO zero (1971) PR:C
CRY DOUBLE CROSS
  (SEE:BOOMERANG)
CRY FOR HAPPY **½ (1961) PR:C
CRY FOR ME, BILLY
  (SEE:COUNT YOUR BULLETS)
CRY FREEDOM ** (1961, Phil.) PR:A
CRY FREEDOM **½ (1987, Brit.) PR:C
CRY FROM THE STREET, A ***½
  (1959, Brit.) PR:A
CRY HAVOC **½ (1943) PR:A
CRY IN THE DARK, A ***½ (1988) PR:C
CRY IN THE NIGHT, A **½ (1956) PR:C
CRY MURDER * (1936) PR:A
CRY OF BATTLE ** (1963, US/Phil.) PR:A
CRY OF THE BANSHEE *½ (1970, Brit.) PR:O
CRY OF THE BEWITCHED
  (SEE:YOUNG AND EVIL)
CRY OF THE CITY ***½ (1948) PR:C
CRY OF THE HUNTED *** (1953) PR:A
CRY OF THE PENGUINS ** (1972, Brit.) PR:A
CRY OF THE WEREWOLF ** (1944) PR:C-O
CRY TERROR *** (1958) PR:A-C
CRY, THE BELOVED COUNTRY ***½
  (1952, Brit.) PR:A
CRY TOUGH **½ (1959) PR:A
CRY VENGEANCE * (1954) PR:A**
CRY WILDERNESS zero (1987) PR:C
CRY WOLF **½ (1947) PR:A
CRY WOLF ** (1968, Brit.) PR:AA
CRYPT OF THE LIVING DEAD zero (1973) PR:C

CRYSTAL BALL, THE **½ (1943) PR:A
CRYSTAL HEART ** (1987) PR:C-O
CUBA * (1979) PR:C**
CUBA CROSSING zero (1980) PR:O
CUBAN FIREBALL ** (1951) PR:A
CUBAN LOVE SONG, THE *** (1931) PR:A
CUBAN PETE **½ (1946) PR:A
CUBAN REBEL GIRLS
  (SEE:ASSAULT OF THE REBEL GIRLS)
CUCKOO CLOCK, THE ** (1938, It.) PR:A
CUCKOO IN THE NEST, THE ** (1933, Brit.) PR:A-C
CUCKOO PATROL zero (1965, Brit.) PR:A
CUCKOOS, THE ***½ (1930) PR:AA
CUJO * (1983) PR:O**
CUL-DE-SAC *** (1966, Brit.) PR:C-O
CULPEPPER CATTLE COMPANY, THE **
(1972) PR:C
CULT OF THE COBRA ** (1955) PR:A-C
CULT OF THE DAMNED
  (SEE:ANGEL, ANGEL, DOWN WE GO)
CUP FEVER *½ (1965, Brit.) PR:AA
CUP OF KINDNESS, A *½ (1934, Brit.) PR:A
CUP-TIE HONEYMOON *½ (1948, Brit.) PR:A
CUPS OF SAN SEBASTIAN, THE
  (SEE:FICKLE FINGER OF FATE, THE)
CURE FOR LOVE, THE *½ (1950, Brit.) PR:A
CURFEW BREAKERS *½ (1957) PR:C
CURIOUS DR. HUMPP * (1967, Arg.) PR:O
CURIOUS FEMALE, THE zero (1969) PR:O
CURLY TOP ** (1935) PR:AA**
CURSE OF BIGFOOT, THE * (1972) PR:C
CURSE OF DRACULA, THE
  (SEE:RETURN OF DRACULA, THE)
CURSE OF FRANKENSTEIN, THE **
(1957, Brit.) PR:O
CURSE OF THE AZTEC MUMMY, THE *
(1965, Mex.) PR:A-C
CURSE OF THE BLOOD GHOULS zero
  (1969, It.) PR:O
CURSE OF THE CAT PEOPLE, THE **
(1944) PR:C-O
CURSE OF THE CRIMSON ALTAR
  (SEE:CRIMSON CULT, THE)
CURSE OF THE CRYING WOMAN, THE zero
  (1969, Mex.) PR:C
CURSE OF THE DEMON ***½ (1958) PR:O
CURSE OF THE DEVIL * (1973, Sp./Mex.) PR:O
CURSE OF THE DOLL PEOPLE, THE **
  (1968, Mex.) PR:C
CURSE OF THE FACELESS MAN * (1958) PR:C
CURSE OF THE FLY *½ (1965, Brit.) PR:C
CURSE OF THE GOLEM
  (SEE:IT!)
CURSE OF THE LIVING CORPSE, THE **
(1964) PR:O
CURSE OF THE MUMMY'S TOMB, THE **
  (1965, Brit.) PR:C
CURSE OF THE MUSHROOM PEOPLE
  (SEE:ATTACK OF THE MUSHROOM PEOPLE)
CURSE OF THE PINK PANTHER zero (1983) PR:A
CURSE OF THE STONE HAND zero
  (1965, Mex./Chile) PR:C
CURSE OF THE SWAMP CREATURE * (1966) PR:C
CURSE OF THE UNDEAD *½ (1959) PR:C
CURSE OF THE VAMPIRE
  (SEE:PLAYGIRLS AND THE VAMPIRE, THE)
CURSE OF THE VAMPIRES ***
  (1970, Phil./US) PR:O
CURSE OF THE VOODOO *½ (1965, Brit.) PR:O
CURSE OF THE WEREWOLF, THE * (1961) PR:O**
CURSE OF THE WRAYDONS, THE *½
  (1946, Brit.) PR:A-C
CURSE, THE *½ (1987) PR:O
CURSES OF THE GHOULS
  (SEE:CURSES OF THE BLOOD-GHOULS)
CURTAIN AT EIGHT *½ (1934) PR:A
CURTAIN CALL *½ (1940) PR:A
CURTAIN CALL AT CACTUS CREEK **
  (1950) PR:AA
CURTAIN FALLS, THE * (1935) PR:A
CURTAIN RISES, THE ** (1939, Fr.) PR:A
CURTAIN UP *½ (1952, Brit.) PR:A
CURTAINS zero (1983, Can.) PR:O
CURUCU, BEAST OF THE AMAZON * (1956) PR:C
CUSTER MASSACRE, THE
  (SEE:GREAT SIOUX MASSACRE, THE)
CUSTER OF THE WEST ** (1968, US/Sp.) PR:C

Finding entries in **THE MOTION PICTURE GUIDE** ™		STAR RATINGS		PARENTAL RECOMMENDATION (PR:)	
Years 1929-83	Volumes I-IX	★★★★★	Masterpiece	AA	Good for Children
1984	Volume IX	★★★★	Excellent	A	Acceptable for Children
1985	1986 ANNUAL	★★★	Good	C	Cautionary, some objectionable scenes
1986	1987 ANNUAL	★★	Fair	O	Objectionable for Children
1987	1988 ANNUAL	★	Poor		
1988	1989 ANNUAL	zero	Without Merit	**BOLD:** Films on Videocassette	

CUSTOMS AGENT ** (1950) PR:A
CUT AND RUN ** (1986, It.) PR:O
CUTTER AND BONE ** (1981) PR:O**
CYBORG 2087 *½ (1966) PR:A
CYCLE SAVAGES *½ (1969) PR:O
CYCLE, THE *** (1979, Iran) PR:A-C
CYCLONE ** (1987) PR:C
CYCLONE FURY ** (1951) PR:A
CYCLONE KID *½ (1931) PR:A
CYCLONE KID, THE *½ (1942) PR:A
CYCLONE OF THE SADDLE * (1935) PR:A
CYCLONE ON HORSEBACK * (1941) PR:A
CYCLONE PRAIRIE RANGERS ** (1944) PR:A
CYCLONE RANGER ** (1935) PR:A
CYCLOPS *½ (1957) PR:C-O
CYCLOTRODE X ** (1946) PR:A
CYNARA ***½ (1932) PR:A-C
CYNTHIA **½ (1947) PR:AA
CYRANO DE BERGERAC ** (1950) PR:AA**
CZAR OF BROADWAY, THE ** (1930) PR:A
CZAR WANTS TO SLEEP ** (1934, US/USSR) PR:A

D

D.C. CAB ** (1983) PR:C
D-DAY, THE SIXTH OF JUNE * (1956) PR:A**
DA ***½ (1988) PR:A-C
DAD AND DAVE COME TO TOWN **½ (1938, Aus.) PR:A
DADDY LONG LEGS **** (1931) PR:AA
DADDY LONG LEGS **** (1955) PR:AA
DADDY-O * (1959) PR:C
DADDY'S DEADLY DARLING zero (1984) PR:O
DADDY'S BOYS ** (1988) PR:O
DADDY'S GIRL (SEE:DADDY'S DEADLY DARLING)
DADDY'S GONE A-HUNTING ** (1969) PR:C
DAD'S ARMY **½ (1971, Brit.) PR:A
DAFFODIL KILLER (SEE:DEVIL'S DAFFODIL, THE)
DAFFY (SEE:WILD SEED)
DAFFY DUCK'S MOVIE: FANTASTIC ISLAND **½ (1983) PR:AA
DAGGERS OF BLOOD (SEE:INVASION SEVENTEEN HUNDRED)
DAGORA THE SPACE MONSTER * (1964, Jap.) PR:A
DAISIES *½ (1967, Czech.) PR:C-O
DAISY KENYON ***½ (1947) PR:A-C
DAISY MILLER * (1974) PR:C-O
DAKOTA **½ (1945) PR:A
DAKOTA INCIDENT **½ (1956) PR:A
DAKOTA KID, THE * (1951) PR:AA
DAKOTA LIL ** (1950) PR:A
DALEKS—INVASION EARTH 2155 A.D. ** (1966, Brit.) PR:A
DALLAS *** (1950) PR:A
DALTON GANG, THE *½ (1949) PR:A
DALTON GIRLS, THE ** (1957) PR:A
DALTON THAT GOT AWAY * (1960) PR:A
DALTONS RIDE AGAIN, THE ** (1945) PR:A
DALTONS' WOMEN, THE * (1950) PR:A
DAM BUSTERS, THE ***½ (1955, Brit.) PR:A
DAMAGED GOODS * (1937) PR:C
DAMAGED LIVES * (1937) PR:C
DAMAGED LOVE * (1931) PR:C
DAMES ***½ (1934) PR:AA
DAMES AHOY * (1930) PR:AA
DAMIEN—OMEN II * (1978) PR:O
DAMN CITIZEN ** (1958) PR:A
DAMN THE DEFIANT! * (1962, Brit.) PR:A**
DAMN YANKEES ** (1958) PR:A**
DAMNATION **** (1988, Hung.) PR:O
DAMNATION ALLEY * (1977) PR:C
DAMNED DON'T CRY, THE *** (1950) PR:A-C
DAMNED, THE *** (1948, Fr.) PR:C
DAMNED, THE (SEE:THESE ARE THE DAMNED)
DAMON AND PYTHIAS ** (1962) PR:A
DAMSEL IN DISTRESS, A * (1937) PR:A**
DAN CANDY'S LAW (SEE:ALIEN THUNDER)
DAN MATTHEWS * (1936) PR:A
DAN'S MOTEL * (1982) PR:O
DANCE BAND *½ (1935, Brit.) PR:A
DANCE HALL ** (1929) PR:A
DANCE HALL ** (1941) PR:AA
DANCE HALL * (1950, Brit.) PR:A
DANCE LITTLE LADY *½ (1954, Brit.) PR:A
DANCE MALL HOSTESS * (1933) PR:A
DANCE OF DEATH, THE *½ (1938, Brit.) PR:A
DANCE OF DEATH, THE **½ (1971, Brit.) PR:C
DANCE OF LIFE, THE **½ (1929) PR:A
DANCE OF THE DWARFS ** (1983, US/Phil.) PR:C
DANCE OF THE VAMPIRES (SEE:FEARLESS VAMPIRE KILLER)
DANCE PRETTY LADY *½ (1932, Brit.) PR:A
DANCE TEAM ** (1932) PR:AA
DANCE WITH A STRANGER ** (1985, Brit.) PR:C-O
DANCE WITH ME, HENRY ** (1956) PR:A
DANCE, CHARLIE, DANCE ** (1937) PR:A
DANCE, FOOLS, DANCE *** (1931) PR:A-C
DANCE, GIRL, DANCE * (1933) PR:A
DANCE, GIRL, DANCE ***½ (1940) PR:A
DANCERS ** (1987) PR:A
DANCERS, THE * (1930) PR:A
DANCERS IN THE DARK * (1932) PR:A
DANCING CO-ED *** (1939) PR:A
DANCING DYNAMITE * (1931) PR:A
DANCING FEET * (1936) PR:A
DANCING HEART, THE *½ (1959, Ger.) PR:A
DANCING IN MANHATTAN * (1945) PR:A
DANCING IN THE DARK *** (1949) PR:A
DANCING IN THE DARK ** (1986, Can.) PR:C
DANCING LADY * (1933) PR:A**
DANCING MAN * (1934) PR:A
DANCING MASTERS, THE ** (1943) PR:A
DANCING ON A DIME * (1940) PR:A
DANCING PIRATE ** (1936) PR:A
DANCING SWEETIES * (1930) PR:A
DANCING WITH CRIME * (1947, Brit.) PR:A
DANCING YEARS, THE * (1950, Brit.) PR:AA
DANDY DICK *½ (1935, Brit.) PR:A
DANDY IN ASPIC, A *½ (1968, Brit.) PR:A
DANDY, THE ALL AMERICAN GIRL ** (1976) PR:A
DANGER AHEAD * (1935) PR:A
DANGER AHEAD * (1940) PR:A
DANGER BY MY SIDE ** (1962, Brit.) PR:A-C
DANGER: DIABOLIK ** (1968, It./Fr.) PR:A
DANGER FLIGHT **½ (1939) PR:AA
DANGER IN THE PACIFIC ** (1942) PR:A
DANGER IS A WOMAN ** (1952, Fr.) PR:C-O
DANGER ISLAND (SEE:MR. MOTO ON DANGER ISLAND)
DANGER LIGHTS * (1930) PR:AA
DANGER—LOVE AT WORK **½ (1937) PR:A
DANGER ON THE AIR ** (1938) PR:A
DANGER ON WHEELS ** (1940) PR:A
DANGER PATROL **½ (1937) PR:A
DANGER ROUTE ** (1968, Brit.) PR:A
DANGER SIGNAL *** (1945) PR:A
DANGER STREET * (1947) PR:A
DANGER TOMORROW ** (1960, Brit.) PR:A-C
DANGER TRAILS * (1935) PR:A
DANGER VALLEY * (1938) PR:AA
DANGER WITHIN (SEE:BREAKOUT)
DANGER WOMAN * (1946) PR:A
DANGER! WOMEN AT WORK ** (1943) PR:A
DANGER ZONE * (1951) PR:C
DANGER ZONE, THE * (1987) PR:O
DANGEROUS * (1936) PR:A-C**
DANGEROUS ADVENTURE, A ** (1937) PR:A
DANGEROUS AFFAIR, A * (1931) PR:A
DANGEROUS AFTERNOON *½ (1961, Brit.) PR:A-C
DANGEROUS AGE, A *½ (1960, Can.) PR:A
DANGEROUS ASSIGNMENT ** (1950, Brit.) PR:A-C
DANGEROUS BLONDES *½ (1943) PR:A
DANGEROUS BUSINESS ** (1946) PR:A
DANGEROUS CARGO ** (1939, Brit.) PR:A
DANGEROUS CARGO *½ (1954, Brit.) PR:C
DANGEROUS CHARTER * (1962 76m Crown International c) PR:A
DANGEROUS CORNER *½ (1935) PR:A
DANGEROUS CROSSING **½ (1953) PR:A
DANGEROUS CURVES **½ (1929) PR:AA
DANGEROUS DAN McGREW ** (1930) PR:A
DANGEROUS DAVIES—THE LAST DETECTIVE ** (1981, Brit.) PR:A
DANGEROUS EXILE **½ (1958, Brit.) PR:A
DANGEROUS FEMALE (SEE:MALTESE FALCON, THE)
DANGEROUS FINGERS (SEE:WANTED BY SCOTLAND YARD)
DANGEROUS FRIEND (SEE:TODD KILLINGS, THE)
DANGEROUS GAME, A * (1941) PR:A
DANGEROUS GROUND *½ (1934, Brit.) PR:A
DANGEROUS HOLIDAY * (1937) PR:AA
DANGEROUS INTRIGUE ** (1936) PR:A
DANGEROUS INTRUDER ** (1945) PR:A
DANGEROUS KISS, THE * (1961, Jap.) PR:A
DANGEROUS LADY * (1941) PR:A
DANGEROUS LIAISONS ***½ (1988) PR:O
DANGEROUS LOVE AFFAIR (SEE:LES LIASONS DANGEREUSES)
DANGEROUS MEDICINE **½ (1938, Brit.) PR:A
DANGEROUS MILLIONS ** (1946) PR:A
DANGEROUS MISSION *½ (1954) PR:A-C
DANGEROUS MONEY ** (1946) PR:A
DANGEROUS MOONLIGHT (SEE:SUICIDE SQUADRON)
DANGEROUS MOVES ***½ (1985, Switz.) PR:C
DANGEROUS NUMBER ** (1937) PR:A
DANGEROUS PARADISE *½ (1930) PR:A
DANGEROUS PARTNERS zero (1945) PR:A
DANGEROUS PASSAGE ** (1944) PR:A
DANGEROUS PROFESSION, A ** (1949) PR:A
DANGEROUS SEAS ** (1931, Brit.) PR:A
DANGEROUS SECRETS **½ (1938, Brit.) PR:A
DANGEROUS TO KNOW * (1938) PR:A
DANGEROUS VENTURE ** (1947) PR:A
DANGEROUS VOYAGE (SEE:TERROR SHIP)
DANGEROUS WATERS *½ (1936) PR:A
DANGEROUS WHEN WET **½ (1953) PR:A
DANGEROUS WOMAN *½ (1929) PR:A
DANGEROUS YEARS * (1947) PR:A
DANGEROUS YOUTH ** (1958, Brit.) PR:A
DANGEROUSLY CLOSE **½ (1986) PR:O
DANGEROUSLY THEY LIVE **½ (1942) PR:A
DANGEROUSLY YOURS ** (1933) PR:A
DANGEROUSLY YOURS *½ (1937) PR:A
DANIEL ** (1983) PR:C
DANIEL BOONE ** (1936) PR:AA
DANIEL BOONE, TRAIL BLAZER *½ (1957) PR:AA
DANIELLA BY NIGHT ** (1962, Fr/Ger.) PR:C
DANNY BOY ** (1934, Brit.) PR:A
DANNY BOY *½ (1941, Brit.) PR:A
DANNY BOY ** (1946) PR:AA
DANS LES GRIFFES DU MANIAQUE (SEE:DIABOLICAL DR. Z, THE)
DANSE MACABRE (SEE:CASTLE OF BLOOD)
DANTE'S INFERNO *** (1935) PR:A
DANTON *** (1931, Ger.) PR:A
DANTON **½ (1983, Fr./Pol.) PR:O
DAPHNE, THE * (1967, Jap.) PR:A-C
DARBY AND JOAN *½ (1937, Brit.) PR:A
DARBY O'GILL AND THE LITTLE PEOPLE *** (1959) PR:AA**
DARBY'S RANGERS **½ (1958) PR:A
DAREDEVIL, THE * (1971) PR:C
DAREDEVIL DRIVERS * (1938) PR:A
DAREDEVIL IN THE CASTLE *** (1969, Jap.) PR:A
DAREDEVILS OF EARTH * (1936, Brit.) PR:A
DAREDEVILS OF THE CLOUDS *½ (1948) PR:A
DARING CABALLERO, THE * (1949) PR:A
DARING DANGER * (1932) PR:A
DARING DAUGHTERS ** (1933) PR:A
DARING DOBERMANS, THE ** (1973) PR:AA
DARING GAME * (1968) PR:A
DARING YOUNG MAN, THE * (1935) PR:A
DARING YOUNG MAN, THE ** (1942) PR:A
DARK, THE * (1979) PR:O
DARK ALIBI *½ (1946) PR:A
DARK ANGEL, THE ***½ (1935) PR:A
DARK AT THE TOP OF THE STAIRS, THE ***½ (1960) PR:C
DARK AVENGER, THE (SEE:WARRIORS, THE)
DARK CITY *** (1950) PR:A
DARK COMMAND, THE ***½ (1940) PR:A
DARK CORNER, THE ***½ (1946) PR:C
DARK CRYSTAL, THE * (1982, Brit.) PR:A**
DARK DELUSION ** (1947) PR:A
DARK END OF THE STREET, THE *½ (1981) PR:O
DARK ENEMY ** (1984, Brit.) PR:A
DARK EYES ** (1938, Fr.) PR:O
DARK EYES ***½ (1987, It.) PR:A-C
DARK EYES OF LONDON (SEE:HUMAN MONSTER, THE)
DARK EYES OF LONDON **½ (1961, Ger.) PR:A
DARK HAZARD *** (1934) PR:A
DARK HORSE, THE ** (1932) PR:A
DARK HORSE, THE *½ (1946) PR:A
DARK HOUR, THE * (1936) PR:A
DARK INTERVAL * (1950, Brit.) PR:C
DARK INTRUDER ** (1965) PR:C
DARK IS THE NIGHT *** (1946, USSR) PR:C-O
DARK JOURNEY ***½ (1937, Brit.) PR:A
DARK LIGHT, THE *½ (1951, Brit.) PR:C
DARK MAN, THE * (1951, Brit.) PR:A
DARK MANHATTAN * (1937) PR:C
DARK MIRROR, THE ***½ (1946) PR:C
DARK MOUNTAIN *½ (1944) PR:A
DARK ODYSSEY ** (1961) PR:C

DARK OF THE SUN ** (1968, Brit.) PR:A
DARK PASSAGE ***½ (1947) PR:A
DARK PAST, THE * (1948) PR:A**
DARK PLACES * (1974, Brit.) PR:A
DARK PURPOSE * (1964) PR:C
DARK RED ROSES ** (1930, Brit.) PR:A
DARK RIVER * (1956, Arg.) PR:O
DARK ROAD, THE * (1948, Brit.) PR:A
DARK SANDS **½ (1938, Brit.) PR:AA
DARK SECRET *½ (1949, Brit.) PR:A

DARK SHADOWS
   (SEE:HOUSE OF DARK SHADOWS)
DARK SIDE OF TOMORROW, THE * (1970) PR:O
DARK SKIES
   (SEE:DARKENED SKIES)
DARK STAIRWAY, THE ** (1938, Brit.) PR:A
DARK STAR **½ (1975) PR:C
DARK STREETS *½ (1929) PR:A
DARK STREETS OF CAIRO * (1940) PR:A
DARK TOWER, THE * (1943, Brit.) PR:A
DARK VENTURE zero (1956) PR:A
DARK VICTORY ** (1939) PR:A**
DARK WATERS **½ (1944) PR:A
DARK WORLD *½ (1935, Brit.) PR:A
DARK, THE,
   (SEE:HORROR HOUSE)
DARKENED ROOMS *½ (1929) PR:A
DARKENED SKIES *½ (1930) PR:A
DARKER THAN AMBER *½ (1970) PR:O
DARKEST AFRICA *½ (1936) PR:A
DARKTOWN STRUTTERS zero (1975) PR:C
DARLING ** (1965, Brit.) PR:O**
DARLING, HOW COULD YOU! *½ (1951) PR:A
DARLING LILI * (1970) PR:C
DARTS ARE TRUMPS **½ (1938, Brit.) PR:A
DARWIN ADVENTURE, THE ** (1972, Brit.) PR:A
D.A.R.Y.L. *½ (1985) PR:AA
DAS HAUS AM FLUSS **½ (1986, E./Ger.) PR:O
DAS LETZTE GEHEIMNIS * (1959, Ger.) PR:C
DATE AT MIDNIGHT ** (1960, Brit.) PR:A-C
DATE BAIT * (1960) PR:O
DATE WITH A DREAM, A ** (1948, Brit.) PR:A
DATE WITH AN ANGEL * (1987) PR:A-C**
DATE WITH DEATH, A zero (1959) PR:A
DATE WITH DISASTER *½ (1957, Brit.) PR:C
DATE WITH JUDY, A ***½ (1948) PR:AA
DATE WITH THE FALCON, A ** (1941) PR:A
DATELINE DIAMONDS * (1966, Brit.) PR:A
DAUGHTER OF CLEOPATRA
   (SEE:CLEOPATRA'S DAUGHTER)
DAUGHTER OF DARKNESS **½ (1948, Brit.) PR:O
DAUGHTER OF DECEIT **½ (1977, Mex.) PR:A-C
DAUGHTER OF DR. JEKYLL * (1957) PR:A**
DAUGHTER OF EVIL ** (1930, Ger.) PR:O
DAUGHTER OF MATA HARI
   (SEE:MATA HARI'S DAUGHTER)
DAUGHTER OF ROSIE O'GRADY, THE **½
   (1950) PR:AA
DAUGHTER OF SHANGHAI **½ (1937) PR:A
DAUGHTER OF THE DRAGON ** (1931) PR:A
DAUGHTER OF THE JUNGLE *½ (1949) PR:A
DAUGHTER OF THE NILE ***½
   (1988, Taiwan) PR:C
DAUGHTER OF THE SANDS *** (1952, Fr.) PR:C-O
DAUGHTER OF THE SUN GOD ** (1962) PR:A
DAUGHTER OF THE TONG * (1939) PR:A
DAUGHTER OF THE WEST **½ (1949) PR:A
DAUGHTERS COURAGEOUS *** (1939) PR:A
DAUGHTERS OF DARKNESS *
   (1971, Bel./Fr./Ger./It.) PR:O**
DAUGHTERS OF DESTINY *** (1954, Fr./It.) PR:C
DAUGHTERS OF SATAN * (1972) PR:C
DAUGHTERS OF TODAY * (1933, Brit.) PR:C
DAVID * (1979, Ger.) PR:C**
DAVID AND BATHSHEBA ***½ (1951) PR:C
DAVID AND GOLIATH *½ (1961, It.) PR:A
DAVID AND LISA ** (1962) PR:A-C**
DAVID COPPERFIELD *** (1935) PR:A**
DAVID COPPERFIELD ** (1970, Brit.) PR:A
DAVID GOLDER ** (1932, Fr.) PR:A
DAVID HARDING, COUNTERSPY ** (1950) PR:A
DAVID HARUM **½ (1934) PR:A

DAVID HOLZMAN'S DIARY *** (1968) PR:C-O
DAVID LIVINGSTONE * (1936, Brit.) PR:A
DAVY ** (1958, Brit.) PR:A
**DAVY CROCKETT AND THE RIVER PIRATES **½
   (1956) PR:AA**
DAVY CROCKETT, INDIAN SCOUT ***
   (1950) PR:AA
**DAVY CROCKETT, KING OF THE WILD FRONTIER
   *** (1955) PR:AA**
DAWN, THE
   (SEE:DAWN OVER IRELAND)
DAWN AT SOCORRO *** (1954) PR:A
DAWN *½ (1979, Aus.) PR:C
DAWN EXPRESS, THE *½ (1942) PR:A
DAWN OF THE DEAD * (1979) PR:O**
DAWN ON THE GREAT DIVIDE **½ (1942) PR:A
DAWN OVER IRELAND ** (1938, Ireland) PR:A
DAWN PATROL, THE * (1930) PR:A**
DAWN PATROL, THE ** (1938) PR:C**
DAWN RIDER * (1935) PR:A**
DAWN TRAIL, THE ** (1931) PR:A
DAY AFTER, THE
   (SEE:UP FROM THE BEACH)
DAY AFTER HALLOWEEN, THE zero
   (1981, Aus.) PR:O
DAY AFTER THE DIVORCE, THE *½
   (1940, Ger.) PR:A
**DAY AND THE HOUR, THE **½
   (1963, Fr./It.) PR:A**
DAY AT THE BEACH, A *½ (1970) PR:O
DAY AT THE RACES, A ***½ (1937) PR:AA
DAY FOR NIGHT *** (1973, Fr.) PR:A-C**
DAY IN COURT, A * (1965, It.) PR:O
**DAY IN THE DEATH OF JOE EGG, A **
   (1972, Brit.) PR:O**
DAY MARS INVADED EARTH, THE ** (1963) PR:C
DAY OF ANGER * (1970, It./Ger.) PR:O
DAY OF FURY, A *** (1956) PR:A
DAY OF RECKONING ** (1933) PR:O
DAY OF THE ANIMALS zero (1977) PR:C
DAY OF THE BAD MAN *** (1958) PR:A
DAY OF THE COBRA, THE ** (1985, It.) PR:O
DAY OF THE DEAD * (1985) PR:O**
DAY OF THE DOLPHIN, THE ** (1973) PR:A
DAY OF THE EVIL GUN ** (1968) PR:A
DAY OF THE HANGING, THE
   (SEE:LAW OF THE LAWLESS)
DAY OF THE JACKAL, THE **
   (1973, Brit./Fr.) PR:C**
DAY OF THE LANDGRABBERS
   (SEE:LAND RAIDERS)
DAY OF THE LOCUST, THE *** (1975) PR:C-O**
DAY OF THE NIGHTMARE * (1965) PR:C
DAY OF THE OUTLAW * (1959) PR:A
DAY OF THE OWL, THE *** (1968, It./Fr.) PR:C
DAY OF THE TRIFFIDS, THE * (1963) PR:C**
DAY OF THE WOLVES ** (1973) PR:A-C
DAY OF TRIUMPH * (1954) PR:A**
DAY OF WRATH ** (1948, Den.) PR:C**
DAY THE BOOKIES WEPT, THE **½ (1939) PR:A
DAY THE EARTH CAUGHT FIRE, THE *
   (1961, Brit.) PR:A**
DAY THE EARTH FROZE, THE **
   (1959, Fin./USSR) PR:AA
DAY THE EARTH STOOD STILL, THE **
   (1951) PR:A**
DAY THE FISH CAME OUT, THE *
   (1967., Brit./Gr.) PR:C
**DAY THE HOTLINE GOT HOT, THE *½
   (1968, Fr./Sp.) PR:A**
DAY THE SCREAMING STOPPED, THE
   (SEE:COMEBACK, THE)
DAY THE SKY EXPLODED, THE *½
   (1958, Fr./It.) PR:A
DAY THE SUN ROSE, THE **½ (1969, Jap.) PR:A
DAY THE WAR ENDED, THE **½
   (1961, USSR) PR:A-C
DAY THE WORLD CHANGED HANDS, THE
   (SEE:COLOSSUS: THE FORBIN PROJECT, THE)
DAY THE WORLD ENDED, THE ** (1956) PR:A
**DAY THEY ROBBED THE BANK OF ENGLAND, THE
   ½ (1960, Brit.) PR:A
DAY TIME ENDED, THE *½ (1980, Sp.) PR:A
DAY-TIME WIFE *** (1939) PR:A-C

DAY TO REMEMBER, A *** (1953, Brit.) PR:A
DAY WILL COME, A ** (1960, Ger.) PR:A
DAY WILL DAWN, THE
   (SEE:AVENGERS, THE)
DAY YOU LOVE ME, THE **
   (1988, Colombia/Venezuela) PR:A
DAYBREAK *½ (1931) PR:A
DAYBREAK *** (1940, Fr.) PR:A**
DAYBREAK ** (1948, Brit.) PR:C-O
DAYDREAMER, THE * (1966) PR:AA**
DAYDREAMER, THE ** (1975, Fr.) PR:A
DAYLIGHT ROBBERY ** (1964, Brit.) PR:AA
DAYS AND NIGHTS **½ (1946, USSR) PR:C
DAYS OF BUFFALO BILL ** (1946) PR:A
DAYS OF GLORY **½ (1944) PR:A
DAYS OF HEAVEN *** (1978) PR:A**
DAYS OF JESSE JAMES *** (1939) PR:A
DAYS OF OLD CHEYENNE *½ (1943) PR:A
DAYS OF 36 **** (1972, Gr.) PR:C
DAYS OF WINE AND ROSES ** (1962) PR:A-C**
DAYTON'S DEVILS *** (1968) PR:A
DAYTONA BEACH WEEKEND zero (1965) PR:A-C
DOCTORS, THE ** (1956, Fr.) PR:A
DE L'AMOUR ** (1968, Fr./Itl.) PR:C
DE SADE zero (1969, US/Ger.) PR:O
DEAD, THE *** (1987) PR:A**
DEAD AND BURIED * (1981) PR:O
DEAD ARE ALIVE, THE *
   (1972, Yugo./Ger./It.) PR:O
DEAD DON'T DREAM, THE *½ (1948) PR:A
DEAD END *** (1937) PR:C**
DEAD-END DRIVE-IN ***½ (1986, Aus.) PR:O
DEAD END KIDS **½ (1986) PR:C-O
DEAD END KIDS ON DRESS PARADE **
   (1939) PR:A
DEAD EYES OF LONDON
   (SEE:DARK EYES OF LONDON)
DEAD HEAT * (1988) PR:O
**DEAD HEAT ON A MERRY-GO-ROUND **½
   (1966) PR:A**
DEAD KIDS ** (1981, Aus./New Zealand) PR:O
DEAD LUCKY *½ (1960, Brit.) PR:C
DEAD MAN WALKING *½ (1988) PR:O
DEAD MAN'S CHEST * (1965, Brit.) PR:A-C
DEAD MAN'S EVIDENCE **½ (1962, Brit.) PR:A-C
DEAD MAN'S EYES *½ (1944) PR:A
DEAD MAN'S FLOAT ** (1980, Aus.) PR:C
DEAD MAN'S GOLD ** (1948) PR:A
DEAD MAN'S GULCH **½ (1943) PR:A
DEAD MAN'S SHOES ** (1939, Brit.) PR:A
DEAD MAN'S TRAIL ** (1952) PR:A
DEAD MARCH, THE * (1937) PR:C
DEAD MELODY * (1938, Ger.) PR:C
DEAD MEN ARE DANGEROUS ** (1939, Brit.) PR:A
DEAD MEN DON'T WEAR PLAID ** (1982) PR:C
DEAD MEN TELL ** (1941) PR:A
DEAD MEN TELL NO TALES ** (1939, Brit.) PR:A
DEAD MEN WALK ** (1943) PR:C
DEAD MOUNTAINEER HOTEL, THE ***
   (1979, USSR) PR:C
DEAD OF NIGHT ** (1946, Brit.) PR:O**
DEAD OF NIGHT
   (SEE:DEATHDREAM)
DEAD OF SUMMER ** (1970, It./Fr.) PR:C-O
DEAD OF WINTER **½ (1987) PR:O
DEAD ON COURSE *½ (1952, Brit.) PR:A-C
DEAD ONE, THE * (1961) PR:C
DEAD OR ALIVE ** (1944) PR:A
DEAD OR ALIVE
   (SEE:MINUTE TO PRAY, A SECOND TO DIE, A)
DEAD PEOPLE zero (1974) PR:O
DEAD PIGEON ON BEETHOVEN STREET ***
   (1972, Ger.) PR:C
DEAD POOL, THE * (1988) PR:O**
DEAD RECKONING ***½ (1947) PR:C
DEAD RINGER ** (1964) PR:C
DEAD RINGERS ** (1988, Can.) PR:O**
DEAD RUN ** (1961, Fr./It./Ger.) PR:C
DEAD TO THE WORLD *½ (1961) PR:A
DEAD WOMAN'S KISS, A * (1951, It.) PR:A
DEAD ZONE, THE **½ (1983) PR:O
DEADFALL *½ (1968, Brit.) PR:C
DEADHEAD MILES *** (1982) PR:A-C
DEADLIER THAN THE MALE *** (1957, Fr.) PR:C

DEADLIER THAN THE MALE **½ (1967, Brit.) PR:C
DEADLIEST SIN, THE **½ (1956, Brit.) PR:A
DEADLINE, THE *½ (1932) PR:A
DEADLINE *½ (1948) PR:A
DEADLINE ** (1987, Brit./Ger./Israel) PR:O
DEADLINE AT DAWN **½ (1946) PR:A
DEADLINE FOR MURDER **½ (1946) PR:A
DEADLINE—U.S.A. ***½ (1952) PR:C
DEADLOCK *½ (1931, Brit.) PR:A
DEADLOCK *½ (1943, Brit.) PR:A
DEADLOCK (SEE:MAN-TRAP)
DEADLY AFFAIR, THE **** (1967, Brit.) PR:A-C
DEADLY AS THE FEMALE (SEE:GUN CRAZY)
DEADLY BEES, THE ** (1967, Brit.) PR:C
DEADLY BLESSING **½ (1981) PR:O
DEADLY CHINA DOLL * (1973, Hong Kong) PR:O
DEADLY CIRCLE, THE (SEE:HONEYMOON OF HORROR)
DEADLY COMPANIONS, THE *** (1961) PR:C
DEADLY DECISION (SEE:CANARIS)
DEADLY DECOYS, THE * (1962, Fr.) PR:A-C
DEADLY DREAMS * (1988) PR:O
DEADLY DUO * (1962) PR:A
DEADLY EYES ** (1982) PR:O
DEADLY FEMALES, THE zero (1976, Brit.) PR:O
DEADLY FORCE * (1983) PR:O
DEADLY FRIEND ** (1986) PR:O
DEADLY GAME, THE * (1941) PR:A
DEADLY GAME, THE ** (1955, Brit.) PR:A
DEADLY HERO *** (1976) PR:O
DEADLY IS THE FEMALE (SEE:GUN CRAZY)
DEADLY MANTIS, THE *½ (1957) PR:A
DEADLY NIGHTSHADE *½ (1953, Brit.) PR:A
DEADLY PASSION ** (1985, South Africa) PR:O
DEADLY RECORD *½ (1959, Brit.) PR:A
DEADLY SILENCE (SEE:TARZAN'S DEADLY SILENCE)
DEADLY SPAWN, THE zero (1983) PR:O
DEADLY STRANGERS ** (1974, Brit.) PR:C
DEADLY TRACKERS *½ (1973) PR:O
DEADLY TRAP, THE *½ (1972, Fr./It.) PR:C
DEADLY TWINS zero (1988) PR:O
DEADTIME STORIES zero (1987) PR:O
DEADWOOD PASS * (1933) PR:A
DEADWOOD '76 zero (1965) PR:C
DEAF SMITH AND JOHNNY EARS * (1973, It.) PR:C
DEAL OF THE CENTURY *½ (1983) PR:C
DEALING: OR THE BERKELEY TO BOSTON FORTY-BRICK LOST-BAG BLUES *½ (1971) PR:O
DEAR BRAT ** (1951) PR:A
DEAR BRIGETTE ***½ (1965) PR:A
DEAR, DEAD DELILAH zero (1972) PR:O
DEAR DETECTIVE ** (1978, Fr.) PR:C
DEAR HEART *** (1964) PR:A
DEAR INSPECTOR (SEE:DEAR DETECTIVE)
DEAR JOHN **½ (1966, Swed.) PR:C
DEAR MARTHA (SEE:HONEYMOON KILLERS, THE)
DEAR MR. PROHACK ** (1949, Brit.) PR:A
DEAR MR. WONDERFUL **½ (1983, Ger.) PR:C
DEAR MURDERER ** (1947, Brit.) PR:C
DEAR OCTOPUS (SEE:RANDOLPH FAMILY, THE)
DEAR RUTH *** (1947) PR:A
DEAR WIFE *** (1949) PR:AA
DEATH AT A BROADCAST ** (1934, Brit.) PR:A
DEATH BEFORE DISHONOR **½ (1987) PR:C
DEATH BITE (SEE:SPASMS)
DEATH BLOW (SEE:TOUCH OF LEATHER)
DEATH COLLECTOR ** (1976) PR:O
DEATH CORDS (SEE:SHOCK WAVES)
DEATH CROONS THE BLUES *½ (1937, Brit.) PR:A
DEATH CURSE OF TARTU * (1967) PR:C-O
DEATH DRIVES THROUGH ** (1935, Brit.) PR:A
DEATH DRUMS ALONG THE RIVER (SEE:SANDERS)
DEATH FLIES EAST ** (1935) PR:A
DEATH FROM A DISTANCE *½ (1936) PR:A
DEATH FROM OUTER SPACE (SEE:DAY THE SKY EXPLODED, THE)
DEATH GAME zero (1977) PR:O
DEATH GOES NORTH *½ (1939) PR:A
DEATH GOES TO SCHOOL ** (1953, Brit.) PR:A
DEATH HUNT **½ (1981) PR:C
DEATH IN SMALL DOSES ** (1957) PR:C
DEATH IN THE GARDEN *** (1961, Fr./Mex.) PR:O
DEATH IN THE SKY * (1937) PR:C
DEATH IN VENICE **** (1971, It./Fr.) PR:C
DEATH IS A NUMBER ** (1951, Brit.) PR:A-C
DEATH IS A WOMAN (SEE:LOVE IS A WOMAN)
DEATH IS CALLED ENGELCHEN *** (1963, Czech.) PR:C
DEATH KISS, THE * (1933) PR:A
DEATH MACHINES zero (1976) PR:O
DEATH OF A BUREAUCRAT *** (1979, Cuba) PR:A-C
DEATH OF A CHAMPION ** (1939) PR:A
DEATH OF A CYCLIST (SEE:AGE OF INFIDELITY)
DEATH OF A GUNFIGHTER **½ (1969) PR:C
DEATH OF A JEW (SEE:SABRA)
DEATH OF A SALESMAN ***** (1952) PR:O
DEATH OF A SCOUNDREL *** (1956) PR:C
DEATH OF A SOLDIER ***½ (1986, Aus.) PR:O
DEATH OF AN ANGEL ** (1952, Brit.) PR:A
DEATH OF AN ANGEL ** (1985) PR:C
DEATH OF EMPEDOCLES, THE *** (1988, Fr./W. Ger.) PR:A
DEATH OF HER INNOCENCE (SEE:OUR TIME)
DEATH OF MARIO RICCI, THE *** (1985, Fr./Switz.) PR:C
DEATH OF MICHAEL TURBIN, THE * (1954, Brit.) PR:A
DEATH OF TARZAN, THE **** (1968, Czech.) PR:C
DEATH OF THE APEMAN (SEE:DEATH OF TARZAN, THE)
DEATH ON THE DIAMOND *½ (1934) PR:A
DEATH ON THE MOUNTAIN * (1961, Jap.) PR:O
DEATH ON THE NILE **** (1978, Brit.) PR:C
DEATH ON THE SET (SEE:MURDER ON THE SET)
DEATH OVER MY SHOULDER ** (1958, Brit.) PR:A-C
DEATH PLAY * (1976) PR:C
DEATH RACE *½ (1978, It.) PR:C-O
DEATH RACE 2000 *** (1975) PR:O
DEATH RIDES A HORSE ** (1969, It.) PR:O
DEATH RIDES THE PLAINS * (1944) PR:A
DEATH RIDES THE RANGE * (1940) PR:A
DEATH SENTENCE * (1967, It.) PR:O
DEATH SENTENCE **½ (1986, Pol.) PR:O
DEATH SHIP * (1980, Can.) PR:O
DEATH TAKES A HOLIDAY **** (1934) PR:C
DEATH TOOK PLACE LAST NIGHT ** (1970, It./Ger.) PR:O
DEATH TRAP *½ (1962, Brit.) PR:C
DEATH TRAP (SEE:TAKE HER BY SURPRISE)
DEATH TRAP (SEE:EATEN ALIVE)
DEATH TRAP (SEE:DEATHTRAP)
DEATH VALLEY *½ (1946) PR:A
DEATH VALLEY *½ (1982) PR:O
DEATH VALLEY GUNFIGHTER ** (1949) PR:A
DEATH VALLEY MANHUNT *½ (1943) PR:A
DEATH VALLEY OUTLAWS *½ (1941) PR:A
DEATH VALLEY RANGERS **½ (1944) PR:A
DEATH VENGEANCE ** (1982) PR:O
DEATH WATCH ***½ (1980, Fr./Ger.) PR:O
DEATH WEEKEND (SEE:HOUSE BY THE LAKE, THE)
DEATH WISH ** (1974) PR:O
DEATH WISH 4: THE CRACKDOWN * (1987) PR:O
DEATH WISH 3 zero (1985) PR:O
DEATH WISH II zero (1982) PR:O
DEATHCHEATERS ** (1976, Aus.) PR:C
DEATHDREAM ** (1972, Can.) PR:O
DEATHLINE *½ (1973, Brit.) PR:O
DEATHMASTER, THE zero (1972) PR:O
DEATHROW GAMESHOW zero (1987) PR:O
DEATHSHEAD VAMPIRE (SEE:VAMPIRE BEAST CRAVES BLOOD, THE)
DEATHSPORT **½ (1978) PR:O
DEATHSTALKER * (1983, Arg./US) PR:O
DEATHSTALKER, THE *½ (1984) PR:O
DEATHTRAP **½ (1982) PR:C
DEATHWATCH ***½ (1966) PR:O
DEBT, THE **** (1988, Arg./Brit.) PR:A
DEBT OF HONOR ** (1936, Brit.) PR:A
DECAMERON NIGHTS *** (1953, Brit.) PR:A
DECEIVER, THE ** (1931) PR:A
DECEIVERS, THE ** (1988, Brit./India) PR:O
DECEIVERS, THE (SEE:INTIMACY)
DECEPTION * (1933) PR:A
DECEPTION *** (1946) PR:A-C
DECISION AGAINST TIME **½ (1957, Brit.) PR:A
DECISION AT SUNDOWN ***½ (1957) PR:C
DECISION BEFORE DAWN ***** (1951) PR:A
DECISION OF CHRISTOPHER BLAKE, THE * (1948) PR:A
DECKS RAN RED, THE **½ (1958) PR:A-C
DECLINE AND FALL. . .OF A BIRD WATCHER ** (1969, Brit.) PR:C
DECLINE OF THE AMERICAN EMPIRE, THE ***½ (1986, Can.) PR:O
DECOY *** (1946) PR:C-O
DECOY (SEE:MYSTERY SUBMARINE)
DECOY FOR TERROR zero (1970, Can.) PR:O
DEDEE ** (1949, Fr.) PR:C
DEEP, THE ** (1977) PR:O
DEEP BLUE SEA, THE ***½ (1955, Brit.) PR:C
DEEP DESIRE OF GODS (SEE:KURAGEJIMA—LEGENDS FROM A SOUTHERN ISLAND)
DEEP END *** (1970, Ger./US) PR:O
DEEP IN MY HEART **** (1954) PR:AA
DEEP IN THE HEART ** (1983) PR:O
DEEP IN THE HEART OF TEXAS ** (1942) PR:A
DEEP RED ** (1976, It.) PR:O
DEEP SIX, THE **½ (1958) PR:A
DEEP THRUST—THE HAND OF DEATH * (1973, Hong Kong) PR:O
DEEP VALLEY ***½ (1947) PR:C
DEEP WATERS **½ (1948) PR:A
DEER HUNTER, THE ***** (1978) PR:O
DEERSLAYER * (1943) PR:A
DEERSLAYER, THE ** (1957) PR:A
DEF-CON 4 *** (1985) PR:O
DEFEAT OF HANNIBAL, THE zero (1937, It.) PR:C
DEFECTOR, THE ** (1966, Ger./Fr.) PR:C
DEFENCE OF THE REALM ***½ (1985, Brit.) PR:C-O
DEFEND MY LOVE **½ (1956, It.) PR:A-C
DEFENDERS OF THE LAW *½ (1931) PR:A
DEFENSE OF VOLOTCHAYEVSK, THE ** (1938, USSR) PR:A
DEFENSE RESTS, THE ** (1934) PR:A
DEFIANCE *** (1980) PR:C
DEFIANT DAUGHTERS (SEE:SHADOWS GROW LONGER, THE)
DEFIANT ONES, THE **** (1958) PR:C
DEGREE OF MURDER, A **½ (1969, Ger.) PR:O
DEJA VU ** (1985, Brit.) PR:O
DELAVINE AFFAIR, THE ** (1954, Brit.) PR:A
DELAY IN MARIENBORN (SEE:STOP TRAIN 349)
DELAYED ACTION ** (1954, Brit.) PR:A
DELICATE BALANCE, A ** (1973) PR:C
DELICATE DELINQUENT, THE **½ (1957) PR:A
DELICIOUS ** (1931) PR:A
DELIGHTFUL ROGUE *½ (1929) PR:A
DELIGHTFULLY DANGEROUS ** (1945) PR:A
DELINQUENT DAUGHTERS * (1944) PR:C
DELINQUENT PARENTS * (1938) PR:A
DELINQUENTS, THE ** (1957) PR:C
DELIRIUM * (1979) PR:O
DELIVERANCE ***½ (1972) PR:O
DELIVERY BOYS * (1984) PR:O
DELOS ADVENTURE, THE * (1987) PR:C-O
DELTA FACTOR, THE ** (1970) PR:C
DELTA FORCE, THE ** (1986) PR:O
DELTA FOX *½ (1979) PR:O
DELUGE ** (1933) PR:A
DELUSION (SEE:HOUSE WHERE DEATH LIVES, THE)
DELUSIONS OF GRANDEUR *** (1971, Fr.) PR:C
DEMENTED ** (1980) PR:O
DEMENTIA *½ (1955) PR:O
DEMENTIA 13 **½ (1963) PR:C
DEMETRIUS AND THE GLADIATORS ***½ (1954) PR:C
DEMI-PARADISE, THE (SEE:ADVENTURE FOR TWO)
DEMOBBED ** (1944, Brit.) PR:A
DEMON, THE (SEE:ONIBABA)
DEMON BARBER OF FLEET STREET, THE *½ (1939, Brit.) PR:O
DEMON FOR TROUBLE, A ** (1934) PR:A
DEMON FROM DEVIL'S LAKE, THE * (1964) PR:A
DEMON LOVER, THE zero (1977) PR:O
DEMON PLANET, THE (SEE:PLANET OF THE VAMPIRES)
DEMON POND ***½ (1980, Jap.) PR:C
DEMON SEED *** (1977) PR:O
DEMON WITCH CHILD * (1974, Sp.) PR:O
DEMON, THE ** (1981, South Africa) PR:O
DEMONIAQUE ** (1958, Fr.) PR:C-O
DEMONIOS EN EL JARDIN (SEE:DEMONS IN THE GARDEN)
DEMONOID *½ (1981) PR:O
DEMONS zero (1985, It.) PR:O
DEMONS **½ (1987, Swed.) PR:O
DEMONS IN THE GARDEN *** (1984, Sp.) PR:O
DEMONS OF LUDLOW, THE ** (1983) PR:O
DEMONS OF THE MIND ** (1972, Brit.) PR:O
DEMONSTRATOR **½ (1971, Aus.) PR:O

DEN OF DOOM
  (SEE:GLASS CAGE, THE)
DENTIST IN THE CHAIR ** (1960, Brit.) PR:A
DENTIST ON THE JOB
  (SEE:GET ON WITH IT)
DENVER AND RIO GRANDE **½ (1952) PR:A
DENVER KID, THE * (1948) PR:A
DEPARTMENT STORE * (1935, Brit.) PR:A
DEPORTED **½ (1950) PR:A
DEPRAVED, THE *½ (1957, Brit.) PR:A-C
DEPTH CHARGE ** (1960, Brit.) PR:A
DEPUTY DRUMMER, THE *½ (1935, Brit.) PR:A
DEPUTY MARSHAL ** (1949) PR:A
DER FREISCHUTZ ** (1970, Ger.) PR:A
DER ROSENKONIG *** (1986, Ger.) PR:O
DERANGED *** (1974, Can.) PR:O
DERBY DAY
  (SEE:FOUR AGAINST FATE)
DERELICT ** (1930) PR:A
DERELICT, THE * (1937, Brit.) PR:A
DERSU UZALA * (1976, Jap./USSR) PR:A**
DESCENDANT OF THE SNOW LEOPARD, THE ****
  (1986, USSR) PR:AA
DESERT ATTACK *** (1958, Brit.) PR:A
DESERT BANDIT *½ (1941) PR:A
DESERT BLOOM **½ (1986) PR:A-C
DESERT DESPERADOES *½ (1959) PR:A
DESERT FOX, THE ** (1951) PR:A**
DESERT FURY ** (1947) PR:C
DESERT GOLD *½ (1936) PR:A
DESERT GUNS * (1936) PR:A
DESERT HAWK, THE ** (1950) PR:A
DESERT HEARTS * (1985) PR:O**
DESERT HELL ** (1958) PR:A
DESERT HORSEMAN, THE ** (1946) PR:A
DESERT JUSTICE *½ (1936) PR:A
DESERT LEGION ** (1953) PR:A
DESERT MESA * (1935) PR:A
DESERT MICE **½ (1960, Brit.) PR:A
DESERT OF LOST MEN * (1951) PR:A
DESERT OF THE TARTARS, THE **½
  (1976, Fr./It./Iranian) PR:C
DESERT PASSAGE ** (1952) PR:A
DESERT PATROL * (1938) PR:A
DESERT PATROL ** (1962, Brit.) PR:C
DESERT PHANTOM ** (1937) PR:A
DESERT PURSUIT * (1952) PR:A
DESERT RATS, THE ***½ (1953) PR:A
DESERT RAVEN, THE *½ (1965) PR:A
DESERT SANDS **½ (1955) PR:A
DESERT SONG, THE **½ (1929) PR:A
DESERT SONG, THE *** (1943) PR:A
DESERT SONG, THE *½ (1953) PR:A
DESERT TRAIL ** (1935) PR:A
DESERT VENGEANCE *½ (1931) PR:A
DESERT VIGILANTE ** (1949) PR:A
DESERT WARRIOR **½ (1961, It./Sp.) PR:A
DESERT WARRIOR zero (1985) PR:O
DESERTER *** (1934, USSR) PR:A
DESERTER, THE ** (1971, It./Yugo.) PR:O
DESERTER AND THE NOMADS, THE **
  (1969, Czech./It.) PR:O
DESERTERS * (1983, Can.) PR:C
DESIGN FOR LIVING *** (1933) PR:A
DESIGN FOR LOVING ** (1962, Brit.) PR:A
DESIGN FOR MURDER ** (1940, Brit.) PR:A
DESIGN FOR SCANDAL *** (1941) PR:A
DESIGNING WOMAN ***½ (1957) PR:A
DESIGNING WOMEN ** (1934, Brit.) PR:A
DESIRABLE **½ (1934) PR:A
DESIRE ** (1936) PR:A**
DESIRE IN THE DUST **½ (1960) PR:C
DESIRE ME ** (1947) PR:A
DESIRE, THE INTERIOR LIFE **
  (1980, Ital./Ger.) PR:O
DESIRE UNDER THE ELMS * (1958) PR:O
DESIREE * (1954) PR:A**
DESIREE **½ (1984, Neth.) PR:O
DESK SET *** (1957) PR:A
DESPAIR **½ (1978, Ger.) PR:O
DESPERADO, THE ** (1954) PR:A
DESPERADO TRAIL, THE **
  (1965, Ger./Yugo.) PR:A
DESPERADOES, THE *** (1943) PR:A
DESPERADOES ARE IN TOWN, THE ** (1956) PR:A
DESPERADOES OF DODGE CITY ** (1948) PR:A
DESPERADOES OUTPOST ** (1952) PR:A

DESPERADOS, THE ** (1969) PR:O
DESPERATE ***½ (1947) PR:C
DESPERATE ADVENTURE, A ** (1938) PR:A
DESPERATE CARGO ** (1941) PR:A
DESPERATE CHANCE FOR ELLERY QUEEN, A *
  (1942) PR:A
DESPERATE CHARACTERS **** (1971) PR:A-C
DESPERATE DECISION *½ (1954, Fr.) PR:O
DESPERATE HOURS, THE ** (1955) PR:C**
DESPERATE JOURNEY **½ (1942) PR:A
DESPERATE MAN, THE *½ (1959, Brit.) PR:A-C
DESPERATE MOMENT *** (1953, Brit.) PR:A
DESPERATE MOVES * (1986, It.) PR:C-O
DESPERATE ONES, THE ** (1968, US/Sp.) PR:C
DESPERATE SEARCH **½ (1952) PR:A
DESPERATE SIEGE
  (SEE:RAWHIDE)
DESPERATE TRAILS *½ (1939) PR:A
DESPERATE WOMEN, THE zero (1954) PR:O
DESPERATELY SEEKING SUSAN **½ (1985) PR:O
DESTINATION BIG HOUSE **½ (1950) PR:A
DESTINATION GOBI * (1953) PR:A**
DESTINATION INNER SPACE *½ (1966) PR:A
DESTINATION MILAN * (1954, Brit.) PR:A
DESTINATION MOON * (1950) PR:A**
DESTINATION MURDER **½ (1950) PR:C
DESTINATION 60,000 ** (1957) PR:A
DESTINATION TOKYO ** (1944) PR:A**
DESTINATION UNKNOWN ** (1933) PR:A
DESTINATION UNKNOWN *½ (1942) PR:A
DESTINEES
  (SEE:DAUGHTERS OF DESTINY)
DESTINY ** (1938) PR:A
DESTINY **½ (1944) PR:A
DESTINY
  (SEE:TIME OF DESTINY, A)
DESTINY OF A MAN ** (1961, USSR) PR:A
DESTROY ALL MONSTERS **½ (1969, Jap.) PR:A
DESTROY, SHE SAID *½ (1969, Fr.) PR:O
DESTROYER *** (1943) PR:A
DESTRUCTION TEST
  (SEE:CIRCLE OF DECEPTION)
DESTRUCTORS, THE *½ (1968) PR:C
DESTRUCTORS, THE *½ (1974, Brit.) PR:C
DESTRY **½ (1954) PR:A
DESTRY RIDES AGAIN ** (1932) PR:A
DESTRY RIDES AGAIN ***½ (1939) PR:A
DETECTIVE ***½ (1985, Fr./Switz.) PR:O
DETECTIVE, THE * (1954, Brit.) PR:A**
DETECTIVE, THE ***½ (1968) PR:C
DETECTIVE BELLI * (1970, It.) PR:O
DETECTIVE KITTY O'DAY ** (1944) PR:A
DETECTIVE SCHOOL DROPOUTS *
  (1986) PR:A-C**
DETECTIVE STORY *** (1951) PR:C**
DETOUR ** (1945) PR:O**
DETOUR, THE **½ (1968, Bulgaria) PR:A
DETROIT 9000 **½ (1973) PR:O
DEVIL, THE **½ (1963, It.) PR:A
DEVIL AND DANIEL WEBSTER, THE **
  (1941) PR:A**
DEVIL AND MAX DEVLIN, THE **½ (1981) PR:A
DEVIL AND MISS JONES, THE ***½ (1941) PR:A
DEVIL AND THE DEEP **½ (1932) PR:C
DEVIL AND THE TEN COMMANDMENTS, THE **½
  (1962, Fr.) PR:C
DEVIL AT FOUR O'CLOCK, THE ***½ (1961) PR:A
DEVIL BAT, THE * (1941) PR:A
DEVIL BAT'S DAUGHTER, THE *½ (1946) PR:A
DEVIL BY THE TAIL, THE *** (1969, Fr./It.) PR:C
DEVIL COMMANDS, THE *** (1941) PR:C
DEVIL DOGS OF THE AIR *** (1935) PR:A
DEVIL DOLL, THE ***½ (1936) PR:C
DEVIL DOLL ** (1964, Brit.) PR:C
DEVIL GIRL FROM MARS ** (1954, Brit.) PR:A
DEVIL GODDESS zero (1955) PR:A
DEVIL GOT ANGRY, THE
  (SEE:MAJIN)
DEVIL IN LOVE, THE * (1968, It.) PR:C
DEVIL IN SILK **½ (1968, Ger.) PR:C
DEVIL IN THE CASTLE
  (SEE:DAREDEVIL IN THE CASTLE)
DEVIL IN THE FLESH **½ (1986, It./Fr.) PR:O
DEVIL IN THE FLESH, THE ** (1949, Fr.) PR:C
DEVIL IS A SISSY, THE ***½ (1936) PR:A
DEVIL IS A WOMAN, THE *½ (1975, Brit./It.) PR:O
DEVIL IS A WOMAN, THE *** (1935) PR:C

DEVIL IS AN EMPRESS, THE **½ (1939, Fr.) PR:A
DEVIL IS DRIVING, THE *½ (1932) PR:A
DEVIL IS DRIVING, THE *½ (1937) PR:A
DEVIL MADE A WOMAN, THE ** (1962, Sp.) PR:A
DEVIL MAKES THREE, THE **½ (1952) PR:A-C
DEVIL MAY CARE **½ (1929) PR:A
DEVIL NEVER SLEEPS, THE
  (SEE:SATAN NEVER SLEEPS)
DEVIL ON HORSEBACK, THE ** (1936) PR:A
DEVIL ON HORSEBACK *** (1954, Brit.) PR:A
DEVIL ON WHEELS, THE ** (1947) PR:A
DEVIL PAYS OFF, THE *** (1941) PR:A
DEVIL PAYS, THE *½ (1932) PR:A
DEVIL PROBABLY, THE *** (1977, FR.) PR:C
DEVIL RIDERS *½ (1944) PR:A
DEVIL RIDES OUT, THE
  (SEE:DEVIL'S BRIDE, THE)
DEVIL SHIP * (1947) PR:A
DEVIL-SHIP PIRATES, THE **½ (1964, Brit.) PR:C
DEVIL STRIKES AT NIGHT, THE ***
  (1959, Ger.) PR:C
DEVIL THUMBS A RIDE, THE ** (1947) PR:A
DEVIL TIGER ** (1934) PR:A
DEVIL TIMES FIVE *½ (1974) PR:C
DEVIL TO PAY, THE *** (1930) PR:A
DEVIL WITH WOMEN, A *½ (1930) PR:A
DEVIL WITHIN HER, THE **½ (1976, Brit.) PR:O
DEVIL WOMAN
  (SEE:ONIBABA)
DEVIL WOMAN zero (1976, Phil.) PR:O
DEVIL'S AGENT, THE **½ (1962, Brit.) PR:C
DEVIL'S ANGELS * (1967) PR:O
DEVIL'S BAIT * (1959, Brit.) PR:A
DEVIL'S BEDROOM, THE * (1964) PR:O
DEVIL'S BRIDE, THE **½ (1968, Brit.) PR:O
DEVIL'S BRIGADE, THE ** (1968) PR:C
DEVIL'S BROTHER, THE *** (1933) PR:AA
DEVIL'S CANYON ** (1953) PR:A
DEVIL'S CARGO, THE *½ (1948) PR:A
DEVIL'S COMMANDMENT, THE zero
  (1956, It.) PR:O
DEVIL'S DAFFODIL, THE ** (1961, Brit./Ger.) PR:A
DEVIL'S DAUGHTER, THE ** (1949, Fr.) PR:A
DEVIL'S DISCIPLE, THE * (1959) PR:A**
DEVIL'S DOLL
  (SEE:DEVIL'S HAND, THE)
DEVIL'S DOORWAY **½ (1950) PR:A
DEVIL'S 8, THE ** (1969) PR:C
DEVIL'S ENVOYS, THE ***½ (1947, Fr.) PR:A
DEVIL'S EYE, THE * (1960, Swed.) PR:C**
DEVIL'S GENERAL, THE **½ (1957, Ger.) PR:A-C
DEVIL'S GODMOTHER, THE *½ (1938, Mex.) PR:A
DEVIL'S HAIRPIN, THE **½ (1957) PR:A
DEVIL'S HAND, THE
  (SEE:CARNIVAL OF SINNERS)
DEVIL'S HAND, THE * (1961) PR:C
DEVIL'S HARBOR ** (1954, Brit.) PR:C
DEVIL'S HENCHMEN, THE ** (1949) PR:A
DEVIL'S HOLIDAY, THE **½ (1930) PR:A
DEVIL'S IMPOSTER, THE
  (SEE:POPE JOAN)
DEVIL'S IN LOVE, THE **½ (1933) PR:A
DEVIL'S ISLAND *** (1940) PR:C
DEVIL'S JEST, THE ** (1954, Brit.) PR:A
DEVIL'S LOTTERY * (1932) PR:A
DEVIL'S MAN, THE * (1967, It.) PR:C
DEVIL'S MASK, THE **½ (1946) PR:A
DEVIL'S MATE *½ (1933) PR:A
DEVIL'S MAZE, THE *½ (1929, Brit.) PR:A-C
DEVIL'S MEN, THE
  (SEE:LAND OF THE MINOTAUR)
DEVIL'S MESSENGER, THE * (1962, US/Swed.) PR:C
DEVIL'S MISTRESS, THE * (1968) PR:O
DEVIL'S NIGHTMARE, THE zero
  (1971, Bel./It.) PR:O
DEVILS OF DARKNESS, THE *½ (1965, Brit.) PR:C
DEVIL'S OWN, THE ** (1967, Brit.) PR:C
DEVIL'S PARTNER, THE ** (1958) PR:C-O
DEVIL'S PARTY, THE ** (1938) PR:C
DEVIL'S PASS, THE *½ (1957, Brit.) PR:AA
DEVIL'S PIPELINE, THE ** (1940) PR:A
DEVIL'S PITCHFORK
  (SEE:ANATAHAN)
DEVIL'S PLAYGROUND **½ (1937) PR:A
DEVIL'S PLAYGROUND, THE *½ (1946) PR:A
DEVIL'S PLAYGROUND, THE * (1976, Aus.) PR:A**

Finding entries in **THE MOTION PICTURE GUIDE** ™   **STAR RATINGS**   **PARENTAL RECOMMENDATION (PR:)**

Years 1929-83	Volumes I-IX			
1984	Volume IX	★★★★★	Masterpiece	AA Good for Children
1985	1986 ANNUAL	★★★★	Excellent	A Acceptable for Children
1986	1987 ANNUAL	★★★	Good	C Cautionary, some objectionable scenes
1987	1988 ANNUAL	★★	Fair	O Objectionable for Children
1988	1989 ANNUAL	★	Poor	
		zero	Without Merit	**BOLD:** Films on Videocassette

DEVIL'S PLOT, THE *** (1948, Brit.) PR:C
DEVIL'S RAIN, THE * (1975, US/Mex.) PR:O
DEVIL'S ROCK * (1938, Brit.) PR:A
DEVIL'S SADDLE LEGION, THE *½ (1937) PR:A
DEVIL'S SISTERS, THE * (1966) PR:O
DEVIL'S SLEEP, THE * (1951) PR:A
DEVIL'S SPAWN, THE
(SEE:LAST GUNFIGHTER, THE)
DEVIL'S SQUADRON ** (1936) PR:A
DEVIL'S TEMPLE *½ (1969, Jap.) PR:C-O
DEVIL'S TRAIL, THE * (1942) PR:A
DEVIL'S TRAP, THE ** (1964, Czech.) PR:A-C
DEVIL'S WANTON, THE ** (1962, Swed.) PR:C
DEVIL'S WEDDING NIGHT, THE zero (1973, It.) PR:O
DEVIL'S WIDOW, THE zero (1972, Brit.) PR:O
DEVIL'S WOMAN, THE
(SEE:EVA)
DEVONSVILLE TERROR, THE **½ (1983) PR:O
DEVOTION **½ (1931) PR:A
DEVOTION ** (1946) PR:A
DEVOTION * (1953, It.) PR:C-O
DEVOTION *½ (1955, USSR) PR:A
D.I., THE * (1957) PR:A**
DIABOLICAL DR. Z, THE *½ (1966, Sp./Fr.) PR:O
DIABOLICAL DR. MABUSE, THE
(SEE:SECRET OF DR. MABUSE, THE)
DIABOLICALLY YOURS **½ (1968, Fr.) PR:C
DIABOLIQUE ** (1955, Fr.) PR:O**
DIAGNOSIS: MURDER **½ (1974, Brit.) PR:C
DIAL M FOR MURDER ***½ (1954) PR:A-C
DIAL 999
(SEE:REVENGE OF SCOTLAND YARD)
DIAL 999
(SEE:WAY OUT, THE)
DIAL 1119 **½ (1950) PR:C
DIAL RED O **½ (1955) PR:C
DIALOGUE *½ (1967, Hung.) PR:A
DIAMOND CITY ** (1949, Brit.) PR:A
DIAMOND COUNTRY
(SEE:RUN LIKE A THIEF)
DIAMOND CUT DIAMOND
(SEE:BLAME THE WOMAN)
DIAMOND EARRINGS
(SEE:EARRINGS OF MADAME DE. . ., THE)
DIAMOND FRONTIER ** (1940) PR:A
DIAMOND HEAD * (1962) PR:C
DIAMOND HORSESHOE *** (1945) PR:A
DIAMOND HUNTERS
(SEE:RUN LIKE A THIEF)
DIAMOND JIM *** (1935) PR:A
DIAMOND QUEEN, THE ** (1953) PR:A
DIAMOND SAFARI ** (1958) PR:A
DIAMOND STUD * (1970) PR:C
DIAMOND TRAIL * (1933) PR:A
DIAMOND WIZARD, THE ** (1954, Brit.) PR:A
DIAMONDS **½ (1975, US/Israel) PR:C
DIAMONDS AND CRIME
(SEE:HI DIDDLE DIDDLE)
DIAMONDS ARE FOREVER * (1971, Brit.) PR:C**
DIAMONDS FOR BREAKFAST **½ (1968, Brit.) PR:C
DIAMONDS OF THE NIGHT ** (1964, Czech.) PR:C
DIANE **½ (1955) PR:A-C
DIANE'S BODY **½ (1969, Fr./Czech.) PR:A
DIARY FOR MY CHILDREN *** (1984, Hung.) PR:O
DIARY OF A BACHELOR * (1964) PR:O
DIARY OF A BAD GIRL *½ (1958, Fr.) PR:C
DIARY OF A CHAMBERMAID ***½ (1946) PR:A
DIARY OF A CHAMBERMAID ** (1964, Fr./It.) PR:O**
DIARY OF A CLOISTERED NUN * (1973, It./Fr./Ger.) PR:O
DIARY OF A COUNTRY PRIEST ** (1954, Fr.) PR:A**
DIARY OF A HIGH SCHOOL BRIDE * (1959) PR:C-O
DIARY OF A MAD HOUSEWIFE ***½ (1970) PR:C-O
DIARY OF A MADMAN ** (1963) PR:C-O
DIARY OF A NAZI ** (1943, USSR) PR:C
DIARY OF A REVOLUTIONIST * (1932, USSR) PR:A
DIARY OF A SCHIZOPHRENIC GIRL **½ (1970, It.) PR:A
DIARY OF A SHINJUKU BURGLAR **½ (1969, Jap.) PR:O
DIARY OF AN ITALIAN **½ (1972, It.) PR:C
DIARY OF ANNE FRANK, THE ** (1959) PR:A**
DIARY OF FORBIDDEN DREAMS
(SEE:WHAT?)
DIARY OF MAJOR THOMPSON, THE
(SEE:FRENCH, THEY ARE A FUNNY RACE, THE)
DIARY OF OHARU
(SEE:LIFE OF OHARU, THE)
DICK BARTON AT BAY ** (1950, Brit.) PR:A
DICK BARTON—SPECIAL AGENT *½ (1948, Brit.) PR:A
DICK BARTON STRIKES BACK **½ (1949, Brit.) PR:A
DICK TRACY **½ (1945) PR:A-C
DICK TRACY MEETS GRUESOME **½ (1947) PR:A-C
DICK TRACY VS. CUEBALL ** (1946) PR:C
DICK TRACY'S DILEMMA ** (1947) PR:C
DICK TURPIN ** (1933, Brit.) PR:A
DICTATOR, THE **½ (1935, Brit./Ger.) PR:A
DID I BETRAY?
(SEE:BLACK ROSES)
DID YOU HEAR THE ONE ABOUT THE TRAVELING SALESLADY? zero (1968) PR:A-C
DIE, DIE, MY DARLING * (1965, Brit.) PR:O**
DIE FASTNACHTSBEICHTE ** (1962, Ger.) PR:A
DIE FLAMBIERTE FRAU
(SEE:WOMAN IN FLAMES, A)
DIE FLEDERMAUS **½ (1964, Aust.) PR:A
DIE GANS VON SEDAN ** (1962, Fr/Ger.) PR:A
DIE HAMBURGER KRANKHEIT *½ (1979, Ger./Fr.) PR:C
DIE HARD * (1988) PR:O**
DIE LAUGHING zero (1980) PR:O
DIE MANNER UM LUCIE ** (1931) PR:A
DIE, MONSTER, DIE * (1965, Brit.) PR:C**
DIE SCREAMING, MARIANNE ** (1970, Brit.) PR:O
DIE UNENDLICHE GESCHICHTE
(SEE:NEVERENDING STORY, THE)
DIFFERENT SONS * (1962, Jap.) PR:O
DIFFERENT STORY, A ** (1978) PR:O
DIFFICULT LOVE, A
(SEE:CLOSELY WATCHED TRAINS)
DIFFICULT YEARS **½ (1950, It.) PR:C
DIG THAT JULIET
(SEE:ROMANOFF AND JULIET)
DIG THAT URANIUM ** (1956) PR:A
DIGBY, THE BIGGEST DOG IN THE WORLD * (1974, Brit.) PR:AA
DILLINGER ** (1945) PR:C-O
DILLINGER zero (1973) PR:O
DILLINGER IS DEAD ** (1969, It.) PR:O
DIM SUM: A LITTLE BIT OF HEART * (1985) PR:A**
DIMBOOLA ***½ (1979, Aus.) PR:O
DIME WITH A HALO **½ (1963) PR:A
DIMENSION 5 *½ (1966) PR:A
DIMKA **½ (1964, USSR) PR:AA
DIMPLES * (1936) PR:AA**
DINER ** (1982) PR:C-O**
DING DONG WILLIAMS ** (1946) PR:A
DINGAKA ** (1965, South Africa) PR:A
DINKY *½ (1935) PR:A
DINNER AT EIGHT *** (1933) PR:C**
DINNER AT THE RITZ ** (1937, Brit.) PR:A
DINNER FOR ADELE
(SEE:ADELE HASN'T HAD HER SUPPER YET)
DINO * (1957) PR:A**
DINOSAURUS ** (1960) PR:AA
DION BROTHERS, THE
(SEE:GRAVY TRAIN, THE)
DIPLOMANIACS **½ (1933) PR:A
DIPLOMAT'S MANSION, THE * (1961, Jap.) PR:C
DIPLOMATIC CORPSE, THE ** (1958, Brit.) PR:A
DIPLOMATIC COURIER * (1952) PR:A**
DIPLOMATIC LOVER, THE *½ (1934, Brit.) PR:A
DIPLOMATIC PASSPORT ** (1954, Brit.) PR:A
DIRIGIBLE *** (1931) PR:A
DIRT BIKE KID, THE ** (1986) PR:A
DIRT GANG, THE * (1972) PR:O
DIRTY DANCING ***½ (1987) PR:C
DIRTY DINGUS MAGEE ** (1970) PR:C
DIRTY DOZEN, THE * (1967, Brit.) PR:C-O**
DIRTY GAME, THE **½ (1966, Fr./It./Ger.) PR:C
DIRTY HANDS * (1976, Fr/It./Ger.) PR:O**
DIRTY HARRY ***½ (1971) PR:O
DIRTY HEROES ** (1971, It./Fr./Ger.) PR:A
DIRTY KNIGHT'S WORK **½ (1976, Brit.) PR:C
DIRTY LAUNDRY zero (1987) PR:A-C
DIRTY LITTLE BILLY **½ (1972) PR:C-O
DIRTY MARY, CRAZY LARRY * (1974) PR:O
DIRTY MONEY ** (1977, Fr.) PR:C
DIRTY O'NEIL zero (1974) PR:O
DIRTY OUTLAWS, THE ** (1971, It.) PR:O
DIRTY ROTTEN SCOUNDRELS **½ (1988) PR:C
DIRTY TRICKS *½ (1981, Can.) PR:C
DIRTY WORK ** (1934, Brit.) PR:A
DIRTYMOUTH ** (1970) PR:O
DISAPPEARANCE, THE * (1981, Brit./Can.) PR:C
DISASTER * (1948) PR:A
DISBARRED ** (1939) PR:A
DISC JOCKEY ** (1951) PR:A
DISC JOCKEY JAMBOREE
(SEE:JAMBOREE)
DISCARDED LOVERS **½ (1932) PR:A
DISCIPLE OF DEATH * (1972, Brit.) PR:O
DISCORD ** (1933, Brit.) PR:A
DISCOVERIES **½ (1939, Brit.) PR:A
DISCREET CHARM OF THE BOURGEOISIE, THE ** (1972, Fr./It./Sp.) PR:C
DISEMBODIED, THE * (1957) PR:C
DISGRACED * (1933) PR:A
DISHONOR BRIGHT ** (1936, Brit.) PR:A
DISHONORED *** (1931) PR:C
DISHONORED *½ (1950, It.) PR:A
DISHONORED LADY ** (1947) PR:C
DISILLUSION ** (1949, It.) PR:A
DISOBEDIENT ** (1953, Brit.) PR:O
DISORDER *½ (1964, Fr./It.) PR:A
DISORDER AND EARLY TORMENT *** (1977, Ger.) PR:A
DISORDERLIES ** (1987) PR:A-C
DISORDERLY CONDUCT **½ (1932) PR:A
DISORDERLY ORDERLY, THE * (1964) PR:A**
DISPATCH FROM REUTERS, A *** (1940) PR:A
DISPUTED PASSAGE ** (1939) PR:A
DISRAELI ***½ (1929) PR:A
DISTANCE *** (1975) PR:O
DISTANT DRUMS ***½ (1951) PR:A
DISTANT JOURNEY *** (1950, Czech.) PR:C
DISTANT THUNDER ** (1988, US/Can.) PR:O
DISTANT TRUMPET ** (1952, Brit.) PR:A
DISTANT TRUMPET, A ** (1964) PR:A
DITES 33
(SEE:LADY DOCTOR, THE)
DIVA ** (1982, Fr.) PR:C**
DIVE BOMBER *** (1941) PR:A-C
DIVIDED HEART, THE *** (1955, Brit.) PR:A
DIVINE EMMA, THE * (1983, Czech.) PR:A
DIVINE MR. J., THE zero (1974) PR:O
DIVINE NYMPH, THE ** (1979, It.) PR:O
DIVINE SPARK, THE *½ (1935, Brit./It.) PR:A
DIVING GIRLS OF JAPAN
(SEE:VIOLATED PARADISE)
DIVING GIRLS' ISLAND, THE
(SEE:VIOLATED PARADISE)
DIVORCE *½ (1945) PR:A
DIVORCE AMERICAN STYLE * (1967) PR:C**
DIVORCE AMONG FRIENDS *½ (1931) PR:C
DIVORCE IN THE FAMILY **½ (1932) PR:A
DIVORCE OF LADY X, THE * (1938, Brit.) PR:A**
DIVORCE, ITALIAN STYLE **** (1962, It.) PR:A
DIVORCEE, THE ***½ (1930) PR:C
DIXIANA * (1930) PR:A
DIXIE *** (1943) PR:A
DIXIE DUGAN *½ (1943) PR:A
DIXIE DYNAMITE ** (1976) PR:C
DIXIE JAMBOREE *½ (1945) PR:A
DIXIELAND DAIMYO *** (1988, Jap.) PR:A
DIZZY DAMES *½ (1936) PR:A
DJANGO **½ (1966, It./Sp.) PR:O
DJANGO KILL ** (1967, It./Sp.) PR:O
DO NOT DISTURB **½ (1965) PR:A
DO NOT THROW CUSHIONS INTO THE RING **½ (1970) PR:O
DO YOU KEEP A LION AT HOME? *** (1966, Czech.) PR:AA
DO YOU LIKE WOMEN?
(SEE:TASTE FOR WOMEN, A)
DO YOU LOVE ME? *** (1946) PR:A
DO YOU REMEMBER DOLLY BELL? *** (1986, Yugo.) PR:O
D.O.A. ***½ (1950) PR:A
D.O.A. ***½ (1988) PR:C-O
DOBERMAN GANG, THE ** (1972) PR:C
DOC ** (1971) PR:O
DOC SAVAGE. . .THE MAN OF BRONZE *½ (1975) PR:A
DOCK BRIEF, THE
(SEE:TRIAL AND ERROR)
DOCKS OF NEW ORLEANS * (1948) PR:A
DOCKS OF NEW YORK ** (1945) PR:A
DOCKS OF SAN FRANCISCO *½ (1932) PR:A
DOCTEUR LAENNEC **½ (1949, Fr.) PR:A
DOCTEUR POPAUL *** (1972, Fr.) PR:O
DOCTOR AND THE DEVILS, THE ** (1985, Brit.) PR:O
DOCTOR AND THE GIRL, THE ** (1949) PR:C
DOCTOR AT LARGE **½ (1957, Brit.) PR:A
DOCTOR AT SEA **½ (1955, Brit.) PR:A
DOCTOR BEWARE *** (1951, It.) PR:C
DR. BROADWAY ** (1942) PR:C
DR. BULL ***½ (1933) PR:A
DR. BUTCHER, M.D. * (1982, It.) PR:O
DR. CHRISTIAN MEETS THE WOMEN * (1940) PR:A
DR. COPPELIUS *** (1968, US/Sp.) PR:AA
DOCTOR CRIMEN ** (1953, Mex.) PR:C
DR. CRIPPEN ** (1963, Brit.) PR:C
DR. CYCLOPS **½ (1940) PR:A
DOCTOR DEATH: SEEKER OF SOULS *½ (1973) PR:O
DOCTOR DETROIT zero (1983) PR:O
DOCTOR DOLITTLE * (1967) PR:AA**
DR. EHRLICH'S MAGIC BULLET **** (1940) PR:A
DOCTOR FAUSTUS * (1967, Brit.) PR:C
DR. FRANKENSTEIN ON CAMPUS * (1970, Can.) PR:O

DOCTOR FROM SEVEN DIALS, THE (SEE:CORRIDORS OF BLOOD)
DR. GILLESPIE'S CRIMINAL CASE ** (1943) PR:A
DR. GILLESPIE'S NEW ASSISTANT ** (1942) PR:A
DR. GOLDFOOT AND THE BIKINI MACHINE *½ (1965 88m AI c) PR:C
DR. GOLDFOOT AND THE GIRL BOMBS * (1966, It.) PR:O
__DR. HECKYL AND MR. HYPE **½ (1980) PR:O__
DOCTOR IN CLOVER (SEE:CARNABY, M.D.)
__DOCTOR IN DISTRESS ** (1963, Brit.) PR:A__
DOCTOR IN LOVE **½ (1960, Brit.) PR:A
__DOCTOR IN THE HOUSE *** (1954, Brit.) PR:A__
__DOCTOR IN TROUBLE *½ (1970, Brit.) PR:A__
DR. JEKYLL * (1985, Fr.) PR:O
DR. JEKYLL AND MR. HYDE **** (1932) PR:O
__DR. JEKYLL AND MR. HYDE *** (1941) PR:C-O__
__DR. JEKYLL AND SISTER HYDE **½ (1971, Brit.) PR:A__
DR. JEKYLL AND THE WOLFMAN zero (1971, Sp.) PR:O
__DR. JEKYLL'S DUNGEON OF DEATH zero (1982) PR:O__
DR. JOSSER KC ** (1931, Brit.) PR:A
DR. KILDARE GOES HOME *½ (1940) PR:A
DR. KILDARE'S CRISIS ** (1940) PR:A
__DR. KILDARE'S STRANGE CASE ** (1940) PR:A__
DR. KILDARE'S VICTORY ** (1941) PR:A
DR. KILDARE'S WEDDING DAY ** (1941) PR:A
DR. KNOCK **½ (1936, Fr.) PR:A
DR. MABUSE'S RAYS OF DEATH *½ (1964, Ger./Fr./It.) PR:A
__DR. MINX zero (1975) PR:O__
DOCTOR MONICA *½ (1934) PR:A
DR. MORELLE—THE CASE OF THE MISSING HEIRESS *½ (1949, Brit.) PR:A
__DR. NO ***½ (1962, Brit.) PR:C__
DR. O'DOWD * (1940, Brit.) PR:A
DOCTOR OF DOOM ** (1962, Mex.) PR:O
DOCTOR OF ST. PAUL, THE *½ (1969, Ger.) PR:C
__DR. OTTO AND THE RIDDLE OF THE GLOOM BEAM ** (1986) PR:A__
__DOCTOR PHIBES RISES AGAIN *** (1972, Brit.) PR:C-O__
DR. POPAUL (SEE:HIGH HEELS)
DR. RENAULT'S SECRET ** (1942) PR:C
DR. RHYTHM ** (1938) PR:AA
DR. SIN FANG ** (1937, Brit.) PR:A
DR. SOCRATES ** (1935) PR:A-C
__DR. STRANGELOVE: OR HOW I LEARNED TO STOP WORRYING AND LOVE THE BOMB ***½ (1964, Brit.) PR:C__
__DOCTOR SYN ** (1937, Brit.) PR:A__
__DR. SYN, ALIAS THE SCARECROW ** (1975) PR:AA__
__DOCTOR TAKES A WIFE **½ (1940) PR:AA__
__DR. TARR'S TORTURE DUNGEON ** (1972, Mex.) PR:O__
DR. TERROR'S GALLERY OF HORRORS zero (1967) PR:O
__DR. TERROR'S HOUSE OF HORRORS **½ (1965, Brit.) PR:O__
__DR. WHO AND THE DALEKS **½ (1965, Brit.) PR:A__
__DOCTOR X **** (1932) PR:A__
DOCTOR, YOU'VE GOT TO BE KIDDING ** (1967) PR:A
__DOCTOR ZHIVAGO **** (1965) PR:A-C__
DOCTOR'S DIARY, A * (1937) PR:A
DOCTOR'S DILEMMA, THE **½ (1958, Brit.) PR:A
DOCTORS DON'T TELL *½ (1941) PR:A
DOCTOR'S ORDERS ** (1934, Brit.) PR:A
DOCTOR'S SECRET * (1929) PR:A
DOCTORS WEAR SCARLET (SEE:INCENSE FOR THE DAMNED)
DOCTORS' WIVES ** (1931) PR:C
__DOCTORS' WIVES * (1971) PR:O__
__DODES 'KA-DEN *** (1970, Jap.) PR:C__
__DODGE CITY **** (1939) PR:A__
DODGE CITY TRAIL * (1937) PR:A
DODGING THE DOLE ** (1936, Brit.) PR:A
__DODSWORTH ***** (1936) PR:A__
DOG, A MOUSE AND A SPUTNIK, A (SEE:SPUTNIK)
DOG AND THE DIAMONDS, THE *** (1962, Brit.) PR:AA
DOG DAY zero (1984, Fr.) PR:O
__DOG DAY AFTERNOON **** (1975) PR:O__
DOG EAT DOG *½ (1963, US/Ger./It.) PR:A
DOG OF FLANDERS, A ** (1935) PR:AA
__DOG OF FLANDERS, A ***½ (1959) PR:AA__
__DOGPOUND SHUFFLE ** (1975, Can.) PR:A__
DOGS zero (1976) PR:O
DOG'S BEST FRIEND, A ** (1960) PR:AA
DOGS OF HELL (SEE:ROTWEILER: DOGS OF HELL)
__DOGS OF WAR, THE ** (1980, Brit.) PR:O__
__DOIN' TIME zero (1985) PR:O__
DOING TIME **½ (1979, Brit.) PR:A
DOLEMITE * (1975) PR:O
DOLL, THE **½ (1962, Fr.) PR:A
DOLL, THE ** (1964, Swed.) PR:C
__DOLL FACE **½ (1945) PR:A__
__DOLL SQUAD, THE zero (1973) PR:O__
DOLL THAT TOOK THE TOWN, THE ** (1965, It.) PR:A
DOLLAR **½ (1938, Swed.) PR:A
__$ (DOLLARS) **½ (1971) PR:O__
DOLLARS FOR A FAST GUN * (1969, It./Sp.) PR:A
__DOLLS *½ (1987) PR:O__
__DOLL'S HOUSE, A *** (1973) PR:A__
__DOLL'S HOUSE, A ** (1973, Brit.) PR:A__
DOLLS, THE (SEE:BAMBOLE!)
DOLLY GETS AHEAD * (1931, Ger.) PR:A
DOLLY SISTERS, THE ** (1945) PR:AA
DOLORES **½ (1949, Sp.) PR:A
DOLWYN (SEE:LAST DAYS OF DOLWYN, THE)
DOMANI A TROPPO TARDI (SEE:TOMORROW IS TOO LATE)
DOMENICA D'AGOSTO (SEE:SUNDAY IN AUGUST)
DOMINANT SEX, THE * (1937, Brit.) PR:A
__DOMINICK AND EUGENE *** (1988) PR:C__
__DOMINIQUE ** (1978, Brit.) PR:C__
DOMINO KID **½ (1957) PR:A
__DOMINO PRINCIPLE, THE *½ (1977) PR:O__
DON CHICAGO ** (1945, Brit.) PR:A
DON GIOVANNI **½ (1955, Brit.) PR:A
DON GIOVANNI **½ (1979, Fr./It./Ger.) PR:A
__DON IS DEAD, THE ** (1973) PR:O__
DON JUAN (SEE:PRIVATE LIFE OF DON JUAN, THE)
DON JUAN * (1956, Aust.) PR:A
DON JUAN QUILLIGAN * (1945) PR:A
DON QUIXOTE **** (1935, Fr.) PR:A
DON QUIXOTE **** (1961, USSR) PR:A
__DON QUIXOTE *** (1973, Aus.) PR:A__
DON RICARDO RETURNS * (1946) PR:A
__DONA FLOR AND HER TWO HUSHANDS *** (1977, Braz.) PR:O__
DONA HERLINDA AND HER SON **** (1986, Mex.) PR:O
DONATELLA ** (1956, It.) PR:A
DONDI **½ (1961) PR:AA
__DONKEY SKIN *** (1975, Fr.) PR:C-O__
DONOVAN AFFAIR, THE **½ (1929) PR:A
__DONOVAN'S BRAIN *** (1953) PR:C__
__DONOVAN'S REEF *** (1963) PR:A__
__DON'S PARTY **** (1976, Aus.) PR:C-O__
__DON'T ANSWER THE PHONE * (1980) PR:O__
DON'T BE A DUMMY * (1932, Brit.) PR:A
DON'T BET ON BLONDES *½ (1935) PR:A
DON'T BET ON LOVE ** (1933) PR:A
DON'T BET ON WOMEN *½ (1931) PR:A
DON'T BLAME THE STORK * (1954, Brit.) PR:A
DON'T BOTHER TO KNOCK *** (1952) PR:O
DON'T BOTHER TO KNOCK (SEE:WHY BOTHER TO KNOCK)
DON'T CALL ME A CON MAN ** (1966, Jap.) PR:A
__DON'T CRY, IT'S ONLY THUNDER *** (1982) PR:O__
DON'T CRY WITH YOUR MOUTH FULL **½ (1974, Fr.) PR:A
__DON'T DRINK THE WATER ** (1969) PR:A__
DON'T EVER LEAVE ME *½ (1949, Brit.) PR:A
__DON'T FENCE ME IN **½ (1945) PR:A__
DON'T GAMBLE WITH LOVE ** (1936) PR:A
DON'T GAMBLE WITH STRANGERS * (1946) PR:A
DON'T GET ME WRONG ** (1937, Brit.) PR:A
DON'T GET PERSONAL *½ (1936) PR:A
DON'T GET PERSONAL *½ (1941) PR:A
DON'T GIVE UP THE SHIP ** (1959) PR:A
__DON'T GO IN THE HOUSE zero (1980) PR:O__
DON'T GO NEAR THE WATER ***½ (1957) PR:A
DON'T JUST LIE THERE, SAY SOMETHING! * (1973, Brit.) PR:O
DON'T JUST STAND THERE *½ (1968) PR:A
DON'T KNOCK THE ROCK **½ (1956) PR:A
DON'T KNOCK THE TWIST ** (1962) PR:A
DON'T LET THE ANGELS FALL **½ (1969, Can.) PR:A
__DON'T LOOK IN THE BASEMENT zero (1973) PR:O__
DON'T LOOK NOW ** (1969, Brit./Fr.) PR:A
__DON'T LOOK NOW ***½ (1973, Brit./It.) PR:O__
DON'T LOSE YOUR HEAD *½ (1967, Brit.) PR:C
DON'T MAKE WAVES ** (1967) PR:A
DON'T OPEN THE WINDOW zero (1974, It.) PR:O
__DON'T OPEN TILL CHRISTMAS zero (1984, Brit.) PR:O__
DON'T PANIC CHAPS! * (1959, Brit.) PR:A
DON'T PLAY WITH MARTIANS * (1967, Fr.) PR:A
__DON'T RAISE THE BRIDGE, LOWER THE RIVER * (1968, Brit.) PR:A__
DON'T RUSH ME ** (1936, Brit.) PR:A
DON'T SAY DIE *½ (1950, Brit.) PR:A
DON'T SCREAM, DORIS MAYS! (SEE:DAY OF THE NIGHTMARE)
DON'T TAKE IT TO HEART *** (1944, Brit.) PR:A
DON'T TALK TO STRANGE MEN * (1962, Brit.) PR:C
DON'T TELL THE WIFE ** (1937) PR:A
DON'T TEMPT THE DEVIL ** (1964, Fr./It.) PR:A
DON'T TOUCH MY SISTER (SEE:GLASS CAGE, THE)
DON'T TOUCH THE LOOT (SEE:GRISBI)
DON'T TOUCH WHITE WOMEN! **½ (1974, Fr.) PR:C
DON'T TRUST YOUR HUSBAND ** (1948) PR:C
DON'T TURN 'EM LOOSE * (1936) PR:A
__DON'T TURN THE OTHER CHEEK ** (1974, It./Ger./Sp.) PR:C__
DON'T WORRY, WE'LL THINK OF A TITLE * (1966) PR:A
DON'T YOU CRY (SEE:MY LOVER, MY SON)
DONZOKO (SEE:LOWER DEPTHS, THE)
DOOLINS OF OKLAHOMA, THE *** (1949) PR:A
DOOMED AT SUNDOWN **½ (1937) PR:AA
DOOMED BATTALION, THE ** (1932) PR:A
DOOMED CARAVAN *** (1941) PR:A
DOOMED CARGO ** (1936, Brit.) PR:A
__DOOMED TO DIE *½ (1940) PR:A__
DOOMED TO DIE zero (1985, It.) PR:O
DOOMSDAY AT ELEVEN *½ (1963, Brit.) PR:A-C
DOOMSDAY MACHINE zero (1967) PR:A
DOOMSDAY VOYAGE * (1972) PR:O
__DOOMWATCH ** (1972, Brit.) PR:C__
__DOOR TO DOOR ** (1984) PR:C__
DOOR-TO-DOOR MANIAC (SEE:FIVE MINUTES TO LIVE)
DOOR WITH SEVEN LOCKS, THE (SEE:CHAMBER OF HORRORS)
DOORWAY TO HELL ***½ (1930) PR:O
__DORIAN GRAY *½ (1970, It./Brit./Ger./Liechtenstein) PR:O__
__DORM THAT DRIPPED BLOOD, THE * (1983) PR:O__
DORMIRE * (1985, Ger.) PR:C
DOS COSMONAUTAS A LA FUERZA * (1967, Sp./It.) PR:A
DOSS HOUSE *** (1933, Brit.) PR:A-C
DOT AND THE BUNNY **½ (1983, Aus.) PR:AA
DOT AND THE KOALA *** (1985, Aus.) PR:AA
DOUBLE, THE *½ (1963, Brit.) PR:A
DOUBLE AFFAIR, THE (SEE:SPY WITH MY FACE, THE)
DOUBLE AGENTS, THE (SEE:NIGHT ENCOUNTER)
DOUBLE ALIBI ** (1940) PR:A
DOUBLE-BARRELLED DETECTIVE STORY, THE ** (1965) PR:A
DOUBLE BED, THE * (1965, Fr./It.) PR:C
__DOUBLE BUNK * (1961, Brit.) PR:A__
DOUBLE CON, THE (SEE:TRICK BABY)
DOUBLE CONFESSION ** (1953, Brit.) PR:C

DOUBLE CRIME IN THE MAGINOT LINE *½ (1939, Fr.) PR:A
DOUBLE CROSS ** (1941) PR:A
DOUBLE CROSS ** (1956, Brit.) PR:A-C
DOUBLE CROSS ROADS **½ (1930) PR:A
DOUBLE CROSSBONES ** (1950) PR:AA
DOUBLE DANGER ** (1938) PR:AA
DOUBLE DATE ** (1941) PR:AA
DOUBLE DEAL ** (1950) PR:A
DOUBLE DECEPTION ** (1963, Fr.) PR:A-C
DOUBLE DOOR * (1934) PR:C-O
DOUBLE DYNAMITE ** (1951) PR:A
DOUBLE EVENT, THE * (1934, Brit.) PR:A
DOUBLE EXPOSURE ** (1944) PR:A
DOUBLE EXPOSURE *½ (1954, Brit.) PR:A-C
DOUBLE EXPOSURE zero (1982) PR:O
DOUBLE EXPOSURES *½ (1937, Brit.) PR:A
DOUBLE HARNESS *** (1933) PR:A-C
DOUBLE INDEMNITY ***** (1944) PR:C
DOUBLE JEOPARDY * (1955) PR:A
DOUBLE LIFE, A ***** (1947) PR:C-O
DOUBLE MAN, THE ** (1967) PR:C
DOUBLE McGUFFIN, THE ** (1979) PR:A
DOUBLE NEGATIVE *½ (1980, Can.) PR:O
DOUBLE NICKELS *½ (1977) PR:C
DOUBLE OR NOTHING ** (1937) PR:A
DOUBLE OR QUITS ** (1938, Brit.) PR:A
DOUBLE STOP ** (1968) PR:C
DOUBLE SUICIDE *** (1970, Jap.) PR:O
DOUBLE TROUBLE **½ (1941) PR:A
DOUBLE TROUBLE (SEE:SWINGIN' ALONG)
DOUBLE TROUBLE * (1967) PR:A
DOUBLE WEDDING **½ (1937) PR:A
DOUBLES ** (1978) PR:C
DOUBTING THOMAS **½ (1935) PR:A
DOUCE (SEE:LOVE STORY)
DOUGH BOYS **** (1930) PR:AA
DOUGHBOYS IN IRELAND *½ (1943) PR:A
DOUGHGIRLS, THE **½ (1944) PR:A
DOUGHNUTS AND SOCIETY * (1936) PR:A
DOULOS—THE FINGER MAN ** (1964, Fr./It.) PR:C
DOVE, THE *** (1974, Brit.) PR:AA
DOWN AMONG THE SHELTERING PALMS **½ (1953) PR:A
DOWN AMONG THE Z MEN ** (1952, Brit.) PR:A
DOWN AND OUT IN BEVERLY HILLS **** (1986) PR:C-O
DOWN ARGENTINE WAY ***½ (1940) PR:AA
DOWN BY LAW **½ (1986) PR:O
DOWN DAKOTA WAY **½ (1949) PR:A
DOWN IN ARKANSAW * (1938) PR:A
DOWN IN SAN DIEGO ** (1941) PR:A
DOWN LAREDO WAY *½ (1953) PR:A
DOWN MEMORY LANE *** (1949) PR:A
DOWN MEXICO WAY **½ (1941) PR:A
DOWN MISSOURI WAY **½ (1946) PR:A
DOWN ON THE FARM ** (1938) PR:A
DOWN OUR ALLEY * (1939, Brit.) PR:A
DOWN OUR STREET ** (1932, Brit.) PR:A
DOWN RIO GRANDE WAY **½ (1942) PR:A
DOWN RIVER ** (1931, Brit.) PR:A
DOWN TEXAS WAY ** (1942) PR:A
DOWN THE ANCIENT STAIRCASE ** (1975, It.) PR:O
DOWN THE STRETCH ** (1936) PR:A
DOWN THE WYOMING TRAIL * (1939) PR:A
DOWN THREE DARK STREETS ** (1954) PR:C
DOWN TO EARTH ** (1932) PR:A
DOWN TO EARTH ** (1947) PR:A
DOWN TO THE SEA * (1936) PR:A
DOWN TO THE SEA IN SHIPS (SEE:LAST ADVENTURERS, THE)
DOWN TO THE SEA IN SHIPS *** (1949) PR:AA
DOWN TO THEIR LAST YACHT * (1934) PR:A
DOWN UNDER THE SEA (SEE:DOWN TO THE SEA)
DOWNFALL ** (1964, Brit.) PR:C
DOWNHILL RACER ***½ (1969) PR:C
DOWNSTAIRS *½ (1932) PR:A
DOZENS, THE ** (1981) PR:C
DR. BLACK AND MR. HYDE **½ (1976) PR:O
DR. BLOOD'S COFFIN ** (1961) PR:O
DRACULA **** (1931) PR:C-O
DRACULA (SEE:HORROR OF DRACULA)
DRACULA ** (1979) PR:C
DRACULA A.D. 1972 * (1972, Brit.) PR:O
DRACULA AND SON **½ (1976, Fr.) PR:C
DRACULA AND THE SEVEN GOLDEN VAMPIRES *½ (1978, Brit./Chi.) PR:O
DRACULA HAS RISEN FROM HIS GRAVE **½ (1968, Brit.) PR:O
DRACULA—PRINCE OF DARKNESS **½ (1966, Brit.) PR:O
DRACULA (THE DIRTY OLD MAN) ** (1969) PR:O
DRACULA TODAY (SEE:DRACULA A.D. 1972)
DRACULA VERSUS FRANKENSTEIN zero (1972, Sp.) PR:O
DRACULA'S DAUGHTER ** (1936) PR:O
DRACULA'S DOG * (1978) PR:O
DRACULA'S GREAT LOVE * (1972, Sp.) PR:O
DRACULA'S WIDOW * (1988) PR:O
DRAEGERMAN COURAGE *** (1937) PR:A
DRAG ** (1929) PR:A
DRAGNET **½ (1947) PR:A
DRAGNET *** (1954) PR:A
DRAGNET **½ (1987) PR:C
DRAGNET NIGHT * (1931, Fr.) PR:A
DRAGNET PATROL * (1932) PR:A
DRAGON CHOW ***½ (1988, W. Ger./Switz.) PR:C
DRAGON FLIES, THE (SEE:MAN FROM HONG KONG, THE)
DRAGON INN *½ (1968, Chi.) PR:C
DRAGON MASTER (SEE:CANNON FOR CORDOBA)
DRAGON MURDER CASE, THE * (1934) PR:A
DRAGON OF PENDRAGON CASTLE, THE * (1950, Brit.) PR:AA
DRAGON SEED *** (1944) PR:A
DRAGON SKY ** (1964, Fr.) PR:A
DRAGON WELLS MASSACRE **½ (1957) PR:A
DRAGONFLY, THE ** (1955, USSR) PR:A
DRAGONFLY (SEE:ONE SUMMER LOVE)
DRAGONFLY SQUADRON *½ (1953) PR:A
DRAGON'S GOLD *½ (1954) PR:A
DRAGONSLAYER ***½ (1981) PR:C-O
DRAGONWYCH *** (1946) PR:A
DRAGSTRIP GIRL ** (1957) PR:A
DRAGSTRIP RIOT ** (1958) PR:C
DRAKE CASE, THE ** (1929) PR:A
DRAKE THE PIRATE *** (1935, Brit.) PR:A
DRAMA OF JEALOUSY, A (SEE:PIZZA TRIANGLE, THE)
DRAMA OF THE RICH *** (1975, It./Fr.) PR:A-C
DRAMATIC SCHOOL **½ (1938) PR:A-C
DRANGO *** (1957) PR:A
DRAUGHTSMAN'S CONTRACT, THE *** (1983, Brit.) PR:O
DREAM COME TRUE, A ** (1963, USSR) PR:A
DREAM GIRL **½ (1947) PR:A
DREAM LOVER * (1986) PR:C
DREAM MAKER, THE ** (1963, Brit.) PR:A
DREAM NO MORE * (1950, Palestine) PR:A
DREAM OF A COSSACK ** (1982, USSR) PR:A
DREAM OF BUTTERFLY, THE ** (1941, It.) PR:A
DREAM OF KINGS, A *** (1969) PR:C
DREAM OF PASSION, A **½ (1978, Gr.) PR:C
DREAM OF SCHONBRUNN ** (1933, Aus.) PR:A
DREAM OF THE RED CHAMBER, THE ** (1966, Chi.) PR:A
DREAM ON * (1981) PR:O
DREAM ONE **½ (1984, Brit./Fr.) PR:A
DREAM TOWN * (1973, Ger.) PR:C
DREAM WIFE **½ (1953) PR:A
DREAMANIAC zero (1987) PR:O
DREAMBOAT ***½ (1952) PR:AA
DREAMCHILD **½ (1985, Brit.) PR:A
DREAMER, THE ** (1936, Ger.) PR:A
DREAMER, THE ** (1970, Israel) PR:O
DREAMER *½ (1979) PR:A
DREAMING *½ (1944, Brit.) PR:A
DREAMING LIPS *** (1937, Brit.) PR:C
DREAMING LIPS *½ (1958, Ger.) PR:C
DREAMING OUT LOUD ** (1940) PR:A
DREAMS ** (1960, Swed.) PR:C
DREAMS COME TRUE **½ (1936, Brit.) PR:A
DREAMS IN A DRAWER **½ (1957, Fr./It.) PR:A
DREAMS OF GLASS ** (1969) PR:C
DREAMS THAT MONEY CAN BUY *½ (1948) PR:C
DREAMSCAPE *** (1984) PR:C-O
DREAMWORLD (SEE:COVERGIRL)
DREI GEGEN DREI zero (1985, Ger.) PR:C
DREI VON DER TANKSTELLE (SEE:FROM THE GAS STATION)
DRESSED TO KILL *** (1941) PR:A
DRESSED TO KILL ** (1946) PR:A
DRESSED TO KILL *** (1980) PR:O
DRESSED TO THRILL * (1935) PR:A
DRESSER, THE ** (1983) PR:C
DREYFUS CASE, THE **** (1931, Brit.) PR:A
DREYFUS CASE, THE ** (1940, Ger.) PR:A
DRIFT FENCE **½ (1936) PR:A
DRIFTER, THE * (1988) PR:O
DRIFTER *** (1975) PR:O
DRIFTER, THE *½ (1932) PR:A
DRIFTER, THE * (1944) PR:A
DRIFTER, THE ** (1966) PR:C
DRIFTERS, THE (SEE:HALLUCINATION GENERATION)
DRIFTIN' KID, THE * (1941) PR:A
DRIFTIN' RIVER ** (1946) PR:A
DRIFTING * (1932) PR:A
DRIFTING *** (1984, Israel) PR:O
DRIFTING ALONG **½ (1946) PR:A
DRIFTING WEEDS (SEE:FLOATING WEEDS)
DRIFTING WESTWARD ** (1939) PR:A
DRIFTWOOD *** (1947) PR:A
DRILLER KILLER *½ (1979) PR:O
DRIVE A CROOKED ROAD *** (1954) PR:C
DRIVE, HE SAID ** (1971) PR:O
DRIVE-IN ***½ (1976) PR:O
DRIVE-IN MASSACRE ** (1976) PR:O
DRIVER, THE **** (1978) PR:O
DRIVER'S SEAT, THE * (1975, It.) PR:O
DRIVERS TO HELL (SEE:WILD ONES ON WHEELS)
DROLE DE DRAME (SEE:BIZARRE, BIZARRE)
DROP DEAD, DARLING (SEE:ARRIVEDERCI, BABY!)
DROP DEAD, MY LOVE * (1968, It.) PR:C
DROP THEM OR I'LL SHOOT *½ (1969, Fr./Ger./Sp.) PR:O
DROWNING BY NUMBERS *** (1988, Brit.) PR:O
DROWNING POOL, THE *** (1975) PR:C
DRUM zero (1976) PR:O
DRUM BEAT *** (1954) PR:A
DRUM TAPS ** (1933) PR:A
DRUMMER OF VENGEANCE *½ (1974, Brit.) PR:O
DRUMS **** (1938, Brit.) PR:A
DRUMS ACROSS THE RIVER ** (1954) PR:A
DRUMS ALONG THE MOHAWK ***** (1939) PR:AA
DRUMS IN THE DEEP SOUTH *** (1951) PR:A
DRUMS O' VOODOO * (1934) PR:A
DRUMS OF AFRICA * (1963) PR:A
DRUMS OF DESTINY * (1937) PR:A
DRUMS OF FU MANCHU ** (1943) PR:A
DRUMS OF JEOPARDY * (1931) PR:A
DRUMS OF TABU, THE zero (1967, It./Sp.) PR:A
DRUMS OF TAHITI * (1954) PR:A
DRUMS OF THE CONGO **½ (1942) PR:A
DRUMS OF THE DESERT * (1940) PR:A
DRUNKEN ANGEL **** (1948, Jap.) PR:C
DRY BIKINI, THE (SEE:HER BIKINI NEVER GOT WET)
DRY ROT ** (1956, Brit.) PR:A
DRY SUMMER ** (1967, Turk.) PR:A
DRYLANDERS **½ (1963, Can.) PR:A
DU BARRY WAS A LADY ** (1943) PR:A
DU BARRY, WOMAN OF PASSION * (1930) PR:A-C
DUAL ALIBI ** (1947, Brit.) PR:A
DUBEAT-E-O *½ (1984) PR:O
DUBLIN NIGHTMARE ** (1958, Brit.) PR:A-C
DUCHESS AND THE DIRTWATER FOX, THE ** (1976) PR:C
DUCHESS OF IDAHO, THE **½ (1950) PR:A
DUCK IN ORANGE SAUCE ** (1976, It.) PR:C
DUCK RINGS AT HALF PAST SEVEN, THE ** (1969, Ger./It.) PR:O
DUCK SOUP **** (1933) PR:AA
DUCK, YOU SUCKER! *** (1972, It.) PR:C
DUDE BANDIT, THE ** (1933) PR:A
DUDE COWBOY **½ (1941) PR:A
DUDE GOES WEST, THE *** (1948) PR:A
DUDE RANCH ** (1931) PR:A
DUDE RANGER, THE **½ (1934) PR:A
DUDE WRANGLER, THE * (1930) PR:A
DUDES **½ (1988) PR:O
DUE SOLDI DI SPERANZA (SEE:TWO PENNY WORTH OF HOPE)
DUEL, THE **½ (1964, USSR) PR:A
DUEL AT APACHE WELLS **½ (1957) PR:A
DUEL AT DIABLO **½ (1966) PR:A
DUEL AT EZO ** (1970, Jap.) PR:C
DUEL AT SILVER CREEK, THE **½ (1952) PR:A
DUEL IN DURANGO (SEE:GUN DUEL IN DURANGO)
DUEL IN THE JUNGLE **½ (1954, Brit.) PR:A
DUEL IN THE SUN ***½ (1946) PR:C-O
DUEL OF CHAMPIONS zero (1964, It./Sp.) PR:A
DUEL OF THE TITANS ** (1963, It.) PR:A
DUEL ON THE MISSISSIPPI ** (1955) PR:A
DUEL WITHOUT HONOR * (1953, It.) PR:A
DUELLISTS, THE *** (1977, Brit.) PR:C
DUET FOR CANNIBALS ** (1969, Swed.) PR:O
DUET FOR FOUR * (1982, Aus.) PR:C
DUET FOR ONE *** (1986) PR:O
DUFFY *½ (1968, Brit.) PR:C
DUFFY OF SAN QUENTIN ** (1954) PR:A
DUFFY'S TAVERN *** (1945) PR:A
DUGAN OF THE BAD LANDS *½ (1931) PR:A
DUGI BRODOVI (SEE:LONG SHIPS, THE)
DUKE COMES BACK, THE *½ (1937) PR:A
DUKE IS THE TOPS, THE ** (1938) PR:A
DUKE OF CHICAGO ** (1949) PR:A
DUKE OF THE NAVY *½ (1942) PR:A

DUKE OF WEST POINT, THE **½ (1938) PR:A
DUKE WORE JEANS, THE ** (1958, Brit.) PR:A
DULCIMA ** (1971, Brit.) PR:A
DULCIMER STREET ** (1948, Brit.) PR:A
DULCINEA **½ (1962, Sp.) PR:C
DULCY *** (1940) PR:A
DUMB DICKS
    (SEE:DETECTIVE SCHOOL DROPOUTS)
DUMBBELLS IN ERMINE ** (1930) PR:A
DUMBO *** (1941) PR:AA**
DUMMY, THE * (1929) PR:A-C
DUMMY TALKS, THE ** (1943, Brit.) PR:A
DUNE ** (1984) PR:C-O
DUNGEONMASTER * (1985) PR:C-O
DUNGEONS OF HARROW zero (1964) PR:O
DUNKIRK *** (1958, Brit.) PR:A
DUNWICH HORROR, THE **½ (1970) PR:C
DURANGO KID, THE **½ (1940) PR:A
DURANGO VALLEY RAIDERS * (1938) PR:A
DURANT AFFAIR, THE ** (1962, Brit.) PR:A-C
DURING ONE NIGHT * (1962, Brit.) PR:A
DUST * (1985, Fr./Bel.) PR:O
DUST BE MY DESTINY *** (1939) PR:A
DUSTY AND SWEETS MCGEE * (1971) PR:O
DUSTY ERMINE
    (SEE:HIDEOUT IN THE ALPS)
DUTCH TREAT ** (1987) PR:C-O
DUTCHMAN *** (1966, Brit.) PR:C
DYBBUK, THE * (1938, Pol.) PR:A**
DYNAMITE *** (1930) PR:A
DYNAMITE ** (1948) PR:A
DYNAMITE CANYON ** (1941) PR:A
DYNAMITE DELANEY *½ (1938) PR:A
DYNAMITE DENNY * (1932) PR:A
DYNAMITE JACK zero (1961, Fr.) PR:A
DYNAMITE JOHNSON zero (1978, Phil.) PR:A
DYNAMITE PASS ** (1950) PR:A
DYNAMITE RANCH *½ (1932) PR:A
DYNAMITERS, THE * (1956, Brit.) PR:A

E

EACH DAWN I DIE ***½ (1939) PR:A
EACH MAN FOR HIMSELF
    (SEE:RUTHLESS FOUR, THE)
EADIE WAS A LADY ** (1945) PR:A
EAGER BEAVERS
    (SEE:SWINGING BARMAIDS, THE)
EAGLE AND THE HAWK, THE ***½ (1933) PR:C
EAGLE AND THE HAWK, THE **½ (1950) PR:A
EAGLE HAS LANDED, THE * (1976, Brit.) PR:C**
EAGLE IN A CAGE *** (1971, US/Yugo.) PR:A
EAGLE OVER LONDON ** (1973, It.) PR:C
EAGLE ROCK * (1964, Brit.) PR:A
EAGLE SQUADRON ***½ (1942) PR:A
EAGLE WITH TWO HEADS ***½ (1948, Fr.) PR:A
EAGLE'S BROOD, THE **½ (1936) PR:A
EAGLE'S WING *½ (1979, Brit.) PR:A
EARL CARROLL SKETCHBOOK ** (1946) PR:A
EARL CARROLL'S VANITIES ** (1945) PR:A
EARL OF CHICAGO, THE *** (1940) PR:A
EARL OF PUDDLESTONE ** (1940) PR:A
EARLY AUTUMN ** (1962, Jap.) PR:C
EARLY BIRD, THE *½ (1936, Brit.) PR:A
EARLY BIRD, THE ** (1965, Brit.) PR:A
EARLY TO BED ** (1933, Brit./Ger.) PR:A
EARLY TO BED **½ (1936) PR:A
EARLY WORKS **½ (1970, Yugo.) PR:O
EARRINGS OF MADAME DE..., THE **
    (1954, Fr./It.) PR:A
EARTH CRIES OUT, THE *½ (1949, It.) PR:A
EARTH DIES SCREAMING, THE **
    (1964, Brit.) PR:A
EARTH ENTRANCED *** (1970, Braz.) PR:C
EARTH VS. THE FLYING SAUCERS * (1956) PR:A**
EARTH VS. THE SPIDER * (1958) PR:A
EARTHBOUND **½ (1940) PR:A
EARTHBOUND * (1981) PR:C
EARTHLING, THE *½ (1980) PR:C
EARTHQUAKE zero (1974) PR:C
EARTHWORM TRACTORS **½ (1936) PR:A
EASIEST WAY, THE **½ (1931) PR:C

EAST CHINA SEA ** (1969, Jap.) PR:C
EAST END CHANT
    (SEE:LIMEHOUSE BLUES)
EAST IS WEST *½ (1930) PR:C
EAST LYNNE ** (1931) PR:C
EAST LYNNE ON THE WESTERN FRONT **
    (1931, Brit.) PR:A
EAST MEETS WEST ** (1936, Brit.) PR:A
EAST OF BORNEO ** (1931) PR:A
EAST OF EDEN *** (1955) PR:C-O**
EAST OF ELEPHANT ROCK * (1976, Brit.) PR:O
EAST OF FIFTH AVE. *½ (1933) PR:C
EAST OF JAVA ** (1935) PR:A
EAST OF KILIMANJARO ** (1962, Brit./It.) PR:A
EAST OF PICADILLY
    (SEE:STRANGLER, THE)
EAST OF SHANGHAI
    (SEE:RICH AND STRANGE)
EAST OF SUDAN ** (1964, Brit.) PR:A
EAST OF SUMATRA *** (1953) PR:A
EAST OF THE RIVER ** (1940) PR:A
EAST OF THE WALL ** (1986, Ger.) PR:C
EAST SIDE KIDS * (1940) PR:A
EAST SIDE KIDS MEET BELA LUGOSI, THE
    (SEE:GHOSTS ON THE LOOSE)
EAST SIDE OF HEAVEN **½ (1939) PR:A
EAST SIDE SADIE ** (1929) PR:A
EAST SIDE, WEST SIDE **½ (1949) PR:A-C
EASTER PARADE ** (1948) PR:AA**
EASTER SUNDAY
    (SEE:BEING, THE)
EASY COME, EASY GO ** (1947) PR:A
EASY COME, EASY GO ** (1967) PR:A
EASY GO
    (SEE:FREE AND EASY)
EASY LIFE, THE ***½ (1963, It.) PR:C
EASY LIFE, THE *** (1971, Fr.) PR:C
EASY LIVING *** (1937) PR:A
EASY LIVING **½ (1949) PR:A
EASY MILLIONS *½ (1933) PR:A
EASY MONEY ** (1934, Brit.) PR:A
EASY MONEY ** (1936) PR:A
EASY MONEY ** (1948, Brit.) PR:A
EASY MONEY ***½ (1983) PR:C-O
EASY RICHES *½ (1938, Brit.) PR:A
EASY RIDER ** (1969) PR:O**
EASY TO LOOK AT ** (1945) PR:A
EASY TO LOVE ** (1934) PR:A
EASY TO LOVE *** (1953) PR:A
EASY TO TAKE **½ (1936) PR:A
EASY TO WED *** (1946) PR:A
EASY WAY
    (SEE:ROOM FOR ONE MORE)
EAT AND RUN * (1986) PR:O
EAT MY DUST! ** (1976) PR:A
EAT THE PEACH * (1987, Brit.) PR:A-C**
EATEN ALIVE ** (1976) PR:O
EATING RAOUL zero (1982) PR:O
EAVESDROPPER, THE ** (1966, US/Arg.) PR:C
EBB TIDE ** (1932, Brit.) PR:A
EBB TIDE *** (1937) PR:A
EBIRAH, HORROR OF THE DEEP
    (SEE:GODZILLA VS THE SEA MONSTER)
EBOLI **½ (1980, It./Fr.) PR:A
ECHO, THE ** (1964, Pol.) PR:C
ECHO MURDERS, THE *½ (1945, Brit.) PR:A
ECHO OF A DREAM * (1930, Ger.) PR:A-C
ECHO OF BARBARA **½ (1961, Brit.) PR:C
ECHO OF DIANA *½ (1963, Brit.) PR:A-C
ECHO PARK * (1986, Aust.) PR:O
ECHOES ** (1983) PR:O
ECHOES OF A SUMMER ** (1976) PR:A
ECHOES OF SILENCE ** (1966) PR:C
ECLIPSE *** (1962, Fr./It.) PR:A
ECSTACY OF YOUNG LOVE *** (1936, Czech.) PR:A
ECSTASY * (1940, Czech.) PR:O**
EDDIE AND THE CRUISERS *½ (1983) PR:C
EDDIE CANTOR STORY, THE *½ (1953) PR:AA
EDDIE MACON'S RUN * (1983) PR:A-C
EDDY DUCHIN STORY, THE **½ (1956) PR:A
EDEN CRIED *½ (1967) PR:A
EDGAR ALLAN POE'S CASTLE OF BLOOD
    (SEE:CASTLE OF BLOOD)
EDGAR ALLAN POE'S CONQUEROR WORM
    (SEE:CONQUEROR WORM)
EDGAR ALLAN POE'S "THE OBLONG BOX"
    (SEE:OBLONG BOX, THE)

EDGE, THE *** (1968) PR:C
EDGE OF DARKNESS ***½ (1943) PR:A
EDGE OF DIVORCE
    (SEE:BACKGROUND)
EDGE OF DOOM *** (1950) PR:C
EDGE OF ETERNITY *** (1959) PR:A
EDGE OF FURY zero (1958) PR:O
EDGE OF HELL ** (1956) PR:A
EDGE OF THE CITY *** (1957) PR:A
EDGE OF THE WORLD, THE *** (1937, Brit.) PR:A
EDISON, THE MAN *** (1940) PR:A
EDITH AND MARCEL **½ (1984, Fr.) PR:A
EDUCATED EVANS ** (1936, Brit.) PR:A
EDUCATING FATHER ** (1936) PR:A
EDUCATING RITA **½ (1983) PR:A
EDUCATION OF SONNY CARSON, THE **½
    (1974) PR:C
EDVARD MUNCH *** (1976, Norway/Swed.) PR:C
EDWARD AND CAROLINE **½ (1952, Fr.) PR:A
EDWARD, MY SON *** (1949, US/Brit.) PR:C
EEGAH! * (1962) PR:C
EERIE WORLD OF DR. JORDAN, THE
    (SEE:SOMETHING WEIRD)
EFFECT OF GAMMA RAYS ON MAN-IN-THE-MOON
    MARIGOLDS, THE *** (1972) PR:C
EFFECTS *½ (1980) PR:O
EFFI BRIEST **** (1974, Ger.) PR:O
EGG AND I, THE ** (1947) PR:AA**
EGGHEAD'S ROBOT ** (1970, Brit.) PR:A
EGLANTINE *** (1972, Fr.) PR:A
EGON SCHIELE—EXCESS AND PUNISHMENT **½
    (1981, Ger.) PR:O
EGYPT BY THREE ** (1953) PR:A
EGYPTIAN, THE ** (1954) PR:A-C
EIGER SANCTION, THE ** (1975) PR:C
8 1/2 ** (1963, It.) PR:C**
EIGHT ARMS TO HOLD YOU
    (SEE:HELP!)
EIGHT BELLS **½ (1935) PR:A
EIGHT GIRLS IN A BOAT ** (1932, Ger.) PR:A
EIGHT GIRLS IN A BOAT *** (1934) PR:C
EIGHT IRON MEN **½ (1952) PR:A
EIGHT MEN OUT * (1988) PR:C-O**
8 MILLION WAYS TO DIE * (1986) PR:O
EIGHT O'CLOCK WALK ***½ (1954, Brit.) PR:A
EIGHT ON THE LAM * (1967) PR:A
18 AGAIN! * (1988) PR:C
EIGHTEEN AND ANXIOUS *½ (1957) PR:C
1812 *** (1944, USSR) PR:A
EIGHTEEN IN THE SUN * (1964, It.) PR:C
18 MINUTES *** (1935, Brit.) PR:A
EIGHTH DAY OF THE WEEK, THE ***½
    (1959, Pol./Ger.) PR:C-O
84 CHARING CROSS ROAD * (1987) PR:A-C**
80 STEPS TO JONAH ** (1969) PR:A
80,000 SUSPECTS *** (1963, Brit.) PR:C
EIN BLICK-UND DIE LIEBE BRICHT AUS ***
    (1987, Ger.) PR:O
EINE LIEBE IN DEUTSCHLAND
    (SEE:LOVE IN GERMANY, A)
EL **** (1955, Mex.) PR:C-O
EL ALAMEIN ** (1954) PR:A-C
EL AMOR BRUJO * (1986, Sp.) PR:A**
EL ANO DE LAS LUCES
    (SEE:YEAR OF AWAKENING, THE)
EL BRUTO
    (SEE:BRUTE, THE)
EL CID * (1961, US/It.) PR:A**
EL CONDOR * (1970) PR:O
EL DIABLO RIDES * (1939) PR:A
EL DIPUTADO **½ (1985, Sp.) PR:O
EL DORADO * (1967) PR:A-C**
EL DORADO PASS *½ (1949) PR:A
EL GRECO ** (1966, Ital./Fr.) PR:A
EL HOMBRE Y EL MONSTRUO
    (SEE:MAN AND THE MONSTER, THE)
EL IMPERIO DE LA FORTUNA
    (SEE:REALM OF FORTUNE, THE)
EL NORTE ** (1984) PR:O**
EL PASO *** (1949) PR:A
EL PASO KID, THE ** (1946) PR:A
EL PASO STAMPEDE ** (1953) PR:A
EL TOPO * (1971, Mex.) PR:O
ELDER BROTHER, THE * (1937, Brit.) PR:A
ELECTRA ** (1962, Gr.) PR:A
ELECTRA GLIDE IN BLUE ** (1973) PR:C
ELECTRIC BLUE ** (1988, It.) PR:A-C

ELECTRIC BOOGALOO: BREAKIN' 2 (SEE:BREAKIN' 2 ELECTRIC BOOGALOO)
ELECTRIC DREAMS * (1984) PR:A-C**
ELECTRIC HORSEMAN, THE **½ (1979) PR:A-C
ELECTRONIC MONSTER, THE ***½ (1960, Brit.) PR:C
ELEMENT OF CRIME, THE ** (1984, Den.) PR:O
ELENI * (1985) PR:A-C
ELEPHANT BOY * (1937, Brit.) PR:AA**
ELEPHANT CALLED SLOWLY, AN ** (1970, Brit.) PR:A
ELEPHANT GUN ** (1959, Brit.) PR:A
ELEPHANT MAN, THE ** (1980, Brit.) PR:A-C**
ELEPHANT STAMPEDE *½ (1951) PR:A
ELEPHANT WALK **½ (1954) PR:A
11 HARROWHOUSE ** (1974, Brit.) PR:C
ELEVENTH COMMANDMENT *½ (1933) PR:A
ELI ELI *½ (1940) PR:A
ELIMINATOR, THE (SEE:DANGER ROUTE)
ELIMINATORS ** (1986) PR:A-C
ELINOR NORTON *½ (1935) PR:A
ELISABETH OF AUSTRIA **½ (1931, Ger.) PR:A
ELIZA COMES TO STAY *½ (1936, Brit.) PR:A
ELIZA FRASER ***½ (1976, Aus.) PR:C
ELIZABETH OF ENGLAND (SEE:DRAKE THE PIRATE)
ELIZABETH OF LADYMEAD *½ (1949, Brit.) PR:A
ELIZABETH THE QUEEN (SEE:PRIVATE LIVES OF ELIZABETH AND ESSEX, THE)
ELIZA'S HOROSCOPE ** (1975, Can.) PR:O
ELLERY QUEEN AND THE MURDER RING ** (1941) PR:A
ELLERY QUEEN AND THE PERFECT CRIME * (1941) PR:A
ELLERY QUEEN, MASTER DETECTIVE ** (1940) PR:A
ELLERY QUEEN'S PENTHOUSE MYSTERY ** (1941) PR:A
ELLIE zero (1984) PR:O
ELMER AND ELSIE ** (1934) PR:A
ELMER GANTRY ** (1960) PR:C**
ELMER THE GREAT * (1933) PR:A**
ELOPEMENT ** (1951) PR:A
ELUSIVE CORPORAL, THE * (1963, Fr.) PR:A**
ELUSIVE PIMPERNEL, THE (SEE:FIGHTING PIMPERNEL, THE)
ELVIRA MADIGAN ** (1967, Swed.) PR:A-C**
ELVIRA: MISTRESS OF THE DARK ** (1988) PR:C
ELVIS! ELVIS! ** (1977, Swed.) PR:A
EMANON * (1987) PR:A-C
EMBALMER, THE zero (1966, It.) PR:C
EMBARRASSING MOMENTS **½ (1930) PR:A
EMBARRASSING MOMENTS *½ (1934) PR:A
EMBASSY **½ (1972, Brit.) PR:C
EMBEZZLED HEAVEN ** (1959, Ger.) PR:A
EMBEZZLER, THE *½ (1954, Brit.) PR:A
EMBRACEABLE YOU **½ (1948) PR:A
EMBRACERS, THE * (1966) PR:C
EMBRYO * (1976) PR:C
EMBRYOS ** (1985, Hung.) PR:O
EMERALD FOREST, THE ** (1985) PR:C-O**
EMERGENCY! (SEE:HUNDRED HOUR HUNT)
EMERGENCY ** (1962, Brit.) PR:A
EMERGENCY CALL ** (1933) PR:A
EMERGENCY CALL (SEE:HUNDRED HOUR HUNT)
EMERGENCY HOSPITAL **½ (1956) PR:A
EMERGENCY LANDING * (1941) PR:A
EMERGENCY SQUAD ** (1940) PR:A
EMERGENCY WARD (SEE:CAREY TREATMENT, THE)
EMERGENCY WEDDING ** (1950) PR:A
EMIGRANTS, THE ** (1972, Swed.) PR:A**
EMIL *** (1938, Brit.) PR:AA
EMIL AND THE DETECTIVE ***½ (1931, Ger.) PR:AA
EMIL AND THE DETECTIVES ** (1964) PR:AA
EMILY * (1976, Brit.) PR:O
EMILY (SEE:AMERICANIZATION OF EMILY, THE)
EMMA ***½ (1932) PR:A
EMMA MAE ** (1976) PR:O
EMMANUELLE 5 * (1987, Fr.) PR:O
EMPEROR AND A GENERAL, THE **½ (1968, Jap.) PR:O
EMPEROR AND THE GOLEM, THE ** (1955, Czech.) PR:A
EMPEROR AND THE NIGHTINGALE, THE *** (1949, Czech.) PR:AA
EMPEROR JONES, THE ** (1933) PR:C**
EMPEROR OF PERU (SEE:ODYSSEY IN THE PACIFIC)
EMPEROR OF THE NORTH POLE * (1973) PR:C**
EMPEROR WALTZ, THE *** (1948) PR:AA
EMPEROR'S CANDLESTICKS, THE ** (1937) PR:A
EMPIRE OF THE ANTS * (1977) PR:C
EMPIRE OF NIGHT, THE *** (1963, Fr.) PR:C
EMPIRE OF THE SUN ** (1987) PR:A**
EMPIRE STRIKES BACK, THE ***½ (1980) PR:A
EMPLOYEE'S ENTRANCE ***½ (1933) PR:A
EMPRESS AND I, THE *** (1933, Ger.) PR:A
EMPRESS WU ** (1965, Hong Kong) PR:A
EMPTY CANVAS, THE * (1964, Fr./It.) PR:O
EMPTY HOLSTERS *½ (1937) PR:A
EMPTY SADDLES ** (1937) PR:A
EMPTY STAR, THE ** (1962, Mex.) PR:A
ENCHANTED APRIL * (1935) PR:A
ENCHANTED COTTAGE, THE ***** (1945) PR:A
ENCHANTED FOREST, THE ***½ (1945) PR:AA
ENCHANTED ISLAND ** (1958) PR:A
ENCHANTED VALLEY, THE ** (1948) PR:A
ENCHANTING SHADOW, THE ** (1965, Hong Kong) PR:A
ENCHANTMENT *** (1948) PR:A
ENCORE * (1951, Brit.) PR:A**
ENCOUNTER WITH THE UNKNOWN *½ (1973) PR:C
ENCOUNTERS IN SALZBURG **½ (1964, Ger.) PR:C
END, THE ** (1978) PR:O
END OF A DAY, THE *** (1939, Fr.) PR:A
END OF A PRIEST ** (1970, Czech.) PR:C
END OF AUGUST, THE * (1982) PR:C-O
END OF AUGUST AT THE HOTEL OZONE, THE ** (1967, Czech.) PR:C
END OF BELLE, THE (SEE:PASSION OF SLOW FIRE, THE)
END OF DESIRE ** (1962, Fr./It.) PR:A
END OF INNOCENCE **** (1960, Arg.) PR:O
END OF MRS. CHENEY **½ (1963, Ger.) PR:A
END OF SUMMER, THE (SEE:EARLY AUTUMN)
END OF THE AFFAIR, THE ** (1955, Brit.) PR:A
END OF THE GAME **½ (1976, Ger./It.) PR:C-O
END OF THE LINE, THE * (1959, Brit.) PR:A-C
END OF THE LINE * (1988) PR:A-C**
END OF THE RIVER, THE ** (1947, Brit.) PR:A
END OF THE ROAD ** (1944) PR:A
END OF THE ROAD, THE *** (1954, Brit.) PR:A
END OF THE ROAD, THE **½ (1936, Brit.) PR:A
END OF THE TRAIL ***½ (1932) PR:A
END OF THE TRAIL *** (1936) PR:A
END OF THE WORLD, THE * (1930, Fr.) PR:A
END OF THE WORLD, THE (SEE:PANIC IN YEAR ZERO!)
END OF THE WORLD * (1977) PR:C
END OF THE WORLD (IN OUR USUAL BED IN A NIGHT FULL OF RAIN), THE *½ (1978, It.) PR:C
END PLAY *** (1975, Aus.) PR:C
ENDANGERED SPECIES zero (1982) PR:O
ENDLESS LOVE zero (1981) PR:O
ENDLESS NIGHT, THE **½ (1963, Ger.) PR:C
ENDLESS NIGHT ** (1971, Brit.) PR:C
ENDSTATION 13 SAHARA (SEE:STATION SIX-SAHARA)
ENEMIES OF PROGRESS **½ (1934, USSR) PR:A
ENEMIES OF THE LAW * (1931) PR:A
ENEMY, THE (SEE:HELL IN THE PACIFIC)
ENEMY AGENT **½ (1940) PR:A
ENEMY AGENTS MEET ELLERY QUEEN * (1942) PR:A
ENEMY BELOW, THE **** (1957) PR:A
ENEMY FROM SPACE ***½ (1957, Brit.) PR:A
ENEMY GENERAL, THE ** (1960) PR:A
ENEMY MINE *½ (1985) PR:A-C
ENEMY OF THE LAW ** (1945) PR:A
ENEMY OF THE PEOPLE, AN ** (1978) PR:A
ENEMY OF THE POLICE * (1933, Brit.) PR:A
ENEMY OF WOMEN ** (1944) PR:C
ENEMY, THE SEA, THE (SEE:MY ENEMY, THE SEA)
ENFORCER, THE ** (1951) PR:C**
ENFORCER, THE ** (1976) PR:O
ENGAGEMENT ITALIANO ** (1966, Fr./It.) PR:A
ENGLAND MADE ME ***½ (1973, Brit.) PR:C
ENGLISH WITHOUT TEARS (SEE:HER MAN GILBY)
ENGLISHMAN'S HOME, AN (SEE:MAD MEN OF EUROPE)
ENIGMA *½ (1983) PR:C
ENJO *** (1959, Jap.) PR:O
ENLIGHTEN THY DAUGHTER * (1934) PR:A
ENORMOUS CHANGES AT THE LAST MINUTE **½ (1985) PR:A
ENOUGH ROPE ** (1966, Fr./It./Ger.) PR:A
ENSIGN PULVER **½ (1964) PR:A
ENTENTE CORDIALE *** (1939, Fr.) PR:A
ENTER ARSENE LUPIN ** (1944) PR:A
ENTER INSPECTOR DUVAL ** (1961, Brit.) PR:A-C
ENTER LAUGHING **½ (1967) PR:A
ENTER MADAME **½ (1935) PR:A
ENTER THE DRAGON * (1973) PR:O**
ENTER THE NINJA * (1982) PR:O
ENTERTAINER, THE ** (1960, Brit.) PR:A**
ENTERTAINER, THE ***½ (1975) PR:A-C
ENTERTAINING MR. SLOANE ***½ (1970, Brit.) PR:O
ENTITY, THE **½ (1982) PR:O
ENTRE NOUS * (1983, Fr.) PR:C**
EPILOGUE ** (1967, Den.) PR:A
EPISODE ** (1937, Aust.) PR:A
EQUALIZER 2000 * (1987) PR:O
EQUINOX * (1970) PR:C-O**
EQUUS ** (1977) PR:C-O**
ERASERHEAD * (1978) PR:O**
ERASMUS WITH FRECKLES (SEE:DEAR BRIGITTE)
ERENDIRA **½ (1984, Mex./Fr./Ger.) PR:O
ERIC SOYA'S "17" ** (1967, Den.) PR:O
ERIK THE CONQUEROR *½ (1963, Fr./It.) PR:C
ERNEST GOES TO CAMP * (1987) PR:A-C
ERNEST HEMINGWAY'S ADVENTURES OF A YOUNG MAN (SEE:ADVENTURES OF A YOUNG MAN)
ERNEST HEMINGWAY'S THE KILLERS (SEE:KILLERS, THE)
ERNEST SAVES CHRISTMAS **½ (1988) PR:A
ERNESTO * (1979, It.) PR:O
EROICA *** (1966, Pol.) PR:C
EROTIQUE *½ (1969, Fr.) PR:C
ERRAND BOY, THE **½ (1961) PR:A
ESCAPADE *½ (1932) PR:A
ESCAPADE ***½ (1935) PR:A
ESCAPADE **½ (1955, Brit.) PR:A
ESCAPADE IN JAPAN ** (1957) PR:A
ESCAPE ** (1930, Brit.) PR:A
ESCAPE ARTIST, THE **½ (1982) PR:C
ESCAPE *** (1940) PR:A
ESCAPE BY NIGHT *½ (1937) PR:A
ESCAPE BY NIGHT ** (1954, Brit.) PR:A-C
ESCAPE BY NIGHT ** (1965, Brit.) PR:C
ESCAPE *** (1948, Brit.) PR:A
ESCAPE, THE **½ (1939) PR:A
ESCAPE DANGEROUS *½ (1947, Brit.) PR:A
ESCAPE FROM ALCATRAZ ***½ (1979) PR:C
ESCAPE FROM CRIME ** (1942) PR:A
ESCAPE FROM DEVIL'S ISLAND ** (1935) PR:A
ESCAPE FROM EAST BERLIN **½ (1962) PR:A
ESCAPE FROM FORT BRAVO * (1953) PR:A**
ESCAPE FROM HELL ISLAND (SEE:MAN IN THE WATER, THE)
ESCAPE FROM HONG KONG *** (1942) PR:A
ESCAPE FROM NEW YORK **½ (1981) PR:O
ESCAPE FROM RED ROCK **½ (1958) PR:A
ESCAPE FROM SAN QUENTIN ** (1957) PR:A
ESCAPE FROM SEGOVIA *** (1984, Sp.) PR:C
ESCAPE FROM TERROR ** (1960) PR:A
ESCAPE FROM THE BRONX * (1985, It.) PR:O
ESCAPE FROM THE DARK (SEE:LITTLEST HORSE THIEVES)
ESCAPE FROM THE PLANET OF THE APES **½ (1971) PR:C
ESCAPE FROM THE SEA * (1968, Brit.) PR:AA
ESCAPE FROM YESTERDAY **½ (1939, Fr.) PR:A
ESCAPE FROM ZAHRAIN ** (1962) PR:A
ESCAPE IN THE DESERT **½ (1945) PR:A
ESCAPE IN THE FOG ** (1945) PR:A
ESCAPE IN THE SUN **½ (1956, Brit.) PR:A
ESCAPE LIBRE (SEE:BACKFIRE)
ESCAPE ME NEVER *½ (1935, Brit.) PR:A
ESCAPE ME NEVER **½ (1947) PR:A
ESCAPE ROUTE (SEE:I'LL GET YOU)
ESCAPE TO ATHENA ** (1979, Brit.) PR:C
ESCAPE TO BERLIN ** (1962, US/Switz./Ger.) PR:A
ESCAPE TO BURMA ** (1955) PR:A
ESCAPE TO DANGER *½ (1943, Brit.) PR:A
ESCAPE TO GLORY *½ (1940) PR:A
ESCAPE TO PARADISE *½ (1939) PR:A
ESCAPE TO THE SUN ** (1972, Fr./Ger./Israel) PR:C
ESCAPE TO WITCH MOUNTAIN **½ (1975) PR:AA
ESCAPE 2000 * (1983, Aus.) PR:O
ESCAPED FROM DARTMOOR ** (1930, Brit.) PR:C
ESCAPES zero (1987, Brit.) PR:A
ESCORT FOR HIRE *½ (1960, Brit.) PR:A-C
ESCORT WEST **½ (1959) PR:A
ESPIONAGE ** (1937) PR:A
ESPIONAGE AGENT **½ (1939) PR:A
ESTHER AND THE KING * (1960, US/It.) PR:A
ESTHER WATERS **½ (1948, Brit.) PR:C
E.T. THE EXTRA-TERRESTRIAL ** (1982) PR:AA**
ETERNAL FEMININE, THE *½ (1931, Brit.) PR:A
ETERNAL HUSBAND, THE *** (1946, Fr.) PR:C
ETERNAL LOVE * (1960, Ger.) PR:A
ETERNAL MASK, THE **** (1937, Switz.) PR:A-C
ETERNAL MELODIES * (1948, It.) PR:A
ETERNAL RETURN, THE ***½ (1943, Fr.) PR:A
ETERNAL SEA, THE **½ (1955) PR:A
ETERNAL SUMMER * (1961) PR:A

ETERNAL WALTZ, THE ** (1959, Ger.) PR:A
ETERNALLY YOURS ** (1939) PR:A
ETERNITY OF LOVE *** (1961, Jap.) PR:C
EUREKA ** (1983, Brit.) PR:O
EUREKA STOCKADE
(SEE:MASSACRE HILL)
EUROPE 51
(SEE:GREATEST LOVE, THE)
EUROPEANS, THE ** (1979, Brit.) PR:A
EVA *** (1962, Fr./It.) PR:O
EVANGELINE ** (1929) PR:A
EVE * (1968, Brit./Sp.) PR:O
EVE KNEW HER APPLES ** (1945) PR:A
EVE OF ST. MARK, THE *** (1944) PR:A-C
EVE WANTS TO SLEEP *** (1961, Pol.) PR:A
EVEL KNIEVEL **½ (1971) PR:A
EVELYN PRENTICE **½ (1934) PR:C
EVENINGS FOR SALE ** (1932) PR:A
EVENSONG **½ (1934, Brit.) PR:A
EVENT, AN *** (1970, Yugo.) PR:C
EVENTS **½ (1970) PR:O
EVER IN MY HEART **½ (1933) PR:C
EVER SINCE EVE ** (1934) PR:A
EVER SINCE EVE ** (1937) PR:A
EVER SINCE VENUS *** (1944) PR:A
EVERGREEN *** (1934, Brit.) PR:A
EVERY BASTARD A KING **½ (1968, Israel) PR:C
EVERY DAY IS A HOLIDAY ** (1966, Sp.) PR:A
EVERY DAY'S A HOLIDAY ** (1938) PR:A
EVERY DAY'S A HOLIDAY
(SEE:GOLD OF NAPLES)
EVERY DAY'S A HOLIDAY
(SEE:SEASIDE SWINGERS)
**EVERY GIRL SHOULD BE MARRIED **½
(1948) PR:A**
EVERY HOME SHOULD HAVE ONE
(SEE:THINK DIRTY)
EVERY LITTLE CROOK AND NANNY *½
(1972) PR:C
EVERY MAN A KING
(SEE:EVERY BASTARD A KING)
EVERY MAN FOR HIMSELF *** (1980, Fr.) PR:O
**EVERY MAN FOR HIMSELF AND GOD AGAINST
ALL ***½ (1975, Ger.) PR:A**
EVERY NIGHT AT EIGHT **½ (1935) PR:A
EVERY PICTURE TELLS A STORY **½
(1984, Brit.) PR:C
EVERY SATURDAY NIGHT ** (1936) PR:A
EVERY SPARROW MUST FALL * (1964) PR:C
EVERY TIME WE SAY GOODBYE **½ (1986) PR:C
EVERY WHICH WAY BUT LOOSE **½ (1978) PR:C
EVERYBODY DANCE ** (1936, Brit.) PR:A
EVERYBODY DOES IT *** (1949) PR:A
EVERYBODY GO HOME! ** (1962, Fr./It.) PR:A
EVERYBODY SING ** (1938) PR:A
EVERYBODY'S ALL-AMERICAN **½ (1988) PR:C-O
EVERYBODY'S BABY ** (1939) PR:A
EVERYBODY'S DANCIN' ** (1950) PR:A
EVERYBODY'S DOING IT ** (1938) PR:A
EVERYBODY'S HOBBY *½ (1939) PR:A
EVERYBODY'S OLD MAN ** (1936) PR:A
EVERYMAN'S LAW *½ (1936) PR:A
EVERYTHING BUT THE TRUTH ** (1956) PR:AA
**EVERYTHING HAPPENS AT NIGHT **½
(1939) PR:A**
EVERYTHING HAPPENS TO ME **
(1938, Brit.) PR:A
EVERYTHING I HAVE IS YOURS **½ (1952) PR:A
EVERYTHING IN LIFE *½ (1936, Brit.) PR:A
EVERYTHING IS RHYTHM ** (1940, Brit.) PR:A
EVERYTHING IS THUNDER ** (1936, Brit.) PR:A
EVERYTHING OKAY * (1936, Brit.) PR:A
**EVERYTHING YOU ALWAYS WANTED TO KNOW
ABOUT SEX BUT WERE AFRAID TO ASK **½
(1972) PR:O**
EVERYTHING'S DUCKY zero (1961) PR:A
EVERYTHING'S ON ICE ** (1939) PR:A
EVERYTHING'S ROSIE ** (1931) PR:A
EVICTORS, THE zero (1979) PR:O
EVIDENCE ** (1929) PR:A
EVIL, THE ** (1978) PR:O
EVIL COME, EVIL GO
(SEE:YELLOW CANARY, THE)
EVIL DEAD, THE ***½ (1983) PR:O
EVIL DEAD 2: DEAD BY DAWN * (1987) PR:O**
EVIL EYE ** (1964, It.) PR:A

EVIL GUN
(SEE:DAY OF THE EVIL GUN)
EVIL IN THE DEEP
(SEE:TREASURE OF JAMAICA REEF, THE)
EVIL MIND
(SEE:CLAIRVOYANT, THE)
**EVIL OF FRANKENSTEIN, THE *½
(1964, Brit.) PR:A**
EVIL THAT MEN DO, THE * (1984) PR:O
EVIL UNDER THE SUN ** (1982, Brit.) PR:A
EVILS OF THE NIGHT zero (1985) PR:O
EVILSPEAK *½ (1982) PR:O
EX-BAD BOY ** (1931) PR:A
EX-CHAMP ** (1939) PR:A
EX-FLAME * (1931) PR:A
EX-LADY *½ (1933) PR:A
EX-MRS. BRADFORD, THE ***½ (1936) PR:A
EXCALIBUR ** (1981) PR:C-O**
EXCESS BAGGAGE ** (1933, Brit.) PR:A
EXCLUSIVE **½ (1937) PR:A
EXCLUSIVE STORY ** (1936) PR:A
EXCUSE MY DUST ***½ (1951) PR:AA
EXCUSE MY GLOVE *½ (1936, Brit.) PR:A
EXECUTIONER, THE *½ (1970, Brit.) PR:C
EXECUTIONER PART II, THE zero (1984) PR:O
EXECUTIVE ACTION **½ (1973) PR:C
EXECUTIVE SUITE *** (1954) PR:A**
EXILE, THE * (1931) PR:C-O
EXILE, THE ** (1947) PR:A
EXILE EXPRESS **½ (1939) PR:A
EXILED TO SHANGHAI **½ (1937) PR:A
EXILES, THE **½ (1966) PR:A
**EXIT THE DRAGON, ENTER THE TIGER *
(1977, Hong Kong) PR:O**
EXODUS ** (1960) PR:C**
EXORCISM AT MIDNIGHT * (1966, Brit./US) PR:C-O
EXORCISM'S DAUGHTER zero (1974, Sp.) PR:O
EXORCIST, THE ** (1973) PR:O**
EXORCIST II: THE HERETIC * (1977) PR:O
EXOTIC ONES, THE zero (1968) PR:O
EXPENSIVE HUSBANDS **½ (1937) PR:A
EXPENSIVE WOMEN * (1931) PR:C
**EXPERIENCE PREFERRED... BUT NOT ESSENTIAL
***½ (1983, Brit.) PR:C**
EXPERIMENT ALCATRAZ ** (1950) PR:A
EXPERIMENT IN TERROR * (1962) PR:C**
EXPERIMENT PERILOUS ***½ (1944) PR:A
EXPERT, THE ** (1932) PR:A
EXPERT'S OPINION *½ (1935, Brit.) PR:A
EXPLORERS ** (1985) PR:C
EXPLOSION ** (1969, Can.) PR:O
EXPLOSIVE GENERATION, THE ** (1961) PR:C
EXPOSED *½ (1932) PR:A
EXPOSED * (1938) PR:A
EXPOSED ** (1947) PR:A
EXPOSED * (1983) PR:O**
EXPRESSO BONGO *½ (1959, Brit.) PR:C
EXTERMINATING ANGEL, THE **
(1967, Mex.) PR:O**
EXTERMINATOR, THE zero (1980) PR:O
EXTERMINATOR 2 zero (1984) PR:O
EXTERMINATORS, THE * (1965, Fr.) PR:A-C
**EXTERMINATORS OF THE YEAR 3000, THE *
(1985, It./Sp.) PR:O**
EXTORTION * (1938) PR:A
EXTRA DAY, THE *½ (1956, Brit.) PR:A
EXTRAORDINARY SEAMAN, THE zero (1969) PR:A
EXTRAVAGANCE * (1930) PR:A
EXTREME PREJUDICE * (1987) PR:O**
EXTREMITIES * (1986) PR:O**
EYE CREATURES, THE zero (1965) PR:A-C
EYE FOR AN EYE, AN **½ (1966) PR:C
EYE FOR AN EYE, AN *½ (1981) PR:O
EYE OF THE CAT *½ (1969) PR:C
EYE OF THE DEVIL ** (1967, Brit.) PR:C
EYE OF THE NEEDLE, THE ** (1965, It./Fr.) PR:C
EYE OF THE NEEDLE ***½ (1981, Brit.) PR:C-O
EYE OF THE TIGER *½ (1986) PR:O
EYE WITNESS ** (1950, Brit.) PR:A-C
EYEBALL zero (1978, It.) PR:O
EYES IN THE NIGHT ** (1942) PR:A
EYES OF A STRANGER zero (1980) PR:O
EYES OF ANNIE JONES, THE ** (1963, Brit.) PR:A
EYES OF FATE ** (1933, Brit.) PR:A
EYES OF FIRE *½ (1984) PR:O
EYES OF HELL
(SEE:MASK, THE)

EYES OF LAURA MARS ** (1978) PR:O
EYES OF TEXAS * (1948) PR:A**
EYES OF THE AMARYLLIS, THE *½ (1982) PR:A-C
EYES OF THE UNDERWORLD * (1943) PR:A
EYES OF THE WORLD, THE *½ (1930) PR:C
EYES THAT KILL *½ (1947, Brit.) PR:A
EYES, THE MOUTH, THE **½ (1982, It./Fr.) PR:O
EYES, THE SEA AND A BALL **½ (1968, Jap.) PR:A
EYES WITHOUT A FACE
(SEE:HORROR CHAMBER OF DR. FAUSTUS)
EYEWITNESS ** (1956, Brit.) PR:A
EYEWITNESS
(SEE:SUDDEN TERROR)
EYEWITNESS * (1981) PR:O**

F

F MAN ** (1936) PR:A
FABIAN OF THE YARD ** (1954, Brit.) PR:A
FABIOLA **½ (1951, It.) PR:A-C
FABLE, A **½ (1971) PR:O
FABULOUS ADVENTURES OF MARCO POLO, THE
(SEE:MARCO THE MAGNIFICENT)
FABULOUS BARON MUNCHHAUSEN, THE
(SEE:BARON MUNCHAUSEN)
FABULOUS DORSEYS, THE **½ (1947) PR:A
FABULOUS SENORITA, THE *½ (1952) PR:A
FABULOUS SUZANNE, THE ** (1946) PR:A
FABULOUS TEXAN, THE ** (1947) PR:A
FABULOUS WORLD OF JULES VERNE, THE ***
(1961, Czech.) PR:AA
FACE, THE
(SEE:MAGICIAN, THE)
FACE AT THE WINDOW, THE ** (1932, Brit.) PR:C
FACE AT THE WINDOW, THE ** (1939, Brit.) PR:C
FACE BEHIND THE MASK, THE **½ (1941) PR:A
FACE BEHIND THE SCAR ** (1940, Brit.) PR:A
FACE IN THE CROWD, A ** (1957) PR:C**
FACE IN THE FOG, A ** (1936) PR:A
FACE IN THE NIGHT
(SEE:MENACE IN THE NIGHT)
FACE IN THE RAIN, A **½ (1963) PR:A
FACE IN THE SKY ** (1933) PR:A
FACE OF A FUGITIVE ** (1959) PR:A
FACE OF A STRANGER (1964, Brit.) PR:A-C
FACE OF ANOTHER, THE *½ (1967, Jap.) PR:O
FACE OF EVE, THE
(SEE:EVE)
FACE OF EVIL
(SEE:DOCTOR BLOOD'S COFFIN)
FACE OF FEAR
(SEE:PEEPING TOM)
FACE OF FEAR
(SEE:FACE OF TERROR)
FACE OF FIRE ** (1959, US/Brit.) PR:C
FACE OF FU MANCHU, THE **½ (1965, Brit.) PR:O
FACE OF MARBLE, THE *½ (1946) PR:A
FACE OF TERROR ** (1964, Sp.) PR:C
FACE OF THE SCREAMING WEREWOLF *
(1959, Mex.) PR:A
FACE ON THE BARROOM FLOOR, THE *
(1932) PR:A
FACE TO FACE *** (1952) PR:A
FACE TO FACE ** (1967, It.) PR:A
FACE TO FACE **** (1976, Swed.) PR:O
FACE TO THE WIND
(SEE:COUNT YOUR BULLETS)
FACELESS MAN, THE
(SEE:COUNTERFEIT KILLER, THE)
FACELESS MEN, THE
(SEE:INCIDENT AT PHANTOM HILL)
FACELESS MONSTERS
(SEE:NIGHTMARE CASTLE)
FACES * (1934, Brit.) PR:A
FACES ** (1968) PR:O**
FACES IN THE DARK **½ (1960, Brit.) PR:A
FACES IN THE FOG ** (1944) PR:A
FACING THE MUSIC *½ (1933, Brit.) PR:A
FACING THE MUSIC * (1941, Brit.) PR:A
FACTS OF LIFE, THE
(SEE:QUARTET)
FACTS OF LIFE, THE **½ (1960) PR:A

FACTS OF LOVE ** (1949, Brit.) PR:A
FACTS OF MURDER, THE **½ (1965, It.) PR:O
FADE TO BLACK * (1980) PR:O
FAHRENHEIT 451 * (1966, Brit.) PR:C**
FAIL SAFE ** (1964) PR:C**
FAILURE, THE ** (1986, Neth.) PR:O
FAIR EXCHANGE **½ (1936, Brit.) PR:A
FAIR GAME zero (1985) PR:O
FAIR GAME ** (1986, Aus.) PR:O
FAIR WARNING **½ (1931) PR:A
FAIR WARNING ** (1937) PR:A
FAIR WIND TO JAVA **½ (1953) PR:A
FAITHFUL ** (1936, Brit.) PR:A
FAITHFUL CITY **½ (1952, Israel) PR:A
FAITHFUL HEART * (1933, Brit.) PR:A
FAITHFUL HEARTS
    (SEE:FAITHFUL HEART)
FAITHFUL IN MY FASHION *** (1946) PR:A
FAITHLESS ** (1932) PR:A
FAKE, THE ** (1953, Brit.) PR:A
FAKERS, THE
    (SEE:HELL'S BLOODY DEVILS)
FAKE'S PROGRESS * (1950, Brit.) PR:A
FALCON AND THE CO-EDS, THE *** (1943) PR:A
FALCON AND THE SNOWMAN, THE * (1985) PR:O**
FALCON FIGHTERS, THE ** (1970, Jap.) PR:C
FALCON IN DANGER, THE **½ (1943) PR:A
FALCON IN HOLLYWOOD, THE **½ (1944) PR:A
FALCON IN MEXICO, THE * (1944) PR:A**
FALCON IN SAN FRANCISCO, THE ** (1945) PR:A
FALCON OUT WEST, THE **½ (1944) PR:A
FALCON STRIKES BACK, THE **½ (1943) PR:A
FALCON TAKES OVER, THE * (1942) PR:A**
FALCON'S ADVENTURE, THE **½ (1946) PR:A
FALCON'S ALIBI, THE *** (1946) PR:A
FALCON'S BROTHER, THE * (1942) PR:A**
FALL GIRL, THE
    (SEE:LISETTE)
FALL GUY **½ (1947) PR:C
FALL GUY *** (1985, Jap.) PR:C
FALL GUY, THE ** (1930) PR:A
FALL GUY, THE
    (SEE:FALLGUY, THE)
FALL OF EVE, THE ** (1929) PR:A
FALL OF ROME, THE ** (1963, It.) PR:C
FALL OF THE HOUSE OF USHER, THE * (1952, Brit.) PR:C
FALL OF THE HOUSE OF USHER, THE
    (SEE:HOUSE OF USHER)
FALL OF THE HOUSE OF USHER, THE * (1980) PR:O
FALL OF THE ROMAN EMPIRE, THE **½ (1964) PR:O
FALLEN ANGEL ***½ (1945) PR:A
FALLEN IDOL, THE *** (1949, Brit.) PR:A**
FALLEN SPARROW, THE ***½ (1943) PR:C
FALLGUY *½ (1962) PR:A
FALLING FOR YOU ** (1933, Brit.) PR:A
FALLING IN LOVE
    (SEE:TROUBLE AHEAD)
FALLING IN LOVE ** (1984) PR:C
FALLING IN LOVE AGAIN *½ (1980) PR:C
FALSE COLORS ** (1943) PR:A
FALSE EVIDENCE ** (1937, Brit.) PR:A-C
FALSE FACE
    (SEE:SCALPEL)
FALSE FACES *½ (1932) PR:A
FALSE FACES * (1943) PR:A
FALSE MADONNA * (1932) PR:A
FALSE PARADISE ** (1948) PR:A
FALSE PRETENSES *½ (1935) PR:A
FALSE RAPTURE *½ (1941) PR:A
FALSE WITNESS
    (SEE:ZIGZAG)
FALSTAFF
    (SEE:CHIMES AT MIDNIGHT)
FAME ** (1936, Brit.) PR:A
FAME **½ (1980) PR:C
FAME IS THE SPUR *½ (1947, Brit.) PR:A
FAME STREET *½ (1932) PR:A
FAMILY, THE ** (1974, Fr./It.) PR:O
FAMILY, THE ***½ (1987, It./Fr.) PR:A
FAMILY AFFAIR ** (1954, Brit.) PR:A
FAMILY AFFAIR, A *** (1937) PR:AA
FAMILY BUSINESS (1987, Fr.) PR:C
FAMILY DIARY ** (1963, It.) PR:A
FAMILY DOCTOR
    (SEE:RX MURDER)
FAMILY GAME, THE * (1984, Jap.) PR:C**
FAMILY HONEYMOON **½ (1948) PR:A
FAMILY HONOR *½ (1973) PR:O
FAMILY JEWELS, THE **½ (1965) PR:A
FAMILY LIFE **½ (1971, Brit.) PR:O
FAMILY NEXT DOOR, THE * (1939) PR:A
FAMILY PLOT ***½ (1976) PR:C
FAMILY SECRET, THE *** (1951) PR:A
FAMILY WAY, THE ***½ (1966, Brit.) PR:O

FAMOUS FERGUSON CASE, THE * (1932) PR:A
FAN, THE ** (1949) PR:A
FAN, THE ** (1981) PR:C-O
FANATIC, THE
    (SEE:LAST HORROR FILM, THE)
FANATIC
    (SEE:DIE! DIE! MY DARLING)
FANCY BAGGAGE ** (1929) PR:A
FANCY PANTS **½ (1950) PR:A
FANDANGO ** (1970) PR:O
FANDANGO ** (1985) PR:C
FANFAN THE TULIP **** (1952, Fr.) PR:A
FANGELSE
    (SEE:DEVIL'S WANTON, THE)
FANGS OF THE ARCTIC ** (1953) PR:A
FANGS OF THE WILD ** (1954) PR:A
FANNY ***½ (1948, Fr.) PR:A-C
FANNY * (1961) PR:A-C**
FANNY AND ALEXANDER ** (1983, Swed./Fr./Ger.) PR:C-O**
FANNY BY GASLIGHT
    (SEE:MAN OF EVIL)
FANNY FOLEY HERSELF *½ (1931) PR:A
FANNY HILL: MEMOIRS OF A WOMAN OF PLEASURE zero (1965) PR:O
FAN'S NOTES, A ** (1972, Can.) PR:C
FANTASIA *** (1940) PR:AA**
FANTASIES zero (1981) PR:O
FANTASM zero (1976, Aus.) PR:O
FANTASTIC COMEDY, A **½ (1975, Rum.) PR:C
FANTASTIC INVASION OF THE PLANET EARTH, THE
    (SEE:BUBBLE, THE)
FANTASTIC INVENTION, THE
    (SEE:FABULOUS WORLD OF JULES, THE)
FANTASTIC PLANET * (1973, Fr./Czech.) PR:A**
FANTASTIC THREE, THE *** (1967, It./Ger./Fr./Yugo.) PR:A
FANTASTIC VOYAGE * (1966) PR:A**
FANTASTICA *½ (1980, Can./Fr.) PR:C-O
FANTASY MAN * (1984, Aus.) PR:O
FANTOMAS *** (1966, Fr./It.) PR:AA
FANTOMAS STRIKES BACK ** (1965, Fr./It.) PR:A
FAR COUNTRY, THE ** (1955) PR:A**
FAR FROM DALLAS ** (1972, Fr.) PR:C
FAR FROM POLAND ** (1984) PR:C
FAR FROM THE MADDING CROWD **½ (1967, Brit.) PR:A
FAR FRONTIER, THE ** (1949) PR:A
FAR HORIZONS, THE ***½ (1955) PR:A
FAR NORTH *½ (1988) PR:C
FAR SHORE, THE *** (1976, Can.) PR:O
FARARUV KONEC
    (SEE:END OF A PRIEST)
FAREWELL AGAIN
    (SEE:TROOPSHIP)
FAREWELL, DOVES *½ (1962, USSR) PR:A
FAREWELL, FRIEND ** (1968, Fr./It.) PR:O
FAREWELL, MY BELOVED ** (1969, Jap.) PR:O
FAREWELL, MY LOVELY
    (SEE:MURDER, MY SWEET)
FAREWELL, MY LOVELY * (1975) PR:C-O**
FAREWELL PERFORMANCE ** (1963, Brit.) PR:A-C
FAREWELL TO ARMS, A **½ (1957) PR:C
FAREWELL TO CINDERELLA ** (1937, Brit.) PR:A
FAREWELL TO LOVE **½ (1931, Brit.) PR:A
FARGO ** (1952) PR:A
FARGO
    (SEE:WILD SEED)
FARGO EXPRESS *½ (1933) PR:A
FARGO KID, THE ** (1941) PR:A
FARM, THE
    (SEE:CURSE, THE)
FARM GIRL
    (SEE:FARMER'S OTHER DAUGHTER, THE)
FARMER, THE zero (1977) PR:O
FARMER IN THE DELL, THE ** (1936) PR:A
FARMER TAKES A WIFE, THE *** (1935) PR:A
FARMER TAKES A WIFE, THE ** (1953) PR:A
FARMER'S DAUGHTER, THE **½ (1940) PR:A
FARMER'S DAUGHTER, THE ***½ (1947) PR:AA
FARMER'S OTHER DAUGHTER, THE ** (1965) PR:A
FARMER'S WIFE, THE *½ (1941, Brit.) PR:A
FAREWELL TO ARMS, A ** (1932) PR:A**
FASCINATION *½ (1931, Brit.) PR:A
FASCIST, THE *** (1965, It.) PR:A
FASHION HOUSE OF DEATH
    (SEE:BLOOD AND BLACK LACE)
FASHION MODEL **½ (1945) PR:A
FASHIONS IN LOVE ** (1929) PR:A-C
FASHIONS OF 1934 **½ (1934) PR:A
FAST AND FURIOUS **½ (1939) PR:A
FAST AND LOOSE * (1930) PR:A
FAST AND LOOSE *** (1939) PR:A
FAST AND LOOSE ** (1954, Brit.) PR:A
FAST AND SEXY ** (1960, Fr./It.) PR:A
FAST AND THE FURIOUS, THE ** (1954) PR:A

FAST BREAK *½ (1979) PR:A
FAST BULLETS ** (1936) PR:A
FAST CHARLIE... THE MOONBEAM RIDER * (1979) PR:C
FAST COMPANIONS ** (1932) PR:A
FAST COMPANY ** (1929) PR:A
FAST COMPANY ** (1938) PR:A
FAST COMPANY ** (1953) PR:A
FAST FORWARD ** (1985) PR:A-C
FAST LADY, THE ** (1963, Brit.) PR:A
FAST LIFE *½ (1929) PR:A
FAST LIFE *½ (1932) PR:A
FAST ON THE DRAW * (1950) PR:A
FAST TIMES AT RIDGEMONT HIGH **½ (1982) PR:O
FAST-WALKING *½ (1982) PR:O
FAST WORKERS * (1933) PR:A
FASTEST GUITAR ALIVE, THE * (1967) PR:A
FASTEST GUN ALIVE **½ (1956) PR:A
FASTEST GUN, THE
    (SEE:QUICK GUN, THE)
FAT CITY ** (1972) PR:C**
FAT GUY GOES NUTZOID!! * (1986) PR:O
FAT MAN, THE ** (1951) PR:A
FAT SPY * (1966) PR:A
FATAL ATTRACTION **½ (1987) PR:O
FATAL BEAUTY *½ (1987) PR:O
FATAL DESIRE ** (1953) PR:C
FATAL HOUR, THE ** (1937, Brit.) PR:A
FATAL LADY * (1936) PR:A
FATAL NIGHT, THE ** (1948, Brit.) PR:A
FATAL WITNESS, THE * (1945) PR:A
FATE IS THE HUNTER *** (1964) PR:A
FATE TAKES A HAND **½ (1962, Brit.) PR:A
FATHER * (1967, Hung.) PR:C**
FATHER AND SON ** (1929) PR:A
FATHER BROWN
    (SEE:DETECTIVE, THE)
FATHER BROWN, DETECTIVE ** (1935) PR:A
FATHER CAME TOO ** (1964, Brit.) PR:A
FATHER GOOSE ***½ (1964) PR:AA
FATHER IS A BACHELOR *½ (1950) PR:A
FATHER IS A PRINCE ** (1940) PR:A
FATHER MAKES GOOD ** (1950) PR:A
FATHER OF A SOLDIER **½ (1966, USSR) PR:C
FATHER OF THE BRIDE ***½ (1950) PR:AA
FATHER O'FLYNN *½ (1938, Ireland) PR:A
FATHER STEPS OUT ** (1937, Brit.) PR:A
FATHER TAKES A WIFE *½ (1941) PR:A
FATHER TAKES THE AIR **½ (1951) PR:A
FATHER WAS A FULLBACK **½ (1949) PR:A
FATHERS AND SONS ** (1960, USSR) PR:A
FATHER'S DILEMMA *** (1952, It.) PR:A
FATHER'S DOING FINE ** (1952, Brit.) PR:A
FATHER'S LITTLE DIVIDEND * (1951) PR:AA**
FATHER'S SON ** (1931) PR:A
FATHER'S SON * (1941) PR:A
FATHER'S WILD GAME *½ (1950) PR:A
FATHOM * (1967) PR:A
FATSO * (1980) PR:A
FATTY FINN ** (1980, Aus.) PR:A-C
FAUSSES INGENUES
    (SEE:RED LIPS)
FAUST **½ (1963, Ger.) PR:A
FAUST * (1964) PR:A
FAVORITES OF THE MOON ***½ (1985, Fr./It.) PR:C
FBI CODE 98 * (1964) PR:A
FBI CONTRO DR. MABUSE
    (SEE:RETURN OF DR. MABUSE, THE)
FBI GIRL *½ (1951) PR:A
FBI STORY, THE *** (1959) PR:C
FEAR *** (1946) PR:C
FEAR * (1956, Ger./It.) PR:A**
FEAR, THE ** (1967, Gr.) PR:O
FEAR AND DESIRE *** (1953) PR:C
FEAR CHAMBER, THE * (1968, US/Mex.) PR:C
FEAR CITY **½ (1984) PR:O
FEAR EATS THE SOUL *** (1974, Ger.) PR:O
FEAR IN THE NIGHT *** (1947) PR:C-O
FEAR IN THE NIGHT * (1972, Brit.) PR:C
FEAR IS THE KEY ** (1973) PR:C
FEAR NO EVIL ** (1981) PR:O
FEAR NO MORE ** (1961) PR:C
FEAR SHIP, THE * (1933, Brit.) PR:A
FEAR STRIKES OUT ** (1957) PR:C**
FEARLESS FAGAN *** (1952) PR:AA
FEARLESS FRANK **½ (1967) PR:A
FEARLESS VAMPIRE KILLERS, OR PARDON ME BUT YOUR TEETH ARE IN MY NECK, THE ***½ (1967) PR:C
FEARMAKERS, THE *** (1958) PR:A
FEAST OF FLESH
    (SEE:NIGHT OF THE LIVING DEAD)
FEATHER, THE * (1929, Brit.) PR:A
FEATHER IN HER HAT, A *½ (1935) PR:A
FEATHER YOUR NEST ** (1937, Brit.) PR:A

FEATHERED SERPENT, THE *½ (1934, Brit.) PR:A
FEATHERED SERPENT, THE *½ (1948) PR:A
FEDERAL AGENT *½ (1936) PR:A
FEDERAL AGENT AT LARGE *½ (1950) PR:A
FEDERAL BULLETS ** (1937) PR:A
FEDERAL FUGITIVES *½ (1941) PR:A
FEDERAL MAN ** (1950) PR:A
FEDERAL MAN-HUNT **½ (1939) PR:A
FEDERICO FELLINI'S 8 1/2
(SEE:8 1/2)
FEDERICO FELLINI'S INTERVISTA
(SEE:INTERVISTA)
FEDORA *** (1946, It.) PR:A
FEDORA ** (1978, Ger./Fr.) PR:C
FEEDBACK * (1979) PR:C
FEEL THE HEAT
(SEE:CATCH THE HEAT)
FEELIN' GOOD * (1966) PR:A
FEET FIRST *** (1930) PR:A
FEET OF CLAY * (1960, Brit.) PR:A
FELDMANN CASE, THE ***½ (1987, Norway) PR:O
FELLER NEEDS A FRIEND *½ (1932) PR:A
FELLINI SATYRICON ** (1969, Fr./It.) PR:C-O**
FELLINI'S CASANOVA
(SEE:CASANOVA)
FELLINI'S ROMA
(SEE:ROMA)
FEMALE ** (1933) PR:A
FEMALE, THE ** (1960, Fr.) PR:C
FEMALE ANIMAL, THE *½ (1958) PR:A
FEMALE BUNCH, THE zero (1969) PR:O
FEMALE BUTCHER, THE zero (1972, It./Sp.) PR:O
FEMALE FIENDS **½ (1958, Brit.) PR:A
FEMALE FUGITIVE ** (1938) PR:A
FEMALE JUNGLE, THE * (1955) PR:C
FEMALE ON THE BEACH ** (1955) PR:A-C
FEMALE PRINCE, THE * (1966, Hong Kong) PR:C
FEMALE PRISONER, THE
(SEE:LA PRISONNIERE)
FEMALE RESPONSE, THE * (1972) PR:O
FEMALE TRAP, THE
(SEE:NAME OF THE GAME IS KILL, THE)
FEMALE TROUBLE * (1975) PR:O
FEMININE TOUCH, THE *** (1941, Brit.) PR:A
FEMININE TOUCH, THE
(SEE:GENTLE TOUCH, THE)
FEMMES DE PERSONNE **½ (1986, Fr.) PR:O
FEMMES D'UN ETE
(SEE:LOVE ON THE RIVIERA)
FEMMINA ** (1968, Fr./It./Ger.) PR:C
FEMMINE DI LUSSO
(SEE:LOVE, THE ITALIAN WAY)
FENCE RIDERS * (1950) PR:A
**FERNANDEL THE DRESSMAKER **½
(1957, Fr.) PR:A**
FEROCIOUS PAL * (1934) PR:AA
FERRIS BUELLER'S DAY OFF ** (1986) PR:C
FERRY ACROSS THE MERSEY ** (1964, Brit.) PR:A
FERRY TO HONG KONG ** (1959, Brit.) PR:A
FEUD MAKER *½ (1938) PR:A
FEUD OF THE RANGE *½ (1939) PR:A
FEUD OF THE TRAIL * (1938) PR:A
FEUD OF THE WEST * (1936) PR:A
FEUDIN' FOOLS * (1952) PR:A
FEUDIN', FUSSIN' AND A-FIGHTIN' **½
(1948) PR:A
FEVER HEAT * (1968) PR:A
FEVER IN THE BLOOD, A ** (1961) PR:A
FEVER PITCH * (1985) PR:C-O
FEW BULLETS MORE, A ** (1968, It./Sp.) PR:A
FFOLKES *½ (1980, Brit.) PR:C
FIANCES, THE ** (1964, It.) PR:A
FIASCO IN MILAN ** (1963, Fr./It.) PR:A
FICKLE FINGER OF FATE, THE **½
(1967, Sp./US) PR:A
FIDDLER ON THE ROOF ***½ (1971) PR:AA
FIDDLERS THREE *½ (1944, Brit.) PR:A
FIDDLIN' BUCKAROO, THE *½ (1934) PR:A
FIDELIO **½ (1961, Aust.) PR:A
FIDELIO **½ (1970, Ger.) PR:A
FIELDS OF HONOR
(SEE:SHENANDOAH)
FIEND * (1980) PR:O
FIEND OF DOPE ISLAND *½ (1961) PR:C
FIEND WHO WALKED THE WEST, THE **
(1958) PR:O
FIEND WITH THE SYNTHETIC BRAIN
(SEE:BLOOD OF GHASTLY HORROR)
FIEND WITHOUT A FACE * (1958) PR:C-O**
FIENDISH GHOULS, THE
(SEE:MANIA)
**FIENDISH PLOT OF DR. FU MANCHU, THE *
(1980) PR:C**
FIENDS, THE
(SEE:DIABOLIQUE)
FIERCEST HEART, THE ** (1961) PR:A
FIERY SPUR
(SEE:HOT SPUR)
FIESTA ** (1947) PR:A
15 FROM ROM
(SEE:OPIATE'67)
FIFTEEN MAIDEN LANE * (1936) PR:A
FIFTEEN WIVES * (1934) PR:A
FIFTH AVENUE GIRL **½ (1939) PR:A
FIFTH FLOOR, THE * (1980) PR:O
FIFTH HORSEMAN IS FEAR, THE ***
(1968, Czech.) PR:C
FIFTH MUSKETEER, THE
(SEE:BEHIND THE IRON MASK)
FIFTY FATHOMS DEEP *½ (1931) PR:A
55 DAYS AT PEKING * (1963) PR:A**
FIFTY MILLION FRENCHMEN ** (1931) PR:AA
FIFTY ROADS TO TOWN *** (1937) PR:A
52ND STREET * (1937) PR:A
FIFTY-SHILLING BOXER ** (1937, Brit.) PR:A
50,000 B.C. (BEFORE CLOTHING) * (1963) PR:O
52 MILES TO MIDNIGHT
(SEE:HOT RODS TO HELL)
52 MILES TO TERROR
(SEE:HOT RODS TO HELL)
52 PICK-UP **½ (1986) PR:O
FIGHT FOR ROME **½ (1969, Ger./Rum.) PR:A
FIGHT FOR THE GLORY *½ (1970, Jap.) PR:C
FIGHT FOR YOUR LADY * (1937) PR:A
FIGHT FOR YOUR LIFE zero (1977) PR:O
FIGHT TO THE FINISH, A ** (1937) PR:A
FIGHT TO THE LAST ** (1938, Chi.) PR:C
FIGHTER, THE **½ (1952) PR:A
FIGHTER ATTACK **½ (1953) PR:A
FIGHTER SQUADRON ***½ (1948) PR:A
FIGHTING BACK ** (1948) PR:A
FIGHTING BACK
(SEE:DEATH VENGEANCE)
FIGHTING BACK **½ (1983, Brit.) PR:C
FIGHTING BILL CARSON *½ (1945) PR:A
FIGHTING BILL FARGO ** (1942) PR:A
FIGHTING BUCKAROO, THE *½ (1943) PR:A
FIGHTING CABALLERO *½ (1935) PR:A
FIGHTING CARAVANS ** (1931) PR:A
FIGHTING CHAMP * (1933) PR:A
FIGHTING CHANCE, THE * (1955) PR:A
FIGHTING COAST GUARD ** (1951) PR:A
FIGHTING CODE, THE *½ (1934) PR:A
FIGHTING COWBOY *½ (1933) PR:A
FIGHTING DEPUTY, THE * (1937) PR:A
FIGHTING FATHER DUNNE ** (1948) PR:A
FIGHTING FOOL, THE * (1932) PR:A
FIGHTING FOOLS ** (1949) PR:A
FIGHTING FRONTIER **½ (1943) PR:AA
FIGHTING FURY
(SEE:OUTLAW'S HIGHWAY)
FIGHTING GENTLEMAN, THE * (1932) PR:A
FIGHTING GRINGO, THE **½ (1939) PR:A
FIGHTING GUARDSMAN, THE ** (1945) PR:A
FIGHTING HERO * (1934) PR:A
FIGHTING KENTUCKIAN, THE * (1949) PR:A**
FIGHTING LAWMAN, THE ** (1953) PR:A
FIGHTING LEGION, THE *½ (1930) PR:A
FIGHTING MAD * (1939) PR:A
FIGHTING MAD **½ (1948) PR:A
FIGHTING MAD * (1957, Brit.) PR:A-C
FIGHTING MAD **½ (1976) PR:C
FIGHTING MAN OF THE PLAINS ** (1949) PR:A
FIGHTING MARSHAL, THE ** (1932) PR:AA
FIGHTING O'FLYNN, THE *** (1949) PR:A
FIGHTING PARSON, THE * (1933) PR:A
FIGHTING PIMPERNEL, THE **½ (1950, Brit.) PR:A
FIGHTING PIONEERS ** (1935) PR:A
FIGHTING PLAYBOY zero (1937) PR:A
**FIGHTING PRINCE OF DONEGAL, THE **
(1966, Brit.) PR:AA**
FIGHTING RANGER, THE **½ (1934) PR:A
FIGHTING RANGER, THE *½ (1948) PR:A
FIGHTING REDHEAD, THE ** (1950) PR:A
FIGHTING RENEGADE ** (1939) PR:AA
FIGHTING ROOKIE, THE * (1934) PR:A
FIGHTING SEABEES, THE * (1944) PR:C**
FIGHTING SHADOWS *½ (1935) PR:A
FIGHTING SHERIFF, THE * (1931) PR:A
FIGHTING 69TH, THE ***** (1940) PR:A
FIGHTING STALLION, THE * (1950) PR:A
FIGHTING STOCK ** (1935, Brit.) PR:A
FIGHTING SULLIVANS, THE
(SEE:SULLIVANS, THE)
FIGHTING TEXAN * (1937) PR:A
FIGHTING TEXANS * (1933) PR:A
FIGHTING THOROUGHBREDS **½ (1939) PR:A
FIGHTING THRU ** (1931) PR:A
FIGHTING TROOPER, THE * (1935) PR:A
FIGHTING TROUBLE ** (1956) PR:A
FIGHTING VALLEY * (1943) PR:A
FIGHTING VIGILANTES, THE ** (1947) PR:A
FIGHTING WILDCATS, THE ** (1957, Brit.) PR:A-C
FIGHTING YOUTH ** (1935) PR:A
FIGURES IN A LANDSCAPE ** (1970, Brit.) PR:C
FILE OF THE GOLDEN GOOSE, THE **½
(1969, Brit.) PR:C
FILE ON THELMA JORDAN, THE ***½
(1950) PR:A-C
FILE 113 * (1932) PR:A
FILES FROM SCOTLAND YARD *½
(1951, Brit.) PR:A
FILM WITHOUT A NAME ** (1950, Ger.) PR:A
FINAL APPOINTMENT *½ (1954, Brit.) PR:A
FINAL ASSIGNMENT * (1980, Can.) PR:C
**FINAL CHAPTER—WALKING TALL zero
(1977) PR:O**
FINAL CHORD, THE ** (1936, Ger.) PR:C
FINAL COLUMN, THE * (1955, Brit.) PR:A
FINAL COMEDOWN, THE ** (1972) PR:O
FINAL CONFLICT, THE * (1981) PR:O
FINAL COUNTDOWN, THE ** (1980) PR:C
FINAL CUT, THE ** (1980, Aus.) PR:O
FINAL EDITION ** (1932) PR:A
FINAL EXAM zero (1981) PR:O
FINAL EXECUTIONER, THE * (1986, It.) PR:O
FINAL HOUR, THE * (1936) PR:A
FINAL JUSTICE ** (1985) PR:O
FINAL OPTION, THE * (1982, Brit.) PR:O
FINAL PROGRAMME, THE
(SEE:LAST DAYS OF MAN ON EARTH, THE)
FINAL RECKONING, THE * (1932, Brit.) PR:A
FINAL TAKE: THE GOLDEN AGE OF MOVIES ***
(1986, Jap.) PR:A
FINAL TERROR, THE * (1983) PR:O
FINAL TEST, THE * (1953, Brit.) PR:A**
FINAL WAR, THE *** (1960, Jap.) PR:C
FINALLY SUNDAY
(SEE:CONFIDENTIALLY YOURS)
FINCHE DURA LA TEMPESTA
(SEE:TORPEDO BAY)
FIND THE BLACKMAILER * (1943) PR:A
FIND THE LADY * (1936, Brit.) PR:A
FIND THE LADY ** (1956, Brit.) PR:A
FIND THE WITNESS * (1937) PR:A
FINDERS KEEPERS ** (1951) PR:AA
FINDERS KEEPERS ** (1966, Brit.) PR:A
FINDERS KEEPERS **½ (1984) PR:C-O
FINDERS KEEPERS, LOVERS WEEPERS *
(1968) PR:O
FINE FEATHERS * (1937, Brit.) PR:A
FINE MADNESS, A **½ (1966) PR:C
FINE MESS, A *½ (1986) PR:A-C
FINE PAIR, A ** (1969, It.) PR:C
FINGER MAN * (1955) PR:A
FINGER OF GUILT **½ (1956, Brit.) PR:A
FINGER ON THE TRIGGER ** (1965, US/Sp.) PR:A
FINGER POINTS, THE *** (1931) PR:C
FINGERMAN, THE * (1963, Fr.) PR:C**
FINGERPRINTS DON'T LIE * (1951) PR:A
FINGERS ** (1940, Brit.) PR:A
FINGERS * (1978) PR:O**
FINGERS AT THE WINDOW *** (1942) PR:C
FINIAN'S RAINBOW **½ (1968) PR:A
FINISHING SCHOOL *½ (1934) PR:A
FINN AND HATTIE ** (1931) PR:A
FINNEGANS WAKE *** (1965) PR:A
FINNEY **½ (1969) PR:A
FINO A FARTI MALE ** (1969, Fr./It.) PR:O
FIRE AND ICE *½ (1983) PR:C

Finding entries in **THE MOTION PICTURE GUIDE ™**

Years	Volumes
1929-83	Volumes I-IX
1984	Volume IX
1985	1986 ANNUAL
1986	1987 ANNUAL
1987	1988 ANNUAL
1988	1989 ANNUAL

STAR RATINGS

★★★★★	Masterpiece
★★★★	Excellent
★★★	Good
★★	Fair
★	Poor
zero	Without Merit

PARENTAL RECOMMENDATION (PR:)

AA	Good for Children
A	Acceptable for Children
C	Cautionary, some objectionable scenes
O	Objectionable for Children

BOLD: Films on Videocassette

FIRE AND ICE ** (1987) PR:A
FIRE DOWN BELOW **½ (1957, US/Brit.) PR:C
FIRE HAS BEEN ARRANGED, A **
  (1935, Brit.) PR:A
FIRE IN THE FLESH ** (1964, Fr.) PR:A
FIRE IN THE NIGHT zero (1986) PR:O
FIRE IN THE STONE, THE **½ (1983, Aus.) PR:AA
FIRE IN THE STRAW *** (1943, Fr.) PR:A
FIRE MAIDENS FROM OUTER SPACE **
  (1956, Brit.) PR:A
FIRE OVER AFRICA ** (1954, Brit.) PR:A
FIRE OVER ENGLAND **** (1937, Brit.) PR:A
FIRE RAISERS, THE ** (1933, Brit.) PR:A
FIRE SALE * (1977) PR:A-C
FIRE WITH FIRE * (1986) PR:O
FIRE WITHIN, THE *** (1964, Fr./It.) PR:O
FIREBALL, THE ** (1950) PR:A
FIREBALL 590 ** (1966) PR:A
FIREBALL JUNGLE ** (1968) PR:C
FIREBIRD, THE *½ (1934) PR:A
FIREBIRD 2015 AD *½ (1981) PR:O
FIREBRAND, THE ** (1962) PR:C
FIREBRAND JORDAN * (1930) PR:A
FIREBRANDS OF ARIZONA ** (1944) PR:A
FIRECHASERS, THE * (1970, Brit.) PR:C
FIRECRACKER zero (1981) PR:O
FIRECREEK ** (1968) PR:C
FIRED WIFE * (1943) PR:A
FIREFLY, THE ** (1937) PR:A
FIREFOX ***½ (1982) PR:C
FIREHOUSE zero (1987) PR:O
FIREMAN, SAVE MY CHILD *** (1932) PR:A
FIREMAN SAVE MY CHILD *** (1954) PR:A
FIREMAN'S BALL, THE ***½ (1968, Czech.) PR:C
FIREPOWER *½ (1979, Brit.) PR:O
FIRES OF FATE * (1932, Brit.) PR:A
FIRES ON THE PLAIN *** (1962, Jap.) PR:O
FIRESTARTER **½ (1984) PR:O
FIRETRAP, THE *½ (1935) PR:A
FIREWALKER *½ (1986) PR:A
FIRM MAN, THE ** (1975, Aus.) PR:C
FIRST A GIRL **½ (1935, Brit.) PR:A
FIRST AID * (1931) PR:A
FIRST AND THE LAST, THE
  (SEE:21 DAYS)
FIRST BABY ** (1936) PR:A
FIRST BLOOD zero (1982) PR:O
FIRST COMES COURAGE **½ (1943) PR:A
FIRST DEADLY SIN, THE *½ (1980) PR:O
FIRST FAMILY zero (1980) PR:O
FIRST GENTLEMAN, THE
  (SEE:AFFAIRS OF A ROGUE)
FIRST GREAT TRAIN ROBBERY, THE
  (SEE:GREAT TRAIN ROBBERY)
FIRST HUNDRED YEARS
  (SEE:FIRST ONE HUNDRED YEARS)
FIRST LADY *** (1937) PR:A
FIRST LEGION, THE *** (1951) PR:A
FIRST LOVE **½ (1939) PR:A
FIRST LOVE **½ (1970, Ger./Switz.) PR:C-O
FIRST LOVE * (1977) PR:O
FIRST MAN INTO SPACE **½ (1959, Brit.) PR:A
FIRST MARINES
  (SEE:TRIPOLI)
FIRST MEN IN THE MOON ** (1964, Brit.) PR:A
FIRST MONDAY IN OCTOBER **½ (1981) PR:O
FIRST MRS. FRASER, THE ** (1932, Brit.) PR:A
FIRST NAME: CARMEN ***½ (1984, Fr.) PR:O
FIRST NIGHT * (1937, Brit.) PR:A
FIRST NUDIE MUSICAL, THE * (1976) PR:O
FIRST OF THE FEW, THE
  (SEE:SPITFIRE)
FIRST OFFENCE ** (1936, Brit.) PR:A
FIRST OFFENDERS *½ (1939) PR:A
FIRST 100 YEARS, THE **½ (1938) PR:A
FIRST REBEL, THE
  (SEE:ALLEGHENY UPRISING)
FIRST SPACESHIP ON VENUS ***
  (1960, Ger./Pol.) PR:A
FIRST START ** (1953, Pol.) PR:A
FIRST TASTE OF LOVE ** (1962, Fr.) PR:C
FIRST TEXAN, THE ** (1956) PR:A
FIRST TIME, THE ** (1952) PR:A
FIRST TIME, THE * (1969) PR:C
FIRST TIME, THE *** (1978, Fr.) PR:O
FIRST TIME, THE ** (1983) PR:O
FIRST TO FIGHT *** (1967) PR:C
FIRST TRAVELING SALESLADY, THE * (1956) PR:A
FIRST TURN-ON?, THE zero (1984) PR:O
FIRST WIFE
  (SEE:WIVES AND LOVERS)
FIRST YANK INTO TOKYO ** (1945) PR:C
FIRST YEAR, THE **½ (1932) PR:A
FIRSTBORN *** (1984) PR:C
FISH CALLED WANDA, A ***½ (1988) PR:C-O
FISH HAWK * (1981, Can.) PR:AA
FISH THAT SAVED PITTSBURGH, THE *
  (1979) PR:AA

FISHERMAN'S WHARF *½ (1939) PR:AA
F.I.S.T. *** (1978) PR:A-C
FIST IN HIS POCKET ** (1968, It.) PR:O
FIST OF FEAR, TOUCH OF DEATH zero
  (1980) PR:O
FIST OF FURY
  (SEE:FISTS OF FURY)
FISTFUL OF CHOPSTICKS, A
  (SEE:THEY CALL ME BRUCE)
FISTFUL OF DOLLARS, A ***
  (1964, It./Ger./Span.) PR:C
FISTFUL OF DYNAMITE, A
  (SEE:DUCK, YOU SUCKER)
FISTS OF FURY ** (1973, Chi.) PR:O
FIT FOR A KING ** (1937) PR:A
FITZCARRALDO **** (1982) PR:C
FIVE AND TEN **½ (1931) PR:A
FIVE ANGLES ON MURDER **½ (1950, Brit.) PR:A
FIVE ASHORE IN SINGAPORE
  (SEE:SINGAPORE, SINGAPORE)
FIVE BLOODY GRAVES
  (SEE:GUN RIDERS)
FIVE BOLD WOMEN ** (1960) PR:A
FIVE BRANDED WOMEN ***½ (1960) PR:C
FIVE CAME BACK **½ (1939) PR:A
FIVE CARD STUD ** (1968) PR:C
FIVE CORNERS **½ (1988, US/Brit.) PR:O
FIVE DAYS
  (SEE:PAID TO KILL)
FIVE DAYS FROM HOME *½ (1978) PR:C
FIVE DAYS ONE SUMMER * (1982) PR:A
FIVE EASY PIECES ***** (1970) PR:C-O
FIVE FINGER EXERCISE *½ (1962) PR:A
FIVE FINGERS **** (1952) PR:A
FIVE FINGERS OF DEATH *
  (1973, Hong Kong) PR:O
FIVE GATES TO HELL *** (1959) PR:O
FIVE GIANTS FROM TEXAS ** (1966, It./Sp.) PR:C
FIVE GOLDEN DRAGONS **½ (1967, Brit.) PR:O
FIVE GOLDEN HOURS **½ (1961, Brit.) PR:A
FIVE GRAVES TO CAIRO *** (1943) PR:A
FIVE GUNS TO TOMBSTONE *½ (1961) PR:A
FIVE GUNS WEST ** (1955) PR:A
FIVE LITTLE PEPPERS AND HOW THEY GREW **
  (1939) PR:AA
FIVE LITTLE PEPPERS AT HOME *½ (1940) PR:AA
FIVE LITTLE PEPPERS IN TROUBLE * (1940) PR:A
FIVE MAN ARMY, THE ** (1970, It.) PR:C
FIVE MILES TO MIDNIGHT *
  (1963, US/Fr./It.) PR:O
FIVE MILLION YEARS TO EARTH ***½
  (1968, Brit.) PR:A
FIVE MINUTES TO LIVE ** (1961) PR:C
5 MINUTES TO LOVE
  (SEE:ROTTEN APPLE, THE)
FIVE OF A KIND *½ (1938) PR:AA
FIVE OF THE JAZZBAND
  (SEE:JAZZBAND FIVE)
FIVE ON THE BLACK HAND SIDE ***½
  (1973) PR:A
FIVE PENNIES, THE *** (1959) PR:A
FIVE POUND MAN, THE *½ (1937, Brit.) PR:C
5 SINNERS ** (1961, Ger.) PR:C-O
FIVE STAR FINAL *** (1931) PR:C
FIVE STEPS TO DANGER ** (1957) PR:A
FIVE THE HARD WAY ** (1969) PR:C
5,000 FINGERS OF DR. T. THE **** (1953) PR:AA
FIVE TO ONE *½ (1963, Brit.) PR:C
FIVE WEEKS IN A BALLOON ** (1962) PR:A
FIVE WILD GIRLS *½ (1966, Fr.) PR:O
FIX, THE ** (1985) PR:C-O
FIXATION
  (SEE:SHE-MAN, THE)
FIXED BAYONETS *** (1951) PR:A
FIXER, THE ***½ (1968) PR:O
FIXER DUGAN * (1939) PR:A
F.J. HOLDEN, THE **½ (1977, Aus.) PR:O
FLAG LIEUTENANT, THE ** (1932, Brit.) PR:A
FLAME, THE *½ (1948) PR:A
FLAME ** (1975, Brit.) PR:O
FLAME AND THE ARROW, THE ***½ (1950) PR:A
FLAME AND THE FLESH ** (1954) PR:C
FLAME BARRIER, THE **½ (1958) PR:C
FLAME IN THE HEATHER * (1935, Brit.) PR:A
FLAME IN THE STREETS *** (1961, Brit.) PR:A
FLAME OF ARABY ** (1951) PR:A
FLAME OF CALCUTTA ** (1953) PR:A
FLAME OF LOVE, THE * (1930, Brit.) PR:A
FLAME OF NEW ORLEANS, THE **½
  (1941) PR:A-C
FLAME OF SACRAMENTO
  (SEE:IN OLD SACRAMENTO)
FLAME OF STAMBOUL *½ (1957) PR:A
FLAME OF THE BARBARY COAST ** (1945) PR:A
FLAME OF THE ISLANDS *½ (1955) PR:A
FLAME OF THE WEST *** (1945) PR:A
FLAME OF TORMENT
  (SEE:ENJO)

FLAME OF YOUTH * (1949) PR:A
FLAME OVER INDIA *** (1960, Brit.) PR:A
FLAME OVER VIETNAM **½ (1967, Sp./Ger.) PR:A
FLAME WITHIN, THE ** (1935) PR:C
FLAMES *½ (1932) PR:A
FLAMING BULLETS ** (1945) PR:A
FLAMING DESIRE
  (SEE:SMALL HOURS, THE)
FLAMING FEATHER **½ (1951) PR:A
FLAMING FRONTIER * (1958, Can.) PR:A
FLAMING FRONTIER *½ (1968, Ger./Yugo.) PR:A
FLAMING FURY ** (1949) PR:A
FLAMING GOLD * (1934) PR:A
FLAMING GUNS *½ (1933) PR:A
FLAMING LEAD *½ (1939) PR:A
FLAMING SIGNAL ** (1933) PR:A
FLAMING STAR ***½ (1960) PR:C-O
FLAMING TEEN-AGE, THE * (1956) PR:A
FLAMINGO AFFAIR, THE * (1948, Brit.) PR:A
FLAMINGO KID, THE ****½ (1984) PR:C
FLAMINGO ROAD *** (1949) PR:C
FLANAGAN ** (1985) PR:O
FLANAGAN BOY, THE
  (SEE:BAD BLONDE)
FLANNELFOOT * (1953, Brit.) PR:A
FLAP zero (1970) PR:A
FLAREUP ** (1969) PR:O
FLASH AND THE FIRECAT * (1976) PR:C
FLASH GORDON **** (1936) PR:AA
FLASH GORDON ** (1980) PR:AA
FLASH OF GREEN, A ***½ (1984) PR:A-C
FLASH THE SHEEPDOG * (1967, Brit.) PR:AA
FLASHDANCE * (1983) PR:O
FLASHING GUNS ** (1947) PR:A
FLASHPOINT *½ (1984) PR:O
FLAT TOP *** (1952) PR:A
FLAT TWO * (1962, Brit.) PR:A-C
FLAVOR OF GREEN TEA OVER RICE, THE
  (SEE:TEA AND RICE)
FLAW, THE ** (1933, Brit.) PR:A
FLAW, THE *½ (1955, Brit.) PR:A
FLAXFIELD, THE ** (1985, Bel.) PR:O
FLAXY MARTIN **½ (1949) PR:A
FLEA IN HER EAR, A **½ (1968, Fr.) PR:C
FLEDGLINGS * (1965, Brit.) PR:O
FLEET'S IN, THE *** (1942) PR:AA
FLEMISH FARM, THE **½ (1943, Brit.) PR:A
FLESH *** (1932) PR:C
FLESH AND BLOOD *** (1951, Brit.) PR:C
FLESH AND BLOOD *** (1985) PR:O
FLESH AND BLOOD SHOW, THE *
  (1974, Brit.) PR:O
FLESH AND FANTASY *** (1943) PR:A-C
FLESH AND FLAME
  (SEE:NIGHT OF THE QUARTER MOON)
FLESH AND FURY *** (1952) PR:A
FLESH AND THE FIENDS, THE
  (SEE:MANIA)
FLESH AND THE SPUR * (1957) PR:C
FLESH AND THE WOMAN ** (1954, Fr./It.) PR:O
FLESH EATERS, THE **½ (1964) PR:O
FLESH FEAST ** (1970) PR:O
FLESH IS WEAK, THE * (1957, Brit.) PR:O
FLESH MERCHANT, THE * (1956) PR:O
FLESHBURN zero (1984) PR:O
FLETCH *** (1984) PR:C
FLICK
  (SEE:DR. FRANKENSTEIN ON CAMPUS)
FLICKS * (1987) PR:O
FLIGHT *** (1929) PR:A
FLIGHT *½ (1960) PR:C
FLIGHT ANGELS * (1940) PR:A
FLIGHT AT MIDNIGHT ** (1939) PR:A
FLIGHT COMMAND *** (1940) PR:A
FLIGHT FOR FREEDOM *** (1943) PR:A
FLIGHT FROM ASHIYA ** (1964, US/Jap.) PR:A
FLIGHT FROM DESTINY ***½ (1941) PR:A
FLIGHT FROM FOLLY *½ (1945, Brit.) PR:A
FLIGHT FROM GLORY ***½ (1937) PR:A
FLIGHT FROM SINGAPORE *½ (1962, Brit.) PR:A
FLIGHT FROM TERROR
  (SEE:SATAN NEVER SLEEPS)
FLIGHT FROM VIENNA ** (1956, Brit.) PR:A
FLIGHT INTO NOWHERE **½ (1938) PR:A
FLIGHT LIEUTENANT ** (1942) PR:A
FLIGHT NURSE *½ (1953) PR:A
FLIGHT OF THE DOVES *** (1971) PR:AA
FLIGHT OF THE EAGLE **½
  (1983, Swed./Ger./Norway) PR:A-C
FLIGHT OF THE LOST BALLOON zero (1961) PR:C
FLIGHT OF THE NAVIGATOR *** (1986) PR:A
FLIGHT OF THE PHOENIX, THE **** (1965) PR:C
FLIGHT OF THE SANDPIPER, THE
  (SEE:SANDPIPER, THE)
FLIGHT THAT DISAPPEARED, THE **½
  (1961) PR:A
FLIGHT TO BERLIN **½ (1984, Ger./Brit.) PR:O
FLIGHT TO FAME ** (1938) PR:A

FLIGHT TO FURY **½ (1966, US/Phil.) PR:C
FLIGHT TO HONG KONG **½ (1956) PR:C
FLIGHT TO MARS ** (1951) PR:A
FLIGHT TO NOWHERE zero (1946) PR:C
FLIGHT TO TANGIER *** (1953) PR:A
FLIM-FLAM MAN, THE * (1967) PR:A**
FLIPPER ***½ (1963) PR:AA
FLIPPER'S NEW ADVENTURE *** (1964) PR:AA
FLIRTATION WALK *** (1934) PR:AA
FLIRTING WIDOW, THE ** (1930) PR:A
FLIRTING WITH DANGER **½ (1935) PR:A
FLIRTING WITH FATE *½ (1938) PR:A
FLITTERWOCHEN IN DER HOLLE
   (SEE:ISLE OF SIN)
FLOATING DUTCHMAN, THE ** (1953, Brit.) PR:A
FLOATING WEEDS **½ (1970, Jap.) PR:A
FLOOD, THE * (1931) PR:A
FLOOD, THE * (1963) PR:AA
FLOOD TIDE ** (1935, Brit.) PR:A
FLOOD TIDE ** (1958) PR:C
FLOODS OF FEAR *** (1958, Brit.) PR:A
FLOODTIDE *½ (1949, Brit.) PR:A
FLORENTINE DAGGER, THE *** (1935) PR:A
FLORIAN ** (1940) PR:A
FLORIDA SPECIAL **½ (1936) PR:A
FLORODORA GIRL, THE **½ (1930) PR:A
FLOWER DRUM SONG ** (1961) PR:A
FLOWER THIEF, THE * (1962) PR:O
FLOWERS FOR THE MAN IN THE MOON **
   (1975, Ger.) PR:A
FLOWERS IN THE ATTIC *½ (1987) PR:C-O
FLOWING GOLD **½ (1940) PR:A
FLUCHT NACH BERLIN
   (SEE:ESCAPE TO BERLIN)
FLUFFY **½ (1965) PR:AA
FLY, THE ***½ (1958) PR:O
FLY-AWAY BABY **½ (1937) PR:A
FLY AWAY PETER **½ (1948, Brit.) PR:A
FLY, THE ** (1986) PR:O**
FLY BY NIGHT *** (1942) PR:A
FLY NOW, PAY LATER zero (1969) PR:O
FLY, RAVEN, FLY
   (SEE:DESERT RAVEN, THE)
FLYER, THE **½ (1987, Ger.) PR:O
FLYING BLIND ** (1941) PR:A
FLYING CADETS *½ (1941) PR:A
FLYING DEUCES, THE * (1939) PR:AA
FLYING DEVILS ** (1933) PR:A
FLYING DOCTOR, THE * (1936, Aus.) PR:A
FLYING DOWN TO RIO ** (1933) PR:A**
FLYING EYE, THE **½ (1955, Brit.) PR:AA
FLYING FIFTY-FIVE * (1939, Brit.) PR:A
FLYING FISTS, THE *½ (1938) PR:A
FLYING FONTAINES, THE **½ (1959) PR:A
FLYING FOOL ** (1929) PR:A
FLYING FOOL, THE **½ (1931, Brit.) PR:A
FLYING FORTRESS *½ (1942, Brit.) PR:A
FLYING GUILLOTINE, THE ** (1975, Chi.) PR:O-C
FLYING HIGH *** (1931) PR:A
FLYING HOSTESS **½ (1936) PR:A
FLYING IRISHMAN, THE ** (1939) PR:A
FLYING LEATHERNECKS * (1951) PR:C**
FLYING MARINE, THE *½ (1929) PR:A
FLYING MATCHMAKER, THE ** (1970, Israel) PR:A
FLYING MISSILE **½ (1950) PR:A
FLYING SAUCER, THE **½ (1950) PR:A
FLYING SAUCER, THE **½ (1964, It.) PR:A
FLYING SCOT, THE
   (SEE:MAILBAG ROBBERY)
FLYING SCOTSMAN, THE ** (1929, Brit.) PR:A
FLYING SERPENT, THE * (1946) PR:C
FLYING SORCERER, THE * (1974, Brit.) PR:A
FLYING SQUAD, THE ** (1932, Brit.) PR:A
FLYING SQUAD, THE * (1940, Brit.) PR:A
FLYING TIGERS * (1942) PR:C**
FLYING WILD ** (1941) PR:A
FLYING WITH MUSIC *½ (1942) PR:A
FM ** (1978) PR:C
FOES zero (1977) PR:C
FOG ** (1934) PR:A
FOG
   (SEE:STUDY IN TERROR, A)
FOG, THE ** (1980) PR:C-O
FOG ISLAND *½ (1945) PR:A
FOG OVER FRISCO ***½ (1934) PR:A
FOLIES BERGERE *** (1935) PR:A
FOLIES BERGERE **½ (1958, Fr.) PR:C

FOLKS AT THE RED WOLF INN
   (SEE:TERROR HOUSE)
FOLLIES GIRL ** (1943) PR:A
FOLLOW A STAR ** (1959, Brit.) PR:A
FOLLOW ME, BOYS! * (1966) PR:AA**
FOLLOW ME QUIETLY ***½ (1949) PR:C
FOLLOW THAT CAMEL ** (1967, Brit.) PR:A
FOLLOW THAT DREAM **½ (1962) PR:A
FOLLOW THAT HORSE! **½ (1960, Brit.) PR:A
FOLLOW THAT MAN *½ (1961, Brit.) PR:A
FOLLOW THAT WOMAN ** (1945) PR:A
FOLLOW THE BAND ** (1943) PR:A
FOLLOW THE BOYS ***½ (1944) PR:AA
FOLLOW THE BOYS *½ (1963) PR:A
FOLLOW THE FLEET ***½ (1936) PR:AA
FOLLOW THE HUNTER
   (SEE:FANGS OF THE WILD)
FOLLOW THE LEADER **½ (1930) PR:A
FOLLOW THE LEADER ** (1944) PR:A
FOLLOW THE SUN **½ (1951) PR:A
FOLLOW THRU **½ (1930) PR:A
FOLLOW YOUR HEART ** (1936) PR:A
FOLLOW YOUR STAR **½ (1938, Brit.) PR:A
FOLLOWING THE FUHRER **½ (1986, Ger.) PR:C
FOLLY TO BE WISE *** (1953) PR:A
FOND MEMORIES *** (1982, Can.) PR:C
FOOD OF THE GODS, THE zero (1976) PR:O
FOOL AND THE PRINCESS, THE **½
   (1948, Brit.) PR:A
FOOL FOR LOVE ** (1985) PR:O
FOOL KILLER, THE ** (1965) PR:O
FOOLIN' AROUND ** (1980) PR:C
FOOLISH HUSBANDS *½ (1948, Fr.) PR:A
FOOLS * (1970) PR:O
FOOLS FOR SCANDAL ** (1938) PR:A
FOOL'S GOLD ** (1946) PR:A
FOOLS OF DESIRE * (1941) PR:C
FOOLS' PARADE *** (1971) PR:C
FOOLS RUSH IN * (1949, Brit.) PR:A
FOOTLIGHT FEVER *½ (1941) PR:A
FOOTLIGHT GLAMOUR ** (1943) PR:A
FOOTLIGHT PARADE ** (1933) PR:A**
FOOTLIGHT SERENADE **½ (1942) PR:A
FOOTLIGHTS AND FOOLS *½ (1929) PR:A
FOOTLOOSE **½ (1984) PR:A-C
FOOTLOOSE HEIRESS, THE *½ (1937) PR:A
FOOTSTEPS IN THE DARK **½ (1941) PR:A
FOOTSTEPS IN THE FOG ***½ (1955, Brit.) PR:A
FOOTSTEPS IN THE NIGHT *½ (1932, Brit.) PR:A
FOOTSTEPS IN THE NIGHT ** (1957) PR:A
FOR A DOLLAR IN THE TEETH
   (SEE:STRANGER IN TOWN, A)
FOR A FEW BULLETS MORE
   (SEE:ANY GUN CAN PLAY)
FOR A FEW DOLLARS MORE ***½
   (1967, It./Ger./Sp.) PR:C
FOR A FISTFUL OF DOLLARS
   (SEE:FISTFUL OF DOLLARS)
FOR A NIGHT OF LOVE
   (SEE:MANIFESTO)
FOR ATT INTE TALA OM ALLA DESSA KVINNOR
   (SEE:ALL THESE WOMEN)
FOR BEAUTY'S SAKE *½ (1941) PR:A
FOR BETTER FOR WORSE *** (1954, Brit.) PR:A
FOR BETTER FOR WORSE
   (SEE:ZANDY'S BRIDE)
FOR FREEDOM *** (1940, Brit.) PR:A
FOR HE'S A JOLLY BAD FELLOW
   (SEE:THEY ALL DIED LAUGHING)
FOR HEAVEN'S SAKE **½ (1950) PR:A
FOR KEEPS * (1988) PR:A-C
FOR LOVE AND MONEY zero (1967) PR:O
FOR LOVE OF IVY **½ (1968) PR:A
FOR LOVE OF MONEY
   (SEE:FOR LOVE AND MONEY)
FOR LOVE OF YOU * (1933, Brit.) PR:A
FOR LOVE OR MONEY **½ (1934, Brit.) PR:A
FOR LOVE OR MONEY *** (1939) PR:A
FOR LOVE OR MONEY ** (1963) PR:A
FOR ME AND MY GAL ***½ (1942) PR:A
FOR MEN ONLY *** (1952) PR:A
FOR PETE'S SAKE! * (1966) PR:A
FOR PETE'S SAKE ** (1977) PR:C
FOR SINGLES ONLY zero (1968) PR:O
FOR THE DEFENSE ***½ (1930) PR:A-C
FOR THE FIRST TIME *** (1959, US/Ger./It.) PR:A
FOR THE LOVE OF BENJI **½ (1977) PR:AA

FOR THE LOVE OF MARY **½ (1948) PR:A
FOR THE LOVE OF MIKE ** (1933, Brit.) PR:A
FOR THE LOVE OF MIKE ** (1960) PR:AA
FOR THE LOVE OF RUSTY ** (1947) PR:AA
FOR THE LOVE O'LIL * (1930) PR:A
FOR THE SERVICE ** (1936) PR:A
FOR THEM THAT TRESPASS **½ (1949, Brit.) PR:A
FOR THOSE IN PERIL **½ (1944, Brit.) PR:A
FOR THOSE WHO THINK YOUNG ** (1964) PR:A
FOR VALOR *** (1937, Brit.) PR:A
FOR WHOM THE BELL TOLLS **** (1943) PR:C
FOR YOU ALONE *½ (1945, Brit.) PR:A
FOR YOU I DIE * (1947) PR:A
FOR YOUR EYES ONLY * (1981) PR:A**
FORBIDDEN *** (1932) PR:A-C
FORBIDDEN **½ (1949, Brit.) PR:A-C
FORBIDDEN **½ (1953) PR:A
FORBIDDEN ALLIANCE
   (SEE:BARRETTS OF WIMPOLE STREET)
FORBIDDEN CARGO ** (1954, Brit.) PR:A
FORBIDDEN COMPANY ** (1932) PR:A
FORBIDDEN FRUIT *** (1959, Fr.) PR:C
FORBIDDEN GAMES ** (1953, Fr.) PR:C**
FORBIDDEN HEAVEN * (1936) PR:A
FORBIDDEN ISLAND **½ (1959) PR:C
FORBIDDEN JOURNEY * (1950, Can.) PR:A
FORBIDDEN JUNGLE * (1950) PR:A
FORBIDDEN LOVE AFFAIR
   (SEE:FOREVER YOUNG, FOREVER FREE)
FORBIDDEN MUSIC *** (1936, Brit.) PR:A
FORBIDDEN PARADISE
   (SEE:HURRICANE)
FORBIDDEN PLANET ** (1956) PR:C**
FORBIDDEN RELATIONS ** (1983, Hung.) PR:O
FORBIDDEN STREET, THE
   (SEE:AFFAIRS OF ADELAIDE)
FORBIDDEN TERRITORY **½ (1938, Brit.) PR:A
FORBIDDEN TRAIL ** (1936) PR:A
FORBIDDEN TRAILS ** (1941) PR:A
FORBIDDEN VALLEY *½ (1938) PR:A-AA
FORBIDDEN WORLD * (1982) PR:O
FORBIDDEN ZONE *½ (1980) PR:C
FORBIN PROJECT
   (SEE:COLOSSUS, THE FORBIN PROJECT)
FORBRYDELSENS ELEMENT
   (SEE:ELEMENT OF CRIME, THE)
FORCE BEYOND, THE zero (1978) PR:C
FORCE: FIVE * (1981) PR:O
FORCE OF ARMS ***½ (1951) PR:A
FORCE OF EVIL ***½ (1948) PR:C
FORCE OF IMPULSE * (1961) PR:A
FORCE OF ONE, A ** (1979) PR:C-O
FORCE 10 FROM NAVARONE ***½
   (1978, Brit.) PR:A-C
FORCED ENTRY * (1975) PR:O
FORCED LANDING * (1935) PR:A
FORCED LANDING ** (1941) PR:A
FORCED VENGEANCE * (1982) PR:O
FORCES' SWEETHEART * (1953, Brit.) PR:A
FOREIGN AFFAIR, A *** (1948) PR:C
FOREIGN AFFAIRES **½ (1935, Brit.) PR:A
FOREIGN AGENT **½ (1942) PR:A
FOREIGN BODY ** (1986, Brit.) PR:C-O
FOREIGN CITY, A ** (1988, Fr.) PR:C
FOREIGN CORRESPONDENT *** (1940) PR:A**
FOREIGN INTRIGUE **½ (1956) PR:A
FOREIGNER, THE *½ (1978) PR:C
FOREMAN WENT TO FRANCE, THE
   (SEE:SOMEWHERE IN FRANCE)
FOREPLAY zero (1975) PR:O
FOREST RANGERS, THE **½ (1942) PR:A
FOREST, THE * (1983) PR:O
FOREVER AMBER **½ (1947) PR:C-O
FOREVER AND A DAY **** (1943) PR:A
FOREVER DARLING * (1956) PR:A
FOREVER ENGLAND
   (SEE:BORN FOR GLORY)
FOREVER FEMALE *** (1953) PR:A
FOREVER MY HEART * (1954, Brit.) PR:C
FOREVER MY LOVE *** (1962) PR:A
FOREVER YOUNG *½ (1984, Brit.) PR:C
FOREVER YOUNG, FOREVER FREE **
   (1976, South Africa) PR:A
FOREVER YOURS ** (1937, Brit.) PR:A
FOREVER YOURS ** (1945) PR:A
FORGED PASSPORT ** (1939) PR:A

Finding entries in **THE MOTION PICTURE GUIDE** ™	**STAR RATINGS**		**PARENTAL RECOMMENDATION (PR:)**	
Years 1929-83 Volumes I-IX	★★★★★	Masterpiece	AA	Good for Children
1984 Volume IX	★★★★	Excellent	A	Acceptable for Children
1985 1986 ANNUAL	★★★	Good	C	Cautionary, some objectionable scenes
1986 1987 ANNUAL	★★	Fair	O	Objectionable for Children
1987 1988 ANNUAL	★	Poor		
1988 1989 ANNUAL	zero	Without Merit	**BOLD:** Films on Videocassette	

FORGET ME NOT
(SEE:FOREVER YOURS)
FORGET MOZART! ** (1985, Czech./Ger.) PR:A
FORGOTTEN * (1933) PR:A
FORGOTTEN COMMANDMENTS zero (1932) PR:A
FORGOTTEN FACES * (1936) PR:A
FORGOTTEN GIRLS * (1940) PR:A
FORGOTTEN WOMAN, THE ** (1939) PR:A
FORGOTTEN WOMEN ** (1932) PR:A
FORGOTTEN WOMEN * (1949) PR:A
FORLORN RIVER *½ (1937) PR:AA
FORMULA, THE *½ (1980) PR:C
FORSAKEN GARDEN, THE
(SEE:OF LOVE AND DESIRE)
FORSAKING ALL OTHERS ***½ (1935) PR:A
FORT ALGIERS ** (1953) PR:A
FORT APACHE *** (1948) PR:A**
FORT APACHE, THE BRONX **½ (1981) PR:O
FORT BOWIE **½ (1958) PR:A
FORT COURAGEOUS **½ (1965) PR:A
FORT DEFIANCE **½ (1951) PR:A
FORT DOBBS ** (1958) PR:A
FORT DODGE STAMPEDE ** (1951) PR:AA
FORT GRAVEYARD **½ (1966, Jap.) PR:C
FORT MASSACRE *** (1958) PR:C
FORT OSAGE * (1952) PR:A
FORT SAVAGE RAIDERS **½ (1951) PR:A
FORT TI *½ (1953) PR:AA
FORT UTAH * (1967) PR:A
FORT VENGEANCE ** (1953) PR:A
FORT WORTH ** (1951) PR:A
FORT YUMA ** (1955) PR:A
FORTRESS, THE ** (1979, Hung.) PR:C
FORTUNATE FOOL, THE * (1933, Brit.) PR:A
FORTUNE AND MEN'S EYES *
(1971, US/Can.) PR:O
FORTUNE COOKIE, THE * (1966) PR:A-C**
FORTUNE IN DIAMONDS
(SEE:ADVENTURERS, THE)
FORTUNE IS A WOMAN
(SEE:SHE PLAYED WITH FIRE)
FORTUNE LANE ** (1947, Brit.) PR:AA
FORTUNE TELLER, THE * (1961, Gr.) PR:A-C
FORTUNE, THE **** (1975) PR:C
FORTUNES OF CAPTAIN BLOOD *½ (1950) PR:A
FORTY ACRE FEUD *½ (1965) PR:A
FORTY CARATS **½ (1973) PR:A-C
FORTY DEUCE ** (1982) PR:O
48 HOURS TO LIVE ** (1960, Brit./Swed.) PR:A
45 FATHERS ** (1937) PR:AA
FORTY GUNS **½ (1957) PR:A-C
FORTY LITTLE MOTHERS **½ (1940) PR:A
FORTY NAUGHTY GIRLS * (1937) PR:A
FORTY-NINE DAYS ** (1964, USSR) PR:A
FORTY-NINERS, THE * (1932) PR:A
FORTY-NINTH MAN, THE ** (1953) PR:A
FORTY NINTH PARALLEL
(SEE:INVADERS, THE)
FORTY POUNDS OF TROUBLE **½ (1962) PR:AA
42ND STREET *** (1933) PR:A**
FORTY SQUARE METERS OF GERMANY ***
(1986, Ger.) PR:A
FORTY THIEVES ** (1944) PR:A
FORTY THOUSAND HORSEMEN **½
(1941, Aus.) PR:A
FORTYNINERS, THE *½ (1954) PR:A
FORWARD PASS, THE **½ (1929) PR:A
FOUETTE *** (1986, USSR) PR:O
FOUL PLAY ** (1978) PR:A-C**
FOUND ALIVE * (1934) PR:A
FOUNTAIN, THE *½ (1934) PR:A
FOUNTAIN OF LOVE, THE ** (1968, Aust.) PR:C
FOUNTAINHEAD, THE **½ (1949) PR:A
FOUR AGAINST FATE **½ (1952, Brit.) PR:A
FOUR BAGS FULL * (1957, Fr./It.) PR:A-C**
FOUR BOYS AND A GUN ** (1957) PR:C
FOUR COMPANIONS, THE ** (1938, Ger.) PR:A
FOUR CORNERED TRIANGLE
(SEE:SCREAM OF THE BUTTERFLY)
4D MAN * (1959) PR:A**
FOUR DARK HOURS
(SEE:GREEN COCKATOO, THE)
FOUR DAUGHTERS **** (1938) PR:A
FOUR DAYS ** (1951, Brit.) PR:A
FOUR DAYS IN JULY **½ (1984) PR:C-O
FOUR DAYS LEAVE ** (1950, Switz.) PR:A
FOUR DAYS OF NAPLES, THE **
(1963, US/It.) PR:A
FOUR DAYS WONDER **½ (1936) PR:AA
FOUR DESPERATE MEN ** (1960, Brit.) PR:C
FOUR DEUCES, THE ** (1976) PR:O
FOUR DEVILS ** (1929) PR:A
FOUR FACES WEST * (1948) PR:A**
FOUR FAST GUNS ** (1959) PR:A
FOUR FEATHERS, THE *** (1939, Brit.) PR:A**
FOUR FLIES ON GREY VELVET **½
(1972, It.) PR:C
FOUR FOR TEXAS * (1963) PR:C
FOUR FOR THE MORGUE *½ (1962) PR:C
FOUR FRIENDS ***½ (1981) PR:O
FOUR FRIGHTENED PEOPLE *** (1934) PR:C
FOUR GIRLS IN TOWN * (1956) PR:A
FOUR GIRLS IN WHITE ** (1939) PR:A
FOUR GUNS TO THE BORDER ** (1954) PR:A
FOUR HORSEMEN OF THE APOCALYPSE, THE **
(1962) PR:A
FOUR HOURS TO KILL ** (1935) PR:A
FOUR HUNDRED BLOWS, THE *****
(1959) PR:A-C
FOUR IN A JEEP ** (1951, Switz.) PR:A
FOUR IN THE MORNING ** (1965, Brit.) PR:C
FOUR JACKS AND A JILL **½ (1941) PR:A
FOUR JILLS IN A JEEP **½ (1944) PR:A
FOUR JUST MEN, THE
(SEE:SECRET FOUR, THE)
FOUR KINDS OF LOVE
(SEE:BAMBOLE!)
FOUR MASKED MEN ** (1934, Brit.) PR:A
FOUR MEN AND A PRAYER **½ (1938) PR:A
FOUR MOTHERS **½ (1941) PR:A
FOUR MUSKETEERS, THE ***½ (1975) PR:A-C
FOUR NIGHTS OF A DREAMER ***½
(1972, Fr.) PR:O
FOUR POSTER, THE *** (1952) PR:A
FOUR RODE OUT * (1969, US/Sp.) PR:O
FOUR SEASONS, THE * (1981) PR:C**
FOUR SIDED TRIANGLE *½ (1953, Brit.) PR:C
FOUR SKULLS OF JONATHAN DRAKE, THE **½
(1959) PR:C-O
FOUR SONS **½ (1940) PR:A
FOUR WAYS OUT ** (1954, It.) PR:C
FOUR WIVES ** (1939) PR:A
FOUR'S A CROWD **½ (1938) PR:A
FOURTEEN HOURS ***½ (1951) PR:C
FOURTEEN, THE *** (1973, Brit.) PR:A
FOURTH ALARM, THE **½ (1930) PR:A
FOURTH FOR MARRIAGE, A
(SEE:WHAT'S UP FRONT)
FOURTH HORSEMAN, THE **½ (1933) PR:AA
FOURTH MAN, THE **½ (1984, Neth.) PR:O
FOURTH PROTOCOL, THE ** (1987, Brit.) PR:C
FOURTH SQUARE, THE ** (1961, Brit.) PR:A-C
48 HOURS *½ (1944, Brit.) PR:A
48 HOURS *** (1982) PR:O
48 HOURS TO ACAPULCO ** (1968, Ger.) PR:C
40 GUNS TO APACHE PASS *½ (1967) PR:A
47 SAMURAI
(SEE:CHUSHINGURA)
FOX AND HIS FRIENDS *** (1976, Ger.) PR:O
FOX AND THE HOUND, THE **** (1981) PR:AA
FOX MOVIETONE FOLLIES **½ (1929) PR:A
FOX MOVIETONE FOLLIES OF 1930 ** (1930) PR:A
FOX WITH NINE TAILS, THE **½
(1969, Jap.) PR:AA
FOX, THE *** (1967) PR:O
FOXES **½ (1980) PR:O
FOXES OF HARROW, THE ***½ (1947) PR:A
FOXFIRE ** (1955) PR:C
FOXHOLE IN CAIRO ** (1960, Brit.) PR:A
FOXTROT ** (1977, Mex./Swiss) PR:C-O
FOXY BROWN * (1974) PR:O
FOXY LADY *½ (1971, Can.) PR:A
F.P. 1 **½ (1933, Brit.) PR:A
F.P. 1 DOESN'T ANSWER * (1933, Ger.) PR:A**
FRA DIAVOLO
(SEE:DEVIL'S BROTHER, THE)
FRAGE 7
(SEE:QUESTION 7)
FRAGMENT OF FEAR *** (1971, Brit.) PR:C-O
FRAGRANCE OF WILD FLOWERS, THE ***
(1979, Yugo.) PR:C
FRAIL WOMEN **½ (1932, Brit.) PR:C
FRAME-UP THE **½ (1937) PR:A
FRAMED ** (1930) PR:A
FRAMED *½ (1940) PR:A
FRAMED **½ (1947) PR:C
FRAMED ** (1975) PR:O
FRANCES **½ (1982) PR:O
FRANCESCA ***½ (1987, Ger.) PR:O
FRANCHETTE; LES INTRIGUES *½ (1969) PR:O
FRANCHISE AFFAIR, THE ** (1952, Brit.) PR:A
FRANCIS * (1949) PR:AA**
FRANCIS COVERS THE BIG TOWN ** (1953) PR:AA
FRANCIS GOES TO THE RACES ** (1951) PR:AA
FRANCIS GOES TO WEST POINT ** (1952) PR:AA
FRANCIS IN THE HAUNTED HOUSE *½
(1956) PR:AA
FRANCIS IN THE NAVY ** (1955) PR:AA
FRANCIS JOINS THE WACS ** (1954) PR:AA
FRANCIS OF ASSISI ** (1961) PR:A
FRANCOISE
(SEE:ANATOMY OF A MARRIAGE, MY DAYS WITH JEAN-MARC, MY NIGHTS WITH FRANCOISE)
FRANK'S GREATEST ADVENTURE
(SEE:FEARLESS FRANK)
FRANKENSTEIN ** (1931) PR:C-O**
FRANKENSTEIN AND THE MONSTER FROM HELL
** (1974, Brit.) PR:O
FRANKENSTEIN CONQUERS THE WORLD zero
(1964, Jap./US) PR:C
FRANKENSTEIN CREATED WOMAN ***
(1965, Brit.) PR:O
FRANKENSTEIN GENERAL HOSPITAL zero
(1988) PR:O
FRANKENSTEIN-ITALIAN STYLE zero
(1977, It.) PR:O
FRANKENSTEIN MEETS THE SPACE MONSTER
zero (1965) PR:C
FRANKENSTEIN MEETS THE WOLF MAN ***
(1943) PR:C
FRANKENSTEIN MUST BE DESTROYED! ***
(1969, Brit.) PR:C-O
FRANKENSTEIN 1970 ** (1958) PR:C
FRANKENSTEIN VS. THE GIANT DEVILFISH
(SEE:FRANKENSTEIN CONQUERS THE WORLD)
FRANKENSTEIN'S BLOODY TERROR *
(1968, Sp.) PR:C
FRANKENSTEIN'S DAUGHTER zero (1958) PR:C-O
FRANKENSTEIN, THE VAMPIRE AND CO. *
(1961, Mex.) PR:C
FRANKIE AND JOHNNY * (1936) PR:A-C
FRANKIE AND JOHNNY ** (1966) PR:A
FRANTIC * (1961, Fr.) PR:C**
FRANTIC ** (1988) PR:A-C**
FRASIER, THE SENSUOUS LION * (1973) PR:AA
FRATERNITY ROW ***½ (1977) PR:O
FRATERNITY VACATION *½ (1985) PR:C
FRAULEIN **½ (1958) PR:C
FRAULEIN DOKTOR **½ (1969, It./Yugo.) PR:C-O
FREAKS ** (1932) PR:O**
FREAKS!
(SEE:SHE FREAK)
FREAKY FRIDAY ***½ (1976) PR:AA
FRECKLES ** (1935) PR:A
FRECKLES ** (1960) PR:A
FRECKLES COMES HOME ** (1942) PR:A
FREDDIE STEPS OUT ** (1946) PR:A
FREDDY UNTER FREMDEN STERNEN *½
(1962, Ger.) PR:A
FREE AND EASY ***½ (1930) PR:A
FREE AND EASY * (1941) PR:A
FREE, BLONDE AND 21 ** (1940) PR:A
FREE FOR ALL **½ (1949) PR:A
FREE GRASS * (1969) PR:O
FREE LOVE *½ (1930) PR:C
FREE RIDE zero (1986) PR:O
FREE SOUL, A ***½ (1931) PR:C
FREE SPIRIT
(SEE:BELSTONE FOX)
FREE, WHITE AND 21 * (1963) PR:C
FREEBIE AND THE BEAN **½ (1974) PR:O
FREEDOM FOR US
(SEE:A NOUS LA LIBERTE)
FREEDOM OF THE SEAS ** (1934, Brit.) PR:A
FREEDOM RADIO
(SEE:VOICE IN THE NIGHT, A)
FREEDOM TO DIE ** (1962, Brit.) PR:A
FREEWHEELIN' *½ (1976) PR:A
FREIGHTERS OF DESTINY ** (1932) PR:A
FRENCH CANCAN ** (1956, Fr.) PR:A**
FRENCH CONNECTION II ***½ (1975) PR:O
FRENCH CONNECTION, THE *** (1971) PR:O**
FRENCH CONSPIRACY, THE *½ (1973, Fr.) PR:A
FRENCH DRESSING ** (1964, Brit.) PR:A
FRENCH GAME, THE ** (1963, Fr.) PR:C
FRENCH KEY, THE ** (1946) PR:A
FRENCH LEAVE * (1931, Brit.) PR:A
FRENCH LEAVE ** (1937, Brit.) PR:A
FRENCH LEAVE ** (1948) PR:A
FRENCH LESSON **½ (1986, Brit.) PR:C
FRENCH LIEUTENANT'S WOMAN, THE *
(1981) PR:O
FRENCH LINE, THE ** (1954) PR:C
FRENCH MISTRESS **½ (1960, Brit.) PR:A
FRENCH POSTCARDS ** (1979) PR:A-C
FRENCH QUARTER **½ (1978) PR:O
FRENCH, THEY ARE A FUNNY RACE, THE **
(1956, Fr.) PR:A
FRENCH TOUCH, THE **½ (1954, Fr.) PR:A
FRENCH WAY, THE ** (1952, Fr.) PR:A
FRENCH WAY, THE ** (1975, Fr.) PR:O
FRENCH WITHOUT TEARS ** (1939, Brit.) PR:A
FRENCHIE ** (1950) PR:A
FRENCHMAN'S CREEK *** (1944) PR:A
FRENZY **½ (1946, Brit.) PR:A
FRENZY ***½ (1972, Brit.) PR:C-O
FRESH FROM PARIS *½ (1955) PR:A
FRESH HORSES zero (1988) PR:C
FRESHMAN LOVE **½ (1936) PR:A
FRESHMAN YEAR ** (1938) PR:A
FRESHMAN, THE
(SEE:BACHELOR OF HEARTS)
FREUD **½ (1962) PR:A-C

FRIC FRAC **½ (1939, FR.) PR:A
FRIDAY FOSTER ** (1975) **PR:O**
FRIDAY THE 13TH *** (1934, Brit.) PR:A
FRIDAY THE 13TH zero (1980) **PR:O**
FRIDAY THE 13TH, PART V—A NEW BEGINNING
zero (1985) **PR:O**
FRIDAY THE 13TH PART VI: JASON LIVES *
(1986) **PR:O**
FRIDAY THE 13TH PART VII—THE NEW BLOOD
zero (1988) **PR:O**
FRIDAY THE 13TH PART III * (1982) **PR:O**
FRIDAY THE 13TH PART II zero (1981) **PR:O**
FRIDAY THE 13TH—THE FINAL CHAPTER zero
(1984) **PR:O**
FRIDAY THE 13TH... THE ORPHAN * (1979) PR:O
FRIEDA *** (1947, Brit.) **PR:A**
FRIEND OF THE FAMILY ** (1965, Fr./It.) PR:A
FRIEND WILL COME TONIGHT, A ***
(1948, Fr.) PR:A
FRIENDLIEST GIRLS IN THE WORLD, THE
(SEE:COME FLY WITH ME)
FRIENDLY ENEMIES *½ (1942) PR:A
FRIENDLY KILLER, THE ** (1970, Jap.) PR:C-O
FRIENDLY NEIGHBORS *** (1940) PR:A
FRIENDLY PERSUASION ***½ (1956) **PR:A**
FRIENDS * (1971, Brit.) PR:O
FRIENDS AND HUSBANDS *** (1983, Ger.) PR:C
FRIENDS AND LOVERS *½ (1931) PR:A
FRIENDS AND LOVERS
(SEE:VIXENS, THE)
FRIENDS AND NEIGHBORS ** (1963, Brit.) PR:A
FRIENDS FOR LIFE ** (1964, It.) PR:A
FRIENDS OF EDDIE COYLE, THE ***½ (1973) PR:O
FRIENDS OF MR. SWEENEY *** (1934) PR:A
FRIENDSHIP'S DEATH *** (1988, Brit.) PR:A
FRIGHT
(SEE:SPELL OF THE HYPNOTIST)
FRIGHT **½ (1971, Brit.) PR:O
FRIGHT NIGHT ***½ (1985) **PR:O**
FRIGHTENED BRIDE, THE ** (1952, Brit.) PR:A
FRIGHTENED CITY, THE *** (1961, Brit.) PR:A
FRIGHTENED LADY, THE
(SEE:CRIMINAL AT LARGE)
FRIGHTENED LADY
(SEE:CASE OF THE FRIGHTENED LADY, THE)
FRIGHTENED MAN, THE ** (1952, Brit.) PR:A
FRIGHTMARE ** (1974, Brit.) **PR:O**
FRIGHTMARE * (1983) **PR:O**
FRIGID WIFE
(SEE:MODERN MARRIAGE, A)
FRINGE DWELLERS, THE *** (1986, Aus.) **PR:A-C**
FRISCO JENNY **½ (1933) PR:A
FRISCO KID *** (1935) PR:A
FRISCO KID, THE ** (1979) **PR:C**
FRISCO LILL *½ (1942) PR:A
FRISCO SAL ** (1945) PR:A
FRISCO TORNADO *½ (1950) PR:A
FRISCO WATERFRONT ** (1935) PR:A
FRISKY *½ (1955, It.) PR:A
FROG, THE ** (1937, Brit.) PR:A
FROGMEN, THE *** (1951) PR:A
FROGS **½ (1972) **PR:C**
FROM A ROMAN BALCONY *½ (1961, Fr./It.) PR:C
FROM A WHISPER TO A SCREAM
(SEE:OFFSPRING, THE)
FROM BEYOND **½ (1986) **PR:O**
FROM BEYOND THE GRAVE ** (1974, Brit.) **PR:C**
FROM HEADQUARTERS * (1929) PR:A
FROM HEADQUARTERS ** (1933) PR:A
FROM HELL IT CAME ** (1957) PR:C
FROM HELL TO HEAVEN **½ (1933) **PR:C**
FROM HELL TO TEXAS ***½ (1958) PR:C
FROM HELL TO VICTORY **
(1979, Fr./It./Sp.) PR:C
FROM HERE TO ETERNITY ***** (1953) **PR:C**
FROM NASHVILLE WITH MUSIC * (1969) PR:AA
FROM NOON TO THREE **½ (1976) PR:C
FROM RUSSIA WITH LOVE **** (1963, Brit.) **PR:A**
FROM THE EARTH TO THE MOON *½
(1958) **PR:A**
FROM THE HIP * (1987) PR:C
FROM THE LIFE OF THE MARIONETTES **½
(1980, Ger.) PR:O
FROM THE MIXED-UP FILES OF MRS. BASIL E.
FRANKWEILER **½ (1973) PR:AA
FROM THE TERRACE ** (1960) PR:C
FROM THIS DAY FORWARD **½ (1946) PR:A

FROM TOP TO BOTTOM **½ (1933, Fr.) PR:A
FRONT LINE KIDS ** (1942, Brit.) PR:AA
FRONT PAGE STORY **½ (1954, Brit.) PR:A
FRONT PAGE WOMAN **½ (1935) PR:A
FRONT PAGE, THE ***** (1931) **PR:A**
FRONT PAGE, THE *** (1974) PR:C-O
FRONT, THE *½ (1976) **PR:C**
FRONTIER AGENT *½ (1948) PR:A
FRONTIER BADMEN **½ (1943) PR:A
FRONTIER CRUSADER *½ (1940) PR:A
FRONTIER DAYS ** (1934) PR:A
FRONTIER FEUD ** (1945) PR:A
FRONTIER FUGITIVES * (1945) PR:A
FRONTIER FURY ** (1943) PR:A
FRONTIER GAL ** (1945) PR:A
FRONTIER GAMBLER * (1956) PR:A
FRONTIER GUN ** (1958) PR:A
FRONTIER HELLCAT **
(1966, Fr./It./Ger./Yugo.) PR:A
FRONTIER INVESTIGATOR ** (1949) PR:A
FRONTIER JUSTICE *½ (1936) PR:A
FRONTIER LAW *½ (1943) PR:A
FRONTIER MARSHAL **½ (1934) PR:A
FRONTIER MARSHAL *** (1939) PR:A
FRONTIER MARSHAL IN PRAIRIE PALS
(SEE:PRAIRIE PALS)
FRONTIER OUTLAWS ** (1944) PR:A
FRONTIER OUTPOST **½ (1950) PR:A
FRONTIER PHANTOM, THE ** (1952) PR:A
FRONTIER PONY EXPRESS ** (1939) **PR:A**
FRONTIER REVENGE ** (1948) PR:A
FRONTIER SCOUT * (1939) PR:A
FRONTIER TOWN * (1938) PR:A
FRONTIER UPRISING *½ (1961) PR:A
FRONTIER VENGEANCE * (1939) PR:A
FRONTIERS OF '49 *½ (1939) PR:A
FRONTIERSMAN, THE
(SEE:BUCKSKIN)
FRONTIERSMAN, THE ** (1938) **PR:A**
FROU-FROU ** (1955, Fr.) PR:A
FROZEN ALIVE * (1966, Brit./Ger.) PR:A
FROZEN DEAD, THE *½ (1967, Brit.) PR:C
FROZEN GHOST, THE ** (1945) PR:C
FROZEN JUSTICE ** (1929) PR:A
FROZEN LIMITS, THE *** (1939, Brit.) PR:A
FROZEN RIVER * (1929) PR:A
FRUIT IS RIPE, THE ** (1961, Fr./It.) PR:C
FRUSTRATIONS * (1967, Fr./It.) PR:O
FU MANCHU AND THE KISS OF DEATH
(SEE:KISS & KILL)
FUEGO
(SEE:PYRO)
FUGITIVE, THE **½ (1940, Brit.) PR:A
FUGITIVE AT LARGE ** (1939) PR:A
FUGITIVE FROM A PRISON CAMP * (1940) PR:A
FUGITIVE FROM JUSTICE, A *** (1940) PR:A
FUGITIVE FROM SONORA **½ (1943) PR:A
FUGITIVE IN THE SKY ** (1937) PR:A
FUGITIVE KIND, THE ** (1960) PR:C
FUGITIVE LADY **½ (1934) PR:C
FUGITIVE LADY **½ (1951) PR:O
FUGITIVE LOVERS ** (1934) PR:A
FUGITIVE ROAD ** (1934) PR:A
FUGITIVE SHERIFF, THE ** (1936) PR:A
FUGITIVE VALLEY *½ (1941) PR:A
FUGITIVE, THE ** (1933) PR:A
FUGITIVE, THE ***** (1947) PR:C
FUGITIVES FOR A NIGHT ** (1938) PR:C
FULL CIRCLE zero (1935, Brit.) PR:A
FULL CONFESSION *** (1939) PR:C
FULL METAL JACKET **** (1987) **PR:O**
FULL MOON HIGH * (1982) PR:A-C
FULL MOON IN BLUE WATER ***½ (1988) PR:A
FULL MOON IN PARIS ***½ (1984, Fr.) **PR:O**
FULL OF LIFE *** (1956) PR:A
FULL SPEED AHEAD * (1936, Brit.) PR:A
FULL SPEED AHEAD ** (1939, Brit.) PR:A
FULL TREATMENT, THE
(SEE:STOP ME BEFORE I KILL!)
FULLER BRUSH GIRL, THE *** (1950) **PR:AA**
FULLER BRUSH MAN ***½ (1948) **PR:AA**
FUN AND FANCY FREE ** (1947) PR:AA
FUN AT ST. FANNY'S *** (1956, Brit.) PR:AA
FUN IN ACAPULCO ** (1963) **PR:A**
FUN LOVING
(SEE:QUACKSER FORTUNE HAS A COUSIN IN THE
BRONX)

FUN ON A WEEKEND *** (1979) PR:AA
FUN WITH DICK AND JANE ** (1977) **PR:C-O**
FUNDOSHI ISHA
(SEE:LIFE OF A COUNTRY DOCTOR)
FUNERAL FOR AN ASSASSIN *½ (1977) **PR:A**
FUNERAL HOME * (1982, Can.) PR:O
FUNERAL IN BERLIN ***½ (1966, Brit.) PR:C
FUNHOUSE, THE ** (1981) **PR:O**
FUNNY FACE ***½ (1957) PR:AA
FUNNY FARM *½ (1988) **PR:C**
FUNNY FARM, THE ** (1982, Can.) **PR:C**
FUNNY GIRL **** (1968) **PR:A**
FUNNY LADY ***½ (1975) **PR:A**
FUNNY MONEY zero (1983, Brit.) PR:O
FUNNY PARISHIONER, THE
(SEE:THANK HEAVEN FOR SMALL FAVORS)
**FUNNY THING HAPPENED ON THE WAY TO THE
FORUM, A** *** (1966) **PR:C**
FUNNYMAN **½ (1967) PR:C
FUOCO FATUO
(SEE:FIRE WITHIN, THE)
FUR COLLAR, THE * (1962, Brit.) PR:A
FURESSHUMAN WAKADAISHO
(SEE:YOUNG GUY GRADUATES)
FURIA *** (1947, It.) PR:O
FURIES, THE *½ (1930) PR:A
FURIES, THE *** (1950) PR:C
FURIN KAZAN
(SEE:UNDER THE BANNER OF SAMURAI)
**FURTHER ADVENTURES OF TENNESSEE BUCK,
THE** ** (1988) **PR:O**
FURTHER ADVENTURES OF THE WILDERNESS
FAMILY—PART II **½ (1978) PR:AA
FURTHER UP THE CREEK! *** (1958, Brit.) PR:AA
FURY ***** (1936) PR:C
FURY, THE *½ (1978) **PR:O**
FURY AND THE WOMAN ** (1937) PR:A
FURY AT FURNACE CREEK *** (1948) PR:A
FURY AT GUNSIGHT PASS **½ (1956) PR:O
FURY AT SHOWDOWN *** (1957) PR:O
FURY AT SMUGGLERS BAY ** (1963, Brit.) PR:A
FURY BELOW *½ (1938) PR:A
FURY IN PARADISE * (1955, US/Mex.) PR:A
FURY OF HERCULES, THE *½ (1961, It.) **PR:A**
FURY OF THE CONGO **½ (1951) PR:AA
FURY OF THE JUNGLE * (1934) PR:O
FURY OF THE PAGANS *½ (1963, It.) PR:C
FURY OF THE VIKINGS
(SEE:ERIK THE CONQUEROR)
FUSS OVER FEATHERS *** (1954, Brit.) PR:AA
FUTARI NO MUSUCKO
(SEE:DIFFERENT SONS)
FUTURE-KILL ** (1985) **PR:O**
FUTUREWORLD *** (1976) **PR:C**
FUZZ *** (1972) **PR:O**
FUZZY PINK NIGHTGOWN, THE ** (1957) PR:A
FUZZY SETTLES DOWN * (1944) PR:A
F/X ***½ (1986) **PR:C-O**

G

G.I. BLUES ** (1960) PR:A
G.I. WAR BRIDES *½ (1946) PR:A
G-MAN'S WIFE
(SEE:PUBLIC ENEMY'S WIFE)
G-MEN **** (1935) PR:A
GABLE AND LOMBARD * (1976) PR:O
GABLES MYSTERY, THE *½ (1931, Brit.) PR:A
GABLES MYSTERY, THE * (1938, Brit.) PR:A
GABRIEL OVER THE WHITE HOUSE ***
(1933) PR:C
GABRIELA ** (1984, Braz.) **PR:O**
GABY ** (1956) PR:A
GAIETY GEORGE
(SEE:SHOWTIME)
GAIETY GIRLS, THE ** (1938, Brit.) PR:A
GAILY, GAILY *** (1969) PR:C-O
GAL WHO TOOK THE WEST, THE ** (1949) PR:A
GAL YOUNG UN **½ (1979) **PR:C**
GALACTIC GIGOLO zero (1988) **PR:O**
GALAXINA * (1980) **PR:O**
GALAXY EXPRESS **½ (1982, Jap.) PR:A

GALAXY OF TERROR * (1981) PR:O
GALIA ** (1966, Fr./It.) PR:C
GALILEO **½ (1968, It./Bul.) PR:A
GALILEO *** (1975, Brit.) PR:A
GALLANT BESS ** (1946) PR:A
GALLANT BLADE, THE ** (1948) PR:A
GALLANT DEFENDER *½ (1935) PR:A
GALLANT FOOL, THE *½ (1933) PR:A
GALLANT HOURS, THE *** (1960) PR:A
GALLANT JOURNEY *½ (1946) PR:A
GALLANT LADY ** (1934) PR:A
GALLANT LADY *½ (1942) PR:A
GALLANT LEGION, THE ** (1948) PR:A
GALLANT ONE, THE ** (1964, US/Peru) PR:A
GALLANT SONS ** (1940) PR:A
GALLERY OF HORRORS
(SEE:DR. TERROR'S GALLERY OF HORRORS)
GALLIPOLI ** (1981, Aus.) PR:A-C**
GALLOPING DYNAMITE *½ (1937) PR:A
GALLOPING MAJOR, THE ** (1951, Brit.) PR:A
GALLOPING ROMEO *½ (1933) PR:A
GALLOPING THRU **½ (1932) PR:A
GALS, INCORPORATED *½ (1943) PR:A
GAMBIT * (1966) PR:A-C**
GAMBLER AND THE LADY, THE *½
(1952, Brit.) PR:A
GAMBLER FROM NATCHEZ, THE **½ (1954) PR:A
GAMBLER WORE A GUN, THE *½ (1961) PR:A
GAMBLER, THE *½ (1958, Fr.) PR:C
GAMBLER, THE * (1974) PR:O**
GAMBLERS, THE
(SEE:JUDGE, THE)
GAMBLER'S CHOICE ** (1944) PR:A
GAMBLERS, THE ** (1929) PR:A
GAMBLERS, THE ** (1969) PR:A
GAMBLIN' MAN
(SEE:BORN TO KILL)
GAMBLING *½ (1934) PR:A
GAMBLING DAUGHTERS *½ (1941) PR:A
GAMBLING HOUSE **½ (1950) PR:A
GAMBLING LADY **½ (1934) PR:A
GAMBLING ON THE HIGH SEAS ** (1940) PR:A
GAMBLING SAMURAI, THE *** (1966, Jap.) PR:C
GAMBLING SEX *½ (1932) PR:A
GAMBLING SHIP **½ (1933) PR:A
GAMBLING SHIP *½ (1939) PR:A
GAMBLING TERROR, THE ** (1937) PR:A
GAME FOR SIX LOVERS, A ** (1962, Fr.) PR:A
GAME FOR THREE LOSERS ** (1965, Brit.) PR:A
GAME FOR VULTURES, A * (1980, Brit.) PR:O
GAME IS OVER, THE * (1967, Fr.) PR:O**
GAME OF CHANCE, A * (1932, Brit.) PR:A
GAME OF DANGER
(SEE:BANG! YOU'RE DEAD)
GAME OF DEATH, A **½ (1945) PR:A
GAME OF DEATH, THE * (1979) PR:O
GAME OF LOVE, THE ** (1954, Fr.) PR:C
GAME OF TRUTH, THE ** (1961, Fr.) PR:C
GAME THAT KILLS, THE *½ (1937) PR:A
GAMEKEEPER, THE **½ (1980, Brit.) PR:A
GAMERA THE INVINCIBLE zero (1966, Jap.) PR:A
GAMERA VERSUS BARUGON *½
(1966, Jap./US) PR:A
GAMERA VERSUS GAOS *½ (1967, Jap.) PR:A
GAMERA VERSUS GUIRON *½ (1969, Jap.) PR:A
GAMERA VERSUS MONSTER K *½
(1970, Jap.) PR:A
GAMERA VERSUS VIRAS *½ (1968, Jap.) PR:A
GAMERA VERSUS ZIGRA *½ (1971, Jap.) PR:A
GAMES **½ (1967) PR:O
GAMES, THE ** (1970) PR:A
GAMES FOR SIX LOVERS
(SEE:GAME FOR SIX LOVERS, A)
GAMES MEN PLAY, THE * (1968, Arg.) PR:O
GAMES THAT LOVERS PLAY *½ (1971, Brit.) PR:O
GAMLET
(SEE:HAMLET)
GAMMA PEOPLE, THE ** (1956) PR:A
GAMMERA THE INVINCIBLE
(SEE:GAMERA THE INVINCIBLE)
GANDAHAR
(SEE:LIGHT YEARS)
GANDHI *** (1982) PR:A**
GANG BULLETS * (1938) PR:A
GANG BUSTER, THE **½ (1931) PR:A
GANG BUSTERS * (1955) PR:A
GANG SHOW, THE
(SEE:GANG, THE)
GANG THAT COULDN'T SHOOT STRAIGHT, THE *
(1971) PR:A-C
GANG WAR *½ (1928) PR:A
GANG WAR * (1940) PR:C
GANG WAR *** (1958) PR:C-O
GANG WAR *½ (1962, Brit.) PR:A
GANG'S ALL HERE *½ (1941) PR:A
GANG'S ALL HERE, THE
(SEE:AMAZING MR. FORREST, THE)
GANG, THE ** (1938, Brit.) PR:A
GANGA
(SEE:RIVER, THE)
GANG'S ALL HERE, THE *** (1943) PR:A
GANGS INCORPORATED
(SEE:PAPER BULLETS)
GANGS OF CHICAGO ** (1940) PR:A
GANGS OF NEW YORK **½ (1938) PR:A
GANGS OF SONORA ** (1941) PR:A
GANGS OF THE WATERFRONT *½ (1945) PR:A
GANGSTER STORY **½ (1959) PR:A
GANGSTER VIP, THE * (1968, Jap.) PR:C
GANGSTER'S BRIDE, THE
(SEE:SECRET VALLEY)
GANGSTER'S REVENGE
(SEE:GET OUTTA TOWN)
GANGSTER, THE *** (1947) PR:C
GANGSTER'S BOY *½ (1938) PR:A
GANGSTER'S ENEMY NO. 1
(SEE:TRAIL OF TERROR)
GANGSTERS OF THE FRONTIER *½ (1944) PR:A
GANGWAY *½ (1937, Brit.) PR:A
GANGWAY FOR TOMORROW **½ (1943) PR:A
GANJA AND HESS * (1973) PR:O
GAOL BREAK **½ (1936, Brit.) PR:A
GAOLBREAK *½ (1962, Brit.) PR:A
GAP, THE
(SEE:JOE)
GAPPA THE TRIFIBIAN MONSTER *½
(1967, Jap.) PR:A
GARAKUTA
(SEE:RABBLE, THE)
GARBAGE MAN, THE ** (1963) PR:C
GARBAGE PAIL KIDS MOVIE, THE zero
(1987) PR:C
GARBO TALKS * (1984) PR:C**
GARCON! **½ (1985, Fr.) PR:C
GARDEN MURDER CASE, THE *½ (1936) PR:A
GARDEN OF ALLAH, THE ** (1936) PR:C**
GARDEN OF EDEN *½ (1954) PR:O
GARDEN OF EVIL **½ (1954) PR:C
GARDEN OF THE DEAD zero (1972) PR:O
GARDEN OF THE FINZI-CONTINIS, THE ****
(1971, It./Ger.) PR:C
GARDEN OF THE MOON ** (1938) PR:A
GARDENER, THE
(SEE:SEEDS OF EVIL)
GARDENS OF STONE ** (1987) PR:O
GARMENT JUNGLE, THE *** (1957) PR:A
GARNET BRACELET, THE *** (1966, USSR) PR:A
GARRISON FOLLIES ** (1940, Brit.) PR:A
GARU, THE MAD MONK
(SEE:GURU, THE MAD MONK)
GAS zero (1981, Can.) PR:O
GAS HOUSE KIDS *½ (1946) PR:A
GAS HOUSE KIDS GO WEST * (1947) PR:A
GAS HOUSE KIDS IN HOLLYWOOD * (1947) PR:A
GAS-S-S-S! * (1970) PR:O**
GASBAGS **½ (1940, Brit.) PR:A
GASLIGHT ***** (1940) PR:C
GASLIGHT *** (1944) PR:C**
GASOLINE ALLEY **½ (1951) PR:AA
GASU NINGEN DAIICHIGO
(SEE:HUMAN VAPOR, THE)
GATE OF FLESH * (1964, Jap.) PR:O
GATE OF HELL ** (1954, Jap.) PR:C-O**
GATE, THE **½ (1987, Can.) PR:C
GATES OF HELL, THE zero (1983, US/It.) PR:O
GATES OF PARIS *** (1958, Fr./It.) PR:C
GATES OF THE NIGHT *** (1950, Fr.) PR:C-O
GATES TO PARADISE ** (1968, Brit./Ger.) PR:C
GATEWAY *** (1938) PR:A
GATEWAY TO GLORY * (1970, Jap.) PR:C
GATHERING OF EAGLES, A ** (1963) PR:A
GATLING GUN, THE *½ (1972) PR:C
GATOR ** (1976) PR:C
GATOR BAIT * (1974) PR:O
GAUCHO SERENADE ** (1940) PR:A
GAUCHOS OF EL DORADO *½ (1941) PR:A
GAUNT STRANGER, THE
(SEE:PHANTOM STRIKES, THE)
GAUNTLET, THE ** (1977) PR:O
GAVILAN ** (1968) PR:C
GAWAIN AND THE GREEN KNIGHT **½
(1973, Brit.) PR:C-O
GAY ADVENTURE, THE * (1936, Brit.) PR:A
GAY ADVENTURE, THE * (1953, Brit.) PR:A
GAY AMIGO, THE ** (1949) PR:A
GAY BLADES ** (1946) PR:A
GAY BRIDE, THE ** (1934) PR:A-C
GAY BUCKAROO, THE *½ (1932) PR:A
GAY CABALLERO, THE ** (1932) PR:A
GAY CABALLERO, THE ** (1940) PR:A
GAY CITY, THE
(SEE:LAS VEGAS NIGHTS)
GAY DECEIVERS, THE *½ (1969) PR:O
GAY DECEPTION, THE **½ (1935) PR:A
GAY DESPERADO, THE ***½ (1936) PR:A
GAY DIPLOMAT, THE * (1931) PR:A
GAY DIVORCEE, THE ** (1934) PR:AA**
GAY DOG, THE *½ (1954, Brit.) PR:A
GAY FALCON, THE **½ (1941) PR:A
GAY IMPOSTERS, THE
(SEE:GOLD DIGGERS IN PARIS)
GAY INTRUDERS, THE *** (1946, Brit.) PR:A
GAY INTRUDERS, THE *½ (1948) PR:A
GAY LADY, THE
(SEE:LADY TUBBS)
GAY LADY, THE ** (1949, Brit.) PR:A
GAY LOVE **½ (1936, Brit.) PR:A
GAY NINETIES
(SEE:FLORO DORA GIRL, THE)
GAY OLD DOG *½ (1936, Brit.) PR:A
GAY PURR-EE **½ (1962) PR:AA
GAY RANCHERO, THE **½ (1948) PR:A
GAY SENORITA, THE ** (1945) PR:A
GAY SISTERS, THE *½ (1942) PR:A-C
GAY VAGABOND, THE *½ (1941) PR:A
GAZEBO, THE *** (1959) PR:A
GEEK MAGGOT BINGO zero (1983) PR:O
GEHEIMINISSE IN GOLDEN NYLONS
(SEE:DEAD RUN)
GEISHA BOY, THE *** (1958) PR:A
GEISHA GIRL *½ (1952) PR:A
GEISHA, A *** (1978, Jap.) PR:A
GELIEBTE BESTIE
(SEE:HIPPODROME)
GELIGNITE GANG
(SEE:DYNAMITERS, THE)
GEN TO FUDO-MYOH
(SEE:YOUTH AND HIS AMULET, THE)
GENDARME OF ST. TROPEZ, THE *
(1966, Fr./It.) PR:O
GENE AUTRY AND THE MOUNTIES **½
(1951) PR:A
GENE KRUPA STORY, THE **½ (1959) PR:A-C
GENERAL CRACK ** (1929) PR:A-C
GENERAL DELLA ROVERE ***½
(1960, It./Fr.) PR:C
GENERAL DIED AT DAWN, THE ***½ (1936) PR:C
GENERAL JOHN REGAN ** (1933, Brit.) PR:A
GENERAL MASSACRE ** (1973, US/Bel.) PR:O
GENERAL SPANKY **½ (1937) PR:AA
GENERAL SUVOROV *** (1941, USSR) PR:A
GENERALS OF TOMORROW
(SEE:TOUCHDOWN ARMY)
GENERALS WITHOUT BUTTONS **½
(1938, Fr.) PR:A
GENERATION *½ (1969) PR:C
GENEVIEVE ***½ (1953, Brit.) PR:A
GENGHIS KHAN **½
(1965, US/Brit./Ger./Yugo.) PR:C
GENIE, THE ** (1953, Brit.) PR:A
GENIUS AT WORK *½ (1946) PR:A
GENIUS, THE **½ (1976, It./Fr./Ger.) PR:C
GENTLE ANNIE ** (1944) PR:A
GENTLE ART OF MURDER
(SEE:CRIME DOES NOT PAY)
GENTLE CREATURE, A **** (1971, Fr.) PR:C
GENTLE GANGSTER, A ** (1943) PR:A
GENTLE GIANT * (1967) PR:AA**
GENTLE GUNMAN, THE *** (1952, Brit.) PR:C
GENTLE JULIA *** (1936) PR:A
GENTLE PEOPLE AND THE QUIET LAND, THE *½
(1972) PR:A
GENTLE RAIN, THE *½ (1966, Braz.) PR:O
GENTLE SEX, THE **½ (1943, Brit.) PR:A
GENTLE TERROR, THE *½ (1962, Brit.) PR:A
GENTLE TOUCH, THE ** (1956, Brit.) PR:A
GENTLE TRAP, THE * (1960, Brit.) PR:A
GENTLEMAN AFTER DARK, A ** (1942) PR:A
GENTLEMAN AT HEART, A *** (1942) PR:A
GENTLEMAN CHAUFFEUR
(SEE:WHAT A MAN)
GENTLEMAN FROM ARIZONA, THE **
(1940) PR:A
GENTLEMAN FROM CALIFORNIA, THE
(SEE:CALIFORNIAN, THE)
GENTLEMAN FROM DIXIE ** (1941) PR:A
GENTLEMAN FROM LOUISIANA *** (1936) PR:A
GENTLEMAN FROM NOWHERE, THE **½
(1948) PR:A
GENTLEMAN FROM TEXAS * (1946) PR:A
GENTLEMAN JIM ** (1942) PR:A**
GENTLEMAN JOE PALOOKA
(SEE:JOE PALOOKA, CHAMP)
GENTLEMAN MISBEHAVES, THE * (1946) PR:A
GENTLEMAN OF PARIS, A *½ (1931) PR:A
GENTLEMAN OF VENTURE
(SEE:IT HAPPENED TO ONE MAN)
GENTLEMAN'S AGREEMENT * (1935, Brit.) PR:A
GENTLEMAN'S AGREEMENT **** (1947) PR:A
GENTLEMAN'S FATE **½ (1931) PR:C
GENTLEMAN'S GENTLEMAN, A *½
(1939, Brit.) PR:A
GENTLEMEN ARE BORN ** (1934) PR:A

GENTLEMEN MARRY BRUNETTES **½ (1955) PR:A
GENTLEMEN OF THE NAVY (SEE:ANNAPOLIS FAREWELL)
GENTLEMEN OF THE PRESS **½ (1929) PR:A
GENTLEMEN PREFER BLONDES * (1953) PR:A**
GENTLEMEN WITH GUNS *½ (1946) PR:A
GEORDIE (SEE:WEE GEORDIE)
GEORG **½ (1964) PR:C
GEORGE ** (1973, US/Switz.) PR:A
GEORGE AND MARGARET *** (1940, Brit.) PR:A
GEORGE AND MILDRED * (1980, Brit.) PR:A-C
GEORGE IN CIVVY STREET *½ (1946, Brit.) PR:A
GEORGE RAFT STORY, THE **½ (1961) PR:A
GEORGE TAKES THE AIR (SEE:IT'S IN THE AIR)
GEORGE WASHINGTON CARVER ** (1940) PR:A
GEORGE WASHINGTON SLEPT HERE **** (1942) PR:A
GEORGE WHITE'S 1935 SCANDALS ** (1935) PR:A
GEORGE WHITE'S SCANDALS **½ (1934) PR:AA
GEORGE WHITE'S SCANDALS ** (1945) PR:A
GEORGIA, GEORGIA * (1972) PR:O
GEORGY GIRL ** (1966, Brit.) PR:A-C**
GERALDINE ** (1929) PR:A
GERALDINE ** (1953) PR:A
GERMAN SISTERS, THE ** (1982, Ger.) PR:C-O
GERMANY IN AUTUMN ** (1978, Ger.) PR:O
GERMANY PALE MOTHER ***½ (1984, Ger.) PR:O
GERMANY, YEAR ZERO * (1949, It./Fr./Ger.) PR:C**
GERMINAL ** (1963, Fr.) PR:A
GERONIMO *** (1939) PR:C
GERONIMO **½ (1962) PR:C
GERT AND DAISY CLEAN UP ** (1942, Brit.) PR:A
GERT AND DAISY'S WEEKEND ** (1941, Brit.) PR:A
GERTRUD **½ (1966, Den.) PR:A
GERVAISE * (1956, Fr.) PR:C**
GESTAPO (SEE:NIGHT TRAIN)
GET-AWAY, THE ** (1941) PR:C
GET BACK ** (1973, Can.) PR:C
GET CARTER *** (1971, Brit.) PR:O
GET CHARLIE TULLY ** (1976, Brit.) PR:C
GET CRACKING **½ (1943, Brit.) PR:A
GET CRAZY **½ (1983) PR:O
GET GOING *** (1943) PR:A
GET HEP TO LOVE **½ (1942) PR:A
GET MEAN *½ (1976, It.) PR:C
GET OFF MY FOOT * (1935, Brit.) PR:A
GET ON WITH IT ** (1963, Brit.) PR:A
GET OUT OF TOWN (SEE:GET OUTTA TOWN)
GET OUT YOUR HANDKERCHIEFS **½ (1978, Fr./Bel.) PR:O
GET OUTTA TOWN *½ (1960) PR:C
GET THAT GIRL * (1932) PR:C
GET THAT GIRL, 1936 (SEE:CARYL OF THE MOUNTAINS)
GET THAT MAN *½ (1935) PR:A
GET TO KNOW YOUR RABBIT ** (1972) PR:O
GET YOUR MAN * (1934, Brit.) PR:A
GET YOURSELF A COLLEGE GIRL * (1964) PR:A
GETAWAY, THE ***½ (1972) PR:O
GETTING AWAY WITH MUROER (SEE:END OF THE GAME)
GETTING EVEN * (1981) PR:C
GETTING EVEN *½ (1986) PR:O
GETTING GERTIE'S GARTER *** (1945) PR:A
GETTING OF WISDOM, THE * (1977, Aus.) PR:C**
GETTING OVER * (1981) PR:A-C
GETTING STRAIGHT ***½ (1970) PR:C-O
GETTING TOGETHER zero (1976) PR:O
GHARBAR (SEE:HOUSEHOLDER, THE)
GHARE BAIRE (SEE:HOME AND THE WORLD, THE)
GHASTLY ONES, THE zero (1968) PR:O
GHETTO FREAKS (SEE:SIGN OF AQUARIUS)
GHIDRAH, THE THREE-HEADED MONSTER **½ (1965, Jap.) PR:A
GHOST, THE zero (1965, It.) PR:O
GHOST AND MR. CHICKEN, THE *** (1966) PR:A
GHOST AND MRS. MUIR, THE **** (1942) PR:A
GHOST AND THE GUEST *** (1943) PR:A
GHOST BREAKERS, THE ***½ (1940) PR:A
GHOST CAMERA, THE **½ (1933, Brit.) PR:A
GHOST CATCHERS *** (1944) PR:A
GHOST CHASERS ** (1951) PR:A
GHOST CITY * (1932) PR:A
GHOST COMES HOME, THE **½ (1940) PR:A
GHOST CREEPS, THE (SEE:BOYS OF THE CITY)
GHOST DANCE *½ (1984, Brit.) PR:O
GHOST DIVER ** (1957) PR:A
GHOST FEVER zero (1987) PR:C
GHOST GOES WEST, THE ** (1936) PR:A**
GHOST GOES WILD, THE ** (1947) PR:A
GHOST GUNS ** (1944) PR:A
GHOST IN THE INVISIBLE BIKINI *½ (1966) PR:C
GHOST OF DRAGSTRIP HOLLOW zero (1959) PR:C
GHOST OF FRANKENSTEIN, THE *** (1942) PR:C
GHOST OF HIDDEN VALLEY *½ (1946) PR:A
GHOST OF JOHN HOLLING (SEE:MYSTERY LINER)
GHOST OF ST. MICHAEL'S. THE **½ (1941, Brit.) PR:A
GHOST OF THE CHINA SEA ** (1958) PR:A
GHOST OF ZORRO ** (1959) PR:A
GHOST PATROL ** (1936) PR:A
GHOST RIDER, THE * (1935) PR:A
GHOST SHIP ** (1953, Brit.) PR:A
GHOST SHIP, THE ***½ (1943) PR:C
GHOST STORIES (SEE:KWAIDAN)
GHOST STORY ** (1974, Brit.) PR:C
GHOST STORY **½ (1981) PR:O
GHOST TALKS, THE ** (1929) PR:A
GHOST THAT WALKS ALONE, THE * (1944) PR:A
GHOST TOWN *½ (1937) PR:A
GHOST TOWN ** (1956) PR:A
GHOST TOWN ** (1988) PR:C-O
GHOST TOWN GOLD ** (1937) PR:A
GHOST TOWN LAW *** (1942) PR:C
GHOST TOWN RENEGADES ** (1947) PR:A
GHOST TOWN RIDERS *½ (1938) PR:A
GHOST TRAIN, THE ** (1933, Brit.) PR:A
GHOST TRAIN, THE ** (1941, Brit.) PR:A
GHOST VALLEY **½ (1932) PR:A
GHOST VALLEY RAIDERS ** (1940) PR:A
GHOST WALKS, THE ***½ (1935) PR:A
GHOSTBUSTERS ***½ (1984) PR:A-C
GHOSTS IN THE NIGHT (SEE:GHOSTS ON THE LOOSE)
GHOSTS, ITALIAN STYLE ** (1969, It./Fr.) PR:C
GHOSTS OF BERKELEY SQUARE **½ (1947, Brit.) PR:A
GHOSTS ON THE LOOSE ** (1943) PR:A
GHOUL, THE * (1934, Brit.) PR:C**
GHOUL IN SCHOOL, THE (SEE:WEREWOLF IN A GIRLS' DORMITORY)
GHOUL, THE **½ (1975, Brit.) PR:O
GHOULIES *½ (1985) PR:O
GHOULIES II * (1988) PR:C-O
G.I. EXECUTIONER, THE ** (1985) PR:O
G.I. HONEYMOON ** (1945) PR:A
G.I. JANE ** (1951) PR:A
GIANT ** (1956) PR:A**
GIANT BEHEMOTH, THE (SEE:BEHEMOTH, THE SEA MONSTER)
GIANT CLAW, THE * (1957) PR:A
GIANT FROM THE UNKNOWN zero (1958) PR:C
GIANT GILA MONSTER, THE **½ (1959) PR:A
GIANT LEECHES, THE (SEE:ATTACK OF THE GIANT LEECHES)
GIANT OF MARATHON, THE ** (1960, It.) PR:O
GIANT OF METROPOLIS, THE *½ (1963, It.) PR:A
GIANT SPIDER INVASION, THE zero (1975) PR:A
GIANTS A' FIRE (SEE:ROYAL MOUNTED PATROL)
GIBRALTAR (SEE:IT HAPPENED IN GIBRALTAR)
GIBRALTAR ADVENTURE (SEE:CLUE OF THE MISSING APE, THE)
GIDEON OF SCOTLAND YARD *** (1959, Brit.) PR:A
GIDEON'S DAY (SEE:GIDEON OF SCOTLAND YARD)
GIDGET * (1959) PR:A**
GIDGET GOES HAWAIIAN ** (1961) PR:A
GIDGET GOES TO ROME *½ (1963) PR:A
GIFT (SEE:VENOM)
GIFT HORSE, THE (SEE:GLORY AT SEA)
GIFT OF GAB **½ (1934) PR:A
GIFT OF LOVE, THE ** (1958) PR:A
GIFT, THE ** (1983, Fr./It.) PR:O
GIG, THE ** (1985) PR:A-C**
GIGANTES PLANETARIOS ** (1965, Mex.) PR:A
GIGANTIS *½ (1959, Jap./US) PR:A
GIGI *** (1958) PR:A**
GIGOLETTE *½ (1935) PR:A-C
GIGOLETTES OF PARIS * (1933) PR:A
GIGOT ***½ (1962) PR:A
GILBERT AND SULLIVAN (SEE:GREAT GILBERT AND SULLIVAN, THE)
GILDA ** (1946) PR:C**
GILDED CAGE, THE ** (1954, Brit.) PR:A
GILDED LILY, THE ***½ (1935) PR:AA
GILDERSLEEVE ON BROADWAY **½ (1943) PR:A
GILDERSLEEVE'S BAD DAY ** (1943) PR:A
GILDERSLEEVE'S GHOST ** (1944) PR:A
GILSODOM ***½ (1986, S.K.) PR:O
GIMME AN 'F' zero (1984) PR:O
GINA (SEE:DEATH IN THE GARDEN)
GINGER ** (1935) PR:A
GINGER ** (1947) PR:A
GINGER & FRED * (1986, It./Fr./Ger.) PR:A-C**
GINGER IN THE MORNING ** (1973) PR:A
GION MATSURI (SEE:DAY THE SUN ROSE, THE)
GIORDANO BRUNO *** (1973, It.) PR:O
GIORNI DI FUOCO (SEE:LAST OF THE RENEGADES)
GIPSY BLOOD (SEE:CARMEN)
GIRARA *½ (1967, Jap.) PR:A
GIRDLE OF GOLD *½ (1952, Brit.) PR:A
GIRL, A GUY AND A GOB, A *** (1941) PR:A
GIRL AGAINST NAPOLEON, A (SEE:DEVIL MADE A WOMAN, THE)
GIRL AND THE BURGLER, THE *** (1967, USSR) PR:AA
GIRL AND THE GAMBLER, THE ** (1939) PR:A
GIRL AND THE GENERAL, THE ** (1967, Fr./It.) PR:C
GIRL AND THE LEGEND, THE *½ (1966, Ger.) PR:A
GIRL AND THE PALIO, THE (SEE:LOVE SPECIALIST, THE)
GIRL CAN'T HELP IT, THE ** (1956) PR:C
GIRL CAN'T STOP, THE *½ (1966, Fr./Gr.) PR:C
GIRL CRAZY **½ (1932) PR:A
GIRL CRAZY ** (1943) PR:AA**
GIRL CRAZY, 1965 (SEE:WHEN THE BOYS MEET THE GIRLS)
GIRL DOWNSTAIRS, THE **½ (1938) PR:A
GIRL FEVER * (1961) PR:A
GIRL FOR JOE, A (SEE:FORCE OF ARMS)
GIRL FRIEND, THE **½ (1935) PR:A
GIRL FRIENDS, THE (SEE:LE AMICHE)
GIRL FROM ALASKA ** (1942) PR:A
GIRL FROM AVENUE A ** (1940) PR:A
GIRL FROM CALGARY ** (1932) PR:A
GIRL FROM CHINA, THE (SEE:SHANGHAI LADY)
GIRL FROM GOD'S COUNTRY ** (1940) PR:A
GIRL FROM HAVANA ** (1940) PR:A
GIRL FROM HAVANA, THE **** (1929) PR:A
GIRL FROM HONG KONG ** (1966, Ger.) PR:A
GIRL FROM IRELAND (SEE:KATHLEEN MAVOURNEEN)
GIRL FROM JONES BEACH, THE **½ (1949) PR:AA
GIRL FROM LORRAINE, A *** (1982, Fr./Switz.) PR:O
GIRL FROM MANDALAY * (1936) PR:A
GIRL FROM MANHATTAN ** (1948) PR:A
GIRL FROM MAXIM'S THE ** (1936, Brit.) PR:A
GIRL FROM MEXICO, 1930 (SEE:MEXICALI ROSE)
GIRL FROM MEXICO, THE **½ (1939) PR:A
GIRL FROM MISSOURI, THE *** (1934) PR:A-C
GIRL FROM MONTEREY, THE ** (1943) PR:A

Finding entries in **THE MOTION PICTURE GUIDE ™**

Years	Volumes
Years 1929-83	Volumes I-IX
1984	Volume IX
1985	1986 ANNUAL
1986	1987 ANNUAL
1987	1988 ANNUAL
1988	1989 ANNUAL

STAR RATINGS

★★★★★	Masterpiece
★★★★	Excellent
★★★	Good
★★	Fair
★	Poor
zero	Without Merit

PARENTAL RECOMMENDATION (PR:)

AA	Good for Children
A	Acceptable for Children
C	Cautionary, some objectionable scenes
O	Objectionable for Children

BOLD: Films on Videocassette

GIRL FROM PARIS, THE
(SEE:THAT GIRL FROM PARIS)
GIRL FROM PETROVKA, THE *½ (1974) PR:A
GIRL FROM POLTAVA **½ (1937) PR:A
GIRL FROM RIO, THE ** (1939) PR:A
GIRL FROM SAN LORENZO, THE ** (1950) PR:A
GIRL FROM SCOTLAND YARD, THE ** (1937) PR:A
GIRL FROM STARSHIP VENUS, THE zero (1975, Brit.) PR:O
GIRL FROM TENTH AVENUE, THE **½ (1935) PR:A
GIRL FROM THE MARSH CROFT, THE ** (1935, Ger.) PR:A
GIRL FROM TRIESTE, THE * (1983, It.) PR:C
GIRL FROM VALLADOLIO *½ (1958, Sp.) PR:A
GIRL FROM WOOLWORTH'S, THE *½ (1929) PR:A
GIRL GAME * (1968, Braz./Fr./It.) PR:C
GIRL GETTERS, THE **½ (1966, Brit.) PR:C
GIRL GRABBERS, THE zero (1968) PR:O
GIRL HABIT *½ (1931) PR:A
GIRL HAPPY ** (1965) PR:A
GIRL HE LEFT BEHIND, THE **½ (1956) PR:A
GIRL HUNTERS, THE **½ (1963, Brit.) PR:C-O
GIRL I ABANDONED, THE *½ (1970, Jap.) PR:C-O
GIRL I MADE, THE
(SEE:MADE ON BROADWAY)
GIRL IN A MILLION, A ** (1946, Brit.) PR:A
GIRL IN BLACK STOCKINGS ** (1957) PR:C
GIRL IN DANGER ** (1934) PR:A
GIRL IN DISTRESS **½ (1941, Brit.) PR:A
GIRL IN EVERY PORT, A **½ (1952) PR:A
GIRL IN 419 **½ (1933) PR:A
GIRL IN GOLD BOOTS * (1968) PR:O
GIRL IN HIS POCKET
(SEE:NUDE IN HIS POCKET)
GIRL IN LOVER'S LANE, THE zero (1960) PR:A
GIRL IN OVERALLS, THE
(SEE:SWINGSHIFT MAISIE)
GIRL IN PAWN
(SEE:LITTLE MISS MARKER)
GIRL IN POSSESSION ** (1934, Brit.) PR:A
GIRL IN ROOM 17, THE
(SEE:VICE SQUAD)
GIRL IN ROOM 13 * (1961, US/Braz.) PR:A
GIRL IN THE BIKINI, THE *½ (1958, Fr.) PR:C
GIRL IN THE CASE ** (1944) PR:A
GIRL IN THE CROWD, THE *½ (1934, Brit.) PR:A
GIRL IN THE FLAT, THE * (1934, Brit.) PR:A
GIRL IN THE GLASS CAGE, THE *½ (1929) PR:A
GIRL IN THE HEADLINES, THE
(SEE:MODEL MURDER CASE, THE)
GIRL IN THE INVISIBLE BIKINI, THE
(SEE:GHOST IN THE INVISIBLE BIKINI, THE)
GIRL IN THE KREMLIN, THE zero (1957) PR:A
GIRL IN THE LEATHER SUIT
(SEE:HELLS BELLES)
GIRL IN THE NEWS, THE **½ (1941, Brit.) PR:A
GIRL IN THE NIGHT, THE ** (1931, Brit.) PR:A
GIRL IN THE PAINTING, THE *** (1948, Brit.) PR:A
GIRL IN THE PICTURE, THE ** (1956, Brit.) PR:A
GIRL IN THE PICTURE, THE * (1985, Brit.) PR:C**
GIRL IN THE RED VELVET SWING, THE **½ (1955) PR:C
GIRL IN THE SHOW, THE *½ (1929) PR:A
GIRL IN THE STREET ** (1938, Brit.) PR:A
GIRL IN THE TAXI * (1937, Brit.) PR:A
GIRL IN THE WOODS ** (1958) PR:A
GIRL IN 313 ** (1940) PR:A
GIRL IN TROUBLE * (1963) PR:C
GIRL IN WHITE, THE **** (1952) PR:A
GIRL IS MINE, THE ** (1950, Brit.) PR:A
GIRL LOVES BOY ** (1937) PR:A
GIRL MADNESS
(SEE:BEAST OF YUCCA FLATS, THE)
GIRL MERCHANTS
(SEE:SELLERS OF GIRLS)
GIRL MISSING * (1933) PR:A
GIRL MOST LIKELY, THE **½ (1957) PR:AA
GIRL MUST LIVE, A *** (1941, Brit.) PR:A
GIRL NAMED TAMIKO, A **½ (1962) PR:A
GIRL NEXT DOOR, THE **½ (1953) PR:A
GIRL O' MY DREAMS ** (1935) PR:A
GIRL OF MY DREAMS
(SEE:SWEETHEART OF SIGMA CHI, THE)
GIRL OF THE GOLDEN WEST **½ (1930) PR:A
GIRL OF THE GOLDEN WEST, THE **½ (1938) PR:AA
GIRL OF THE LIMBERLOST ** (1934) PR:A
GIRL OF THE LIMBERLOST, THE ** (1945) PR:A
GIRL OF THE MOORS, THE ** (1961, Ger.) PR:C-O
GIRL OF THE MOUNTAINS ** (1958, Gr.) PR:C-O
GIRL OF THE NIGHT ** (1960) PR:C-O
GIRL OF THE OZARKS **½ (1936) PR:A
GIRL OF THE PORT * (1930) PR:A
GIRL OF THE RIO ** (1932) PR:A
GIRL OF THE YEAR
(SEE:PRETTY GIRL, THE)
GIRL ON A CHAIN GANG * (1966) PR:O
GIRL ON A MOTORCYCLE, THE ** (1968, Fr./Brit.) PR:O
GIRL ON APPROVAL *½ (1962, Brit.) PR:A
GIRL ON THE BARGE, THE *½ (1929) PR:A
GIRL ON THE BOAT, THE ** (1962, Brit.) PR:A
GIRL ON THE BRIDGE, THE zero (1951) PR:A
GIRL ON THE CANAL, THE ** (1947, Brit.) PR:A
GIRL ON THE FRONT PAGE, THE ** (1936) PR:A
GIRL ON THE PIER, THE * (1953, Brit.) PR:A
GIRL ON THE RUN * (1961) PR:A
GIRL ON THE SPOT ** (1946) PR:A
GIRL OVERBOARD *½ (1929) PR:A
GIRL OVERBOARD * (1937) PR:A
GIRL RUSH ** (1944) PR:A
GIRL RUSH, THE **½ (1955) PR:A
GIRL SAID NO, THE *½ (1937) PR:A
GIRL SAID NO, THE * (1930) PR:A
GIRL SMUGGLERS * (1967) PR:O
GIRL STROKE BOY **½ (1971, Brit.) PR:C
GIRL SWAPPERS, THE
(SEE:TWO AND TWO MAKE SIX)
GIRL, THE BODY, AND THE PILL, THE zero (1967) PR:O
GIRL THIEF, THE * (1938) PR:AA
GIRL TROUBLE **½ (1942) PR:A
GIRL WAS YOUNG, THE
(SEE:YOUNG AND INNOCENT)
GIRL WHO CAME BACK, THE *½ (1935) PR:A
GIRL WHO COULDN'T QUITE, THE ** (1949, Brit.) PR:A
GIRL WHO COULDN'T SAY NO, THE ** (1969, It.) PR:A
GIRL WHO DARED, THE *½ (1944) PR:A
GIRL WHO FORGOT, THE * (1939, Brit.) PR:A
GIRL WHO HAD EVERYTHING, THE **½ (1953) PR:A
GIRL WHO KNEW TOO MUCH, THE * (1969) PR:O
GIRL WITH A PISTOL, THE **½ (1968, It.) PR:A
GIRL WITH A SUITCASE ***½ (1961, Fr./It.) PR:A
GIRL WITH GREEN EYES ***½ (1964, Brit.) PR:A-C
GIRL WITH IDEAS, A *** (1937) PR:A
GIRL WITH THE GOLDEN EYES, THE *½ (1962, Fr.) PR:C
GIRL WITH THE RED HAIR, THE ** (1983, Neth.) PR:A
GIRL WITH THREE CAMELS, THE ** (1968, Czech.) PR:A
GIRL WITHOUT A ROOM ** (1933) PR:A
GIRL, THE *½ (1987, Brit.) PR:O
GIRLFRIENDS ***½ (1978) PR:A-C
GIRLS ABOUT TOWN **½ (1931) PR:O
GIRLS AT SEA ** (1958, Brit.) PR:A
GIRLS CAN PLAY ** (1937) PR:A
GIRLS DEMAND EXCITEMENT * (1931) PR:A
GIRLS DISAPPEAR
(SEE:ROAD TO SHAME, THE)
GIRLS' DORMITORY *** (1936) PR:A
GIRLS FROM THUNDER STRIP, THE zero (1966) PR:O
GIRLS! GIRLS! GIRLS! **½ (1962) PR:A
GIRLS HE LEFT BEHIND, THE
(SEE:GANG'S ALL HERE, THE)
GIRLS IN ACTION
(SEE:OPERATION DAMES)
GIRLS IN ARMS
(SEE:OPERATION BULLSHINE)
GIRLS IN CHAINS *½ (1943) PR:A
GIRLS IN PRISON *½ (1956) PR:C
GIRLS IN THE NIGHT *½ (1953 83m UNIV bw) PR:C
GIRLS IN THE STREET *½ (1937, Brit.) PR:A
GIRLS IN UNIFORM
(SEE:MAEDCHEN IN UNIFORM)
GIRLS IN UNIFORM
(SEE:MAEDCHEN IN UNIFORM)
GIRLS JUST WANT TO HAVE FUN ** (1985) PR:C
GIRLS NEVER TELL
(SEE:HER FIRST ROMANCE)
GIRLS NIGHT OUT zero (1984) PR:O
GIRLS OF LATIN QUARTER * (1960, Brit.) PR:A
GIRLS OF PLEASURE ISLAND, THE **½ (1953) PR:A
GIRLS OF SPIDER ISLAND
(SEE:IT'S HOT IN PARADISE)
GIRLS OF THE BIG HOUSE ** (1945) PR:A
GIRLS OF THE ROAD *½ (1940) PR:C
GIRLS ON PROBATION * (1938) PR:A
GIRLS ON THE BEACH ** (1965) PR:A
GIRLS ON THE LOOSE **½ (1958) PR:O
GIRLS PLEASE! *½ (1934, Brit.) PR:A
GIRLS' SCHOOL **½ (1938) PR:A
GIRLS' SCHOOL * (1950) PR:A
GIRLS SCHOOL SCREAMERS *½ (1986) PR:O
GIRLS' TOWN ** (1942) PR:A
GIRLS' TOWN * (1959) PR:C
GIRLS UNDER TWENTY-ONE **½ (1940) PR:A
GIRLS WILL BE BOYS **½ (1934, Brit.) PR:A
GIRLS, THE ** (1972, Swed.) PR:O
GIRLY
(SEE:MUMSY, NANNY, SONNY AND GIRLY)
GIRO CITY * (1982, Brit.) PR:C
GIT! **½ (1965) PR:AA
GIT ALONG, LITTLE DOGIES * (1937) PR:A
GIU LA TESTA
(SEE:DUCK, YOU SUCKER!)
GIULIETTA DEGLI SPIRITI
(SEE:JULIET OF THE SPIRITS)
GIULIO CEASRE IL CONQUISTATORE DELLE GALLIE
(SEE:CAESAR THE CONQUEROR)
GIUSEPPE VENDUTO DAI FRATELLI
(SEE:STORY OF JOSEPH AND HIS BRETHREN, THE)
GIVE A DOG A BONE * (1967, Brit.) PR:A
GIVE A GIRL A BREAK **½ (1953) PR:A
GIVE AND TAKE *½ (1929) PR:A
GIVE AND TAKE
(SEE:SINGING IN THE CORN)
GIVE HER A RING * (1936, Brit.) PR:A
GIVE HER THE MOON *** (1970, Fr./It.) PR:A
GIVE ME A SAILOR **½ (1938) PR:A
GIVE ME MY CHANCE ** (1958, Fr.) PR:C
GIVE ME THE STARS ** (1944, Brit.) PR:A
GIVE ME YOUR HEART **½ (1936) PR:A
GIVE MY REGARDS TO BROAD STREET ** (1984, Brit.) PR:A-C
GIVE MY REGARDS TO BROADWAY *** (1948) PR:A
GIVE OUT, SISTERS ** (1942) PR:A
GIVE US THE MOON ** (1944, Brit.) PR:A
GIVE US THIS DAY
(SEE:SALT TO THE DEVIL)
GIVE US THIS NIGHT ** (1936) PR:A
GIVE US WINGS ** (1940) PR:A
GIVE'EM HELL, HARRY! * (1975) PR:A**
GIVEN WORD, THE **½ (1964, Braz.) PR:A
GLAD RAG DOLL, THE ** (1929) PR:O
GLAD TIDINGS *½ (1953, Brit.) PR:A
GLADIATOR, THE ***½ (1938) PR:AA
GLADIATOR OF ROME * (1963, It.) PR:C
GLADIATORERNA
(SEE:GLADIATORS, THE)
GLADIATORS 7 *½ (1964, Sp./It.) PR:O
GLADIATORS, THE *½ (1970, Swed.) PR:C-O
GLAMOROUS NIGHT **½ (1937, Brit.) PR:C
GLAMOUR *½ (1931, Brit.) PR:A
GLAMOUR *½ (1934) PR:C
GLAMOUR BOY
(SEE:MILLIONAIRE PLAYBOY)
GLAMOUR BOY ***½ (1941) PR:AA
GLAMOUR FOR SALE ** (1940) PR:A
GLAMOUR GIRL ** (1938, Brit.) PR:A
GLAMOUR GIRL **½ (1947) PR:A
GLASS ALIBI, THE *** (1946) PR:A
GLASS BOTTOM BOAT, THE *** (1966) PR:A
GLASS CAGE, THE
(SEE:GLASS TOMB, THE)
GLASS CAGE, THE ** (1964) PR:O
GLASS HOUSES **½ (1972) PR:O
GLASS KEY, THE *** (1935) PR:C
GLASS KEY, THE ***½ (1942) PR:O
GLASS MENAGERIE, THE *** (1950) PR:A
GLASS MENAGERIE, THE ***½ (1987) PR:C
GLASS MOUNTAIN, THE ** (1950, Brit.) PR:A
GLASS OF WATER, A *½ (1962, Ger.) PR:A
GLASS SLIPPER, THE ** (1955) PR:A
GLASS SPHINX, THE * (1968, Egypt/It./Sp.) PR:A
GLASS TOMB, THE * (1955, Brit.) PR:A
GLASS TOWER, THE ** (1959, Ger.) PR:A
GLASS WALL, THE **½ (1953) PR:A
GLASS WEB, THE **½ (1953) PR:A
GLEN OR GLENDA zero (1953) PR:O
GLENN MILLER STORY, THE ** (1953) PR:AA**
GLENROWAN AFFAIR, THE *½ (1951, Aus.) PR:C
GLIMPSE OF PARADISE, A *½ (1934, Brit.) PR:A
GLITTERBALL, THE *** (1977, Brit.) PR:AA
GLOBAL AFFAIR, A ** (1964) PR:A
GLORIA ***½ (1980) PR:O
GLORIFYING THE AMERICAN GIRL **½ (1930) PR:A
GLORIOUS SACRIFICE
(SEE:GLORY TRAIL, THE)
GLORY **½ (1955) PR:AA
GLORY ALLEY ** (1952) PR:C
GLORY AT SEA **½ (1952, Brit.) PR:A
GLORY BOY *½ (1971) PR:O
GLORY BRIGADE, THE *** (1953) PR:C
GLORY GUYS, THE ** (1965) PR:C
GLORY OF FAITH, THE **½ (1938, Fr.) PR:A
GLORY STOMPERS, THE zero (1967) PR:O
GLORY TRAIL, THE *½ (1937) PR:A
GLOVE, THE *½ (1980) PR:O
GLOWING AUTUMN ** (1981, Jap.) PR:A-C
GNOME-MOBILE, THE ** (1967) PR:AA**
GO-BETWEEN, THE **** (1971, Brit.) PR:A-C
GO CHASE YOURSELF *** (1938) PR:A

GO FOR BROKE * (1951) PR:A**
GO-GETTER, THE ** (1937) PR:A
GO-GO SET (SEE:GET YOURSELF A COLLEGE GIRL)
GO INTO YOUR DANCE **½ (1935) PR:A
GO, JOHNNY, GO! **½ (1959) PR:A
GO KART GO ** (1964, Brit.) PR:AA
GO, MAN, GO! * (1954) PR:A**
GO MASTERS, THE * (1985, Jap./Chi.) PR:C**
GO NAKED IN THE WORLD ** (1961) PR:O
GO TELL IT ON THE MOUNTAIN *** (1984) PR:A
GO TELL THE SPARTANS ***½ (1978) PR:O
GO TO BLAZES **½ (1962, Brit.) PR:A
GO WEST **½ (1940) PR:A
GO WEST, YOUNG LADY ** (1941) PR:A
GO WEST, YOUNG MAN ** (1936) PR:C
GOBEN NO TSUBAKI (SEE:SCARLET CAMELLIA, THE)
GOBOTS: BATTLE OF THE ROCKLORDS * (1986) PR:AA
GOBS AND GALS ** (1952) PR:A
GOD FORGIVES—I DON'T! *½ (1969, It./Sp.) PR:O
GOD GAME, THE (SEE:MAGUS, THE)
GOD GAVE HIM A DOG (SEE:BISCUIT EATER, THE)
GOD IS MY CO-PILOT ***½ (1945) PR:A
GOD IS MY PARTNER *½ (1957) PR:A
GOD TOLD ME TO * (1976) PR:O**
GODDESS, THE *** (1962, India) PR:C
GODDESS OF LOVE, THE ** (1960, It./Fr.) PR:O
GODDESS, THE **½ (1958) PR:C-O
GODFATHER, THE *** (1972) PR:O**
GODFATHER, THE, PART II *** (1974) PR:O**
GODLESS GIRL, THE ** (1929) PR:C
GOD'S COUNTRY *½ (1946) PR:A
GOD'S COUNTRY AND THE MAN *½ (1931) PR:A
GOD'S COUNTRY AND THE MAN ** (1937) PR:A
GOD'S COUNTRY AND THE WOMAN ** (1937) PR:A
GOD'S GIFT TO WOMEN ** (1931) PR:A
GOD'S GUN *½ (1977) PR:O
GOD'S LITTLE ACRE * (1958) PR:O**
GODS MUST BE CRAZY, THE ** (1984, Botswana) PR:C**
GODSEND, THE * (1980, Can.) PR:O
GODSON, THE *** (1972, It./Fr.) PR:C-O
GODSPELL ** (1973) PR:C
GODY MOLODYYE (SEE:TRAIN GOES TO KIEV, THE)
GODZILLA (SEE:GODZILLA, KING OF THE MONSTERS)
GODZILLA, KING OF THE MONSTERS **½ (1956, Jap.) PR:C
GODZILLA 1985 *½ (1985, Jap.) PR:C
GODZILLA TAI MOTHRA (SEE:GODZILLA VS. THE THING)
GODZILLA VERSUS THE COSMIC MONSTER *½ (1974, Jap.) PR:C
GODZILLA VERSUS THE SEA MONSTER *½ (1966, Jap.) PR:C
GODZILLA VERSUS THE SMOG MONSTER zero (1972, Jap.) PR:C
GODZILLA VS. MEGALON *½ (1976, Jap.) PR:C
GODZILLA VS. THE THING *½ (1964, Jap.) PR:C
GODZILLA'S REVENGE * (1969) PR:C
GOFORTH (SEE:BOOM!)
GOG ** (1954) PR:A
GOHA **½ (1958, Tunisia) PR:O
GOIN' COCONUTS **½ (1978) PR:AA
GOIN' DOWN THE ROAD ***½ (1970, Can.) PR:O
GOIN' HOME **½ (1976) PR:AA
GOIN' SOUTH ** (1978) PR:O
GOIN' TO TOWN ** (1935) PR:C
GOIN' TO TOWN **½ (1944) PR:A
GOING AND COMING BACK ** (1985, Fr.) PR:O
GOING APE! *½ (1981) PR:A
GOING BERSERK zero (1983) PR:O
GOING GAY (SEE:KISS ME GOODBYE)
GOING HIGHBROW ** (1935) PR:A
GOING HOLLYWOOD *** (1933) PR:A
GOING HOME ** (1971) PR:O
GOING HOME ** (1988, Brit./Can.) PR:C
GOING IN STYLE ** (1979) PR:C**
GOING MY WAY *** (1944) PR:AA**
GOING PLACES ** (1939) PR:A
GOING PLACES **½ (1974, Fr.) PR:O
GOING STEADY ** (1958) PR:A
GOING STRAIGHT * (1933, Brit.) PR:A
GOING TO TOWN (SEE:MA AND PA KETTLE GO TO TOWN)
GOING WILD ** (1931) PR:A
GOJIRA TAI MOSUHA (SEE:GODZILLA VS. THE THING)
GOJUMAN-NIN NO ISAN (SEE:LEGACY OF THE 500,000, THE)
GOKE, BODYSNATCHER FROM HELL * (1968, Jap.) PR:O
GOLD ** (1932) PR:A
GOLD ** (1934, Ger.) PR:C
GOLD ** (1974, Brit.) PR:O
GOLD DIGGERS IN PARIS **½ (1938) PR:A
GOLD DIGGERS OF 1933 ** (1933) PR:A**
GOLD DIGGERS OF 1935 *** (1935) PR:A
GOLD DIGGERS OF 1937 *** (1936) PR:A
GOLD DIGGERS OF BROADWAY **½ (1929) PR:A
GOLD DUST GERTIE *½ (1931) PR:A
GOLD EXPRESS, THE * (1955, Brit.) PR:A
GOLD FEVER ** (1952) PR:A
GOLD FOR THE CAESARS *½ (1964) PR:C
GOLD GUITAR, THE *½ (1966) PR:A
GOLD IS WHERE YOU FIND IT *** (1938) PR:A
GOLD MINE IN THE SKY ** (1938) PR:A
GOLD OF NAPLES ** (1957, It.) PR:C-O
GOLD OF THE SEVEN SAINTS ** (1961) PR:A
GOLD RACKET, THE * (1937) PR:A
GOLD RAIDERS, THE * (1952) PR:A
GOLD RUSH MAISIE ** (1940) PR:A
GOLDBERGS, THE **½ (1950) PR:A
GOLDEN APPLES OF THE SUN zero (1971, Can.) PR:O
GOLDEN ARROW, THE **½ (1936) PR:A
GOLDEN ARROW, THE (SEE:GAY ADVENTURE, THE)
GOLDEN ARROW, THE *½ (1964, It.) PR:A
GOLDEN BLADE, THE **½ (1953) PR:A
GOLDEN BOX, THE ** (1970) PR:O
GOLDEN BOY ** (1939) PR:A**
GOLDEN BULLET (SEE:IMPASSE)
GOLDEN CAGE, THE ** (1933, Brit.) PR:A
GOLDEN CALF, THE ** (1930) PR:AA
GOLDEN CHILD, THE * (1986) PR:C
GOLDEN COACH, THE **½ (1953, Fr./It.) PR:A
GOLDEN DAWN ** (1930) PR:A
GOLDEN DEMON **½ (1956, Jap.) PR:C
GOLDEN DISK (SEE:INBETWEEN AGE, THE)
GOLDEN EARRINGS **½ (1947) PR:C
GOLDEN EIGHTIES ***½ (1986, Fr./Bel./Switz.) PR:A
GOLDEN EYE, THE (SEE:MYSTERY OF THE GOLDEN EYE)
GOLDEN FLEECING, THE ** (1940) PR:A
GOLDEN GATE GIRL ** (1941) PR:C
GOLDEN GIRL *** (1951) PR:AA
GOLDEN GLOVES (SEE:EX-CHAMP)
GOLDEN GLOVES ** (1940) PR:A
GOLDEN GLOVES STORY, THE ** (1950) PR:A
GOLDEN GOOSE, THE **½ (1966, E. Ger.) PR:AA
GOLDEN HARVEST **½ (1933) PR:A
GOLDEN HAWK, THE **½ (1952) PR:A
GOLDEN HEAD, THE ** (1965, Hung./US) PR:A
GOLDEN HEIST, THE (SEE:INSIDE OUT)
GOLDEN HELMET (SEE:CASQUE D'OR)
GOLDEN HOOFS **½ (1941) PR:AA
GOLDEN HORDE, THE **½ (1951) PR:A
GOLDEN IDOL, THE ** (1954) PR:AA
GOLDEN IVORY (SEE:WHITE HUNTRESS)
GOLDEN LADY, THE * (1979, Brit.) PR:O
GOLDEN LINK, THE *** (1954, Brit.) PR:A
GOLDEN MADONNA, THE **½ (1949, Brit.) PR:A
GOLDEN MARIE (SEE:CASQUE D'OR)
GOLDEN MASK, THE **½ (1954, Brit.) PR:A
GOLDEN MISTRESS, THE ** (1954) PR:A
GOLDEN MOUNTAINS **½ (1958, Den.) PR:A
GOLDEN NEEDLES *½ (1974) PR:O
GOLDEN NYMPHS, THE (SEE:HONEYMOON OF HORROR)
GOLDEN PLAGUE, THE *½ (1963, Ger.) PR:A
GOLDEN RABBIT, THE * (1962, Brit.) PR:A
GOLDEN RENDEZVOUS * (1977) PR:O
GOLDEN SALAMANDER *** (1950, Brit.) PR:A
GOLDEN SEAL, THE ** (1983) PR:AA
GOLDEN STALLION, THE **½ (1949) PR:A
GOLDEN TRAIL, THE (SEE:RIDERS OF THE WHISTLING SKULL, THE)
GOLDEN TRAIL, THE ** (1940) PR:A
GOLDEN VOYAGE OF SINBAD, THE ***½ (1974, Brit.) PR:AA
GOLDEN WEST, THE ** (1932) PR:A
GOLDENGIRL zero (1979) PR:O
GOLDFINGER ** (1964, Brit.) PR:C-O**
GOLDIE * (1931) PR:A
GOLDIE GETS ALONG ** (1933) PR:A
GOLDSTEIN **½ (1964) PR:O
GOLDTOWN GHOST RIDERS ** (1953) PR:A
GOLDWYN FOLLIES, THE ** (1938) PR:A
GOLEM, THE *** (1937, Czech./Fr.) PR:C
GOLEM ** (1980, Pol.) PR:C
GOLFO (SEE:GIRL OF THE MOUNTAINS)
GOLGOTHA **½ (1937, Fr.) PR:A
GOLIATH AGAINST THE GIANTS * (1963, It./Sp.) PR:A
GOLIATH AND THE BARBARIANS ** (1960, It.) PR:A
GOLIATH AND THE DRAGON *½ (1961, It./Fr.) PR:A
GOLIATH AND THE SINS OF BABYLON ** (1964, It.) PR:A
GOLIATH AND THE VAMPIRES * (1964, It.) PR:C
GOLIATHON zero (1979, Hong Kong) PR:C
GONE ARE THE DAYS * (1963) PR:A**
GONE IN 60 SECONDS ** (1974) PR:C
GONE TO EARTH (SEE:WILD HEART, THE)
GONE TO THE DOGS *½ (1939, Aus.) PR:A
GONE WITH THE WIND *** (1939) PR:A**
GONG SHOW MOVIE, THE zero (1980) PR:C
GONKS GO BEAT *½ (1965, Brit.) PR:A
GOOD BAD GIRL, THE ** (1931) PR:C
GOOD BEGINNING, THE * (1953, Brit.) PR:A
GOOD COMPANIONS ** (1933, Brit.) PR:A
GOOD COMPANIONS, THE **½ (1957, Brit.) PR:A
GOOD DAME * (1934) PR:A
GOOD DAY FOR A HANGING **½ (1958) PR:A
GOOD DAY FOR FIGHTING (SEE:CUSTER OF THE WEST)
GOOD DIE YOUNG, THE **½ (1954, Brit.) PR:C
GOOD DISSONANCE LIKE A MAN, A ***½ (1977) PR:C
GOOD EARTH, THE *** (1937) PR:A**
GOOD FAIRY, THE ***½ (1935) PR:A
GOOD FATHER, THE * (1986, Brit.) PR:O**
GOOD FELLOWS, THE ** (1943) PR:A
GOOD GIRLS GO TO PARIS **½ (1939) PR:A
GOOD GUYS AND THE BAD GUYS, THE *½ (1969) PR:A-C
GOOD GUYS WEAR BLACK **½ (1978) PR:O
GOOD HUMOR MAN, THE *** (1950) PR:A
GOOD INTENTIONS ** (1930) PR:A
GOOD LUCK, MISS WYCKOFF zero (1979) PR:O
GOOD LUCK, MR. YATES ** (1943) PR:A
GOOD MORNING. . . AND GOODBYE zero (1967) PR:O
GOOD MORNING BABYLON **½ (1987, It./Fr./USA) PR:C-O
GOOD MORNING, BOYS (SEE:WHERE THERE'S A WILL)
GOOD MORNING, DOCTOR (SEE:YOU BELONG TO ME)
GOOD MORNING, JUDGE **½ (1943) PR:A
GOOD MORNING, MISS DOVE *** (1955) PR:A
GOOD MORNING, VIETNAM ***½ (1987) PR:O
GOOD MOTHER, THE ** (1988) PR:O
GOOD NEIGHBOR SAM ***½ (1964) PR:A-C
GOOD NEWS ** (1930) PR:A
GOOD NEWS ** (1947) PR:AA**
GOOD OLD DAYS, THE ** (1939, Brit.) PR:A
GOOD OLD SOAK, THE ** (1937) PR:A
GOOD SAM **½ (1948) PR:A
GOOD SOLDIER SCHWEIK, THE *** (1963, Ger.) PR:C

Finding entries in **THE MOTION PICTURE GUIDE ™**

Years	Volume
1929-83	Volumes I-IX
1984	Volume IX
1985	1986 ANNUAL
1986	1987 ANNUAL
1987	1988 ANNUAL
1988	1989 ANNUAL

STAR RATINGS

★★★★★	Masterpiece
★★★★	Excellent
★★★	Good
★★	Fair
★	Poor
zero	Without Merit

PARENTAL RECOMMENDATION (PR:)

AA	Good for Children
A	Acceptable for Children
C	Cautionary, some objectionable scenes
O	Objectionable for Children

BOLD: Films on Videocassette

GOOD SPORT **½ (1931) PR:A
GOOD, THE BAD, AND THE UGLY, THE **** (1967, It./Sp.) PR:O
GOOD TIME GIRL **½ (1950, Brit.) PR:O
GOOD TIMES *½ (1967) PR:A
GOOD WIFE, THE ** (1987, Aus.) PR:C-O
GOODBYE AGAIN **½ (1933) PR:A
GOODBYE AGAIN *** (1961) PR:A
GOODBYE BROADWAY ** (1938) PR:A
GOODBYE BRUCE LEE: HIS LAST GAME OF DEATH
   (SEE:GAME OF DEATH)
GOODBYE CHARLIE **½ (1964) PR:C
GOODBYE COLUMBUS * (1969) PR:O
GOODBYE EMMANUELLE zero (1980, Fr.) PR:O
GOODBYE FRANKLIN HIGH **½ (1978) PR:A
GOODBYE GEMINI * (1970, Brit.) PR:O
GOODBYE GIRL, THE **** (1977) PR:C
GOODBYE LOVE *½ (1934) PR:A
GOODBYE MR. CHIPS **** (1939, Brit.) PR:AA
GOODBYE MR. CHIPS **½ (1969, US/Brit.) PR:A
GOODBYE, MOSCOW ** (1968, Jap.) PR:O
GOODBYE, MY FANCY ** (1951) PR:A
GOODBYE, MY LADY *** (1956) PR:AA
GOODBYE NEW YORK *** (1985, Israel) PR:O
GOODBYE, NORMA JEAN zero (1976) PR:O
GOODBYE PEOPLE, THE *** (1984) PR:A-C
GOODBYE PORK PIE **½ (1981, New Zealand) PR:C
GOODBYE TO THE HILL
   (SEE:PADDY)
GOODBYE, CHILDREN
   (SEE:AU REVOIR LES ENFANTS)
GOODNIGHT, LADIES AND GENTLEMEN **½ (1977, It.) PR:C-O
GOODNIGHT SWEETHEART *½ (1944) PR:A
GOODNIGHT VIENNA
   (SEE:MAGIC NIGHT)
GOOFBALLS * (1987) PR:C
GOONIES, THE * (1985) PR:C
GOOSE AND THE GANDER, THE ** (1935) PR:A
GOOSE GIRL, THE **½ (1967, Ger.) PR:C-O
GOOSE STEP
   (SEE:BEASTS OF BERLIN)
GOOSE STEPS OUT, THE ** (1942, Brit.) PR:A
GORATH *½ (1964, Jap.) PR:C
GORBALS STORY, THE *½ (1950, Brit.) PR:C
GORDEYEV FAMILY, THE **½ (1961, USSR) PR:O)
GORDON IL PIHATA NERO
   (SEE:RAGE OF THE BUCCANEERS)
GORDON'S WAR * (1973) PR:O
GORGEOUS HUSSY, THE **½ (1936) PR:AA
GORGO **½ (1961, Brit.) PR:C
GORGON, THE **½ (1964, Brit.) PR:C-O
GORILLA, THE *½ (1931) PR:A
GORILLA, THE ** (1939) PR:A
GORILLA
   (SEE:NABONGA)
GORILLA ** (1964, Swed.) PR:C
GORILLA AT LARGE **½ (1954) PR:C
GORILLA GREETS YOU, THE **½ (1958, Fr.) PR:C
GORILLA MAN ** (1942) PR:A
GORILLA SHIP, THE * (1932) PR:A
GORILLAS IN THE MIST *** (1988) PR:C
GORKY PARK *** (1983) PR:O
GORP zero (1980) PR:O
GOSPEL ACCORDING TO ST. MATTHEW, THE *** (1966, Fr./It.) PR:A
GOSPEL ACCORDING TO VIC, THE *** (1986, Brit.) PR:C
GOSPEL ROAD, THE ** (1973) PR:A
GOT IT MADE ** (1974, Brit.) PR:C-O
GOT WHAT SHE WANTED * (1930) PR:A
GOTCHA! ** (1985) PR:O
GOTHIC *½ (1987, Brit.) PR:O
GOUPI MAINS ROUGES
   (SEE:IT HAPPENED AT THE INN)
GOVERNMENT GIRL ** (1943) PR:A
GOYOKIN ** (1969, Jap.) PR:O
GRACE QUIGLEY
   (SEE:ULTIMATE SOLUTION OF GRACE QUIGLEY, THE)
GRACIE ALLEN MURDER CASE ** (1939) PR:A
GRADUATE, THE ***** (1967) PR:A
GRADUATION DAY * (1981) PR:O
GRAFT ** (1931) PR:C
GRAN VARIETA *** (1955, It.) PR:A
GRANATOVYY BRASLET
   (SEE:GARNET BRACELET, THE)
GRAND CANARY *½ (1934) PR:A
GRAND CANYON ** (1949) PR:A
GRAND CANYON TRAIL **½ (1948) PR:A
GRAND CENTRAL MURDER *** (1942) PR:A
GRAND DUKE AND MR. PIMM
   (SEE:LOVE IS A BALL)
GRAND ESCAPADE, THE ** (1946, Brit.) PR:A
GRAND EXIT ** (1935) PR:A
GRAND FINALE * (1936, Brit.) PR:A
GRAND HIGHWAY, THE **½ (1988, Fr.) PR:O

GRAND HOTEL ***** (1932) PR:A
GRAND ILLUSION ***** (1938, Fr.) PR:A
GRAND JURY *½ (1936) PR:A
GRAND JURY SECRETS *½ (1939) PR:A
GRAND MANEUVER, THE **** (1956, Fr.) PR:C
GRAND NATIONAL NIGHT
   (SEE:WICKED WIFE, THE)
GRAND OLD GIRL * (1935) PR:A
GRAND OLE OPRY ** (1940) PR:A
GRAND PARADE, THE *½ (1930) PR:A
GRAND PRIX ** (1934, Brit.) PR:A
GRAND PRIX *½ (1966) PR:O
GRAND SLAM **½ (1933) PR:A
GRAND SLAM *** (1968, It./Sp./Ger.) PR:A-C
GRAND SUBSTITUTION, THE **½ (1965, Hong Kong) PR:C
GRAND THEFT AUTO **½ (1977) PR:C
GRANDAD RUDD **½ (1935, Aus.) PR:A
GRANDPA GOES TO TOWN ** (1940) PR:A
GRANDVIEW, U.S.A. **½ (1984) PR:O
GRANNY GET YOUR GUN * (1940) PR:A
GRAPES OF WRATH ***** (1940) PR:A
GRASS EATER, THE * (1961) PR:C
GRASS IS GREENER, THE ** (1960) PR:A
GRASS IS SINGING, THE ** (1982, Brit./Swed.) PR:A
GRASS IS SINGING, THE
   (SEE:KILLING HEAT)
GRASSHOPPER, THE *** (1970) PR:O
GRAVE OF THE VAMPIRE zero (1972) PR:O
GRAVE ROBBERS FROM OUTER SPACE
   (SEE:PLAN 9 FROM OUTER SPACE)
GRAVESIDE STORY, THE
   (SEE:COMEDY OF TERRORS, THE)
GRAVEYARD OF HORROR zero (1971, Sp.) PR:O
GRAVEYARD SHIFT *½ (1987) PR:C-O
GRAVY TRAIN, THE *** (1974) PR:O
GRAY LADY DOWN * (1978) PR:A
GRAYEAGLE ** (1977) PR:C
GRAZIE ZIA
   (SEE:THANK YOU, AUNT)
GREASE ***½ (1978) PR:A
GREASE 2 **½ (1982) PR:C-O
GREASED LIGHTNING *** (1977) PR:C
GREASER'S PALACE **½ (1972) PR:C
GREAT ADVENTURE, THE *** (1955, Swed.) PR:AA
GREAT ADVENTURE, THE *½ (1976, Sp./It.) PR:A
GREAT ALLIGATOR * (1980, It.) PR:O
GREAT AMERICAN BROADCAST, THE *** (1941) PR:A
GREAT AMERICAN BUGS BUNNY-ROAD RUNNER CHASE ** (1979) PR:AA
GREAT AMERICAN PASTIME, THE **½ (1956) PR:A
GREAT ARMORED CAR SWINDLE, THE ** (1964) PR:A
GREAT AWAKENING, THE
   (SEE:NEW WINE)
GREAT BALLOON ADVENTURE, THE
   (SEE:OLLY, OLLY OXEN FREE)
GREAT BANK HOAX, THE **½ (1977) PR:C
GREAT BANK ROBBERY, THE ** (1969) PR:A
GREAT BARRIER, THE
   (SEE:SILENT BARRIERS)
GREAT BIG THING, A * (1968, US/Can.) PR:C
GREAT BIG WORLD AND LITTLE CHILDREN, THE *** (1962, Pol.) PR:A
GREAT BRAIN, THE ** (1978) PR:AA
GREAT BRAIN MACHINE, THE
   (SEE:BRAIN MACHINE, THE)
GREAT BRITISH TRAIN ROBBERY, THE *** (1967, Ger.) PR:A
GREAT CARUSO, THE ***½ (1951) PR:A
GREAT CATHERINE ** (1968, Brit.) PR:A
GREAT CHICAGO CONSPIRACY CIRCUS, THE
   (SEE:CHICAGO '70)
GREAT CITIZEN, THE *½ (1939, USSR) PR:A
GREAT COMMANDMENT, THE *½ (1941) PR:A
GREAT DAN PATCH, THE **½ (1949) PR:AA
GREAT DAWN, THE ** (1947, It.) PR:A
GREAT DAY *½ (1945, Brit.) PR:A
GREAT DAY, THE
   (SEE:SPECIAL DAY, A)
GREAT DAY IN THE MORNING **½ (1956) PR:A
GREAT DEFENDER, THE * (1934, Brit.) PR:A
GREAT DIAMOND ROBBERY ** (1953) PR:A
GREAT DICTATOR, THE **** (1940) PR:AA
GREAT DIVIDE, THE *½ (1930) PR:A
GREAT DREAM, THE
   (SEE:EMBRACERS, THE)
GREAT ESCAPE, THE **** (1963) PR:A
GREAT EXPECTATIONS **½ (1934) PR:AA
GREAT EXPECTATIONS ***** (1946, Brit.) PR:AA
GREAT EXPECTATIONS *** (1975, Brit.) PR:AA
GREAT FEED, THE
   (SEE:LA GRANDE BOUFFE)
GREAT FLAMARION, THE *** (1945) PR:A-C
GREAT FLIRTATION, THE *½ (1934) PR:A
GREAT GABBO, THE *** (1929) PR:C

GREAT GAMBINI, THE ** (1937) PR:A
GREAT GAME, THE * (1930) PR:A
GREAT GAME, THE ** (1953, Brit.) PR:A
GREAT GARRICK, THE *** (1937) PR:A
GREAT GATSBY, THE *** (1949) PR:A
GREAT GATSBY, THE * (1974) PR:A
GREAT GAY ROAD, THE **½ (1931, Brit.) PR:A
GREAT GENERATION, THE ***½ (1986, Hung.) PR:O
GREAT GEORGIA BANK HOAX
   (SEE:GREAT BANK HOAX)
GREAT GILBERT AND SULLIVAN, THE **½ (1953, Brit.) PR:AA
GREAT GILDERSLEEVE, THE ** (1942) PR:A
GREAT GOD GOLD ** (1935) PR:A
GREAT GUNDOWN, THE *½ (1977) PR:O
GREAT GUNFIGHTER, THE
   (SEE:GUNFIGHT AT COMMANCHE)
GREAT GUNS **½ (1941) PR:AA
GREAT GUY **½ (1936) PR:A
GREAT HOPE, THE **½ (1954, It.) PR:C
GREAT HOSPITAL MYSTERY, THE ** (1937) PR:A
GREAT HOTEL MURDER ** (1935) PR:A
GREAT IMPERSONATION, THE ** (1935) PR:A
GREAT IMPERSONATION, THE ** (1942) PR:A
GREAT IMPOSTOR, THE **½ (1960) PR:A
GREAT JASPER, THE **½ (1933) PR:A
GREAT JESSE JAMES RAID, THE *½ (1953) PR:A
GREAT JEWEL ROBBER, THE *** (1950) PR:A
GREAT JOHN L. THE *** (1945) PR:A
GREAT LIE, THE *** (1941) PR:A
GREAT LOCOMOTIVE CHASE, THE *** (1956) PR:AA
GREAT LOVER, THE **½ (1931) PR:A
GREAT LOVER, THE **½ (1949) PR:A
GREAT MACARTHY, THE **½ (1975, Aus.) PR:C-O
GREAT MAN, THE *** (1957) PR:A
GREAT MAN VOTES, THE *** (1939) PR:A
GREAT MANHUNT, THE
   (SEE:DOOLINS OF OKLAHOMA)
GREAT MANHUNT, THE ***½ (1951, Brit.) PR:A
GREAT MAN'S LADY, THE **½ (1942) PR:A
GREAT McGINTY, THE **** (1940) PR:A
GREAT McGONAGALL, THE * (1975, Brit.) PR:O
GREAT MEADOW, THE *½ (1931) PR:A
GREAT MIKE, THE **½ (1944) PR:A
GREAT MISSOURI RAID, THE **½ (1950) PR:A
GREAT MR. HANDEL, THE *½ (1942, Brit.) PR:A
GREAT MR. NOBODY, THE **½ (1941) PR:A
GREAT MOMENT, THE *** (1944) PR:A
GREAT MOUSE DETECTIVE, THE **** (1986) PR:AA
GREAT MUPPET CAPER, THE *** (1981) PR:AA
GREAT NORTHFIELD, MINNESOTA RAID, THE **** (1972) PR:O
GREAT O'MALLEY, THE *** (1937) PR:A
GREAT OUTDOORS, THE * (1988) PR:A-C
GREAT PLANE ROBBERY, THE ** (1940) PR:A
GREAT PLANE ROBBERY, THE *½ (1950) PR:A
GREAT PONY RAID, THE **½ (1968, Brit.) PR:AA
GREAT POWER, THE zero (1929) PR:A
GREAT PROFILE, THE ** (1940) PR:A
GREAT RACE, THE *** (1965) PR:A-C
GREAT RADIO MYSTERY, THE
   (SEE:TAKE THE STAND)
GREAT RUPERT, THE *** (1950) PR:AA
GREAT ST. LOUIS BANK ROBBERY, THE *½ (1959) PR:C-O
GREAT ST. TRINIAN'S TRAIN ROBBERY, THE **½ (1966, Brit.) PR:AA
GREAT SANTINI, THE **** (1979) PR:C
GREAT SCHNOZZLE, THE
   (SEE:PALOOKA)
GREAT SCOUT AND CATHOUSE THURSDAY, THE * (1976) PR:O
GREAT SINNER, THE ***½ (1949) PR:A
GREAT SIOUX MASSACRE, THE **½ (1965) PR:A
GREAT SIOUX UPRISING, THE ** (1953) PR:A
GREAT SMOKEY ROADBLOCK, THE **½ (1978) PR:C
GREAT SPY CHASE, THE **½ (1966, Fr.) PR:C
GREAT SPY MISSION, THE
   (SEE:OPERATION CROSSBOW)
GREAT STAGECOACH ROBBERY ** (1945) PR:A
GREAT STUFF * (1933, Brit.) PR:A
GREAT SWINDLE, THE *½ (1941) PR:A
GREAT TEXAS DYNAMITE CHASE, THE **½ (1976) PR:O
GREAT TRAIN ROBBERY, THE *** (1979, Brit.) PR:A
GREAT TRAIN ROBBERY, THE *½ (1941) PR:A
GREAT VAN ROBBERY, THE **½ (1963, Brit.) PR:O
GREAT VICTOR HERBERT, THE *** (1939) PR:AA
GREAT WALDO PEPPER, THE *** (1975) PR:C
GREAT WALL, A **½ (1986) PR:A
GREAT WALL OF CHINA, THE zero (1970, Brit.) PR:C-O
GREAT WALL, THE **½ (1965, Jap.) PR:O

GREAT WALTZ, THE *** (1938) PR:AA
GREAT WALTZ, THE ** (1972) PR:AA
GREAT WAR, THE ** (1961, Fr./It.) PR:O
GREAT WHITE HOPE, THE ***½ (1970) PR:C-O
GREAT WHITE, THE * (1982, It.) PR:O
GREAT YEARNING, THE ** (1930, Ger.) PR:A
GREAT ZIEGFELD, THE *** (1936) PR:AA**
GREATEST LOVE, THE *** (1954, It.) PR:C
GREATEST SHOW ON EARTH, THE ** (1952) PR:AA**
GREATEST STORY EVER TOLD, THE ***½ (1965) PR:AA
GREATEST, THE zero (1977, US/Brit.) PR:C-O
GREED IN THE SUN **½ (1965, Fr./It.) PR:O
GREED OF WILLIAM HART, THE **½ (1948, Brit.) PR:C-O
GREEK STREET
(SEE:LATIN LOVE)
GREEK TYCOON, THE * (1978) PR:C
GREEKS HAD A WORD FOR THEM *** (1932) PR:A
GREEN BERETS, THE * (1968) PR:C**
GREEN BUDDHA, THE * (1954, Brit.) PR:A
GREEN CARNATION
(SEE:TRIALS OF OSCAR WILDE, THE)
GREEN COCKATOO, THE * (1947, Brit.) PR:A
GREEN DOLPHIN STREET * (1947) PR:A-C**
GREEN-EYED BLONDE, THE *½ (1957) PR:C
GREEN EYES *½ (1934) PR:A
GREEN FIELDS ** (1937) PR:A
GREEN FINGERS ** (1947) PR:A
GREEN FIRE ** (1955) PR:C
GREEN FOR DANGER ** (1946, Brit.) PR:A
GREEN GLOVE, THE ** (1952) PR:A
GREEN GODDESS, THE **½ (1930) PR:A
GREEN GRASS OF WYOMING **½ (1948) PR:AA
GREEN GROW THE RUSHES **½ (1951, Brit.) PR:A
GREEN HELL ** (1940) PR:A
GREEN HELMET, THE *½ (1961, Brit.) PR:A
GREEN ICE *½ (1981, Brit.) PR:C
GREEN LIGHT **½ (1937) PR:A
GREEN MAN, THE **** (1957, Brit.) PR:A
GREEN MANSIONS ** (1959) PR:A
GREEN MARE, THE **½ (1961, Fr./It.) PR:O
GREEN PACK, THE **½ (1934, Brit.) PR:C
GREEN PASTURES ***½ (1936) PR:AA
GREEN PROMISE, THE ** (1949) PR:A
GREEN ROOM, THE ***½ (1979, Fr.) PR:C-O
GREEN SCARF, THE ** (1954, Brit.) PR:A
GREEN SLIME, THE * (1969, US/Jap.) PR:C
GREEN TREE, THE **½ (1965, It.) PR:A
GREEN YEARS, THE ** (1946) PR:A
GREENE MURDER CASE, THE *** (1929) PR:A
GREENGAGE SUMMER, THE
(SEE:LOSS OF INNOCENCE)
GREENWICH VILLAGE ** (1944) PR:A
GREENWICH VILLAGE STORY **½ (1963) PR:C
GREENWOOD TREE, THE
(SEE:UNDER THE GREENWOOD TREE)
GREGORY'S GIRL * (1982, Brit.) PR:C**
GREH ** (1962, Ger./Yugo.) PR:O
GREMLINS * (1984) PR:O
GRENDEL GRENDEL GRENDEL ** (1981, Aus.) PR:AA
GREY FOX, THE ** (1983, Can.) PR:C**
GREYFRIARS BOBBY **½ (1961, Brit.) PR:AA
GREYHOUND LIMITED, THE ** (1929) PR:A
GREYSTOKE: THE LEGEND OF TARZAN, LORD OF THE APES ** (1984) PR:C**
GRIDIRON FLASH *½ (1935) PR:A
GRIEF STREET *½ (1931) PR:A
GRIGSBY
(SEE:LAST GRENADE, THE)
GRIM REAPER, THE *½ (1981, It.) PR:O
GRINGO ** (1963, Sp./It.) PR:O
GRIP OF THE STRANGLER
(SEE:HAUNTED STRANGLER, THE)
GRISSLY'S MILLIONS ** (1945) PR:A
GRISSOM GANG, THE * (1971) PR:C-O
GRITOS EN LA NOCHE
(SEE:AWFUL DR. ORLOFF, THE)
GRIZZLY *½ (1976) PR:C
GROOM WORE SPURS, THE ** (1951) PR:A
GROOVE TUBE, THE * (1974) PR:O**
GROUCH, THE *½ (1961, Gr.) PR:A
GROUND ZERO zero (1973) PR:O
GROUNDS FOR MARRIAGE *** (1950) PR:A
GROUNDSTAR CONSPIRACY, THE **½ (1972, Can.) PR:C
GROUP, THE * (1966) PR:O**
GROUPIE GIRL
(SEE:I AM A GROUPIE)
GROVE, THE
(SEE:NAKED ZOO, THE)
GROWING PAINS
(SEE:BAD MANNERS)
GROWN-UP CHILDREN **½ (1963, USSR) PR:A
GRUESOME TWOSOME zero (1968) PR:O
GRUMPY **½ (1930) PR:A
GRUNT! THE WRESTLING MOVIE zero (1985) PR:O
GUADALAJARA *½ (1943, Mex.) PR:A
GUADALCANAL DIARY ** (1943) PR:C**
GUARD THAT GIRL *½ (1935) PR:A
GUARDIAN OF HELL zero (1985, It.) PR:O
GUARDIAN OF THE WILDERNESS ** (1977) PR:AA
GUARDSMAN, THE **** (1931) PR:A
GUDRUN
(SEE:SUDDENLY, A WOMAN)
GUERRE SECRET
(SEE:DIRTY GAME, THE)
GUERRILLA GIRL zero (1953) PR:C
GUESS WHAT!?!
(SEE:GUESS WHAT WE LEARNED IN SCHOOL TODAY?)
GUESS WHAT HAPPENED TO COUNT DRACULA * (1970) PR:O
GUESS WHAT WE LEARNED IN SCHOOL TODAY? zero (1970) PR:O
GUESS WHO'S COMING TO DINNER **½ (1967) PR:C
GUEST, THE *** (1963, Brit.) PR:C
GUEST HOUSE, THE
(SEE:IN OLD CHEYENNE)
GUEST IN THE HOUSE ** (1944) PR:A
GUEST OF HONOR * (1934, Brit.) PR:A
GUEST WIFE **½ (1945) PR:A
GUEST, THE *** (1984, South Africa) PR:O
GUESTS ARE COMING * (1965, Pol.) PR:A
GUEULE D'ANGE
(SEE:PLEASURES AND VICES)
GUIDE, THE **½ (1965, US/India) PR:A
GUIDE FOR THE MARRIED MAN, A * (1967) PR:C**
GUILIA E GUILIA
(SEE:JULIA AND JULIA)
GUILT * (1930, Brit.) PR:A
GUILT **½ (1967, Swed.) PR:O
GUILT IS MY SHADOW ** (1950, Brit.) PR:O
GUILT IS NOT MINE **½ (1968, It.) PR:A
GUILT OF JANET AMES, THE **½ (1947) PR:A
GUILTY? *½ (1930) PR:A
GUILTY? *** (1956, Brit.) PR:A
GUILTY AS CHARGED
(SEE:GUILTY AS HELL)
GUILTY AS HELL **½ (1932) PR:A
GUILTY BYSTANDER ** (1950) PR:C
GUILTY GENERATION, THE *** (1931) PR:A
GUILTY HANDS **½ (1931) PR:C
GUILTY MELODY *½ (1936, Brit.) PR:A
GUILTY OF TREASON **½ (1950) PR:C
GUILTY PARENTS *½ (1934) PR:C
GUILTY TRAILS ** (1938) PR:A
GUILTY, THE ** (1947) PR:C
GUINEA PIG, THE
(SEE:OUTSIDER, THE)
GUINGUETTE ** (1959, Fr.) PR:C
GULLIVER'S TRAVELS **½ (1939) PR:AA
GULLIVER'S TRAVELS *½ (1977, Brit./Bel.) PR:AA
GULLIVER'S TRAVELS BEYOND THE MOON ** (1966, Jap.) PR:AA
GUMBALL RALLY, THE *½ (1976) PR:A
GUMBO YA-YA
(SEE:GIRLS! GIRLS! GIRLS!)
GUMSHOE * (1972, Brit.) PR:C**
GUN, THE *½ (1978, It.) PR:O
GUN BATTLE AT MONTEREY * (1957) PR:C
GUN BELT **½ (1953) PR:A
GUN BROTHERS **½ (1956) PR:A
GUN CODE *½ (1940) PR:A
GUN CRAZY ** (1949) PR:O
GUN DUEL IN DURANGO **½ (1957) PR:A
GUN FEVER * (1958) PR:O
GUN FIGHT **½ (1961) PR:C
GUN FOR A COWARD **½ (1957) PR:O
GUN FURY **½ (1953) PR:A
GUN GLORY **½ (1957) PR:A
GUN HAND, THE
(SEE:HE RIDES TALL)
GUN HAWK, THE *½ (1963) PR:C
GUN JUSTICE **½ (1934) PR:A
GUN LAW *½ (1933) PR:A
GUN LAW *** (1938) PR:A
GUN LAW JUSTICE *½ (1949) PR:A
GUN LORDS OF STIRRUP BASIN ** (1937) PR:A
GUN MAN FROM BODIE, THE ** (1941) PR:A
GUN MOLL
(SEE:JIGSAW)
GUN PACKER **½ (1938) PR:A
GUN PLAY ** (1936) PR:A
GUN RANGER, THE ** (1937) PR:A
GUN RIDERS, THE ** (1969) PR:O
GUN RUNNER *½ (1949) PR:A
GUN RUNNER ** (1969) PR:O
GUN RUNNER, THE
(SEE:SANTIAGO)
GUN RUNNERS, THE **½ (1958) PR:A
GUN SMOKE *½ (1931) PR:A
GUN SMOKE * (1936) PR:A
GUN SMUGGLERS ** (1948) PR:A
GUN STREET * (1962) PR:C
GUN TALK ** (1948) PR:A
GUN THAT WON THE WEST, THE ** (1955) PR:C
GUN THE MAN DOWN *** (1957) PR:C
GUN TOWN *½ (1946) PR:A
GUNFIGHT AT ABILENE
(SEE:GUNFIGHT IN ABILENE)
GUNFIGHT AT COMANCHE CREEK ** (1964) PR:A
GUNFIGHT AT DODGE CITY, THE **½ (1959) PR:A
GUNFIGHT AT RED SANDS
(SEE:GRINGO)
GUNFIGHT AT THE O.K. CORRAL *** (1957) PR:C**
GUNFIGHT IN ABILENE **½ (1967) PR:C
GUNFIGHT, A * (1971) PR:O**
GUNFIGHTER, THE *** (1950) PR:C**
GUNFIGHTERS OF ABILENE *½ (1960) PR:A
GUNFIGHTERS OF CASA GRANDE ** (1965, US/Sp.) PR:C
GUNFIGHTERS, THE *½ (1947) PR:A
GUNFIRE *½ (1950) PR:A
GUNFIRE AT INDIAN GAP *½ (1957) PR:A
GUNG HO! * (1943) PR:C**
GUNG HO **½ (1986) PR:C
GUNGA DIN *** (1939) PR:C**
GUNMAN FROM BODIE
(SEE:GUN MAN FROM BODIE)
GUNMAN HAS ESCAPED, A ** (1948, Brit.) PR:C
GUNMAN'S CODE * (1946) PR:A
GUNMAN'S WALK *** (1958) PR:C
GUNMEN FROM LAREDO *½ (1959) PR:O
GUNMEN OF ABILENE ** (1950) PR:A
GUNMEN OF THE RIO GRANDE ** (1965, Fr./It./Sp.) PR:C
GUNN **½ (1967) PR:C
GUNNING FOR JUSTICE *½ (1948) PR:A
GUNPLAY * (1951) PR:A
GUNPOINT!
(SEE:AT GUNPOINT)
GUNPOINT ** (1966) PR:A
GUNPOWDER ** (1987, Brit.) PR:C
GUNRUNNERS, THE
(SEE:GUN RUNNER)
GUNS ** (1980, Fr.) PR:O
GUNS A'BLAZING
(SEE:LAW AND ORDER)
GUNS AND GUITARS *½ (1936) PR:A
GUNS AND THE FURY, THE *½ (1983) PR:O
GUNS AT BATASI *** (1964, Brit.) PR:C
GUNS FOR SAN SEBASTIAN ** (1968, US/Fr./Mex./It.) PR:O
GUNS, GIRLS AND GANGSTERS *½ (1958) PR:C
GUNS IN THE AFTERNOON
(SEE:RIDE THE HIGH COUNTRY)
GUNS IN THE DARK ** (1937) PR:A
GUNS IN THE HEATHER ** (1968, Brit.) PR:AA
GUNS OF A STRANGER * (1973) PR:A
GUNS OF DARKNESS ** (1962, Brit.) PR:C
GUNS OF DIABLO *½ (1964) PR:C
GUNS OF FORT PETTICOAT, THE ** (1957) PR:A
GUNS OF HATE ** (1948) PR:A

Finding entries in **THE MOTION PICTURE GUIDE ™**

Years 1929-83	Volumes I-IX
1984	Volume IX
1985	1986 ANNUAL
1986	1987 ANNUAL
1987	1988 ANNUAL
1988	1989 ANNUAL

STAR RATINGS

★★★★★	Masterpiece
★★★★	Excellent
★★★	Good
★★	Fair
★	Poor
zero	Without Merit

PARENTAL RECOMMENDATION (PR:)

AA	Good for Children
A	Acceptable for Children
C	Cautionary, some objectionable scenes
O	Objectionable for Children

BOLD: Films on Videocassette

GUNS OF NAVARONE, THE ***½ (1961, Brit.) PR:C
GUNS OF THE BLACK WITCH ** (1961, Fr./It.) PR:C
GUNS OF THE LAW *½ (1944) PR:A
GUNS OF THE MAGNIFICENT SEVEN ** (1969) PR:C
GUNS OF THE PECOS *½ (1937) PR:A
GUNS OF THE TIMBERLAND ** (1960) PR:A
GUNS OF THE TREES * (1964) PR:O
GUNS OF WYOMING
(SEE:CATTLE KING)
GUNS, SIN AND BATHTUB GIN
(SEE:LADY IN RED, THE)
GUNSIGHT RIDGE ** (1957) PR:A
GUNSLINGER ** (1956) PR:C
GUNSLINGERS *½ (1950) PR:A
GUNSMOKE **½ (1953) PR:A
GUNSMOKE IN TUCSON ** (1958) PR:A
GUNSMOKE MESA ** (1944) PR:A
GUNSMOKE RANCH * (1937) PR:A
GUNSMOKE TRAIL ** (1938) PR:A
GURU, THE MAD MONK * (1971) PR:O
GURU, THE **½ (1969, US/India) PR:C
GUS ** (1976) PR:AA
GUSARSKAYA BALLADA
(SEE:BALLAD OF A HUSSAR, THE)
GUTS IN THE SUN * (1959, Fr.) PR:O
GUTTER GIRLS **½ (1964, Brit.) PR:O
GUV'NOR, THE
(SEE:MISTER HOBO)
GUY, A GAL AND A PAL, A *½ (1945) PR:A
GUY CALLED CAESAR, A *½ (1962, Brit.) PR:A
GUY COULD CHANGE, A *½ (1946) PR:A
GUY NAMED JOE, A **** (1943) PR:A
GUY WHO CAME BACK, THE **½ (1951) PR:A
GUYANA, CULT OF THE DAMNED zero (1980, Mex./Sp./Pan.) PR:O
GUYS AND DOLLS ***½ (1955) PR:A
GWENDOLINE
(SEE:PERILS OF GWENDOLINE, THE)
GYMKATA *½ (1985) PR:O
GYPSY **½ (1937, Brit.) PR:A
GYPSY **** (1962) PR:C
GYPSY AND THE GENTLEMAN, THE *½ (1958, Brit.) PR:O
GYPSY COLT **½ (1954) PR:AA
GYPSY FURY ** (1950, Fr.) PR:C
GYPSY GIRL **½ (1966, Brit.) PR:C
GYPSY MELODY **½ (1936, Brit.) PR:A
GYPSY MOTHS, THE *** (1969) PR:O
GYPSY WILDCAT ** (1944) PR:A

H

H-MAN, THE *** (1959, Jap.) PR:O
HA' PENNY BREEZE ** (1950, Brit.) PR:A
HADAKA NO SHIMA
(SEE:ISLAND, THE)
HADAKA NO TAISHO
(SEE:NAKED GENERAL, THE)
HADLEY'S REBELLION ** (1984) PR:C
HAGBARD AND SIGNE *** (1968, Den./Iceland/Swed.) PR:C-O
HAIL ** (1973) PR:O
HAIL AND FAREWELL **½ (1936, Brit.) PR:A
HAIL, HERO! **½ (1969) PR:C
HAIL MAFIA **½ (1965, Fr./It.) PR:O
HAIL, MARY **** (1985, Fr./Switz./Brit.) PR:O
HAIL THE CONQUERING HERO **** (1944) PR:A
HAIL TO THE CHIEF
(SEE:HAIL)
HAIL TO THE RANGERS *½ (1943) PR:A
HAIR **** (1979) PR:C-O
HAIR OF THE DOG *½ (1962, Brit.) PR:A
HAIRSPRAY ***½ (1988) PR:A-C
HAIRY APE, THE *** (1944) PR:A
HAKUCHI
(SEE:IDIOT, THE)
HAKUJA DEN
(SEE:PANDA AND MAGIC SERPENT)
HALCON Y LA PRESA, EL
(SEE:BIG GUNDOWN, THE)
HALF A HERO **½ (1953) PR:AA
HALF A SINNER ** (1934) PR:A
HALF A SINNER *½ (1940) PR:A
HALF A SIXPENCE *** (1967, Brit.) PR:A
HALF ANGEL ** (1936) PR:C
HALF ANGEL **½ (1951) PR:A
HALF-BREED, THE ** (1952) PR:A
HALF HUMAN *½ (1955, Jap.) PR:C-O
HALF-MARRIAGE ** (1929) PR:A
HALF MOON STREET * (1986) PR:O
HALF-NAKED TRUTH, THE *** (1932) PR:A
HALF PAST MIDNIGHT ** (1948) PR:A
HALF PINT, THE ** (1960) PR:AA
HALF SHOT AT SUNRISE *** (1930) PR:A
HALF-WAY HOUSE, THE *** (1945, Brit.) PR:C
HALF WAY TO HEAVEN *½ (1929) PR:A
HALF WAY TO SHANGHAI *½ (1942) PR:C
HALLELUJAH **** (1929) PR:A
HALLELUJAH, I'M A BUM *** (1933) PR:A
HALLELUJAH THE HILLS **½ (1963) PR:C
HALLELUJAH TRAIL, THE **½ (1965) PR:A
HALLIDAY BRAND, THE *** (1957) PR:C
HALLOWEEN **** (1978) PR:O
HALLOWEEN IV: THE RETURN OF MICHAEL MYERS *** (1988) PR:O
HALLOWEEN III: SEASON OF THE WITCH ** (1982) PR:O
HALLOWEEN II *½ (1981) PR:O
HALLS OF ANGER *** (1970) PR:O
HALLS OF MONTEZUMA ***½ (1951) PR:C
HALLUCINATION GENERATION *½ (1966) PR:C
HALLUCINATORS, THE
(SEE:NAKED ZOO, THE)
HAMBONE AND HILLIE ** (1984) PR:A
HAMBURGER zero (1986) PR:O
HAMBURGER HILL ***½ (1987) PR:O
HAMILE * (1965, Ghana) PR:C
HAMLET **** (1948, Brit.) PR:A
HAMLET ***½ (1962, Ger.) PR:A
HAMLET **** (1964) PR:A
HAMLET ** (1966, USSR) PR:C
HAMLET ***½ (1969, Brit.) PR:A
HAMLET ** (1976, Brit.) PR:O
HAMMER ** (1972) PR:O
HAMMER THE TOFF ** (1952, Brit.) PR:A
HAMMERHEAD ** (1968) PR:C
HAMMERSMITH IS OUT *½ (1972) PR:C
HAMMETT ***½ (1982) PR:C
HAMNSTED
(SEE:PORT OF CALL)
HAMP
(SEE:KING AND COUNTRY)
HAMPSTER OF HAPPINESS
(SEE:SECOND-HAND HEARTS)
HANA TO NAMIDA TO HONOO
(SEE:PERFORMERS, THE)
HAND, THE ** (1981) PR:O
HAND IN HAND *** (1960, Brit.) PR:AA
HAND IN THE TRAP, THE **½ (1963, Arg./Sp.) PR:C
HAND OF DEATH *½ (1962) PR:C
HAND OF NIGHT, THE **½ (1968, Brit.) PR:C
HAND, THE ** (1960, Brit.) PR:C
HANDCUFFED ** (1929) PR:A
HANDCUFFS, LONDON ** (1955, Brit.) PR:A
HANDFUL OF DUST, A **½ (1988, Brit.) PR:C
HANDGUN
(SEE:DEEP IN THE HEART)
HANDLE WITH CARE *½ (1932) PR:A
HANDLE WITH CARE * (1935, Brit.) PR:A
HANDLE WITH CARE ** (1958) PR:A
HANDLE WITH CARE ** (1964) PR:A
HANDLE WITH CARE
(SEE:CITIZENS BAND)
HANDS ACROSS THE BORDER **½ (1943) PR:A
HANDS ACROSS THE TABLE ***½ (1935) PR:A
HANDS OF A STRANGER **½ (1962) PR:C
HANDS OF DESTINY *½ (1954, Brit.) PR:A
HANDS OF ORLAC, THE ** (1964, Brit./Fr.) PR:A
HANDS OF STEEL * (1986, It.) PR:O
HANDS OF THE RIPPER *** (1971, Brit.) PR:O
HANDS OF THE STRANGLER
(SEE:HANDS OF ORLAC)
HANDSOME SERGE
(SEE:LE BEAU SERGE)
HANDY ANDY **½ (1934) PR:A
HANGAR 18 * (1980) PR:A
HANG'EM HIGH **½ (1968) PR:C
HANGING TREE, THE *** (1959) PR:C
HANGMAN WAITS, THE ** (1947, Brit.) PR:C
HANGMAN, THE *** (1959) PR:A
HANGMAN'S KNOT *** (1952) PR:C
HANGMAN'S WHARF *½ (1950, Brit.) PR:A
HANGMEN ALSO DIE ***½ (1943) PR:C-O
HANGOVER
(SEE:FEMALE JUNGLE)
HANGOVER SQUARE *** (1945) PR:C
HANGUP * (1974) PR:O
HANK WILLIAMS STORY, THE
(SEE:YOUR CHEATIN' HEART)
HANK WILLIAMS: THE SHOW HE NEVER GAVE ***½ (1982, Can.) PR:C
HANKY-PANKY * (1982) PR:A-C
HANNAH AND HER SISTERS ***** (1986) PR:C
HANNAH K. ** (1983, Fr.) PR:C
HANNAH LEE **½ (1953) PR:A
HANNA'S WAR **½ (1988) PR:C-O
HANNIBAL * (1960, It.) PR:A
HANNIBAL BROOKS **½ (1969, Brit.) PR:C
HANNIE CALDER ** (1971, Brit.) PR:O
HANOI HANNA—QUEEN OF CHINA
(SEE:CHELSEA GIRLS, THE)
HANOI HILTON, THE **½ (1987) PR:O
HANOVER STREET **½ (1979, Brit.) PR:C
HANS CHRISTIAN ANDERSEN *** (1952) PR:AA
HANSEL AND GRETEL ** (1954) PR:AA
HANSEL AND GRETEL **½ (1965, Ger.) PR:AA
HAPPENING, THE **½ (1967) PR:C
HAPPIDROME * (1943, Brit.) PR:A
HAPPIEST DAYS OF YOUR LIFE ***½ (1950, Brit.) PR:A
HAPPIEST MILLIONAIRE, THE * (1967) PR:AA
HAPPILY EVER AFTER
(SEE:MORE THAN A MIRACLE)
HAPPINESS
(SEE:LE BONHEUR)
HAPPINESS AHEAD *** (1934) PR:A
HAPPINESS CAGE, THE ** (1972) PR:C
HAPPINESS C.O.D. ** (1935) PR:A
HAPPINESS OF THREE WOMEN, THE **½ (1954, Brit.) PR:A
HAPPINESS OF US ALONE **½ (1962, Jap.) PR:A
HAPPY ** (1934, Brit.) PR:A
HAPPY ALEXANDER
(SEE:VERY HAPPY ALEXANDER)
HAPPY ANNIVERSARY *** (1959) PR:C
HAPPY AS THE GRASS WAS GREEN * (1973) PR:A
HAPPY BIRTHDAY, DAVY zero (1970) PR:O
HAPPY BIRTHDAY, GEMINI *½ (1980) PR:O
HAPPY BIRTHDAY TO ME *½ (1981) PR:O
HAPPY BIRTHDAY, WANDA JUNE ***½ (1971) PR:C
HAPPY DAYS *** (1930) PR:A
HAPPY DAYS ARE HERE AGAIN *½ (1936, Brit.) PR:A
HAPPY DEATHDAY *½ (1969, Brit.) PR:C
HAPPY END ** (1968, Czech.) PR:C-O
HAPPY ENDING, THE * (1931, Brit.) PR:A
HAPPY ENDING, THE ** (1969) PR:C
HAPPY EVER AFTER **½ (1932, Ger./Brit.) PR:A
HAPPY EVER AFTER
(SEE:TONIGHT'S THE NIGHT)
HAPPY FAMILY, THE * (1936, Brit.) PR:A
HAPPY FAMILY, THE
(SEE:MR. LORD SAYS NO)
HAPPY GO LOVELY *** (1951, Brit.) PR:A
HAPPY-GO-LUCKY **½ (1937) PR:A
HAPPY GO LUCKY ** (1943) PR:AA
HAPPY GYPSIES
(SEE:I EVEN MET HAPPY GYPSIES)
HAPPY HOOKER GOES TO HOLLYWOOD, THE zero (1980) PR:O
HAPPY HOOKER GOES TO WASHINGTON, THE * (1977) PR:O
HAPPY HOOKER, THE * (1975) PR:O
HAPPY HOUR zero (1987) PR:O
HAPPY IS THE BRIDE ** (1958, Brit.) PR:A
HAPPY LAND *** (1943) PR:A
HAPPY LANDING ** (1934) PR:A
HAPPY LANDING **½ (1938) PR:A
HAPPY MOTHER'S DAY . . . LOVE, GEORGE ** (1973) PR:C
HAPPY NEW YEAR **½ (1987) PR:C
HAPPY ROAD, THE *** (1957) PR:A
HAPPY THIEVES, THE **½ (1962) PR:C
HAPPY TIME, THE ***½ (1952) PR:AA
HAPPY YEARS, THE **½ (1950) PR:A
HAR HAR DU DITT LIV
(SEE:HERE'S YOUR LIFE)
HARAKIRI *** (1963, Jap.) PR:O
HARASSED HERO, THE *½ (1954, Brit.) PR:A
HARBOR LIGHT YOKOHAMA ** (1970, Jap.) PR:C-O
HARBOR LIGHTS ** (1963) PR:A
HARBOR OF MISSING MEN **½ (1950) PR:A
HARD-BOILED CANARY
(SEE:THERE'S MAGIC IN MUSIC)
HARD BOILED MAHONEY ** (1947) PR:A
HARD BUNCH, THE
(SEE:HARD TRAIL)
HARD CHOICES *** (1984) PR:O
HARD CONTRACT *** (1969) PR:C
HARD COUNTRY *** (1981) PR:O
HARD DAY'S NIGHT, A **** (1964, Brit.) PR:A
HARD DRIVER
(SEE:LAST AMERICAN HERO, THE)
HARD, FAST, AND BEAUTIFUL **½ (1951) PR:A
HARD GUY ** (1941) PR:A
HARD HOMBRE *** (1931) PR:A
HARD KNOCKS ***½ (1980, Aus.) PR:O
HARD MAN, THE ** (1957) PR:A
HARD ON THE TRAIL
(SEE:HARD TRAIL)
HARD PART BEGINS, THE *** (1973, Can.) PR:C
HARD RIDE, THE **½ (1971) PR:C
HARD ROAD, THE * (1970) PR:O
HARD ROCK HARRIGAN **½ (1935) PR:A
HARD STEEL *½ (1941, Brit.) PR:A

HARD TIMES * (1975) PR:A-C**
HARD TIMES *** (1988, Portugal) PR:A
HARD TO GET **½ (1929) PR:A
HARD TO GET **½ (1938) PR:A
HARD TO HANDLE *** (1933) PR:A
HARD TO HOLD * (1984) PR:A-C
HARD TRAIL zero (1969) PR:O
HARD TRAVELING **½ (1985) PR:C
HARD WAY, THE ***½ (1942) PR:A-C
HARDBODIES * (1984) PR:O
HARDBODIES 2 * (1986) PR:O
HARDBOILED ROSE *½ (1929) PR:A
HARDCORE zero (1979) PR:O
HARDER THEY COME, THE * (1973, Jamaica) PR:C**
HARDER THEY FALL, THE ** (1956) PR:O**
HARDLY WORKING * (1981) PR:A
HARDYS RIDE HIGH, THE *** (1939) PR:AA
HAREM ** (1985, Fr.) PR:O
HAREM BUNCH; OR WAR AND PIECE, THE *½ (1969) PR:C-O
HAREM GIRL ** (1952) PR:A
HAREM HOLIDAY (SEE:HARUM SCARUM)
HARLEM GLOBETROTTERS, THE **½ (1951) PR:A
HARLEM IS HEAVEN *** (1932) PR:A
HARLEM ON THE PRAIRIE * (1938) PR:A
HARLEM RIDES THE RANGE *½ (1939) PR:A
HARLEQUIN **½ (1980, Aus.) PR:C-O
HARLOW * (1965) PR:C
HARLOW *½ (1965) PR:C
H.A.R.M. MACHINE, THE (SEE:AGENT FOR H.A.R.M.)
HARMON OF MICHIGAN ** (1941) PR:A
HARMONY AT HOME *½ (1930) PR:A
HARMONY HEAVEN * (1930, Brit.) PR:A
HARMONY LANE *** (1935) PR:A
HARMONY ROW *½ (1933, Aus.) PR:A
HARMONY TRAIL (SEE:WHITE STALLION)
HAROLD AND MAUDE ***½ (1971) PR:A-C
HAROLD ROBBINS' THE BETSY (SEE:BETSY, THE)
HAROLD TEEN ** (1934) PR:A
HARP OF BURMA ***½ (1967, Jap.) PR:C-O
HARPER **½ (1966) PR:C
HARPER VALLEY, P.T.A. zero (1978) PR:C
HARPOON ** (1948) PR:A
HARRAD EXPERIMENT, THE *½ (1973) PR:O
HARRAD SUMMER, THE * (1974) PR:O)
HARRIET CRAIG ***½ (1950) PR:A-C
HARRIGAN'S KID ** (1943) PR:A
HARRY AND SON **½ (1984) PR:C
HARRY AND THE HENDERSONS ** (1987) PR:A-C
HARRY AND TONTO * (1974) PR:C**
HARRY AND WALTER GO TO NEW YORK ** (1976) PR:C
HARRY BLACK AND THE TIGER *** (1958, Brit.) PR:C
HARRY FRIGG (SEE:SECRET WAR OF HARRY FRIGG, THE)
HARRY IN YOUR POCKET ** (1973) PR:C
HARRY TRACY—DESPERADO ** (1982, Can.) PR:C
HARRY'S WAR **½ (1981) PR:C
HARUM SCARUM * (1965) PR:A
HARVARD, HERE I COME ** (1942) PR:A
HARVEST ***½ (1939, Fr.) PR:O
HARVEST MELODY ** (1943) PR:A
HARVESTER, THE * (1936) PR:A
HARVEY **** (1950) PR:A
HARVEY GIRLS, THE * (1946) PR:AA**
HARVEY MIDDLEMAN, FIREMAN ** (1965) PR:C
HAS ANYBODY SEEN MY GAL? *** (1952) PR:A
HASSAN, TERRORIST **½ (1968, Algeria) PR:O
HASTY HEART, THE **** (1949) PR:A
HAT CHECK GIRL **½ (1932) PR:C
HAT CHECK HONEY *½ (1944) PR:A
HAT, COAT AND GLOVE ** (1934) PR:A
HATARI! **½ (1962) PR:A
HATCHET FOR A HONEYMOON * (1969, Sp./It.) PR:O
HATCHET MAN, THE **½ (1932) PR:C-O
HATE FOR HATE ** (1967, It.) PR:C
HATE IN PARADISE *½ (1938, Brit.) PR:A
HATE SHIP, THE *½ (1930, Brit.) PR:A
HATE WITHIN (SEE:STARK FEAR)
HATFUL OF RAIN, A *** (1957) PR:C
HATRED **½ (1941, Fr.) PR:A
HATS OFF * (1937) PR:A
HATS OFF TO RHYTHM (SEE:EARL CARROLL SKETCHBOOK)
HATTER'S CASTLE ***½ (1948, Brit.) PR:C
HATTER'S GHOST, THE **½ (1982, Fr.) PR:C
HAUNTED * (1976) PR:O
HAUNTED AND THE HUNTED (SEE:DEMENTIA 13)
HAUNTED GOLD ** (1932) PR:A
HAUNTED HONEYMOON (SEE:BUSMAN'S HONEYMOON)
HAUNTED HONEYMOON *½ (1986) PR:A
HAUNTED HOUSE OF HORROR (SEE:HORROR HOUSE)
HAUNTED HOUSE, THE *½ (1928) PR:A
HAUNTED HOUSE, THE ** (1940) PR:A
HAUNTED PALACE, THE **½ (1963) PR:C-O
HAUNTED RANCH, THE ** (1943) PR:A
HAUNTED STRANGLER, THE * (1958, Brit.) PR:O**
HAUNTING, THE ***½ (1963) PR:C-O
HAUNTING OF CASTLE MONTEGO (SEE:CASTLE OF EVIL)
HAUNTING OF HAMILTON HIGH, THE (SEE:HELLO MARY LOU: PROM NIGHT II)
HAUNTING OF JULIA, THE * (1981, Brit./Can.) PR:O**
HAUNTING OF M, THE *** (1979) PR:C
HAUNTS * (1977) PR:O
HAVANA ROSE *½ (1951) PR:A
HAVANA WIDOWS ** (1933) PR:A
HAVE A HEART *½ (1934) PR:A
HAVE A NICE WEEKEND *½ (1975) PR:O
HAVE ROCKET, WILL TRAVEL ** (1959) PR:A
HAVING A WILD WEEKEND *** (1965, Brit.) PR:A
HAVING WONDERFUL CRIME * (1945) PR:A**
HAVING WONDERFUL TIME * (1938) PR:A**
HAWAII * (1966) PR:C**
HAWAII BEACH BOY (SEE:BLUE HAWAII)
HAWAII CALLS ** (1938) PR:A
HAWAIIAN BUCKAROO ** (1938) PR:A
HAWAIIAN NIGHTS (SEE:DOWN TO THEIR LAST YACHT)
HAWAIIAN NIGHTS ** (1939) PR:A
HAWAIIANS, THE ** (1970) PR:C
HAWK OF POWDER RIVER, THE * (1948) PR:A
HAWK OF WILD RIVER, THE **½ (1952) PR:A
HAWK THE SLAYER ** (1980, Brit.) PR:A
HAWKS * (1988, Brit.) PR:C
HAWKS AND THE SPARROWS, THE *** (1967, It.) PR:C
HAWLEY'S OF HIGH STREET ** (1933, Brit.) PR:A
HAWMPS! *½ (1976) PR:A
HAZARD ** (1948) PR:A
HAZEL'S PEOPLE zero (1978) PR:C
HAZING, THE ** (1978) PR:C
HE COULDN'T SAY NO **½ (1938) PR:A
HE COULDN'T TAKE IT * (1934) PR:A
HE FOUND A STAR ** (1941, Brit.) PR:A
HE HIRED THE BOSS ** (1943) PR:A
HE KNEW WOMEN **½ (1930) PR:A
HE KNOWS YOU'RE ALONE * (1980) PR:O
HE LAUGHED LAST **½ (1956) PR:A
HE LEARNED ABOUT WOMEN *½ (1933) PR:A
HE LOVED AN ACTRESS ** (1938, Brit.) PR:A
HE MARRIED HIS WIFE **½ (1940) PR:A
HE RAN ALL THE WAY ***½ (1951) PR:C
HE RIDES TALL ** (1964) PR:A
HE, SHE OR IT! (SEE:DOLL, THE)
HE SNOOPS TO CONQUER *½ (1944, Brit.) PR:A
HE STAYED FOR BREAKFAST ** (1940) PR:A
HE WALKED BY NIGHT ** (1948) PR:C**
HE WAS HER MAN **½ (1934) PR:A-C
HE WHO RIDES A TIGER **½ (1966, Brit.) PR:A
HE WHO SHOOTS FIRST *½ (1966, It.) PR:C
HEAD, THE * (1961, Ger.) PR:O
HEAD * (1968) PR:A**
HEAD FOR THE DEVIL (SEE:HEAD, THE)
HEAD FOR THE HILLS (SEE:SOD SISTERS)
HEAD OF A TYRANT **½ (1960, Fr./It.) PR:C
HEAD OF THE FAMILY ** (1933, Brit.) PR:A
HEAD OF THE FAMILY * (1967, It./Fr.) PR:C**
HEAD OFFICE ** (1936, Brit.) PR:A
HEAD OFFICE zero (1986) PR:C
HEAD ON * (1971) PR:O
HEAD ON **½ (1981, Can.) PR:O
HEAD OVER HEELS (SEE:CHILLY SCENES OF WINTER)
HEAD OVER HEELS IN LOVE ** (1937, Brit.) PR:A
HEAD THAT WOULDN'T DIE (SEE:BRAIN THAT WOULDN'T DIE, THE)
HEADIN' EAST ** (1937) PR:A
HEADIN' FOR BROADWAY zero (1980) PR:C
HEADIN' FOR GOD'S COUNTRY ** (1943) PR:A
HEADIN' FOR THE RIO GRANDE **½ (1937) PR:A
HEADIN' FOR TROUBLE * (1931) PR:A
HEADIN' NORTH ** (1930) PR:A
HEADING FOR HEAVEN ** (1947) PR:A
HEADLESS GHOST, THE ** (1959, Brit.) PR:A
HEADLEYS AT HOME, THE ** (1939) PR:A
HEADLINE ** (1943, Brit.) PR:A
HEADLINE CRASHER * (1937) PR:A
HEADLINE HUNTERS ** (1955) PR:A
HEADLINE HUNTERS ** (1968, Brit.) PR:AA
HEADLINE SHOOTER *** (1933) PR:A
HEADLINE WOMAN, THE **½ (1935) PR:A
HEADS UP ** (1930) PR:A
HEADS WE GO (SEE:CHARMING DECEIVER, THE)
HEALER, THE *½ (1935) PR:A
H.E.A.L.T.H. (SEE:HEALTH)
HEALTH * (1980) PR:C-O
HEAR ME GOOD *½ (1957) PR:A
HEARSE, THE *½ (1980) PR:A
HEART AND SOUL ***½ (1950, It.) PR:A
HEART BEAT ** (1979) PR:O
HEART IS A LONELY HUNTER, THE **½ (1968) PR:O
HEART LIKE A WHEEL **½ (1983) PR:C
HEART OF A CHILD *½ (1958, Brit.) PR:C
HEART OF A MAN, THE ** (1959, Brit.) PR:A
HEART OF A NATION, THE *** (1943, Fr.) PR:A
HEART OF ARIZONA **½ (1938) PR:A
HEART OF NEW YORK ** (1932) PR:A
HEART OF PARIS *** (1939, Fr.) PR:A
HEART OF THE GOLDEN WEST **½ (1942) PR:A
HEART OF THE MATTER, THE **½ (1954, Brit.) PR:A-C
HEART OF THE NORTH *** (1938) PR:A
HEART OF THE RIO GRANDE *½ (1942) PR:A
HEART OF THE ROCKIES ** (1937) PR:A
HEART OF THE ROCKIES **½ (1951) PR:A
HEART OF THE STAG **½ (1984, New Zealand) PR:O
HEART OF THE WEST **½ (1937) PR:A
HEART OF VIRGINIA ** (1948) PR:A
HEART PUNCH ** (1932) PR:A
HEART SONG ** (1933, Brit.) PR:A
HEART WITHIN, THE **½ (1957, Brit.) PR:A
HEARTACHES ** (1947) PR:A
HEARTACHES * (1981, Can.) PR:O**
HEARTBEAT **½ (1946) PR:A
HEARTBEEPS ** (1981) PR:A
HEARTBREAK ** (1931) PR:A
HEARTBREAK HOTEL * (1988) PR:C
HEARTBREAK KID, THE ** (1972) PR:C-O
HEARTBREAK RIDGE ** (1986) PR:O**
HEARTBREAKER **½ (1983) PR:C
HEARTBREAKERS * (1984) PR:C-O**
HEARTBURN ** (1986) PR:C-O
HEARTLAND ** (1980) PR:A**
HEART'S DESIRE ** (1937, Brit.) PR:A
HEARTS DIVIDED *½ (1936) PR:A
HEARTS IN BONDAGE ** (1936) PR:A
HEARTS IN DIXIE **½ (1929) PR:A
HEARTS IN EXILE ** (1929) PR:A
HEARTS OF HUMANITY ** (1932) PR:A
HEARTS OF HUMANITY ** (1936, Brit.) PR:A
HEARTS OF THE WEST ***½ (1975) PR:A
HEAT *½ (1970, Arg.) PR:O
HEAT ** (1987) PR:O
HEAT AND DUST * (1983, Brit.) PR:C**
HEAT AND SUNLIGHT **** (1988) PR:O
HEAT LIGHTNING ** (1934) PR:A
HEAT OF DESIRE ** (1984, Fr./Sp.) PR:O
HEAT OF MIDNIGHT * (1966, Fr.) PR:O
HEAT OF THE SUMMER ** (1961, Fr.) PR:A
HEAT WAVE ** (1935, Brit.) PR:A

Finding entries in **THE MOTION PICTURE GUIDE ™**

Years	Volumes
Years 1929-83	Volumes I-IX
1984	Volume IX
1985	1986 ANNUAL
1986	1987 ANNUAL
1987	1988 ANNUAL
1988	1989 ANNUAL

STAR RATINGS

★★★★★	Masterpiece
★★★★	Excellent
★★★	Good
★★	Fair
★	Poor
zero	Without Merit

PARENTAL RECOMMENDATION (PR:)

AA	Good for Children
A	Acceptable for Children
C	Cautionary, some objectionable scenes
O	Objectionable for Children

BOLD: Films on Videocassette

HEATHCLIFF: THE MOVIE ** (1986) PR:AA
HEAT'S ON, THE **½ (1943) PR:A-C
HEATWAVE ** (1954, Brit.) PR:A
HEATWAVE ** (1983, Aus.) PR:O
HEAVEN CAN WAIT ***½ (1943) PR:A
HEAVEN CAN WAIT * (1978) PR:C**
HEAVEN HELP US ***½ (1985) PR:O
HEAVEN IS ROUND THE CORNER * (1944, Brit.) PR:A
HEAVEN KNOWS, MR. ALLISON *** (1957) PR:A
HEAVEN ON EARTH ** (1931) PR:A
HEAVEN ON EARTH *½ (1960, It./US) PR:A
HEAVEN ONLY KNOWS *** (1947) PR:A
HEAVEN SENT
(SEE:THANK HEAVEN FOR SMALL FAVORS)
HEAVEN WITH A BARBED WIRE FENCE ** (1939) PR:A
HEAVEN WITH A GUN ** (1969) PR:C
HEAVENLY BODIES * (1985) PR:O
HEAVENLY BODY, THE **½ (1943) PR:A
HEAVENLY DAYS ** (1944) PR:A
HEAVENLY KID, THE * (1985) PR:O
HEAVENLY PURSUITS
(SEE:GOSPEL ACCORDING TO VIC, THE)
HEAVENS ABOVE! * (1963, Brit.) PR:AA**
HEAVEN'S GATE * (1980) PR:O
HEAVY METAL * (1981, Can.) PR:O
HEDDA * (1975, Brit.) PR:A-C**
HEIDI ***½ (1937) PR:AA
HEIDI AND PETER ** (1955, Switz.) PR:AA
HEIDI **½ (1954, Switz.) PR:AA
HEIDI ***½ (1968, Aust.) PR:AA
HEIDI'S SONG ** (1982) PR:AA
HEIGHTS OF DANGER *½ (1962, Brit.) PR:A
HEIMAT ***½ (1985, Ger.) PR:C-O
HEINZELMANNCHEN
(SEE:SHOEMAKER AND THE ELVES, THE)
HEIR TO TROUBLE ** (1936) PR:A
HEIRESS, THE *** (1949) PR:A**
HEIRLOOM MYSTERY, THE ** (1936, Brit.) PR:A
HEIST, THE * (1979, It.) PR:A
HELD FOR RANSOM * (1938) PR:A
HELD IN TRUST *½ (1949, Brit.) PR:A
HELDEN
(SEE:ARMS AND THE MAN)
HELDEN—HIMMEL UND HOLLE
(SEE:CAVERN, THE)
HELDINNEN ** (1962, Ger.) PR:A
HELDORADO
(SEE:HELLDORADO)
HELEN MORGAN STORY, THE *** (1959) PR:A
HELEN OF TROY * (1956, It.) PR:A
HELICOPTER SPIES, THE *½ (1968) PR:A
HELL AND HIGH WATER zero (1933) PR:A
HELL AND HIGH WATER *** (1954) PR:A
HELL BELOW *** (1933) PR:A
HELL BELOW ZERO *** (1954, Brit.) PR:A
HELL BENT FOR 'FRISCO * (1931) PR:A
HELL BENT FOR GLORY
(SEE:LAFAYETTE ESCADRILLE)
HELL BENT FOR LEATHER *½ (1960) PR:A
HELL BENT FOR LOVE ** (1934) PR:A
HELL BOATS ** (1970, Brit.) PR:A
HELL BOUND * (1931) PR:A
HELL BOUND ** (1957) PR:A
HELL CANYON OUTLAWS ** (1957) PR:A
HELL CAT, THE * (1934) PR:A
HELL COMES TO FROGTOWN ** (1988) PR:O
HELL DIVERS **½ (1932) PR:A
HELL DRIVERS *** (1958, Brit.) PR:A
HELL FIRE AUSTIN ** (1932) PR:A
HELL HARBOR ** (1930) PR:A
HELL, HEAVEN OR HOBOKEN *** (1958, Brit.) PR:A
HELL IN KOREA ***½ (1956, Brit.) PR:C
HELL IN THE CITY
(SEE:AND THE WILD, WILD WOMEN)
HELL IN THE HEAVENS * (1934) PR:A
HELL IN THE PACIFIC ** (1968) PR:O
HELL IS A CITY **½ (1960, Brit.) PR:A
HELL IS EMPTY *½ (1967, Brit./It.) PR:C
HELL IS FOR HEROES ***½ (1962) PR:C
HELL IS SOLD OUT **½ (1951, Brit.) PR:A
HELL NIGHT zero (1981) PR:O
HELL ON DEVIL'S ISLAND ** (1957) PR:A
HELL ON EARTH **½ (1934, Ger.) PR:A
HELL ON FRISCO BAY * (1956) PR:C**
HELL ON WHEELS *½ (1967) PR:A
HELL RAIDERS * (1968) PR:A-C
HELL RAIDERS OF THE DEEP ** (1954, It.) PR:A
HELL-SHIP MORGAN *½ (1936) PR:A
HELL SHIP MUTINY * (1957) PR:A
HELL SQUAD *½ (1958) PR:A
HELL SQUAD zero (1986) PR:O
HELL TO ETERNITY ** (1960) PR:A
HELL TO MACAO
(SEE:CORRUPT ONES, THE)
HELL UP IN HARLEM zero (1973) PR:O
HELL WITH HEROES, THE * (1968) PR:C
HELLBENDERS, THE ** (1967, US/It./Sp.) PR:A
HELLBOUND: HELLRAISER II ** (1988) PR:O
HELLCATS, THE zero (1968) PR:O
HELLCATS OF THE NAVY ** (1957) PR:A
HELLDORADO ** (1935) PR:A
HELLDORADO **½ (1946) PR:A
HELLER IN PINK TIGHTS ** (1960) PR:C
HELLFIGHTERS ** (1968) PR:A
HELLFIRE ** (1949) PR:A
HELLFIRE CLUB, THE ** (1963, Brit.) PR:C
HELLGATE ** (1952) PR:A
HELLHOLE * (1985) PR:O
HELLIONS, THE ** (1962, Brit.) PR:O
HELLO AGAIN * (1987) PR:A-C
HELLO ANNAPOLIS * (1942) PR:A
HELLO BEAUTIFUL
(SEE:POWERS GIRL, THE)
HELLO, DOLLY! * (1969) PR:AA**
HELLO DOWN THERE ** (1969) PR:A
HELLO, ELEPHANT *½ (1954, It.) PR:A
HELLO, EVERYBODY ** (1933) PR:A
HELLO, FRISCO, HELLO *** (1943) PR:A
HELLO GOD * (1951, US/It.) PR:A
HELLO—GOODBYE ** (1970) PR:O
HELLO LONDON zero (1958, Brit.) PR:A
HELLO MARY LOU, PROM NIGHT II * (1987, Can.) PR:O
HELLO SISTER *½ (1930) PR:A
HELLO SISTER! **½ (1933) PR:C-O
HELLO SUCKER zero (1941) PR:A
HELLO SWEETHEART *½ (1935, Brit.) PR:A
HELLO TROUBLE ** (1932) PR:A
HELLRAISER **½ (1987, Brit.) PR:O
HELL'S ANGELS ***½ (1930) PR:C
HELL'S ANGELS ON WHEELS zero (1967) PR:O
HELL'S ANGELS '69 zero (1969) PR:O
HELL'S BELLES *½ (1969) PR:O
HELL'S BLOODY DEVILS * (1970) PR:O
HELL'S CARGO ** (1935, Brit.) PR:A
HELL'S CARGO
(SEE:DANGEROUS CARGO)
HELL'S CHOSEN FEW zero (1968) PR:O
HELL'S CROSSROADS *½ (1957) PR:A
HELL'S FIVE HOURS ** (1958) PR:A
HELL'S HALF ACRE *½ (1954) PR:A
HELL'S HEADQUARTERS * (1932) PR:A
HELL'S HEROES **** (1930) PR:A
HELL'S HIGHWAY **½ (1932) PR:A
HELL'S HORIZON *½ (1955) PR:A
HELL'S HOUSE ** (1932) PR:A
HELL'S ISLAND ** (1930) PR:A
HELL'S ISLAND ** (1955) PR:A
HELL'S KITCHEN ** (1939) PR:A
HELL'S OUTPOST ** (1955) PR:A
HELL'S PLAYGROUND * (1967) PR:A
HELLZAPOPPIN' *** (1941) PR:A
HELP! **½ (1965, Brit.) PR:A
HELP I'M INVISIBLE * (1952, Ger.) PR:A
HELP YOURSELF *½ (1932, Brit.) PR:A
HELTER SKELTER * (1949, Brit.) PR:A
HEMINGWAY'S ADVENTURES OF A YOUNG MAN
(SEE:ADVENTURES OF A YOUNG MAN)
HENNESSY **½ (1975, Brit.) PR:C
HENRY ALDRICH, BOY SCOUT ** (1944) PR:A
HENRY ALDRICH, EDITOR * (1942) PR:A
HENRY ALDRICH FOR PRESIDENT **½ (1941) PR:A
HENRY ALDRICH GETS GLAMOUR *** (1942) PR:A
HENRY ALDRICH HAUNTS A HOUSE **½ (1943) PR:A
HENRY ALDRICH PLAYS CUPID ** (1944) PR:A
HENRY ALDRICH SWINGS IT ** (1943) PR:A
HENRY ALDRICH'S LITTLE SECRET ** (1944) PR:A
HENRY AND DIZZY * (1942) PR:A
HENRY VIII
(SEE:PRIVATE LIFE OF HENRY VIII, THE)
HENRY VIII AND HIS SIX WIVES *** (1972, Brit.) PR:A
HENRY V *** (1944, Brit.) PR:A**
HENRY GOES ARIZONA ** (1939) PR:A
HENRY LIMPET
(SEE:INCREDIBLE MR. LIMPET, THE)
HENRY STEPS OUT * (1940, Brit.) PR:A
HENRY IV **½ (1985, It.) PR:C
HENRY, THE RAINMAKER ** (1949) PR:A
HENTAI ** (1966, Jap.) PR:O
HER ADVENTUROUS NIGHT *½ (1946) PR:A
HER BODYGUARD *½ (1933) PR:A
HER CARDBOARD LOVER **½ (1942) PR:A
HER ENLISTED MAN
(SEE:RED SALUTE)
HER FAVORITE HUSBAND
(SEE:TAMING OF DOROTHY)
HER FIRST AFFAIR *** (1947, Fr.) PR:A
HER FIRST AFFAIRE *½ (1932, Brit.) PR:A
HER FIRST BEAU ** (1941) PR:A
HER FIRST MATE ** (1933) PR:A
HER FIRST ROMANCE **½ (1940) PR:A
HER FIRST ROMANCE *½ (1951) PR:A
HER FORGOTTEN PAST * (1933) PR:A
HER HIGHNESS AND THE BELLBOY ** (1945) PR:A
HER HUSBAND LIES ** (1937) PR:A
HER HUSBAND'S AFFAIRS ***½ (1947) PR:A
HER HUSBAND'S SECRETARY * (1937) PR:A
HER IMAGINARY LOVER ** (1933, Brit.) PR:A
HER JUNGLE LOVE ** (1938) PR:A
HER KIND OF MAN ** (1946) PR:A
HER LAST AFFAIRE *½ (1935, Brit.) PR:A
HER LUCKY NIGHT ** (1945) PR:A
HER MAD NIGHT * (1932) PR:A
HER MAJESTY LOVE *½ (1931) PR:A
HER MAN ** (1930) PR:C
HER MAN GILBEY **½ (1949, Brit.) PR:A
HER MASTER'S VOICE ** (1936) PR:A
HER NIGHT OUT *½ (1932, Brit.) PR:A
HER PANELLED DOOR ** (1951, Brit.) PR:A
HER PRIMITIVE MAN ***½ (1944) PR:A
HER PRIVATE AFFAIR ** (1930) PR:A
HER PRIVATE LIFE ** (1929) PR:A
HER REPUTATION * (1931, Brit.) PR:A
HER RESALE VALUE * (1933) PR:A
HER SISTER'S SECRET *** (1946) PR:A
HER SPLENDID FOLLY *½ (1933) PR:A
HER STRANGE DESIRE ** (1931, Brit.) PR:A
HER TWELVE MEN *½ (1954) PR:A
HER WEDDING NIGHT ** (1930) PR:A
HERBIE GOES BANANAS ** (1980) PR:AA
HERBIE GOES TO MONTE CARLO ** (1977) PR:AA
HERBIE RIDES AGAIN ***½ (1974) PR:AA
HERCULE CONTRE MOLOCH
(SEE:CONQUEST OF MYCENE)
HERCULES ** (1959, It.) PR:C-O
HERCULES AGAINST THE MOON MEN *½ (1965, Fr./It.) PR:A
HERCULES AGAINST THE SONS OF THE SUN * (1964, Sp./It.) PR:A
HERCULES AND THE CAPTIVE WOMEN * (1963, Fr./It.) PR:A
HERCULES zero (1983) PR:A
HERCULES IN NEW YORK * (1970) PR:A
HERCULES IN THE HAUNTED WORLD ** (1964, It.) PR:C
HERCULES' PILLS *** (1960, It.) PR:C
HERCULES, SAMSON & ULYSSES * (1964, It.) PR:A
HERCULES II zero (1985) PR:C
HERCULES UNCHAINED * (1960, It./Fr.) PR:A
HERCULES VS-THE GIANT WARRIORS * (1965, Fr./It.) PR:A
HERE COME THE CO-EDS ***½ (1945) PR:AA
HERE COME THE GIRLS ** (1953) PR:A
HERE COME THE HUGGETTS * (1948, Brit.) PR:A
HERE COME THE JETS **½ (1959) PR:A
HERE COME THE LITTLES ** (1985) PR:AA
HERE COME THE MARINES ** (1952) PR:A
HERE COME THE NELSONS **½ (1952) PR:A
HERE COME THE TIGERS * (1978) PR:C
HERE COME THE WAVES ***½ (1944) PR:A
HERE COMES CARTER ** (1936) PR:A
HERE COMES COOKIE *** (1935) PR:A
HERE COMES ELMER **½ (1943) PR:A
HERE COMES HAPPINESS ** (1941) PR:A
HERE COMES KELLY **½ (1943) PR:A
HERE COMES MR. JORDAN ** (1941) PR:A**
HERE COMES SANTA CLAUS **½ (1984) PR:AA
HERE COMES THAT NASHVILLE SOUND
(SEE:COUNTRY BOY)
HERE COMES THE BAND *½ (1935) PR:A
HERE COMES THE GROOM *½ (1934) PR:A
HERE COMES THE GROOM **** (1951) PR:A
HERE COMES THE NAVY *** (1934) PR:A
HERE COMES THE SUN ** (1945, Brit.) PR:A
HERE COMES TROUBLE *½ (1936) PR:A
HERE COMES TROUBLE *½ (1948) PR:A
HERE I AM A STRANGER **** (1939) PR:A
HERE IS A MAN
(SEE:DEVIL AND DANIEL WEBSTER, THE)
HERE IS MY HEART **½ (1934) PR:A
HERE WE GO AGAIN **½ (1942) PR:AA
HERE WE GO ROUND THE MULBERRY BUSH *** (1968, Brit.) PR:C
HERE'S FLASH CASEY * (1937) PR:A
HERE'S GEORGE **½ (1932, Brit.) PR:A
HERE'S THE KNIFE, DEAR: NOW USE IT
(SEE:NIGHTMARE)
HERE'S TO ROMANCE * (1935) PR:A
HERE'S YOUR LIFE **½ (1968, Swed.) PR:C-O
HERETIC
(SEE:EXORCIST, PART 2)
HERITAGE ** (1935, Aus.) PR:A
HERITAGE OF THE DESERT **½ (1933) PR:A
HERITAGE OF THE DESERT *** (1939) PR:A
HERKER VON LONDON, DER
(SEE:MAD EXECUTIONERS, THE)

HERO, THE
(SEE:BLOOMFIELD)
HERO ** (1982, Brit.) PR:C
HERO AIN'T NOTHIN' BUT A SANDWICH, A ** (1977) PR:C-O
HERO AND THE TERROR ** (1988) PR:O
HERO AT LARGE **½ (1980) PR:A
HERO FOR A DAY zero (1939) PR:A
HERO OF BABYLON *½ (1963, It.) PR:A
HEROD THE GREAT *½ (1960, It.) PR:C
HEROES, THE
(SEE:INVINCIBLE SIX)
HEROES ARE MADE ** (1944, USSR) PR:C-O
HEROES *½ (1977) PR:A
HEROES DIE YOUNG *** (1960) PR:C
HEROES FOR SALE zero (1933) PR:A
HEROES IN BLUE ** (1939) PR:A
HEROES OF TELEMARK, THE *** (1965, Brit.) PR:C
HEROES OF THE ALAMO zero (1938) PR:A
HEROES OF THE HILLS **½ (1938) PR:A
HEROES OF THE RANGE ** (1936) PR:A
HEROES OF THE SADDLE *½ (1940) PR:A
HEROES OF THE SEA ** (1941) PR:A
HEROINA ** (1965) PR:C
HERO'S ISLAND **½ (1962) PR:A
HEROS SANS RETOUR
(SEE:COMMANDO)
HEROSTRATUS * (1968, Brit.) PR:C
HERRSCHER OHNE KRONE
(SEE:KING IN SHADOW)
HERS TO HOLD **½ (1943) PR:A
HE'S A COCKEYED WONDER **½ (1950) PR:A
HE'S MY GIRL * (1987) PR:C
HE'S MY GUY ** (1943) PR:A
HESTER STREET ***½ (1975) PR:C
HEX *½ (1973) PR:O
HEY BABE? * (1984, Can.) PR:A
HEY BABU RIBA * (1987, Yugo.) PR:C**
HEY BOY! HEY GIRL! **½ (1959) PR:A
HEY, GOOD LOOKIN' *½ (1982) PR:O
HEY! HEY! U.S.A. *½ (1938, Brit.) PR:A
HEY, LET'S TWIST! ** (1961) PR:A
HEY, ROOKIE ** (1944) PR:A
HEY THERE, IT'S YOGI BEAR ** (1964) PR:AA
HI BEAUTIFUL ** (1944) PR:A
HI, BUDDY ** (1943) PR:A
HI-DE-HO **½ (1947) PR:A
HI DIDDLE DIDDLE *** (1943) PR:A
HI, GANG! ** (1941, Brit.) PR:A
HI GAUCHO! * (1936) PR:A
HI, GOOD-LOOKIN' ** (1944) PR:A
HI IN THE CELLAR
(SEE:UP IN THE CELLAR)
HI-JACKED *½ (1950) PR:A
HI-JACKERS, THE *½ (1963, Brit.) PR:A
HI, MOM! ** (1970) PR:O
HI, NEIGHBOR *½ (1942) PR:A
HI, NELLIE! ** (1934) PR:A
HI-RIDERS * (1978) PR:O
HI 'YA, CHUM * (1943) PR:A
HI' YA, SAILOR ** (1943) PR:A
HI-YO SILVER **½ (1940) PR:AA
HIAWATHA ** (1952) PR:AA
HICKEY AND BOGGS *** (1972) PR:C
HIDDEN, THE ***½ (1987) PR:O
HIDDEN DANGER ** (1949) PR:A
HIDDEN ENEMY *½ (1940) PR:A
HIDDEN EYE, THE *** (1945) PR:A
HIDDEN FEAR * (1957) PR:C
HIDDEN FORTRESS, THE ** (1959, Jap.) PR:C**
HIDDEN GOLD ** (1933) PR:A
HIDDEN GOLD **½ (1940) PR:A
HIDDEN GUNS *** (1956) PR:C
HIDDEN HAND, THE **½ (1942) PR:C
HIDDEN HOMICIDE ** (1959, Brit.) PR:C
HIDDEN MENACE, THE ** (1940, Brit.) PR:A
HIDDEN POWER * (1939) PR:A
HIDDEN ROOM, THE *** (1949, Brit.) PR:A
HIDDEN ROOM OF 1,000 HORRORS
(SEE:TELL-TALE HEART)
HIDDEN VALLEY ** (1932) PR:A
HIDDEN VALLEY OUTLAWS ** (1944) PR:A
HIDE AND SEEK *½ (1964, Brit.) PR:A
HIDE IN PLAIN SIGHT ***½ (1980) PR:C
HIDEAWAY * (1937) PR:A
HIDEAWAY GIRL ** (1937) PR:A
HIDEAWAYS, THE
(SEE:FROM THE MIXED-UP FILES OF MRS. BASIL E. FRANKWEILER)
HIDE-OUT ** (1934) PR:A
HIDEOUS SUN DEMON, THE *½ (1959) PR:C
HIDE-OUT, THE ** (1930) PR:A
HIDEOUT * (1948, Brit.) PR:C**
HIDEOUT ** (1949) PR:A
HIDEOUT, THE ** (1956, Brit.) PR:C
HIDEOUT IN THE ALPS **½ (1938, Brit.) PR:A
HIDING OUT *** (1987) PR:C
HIDING PLACE, THE * (1975) PR:C-O**
HIGGINS FAMILY, THE ** (1938) PR:A
HIGH *½ (1968, Can.) PR:O
HIGH AND DRY ** (1954, Brit.) PR:A
HIGH AND LOW ** (1963, Jap.) PR:C-O**
HIGH AND THE MIGHTY, THE *** (1954) PR:A
HIGH ANXIETY * (1977) PR:C**
HIGH-BALLIN' * (1978) PR:C
HIGH BARBAREE * (1947) PR:A
HIGH BRIGHT SUN, THE
(SEE:MC GUIRE GO HOME)
HIGH COMMAND *½ (1938, Brit.) PR:A
HIGH COMMISSIONER, THE ** (1968, US/Brit.) PR:C-O
HIGH CONQUEST **½ (1947) PR:A
HIGH COST OF LOVING, THE *** (1958) PR:A
HIGH COUNTRY, THE zero (1981, Can.) PR:A
HIGH EXPLOSIVE **½ (1943) PR:A
HIGH FINANCE * (1933, Brit.) PR:A
HIGH FLIGHT ** (1957, Brit.) PR:A
HIGH FLYERS *½ (1937) PR:A
HIGH FURY ** (1947, Brit.) PR:A
HIGH GEAR * (1933) PR:A
HIGH HAT * (1937) PR:A
HIGH HELL ** (1958) PR:C
HIGH INFIDELITY ** (1965, Fr./It.) PR:O
HIGH JINKS IN SOCIETY ** (1949, Brit.) PR:A
HIGH JUMP *½ (1959, Brit.) PR:A
HIGH LONESOME **½ (1950) PR:A
HIGH NOON *** (1952) PR:C**
HIGH PLAINS DRIFTER ***½ (1973) PR:O
HIGH POWERED *½ (1945) PR:A
HIGH-POWERED RIFLE, THE **½ (1960) PR:A
HIGH PRESSURE *** (1932) PR:A
HIGH RISK *½ (1981) PR:O
HIGH ROAD TO CHINA ** (1983) PR:C
HIGH ROLLING ** (1977, Aus.) PR:O
HIGH SCHOOL ** (1940) PR:A
HIGH SCHOOL BIG SHOT ** (1959) PR:C
HIGH SCHOOL CAESAR ** (1960) PR:C
HIGH SCHOOL CONFIDENTIAL **½ (1958) PR:O
HIGH SCHOOL GIRL *½ (1935) PR:A
HIGH SCHOOL HELLCATS * (1958) PR:O
HIGH SCHOOL HERO * (1946) PR:A
HIGH SCHOOL HONEYMOON
(SEE:TOO SOON TO LOVE)
HIGH SEAS *½ (1929, Brit.) PR:A
HIGH SEASON ***½ (1988, Brit.) PR:C-O
HIGH SIERRA ** (1941) PR:C**
HIGH SOCIETY *½ (1932, Brit.) PR:A
HIGH SOCIETY * (1955) PR:AA
HIGH SOCIETY * (1956) PR:A**
HIGH SOCIETY BLUES ** (1930) PR:A
HIGH SPEED *½ (1932) PR:A
HIGH SPEED ** (1986, Fr.) PR:O
HIGH SPIRITS ** (1988) PR:C
HIGH STAKES ** (1931) PR:A
HIGH TENSION **½ (1936) PR:A
HIGH TERRACE **½ (1957, Brit.) PR:A
HIGH TIDE ** (1947) PR:A
HIGH TIDE **½ (1987, Aus.) PR:A-C
HIGH TIDE AT NOON **½ (1957, Brit.) PR:A
HIGH TIME ** (1960) PR:A
HIGH TREASON * (1929, Brit.) PR:A
HIGH TREASON *½ (1937, Brit.) PR:A
HIGH TREASON ** (1951, Brit.) PR:A
HIGH VELOCITY ** (1977) PR:C
HIGH VOLTAGE *½ (1929) PR:A
HIGH WALL, THE ***½ (1947) PR:C
HIGH, WIDE AND HANDSOME ***½ (1937) PR:A
HIGH WIND IN JAMAICA, A *** (1965) PR:A
HIGH YELLOW * (1965) PR:C-O
HIGHER AND HIGHER ** (1943) PR:A
HIGHLAND FLING * (1936, Brit.) PR:A
HIGHLANDER ** (1986) PR:O
HIGHLY DANGEROUS *½ (1950, Brit.) PR:A
HIGHPOINT ** (1984, Can.) PR:C
HIGHWAY DRAGNET *½ (1954) PR:A
HIGHWAY PATROL *½ (1938) PR:A
HIGHWAY PICKUP **½ (1965, Fr./It.) PR:C
HIGHWAY 13 * (1948) PR:A
HIGHWAY 301 ** (1950) PR:C
HIGHWAY TO BATTLE ** (1961, Brit.) PR:A
HIGHWAY TO HELL * (1984) PR:O
HIGHWAY WEST *½ (1941) PR:A
HIGHWAYMAN, THE **½ (1951) PR:C
HIGHWAYMAN RIDES, THE
(SEE:BILLY THE KID)
HIGHWAYS BY NIGHT *½ (1942) PR:A
HIKEN
(SEE:YOUNG SWORDSMAN)
HIKEN YABURI **½ (1969, Jap.) PR:C
HILDA CRANE ** (1956) PR:A
HILDUR AND THE MAGICIAN *** (1969) PR:AA
HILL, THE *** (1965, Brit.) PR:O
HILL IN KOREA, A
(SEE:HELL IN KOREA)
HILL 24 DOESN'T ANSWER * (1955, Israel) PR:A**
HILLBILLY BLITZKRIEG zero (1942) PR:A
HILLBILLYS IN A HAUNTED HOUSE *½ (1967) PR:A
HILLS HAVE EYES, THE * (1978) PR:O**
HILLS HAVE EYES II, THE *½ (1985) PR:O
HILLS OF DONEGAL, THE * (1947, Brit.) PR:A
HILLS OF HOME *** (1948) PR:AA
HILLS OF OKLAHOMA ** (1950) PR:A
HILLS OF OLD WYOMING ** (1937) PR:A
HILLS OF UTAH ** (1951) PR:A
HILLS RUN RED, THE ** (1967, It.) PR:C
HIM
(SEE:EL)
HIMATSURI ** (1985, Jap.) PR:O**
HIMMO, KING OF JERUSALEM **½ (1988, Israel) PR:C-O
HINDENBURG, THE **½ (1975) PR:C
HINDLE WAKES ** (1931, Brit.) PR:A
HINDLE WAKES
(SEE:HOLIDAY WEEK)
HINDU, THE **½ (1953, Brit.) PR:AA
HINOTORI *** (1980, Jap.) PR:O
HIPPODROME ** (1961, Aust./Ger.) PR:C-O
HIPPOLYT, THE LACKEY ** (1932, Hung.) PR:A
HIPS, HIPS, HOORAY ** (1934) PR:A
HIRED GUN, THE **½ (1957) PR:A
HIRED GUN
(SEE:LAST GUNFIGHTER, THE)
HIRED HAND, THE **½ (1971) PR:A
HIRED KILLER, THE ** (1967, Fr./It.) PR:C
HIRED WIFE ** (1934) PR:A
HIRED WIFE **½ (1940) PR:A
HIRELING, THE ***½ (1973, Brit.) PR:C
HIROSHIMA, MON AMOUR ** (1959, Fr./Jap.) PR:C-O**
HIS AND HERS ** (1961, Brit.) PR:A
HIS AND HIS
(SEE:HONEYMOON HOTEL)
HIS BROTHER'S GHOST ** (1945) PR:A
HIS BROTHER'S KEEPER *½ (1939, Brit.) PR:A-C
HIS BROTHER'S WIFE ** (1936) PR:A-C
HIS BUTLER'S SISTER ** (1943) PR:A
HIS CAPTIVE WOMAN * (1929) PR:A
HIS DOUBLE LIFE **½ (1933) PR:A
HIS EXCELLENCY **½ (1952, Brit.) PR:A
HIS EXCITING NIGHT ** (1938) PR:A
HIS FAMILY TREE ** (1936) PR:A
HIS FIGHTING BLOOD * (1935) PR:A
HIS FIRST COMMAND *½ (1929) PR:A
HIS GIRL FRIDAY *** (1940) PR:C**
HIS GLORIOUS NIGHT ** (1929) PR:C
HIS GRACE GIVES NOTICE *½ (1933, Brit.) PR:A
HIS GREATEST GAMBLE * (1934) PR:A
HIS, HERS AND THEIRS
(SEE:YOURS, MINE AND OURS)
HIS KIND OF WOMAN * (1951) PR:C-O**
HIS LAST TWELVE HOURS ** (1953, It.) PR:A
HIS LORDSHIP * (1932, Brit.) PR:A
HIS LORDSHIP
(SEE:MAN OF AFFAIRS)
HIS LORDSHIP GOES TO PRESS * (1939, Brit.) PR:A
HIS LORDSHIP REGRETS * (1938, Brit.) PR:A
HIS LUCKY DAY *½ (1929) PR:A
HIS MAJESTY AND CO *½ (1935, Brit.) PR:A

Finding entries in **THE MOTION PICTURE GUIDE ™**

Years	Volumes
1929-83	Volumes I-IX
1984	Volume IX
1985	1986 ANNUAL
1986	1987 ANNUAL
1987	1988 ANNUAL
1988	1989 ANNUAL

STAR RATINGS

★★★★★	Masterpiece
★★★★	Excellent
★★★	Good
★★	Fair
★	Poor
zero	Without Merit

PARENTAL RECOMMENDATION (PR:)

AA	Good for Children
A	Acceptable for Children
C	Cautionary, some objectionable scenes
O	Objectionable for Children

BOLD: Films on Videocassette

HIS MAJESTY BUNKER BEAN
(SEE:BUNKER BEAN)
HIS MAJESTY, KING BALLYHOO **
(1931, Ger.) PR:A
HIS MAJESTY O'KEEFE *** (1953) PR:A
HIS NIGHT OUT ** (1935) PR:A
HIS OTHER WOMAN
(SEE:DESK SET)
HIS PRIVATE SECRETARY *½ (1933) PR:A
HIS ROYAL HIGHNESS * (1932, Aus.) PR:A
HIS WIFE'S MOTHER * (1932, Brit.) PR:A
HIS WOMAN ** (1931) PR:A
HISTOIRE D'ADELE H
(SEE:STORY OF ADELE H. THE)
HISTOIRE D'AIMER
(SEE:LOVE IS A FUNNY THING)
HISTORY ** (1988, It.) PR:O
HISTORY IS MADE AT NIGHT ** (1937) PR:C**
HISTORY OF MR. POLLY, THE **½
(1949, Brit.) PR:A
HISTORY OF THE WORLD, PART 1 **
(1981) PR:C-O
HIT ** (1973) PR:O
HIT, THE ** (1985, Brit.) PR:O**
HIT AND RUN * (1957) PR:C
HIT AND RUN ** (1982) PR:C-O
HIT MAN zero (1972) PR:O
HIT PARADE, THE ** (1937) PR:A
HIT PARADE OF 1951 ** (1950) PR:A
HIT PARADE OF 1947 ** (1947) PR:A
HIT PARADE OF 1943 **½ (1943) PR:A
HIT PARADE OF 1941 ** (1940) PR:A
HIT THE DECK ** (1930) PR:A
HIT THE DECK * (1955) PR:AA**
HIT THE HAY *½ (1945) PR:A
HIT THE ICE * (1943) PR:A**
HIT THE ROAD *½ (1941) PR:A
HIT THE SADDLE ** (1937) PR:A
HITCH HIKE LADY ** (1936) PR:A
HITCH HIKE TO HEAVEN * (1936) PR:A
HITCH-HIKER, THE *** (1953) PR:C-O
HITCH IN TIME, A *** (1978, Brit.) PR:AA
HITCHER, THE * (1986) PR:O
HITCHHIKE TO HAPPINESS **½ (1945) PR:A
HITCHHIKERS, THE zero (1972) PR:O
HITLER *½ (1962) PR:C
HITLER, A FILM FROM GERMANY
(SEE:OUR HITLER)
HITLER—DEAD OR ALIVE ** (1942) PR:A
HITLER GANG, THE **½ (1944) PR:A
HITLER: THE LAST TEN DAYS **
(1973, Brit./It.) PR:C
HITLER'S CHILDREN **½ (1942) PR:C
HITLER'S GOLD
(SEE:INSIDE OUT)
HITLER'S MADMAN *** (1943) PR:A
HITOKIRI
(SEE:TENCHU!)
HITTIN' THE TRAIL * (1937) PR:A
HITTING A NEW HIGH *½ (1937) PR:A
HIYA, CHUM
(SEE:HI'YA, CHUM)
H.M. PULHAM, ESQ. ***½ (1941) PR:A
H.M.S. DEFIANT
(SEE:DAMN THE DEFIANT)
HO *½ (1968, Fr.) PR:O
HOA-BINH *** (1971, Fr.) PR:C-O
HOAX, THE ** (1972) PR:C
HOBSON'S CHOICE *½ (1931, Brit.) PR:A
HOBSON'S CHOICE ** (1954, Brit.) PR:A**
HOEDOWN *½ (1950) PR:A
HOFFMAN *½ (1970, Brit.) PR:A
HOG WILD zero (1980, Can.) PR:O
HOLCROFT COVENANT, THE ** (1985, Brit.) PR:O
HOLD BACK THE DAWN **** (1941) PR:A
HOLD BACK THE NIGHT *** (1956) PR:A
HOLD BACK TOMORROW **½ (1955) PR:O
HOLD 'EM JAIL ** (1932) PR:A
HOLD 'EM NAVY! ** (1937) PR:A
HOLD 'EM YALE **½ (1935) PR:A
HOLD EVERYTHING * (1930) PR:AA**
HOLD ME TIGHT *½ (1933) PR:A
HOLD MY HAND ** (1938, Brit.) PR:A
HOLD ON ** (1966) PR:A
HOLD THAT BABY! ** (1949) PR:A
HOLD THAT BLONDE ** (1945) PR:A
HOLD THAT CO-ED ** (1938) PR:A
HOLD THAT GHOST * (1941) PR:AA**
HOLD THAT GIRL **½ (1934) PR:A
HOLD THAT HYPNOTIST ** (1957) PR:A
HOLD THAT KISS ** (1938) PR:A
HOLD THAT LINE ** (1952) PR:A
HOLD THAT WOMAN * (1940) PR:A
HOLD THE PRESS ** (1933) PR:C
HOLD-UP A LA MILANAISE
(SEE:FIASCO IN MILAN)
HOLD YOUR MAN * (1929) PR:C
HOLD YOUR MAN *** (1933) PR:C
HOLE IN THE HEAD, A **½ (1959) PR:A
HOLE IN THE WALL **½ (1929) PR:A-C
HOLIDAY *** (1930) PR:A
HOLIDAY ***½ (1938) PR:A
HOLIDAY AFFAIR **½ (1949) PR:A
HOLIDAY CAMP **½ (1947, Brit.) PR:C
HOLIDAY FOR HENRIETTA **** (1955, Fr.) PR:A
HOLIDAY FOR LOVERS ** (1959) PR:A
HOLIDAY FOR SINNERS ** (1952) PR:C
HOLIDAY IN HAVANA **½ (1949) PR:A
HOLIDAY IN MEXICO ** (1946) PR:A
HOLIDAY IN SPAIN
(SEE:SCENT OF MYSTERY)
HOLIDAY INN ** (1942) PR:A**
HOLIDAY RHYTHM ** (1950) PR:A
HOLIDAY WEEK *½ (1952, Brit.) PR:A
HOLIDAY'S END ** (1937, Brit.) PR:A
HOLIDAYS WITH PAY * (1948, Brit.) PR:A
HOLLOW TRIUMPH ***½ (1948) PR:A
HOLLY AND THE IVY, THE ***½ (1954, Brit.) PR:A
HOLLYWOOD AND VINE **½ (1945) PR:AA
HOLLYWOOD BARN DANCE *½ (1947) PR:A
HOLLYWOOD BOULEVARD ** (1936) PR:A
HOLLYWOOD BOULEVARD * (1976) PR:O**
HOLLYWOOD CANTEEN **** (1944) PR:A
HOLLYWOOD CAVALCADE *** (1939) PR:A
HOLLYWOOD COWBOY *** (1937) PR:A
HOLLYWOOD COWBOY
(SEE:HEARTS OF THE WEST)
HOLLYWOOD HARRY * (1985) PR:O
HOLLYWOOD HIGH zero (1977) PR:O
HOLLYWOOD HIGH PART II zero (1984) PR:O
HOLLYWOOD HOODLUM
(SEE:HOLLYWOOD MYSTERY)
HOLLYWOOD HOT TUBS zero (1984) PR:O
HOLLYWOOD HOTEL ***½ (1937) PR:AA
HOLLYWOOD KNIGHTS, THE zero (1980) PR:O
HOLLYWOOD MYSTERY *½ (1934) PR:C
HOLLYWOOD OR BUST *½ (1956) PR:A
HOLLYWOOD PARTY ** (1934) PR:AA
HOLLYWOOD ROUNDUP *** (1938) PR:A
HOLLYWOOD SHUFFLE **½ (1987) PR:O
HOLLYWOOD SPEAKS ** (1932) PR:C-O
HOLLYWOOD STADIUM MYSTERY ** (1938) PR:A
HOLLYWOOD STORY ** (1951) PR:A
HOLLYWOOD STRANGLER, THE
(SEE:DON'T ANSWER THE PHONE)
HOLLYWOOD THRILLMAKERS
(SEE:MOVIE STUNT MEN)
HOLLYWOOD VICE SQUAD ** (1986) PR:O
HOLLYWOOD ZAP! * (1986) PR:O
HOLOCAUST 2000
(SEE:CHOSEN, THE)
HOLY INNOCENTS, THE * (1984, Sp.) PR:O**
HOLY MATRIMONY ***½ (1943) PR:A
HOLY MOUNTAIN, THE ** (1973, US/Mex.) PR:O
HOLY TERROR, A ** (1931) PR:A
HOLY TERROR, THE **½ (1937) PR:A
HOLY TERROR
(SEE:ALICE, SWEET ALICE)
HOMBRE * (1967) PR:C**
HOME AND AWAY *½ (1956, Brit.) PR:A
HOME AND THE WORLD, THE ***
(1984, India) PR:C
HOME AT SEVEN
(SEE:MURDER ON MONDAY)
HOME BEFORE DARK *** (1958) PR:C
HOME FOR TANYA, A ** (1961, USSR) PR:A
HOME FREE ALL ** (1983) PR:A
HOME FREE ALL *½ (1984) PR:O
HOME FROM HOME ** (1939, Brit.) PR:A
HOME FROM THE HILL *** (1960) PR:O
HOME IN INDIANA * (1944) PR:AA**
HOME IN OKLAHOMA **½ (1946) PR:A
HOME IN WYOMIN' ** (1942) PR:A
HOME IS THE HERO *** (1959, Ireland) PR:C
HOME IS WHERE THE HART IS zero
(1987, Can.) PR:C
HOME MOVIES **½ (1979) PR:C
HOME OF THE BRAVE * (1949) PR:C**
HOME ON THE PRAIRIE ** (1939) PR:A
HOME ON THE RANGE *½ (1935) PR:A
HOME ON THE RANGE ** (1946) PR:A
HOME, SWEET HOME ** (1933, Brit.) PR:A
HOME SWEET HOME *½ (1945, Brit.) PR:A
HOME SWEET HOME *½ (1981) PR:O
HOME SWEET HOMICIDE *** (1946) PR:AA
HOME TO DANGER *½ (1951, Brit.) PR:A
HOME TOWN STORY *½ (1951) PR:C
HOME TOWNERS, THE **½ (1928) PR:A
HOMEBODIES **½ (1974) PR:O
HOMECOMING ** (1948) PR:A
HOMECOMING, THE ** (1973) PR:C**
HOMER ** (1970) PR:C
HOMESTEADERS, THE ** (1953) PR:A
HOMESTEADERS OF PARADISE VALLEY *½
(1947) PR:A
HOMESTRETCH, THE **½ (1947) PR:A
HOMETOWN U.S.A. ** (1979) PR:C
HOMEWORK zero (1982) PR:O
HOMICIDAL **½ (1961) PR:O
HOMICIDE ** (1949) PR:C
HOMICIDE BUREAU * (1939) PR:O
HOMICIDE FOR THREE ** (1948) PR:C
HOMICIDE SQUAD ** (1931) PR:A
HONDO *** (1953) PR:C
HONEY **½ (1930) PR:A
HONEY POT, THE ** (1967, Brit.) PR:A
HONEYBABY, HONEYBABY * (1974) PR:C
HONEYCHILE ** (1951) PR:A
HONEYMOON **½ (1947) PR:A
HONEYMOON ADVENTURE, A
(SEE:FOOTSTEPS IN THE NIGHT)
HONEYMOON AHEAD **½ (1945) PR:A
HONEYMOON DEFERRED *½ (1940) PR:A
HONEYMOON DEFERRED ** (1951, Brit.) PR:A
HONEYMOON FOR THREE **½ (1935, Brit.) PR:A
HONEYMOON FOR THREE *½ (1941) PR:A
HONEYMOON HOTEL ** (1946, Brit.) PR:A
HONEYMOON HOTEL *½ (1964) PR:C
HONEYMOON IN BALI **½ (1939) PR:A
HONEYMOON KILLERS, THE * (1969) PR:O**
HONEYMOON LANE * (1931) PR:A
HONEYMOON LIMITED * (1936) PR:A
HONEYMOON LODGE ** (1943) PR:A
HONEYMOON MACHINE, THE **½ (1961) PR:A
HONEYMOON MERRY-GO-ROUND **½
(1939, Brit.) PR:AA
HONEYMOON OF HORROR * (1964) PR:O
HONEYMOON OF TERROR zero (1961) PR:O
HONEYMOON'S OVER, THE ** (1939) PR:C
HONEYSUCKLE ROSE * (1980) PR:C**
HONG KONG **½ (1951) PR:A
HONG KONG AFFAIR ** (1958) PR:A
HONG KONG CONFIDENTIAL **½ (1958) PR:A
HONG KONG NIGHTS **½ (1935) PR:A
HONKERS, THE **½ (1972) PR:C
HONKY ** (1971) PR:O
HONKY TONK ** (1929) PR:A
HONKY TONK *** (1941) PR:C
HONKY TONK FREEWAY ** (1981) PR:C
HONKYTONK MAN **½ (1982) PR:A-C
HONOLULU **½ (1939) PR:A
HONOLULU LU *½ (1941) PR:A
HONOLULU-TOKYO-HONG KONG *½
(1963, Hong Kong/Jap.) PR:A
HONOR AMONG LOVERS *** (1931) PR:A
HONOR OF THE FAMILY *½ (1931) PR:A
HONOR OF THE MOUNTED *½ (1932) PR:A
HONOR OF THE PRESS *½ (1932) PR:A
HONOR OF THE RANGE ** (1934) PR:A
HONOR OF THE WEST ** (1939) PR:A
HONOURABLE MURDER, AN * (1959, Brit.) PR:C
HONOURS EASY ** (1935, Brit.) PR:A
HOODLUM, THE ** (1951) PR:C
HOODLUM EMPIRE **½ (1952) PR:A
HOODLUM PRIEST, THE *** (1961) PR:C
HOODLUM SAINT, THE **½ (1946) PR:A
HOODWINK *** (1981, Aus.) PR:C
HOOK, THE ** (1962) PR:C
HOOK, LINE AND SINKER ** (1930) PR:A
HOOK, LINE AND SINKER * (1969) PR:A
HOOKED GENERATION, THE zero (1969) PR:O
HOOPER * (1978) PR:A
HOOPLA ** (1933) PR:C
HOORAY FOR LOVE ** (1935) PR:A
HOOSIER HOLIDAY ** (1943) PR:A
HOOSIER SCHOOLBOY ** (1937) PR:A
HOOSIER SCHOOLMASTER ** (1935) PR:A
HOOSIERS ** (1986) PR:A-C**
HOOTENANNY HOOT ** (1963) PR:A
HOOTS MON! **½ (1939, Brit.) PR:A
HOPALONG CASSIDY *** (1935) PR:A
HOPALONG CASSIDY RETURNS **½ (1936) PR:C
HOPALONG RIDES AGAIN ** (1937) PR:A
HOPE AND GLORY *** (1987, Brit.) PR:C**
HOPE OF HIS SIDE ** (1935, Brit.) PR:A
HOPELESS ONES, THE
(SEE:ROUND UP, THE)
HOPPITY GOES TO TOWN
(SEE:MR. BUG GOES TO TOWN)
HOPPY'S HOLIDAY *½ (1947) PR:A
HOPPY SERVES A WRIT ** (1943) PR:A
HOPSCOTCH ***½ (1980) PR:C
HORIZONS WEST **½ (1952) PR:A
HORIZONTAL LIEUTENANT, THE ** (1962) PR:A
HORLA, THE
(SEE:DIARY OF A MADMAN)
HORN BLOWS AT MIDNIGHT, THE ***
(1945) PR:AA
HORNET'S NEST, THE *½ (1955, Brit.) PR:A
HORNET'S NEST ** (1970) PR:O
HOROSCOPE *½ (1950, Yugo.) PR:O
HORRIBLE DR. HICHCOCK, THE **
(1964, It.) PR:O

HORRIBLE HOUSE ON THE HILL, THE
  (SEE:DEVIL TIMES FIVE)
HORRIBLE MILL WOMEN, THE
  (SEE:MILL OF THE STONE WOMEN)
HORROR CASTLE ** (1965, It.) PR:O
HORROR CHAMBER OF DR. FAUSTUS, THE ***½
  (1962, Fr./It.) PR:O
HORROR CREATURES OF THE PREHISTORIC
  PLANET
  (SEE:HORROR OF THE BLOOD MONSTERS)
HORROR EXPRESS *** (1972, Sp./Brit.) PR:C
HORROR HIGH zero (1974) PR:O
HORROR HOSPITAL *½ (1973, Brit.) PR:O
HORROR HOTEL **½ (1960, Brit.) PR:C
HORROR HOTEL
  (SEE:EATEN ALIVE!)
HORROR HOUSE *½ (1970, Brit.) PR:O
HORROR ISLAND zero (1941) PR:A
HORROR MANIACS
  (SEE:GREED OF WILLIAM HART, THE)
HORROR OF DRACULA, THE ****
  (1958, Brit.) PR:O
HORROR OF FRANKENSTEIN, THE *
  (1970, Brit.) PR:O
HORROR OF IT ALL, THE ** (1964, Brit.) PR:A
HORROR OF PARTY BEACH, THE * (1964) PR:C
HORROR OF THE BLOOD MONSTERS zero
  (1970, US/Phil.) PR:O
HORROR OF THE STONE WOMEN
  (SEE:MILL OF THE STONE WOMEN)
HORROR OF THE ZOMBIES * (1974, Sp.) PR:C
HORROR ON SNAPE ISLAND
  (SEE:BEYOND THE FOG)
HORROR PLANET zero (1982, Brit.) PR:O
HORRORS OF SPIDER ISLAND
  (SEE:IT'S HOT IN PARADISE)
HORRORS OF THE BLACK MUSEUM **
  (1959, US/Brit.) PR:O
HORRORS OF THE BLACK ZOO
  (SEE:BLACK ZOO)
HORSE, THE *** (1984, Turk.) PR:O
HORSE FEATHERS **** (1932) PR:A
HORSE IN THE GRAY FLANNEL SUIT, THE *½
  (1968) PR:AA
HORSE, MY HORSE
  (SEE:HORSE, THE)
HORSE NAMED COMANCHE, A
  (SEE:TONKA)
HORSE OF PRIDE **½ (1980, Fr.) PR:A
HORSE SOLDIERS, THE **** (1959) PR:C
HORSEMEN, THE ** (1971) PR:C
HORSEMEN OF THE SIERRAS ** (1950) PR:A
HORSEPLAY *½ (1933) PR:A
HORSE'S MOUTH, THE *½ (1953, Brit.) PR:A
HORSE'S MOUTH, THE **** (1958, Brit.) PR:A
HOSPITAL, THE *** (1971) PR:C
HOSPITAL MASSACRE zero (1982) PR:O
HOSPITAL MASSACRE zero (1984) PR:O
HOSTAGE *½ (1987) PR:C-O
HOSTAGE, THE * (1956, Brit.) PR:A
HOSTAGE, THE **½ (1966) PR:A
HOSTAGE: DALLAS
  (SEE:GETTING EVEN)
HOSTAGES ** (1943) PR:A
HOSTILE COUNTRY ** (1950) PR:A
HOSTILE GUNS **½ (1967) PR:A
HOSTILE WITNESS *½ (1968, Brit.) PR:A
HOT ANGEL, THE *½ (1958) PR:C
HOT BLOOD *** (1956) PR:A
HOT BOX, THE **½ (1972, US/Phil.) PR:O
HOT CAR GIRL *½ (1958) PR:A
HOT CARGO ** (1946) PR:A
HOT CARS ** (1956) PR:A
HOT CHILD IN THE CITY * (1987) PR:O
HOT CHILI zero (1986) PR:O
HOT CURVES ** (1930) PR:A
HOT DOG...THE MOVIE * (1984) PR:O
HOT ENOUGH FOR JUNE
  (SEE:AGENT 8 3/4)
HOT FOR PARIS ** (1930) PR:A
HOT FRUSTRATIONS
  (SEE:FRUSTRATIONS)
HOT HEIRESS ** (1931) PR:A
HOT HORSE
  (SEE:ONCE UPON A HORSE)
HOT HOURS **½ (1963, Fr.) PR:O
HOT ICE **½ (1952, Brit.) PR:A

HOT IN PARADISE
  (SEE:IT'S HOT IN PARADISE)
HOT LEAD ** (1951) PR:A
HOT LEAD AND COLD FEET **½ (1978) PR:AA
HOT MILLIONS ***½ (1968, Brit.) PR:C
HOT MONEY *½ (1936) PR:A
HOT MONEY GIRL ** (1962, Brit./Ger.) PR:C
HOT MONTH OF AUGUST, THE * (1969, Gr.) PR:C
HOT MOVES * (1984) PR:O
HOT NEWS *½ (1936, Brit.) PR:A
HOT NEWS ** (1953) PR:A
HOT PEPPER ** (1933) PR:A
HOT POTATO *½ (1976) PR:O
HOT PURSUIT ** (1987) PR:C-O
HOT RESORT *½ (1985) PR:O
HOT RHYTHM ** (1944) PR:A
HOT ROCK, THE *** (1972) PR:A-C
HOT ROD *½ (1950) PR:A
HOT ROD GANG **½ (1958) PR:A
HOT ROD GIRL *½ (1956) PR:A
HOT ROD HULLABALOO * (1966) PR:C
HOT ROD RUMBLE *½ (1957) PR:C
HOT RODS TO HELL **½ (1967) PR:C-O
HOT SATURDAY ** (1932) PR:A
HOT SHOT * (1987) PR:A
HOT SHOTS * (1956) PR:A
HOT SPELL ** (1958) PR:C-O
HOT SPOT
  (SEE:I WAKE UP SCREAMING)
HOT SPUR zero (1968) PR:O
HOT STEEL * (1940) PR:A
HOT STUFF *½ (1929) PR:A
HOT STUFF * (1979) PR:C
HOT SUMMER NIGHT ** (1957) PR:A
HOT SUMMER WEEK * (1973, Can.) PR:O
HOT TARGET ** (1985, New Zealand) PR:C-O
HOT TIMES *½ (1974) PR:O
HOT TIP **½ (1935) PR:A
HOT TO TROT * (1988) PR:C
HOT TOMORROWS *** (1978) PR:C
HOT WATER ** (1937) PR:A
HOTEL *** (1967) PR:A
HOTEL BERLIN *** (1945) PR:A
HOTEL COLONIAL * (1987, US/It.) PR:O
HOTEL CONTINENTAL ** (1932) PR:A
HOTEL FOR WOMEN ** (1939) PR:A
HOTEL HAYWIRE ** (1937) PR:A
HOTEL IMPERIAL **½ (1939) PR:A
HOTEL NEW HAMPSHIRE, THE **½
  (1984) PR:C-O
HOTEL NEW YORK ** (1985) PR:O
HOTEL PARADISO **½ (1966, US/Brit.) PR:C
HOTEL RESERVE *** (1946, Brit.) PR:A
HOTEL SAHARA **½ (1951, Brit.) PR:A
HOTEL SPLENDIDE *½ (1932, Brit.) PR:A
HOTEL VARIETY *½ (1933) PR:A
HOTHEAD * (1963) PR:C
HOTSPRINGS HOLIDAY **½ (1970, Jap.) PR:A
HOTTENTOT, THE ** (1929) PR:A
HOUDINI *** (1953) PR:A
HOUND-DOG MAN *** (1959) PR:A
HOUND OF THE BASKERVILLES **½
  (1932, Brit.) PR:A
HOUND OF THE BASKERVILLES, THE ****
  (1939) PR:A
HOUND OF THE BASKERVILLES, THE ***
  (1959, Brit.) PR:C
HOUND OF THE BASKERVILLES, THE *
  (1980, Brit.) PR:C
HOUND OF THE BASKERVILLES, THE **
  (1983, Brit.) PR:C
HOUNDS... OF NOTRE DAME, THE **½
  (1980, Can.) PR:A
HOUR BEFORE THE DAWN, THE *½ (1944) PR:A
HOUR OF DECISION *½ (1957, Brit.) PR:A
HOUR OF GLORY **½ (1949, Brit.) PR:A
HOUR OF THE ASSASSIN ** (1987) PR:O
HOUR OF THE GUN ***½ (1967) PR:C
HOUR OF THE STAR, THE *** (1986, Braz.) PR:O
HOUR OF THE WOLF, THE ** (1968, Swed.) PR:O
HOUR OF THIRTEEN, THE *** (1952) PR:A
HOURS OF LONELINESS * (1930, Brit.) PR:C
HOURS OF LOVE, THE **½ (1965, It.) PR:A
HOUSE * (1986) PR:C-O
HOUSE ACROSS THE BAY, THE **½ (1940) PR:A

HOUSE ACROSS THE LAKE, THE
  (SEE:HEAT WAVE)
HOUSE ACROSS THE STREET, THE *½ (1949) PR:A
HOUSE AT THE END OF THE WORLD
  (SEE:DIE, MONSTER, DIE)
HOUSE AT THE END OF THE WORLD
  (SEE:TOMB OF LIGEIA)
HOUSE II: THE SECOND STORY * (1987) PR:C-O
HOUSE BROKEN ** (1936, Brit.) PR:A
HOUSE BY THE CEMETERY, THE zero
  (1984, It.) PR:O
HOUSE BY THE LAKE, THE ** (1977, Can.) PR:O
HOUSE BY THE RIVER **½ (1950) PR:C
HOUSE CALLS **½ (1978) PR:C
HOUSE DIVIDED, A **½ (1932) PR:C
HOUSE IN MARSH ROAD, THE ** (1960, Brit.) PR:A
HOUSE IN NIGHTMARE PARK, THE
  (SEE:NIGHT OF THE LAUGHING DEAD)
HOUSE IN THE SQUARE, THE
  (SEE:I'LL NEVER FORGET YOU)
HOUSE IN THE WOODS, THE **½ (1957, Brit.) PR:C
HOUSE IS NOT A HOME, A *½ (1964) PR:O
HOUSE OF A THOUSAND CANDLES, THE **
  (1936) PR:A
HOUSE OF BAMBOO ***½ (1955) PR:C
HOUSE OF BLACKMAIL ** (1953, Brit.) PR:C
HOUSE OF CARDS
  (SEE:DESIGNING WOMEN)
HOUSE OF CARDS *** (1969) PR:C
HOUSE OF CONNELLY
  (SEE:CAROLINA)
HOUSE OF CRAZIES
  (SEE:ASYLUM)
HOUSE OF DANGER * (1934) PR:A
HOUSE OF DARK SHADOWS **½ (1970) PR:C-O
HOUSE OF DARKNESS ** (1948, Brit.) PR:O
HOUSE OF DEATH ** (1932, USSR) PR:C
HOUSE OF DRACULA **½ (1945) PR:A
HOUSE OF ERRORS *½ (1942) PR:A
HOUSE OF EVIL *½ (1968, US/Mex.) PR:O
HOUSE OF EXORCISM, THE zero (1976, It.) PR:O
HOUSE OF FEAR
  (SEE:LAST WARNING, THE)
HOUSE OF FEAR, THE *½ (1939) PR:A
HOUSE OF FEAR, THE **½ (1945) PR:A
HOUSE OF FRANKENSTEIN **½ (1944) PR:A
HOUSE OF FREAKS zero (1973, It.) PR:O
HOUSE OF FRIGHT ** (1961) PR:A
HOUSE OF GAMES **** (1987) PR:O
HOUSE OF GOD, THE ** (1984) PR:O
HOUSE OF GREED * (1934, USSR) PR:A
HOUSE OF HORROR * (1929) PR:A
HOUSE OF HORRORS **½ (1946) PR:C
HOUSE OF INTRIGUE, THE ** (1959, It.) PR:A
HOUSE OF LIFE *½ (1953, Ger.) PR:A
HOUSE OF LONG SHADOWS, THE **
  (1983, Brit.) PR:O
HOUSE OF MORTAL SIN, THE
  (SEE:CONFESSIONAL)
HOUSE OF MYSTERY ** (1934) PR:A
HOUSE OF MYSTERY ** (1941, Brit.) PR:A
HOUSE OF MYSTERY ** (1961, Brit.) PR:C
HOUSE OF NUMBERS **½ (1957) PR:A
HOUSE OF 1,000 DOLLS * (1967, Ger./Sp./Brit.) PR:O
HOUSE OF PLEASURE
  (SEE:LE PLAISIR)
HOUSE OF PSYCHOTIC WOMEN, THE zero
  (1973, Sp.) PR:O
HOUSE OF ROTHSCHILD, THE **** (1934) PR:A
HOUSE OF SECRETS * (1929) PR:O
HOUSE OF SECRETS, THE ** (1937) PR:A
HOUSE OF SECRETS
  (SEE:TRIPLE DECEPTION)
HOUSE OF SEVEN CORPSES, THE **
  (1974) PR:C-O
HOUSE OF SEVEN GABLES
  (SEE:HOUSE OF THE SEVEN GABLES)
HOUSE OF SEVEN JOYS
  (SEE:WRECKING CREW, THE)
HOUSE OF STRANGE LOVES, THE *½
  (1969, Jap.) PR:C
HOUSE OF STRANGERS *** (1949) PR:C
HOUSE OF THE ARROW, THE **½
  (1930, Brit.) PR:A
HOUSE OF THE ARROW, THE
  (SEE:CASTLE OF CRIMES)
HOUSE OF THE ARROW, THE *** (1953, Brit.) PR:A

Finding entries in **THE MOTION PICTURE GUIDE** ™

Years 1929-83	Volumes I-IX
1984	Volume IX
1985	1986 ANNUAL
1986	1987 ANNUAL
1987	1988 ANNUAL
1988	1989 ANNUAL

STAR RATINGS

★★★★★ Masterpiece
★★★★ Excellent
★★★ Good
★★ Fair
★ Poor
zero Without Merit

PARENTAL RECOMMENDATION (PR:)

AA Good for Children
A Acceptable for Children
C Cautionary, some objectionable scenes
O Objectionable for Children

BOLD: Films on Videocassette

HOUSE OF THE BLACK DEATH ** (1965) PR:O
HOUSE OF THE DAMNED * (1963) PR:C
HOUSE OF THE LIVING DEAD * (1973, South Africa) PR:C
HOUSE OF THE SEVEN GABLES, THE **½ (1940) PR:A
HOUSE OF THE SEVEN HAWKS, THE ** (1959) PR:A
HOUSE OF THE SPANIARD, THE ** (1936, Brit.) PR:A
HOUSE OF THE THREE GIRLS, THE ** (1961, Aust.) PR:A
HOUSE OF TRENT, THE ** (1933, Brit.) PR:A
HOUSE OF UNREST, THE *½ (1931, Brit.) PR:A
HOUSE OF USHER ***½ (1960) PR:O
HOUSE OF WAX * (1953) PR:C**
HOUSE OF WHIPCORD zero (1974, Brit.) PR:O
HOUSE OF WOMEN ** (1962) PR:O
HOUSE ON CARROLL STREET, THE * (1988) PR:C**
HOUSE ON 56TH STREET, THE **½ (1933) PR:C
HOUSE ON HAUNTED HILL * (1958) PR:C**
HOUSE ON 92ND STREET, THE **** (1945) PR:A
HOUSE ON SKULL MOUNTAIN, THE * (1974) PR:C
HOUSE ON SORORITY ROW, THE ** (1983) PR:O
HOUSE ON TELEGRAPH HILL *** (1951) PR:C
HOUSE ON THE EDGE OF THE PARK zero (1985, It.) PR:O
HOUSE ON THE FRONT LINE, THE *** (1963, USSR) PR:A
HOUSE ON THE SAND *½ (1967) PR:C
HOUSE ON THE SQUARE, THE
(SEE:I'LL NEVER FORGET YOU)
HOUSE OPPOSITE, THE *½ (1931, Brit.) PR:A
HOUSE THAT CRIED MURDER, THE
(SEE:BRIDE, THE)
HOUSE THAT DRIPPED BLOOD, THE **½ (1971, Brit.) PR:O
HOUSE THAT SCREAMED, THE **½ (1970, Sp.) PR:O
HOUSE THAT VANISHED, THE * (1974, Brit.) PR:O
HOUSE WHERE DEATH LIVES, THE * (1984) PR:O
HOUSE WHERE EVIL DWELLS, THE *½ (1982) PR:O
HOUSE WITH AN ATTIC, THE **½ (1964, USSR) PR:A
HOUSEBOAT * (1958) PR:A**
HOUSEHOLDER, THE * (1963, US/India) PR:A
HOUSEKEEPER, THE * (1987, Can.) PR:C
HOUSEKEEPER'S DAUGHTER **½ (1939) PR:A
HOUSEKEEPING ***½ (1987) PR:A-C
HOUSEMASTER **½ (1938, Brit.) PR:A
HOUSEWIFE ** (1934) PR:A
HOUSTON STORY, THE **½ (1956) PR:A
HOVERBUG ** (1970, Brit.) PR:AA
HOW ABOUT US?
(SEE:EPILOGUE)
HOW COME NOBODY'S ON OUR SIDE? * (1975) PR:A
HOW DO I LOVE THEE? *½ (1970) PR:C
HOW DO YOU DO? *½ (1946) PR:A
HOW GREEN WAS MY VALLEY *** (1941) PR:A**
HOW I WON THE WAR ***½ (1967, Brit.) PR:C
HOW LOW CAN YOU FALL?
(SEE:TILL MARRIAGE DO US PART)
HOW MANY ROADS
(SEE:LOST MAN, THE)
HOW NOT TO ROB A DEPARTMENT STORE *** (1965, Fr./It.) PR:A
HOW SWEET IT IS **½ (1968) PR:C-O
HOW THE WEST WAS WON ** (1962) PR:AA**
HOW TO BE VERY, VERY, POPULAR **½ (1955) PR:A
HOW TO BEAT THE HIGH COST OF LIVING * (1980) PR:A
HOW TO COMMIT MARRIAGE **½ (1969) PR:A
HOW TO FRAME A FIGG ** (1971) PR:AA
HOW TO MAKE A MONSTER **½ (1958) PR:C
HOW TO MAKE IT
(SEE:TARGET: HARRY)
HOW TO MARRY A MILLIONAIRE * (1953) PR:A**
HOW TO MURDER A RICH UNCLE **½ (1957, Brit.) PR:A
HOW TO MURDER YOUR WIFE ***½ (1965) PR:A
HOW TO SAVE A MARRIAGE—AND RUIN YOUR LIFE ** (1968) PR:A
HOW TO SEDUCE A PLAYBOY * (1968, Aust./Fr./It.) PR:C
HOW TO SEDUCE A WOMAN ** (1974) PR:O
HOW TO STEAL A MILLION ***½ (1966) PR:A
HOW TO STUFF A WILD BIKINI ** (1965) PR:A
HOW TO SUCCEED IN BUSINESS WITHOUT REALLY TRYING **** (1967) PR:A
HOW WILLINGLY YOU SING **½ (1975, Aus.) PR:A-C
HOWARD CASE, THE *½ (1936, Brit.) PR:A
HOWARD THE DUCK *½ (1986) PR:A-C
HOWARDS OF VIRGINIA, THE * (1940) PR:A**
HOWLING, THE ***½ (1981) PR:O
HOWLING TWO: YOUR SISTER IS A WEREWOLF *½ (1985) PR:O
HOWLING III, THE *½ (1987, Aus.) PR:C-O
HOWLING IV: THE ORIGINAL NIGHTMARE ** (1988, Brit.) PR:O
HOW'S ABOUT IT? ** (1943) PR:A
HOW'S CHANCES
(SEE:DIPLOMATIC LOVER, THE)
HOWZER ** (1973) PR:A
HU-MAN *** (1975, Fr.) PR:C
HUCKLEBERRY FINN *** (1931) PR:AA
HUCKLEBERRY FINN ***½ (1939) PR:AA
HUCKLEBERRY FINN
(SEE:ADVENTURES OF HUCKLEBERRY FINN, THE)
HUCKLEBERRY FINN *½ (1974) PR:AA
HUCKSTERS, THE **** (1947) PR:A
HUD **½ (1963) PR:O
HUDDLE *½ (1932) PR:A
HUDSON'S BAY **½ (1940) PR:A
HUE AND CRY ** (1950, Brit.) PR:A
HUGGETTS ABROAD, THE *½ (1949, Brit.) PR:A
HUGO THE HIPPO ***½ (1976, Hung./US) PR:AA
HUGS AND KISSES **½ (1968, Swed.) PR:O
HUK *½ (1956) PR:O
HULLABALOO **½ (1940) PR:A
HULLABALOO OVER GEORGIE AND BONNIE'S PICTURES ** (1979, Brit.) PR:A
HUMAN BEAST, THE
(SEE:LA BETE HUMAINE)
HUMAN CARGO *½ (1936) PR:A
HUMAN COMEDY, THE ***½ (1943) PR:A
HUMAN CONDITION, THE * (1959, Jap.) PR:O**
HUMAN DESIRE **½ (1954) PR:C
HUMAN DUPLICATORS, THE * (1965) PR:A
HUMAN EXPERIMENTS *½ (1980) PR:O
HUMAN FACTOR, THE * (1975) PR:O
HUMAN FACTOR, THE ** (1979, Brit.) PR:C
HUMAN HIGHWAY * (1982) PR:O
HUMAN JUNGLE, THE **½ (1954) PR:A
HUMAN MONSTER, THE * (1940, Brit.) PR:O**
HUMAN SIDE, THE *** (1934) PR:A
HUMAN TARGETS ** (1932) PR:A
HUMAN TORNADO, THE *½ (1976) PR:O
HUMAN VAPOR, THE *½ (1964, Jap.) PR:A
HUMANITY * (1933) PR:A
HUMANOID, THE ** (1979, It.) PR:C
HUMANOIDS FROM THE DEEP **½ (1980) PR:O
HUMONGOUS * (1982, Can.) PR:O
HUMORESQUE ***½ (1946) PR:A-C
HUMPHREY TAKES A CHANCE * (1950) PR:A
HUNCH, THE ** (1967, Brit.) PR:AA
HUNCHBACK OF NOTRE DAME, THE *** (1939) PR:A-C**
HUNCHBACK OF NOTRE DAME, THE ** (1957, Fr.) PR:A-C
HUNCHBACK OF ROME, THE **½ (1963, It.) PR:C
HUNCHBACK OF THE MORGUE, THE zero (1972, Sp.) PR:O
HUNDRA ** (1984, It.) PR:C
HUNDRED HOUR HUNT **½ (1953, Brit.) PR:A
HUNDRED POUND WINDOW, THE *½ (1943, Brit.) PR:A
HUNGER * (1968, Den./Norway/Swed.) PR:O**
HUNGER, THE zero (1983) PR:O
HUNGRY HILL ** (1947, Brit.) PR:C
HUNGRY WIVES * (1973) PR:O
HUNK *½ (1987) PR:C
HUNS, THE * (1962, Fr./It.) PR:C
HUNT, THE **** (1967, Sp.) PR:O
HUNT THE MAN DOWN * (1950) PR:A**
HUNT TO KILL
(SEE:WHITE BUFFALO, THE)
HUNTED
(SEE:STRANGER IN BETWEEN, THE)
HUNTED, THE *½ (1948) PR:A
HUNTED, THE
(SEE:TOUCH ME NOT)
HUNTED IN HOLLAND ** (1961, Brit.) PR:AA
HUNTED MEN **½ (1938) PR:A
HUNTER, THE * (1980) PR:C
HUNTER OF THE APOCALYPSE
(SEE:LAST HUNTER, THE)
HUNTERS, THE *** (1958) PR:A-C
HUNTER'S BLOOD **½ (1987) PR:O
HUNTERS OF THE GOLDEN COBRA, THE ** (1984, It.) PR:A
HUNTING IN SIBERIA ** (1962, USSR) PR:A
HUNTING PARTY, THE * (1977, Brit.) PR:O
HURRICANE * (1929) PR:A
HURRICANE, THE ** (1937) PR:A**
HURRICANE, THE
(SEE:VOICE OF THE HURRICANE)
HURRICANE zero (1979) PR:A
HURRICANE HORSEMAN *½ (1931) PR:A
HURRICANE ISLAND ** (1951) PR:A
HURRICANE SMITH ** (1942) PR:A
HURRICANE SMITH *½ (1952) PR:A
HURRY, CHARLIE, HURRY ** (1941) PR:A
HURRY SUNDOWN * (1967) PR:O
HURRY UP OR I'LL BE 30 **½ (1973) PR:C
HUSBANDS **½ (1970) PR:C
HUSBAND'S HOLIDAY *½ (1931) PR:A
HUSH-A-BYE MURDER
(SEE:MY LOVER, MY SON)
HUSH... HUSH, SWEET CHARLOTTE ***½ (1964) PR:O
HUSH MONEY *½ (1931) PR:A
HUSTLE ***½ (1975) PR:O
HUSTLER, THE *** (1961) PR:C**
HUSTLER SQUAD, THE
(SEE:DOLL SQUAD, THE)
HYDE PARK CORNER **½ (1935, Brit.) PR:A
HYPERBOLOID OF ENGINEER GARIN, THE ** (1965, USSR) PR:A
HYPNOSIS * (1966, Ger./Sp./It.) PR:C-O
HYPNOTIC EYE, THE *½ (1960) PR:O
HYPNOTIST, THE
(SEE:SCOTLAND YARD DRAGNET)
HYPNOTIZED zero (1933) PR:A
HYSTERIA * (1965, Brit.) PR:O**
HYSTERICAL zero (1983) PR:O

I

I ACCUSE
(SEE:J'ACCUSE)
I ACCUSE! ***½ (1958, Brit.) PR:A
I ACCUSE MY PARENTS * (1945) PR:A
I ADORE YOU ** (1933, Brit.) PR:A
I AIM AT THE STARS **½ (1960) PR:A
I AM A CAMERA ** (1955, Brit.) PR:A
I AM A CRIMINAL ** (1939) PR:A
I AM A FUGITIVE FROM A CHAIN GANG *** (1932) PR:O**
I AM A GROUPIE * (1970, Brit.) PR:O
I AM A THIEF ** (1935) PR:A
I AM CURIOUS GAY
(SEE:HAPPY BIRTHDAY, DAVY)
I AM NOT AFRAID *½ (1939) PR:A
I AM SUZANNE ** (1934) PR:A
I AM THE CHEESE * (1983) PR:A
I AM THE LAW * (1938) PR:A**
I BECAME A CRIMINAL ** (1947) PR:A
I BELIEVE IN YOU *** (1953, Brit.) PR:A
I BELIEVED IN YOU * (1934) PR:A
I BOMBED PEARL HARBOR ** (1961, Jap.) PR:A
I BURY THE LIVING ** (1958) PR:A
I CALL FIRST
(SEE:WHO'S THAT KNOCKING AT MY DOOR?)
I CAN GET IT FOR YOU WHOLESALE ***½ (1951) PR:A
I CAN'T ESCAPE *½ (1934) PR:A
I CAN'T GIVE YOU ANYTHING BUT LOVE, BABY zero (1940) PR:A
I CAN'T ... I CAN'T
(SEE:WEDDING NIGHT)
I CHANGED MY SEX
(SEE:GLEN OR GLENDA)
I CHEATED THE LAW *½ (1949) PR:A
I COLTELLI DEL VENDICATORE
(SEE:KNIVES OF THE AVENGER)
I COMPAGNI
(SEE:ORGANIZER, THE)
I CONFESS * (1953) PR:A**
I CONQUER THE SEA * (1936) PR:A
I COULD GO ON SINGING ** (1963) PR:A
I COULD NEVER HAVE SEX WITH ANY MAN WHO HAS SO LITTLE REGARD FOR MY HUSBAND zero (1973) PR:O
I COVER BIG TOWN ** (1947) PR:A
I COVER CHINATOWN *½ (1938) PR:A
I COVER THE UNDERWORLD
(SEE:I COVER BIG TOWN)
I COVER THE UNDERWORLD ** (1955) PR:A
I COVER THE WAR **½ (1937) PR:A
I COVER THE WATERFRONT ** (1933) PR:A
I CROSSED THE COLOR LINE
(SEE:BLACK KLANSMAN, THE)
I DEAL IN DANGER *½ (1966) PR:A
I DEMAND PAYMENT *½ (1938) PR:A
I DIDN'T DO IT **½ (1945, Brit.) PR:A
I DIED A THOUSAND TIMES ** (1955) PR:A-C
I DISMEMBER MAMA zero (1974) PR:O
I DON'T CARE GIRL, THE ** (1952) PR:A
I DON'T WANT TO BE BORN
(SEE:DEVIL WITHIN HER, THE)
I DOOD IT ** (1943) PR:A
I DREAM OF JEANIE * (1952) PR:A

__I DREAM TOO MUCH ** (1935) PR:A__
__I DRINK YOUR BLOOD * (1971) PR:O__
__I EAT YOUR SKIN zero (1971) PR:O__
I ESCAPED FROM DEVIL'S ISLAND zero (1973) PR:O
I ESCAPED FROM THE GESTAPO ** (1943) PR:A
I EVEN MET HAPPY GYPSIES ** (1968, Yugo.) PR:A
I FOUND STELLA PARISH ** (1935) PR:A
I GIORNI DELL'IRA
(SEE:DAY OF ANGER)
I GIVE MY HEART
(SEE:LOVES OF MADAME DUBARRY, THE)
I GIVE MY LOVE ** (1934) PR:A
I HAD SEVEN DAUGHTERS
(SEE:MY SEVEN LITTLE SINS)
__I HATE BLONDES ** (1981, It.) PR:A__
I HATE MY BODY *½ (1975, Sp./Switz.) PR:A
I HATE YOUR GUTS!
(SEE:INTRUDER, THE)
I HAVE LIVED * (1933) PR:A
I HAVE SEVEN DAUGHTERS
(SEE:MY SEVEN LITTLE SINS)
I, JANE DOE ** (1948) PR:A
I KILLED EINSTEIN, GENTLEMEN ** (1970, Czech.) PR:A
I KILLED GERONIMO *½ (1950) PR:A
I KILLED THAT MAN **½ (1942) PR:A
I KILLED THE COUNT
(SEE:WHO IS GUILTY?)
I KILLED WILD BILL HICKOK *½ (1956) PR:A
I KNOW WHERE I'M GOING *** (1947, Brit.) PR:A
I LED TWO LIVES
(SEE:GLEN OR GLENDA)
I LIKE IT THAT WAY ** (1934) PR:A
I LIKE MONEY **½ (1962, Brit.) PR:A
I LIKE YOUR NERVE *½ (1931) PR:A
I LIVE FOR LOVE ** (1935) PR:A
I LIVE FOR YOU
(SEE:I LIVE FOR LOVE)
I LIVE IN FEAR ***½ (1967, Jap.) PR:A
I LIVE IN GROSVENOR SQUARE
(SEE:YANK IN LONDON, A)
I LIVE MY LIFE *** (1935) PR:A
I LIVE ON DANGER **½ (1942) PR:A
I LIVED WITH YOU **½ (1933, Brit.) PR:A
I LOVE A BANDLEADER ** (1945) PR:A
I LOVE A MYSTERY ** (1945) PR:A
I LOVE A SOLDIER ** (1944) PR:A
I LOVE IN JERUSALEM
(SEE:MY MARGO)
I LOVE MELVIN **½ (1953) PR:A
__I LOVE MY WIFE *½ (1970) PR:O__
I LOVE N.Y. * (1987) PR:C
I LOVE THAT MAN *½ (1933) PR:A
I LOVE TROUBLE ** (1947) PR:A
I LOVE YOU
(SEE:JE T'AIME)
I LOVE YOU AGAIN ***½ (1940) PR:A
__I LOVE YOU, ALICE B. TOKLAS! **** (1968) PR:O__
I LOVE YOU, I KILL YOU ** (1972, Ger.) PR:O
I LOVE YOU, I LOVE YOU NOT
(SEE:TOGETHER)
I LOVED A WOMAN **½ (1933) PR:A
I LOVED YOU WEDNESDAY *½ (1933) PR:A
I MARRIED A COMMUNIST
(SEE:WOMAN ON PIER 13)
I MARRIED A DOCTOR **½ (1936) PR:A
__I MARRIED A MONSTER FROM OUTER SPACE *** (1958) PR:O__
I MARRIED A NAZI
(SEE:MAN I MARRIED, THE)
I MARRIED A SPY ** (1938) PR:A
__I MARRIED A WITCH ***½ (1942) PR:A__
I MARRIED A WOMAN * (1958) PR:A
__I MARRIED AN ANGEL ** (1942) PR:A__
I MARRIED TOO YOUNG
(SEE:MARRIED TOO YOUNG)
I, MAUREEN *½ (1978, Can.) PR:A
I MET A MURDERER **½ (1939, Brit.) PR:C-O
I MET HIM IN PARIS *** (1937) PR:A
I MET MY LOVE AGAIN **½ (1938) PR:A
I MISS YOU, HUGS AND KISSES ** (1978, Can.) PR:C-O
I MISTERI DELLA GIUNGLA NERA
(SEE:MYSTERY OF THUG ISLAND, THE)
I, MOBSTER *** (1959) PR:C-O
I, MONSTER **½ (1971, Brit.) PR:C

__I NEVER PROMISED YOU A ROSE GARDEN ***½ (1977) PR:O__
__I NEVER SANG FOR MY FATHER ***½ (1970) PR:A-C__
I NUOVI BARBARI
(SEE:WARRIORS OF THE WASTELAND)
I NUOVI MOSTRI
(SEE:VIVA ITALIA)
I ONLY ASKED! *** (1958, Brit.) PR:A
__I OUGHT TO BE IN PICTURES ***½ (1982) PR:C__
I PASSED FOR WHITE ** (1960) PR:A
I PHOTOGRAPHIA
(SEE:PHOTOGRAPH, THE)
I PROMISE TO PAY **½ (1937) PR:A
I PROMISE TO PAY
(SEE:PAYROLL)
__I REMEMBER MAMA **** (1948) PR:AA__
I RING DOORBELLS *½ (1946) PR:A
I SAILED TO TAHITI WITH AN ALL GIRL CREW * (1969) PR:A
I SAW WHAT YOU DID *** (1965) PR:C-O
I SEE A DARK STRANGER
(SEE:ADVENTURESS, THE)
I SEE ICE **½ (1938) PR:A
I SELL ANYTHING *½ (1934) PR:A
__I SENT A LETTER TO MY LOVE *** (1981, Fr.) PR:A__
I SHALL RETURN
(SEE:AMERICAN GUERRILLA IN THE PHILIPPINES, AN)
I SHOT BILLY THE KID *½ (1950) PR:A
I SHOT JESSE JAMES *** (1949) PR:A
I SPIT ON YOUR GRAVE * (1962, Fr.) PR:O
__I SPIT ON YOUR GRAVE zero (1983) PR:O__
I SPY *½ (1933, Brit.) PR:A
I SPY, YOU SPY
(SEE:BANG, BANG, YOU'RE DEAD)
I STAND ACCUSED ** (1938) PR:A
__I STAND CONDEMNED ** (1936, Brit.) PR:A__
I START COUNTING ** (1970, Brit.) PR:O
I STOLE A MILLION *** (1939) PR:A
I SURRENDER DEAR *½ (1948) PR:A
I TAKE THIS OATH * (1940) PR:A
I TAKE THIS WOMAN ** (1931) PR:A
I TAKE THIS WOMAN *½ (1940) PR:A
I THANK A FOOL ** (1962, Brit.) PR:A-C
I THANK YOU ** (1941, Brit.) PR:A
I, THE JURY *** (1953) PR:C-O
__I, THE JURY *½ (1982) PR:O__
I TITANI
(SEE:MY SON, THE HERO)
I, TOO, AM ONLY A WOMAN *½ (1963, Ger.) PR:C
I TRE VOLTI
(SEE:THREE FACES OF A WOMAN)
I TRE VOLTI DELLA PAURA
(SEE:BLACK SABBATH)
I VAMPIRI
(SEE:DEVIL'S COMMANDMENT, THE)
I VITELLONI
(SEE:VITELLONI)
__I WAKE UP SCREAMING *** (1942) PR:A__
I WALK ALONE *** (1948) PR:C
I WALK THE LINE *** (1970) PR:A
__I WALKED WITH A ZOMBIE *** (1943) PR:C-O__
I WANNA HOLD YOUR HAND *** (1978) PR:A
I WANT A DIVORCE ** (1940) PR:A
I WANT HER DEAD
(SEE:W)
__I WANT TO LIVE! *** (1958) PR:O__
__I WANT WHAT I WANT ** (1972, Brit.) PR:O__
I WANT YOU *** (1951) PR:A
I WANTED WINGS *** (1941) PR:A
I WAS A CAPTIVE IN NAZI GERMANY *½ (1936) PR:A
I WAS A COMMUNIST FOR THE F.B.I. ** (1951) PR:C
I WAS A CONVICT *½ (1939) PR:A
I WAS A MALE WAR BRIDE *** (1949) PR:A
I WAS A PRISONER ON DEVIL'S ISLAND * (1941) PR:A
I WAS A SHOPLIFTER *½ (1950) PR:A
I WAS A SPY **½ (1934, Brit.) PR:A
I WAS A TEENAGE FRANKENSTEIN *½ (1958) PR:C-O
__I WAS A TEENAGE T.V. TERRORIST zero (1987) PR:C__
I WAS A TEENAGE WEREWOLF *** (1957) PR:C-O

__I WAS A TEENAGE ZOMBIE *½ (1987) PR:O__
I WAS AN ADVENTURESS *** (1940) PR:A
I WAS AN AMERICAN SPY ** (1951) PR:A
I WAS FAITHLESS
(SEE:CYNARA)
I WAS FRAMED ** (1942) PR:A
I WAS HAPPY HERE
(SEE:TIME LOST AND TIME REMEMBERED)
I WAS MONTY'S DOUBLE
(SEE:HELL, HEAVEN OR HOBOKEN)
__I WILL . . . I WILL . . . FOR NOW *½ (1976) PR:C__
I WONDER WHO'S KISSING HER NOW **½ (1947) PR:A
I WOULDN'T BE IN YOUR SHOES ** (1948) PR:A
ICARUS XB-1
(SEE:VOYAGE TO THE END OF THE UNIVERSE)
ICE zero (1970) PR:O
ICE-CAPADES ** (1941) PR:A
ICE-CAPADES REVUE **½ (1942) PR:A
__ICE CASTLES ** (1978) PR:A__
ICE COLD IN ALEX
(SEE:DESERT ATTACK)
ICE FOLLIES OF 1939 **½ (1939) PR:A
ICE HOUSE, THE ** (1969) PR:O
__ICE PALACE **½ (1960) PR:A-C__
ICE PALACE, THE **½ (1988, Norway) PR:C
__ICE PIRATES, THE ** (1984) PR:A-C__
__ICE STATION ZEBRA **½ (1968) PR:A__
ICELAND ** (1942) PR:A
__ICEMAN **½ (1984) PR:A-C__
ICEMAN COMETH, THE *** (1973) PR:C
ICHABOD AND MR. TOAD
(SEE:ADVENTURES OF ICHABOD AND MR. TOAD, THE)
ICHIJOJI NO KETTO
(SEE:SAMURAI, PART II)
I'D CLIMB THE HIGHEST MOUNTAIN *** (1951) PR:A
I'D GIVE MY LIFE *½ (1936) PR:A
I'D RATHER BE RICH **½ (1964) PR:A
IDAGINE SU UN CITTADINO AL DI DOPRA DI OGNI SOSPETTO
(SEE:INVESTIGATION OF A CITIZEN ABOVE SUSPICION)
__IDAHO **½ (1943) PR:A__
IDAHO KID, THE * (1937) PR:A
__IDAHO TRANSFER * (1975) PR:C__
IDEA GIRL ** (1946) PR:A
IDEAL HUSBAND, AN ** (1948, Brit.) PR:A
IDEAL LODGER, THE * (1957, Ger.) PR:O
IDENTIFICATION MARKS: NONE **½ (1969, Pol.) PR:A
IDENTIFICATION OF A WOMAN *** (1983, It.) PR:C-O
IDENTIKIT
(SEE:DRIVER'S SEAT, THE)
IDENTITY PARADE
(SEE:LINE-UP, THE)
IDENTITY UNKNOWN *** (1945) PR:A
IDENTITY UNKNOWN * (1960, Brit.) PR:A
IDIOT, THE ***½ (1948, Fr.) PR:A
IDIOT, THE *** (1960, USSR) PR:O
IDIOT, THE ** (1963, Jap.) PR:C-O
__IDIOT'S DELIGHT ***½ (1939) PR:A__
IDLE ON PARADE
(SEE:IDOL ON PARADE)
IDLE RICH, THE **½ (1929) PR:A
IDO ZERO DAISAKUSEN
(SEE:LATITUDE ZERO)
IDOL, THE ** (1966, Brit.) PR:O
IDOL OF PARIS *½ (1948, Brit.) PR:A
__IDOL OF THE CROWDS **½ (1937) PR:A__
IDOL ON PARADE **½ (1959, Brit.) PR:A
__IDOLMAKER, THE ***½ (1980) PR:A-C__
IDOLS IN THE DUST
(SEE:SATURDAY'S HERO)
IERI, OGGI E DOMANI
(SEE:YESTERDAY, TODAY AND TOMORROW)
__IF . . . *** (1968, Brit.) PR:O__
IF A MAN ANSWERS ** (1962) PR:A
__IF EVER I SEE YOU AGAIN zero (1978) PR:C__
IF HE HOLLERS, LET HIM GO * (1968) PR:O
IF I HAD A MILLION ***½ (1932) PR:A
IF I HAD MY WAY ** (1940) PR:A
IF I WERE BOSS * (1938, Brit.) PR:A
IF I WERE FREE *½ (1933) PR:A

IF I WERE KING
  (SEE:VAGABOND KING)
IF I WERE KING ***½ (1938) PR:A
IF I WERE RICH ** (1936) PR:A
IF I'M LUCKY ** (1946) PR:A
IF IT'S TUESDAY, THIS MUST BE BELGIUM ***
  (1969) PR:A
IF PARIS WERE TOLD TO US **½ (1956, Fr.) PR:A
IF THIS BE SIN ** (1950, Brit.) PR:A
IF WINTER COMES **½ (1947) PR:A
IF YOU COULD ONLY COOK *** (1936) PR:A
IF YOU COULD SEE WHAT I HEAR *½
  (1982) PR:A
IF YOU FEEL LIKE SINGING
  (SEE:SUMMER STOCK)
IF YOU KNEW SUSIE **½ (1948) PR:A
IGOROTA, THE LEGEND OF THE TREE OF LIFE **
  (1970, Phil.) PR:O
IKARIE XB 1
  (SEE:VOYAGE TO THE END OF THE UNIVERSE)
IKIMONO NO KIROUKU
  (SEE:I LIVE IN FEAR)
IKIRU * (1960, Jap.) PR:A**
IL BIDONE
  (SEE:SWINDLE, THE)
IL BODONE
  (SEE:SWINDLER, THE)
IL BUONO, IL BRUTTO, IL CATTIVO
  (SEE:GOOD, THE BAD, AND THE UGLY, THE)
IL CASO MORO
  (SEE:MORO AFFAIR, THE)
IL COBRA
  (SEE:COBRA, THE)
IL CONFORMIST
  (SEE:CONFORMIST, THE)
IL CONTE DI MONTECRISTO
  (SEE:STORY OF THE COUNT OF MONTE CRISTO,
  THE)
IL DESERTO ROSSO
  (SEE:RED DESERT)
IL DESTINO
  (SEE:DESTINY)
IL DIABOLICO DR. MABUSE
  (SEE:THOUSAND EYES OF DR. MABUSE)
IL DISPREZZO
  (SEE:CONTEMPT)
IL GATTOPARDO
  (SEE:LEOPARD, THE)
IL GENERALE DELA-ROVERE
  (SEE:GENERALE DELLA-ROVERE)
IL GIORNO DELLA CIVETTA
  (SEE:DAY OF THE OWL, THE)
IL GIORNO E L'ORA
  (SEE:DAY AND THE HOUR, THE)
IL GRIDO **½ (1962, US/It.) PR:C
IL MAESTRO
  (SEE:TEACHER AND THE MIRACLE, THE)
IL MAESTRO DI DON GIOVANNI
  (SEE:CROSSED SWORDS)
IL MAGNIFICO CORNUTO
  (SEE:MAGNIFICENT CUCKHOLD, THE)
IL MITO
  (SEE:MYTH, THE)
IL NEMICO DI MIA MOGLIE
  (SEE:MY WIFE'S ENEMY)
IL POZZO DELLE TRE VERITA
  (SEE:THREE FACES OF SIN)
IL RE DEI FAISARI
  (SEE:COUNTERFEITERS OF PARIS, THE)
IL SEGNO DI VENERA
  (SEE:SIGN OF VENUS)
IL SEME DELL'UOMO
  (SEE:SEED OF MAN, THE)
IL SEPOLCRO DEI RE
  (SEE:CLEOPATRA'S DAUGHTER)
IL SOGNO DI BUTTERFLY
  (SEE:DREAM OF THE BUTTERFLY, THE)
IL SUFFIT D'AIMER
  (SEE:BERNADETTE OF LOURDES)
IL TESORO DI ROMMEL
  (SEE:ROMMEL'S TREASURE)
IL VANGELO SECONDE MATTEO
  (SEE:GOSPEL ACCORDING TO ST. MATTHEW,
  THE)
I'LL BE SEEING YOU ***½ (1944) PR:A
I'LL BE YOUR SWEETHEART *½ (1945, Brit.) PR:A
I'LL BE YOURS **½ (1947) PR:A
I'LL CRY TOMORROW ** (1955) PR:A-C**
I'LL FIX IT * (1934) PR:A
I'LL GET BY **½ (1950) PR:A
I'LL GET YOU ** (1953, Brit.) PR:A
I'LL GET YOU FOR THIS
  (SEE:LUCKY NICK CAIN)
I'LL GIVE A MILLION **½ (1938) PR:A
I'LL GIVE MY LIFE * (1959) PR:A
I'LL LOVE YOU ALWAYS *½ (1935) PR:A
ILL MET BY MOONLIGHT
  (SEE:NIGHT AMBUSH)

I'LL NEVER FORGET WHAT'S 'IS NAME **
  (1967, Brit.) PR:AC
I'LL NEVER FORGET YOU *** (1951) PR:A
I'LL REMEMBER APRIL *½ (1945) PR:A
I'LL SAVE MY LOVE
  (SEE:TWO LOVES)
I'LL SEE YOU IN MY DREAMS **½ (1951) PR:A
I'LL SELL MY LIFE *½ (1941) PR:A
I'LL STICK TO YOU *½ (1933, Brit.) PR:A
I'LL TAKE ROMANCE **½ (1937) PR:A
I'LL TAKE SWEDEN **½ (1965) PR:A
I'LL TELL THE WORLD * (1934) PR:A
I'LL TELL THE WORLD *½ (1945) PR:AA
I'LL TURN TO YOU **½ (1946, Brit.) PR:A
I'LL WAIT FOR YOU * (1941) PR:A
I'LL WALK BESIDE YOU ** (1943, Brit.) PR:A
ILLEGAL *½ (1932, Brit.) PR:A
ILLEGAL *** (1955) PR:C
ILLEGAL DIVORCE, THE
  (SEE:SECOND HAND WIFE)
ILLEGAL ENTRY **½ (1949) PR:A
ILLEGAL RIGHTS
  (SEE:HAIL TO THE RANGERS)
ILLEGAL TRAFFIC ** (1938) PR:A
ILLEGALLY YOURS **½ (1988) PR:A
ILLIAC PASSION, THE zero (1968) PR:O
ILLICIT **½ (1931) PR:C
ILLICIT INTERLUDE * (1954, Swed.) PR:O**
ILLUMINATIONS ** (1976, Aus.) PR:O
ILLUSION ** (1929) PR:A
ILLUSION OF BLOOD ** (1966, Jap.) PR:O
ILLUSION TRAVELS BY STREETCAR, THE ***
  (1977, Mex.) PR:C
ILLUSIONIST, THE ** (1985, Neth.) PR:C
ILLUSIONIST, THE ** (1985, Neth.) PR:C
ILLUSTRATED MAN, THE ** (1969) PR:O
ILLUSTRIOUS ENERGY ***
  (1988, New Zealand) PR:C
I'M A STRANGER *½ (1952, Brit.) PR:A
I'M ALL RIGHT, JACK ** (1959, Brit.) PR:A**
I'M AN EXPLOSIVE ** (1933, Brit.) PR:A
I'M CRAZY ABOUT YOU
  (SEE:TE QUIERO CON LOCURA)
I'M DANCING AS FAST AS I CAN ** (1982) PR:C-O
I'M FROM ARKANSAS * (1944) PR:A
I'M FROM MISSOURI *½ (1939) PR:A
I'M FROM THE CITY ** (1938) PR:A
I'M GOING TO GET YOU ... ELLIOT BOY zero
  (1971, Can.) PR:O
I'M GONNA GIT YOU SUCKA * (1988) PR:O**
IM LAUF DER ZEIT
  (SEE:KINGS OF THE ROAD)
I'M NO ANGEL **** (1933) PR:C
I'M NOBODY'S SWEETHEART NOW ***
  (1940) PR:A
IM STAHLNETZ DES DR. MABUSE
  (SEE:RETURN OF DR. MABUSE, THE)
I'M STILL ALIVE **½ (1940) PR:A
IMAGEMAKER, THE * (1986) PR:C-O
IMAGES * (1972, Ireland) PR:C-O
IMAGINARY SWEETHEART
  (SEE:PROFESSIONAL SWEETHEART)
IMERES TOU 36
  (SEE:DAYS OF 36)
IMITATION GENERAL *** (1958) PR:A
IMITATION OF LIFE ***½ (1934) PR:A
IMITATION OF LIFE * (1959) PR:A**
IMMEDIATE DISASTER
  (SEE:STRANGER FROM VENUS)
IMMORAL CHARGE *** (1962, Brit.) PR:A
IMMORAL MOMENT, THE ** (1967, Fr.) PR:C
IMMORTAL BACHELOR, THE **½ (1980, It.) PR:O
IMMORTAL BATTALION, THE **½
  (1944, Brit.) PR:A
IMMORTAL GARRISON, THE ** (1957, USSR) PR:A
IMMORTAL GENTLEMAN **½ (1935, Brit.) PR:A
IMMORTAL MONSTER
  (SEE:CALTIKI, THE IMMORTAL MONSTER)
IMMORTAL SERGEANT, THE **½ (1943) PR:A
IMMORTAL STORY, THE ***½ (1969, Fr.) PR:C
IMMORTAL VAGABOND **½ (1931, Ger.) PR:A
IMPACT *** (1949) PR:A
IMPACT ** (1963, Brit.) PR:C
IMPASSE **½ (1969) PR:O
IMPASSE DES VERTUS
  (SEE:LOVE AT NIGHT)
IMPASSIVE FOOTMAN, THE
  (SEE:WOMAN IN BONDAGE)
IMPATIENT MAIDEN **½ (1932) PR:C
IMPATIENT YEARS, THE **½ (1944) PR:A
IMPERFECT LADY, THE ** (1947) PR:A
IMPERFECT LADY, THE
  (SEE:PERFECT GENTLEMAN, THE)
IMPERIAL VENUS ** (1963, It./Fr.) PR:A
IMPERSONATOR, THE ** (1962, Brit.) PR:C
IMPORTANCE OF BEING EARNEST, THE **
  (1952, Brit.) PR:A**
IMPORTANT MAN, THE *** (1961, Mex.) PR:O

IMPORTANT WITNESS, THE ** (1933) PR:A
IMPOSSIBLE LOVER
  (SEE:HUDDLE)
IMPOSSIBLE OBJECT *** (1973, Fr.) PR:C-O
IMPOSSIBLE ON SATURDAY **
  (1966, Fr./Israel) PR:A
IMPOSSIBLE YEARS, THE ***½ (1968) PR:A
IMPOSTER, THE **½ (1944) PR:A
IMPOSTORS * (1979) PR:O
"IMP"PROBABLE MR. WEE GEE, THE *
  (1966) PR:A
IMPRESSIVE FOOTMAN, THE
  (SEE:WOMAN IN CHAINS)
IMPROPER CHANNELS ** (1981, Can.) PR:C
IMPROPER DUCHESS, THE *½ (1936, Brit.) PR:A
IMPULSE **½ (1955, Brit.) PR:C
IMPULSE zero (1975) PR:O
IMPULSE **½ (1984) PR:O
IN
  (SEE:HIGH)
IN A LONELY PLACE *** (1950) PR:C**
IN A MONASTERY GARDEN ** (1935) PR:A
IN A SECRET GARDEN
  (SEE:OF LOVE AND DESIRE)
IN A YEAR OF THIRTEEN MOONS **
  (1980, Ger.) PR:O
IN CALIENTE **½ (1935) PR:A
IN CASE OF ADVERSITY
  (SEE:LOVE IS MY PROFESSION)
IN CELEBRATION **½ (1975, Brit.) PR:O
IN COLD BLOOD * (1967) PR:O
IN DARKNESS WAITING
  (SEE:STRATEGY OF TERROR)
IN DER HOLLE IST NOCH PLATZ
  (SEE:THERE IS STILL ROOM IN HELL)
IN EARLY ARIZONA ** (1938) PR:A
IN ENEMY COUNTRY ** (1968) PR:A-C
IN FAST COMPANY ** (1946) PR:A
IN GAY MADRID ** (1930) PR:A
IN GOD WE TRUST zero (1980) PR:C-O
IN HARM'S WAY * (1965) PR:A**
IN HIS STEPS ** (1936) PR:A
IN-LAWS, THE * (1979) PR:A**
IN LIKE FLINT *½ (1967) PR:A
IN LOVE AND WAR **½ (1958) PR:A
IN LOVE WITH LIFE ** (1934) PR:A
IN MACARTHUR PARK *½ (1977) PR:C-O
IN NAME ONLY * (1939) PR:A**
IN OLD AMARILLO **½ (1951) PR:A
IN OLD ARIZONA *** (1929) PR:A
IN OLD CALIENTE ** (1939) PR:A
IN OLD CALIFORNIA *½ (1929) PR:A
IN OLD CALIFORNIA ** (1942) PR:A
IN OLD CHEYENNE ** (1931) PR:A
IN OLD CHEYENNE ** (1941) PR:A
IN OLD CHICAGO **** (1938) PR:A
IN OLD COLORADO **½ (1941) PR:A
IN OLD KENTUCKY *** (1935) PR:A
IN OLD MEXICO **½ (1938) PR:A
IN OLD MISSOURI ** (1940) PR:A
IN OLD MONTANA *½ (1939) PR:A
IN OLD MONTEREY ** (1939) PR:A
IN OLD NEW MEXICO **½ (1945) PR:AA
IN OLD OKLAHOMA ** (1943) PR:A
IN OLD SACRAMENTO ** (1946) PR:C
IN OLD SANTA FE *** (1935) PR:A
IN OUR TIME ** (1944) PR:C
IN PERSON ** (1935) PR:A
IN PIENO SOLE
  (SEE:PURPLE NOON)
IN PRAISE OF OLDER WOMEN *
  (1978, Can.) PR:O**
IN ROSIE'S ROOM
  (SEE:ROSIE, THE RIVETER)
IN SEARCH OF ANNA *½ (1978, Aus.) PR:O
IN SEARCH OF GREGORY ** (1970, Brit./It.) PR:O
IN SEARCH OF HISTORIC JESUS * (1980) PR:AA
IN SEARCH OF THE CASTAWAYS **½
  (1962, Brit.) PR:AA
IN SOCIETY **½ (1944) PR:AA
IN SPITE OF DANGER *½ (1935) PR:A
IN STRANGE COMPANY
  (SEE:FIRST AID)
IN THE COOL OF THE DAY *½ (1963) PR:C
IN THE COUNTRY ** (1967) PR:O
IN THE DAYS OF THE THUNDERING HERD
  (SEE:THUNDERING HERD, THE)
IN THE DEVIL'S GARDEN
  (SEE:ASSAULT)
IN THE DOGHOUSE ** (1964, Brit.) PR:A
IN THE FALL OF '55 EDEN CRIED
  (SEE:EDEN CRIED)
IN THE FRENCH STYLE *** (1963, US/Fr.) PR:O
IN THE GOOD OLD SUMMERTIME ***½
  (1949) PR:AA
IN THE HEADLINES ** (1929) PR:A
IN THE HEAT OF THE NIGHT ** (1967) PR:C**
IN THE LINE OF DUTY ** (1931) PR:A

IN THE MEANTIME, DARLING ** (1944) PR:A
IN THE MONEY * (1934) PR:A
IN THE MONEY **½ (1958) PR:AA
IN THE MOOD * (1987) PR:C**
IN THE MOUTH OF THE WOLF **½
(1988, Peru/Sp.) PR:O
IN THE NAME OF LIFE **½ (1947, USSR) PR:O
IN THE NAVY **½ (1941) PR:AA
IN THE NEXT ROOM *½ (1930) PR:A
IN THE NICK ** (1960, Brit.) PR:A
IN THE NIGHT
(SEE:GANG'S ALL HERE, THE)
**IN THE SHADOW OF KILIMANJARO **
(1986) PR:O**
IN THE SOUP *** (1936, Brit.) PR:A
IN THE WAKE OF A STRANGER **
(1960, Brit.) PR:C
IN THE WAKE OF THE BOUNTY *
(1933, Aus.) PR:A
IN THE WHITE CITY ***½
(1983, Switz./Portugal) PR:C-O
IN THE WILD MOUNTAINS ***½ (1986, Chi.) PR:C
IN THE WOODS
(SEE:RASHOMON)
IN THE YEAR 2889 *½ (1966) PR:C
IN THIS CORNER ** (1948) PR:A
IN THIS OUR LIFE **½ (1942) PR:C-O
IN TROUBLE WITH EVE *½ (1964, Brit.) PR:A
IN WALKED EVE
(SEE:IN TROUBLE WITH EVE)
IN WHICH WE SERVE ** (1942, Brit.) PR:A**
INADMISSIBLE EVIDENCE ** (1968, Brit.) PR:C
INBETWEEN AGE, THE ** (1958, Brit.) PR:A
INBREAKER, THE *½ (1974, Can.) PR:O
INCENDIARY BLONDE ** (1945) PR:A
INCENSE FOR THE DAMNED ** (1970, Brit.) PR:O
INCHON zero (1981) PR:O
INCIDENT **** (1948) PR:C
INCIDENT, THE **½ (1967) PR:O
INCIDENT AT MIDNIGHT ** (1966, Brit.) PR:A
INCIDENT AT PHANTOM HILL ** (1966) PR:A
INCIDENT IN AN ALLEY ** (1962) PR:A
INCIDENT IN SHANGHAI * (1937, Brit.) PR:A
INCORRIGIBLE ** (1980, Fr.) PR:A
INCREDIBLE INVASION, THE zero
(1971, Mex./US) PR:C-O
INCREDIBLE JOURNEY, THE * (1963) PR:AA**
INCREDIBLE MELTING MAN, THE ** (1978) PR:O
INCREDIBLE MR. LIMPET, THE **½ (1964) PR:AA
**INCREDIBLE PETRIFIED WORLD, THE *½
(1959) PR:A**
INCREDIBLE PRAYING MANTIS, THE
(SEE:DEADLY MANTIS, THE)
INCREDIBLE SARAH, THE *½ (1976, Brit.) PR:C
INCREDIBLE SHRINKING MAN, THE **
(1957) PR:A**
**INCREDIBLE SHRINKING WOMAN, THE **
(1981) PR:C**
**INCREDIBLE TWO-HEADED TRANSPLANT, THE *
(1971) PR:O**
**INCREDIBLY STRANGE CREATURES WHO
STOPPED LIVING AND BECAME CRAZY
MIXED-UP ZOMBIES, THE **½ (1965) PR:O**
INCREDIBLY STRANGE CREATURES, THE
(SEE:INCREDIBLY STRANGE CREATURES WHO
STOPPED LIVING AND BECAME CRAZY
MIXED-UP ZOMBIES, THE)
INCUBUS *½ (1966) PR:O
INCUBUS, THE * (1982, Can.) PR:O
INDECENT ** (1962, Ger.) PR:O
INDECENT OBSESSION, AN ** (1985, Aus.) PR:C-O
INDEPENDENCE DAY **½ (1976) PR:C-O
INDEPENDENCE DAY ** (1983) PR:O
INDESTRUCTIBLE MAN, THE * (1956) PR:A
INDIAN AGENT *** (1948) PR:A
INDIAN FIGHTER, THE ***½ (1955) PR:C
INDIAN LOVE CALL
(SEE:ROSE MARIE)
INDIAN PAINT **½ (1965) PR:AA
INDIAN SCOUT
(SEE:DAVY CROCKETT, INDIAN SCOUT)
INDIAN SUMMER
(SEE:JUDGE STEPS OUT, THE)
INDIAN TERRITORY **½ (1950) PR:A
INDIAN TOMB, THE
(SEE:JOURNEY TO THE LOST CITY)
INDIAN UPRISING ** (1951) PR:A

INDIANA JONES AND THE TEMPLE OF DOOM
***½ (1984) PR:C-O
INDIANAPOLIS SPEEDWAY ** (1939) PR:A
INDISCREET ** (1931) PR:C
INDISCREET ***½ (1958) PR:A-C
**INDISCRETION OF AN AMERICAN WIFE **½
(1954, US/It.) PR:A-C**
INDISCRETIONS OF EVE ** (1932, Brit.) PR:A
INFAMOUS
(SEE:CHILDREN'S HOUR, THE)
INFERNAL IDOL
(SEE:CRAZE, THE)
INFERNAL MACHINE *½ (1933) PR:A
INFERNO *** (1953) PR:O
INFERNO ** (1980, It.) PR:O
INFERNO DEI MORTI-VIVENTI
(SEE:ZOMBIE CREEPING FLESH)
INFORMATION KID
(SEE:FAST COMPANIONS)
INFORMATION RECEIVED ** (1962, Brit.) PR:C
INFORMER, THE *½ (1929, Brit.) PR:A
INFORMER, THE *** (1935) PR:C**
INFORMERS, THE
(SEE:UNDERWORLD INFORMERS)
INFRA-MAN * (1975, Hong Kong) PR:C**
INFRA SUPERMAN, THE
(SEE:INFRA-MAN)
INGAGI * (1931) PR:C
INGLORIOUS BASTARDS
(SEE:COUNTERFEIT COMMANDOS)
INHERIT THE WIND *** (1960) PR:A**
INHERITANCE, THE ** (1951, Brit.) PR:A
INHERITANCE, THE ** (1964, Jap.) PR:C
INHERITANCE, THE * (1978, It.) PR:O**
INHERITANCE IN PRETORIA * (1936, Ger.) PR:C
INHERITORS, THE ** (1985, Aust.) PR:O
INITIATION, THE *½ (1984) PR:O
INJUN FENDER ** (1973) PR:O
INJUSTICE
(SEE:ROAD GANG)
INN FOR TROUBLE **½ (1960, Brit.) PR:A
INN OF THE DAMNED ** (1974, Aus.) PR:O
INN OF THE FRIGHTENED PEOPLE
(SEE:TERROR FROM UNDER THE HOUSE)
**INN OF THE SIXTH HAPPINESS, THE ***½
(1958, Brit.) PR:AA**
INNER CIRCLE, THE *½ (1946) PR:A
INNER SANCTUM * (1948) PR:A
INNERSPACE ** (1987) PR:C
INNERVIEW, THE zero (1974) PR:O
INNOCENCE IS BLISS
(SEE:MISS GRANT TAKES RICHMOND)
INNOCENCE UNPROTECTED ****
(1971, Yugo.) PR:C
INNOCENT, THE * (1979, It.) PR:O**
INNOCENT, THE ** (1988, Fr.) PR:O
INNOCENT AFFAIR, AN
(SEE:DON'T TRUST YOUR HUSBAND)
INNOCENT AND THE DAMNED
(SEE:GIRLS TOWN)
INNOCENT BYSTANDERS **½ (1973, Brit.) PR:O
INNOCENT MEETING **½ (1959, Brit.) PR:C
INNOCENT SINNERS *½ (1958, Brit.) PR:AA
INNOCENTS, THE **** (1961, US/Brit.) PR:A-C
INNOCENTS IN PARIS **½ (1955, Brit.) PR:A
INNOCENTS OF CHICAGO, THE
(SEE:WHY SAPS LEAVE HOME)
INNOCENTS OF PARIS ** (1929) PR:A
INNOCENTS WITH DIRTY HANDS
(SEE:DIRTY HANDS)
INQUEST ** (1931, Brit.) PR:C
INQUEST *½ (1939, Brit.) PR:C
INQUISITOR, THE *** (1982, Fr.) PR:C-O
INSECT, THE
(SEE:INSECT WOMAN, THE)
INSECT WOMAN, THE *** (1964, Jap.) PR:C
INSEL DER AMAZONEN
(SEE:SEVEN DARING GIRLS)
INSEMINOID
(SEE:HORROR PLANET)
INSIDE AMY zero (1975) PR:O
INSIDE DAISY CLOVER *½ (1965) PR:O
INSIDE DETROIT ** (1955) PR:O
INSIDE INFORMATION *½ (1934) PR:A
INSIDE INFORMATION ** (1939) PR:A
INSIDE INFORMATION
(SEE:LONE PRAIRIE, THE)

INSIDE JOB *½ (1946) PR:A
INSIDE LOOKING OUT ** (1977, Aus.) PR:C
INSIDE MOVES **½ (1980) PR:C
INSIDE OUT
(SEE:LIFE UPSIDE DOWN)
INSIDE OUT **½ (1975, Brit.) PR:C
INSIDE OUT ** (1986) PR:O
INSIDE STORY **½ (1939) PR:A
INSIDE STORY, THE ** (1948) PR:A
INSIDE STRAIGHT ** (1951) PR:O
INSIDE THE LAW ** (1942) PR:A
INSIDE THE LINES *½ (1930) PR:A
INSIDE THE MAFIA **½ (1959) PR:O
INSIDE THE ROOM **½ (1935, Brit.) PR:C
INSIDE THE WALLS OF FOLSOM PRISON ***
(1951) PR:C
INSIDIOUS DR. FU MANCHU, THE
(SEE:MYSTERIOUS DR. FU MANCHU)
INSIGNIFICANCE *½ (1985, Brit.) PR:O
INSOMNIACS ** (1986, Arg.) PR:O
INSPECTOR, THE
(SEE:LISA)
INSPECTOR CALLS, AN *** (1954, Brit.) PR:O
INSPECTOR CLOUSEAU *** (1968, Brit.) PR:A
INSPECTOR GENERAL, THE *** (1937, Czech.) PR:A
INSPECTOR GENERAL, THE * (1949) PR:AA**
INSPECTOR HORNLEIGH **½ (1939, Brit.) PR:A
INSPECTOR HORNLEIGH GOES TO IT
(SEE:MAIL TRAIN)
INSPECTOR HORNLEIGH ON HOLIDAY ***
(1939, Brit.) PR:A
INSPECTOR MAIGRET
(SEE:MAIGRET LAYS A TRAP)
INSPIRATION ** (1931) PR:C
INSTANT JUSTICE zero (1986) PR:O
INSULT **½ (1932, Brit.) PR:C
INSURANCE INVESTIGATOR ** (1951) PR:C
INTELLIGENCE MEN, THE
(SEE:SPYLARKS)
INTENT TO KILL *** (1958, Brit.) PR:A
INTERFERENCE ** (1928) PR:A
INTERIORS ** (1978) PR:C-O**
INTERLUDE
(SEE:INTERMEZZO)
INTERLUDE *½ (1957) PR:A
INTERLUDE **½ (1968, Brit.) PR:C
INTERMEZZO **½ (1937, Ger.) PR:A
INTERMEZZO ** (1937, Swed.) PR:A
INTERMEZZO: A LOVE STORY *** (1939) PR:A**
INTERNATIONAL CRIME **½ (1938) PR:A
INTERNATIONAL HOUSE ** (1933) PR:A**
INTERNATIONAL LADY **½ (1941) PR:A
INTERNATIONAL POLICE
(SEE:PICK-UP ALLEY)
INTERNATIONAL SETTLEMENT **½ (1938) PR:A
INTERNATIONAL SQUADRON *** (1941) PR:A
INTERNATIONAL VELVET **½ (1978, Brit.) PR:AA
**INTERNECINE PROJECT, THE **
(1974, Brit.) PR:O**
INTERNES CAN'T TAKE MONEY **½ (1937) PR:A
INTERNS, THE **½ (1962) PR:O
INTERPOL
(SEE:PICK-UP ALLEY)
INTERRUPTED HONEYMOON, THE ***
(1936, Brit.) PR:A
INTERRUPTED HONEYMOON, AN
(SEE:HOMICIDE FOR THREE)
INTERRUPTED JOURNEY, THE **
(1949, Brit.) PR:A-C
INTERRUPTED MELODY ***½ (1955) PR:A
INTERVAL ** (1973, Mex./US) PR:C
INTERVISTA ** (1987, It.) PR:C**
INTIMACY ** (1966) PR:O
INTIMATE LIGHTING ***½ (1969, Czech.) PR:A
INTIMATE POWER * (1986, Can.) PR:C-O**
INTIMATE RELATIONS ** (1937, Brit.) PR:A
INTIMATE RELATIONS
(SEE:LES PARENTS TERRIBLES)
INTIMATE RELATIONS
(SEE:DISOBEDIENT)
INTIMATE STRANGER, THE
(SEE:FINGER OF GUILT)
INTIMNI OSVETLENI
(SEE:INTIMATE LIGHTING)
INTO THE BLUE
(SEE:MAN IN THE DINGHY, THE)
INTO THE NIGHT **½ (1985) PR:O

INTO THE STRAIGHT ** (1950, Aus.) PR:C
INTRAMUROS
(SEE:WALLS OF HELL, THE)
INTRIGUE *½ (1947) PR:A
INTRIGUE IN PARIS
(SEE:MISS V FROM MOSCOW)
INTRUDER, THE *½ (1932) PR:A
INTRUDER, THE **½ (1955, Brit.) PR:C
INTRUDER, THE ***½ (1962) PR:C
INTRUDER IN THE DUST **** (1949) PR:C-O
INVADER, THE
(SEE:OLD SPANISH CUSTOM, AN)
INVADERS, THE *** (1941, Brit.) PR:A**
INVADERS FROM MARS * (1953) PR:A**
INVADERS FROM MARS *½ (1986) PR:C
INVASION **½ (1965, Brit.) PR:A
INVASION EARTH 2150 A.D.
(SEE:DALEKS—INVASION EARTH 2150 A.D.)
INVASION FORCE
(SEE:HANGAR 18)
INVASION FROM THE MOON
(SEE:MUTINY IN OUTER SPACE)
INVASION OF ASTRO-MONSTERS
(SEE:MONSTER ZERO)
INVASION OF THE ANIMAL PEOPLE *½ (1962, US/Swed.) PR:A
INVASION OF THE ASTROS
(SEE:MONSTER ZERO)
INVASION OF THE BEE GIRLS * (1973) PR:O**
INVASION OF THE BLOOD FARMERS * (1972) PR:O
INVASION OF THE BODY SNATCHERS ** (1956) PR:A**
INVASION OF THE BODY SNATCHERS **½ (1978) PR:C-O
INVASION OF THE BODY STEALERS
(SEE:BODY STEALERS, THE)
INVASION OF THE FLYING SAUCERS
(SEE:EARTH VERSUS THE FLYING SAUCERS)
INVASION OF THE HELL CREATURES
(SEE:INVASION OF THE SAUCER MEN)
INVASION OF THE SAUCER MEN *½ (1957) PR:C
INVASION OF THE STAR CREATURES * (1962) PR:A
INVASION OF THE VAMPIRES, THE * (1961, Mex.) PR:O
INVASION OF THE ZOMBIES
(SEE:HORROR OF PARTY BEACH, THE)
INVASION QUARTET ** (1961, Brit.) PR:A
INVASION 1700 *½ (1965, Fr./It./Yugo.) PR:C
INVASION U.S.A. ** (1952) PR:A
INVASION U.S.A. ** (1985) PR:O
INVESTIGATION OF A CITIZEN ABOVE SUSPICION ***½ (1970, It.) PR:O
INVESTIGATION OF MURDER, AN
(SEE:LAUGHING POLICEMAN, THE)
INVINCIBLE GLADIATOR, THE *½ (1963, It./Sp.) PR:C
INVINCIBLE SIX, THE zero (1970, US/Iran) PR:A
INVISIBLE AGENT **½ (1942) PR:A
INVISIBLE AVENGER, THE **½ (1958) PR:A
INVISIBLE BOY, THE *** (1957) PR:AA
INVISIBLE CREATURE, THE
(SEE:HOUSE IN MARSH ROAD, THE)
INVISIBLE DR. MABUSE, THE *** (1965, Ger.) PR:C
INVISIBLE ENEMY *½ (1938) PR:A
INVISIBLE GHOST, THE * (1941) PR:C
INVISIBLE HORROR, THE
(SEE:INVISIBLE DR. MABUSE, THE)
INVISIBLE INFORMER *½ (1946) PR:A
INVISIBLE INVADERS *½ (1959) PR:C
INVISIBLE KID, THE zero (1988) PR:C
INVISIBLE KILLER, THE *½ (1940) PR:A
INVISIBLE MAN, THE ***½ (1933) PR:C
INVISIBLE MAN, THE *½ (1958, Mex.) PR:A
INVISIBLE MAN, THE ** (1963, Ger.) PR:A
INVISIBLE MAN RETURNS, THE *** (1940) PR:A
INVISIBLE MAN'S REVENGE ** (1944) PR:A
INVISIBLE MENACE, THE ** (1938) PR:A
INVISIBLE MESSAGE, THE
(SEE:GUN PLAY)
INVISIBLE OPPONENT ** (1933, Ger.) PR:A
INVISIBLE POWER
(SEE:WASHINGTON MERRY-GO-ROUND)
INVISIBLE RAY, THE **½ (1936) PR:C
INVISIBLE STRANGLER *½ (1984) PR:C-O
INVISIBLE STRIPES *** (1940) PR:A
INVISIBLE WALL, THE *½ (1947) PR:A
INVISIBLE WOMAN, THE **½ (1941) PR:A
INVITATION *** (1952) PR:A
INVITATION, THE ***½ (1975, Fr./Switz.) PR:C-O
INVITATION TO A GUNFIGHTER * (1964) PR:C**
INVITATION TO A HANGING
(SEE:LAW OF THE LAWLESS)
INVITATION TO HAPPINESS *** (1939) PR:A
INVITATION TO MURDER ** (1962, Brit.) PR:C
INVITATION TO THE DANCE ***½ (1956) PR:A
INVITATION TO THE WALTZ *½ (1935, Brit.) PR:A
IO . . . TU . . . Y . . . ELLA *½ (1933) PR:A
IOLANTA
(SEE:YOLANTA)
IPCRESS FILE, THE ***½ (1965, Brit.) PR:A-C
IPHIGENIA **½ (1977, Gr.) PR:A
IPNOSI
(SEE:HYPNOSIS)
IRELAND'S BORDER LINE ** (1939, Ireland) PR:A
IRENE *** (1940) PR:A
IRISH AND PROUD OF IT *½ (1938, Ireland) PR:A
IRISH EYES ARE SMILING *** (1944) PR:A
IRISH FOR LUCK *½ (1936, Brit.) PR:A
IRISH HEARTS
(SEE:NORAH O'NEALE)
IRISH IN US, THE *** (1935) PR:A
IRISH LUCK ** (1939) PR:A
IRISH WHISKEY REBELLION ** (1973) PR:C
IRISHMAN, THE * (1978, Aus.) PR:A**
IRMA LA DOUCE * (1963) PR:C-O**
IRO
(SEE:SPOILS OF THE NIGHT)
IRON ANGEL *½ (1964) PR:A
IRON COLLAR, THE
(SEE:SHOWDOWN)
IRON CURTAIN, THE *** (1948) PR:A
IRON DUKE, THE **½ (1935, Brit.) PR:A
IRON EAGLE *½ (1986) PR:C
IRON EAGLE II * (1988) PR:C
IRON FIST
(SEE:AWAKENING OF JIM BURKE)
IRON GLOVE, THE **½ (1954) PR:A
IRON KISS, THE
(SEE:NAKED KISS, THE)
IRON MAIDEN, THE
(SEE:SWINGING MAIDEN, THE)
IRON MAJOR, THE * (1943) PR:A**
IRON MAN, THE * (1931) PR:A**
IRON MAN, THE **½ (1951) PR:C
IRON MASK, THE * (1929) PR:A**
IRON MASTER, THE ** (1933) PR:A
IRON MISTRESS, THE **½ (1952) PR:C
IRON MOUNTAIN TRAIL ** (1953) PR:A
IRON PETTICOAT, THE *½ (1956, Brit.) PR:A
IRON ROAD, THE
(SEE:BUCKSKIN FRONTIER)
IRON SHERIFF, THE **½ (1957) PR:A
IRON STAIR, THE * (1933, Brit.) PR:A
IRONWEED *½ (1987) PR:C-O
IROQUOIS TRAIL, THE ** (1950) PR:A
IRRECONCILABLE DIFFERENCES * (1984) PR:A-C**
IS EVERYBODY HAPPY? * (1929) PR:A
IS EVERYBODY HAPPY? ** (1943) PR:A
IS MY FACE RED? **½ (1932) PR:A
IS PARIS BURNING? ***½ (1966, US/Fr.) PR:A
IS THERE JUSTICE? *½ (1931) PR:A
IS THIS TRIP REALLY NECESSARY? zero (1970) PR:O
IS YOUR HONEYMOON REALLY NECESSARY? ** (1953, Brit.) PR:A
ISAAC LITTLEFEATHERS *½ (1984, Can.) PR:C
ISABEL **½ (1968, Can.) PR:O
ISADORA * (1968, Brit.) PR:O
ISHTAR * (1987) PR:A-C**
ISLAND, THE **½ (1962, Jap.) PR:C
ISLAND, THE zero (1980) PR:O
ISLAND AT THE TOP OF THE WORLD, THE * (1974) PR:AA**
ISLAND CAPTIVES zero (1937) PR:A
ISLAND CLAWS zero (1981) PR:O
ISLAND IN THE SKY ** (1938) PR:A
ISLAND IN THE SKY *** (1953) PR:A
ISLAND IN THE SUN *½ (1957) PR:C
ISLAND MAN
(SEE:MEN OF IRELAND)
ISLAND OF ALLAH * (1956) PR:A
ISLAND OF DESIRE
(SEE:LOVE TRADER, THE)
ISLAND OF DESIRE * (1952, Brit.) PR:C**
ISLAND OF DR. MOREAU, THE * (1977) PR:C
ISLAND OF DOOM **½ (1933, USSR) PR:A
ISLAND OF DOOMED MEN **½ (1940) PR:C
ISLAND OF LOST MEN ** (1939) PR:A
ISLAND OF LOST SOULS **** (1933) PR:C
ISLAND OF LOST WOMEN *½ (1959) PR:A
ISLAND OF LOVE **½ (1963) PR:A
ISLAND OF MONTE CRISTO
(SEE:SWORD OF VENUS)
ISLAND OF PROCIDA, THE *** (1952, It.) PR:C
ISLAND OF TERROR **½ (1967, Brit.) PR:C
ISLAND OF THE BLUE DOLPHINS **½ (1964) PR:AA
ISLAND OF THE BURNING DAMNED ** (1971, Brit.) PR:C
ISLAND OF THE BURNING DOOMED
(SEE:ISLAND OF THE BURNING DAMNED)
ISLAND OF THE DAMNED *½ (1976, Sp.) PR:O
ISLAND OF THE DOOMED *½ (1968, Sp./Ger.) PR:C
ISLAND OF THE FISHMEN, THE
(SEE:SCREAMERS)
ISLAND RESCUE **½ (1952, Brit.) PR:A
ISLAND WOMAN
(SEE:ISLAND WOMEN)
ISLAND WOMEN * (1958) PR:A
ISLANDS IN THE STREAM * (1977) PR:C**
ISLE OF DESTINY *½ (1940) PR:A
ISLE OF ESCAPE *½ (1930) PR:C
ISLE OF FORGOTTEN SINS ** (1943) PR:A
ISLE OF FURY ** (1936) PR:A
ISLE OF LOST SHIPS **½ (1929) PR:A
ISLE OF LOST WRANGLERS
(SEE:99 WOUNDS)
ISLE OF MISSING MEN *½ (1942) PR:A
ISLE OF SIN *½ (1963, Ger.) PR:C-O
ISLE OF THE DEAD * (1945) PR:C**
ISLE OF THE SNAKE PEOPLE
(SEE:SNAKE PEOPLE)
ISN'T IT ROMANTIC? *½ (1948) PR:A
ISN'T LIFE A BITCH?
(SEE:LA CHIENNE)
ISN'T LIFE WONDERFUL! **½ (1953, Brit.) PR:A
ISTANBUL ** (1957) PR:A
IT! * (1967, Brit.) PR:O
IT AIN'T EASY *½ (1972) PR:C-O
IT AIN'T HAY **½ (1943) PR:AA
IT ALL CAME TRUE ** (1940) PR:A-C
IT ALWAYS RAINS ON SUNDAY ** (1949, Brit.) PR:C
IT CAME FROM BENEATH THE SEA **½ (1955) PR:A
IT CAME FROM OUTER SPACE ***½ (1953) PR:A
IT CAME WITHOUT WARNING
(SEE:WITHOUT WARNING)
IT CAN BE DONE ** (1929) PR:A
IT CAN'T LAST FOREVER *½ (1937) PR:A
IT COMES UP LOVE **½ (1943) PR:A
IT COMES UP MURDER
(SEE:HONEY POT, THE)
IT CONQUERED THE WORLD **½ (1956) PR:A
IT COULD HAPPEN TO YOU *½ (1937) PR:A
IT COULD HAPPEN TO YOU **½ (1939) PR:A
IT COULDN'T HAPPEN HERE * (1988, Brit.) PR:C-O
IT COULDN'T HAVE HAPPENED
(SEE:IT COULDN'T HAVE HAPPENED—BUT IT DID)
IT COULDN'T HAVE HAPPENED—BUT IT DID * (1936) PR:A
IT DON'T PAY TO BE AN HONEST CITIZEN ** (1985) PR:O
IT FELL FROM THE SKY * (1980) PR:C
IT GROWS ON TREES **½ (1952) PR:A
IT HAD TO BE YOU ** (1947) PR:A
IT HAD TO HAPPEN *** (1936) PR:A
IT HAPPENED AT THE INN ***½ (1945, Fr.) PR:A
IT HAPPENED AT THE WORLD'S FAIR **½ (1963) PR:A
IT HAPPENED HERE ***½ (1966, Brit.) PR:C
IT HAPPENED IN ATHENS * (1962) PR:A
IT HAPPENED IN BROAD DAYLIGHT *½ (1960, Ger./Switz.) PR:A
IT HAPPENED IN BROOKLYN *** (1947) PR:A
IT HAPPENED IN CANADA ** (1962, Can.) PR:A
IT HAPPENED IN FLATBUSH **½ (1942) PR:A
IT HAPPENED IN GIBRALTAR *** (1943, Fr.) PR:A
IT HAPPENED IN HOLLYWOOD
(SEE:ANOTHER FACE)
IT HAPPENED IN HOLLYWOOD ** (1937) PR:A
IT HAPPENED IN NEW YORK ** (1935) PR:A
IT HAPPENED IN PARIS *½ (1935, Brit.) PR:A
IT HAPPENED IN PARIS
(SEE:DESPERATE ADVENTURE, A)
IT HAPPENED IN PARIS
(SEE:LADY IN QUESTION, THE)
IT HAPPENED IN PARIS ** (1953, Fr.) PR:A
IT HAPPENED IN ROME ** (1959, It.) PR:A
IT HAPPENED IN SOHO * (1948, Brit.) PR:C
IT HAPPENED ON 5TH AVENUE ** (1947) PR:A
IT HAPPENED ONE NIGHT *** (1934) PR:A**
IT HAPPENED ONE SUMMER
(SEE:STATE FAIR)
IT HAPPENED ONE SUNDAY * (1944, Brit.) PR:A
IT HAPPENED OUT WEST ** (1937) PR:A
IT HAPPENED TO JANE **½ (1959) PR:A
IT HAPPENED TO ONE MAN ** (1941, Brit.) PR:A
IT HAPPENED TOMORROW ***½ (1944) PR:A
IT HAPPENS EVERY SPRING ** (1949) PR:AA**
IT HAPPENS EVERY THURSDAY *** (1953) PR:A
IT HAPPENS IN ROME
(SEE:IT HAPPENED IN ROME)
IT HURTS ONLY WHEN I LAUGH
(SEE:ONLY WHEN I LAUGH)
IT ISN'T DONE ** (1937, Aus.) PR:A
IT LIVES AGAIN * (1978) PR:O**

IT LIVES BY NIGHT
(SEE:BAT PEOPLE, THE)
IT ONLY HAPPENS TO OTHERS **½
(1971, Fr./It.) PR:C
IT ONLY TAKES 5 MINUTES
(SEE:ROTTEN APPLE, THE)
IT PAYS TO ADVERTISE **½ (1931) PR:A
IT SEEMED LIKE A GOOD IDEA AT THE TIME zero
(1975, Can.) PR:O
IT SHOULD HAPPEN TO YOU ** (1954) PR:A**
IT SHOULDN'T HAPPEN TO A DOG **½
(1946) PR:A
IT SHOULDN'T HAPPEN TO A VET
(SEE:ALL THINGS BRIGHT AND BEAUTIFUL)
IT STALKED THE OCEAN FLOOR
(SEE:MONSTER FROM THE OCEAN FLOOR, THE)
IT STARTED AT MIDNIGHT
(SEE:SCHWEIK'S NEW ADVENTURES)
IT STARTED IN NAPLES ** (1960) PR:C
IT STARTED IN PARADISE ** (1952) PR:A
IT STARTED IN THE ALPS *½ (1966, Jap.) PR:A
IT STARTED WITH A KISS **½ (1959) PR:C
IT STARTED WITH EVE **½ (1941) PR:A
IT TAKES A THIEF ** (1960, Brit.) PR:C
IT TAKES ALL KINDS ** (1969, US/Aus.) PR:C
IT! THE TERROR FROM BEYOND SPACE **½
(1958) PR:C
IT! THE VAMPIRE FROM BEYOND SPACE
(SEE:IT! THE TERROR FROM BEYOND SPACE)
IT WON'T RUB OFF, BABY!
(SEE:SWEET LOVE, BITTER)
ITALIAN CONNECTION, THE **
(1973, US/It./Ger.) PR:O
ITALIAN JOB, THE **½ (1969, Brit.) PR:A
ITALIAN MOUSE, THE
(SEE:MAGIC WORLD OF TOPO GIGIO, THE)
ITALIAN SECRET SERVICE ** (1968, It.) PR:C
ITALIANI BRAVA GENTE
(SEE:ITALIANO BRAVA GENTE)
ITALIANO BRAVA GENTE ** (1965, It./USSR) PR:A
IT'S A BET **½ (1935, Brit.) PR:A
IT'S A BIG COUNTRY ** (1951) PR:AA
IT'S A BIKINI WORLD *½ (1967) PR:A
IT'S A BOY **½ (1934, Brit.) PR:A
IT'S A COP * (1934, Brit.) PR:A
IT'S A DATE ** (1940) PR:A
IT'S A DEAL *** (1930) PR:A-C
IT'S A DOG'S LIFE
(SEE:BAR SINISTER, THE)
IT'S A GIFT *** (1934) PR:AA**
IT'S A GRAND LIFE * (1953, Brit.) PR:A
IT'S A GRAND OLD WORLD *½ (1937, Brit.) PR:A
IT'S A GREAT DAY * (1956, Brit.) PR:A
IT'S A GREAT FEELING *** (1949) PR:A
IT'S A GREAT LIFE * (1930) PR:A
IT'S A GREAT LIFE * (1936) PR:A
IT'S A GREAT LIFE ** (1943) PR:AA
IT'S A JOKE, SON! *½ (1947) PR:A
IT'S A KING * (1933, Brit.) PR:A
IT'S A MAD, MAD, MAD, MAD WORLD **
(1963) PR:AA**
IT'S A PLEASURE ** (1945) PR:A
IT'S A SMALL WORLD *½ (1935) PR:A
IT'S A SMALL WORLD ** (1950) PR:A
IT'S A 2'6" ABOVE THE GROUND WORLD *
(1972, Brit.) PR:O
IT'S A WISE CHILD ** (1931) PR:A
IT'S A WONDERFUL WORLD ***½ (1939) PR:A
IT'S A WONDERFUL DAY *½ (1949, Brit.) PR:A
IT'S A WONDERFUL LIFE *** (1946) PR:AA**
IT'S A WONDERFUL WORLD ** (1956, Brit.) PR:A
IT'S ALIVE *½ (1968) PR:C
IT'S ALIVE ** (1974) PR:O
**IT'S ALIVE III: ISLAND OF THE ALIVE **½
(1988) PR:O**
IT'S ALIVE II
(SEE:IT LIVES AGAIN)
IT'S ALL HAPPENING
(SEE:DREAM MAKER, THE)
IT'S ALL OVER TOWN ** (1963, Brit.) PR:A
IT'S ALL YOURS ** (1937) PR:A
IT'S ALWAYS FAIR WEATHER ** (1955) PR:A**
IT'S GREAT TO BE ALIVE **½ (1933) PR:A
IT'S GREAT TO BE YOUNG *½ (1946) PR:A
IT'S GREAT TO BE YOUNG *** (1956, Brit.) PR:A
IT'S HARD TO BE GOOD ** (1950, Brit.) PR:A

IT'S HOT IN HELL
(SEE:MONKEY IN WINTER, A)
IT'S HOT IN PARADISE zero (1962, Ger./Yugo.) PR:C
IT'S IN THE AIR *½ (1935) PR:A
IT'S IN THE AIR * (1940, Brit.) PR:A
IT'S IN THE BAG * (1936, Brit.) PR:A
IT'S IN THE BAG ** (1943, Brit.) PR:A
IT'S IN THE BAG **½ (1945) PR:A
IT'S IN THE BLOOD *** (1938, Brit.) PR:A
IT'S LOVE AGAIN **½ (1936, Brit.) PR:A
IT'S LOVE I'M AFTER ***** (1937) PR:A
IT'S MAGIC
(SEE:ROMANCE ON THE HIGH SEAS)
IT'S MY LIFE
(SEE:MY LIFE TO LIVE)
IT'S MY TURN * (1980) PR:C**
IT'S NEVER TOO LATE ** (1958, Brit.) PR:A
IT'S NEVER TOO LATE *** (1984, Sp.) PR:O
IT'S NEVER TOO LATE TO MEND **½
(1937, Brit.) PR:A
IT'S NOT CRICKET **½ (1937, Brit.) PR:A
IT'S NOT CRICKET **½ (1949, Brit.) PR:A
IT'S NOT THE SIZE THAT COUNTS *½
(1979, Brit.) PR:O
IT'S ONLY MONEY
(SEE:DOUBLE DYNAMITE)
IT'S ONLY MONEY *** (1962) PR:A
IT'S SAM SMALL AGAIN
(SEE:SAM SMALL LEAVES HOME)
IT'S THAT MAN AGAIN ** (1943, Brit.) PR:A
IT'S TOUGH TO BE FAMOUS ** (1932) PR:A
IT'S TRAD, DAD!
(SEE:RING-A-DING RHYTHM)
IT'S TURNED OUT NICE AGAIN
(SEE:TURNED OUT NICE AGAIN)
IT'S WHAT'S HAPPENING
(SEE:HAPPENING, THE)
IT'S YOU I WANT ** (1936, Brit.) PR:A
IVAN GROZNYI
(SEE:IVAN THE TERRIBLE, PARTS I & II)
IVAN THE TERRIBLE, PARTS I & II **
(1947, USSR) PR:A**
IVANOVO DETSTVO
(SEE:MY NAME IS IVAN)
IVAN'S CHILDHOOD
(SEE:MY NAME IS IVAN)
I'VE ALWAYS LOVED YOU ** (1946) PR:A
I'VE BEEN AROUND * (1935) PR:A
I'VE GOT A HORSE ** (1938, Brit.) PR:A
I'VE GOT YOUR NUMBER ** (1934) PR:A
I'VE GOTTA HORSE ** (1965, Brit.) PR:A
I'VE LIVED BEFORE **½ (1956) PR:A
IVORY-HANDLED GUN ** (1935) PR:A
IVORY HUNTER **½ (1952, Brit.) PR:A
IVORY HUNTERS, THE
(SEE:IVORY HUNTER)
IVY **½ (1947) PR:A

J

J.D.'S REVENGE **½ (1976) PR:O
J-MEN FOREVER **½ (1980) PR:C
J.R.
(SEE:WHO'S THAT KNOCKING AT MY DOOR!)
J.W. COOP * (1971) PR:A**
JABBERWOCKY ** (1977, Brit.) PR:O
J'ACCUSE ***½ (1939, Fr.) PR:C-O
JACK AHOY! *½ (1935, Brit.) PR:A
JACK AND THE BEANSTALK **½ (1952) PR:AA
JACK AND THE BEANSTALK * (1970) PR:AA
JACK FROST *** (1966, USSR) PR:AA
JACK KEROUAC'S AMERICA
(SEE:KEROUAC)
JACK LONDON **½ (1943) PR:A
JACK LONDON'S KLONDIKE FEVER
(SEE:KLONDIKE FEVER)
JACK MCCALL, DESPERADO ** (1953) PR:A
JACK OF ALL TRADES
(SEE:TWO OF US, THE)
JACK OF DIAMONDS, THE ** (1949, Brit.) PR:A
JACK OF DIAMONDS *½ (1967, US/Ger.) PR:A
JACK SLADE *½ (1953) PR:C

JACK THE GIANT KILLER *** (1962) PR:AA
JACK THE RIPPER *½ (1959, Brit.) PR:O
JACKALS, THE ** (1967, South Africa) PR:A
JACKASS MAIL **½ (1942) PR:A
JACKIE ROBINSON STORY, THE ** (1950) PR:AA
JACKPOT, THE *** (1950) PR:A
JACKPOT *½ (1960, Brit.) PR:A
JACK'S BACK * (1988) PR:O**
JACK'S WIFE
(SEE:HUNGRY WIVES)
JACKSON COUNTY JAIL **½ (1976) PR:O
JACKTOWN ** (1962) PR:A
**JACOB TWO-TWO MEETS THE HOODED FANG **½
(1979, Can.) PR:AA**
JACQUELINE **½ (1956, Brit.) PR:A
JACQUELINE SUSANN'S ONCE IS NOT ENOUGH
(SEE:ONCE IS NOT ENOUGH)
JACQUES AND NOVEMBER *** (1985, Can.) PR:C
JACQUES BREL IS ALIVE AND WELL AND LIVING
IN PARIS ** (1975) PR:A
JADA, GOSCIE, JADA
(SEE:GUESTS ARE COMING)
JADE MASK, THE ** (1945) PR:A
JAGA WA HASHITTA
(SEE:CREATURE CALLED MAN, THE)
JAGGED EDGE, THE * (1985) PR:O**
JAGUAR ** (1956) PR:A
JAGUAR *** (1980, Phil.) PR:A
JAGUAR LIVES zero (1979) PR:C
JAIL BAIT * (1954) PR:C
JAIL BAIT *** (1977, Ger.) PR:O
JAIL BUSTERS **½ (1955) PR:AA
JAIL HOUSE BLUES ** (1942) PR:A
JAILBIRD ROCK ** (1988) PR:O
JAILBIRDS
(SEE:PARDON US)
JAILBIRDS **½ (1939, Brit.) PR:A
JAILBREAK * (1936) PR:A
JAILBREAKERS, THE zero (1960) PR:A
JAILHOUSE ROCK **½ (1957) PR:A
JAK BYC KOCHANA
(SEE:HOW TO BE LOVED)
JAKE SPEED **½ (1986) PR:A-C
JALNA ** (1935) PR:A
JALOPY *** (1953) PR:AA
JALSAGHAR
(SEE:MUSIC ROOM, THE)
JAM SESSION **½ (1944) PR:A
JAMAICA INN ** (1939, Brit.) PR:C
JAMAICA RUN ** (1953) PR:A
JAMBOREE
(SEE:ROOKIES ON PARADE)
JAMBOREE ** (1944) PR:A
JAMBOREE **½ (1957) PR:A
JAMES BROTHERS, THE
(SEE:TRUE STORY OF JESSE JAMES, THE)
JAMES JOYCE'S WOMEN * (1985) PR:O**
JANE AUSTEN IN MANHATTAN ** (1980) PR:A
JANE EYRE * (1935) PR:A
JANE EYRE **** (1944) PR:A
JANE EYRE ** (1971, Brit.) PR:A
JANE STEPS OUT ** (1938, Brit.) PR:A
JANIE **½ (1944) PR:AA
JANIE GETS MARRIED *½ (1946) PR:A
JANITOR, THE
(SEE:EYEWITNESS)
JAPANESE WAR BRIDE *** (1952) PR:A
JASON AND THE ARGONAUTS **
(1963, Brit.) PR:AA**
JASSY **½ (1948, Brit.) PR:A
JAVA HEAD *½ (1935, Brit.) PR:C
JAVA SEAS
(SEE:EAST OF JAVA)
J'AVAIS SEPT FILLES
(SEE:MY SEVEN LITTLE SINS)
JAWS ** (1975) PR:C-O**
JAWS II * (1978) PR:A**
JAWS 3-D ** (1983) PR:C-O
JAWS OF DEATH, THE
(SEE:MAKO: THE JAWS OF DEATH)
JAWS OF JUSTICE ** (1933) PR:A
JAWS OF SATAN * (1980) PR:O
JAWS OF THE JUNGLE ** (1936) PR:C
JAWS: THE REVENGE * (1987) PR:O
JAYHAWKERS, THE ** (1959) PR:A
JAZZ AGE, THE **½ (1929) PR:A
JAZZ BOAT ** (1960, Brit.) PR:A

Finding entries in **THE MOTION PICTURE GUIDE** ™

Years 1929-83	Volumes I-IX
1984	Volume IX
1985	1986 ANNUAL
1986	1987 ANNUAL
1987	1988 ANNUAL
1988	1989 ANNUAL

STAR RATINGS

★★★★★ Masterpiece
★★★★ Excellent
★★★ Good
★★ Fair
★ Poor
zero Without Merit

PARENTAL RECOMMENDATION (PR:)

AA Good for Children
A   Acceptable for Children
C   Cautionary, some objectionable scenes
O   Objectionable for Children

BOLD: Films on Videocassette

JAZZ CINDERELLA *½ (1930) PR:A
JAZZ HEAVEN **½ (1929) PR:A
JAZZ SINGER, THE * (1927) PR:A**
JAZZ SINGER, THE **½ (1953) PR:A
JAZZ SINGER, THE * (1980) PR:C
JAZZBAND FIVE, THE ***½ (1932, Ger.) PR:A
JAZZBOAT
(SEE:JAZZ BOAT)
JAZZMAN *½ (1984, USSR) PR:C
JE T'AIME * (1974, Can.) PR:C
JE T'AIME, JE T'AIME *** (1972, Fr./Swed.) PR:C
JE VOUS SALUE, MAFIA
(SEE:HAIL MAFIA)
JEALOUSY * (1929) PR:C
JEALOUSY *½ (1931, Brit.) PR:A
JEALOUSY *½ (1934) PR:C
JEALOUSY ** (1945) PR:A
JEALOUSY
(SEE:EMERGENCY WEDDING)
JEAN DE FLORETTE ***½ (1987, Fr.) PR:A
JEAN MARC OR CONJUGAL LIFE
(SEE:ANATOMY OF A MARRIAGE)
JEANNE EAGELS **½ (1957) PR:C
JEANNIE
(SEE:GIRL IN DISTRESS)
JEDDA, THE UNCIVILIZED ** (1956, Aus.) PR:A
JEDER FUR SICH UND GOTT GEGEN ALLE
(SEE:EVERY MAN FOR HIMSELF AND GOD AGAINST ALL)
JEEPERS CREEPERS ** (1939) PR:A
JEKYLL AND HYDE. . .TOGETHER AGAIN *½ (1982) PR:O
JEKYLL'S INFERNO
(SEE:HOUSE OF FRIGHT)
JENATSCH *** (1987, Switz./Fr.) PR:C
JENIFER HALE ** (1937, Brit.) PR:A
JENNIE *½ (1941) PR:A
JENNIE
(SEE:PORTRAIT OF JENNIE)
JENNIE GERHARDT *** (1933) PR:A
JENNIE LESS HA UNA NUOVA PISTOLA
(SEE:GUNMEN OF THE RIO GRANDE)
JENNIFER *½ (1953) PR:A
JENNIFER zero (1978) PR:C-O
JENNIFER ON MY MIND zero (1971) PR:O
JENNIFER (THE SNAKE GODDESS)
(SEE:JENNIFER)
JENNY * (1969) PR:A
JENNY KISSED ME ** (1985, Aus.) PR:C
JENNY LAMOUR *** (1948, Fr.) PR:A
JENNY LIND
(SEE:LADY'S MORALS, A)
JENSEITS DES RHIENS
(SEE:TOMORROW IS MY TURN)
JEOPARDY **½ (1953) PR:A
JEREMIAH JOHNSON ***½ (1972) PR:C-O
JEREMY ** (1973) PR:A
JERICHO
(SEE:DARK SANDS)
JERK, THE ** (1979) PR:O
JERRICO, THE WONDER CLOWN
(SEE:THREE RING CIRCUS)
JERUSALEM FILE, THE *½ (1972, US/Israel) PR:C
JESSE AND LESTER, TWO BROTHERS IN A PLACE CALLED TRINITY ** (1972, It.) PR:A
JESSE JAMES *** (1939) PR:A**
JESSE JAMES AT BAY **½ (1941) PR:A
JESSE JAMES, JR. * (1942) PR:A
JESSE JAMES MEETS FRANKENSTEIN'S DAUGHTER *½ (1966) PR:A
JESSE JAMES VERSUS THE DALTONS *½ (1954) PR:A
JESSE JAMES' WOMEN * (1954) PR:A
JESSICA *½ (1962, US/It./Fr.) PR:C
JESSICA
(SEE:MISS JESSICA IS PREGNANT)
JESSIE'S GIRLS * (1976) PR:O
JEST OF GOD, A
(SEE:RACHEL, RACHEL)
JESTER, THE ***½ (1987, Portugal) PR:O
JESUS zero (1979) PR:A
JESUS CHRIST, SUPERSTAR ** (1973) PR:A
JESUS TRIP, THE * (1971) PR:C
JET ATTACK zero (1958) PR:A
JET JOB *½ (1952) PR:A
JET MEN OF THE AIR
(SEE:AIR CADET)
JET OVER THE ATLANTIC ** (1960) PR:A
JET PILOT ** (1957) PR:C
JET SQUAD
(SEE:JET ATTACK)
JET STORM ** (1961, Brit.) PR:A
JETLAG ** (1981, US/Sp.) PR:C
JETSTREAM
(SEE:JET STORM)
JEU DE MASSACRE
(SEE:KILLING GAME, THE)
JEUNE FILLE, UN SEUL AMOUR, UNE
(SEE:MAGNIFICENT SINNER)
JEUNES FILLES EN UNIFORME
(SEE:MAEDCHEN IN UNIFORM)
JEUX D'ADULTES
(SEE:HEAD OF THE FAMILY)
JEUX PRECOCES
(SEE:LIPSTICK)
JEW SUSS
(SEE:POWER)
JEWEL, THE * (1933, Brit.) PR:A
JEWEL OF THE NILE, THE * (1985) PR:C**
JEWEL ROBBERY *** (1932) PR:A
JEWELS OF BRANDENBURG *½ (1947) PR:A
JEZEBEL ** (1938) PR:A**
JEZEBELS, THE
(SEE:SWITCHBLADE SISTERS)
JIG SAW **½ (1965, Brit.) PR:A
JIGGS AND MAGGIE IN SOCIETY *½ (1948) PR:AA
JIGGS AND MAGGIE OUT WEST *½ (1950) PR:AA
JIGOKUHEN
(SEE:PORTRAIT OF HELL)
JIGOKUMEN
(SEE:GATE OF HELL)
JIGSAW **½ (1949) PR:A
JIGSAW
(SEE:JIG SAW)
JIGSAW *½ (1968) PR:O
JIGSAW MAN, THE ** (1984, Brit.) PR:C
JIM HANVEY, DETECTIVE *½ (1937) PR:A
JIM, THE WORLD'S GREATEST ** (1976) PR:A
JIM THORPE—ALL AMERICAN ** (1951) PR:A**
JIMMY AND SALLY *½ (1933) PR:A
JIMMY BOY * (1935, Brit.) PR:A
JIMMY ORPHEUS *½ (1966, Ger.) PR:C
JIMMY THE GENT **½ (1934) PR:A
JIMMY THE KID * (1982) PR:A
JIMMY VALENTINE
(SEE:ALIAS JIMMY VALENTINE)
JINCHOGE
(SEE:DAPHNE, THE)
JINX MONEY **½ (1948) PR:A
JINXED! * (1982) PR:O
J'IRAI CRACHER SUR VOS TOMBES
(SEE:I SPIT ON YOUR GRAVE)
JITTERBUGS ** (1943) PR:AA
JIVARO **½ (1954) PR:A
JIVE JUNCTION ** (1944) PR:A
JO JO DANCER, YOUR LIFE IS CALLING ** (1986) PR:C-O
JOAN AT THE STAKE * (1954, It./Fr.) PR:A
JOAN BEDFORD IS MISSING
(SEE:HOUSE OF HORRORS)
JOAN OF ARC ***½ (1948) PR:A
JOAN OF OZARK **½ (1942) PR:A
JOAN OF PARIS *** (1942) PR:A
JOAN OF THE ANGELS **½ (1962, Pol.) PR:O
JOANNA **½ (1968, Brit.) PR:O
JOAQUIN MARRIETA
(SEE:MURIETA)
JOB LAZADASA
(SEE:REVOLT OF JOB, THE)
JOCK PETERSEN
(SEE:PETERSEN)
JOCKS zero (1987) PR:O
JOE * (1970) PR:O**
JOE AND ETHEL TURP CALL ON THE PRESIDENT *** (1939) PR:A
JOE BUTTERFLY ** (1957) PR:A
JOE DAKOTA ** (1957) PR:C
JOE, EL IMPLACABLE
(SEE:NAVAJO JOE)
JOE HILL **½ (1971, Swed./US) PR:C
JOE KIDD ** (1972) PR:C
JOE LOUIS STORY, THE ***½ (1953) PR:A
JOE MACBETH **½ (1955) PR:C
JOE NAVIDAD
(SEE:CHRISTMAS KID, THE)
JOE PALOOKA
(SEE:PALOOKA)
JOE PALOOKA, CHAMP **½ (1946) PR:AA
JOE PALOOKA IN FIGHTING MAD
(SEE:FIGHTING MAD)
JOE PALOOKA IN HUMPHREY TAKES A CHANCE
(SEE:HUMPHREY TAKES A CHANCE)
JOE PALOOKA IN THE BIG FIGHT **½ (1949) PR:AA
JOE PALOOKA IN THE COUNTERPUNCH **½ (1949) PR:AA
JOE PALOOKA IN THE SQUARED CIRCLE **½ (1950) PR:A
JOE PALOOKA IN TRIPLE CROSS ** (1951) PR:AA
JOE PALOOKA IN WINNER TAKE ALL **½ (1948) PR:AA
JOE PALOOKA MEETS HUMPHREY **½ (1950) PR:AA
JOE PANTHER **½ (1976) PR:AA
JOE SMITH, AMERICAN ***½ (1942) PR:A
JOEY BOY *½ (1965, Brit.) PR:O
JOHANSSON GETS SCOLDED *½ (1945, Swed.) PR:A
JOHN AND JULIE *** (1957, Brit.) PR:AA
JOHN AND MARY ***½ (1969) PR:O
JOHN GOLDFARB, PLEASE COME HOME ** (1964) PR:A-C
JOHN HALIFAX—GENTLEMAN * (1938, Brit.) PR:A
JOHN LOVES MARY **½ (1949) PR:A
JOHN MEADE'S WOMAN ** (1937) PR:C
JOHN OF THE FAIR **½ (1962, Brit.) PR:AA
JOHN PAUL JONES *** (1959) PR:A
JOHN WESLEY *** (1954, Brit.) PR:AA
JOHNNY ALLEGRO ** (1949) PR:A-C
JOHNNY ANGEL ** (1945) PR:A
JOHNNY APOLLO ***½ (1940) PR:A
JOHNNY BANCO *½ (1969, Fr./It./Ger.) PR:O
JOHNNY BE GOOD zero (1988) PR:O
JOHNNY BELINDA *** (1948) PR:C**
JOHNNY COME LATELY ** (1943) PR:A
JOHNNY COMES FLYING HOME ** (1946) PR:A
JOHNNY CONCHO *½ (1956) PR:A
JOHNNY COOL * (1963) PR:O
JOHNNY DANGEROUSLY **½ (1984) PR:C
JOHNNY DARK **½ (1954) PR:A
JOHNNY DOESN'T LIVE HERE ANY MORE **½ (1944) PR:A
JOHNNY DOUGHBOY ** (1943) PR:AA
JOHNNY EAGER ***½ (1942) PR:C
JOHNNY FRENCHMAN ** (1946, Brit.) PR:A
JOHNNY GOT HIS GUN ** (1971) PR:O
JOHNNY GUITAR * (1954) PR:C**
JOHNNY HAMLET *½ (1972, It.) PR:O
JOHNNY HOLIDAY *** (1949) PR:A
JOHNNY IN THE CLOUDS ***½ (1945, Brit.) PR:A
JOHNNY NOBODY ** (1965, Brit.) PR:O
JOHNNY NORTH
(SEE:KILLERS, THE)
JOHNNY O'CLOCK ***½ (1947) PR:A
JOHNNY ON THE RUN *** (1953, Brit.) PR:AA
JOHNNY ON THE SPOT * (1954, Brit.) PR:A
JOHNNY ONE-EYE **½ (1950) PR:A
JOHNNY ORO
(SEE:RINGO AND HIS GOLDEN PISTOL)
JOHNNY RENO **½ (1966) PR:O
JOHNNY ROCCO ** (1958) PR:A
JOHNNY STEALS EUROPE *** (1932, Ger.) PR:A
JOHNNY STOOL PIGEON **½ (1949) PR:C
JOHNNY THE GIANT KILLER ** (1953, Fr.) PR:AA
JOHNNY TIGER **½ (1966) PR:A
JOHNNY TREMAIN ***½ (1957) PR:AA
JOHNNY TROUBLE *** (1957) PR:A
JOHNNY VAGABOND
(SEE:JOHNNY COME LATELY)
JOHNNY VIK **½ (1973) PR:C
JOHNNY, YOU'RE WANTED ** (1956, Brit.) PR:A
JOHNNY YUMA *½ (1967, It.) PR:O
JOI-UCHI
(SEE:REBELLION)
JOIN THE MARINES *** (1937) PR:A
JOKE OF DESTINY, A
(SEE:JOKE OF DESTINY LYING IN WAIT AROUND THE CORNER LIKE A STREET BANDIT, A)
JOKE OF DESTINY LYING IN WAIT AROUND THE CORNER LIKE A STREET BANDIT, A * (1984, It.) PR:C
JOKER, THE **½ (1961, Fr.) PR:O
JOKER IS WILD, THE ***½ (1957) PR:C
JOKERS, THE ***½ (1967, Brit.) PR:A-C
JOLLY BAD FELLOW, A **½ (1964, Brit.) PR:C
JOLLY OLD HIGGINS
(SEE:EARL OF PUDDLESTONE)
JOLSON SINGS AGAIN ***½ (1949) PR:A
JOLSON STORY, THE ***½ (1946) PR:A
JONAH—WHO WILL BE 25 IN THE YEAR 2000 ***½ (1976, Switz.) PR:C
JONAS: QUI AURA 25 ANS EN L'AN 2000
(SEE:JONAH: WHO WILL BE 25 IN THE YEAR 2000)
JONATHAN *** (1973, Ger.) PR:O
JONATHAN LIVINGSTON SEAGULL * (1973) PR:A
JONES FAMILY IN HOLLYWOOD, THE ** (1939) PR:A
JONI **½ (1980) PR:A
JONIKO
(SEE:JONIKO AND THE KUSH TA KA)
JONIKO AND THE KUSH TA KA **½ (1969) PR:AA
JORY * (1972) PR:A
JOSEPH AND HIS BRETHREN
(SEE:STORY OF JOSEPH AND HIS BRETHREN)
JOSEPH ANDREWS ** (1977, Brit.) PR:O
JOSEPH SOLD BY HIS BROTHERS
(SEE:STORY OF JOSEPH AND HIS BRETHREN, THE)
JOSEPHINE AND MEN ** (1955, Brit.) PR:A
JOSETTE **½ (1938) PR:A
JOSHUA * (1976) PR:O
JOSHUA THEN AND NOW * (1985, Can.) PR:O**
JOSSER IN THE ARMY ** (1932, Brit.) PR:A

JOSSER JOINS THE NAVY ** (1932, Brit.) PR:A
JOSSER ON THE FARM *½ (1934, Brit.) PR:A
JOSSER ON THE RIVER * (1932, Brit.) PR:A
JOTAI
  (SEE:VIXEN)
JOUR DE FETE **** (1952, Fr.) PR:A**
JOURNAL OF A CRIME ** (1934) PR:C
JOURNEY * (1977, Can.) PR:O
JOURNEY, THE **½ (1959, US/Aust.) PR:A-C
JOURNEY, THE *** (1986, Ger./Switz.) PR:O
JOURNEY AHEAD ** (1947, Brit.) PR:A
JOURNEY AMONG WOMEN ** (1977, Aus.) PR:O
JOURNEY BACK TO OZ ** (1974) PR:AA
JOURNEY BENEATH THE DESERT **
  (1967, Fr./It.) PR:A**
JOURNEY FOR MARGARET ***½ (1942) PR:AA
JOURNEY INTO DARKNESS ** (1968, Brit.) PR:A
JOURNEY INTO FEAR **** (1942) PR:A**
JOURNEY INTO FEAR ** (1976, Can.) PR:O
JOURNEY INTO LIGHT **½ (1951) PR:C
JOURNEY INTO MIDNIGHT ** (1968, Brit.) PR:A
JOURNEY INTO NOWHERE **½ (1963, Brit.) PR:O
JOURNEY OF NATTY GANN, THE * (1985) PR:C**
JOURNEY THROUGH ROSEBUD ** (1972) PR:O
JOURNEY TO FREEDOM ** (1957) PR:A
JOURNEY TO ITALY
  (SEE:STRANGERS)
JOURNEY TO LOVE ** (1953, It.) PR:A
JOURNEY TO SHILOH *** (1968) PR:C
JOURNEY TO SPIRIT ISLAND **½ (1988) PR:AA
JOURNEY TO THE BEGINNING OF TIME **½
  (1966, Czech.) PR:AA
**JOURNEY TO THE CENTER OF THE EARTH ***½
  (1959) PR:AA**
**JOURNEY TO THE CENTER OF TIME **
  (1967) PR:A**
**JOURNEY TO THE FAR SIDE OF THE SUN **
  (1969, Brit.) PR:A**
JOURNEY TO THE LOST CITY *
  (1960, Ger./Fr./It.) PR:A
JOURNEY TO THE SEVENTH PLANET **
  (1962, US/Swed.) PR:C
JOURNEY TOGETHER ***½ (1946, Brit.) PR:A
JOURNEY'S END *** (1930) PR:A
JOURNEYS FROM BERLIN—1971 **½ (1980) PR:O
JOVITA **½ (1970, Pol.) PR:O
JOY '?!- 0 (1983, Fr./Can.) PR:O
JOY HOUSE ** (1964, Fr.) PR:O
JOY IN THE MORNING ** (1965) PR:O
JOY OF LEARNING, THE
  (SEE:LE GAI SAVOIR)
JOY OF LIVING *½ (1938) PR:A
JOY OF SEX zero (1984) PR:O
JOY PARADE, THE
  (SEE:LIFE BEGINS IN COLLEGE)
JOY RIDE *½ (1935, Brit.) PR:A
JOY RIDE ** (1958) PR:C
JOYRIDE ** (1977) PR:O
JOYSTICKS * (1983) PR:O
JUAREZ **** (1939) PR:A**
JUAREZ AND MAXIMILLIAN
  (SEE:MAD EMPRESS, THE)
JUBAL ***½ (1956) PR:C
JUBILEE ***½ (1978, Brit.) PR:O
JUBILEE TRAIL **½ (1954) PR:A
JUBILEE WINDOW * (1935, Brit.) PR:A
JUD * (1971) PR:O
JUDAS CITY
  (SEE:SATAN'S BED)
JUDAS WAS A WOMAN
  (SEE:LA BETE HUMAINE)
JUDEX ***½ (1966, Fr./It.) PR:C
JUDGE, THE ** (1949) PR:O
JUDGE AND THE ASSASSIN, THE ***
  (1979, Fr.) PR:C
JUDGE AND THE SINNER, THE **½
  (1964, Ger.) PR:C
JUDGE HARDY AND SON *** (1939) PR:AA
JUDGE HARDY'S CHILDREN ***½ (1938) PR:AA
JUDGE PRIEST **½ (1934) PR:AA
JUDGE STEPS OUT, THE **½ (1949) PR:A
JUDGMENT AT NUREMBERG ***½ (1961) PR:C
JUDGMENT DEFERRED **½ (1952, Brit.) PR:A
JUDGMENT IN BERLIN *½ (1988) PR:A
JUDGMENT IN THE SUN
  (SEE:OUTRAGE, THE)
JUDITH * (1965) PR:C-O

JUDO SAGA **½ (1965, Jap.) PR:C
JUDO SHOWDOWN **½ (1966, Jap.) PR:C
JUDY GOES TO TOWN
  (SEE:PUDDIN' HEAD)
JUDY'S LITTLE NO-NO *½ (1969) PR:O
JUGGERNAUT ** (1937, Brit.) PR:O
JUGGERNAUT * (1974, Brit.) PR:A-C**
JUGGLER, THE **** (1953) PR:C-O
JUKE BOX JENNY **½ (1942) PR:AA
JUKE BOX RACKET *½ (1960) PR:A
JUKE BOX RHYTHM **½ (1959) PR:A
JUKE GIRL ** (1942) PR:A
JULES AND JIM **** (1962, Fr.) PR:C-O**
JULES VERNE'S ROCKET TO THE MOON
  (SEE:THOSE FANTASTIC FLYING FOOLS)
JULIA *** (1977) PR:A-C**
JULIA AND JULIA *½ (1988, It.) PR:C-O
JULIA, DU BIST ZAUBER-HAFT
  (SEE:ADORABLE JULIA)
JULIA MISBEHAVES ***½ (1948) PR:A
JULIE ** (1956) PR:A
JULIE DARLING * (1982, Can./Ger.) PR:O
JULIE THE REDHEAD **½ (1963, Fr.) PR:A
JULIET OF THE SPIRITS **
  (1965, Fr./It./W.Ger.) PR:A-C**
JULIETTA *½ (1957, Fr.) PR:A
JULIUS CAESAR ** (1952) PR:A
JULIUS CAESAR ***** (1953) PR:C
JULIUS CAESAR ** (1970, Brit.) PR:A
JULY PORK BELLIES
  (SEE:FOR PETE'S SAKE)
JUMBO ** (1962) PR:AA
JUMP *½ (1971) PR:A
JUMP FOR GLORY
  (SEE:WHEN THIEF MEETS THIEF)
JUMP INTO HELL *½ (1955) PR:A
JUMPIN' JACK FLASH ** (1986) PR:O
JUMPING FOR JOY ** (1956, Brit.) PR:A
JUMPING JACKS ** (1952) PR:A
JUNCTION CITY * (1952) PR:A
JUNE BRIDE *** (1948) PR:A
JUNE MOON * (1931) PR:A
JUNGE LORD, DER
  (SEE:YOUNG LORD, THE)
JUNGE SCHRIE MORD, EIN
  (SEE:BOY CRIED MURDER, THE)
JUNGE TORLESS, DER
  (SEE:YOUNG TORLESS)
JUNGLE, THE zero (1952) PR:AA
JUNGLE ATTACK
  (SEE:CROSSWINDS)
JUNGLE BOOK **** (1942) PR:AA**
JUNGLE BOOK, THE ***½ (1967) PR:AA
JUNGLE BRIDE * (1933) PR:A
JUNGLE CAPTIVE ** (1945) PR:A
JUNGLE FIGHTERS
  (SEE:LONG, AND THE SHORT, AND THE TALL,
  THE)
JUNGLE FLIGHT ** (1947) PR:A
JUNGLE GENTS *½ (1954) PR:AA
JUNGLE GODDESS *½ (1948) PR:A
JUNGLE HEAT * (1957) PR:A
JUNGLE ISLAND
  (SEE:WOLVES OF THE SEA)
JUNGLE JIM ** (1948) PR:AA
JUNGLE JIM IN THE FORBIDDEN LAND **
  (1952) PR:AA
JUNGLE MAN * (1941) PR:A
JUNGLE MAN-EATERS ** (1954) PR:AA
JUNGLE MANHUNT ** (1951) PR:AA
JUNGLE MOON MEN ** (1955) PR:AA
JUNGLE OF CHANG * (1951) PR:A
JUNGLE PATROL **½ (1948) PR:A
JUNGLE PRINCESS, THE **½ (1936) PR:A
JUNGLE RAIDERS * (1986, It.) PR:A-C
JUNGLE RAMPAGE
  (SEE:RAMPAGE)
JUNGLE SIREN ** (1942) PR:A
JUNGLE STREET
  (SEE:JUNGLE STREET GIRLS)
JUNGLE STREET GIRLS *½ (1963, Brit.) PR:A
JUNGLE TERROR
  (SEE:FIREBALL JUNGLE)
JUNGLE VIRGIN
  (SEE:JAWS OF THE JUNGLE)
JUNGLE WARRIORS ** (1984, US/Ger./Mex.) PR:O
JUNGLE WOMAN * (1944) PR:A

JUNGLE WOMAN
  (SEE:NABONGA)
JUNIOR ARMY *½ (1943) PR:AA
JUNIOR BONNER * (1972) PR:A-C**
JUNIOR MISS *** (1945) PR:AA
JUNIOR PROM ** (1946) PR:AA
JUNKET 89 ** (1970, Brit.) PR:AA
JUNKMAN, THE * (1982) PR:C-O
JUNO AND THE PAYCOCK **½ (1930, Brit.) PR:A
JUPITER * (1952, Fr.) PR:A
JUPITER'S DARLING *½ (1955) PR:A
JURY OF ONE
  (SEE:VERDICT, THE)
JURY OF THE JUNGLE
  (SEE:FURY OF THE JUNGLE)
JURY'S EVIDENCE *½ (1936, Brit.) PR:A
JURY'S SECRET, THE ** (1938) PR:A
JUST A BIG, SIMPLE GIRL * (1949, Fr.) PR:A
JUST A GIGOLO * (1931) PR:A
JUST A GIGOLO *** (1979, Ger.) PR:O
JUST ACROSS THE STREET ** (1952) PR:A
JUST AROUND THE CORNER ** (1938) PR:AA
JUST BEFORE DAWN ** (1946) PR:A
JUST BEFORE DAWN *½ (1980) PR:O
JUST BEFORE NIGHTFALL ** (1975, Fr./It.) PR:A-C
JUST BETWEEN FRIENDS ** (1986) PR:O
JUST FOR A SONG *½ (1930, Brit.) PR:A
JUST FOR FUN * (1963, Brit.) PR:AA
JUST FOR THE HELL OF IT zero (1968) PR:O
JUST FOR YOU **½ (1952) PR:A
JUST GREAT
  (SEE:TOUT VA BIEN)
JUST IMAGINE **½ (1930) PR:A
JUST JOE * (1960, Brit.) PR:A
JUST LIKE A WOMAN ** (1939, Brit.) PR:A
JUST LIKE A WOMAN ** (1967, Brit.) PR:C
JUST LIKE HEAVEN * (1930) PR:A
JUST ME *½ (1950, Fr.) PR:A
JUST MY LUCK ** (1933, Brit.) PR:A
JUST MY LUCK ** (1957, Brit.) PR:A
JUST OFF BROADWAY **½ (1942) PR:A
JUST ONCE MORE ** (1963, Swed.) PR:O
JUST ONE MORE
  (SEE:JUST ONCE MORE)
JUST ONE OF THE GUYS **½ (1985) PR:C
JUST OUT OF REACH *½ (1979, Aus.) PR:A
JUST SMITH
  (SEE:LEAVE IT TO SMITH)
JUST TELL ME WHAT YOU WANT ** (1980) PR:C
JUST THE WAY YOU ARE * (1984) PR:C
JUST THIS ONCE **½ (1952) PR:A
JUST TO BE LOVED
  (SEE:NEW LIFE STYLE, THE)
JUST WILLIAM ** (1939, Brit.) PR:AA
JUST WILLIAM'S LUCK * (1948, Brit.) PR:A
JUST YOU AND ME, KID * (1979) PR:C
JUSTE AVANT LA NUIT
  (SEE:JUST BEFORE NIGHTFALL)
JUSTICE CAIN
  (SEE:CAIN'S WAY)
JUSTICE FOR SALE
  (SEE:NIGHT COURT)
JUSTICE OF THE RANGE ** (1935) PR:A
JUSTICE TAKES A HOLIDAY * (1933) PR:A
JUSTINE ** (1969) PR:C
JUSTINE ** (1969, It./Sp.) PR:O
JUVENILE COURT ** (1938) PR:A
JUVENILE JUNGLE *½ (1958) PR:A
JUVENTUD A LA IMTEMPERIE
  (SEE:UNSATISFIED, THE)

K

KADOYNG *** (1974, Brit.) PR:AA
KAGEMUSHA *** (1980, Jap.) PR:C**
KAGI
  (SEE:ODD OBSESSION)
KAIDAN
  (SEE:KWAIDAN)
KAIJU DAISENSO
  (SEE:MONSTER ZERO)

Finding entries in **THE MOTION PICTURE GUIDE** ™		STAR RATINGS		PARENTAL RECOMMENDATION (PR:)	
Years 1929-83	Volumes I-IX	★★★★★	Masterpiece	AA	Good for Children
1984	Volume IX	★★★★	Excellent	A	Acceptable for Children
1985	1986 ANNUAL	★★★	Good	C	Cautionary, some objectionable scenes
1986	1987 ANNUAL	★★	Fair	O	Objectionable for Children
1987	1988 ANNUAL	★	Poor		
1988	1989 ANNUAL	zero	Without Merit	**BOLD:** Films on Videocassette	

KAIJU SOSHINGEKI
(SEE:DESTROY ALL MONSTERS)
KAITEI GUNKA
(SEE:ATRAGON, THE FLYING SUPERSUB)
KAJA, UBIT CU TE
(SEE:KAYA I'LL KILL YOU)
KAJIKKO
(SEE:ANGRY ISLAND)
KALEIDOSCOPE ** (1966, Brit.) PR:A-C
KAMERADSCHAFT **** (1931, Ger.) PR:A-C
KAMIGAMI NO FUKAKI YOKUBO
(SEE:KURAGEJIMA—LEGENDS FROM A SOUTHERN ISLAND)
KAMIKAZE '89 ** (1983, Ger.) PR:O
KAMILLA ***½ (1984, Norway) PR:A-C
KAMOURASKA **½ (1973, Can./Fr.) PR:O
KANAL ***½ (1961, Pol.) PR:C
KANCHENJUNGHA *** (1966, India) PR:A
KANDYLAND * (1988) PR:O
KANGAROO **½ (1952) PR:A
KANGAROO ** (1986, Aus.) PR:C
KANGAROO KID, THE ** (1950, Aus./US) PR:A
KANOJO
(SEE:SHE AND HE)
KANSAN, THE ** (1943) PR:A
KANSAS * (1988) PR:C-O
KANSAS CITY BOMBER * (1972) PR:O
KANSAS CITY CONFIDENTIAL *** (1952) PR:C-O
KANSAS CITY KITTY **½ (1944) PR:A
KANSAS CITY PRINCESS ** (1934) PR:A
KANSAS CYCLONE **½ (1941) PR:A
KANSAS PACIFIC ** (1953) PR:A
KANSAS RAIDERS **½ (1950) PR:A
KANSAS TERRITORY **½ (1952) PR:A
KANSAS TERRORS, THE ** (1939) PR:A
KAOS *** (1985, It.) PR:O
KAPHETZOU
(SEE:FORTUNE TELLER, THE)
KAPITANLEUTENANT PRIEN—DER STIER VON SCAPA FLOW
(SEE:U-47 LT. COMMANDER PRIEN)
KAPO *** (1964, It./Fr./Yugo.) PR:O
KARAMAZOV **½ (1931, Ger.) PR:C
KARAMI-AI
(SEE:INHERITANCE, THE)
KARATE KID, THE ***½ (1984) PR:A-C
KARATE KID PART II, THE **½ (1986) PR:A-C
KARATE KILLERS, THE ** (1967) PR:A
KARATE, THE HAND OF DEATH ** (1961) PR:C
KARE JOHN
(SEE:DEAR JOHN)
KAREN, THE LOVEMAKER * (1970) PR:O
KARMA ** (1933, Brit./India) PR:A
KARMA *** (1986, Switz.) PR:O
KATE PLUS TEN ** (1938, Brit.) PR:A
KATERINA IZMAILOVA ***½ (1969, USSR) PR:A
KATHLEEN **½ (1938, Ireland) PR:A
KATHLEEN ** (1941) PR:AA
KATHLEEN MAVOUREEN
(SEE:KATHLEEN)
KATHLEEN MAVOURNEEN ** (1930) PR:A
KATHY O' **½ (1958) PR:A
KATHY'S LOVE AFFAIR
(SEE:COURTNEY AFFAIR)
KATIA
(SEE:MAGNIFI-SINNER)
KATIE DID IT ** (1951) PR:A
KATINA
(SEE:ICELAND)
KATOK I SKRIPKA
(SEE:VIOLIN AND ROLLER)
KAWAITA MIZUUMI
(SEE:YOUTH IN FURY)
KAYA, I'LL KILL YOU **½ (1969, Yugo./Fr.) PR:A
KAZABLAN *** (1974, Israel) PR:A
KAZAN * (1949) PR:AA
KEELER AFFAIR, THE
(SEE:CHRISTINE KEELER AFFAIR, THE)
KEEP, THE ** (1983) PR:O
KEEP 'EM FLYING ** (1941) PR:AA
KEEP 'EM ROLLING *½ (1934) PR:A
KEEP 'EM SLUGGING ** (1943) PR:AA
KEEP FIT ** (1937, Brit.) PR:A
KEEP HIM ALIVE
(SEE:GREAT PLANE ROBBERY, THE)
KEEP IT CLEAN *½ (1956, Brit.) PR:A
KEEP IT COOL
(SEE:LET'S ROCK)
KEEP IT QUIET *½ (1934, Brit.) PR:A
KEEP MY GRAVE OPEN * (1980) PR:O
KEEP SMILING ** (1938) PR:A
KEEP SMILING
(SEE:SMILING ALONG)
KEEP YOUR POWDER DRY ** (1945) PR:A
KEEP YOUR SEATS PLEASE **½ (1936, Brit.) PR:A
KEEPER, THE * (1976, Can.) PR:A
KEEPER OF THE BEES *½ (1935) PR:A
KEEPER OF THE BEES * (1947) PR:A
KEEPER OF THE FLAME *** (1942) PR:A
KEEPERS OF YOUTH ** (1931, Brit.) PR:A
KEEPING COMPANY *½ (1941) PR:A
KEK BALVANY
(SEE:BLUE IDOL, THE)
KELLY AND ME ** (1957) PR:AA
KELLY OF THE SECRET SERVICE ** (1936) PR:A
KELLY OF THE U.S.A.
(SEE:KING KELLY OF THE USA)
KELLY THE SECOND *½ (1936) PR:A
KELLY'S HEROES **½ (1970, US/Yugo.) PR:C-O
KEMPO SAMURAI
(SEE:SAMURAI FROM NOWHERE)
KENNEL MURDER CASE, THE ***½ (1933) PR:A
KENNER *½ (1969) PR:C
KENNY AND CO. **½ (1976) PR:C
KENTUCKIAN, THE **½ (1955) PR:A
KENTUCKY ***½ (1938) PR:AA
KENTUCKY BLUE STREAK *½ (1935) PR:A
KENTUCKY FRIED MOVIE, THE ** (1977) PR:O
KENTUCKY JUBILEE ** (1951) PR:A
KENTUCKY KERNELS ** (1935) PR:A
KENTUCKY MINSTRELS * (1934, Brit.) PR:A
KENTUCKY MOONSHINE **½ (1938) PR:AA
KENTUCKY RIFLE ** (1956) PR:A
KEPT HUSBANDS ** (1931) PR:C
KEROUAC ** (1985) PR:O
KES **½ (1970, Brit.) PR:C
KETTLE CREEK
(SEE:MOUNTAIN JUSTICE)
KETTLES IN THE OZARKS, THE **½ (1956) PR:AA
KETTLES ON OLD MACDONALD'S FARM, THE **½ (1957) PR:AA
KETTO GENRYU JIMA
(SEE:SAMURAI III)
KEY, THE *** (1934) PR:A
KEY, THE **½ (1958, Brit.) PR:O
KEY EXCHANGE * (1985) PR:O
KEY LARGO ***** (1948) PR:C
KEY MAN, THE *½ (1957, Brit.) PR:A
KEY TO HARMONY * (1935, Brit.) PR:A
KEY TO THE CITY **½ (1950) PR:A
KEY WITNESS * (1947) PR:C
KEY WITNESS **½ (1960) PR:O
KEYHOLE, THE ** (1933) PR:A
KEYS OF THE KINGDOM, THE *** (1944) PR:A
KHARTOUM **** (1966, Brit.) PR:C
KHYBER PATROL **½ (1954) PR:A
KIBITZER, THE ** (1929) PR:A
KICK IN *½ (1931) PR:C
KICKING THE MOON AROUND
(SEE:PLAYBOY, THE)
KID BLUE *** (1973) PR:C
KID COLOSSUS, THE
(SEE:ROOGIE'S BUMP)
KID COMES BACK, THE **½ (1937) PR:A
KID COURAGEOUS *½ (1935) PR:A
KID DYNAMITE * (1943) PR:AA
KID FOR TWO FARTHINGS, A **** (1956, Brit.) PR:A
KID FROM AMARILLO, THE'!- 0 (1951) PR:A
KID FROM ARIZONA, THE * (1931) PR:A
KID FROM BROKEN GUN, THE * (1952) PR:A
KID FROM BROOKLYN, THE *** (1946) PR:AA
KID FROM CANADA, THE ** (1957, Brit.) PR:AA
KID FROM CLEVELAND, THE ** (1949) PR:A
KID FROM GOWER GULCH, THE *½ (1949) PR:A
KID FROM KANSAS, THE *½ (1941) PR:C
KID FROM KOKOMO, THE ** (1939) PR:A
KID FROM LEFT FIELD, THE **½ (1953) PR:AA
KID FROM SANTA FE, THE *½ (1940) PR:AA
KID FROM SPAIN, THE ***½ (1932) PR:AA
KID FROM TEXAS, THE ** (1939) PR:AA
KID FROM TEXAS, THE *½ (1950) PR:C
KID GALAHAD ***½ (1937) PR:A-C
KID GALAHAD ** (1962) PR:A
KID GLOVE KILLER *** (1942) PR:C
KID GLOVES ** (1929) PR:C
KID MILLIONS **½ (1934) PR:AA
KID MONK BARONI ** (1952) PR:C
KID NIGHTINGALE **½ (1939) PR:A
KID RANGER, THE *½ (1936) PR:A
KID RIDES AGAIN, THE *½ (1943) PR:A
KID RODELO * (1966, US/Sp.) PR:C
KID SISTER, THE **½ (1945) PR:A
KID VENGEANCE * (1977) PR:C
KIDCO **½ (1984) PR:C
KIDNAP OF MARY LOU, THE
(SEE:ALMOST HUMAN)
KIDNAPPED
(SEE:MISS FANE'S BABY IS STOLEN)
KIDNAPPED *** (1938) PR:AA
KIDNAPPED ** (1948) PR:AA
KIDNAPPED ** (1960) PR:AA
KIDNAPPED ***½ (1971, Brit.) PR:AA
KIDNAPPERS, THE
(SEE:THE LITTLE KIDNAPPERS)
KIDNAPPERS, THE ** (1964, US/Phil.) PR:A
KIDNAPPING OF THE PRESIDENT, THE **½ (1980, Can.) PR:O
KID'S LAST FIGHT, THE
(SEE:LIFE OF JIMMY DOLAN, THE)
KID'S LAST RIDE, THE *½ (1941) PR:A
KIEV COMEDY, A *** (1963, USSR) PR:C
KIGEKI DAI SHOGEKI
(SEE:HOT-SPRINGS HOLIDAY)
KIKI * (1931) PR:A
KIL 1
(SEE:SKIN GAME, THE)
KILL **½ (1968, Jap.) PR:C
KILL, THE ** (1968) PR:O
KILL
(SEE:KILL! KILL! KILL!)
KILL A DRAGON *½ (1967) PR:O
KILL AND GO HIDE
(SEE:CHILD, THE)
KILL AND KILL AGAIN ** (1981) PR:O
KILL BABY KILL *** (1966, It.) PR:O
KILL CASTRO
(SEE:CUBA CROSSING)
KILL HER GENTLY *½ (1958, Brit.) PR:O
KILL! KILL! KILL! ** (1972, Fr./Ger./It./Sp.) PR:O
KILL ME TOMORROW ** (1958, Brit.) PR:C
KILL OR BE KILLED ** (1950) PR:C
KILL OR BE KILLED ** (1967, It.) PR:C
KILL OR BE KILLED ** (1980) PR:C
KILL OR CURE ** (1962, Brit.) PR:C
KILL SQUAD zero (1982) PR:O
KILL THE UMPIRE **½ (1950) PR:AA
KILL THEM ALL AND COME BACK ALONE **½ (1970, It./Sp.) PR:O
KILL ZONE zero (1985) PR:O
KILLER, THE
(SEE:MYSTERY RANCH)
KILLER, THE
(SEE:SACRED KNIVES OF VENGEANCE, THE)
KILLER APE ** (1953) PR:AA
KILLER AT LARGE *½ (1936) PR:O
KILLER AT LARGE **½ (1947) PR:O
KILLER BATS
(SEE:DEVIL BAT, THE)
KILLER BEHIND THE MASK, THE
(SEE:SAVAGE WEEKEND)
KILLER DILL * (1947) PR:C
KILLER DINO
(SEE:DINO)
KILLER ELITE, THE ** (1975) PR:O
KILLER FISH zero (1979, It./Braz.) PR:O
KILLER FORCE ** (1975, Switz./Ireland) PR:O
KILLER GRIZZLY
(SEE:GRIZZLY)
KILLER INSIDE ME, THE **½ (1976) PR:O
KILLER IS LOOSE, THE **½ (1956) PR:O
KILLER KLOWNS FROM OUTER SPACE *½ (1988) PR:C-O
KILLER LEOPARD ** (1954) PR:A
KILLER McCOY **½ (1947) PR:A
KILLER ON A HORSE
(SEE:WELCOME TO HARD TIMES)
KILLER PARTY *½ (1986) PR:O
KILLER SHARK *½ (1950) PR:A
KILLER SHREWS, THE *½ (1959) PR:C
KILLER THAT STALKED NEW YORK, THE **½ (1950) PR:O
KILLER WALKS, A * (1952, Brit.) PR:A
KILLER WITH A LABEL
(SEE:ONE TOO MANY)
KILLER WORKOUT zero (1987) PR:O
KILLERS, THE **** (1946) PR:C
KILLERS, THE *** (1964) PR:C-O
KILLERS, THE **½ (1984) PR:O
KILLERS ARE CHALLENGED
(SEE:SECRET AGENT FIREBALL)
KILLER'S CAGE
(SEE:CODE OF SILENCE)
KILLERS FROM KILIMANJARO
(SEE:KILLERS OF KILIMANJARO)
KILLERS FROM SPACE * (1954) PR:A
KILLER'S KISS **½ (1955) PR:C
KILLERS OF KILIMANJARO ** (1960, Brit.) PR:A
KILLERS OF THE PRAIRIE
(SEE:KING OF THE SIERRAS)
KILLERS OF THE WILD *½ (1940) PR:AA
KILLERS THREE * (1968) PR:O
KILLING, THE **** (1956) PR:C
KILLING FIELDS, THE ***½ (1984, Brit.) PR:O
KILLING GAME, THE **½ (1968, Fr.) PR:C
KILLING HEAT ** (1984) PR:O
KILLING HOUR, THE * (1982) PR:O
KILLING KIND, THE **½ (1973) PR:O
KILLING OF A CHINESE BOOKIE, THE *½ (1976) PR:C
KILLING OF ANGEL STREET, THE **½ (1983, Aus.) PR:A
KILLING URGE
(SEE:JET STORM)

KILLPOINT zero (1984) PR:O
KILROY ON DECK
(SEE:FRENCH LEAVE)
KILROY WAS HERE ** (1947) PR:AA
KIM * (1950) PR:AA**
KIMBERLEY JIM ** (1965, South Africa) PR:A
KIN FOLK
(SEE:KINFOLK)
KIND HEARTS AND CORONETS *** (1949, Brit.) PR:A-C**
KIND LADY * (1935) PR:A
KIND LADY *** (1951) PR:O
KIND OF LOVING, A ***½ (1962, Brit.) PR:A-C
KIND STEPMOTHER *½ (1936, Hung.) PR:AA
KINDRED, THE *½ (1987) PR:O
KINEMA NO TENCHI *** (1986, Jap.) PR:A
KINFOLK zero (1970) PR:O
KING, THE
(SEE:ROYAL AFFAIR, A)
KING AND COUNTRY **** (1964, Brit.) PR:C
KING AND FOUR QUEENS, THE ** (1956) PR:A
KING AND HIS MOVIE, A ***½ (1986, Arg.) PR:C
KING AND I, THE *** (1956) PR:AA**
KING AND THE CHORUS GIRL, THE **½ (1937) PR:AA
KING ARTHUR WAS A GENTLEMAN ** (1942, Brit.) PR:A
KING BLANK * (1983) PR:O
KING COBRA
(SEE:JAWS OF SATAN)
KING CREOLE * (1958) PR:A**
KING DAVID ** (1985) PR:C
KING DINOSAUR * (1955) PR:AA
KING FOR A NIGHT **½ (1933) PR:C
KING IN NEW YORK, A **½ (1957, Brit.) PR:A
KING IN SHADOW *** (1961, Ger.) PR:A
KING KELLY OF THE U.S.A * (1934) PR:A
KING KONG *** (1933) PR:A-C**
KING KONG *½ (1976) PR:C-O
KING KONG ESCAPES *½ (1968, Jap.) PR:C
KING KONG LIVES * (1986) PR:C
KING KONG VERSUS GODZILLA *½ (1963, Jap.) PR:C
KING KONG'S COUNTERATTACK
(SEE:KING KONG ESCAPES)
KING LEAR * (1971, Brit./Den.) PR:C**
KING LEAR **** (1988, US/Fr.) PR:A-C
KING MURDER, THE ** (1932) PR:O
KING, MURRAY ** (1969) PR:O
KING OEDIPUS
(SEE:OEDIPUS REX)
KING OF AFRICA
(SEE:ONE STEP TO HELL)
KING OF ALCATRAZ ***½ (1938) PR:C
KING OF BURLESQUE *** (1936) PR:A
KING OF CHINATOWN **½ (1939) PR:O
KING OF COMEDY, THE ** (1983) PR:C**
KING OF DODGE CITY ** (1941) PR:A
KING OF GAMBLERS ** (1937) PR:A
KING OF HEARTS ** (1936, Brit.) PR:AA
KING OF HEARTS **½ (1967, Fr./It.) PR:C
KING OF HOCKEY * (1936) PR:AA
KING OF KINGS ***½ (1961) PR:AA
KING OF MARVIN GARDENS, THE **½ (1972) PR:C-O
KING OF PARIS, THE ** (1934, Brit.) PR:A
KING OF THE ALCATRAZ
(SEE:KING OF ALCATRAZ)
KING OF THE ARENA ** (1933) PR:A
KING OF THE BANDITS **½ (1948) PR:A
KING OF THE BULLWHIP ** (1950) PR:C
KING OF THE CASTLE *½ (1936, Brit.) PR:A
KING OF THE CORAL SEA * (1956, Aus.) PR:C
KING OF THE COWBOYS * (1943) PR:AA**
KING OF THE DAMNED *½ (1936, Brit.) PR:C
KING OF THE GAMBLERS *½ (1948) PR:A
KING OF THE GRIZZLIES ** (1970) PR:AA
KING OF THE GYPSIES ***½ (1978) PR:O
KING OF THE ICE RINK
(SEE:KING OF HOCKEY)
KING OF THE JUNGLE ** (1933) PR:A
KING OF THE JUNGLELAND
(SEE:DARKEST AFRICA)
KING OF THE KHYBER RIFLES
(SEE:BLACK WATCH, THE)
KING OF THE KHYBER RIFLES ***½ (1953) PR:A
KING OF THE LUMBERJACKS *½ (1940) PR:A
KING OF THE MOUNTAIN
(SEE:BEDTIME STORY)
KING OF THE MOUNTAIN ** (1981) PR:O
KING OF THE NEWSBOYS ** (1938) PR:A
KING OF THE PECOS *** (1936) PR:A
KING OF THE RITZ *½ (1933, Brit.) PR:A
KING OF THE ROARING TWENTIES—THE STORY OF ARNOLD ROTHSTEIN **½ (1961) PR:C
KING OF THE ROYAL MOUNTED **½ (1936) PR:A
KING OF THE SIERRAS ** (1938) PR:A
KING OF THE STALLIONS *½ (1942) PR:A
KING OF THE STREETS * (1986) PR:O
KING OF THE TURF * (1939) PR:A**
KING OF THE UNDERWORLD **½ (1939) PR:A-C
KING OF THE UNDERWORLD *½ (1952, Brit.) PR:A
KING OF THE WILD
(SEE:KING OF THE WILD HORSES, THE)
KING OF THE WILD HORSES, THE * (1934) PR:A
KING OF THE WILD HORSES ** (1947) PR:A
KING OF THE WILD STALLIONS **½ (1959) PR:AA
KING OF THE ZOMBIES * (1941) PR:C
KING, QUEEN, KNAVE ** (1972, Ger./US) PR:O
KING RAT **½ (1965) PR:O
KING RICHARD AND THE CRUSADERS ** (1954) PR:A
KING SOLOMON OF BROADWAY ** (1935) PR:A
KING SOLOMON'S MINES *** (1937, Brit.) PR:A
KING SOLOMON'S MINES ** (1950) PR:A**
KING SOLOMON'S MINES **½ (1985) PR:C
KING SOLOMON'S TREASURE * (1978, Can.) PR:A
KING STEPS OUT, THE *** (1936) PR:A
KINGDOM OF THE SPIDERS * (1977) PR:C**
KINGFISH CAPER, THE *½ (1976, South Africa) PR:A
KINGFISHER CAPER, THE
(SEE:KINGFISH CAPER, THE)
KINGS AND DESPERATE MEN ** (1984, Brit.) PR:C
KING'S CUP, THE *½ (1933, Brit.) PR:A
KINGS GO FORTH *** (1958) PR:A
KING'S JESTER, THE ***½ (1947, It.) PR:O
KINGS OF THE ROAD ***½ (1976, Ger.) PR:C
KINGS OF THE SUN ** (1963) PR:O
KING'S PIRATE ** (1967) PR:A
KING'S RHAPSODY **½ (1955, Brit.) PR:A
KINGS ROW ** (1942) PR:C-O**
KING'S THIEF, THE **½ (1955) PR:A
KING'S VACATION, THE **½ (1933) PR:A
KIPPERBANG * (1984, Brit.) PR:A-C**
KIPPS
(SEE:REMARKABLE MR. KIPPS, THE)
KIRI NI MUSEBU YORU
(SEE:HARBOR LIGHT YOKOHAMA)
KIRLIAN WITNESS, THE * (1978) PR:O**
KIRU
(SEE:KILL)
KISENGA, MAN OF AFRICA ** (1952, Brit.) PR:C
KISMET *** (1930) PR:A
KISMET *** (1944) PR:A
KISMET **½ (1955) PR:A
KISS AND KILL
(SEE:BLOOD OF FU MANCHU, THE)
KISS AND MAKE UP ** (1934) PR:A
KISS AND TELL **½ (1945) PR:A
KISS BEFORE DYING, A *** (1956) PR:A
KISS BEFORE THE MIRROR, THE ** (1933) PR:A
KISS FOR CORLISS, A *½ (1949) PR:A
KISS FROM EDDIE, A
(SEE:AROUSERS, THE)
KISS IN THE DARK, A **½ (1949) PR:A
KISS ME
(SEE:LOVE KISS, THE)
KISS ME AGAIN ** (1931) PR:A
KISS ME DEADLY **** (1955) PR:O
KISS ME GOODBYE ** (1935, Brit.) PR:A
KISS ME GOODBYE *½ (1982) PR:C
KISS ME KATE ** (1953) PR:AA**
KISS ME, SERGEANT * (1930, Brit.) PR:A
KISS ME, STUPID *½ (1964) PR:C
KISS MY BUTTERFLY
(SEE:I LOVE YOU, ALICE B. TOKLAS)
KISS OF DEATH **** (1947) PR:C-O
KISS OF EVIL *** (1963, Brit.) PR:C
KISS OF FIRE, THE *** (1940, Fr.) PR:A
KISS OF FIRE ** (1955) PR:A
KISS OF THE SPIDER WOMAN ** (1985, US/Braz.) PR:O**
KISS OF THE TARANTULA * (1975) PR:O
KISS OF THE VAMPIRE, THE
(SEE:KISS OF EVIL)
KISS THE BLOOD OFF MY HANDS *** (1948) PR:C-O
KISS THE BOYS GOODBYE **½ (1941) PR:A
KISS THE BRIDE GOODBYE ** (1944, Brit.) PR:A
KISS THE GIRLS AND MAKE THEM DIE * (1967, US/It.) PR:O
KISS THE OTHER SHEIK * (1968, Fr./It.) PR:C
KISS THEM FOR ME ** (1957) PR:A
KISS TOMORROW GOODBYE * (1950) PR:C-O**
KISSES FOR BREAKFAST ** (1941) PR:A
KISSES FOR MY PRESIDENT **½ (1964) PR:A
KISSES FOR THE PRESIDENT
(SEE:KISSES FOR MY PRESIDENT)
KISSIN' COUSINS ** (1964) PR:A
KISSING BANDIT, THE * (1948) PR:A
KISSING CUP'S RACE *½ (1930, Brit.) PR:A
KIT CARSON ***½ (1940) PR:A
KITCHEN, THE *** (1961, Brit.) PR:A
KITTEN WITH A WHIP zero (1964) PR:C-O
KITTY * (1929, Brit.) PR:A
KITTY *** (1945) PR:A
KITTY AND THE BAGMAN ** (1983, Aus.) PR:O
KITTY FOYLE **½ (1940) PR:A-C
KLANSMAN, THE * (1974) PR:C
KLASSENVERHALTNISSE
(SEE:CLASS RELATIONS)
KLAUN FERDINAND A RAKETA
(SEE:ROCKET TO NOWHERE)
KLEINES ZELT UND GROSSE LIEBE
(SEE:TWO IN A SLEEPING BAG)
KLONDIKE ** (1932) PR:A
KLONDIKE ANNIE **½ (1936) PR:A-C
KLONDIKE FEVER *½ (1980) PR:A
KLONDIKE FURY ** (1942) PR:A
KLONDIKE KATE *½ (1944) PR:A
KLUTE ** (1971) PR:O
KNACK, THE
(SEE:KNACK . . . AND HOW TO GET IT, THE)
KNACK . . . AND HOW TO GET IT, THE **** (1965, Brit.) PR:C
KNAVE OF HEARTS
(SEE:LOVERS HAPPY LOVERS)
KNICKERBOCKER HOLIDAY ** (1944) PR:A
KNIFE IN THE BODY, THE
(SEE:MURDER CLINIC, THE)
KNIFE IN THE WATER ** (1963, Pol.) PR:O**
KNIGHT IN LONDON, A ** (1930, Brit./Ger.) PR:A
KNIGHT OF THE PLAINS ** (1939) PR:A
KNIGHT WITHOUT ARMOR *** (1937, Brit.) PR:A**
KNIGHTRIDERS * (1981) PR:C**
KNIGHTS FOR A DAY *½ (1937, Brit.) PR:A
KNIGHTS OF THE BLACK CROSS
(SEE:KNIGHTS OF THE TEUTONIC ORDER)
KNIGHTS OF THE CITY * (1985) PR:O
KNIGHTS OF THE RANGE **½ (1940) PR:A
KNIGHTS OF THE ROUND TABLE * (1953) PR:A**
KNIGHTS OF THE TEUTONIC ORDER, THE *** (1962, Pol.) PR:A
KNIVES OF THE AVENGER *** (1967, It.) PR:A
KNOCK *½ (1955, Fr.) PR:A
KNOCK ON ANY DOOR ***½ (1949) PR:C
KNOCK ON WOOD *** (1954) PR:A
KNOCKOUT **½ (1941) PR:A
KNOWING MEN ** (1930, Brit.) PR:A
KNUTE ROCKNE—ALL AMERICAN ** (1940) PR:AA**
KOENIGSMARK *** (1935, Fr.) PR:A
KOGDA DEREVYA BYLI BOLSHIMI
(SEE:WHEN THE TREES WERE TALL)
KOHAYAGAWA-KE NO AKI
(SEE:EARLY AUTUMN)
KOJIRO * (1967, Jap.) PR:A**
KOKKINA PHANARIA
(SEE:RED LANTERNS, THE)
KOKOSEI BANCHO
(SEE:WAY OUT, WAY IN)
KOL MAMZER MELECH
(SEE:EVERY BASTARD A KING)
KOLBERG * (1945, Ger.) PR:O
KOLYBELNAYA
(SEE:LULLABY)
KOMMANDO SINAI
(SEE:SINAI COMMANDOS)
KONA COAST ** (1968) PR:C

Finding entries in **THE MOTION PICTURE GUIDE ™**

Years	Volumes
1929-83	Volumes I-IX
1984	Volume IX
1985	1986 ANNUAL
1986	1987 ANNUAL
1987	1988 ANNUAL
1988	1989 ANNUAL

STAR RATINGS

★★★★★	Masterpiece
★★★★	Excellent
★★★	Good
★★	Fair
★	Poor
zero	Without Merit

PARENTAL RECOMMENDATION (PR:)

AA	Good for Children
A	Acceptable for Children
C	Cautionary, some objectionable scenes
O	Objectionable for Children

BOLD: Films on Videocassette

KONEC SPRNA V HOTELU OZON
  (SEE:END OF AUGUST AT THE HOTEL OZONE,
  THE)
KONGA
  (SEE:KONGA, THE WILD STALLION)
KONGA ** (1961, Brit.) PR:C
KONGA, THE WILD STALLION *** (1939) PR:AA
KONGI'S HARVEST ** (1971, US/Nigeria) PR:A
KONGO *** (1932) PR:O
KONSKA OPERA
  (SEE:LEMONADE JOE)
KOREA PATROL ** (1951) PR:C
KORT AR SOMMAREN
  (SEE:SHORT IS THE SUMMER)
KOSHOKU ICHIDAI ONNA
  (SEE:LIFE OF OHARU)
KOTCH *** (1971) PR:A-C
KOTO
  (SEE:TWIN SISTERS OF KYOTO)
KOTO NO TAIYO
  (SEE:NO GREATER LOVE THAN THIS)
KRADETSUT NA PRASKOVI
  (SEE:PEACH THIEF, THE)
KRAKATIT **½ (1948, Czech.) PR:C
KRAKATOA, EAST OF JAVA **½ (1969) PR:A
KRALJ PETROLEJA
  (SEE:RAMPAGE AT APACHE WELLS)
KRAMER VS. KRAMER **** (1979) PR:A
KRASNAYA PALATKA
  (SEE:RED TENT, THE)
KREMLIN LETTER, THE *** (1970) PR:C-O
KRIEGSGERICHT
  (SEE:COURT MARTIAL)
KRIVI PUT
  (SEE:CROOKED ROAD, THE)
KRONOS *** (1957) PR:A
KRONOS
  (SEE:CAPTAIN KRONOS: VAMPIRE HUNTER)
KRUEZER EMDEN
  (SEE:CRUISER EMDEN)
KRULL *½ (1983) PR:A
KRUSH GROOVE ** (1985) PR:O
KUMONOSUJO
  (SEE:THRONE OF BLOOD)
KUNGSLEDEN
  (SEE:OBSESSION)
KUNISADA CHUJI
  (SEE:GAMBLING SAMURAI, THE)
KURAGEJIMA—LEGENDS FROM A SOUTHERN
  ISLAND **½ (1970, Jap.) PR:O
KUREIZI OGON SAKUSEN
  (SEE:LAS VEGAS FREE-FOR-ALL)
KUROBE NO TAIYO
  (SEE:TUNNEL TO THE SUN)
KUROENKO ** (1968, Jap.) PR:O
KVARTERET KORPEN
  (SEE:RAVEN'S END)
KVINNORS VANTAN
  (SEE:SECRETS OF WOMEN)
KWAIDAN **** (1965, Jap.) PR:O
KYOMO WARE OZORANI ARI
  (SEE:TIGER FLIGHT)
KYONETSU NO KISETSU
  (SEE:WEIRD LOVE MAKERS, THE)
KYUBI NO KITSUNE TO TOBIMARU
  (SEE:FOX WITH NINE TAILS, THE)

L

L-SHAPED ROOM, THE **** (1962, Brit.) PR:C
LA BABY SITTER ** (1975, Fr./It./Ger.) PR:O
LA BAI DES ANGES
  (SEE:BAY OF ANGELS)
LA BALANCE **½ (1983, Fr.) PR:O
LA BAMBA **** (1987) PR:C
LA BATAILLE DU RAIL
  (SEE:BATTLE OF THE RAILS)
LA BEAUTE DU DIABLE
  (SEE:BEAUTY AND THE DEVIL)
LA BELLA MUGNAIA
  (SEE:MILLER'S WIFE, THE)
LA BELLE AMERICAINE *** (1961, Fr.) PR:A
LA BELLE CAPTIVE
  (SEE:BEAUTIFUL PRISONER, THE)
LA BELLE EQUIPE
  (SEE:THEY WERE FIVE)
LA BELLE ET LA BETE
  (SEE:BEAUTY AND THE BEAST)
LA BELLE ET LE CAVALIER
  (SEE:MORE THAN A MIRACLE)
LA BETE HUMAINE ***½ (1938, Fr.) PR:A
LA BISBETICA DOMATA
  (SEE:TAMING OF THE SHREW, THE)

LA BOHEME ***½ (1965, It.) PR:A
LA BONNE SOUPE ** (1964, Fr./It.) PR:C
LA BOUM **½ (1983, Fr.) PR:A
LA CAGE ** (1975, Fr.) PR:C
LA CAGE AUX FOLLES **** (1979, Fr./It.) PR:O
LA CAGE AUX FOLLES II ** (1981, It./Fr.) PR:C-O
LA CAGE AUX FOLLES 3: THE WEDDING **
  (1985, Fr./It.) PR:C
LA CASSE
  (SEE:BURGLARS, THE)
LA CHAMBRE VERTE
  (SEE:GREEN ROOM, THE)
LA CHASSE A L'HOMME
  (SEE:MALE HUNT)
LA CHEVRE *** (1985, Fr.) PR:A
LA CHIENNE ***½ (1975, Fr.) PR:C-O
LA CHINOISE *** (1967, Fr.) PR:C-O
LA CINTURA DI CASTITA
  (SEE:ON MY WAY TO THE CRUSADES, I MET A
  GIRL WHO . . .)
LA CITTA PRIGIONIERA
  (SEE:CONQUERED CITY)
LA CITTA SI DIFENDE
  (SEE:FOUR WAYS OUT)
LA COLLECTIONNEUSE *** (1971, Fr.) PR:C-O
LA CONGA NIGHTS *½ (1940) PR:A
LA CONGIUNTURA
  (SEE:ONE MILLION DOLLARS)
LA CROIX DES VIVANTS
  (SEE:CROSS OF THE LIVING)
LA CUCARACHA *½ (1961, Mex.) PR:A
LA DECADE PRODIGIEUSE
  (SEE:TEN DAYS' WONDER)
LA DENTELLIERE
  (SEE:LACEMAKER, THE)
LA DOLCE VITA ***** (1961, It./Fr.) PR:C
LA FABULEUSE AVENTURE DE MARCO POLO
  (SEE:MARCO THE MAGNIFICENT)
LA FAMIGLIA
  (SEE:FAMILY, THE)
LA FEMME D'A COTE
  (SEE:WOMAN NEXT DOOR, THE)
LA FEMME AUX BOTTES ROUGES
  (SEE:WOMAN WITH RED BOOTS, THE)
LA FEMME DE MON POTE
  (SEE:MY BEST FRIEND'S GIRL)
LA FEMME DU BOULANGERS
  (SEE:BAKER'S WIFE, THE)
LA FEMME INFIDELE *** (1969, Fr./It.) PR:C
LA FERME DU PENDU *½ (1946, Fr.) PR:C
LA FETE A HENRIETTE
  (SEE:HOLIDAY FOR HENRIETTE)
LA FEU FOLLET
  (SEE:FIRE WITHIN, THE)
LA FILLE DE MATA HARI
  (SEE:MATA HARI'S DAUGHTER)
LA FILLE DE PUISATIER
  (SEE:WELL-DIGGERS DAUGHTER, THE)
LA FILLE DU DIABLE
  (SEE:DEVIL'S DAUGHTER)
LA FILLE SANS VOILE
  (SEE:GIRL IN THE BIKINI, THE)
LA FIN DU MONDE
  (SEE:THE END OF THE WORLD)
LA FLUTE A SIX SCHTROUMPFS
  (SEE:SMURFS AND THE MAGIC FLUTE, THE)
LA FOLLE DES GRANDEURS
  (SEE:DELUSIONS OF GRANDEUR)
LA FORTUNA DI ESSERE DONNA
  (SEE:LUCKY TO BE A WOMAN)
LA FUGA ** (1966, It.) PR:O
LA GRANDE BOUFFE ** (1973, Fr.) PR:C-O
LA GRANDE BOURGEOISE ** (1977, It.) PR:C
LA GRANDE ILLUSION
  (SEE:GRAND ILLUSION)
LA GUERRE EST FINIE ** (1967, Fr./Swed.) PR:C-O
LA HABANERA ** (1937, Ger.) PR:A
LA HIJA DEL ENGANO
  (SEE:DAUGHTER OF DECEIT)
LA JOVEN
  (SEE:YOUNG ONE, THE)
LA KERMESSE HEROIQUE
  (SEE:CARNIVAL IN FLANDERS)
LA LAMA NEL CORPO
  (SEE:MURDER CLINIC, THE)
LA LEI DEL DESEO
  (SEE:LAW OF DESIRE, THE)
LA LINEA DEL CIELO
  (SEE:SKYLINE)
LA LUNE DANS LE CANIVEAU
  (SEE:THE MOON IN THE GUTTER)
LA MALDICION DE LA MOMIA AZTECA
  (SEE:CURSE OF THE AZTEC MUMMY, THE)
LA MAMAM ET LA PUTAIN
  (SEE:THE MOTHER AND THE WHORE)
LA MANDARINE
  (SEE:SWEET DECEPTION)

LA MANDRAGOLA
  (SEE:MANDRAGOLA)
LA MARCA DEL MUERTO
  (SEE:CREATURE OF THE WALKING DEAD)
LA MARIE DU PORT *** (1951, Fr.) PR:C
LA MARIEE ETAIT EN NOIR
  (SEE:BRIDE WORE BLACK, THE)
LA MARSEILLAISE ***½ (1938, Fr.) PR:A
LA MATERNELLE **½ (1933, Fr.) PR:A
LA MORT EN CE JARDIN
  (SEE:DEATH IN THE GARDEN)
LA MORTADELLA
  (SEE:LADY LIBERTY)
LA MORTE EN DIRECT
  (SEE:DEATHWATCH)
LA MORTE RISALE A IERI SERA
  (SEE:DEATH TOOK PLACE LAST NIGHT)
LA MORTE VIENE DALLA SPAZIO
  (SEE:DAY THE SKY EXPLODED, THE)
LA MUERTA EN EST JARDIN
  (SEE:DEATH IN THE GARDEN)
LA NAVE DE LOS MONSTRUOS zero
  (1959, Mex.) PR:C-O
LA NOTTE ***½ (1961, Fr./It.) PR:C-O
LA NOTTE BRAVA **½ (1962, Fr./It.) PR:O
LA NOTTI BIANCHE
  (SEE:WHITE NIGHTS)
LA NUIT AMERICAINE
  (SEE:DAY FOR NIGHT)
LA NUIT DE VARENNES *** (1983, Fr./It.) PR:O
LA NUIT DES GENERAUX
  (SEE:NIGHT OF THE GENERALS, THE)
LA PARISIENNE *** (1958, Fr./It.) PR:C-O
LA PART DE L'OMBRE
  (SEE:BLIND DESIRE)
LA PASSANTE *** (1983, Fr./Ger.) PR:C
LA PASSION BEATRICE
  (SEE:BEATRICE)
LA PEAU DOUCE
  (SEE:SOFT SKIN, THE)
LA PERMISSION
  (SEE:STORY OF A THREE DAY PASS, THE)
LA PETIT SIRENE *** (1984, Fr.) PR:C
LA PETITE CAFE
  (SEE:PLAYBOY OF PARIS)
LA PLANETE SAUVAGE
  (SEE:FANTASTIC PLANET)
LA POUPEE
  (SEE:DOLL, THE)
LA PRISE DE POUVOIR PAR LOUIS XIV
  (SEE:RISE OF LOUIS XIV, THE)
LA PRISONNIERE ** (1969, Fr./It.) PR:O
LA PROMISE DE L'AUBE
  (SEE:PROMISE AT DAWN)
LA PROVINCIALE
  (SEE:GIRL FROM LORRAINE, THE)
LA QUESTION
  (SEE:QUESTION, THE)
LA RESIDENCIA
  (SEE:HOUSE THAT SCREAMED, THE)
LA RONDE **** (1954, Fr.) PR:O
LA ROSE ESCORCHEE
  (SEE:BLOOD ROSE, THE)
LA ROUTE EST BELLE
  (SEE:ROAD IS FINE, THE)
LA RUE DES AMOURS FACILES
  (SEE:RUN WITH THE DEVIL)
LA SCARLATINE ** (1985, Fr.) PR:C
LA SEGUA *½ (1985, Costa Rica/Mex.) PR:O
LA SIGNORA SENZA CAMELIE
  (SEE:LADY WITHOUT CAMELLIAS, THE)
LA SIRENE DU MISSISSIPPI
  (SEE:MISSISSIPPI MERMAID)
LA STRADA ***** (1956, It.) PR:A-C
LA STRADA PER FORT ALAMO
  (SEE:ROAD TO FORT ALAMO, THE)
LA SYMPHONIE PASTORALE
  (SEE:SYMPHONIE PASTORALE)
LA TENDA ROSSA
  (SEE:RED TENT, THE)
LA TERRA TREMA **** (1947, It.) PR:A
LA TERRAZA
  (SEE:TERRACE, THE)
LA TRAVIATA ** (1968, It.) PR:A
LA TRAVIATA **** (1982) PR:A
LA TRUITE
  (SEE:TROUT, THE)
LA VACCA E IL PRIGIONIERO
  (SEE:COW AND I, THE)
LA VACHE ET LE PRISONNIER
  (SEE:COW AND I, THE)
LA VALLEE DES PHARAOHS
  (SEE:CLEOPATRA'S DAUGHTER)
LA VENGANZA DEL SEXO
  (SEE:CURIOUS DR. HUMPP)
LA VIA LATTEA
  (SEE:THE MILKY WAY)
LA VIACCIA **½ (1962, Fr./It.) PR:C-O

LA VICTOIRE EN CHANTANT
 (SEE:BLACK AND WHITE IN COLOR)
LA VIE CONTINUE ** (1982, Fr.) PR:A
LA VIE DE CHATEAU **½ (1967, Fr.) PR:A
LA VIE DEVANT SOI
 (SEE:MADAME ROSA)
LA VIE EST UN ROMAN
 (SEE:LIFE IS A BED OF ROSES)
LA VIOLENZA E L'MORE
 (SEE:MYTH, THE)
LA VISITA ** (1966, It./Fr.) PR:O
LA VOGLIA MATTA
 (SEE:CRAZY DESIRE)
LA VOIE LACTEE
 (SEE:THE MILKY WAY)
LABBRA ROSSE
 (SEE:RED LIPS)
LABURNUM GROVE ** (1936, Brit.) PR:A
LABYRINTH
 (SEE:REFLECTION OF FEAR, A)
LABYRINTH ****½ (1986) PR:AA
LACEMAKER, THE ***½ (1977, Fr.) PR:O
LACOMBE, LUCIEN *** (1974) PR:O
LAD, THE * (1935, Brit.) PR:A
LAD: A DOG **½ (1962) PR:AA
LAD FROM OUR TOWN ** (1941, USSR) PR:A
LADDIE **½ (1940) PR:AA
LADDIE *** (1935) PR:AA
L'ADDITION *** (1985, Fr.) PR:O
LADIES AND GENTLEMEN, THE FABULOUS STAINS
 **½ (1982) PR:O
LADIES CLUB, THE **½ (1986) PR:O
LADIES COURAGEOUS ** (1944) PR:A
LADIES CRAVE EXCITEMENT ** (1935) PR:A
LADIES' DAY ** (1943) PR:A
LADIES IN DISTRESS *½ (1938) PR:A
LADIES IN LOVE ** (1930) PR:A
LADIES IN LOVE **½ (1936) PR:A
LADIES IN RETIREMENT ***½ (1941) PR:C
LADIES IN WASHINGTON
 (SEE:LADIES OF WASHINGTON)
LADIES LOVE BRUTES ** (1930) PR:A
LADIES LOVE DANGER ** (1935) PR:A
LADIES' MAN **½ (1931) PR:C
LADIES MAN, THE **½ (1961) PR:A
LADIES' MAN ** (1947) PR:A
LADIES MUST LIVE ** (1940) PR:A
LADIES MUST LOVE * (1933) PR:A
LADIES MUST PLAY * (1930) PR:A
LADIES OF LEISURE **½ (1930) PR:A-C
LADIES OF THE BIG HOUSE **½ (1932) PR:A
LADIES OF THE CHORUS ** (1948) PR:A
LADIES OF THE JURY ** (1932) PR:A
LADIES OF THE LOTUS zero (1987, Can.) PR:O
LADIES OF THE MOB
 (SEE:HOUSE OF WOMEN)
LADIES OF THE PARK *** (1964, Fr.) PR:C
LADIES OF WASHINGTON ** (1944, Brit.) PR:A
LADIES ON THE ROCKS *** (1985, Den.) PR:C-O
LADIES SHOULD LISTEN ** (1934) PR:A
LADIES THEY TALK ABOUT ** (1933) PR:A
LADIES WHO DO ** (1964, Brit.) PR:A
L'ADOLESCENT
 (SEE:ADOLESCENT, THE)
LADY AND GENT ** (1932) PR:A
LADY AND THE BANDIT, THE ** (1951) PR:A
LADY AND THE DOCTOR, THE
 (SEE:LADY AND THE MONSTER, THE)
LADY AND THE MOB, THE *** (1939) PR:A
LADY AND THE MONSTER, THE **½ (1944) PR:C
LADY AND THE OUTLAW, THE
 (SEE:BILLY TWO HATS)
LADY AND THE TRAMP ***½ (1955) PR:AA
LADY AT MIDNIGHT ** (1948) PR:A
LADY BE CAREFUL * (1936) PR:A
LADY BE GAY
 (SEE:LAUGH IT OFF)
LADY BE GOOD *** (1941) PR:A
LADY BEHAVE *½ (1937) PR:A
LADY BEWARE
 (SEE:THIRTEENTH GUEST, THE)
LADY BODYGUARD ** (1942) PR:A
LADY BY CHOICE *** (1934) PR:A
LADY CAROLINE LAMB * (1972, Brit./It.) PR:A
LADY CHASER *½ (1946) PR:A
LADY CHATTERLEY'S LOVER ** (1959, Fr.) PR:A

LADY CHATTERLEY'S LOVER zero
 (1981, Fr./Brit.) PR:O
LADY CONFESSES, THE ** (1945) PR:A
LADY CONSENTS, THE **½ (1936) PR:A
LADY CRAVED EXCITEMENT, THE *
 (1950, Brit.) PR:A
LADY DANCES, THE
 (SEE:MERRY WIDOW, THE)
LADY DOCTOR, THE ** (1963, Fr./It./Sp.) PR:C
LADY DRACULA, THE * (1974) PR:O
LADY ESCAPES, THE ** (1937) PR:A
LADY EVE, THE ***** (1941) PR:A
LADY FIGHTS BACK ** (1937) PR:A
LADY FOR A DAY ***½ (1933) PR:A
LADY FOR A NIGHT ** (1941) PR:A
LADY FRANKENSTEIN zero (1971, It.) PR:O
LADY FROM BOSTON, THE
 (SEE:PARDON MY FRENCH)
LADY FROM CHEYENNE **½ (1941) PR:A
LADY FROM CHUNGKING ** (1943) PR:A
LADY FROM LISBON **½ (1942, Brit.) PR:A
LADY FROM LOUISIANA **½ (1941) PR:A
LADY FROM NOWHERE ** (1936) PR:A
LADY FROM NOWHERE zero (1931) PR:A
LADY FROM SHANGHAI, THE ****½ (1948) PR:C
LADY FROM TEXAS, THE **½ (1951) PR:A
LADY FROM THE SEA, THE ** (1929, Brit.) PR:A
LADY GAMBLES, THE **½ (1949) PR:A
LADY GANGSTER * (1942) PR:A
LADY GENERAL, THE ** (1965, Hong Kong) PR:A
LADY GODIVA *½ (1955) PR:A
LADY GODIVA RIDES AGAIN ** (1955, Brit.) PR:A
LADY GREY zero (1980) PR:O
LADY HAMILTON
 (SEE:THAT HAMILTON WOMAN)
LADY HAMILTON *½ (1969, Ger./It./Fr.) PR:O
LADY HAS PLANS, THE **½ (1942) PR:A
LADY ICE *½ (1973) PR:A-C
LADY IN A CAGE *** (1964) PR:O
LADY IN A JAM **½ (1942) PR:A
LADY IN CEMENT ** (1968) PR:O
LADY IN DANGER *½ (1934, Brit.) PR:A
LADY IN DISTRESS **½ (1942, Brit.) PR:A
LADY IN QUESTION, THE *** (1940) PR:A
LADY IN RED, THE *** (1979) PR:O
LADY IN SCARLET, THE * (1935) PR:A
LADY IN THE CAR WITH GLASSES AND A GUN,
 THE **½ (1970, US/Fr.) PR:O
LADY IN THE DARK ***½ (1944) PR:A
LADY IN THE DEATH HOUSE * (1944) PR:A
LADY IN THE FOG
 (SEE:SCOTLAND YARD INVESTIGATOR)
LADY IN THE IRON MASK **½ (1952) PR:A
LADY IN THE LAKE **** (1947) PR:A
LADY IN THE MORGUE **½ (1938) PR:A
LADY IN WHITE ***½ (1988) PR:C
LADY IS A SQUARE, THE ** (1959, Brit.) PR:A
LADY IS FICKLE, THE ** (1948, It.) PR:A
LADY IS WILLING, THE *** (1942) PR:A
LADY IS WILLING, THE **½ (1934, Brit.) PR:A
LADY JANE ***½ (1986) PR:C
LADY JANE GREY *** (1936, Brit.) PR:A
LADY KILLER ***½ (1933) PR:A
LADY KILLERS, THE
 (SEE:LADYKILLERS, THE)
LADY L * (1965, Fr./It.) PR:C
LADY, LET'S DANCE **½ (1944) PR:A
LADY LIBERTY * (1972, It./Fr.) PR:C
LADY LIES, THE *** (1929) PR:A
LADY LUCK ** (1936) PR:A
LADY LUCK ** (1946) PR:A
LADY MISLAID, A ** (1958, Brit.) PR:A
LADY OBJECTS, THE *½ (1938) PR:A
LADY OF BURLESQUE **½ (1943) PR:C
LADY OF CHANCE, A ** (1928) PR:A
LADY OF DECEIT
 (SEE:BORN TO KILL)
LADY OF MONZA, THE * (1970, It.) PR:O
LADY OF MYSTERY
 (SEE:CLOSE CALL FOR BOSTON BLACKIE, A)
LADY OF SCANDAL, THE ** (1930) PR:A
LADY OF SECRETS ** (1936) PR:A
LADY OF THE BOULEVARDS
 (SEE:NANA)
LADY OF THE CAMELIAS *** (1987, Ger.) PR:C
LADY OF THE PAVEMENTS ** (1929) PR:A

LADY OF THE ROSE
 (SEE:BRIDE OF THE REGIMENT)
LADY OF THE SHADOWS
 (SEE:TERROR, THE)
LADY OF THE TROPICS *½ (1939) PR:C
LADY OF VENGEANCE * (1957, Brit.) PR:A
LADY ON A TRAIN ***½ (1945) PR:A
LADY ON THE TRACKS, THE ** (1968, Czech.) PR:A
LADY OSCAR ** (1979, Fr./Jap.) PR:C
LADY PAYS OFF, THE ** (1951) PR:A
LADY POSSESSED * (1952) PR:A
LADY REFUSES, THE * (1931) PR:A
LADY REPORTER
 (SEE:BULLDOG EDITION)
LADY SAYS NO, THE ** (1951) PR:A
LADY SCARFACE ** (1941) PR:A
LADY SINGS THE BLUES ***½ (1972) PR:O
LADY, STAY DEAD zero (1982, Aus.) PR:O
LADY SURRENDERS, A ** (1947, Brit.) PR:A
LADY SURRENDERS, A * (1930) PR:A
LADY TAKES A CHANCE, A **½ (1943) PR:A
LADY TAKES A FLYER, THE ** (1958) PR:A
LADY TAKES A SAILOR, THE ** (1949) PR:A
LADY TO LOVE, A **½ (1930) PR:A
LADY TUBBS ** (1935) PR:A
LADY VANISHES, THE ***** (1938, Brit.) PR:A
LADY VANISHES, THE *½ (1980, Brit.) PR:C
LADY WANTS MINK, THE *½ (1953) PR:A
LADY WHO DARED, THE * (1931) PR:A
LADY WINDERMERE'S FAN
 (SEE:FAN, THE)
LADY WITH A LAMP, THE *** (1951, Brit.) PR:A
LADY WITH A PAST ** (1932) PR:A
LADY WITH RED HAIR ** (1940) PR:A
LADY WITH THE DOG, THE **½
 (1962, USSR) PR:A
LADY WITH THE LAMP, THE
 (SEE:LADY WITH A LAMP, THE)
LADY WITHOUT CAMELLIAS, THE ***
 (1981) PR:C-O
LADY WITHOUT PASSPORT, A ** (1950) PR:A
LADYBUG, LADYBUG **½ (1963) PR:C
LADYHAWKE *** (1985) PR:C
LADYKILLERS, THE **** (1956, Brit.) PR:A-C
LADY'S FROM KENTUCKY, THE ** (1939) PR:A
LADY'S MORALS, A *** (1930) PR:A
LADY'S PROFESSION, A * (1933) PR:A
LAFAYETTE *½ (1963, Fr.) PR:AA
LAFAYETTE ESCADRILLE **½ (1958) PR:A
L'AFRICAN
 (SEE:AFRICAN, THE)
L'AGE D'OR **** (1979, Fr.) PR:C
LAILA
 (SEE:MAKE WAY FOR LILA)
LAIR OF THE WHITE WORM, THE **½
 (1988, Brit.) PR:O
LAKE, THE * (1970, Jap.) PR:O
LAKE OF DRACULA ** (1973, Jap.) PR:O
LAKE PLACID SERENADE ** (1944) PR:A
LAMA NEL CORPO, LA
 (SEE:MURDER CLINIC, THE)
L'AMANT DE LADY CHATTERLEY
 (SEE:LADY CHATTERLEY'S LOVER)
LAMBETH WALK, THE *½ (1940, Brit.) PR:A
LAMENT OF THE PATH, THE
 (SEE:PANTHER PANCHALI)
L'AMORE
 (SEE:WAYS OF LOVE)
L'AMORE DIFFICILE
 (SEE:OF WAYWARD LOVE)
L'AMOUR zero (1973) PR:O
L'AMOUR PAR TERRE
 (SEE:LOVE ON THE GROUND)
LAMP, THE
 (SEE:OUTING, THE)
LAMP IN ASSASSIN MEWS, THE *½
 (1962, Brit.) PR:A
LAMP STILL BURNS, THE *** (1943, Brit.) PR:A
L'ANATRA ALL'ARANCIA
 (SEE:DUCK IN ORANGE SAUCE)
LANCASHIRE LUCK *½ (1937, Brit.) PR:A
LANCELOT AND GUINEVERE
 (SEE:SWORD AND LANCELOT)
LANCELOT DU LAC
 (SEE:LANCELOT OF THE LAKE)
LANCELOT OF THE LAKE *** (1975, Fr.) PR:C
LANCER SPY *** (1937) PR:A

Finding entries in THE MOTION PICTURE GUIDE ™

Years 1929-83	Volumes I-IX
1984	Volume IX
1985	1986 ANNUAL
1986	1987 ANNUAL
1987	1988 ANNUAL
1988	1989 ANNUAL

STAR RATINGS

★★★★★ Masterpiece
★★★★ Excellent
★★★ Good
★★ Fair
★ Poor
zero Without Merit

PARENTAL RECOMMENDATION (PR:)

AA Good for Children
A Acceptable for Children
C Cautionary, some objectionable scenes
O Objectionable for Children

BOLD: Films on Videocassette

LAND AND THE LAW
   (SEE:BLACK MARKET RUSTLERS)
LAND BEFORE TIME, THE ***½ (1988) PR:AA
LAND BEYOND THE LAW **½ (1937) PR:A
LAND OF DOOM zero (1986) PR:C
LAND OF FIGHTING MEN ** (1938) PR:A
LAND OF FURY ** (1955, Brit.) PR:A
LAND OF HUNTED MEN ** (1943) PR:A
LAND OF MISSING MEN, THE ** (1930) PR:A
LAND OF NO RETURN, THE *½ (1981) PR:A
LAND OF OZ
   (SEE:WONDERFUL LAND OF OZ)
LAND OF THE LAWLESS ** (1947) PR:A
LAND OF THE MINOTAUR *½ (1976, Gr.) PR:O
LAND OF THE MISSING MEN
   (SEE:LAND OF MISSING MEN)
LAND OF THE OPEN RANGE ** (1941) PR:A
LAND OF THE OUTLAWS ** (1944) PR:A
LAND OF THE PHARAOHS ** (1955) PR:A-C
LAND OF THE SILVER FOX ** (1928) PR:AA
LAND OF THE SIX GUNS *½ (1940) PR:A
LAND OF WANTED MEN ** (1932) PR:A
LAND RAIDERS ** (1969) PR:C
LAND THAT TIME FORGOT, THE **
   (1975, Brit.) PR:A
LAND UNKNOWN, THE **½ (1957) PR:A
LAND WE LOVE, THE
   (SEE:HERO'S ISLAND)
LAND WITHOUT MUSIC
   (SEE:FORBIDDEN MUSIC)
LANDFALL ** (1953, Brit.) PR:A
LANDLORD, THE *** (1970) PR:C
LANDRU **½ (1963, Fr./It.) PR:O
LANDRUSH * (1946) PR:A
LANDSCAPE IN THE MIST ***½
   (1988, Gr./Fr./It.) PR:C
LANDSCAPE SUICIDE *½ (1986) PR:O
LANDSLIDE ** (1937, Brit.) PR:A
LANGTAN
   (SEE:NIGHT GAMES)
L'ANNEE DERNIERE A MARIENBAD
   (SEE:LAST YEAR AT MARIENBAD)
L'ANNEE DES MEDUSES zero (1987, Fr.) PR:O
LARAMIE *½ (1949) PR:A
LARAMIE MOUNTAINS *½ (1952) PR:A
LARAMIE TRAIL, THE **½ (1944) PR:A
LARCENY *** (1948) PR:A-C
LARCENY IN HER HEART ** (1946) PR:A
LARCENY, INC. *** (1942) PR:A
LARCENY LANE
   (SEE:BLONDE CRAZY)
LARCENY ON THE AIR ** (1937) PR:A
LARCENY STREET *½ (1941, Brit.) PR:A
LARCENY WITH MUSIC ** (1943) PR:A
LARGE ROPE, THE * (1953, Brit.) PR:A
LARGE ROPE, THE
   (SEE:LONG ROPE)
L'ARGENT ***** (1984, Fr./Switz.) PR:O
L'ARMEE DES OMBRES ***½ (1969, Fr./It.) PR:C
LAS CUATRO VERDADES
   (SEE:THREE FABLES OF LOVE)
L'AS DES AS
   (SEE:ACE OF ACES)
LAS RATAS NO DUERMEN DE NOCHE *
   (1974, Sp./Fr.) PR:O
LAS VEGAS 500 MILLIONS
   (SEE:THEY CAME TO ROB LAS VEGAS)
LAS VEGAS FREE-FOR-ALL *½ (1968, Jap.) PR:C
LAS VEGAS HILLBILLYS * (1966) PR:A
LAS VEGAS LADY *½ (1976) PR:A
LAS VEGAS NIGHTS *½ (1941) PR:A
LAS VEGAS SHAKEDOWN **½ (1955) PR:A
LAS VEGAS STORY, THE * (1952) PR:A
LAS VEGAS WEEKEND zero (1985) PR:O
LASCA OF THE RIO GRANDE **½ (1931) PR:A
LASER MAN, THE ** (1988) PR:O
LASERBLAST *½ (1978) PR:C
LASH, THE ** (1930) PR:A
LASH, THE **½ (1934, Brit.) PR:C
LASH OF THE PENITENTES
   (SEE:PENITENTE MURDER CASE)
LASKY JEDNE PLAVOLASKY
   (SEE:LOVES OF A BLONDE)
L'ASSASSIN HABITE AU 21
   (SEE:MURDERER LIVES AT NUMBER 21, THE)
LASSIE, COME HOME **** (1943) PR:AA
LASSIE FROM LANCASHIRE **½
   (1938, Brit.) PR:AA
LASSIE'S GREAT ADVENTURE ** (1963) PR:AA
LASSITER **½ (1984) PR:O
L'ASSOCIE
   (SEE:ASSOCIATE, THE)
LAST ACT OF MARTIN WESTON, THE *½
   (1970, Can./Czech.) PR:C
LAST ADVENTURE, THE *½ (1968, Fr./It.) PR:A
LAST ADVENTURERS, THE *** (1937, Brit.) PR:A
LAST AFFAIR, THE * (1976) PR:A
LAST AMERICAN HERO, THE *** (1973) PR:C

LAST AMERICAN VIRGIN, THE * (1982) PR:O
LAST ANGRY MAN, THE ***½ (1959) PR:A
LAST BANDIT, THE **½ (1949) PR:A
LAST BARRICADE, THE ** (1938, Brit.) PR:C
LAST BATTLE, THE
   (SEE:LE DERNIER COMBAT)
LAST BLITZKRIEG, THE **½ (1958) PR:A
LAST BRIDGE, THE ***½ (1957, Aust.) PR:O
LAST CASTLE, THE
   (SEE:ECHOES OF A SUMMER)
LAST CHALLENGE, THE **½ (1967) PR:A
LAST CHANCE, THE **½ (1937, Brit.) PR:A
LAST CHANCE, THE ***½ (1945, Switz.) PR:A
LAST CHASE, THE ** (1981) PR:A
LAST COMMAND, THE ***½ (1955) PR:A
LAST COMMAND, THE
   (SEE:PRISONER OF JAPAN)
LAST COUPON, THE **½ (1932, Brit.) PR:A
LAST CROOKED MILE, THE **½ (1946) PR:A
LAST CURTAIN, THE *½ (1937, Brit.) PR:A
LAST DANCE, THE ** (1930) PR:A
LAST DAY OF THE WAR, THE **
   (1969, US/It./Sp.) PR:A
LAST DAYS OF BOOT HILL ** (1947) PR:A
LAST DAYS OF DOLWYN, THE **½
   (1949, Brit.) PR:A
LAST DAYS OF MAN ON EARTH, THE *½
   (1975, Brit.) PR:O
LAST DAYS OF MUSSOLINI *** (1974, It.) PR:A
LAST DAYS OF PLANET EARTH
   (SEE:PROPHECIES OF NOSTRADAMUS:
   CATASTROPHE 1999)
LAST DAYS OF POMPEII, THE **½
   (1960, It.) PR:A
LAST DAYS OF POMPEII, THE *** (1935) PR:A
LAST DAYS OF SODOM AND GOMORRAH, THE
   (SEE:SODOM AND GOMORRAH)
LAST DETAIL, THE **** (1973) PR:O
LAST DRAGON, THE **½ (1985) PR:C
LAST EMBRACE **½ (1979) PR:O
LAST EMPEROR, THE **** (1987) PR:C
LAST ESCAPE, THE ** (1970, Brit.) PR:A
LAST EXPRESS, THE ** (1938) PR:A
LAST FIGHT, THE *½ (1983) PR:O
LAST FIGHT, THE *** (1931) PR:A
LAST FLIGHT OF NOAH'S ARK, THE **
   (1980) PR:AA
LAST FOUR DAYS, THE
   (SEE:LAST DAYS OF MUSSOLINI)
LAST FRONTIER, THE ** (1955) PR:A
LAST FRONTIER UPRISING *½ (1947) PR:A
LAST GAME, THE *** (1964, USSR) PR:C
LAST GANGSTER, THE *** (1937) PR:A
LAST GANGSTER, THE
   (SEE:ROGER TOUHY, GANGSTER)
LAST GENTLEMAN, THE **½ (1934) PR:A
LAST GLORY OF TROY
   (SEE:AVENGER, THE)
LAST GRAVE, THE
   (SEE:NAVAJO RUN)
LAST GREAT TREASURE, THE
   (SEE:MOTHER LODE)
LAST GRENADE, THE ** (1970, Brit.) PR:C
LAST GUNFIGHTER, THE * (1961, Can.) PR:A
LAST GUNFIGHTER, THE
   (SEE:DEATH OF A GUNFIGHTER)
LAST HARD MEN, THE **½ (1976) PR:O
LAST HERO
   (SEE:LONELY ARE THE BRAVE)
LAST HILL, THE ** (1945, USSR) PR:A
LAST HOLIDAY *** (1950, Brit.) PR:A
LAST HORROR FILM, THE zero (1984) PR:O
LAST HORSEMAN, THE ** (1944) PR:A
LAST HOUR, THE **½ (1930, Brit.) PR:A
LAST HOUSE ON DEAD END STREET zero
   (1977) PR:O
LAST HOUSE ON THE LEFT **½ (1972) PR:O
LAST HOUSE ON THE LEFT, PART II
   (SEE:TWITCH OF THE DEATH NERVE)
LAST HUNT, THE ***½ (1956) PR:C
LAST HUNTER, THE * (1984, It.) PR:O
LAST HURRAH, THE ****½ (1958) PR:A
LAST JOURNEY, THE ** (1936, Brit.) PR:A
LAST LOAD, THE ** (1948, Brit.) PR:AA
LAST MAN ** (1932) PR:A
LAST MAN, THE **½ (1968, Fr.) PR:C
LAST MAN ON EARTH, THE ** (1964, US/It.) PR:O
LAST MAN TO HANG, THE *½ (1956, Brit.) PR:C
LAST MARRIED COUPLE IN AMERICA, THE **
   (1980) PR:O
LAST MERCENARY, THE **
   (1969, It./Sp./Ger.) PR:C
LAST METRO, THE ***½ (1981, Fr.) PR:C-O
LAST MILE, THE ***½ (1932) PR:A
LAST MILE, THE *** (1959) PR:C
LAST MOMENT, THE * (1954, Brit.) PR:A
LAST MOMENT, THE zero (1966) PR:C
LAST MOVIE, THE * (1971) PR:O

LAST MUSKETEER, THE ** (1952) PR:A
LAST NIGHT AT THE ALAMO *** (1984) PR:O
LAST OF MRS. CHEYNEY, THE **½ (1929) PR:A
LAST OF MRS. CHEYNEY, THE ** (1937) PR:A
LAST OF SHEILA, THE * (1973) PR:C
LAST OF SUMMER
   (SEE:EARLY AUTUMN)
LAST OF THE BADMEN ** (1957) PR:A
LAST OF THE BUCCANEERS **½ (1950) PR:A
LAST OF THE CAVALRY, THE
   (SEE:ARMY GIRL)
LAST OF THE CLINTONS, THE * (1935) PR:A
LAST OF THE COMANCHES ** (1952) PR:A
LAST OF THE COWBOYS, THE
   (SEE:GREAT SMOKEY ROADBLOCK, THE)
LAST OF THE DESPERADOES **½ (1956) PR:A
LAST OF THE DUANES *½ (1930) PR:A
LAST OF THE DUANES ** (1941) PR:A
LAST OF THE FAST GUNS, THE ** (1958) PR:A
LAST OF THE KNUCKLEMEN, THE ***
   (1981, Aus.) PR:A
LAST OF THE LONE WOLF ** (1930) PR:A
LAST OF THE MOHICANS, THE **** (1936) PR:A
LAST OF THE PAGANS ** (1936) PR:A
LAST OF THE PONY RIDERS ** (1953) PR:A
LAST OF THE RED HOT LOVERS *½ (1972) PR:A
LAST OF THE REDMEN **½ (1947) PR:AA
LAST OF THE REDSKINS
   (SEE:LAST OF THE REDMEN)
LAST OF THE RENEGADES **
   (1966, Fr./It./Ger./Yugo.) PR:A
LAST OF THE SECRET AGENTS?, THE *
   (1966) PR:A
LAST OF THE VIKINGS, THE *½ (1962, Fr./It.) PR:A
LAST OF THE WARRENS, THE * (1936) PR:A
LAST OF THE WILD HORSES ** (1948) PR:A
LAST OUTLAW, THE *** (1936) PR:A
LAST OUTPOST, THE **½ (1935) PR:A
LAST OUTPOST, THE *** (1951) PR:A
LAST PAGE, THE
   (SEE:MAN BAIT)
LAST PARADE, THE ** (1931) PR:A
LAST PERFORMANCE, THE *** (1929) PR:C
LAST PICTURE SHOW, THE ***** (1971) PR:C-O
LAST PORNO FLICK, THE zero (1974) PR:O
LAST POSSE, THE **½ (1953) PR:A
LAST POST, THE *½ (1929, Brit.) PR:C
LAST REBEL, THE * (1971) PR:C
LAST REBEL, THE ** (1961, Mex.) PR:C
LAST REMAKE OF BEAU GESTE, THE *½
   (1977) PR:C
LAST RESORT, THE zero (1986) PR:O
LAST RHINO, THE ** (1961, Brit.) PR:AA
LAST RIDE, THE * (1944) PR:A
LAST RIDE, THE zero (1932) PR:A
LAST RITES zero (1980) PR:O
LAST RITES * (1988) PR:O
LAST ROMAN, THE
   (SEE:FIGHT FOR ROME-PART 1)
LAST ROSE OF SUMMER, THE *½ (1937, Brit.) PR:A
LAST ROUND-UP, THE *½ (1934) PR:A
LAST ROUND-UP, THE ***½ (1947) PR:AA
LAST RUN, THE ** (1971) PR:A
LAST SAFARI, THE ** (1967, Brit.) PR:A
LAST SHOT YOU HEAR, THE * (1969, Brit.) PR:C
LAST STAGE, THE
   (SEE:LAST STOP, THE)
LAST STAGECOACH WEST, THE ** (1957) PR:A
LAST STAND, THE ** (1938) PR:A
LAST STARFIGHTER, THE ****½ (1984) PR:C
LAST STOP, THE **** (1949, Pol.) PR:O
LAST STRAW, THE *** (1987, Can.) PR:O
LAST SUMMER *** (1969) PR:O
LAST SUNSET, THE *** (1961) PR:C-O
LAST TEMPTATION OF CHRIST, THE ****
   (1988) PR:O
LAST TEN DAYS, THE *** (1956, Ger.) PR:A
LAST TIME I SAW ARCHIE, THE **½ (1961) PR:A
LAST TIME I SAW PARIS, THE ***½ (1954) PR:A
LAST TOMAHAWK, THE ** (1965, Ger./It./Sp.) PR:A
LAST TOMB OF LIGEIA
   (SEE:TOMB OF LIGEIA, THE)
LAST TRAIL, THE *½ (1934) PR:A
LAST TRAIN FROM BOMBAY *½ (1952) PR:A
LAST TRAIN FROM GUN HILL ***½ (1959) PR:C
LAST TRAIN FROM MADRID, THE *** (1937) PR:A
LAST TYCOON, THE **½ (1976) PR:C
LAST UNICORN, THE **½ (1982) PR:AA
LAST VALLEY, THE ** (1971, Brit.) PR:A
LAST VICTIM, THE
   (SEE:FORCED ENTRY)
LAST VOYAGE, THE ** (1960) PR:A
LAST WAGON, THE *** (1956) PR:C
LAST WALTZ, THE ** (1936, Brit.) PR:A
LAST WAR, THE ** (1962, Jap.) PR:C
LAST WARNING, THE *½ (1929) PR:A
LAST WARNING, THE *½ (1938) PR:A

LAST WARRIOR, THE
(SEE:FLAP)
LAST WAVE, THE **** (1978, Aus.) PR:A
LAST WILL OF DR. MABUSE, THE
(SEE:TESTAMENT OF DR. MABUSE, THE)
LAST WOMAN OF SHANG, THE **
(1964, Hong Kong) PR:A
LAST WOMAN ON EARTH, THE *½ (1960) PR:A
LAST WORD, THE **½ (1979) PR:A
LAST YEAR AT MARIENBAD ****
(1962, Fr./It.) PR:C
L'ATALANTE ***** (1947, Fr.) PR:C
LATE AT NIGHT * (1946, Brit.) PR:A
LATE AUTUMN *** (1973, Jap.) PR:A
LATE EDWINA BLACK, THE
(SEE:OBSESSED)
LATE EXTRA *½ (1935, Brit.) PR:A
LATE GEORGE APLEY, THE **** (1947) PR:A
LATE LIZ, THE zero (1971) PR:A
LATE SHOW, THE ***½ (1977) PR:A-C
LATE SUMMER BLUES *** (1988, Israel) PR:C
LATENT IMAGE *** (1988, Chile) PR:O
LATIN LOVE **½ (1930, Brit.) PR:A
LATIN LOVERS *** (1953) PR:A
LATIN QUARTER
(SEE:FRENZY)
LATINO ** (1985) PR:C-O
LATITUDE ZERO ** (1969, US/Jap.) PR:AA
L'ATLANTIDE
(SEE:JOURNEY BENEATH THE DESERT)
L'ATLANTIDE
(SEE:MISTRESS OF ATLANTIS, THE)
L'ATTENTAT
(SEE:FRENCH CONSPIRACY, THE)
LAUGH AND GET RICH ** (1931) PR:A
LAUGH IT OFF **½ (1940, Brit.) PR:A
LAUGH IT OFF * (1939) PR:A
LAUGH PAGLIACCI ** (1948, It.) PR:A
LAUGH YOUR BLUES AWAY * (1943) PR:A
LAUGHING ANNE zero (1954, Brit./US) PR:A
LAUGHING AT DANGER *½ (1940) PR:A
LAUGHING AT LIFE *½ (1933) PR:A
LAUGHING AT TROUBLE ** (1937) PR:A
LAUGHING BOY * (1934) PR:A
LAUGHING IN THE SUNSHINE *½
(1953, Brit./Swed.) PR:A
LAUGHING IRISH EYES ** (1936) PR:A
LAUGHING LADY, THE ** (1930) PR:A
LAUGHING LADY, THE ** (1950, Brit.) PR:A
LAUGHING POLICEMAN, THE **½ (1973) PR:O
LAUGHING SINNERS ** (1931) PR:C
LAUGHTER ***** (1930) PR:A-C
LAUGHTER HOUSE ** (1984, Brit.) PR:C
LAUGHTER IN HELL * (1933) PR:A
LAUGHTER IN PARADISE **½ (1951, Brit.) PR:AA
LAUGHTER IN THE AIR
(SEE:MYRT AND MARGE)
LAURA ***** (1944) PR:A
LAUTLOSE WAFFEN
(SEE:DEFECTOR, THE)
LAVENDER HILL MOB, THE **** (1951, Brit.) PR:A
L'AVEU
(SEE:CONFESSION, THE)
LAVIRINT SMRTI
(SEE:FLAMING FRONTIER)
L'AVVENTURA **** (1960, It./Fr.) PR:A
L'AVVENTURIERO
(SEE:ROVER, THE)
LAW, THE
(SEE:LAW AND ORDER)
LAW AND DISORDER **½ (1940, Brit.) PR:A
LAW AND DISORDER *** (1958, Brit.) PR:A
LAW AND DISORDER *** (1974) PR:O
LAW AND JAKE WADE, THE *** (1958) PR:A
LAW AND LAWLESS ** (1932) PR:A
LAW AND LEAD ** (1937) PR:A
LAW AND ORDER ***½ (1932) PR:A
LAW AND ORDER
(SEE:FUGITIVE SHERIFF, THE)
LAW AND ORDER
(SEE:FAST BULLETS)
LAW AND ORDER ** (1940) PR:A
LAW AND ORDER *½ (1942) PR:A
LAW AND ORDER *½ (1953) PR:A
LAW AND THE LADY, THE *½ (1951) PR:A
LAW AND TOMBSTONE, THE
(SEE:HOUR OF THE GUN)

LAW, THE
(SEE:WHERE THE HOT WIND BLOWS)
LAW BEYOND THE RANGE ** (1935) PR:A
LAW COMES TO TEXAS, THE **½ (1939) PR:A
LAW COMMANDS, THE * (1938) PR:A
LAW DEMANDS, THE
(SEE:RECKLESS RIDER)
LAW FOR TOMBSTONE *½ (1937) PR:A
LAW IN HER HANDS, THE * (1936) PR:A
LAW IS THE LAW, THE **½ (1959, Fr.) PR:A
LAW MEN * (1944) PR:A
LAW OF DESIRE **½ (1987, Sp.) PR:O
LAW OF THE BADLANDS ** (1950) PR:A
LAW OF THE BARBARY COAST *½ (1949) PR:A
LAW OF THE GOLDEN WEST **½ (1949) PR:A
LAW OF THE JUNGLE *½ (1942) PR:A
LAW OF THE LASH ** (1947) PR:A
LAW OF THE LAWLESS **½ (1964) PR:A
LAW OF THE NORTH * (1932) PR:AA
LAW OF THE NORTHWEST *½ (1943) PR:A
LAW OF THE PAMPAS ** (1939) PR:A
LAW OF THE PANHANDLE *½ (1950) PR:A
LAW OF THE PLAINS *** (1938) PR:A
LAW OF THE RANGE ** (1941) PR:A
LAW OF THE RANGER * (1937) PR:A
LAW OF THE RIO
(SEE:RIDERS OF THE RIO)
LAW OF THE RIO GRANDE * (1931) PR:A
LAW OF THE SADDLE * (1944) PR:A
LAW OF THE SEA zero (1932) PR:A
LAW OF THE TEXAN * (1938) PR:A
LAW OF THE TIMBER *½ (1941) PR:A
LAW OF THE TONG zero (1931) PR:A
LAW OF THE TROPICS *½ (1941) PR:A
LAW OF THE UNDERWORLD *½ (1938) PR:A
LAW OF THE VALLEY ** (1944) PR:A
LAW OF THE WEST zero (1949) PR:A
LAW RIDES, THE ** (1936) PR:A
LAW RIDES AGAIN, THE *½ (1943) PR:A
LAW RIDES WEST, THE
(SEE:SANTA FE TRAIL, THE)
LAW VS. BILLY THE KID, THE ** (1954) PR:A
LAW WEST OF TOMBSTONE, THE **½ (1938) PR:A
LAWFUL LARCENY ** (1930) PR:A
LAWLESS, THE *** (1950) PR:A-C
LAWLESS BORDER ** (1935) PR:A
LAWLESS BREED, THE ** (1946) PR:AA
LAWLESS BREED, THE *** (1952) PR:A
LAWLESS CLAN
(SEE:LAWLESS BREED, THE)
LAWLESS CODE ** (1949) PR:A
LAWLESS COWBOYS * (1952) PR:A
LAWLESS EIGHTIES, THE **½ (1957) PR:C
LAWLESS EMPIRE * (1946) PR:A
LAWLESS FRONTIER, THE ** (1935) PR:A
LAWLESS LAND *½ (1937) PR:A
LAWLESS NINETIES, THE ** (1936) PR:A
LAWLESS PLAINSMEN *½ (1942) PR:A
LAWLESS RANGE ** (1935) PR:A
LAWLESS RIDER, THE ** (1954) PR:A
LAWLESS RIDERS * (1936) PR:A
LAWLESS STREET, A *** (1955) PR:A
LAWLESS VALLEY **½ (1938) PR:A
LAWLESS WOMAN, THE *½ (1931) PR:A
LAWMAN * (1971) PR:C
LAWMAN IS BORN, A *** (1937) PR:A
LAWRENCE OF ARABIA ***** (1962, Brit.) PR:C
LAWTON STORY, THE ** (1949) PR:A
LAWYER, THE ** (1969) PR:O
LAWYER MAN ** (1933) PR:A
LAWYER'S SECRET, THE *½ (1931) PR:A
LAXDALE HALL
(SEE:SCOTCH ON THE ROCKS)
LAY THAT RIFLE DOWN *½ (1955) PR:A
LAZARILLO * (1963, Sp.) PR:A
LAZY BONES
(SEE:HALLELUJAH, I'M A BUM)
LAZY RIVER *½ (1934) PR:A
LAZYBONES **½ (1935, Brit.) PR:A
LE AMICHE *** (1962, It.) PR:C
LE AVVENTURE E GLI AMORI DI MIGUEL
CERVANTES
(SEE:YOUNG REBEL, THE)
LE BAL **½ (1984, Fr./It./Algeria) PR:A
LE BEAU MARIAGE **** (1982, Fr.) PR:C-O
LE BEAU SERGE ***½ (1959, Fr.) PR:C-O

LE BLE EN HERBE
(SEE:GAME OF LOVE, THE)
LE BON PLAISIR **½ (1984, Fr.) PR:A-C
LE BONHEUR **½ (1966, Fr.) PR:C
LE BOUCHER **½ (1971, Fr./It.) PR:O
LE CAPORAL EPINGLE
(SEE:ELUSIVE CORPORAL, THE)
LE CAVE SE REBIFFE
(SEE:COUNTERFEITERS OF PARIS, THE)
LE CERVEAU
(SEE:BRAIN, THE)
LE CHARME DISCRET DE LA BOURGEOISIE
(SEE:DISCREET CHARM OF THE BOURGEOISIE,
THE)
LE CHAT
(SEE:CAT, THE)
LE CHAT DANS LE SAC
(SEE:CAT IN THE SACK, THE)
LE CHEVAL D'ORGEUIL
(SEE:HORSE OF PRIDE)
LE CIEL EST A VOUS *** (1957, Fr.) PR:A
LE CLOCHARD
(SEE:MAGNIFICENT TRAMP, THE)
LE COMTE DE MONTE CRISTO
(SEE:STORY OF THE COUNT OF MONTE CRISTO,
THE)
LE CORBEAU
(SEE:RAVEN, THE)
LE CORNIAUD
(SEE:SUCKER, THE)
LE CRABE TAMBOUR *** (1984, Fr.) PR:O
LE CRIME DE MONSIEUR LANGE
(SEE:CRIME OF MONSIEUR LANGE, THE)
LE DANGER VIENT DE L'ESCAPE
(SEE:DAY THE SKY EXPLODED, THE)
LE DENIER MILLIARDAIRE **½ (1934, Fr.) PR:A
LE DERNIER COMBAT *** (1984, Fr.) PR:O
LE DESERT DES TARTARES
(SEE:DESERT OF THE TARTARS, THE)
LE DESERT ROUGE
(SEE:RED DESERT)
LE DIABLE AU CORPS
(SEE:DEVIL IN THE FLESH, THE)
LE DIABLE PAR LA QUEUE
(SEE:DEVIL BY THE TAIL, THE)
LE DIABLE PROBABLEMENT
(SEE:DEVIL PROBABLY, THE)
LE DIABOLIQUE DOCTEUR MABUSE
(SEE:THOUSAND EYES OF DR. MABUSE, THE)
LE DISTRAIT
(SEE:DAYDREAMER, THE)
LE FANTOME DE LA LIBERTE
(SEE:PHANTOM OF LIBERTY, THE)
LE FARCEUR
(SEE:JOKER, THE)
LE FATE
(SEE:QUEENS, THE)
LE GAI SAVOIR **** (1968, Fr.) PR:A
LE GENDARME ET LES EXTRATERRESTRES zero
(1978, Fr.) PR:C
LE GENTLEMAN DE COCODY
(SEE:MAN FROM COCODY)
LE GORILLE A MORDU L'ARCHEVEQUE
(SEE:DEADLY DECOYS, THE)
LE GRAND BLEU
(SEE:BIG BLUE, THE)
LE GRAND CHEF
(SEE:BIG CHIEF, THE)
LE GRAND CHEMIN
(SEE:GRAND HIGHWAY, THE)
LE GRAND JEU
(SEE:BIG GAME, THE)
LE JEUNE FOLLE
(SEE:DESPERATE DECISION)
LE JEUNE MARIE ** (1985, Fr.) PR:C
LE JOUER D'ECHECS
(SEE:DEVIL IS AN EMPRESS, THE)
LE JOUEUR
(SEE:GAMBLER, THE)
LE JOUR ET L'HEURE
(SEE:DAY AND THE HOUR, THE)
LE JOUR SE LEVE
(SEE:DAYBREAK)
LE JOURNAL D'UNE CURE DE CAMPAGNE
(SEE:DIARY OF A COUNTRY PRIEST)
LE JUGE ET L'ASSASSIN
(SEE:JUDGE AND THE ASSASSIN, THE)

Finding entries in THE MOTION PICTURE GUIDE ™

Years 1929-83	Volumes I-IX
1984	Volume IX
1985	1986 ANNUAL
1986	1987 ANNUAL
1987	1988 ANNUAL
1988	1989 ANNUAL

STAR RATINGS

★★★★★ Masterpiece
★★★★ Excellent
★★★ Good
★★ Fair
★ Poor
zero Without Merit

PARENTAL RECOMMENDATION (PR:)

AA Good for Children
A Acceptable for Children
C Cautionary, some objectionable scenes
O Objectionable for Children

BOLD: Films on Videocassette

LE JUPON ROUGE
  (SEE:MANUELA'S LOVES)
LE LEOPARD ** (1985, Fr.) PR:O
LE LONG DES TROITTORS
  (SEE:DIARY OF A BAD GIRL)
LE MAGNIFIQUE
  (SEE:MAGNIFICENT ONE, THE)
LE MANS * (1971) PR:A**
LE MARIAGE DE FIGARO
  (SEE:MARRIAGE OF FIGARO, THE)
LE MEPRIS
  (SEE:CONTEMPT)
LE MERAVIGLIOSE AVVENTURE DI MARCO POLO
  (SEE:MARCO THE MAGNIFICENT)
LE MERCENARIRE
  (SEE:SWORDSMAN OF SIENA, THE)
LE MILLION
  (SEE:THE MILLION)
LE MIROIR A DEUX FACES
  (SEE:MIRROR HAS TWO FACES, THE)
LE MONDAT
  (SEE:MANDABI)
LE MONDE TREMBLERA ** (1939, Fr.) PR:A
LE NOTTI BIANCHE
  (SEE:WHITE NIGHTS)
LE PASSAGER DE LA PLUIE
  (SEE:RIDER ON THE RAIN)
LE PASSE MURAILLE
  (SEE:MR. PEEK-A-BOO)
LE PAYS BLEU
  (SEE:BLUE COUNTRY, THE)
LE PERE TRANQUILLE
  (SEE:MR. ORCHID)
LE PETIT SOLDAT **½ (1965, Fr.) PR:C
LE PETIT THEATRE DE JEAN RENOIR ****
  (1974, Fr.) PR:C
LE PLAISIR ***½ (1954, Fr.) PR:C-O
LE PUITS AUX TROIS VERITES
  (SEE:THREE FACES OF SIN)
LE QUATTRO VERITA
  (SEE:THREE FABLES OF LOVE)
LE ROI DE COEUR
  (SEE:KING OF HEARTS)
LE ROMAN D'UN TRICHEUR
  (SEE:STORY OF A CHEAT, THE)
LE ROUBLE A DEUX FACES
  (SEE:DAY THE HOTLINE GOT HOT, THE)
LE ROUGE AUX LEVRES
  (SEE:DAUGHTERS OF DARKNESS)
LE ROUGE ET LA NOIR
  (SEE:THE RED AND THE BLACK)
LE ROUTE DE CORINTH
  (SEE:WHO'S GOT THE BLACK BOX?)
LE SANG D'UN POETE
  (SEE:BLOOD OF A POET)
LE SERPENT
  (SEE:SERPENT, THE)
LE SILENCE EST D'OR
  (SEE:MAN ABOUT TOWN)
LE SOUFFLE AU COEUR
  (SEE:MURMUR OF THE HEART)
LE TEMPS DES ASSASSINS
  (SEE:DEADLIER THAN THE MALE)
LE TESTAMENT DU DR. MABUSE
  (SEE:TESTAMENT OF DR. MABUSE, THE)
LE VENT D'EST
  (SEE:WIND FROM THE EAST)
LE VICOMTE REGLE SES COMPTES
  (SEE:VISCOUNT, THE)
LE VIOL *** (1968, Fr./Swed.) PR:O
LE VOILE BLEU
  (SEE:BLUE VEIL, THE)
LE VOLEUR
  (SEE:THIEF OF PARIS, THE)
LE VOYAGE EN AMERIQUE
  (SEE:VOYAGE TO AMERICA)
LE VOYOU
  (SEE:CROOK, THE)
LEAD LAW
  (SEE:CROOKED TRAIL)
LEADBELLY ***½ (1976) PR:C-O
LEADVILLE GUNSLINGER *½ (1952) PR:A
LEAGUE OF FRIGHTENED MEN * (1937) PR:A
LEAGUE OF GENTLEMEN, THE ***½
  (1961, Brit.) PR:A-C
LEAP INTO THE VOID *** (1982, It.) PR:O
LEAP OF FAITH *** (1931, Brit.) PR:A
LEAP YEAR *½ (1932, Brit.) PR:A
LEARN, BABY, LEARN
  (SEE:LEARNING TREE, THE)
LEARNING TREE, THE **½ (1969) PR:O
LEASE OF LIFE *** (1954, Brit.) PR:A
LEATHER AND NYLON ** (1969, Fr./It.) PR:A-C
LEATHER BOYS, THE * (1965, Brit.) PR:O**
LEATHER BURNERS, THE ** (1943) PR:A
LEATHER GLOVES ** (1948) PR:A
LEATHER-PUSHERS, THE *½ (1940) PR:A
LEATHER SAINT, THE ** (1956) PR:A

LEATHERNECK, THE *½ (1929) PR:A
LEATHERNECKING *½ (1930) PR:A
LEATHERNECKS HAVE LANDED, THE *½
  (1936) PR:A
LEAVE HER TO HEAVEN *** (1946) PR:O
LEAVE IT TO BLANCHE * (1934, Brit.) PR:A
LEAVE IT TO BLONDIE ** (1945) PR:A
LEAVE IT TO HENRY ** (1949) PR:A
LEAVE IT TO ME **½ (1933, Brit.) PR:A
LEAVE IT TO ME ** (1937, Brit.) PR:A
LEAVE IT TO SMITH *½ (1934) PR:A
LEAVE IT TO THE IRISH *½ (1944) PR:A
LEAVE IT TO THE MARINES * (1951) PR:A
LEAVENWORTH CASE, THE * (1936) PR:A
LEBENSBORN
  (SEE:ORDERED TO LOVE)
LEBENSZEICHEN
  (SEE:SIGNS OF LIFE)
L'ECLIPSE
  (SEE:ECLIPSE)
L'ECLISSE
  (SEE:ECLIPSE)
L'ECOLE BUISSONIERE
  (SEE:PASSION FOR LIFE)
LEDA
  (SEE:WEB OF PASSION)
LEECH WOMAN, THE ** (1960) PR:C
LEFT HAND OF GOD, THE ***½ (1955) PR:A
LEFT-HANDED GUN, THE ***½ (1958) PR:C
LEFT-HANDED LAW *½ (1937) PR:A
LEFT-HANDED WOMAN, THE ***
  (1980, Ger.) PR:C-O
LEFT, RIGHT AND CENTRE **½ (1959) PR:A
LEFTOVER LADIES * (1931) PR:A
LEGACY **½ (1976) PR:O
LEGACY, THE *½ (1979, Brit.) PR:O
LEGACY OF A SPY
  (SEE:A DOUBLE MAN)
LEGACY OF BLOOD * (1973) PR:O
LEGACY OF BLOOD zero (1978) PR:O
LEGACY OF MAGGIE WALSH
  (SEE:LEGACY, THE)
LEGACY OF THE 500,000, THE **½
  (1964, Jap.) PR:A
LEGAL EAGLES ** (1986) PR:C
LEGAL LARCENY
  (SEE:SILVER CITY RAIDERS)
LEGEND * (1985, Brit.) PR:A**
LEGEND IN LEOTARDS
  (SEE:RETURN OF CAPTAIN INVINCIBLE, THE)
LEGEND OF A BANDIT, THE ** (1945, Mex.) PR:A
LEGEND OF BILLIE JEAN, THE * (1985) PR:O
LEGEND OF BLOOD MOUNTAIN, THE *
  (1965) PR:O
LEGEND OF BOGGY CREEK, THE ** (1973) PR:A-C
LEGEND OF COUGAR CANYON ** (1974) PR:A
LEGEND OF FRENCHIE KING, THE *
  (1971, Fr./It./Sp./Brit.) PR:C**
LEGEND OF HELL HOUSE, THE *
  (1973, Brit.) PR:C**
LEGEND OF HILLBILLY JOHN, THE
  (SEE:WHO FEARS THE DEVIL)
LEGEND OF LOBO, THE **½ (1962) PR:AA
LEGEND OF LYLAH CLARE, THE **½
  (1968) PR:A-C
LEGEND OF NIGGER CHARLEY, THE **
  (1972) PR:C
LEGEND OF ROBIN HOOD, THE
  (SEE:CHALLENGE FOR ROBIN HOOD)
LEGEND OF SPIDER FOREST, THE *
  (1976, Brit.) PR:C**
LEGEND OF SURAM FORTRESS *
  (1985, USSR) PR:C
LEGEND OF THE BAYOU
  (SEE:EATEN ALIVE!)
LEGEND OF THE LONE RANGER, THE'!- 0
  (1981) PR:C
LEGEND OF THE LOST *
  (1957, US/Panama/It.) PR:C
LEGEND OF THE SEA WOLF
  (SEE:WOLF LARSEN)
LEGEND OF THE SEVEN GOLDEN VAMPIRES, THE
  (SEE:DRACULA AND THE SEVEN GOLDEN
  VAMPIRES)
LEGEND OF THE TREE OF LIFE
  (SEE:IGOROTA, THE LEGEND OF THE TREE OF
  LIFE)
**LEGEND OF THE WOLF WOMAN, THE'!- 0
  (1977, Sp.) PR:O**
LEGEND OF TOM DOOLEY, THE *** (1959) PR:A
LEGEND OF WITCH HOLLOW
  (SEE:WITCHMAKER, THE)
LEGENDARY CURSE OF LEMORA
  (SEE:LADY DRACULA)
LEGION OF LOST FLYERS *½ (1939) PR:A
LEGION OF MISSING MEN * (1937) PR:A
LEGION OF TERROR ** (1936) PR:A
LEGION OF THE DOOMED * (1958) PR:A

LEGION OF THE LAWLESS ** (1940) PR:A
LEGIONS OF THE NILE ** (1960, It.) PR:A
L'ELISIR D'AMORE
  (SEE:THIS WINE OF LOVE)
LEMON DROP KID, THE *** (1934) PR:A
LEMON DROP KID, THE * (1951) PR:A**
LEMON GROVE KIDS MEET THE MONSTERS, THE
  **½ (1966) PR:C
LEMONADE JOE *** (1966, Czech.) PR:A
LEMORA THE LADY DRACULA
  (SEE:LADY DRACULA)
LENA RIVERS *½ (1932) PR:A
LEND ME YOUR EAR
  (SEE:THE LIVING GHOST)
LEND ME YOUR HUSBAND *½ (1935, Brit.) PR:A
LEND ME YOUR WIFE ** (1935, Brit.) PR:A
L'ENFANCE NUE
  (SEE:ME)
L'ENIGMATIQUE MONSIEUR PARKES **
  (1930) PR:A
LENNY * (1974) PR:C-O**
LEO AND LOREE ** (1980) PR:A
LEO THE LAST *½ (1970, Brit.) PR:O
LEONARD PART 6 zero (1987) PR:A-C
LEONOR * (1977, Fr./Sp./It.) PR:O
LEOPARD, THE **½ (1963, It.) PR:A-C
**LEOPARD IN THE SNOW **½
  (1979, Brit./Can.) PR:A**
LEOPARD MAN, THE ***½ (1943) PR:O
LEPKE **½ (1975, US/Israel) PR:O
LES ABYSSES *½ (1964, Fr.) PR:O
LES AMANTS
  (SEE:LOVERS, THE)
LES AMANTS DE VERONE
  (SEE:LOVERS OF VERONA)
LES ANGES DU PECHE
  (SEE:ANGELS OF THE STREET)
LES AVENTURES EXTRAORDINAIRES DE
  CERVANTES
  (SEE:YOUNG REBEL, THE)
LES BAS FONDS
  (SEE:LOWER DEPTHS, THE)
LES BELLES-DE-NUIT **½ (1952, Fr.) PR:C
LES BICHES ***½ (1968, Fr.) PR:O
LES CAMARADES
  (SEE:ORGANIZER, THE)
LES CAPRICES DE MARIE
  (SEE:GIVE HER THE MOON)
LES CARABINIERS **½ (1968, Fr./It.) PR:O
LES CHOSES DE LA VIE
  (SEE:THINGS OF LIFE, THE)
LES CLANDESTINS
  (SEE:CLANDESTINE)
LES COMPERES ***½ (1984, Fr.) PR:A
LES COUSINS
  (SEE:COUSINS, THE)
LES CREATURES *** (1969, Fr./Swed.) PR:A
LES DAMES DE BOIS DE BOULOGNE
  (SEE:LADIES OF THE PARK)
LES DEMOISELLES DE ROCHEFORT
  (SEE:YOUNG GIRLS OF ROCHEFORT)
LES DEMONS DE MINUIT
  (SEE:MIDNIGHT FOLLY)
LES DERNIERES VACANCES *** (1947, Fr.) PR:A-C
LES DIABOLIQUES
  (SEE:DIABOLIQUE)
LES DOIGTS CROISES
  (SEE:CATCH ME A SPY)
LES ENFANTS DU PARADIS
  (SEE:CHILDREN OF PARADISE)
LES ENFANTS TERRIBLES * (1952, Fr.) PR:A-C**
LES ESPIONS
  (SEE:SPIES, THE)
LES FELINS
  (SEE:JOY HOUSE)
LES GARCONS
  (SEE:LA NOTTE BRAVA)
LES GAULOISES BLEUES * (1969, Fr.) PR:A
LES GIRLS * (1957) PR:A**
LES GRANDES MANOEUVRES
  (SEE:GRAND MANUEVERS)
LES HOMMES EN BLANC
  (SEE:DOCTORS, THE)
LES INNOCENTS AUX MAINS SALES
  (SEE:DIRTY HANDS)
LES JEUX INTERDIT
  (SEE:FORBIDDEN GAMES)
LES JEUX SONT FAITS ** (1947, Fr.) PR:A-C
LES LACHES VIVENT D'ESPOIR
  (SEE:MY BABY IS BLACK!)
LES LETTRES DE MON MOULIN
  (SEE:LETTERS FROM MY WINDMILL)
LES LIAISONS DANGEREUSES **
  (1961, Fr./It.) PR:O
LES LIENS DE SANG
  (SEE:BLOOD RELATIVES)
LES LOUVES
  (SEE:DEMONIAQUE)

LES MAINS SALES ** (1954, Fr.) PR:A-C
LES MAITRES DU TEMPS **½
  (1982, Fr./Switz./Ger.) PR:A
LES MAUDITS
  (SEE:DAMNED, THE)
LES MISERABLES *** (1935) PR:A**
LES MISERABLES *** (1936, Fr.) PR:A
LES MISERABLES *** (1952) PR:A
LES MISERABLES ** (1982, Fr.) PR:A
LES NOCES DU SABLE
  (SEE:DAUGHTER OF THE SANDS)
LES NUITS DE L'EVPOUVANTE
  (SEE:MURDER CLINIC, THE)
LES NUITS DE LA PLEINE LUNE
  (SEE:FULL MOON IN PARIS)
LES OGRESSES
  (SEE:QUEENS, THE)
LES PARENTS TERRIBLES **** (1950, Fr.) PR:A
LES PEMPS DES AMANTS
  (SEE:PLACE FOR LOVERS, A)
LES PERLES DES COURONNE
  (SEE:PEARLS OF THE CROWN)
LES PETROLEUSES
  (SEE:LEGEND OF FRENCHIE KING, THE)
LES PLOUFFE ** (1985, Can.) PR:C
LES PORTES DE LA NUIT
  (SEE:GATES OF THE NIGHT)
LES QUATRES CENTS COUPS
  (SEE:FOUR HUNDRED BLOWS, THE)
LES QUATRES VERITES
  (SEE:THREE FABLES OF LOVE)
LES RIPOUX
  (SEE:MY NEW PARTNER)
LES SOMNAMBULES
  (SEE:MON ONCLE D'AMERIQUE)
LES TITANS
  (SEE:MY SON, THE HERO)
LES TRICHEURS
  (SEE:CHEATERS, THE)
LES TRIPES AU SOLEIL
  (SEE:CHECKERBOARD)
LES TROIS COURONNES DU MATELOT
  (SEE:THREE CROWNS OF THE SAILOR)
LES VACANCES DE MONSIEUR HULOT
  (SEE:MR. HULOT'S HOLIDAY)
LES VALSEUSES
  (SEE:GOING PLACES)
LES VISITEURS DU SOIR
  (SEE:DEVIL'S ENVOYS, THE)
LES YEUX SANS VISAGE
  (SEE:HORROR CHAMBER OF DR. FAUSTUS, THE)
LESBIAN TWINS
  (SEE:VIRGIN WITCH, THE)
LESNAYA PESNYA
  (SEE:SONG OF THE FOREST)
L'ESPION
  (SEE:DEFECTOR, THE)
LESS THAN ZERO *½ (1987) PR:O
LESSON IN LOVE, A * (1960, Swed.) PR:C**
LEST WE FORGET ** (1934, Brit.) PR:C
LET 'EM HAVE IT * (1935) PR:A**
LET FREEDOM RING *** (1939) PR:A
LET GEORGE DO IT ** (1940, Brit.) PR:A
LET JOY REIGN SUPREME *** (1977, Fr.) PR:C
LET ME EXPLAIN, DEAR **½ (1932) PR:A
LET NO MAN WRITE MY EPITAPH ** (1960) PR:A
LET THE BALLOON GO * (1977, Aus.) PR:A
LET THE PEOPLE LAUGH
  (SEE:SING AS YOU SWING)
LET THE PEOPLE SING ** (1942, Brit.) PR:A
LET THEM LIVE ** (1937) PR:A
LET US BE GAY ** (1930) PR:A
LET US LIVE *** (1939) PR:A
L'ETE MEURTRIER
  (SEE:ONE DEADLY SUMMER)
LETHAL OBSESSION ** (1988, W. Ger.) PR:O
LETHAL WEAPON **½ (1987) PR:O
L'ETOILE DU NORD * (1983, Fr.) PR:O
L'ETRANGER
  (SEE:STRANGER, THE)
LET'S BE FAMOUS **½ (1939, Brit.) PR:A
LET'S BE HAPPY ** (1957, Brit.) PR:A
LET'S BE RITZY ** (1934) PR:A
LET'S DANCE **½ (1950) PR:A
LET'S DO IT
  (SEE:JUDY'S LITTLE NO-NO)
LET'S DO IT AGAIN ** (1953) PR:A

LET'S DO IT AGAIN * (1975) PR:A**
LET'S FACE IT **½ (1943) PR:A
LET'S FALL IN LOVE ** (1934) PR:A
LET'S GET HARRY ** (1987) PR:O
LET'S GET MARRIED ** (1937) PR:A
LET'S GET MARRIED ** (1960, Brit.) PR:A
LET'S GET TOUGH ** (1942) PR:A
LET'S GO COLLEGIATE *½ (1941) PR:A
LET'S GO NATIVE *½ (1930) PR:A
LET'S GO NAVY *** (1951) PR:A
LET'S GO PLACES ** (1930) PR:A
LET'S GO STEADY ** (1945) PR:A
LET'S GO, YOUNG GUY! * (1967, Jap.) PR:A
LET'S HAVE A MURDER
  (SEE:STICK 'EM UP)
LET'S HAVE FUN
  (SEE:LAUGH YOUR BLUES AWAY)
LET'S KILL UNCLE *** (1966) PR:C
LET'S LIVE A LITTLE ** (1948) PR:A
LET'S LIVE AGAIN ** (1948) PR:A
LET'S LIVE TONIGHT *½ (1935) PR:A
LET'S LOVE AND LAUGH
  (SEE:BRIDEGROOM FOR TWO)
LET'S MAKE A NIGHT OF IT *½ (1937, Brit.) PR:A
LET'S MAKE A MILLION *½ (1937) PR:A
LET'S MAKE IT LEGAL **½ (1951) PR:A
LET'S MAKE LOVE **½ (1960) PR:AA
LET'S MAKE MUSIC ** (1940) PR:A
LET'S MAKE UP ** (1955, Brit.) PR:A
LET'S ROCK *½ (1958) PR:A
LET'S SCARE JESSICA TO DEATH ** (1971) PR:C
LET'S SING AGAIN ** (1936) PR:A
LET'S TALK ABOUT WOMEN ***
  (1964, Fr./It.) PR:C
LET'S TALK IT OVER *½ (1934) PR:A
LET'S TRY AGAIN ** (1934) PR:A
LETTER, THE * (1929) PR:A
LETTER, THE ** (1940) PR:A**
LETTER FOR EVIE, A ** (1945) PR:A
LETTER FROM A NOVICE
  (SEE:RITA)
**LETTER FROM AN UNKNOWN WOMAN ***½
  (1948) PR:A**
LETTER FROM KOREA
  (SEE:YANK IN KOREA, A)
LETTER OF INTRODUCTION **½ (1938) PR:A
LETTER THAT WAS NEVER SENT, THE **
  (1962, USSR) PR:A
LETTER TO BREZHNEV ***½ (1986, Brit.) PR:C-O
LETTER TO THREE WIVES, A ** (1948) PR:A**
LETTERS FROM MY WINDMILL ***½
  (1955, Fr.) PR:A
LETTING IN THE SUNSHINE ** (1933, Brit.) PR:A
LETTY LYNTON **½ (1932) PR:A-C
LETYAT ZHURAVIT
  (SEE:CRANES ARE FLYING, THE)
L'EVANGILE SELON SAINT MATTHIEU
  (SEE:GOSPEL ACCORDING TO SAINT MATTHEW,
  THE)
LEVIATHAN *** (1961, Fr.) PR:O
L'HOMME AU CHAPEAU ROND
  (SEE:ETERNAL HUSBAND, THE)
L'HOMME BLESSE ** (1985, Fr.) PR:O
L'HOMME DE RIO
  (SEE:THAT MAN FROM RIO)
L'HOMME DU MINNESOTA
  (SEE:MINNESOTA CLAY)
L'HOMME EN COLERE
  (SEE:ANGRY MAN, THE)
L'HOMME QUI AIMAT LES FEMMES
  (SEE:MAN WHO LOVED WOMEN, THE)
LIANG SHAN-PO YU CHU YING-TAI
  (SEE:LOVE ETERNE, THE)
LIANNA *** (1983) PR:O
LIARS, THE ** (1964, Fr.) PR:A
LIAR'S DICE **½ (1980) PR:O
LIAR'S MOON * (1982) PR:C
LIBEL **½ (1959, Brit.) PR:A
LIBELED LADY ** (1936) PR:A**
LIBERATION OF L.B. JONES, THE ** (1970) PR:O
LIBIDO **½ (1973, Aus.) PR:O
LICENSE TO DRIVE * (1988) PR:O
LICENSED TO KILL
  (SEE:SECOND BEST AGENT IN THE WHOLE WIDE
  WORLD, THE)
L'IDIOT
  (SEE:IDIOT, THE)

LIDO MYSTERY, THE
  (SEE:ENEMY AGENTS MEET ELLERY QUEEN)
LIE DETECTOR, THE
  (SEE:TRUTH ABOUT MURDER, THE)
LIEBESSPIELE
  (SEE:SKI FEVER)
LIES * (1984, Brit.) PR:C
LIES MY FATHER TOLD ME ***½ (1975, Can.) PR:A
LIES MY FATHER TOLD ME ** (1960, Brit.) PR:A
LIEUTENANT DARING, RN *** (1935, Brit.) PR:A
LT. ROBIN CRUSOE, U.S.N. * (1966) PR:AA
LIEUTENANT WORE SKIRTS, THE *** (1956) PR:A
LIFE AFTER DARK
  (SEE:GIRLS IN THE NIGHT)
LIFE AND DEATH OF COLONEL BLIMP, THE ****
  (1945, Brit.) PR:A
LIFE AND LOVES OF BEETHOVEN, THE ***½
  (1937, Fr.) PR:A
LIFE AND LOVES OF MOZART, THE ***
  (1959, Ger.) PR:C
LIFE AND TIMES OF CHESTER-ANGUS RAMSGOOD,
  THE ** (1971, Can.) PR:C
**LIFE AND TIMES OF GRIZZLY ADAMS, THE *½
  (1974) PR:AA**
**LIFE AND TIMES OF JUDGE ROY BEAN, THE *
  (1972) PR:C**
LIFE AT STAKE, A
  (SEE:KEY MAN)
LIFE AT THE TOP ***½ (1965, Brit.) PR:C
LIFE BEGINS *** (1932) PR:C
LIFE BEGINS ANEW **½ (1938, Ger.) PR:A
LIFE BEGINS AT COLLEGE
  (SEE:LIFE BEGINS IN COLLEGE)
LIFE BEGINS AT 8:30 ** (1942) PR:A
LIFE BEGINS AT 40 *** (1935) PR:AA
LIFE BEGINS AT 17 **½ (1958) PR:C
LIFE BEGINS FOR ANDY HARDY ***½ (1941) PR:A
LIFE BEGINS IN COLLEGE **½ (1937) PR:AA
LIFE BEGINS TOMORROW ** (1952, Fr.) PR:C
LIFE BEGINS WITH LOVE ** (1937) PR:A
LIFE DANCES ON, CHRISTINE
  (SEE:UN CARNET DE BAL)
LIFE FOR RUTH
  (SEE:WALK IN THE SHADOW)
LIFE GOES ON ** (1932, Brit.) PR:A-C
LIFE IN DANGER * (1964, Brit.) PR:A
LIFE IN EMERGENCY WARD 10 ***
  (1959, Brit.) PR:C
LIFE IN HER HANDS **½ (1951, Brit.) PR:C
LIFE IN THE BALANCE, A **½ (1955) PR:O
LIFE IN THE RAW **½ (1933) PR:A
LIFE IS A BED OF ROSES *** (1984, Fr.) PR:C
LIFE IS A CIRCUS **½ (1962, Brit.) PR:A
LIFE LOVE DEATH * (1969, Fr./It.) PR:O
LIFE OF A COUNTRY DOCTOR ** (1961, Jap.) PR:A
LIFE OF BRIAN
  (SEE:MONTY PYTHON'S LIFE OF BRIAN)
LIFE OF EMILE ZOLA, THE *** (1937) PR:AA**
LIFE OF HER OWN, A ** (1950) PR:C
LIFE OF JIMMY DOLAN, THE **½ (1933) PR:A
LIFE OF OHARU ***½ (1964, Jap.) PR:C
LIFE OF RILEY, THE *** (1949) PR:A
LIFE OF THE COUNTRY DOCTOR
  (SEE:LIFE OF A COUNTRY DOCTOR)
LIFE OF THE PARTY ** (1934, Brit.) PR:A
LIFE OF THE PARTY, THE **½ (1930) PR:A
LIFE OF THE PARTY, THE ** (1937) PR:A
LIFE OF VERGIE WINTERS, THE **½ (1934) PR:C
LIFE RETURNS *½ (1939) PR:C
LIFE STUDY ** (1973) PR:O
LIFE UPSIDE DOWN ** (1965, Fr.) PR:C
LIFE WITH BLONDIE **½ (1946) PR:AA
LIFE WITH FATHER ** (1947) PR:AA**
LIFE WITH HENRY ** (1941) PR:AA
LIFE WITH THE LYONS
  (SEE:FAMILY AFFAIR)
LIFEBOAT *** (1944) PR:A**
LIFEFORCE *½ (1985) PR:O
LIFEGUARD * (1976) PR:C**
LIFESPAN ** (1975, US/Brit./Neth.) PR:C
LIFT, THE *½ (1965, Brit./Can.) PR:O
LIFT, THE ** (1983, Neth.) PR:C
LIGEA
  (SEE:TOMB OF LIGEA)
LIGHT
  (SEE:LUMIMERE)

LIGHT ACROSSS THE STREET, THE **½ (1957, Fr.) PR:O
LIGHT AT THE EDGE OF THE WORLD, THE *½ (1971, US/Sp./Lichtenstein) PR:O
LIGHT BLUE (SEE:BACHELOR OF HEARTS)
LIGHT FANTASTIC, THE (SEE:LOVE IS BETTER THAN EVER)
LIGHT FANTASTIC ** (1964) PR:A
LIGHT FINGERS ** (1929) PR:A
LIGHT FINGERS *½ (1957, Brit.) PR:A
LIGHT IN THE FOREST, THE * (1958) PR:AA**
LIGHT IN THE PIAZZA ***½ (1962) PR:A
LIGHT OF DAY ** (1987) PR:C
LIGHT OF HEART, THE (SEE:LIFE BEGINS AT 8:30)
LIGHT OF WESTERN STARS, THE *** (1930) PR:A
LIGHT OF WESTERN STARS, THE ** (1940) PR:A
LIGHT THAT FAILED, THE **** (1939) PR:A
LIGHT TOUCH, THE ** (1951) PR:C
LIGHT TOUCH, THE * (1955, Brit.) PR:A
LIGHT UP THE SKY ** (1960, Brit.) PR:A
LIGHT YEARS ** (1988, Fr.) PR:C
LIGHT YEARS AWAY ** (1982, Fr./Switz.) PR:C
LIGHTHORSEMEN, THE **½ (1988, Aus.) PR:A-C
LIGHTHOUSE ** (1947) PR:A
LIGHTHOUSE KEEPER'S DAUGHTER, THE (SEE:GIRL IN THE BIKINI, THE)
LIGHTNIN' *** (1930) PR:A
LIGHTNIN' CRANDALL ** (1937) PR:A
LIGHTNIN' IN THE FOREST ** (1948) PR:C
LIGHTNING BILL CARSON * (1936) PR:A
LIGHTNING BOLT * (1967, It./Sp.) PR:A
LIGHTNING CONDUCTOR **½ (1938, Brit.) PR:A
LIGHTNING FLYER ** (1931) PR:A
LIGHTNING GUNS **½ (1950) PR:A
LIGHTNING RAIDERS ** (1945) PR:A
LIGHTNING RANGE ** (1934) PR:A
LIGHTNING STRIKES TWICE * (1935) PR:A
LIGHTNING STRIKES TWICE ** (1951) PR:C
LIGHTNING STRIKES WEST ** (1940) PR:A
LIGHTNING SWORDS OF DEATH (SEE:SHOGUN ASSASSIN)
LIGHTNING—THE WHITE STALLION ** (1986) PR:A
LIGHTS AND SHADOWS (SEE:WOMAN RACKET, THE)
LIGHTS OF NEW YORK ** (1928) PR:A
LIGHTS OF OLD SANTA FE **½ (1944) PR:A
LIGHTS OF VARIETY (SEE:VARIETY LIGHTS)
LIGHTS OUT (SEE:BRIGHT VICTORY)
LIGHTSHIP, THE * (1986) PR:C**
LIKE A CROW ON A JUNE BUG *** (1972) PR:C
LIKE A TURTLE ON ITS BACK **½ (1981, Fr.) PR:O
LIKE FATHER LIKE SON ** (1961) PR:C
LIKE FATHER, LIKE SON (SEE:YOUNG SINNER, THE)
LIKE FATHER, LIKE SON ** (1987) PR:C
LIKELY LADS, THE * (1976, Brit.) PR:A
LIKELY STORY, A ** (1947) PR:A
LI'L ABNER ** (1940) PR:AA
LI'L ABNER *** (1959) PR:AA
LILA (SEE:MAKE WAY FOR LILA)
LILA (SEE:MANTIS IN LACE)
LILA—LOVE UNDER THE MIDNIGHT SUN (SEE:MAKE WAY FOR LILA)
LILAC DOMINO, THE * (1940, Brit.) PR:A
LILACS IN THE SPRING (SEE:LET'S MAKE UP)
LILI ***½ (1953) PR:AA
LILI MARLEEN ** (1981, Ger.) PR:O
LILI MARLENE (SEE:LILLI MARLENE)
LILIES OF THE FIELD *** (1930) PR:O
LILIES OF THE FIELD ** (1934, Brit.) PR:A
LILIES OF THE FIELD ***½ (1963) PR:A
LILIOM ** (1930) PR:C
LILIOM *** (1935, Fr.) PR:A
LILITH ** (1964) PR:C
LILLI MARLENE *½ (1951, Brit.) PR:C
LILLIAN RUSSELL **½ (1940) PR:A
LILLY TURNER * (1933) PR:C
LILY CHRISTINE * (1932, Brit.) PR:C
LILY IN LOVE ** (1985, US/Hung.) PR:C
LILY OF KILARNEY (SEE:BRIDE OF THE LAKE)
LILY OF LAGUNA *½ (1938, Brit.) PR:C
LIMBO (SEE:REBEL ROUSERS)
LIMBO *** (1972) PR:O
LIMBO LINE, THE ** (1969, Brit.) PR:O
LIMEHOUSE BLUES * (1934) PR:A-C
LIMELIGHT (SEE:BACKSTAGE)
LIMELIGHT ** (1952) PR:A**
LIMIT, THE ** (1972) PR:C
L'IMMORTELLE *** (1969, Fr./It./Turkey) PR:C
LIMONADOVY JOE (SEE:LEMONADE JOE)
LIMPING MAN, THE *½ (1931, Brit.) PR:A
LIMPING MAN, THE *½ (1936, Brit.) PR:A
LIMPING MAN, THE ** (1953, Brit.) PR:A
LINCOLN CONSPIRACY, THE * (1977) PR:A
LINDA ** (1960, Brit.) PR:A
LINDA BE GOOD ** (1947) PR:A
LINE (SEE:PASSIONATE DEMONS, THE)
LINE, THE * (1982) PR:C
LINE ENGAGED ** (1935, Brit.) PR:A
LINE OF DUTY (SEE:INCIDENT IN AN ALLEY)
LINEUP, THE ** (1934) PR:A
LINEUP, THE *** (1958) PR:O
LINK ** (1986, Brit.) PR:O
LINKS OF JUSTICE ** (1958) PR:A
L'INTRIGO (SEE:DARK PURPOSE)
LIOLA (SEE:VERY HANDY MAN, A)
LION, THE *** (1962, Brit.) PR:A
LION AND THE HORSE, THE *½ (1952) PR:A
LION AND THE LAMB * (1931) PR:A
LION AND THE MOUSE, THE * (1928) PR:A
LION HAS WINGS, THE ** (1940, Brit.) PR:A
LION HUNTERS, THE *½ (1951) PR:AA
LION IN THE STREETS, A (SEE:LION IS IN THE STREETS, A)
LION IN WINTER, THE ** (1968, Brit.) PR:A**
LION IS IN THE STREETS, A ***½ (1953) PR:A
LION OF ST. MARK ** (1967, It.) PR:A
LION OF SPARTA (SEE:300 SPARTANS, THE)
LION OF THE DESERT *½ (1981, Libya/Brit.) PR:O
LIONHEART ** (1968, Brit.) PR:AA
LION'S DEN, THE ** (1936) PR:A
LIONS LOVE *** (1969) PR:O
LIPSTICK ** (1965, Fr./It.) PR:C-O
LIPSTICK zero (1976) PR:O
LIQUID SKY ***½ (1982) PR:O
LIQUIDATOR, THE **½ (1966, Brit.) PR:C
LISA **½ (1962, Brit.) PR:O
LISA AND THE DEVIL (SEE:HOUSE OF EXORCISM, THE)
LISA, TOSCA OF ATHENS *½ (1961, Gr.) PR:A
LISBON ** (1956) PR:O
LISBON STORY, THE **½ (1946, Brit.) PR:A
LISETTE *½ (1961) PR:C
LIST OF ADRIAN MESSENGER, THE ***½ (1963) PR:A
LISTEN, DARLING *** (1938) PR:AA
LISTEN, LET'S MAKE LOVE *½ (1969, Fr./It.) PR:O
LISTEN TO THE CITY *½ (1984, Can.) PR:O
LISZTOMANIA *½ (1975, Brit.) PR:O
LITTLE ACCIDENT ** (1930) PR:A
LITTLE ACCIDENT ** (1939) PR:A
LITTLE ADVENTURESS, THE *½ (1938) PR:AA
LITTLE ANGEL ** (1961, Mex.) PR:A
LITTLE ARK, THE *** (1972) PR:AA
LITTLE AUSTRALIANS zero (1940, Aus.) PR:C
LITTLE BALLERINA, THE ** (1951, Brit.) PR:AA
LITTLE BIG HORN *** (1951) PR:C
LITTLE BIG MAN **½ (1970) PR:C-O
LITTLE BIG SHOT ** (1935) PR:AA
LITTLE BIG SHOT *½ (1952, Brit.) PR:A
LITTLE BIT OF BLUFF, A *½ (1935, Brit.) PR:A
LITTLE BIT OF HEAVEN, A ** (1940) PR:AA
LITTLE BOY BLUE * (1963, Mex.) PR:A
LITTLE BOY LOST *** (1953) PR:A
LITTLE CAESAR ** (1931) PR:C**
LITTLE CIGARS **½ (1973) PR:A
LITTLE COLONEL, THE ***½ (1935) PR:AA
LITTLE CONVICT, THE ** (1980, Aus.) PR:AA
LITTLE DAMOZEL, THE ** (1933, Brit.) PR:A
LITTLE DARLINGS ** (1980) PR:O
LITTLE DOLLY DAYDREAM *½ (1938, Brit.) PR:AA
LITTLE DORRIT **** (1988, Brit.) PR:A
LITTLE DRAGONS, THE *½ (1980) PR:A-C
LITTLE DRUMMER GIRL, THE *½ (1984) PR:C-O
LITTLE EGYPT **½ (1951) PR:A
LITTLE FAUSS AND BIG HALSY ** (1970) PR:O
LITTLE FLAMES **½ (1985, It.) PR:O
LITTLE FOXES, THE *** (1941) PR:A-C**
LITTLE FRIEND *** (1934, Brit.) PR:C
LITTLE FUGITIVE, THE ***½ (1953) PR:A
LITTLE GEL (SEE:KING OF HEARTS)
LITTLE GIANT, THE *** (1933) PR:A
LITTLE GIANT ** (1946) PR:A
LITTLE GIRL WHO LIVES DOWN THE LANE, THE ***½ (1977, Can.) PR:O
LITTLE HUMPBACKED HORSE, THE **½ (1962, USSR) PR:A
LITTLE HUT, THE ** (1957) PR:A
LITTLE IODINE ** (1946) PR:A
LITTLE JOE, THE WRANGLER *½ (1942) PR:A
LITTLE JOHNNY JONES ** (1930) PR:A
LITTLE JUNGLE BOY *½ (1969, Aus.) PR:A
LITTLE KIDNAPPERS, THE ***½ (1954, Brit.) PR:AA
LITTLE LAURA AND BIG JOHN ** (1973) PR:O
LITTLE LORD FAUNTLEROY * (1936) PR:AA**
LITTLE MALCOLM *** (1974, Brit.) PR:C
LITTLE MAN, WHAT NOW? ***½ (1934) PR:A
LITTLE MARTYR, THE *** (1947, It.) PR:A
LITTLE MELODY FROM VIENNA ** (1948, Aust.) PR:A
LITTLE MEN ** (1935) PR:A
LITTLE MEN * (1940) PR:AA
LITTLE MINISTER, THE * (1934) PR:A**
LITTLE MISS MARKER ***½ (1934) PR:AA
LITTLE MISS BIG *½ (1946) PR:A
LITTLE MISS BROADWAY **½ (1938) PR:A
LITTLE MISS BROADWAY *½ (1947) PR:A
LITTLE MISS DEVIL *½ (1951, Egypt) PR:A
LITTLE MISS MARKER *½ (1980) PR:C
LITTLE MISS MOLLY ** (1940) PR:A
LITTLE MISS NOBODY ** (1933, Brit.) PR:A
LITTLE MISS NOBODY *½ (1936) PR:AA
LITTLE MISS ROUGHNECK * (1938) PR:AA
LITTLE MISS SOMEBODY * (1937, Brit.) PR:A
LITTLE MISS THOROUGHBRED *½ (1938) PR:AA
LITTLE MISTER JIM *½ (1946) PR:A
LITTLE MOTHER *½ (1973, US/Yugo./Ger.) PR:O
LITTLE MURDERS ***½ (1971) PR:O
LITTLE NELLIE KELLY **½ (1940) PR:A
LITTLE NIGHT MUSIC, A ** (1977, Aust./US/Ger.) PR:C
LITTLE NIKITA **½ (1988) PR:A-C
LITTLE NUNS, THE **½ (1965, It.) PR:A
LITTLE OF WHAT YOU FANCY, A *½ (1968, Brit.) PR:A
LITTLE OLD NEW YORK **½ (1940) PR:A
LITTLE ONES, THE ** (1965, Brit.) PR:AA
LITTLE ORPHAN ANNIE ** (1932) PR:AA
LITTLE ORPHAN ANNIE * (1938) PR:A
LITTLE ORVIE *½ (1940) PR:AA
LITTLE PRINCE, THE ** (1974, Brit.) PR:AA
LITTLE PRINCESS, THE ***½ (1939) PR:AA
LITTLE RED MONKEY (SEE:CASE OF THE RED MONKEY)
LITTLE RED RIDING HOOD **½ (1963, Mex.) PR:A
LITTLE RED RIDING HOOD AND HER FRIENDS ** (1964, Mex.) PR:A
LITTLE RED RIDING HOOD AND THE MONSTERS ** (1965, Mex.) PR:C
LITTLE RED SCHOOLHOUSE *½ (1936) PR:AA
LITTLE ROMANCE, A ** (1979, US/Fr.) PR:A**
LITTLE SAVAGE, THE ** (1959) PR:A
LITTLE SEX, A * (1982) PR:O
LITTLE SHEPHERD OF KINGDOM COME **½ (1961) PR:A
LITTLE SHOP OF HORRORS * (1961) PR:C-O**
LITTLE SHOP OF HORRORS * (1986) PR:C**
LITTLE SISTER (SEE:MARLOWE)
LITTLE SISTER, THE ** (1985) PR:O
LITTLE SOLDIER, THE (SEE:LE PETIT SOLDAT)
LITTLE STRANGER * (1934, Brit.) PR:A
LITTLE THEATER OF JEAN RENOIR, THE (SEE:LE PETIT THEATRE DE JEAN RENOIR)
LITTLE TOKYO, U.S.A. * (1942) PR:A
LITTLE TOUGH GUY ** (1938) PR:A
LITTLE TOUGH GUYS IN SOCIETY *½ (1938) PR:A
LITTLE TREASURE *½ (1985) PR:O
LITTLE WILDCAT, THE ** (1928) PR:A
LITTLE WOMEN *** (1933) PR:AA**
LITTLE WOMEN **½ (1949) PR:AA
LITTLE WORLD OF DON CAMILLO, THE *** (1953, Fr./It.) PR:A
LITTLEST HOBO, THE **½ (1958) PR:AA
LITTLEST HORSE THIEVES, THE * (1977) PR:AA**
LITTLEST OUTLAW, THE * (1955) PR:AA**
LITTLEST REBEL, THE ***½ (1935) PR:AA
LIVE A LITTLE, LOVE A LITTLE *½ (1968) PR:A
LIVE A LITTLE, STEAL A LOT (SEE:MURPH THE SURF)
LIVE AGAIN * (1936, Brit.) PR:A
LIVE AND LET DIE **½ (1973, Brit.) PR:C
LIVE FAST, DIE YOUNG *½ (1958) PR:A
LIVE FOR LIFE ** (1967, Fr./It.) PR:A
LIVE IT UP (SEE:SING AND SWING)
LIVE, LOVE AND LEARN ** (1937) PR:A
LIVE NOW—PAY LATER ** (1962, Brit.) PR:A
LIVE TO LOVE (SEE:DEVIL'S HAND, THE)
LIVE TODAY FOR TOMORROW (SEE:ACT OF MURDER, AN)
LIVE WIRE, THE ** (1937, Brit.) PR:A
LIVE WIRES **½ (1946) PR:A

LIVE YOUR OWN WAY ** (1970, Jap.) PR:A
LIVELY SET, THE ** (1964) PR:A
LIVER EATERS, THE
  (SEE:SPIDER BABY)
LIVES OF A BENGAL LANCER ** (1935) PR:A**
LIVING
  (SEE:IKIRU)
LIVING BETWEEN TWO WORLDS ** (1963) PR:A
LIVING COFFIN, THE *½ (1965, Mex.) PR:C
LIVING CORPSE, THE ** (1940, Fr.) PR:A
LIVING DANGEROUSLY ** (1936, Brit.) PR:A
LIVING DANGEROUSLY ** (1988, Cuba) PR:A
LIVING DAYLIGHTS, THE ***½ (1987) PR:C
LIVING DEAD, THE * (1936, Brit.) PR:A
LIVING DEAD AT MANCHESTER MORGUE
  (SEE:DON'T OPEN THE WINDOW)
LIVING FREE **½ (1972, Brit.) PR:A
LIVING GHOST, THE * (1942) PR:A
LIVING HEAD, THE *½ (1969, Mex.) PR:O
LIVING IDOL, THE *½ (1957) PR:C-O
LIVING IN A BIG WAY ** (1947) PR:A
LIVING IT UP ***½ (1954) PR:A
LIVING LEGEND zero (1980) PR:O
LIVING ON LOVE ** (1937) PR:A
LIVING ON TOKYO TIME ** (1987) PR:C
LIVING ON VELVET **½ (1935) PR:A
LIVING VENUS zero (1961) PR:A
LIZA zero (1976, Fr./It.) PR:O
LIZZIE **½ (1957) PR:C
LJUBAVNI SLUJAC ILI TRAGEDIJA SLUZBENICE
  P.T.T.
  (SEE:LOVE AFFAIR; OR THE CASE OF THE
  MISSING SWITCHBOARD OPERATOR)
LLANO KID, THE *½ (1940) PR:A
LLOYDS OF LONDON ***½ (1936) PR:A
LO STRANIERO
  (SEE:STRANGER, THE)
LOADED DICE
  (SEE:CROSS MY HEART)
LOADED PISTOLS **½ (1948) PR:A
LOAN SHARK ** (1952) PR:A
LOCAL BAD MAN *½ (1932) PR:A
LOCAL BOY MAKES GOOD ** (1931) PR:A
LOCAL COLOR zero (1978) PR:O
LOCAL HERO **** (1983, Brit.) PR:A-C
LOCK UP YOUR DAUGHTERS zero
  (1969, Brit.) PR:C-O
LOCK YOUR DOORS
  (SEE:APE MAN, THE)
LOCKED DOOR, THE *½ (1929) PR:A
LOCKER 69 *½ (1962, Brit.) PR:A
LOCKET, THE ** (1946) PR:C
LODGER, THE
  (SEE:PHANTOM FIEND, THE)
LODGER, THE ** (1944) PR:C-O**
L'OEIL DU MALIN
  (SEE:THIRD LOVER, THE)
LONG ROPE, THE ** (1961) PR:A
LOGAN'S RUN **½ (1976) PR:A
LOLA
  (SEE:YOUNG BLOOD)
LOLA *** (1961, Fr./It.) PR:C
LOLA * (1971, Brit./It.) PR:C-O
LOLA ***½ (1982, Ger.) PR:O
LOLA MONTES *** (1955, Fr./Ger.) PR:C**
LOLA'S MISTAKE
  (SEE:THIS REBEL BREED)
LOLITA ***½ (1962) PR:C-O
LOLLIPOP
  (SEE:FOREVER YOUNG, FOREVER FREE)
LOLLIPOP ** (1966, Braz.) PR:O
LOLLIPOP COVER, THE **½ (1965) PR:A
LOLLY MADONNA WAR, THE
  (SEE:LOLLY MADONNA XXX)
LOLLY-MADONNA XXX ** (1973) PR:A
LONDON BELONGS TO ME
  (SEE:DULCIMER STREET)
LONDON BLACKOUT MURDERS ** (1942) PR:A
LONDON BY NIGHT *½ (1937) PR:A
LONDON CALLING
  (SEE:HELLO LONDON)
LONDON MELODY * (1930, Brit.) PR:A
LONDON MELODY
  (SEE:GIRL IN THE STREET)
LONDON TOWN
  (SEE:MY HEART GOES CRAZY)
LONE AVENGER, THE ** (1933) PR:A

LONE CLIMBER, THE **½ (1950, Brit./Aust.) PR:AA
LONE COWBOY *½ (1934) PR:A
LONE GUN, THE *½ (1954) PR:A
LONE HAND, THE **½ (1953) PR:A
LONE HAND TEXAN, THE ** (1947) PR:A
LONE PRAIRIE, THE *½ (1942) PR:A
LONE RANGER, THE **½ (1955) PR:AA
**LONE RANGER AND THE LOST CITY OF GOLD, THE
  ** (1958) PR:AA**
LONE RIDER, THE *½ (1930) PR:A
LONE RIDER AMBUSHED, THE *½ (1941) PR:A
LONE RIDER AND THE BANDIT, THE *½
  (1942) PR:A
LONE RIDER CROSSES THE RIO, THE *½
  (1941) PR:A
LONE RIDER FIGHTS BACK, THE *½ (1941) PR:A
LONE RIDER IN CHEYENNE, THE *½ (1942) PR:A
LONE RIDER IN GHOST TOWN, THE *½
  (1941) PR:A
LONE STAR **½ (1952) PR:A
LONE STAR LAW MEN * (1942) PR:A
LONE STAR LAWMAN
  (SEE:TEXAS LAWMEN)
LONE STAR PIONEERS ** (1939) PR:A
LONE STAR RAIDERS * (1940) PR:A
LONE STAR RANGER, THE *½ (1930) PR:A
LONE STAR RANGER *½ (1942) PR:A
LONE STAR TRAIL, THE **½ (1943) PR:A
LONE STAR VIGILANTES, THE ** (1942) PR:A
LONE TEXAN **½ (1959) PR:A
LONE TEXAS RANGER *½ (1945) PR:A
LONE TRAIL, THE *½ (1932) PR:A
LONE TROUBADOR, THE
  (SEE:TWO-GUN TROUBADOR)
LONE WOLF AND HIS LADY, THE ** (1949) PR:A
LONE WOLF IN LONDON *½ (1947) PR:A
LONE WOLF IN MEXICO, THE *½ (1947) PR:A
LONE WOLF IN PARIS, THE ** (1938) PR:A
LONE WOLF KEEPS A DATE, THE *½ (1940) PR:A
LONE WOLF McQUADE ** (1983) PR:C-O
LONE WOLF MEETS A LADY, THE ** (1940) PR:A
LONE WOLF RETURNS, THE **½ (1936) PR:A
LONE WOLF SPY HUNT, THE *** (1939) PR:A
LONE WOLF STRIKES, THE ** (1940) PR:A
LONE WOLF TAKES A CHANCE, THE **
  (1941) PR:A
LONE WOLF'S DAUGHTER, THE *½ (1929) PR:A
LONE WOLF'S DAUGHTER, THE
  (SEE:LONE WOLF SPY HUNT, THE)
**LONELINESS OF THE LONG DISTANCE RUNNER,
  THE **** (1962, Brit.) PR:C-O**
LONELY ARE THE BRAVE ** (1962) PR:C**
LONELY GUY, THE *½ (1984) PR:O
LONELY HEART BANDITS
  (SEE:LONELY HEARTS BANDITS)
LONELY HEARTS **½ (1983, Aus.) PR:O
LONELY HEARTS BANDITS ** (1950) PR:A
LONELY HEARTS KILLER
  (SEE:HONEYMOON KILLERS, THE)
LONELY HEARTS KILLERS
  (SEE:HONEYMOON KILLERS, THE)
LONELY LADY, THE
  (SEE:STRANGERS, THE)
LONELY LADY, THE zero (1983) PR:O
LONELY LANE *** (1963, Jap.) PR:O
LONELY MAN, THE
  (SEE:GUN RIDERS)
LONELY MAN, THE **½ (1957) PR:A
LONELY PASSION OF JUDITH HEARNE, THE *
  (1988, Brit.) PR:O**
LONELY ROAD, THE
  (SEE:SCOTLAND YARD COMMANDS)
LONELY STAGE
  (SEE:I COULD GO ON SINGING)
LONELY TRAIL, THE * (1936) PR:A
LONELY WIVES *½ (1931) PR:A
LONELY WOMAN, THE
  (SEE:STRANGERS, THE)
LONELYHEARTS ***½ (1958) PR:C
LONER, THE
  (SEE:RUCKUS)
LONERS, THE *½ (1972) PR:O
LONESOME ** (1928) PR:A
LONESOME COWBOYS zero (1968) PR:O
LONESOME TRAIL, THE *½ (1930) PR:A
LONESOME TRAIL, THE ** (1955) PR:A
LONG ABSENCE, THE *** (1962, Fr./It.) PR:A

LONG AGO, TOMORROW * (1971, Brit.) PR:C**
LONG AND THE SHORT AND THE TALL, THE ***
  (1961, Brit.) PR:A
LONG ARM, THE
  (SEE:THIRD KEY, THE)
LONG CORRIDOR
  (SEE:SHOCK CORRIDOR)
LONG DARK HALL, THE ** (1951, Brit.) PR:A-C
LONG, DARK NIGHT, THE
  (SEE:PACK, THE)
LONG DAY'S DYING, THE * (1968, Brit.) PR:C-O
LONG DAY'S JOURNEY INTO NIGHT ***
  (1962) PR:C**
LONG DISTANCE
  (SEE:HOT MONEY GIRL)
LONG DUEL, THE ** (1967, Brit.) PR:A
LONG GOOD FRIDAY, THE ***½ (1982, Brit.) PR:O
LONG GOODBYE, THE * (1973) PR:O
LONG GRAY LINE, THE ***½ (1955) PR:A
LONG HAUL, THE ** (1957, Brit.) PR:A
LONG, HOT SUMMER, THE **** (1958) PR:A-C
LONG IS THE ROAD *** (1948, Ger.) PR:A
LONG JOHN SILVER **½ (1954, Aus.) PR:A
LONG JOHN SILVER RETURNS TO TREASURE
  ISLAND
  (SEE:LONG JOHN SILVER)
LONG KNIFE, THE ** (1958, Brit.) PR:C
LONG, LONG TRAIL, THE *½ (1929) PR:A
LONG, LONG TRAIL, THE
  (SEE:TEXAS TO BATAAN)
LONG, LONG TRAILER, THE *** (1954) PR:A
LONG LOST FATHER **½ (1934) PR:A
LONG MEMORY, THE ** (1953, Brit.) PR:A
LONG NIGHT, THE *** (1947) PR:A
LONG NIGHT, THE **½ (1976) PR:A
LONG RIDE, THE
  (SEE:BRADY'S ESCAPE)
LONG RIDE FROM HELL, A *½ (1970, It.) PR:O
LONG RIDE HOME, THE
  (SEE:TIME FOR KILLING, A)
LONG RIDERS, THE *** (1980) PR:O**
LONG SHADOW, THE ** (1961, Brit.) PR:A
LONG SHIPS, THE zero (1964, Brit./Yugo.) PR:C
LONG SHOT, THE ** (1939) PR:A
LONG SHOT * (1981, Brit.) PR:C**
LONG VOYAGE HOME, THE *** (1940) PR:A**
LONG WAIT, THE **½ (1954) PR:A
LONG WEEKEND **½ (1978, Aus.) PR:C-O
LONGEST DAY, THE ** (1962) PR:C**
LONGEST NIGHT, THE *½ (1936) PR:A
LONGEST SPUR
  (SEE:HOT SPUR)
LONGEST YARD, THE ***½ (1974) PR:O
LONGHORN, THE ** (1951) PR:A
LONGING FOR LOVE ** (1966, Jap.) PR:O
LONGSHOT, THE zero (1986) PR:O
LONNIE * (1963) PR:C
LOOK BACK IN ANGER * (1959) PR:C-O**
LOOK BEFORE YOU LAUGH
  (SEE:MAKE MINE A MILLION)
LOOK BEFORE YOU LOVE ** (1948, Brit.) PR:A
LOOK DOWN AND DIE, MEN OF STEEL
  (SEE:STEEL)
LOOK FOR THE SILVER LINING *½ (1949) PR:A
LOOK IN ANY WINDOW ** (1961) PR:A
LOOK OUT FOR LOVE
  (SEE:GIRLS IN THE STREET)
LOOK OUT SISTER *** (1948) PR:A
LOOK UP AND LAUGH *½ (1935, Brit.) PR:A
LOOK WHO'S LAUGHING **½ (1941) PR:A
LOOKER *½ (1981) PR:O
LOOKIN' FOR SOMEONE
  (SEE:SINGING ON THE TRAIL)
LOOKIN' GOOD
  (SEE:CORKY)
LOOKIN' TO GET OUT ** (1982) PR:O
LOOKING FOR DANGER ** (1957) PR:A
LOOKING FOR EILEEN **½ (1987, Neth.) PR:O
LOOKING FOR LOVE ** (1964) PR:A
LOOKING FOR MR. GOODBAR ***½ (1977) PR:C-O
LOOKING FOR TROUBLE
  (SEE:TIP-OFF, THE)
LOOKING FOR TROUBLE *½ (1934) PR:A
LOOKING FORWARD ** (1933) PR:A
LOOKING GLASS WAR, THE ** (1970, Brit.) PR:C
LOOKING ON THE BRIGHT SIDE **
  (1932, Brit.) PR:A

Finding entries in **THE MOTION PICTURE GUIDE** ™

		STAR RATINGS		PARENTAL RECOMMENDATION (PR:)
Years 1929-83	Volumes I-IX	★★★★★	Masterpiece	AA Good for Children
1984	Volume IX	★★★★	Excellent	A Acceptable for Children
1985	1986 ANNUAL	★★★	Good	C Cautionary, some objectionable scenes
1986	1987 ANNUAL	★★	Fair	O Objectionable for Children
1987	1988 ANNUAL	★	Poor	
1988	1989 ANNUAL	zero	Without Merit	**BOLD:** Films on Videocassette

LOOKING UP ** (1977) PR:C
LOOKS AND SMILES *** (1982, Brit.) PR:C
LOONIES ON BROADWAY
(SEE:ZOMBIES ON BROADWAY)
LOOPHOLE * (1981, Brit.) PR:C
LOOPHOLE *½ (1954) PR:A
LOOSE ANKLES **½ (1930) PR:A
LOOSE CONNECTIONS ** (1984, Brit.) PR:C
LOOSE ENDS *½ (1930, Brit.) PR:A
LOOSE ENDS *½ (1975) PR:C
LOOSE IN LONDON **½ (1953) PR:A
LOOSE PLEASURES
(SEE:TIGHT SKIRTS, LOOSE PLEASURES)
LOOSE SCREWS zero (1985) PR:O
LOOSE SHOES ** (1980) PR:C
LOOT *** (1971, Brit.) PR:C
LOOTERS, THE ** (1955) PR:A
LOPERJENTEN
(SEE:KAMILLA)
L'OR ET L'AMOUR
(SEE:GREAT DAY IN THE MORNING)
LORD BABS ** (1932, Brit.) PR:A
LORD BYRON OF BROADWAY ** (1930) PR:A
LORD CAMBER'S LADIES ** (1932, Brit.) PR:A
LORD EDGEWARE DIES ** (1934, Brit.) PR:A
LORD JEFF **½ (1938) PR:AA
LORD JIM ** (1965, Brit.) PR:A**
LORD LOVE A DUCK *** (1966) PR:A
LORD MOUNTDRAGO
(SEE:THREE CASES OF MURDER)
LORD OF THE FLIES ** (1963, Brit.) PR:A-C
LORD OF THE JUNGLE * (1955) PR:A
LORD OF THE MANOR **½ (1933, Brit.) PR:A
LORD OF THE RINGS, THE **½ (1978) PR:A
LORD RICHARD IN THE PANTRY *½ (1930, Brit.) PR:A
LORD SHANGO ** (1975) PR:O
LORDS OF DISCIPLINE, THE **½ (1983) PR:O
LORDS OF FLATBUSH, THE * (1974) PR:C**
LORNA DOONE ** (1935, Brit.) PR:A
LORNA DOONE ** (1951) PR:A
LOS AMANTES DE VERONA
(SEE:ROMEO AND JULIET)
LOS AMIGOS
(SEE:DEAF SMITH AND JOHNNY EARS)
LOS ASTRONAUTAS ** (1960, Mex.) PR:A
LOS AUTOMATAS DE LA MUERTE * (1960, Mex.) PR:A
LOS INVISIBLES * (1961, Mex.) PR:A
LOS OLVIDADOS ** (1950, Mex.) PR:O**
LOS PLATILLOS VOLADORES zero (1955, Mex.) PR:A
LOS SANTOS INOCENTES
(SEE:HOLY INNOCENTS, THE)
LOSER TAKE ALL
(SEE:LEATHER GLOVES)
LOSER TAKES ALL ** (1956, Brit.) PR:A
LOSER, THE HERO, THE * (1985, Taiwan) PR:A
LOSERS, THE zero (1968) PR:O
LOSERS, THE zero (1970) PR:O
LOSIN' IT * (1983) PR:O
LOSING GAME, THE
(SEE:PAY-OFF, THE)
LOSS OF FEELING **½ (1935, USSR) PR:A
LOSS OF INNOCENCE ** (1961, Brit.) PR:C
LOST
(SEE:TEARS FOR SIMON)
LOST AND FOUND **½ (1979) PR:A-C
LOST ANGEL *** (1944) PR:A
LOST BATTALION *½ (1961, US/Phil.) PR:A
LOST BOUNDARIES *** (1949) PR:A
LOST BOYS, THE **½ (1987) PR:O
LOST CANYON ** (1943) PR:A
LOST CHORD, THE *½ (1937, Brit.) PR:A
LOST COMMAND, THE **½ (1966) PR:A-C
LOST CONTINENT *½ (1951) PR:A
LOST CONTINENT, THE ** (1968, Brit.) PR:A
LOST EMPIRE, THE * (1985) PR:O
LOST FACE, THE ** (1965, Czech.) PR:C
LOST HAPPINESS *½ (1948, It.) PR:A
LOST HONEYMOON **½ (1947) PR:A
LOST HONOR OF KATHARINA BLUM, THE **½ (1975, Ger.) PR:C
LOST HORIZON *** (1937) PR:A**
LOST HORIZON zero (1973) PR:A
LOST ILLUSION, THE
(SEE:FALLEN IDOL, THE)
LOST IN A HAREM ** (1944) PR:A
LOST IN ALASKA ** (1952) PR:AA
LOST IN AMERICA **½ (1985) PR:O
LOST IN THE LEGION *½ (1934, Brit.) PR:A
LOST IN THE STARS ** (1974) PR:A
LOST IN THE STRATOSPHERE * (1935) PR:A
LOST JUNGLE, THE *½ (1934) PR:A
LOST LADY, THE
(SEE:SAFE IN HELL)
LOST LADY, A ** (1934) PR:A
LOST LAGOON *½ (1958) PR:A
LOST, LONELY AND VICIOUS *½ (1958) PR:A
LOST MAN, THE **½ (1969) PR:C
LOST MEN
(SEE:HOMICIDE SQUAD, THE)
LOST MISSILE, THE ** (1958, US/Can.) PR:A
LOST MOMENT, THE **½ (1947) PR:A
LOST ON THE WESTERN FRONT **½ (1940, Brit.) PR:A
LOST ONE, THE ***½ (1951, Ger.) PR:C
LOST PATROL, THE ***½ (1934) PR:C
LOST PEOPLE, THE **½ (1950, Brit.) PR:A
LOST RANCH * (1937) PR:A
LOST RIVER
(SEE:TRAIL OF THE RUSTLERS)
LOST SEX **½ (1968, Jap.) PR:O
LOST SOULS *½ (1961, It.) PR:O
LOST SQUADRON, THE * (1932) PR:C**
LOST STAGE VALLEY
(SEE:STAGE TO TUCSON)
LOST TRAIL, THE *½ (1945) PR:A
LOST TREASURE OF THE AMAZON
(SEE:JIVARO)
LOST TRIBE, THE ** (1949) PR:A
LOST VOLCANO, THE ** (1950) PR:AA
LOST WEEKEND, THE *** (1945) PR:C-O**
LOST WOMEN
(SEE:MESA OF LOST WOMEN)
LOST WORLD, THE *½ (1960) PR:A
LOST WORLD OF SINBAD, THE ** (1965, Jap.) PR:A
LOST ZEPPELIN ** (1930) PR:A
LOTNA *** (1966, Pol.) PR:C
LOTTERY BRIDE, THE zero (1930) PR:A
LOTTERY LOVER *½ (1935) PR:A
LOTUS LADY * (1930) PR:A
LOUDEST WHISPER, THE
(SEE:CHILDREN'S HOUR, THE)
LOUDSPEAKER, THE ** (1934) PR:A
LOUIE, THERE'S A CROWD DOWNSTAIRS
(SEE:START THE REVOLUTION WITHOUT ME)
LOUISA *** (1950) PR:A
LOUISE *½ (1940, Fr.) PR:A
LOUISIANA ** (1947) PR:A
LOUISIANA GAL
(SEE:OLD LOUISIANA)
LOUISIANA HAYRIDE * (1944) PR:A
LOUISIANA HUSSY * (1960) PR:C
LOUISIANA PURCHASE **½ (1941) PR:A
LOUISIANA TERRITORY *½ (1953) PR:A
LOUISIANE ** (1984, Fr./Can.) PR:A-C
LOULOU *** (1980, Fr.) PR:O
L'OURS
(SEE:BEAR, THE)
LOVABLE AND SWEET
(SEE:RUNAROUND, THE)
LOVABLE CHEAT, THE ** (1949) PR:A
LOVE A LA CARTE **½ (1965, It.) PR:O
LOVE *** (1972, Hung.) PR:C
LOVE AFFAIR ** (1932) PR:A
LOVE AFFAIR **** (1939) PR:A
LOVE AFFAIR OF THE DICTATOR, THE
(SEE:DICTATOR, THE)
LOVE AFFAIR; OR THE CASE OF THE MISSING SWITCHBOARD OPERATOR * (1968, Yugo.) PR:O**
LOVE AMONG THE MILLIONAIRES *½ (1930) PR:A
LOVE AND ANARCHY **½ (1974, It.) PR:O
LOVE AND BULLETS *½ (1979, Brit.) PR:C
LOVE AND DEATH ***½ (1975) PR:A-C
LOVE AND HISSES ** (1937) PR:A
LOVE AND KISSES ** (1965) PR:A
LOVE AND LARCENY *** (1963, Fr./It.) PR:A
LOVE AND LEARN *½ (1947) PR:A
LOVE AND MARRIAGE **½ (1966, It.) PR:C
LOVE AND MONEY *** (1982) PR:O
LOVE AND PAIN AND THE WHOLE DAMN THING *** (1973) PR:C
LOVE AND THE FRENCHWOMAN *** (1961, Fr.) PR:C-O
LOVE AND THE MIDNIGHT AUTO SUPPLY * (1978) PR:C-O
LOVE AT FIRST BITE **½ (1979) PR:C
LOVE AT FIRST SIGHT ** (1930) PR:A
LOVE AT FIRST SIGHT *½ (1977, Can.) PR:A
LOVE AT NIGHT ** (1961, Fr.) PR:C-O
LOVE AT SEA *½ (1936, Brit.) PR:A
LOVE AT SECOND SIGHT
(SEE:GIRL THIEF, THE)
LOVE AT TWENTY *** (1963, Fr./It./Jap./Pol./Ger.) PR:C
LOVE **½ (1982, Can.) PR:C
LOVE BAN, THE
(SEE:IT'S A 2'6" ABOVE THE GROUND WORLD)
LOVE BEFORE BREAKFAST **½ (1936) PR:A
LOVE BEGINS AT TWENTY ** (1936) PR:A
LOVE BIRDS *½ (1934) PR:A
LOVE BOUND * (1932) PR:A
LOVE BUG, THE * (1968) PR:AA**
LOVE BUTCHER, THE *½ (1982) PR:O
LOVE CAGE, THE
(SEE:JOY HOUSE)
LOVE CAPTIVE, THE **½ (1934) PR:A
LOVE CHILD **½ (1982) PR:O
LOVE CHILDREN
(SEE:PSYCHOUT)
LOVE COMES ALONG *½ (1930) PR:A
LOVE CONTRACT, THE ** (1932, Brit.) PR:A
LOVE CRAZY **** (1941) PR:A
LOVE CYCLES ** (1969, Gr.) PR:C
LOVE DOCTOR, THE *½ (1929) PR:A
LOVE ETERNAL
(SEE:ETERNAL RETURN, THE)
LOVE ETERNE, THE **½ (1964, Hong Kong) PR:A
LOVE FACTORY ** (1969, It.) PR:C-O
LOVE FEAST, THE *½ (1966, Ger.) PR:O
LOVE FINDS A WAY
(SEE:ALIAS FRENCH GERTIE)
LOVE FINDS ANDY HARDY *** (1938) PR:AA
LOVE FROM A STRANGER **** (1937, Brit.) PR:C
LOVE FROM A STRANGER **½ (1947) PR:A
LOVE GOD?, THE *½ (1969) PR:A
LOVE HABIT, THE **½ (1931, Brit.) PR:A
LOVE HAPPY **½ (1949) PR:A
LOVE HAS MANY FACES ** (1965) PR:C
LOVE, HONOR AND BEHAVE **½ (1938) PR:A
LOVE, HONOR AND GOODBYE *½ (1945) PR:A
LOVE, HONOR, AND OH BABY! *½ (1933) PR:A
LOVE, HONOR AND OH, BABY *½ (1940) PR:A
LOVE HUNGER * (1965, Arg.) PR:O
LOVE IN A BUNGALOW * (1937) PR:A
LOVE IN A FOUR LETTER WORLD * (1970, Can.) PR:O
LOVE IN A GOLDFISH BOWL **½ (1961) PR:A
LOVE IN A HOT CLIMATE ** (1958, Fr./Sp.) PR:A
LOVE IN A TAXI *** (1980) PR:A
LOVE IN BLOOM *½ (1935) PR:A
LOVE IN COLD BLOOD
(SEE:ICE HOUSE, THE)
LOVE IN EXILE ** (1936, Brit.) PR:A
LOVE IN 4 DIMENSIONS **½ (1965, Fr./It.) PR:C
LOVE IN GERMANY, A **½ (1984, Fr./Ger.) PR:O
LOVE IN LAS VEGAS
(SEE:VIVA LAS VEGAS)
LOVE IN MOROCCO * (1933, Fr.) PR:A
LOVE IN PAWN **½ (1953, Brit.) PR:A
LOVE IN THE AFTERNOON * (1957) PR:A**
LOVE IN THE DESERT *½ (1929) PR:A
LOVE IN THE ROUGH *½ (1930) PR:A
LOVE IN WAITING * (1948, Brit.) PR:A
LOVE-INS, THE ** (1967) PR:C
LOVE IS A BALL ** (1963) PR:A
LOVE IS A CAROUSEL * (1970) PR:O
LOVE IS A FAT WOMAN *** (1988, Arg.) PR:O
LOVE IS A FUNNY THING ** (1970, Fr./It.) PR:C
LOVE IS A HEADACHE ** (1938) PR:A
LOVE IS A MANY-SPLENDORED THING ** (1955) PR:A
LOVE IS A RACKET *** (1932) PR:A
LOVE IS A SPLENDID ILLUSION *½ (1970, Brit.) PR:O
LOVE IS A WEAPON
(SEE:HELL'S ISLAND)
LOVE IS A WOMAN *½ (1967, Brit.) PR:C
LOVE IS BETTER THAN EVER **½ (1952) PR:A
LOVE IS A DAY'S WORK
(SEE:FROM A ROMAN BALCONY)
LOVE IS LIKE THAT
(SEE:JAZZ CINDERELLA)
LOVE IS LIKE THAT * (1933) PR:A
LOVE IS MY PROFESSION **½ (1959, Fr.) PR:O
LOVE IS NEWS *** (1937) PR:A
LOVE IS ON THE AIR ** (1937) PR:A
LOVE ISLAND *½ (1952) PR:A
LOVE ITALIAN STYLE
(SEE:LOVE, THE ITALIAN WAY)
LOVE KISS, THE *½ (1930) PR:A
LOVE LAUGHS AT ANDY HARDY *½ (1946) PR:A
LOVE LETTERS **½ (1945) PR:A
LOVE LETTERS * (1983) PR:C**
LOVE LETTERS OF A STAR **½ (1936) PR:A
LOVE LIES ** (1931, Brit.) PR:A
LOVE, LIFE AND LAUGHTER ** (1934, Brit.) PR:A
LOVE, LIVE AND LAUGH * (1929) PR:A
LOVE LOTTERY, THE **½ (1954, Brit.) PR:A
LOVE MACHINE, THE *½ (1971) PR:O
LOVE MADNESS
(SEE:REEFER MADNESS)
LOVE MAKERS, THE
(SEE:LA VIACCIA)
LOVE MATCH, THE **½ (1955, Brit.) PR:A
LOVE MATES * (1967, Swed.) PR:A
LOVE MATES, THE
(SEE:MADLY)
LOVE ME DEADLY * (1972) PR:O
LOVE ME FOREVER **½ (1935) PR:A
LOVE ME OR LEAVE ME ** (1955) PR:A**

LOVE ME TENDER *½ (1956) PR:A
LOVE ME TONIGHT ***** (1932) PR:A
LOVE MERCHANT, THE * (1966) PR:O
LOVE MERCHANTS
(SEE:LOVE MERCHANT, THE)
LOVE NEST, THE ** (1933, Brit.) PR:A
LOVE NEST ** (1951) PR:A
LOVE NOW...PAY LATER zero (1966) PR:O
LOVE NOW . . . PAY LATER ** (1966, It.) PR:C
LOVE OF THREE QUEENS
(SEE:LOVES OF THREE QUEENS)
LOVE ON A BET ** (1936) PR:A
LOVE ON A BUDGET ** (1938) PR:A
LOVE ON A PILLOW ** (1963, Fr./It.) PR:O
LOVE ON SKIS *½ (1933, Brit.) PR:A
LOVE ON THE DOLE *** (1945, Brit.) PR:A
LOVE ON THE GROUND * (1984,Fr.) PR:C
LOVE ON THE RIVIERA ** (1964, Fr./It.) PR:C
LOVE ON THE RUN *** (1936) PR:A
LOVE ON THE RUN ***½ (1980, Fr.) PR:A-C
LOVE ON THE SPOT ** (1932, Brit.) PR:A
LOVE ON TOAST *½ (1937) PR:A
LOVE ON WHEELS *½ (1932, Brit.) PR:A
LOVE PARADE, THE ***½ (1929) PR:A-C
LOVE PAST THIRTY *½ (1934) PR:A
LOVE PLAY
(SEE:PLAYTIME)
LOVE PROBLEMS ** (1970, It.) PR:C
LOVE RACE, THE ** (1931, Brit.) PR:A
LOVE RACE
(SEE:GIRL O' MY DREAMS)
LOVE RACKET, THE *½ (1929) PR:A
LOVE REDEEMED
(SEE:DRAGNET PATROL)
LOVE ROBOTS, THE * (1965, Jap.) PR:C
LOVE ROOT, THE
(SEE:MANDRAGOLA)
LOVE SLAVES OF THE AMAZONS * (1957) PR:A
LOVE, SOLDIERS AND WOMEN
(SEE:DAUGHTERS OF DESTINY)
LOVE SONGS *½ (1986, Fr./Can.) PR:C
LOVE SPECIALIST, THE * (1959, It.) PR:A
LOVE STARVED
(SEE:YOUNG BRIDE)
LOVE STORM, THE *½ (1931, Brit.) PR:A
LOVE STORY
(SEE:LADY SURRENDERS, A)
LOVE STORY *** (1949, Fr.) PR:C
LOVE STORY * (1970) PR:A-C**
LOVE STREAMS ***½ (1984) PR:C
LOVE—TAHITI STYLE
(SEE:NUDE ODYSSEY)
LOVE TAKES FLIGHT * (1937) PR:A
LOVE TEST, THE ** (1935, Brit.) PR:A
LOVE THAT BRUTE **½ (1950) PR:A
LOVE, THE ITALIAN WAY ** (1964, It.) PR:C
LOVE THY NEIGHBOR ** (1940) PR:A
LOVE TILL FIRST BLOOD ** (1985, Hung.) PR:C-O
LOVE TIME * (1934) PR:A
LOVE TRADER * (1930) PR:A
LOVE TRAP, THE ** (1929) PR:A
LOVE UNDER FIRE *½ (1937) PR:A
LOVE UNDER THE CRUCIFIX ** (1965, Jap.) PR:A
LOVE UP THE POLE *½ (1936, Brit.) PR:A
LOVE WAGER, THE ** (1933, Brit.) PR:A
LOVE WALTZ, THE ** (1930, Ger.) PR:A
LOVE WITH THE PROPER STRANGER ***
(1963) PR:C
LOVED ONE, THE *** (1965) PR:C
LOVELESS, THE **½ (1982) PR:O
LOVELINES zero (1984) PR:O
LOVELY TO LOOK AT
(SEE:THIN ICE)
LOVELY TO LOOK AT *** (1952) PR:A
LOVELY WAY TO DIE, A ** (1968) PR:C
LOVELY WAY TO GO, A
(SEE:A LOVELY WAY TO DIE)
LOVEMAKER, THE
(SEE:MAIN STREET)
LOVEMAKERS, THE
(SEE:LA VIACCIA)
LOVER BOY
(SEE:LOVERS, HAPPY LOVERS!)
LOVER COME BACK **½ (1946) PR:A
LOVER COME BACK ***½ (1961) PR:A
LOVER FOR THE SUMMER, A
(SEE:MISTRESS FOR THE SUMMER, A)

LOVER COME BACK *½ (1931) PR:A
LOVER, WIFE
(SEE:WIFE MISTRESS)
LOVERS, THE ** (1959, Fr.) PR:O
LOVERS AND LIARS *½ (1981, It.) PR:O
LOVERS AND LOLLIPOPS **½ (1956) PR:A
LOVERS AND LUGGERS *** (1938, Aus.) PR:A
LOVERS AND OTHER STRANGERS ***½ (1970) PR:C
LOVERS, THE *½ (1972, Brit.) PR:C
LOVERS COURAGEOUS ** (1932) PR:A
LOVERS, HAPPY LOVERS! ** (1955, Brit.) PR:C
LOVERS IN LIMBO
(SEE:NAME OF THE GAME IS KILL, THE)
LOVERS LIKE US
(SEE:SAVAGE, THE)
LOVERS MUST LEARN
(SEE:ROME ADVENTURE)
LOVER'S NET *** (1957, Fr.) PR:C
LOVERS OF LISBON
(SEE:LOVER'S NET)
LOVERS OF MONTPARNASSE, THE
(SEE:MODIGLIANI OF MONTPARNASSE)
LOVERS OF TERUEL, THE *** (1962, Fr.) PR:A
LOVERS OF TOLEDO, THE *½
(1954, Fr./Sp./It.) PR:A
LOVERS OF VERONA, THE *** (1951, Fr.) PR:A
LOVERS ON A TIGHTROPE ** (1962, Fr.) PR:A
LOVERS' ROCK ** (1966, Chi.) PR:A
LOVE'S A LUXURY
(SEE:CARETAKER'S DAUGHTER, THE)
LOVES AND TIMES OF SCARAMOUCHE, THE *½
(1976, It.) PR:C
LOVES OF A BLONDE ***½ (1966, Czech.) PR:A
LOVES OF A DICTATOR
(SEE:DICTATOR, THE)
LOVES OF ARIANE, THE
(SEE:ARIANE)
LOVES OF CARMEN, THE **½ (1948) PR:C
LOVES OF EDGAR ALLAN POE, THE **
(1942) PR:A
LOVES OF HERCULES, THE * (1960, Ital./Fr.) PR:A
LOVES OF ISADORA, THE
(SEE:ISADORA)
LOVES OF JOANNA GODDEN, THE *½
(1947, Brit.) PR:A
LOVES OF MADAME DUBARRY, THE **
(1938, Brit.) PR:A
LOVES OF ROBERT BURNS, THE **
(1930, Brit.) PR:A
LOVES OF SALAMMBO, THE * (1962, Fr./It.) PR:A
LOVES OF THREE QUEENS, THE **½
(1954, It./Fr.) PR:A
LOVE'S OLD SWEET SONG ** (1933, Brit.) PR:A
LOVESICK ** (1983) PR:C
LOVIN' MOLLY ** (1974) PR:O
LOVIN' THE LADIES ** (1930) PR:A
LOVING ** (1970) PR:C
LOVING COUPLES ** (1980) PR:O
LOVING COUPLES ** (1966, Swed.) PR:O
LOVING MEMORY *½ (1970, Brit.) PR:O
LOVING YOU * (1957) PR:A**
LOW BLOW * (1986) PR:O
LOWER DEPTHS, THE * (1937, Fr.) PR:C**
LOWER DEPTHS, THE * (1962, Jap.) PR:C**
LOYAL HEART ** (1946, Brit.) PR:AA
LOYALTIES **½ (1934, Brit.) PR:A
LOYALTIES * (1986, Brit./Can.) PR:O**
LOYALTY OF LOVE ** (1937, It.) PR:A
LSD, I HATE YOU
(SEE:MOVIE STAR, AMERICAN STYLE OR, LSD, I HATE YOU)
LUCAS * (1986) PR:A**
LUCI DEL VARIETA
(SEE:VARIETY LIGHTS)
LUCIANO ** (1963, It.) PR:C
LUCIFER PROJECT, THE
(SEE:BARRACUDA)
LUCK OF A SAILOR, THE ** (1934, Brit.) PR:A
LUCK OF GINGER COFFEY, THE ***
(1964, US/Can.) PR:A-C
LUCK OF ROARING CAMP, THE *½ (1937) PR:A
LUCK OF THE GAME
(SEE:GRIDIRON FLASH)
LUCK OF THE IRISH *** (1948) PR:A
LUCK OF THE IRISH, THE *** (1937, Ireland) PR:A

LUCK OF THE NAVY
(SEE:NORTH SEA PATROL)
LUCK OF THE TURF **½ (1936, Brit.) PR:A
LUCKIEST GIRL IN THE WORLD, THE **
(1936) PR:A
LUCKY
(SEE:BOY, A GIRL, AND A DOG, A)
LUCKY BOOTS
(SEE:GUN PLAY)
LUCKY BOY ** (1929) PR:A
LUCKY BRIDE, THE **½ (1948, USSR) PR:AA
LUCKY CISCO KID **½ (1940) PR:A
LUCKY DAYS *½ (1935, Brit.) PR:A
LUCKY DAYS
(SEE:SING A JINGLE)
LUCKY DEVILS *** (1933) PR:A
LUCKY DEVILS ** (1941) PR:C
LUCKY DOG **½ (1933) PR:AA
LUCKY GIRL *½ (1932, Brit.) PR:A
LUCKY IN LOVE *½ (1929) PR:A
LUCKY JADE ** (1937, Brit.) PR:A
LUCKY JIM **½ (1957, Brit.) PR:C
LUCKY JORDAN *** (1942) PR:A
LUCKY LADIES *½ (1932, Brit.) PR:A
LUCKY LADY *½ (1975) PR:C-O
LUCKY LARRIGAN *½ (1933) PR:A
LUCKY LEGS *½ (1942) PR:A
LUCKY LOSER ** (1934, Brit.) PR:A
LUCKY LOSERS ** (1950) PR:C
LUCKY LUCIANO
(SEE:RE: LUCKY LUCIANO)
LUCKY LUKE ** (1971, Fr./Bel.) PR:A
LUCKY MASCOT, THE *½ (1951, Brit.) PR:A
LUCKY ME ** (1954) PR:A
LUCKY NICK CAIN **½ (1951) PR:A
LUCKY NIGHT * (1939) PR:A
LUCKY NUMBER, THE ** (1933, Brit.) PR:A
LUCKY PARTNERS *½ (1940) PR:A
LUCKY RALSTON
(SEE:LAW AND ORDER)
LUCKY STAR ** (1929) PR:A
LUCKY STAR, THE *** (1980, Can.) PR:A
LUCKY STIFF, THE ** (1949) PR:A
LUCKY SWEEP, A * (1932, Brit.) PR:A
LUCKY TERROR * (1936) PR:A
LUCKY TEXAN, THE **½ (1934) PR:A
LUCKY 13
(SEE:RUNNING HOT)
LUCKY TO BE A WOMAN * (1955, It.) PR:C-O
LUCKY TO ME *½ (1939, Brit.) PR:AA
LUCRECE BORGIA **½ (1953, It./Fr.) PR:O
LUCRETIA BORGIA
(SEE:LUCRECE BORGIA)
LUCREZIA BORGIA **½ (1937, Fr.) PR:A
LUCY GALLANT ** (1955) PR:C
LUDWIG ** (1973, It./Ger./Fr.) PR:O
LUGGAGE OF THE GODS **½ (1983) PR:C
LULLABY ** (1961, USSR) PR:A
LULLABY, THE
(SEE:SIN OF MADELON CLAUDET)
LULLABY OF BROADWAY, THE **½ (1951) PR:A
L'ULTIMO UOMO DELLA TERRA
(SEE:LAST MAN ON EARTH, THE)
LULU *½ (1978) PR:O
LULU ** (1962, Aus.) PR:O
LULU BELLE *½ (1948) PR:A
LUM AND ABNER ABROAD * (1956) PR:AA
LUMBERJACK ** (1944) PR:A
LUMIERE **½ (1976, Fr.) PR:O
LUMIERE D'ETE *** (1943, Fr.) PR:C
LUMIKUNINGATAR
(SEE:SNOW QUEEN)
LUMMOX ** (1930) PR:A
L'UN ET L'AUTRE
(SEE:OTHER ONE, THE)
LUNA *½ (1979, It.) PR:O
LUNATICS, THE *** (1986, Hong Kong) PR:O
LUNCH HOUR ** (1962, Brit.) PR:C
LUNCH ON THE GRASS
(SEE:PICNIC ON THE GRASS)
LUNCH WAGON ** (1981) PR:O
LUNCH WAGON GIRLS
(SEE:LUNCH WAGON)
L'UNE CHANTE L'AUTRE PAS
(SEE:ONE SINGS, THE OTHER DOESN'T)
LUNG-MEN K'O-CHAN
(SEE:DRAGON INN)

L'UOMO DALLE DUE OMBRE
  (SEE:COLD SWEAT)
LUPE zero (1967) PR:O
LURE, THE ** (1933, Brit.) PR:A
LURE OF THE ISLANDS * (1942) PR:A
LURE OF THE JUNGLE, THE **½
  (1970, Den.) PR:AA
LURE OF THE SWAMP ** (1957) PR:C
LURE OF THE WASTELAND ** (1939) PR:A
LURE OF THE WILDERNESS ** (1952) PR:C
LURED *** (1947) PR:A
LUST FOR A VAMPIRE ** (1971, Brit.) PR:O
LUST FOR EVIL
  (SEE:PURPLE NOON)
LUST FOR GOLD ** (1949) PR:O
LUST FOR LIFE ***** (1956) PR:C
LUST IN THE DUST zero (1985) PR:O
LUST OF EVIL
  (SEE:PURPLE NOON)
LUSTY BRAWLERS
  (SEE:THIS MAN CAN'T DIE)
LUSTY MEN, THE ***** (1952) PR:C
LUTHER **½ (1974) PR:C
LUTRING
  (SEE:WAKE UP AND DIE)
LUV * (1967) PR:A-C
LUXURY GIRLS ** (1953, It.) PR:C
LUXURY LINER zero (1933) PR:A
LUXURY LINER ** (1948) PR:A
LYCANTHROPUS
  (SEE:WEREWOLF IN A GIRL'S DORMITORY)
LYDIA **½ (1941) PR:A
LYDIA ** (1964, Can.) PR:O
LYDIA ATE THE APPLE
  (SEE:PARTINGS)
LYDIA BAILEY **½ (1952) PR:A
LYONS IN PARIS, THE **½ (1955, Brit.) PR:A
LYONS MAIL, THE ** (1931, Brit.) PR:A
LYSISTRATA
  (SEE:DAUGHTERS OF DESTINY)

M

M ***** (1933, Ger.) PR:O
M *** (1951) PR:C
MA AND PA KETTLE **½ (1949) PR:A
MA AND PA KETTLE AT HOME ** (1954) PR:A
MA AND PA KETTLE AT THE FAIR ** (1952) PR:A
MA AND PA KETTLE AT WAIKIKI ** (1955) PR:A
MA AND PA KETTLE BACK ON THE FARM **
  (1951) PR:A
MA AND PA KETTLE GO TO PARIS
  (SEE:MA AND PA KETTLE ON VACATION)
MA AND PA KETTLE GO TO TOWN ** (1950) PR:A
MA AND PA KETTLE ON VACATION **
  (1953) PR:A
MA BARKER'S KILLER BROOD ** (1960) PR:O
MA, HE'S MAKING EYES AT ME *½ (1940) PR:A
MA NUIT CHEZ MAUD
  (SEE:MY NIGHT AT MAUD'S)
MA POMME
  (SEE:JUST ME)
MAARAKAT ALGER
  (SEE:BATTLE OF ALGIERS, THE)
MAC ARTHUR ***½ (1977) PR:A
MACABRE ** (1958) PR:C
MACAO *** (1952) PR:C
MACARIO ** (1961, Mex.) PR:AA
MACARONI ** (1985, It.) PR:C
MACARTHUR'S CHILDREN *** (1985, Jap.) PR:C
MACBETH ** (1948) PR:A
MACBETH **½ (1963) PR:A
MACBETH ***½ (1971, Brit.) PR:O
MACDONALD OF THE CANADIAN MOUNTIES
  (SEE:PONY SOLDIER)
MACHETE * (1958) PR:A
MACHINE GUN KELLY **½ (1958) PR:C-O
MACHINE GUN MAMA zero (1944) PR:A
MACHINE GUN McCAIN ** (1970, It.) PR:O
MACHISMO—40 GRAVES FOR 40 GUNS **½
  (1970) PR:O
MACHISTE AGAINST THE CZAR
  (SEE:ATLAS AGAINST THE CZAR)
MACHO CALLAHAN * (1970) PR:O
MACISTE NELLA TERRA DEI CICLOPI
  (SEE:ATLAS AGAINST THE CZAR)
MACK, THE *½ (1973) PR:O
MACKENNA'S GOLD **½ (1969) PR:C
MACKINTOSH & T.J. ** (1975) PR:C-O
MACKINTOSH MAN, THE **½ (1973, Brit.) PR:C
MACOMBER AFFAIR, THE ***½ (1947) PR:C
MACON COUNTY LINE ** (1974) PR:O
MACUMBA LOVE * (1960) PR:A

MACUSHLA ** (1937, Brit.) PR:A
MAD ABOUT MEN ** (1954, Brit.) PR:A
MAD ABOUT MONEY
  (SEE:HE LOVED AN ACTRESS)
MAD ABOUT MUSIC *** (1938) PR:A
MAD ADVENTURES OF '"RABBI" JACOB, THE
  (SEE:ADVENTURES OF RABBI JACOB, THE)
MAD AT THE WORLD ** (1955) PR:C
MAD ATLANTIC, THE **½ (1967, Jap.) PR:O
MAD BOMBER, THE ** (1973) PR:O
MAD CAGE, THE
  (SEE:LA CAGE AUX FOLLES)
MAD DOCTOR, THE ** (1941) PR:A
MAD DOCTOR OF BLOOD ISLAND, THE *
  (1969, Phil./US) PR:O
MAD DOCTOR OF MARKET STREET, THE *
  (1942) PR:A
MAD DOG
  (SEE:MAD DOG MORGAN)
MAD DOG COLL ** (1961) PR:C
MAD DOG MORGAN *** (1976,Aus.) PR:O
MAD EMPRESS, THE ** (1940) PR:A
MAD EXECUTIONERS, THE ** (1965, Ger.) PR:O
MAD GAME, THE **½ (1933) PR:A
MAD GENIUS, THE **½ (1931) PR:A-C
MAD GHOUL, THE **½ (1943) PR:C
MAD HATTER, THE
  (SEE:BREAKFAST IN HOLLYWOOD)
MAD HATTERS, THE ** (1935, Brit.) PR:A
MAD HOLIDAY *½ (1936) PR:A
MAD LITTLE ISLAND **½ (1958, Brit.) PR:A
MAD LOVE **** (1935) PR:C
MAD, MAD MOVIE MAKERS, THE
  (SEE:LAST PORNO FLICK, THE)
MAD MAGAZINE PRESENTS UP THE ACADEMY
  (SEE:UP THE ACADEMY)
MAD MAGICIAN, THE ** (1954) PR:C
MAD MARTINDALES, THE ** (1942) PR:A
MAD MASQUERADE
  (SEE:WASHINGTON MASQUERADE, THE)
MAD MAX ***½ (1979, Aus.) PR:O
MAD MAX BEYOND THUNDERDOME ***
  (1985, Aus.) PR:C-O
MAD MAX 2
  (SEE:ROAD WARRIOR, THE)
MAD MEN OF EUROPE ** (1940, Brit.) PR:A
MAD MISS MANTON, THE **½ (1938) PR:A-C
MAD MONSTER PARTY **½ (1967) PR:AA
MAD MONSTER, THE * (1942) PR:A
MAD PARADE, THE ** (1931) PR:A
MAD QUEEN, THE ** (1950, Sp.) PR:A
MAD ROOM, THE ** (1969) PR:O
MAD WEDNESDAY *** (1950) PR:A
MAD YOUTH * (1940) PR:A
MADALENA **½ (1965, Gr.) PR:A
MADAM SATAN
  (SEE:MADAME SATAN)
MADAME **½ (1963, Fr./It./Sp.) PR:A-C
MADAME AKI *** (1963, Jap.) PR:O
MADAME BOVARY *** (1949) PR:A
MADAME BUTTERFLY **½ (1932) PR:A
MADAME BUTTERFLY *** (1955, It./Jap.) PR:A
MADAME CURIE **** (1943) PR:AA
MADAME DE
  (SEE:EARRINGS OF MADAME DE, THE)
MADAME DEATH zero (1968, Mex.) PR:O
MADAME DU BARRY *½ (1934) PR:A
MADAME DU BARRY ** (1954, Fr./It.) PR:C
MADAME FRANKENSTEIN
  (SEE:LADY FRANKENSTEIN)
MADAME GUILLOTINE *½ (1931, Brit.) PR:A
MADAME JULIE
  (SEE:WOMAN BETWEEN, THE)
MADAME LOUISE *½ (1951, Brit.) PR:A
MADAME PIMPERNEL
  (SEE:PARIS UNDERGROUND)
MADAME RACKETEER ** (1932) PR:A
MADAME ROSA ***½ (1977, Fr.) PR:O
MADAME SANS-GENE
  (SEE:MADAME)
MADAME SATAN **½ (1930) PR:A
MADAME SOUSATZKA *** (1988, Brit.) PR:A-C
MADAME SPY ** (1934) PR:A
MADAME SPY *½ (1942) PR:A
MADAME WHITE SNAKE **½
  (1963, Hong Kong) PR:C
MADAME X ** (1929) PR:A
MADAME X **½ (1937) PR:A
MADAME X ** (1966) PR:A
MADCAP
  (SEE:TAMING THE WILD)
MADCAP OF THE HOUSE *½ (1950, Mex.) PR:A
MADCHEN FUR DIE MAMBO-BAR
  (SEE:$100 A NIGHT)
MADCHEN IN UNIFORM
  (SEE:MAEDCHEN IN UNIFORM)
MADDEST CAR IN THE WORLD, THE *
  (1974, Ger.) PR:AA

MADDEST STORY EVER TOLD, THE
  (SEE:SPIDER BABY)
MADE *½ (1972, Brit.) PR:C
MADE FOR EACH OTHER ***½ (1939) PR:AA
MADE FOR EACH OTHER *** (1971) PR:C
MADE IN HEAVEN ** (1952, Brit.) PR:A
MADE IN HEAVEN *** (1987) PR:A
MADE IN ITALY *** (1967, Fr./It.) PR:C
MADE IN PARIS ** (1966) PR:A
MADE IN U.S.A. **½ (1966, Fr.) PR:C
MADE ON BROADWAY ** (1933) PR:A
MADELEINE ***½ (1950, Brit.) PR:A
MADELEINE IS *½ (1971, Can.) PR:O
MADEMOISELLE **½ (1966, Fr./Brit.) PR:C
MADEMOISELLE DOCTEUR
  (SEE:UNDER SECRET ORDERS)
MADEMOISELLE FIFI **½ (1944) PR:A
MADEMOISELLE FRANCE
  (SEE:REUNION IN FRANCE)
MADHOUSE *½ (1974, Brit.) PR:C
MADIGAN ***½ (1968) PR:C
MADIGAN'S MILLIONS * (1970, Sp./It.) PR:A
MADISON AVENUE ** (1962) PR:A
MADISON SQUARE GARDEN ** (1932) PR:A
MADLY *½ (1970, Fr.) PR:O
MADMAN zero (1982) PR:O
MADMAN OF LAB 4, THE ** (1967, Fr.) PR:A
MADMEN OF MANDORAS
  (SEE:THEY SAVED HITLER'S BRAIN)
MADNESS OF THE HEART ** (1949, Brit.) PR:A
MADONNA OF AVENUE A *½ (1929) PR:A
MADONNA OF THE DESERT ** (1948) PR:A
MADONNA OF THE SEVEN MOONS **½
  (1945, Brit.) PR:C
MADONNA OF THE STREETS *½ (1930) PR:A
MADONNA'S SECRET, THE ** (1946) PR:A
MADRON * (1970, US/Israel) PR:O
MADWOMAN OF CHAILLOT, THE * (1969) PR:A
MAEDCHEN IN UNIFORM ***** (1932, Ger.) PR:C
MAEDCHEN IN UNIFORM ** (1965, Ger./Fr.) PR:C
MAEVA * (1961) PR:O
MAEVA—PORTRAIT OF A TAHITIAN GIRL
  (SEE:MAEVA)
MAFIA ** (1969, Fr./It.) PR:C
MAFIA, THE ** (1972, Arg.) PR:C
MAFIA GIRLS, THE * (1969) PR:C-O
MAFIOSO **½ (1962, It.) PR:C
MAFU CAGE, THE ** (1978) PR:O
MAGGIE, THE
  (SEE:HIGH AND DRY)
MAGIC *** (1978) PR:O
MAGIC BOW, THE *½ (1947, Brit.) PR:A
MAGIC BOX, THE **** (1952, Brit.) PR:AA
MAGIC BOY, THE
  (SEE:GIRL WITH THE FABULOUS BOX, THE)
MAGIC BOY ** (1960, Jap.) PR:A
MAGIC CARPET, THE ** (1951) PR:A
MAGIC CHRISTIAN, THE ***½ (1970, Brit.) PR:C-O
MAGIC CHRISTMAS TREE ** (1964) PR:A
MAGIC FACE, THE ** (1951, Aust.) PR:A
MAGIC FIRE ** (1956) PR:A
MAGIC FOUNTAIN, THE ** (1961) PR:A
MAGIC GARDEN, THE
  (SEE:PENNYWHISTLE BLUES, THE)
MAGIC GARDEN OF STANLEY SWEETHART, THE *
  (1970) PR:O
MAGIC NIGHT ** (1932, Brit.) PR:A
MAGIC OF LASSIE, THE * (1978) PR:AA
MAGIC SPECTACLES zero (1961) PR:O
MAGIC SWORD, THE *** (1962) PR:A
MAGIC TOWN **½ (1947) PR:AA
MAGIC VOYAGE OF SINBAD, THE **
  (1962, USSR) PR:A
MAGIC WEAVER, THE ** (1965, USSR) PR:A
MAGIC WORLD OF TOPO GIGIO, THE **½
  (1961, It.) PR:A
MAGICAL SPECTACLES
  (SEE:MAGIC SPECTACLES)
MAGICIAN, THE ***½ (1959, Swed.) PR:C
MAGICIAN OF LUBLIN, THE **½
  (1979, Israel/Ger.) PR:C
MAGNET, THE ** (1950, Brit.) PR:A
MAGNETIC MONSTER, THE *** (1953) PR:C
MAGNIFICENT AMBERSONS, THE *****
  (1942) PR:A
MAGNIFICENT BANDITS, THE *½
  (1969, It./Sp.) PR:C
MAGNIFICENT BRUTE, THE ** (1936) PR:A
MAGNIFICENT CONCUBINE, THE **
  (1964, Hong Kong) PR:A
MAGNIFICENT CUCKOLD, THE **½
  (1965, Fr./It.) PR:A
MAGNIFICENT DOLL ** (1946) PR:A
MAGNIFICENT DOPE, THE ** (1942) PR:A
MAGNIFICENT FRAUD, THE *½ (1939) PR:A
MAGNIFICENT LIE ** (1931) PR:A
MAGNIFICENT MATADOR, THE ** (1955) PR:A
MAGNIFICENT OBSESSION *** (1935) PR:A

MAGNIFICENT OBSESSION **½ (1954) PR:A
MAGNIFICENT ONE, THE **½ (1974, Fr./It.) PR:A
MAGNIFICENT OUTCAST
  (SEE:ALMOST A GENTLEMAN)
MAGNIFICENT ROGUE, THE *½ (1946) PR:A
MAGNIFICENT ROUGHNECKS *½ (1956) PR:A
MAGNIFICENT SEVEN, THE
  (SEE:SEVEN SAMURAI, THE)
MAGNIFICENT SEVEN, THE **** (1960) PR:C
MAGNIFICENT SEVEN DEADLY SINS, THE **½
  (1971, Brit.) PR:A-C
MAGNIFICENT SEVEN RIDE, THE ** (1972) PR:A
MAGNIFICENT SHOWMAN, THE
  (SEE:CIRCUS WORLD)
MAGNIFICENT SINNER **½ (1963, Fr.) PR:A
MAGNIFICENT TRAMP, THE ** (1962, Fr./It.) PR:A
MAGNIFICENT TWO, THE ** (1967, Brit.) PR:A
MAGNIFICENT YANKEE, THE **** (1950) PR:AA
MAGNUM FORCE *** (1973) PR:C-O
MAGOICHI SAGA, THE ** (1970, Jap.) PR:C
MAGUS, THE * (1968, Brit.) PR:C
MAHANAGAR
  (SEE:BIG CITY, THE)
MAHLER **½ (1974, Brit.) PR:A-C
MAHOGANY *½ (1975) PR:C
MAID AND THE MARTIAN, THE
  (SEE:PAJAMA PARTY)
MAID FOR MURDER ** (1963, Brit.) PR:A
MAID HAPPY ** (1933, Brit.) PR:A
MAID OF SALEM ** (1937) PR:A
MAID OF THE MOUNTAINS, THE *½
  (1932, Brit.) PR:A
MAID TO ORDER *½ (1932) PR:A
MAID TO ORDER **½ (1987) PR:C
MAIDEN, THE ** (1961, Fr.) PR:A
MAIDEN FOR A PRINCE, A ** (1967, Fr./It.) PR:A
MAIDS, THE ** (1975, Brit.) PR:C
MAID'S NIGHT OUT **½ (1938) PR:A
MAIDSTONE zero (1970) PR:C
MAIGRET LAYS A TRAP ** (1958, Fr.) PR:C
MAIL ORDER BRIDE ** (1964) PR:A
MAIL TRAIN ** (1941, Brit.) PR:A
MAILBAG ROBBERY *** (1957, Brit.) PR:A-C
MAIN ATTRACTION, THE *½ (1962, Brit.) PR:A
MAIN CHANCE, THE * (1966, Brit.) PR:A
MAIN EVENT, THE zero (1938) PR:A
MAIN EVENT, THE ** (1979) PR:A-C
MAIN STREET
  (SEE:I MARRIED A DOCTOR)
MAIN STREET AFTER DARK ** (1944) PR:A
MAIN STREET ** (1956, Sp.) PR:A
MAIN STREET GIRL
  (SEE:PAROLED FROM THE BIG HOUSE)
MAIN STREET KID, THE ** (1947) PR:A
MAIN STREET LAWYER * (1939) PR:A
MAIN STREET TO BROADWAY *½ (1953) PR:A
MAIN THING IS TO LOVE, THE **½
  (1975, It./Fr.) PR:C
MAIS OU ET DONC ORNICAR **½ (1979, Fr.) PR:C
MAISIE ** (1939) PR:A
MAISIE GETS HER MAN ** (1942) PR:A
MAISIE GOES TO RENO ** (1944) PR:A
MAISIE WAS A LADY **½ (1941) PR:A
MAJDHAR **½ (1984, Brit.) PR:C
MAJIN ** (1968, Jap.) PR:A
MAJIN, THE HIDEOUS IDOL
  (SEE:MAJIN)
MAJIN, THE MONSTER OF TERROR
  (SEE:MAJIN)
MAJOR AND THE MINOR, THE **** (1942) PR:A
MAJOR BARBARA ***** (1941, Brit.) PR:A
MAJOR DUNDEE *** (1965) PR:C-O
MAJORITY OF ONE, A *** (1961) PR:A
MAKE A FACE ** (1971) PR:C
MAKE A MILLION *½ (1935) PR:A
MAKE A WISH ** (1937) PR:A
MAKE AND BREAK
  (SEE:TELL ME LIES)
MAKE BELIEVE BALLROOM ** (1949) PR:A
MAKE HASTE TO LIVE ** (1954) PR:A
MAKE IT THREE * (1938, Brit.) PR:A
MAKE LIKE A THIEF ** (1966, Fin.) PR:A
MAKE ME A STAR *** (1932) PR:A
MAKE ME AN OFFER *½ (1954, Brit.) PR:A
MAKE MINE A DOUBLE ** (1962, Brit.) PR:A
MAKE MINE A MILLION **½ (1965, Brit.) PR:A
MAKE MINE MINK *** (1960, Brit.) PR:A

MAKE MINE MUSIC *** (1946) PR:AA
MAKE-UP * (1937, Brit.) PR:A
MAKE WAY FOR A LADY ** (1936) PR:A
MAKE WAY FOR LILA ** (1962, Swed./Ger.) PR:A
MAKE WAY FOR TOMORROW ***½ (1937) PR:A
MAKE YOUR OWN BED ** (1944) PR:A
MAKER OF MEN *½ (1931) PR:A
MAKING IT *½ (1971) PR:O
MAKING LOVE * (1982) PR:O
MAKING MR. RIGHT * (1987) PR:C-O
MAKING OF A LADY, THE
  (SEE:LADY HAMILTON)
MAKING THE GRADE *½ (1929) PR:A
MAKING THE GRADE ** (1984) PR:O
MAKING THE HEADLINES * (1938) PR:A
MAKIOKA SISTERS, THE ***½ (1985, Jap.) PR:C-O
MAKO: THE JAWS OF DEATH * (1976) PR:C
MAKUCHI
  (SEE:IDIOT, THE)
MALACHI'S COVE **½ (1973, Brit.) PR:AA
MALAGA
  (SEE:FIRE OVER AFRICA)
MALAGA * (1962, Brit.) PR:A
MALANDRO **½ (1986, Braz./Fr.) PR:C
MALATESTA'S CARNIVAL *½ (1973) PR:O
MALAY NIGHTS zero (1933) PR:A
MALAYA *** (1950) PR:A
MALCOLM *** (1986, Aus.) PR:C
MALE AND FEMALE
  (SEE:MALE AND FEMALE SINCE ADAM AND
  EVE)
MALE AND FEMALE SINCE ADAM AND EVE **
  (1961, Arg.) PR:A
MALE ANIMAL, THE **** (1942) PR:A
MALE COMPANION ** (1965, Fr./It.) PR:A
MALE HUNT ** (1965, Fr./It.) PR:A
MALE SERVICE zero (1966) PR:O
MALEFICES
  (SEE:WHERE THE TRUTH LIES)
MALENKA, THE VAMPIRE zero (1972, Sp./It.) PR:O
MALEVIL ** (1981, Fr./Ger.) PR:C
MALIBU
  (SEE:SEQUOIA)
MALIBU BEACH * (1978) PR:C
MALIBU BIKINI SHOP, THE * (1987) PR:O
MALIBU HIGH zero (1979) PR:O
MALICE
  (SEE:MALICIOUS)
MALICIOUS *** (1974, It.) PR:O
MALIZIA
  (SEE:MALICIOUS)
MALONE **½ (1987) PR:O
MALOU *** (1983) PR:C
MALPAS MYSTERY, THE ** (1967, Brit.) PR:A
MALPERTIUS *½ (1972, Bel./Fr.) PR:C
MALTA STORY *** (1954, Brit.) PR:A-C
MALTESE BIPPY, THE *½ (1969) PR:A
MALTESE FALCON, THE ***** (1941) PR:A
MALTESE FALCON, THE *** (1931) PR:A
MAMA LOVES PAPA ** (1933) PR:A
MAMA LOVES PAPA *½ (1945) PR:A
MAMA RUNS WILD * (1938) PR:A
MAMA STEPS OUT * (1937) PR:A
MAMBA * (1930) PR:A
MAMBO **½ (1955, It.) PR:C
MAME **½ (1974) PR:A
MAMI
  (SEE:MAMMY)
MAMMA DRACULA * (1980, Bel./Fr.) PR:O
MAMMA ROMA **** (1962, It.) PR:C
MAMMY **½ (1930) PR:A
MAN, THE ** (1972) PR:A
MAN, A WOMAN, AND A BANK, A **½
  (1979, Can.) PR:C
MAN, A WOMAN AND A KILLER, A **½
  (1975) PR:O
MAN ABOUT THE HOUSE, A ** (1947, Brit.) PR:A
MAN ABOUT TOWN *½ (1932) PR:A
MAN ABOUT TOWN **½ (1939) PR:AA
MAN ABOUT TOWN ** (1947, Fr.) PR:A
MAN ACCUSED * (1959) PR:C
MAN AFRAID ** (1957) PR:A
MAN AGAINST MAN ** (1961, Jap.) PR:C
MAN AGAINST WOMAN *½ (1932) PR:A
MAN ALIVE *½ (1945) PR:A
MAN ALONE, A *** (1955) PR:A
MAN AND A WOMAN, A ***½ (1966, Fr.) PR:A-C

MAN AND A WOMAN: 20 YEARS LATER, A ***
  (1986, Fr.) PR:C
MAN AND BOY *½ (1972) PR:A
MAN AND HIS MATE
  (SEE:ONE MILLION B.C.)
MAN AND THE BEAST, THE **½ (1951, Arg.) PR:A
MAN AND THE MOMENT, THE ** (1929) PR:A
MAN AND THE MONSTER, THE *
  (1965, Mex.) PR:A
MAN AT LARGE *½ (1941) PR:A
MAN AT SIX
  (SEE:GABLES MYSTERY, THE)
MAN AT THE CARLTON TOWER **
  (1961, Brit.) PR:C
MAN AT THE TOP ** (1973, Brit.) PR:A
MAN BAIT ** (1952, Brit.) PR:A
MAN BEAST *½ (1956) PR:A
MAN BEHIND THE GUN, THE ** (1952) PR:A
MAN BEHIND THE MASK, THE **½
  (1936, Brit.) PR:A
MAN BETRAYED, A * (1937) PR:A
MAN BETRAYED, A *½ (1941) PR:A
MAN BETWEEN, THE *** (1953, Brit.) PR:A
MAN CALLED ADAM, A ** (1966) PR:C
MAN CALLED BACK, THE * (1932) PR:C
MAN CALLED DAGGER, A * (1967) PR:A
MAN CALLED FLINTSTONE, THE **½
  (1966) PR:AA
MAN CALLED GANNON, A ** (1969) PR:A
MAN CALLED HORSE, A **½ (1970) PR:O
MAN CALLED NOON, THE ** (1973, Brit.) PR:C
MAN CALLED PETER, THE ***½ (1955) PR:AA
MAN CALLED SLEDGE, A **½ (1971, It.) PR:O
MAN CALLED SULLIVAN, A
  (SEE:GREAT JOHN L., THE)
MAN COULD GET KILLED, A ** (1966) PR:A
MAN CRAZY ** (1953) PR:A
MAN DETAINED **½ (1961, Brit.) PR:C
MAN-EATER
  (SEE:SHARK!)
MAN EATER OF HYDRA
  (SEE:ISLAND OF THE DOOMED)
MAN-EATER OF HYDRA
  (SEE:ISLAND OF THE DOOMED)
MAN-EATER OF KUMAON *** (1948) PR:A
MAN ESCAPED, A **** (1957, Fr.) PR:A
MAN FACING SOUTHEAST **** (1986, Arg.) PR:O
MAN FOLLOWING THE SUN
  (SEE:SANDU FOLLOWS THE SUN)
MAN FOR ALL SEASONS, A ***** (1966, Brit.) PR:A
MAN FRIDAY **½ (1975, Brit.) PR:A-C
MAN FROM BITTER RIDGE, THE **½ (1955) PR:A
MAN FROM BLACK HILLS, THE ** (1952) PR:A
MAN FROM BLANKLEY'S, THE ** (1930) PR:A
MAN FROM BUTTON WILLOW, THE **
  (1965) PR:AA
MAN FROM CAIRO, THE *½ (1953) PR:A
MAN FROM CHEYENNE ** (1942) PR:A
MAN FROM CHICAGO, THE *½ (1931, Brit.) PR:A
MAN FROM COCODY *½ (1966, Fr./It.) PR:A
MAN FROM COLORADO, THE ** (1948) PR:A-C
MAN FROM C.O.T.T.O.N.
  (SEE:GONE ARE THE DAYS)
MAN FROM DAKOTA, THE ** (1940) PR:A
MAN FROM DEATH VALLEY, THE *½ (1931) PR:A
MAN FROM DEL RIO *** (1956) PR:A
MAN FROM DOWN UNDER, THE ** (1943) PR:A-C
MAN FROM FRISCO ** (1944) PR:A
MAN FROM GALVESTON, THE ** (1964) PR:A
MAN FROM GOD'S COUNTRY ** (1958) PR:A
MAN FROM GUN TOWN, THE ** (1936) PR:A
MAN FROM HEADQUARTERS ** (1942) PR:A
MAN FROM HELL, THE * (1934) PR:A
MAN FROM HELL'S EDGES * (1932) PR:A
MAN FROM HONG KONG *½ (1975) PR:O
MAN FROM LARAMIE, THE **** (1955) PR:C
MAN FROM MONTANA *½ (1941) PR:A
MAN FROM MONTEREY, THE ** (1933) PR:A
MAN FROM MONTREAL, THE ** (1940) PR:A
MAN FROM MOROCCO, THE **½ (1946, Brit.) PR:A
MAN FROM MUSIC MOUNTAIN **½ (1938) PR:A
MAN FROM MUSIC MOUNTAIN **½ (1943) PR:A
MAN FROM NEVADA, THE
  (SEE:NEVADAN, THE)
MAN FROM NEW MEXICO, THE ** (1932) PR:A
MAN FROM NOWHERE, THE
  (SEE:ARIZONA COLT)

MAN FROM OKLAHOMA, THE ** (1945) PR:AA
MAN FROM O.R.G.Y., THE zero (1970) PR:O
MAN FROM PLANET X, THE **½ (1951) PR:A
MAN FROM RAINBOW VALLEY, THE **½
   (1946) PR:A
MAN FROM SNOWY RIVER, THE *
   (1983, Aus.) PR:C**
MAN FROM SUNDOWN, THE *½ (1939) PR:A
MAN FROM TANGIER
   (SEE:THUNDER OVER TANGIER)
MAN FROM TEXAS, THE **½ (1939) PR:A
MAN FROM TEXAS, THE * (1948) PR:A
MAN FROM THE ALAMO, THE * (1953) PR:A**
MAN FROM THE BIG CITY, THE
   (SEE:IT HAPPENED OUT WEST)
MAN FROM THE DINERS' CLUB, THE ***
   (1963) PR:A
MAN FROM THE EAST, THE ** (1961, Jap.) PR:A
MAN FROM THE EAST, A *** (1974, It./Fr.) PR:C-O
MAN FROM THE FIRST CENTURY, THE *
   (1961, Czech.) PR:A
MAN FROM THE FOLIES BERGERE, THE
   (SEE:FOLIES BERGERE)
MAN FROM THE PAST, THE
   (SEE:MAN FROM THE FIRST CENTURY, THE)
MAN FROM THE RIO GRANDE, THE *½
   (1943) PR:A
MAN FROM THUNDER RIVER, THE **½
   (1943) PR:A
MAN FROM TORONTO, THE ** (1933, Brit.) PR:A
MAN FROM TUMBLEWEEDS, THE **½ (1940) PR:A
MAN FROM UTAH, THE * (1934) PR:A
MAN FROM WYOMING, A * (1930) PR:A
MAN FROM YESTERDAY, THE *** (1932) PR:A
MAN FROM YESTERDAY, THE *½
   (1949, Brit.) PR:O
MAN GOES THROUGH THE WALL, A
   (SEE:MAN WHO WALKED THROUGH THE WALL)
MAN HE FOUND, THE
   (SEE:WHIP HAND, THE)
MAN HUNT ** (1933) PR:A
MAN HUNT ** (1936) PR:A
MAN HUNT **** (1941) PR:A
MAN HUNTER, THE * (1930) PR:A
MAN HUNTERS OF THE CARIBBEAN zero
   (1938) PR:A
MAN I KILLED
   (SEE:BROKEN LULLABY)
MAN I LOVE, THE ** (1929) PR:A
MAN I LOVE, THE *** (1946) PR:A
MAN I MARRIED, THE *** (1940) PR:A
MAN I MARRY, THE ** (1936) PR:A
MAN I WANT, THE * (1934, Brit.) PR:A
MAN IN A COCKED HAT ** (1960, Brit.) PR:A
MAN IN BLACK, THE * (1950, Brit.) PR:C-O
MAN IN BLUE, THE **½ (1937) PR:A
MAN IN GREY, THE * (1943, Brit.) PR:A-C**
MAN IN HALF-MOON STREET, THE ***
   (1944) PR:A
MAN IN HIDING
   (SEE:MAN-TRAP)
MAN IN LOVE, A ***½ (1987, Fr.) PR:O
MAN IN OUTER SPACE
   (SEE:MAN FROM THE FIRST CENTURY, THE)
MAN IN POSSESSION, THE ** (1931) PR:A-C
MAN IN POSSESSION, THE
   (SEE:PERSONAL PROPERTY)
MAN IN THE ATTIC **½ (1953) PR:C
MAN IN THE BACK SEAT, THE ** (1961, Brit.) PR:A
MAN IN THE DARK **½ (1953) PR:A
MAN IN THE DARK * (1963, Brit.) PR:A
MAN IN THE DINGHY, THE ** (1951, Brit.) PR:A
MAN IN THE GLASS BOOTH, THE ***½
   (1975) PR:A
MAN IN THE GREY FLANNEL SUIT, THE ***½
   (1956) PR:A
MAN IN THE IRON MASK, THE * (1939) PR:A**
MAN IN THE MIDDLE *** (1964, US/Brit.) PR:A-C
MAN IN THE MIRROR, THE ** (1936, Brit.) PR:A
MAN IN THE MOON *** (1961, Brit.) PR:A
MAN IN THE MOONLIGHT MASK, THE *½
   (1958, Jap.) PR:A
MAN IN THE NET, THE *½ (1959) PR:A
MAN IN THE ROAD, THE ** (1957, Brit.) PR:A
MAN IN THE SADDLE **½ (1951) PR:A
MAN IN THE SHADOW **½ (1957) PR:A
MAN IN THE SHADOW
   (SEE:VIOLENT STRANGER)
MAN IN THE SKY
   (SEE:DECISION AGAINST TIME)
MAN IN THE STORM, THE ** (1969, Jap.) PR:A
MAN IN THE TRUNK, THE * (1942) PR:A
MAN IN THE VAULT *½ (1956) PR:A
MAN IN THE WATER, THE *½ (1963) PR:A
MAN IN THE WHITE SUIT, THE ** (1952) PR:A**
MAN IN THE WILDERNESS **½
   (1971, US/Sp.) PR:O
MAN INSIDE, THE **½ (1958, Brit.) PR:C

MAN IS ARMED, THE * (1956) PR:A
MAN IS TEN FEET TALL, A
   (SEE:EDGE OF THE CITY)
MAN KILLER
   (SEE:PRIVATE DETECTIVE 62)
MAN-KILLER
   (SEE:OTHER LOVE, THE)
MAN LIKE EVA, A ** (1985, Ger.) PR:O
MAN MAD
   (SEE:NO PLACE TO LAND)
MAN MADE MONSTER *** (1941) PR:A
MAN MISSING
   (SEE:YOU HAVE TO RUN FAST)
MAN OF A THOUSAND FACES ***½ (1957) PR:A
MAN OF AFFAIRS * (1937, Brit.) PR:A
MAN OF AFRICA ** (1956, Brit.) PR:A
MAN OF BRONZE
   (SEE:JIM THORPE—ALL AMERICAN)
MAN OF CONFLICT ** (1953) PR:A
MAN OF CONQUEST *** (1939) PR:A
MAN OF COURAGE * (1943) PR:A
MAN OF EVIL **½ (1948, Brit.) PR:A
MAN OF FLOWERS ***½ (1984, Aus.) PR:O
MAN OF IRON
   (SEE:RAILROAD MAN, THE)
MAN OF IRON * (1935) PR:A
MAN OF IRON **** (1981, Pol.) PR:C
MAN OF LA MANCHA *½ (1972) PR:C
MAN OF MARBLE ***½ (1979, Pol.) PR:C-O
MAN OF MAYFAIR *½ (1931, Brit.) PR:A
MAN OF MUSIC ** (1953, USSR) PR:A
MAN OF SENTIMENT, A *½ (1933) PR:A
MAN OF THE FAMILY
   (SEE:TOP MAN)
MAN OF THE FOREST **½ (1933) PR:A
MAN OF THE HOUR
   (SEE:COLONEL EFFINGHAM'S RAID)
MAN OF THE HOUR, THE *** (1940, Fr.) PR:A
MAN OF THE MOMENT **½ (1955, Brit.) PR:A
MAN OF THE MOMENT **½ (1935, Brit.) PR:A
MAN OF THE PEOPLE ** (1937) PR:A
MAN OF THE WEST ***** (1958) PR:C-O
MAN OF THE WORLD ** (1931) PR:A
MAN OF TWO WORLDS * (1934) PR:A
MAN OF VIOLENCE zero (1970, Brit.) PR:O
MAN ON A STRING ** (1960) PR:A
MAN ON A SWING *** (1974) PR:C
MAN ON A TIGHTROPE **** (1953) PR:A
MAN ON AMERICA'S CONSCIENCE, THE
   (SEE:TENNESSEE JOHNSON)
MAN ON FIRE *** (1957) PR:A
MAN ON FIRE ** (1987, It./Fr.) PR:O
MAN ON THE EIFFEL TOWER, THE **
   (1949) PR:A**
MAN ON THE FLYING TRAPEZE, THE ****
   (1935) PR:A
MAN ON THE PROWL * (1957) PR:A
MAN ON THE RUN
   (SEE:KIDNAPPERS, THE)
MAN ON THE RUN *½ (1949, Brit.) PR:A
MAN OR GUN *½ (1958) PR:A
MAN OUTSIDE, THE *½ (1933, Brit.) PR:A
MAN OUTSIDE, THE ** (1968, Brit.) PR:A
MAN OUTSIDE * (1988) PR:C
MAN-PROOF *½ (1938) PR:A
MAN STOLEN **½ (1934, Fr.) PR:A
**MAN THEY COULD NOT HANG, THE **½
   (1939) PR:C**
MAN THEY COULDN'T ARREST, THE *
   (1933, Brit.) PR:A
MAN TO MAN **½ (1931) PR:A
MAN TO REMEMBER, A *** (1938) PR:A
MAN TRAILER, THE **½ (1934) PR:A
MAN-TRAP ** (1961) PR:A
MAN TROUBLE ** (1930) PR:A
MAN UNDER SUSPICION *** (1985, Ger.) PR:C
MAN UPSTAIRS, THE *** (1959, Brit.) PR:A
MAN WANTED *½ (1932, Brit.) PR:A
MAN WHO BROKE THE BANK AT MONTE CARLO,
   THE ** (1935) PR:A
MAN WHO CAME BACK, THE * (1931) PR:C
MAN WHO CAME FOR COFFEE, THE ***
   (1970, It.) PR:O
MAN WHO CAME TO DINNER, THE ****
   (1942) PR:A
MAN WHO CHANGED, THE
   (SEE:MAN WHO CHANGED HIS NAME)
MAN WHO CHANGED HIS MIND
   (SEE:MAN WHO LIVED AGAIN, THE)
MAN WHO CHANGED HIS NAME, THE *
   (1934, Brit.) PR:A
MAN WHO CHEATED HIMSELF, THE **½
   (1951) PR:A
MAN WHO COULD CHEAT DEATH, THE **½
   (1959, Brit.) PR:C
**MAN WHO COULD WORK MIRACLES, THE ***½
   (1937, Brit.) PR:A**

MAN WHO COULDN'T WALK, THE **½
   (1964, Brit.) PR:A
MAN WHO CRIED WOLF, THE **½ (1937) PR:A
MAN WHO DARED, THE ** (1939) PR:A
MAN WHO DARED, THE ** (1933) PR:AA
MAN WHO DARED, THE **½ (1946) PR:A
MAN WHO DIED TWICE, THE *½ (1958) PR:A
MAN WHO ENVIED WOMEN, THE **½ (1985) PR:C
**MAN WHO FELL TO EARTH, THE ***½
   (1976, Brit.) PR:C-O**
MAN WHO FINALLY DIED, THE *½
   (1967, Brit.) PR:A
MAN WHO FOUND HIMSELF, THE ** (1937) PR:A
**MAN WHO HAD POWER OVER WOMEN, THE **
   (1970, Brit.) PR:C**
**MAN WHO HAUNTED HIMSELF, THE **
   (1970, Brit.) PR:A**
MAN WHO KILLED BILLY THE KID, THE *
   (1967, Span./It.) PR:A
MAN WHO KNEW TOO MUCH, THE **
   (1935, Brit.) PR:C**
MAN WHO KNEW TOO MUCH, THE **
   (1956) PR:A**
MAN WHO LAUGHS, THE * (1966, It.) PR:O
MAN WHO LIES, THE **½ (1970, Czech./Fr.) PR:C
MAN WHO LIKED FUNERALS, THE *½
   (1959, Brit.) PR:A
MAN WHO LIVED AGAIN, THE ***
   (1936, Brit.) PR:A
MAN WHO LIVED TWICE **½ (1936) PR:A
MAN WHO LOST HIMSELF, THE ** (1941) PR:A
MAN WHO LOST HIS WAY, THE
   (SEE:CROSSROADS)
**MAN WHO LOVED CAT DANCING, THE **
   (1973) PR:C-O**
MAN WHO LOVED REDHEADS, THE ***
   (1955, Brit.) PR:A
MAN WHO LOVED WOMEN, THE *
   (1977, Fr.) PR:O**
MAN WHO LOVED WOMEN, THE *½ (1983) PR:O
MAN WHO MADE DIAMONDS, THE **½
   (1937, Brit.) PR:A
MAN WHO NEVER WAS, THE *** (1956, Brit.) PR:A
MAN WHO PAWNED HIS SOUL
   (SEE:UNKNOWN BLOND)
MAN WHO PLAYED GOD, THE **½ (1932) PR:A
MAN WHO RECLAIMED HIS HEAD, THE ***
   (1935) PR:A
MAN WHO RETURNED TO LIFE, THE **
   (1942) PR:A
MAN WHO SHOT LIBERTY VALANCE, THE *
   (1962) PR:A**
MAN WHO STOLE THE SUN, THE **
   (1980, Jap.) PR:C
MAN WHO TALKED TOO MUCH, THE *½
   (1940) PR:A
MAN WHO THOUGHT LIFE, THE *½
   (1969, Den.) PR:A
MAN WHO TURNED TO STONE, THE zero
   (1957) PR:A
MAN WHO UNDERSTOOD WOMEN, THE **½
   (1959) PR:A-C
MAN WHO WAGGED HIS TAIL, THE **½
   (1961, It./Span.) PR:A
MAN WHO WALKED ALONE, THE * (1945) PR:A
MAN WHO WALKED THROUGH THE WALL, THE **
   (1964, Ger.) PR:A
MAN WHO WAS NOBODY, THE **
   (1960, Brit.) PR:C
MAN WHO WAS SHERLOCK HOLMES, THE ***
   (1937, Ger.) PR:A
MAN WHO WASN'T THERE, THE zero (1983) PR:C
MAN WHO WATCHED TRAINS GO BY, THE
   (SEE:PARIS EXPRESS)
MAN WHO WON, THE * (1933, Brit.) PR:A
MAN WHO WOULD BE KING, THE ***
   (1975, Brit.) PR:A-C**
MAN WHO WOULD NOT DIE, THE *½ (1975) PR:C
MAN WHO WOULDN'T DIE, THE ** (1942) PR:A
MAN WHO WOULDN'T TALK, THE ** (1940) PR:A
MAN WHO WOULDN'T TALK, THE **½
   (1958, Brit.) PR:A
MAN WITH A CLOAK, THE *** (1951) PR:A
MAN WITH A GUN * (1958, Brit.) PR:C
MAN WITH A MILLION *** (1954, Brit.) PR:A
**MAN WITH BOGART'S FACE, THE ***½
   (1980) PR:A-C**
MAN WITH CONNECTIONS, THE **
   (1970, Fr.) PR:C
MAN WITH MY FACE, THE ** (1951) PR:A
MAN WITH NINE LIVES, THE *** (1940) PR:A
MAN WITH 100 FACES, THE ** (1938, Brit.) PR:A
MAN WITH ONE RED SHOE, THE *½ (1985) PR:C
MAN WITH THE BALLOONS, THE **
   (1968, It./Fr.) PR:A
MAN WITH THE DEADLY LENS, THE
   (SEE:WRONG IS RIGHT)

MAN WITH THE ELECTRIC VOICE, THE
  (SEE:FIFTEEN WIVES)
MAN WITH THE GOLDEN ARM, THE **½
(1955)   PR:O
MAN WITH THE GOLDEN GUN, THE **
(1974, Brit.)   PR:A
MAN WITH THE GREEN CARNATION, THE ***
  (1960, Brit.)   PR:A
MAN WITH THE GREEN CARNATION, THE
  (SEE:GREEN BUDDHA, THE)
MAN WITH THE GUN *** (1955)   PR:C
MAN WITH THE MAGNETIC EYES, THE *½
  (1945, Brit.)   PR:C
MAN WITH THE SYNTHETIC BRAIN
  (SEE:PSYCHO A GO-GO)
MAN WITH THE TRANSPLANTED BRAIN, THE **½
  (1972, Fr./It./Ger.)   PR:A
MAN WITH THE X-RAY EYES, THE
  (SEE:"X"—THE MAN WITH THE X-RAY EYES)
MAN WITH THE YELLOW EYES
  (SEE:PLANETS AGAINST US, THE)
MAN WITH THIRTY SONS, THE
  (SEE:MAGNIFICENT YANKEE, THE)
MAN WITH TWO BRAINS, THE ** (1983)   PR:O
MAN WITH TWO FACES, THE *** (1934)   PR:A-C
MAN WITH TWO HEADS, THE zero (1972)   PR:O
MAN WITH TWO LIVES, THE *½ (1942)   PR:A
MAN WITH X-RAY EYES, THE
  (SEE:"X"—THE MAN WITH THE X-RAY EYES)
MAN WITHIN, THE
  (SEE:SMUGGLERS, THE)
MAN WITHOUT A BODY, THE * (1957, Brit.)   PR:A
MAN WITHOUT A FACE, THE * (1935, Brit.)   PR:A
MAN WITHOUT A FACE
  (SEE:PYRO)
MAN WITHOUT A FACE, THE
  (SEE:SHADOWMAN)
MAN WITHOUT A GUN
  (SEE:MAN WITH THE GUN)
MAN WITHOUT A STAR ***½ (1955)   PR:C
MAN, WOMAN AND CHILD ** (1983)   PR:A
MANCHU EAGLE MURDER CAPER MYSTERY, THE
  *½ (1975)   PR:A
MANCHURIAN AVENGER * (1985)   PR:O
MANCHURIAN CANDIDATE, THE ***½
(1962)   PR:C-O
MANDABI ** (1970, Fr./Senegal)   PR:A
MANDALAY *½ (1934)   PR:A-C
MANDARIN MYSTERY, THE *½ (1937)   PR:A
MANDINGO ** (1975)   PR:O
MANDRAGOLA ** (1966, Fr./It.)   PR:A
MANDRAGOLA/THE LOVE ROOT
  (SEE:MANDRAGOLA)
MANDY
  (SEE:CRASH OF SILENCE)
MANFISH *½ (1956)   PR:A
MANGANINNIE **½ (1982, Aus.)   PR:A
MANGO TREE, THE **½ (1981, Aus.)   PR:O
MANHANDLED ** (1949)   PR:A
MANHATTAN ***** (1979)   PR:C
MANHATTAN ANGEL *½ (1948)   PR:A
MANHATTAN BABY zero (1986, It.)   PR:O
MANHATTAN COCKTAIL ** (1928)   PR:A
MANHATTAN HEARTBEAT ** (1940)   PR:A
MANHATTAN LOVE SONG ** (1934)   PR:A
MANHATTAN MADNESS
  (SEE:ADVENTURE IN MANHATTAN)
MANHATTAN MADNESS
  (SEE:ADVENTURE IN BLACKMAIL)
MANHATTAN MELODRAMA **** (1934)   PR:A
MANHATTAN MERRY-GO-ROUND * (1937)   PR:A
MANHATTAN MOON ** (1935)   PR:A
MANHATTAN MUSIC BOX
  (SEE:MANHATTAN MERRY-GO-ROUND)
MANHATTAN PARADE *½ (1931)   PR:A
MANHATTAN PROJECT, THE ** (1986)   PR:A
MANHATTAN SHAKEDOWN * (1939)   PR:A
MANHATTAN TOWER *½ (1932)   PR:A
MANHUNT
  (SEE:FROM HELL TO TEXAS)
MANHUNT
  (SEE:ITALIAN CONNECTION, THE)
MANHUNT, THE * (1986, It.)   PR:O
MANHUNT IN THE JUNGLE ** (1958)   PR:A
MANHUNTER *** (1986)   PR:O
MANIA ** (1961, Brit.)   PR:O
MANIAC zero (1934)   PR:O

MANIAC ** (1963, Brit.)   PR:C
MANIAC! zero (1977)   PR:C
MANIAC COP *½ (1988)   PR:O
MANIAC
  (SEE:MANIAC MANSION)
MANIAC * (1980)   PR:O
MANIAC MANSION zero (1978, It.)   PR:O
MANIACS ARE LOOSE, THE
  (SEE:THRILL KILLERS, THE)
MANIACS ON WHEELS ** (1951, Brit.)   PR:A
MANIFESTO *** (1988)   PR:O
MANILA CALLING *** (1942)   PR:A
MANINA
  (SEE:GIRL IN THE BIKINI)
MANITOU, THE ** (1978)   PR:C
MANJI
  (SEE:PASSION)
MANKILLERS zero (1987)   PR:O
MANNEQUIN * (1933, Brit.)   PR:A
MANNEQUIN **½ (1937)   PR:A
MANNEQUIN * (1987)   PR:A-C
MANNER MUSSEN SO SIEN
  (SEE:HIPPODROME)
MANNISKOR MOTS OCH LJUV MUSIK UPPSTAR I
HJARTAT
  (SEE:PEOPLE MEET AND SWEET MUSIC FILLS
  THE HEART)
MANNY'S ORPHANS
  (SEE:HERE COME THE TIGERS)
MANOLETE ** (1950, Sp.)   PR:A
MANOLIS ** (1962, Brit.)   PR:A
MANON ** (1987, Venezuela)   PR:O
MANON OF THE SPRING ***½ (1987, Fr.)   PR:C
MANON 70 ** (1968, Fr.)   PR:O
MANOS, THE HANDS OF FATE zero (1966)   PR:C
MANPOWER *** (1941)   PR:A
MAN'S AFFAIR, A ** (1949, Brit.)   PR:A
MAN'S CASTLE, A *** (1933)   PR:A
MAN'S COUNTRY ** (1938)   PR:A
MAN'S FAVORITE SPORT (?) **½ (1964)   PR:A
MAN'S GAME, A *½ (1934)   PR:A
MAN'S HERITAGE
  (SEE:SPIRIT OF CULVER)
MAN'S HOPE **** (1947, Sp.)   PR:A
MAN'S LAND, A ** (1932)   PR:A
MAN'S WORLD, A ** (1942)   PR:A
MANSION OF THE DOOMED zero (1976)   PR:O
MANSLAUGHTER ** (1930)   PR:A
MANSTER, THE zero (1962, Jap.)   PR:A
MANSTER—HALF MAN, HALF MONSTER, THE
  (SEE:MANSTER, THE)
MANTIS IN LACE *½ (1968)   PR:O
MANTRAP, THE *½ (1943)   PR:A
MANTRAP
  (SEE:WOMAN IN HIDING)
MANTRAP
  (SEE:MAN-TRAP)
MANUELA
  (SEE:STOWAWAY GIRL)
MANUELA'S LOVES ** (1987, Fr.)   PR:C-O
MANULESCU **½ (1933, Ger.)   PR:A
MANUSCRIPT FOUND IN SARAGOSSA
  (SEE:SARAGOSSA MANUSCRIPT, THE)
MANY A SLIP * (1931)   PR:A
MANY HAPPY RETURNS *½ (1934)   PR:A
MANY RIVERS TO CROSS **½ (1955)   PR:A
MANY TANKS MR. ATKINS **½ (1938, Brit.)   PR:A
MANY WATERS ** (1931, Brit.)   PR:A
MAOS SANGRENTAS
  (SEE:VIOLENT AND THE DAMNED, THE)
MARA MARU **½ (1952)   PR:A
MARA OF THE WILDERNESS **½ (1966)   PR:A
MARACAIBO **½ (1958)   PR:A
MARAT/SADE
  (SEE:PERSECUTION AND ASSASSINATION OF
  JEAN-PAUL MARAT AS PERFORMED BY THE
  INMATES OF THE ASYLUM OF CHARENTON
  UNDER THE DIRECTION OF THE MARQUIS DE
  SADE)
MARATHON MAN **** (1976)   PR:O
MARAUDERS, THE *** (1947)   PR:A
MARAUDERS, THE ** (1955)   PR:A
MARAUDERS, THE
  (SEE:MERRILL'S MARAUDERS)
MARCH HARE, THE *** (1956, Brit.)   PR:A
MARCH OF THE SPRING HARE *½ (1969)   PR:O

MARCH OF THE WOODEN SOLDIERS, THE
  (SEE:BABES IN TOYLAND)
MARCH ON PARIS 1914—OF GENERALOBERST
  ALEXANDER VON KLUCK—AND HIS MEMORY
  OF JESSIE HOLLADAY ***½ (1977)   PR:C
MARCH OR DIE *** (1977, Brit.)   PR:C-O
MARCHA O MUERE
  (SEE:COMMANDO)
MARCHANDES D'ILLUSIONS
  (SEE:NIGHTS OF SHAME)
MARCHANDS DE FILLES
  (SEE:SELLERS OF GIRLS)
MARCIA O CREPA
  (SEE:COMMANDO)
MARCO *** (1973)   PR:A
MARCO POLO ** (1962, Fr./It.)   PR:A
MARCO POLO JUNIOR * (1973, Aus.)   PR:A
MARCO THE MAGNIFICENT
  (1966, It./Fr./Yugo./Egypt/Afghanistan)   PR:C
MARDI GRAS **½ (1958)   PR:A
MARDI GRAS MASSACRE zero (1978)   PR:O
MARGEM, A
  (SEE:MARGIN, THE)
MARGIE ** (1940)   PR:A
MARGIE **** (1946)   PR:AA
MARGIN, THE ** (1969, Braz.)   PR:A
MARGIN FOR ERROR ** (1943)   PR:A
MARIA CANDELARIA
  (SEE:PORTRAIT OF MARIA)
MARIA CHAPDELAINE
  (SEE:THE NAKED HEART)
MARIA ELENA
  (SEE:SHE-DEVIL ISLAND)
MARIA MARTEN
  (SEE:MURDER IN THE OLD RED BARN)
MARIA, THE WONDERFUL WEAVER
  (SEE:MAGIC WEAVER, THE)
MARIAGE A L'ITALIENNE
  (SEE:MARRIAGE ITALIAN STYLE)
MARIANNE ** (1929)   PR:A
MARIANNE
  (SEE:MIRRORS)
MARIA'S LOVERS **½ (1985)   PR:O
MARIE ***½ (1985)   PR:C
MARIE-ANN ** (1978, Can.)   PR:A
MARIE ANTOINETTE **** (1938)   PR:A
MARIE DES ILES
  (SEE:MARIE OF THE ISLES)
MARIE GALANTE *** (1934)   PR:A
MARIE OF THE ISLES ** (1960, Fr.)   PR:A
MARIE WALEWSKA
  (SEE:CONQUEST)
MARIGOLD **½ (1938, Brit.)   PR:A
MARIGOLD MAN zero (1970)   PR:C
MARIGOLDS IN AUGUST ***½
  (1984, South Africa)   PR:C
MARILYN * (1953, Brit.)   PR:O
MARINE BATTLEGROUND *½
  (1966, US/S.K.)   PR:A
MARINE RAIDERS **½ (1944)   PR:A
MARINES ARE COMING, THE ** (1935)   PR:A
MARINES ARE HERE, THE ** (1938)   PR:A
MARINES COME THROUGH, THE * (1943)   PR:A
MARINES FLY HIGH, THE ** (1940)   PR:A
MARINES, LET'S GO **½ (1961)   PR:A
MARIUS ***½ (1933, Fr.)   PR:C
MARIZINIA ** (1962, US/Braz.)   PR:A
MARIZINIA, THE WITCH BENEATH THE SEA
  (SEE:MARIZINIA)
MARJORIE MORNINGSTAR **½ (1958)   PR:A-C
MARK, THE ***½ (1961, Brit.)   PR:A
MARK IT PAID ** (1933)   PR:A
MARK OF CAIN, THE ** (1948, Brit.)   PR:A
MARK OF THE APACHE
  (SEE:TOMAHAWK TRAIL)
MARK OF THE AVENGER
  (SEE:MYSTERIOUS RIDER, THE)
MARK OF THE CLAW
  (SEE:DICK TRACY'S DILEMMA)
MARK OF THE DEVIL * (1970, Ger./Brit.)   PR:O
MARK OF THE DEVIL II * (1975, Ger./Brit.)   PR:O
MARK OF THE GORILLA ** (1950)   PR:A
MARK OF THE HAWK, THE *** (1958)   PR:A
MARK OF THE LASH *½ (1948)   PR:A
MARK OF THE PHOENIX *½ (1958, Brit.)   PR:C
MARK OF THE RENEGADE ** (1951)   PR:A
MARK OF THE VAMPIRE *** (1935)   PR:C

Finding entries in **THE MOTION PICTURE GUIDE** ™

Years 1929-83	Volumes I-IX
1984	Volume IX
1985	1986 ANNUAL
1986	1987 ANNUAL
1987	1988 ANNUAL
1988	1989 ANNUAL

STAR RATINGS

★★★★★   Masterpiece
★★★★   Excellent
★★★   Good
★★   Fair
★   Poor
zero   Without Merit

PARENTAL RECOMMENDATION (PR:)

AA   Good for Children
A   Acceptable for Children
C   Cautionary, some objectionable scenes
O   Objectionable for Children

BOLD: Films on Videocassette

MARK OF THE VAMPIRE
  (SEE:VAMPIRE, THE)
MARK OF THE WHISTLER, THE **½ (1944) PR:A
MARK OF THE WITCH *½ (1970) PR:C
MARK OF ZORRO, THE **** (1940) PR:A
MARK TWAIN
  (SEE:ADVENTURES OF MARK TWAIN, THE)
MARKED BULLET, THE
  (SEE:PRAIRIE STRANGER)
MARKED FOR MURDER ** (1945) PR:A
MARKED GIRLS *½ (1949, Fr.) PR:A
MARKED MAN, THE
  (SEE:MARK OF THE WHISTLER, THE)
MARKED MEN * (1940) PR:A
MARKED ONE, THE *½ (1963, Brit.) PR:A
MARKED TRAILS ** (1944) PR:A
MARKED WOMAN ***½ (1937) PR:C
MARKETA LAZAROVA **** (1968, Czech.) PR:O
MARKO POLO
  (SEE:MARCO THE MAGNIFICENT)
MARKOPOULOS PASSION, THE
  (SEE:ILLIAC PASSION, THE)
MARKSMAN, THE ** (1953) PR:C
MARLOWE *** (1969) PR:A
MARNIE **½ (1964) PR:C
MAROC 7 *** (1967, Brit.) PR:A
MAROONED *** (1969) PR:A
MAROONED *½ (1933, Brit.) PR:C
MARQUIS DE SADE: JUSTINE
  (SEE:JUSTINE)
MARRIAGE, A *** (1983) PR:C
MARRIAGE BOND, THE ** (1932, Brit.) PR:A
MARRIAGE BY CONTRACT *** (1928) PR:A
MARRIAGE CAME TUMBLING DOWN, THE **
  (1968, Fr.) PR:A
MARRIAGE FORBIDDEN
  (SEE:DAMAGED GOODS)
MARRIAGE-GO-ROUND, THE *½ (1960) PR:A
MARRIAGE IN THE SHADOWS ** (1948, Ger.) PR:A
MARRIAGE IS A PRIVATE AFFAIR ** (1944) PR:A
MARRIAGE—ITALIAN STYLE ***
  (1964, Fr./It.) PR:O
MARRIAGE OF A YOUNG STOCKBROKER, THE
  ***½ (1971) PR:A
MARRIAGE OF BALZAMINOV, THE **½
  (1966, USSR) PR:A
MARRIAGE OF CONVENIENCE
  (SEE:HIRED WIFE)
MARRIAGE OF CONVENIENCE **
  (1970, Brit.) PR:A
MARRIAGE OF CORBAL
  (SEE:PRISONER OF CORBAL)
MARRIAGE OF FIGARO, THE ** (1963, Fr.) PR:A
MARRIAGE OF FIGARO, THE ** (1949, Ger.) PR:A
MARRIAGE OF MARIA BRAUN, THE ****
  (1979, Ger.) PR:O
MARRIAGE ON APPROVAL * (1934) PR:A
MARRIAGE ON THE ROCKS ** (1965) PR:A-C
MARRIAGE PLAYGROUND, THE *** (1929) PR:A
MARRIAGE SYMPHONY
  (SEE:LET'S TRY AGAIN)
MARRIED AND IN LOVE ** (1940) PR:A
MARRIED BACHELOR *** (1941) PR:A
MARRIED BEFORE BREAKFAST ** (1937) PR:A
MARRIED BUT SINGLE
  (SEE:THIS THING CALLED LOVE)
MARRIED COUPLE, A *** (1969, Can.) PR:O
MARRIED IN HASTE
  (SEE:CONSOLATION MARRIAGE)
MARRIED IN HASTE
  (SEE:MARRIAGE ON APPROVAL)
MARRIED IN HOLLYWOOD ** (1929) PR:A
MARRIED TO THE MOB *** (1988) PR:O
MARRIED TOO YOUNG ** (1962) PR:A
MARRIED WOMAN, THE ***½ (1965, Fr.) PR:C
MARRY ME *½ (1932, Brit.) PR:A
MARRY ME AGAIN **½ (1953) PR:A
MARRY ME! ** (1949, Brit.) PR:A
MARRY ME! MARRY ME! ** (1969, Fr.) PR:A
MARRY THE BOSS' DAUGHTER *½ (1941) PR:A
MARRY THE GIRL *½ (1935, Brit.) PR:A
MARRY THE GIRL *½ (1937) PR:A
MARRYING KIND, THE **½ (1952) PR:A
MARRYING WIDOWS * (1934) PR:C
MARS NEEDS WOMEN zero (1966) PR:A
MARSCHIER ODER KREIPER
  (SEE:COMMANDO)
MARSEILLAISE
  (SEE:LA MARSEILLAISE)
MARSEILLES CONTRACT, THE
  (SEE:DESTRUCTORS, THE)
MARSHAL OF AMARILLO **½ (1948) PR:A
MARSHAL OF CEDAR ROCK **½ (1953) PR:A
MARSHAL OF CRIPPLE CREEK, THE ** (1947) PR:A
MARSHAL OF GUNSMOKE **½ (1944) PR:A
MARSHAL OF HELDORADO ** (1950) PR:A
MARSHAL OF LAREDO ** (1945) PR:A
MARSHAL OF MESA CITY, THE *** (1939) PR:A

MARSHAL OF RENO *** (1944) PR:A
MARSHAL'S DAUGHTER, THE *½ (1953) PR:A
MARSHMALLOW MOON
  (SEE:AARON SLICK FROM PUNKIN CRICK)
MARSUPIALS: THE HOWLING III
  (SEE:HOWLING III, THE)
MARTHA JELLNECK **½ (1988, W. Ger.) PR:C
MARTIAN IN PARIS, A * (1961, Fr.) PR:A
MARTIN ***½ (1979) PR:O
MARTIN LUTHER **½ (1953) PR:AA
MARTIN ROUMAGNAC
  (SEE:ROOM UPSTAIRS, THE)
MARTIN'S DAY * (1985, Can.) PR:C
MARTY **** (1955) PR:A
MARTYR, THE *** (1976, Ger./Israel) PR:C
MARTYRS OF LOVE ** (1968, Czech.) PR:A
MARUSA NO ONNA
  (SEE:TAXING WOMAN, A)
MARVIN AND TIGE ** (1983) PR:C
MARX BROTHERS AT THE CIRCUS
  (SEE:AT THE CIRCUS)
MARX BROTHERS GO WEST
  (SEE:GO WEST)
MARY
  (SEE:MURDER)
MARY BURNS, FUGITIVE *** (1935) PR:A
MARY HAD A LITTLE ** (1961, Brit.) PR:C
MARY JANE'S PA **½ (1935) PR:A
MARY LOU ** (1948) PR:A
MARY, MARY **½ (1963) PR:A-C
MARY, MARY, BLOODY MARY *
  (1975, US/Mex.) PR:O
MARY NAMES THE DAY
  (SEE:DR. KILDARE'S WEDDING DAY)
MARY OF SCOTLAND **½ (1936) PR:A
MARY POPPINS ***** (1964) PR:AA
MARY, QUEEN OF SCOTS ** (1971, Brit.) PR:A-C
MARY RYAN, DETECTIVE ** (1949) PR:C
MARY STEVENS, M.D. ** (1933) PR:A
MARYA-ISKUSNITSA
  (SEE:MAGIC WEAVER, THE)
MARYJANE * (1968) PR:O
MARYLAND ** (1940) PR:A
MAS ALLA DE LAS MONTANAS
  (SEE:DESPERATE ONES, THE)
MASCARA ***½ (1987, US/Belg./Neth./Fr.) PR:O
MASCULINE FEMININE ****
  (1966, Fr./Swed.) PR:C-O
M*A*S*H **** (1970) PR:C-O
MASK, THE *½ (1961, Can.) PR:O
MASK *** (1985) PR:C
MASK OF DIIJON, THE *½ (1946) PR:A-C
MASK OF DIMITRIOS, THE ***** (1944) PR:A
MASK OF DUST
  (SEE:RACE FOR LIFE)
MASK OF FU MANCHU, THE *** (1932) PR:C
MASK OF FURY
  (SEE:FIRST YANK INTO TOKYO)
MASK OF KOREA *½ (1950, Fr.) PR:A
MASK OF THE AVENGER **½ (1951) PR:A
MASK OF THE DRAGON *½ (1951) PR:A
MASK OF THE HIMALAYAS
  (SEE:STORM OVER TIBET)
MASKED PIRATE, THE
  (SEE:PIRATES OF CAPRI, THE)
MASKED RAIDERS **½ (1949) PR:A
MASKED RIDER, THE **½ (1941) PR:A
MASKED STRANGER
  (SEE:DURANGO KID, THE)
MASOCH ***½ (1980, It.) PR:O
MASON OF THE MOUNTED ** (1932) PR:A
MASQUE OF THE RED DEATH, THE ***½
  (1964, US/Brit.) PR:A
MASQUERADE zero (1929) PR:A
MASQUERADE *** (1965, Brit.) PR:A
MASQUERADE *½ (1988) PR:O
MASQUERADE IN MEXICO ** (1945) PR:C
MASQUERADER, THE **½ (1933) PR:A
MASS APPEAL *** (1984) PR:C
MASS IS ENDED, THE ***½ (1988, It.) PR:C
MASSACRE ** (1934) PR:A
MASSACRE * (1956) PR:A
MASSACRE AT CENTRAL HIGH *** (1976) PR:O
MASSACRE AT FORT HOLMAN
  (SEE:REASON TO LIVE, A REASON TO DIE, A)
MASSACRE AT THE ROSEBUD
  (SEE:GREAT SIOUX MASSACRE, THE)
MASSACRE CANYON * (1954) PR:A
MASSACRE HILL ** (1949, Brit.) PR:A
MASSACRE IN ROME *** (1973, It.) PR:C
MASSACRE RIVER *½ (1949) PR:A
MASSIVE RETALIATION * (1984) PR:O
MASTER AND MAN *½ (1934, Brit.) PR:A
MASTER GUNFIGHTER, THE zero (1975) PR:C
MASTER MINDS * (1949) PR:A
MASTER OF BALLANTRAE, THE ***
  (1953, US/Brit.) PR:A
MASTER OF BANKDAM, THE *** (1947, Brit.) PR:C

MASTER OF HORROR *½ (1965, Arg.) PR:C-O
MASTER OF LASSIE
  (SEE:HILLS OF HOME)
MASTER OF MEN * (1933) PR:A
MASTER OF TERROR
  (SEE:4D MAN, THE)
MASTER OF THE ISLANDS
  (SEE:HAWAIIANS, THE)
MASTER OF THE WORLD *½ (1935, Ger.) PR:A
MASTER OF THE WORLD ** (1961) PR:A
MASTER PLAN, THE ** (1955, Brit.) PR:A
MASTER RACE, THE ** (1944) PR:C
MASTER SPY ** (1964, Brit.) PR:A
MASTER TOUCH, THE ** (1974, It./Ger.) PR:C
MASTERBLASTER * (1987) PR:C-O
MASTERMIND **½ (1977) PR:A
MASTERS OF THE UNIVERSE **½ (1987) PR:C-O
MASTERSON OF KANSAS **½ (1954) PR:A
MATA HARI ***½ (1931) PR:A
MATA HARI *** (1965, Fr./It.) PR:C
MATA HARI *½ (1985) PR:O
MATA HARI'S DAUGHTER ** (1954, Fr./It.) PR:A
MATALOS Y VUELVE
  (SEE:KILL THEM ALL AND COME BACK ALONE)
MATCH KING, THE ***½ (1932) PR:C
MATCHLESS ** (1967, It.) PR:C
MATCHLESS **½ (1974, Aus.) PR:O
MATCHMAKER, THE ***½ (1958) PR:A
MATCHMAKING OF ANNA, THE ****
  (1972, Gr.) PR:O
MATE DOMA IVA?
  (SEE:DO YOU KEEP A LION AT HOME?)
MATEWAN **** (1987) PR:C
MATHIAS SANDORF ** (1963, Fr.) PR:A
MATILDA ***½ (1978) PR:A
MATINEE IDOL *½ (1933, Brit.) PR:A
MATING GAME, THE *** (1959) PR:A
MATING OF MILLIE, THE **½ (1948) PR:A
MATING OF THE SABINE WOMEN, THE
  (SEE:SHAME OF THE SABINE WOMEN, THE)
MATING SEASON, THE **½ (1951) PR:A
MATKA JOANNA OD ANIOLOW
  (SEE:JOAN OF THE ANGELS)
MATRIMONIAL BED, THE * (1930) PR:A
MATRIMONIAL PROBLEM, A
  (SEE:MATRIMONIAL BED, THE)
MATRIMONIO ALL'ITALIANA
  (SEE:MARRIAGE, ITALIAN STYLE)
MATTER OF CHOICE, A ** (1963, Brit.) PR:A
MATTER OF CONVICTION, A
  (SEE:YOUNG SAVAGES, THE)
MATTER OF DAYS, A *** (1969, Fr./Czech.) PR:O
MATTER OF HONOR, A **½ (1988, Colombia) PR:C
MATTER OF INNOCENCE, A ** (1968, Brit.) PR:A
MATTER OF LIFE AND DEATH, A
  (SEE:STAIRWAY TO HEAVEN)
MATTER OF MORALS, A **½
  (1961, US/Swed.) PR:A
MATTER OF MURDER, A * (1949, Brit.) PR:A
MATTER OF RESISTANCE, A
  (SEE:LA VIE DE CHATEAU)
MATTER OF TIME, A * (1976, It./US) PR:A-C
MATTER OF WHO, A ** (1962, Brit.) PR:A
MAURICE **½ (1987, Brit.) PR:O
MAURIE *½ (1973) PR:A
MAUSOLEUM zero (1983) PR:O
MAUVAIS SANG
  (SEE:BAD BLOOD)
MAVERICK, THE *½ (1952) PR:A
MAVERICK QUEEN, THE *** (1956) PR:A
MAX DUGAN RETURNS ** (1983) PR:A
MAXIE ** (1985) PR:C
MAXIME ** (1962, Fr.) PR:A
MAXIMUM OVERDRIVE zero (1986) PR:O
MAXWELL ARCHER, DETECTIVE *
  (1942, Brit.) PR:C
MAYA *½ (1966) PR:A
MAYA zero (1982) PR:C
MAYBE IT'S LOVE ** (1930) PR:A
MAYBE IT'S LOVE * (1935) PR:A
MAYERLING ***** (1937, Fr.) PR:C-O
MAYERLING ** (1968, Brit./Fr.) PR:C
MAYFAIR GIRL * (1933, Brit.) PR:A
MAYFAIR MELODY ** (1937, Brit.) PR:A
MAYHEM
  (SEE:SCREAM, BABY, SCREAM)
MAYOR OF 44TH STREET, THE * (1942) PR:A
MAYOR OF HELL, THE *** (1933) PR:C
MAYOR'S NEST, THE *½ (1932, Brit.) PR:A
MAYOR'S NEST, THE
  (SEE:RETURN OF DANIEL BOONE, THE)
MAYTIME **** (1937) PR:A
MAYTIME IN MAYFAIR ** (1952, Brit.) PR:A
MAZE, THE **½ (1953) PR:C
MAZEL TOV OU LE MARIAGE
  (SEE:MARRY ME—MARRY ME—)
M'BLIMEY zero (1931, Brit.) PR:A
MC CABE AND MRS. MILLER * (1971) PR:O

MC CONNELL STORY, THE **½ (1955) PR:A
MC CORD
　(SEE:MINUTE TO PRAY, A SECOND TO DIE, A)
MC CULLOCHS, THE
　(SEE:WILD MCCULLOCHS, THE)
MC FADDEN'S FLATS * (1935) PR:A
MC GLUSKY THE SEA ROVER
　(SEE:HELL'S CARGO)
MC GUFFIN, THE * (1985, Brit.) PR:A-C
MC GUIRE, GO HOME! ** (1966, Brit.) PR:A
MC HALE'S NAVY **½ (1964) PR:A
MC HALE'S NAVY JOINS THE AIR FORCE **½
　(1965) PR:A
MC KENNA OF THE MOUNTED *½ (1932) PR:A
MC KENZIE BREAK, THE ***½ (1970) PR:C
MC LINTOCK! **½ (1963) PR:A
MC MASTERS, THE ** (1970) PR:O
MC Q ** (1974) PR:O
MC VICAR **½ (1982, Brit.) PR:C
ME **½ (1970, Fr.) PR:A
ME AND MARLBOROUGH **½ (1935, Brit.) PR:A
ME AND MY BROTHER zero (1969) PR:O
ME AND MY GAL ** (1932) PR:A
ME AND MY PAL ** (1939, Brit.) PR:A
ME AND THE COLONEL ** (1958) PR:A
ME, NATALIE ** (1969) PR:C
MEAL, THE *** (1975) PR:O
MEAN DOG BLUES *½ (1978) PR:O
MEAN FRANK AND CRAZY TONY **
**　(1976, It.) PR:O**
MEAN JOHNNY BARROWS ** (1976) PR:O
MEAN SEASON, THE **½ (1985) PR:O
MEAN STREETS ** (1973) PR:O**
MEANEST GAL IN TOWN, THE * (1934) PR:A
MEANEST MAN IN THE WORLD, THE **
　(1943) PR:A
MEANWHILE BACK AT THE RANCH
　(SEE:BALLAD OF JOSIE, THE)
MEANWHILE, FAR FROM THE FRONT
　(SEE:SECRET WAR OF HARRY FRIGG, THE)
MEAT CLEAVER MASSACRE zero (1977) PR:O
MEATBALLS *½ (1979, Can.) PR:C
MEATBALLS PART II * (1984) PR:C
MEATBALLS III *½ (1987) PR:O
MECHANIC, THE ** (1972) PR:O
MED MORD I BAGAGET
　(SEE:NO TIME TO KILL)
MEDAL FOR BENNY, A **½ (1945) PR:A
MEDAL FOR THE GENERAL
　(SEE:GAY INTRUDERS, THE)
MEDALS
　(SEE:SEVEN DAYS LEAVE)
MEDEA * (1971, It./Fr./Ger.) PR:O**
MEDICINE MAN, THE * (1930) PR:A
MEDICINE MAN, THE * (1933, Brit.) PR:A
MEDICO OF PAINTED SPRINGS, THE **
**　(1941) PR:A**
MEDIUM, THE * (1951) PR:A**
MEDIUM COOL ** (1969) PR:O**
MEDJU JASTREBOVIMA
　(SEE:FRONTIER HELLCAT)
MEDUSA TOUCH, THE * (1978, Brit.) PR:C
MEET BOSTON BLACKIE **½ (1941) PR:A
MEET DANNY WILSON *** (1952) PR:A
MEET DR. CHRISTIAN **½ (1939) PR:A
MEET JOHN DOE *** (1941) PR:A**
MEET MAXWELL ARCHER
　(SEE:MAXWELL ARCHER, DETECTIVE)
MEET ME AFTER THE SHOW *** (1951) PR:A
MEET ME AT DAWN ** (1947, Brit.) PR:A
MEET ME AT THE FAIR **½ (1952) PR:A
MEET ME IN LAS VEGAS *** (1956) PR:A
MEET ME IN MOSCOW ** (1966, USSR) PR:A
MEET ME IN ST. LOUIS *** (1944) PR:AA**
MEET ME ON BROADWAY ** (1946) PR:A
MEET ME TONIGHT
　(SEE:TONIGHT AT 8:30)
MEET MISS BOBBY SOCKS * (1944) PR:A
MEET MISS MARPLE
　(SEE:MURDER SHE SAID)
MEET MR. CALLAGHAN ** (1954, Brit.) PR:A
MEET MR. LUCIFER ** (1953, Brit.) PR:A
MEET MR. MALCOLM *½ (1954, Brit.) PR:A
MEET MR. PENNY *½ (1938, Brit.) PR:A
MEET MY SISTER **½ (1933, Brit.) PR:A
MEET NERO WOLFE *** (1936) PR:A
MEET SEXTON BLAKE ** (1944, Brit.) PR:A

MEET SIMON CHERRY ** (1949, Brit.) PR:A
MEET THE BARON **½ (1933) PR:A
MEET THE BOY FRIEND * (1937) PR:A
MEET THE CHUMP ** (1941) PR:A
MEET THE DUKE *½ (1949, Brit.) PR:A
MEET THE GIRLS *½ (1938) PR:A
MEET THE MAYOR * (1938) PR:A
MEET THE MISSUS ** (1937) PR:A
MEET THE MISSUS **½ (1940) PR:A
MEET THE MOB ** (1942) PR:A
MEET THE NAVY **½ (1946, Brit.) PR:A
MEET THE NELSONS
　(SEE:HERE COME THE NELSONS)
MEET THE PEOPLE ** (1944) PR:A
MEET THE STEWARTS **½ (1942) PR:A
MEET THE WIFE ** (1931) PR:A
MEET THE WILDCAT * (1940) PR:A
MEET WHIPLASH WILLIE
　(SEE:FORTUNE COOKIE, THE)
MEETING AT MIDNIGHT
　(SEE:CHARLIE CHAN IN BLACK MAGIC)
MEETINGS WITH REMARKABLE MEN **
　(1979, Brit.) PR:A
MEGAFORCE zero (1982) PR:C
MEGLIO VEDOVA
　(SEE:BETTER A WIDOW)
MEIER *** (1987, Ger.) PR:O
MEIN KAMPF—MY CRIMES ** (1940, Brit.) PR:C
MELANIE ** (1982, Can.) PR:A
MELBA **½ (1953, Brit.) PR:A
MELINDA *½ (1972) PR:O
MELO ***** (1988, Fr.) PR:A
MELODIE EN SOUS-SOL
　(SEE:ANY NUMBER CAN WIN)
MELODY * (1971, Brit.) PR:AA**
MELODY AND MOONLIGHT *½ (1940) PR:A
MELODY AND ROMANCE ** (1937, Brit.) PR:A
MELODY CLUB * (1949, Brit.) PR:A
MELODY CRUISE ** (1933) PR:A
MELODY FOR THREE **½ (1941) PR:A
MELODY FOR TWO *½ (1937) PR:A
MELODY GIRL
　(SEE:SING, DANCE, PLENTY HOT)
MELODY IN SPRING ** (1934) PR:A
MELODY IN THE DARK * (1948, Brit.) PR:A
MELODY INN
　(SEE:RIDING HIGH)
MELODY LANE *½ (1929) PR:A
MELODY LANE * (1941) PR:A
MELODY LINGERS ON, THE ** (1935) PR:A
MELODY MAKER, THE *½ (1933, Brit.) PR:A
MELODY MAKER
　(SEE:DING DONG WILLIAMS)
MELODY MAN ** (1930) PR:A
MELODY OF LIFE
　(SEE:SYMPHONY OF SIX MILLION)
MELODY OF LOVE, THE ** (1928) PR:A
MELODY OF LOVE * (1954, It.) PR:A
MELODY OF MY HEART *½ (1936, Brit.) PR:A
MELODY OF THE PLAINS * (1937) PR:A
MELODY OF YOUTH
　(SEE:THEY SHALL HAVE MUSIC)
MELODY PARADE ** (1943) PR:A
MELODY RANCH ** (1940) PR:A
MELODY TIME ***½ (1948) PR:AA
MELODY TRAIL ** (1935) PR:AA
MELTING POT, THE
　(SEE:BETTY CO-ED)
MELVIN AND HOWARD ***½ (1980) PR:C-O
MELVIN, SON OF ALVIN *½ (1984, Aus.) PR:O
MEMBER OF THE JURY * (1937, Brit.) PR:A
MEMBER OF THE WEDDING, THE *** (1952) PR:A
MEMED MY HAWK ** (1984, Brit.) PR:A
MEMENTO MEI * (1963) PR:C
MEMOIRS * (1984, Can.) PR:O
MEMOIRS OF A SURVIVOR *½ (1981, Brit.) PR:C
MEMOIRS OF PRISON ** (1984, Braz.) PR:O
MEMORIAS DO CARCERE
　(SEE:MEMOIRS OF PRISON)
MEMORIES OF ME ** (1988) PR:C
MEMORY EXPERT, THE
　(SEE:MAN ON THE FLYING TRAPEZE)
MEMORY FOR TWO
　(SEE:I LOVE A BANDLEADER)
MEMORY OF US ** (1974) PR:A
MEN, THE ** (1950) PR:C**
MEN AGAINST THE SKY ** (1940) PR:A

MEN AGAINST THE SUN **½ (1953, Brit.) PR:A
MEN ARE CHILDREN TWICE *** (1953, Brit.) PR:A
MEN ARE LIKE THAT *½ (1930) PR:A
MEN ARE LIKE THAT *½ (1931) PR:A
MEN ARE NOT GODS * (1937, Brit.) PR:A-C
MEN ARE SUCH FOOLS * (1933) PR:A
MEN ARE SUCH FOOLS ** (1938) PR:A
MEN ***½ (1985, Ger.) PR:O
MEN BEHIND BARS
　(SEE:DUFFY OF SAN QUENTIN)
MEN CALL IT LOVE * (1931) PR:C
MEN IN EXILE ** (1937) PR:A
MEN IN HER DIARY **½ (1945) PR:A
MEN IN HER LIFE ** (1931) PR:A
MEN IN HER LIFE, THE *** (1941) PR:A
MEN IN WAR ***½ (1957) PR:A-C
MEN IN WHITE *** (1934) PR:A
MEN LIKE THESE
　(SEE:TRAPPED IN A SUBMARINE)
MEN MUST FIGHT * (1933) PR:A
MEN OF AMERICA * (1933) PR:A
MEN OF BOYS TOWN **½ (1941) PR:AA
MEN OF CHANCE *½ (1932) PR:A
MEN OF DESTINY
　(SEE:MEN OF TEXAS)
MEN OF IRELAND ** (1938, Ireland) PR:A
MEN OF SAN QUENTIN * (1942) PR:A
MEN OF SHERWOOD FOREST **½
　(1957, Brit.) PR:A
MEN OF STEEL *½ (1932, Brit.) PR:A
MEN OF STEEL
　(SEE:BILL CRACKS DOWN)
MEN OF STEEL
　(SEE:STEEL)
MEN OF TEXAS **½ (1942) PR:A
MEN OF THE DEEP
　(SEE:ROUGH, TOUGH, AND READY)
MEN OF THE FIGHTING LADY **** (1954) PR:A
MEN OF THE HOUR * (1935) PR:A
MEN OF THE NIGHT ** (1934) PR:A
MEN OF THE NORTH ** (1930) PR:A
MEN OF THE PLAINS *½ (1936) PR:A
MEN OF THE SEA *½ (1938, USSR) PR:A
MEN OF THE SEA *** (1951, Brit.) PR:A
MEN OF THE SKY ** (1931) PR:A
MEN OF THE TENTH
　(SEE:RED, WHITE, AND BLACK, THE)
MEN OF THE TIMBERLAND *½ (1941) PR:A
MEN OF TOMORROW ** (1935, Brit.) PR:A
MEN OF TWO WORLDS
　(SEE:KISENGA, MAN OF AFRICA)
MEN OF YESTERDAY **½ (1936, Brit.) PR:A
MEN ON CALL * (1931) PR:A
MEN ON HER MIND
　(SEE:GIRL FROM TENTH AVENUE, THE)
MEN ON HER MIND ** (1944) PR:A
MEN PREFER FAT GIRLS ** (1981, Fr.) PR:C
MEN WITH WINGS **½ (1938) PR:A
MEN WITHOUT HONOUR * (1939, Brit.) PR:A
MEN WITHOUT LAW ** (1930) PR:A
MEN WITHOUT NAMES ** (1935) PR:A
MEN WITHOUT SOULS ** (1940) PR:A
MEN WITHOUT WOMEN *** (1930) PR:A
MEN WOMEN LOVE
　(SEE:SALVATION NELL)
MENACE, THE *½ (1932) PR:A-C
MENACE ** (1934) PR:A
MENACE
　(SEE:WHEN LONDON SLEEPS)
MENACE IN THE NIGHT ** (1958, Brit.) PR:A
MENNESKER MODES OG SOD MUSIK OPSTAR I
　HJERTET
　(SEE:PEOPLE MEET AND SWEET MUSIC FILLS
　THE HEART)
MEN'S CLUB, THE *½ (1986) PR:C-O
MENSCHEN IM NETZ
　(SEE:UNWILLING AGENT)
MEPHISTO ** (1981, Ger.) PR:O**
MEPHISTO WALTZ, THE * (1971) PR:C-O**
MERCENARIES, THE
　(SEE:DARK OF THE SUN)
MERCENARY FIGHTERS * (1988) PR:O
MERCENARY, THE **½ (1970, It./Sp.) PR:C
MERCHANT OF SLAVES * (1949, It.) PR:C
MERCY ISLAND ** (1941) PR:A
MERCY PLANE ** (1940) PR:A
MERELY MARY ANN **½ (1931) PR:A

Finding entries in **THE MOTION PICTURE GUIDE** ™

Years 1929-83	Volumes I-IX
1984	Volume IX
1985	1986 ANNUAL
1986	1987 ANNUAL
1987	1988 ANNUAL
1988	1989 ANNUAL

STAR RATINGS

★★★★★　Masterpiece
★★★★　Excellent
★★★　Good
★★　Fair
★　Poor
zero　Without Merit

PARENTAL RECOMMENDATION (PR:)

AA　Good for Children
A　Acceptable for Children
C　Cautionary, some objectionable scenes
O　Objectionable for Children

BOLD: Films on Videocassette

MERELY MR. HAWKINS * (1938, Brit.) PR:A
MERMAID, THE ** (1966, Hong Kong) PR:A
MERMAIDS OF TIBURON, THE * (1962) PR:A-C
MERRILL'S MARAUDERS ***½ (1962) PR:C-O
MERRILY WE GO TO HELL *½ (1932) PR:A-C
MERRILY WE LIVE *** (1938) PR:A
MERRY ANDREW **½ (1958) PR:AA
MERRY CHRISTMAS, MR. LAWRENCE ** (1983, Jap./Brit.) PR:O**
MERRY COMES TO STAY ** (1937, Brit.) PR:A
MERRY COMES TO TOWN (SEE:MERRY COMES TO STAY)
MERRY FRINKS, THE ** (1934) PR:A
MERRY-GO-ROUND OF 1938 ** (1937) PR:A
MERRY MONAHANS, THE **½ (1944) PR:A
MERRY WIDOW, THE *** (1934) PR:A-C**
MERRY WIDOW, THE ** (1952) PR:A
MERRY WIVES OF RENO, THE *½ (1934) PR:A
MERRY WIVES OF TOBIAS ROUKE, THE * (1972, Can.) PR:A
MERRY WIVES OF WINDSOR, THE ** (1952, Ger.) PR:A
MERRY WIVES OF WINDSOR, THE **½ (1966, Aust.) PR:A
MERRY WIVES, THE ** (1940, Czech.) PR:C
MERRY-G0-ROUND zero (1948, Brit.) PR:A
MERTON OF THE MOVIES *** (1947) PR:A
MES FEMMES AMERICAINES (SEE:RUN FOR YOUR WIFE)
MESA OF LOST WOMEN, THE zero (1956) PR:A
MESDAMES ET MESSIEURS (SEE:BIRDS, THE BEES, AND THE ITALIANS, THE)
MESQUITE BUCKAROO * (1939) PR:A
MESSAGE, THE (SEE:MOHAMMAD, MESSENGER OF GOD)
MESSAGE FROM SPACE **½ (1978, Jap.) PR:A
MESSAGE TO GARCIA, A *½ (1936) PR:A
MESSALINE **½ (1952, Fr./It.) PR:A
MESSENGER OF PEACE *½ (1950) PR:A
MESSIAH OF EVIL (SEE:DEAD PEOPLE)
METALSTORM: THE DESTRUCTION OF JARED-SYN zero (1983) PR:C
METAMORPHOSES *½ (1978) PR:A
METEMPSYCO (SEE:TOMB OF TORTURE)
METEOR * (1979) PR:C
METEOR MONSTER (SEE:TEENAGE MONSTER)
METROPOLITAN ** (1935) PR:A
MEURTRE EN 45 TOURS (SEE:MURDER AT 45 RPM)
MEXICALI KID, THE *½ (1938) PR:A
MEXICALI ROSE *½ (1929) PR:A
MEXICALI ROSE **½ (1939) PR:A
MEXICAN, THE (SEE:HURRICANE HORSEMAN)
MEXICAN HAYRIDE *½ (1948) PR:A
MEXICAN MANHUNT * (1953) PR:A
MEXICAN SPITFIRE **½ (1939) PR:A
MEXICAN SPITFIRE AT SEA *½ (1942) PR:A
MEXICAN SPITFIRE OUT WEST ** (1940) PR:A
MEXICAN SPITFIRE SEES A GHOST * (1942) PR:A
MEXICAN SPITFIRE'S BABY *½ (1941) PR:A
MEXICAN SPITFIRE'S BLESSED EVENT *½ (1943) PR:A
MEXICAN SPITFIRE'S ELEPHANT ** (1942) PR:A
MEXICANA ** (1945) PR:A
MEXICO IN FLAMES *½ (1982, USSR/Mex./It.) PR:O
MI GENERAL (SEE:MY GENERAL)
MI MUJER ES DOCTOR (SEE:LADY DOCTOR, THE)
MIAMI EXPOSE ** (1956) PR:A
MIAMI RENDEZVOUS (SEE:PASSION HOLIDAY)
MIAMI STORY, THE ** (1954) PR:A
MICHAEL AND MARY ** (1932, Brit.) PR:A
MICHAEL O'HALLORAN ** (1937) PR:A
MICHAEL O'HALLORAN ** (1948) PR:A
MICHAEL SHAYNE, PRIVATE DETECTIVE **½ (1940) PR:A
MICHAEL STROGOFF (SEE:SOLDIER AND THE LADY, THE)
MICHAEL STROGOFF *½ (1960, Fr./It./Yugo.) PR:A
MICHELLE * (1970, Fr.) PR:C
MICHIGAN KID, THE ** (1947) PR:A
MICKEY * (1948) PR:A
MICKEY ONE **½ (1965) PR:C-O
MICKEY, THE KID *½ (1939) PR:A
MICKI AND MAUDE ***½ (1984) PR:C
MICROSCOPIA (SEE:FANTASTIC VOYAGE)
MICROWAVE MASSACRE zero (1983) PR:O
MID-DAY MISTRESS zero (1968) PR:O
MIDAREGUMO (SEE:TWO IN THE SHADOW)
MIDARERU (SEE:YEARNING)
MIDAS RUN ** (1969) PR:C
MIDAS TOUCH, THE *½ (1940, Brit.) PR:A
MIDDLE AGE CRAZY **½ (1980, Can.) PR:O
MIDDLE AGE SPREAD *** (1979, New Zealand) PR:O
MIDDLE COURSE, THE *½ (1961, Brit.) PR:A
MIDDLE OF THE NIGHT ***½ (1959) PR:A-C
MIDDLE WATCH, THE ** (1930, Brit.) PR:A
MIDDLE WATCH, THE *½ (1939, Brit.) PR:A
MIDDLETON FAMILY AT THE N.Y. WORLD'S FAIR *½ (1939) PR:A
MIDNIGHT *½ (1934) PR:A
MIDNIGHT ALIBI *½ (1934) PR:A
MIDNIGHT ANGEL **½ (1941) PR:A
MIDNIGHT AT MADAME TUSSAUD'S (SEE:MIDNIGHT AT THE WAX MUSEUM)
MIDNIGHT AT THE WAX MUSEUM * (1936, Brit.) PR:A
MIDNIGHT AUTO SUPPLY (SEE:LOVE AND MIDNIGHT AUTO SUPPLY)
MIDNIGHT ***½ (1939) PR:A
MIDNIGHT ** (1983) PR:O
MIDNIGHT CLUB *½ (1933) PR:A
MIDNIGHT COURT *½ (1937) PR:A
MIDNIGHT COWBOY ** (1969) PR:O**
MIDNIGHT CROSSING ** (1988) PR:O
MIDNIGHT DADDIES * (1929) PR:A
MIDNIGHT EPISODE ** (1951, Brit.) PR:A
MIDNIGHT EXPRESS ** (1978, Brit.) PR:O**
MIDNIGHT FOLLY ** (1962, Fr.) PR:C
MIDNIGHT INTRUDER ** (1938) PR:A
MIDNIGHT LACE * (1960) PR:C**
MIDNIGHT LADY * (1932) PR:A
MIDNIGHT LIMITED ** (1940) PR:A
MIDNIGHT MADNESS * (1980) PR:C
MIDNIGHT MADONNA *½ (1937) PR:A
MIDNIGHT MAN, THE **½ (1974) PR:O
MIDNIGHT MANHUNT (SEE:ONE EXCITING NIGHT)
MIDNIGHT MARY ** (1933) PR:A-C
MIDNIGHT MEETING ** (1962, Fr.) PR:A
MIDNIGHT MELODY (SEE:MURDER IN THE MUSIC HALL)
MIDNIGHT MENACE (SEE:BOMBS OVER LONDON)
MIDNIGHT MORALS * (1932) PR:A
MIDNIGHT MYSTERY ** (1930) PR:A
MIDNIGHT PATROL, THE *½ (1932) PR:A
MIDNIGHT PLEASURES ** (1975, It.) PR:O
MIDNIGHT RAIDERS (SEE:OKLAHOMA RAIDERS)
MIDNIGHT RUN ***½ (1988) PR:O
MIDNIGHT SPECIAL * (1931) PR:A
MIDNIGHT STORY, THE *** (1957) PR:A
MIDNIGHT TAXI, THE *½ (1928) PR:A
MIDNIGHT TAXI *½ (1937) PR:A
MIDNIGHT WARNING, THE **½ (1932) PR:A
MIDSHIPMAID GOB *½ (1932, Brit.) PR:A
MIDSHIPMAN, THE (SEE:MIDSHIPMAN GOB, THE)
MIDSHIPMAN EASY (SEE:MEN OF THE SEA)
MIDSHIPMAN JACK *½ (1933) PR:A
MIDSTREAM *½ (1929) PR:A
MIDSUMMER NIGHT'S DREAM, A **½ (1969, Brit.) PR:A
MIDSUMMER NIGHT'S DREAM, A **½ (1984, Brit./Sp.) PR:O
MIDSUMMER NIGHT'S SEX COMEDY, A **½ (1982) PR:C-O
MIDSUMMER'S NIGHT'S DREAM, A ***½ (1935) PR:A
MIDSUMMERS NIGHT'S DREAM, A **** (1961, Czech.) PR:AA
MIDSUMMER NIGHT'S DREAM, A *** (1966) PR:A
MIDWAY ** (1976) PR:A
MIDWIFE, THE * (1961, Gr.) PR:A
MIGHT MAKES RIGHT (SEE:FOX AND HIS FRIENDS)
MIGHTY, THE *½ (1929) PR:A
MIGHTY BARNUM, THE **½ (1934) PR:A
MIGHTY CRUSADERS, THE * (1961, It.) PR:A
MIGHTY GORGA, THE zero (1969) PR:A
MIGHTY JOE YOUNG ** (1949) PR:A
MIGHTY JUNGLE, THE * (1965, US/Mex.) PR:A
MIGHTY MCGURK, THE ** (1946) PR:A
MIGHTY MOUSE IN THE GREAT SPACE CHASE *** (1983) PR:AA
MIGHTY TREVE, THE **½ (1937) PR:AA
MIGHTY TUNDRA, THE (SEE:TUNDRA)
MIGHTY URSUS *½ (1962, It./Sp.) PR:A
MIGHTY WARRIOR, THE (SEE:TROJAN HORSE, THE)
MIKADO, THE **½ (1939, Brit.) PR:A
MIKADO, THE **½ (1967, Brit.) PR:AA
MIKE'S MURDER ** (1984) PR:O
MIKEY AND NICKY **½ (1976) PR:C-O
MILAGRO BEANFIELD WAR, THE **½ (1988) PR:C
MILCZACA GWIAZDA (SEE:FIRST SPACESHIP ON VENUS)
MILDRED PIERCE *** (1945) PR:A**
MILE A MINUTE (SEE:RIDERS OF THE SANTA FE)
MILE A MINUTE LOVE * (1937) PR:A
MILES FROM HOME * (1988) PR:C**
MILESTONES *** (1975) PR:C
MILITARY ACADEMY ** (1940) PR:A
MILITARY ACADEMY WITH THAT TENTH AVENUE GANG * (1950) PR:A
MILITARY POLICEMAN (SEE:OFF LIMITS)
MILITARY SECRET **½ (1945, USSR) PR:A
MILKMAN, THE ** (1950) PR:A
MILKY WAY, THE ***½ (1936) PR:AA
MILKY WAY, THE ***½ (1969, Fr./It.) PR:C
MILL OF THE STONE WOMEN ** (1963, Fr./It.) PR:O
MILL ON THE FLOSS **½ (1939, Brit.) PR:A
MILLER'S WIFE, THE *½ (1957, It.) PR:O
MILLERSON CASE, THE *½ (1947) PR:A
MILLIE *½ (1931) PR:A
MILLIE'S DAUGHTER *½ (1947) PR:A
MILLION, THE * (1931, Fr.) PR:A**
MILLION DOLLAR BABY *½ (1935) PR:A
MILLION DOLLAR BABY ** (1941) PR:A
MILLION DOLLAR COLLAR, THE ** (1929) PR:A
MILLION DOLLAR DUCK (SEE:$1,000,000 DUCK)
MILLION DOLLAR KID ** (1944) PR:A
MILLION DOLLAR LEGS * (1932) PR:A**
MILLION DOLLAR LEGS **½ (1939) PR:A
MILLION DOLLAR MANHUNT * (1962, Brit.) PR:A
MILLION DOLLAR MERMAID * (1952) PR:A**
MILLION DOLLAR MYSTERY * (1987) PR:A-C
MILLION DOLLAR PURSUIT ** (1951) PR:A
MILLION DOLLAR RACKET (SEE:$1,000,000 RACKET)
MILLION DOLLAR RANSOM *½ (1934) PR:A
MILLION DOLLAR WEEKEND *½ (1948) PR:A
MILLION EYES OF SU-MURU, THE * (1967, Brit.) PR:A
MILLION POUND NOTE (SEE:MAN WITH A MILLION)
MILLION TO ONE, A * (1938) PR:A
MILLIONAIRE, THE *** (1931) PR:A
MILLIONAIRE FOR A DAY (SEE:LET'S BE RITZY)
MILLIONAIRE FOR CHRISTY, A ** (1951) PR:A
MILLIONAIRE KID *½ (1936) PR:A
MILLIONAIRE MERRY-GO-ROUND (SEE:PLAYBOY, THE)
MILLIONAIRE PLAYBOY (SEE:PARK AVENUE LOGGER)
MILLIONAIRE PLAYBOY ** (1940) PR:A
MILLIONAIRES IN PRISON *½ (1940) PR:A
MILLIONAIRESS, THE *** (1960, Brit.) PR:A
MILLIONS *½ (1936, Brit.) PR:A
MILLIONS IN THE AIR ** (1935) PR:A
MILLIONS LIKE US *** (1943, Brit.) PR:A
MILLS OF THE GODS *½ (1935) PR:A
MILOSC DWUDZIESTOLATKOW (SEE:LOVE AT TWENTY)
MILWR BYCHAN (SEE:BOY SOLDIER)
MIMI ** (1935, Brit.) PR:A
MIN AND BILL ** (1930) PR:A**
MIN VAN BALTHAZAR (SEE:AU HASARD, BALTHAZAR)
MINAMI NO SHIMA NI YUKI GA FURA (SEE:SNOW IN THE SOUTH SEAS)
MIND BENDERS, THE *** (1963, Brit.) PR:C-O
MIND OF MR. REEDER, THE (SEE:MYSTERIOUS MR. REEDER, THE)
MIND OF MR. SOAMES, THE *** (1970, Brit.) PR:A
MIND READER, THE *½ (1933) PR:A
MIND SNATCHERS, THE (SEE:HAPPINESS CAGE, THE)
MIND YOUR OWN BUSINESS *½ (1937) PR:A
MINDWARP: AN INFINITY OF TERROR (SEE:GALAXY OF TERROR)
MINE OWN EXECUTIONER * (1948, Brit.) PR:C-O**
MINE WITH THE IRON DOOR, THE ** (1936) PR:A
MINESWEEPER ** (1943) PR:A
MINI-AFFAIR, THE * (1968, Brit.) PR:A
MINI-SKIRT MOB, THE *½ (1968) PR:O
MINI WEEKEND (SEE:TOMCAT, THE)
MINISTRY OF FEAR **** (1945) PR:C
MINIVER STORY, THE ** (1950, Brit./US) PR:A
MINNESOTA CLAY **½ (1966, It./Fr./Sp.) PR:C
MINNIE AND MOSKOWITZ ** (1971) PR:C

MINOTAUR
(SEE:LAND OF THE MINOTAUR)
MINOTAUR, THE * (1961, It.) PR:A
MINOTAUR
(SEE:LAND OF THE MINOTAUR)
MINOTAUR, WILD BEAST OF CRETE
(SEE:MINOTAUR, THE)
MINSTREL BOY, THE * (1937, Brit.) PR:A
MINSTREL MAN ** (1944) PR:A
MINUTE TO PRAY, A SECOND TO DIE, A ** (1968, It.) PR:C
MINX, THE *½ (1969) PR:O
MIO FIGILIO NERONE
(SEE:NERO'S MISTRESS)
MIR VKHODYASHCHEMU
(SEE:PEACE TO HIM WHO ENTERS)
MIRACLE, THE ** (1959) PR:A
MIRACLE, THE
(SEE:WAYS OF LOVE)
MIRACLE CAN HAPPEN, A
(SEE:ON OUR MERRY WAY)
MIRACLE IN HARLEM ** (1948) PR:A
MIRACLE IN MILAN ** (1951, It.) PR:A**
MIRACLE IN SOHO **½ (1957, Brit.) PR:A
MIRACLE IN THE RAIN ** (1956) PR:A
MIRACLE IN THE SAND
(SEE:THREE GODFATHERS)
MIRACLE KID * (1942) PR:A
MIRACLE MAN, THE **½ (1932) PR:A
MIRACLE OF FATIMA
(SEE:MIRACLE OF OUR LADY OF FATIMA, THE)
MIRACLE OF LIFE
(SEE:OUR DAILY BREAD)
MIRACLE OF MORGAN'S CREEK, THE *** (1944) PR:C**
MIRACLE OF OUR LADY OF FATIMA, THE * (1952) PR:A**
MIRACLE OF SAN SEBASTIAN
(SEE:GUNS FOR SAN SEBASTIAN)
MIRACLE OF SANTA'S WHITE REINDEER, THE * (1963) PR:A
MIRACLE OF THE BELLS, THE ***½ (1948) PR:A
MIRACLE OF THE HILLS, THE **½ (1959) PR:A
MIRACLE OF THE WHITE REINDEER, THE
(SEE:MIRACLE OF SANTA'S WHITE REINDEER, THE)
MIRACLE OF THE WHITE STALLIONS ** (1963) PR:AA
MIRACLE ON MAIN STREET, A ** (1940) PR:A
MIRACLE ON 34TH STREET, THE *** (1947) PR:AA**
MIRACLE WOMAN, THE ***½ (1931) PR:A-C
MIRACLE WORKER, THE *** (1962) PR:A**
MIRACLES **½ (1987) PR:C
MIRACLES DO HAPPEN * (1938, Brit.) PR:A
MIRACLES FOR SALE *** (1939) PR:A
MIRACOLO A MILANO
(SEE:MIRACLE IN MILAN)
MIRACULOUS JOURNEY ** (1948) PR:A
MIRAGE **½ (1965) PR:A-C
MIRAGE **** (1972, Peru) PR:C
MIRANDA *** (1949, Brit.) PR:A
MIRIAM
(SEE:TRILOGY)
MIRROR CRACK'D, THE * (1980, Brit.) PR:A-C**
MIRROR HAS TWO FACES, THE **½ (1959, Fr.) PR:A
MIRRORS * (1984) PR:O
MIRTH AND MELODY
(SEE:LET'S GO PLACES)
MISADVENTURES OF MERLIN JONES, THE **½ (1964) PR:AA
MISBEHAVING HUSBANDS *½ (1941) PR:A
MISBEHAVING LADIES *½ (1931) PR:A
MISCHIEF * (1969, Brit.) PR:A
MISCHIEF *** (1931, Brit.) PR:A
MISCHIEF ** (1985) PR:O
MISFIT BRIGADE, THE ** (1988) PR:O
MISFITS, THE * (1961) PR:C**
MISHIMA ***½ (1985) PR:O
MISHPACHAT SIMCHON
(SEE:SIMCHON FAMILY, THE)
MISLEADING LADY, THE ** (1932) PR:A
MISS ANNIE ROONEY ** (1942) PR:A
MISS FANE'S BABY IS STOLEN *** (1934) PR:A
MISS FIX-IT
(SEE:KEEP SMILING)
MISS GRANT TAKES RICHMOND ***½ (1949) PR:A
MISS JESSICA IS PREGNANT ** (1970) PR:O
MISS JUDE
(SEE:TRUTH ABOUT SPRING, THE)
MISS LONDON LTD. ** (1943, Brit.) PR:A
MISS MARY ** (1987, Arg.) PR:O
MISS MINK OF 1949 ** (1949) PR:A
MISS MONA ***½ (1987, Fr.) PR:O
MISS MUERTE
(SEE:DIABOLICAL DR. Z, THE)
MISS PACIFIC FLEET *½ (1935) PR:A
MISS PILGRIM'S PROGRESS ** (1950, Brit.) PR:A
MISS PINKERTON *½ (1932) PR:A
MISS PRESIDENT **½ (1935, Hung.) PR:A
MISS ROBIN CRUSOE ** (1954) PR:A
MISS ROBIN HOOD * (1952, Brit.) PR:A
MISS SADIE THOMPSON * (1953) PR:O**
MISS SUSIE SLAGLE'S **½ (1945) PR:A
MISS TATLOCK'S MILLIONS *** (1948) PR:A
MISS TULIP STAYS THE NIGHT * (1955, Brit.) PR:A
MISS V FROM MOSCOW *½ (1942) PR:A
MISSILE FROM HELL **½ (1960, Brit.) PR:A
MISSILE TO THE MOON * (1959) PR:A
MISSING ** (1982) PR:A-C**
MISSING, BELIEVED MARRIED * (1937, Brit.) PR:A
MISSING CORPSE, THE *** (1945) PR:A
MISSING DAUGHTERS * (1939) PR:A
MISSING EVIDENCE **½ (1939) PR:A
MISSING GIRLS ** (1936) PR:A
MISSING GUEST, THE * (1938) PR:A
MISSING IN ACTION ** (1984) PR:O
MISSING IN ACTION 2—THE BEGINNING **½ (1985) PR:O
MISSING JUROR, THE *** (1944) PR:A
MISSING LADY, THE ** (1946) PR:A
MISSING MILLION, THE *½ (1942, Brit.) PR:A
MISSING NOTE, THE * (1961, Brit.) PR:AA
MISSING PEOPLE, THE ** (1940, Brit.) PR:A
MISSING PERSONS
(SEE:BUREAU OF MISSING PERSONS)
MISSING REMBRANDT, THE *½ (1932, Brit.) PR:A
MISSING TEN DAYS **½ (1941, Brit.) PR:A
MISSING WITNESS
(SEE:LOVE'S OLD SWEET SONG)
MISSING WITNESSES *** (1937) PR:A
MISSING WOMEN *½ (1951) PR:A
MISSION, THE * (1984) PR:O**
MISSION, THE * (1986, Brit.) PR:C**
MISSION BATANGAS *½ (1968) PR:A
MISSION BLOODY MARY ** (1967, Fr./It./Sp.) PR:A
MISSION GALACTICA: THE CYLON ATTACK * (1979) PR:A
MISSION KILL ** (1987) PR:C-O
MISSION MARS * (1968) PR:A
MISSION OVER KOREA ** (1953) PR:A
MISSION STARDUST * (1968, It./Sp./Ger.) PR:A
MISSION TO HELL
(SEE:SAVAGE!)
MISSION TO HONG KONG
(SEE:RED-DRAGON)
MISSION TO MOSCOW *** (1943) PR:A
MISSIONARY, THE **½ (1982) PR:O
MISSISSIPPI
(SEE:HEAVEN ON EARTH)
MISSISSIPPI **½ (1935) PR:A
MISSISSIPPI BURNING ** (1988) PR:O
MISSISSIPPI GAMBLER ** (1929) PR:A
MISSISSIPPI GAMBLER *½ (1942) PR:A
MISSISSIPPI GAMBLER, THE *** (1953) PR:C
MISSISSIPPI MERMAID ***½ (1970, Fr./It.) PR:A
MISSISSIPPI RHYTHM *½ (1949) PR:A
MISSISSIPPI SUMMER * (1971) PR:C
MISSOURI BREAKS, THE * (1976) PR:C-O**
MISSOURI OUTLAW, A ** (1942) PR:A
MISSOURI TRAVELER, THE *** (1958) PR:A
MISSOURIANS, THE **½ (1950) PR:A
MR. ACE ** (1946) PR:A
MR. AND MRS. NORTH **½ (1941) PR:A
MR. AND MRS. SMITH * (1941) PR:A**
MISTER ANTONIO ** (1929) PR:A
MR. ARKADIN **½ (1962, Brit./Fr./Sp.) PR:C
MR. ASHTON WAS INDISCREET
(SEE:SENATOR WAS INDISCREET, THE)
MR. BELVEDERE RINGS THE BELL *** (1951) PR:A
MR. BELVEDERE GOES TO COLLEGE *** (1949) PR:A
MR. BIG ** (1943) PR:A
MR. BILL THE CONQUEROR
(SEE:MAN WHO WON, THE)
MR. BILLION ** (1977) PR:A
MR. BLANDINGS BUILDS HIS DREAM HOUSE * (1948) PR:A**
MR. BOGGS STEPS OUT *½ (1938) PR:A
MISTER BROWN **½ (1972) PR:C
MR. BROWN COMES DOWN THE HILL ** (1966, Brit.) PR:A
MISTER BUDDWING ** (1966) PR:C
MR. BUG GOES TO TOWN *** (1941) PR:AA
MR. CELEBRITY ** (1942) PR:A
MR. CHEDWORTH STEPS OUT **½ (1939, Aus.) PR:A
MR. CHUMP ** (1938) PR:A
MISTER CINDERELLA *½ (1936) PR:A
MISTER CINDERS ** (1934, Brit.) PR:A
MR. COHEN TAKES A WALK **½ (1936, Brit.) PR:A
MISTER CORY *** (1957) PR:A
MR. DEEDS GOES TO TOWN ***** (1936) PR:A
MR. DENNING DRIVES NORTH *** (1953, Brit.) PR:A
MR. DISTRICT ATTORNEY *½ (1941) PR:A
MR. DISTRICT ATTORNEY ** (1946) PR:A
MR. DISTRICT ATTORNEY IN THE CARTER CASE
(SEE:CARTER CASE, THE)
MR. DODD TAKES THE AIR ** (1937) PR:A
MR. DOODLE KICKS OFF *½ (1938) PR:A
MR. DRAKE'S DUCK **½ (1951, Brit.) PR:A
MR. DREW
(SEE:FOR THEM THAT TRESPASS)
MR. DYNAMITE ** (1935) PR:A
MR. DYNAMITE ** (1941) PR:A
MISTER 880 ***½ (1950) PR:AA
MR. EMMANUEL ** (1945, Brit.) PR:A
MR. FAINTHEART
(SEE:$10 RAISE)
MR. FORBUSH AND THE PENGUINS
(SEE:CRY OF THE PENGUINS)
MR. FOX OF VENICE
(SEE:HONEY POT, THE)
MISTER FREEDOM ** (1970, Fr.) PR:A
MR. GRIGGS RETURNS
(SEE:COCKEYED MIRACLE, THE)
MR. H.C. ANDERSEN * (1950, Brit.) PR:A
MR. HEX ** (1946) PR:A
MR. HOBBS TAKES A VACATION * (1962) PR:AA**
MISTER HOBO *** (1936, Brit.) PR:A
MR. HOT SHOT
(SEE:FLAMINGO KID, THE)
MR. HULOT'S HOLIDAY *** (1954, Fr.) PR:AA**
MR. IMPERIUM ** (1951) PR:A
MR. INNOCENT
(SEE:HAPPENING, THE)
MR. INVISIBLE
(SEE:MR. SUPERINVISIBLE)
MR. JIM—AMERICAN, SOLDIER, AND GENTLEMAN
(SEE:SERGEANT JIM)
MR. KLEIN **½ (1976, Fr.) PR:C
MR. LEMON OF ORANGE *½ (1931) PR:A
MR. LIMPET
(SEE:INCREDIBLE MR. LIMPET, THE)
MR. LORD SAYS NO **½ (1952, Brit.) PR:A
MR. LOVE **½ (1986, Brit.) PR:A
MR. LUCKY * (1943) PR:A**
MR. MAGOO'S HOLIDAY FESTIVAL *** (1970) PR:AA
MR. MAJESTYK * (1974) PR:C**
MR. MOM **½ (1983) PR:A-C
MISTER MOSES **½ (1965) PR:A
MR. MOTO AND THE PERSIAN OIL CASE
(SEE:RETURN OF MR. MOTO, THE)
MR. MOTO IN DANGER ISLAND **½ (1939) PR:A
MR. MOTO ON DANGER ISLAND
(SEE:MR. MOTO IN DANGER ISLAND)
MR. MOTO TAKES A CHANCE ** (1938) PR:A
MR. MOTO TAKES A VACATION ** (1938) PR:A
MR. MOTO'S GAMBLE **½ (1938) PR:A
MR. MOTO'S LAST WARNING **½ (1939) PR:A
MR. MUGGS RIDES AGAIN ** (1945) PR:A
MR. MUGGS STEPS OUT **½ (1943) PR:A
MR. MUSIC **½ (1950) PR:A
MR. NORTH ** (1988) PR:A
MR. ORCHID **½ (1948, Fr.) PR:A
MR. PATMAN *½ (1980, Can.) PR:C

MR. PEABODY AND THE MERMAID **½
  (1948) PR:AA
MR. PEEK-A-BOO ** (1951, Fr.) PR:A
MR. PERRIN AND MR. TRAILL ***
  (1948, Brit.) PR:A
MR. POTTS GOES TO MOSCOW ***
  (1953, Brit.) PR:A
MR. PULVER AND THE CAPTAIN
  (SEE:ENSIGN PULVER)
MR. QUILP *½ (1975, Brit.) PR:A
MR. QUINCEY OF MONTE CARLO **½
  (1933, Brit.) PR:A
MR. RADISH AND MR. CARROT
  (SEE:TWILIGHT PATH)
MR. RECKLESS *½ (1948) PR:A
MR. REEDER IN ROOM 13
  (SEE:MYSTERY OF ROOM 13)
MR. RICCO *½ (1975) PR:C
MISTER ROBERTS ** (1955) PR:A**
MR. ROBINSON CRUSOE * (1932) PR:A
MISTER ROCK AND ROLL *** (1957) PR:A
MR. SARDONICUS *** (1961) PR:C
MR. SATAN ** (1938, Brit.) PR:A
MR. SCOUTMASTER **½ (1953) PR:A
MR. SEBASTIAN
  (SEE:SEBASTIAN)
MR. SKEFFINGTON * (1944) PR:C**
MR. SKITCH *½ (1933) PR:A
MR. SMITH CARRIES ON ** (1937, Brit.) PR:A
MR. SMITH GOES TO WASHINGTON ***
  (1939) PR:AA**
MR. SOFT TOUCH ** (1949) PR:A
MR. STRINGFELLOW SAYS NO ** (1937, Brit.) PR:A
**MR. SUPERINVISIBLE **
  (1974, It./Sp./Ger.) PR:AA**
MR. SYCAMORE * (1975) PR:A
MISTER TEN PERCENT *½ (1967, Brit.) PR:A
MR. TOPAZE
  (SEE:I LIKE MONEY)
MR. UNIVERSE ** (1951) PR:A
MISTER V
  (SEE:PIMPERNEL SMITH)
MR. WALKIE TALKIE ** (1952) PR:A
MR. WASHINGTON GOES TO TOWN ** (1941) PR:A
MR. WHAT'S-HIS-NAME **½ (1935, Brit.) PR:A
MR. WINKLE GOES TO WAR ** (1944) PR:C
MR. WISE GUY ** (1942) PR:A
MR. WONG AT HEADQUARTERS
  (SEE:FATAL HOUR)
MR. WONG, DETECTIVE ** (1938) PR:A
MR. WONG IN CHINATOWN ** (1939) PR:A
MISTER, YOU ARE A WIDOWER
  (SEE:SIR, YOU ARE A WIDOWER)
MISTERIOUS DE ULTRATUMBA
  (SEE:BLACK PIT OF DR. M)
MISTRESS FOR THE SUMMER, A **
  (1964, Fr./It.) PR:C
MISTRESS OF ATLANTIS, THE **½
  (1932, Ger.) PR:A
MISTRESS OF THE APES * (1981) PR:O
**MISTRESS OF THE WORLD **
  (1959, It./Fr./Ger.) PR:A**
MISTY *** (1961) PR:AA
MISUNDERSTOOD ** (1984) PR:C
MIT EVA DIE SUNDE AN
  (SEE:PLAYGIRLS AND THE BELLBOY, THE)
MITCHELL ** (1975) PR:O
MIVTZA KAHIR
  (SEE:TRUNK TO CAIRO)
MIX ME A PERSON *½ (1962, Brit.) PR:C
MIXED BLOOD ***½ (1984) PR:O
MIXED COMPANY **½ (1974) PR:C
MIXED DOUBLES * (1933, Brit.) PR:A
M'LISS ** (1936) PR:A
MOB, THE *** (1951) PR:C-O
MOB TOWN zero (1941) PR:A
MOBS INC * (1956) PR:A
MOBY DICK *** (1956, Brit.) PR:C**
MOBY DICK ***½ (1930) PR:A
MODEL AND THE MARRIAGE BROKER, THE ***
  (1951) PR:A
MODEL FOR MURDER *½ (1960, Brit.) PR:A
MODEL MURDER CASE, THE ** (1964, Brit.) PR:A
MODEL SHOP, THE *** (1969) PR:C-O
MODEL WIFE **½ (1941) PR:A
MODELS, INC. * (1952) PR:C
MODERATO CANTABILE **½ (1964, Fr./It.) PR:C
MODERN GIRLS * (1986) PR:O
MODERN HERO, A ** (1934) PR:A
MODERN HERO, A
  (SEE:KNUTE ROCKNE-ALL AMERICAN)
MODERN LOVE **½ (1929) PR:A
MODERN MADNESS
  (SEE:BIG NOISE, THE)
MODERN MARRIAGE, A *½ (1950) PR:O
MODERN MIRACLE, THE
  (SEE:STORY OF ALEXANDER GRAHAM BELL,
  THE)

MODERN PROBLEMS *½ (1981) PR:A-C
MODERN ROMANCE ***½ (1981) PR:C
MODERN TIMES ** (1936) PR:A**
MODERNS, THE ** (1988) PR:O**
MODESTY BLAISE **½ (1966, Brit.) PR:A
MODIGLIANI OF MONTPARNASSE ***
  (1961, Fr./It.) PR:A
MOGAMBO ** (1953) PR:A**
MOGLIAMANTE
  (SEE:WIFEMISTRESS)
**MOHAMMAD, MESSENGER OF GOD **½
  (1976, Lebanon/Brit.) PR:C-O**
MOHAN JOSHI HAAZIR HO ***½ (1984, India) PR:A
MOHAWK **½ (1956) PR:A
MOJAVE FIREBRAND *½ (1944) PR:A
MOKEY *½ (1942) PR:A
MOLE, THE
  (SEE:EL TOPO)
MOLE PEOPLE, THE * (1956) PR:A
MOLESTER, THE
  (SEE:NEVER TAKE CANDY FROM A STRANGER)
MOLLY
  (SEE:GOLDBERGS, THE)
MOLLY AND LAWLESS JOHN ** (1972) PR:A
MOLLY AND ME ** (1929) PR:A
MOLLY AND ME *** (1945) PR:A
MOLLY LOUVAIN
  (SEE:STRANGE LOVE OF MOLLY LOUVAIN, THE)
MOLLY MAGUIRES, THE * (1970) PR:C-O**
MOM AND DAD * (1948) PR:O
MOMENT BY MOMENT zero (1978) PR:O
MOMENT OF DANGER
  (SEE:MALGA)
MOMENT OF INDISCRETION * (1958, Brit.) PR:A
MOMENT OF TERROR *** (1969, Jap.) PR:C
MOMENT OF TRUTH
  (SEE:NEVER LET GO)
MOMENT OF TRUTH, THE ** (1965, It./Sp.) PR:A
MOMENT TO MOMENT ** (1966) PR:A
MOMENTS **½ (1974, Brit.) PR:O
MOMMAN, LITTLE JUNGLE BOY
  (SEE:LITTLE JUNGLE BOY)
MOMMIE DEAREST zero (1981) PR:C-O
MON ONCLE
  (SEE:MY UNCLE)
MON ONCLE ANTOINE
  (SEE:MY UNCLE ANTOINE)
MON ONCLE D'AMERIQUE ** (1980, Fr.) PR:C**
MON PREMIER AMOUR
  (SEE:MY FIRST LOVE)
MONA KENT
  (SEE:SIN OF MONA KENT)
MONA LISA ***½ (1986, Brit.) PR:O
MONASTERY GARDEN
  (SEE:IN A MONASTERY GARDEN)
MONDAY'S CHILD * (1967, US/Arg.) PR:A-C
MONDO TRASHO zero (1970) PR:O
MONEY, THE ** (1975) PR:O
MONEY AND THE WOMAN * (1940) PR:A
MONEY FOR JAM
  (SEE:IT AIN'T HAY)
MONEY FOR NOTHING ** (1932, Brit.) PR:A
MONEY FOR SPEED ** (1933, Brit.) PR:A
MONEY FROM HOME ** (1953) PR:A
MONEY ISN'T EVERYTHING
  (SEE:JEEPERS CREEPERS)
MONEY JUNGLE, THE ** (1968) PR:A
MONEY MAD * (1934, Brit.) PR:A
MONEY MADNESS * (1948) PR:A
MONEY MEANS NOTHING *½ (1934) PR:A
MONEY MEANS NOTHING * (1932, Brit.) PR:A
MONEY, MONEY, MONEY
  (SEE:COUNTERFEITERS OF PARIS, THE)
MONEY MOVERS **½ (1978, Aus.) PR:O
MONEY ON THE STREET ** (1930, Aust.) PR:A
MONEY ORDER, THE
  (SEE:MANDABI)
MONEY PIT, THE ** (1986) PR:A-C
MONEY TALKS **½ (1933, Brit.) PR:A
MONEY TO BURN *½ (1940) PR:A
MONEY TRAP, THE *½ (1966) PR:C
MONEY, WOMEN AND GUNS ** (1958) PR:A
MONGOLS, THE ** (1966, Fr./It.) PR:A
MONGREL zero (1982) PR:O
MONITORS, THE ** (1969) PR:C
MONKEY BUSINESS * (1931) PR:A**
MONKEY BUSINESS * (1952) PR:A**
MONKEY GRIP *½ (1983, Aus.) PR:A
MONKEY HUSTLE, THE *½ (1976) PR:C-O
MONKEY IN WINTER, A *** (1962, Fr.) PR:A
MONKEY ON MY BACK **½ (1957) PR:C
MONKEY SHINES: AN EXPERIMENT IN FEAR **
  (1988) PR:O**
MONKEYS, GO HOME! ** (1967) PR:AA
MONKEY'S PAW, THE **½ (1933) PR:C
MONKEY'S PAW, THE * (1948, Brit.) PR:A
MONKEY'S UNCLE, THE ** (1965) PR:AA
MOON IS DOWN, THE ***½ (1943) PR:C

MONOLITH MONSTERS, THE ** (1957) PR:A
MONSEIGNEUR ** (1950, Fr.) PR:A
MONSIEUR ** (1964, Fr.) PR:A
MONSIEUR BEAUCAIRE *** (1946) PR:A
MONSIEUR COGNAC
  (SEE:WILD AND WONDERFUL)
MONSIEUR FABRE
  (SEE:AMAZING MONSIEUR FABRE, THE)
MONSIEUR HULOT'S HOLIDAY
  (SEE:MR. HULOT'S HOLIDAY)
MONSIEUR RIPOIS
  (SEE:LOVER'S HAPPY LOVER'S)
MONSIEUR VERDOUX **½ (1947) PR:O
MONSIEUR VINCENT *** (1949, Fr.) PR:A
MONSIGNOR zero (1982) PR:O
MONSOON *½ (1953) PR:C
MONSTER zero (1979) PR:O
MONSTER
  (SEE:HUMANOIDS FROM THE DEEP)
MONSTER A GO-GO zero (1965) PR:C
MONSTER AND THE GIRL, THE **½ (1941) PR:C
MONSTER BARAN, THE
  (SEE:VARAN THE UNBELIEVABLE)
MONSTER CLUB, THE *½ (1981, Brit.) PR:C
MONSTER DOG zero (1986) PR:O
**MONSTER FROM THE GREEN HELL *½
  (1958) PR:A**
**MONSTER FROM THE OCEAN FLOOR, THE zero
  (1954) PR:A**
MONSTER FROM THE SURF
  (SEE:BEACH GIRLS AND THE MONSTER, THE)
MONSTER IN THE CLOSET ** (1987) PR:A-C
MONSTER ISLAND * (1981, Sp./US) PR:C
MONSTER MAKER, THE * (1944) PR:C
MONSTER MAKER
  (SEE:THE MONSTER FROM THE OCEAN FLOOR)
MONSTER MEETS THE GORILLA
  (SEE:BELA LUGOSI MEETS A BROOKLYN
  GORILLA)
MONSTER OF HIGHGATE PONDS, THE **
  (1961, Brit.) PR:AA
MONSTER OF LONDON CITY, THE *
  (1967, Ger.) PR:O
**MONSTER OF PIEDRAS BLANCAS, THE *½
  (1959) PR:C**
MONSTER OF TERROR
  (SEE:DIE, MONSTER, DIE)
MONSTER OF THE ISLAND *½ (1953, It.) PR:A
MONSTER OF THE WAX MUSEUM
  (SEE:NIGHTMARE IN WAX)
MONSTER ON THE CAMPUS ** (1958) PR:C
MONSTER SHARK zero (1986, It./Fr.) PR:O
MONSTER SQUAD, THE ** (1987) PR:A-C
MONSTER THAT CHALLENGED THE WORLD, THE
  **½ (1957) PR:A
MONSTER WALKED, THE
  (SEE:MONSTER WALKS, THE)
MONSTER WALKS, THE ** (1932) PR:A
MONSTER WANGMAGWI * (1967, S.K.) PR:A
MONSTER YONGKARI
  (SEE:YONGKARI MONSTER FROM THE DEEP)
MONSTER ZERO ** (1970, Jap.) PR:A
MONSTERS ARE LOOSE
  (SEE:THRILL KILLERS, THE)
MONSTERS FROM THE MOON
  (SEE:ROBOT MONSTER)
MONSTERS FROM THE UNKNOWN PLANET **
  (1975, Jap.) PR:A
MONSTROSITY
  (SEE:ATOMIC BRAIN, THE)
MONTANA ** (1950) PR:A
MONTANA BELLE * (1952) PR:A
MONTANA DESPERADO ** (1951) PR:A
MONTANA JUSTICE
  (SEE:MAN FROM MONTANA)
MONTANA KID, THE zero (1931) PR:A
MONTANA MIKE
  (SEE:HEAVEN ONLY KNOWS)
MONTANA MOON **½ (1930) PR:A
MONTANA TERRITORY * (1952) PR:A
MONTE CARLO ***½ (1930) PR:AA
MONTE CARLO BABY * (1953, Fr.) PR:A
MONTE CARLO MADNESS
  (SEE:BOMBARDMENT OF MONTE CARLO, THE)
MONTE CARLO NIGHTS * (1934) PR:A
MONTE CARLO OR BUST
  (SEE:THOSE DARING YOUNG MEN IN THEIR
  JAUNTY JALOPIES)
MONTE CARLO STORY, THE ** (1957, It.) PR:A
MONTE CASSINO ** (1948, It.) PR:A
MONTE CRISTO'S REVENGE
  (SEE:RETURN OF MONTE CRISTO, THE)
MONTE WALSH * (1970) PR:C**
MONTENEGRO * (1981, Brit./Swed.) PR:O**
MONTENEGRO—OR PIGS AND PEARLS
  (SEE:MONTENEGRO)
MONTPARNASSE 19
  (SEE:MODIGLIANI OF MONTPARNASSE)

MONTREAL MAIN *½ (1974, Can.) PR:O
MONTY PYTHON AND THE HOLY GRAIL **½
(1975, Brit.) PR:O
MONTY PYTHON'S LIFE OF BRIAN **
(1979, Brit.) PR:O
MONTY PYTHON'S THE MEANING OF LIFE zero
(1983, Brit.) PR:O
MOON AND SIXPENCE, THE **** (1942) PR:A
MOON IN SCORPIO * (1987) PR:O
MOON IN THE GUTTER, THE **
(1983, Fr./It.) PR:O
MOON IS BLUE, THE **½ (1953) PR:A-C
MOON OVER BURMA ** (1940) PR:A
MOON OVER HER SHOULDER ** (1941) PR:A
MOON OVER LAS VEGAS *½ (1944) PR:AA
MOON OVER MIAMI **½ (1941) PR:A
MOON OVER PARADOR ** (1988) PR:C
MOON OVER THE ALLEY zero (1980, Brit.) PR:O
MOON PILOT **½ (1962) PR:AA
MOON-SPINNERS, THE **½ (1964) PR:AA
MOON WALK
   (SEE:TICKLISH AFFAIR, A)
MOON ZERO TWO * (1970, Brit.) PR:A
MOONBEAM MAN, THE
   (SEE:MAN IN THE MOONLIGHT MASK, THE)
MOONCHILD ** (1972) PR:O
MOONFIRE zero (1970) PR:O
MOONFLEET **½ (1955) PR:A
MOONLIGHT AND CACTUS ** (1944) PR:A
MOONLIGHT AND MELODY
   (SEE:MOONLIGHT AND PRETZELS)
MOONLIGHT AND PRETZELS **½ (1933) PR:A
MOONLIGHT IN HAVANA ** (1942) PR:A
MOONLIGHT IN HAWAII * (1941) PR:A
MOONLIGHT IN VERMONT *½ (1943) PR:A
MOONLIGHT MASQUERADE *½ (1942) PR:A
MOONLIGHT MURDER *½ (1936) PR:A
MOONLIGHT ON THE PRAIRIE ** (1936) PR:A
MOONLIGHT ON THE RANGE ** (1937) PR:A
MOONLIGHT RAID
   (SEE:CHALLENGE OF THE RANGE)
MOONLIGHT SONATA *** (1938, Brit.) PR:A
MOONLIGHTER, THE * (1953) PR:A
MOONLIGHTING ** (1982, Brit.) PR:C**
MOONLIGHTING WIVES zero (1966) PR:O
MOONRAKER, THE **½ (1958, Brit.) PR:A
MOONRAKER * (1979, Brit.) PR:A**
MOONRISE ***½ (1948) PR:C
MOONRUNNERS *½ (1975) PR:A
MOON'S OUR HOME, THE *** (1936) PR:A
MOONSHINE COUNTY EXPRESS ** (1977) PR:C
MOONSHINE MOUNTAIN zero (1964) PR:A
MOONSHINE WAR, THE ** (1970) PR:C
MOONSHINER'S WOMAN zero (1968) PR:O
MOONSHOT
   (SEE:COUNTDOWN)
MOONSPINNERS, THE
   (SEE:MOON SPINNERS, THE)
MOONSTONE, THE ** (1934) PR:A
MOONSTRUCK ***½ (1987) PR:C
MOONTIDE **½ (1942) PR:A
MOONWOLF *½ (1966, Fin./Ger.) PR:A
MORALIST, THE ** (1964, It.) PR:A
MORALS FOR WOMEN *½ (1931) PR:A
MORALS OF MARCUS, THE ** (1936, Brit.) PR:A
MORD UND TOTSCHLAG
   (SEE:DEGREE OF MURDER, A)
MORDEI HA'OR
   (SEE:SANDS OF BEERSHEBA)
MORDER UNTER UNS
   (SEE:M)
MORE **½ (1969, Luxembourg) PR:O
MORE AMERICAN GRAFFITI ** (1979) PR:C
MORE DEAD THAN ALIVE **½ (1968) PR:C
MORE DEADLY THAN THE MALE *
   (1961, Brit.) PR:C
MORE THAN A MIRACLE *½ (1967, It./Fr.) PR:O
MORE THAN A SECRETARY ** (1936) PR:A
MORE THE MERRIER, THE ***½ (1943) PR:A
MORGAN! * (1966, Brit.) PR:C**
MORGAN STEWART'S COMING HOME **
   (1987) PR:A-C
MORGAN THE PIRATE ** (1961, Fr./It.) PR:A
MORGAN'S MARAUDERS *½ (1929) PR:A
MORITURI * (1965) PR:C**
MORNING AFTER, THE **½ (1986) PR:C-O

MORNING CALL
   (SEE:STRANGE CASE OF DR. MANNING, THE)
MORNING DEPARTURE
   (SEE:OPERATION DISASTER)
MORNING GLORY * (1933) PR:C**
MORNING STAR ** (1962, USSR) PR:A
MORO AFFAIR, THE ***½ (1986, It.) PR:C-O
MORO WITCH DOCTOR * (1964, US/Phil.) PR:C
MOROCCO ** (1930) PR:C**
MORONS FROM OUTER SPACE **
   (1985, Brit.) PR:C
MOROZKO
   (SEE:JACK FROST)
MORTADELLA
   (SEE:LADY LIBERTY)
MORTAL STORM, THE ***½ (1940) PR:A
MORTE A VENEZIA
   (SEE:DEATH IN VENICE)
MORTON OF THE MOUNTED
   (SEE:TIMBER TERRORS)
MORTUARY zero (1983) PR:O
MOSCOW—CASSIOPEIA **½ (1974, USSR) PR:A
MOSCOW DISTRUSTS TEARS
   (SEE:MOSCOW DOES NOT BELIEVE IN TEARS)
MOSCOW DOES NOT BELIEVE IN TEARS **½
   (1980, USSR) PR:A
MOSCOW NIGHTS
   (SEE:I STAND CONDEMNED)
MOSCOW ON THE HUDSON * (1984) PR:C-O**
MOSCOW SHANGHAI ** (1936, Ger.) PR:A
MOSES ** (1976, Brit./It.) PR:A
MOSES AND AARON *** (1975, Ger./Fr./It.) PR:C
MOSQUITO COAST, THE *½ (1986) PR:O
MOSQUITO SQUADRON ** (1970, Brit.) PR:A
MOSS ROSE *** (1947) PR:A
MOST BEAUTIFUL AGE, THE **½
   (1970, Czech.) PR:C
MOST DANGEROUS GAME, THE * (1932) PR:C-O**
MOST DANGEROUS MAN ALIVE, THE **½
   (1961) PR:A
MOST DANGEROUS MAN IN THE WORLD, THE
   (SEE:CHAIRMAN, THE)
MOST IMMORAL LADY, A * (1929) PR:A
MOST PRECIOUS THING IN LIFE ** (1934) PR:A
MOST WANTED MAN, THE ** (1962, Fr./It.) PR:A
MOST WONDERFUL EVENING OF MY LIFE, THE
   **½ (1972, It./Fr.) PR:A
MOSURA
   (SEE:MOTHRA)
MOTEL HELL zero (1980) PR:O
MOTEL, THE OPERATOR ** (1940) PR:C
MOTH, THE * (1934) PR:A
MOTHER AND DAUGHTER ** (1965, USSR) PR:A
MOTHER AND SON * (1931) PR:A
MOTHER AND THE WHORE, THE ***
   (1973, Fr.) PR:C
MOTHER CAREY'S CHICKENS **½ (1938) PR:A
MOTHER DIDN'T TELL ME **½ (1950) PR:A
MOTHER GOOSE A GO-GO * (1966) PR:A
MOTHER IS A FRESHMAN **½ (1949) PR:A
MOTHER JOAN OF THE ANGELS?
   (SEE:JOAN OF THE ANGELS?)
MOTHER, JUGS & SPEED zero (1976) PR:O
MOTHER KNOWS BEST ** (1928) PR:A
MOTHER KNOWS BEST
   (SEE:MOTHER IS A FRESHMAN)
MOTHER KUSTERS GOES TO HEAVEN **½
   (1976, Ger.) PR:C-O
MOTHER LODE * (1982) PR:C
MOTHER OUGHT TO MARRY
   (SEE:SECOND TIME AROUND, THE)
MOTHER RILEY MEETS THE VAMPIRE
   (SEE:MY SON THE VAMPIRE)
MOTHER SIR
   (SEE:NAVY WIFE)
MOTHER SUPERIOR
   (SEE:TROUBLE WITH ANGELS, THE)
MOTHER WORE TIGHTS *** (1947) PR:A
MOTHER'S BOY ** (1929) PR:A
MOTHERS CRY *½ (1930) PR:A
MOTHER'S DAY zero (1980) PR:O
MOTHER'S MILLIONS
   (SEE:SHE-WOLF, THE)
MOTHERS OF TODAY ** (1939) PR:C
MOTHRA **½ (1962, Jap.) PR:A
MOTIVE FOR REVENGE * (1935) PR:A

MOTIVE WAS JEALOUSY, THE **
   (1970, It./Sp.) PR:C
MOTOR MADNESS *½ (1937) PR:A
MOTOR PATROL * (1950) PR:A
MOTOR PSYCHO zero (1965) PR:O
MOTORCYCLE GANG *½ (1957) PR:C-O
MOTSART I SALVERI
   (SEE:REQUIEM FOR MOZART)
MOUCHETTE ***½ (1970, Fr.) PR:C
MOULIN ROUGE **½ (1934) PR:A
MOULIN ROUGE ** (1944, Fr.) PR:A
MOULIN ROUGE ***½ (1952) PR:A-C
MOUNTAIN, THE * (1935, Brit.) PR:A
MOUNTAIN, THE *½ (1956) PR:A
MOUNTAIN DESPERADOES
   (SEE:LARAMIE MOUNTAINS)
MOUNTAIN FAMILY ROBINSON ** (1979) PR:A
MOUNTAIN JUSTICE ** (1930) PR:A
MOUNTAIN JUSTICE **½ (1937) PR:A
MOUNTAIN MAN
   (SEE:GUARDIAN OF THE WILDERNESS)
MOUNTAIN MEN, THE * (1980) PR:O
MOUNTAIN MOONLIGHT ** (1941) PR:A
MOUNTAIN MUSIC ** (1937) PR:A
MOUNTAIN RHYTHM ** (1942) PR:AA
MOUNTAIN RHYTHM * (1939) PR:A
MOUNTAIN ROAD, THE **½ (1960) PR:A
MOUNTAINS O'MOURNE **½ (1938, Brit.) PR:A
MOUNTAINTOP MOTEL MASSACRE zero
   (1986) PR:O
MOUNTED FURY zero (1931) PR:A
MOUNTED STRANGER, THE * (1930) PR:A
MOURNING BECOMES ELECTRA ** (1947) PR:C
MOURNING SUIT, THE ** (1975, Can.) PR:C
MOUSE AND HIS CHILD, THE * (1977) PR:A
MOUSE AND THE WOMAN, THE **½
   (1981, Brit.) PR:O
MOUSE ON THE MOON, THE **½
   (1963, Brit.) PR:AA
MOUSE THAT ROARED, THE **
   (1959, Brit.) PR:AA
MOUTH TO MOUTH *** (1978, Aus.) PR:C
MOUTHPIECE, THE *** (1932) PR:A
MOVE zero (1970) PR:C
MOVE OVER, DARLING ** (1963) PR:A
MOVERS AND SHAKERS * (1985) PR:C
MOVIE CRAZY ***½ (1932) PR:A
MOVIE HOUSE MASSACRE * (1986) PR:O
MOVIE MOVIE **½ (1978) PR:A-C
MOVIE STAR, AMERICAN STYLE, OR, LSD I HATE
   YOU! * (1966) PR:C
MOVIE STRUCK
   (SEE:PICK A STAR)
MOVIE STUNTMEN * (1953) PR:A
MOVIETONE FOLLIES OF 1929
   (SEE:FOX MOVIETONE FOLLIES)
MOVIETONE FOLLIES OF 1930
   (SEE:FOX MOVIETONE FOLLIES OF 1930)
MOVING * (1988) PR:O
MOVING FINGER, THE ** (1963) PR:C
MOVING IN SOCIETY
   (SEE:MOUNTAIN MOONLIGHT)
MOVING TARGET, THE
   (SEE:HARPER)
MOVING TARGETS * (1987, Aus.) PR:C**
MOVING VIOLATION ** (1976) PR:C
MOVING VIOLATIONS *½ (1985) PR:O
MOZAMBIQUE *½ (1966, Brit.) PR:A
MOZART *½ (1940, Brit.) PR:A
MOZART
   (SEE:LIFE AND LOVES OF MOZART, THE)
MOZART STORY, THE ** (1948, Aust.) PR:A
MRS. BROWN, YOU'VE GOT A LOVELY DAUGHTER
   *½ (1968, Brit.) PR:A
MRS. DANE'S DEFENCE * (1933, Brit.) PR:A
MRS. FITZHERBERT ** (1950, Brit.) PR:A
MRS. GIBBONS' BOYS ** (1962, Brit.) PR:A
MRS. LORING'S SECRET
   (SEE:IMPERFECT LADY, THE)
MRS. MIKE **½ (1949) PR:A
MRS. MINIVER *** (1942) PR:A**
MRS. O'MALLEY AND MR. MALONE **
   (1950) PR:A
MRS. PARKINGTON **½ (1944) PR:A
MRS. POLLIFAX-SPY * (1971) PR:A
MRS. PYM OF SCOTLAND YARD **
   (1939, Brit.) PR:A

Finding entries in **THE MOTION PICTURE GUIDE** ™

Years 1929-83	Volumes I-IX
1984	Volume IX
1985	1986 ANNUAL
1986	1987 ANNUAL
1987	1988 ANNUAL
1988	1989 ANNUAL

STAR RATINGS

★★★★★ Masterpiece
★★★★ Excellent
★★★ Good
★★ Fair
★ Poor
zero Without Merit

PARENTAL RECOMMENDATION (PR:)

AA Good for Children
A Acceptable for Children
C Cautionary, some objectionable scenes
O Objectionable for Children

BOLD: Films on Videocassette

MRS. SOFFEL **½ (1984) PR:C
MRS. WARREN'S PROFESSION ** (1960, Ger.) PR:A
MRS. WIGGS OF THE CABBAGE PATCH ***
 (1934) PR:A
MRS. WIGGS OF THE CABBAGE PATCH *½
 (1942) PR:AA
MS. 45 ** (1981) PR:O
MUCEDNICI LASKY
 (SEE:MARTYRS OF LOVE)
MUCH TOO SHY *½ (1942, Brit.) PR:A
MUD
 (SEE:STICK UP, THE)
MUD HONEY
 (SEE:ROPE OF FLESH)
MUDDY RIVER ***½ (1982, Jap.) PR:A
MUDHONEY
 (SEE:ROPE OF FLESH)
MUDLARK, THE **½ (1950, Brit.) PR:A
MUERTO 4-3-2-1-0
 (SEE:MISSION STARDUST)
MUG TOWN *½ (1943) PR:A
MUGGER, THE ** (1958) PR:A
MUHOMATSU NO ISSHO
 (SEE:RICKSHAW MAN, THE)
MULE TRAIN ** (1950) PR:A
MUMMY, THE **** (1932) PR:C-O
MUMMY, THE *** (1959, Brit.) PR:C
MUMMY'S BOYS *½ (1936) PR:A
MUMMY'S CURSE, THE *½ (1944) PR:A
MUMMY'S GHOST, THE ** (1944) PR:A
MUMMY'S HAND, THE *** (1940) PR:C
MUMMY'S SHROUD, THE * (1967, Brit.) PR:C
MUMMY'S TOMB, THE **½ (1942) PR:C
MUMSY, NANNY, SONNY, AND GIRLY zero
 (1970, Brit.) PR:O
MUMU **½ (1961, USSR) PR:A
MUNCHIES zero (1987) PR:C
MUNECOS INFERNALES
 (SEE:CURSE OF THE DOLL PEOPLE)
MUNKBROGREVEN
 (SEE:COUNT OF THE MONK'S BRIDGE, THE)
MUNSTER, GO HOME ** (1966) PR:A
MUPPET MOVIE, THE *** (1979) PR:AA
MUPPETS TAKE MANHATTAN, THE **½
 (1984) PR:AA
MURDER **** (1930, Brit.) PR:A
MURDER A LA MOD * (1968) PR:C
MURDER AHOY *** (1964, Brit.) PR:A
MURDER AMONG FRIENDS ** (1941) PR:A
MURDER AT COVENT GARDEN *½
 (1932, Brit.) PR:A
MURDER AT DAWN * (1932) PR:A
MURDER AT 45 R.P.M. ** (1965, Fr.) PR:A
MURDER AT GLEN ATHOL *½ (1936) PR:A
MURDER AT MIDNIGHT *½ (1931) PR:A
MURDER AT MONTE CARLO * (1935, Brit.) PR:A
MURDER AT SITE THREE * (1959, Brit.) PR:A
MURDER AT THE BASKERVILLES **½
 (1941, Brit.) PR:A
MURDER AT THE BURLESQUE
 (SEE:MYSTERY AT THE BURLESQUE)
MURDER AT THE CABARET * (1936, Brit.) PR:A
MURDER AT THE GALLOP ***½ (1963, Brit.) PR:A
MURDER AT THE INN * (1934, Brit.) PR:A
MURDER AT THE VANITIES **½ (1934) PR:A
MURDER AT THE WINDMILL
 (SEE:MYSTERY AT THE BURLESQUE)
MURDER AT 3 A.M. * (1953, Brit.) PR:A
MURDER BY AGREEMENT
 (SEE:JOURNEY INTO NOWHERE)
MURDER BY AN ARISTOCRAT *½ (1936) PR:A
MURDER BY CONTRACT ** (1958) PR:C
MURDER BY DEATH **** (1976) PR:A
MURDER BY DECREE *** (1979, Brit.) PR:C
MURDER BY INVITATION *½ (1941) PR:A
MURDER BY MAIL
 (SEE:SCHIZOID)
MURDER BY PHONE
 (SEE:BELLS)
MURDER BY PROXY
 (SEE:BLACKOUT)
MURDER BY ROPE * (1936, Brit.) PR:A
MURDER BY TELEVISION * (1935) PR:A
MURDER BY THE CLOCK **½ (1931) PR:C
MURDER CAN BE DEADLY *½ (1963, Brit.) PR:A
MURDER CLINIC, THE *½ (1967, It./Fr.) PR:C
MURDER CZECH STYLE *** (1968, Czech.) PR:A
MURDER FOR SALE
 (SEE:TEMPORARY WIDOW)
MURDER GAME, THE ** (1966, Brit.) PR:A
MURDER GOES TO COLLEGE ** (1937) PR:A
MURDER, HE SAYS **** (1945) PR:A
MURDER IN EDEN ** (1962, Brit.) PR:A
MURDER IN GREENWICH VILLAGE * (1937) PR:A
MURDER IN MISSISSIPPI zero (1965) PR:C
MURDER IN MOROCCO
 (SEE:SCREAM IN THE NIGHT)
MURDER IN REVERSE *** (1946, Brit.) PR:A

MURDER IN SOHO
 (SEE:MURDER IN THE NIGHT)
MURDER IN THE AIR ** (1940) PR:A
MURDER IN THE BIG HOUSE
 (SEE:JAILBREAK)
MURDER IN THE BIG HOUSE *½ (1942) PR:A
MURDER IN THE BLUE ROOM *½ (1944) PR:A
MURDER IN THE CATHEDRAL ** (1952, Brit.) PR:A
MURDER IN THE CLOUDS **½ (1934) PR:A
MURDER IN THE FAMILY *½ (1938, Brit.) PR:A
MURDER IN THE FAMILY *½ (1938, Brit.) PR:A
MURDER IN THE FOOTLIGHTS
 (SEE:TROJAN BROTHERS, THE)
MURDER IN THE MUSEUM *½ (1934) PR:C
MURDER IN THE MUSIC HALL **½ (1946) PR:O
MURDER IN THE NIGHT zero (1940, Brit.) PR:O
MURDER IN THE OLD RED BARN *
 (1936, Brit.) PR:O
MURDER IN THE PRIVATE CAR *½ (1934) PR:A
MURDER IN THORTON SQUARE
 (SEE:GASLIGHT)
MURDER IN TIMES SQUARE **½ (1943) PR:O
MURDER IN TRINIDAD ** (1934) PR:O
MURDER, INC.
 (SEE:ENFORCER, THE)
MURDER, INC. *** (1960) PR:O
MURDER IS MY BEAT *** (1955) PR:O
MURDER IS MY BUSINESS ** (1946) PR:O
MURDER IS NEWS zero (1939) PR:O
MURDER MAN *** (1935) PR:C
MURDER MISSISSIPPI
 (SEE:MURDER IN MISSISSIPPI)
MURDER MOST FOUL *** (1964, Brit.) PR:A
MURDER, MY SWEET ***** (1945) PR:C-O
MURDER OF DR. HARRIGAN, THE ** (1936) PR:O
MURDER ON A BRIDLE PATH ** (1936) PR:O
MURDER ON A HONEYMOON ** (1935) PR:A
MURDER ON APPROVAL * (1956, Brit.) PR:C
MURDER ON DIAMOND ROW ** (1937, Brit.) PR:C
MURDER ON MONDAY *** (1953, Brit.) PR:C
MURDER ON THE BLACKBOARD *** (1934) PR:A
MURDER ON THE BRIDGE
 (SEE:END OF THE GAME)
MURDER ON THE CAMPUS *** (1934) PR:A
MURDER ON THE CAMPUS *½ (1963, Brit.) PR:A
MURDER ON THE ORIENT EXPRESS ***½
 (1974, Brit.) PR:C
MURDER ON THE ROOF ** (1930) PR:A
MURDER ON THE RUNAWAY TRAIN
 (SEE:MURDER IN THE PRIVATE CAR)
MURDER ON THE SECOND FLOOR *
 (1932, Brit.) PR:A
MURDER ON THE SET * (1936, Brit.) PR:A
MURDER ON THE WATERFRONT zero (1943) PR:A
MURDER ON THE YUKON ** (1940) PR:A
MURDER ONE *** (1988, Can.) PR:A
MURDER OVER NEW YORK **½ (1940) PR:A
MURDER RING, THE
 (SEE:ELLERY QUEEN AND THE MURDER RING)
MURDER REPORTED *½ (1958, Brit./Brit.) PR:O
MURDER SOCIETY, THE
 (SEE:MURDER CLINIC, THE)
MURDER TOMORROW *½ (1938, Brit.) PR:A
MURDER WILL OUT * (1930) PR:A
MURDER WILL OUT ** (1939, Brit.) PR:A
MURDER WILL OUT ** (1953, Brit.) PR:A
MURDER WITH PICTURES ** (1936) PR:A
MURDER WITHOUT CRIME * (1951, Brit.) PR:A
MURDER WITHOUT TEARS * (1953) PR:A
MURDERER, THE
 (SEE:ENOUGH ROPE)
MURDERER AMONG US
 (SEE:M)
MURDERER DMITRI KARAMAZOV, THE
 (SEE:KARAMAZOV)
MURDERER LIVES AT NUMBER 21, THE ***
 (1947, Fr.) PR:A
MURDERERS AMONG US *** (1948, Ger.) PR:O
MURDERERS ARE AMONGST US
 (SEE:MURDERERS AMONG US)
MURDERERS' ROW zero (1966) PR:C
MURDERS IN THE RUE MORGUE ** (1971) PR:O
MURDERS IN THE RUE MORGUE **½ (1932) PR:C
MURDERS IN THE ZOO *** (1933) PR:O
MURIEL **** (1963, Fr./It.) PR:A
MURIEL, OU LE TEMPS D'UN RETOUR
 (SEE:MURIEL)
MURIETA *½ (1965, Sp.) PR:O
MURMUR OF THE HEART ****
 (1971, Fr./It./Ger.) PR:A
MURPH THE SURF *** (1974) PR:C
MURPHY'S LAW ** (1986) PR:O
MURPHY'S ROMANCE **½ (1985) PR:C-O
MURPHY'S WAR **½ (1971, Brit.) PR:C-O
MURRI AFFAIR, THE
 (SEE:LA GRANDE BOURGEOISE)
MUSCLE BEACH PARTY **½ (1964) PR:AA
MUSEUM MYSTERY * (1937, Brit.) PR:A

MUSHROOM EATER, THE ***½ (1976, Mex.) PR:O
MUSIC AND MILLIONS
 (SEE:SUCH IS LIFE)
MUSIC BOX KID, THE ** (1960) PR:C
MUSIC FOR MADAME * (1937) PR:A
MUSIC FOR MILLIONS ** (1944) PR:AA
MUSIC GOES 'ROUND, THE *½ (1936) PR:A
MUSIC HALL ** (1934, Brit.) PR:A
MUSIC HALL PARADE ** (1939, Brit.) PR:A
MUSIC HATH CHARMS *** (1935, Brit.) PR:A
MUSIC IN MANHATTAN ** (1944) PR:A
MUSIC IN MY HEART * (1940) PR:A
MUSIC IN THE AIR **½ (1934) PR:A
MUSIC IS MAGIC ** (1935) PR:A
MUSIC LOVERS, THE zero (1971, Brit.) PR:O
MUSIC MACHINE, THE * (1979, Brit.) PR:O
MUSIC MAKER, THE * (1936, Brit.) PR:A
MUSIC MAN ** (1948) PR:AA
MUSIC MAN, THE ***** (1962) PR:AA
MUSIC ROOM, THE *** (1963, India) PR:A
MUSICAL MUTINY zero (1970) PR:A
MUSIK I MORKER
 (SEE:NIGHT IS MY FUTURE)
MUSS 'EM UP *** (1936) PR:A
MUSTANG zero (1959) PR:A
MUSTANG COUNTRY ** (1976) PR:A
MUSUME TO WATASHI
 (SEE:MY DAUGHTER AND I)
MUTANT
 (SEE:FORBIDDEN WORLD)
MUTANT HUNT zero (1987) PR:O
MUTATIONS, THE * (1974, Brit.) PR:O
MUTILATOR, THE * (1985) PR:O
MUTINEERS, THE
 (SEE:DAMN THE DEFIANT!)
MUTINEERS, THE * (1949) PR:A
MUTINY *½ (1952) PR:A
MUTINY AHEAD ** (1935) PR:A
MUTINY IN OUTER SPACE ** (1965) PR:A
MUTINY IN OUTER SPACE
 (SEE:SPACE MASTER X-7)
MUTINY IN THE ARCTIC **½ (1941) PR:A
MUTINY IN THE BIG HOUSE ** (1939) PR:A
MUTINY OF THE ELSINORE, THE *
 (1939, Brit.) PR:A
MUTINY ON THE BLACKHAWK ** (1939) PR:A
MUTINY ON THE BOUNTY ***** (1935) PR:A
MUTINY ON THE BOUNTY **½ (1962) PR:C-O
MUTINY ON THE SEAS
 (SEE:OUTSIDE THE 3-MILE LIMIT)
MY AIN FOLK * (1944, Brit.) PR:A
MY AIN FOLK ** (1974, Brit.) PR:A
MY AMERICAN COUSIN *** (1985, Can.) PR:A-C
MY AMERICAN UNCLE
 (SEE:MON ONCLE D'AMERICAIN)
MY AMERICAN WIFE ** (1936) PR:A
MY APPLE
 (SEE:JUST ME)
MY BABY IS BLACK! ** (1965, Fr.) PR:A
MY BEAUTIFUL LAUNDRETTE ***½
 (1986, Brit.) PR:O
MY BEST FRIEND'S GIRL ** (1984, Fr.) PR:O
MY BEST GAL * (1944) PR:A
MY BILL ** (1938) PR:A
MY BLOOD RUNS COLD *½ (1965) PR:O
MY BLOODY VALENTINE zero (1981, Can.) PR:O
MY BLUE HEAVEN **½ (1950) PR:A
MY BODY HUNGERS * (1967) PR:O
MY BODYGUARD ***½ (1980) PR:A
MY BOYS ARE GOOD BOYS * (1978) PR:A
MY BREAKFAST WITH BLASSIE ** (1983) PR:O
MY BRILLIANT CAREER **** (1980, Aus.) PR:O
MY BROTHER HAS BAD DREAMS * (1977) PR:O
MY BROTHER JONATHAN ** (1949, Brit.) PR:A
MY BROTHER TALKS TO HORSES *** (1946) PR:AA
MY BROTHER, THE OUTLAW * (1951) PR:A
MY BROTHER'S KEEPER **½ (1949, Brit.) PR:A
MY BROTHER'S WEDDING ***½ (1983) PR:A
MY BUDDY **½ (1944) PR:A
MY CHAUFFEUR ** (1986) PR:O
MY CHILDHOOD **½ (1972, Brit.) PR:A
MY COUSIN RACHEL *** (1952) PR:A
MY DARK LADY **½ (1987) PR:O
MY DARLING CLEMENTINE ***** (1946) PR:A
MY DAUGHTER JOY
 (SEE:OPERATION X)
MY DAYS WITH JEAN MARC
 (SEE:ANATOMY OF A MARRIAGE)
MY DEAR MISS ALDRICH *** (1937) PR:A
MY DEAR SECRETARY **½ (1948) PR:A-C
MY DEATH IS A MOCKERY ** (1952, Brit.) PR:C-O
MY DEMON LOVER *½ (1987) PR:C
MY DINNER WITH ANDRE * (1981) PR:A-C
MY DOG, BUDDY ** (1960) PR:A
MY DOG RUSTY ** (1948) PR:AA
MY DREAM IS YOURS **½ (1949) PR:A
MY ENEMY, THE SEA
 (SEE:ALONE ON THE PACIFIC)

MY FAIR LADY **** (1964) PR:AA
MY FATHER'S HOUSE * (1947, Palestine) PR:A
MY FATHER'S MISTRESS *½ (1970, Swed.) PR:C
MY FAVORITE BLONDE *** (1942) PR:A
MY FAVORITE BRUNETTE **** (1947) PR:A
MY FAVORITE SPY * (1942) PR:A
MY FAVORITE SPY *** (1951) PR:A
MY FAVORITE WIFE *** (1940) PR:A
MY FAVORITE YEAR **** (1982) PR:C
MY FIRST LOVE ** (1978, Fr.) PR:O
MY FIRST WIFE **** (1985, Aus.) PR:O
MY FOOLISH HEART **½ (1949) PR:A-C
MY FORBIDDEN PAST **½ (1951) PR:C
MY FRIEND FLICKA **** (1943) PR:A-A
MY FRIEND IRMA ** (1949) PR:A
MY FRIEND IRMA GOES WEST **½ (1950) PR:A
MY FRIEND THE KING ** (1931, Brit.) PR:A
MY GAL LOVES MUSIC *** (1944) PR:A
MY GAL SAL *** (1942) PR:A
MY GEISHA ** (1962) PR:A
MY GIRL TISA **½ (1948) PR:A
MY GUN IS QUICK *½ (1957) PR:O
MY HANDS ARE CLAY * (1948, Ireland) PR:A
MY HEART BELONGS TO DADDY * (1942) PR:A
MY HEART GOES CRAZY *½ (1953, Brit.) PR:A
MY HEART IS CALLING *½ (1935, Brit.) PR:A
MY HERO
   (SEE:SOUTHERN YANKEE, A)
MY HOBO *** (1963, Jap.) PR:A
MY IRISH MOLLY
   (SEE:LITTLE MISS MOLLY)
MY KIND OF TOWN **½ (1984, Can.) PR:A
MY KINGDOM FOR A COOK *** (1943) PR:A
MY LAST DUCHESS
   (SEE:ARRIVEDERCI, BABY!)
MY LEARNED FRIEND *** (1943, Brit.) PR:A
MY LIFE AS A DOG *** (1987, Swed.) PR:C
MY LIFE IS YOURS
   (SEE:PEOPLE VS. DR. KILDARE, THE)
MY LIFE TO LIVE **** (1963, Fr.) PR:A
MY LIFE WITH CAROLINE *½ (1941) PR:A-C
MY LIPS BETRAY *½ (1933) PR:A
MY LITTLE CHICKADEE **½ (1940) PR:A
MY LITTLE PONY ** (1986) PR:AA
MY LOVE CAME BACK *** (1940) PR:A
MY LOVE FOR YOURS
   (SEE:HONEYMOON IN BALI)
MY LOVE LETTERS
   (SEE:LOVE LETTERS)
MY LOVER, MY SON * (1970, Brit.) PR:O
MY LUCKY STAR ** (1933, Brit.) PR:A
MY LUCKY STAR **½ (1938) PR:A
MY MAIN MAN FROM STONY ISLAND
   (SEE:STONY ISLAND)
MY MAN **½ (1928) PR:A
MY MAN ADAM zero (1986) PR:O
MY MAN AND I **½ (1952) PR:A
MY MAN GODFREY ***** (1936) PR:A
MY MAN GODFREY *** (1957) PR:A
MY MARGO **½ (1969, Israel) PR:C
MY MARRIAGE ** (1936) PR:A
MY MOTHER ** (1933) PR:A
MY NAME IS IVAN ** (1963, USSR) PR:O
MY NAME IS JULIA ROSS ***½ (1945) PR:A
MY NAME IS NOBODY ***
   (1974, It./Fr./Ger.) PR:O
MY NAME IS PECOS *½ (1966, It.) PR:C
MY NAME IS ROCCO PAPALEO
   (SEE:ROCCO PAPALEO)
MY NEW PARTNER **½ (1984, Fr.) PR:O
MY NIGHT AT MAUD'S **** (1970, Fr.) PR:A
MY NIGHT WITH MAUD
   (SEE:MY NIGHT AT MAUD'S)
MY NIGHTS WITH FRANCOISE
   (SEE:ANATOMY OF A MARRIAGE)
MY OLD DUCHESS ** (1933, Brit.) PR:A
MY OLD DUTCH ** (1934, Brit.) PR:A
MY OLD KENTUCKY HOME ** (1938) PR:A
MY OLD MAN'S PLACE
   (SEE:GLORY BOY)
MY OTHER HUSBAND ** (1985, Fr.) PR:C
MY OUTLAW BROTHER
   (SEE:MY BROTHER, THE OUTLAW)
MY OWN TRUE LOVE ** (1948) PR:A
MY PAL GUS ** (1952) PR:A
MY PAL, THE KING *** (1932) PR:A
MY PAL TRIGGER ***½ (1946) PR:AA

MY PAL, WOLF *** (1944) PR:A
MY PARTNER MR. DAVIS
   (SEE:MYSTERIOUS MR. DAVIS, THE)
MY PAST *** (1931) PR:A
MY REPUTATION ** (1946) PR:A-C
MY SCIENCE PROJECT zero (1985) PR:C-O
MY SEVEN LITTLE SINS **½ (1956, Fr./It.) PR:A
MY SIDE OF THE MOUNTAIN *** (1969) PR:AA
MY SIN * (1931) PR:A-C
MY SISTER AND I * (1948, Brit.) PR:C
MY SISTER EILEEN *** (1942) PR:AA
MY SISTER EILEEN ***½ (1955) PR:AA
MY SISTER, MY LOVE
   (SEE:MAFU CAGE, THE)
MY SIX CONVICTS *** (1952) PR:A-C
MY SIX LOVES ** (1963) PR:AA
MY SON ALONE
   (SEE:AMERICAN EMPIRE)
MY SON IS A CRIMINAL **½ (1939) PR:A
MY SON IS GUILTY ** (1940) PR:C
MY SON, JOHN **½ (1952) PR:C
MY SON, MY SON! **** (1940) PR:A
MY SON NERO
   (SEE:NERO'S MISTRESS)
MY SON, THE HERO ** (1943) PR:A
MY SON, THE HERO **½ (1963, It./Fr.) PR:A
MY SON, THE VAMPIRE *½ (1963, Brit.) PR:A
MY SONG FOR YOU *** (1935, Brit.) PR:A
MY SONG GOES ROUND THE WORLD *½
   (1934, Brit.) PR:A
MY SOUL RUNS NAKED
   (SEE:RAT FINK)
MY STEPMOTHER IS AN ALIEN * (1988) PR:C
MY SWEET LITTLE VILLAGE ***
   (1985, Czech.) PR:A
MY TEENAGE DAUGHTER
   (SEE:TEENAGE BAD GIRL)
MY THIRD WIFE BY GEORGE
   (SEE:MY THIRD WIFE GEORGE)
MY THIRD WIFE GEORGE ** (1968) PR:A
MY TRUE STORY *½ (1951) PR:A
MY TUTOR ** (1983) PR:O
MY TWO HUSBANDS
   (SEE:TOO MANY HUSBANDS)
MY UNCLE **** (1958, Fr.) PR:AA
MY UNCLE ANTOINE ***½ (1971, Can.) PR:C
MY UNCLE FROM AMERICA
   (SEE:MON ONCLE D'AMERIQUE)
MY UNCLE, MR. HULOT
   (SEE:MY UNCLE)
MY UNCLE'S LEGACY *** (1988, Yugo.) PR:C
MY UNIVERSITY
   (SEE:UNIVERSITY OF LIFE)
MY WAY ** (1974, South Africa) PR:A
MY WAY HOME zero (1978, Brit.) PR:C
MY WEAKNESS *** (1933) PR:A
MY WIDOW AND I *** (1950, It.) PR:C
MY WIFE'S BEST FRIEND ** (1952) PR:A
MY WIFE'S ENEMY ** (1967, It.) PR:A
MY WIFE'S FAMILY ** (1932, Brit.) PR:A
MY WIFE'S FAMILY ** (1941, Brit.) PR:A
MY WIFE'S FAMILY *½ (1962, Brit.) PR:A
MY WIFE'S HUSBAND ** (1965, Fr./It.) PR:A
MY WIFE'S LODGER ** (1952, Brit.) PR:A
MY WIFE'S RELATIVES * (1939) PR:AA
MY WILD IRISH ROSE **½ (1947) PR:A
MY WOMAN ** (1933) PR:A
MY WORLD DIES SCREAMING ** (1958) PR:C
MYRT AND MARGE zero (1934) PR:A
MYSTERIANS, THE ** (1959, Jap.) PR:A
MYSTERIES zero (1979, Neth.) PR:A
MYSTERIOUS AVENGER, THE *** (1936) PR:A
MYSTERIOUS CROSSING ** (1937) PR:A-C
MYSTERIOUS DESPERADO, THE *** (1949) PR:A
MYSTERIOUS DR. FU MANCHU, THE ***
   (1929) PR:A
MYSTERIOUS DOCTOR, THE zero (1943) PR:C
MYSTERIOUS HOUSE OF DR. C., THE ***½
   (1976) PR:A
MYSTERIOUS INTRUDER *** (1946) PR:A
MYSTERIOUS INVADER, THE
   (SEE:ASTOUNDING SHE-MONSTER, THE)
MYSTERIOUS ISLAND * (1929) PR:A
MYSTERIOUS ISLAND *** (1941, USSR) PR:A
MYSTERIOUS ISLAND *** (1961, US/Brit.) PR:AA

MYSTERIOUS ISLAND, THE
   (SEE:MYSTERIOUS ISLAND OF CAPTAIN NEMO,
   THE)
MYSTERIOUS ISLAND OF CAPTAIN NEMO, THE *
   (1973, Fr./It./Sp./Cameroon) PR:AA
MYSTERIOUS MISS X, THE ** (1939) PR:A
MYSTERIOUS MR. DAVIS, THE * (1936, Brit.) PR:A
MYSTERIOUS MR. MOTO *** (1938) PR:A
MYSTERIOUS MR. MOTO OF DEVIL'S ISLAND
   (SEE:MYSTERIOUS MR. MOTO)
MYSTERIOUS MR. NICHOLSON, THE *½
   (1947, Brit.) PR:A
MYSTERIOUS MR. REEDER, THE **
   (1940, Brit.) PR:A-C
MYSTERIOUS MR. VALENTINE, THE **
   (1946) PR:A
MYSTERIOUS MR. WONG *** (1935) PR:C
MYSTERIOUS RIDER, THE **½ (1933) PR:A
MYSTERIOUS RIDER, THE **½ (1938) PR:A
MYSTERIOUS RIDER, THE ** (1942) PR:A
MYSTERIOUS SATELLITE, THE **½
   (1956, Jap.) PR:A
MYSTERIOUS STRANGER, THE
   (SEE:WESTERN GOLD)
MYSTERIOUS STRANGER, THE
   (SEE:CODE OF THE LAWLESS)
MYSTERY AT MONTE CARLO
   (SEE:REVENGE AT MONTE CARLO)
MYSTERY AT THE BURLESQUE **
   (1950, Brit.) PR:A
MYSTERY AT THE VILLA ROSE **
   (1930, Brit.) PR:A
MYSTERY MAN *½ (1944) PR:A
MYSTERY BROADCAST *** (1943) PR:A
MYSTERY HOUSE * (1938) PR:A
MYSTERY IN MEXICO **½ (1948) PR:A
MYSTERY JUNCTION * (1951, Brit.) PR:A
MYSTERY LAKE **½ (1953) PR:A
MYSTERY LINER *** (1934) PR:A
MYSTERY MAN, THE **½ (1935) PR:A
MYSTERY MANSION ** (1984) PR:C
MYSTERY OF ALEXINA, THE **½ (1985, Fr.) PR:O
MYSTERY OF DIAMOND ISLAND, THE
   (SEE:RIP ROARING RILEY)
MYSTERY OF EDWIN DROOD, THE *** (1935) PR:C
MYSTERY OF KASPAR HAUSER, THE
   (SEE:EVERY MAN FOR HIMSELF AND GOD
   AGAINST ALL)
MYSTERY OF MARIE ROGET, THE ** (1942) PR:A
MYSTERY OF MR. WONG, THE *** (1939) PR:A
MYSTERY OF MR. X, THE *** (1934) PR:C
MYSTERY OF ROOM 13 ** (1941, Brit.) PR:A
MYSTERY OF THE BLACK JUNGLE * (1955) PR:A
MYSTERY OF THE GOLDEN EYE, THE *
   (1948) PR:A
MYSTERY OF THE HOODED HORSEMEN, THE **½
   (1937) PR:A
MYSTERY OF THE MARIE CELESTE
   (SEE:PHANTOM SHIP)
MYSTERY OF THE PINK VILLA, THE
   (SEE:MYSTERY AT THE VILLA ROSE)
MYSTERY OF THE 13TH GUEST, THE * (1943) PR:A
MYSTERY OF THE WAX MUSEUM, THE ****
   (1933) PR:C
MYSTERY OF THE WENTWORTH CASTLE, THE
   (SEE:DOOMED TO DIE)
MYSTERY OF THE WHITE ROOM zero (1939) PR:A
MYSTERY OF THUG ISLAND, THE *½
   (1966, It./Ger.) PR:A
MYSTERY ON BIRD ISLAND *** (1954, Brit.) PR:A
MYSTERY ON MONSTER ISLAND
   (SEE:MONSTER ISLAND)
MYSTERY PLANE ** (1939) PR:A
MYSTERY RANCH *** (1932) PR:A
MYSTERY RANGE ** (1937) PR:A
MYSTERY SEA RAIDER ** (1940) PR:A
MYSTERY SHIP ** (1941) PR:A
MYSTERY STREET ***½ (1950) PR:C
MYSTERY SUBMARINE *½ (1950) PR:A
MYSTERY SUBMARINE ** (1963, Brit.) PR:A
MYSTERY TRAIN * (1931) PR:A
MYSTERY WOMAN ** (1935) PR:A
MYSTIC CIRCLE MURDER * (1939) PR:A
MYSTIC HOUR, THE **½ (1934) PR:A
MYSTIC PIZZA **½ (1988) PR:O
MYSTIFIERS, THE
   (SEE:SYMPHONY FOR A MASSACRE)

Finding entries in **THE MOTION PICTURE GUIDE** ™

Years 1929-83	Volumes I-IX
1984	Volume IX
1985	1986 ANNUAL
1986	1987 ANNUAL
1987	1988 ANNUAL
1988	1989 ANNUAL

STAR RATINGS

★★★★★ Masterpiece
★★★★ Excellent
★★★ Good
★★ Fair
★ Poor
zero Without Merit

PARENTAL RECOMMENDATION (PR:)

AA   Good for Children
A   Acceptable for Children
C   Cautionary, some objectionable scenes
O   Objectionable for Children

BOLD: Films on Videocassette

MYSTIQUE zero (1981) PR:O
MYTH, THE ** (1965, It.) PR:O

N

N. P. ** (1971, It.) PR:A
NA SEMI VETRAKH
(SEE:HOUSE, ON THE WATER FRONT LINE, THE)
NABONGA zero (1944) PR:A
NACHTS, WENN DER TEUFEL KAM
(SEE:DEVIL STRIKES AT NIGHT, THE)
NACKT UNTER WOLFEN
(SEE:NAKED AMONG THE WOLVES)
NADA
(SEE:NADA GAME, THE)
NADA GANG, THE ** (1974, Fr./It.) PR:A
NADA MAS QUE UNA MUJER *½ (1934) PR:A
NADIA ** (1984, US/Yugo.) PR:C
NADINE ** (1987) PR:C
NAGANA ** (1933) PR:A
NAGOOA
(SEE:DRIFTING)
NAIL GUN MASSACRE * (1987) PR:O
NAKED ALIBI *** (1954) PR:A
NAKED AMONG THE WOLVES *** (1967, Ger.) PR:C
NAKED AND THE DEAD, THE * (1958) PR:O
NAKED ANGELS * (1969) PR:O
NAKED APE, THE * (1973) PR:C
NAKED AUTUMN ** (1963, Fr.) PR:A
NAKED BRIGADE, THE ** (1965, US/Gr.) PR:A
NAKED CAGE, THE *½ (1986) PR:O
NAKED CHILDHOOD
(SEE:ME)
NAKED CITY, THE **** (1948) PR:C
NAKED DAWN, THE **½ (1955) PR:A
NAKED EARTH, THE *½ (1958, Brit.) PR:A
NAKED EDGE, THE ** (1961) PR:A-C
NAKED EVIL
(SEE:EXORCISM AT MIDNIGHT)
NAKED FACE, THE **½ (1984) PR:C
NAKED FLAME, THE ** (1970, Can.) PR:C
NAKED FURY **½ (1959, Brit.) PR:C
NAKED FURY, THE
(SEE:PLEASURE LOVERS, THE)
NAKED GENERAL, THE **½ (1964, Jap.) PR:A
NAKED GODDESS, THE
(SEE:DEVIL'S HAND, THE)
NAKED GUN, THE **½ (1988) PR:C-O
NAKED GUN, THE * (1956) PR:A
NAKED HEART, THE *½ (1955, Brit.) PR:A
NAKED HEARTS *½ (1970, Fr.) PR:A
NAKED HILLS, THE ** (1956) PR:A
NAKED HOURS, THE *** (1964, It.) PR:C
NAKED IN THE SUN ** (1957) PR:C
NAKED ISLAND
(SEE:ISLAND, THE)
NAKED JUNGLE, THE ***½ (1953) PR:A-C
NAKED KISS, THE **½ (1964) PR:O
NAKED LOVERS, THE
(SEE:NAKED ZOO, THE)
NAKED MAJA, THE * (1959, It./US) PR:A
NAKED NIGHT, THE *** (1956, Swed.) PR:O
NAKED PARADISE ** (1957) PR:A
NAKED PREY, THE ***½ (1966, US/South Africa) PR:O
NAKED RUNNER, THE * (1967, Brit.) PR:A-C
NAKED SET
(SEE:NAKED ROAD, THE)
NAKED SPUR, THE **** (1953) PR:A-C
NAKED SPUR
(SEE:HOT SPUR)
NAKED STREET, THE *** (1955) PR:C
NAKED TEMPTATION
(SEE:WOMAN AND TEMPTATION)
NAKED TEMPTRESS, THE
(SEE:THE NAKED WITCH)
NAKED TRUTH, THE
(SEE:YOUR PAST IS SHOWING)
NAKED UNDER LEATHER
(SEE:GIRL ON A MOTORCYCLE)
NAKED VENGEANCE * (1986, US/Phil.) PR:O
NAKED WITCH, THE *½ (1964) PR:C
NAKED WOMAN, THE * (1950, Fr.) PR:A
NAKED WORLD OF HARRISON MARKS, THE *½ (1967, Brit.) PR:O
NAKED YOUTH ***½ (1961, Jap.) PR:C-O
NAKED YOUTH
(SEE:WILD YOUTH)
NAKED ZOO, THE zero (1970) PR:C
NAM ANGELS
(SEE:LOSERS, THE)
NAME FOR EVIL, A * (1970) PR:C-O
NAME OF THE GAME IS KILL, THE **½ (1968) PR:C
NAME OF THE ROSE, THE ** (1986) PR:C-O
NAME THE WOMAN * (1934) PR:A
NAMELESS
(SEE:FRAULEIN DOKTOR)
NAMONAKU MAZUSHIKU UTSUKUSHIKU
(SEE:HAPPINESS OF US ALONE)
NAMU, THE KILLER WHALE **½ (1966) PR:A
NANA **½ (1934) PR:C
NANA *½ (1957, Fr./It.) PR:A-C
NANA zero (1983, It.) PR:O
NANCY DREW AND THE HIDDEN STAIRCASE **½ (1939) PR:AA
NANCY DREW—DETECTIVE ** (1938) PR:AA
NANCY DREW—REPORTER ** (1939) PR:AA
NANCY DREW, TROUBLE SHOOTER **½ (1939) PR:AA
NANCY GOES TO RIO **½ (1950) PR:A
NANCY STEELE IS MISSING *** (1937) PR:A
NANNY, THE *** (1965, Brit.) PR:O
NAPLO GYERMEKEIMNEK
(SEE:DIARY FOR MY CHILDREN)
NAPOLEON ** (1955, Fr.) PR:A
NAPOLEON AND SAMANTHA **½ (1972) PR:AA
NARAYAMA-BUSHI-KO
(SEE:BALLAD OF NARAYAMA)
NARCO MEN, THE ** (1969, Sp./It.) PR:O
NARCOTICS STORY, THE zero (1958) PR:O
NARK, THE
(SEE:LA BALANCE)
NARROW CORNER, THE *** (1933) PR:C
NARROW MARGIN, THE *** (1952) PR:A
NARROWING CIRCLE, THE **½ (1956, Brit.) PR:C
NASHVILLE ***** (1975) PR:C-O
NASHVILLE GIRL
(SEE:NEW GIRL IN TOWN)
NASHVILLE REBEL ** (1966) PR:A
NASILJE NA TRGU
(SEE:SQUARE OF VIOLENCE)
NASTY HABITS *** (1976, Brit.) PR:C
NASTY RABBIT, THE ** (1964) PR:A
NATCHEZ TRACE ** (1960) PR:C
NATE AND HAYES **½ (1983, US/New Zealand) PR:C
NATHALIE **½ (1958, Fr.) PR:A
NATHALIE, AGENT SECRET ** (1960, Fr.) PR:A
NATHALIE GRANGER * (1972, Fr.) PR:C
NATHANIEL HAWTHORNE'S ""TWICE TOLD TALES"
(SEE:TWICE TOLD TALES)
NATION AFLAME zero (1937) PR:A
NATIONAL BARN DANCE ** (1944) PR:A
NATIONAL HEALTH, OR NURSE NORTON'S AFFAIR, THE *** (1973, Brit.) PR:C
NATIONAL LAMPOON'S ANIMAL HOUSE ***½ (1978) PR:C
NATIONAL LAMPOON'S CLASS REUNION zero (1982) PR:O
NATIONAL LAMPOON'S EUROPEAN VACATION *** (1985) PR:C
NATIONAL LAMPOON'S VACATION ** (1983) PR:C
NATIONAL VELVET **** (1944) PR:AA
NATIVE LAND **½ (1942) PR:A
NATIVE SON **½ (1951, US/Arg.) PR:C-O
NATIVE SON **½ (1986) PR:C
NATSUKASHIKI FUE YA TAIKO
(SEE:EYES, THE SEA AND A BALL)
NATTLEK
(SEE:NIGHT GAMES)
NATTVARDSGASTERNA
(SEE:WINTER LIGHT)
NATURAL, THE *** (1984) PR:C
NATURAL BORN SALESMAN
(SEE:EARTHWORM TRACTORS)
NATURAL ENEMIES *½ (1979) PR:O
NATURE'S MISTAKES
(SEE:FREAKS)
NAUGHTY ARLETTE ** (1951, Brit.) PR:C-O
NAUGHTY BUT NICE ** (1939) PR:A
NAUGHTY CINDERELLA ** (1933, Brit.) PR:A
NAUGHTY FLIRT, THE * (1931) PR:A
NAUGHTY MARIETTA ***½ (1935) PR:A
NAUGHTY NINETIES, THE ** (1945) PR:AA
NAVAJO *** (1952) PR:A
NAVAJO JOE ** (1967, It./Sp.) PR:C
NAVAJO KID, THE *½ (1946) PR:A
NAVAJO RUN ** (1966) PR:C
NAVAJO TRAIL RAIDERS ** (1949) PR:A
NAVAJO TRAIL, THE ** (1945) PR:A
NAVAL ACADEMY *½ (1941) PR:A
NAVY BLUE AND GOLD ** (1937) PR:A
NAVY BLUES ** (1930) PR:A
NAVY BLUES * (1937) PR:A
NAVY BLUES **½ (1941) PR:A
NAVY BORN * (1936) PR:A
NAVY BOUND *½ (1951) PR:A
NAVY HEROES ** (1959, Brit.) PR:A
NAVY LARK, THE ** (1959, Brit.) PR:A
NAVY SECRETS ** (1939) PR:A
NAVY SPY zero (1937) PR:A
NAVY STEPS OUT, THE
(SEE:GIRL, A GUY, AND A GOB, A)
NAVY VS. THE NIGHT MONSTERS, THE ** (1966) PR:C
NAVY WAY, THE * (1944) PR:A
NAVY WIFE ** (1936) PR:A
NAVY WIFE *½ (1956) PR:A
NAZARIN **½ (1968, Mex.) PR:A
NEAR DARK ***½ (1987) PR:O
'NEATH BROOKLYN BRIDGE **½ (1942) PR:A
'NEATH THE ARIZONA SKIES ** (1934) PR:A
NEBO ZOVYOT
(SEE:BATTLE BEYOND THE SUN)
NEBRASKAN, THE * (1953) PR:A
NECK AND NECK * (1931) PR:A
NECROMANCY * (1972) PR:C
NECROPOLIS zero (1987) PR:O
NED KELLY **½ (1970, Brit.) PR:C
NEFERTITE, REGINA DEL NILO
(SEE:QUEEN OF THE NILE)
NEGATIVES ** (1968, Brit.) PR:C
NEHEZELETUEK
(SEE:THE ROUND UP)
NEIGE
(SEE:SNOW)
NEIGHBORS **½ (1981) PR:C-O
NEIGHBORS' WIVES *½ (1933) PR:A
NEITHER BY DAY NOR BY NIGHT *** (1972, US/Israel) PR:A
NEITHER THE SEA NOR THE SAND * (1974, Brit.) PR:A
NELL GWYN *** (1935, Brit.) PR:A-C
NELLA CITTA L'INFERNO
(SEE:AND THE WILD, WILD WOMEN)
NELLY'S VERSION *½ (1983, Brit.) PR:A
NELSON AFFAIR, THE ** (1973, Brit.) PR:C
NELSON TOUCH, THE
(SEE:CORVETTE K-225)
NEMO
(SEE:DREAM ONE)
NEON MANIACS * (1986) PR:O
NEON PALACE, THE ** (1970, Can.) PR:A
NEPTUNE DISASTER, THE
(SEE:NEPTUNE FACTOR, THE)
NEPTUNE FACTOR, THE *½ (1973, Can.) PR:A
NEPTUNE'S DAUGHTER **½ (1949) PR:A
NERO'S BIG WEEKEND
(SEE:NERO'S MISTRESS)
NERO'S MISTRESS zero (1962, It.) PR:C
NEST, THE **½ (1982, Sp.) PR:A
NEST OF THE CUCKOO BIRDS, THE * (1965) PR:C
NEST OF VIPERS *½ (1979, It.) PR:O
NESTING, THE *½ (1981) PR:O
NET, THE
(SEE:PROJECT M7)
NETWORK ***** (1976) PR:C
NEUNZIG MINUTEN NACH MITTER NACHT
(SEE:TERROR AFTER MIDNIGHT)
NEUTRAL PORT **½ (1941, Brit.) PR:A
NEUTRON CONTRA EL DR. CARONTE * (1962, Mex.) PR:A
NEUTRON EL ENMASCARADO NEGRO * (1962, Mex.) PR:A
NEVADA ** (1936) PR:A
NEVADA **½ (1944) PR:A
NEVADA BADMEN *½ (1951) PR:A
NEVADA CITY ** (1941) PR:A
NEVADA SMITH ***½ (1966) PR:C
NEVADAN, THE **½ (1950) PR:A
NEVER A DULL MOMENT ** (1943) PR:A
NEVER A DULL MOMENT ** (1950) PR:A
NEVER A DULL MOMENT *** (1968) PR:A
NEVER BACK LOSERS ** (1967, Brit.) PR:A
NEVER CRY WOLF ***½ (1983) PR:C
NEVER FEAR *** (1950) PR:A
NEVER GIVE A SUCKER A BREAK
(SEE:NUISANCE, THE)
NEVER GIVE A SUCKER AN EVEN BREAK *** (1941) PR:A
NEVER GIVE AN INCH
(SEE:SOMETIMES A GREAT NOTION)
NEVER LET GO **½ (1960, Brit.) PR:C
NEVER LET ME GO ** (1953, US/Brit.) PR:A
NEVER LOOK BACK ** (1952, Brit.) PR:A
NEVER LOVE A STRANGER *½ (1958) PR:A
NEVER MENTION MURDER *½ (1964, Brit.) PR:A
NEVER NEVER LAND **½ (1982) PR:A
NEVER ON SUNDAY *** (1960, Gr.) PR:O
NEVER PUT IT IN WRITING ** (1964) PR:A
NEVER SAY DIE *½ (1939) PR:A
NEVER SAY DIE
(SEE:DON'T SAY DIE)
NEVER SAY GOODBYE *½ (1946) PR:A
NEVER SAY GOODBYE ** (1956) PR:A
NEVER SAY NEVER AGAIN **½ (1983) PR:A

NEVER SO FEW * (1959) PR:C**
NEVER STEAL ANYTHING SMALL **½ (1959) PR:C
NEVER STEAL ANYTHING WET (SEE:CATALINA CAPER)
NEVER TAKE CANDY FROM A STRANGER *** (1961, Brit.) PR:C-O
NEVER TAKE NO FOR AN ANSWER **½ (1952, Brit./It.) PR:A
NEVER TAKE SWEETS FROM A STRANGER (SEE:NEVER TAKE CANDY FROM A STRANGER)
NEVER THE TWAIN SHALL MEET *½ (1931) PR:A
NEVER TO LOVE (SEE:BILL OF DIVORCEMENT)
NEVER TOO LATE *½ (1965) PR:A
NEVER TOO YOUNG TO DIE **½ (1986) PR:O
NEVER TROUBLE TROUBLE *½ (1931, Brit.) PR:A
NEVER TRUST A GAMBLER *½ (1951) PR:A
NEVER WAVE AT A WAC *** (1952) PR:A
NEVERENDING STORY, THE ***½ (1984, Ger.) PR:C
NEW ADVENTURES OF DR. FU MANCHU, THE (SEE:RETURN OF DR. FU MANCHU)
NEW ADVENTURES OF DON JUAN (SEE:ADVENTURES OF DON JUAN)
NEW ADVENTURES OF GET-RICH-QUICK WALLINGFORD, THE ** (1931) PR:A
NEW ADVENTURES OF PIPPI LONGSTOCKING, THE ** (1988) PR:A
NEW ADVENTURES OF TARZAN *½ (1935) PR:A
NEW BARBARIANS, THE zero (1983, It.) PR:O
NEW CENTURIONS, THE ** (1972) PR:O
NEW EARTH, THE ** (1937, Jap./Ger.) PR:A
NEW FACE IN HELL (SEE:P.J.)
NEW FACES ** (1954) PR:A
NEW FACES OF 1937 *½ (1937) PR:A
NEW FRONTIER, THE *½ (1935) PR:A
NEW FRONTIER *½ (1939) PR:A
NEW GIRL IN TOWN ** (1977) PR:C-O
NEW HORIZONS * (1939, USSR) PR:A
NEW HOTEL, THE *½ (1932, Brit.) PR:A-C
NEW HOUSE ON THE LEFT, THE zero (1978, Brit.) PR:O
NEW INTERNS, THE **½ (1964) PR:C
NEW INVISIBLE MAN, THE (SEE:INVISIBLE MAN, THE)
NEW KIDS, THE zero (1985) PR:O
NEW KIND OF LOVE, A *½ (1963) PR:A-C
NEW LAND, THE *** (1973, Swed.) PR:A
NEW LEAF, A * (1971) PR:C-O**
NEW LIFE, A ** (1988) PR:C
NEW LIFE STYLE, THE *½ (1970, Ger.) PR:O
NEW LOVE *½ (1968, Chile) PR:O
NEW MEXICO ** (1951) PR:A
NEW MONSTERS, THE (SEE:VIVA ITALIA)
NEW MOON *½ (1930) PR:A
NEW MOON ** (1940) PR:A
NEW MORALS FOR OLD ** (1932) PR:A
NEW MOVIETONE FOLLIES OF 1930, THE (SEE:FOX MOVIETONE FOLLIES OF 1930)
NEW ONE-ARMED SWORDSMAN, THE (SEE:TRIPLE IRONS)
NEW ORLEANS ** (1929) PR:A
NEW ORLEANS ** (1947) PR:A
NEW ORLEANS AFTER DARK ** (1958) PR:C
NEW ORLEANS UNCENSORED ** (1955) PR:A
NEW TEACHER, THE *½ (1941, USSR) PR:A
NEW WINE ** (1941) PR:A
NEW YEAR'S EVIL zero (1980) PR:O
NEW YORK (SEE:HALLELUJAH, I'M A BUM)
NEW YORK APPELLE SUPER DRAGON (SEE:SECRET AGENT SUPER DRAGON)
NEW YORK CONFIDENTIAL ** (1955) PR:C
NEW YORK, NEW YORK ***½ (1977) PR:C
NEW YORK NIGHTS ** (1929) PR:A
NEW YORK NIGHTS * (1984) PR:O
NEW YORK TOWN **½ (1941) PR:A
NEW YORK'S FINEST zero (1988) PR:O
NEWLY RICH *½ (1931) PR:AA
NEWMAN'S LAW ** (1974) PR:A
NEWS HOUNDS ** (1947) PR:A
NEWS IS MADE AT NIGHT ** (1939) PR:A
NEWSBOY'S HOME *½ (1939) PR:A
NEWSFRONT * (1979, Aus.) PR:C**
NEXT! * (1971, It./Sp.) PR:O
NEXT IN LINE (SEE:RIDERS OF THE NORTHLAND)
NEXT MAN, THE **½ (1976) PR:O
NEXT OF KIN *½ (1942, Brit.) PR:A
NEXT OF KIN * (1983, Aus.) PR:O
NEXT ONE, THE * (1982, US/Gr.) PR:C
NEXT STOP, GREENWICH VILLAGE **** (1976) PR:C
NEXT TIME I MARRY *½ (1938) PR:A
NEXT TIME WE LOVE *½ (1936) PR:A
NEXT TO NO TIME **½ (1960, Brit.) PR:A
NEXT VOICE YOU HEAR, THE *** (1950) PR:AA
NGATI *** (1987, New Zealand) PR:A
NIAGARA ***½ (1953) PR:C
NICE GIRL? ** (1941) PR:A
NICE GIRL LIKE ME, A **½ (1969, Brit.) PR:C
NICE GIRLS DON'T EXPLODE **½ (1987) PR:C
NICE LITTLE BANK THAT SHOULD BE ROBBED, A *½ (1958) PR:A
NICE PLATE OF SPINACH, A (SEE:WHAT WOULD YOU SAY TO SOME SPINACH)
NICE WOMAN * (1932) PR:A
NICHOLAS AND ALEXANDRA ***½ (1971, Brit.) PR:C
NICHOLAS NICKLEBY ** (1947, Brit.) PR:A
NICHT VERSOHNT ODER ""ES HILFT NUR GEWALT, WO GEWALT HERRSCHT" (SEE:NOT RECONCILED, OR "ONLY VIOLENCE HELPS WHERE IT RULES")
NICK CARTER IN PRAGUE (SEE:ADELE HASN'T HAD HER SUPPER YET)
NICK CARTER, MASTER DETECTIVE *** (1939) PR:A
NICKEL MOUNTAIN ** (1985) PR:C
NICKEL QUEEN, THE ** (1971, Aus.) PR:A
NICKEL RIDE, THE *** (1974) PR:C
NICKELODEON ** (1976) PR:C
NIGHT, THE (SEE:LA NOTTE)
NIGHT AFFAIR ** (1961, Fr.) PR:A
NIGHT AFTER NIGHT *** (1932) PR:C
NIGHT AFTER NIGHT AFTER NIGHT *½ (1970, Brit.) PR:C-O
NIGHT ALARM *½ (1935) PR:A
NIGHT ALONE **½ (1938, Brit.) PR:A
NIGHT AMBUSH *** (1958, Brit.) PR:A
NIGHT AND DAY *½ (1933, Brit.) PR:A
NIGHT AND DAY * (1946) PR:A**
NIGHT AND THE CITY ***½ (1950, Brit.) PR:O
NIGHT ANGEL, THE ** (1931) PR:A
NIGHT ANGELS *** (1987, Braz.) PR:O
NIGHT AT EARL CARROLL'S, A ** (1940) PR:A
NIGHT AT THE OPERA, A ** (1935) PR:A**
NIGHT AT THE RITZ, A ** (1935) PR:A
NIGHT BEAT *½ (1932) PR:A
NIGHT BEAT * (1948, Brit.) PR:A
NIGHT BEFORE CHRISTMAS, A ** (1963, USSR) PR:A
NIGHT BEFORE THE DIVORCE, THE ** (1942) PR:A
NIGHT BIRDS * (1931, Brit.) PR:A
NIGHT BOAT TO DUBLIN ** (1946, Brit.) PR:A
NIGHT CALL NURSES ** (1974) PR:O
NIGHT CALLER, THE (SEE:BLOOD BEAST FROM OUTER SPACE)
NIGHT CALLER FROM OUTER SPACE (SEE:BLOOD BEAST FROM OUTER SPACE)
NIGHT CARGO * (1936) PR:A
NIGHT CHILD * (1975, Brit./It.) PR:O
NIGHT CLUB (SEE:GIGOLETTE)
NIGHT CLUB GIRL ** (1944) PR:A
NIGHT CLUB GIRL (SEE:GLAMOUR GIRL)
NIGHT CLUB HOSTESS (SEE:UNMARRIED)
NIGHT CLUB LADY ** (1932) PR:A
NIGHT CLUB MURDER (SEE:ROMANCE IN RHYTHM)
NIGHT CLUB QUEEN ** (1934, Brit.) PR:A
NIGHT CLUB SCANDAL **½ (1937) PR:A
NIGHT COMERS, THE * (1971, Brit.) PR:C-O
NIGHT COMES TOO SOON ** (1948, Brit.) PR:C
NIGHT COURT *** (1932) PR:A
NIGHT CRAWLERS, THE (SEE:NAVY VS. THE NIGHT MONSTERS, THE)
NIGHT CREATURE * (1979) PR:A
NIGHT CREATURES **½ (1962, Brit.) PR:A
NIGHT CROSSING *½ (1982) PR:C
NIGHT DIGGER, THE ** (1971, Brit.) PR:O
NIGHT EDITOR **½ (1946) PR:A
NIGHT ENCOUNTER **½ (1963, Fr./It.) PR:A
NIGHT EVELYN CAME OUT OF THE GRAVE, THE *½ (1973, It.) PR:O
NIGHT EXPRESS, THE (SEE:WESTERN LIMITED, THE)
NIGHT FIGHTERS, THE *** (1960) PR:A
NIGHT FLIGHT *** (1933) PR:A
NIGHT FLIGHT FROM MOSCOW (SEE:SERPENT, THE)
NIGHT FLOWERS * (1979) PR:O
NIGHT FOR CRIME, A *½ (1942) PR:A
NIGHT FREIGHT *½ (1955) PR:A
NIGHT FULL OF RAIN, A (SEE:END OF THE WORLD IN OUR USUAL BED IN A NIGHT FULL OF RAIN)
NIGHT GAMES ** (1966, Swed.) PR:O
NIGHT GAMES ** (1980) PR:O
NIGHT GOD SCREAMED, THE * (1975) PR:O
NIGHT HAIR CHILD * (1971, Brit.) PR:O
NIGHT HAS A THOUSAND EYES *** (1948) PR:C
NIGHT HAS EYES, THE (SEE:TERROR HOUSE)
NIGHT HEAVEN FELL, THE ** (1958, Fr.) PR:O
NIGHT HOLDS TERROR, THE *** (1955) PR:C
NIGHT HUNT (SEE:IF HE HOLLERS, LET HIM GO!)
NIGHT IN BANGKOK **½ (1966, Jap.) PR:A
NIGHT IN CAIRO, A (SEE:BARBARIAN, THE)
NIGHT IN CASABLANCA, A * (1946) PR:A**
NIGHT IN HAVANA (SEE:BIG BOODLE, THE)
NIGHT IN HEAVEN, A * (1983) PR:O
NIGHT IN HONG KONG, A **½ (1961, Jap.) PR:A
NIGHT IN JUNE, A **½ (1940, Swed.) PR:A
NIGHT IN MONTMARTE, A *½ (1931, Brit.) PR:A
NIGHT IN NEW ORLEANS, A ** (1942) PR:A
NIGHT IN PARADISE, A ** (1946) PR:A
NIGHT IN THE LIFE OF JIMMY REARDON, A * (1988) PR:O**
NIGHT INTO MORNING **½ (1951) PR:A
NIGHT INVADER, THE **½ (1943, Brit.) PR:C
NIGHT IS ENDING, THE (SEE:PARIS AFTER DARK)
NIGHT IS MY FUTURE **½ (1962, Swed.) PR:A
NIGHT IS OURS *½ (1930, Fr.) PR:A
NIGHT IS THE PHANTOM (SEE:WHAT!)
NIGHT IS YOUNG, THE ** (1935) PR:A
NIGHT IS YOUNG, THE (SEE:BAD BLOOD)
NIGHT JOURNEY ** (1938, Brit.) PR:A
NIGHT KEY **½ (1937) PR:A
NIGHT LIFE IN RENO * (1931) PR:A
NIGHT LIFE OF THE GODS **½ (1935) PR:A
NIGHT LIKE THIS, A *** (1932, Brit.) PR:A
NIGHT MAIL **½ (1935, Brit.) PR:C
NIGHT MAYOR, THE **½ (1932) PR:A
NIGHT MONSTER ** (1942) PR:A
'NIGHT, MOTHER ***½ (1986) PR:C
NIGHT MOVES **½ (1975) PR:C
NIGHT MUST FALL **** (1937) PR:O
NIGHT MUST FALL *** (1964, Brit.) PR:O
NIGHT MY NUMBER CAME UP, THE **½ (1955, Brit.) PR:A-C
NIGHT NURSE *** (1931) PR:A-C
NIGHT OF A THOUSAND CATS ** (1974, Mex.) PR:O
NIGHT OF ADVENTURE, A ** (1944) PR:A
NIGHT OF ANUBIS (SEE:NIGHT OF THE LIVING DEAD)
NIGHT OF BLOODY HORROR zero (1969) PR:O
NIGHT OF DARK SHADOWS * (1971) PR:C
NIGHT OF EVIL * (1962) PR:C
NIGHT OF JANUARY 16TH * (1941) PR:A
NIGHT OF JUNE 13 ***½ (1932) PR:A
NIGHT OF LUST *½ (1965, Fr.) PR:C
NIGHT OF MAGIC, A ** (1944, Brit.) PR:A
NIGHT OF MYSTERY * (1937) PR:A
NIGHT OF NIGHTS, THE **½ (1939) PR:A
NIGHT OF PASSION (SEE:DURING ONE NIGHT)

Finding entries in **THE MOTION PICTURE GUIDE ™**

Years	Volumes
Years 1929-83	Volumes I-IX
1984	Volume IX
1985	1986 ANNUAL
1986	1987 ANNUAL
1987	1988 ANNUAL
1988	1989 ANNUAL

STAR RATINGS

★★★★★	Masterpiece
★★★★	Excellent
★★★	Good
★★	Fair
★	Poor
zero	Without Merit

PARENTAL RECOMMENDATION (PR:)

AA	Good for Children
A	Acceptable for Children
C	Cautionary, some objectionable scenes
O	Objectionable for Children

BOLD: Films on Videocassette

NIGHT OF SAN LORENZO, THE
(SEE:NIGHT OF THE SHOOTING STARS)
NIGHT OF TERROR * (1933) PR:A
NIGHT OF TERRORS
(SEE:MURDER CLINIC, THE)
NIGHT OF THE ASKARI **
(1978, Ger./South Africa/African) PR:C
NIGHT OF THE BEAST
(SEE:HOUSE OF THE BLACK DEATH)
NIGHT OF THE BIG HEAT
(SEE:ISLAND OF THE BURNING DOOMED)
NIGHT OF THE BLOOD BEAST *½ (1958) PR:A
NIGHT OF THE BLOODY APES zero
(1968, Mex.) PR:O
NIGHT OF THE CLAW
(SEE:ISLAND CLAWS)
NIGHT OF THE COBRA WOMAN *
(1974, US/Phil.) PR:O
NIGHT OF THE COMET ***½ (1984) PR:C-O
NIGHT OF THE CREEPS ** (1986) PR:O
NIGHT OF THE DARK FULL MOON
(SEE:SILENT NIGHT, BLOODY NIGHT)
NIGHT OF THE DEMON
(SEE:CURSE OF THE DEMON)
NIGHT OF THE DEMON
(SEE:TOUCH OF SATAN, THE)
NIGHT OF THE EAGLE
(SEE:BURN, WITCH, BURN!)
NIGHT OF THE FLESH EATERS
(SEE:NIGHT OF THE LIVING DEAD)
NIGHT OF THE FOLLOWING DAY, THE *
(1969, Brit.) PR:O
NIGHT OF THE FULL MOON, THE *
(1954, Brit.) PR:C
NIGHT OF THE GARTER *½ (1933, Brit.) PR:A
NIGHT OF THE GENERALS, THE **
(1967, Brit./Fr.) PR:O
NIGHT OF THE GHOULS zero (1959) PR:O
NIGHT OF THE GRIZZLY, THE *½ (1966) PR:A
NIGHT OF THE HUNTER, THE *** (1955) PR:O
NIGHT OF THE IGUANA, THE **½ (1964) PR:O
NIGHT OF THE JUGGLER * (1980) PR:O
NIGHT OF THE LAUGHING DEAD
(SEE:HOUSE IN NIGHTMARE PARK)
NIGHT OF THE LEPUS * (1972) PR:C
NIGHT OF THE LIVING DEAD ** (1968) PR:O
NIGHT OF THE PARTY, THE * (1934, Brit.) PR:A
NIGHT OF THE PROWLER ** (1962, Brit.) PR:C
NIGHT OF THE PROWLER, THE zero
(1979, Aus.) PR:O
NIGHT OF THE QUARTER MOON * (1959) PR:C
NIGHT OF THE SEAGULL, THE **½
(1970, Jap.) PR:C
NIGHT OF THE SHOOTING STARS, THE **
(1982, It.) PR:O
NIGHT OF THE SILICATES
(SEE:ISLAND OF TERROR)
NIGHT OF THE STRANGLER * (1975) PR:O
NIGHT OF THE TIGER, THE
(SEE:RIDE BEYOND VENGEANCE)
NIGHT OF THE WITCHES zero (1970) PR:O
NIGHT OF THE ZOMBIES zero (1981) PR:O
NIGHT OF THE ZOMBIES zero (1983, Sp./It.) PR:O
NIGHT PARADE ** (1929, Brit.) PR:A
NIGHT PASSAGE **½ (1957) PR:A
NIGHT PATROL zero (1984) PR:O
NIGHT PEOPLE ***½ (1954) PR:C
NIGHT PLANE FROM CHUNGKING **½
(1942) PR:A
NIGHT PORTER, THE **½ (1974, It./US) PR:O
NIGHT RAIDERS *½ (1952) PR:A
NIGHT RIDE ** (1930) PR:A
NIGHT RIDE ** (1937, Brit.) PR:C
NIGHT RIDER, THE *½ (1932) PR:A
NIGHT RIDERS, THE * (1939) PR:A
NIGHT RIDERS OF MONTANA *½ (1951) PR:A
NIGHT RUNNER, THE *** (1957) PR:A
NIGHT SCHOOL * (1981) PR:O
NIGHT SHADOWS *½ (1984) PR:O
NIGHT SHIFT * (1982) PR:C
NIGHT SONG *½ (1947) PR:A
NIGHT SPOT *½ (1938) PR:A
NIGHT STAGE TO GALVESTON * (1952) PR:A
NIGHT STALKER, THE * (1987) PR:O
NIGHT THE CREATURES CAME
(SEE:ISLAND OF TERROR)
NIGHT THE LIGHTS WENT OUT IN GEORGIA, THE
**** (1981) PR:C**
NIGHT THE SILICATES CAME
(SEE:ISLAND OF TERROR)
NIGHT THE SUN CAME OUT, THE
(SEE:WATERMELON MAN)
NIGHT THE WORLD EXPLODED, THE *½
(1957) PR:A
NIGHT THEY KILLED RASPUTIN, THE **
(1962, Fr./It.) PR:C
NIGHT THEY RAIDED MINSKY'S, THE **
(1968) PR:C-O

NIGHT THEY ROBBED BIG BERTHA'S, THE zero
(1975) PR:O
NIGHT TIDE **½ (1963) PR:C
NIGHT TIME IN NEVADA **½ (1948) PR:A
NIGHT TO REMEMBER, A **½ (1942) PR:A
NIGHT TO REMEMBER, A ** (1958, Brit.) PR:A
NIGHT TRAIN *** (1940, Brit.) PR:A
NIGHT TRAIN FOR INVERNESS **½
(1960, Brit.) PR:C
NIGHT TRAIN TO MEMPHIS *½ (1946) PR:A
NIGHT TRAIN TO MUNDO FINE * (1966) PR:A
NIGHT TRAIN TO MUNICH
(SEE:NIGHT TRAIN)
NIGHT TRAIN TO PARIS ** (1964, Brit.) PR:A
NIGHT UNTO NIGHT ** (1949) PR:A
NIGHT VISITOR, THE *½ (1970, Swed./U.S.) PR:C
NIGHT WAITRESS *½ (1936) PR:A
NIGHT WALK
(SEE:DEATHDREAM)
NIGHT WALKER, THE *½ (1964) PR:C
NIGHT WAS OUR FRIEND *½ (1951, Brit.) PR:C-O
NIGHT WATCH, THE **** (1964, Fr./It.) PR:A
NIGHT WATCH * (1973, Brit.) PR:C
NIGHT WE DROPPED A CLANGER, THE
(SEE:MAKE MINE A DOUBLE)
NIGHT WE GOT THE BIRD, THE *½
(1961, Brit.) PR:C
NIGHT WIND * (1948) PR:A
NIGHT WITHOUT PITY ** (1962, Brit.) PR:C
NIGHT WITHOUT SLEEP ** (1952) PR:C
NIGHT WITHOUT STARS *½ (1953, Brit.) PR:A
NIGHT WON'T TALK, THE **½ (1952, Brit.) PR:C
NIGHT WORK **½ (1930) PR:A
NIGHT WORK ** (1939) PR:A
NIGHT WORLD **½ (1932) PR:A
NIGHT ZOO * (1988, Can.) PR:O
NIGHTBEAST *½ (1982) PR:C-O
NIGHTFALL ***½ (1956) PR:A
NIGHTFLIGHT FROM MOSCOW
(SEE:SERPENT, THE)
NIGHTFORCE * (1987) PR:O
NIGHTHAWKS * (1978, Brit.) PR:O
NIGHTHAWKS ***½ (1981) PR:O
NIGHTMARE
(SEE:CITY OF THE WALKING DEAD)
NIGHTMARE *** (1942) PR:C
NIGHTMARE *** (1956) PR:C
NIGHTMARE ** (1963, Brit.) PR:O
NIGHTMARE zero (1981) PR:O
NIGHTMARE ALLEY **** (1947) PR:C-O
NIGHTMARE CASTLE **½ (1966, It.) PR:C
NIGHTMARE CITY
(SEE:CITY OF THE WALKING DEAD)
NIGHTMARE HONEYMOON * (1973) PR:O
NIGHTMARE IN BLOOD *½ (1978) PR:O
NIGHTMARE IN THE SUN *½ (1964) PR:O
NIGHTMARE IN WAX zero (1969) PR:O
NIGHTMARE ON ELM STREET 4: THE DREAM
MASTER, A **½ (1988) PR:O
NIGHTMARE ON ELM STREET PART 2: FREDDY'S
REVENGE, A **½ (1985) PR:O
NIGHTMARE ON ELM STREET 3: DREAM
WARRIORS, A * (1987) PR:O
NIGHTMARE ON ELM STREET, A ***½
(1984, US) PR:O
NIGHTMARE WEEKEND zero
(1986, Brit./U.S./Fr.) PR:O
NIGHTMARES * (1983) PR:O
NIGHTMARE'S PASSENGERS ***½
(1986, Arg.) PR:O
NIGHTS IN A HAREM
(SEE:SON OF SINBAD)
NIGHTS OF CABIRIA * (1957, It.) PR:C
NIGHTS OF LUCRETIA BORGIA, THE *½
(1960, It.) PR:A
NIGHTS OF PRAGUE, THE *** (1968, Czech.) PR:C
NIGHTS OF SHAME **½ (1961, Fr.) PR:O
NIGHTS WHEN THE DEVIL CAME
(SEE:DEVIL STRIKES AT NIGHT, THE)
NIGHTSONGS **½ (1984) PR:C
NIGHTWARS * (1988) PR:O
NIGHTWING * (1979) PR:O
NIGHT HAWK, THE *½ (1938) PR:A
NIHON NO ICHIBAN NAGAI HI
(SEE:EMPEROR AND A GENERAL, THE)
NIJINSKY ** (1980, Brit.) PR:C-O
NIKKI, WILD DOG OF THE NORTH ***½
(1961, US/Can.) PR:AA
NIKUTAI NO GAKKO
(SEE:SCHOOL OF LOVE)
9 1/2 WEEKS * (1986) PR:O
NINE DAYS A QUEEN
(SEE:LADY JANE GREY)
NINE DAYS OF ONE YEAR *** (1964, USSR) PR:O
9 DEATHS OF THE NINJA * (1985) PR:O
NINE FORTY-FIVE **½ (1934, Brit.) PR:A
NINE GIRLS **½ (1944) PR:C
NINE HOURS TO RAMA *** (1963, U.S./Brit.) PR:C

NINE LIVES ARE NOT ENOUGH **½ (1941) PR:A
NINE MEN ***½ (1943, Brit.) PR:A
NINE MILES TO NOON **½ (1963) PR:C
9/30/55 ***½ (1977) PR:C
NINE TILL SIX ** (1932, Brit.) PR:A
NINE TO FIVE * (1980) PR:C-O
1918 **½ (1985) PR:C
1984 **½ (1956, Brit.) PR:A-C
1984 * (1984, Brit.) PR:O
1941 **½ (1979) PR:C-O
1914 ** (1932, Ger.) PR:C
1900 * (1976, It.) PR:C-O
NINETEEN HUNDRED TWENTY ONE
(SEE:RISING OF THE SUN, THE)
1919 *** (1984, Brit.) PR:C
1990: THE BRONX WARRIORS * (1983, It.) PR:C
1969 ** (1988) PR:C
90 DAYS *** (1986, Can.) PR:O
90 DEGREES IN THE SHADE **½
(1966, Czech./Brit.) PR:O
99 AND 44/100% DEAD * (1974) PR:C-O
99 RIVER STREET *** (1953) PR:C
99 WOUNDS * (1931) PR:A
92 IN THE SHADE * (1975, US/Brit.) PR:C
NINGEN NO JOKEN
(SEE:HUMAN CONDITION, THE)
NINGEN NO JOKEN III
(SEE:SOLDIER'S PRAYER)
NINGEN NO JOKEN II
(SEE:ROAD TO ETERNITY)
NINJA III—THE DOMINATION *½ (1984) PR:O
NINJA TURF zero (1986) PR:O
NINJUTSU, SORYU HIKEN
(SEE:SECRET SCROLLS—PART II)
NINOTCHKA *** (1939) PR:A
NINTH CIRCLE, THE *** (1961, Yugo.) PR:O
NINTH CONFIGURATION, THE * (1980) PR:O
NINTH GUEST, THE **½ (1934) PR:A
NINTH HEART, THE *** (1980, Czech.) PR:A
NIPPER, THE
(SEE:BRAT, THE)
NIPPON KONCHUKI
(SEE:INSECT WOMAN, THE)
NIPPON NO ICHIBAN NAGAI HI
(SEE:EMPEROR AND A GENERAL, THE)
NITWITS, THE **½ (1935) PR:A
NIX ON DAMES ** (1929) PR:A
NO BLADE OF GRASS ** (1970, Brit.) PR:O
NO BRAKES
(SEE:OH, YEAH)
NO DEAD HEROES zero (1987) PR:O
NO DEADLY MACHINE
(SEE:YOUNG DOCTORS, THE)
NO DEFENSE * (1929) PR:A
NO DEPOSIT, NO RETURN * (1976) PR:AA
NO DOWN PAYMENT **½ (1957) PR:C
NO DRUMS, NO BUGLES ***½ (1971) PR:A
NO ESCAPE
(SEE:I ESCAPED FROM THE GESTAPO)
NO ESCAPE **½ (1934, Brit.) PR:C
NO ESCAPE **½ (1936, Brit.) PR:C
NO ESCAPE ** (1953) PR:O
NO EXIT *** (1962, US/Arg.) PR:O
NO EXIT ** (1930, Brit.) PR:A
NO FUNNY BUSINESS * (1934, Brit.) PR:A
NO GREATER GLORY **** (1934) PR:A
NO GREATER LOVE
(SEE:ALOHA)
NO GREATER LOVE ** (1932) PR:A
NO GREATER LOVE * (1944, USSR) PR:O
NO GREATER LOVE
(SEE:HUMAN CONDITION, THE)
NO GREATER LOVE THAN THIS **½
(1969, Jap.) PR:C
NO GREATER SIN * (1941) PR:A
NO GREATER SIN
(SEE:EIGHTEEN AND ANXIOUS)
NO HANDS ON THE CLOCK **½ (1941) PR:A
NO HAUNT FOR A GENTLEMAN **
(1952, Brit.) PR:A
NO HIGHWAY
(SEE:NO HIGHWAY IN THE SKY)
NO HIGHWAY IN THE SKY ***½ (1951, Brit.) PR:A
NO HOLDS BARRED **½ (1952) PR:A
NO KIDDING
(SEE:BEWARE OF CHILDREN)
NO KNIFE
(SEE:FRISCO KID, THE)
NO LADY * (1931, Brit.) PR:A
NO LEAVE, NO LOVE *½ (1946) PR:A
NO LIMIT ** (1931) PR:A
NO LIMIT ***½ (1935, Brit.) PR:A
NO LIVING WITNESS ** (1932) PR:A
NO LONGER ALONE *** (1978) PR:C
NO LOVE FOR JOHNNIE ***½ (1961, Brit.) PR:O
NO LOVE FOR JUDY ** (1955, Brit.) PR:C
NO MAN IS AN ISLAND *** (1962) PR:C
NO MAN OF HER OWN **½ (1933) PR:A

NO MAN OF HER OWN **½ (1950) PR:A
NO MAN WALKS ALONE
  (SEE:BLACK LIKE ME)
NO MAN'S LAND ** (1964) PR:O
NO MAN'S LAND ** (1987) PR:O
NO MAN'S RANGE ** (1935) PR:A
NO MAN'S WOMAN ** (1955) PR:C
NO MARRIAGE TIES ** (1933) PR:A
NO MERCY **½ (1986) PR:O
NO MINOR VICES *** (1948) PR:A
NO MONKEY BUSINESS *½ (1935, Brit.) PR:A
NO MORE EXCUSES ** (1968) PR:O
NO MORE LADIES ** (1935) PR:C
NO MORE ORCHIDS *** (1933) PR:A
NO MORE WOMEN * (1934) PR:A
NO, MY DARLING DAUGHTER **½
  (1964, Brit.) PR:A
NO NAME ON THE BULLET ***½ (1959) PR:A
NO, NO NANETTE *** (1930) PR:A
NO, NO NANETTE *½ (1940) PR:A
NO ONE MAN * (1932) PR:A
NO ORCHIDS FOR MISS BLANDISH zero
  (1948, Brit.) PR:O
NO OTHER WOMAN *½ (1933) PR:A
NO PARKING ** (1938, Brit.) PR:A
NO PLACE FOR A LADY ** (1943) PR:A
NO PLACE FOR JENNIFER ** (1950, Brit.) PR:A
NO PLACE LIKE HOMICIDE
  (SEE:WHAT A CARVE UP!)
NO PLACE TO GO *** (1939) PR:A
NO PLACE TO HIDE ** (1956) PR:A
NO PLACE TO HIDE * (1975) PR:C-O
NO PLACE TO LAND * (1958) PR:A-C
NO QUESTIONS ASKED **½ (1951) PR:A
NO RANSOM ** (1935) PR:A
NO RESTING PLACE ** (1952, Brit.) PR:A
NO RETREAT, NO SURRENDER * (1986) PR:C
NO RETURN ADDRESS **½ (1961) PR:A
NO ROAD BACK *½ (1957, Brit.) PR:A
NO ROOM AT THE INN *** (1950, Brit.) PR:A
NO ROOM FOR THE GROOM * (1952) PR:A
NO ROOM TO DIE ** (1969, It.) PR:O
NO ROSES FOR OSS 117 ** (1968, Fr.) PR:C
NO SAD SONGS FOR ME ** (1950) PR:A-C
NO SAFETY AHEAD * (1959, Brit.) PR:C
NO SEX PLEASE—WE'RE BRITISH **½
  (1979, Brit.) PR:C
NO SLEEP TILL DAWN
  (SEE:BOMBERS B-52)
NO SMALL AFFAIR ** (1984) PR:O
NO SMOKING *½ (1955, Brit.) PR:A
NO SURRENDER ***½ (1986, Brit.) PR:O
NO SURVIVORS, PLEASE * (1963, Ger.) PR:C
NO TIME FOR BREAKFAST *** (1978, Fr.) PR:O
NO TIME FOR COMEDY ***½ (1940) PR:A
NO TIME FOR ECSTASY **½ (1963, Fr.) PR:O
NO TIME FOR FLOWERS *½ (1952) PR:A
NO TIME FOR LOVE *** (1943) PR:A
NO TIME FOR SERGEANTS ***½ (1958) PR:A
NO TIME FOR TEARS
  (SEE:PURPLE HEART DIARY)
NO TIME FOR TEARS ***½ (1957, Brit.) PR:A
NO TIME TO BE YOUNG ** (1957) PR:O
NO TIME TO DIE
  (SEE:TANK FORCE)
NO TIME TO KILL **½ (1963, Brit./Swed./Ger.) PR:C
NO TIME TO MARRY **½ (1938) PR:A
NO TOYS FOR CHRISTMAS
  (SEE:ONCE BEFORE I DIE)
NO TRACE *** (1950, Brit.) PR:A
NO TREE IN THE STREET ** (1964, Brit.) PR:A
NO WAY BACK ** (1949, Brit.) PR:C
NO WAY BACK zero (1976) PR:O
NO WAY OUT *** (1950) PR:A
NO WAY OUT *½ (1975, It./Fr.) PR:O
NO WAY OUT *½ (1987) PR:O
NO WAY TO TREAT A LADY ***½ (1968) PR:C-O
NOAH'S ARK *** (1928) PR:A-C
NOB HILL **½ (1945) PR:A
NOBI
  (SEE:FIRES ON THE PLAIN)
NOBODY IN TOYLAND ** (1958, Brit.) PR:A
NOBODY LIVES FOREVER *** (1946) PR:A
NOBODY LOVES A DRUNKEN INDIAN
  (SEE:FLAP)
NOBODY LOVES A FLAPPING EAGLE
  (SEE:FLAP)

NOBODY RUNS FOREVER
  (SEE:HIGH COMMISSIONER, THE)
NOBODY WAVED GOODBYE ** (1965, Can.) PR:C
NOBODY'S BABY **½ (1937) PR:A
NOBODY'S CHILDREN ** (1940) PR:AA
NOBODY'S DARLING ** (1943) PR:A
NOBODY'S FOOL *** (1936) PR:A
NOBODY'S FOOL ** (1986) PR:C
NOBODY'S PERFECT ** (1968) PR:A
NOBODY'S PERFEKT zero (1981) PR:C
NOBORIRYU TEKKAHADA
  (SEE:FRIENDLY KILLER, THE)
NO MERCY MAN, THE * (1975) PR:O
NOCE IN GALILEE
  (SEE:WEDDING IN GALILEE)
NOCTURNA zero (1979) PR:O
NOCTURNE **½ (1946) PR:C
NOISY NEIGHBORS *** (1929) PR:A
NOMADIC LIVES ** (1977) PR:C
NOMADS **½ (1985) PR:O
NON-STOP NEW YORK **½ (1937, Brit.) PR:A
NON TIRATE IL DIAVOLO PER LA CODA
  (SEE:DEVIL BY THE TAIL, THE)
NONE BUT THE BRAVE ** (1963) PR:C
NONE BUT THE BRAVE
  (SEE:FOR THE LOVE OF MIKE)
NONE BUT THE BRAVE ** (1965, US/Jap.) PR:O
NONE BUT THE LONELY HEART ** (1944) PR:A**
NONE SHALL ESCAPE ***½ (1944) PR:A
NOOSE
  (SEE:SILK NOOSE, THE)
NOOSE FOR A GUNMAN **½ (1960) PR:A
NOOSE FOR A LADY ** (1953, Brit.) PR:A
NOOSE HANGS HIGH, THE *** (1948) PR:AA
NOR THE MOON BY NIGHT
  (SEE:ELEPHANT GUN)
NORA INU
  (SEE:STRAY DOG)
NORA PRENTISS *** (1947) PR:A
NORAH O'NEALE *½ (1934, Brit.) PR:A
NORMA RAE ** (1979) PR:A-C**
NORMAN CONQUEST * (1953, Brit.) PR:A
NORMAN...IS THAT YOU? ** (1976) PR:C
NORMAN LOVES ROSE ** (1982, Aus.) PR:O
NORSEMAN, THE ** (1978) PR:C
NORTH AVENUE IRREGULARS, THE **½
  (1979) PR:A
NORTH BY NORTHWEST *** (1959) PR:A**
NORTH DALLAS FORTY ***½ (1979) PR:C-O
NORTH FROM LONE STAR ** (1941) PR:A
NORTH OF NOME *½ (1937) PR:A
NORTH OF SHANGHAI *½ (1939) PR:A
NORTH OF THE GREAT DIVIDE *½ (1950) PR:A
NORTH OF THE RIO GRANDE ** (1937) PR:A
NORTH OF THE YUKON ** (1939) PR:A
NORTH SEA HIJACK
  (SEE:FFOLKES)
NORTH SEA PATROL * (1939, Brit.) PR:A
NORTH SHORE ** (1987) PR:C
NORTH STAR, THE **½ (1943) PR:A-C
NORTH STAR, THE ** (1982, Fr.) PR:C
NORTH TO ALASKA ***½ (1960) PR:A
NORTH TO THE KLONDIKE ** (1942) PR:A
NORTH WEST FRONTIER
  (SEE:FLAME OVER INDIA)
NORTHERN FRONTIER ** (1935) PR:A
NORTHERN LIGHTS **½ (1978) PR:A
NORTHERN PATROL * (1953) PR:A
NORTHERN PURSUIT * (1943) PR:A**
NORTHFIELD CEMETERY MASSACRE, THE
  (SEE:NORTHVILLE CEMETERY MASSACRE, THE)
**NORTHVILLE CEMETERY MASSACRE, THE zero
  (1976) PR:O**
NORTHWEST MOUNTED POLICE *** (1940) PR:A
NORTHWEST OUTPOST **½ (1947) PR:A
NORTHWEST PASSAGE ***** (1940) PR:A-C
NORTHWEST RANGERS ** (1942) PR:A
NORTHWEST STAMPEDE ** (1948) PR:A
NORTHWEST TERRITORY *½ (1952) PR:A
NORTHWEST TRAIL * (1945) PR:A
NORWOOD ** (1970) PR:A
NOSE ON MY FACE, THE
  (SEE:MODEL MURDER CASE, THE)
NOSFERATU, THE VAMPIRE *
  (1979, Fr./Ger.) PR:C-O**
NOSTALGHIA **** (1984, USSR/It.) PR:O
NOT A HOPE IN HELL * (1960, Brit.) PR:A

NOT AGAINST THE FLESH
  (SEE:VAMPYR)
NOT AS A STRANGER **½ (1955) PR:A-C
NOT DAMAGED *½ (1930) PR:C
NOT EXACTLY GENTLEMEN
  (SEE:THREE ROGUES)
NOT FOR HONOR AND GLORY
  (SEE:LOST COMMAND)
NOT FOR PUBLICATION **½ (1984) PR:C-O
NOT MINE TO LOVE **½ (1969, Israel) PR:A
NOT NOW DARLING *½ (1975, Brit.) PR:O
NOT OF THIS EARTH **½ (1957) PR:A
NOT OF THIS EARTH * (1988) PR:O
NOT ON YOUR LIFE
  (SEE:ISLAND OF LOVE)
NOT ON YOUR LIFE ** (1965, It./Sp.) PR:C-O
NOT QUITE DECENT ** (1929) PR:A
NOT QUITE JERUSALEM ** (1985, Brit.) PR:O
NOT RECONCILED, OR "ONLY VIOLENCE HELPS
  WHERE IT RULES" ** (1969, Ger.) PR:C
NOT SINCE CASANOVA ** (1988) PR:O
NOT SO DUMB * (1930) PR:A
NOT SO DUSTY **½ (1936, Brit.) PR:A
NOT SO DUSTY *½ (1956, Brit.) PR:A
NOT SO QUIET ON THE WESTERN FRONT **½
  (1930, Brit.) PR:A
NOT WANTED **½ (1949) PR:A
NOT WANTED ON VOYAGE
  (SEE:TREACHERY ON THE HIGH SEAS)
NOT WANTED ON VOYAGE ** (1957, Brit.) PR:A
NOT WITH MY WIFE, YOU DON'T! **½
  (1966) PR:A
NOTEBOOKS OF MAJOR THOMPSON
  (SEE:FRENCH THEY ARE A FUNNY RACE, THE)
NOTHING BARRED **½ (1961, Brit.) PR:A
NOTHING BUT A MAN *** (1964) PR:A
NOTHING BUT THE BEST ** (1964, Brit.) PR:C
NOTHING BUT THE NIGHT ** (1975, Brit.) PR:A
NOTHING BUT THE TRUTH **½ (1929) PR:A
NOTHING BUT THE TRUTH *** (1941) PR:A
NOTHING BUT TROUBLE **½ (1944) PR:A
NOTHING IN COMMON * (1986) PR:A-C**
NOTHING LASTS FOREVER ** (1984) PR:C
NOTHING LIKE PUBLICITY **½ (1936, Brit.) PR:A
NOTHING PERSONAL * (1980, Can.) PR:A-C
NOTHING SACRED *** (1937) PR:A**
NOTHING TO LOSE
  (SEE:TIME GENTLEMEN PLEASE)
NOTHING VENTURE **½ (1948, Brit.) PR:AA
NOTORIOUS *** (1946) PR:A**
NOTORIOUS AFFAIR, A *½ (1930) PR:A
NOTORIOUS BUT NICE * (1934) PR:A
NOTORIOUS CLEOPATRA, THE *½ (1970) PR:O
NOTORIOUS GENTLEMAN, A ** (1935) PR:A
NOTORIOUS GENTLEMAN **½ (1945, Brit.) PR:C
NOTORIOUS LANDLADY, THE *** (1962) PR:A-C
NOTORIOUS LONE WOLF, THE ** (1946) PR:A
NOTORIOUS MR. MONKS, THE * (1958) PR:A
NOTORIOUS SOPHIE LANG, THE *½ (1934) PR:A
NOTRE DAME DE PARIS
  (SEE:HUNCHBACK OF NOTRE DAME, THE)
NOUS IRONS A PARIS ** (1949, Fr.) PR:A
NOVEL AFFAIR, A **½ (1957, Brit.) PR:A
NOW AND FOREVER ** (1934) PR:A
NOW AND FOREVER ** (1956, Brit.) PR:A
NOW AND FOREVER ** (1983, Aus.) PR:O
NOW BARABBAS
  (SEE:NOW BARABBAS WAS A ROBBER)
NOW BARABBAS WAS A ROBBER **½
  (1949, Brit.) PR:A
NOW I LAY ME DOWN
  (SEE:RACHEL, RACHEL)
NOW I'LL TELL **½ (1934) PR:A-C
NOW IT CAN BE TOLD
  (SEE:SECRET DOOR, THE)
NOW THAT APRIL'S HERE *½ (1958, Can.) PR:A
NOW, VOYAGER * (1942) PR:A-C**
NOW YOU SEE HIM, NOW YOU DON'T *
  (1972) PR:AA**
NOWHERE TO GO **½ (1959, Brit.) PR:A
NOWHERE TO HIDE ** (1987) PR:O
NOZ W WODZIE
  (SEE:KNIFE IN THE WATER)
NUDE BOMB, THE *½ (1980) PR:A

Finding entries in **THE MOTION PICTURE GUIDE** ™

Years 1929-83	Volumes I-IX
1984	Volume IX
1985	1986 ANNUAL
1986	1987 ANNUAL
1987	1988 ANNUAL
1988	1989 ANNUAL

STAR RATINGS

★★★★★ Masterpiece
★★★★ Excellent
★★★ Good
★★ Fair
★ Poor
zero Without Merit

PARENTAL RECOMMENDATION (PR:)

AA Good for Children
A Acceptable for Children
C Cautionary, some objectionable scenes
O Objectionable for Children

BOLD: Films on Videocassette

NUDE HEAT WAVE
(SEE:TOUCHABLES, THE)
NUDE IN A WHITE CAR **½ (1960, Fr.) PR:C
NUDE IN HIS POCKET ** (1962, Fr.) PR:A
NUDE ODYSSEY ** (1962, Fr./It.) PR:A
NUDE...SI MUORE
(SEE:YOUNG, THE EVIL AND THE SAVAGE, THE)
NUDES ON CREDIT
(SEE:LOVE NOW$e3PAY LATER)
NUISANCE, THE **½ (1933) PR:A
NUITS ROUGES
(SEE:SHADOWMAN)
NO. 96 *½ (1974, Aus.) PR:C
NUMBER ONE *½ (1969) PR:C
NUMBER ONE **½ (1984, Brit.) PR:C
NUMBER ONE WITH A BULLET * (1987) PR:C-O
NUMBER SEVENTEEN *½ (1928, Brit./Ger.) PR:A
NUMBER SEVENTEEN *** (1932, Brit.) PR:A
NUMBER SIX ** (1962, Brit.) PR:A
NO. 13 DEMON STREET
(SEE:DEVIL'S MESSENGER, THE)
NUMBER TWO ** (1975, Fr.) PR:O
NUMBERED MEN ** (1930) PR:A
NUMERO DEUX
(SEE:NUMBER TWO)
NUN, THE ***½ (1971, Fr.) PR:C
NUN AND THE SERGEANT, THE ** (1962) PR:A
NUN AT THE CROSSROADS, A **
(1970, It./Sp.) PR:A
NUN OF MONZA, THE
(SEE:LADY OF MONZA, THE)
NUN'S STORY, THE ***** (1959) PR:A
NUNZIO **½ (1978) PR:O
NUR TOTE ZEUGEN SCHWEIGEN
(SEE:HYPNOSIS)
NUREMBERG * (1961) PR:A
NURSE EDITH CAVELL *** (1939) PR:A
NURSE FROM BROOKLYN ** (1938) PR:A
NURSE ON WHEELS **½ (1964, Brit.) PR:O
NURSE SHERRI ** (1978) PR:O
NURSEMAID WHO DISAPPEARED, THE **½
(1939, Brit.) PR:A
NURSE'S SECRET, THE **½ (1941) PR:A
NUT FARM, THE ** (1935) PR:A
NUTCRACKER zero (1982, Brit.) PR:O
NUTCRACKER FANTASY **½ (1979) PR:AA
NUTCRACKER: THE MOTION PICTURE ***
(1986) PR:AA
NUTS *** (1987) PR:C-O
NUTTY, NAUGHTY CHATEAU **
(1964, Fr./It.) PR:C
NUTTY PROFESSOR, THE ***½ (1963) PR:A
NVUIIRANDO NO WAKADAISHO
(SEE:YOUNG GUY ON MT. COOK)
NYUJIRANDO NO WAKADAISHO
(SEE:YOUNG GUY ON MT. COOK)

O

O BOBO
(SEE:JESTER, THE)
O. HENRY'S FULL HOUSE ***½ (1952) PR:AA
O LUCKY MAN! **** (1973, Brit.) PR:O
O, MY DARLING CLEMENTINE * (1943) PR:A
O SLAVNOSTI A HOSTECH
(SEE:REPORT ON THE PARTY AND THE GUESTS, A)
OASIS, THE * (1984) PR:O
OBEY THE LAW *½ (1933) PR:A
OBJECTIVE, BURMA! **** (1945) PR:C
OBJECTIVE 500 MILLION ** (1966, Fr.) PR:C
OBLIGING YOUNG LADY *½ (1941) PR:A
OBLONG BOX, THE * (1969, Brit.) PR:O
OBSESSED ** (1951, Brit.) PR:C
OBSESSED * (1988, Can.) PR:C
OBSESSION
(SEE:HIDDEN ROOM, THE)
OBSESSION *½ (1954, Fr./It.) PR:C
OBSESSION ** (1968, Swed.) PR:C
OBSESSION ** (1976) PR:C
OBVIOUS SITUATION, AN
(SEE:HOURS OF LONELINESS)
O.C. AND STIGGS * (1987) PR:O
OCCHI SENZA VOLTO
(SEE:HORROR CHAMBER OF DR. FAUSTUS, THE)
OCEAN BREAKERS ** (1949, Swed.) PR:A
OCEAN DRIVE WEEKEND zero (1986) PR:C
OCEAN'S ELEVEN **½ (1960) PR:A
OCHAZUKE NO AJI
(SEE:TEA AND RICE)
OCI CIORNIE
(SEE:DARK EYES)
OCTAGON, THE ** (1980) PR:O
OCTAMAN zero (1971) PR:O
OCTOBER MAN, THE **½ (1948, Brit.) PR:A
OCTOBER MOTH ** (1960, Brit.) PR:O
OCTOMAN
(SEE:OCTAMAN)
OCTOPUSSY ** (1983, Brit.) PR:C
ODD ANGRY SHOT, THE ** (1979, Aus.) PR:C
ODD COUPLE, THE **** (1968) PR:A
ODD JOB, THE ** (1978, Brit.) PR:O
ODD JOBS **½ (1986) PR:C-O
ODD MAN OUT ***** (1947, Brit.) PR:C-O
ODD OBSESSION ** (1961, Jap.) PR:O
ODDO zero (1967) PR:O
ODDS AGAINST TOMORROW *** (1959) PR:C
ODE TO BILLY JOE *** (1976) PR:O
ODESSA FILE, THE ***½ (1974, Brit./Ger.) PR:C
ODETTE *** (1951, Brit.) PR:A-C
ODISSEA NUDA
(SEE:NUDE ODYSSEY)
ODONGO ** (1956, Brit.) PR:A
ODYSSEY OF THE PACIFIC **
(1983, Can./Fr.) PR:AA
OEDIPUS REX ** (1957, Can.) PR:A
OEDIPUS THE KING *** (1968, Brit.) PR:C
OF BEDS AND BROADS
(SEE:TALES OF PARIS)
OF FLESH AND BLOOD ** (1964, Fr./It.) PR:C
OF HUMAN BONDAGE **** (1934) PR:C-O
OF HUMAN BONDAGE **½ (1946) PR:O
OF HUMAN BONDAGE ** (1964, Brit.) PR:O
OF HUMAN HEARTS ***½ (1938) PR:A
OF LOVE AND DESIRE * (1963) PR:O
OF MICE AND MEN ***** (1939) PR:O
OF STARS AND MEN **** (1961) PR:AA
OF UNKNOWN ORIGIN **½ (1983, Can.) PR:O
OF WAYWARD LOVE ** (1964, It./Ger.) PR:O
OFF BEAT ** (1986) PR:C
OFF LIMITS **½ (1953) PR:A
OFF LIMITS ** (1988) PR:O
OFF THE BEATEN TRACK
(SEE:BEHIND THE EIGHT BALL)
OFF THE DOLE **½ (1935, Brit.) PR:A
OFF THE RECORD ** (1939) PR:A
OFF THE WALL *½ (1977) PR:C
OFF THE WALL **½ (1983) PR:O
OFF TO THE RACES ** (1937) PR:A
OFFBEAT **½ (1961, Brit.) PR:A
OFFENDERS, THE zero (1980) PR:O
OFFENSE, THE *** (1973, Brit.) PR:O
OFFERING, THE **½ (1966, Can.) PR:C
OFFICE GIRL, THE * (1932, Brit.) PR:A
OFFICE GIRLS zero (1974) PR:O
OFFICE PICNIC, THE *** (1974, Aus.) PR:C
OFFICE SCANDAL, THE *½ (1929) PR:A
OFFICE WIFE, THE ** (1930) PR:A
OFFICER AND A GENTLEMAN, AN ***½
(1982) PR:O
OFFICER AND THE LADY, THE *½ (1941) PR:A
OFFICER O'BRIEN *½ (1930) PR:A
OFFICER 13 * (1933) PR:A
OFFICER'S MESS, THE **½ (1931, Brit.) PR:A
OFFICIAL STORY, THE ***½ (1985, Arg.) PR:O
OFFSPRING, THE ** (1987) PR:O
O'FLYNN, THE
(SEE:FIGHTING O'FLYNN, THE)
OGGI, DOMANI E DOPODOMANI
(SEE:KISS THE OTHER SHEIK)
OGGI, DOMANI E DOPODOMANI
(SEE:MAN WITH THE BALLOONS, THE)
OGNUNO PER SE
(SEE:RUTHLESS FOUR, THE)
OH, ALFIE
(SEE:ALFIE DARLING)
OH BOY! ** (1938, Brit.) PR:A
OH BROTHERHOOD
(SEE:FRATERNITY ROW)
OH! CALCUTTA! zero (1972) PR:O
OH DAD, POOR DAD, MAMA'S HUNG YOU IN THE CLOSET AND I'M FEELIN' SO SAD *½
(1967) PR:C
OH DADDY! *½ (1935, Brit.) PR:A
OH DOCTOR ** (1937) PR:A
OH, FOR A MAN! **½ (1930) PR:A
OH! FOR A MAN!
(SEE:WILL SUCCESS SPOIL ROCK HUNTER)
OH, GOD! **½ (1977) PR:A-C
OH GOD! BOOK II ** (1980) PR:A-C
OH GOD! YOU DEVIL *** (1984) PR:A-C
OH, HEAVENLY DOG! ** (1980) PR:A
OH JOHNNY, HOW YOU CAN LOVE! *½
(1940) PR:A
OH, MEN! OH, WOMEN! *** (1957) PR:A-C
OH, MR. PORTER! ** (1937, Brit.) PR:A
OH MY DARLING CLEMENTINE
(SEE:O, MY DARLING CLEMENTINE)
OH NO DOCTOR! ** (1934, Brit.) PR:A
OH ROSALINDA **½ (1956, Brit.) PR:A
OH! SAILOR, BEHAVE! **½ (1930) PR:AA
OH, SUSANNA *½ (1937) PR:A
OH! SUSANNA ** (1951) PR:A
OH! THOSE MOST SECRET AGENTS
(SEE:00-2 MOST SECRET AGENTS)
OH WHAT A DUCHESS!
(SEE:MY OLD DUCHESS)
OH! WHAT A LOVELY WAR ***½
(1969, Brit.) PR:A-C
OH, WHAT A NIGHT *½ (1935) PR:A
OH, WHAT A NIGHT *½ (1944) PR:A
OH, YEAH! ** (1929) PR:A
OH, YOU BEAUTIFUL DOLL **½ (1949) PR:A
O'HARA'S WIFE ** (1983) PR:C
OHAYO *** (1962, Jap.) PR:A
OIL FOR THE LAMPS OF CHINA *** (1935) PR:A
OIL GIRLS, THE
(SEE:LEGEND OF FRENCHIE KING, THE)
OIL TOWN
(SEE:LUCY GALLANT)
O.K. CONNERY
(SEE:OPERATION KID BROTHER)
OKAY AMERICA *½ (1932) PR:A
OKAY BILL ** (1971) PR:O
OKAY FOR SOUND ** (1937, Brit.) PR:A
OKEFENOKEE * (1960) PR:O
OKINAWA ** (1952) PR:A
OKLAHOMA **** (1955) PR:AA
OKLAHOMA ANNIE ** (1952) PR:A
OKLAHOMA BADLANDS ** (1948) PR:A
OKLAHOMA BLUES ** (1948) PR:A
OKLAHOMA CRUDE **½ (1973) PR:O
OKLAHOMA CYCLONE ** (1930) PR:A
OKLAHOMA FRONTIER ** (1939) PR:A
OKLAHOMA JIM *½ (1931) PR:A
OKLAHOMA JUSTICE ** (1951) PR:A
OKLAHOMA KID, THE *** (1939) PR:A
OKLAHOMA RAIDERS ** (1944) PR:A
OKLAHOMA RENEGADES ** (1940) PR:A
OKLAHOMA TERRITORY **½ (1960) PR:A
OKLAHOMA TERROR *½ (1939) PR:A
OKLAHOMA WOMAN, THE * (1956) PR:C
OKLAHOMAN, THE **½ (1957) PR:A
OLD ACQUAINTANCE **½ (1943) PR:A-C
OLD BARN DANCE, THE ** (1938) PR:A
OLD BILL AND SON ** (1940, Brit.) PR:A
OLD BONES OF THE RIVER *** (1938, Brit.) PR:A
OLD BOYFRIENDS ** (1979) PR:O
OLD CHISHOLM TRAIL ** (1943) PR:A
OLD CORRAL, THE
(SEE:SONG OF THE GRINGO)
OLD CORRAL, THE * (1937) PR:A
OLD CURIOSITY SHOP, THE
(SEE:MR. QUILP)
OLD CURIOSITY SHOP, THE **½ (1935, Brit.) PR:A
OLD DARK HOUSE, THE ***½ (1932) PR:A
OLD DARK HOUSE, THE **½ (1963, Brit.) PR:A
OLD DRACULA *½ (1975, Brit.) PR:C
OLD ENGLISH **½ (1930) PR:A
OLD ENOUGH *** (1984) PR:C
OLD FAITHFUL **½ (1935, Brit.) PR:A
OLD-FASHIONED GIRL, AN ** (1948) PR:A
OLD-FASHIONED WAY, THE ***½ (1934) PR:A
OLD FRONTIER, THE *½ (1950) PR:A
OLD GREATHEART
(SEE:WAY BACK HOME)
OLD GROUCHY
(SEE:GROUCH, THE)
OLD HOMESTEAD, THE ** (1935) PR:A
OLD HOMESTEAD, THE *½ (1942) PR:A
OLD HUTCH **½ (1936) PR:A
OLD IRON ** (1938, Brit.) PR:A
OLD LOS ANGELES *½ (1948) PR:A
OLD LOUISIANA *½ (1938) PR:A
OLD MAC ** (1961, Brit.) PR:A
OLD MAID, THE ***½ (1939) PR:C
OLD MAN, THE ** (1932, Brit.) PR:A
OLD MAN AND THE BOY, THE
(SEE:THE TWO OF US)
OLD MAN AND THE SEA, THE **** (1958) PR:A
OLD MAN RHYTHM ** (1935) PR:A
OLD MOTHER RILEY *½ (1937, Brit.) PR:A
OLD MOTHER RILEY ** (1952, Brit.) PR:A
OLD MOTHER RILEY AT HOME *½
(1945, Brit.) PR:A
OLD MOTHER RILEY CATCHES A QUISLING
(SEE:OLD MOTHER RILEY IN PARIS)
OLD MOTHER RILEY, DETECTIVE *½
(1943, Brit.) PR:A
OLD MOTHER RILEY, HEADMISTRESS *
(1950, Brit.) PR:A
OLD MOTHER RILEY IN BUSINESS **
(1940, Brit.) PR:A
OLD MOTHER RILEY IN PARIS **½
(1938, Brit.) PR:A
OLD MOTHER RILEY IN SOCIETY *½
(1940, Brit.) PR:A
OLD MOTHER RILEY JOINS UP *½
(1939, Brit.) PR:A

OLD MOTHER RILEY MEETS THE VAMPIRE
(SEE:MY SON, THE VAMPIRE)
OLD MOTHER RILEY MP ** (1939, Brit.) PR:A
OLD MOTHER RILEY OVERSEAS **
(1943, Brit.) PR:A
OLD MOTHER RILEY'S CIRCUS ** (1941, Brit.) PR:A
OLD MOTHER RILEY'S GHOSTS **
(1941, Brit.) PR:A
OLD MOTHER RILEY'S JUNGLE TREASURE **
(1951, Brit.) PR:A
OLD MOTHER RILEY'S NEW VENTURE
(SEE:OLD MOTHER RILEY)
OLD OKLAHOMA PLAINS *½ (1952) PR:A
OLD OVERLAND TRAIL * (1953) PR:A
OLD ROSES *½ (1935, Brit.) PR:A
OLD SCHOOL TIE, THE
(SEE:WE WENT TO COLLEGE)
OLD SHATTERHAND **
(1968, Ger./Yugo./Fr./It.) PR:A
OLD SOLDIERS NEVER DIE *½ (1931, Brit.) PR:A
OLD SPANISH CUSTOM, AN *½ (1936, Brit.) PR:A
OLD SPANISH CUSTOMERS ** (1932, Brit.) PR:A
OLD SUREHAND, 1. TIEL
(SEE:FLAMING FRONTIER)
OLD SWIMMIN' HOLE, THE * (1941) PR:A
OLD TEXAS TRAIL, THE ** (1944) PR:A
OLD WEST, THE *½ (1952) PR:A
OLD WYOMING TRAIL, THE ** (1937) PR:A
OLD YELLER ***½ (1957) PR:A
OLDEST CONFESSION, THE
(SEE:HAPPY THIEVES, THE)
OLDEST PROFESSION, THE *
(1968, Fr./It./Ger.) PR:O
O'LEARY NIGHT
(SEE:TONIGHT'S THE NIGHT)
OLGA'S GIRLS zero (1964) PR:O
OLIVE TREES OF JUSTICE, THE **½
(1967, Fr.) PR:A
OLIVER! *** (1968, Brit.) PR:AA**
OLIVER & COMPANY **½ (1988) PR:AA
OLIVER TWIST ** (1933) PR:A
OLIVER TWIST ** (1951, Brit.) PR:AA**
OLIVER'S STORY * (1978) PR:C
OLLY, OLLY, OXEN FREE *½ (1978) PR:A
OLSEN'S BIG MOMENT *½ (1934) PR:A
OLSEN'S NIGHT OUT
(SEE:OLSEN'S BIG MOMENT)
OLTRAGGIO AL PUDORE
(SEE:ALL THE OTHER GIRLS DO)
OLTRE IL BENE E IL MALE
(SEE:BEYOND GOOD AND EVIL)
OLYMPIC HONEYMOON
(SEE:HONEYMOON MERRY-GO-ROUND)
OMAHA TRAIL, THE ** (1942) PR:A
O'MALLEY OF THE MOUNTED *½ (1936) PR:A
OMAR KHAYYAM ** (1957) PR:A
OMBRE BIANCHE
(SEE:SAVAGE INNOCENTS, THE)
OMEGA MAN, THE ** (1971) PR:C
OMEGA SYNDROME ** (1987) PR:O
OMEN, THE ** (1976) PR:O
O.M.H.S.
(SEE:YOU'RE IN THE ARMY NOW)
OMICRON ** (1963, It.) PR:A
OMOO OMOO, THE SHARK GOD * (1949) PR:A
**ON A CLEAR DAY YOU CAN SEE FOREVER **½
(1970) PR:AA**
ON AGAIN—OFF AGAIN ** (1937) PR:A
ON AN ISLAND WITH YOU *** (1948) PR:A
ON ANY STREET
(SEE:LA NOTTE BRAVA)
ON APPROVAL *½ (1930, Brit.) PR:A
ON APPROVAL **½ (1944, Brit.) PR:A
ON BORROWED TIME *** (1939) PR:A
ON DANGEROUS GROUND *** (1951) PR:C
ON DRESS PARADE
(SEE:DEAD END KIDS ON DRESS PARADE)
ON FRIDAY AT ELEVEN
(SEE:WORLD IN MY POCKET, THE)
ON GOLDEN POND ** (1981) PR:A-C**
ON GUARD
(SEE:OUTPOST OF THE MOUNTIES)
ON HER BED OF ROSES zero (1966) PR:C
**ON HER MAJESTY'S SECRET SERVICE ***½
(1969, Brit.) PR:C**
ON HIS OWN ** (1939, USSR) PR:A
ON MOONLIGHT BAY *** (1951) PR:AA

ON MY WAY TO THE CRUSADES, I MET A GIRL
WHO. . .
(SEE:CHASTITY BELT, THE)
ON OUR LITTLE PLACE
(SEE:ON OUR SELECTION)
ON OUR MERRY WAY ** (1948) PR:A
ON OUR SELECTION **½ (1930, Aus.) PR:A
ON PROBATION *** (1935) PR:A
ON PROBATION
(SEE:DADDY-O)
ON SECRET SERVICE
(SEE:SECRET AGENT)
ON SECRET SERVICE
(SEE:TRAILIN' WEST)
ON SPECIAL DUTY
(SEE:BULLETS FOR RUSTLERS)
ON STAGE EVERYBODY ** (1945) PR:A
ON SUCH A NIGHT ** (1937) PR:A
ON THE AIR ** (1934, Brit.) PR:A
**ON THE AIR LIVE WITH CAPTAIN MIDNIGHT *½
(1979) PR:C**
ON THE AVENUE *** (1937) PR:AA
ON THE BEACH **½ (1959) PR:O
ON THE BEAT ** (1962, Brit.) PR:A
ON THE BRINK
(SEE:THESE ARE THE DAMNED)
ON THE BUSES * (1972, Brit.) PR:C
ON THE CARPET
(SEE:LITTLE GIANT)
ON THE COMET **½ (1970, Czech.) PR:A
ON THE DOUBLE *** (1961) PR:A
ON THE EDGE ** (1985) PR:O
ON THE FIDDLE
(SEE:OPERATION SNAFU)
ON THE GREAT WHITE TRAIL * (1938) PR:A
ON THE ISLE OF SAMOA ** (1950) PR:A
ON THE LEVEL *½ (1930) PR:A
ON THE LINE * (1984, Sp.) PR:O**
ON THE LOOSE ** (1951) PR:A
ON THE MAKE
(SEE:DEVIL WITH WOMEN, A)
ON THE NICKEL *½ (1980) PR:O
ON THE NIGHT OF THE FIRE
(SEE:FUGITIVE, THE)
ON THE OLD SPANISH TRAIL ** (1947) PR:A
ON THE RIGHT TRACK *½ (1981) PR:C
ON THE RIVIERA ** (1951) PR:A
ON THE ROAD AGAIN
(SEE:HONEYSUCKLE ROSE)
ON THE RUN ** (1958, Brit.) PR:A
ON THE RUN ** (1967, Brit.) PR:A
ON THE RUN ** (1969, Brit.) PR:A
ON THE RUN ** (1983, Aus.) PR:C
ON THE SPOT *½ (1940) PR:A
ON THE STROKE OF NINE
(SEE:MURDER ON CAMPUS)
ON THE SUNNY SIDE ** (1942) PR:AA
ON THE SUNNYSIDE ** (1936, Swed.) PR:A
ON THE THRESHOLD OF SPACE *** (1956) PR:A
ON THE TOWN *** (1949) PR:A**
ON THE WATERFRONT *** (1954) PR:O**
ON THE YARD * (1978) PR:O**
ON THEIR OWN ** (1940) PR:A
ON THIN ICE *½ (1933, Brit.) PR:A
ON TOP OF OLD SMOKY *½ (1953) PR:A
ON TOP OF THE WORLD
(SEE:EVERYTHING OKAY)
ON TRIAL ** (1928) PR:A
ON TRIAL **½ (1939) PR:A
ON VALENTINE'S DAY ***½ (1986) PR:A-C
ON VELVET * (1938, Brit.) PR:A
ON WINGS OF SONG
(SEE:LOVE ME FOREVER)
ON WITH THE SHOW **½ (1929) PR:A
ON YOUR BACK *½ (1930) PR:A
ON YOUR TOES *½ (1939) PR:A
ONCE * (1974) PR:C
ONCE A CROOK **½ (1941, Brit.) PR:A
ONCE A DOCTOR ** (1937) PR:A
ONCE A GENTLEMAN ** (1930) PR:A
ONCE A JOLLY SWAGMAN
(SEE:MANIACS ON WHEELS)
ONCE A LADY ** (1931) PR:A
ONCE A RAINY DAY **½ (1968, Jap.) PR:A
ONCE A SINNER *½ (1931) PR:A
ONCE A SINNER *½ (1952, Brit.) PR:A
ONCE A THIEF ** (1935, Brit.) PR:A

ONCE A THIEF * (1950) PR:A
ONCE A THIEF
(SEE:HAPPY THIEVES, THE)
ONCE A THIEF **½ (1965) PR:C
ONCE BEFORE I DIE *½ (1967, US/Phil.) PR:C
ONCE BITTEN * (1985) PR:C
ONCE IN A BLUE MOON * (1936) PR:A
ONCE IN A LIFETIME **½ (1932) PR:A
ONCE IN A MILLION
(SEE:WEEKEND MILLIONAIRE)
ONCE IN A NEW MOON ** (1935, Brit.) PR:A
ONCE IN PARIS ***½ (1978) PR:C
ONCE IS NOT ENOUGH * (1975) PR:O
ONCE MORE, MY DARLING **½ (1949) PR:A
ONCE MORE, WITH FEELING *** (1960) PR:A-C
ONCE THERE WAS A GIRL *** (1945, USSR) PR:C
ONCE TO EVERY BACHELOR ** (1934) PR:A
ONCE TO EVERY WOMAN ** (1934) PR:A
ONCE UPON A COFFEE HOUSE *½ (1965) PR:A
ONCE UPON A DREAM ** (1949, Brit.) PR:A
ONCE UPON A HONEYMOON *½ (1942) PR:A
ONCE UPON A HORSE ** (1958) PR:A
ONCE UPON A SCOUNDREL **½ (1973) PR:A
ONCE UPON A SUMMER
(SEE:GIRL WITH GREEN EYES)
ONCE UPON A THURSDAY
(SEE:AFFAIRS OF MARTHA)
ONCE UPON A TIME *½ (1944) PR:A
ONCE UPON A TIME
(SEE:MORE THAN A MIRACLE)
ONCE UPON A TIME IN AMERICA **
(1984) PR:O**
ONCE UPON A TIME IN THE WEST ***
(1969, US/It.) PR:A**
ONCE YOU KISS A STRANGER * (1969) PR:O
ONDATA DI CALORE
(SEE:DEAD OF SUMMER)
ONE AGAINST SEVEN
(SEE:COUNTER-ATTACK)
ONE AND ONLY, THE * (1978) PR:C**
**ONE AND ONLY GENUINE ORIGINAL FAMILY
BAND, THE *½ (1968) PR:AA**
ONE APRIL 2000 *½ (1952, Aust.) PR:A
ONE BIG AFFAIR ** (1952) PR:A
ONE BODY TOO MANY **½ (1944) PR:A
ONE BORN EVERY MINUTE
(SEE:FLIM-FLAM MAN, THE)
ONE BRIEF SUMMER * (1971, Brit.) PR:A
ONE CRAZY SUMMER **½ (1986) PR:C
ONE CROWDED NIGHT *½ (1940) PR:A
ONE DANGEROUS NIGHT ** (1943) PR:A
ONE DARK NIGHT ** (1939) PR:A
ONE DARK NIGHT **½ (1983) PR:C
**ONE DAY IN THE LIFE OF IVAN DENISOVICH **
(1971, US/Brit./Norway) PR:A**
ONE DEADLY SUMMER ** (1984, Fr.) PR:O
ONE DESIRE **½ (1955) PR:AA
ONE DOWN TWO TO GO *½ (1982) PR:O
ONE EMBARRASSING NIGHT **½
(1930, Brit.) PR:A
1=2? *½ (1975, Fr.) PR:C
ONE EXCITING ADVENTURE **½ (1935) PR:A
ONE EXCITING NIGHT ** (1945) PR:A
ONE EXCITING NIGHT
(SEE:YOU CAN'T DO WITHOUT LOVE)
ONE EXCITING WEEK ** (1946) PR:A
ONE-EYED JACKS ***½ (1961) PR:O
ONE-EYED SOLDIERS **
(1967, US/Brit./Yugo.) PR:C
ONE FAMILY *½ (1930, Brit.) PR:A
ONE FATAL HOUR
(SEE:FIVE STAR FINAL)
ONE FATAL HOUR
(SEE:TWO AGAINST THE WORLD)
ONE FLEW OVER THE CUCKOO'S NEST **
(1975) PR:O**
ONE FOOT IN HEAVEN ***½ (1941) PR:AA
ONE FOOT IN HELL ** (1960) PR:A
ONE FOR ALL
(SEE:PRESIDENT'S MYSTERY, THE)
ONE FOR THE BOOKS
(SEE:VOICE OF THE TURTLE, THE)
ONE FRIGHTENED NIGHT ** (1935) PR:A
ONE FROM THE HEART ** (1982) PR:O
ONE GIRL'S CONFESSION *½ (1953) PR:C
ONE GOOD TURN *½ (1936, Brit.) PR:A
ONE GOOD TURN ** (1955, Brit.) PR:A

ONE HEAVENLY NIGHT ** (1931) PR:A
ONE HORSE TOWN
(SEE:SMALL TOWN GIRL)
ONE HOUR LATE *½ (1935) PR:A
ONE HOUR TO DOOM'S DAY
(SEE:CITY BENEATH THE SEA)
ONE HOUR TO LIVE *½ (1939) PR:A
ONE HOUR WITH YOU *** (1932) PR:A-C
ONE HUNDRED AND ONE DALMATIANS ***½ (1961) PR:AA
$100 A NIGHT **½ (1968, Ger.) PR:C
100 MEN AND A GIRL **½ (1937) PR:AA
ONE HUNDRED PERCENT PURE
(SEE:GIRL FROM MISSOURI, THE)
100 RIFLES ** (1969) PR:O
125 ROOMS OF COMFORT * (1974, Can.) PR:O
ONE HYSTERICAL NIGHT ** (1930) PR:A
ONE IN A MILLION * (1935) PR:A
ONE IN A MILLION ** (1936) PR:AA
ONE IS A LONELY NUMBER *** (1972) PR:C
ONE IS GUILTY ** (1934) PR:A
ONE JUMP AHEAD ** (1955, Brit.) PR:A
ONE JUST MAN * (1955, Brit.) PR:A
ONE LAST FLING * (1949) PR:A
ONE LIFE
(SEE:END OF DESIRE)
ONE LITTLE INDIAN **½ (1973) PR:AA
ONE MAD KISS * (1930) PR:A
ONE MAGIC CHRISTMAS *½ (1985) PR:AA
ONE MAN **½ (1979, Can.) PR:C
ONE MAN JURY * (1978) PR:O
ONE MAN JUSTICE *** (1937) PR:A
ONE-MAN LAW ** (1932) PR:A
ONE-MAN MUTINY
(SEE:COURT-MARTIAL OF BILLY MITCHELL, THE)
ONE MAN'S JOURNEY **½ (1933) PR:A
ONE MAN'S LAW ** (1940) PR:A
ONE MILE FROM HEAVEN ** (1937) PR:A
ONE MILLION B.C. * (1940) PR:A-C**
$1,000,000 DUCK **½ (1971) PR:AA
$1,000,000 RACKET * (1937) PR:A
ONE MILLION DOLLARS ** (1965, It.) PR:A
1,000,000 EYES OF SU-MURU
(SEE:MILLION EYES OF SU-MURU, THE)
ONE MILLION YEARS B.C. ** (1967, Brit./US) PR:A
ONE MINUTE TO ZERO ** (1952) PR:A
ONE MORE RIVER *** (1934) PR:A
ONE MORE SATURDAY NIGHT * (1986) PR:C-O
ONE MORE SPRING *** (1935) PR:A
ONE MORE TIME *½ (1970, Brit.) PR:A
ONE MORE TOMORROW ** (1946) PR:A
ONE MORE TRAIN TO ROB *** (1971) PR:A
ONE MYSTERIOUS NIGHT ** (1944) PR:A
ONE NEW YORK NIGHT **½ (1935) PR:A
ONE NIGHT...A TRAIN ** (1968, Fr./Bel.) PR:C
ONE NIGHT AT SUSIE'S **½ (1930) PR:A
ONE NIGHT IN LISBON **½ (1941) PR:A
ONE NIGHT IN PARIS ** (1940, Brit.) PR:A
ONE NIGHT IN THE TROPICS **½ (1940) PR:A
ONE NIGHT OF LOVE ** (1934) PR:A
ONE NIGHT ONLY zero (1986, Can.) PR:O
ONE NIGHT STAND ** (1976, Fr.) PR:O
ONE NIGHT WITH YOU *½ (1948, Brit.) PR:A
ONE OF OUR AIRCRAFT IS MISSING ***½ (1942, Brit.) PR:A
ONE OF OUR DINOSAURS IS MISSING ** (1975, Brit.) PR:AA
ONE OF OUR SPIES IS MISSING ** (1966) PR:A
ONE OF THE MANY
(SEE:HE COULDN'T TAKE IT)
ONE ON ONE ** (1977) PR:A
ONE-PIECE BATHING SUIT, THE
(SEE:MILLION DOLLAR MERMAID)
ONE PLUS ONE zero (1961, Can.) PR:C-O
ONE PLUS ONE ** (1969, Brit.) PR:O
ONE POTATO, TWO POTATO *** (1964) PR:C
ONE PRECIOUS YEAR ** (1933, Brit.) PR:A
ONE RAINY AFTERNOON ** (1936) PR:A
ONE ROMANTIC NIGHT *½ (1930) PR:A
ONE SINGS, THE OTHER DOESN'T ** (1977, Fr.) PR:C-O
ONE SPY TOO MANY ** (1966) PR:A
ONE STEP TO HELL *½ (1969, US/It./Sp.) PR:C
ONE STOLEN NIGHT *½ (1929) PR:A
ONE SUMMER LOVE * (1976) PR:C
ONE SUNDAY AFTERNOON *** (1933) PR:A
ONE SUNDAY AFTERNOON ** (1948) PR:A
ONE THAT GOT AWAY, THE **½ (1958, Brit.) PR:A
ONE THIRD OF A NATION ** (1939) PR:A
1001 ARABIAN NIGHTS * (1959) PR:AA**
1,000 CONVICTS AND A WOMAN zero (1971, Brit.) PR:O
$1,000 A MINUTE **½ (1935) PR:A
$1,000 A TOUCHDOWN ** (1939) PR:A
1,000 FEMALE SHAPES
(SEE:1,000 SHAPES OF A FEMALE)
1,000 PLANE RAID, THE *½ (1969) PR:A
1,000 SHAPES OF A FEMALE *½ (1963) PR:A

ONE THRILLING NIGHT ** (1942) PR:A
ONE TOO MANY * (1950) PR:A
ONE TOUCH OF VENUS **½ (1948) PR:A
ONE-TRICK PONY * (1980) PR:O**
ONE, TWO, THREE ***½ (1961) PR:A
1 2 3 MONSTER EXPRESS ** (1977, Thai.) PR:C
ONE WAY OUT
(SEE:CONVICTED)
ONE WAY OUT *½ (1955, Brit.) PR:A
ONE WAY PASSAGE *** (1932) PR:A
ONE WAY PENDULUM *** (1965, Brit.) PR:A
ONE WAY STREET *½ (1950) PR:A
ONE-WAY TICKET *½ (1935) PR:A
ONE-WAY TICKET, A **½ (1988, Dominican Republic) PR:C
ONE WAY TICKET TO HELL * (1955) PR:A
ONE WAY TO LOVE *½ (1946) PR:A
ONE WAY TRAIL, THE **½ (1931) PR:A
ONE WAY WAHINI * (1965) PR:C-O
ONE WILD NIGHT * (1938) PR:A
ONE WILD OAT ** (1951, Brit.) PR:A
ONE WISH TOO MANY **½ (1956, Brit.) PR:A
ONE WITH THE FUZZ, THE
(SEE:SOME KIND OF NUT)
ONE WOMAN'S STORY *** (1949, Brit.) PR:A
ONE YEAR LATER ** (1933) PR:A
ONEICHAN MAKARI TORU
(SEE:THREE DOLLS FROM HONG KONG)
ONI NO SUMU YAKATA
(SEE:DEVIL'S TEMPLE, THE)
ONI SHLI NA VOSTOK
(SEE:ITALIANO BRAVA GENTE)
ONIBABA *½ (1965, Jap.) PR:C
ONIMASA ** (1983, Jap.) PR:O
ONION FIELD, THE * (1979) PR:C-O**
ONIONHEAD ** (1958) PR:A
ONKEL TOMS HUTTE
(SEE:UNCLE TOM'S CABIN)
ONLY A WOMAN *½ (1966, Ger.) PR:A
ONLY ANGELS HAVE WINGS ** (1939) PR:A**
ONLY EIGHT HOURS
(SEE:SOCIETY DOCTOR)
ONLY GAME IN TOWN, THE *½ (1970) PR:C
ONLY GIRL, THE
(SEE:HEART SONG)
ONLY GOD KNOWS * (1974, Can.) PR:A
ONLY ONCE IN A LIFETIME * (1979) PR:C
ONLY ONE NIGHT ** (1942, Swed.) PR:C
ONLY SAPS WORK ** (1930) PR:A
ONLY THE BEST
(SEE:I CAN GET IT FOR YOU WHOLESALE)
ONLY THE BRAVE *½ (1930) PR:A
ONLY THE FRENCH CAN
(SEE:FRENCH CAN-CAN)
ONLY THE VALIANT **½ (1951) PR:A
ONLY THING YOU KNOW, THE ** (1971, Can.) PR:C
ONLY TWO CAN PLAY ***½ (1962, Brit.) PR:C
ONLY WAY, THE * (1970, Panama/Den./US) PR:A**
ONLY WAY HOME, THE ** (1972) PR:C
ONLY WHEN I LARF **½ (1968, Brit.) PR:A
ONLY WHEN I LAUGH ***½ (1981) PR:C
ONLY YESTERDAY **½ (1933) PR:C
ONNA GA KAIDAN O AGARUTOKI
(SEE:WHEN A WOMAN ASCENDS THE STAIRS)
ONNA GOROSHI ABURA JIGOKU
(SEE:PRODIGAL SON, THE)
ONNA NO MIZUUMI
(SEE:LAKE, THE)
ONNA NO NAKANI IRU TANIN
(SEE:THIN LINE, THE)
ONNA NO REKISHI
(SEE:WOMAN'S LIFE, A)
ONNA NO UZU TO FUCHI TO NAGARE
(SEE:WHIRLPOOL OF WOMAN)
ONNA NO ZA
(SEE:WISER AGE, THE)
ONNA UKIYOBURO
(SEE:HOUSE OF STRANGE LOVES, THE)
ONE MAN'S WAY ** (1964) PR:A
ONSEN GERIRA DAI SHOGEKI
(SEE:HOTSPRINGS HOLIDAY)
OOH, YOU ARE AWFUL
(SEE:GET CHARLIE TULLY)
OPEN ALL NIGHT ** (1934, Brit.) PR:O
OPEN CITY ** (1945, It.) PR:O**
OPEN HOUSE * (1987) PR:O
OPEN ROAD, THE *½ (1940, Fr.) PR:A
OPEN SEASON * (1974, US/Sp.) PR:O
OPEN SECRET ** (1948) PR:A
OPEN THE DOOR AND SEE ALL THE PEOPLE **½ (1964) PR:A
OPENED BY MISTAKE *½ (1940) PR:A
OPENING NIGHT ** (1977) PR:C
OPERACION GOLDMAN
(SEE:LIGHTNING BOLT)
OPERACION LOTO AZUL
(SEE:MISSION BLOODY MARY)

OPERATION AMSTERDAM ** (1960, Brit.) PR:A
OPERATION BIKINI ** (1963) PR:A
OPERATION BLUE BOOK
(SEE:BAMBOO SAUCER, THE)
OPERATION BOTTLENECK * (1961) PR:A
OPERATION BULLSHINE ** (1963, Brit.) PR:A
OPERATION CAMEL ** (1961, Den.) PR:A
OPERATION CIA *½ (1965) PR:A
OPERATION CONSPIRACY * (1957, Brit.) PR:A
OPERATION CROSS EAGLES ** (1969, US/Yugo.) PR:A
OPERATION CROSSBOW ** (1965, US/It.) PR:A
OPERATION CUPID * (1960, Brit.) PR:A
OPERATION DAMES *½ (1959) PR:C
OPERATION DAYBREAK ** (1976, US/Brit./Czech.) PR:A
OPERATION DELILAH *½ (1966, US/Sp.) PR:A
OPERATION DIAMOND ** (1948, Brit.) PR:A
OPERATION DIPLOMAT ** (1953, Brit.) PR:A
OPERATION DISASTER ** (1951, Brit.) PR:A
OPERATION EICHMANN ** (1961) PR:A
OPERATION ENEMY FORT *½ (1964, Jap.) PR:A
OPERATION GANYMED **½ (1977, Ger.) PR:C
OPERATION HAYLIFT ** (1950) PR:A
OPERATION KID BROTHER *½ (1967, It.) PR:A
OPERATION LOTUS BLEU
(SEE:MISSION BLOODY MARY)
OPERATION LOVEBIRDS * (1968, Den.) PR:A
OPERATION M
(SEE:HELL'S BLOODY DEVILS)
OPERATION MAD BALL *** (1957) PR:A
OPERATION MANHUNT **½ (1954) PR:A
OPERATION MASQUERADE
(SEE:MASQUERADE)
OPERATION MERMAID
(SEE:BAY OF SAINT MICHEL)
OPERATION MURDER * (1957, Brit.) PR:A
OPERATION PACIFIC *** (1951) PR:A
OPERATION PETTICOAT ***½ (1959) PR:A
OPERATION ST. PETER'S * (1968, It.) PR:A
OPERATION SAN GENNARO
(SEE:TREASURE OF SAN GENNARO)
OPERATION SECRET **½ (1952) PR:A
OPERATION SNAFU ** (1965, Brit.) PR:A
OPERATION SNATCH **½ (1962, Brit.) PR:A
OPERATION THIRD FORM ** (1966, Brit.) PR:AA
OPERATION THUNDERBOLT **½ (1978, ISRAEL) PR:C
OPERATION UNDER COVER
(SEE:REPORT TO THE COMMISSIONER)
OPERATION WAR HEAD
(SEE:OPERATION SNAFU)
OPERATION X *½ (1951, Brit.) PR:A-C
OPERATION X ** (1963, Jap.) PR:C
OPERATOR 13 ** (1934) PR:A
OPERAZIA GOLDMAN
(SEE:LIGHTNING BOLT)
OPERAZIONE CROSSBOW
(SEE:OPERATION CROSSBOW)
OPERAZIONE PARADISO
(SEE:KISS THE GIRLS AND MAKE THEM DIE)
OPERAZIONE PAURA
(SEE:KILL BABY KILL)
OPERETTA **½ (1949, Ger.) PR:A
OPHELIA zero (1964, Fr.) PR:C
OPIATE '67 ** (1967, Fr./It.) PR:C
OPPOSING FORCE **½ (1987) PR:O
OPPOSITE SEX, THE ** (1956) PR:A
OPTIMIST, THE
(SEE:BIG SHOT, THE)
OPTIMISTIC TRAGEDY, THE *½ (1964, USSR) PR:A
OPTIMISTS, THE *** (1973, Brit.) PR:A
OPTIMISTS OF NINE ELMS, THE
(SEE:OPTIMISTS, THE)
OR POUR LES CESARS
(SEE:GOLD FOR THE CAESARS)
ORACLE, THE
(SEE:HORSE'S MOUTH, THE)
ORAZIO E COURIAZI
(SEE:DUEL OF CHAMPIONS)
ORBITA MORTAL
(SEE:MISSION STARDUST)
ORCA * (1977) PR:C
ORCHESTRA WIVES **** (1942) PR:A
ORCHIDS TO YOU ** (1935) PR:A
ORDEAL BY INNOCENCE ** (1984, Brit.) PR:C
ORDER OF DEATH
(SEE:CORRUPT)
ORDERED TO LOVE ** (1963, Ger.) PR:O
ORDERS, THE *** (1977, Can.) PR:C-O
ORDERS ARE ORDERS *½ (1959, Brit.) PR:A
ORDERS IS ORDERS *** (1934, Brit.) PR:A
ORDERS TO KILL ** (1958, Brit.) PR:A
ORDET **½ (1957, Den.) PR:A-C
ORDINARY PEOPLE ***½ (1980) PR:O
OREGON PASSAGE ** (1958) PR:A
OREGON TRAIL, THE **½ (1936) PR:A
OREGON TRAIL *½ (1945) PR:A

OREGON TRAIL, THE ** (1959) PR:A
OREGON TRAIL SCOUTS ** (1947) PR:A
ORFEU NEGRO
  (SEE:BLACK ORPHEUS)
ORGANIZATION, THE ** (1971) PR:C
ORGANIZER, THE *** (1964, Fr./It./Yugo.) PR:A
ORGY OF BLOOD
  (SEE:BRIDES OF BLOOD)
ORGY OF THE DEAD zero (1965) PR:O
ORGY OF THE GOLDEN NUDES
  (SEE:HONEYMOON OF HORROR)
ORIANE **½ (1985, Fr./Venezuela) PR:O
ORIENT EXPRESS *½ (1934) PR:A
ORIENTAL DREAM
  (SEE:KISMET)
ORIGINAL OLD MOTHER RILEY, THE
  (SEE:OLD MOTHER RILEY)
O'RILEY'S LUCK
  (SEE:ROSE BOWL)
ORLAK, THE HELL OF FRANKENSTEIN *
  (1960, Mex.) PR:C-O
ORMENS VAG PA HALLEBERGET
  (SEE:SERPENT'S WAY)
O'ROURKE OF THE ROYAL MOUNTED
  (SEE:SASKATCHEWAN)
ORPHAN OF THE PECOS ** (1938) PR:A
ORPHAN OF THE RING
  (SEE:KID FROM KOKOMO, THE)
ORPHAN OF THE WILDERNESS **½
  (1937, Aus.) PR:A
ORPHANS ** (1987) PR:A-C**
ORPHANS OF THE NORTH * (1940) PR:AA
ORPHANS OF THE STREET **½ (1939) PR:AA
ORPHEE
  (SEE:ORPHEUS)
ORPHEUS *** (1950, Fr.) PR:A**
OSA *½ (1985) PR:O
OSAKA MONOGATARI
  (SEE:DAREDEVIL IN THE CASTLE)
OSCAR, THE * (1966) PR:A
OSCAR WILDE ***½ (1960, Brit.) PR:C
OSETROVNA
  (SEE:SIGN OF THE VIRGIN)
O'SHAUGHNESSY'S BOY **½ (1935) PR:A
O.S.S. ***½ (1946) PR:C
OSS 117—MISSION FOR A KILLER **½
  (1966, Fr./It.) PR:C
OSSESSIONE * (1959, It.) PR:C**
OSTATNI ETAP
  (SEE:LAST STOP, THE)
OSTERMAN WEEKEND, THE ** (1983) PR:C-O
OSTRE SLEDOVANE VLAKY
  (SEE:CLOSELY WATCHED TRAINS)
OTCHI TCHORNIA
  (SEE:DARK EYES)
OTCHIY DOM
  (SEE:HOME FOR TANYA, A)
OTEL U POGIBSHCHEGO ALPINISTA
  (SEE:DEAD MOUTAINEER HOTEL, THE)
OTELLO ***½ (1986, It.) PR:A-C
OTETS SOLDATA
  (SEE:FATHER OF A SOLDIER)
OTHELLO ** (1955, US/Fr./It.) PR:C
OTHELLO **½ (1960, USSR) PR:A
OTHELLO **½ (1965, Brit.) PR:A
OTHER, THE * (1972) PR:O**
OTHER LOVE, THE *½ (1947) PR:A
OTHER MEN'S WOMEN *½ (1931) PR:A-C
OTHER ONE, THE **½ (1967, Fr.) PR:C
OTHER PEOPLE'S BUSINESS
  (SEE:WAY BACK HOME)
OTHER PEOPLE'S SINS ** (1931, Brit.) PR:A
OTHER SIDE OF BONNIE AND CLYDE, THE *
  (1968) PR:O
OTHER SIDE OF MIDNIGHT, THE * (1977) PR:O
OTHER SIDE OF PARADISE, THE
  (SEE:FOXTROT)
OTHER SIDE OF THE MOUNTAIN—PART 2, THE *½
  (1978) PR:A
**OTHER SIDE OF THE MOUNTAIN, THE *½
  (1975) PR:A**
OTHER SIDE OF THE UNDERNEATH, THE *
  (1972, Brit.) PR:O
OTHER TOMORROW, THE **½ (1930) PR:A
OTHER WOMAN, THE * (1931, Brit.) PR:A
OTHER WOMAN, THE *½ (1954) PR:C-O

OTKLONENIE
  (SEE:DETOUR)
OTLEY **½ (1969, Brit.) PR:C
OTOKO TAI OTOKO
  (SEE:MAN AGAINST MAN)
OTROKI VO VSELENNOI
  (SEE:TEENAGERS IN SPACE)
OTTO E MEZZO
  (SEE:8$fr;1;2$)
OUANGA *½ (1936, Brit.) PR:A
OUR BETTERS ***½ (1933) PR:C
OUR BLUSHING BRIDES **½ (1930) PR:A
OUR DAILY BREAD * (1934) PR:A**
OUR DAILY BREAD **½ (1950, Ger.) PR:O
OUR FATHER **½ (1985, Sp.) PR:O
OUR FIGHTING NAVY
  (SEE:TORPEDOED)
OUR GIRL FRIDAY
  (SEE:ADVENTURES OF SADIE, THE)
OUR HEARTS WERE GROWING UP **½
  (1946) PR:A
OUR HEARTS WERE YOUNG AND GAY **½
  (1944) PR:A
OUR HITLER, A FILM FROM GERMANY ***
  (1980, Ger.) PR:O
OUR LADY OF FATIMA
  (SEE:MIRACLE OF OUR LADY OF FATIMA, THE)
OUR LEADING CITIZEN *½ (1939) PR:A
OUR LITTLE GIRL **½ (1935) PR:AA
OUR MAN FLINT *** (1966) PR:A
OUR MAN IN HAVANA *** (1960, Brit.) PR:A
OUR MAN IN MARRAKESH
  (SEE:BANG! BANG!YOU'RE DEAD)
OUR MAN IN MARRAKESH, 1967
  (SEE:THAT MAN GEORGE)
OUR MISS BROOKS **½ (1956) PR:AA
OUR MISS FRED * (1972, Brit.) PR:C
OUR MODERN MAIDENS **½ (1929) PR:A
OUR MOTHER'S HOUSE ***½ (1967, Brit.) PR:O
OUR NEIGHBORS—THE CARTERS ** (1939) PR:AA
OUR RELATIONS ** (1936) PR:AA**
OUR SILENT LOVE **½ (1969, Jap.) PR:A
OUR TOWN ** (1940) PR:A**
OUR VERY OWN ** (1950) PR:A
OUR VINES HAVE TENDER GRAPES ****
  (1945) PR:A
OUR WIFE *** (1941) PR:A
OUR WINNING SEASON *½ (1978) PR:C
OURSELVES ALONE
  (SEE:RIVER OF UNREST)
OUT **½ (1982) PR:C-O
OUT ALL NIGHT ** (1933) PR:A
OUT CALIFORNIA WAY ** (1946) PR:A
OUT OF AFRICA **½ (1985) PR:C
OUT OF BOUNDS zero (1986) PR:O
OUT OF CONTROL *½ (1985) PR:O
OUT OF IT **½ (1969) PR:A
OUT OF ORDER ** (1985, Ger.) PR:C
OUT OF ROSENHEIM
  (SEE:BAGDAD CAFE)
OUT OF SEASON * (1975, Brit.) PR:C-O**
OUT OF SIGHT *½ (1966) PR:A
OUT OF SINGAPORE **½ (1932) PR:C
OUT OF THE BLUE ** (1931, Brit.) PR:A
OUT OF THE BLUE * (1947) PR:A**
OUT OF THE BLUE **½ (1982) PR:O
OUT OF THE CLOUDS *** (1957, Brit.) PR:A
OUT OF THE DARKNESS
  (SEE:TEENAGE CAVEMAN)
OUT OF THE DARKNESS
  (SEE:NIGHT CREATURE)
OUT OF THE DEPTHS *½ (1946) PR:A
OUT OF THE FOG ***½ (1941) PR:C
OUT OF THE FOG * (1962, Brit.) PR:A
OUT OF THE FRYING PAN
  (SEE:YOUNG AND WILLING)
OUT OF THE NIGHT
  (SEE:STRANGE ILLUSIONS)
OUT OF THE PAST ** (1933, Brit.) PR:A
OUT OF THE PAST *** (1947) PR:C**
OUT OF THE SHADOW
  (SEE:MURDER ON THE CAMPUS)
OUT OF THE STORM ** (1948) PR:A
OUT OF THE TIGER'S MOUTH ** (1962) PR:A
OUT OF THIS WORLD **½ (1945) PR:A

OUT OF TOWNERS, THE
  (SEE:DEAR HEART)
OUT OF TOWNERS, THE ** (1970) PR:A**
OUT WEST WITH THE HARDYS ***½ (1938) PR:AA
OUT WEST WITH THE PEPPERS *½ (1940) PR:AA
OUTBACK **½ (1971, Aus.) PR:O
OUTCAST, THE ** (1934, Brit.) PR:A
OUTCAST **½ (1937) PR:A
OUTCAST, THE
  (SEE:MAN IN THE SADDLE)
OUTCAST, THE **½ (1954) PR:A
OUTCAST LADY *½ (1934) PR:A
OUTCAST OF BLACK MESA ** (1950) PR:A
OUTCAST OF THE ISLANDS ***½ (1952, Brit.) PR:A
OUTCASTS OF POKER FLAT, THE ** (1937) PR:A
OUTCASTS OF POKER FLAT, THE **½ (1952) PR:A
OUTCASTS OF THE CITY ** (1958) PR:A
OUTCASTS OF THE TRAIL ** (1949) PR:A
OUTCRY ***½ (1949, It.) PR:C-O
OUTCRY, THE
  (SEE:IL GRIDO)
OUTER GATE, THE ** (1937) PR:A
OUTFIT, THE ** (1973) PR:C-O
OUTING, THE *½ (1987) PR:O
OUTLAND ** (1981) PR:O
OUTLAW, THE * (1943) PR:O
OUTLAW AND THE LADY, THE
  (SEE:WACO)
OUTLAW BLUES **½ (1977) PR:A
OUTLAW BRAND *½ (1948) PR:A
OUTLAW COUNTRY **½ (1949) PR:A
OUTLAW DEPUTY, THE **½ (1935) PR:A
OUTLAW EXPRESS *½ (1938) PR:A
OUTLAW GOLD *½ (1950) PR:A
OUTLAW JOSEY WALES, THE *** (1976) PR:O**
OUTLAW JUSTICE ** (1933) PR:A
OUTLAW MOTORCYCLES * (1967) PR:O
OUTLAW OF THE PLAINS * (1946) PR:A
OUTLAW STALLION, THE ** (1954) PR:A
OUTLAW TERRITORY
  (SEE:HANNAH LEE)
OUTLAW: THE SAGE OF GISLI **
  (1982, Iceland) PR:C
OUTLAW TRAIL ** (1944) PR:A
OUTLAW TREASURE * (1955) PR:A
OUTLAW WOMEN ** (1952) PR:A
OUTLAWED GUNS ** (1935) PR:A
OUTLAW'S DAUGHTER, THE ** (1954) PR:A
OUTLAWS IS COMING, THE **½ (1965) PR:A
OUTLAWS OF PINE RIDGE **½ (1942) PR:A
OUTLAWS OF SANTA FE ** (1944) PR:A
OUTLAWS OF SONORA ** (1938) PR:A
OUTLAWS OF STAMPEDE PASS *½ (1943) PR:A
OUTLAWS OF TEXAS **½ (1950) PR:A
OUTLAWS OF THE CHEROKEE TRAIL *½
  (1941) PR:A
OUTLAWS OF THE DESERT *½ (1941) PR:A
OUTLAWS OF THE ORIENT ** (1937) PR:A
OUTLAWS OF THE PANHANDLE ** (1941) PR:A
OUTLAWS OF THE PRAIRIE **½ (1938) PR:A
OUTLAWS OF THE RIO GRANDE ** (1941) PR:A
OUTLAWS OF THE ROCKIES *½ (1945) PR:A
OUTLAWS OF THE WEST
  (SEE:CALL THE MESQUITEERS)
OUTLAW'S PARADISE ** (1939) PR:A
OUTLAW'S SON ** (1957) PR:A
OUTPOST IN MALAYA **½ (1952, Brit.) PR:A
OUTPOST IN MOROCCO ** (1949) PR:A
OUTPOST OF HELL ** (1966, Jap.) PR:A
OUTPOST OF THE MOUNTIES *½ (1939) PR:A
OUTRAGE **½ (1950) PR:C
OUTRAGE, THE *½ (1964) PR:C
OUTRAGEOUS! ***½ (1977, Can.) PR:O
OUTRAGEOUS FORTUNE ** (1987) PR:O
OUTRIDERS, THE ** (1950) PR:A
OUTSIDE IN *½ (1972) PR:C
OUTSIDE MAN, THE **½ (1973, US/FR.) PR:C
OUTSIDE OF PARADISE **½ (1938) PR:A
OUTSIDE THE LAW * (1930) PR:A
OUTSIDE THE LAW
  (SEE:CITADEL OF CRIME)
OUTSIDE THE LAW *½ (1956) PR:A
OUTSIDE THE 3-MILE LIMIT *½ (1940) PR:A
OUTSIDE THE WALL **½ (1950) PR:A
OUTSIDE THESE WALLS **½ (1939) PR:A
OUTSIDER, THE ** (1933, Brit.) PR:A
OUTSIDER, THE ** (1940, Brit.) PR:A

Finding entries in **THE MOTION PICTURE GUIDE** ™		**STAR RATINGS**		**PARENTAL RECOMMENDATION (PR:)**	
Years 1929-83	Volumes I-IX	★★★★★	Masterpiece	AA	Good for Children
1984	Volume IX	★★★★	Excellent	A	Acceptable for Children
1985	1986 ANNUAL	★★★	Good	C	Cautionary, some objectionable scenes
1986	1987 ANNUAL	★★	Fair	O	Objectionable for Children
1987	1988 ANNUAL	★	Poor		
1988	1989 ANNUAL	zero	Without Merit	**BOLD:** Films on Videocassette	

OUTSIDER, THE **½ (1949, Brit.) PR:A
OUTSIDER, THE ** (1962) PR:A-C
OUTSIDER, THE ***½ (1980) PR:O
OUTSIDER IN AMSTERDAM ** (1983, Neth.) PR:O
OUTSIDERS, THE
(SEE:BAND OF OUTSIDERS)
OUTSIDERS, THE * (1983) PR:C**
OUTSIDERS, THE *** (1987, Taiwan) PR:O
OUTWARD BOUND **½ (1930) PR:C
OVER-EXPOSED *½ (1956) PR:C
OVER GRENSEN
(SEE:FELDMANN CASE, THE)
OVER MY DEAD BODY *** (1942) PR:A
OVER SHE GOES *** (1937, Brit.) PR:A
OVER THE BORDER *½ (1950) PR:A
OVER THE BROOKLYN BRIDGE **½ (1984) PR:O
OVER THE EDGE **½ (1979) PR:O
OVER THE GARDEN WALL ** (1934, Brit.) PR:A
OVER THE GARDEN WALL * (1950, Brit.) PR:A
OVER THE GOAL ** (1937) PR:A
OVER THE HILL ***½ (1931) PR:C
OVER THE MOON ** (1940, Brit.) PR:A
OVER THE ODDS *** (1961, Brit.) PR:A
OVER THE RIVER
(SEE:ONE MORE RIVER)
OVER THE SUMMER **½ (1986) PR:O
OVER THE TOP * (1987) PR:C
OVER THE WALL ** (1938) PR:A
OVER 21 *** (1945) PR:C
OVER-UNDER, SIDEWAYS-DOWN * (1977) PR:C
OVERBOARD ** (1987) PR:C
OVERCOAT, THE **½ (1965, USSR) PR:O
OVERKILL zero (1987) PR:O
OVERLAND BOUND ** (1929) PR:A
OVERLAND EXPRESS, THE *½ (1938) PR:A
OVERLAND MAIL **½ (1939) PR:A
OVERLAND MAIL ROBBERY *½ (1943) PR:A
OVERLAND PACIFIC **½ (1954) PR:A
OVERLAND RIDERS ** (1946) PR:A
OVERLAND STAGE COACH
(SEE:OVERLAND STAGECOACH)
OVERLAND STAGE RAIDERS *** (1938) PR:A
OVERLAND STAGECOACH ** (1942) PR:A
OVERLAND TELEGRAPH **½ (1951) PR:A
OVERLANDERS, THE ***½ (1946, Brit./Aus.) PR:C
OVERLORD ***½ (1975, Brit.) PR:O
OVERNIGHT **½ (1933, Brit.) PR:C
OVERTURE TO GLORY * (1940) PR:C**
OWD BOB
(SEE:TO THE VICTOR)
OWL AND THE PUSSYCAT, THE **½ (1970) PR:C
OX-BOW INCIDENT, THE *** (1943) PR:C-O**
OXFORD BLUES * (1984) PR:O
OZ
(SEE:20TH CENTURY OZ)

P

PACE THAT THRILLS, THE ** (1952) PR:C
PACIFIC ADVENTURE * (1947, Aus.) PR:A
PACIFIC BLACKOUT *½ (1942) PR:A
PACIFIC DESTINY ** (1956, Brit.) PR:A
PACIFIC LINER ** (1939) PR:C
PACIFIC RENDEZVOUS ** (1942) PR:A
PACK, THE **½ (1977) PR:O
PACK TRAIN ** (1953) PR:A
PACK UP YOUR TROUBLES **½ (1932) PR:AA
PACK UP YOUR TROUBLES *** (1939) PR:AA
PACK UP YOUR TROUBLES ** (1940, Brit.) PR:A
PAD...AND HOW TO USE IT, THE *
(1966, Brit.) PR:O
PADDY * (1970, Ireland) PR:O**
PADDY O'DAY *** (1935) PR:A
PADDY, THE NEXT BEST THING *** (1933) PR:A
PADRE PADRONE ***½ (1977, It.) PR:C
PAGAN, THE **½ (1929) PR:A-C
PAGAN HELLCAT
(SEE:MAEVA)
PAGAN ISLAND ** (1961) PR:A
PAGAN LADY * (1931) PR:A
PAGAN LOVE SONG ** (1950) PR:A
PAGE MISS GLORY **½ (1935) PR:A
PAGLIACCI
(SEE:CLOWN MUST LAUGH, A)
PAI-SHE CHUAN
(SEE:MADAME WHITESNAKE)
PAID *** (1930) PR:A
PAID IN ERROR ** (1938, Brit.) PR:A
PAID IN FULL **½ (1950) PR:A
PAID TO DANCE * (1937) PR:C
PAID TO KILL ** (1954, Brit.) PR:C
PAINT YOUR WAGON ** (1969) PR:C
PAINTED ANGEL, THE **½ (1929) PR:A
PAINTED BOATS
(SEE:GIRL ON THE CANAL, THE)
PAINTED DESERT, THE **½ (1931) PR:A
PAINTED DESERT, THE *½ (1938) PR:A
PAINTED FACES ** (1929) PR:A
PAINTED HILLS, THE * (1951) PR:AA**
PAINTED SMILE, THE
(SEE:MURDER CAN BE DEADLY)
PAINTED TRAIL, THE *** (1938) PR:A
PAINTED VEIL, THE *** (1934) PR:A
PAINTED WOMAN * (1932) PR:A
PAINTING THE CLOUDS WITH SUNSHINE **
(1951) PR:A
PAIR OF BRIEFS, A ** (1963, Brit.) PR:A
PAISA
(SEE:PAISAN)
PAISAN ** (1948, It.) PR:C**
PAJAMA GAME, THE **** (1957) PR:A
PAJAMA PARTY **½ (1964) PR:AA
PAJAMA PARTY IN THE HAUNTED HOUSE
(SEE:GHOST IN THE INVISIBLE BIKINI, THE)
PAL FROM TEXAS, THE ** (1939) PR:A
PAL JOEY ** (1957) PR:C**
PALACE OF NUDES *½ (1961, Fr./It.) PR:C
PALE ARROW
(SEE:PAWNEE)
PALE RIDER ***½ (1985) PR:O
PALEFACE, THE ***½ (1948) PR:A
PALLET ON THE FLOOR *½
(1984, New Zealand) PR:O
PALM BEACH * (1979, Aus.) PR:O**
PALM BEACH STORY, THE ** (1942) PR:A**
PALM SPRINGS ** (1936) PR:A
PALM SPRINGS AFFAIR
(SEE:PALM SPRINGS)
PALM SPRINGS WEEKEND **½ (1963) PR:C
PALMY DAYS *** (1931) PR:A
PALOMINO, THE **½ (1950) PR:AA
PALOOKA * (1934) PR:AA**
PALS OF THE GOLDEN WEST ** (1952) PR:A
PALS OF THE PECOS **½ (1941) PR:A
PALS OF THE RANGE ** (1935) PR:A
PALS OF THE SADDLE **½ (1938) PR:A
PALS OF THE SILVER SAGE ** (1940) PR:A
PAMPA SALVAJE
(SEE:SAVAGE PAMPAS)
PAN-AMERICANA **½ (1945) PR:A
PANAMA FLO * (1932) PR:A
PANAMA HATTIE ** (1942) PR:A
PANAMA LADY *½ (1939) PR:A
PANAMA PATROL **½ (1939) PR:A
PANAMA SAL *½ (1957) PR:A
PANAMINT'S BAD MAN *½ (1938) PR:A
PANCHO VILLA *½ (1975, Sp.) PR:C
PANCHO VILLA RETURNS ** (1950, Mex.) PR:A
**PANDA AND THE MAGIC SERPENT **
(1961, Jap.) PR:A**
PANDEMONIUM zero (1982) PR:C
PANDORA AND THE FLYING DUTCHMAN **
(1951, Brit.) PR:A-C
PANHANDLE *** (1948) PR:A
PANIC
(SEE:PANIQUE)
PANIC *½ (1966, Brit.) PR:A
PANIC BUTTON **½ (1964) PR:A
PANIC IN NEEDLE PARK *½ (1971) PR:O
PANIC IN THE CITY *½ (1968) PR:O
PANIC IN THE PARLOUR ** (1957, Brit.) PR:A
PANIC IN THE STREETS *** (1950) PR:C
PANIC IN YEAR ZERO! *** (1962) PR:O
PANIC ON THE AIR
(SEE:YOU MAY BE NEXT!)
PANIC ON THE TRANS-SIBERIAN TRAIN
(SEE:HORROR EXPRESS)
PANIQUE ** (1947, Fr.) PR:C
PANTHER ISLAND
(SEE:BOMBA ON PANTHER ISLAND)
PANTHER SQUAD zero (1986, Fr./Belg.) PR:A
PANTHER'S CLAW, THE **½ (1942) PR:A
PANTHER'S MOON
(SEE:SPY HUNT)
PAPA'S DELICATE CONDITION * (1963) PR:A**
PAPER BULLETS *** (1941) PR:A
PAPER CHASE, THE **½ (1973) PR:A-C
PAPER GALLOWS *** (1950, Brit.) PR:A
PAPER LION * (1968) PR:A**
PAPER MOON ***½ (1973) PR:C
PAPER ORCHID **½ (1949, Brit.) PR:C
PAPER TIGER * (1975, Brit.) PR:A-C
PAPERBACK HERO **½ (1973, Can.) PR:O
PAPERHOUSE ** (1988, Brit.) PR:C
PAPILLON ** (1973) PR:O**
PAR LE FER ET PAR LE FEU
(SEE:INVASION 1700)
PAR OU T'ES RENTRE? ON T'A PAS VUE SORTIR
zero (1984, Fr./Tunisia) PR:A
PARACHUTE BATTALION ** (1941) PR:A
PARACHUTE JUMPER **½ (1933) PR:A
PARACHUTE NURSE ** (1942) PR:A
PARADE D'AMOUR
(SEE:LOVE PARADE, THE)
PARADE OF THE WEST *½ (1930) PR:A
PARADES ** (1972) PR:O
PARADINE CASE, THE * (1947) PR:A-C**
PARADISE zero (1982) PR:O
PARADISE ALLEY ** (1962) PR:A
PARADISE ALLEY ** (1978) PR:O**
PARADISE CANYON **½ (1935) PR:A
PARADISE EXPRESS **½ (1937) PR:A
PARADISE FOR THREE * (1938) PR:A**
PARADISE FOR TWO
(SEE:GAIETY GIRLS, THE)
PARADISE, HAWAIIAN STYLE ** (1966) PR:A
PARADISE ISLAND * (1930) PR:A
PARADISE ISLE *** (1937) PR:A
PARADISE LAGOON
(SEE:ADMIRABLE CRICHTON, THE)
PARADISE MOTEL * (1985) PR:O
PARADISE POUR TOUS ** (1982, Fr.) PR:C-O
PARADISE ROAD
(SEE:BIG DADDY)
PARADISIO * (1962, Brit.) PR:O
PARADISO DELL'UOMO
(SEE:MAN'S PARADISE)
PARALLAX VIEW, THE ***½ (1974) PR:O
PARALLELS ** (1980, Can.) PR:A-C
PARANOIA
(SEE:KISS THE OTHER SHEIK)
PARANOIA
(SEE:MAN WITH THE BALLOONS, THE)
PARANOIAC ***½ (1963, Brit.) PR:O
PARASITE zero (1982) PR:O
PARASITE MURDERS, THE
(SEE:THEY CAME FROM WITHIN)
PARATROOP COMMAND ** (1959) PR:A
PARATROOPER **½ (1954, Brit.) PR:A
PARBESZED
(SEE:DIALOGUE)
PARDNERS ** (1956) PR:A
PARDON MY BRUSH zero (1964) PR:O
PARDON MY FRENCH *½ (1951, US/Fr.) PR:A
PARDON MY GUN * (1930) PR:A
PARDON MY GUN *½ (1942) PR:A
PARDON MY PAST **½ (1945) PR:A
PARDON MY RHYTHM ** (1944) PR:A
PARDON MY SARONG **½ (1942) PR:AA
PARDON MY STRIPES *½ (1942) PR:A
PARDON MY TRUNK
(SEE:HELLO, ELEPHANT)
PARDON OUR NERVE ** (1939) PR:A
PARDON US **½ (1931) PR:AA
PARENT TRAP, THE * (1961) PR:AA**
PARENTS ON TRIAL * (1939) PR:A
PARIS ** (1929) PR:A
PARIS AFTER DARK **½ (1943) PR:A
PARIS AU MOIS D'AOUT
(SEE:PARIS IN THE MONTH OF AUGUST)
PARIS BELONGS TO US *** (1962, Fr.) PR:A-C
PARIS BLUES **½ (1961) PR:O
PARIS BOUND ** (1929) PR:A
PARIS BRULE-T-IL?
(SEE:IS PARIS BURNING?)
PARIS CALLING ** (1941) PR:A
**PARIS DOES STRANGE THINGS ***½
(1957, Fr./It.) PR:A**
PARIS EROTIKA
(SEE:PARIS OOH-LA-LA)
PARIS EXPRESS, THE **½ (1953, Brit.) PR:A
PARIS FOLLIES OF 1956 ** (1955) PR:A
PARIS HOLIDAY **½ (1958) PR:A
PARIS HONEYMOON **½ (1939) PR:A
PARIS IN SPRING * (1935) PR:A
PARIS IN THE MONTH OF AUGUST **½
(1968, Fr.) PR:A
PARIS INTERLUDE *½ (1934) PR:A
PARIS IS OURS
(SEE:PARIS BELONGS TO US)
PARIS LOVE SONG
(SEE:PARIS IN SPRING)
PARIS MODEL ** (1953) PR:A
PARIS NOUS APPARTIENT
(SEE:PARIS BELONGS TO US)
PARIS OOH-LA-LA! ** (1963, US/Fr.) PR:O
PARIS PICK-UP ** (1963, Fr./It.) PR:C
PARIS PLANE ** (1933, Brit.) PR:A
PARIS PLAYBOYS ** (1954) PR:A
PARIS, TEXAS ** (1984, Ger./Fr.) PR:C-O**
PARIS UNDERGROUND ** (1945) PR:A
PARIS VU PAR
(SEE:SIX IN PARIS)
PARIS WAS MADE FOR LOVERS
(SEE:TIME FOR LOVING, A)
PARIS WHEN IT SIZZLES ** (1964) PR:A
PARISIAN, THE **½ (1931, Fr.) PR:A
PARISIAN ROMANCE, A *½ (1932) PR:A

PARISIENNE
(SEE:LA PARISIENNE)
PARK AVENUE LOGGER ** (1937) PR:A
PARK PLAZA 605
(SEE:NORMAN CONQUEST)
PARK ROW ** (1952) PR:A
PARKING **½ (1985, Fr.) PR:C
PARLIAMO DI DONNE
(SEE:LET'S TALK ABOUT WOMEN)
PARLOR, BEDROOM AND BATH **½ (1931) PR:A
PARMI LES VAUTOURS
(SEE:FRONTIER HELLCAT)
PARNELL * (1937) PR:A-C
PAROLE *½ (1936) PR:A
PAROLE FIXER ** (1940) PR:A
PAROLE GIRL *½ (1933) PR:A
PAROLE, INC. * (1949) PR:A
PAROLE RACKET * (1937) PR:A
PAROLED FROM THE BIG HOUSE * (1938) PR:A
PAROLED—TO DIE *½ (1938) PR:A
PAROXISMUS
(SEE:VENUS IN FURS)
PARRISH *½ (1961) PR:A
PARSIFAL ** (1983, Fr.) PR:A
PARSON AND THE OUTLAW, THE ** (1957) PR:A
PARSON OF PANAMINT, THE ** (1941) PR:A
PART TIME WIFE **½ (1930) PR:A
PART-TIME WIFE * (1961, Brit.) PR:A
PART 2, SOUNDER
(SEE:SOUNDER, PART 2)
PART 2, WALKING TALL
(SEE:WALKING TALL, PART 2)
PARTING GLANCES * (1986) PR:O**
PARTINGS ** (1962, Pol.) PR:A
PARTLY CONFIDENTIAL
(SEE:THANKS FOR LISTENING)
PARTNER, THE *½ (1966, Brit.) PR:A
PARTNERS *½ (1932) PR:A
PARTNERS ** (1976, Can.) PR:C
PARTNERS * (1982) PR:O
PARTNERS IN CRIME * (1937) PR:A
PARTNERS IN FORTUNE
(SEE:ROCKIN' IN THE ROCKIES)
PARTNERS IN TIME *½ (1946) PR:A
PARTNERS OF THE PLAINS **½ (1938) PR:A
PARTNERS OF THE SUNSET * (1948) PR:A
PARTNERS OF THE TRAIL *½ (1931) PR:A
PARTNERS OF THE TRAIL ** (1944) PR:A
PARTS: THE CLONUS HORROR
(SEE:CLONUS HORROR, THE)
PARTY, THE ** (1968) PR:A
PARTY CAMP * (1987) PR:O
PARTY CRASHERS, THE *½ (1958) PR:A
PARTY GIRL *½ (1930) PR:A
PARTY GIRL ***½ (1958) PR:C
PARTY GIRLS FOR THE CANDIDATE
(SEE:CANDIDATE, THE)
PARTY HUSBAND * (1931) PR:A
PARTY PARTY zero (1983, Brit.) PR:C
PARTY WIRE ** (1935) PR:A
PARTY'S OVER, THE * (1966, Brit.) PR:O
PARTY'S OVER, THE *½ (1934) PR:A
PAS DE MENTALITE
(SEE:WORLD IN MY POCKET, THE)
PAS QUESTION LE SEMEDI
(SEE:IMPOSSIBLE ON SATURDAY)
PASAZERKA
(SEE:PASSENGER, THE)
PASCALI'S ISLAND *½ (1988, Brit.) PR:C-O
PASQUALINO SETTEBELLEZZE
(SEE:SEVEN BEAUTIES)
PASQUALINO: SEVEN BEAUTIES
(SEE:SEVEN BEAUTIES)
PASS THE AMMO **½ (1988) PR:O
PASS TO ROMANCE
(SEE:HI, BEAUTIFUL)
PASSAGE, THE zero (1979, Brit.) PR:O
PASSAGE FROM HONG KONG ** (1941) PR:A
PASSAGE HOME **½ (1955, Brit.) PR:A
PASSAGE OF LOVE
(SEE:TIME LOST AND TIME REMEMBERED)
PASSAGE TO INDIA, A ***½ (1984, Brit.) PR:C
PASSAGE TO MARSEILLE ***½ (1944) PR:A
PASSAGE WEST **½ (1951) PR:A
PASSAGES FROM JAMES JOYCE'S FINNEGANS WAKE
(SEE:FINNEGAN'S WAKE)
PASSENGER, THE ***½ (1970, Pol.) PR:O
PASSENGER, THE ** (1975, It.) PR:C**
PASSENGER TO LONDON * (1937, Brit.) PR:A
PASSING OF THE THIRD FLOOR BACK, THE *** (1936, Brit.) PR:A
PASSING SHADOWS ** (1934, Brit.) PR:A
PASSING SHOW, THE
(SEE:HOTEL VARIETY)
PASSING STRANGER, THE ** (1954, Brit.) PR:A
PASSING THROUGH **½ (1977) PR:O
PASSION ** (1954) PR:A
PASSION ** (1968, Jap.) PR:O
PASSION
(SEE:PASSION OF ANNA, THE)
PASSION ***½ (1983, Fr./Switz.) PR:O
PASSION FLOWER *½ (1930) PR:A
PASSION FOR LIFE **½ (1951, Fr.) PR:A
PASSION HOLIDAY * (1963) PR:C
PASSION IN THE SUN * (1964) PR:O
PASSION ISLAND **½ (1943, Mex.) PR:A
PASSION OF ANNA, THE *** (1970, Swed.) PR:C
PASSION OF LOVE ** (1982, It./Fr.) PR:O
PASSION OF SLOW FIRE, THE **½ (1962, Fr.) PR:C
PASSION OF THE SUN
(SEE:PASSION IN THE SUN)
PASSION PIT, THE
(SEE:SCREAM OF THE BUTTERFLY)
PASSION PIT, THE
(SEE:ICE HOUSE, THE)
PASSION STREET, U.S.A. * (1964) PR:C
PASSIONATE DEMONS, THE ** (1962, Norway) PR:A
PASSIONATE FRIENDS, THE
(SEE:ONE WOMAN'S STORY)
PASSIONATE PLUMBER **½ (1932) PR:A
PASSIONATE SENTRY, THE *** (1952, Brit.) PR:C
PASSIONATE STRANGER, THE
(SEE:NOVEL AFFAIR, A)
PASSIONATE STRANGERS, THE * (1968, Phil.) PR:C
PASSIONATE SUMMER ** (1959, Brit.) PR:A
PASSIONATE SUNDAY
(SEE:DARK ODYSSEY)
PASSIONATE THIEF, THE * (1963, It.) PR:A**
PASSIONE D'AMORE
(SEE:PASSION OF LOVE)
PASSKEY TO DANGER ** (1946) PR:A
PASSOVER PLOT, THE * (1976, Israel) PR:C
PASSPORT HUSBAND *½ (1938) PR:A
PASSPORT TO ADVENTURE
(SEE:PASSPORT TO DESTINY)
PASSPORT TO ALCATRAZ *½ (1940) PR:A
PASSPORT TO CHINA ** (1961, Brit.) PR:A
PASSPORT TO DESTINY ** (1944) PR:A
PASSPORT TO HELL *½ (1932, Brit.) PR:A
PASSPORT TO HELL
(SEE:PASSPORT TO ALCATRAZ)
PASSPORT TO OBLIVION
(SEE:WHERE THE SPIES ARE)
PASSPORT TO PIMLICO * (1949, Brit.) PR:A**
PASSPORT TO SHAME
(SEE:ROOM 43)
PASSPORT TO SUEZ ** (1943) PR:A
PASSPORT TO TREASON *½ (1956, Brit.) PR:A
PASSWORD IS COURAGE, THE **½ (1962, Brit.) PR:A
PAST OF MARY HOLMES, THE * (1933) PR:A
PASTEUR * (1936, Fr.) PR:A
PASTOR HALL **½ (1940, Brit.) PR:A
PAT AND MIKE ** (1952) PR:A**
PAT GARRETT AND BILLY THE KID ** (1973) PR:C
PATAKIN *** (1985, Cuba) PR:A
PATATE
(SEE:FRIEND OF THE FAMILY)
PATCH
(SEE:DEATH OF A GUNFIGHTER)
PATCH OF BLUE, A *** (1965) PR:A
PATERNITY ** (1981) PR:C
PATH OF GLORY, THE ** (1934, Brit.) PR:A
PATHER PANCHALI ***½ (1958, India) PR:A
PATHFINDER, THE ** (1952) PR:A
PATHS OF GLORY *** (1957) PR:C**
PATIENT IN ROOM 18, THE ** (1938) PR:A
PATIENT VANISHES, THE *½ (1947, Brit.) PR:A
PATRICIA GETS HER MAN *½ (1937, Brit.) PR:A
PATRICK * (1979, Aus.) PR:O**
PATRICK THE GREAT ** (1945) PR:A
PATRIOT, THE ***½ (1928) PR:C
PATRIOT, THE * (1986) PR:O
PATSY, THE *½ (1964) PR:A
PATTERN FOR PLUNDER
(SEE:BAY OF SAINT MICHEL)
PATTERN OF EVIL
(SEE:SATAN IN HIGH HEELS)
PATTERNS **** (1956) PR:A
PATTERNS OF POWER
(SEE:PATTERNS)
PATTI ROCKS * (1988) PR:O**
PATTON *** (1970) PR:C**
PATTY HEARST **½ (1988) PR:O
PAUL AND MICHELLE *½ (1974, Fr./Brit.) PR:O
PAUL TEMPLE RETURNS ** (1952, Brit.) PR:A
PAUL TEMPLE'S TRIUMPH *½ (1951, Brit.) PR:A
PAULA
(SEE:FRAMED)
PAULA ** (1952) PR:A
PAULINE A LA PLAGE
(SEE:PAULINE AT THE BEACH)
PAULINE AT THE BEACH ***½ (1983, Fr.) PR:O
PAVLOVA—A WOMAN FOR ALL TIME ** (1985, Brit./USSR) PR:A-C
PAWNBROKER, THE ** (1965) PR:C**
PAWNEE zero (1957) PR:A
PAY BOX ADVENTURE * (1936, Brit.) PR:A
PAY OFF, THE * (1930) PR:A
PAY OR DIE * (1960) PR:C**
PAY THE DEVIL
(SEE:MAN IN THE SHADOW)
PAYDAY ** (1972) PR:O**
PAYMENT DEFERRED **½ (1932) PR:A
PAYMENT IN BLOOD * (1968, It.) PR:O
PAYMENT ON DEMAND *** (1951) PR:A-C
PAYOFF, THE *½ (1935) PR:A
PAYOFF, THE *½ (1943) PR:A
PAYROLL ** (1962, Brit.) PR:A
P.C. JOSSER **½ (1931, Brit.) PR:A
PEACE FOR A GUNFIGHTER * (1967) PR:C
PEACE KILLERS, THE * (1971) PR:O
PEACE TO HIM WHO ENTERS *** (1963, USSR) PR:A
PEACEMAKER
(SEE:AMBASSADOR, THE)
PEACEMAKER, THE ** (1956) PR:A
PEACH O'RENO ** (1931) PR:A
PEACH THIEF, THE *** (1969, Bulgaria) PR:C
PEACOCK ALLEY *½ (1930) PR:A
PEACOCK FEATHERS
(SEE:OPEN THE DOOR AND SEE ALL THE PEOPLE)
PEARL, THE ***½ (1948, US/Mex.) PR:A
PEARL OF DEATH, THE * (1944) PR:A**
PEARL OF THE SOUTH PACIFIC *½ (1955) PR:A
PEARL OF TLAYUCAN, THE ** (1964, Mex.) PR:A
PEARLS BRING TEARS **½ (1937, Brit.) PR:A
PEARLS OF THE CROWN ***½ (1938, Fr.) PR:A
PEAU DE BANANE
(SEE:BANANA PEEL)
PEAU D'ESPION
(SEE:TO COMMIT A MURDER)
PECCATORI IN BLUE-JEANS
(SEE:CHEATERS, THE)
PECK'S BAD BOY **½ (1934) PR:AA
PECK'S BAD BOY WITH THE CIRCUS ** (1938) PR:AA
PECOS RIVER ** (1951) PR:A
PEDDLIN' IN SOCIETY ** (1949, It.) PR:A
PEDESTRIAN, THE ***½ (1974, Ger.) PR:C
PEE-WEE'S BIG ADVENTURE ***½ (1985) PR:A
PEEK-A-BOO * (1961, Fr.) PR:O
PEEPER * (1975) PR:A
PEEPING TOM **½ (1960, Brit.) PR:O
PEER GYNT *½ (1965) PR:A
PEG O' MY HEART **½ (1933) PR:A
PEG OF OLD DRURY *** (1936, Brit.) PR:A
PEGGY **½ (1950) PR:A
PEGGY SUE GOT MARRIED ***½ (1986) PR:C
PEKING BLONDE
(SEE:BLONDE FROM PEKING, THE)
PEKING EXPRESS **½ (1951) PR:A
PEKING MEDALLION, THE
(SEE:CORRUPT ONES, THE)
PEKING OPERA BLUES ***½ (1986, Hong Kong) PR:C
PENAL CODE, THE * (1933) PR:A
PENALTY, THE ** (1941) PR:C

Finding entries in **THE MOTION PICTURE GUIDE ™**

Years 1929-83	Volumes I-IX
1984	Volume IX
1985	1986 ANNUAL
1986	1987 ANNUAL
1987	1988 ANNUAL
1988	1989 ANNUAL

STAR RATINGS

★★★★★	Masterpiece
★★★★	Excellent
★★★	Good
★★	Fair
★	Poor
zero	Without Merit

PARENTAL RECOMMENDATION (PR:)

AA	Good for Children
A	Acceptable for Children
C	Cautionary, some objectionable scenes
O	Objectionable for Children

BOLD: Films on Videocassette

PENALTY OF FAME
(SEE:OKAY AMERICA)
PENDULUM **½ (1969) PR:A-C
PENELOPE ** (1966) PR:A
PENGUIN POOL MURDER, THE *** (1932) PR:A
PENGUIN POOL MYSTERY, THE
(SEE:PENGUIN POOL MURDER, THE)
PENITENT, THE **½ (1988) PR:C-O
PENITENTE MURDER CASE, THE ** (1936) PR:O
PENITENTIARY ** (1938) PR:A
PENITENTIARY **½ (1979) PR:O
PENITENTIARY II zero (1982) PR:O
PENITENTIARY III **½ (1987) PR:O
PENN OF PENNSYLVANIA
(SEE:COURAGEOUS MR. PENN)
PENNIES FROM HEAVEN *** (1936) PR:A
PENNIES FROM HEAVEN **½ (1981) PR:C-O
PENNY PARADISE ** (1938, Brit.) PR:A
PENNY POINTS TO PARADISE *½
(1951, Brit.) PR:A
PENNY POOL, THE **½ (1937, Brit.) PR:A
PENNY PRINCESS *** (1953, Brit.) PR:A
PENNY SERENADE **½ (1941) PR:A
PENNYWHISTLE BLUES, THE **
(1952, South Africa) PR:A
PENROD AND HIS TWIN BROTHER **
(1938) PR:AA
PENROD AND SAM ** (1931) PR:AA
PENROD AND SAM ** (1937) PR:AA
PENROD'S DOUBLE TROUBLE ** (1938) PR:AA
PENTHOUSE *** (1933) PR:A
PENTHOUSE, THE zero (1967, Brit.) PR:O
PENTHOUSE PARTY ** (1936) PR:A
PENTHOUSE RHYTHM * (1945) PR:A
PEOPLE AGAINST O'HARA, THE *** (1951) PR:C
PEOPLE ARE FUNNY *½ (1945) PR:A
PEOPLE MEET AND SWEET MUSIC FILLS THE
HEART ** (1969, Den./Swed.) PR:O
PEOPLE NEXT DOOR, THE * (1970) PR:O
PEOPLE THAT TIME FORGOT, THE *
(1977, Brit.) PR:AA
PEOPLE TOYS
(SEE:DEVIL TIMES FIVE)
PEOPLE VS. DR. KILDARE, THE ** (1941) PR:A
PEOPLE WHO OWN THE DARK * (1975, Sp.) PR:O
PEOPLE WILL TALK **½ (1935) PR:A
PEOPLE WILL TALK **** (1951) PR:A-C
PEOPLE'S ENEMY, THE ** (1935) PR:A
PEPE **½ (1960) PR:AA
PEPE LE MOKO ***** (1937, Fr.) PR:C
PEPPER ** (1936) PR:AA
PEPPERMINT SODA ***½ (1979, Fr.) PR:C
PER IL BENE E PER IL MALE
(SEE:ANATOMY OF A MARRIAGE)
PER QUALCHE DOLLARO IN PIU
(SEE:FOR A FEW DOLLARS MORE)
PER UN PUGNO DI DOLLARI
(SEE:FISTFUL OF DOLLARS, A)
PERCY * (1971, Brit.) PR:O
PERCY'S PROGRESS
(SEE:IT'S NOT THE SIZE THAT COUNTS)
PERFECT *½ (1985) PR:O
PERFECT ALIBI, THE ** (1931, Brit.) PR:A
PERFECT CLUE, THE ** (1935) PR:A
PERFECT COUPLE, A *½ (1979) PR:A-C
PERFECT CRIME, THE ** (1928) PR:A-C
PERFECT CRIME, THE
(SEE:ELLERY QUEEN AND THE PERFECT CRIME)
PERFECT CRIME, THE **½ (1937, Brit.) PR:A
PERFECT FLAW, THE *½ (1934, Brit.) PR:A
PERFECT FRIDAY *** (1970, Brit.) PR:C
PERFECT FURLOUGH, THE **½ (1958) PR:A
PERFECT GENTLEMAN, THE ** (1935) PR:A
PERFECT LADY, THE ** (1931, Brit.) PR:A
PERFECT MARRIAGE, THE *½ (1946) PR:A
PERFECT MATCH, THE ** (1987) PR:C
PERFECT SET-UP, THE
(SEE:ONCE YOU KISS A STRANGER)
PERFECT SNOB, THE ** (1941) PR:A
PERFECT SPECIMEN, THE *** (1937) PR:A
PERFECT STRANGERS
(SEE:VACATION FROM MARRIAGE)
PERFECT STRANGERS ** (1950) PR:A
PERFECT STRANGERS ** (1984) PR:O
PERFECT UNDERSTANDING *½
(1933, Brit.) PR:A-C
PERFECT WEEKEND, A
(SEE:ST. LOUIS KID, THE)
PERFECT WOMAN, THE **½ (1950, Brit.) PR:A
PERFECTIONIST, THE ** (1952, Fr.) PR:A
PERFORMERS, THE **½ (1970, Jap.) PR:C
PERIL **½ (1985, Fr.) PR:O
PERIL FOR THE GUY ** (1956, Brit.) PR:A
PERILOUS HOLIDAY **½ (1946) PR:A
PERILOUS JOURNEY, A
(SEE:BAD BOY)
PERILOUS JOURNEY, A **½ (1953) PR:A
PERILOUS WATERS ** (1948) PR:A
PERILS OF GWENDOLINE IN THE LAND OF THE
YIK-YAK, THE
(SEE:PERILS OF GWENDOLINE, THE)
PERILS OF GWENDOLINE, THE *½
(1984, Fr.) PR:O
PERILS OF PAULINE, THE ***½ (1947) PR:A
PERILS OF PAULINE, THE ** (1967) PR:A
PERILS OF P.K., THE zero (1986) PR:O
PERIOD OF ADJUSTMENT *** (1962) PR:A-C
PERMANENT RECORD **½ (1988) PR:A-C
PERMANENT VACATION **½ (1982) PR:C
PERMETTE SIGNORA CHE AMI VOSTRA FIGLIA
(SEE:CLARETTA AND BEN)
PERMISSION TO KILL *½ (1975, US/Aust.) PR:C
PERRY RHODAN-SOS AUS DEM WELTALLO
(SEE:MISSION STARDUST)
PERSECUTION *½ (1974, Brit.) PR:C
PERSECUTION AND ASSASSINATION OF
JEAN-PAUL MARAT AS PERFORMED BY THE
INMATES OF THE ASYLUM OF CHARENTON
UNDER THE DIRECTION OF THE MARQUIS DE
SADE, THE ** (1967, Brit.) PR:C
PERSECUTION OF HASTA VALENCIA
(SEE:NARCO MEN, THE)
PERSONA **** (1967, Swed.) PR:O
PERSONAL AFFAIR **½ (1954, Brit.) PR:C
PERSONAL BEST ** (1982) PR:C-O
PERSONAL COLUMN *** (1939, Fr.) PR:C
PERSONAL COLUMN
(SEE:LURED)
PERSONAL FOUL **½ (1987) PR:A-C
PERSONAL HONOR
(SEE:HELLO ANNAPOLIS)
PERSONAL MAID **½ (1931) PR:A
PERSONAL MAID'S SECRET ** (1935) PR:A
PERSONAL PROPERTY **½ (1937) PR:A
PERSONAL SECRETARY ** (1938) PR:A
PERSONAL SERVICES *** (1987, Brit.) PR:O
PERSONALITY ** (1930) PR:A
PERSONALITY KID, THE ** (1934) PR:A
PERSONALITY KID *½ (1946) PR:AA
PERSONALS, THE *** (1982) PR:C
PERSONS IN HIDING **½ (1939) PR:A-C
PERSONS UNKNOWN
(SEE:BIG DEAL ON MADONNA STREET)
PERSUADER, THE ** (1957) PR:A
PERVYY DEN MIRA
(SEE:DAY THE WAR ENDED, THE)
PETE KELLY'S BLUES *** (1955) PR:C
PETE 'N' TILLIE ***½ (1972) PR:A-C
PETER IBBETSON ***½ (1935) PR:A
PETER PAN **** (1953) PR:AA
PETER RABBIT AND TALES OF BEATRIX POTTER
*** (1971, Brit.) PR:AA
PETER THE CRAZY
(SEE:PIERROT LE FOU)
PETERSEN **½ (1974, Aus.) PR:C
PETERVILLE DIAMOND, THE **½
(1942, Brit.) PR:A
PETE'S DRAGON ** (1977) PR:AA
PETEY WHEATSTRAW zero (1978) PR:O
PETIT CON **½ (1985, Fr.) PR:C-O
PETRIFIED FOREST, THE **** (1936) PR:A
PETS zero (1974) PR:O
PETTICOAT FEVER ** (1936) PR:A
PETTICOAT LARCENY *½ (1943) PR:A
PETTICOAT PIRATES ** (1961, Brit.) PR:A
PETTICOAT POLITICS ** (1941) PR:A
PETTICOATS AND BLUEJEANS
(SEE:PARENT TRAP, THE)
PETTY GIRL, THE *** (1950) PR:A
PETULIA *** (1968, US/Brit.) PR:C
PEYTON PLACE ***½ (1957) PR:C
PHAEDRA **½ (1962, US/Gr./Fr.) PR:C
PHANTASM ***½ (1979) PR:O
PHANTASM II ** (1988) PR:O
PHANTOM BROADCAST, THE *½ (1933) PR:A
PHANTOM COWBOY, THE ** (1941) PR:A
PHANTOM EXPRESS, THE *½ (1932) PR:A
PHANTOM FIEND, THE *½ (1935, Brit.) PR:A
PHANTOM FIEND
(SEE:RETURN OF DR. MABUSE, THE)
PHANTOM FROM SPACE *½ (1953) PR:A
PHANTOM FROM 10,000 LEAGUES, THE *
(1956) PR:A
PHANTOM GOLD ** (1938) PR:A
PHANTOM HORSEMAN, THE
(SEE:BORDER OUTLAW)
PHANTOM IN THE HOUSE, THE ** (1929) PR:A
PHANTOM KILLER ** (1942) PR:A
PHANTOM LADY ***½ (1944) PR:C
PHANTOM LIGHT, THE *** (1935, Brit.) PR:C
PHANTOM OF CHINATOWN ** (1940) PR:A
PHANTOM OF CRESTWOOD, THE ** (1932) PR:A
PHANTOM OF 42ND STREET, THE ** (1945) PR:A
PHANTOM OF LIBERTY, THE **** (1974, Fr.) PR:O
PHANTOM OF PARIS
(SEE:MYSTERY OF MARIE ROGET, THE)
PHANTOM OF PARIS, THE **½ (1931) PR:A
PHANTOM OF SANTA FE ** (1937) PR:A
PHANTOM OF SOHO, THE ** (1967, Ger.) PR:C
PHANTOM OF TERROR, THE
(SEE:BIRD WITH THE CRYSTAL PLUMAGE, THE)
PHANTOM OF THE AIS
(SEE:PHANTOM BROADCAST)
PHANTOM OF THE DESERT * (1930) PR:A
PHANTOM OF THE JUNGLE ** (1955) PR:A
PHANTOM OF THE OPERA, THE **** (1929) PR:A
PHANTOM OF THE OPERA *** (1943) PR:A
PHANTOM OF THE OPERA, THE ***
(1962, Brit.) PR:C-O
PHANTOM OF THE PARADISE **½ (1974) PR:C
PHANTOM OF THE PLAINS ** (1945) PR:A
PHANTOM OF THE RANGE, THE ** (1938) PR:A
PHANTOM OF THE RUE MORGUE *½ (1954) PR:C
PHANTOM PATROL * (1936) PR:A
PHANTOM PLAINSMEN, THE ** (1942) PR:A
PHANTOM PLANET, THE ** (1961) PR:A
PHANTOM PRESIDENT, THE **½ (1932) PR:A
PHANTOM RAIDERS *** (1940) PR:A
PHANTOM RANCHER ** (1940) PR:A
PHANTOM RANGER *½ (1938) PR:A
PHANTOM SHIP ** (1937, Brit.) PR:A
PHANTOM SPEAKS, THE *½ (1945) PR:A
PHANTOM STAGE, THE ** (1939) PR:A
PHANTOM STAGECOACH, THE *½ (1957) PR:A
PHANTOM STALLION, THE ** (1954) PR:A
PHANTOM STOCKMAN, THE ** (1953, Aus.) PR:A
PHANTOM STRIKES, THE **½ (1939, Brit.) PR:A
PHANTOM SUBMARINE, THE * (1941) PR:A
PHANTOM THIEF, THE **½ (1946) PR:A
PHANTOM THUNDERBOLT, THE *½ (1933) PR:A
PHANTOM TOLLBOOTH, THE ***½ (1970) PR:AA
PHANTOM VALLEY *½ (1948) PR:A
PHAR LAP ***½ (1984, Aus.) PR:C
PHARAOH'S CURSE *½ (1957) PR:A
PHAROAH'S WOMAN, THE * (1961, It.) PR:A
PHASE IV **½ (1974) PR:A
PHENIX CITY STORY, THE **½ (19.5) PR:C
PHFFFT! *** (1954) PR:A
PHILADELPHIA ATTRACTION, THE **½
(1985, Hung.) PR:A
PHILADELPHIA EXPERIMENT, THE **½
(1984) PR:C
PHILADELPHIA STORY, THE ***** (1940) PR:A
PHILIP
(SEE:RUN WILD, RUN FREE)
PHILO VANCE RETURNS ** (1947) PR:A
PHILO VANCE'S GAMBLE ** (1947) PR:A
PHILO VANCE'S SECRET MISSION **½ (1947) PR:A
PHOBIA *½ (1980, Can.) PR:O
PHOBIA
(SEE:THE NESTING)
PHOBIA ***½ (1988, Aus.) PR:O
PHOENIX CITY STORY
(SEE:PHENIX CITY STORY)
PHONE CALL FROM A STRANGER ***
(1952) PR:A-C
PHONY AMERICAN, THE ** (1964, Ger.) PR:A
PHOTOGRAPH, THE *** (1987, Gr.) PR:C
PHYNX, THE zero (1970) PR:C
PIAF—THE EARLY YEARS ***
(1982, US/Fr.) PR:A-C
PICCADILLY *½ (1932, Brit.) PR:A-C
PICCADILLY INCIDENT ** (1948, Brit.) PR:A
PICCADILLY JIM **½ (1936) PR:A
PICCADILLY NIGHTS ** (1930, Brit.) PR:A
PICCADILLY THIRD STOP ** (1960, Brit.) PR:A
PICK A STAR ** (1937) PR:AA
PICK-UP *½ (1933) PR:A
PICK-UP ARTIST, THE ** (1987) PR:A-C
PICK-UP SUMMER zero (1981) PR:O
PICKPOCKET **** (1963, Fr.) PR:A
PICKUP * (1951) PR:A
PICKUP ALLEY ** (1957, Brit.) PR:A
PICKUP IN ROME
(SEE:FROM A ROMAN BALCONY)
PICKUP ON 101 **½ (1972) PR:C
PICKUP ON SOUTH STREET ***½ (1953) PR:C
PICKWICK PAPERS, THE *** (1952, Brit.) PR:AA
PICNIC **** (1955) PR:A
PICNIC AT HANGING ROCK ***
(1975, Aus.) PR:C-O
PICNIC ON THE GRASS *** (1960, Fr.) PR:C
PICTURE BRIDES * (1934) PR:A
PICTURE MOMMY DEAD **½ (1966) PR:O
PICTURE OF DORIAN GRAY, THE ***½
(1945) PR:C
PICTURE SHOW MAN, THE *** (1980, Aus.) PR:A
PICTURE SNATCHER **½ (1933) PR:A-C
PICTURES ** (1982, New Zealand) PR:A-C
PIE IN THE SKY *** (1964) PR:A
PIECE OF THE ACTION, A **½ (1977) PR:C
PIECES * (1983, Sp./Puerto/Rico) PR:O
PIECES OF DREAMS ** (1970) PR:C
PIED PIPER, THE ***½ (1942) PR:C

PIED PIPER, THE
(SEE:CLOWN AND THE KIDS)
PIED PIPER, THE *** (1972, Brit.) PR:C
PIEGES
(SEE:PERSONAL COLUMN)
PIEL DE VERANO
(SEE:SUMMERSKIN)
PIER 5, HAVANA *½ (1959) PR:A
PIER 13
(SEE:ME AND MY GAL)
PIER 13 ** (1940) PR:A
PIER 23 *½ (1951) PR:A
PIERRE OF THE PLAINS ** (1942) PR:A
PIERROT LE FOU ** (1968, Fr./It.) PR:O
PIGEON THAT TOOK ROME, THE ** (1962) PR:C
PIGEONS
(SEE:SIDELONG GLANCES OF A PIGEON KICKER)
PIGS ** (1984, Ireland) PR:C
PIGS, THE
(SEE:DADDY'S DEADLY DARLING)
PIGSKIN PARADE *** (1936) PR:A
PIKOVAYA DAMA
(SEE:QUEEN OF SPADES)
PILGRIM, FAREWELL ** (1980) PR:C
PILGRIM LADY, THE ** (1947) PR:A
PILGRIMAGE ***½ (1933) PR:A-C
PILGRIMAGE ** (1972) PR:C
PILL, THE
(SEE:GIRL, THE BODY, AND THE PILL, THE)
PILLAR OF FIRE, THE ** (1963, Israel) PR:A
PILLARS OF SOCIETY **½ (1936, Ger.) PR:A
PILLARS OF THE SKY **½ (1956) PR:A
PILLOW OF DEATH ** (1945) PR:A
PILLOW TALK ***½ (1959) PR:A
PILLOW TO POST **½ (1945) PR:A
PILOT, THE ** (1979) PR:C
PILOT NO. 5 ** (1943) PR:A
PIMPERNEL SMITH ***½ (1942, Brit.) PR:A
PIMPERNEL SVENSSON *½ (1953, Swed.) PR:A
PIN UP GIRL ** (1944) PR:A
PINBALL PICK-UP
(SEE:PICK-UP SUMMER)
PINBALL SUMMER
(SEE:PICK-UP SUMMER)
PINK FLOYD—THE WALL ** (1982, Brit.) PR:O
PINK JUNGLE, THE **½ (1968) PR:A
PINK MOTEL zero (1983) PR:O
PINK NIGHTS **½ (1985) PR:A
PINK PANTHER, THE ***½ (1964) PR:A
PINK PANTHER STRIKES AGAIN, THE ***
(1976, Brit.) PR:A
PINK STRING AND SEALING WAX **
(1950, Brit.) PR:A
PINKY **** (1949) PR:A
PINOCCHIO ***** (1940) PR:AA
PINOCCHIO ** (1969, E./Ger.) PR:AA
PINOCCHIO AND THE EMPEROR OF THE NIGHT
*** (1987) PR:AA
PINOCCHIO IN OUTER SPACE **
(1965, US/Bel.) PR:AA
PINTO BANDIT, THE ** (1944) PR:A
PINTO CANYON ** (1940) PR:AA
PINTO KID, THE *½ (1941) PR:A
PINTO RUSTLERS *½ (1937) PR:A
PIONEER BUILDERS
(SEE:CONQUERORS, THE)
PIONEER DAYS *½ (1940) PR:A
PIONEER, GO HOME
(SEE:FOLLOW THAT DREAM)
PIONEER JUSTICE **½ (1947) PR:A
PIONEER MARSHAL * (1950) PR:A
PIONEER TRAIL ** (1938) PR:A
PIONEERS, THE *½ (1941) PR:A
PIONEERS OF THE FRONTIER ** (1940) PR:A
PIONEERS OF THE WEST ** (1940) PR:A
PIPE DREAMS **½ (1976) PR:C
PIPER, THE
(SEE:CLOWN AND THE KIDS, THE)
PIPER'S TUNE, THE **½ (1962, Brit.) PR:AA
PIPPI IN THE SOUTH SEAS **½
(1974, Swed./Ger.) PR:AA
PIPPI ON THE RUN **½ (1977) PR:AA
PIRANHA **½ (1978) PR:O
PIRAHANA II: FLYING KILLERS
(SEE:PIRAHNA II: THE SPAWNING)
PIRANHA II: THE SPAWNING *½
(1981, Neth.) PR:O

PIRATE, THE ***½ (1948) PR:A
PIRATE AND THE SLAVE GIRL, THE *½
(1961, Fr./It.) PR:A
PIRATE MOVIE, THE zero (1982, Aus.) PR:C
PIRATE OF THE BLACK HAWK, THE **
(1961, Fr./It.) PR:A
PIRATE SHIP
(SEE:MUTINEERS, THE)
PIRATES *** (1986, Fr./Tunisia) PR:C
PIRATES OF BLOOD RIVER, THE **½
(1962, Brit.) PR:A
PIRATES OF CAPRI, THE **½ (1949) PR:A
PIRATES OF MONTEREY *½ (1947) PR:A
PIRATES OF PENZANCE, THE *** (1983) PR:A
PIRATES OF THE PRAIRIE ** (1942) PR:A
PIRATES OF THE SEVEN SEAS ** (1941, Brit.) PR:A
PIRATES OF THE SKIES ** (1939) PR:A
PIRATES OF TORTUGA ** (1961) PR:A
PIRATES OF TRIPOLI ** (1955) PR:A
PIRATES ON HORSEBACK *½ (1941) PR:A
PISTOL FOR RINGO, A **½ (1966, It./Sp.) PR:C
PISTOL HARVEST ** (1951) PR:A
PISTOL PACKIN' MAMA *½ (1943) PR:A
PISTOLERO
(SEE:LAST CHALLENGE, THE)
PIT, THE
(SEE:FIVE MILLION YEARS TO EARTH)
PIT AND THE PENDULUM, THE ***½ (1961) PR:C
PIT OF DARKNESS **½ (1961, Brit.) PR:A
PIT STOP zero (1969) PR:O
PITFALL ***½ (1948) PR:C
PITTSBURGH *** (1942) PR:A
PITTSBURGH KID, THE *½ (1941) PR:A
PIXOTE **** (1981, Braz.) PR:O
PIZZA TRIANGLE, THE **½ (1970, It./Sp.) PR:O
P.J. * (1968) PR:O
P.K. & THE KID **½ (1987) PR:A
PLACE CALLED GLORY, A **½
(1966, Sp./Ger.) PR:C
PLACE FOR LOVERS, A zero (1969, It./Fr.) PR:C-O
PLACE IN THE SUN, A ***** (1951) PR:C
PLACE OF ONE'S OWN, A *** (1945, Brit.) PR:A
PLACE OF WEEPING ***
(1986, South Africa) PR:C-O
PLACE TO GO, A ** (1964, Brit.) PR:A
PLACES IN THE HEART ***½ (1984) PR:A-C
PLAGUE * (1978, Can.) PR:C
PLAGUE DOGS, THE ** (1984, US/Brit.) PR:C-O
PLAGUE-M3: THE GEMINI STRAIN
(SEE:PLAGUE)
PLAGUE OF THE ZOMBIES, THE ***
(1966, Brit.) PR:C
PLAINSMAN, THE ***½ (1937) PR:C
PLAINSMAN, THE
(SEE:RAIDERS, THE)
PLAINSMAN, THE ** (1966) PR:A
PLAINSMAN AND THE LADY ** (1946) PR:A
PLAINSONG ** (1982) PR:C
PLAN 9 FROM OUTER SPACE zero (1959) PR:A
PLANES, TRAINS AND AUTOMOBILES ***
(1987) PR:O
PLANET OF BLOOD
(SEE:PLANET OF THE VAMPIRES)
PLANET OF BLOOD
(SEE:QUEEN OF BLOOD)
PLANET OF DINOSAURS ** (1978) PR:A
PLANET OF HORRORS
(SEE:MINDWARP: AN INFINITY OF TERROR)
PLANET OF STORMS
(SEE:STORM PLANET)
PLANET OF THE APES **** (1968) PR:C
PLANET OF THE VAMPIRES ***
(1965, US/It./Sp.) PR:C
PLANET ON THE PROWL
(SEE:WAR BETWEEN THE PLANETS)
PLANETS AGAINST US, THE ** (1961, It./Fr.) PR:C
PLANK, THE **½ (1967, Brit.) PR:A
PLANTER'S WIFE, THE
(SEE:OUTPOST IN MALAYA)
PLANTS ARE WATCHING US, THE
(SEE:KIRLIAN WITNESS, THE)
PLASTIC DOME OF NORMA JEAN, THE *½
(1966) PR:C
PLATINUM BLONDE *** (1931) PR:A
PLATINUM HIGH SCHOOL *½ (1960) PR:A
PLATOON **** (1986) PR:O
PLATOON LEADER ** (1988) PR:O

PLAY DEAD * (1981) PR:O
PLAY DIRTY *** (1969, Brit.) PR:C
PLAY GIRL * (1932) PR:A
PLAY GIRL **½ (1940) PR:A
PLAY IT AGAIN, SAM ***½ (1972) PR:C
PLAY IT AS IT LAYS * (1972) PR:O
PLAY IT COOL *½ (1963, Brit.) PR:A
PLAY IT COOL **½ (1970, Jap.) PR:A
PLAY MISTY FOR ME ***½ (1971) PR:O
PLAY UP THE BAND ** (1935, Brit.) PR:A
PLAYBACK ** (1962, Brit.) PR:A
PLAYBOY, THE *** (1942, Brit.) PR:AA
PLAYBOY OF PARIS **½ (1930) PR:A
PLAYBOY OF THE WESTERN WORLD, THE ***
(1963, Ireland) PR:C
PLAYERS zero (1979) PR:O
PLAYERS
(SEE:CLUB, THE)
PLAYGIRL **½ (1954) PR:A
PLAYGIRL
(SEE:THAT WOMAN)
PLAYGIRL AFTER DARK
(SEE:TOO HOT TO HANDLE)
PLAYGIRL AND THE WAR MINISTER, THE
(SEE:AMOROUS MR. PRAWN, THE)
PLAYGIRL KILLER
(SEE:DECOY FOR TERROR)
PLAYGIRLS AND THE BELLBOY, THE zero
(1962, Ger.) PR:O
PLAYGIRLS AND THE VAMPIRE * (1964, It.) PR:O
PLAYGROUND, THE zero (1965) PR:O
PLAYING AROUND *½ (1930) PR:A
PLAYING FOR KEEPS *½ (1986) PR:C
PLAYING THE GAME
(SEE:TOUCHDOWN)
PLAYMATES ** (1941) PR:A
PLAYMATES *½ (1969, Fr./It.) PR:O
PLAYTHING, THE *½ (1929, Brit.) PR:A
PLAYTIME *** (1963, Fr.) PR:C
PLAYTIME ***½ (1973, Fr.) PR:AA
PLAZA SUITE **** (1971) PR:A-C
PLEASANTVILLE ** (1976) PR:A
PLEASE BELIEVE ME **½ (1950) PR:A
PLEASE DON'T EAT THE DAISIES *** (1960) PR:A
PLEASE! MR. BALZAC *½ (1957, Fr.) PR:C
PLEASE MURDER ME *½ (1956) PR:A
PLEASE, NOT NOW! ** (1963, Fr./It.) PR:C
PLEASE SIR *½ (1971, Brit.) PR:A
PLEASE STAND BY * (1972) PR:C
PLEASE TEACHER ** (1937, Brit.) PR:A
PLEASE TURN OVER *** (1960, Brit.) PR:C
PLEASURE zero (1933) PR:A
PLEASURE CRAZED *½ (1929) PR:A
PLEASURE CRUISE *½ (1933) PR:A
PLEASURE GIRL
(SEE:GIRL WITH A SUITCASE)
PLEASURE GIRLS, THE *½ (1966, Brit.) PR:C
PLEASURE LOVER
(SEE:PLEASURE LOVERS, THE)
PLEASURE LOVERS, THE ** (1964, Brit.) PR:C
PLEASURE OF HIS COMPANY, THE *** (1961) PR:A
PLEASURE PLANTATION zero (1970) PR:O
PLEASURE SEEKERS, THE **½ (1964) PR:A
PLEASURES AND VICES ** (1962, Fr.) PR:C
PLEASURES OF THE FLESH, THE **½ (1965) PR:C
PLEDGEMASTERS, THE zero (1971) PR:O
PLEIN SOLEIL
(SEE:PURPLE NOON)
PLEIN SUD
(SEE:HEAT OF DESIRE)
PLENTY *** (1985) PR:O
PLEURE PAS LA BOUCHE PLEINE
(SEE:DON'T CRY WITH YOUR MOUTH FULL)
PLOT THICKENS, THE
(SEE:HERE COMES COOKIE)
PLOT THICKENS, THE *½ (1936) PR:A
PLOT TO KILL ROOSEVELT, THE
(SEE:CONSPIRACY IN TEHERAN)
PLOUGH AND THE STARS, THE *** (1936) PR:A
PLOUGHMAN'S LUNCH, THE ****
(1984, Brit.) PR:O
PLUCKED ** (1969, Fr./It.) PR:C-O
PLUMBER, THE ***½ (1980, Aus.) PR:C-O
PLUNDER ** (1931, Brit.) PR:A
PLUNDER OF THE SUN ** (1953) PR:C
PLUNDER ROAD *** (1957) PR:A
PLUNDERERS, THE *** (1948) PR:A

Finding entries in **THE MOTION PICTURE GUIDE** ™

Years 1929-83	Volumes I-IX
1984	Volume IX
1985	1986 ANNUAL
1986	1987 ANNUAL
1987	1988 ANNUAL
1988	1989 ANNUAL

STAR RATINGS

★★★★★ Masterpiece
★★★★   Excellent
★★★   Good
★★   Fair
★   Poor
zero   Without Merit

PARENTAL RECOMMENDATION (PR:)

AA Good for Children
A   Acceptable for Children
C   Cautionary, some objectionable scenes
O   Objectionable for Children

BOLD: Films on Videocassette

PLUNDERERS, THE *** (1960) PR:A
PLUNDERERS OF PAINTED FLATS ** (1959) PR:A
PLYMOUTH ADVENTURE **½ (1952) PR:AA
POACHER'S DAUGHTER, THE **½
 (1960, Brit.) PR:A
POCATELLO KID *½ (1932) PR:A
POCKET MONEY ** (1972) PR:A-C
POCKETFUL OF MIRACLES ***½ (1961) PR:AA
POCOLITTLE DOG LOST ** (1977) PR:A
POCOMANIA ** (1939) PR:C
POE'S TALES OF HORROR
 (SEE:TALES OF TERROR)
POET'S PUB ** (1949, Brit.) PR:A
POET'S SILENCE, THE *** (1987, Ger.) PR:C
POI TI SPOSERO
 (SEE:MALE COMPANION)
POIL DE CAROTTE ** (1932, Fr.) PR:A**
POINT BLANK
 (SEE:PRESSURE POINT)
POINT BLANK **½ (1967, US) PR:O
POINT OF TERROR * (1971) PR:O
POINTED HEELS **½ (1930) PR:A
POINTING FINGER, THE ** (1934, Brit.) PR:A
POISON PEN *** (1941, Brit.) PR:A
POISONED DIAMOND, THE ** (1934, Brit.) PR:A
POITIN ** (1979, Ireland) PR:A
POKAYANIYE
 (SEE:REPENTANCE)
POLICE *** (1986, Fr.) PR:O
POLICE ACADEMY * (1984) PR:O
**POLICE ACADEMY 5: ASSIGNMENT MIAMI BEACH
 * (1988) PR:C**
**POLICE ACADEMY 4: CITIZENS ON PATROL *
 (1987) PR:C**
**POLICE ACADEMY 3: BACK IN TRAINING *½
 (1986) PR:C-O**
**POLICE ACADEMY 2: THEIR FIRST ASSIGNMENT
 zero (1985) PR:O**
POLICE BULLETS ** (1942) PR:A
POLICE CALL * (1933) PR:A
POLICE CAR 17 ** (1933) PR:A
POLICE CONNECTION: DETECTIVE GERONIMO
 (SEE:MAD BOMBER, THE)
POLICE COURT
 (SEE:FAME STREET)
POLICE DOG ** (1955, Brit.) PR:A
POLICE DOG STORY, THE ** (1961) PR:A
POLICE NURSE **½ (1963) PR:A
POLICE PYTHON 357 *** (1976, Fr.) PR:C
POLICEMAN OF THE 16TH PRECINCT, THE zero
 (1963, Gr.) PR:A
POLICEWOMAN * (1974) PR:O
POLITICAL ASYLUM ** (1975, Mex./Guat.) PR:A
POLITICAL PARTY, A **½ (1933, Brit.) PR:A
POLITICS ** (1931) PR:A
POLLY FULTON
 (SEE:B.F.'S DAUGHTER)
POLLY OF THE CIRCUS *½ (1932) PR:A
POLLYANNA ** (1960) PR:AA**
POLO JOE * (1936) PR:A
POLTERGEIST ** (1982) PR:C-O
POLTERGEIST III *½ (1988) PR:C-O
POLTERGEIST II **½ (1986) PR:O
POLYESTER ** (1981) PR:O
POM POM GIRLS, THE *½ (1976) PR:O
POMOCNIK
 (SEE:ASSISTANT, THE)
PONCOMANIA
 (SEE:POCOMANIA)
PONTIUS PILATE ** (1967, Fr./It.) PR:A
PONY EXPRESS * (1953) PR:A**
PONY EXPRESS RIDER **½ (1976) PR:A
PONY POST * (1940) PR:A
PONY SOLDIER *** (1952) PR:A
POOKIE
 (SEE:STERILE CUCKOO, THE)
POOL OF LONDON **½ (1951, Brit.) PR:A
POOR ALBERT AND LITTLE ANNIE
 (SEE:I DISMEMBER MAMA)
POOR COW *** (1968, Brit.) PR:C
POOR LITTLE RICH GIRL ** (1936) PR:A
POOR OLD BILL *½ (1931, Brit.) PR:A
POOR OUTLAWS, THE
 (SEE:ROUND UP, THE)
POOR RICH, THE *½ (1934) PR:A
POOR WHITE TRASH
 (SEE:BAYOU)
POOR WHITE TRASH II
 (SEE:SCUM OF THE EARTH)
POP ALWAYS PAYS ** (1940) PR:A
P.O.W., THE *½ (1973) PR:C
POPDOWN ** (1968, Brit.) PR:A
POPE JOAN * (1972, Brit.) PR:C
**POPE OF GREENWICH VILLAGE, THE **½
 (1984) PR:O**
POPE ONDINE STORY, THE
 (SEE:CHELSEA GIRLS, THE)
POPEYE ** (1980) PR:A
POPI *** (1969) PR:A

POPIOL Y DIAMENT
 (SEE:ASHES AND DIAMONDS)
POPPY *** (1936) PR:A
POPPY IS ALSO A FLOWER, THE * (1966) PR:C**
POPSY POP ** (1971, Fr.) PR:A
POR MIS PISTOLAS **½ (1969, Mex.) PR:A
POR UN PUNADO DE DOLARES
 (SEE:FISTFUL OF DOLLARS, A)
PORGY AND BESS ***½ (1959) PR:A-C
PORK CHOP HILL ** (1959) PR:C**
PORKY'S * (1982) PR:O
PORKY'S REVENGE * (1985) PR:O
PORKY'S II: THE NEXT DAY *½ (1983) PR:O
PORRIDGE
 (SEE:DOING TIME)
PORT AFRIQUE *½ (1956, Brit.) PR:A
PORT DES LILAS
 (SEE:GATES OF PARIS)
PORT O' DREAMS
 (SEE:GIRL OUTBOARD)
PORT OF CALL **½ (1963, Swed.) PR:C
PORT OF DESIRE *½ (1960, Fr.) PR:C
PORT OF ESCAPE ** (1955, Brit.) PR:A
PORT OF 40 THIEVES, THE *** (1944) PR:A
PORT OF HATE * (1939) PR:A
PORT OF HELL ** (1955) PR:A
PORT OF LOST DREAMS ** (1935) PR:A
PORT OF MISSING GIRLS * (1938) PR:A
PORT OF NEW YORK * (1949) PR:A**
PORT OF SEVEN SEAS *** (1938) PR:A
PORT OF SHADOWS **** (1938, Fr.) PR:A
PORT OF SHAME
 (SEE:LOVER'S NET)
PORT SAID ** (1948) PR:A
PORT SINISTER * (1953) PR:A
PORTIA ON TRIAL **½ (1937) PR:A
PORTLAND EXPOSE **½ (1957) PR:A
PORTNOY'S COMPLAINT * (1972) PR:O
PORTRAIT FROM LIFE
 (SEE:GIRL IN THE PAINTING, THE)
PORTRAIT IN BLACK ** (1960) PR:A-C
PORTRAIT IN SMOKE ** (1957, Brit.) PR:O
PORTRAIT IN TERROR *½ (1965) PR:O
PORTRAIT OF A MOBSTER ** (1961) PR:C
PORTRAIT OF A SINNER ** (1961, Brit.) PR:C
PORTRAIT OF A WOMAN *** (1946, Fr.) PR:A
PORTRAIT OF ALISON
 (SEE:POSTMARK FOR DANGER)
PORTRAIT OF CHIEKO **½ (1968, Jap.) PR:A
PORTRAIT OF CLARE ** (1951, Brit.) PR:A
PORTRAIT OF HELL *** (1969, Jap.) PR:A
PORTRAIT OF INNOCENCE ** (1948, Fr.) PR:A
PORTRAIT OF JENNIE **** (1949) PR:A
PORTRAIT OF LENIN *** (1967, Pol./USSR) PR:A
PORTRAIT OF MARIA ** (1946, Mex.) PR:C
**PORTRAIT OF THE ARTIST AS A YOUNG MAN, A
 ½ (1979, Ireland) PR:A
POSEIDON ADVENTURE, THE **½ (1972) PR:A
POSITIONS
 (SEE:PUT UP OR SHUT UP)
POSITIONS OF LOVE
 (SEE:PUT UP OR SHUT UP)
POSSE *** (1975) PR:C
POSSE FROM HELL *** (1961) PR:A
POSSESSED **½ (1931) PR:A
POSSESSED ***½ (1947) PR:A-C
POSSESSION * (1981, Fr./Ger.) PR:O
POSSESSION OF JOEL DELANEY, THE *
 (1972) PR:O
POST OFFICE INVESTIGATOR ** (1949) PR:A
POSTAL INSPECTOR *½ (1936) PR:A
POSTMAN ALWAYS RINGS TWICE, THE ***
 (1946) PR:O**
**POSTMAN ALWAYS RINGS TWICE, THE *½
 (1981) PR:O**
POSTMAN DIDN'T RING, THE ** (1942) PR:A
POSTMAN GOES TO WAR, THE ** (1968, Fr.) PR:A
POSTMAN'S KNOCK ** (1962, Brit.) PR:A
POSTMARK FOR DANGER **½ (1956, Brit.) PR:A
POSTORONNIM VKHOD VOSPRESHCHEN
 (SEE:WELCOME KOSTYA!)
POT CARRIERS, THE *** (1962, Brit.) PR:A
POT LUCK **½ (1936, Brit.) PR:A
POT O' GOLD *½ (1941) PR:A
POTIPHAR'S WIFE
 (SEE:HER STRANGE DESIRE)
**POUND PUPPIES AND THE LEGEND OF BIG PAW
 ** (1988) PR:AA**
POURQUOI PAS! *** (1979, Fr.) PR:C
P.O.W. THE ESCAPE ** (1986) PR:O
POWDER RIVER *** (1953) PR:A
POWDER RIVER RUSTLERS **½ (1949) PR:A
POWDER TOWN *½ (1942) PR:A
POWDERSMOKE RANGE **½ (1935) PR:A
POWER **½ (1934, Brit.) PR:A
POWER * (1986) PR:O**
POWER, THE **½ (1968) PR:A

POWER, THE * (1984) PR:O
POWER AND GLORY
 (SEE:POWER AND THE GLORY, THE)
POWER AND THE GLORY, THE *** (1933) PR:A-C
POWER AND THE PRIZE, THE **½ (1956) PR:A
POWER DIVE **½ (1941) PR:A
POWER OF EVIL, THE ** (1985, Fr./It.) PR:O
POWER OF JUSTICE
 (SEE:BEYOND THE SACRAMENTO)
POWER OF POSSESSION
 (SEE:LAWLESS EMPIRE)
POWER OF THE PRESS * (1943) PR:A
POWER OF THE WHISTLER, THE ** (1945) PR:A
POWER PLAY ** (1978, Brit./Can.) PR:C
POWERFORCE * (1983) PR:O
POWERS GIRL, THE *½ (1942) PR:A
POZEGNANIA
 (SEE:PARTINGS)
PRACTICALLY YOURS **½ (1944) PR:A
PRAIRIE, THE ** (1948) PR:A
PRAIRIE BADMEN ** (1946) PR:A
PRAIRIE EXPRESS *½ (1947) PR:A
PRAIRIE JUSTICE ** (1938) PR:A
PRAIRIE LAW ** (1940) PR:A
PRAIRIE MOON **½ (1938) PR:A
PRAIRIE OUTLAWS ** (1948) PR:A
PRAIRIE PALS * (1942) PR:A
PRAIRIE PIONEERS ** (1941) PR:A
PRAIRIE ROUNDUP **½ (1951) PR:A
PRAIRIE RUSTLERS ** (1945) PR:A
PRAIRIE SCHOONERS *½ (1940) PR:A
PRAIRIE STRANGER * (1941) PR:A
PRAIRIE THUNDER *½ (1937) PR:A
PRAISE MARX AND PASS THE AMMUNITION **
 (1970, Brit.) PR:A
PRATLDWANDI
 (SEE:ADVERSARY, THE)
PRAY FOR DEATH **½ (1986) PR:O
PRAYER FOR THE DYING, A ** (1987) PR:C-O
PRAYING MANTIS ** (1982, Brit.) PR:C
PREACHERMAN zero (1971) PR:O
PRECIOUS JEWELS * (1969) PR:C
PREDATOR ** (1987) PR:O
PREHISTORIC PLANET WOMEN
 (SEE:WOMEN OF THE PREHISTORIC PLANET)
PREHISTORIC WOMEN * (1950) PR:C
PREHISTORIC WOMEN * (1967, Brit.) PR:O
PREHISTORIC WORLD
 (SEE:TEENAGE CAVEMAN)
PREJUDICE *½ (1949) PR:A
PRELUDE TO ECSTASY ** (1963, Fin.) PR:C
PRELUDE TO FAME *** (1950, Brit.) PR:A
PREMATURE BURIAL, THE **½ (1962) PR:C
PREMIERE
 (SEE:ONE NIGHT IN PARIS)
PREMONITION, THE ** (1976) PR:C
PRENOM: CARMEN
 (SEE:FIRST NAME: CARMEN)
PREPPIES ** (1984) PR:O
PREPPIES
 (SEE:MAKING THE GRADE)
PRESCOTT KID, THE ** (1936) PR:A
PRESCRIPTION FOR ROMANCE ** (1937) PR:A
PRESENT ARMS
 (SEE:LEATHERNECKING)
PRESENTING LILY MARS **½ (1943) PR:A
PRESIDENT VANISHES, THE ** (1934) PR:A
PRESIDENT'S ANALYST, THE ***½ (1967) PR:O
PRESIDENT'S LADY, THE *** (1953) PR:A-C
PRESIDENT'S MYSTERY, THE *½ (1936) PR:A
PRESIDIO, THE *½ (1988) PR:C-O
PRESS FOR TIME **½ (1966, Brit.) PR:A
PRESSURE **½ (1976, Brit.) PR:C
PRESSURE OF GUILT *** (1964, Jap.) PR:C
PRESSURE POINT ***½ (1962) PR:C
PRESTIGE ** (1932) PR:A
PRETENDER, THE *** (1947) PR:A
PRETTY BABY ** (1950) PR:A
PRETTY BABY ***½ (1978) PR:O
PRETTY BOY FLOYD **½ (1960) PR:C-O
PRETTY BUT WICKED zero (1965, Braz.) PR:O
PRETTY IN PINK ** (1986) PR:C
PRETTY MAIDS ALL IN A ROW **½ (1971) PR:O
PRETTY POISON ***½ (1968) PR:C-O
PRETTY POLLY
 (SEE:MATTER OF INNOCENCE, A)
PRETTY SMART zero (1987) PR:O
PRETTYKILL * (1987) PR:O
PREVIEW MURDER MYSTERY **½ (1936) PR:A
PREY, THE * (1984) PR:O
PRICE OF A SONG, THE ** (1935, Brit.) PR:A
PRICE OF FEAR, THE **½ (1956) PR:A
PRICE OF FLESH, THE * (1962, Fr.) PR:O
PRICE OF FOLLY, THE * (1937, Brit.) PR:A
PRICE OF FREEDOM, THE
 (SEE:OPERATION DAYBREAK)
PRICE OF POWER, THE ** (1969, It./Sp.) PR:C
PRICE OF SILENCE, THE * (1960, Brit.) PR:A

PRICE OF THINGS, THE * (1930, Brit.) PR:A
PRICE OF WISDOM, THE * (1935, Brit.) PR:A
PRICK UP YOUR EARS ***½ (1987, Brit.) PR:O
PRIDE AND PREJUDICE ** (1940) PR:A**
PRIDE AND THE PASSION, THE **½ (1957) PR:C
PRIDE OF KENTUCKY
(SEE:STORY OF SEABISCUIT, THE)
PRIDE OF MARYLAND ** (1951) PR:A
PRIDE OF ST. LOUIS, THE ***½ (1952) PR:AA
PRIDE OF THE ARMY ** (1942) PR:AA
PRIDE OF THE BLUE GRASS ** (1954) PR:A
PRIDE OF THE BLUEGRASS ** (1939) PR:AA
PRIDE OF THE BOWERY *½ (1941) PR:A
PRIDE OF THE BOWERY, THE
(SEE:MR. HEX)
PRIDE OF THE FORCE, THE ** (1933, Brit.) PR:A
PRIDE OF THE LEGION, THE ** (1932) PR:A
PRIDE OF THE MARINES ** (1936) PR:A
PRIDE OF THE MARINES **** (1945) PR:C
PRIDE OF THE NAVY *½ (1939) PR:A
PRIDE OF THE PLAINS ** (1944) PR:A
PRIDE OF THE WEST **½ (1938) PR:A
PRIDE OF THE YANKEES, THE *** (1942) PR:AA**
PRIEST OF LOVE **½ (1981, Brit.) PR:O
PRIEST OF ST. PAULI, THE ** (1970, Ger.) PR:C
PRIEST'S WIFE, THE * (1971, It./Fr.) PR:O
PRIMA DELLA REVOLUTIONA
(SEE:BEFORE THE REVOLUTION)
PRIMAL SCREAM * (1988) PR:O
PRIME CUT * (1972) PR:O**
PRIME MINISTER, THE * (1941, Brit.) PR:A
PRIME OF MISS JEAN BRODIE, THE ***½
(1969, Brit.) PR:C
PRIME RISK **½ (1985) PR:C
PRIME TIME, THE zero (1960) PR:O
PRIMITIVE LOVE * (1966, It.) PR:O
PRIMITIVES, THE ** (1962, Brit.) PR:A
PRIMROSE PATH, THE ** (1934, Brit.) PR:A
PRIMROSE PATH *** (1940) PR:C
PRINCE AND THE PAUPER, THE ***½
(1937) PR:AA
PRINCE AND THE PAUPER, THE *½ (1969) PR:AA
PRINCE AND THE PAUPER, THE
(SEE:CROSSED SWORDS)
PRINCE AND THE SHOWGIRL, THE ***½
(1957, Brit.) PR:A
PRINCE JACK ** (1985) PR:A
PRINCE OF ARCADIA **½ (1933, Brit.) PR:AA
PRINCE OF DARKNESS * (1987) PR:O**
PRINCE OF DIAMONDS ** (1930) PR:A
PRINCE OF FOXES **** (1949) PR:C
PRINCE OF PEACE, THE *½ (1951) PR:AA
PRINCE OF PIRATES **½ (1953) PR:A
PRINCE OF PLAYERS ***½ (1955) PR:C
PRINCE OF THE BLUE GRASS
(SEE:PRIDE OF THE BLUE GRASS)
PRINCE OF THE CITY ***½ (1981) PR:O
PRINCE OF THE PLAINS ** (1949) PR:A
PRINCE OF THIEVES, THE ** (1948) PR:A
PRINCE VALIANT **½ (1954) PR:A
PRINCE WHO WAS A THIEF, THE **½ (1951) PR:A
PRINCESS, THE
(SEE:TIME IN THE SUN)
PRINCESS ACADEMY, THE zero
(1987, US/Yugo./Fr.) PR:C-O
PRINCESS AND THE MAGIC FROG, THE **
(1965) PR:AA
PRINCESS AND THE PIRATE, THE * (1944) PR:A**
PRINCESS AND THE PLUMBER, THE **
(1930) PR:A
PRINCESS BRIDE, THE ***½ (1987) PR:A-C
PRINCESS CHARMING ** (1935, Brit.) PR:A
PRINCESS COMES ACROSS, THE *** (1936) PR:A
PRINCESS OF THE NILE *½ (1954) PR:AA
PRINCESS O'HARA ** (1935) PR:A
PRINCESS O'ROURKE *** (1943) PR:A
PRINCIPAL, THE *½ (1987) PR:O
PRINSESSAN
(SEE:TIME IN THE SUN, A)
PRIORITIES ON PARADE *½ (1942) PR:A
PRISM ** (1971) PR:C
PRISON **½ (1988) PR:O
PRISON BREAK ** (1938) PR:A
PRISON BREAKER ** (1936, Brit.) PR:A
PRISON CAMP
(SEE:FUGITIVE FROM A PRISON CAMP)
PRISON FARM ** (1938) PR:A

PRISON GIRL *½ (1942) PR:A
PRISON NURSE ** (1938) PR:A
PRISON SHADOWS * (1936) PR:A
PRISON SHIP ** (1945) PR:C
PRISON TRAIN *½ (1938) PR:A
PRISON WARDEN ** (1949) PR:A
PRISON WITHOUT BARS ** (1939, Brit.) PR:A
PRISONER, THE ***½ (1955, Brit.) PR:A
PRISONER OF CORBAL ** (1939, Brit.) PR:C
PRISONER OF JAPAN *½ (1942) PR:A
PRISONER OF SECOND AVENUE, THE *
(1975) PR:A-C**
PRISONER OF SHARK ISLAND, THE ****
(1936) PR:A
PRISONER OF THE IRON MASK **
(1962, Fr./It.) PR:A
PRISONER OF THE VOLGA *½ (1960, Fr./It.) PR:C
PRISONER OF WAR ** (1954) PR:C
PRISONER OF ZENDA, THE *** (1937) PR:A**
PRISONER OF ZENDA, THE * (1952) PR:A**
PRISONER OF ZENDA, THE ** (1979) PR:A
PRISONERS *½ (1929) PR:A
PRISONERS IN PETTICOATS *½ (1950) PR:A
PRISONERS OF THE CASBAH * (1953) PR:A
PRIVATE ACCESS * (1988, It.) PR:C-O**
PRIVATE AFFAIRS
(SEE:PUBLIC STENOGRAPHER)
PRIVATE AFFAIRS ** (1940) PR:A
PRIVATE AFFAIRS OF BEL AMI, THE ***
(1947) PR:A
PRIVATE ANGELO **½ (1949, Brit.) PR:A
PRIVATE BENJAMIN **½ (1980) PR:O
PRIVATE BUCKAROO ** (1942) PR:A
PRIVATE COLLECTION **½ (1972, Aus.) PR:O
PRIVATE DETECTIVE ** (1939) PR:A
PRIVATE DETECTIVE 62 ** (1933) PR:A
PRIVATE DUTY NURSES ** (1972) PR:O
PRIVATE ENTERPRISE, A *½ (1975, Brit.) PR:A
PRIVATE EYES **½ (1953) PR:A
PRIVATE EYES, THE **½ (1980) PR:A
PRIVATE FILES OF J. EDGAR HOOVER, THE **½
(1978) PR:C
PRIVATE FUNCTION, A * (1985, Brit.) PR:O**
PRIVATE HELL 36 **½ (1954) PR:C
PRIVATE INFORMATION *½ (1952, Brit.) PR:A
PRIVATE JONES ** (1933) PR:A
PRIVATE LESSONS * (1981) PR:O
PRIVATE LIFE
(SEE:VERY PRIVATE AFFAIR, A)
**PRIVATE LIFE OF DON JUAN, THE **
(1934, Brit.) PR:A**
PRIVATE LIFE OF HENRY VIII, THE **
(1933) PR:A-C**
PRIVATE LIFE OF LOUIS XIV ** (1936, Ger.) PR:A
PRIVATE LIFE OF SHERLOCK HOLMES, THE ***½
(1970, Brit.) PR:C
PRIVATE LIVES *** (1931) PR:A
PRIVATE LIVES OF ADAM AND EVE, THE *½
(1961) PR:C
PRIVATE LIVES OF ELIZABETH AND ESSEX, THE
*****½ (1939) PR:A**
PRIVATE NAVY OF SGT. O'FARRELL, THE *
(1968) PR:A
PRIVATE NUMBER ** (1936) PR:A
PRIVATE NURSE * (1941) PR:A
PRIVATE PARTS * (1972) PR:O
PRIVATE POOLEY ** (1962, Brit./E./Ger.) PR:C
PRIVATE POTTER ** (1963, Brit.) PR:A-C
PRIVATE PROPERTY *** (1960) PR:O
PRIVATE RESORT * (1985) PR:O
PRIVATE RIGHT, THE ** (1967, Brit.) PR:A
PRIVATE ROAD *½ (1971, Brit.) PR:O
PRIVATE SCANDAL, A *½ (1932) PR:A
PRIVATE SCANDAL ** (1934) PR:A
PRIVATE SCHOOL zero (1983) PR:O
PRIVATE SECRETARY, THE ** (1935, Brit.) PR:A
PRIVATE SHOW *½ (1985, Phil.) PR:O
PRIVATE SNUFFY SMITH
(SEE:SNUFFY SMITH, YARDBIRD)
PRIVATE WAR OF MAJOR BENSON, THE **½
(1955) PR:A
PRIVATE WORE SKIRTS, THE
(SEE:NEVER WAVE AT A WAC)
PRIVATE WORLDS *** (1935) PR:A-C
PRIVATE'S AFFAIR, A ** (1959) PR:A
PRIVATES ON PARADE * (1984, Brit.) PR:O
PRIVATE'S PROGRESS ** (1956, Brit.) PR:A

PRIVATKLINIK PROF. LUND
(SEE:DAS LETZTE GEHEIMNIS)
PRIVILEGE *½ (1967, Brit.) PR:A
PRIVILEGED *½ (1982, Brit.) PR:C-O
PRIZE, THE ** (1952, Fr.) PR:A
PRIZE, THE **½ (1963) PR:C
PRIZE FIGHTER, THE *½ (1979) PR:C
PRIZE OF ARMS, A ** (1962, Brit.) PR:A
PRIZE OF GOLD, A *** (1955) PR:A
PRIZED AS A MATE!
(SEE:SPOILED ROTTEN)
PRIZEFIGHTER AND THE LADY, THE *
(1933) PR:A**
PRIZZI'S HONOR * (1985) PR:O**
PRO, THE
(SEE:NUMBER ONE)
PROBATION ** (1932) PR:A
PROBLEM GIRLS ** (1953) PR:A
PROCES DE JEANNE D'ARC
(SEE:TRIAL OF JOAN OF ARC)
PRODIGAL, THE *½ (1931) PR:A
PRODIGAL, THE * (1955) PR:A-C
PRODIGAL, THE ** (1984) PR:A
PRODIGAL GUN
(SEE:MINUTE TO PRAY, A SECOND TO DIE, A)
PRODIGAL SON, THE ** (1935) PR:A
PRODIGAL SON, THE ** (1964, Jap.) PR:C
PRODUCERS, THE ** (1967) PR:O**
PROFESSIONAL BLONDE
(SEE:BLONDE FROM PEKING)
PROFESSIONAL BRIDE
(SEE:HEAD GUY)
PROFESSIONAL GUN, A
(SEE:MERCENARY, THE)
PROFESSIONAL SOLDIER **½ (1936) PR:A
PROFESSIONAL SWEETHEART *** (1933) PR:A
PROFESSIONALS, THE *½ (1960, Brit.) PR:A
PROFESSIONALS, THE ***½ (1966) PR:O
PROFESSOR BEWARE **½ (1938) PR:A
PROFESSOR TIM **½ (1957, Ireland) PR:A
PROFILE *½ (1954, Brit.) PR:A
PROFILE OF TERROR, THE
(SEE:SADIST, THE)
PROJECT: KILL * (1976) PR:O
PROJECT MOONBASE * (1953) PR:A
PROJECT M7 *** (1953, Brit.) PR:A
PROJECT X * (1949) PR:A
PROJECT X **½ (1968) PR:A
PROJECT X * (1987) PR:A**
PROJECTED MAN, THE ** (1967, Brit.) PR:A
PROJECTIONIST, THE ***½ (1970) PR:A-C
PROLOGUE *** (1970, Can.) PR:C
PROM NIGHT * (1980) PR:O
PROMISE, THE * (1969, Brit.) PR:A
PROMISE, THE *½ (1979) PR:A-C
PROMISE AT DAWN **½ (1970, US/Fr.) PR:A
PROMISE HER ANYTHING
(SEE:PROMISES! PROMISES!)
PROMISE HER ANYTHING ** (1966, Brit.) PR:A
PROMISE OF A BED, A
(SEE:THIS, THAT AND THE OTHER)
PROMISED LAND * (1988) PR:O**
PROMISES IN THE DARK ** (1979) PR:C
PROMISES, PROMISES zero (1963) PR:O
PROMOTER, THE *** (1952, Brit.) PR:A
PROPER TIME, THE *½ (1959) PR:A
PROPERTY ** (1979) PR:A-C
PROPHECIES OF NOSTRADAMUS **½
(1974, Jap.) PR:A
PROPHECY * (1979) PR:C-O
PROSPERITY ** (1932) PR:A
PROSTITUTE **½ (1980, Brit.) PR:O
PROSTITUTION **½ (1965, Fr.) PR:C
PROTECTOR, THE ** (1985, Hong Kong/US) PR:O
PROTECTORS, THE
(SEE:COMPANY OF KILLERS)
PROTECTORS, BOOK 1, THE * (1981) PR:O
PROTOCOL ** (1984) PR:A-C
PROUD AND THE DAMNED, THE *½
(1972) PR:C-O
PROUD AND THE PROFANE, THE *½
(1956) PR:A-C
PROUD, DAMNED AND DEAD
(SEE:PROUD AND THE DAMNED, THE)
PROUD ONES, THE *** (1956) PR:A
PROUD REBEL, THE ***½ (1958) PR:A
PROUD RIDER, THE *** (1971, Can.) PR:C

Finding entries in **THE MOTION PICTURE GUIDE** ™

Years 1929-83	Volumes I-IX
1984	Volume IX
1985	1986 ANNUAL
1986	1987 ANNUAL
1987	1988 ANNUAL
1988	1989 ANNUAL

STAR RATINGS

★★★★★ Masterpiece
★★★★ Excellent
★★★ Good
★★ Fair
★ Poor
zero Without Merit

PARENTAL RECOMMENDATION (PR:)

AA Good for Children
A   Acceptable for Children
C   Cautionary, some objectionable scenes
O   Objectionable for Children

BOLD: Films on Videocassette

PROUD VALLEY, THE ** (1941, Brit.) PR:A
PROVIDENCE **** (1977, Fr.) PR:O
PROWL GIRLS zero (1968) PR:O
PROWLER, THE *** (1951) PR:C-O
PROWLER, THE * (1981) PR:O
PRUDENCE AND THE PILL **½ (1968, Brit.) PR:O
PRZYPADEK
  (SEE:BLIND CHANCE)
PSYCH-OUT **½ (1968) PR:O
PSYCHE 59 *½ (1964, Brit.) PR:C
PSYCHIC, THE * (1979, It.) PR:O
PSYCHIC KILLER *½ (1975) PR:O
PSYCHIC LOVER, THE
  (SEE:SWEET SMELL OF LOVE)
PSYCHO ***** (1960) PR:O
PSYCHO A GO-GO! * (1965) PR:O
PSYCHO-CIRCUS ** (1967, Brit.) PR:O
PSYCHO FROM TEXAS zero (1982) PR:O
PSYCHO KILLERS
  (SEE:MANIA)
PSYCHO III *** (1986) PR:O
PSYCHO II **½ (1983) PR:O
PSYCHOMANIA *½ (1964) PR:O
PSYCHOMANIA ** (1974, Brit.) PR:O
PSYCHOPATH, THE *** (1966, Brit.) PR:O
PSYCHOPATH, THE * (1973) PR:O
PSYCHOS IN LOVE *½ (1987) PR:O
PSYCHOTRONIC MAN, THE * (1980) PR:O
PSYCHOUT FOR MURDER ** (1971, Arg./It.) PR:O
PSYCOSISSIMO ** (1962, It.) PR:O
PT 109 *** (1963) PR:A
PT RAIDERS
  (SEE:SHIP THAT DIED OF SHAME, THE)
PT RAIDERS
  (SEE:SHIP THAT DIED OF SHAME)
P'TANG, YANG, KIPPERBANG
  (SEE:KIPPERBANG)
PUBERTY BLUES **½ (1983, Aus.) PR:O
PUBLIC AFFAIR, A *** (1962) PR:C
PUBLIC BE HANGED, THE
  (SEE:WORLD GONE MAD, THE)
PUBLIC COWBOY NO. 1 *** (1937) PR:A
PUBLIC DEB NO. 1 *½ (1940) PR:C
PUBLIC DEFENDER, THE *** (1931) PR:A
PUBLIC ENEMIES *** (1941) PR:A
PUBLIC ENEMY, THE ***** (1931) PR:O
PUBLIC ENEMY'S WIFE *** (1936) PR:A
PUBLIC EYE, THE *½ (1972, Brit.) PR:A
PUBLIC HERO NO. 1 ***½ (1935) PR:A
PUBLIC LIFE OF HENRY THE NINTH, THE **
  (1934, Brit.) PR:A
PUBLIC MENACE **½ (1935) PR:C
PUBLIC NUISANCE NO. 1 *½ (1936, Brit.) PR:A
PUBLIC OPINION ** (1935) PR:A
PUBLIC PIGEON NO. 1 **½ (1957) PR:A
PUBLIC STENOGRAPHER * (1935) PR:C
PUBLIC WEDDING ** (1937) PR:A
PUDDIN' HEAD ** (1941) PR:AA
PUFNSTUF ** (1970) PR:AA
PULGARCITO
  (SEE:TOM THUMB)
PULP ***½ (1972, Brit.) PR:C
PULSE *** (1988) PR:C
PULSEBEAT * (1986, Sp.) PR:O
PUMPKIN EATER, THE **** (1964, Brit.) PR:O
PUMPKINHEAD ** (1988) PR:O
PUNCH AND JUDY MAN, THE ** (1963, Brit.) PR:A
PUNCHLINE ***½ (1988) PR:C
PUNISHMENT PARK **½ (1971) PR:O
PUO UNA MORTA RIVIVERE PER AMORE?
  (SEE:VENUS IN FURS)
PUPPET ON A CHAIN *½ (1971, Brit.) PR:O
PUPPETS OF FATE
  (SEE:WOLVES OF THE UNDERWORLD)
PURCHASE PRICE, THE * (1932) PR:O
PURE HELL OF ST. TRINIAN'S, THE ***
  (1961, Brit.) PR:C
PURE S **½ (1976, Aus.) PR:O
PURLIE VICTORIOUS
  (SEE:GONE ARE THE DAYS)
PURPLE GANG, THE **½ (1960) PR:O
PURPLE HAZE **½ (1982) PR:O
PURPLE HEART, THE **** (1944) PR:C-O
PURPLE HEART DIARY **½ (1951) PR:A
PURPLE HEARTS ** (1984) PR:C-O
PURPLE HILLS, THE ** (1961) PR:O
PURPLE MASK, THE **½ (1955) PR:A
PURPLE NOON *** (1961, Fr./It.) PR:O
PURPLE PLAIN, THE *** (1954, Brit.) PR:A-C
PURPLE RAIN ** (1984) PR:O
PURPLE RIDERS, THE
  (SEE:PURPLE VIGILANTES, THE)
PURPLE ROSE OF CAIRO, THE *** (1985) PR:C
PURPLE TAXI, THE * (1977, Fr./It./Ireland) PR:O
PURPLE V, THE ** (1943) PR:O
PURPLE VIGILANTES, THE *** (1938) PR:A
PURSE STRINGS * (1933, Brit.) PR:A
PURSUED **½ (1934) PR:A

PURSUED ***½ (1947) PR:C-O
PURSUERS, THE ** (1961, Brit.) PR:A
PURSUIT ** (1935) PR:A
PURSUIT *½ (1975) PR:O
PURSUIT OF D.B. COOPER, THE * (1981) PR:C
PURSUIT OF HAPPINESS, THE *** (1934) PR:C
PURSUIT OF HAPPINESS, THE **½ (1971) PR:O
PURSUIT OF THE GRAF SPEE *½
  (1957, Brit.) PR:A
PURSUIT TO ALGIERS **½ (1945) PR:A
PUSHER, THE ** (1960) PR:O
PUSHERS, THE
  (SEE:HOOKED GENERATION, THE)
PUSHOVER ***½ (1954) PR:A
PUSHOVER, THE
  (SEE:MYTH, THE)
PUSS AND KRAM
  (SEE:HUGS AND KISSES)
PUSS "N' BOOTS ** (1964, Mex.) PR:AA
PUSS "N' BOOTS ** (1967, Ger.) PR:AA
PUSS OCH KRAM
  (SEE:HUGS AND KISSES)
PUSSYCAT ALLEY **½ (1965, Brit.) PR:O
PUSSYCAT, PUSSYCAT, I LOVE YOU * (1970) PR:O
PUT ON THE SPOT ** (1936) PR:A
PUT UP OR SHUT UP * (1968, Arg.) PR:O
PUTNEY SWOPE ** (1969) PR:O
PUTTIN' ON THE RITZ ** (1930) PR:A
PUTYOVKA V ZHIZN
  (SEE:ROAD TO LIFE)
PUZZLE OF A DOWNFALL CHILD **½ (1970) PR:O
PYGMALION ***** (1938, Brit.) PR:A
PYGMY ISLAND ** (1950) PR:A
PYRO ** (1964, US/Sp.) PR:O
PYRO-THE THING WITHOUT A FACE
  (SEE:PYRO)
PYX, THE *** (1973, Can.) PR:O

Q ***½ (1982) PR:O
Q PLANES
  (SEE:CLOUDS OVER EUROPE)
Q-SHIPS
  (SEE:BLOCKADE)
QUACKSER FORTUNE HAS A COUSIN IN THE
  BRONX ** (1970) PR:A-C
QUADROON * (1972) PR:O
QUADROPHENIA **** (1979, Brit.) PR:O
QUAI DE GRENELLE
  (SEE:DANGER IS A WOMAN)
QUAI DES BRUMES
  (SEE:PORT OF SHADOWS)
QUALCOSA DI BIONDO ** (1985, It.) PR:O
QUALITY STREET *½ (1937) PR:A
QUANDO EL AMOR RIE *½ (1933) PR:A
QUANTEZ ** (1957) PR:A
QUANTRILL'S RAIDERS **½ (1958) PR:A
QUARE FELLOW, THE *** (1962, Brit.) PR:C-O
QUARTERBACK, THE ** (1940) PR:A
QUARTET **** (1949, Brit.) PR:C
QUARTET ** (1981, Brit./Fr.) PR:C
QUARTIERE ** (1987, It.) PR:O
QUATERMASS AND THE PIT
  (SEE:FIVE MILLION YEARS TO EARTH)
QUATERMASS CONCLUSION **½
  (1980, Brit.) PR:C
QUATERMASS EXPERIMENT, THE
  (SEE:CREEPING UNKNOWN, THE)
QUATERMASS II
  (SEE:ENEMY FROM SPACE)
QUE LA BETE MEURE
  (SEE:THIS MAN MUST DIE)
QUE LA FETE COMMENCE
  (SEE:LET JOY REIGN SUPREME)
QUEBEC **½ (1951) PR:A
QUEEN BEE *** (1955) PR:C
QUEEN BEE
  (SEE:CONJUGAL BED, THE)
QUEEN CHRISTINA ***** (1933) PR:A
QUEEN FOR A DAY **½ (1951) PR:A
QUEEN HIGH **½ (1930) PR:A
QUEEN OF ATLANTIS
  (SEE:SIREN OF ATLANTIS)
QUEEN OF BABYLON, THE ** (1956, It.) PR:A
QUEEN OF BLOOD *** (1966) PR:O
QUEEN OF BROADWAY *½ (1942) PR:A
QUEEN OF BROADWAY
  (SEE:KID DYNAMITE)
QUEEN OF BURLESQUE ** (1946) PR:C
QUEEN OF CLUBS
  (SEE:LOVE CYCLES)

QUEEN OF CRIME
  (SEE:KATE PLUS TEN)
QUEEN OF DESTINY
  (SEE:SIXTY GLORIOUS YEARS)
QUEEN OF HEARTS **½ (1936, Brit.) PR:A
QUEEN OF OUTER SPACE ** (1958) PR:A
QUEEN OF SHEBA * (1953, It.) PR:A
QUEEN OF SPADES ***½ (1948, Brit.) PR:A-C
QUEEN OF SPADES *** (1961, USSR) PR:C
QUEEN OF SPIES
  (SEE:JOAN OF OZARK)
QUEEN OF THE AMAZONS ** (1947) PR:A
QUEEN OF THE CANNIBALS
  (SEE:DR. BUTCHER M.D.)
QUEEN OF THE MOB **½ (1940) PR:C
QUEEN OF THE NIGHTCLUBS **½ (1929) PR:A-C
QUEEN OF THE NILE ** (1964, It.) PR:C
QUEEN OF THE PIRATES ** (1961, It./Ger.) PR:C
QUEEN OF THE WEST
  (SEE:CATTLE QUEEN)
QUEEN OF THE YUKON ** (1940) PR:A
QUEENS, THE *½ (1968, It./Fr.) PR:O
QUEEN'S AFFAIR, THE
  (SEE:RUNAWAY QUEEN, THE)
QUEEN'S GUARDS, THE ** (1963, Brit.) PR:C
QUEEN'S HUSBAND, THE
  (SEE:ROYAL BED, THE)
QUEEN'S SWORDSMEN, THE **½
  (1963, Mex.) PR:AA
QUEER CARGO
  (SEE:PIRATES OF THE SEVEN SEAS)
QUEI DISPERATI CHE PUZZANO DI SUDORE E DI
  MORTE
  (SEE:BULLET FOR SANDOVAL, A)
QUEI TEMERARI SULLE LORO PAZZE, SCATENATE,
  SCALCINATE CARRIOLE
  (SEE:THOSE DARING YOUNG MEN IN THEIR
  JAUNTY JALOPIES)
QUEIMADA
  (SEE:BURN!)
QUELLA VILLA ACCANTO AL CIMITERO
  (SEE:HOUSE BY THE CEMETERY, THE)
QUELLI CHE NON MUOIONO
  (SEE:GUILT IS NOT MINE)
QUELQUES JOURS PRES
  (SEE:MATTER OF DAYS, A)
QUELQU'UN DERRIERE LA PORTE
  (SEE:SOMEONE BEHIND THE DOOR)
QUEMADA!
  (SEE:BURN!)
QUENTIN DURWARD *** (1955) PR:A
QUERELLE ** (1983, Ger./Fr.) PR:O
QUERY *** (1945, Brit.) PR:O
QUEST FOR FIRE *** (1982, Fr./Can.) PR:O
QUEST FOR LOVE *** (1971, Brit.) PR:C
QUESTI FANTASMI
  (SEE:GHOSTS—ITALIAN STYLE)
QUESTION, THE ***½ (1977, Fr.) PR:O
QUESTION OF ADULTERY, A ** (1959, Brit.) PR:C
QUESTION OF SILENCE ***½ (1984, Neth.) PR:O
QUESTION OF SUSPENSE, A ** (1961, Brit.) PR:C
QUESTION 7 **½ (1961, US/Ger.) PR:C
QUESTIONE DI PELLE
  (SEE:CHECKERBOARD)
QUICK AND THE DEAD, THE ** (1963) PR:O
QUICK, BEFORE IT MELTS **½ (1964) PR:A
QUICK GUN, THE **½ (1964) PR:A
QUICK, LET'S GET MARRIED zero (1965) PR:C
QUICK MILLIONS *** (1931) PR:C
QUICK MILLIONS **½ (1939) PR:A
QUICK MONEY ** (1938) PR:A
QUICK ON THE TRIGGER ** (1949) PR:A
QUICKSAND *** (1950) PR:C
QUICKSILVER * (1986) PR:A-C
QUIEN SABE?
  (SEE:BULLET FOR THE GENERAL, A)
QUIET AMERICAN, THE **½ (1958) PR:A
QUIET COOL **½ (1986) PR:O
QUIET DAY IN BELFAST, A **½ (1974, Can.) PR:C
QUIET EARTH, THE **½ (1985, New Zealand) PR:O
QUIET GUN, THE **½ (1957) PR:A
QUIET MAN, THE ***** (1952) PR:A
QUIET PLACE IN THE COUNTRY, A **½
  (1970, It./Fr.) PR:O
QUIET PLEASE ** (1938, Brit.) PR:A
QUIET PLEASE, MURDER **½ (1942) PR:A
QUIET WEDDING *** (1941, Brit.) PR:A
QUIET WEEKEND **½ (1948, Brit.) PR:A
QUIET WOMAN, THE ** (1951, Brit.) PR:A
QUILLER MEMORANDUM, THE ***
  (1966, Brit.) PR:C
QUILOMBO *** (1986, Braz.) PR:O
QUINCANNON, FRONTIER SCOUT * (1956) PR:A
QUINTET zero (1979) PR:C-O
QUITTER, THE
  (SEE:QUITTERS, THE)
QUITTERS, THE * (1934) PR:A
QUO VADIS ***½ (1951) PR:C

R

RABBI AND THE SHIKSE, THE ** (1976, Israel) PR:A
RABBIT, RUN * (1970) PR:O
RABBIT TEST * (1978) PR:C-O
RABBIT TRAP, THE ** (1959) PR:A
RABBLE, THE **½ (1965, Jap.) PR:A
RABID * (1976, Can.) PR:O
RACCONTI D'ESTATE
(SEE:LOVE ON THE RIVIERA)
RACE FOR LIFE, A *½ (1955, Brit.) PR:A
RACE FOR THE YANKEE ZEPHYR
(SEE:TREASURE OF THE YANKEE ZEPHYR)
RACE FOR YOUR LIFE, CHARLIE BROWN **½ (1977) PR:AA
RACE GANG
(SEE:GREEN COCKATOO, THE)
RACE STREET **½ (1948) PR:C
RACE WITH THE DEVIL **½ (1975) PR:C
RACERS, THE * (1955) PR:A**
RACETRACK ** (1933) PR:A
RACHEL AND THE STRANGER * (1948) PR:A**
RACHEL CADE
(SEE:SINS OF RACHEL CADE, THE)
RACHEL, RACHEL ***½ (1968) PR:A-C
RACING BLOOD zero (1938) PR:A
RACING BLOOD *½ (1954) PR:A
RACING FEVER zero (1964) PR:C
RACING LADY *½ (1937) PR:A
RACING LUCK *½ (1935) PR:A
RACING LUCK
(SEE:RED HOT TIRES)
RACING LUCK zero (1948) PR:A
RACING ROMANCE ** (1937, Brit.) PR:A
RACING STRAIN, THE * (1933) PR:A
RACING WITH THE MOON **½ (1984) PR:C
RACING YOUTH * (1932) PR:A
RACK, THE **½ (1956) PR:A
RACKET, THE ** (1951) PR:C**
RACKET BUSTERS *** (1938) PR:A
RACKET MAN, THE ** (1944) PR:A
RACKETEER, THE ** (1929) PR:A
RACKETEERS IN EXILE *½ (1937) PR:A
RACKETEERS OF THE RANGE **½ (1939) PR:A
RACKETY RAX **½ (1932) PR:A
RACQUET zero (1979) PR:O
RAD * (1986) PR:A-C
RADAN
(SEE:RODAN)
RADAR SECRET SERVICE * (1950) PR:A
RADIO CAB MURDER ** (1954, Brit.) PR:A
RADIO CITY REVELS ** (1938) PR:A
RADIO DAYS ***½ (1987) PR:A-C
RADIO FOLLIES **½ (1935, Brit.) PR:A
RADIO LOVER ** (1936, Brit.) PR:A
RADIO MURDER MYSTERY, THE
(SEE:LOVE IS ON THE AIR)
RADIO ON **½ (1980, Brit./Ger.) PR:C
RADIO PARADE OF 1935
(SEE:RADIO FOLLIES)
RADIO PATROL * (1932) PR:A
RADIO PIRATES ** (1935, Brit.) PR:A
RADIO REVELS OF 1942
(SEE:SWING IT SOLDIER)
RADIO STARS ON PARADE *½ (1945) PR:A
RADIOACTIVE DREAMS *½ (1986) PR:O
RADIOGRAFIA D'UN COLPO D'ORO
(SEE:THEY CAME TO ROB LAS VEGAS)
RADISHES AND CARROTS
(SEE:TWILIGHT PATH)
RADON
(SEE:RODAN)
RADON THE FLYING MONSTER
(SEE:RODAN)
RADIO STAR, THE
(SEE:LOUDSPEAKER, THE)
RAFFERTY AND THE GOLD DUST TWINS ** (1975) PR:C-O
RAFFICA DI COLTELLI
(SEE:KNIVES OF THE AVENGER)
RAFFLES ***½ (1930) PR:A
RAFFLES *** (1939) PR:A
RAFTER ROMANCE ** (1934) PR:A
RAG DOLL
(SEE:YOUNG, WILLING AND EAGER)
RAGE, THE zero (1963, US/Mex.) PR:O
RAGE **½ (1966, US/Mex.) PR:C
RAGE *½ (1972) PR:C
RAGE
(SEE:RABID)
RAGE AT DAWN **½ (1955) PR:A
RAGE IN HEAVEN ** (1941) PR:C
RAGE OF HONOR ** (1987) PR:O
RAGE OF PARIS, THE **½ (1938) PR:A
RAGE OF THE BUCCANEERS * (1963, It.) PR:A
RAGE TO LIVE, A *½ (1965) PR:C
RAGE WITHIN, THE
(SEE:RAGE, THE)
RAGGED ANGELS
(SEE:THEY SHALL HAVE MUSIC)
RAGGEDY ANN AND ANDY ** (1977) PR:AA
RAGGEDY MAN * (1981) PR:C**
RAGING BULL *** (1980) PR:O**
RAGING MOON, THE
(SEE:LONG AGO TOMORROW)
RAGING TIDE, THE ** (1951) PR:A
RAGING WATERS
(SEE:GREEN PROMISE, THE)
RAGMAN'S DAUGHTER, THE **½ (1974, Brit.) PR:C
RAGS TO RICHES *½ (1941) PR:A
RAGTIME * (1981) PR:C**
RAGTIME COWBOY JOE ** (1940) PR:A
RAID, THE *** (1954) PR:A-C
RAID ON ROMMEL * (1971) PR:C
RAIDERS, THE **½ (1952) PR:A
RAIDERS, THE **½ (1964) PR:A
RAIDERS FROM BENEATH THE SEA ** (1964) PR:A
RAIDERS OF LEYTE GULF *½ (1963, US/Phil.) PR:A
RAIDERS OF OLD CALIFORNIA *½ (1957) PR:A
RAIDERS OF RED GAP ** (1944) PR:A
RAIDERS OF SAN JOAQUIN ** (1943) PR:A
RAIDERS OF SUNSET PASS ** (1943) PR:A
RAIDERS OF THE BORDER ** (1944) PR:A
RAIDERS OF THE DESERT ** (1941) PR:A
RAIDERS OF THE LOST ARK *** (1981) PR:C-O**
RAIDERS OF THE RANGE ** (1942) PR:A
RAIDERS OF THE SEVEN SEAS ** (1953) PR:A
RAIDERS OF THE SOUTH * (1947) PR:A
RAIDERS OF THE WEST *½ (1942) PR:A
RAIDERS OF TOMAHAWK CREEK **½ (1950) PR:A
RAILROAD MAN, THE **½ (1965, It.) PR:A
RAILROAD WORKERS **½ (1948, Swed.) PR:A
RAILROADED * (1947) PR:C**
RAILS INTO LARAMIE **½ (1954) PR:A
RAILWAY CHILDREN, THE *** (1971, Brit.) PR:A
RAIN **½ (1932) PR:C-O
RAIN FOR A DUSTY SUMMER *½ (1971, US/Sp.) PR:C
RAIN MAN ***½ (1988) PR:C-O
RAIN OR SHINE **½ (1930) PR:A
RAIN PEOPLE, THE * (1969) PR:C-O**
RAINBOW, THE ** (1944, USSR) PR:C
RAINBOW BOYS, THE **½ (1973, Can.) PR:A
RAINBOW BRITE AND THE STAR STEALER *½ (1985) PR:AA
RAINBOW ISLAND **½ (1944) PR:A
RAINBOW JACKET, THE ** (1954, Brit.) PR:A
RAINBOW MAN *½ (1929) PR:A
RAINBOW ON THE RIVER ** (1936) PR:A
RAINBOW OVER BROADWAY ** (1933) PR:A
RAINBOW OVER TEXAS ** (1946) PR:A
RAINBOW OVER THE RANGE *½ (1940) PR:A
RAINBOW OVER THE ROCKIES *½ (1947) PR:A
RAINBOW RANCH * (1933) PR:A
RAINBOW 'ROUND MY SHOULDER ** (1952) PR:A
RAINBOW TRAIL ** (1932) PR:A
RAINBOW VALLEY ** (1935) PR:A
RAINBOW'S END ** (1935) PR:A
RAINMAKER, THE * (1956) PR:A**
RAINMAKERS, THE *½ (1935) PR:A
RAINS CAME, THE ***½ (1939) PR:A
RAINS OF RANCHIPUR, THE *** (1955) PR:A
RAINTREE COUNTY * (1957) PR:C**
RAISE THE ROOF ** (1930) PR:A
RAISE THE TITANIC * (1980, Brit.) PR:A-C
RAISIN IN THE SUN, A ***½ (1961) PR:A
RAISING A RIOT ** (1957, Brit.) PR:A
RAISING ARIZONA * (1987) PR:C**
RAISING THE WIND
(SEE:BIG RACE, THE)
RAISING THE WIND
(SEE:ROOMMATES)
RAKE'S PROGRESS, THE
(SEE:NOTORIOUS GENTLEMAN)
RALLY 'ROUND THE FLAG, BOYS! ** (1958) PR:C
RAMBO: FIRST BLOOD, PART II zero (1985) PR:O
RAMBO III *½ (1988) PR:O
RAMONA ** (1936) PR:A
RAMPAGE ** (1963) PR:A
RAMPAGE AT APACHE WELLS ** (1966, Ger./Yugo.) PR:A
RAMPANT AGE, THE *½ (1930) PR:A
RAMPARTS WE WATCH, THE ** (1940) PR:A
RAMROD *** (1947) PR:A
RAMRODDER, THE * (1969) PR:O
RAMSBOTTOM RIDES AGAIN *½ (1956, Brit.) PR:A
RAN *** (1985, Jap./Fr.) PR:O**
RANCHO DELUXE **½ (1975) PR:C
RANCHO GRANDE *½ (1938, Mex.) PR:A
RANCHO GRANDE *½ (1940) PR:A
RANCHO NOTORIOUS ** (1952) PR:A**
RANDOLPH FAMILY, THE ** (1945, Brit.) PR:A
RANDOM HARVEST ***½ (1942) PR:A
RANDY RIDES ALONE **½ (1934) PR:A
RANDY STRIKES OIL
(SEE:FIGHTING TEXANS)
RANGE BEYOND THE BLUE *½ (1947) PR:A
RANGE BUSTERS, THE ** (1940) PR:A
RANGE DEFENDERS ** (1937) PR:A
RANGE FEUD, THE ** (1931) PR:A
RANGE JUSTICE ** (1949) PR:A
RANGE LAND ** (1949) PR:A
RANGE LAW ** (1931) PR:A
RANGE LAW * (1944) PR:A
RANGE RENEGADES *½ (1948) PR:A
RANGE WAR *½ (1939) PR:A
RANGER AND THE LADY, THE ** (1940) PR:A
RANGER COURAGE *½ (1937) PR:A
RANGER OF CHEROKEE STRIP ** (1949) PR:A
RANGER'S CODE, THE * (1933) PR:A
RANGERS OF CHEROKEE STRIP
(SEE:RANGER OF CHEROKEE STRIP)
RANGERS OF FORTUNE **½ (1940) PR:AA
RANGERS RIDE, THE *½ (1948) PR:A
RANGER'S ROUNDUP, THE *½ (1938) PR:A
RANGERS STEP IN, THE * (1937) PR:A
RANGERS TAKE OVER, THE *½ (1942) PR:A
RANGLE RIVER ** (1939, Aus.) PR:A
RANGO * (1931) PR:A
RANI RADOVI
(SEE:EARLY WORKS)
RANSOM
(SEE:TERRORISTS, THE)
RANSOM
(SEE:MANIAC!)
RANSOM *** (1956) PR:A
RAPE, THE **½ (1965, Gr.) PR:O
RAPE OF MALAYA
(SEE:TOWN LIKE ALICE, A)
RAPE OF THE SABINES, THE
(SEE:SHAME OF THE SABINE WOMEN, THE)
RAPE SQUAD
(SEE:ACT OF VENGEANCE)
RAPE, THE
(SEE:LE VIOL)
RAPPIN' ** (1985) PR:O
RAPTURE **½ (1950, It.) PR:A
RAPTURE **½ (1965) PR:C
RAQ LO B'SHABBAT
(SEE:IMPOSSIBLE ON SATURDAY)
RARE BREED, THE * (1966) PR:A**
RARE BREED ** (1984) PR:A
RASCAL *** (1969) PR:AA
RASCALS ** (1938) PR:AA
RASHOMON *** (1951, Jap.) PR:A-C**
RASPOUTINE ** (1954, Fr.) PR:C
RASPUTIN
(SEE:RASPUTIN AND THE EMPRESS)
RASPUTIN ** (1932, Ger.) PR:A
RASPUTIN **½ (1939, Fr.) PR:A
RASPUTIN *** (1985, USSR) PR:O
RASPUTIN AND THE EMPRESS **** (1932) PR:C
RASPUTIN THE MAD MONK
(SEE:RASPUTIN AND THE EMPRESS)

RASPUTIN—THE MAD MONK **½ (1966, Brit.) PR:C
RAT, THE *½ (1938, Brit.) PR:A
RAT *** (1960, Yugo.) PR:A
RAT FINK *** (1965) PR:C
RAT PFINK AND BOO BOO ** (1966) PR:A
RAT RACE, THE **½ (1960) PR:A
RAT SAVIOUR, THE *** (1977, Yugo.) PR:A
RATATAPLAN **½ (1979, It.) PR:A
RATBOY **½ (1986) PR:C
RATIONING ** (1944) PR:A
RATON PASS **½ (1951) PR:A
RATS, THE *** (1955, Ger.) PR:A
RATS ARE COMING! THE WEREWOLVES ARE HERE!, THE zero (1972) PR:O
RATS OF TOBRUK *½ (1951, Aus.) PR:A
RATS, THE (SEE:DEADLY EYES)
RATTLE OF A SIMPLE MAN **½ (1964, Brit.) PR:C
RATTLERS * (1976) PR:C
RAUTHA SKIKKJAN (SEE:HAGBARD AND SIGNE)
RAVAGER, THE * (1970) PR:O
RAVAGERS, THE ** (1965, U.S./Phil.) PR:A
RAVAGERS, THE * (1979) PR:A
RAVEN, THE * (1935) PR:A**
RAVEN, THE * (1948, Fr.) PR:A**
RAVEN, THE ***½ (1963) PR:C
RAVEN'S END **½ (1970, Swed.) PR:A
RAVISHING IDIOT, A ** (1966, It./Fr.) PR:A
RAW COURAGE zero (1984) PR:O
RAW DEAL *** (1948) PR:A-C
RAW DEAL **½ (1977, Aus.) PR:A
RAW DEAL ** (1986) PR:O
RAW EDGE ** (1956) PR:A
RAW FORCE zero (1982) PR:O
RAW MEAT (SEE:DEATHLINE)
RAW TIMBER * (1937) PR:A
RAW WEEKEND * (1964) PR:O
RAW WIND IN EDEN *½ (1958) PR:A
RAWHEAD REX * (1987, Brit.) PR:O
RAWHIDE **½ (1938) PR:A
RAWHIDE * (1951) PR:A**
RAWHIDE HALO, THE (SEE:SHOOT OUT AT BIG SAC)
RAWHIDE RANGERS ** (1941) PR:A
RAWHIDE TRAIL, THE *½ (1958) PR:A
RAWHIDE YEARS, THE ** (1956) PR:A
RAYMIE **½ (1960) PR:AA
RAZORBACK **½ (1984, Aus.) PR:O
RAZOR'S EDGE, THE ** (1946) PR:C**
RAZOR'S EDGE, THE **½ (1984) PR:C-O
RE-ANIMATOR **½ (1985) PR:O
RE: LUCKY LUCIANO *** (1974, Fr./It.) PR:O
RE-UNION (SEE:IN LOVE WITH LIFE)
REACH FOR GLORY **½ (1963, Brit.) PR:A
REACH FOR THE SKY *** (1957, Brit.) PR:A
REACHING FOR THE MOON ** (1931) PR:A
REACHING FOR THE SUN **½ (1941) PR:A
REACHING OUT *½ (1983) PR:O
READY FOR LOVE **½ (1934) PR:A
READY FOR THE PEOPLE ** (1964) PR:A
READY, WILLING AND ABLE *½ (1937) PR:A
REAL BLOKE, A ** (1935, Brit.) PR:A
REAL GENIUS ** (1985) PR:C
REAL GLORY, THE ***½ (1939) PR:A
REAL GONE GIRLS, THE (SEE:MAN FROM O.R.G.Y., THE)
REAL LIFE *** (1979) PR:C**
REAL LIFE ** (1984, Brit.) PR:C
REALM OF FORTUNE, THE *** (1986, Mex.) PR:O
REAP THE WILD WIND ***½ (1942) PR:A
REAR WINDOW *** (1954) PR:C**
REASON TO LIVE, A REASON TO DIE, A *½ (1974, It./Fr./Ger./Span.) PR:A
REASONABLE DOUBT *½ (1936, Brit.) PR:A
REBECCA ** (1940) PR:C**
REBECCA OF SUNNYBROOK FARM ** (1932) PR:A
REBECCA OF SUNNYBROOK FARM ** (1938) PR:AA
REBEL *½ (1985, Aus.) PR:O
REBEL, THE ** (1933, Ger.) PR:A
REBEL, THE (SEE:CALL ME GENIUS)
REBEL ANGEL *½ (1962) PR:C
REBEL CITY *½ (1953) PR:A
REBEL GLADIATORS, THE ** (1963, It.) PR:A
REBEL IN TOWN *** (1956) PR:A
REBEL LOVE *½ (1986) PR:C-O
REBEL ROUSERS **½ (1970) PR:O
REBEL SET, THE **½ (1959) PR:A
REBEL SON, THE *½ (1939, Brit.) PR:A
REBEL WITH A CAUSE (SEE:LONELINESS OF THE LONG DISTANCE RUNNER, THE)
REBEL WITHOUT A CAUSE ** (1955) PR:C-O**
REBELLION ** (1938) PR:A
REBELLION *** (1967, Jap.) PR:C
REBELLION IN CUBA * (1961) PR:A
REBELLION OF THE HANGED, THE **½ (1954, Mex.) PR:C
REBELLIOUS DAUGHTERS * (1938) PR:A
REBELLIOUS ONE, THE (SEE:WILD SEED)
REBELS AGAINST THE LIGHT **½ (1964) PR:A
REBELS DIE YOUNG (SEE:TOO YOUNG, TOO IMMORAL!)
REBOUND **½ (1931) PR:A
RECAPTURED LOVE ** (1930) PR:A
RECESS **½ (1967) PR:A
RECKLESS **½ (1935) PR:A
RECKLESS ** (1984) PR:O
RECKLESS AGE **½ (1944) PR:A
RECKLESS AGE, THE (SEE:DRAGSTRIP RIOT)
RECKLESS HOUR, THE ** (1931) PR:A
RECKLESS LIVING ** (1931) PR:A
RECKLESS LIVING *½ (1938) PR:A
RECORD CITY * (1978) PR:A-C
RECORD 413 *½ (1936, Fr.) PR:A
RECORD OF A LIVING BEING (SEE:I LIVE IN FEAR)
RECRUITS zero (1986) PR:O
RED *** (1970, Can.) PR:C
RED AND THE BLACK, THE **½ (1954, Fr./It.) PR:A
RED AND THE WHITE, THE **½ (1969, Hung./USSR) PR:A
RED BADGE OF COURAGE, THE *** (1951) PR:C**
RED BALL EXPRESS **½ (1952) PR:A
RED BEARD * (1966, Jap.) PR:C-O**
RED BERET, THE (SEE:PARATROOPER)
RED BLOOD OF COURAGE ** (1935) PR:A
RED CANYON **½ (1949) PR:A
RED CLOAK, THE ** (1961, It./Fr.) PR:A
RED DANUBE, THE ** (1949) PR:A
RED DAWN * (1984) PR:O
RED DESERT **½ (1949) PR:A
RED DESERT ***½ (1965, Fr./It.) PR:O
RED DRAGON, THE *½ (1946) PR:A
RED-DRAGON **½ (1967, It./Ger./US) PR:A
RED DRESS, THE ** (1954, Brit.) PR:A
RED DUST ***½ (1932) PR:C
RED ENSIGN (SEE:STRIKE!)
RED FORK RANGE * (1931) PR:A
RED GARTERS **½ (1954) PR:A
RED-HAIRED ALIBI, THE ** (1932) PR:A
RED HANGMAN, THE (SEE:BLOODY PIT OF HORROR)
RED HEAD, THE (SEE:POIL DE CAROTTE)
RED HEAD ** (1934) PR:A
RED HEADED STRANGER ** (1987) PR:C-O
RED HEADED WOMAN *** (1932) PR:A
RED HEAT * (1988) PR:O**
RED HEAT zero (1988, US/W. Ger.) PR:O
RED, HOT AND BLUE **½ (1949) PR:A
RED HOT RHYTHM *½ (1930) PR:A
RED HOT SPEED *½ (1929) PR:A
RED HOT TIRES ** (1935) PR:A
RED HOUSE, THE * (1947) PR:A**
RED INN, THE *** (1954, Fr.) PR:A
RED KISS ***½ (1985, Fr./Ger.) PR:O
RED LANTERNS *** (1965, Gr.) PR:C
RED LIGHT ** (1949) PR:A-C
RED LIGHTS AHEAD * (1937) PR:A
RED LINE 7000 **½ (1965) PR:C
RED LION ** (1971, Jap.) PR:A
RED LIPS *½ (1964, Fr./It.) PR:O
RED MANTLE, THE (SEE:HAGBARD AND SIGNE)
RED MENACE, THE * (1949) PR:A
RED MONARCH *½ (1983, Brit.) PR:C
RED MORNING * (1935) PR:A
RED MOUNTAIN *** (1951) PR:A-C
RED ON RED (SEE:SCARRED)
RED OVER RED (SEE:COME SPY WITH ME)
RED PLANET MARS * (1952) PR:A
RED PONY, THE **½ (1949) PR:AA
RED RIVER *** (1948) PR:A**
RED RIVER RANGE ** (1938) PR:A
RED RIVER RENEGADES *½ (1946) PR:A
RED RIVER ROBIN HOOD ** (1943) PR:A
RED RIVER SHORE *½ (1953) PR:A
RED RIVER VALLEY ** (1936) PR:A
RED RIVER VALLEY **½ (1941) PR:A
RED ROCK OUTLAW * (1950) PR:A
RED ROPE, THE ** (1937) PR:A
RED RUNS THE RIVER *½ (1963) PR:A
RED SALUTE ** (1935) PR:A
RED SHEIK, THE ** (1963, It.) PR:A
RED SHOES, THE *** (1948, Brit.) PR:A**
RED SKIES OF MONTANA **½ (1952) PR:A
RED SKY AT MORNING *½ (1971) PR:C
RED SNOW ** (1952) PR:A
RED SONJA *½ (1985) PR:C-O
RED SORGHUM **** (1988, Chi.) PR:O
RED STALLION, THE ** (1947) PR:A
RED STALLION IN THE ROCKIES **½ (1949) PR:AA
RED SUN ** (1972, Fr./It./Sp.) PR:A
RED SUNDOWN ** (1956) PR:A
RED TENT, THE * (1971, It./USSR) PR:A**
RED TOMAHAWK ** (1967) PR:A
RED WAGON ** (1936) PR:A
RED, WHITE AND BLACK, THE **½ (1970) PR:C
REDEEMER, THE ** (1965, Sp.) PR:A
REDEEMER, THE (SEE:RAT SAVIOUR, THE)
REDEEMER, THE zero (1978) PR:O
REDEEMING SIN, THE *½ (1929) PR:A
REDEMPTION * (1930) PR:A
REDHEAD (SEE:RED HEAD)
REDHEAD * (1941) PR:A
REDHEAD AND THE COWBOY, THE **½ (1950) PR:A
REDHEAD FROM MANHATTAN *½ (1954) PR:A
REDHEAD FROM WYOMING, THE **½ (1953) PR:A
REDHEADS ON PARADE *½ (1935) PR:A
REDNECK zero (1975, It./Sp.) PR:O
REDS ***½ (1981) PR:C-O
REDUCING ** (1931) PR:A
REDWOOD FOREST TRAIL ** (1950) PR:A
REEFER MADNESS * (1936) PR:C-O
REFLECTION OF FEAR, A ** (1973) PR:C
REFLECTIONS ** (1984, Brit.) PR:C
REFLECTIONS IN A GOLDEN EYE * (1967) PR:O
REFORM GIRL *½ (1933) PR:A
REFORM SCHOOL ** (1939) PR:A
REFORM SCHOOL GIRL **½ (1957) PR:A
REFORM SCHOOL GIRLS * (1986) PR:O
REFORMATORY *½ (1938) PR:A
REFORMER AND THE REDHEAD, THE *** (1950) PR:A
REFUGE * (1981) PR:O
REFUGEE, THE (SEE:THREE FACES WEST)
REGAL CAVALCADE **½ (1935, Brit.) PR:A
REGISTERED NURSE * (1934) PR:A
REG'LAR FELLERS *½ (1941) PR:A
REHEARSAL FOR A CRIME (SEE:CRIMINAL LIFE OF ARCHIBALDO DE LA CRUZ, THE)
REIGN OF TERROR (SEE:BLACK BOOK, THE)
REINCARNATE, THE *½ (1971, Can.) PR:C
REINCARNATION OF PETER PROUD, THE **½ (1975) PR:C-O
REIVERS, THE *½ (1969) PR:C
REKOPIS ZNALEZIONY W SARAGOSSIE (SEE:SARAGOSSA MANUSCRIPT, THE)
RELAZIONI PERICOLOSE (SEE:LES LIAISONS DANGEREUSES)
RELENTLESS *** (1948) PR:A
RELIGIOUS RACKETEERS (SEE:MYSTIC CIRCLE MURDERS)
RELUCTANT ASTRONAUT, THE **½ (1967) PR:A
RELUCTANT BRIDE (SEE:TWO GROOMS FOR A BRIDE)
RELUCTANT DEBUTANTE, THE ***½ (1958) PR:A
RELUCTANT DRAGON, THE **½ (1941) PR:AA
RELUCTANT HEROES ** (1951, Brit.) PR:A
RELUCTANT SAINT, THE ** (1962, US/It.) PR:A
RELUCTANT WIDOW, THE *½ (1951, Brit.) PR:A
REMAINS TO BE SEEN ** (1953) PR:A
REMARKABLE ANDREW, THE ** (1942) PR:A
REMARKABLE MR. KIPPS ** (1942, Brit.) PR:A
REMARKABLE MR. PENNYPACKER, THE **½ (1959) PR:A
REMBETIKO ** (1985, Gr.) PR:C
REMBRANDT ** (1936, Brit.) PR:A**
REMEDY FOR RICHES **½ (1941) PR:A
REMEMBER? * (1939) PR:A
REMEMBER LAST NIGHT *½ (1935) PR:A
REMEMBER MY NAME **½ (1978) PR:O
REMEMBER PEARL HARBOR ** (1942) PR:A
REMEMBER THAT FACE (SEE:MOB, THE)
REMEMBER THE DAY *** (1941) PR:A
REMEMBER THE NIGHT ***½ (1940) PR:A
REMEMBER WHEN (SEE:RIDING HIGH)
REMEMBRANCE **½ (1982, Brit.) PR:C-O
REMO WILLIAMS: THE ADVENTURE BEGINS * (1985) PR:C**

REMORQUES
(SEE:STORMY WATERS)
REMOTE CONTROL ** (1930) PR:A
REMOTE CONTROL * (1988) PR:C
REMOVALISTS, THE **½ (1975, Aus.) PR:C
RENALDO AND CLARA *½ (1978) PR:O
RENDEZ-VOUS **½ (1932, Ger.) PR:A
RENDEZVOUS *** (1935) PR:A
RENDEZVOUS
(SEE:DARLING, HOW COULD YOU?)
RENDEZVOUS *** (1985, Fr.) PR:O
RENDEZVOUS AT MIDNIGHT *½ (1935) PR:A
RENDEZVOUS 24 ** (1946) PR:A
RENDEZVOUS WITH ANNIE **½ (1946) PR:A
RENEGADE GIRL ** (1946) PR:A
RENEGADE GIRLS *½ (1974) PR:O
RENEGADE POSSE
(SEE:BULLET FOR A BADMAN)
RENEGADE RANGER **½ (1938) PR:A
RENEGADE TRAIL ** (1939) PR:A
RENEGADES ** (1930) PR:A
RENEGADES **½ (1946) PR:A
RENEGADES OF SONORA ** (1948) PR:A
RENEGADES OF THE RIO GRANDE ** (1945) PR:A
RENEGADES OF THE SAGE ** (1949) PR:A
RENEGADES OF THE WEST * (1932) PR:A
RENFREW OF THE ROYAL MOUNTED *½ (1937) PR:A
RENFREW OF THE ROYAL MOUNTED ON THE GREAT WHITE TRAIL
(SEE:ON THE GREAT WHITE TRAIL)
RENFREW ON THE GREAT WHITE TRAIL
(SEE:ON THE GREAT WHITE TRAIL)
RENO * (1930) PR:A
RENO **½ (1939) PR:A
RENO AND THE DOC * (1984, Can.) PR:O
RENT-A-COP ** (1988) PR:C
"RENT-A-GIRL" * (1965) PR:O
RENT CONTROL *** (1981) PR:C
RENTADICK ** (1972, Brit.) PR:O
RENTED
(SEE:""RENT-A-GIRL")
RENTED LIPS zero (1988) PR:O
REPEAT PERFORMANCE **½ (1947) PR:A
REPENT AT LEISURE *½ (1941) PR:A
REPENTANCE ** (1988, USSR) PR:C**
REPLICA OF A CRIME
(SEE:MANIAC MANSION)
REPO MAN ***½ (1984) PR:O
REPORT ON THE PARTY AND THE GUESTS, A ** (1968, Czech.) PR:A
REPORT TO THE COMMISSIONER **½ (1975) PR:C
REPORTED MISSING *½ (1937) PR:A
REPRIEVE
(SEE:CONVICTS FOUR)
REPRIEVED
(SEE:SING SING NIGHTS)
REPRISAL ** (1956) PR:A
REPTILE, THE *½ (1966, Brit.) PR:C
REPTILICUS * (1962, US/Den.) PR:A
REPULSION *** (1965, Brit.) PR:O**
REPUTATION
(SEE:LADY WITH A PAST)
REQUIEM FOR A GUNFIGHTER **½ (1965) PR:A
REQUIEM FOR A HEAVYWEIGHT ***½ (1962) PR:C
REQUIEM FOR A SECRET AGENT * (1966, It.) PR:A
RESCUE, THE * (1988) PR:A-C
RESCUE SQUAD * (1935) PR:A
RESCUE SQUAD, THE ** (1963, Brit.) PR:A
RESCUERS, THE *** (1977) PR:AA
RESERVED FOR LADIES *** (1932, Brit.) PR:AA
REST IS SILENCE, THE **½ (1960, Ger.) PR:C
RESTLESS
(SEE:MAN-TRAP)
RESTLESS BREED, THE ** (1957) PR:A
RESTLESS NIGHT, THE ** (1964, Ger.) PR:C
RESTLESS ONES, THE ** (1965) PR:A
RESTLESS YEARS, THE *½ (1958) PR:A
RESURRECTION ** (1931) PR:A
RESURRECTION *** (1963, USSR) PR:A
RESURRECTION ** (1980) PR:C
RESURRECTION OF ZACHARY WHEELER, THE **½ (1971) PR:A
RESURRECTION SYNDICATE
(SEE:NOTHING BUT THE NIGHT)

RETENEZ MOI. . .OU JE FAIS UN MALHEUR
(SEE:TO CATCH A COP)
RETRIBUTION * (1988) PR:O
RETRIEVERS, THE
(SEE:HOT AND DEADLY)
RETURN ** (1986) PR:O
RETURN, THE * (1980) PR:C
RETURN FROM THE ASHES ** (1965, US/Brit.) PR:A
RETURN FROM THE PAST
(SEE:DR. TERROR'S GALLERY OF HORRORS)
RETURN FROM THE SEA **½ (1954) PR:A
RETURN FROM WITCH MOUNTAIN **½ (1978) PR:AA
RETURN OF A MAN CALLED HORSE, THE ** (1976) PR:C
RETURN OF A STRANGER
(SEE:FACE BEHIND THE SCAR)
RETURN OF A STRANGER **½ (1962, Brit.) PR:C
RETURN OF BULLDOG DRUMMOND, THE ** (1934, Brit.) PR:A
RETURN OF CAPTAIN INVINCIBLE, THE ** (1983, Aus./US) PR:C
RETURN OF CAROL DEANE, THE ** (1938, Brit.) PR:A
RETURN OF CASEY JONES ** (1933) PR:A
RETURN OF COUNT YORGA, THE ** (1971) PR:C
RETURN OF DANIEL BOONE, THE ** (1941) PR:A
RETURN OF DR. FU MANCHU, THE ** (1930) PR:A
RETURN OF DR. MABUSE, THE **½ (1961, Ger./Fr./It.) PR:C
RETURN OF DR. X, THE **½ (1939) PR:C
RETURN OF DRACULA, THE ** (1958) PR:C
RETURN OF FRANK JAMES, THE ***½ (1940) PR:A
RETURN OF JACK SLADE, THE *½ (1955) PR:A
RETURN OF JESSE JAMES, THE **½ (1950) PR:A
RETURN OF JIMMY VALENTINE, THE **½ (1936) PR:A
RETURN OF JOSEY WALES, THE *½ (1987) PR:C
RETURN OF MARTIN GUERRE, THE ***½ (1983, Fr.) PR:C
RETURN OF MAXWELL SMART, THE
(SEE:NUDE BOMB, THE)
RETURN OF MR. H, THE
(SEE:THEY SAVED HITLER'S BRAIN)
RETURN OF MR. MOTO, THE **½ (1965, Brit.) PR:A
RETURN OF MONTE CRISTO, THE **½ (1946) PR:A
RETURN OF OCTOBER, THE ** (1948) PR:A
RETURN OF OLD MOTHER RILEY, THE
(SEE:OLD MOTHER RILEY)
RETURN OF PETER GRIMM, THE *** (1935) PR:A
RETURN OF RAFFLES, THE ** (1932, Brit.) PR:A
RETURN OF RIN TIN TIN, THE **½ (1947) PR:AA
RETURN OF RINGO, THE *½ (1966, It./Sp.) PR:A
RETURN OF SABATA zero (1972, It./Fr./Ger.) PR:C
RETURN OF SHERLOCK HOLMES, THE **½ (1929) PR:A
RETURN OF SOPHIE LANG, THE ** (1936) PR:A
RETURN OF THE APE MAN *½ (1944) PR:A
RETURN OF THE BADMEN * (1948) PR:C**
RETURN OF THE BLACK EAGLE **½ (1949, It.) PR:A
RETURN OF THE CISCO KID *½ (1939) PR:A
RETURN OF THE CORSICAN BROTHERS
(SEE:BANDITS OF CORSICA, THE)
RETURN OF THE DRAGON **½ (1974, Chi.) PR:O
RETURN OF THE FLY *½ (1959) PR:A
RETURN OF THE FROG, THE * (1938, Brit.) PR:A
RETURN OF THE FRONTIERSMAN ** (1950) PR:A
RETURN OF THE JEDI ***½ (1983) PR:A-C
RETURN OF THE LASH zero (1947) PR:A
RETURN OF THE LIVING DEAD
(SEE:DEAD PEOPLE)
RETURN OF THE LIVING DEAD ** (1985) PR:O
RETURN OF THE LIVING DEAD PART II ** (1988) PR:O
RETURN OF THE PINK PANTHER, THE ***½ (1975, Brit.) PR:A-C
RETURN OF THE RANGERS, THE * (1943) PR:A
RETURN OF THE RAT, THE **½ (1929, Brit.) PR:A
RETURN OF THE SCARLET PIMPERNEL ** (1938, Brit.) PR:A
RETURN OF THE SECAUCUS SEVEN ***½ (1980) PR:O
RETURN OF THE SEVEN *½ (1966, Sp.) PR:A

RETURN OF THE SOLDIER, THE * (1983, Brit.) PR:C**
RETURN OF THE TERROR * (1934) PR:C
RETURN OF THE TEXAN *** (1952) PR:A
RETURN OF THE VAMPIRE, THE **½ (1944) PR:A
RETURN OF THE VIGILANTES, THE
(SEE:VIGILANTES RETURN, THE)
RETURN OF THE WHISTLER, THE ** (1948) PR:A
RETURN OF WILD BILL, THE ** (1940) PR:A
RETURN OF WILDFIRE, THE *** (1948) PR:A
RETURN TO BOGGY CREEK *½ (1977) PR:AA
RETURN TO CAMPUS *½ (1975) PR:C
RETURN TO HORROR HIGH *½ (1987) PR:O
RETURN TO MACON COUNTY * (1975) PR:C-O
RETURN TO OZ **½ (1985) PR:C
RETURN TO PARADISE ** (1953) PR:A
RETURN TO PEYTON PLACE **½ (1961) PR:A
RETURN TO SALEM'S LOT, A **½ (1988) PR:O
RETURN TO SENDER ** (1963, Brit.) PR:A
RETURN TO SNOWY RIVER: PART II * (1988, Aus.) PR:A**
RETURN TO THE HORRORS OF BLOOD ISLAND
(SEE:BEAST OF BLOOD)
RETURN TO TREASURE ISLAND ** (1954) PR:A
RETURN TO WARBOW *½ (1958) PR:A
RETURN TO WATERLOO ** (1985, Brit.) PR:C
RETURN TO YESTERDAY ** (1940, Brit.) PR:A
RETURNING, THE zero (1983) PR:O
REUBEN, REUBEN ** (1983) PR:O
REUNION ***½ (1932, Brit.) PR:A
REUNION **½ (1936) PR:A
REUNION IN FRANCE **½ (1942) PR:A
REUNION IN RENO **½ (1951) PR:A
REUNION IN VIENNA ** (1933) PR:A-C
REVEILLE-TOI ET MEURS
(SEE:WAKE UP AND DIE)
REVEILLE WITH BEVERLY ** (1943) PR:A
REVENGE
(SEE:END OF THE TRAIL)
REVENGE AT EL PASO ** (1968, It.) PR:A
REVENGE AT MONTE CARLO *½ (1933) PR:A
REVENGE
(SEE:TERROR FROM UNDER THE HOUSE)
REVENGE
(SEE:BLOOD FEUD)
REVENGE zero (1986) PR:O
REVENGE OF DRACULA
(SEE:DRACULA—PRINCE OF DARKNESS)
REVENGE OF FRANKENSTEIN, THE **½ (1958, Brit.) PR:C
REVENGE OF GENERAL LING
(SEE:WIFE OF GENERAL LING, THE)
REVENGE OF KING KONG
(SEE:KING KONG ESCAPES)
REVENGE OF MILADY, THE
(SEE:FOUR MUSKETEERS, THE)
REVENGE OF THE BLOOD BEAST, THE
(SEE:SHE BEAST, THE)
REVENGE OF THE CHEERLEADERS zero (1976) PR:O
REVENGE OF THE CREATURE ** (1955) PR:A
REVENGE OF THE DEAD
(SEE:NIGHT OF THE GHOULS)
REVENGE OF THE GLADIATORS *½ (1965, It.) PR:A
REVENGE OF THE LIVING DEAD
(SEE:MURDER CLINIC, THE)
REVENGE OF THE NERDS ***½ (1984) PR:C-O
REVENGE OF THE NERDS II: NERDS IN PARADISE * (1987) PR:C
REVENGE OF THE NINJA * (1983) PR:A
REVENGE OF THE PINK PANTHER * (1978) PR:A-C**
REVENGE OF THE SCREAMING DEAD
(SEE:DEAD PEOPLE)
REVENGE OF THE SHOGUN WOMEN zero (1982, Taiwan) PR:O
REVENGE OF THE TEENAGE VIXENS FROM OUTER SPACE, THE *½ (1986) PR:C
REVENGE OF THE ZOMBIES *½ (1943) PR:A
REVENGE OF UKENO-JO, THE
(SEE:ACTOR'S REVENGE, AN)
REVENGE RIDER, THE ** (1935) PR:A
REVENGERS, THE **½ (1972, US/Mex.) PR:A-C
REVENUE AGENT *** (1950) PR:A
REVERSE BE MY LOT, THE * (1938, Brit.) PR:A
REVOLT AT FORT LARAMIE **½ (1957) PR:A

REVOLT IN THE BIG HOUSE *** (1958) PR:A
REVOLT OF JOB, THE ***½ (1984, Hung./Ger.) PR:O
REVOLT OF MAMIE STOVER, THE **½ (1956) PR:A
REVOLT OF THE BOYARS, THE (SEE:IVAN THE TERRIBLE, PART II)
REVOLT OF THE MERCENARIES **½ (1964, It./Sp.) PR:A
REVOLT OF THE SLAVES, THE ** (1961, It./Sp./Ger.) PR:C
REVOLT OF THE ZOMBIES * (1936) PR:C
REVOLUTION ** (1985, Brit./Norway) PR:C
REVOLUTIONARY, THE ***½ (1970, Brit.) PR:A-C
REVOLUTIONS PER MINUTE (SEE:R.P.M.)
REVOLVING DOORS, THE **½ (1988, Can./Fr.) PR:A
REWARD, THE **½ (1965) PR:A
REY DE AFRICA (SEE:ONE STEP TO HELL)
RHAPSODIE IN BLEI (SEE:HOT MONEY GIRL)
RHAPSODY *** (1954) PR:A
RHAPSODY IN BLUE ***½ (1945) PR:AA
RHINESTONE zero (1984) PR:C
RHINO *** (1964) PR:A
RHINOCEROS ** (1974) PR:A-C
RHODES ***½ (1936, Brit.) PR:A
RHODES OF AFRICA (SEE:RHODES)
RHUBARB **½ (1951) PR:A
RHYTHM HITS THE ICE (SEE:ICE-CAPADES REVUE)
RHYTHM IN THE AIR ** (1936, Brit.) PR:A
RHYTHM IN THE CLOUDS ** (1937) PR:A
RHYTHM INN *½ (1951) PR:A
RHYTHM OF THE ISLANDS ** (1943) PR:A
RHYTHM OF THE RIO GRANDE ** (1940) PR:A
RHYTHM OF THE SADDLE *½ (1938) PR:A
RHYTHM ON THE RANGE *** (1936) PR:A
RHYTHM ON THE RANGE (SEE:ROOTIN' TOOTIN' RHYTHM)
RHYTHM ON THE RIVER (SEE:FRESHMAN LOVE)
RHYTHM ON THE RIVER ***½ (1940) PR:A
RHYTHM PARADE ** (1943) PR:A
RHYTHM RACKETEER * (1937, Brit.) PR:A
RHYTHM ROMANCE (SEE:SOME LIKE IT HOT)
RHYTHM SERENADE ** (1943, Brit.) PR:A
RICE GIRL *** (1963, Fr./It.) PR:C-O
RICH AND FAMOUS * (1981) PR:O
RICH AND STRANGE * (1932, Brit.) PR:C**
RICH ARE ALWAYS WITH US, THE **½ (1932) PR:A
RICH BRIDE, THE (SEE:COUNTRY BRIDE)
RICH, FULL LIFE, THE (SEE:CYNTHIA)
RICH KIDS * (1979) PR:C**
RICH MAN, POOR GIRL **½ (1938) PR:A
RICH MAN'S FOLLY *** (1931) PR:A
RICH PEOPLE **½ (1929) PR:A
RICH, YOUNG AND DEADLY (SEE:PLATINUM HIGH SCHOOL)
RICH, YOUNG AND PRETTY *** (1951) PR:A-C
RICHARD *** (1972) PR:C
RICHARD TAUBER STORY, THE (SEE:YOU ARE THE WORLD FOR ME)
RICHARD III *** (1956, Brit.) PR:A-C**
RICHARD'S THINGS ** (1981, Brit.) PR:O
RICHELIEU (SEE:CARDINAL RICHELIEU)
RICHES AND ROMANCE (SEE:ROMANCE AND RICHES)
RICHEST GIRL IN THE WORLD, THE ***½ (1934) PR:A
RICHEST MAN IN THE WORLD, THE (SEE:SINS OF THE CHILDREN)
RICHEST MAN IN TOWN *½ (1941) PR:A
RICKSHAW MAN, THE ***½ (1960, Jap.) PR:C-O
RICOCHET **½ (1966, Brit.) PR:C
RICOCHET ROMANCE **½ (1954) PR:AA
RIDDLE OF THE SANDS, THE ** (1984, Brit.) PR:C
RIDE A CROOKED MILE ***½ (1938) PR:C
RIDE A CROOKED TRAIL ** (1958) PR:A-C
RIDE A NORTHBOUND HORSE ** (1969) PR:AA
RIDE A VIOLENT MILE * (1957) PR:C
RIDE A WILD PONY **½ (1976, US/Aus.) PR:AA
RIDE BACK, THE ***½ (1957) PR:C
RIDE BEYOND VENGEANCE zero (1966) PR:O
RIDE CLEAR OF DIABLO *** (1954) PR:C
RIDE 'EM COWBOY **½ (1936) PR:A
RIDE 'EM COWBOY *** (1942) PR:AA
RIDE 'EM COWGIRL ** (1939) PR:A
RIDE HIM, COWBOY *** (1932) PR:A
RIDE IN A PINK CAR *½ (1974, Can.) PR:C-O
RIDE IN THE WHIRLWIND * (1966) PR:C
RIDE, KELLY, RIDE *½ (1941) PR:A
RIDE LONESOME *** (1959) PR:C
RIDE ON VAQUERO *** (1941) PR:A
RIDE OUT FOR REVENGE ** (1957) PR:C
RIDE, RANGER, RIDE * (1936) PR:A**
RIDE, RYDER, RIDE! ** (1949) PR:A
RIDE, TENDERFOOT, RIDE *** (1940) PR:A
RIDE THE HIGH COUNTRY *** (1962) PR:C**
RIDE THE HIGH IRON ** (1956) PR:A
RIDE THE HIGH WIND **½ (1967, South Africa) PR:A
RIDE THE MAN DOWN ** (1952) PR:C
RIDE THE PINK HORSE ***½ (1947) PR:C
RIDE THE WILD SURF **½ (1964) PR:A
RIDE TO HANGMAN'S TREE, THE **½ (1967) PR:A
RIDE, VAQUERO! ** (1953) PR:A
RIDER FROM NOWHERE (SEE:RIDERS FROM NOWHERE)
RIDER FROM TUCSON *** (1950) PR:A
RIDER IN THE NIGHT, THE * (1968, South Africa) PR:C
RIDER OF DEATH VALLEY ***½ (1932) PR:A
RIDER OF THE LAW, THE ** (1935) PR:A
RIDER OF THE PLAINS ** (1931) PR:A
RIDER ON A DEAD HORSE ** (1962) PR:C
RIDER ON THE RAIN ***½ (1970, Fr./It.) PR:C
RIDERS FROM NOWHERE ** (1940) PR:A
RIDERS FROM THE DUSK (SEE:RIDERS OF THE DUSK)
RIDERS IN THE SKY **½ (1949) PR:A
RIDERS OF BLACK HILLS (SEE:RIDERS OF THE BLACK HILLS)
RIDERS OF BLACK MOUNTAIN * (1941) PR:A
RIDERS OF BLACK RIVER ** (1939) PR:A
RIDERS OF DESTINY * (1933) PR:A**
RIDERS OF PASCO BASIN ** (1940) PR:A
RIDERS OF THE BADLANDS **½ (1941) PR:A
RIDERS OF THE BLACK HILLS **½ (1938) PR:A
RIDERS OF THE CACTUS * (1931) PR:A
RIDERS OF THE DAWN ** (1937) PR:A
RIDERS OF THE DAWN *½ (1945) PR:A
RIDERS OF THE DEADLINE **½ (1943) PR:A
RIDERS OF THE DESERT ** (1932) PR:A
RIDERS OF THE DUSK ** (1949) PR:A
RIDERS OF THE FRONTIER *½ (1939) PR:A
RIDERS OF THE GOLDEN GULCH ** (1932) PR:A
RIDERS OF THE NORTH ** (1931) PR:A
RIDERS OF THE NORTHLAND **½ (1942) PR:A
RIDERS OF THE NORTHWEST MOUNTED *½ (1943) PR:A
RIDERS OF THE PURPLE SAGE **½ (1931) PR:A
RIDERS OF THE PURPLE SAGE ** (1941) PR:A
RIDERS OF THE RANGE *** (1949) PR:A
RIDERS OF THE RIO GRANDE **½ (1943) PR:A
RIDERS OF THE ROCKIES * (1937) PR:A**
RIDERS OF THE SANTA FE *½ (1944) PR:A
RIDERS OF THE STORM ** (1988, Brit.) PR:O
RIDERS OF THE WEST * (1942) PR:A
RIDERS OF THE WHISTLING PINES *½ (1949) PR:A
RIDERS OF THE WHISTLING SKULL *** (1937) PR:A-C
RIDERS OF VENGEANCE (SEE:RAIDERS, THE)
RIDERS TO THE STARS ** (1954) PR:A
RIDIN' DOWN THE CANYON **½ (1942) PR:A
RIDIN' DOWN THE TRAIL *½ (1947) PR:A
RIDIN' FOR JUSTICE **½ (1932) PR:A
RIDIN' LAW zero (1930) PR:A
RIDIN' ON A RAINBOW ** (1941) PR:A
RIDIN' THE LONE TRAIL zero (1937) PR:A
RIDIN' THE OUTLAW TRAIL *** (1951) PR:A
RIDING AVENGER, THE ** (1936) PR:A
RIDING HIGH ** (1937, Brit.) PR:A
RIDING HIGH *½ (1943) PR:A
RIDING HIGH ***½ (1950) PR:A
RIDING ON *½ (1937) PR:A
RIDING ON AIR **½ (1937) PR:AA
RIDING SHOTGUN ** (1954) PR:A
RIDING SPEED * (1934) PR:A
RIDING TALL (SEE:SQUARES)
RIDING THE CHEROKEE TRAIL ** (1941) PR:A
RIDING THE SUNSET TRAIL *** (1941) PR:A
RIDING THE WIND **½ (1942) PR:A
RIDING TORNADO, THE **½ (1932) PR:A
RIDING WEST **½ (1944) PR:A
RIFF-RAFF *** (1936) PR:A
RIFF RAFF GIRLS **½ (1962, Fr./It.) PR:O
RIFFRAFF **½ (1947) PR:A
RIFIFFI A TOKYO (SEE:RIFIFI IN TOKYO)
RIFIFI *** (1956, Fr.) PR:A-C**
RIFIFI FOR GIRLS (SEE:RIFF RAFF GIRLS)
RIFIFI FRA LE DONNE (SEE:RIFF RAFF GIRLS)
RIFIFI IN PARIS (SEE:UPPER HAND, THE)
RIFIFI IN TOKYO **½ (1963, Fr./It.) PR:A-C
RIFIFI INTERNAZIONALE (SEE:UPPER HAND, THE)
RIGHT AGE TO MARRY, THE ** (1935, Brit.) PR:A
RIGHT APPROACH, THE ** (1961) PR:A
RIGHT CROSS * (1950) PR:A-C**
RIGHT HAND OF THE DEVIL, THE * (1963) PR:C
RIGHT MAN, THE (SEE:HER FIRST ROMANCE)
RIGHT OF WAY, THE * (1931) PR:A
RIGHT STUFF, THE *** (1983) PR:A-C**
RIGHT TO LIVE, THE * (1933, Brit.) PR:A
RIGHT TO LIVE, THE ** (1935) PR:A
RIGHT TO LIVE, THE (SEE:FOREVER YOURS)
RIGHT TO LOVE, THE *** (1931) PR:C
RIGHT TO ROMANCE ** (1933) PR:A-C
RIGHT TO THE HEART **½ (1942) PR:A
RIGOLETTO **½ (1949) PR:A
RIKKY AND PETE **½ (1988, Aus.) PR:O
RIM OF THE CANYON **½ (1949) PR:A
RIMFIRE ** (1949) PR:A
RING, THE * (1952) PR:A**
RING-A-DING RHYTHM **½ (1962, Brit.) PR:A
RING AROUND THE CLOCK **½ (1953, It.) PR:A
RING AROUND THE MOON * (1936) PR:A
RING OF BRIGHT WATER * (1969, Brit.) PR:A**
RING OF FEAR ** (1954) PR:A
RING OF FIRE *** (1961) PR:A-C
RING OF SPIES (SEE:RING OF TREASON)
RING OF SPIES **½ (1964, Brit.) PR:A
RING OF TERROR **½ (1962) PR:A
RING UP THE CURTAIN (SEE:BROADWAY TO HOLLYWOOD)
RINGER, THE *½ (1932, Brit.) PR:A
RINGER, THE ** (1953, Brit.) PR:A
RINGO AND HIS GOLDEN PISTOL ** (1966, It.) PR:A
RINGS ON HER FINGERS ** (1942) PR:A
RINGSIDE **½ (1949) PR:A
RINGSIDE MAISIE ** (1941) PR:A
RIO **½ (1939) PR:A
RIO ABAJO (SEE:ON THE LINE)
RIO BRAVO ** (1959) PR:A**
RIO CONCHOS * (1964) PR:A**
RIO GRANDE ** (1939) PR:A
RIO GRANDE ** (1950) PR:A**
RIO GRANDE PATROL *½ (1950) PR:A
RIO GRANDE RAIDERS **½ (1946) PR:A
RIO GRANDE RANGER * (1937) PR:A
RIO GRANDE ROMANCE *½ (1936) PR:A
RIO LOBO *½ (1970) PR:A
RIO RITA ***½ (1929) PR:A
RIO RITA **½ (1942) PR:AA
RIO 70 * (1970, US/Ger./Sp.) PR:C
RIO VENGENCE (SEE:MOTOR PSYCHO)
RIOT **½ (1969) PR:O
RIOT AT LAUDERDALE (SEE:HELL'S PLAYGROUND)
RIOT IN CELL BLOCK 11 ***½ (1954) PR:C
RIOT IN JUVENILE PRISON ** (1959) PR:C
RIOT ON PIER 6 (SEE:NEW ORLEANS UNCENSORED)
RIOT ON SUNSET STRIP *** (1967) PR:C
RIOT SQUAD ** (1941) PR:A
RIOTOUS BRUIN, THE (SEE:RUINED BRUIN, THE)
RIP-OFF *** (1971, Can.) PR:O
RIP ROARIN' BUCKAROO *½ (1936) PR:A
RIP ROARING RILEY *½ (1935) PR:A
RIP TIDE *** (1934) PR:A
RIPPED-OFF ** (1971, It.) PR:C-O
RISATE DI GIOLA (SEE:PASSIONATE THIEF, THE)
RISE AGAINST THE SWORD **½ (1966, Jap.) PR:A
RISE AND FALL OF LEGS DIAMOND, THE ***½ (1960) PR:C
RISE AND RISE OF MICHAEL RIMMER, THE **½ (1970, Brit.) PR:C
RISE AND SHINE **½ (1941) PR:A
RISE OF CATHERINE THE GREAT (SEE:CATHERINE THE GREAT)
RISE OF HELGA, THE (SEE:SUSAN LENOX: HER FALL AND RISE)
RISE OF LOUIS XIV, THE * (1970, Fr.) PR:A**
RISING DAMP *** (1980, Brit.) PR:C
RISING OF THE MOON, THE *** (1957, Ireland) PR:A
RISING TO FAME (SEE:SUSAN LENOX: HER FALL AND RISE)
RISK, THE **½ (1961, Brit.) PR:A
RISKY BUSINESS **½ (1939) PR:A
RISKY BUSINESS * (1983) PR:O**

RITA ** (1963, Fr./It.) PR:C
RITA, SUE AND BOB TOO! *** (1987, Brit.) **PR:O**
RITEN
(SEE:RITUAL, THE)
RITUAL, THE ** (1970, Swed.) PR:O
RITUALS
(SEE:CREEPER)
RITZ, THE ***½ (1976) **PR:C-O**
RIVALEN DER MANEGE
(SEE:BIMBO THE GREAT)
RIVALS, THE ** (1963, Brit.) PR:A
RIVALS ** (1972) PR:O
RIVER, THE **½ (1928) PR:A
RIVER, THE ***½ (1951) **PR:A**
RIVER, THE **½ (1961, India) PR:A
RIVER, THE *** (1984) **PR:A-C**
RIVER BEAT ** (1954) PR:A
RIVER CHANGES, THE *** (1956) PR:A
RIVER GANG *½ (1945) PR:A
RIVER HOUSE GHOST, THE *½ (1932, Brit.) PR:A
RIVER HOUSE MYSTERY, THE * (1935, Brit.) PR:A
RIVER LADY **½ (1948) PR:A
RIVER NIGER, THE ** (1976) **PR:O**
RIVER OF FOREVER * (1967, Jap.) PR:A-C
RIVER OF MISSING MEN
(SEE:TRAPPED BY G-MEN)
RIVER OF NO RETURN ***½ (1954) **PR:A**
RIVER OF POISON
(SEE:SOUTH OF DEATH VALLEY)
RIVER OF ROMANCE ** (1929) PR:A
RIVER OF UNREST **½ (1937, Brit.) **PR:A**
RIVER RAT, THE **½ (1984) **PR:A**
RIVER WOLVES, THE * (1934, Brit.) PR:A
RIVER WOMAN, THE ** (1928) PR:A
RIVERBOAT RHYTHM *½ (1946) PR:A
RIVERRUN ** (1968) PR:O
RIVER'S EDGE, THE **½ (1957) PR:C
RIVER'S EDGE ***½ (1987) **PR:O**
RIVER'S END **½ (1931) PR:A
RIVER'S END **½ (1940) PR:A
RIVERSIDE MURDER, THE ** (1935, Brit.) PR:A
ROAD, THE
(SEE:LA STRADA)
ROAD AGENT ** (1941) PR:A
ROAD AGENT ** (1952) **PR:A**
ROAD BACK, THE *** (1937) PR:A
ROAD DEMON ** (1938) **PR:A**
ROAD GAMES **½ (1981, Aus.) **PR:O**
ROAD GANG ** (1936) PR:C
ROAD GANGS, ADVENTURES IN THE CREEP ZONE
(SEE:SPACEHUNTER: ADVENTURES IN THE
FORBIDDEN ZONE)
ROAD HOME, THE ** (1947, USSR) PR:A
ROAD HOUSE ** (1934, Brit.) PR:A
ROAD HOUSE *** (1948) PR:C
ROAD HUSTLERS, THE *½ (1968) PR:C
ROAD IS FINE, THE ** (1930, Fr.) PR:A
ROAD MOVIE *** (1974) PR:O
ROAD SHOW **½ (1941) PR:A
ROAD TO ALCATRAZ ** (1945) PR:A
ROAD TO BALI **½ (1952) **PR:AA**
ROAD TO DENVER, THE **½ (1955) PR:A
ROAD TO ETERNITY *** (1962, Jap.) PR:O
ROAD TO FORT ALAMO, THE *½
(1966, Fr./It.) PR:C
ROAD TO FORTUNE, THE * (1930, Brit.) PR:A
ROAD TO FRISCO
(SEE:THEY DRIVE BY NIGHT)
ROAD TO GLORY, THE **½ (1936) PR:A-C
ROAD TO HAPPINESS * (1942) PR:A
ROAD TO HONG KONG, THE **
(1962, US/Brit.) PR:AA
ROAD TO LIFE ***½ (1932, USSR) PR:A
ROAD TO MOROCCO *** (1942) PR:AA
ROAD TO PARADISE ** (1930) PR:A
ROAD TO RENO ** (1931) PR:A
ROAD TO RENO, THE **½ (1938) PR:A
ROAD TO RIO ***½ (1947) **PR:AA**
ROAD TO RUIN *½ (1934) PR:O
ROAD TO SALINA **½ (1971, Fr./It.) **PR:O**
ROAD TO SHAME, THE ** (1962, Fr.) PR:C-O
ROAD TO SINGAPORE **½ (1931) PR:A
ROAD TO SINGAPORE **½ (1940) PR:AA
ROAD TO THE BIG HOUSE *½ (1947) PR:A
ROAD TO UTOPIA ***½ (1945) **PR:AA**
ROAD TO ZANZIBAR ***½ (1941) PR:AA
ROAD WARRIOR, THE ***½ (1982, Aus.) **PR:O**

ROADBLOCK *** (1951) PR:A
ROADHOUSE GIRL
(SEE:MARILYN)
ROADHOUSE MURDER, THE **½ (1932) PR:A
ROADHOUSE NIGHTS **½ (1930) PR:A
ROADHOUSE 66 * (1984) **PR:C**
ROADIE * (1980) PR:A-C
ROADRACERS, THE * (1959) **PR:A**
ROAMING COWBOY, THE ** (1937) PR:A
ROAMING LADY **½ (1936) PR:A
ROAR *½ (1981) PR:A
ROAR OF THE CROWD *½ (1953) PR:A
ROAR OF THE DRAGON ** (1932) PR:A
ROAR OF THE PRESS *½ (1941) PR:A
ROARIN' GUNS *½ (1936) **PR:A**
ROARIN' LEAD ** (1937) PR:A
ROARING CITY * (1951) PR:A
ROARING RANCH *½ (1930) PR:A
ROARING ROADS * (1935) PR:A
ROARING SIX GUNS *½ (1937) PR:A
ROARING TIMBER ** (1937) PR:A
ROARING TIMBERS
(SEE:COME AND GET IT)
ROARING TWENTIES, THE **** (1939) **PR:C**
ROARING WESTWARD * (1949) PR:A
ROB ROY
(SEE:ROB ROY, THE HIGHLAND ROGUE)
ROB ROY, THE HIGHLAND ROGUE *
(1954, Brit.) **PR:A**
ROBBER SYMPHONY, THE *** (1937, Brit.) PR:A
ROBBERS OF THE RANGE **½ (1941) PR:A
ROBBERS' ROOST *** (1933) PR:A
ROBBERY *** (1967, Brit.) **PR:A-C**
ROBBERY UNDER ARMS ** (1958, Brit.) PR:A
ROBBERY WITH VIOLENCE * (1958, Brit.) PR:A
ROBBO
(SEE:ROBIN AND THE 7 HOODS)
ROBBY *½ (1968) PR:AA
ROBE, THE ***½ (1953) **PR:A**
ROBERTA **** (1935) **PR:A**
ROBIN AND MARIAN *** (1976, Brit.) **PR:A-C**
ROBIN AND THE SEVEN HOODS ***
(1964) **PR:A-C**
ROBIN HOOD
(SEE:ADVENTURES OF ROBIN HOOD, THE)
ROBIN HOOD
(SEE:STORY OF ROBIN HOOD, THE)
ROBIN HOOD *** (1973) **PR:AA**
ROBIN HOOD OF EL DORADO **½ (1936) PR:C
ROBIN HOOD OF THE PECOS ** (1941) PR:A
ROBIN HOOD OF THE RANGE ** (1943) PR:A
ROBIN OF TEXAS *** (1947) **PR:A**
ROBINSON CRUSOE
(SEE:ADVENTURES OF ROBINSON CRUSOE, THE)
ROBINSON CRUSOE ON MARS *** (1964) PR:A
ROBINSON CRUSOELAND
(SEE:UTOPIA)
ROBINSON SOLL NICHT STERBEN
(SEE:GIRL AND THE LEGEND, THE)
ROBINSON'S GARDEN ***½ (1988, Jap.) PR:O
ROBO DE DIAMANTES
(SEE:RUN LIKE A THIEF)
ROBO NO ISHI
(SEE:WAYSIDE PEBBLE, THE)
ROBOCOP ***½ (1987) **PR:O**
ROBOT HOLOCAUST zero (1987) **PR:O**
ROBOT MONSTER zero (1953) **PR:A**
ROBOT VS. THE AZTEC MUMMY, THE zero
(1965, Mex.) **PR:O**
ROCCO AND HIS BROTHERS ***½
(1961, Fr./It.) PR:C
ROCCO E I SUOI FRATELLI
(SEE:ROCCO AND HIS BROTHERS)
ROCCO PAPALEO *** (1974, It./Fr.) PR:O
ROCK-A-BYE BABY *** (1958) PR:A
ROCK ALL NIGHT ** (1957) PR:A
ROCK AROUND THE CLOCK *** (1956) PR:A
ROCK AROUND THE WORLD *½ (1957, Brit.) PR:A
ROCK BABY, ROCK IT zero (1957) **PR:A**
ROCK ISLAND TRAIL **½ (1950) PR:A
ROCK 'N' ROLL HIGH SCHOOL **** (1979) **PR:C**
ROCK 'N' ROLL NIGHTMARE zero
(1987, Can.) **PR:O**
ROCK, PRETTY BABY * (1956) **PR:A**
ROCK RIVER RENEGADES *½ (1942) PR:A
ROCK, ROCK, ROCK! **½ (1956) **PR:A**
ROCK YOU SINNERS * (1957, Brit.) PR:A

ROCKABILLY BABY ** (1957) PR:A
ROCKABYE ** (1932) PR:A
ROCKERS *** (1980) **PR:O**
ROCKET ATTACK, U.S.A. zero (1961) **PR:A**
ROCKET FROM CALABUCH, THE
(SEE:CALABUCH)
ROCKET MAN, THE *½ (1954) PR:A
ROCKET TO NOWHERE **½ (1962, Czech.) PR:AA
ROCKET TO THE MOON
(SEE:CAT WOMEN OF THE MOON)
ROCKETS GALORE
(SEE:MAD LITTLE ISLAND)
ROCKETS IN THE DUNES **½ (1960, Brit.) PR:AA
ROCKETSHIP X-M *** (1950) **PR:A**
ROCKIN' IN THE ROCKIES * (1945) PR:A
ROCKIN' ROAD TRIP ** (1986) **PR:C-O**
ROCKING HORSE WINNER, THE ***½
(1950, Brit.) PR:C-O
ROCKS OF VALPRE, THE
(SEE:HIGH TREASON)
ROCKY * (1948) PR:A
ROCKY **** (1976) **PR:A-C**
ROCKY II ***½ (1979) **PR:A-C**
ROCKY III *** (1982) **PR:A-C**
ROCKY IV *½ (1985) **PR:C**
ROCKY HORROR PICTURE SHOW, THE *
(1975, Brit.) PR:O
ROCKY MOUNTAIN *** (1950) PR:A
ROCKY MOUNTAIN MYSTERY **½ (1935) PR:A
ROCKY MOUNTAIN RANGERS ** (1940) **PR:A**
ROCKY RHODES ** (1934) PR:A
RODAN *½ (1958, Jap.) **PR:A**
RODEO ** (1952) **PR:A**
RODEO KING AND THE SENORITA ** (1951) PR:A
RODEO RHYTHM *½ (1941) PR:AA
ROGER TOUHY, GANGSTER! ** (1944) PR:A
ROGUE COP *** (1954) PR:A
ROGUE OF THE RANGE *½ (1937) PR:A
ROGUE OF THE RIO GRANDE ** (1930) PR:A
ROGUE RIVER **½ (1951) PR:A
ROGUE SONG, THE *** (1930) PR:A
ROGUE'S GALLERY
(SEE:DEVIL'S TRAIL, THE)
ROGUES GALLERY ** (1945) PR:A
ROGUE'S MARCH ** (1952) PR:A
ROGUES OF SHERWOOD FOREST ** (1950) PR:A
ROGUES' REGIMENT ** (1948) PR:A
ROGUES' TAVERN, THE ** (1936) PR:A
ROGUE'S YARN ** (1956, Brit.) **PR:A**
ROLL ALONG, COWBOY * (1938) **PR:A**
ROLL ON
(SEE:LAWLESS PLAINSMEN)
ROLL ON TEXAS MOON **½ (1946) PR:A
ROLL, THUNDER, ROLL *½ (1949) PR:A
ROLL, WAGONS, ROLL **½ (1939) PR:A
ROLLER BLADE zero (1986) **PR:O**
ROLLER BOOGIE zero (1979) **PR:C**
ROLLERBALL *** (1975) **PR:O**
ROLLERCOASTER *** (1977) **PR:C-O**
ROLLIN' HOME TO TEXAS ** (1941) PR:A
ROLLIN' PLAINS *½ (1938) PR:A
ROLLIN' WESTWARD *½ (1939) PR:A
ROLLING CARAVANS *½ (1938) PR:A
ROLLING DOWN THE GREAT DIVIDE **
(1942) PR:A
ROLLING HOME * (1935, Brit.) PR:A
ROLLING IN MONEY * (1934, Brit.) PR:A
ROLLING THUNDER *** (1977) **PR:O**
ROLLOVER ** (1981) **PR:O**
ROMA ***½ (1972, It./Fr.) PR:O
ROMA, CITTA APERTA
(SEE:ROME, OPEN CITY)
ROMA CONTRO ROMA
(SEE:WAR OF THE ZOMBIES, THE)
ROMA RIVUOLE CESARE
(SEE:ROME WANTS ANOTHER CAESAR)
ROMAN HOLIDAY **** (1953) **PR:A**
ROMAN SCANDALS ***½ (1933) **PR:A-C**
ROMAN SPRING OF MRS. STONE, THE ***½
(1961, US/Brit.) PR:C
ROMANCE *** (1930) PR:A
ROMANCE A LA CARTE * (1938, Brit.) PR:A
ROMANCE AND RHYTHM
(SEE:COWBOY FROM BROOKLYN)
ROMANCE AND RICHES **½ (1937, Brit.) PR:A
ROMANCE FOR THREE
(SEE:PARADISE FOR THREE)

Finding entries in **THE MOTION PICTURE GUIDE** ™
Years 1929-83   Volumes I-IX
1984   Volume IX
1985   1986 ANNUAL
1986   1987 ANNUAL
1987   1988 ANNUAL
1988   1989 ANNUAL

STAR RATINGS
★★★★★ Masterpiece
★★★★ Excellent
★★★ Good
★★ Fair
★ Poor
zero Without Merit

PARENTAL RECOMMENDATION (PR:)
AA   Good for Children
A   Acceptable for Children
C   Cautionary, some objectionable scenes
O   Objectionable for Children

BOLD: Films on Videocassette

ROMANCE IN FLANDERS, A
(SEE:LOST ON THE WESTERN FRONT)
ROMANCE IN MANHATTAN ** (1935) PR:A
ROMANCE IN RHYTHM ** (1934, Brit.) PR:C
ROMANCE IN THE DARK *½ (1938) PR:A
ROMANCE IN THE RAIN ** (1934) PR:A
ROMANCE IS SACRED
(SEE:KING AND THE CHORUS GIRL, THE)
ROMANCE OF A HORSE THIEF ** (1971) PR:A
ROMANCE OF RIO GRANDE
(SEE:ROMANCE OF THE RIO GRANDE)
ROMANCE OF ROSY RIDGE, THE *** (1947) PR:A
ROMANCE OF SEVILLE, A *½ (1929, Brit.) PR:A
ROMANCE OF THE LIMBERLOST ** (1938) PR:A
ROMANCE OF THE REDWOODS *½ (1939) PR:A
ROMANCE OF THE RIO GRANDE **½ (1929) PR:A
ROMANCE OF THE RIO GRANDE ** (1941) PR:A
ROMANCE OF THE ROCKIES ** (1938) PR:A
ROMANCE OF THE WEST *½ (1946) PR:A
ROMANCE ON THE BEACH
(SEE:SIN ON THE BEACH)
ROMANCE ON THE HIGH SEAS *** (1948) PR:A
ROMANCE ON THE RANGE ** (1942) PR:A
ROMANCE ON THE RUN *½ (1938) PR:A
ROMANCE RIDES THE RANGE * (1936) PR:A
ROMANCING THE STONE ***½ (1984) PR:C-O
ROMANOFF AND JULIET ***½ (1961) PR:A
ROMANTIC AGE, THE
(SEE:SISTERS UNDER THE SKIN)
ROMANTIC AGE, THE
(SEE:NAUGHTY ARLETTE)
ROMANTIC COMEDY **½ (1983) PR:A-C
ROMANTIC ENGLISHWOMAN, THE ***½
(1975, Brit./Fr.) PR:O
ROMANY LOVE * (1931, Brit.) PR:A
ROME ADVENTURE ** (1962) PR:A
ROME EXPRESS *** (1933, Brit.) PR:A
ROME, OPEN CITY
(SEE:OPEN CITY)
ROME WANTS ANOTHER CAESAR ***
(1974, It.) PR:A
ROMEO AND JULIET **** (1936) PR:C
ROMEO AND JULIET ** (1954, Brit.) PR:A**
ROMEO AND JULIET ** (1955, USSR) PR:A
ROMEO AND JULIET * (1966, Brit.) PR:A**
ROMEO AND JULIET ***½ (1968, Brit./It.) PR:C
ROMEO AND JULIET ***½ (1968, It./Sp.) PR:A-C
ROMEO IN PYJAMAS
(SEE:PARLOR, BEDROOM & BATH)
ROMEO, JULIET AND DARKNESS
(SEE:SWEET LIGHT IN A DARK ROOM)
ROMMEL-DESERT FOX
(SEE:DESERT FOX)
ROMMEL'S TREASURE *½ (1962, It.) PR:A
ROMOLO E REMO
(SEE:DUEL OF THE TITANS)
ROOF, THE ** (1933, Brit.) PR:A
ROOGIE'S BUMP * (1954) PR:A
ROOK, THE
(SEE:SOMETHING FOR EVERYONE)
ROOKERY NOOK
(SEE:ONE EMBARRASSING NIGHT)
ROOKIE, THE * (1959) PR:A
ROOKIE COP, THE ** (1939) PR:A
ROOKIE FIREMAN ** (1950) PR:A
ROOKIES
(SEE:BUCK PRIVATES)
ROOKIES COME HOME
(SEE:BUCK PRIVATES COME HOME)
ROOKIES IN BURMA ** (1943) PR:A
ROOKIES ON PARADE ** (1941) PR:A
ROOM AT THE TOP ** (1959, Brit.) PR:O**
ROOM FOR ONE MORE ***½ (1952) PR:AA
ROOM FOR TWO * (1940, Brit.) PR:A
ROOM 43 ** (1959, Brit.) PR:A
ROOM IN THE HOUSE ** (1955, Brit.) PR:A
ROOM SERVICE * (1938) PR:A**
ROOM TO LET ** (1949, Brit.) PR:A
ROOM UPSTAIRS, THE **½ (1948, Fr.) PR:C
ROOM WITH A VIEW, A ** (1986, Brit.) PR:C**
ROOMATES
(SEE:MARCH OF THE SPRING HARE)
ROOMMATES ** (1962, Brit.) PR:AA
ROOMMATES zero (1971) PR:O
ROOMMATES, THE * (1973) PR:O
ROONEY *** (1958, Brit.) PR:A
ROOSTER COGBURN *½ (1975) PR:A
ROOT OF ALL EVIL, THE * (1947, Brit.) PR:A
ROOTIN' TOOTIN' RHYTHM * (1937) PR:A**
ROOTS OF HEAVEN, THE *** (1958) PR:C
ROPE * (1948) PR:C-O**
ROPE
(SEE:ROPE OF FLESH)
ROPE OF FLESH *½ (1965) PR:O
ROPE OF SAND *** (1949) PR:A
ROSALIE * (1937) PR:A**
ROSARY, THE *½ (1931, Brit.) PR:O
ROSARY MURDERS, THE ** (1987) PR:O
ROSE, THE * (1979) PR:O**
ROSE BOWL * (1936) PR:A
ROSE BOWL STORY, THE ** (1952) PR:A
ROSE FOR EVERYONE, A **½ (1967, It.) PR:O
ROSE MARIE ** (1936) PR:AA**
ROSE MARIE *** (1954) PR:AA
ROSE OF CIMARRON **½ (1952) PR:A
ROSE OF THE RANCHO *½ (1936) PR:A
ROSE OF THE RIO GRANDE
(SEE:GOD'S COUNTRY AND THE MAN)
ROSE OF THE RIO GRANDE * (1938) PR:A
ROSE OF THE YUKON ** (1949) PR:A
ROSE OF TRALEE * (1938, Ireland) PR:A
ROSE OF TRALEE *½ (1942, Brit.) PR:A
ROSE OF WASHINGTON SQUARE *** (1939) PR:A
ROSE TATTOO, THE **** (1955) PR:C-O
ROSEANNA McCOY *** (1949) PR:AA
ROSEBUD * (1975) PR:C
ROSEBUD BEACH HOTEL ** (1984) PR:C-O
ROSELAND * (1977) PR:C**
ROSEMARY ***½ (1960, Ger.) PR:C
ROSEMARY'S BABY ** (1968) PR:O**
ROSEMARY'S KILLER
(SEE:THE PROWLER)
ROSEN FUR DEN STAATSANWALT
(SEE:ROSES FOR THE PROSECUTOR)
ROSES ARE RED ** (1947) PR:A
ROSES FOR THE PROSECUTOR ***
(1961, Ger.) PR:A
ROSIE! *½ (1967) PR:A
ROSIE THE RIVETER ** (1944) PR:A
ROSMUNDA E ALBOINO
(SEE:SWORD OF THE CONQUEROR)
ROSSINI ** (1948, It.) PR:A
ROSSITER CASE, THE *½ (1950, Brit.) PR:A
ROTHSCHILD ** (1938, Fr.) PR:A
R.O.T.O.R. zero (1988) PR:O
ROTTEN APPLE, THE * (1963) PR:O
ROTTEN TO THE CORE **½ (1956, Brit.) PR:C
ROTWEILER: DOGS OF HELL zero (1984) PR:O
ROUGE OF THE NORTH *** (1988, Taiwan) PR:C
ROUGH AND THE SMOOTH, THE
(SEE:PORTRAIT OF A SINNER)
ROUGH COMPANY
(SEE:VIOLENT MEN, THE)
ROUGH CUT **½ (1980, Brit.) PR:C
ROUGH NIGHT IN JERICHO *½ (1967) PR:O
ROUGH RIDERS OF CHEYENNE ** (1945) PR:A
ROUGH RIDERS OF DURANGO ** (1951) PR:A
ROUGH RIDERS' ROUNDUP **½ (1939) PR:A
ROUGH RIDIN' RHYTHM *½ (1937) PR:A
ROUGH RIDING RANGER * (1935) PR:A
ROUGH RIDING ROMEO
(SEE:FLAMING GUNS)
ROUGH ROMANCE *½ (1930) PR:A
ROUGH SHOOT
(SEE:SHOOT FIRST)
ROUGH, TOUGH AND READY ** (1945) PR:A
ROUGH, TOUGH WEST, THE ** (1952) PR:A
ROUGH WATERS **½ (1930) PR:AA
ROUGHLY SPEAKING ** (1945) PR:A
ROUGHSHOD *** (1949) PR:A
'ROUND MIDNIGHT *** (1986, Fr./US) PR:C**
ROUND TRIP * (1967) PR:C
ROUND UP, THE ***½ (1969, Hung.) PR:O
ROUNDERS, THE ***½ (1965) PR:A-C
ROUNDTRIP
(SEE:ROUND TRIP)
ROUNDUP, THE * (1941) PR:A
ROUNDUP TIME IN TEXAS **½ (1937) PR:A
ROUSTABOUT **½ (1964) PR:A
ROVER, THE * (1967, It.) PR:C
ROVIN' TUMBLEWEEDS * (1939) PR:A
ROVING ROGUE, A
(SEE:OUTLAWS OF THE ROCKIES)
ROWDYMAN, THE **½ (1973, Can.) PR:C
ROWING WITH THE WIND *** (1988, Sp.) PR:C
ROXANNE ***½ (1987) PR:A-C
ROXIE HART *** (1942) PR:A
ROYAL AFFAIR, A *** (1950) PR:A
ROYAL AFFAIRS IN VERSAILLES ***
(1957, Fr.) PR:A
ROYAL AFRICAN RIFLES, THE ** (1953) PR:A
ROYAL BED, THE ** (1931) PR:A
ROYAL BOX, THE * (1930) PR:A
ROYAL CAVALCADE
(SEE:REGAL CAVALCADE)
ROYAL DEMAND, A * (1933, Brit.) PR:A
ROYAL DIVORCE, A ** (1938, Brit.) PR:A
ROYAL EAGLE ** (1936, Brit.) PR:A
ROYAL FAMILY OF BROADWAY, THE ****
(1930) PR:A
ROYAL FLASH *** (1975, Brit.) PR:A-C
ROYAL FLUSH
(SEE:TWO GUYS FROM MILWAUKEE)
ROYAL GAME, THE
(SEE:BRAINWASHED)
ROYAL HUNT OF THE SUN, THE **½
(1969, Brit.) PR:A
ROYAL MOUNTED PATROL, THE *** (1941) PR:A
ROYAL ROMANCE, A *½ (1930) PR:A
ROYAL SCANDAL, A *** (1945) PR:C-O
ROYAL TRACK, THE
(SEE:OBSESSION)
ROYAL WALTZ, THE ** (1936) PR:A
ROYAL WEDDING ** (1951) PR:A**
ROZMARNE LETO
(SEE:CAPRICIOUS SUMMER)
R.P.M. zero (1970) PR:C
RUBA AL PROSSIMO TUO
(SEE:FINE PAIR, A)
RUBBER GUN, THE ** (1977, Can.) PR:C
RUBBER RACKETEERS *½ (1942) PR:A
RUBY **½ (1971) PR:C
RUBY * (1977) PR:O
RUBY GENTRY ** (1952) PR:C-O
RUBY VIRGIN, THE
(SEE:HELL'S ISLAND)
RUCKUS **½ (1981) PR:C
RUDE BOY * (1980, Brit.) PR:O**
RUDYARD KIPLING'S JUNGLE BOOK
(SEE:JUNGLE BOOK)
RUE CASES NEGRES
(SEE:SUGAR CANE ALLEY)
RUGGED O'RIORDANS, THE ** (1949, Aus.) PR:A
RUGGLES OF RED GAP ** (1935) PR:A**
RULER OF THE WORLD
(SEE:MASTER OF THE WORLD)
RULERS OF THE SEA ** (1939) PR:A
RULES OF THE GAME, THE *** (1939, Fr.) PR:C**
RULING CLASS, THE ***½ (1972, Brit.) PR:O
RULING VOICE, THE *½ (1931) PR:A
RUMBA ** (1935) PR:A
RUMBLE FISH ** (1983) PR:O**
RUMBLE ON THE DOCKS ** (1956) PR:A
RUMPELSTILTSKIN ** (1965, Ger.) PR:A
RUMPELSTILTSKIN **½ (1987) PR:AA
RUMPELSTILZCHEN
(SEE:RUMPELSTILTSKIN)
RUN ACROSS THE RIVER * (1961) PR:A
RUN, ANGEL, RUN ** (1969) PR:O
RUN FOR COVER ***½ (1955) PR:A-C
RUN FOR THE HILLS zero (1953) PR:A
RUN FOR THE ROSES *½ (1978) PR:C
RUN FOR THE SUN ** (1956) PR:A
RUN FOR YOUR MONEY, A *** (1950, Brit.) PR:A
RUN FOR YOUR WIFE **½ (1966, Fr./It.) PR:C
RUN HERO RUN
(SEE:HELL WITH HEROS, THE)
RUN HOME SLOW ** (1965) PR:C
RUN LIKE A THIEF
(SEE:MAKE LIKE A THIEF)
RUN LIKE A THIEF *½ (1968, Sp.) PR:C
RUN OF THE ARROW * (1957) PR:C-O**
RUN ON GOLD, A
(SEE:MIDAS RUN)
RUN SHADOW RUN
(SEE:COVER ME BABE)
RUN SILENT, RUN DEEP * (1958) PR:A-C**
RUN, STRANGER, RUN
(SEE:HAPPY MOTHER'S DAY$e3LOVE, GEORGE)
RUN WILD, RUN FREE **½ (1969, Brit.) PR:A
RUN WITH THE DEVIL *½ (1963, Fr./It.) PR:A
RUN WITH THE WIND * (1966, Brit.) PR:O
RUNAROUND, THE * (1931) PR:A
RUNAROUND, THE ** (1946) PR:A
RUNAWAY **½ (1984) PR:C-O
RUNAWAY BRIDE * (1930) PR:A
RUNAWAY BUS, THE **½ (1954, Brit.) PR:A
RUNAWAY DAUGHTER
(SEE:RED SALUTE)
RUNAWAY DAUGHTERS ** (1957) PR:A
RUNAWAY DAUGHTERS
(SEE:PROWL GIRLS)
RUNAWAY GIRL ** (1966) PR:C
RUNAWAY LADIES ** (1935, Brit.) PR:A
RUNAWAY QUEEN, THE ** (1935, Brit.) PR:A
RUNAWAY RAILWAY ** (1965, Brit.) PR:AA
RUNAWAY TRAIN ***½ (1985) PR:O
RUNAWAY, THE *½ (1964, Brit.) PR:A
RUNNER STUMBLES, THE ** (1979) PR:C
RUNNERS * (1983, Brit.) PR:A
RUNNING *½ (1979, Can.) PR:C
RUNNING BRAVE *½ (1983, Can.) PR:C
RUNNING HOT * (1984) PR:O
RUNNING MAN, THE *** (1963, Brit.) PR:A-C
RUNNING MAN, THE ** (1987) PR:O
RUNNING ON EMPTY * (1988) PR:C**
RUNNING OUT OF LUCK zero (1986) PR:O
RUNNING SCARED
(SEE:GHOST AND MR. CHICKEN, THE)
RUNNING SCARED **½ (1972, Brit.) PR:C-O
RUNNING SCARED **½ (1986) PR:C-O
RUNNING TARGET *** (1956) PR:A
RUNNING WILD *½ (1955) PR:A

RUNNING WILD **½ (1973) PR:AA
RUSH * (1984, It.) PR:C-O
RUSSIAN ROULETTE ** (1975) PR:C
RUSSIANS ARE COMING, THE, RUSSIANS ARE
COMING, THE ***½ (1966) PR:A
RUSSKIES * (1987) PR:A
RUSTLERS ** (1949) PR:A
RUSTLER'S HIDEOUT * (1944) PR:A
RUSTLERS OF DEVIL'S CANYON **½ (1947) PR:A
RUSTLERS ON HORSEBACK ** (1950) PR:A
RUSTLER'S PARADISE ** (1935) PR:A
RUSTLER'S RHAPSODY **½ (1985) PR:C
RUSTLERS' ROUNDUP ** (1933) PR:A
RUSTLER'S ROUNDUP *½ (1946) PR:A
RUSTLER'S VALLEY * (1937) PR:A
RUSTY LEADS THE WAY *½ (1948) PR:A
RUSTY RIDES ALONE *½ (1933) PR:A
RUSTY SAVES A LIFE *½ (1949) PR:A
RUSTY'S BIRTHDAY *½ (1949) PR:A
RUTHLESS * (1948) PR:A
RUTHLESS FOUR, THE ** (1969, It./Ger.) PR:C
RUTHLESS PEOPLE ***½ (1986) PR:C-O
RUUSUJEN AIKA
(SEE:TIME OF ROSES)
RUY BLAS **½ (1948, Fr.) PR:A
RX MURDER ** (1958, Brit.) PR:A
RYAN'S DAUGHTER **½ (1970, Brit.) PR:O
RYDER, P.I. zero (1986) PR:C-O
RYMDINVASION I LAPPLAND
(SEE:INVASION OF THE ANIMAL PEOPLE)
RYSOPIS
(SEE:IDENTIFICATION MARKS: NONE)

S

SAADIA *½ (1953) PR:A
SABAKA
(SEE:HINDU, THE)
SABALEROS
(SEE:PUT UP OR SHUT UP)
SABATA **½ (1969, It.) PR:C
SABINA, THE * (1979, Sp./Swed.) PR:O
SABOTAGE
(SEE:WHEN LONDON SLEEPS)
SABOTAGE ***½ (1937, Brit.) PR:O
SABOTAGE ** (1939) PR:A
SABOTAGE AT SEA *½ (1942, Brit.) PR:A
SABOTAGE SQUAD * (1942) PR:A
SABOTEUR ** (1942) PR:A**
SABOTEUR, CODE NAME MORITURI
(SEE:MORITURI)
SABRA **½ (1970, Fr./It./Israel) PR:C
SABRE AND THE ARROW, THE
(SEE:LAST OF THE COMANCHES, THE)
SABRE JET *½ (1953) PR:A
SABRINA ** (1954) PR:A**
SABRINA FAIR
(SEE:SABRINA)
SABU AND THE MAGIC RING * (1957) PR:A
SACCO AND VANZETTI * (1971, It./Fr.) PR:C**
SACRED FLAME, THE *½ (1929) PR:A
SACRED FLAME, THE
(SEE:RIGHT TO LIVE, THE)
SACRED GROUND **½ (1984) PR:C
SACRED HEARTS **½ (1984, Brit.) PR:A
SACRED KNIVES OF VENGEANCE, THE *
(1974, Hong Kong) PR:O
SACRIFICE OF HONOR ** (1938, Fr.) PR:A
SACRIFICE, THE ** (1986, Fr./Swed.) PR:C**
SAD HORSE, THE **½ (1959) PR:A
SAD SACK, THE * (1957) PR:A**
SAD SACK, THE
(SEE:ARMY GAME, THE)
SADDLE BUSTER, THE *½ (1932) PR:A
SADDLE LEGION ** (1951) PR:A
SADDLE MOUNTAIN ROUNDUP ** (1941) PR:A
SADDLE PALS ** (1947) PR:A
SADDLE THE WIND *** (1958) PR:A
SADDLE TRAMP *** (1950) PR:A
SADDLEMATES ** (1941) PR:A
SADIE MCKEE *** (1934) PR:A
SADIST, THE *½ (1963) PR:A

SADKO
(SEE:MAGIC VOYAGE OF SINBAD, THE)
SAFARI *½ (1940) PR:A
SAFARI ** (1956) PR:A
SAFARI DRUMS ** (1953) PR:A
SAFARI 3000 ** (1982) PR:A-C
SAFE AFFAIR, A *½ (1931, Brit.) PR:A
SAFE AT HOME ** (1962) PR:A
SAFE IN HELL ** (1931) PR:A
SAFE PLACE, A ** (1971) PR:A
SAFECRACKER, THE **½ (1958, Brit.) PR:A
SAFETY IN NUMBERS ** (1930) PR:A
SAFETY IN NUMBERS ** (1938) PR:A
SAFFO, VENERE DE LESBO
(SEE:WARRIOR EMPRESS, THE)
SAGA OF DEATH VALLEY ** (1939) PR:A
SAGA OF DRACULA, THE * (1975, Sp.) PR:O
SAGA OF HEMP BROWN, THE ** (1958) PR:A
SAGA OF THE FLYING HOSTESS
(SEE:GIRL GAME)
SAGA OF THE ROAD, THE
(SEE:PATHER PANCHALI)
SAGA OF THE VAGABONDS *** (1964, Jap.) PR:A
SAGA OF THE VIKING WOMEN AND THEIR
VOYAGE TO THE WATERS OF THE GREAT SEA
SERPENT, THE zero (1957) PR:A
SAGEBRUSH FAMILY TRAILS WEST, THE *
(1940) PR:A
SAGEBRUSH LAW *½ (1943) PR:A
SAGEBRUSH POLITICS * (1930) PR:A
SAGEBRUSH TRAIL ** (1934) PR:A
SAGEBRUSH TROUBADOR ** (1935) PR:A
SAGINAW TRAIL ** (1953) PR:A
SAHARA *** (1943) PR:A**
SAHARA * (1984) PR:C
SAID O'REILLY TO MACNAB
(SEE:SEZ O'REILLY TO MACNAB)
SAIGON *** (1948) PR:A
SAIKAKU ICHIDAI ONNA
(SEE:LIFE OF OHARU)
SAIL A CROOKED SHIP ** (1961) PR:A
SAIL INTO DANGER ** (1957, Brit.) PR:A
SAILING ALONG ** (1938, Brit.) PR:A
SAILOR BE GOOD *½ (1933) PR:A
SAILOR BEWARE ** (1951) PR:A
SAILOR BEWARE?
(SEE:PANIC IN THE PARLOUR)
SAILOR FROM GIBRALTAR, THE *
(1967, Brit.) PR:O
SAILOR OF THE KING ** (1953, Brit.) PR:A
SAILOR TAKES A WIFE, THE ** (1946) PR:A
**SAILOR WHO FELL FROM GRACE WITH THE SEA,
THE ** (1976, Brit.) PR:O**
SAILOR'S DON'T CARE ** (1940, Brit.) PR:A
SAILORS' HOLIDAY *½ (1929) PR:A
SAILOR'S HOLIDAY ** (1944) PR:A
SAILOR'S LADY ** (1940) PR:A
SAILOR'S LUCK ** (1933) PR:A
SAILORS ON LEAVE ** (1941) PR:A
SAILOR'S RETURN, THE * (1978, Brit.) PR:O
SAILORS THREE
(SEE:THREE COCKEYED SAILORS)
ST. BENNY THE DIP **½ (1951) PR:A
ST. ELMO'S FIRE * (1985) PR:O
ST. GEORGE AND THE 7 CURSES
(SEE:MAGIC SWORD, THE)
ST. HELENS ** (1981) PR:A
SAINT IN LONDON, THE ***½ (1939, Brit.) PR:A
SAINT IN NEW YORK, THE * (1938) PR:A**
SAINT IN PALM SPRINGS, THE *** (1941) PR:A
ST. IVES ** (1976) PR:O
SAINT JACK **½ (1979) PR:O
SAINT JOAN **½ (1957) PR:A-C
ST. LOUIS BLUES **½ (1939) PR:A
ST. LOUIS BLUES ** (1958) PR:A
ST. LOUIS KID, THE *** (1934) PR:A
ST. MARTIN'S LANE
(SEE:SIDEWALKS OF LONDON)
SAINT MEETS THE TIGER, THE **
(1943, Brit.) PR:A
SAINT STRIKES BACK, THE ***½ (1939) PR:A
SAINT TAKES OVER, THE *** (1940) PR:A
ST. VALENTINE'S DAY MASSACRE, THE ***½
(1967) PR:O
SAINTED SISTERS, THE ** (1948) PR:A
SAINTLY SINNERS **½ (1962) PR:A
SAINTS AND SINNERS ** (1949, Brit.) PR:A

SAINT'S DOUBLE TROUBLE, THE **½ (1940) PR:A
SAINT'S GIRL FRIDAY, THE ***½ (1954, Brit.) PR:A
SAINT'S RETURN, THE
(SEE:SAINT'S GIRL FRIDAY, THE)
SAINT'S VACATION, THE * (1941, Brit.) PR:A**
SAL OF SINGAPORE **½ (1929) PR:A
SALAAM BOMBAY * (1988, India) PR:O**
SALAMANDER, THE * (1983, US/It./Brit.) PR:O
SALAMMBO
(SEE:LOVE OF SALAMMBO, THE)
SALARIO PARA MATAR
(SEE:MERCENARY, THE)
SALESLADY **½ (1938) PR:A
SALLAH **½ (1965, Israel) PR:C
SALLY **½ (1929) PR:A
SALLY AND SAINT ANNE *** (1952) PR:A
SALLY BISHOP ** (1932, Brit.) PR:A
SALLY FIELDGOOD & CO. * (1975, Can.) PR:C-O
SALLY IN OUR ALLEY **½ (1931, Brit.) PR:A
SALLY, IRENE AND MARY ** (1938) PR:A
SALLY OF THE SUBWAY *½ (1932) PR:C
SALLY'S HOUNDS * (1968) PR:C
SALLY'S IRISH ROGUE
(SEE:POACHER'S DAUGHTER, THE)
SALOME * (1953) PR:C**
SALOME zero (1986, Fr./It.) PR:O
SALOME, WHERE SHE DANCED * (1945) PR:C
SALOME'S LAST DANCE ***½ (1988) PR:O
SALOON BAR *** (1940, Brit.) PR:C
SALSA * (1988) PR:C**
SALT & PEPPER ** (1968, Brit.) PR:C
SALT AND THE DEVIL
(SEE:SALT TO THE DEVIL)
SALT LAKE RAIDERS *** (1950) PR:A
SALT OF THE EARTH *** (1954) PR:C**
SALT TO THE DEVIL *** (1949, Brit.) PR:A
SALTO *** (1966, Pol.) PR:O
SALTY * (1975) PR:A
SALTY O'ROURKE * (1945) PR:A-C**
SALUTE **½ (1929) PR:A
SALUTE FOR THREE ** (1943) PR:A
SALUTE JOHN CITIZEN **½ (1942, Brit.) PR:A
SALUTE THE TOFF ** (1952, Brit.) PR:A
SALUTE TO A REBEL
(SEE:PATTON)
SALUTE TO COURAGE
(SEE:NAZI AGENT)
SALUTE TO ROMANCE
(SEE:ANNAPOLIS SALUTE)
SALUTE TO THE MARINES **½ (1943) PR:C
SALVADOR ** (1986, Brit.) PR:O**
SALVAGE GANG, THE **½ (1958, Brit.) PR:AA
SALVARE LA FACCIA
(SEE:PSYCHOUT FOR MURDER)
SALVATION! **½ (1987) PR:O
SALVATION NELL **½ (1931) PR:A
SALVATORE GIULIANO *** (1966, It.) PR:O
SALZBURG CONNECTION, THE * (1972) PR:C
SAM COOPER'S GOLD
(SEE:RUTHLESS FOUR, THE)
SAM MARLOW, PRIVATE EYE
(SEE:MAN WITH BOGART'S FACE, THE)
SAM SMALL LEAVES TOWN ** (1937, Brit.) PR:A
SAM WHISKEY **½ (1969) PR:C-O
SAMANTHA
(SEE:A NEW KIND OF LOVE)
SAMAR **½ (1962) PR:C
SAMARITAN, THE
(SEE:SOUL OF THE SLUMS)
SAME TIME, NEXT YEAR ***½ (1978) PR:A-C
SAME TO YOU ** (1987, Ger./Switz) PR:O
**SAMMY AND ROSIE GET LAID ***½
(1987, Brit.) PR:O**
SAMMY GOING SOUTH
(SEE:BOY TEN FEET TALL, A)
SAMMY STOPS THE WORLD zero (1978) PR:C
SAMPO
(SEE:DAY THE EARTH FROZE, THE)
SAM'S SON **½ (1984) PR:A-C
SAM'S SONG * (1971) PR:O
SAMSON * (1961, It.) PR:A
SAMSON AND DELILAH ***½ (1949) PR:C
SAMSON AND THE SEVEN MIRACLES OF THE
WORLD ** (1963, Fr./It.) PR:A
SAMSON AND THE SLAVE QUEEN **
(1963, It.) PR:A

Finding entries in **THE MOTION PICTURE GUIDE** ™

Years 1929-83	Volumes I-IX
1984	Volume IX
1985	1986 ANNUAL
1986	1987 ANNUAL
1987	1988 ANNUAL
1988	1989 ANNUAL

STAR RATINGS
★★★★★ Masterpiece
★★★★ Excellent
★★★ Good
★★ Fair
★ Poor
zero Without Merit

PARENTAL RECOMMENDATION (PR:)
AA Good for Children
A Acceptable for Children
C Cautionary, some objectionable scenes
O Objectionable for Children

BOLD: Films on Videocassette

SAMSON IN THE WAX MUSEUM
  (SEE:SANTO EN EL MUSEO DE CERA)
SAMSON VS. THE GIANT KING
  (SEE:ATLAS AGAINST THE CZAR)
SAMURAI * (1945) PR:A-C
SAMURAI ASSASSIN **½ (1965, Jap.) PR:O
SAMURAI * (1955, Jap.) PR:O**
SAMURAI BANNERS
  (SEE:UNDER THE BANNER OF SAMURAI)
SAMURAI
  (SEE:SAMURAI ASSASSIN)
SAMURAI FROM NOWHERE **½ (1964, Jap.) PR:C
SAMURAI (PART II) ** (1967, Jap.) PR:C-O
SAMURAI (PART III) ** (1967, Jap.) PR:C-O
SAMURAI PIRATE
  (SEE:LOST WORLD OF SINBAD, THE)
SAN ANTONE ** (1953) PR:C
SAN ANTONE AMBUSH ** (1949) PR:A
SAN ANTONIO *** (1945) PR:A-C
SAN ANTONIO KID, THE **½ (1944) PR:A
SAN ANTONIO ROSE **½ (1941) PR:A
SAN DEMETRIO, LONDON **½ (1947, Brit.) PR:C
SAN DIEGO, I LOVE YOU ***½ (1944) PR:A
SAN FERNANDO VALLEY ** (1944) PR:A
SAN FERRY ANN ** (1965, Brit.) PR:A
SAN FRANCISCO *** (1936) PR:A**
SAN FRANCISCO DOCKS ** (1941) PR:A
SAN FRANCISCO STORY, THE **½ (1952) PR:A
SAN QUENTIN *** (1937) PR:C
SAN QUENTIN **½ (1946) PR:A
SANCTUARY * (1961) PR:O
SAND **½ (1949) PR:A
SAND CASTLE, THE *** (1961) PR:AA
SAND PEBBLES, THE ** (1966) PR:C-O**
SANDA TAI GAILAH
  (SEE:WAR OF THE GARGANTUAS, THE)
SANDAI KAIJU CHIKYU SAIDAI NO KESSEN
  (SEE:GHIDRAH, THE THREE-HEADED MONSTER)
SANDERS ** (1963, Brit.) PR:A
SANDERS OF THE RIVER * (1935, Brit.) PR:A-C**
SANDFLOW *** (1937) PR:A
SANDOKAN THE GREAT ** (1964, Fr./It./Sp.) PR:A
SANDPIPER, THE * (1965) PR:C-O
SANDPIT GENERALS, THE
  (SEE:WILD PACK, THE)
SANDRA **½ (1966, It.) PR:O
SANDS OF BEERSHEBA **½ (1966, US/Israel) PR:O
SANDS OF IWO JIMA ** (1949) PR:C**
SANDS OF THE DESERT *½ (1960, Brit.) PR:A
SANDS OF THE KALAHARI **½ (1965, Brit.) PR:O
SANDU FOLLOWS THE SUN **½
  (1965, USSR) PR:AA
SANDWICH MAN, THE **½ (1966, Brit.) PR:A
SANDY GETS HER MAN **½ (1940) PR:AA
SANDY IS A LADY ** (1940) PR:AA
SANDY TAKES A BOW
  (SEE:UNEXPECTED FATHER)
SANDY THE SEAL ** (1969, Brit.) PR:AA
SANG D'UN POETE
  (SEE:BLOOD OF A POET, THE)
SANG ET LUMIERES
  (SEE:LOVE IN A HOT CLIMATE)
SANGAREE ** (1953) PR:C
SANITORIUM
  (SEE:TRIO)
SANJURO **½ (1962, Jap.) PR:C
SANSHO THE BAILIFF *** (1969, Jap.) PR:A**
SANSONE
  (SEE:SAMSON)
SANTA * (1932, Mex.) PR:O
SANTA AND THE THREE BEARS ** (1970) PR:AA
SANTA CLAUS * (1960, Mex.) PR:AA
SANTA CLAUS CONQUERS THE MARTIANS zero (1964) PR:A
SANTA CLAUS: THE MOVIE * (1985) PR:A
SANTA FE **½ (1951) PR:A
SANTA FE BOUND ** (1937) PR:A
SANTA FE MARSHAL ** (1940) PR:A
SANTA FE PASSAGE *** (1955) PR:O
SANTA FE SADDLEMATES ** (1945) PR:A
SANTA FE SATAN
  (SEE:CATCH MY SOUL)
SANTA FE SCOUTS ** (1943) PR:A
SANTA FE STAMPEDE **½ (1938) PR:C
SANTA FE TRAIL ***½ (1940) PR:C
SANTA FE TRAIL, THE ** (1930) PR:A
SANTA FE UPRISING ** (1946) PR:A
SANTA'S CHRISTMAS CIRCUS *½ (1966) PR:AA
SANTEE **½ (1973) PR:O
SANTIAGO *** (1956) PR:A
SANTO AND THE BLUE DEMON VS. THE MONSTERS
  (SEE:SANTO Y BLUE DEMON CONTRA LOS MONSTROUS)
SANTO CONTRA BLUE DEMON EN LA ATLANTIDA * (1968, Mex.) PR:O
SANTO CONTRA EL CEREBRO DIABOLICO zero (1962, Mex.) PR:C

SANTO CONTRA EL DOCTOR MUERTE * (1974, Sp./Mex.) PR:O
SANTO CONTRA LA HIJA DE FRANKENSTEIN * (1971, Mex.) PR:O
SANTO CONTRA LA INVASION DE LOS MARCIANOS * (1966, Mex.) PR:O
SANTO EN EL MUSEO DE CERA * (1963, Mex.) PR:O
SANTO VERSUS THE MARTIAN INVASION
  (SEE:SANTO CONTRA LA INVASION DE LOS MARCIANOS)
SANTO VS. FRANKENSTEIN'S DAUGHTER
  (SEE:SANTO CONTRA LA HIJA DE FRANKENSTEIN)
SANTO Y BLUE DEMON CONTRA LOS MONSTRUOS zero (1968, Mex.) PR:O
SAP FROM ABROAD, THE
  (SEE:SAP FROM SYRACUSE, THE)
SAP FROM SYRACUSE, THE **½ (1930) PR:A
SAP, THE *½ (1929) PR:A
SAPHO
  (SEE:WARRIOR EMPRESS, THE)
SAPPHIRE *** (1959, Brit.) PR:A
SAPS AT SEA **½ (1940) PR:A
SARABA MOSUKUWA GURENTAI
  (SEE:GOODBYE MOSCOW)
SARABAND *** (1949, Brit.) PR:A
SARABAND FOR DEAD LOVERS
  (SEE:SARABAND)
SARACEN BLADE, THE **½ (1954) PR:A
SARAGOSSA MANUSCRIPT, THE **½ (1972, Pol.) PR:A
SARAH AND SON **½ (1930) PR:A
SARATOGA ***½ (1937) PR:A
SARATOGA TRUNK *** (1945) PR:A-C
SARDINIA: RANSOM *** (1968, It.) PR:C
SARDONICUS
  (SEE:MR. SARDONICUS)
SARGE GOES TO COLLEGE *½ (1947) PR:A
SARONG GIRL ** (1943) PR:A
SARUMBA *½ (1950) PR:A
SASAKI KOJIRO
  (SEE:KOJIRO)
SASAYASHI NO JOE
  (SEE:WHISPERING JOE)
SASKATCHEWAN *** (1954) PR:A-C
SASOM I EN SPEGEL
  (SEE:THROUGH A GLASS DARKLY)
SASQUATCH *½ (1978) PR:A
SATAN BUG, THE **½ (1965) PR:A
SATAN IN HIGH HEELS zero (1962) PR:O
SATAN MET A LADY **½ (1936) PR:A
SATAN NEVER SLEEPS ** (1962) PR:C
SATANIC RITES OF DRACULA, THE
  (SEE:COUNT DRACULA AND HIS VAMPIRE BRIDE)
SATAN'S BED *½ (1965) PR:O
SATAN'S CHEERLEADERS zero (1977) PR:O
SATAN'S CLAW
  (SEE:BLOOD ON SATAN'S CLAW)
SATAN'S CRADLE ** (1949) PR:A
SATAN'S MISTRESS zero (1982) PR:O
SATAN'S SADIST zero (1969) PR:O
SATAN'S SATELLITES *½ (1958) PR:AA
SATAN'S SKIN
  (SEE:BLOOD ON SATAN'S CLAW)
SATAN'S SLAVE zero (1976, Brit.) PR:O
SATELLITE IN THE SKY *½ (1956) PR:A
SATIN MUSHROOM, THE *½ (1969) PR:C
SATISFACTION * (1988) PR:C-O
SATURDAY ISLAND
  (SEE:ISLAND OF DESIRE)
SATURDAY NIGHT AND SUNDAY MORNING ***** (1961, Brit.) PR:O
SATURDAY NIGHT AT THE BATHS ** (1975) PR:O
SATURDAY NIGHT AT THE PALACE ** (1988, South Africa) PR:C
SATURDAY NIGHT BATH IN APPLE VALLEY
  (SEE:SATURDAY NIGHT IN APPLE VALLEY)
SATURDAY NIGHT FEVER ***½ (1977) PR:C-O
SATURDAY NIGHT IN APPLE VALLEY *½ (1965) PR:C
SATURDAY NIGHT KID, THE ** (1929) PR:A
SATURDAY NIGHT OUT ** (1964, Brit.) PR:A
SATURDAY NIGHT REVUE ** (1937, Brit.) PR:A
SATURDAY THE 14TH * (1981) PR:A
SATURDAY'S CHILDREN *** (1929) PR:A
SATURDAY'S CHILDREN *** (1940) PR:A
SATURDAY'S HERO * (1951) PR:A**
SATURDAY'S HEROES ** (1937) PR:A
SATURDAY'S MILLIONS **½ (1933) PR:A
SATURN 3 * (1980) PR:C
SATYRICON
  (SEE:FELLINI SATYRICON)
SAUL AND DAVID **½ (1968, It./Sp.) PR:A
SAUTERELLE
  (SEE:FEMMINA)

SAUVE QUI PEUT/LA VIE
  (SEE:EVERY MAN FOR HIMSELF)
SAVAGE? ** (1962) PR:A
SAVAGE ABDUCTION zero (1975) PR:O
SAVAGE AMERICAN, THE
  (SEE:TALISMAN, THE)
SAVAGE BRIGADE *½ (1948, Fr.) PR:A
SAVAGE DAWN * (1984) PR:O
SAVAGE DRUMS * (1951) PR:A
SAVAGE EYE, THE *** (1960) PR:C-O
SAVAGE FRONTIER *½ (1953) PR:A
SAVAGE GIRL, THE * (1932) PR:A
SAVAGE GOLD **½ (1933) PR:C
SAVAGE GUNS, THE **½ (1962, US/Sp.) PR:A
SAVAGE HARVEST * (1981) PR:A
SAVAGE HORDE, THE ** (1950) PR:A
SAVAGE INNOCENTS, THE *** (1960, Brit.) PR:A
SAVAGE IS LOOSE, THE **½ (1974) PR:C
SAVAGE ISLAND zero (1985, US/It./Sp.) PR:O
SAVAGE MESSIAH *** (1972, Brit.) PR:O
SAVAGE MUTINY *½ (1953) PR:A
SAVAGE PAMPAS *** (1967, Sp./Arg.) PR:C
SAVAGE SAM ** (1963) PR:A
SAVAGE SEVEN, THE **½ (1968) PR:O
SAVAGE SISTERS * (1974) PR:O
SAVAGE STREETS * (1984) PR:O
SAVAGE WEEKEND zero (1983) PR:O
SAVAGE WILD, THE *½ (1970) PR:A
SAVAGE WILDERNESS
  (SEE:LAST FRONTIER, THE)
SAVAGE, THE **½ (1953) PR:A
SAVAGE, THE ** (1975, Fr.) PR:C
SAVAGES * (1972) PR:O**
SAVAGES FROM HELL * (1968) PR:O
SAVANNAH SMILES **½ (1983) PR:AA
SAVE A LITTLE SUNSHINE *½ (1938, Brit.) PR:A
SAVE THE TIGER ** (1973) PR:C-O**
SAVING GRACE * (1986) PR:A**
SAWDUST AND TINSEL
  (SEE:THE NAKED NIGHT)
SAXO * (1988, Fr.) PR:O
SAXON CHARM, THE **½ (1948) PR:A
SAY HELLO TO YESTERDAY * (1971, Brit.) PR:C
SAY IT IN FRENCH ** (1938) PR:A
SAY IT WITH DIAMONDS *½ (1935, Brit.) PR:A
SAY IT WITH FLOWERS ** (1934, Brit.) PR:A
SAY IT WITH MUSIC **½ (1932, Brit.) PR:A
SAY IT WITH SONGS **½ (1929) PR:A
SAY ONE FOR ME * (1959) PR:C
SAY YES * (1986) PR:O
SAYONARA ** (1957) PR:C**
SAYS O'REILLY TO MCNAB
  (SEE:SEZ O'REILLY TO MCNAB)
SCALAWAG *½ (1973, Yugo.) PR:A
SCALPEL ** (1976) PR:O
SCALPHUNTERS, THE *** (1968) PR:C-O
SCALPS zero (1983) PR:O
SCAMP, THE
  (SEE:STRANGE AFFECTION)
SCANDAL ** (1929) PR:A
SCANDAL *** (1964, Jap.) PR:A
SCANDAL AT SCOURIE ** (1953) PR:A
SCANDAL FOR SALE ** (1932) PR:A
SCANDAL IN DENMARK *½ (1970, Den.) PR:O
SCANDAL IN PARIS, A *** (1946) PR:A
SCANDAL IN SORRENTO ** (1957, It./Fr.) PR:O
SCANDAL INCORPORATED * (1956) PR:A
SCANDAL SHEET *½ (1931) PR:A
SCANDAL SHEET *½ (1940) PR:A
SCANDAL SHEET ***½ (1952) PR:C
SCANDAL '64
  (SEE:CHRISTINE KEELER AFFAIR, THE)
SCANDAL STREET ** (1938) PR:A
SCANDALOUS ** (1984) PR:C
SCANDALOUS ADVENTURES OF BURAIKAN, THE ** (1970, Jap.) PR:C
SCANDALOUS JOHN **½ (1971) PR:AA
SCANDALS
  (SEE:GEORGE WHITE'S SCANDALS)
SCANDALS OF PARIS ** (1935, Brit.) PR:A
SCANNERS * (1981, Can.) PR:O**
SCAPEGOAT, THE **½ (1959, Brit.) PR:A
SCAPPAMENTO APERTO
  (SEE:BACKFIRE)
SCAR, THE
  (SEE:HOLLOW TRIUMPH)
SCARAB * (1982, US/Sp.) PR:O
SCARAB MURDER CASE, THE * (1936, Brit.) PR:A
SCARAMOUCHE ***½ (1952) PR:A
SCARAMOUCHE
  (SEE:ADVENTURES OF SCARAMOUCHE, THE)
SCARECROW * (1973) PR:C-O**
SCARECROW, THE ** (1982, New Zealand) PR:C
SCARECROW IN A GARDEN OF CUCUMBERS **½ (1972) PR:C
SCARECROWS ** (1988) PR:O
SCARED STIFF ** (1945) PR:A
SCARED STIFF **½ (1953) PR:A

SCARED TO DEATH *½ (1947) PR:A
SCARED TO DEATH * (1981) PR:O
SCAREHEADS * (1931) PR:A
SCAREMAKER, THE
  (SEE:GIRLS NIGHT OUT)
SCARF, THE **½ (1951) PR:A
SCARFACE ***** (1932) PR:O
SCARFACE zero (1983) PR:O
SCARFACE MOB, THE **½ (1962) PR:A
SCARLET ANGEL ** (1952) PR:A
SCARLET BLADE, THE
  (SEE:CRIMSON BLADE, THE)
SCARLET BRAND *½ (1932) PR:A
SCARLET BUCCANEER, THE
  (SEE:SWASHBUCKLER)
SCARLET CAMELLIA, THE **½ (1965, Jap.) PR:C
SCARLET CLAW, THE *** (1944) PR:A
SCARLET CLUE, THE **½ (1945) PR:A
SCARLET COAT, THE **½ (1955) PR:A
SCARLET DAWN **½ (1932) PR:A
SCARLET EMPRESS, THE **** (1934) PR:C
SCARLET HOUR, THE ** (1956) PR:A
SCARLET LETTER, THE ** (1934) PR:A
SCARLET PAGES **½ (1930) PR:A
SCARLET PIMPERNEL, THE **** (1935, Brit.) PR:A
SCARLET RIVER **½ (1933) PR:A
SCARLET SPEAR, THE * (1954, Brit.) PR:A
SCARLET STREET *** (1945) PR:C
SCARLET THREAD ** (1951, Brit.) PR:A
SCARLET WEB, THE ** (1954, Brit.) PR:A
SCARLET WEEKEND, A * (1932) PR:A
SCARRED **½ (1984) PR:O
SCARS OF DRACULA, THE *½ (1970, Brit.) PR:O
SCATTERBRAIN ** (1940) PR:A
SCATTERGOOD BAINES **½ (1941) PR:A
SCATTERGOOD MEETS BROADWAY **
  (1941) PR:A
SCATTERGOOD PULLS THE STRINGS **
  (1941) PR:A
SCATTERGOOD RIDES HIGH ** (1942) PR:A
SCATTERGOOD SURVIVES A MURDER **
  (1942) PR:A
SCAVENGER HUNT * (1979) PR:C
SCAVENGERS * (1988) PR:C
SCAVENGERS, THE ** (1959, US/Phil.) PR:A
SCAVENGERS, THE zero (1969) PR:O
SCENE OF THE CRIME *** (1949) PR:A
SCENE OF THE CRIME *** (1986, Fr.) PR:C-O
SCENES FROM A MARRIAGE ***
  (1974, Swed.) PR:C-O
SCENIC ROUTE, THE ** (1978) PR:A
SCENT OF A WOMAN **½ (1976, It.) PR:O
SCENT OF MYSTERY **½ (1960) PR:A
SCHATTEN UBER TIRAN-KOMMANDO SINAI
  (SEE:SINAI COMMANDOES)
SCHEHERAZADE *½ (1965, Fr./It./Sp.) PR:A
SCHIZO * (1977, Brit.) PR:O
SCHIZOID ** (1980) PR:O
SCHLAGER-PARADE (1953, Ger.) PR:A
SCHLOCK ** (1973) PR:A
SCHNEEWEISSCHEN UND ROSENROT
  (SEE:SNOW WHITE AND ROSE RED)
SCHNEEWITTCHEN UND DIE SIEBEN ZWERGE
  (SEE:SNOW WHITE)
SCHNOOK, THE
  (SEE:SWINGIN' ALONG)
SCHOOL DAZE *½ (1988) PR:O
SCHOOL FOR BRIDES ** (1952, Brit.) PR:A
SCHOOL FOR DANGER * (1947, Brit.) PR:A
SCHOOL FOR GIRLS *½ (1935) PR:A
SCHOOL FOR HUSBANDS ** (1939, Brit.) PR:A
SCHOOL FOR RANDLE ** (1949, Brit.) PR:A
SCHOOL FOR SCANDAL, THE *½ (1930, Brit.) PR:A
SCHOOL FOR SCOUNDRELS ****
  (1960, Brit.) PR:AA
SCHOOL FOR SECRETS **½ (1946, Brit.) PR:A
SCHOOL FOR SEX **½ (1966, Jap.) PR:O
SCHOOL FOR SEX * (1969, Brit.) PR:O
SCHOOL FOR STARS * (1935, Brit.) PR:A
SCHOOL FOR UNCLAIMED GIRLS **
  (1973, Brit.) PR:O
SCHOOL FOR VIOLENCE
  (SEE:HIGH SCHOOL HELLCATS)
SCHOOL OF LOVE
  (SEE:SCHOOL FOR SEX)
SCHOOL SPIRIT zero (1985) PR:C-O

SCHOOLBOY PENITENTIARY
  (SEE:LITTLE RED SCHOOLHOUSE, THE)
SCHOOLGIRL DIARY **½ (1947, It.) PR:A
SCHOOLMASTER, THE
  (SEE:HOOSIER SCHOOLMASTER, THE)
SCHOONER GANG, THE * (1937, Brit.) PR:A
SCHWARZE NYLONS-HEISSE NACHTE
  (SEE:INDECENT)
SCHWEIK'S NEW ADVENTURES *½
  (1943, Brit.) PR:A
SCHWESTERN, ODER DIE BALANCE DES GLUECKS
  (SEE:SISTERS, OR THE BALANCE OF HAPPINESS)
SCIENTIFIC CARDPLAYER, THE ** (1972, It.) PR:A
SCINTILLATING SIN
  (SEE:VIOLATED PARADISE)
SCIPIO
  (SEE:DEFEAT OF HANNIBAL, THE)
SCOBIE MALONE ** (1975, Aus.) PR:O
SCOOP, THE
  (SEE:HONOR OF THE PRESS)
SCOOP, THE * (1934, Brit.) PR:A
SCORCHY zero (1976) PR:O
SCORPIO * (1973) PR:C
SCOTCH ON THE ROCKS **½ (1954, Brit.) PR:A
SCOTLAND YARD ** (1930) PR:A
SCOTLAND YARD ** (1941) PR:A
SCOTLAND YARD COMMANDS * (1937, Brit.) PR:A
SCOTLAND YARD DRAGNET *½ (1957, Brit.) PR:A
SCOTLAND YARD HUNTS DR. MABUSE **½
  (1963, Ger.) PR:A
SCOTLAND YARD INSPECTOR *½
  (1952, Brit.) PR:A
SCOTLAND YARD INVESTIGATOR ***
  (1945, Brit.) PR:A
SCOTLAND YARD MYSTERY, THE
  (SEE:LIVING DEAD, THE)
SCOTT JOPLIN *** (1977) PR:C
SCOTT OF THE ANTARCTIC ***½
  (1949, Brit.) PR:A
SCOUNDREL IN WHITE
  (SEE:DOCTEUR POPAUL)
SCOUNDREL, THE ***½ (1935) PR:C
SCOUTS OF THE AIR
  (SEE:DANGER FLIGHT)
SCRAMBLE ** (1970, Brit.) PR:AA
SCRATCH HARRY ** (1969) PR:O
SCREAM AND DIE
  (SEE:HOUSE THAT VANISHED, THE)
SCREAM AND SCREAM AGAIN ***
  (1970, Brit.) PR:O
SCREAM, BABY, SCREAM * (1969) PR:O
SCREAM BLACULA SCREAM ** (1973) PR:O
SCREAM BLOODY MURDER zero (1972) PR:O
SCREAM FOR HELP zero (1984) PR:O
SCREAM FREE
  (SEE:FREE GRASS)
SCREAM IN THE DARK, A ** (1943) PR:A
SCREAM IN THE NIGHT *½ (1943) PR:A
SCREAM OF FEAR ****½ (1961, Brit.) PR:C
SCREAM OF THE BUTTERFLY *½ (1965) PR:O
SCREAMERS *½ (1978, It.) PR:A
SCREAMING EAGLES ** (1956) PR:A
SCREAMING HEAD, THE
  (SEE:HEAD, THE)
SCREAMING MIMI **½ (1958) PR:O
SCREAMING SKULL, THE ** (1958) PR:A
SCREAMPLAY *½ (1986) PR:O
SCREAMS OF A WINTER NIGHT zero (1979) PR:A
SCREAMTIME ** (1986, Brit.) PR:O
SCREEN TEST zero (1986) PR:O
SCREWBALLS zero (1983) PR:O
SCROOGE *** (1935, Brit.) PR:AA
SCROOGE
  (SEE:CHRISTMAS CAROL, A)
SCROOGE ***½ (1970, Brit.) PR:AA
SCROOGED *½ (1988) PR:C
SCRUBBERS **½ (1984, Brit.) PR:O
SCRUFFY ** (1938, Brit.) PR:AA
SCUDDA-HOO? SCUDDA-HAY? ***½ (1948) PR:A
SCUM *** (1979, Brit.) PR:O
SCUM OF THE EARTH zero (1963) PR:O
SCUM OF THE EARTH zero (1974) PR:O
SCUSI, FACCIAMO L'AMORE?
  (SEE:LISTEN LET'S MAKE LOVE)
SE PERMETTETE, PARLIAMO DI DONNE
  (SEE:LET'S TALK ABOUT WOMEN)

SE TUTTE LE DONNE DEL MONDO
  (SEE:KISS THE GIRLS AND MAKE THEM DIE)
SEA BAT, THE **½ (1930) PR:A
SEA CHASE, THE ** (1955) PR:A-C
SEA DEVILS * (1931) PR:A
SEA DEVILS **½ (1937) PR:A
SEA DEVILS ** (1953) PR:A
SEA FURY *½ (1929) PR:A
SEA FURY **½ (1959, Brit.) PR:A
SEA GHOST, THE ** (1931) PR:A
SEA GOD, THE ** (1930) PR:A
SEA GULL, THE ***½ (1968) PR:A-C
SEA GYPSIES, THE *** (1978) PR:AA
SEA HAWK, THE ***** (1940) PR:A
SEA HORNET, THE *½ (1951) PR:A
SEA LEGS ** (1930) PR:A
SEA NYMPHS
  (SEE:VIOLATED PARADISE)
SEA OF GRASS, THE **½ (1947) PR:A-C
SEA OF LOST SHIPS **½ (1953) PR:A
SEA OF SAND
  (SEE:DESERT PATROL)
SEA PIRATE, THE * (1967, Fr./Sp./It.) PR:A
SEA SERPENT, THE * (1937, Sp.) PR:A
SEA SHALL NOT HAVE THEM, THE ***
  (1955, Brit.) PR:A-C
SEA SPOILERS, THE *½ (1936) PR:A
SEA TIGER ** (1952) PR:A
SEA WALL, THE
  (SEE:THIS ANGRY AGE)
SEA WIFE ** (1957, Brit.) PR:A
SEA WOLF, THE **½ (1930) PR:A
SEA WOLF, THE **** (1941) PR:C
SEA WOLVES, THE *** (1981, Brit.) PR:A
SEA WYF AND BUSCUIT
  (SEE:SEA WIFE)
SEABO *½ (1978) PR:O
SEAFIGHTERS, THE
  (SEE:OPERATION BIKINI)
SEAGULLS OVER SORRENTO
  (SEE:CREST OF THE WAVE)
SEALED CARGO *** (1951) PR:A
SEALED LIPS
  (SEE:AFTER TOMORROW)
SEALED LIPS ** (1941) PR:A
SEALED VERDICT ** (1948) PR:A
SEANCE ON A WET AFTERNOON ****
  (1964, Brit.) PR:C
SEARCH AND DESTROY *½ (1981) PR:C
SEARCH FOR BEAUTY *½ (1934) PR:A
SEARCH FOR BRIDEY MURPHY, THE **
  (1956) PR:A
SEARCH FOR DANGER *½ (1949) PR:A
SEARCH FOR THE MOTHER LODE
  (SEE:MOTHER LODE)
SEARCH OF THE CASTAWAYS
  (SEE:IN SEARCH OF THE CASTAWAYS)
SEARCH, THE **** (1948) PR:A
SEARCHERS, THE ***** (1956) PR:C
SEARCHING WIND, THE ***½ (1946) PR:A-C
SEAS BENEATH, THE **½ (1931) PR:A
SEASIDE SWINGERS *½ (1965, Brit.) PR:AA
SEASON FOR LOVE, THE ** (1963, Fr.) PR:A-C
SEASON OF DREAMS
  (SEE:STACKING)
SEASON OF PASSION *** (1961, Aus./Brit.) PR:C
SEASON OF THE WITCH
  (SEE:HUNGRY WIVES)
SEATED AT HIS RIGHT ** (1968, It.) PR:O
SEAWEED CHILDREN, THE
  (SEE:MALACHI'S COVE)
SEBASTIAN **½ (1968, Brit.) PR:A
SECOND BEST BED **½ (1937, Brit.) PR:A
SECOND BEST SECRET AGENT IN THE WHOLE
  WIDE WORLD, THE *½ (1965, Brit.) PR:A-C
SECOND BUREAU ** (1936, Fr.) PR:A
SECOND BUREAU ** (1937, Brit.) PR:A
SECOND CHANCE ** (1947) PR:A
SECOND CHANCE *** (1953) PR:A-C
SECOND CHANCES
  (SEE:PROBATION)
SECOND CHOICE ** (1930) PR:A
SECOND CHORUS *** (1940) PR:A
SECOND COMING OF SUZANNE, THE *½
  (1974) PR:C
SECOND COMING, THE
  (SEE:DEAD PEOPLE)

SECOND FACE, THE * (1950) PR:A
SECOND FIDDLE *** (1939) PR:A
SECOND FIDDLE ** (1957, Brit.) PR:A
SECOND FIDDLE TO A STEEL GUITAR **
 (1965) PR:A
SECOND FLOOR MYSTERY, THE ** (1930) PR:A
SECOND GREATEST SEX, THE ** (1955) PR:A
SECOND-HAND HEARTS * (1981) PR:A-C
SECOND HAND WIFE * (1933) PR:A
SECOND HONEYMOON ** (1931) PR:A
SECOND HONEYMOON **½ (1937) PR:C
SECOND HOUSE FROM THE LEFT
 (SEE:NEW HOUSE ON THE LEFT, THE)
SECOND MATE, THE *½ (1950, Brit.) PR:A
SECOND MR. BUSH, THE *½ (1940, Brit.) PR:A
SECOND MRS. TANQUERAY, THE **½
 (1952, Brit.) PR:A
SECOND STORY MURDER, THE
 (SEE:SECOND FLOOR MYSTERY)
SECOND THOUGHTS
 (SEE:CRIME OF PETER FRAME, THE)
SECOND THOUGHTS zero (1983) PR:C
SECOND TIME AROUND, THE **½ (1961) PR:A
SECOND TIME LUCKY *½
 (1984, Aus./New Zealand) PR:C
SECOND WIFE ** (1930) PR:A
SECOND WIFE zero (1936) PR:A
SECOND WIND ** (1976, Can.) PR:A
SECOND WIND, A ** (1978, Fr.) PR:C
SECOND WOMAN, THE **½ (1951) PR:A-C
SECONDS ***½ (1966) PR:C
SECRET ADMIRER * (1985) PR:C
SECRET AGENT **½ (1933, Brit.) PR:A
SECRET AGENT FIREBALL ** (1965, Fr./It.) PR:A-C
SECRET AGENT OF JAPAN ** (1942) PR:A
SECRET AGENT SUPER DRAGON zero
 (1966, Fr./It./Ger./Monaco) PR:A
SECRET AGENT, THE ***½ (1936, Brit.) PR:C
SECRET BEYOND THE DOOR, THE *** (1948) PR:C
SECRET BRIDE, THE **½ (1935) PR:A
SECRET BRIGADE, THE ** (1951, USSR) PR:A
SECRET CALL, THE ** (1931) PR:A
SECRET CAVE, THE * (1953, Brit.) PR:A
SECRET CEREMONY * (1968, Brit.) PR:O
SECRET COMMAND **½ (1944) PR:A
SECRET DIARY OF SIGMUND FREUD, THE *
 (1984) PR:O
SECRET DOCUMENT—VIENNA **½
 (1954, Fr.) PR:A
SECRET DOOR, THE ** (1964) PR:A
SECRET ENEMIES ** (1942) PR:A
SECRET ENEMY
 (SEE:ENEMY AGENT)
SECRET EVIDENCE ** (1941) PR:A
SECRET FILE: HOLLYWOOD * (1962) PR:A-C
SECRET FILE OF HOLLYWOOD
 (SEE:SECRET FILE: HOLLYWOOD)
SECRET FLIGHT
 (SEE:SCHOOL FOR SECRETS)
SECRET FOUR, THE **½ (1940, Brit.) PR:A
SECRET FOUR, THE
 (SEE:KANSAS CITY CONFIDENTIAL)
SECRET FURY, THE **½ (1950) PR:A
SECRET GARDEN, THE *** (1949) PR:AA
SECRET HEART, THE *** (1946) PR:C
SECRET HONOR: A POLITICAL MYTH
 (SEE:SECRET HONOR)
SECRET HONOR ** (1984) PR:C
SECRET HONOR: THE LAST TESTAMENT OF
 RICHARD M. NIXON
 (SEE:SECRET HONOR)
SECRET INTERLUDE
 (SEE:PRIVATE NUMBER)
SECRET INTERLUDE
 (SEE:VIEW FROM POMPEY'S HEAD)
SECRET INVASION, THE **½ (1964) PR:A
SECRET JOURNEY
 (SEE:AMONG HUMAN WOLVES)
SECRET LIFE OF AN AMERICAN WIFE, THE ***
 (1968) PR:C-O
SECRET LIFE OF WALTER MITTY, THE ****
 (1947) PR:A
SECRET LIVES
 (SEE:I MARRIED A SPY)
SECRET MAN, THE ** (1958, Brit.) PR:A
SECRET MARK OF D'ARTAGNAN, THE **
 (1963, Fr./It.) PR:A
SECRET MENACE * (1931) PR:A
SECRET MISSION **½ (1944, Brit.) PR:A
SECRET MISSION ** (1949, USSR) PR:A
SECRET MOTIVE
 (SEE:LONDON BLACKOUT MURDERS)
SECRET OF BLOOD ISLAND, THE **½
 (1965, Brit.) PR:A
SECRET OF CONVICT LAKE, THE **½ (1951) PR:A
SECRET OF DEEP HARBOR *½ (1961) PR:C
SECRET OF DR. ALUCARD, THE
 (SEE:TASTE OF BLOOD, A)

SECRET OF DR. KILDARE, THE **½ (1939) PR:A
SECRET OF DORIAN GRAY, THE
 (SEE:DORIAN GRAY)
SECRET OF G.32
 (SEE:FLY BY NIGHT)
SECRET OF LINDA HAMILTON
 (SEE:SECRETS OF A SORORITY GIRL)
SECRET OF MADAME BLANCHE, THE **½
 (1933) PR:A
SECRET OF MAGIC ISLAND, THE **
 (1964, Fr./It.) PR:AA
SECRET OF MONTE CRISTO, THE **
 (1961, Brit.) PR:A
SECRET OF MY SUCCESS, THE *
 (1965, Brit.) PR:A-C
SECRET OF MY SUCCESS, THE * (1987) PR:O
SECRET OF NIKOLA TESLA, THE **½
 (1985, Yugo.) PR:A
SECRET OF NIMH, THE *** (1982) PR:AA
SECRET OF OUTER SPACE ISLAND
 (SEE:SECRET OF MAGIC ISLAND, THE)
SECRET OF ST. IVES, THE *½ (1949) PR:A
SECRET OF SANTA VITTORIA, THE **½
 (1969) PR:A
SECRET OF STAMBOUL, THE ** (1936, Brit.) PR:A
SECRET OF THE BLUE ROOM **½ (1933) PR:A
SECRET OF THE CHATEAU *½ (1935) PR:A
SECRET OF THE FOREST, THE **
 (1955, Brit.) PR:A
SECRET OF THE INCAS **½ (1954) PR:A
SECRET OF THE LOCH, THE *½ (1934, Brit.) PR:A
SECRET OF THE PURPLE REEF, THE **
 (1960) PR:A
SECRET OF THE SACRED FOREST, THE *½
 (1970) PR:A
SECRET OF THE SWORD, THE *½ (1985) PR:AA
SECRET OF THE TELEGIAN, THE **½
 (1961, Jap.) PR:A
SECRET OF THE WHISTLER *** (1946) PR:A
SECRET OF TREASURE MOUNTAIN *½
 (1956) PR:A
SECRET PARTNER, THE ** (1961, Brit.) PR:A
SECRET PASSION, THE
 (SEE:FREUD)
SECRET PATROL *½ (1936) PR:A
SECRET PEOPLE *½ (1952, Brit.) PR:A
SECRET PLACE, THE ** (1958, Brit.) PR:A
SECRET PLACES **½ (1984, Brit.) PR:C
SECRET SCROLLS (PART I) **½ (1968, Jap.) PR:A-C
SECRET SCROLLS (PART II) **½ (1968, Jap.) PR:A-C
SECRET SERVICE ** (1931) PR:A
SECRET SERVICE INVESTIGATOR ** (1948) PR:A
SECRET SERVICE OF THE AIR **½ (1939) PR:A
SECRET SEVEN, THE ** (1940) PR:A
SECRET SEVEN, THE *½ (1966, It./Sp.) PR:A
SECRET SINNERS * (1933) PR:A
SECRET SIX, THE ***½ (1931) PR:C
SECRET STRANGER, THE
 (SEE:ROUGH RIDING RANGER)
SECRET TENT, THE *½ (1956, Brit.) PR:A
SECRET VALLEY ** (1937) PR:A
SECRET VENTURE *½ (1955, Brit.) PR:A
SECRET VOICE, THE *½ (1936, Brit.) PR:A
SECRET WAR OF HARRY FRIGG, THE **½
 (1968) PR:A-C
SECRET WAR, THE
 (SEE:DIRTY GAME, THE)
SECRET WAYS, THE ** (1961) PR:A-C
SECRET WEAPON, THE
 (SEE:SHERLOCK HOLMES AND THE SECRET
 WEAPON)
SECRET WITNESS, THE * (1931) PR:A
SECRET WORLD **½ (1969, Fr.) PR:C
SECRET, THE ** (1955, Brit.) PR:A
SECRET, THE **½ (1979, Hong Kong) PR:C-O
SECRETS ** (1933) PR:A-C
SECRETS
 (SEE:SECRETS OF THE LONE WOLF)
SECRETS * (1971) PR:O
SECRETS **½ (1984, Brit.) PR:A-C
SECRETS D'ALCOVE **½ (1954, Fr./It.) PR:C
SECRETS OF A CO-ED *½ (1942) PR:A
SECRETS OF A MODEL * (1940) PR:C
SECRETS OF A NURSE * (1938) PR:A
SECRETS OF A SECRETARY ** (1931) PR:A
SECRETS OF A SORORITY GIRL *½ (1946) PR:A
SECRETS OF A SOUL
 (SEE:CONFESSIONS OF AN OPIUM EATER)
SECRETS OF A WINDMILL GIRL *½
 (1966, Brit.) PR:O
SECRETS OF A WOMAN'S TEMPLE **
 (1969, Jap.) PR:O
SECRETS OF AN ACTRESS * (1938) PR:A-C
SECRETS OF CHINATOWN * (1935) PR:A
SECRETS OF MONTE CARLO ** (1951) PR:A
SECRETS OF SCOTLAND YARD ** (1944) PR:A
SECRETS OF SEX zero (1970, Brit.) PR:O

SECRETS OF THE CITY
 (SEE:CITY OF SECRETS)
SECRETS OF THE FRENCH POLICE *½ (1932) PR:A
SECRETS OF THE LONE WOLF *** (1941) PR:A
SECRETS OF THE MARIE CELESTE, THE
 (SEE:MYSTERY OF THE MARIE CELESTE)
SECRETS OF THE UNDERGROUND ** (1943) PR:A
SECRETS OF THE WASTELANDS ** (1941) PR:A
SECRETS OF WOMEN ***½ (1961, Swed.) PR:C
SECRETS OF WU SIN *½ (1932) PR:A
SECRETS SECRETS **½ (1985, It.) PR:O
SECURITY RISK ** (1954) PR:A
SEDDOK, L'EREDE DI SATANA
 (SEE:ATOM AGE VAMPIRE)
SEDMI KONTINENT
 (SEE:SEVENTH CONTINENT, THE)
SEDMIKRASKY
 (SEE:DAISIES)
SEDUCED AND ABANDONED **
 (1964, Fr./It.) PR:C
SEDUCERS, THE *½ (1962) PR:C
SEDUCTION BY THE SEA **
 (1967, Ger./Yugo.) PR:C
SEDUCTION OF JOE TYNAN, THE ***½
 (1979) PR:C-O
SEDUCTION, THE zero (1982) PR:O
SEE AMERICA THIRST ** (1930) PR:A
SEE HERE, PRIVATE HARGROVE **½ (1944) PR:A
SEE HOW THEY RUN ** (1955, Brit.) PR:A
SEE MY LAWYER ** (1945) PR:A
SEE NO EVIL *** (1971, Brit.) PR:C
SEE YOU IN HELL, DARLING
 (SEE:AMERICAN DREAM, AN)
SEED *½ (1931) PR:A
SEED OF INNOCENCE * (1980) PR:O
SEED OF MAN, THE ** (1970, It.) PR:C-O
SEED OF TERROR
 (SEE:GRAVE OF THE VAMPIRE)
SEEDS OF DESTRUCTION * (1952) PR:A
SEEDS OF EVIL zero (1981) PR:O
SEEDS OF FREEDOM ** (1943, USSR) PR:A
SEEING IS BELIEVING * (1934, Brit.) PR:A
SEEING IT THROUGH
 (SEE:MOTH, THE)
SEEKERS, THE
 (SEE:LAND OF FURY)
SEEMS LIKE OLD TIMES *** (1980) PR:A-C
SEGRETI CHE SCOTTANO
 (SEE:DEAD RUN)
SEI DONNE PER L'ASSASSINO
 (SEE:BLOOD AND BLACK LACE)
SEISHUN MONOTOGARI
 (SEE:NAKED YOUTH)
SEISHUN ZANKOKU MONOTOGARI
 (SEE:NAKED YOUTH)
SEIZURE *½ (1974) PR:C
SELF-MADE LADY *½ (1932, Brit.) PR:A
SELF-PORTRAIT zero (1973, US/Chile) PR:O
SELL OUT, THE ** (1976) PR:C
SELLERS OF GIRLS * (1967, Fr.) PR:O
SELLOUT, THE ** (1951) PR:A
SEMBAZURU
 (SEE:THOUSAND CRANES)
SEMI-TOUGH *** (1977) PR:C-O
SEMINOLE **½ (1953) PR:C
SEMINOLE UPRISING *½ (1955) PR:A
SEN NOCI SVATOJANSKE
 (SEE:MIDSUMMER NIGHT'S DREAM, A)
SENATOR WAS INDISCREET, THE ***½
 (1947) PR:A
SEND FOR PAUL TEMPLE ** (1946, Brit.) PR:A
SEND ME NO FLOWERS **½ (1964) PR:A
SENDER, THE *** (1982, Brit.) PR:O
SENGOKU GUNTO-DEN
 (SEE:SAGA OF THE VAGABONDS)
SENGOKU YARO
 (SEE:WARRING CLANS)
SENIOR PROM * (1958) PR:A
SENIORS, THE ** (1978) PR:O
SENJO NI NAGARERU UTA
 (SEE:WE WILL REMEMBER)
SENOR AMERICANO ** (1929) PR:A
SENORA CASADA NECEISITA MARIDO **
 (1935) PR:A
SENORITA FROM THE WEST ** (1945) PR:A
SENSATION *½ (1936, Brit.) PR:A
SENSATION
 (SEE:SEDUCERS, THE)
SENSATION HUNTERS ** (1934) PR:A
SENSATION HUNTERS *½ (1945) PR:A
SENSATIONS
 (SEE:SENSATIONS OF 1945)
SENSATIONS OF 1945 ** (1944) PR:A
SENSE OF FREEDOM, A **½ (1985, Brit.) PR:C
SENSO ***½ (1968, It.) PR:A
SENSUALITA **½ (1954, It.) PR:A
SENSUOUS VAMPIRES
 (SEE:VAMPIRE HOOKERS, THE)

SENTENCE SUSPENDED (SEE:MILITARY ACADEMY WITH THAT 10TH AVENUE GANG)
SENTENCED FOR LIFE *½ (1960, Brit.) PR:A
SENTENZA DI MORTE (SEE:DEATH SENTENCE)
SENTIMENTAL BLOKE ** (1932, Aus.) PR:A
SENTIMENTAL JOURNEY *** (1946) PR:A
SENTIMIENTOS: MIRTA DE LINIERS A ESTAMBUL ***½ (1987, Arg.) PR:O
SENTINEL, THE * (1977) PR:O
SEPARATE PEACE, A * (1972) PR:A**
SEPARATE TABLES ** (1958) PR:A-C**
SEPARATE VACATIONS *½ (1986, Can.) PR:O
SEPARATE WAYS **½ (1981) PR:O
SEPARATION *½ (1968, Brit.) PR:A
SEPIA CINDERELLA ** (1947) PR:A
SEPPUKU (SEE:HARAKIRI)
SEPT FOIS FEMME (SEE:WOMAN TIMES SEVEN)
SEPT HOMMES EN OR (SEE:SEVEN GOLDEN MEN)
SEPTEMBER ** (1987) PR:A**
SEPTEMBER AFFAIR * (1950) PR:A**
SEPTEMBER STORM ** (1960) PR:A
SEPTEMBER 30, 1955 (SEE:9/30/55)
SEQUOIA *** (1934) PR:A
SERAFINO **½ (1970, Fr./It.) PR:A
SERDTSE MATERI (SEE:SONS AND MOTHERS)
SERE CUALQUIER COSA PERO TE QUIERO ** (1986, Arg.) PR:C-O
SERENA ** (1962, Brit.) PR:A-C
SERENADE *** (1956) PR:A
SERENADE FOR TWO SPIES **½ (1966, It./Ger.) PR:A
SERENADE OF THE WEST (SEE:GIT ALONG LITTLE DOGIE)
SERENADE OF THE WEST (SEE:COWBOY SERENADE)
SERENITY **½ (1962) PR:A
SERGEANT BERRY ** (1938, Ger.) PR:A
SERGEANT DEADHEAD *½ (1965) PR:A
SERGEANT DEADHEAD THE ASTRONAUT (SEE:SERGEANT DEADHEAD)
SERGEANT JIM *** (1962, Yugo.) PR:A
SERGEANT MADDEN **½ (1939) PR:A
SERGEANT MIKE ** (1945) PR:A
SERGEANT MURPHY *½ (1938) PR:A
SGT. PEPPER'S LONELY HEARTS CLUB BAND zero (1978) PR:A
SERGEANT RUTLEDGE ***½ (1960) PR:C
SERGEANT RYKER * (1968) PR:A**
SERGEANT STEINER (SEE:BREAKTHROUGH)
SERGEANT WAS A LADY, THE ** (1961) PR:A
SERGEANT YORK *** (1941) PR:A**
SERGEANT, THE zero (1968) PR:O
SERGEANTS 3 ** (1962) PR:A
SERIAL * (1980) PR:O**
SERIOUS CHARGE (SEE:IMMORAL CHARGE)
SERPENT AND THE RAINBOW, THE * (1988) PR:O**
SERPENT ISLAND *½ (1954) PR:A
SERPENT OF THE NILE ** (1953) PR:A
SERPENT, THE ***½ (1973, Fr./It./Ger.) PR:A-C
SERPENT'S EGG, THE ** (1977, Ger./US) PR:O
SERPENTS OF THE PIRATE MOON, THE **½ (1973) PR:O
SERPENT'S WAY, THE ***½ (1987, Swed.) PR:O
SERPICO ** (1973) PR:C-O**
SERVANT, THE * (1964, Brit.) PR:C**
SERVANTS' ENTRANCE ** (1934) PR:A
SERVICE (SEE:LOOKING FORWARD)
SERVICE DE LUXE **½ (1938) PR:A
SERVICE FOR LADIES (SEE:RESERVED FOR LADIES)
SERYOZHA (SEE:SUMMER TO REMEMBER, A)
SESAME STREET PRESENTS: FOLLOW THE BIRD **½ (1985) PR:AA
SESSION WITH THE COMMITTEE (SEE:COMMITTEE, THE)

SET-UP, THE ** (1949) PR:C**
SET-UP, THE ** (1963, Brit.) PR:A
SET, THE * (1970, Aus.) PR:O
SETTE CONTRO LA MORTE (SEE:CAVERN, THE)
SETTE DONNE PER I MAC GREGOR (SEE:UP THE MAC GREGORS)
SETTE PISTOLE PER I MAC GREGOR (SEE:SEVEN GUNS FOR THE MAC GREGORS)
SETTE UOMINI D'ORO (SEE:SEVEN GOLDEN MEN)
SETTE VOLTE DONNA (SEE:WOMAN TIMES SEVEN)
SETTE WINCHESTER PER UN MASSACRO (SEE:PAYMENT IN BLOOD)
SEVEN ** (1979) PR:O
SEVEN AGAINST THE SUN **½ (1968, South Africa) PR:A
SEVEN ALONE ** (1975) PR:AA
SEVEN ANGRY MEN *** (1955) PR:A
SEVEN BAD MEN (SEE:RAGE AT DAWN)
SEVEN BEAUTIES ***½ (1976, It.) PR:O
SEVEN BRAVE MEN ** (1936, USSR) PR:A
SEVEN BRIDES FOR SEVEN BROTHERS *** (1954) PR:AA**
SEVEN BROTHERS MEET DRACULA, THE (SEE:DRACULA & THE GOLDEN VAMPIRES)
SEVEN CAPITAL SINS *** (1962, Fr./It.) PR:O
SEVEN CITIES OF GOLD * (1955) PR:A-C**
SEVEN CITIES TO ATLANTIS (SEE:WARLORDS OF ATLANTIS)
SEVEN DARING GIRLS **½ (1962, Ger.) PR:A
SEVEN DAYS ASHORE *½ (1944) PR:A
SEVEN DAYS IN MAY ** (1964) PR:C**
SEVEN DAYS LEAVE ** (1930) PR:A
SEVEN DAYS LEAVE ** (1942) PR:A
SEVEN DAYS TO NOON ***½ (1950, Brit.) PR:C
SEVEN DEADLY SINS, THE *** (1953, Fr./It.) PR:A
SEVEN DIFFERENT WAYS (SEE:QUICK, LET'S GET MARRIED)
SEVEN DOORS TO DEATH *½ (1944) PR:A
SEVEN DWARFS TO THE RESCUE, THE **½ (1965, It.) PR:A
SEVEN FACES *½ (1929) PR:A
SEVEN FACES OF DR. LAO ***½ (1964) PR:A
SEVEN FOOTPRINTS TO SATAN *½ (1929) PR:C
SEVEN GOLDEN MEN *½ (1969, Fr./It./Sp.) PR:A
SEVEN GRAVES FOR ROGAN (SEE:TIME TO DIE, A)
SEVEN GUNS FOR THE MACGREGORS **½ (1968, It./Sp.) PR:A
SEVEN GUNS TO MESA *½ (1958) PR:A
SEVEN HILLS OF ROME, THE ** (1958) PR:A
SEVEN HOURS TO JUDGEMENT zero (1988) PR:O
711 OCEAN DRIVE *** (1950) PR:C
SEVEN KEYS *½ (1962, Brit.) PR:A
SEVEN KEYS TO BALDPATE ** (1930) PR:A
SEVEN KEYS TO BALDPATE **½ (1935) PR:A
SEVEN KEYS TO BALDPATE ** (1947) PR:A
SEVEN LITTLE FOYS, THE ***½ (1955) PR:AA
SEVEN MEN FROM NOW ***½ (1956) PR:A
SEVEN MILES FROM ALCATRAZ * (1942) PR:A**
SEVEN MINUTES IN HEAVEN **½ (1986) PR:C
SEVEN MINUTES, THE * (1971) PR:O
SEVEN NIGHTS IN JAPAN ** (1976, Brit./Fr.) PR:C
SEVEN-PER-CENT SOLUTION, THE * (1977, Brit.) PR:C**
SEVEN REVENGES, THE * (1967, It.) PR:C
SEVEN SAMURAI, THE *** (1956, Jap.) PR:C**
SEVEN SEAS TO CALAIS ** (1963, It.) PR:A
SEVEN SECRETS OF SU-MARU, THE (SEE:RIO 70)
SEVEN SINNERS (SEE:DOOMED CARGO)
SEVEN SINNERS ***½ (1940) PR:A
SEVEN SISTERS (SEE:HOUSE ON SORORITY ROW)
SEVEN SLAVES AGAINST THE WORLD ** (1965, It.) PR:A
SEVEN SWEETHEARTS ** (1942) PR:A
SEVEN TASKS OF ALI BABA, THE ** (1963, It.) PR:A
SEVEN THIEVES **** (1960) PR:A-C
SEVEN THUNDERS (SEE:BEASTS OF MARSEILLES, THE)
7254 zero (1971) PR:O

SEVEN UPS, THE * (1973) PR:C**
SEVEN WAVES AWAY (SEE:ABANDON SHIP)
SEVEN WAYS FROM SUNDOWN *½ (1960) PR:A
SEVEN WERE SAVED * (1947) PR:A
SEVEN WOMEN *** (1966) PR:C
SEVEN WOMEN FROM HELL * (1961) PR:A
SEVEN YEAR ITCH, THE ** (1955) PR:A-C**
SEVENTEEN **½ (1940) PR:A
1776 ** (1972) PR:A
SEVENTH CAVALRY **½ (1956) PR:A
7TH COMMANDMENT, THE *½ (1961) PR:A
SEVENTH CONTINENT, THE *** (1968, Czech./Yugo.) PR:A
SEVENTH CROSS, THE ***½ (1944) PR:C
SEVENTH DAWN, THE ** (1964) PR:A-C
SEVENTH HEAVEN **½ (1937) PR:A-C
SEVENTH JUROR, THE ** (1964, Fr.) PR:A
SEVENTH SEAL, THE ** (1958, Swed.) PR:C**
SEVENTH SIGN, THE * (1988) PR:C
SEVENTH SIN, THE *½ (1957) PR:A
SEVENTH SURVIVOR, THE **½ (1941, Brit.) PR:A
SEVENTH VEIL, THE ** (1946, Brit.) PR:A-C**
SEVENTH VICTIM, THE * (1943) PR:A**
SEVENTH VOYAGE OF SINBAD, THE ***½ (1958) PR:AA
SEVENTY DEADLY PILLS ** (1964, Brit.) PR:AA
77 PARK LANE ** (1931, Brit.) PR:A
70,000 WITNESSES ** (1932) PR:A
SEVERED HEAD, A *½ (1971, Brit.) PR:O
SEX AGENT (SEE:THERE IS A STILL ROOM IN HELL)
SEX AND THE SINGLE GIRL *** (1964) PR:C
SEX AND THE TEENAGER (SEE:TO FIND A MAN)
SEX APPEAL ** (1986) PR:O
SEX AT NIGHT (SEE:LOVE AT NIGHT)
SEX IS A WOMAN (SEE:LOVE IS A WOMAN)
SEX KITTENS GO TO COLLEGE * (1960) PR:A
SEX O'CLOCK NEWS, THE zero (1986) PR:O
SEX RACKETEERS, THE (SEE:MAN OF VIOLENCE)
SEXORCISTS, THE (SEE:TORMENTED, THE)
SEXTETTE * (1978) PR:C
SEXTON BLAKE AND THE BEARDED DOCTOR * (1935, Brit.) PR:A
SEXTON BLAKE AND THE HOODED TERROR **½ (1938, Brit.) PR:A
SEXTON BLAKE AND THE MADEMOISELLE ** (1935, Brit.) PR:A
SEXY GANG (SEE:MICHELLE)
SEZ O'REILLY TO MACNAB *** (1938, Brit.) PR:A
SFIDA A RIO BRAVO (SEE:GUNMEN OF THE RIO GRANDE)
SH! THE OCTOPUS *½ (1937) PR:A
SHABBY TIGER, THE (SEE:MASQUERADE)
SHACK OUT ON 101 *½ (1955) PR:A
SHADES OF SILK **½ (1979, Can.) PR:O
SHADEY ** (1987, Brit.) PR:C
SHADOW AND THE MISSING LADY, THE (SEE:MISSING LADY, THE)
SHADOW BETWEEN, THE **½ (1932, Brit.) PR:A
SHADOW IN THE SKY **½ (1951) PR:A
SHADOW MAN ** (1953, Brit.) PR:A
SHADOW OF A DOUBT ** (1935) PR:A
SHADOW OF A DOUBT *** (1943) PR:C**
SHADOW OF A MAN ** (1955, Brit.) PR:A-C
SHADOW OF A WOMAN ** (1946) PR:A
SHADOW OF CHIKARA (SEE:WISHBONE CUTTER)
SHADOW OF EVIL ** (1967, Fr./It.) PR:A
SHADOW OF FEAR ** (1956, Brit.) PR:A
SHADOW OF FEAR **½ (1963, Brit.) PR:A
SHADOW OF MIKE EMERALD, THE ** (1935, Brit.) PR:A
SHADOW OF SUSPICION ** (1944) PR:A
SHADOW OF TERROR ** (1945) PR:A
SHADOW OF THE CAT, THE ** (1961, Brit.) PR:A
SHADOW OF THE EAGLE **½ (1955, Brit.) PR:A
SHADOW OF THE HAWK *½ (1976, Can.) PR:A
SHADOW OF THE LAW *** (1930) PR:A
SHADOW OF THE PAST ** (1950, Brit.) PR:A

Finding entries in **THE MOTION PICTURE GUIDE ™**

Years	Volumes
1929-83	Volumes I-IX
1984	Volume IX
1985	1986 ANNUAL
1986	1987 ANNUAL
1987	1988 ANNUAL
1988	1989 ANNUAL

STAR RATINGS

★★★★★	Masterpiece
★★★★	Excellent
★★★	Good
★★	Fair
★	Poor
zero	Without Merit

PARENTAL RECOMMENDATION (PR:)

AA	Good for Children
A	Acceptable for Children
C	Cautionary, some objectionable scenes
O	Objectionable for Children

BOLD: Films on Videocassette

SHADOW OF THE THIN MAN * (1941) PR:A**
SHADOW OF VICTORY *** (1986, Neth.) PR:O
SHADOW ON THE WALL **½ (1950) PR:A
SHADOW ON THE WINDOW, THE **½ (1957) PR:A
SHADOW PLAY * (1986) PR:O
SHADOW RANCH ** (1930) PR:A
SHADOW RETURNS, THE ** (1946) PR:A
SHADOW STRIKES, THE *½ (1937) PR:A
SHADOW VALLEY *½ (1947) PR:A
SHADOW VERSUS THE THOUSAND EYES OF DR. MABUSE, THE
(SEE:THOUSAND EYES OF DR. MABUSE, THE)
SHADOW WARRIOR, THE
(SEE:KAGEMUSHA)
SHADOW, THE *½ (1936, Brit.) PR:A
SHADOW, THE **½ (1937) PR:A
SHADOWED *½ (1946) PR:A
SHADOWED EYES *½ (1939, Brit.) PR:A-C
SHADOWMAN * (1974, Fr./It.) PR:A**
SHADOWS *½ (1931, Brit.) PR:A-C
SHADOWS **** (1960) PR:O
SHADOWS GROW LONGER, THE **½ (1962, Switz./Ger.) PR:A
SHADOWS IN AN EMPTY ROOM
(SEE:STRANGE SHADOWS IN AN EMPTY ROOM)
SHADOWS IN THE NIGHT ** (1944) PR:A
SHADOWS OF DEATH *½ (1945) PR:A
SHADOWS OF FORGOTTEN ANCESTORS * (1967, USSR) PR:A**
SHADOWS OF OUR FORGOTTEN ANCESTORS
(SEE:SHADOWS OF FORGOTTEN ANCESTORS)
SHADOWS OF SING SING *½ (1934) PR:A
SHADOWS OF SINGAPORE
(SEE:MALAY NIGHTS)
SHADOWS OF THE ORIENT * (1937) PR:A
SHADOWS OF THE WEST ** (1949) PR:A
SHADOWS OF TOMBSTONE *½ (1953) PR:A
SHADOWS ON THE SAGE ** (1942) PR:A
SHADOWS ON THE STAIRS ** (1941) PR:A
SHADOWS OVER CHINATOWN ** (1946) PR:A
SHADOWS OVER SHANGHAI *½ (1938) PR:A
SHADOWS RUN BLACK zero (1986) PR:O
SHADY LADY **½ (1945) PR:A
SHADY LADY, THE ** (1929) PR:A
SHAFT * (1971) PR:O**
SHAFT IN AFRICA ** (1973) PR:O
SHAFT'S BIG SCORE **½ (1972) PR:O
SHAGGY **½ (1948) PR:AA
SHAGGY D.A., THE * (1976) PR:AA**
SHAGGY DOG, THE * (1959) PR:AA**
SHAKE HANDS WITH MURDER ** (1944) PR:A
SHAKE HANDS WITH THE DEVIL ***½ (1959, Ireland) PR:C
SHAKE, RATTLE, AND ROCK? **½ (1957) PR:A
SHAKEDOWN, THE ** (1929) PR:A
SHAKEDOWN
(SEE:BIG SHAKEDOWN, THE)
SHAKEDOWN *½ (1936) PR:A
SHAKEDOWN ***½ (1950) PR:C
SHAKEDOWN **½ (1988) PR:O
SHAKEDOWN, THE **½ (1960, Brit.) PR:C
SHAKESPEARE WALLAH * (1966, India) PR:A**
SHAKIEST GUN IN THE WEST, THE *½ (1968) PR:A
SHALAKO ** (1968, Brit.) PR:O
SHALL THE CHILDREN PAY?
(SEE:WHAT PRICE INNOCENCE)
SHALL WE DANCE ***½ (1937) PR:A
SHAME
(SEE:INTRUDER, THE)
SHAME ***½ (1968, Swed.) PR:O
SHAME ***½ (1988, Aus.) PR:O
SHAME OF MARY BOYLE, THE
(SEE:JUNO AND THE PAYCOCK)
SHAME OF PATTY SMITH, THE
(SEE:CASE OF PATTY SMITH, THE)
SHAME OF THE SABINE WOMEN, THE *½ (1962, Mex.) PR:A
SHAME, SHAME, EVERYBODY KNOWS HER NAME * (1969) PR:O
SHAMELESS OLD LADY, THE *** (1966, Fr.) PR:A
SHAMPOO * (1975) PR:O**
SHAMROCK HILL **½ (1949) PR:AA
SHAMUS ** (1959, Brit.) PR:AA
SHAMUS ** (1973) PR:C
SHAN-KO LIEN
(SEE:SHEPHERD GIRL, THE)
SHANE *** (1953) PR:C**
SHANGHAI ** (1935) PR:A
SHANGHAI CHEST, THE *½ (1948) PR:A
SHANGHAI COBRA, THE *½ (1945) PR:A
SHANGHAI DRAMA, THE *** (1945, Fr.) PR:A
SHANGHAI EXPRESS **** (1932) PR:O
SHANGHAI GESTURE, THE ***½ (1941) PR:C
SHANGHAI LADY ** (1929) PR:A
SHANGHAI MADNESS ** (1933) PR:A
SHANGHAI STORY, THE ** (1954) PR:A
SHANGHAI SURPRISE ** (1986, Brit.) PR:C
SHANGHAIED LOVE ** (1931) PR:A
SHANGRI-LA * (1961) PR:O
SHANKS ** (1974) PR:A
SHANNONS OF BROADWAY, THE ** (1929) PR:A
SHANTY TRAMP * (1967) PR:O
SHANTYTOWN ** (1943) PR:A
SHAPE OF THINGS TO COME, THE * (1979, Can.) PR:A
SHARE OUT, THE **½ (1966, Brit.) PR:A
SHARK * (1970, US/Mex.) PR:C**
SHARK GOD, THE
(SEE:OMOO OMOO, THE SHARK GOD)
SHARK REEF
(SEE:SHE-GODS OF SHARK REEF)
SHARK RIVER ** (1953) PR:A
SHARK WOMAN, THE ** (1941) PR:A
SHARKFIGHTERS, THE *½ (1956) PR:A
SHARK'S TREASURE *½ (1975) PR:A
SHARKY'S MACHINE * (1981) PR:O**
SHARPSHOOTERS **½ (1938) PR:A
SHATTER
(SEE:CALL HIM MR. SHATTER)
SHATTERHAND
(SEE:OLD SHATTERHAND)
SHE *** (1935) PR:A
SHE **½ (1965, Brit.) PR:A-C
SHE zero (1985, It.) PR:O
SHE ALWAYS GETS THEIR MAN * (1962, Brit.) PR:A
SHE AND HE **½ (1967, Jap.) PR:A
SHE AND HE ** (1969, It.) PR:O
SHE ASKED FOR IT *½ (1937) PR:A
SHE BEAST, THE **½ (1966, Brit./It./Yugo.) PR:C
SHE COULDN'T SAY NO ** (1930) PR:A
SHE COULDN'T SAY NO ** (1939, Brit.) PR:A
SHE COULDN'T SAY NO ** (1941) PR:A
SHE COULDN'T SAY NO *½ (1954) PR:A
SHE COULDN'T TAKE IT ** (1935) PR:A
SHE-CREATURE, THE *½ (1956) PR:A
SHE DANCES ALONE **½ (1981, Aust./US) PR:A
SHE DEMONS * (1958) PR:A
SHE DEVIL *½ (1957) PR:A
SHE-DEVIL ISLAND *½ (1936, Mex.) PR:A
SHE-DEVILS ON WHEELS zero (1968) PR:O
SHE DIDN'T SAY NO? *** (1962, Brit.) PR:A
SHE DONE HIM WRONG ** (1933) PR:C**
SHE FREAK *½ (1967) PR:O
SHE GETS HER MAN *½ (1935) PR:A
SHE GETS HER MAN ** (1945) PR:A
SHE-GODS OF SHARK REEF *½ (1958) PR:A
SHE GOES TO WAR *** (1929) PR:A
SHE GOT HER MAN
(SEE:MAISIE GETS HER MAN)
SHE GOT WHAT SHE WANTED ** (1930) PR:A
SHE HAD TO CHOOSE *½ (1934) PR:A
SHE HAD TO EAT * (1937) PR:A
SHE HAD TO SAY YES
(SEE:SHE COULDN'T SAY NO)
SHE HAD TO SAY YES ** (1933) PR:A
SHE HAS WHAT IT TAKES *½ (1943) PR:A
SHE KNEW ALL THE ANSWERS ** (1941) PR:A
SHE KNEW WHAT SHE WANTED *½ (1936, Brit.) PR:A
SHE KNOWS Y'KNOW ** (1962, Brit.) PR:C
SHE LEARNED ABOUT SAILORS ** (1934) PR:A
SHE LET HIM CONTINUE
(SEE:PRETTY POISON)
SHE LOVED A FIREMAN ** (1937) PR:A
SHE LOVES ME NOT **½ (1934) PR:A
SHE MADE HER BED * (1934) PR:A
SHE MAN, THE zero (1967) PR:C
SHE MARRIED A COP ** (1939) PR:A
SHE MARRIED AN ARTIST *½ (1938) PR:A
SHE MARRIED HER BOSS *** (1935) PR:A
SHE MONSTER OF THE NIGHT
(SEE:FRANKENSTEIN'S DAUGHTER)
SHE PLAYED WITH FIRE *½ (1957, Brit.) PR:C
SHE SHALL HAVE MURDER * (1950, Brit.) PR:A
SHE SHALL HAVE MUSIC ** (1935, Brit.) PR:A
SHE SHOULDA SAID NO
(SEE:WILD WEED)
SHE STEPS OUT
(SEE:HARMONY AT HOME)
SHE WANTED A MILLIONAIRE *½ (1932) PR:A
SHE WAS A HIPPY VAMPIRE
(SEE:WILD WORLD OF BATWOMAN, THE)
SHE WAS A LADY *½ (1934) PR:A
SHE WAS ONLY A VILLAGE MAIDEN ** (1933, Brit.) PR:A
SHE WENT TO THE RACES *½ (1945) PR:A
SHE WHO DARES
(SEE:THREE RUSSIAN GIRLS)
SHE-WOLF, THE ** (1931) PR:A
SHE-WOLF, THE ** (1963, USSR) PR:A
SHE-WOLF OF LONDON *½ (1946) PR:A
SHE WORE A YELLOW RIBBON ** (1949) PR:A**
SHE WOULDN'T SAY YES **½ (1945) PR:A
SHE WROTE THE BOOK **½ (1946) PR:A
SHEBA BABY * (1975) PR:C
SHED NO TEARS *½ (1948) PR:A
SHEENA **½ (1984) PR:C-O
SHEEPDOG OF THE HILLS ** (1941, Brit.) PR:A
SHEEPMAN, THE *** (1958) PR:A
SHEHERAZADE
(SEE:SCHEHERAZADE)
SHEIK STEPS OUT, THE *½ (1937) PR:A
SHEILA LEVINE IS DEAD AND LIVING IN NEW YORK ** (1975) PR:A-C
SHE'LL HAVE TO GO
(SEE:MAID FOR MURDER)
SHELL SHOCK * (1964) PR:C
SHENANDOAH ***½ (1965) PR:C
SHENANIGANS
(SEE:GREAT BANK HOAX, THE)
SHEP COMES HOME ** (1949) PR:AA
SHEPHERD GIRL, THE **½ (1965, Hong Kong) PR:A
SHEPHERD OF THE HILLS, THE *** (1941) PR:A
SHEPHERD OF THE HILLS, THE ** (1964) PR:A
SHEPHERD OF THE OZARKS **½ (1942) PR:A
SHEPPER-NEWFOUNDER, THE
(SEE:PART-TIME WIFE)
SHERIFF OF CIMARRON **½ (1945) PR:A
SHERIFF OF FRACTURED JAW, THE *** (1958, Brit.) PR:A
SHERIFF OF LAS VEGAS ** (1944) PR:A
SHERIFF OF REDWOOD VALLEY ** (1946) PR:A
SHERIFF OF SAGE VALLEY ** (1942) PR:A
SHERIFF OF SUNDOWN ** (1944) PR:A
SHERIFF OF TOMBSTONE ** (1941) PR:A
SHERIFF OF WICHITA **½ (1949) PR:A
SHERLOCK HOLMES
(SEE:ADVENTURES OF SHERLOCK HOLMES, THE)
SHERLOCK HOLMES *** (1932) PR:A
SHERLOCK HOLMES AND THE DEADLY NECKLACE **½ (1962, Ger.) PR:A
SHERLOCK HOLMES AND THE SECRET CODE
(SEE:DRESSED TO KILL)
SHERLOCK HOLMES AND THE SECRET WEAPON * (1942) PR:A**
SHERLOCK HOLMES AND THE SPIDER WOMAN **½ (1944) PR:A
SHERLOCK HOLMES AND THE VOICE OF TERROR **½ (1942) PR:A
SHERLOCK HOLMES FACES DEATH * (1943) PR:O**
SHERLOCK HOLMES' FATAL HOUR **½ (1931, Brit.) PR:A
SHERLOCK HOLMES GROSSTER FALL
(SEE:STUDY IN TERROR, A)
SHERLOCK HOLMES IN WASHINGTON ** (1943) PR:A
SHE'S A SOLDIER TOO ** (1944) PR:A
SHE'S A SWEETHEART ** (1944) PR:A
SHE'S BACK ON BROADWAY ** (1953) PR:A
SHE'S DANGEROUS *½ (1937) PR:A
SHE'S FOR ME ** (1943) PR:A
SHE'S GOT EVERYTHING *½ (1938) PR:A
SHE'S GOTTA HAVE IT * (1986) PR:O**
SHE'S HAVING A BABY ** (1988) PR:C-O
SHE'S IN THE ARMY **½ (1942) PR:A
SHE'S MY LOVELY
(SEE:GET HEP TO LOVE)
SHE'S MY WEAKNESS *½ (1930) PR:A
SHE'S NO LADY * (1937) PR:A
SHE'S WORKING HER WAY THROUGH COLLEGE *** (1952) PR:A
SHICHININ NO SAMURAI
(SEE:SEVEN SAMURAI, THE)
SHIELD FOR MURDER **½ (1954) PR:A
SHIELD OF FAITH, THE ** (1956, Brit.) PR:A
SHILLINGBURY BLOWERS, THE **½ (1980, Brit.) PR:A
SHIN NO SHIKOTEI
(SEE:GREAT WALL, THE)
SHINBONE ALLEY ** (1971) PR:A
SHINE ON, HARVEST MOON *½ (1938) PR:A
SHINE ON, HARVEST MOON ** (1944) PR:A
SHINEL
(SEE:OVERCOAT, THE)
SHINING, THE * (1980) PR:C-O**
SHINING HOUR, THE **½ (1938) PR:A-C
SHINING STAR
(SEE:THAT'S THE WAY OF THE WORLD)
SHINING VICTORY ** (1941) PR:A
SHINJU TEN NO AMIJIMA
(SEE:DOUBLE SUICIDE)
SHIP AHOY ** (1942) PR:A
SHIP CAFE *½ (1935) PR:A
SHIP FROM SHANGHAI, THE ** (1930) PR:A
SHIP OF CONDEMNED WOMEN, THE **½ (1963, It.) PR:A
SHIP OF FOOLS ** (1965) PR:C**
SHIP OF WANTED MEN ** (1933) PR:A
SHIP THAT DIED OF SHAME, THE ***½ (1956, Brit.) PR:A

SHIP WAS LOADED, THE (SEE:CARRY ON ADMIRAL)
SHIPBUILDERS, THE **½ (1943, Brit.) PR:A
SHIPMATES ** (1931) PR:A
SHIPMATES FOREVER **½ (1935) PR:A
SHIPMATES O' MINE ** (1936, Brit.) PR:A
SHIPS OF HATE * (1931) PR:A
SHIPS WITH WINGS ** (1942, Brit.) PR:A
SHIPWRECK (SEE:SEA GYPSIES, THE)
SHIPYARD SALLY ** (1940, Brit.) PR:A
SHIRALEE, THE **½ (1957, Brit.) PR:C
SHIRIKURAE MAGOICHI (SEE:MAGOICHI SAGA, THE)
SHIRLEY THOMPSON VERSUS THE ALIENS *** (1968, Aus.) PR:O
SHIRO TO KURO (SEE:PRESSURE OF GUILT)
SHIVERS (SEE:THEY CAME FROM WITHIN)
SHIVERS ***½ (1984, Pol.) PR:C
SHLOSHA YAMIN VE' YELED (SEE:NOT MINE TO LOVE)
SHNEI KUNI LEMEL (SEE:FLYING MATCHMAKER, THE)
SHOCK ** (1934) PR:C
SHOCK ** (1946) PR:O
SHOCK (SEE:BEYOND THE DOOR II)
SHOCK CORRIDOR **½ (1963) PR:O
SHOCK TREATMENT ** (1964) PR:O
SHOCK TREATMENT ** (1973, Fr.) PR:O
SHOCK TREATMENT zero (1981) PR:O
SHOCK TROOPS *** (1968, It./Fr.) PR:O
SHOCK WAVES **½ (1977) PR:O
SHOCKER (SEE:TOWN WITHOUT PITY)
SHOCKING MISS PILGRIM, THE ** (1947) PR:A
SHOCKPROOF *** (1949) PR:C
SHOEMAKER AND THE ELVES, THE **½ (1967, Ger.) PR:AA
SHOES OF THE FISHERMAN, THE * (1968) PR:A**
SHOESHINE ***½ (1947, It.) PR:C
SHOGUN ASSASSIN * (1980, Jap.) PR:O**
SHOGUN ISLAND (SEE:RAW FORCE)
SHONEN SARUTOBI SASUKE (SEE:MAGIC BOY)
SHOOT * (1976, Can.) PR:O
SHOOT FIRST *** (1953, Brit.) PR:C-O
SHOOT FIRST, LAUGH LAST ** (1967, It./Ger./US) PR:O
SHOOT FOR THE SUN ** (1986, Brit.) PR:C-O
SHOOT IT: BLACK, SHOOT IT: BLUE * (1974) PR:O
SHOOT LOUD, LOUDER... I DON'T UNDERSTAND ** (1966, It.) PR:O
SHOOT OUT ** (1971) PR:C
SHOOT OUT AT BIG SAG ** (1962) PR:C
SHOOT-OUT AT MEDICINE BEND **½ (1957) PR:A
SHOOT THE MOON ** (1982) PR:C-O
SHOOT THE PIANO PLAYER *** (1962, Fr.) PR:C**
SHOOT THE WORKS ** (1934) PR:A
SHOOT TO KILL *** (1947) PR:C
SHOOT TO KILL ** (1961, Brit.) PR:A
SHOOT TO KILL * (1988) PR:O**
SHOOTIN' IRONS (SEE:WEST OF TEXAS)
SHOOTING HIGH *½ (1940) PR:A
SHOOTING PARTY, THE **½ (1985, Brit.) PR:O
SHOOTING STRAIGHT **½ (1930) PR:A
SHOOTING, THE ** (1971) PR:O**
SHOOTIST, THE ** (1976) PR:O**
SHOOTOUT (SEE:SHOOT OUT)
SHOOTOUT AT MEDICINE BEND (SEE:SHOOT OUT AT MEDICINE BEND)
SHOP ANGEL ** (1932) PR:C
SHOP AROUND THE CORNER, THE *** (1940) PR:A**
SHOP AT SLY CORNER, THE (SEE:CODE OF SCOTLAND YARD)
SHOP ON HIGH STREET, THE (SEE:SHOP ON MAIN STREET, THE)
SHOP ON MAIN STREET, THE ***½ (1966, Czech.) PR:C-O
SHOPWORN ** (1932) PR:A
SHOPWORN ANGEL ***½ (1938) PR:A
SHOPWORN ANGEL, THE **½ (1928) PR:A
SHORT CIRCUIT *½ (1986) PR:A-C
SHORT CIRCUIT 2 * (1988) PR:A
SHORT CUT TO HELL *** (1957) PR:O
SHORT EYES ***½ (1977) PR:O
SHORT GRASS *** (1950) PR:C
SHORT IS THE SUMMER **½ (1968, Swed.) PR:O
SHOT AT DAWN, A *** (1934, Ger.) PR:C
SHOT GUN PASS (SEE:SHOTGUN PASS)
SHOT IN THE DARK, A *½ (1933, Brit.) PR:A
SHOT IN THE DARK, A ** (1935) PR:C
SHOT IN THE DARK, A ** (1964) PR:A-C**
SHOT IN THE DARK, THE **½ (1941) PR:C
SHOTGUN *** (1955) PR:O
SHOTGUN PASS * (1932) PR:A
SHOTGUN WEDDING, THE ** (1963) PR:A-C
SHOULD A DOCTOR TELL? zero (1931, Brit.) PR:C
SHOULD A GIRL MARRY? *½ (1929) PR:A
SHOULD A GIRL MARRY? * (1939) PR:A
SHOULD HUSBANDS WORK? ** (1939) PR:AA
SHOULD LADIES BEHAVE? ** (1933) PR:C-O
SHOUT, THE * (1978, Brit.) PR:O**
SHOUT AT THE DEVIL **½ (1976, Brit.) PR:C
SHOW BOAT ** (1929) PR:A
SHOW BOAT **** (1936) PR:A
SHOW BOAT ***½ (1951) PR:A
SHOW BUSINESS * (1944) PR:AA**
SHOW FLAT * (1936, Brit.) PR:A
SHOW FOLKS ** (1928) PR:A
SHOW GIRL ** (1928) PR:A
SHOW GIRL IN HOLLYWOOD ** (1930) PR:A
SHOW GOES ON, THE **½ (1937, Brit.) PR:A
SHOW GOES ON, THE ** (1938, Brit.) PR:C
SHOW-OFF, THE *** (1934) PR:A
SHOW-OFF, THE ** (1946) PR:A
SHOW THEM NO MERCY *** (1935) PR:C
SHOWDOWN, THE *** (1950) PR:A
SHOWDOWN ** (1963) PR:A
SHOWDOWN **½ (1973) PR:A
SHOWDOWN AT ABILENE *** (1956) PR:A
SHOWDOWN AT BOOT HILL ***½ (1958) PR:A
SHOWDOWN FOR ZATOICHI **½ (1968, Jap.) PR:C-O
SHOWDOWN, THE **½ (1940) PR:A
SHOWDOWN, THE (SEE:WEST OF ABILENE)
SHOWGIRL IN HOLLYWOOD (SEE:SHOW GIRL IN HOLLYWOOD)
SHOWOFF (SEE:SHOW-OFF, THE)
SHOWTIME **½ (1948, Brit.) PR:A
SHRIEK IN THE NIGHT, A *½ (1933) PR:A
SHRIEK OF THE MUTILATED zero (1974) PR:O
SHRIKE, THE ** (1955) PR:C
SHUBIN (SEE:SCANDAL)
SHUT MY BIG MOUTH *** (1942) PR:AA
SHUTTERED ROOM, THE *** (1968, Brit.) PR:C-O
SHY PEOPLE ***½ (1988) PR:O
SI PARIS NOUS ETAIT CONTE (SEE:IF PARIS WERE TOLD TO US)
SI VERSAILLES M'ETAIT CONTE (SEE:ROYAL AFFAIRS IN VERSAILLES)
SIAVASH IN PERSEPOLIS **½ (1966, Iran) PR:C
SICILIAN CLAN, THE ***½ (1970, Fr.) PR:O
SICILIAN CONNECTION, THE * (1977) PR:O
SICILIAN, THE ** (1987) PR:O
SICILIANS, THE ** (1964, Brit.) PR:A
SID AND NANCY ** (1986, Brit.) PR:O**
SIDDHARTHA *** (1972) PR:C
SIDE SHOW ** (1931) PR:A
SIDE STREET **½ (1929) PR:A
SIDE STREET **½ (1950) PR:C
SIDE STREET ANGEL **½ (1937, Brit.) PR:A
SIDE STREETS ** (1934) PR:A
SIDECAR RACERS * (1975, Aus.) PR:A
SIDEHACKERS, THE (SEE:FIVE THE HARD WAY)
SIDELONG GLANCES OF A PIGEON KICKER, THE ** (1970) PR:O
SIDESHOW ** (1950) PR:C
SIDEWALKS OF LONDON * (1940, Brit.) PR:AA**
SIDEWALKS OF NEW YORK ** (1931) PR:AA
SIDEWINDER ONE * (1977) PR:C
SIDNEY SHELDON'S BLOODLINE (SEE:BLOODLINE)
SIEGE *** (1983, Can.) PR:O
SIEGE AT RED RIVER, THE *** (1954) PR:C
SIEGE OF FORT BISMARK **½ (1968, Jap.) PR:C-O
SIEGE OF HELL STREET, THE (SEE:SIEGE OF SIDNEY STREET, THE)
SIEGE OF PINCHGUT (SEE:FOUR DESPERATE MEN)
SIEGE OF RED RIVER, THE (SEE:SIEGE AT RED RIVER THE)
SIEGE OF SIDNEY STREET, THE **½ (1960, Brit.) PR:O
SIEGE OF SYRACUSE ** (1962, Fr./It.) PR:C
SIEGE OF THE SAXONS **½ (1963, Brit.) PR:A
SIERRA *½ (1950) PR:A
SIERRA BARON **½ (1958) PR:A
SIERRA DE TERUEL (SEE:MAN'S HOPE)
SIERRA PASSAGE ** (1951) PR:A
SIERRA STRANGER * (1957) PR:C
SIERRA SUE **½ (1941) PR:A
SIETE HOMBRES DE ORO (SEE:SEVEN GOLDEN MEN)
SIGN OF AQUARIUS ** (1970) PR:O
SIGN OF FOUR, THE **½ (1932, Brit.) PR:C
SIGN OF FOUR, THE * (1983, Brit.) PR:C
SIGN OF THE CROSS ***½ (1932) PR:C-O
SIGN OF THE GLADIATOR * (1959, Fr./Ger./It.) PR:C
SIGN OF THE PAGAN *½ (1954) PR:C
SIGN OF THE RAM, THE ** (1948) PR:A
SIGN OF THE VIRGIN **½ (1969, Czech.) PR:O
SIGN OF THE WOLF ** (1941) PR:AA
SIGN OF VENUS, THE * (1955, It.) PR:C
SIGN OF ZORRO, THE *½ (1960) PR:AA
SIGNAL 7 * (1984) PR:O**
SIGNALS-AN ADVENTURE IN SPACE ** (1970, E. Ger./Pol.) PR:A
SIGNED JUDGEMENT (SEE:COWBOY FROM LONESOME RIVER)
SIGNORA SENZA CAMELIE (SEE:LADY WITHOUT CAMELLIAS)
SIGNORE E SIGNORI (SEE:BIRDS, THE BEES, AND THE ITALIANS, THE)
SIGNPOST TO MURDER *** (1964) PR:O
SIGNS OF LIFE *** (1981, Ger.) PR:O
SILENCE **½ (1931) PR:O
SILENCE **½ (1974) PR:AA
SILENCE HAS NO WINGS **½ (1971, Jap.) PR:A
SILENCE OF DEAN MAITLAND, THE **½ (1934, Aus.) PR:C-O
SILENCE OF DR. EVANS, THE **½ (1973, USSR) PR:C
SILENCE OF THE NORTH ** (1981, Can.) PR:C
SILENCE, THE * (1964, Swed.) PR:O**
SILENCERS, THE ** (1966) PR:O
SILENT ASSASSINS ** (1988) PR:O
SILENT BARRIERS ** (1937, Brit.) PR:A
SILENT BATTLE, THE (SEE:CONTINENTAL EXPRESS)
SILENT CALL, THE **½ (1961) PR:A
SILENT CONFLICT *½ (1948) PR:A
SILENT DEATH (SEE:VOODOO ISLAND)
SILENT DUST ***½ (1949, Brit.) PR:A
SILENT ENEMY, THE * (1930) PR:C
SILENT ENEMY, THE **½ (1959, Brit.) PR:C
SILENT FLUTE, THE (SEE:CIRCLE OF IRON)
SILENT INVASION, THE ** (1962, Brit.) PR:A
SILENT MADNESS * (1984) PR:O
SILENT MOVIE ***½ (1976) PR:A-C
SILENT NIGHT, BLOODY NIGHT ** (1974) PR:O
SILENT NIGHT, DEADLY NIGHT * (1984) PR:O
SILENT NIGHT, DEADLY NIGHT PART II zero (1987) PR:O
SILENT NIGHT, EVIL NIGHT (SEE:BLACK CHRISTMAS)
SILENT ONE, THE **½ (1984, New Zealand) PR:A
SILENT PARTNER ** (1944) PR:C
SILENT PARTNER, THE ***½ (1979, Can.) PR:C-O
SILENT PASSENGER, THE **½ (1935, Brit.) PR:A
SILENT PLAYGROUND, THE *** (1964, Brit.) PR:C-O
SILENT RAGE *½ (1982) PR:O
SILENT RAIDERS ** (1954) PR:C
SILENT RUNNING * (1972) PR:C**
SILENT SCREAM *½ (1980) PR:O

Finding entries in **THE MOTION PICTURE GUIDE** ™

Years	Volumes
1929-83	Volumes I-IX
1984	Volume IX
1985	1986 ANNUAL
1986	1987 ANNUAL
1987	1988 ANNUAL
1988	1989 ANNUAL

STAR RATINGS

★★★★★	Masterpiece
★★★★	Excellent
★★★	Good
★★	Fair
★	Poor
zero	Without Merit

PARENTAL RECOMMENDATION (PR:)

AA	Good for Children
A	Acceptable for Children
C	Cautionary, some objectionable scenes
O	Objectionable for Children

BOLD: Films on Videocassette

SILENT STAR
(SEE:FIRST SPACESHIP ON VENUS)
SILENT VOICE, THE
(SEE:MAN WHO PLAYED GOD, THE)
SILENT VOICE, THE
(SEE:PAULA)
SILENT WITNESS
(SEE:SECRETS OF A CO-ED)
SILENT WITNESS, THE ** (1962) PR:O
SILENT WITNESS, THE *** (1932) PR:C
SILHOUETTES zero (1982) PR:C
SILICATES
(SEE:ISLAND OF TERROR)
SILIP zero (1985, Phil.) PR:O
SILK * (1986, Phil.) PR:O
SILK EXPRESS, THE ** (1933) PR:A
SILK HAT KID * (1935) PR:A
SILK NOOSE, THE **½ (1950, Brit.) PR:A
SILK STOCKINGS ** (1957) PR:A**
SILKEN AFFAIR, THE ** (1957, Brit.) PR:A
SILKEN SKIN
(SEE:SOFT SKIN, THE)
SILKEN TRAP, THE
(SEE:THE MONEY JUNGLE)
SILKWOOD ** (1983) PR:C-O**
SILLY BILLIES * (1936) PR:A
SILVER BANDIT, THE zero (1950) PR:A
SILVER BEARS ** (1978, Brit.) PR:C
SILVER BLAZE
(SEE:MURDER AT THE BASKERVILLES)
SILVER BULLET, THE ***½ (1942) PR:C
SILVER CANYON **½ (1951) PR:A
SILVER CHAINS
(SEE:KID FROM AMARILLO, THE)
SILVER CHALICE, THE * (1954) PR:A
SILVER CITY
(SEE:ALBUQUERQUE)
SILVER CITY **½ (1951) PR:C
SILVER CITY **½ (1985, Aus.) PR:C
SILVER CITY BONANZA **½ (1951) PR:A
SILVER CITY KID ** (1944) PR:A
SILVER CITY RAIDERS *** (1943) PR:A
SILVER CORD **½ (1933) PR:A
SILVER DARLINGS, THE ** (1947, Brit.) PR:A
SILVER DEVIL
(SEE:WILD HORSE)
SILVER DOLLAR ***½ (1932) PR:A
SILVER DREAM RACER * (1982, Brit.) PR:C
SILVER DUST *** (1953, USSR) PR:C
SILVER FLEET, THE **½ (1945, Brit.) PR:A
SILVER HORDE, THE **½ (1930) PR:A
SILVER KEY, THE
(SEE:GIRL IN THE CASE)
SILVER LINING ** (1932) PR:A
SILVER LODE * (1954) PR:A**
SILVER ON THE SAGE **½ (1939) PR:A
SILVER QUEEN ** (1942) PR:A
SILVER RAIDERS ** (1950) PR:A
SILVER RIVER ** (1948) PR:A
SILVER SKATES **½ (1943) PR:A
SILVER SPOON, THE * (1934, Brit.) PR:A
SILVER SPURS ** (1936) PR:A
SILVER SPURS * (1943) PR:A**
SILVER STALLION * (1941) PR:A
SILVER STAR, THE * (1955) PR:A
SILVER STREAK **½ (1976) PR:C
SILVER STREAK, THE ** (1935) PR:A
SILVER TOP *½ (1938, Brit.) PR:A
SILVER TRAIL, THE *½ (1937) PR:A
SILVER TRAILS **½ (1948) PR:A
SILVER WHIP, THE **½ (1953) PR:A
SILVERADO ** (1985) PR:C
SILVERSPURS
(SEE:SILVER SPURS)
SIMBA **½ (1955, Brit.) PR:O
SIMCHON FAMILY, THE **½ (1969, Israel) PR:C
SIMON * (1980) PR:A-C**
SIMON AND LAURA *** (1956, Brit.) PR:C-O
SIMON, KING OF THE WITCHES * (1971) PR:O
SIMPLE CASE OF MONEY, A **½ (1952, Fr.) PR:A
SIMPLY TERRIFIC *½ (1938, Brit.) PR:A
SIN FLOOD
(SEE:WAY OF ALL MEN, THE)
SIN NOW...PAY LATER
(SEE:LOVE NOW...PAY LATER)
SIN OF HAROLD DIDDLEBOCK, THE
(SEE:MAD WEDNESDAY)
SIN OF MADELON CLAUDET, THE ****
(1931) PR:C
SIN OF MONA KENT, THE ** (1961) PR:O
SIN OF NORA MORAN * (1933) PR:A
SIN ON THE BEACH ** (1964, Fr.) PR:O
SIN SHIP *½ (1931) PR:A
SIN TAKES A HOLIDAY **½ (1930) PR:A
SIN TOWN ** (1942) PR:A
SIN YOU SINNERS * (1963) PR:O
SIN, THE
(SEE:GOOD LUCK MISS WYCOFF)

SINAI COMMANDOS: THE STORY OF THE SIX DAY WAR **½ (1968, Israel/Ger.) PR:C
SINAIA
(SEE:CLOUDS OVER ISRAEL)
SINBAD AND THE EYE OF THE TIGER ** (1977, US/Brit.) PR:AA
SINBAD THE SAILOR * (1947) PR:A**
SINCE YOU WENT AWAY **** (1944) PR:A
SINCERELY CHARLOTTE * (1986, Fr.) PR:C-O**
SINCERELY YOURS zero (1955) PR:A
SINFONIA PER DUE SPIE
(SEE:SERENADE FOR TWO SPIES)
SINFONIA PER UN MASSACRO
(SEE:SYMPHONY FOR A MASSACRE)
SINFUL DAVEY **½ (1969, Brit.) PR:O
SING A JINGLE ** (1943) PR:A
SING ALONG WITH ME *½ (1952, Brit.) PR:A
SING AND BE HAPPY ** (1937) PR:A
SING AND LIKE IT ** (1934) PR:A
SING AND SWING ** (1964, Brit.) PR:C
SING ANOTHER CHORUS ** (1941) PR:A
SING AS WE GO *** (1934, Brit.) PR:A
SING AS YOU SWING ** (1937, Brit.) PR:A
SING, BABY, SING *** (1936) PR:A
SING, BOY, SING ** (1958) PR:C
SING, COWBOY, SING *** (1937) PR:A
SING, DANCE, PLENTY HOT ** (1940) PR:A
SING FOR YOUR SUPPER ** (1941) PR:AA
SING ME A LOVE SONG
(SEE:MANHATTAN MOON)
SING ME A LOVE SONG *½ (1936) PR:A
SING, NEIGHBOR, SING *½ (1944) PR:A
SING SING NIGHTS *½ (1935) PR:C
SING SINNER, SING zero (1933) PR:C
SING WHILE YOU DANCE ** (1946) PR:A
SING WHILE YOU'RE ABLE * (1937) PR:A
SING YOU SINNERS ***½ (1938) PR:AA
SING YOUR WAY HOME * (1945) PR:A
SING YOUR WORRIES AWAY ** (1942) PR:A
SINGAPORE * (1947) PR:A
SINGAPORE, SINGAPORE ** (1969, Fr./It.) PR:C
SINGAPORE WOMAN ** (1941) PR:A
SINGER AND THE DANCER, THE ***
(1977, Aus.) PR:C
SINGER NOT THE SONG, THE *** (1961, Brit.) PR:O
SINGIN' IN THE CORN zero (1946) PR:A
SINGIN' IN THE RAIN *** (1952) PR:A**
SINGING BLACKSMITH *** (1938) PR:C
SINGING BUCKAROO, THE ** (1937) PR:AA
SINGING COP, THE ** (1938, Brit.) PR:A
SINGING COWBOY, THE **½ (1936) PR:A
SINGING COWGIRL, THE * (1939) PR:A
SINGING FOOL, THE *** (1928) PR:A
SINGING GUNS ** (1950) PR:A
SINGING HILL, THE ** (1941) PR:AA
SINGING IN THE DARK * (1956) PR:A
SINGING KID, THE ** (1936) PR:A
SINGING MARINE, THE ** (1937) PR:A
SINGING NUN, THE ** (1966) PR:A
SINGING OUTLAW **½ (1937) PR:A
SINGING PRINCESS, THE **½ (1967, It.) PR:A
SINGING SHERIFF, THE ** (1944) PR:A
SINGING TAXI DRIVER *½ (1953, It.) PR:A
SINGING THROUGH ** (1935, Brit.) PR:A
SINGING VAGABOND, THE ** (1935) PR:A
SINGLE-HANDED
(SEE:SAILOR OF THE KING)
SINGLE-HANDED SANDERS * (1932) PR:A
SINGLE ROOM FURNISHED * (1968) PR:O
SINGLE SIN *½ (1931) PR:A
SINGLETON'S PLUCK
(SEE:LAUGHTER HOUSE)
SINISTER HANDS * (1932) PR:A
SINISTER HOUSE
(SEE:WHO KILLED "DOC" ROBBIN?)
SINISTER JOURNEY ** (1948) PR:A
SINISTER MAN, THE **½ (1965, Brit.) PR:C
SINISTER URGE, THE zero (1961) PR:O
SINK THE BISMARCK **** (1960, Brit.) PR:A
SINNER TAKE ALL *** (1936) PR:C
SINNER, THE
(SEE:DESERT DESPERADOES)
SINNERS GO TO HELL
(SEE:NO EXIT)
SINNER'S HOLIDAY *** (1930) PR:A
SINNERS IN PARADISE * (1938) PR:C
SINNERS IN THE SUN ** (1932) PR:C
SINNERS, THE
(SEE:FIVE SINNERS)
SINS OF JEZEBEL ** (1953) PR:C
SINS OF LOLA MONTES, THE
(SEE:LOLA MONTES)
SINS OF MAN * (1936) PR:A
SINS OF RACHEL CADE, THE **½ (1960) PR:O
SINS OF ROSE BERND, THE ** (1959, Ger.) PR:O
SINS OF THE BORGIAS
(SEE:LUCRECE BORGIA)
SINS OF THE CHILDREN *** (1930) PR:A

SINS OF THE FATHERS **½ (1928) PR:A
SINS OF THE FATHERS **½ (1948, Can.) PR:C
SINS PAYDAY * (1932) PR:A
SIOUX CITY SUE **½ (1946) PR:A
SIR GAWAIN AND THE GREEN KNIGHT
(SEE:GAWAIN AND THE GREEN KNIGHT)
SIR HENRY AT RAWLINSON END ***
(1980, Brit.) PR:O
SIR, YOU ARE A WIDOWER ***½
(1971, Czech.) PR:O
SIREN OF ATLANTIS * (1948) PR:A
SIREN OF BAGDAD **½ (1953) PR:A
SIRENE DU MISSISSIPPI
(SEE:MISSISSIPPI MERMAID)
SIROCCO * (1951) PR:A**
SIROCCO D'HIVER
(SEE:WINTER WIND)
SIS HOPKINS ** (1941) PR:A
SISSI
(SEE:FOREVER MY LOVE)
SISTER-IN-LAW, THE ** (1975) PR:O
SISTER KENNY ***½ (1946) PR:A
SISTER SISTER ** (1988) PR:O
SISTER TO ASSIST'ER, A *½ (1930, Brit.) PR:A
SISTER TO ASSIST'ER, A *½ (1938, Brit.) PR:A
SISTER TO ASSIST'ER, A *½ (1948, Brit.) PR:A
SISTERS ** (1930) PR:A
SISTERS * (1973) PR:O**
SISTERS, OR THE BALANCE OF HAPPINESS **½
(1982, Ger.) PR:O
SISTERS UNDER THE SKIN ** (1934) PR:C
SISTERS, THE ***½ (1938) PR:A
SISTERS, THE ** (1969, Gr.) PR:C
SIT TIGHT *½ (1931) PR:A
SITTING BULL **½ (1954) PR:C
SITTING DUCKS * (1979) PR:C**
SITTING ON THE MOON *** (1936) PR:A
SITTING PRETTY *** (1933) PR:A
SITTING PRETTY **** (1948) PR:AA
SITTING TARGET ** (1972, Brit.) PR:O
SITUATION HOPELESS—BUT NOT SERIOUS **½
(1965) PR:A
SIX BLACK HORSES ** (1962) PR:A
SIX BRIDGES TO CROSS **½ (1955) PR:A
SIX CYLINDER LOVE ** (1931) PR:A
SIX-DAY BIKE RIDER * (1934) PR:A
SIX DAYS A WEEK ** (1966, Fr./It./Sp.) PR:O
SIX FEMMES POUR L'ASSASSIN
(SEE:BLOOD AND BLACK LACE)
6.5 SPECIAL ** (1958, Brit.) PR:A
SIX GUN GOLD *** (1941) PR:A
SIX GUN GOSPEL ** (1943) PR:A
SIX-GUN LAW **½ (1948) PR:AA
SIX GUN MAN *½ (1946) PR:A
SIX-GUN RHYTHM ** (1939) PR:A
SIX GUN SERENADE ** (1947) PR:A
SIX HOURS TO LIVE *½ (1932) PR:C
SIX IN PARIS *** (1968, Fr.) PR:C-O
SIX INCHES TALL
(SEE:ATTACK OF THE PUPPET PEOPLE)
SIX LESSONS FROM MADAME LA ZONGA *½
(1941) PR:A
SIX MEN, THE *½ (1951, Brit.) PR:A
SIX OF A KIND *** (1934) PR:A
SIX PACK ** (1982) PR:C
SIX PACK ANNIE *** (1975) PR:O
SIX P.M. ** (1946, USSR) PR:A
SIX SHOOTIN' SHERIFF **½ (1938) PR:A
6000 ENEMIES *** (1939) PR:C
SIX WEEKS *½ (1982) PR:C
SIXTEEN
(SEE:LIKE A CROW ON A JUNE BUG)
SIXTEEN CANDLES * (1984) PR:A-C**
SIXTEEN FATHOMS DEEP ** (1934) PR:A
SIXTEEN FATHOMS DEEP ** (1948) PR:A
SIXTH AND MAIN **½ (1977) PR:C
SIXTH MAN, THE
(SEE:OUTSIDER, THE)
SIXTH OF JUNE, THE
(SEE:D-DAY, THE SIXTH OF JUNE)
'68 *½ (1988) PR:O
SIXTY GLORIOUS YEARS *** (1938, Brit.) PR:A
SIZZLE BEACH, U.S.A. zero (1986) PR:O
SKAMMEN
(SEE:SHAME)
SKATEBOARD * (1978) PR:C
SKATETOWN, U.S.A. * (1979) PR:A
SKATING-RINK AND THE VIOLIN, THE
(SEE:VIOLIN AND ROLLER)
SKAZA O KONKE-GORBUNKE
(SEE:LITTLE HUMPBACKED HORSE, THE)
SKELETON ON HORSEBACK **½
(1940, Czech.) PR:C
SKI BATTALION **½ (1938, USSR) PR:C
SKI BUM, THE zero (1971) PR:O
SKI FEVER * (1969, US/Aust./Czech.) PR:C
SKI PARTY ** (1965) PR:A
SKI PATROL ** (1940) PR:A

SKI RAIDERS, THE
(SEE:SNOW JOB)
SKI TROOP ATTACK ** (1960) PR:C
SKID KIDS ** (1953, Brit.) PR:AA
SKIDOO zero (1968) PR:C
SKIES ABOVE
(SEE:SKY ABOVE HEAVEN)
SKIMPY IN THE NAVY * (1949, Brit.) PR:A
SKIN DEEP * (1929) PR:C
SKIN DEEP ***½ (1978, New Zealand) PR:O
SKIN GAME ***½ (1971) PR:C
SKIN GAME, THE ** (1931, Brit.) PR:C
SKIN GAME, THE ** (1965, Brit.) PR:O
SKINNER STEPS OUT *½ (1929) PR:A
SKIP TRACER, THE *** (1979, Can.) PR:C
SKIPALONG ROSENBLOOM *** (1951) PR:A
SKIPPER SURPRISED HIS WIFE, THE ** (1950) PR:A
SKIPPY ***½ (1931) PR:AA
SKIRTS AHOY! ** (1952) PR:A
SKULL, THE **½ (1965, Brit.) PR:O
SKULL AND CROWN * (1938) PR:AA
SKULLDUGGERY ** (1970) PR:C
SKUPLIJACI PERJA
(SEE:I EVEN MET HAPPY GYPSIES)
SKY ABOVE HEAVEN **½ (1964, Fr./It.) PR:C
SKY BANDITS ** (1986, Brit.) PR:A-C
SKY BANDITS, THE ** (1940) PR:A
SKY BEYOND HEAVEN
(SEE:SKY ABOVE HEAVEN)
SKY BIKE, THE ** (1967, Brit.) PR:AA
SKY BRIDE ** (1932) PR:A
SKY CALLS, THE **½ (1959, USSR) PR:A
SKY COMMANDO *½ (1953) PR:A
SKY DEVILS ** (1932) PR:A
SKY DRAGON **½ (1949) PR:A
SKY FULL OF MOON **½ (1952) PR:A
SKY GIANT *** (1938) PR:A
SKY HAWK **½ (1929) PR:A
SKY HIGH * (1952) PR:A
SKY IS RED, THE * (1952, It.) PR:O
SKY IS YOURS, THE
(SEE:LE CIEL EST A VOUS)
SKY LINER ** (1949) PR:A
SKY MURDER *½ (1940) PR:A
SKY PARADE *½ (1936) PR:A
SKY PATROL *½ (1939) PR:A
SKY PIRATE, THE ** (1970) PR:C
SKY RAIDERS * (1931) PR:A
SKY RAIDERS, THE * (1938, Brit.) PR:A
SKY RIDERS ** (1976, US/Gr.) PR:C
SKY SPIDER, THE ** (1931) PR:A
SKY TERROR
(SEE:SKYJACKED)
SKY WEST AND CROOKED
(SEE:GYPSY GIRL)
SKYDIVERS, THE * (1963) PR:C
SKYJACKED ** (1972) PR:A
SKYLARK **½ (1941) PR:A
SKYLARKS * (1936, Brit.) PR:A
SKYLINE ** (1931) PR:A
SKYLINE * (1984, Sp.) PR:C**
SKY'S THE LIMIT, THE **½ (1937, Brit.) PR:A
SKY'S THE LIMIT, THE **½ (1943) PR:A
SKYSCRAPER SOULS *½ (1932) PR:A
SKYSCRAPER WILDERNESS
(SEE:BIG CITY)
SKYWATCH
(SEE:LIGHT UP THE SKIES)
SKYWAY * (1933) PR:A
SLA FORST, FREDE?
(SEE:OPERATION LOVEBIRDS)
SLADE
(SEE:JACK SLADE)
SLAMDANCE * (1987, US/Brit.) PR:O**
SLAMMER
(SEE:SHORT EYES)
SLAMS, THE * (1973) PR:O
SLANDER **½ (1956) PR:A
SLANDER HOUSE *½ (1938) PR:A
SLAP SHOT * (1977) PR:O**
SLAPSTICK OF ANOTHER KIND * (1984) PR:A-C
SLASHER, THE ** (1953, Brit.) PR:O
SLASHER, THE * (1975) PR:O
SLATTERY'S HURRICANE **½ (1949) PR:C
SLAUGHTER *½ (1972) PR:O
SLAUGHTER HIGH **½ (1987) PR:O
SLAUGHTER HOTEL * (1971, It.) PR:O
SLAUGHTER IN SAN FRANCISCO * (1981) PR:O
SLAUGHTER OF THE VAMPIRES, THE
(SEE:CURSE OF THE BLOOD GHOULS)
SLAUGHTER ON TENTH AVENUE ***
(1957) PR:A-C
SLAUGHTER TRAIL *½ (1951) PR:A
SLAUGHTERHOUSE *½ (1988) PR:O
SLAUGHTERHOUSE-FIVE **½ (1972) PR:O
SLAUGHTERHOUSE ROCK * (1988) PR:O
SLAUGHTER'S BIG RIP-OFF *½ (1973) PR:O
SLAVE GIRL *½ (1947) PR:A
SLAVE GIRLS
(SEE:PREHISTORIC WOMEN)
SLAVE OF THE CANNIBAL GOD * (1979, It.) PR:O
SLAVE SHIP ** (1937) PR:A
SLAVE, THE *½ (1963, It.) PR:A
SLAVERS * (1977, Ger.) PR:O**
SLAVES ** (1969) PR:O
SLAVES OF BABYLON *½ (1953) PR:A
SLAYER, THE *½ (1982) PR:O
SLAYGROUND *½ (1984, Brit.) PR:O
SLEEP, MY LOVE *** (1948) PR:A
SLEEPAWAY CAMP *½ (1983) PR:O
SLEEPAWAY CAMP 2: UNHAPPY CAMPERS zero
(1988) PR:O
SLEEPER ***½ (1973) PR:A-C
SLEEPERS EAST *½ (1934) PR:A
SLEEPERS WEST *½ (1941) PR:A
SLEEPING BEAUTY ***½ (1959) PR:AA
SLEEPING BEAUTY **½ (1965, Ger.) PR:AA
SLEEPING BEAUTY, THE **½ (1966, USSR) PR:AA
SLEEPING CAR ** (1933, Brit.) PR:A
SLEEPING CAR MURDER, THE ***½
(1966, Fr.) PR:C-O
SLEEPING CAR TO TRIESTE ** (1949, Brit.) PR:A
SLEEPING CARDINAL, THE
(SEE:SHERLOCK HOLMES' FATAL HOUR)
SLEEPING CITY, THE *** (1950) PR:C
SLEEPING DOGS **½ (1977, New Zealand) PR:C
SLEEPING PARTNER
(SEE:SECRET AFFAIR, THE)
SLEEPING PARTNERS *½ (1930, Brit.) PR:A
SLEEPING PARTNERS
(SEE:CARNIVAL OF CRIME)
SLEEPING TIGER, THE **½ (1954, Brit.) PR:C
SLEEPLESS NIGHTS **½ (1933, Brit.) PR:A
SLEEPY LAGOON *½ (1943) PR:A
SLEEPYTIME GAL *½ (1942) PR:A
SLENDER THREAD, THE *** (1965) PR:C
SLEPOY MUZYKANT
(SEE:SOUND OF LIFE)
SLEUTH ** (1972, Brit.) PR:C-O**
SLIGHT CASE OF LARCENY, A ** (1953) PR:A
SLIGHT CASE OF MURDER, A **** (1938) PR:A
SLIGHTLY DANGEROUS *** (1943) PR:A
SLIGHTLY FRENCH ** (1949) PR:A
SLIGHTLY HONORABLE **½ (1940) PR:A
SLIGHTLY MARRIED *½ (1933) PR:A
SLIGHTLY SCANDALOUS *½ (1946) PR:A
SLIGHTLY SCARLET ** (1930) PR:A
SLIGHTLY SCARLET * (1956) PR:C**
SLIGHTLY TEMPTED * (1940) PR:A
SLIGHTLY TERRIFIC *½ (1944) PR:A
SLIM **½ (1937) PR:A
SLIM CARTER **½ (1957) PR:A
SLIME PEOPLE, THE * (1963) PR:A
SLIPPER AND THE ROSE, THE ***
(1976, Brit.) PR:AA
SLIPPER EPISODE, THE ** (1938, Fr.) PR:A
SLIPPY MCGEE ** (1948) PR:A
SLIPSTREAM **½ (1974, Can.) PR:O
SLITHER *** (1973) PR:C
SLITHIS * (1978) PR:C
SLOGAN ** (1970, Fr.) PR:C
SLOW DANCING IN THE BIG CITY **½
(1978) PR:C
SLOW MOTION
(SEE:EVERY MAN FOR HIMSELF)
SLOW MOVES **½ (1984) PR:O
SLOW RUN * (1968) PR:O
SLUGGER'S WIFE, THE *½ (1985) PR:C-O
SLUMBER PARTY '57 zero (1977) PR:O
SLUMBER PARTY IN A HAUNTED HOUSE
(SEE:GHOST IN THE INVISIBLE BIKINI, THE)
SLUMBER PARTY IN HORROR HOUSE
(SEE:GHOST IN THE INVISIBLE BIKINI, THE)
SLUMBER PARTY MASSACRE II **½ (1987) PR:O
SLUMBER PARTY MASSACRE, THE *½
(1982) PR:O
SMALL BACK ROOM, THE
(SEE:HOUR OF GLORY)
SMALL CHANGE ** (1976, Fr.) PR:C**
SMALL CIRCLE OF FRIENDS, A ** (1980) PR:O
SMALL HOTEL ** (1957, Brit.) PR:A
SMALL HOURS, THE * (1962) PR:O
SMALL MAN, THE **½ (1935, Brit.) PR:A
SMALL MIRACLE, THE
(SEE:NEVER TAKE NO FOR AN ANSWER)
SMALL TOWN BOY *½ (1937) PR:A
SMALL TOWN DEB ** (1941) PR:A
SMALL TOWN GIRL **½ (1936) PR:A
SMALL TOWN GIRL **½ (1953) PR:A
SMALL TOWN IN TEXAS, A **½ (1976) PR:C
SMALL TOWN LAWYER
(SEE:MAIN STREET LAWYER)
SMALL TOWN STORY * (1953, Brit.) PR:A
SMALL VOICE, THE
(SEE:HIDEOUT)
SMALL WORLD OF SAMMY LEE, THE ***
(1963, Brit.) PR:C
SMALLEST SHOW ON EARTH, THE ***
(1957, Brit.) PR:A
SMART ALEC * (1951, Brit.) PR:A
SMART ALECKS *½ (1942) PR:A
SMART BLONDE *½ (1937) PR:A
SMART GIRL ** (1935) PR:A
SMART GIRLS DON'T TALK *½ (1948) PR:A
SMART GUY *½ (1943) PR:A
SMART MONEY ***½ (1931) PR:A
SMART POLITICS **½ (1948) PR:A
SMART WOMAN ** (1931) PR:A
SMART WOMAN ** (1948) PR:A
SMARTEST GIRL IN TOWN ** (1936) PR:A
SMARTY ** (1934) PR:A
SMASH AND GRAB
(SEE:LARCENY STREET)
SMASH PALACE * (1982, New Zealand) PR:O**
SMASH-UP, THE STORY OF A WOMAN ***
(1947) PR:C
SMASHING BIRD I USED TO KNOW, THE
(SEE:SCHOOL FOR UNCLAIMED GIRLS)
SMASHING THE CRIME SYNDICATE
(SEE:HELL'S BLOODY DEVILS)
SMASHING THE MONEY RING **½ (1939) PR:A
SMASHING THE RACKETS ** (1938) PR:A
SMASHING THE SPY RING *½ (1939) PR:A
SMASHING THROUGH
(SEE:CHEYENNE CYCLONE)
SMASHING TIME ** (1967, Brit.) PR:C
SMELL OF HONEY, A SWALLOW OF BRINE? A *
(1966) PR:O
SMELL OF HONEY? THE
(SEE:SMELL OF HONEY, A SWALLOW OF BRINE, A)
SMILE ***½ (1975) PR:C-O
SMILE OF THE LAMB, THE *** (1986, Israel) PR:O
SMILE ORANGE ** (1976, Jamaica) PR:C
SMILES OF A SUMMER NIGHT ***
(1957, Swed.) PR:A
SMILEY ***½ (1957, Brit.) PR:A
SMILEY GETS A GUN **½ (1959, Brit.) PR:A
SMILIN' THROUGH ***½ (1932) PR:A
SMILIN' THROUGH * (1941) PR:A**
SMILING ALONG **½ (1938, Brit.) PR:A
SMILING GHOST, THE *½ (1941) PR:A
SMILING IRISH EYES **½ (1929) PR:A
SMILING LIEUTENANT, THE **** (1931) PR:A-C
SMITH **½ (1969) PR:A
SMITHEREENS **½ (1982) PR:O
SMITH'S WIVES * (1935, Brit.) PR:A
SMITHY ** (1933, Brit.) PR:A
SMITHY **½ (1946, Aus.) PR:A
SMOKE IN THE WIND * (1975) PR:C
SMOKE JUMPERS
(SEE:RED SKIES OF MONTANA)
SMOKE SIGNAL ** (1955) PR:A
SMOKE TREE RANGE **½ (1937) PR:A
SMOKESCREEN *½ (1964, Brit.) PR:A
SMOKEY AND THE BANDIT *½ (1977) PR:C-O
SMOKEY AND THE BANDIT—PART 3 zero
(1983) PR:C-O
SMOKEY AND THE BANDIT II * (1980) PR:C-O
SMOKEY BITES THE DUST zero (1981) PR:C
SMOKEY SMITH *½ (1935) PR:A

Finding entries in **THE MOTION PICTURE GUIDE** ™

Years 1929-83	Volumes I-IX
1984	Volume IX
1985	1986 ANNUAL
1986	1987 ANNUAL
1987	1988 ANNUAL
1988	1989 ANNUAL

STAR RATINGS

★★★★★	Masterpiece
★★★★	Excellent
★★★	Good
★★	Fair
★	Poor
zero	Without Merit

PARENTAL RECOMMENDATION (PR:)

AA	Good for Children
A	Acceptable for Children
C	Cautionary, some objectionable scenes
O	Objectionable for Children

BOLD: Films on Videocassette

SMOKING GUNS zero (1934) PR:A
SMOKY ** (1933) PR:A
SMOKY *** (1946) PR:A
SMOKY ** (1966) PR:A
SMOKY CANYON ** (1952) PR:A
SMOKY MOUNTAIN MELODY ** (1949) PR:A
SMOKY TRAILS * (1939) PR:A
SMOOTH AS SILK **½ (1946) PR:A
SMOOTH TALK ** (1985) PR:C-O
SMORGASBORD *½ (1983) PR:C
SMUGGLED CARGO ** (1939) PR:A
SMUGGLERS' COVE *** (1948) PR:A
SMUGGLER'S GOLD ** (1951) PR:A
SMUGGLER'S ISLAND ** (1951) PR:A
SMUGGLERS, THE **½ (1948, Brit.) PR:A
SMUGGLERS, THE * (1969, Fr.) PR:C
SMURFS AND THE MAGIC FLUTE, THE *½
(1984, Fr./Belg.) PR:AA
SNAFU ** (1945) PR:A
SNAKE PEOPLE, THE * (1968, Mex./US) PR:O
SNAKE PIT, THE ***½ (1948) PR:C
SNAKE RIVER DESPERADOES ** (1951) PR:A
SNAKE WOMAN, THE * (1961, Brit.) PR:C
SNAPSHOT
(SEE:DAY AFTER HALLOWEEN, THE)
SNIPER, THE *** (1952) PR:O
SNIPER'S RIDGE **½ (1961) PR:A
SNO-LINE * (1986) PR:O
SNOOPY, COME HOME ***½ (1972) PR:AA
SNORKEL, THE *** (1958, Brit.) PR:A
SNOUT, THE
(SEE:UNDERWORLD INFORMERS)
SNOW **½ (1983, Fr.) PR:O
SNOW COUNTRY ** (1969, Jap.) PR:O
SNOW CREATURE, THE zero (1954) PR:A
SNOW DEMONS
(SEE:SNOW DEVILS, THE)
SNOW DEVILS, THE zero (1965, It.) PR:A
SNOW DOG ** (1950) PR:AA
SNOW IN THE SOUTH SEAS ** (1963, Jap.) PR:C
SNOW JOB * (1972) PR:A
SNOW QUEEN, THE **½ (1959, USSR) PR:AA
SNOW TREASURE * (1968) PR:A
SNOW WHITE ** (1965, Ger.) PR:AA
SNOW WHITE AND ROSE RED **
(1966, Ger.) PR:AA
SNOW WHITE AND THE SEVEN DWARFS ***
(1937) PR:AA
SNOW WHITE AND THE THREE CLOWNS
(SEE:SNOW WHITE AND THE THREE STOOGES)
SNOW WHITE AND THE THREE STOOGES *
(1961) PR:A
SNOWBALL ** (1960, Brit.) PR:A
SNOWBALL EXPRESS ** (1972) PR:AA
SNOWBOUND ** (1949, Brit.) PR:A
SNOWED UNDER *½ (1936) PR:A
SNOWFIRE ** (1958) PR:AA
SNOWMAN
(SEE:LAND OF NO RETURN, THE)
SNOWS OF KILIMANJARO, THE ***½ (1952) PR:C
SNUFFY SMITH
(SEE:SNUFFY SMITH, YARD BIRD)
SNUFFY SMITH, YARD BIRD *½ (1942) PR:A
SO BIG ** (1932) PR:A
SO BIG *** (1953) PR:A
SO BRIGHT THE FLAME
(SEE:GIRL IN WHITE, THE)
SO DARK THE NIGHT ***½ (1946) PR:C
SO DEAR TO MY HEART ** (1949) PR:AA**
SO ENDS OUR NIGHT *** (1941) PR:A
SO EVIL MY LOVE ***½ (1948, Brit.) PR:C
SO EVIL SO YOUNG ** (1961, Brit.) PR:A
SO FINE * (1981) PR:C-O**
SO GOES MY LOVE **½ (1946) PR:A
SO IT'S SUNDAY **½ (1932) PR:A
SO LITTLE TIME **½ (1953, Brit.) PR:A
SO LONG AT THE FAIR ***½ (1951, Brit.) PR:A
SO LONG, BLUE BOY ** (1973) PR:O
SO LONG LETTY ** (1929) PR:A
SO LONG PHILIPPINE
(SEE:ADIEU PHILIPPINE)
SO PROUDLY WE HAIL **** (1943) PR:A
SO RED THE ROSE **½ (1935) PR:A
SO SAD ABOUT GLORIA zero (1973) PR:C-O
SO THIS IS AFRICA * (1933) PR:A
SO THIS IS COLLEGE ** (1929) PR:A
SO THIS IS LONDON **½ (1930) PR:A
SO THIS IS LONDON **½ (1940, Brit.) PR:A
SO THIS IS LOVE **½ (1953) PR:A
SO THIS IS NEW YORK *** (1948) PR:A
SO THIS IS PARIS **½ (1954) PR:A
SO THIS IS WASHINGTON **½ (1943) PR:A
SO THIS WAS PARIS
(SEE:THIS WAS PARIS)
SO WELL REMEMBERED **½ (1947, Brit.) PR:A-C
SO YOU WON'T TALK? ** (1935, Brit.) PR:A
SO YOU WON'T TALK ** (1940) PR:A
SO YOUNG, SO BAD **½ (1950) PR:A

SOAK THE RICH ** (1936) PR:A
SOAPBOX DERBY **½ (1958, Brit.) PR:AA
S.O.B. ** (1981) PR:O
SOB SISTER ** (1931) PR:A
SOCIAL ENEMY NO. 1
(SEE:NO GREATER SIN)
SOCIAL LION, THE *½ (1930) PR:A
SOCIAL REGISTER *½ (1934) PR:A
SOCIETY DOCTOR ** (1935) PR:A
SOCIETY FEVER *½ (1935) PR:A
SOCIETY GIRL ** (1932) PR:A
SOCIETY LAWYER ** (1939) PR:A
SOCIETY SMUGGLERS * (1939) PR:A
SOD SISTERS zero (1969) PR:O
SODOM AND GOMORRAH **½
(1962, US/Fr./It.) PR:C
SODOMA E GOMORRA
(SEE:SODOM AND GOMORRAH)
SOFI ** (1967) PR:A
SOFIA ** (1948) PR:A
SOFIA ***½ (1987, Arg.) PR:O
SOFT BEDS AND HARD BATTLES
(SEE:UNDERCOVERS HERO)
SOFT BODY OF DEBORAH, THE
(SEE:SWEET BODY OF DEBORAH, THE)
SOFT SKIN AND BLACK LACE
(SEE:SOFT SKIN ON BLACK SILK)
SOFT SKIN ON BLACK SILK * (1964, Fr./Sp.) PR:O
SOFT SKIN, THE **½ (1964, Fr.) PR:C-O
SOFT WARM EXPERIENCE, A
(SEE:SATIN MUSHROOM, THE)
SOGEKI
(SEE:SUN ABOVE, DEATH BELOW)
SOGGY BOTTOM U.S.A. ** (1982) PR:C
SOHO CONSPIRACY * (1951, Brit.) PR:A
SOHO INCIDENT
(SEE:SPIN A DARK WEB)
SOL MADRID **½ (1968) PR:C
SOLANGE DU DA BIST
(SEE:AS LONG AS YOU'RE NEAR ME)
SOLARBABIES zero (1986) PR:A-C
SOLARIS ***½ (1972, USSR) PR:C
SOLDATERKAMMERATER PA VAGT
(SEE:OPERATION CAMEL)
SOLDIER AND THE LADY, THE **½ (1937) PR:C
SOLDIER BLUE * (1970) PR:O
SOLDIER IN LOVE
(SEE:FANFAN THE TULIP)
SOLDIER IN SKIRTS
(SEE:TRIPLE ECHO)
SOLDIER IN THE RAIN **½ (1963) PR:C
SOLDIER OF FORTUNE **½ (1955) PR:C
SOLDIER OF LOVE
(SEE:FANFAN THE TULIP)
SOLDIER OF ORANGE ***½ (1979, Neth.) PR:O
SOLDIER, SAILOR ** (1944, Brit.) PR:A
SOLDIER, THE * (1982) PR:O
SOLDIERS AND WOMEN ** (1930) PR:A
SOLDIERS OF FORTUNE
(SEE:WAR CORRESPONDENT)
SOLDIERS OF PANCHO VILLA, THE
(SEE:LA CUCARACHA)
SOLDIERS OF THE KING
(SEE:WOMAN IN COMMAND)
SOLDIERS OF THE STORM *½ (1933) PR:A
SOLDIER'S PLAYTHING, A *½ (1931) PR:A
SOLDIER'S PRAYER, A *** (1970, Jap.) PR:C
SOLDIER'S REVENGE *½ (1986) PR:C
SOLDIER'S STORY, A ***½ (1984) PR:C
SOLDIER'S TALE, THE ** (1964, Brit.) PR:A
SOLDIERS THREE **½ (1951) PR:A
SOLDIERS 3
(SEE:SERGEANTS 3)
SOLDIERS, THE
(SEE:LES CARABINIERS)
SOLE SURVIVOR * (1984) PR:O
SOLID GOLD CADILLAC, THE **** (1956) PR:A
SOLIMANO IL CONQUISTATORE
(SEE:SULEIMAN THE CONQUEROR)
SOLITAIRE MAN, THE ** (1933) PR:A
SOLITARY CHILD, THE **½ (1958, Brit.) PR:A
SOLNTSE SVETIT VSEM
(SEE:SUN SHINES FOR ALL, THE)
SOLO ** (1970, Fr.) PR:O
SOLO ** (1978, New Zealand/Aus.) PR:O
SOLO CONTRO ROMA
(SEE:ALONE AGAINST ROME)
SOLO FOR SPARROW ** (1966, Brit.) PR:A
SOLOMON AND SHEBA ** (1959) PR:C
SOLOMON KING zero (1974) PR:O
SOLUTION BY PHONE *½ (1954, Brit.) PR:A
SOMBRERO **½ (1953) PR:A-C
SOMBRERO KID, THE ** (1942) PR:A
SOME BLONDES ARE DANGEROUS * (1937) PR:A
SOME CALL IT LOVING **½ (1973) PR:O
SOME CAME RUNNING ***½ (1959) PR:C
SOME DAY ** (1935, Brit.) PR:A
SOME GIRLS DO ** (1969, Brit.) PR:C

SOME KIND OF A NUT
(SEE:DOWN AMONG THE Z-MEN)
SOME KIND OF A NUT zero (1969) PR:C
SOME KIND OF HERO * (1982) PR:O**
SOME KIND OF WONDERFUL * (1987) PR:C**
SOME LIKE IT COOL *
(1979, Ger./Aust./It./Fr.) PR:O
SOME LIKE IT HOT *** (1959) PR:C**
SOME LIKE IT HOT **½ (1939) PR:A
SOME MAY LIVE *½ (1967, Brit.) PR:A
SOME OF MY BEST FRIENDS ARE... *½
(1971) PR:O
SOME PEOPLE * (1964, Brit.) PR:A
SOME WILL, SOME WON'T *½ (1970, Brit.) PR:A
SOMEBODY ELSE'S CHILDREN
(SEE:STEPCHILDREN)
SOMEBODY KILLED HER HUSBAND * (1978) PR:A
SOMEBODY LOVES ME *** (1952) PR:A
SOMEBODY UP THERE LIKES ME ***½
(1956) PR:C
SOMEONE *½ (1968) PR:O
SOMEONE AT THE DOOR * (1936, Brit.) PR:A
SOMEONE AT THE DOOR ** (1950, Brit.) PR:A
SOMEONE BEHIND THE DOOR *
(1971, Fr./Brit.) PR:C
SOMEONE TO LOVE ** (1988) PR:A**
SOMEONE TO REMEMBER *** (1943) PR:A
SOMEONE TO WATCH OVER ME * (1987) PR:O**
SOMETHING ALWAYS HAPPENS **
(1934, Brit.) PR:A
SOMETHING BIG **½ (1971) PR:A
SOMETHING FOR EVERYONE * (1970) PR:O**
SOMETHING FOR THE BIRDS **½ (1952) PR:A
SOMETHING FOR THE BOYS **½ (1944) PR:A
SOMETHING IN THE CITY ** (1950, Brit.) PR:A
SOMETHING IN THE WIND **½ (1947) PR:A
SOMETHING IS OUT THERE
(SEE:DAY OF THE ANIMALS)
SOMETHING MONEY CAN'T BUY **
(1952, Brit.) PR:A
SOMETHING OF VALUE ***½ (1957) PR:O
SOMETHING SHORT OF PARADISE *½
(1979) PR:C-O
SOMETHING SPECIAL! **½ (1987) PR:C
SOMETHING TO HIDE ** (1972, Brit.) PR:C-O
SOMETHING TO LIVE FOR **½ (1952) PR:A
SOMETHING TO SHOUT ABOUT *½ (1943) PR:A
SOMETHING TO SING ABOUT ***½ (1937) PR:A
SOMETHING WAITS IN THE DARK
(SEE:SCREAMERS)
SOMETHING WEIRD * (1967) PR:O
SOMETHING WICKED THIS WAY COMES **½
(1983) PR:C
SOMETHING WILD ** (1961) PR:A
SOMETHING WILD ***½ (1986) PR:O
SOMETHING'S ROTTEN * (1979, Can.) PR:C
SOMETIMES A GREAT NOTION ***½ (1971) PR:O
SOMETIMES GOOD * (1934, Brit.) PR:A
SOMEWHERE I'LL FIND YOU *** (1942) PR:A
SOMEWHERE IN BERLIN ** (1949, E./Ger.) PR:A
SOMEWHERE IN CAMP **½ (1942, Brit.) PR:A
SOMEWHERE IN CIVVIES * (1943, Brit.) PR:A
SOMEWHERE IN ENGLAND ** (1940, Brit.) PR:A
SOMEWHERE IN FRANCE ** (1943, Brit.) PR:A
SOMEWHERE IN POLITICS ** (1949, Brit.) PR:A
SOMEWHERE IN SONORA ** (1933) PR:A
SOMEWHERE IN THE NIGHT *** (1946) PR:C
SOMEWHERE IN TIME **½ (1980) PR:C
SOMEWHERE ON LEAVE *½ (1942, Brit.) PR:A
SOMMARLEK
(SEE:ILLICIT INTERLUDE)
SON COMES HOME, A ** (1936) PR:A
SON-DAUGHTER, THE *½ (1932) PR:A
SON OF A BADMAN **½ (1949) PR:A
SON OF A GUNFIGHTER ** (1966, US/Sp.) PR:A
SON OF A SAILOR *½ (1933) PR:A
SON OF A STRANGER * (1957, Brit.) PR:O
SON OF ALI BABA ** (1952) PR:A
SON OF BELLE STARR **½ (1953) PR:A
SON OF BILLY THE KID ** (1949) PR:A
SON OF BLOB
(SEE:BEWARE THE BLOB)
SON OF CAPTAIN BLOOD, THE *½
(1964, US/It./Sp.) PR:A
SON OF DAVY CROCKETT, THE *½ (1941) PR:A
SON OF DR. JEKYLL, THE *½ (1951) PR:A
SON OF DRACULA **½ (1943) PR:C
SON OF DRACULA * (1974, Brit.) PR:C
SON OF FLUBBER **½ (1963) PR:AA
SON OF FRANKENSTEIN ** (1939) PR:C**
SON OF FURY * (1942) PR:A**
SON OF GOD'S COUNTRY *½ (1948) PR:A
SON OF GODZILLA * (1967, Jap.) PR:C
SON OF GREETINGS
(SEE:HI, MOM!)
SON OF INDIA ** (1931) PR:A
SON OF INGAGI *½ (1940) PR:A
SON OF KONG * (1933) PR:A**

SON OF LASSIE **½ (1945) PR:AA
SON OF MINE
 (SEE:POLICE COURT)
SON OF MONGOLIA ** (1936, USSR) PR:A
SON OF MONTE CRISTO ** (1940) PR:A
SON OF OKLAHOMA ** (1932) PR:A
SON OF PALEFACE ***½ (1952) PR:A
SON OF ROARING DAN **½ (1940) PR:A
SON OF ROBIN HOOD ** (1959, Brit.) PR:A
SON OF SAMSON *½ (1962, Fr./It./Yugo.) PR:A
SON OF SINBAD *½ (1955) PR:A
SON OF SPARTACUS
 (SEE:SLAVE, THE)
SON OF THE BLOB
 (SEE:BEWARE THE BLOB)
SON OF THE BORDER *½ (1933) PR:A
SON OF THE GODS ** (1930) PR:A
SON OF THE NAVY ** (1940) PR:A
SON OF THE PLAINS **½ (1931) PR:A
SON OF THE RED CORSAIR ** (1963, It.) PR:A
SON OF THE REGIMENT *½ (1948, USSR) PR:A
SON OF THE RENEGADE *½ (1953) PR:A
SONG AND DANCE MAN, THE ** (1936) PR:A
SONG AND THE SILENCE, THE *½ (1969) PR:A
SONG AT EVENTIDE ** (1934, Brit.) PR:C
SONG FOR MISS JULIE, A *½ (1945) PR:A
SONG FOR TOMORROW, A * (1948, Brit.) PR:A
SONG FROM MY HEART, THE **½
 (1970, Jap.) PR:A
SONG IS BORN, A ***½ (1948) PR:A
SONG O' MY HEART *** (1930) PR:A
SONG OF ARIZONA ** (1946) PR:A
SONG OF BERNADETTE, THE ** (1943) PR:AA**
SONG OF FREEDOM * (1938, Brit.) PR:A**
SONG OF IDAHO ** (1948) PR:A
SONG OF INDIA ** (1949) PR:A
SONG OF KENTUCKY *½ (1929) PR:A
SONG OF LIFE, THE ** (1931, Ger.) PR:A
SONG OF LOVE **½ (1947) PR:A
SONG OF LOVE, THE ** (1929) PR:A
SONG OF MEXICO * (1945) PR:A
SONG OF MY HEART ** (1947) PR:A
SONG OF NEVADA **½ (1944) PR:A
SONG OF NORWAY **½ (1970) PR:A
SONG OF OLD WYOMING *½ (1945) PR:A
SONG OF PARIS
 (SEE:BACHELOR IN PARIS)
SONG OF RUSSIA ** (1943) PR:A
SONG OF SCHEHERAZADE ** (1947) PR:A
SONG OF SOHO * (1930, Brit.) PR:A
SONG OF SONGS **½ (1933) PR:A-C
SONG OF SURRENDER ** (1949) PR:A
SONG OF TEXAS **½ (1943) PR:A
SONG OF THE BUCKAROO *** (1939) PR:A
SONG OF THE CABELLERO ** (1930) PR:A
SONG OF THE CITY *½ (1937) PR:A
SONG OF THE DRIFTER ** (1948) PR:A
SONG OF THE EAGLE ** (1933) PR:A
SONG OF THE FLAME *½ (1930) PR:A
SONG OF THE FOREST ** (1963, USSR) PR:A
SONG OF THE FORGE ** (1937, Brit.) PR:A
SONG OF THE GRINGO ** (1936) PR:A
SONG OF THE ISLANDS ** (1942) PR:A
SONG OF THE LITTLE ROAD
 (SEE:PATHER PANCHALI)
SONG OF THE LOON ** (1970) PR:O
SONG OF THE OPEN ROAD ** (1944) PR:A
SONG OF THE PLOUGH
 (SEE:COUNTY FAIR)
SONG OF THE ROAD
 (SEE:END OF THE ROAD)
SONG OF THE ROAD *½ (1937, Brit.) PR:A
SONG OF THE ROAD, THE
 (SEE:PATHER PANCHALI)
SONG OF THE SADDLE ** (1936) PR:A
SONG OF THE SARONG *½ (1945) PR:A
SONG OF THE SIERRAS *½ (1946) PR:A
SONG OF THE SIERRAS
 (SEE:SPRINGTIME IN THE SIERRAS)
SONG OF THE SOUTH (1946) PR:AA
SONG OF THE THIN MAN * (1947) PR:A**
SONG OF THE TRAIL *½ (1936) PR:A
SONG OF THE WASTELAND *½ (1947) PR:A
SONG OF THE WEST ** (1930) PR:A
SONG OVER MOSCOW ** (1964, USSR) PR:A
SONG TO REMEMBER, A ***½ (1945) PR:A
SONG WITHOUT END ***½ (1960) PR:A

SONG YOU GAVE ME, THE *½ (1934, Brit.) PR:A
SONGS AND BULLETS *½ (1938) PR:A
SONGWRITER * (1984) PR:C-O**
SONNY AND JED * (1974, It.) PR:O
SONNY BOY ** (1929) PR:A
SONORA STAGECOACH ** (1944) PR:A
SONS AND LOVERS ***½ (1960, Brit.) PR:C
SONS AND MOTHERS *** (1967, USSR) PR:A
SONS O' GUNS *½ (1936) PR:A
SONS OF ADVENTURE **½ (1948) PR:A
SONS OF GOOD EARTH *½
 (1967, Hong Kong) PR:A-C
SONS OF KATIE ELDER, THE * (1965) PR:A**
SONS OF MATTHEW
 (SEE:RUGGED O'RIORDANS, THE)
SONS OF NEW MEXICO ** (1949) PR:A
SONS OF SATAN *½ (1969, It./Fr./Ger.) PR:C
SONS OF STEEL ** (1935) PR:A
SONS OF THE DESERT ***½ (1933) PR:A
SONS OF THE LEGION
 (SEE:SONS OF THE DESERT)
SONS OF THE LEGION *½ (1938) PR:A
SONS OF THE MUSKETEERS
 (SEE:AT SWORD'S POINT)
SONS OF THE PIONEERS ** (1942) PR:A
SONS OF THE SADDLE ** (1930) PR:A
SONS OF THE SEA ** (1939, Brit.) PR:A
SONS OF THE SEA
 (SEE:ATLANTIC FERRY)
SOOKY ** (1931) PR:A
SOPHIE LANG
 (SEE:NOTORIOUS SOPHIE LANG, THE)
SOPHIE LANG GOES WEST * (1937) PR:A
SOPHIE'S CHOICE ***½ (1982) PR:O
SOPHIE'S PLACE **½ (1970) PR:C
SOPHIE'S WAYS **½ (1970, Fr.) PR:O
SOPHOMORE, THE *½ (1929) PR:A
SORCERER ***½ (1977) PR:O
SORCERERS, THE *** (1967, Brit.) PR:C
SORCERESS * (1983) PR:O
SORORITY GIRL *½ (1957) PR:C
SORORITY HOUSE **½ (1939) PR:A
SORORITY HOUSE MASSACRE zero (1986) PR:O
SORROWFUL JONES * (1949) PR:A**
SORRY, WRONG NUMBER ** (1948) PR:C**
SORRY YOU'VE BEEN TROUBLED
 (SEE:LIFE GOES ON)
SORYU HIKEN
 (SEE:SECRET SCROLLS, PART II)
S.O.S. ICEBERG ** (1933) PR:A
S.O.S. PACIFIC ** (1960, Brit.) PR:A
S.O.S. TIDAL WAVE ** (1939) PR:A
SO'S YOUR AUNT EMMA
 (SEE:MEET THE MOB)
SO'S YOUR UNCLE ** (1943) PR:A
SOTTO IL TALLONE
 (SEE:CLOPORTES)
SOTTO...SOTTO **½ (1985, It.) PR:O
SOUHVEZDI PANNY
 (SEE:SIGN OF THE VIRGIN)
SOUL KISS
 (SEE:LADY'S MORALS, A)
SOUL MAN **½ (1986) PR:C
SOUL OF A MONSTER, THE *½ (1944) PR:A
SOUL OF NIGGER CHARLEY, THE ** (1973) PR:O
SOUL OF THE SLUMS * (1931) PR:A
SOUL SOLDIERS
 (SEE:RED, WHITE, AND BLACK, THE)
SOULS AT SEA ***½ (1937) PR:A
SOULS FOR SABLES
 (SEE:LOVEBOUND)
SOULS FOR SALE
 (SEE:CONFESSIONS OF AN OPIUM EATER)
SOULS IN CONFLICT *½ (1955, Brit.) PR:A
SOULS OF SIN
 (SEE:MALE AND FEMALE SINCE ADAM AND
 EVE)
SOUND AND FURY ***½ (1988, Fr.) PR:O
SOUND AND THE FURY, THE ***½ (1959) PR:C-O
SOUND BARRIER, THE
 (SEE:BREAKING THE SOUND BARRIER)
SOUND OF FURY, THE * (1950) PR:C**
SOUND OF HORROR * (1966, Sp.) PR:C
SOUND OF LIFE, THE *** (1962, USSR) PR:A
SOUND OF MUSIC, THE ** (1965) PR:AA**
SOUND OF TRUMPETS, THE *** (1963, It.) PR:A

SOUND OFF **½ (1952) PR:A
SOUNDER ***½ (1972) PR:AA
SOUNDER, PART 2 *** (1976) PR:AA
SOUP FOR ONE ** (1982) PR:O
SOUP TO NUTS * (1930) PR:A
SOUP TO NUTS
 (SEE:WAITRESS)
SOURDOUGH *½ (1977) PR:AA
SOURSWEET **½ (1988, Brit.) PR:C-O
SOUS LE SOLEIL DE SATAN
 (SEE:UNDER SATAN'S SUN)
SOUS LES TOITS DE PARIS
 (SEE:UNDER THE ROOFS OF PARIS)
SOUTH ***½ (1988, Arg./Fr.) PR:O
SOUTH AMERICAN GEORGE ** (1941, Brit.) PR:A
SOUTH BRONX HEROES ** (1985) PR:O
SOUTH OF ALGIERS
 (SEE:GOLDEN MASK, THE)
SOUTH OF ARIZONA *½ (1938) PR:A
SOUTH OF CALIENTE * (1951) PR:A
SOUTH OF DEATH VALLEY *½ (1949) PR:A
SOUTH OF DIXIE *½ (1944) PR:A
SOUTH OF PAGO PAGO **½ (1940) PR:A
SOUTH OF PANAMA * (1941) PR:A
SOUTH OF RIO *½ (1949) PR:A
SOUTH OF ST. LOUIS ***½ (1949) PR:A
SOUTH OF SANTA FE * (1932) PR:A
SOUTH OF SANTA FE ** (1942) PR:A
SOUTH OF SONORA * (1930) PR:A
SOUTH OF SUEZ **½ (1940) PR:A
SOUTH OF TAHITI **½ (1941) PR:A
SOUTH OF THE BORDER * (1939) PR:A
SOUTH OF THE RIO GRANDE ** (1932) PR:A
SOUTH OF THE RIO GRANDE * (1945) PR:A
SOUTH PACIFIC ** (1958) PR:A**
SOUTH PACIFIC TRAIL ** (1952) PR:A
SOUTH RIDING *** (1938, Brit.) PR:A
SOUTH SEA ROSE ** (1929) PR:A
SOUTH SEA SINNER *½ (1950) PR:A
SOUTH SEA WOMAN **½ (1953) PR:A
SOUTH SEAS FURY
 (SEE:HELL'S ISLAND)
SOUTH TO KARANGA * (1940) PR:A
SOUTHERN COMFORT ***½ (1981) PR:O
SOUTHERN MAID, A ** (1933, Brit.) PR:A
SOUTHERN ROSES *½ (1936, Brit.) PR:A
SOUTHERN STAR, THE ** (1969, Fr./Brit.) PR:C
SOUTHERN YANKEE, A *** (1948) PR:AA
SOUTHERNER, THE ** (1945) PR:A**
SOUTHERNER, THE
 (SEE:PRODIGAL, THE)
SOUTHSIDE 1-1000 **½ (1950) PR:A
SOUTHWARD HO? ** (1939) PR:A
SOUTHWEST PASSAGE ** (1954) PR:A
SOUTHWEST TO SONORA
 (SEE:APPALOOSA, THE)
SOYLENT GREEN **½ (1973) PR:C
SPACE AMOEBA, THE * (1970, Jap.) PR:A
SPACE CHILDREN, THE **½ (1958) PR:A
SPACE CRUISER ** (1977, Jap.) PR:A
SPACE DEVILS
 (SEE:SNOW DEVILS, THE)
SPACE FIREBIRD 2772 ** (1979, Jap.) PR:A
SPACE HUNTER: ADVENTURES IN THE FORBIDDEN
 ZONE
 (SEE:SPACEHUNTER: ADVENTURES IN THE
 FORBIDDEN ZONE)
SPACE INVASION FROM LAPLAND
 (SEE:INVASION OF THE SPACE PEOPLE)
SPACE MASTER X-7 ** (1958) PR:A
SPACE MEN
 (SEE:ASSIGNMENT-OUTER SPACE)
SPACE MEN APPEAR IN TOKYO
 (SEE:MYSTERIOUS SATELLITE, THE)
SPACE MISSION OF THE LOST PLANET
 (SEE:HORROR OF THE BLOOD MONSTERS)
SPACE MONSTER * (1965) PR:A
SPACE RAGE ** (1987) PR:O
SPACE RAIDERS zero (1983) PR:C
SPACE SHIP, THE **½ (1935, USSR) PR:A
SPACE STATION X
 (SEE:MUTINY IN OUTER SPACE)
SPACE STATION X-14
 (SEE:MUTINY IN OUTER SPACE)
SPACEBALLS ** (1987) PR:C
SPACECAMP ** (1986) PR:A
SPACED OUT zero (1981, Brit.) PR:O

Finding entries in **THE MOTION PICTURE GUIDE** ™		**STAR RATINGS**		**PARENTAL RECOMMENDATION (PR:)**	
Years 1929-83	Volumes I-IX	★★★★★	Masterpiece	AA	Good for Children
1984	Volume IX	★★★★	Excellent	A	Acceptable for Children
1985	1986 ANNUAL	★★★	Good	C	Cautionary, some objectionable scenes
1986	1987 ANNUAL	★★	Fair	O	Objectionable for Children
1987	1988 ANNUAL	★	Poor		
1988	1989 ANNUAL	zero	Without Merit	**BOLD:** Films on Videocassette	

SPACEFLIGHT IC-1 ** (1965, Brit.) PR:A
SPACEHUNTER: ADVENTURES IN THE
FORBIDDEN ZONE ** (1983) PR:C
SPACEMAN AND KING ARTHUR, THE
  (SEE:UNIDENTIFIED FLYING ODDBALL)
SPACEMEN SATURDAY NIGHT
  (SEE:INVASION OF THE SAUCER MEN)
SPACESHIP
  (SEE:DAY MARS INVADED THE EARTH, THE)
SPACESHIP
  (SEE:CREATURE WASN'T NICE)
SPACESHIP TO VENUS
  (SEE:FIRST SPACESHIP ON VENUS)
SPACEWAYS ** (1953, Brit.) PR:A
SPANIARD'S CURSE, THE **½ (1958, Brit.) PR:A
SPANISH AFFAIR **½ (1958, Sp.) PR:A
SPANISH CAPE MYSTERY ** (1935) PR:A
SPANISH EYES * (1930, Brit.) PR:A
SPANISH FLY zero (1975, Brit.) PR:O
SPANISH GARDENER, THE *** (1957, Sp.) PR:A
SPANISH MAIN, THE **½ (1945) PR:A
SPANISH SWORD, THE *½ (1962, Brit.) PR:A
SPARA FORTE, PIU FORTE...NON CAPISCO
  (SEE:SHOOT LOUD, LOUDER...I DON'T
  UNDERSTAND)
SPARE A COPPER ** (1940, Brit.) PR:A
SPARE THE ROD ** (1961, Brit.) PR:A
SPARKLE ** (1976) PR:C-O
SPARROWS CAN'T SING ** (1963, Brit.) PR:A
SPARTACUS ** (1960) PR:C**
SPASMS zero (1983, Can.) PR:O
SPATS TO SPURS
  (SEE:HENRY GOES TO ARIZONA)
SPAWN OF THE NORTH ***½ (1938) PR:A
SPEAK EASILY **½ (1932) PR:A
SPEAKEASY *½ (1929) PR:A
SPECIAL AGENT *** (1935) PR:A-C
SPECIAL AGENT ** (1949) PR:A
SPECIAL AGENT K-7 * (1937) PR:A
SPECIAL DAY, A * (1977, It./Can.) PR:C
SPECIAL DELIVERY **½ (1955, Ger.) PR:A
SPECIAL DELIVERY **½ (1976) PR:C
SPECIAL EDITION ** (1938, Brit.) PR:A
SPECIAL EFFECTS * (1984) PR:O**
SPECIAL INSPECTOR * (1939) PR:A
SPECIAL INVESTIGATOR **½ (1936) PR:A
SPECIALIST, THE *½ (1975) PR:O
SPECKLED BAND, THE * (1931, Brit.) PR:A**
SPECTER OF FREEDOM, THE
  (SEE:PHANTOM OF LIBERTY)
SPECTER OF THE ROSE *** (1946) PR:C
SPECTOR OF FREEDOM
  (SEE:PHANTOM LIBERTY, THE)
SPECTRE OF EDGAR ALLAN POE, THE *½
  (1974) PR:O
SPEED ** (1936) PR:A
SPEED BRENT WINS
  (SEE:BREED OF THE BORDER)
SPEED CRAZY zero (1959) PR:C
SPEED DEVILS * (1935) PR:A
SPEED LIMIT 65
  (SEE:LIMIT, THE)
SPEED LIMITED zero (1940) PR:A
SPEED LOVERS zero (1968) PR:A
SPEED MADNESS *½ (1932) PR:A
SPEED REPORTER
  (SEE:SCAREHEADS)
SPEED REPORTER zero (1936) PR:A
SPEED TO BURN ** (1938) PR:A
SPEED TO SPARE * (1937) PR:A
SPEED TO SPARE *½ (1948) PR:A
SPEED WINGS ** (1934) PR:A
SPEEDTRAP ** (1978) PR:A
SPEEDWAY ** (1968) PR:A
SPELL OF AMY NUGENT, THE ** (1945, Brit.) PR:A
SPELL OF THE HYPNOTIST * (1956) PR:A
SPELLBINDER, THE *½ (1939) PR:A
SPELLBOUND
  (SEE:SPELL OF AMY NUGENT, THE)
SPELLBOUND ** (1945) PR:A-C**
SPENCER'S MOUNTAIN *** (1963) PR:C
SPENDTHRIFT **½ (1936) PR:A
SPESSART INN, THE ** (1961, Ger.) PR:A
SPETTERS * (1983, Neth.) PR:O**
SPHINX zero (1981) PR:C
SPHINX, THE **½ (1933) PR:A
SPICE OF LIFE ** (1954, Fr.) PR:A
SPIDER, THE *½ (1958) PR:A
SPIDER AND THE FLY, THE **½ (1952, Brit.) PR:A
SPIDER BABY zero (1968) PR:O
SPIDER BABY, OR THE MADDEST STORY EVER
  TOLD
  (SEE:SPIDER BABY)
SPIDER WOMAN
  (SEE:SHERLOCK HOLMES AND THE SPIDER
  WOMAN)
SPIDER WOMAN STRIKES BACK, THE **
  (1946) PR:A

SPIDER, THE *½ (1931) PR:A
SPIDER, THE *½ (1940, Brit.) PR:A
SPIDER, THE ** (1945) PR:A
SPIDER'S WEB, THE ** (1960, Brit.) PR:A
SPIDER'S WEB, THE
  (SEE:IT'S HOT IN PARADISE)
SPIELER, THE *½ (1929) PR:A
SPIES A GO-GO
  (SEE:NASTY RABBIT, THE)
SPIES AT WORK
  (SEE:SABOTAGE)
SPIES LIKE US * (1985) PR:C
SPIES OF THE AIR **½ (1940, Brit.) PR:A
SPIKE OF BENSONHURST **½ (1988) PR:C
SPIKER * (1986) PR:C-O
SPIKES GANG, THE **½ (1974) PR:C
SPIN A DARK WEB ** (1956, Brit.) PR:A
SPIN OF A COIN
  (SEE:GEORGE RAFT STORY, THE)
SPINAL TAP
  (SEE:THIS IS SPINAL TAP)
SPINOUT ** (1966) PR:A
SPIONE UNTER SICHE
  (SEE:DIRTY GAME, THE)
SPIRAL ROAD, THE * (1962) PR:A
SPIRAL STAIRCASE, THE ** (1946) PR:C**
SPIRAL STAIRCASE, THE * (1975, Brit.) PR:C-O
SPIRIT AND THE FLESH, THE ** (1948, It.) PR:A
SPIRIT IS WILLING, THE ** (1967) PR:A
SPIRIT OF CULVER, THE *½ (1939) PR:A
SPIRIT OF NOTRE DAME, THE ** (1931) PR:A
SPIRIT OF ST. LOUIS, THE ** (1957) PR:AA**
SPIRIT OF STANFORD, THE * (1942) PR:A
SPIRIT OF THE BEEHIVE, THE ***½
  (1976, Sp.) PR:C
SPIRIT OF THE DEAD
  (SEE:ASPHYX, THE)
SPIRIT OF THE PEOPLE
  (SEE:ABE LINCOLN IN ILLINOIS)
SPIRIT OF THE WEST *½ (1932) PR:A
SPIRIT OF THE WIND ** (1979) PR:C
SPIRIT OF WEST POINT, THE *½ (1947) PR:A
SPIRIT OF YOUTH * (1937) PR:A
SPIRITISM ** (1965, Mex.) PR:C
SPIRITS OF THE DEAD *** (1969, Fr./It.) PR:O
SPIRITUALIST, THE **½ (1948) PR:A
SPITFIRE * (1934) PR:A**
SPITFIRE ***½ (1943, Brit.) PR:A
SPLASH ***½ (1984) PR:A-C
SPLENDID FELLOWS *½ (1934, Aus.) PR:A
SPLENDOR ** (1935) PR:A
SPLENDOR IN THE GRASS * (1961) PR:C**
SPLINTERS *½ (1929, Brit.) PR:A
SPLINTERS IN THE AIR *½ (1937, Brit.) PR:A
SPLINTERS IN THE NAVY ** (1931, Brit.) PR:A
SPLIT DECISIONS ** (1988) PR:C
SPLIT IMAGE * (1982) PR:O**
SPLIT SECOND * (1953) PR:A**
SPLIT, THE
  (SEE:MANSTER, THE)
SPLIT, THE **½ (1968) PR:O
SPLITFACE
  (SEE:DICK TRACY)
SPLITTING UP ** (1981, Neth.) PR:C
SPLITZ zero (1984) PR:O
SPOILED ROTTEN zero (1968, Gr.) PR:C-O
SPOILERS, THE ***½ (1942) PR:A
SPOILERS OF THE FOREST *½ (1957) PR:A
SPOILERS OF THE NORTH *½ (1947) PR:A
SPOILERS OF THE PLAINS ** (1951) PR:A
SPOILERS OF THE RANGE * (1939) PR:A
SPOILERS, THE *** (1930) PR:A
SPOILERS, THE **½ (1955) PR:C
SPOILS OF THE NIGHT **½ (1969, Jap.) PR:C-O
SPOOK BUSTERS **½ (1946) PR:A
SPOOK CHASERS *½ (1957) PR:A
SPOOK TOWN ** (1944) PR:A
SPOOK WHO SAT BY THE DOOR, THE zero
  (1973) PR:O
SPOOKS RUN WILD **½ (1941) PR:A
SPORT OF A NATION
  (SEE:ALL AMERICAN, THE)
SPORT OF KINGS, THE *½ (1931, Brit.) PR:A
SPORT OF KINGS *½ (1947) PR:A
SPORT PARADE, THE ** (1932) PR:A
SPORTING BLOOD * (1931) PR:A**
SPORTING BLOOD ** (1940) PR:A
SPORTING CHANCE *½ (1931) PR:A
SPORTING CHANCE, A ** (1945) PR:A
SPORTING CLUB, THE zero (1971) PR:O
SPORTING LIFE
  (SEE:NIGHT PARADE)
SPORTING LOVE ** (1936, Brit.) PR:A
SPORTING WIDOW, THE
  (SEE:MADAME RACKETEER)
SPOT
  (SEE:DOGPOUND SHUFFLE)

SPOT OF BOTHER, A ** (1938, Brit.) PR:A
SPOTLIGHT SCANDALS **½ (1943) PR:A
SPOTS ON MY LEOPARD, THE **½
  (1974, South Africa) PR:A
SPRING *½ (1948, USSR) PR:A
SPRING AFFAIR ** (1960) PR:A
SPRING AND PORT WINE **½ (1970, Brit.) PR:C-O
SPRING BREAK * (1983) PR:O
SPRING FEVER *½ (1983, Can.) PR:C
SPRING FOR THE THIRSTY, A ***½
  (1988, USSR) PR:A-C
SPRING HANDICAP * (1937, Brit.) PR:A
SPRING IN PARK LANE ***½ (1949, Brit.) PR:A
SPRING IN THE AIR * (1934, Brit.) PR:A
SPRING IS HERE ** (1930) PR:A
SPRING MADNESS ** (1938) PR:A
SPRING MEETING **½ (1941, Brit.) PR:A
SPRING NIGHT, SUMMER NIGHT
  (SEE:MISS JESSICA IS PREGNANT)
SPRING PARADE *** (1940) PR:A
SPRING REUNION *½ (1957) PR:A
SPRING SHOWER *** (1932, Hung.) PR:A
SPRING SONG
  (SEE:SPRINGTIME)
SPRING SYMPHONY **½
  (1986, W. Ger./E. Ger.) PR:A-C
SPRING TONIC * (1935) PR:A
SPRINGFIELD RIFLE *** (1952) PR:A
SPRINGTIME ** (1948, Brit.) PR:A
SPRINGTIME FOR HENRY *½ (1934) PR:A
SPRINGTIME IN THE ROCKIES *½ (1937) PR:A
SPRINGTIME IN THE ROCKIES **½ (1942) PR:A
SPRINGTIME IN THE SIERRAS **½ (1947) PR:A
SPRINGTIME ON THE VOLGA **
  (1961, USSR) PR:A
SPURS ** (1930) PR:A
SPUTNIK *½ (1960, Fr.) PR:A
SPY BUSTERS
  (SEE:GUNS IN THE HEATHER)
SPY CHASERS ** (1956) PR:A
SPY FOR A DAY **½ (1939, Brit.) PR:A
SPY HUNT ** (1950) PR:A
SPY IN BLACK, THE * (1939, Brit.) PR:A**
SPY IN THE GREEN HAT, THE *½ (1966) PR:A
SPY IN THE PANTRY
  (SEE:MISSING TEN DAYS)
SPY IN THE SKY *½ (1958) PR:A
SPY IN WHITE, THE
  (SEE:SECRET OF STAMBOUL, THE)
SPY IN YOUR EYE ** (1966, It.) PR:A
SPY OF NAPOLEON ** (1939, Brit.) PR:A
SPY RING, THE *½ (1938) PR:A
SPY 77
  (SEE:SECRET AGENT)
SPY SHIP *½ (1942) PR:A
SPY 13
  (SEE:OPERATION 13)
SPY TRAIN ** (1943) PR:A
SPY WHO CAME IN FROM THE COLD, THE **
  (1965, Brit.) PR:A-C**
SPY WHO LOVED ME, THE ** (1977, Brit.) PR:C
SPY WITH A COLD NOSE, THE **½
  (1966, Brit.) PR:A
SPY WITH MY FACE, THE *½ (1966) PR:A
SPYASHCHAYA KRASAVITSA
  (SEE:SLEEPING BEAUTY)
SPYLARKS ** (1965, Brit.) PR:A
S*P*Y*S * (1974) PR:C
SPYS
  (SEE:S.P.Y.S.)
SQUAD CAR ** (1961) PR:A
SQUADRON LEADER X ** (1943, Brit.) PR:A
SQUADRON OF HONOR *½ (1938) PR:A
SQUADRON 633 **½ (1964, US/Brit.) PR:C
SQUALL, THE * (1929) PR:A
SQUAMISH FIVE, THE **½ (1988, Can.) PR:C
SQUARE DANCE ** (1987) PR:C
SQUARE DANCE JUBILEE *½ (1949) PR:A
SQUARE DANCE KATY *½ (1950) PR:A
SQUARE JUNGLE, THE **½ (1955) PR:A
SQUARE OF VIOLENCE *** (1963, US/Yugo.) PR:A
SQUARE PEG, THE ** (1958, Brit.) PR:A
SQUARE RING, THE **½ (1955, Brit.) PR:A
SQUARE ROOT OF ZERO, THE *½ (1964) PR:C
SQUARE SHOOTER
  (SEE:SKIPALONG ROSENBLOOM)
SQUARE SHOULDERS **½ (1929) PR:A
SQUARED CIRCLE, THE
  (SEE:JOE PALOOKA IN THE SQUARED CIRCLE)
SQUARES **½ (1972) PR:A
SQUATTER'S DAUGHTER ** (1933, Aus.) PR:A
SQUAW MAN, THE ** (1931) PR:A
SQUEAKER, THE, 1937
  (SEE:MURDER ON DIAMOND ROW)
SQUEAKER, THE ** (1930, Brit.) PR:A
SQUEALER, THE ** (1930) PR:A
SQUEEZE, THE ** (1977, Brit.) PR:O
SQUEEZE A FLOWER ** (1970, Aus.) PR:A

__SQUEEZE, THE ** (1987) PR:O__
__SQUEEZE PLAY * (1981) PR:O__
SQUEEZE, THE *½ (1980, It.) PR:O
SQUIBS *½ (1935, Brit.) PR:A
__SQUIRM * (1976) PR:C__
__SQUIZZY TAYLOR ** (1984, Aus.) PR:O__
SSSSNAKE
(SEE:SSSSSSSS)
SSSSSSSS **½ (1973) PR:C
S.T.A.B. * (1976, Hong Kong/Thai.) PR:O
STABLEMATES *** (1938) PR:A
__STACEY! *½ (1973) PR:O__
STACEY AND HER GANGBUSTERS
(SEE:STACEY!)
__STACKING **½ (1987) PR:A-C__
STACY'S KNIGHTS * (1983) PR:C
STADIUM MURDERS, THE
(SEE:HOLLYWOOD STADIUM MYSTERY)
__STAGE DOOR ***** (1937) PR:A-C__
__STAGE DOOR CANTEEN **** (1943) PR:A__
__STAGE FRIGHT *** (1950, Brit.) PR:A-c__
STAGE FROM BLUE RIVER
(SEE:STAGE TO BLUE RIVER)
STAGE MOTHER ** (1933) PR:A
__STAGE STRUCK ** (1936) PR:A__
STAGE STRUCK *½ (1948) PR:C
__STAGE STRUCK **½ (1958) PR:A-C__
STAGE TO BLUE RIVER *½ (1951) PR:A
STAGE TO CHINO ** (1940) PR:A
__STAGE TO MESA CITY *½ (1947) PR:A__
STAGE TO THUNDER ROCK **½ (1964) PR:A
STAGE TO TUCSON ** (1950) PR:A
STAGE WHISPERS
(SEE:GRIEF STREET)
__STAGECOACH ***** (1939) PR:C__
STAGECOACH ** (1966) PR:A-C
STAGECOACH BUCKAROO **½ (1942) PR:A
STAGECOACH DAYS * (1938) PR:A
STAGECOACH EXPRESS *½ (1942) PR:A
STAGECOACH KID * (1949) PR:A
STAGECOACH LINE
(SEE:OLD TEXAS TRAIL, THE)
STAGECOACH OUTLAWS *½ (1945) PR:A
STAGECOACH TO DANCER'S PARK **½ (1962) PR:A
__STAGECOACH TO DENVER *½ (1946) PR:A__
STAGECOACH TO FURY ** (1956) PR:A
STAGECOACH TO HELL
(SEE:STAGE TO THUNDER ROCK)
STAGECOACH TO MONTEREY ** (1944) PR:A
STAGECOACH WAR * (1940) PR:A
STAIRCASE **½ (1969, US/Brit./Fr.) PR:C-O
STAIRWAY TO HEAVEN **** (1946, Brit.) PR:A
STAKEOUT! ** (1962) PR:A
__STAKEOUT ***½ (1987) PR:O__
STAKEOUT ON DOPE STREET **½ (1958) PR:C
__STALAG 17 ***** (1953) PR:C__
STALKER ***½ (1982, USSR) PR:C
STALKING MOON, THE *½ (1969) PR:A
STALLION CANYON ** (1949) PR:A
STALLION ROAD ** (1947) PR:A
STAMBOUL ** (1931, Brit.) PR:A
STAMBOUL QUEST ***½ (1934) PR:A
STAMMHEIM **** (1986, Ger.) PR:C
STAMPEDE *½ (1936) PR:A
STAMPEDE ** (1949) PR:A
STAMPEDE
(SEE:GUNS OF THE TIMBERLAND)
STAMPEDED
(SEE:BIG LAND, THE)
__STAND ALONE zero (1985) PR:O__
STAND AND DELIVER
(SEE:BOWERY BLITZKRIEG)
__STAND AND DELIVER ***½ (1988) PR:A__
STAND AT APACHE RIVER, THE *½ (1953) PR:A
STAND BY FOR ACTION *** (1942) PR:A
__STAND BY ME ***½ (1986) PR:C__
STAND EASY
(SEE:DOWN AMONG THE Z-MEN)
__STAND-IN ***½ (1937) PR:A__
__STAND-IN, THE **½ (1985) PR:C-O__
STAND UP AND BE COUNTED *½ (1972) PR:C
__STAND UP AND CHEER **½ (1934 80m FOX bw) PR:A__
STAND UP AND FIGHT *** (1939) PR:A-C
STAND UP VIRGIN SOLDIERS *½ (1977, Brit.) PR:O
STANDING ROOM ONLY *** (1944) PR:A

__STANLEY zero (1973) PR:O__
__STANLEY AND LIVINGSTONE *** (1939) PR:AA__
STAR, THE *** (1953) PR:A
STAR! ***½ (1968) PR:A-C
__STAR CHAMBER, THE *** (1983) PR:C-O__
STAR CHILD
(SEE:SPACE RAIDERS)
STAR CRASH
(SEE:STARCRASH)
__STAR CRYSTAL *½ (1986) PR:O__
STAR DUST *** (1940) PR:A
__STAR 80 *** (1983) PR:O__
STAR FELL FROM HEAVEN, A ** (1936, Brit.) PR:AA
STAR FOR A NIGHT **½ (1936) PR:A
STAR IN THE DUST **½ (1956) PR:A
STAR IN THE WEST
(SEE:SECOND TIME AROUND)
STAR INSPECTOR, THE *½ (1980, USSR) PR:A
__STAR IS BORN, A ***** (1937) PR:C__
__STAR IS BORN, A **** (1954) PR:A-C__
__STAR IS BORN, A *** (1976) PR:C-O__
STAR MAKER, THE *** (1939) PR:AA
STAR OF HONG KONG ** (1962, Jap.) PR:A
STAR OF INDIA *½ (1956, Brit.) PR:A
__STAR OF MIDNIGHT *** (1935) PR:A__
STAR OF MY NIGHT ** (1954, Brit.) PR:C
STAR OF TEXAS ** (1953) PR:A
STAR OF THE CIRCUS
(SEE:HIDDEN MENACE)
__STAR PACKER, THE * (1934) PR:A__
STAR PILOT * (1977, It.) PR:A
STAR REPORTER *½ (1939) PR:A
STAR SAID NO, THE
(SEE:CALLAWAY WENT THATAWAY)
__STAR SLAMMER: THE ESCAPE ** (1988) PR:O__
STAR SPANGLED GIRL * (1971) PR:A
STAR SPANGLED RHYTHM ***½ (1942) PR:A
__STAR TREK IV: THE VOYAGE HOME **** (1986) PR:A-C__
__STAR TREK: THE MOTION PICTURE **½ (1979) PR:A__
__STAR TREK III: THE SEARCH FOR SPOCK *** (1984) PR:A-C__
__STAR TREK II: THE WRATH OF KHAN *** (1982) PR:A__
__STAR WARS ***** (1977) PR:A-C__
STAR WITNESS *** (1931) PR:A
__STARCHASER: THE LEGEND OF ORIN ** (1985) PR:C__
__STARCRASH *½ (1979) PR:C__
STARDUST
(SEE:HE LOVED AN ACTRESS)
STARDUST **½ (1974, Brit.) PR:O
__STARDUST MEMORIES **½ (1980) PR:C__
STARDUST ON THE SAGE *½ (1942) PR:A
__STARFIGHTERS, THE *½ (1964) PR:A__
__STARHOPS ** (1978) PR:O__
STARK FEAR * (1963) PR:C
STARK MAD *½ (1929) PR:A
STARLIFT **½ (1951) PR:A
__STARLIGHT HOTEL *** (1987, New Zealand) PR:A__
STARLIGHT OVER TEXAS ** (1938) PR:A
STARLIGHT SLAUGHTER
(SEE:EATEN ALIVE)
__STARMAN *** (1984) PR:C__
__STARS AND BARS * (1988) PR:C-O__
STARS AND STRIPES FOREVER *** (1952) PR:AA
STARS ARE SINGING, THE **½ (1953) PR:A
STARS IN MY CROWN **½ (1950) PR:A
STARS IN YOUR BACKYARD
(SEE:PARADISE ALLEY)
STARS IN YOUR EYES *½ (1956, Brit.) PR:A
__STARS LOOK DOWN, THE **** (1940, Brit.) PR:A-C__
STARS ON PARADE ** (1944) PR:A
STARS OVER ARIZONA ** (1937) PR:A
STARS OVER BROADWAY ** (1935) PR:A
STARS OVER TEXAS ** (1946) PR:A
STARSHIP INVASIONS ** (1978, Can.) PR:AA
__STARSTRUCK **½ (1982, Aus.) PR:C__
START CHEERING **½ (1938) PR:A
__START THE REVOLUTION WITHOUT ME *** (1970) PR:C-O__
__STARTING OVER ***½ (1979) PR:C-O__
STASTNY KONEC
(SEE:HAPPY END)
STATE DEPARTMENT—FILE 649 ** (1949) PR:A

STATE FAIR *** (1933) PR:A
STATE FAIR **** (1945) PR:A
__STATE FAIR **½ (1962) PR:A__
__STATE OF SIEGE ***½ (1973, Fr./US/It./Ger.) PR:C__
__STATE OF THE UNION **** (1948) PR:A__
__STATE OF THINGS, THE ***½ (1983) PR:A__
STATE PENITENTIARY ** (1950) PR:A
STATE POLICE *½ (1938) PR:A
STATE POLICE
(SEE:WHIRLWIND RAIDERS)
STATE SECRET
(SEE:GREAT MANHUNT, THE)
STATE STREET SADIE ** (1928) PR:C
STATE TROOPER ** (1933) PR:A
STATELESS
(SEE:NO EXIT)
__STATELINE MOTEL * (1976, It.) PR:O__
STATE'S ATTORNEY **** (1932) PR:A
STATIC **½ (1985) PR:C-O
STATION SIX-SAHARA ** (1964, Brit./Ger.) PR:C
__STATION WEST *** (1948) PR:A__
__STATUE, THE zero (1971, Brit.) PR:O__
STAVISKY ***½ (1974, Fr.) PR:C
__STAY AWAY, JOE * (1968) PR:A__
__STAY HUNGRY ** (1976) PR:O__
__STAYING ALIVE zero (1983) PR:C__
__STEADY COMPANY ** (1932) PR:A__
__STEAGLE, THE *½ (1971) PR:O__
__STEALING HOME * (1988) PR:C__
STEAMBOAT ROUND THE BEND ** (1935) PR:A
__STEAMING **½ (1985, Brit.) PR:O__
__STEEL **½ (1980) PR:C__
STEEL AGAINST THE SKY *½ (1941) PR:A
__STEEL ARENA *½ (1973) PR:C__
STEEL BAYONET, THE * (1958, Brit.) PR:A
STEEL CAGE, THE ** (1954) PR:A
__STEEL CLAW, THE * (1961) PR:A__
STEEL FIST, THE ** (1952) PR:A
STEEL HELMET, THE **** (1951) PR:C
STEEL HIGHWAY, THE
(SEE:OTHER MEN'S WOMEN)
STEEL JUNGLE, THE *½ (1956) PR:A
STEEL KEY, THE ** (1953, Brit.) PR:A
STEEL LADY, THE *½ (1953) PR:A
STEEL TOWN ** (1952) PR:A
STEEL TRAP, THE ***½ (1952) PR:A
__STEELE JUSTICE * (1987) PR:O__
__STEELYARD BLUES ** (1973) PR:C__
STEFANIA ** (1968, Gr.) PR:O
STELLA **½ (1950) PR:A
__STELLA DALLAS **** (1937) PR:A__
STELLA PARISH
(SEE:I FOUND STELLA PARISH)
STELLA STAR
(SEE:STARCRASH)
STEP BY STEP ** (1946) PR:A
STEP DOWN TO TERROR ** (1958) PR:A
__STEP LIVELY *** (1944) PR:A__
STEP LIVELY, JEEVES *½ (1937) PR:A
STEPCHILD * (1947) PR:A
STEPCHILDREN *** (1962, USSR) PR:A
__STEPFATHER, THE ***½ (1987) PR:O__
STEPFORD WIVES, THE **½ (1975) PR:A-C
STEPHANIA
(SEE:STEFANIA)
__STEPHEN KING'S SILVER BULLET zero (1985) PR:O__
STEPPE, THE ** (1963, Fr./It.) PR:A
__STEPPENWOLF ** (1974) PR:O__
STEPPIN' IN SOCIETY *½ (1945) PR:A
STEPPING INTO SOCIETY
(SEE:DOUGHNUTS AND SOCIETY)
STEPPING SISTERS * (1932) PR:A
STEPPING TOES *½ (1938, Brit.) PR:A
STEPS TO THE MOON **½ (1963, Rum.) PR:A
STEPTOE AND SON * (1972, Brit.) PR:A-C
STEREO * (1969, Can.) PR:O
__STERILE CUCKOO, THE ***½ (1969) PR:C__
__STEVIE *½ (1978, Brit.) PR:A__
__STEWARDESS SCHOOL zero (1986) PR:O__
__STICK ** (1985) PR:O__
STICK 'EM UP ** (1950, Brit.) PR:A
STICK TO YOUR GUNS ** (1941) PR:A
__STICK UP, THE * (1978, Brit.) PR:A__
__STICKY FINGERS *½ (1988) PR:C__
STIGMA zero (1972) PR:O
__STILETTO * (1969) PR:O__

Finding entries in **THE MOTION PICTURE GUIDE ™**

Years 1929-83	Volumes I-IX
1984	Volume IX
1985	1986 ANNUAL
1986	1987 ANNUAL
1987	1988 ANNUAL
1988	1989 ANNUAL

STAR RATINGS

★★★★★	Masterpiece
★★★★	Excellent
★★★	Good
★★	Fair
★	Poor
zero	Without Merit

PARENTAL RECOMMENDATION (PR:)

AA	Good for Children
A	Acceptable for Children
C	Cautionary, some objectionable scenes
O	Objectionable for Children

BOLD: Films on Videocassette

STILL OF THE NIGHT ** (1982) PR:O
STILL ROOM IN HELL
    (SEE:THERE IS STILL ROOM IN HELL)
STILL SMOKIN' * (1983) PR:O
STING OF DEATH zero (1966) PR:C
STING II, THE * (1983) PR:C
STING, THE ***** (1973) PR:C
STINGAREE ** (1934) PR:A
STINGRAY ** (1978) PR:C
STIR *** (1980, Aus.) PR:O
STIR CRAZY *** (1980) PR:C-O
STITCH IN TIME, A *** (1967, Brit.) PR:A
STITCHES zero (1985) PR:O
STOCK CAR ** (1955, Brit.) PR:A
STOKER, THE ** (1932) PR:A
STOKER, THE ** (1935, Brit.) PR:A
STOLEN AIRLINER, THE ** (1962, Brit.) PR:A
STOLEN ASSIGNMENT * (1955, Brit.) PR:A
STOLEN DIRIGIBLE, THE *** (1966, Czech.) PR:AA
STOLEN FACE ***½ (1952, Brit.) PR:A
STOLEN HARMONY **½ (1935) PR:A
STOLEN HEAVEN *½ (1931) PR:A
STOLEN HEAVEN **½ (1938) PR:A
STOLEN HOLIDAY **½ (1937) PR:A
STOLEN HOURS *** (1963) PR:A-C
STOLEN IDENTITY ** (1953) PR:A
STOLEN KISSES ** (1929) PR:A
STOLEN KISSES **** (1969, Fr.) PR:O
STOLEN LIFE ** (1939, Brit.) PR:A
STOLEN LIFE, A *** (1946) PR:A-C
STOLEN PLANS, THE ** (1962, Brit.) PR:AA
STOLEN SWEETS *½ (1934) PR:A
STOLEN TIME
    (SEE:BLONDE BLACKMAILER)
STOLEN WEALTH
    (SEE:BLAZING SIX SHOOTERS)
STONE *½ (1974, Aus.) PR:O
STONE BOY, THE ***½ (1984) PR:C
STONE COLD DEAD *½ (1980, Can.) PR:O
STONE KILLER, THE **½ (1973) PR:O
STONE OF SILVER CREEK **½ (1935) PR:A
STONY ISLAND *** (1978) PR:C
STOOGE, THE ** (1952) PR:A
STOOGEMANIA * (1986) PR:A
STOOGES GO WEST
    (SEE:GOLD RAIDERS)
STOOLIE, THE **½ (1972) PR:C
STOP ME BEFORE I KILL! **½ (1961, Brit.) PR:C
STOP PRESS GIRL * (1949, Brit.) PR:A
STOP THAT CAB *½ (1951) PR:A
STOP THE WORLD—I WANT TO GET OFF **
    (1966, Brit.) PR:A
STOP THE WORLD I WANT TO GET OFF
    (SEE:SAMMY STOPS THE WORLD)
STOP TRAIN 349 ** (1964, Fr./It./Ger.) PR:A
STOP, YOU'RE KILLING ME ** (1952) PR:A
STOP, LOOK, AND LOVE ** (1939) PR:A
STOPOVER FOREVER ** (1964, Brit.) PR:A
STOPOVER TOKYO **½ (1957) PR:A
STORIA DI UNA DONNA
    (SEE:STORY OF A WOMAN)
STORIES FROM A FLYING TRUNK **
    (1979, Brit.) PR:A
STORK **½ (1971, Aus.) PR:O
STORK BITES MAN ** (1947) PR:A
STORK CLUB, THE **½ (1945) PR:A
STORK PAYS OFF, THE ** (1941) PR:A
STORK TALK ** (1964, Brit.) PR:O
STORM AT DAYBREAK *½ (1933) PR:A
STORM BOY *** (1976, Aus.) PR:AA
STORM CENTER ** (1956) PR:A
STORM FEAR **½ (1956) PR:A
STORM IN A TEACUP *** (1937, Brit.) PR:A
STORM IN A WATER GLASS ** (1931, Aust.) PR:A
STORM OVER AFRICA
    (SEE:ROYAL AFRICAN RIFLES)
STORM OVER BENGAL ** (1938) PR:A
STORM OVER LISBON **½ (1944) PR:A
STORM OVER THE ANDES **½ (1935) PR:A
STORM OVER THE NILE ** (1955, Brit.) PR:A
STORM OVER THE PACIFIC
    (SEE:I BOMBED PEARL HARBOR)
STORM OVER TIBET *½ (1952) PR:A
STORM OVER WYOMING ** (1950) PR:A
STORM PLANET * (1962, USSR) PR:A
STORM RIDER, THE ** (1957) PR:A
STORM WARNING *** (1950) PR:C-O
STORM WITHIN, THE
    (SEE:LES PARENTS TERRIBLES)
STORM, THE **½ (1930) PR:A
STORM, THE **½ (1938) PR:A
STORMBOUND * (1951, It.) PR:A
STORMS OF AUGUST, THE ***
    (1988, Wales/Brit.) PR:C
STORMY ** (1935) PR:A
STORMY CROSSING ** (1958, Brit.) PR:A-C
STORMY MONDAY ***½ (1988, Brit.) PR:O
STORMY TRAILS ** (1936) PR:A

STORMY WATERS *** (1946, Fr.) PR:A
STORMY WEATHER *** (1935, Brit.) PR:A
STORMY WEATHER ***½ (1943) PR:A
STORY OF A CHEAT, THE **** (1938, Fr.) PR:O
STORY OF A CITIZEN ABOVE ALL SUSPICION
    (SEE:INVESTIGATION OF A CITIZEN ABOVE
    SUSPICION)
STORY OF A DRAFT DODGER
    (SEE:WINDFLOWERS, THE STORY OF A DRAFT
    DODGER)
STORY OF A LOVE STORY
    (SEE:IMPOSSIBLE OBJECT)
STORY OF A TEENAGER
    (SEE:JIM, THE WORLD'S GREATEST)
STORY OF A THREE DAY PASS, THE ***½
    (1968, Fr.) PR:O
STORY OF A WOMAN * (1970, US/It.) PR:O
STORY OF ADELE H., THE **** (1975, Fr.) PR:C-O
STORY OF ALEXANDER GRAHAM BELL, THE ***½
    (1939) PR:A
STORY OF ARNOLD ROTHSTEIN
    (SEE:KING OF THE ROARING 20'S, THE STORY OF
    ARNOLD ROTHSTEIN)
STORY OF CINDERELLA, THE
    (SEE:SLIPPER AND THE ROSE, THE)
STORY OF DAVID, A ** (1960, Brit.) PR:A
STORY OF DR. EHRLICH'S MAGIC BULLET, THE
    (SEE:DR. EHRLICH'S MAGIC BULLET)
STORY OF DR. WASSELL, THE *** (1944) PR:A-C
STORY OF ESTHER COSTELLO, THE ****
    (1957, Brit.) PR:C
STORY OF FAUSTA, THE *** (1988, Braz.) PR:C
STORY OF G.I. JOE, THE **** (1945) PR:A-C
STORY OF GILBERT AND SULLIVAN, THE
    (SEE:GREAT GILBERT AND SULLIVAN, THE)
STORY OF JOSEPH AND HIS BRETHREN THE *½
    (1962, It.) PR:A
STORY OF LOUIS PASTEUR, THE **** (1936) PR:AA
STORY OF MANDY, THE
    (SEE:CRASH OF SILENCE)
STORY OF MANKIND, THE zero (1957) PR:A
STORY OF MOLLY X, THE ** (1949) PR:A
STORY OF MONTE CRISTO, THE
    (SEE:STORY OF THE COUNT OF MONTE CRISTO,
    THE)
STORY OF ROBIN HOOD AND HIS MERRIE MEN,
    THE
    (SEE:STORY OF ROBIN HOOD, THE)
STORY OF ROBIN HOOD, THE ***½
    (1952, Brit.) PR:AA
STORY OF RUTH, THE ** (1960) PR:A
STORY OF SEABISCUIT, THE **½ (1949) PR:A
STORY OF SHIRLEY YORKE, THE **
    (1948, Brit.) PR:A
STORY OF TEMPLE DRAKE, THE ***½ (1933) PR:O
STORY OF THE COUNT OF MONTE CRISTO, THE *
    (1962, Fr./It.) PR:A
STORY OF THE CRUELTIES OF YOUTH, A
    (SEE:NAKED YOUTH)
STORY OF THREE LOVES, THE *** (1953) PR:A
STORY OF VERNON AND IRENE CASTLE, THE
    ***½ (1939) PR:A
STORY OF VICKIE, THE **½ (1958, Aust.) PR:A
STORY OF WILL ROGERS, THE *** (1952) PR:A
STORY ON PAGE ONE, THE ** (1959) PR:C
STORY WITHOUT A NAME
    (SEE:WITHOUT WARNING)
STORY WITHOUT WORDS **½ (1981, It.) PR:A
STOWAWAY ** (1932) PR:A
STOWAWAY *** (1936) PR:AA
STOWAWAY GIRL *** (1957, Brit.) PR:A
STOWAWAY IN THE SKY ** (1962, Fr.) PR:AA
STRAIGHT FROM THE HEART ** (1935) PR:A
STRAIGHT FROM THE SHOULDER ** (1936) PR:A
STRAIGHT IS THE WAY * (1934) PR:A
STRAIGHT ON TILL MORNING ** (1974, Brit.) PR:O
STRAIGHT, PLACE AND SHOW ** (1938) PR:A
STRAIGHT SHOOTER * (1940) PR:A
STRAIGHT THROUGH THE HEART ***½
    (1985, Ger.) PR:O
STRAIGHT TIME **** (1978) PR:O
STRAIGHT TO HEAVEN ** (1939) PR:A
STRAIGHT TO HELL * (1987, Brit.) PR:O
STRAIGHT TO THE HEART **
    (1988, Can./Switz.) PR:O
STRAIGHTAWAY * (1934) PR:A
STRAIT-JACKET **½ (1964) PR:O
STRAITJACKET, 1963
    (SEE:SHOCK CORRIDOR)
STRANDED ** (1935) PR:A
STRANDED **½ (1965) PR:O
STRANDED **½ (1987) PR:A-C
STRANDED IN PARIS
    (SEE:ARTISTS AND MODELS ABROAD)
STRANDED, 1967
    (SEE:VALLEY OF MYSTERY)
STRANGE ADVENTURE * (1932) PR:A
STRANGE ADVENTURE, A *½ (1956) PR:A

STRANGE ADVENTURES OF MR. SMITH, THE *½
    (1937, Brit.) PR:A
STRANGE AFFAIR ** (1944) PR:A
STRANGE AFFAIR OF UNCLE HARRY, THE
    (SEE:UNCLE HARRY)
STRANGE AFFAIR, THE ** (1968, Brit.) PR:O
STRANGE AFFECTION **½ (1959, Brit.) PR:A
STRANGE ALIBI ** (1941) PR:A
STRANGE AWAKENING, THE
    (SEE:FEMALE FIENDS)
STRANGE BARGAIN **½ (1949) PR:A
STRANGE BEDFELLOWS **½ (1965) PR:A-C
STRANGE BEHAVIOR
    (SEE:DEAD KIDS)
STRANGE BOARDERS *½ (1938, Brit.) PR:A
STRANGE BREW *** (1983) PR:C
STRANGE CARGO ** (1929) PR:A
STRANGE CARGO *½ (1936, Brit.) PR:A
STRANGE CARGO *** (1940) PR:C
STRANGE CASE OF CLARA DEANE, THE *
    (1932) PR:A
STRANGE CASE OF DR. MANNING, THE *
    (1958, Brit.) PR:A
STRANGE CASE OF DR. MEADE ** (1939) PR:A
STRANGE CASE OF DR. RX, THE * (1942) PR:A
STRANGE CONFESSION
    (SEE:IMPOSTER, THE)
STRANGE CONFESSION ** (1945) PR:A
STRANGE CONQUEST ** (1946) PR:A
STRANGE CONSPIRACY, THE
    (SEE:PRESIDENT VANISHES, THE)
STRANGE DEATH OF ADOLF HITLER, THE *½
    (1943) PR:A
STRANGE DECEPTION ***½ (1953, It.) PR:O
STRANGE DOOR, THE *½ (1951) PR:A
STRANGE EVIDENCE * (1933, Brit.) PR:A
STRANGE EXPERIMENT *½ (1937, Brit.) PR:A
STRANGE FACES * (1938) PR:A
STRANGE FASCINATION *½ (1952) PR:A
STRANGE FETISHES OF THE GO-GO GIRLS
    (SEE:STRANGE FETISHES, THE)
STRANGE FETISHES, THE zero (1967) PR:O
STRANGE GAMBLE ** (1948) PR:A
STRANGE HOLIDAY ** (1945) PR:A
STRANGE HOLIDAY *½ (1969, Aus.) PR:A
STRANGE ILLUSION ** (1945) PR:A
STRANGE IMPERSONATION ** (1946) PR:A
STRANGE INCIDENT
    (SEE:OX-BOW INCIDENT, THE)
STRANGE INTERLUDE *** (1932) PR:C
STRANGE INTERVAL
    (SEE:STRANGE INTERLUDE)
STRANGE INTRUDER ** (1956) PR:A
STRANGE INVADERS *** (1983) PR:O
STRANGE JOURNEY * (1946) PR:A
STRANGE JOURNEY, 1966
    (SEE:FANTASTIC VOYAGE)
STRANGE JUSTICE * (1932) PR:A
STRANGE LADY IN TOWN **½ (1955) PR:A
STRANGE LAWS
    (SEE:CHEROKEE STRIP, THE)
STRANGE LOVE OF MARTHA IVERS, THE ***½
    (1946) PR:C
STRANGE LOVE OF MOLLY LOUVAIN, THE *½
    (1932) PR:A
STRANGE LOVERS * (1963) PR:O
STRANGE MR. GREGORY, THE ** (1945) PR:A
STRANGE MRS. CRANE, THE * (1948) PR:A
STRANGE ONE, THE *** (1957) PR:O
STRANGE ONES, THE,
    (SEE:LES ENFANTS TERRIBLES)
STRANGE PEOPLE * (1933) PR:A
STRANGE ROADS
    (SEE:EXPOSED)
STRANGE SHADOWS IN AN EMPTY ROOM *
    (1977, Can./It.) PR:O
STRANGE TRIANGLE **½ (1946) PR:A
STRANGE VENGEANCE OF ROSALIE, THE **
    (1972) PR:C
STRANGE VOYAGE ** (1945) PR:A
STRANGE WIVES *½ (1935) PR:A
STRANGE WOMAN, THE *** (1946) PR:C
STRANGE WORLD * (1952) PR:A
STRANGE WORLD OF PLANET X, THE
    (SEE:COSMIC MONSTERS)
STRANGER, THE * (1967, Algeria/Fr./It.) PR:C-O
STRANGER AT MY DOOR ** (1950, Brit.) PR:A
STRANGER AT MY DOOR *** (1956) PR:A
STRANGER CAME HOME, THE
    (SEE:UNHOLY FOUR, THE)
STRANGER FROM ARIZONA, THE **½ (1938) PR:A
STRANGER FROM PECOS, THE ** (1943) PR:A
STRANGER FROM TEXAS, THE ** (1940) PR:A
STRANGER FROM VENUS, THE *½
    (1954, Brit.) PR:A
STRANGER IN BETWEEN, THE **½
    (1952, Brit.) PR:A
STRANGER IN HOLLYWOOD * (1968) PR:A-C

STRANGER IN MY ARMS **½ (1959) PR:A
STRANGER IN THE HOUSE, 1967
(SEE:COP-OUT)
STRANGER IN THE HOUSE, 1975
(SEE:BLACK CHRISTMAS)
STRANGER IN TOWN ** (1932) PR:A
STRANGER IN TOWN ** (1957, Brit.) PR:A
STRANGER IN TOWN, A ** (1943) PR:A
STRANGER IN TOWN, A * (1968, US/It.) PR:C
__STRANGER IS WATCHING, A ** (1982) PR:O__
STRANGER KNOCKS, A ** (1963, Den.) PR:C
STRANGER ON HORSEBACK ** (1955) PR:A
STRANGER ON THE PROWL **½ (1953, It.) PR:A-C
__STRANGER ON THE THIRD FLOOR ***½__
__(1940) PR:C__
STRANGER RETURNS, THE **
(1968, US/It./Ger./Sp.) PR:A
STRANGER THAN LOVE
(SEE:STRANGE LOVERS)
__STRANGER THAN PARADISE **½__
__(1984, US/Ger.) PR:O__
STRANGER, THE, 1940
(SEE:STRANGER FROM TEXAS, THE)
STRANGER WALKED IN, A
(SEE:LOVE FROM A STRANGER)
STRANGER WORE A GUN, THE **½ (1953) PR:A
STRANGER'S GUNDOWN, THE *½ (1974, It.) PR:C
STRANGER'S MEETING * (1957, Brit.) PR:A
STRANGER'S RETURN ** (1933) PR:A
__STRANGER, THE **** (1946) PR:C__
__STRANGER, THE * (1987, US/Arg.) PR:O__
STRANGER, THE, 1962
(SEE:INTRUDER, THE)
STRANGERS ALL * (1935) PR:A
STRANGERS CAME, THE
(SEE:YOU CAN'T FOOL AN IRISHMAN)
STRANGER'S HAND, THE **½ (1955, Brit.) PR:A
STRANGERS HONEYMOON
(SEE:STRANGERS ON A HONEYMOON)
STRANGERS IN LOVE ** (1932) PR:A
__STRANGERS IN THE CITY **½ (1962) PR:A__
STRANGERS IN THE HOUSE *** (1949, Fr.) PR:C
STRANGERS IN THE NIGHT *** (1944) PR:A-C
__STRANGERS KISS **** (1984) PR:C__
STRANGERS MAY KISS ***½ (1931) PR:A
STRANGERS, 1970
(SEE:I NEVER SANG FOR MY FATHER)
STRANGERS OF THE EVENING ** (1932) PR:A
STRANGERS ON A HONEYMOON **½
(1937, Brit.) PR:A
__STRANGERS ON A TRAIN ***** (1951) PR:C-O__
__STRANGERS WHEN WE MEET **½ (1960) PR:C__
STRANGERS, THE ** (1955, It.) PR:A
STRANGEST CASE, THE
(SEE:CRIME DOCTOR'S STRANGEST CASE)
STRANGLEHOLD ** (1931, Brit.) PR:A
STRANGLEHOLD ** (1962, Brit.) PR:A
__STRANGLER OF THE SWAMP ** (1945) PR:A__
STRANGLER'S WEB *½ (1966, Brit.) PR:A-C
STRANGLER, THE * (1941, Brit.) PR:C
__STRANGLER, THE *½ (1964) PR:C__
STRANGLERS OF BOMBAY, THE **
(1960, Brit.) PR:C
__STRATEGIC AIR COMMAND *** (1955) PR:A__
STRATEGY OF TERROR *½ (1969) PR:A
__STRATTON STORY, THE ***½ (1949) PR:AA__
STRAUSS' GREAT WALTZ *½ (1934, Brit.) PR:A
__STRAW DOGS zero (1971, Brit.) PR:O__
STRAW MAN, THE ** (1953, Brit.) PR:A
__STRAWBERRY BLONDE, THE ***½ (1941) PR:A__
STRAWBERRY ROAN ** (1933) PR:A
STRAWBERRY ROAN *½ (1945, Brit.) PR:A
STRAWBERRY ROAN, THE **½ (1948) PR:A
__STRAWBERRY STATEMENT, THE ** (1970) PR:C__
__STRAY DOG ***½ (1963, Jap.) PR:A-C__
__STREAMERS ***½ (1983) PR:O__
STREAMLINE EXPRESS ** (1935) PR:A
STREET ANGEL ** (1928) PR:A
STREET BANDITS ** (1951) PR:A
STREET CORNER * (1948) PR:C
STREET CORNER
(SEE:BOTH SIDES OF THE LAW)
STREET FIGHTER ** (1959) PR:A
STREET GANG
(SEE:VIGILANTE)
STREET GIRL ** (1929) PR:A
STREET IS MY BEAT, THE *½ (1966) PR:C
__STREET MUSIC **½ (1982) PR:A-C__
STREET OF CHANCE ** (1930) PR:A
STREET OF CHANCE *** (1942) PR:A
STREET OF DARKNESS *½ (1958) PR:A
STREET OF MEMORIES ** (1940) PR:A
STREET OF MISSING MEN ** (1939) PR:A
STREET OF MISSING WOMEN
(SEE:CAFE HOSTESS)
STREET OF SHADOWS
(SEE:SHADOW MAN)
STREET OF SINNERS *** (1957) PR:A
STREET OF WOMEN *½ (1932) PR:A
STREET PARTNER, THE
(SEE:SECRET PARTNER, THE)
__STREET PEOPLE zero (1976, US/It.) PR:O__
__STREET SCENE **** (1931) PR:C__
STREET SINGER, THE ** (1937, Brit.) PR:A
__STREET SMART *½ (1987) PR:O__
STREET SONG *½ (1935, Brit.) PR:A
__STREET TRASH ** (1987) PR:O__
STREET WITH NO NAME, THE ***½ (1948) PR:C-O
__STREETCAR NAMED DESIRE, A *****__
__(1951) PR:C-O__
STREETFIGHTER, THE
(SEE:HARD TIMES)
__STREETS OF FIRE **½ (1984) PR:C__
STREETS OF GHOST TOWN * (1950) PR:A
__STREETS OF GOLD **½ (1986) PR:C__
STREETS OF LAREDO **½ (1949) PR:A-C
STREETS OF NEW YORK *½ (1939) PR:A
STREETS OF SAN FRANCISCO ** (1949) PR:A
STREETS OF SIN
(SEE:NOT WANTED)
STREETS OF SINNERS
(SEE:STREET OF SINNER)
__STREETWALKIN' *** (1985) PR:O__
STRICTLY CONFIDENTIAL
(SEE:BROADWAY BILL)
STRICTLY CONFIDENTIAL zero (1959, Brit.) PR:A
STRICTLY DISHONORABLE ***½ (1931) PR:A-C
STRICTLY DISHONORABLE *** (1951) PR:A
STRICTLY DYNAMITE zero (1934) PR:A
STRICTLY FOR PLEASURE
(SEE:PERFECT FURLOUGH, THE)
STRICTLY FOR THE BIRDS ** (1963, Brit.) PR:C
STRICTLY ILLEGAL ** (1935, Brit.) PR:A
STRICTLY IN THE GROOVE zero (1942) PR:A
STRICTLY MODERN ** (1930) PR:A
STRICTLY PERSONAL * (1933) PR:A
STRICTLY UNCONVENTIONAL * (1930) PR:A
__STRIKE! ** (1934, Brit.) PR:A__
STRIKE IT RICH * (1933, Brit.) PR:A
STRIKE IT RICH ** (1948) PR:A
STRIKE ME DEADLY
(SEE:CRAWLING HAND, THE)
STRIKE ME PINK *** (1936) PR:A
__STRIKE UP THE BAND ***½ (1940) PR:AA__
STRIKEBOUND ** (1984, Aus.) PR:C-O
STRIKERS, THE
(SEE:ORGANIZER, THE)
STRIP-TEASE
(SEE:SWEET SKIN)
STRIP TEASE MURDER * (1961, Brit.) PR:C-O
STRIP, THE *** (1951) PR:C
__STRIPES *** (1981) PR:O__
__STRIPPED TO KILL ** (1987) PR:O__
__STRIPPER *½ (1986) PR:O__
__STRIPPER, THE ** (1963) PR:O__
STRIPTEASE LADY
(SEE:LADY OF BURLESQUE)
__STROKER ACE zero (1983) PR:C__
__STROMBOLI ** (1950, It.) PR:C-O__
STRONGER SEX, THE ** (1931, Brit.) PR:A
STRONGER THAN DESIRE *½ (1939) PR:A
STRONGER THAN FEAR
(SEE:EDGE OF DOOM)
STRONGER THAN THE SUN ** (1980, Brit.) PR:A
STRONGEST MAN IN THE WORLD, THE ***
(1975) PR:A
STRONGHOLD ** (1952, Mex.) PR:A
STRONGROOM ** (1962, Brit.) PR:A
STRUGGLE, THE * (1931) PR:A-C
__STRYKER * (1983, Phil.) PR:O__
__STUCK ON YOU zero (1983) PR:O__
__STUCKEY'S LAST STAND * (1980) PR:C__
__STUD, THE ** (1979, Brit.) PR:O__
__STUDENT BODIES * (1981) PR:O__
__STUDENT BODY, THE * (1976) PR:O__
__STUDENT NURSES, THE * (1970) PR:O__
STUDENT PRINCE, THE **½ (1954) PR:A
STUDENT ROMANCE
(SEE:STUDENT'S ROMANCE, THE)
__STUDENT TEACHERS, THE ** (1973) PR:O__
STUDENT TOUR ** (1934) PR:A
STUDENT'S ROMANCE, THE * (1936, Brit.) PR:A
STUDIO MURDER MYSTERY, THE * (1929) PR:A
STUDIO ROMANCE
(SEE:TALENT SCOUT)
__STUDS LONIGAN *½ (1960) PR:A__
__STUDY IN SCARLET, A ** (1933) PR:A__
__STUDY IN TERROR, A ** (1966, Brit./Ger.) PR:A__
STUETZEN DER GESELLSCHAFT
(SEE:PILLARS OF SOCIETY)
__STUFF, THE ** (1985) PR:C__
__STUNT MAN, THE **** (1980) PR:O__
STUNT PILOT ** (1939) PR:A
__STUNTS **½ (1977) PR:C-O__
SUB-A-DUB-DUB
(SEE:HELLO DOWN THERE)
SUBJECT WAS ROSES, THE **** (1968) PR:C
SUBMARINE ALERT * (1943) PR:A
SUBMARINE BASE * (1943) PR:A
SUBMARINE COMMAND **½ (1951) PR:A
SUBMARINE D-1 ** (1937) PR:A
SUBMARINE PATROL ** (1938) PR:A
SUBMARINE RAIDER * (1942) PR:A
SUBMARINE SEAHAWK **½ (1959) PR:A
SUBMARINE X-1 **½ (1969, Brit.) PR:A
SUBMARINE ZONE
(SEE:ESCAPE TO GLORY)
SUBMERSION OF JAPAN, THE
(SEE:TIDAL WAVE)
SUBSTITUTION * (1970) PR:O
__SUBTERFUGE * (1969, US/Brit.) PR:A__
SUBTERRANEANS, THE * (1960) PR:C
SUBURBAN WIVES * (1973, Brit.) PR:O
__SUBURBIA *** (1984) PR:O__
SUBVERSIVES, THE *** (1967, It.) PR:C
__SUBWAY ** (1985, Fr.) PR:C-O__
SUBWAY EXPRESS * (1931) PR:A
SUBWAY IN THE SKY **½ (1959, Brit.) PR:C
SUBWAY RIDERS ** (1981) PR:O
SUCCESS
(SEE:AMERICAN SUCCESS COMPANY, THE)
SUCCESS AT ANY PRICE ** (1934) PR:A
__SUCCESS IS THE BEST REVENGE ***__
__(1984, Brit.) PR:O__
SUCCESSFUL CALAMITY, A **½ (1932) PR:A
SUCCESSFUL FAILURE, A *½ (1934) PR:A
SUCCESSFUL MAN, A **½ (1987, Cuba) PR:O
SUCH A GORGEOUS KID LIKE ME ***
(1973, Fr.) PR:O
SUCH GOOD FRIENDS * (1971) PR:O
SUCH IS LIFE **½ (1936, Brit.) PR:A
SUCH IS THE LAW ** (1930, Brit.) PR:A
SUCH MEN ARE DANGEROUS ** (1930) PR:A
SUCH MEN ARE DANGEROUS
(SEE:RACERS, THE)
SUCH THINGS HAPPEN
(SEE:LOVE IS A RACKET)
SUCH WOMEN ARE DANGEROUS *½ (1934) PR:A
SUCKER MONEY *½ (1933) PR:A
SUCKER . . . OR HOW TO BE GLAD WHEN YOU'VE
BEEN HAD!, THE
(SEE:SUCKER, THE)
SUCKER, THE *** (1966, Fr./It.) PR:A
SUDAN **½ (1945) PR:A-C
SUDDEN BILL DORN *½ (1938) PR:A
SUDDEN DANGER **½ (1955) PR:A
__SUDDEN DEATH * (1985) PR:O__
SUDDEN FEAR ***½ (1952) PR:A-C
SUDDEN FURY *** (1975, Can.) PR:C
__SUDDEN IMPACT ***½ (1983) PR:O__
SUDDEN MONEY *½ (1939) PR:A
__SUDDEN TERROR **½ (1970, Brit.) PR:A__
__SUDDENLY ***½ (1954) PR:C__
SUDDENLY, A WOMAN! ** (1967, Den.) PR:O
SUDDENLY IT'S SPRING **½ (1947) PR:A
__SUDDENLY, LAST SUMMER **½ (1959, Brit.) PR:O__
SUED FOR LIBEL ** (1940) PR:A
SUENO DE NOCHE DE VERANO
(SEE:MIDSUMMER NIGHT'S DREAM, A)
SUEZ ***½ (1938) PR:A
__SUGAR CANE ALLEY *** (1984, Fr.) PR:C__

Finding entries in **THE MOTION PICTURE GUIDE ™**

Years	Volumes
Years 1929-83	Volumes I-IX
1984	Volume IX
1985	1986 ANNUAL
1986	1987 ANNUAL
1987	1988 ANNUAL
1988	1989 ANNUAL

STAR RATINGS

★★★★★	Masterpiece
★★★★	Excellent
★★★	Good
★★	Fair
★	Poor
zero	Without Merit

PARENTAL RECOMMENDATION (PR:)

AA	Good for Children
A	Acceptable for Children
C	Cautionary, some objectionable scenes
O	Objectionable for Children

BOLD: Films on Videocassette

SUGAR HILL ** (1974) PR:C
SUGARBABY ***½ (1985, Ger.) PR:C-O
SUGARFOOT **½ (1951) PR:A
SUGARLAND EXPRESS, THE *** (1974) PR:C
SUGATA SANSHIRO
    (SEE:JUDO SAGA)
SUICIDE BATTALION **½ (1958) PR:A
SUICIDE CLUB, THE
    (SEE:TROUBLE FOR TWO)
SUICIDE CLUB, THE * (1988) PR:C
SUICIDE FLEET ** (1931) PR:A
SUICIDE LEGION **½ (1940, Brit.) PR:C
SUICIDE MISSION **½ (1956, Brit.) PR:C
SUICIDE RUN
    (SEE:TOO LATE THE HERO)
SUICIDE SQUADRON *½ (1942, Brit.) PR:A
SUITABLE CASE FOR TREATMENT, A
    (SEE:MORGAN)
SUITOR, THE **½ (1963, Fr.) PR:C
SULEIMAN THE CONQUEROR *½ (1963, It.) PR:A
SULLIVANS, THE **** (1944) PR:A
SULLIVAN'S EMPIRE * (1967) PR:A
SULLIVAN'S TRAVELS ***** (1941) PR:C
SULT
    (SEE:HUNGER)
SULTAN'S DAUGHTER, THE *½ (1943) PR:A
SUMMER ***½ (1986, Fr.) PR:O
SUMMER ** (1988, W. Ger.) PR:A
SUMMER AND SMOKE *** (1961) PR:C-O
SUMMER CAMP zero (1979) PR:O
SUMMER CAMP NIGHTMARE ** (1987) PR:C
SUMMER FIRES
    (SEE:MADEMOISELLE)
SUMMER FLIGHT
    (SEE:STOLEN HOURS)
SUMMER HEAT ** (1987) PR:O
SUMMER HOLIDAY ***½ (1948) PR:AA
SUMMER HOLIDAY **½ (1963, Brit.) PR:A
SUMMER INTERLUDE
    (SEE:ILLICIT INTERLUDE)
SUMMER LIGHTNING
    (SEE:SCUDDA-HOO SCUDDA-HAY)
SUMMER LIGHTNING ** (1933, Brit.) PR:A
SUMMER LOVE **½ (1958) PR:A
SUMMER LOVERS *½ (1982) PR:O
SUMMER MADNESS
    (SEE:SUMMERTIME)
SUMMER MAGIC **½ (1963) PR:AA
SUMMER OF '42 **** (1971) PR:O
SUMMER OF SECRETS ** (1976, Aus.) PR:O
SUMMER OF '64
    (SEE:GIRLS ON THE BEACH)
SUMMER OF THE SEVENTEENTH DOLL
    (SEE:SEASON OF PASSION)
SUMMER PLACE, A ** (1959) PR:C
SUMMER RENTAL ** (1985) PR:C
SUMMER RUN **½ (1974) PR:A
SUMMER SCHOOL * (1987) PR:C
SUMMER SCHOOL TEACHERS ** (1977) PR:C
SUMMER SOLDIERS **½ (1972, Jap.) PR:C
SUMMER STOCK ***½ (1950) PR:A
SUMMER STORM *** (1944) PR:C
SUMMER STORY, A *½ (1988, US/Brit.) PR:C-O
SUMMER TALES
    (SEE:LOVE ON THE RIVIERA)
SUMMER TO REMEMBER, A ***
    (1961, USSR) PR:A
SUMMER WISHES, WINTER DREAMS **
    (1973) PR:A
SUMMER'S CHILDREN *½ (1979, Can.) PR:O
SUMMERDOG ** (1977) PR:AA
SUMMERFIELD **½ (1977, Aus.) PR:O
SUMMERPLAY
    (SEE:ILLICIT INTERLUDE)
SUMMERSKIN *** (1962, Arg.) PR:C
SUMMERSPELL *** (1983) PR:C
SUMMERTIME **** (1955) PR:A-C
SUMMERTIME KILLER ** (1973) PR:C
SUMMERTREE ** (1971) PR:A
SUMURU
    (SEE:MILLION EYES OF SUMURU, THE)
SUN ABOVE, DEATH BELOW **½ (1969, Jap.) PR:C
SUN ALSO RISES, THE **** (1957) PR:C
SUN ALWAYS RISES, THE
    (SEE:OUTCRY)
SUN COMES UP, THE ** (1949) PR:AA
SUN DEMON, THE
    (SEE:HIDEOUS SUN DEMON, THE)
SUN IS UP, THE
    (SEE:A BOY...A GIRL)
SUN NEVER SETS, THE * (1939) PR:A
SUN RISES AGAIN, THE
    (SEE:OUTCRY)
SUN SETS AT DAWN, THE *½ (1950) PR:A
SUN SHINES BRIGHT, THE ** (1953) PR:A
SUN SHINES FOR ALL, THE **½ (1961, USSR) PR:A
SUN SHINES FOR EVERYBODY, THE
    (SEE:SUN SHINES FOR ALL, THE)

SUN SHINES, THE *½ (1939, Hung.) PR:A
SUN VALLEY CYCLONE *½ (1946) PR:A
SUN VALLEY SERENADE ***½ (1941) PR:AA
SUNA NO KAORI
    (SEE:NIGHT OF THE SEAGULL, THE)
SUNA NO ONNA
    (SEE:WOMAN IN THE DUNES)
SUNBONNET SUE **½ (1945) PR:A
SUNBURN ** (1979) PR:C
SUNDAY BLOODY SUNDAY ***½
    (1971, Brit.) PR:O
SUNDAY DINNER FOR A SOLDIER **½
    (1944) PR:A
SUNDAY IN NEW YORK *** (1963) PR:C
SUNDAY IN THE COUNTRY *½ (1975, Can.) PR:O
SUNDAY IN THE COUNTRY, A ****
    (1984, Fr.) PR:A
SUNDAY LOVERS ** (1980, It./Fr.) PR:O
SUNDAY PUNCH **½ (1942) PR:A
SUNDAY TOO FAR AWAY *** (1975, Aus.) PR:C
SUNDAYS AND CYBELE *** (1962, Fr.) PR:C
SUNDOWN **½ (1941) PR:C
SUNDOWN IN SANTA FE *½ (1948) PR:A
SUNDOWN JIM **½ (1942) PR:A
SUNDOWN KID, THE ** (1942) PR:A
SUNDOWN ON THE PRAIRIE * (1939) PR:A
SUNDOWN RIDER, THE **½ (1933) PR:AA
SUNDOWN RIDERS ** (1948) PR:A
SUNDOWN SAUNDERS ** (1937) PR:A
SUNDOWN TRAIL ** (1931) PR:A
SUNDOWN VALLEY ** (1944) PR:A
SUNDOWNERS, THE **** (1960) PR:A
SUNDOWNERS, THE **½ (1950) PR:A
SUNFLOWER *½ (1970, Fr./It.) PR:A
SUNNY **½ (1930) PR:A
SUNNY ** (1941) PR:A
SUNNY SIDE OF THE STREET ** (1951) PR:A
SUNNY SIDE UP *** (1929) PR:A
SUNNY SKIES * (1930) PR:A
SUNNYSIDE * (1979) PR:O
SUNRISE AT CAMPOBELLO **** (1960) PR:A
SUNRISE TRAIL **½ (1931) PR:A
SUNSCORCHED ** (1966, Sp./Ger.) PR:O
SUNSET * (1988) PR:C
SUNSET BOULEVARD ***** (1950) PR:C-O
SUNSET COVE * (1978) PR:A
SUNSET IN EL DORADO *½ (1945) PR:A
SUNSET IN THE WEST **½ (1950) PR:A
SUNSET IN VIENNA
    (SEE:SUICIDE LEGION)
SUNSET IN WYOMING *½ (1941) PR:A
SUNSET MURDER CASE * (1941) PR:C
SUNSET OF A CLOWN
    (SEE:THE NAKED NIGHT)
SUNSET OF POWER **½ (1936) PR:A
SUNSET ON THE DESERT ** (1942) PR:AA
SUNSET PASS **½ (1933) PR:A
SUNSET PASS ** (1946) PR:A
SUNSET RANGE ** (1935) PR:A
SUNSET SERENADE *** (1942) PR:A
SUNSET STRIP zero (1985) PR:O
SUNSET TRAIL ** (1932) PR:A
SUNSET TRAIL ** (1938) PR:A
SUNSHINE AHEAD ** (1936, Brit.) PR:A
SUNSHINE BOYS, THE **** (1975) PR:A-C
SUNSHINE SUSIE
    (SEE:OFFICE GIRL, THE)
SUNSTRUCK **½ (1973, Aus.) PR:A
SUPER COPS, THE *** (1974) PR:O
SUPER DRAGON
    (SEE:SECRETA AGENT SUPER DRAGON)
SUPER DUDE
    (SEE:HANGUP)
SUPER FUZZ * (1981) PR:C
SUPER INFRAMAN, THE
    (SEE:INFRA-MAN)
SUPER SLEUTH *** (1937) PR:A
SUPER SPOOK ** (1975) PR:O
SUPER VAN * (1977) PR:C
SUPERARGO ** (1968, It./Sp.) PR:A
SUPERARGO VERSUS DIABOLICUS **
    (1966, It./Sp.) PR:A
SUPERBEAST zero (1972) PR:O
SUPERBUG, SUPER AGENT * (1976, Ger.) PR:AA
SUPERCHICK zero (1973) PR:O
SUPERDAD *½ (1974) PR:AA
SUPERFANTAGENIO
    (SEE:ALADDIN)
SUPERFLY *** (1972) PR:O
SUPERFLY T.N.T. * (1973) PR:O
SUPERGIRL * (1984) PR:C
SUPERMAN *** (1978) PR:AA
SUPERMAN AND THE MOLE MEN ** (1951) PR:A
SUPERMAN AND THE STRANGE PEOPLE
    (SEE:SUPERMAN AND THE MOLE MEN)
SUPERMAN II ***½ (1980) PR:A
SUPERMAN IV: THE QUEST FOR PEACE *
    (1987) PR:C

SUPERMAN III ** (1983) PR:A
SUPERNATURAL **½ (1933) PR:A-C
SUPERNATURALS, THE ** (1987) PR:O
SUPERSNOOPER
    (SEE:SUPER FUZZ)
SUPERSONIC MAN * (1979, Sp.) PR:A
SUPERSPEED **½ (1935) PR:A
SUPERSTITION zero (1985) PR:O
SUPERZAN AND THE SPACE BOY ***
    (1972, Mex.) PR:AA
SUPPORT YOUR LOCAL GUNFIGHTER ***
    (1971) PR:A
SUPPORT YOUR LOCAL SHERIFF ***½
    (1969) PR:A
SUPPOSE THEY GAVE A WAR AND NOBODY
    CAME? ** (1970) PR:A
SUPREME KID, THE **½ (1976, Can.) PR:C
SUPREME SECRET, THE ** (1958, Brit.) PR:A
SUR LA COUR
    (SEE:CRIME OF MONSIEUR LANGE, THE)
SUR LA ROUTE DE SALINA
    (SEE:ROAD TO SALINA)
SURCOUF, LE DERNIER CORSAIRE
    (SEE:SEA PIRATE, THE)
SURE THING, THE *** (1985) PR:C
SURF NAZIS MUST DIE ** (1987) PR:C-O
SURF PARTY * (1964) PR:C
SURF TERROR
    (SEE:BEACH GIRLS AND THE MONSTER, THE)
SURF II zero (1984) PR:O
SURF, THE
    (SEE:OCEAN BREAKERS)
SURFTIDE 777
    (SEE:SURFTIDE 77)
SURFTIDE 77 * (1962) PR:O
SURGEON'S KNIFE, THE ** (1957, Brit.) PR:C
SURPRISE PACKAGE ** (1960) PR:C
SURPRISE PARTY ** (1985, Fr.) PR:C
SURRENDER *½ (1931) PR:A
SURRENDER **½ (1950) PR:C
SURRENDER **½ (1987) PR:A-C
SURRENDER—HELL! ** (1959) PR:C
SURROGATE, THE zero (1984, Can.) PR:O
SURVIVAL zero (1976) PR:C
SURVIVAL, 1962
    (SEE:PANIC IN YEAR ZERO)
SURVIVAL RUN * (1980) PR:O
SURVIVAL, 1965
    (SEE:GUIDE, THE)
SURVIVE! zero (1977, Mex.) PR:O
SURVIVOR *** (1980, Aus.) PR:O
SURVIVORS, THE ** (1983) PR:C-O
SUSAN AND GOD *** (1940) PR:A
SUSAN LENOX—HER FALL AND RISE ***½
    (1931) PR:C
SUSAN SLADE **½ (1961) PR:C
SUSAN SLEPT HERE ** (1954) PR:C
SUSANNA
    (SEE:SHEPHERD OF THE OZARKS)
SUSANNA PASS *½ (1949) PR:A
SUSANNAH OF THE MOUNTIES **½ (1939) PR:AA
SUSIE STEPS OUT ** (1946) PR:A
SUSPECT
    (SEE:RISK, THE)
SUSPECT **½ (1987, US) PR:O
SUSPECT, THE *** (1944) PR:C
SUSPECTED
    (SEE:TEXAS DYNAMO)
SUSPECTED ALIBI
    (SEE:SUSPENDED ALIBI)
SUSPECTED PERSON **½ (1943, Brit.) PR:A
SUSPENDED ALIBI ** (1957, Brit.) PR:A
SUSPENSE ** (1930, Brit.) PR:C
SUSPENSE **½ (1946) PR:A-C
SUSPICION ***½ (1941) PR:A-C
SUSPIRIA *** (1977, It.) PR:O
SUSUZ YAZ
    (SEE:DRY SUMMER)
SUTTER'S GOLD ** (1936) PR:A
SUZANNE * (1980, Can.) PR:C
SUZY *** (1936) PR:C
SVALT
    (SEE:HUNGER)
SVEGLIATI E UCCIDI
    (SEE:WAKE UP AND DIE)
SVENGALI **½ (1931) PR:A-C
SVENGALI ** (1955, Brit.) PR:C
SVIRACHUT
    (SEE:CLOWN AND THE KIDS, THE)
S.W.A.L.K.
    (SEE:MELODY)
SWALLOWS AND AMAZONS *** (1977, Brit.) PR:AA
SWAMP COUNTRY ** (1966) PR:O
SWAMP DIAMONDS
    (SEE:SWAMP WOMEN)
SWAMP FIRE *½ (1946) PR:A
SWAMP THING ** (1982) PR:C
SWAMP WATER **½ (1941) PR:A

SWAMP WOMAN zero (1941) PR:A
SWAMP WOMEN * (1956) PR:A
SWAN LAKE, THE ** (1967) PR:AA**
SWAN, THE *** (1956) PR:A
SWANEE RIVER *** (1939) PR:A-C
SWANN IN LOVE **½ (1984, Fr./Ger.) PR:C-O
SWAP MEET zero (1979) PR:O
SWAPPERS, THE zero (1970, Brit.) PR:O
SWARM, THE * (1978) PR:C
SWASHBUCKLER * (1976) PR:O
SWASTIKA SAVAGES
 (SEE:HELL'S BLOODY DEVILS)
SWEATER GIRL *½ (1942) PR:A
SWEDENHIELMS ***½ (1935, Swed.) PR:A
SWEDISH MISTRESS, THE *** (1964, Swed.) PR:O
SWEDISH WEDDING NIGHT **½
 (1965, Swed.) PR:C
SWEENEY ** (1977, Brit.) PR:O
SWEENEY TODD. THE DEMON BARBER OF FLEET
 STREET
 (SEE:DEMON BARBER OF FLEET STREET, THE)
SWEENEY 2 ***½ (1978, Brit.) PR:O
SWEEPINGS * (1933) PR:A
SWEEPSTAKE ANNIE ** (1935) PR:A
SWEEPSTAKE RACKETEERS
 (SEE:UNDERCOVER AGENT)
SWEEPSTAKES ** (1931) PR:A
SWEEPSTAKES WINNER **½ (1939) PR:A
SWEET ADELINE **½ (1935) PR:A
SWEET ALOES
 (SEE:GIVE ME YOUR HEART)
SWEET AND LOWDOWN *½ (1944) PR:A
SWEET AND SOUR **½ (1964, Fr./It.) PR:A
SWEET BEAT * (1962, Brit.) PR:A
SWEET BIRD OF YOUTH ***½ (1962) PR:O
SWEET BODY OF DEBORAH, THE *
 (1969, It./Fr.) PR:O
SWEET BODY, THE
 (SEE:SWEET BODY OF DEBORAH, THE)
SWEET CHARITY ***½ (1969) PR:A
SWEET COUNTRY ** (1987) PR:O
SWEET CREEK COUNTY WAR, THE *½
 (1979) PR:A
SWEET DEVIL **½ (1937, Brit.) PR:A
SWEET DIRTY TONY
 (SEE:CUBA CROSSING)
SWEET DREAMS * (1985) PR:C-O**
SWEET ECSTASY ** (1962, Fr.) PR:C
SWEET GINGER BROWN
 (SEE:FLAMINGO KID, THE)
SWEET HEART'S DANCE ** (1988) PR:C-O
SWEET HUNTERS ** (1969, Panama) PR:C
SWEET INNISCARRA *½ (1934, Brit.) PR:A
SWEET JESUS, PREACHER MAN * (1973) PR:O
SWEET KILL
 (SEE:AROUSERS, THE)
SWEET KITTY BELLAIRS ** (1930) PR:A
SWEET LIBERTY **½ (1986) PR:A-C
SWEET LIGHT IN A DARK ROOM ***
 (1966, Czech.) PR:A
SWEET LORRAINE * (1987) PR:C**
SWEET LOVE, BITTER ** (1967) PR:C
SWEET MAMA * (1930) PR:A
SWEET MUSIC *½ (1935) PR:A
SWEET NOVEMBER ** (1968) PR:A
SWEET REVENGE
 (SEE:DANDY, THE ALL AMERICAN GIRL)
SWEET REVENGE **½ (1987) PR:O
SWEET RIDE, THE *½ (1968) PR:C
SWEET ROSIE O'GRADY *** (1943) PR:A
SWEET SIXTEEN * (1983) PR:O
SWEET SKIN ** (1965, Fr./It.) PR:O
SWEET SMELL OF LOVE ** (1966, It./Ger.) PR:A
SWEET SMELL OF SUCCESS ** (1957) PR:C-O**
SWEET STEPMOTHER
 (SEE:KIND STEPMOTHER)
SWEET SUBSTITUTE ** (1964, Can.) PR:C
SWEET SUGAR zero (1972) PR:O
SWEET SURRENDER * (1935) PR:A
SWEET SUZY * (1973) PR:O
SWEET TRASH *½ (1970) PR:O
SWEET VIOLENCE
 (SEE:SWEET ECSTASY)
SWEET WILLIAM **½ (1980, Brit.) PR:O
SWEETHEART OF SIGMA CHI ** (1933) PR:A
SWEETHEART OF SIGMA CHI ** (1946) PR:A
SWEETHEART OF THE CAMPUS (1941) PR:A

SWEETHEART OF THE FLEET ** (1942) PR:A
SWEETHEART OF THE NAVY *½ (1937) PR:A
SWEETHEARTS ***½ (1938) PR:A
SWEETHEARTS AND WIVES *½ (1930) PR:A
SWEETHEARTS OF THE U.S.A. * (1944) PR:A
SWEETHEARTS ON PARADE *½ (1930) PR:A
SWEETHEARTS ON PARADE
 (SEE:SWEETHEARTS OF THE U.S.A.)
SWEETHEARTS ON PARADE *½ (1953) PR:A
SWEETIE ** (1929) PR:A
SWELL GUY ** (1946) PR:A
SWELL-HEAD * (1935) PR:A
SWELLHEAD, THE ** (1930) PR:A
SWEPT AWAY...BY AN UNUSUAL DESTINY IN THE
 BLUE SEA OF AUGUST ***½ (1975, It.) PR:O
SWIFT VENGEANCE
 (SEE:ROOKIE COP, THE)
SWIFTY *½ (1936) PR:A
SWIMMER, THE **** (1988, USSR) PR:A
SWIMMER, THE **½ (1968) PR:C
SWINDLE, THE ***½ (1962, Fr./It.) PR:A
SWING AND SWAY
 (SEE:SWING IN THE SADDLE)
SWING FEVER *½ (1943) PR:A
SWING HIGH * (1930) PR:A
SWING HIGH, 1944
 (SEE:JIVE JUNCTION)
SWING HIGH, SWING LOW * (1937) PR:A-C**
SWING HOSTESS *½ (1944) PR:A
SWING IN THE SADDLE ** (1944) PR:A
SWING IT BUDDY
 (SEE:SWING IT, PROFESSOR)
SWING IT, PROFESSOR **½ (1937) PR:A
SWING IT SAILOR * (1937) PR:A
SWING IT SOLDIER *½ (1941) PR:A
SWING OUT, SISTER ** (1945) PR:A
SWING OUT THE BLUES ** (1943) PR:A
SWING PARADE OF 1946 ** (1946) PR:A
SWING SHIFT ** (1984) PR:A-C
SWING SHIFT MAISIE *½ (1943) PR:A
SWING, SISTER, SWING ** (1938) PR:A
SWING THAT CHEER * (1938) PR:A
SWING TIME ***½ (1936) PR:AA
SWING YOUR LADY * (1938) PR:A
SWING YOUR PARTNER *½ (1943) PR:A
SWING, TEACHER, SWING
 (SEE:COLLEGE SWING)
SWINGER, THE **½ (1966) PR:A
SWINGER'S PARADISE ** (1965, Brit.) PR:A
SWINGIN' AFFAIR, A * (1963) PR:A
SWINGIN' SUMMER, A ** (1965) PR:A
SWINGIN' ALONG *½ (1962) PR:A
SWINGIN' MAIDEN, THE ** (1963, Brit.) PR:A
SWINGIN' ON A RAINBOW * (1945) PR:A
SWINGING BARMAIDS, THE *½ (1976) PR:O
SWINGING FINK
 (SEE:RAT FINK)
SWINGING PEARL MYSTERY, THE
 (SEE:PLOT THICKENS, THE)
SWINGING SET
 (SEE:GET YOURSELF A COLLEGE GIRL)
SWINGING THE LEAD ** (1934, Brit.) PR:A
SWINGTIME JOHNNY * (1944) PR:A
SWIRL OF GLORY
 (SEE:SUGARFOOT)
SWISS CONSPIRACY, THE * (1976, US/Ger.) PR:C
SWISS FAMILY ROBINSON **½ (1940) PR:AA
SWISS FAMILY ROBINSON ***½ (1960) PR:AA
SWISS HONEYMOON * (1947, Brit.) PR:A
SWISS MISS ** (1938) PR:AA
SWISS TOUR
 (SEE:FOUR DAYS LEAVE)
SWITCH, THE * (1963, Brit.) PR:C
SWITCHBLADE SISTERS ** (1975) PR:O
SWITCHING CHANNELS **½ (1988) PR:A
SWORD AND THE DRAGON, THE *
 (1960, USSR) PR:A**
SWORD AND THE ROSE, THE * (1953) PR:A**
SWORD AND THE SORCERER, THE * (1982) PR:O
SWORD IN THE DESERT ***½ (1949) PR:A
SWORD IN THE STONE, THE **½ (1963) PR:AA
SWORD OF ALI BABA, THE * (1965) PR:A
SWORD OF DOOM, THE ** (1967, Jap.) PR:C-O
SWORD OF EL CID, THE ** (1965, Sp./It.) PR:A
SWORD OF HEAVEN zero (1985) PR:O
SWORD OF HONOUR *½ (1938, Brit.) PR:A
SWORD OF LANCELOT ** (1963, Brit.) PR:A

SWORD OF MONTE CRISTO, THE **½ (1951) PR:A
SWORD OF SHERWOOD FOREST **½
 (1961, Brit.) PR:A
SWORD OF THE AVENGER * (1948) PR:A
SWORD OF THE CONQUEROR *½ (1962, It.) PR:C
SWORD OF THE VALIANT * (1984, Brit.) PR:C
SWORD OF VENUS * (1953) PR:A
SWORDKILL **½ (1984) PR:C
SWORDSMAN OF SIENA, THE **
 (1962, Fr./It.) PR:A
SWORDSMAN, THE *½ (1947) PR:A
SWORN ENEMY **½ (1936) PR:A
SYLVESTER * (1985) PR:A**
SYLVIA *** (1965) PR:O
SYLVIA * (1985, New Zealand) PR:A-C**
SYLVIA AND THE GHOST
 (SEE:SYLVIA AND THE PHANTOM)
SYLVIA AND THE PHANTOM **½ (1950, Fr.) PR:A
SYLVIA SCARLETT **½ (1936) PR:A-C
SYLVIE AND THE PHANTOM
 (SEE:SYLVIA AND THE PHANTOM)
SYMPATHY FOR THE DEVIL
 (SEE:ONE PLUS ONE)
SYMPHONIE FANTASTIQUE *½ (1947, Fr.) PR:A
SYMPHONIE PASTORALE ***½ (1948, Fr.) PR:C
SYMPHONY FOR A MASSACRE **½
 (1965, Fr./It.) PR:A
SYMPHONY IN TWO FLATS *½ (1930, Brit.) PR:A
SYMPHONY OF LIFE **½ (1949, USSR) PR:A
SYMPHONY OF LIVING **½ (1935) PR:A
SYMPHONY OF SIX MILLION ** (1932) PR:A
SYMPTOMS *½ (1976, Brit.) PR:O
SYNANON *** (1965) PR:C
SYNCOPATION *½ (1929) PR:A
SYNCOPATION ** (1942) PR:A
SYNDICATE, THE ** (1968, Brit.) PR:A
SYSTEM, THE, 1966
 (SEE:GIRL GETTERS, THE)
SYSTEM, THE ** (1953) PR:A
SZAMARKOHOGES
 (SEE:WHOOPING COUGH)
SZEGENYLEGENYEK (NEHEZELETUEK)
 (SEE:ROUND UP, THE)

T

T-BIRD GANG *½ (1959) PR:C
T-MEN ** (1947) PR:C**
T.P.A.
 (SEE:PRESIDENT'S ANALYST, THE)
TA CHI
 (SEE:LAST WOMEN OF SHANG)
TABLE BAY
 (SEE:CODE 7, VICTIM 5)
TABLE FOR FIVE * (1983) PR:C**
TABU (FUGITIVOS DE LAS ISLAS DEL SUR)
 (SEE:DRUMS OF TABU)
TAFFIN ** (1988, US/Brit.) PR:C
TAFFY AND THE JUNGLE HUNTER **
 (1965) PR:A
T.A.G.: THE ASSASSINATION GAME *½
 (1982) PR:C
TAGGART ** (1964) PR:C
TAHITI HONEY ** (1943) PR:A
TAHITI NIGHTS ** (1945) PR:A
TAHITIAN, THE * (1956) PR:A
TAI-PAN * (1986) PR:O
TAIHEIYO HITORIBOTCHI
 (SEE:ALONE ON THE PACIFIC)
TAIHEIYO NO ARASHI
 (SEE:I BOMBED PEARL HARBOR)
TAIL OF THE TIGER **½ (1984, Aus.) PR:AA
TAIL SPIN ** (1939) PR:A
TAILOR MADE MAN, A *½ (1931) PR:A
TAINTED MONEY
 (SEE:SHOW THEM NO MERCY)
TAKE A CHANCE *½ (1933) PR:A
TAKE A CHANCE ** (1937, Brit.) PR:A
TAKE A GIANT STEP ** (1959) PR:A
TAKE A GIRL LIKE YOU ** (1970, Brit.) PR:O
TAKE A HARD RIDE ** (1975, US/It.) PR:C
TAKE A LETTER, DARLING ***½ (1942) PR:A

Years 1929-83	Volumes I-IX
1984	Volume IX
1985	1986 ANNUAL
1986	1987 ANNUAL
1987	1988 ANNUAL
1988	1989 ANNUAL

STAR RATINGS

★★★★★ Masterpiece
★★★★ Excellent
★★★ Good
★★ Fair
★ Poor
zero Without Merit

PARENTAL RECOMMENDATION (PR:)

AA Good for Children
A Acceptable for Children
C Cautionary, some objectionable scenes
O Objectionable for Children

BOLD: Films on Videocassette

TAKE A POWDER * (1953, Brit.) PR:A
TAKE ALL OF ME *½ (1978, It.) PR:O
TAKE CARE OF MY LITTLE GIRL ** (1951) PR:A
TAKE DOWN **½ (1979) PR:C
TAKE HER BY SURPRISE **½ (1967, Can.) PR:A
TAKE HER, SHE'S MINE **½ (1963) PR:A
TAKE IT ALL *** (1966, Can.) PR:A
TAKE IT BIG ** (1944) PR:A
TAKE IT FROM ME *½ (1937, Brit.) PR:A
TAKE IT OR LEAVE IT ** (1944) PR:A
TAKE ME AWAY, MY LOVE * (1962, Gr.) PR:O
TAKE ME HIGH ** (1973, Brit.) PR:A
TAKE ME OUT TO THE BALL GAME ** (1949) PR:AA**
TAKE ME OVER ** (1963, Brit.) PR:A
TAKE ME TO PARIS ** (1951, Brit.) PR:A
TAKE ME TO THE FAIR
(SEE:IT HAPPENED AT THE WORLD'S FAIR)
TAKE ME TO TOWN ** (1953) PR:A
TAKE MY LIFE *½ (1942) PR:A
TAKE MY LIFE *½ (1948, Brit.) PR:A
TAKE MY TIP ** (1937, Brit.) PR:A
TAKE OFF THAT HAT ** (1938, Brit.) PR:A
TAKE ONE FALSE STEP *** (1949) PR:C
TAKE THE HEIR ** (1930) PR:AA
TAKE THE HIGH GROUND *** (1953) PR:A
TAKE THE MONEY AND RUN ***½ (1969) PR:C
TAKE THE STAGE
(SEE:CURTAIN CALL AT CACTUS CREEK)
TAKE THE STAND *½ (1934) PR:A
TAKE THIS JOB AND SHOVE IT ** (1981) PR:C-O
TAKE, THE ** (1974) PR:C
TAKEN BY SURPRISE
(SEE:TAKE HER BY SURPRISE)
TAKERS, THE
(SEE:MALAGA)
TAKING OF PELHAM ONE, TWO, THREE, THE ***½ (1974) PR:O
TAKING OFF **** (1971) PR:O
TAKING SIDES
(SEE:LIGHTNING GUNS)
TAKING TIGER MOUNTAIN ** (1983, US/Welsh) PR:O
TALE OF FIVE CITIES, A
(SEE:TALE OF FIVE WOMEN, A)
TALE OF FIVE WOMEN, A ** (1951, Brit.) PR:A
TALE OF RUBY ROSE, THE *** (1987, Aus.) PR:C
TALE OF THE COCK
(SEE:CHILDISH THINGS)
TALE OF THREE WOMEN, A * (1954, Brit.) PR:A
TALE OF TWO CITIES, A ** (1935) PR:A**
TALE OF TWO CITIES, A * (1958, Brit.) PR:A**
TALENT SCOUT ** (1937) PR:A
TALES AFTER THE RAIN
(SEE:UGETSU MONOGATARI)
TALES FROM THE CRYPT * (1972, Brit.) PR:C**
TALES FROM THE CRYPT PART II
(SEE:VAULT OF HORROR)
TALES OF A SALESMAN *½ (1965) PR:C
TALES OF A TRAVELING SALESMAN
(SEE:TALES OF A SALESMAN)
TALES OF BEATRIX POTTER
(SEE:PETER RABBIT AND TALES OF BEATRIX POTTER)
TALES OF HOFFMANN, THE **½ (1951, Brit.) PR:A
TALES OF MANHATTAN **** (1942) PR:AA
TALES OF ORDINARY MADNESS ** (1983, It.) PR:O
TALES OF PARIS **½ (1962, Fr./It.) PR:A
TALES OF ROBIN HOOD **½ (1951) PR:A
TALES OF TERROR ***½ (1962) PR:C
TALES OF THE THIRD DIMENSION ** (1985) PR:O
TALES OF THE UNCANNY *** (1932, Ger.) PR:C
TALES THAT WITNESS MADNESS **½ (1973, Brit.) PR:O
TALISMAN, THE **½ (1966) PR:C
TALK ABOUT A LADY *½ (1946) PR:A
TALK ABOUT A STRANGER ** (1952) PR:A
TALK ABOUT JACQUELINE ** (1942, Brit.) PR:A
TALK OF A MILLION
(SEE:YOU CAN'T BEAT THE IRISH)
TALK OF HOLLYWOOD, THE *½ (1929) PR:A
TALK OF THE DEVIL ** (1937, Brit.) PR:A
TALK OF THE TOWN ** (1942) PR:AA**
TALK RADIO ***½ (1988) PR:O
TALKING BEAR, THE
(SEE:BEAR, THE)
TALKING FEET *½ (1937, Brit.) PR:A
TALKING TO STRANGERS ** (1988) PR:O
TALKING WALLS ** (1987) PR:O
TALL BLOND MAN WITH ONE BLACK SHOE, THE **½ (1973, Fr.) PR:C
TALL, DARK AND HANDSOME *** (1941) PR:A
TALL HEADLINES
(SEE:FRIGHTENED BRIDE, THE)
TALL IN THE SADDLE * (1944) PR:A**
TALL LIE, THE
(SEE:FOR MEN ONLY)
TALL MAN RIDING ** (1955) PR:A
TALL MEN, THE ***½ (1955) PR:A
TALL STORY *½ (1960) PR:C
TALL STRANGER, THE ** (1957) PR:A
TALL T, THE **** (1957) PR:A
TALL TARGET, THE ** (1951) PR:A
TALL TEXAN, THE ** (1953) PR:A
TALL TIMBER
(SEE:BIG TIMBER)
TALL TIMBERS ***½ (1937, Aus.) PR:A
TALL TROUBLE, THE
(SEE:HELL CANYON OUTLAWS)
TALL WOMEN, THE ** (1967, Aust./It./Sp.) PR:A
TAM-LIN
(SEE:DEVIL'S WIDOW, THE)
TAMAHINE ** (1964, Brit.) PR:C
TAMANGO **½ (1959, Fr.) PR:C
TAMARIND SEED, THE *½ (1974, Brit.) PR:C
TAMING OF DOROTHY, THE *½ (1950, Brit.) PR:A
TAMING OF THE SHREW, THE **½ (1929) PR:A
TAMING OF THE SHREW, THE ***½ (1967, US/It.) PR:A-C
TAMING OF THE WEST, THE ** (1939) PR:A
TAMING SUTTON'S GAL *½ (1957) PR:A
TAMING THE WILD *½ (1937) PR:A
TAMMY
(SEE:TAMMY AND THE BACHELOR)
TAMMY AND THE BACHELOR * (1957) PR:A**
TAMMY AND THE DOCTOR ** (1963) PR:A
TAMMY AND THE MILLIONAIRE ** (1967) PR:A
TAMMY, TELL ME TRUE ** (1961) PR:A
TAMPICO * (1944) PR:A
TAMPOPO ***½ (1986, Jap.) PR:C-O
TANGA-TIKA ** (1953) PR:A
TANGANYIKA ** (1954) PR:A
TANGIER *½ (1946) PR:A
TANGIER ASSIGNMENT * (1954, Brit.) PR:A
TANGIER INCIDENT ** (1953) PR:A
TANGLED DESTINIES *** (1932) PR:A
TANGLED EVIDENCE *½ (1934, Brit.) PR:A
TANGO *½ (1936) PR:A
TANGO BAR ** (1935) PR:A
TANIN NO KAO
(SEE:FACE OF ANOTHER, THE)
TANK **½ (1984) PR:C
TANK BATTALION ** (1958) PR:A
TANK COMMANDO
(SEE:TANK COMMANDOS)
TANK COMMANDOS ** (1959) PR:A
TANK FORCE ** (1958, Brit.) PR:A
TANKS A MILLION ** (1941) PR:A
TANKS ARE COMING, THE ** (1951) PR:A
TANNED LEGS ** (1929) PR:A
TANTE ZITA
(SEE:ZITA)
TANYA'S ISLAND **½ (1981, Can.) PR:O
TAP ROOTS ***½ (1948) PR:C
TAPEHEADS *½ (1988) PR:O
TAPS ***½ (1981) PR:C
TARANTULA *** (1955) PR:A
TARAS BULBA *½ (1962) PR:A
TARAS FAMILY, THE ** (1946, USSR) PR:A
TARAWA BEACHHEAD *** (1958) PR:A
TARGET ** (1952) PR:A
TARGET **½ (1985) PR:O
TARGET EARTH *½ (1954) PR:A
TARGET FOR SCANDAL
(SEE:WASHINGTON STORY)
TARGET: HARRY *½ (1980) PR:C
TARGET HONG KONG **½ (1952) PR:A
TARGET IN THE SUN
(SEE:MAN WHO WOULD NOT DIE, THE)
TARGET UNKNOWN ** (1951) PR:A
TARGET ZERO ** (1955) PR:A
TARGETS ***½ (1968) PR:O
TARNISHED ** (1950) PR:A
TARNISHED ANGEL ** (1938) PR:A
TARNISHED ANGELS, THE **** (1957) PR:C
TARNISHED HEROES ** (1961, Brit.) PR:A
TARNISHED LADY ** (1931) PR:A
TAROT *** (1987, Ger.) PR:C
TARS AND SPARS ** (1946) PR:A
TARTARS, THE *½ (1962, It./Yugo.) PR:A
TARTU
(SEE:ADVENTURES OF TARTU)
TARZAN AND HIS MATE ***½ (1934) PR:A-C
TARZAN AND THE AMAZONS **½ (1945) PR:A
TARZAN AND THE GREAT RIVER *½ (1967, US/Switz.) PR:A
TARZAN AND THE GREEN GODDESS * (1938) PR:AA
TARZAN AND THE HUNTRESS **½ (1947) PR:AA
TARZAN AND THE JUNGLE BOY *½ (1968, US/Switz.) PR:AA
TARZAN AND THE JUNGLE QUEEN
(SEE:TARZAN'S PERIL)
TARZAN AND THE LEOPARD WOMAN **½ (1946) PR:AA
TARZAN AND THE LOST SAFARI **½ (1957, Brit.) PR:AA
TARZAN AND THE MERMAIDS *** (1948) PR:AA
TARZAN AND THE SHE-DEVIL * (1953) PR:AA
TARZAN AND THE SLAVE GIRL ** (1950) PR:AA
TARZAN AND THE VALLEY OF GOLD ** (1966, US/Switz.) PR:AA
TARZAN ESCAPES *** (1936) PR:A
TARZAN FINDS A SON *** (1939) PR:AA
TARZAN GOES TO INDIA ** (1962, US/Brit./Switz.) PR:AA
TARZAN NO. 22
(SEE:TARZAN AND THE JUNGLE BOY)
TARZAN '65
(SEE:TARZAN AND THE VALLEY OF GOLD)
TARZAN '66
(SEE:TARZAN AND THE VALLEY OF GOLD)
TARZAN, THE APE MAN ***½ (1932) PR:AA
TARZAN, THE APE MAN * (1959) PR:A
TARZAN, THE APE MAN zero (1981) PR:O
TARZAN THE FEARLESS ** (1933) PR:AA
TARZAN THE MAGNIFICENT *½ (1960, Brit.) PR:A
TARZAN TRIUMPHS **½ (1943) PR:AA
TARZAN VERSUS I.B.M.
(SEE:ALPHAVILLE)
TARZANA, THE WILD GIRL * (1973) PR:O
TARZANOVA SMRT
(SEE:DEATH OF TARZAN, THE)
TARZAN'S DEADLY SILENCE * (1970) PR:AA
TARZAN'S DESERT MYSTERY ** (1943) PR:AA
TARZAN'S FIGHT FOR LIFE **½ (1958) PR:AA
TARZAN'S GREATEST ADVENTURE *** (1959, Brit.) PR:AA
TARZAN'S HIDDEN JUNGLE ** (1955) PR:AA
TARZAN'S JUNGLE REBELLION * (1970) PR:AA
TARZAN'S MAGIC FOUNTAIN ** (1949) PR:AA
TARZAN'S NEW YORK ADVENTURE **½ (1942) PR:AA
TARZAN'S PERIL **½ (1951) PR:A
TARZAN'S REVENGE * (1938) PR:AA
TARZAN'S SAVAGE FURY *½ (1952) PR:AA
TARZAN'S SECRET TREASURE **½ (1941) PR:AA
TARZAN'S THREE CHALLENGES *** (1963) PR:AA
TASK FORCE ***½ (1949) PR:A
TASTE FOR WOMEN, A ** (1966, Fr./It.) PR:O
TASTE OF BLOOD, A zero (1967) PR:O
TASTE OF EXCITEMENT ** (1969, Brit.) PR:C
TASTE OF FEAR
(SEE:SCREAM OF FEAR)
TASTE OF FLESH, A zero (1967) PR:O
TASTE OF HELL, A * (1973) PR:C
TASTE OF HONEY, A SWALLOW OF BRINE!, A
(SEE:SMELL OF HONEY, A SWALLOW OF BRINE!, A)
TASTE OF HONEY, A ** (1962, Brit.) PR:C**
TASTE OF HOT LEAD, A
(SEE:HOT LEAD)
TASTE OF MONEY, A ** (1960, Brit.) PR:A
TASTE OF SIN, A *** (1983) PR:O
TASTE THE BLOOD OF DRACULA **½ (1970, Brit.) PR:O
TATSU **½ (1962, Jap.) PR:C
TATTERED DRESS, THE **½ (1957) PR:C
TATTOO zero (1981) PR:O
TATTOOED STRANGER, THE *** (1950) PR:O
TAWNY PIPIT **½ (1947, Brit.) PR:A
TAXI ** (1953) PR:A
TAXI! ***½ (1932) PR:A
TAXI DRIVER * (1976) PR:O
TAXI FOR TOBRUK ** (1965, Fr./Sp./Ger.) PR:A
TAXI FOR TWO ** (1929, Brit.) PR:A
TAXI NACH TOBRUK
(SEE:TAXI FOR TOBRUK)
TAXI 13 **½ (1928) PR:AA
TAXI TO HEAVEN ** (1944, USSR) PR:A
TAXING WOMAN, A ***½ (1988, Jap.) PR:C-O
TAXING WOMAN'S RETURN, A **½ (1988, Jap.) PR:C-O
TAZA, SON OF COCHISE **½ (1954) PR:A
TE QUIERO CON LOCURA ** (1935) PR:A
TEA AND RICE *** (1964, Jap.) PR:A
TEA AND SYMPATHY ***½ (1956) PR:C-O
TEA FOR TWO ***½ (1950) PR:A
TEA IN THE HAREM OF ARCHIMEDE ***½ (1985, Fr.) PR:C-O
TEA LEAVES IN THE WIND
(SEE:HATE IN PARADISE)
TEACHER AND THE MIRACLE, THE **½ (1961, It./Sp.) PR:A
TEACHER'S PET * (1958) PR:A**
TEACHER, THE ** (1974) PR:C
TEACHERS **½ (1984) PR:C-O
TEAHOUSE OF THE AUGUST MOON, THE **** (1956) PR:AA
TEAR GAS SQUAD * (1940) PR:A
TEARS FOR SIMON *** (1957, Brit.) PR:A

TEARS OF HAPPINESS * (1974) PR:A
TECHNIQUE D'UN MEUTRE
  (SEE:HIRED KILLER, THE)
TECKMAN MYSTERY, THE **½ (1955, Brit.) PR:A
TECNICA DI UN OMICIDO
  (SEE:HIRED KILLER, THE)
TEDDY BEAR, THE
  (SEE:MY FATHER'S MISTRESS)
TEEN-AGE CRIME WAVE * (1955) PR:C
TEEN-AGE STRANGLER zero (1967) PR:O
TEEN AGE TRAMP
  (SEE:THAT KIND OF GIRL)
TEEN KANYA
  (SEE:TWO DAUGHTERS)
TEEN WOLF **½ (1985) **PR:A-C**
TEEN WOLF TOO * (1987) **PR:A-C**
TEENAGE BAD GIRL **½ (1959, Brit.) PR:O
TEENAGE CAVEMAN ** (1958) PR:A
TEENAGE DELINQUENTS
  (SEE:NO TIME TO BE YOUNG)
TEENAGE DOLL ** (1957) PR:O
TEENAGE FRANKENSTEIN
  (SEE:I WAS A TEENAGE FRANKENSTEIN)
TEENAGE GANG DEBS * (1966) PR:O
TEENAGE LOVERS
  (SEE:TOO SOON TO LOVE)
TEENAGE MILLIONAIRE ** (1961) PR:A
TEENAGE MONSTER zero (1958) PR:A
TEENAGE MOTHER zero (1967) PR:O
TEENAGE PSYCHO MEETS BLOODY MARY
  (SEE:INCREDIBLY STRANGE CREATURES WHO
  STOPPED LIVING AND BECAME CRAZY
  MIXED-UP ZOMBIES)
TEENAGE REBEL ** (1956) PR:A
TEENAGE THUNDER * (1957) PR:A
TEENAGE ZOMBIES zero (1960) **PR:C**
TEENAGERS FROM OUTER SPACE zero
  (1959) PR:A
TEENAGERS IN SPACE **½ (1975, USSR) PR:AA
TEHERAN
  (SEE:PLOT TO KILL ROOSEVELT, THE)
TEL AVIV TAXI zero (1957, Israel) PR:A
TELEFON *** (1977) **PR:C-O**
TELEGIAN, THE
  (SEE:SECRET OF THE TELEGIAN)
TELEGRAPH TRAIL, THE *½ (1933) PR:A
TELEPHONE, THE * (1988) **PR:C**
TELEPHONE OPERATOR * (1938) PR:A
TELEVISION SPY *½ (1939) PR:A
TELEVISION TALENT ** (1937, Brit.) PR:A
TELI SIROKKO
  (SEE:WINTER WIND)
TELL ENGLAND
  (SEE:BATTLE OF GALLIPOLI)
TELL IT TO A STAR ** (1945) PR:A
TELL IT TO THE JUDGE **½ (1949) PR:A
TELL IT TO THE MARINES
  (SEE:HERE COME THE MARINES)
TELL ME A RIDDLE **½ (1980) PR:A
TELL ME IN THE SUNLIGHT ** (1967) PR:C-O
TELL ME LIES ** (1968, Brit.) PR:O
TELL ME THAT YOU LOVE ME, JUNIE MOON **
  (1970) PR:A-C
TELL NO TALES ** (1939) PR:A
TELL-TALE HEART, THE **½ (1962, Brit.) **PR:O**
TELL-TALE HEART, THE, 1934
  (SEE:BUCKET OF BLOOD)
TELL THEM WILLIE BOY IS HERE ***½
  (1969) PR:C
TELL YOUR CHILDREN
  (SEE:REEFER MADNESS)
TEMPEST **½ (1932, Ger.) PR:C
TEMPEST ***½ (1958, It./Yugo./Fr.) PR:C
TEMPEST ** (1982) **PR:C-O**
TEMPLE DRAKE
  (SEE:STORY OF TEMPLE DRAKE)
TEMPLE TOWER *½ (1930) PR:A
TEMPO DI MASSACRO
  (SEE:BRUTE AND THE BEAST, THE)
TEMPORARY WIDOW, THE **
  (1930, Ger./Brit.) PR:C
TEMPTATION *½ (1935, Brit.) PR:A
TEMPTATION ** (1936) PR:A
TEMPTATION ** (1946) PR:A
TEMPTATION * (1962, Fr.) PR:C
TEMPTATION HARBOR ** (1949, Brit.) PR:A

TEMPTER, THE
  (SEE:DEVIL IS A WOMAN, THE)
TEMPTER, THE zero (1978, It.) **PR:O**
TEMPTRESS AND THE MONK, THE **
  (1963, Jap.) PR:C
TEMPTRESS, THE ** (1949, Brit.) PR:A
10 *** (1979) **PR:O**
TEN CENTS A DANCE ** (1931) PR:A
TEN CENTS A DANCE ** (1945) PR:A
TEN COMMANDMENTS, THE **** (1956) **PR:AA**
TEN DAYS IN PARIS
  (SEE:MISSING TEN DAYS)
TEN DAYS THAT SHOOK THE WORLD, THE *½
  (1977, Yugo./Czech.) PR:A-C
TEN DAYS TO TULARA * (1958) PR:A
TEN DAYS' WONDER *½ (1972, Fr.) PR:O
TEN GENTLEMEN FROM WEST POINT **
  (1942) PR:A
TEN LAPS TO GO * (1938) **PR:A**
TEN LITTLE INDIANS * (1965, Brit.) **PR:A**
TEN LITTLE INDIANS *½
  (1975, It./Fr./Sp./Ger.) PR:C
TEN LITTLE NIGGERS
  (SEE:AND THEN THERE WERE NONE)
TEN MINUTE ALIBI ** (1935, Brit.) PR:A
TEN NIGHTS IN A BARROOM * (1931) **PR:A**
10 NORTH FREDERICK **½ (1958) PR:A-C
$10 RAISE * (1935) PR:A
10 RILLINGTON PLACE *** (1971, Brit.) **PR:O**
TEN SECONDS TO HELL **½ (1959) PR:A
TEN TALL MEN **½ (1951) PR:AA
10:30 P.M. SUMMER *½ (1966, US/Sp.) PR:O
TEN THOUSAND BEDROOMS ** (1957) PR:A
10,000 DOLLARS BLOOD MONEY *½
  (1966, It.) PR:O
10 TO MIDNIGHT * (1983) **PR:O**
10 VIOLENT WOMEN ** (1982) PR:O
TEN WANTED MEN ** (1955) **PR:A-C**
TEN WHO DARED zero (1960) **PR:A**
TENANT, THE *** (1976, Fr.) **PR:O**
TENCHU ** (1970, Jap.) PR:O
TENDER COMRADE ** (1943) PR:A
TENDER FLESH *½ (1976) PR:O
TENDER HEARTS ** (1955) PR:A
TENDER IS THE NIGHT ***½ (1961) PR:C
TENDER MERCIES **½ (1982) **PR:A**
TENDER SCOUNDREL ** (1967, Fr./It.) PR:C
TENDER TRAP, THE **½ (1955) PR:A
TENDER WARRIOR, THE ** (1971) **PR:AA**
TENDER YEARS, THE ** (1947) **PR:A-C**
TENDERFOOT GOES WEST, A ** (1937) PR:A
TENDERFOOT, THE **½ (1932) PR:A
TENDERLOIN ** (1928) PR:A
TENDERLY
  (SEE:GIRL WHO COULDN'T SAY NO)
TENDRE POULET
  (SEE:DEAR DETECTIVE)
TENDRE VOYOU
  (SEE:TENDER SCOUNDREL)
TENNESSEE BEAT, THE
  (SEE:THAT TENNESSEE BEAT)
TENNESSEE CHAMP **½ (1954) **PR:A**
TENNESSEE JOHNSON *** (1942) PR:A
TENNESSEE'S PARTNER *** (1955) **PR:C**
TENSION **** (1949) PR:O
TENSION AT TABLE ROCK **½ (1956) PR:A
TENTACLES * (1977, It.) **PR:C**
TENTH AVENUE ANGEL * (1948) PR:A
TENTH AVENUE KID ** (1938) PR:A
TENTH MAN, THE ** (1937, Brit.) PR:A
TENTH VICTIM, THE *** (1965, Fr./It.) **PR:O**
TENTING TONIGHT ON THE OLD CAMP GROUND
  **½ (1943) PR:A
TEOREMA *** (1969, It.) PR:O
TEQUILA SUNRISE **½ (1988) **PR:O**
TERESA *** (1951) PR:A
TERM OF TRIAL **½ (1962, Brit.) PR:C
TERMINAL CHOICE *½ (1985, Can.) **PR:O**
TERMINAL ISLAND ** (1973) **PR:O**
TERMINAL MAN, THE ** (1974) **PR:C**
TERMINAL STATION
  (SEE:INDISCRETION OF AN AMERICAN WIFE)
TERMINATOR, THE *** (1984) **PR:O**
TERMS OF ENDEARMENT ***½ (1983) **PR:A-C**
TERRA EM TRANSE
  (SEE:EARTH ENTRANCED)
TERRACE, THE *** (1964, Arg.) PR:O

TERRIBLE BEAUTY, A
  (SEE:NIGHT FIGHTERS)
TERRIFIED * (1963) PR:O
TERROR, THE **½ (1928) PR:A
TERROR, THE ** (1941, Brit.) PR:A
TERROR, THE ** (1963) **PR:C**
TERROR * (1979, Brit.) **PR:O**
TERROR ABOARD ** (1933) PR:A
TERROR AFTER MIDNIGHT ** (1965, Ger.) PR:C
TERROR AT BLACK FALLS * (1962) PR:C
TERROR AT HALFDAY
  (SEE:MONSTER A GO-GO)
TERROR AT MIDNIGHT *½ (1956) PR:A
TERROR BENEATH THE SEA *½ (1966, Jap.) PR:C
TERROR BY NIGHT ** (1946) **PR:A**
TERROR BY NIGHT, 1931
  (SEE:SECRET WITNESS)
TERROR CASTLE
  (SEE:HORROR CASTLE)
TERROR CIRCUS
  (SEE:BARN OF THE NAKED DEAD)
TERROR-CREATURES FROM THE GRAVE zero
  (1967, US/It.) PR:O
TERROR EN EL ESPACIO
  (SEE:PLANET OF THE VAMPIRES, 2)
TERROR EYES * (1981) PR:O
TERROR FACTOR, THE
  (SEE:SCARED TO DEATH)
TERROR FROM THE SUN
  (SEE:HIDEOUS SUN DEMON, THE)
TERROR FROM THE YEAR 5,000 * (1958) PR:A
TERROR FROM UNDER THE HOUSE **
  (1971, Brit.) PR:C
TERROR HOUSE ***½ (1942, Brit.) PR:C
TERROR HOUSE *½ (1972) **PR:O**
TERROR IN A TEXAS TOWN **½ (1958) PR:A
TERROR IN THE CITY
  (SEE:PIE IN THE SKY)
TERROR IN THE HAUNTED HOUSE
  (SEE:MY WORLD DIES SCREAMING)
TERROR IN THE JUNGLE zero (1968) PR:A
TERROR IN THE MIDNIGHT SUN
  (SEE:INVASION OF THE ANIMAL PEOPLE)
TERROR IN THE WAX MUSEUM *½ (1973) **PR:C**
TERROR IS A MAN ** (1959, US/Phil.) PR:C
TERROR OF DR. CHANEY, THE
  (SEE:MANSION OF THE DOOMED)
TERROR OF DR. MABUSE, THE ** (1965, Ger.) PR:C
TERROR OF FRANKENSTEIN
  (SEE:VICTOR FRANKENSTEIN)
TERROR OF GODZILLA
  (SEE:MONSTERS FROM THE UNKNOWN PLANET)
TERROR OF SHEBA
  (SEE:PERSECUTION)
TERROR OF THE BLACK MASK *½
  (1967, Fr./It.) PR:A
TERROR OF THE BLOODHUNTERS * (1962) PR:A
TERROR OF THE HATCHET MEN
  (SEE:TERROR OF THE TONGS, THE)
TERROR OF THE MAD DOCTOR, THE
  (SEE:TERROR OF DR. MABUSE, THE)
TERROR OF THE TONGS, THE **½
  (1961, Brit.) PR:O
TERROR OF TINY TOWN, THE * (1938) **PR:A**
TERROR ON A TRAIN *½ (1953) PR:A
TERROR ON BLOOD ISLAND
  (SEE:BRIDES OF BLOOD)
TERROR ON TIPTOE *½ (1936, Brit.) PR:A
TERROR ON TOUR zero (1980) **PR:O**
TERROR SHIP ** (1954, Brit.) PR:A
TERROR STREET * (1953) PR:A
TERROR STRIKES, THE
  (SEE:WAR OF THE COLOSSAL BEAST)
TERROR TRAIL ** (1933) PR:A
TERROR TRAIN ** (1980, Can.) **PR:O**
TERRORE NELLO SPAZIO
  (SEE:PLANET OF THE VAMPIRES)
TERRORISTS, THE * (1975, Brit.) **PR:C**
TERRORIZERS, THE **½ (1987, Taiwan) PR:O
TERRORNAUTS, THE *½ (1967, Brit.) **PR:A**
TERRORS ON HORSEBACK ** (1946) PR:A
TERRORVISION **½ (1986) **PR:O**
TESEO CONTRO IL MINOTAURO
  (SEE:MINOTAUR, THE)
TESHA ** (1929, Brit.) PR:A
TESS *** (1980, Fr./Brit.) **PR:A-C**
TESS OF THE STORM COUNTRY **½ (1932) PR:A

Finding entries in **THE MOTION PICTURE GUIDE** ™

Years 1929-83	Volumes I-IX
1984	Volume IX
1985	1986 ANNUAL
1986	1987 ANNUAL
1987	1988 ANNUAL
1988	1989 ANNUAL

STAR RATINGS

★★★★★ Masterpiece
★★★★ Excellent
★★★ Good
★★ Fair
★ Poor
zero Without Merit

PARENTAL RECOMMENDATION (PR:)

AA Good for Children
A Acceptable for Children
C Cautionary, some objectionable scenes
O Objectionable for Children

BOLD: Films on Videocassette

TESS OF THE STORM COUNTRY ** (1961) PR:A
TEST OF PILOT PIRX, THE ** (1978, Pol./USSR) PR:C
TEST PILOT **** (1938) PR:A
TESTAMENT **½ (1983) PR:A
TESTAMENT **½ (1988, Brit.) PR:C
TESTAMENT OF DR. MABUSE, THE (SEE:TERROR OF DR. MABUSE, THE)
TESTAMENT OF DR. MABUSE, THE ***½ (1943, Ger.) PR:C
TESTAMENT OF ORPHEUS, THE *** (1962, Fr.) PR:C**
TESTIGO PARA UN CRIMEN (SEE:VIOLATED LOVE)
TEUFEL IN SEIDE (SEE:DEVIL IN SILK)
TEVYA **½ (1939) PR:A
TEX * (1982) PR:A**
TEX RIDES WITH THE BOY SCOUTS * (1937) PR:A
TEX TAKES A HOLIDAY * (1932) PR:A
TEXAN MEETS CALAMITY JANE, THE * (1950) PR:A
TEXAN, THE *** (1930) PR:A
TEXANS NEVER CRY ** (1951) PR:A
TEXANS, THE **½ (1938) PR:A
TEXAS ***½ (1941) PR:A
TEXAS ACROSS THE RIVER ** (1966) PR:A
TEXAS BAD MAN **½ (1932) PR:A
TEXAS BAD MAN ** (1953) PR:A
TEXAS, BROOKLYN AND HEAVEN ** (1948) PR:A
TEXAS BUDDIES *½ (1932) PR:A
TEXAS CARNIVAL ** (1951) PR:A
TEXAS CHAIN SAW MASSACRE, THE * (1974) PR:O**
TEXAS CHAINSAW MASSACRE PART 2, THE zero (1986) PR:O
TEXAS CITY *½ (1952) PR:A
TEXAS CYCLONE ** (1932) PR:A
TEXAS DESPERADOS (SEE:DRIFT FENCE)
TEXAS DYNAMO *½ (1950) PR:A
TEXAS GUN FIGHTER *½ (1932) PR:A
TEXAS KID (SEE:TEXICAN, THE)
TEXAS KID, OUTLAW (SEE:KID FROM TEXAS, THE)
TEXAS KID, THE ** (1944) PR:A
TEXAS LADY ** (1955) PR:A
TEXAS LAWMEN ** (1951) PR:A
TEXAS LIGHTNING ** (1981) PR:O
TEXAS MAN HUNT ** (1942) PR:A
TEXAS MARSHAL, THE ** (1941) PR:A
TEXAS MASQUERADE **½ (1944) PR:A
TEXAS PIONEERS ** (1932) PR:A
TEXAS RANGER, THE **½ (1931) PR:A
TEXAS RANGERS RIDE AGAIN **½ (1940) PR:A
TEXAS RANGERS, THE **½ (1936) PR:A
TEXAS RANGERS, THE **½ (1951) PR:A
TEXAS ROAD AGENT (SEE:ROAD AGENT)
TEXAS ROSE (SEE:RETURN OF JACK SLADE, THE)
TEXAS SERENADE (SEE:OLD CORRAL, THE)
TEXAS STAGECOACH **½ (1940) PR:A
TEXAS STAMPEDE ** (1939) PR:A
TEXAS TERROR **½ (1935) PR:A
TEXAS TERRORS * (1940) PR:A
TEXAS TO BATAAN * (1942) PR:A
TEXAS TORNADO ** (1934) PR:A
TEXAS TRAIL ** (1937) PR:A
TEXAS WILDCATS ** (1939) PR:A
TEXICAN, THE * (1966, US/Sp.) PR:A
THANK EVANS *½ (1938, Brit.) PR:A
THANK GOD IT'S FRIDAY zero (1978) PR:C
THANK HEAVEN FOR SMALL FAVORS **½ (1965, Fr.) PR:A
THANK YOU ALL VERY MUCH *** (1969, Brit.) PR:C
THANK YOU, AUNT *** (1969, It.) PR:O
THANK YOU, JEEVES ** (1936) PR:A
THANK YOU, MR. MOTO **½ (1937) PR:A
THANK YOUR LUCKY STARS ***½ (1943) PR:A
THANK YOUR STARS (SEE:SHOOT THE WORKS)
THANKS A MILLION *** (1935) PR:A
THANKS FOR EVERYTHING **½ (1938) PR:A
THANKS FOR LISTENING * (1937) PR:A
THANKS FOR THE MEMORY ** (1938) PR:A
THANOS AND DESPINA ** (1970, Fr./Gr.) PR:C
THARK *** (1932, Brit.) PR:A
THAT BRENNAN GIRL *½ (1946) PR:A
THAT CERTAIN AGE **½ (1938) PR:A
THAT CERTAIN FEELING * (1956) PR:A
THAT CERTAIN SOMETHING ** (1941, Aus.) PR:A
THAT CERTAIN WOMAN **½ (1937) PR:A-C
THAT CHAMPIONSHIP SEASON ** (1982) PR:O
THAT COLD DAY IN THE PARK ** (1969, US/Can.) PR:O
THAT DANGEROUS AGE (SEE:IF THIS BE SIN)
THAT DARN CAT * (1965) PR:AA**
THAT FORSYTE WOMAN *** (1949) PR:A-C
THAT FUNNY FEELING ** (1965) PR:C
THAT GANG OF MINE *½ (1940) PR:A
THAT GIRL FROM BEVERLY HILLS (SEE:CORPSE OF BEVERLY HILLS, THE)
THAT GIRL FROM COLLEGE (SEE:SORORITY HOUSE)
THAT GIRL FROM PARIS *** (1937) PR:A
THAT HAGEN GIRL zero (1947) PR:A-C
THAT HAMILTON WOMAN **½ (1941) PR:A
THAT HOUSE IN THE OUTSKIRTS **½ (1980, Sp.) PR:C-O
THAT I MAY LIVE ** (1937) PR:A
THAT KIND OF GIRL (SEE:MODELS, INC.)
THAT KIND OF GIRL zero (1963, Brit.) PR:O
THAT KIND OF WOMAN ** (1959) PR:C
THAT LADY ** (1955, Brit.) PR:C
THAT LADY IN ERMINE **½ (1948) PR:A
THAT LUCKY TOUCH * (1975, Brit.) PR:A-C
THAT MAD MR. JONES (SEE:FULLER BRUSH MAN, THE)
THAT MAN BOLT zero (1973) PR:O
THAT MAN FLINTSTONE (SEE:MAN CALLED FLINTSTONE, THE)
THAT MAN FROM RIO *** (1964, Fr./It.) PR:A
THAT MAN FROM TANGIER ** (1953) PR:A
THAT MAN GEORGE ** (1967, Fr./It./Sp.) PR:A-C
THAT MAN IN ISTANBUL ** (1966, Fr./It./Sp.) PR:A-C
THAT MAN MR. JONES (SEE:FULLER BRUSH MAN)
THAT MAN'S HERE AGAIN *½ (1937) PR:A
THAT MIDNIGHT KISS *** (1949) PR:A
THAT NAVY SPIRIT (SEE:HOLD 'EM NAVY)
THAT NAZTY NUISANCE *½ (1943) PR:A
THAT NIGHT *** (1957) PR:A
THAT NIGHT IN LONDON (SEE:OVERNIGHT)
THAT NIGHT IN RIO *** (1941) PR:A-C
THAT NIGHT WITH YOU ** (1945) PR:A
THAT OBSCURE OBJECT OF DESIRE ***½ (1977, Fr./Sp.) PR:O
THAT OTHER WOMAN ** (1942) PR:A
THAT RIVIERA TOUCH ** (1968, Brit.) PR:A
THAT SINKING FEELING * (1979, Brit.) PR:A**
THAT SPLENDID NOVEMBER * (1971, It./Fr.) PR:C-O
THAT SUMMER ** (1979, Brit.) PR:A-C
THAT TENDER AGE (SEE:ADOLESCENTS, THE)
THAT TENDER TOUCH * (1969) PR:O
THAT TENNESSEE BEAT *½ (1966) PR:A
THAT THEY MAY LIVE (SEE:J'ACCUSE)
THAT TOUCH OF MINK ***½ (1962) PR:C
THAT UNCERTAIN FEELING **½ (1941) PR:A
THAT WAS THEN...THIS IS NOW **½ (1985) PR:O
THAT WAY WITH WOMEN ** (1947) PR:A
THAT WOMAN ** (1968, Ger.) PR:C-O
THAT WOMAN OPPOSITE (SEE:CITY AFTER MIDNIGHT)
THAT WONDERFUL URGE *** (1948) PR:A
THAT'S LIFE **½ (1986) PR:C
THAT'S MY STORY * (1937) PR:A
THAT'S MY WIFE **½ (1933, Brit.) PR:A
THAT'S THE SPIRIT **½ (1945) PR:A
THAT'S THE WAY OF THE WORLD ** (1975) PR:C
THAT'LL BE THE DAY * (1974, Brit.) PR:C**
THAT'S A GOOD GIRL * (1933, Brit.) PR:A
THAT'S GRATITUDE * (1934) PR:A
THAT'S MY BABY *½ (1944) PR:A
THAT'S MY BOY *½ (1932) PR:A
THAT'S MY BOY ** (1951) PR:A
THAT'S MY GAL *½ (1947) PR:A
THAT'S MY MAN ** (1947) PR:A
THAT'S MY UNCLE * (1935, Brit.) PR:A
THAT'S RIGHT—YOU'RE WRONG ** (1939) PR:A
THAT'S THE TICKET *½ (1940, Brit.) PR:A
THEATRE OF BLOOD * (1973, Brit.) PR:O**
THEATRE OF DEATH ** (1967, Brit.) PR:C-O
THEATRE ROYAL *** (1943, Brit.) PR:A
THEATRE ROYAL, 1930 (SEE:ROYAL FAMILIES OF BROADWAY, THE)
THEIR BIG MOMENT *½ (1934) PR:A
THEIR NIGHT OUT ** (1933, Brit.) PR:A
THEIR OWN DESIRE **½ (1929) PR:A
THEIR SECRET AFFAIR (SEE:TOP SECRET AFFAIR)
THELMA JORDAN (SEE:FILE ON THELMA JORDAN, THE)
THEM! ***½ (1954) PR:C
THEM NICE AMERICANS ** (1958, Brit.) PR:A
THEN THERE WERE THREE *½ (1961) PR:A-C
THEODORA GOES WILD **½ (1936) PR:A
THEOREM (SEE:TEOREMA)
THERE AIN'T NO JUSTICE * (1939, Brit.) PR:A
THERE GOES KELLY * (1945) PR:A
THERE GOES MY GIRL ** (1937) PR:A
THERE GOES MY HEART **½ (1938) PR:A
THERE GOES SUSIE (SEE:SCANDALS OF PARIS)
THERE GOES THE BRIDE *½ (1933, Brit.) PR:A
THERE GOES THE BRIDE zero (1980, Brit.) PR:C
THERE GOES THE GROOM ** (1937) PR:A
THERE IS ANOTHER SUN (SEE:WALL OF DEATH)
THERE IS NO 13 ** (1977) PR:O
THERE IS STILL ROOM IN HELL *½ (1963, Ger.) PR:C-O
THERE WAS A CROOKED MAN *** (1962, Brit.) PR:A
THERE WAS A CROOKED MAN * (1970) PR:C**
THERE WAS A YOUNG LADY ** (1953, Brit.) PR:A
THERE WAS A YOUNG MAN * (1937, Brit.) PR:A
THERE WAS AN OLD COUPLE *** (1967, USSR) PR:A
THERE'S A GIRL IN MY HEART ** (1949) PR:A
THERE'S A GIRL IN MY SOUP **½ (1970, Brit.) PR:C
THERE'S ALWAYS A THURSDAY **½ (1957, Brit.) PR:A
THERE'S ALWAYS TOMORROW (SEE:ALWAYS TOMORROW)
THERE'S ALWAYS TOMORROW ***½ (1956) PR:A
THERE'S ALWAYS VANILLA *½ (1972) PR:C
THERE'S MAGIC IN MUSIC ** (1941) PR:A
THERE'S NO BUSINESS LIKE SHOW BUSINESS ***½ (1954) PR:A
THERE'S NO PLACE BY SPACE (SEE:HOLD ON)
THERE'S SOMETHING ABOUT A SOLDIER *½ (1943) PR:A
THERE'S SOMETHING FUNNY GOING ON (SEE:MAIDEN FOR A PRINCE, A)
THERE'S THAT WOMAN AGAIN ** (1938) PR:AA
THERE'S ALWAYS A WOMAN *** (1938) PR:A
THERE'S ONE BORN EVERY MINUTE **½ (1942) PR:A
THERESE *** (1963, Fr.) PR:O
THERESE ** (1986, Fr.) PR:C**
THERESE AND ISABELLE ** (1968, US/Ger.) PR:O
THERESE DESQUEYROUX (SEE:THERESE)
THERESE UND ISABELL (SEE:THERESE AND ISABELLE)
THESE ARE THE DAMNED * (1965, Brit.) PR:C**
THESE CHARMING PEOPLE *½ (1931, Brit.) PR:A
THESE DANGEROUS YEARS (SEE:DANGEROUS YOUTH)
THESE GLAMOUR GIRLS ** (1939) PR:A
THESE THIRTY YEARS ** (1934) PR:A
THESE THOUSAND HILLS *** (1959) PR:A
THESE THREE ** (1936) PR:C**
THESE WILDER YEARS *** (1956) PR:C
THESEUS AGAINST THE MINOTAUR (SEE:MINOTAUR, THE)
THEY ALL COME OUT **½ (1939) PR:A
THEY ALL DIED LAUGHING (SEE:JOLLY BAD FELLOW, A)
THEY ALL KISSED THE BRIDE ***½ (1942) PR:A-C
THEY ALL LAUGHED * (1981) PR:A**
THEY ARE GUILTY (SEE:ARE THESE OUR PARENTS?)
THEY ARE NOT ANGELS **½ (1948, Fr.) PR:A
THEY ASKED FOR IT *½ (1939) PR:A
THEY CALL HER ONE EYE zero (1974, Swed.) PR:O
THEY CALL IT SIN *½ (1932) PR:A
THEY CALL ME BRUCE zero (1982) PR:C
THEY CALL ME MISTER TIBBS **½ (1970) PR:C
THEY CALL ME ROBERT **½ (1967, USSR) PR:A
THEY CALL ME TRINITY ** (1971, It.) PR:A
THEY CAME BY NIGHT *½ (1940, Brit.) PR:A
THEY CAME FROM BEYOND SPACE *½ (1967, Brit.) PR:A
THEY CAME FROM WITHIN *½ (1976, Can.) PR:O
THEY CAME TO A CITY **½ (1944, Brit.) PR:A
THEY CAME TO BLOW UP AMERICA **½ (1943) PR:A
THEY CAME TO CORDURA ***½ (1959) PR:C-O
THEY CAME TO ROB LAS VEGAS * (1969, Fr./It./Sp./Ger.) PR:O
THEY CAN'T HANG ME ** (1955, Brit.) PR:A
THEY DARE NOT LOVE *½ (1941) PR:A
THEY DIDN'T KNOW * (1936, Brit.) PR:A
THEY DIED WITH THEIR BOOTS ON ** (1942) PR:A**
THEY DON'T WEAR PAJAMAS AT ROSIE'S (SEE:FIRST TIME, THE)

THEY DRIVE BY NIGHT ***½ (1938, Brit.) PR:C
THEY DRIVE BY NIGHT ** (1940) PR:A-C**
THEY FLEW ALONE
(SEE:WINGS AND THE WOMAN)
THEY GAVE HIM A GUN *** (1937) PR:A
THEY GOT ME COVERED ** (1943) PR:A
THEY HAD TO SEE PARIS **½ (1929) PR:A
THEY JUST HAD TO GET MARRIED *½
(1933) PR:A
THEY KNEW MR. KNIGHT * (1945, Brit.) PR:A
**THEY KNEW WHAT THEY WANTED ***½
(1940) PR:C**
THEY LEARNED ABOUT WOMEN ** (1930) PR:A
THEY LIVE ***½ (1988) PR:O
THEY LIVE BY NIGHT ** (1949) PR:C**
THEY LIVE IN FEAR ** (1944) PR:A
THEY LOVE AS THEY PLEASE
(SEE:GREENWICH VILLAGE STORY)
THEY LOVED LIFE
(SEE:KANAL)
THEY MADE HER A SPY ** (1939) PR:A
THEY MADE ME A CRIMINAL
(SEE:I BECAME A CRIMINAL)
THEY MADE ME A CRIMINAL * (1939) PR:A**
THEY MADE ME A FUGITIVE
(SEE:I BECAME A CRIMINAL)
THEY MADE ME A KILLER * (1946) PR:A
THEY MEET AGAIN *½ (1941) PR:A
THEY MET AT MIDNIGHT
(SEE:PICADILLY INCIDENT)
THEY MET IN A TAXI ** (1936) PR:A
THEY MET IN ARGENTINA *½ (1941) PR:A
THEY MET IN BOMBAY *** (1941) PR:A
THEY MET IN THE DARK ** (1945, Brit.) PR:A
THEY MET ON SKIS *½ (1940, Fr.) PR:A
THEY MIGHT BE GIANTS **½ (1971) PR:A
THEY NEVER COME BACK *½ (1932) PR:A
THEY ONLY KILL THEIR MASTERS *½ (1972) PR:C
THEY PASS THIS WAY
(SEE:FOUR FACES WEST)
THEY RAID BY NIGHT * (1942) PR:A
THEY RAN FOR THEIR LIVES *½ (1968) PR:A
THEY RODE WEST ** (1954) PR:A
THEY SAVED HITLER'S BRAIN zero (1964) PR:C
THEY SHALL HAVE MUSIC ** (1939) PR:A
**THEY SHOOT HORSES, DON'T THEY? ***½
(1969) PR:O**
THEY STILL CALL ME BRUCE **½ (1987) PR:A-C
THEY WANTED PEACE *½ (1940, USSR) PR:A
THEY WANTED TO MARRY ** (1937) PR:A
**THEY WENT THAT-A-WAY AND THAT-A-WAY *
(1978) PR:C**
THEY WERE EXPENDABLE *** (1945) PR:A**
THEY WERE FIVE *** (1938, Fr.) PR:A
THEY WERE NOT DIVIDED ** (1951, Brit.) PR:A
THEY WERE SISTERS **½ (1945, Brit.) PR:A
THEY WERE SO YOUNG ** (1955) PR:A
THEY WERE TEN ** (1961, Israel) PR:A
THEY WHO DARE **½ (1954, Brit.) PR:A
THEY WON'T BELIEVE ME ***½ (1947) PR:C
THEY WON'T FORGET **** (1937) PR:C
THEY'RE A WEIRD MOB **½ (1966, Aus.) PR:A
THEY'RE OFF
(SEE:STRAIGHT, PLACE AND SHOW)
THEY'RE PLAYING WITH FIRE * (1984) PR:O
THIEF, THE *** (1952) PR:C
THIEF ***½ (1981) PR:O
THIEF OF BAGHDAD, THE ***
(1940, Brit.) PR:AA**
THIEF OF BAGHDAD, THE ** (1961, It./Fr.) PR:A
THIEF OF DAMASCUS *½ (1952) PR:A
THIEF OF HEARTS * (1984) PR:C-O**
THIEF OF PARIS, THE *** (1967, Fr./It.) PR:A
THIEF OF VENICE, THE **½ (1952) PR:A
**THIEF WHO CAME TO DINNER, THE **
(1973) PR:A**
THIEVES *½ (1977) PR:A
THIEVES FALL OUT **½ (1941) PR:A
THIEVES' HIGHWAY *** (1949) PR:C
THIEVES' HOLIDAY
(SEE:SCANDAL IN PARIS)
THIEVES LIKE US ***½ (1974) PR:C
THIN AIR
(SEE:BODY STEALERS, THE)
THIN ICE ***½ (1937) PR:A
THIN LINE, THE *** (1967, Jap.) PR:C
THIN MAN, THE ** (1934) PR:A**
THIN MAN GOES HOME, THE **½ (1944) PR:A
THIN RED LINE, THE **½ (1964) PR:O
THING, THE *** (1951) PR:C**
THING, THE ** (1982) PR:O
THING THAT CAME FROM ANOTHER WORLD,
THE
(SEE:THING, THE)
THING THAT COULDN'T DIE, THE * (1958) PR:C
THING WITH TWO HEADS, THE ** (1972) PR:C
THING WITHOUT A FACE, A
(SEE:PYRO)
THINGS ARE LOOKING UP **½ (1934, Brit.) PR:A
THINGS ARE TOUGH ALL OVER zero (1982) PR:O
THINGS CHANGE ***½ (1988) PR:C
THINGS HAPPEN AT NIGHT * (1948, Brit.) PR:A
THINGS OF LIFE, THE *** (1970, Fr./It./Switz.) PR:C
THINGS TO COME ** (1936, Brit.) PR:C**
THINK DIRTY zero (1970, Brit.) PR:O
THINK FAST, MR. MOTO *** (1937) PR:A
THIRD ALARM, THE ** (1930) PR:A
THIRD ALIBI, THE **½ (1961, Brit.) PR:A
THIRD CLUE, THE *½ (1934, Brit.) PR:A
THIRD DAY, THE **½ (1965) PR:C
THIRD FINGER, LEFT HAND ** (1940) PR:A
THIRD KEY, THE *** (1957, Brit.) PR:A
THIRD LOVER, THE *** (1963, Fr./It.) PR:O
THIRD MAN, THE *** (1950, Brit.) PR:C**
THIRD MAN ON THE MOUNTAIN **
(1959) PR:A**
THIRD OF A MAN ** (1962) PR:C
THIRD PARTY RISK
(SEE:DEADLY MANTIS, THE)
THIRD ROAD, THE
(SEE:7TH DAWN, THE)
THIRD SECRET, THE **½ (1964, Brit.) PR:C
THIRD STRING, THE *½ (1932, Brit.) PR:A
THIRD TIME LUCKY **½ (1931, Brit.) PR:A
THIRD TIME LUCKY ** (1950, Brit.) PR:A
THIRD VISITOR, THE *½ (1951, Brit.) PR:A
THIRD VOICE, THE *** (1960) PR:O
THIRD WALKER, THE ** (1978, Can.) PR:C
THIRST ** (1979, Aus.) PR:O
THIRSTY DEAD, THE zero (1975) PR:O
13
(SEE:EYE OF THE DEVIL, THE)
THIRTEEN, THE *** (1937, USSR) PR:A
13 EAST STREET
(SEE:13 WEST STREET)
13 EAST STREET **½ (1952, Brit.) PR:A
THIRTEEN FIGHTING MEN ** (1960) PR:C
THIRTEEN FRIGHTENED GIRLS * (1963) PR:A
THIRTEEN GHOSTS **½ (1960) PR:A
THIRTEEN HOURS BY AIR **½ (1936) PR:A
THIRTEEN LEAD SOLDIERS **½ (1948) PR:A
13 MEN AND A GUN *** (1938, Brit.) PR:A
13 NUNS
(SEE:REVENGE OF THE SHOGUN WOMEN)
13 RUE MADELEINE ***½ (1946) PR:A-C
THIRTEEN WEST STREET ** (1962) PR:O
THIRTEEN WOMEN ** (1932) PR:C
THIRTEENTH CANDLE, THE *½ (1933, Brit.) PR:A
THIRTEENTH CHAIR, THE ** (1930) PR:A
THIRTEENTH CHAIR, THE ** (1937) PR:A
THIRTEENTH GUEST, THE **½ (1932) PR:A
13TH HOUR, THE *½ (1947) PR:A
THIRTEENTH LETTER, THE *** (1951) PR:C
THIRTEENTH MAN, THE ** (1937) PR:A
—30— *** (1959) PR:A-C
THIRTY-DAY PRINCESS **½ (1934) PR:A
THIRTY DAYS
(SEE:SILVER LINING)
THIRTY FOOT BRIDE OF CANDY ROCK, THE **
(1959) PR:AA
**30 IS A DANGEROUS AGE, CYNTHIA ***½
(1968, Brit.) PR:A-C**
39 STEPS, THE *** (1935, Brit.) PR:A**
THIRTY NINE STEPS, THE ** (1960, Brit.) PR:C
THIRTY NINE STEPS, THE **½ (1978, Brit.) PR:C
THIRTY SECONDS OVER TOKYO ** (1944) PR:A**
36 FILLETTE *½ (1988, Fr.) PR:O
THIRTY-SIX HOURS
(SEE:TERROR STREET)
36 HOURS *** (1965) PR:C
THIRTY SIX HOURS TO KILL **½ (1936) PR:A
THIRTY-SIX HOURS TO LIVE
(SEE:THIRTY-SIX HOURS TO KILL)
THIS ABOVE ALL ***½ (1942) PR:A
THIS ACTING BUSINESS *½ (1933, Brit.) PR:A
THIS ANGRY AGE ** (1958, It./Fr.) PR:C
THIS COULD BE THE NIGHT **½ (1957) PR:AA
THIS DAY AND AGE **½ (1933) PR:A
THIS EARTH IS MINE ** (1959) PR:O
THIS ENGLAND * (1941, Brit.) PR:A
THIS GREEN HELL *** (1936, Brit.) PR:A
THIS GUN FOR HIRE ** (1942) PR:C-O**
THIS HAPPY BREED ***½ (1944, Brit.) PR:A
THIS HAPPY FEELING **½ (1958) PR:A
THIS IMMORAL AGE
(SEE:SQUARE ROOT OF ZERO, THE)
THIS IS A HIJACK zero (1973) PR:C
THIS IS ELVIS **½ (1982) PR:A
THIS IS HEAVEN ** (1929) PR:A
THIS IS MY AFFAIR **½ (1937) PR:A
THIS IS MY LOVE *½ (1954) PR:O
THIS IS MY STREET **½ (1964, Brit.) PR:O
THIS IS NOT A TEST zero (1962) PR:A
THIS IS SPINAL TAP ***½ (1984) PR:C-O
THIS IS THE ARMY * (1943) PR:AA**
THIS IS THE LIFE *** (1933, Brit.) PR:A
THIS IS THE LIFE **½ (1935) PR:A
THIS IS THE LIFE **½ (1944) PR:A
THIS IS THE NIGHT **** (1932) PR:A
THIS ISLAND EARTH * (1955) PR:A**
THIS LAND IS MINE ***½ (1943) PR:A
THIS LOVE OF OURS **½ (1945) PR:C
THIS MAD WORLD ** (1930) PR:C
THIS MADDING CROWD **½ (1964, Jap.) PR:C
THIS MAN CAN'T DIE ** (1970, It.) PR:O
THIS MAN IN PARIS **½ (1939, Brit.) PR:A
THIS MAN IS DANGEROUS
(SEE:PATIENT VANISHES, THE)
THIS MAN IS MINE **½ (1934) PR:A
THIS MAN IS MINE **½ (1946, Brit.) PR:A
THIS MAN IS NEWS **½ (1939, Brit.) PR:A
THIS MAN MUST DIE ***½ (1970, Fr./It.) PR:O
THIS MAN REUTER
(SEE:DISPATCH FROM REUTERS, A)
THIS MAN'S NAVY **½ (1945) PR:AA
THIS MARRIAGE BUSINESS ** (1938) PR:A
THIS MODERN AGE **½ (1931) PR:A-C
THIS OTHER EDEN ** (1959, Brit.) PR:A
**THIS PROPERTY IS CONDEMNED **½
(1966) PR:O**
THIS REBEL AGE
(SEE:BEAT GENERATION, THE)
THIS REBEL BREED *½ (1960) PR:O
THIS RECKLESS AGE *½ (1932) PR:A
THIS SAVAGE LAND **½ (1969) PR:A
THIS SIDE OF HEAVEN **½ (1934) PR:AA
THIS SIDE OF THE LAW ** (1950) PR:C
THIS SPECIAL FRIENDSHIP * (1967, Fr.) PR:O**
THIS SPORTING AGE *½ (1932) PR:A
THIS SPORTING LIFE ***½ (1963, Brit.) PR:O
THIS STRANGE PASSION TORMENTS
(SEE:EL)
THIS STUFF'LL KILL YA! zero (1971) PR:O
THIS THING CALLED LOVE ** (1929) PR:C
THIS THING CALLED LOVE *** (1940) PR:O
THIS TIME FOR KEEPS * (1942) PR:A
THIS TIME FOR KEEPS ** (1947) PR:AA
THIS WAS A WOMAN ** (1949, Brit.) PR:O
THIS WAS PARIS ** (1942, Brit.) PR:C
THIS WAY PLEASE ** (1937) PR:AA
THIS WEEK OF GRACE **½ (1933, Brit.) PR:A
THIS WINE OF LOVE *** (1948, It.) PR:AA
THIS WOMAN IS DANGEROUS **½ (1952) PR:A-C
THIS WOMAN IS MINE
(SEE:18 MINUTES)
THIS WOMAN IS MINE * (1941) PR:A
THIS, THAT AND THE OTHER * (1970, Brit.) PR:O
THIS'LL MAKE YOU WHISTLE ** (1938, Brit.) PR:A
THISTLEDOWN * (1938, Brit.) PR:A
THOMAS CROWN AFFAIR, THE * (1968) PR:C**
THOMASINE AND BUSHROD **½ (1974) PR:O
THOROUGHBRED * (1932, Brit.) PR:A
THOROUGHBRED *½ (1936, Aus.) PR:C
THOROUGHBRED, THE ** (1930) PR:A
THOROUGHBREDS ** (1945) PR:AA
THOROUGHBREDS DON'T CRY **½ (1937) PR:AA
THOROUGHLY MODERN MILLIE * (1967) PR:A**
THOSE CALLOWAYS * (1964) PR:AA**
THOSE DARING YOUNG MEN IN THEIR JAUNTY
JALOPIES *½ (1969, Fr./Brit./It.) PR:A
THOSE DIRTY DOGS * (1974, US/It./Sp.) PR:C

THOSE ENDEARING YOUNG CHARMS ** (1945) PR:A
THOSE FANTASTIC FLYING FOOLS ** (1967, Brit.) PR:AA
THOSE HIGH GREY WALLS *** (1939) PR:C
THOSE KIDS FROM TOWN ** (1942, Brit.) PR:A
THOSE LIPS, THOSE EYES *** (1980) PR:O
THOSE MAGNIFICENT MEN IN THEIR FLYING MACHINES; OR HOW I FLEW FROM LONDON TO PARIS IN 25 HOURS AND 11 MINUTES ***½ (1965, Brit.) PR:A
THOSE PEOPLE NEXT DOOR * (1952, Brit.) PR:A
THOSE REDHEADS FROM SEATTLE **½ (1953) PR:AA
THOSE THREE FRENCH GIRLS *½ (1930) PR:A
THOSE WE LOVE **½ (1932) PR:C
THOSE WERE THE DAYS *** (1934, Brit.) PR:A
THOSE WERE THE DAYS *** (1940) PR:A
THOSE WERE THE HAPPY TIMES (SEE:STAR?)
THOSE WHO DANCE ** (1930) PR:A
THOSE WHO LOVE *½ (1929, Brit.) PR:A
THOU SHALT NOT KILL * (1939) PR:A
THOUSAND AND ONE NIGHTS, A *** (1945) PR:A
THOUSAND CLOWNS, A ** (1965) PR:A-C**
THOUSAND CRANES * (1969, Jap.) PR:O**
THOUSAND EYES OF DR. MABUSE, THE ***½ (1960, Fr./It./Ger.) PR:O
THOUSAND PLANE RAID, THE (SEE:1,000 PLANE RAID, THE)
THOUSANDS CHEER ***½ (1943) PR:A
THRASHIN' **½ (1986) PR:A-C
THREADS * (1932, Brit.) PR:A
THREAT, THE ** (1949) PR:O**
THREAT, THE ** (1960) PR:O
THREE *** (1967, Yugo.) PR:C
THREE *** (1969, Brit.) PR:O
THREE AMIGOS * (1986) PR:C
THREE BAD MEN IN THE HIDDEN FORTRESS (SEE:HIDDEN FORTRESS, THE)
THREE BAD SISTERS *½ (1956) PR:C
THREE BITES OF THE APPLE *½ (1967) PR:A
THREE BLIND MICE *** (1938) PR:A
THREE BLONDES IN HIS LIFE * (1961) PR:C
THREE BRAVE MEN **½ (1957) PR:A
THREE BROADWAY GIRLS (SEE:GREEKS HAD A WORD FOR THEM)
THREE BROTHERS (SEE:SIDE STREET)
THREE BROTHERS * (1982, It.) PR:C**
THREE CABALLEROS, THE ** (1944) PR:AA**
THREE CAME HOME **** (1950) PR:O
THREE CAME TO KILL * (1960) PR:C
THREE CARD MONTE ** (1978, Can.) PR:C
THREE CASES OF MURDER *** (1955, Brit.) PR:A
THREE CHEERS FOR LOVE *½ (1936) PR:A
THREE CHEERS FOR THE IRISH **½ (1940) PR:A
THREE COCKEYED SAILORS **½ (1940, Brit.) PR:A
THREE COINS IN THE FOUNTAIN *** (1954) PR:C
THREE COMRADES **** (1938) PR:A
THREE CORNERED FATE *½ (1954, Brit.) PR:A
THREE-CORNERED MOON *** (1933) PR:A
THREE CRAZY LEGIONNAIRES, THE (SEE:THREE LEGIONNAIRES, THE)
THREE CROOKED MEN ** (1958, Brit.) PR:A
THREE CROWNS OF THE SAILOR *** (1984, Fr.) PR:O
THREE DARING DAUGHTERS **½ (1948) PR:A
THREE DAYS AND A CHILD (SEE:NOT MINE TO LOVE)
THREE DAYS OF THE CONDOR ***½ (1975) PR:C-O
THREE DAYS OF VIKTOR TSCHERNIKOFF ** (1968, USSR) PR:C
THREE DESPERATE MEN ** (1951) PR:A
THREE DOLLS FROM HONG KONG *½ (1966, Jap.) PR:C
THREE DOLLS GO TO HONG KONG (SEE:THREE DOLLS FROM HONG KONG)
THREE FABLES OF LOVE ** (1963, Fr./It./Sp.) PR:C
THREE FACES EAST **½ (1930) PR:A
THREE FACES OF A WOMAN ** (1965, It.) PR:C
THREE FACES OF EVE, THE ***½ (1957) PR:A-C
THREE FACES OF SIN *½ (1963, Fr./It.) PR:O
THREE FACES WEST **½ (1940) PR:A
3:15, THE MOMENT OF TRUTH ** (1986) PR:O
THREE FOR BEDROOM C * (1952) PR:A
THREE FOR JAMIE DAWN ** (1956) PR:A
THREE FOR THE ROAD * (1987) PR:C
THREE FOR THE SHOW **½ (1955) PR:A
THREE GIRLS ABOUT TOWN ** (1941) PR:A
THREE GIRLS LOST *½ (1931) PR:A
THREE GODFATHERS **½ (1936) PR:A
THREE GODFATHERS, THE ***** (1948) PR:A
THREE GUNS FOR TEXAS * (1968) PR:A
THREE GUYS NAMED MIKE **½ (1951) PR:A
THREE HATS FOR LISA **½ (1965, Brit.) PR:A
THREE HEARTS FOR JULIA *½ (1943) PR:A
THREE HOURS **½ (1944, Fr.) PR:A
THREE HOURS TO KILL *** (1954) PR:A
365 NIGHTS IN HOLLYWOOD **½ (1934) PR:A
300 SPARTANS, THE * (1962) PR:A
300 YEAR WEEKEND zero (1971) PR:C
THREE HUSBANDS **½ (1950) PR:A
THREE IN EDEN (SEE:ISLE OF FURY)
THREE IN ONE **½ (1956, Aus.) PR:A
THREE IN THE ATTIC *½ (1968) PR:O
THREE IN THE CELLAR (SEE:UP IN THE CELLAR)
THREE IN THE SADDLE ** (1945) PR:A
THREE INTO TWO WON'T GO **** (1969, Brit.) PR:O
3 IS A FAMILY **½ (1944) PR:A
THREE KIDS AND A QUEEN ** (1935) PR:A
THREE LEGIONNAIRES, THE * (1937) PR:A
THREE LITTLE GIRLS IN BLUE *** (1946) PR:A
THREE LITTLE SISTERS **½ (1944) PR:A
THREE LITTLE WORDS ** (1950) PR:AA**
THREE LIVE GHOSTS *½ (1929) PR:A
THREE LIVE GHOSTS *½ (1935) PR:A
THREE LIVES OF THOMASINA, THE * (1963, US/Brit.) PR:AA**
THREE LOVES HAS NANCY **½ (1938) PR:A
THREE MARRIED MEN ** (1936) PR:A
THREE MAXIMS, THE (SEE:SHOW GOES ON, THE)
THREE MEN AND A BABY **½ (1987) PR:A-C
THREE MEN AND A CRADLE * (1985, Fr.) PR:C
THREE MEN AND A GIRL (SEE:KENTUCKY MOONSHINE)
THREE MEN AND A GIRL (SEE:GAY ADVENTURE, THE)
THREE MEN FROM TEXAS *** (1940) PR:A
THREE MEN IN A BOAT *½ (1933, Brit.) PR:A
THREE MEN IN A BOAT ** (1958, Brit.) PR:A
THREE MEN IN WHITE *½ (1944) PR:A
THREE MEN ON A HORSE *** (1936) PR:A
THREE MEN TO DESTROY ** (1980, Fr.) PR:O
THREE MESQUITEERS, THE **½ (1936) PR:A
THREE MOVES TO FREEDOM **½ (1960, Ger.) PR:A
THREE MUSKETEERS, THE **½ (1939) PR:A
THREE MUSKETEERS, THE ** (1948) PR:C**
THREE MUSKETEERS, THE ** (1974) PR:C**
THREE NIGHTS OF LOVE **½ (1969, It.) PR:O
THREE NUTS IN SEARCH OF A BOLT * (1964) PR:O
THREE O'CLOCK HIGH ** (1987) PR:C
THREE OF A KIND ** (1936) PR:A
THREE ON A COUCH zero (1966) PR:A
THREE ON A HONEYMOON * (1934) PR:A
THREE ON A MATCH *** (1932) PR:C
THREE ON A SPREE * (1961, Brit.) PR:A
THREE ON A TICKET **½ (1947) PR:A
THREE ON THE TRAIL ** (1936) PR:A
THREE OUTLAWS, THE ** (1956) PR:A
THREE PENNY OPERA ** (1963, Fr./Ger.) PR:A
THREE RASCALS IN THE HIDDEN FORTRESS (SEE:HIDDEN FORTRESS, THE)
THREE RING CIRCUS ** (1954) PR:A
THREE ROGUES ** (1931) PR:A
THREE RUSSIAN GIRLS *½ (1943) PR:A
THREE SAILORS AND A GIRL ** (1953) PR:A
THREE SECRETS **½ (1950) PR:A
THREE SHADES OF LOVE (SEE:THIS REBEL BREED)
THREE SILENT MEN ** (1940, Brit.) PR:A
THREE SINNERS (SEE:THREE FACES OF SIN)
THREE SISTERS, THE ** (1930) PR:A
THREE SISTERS, THE ** (1969, USSR) PR:C
THREE SISTERS ***½ (1974, Brit.) PR:C
THREE SISTERS, THE ** (1977) PR:A
THREE SMART GIRLS *** (1937) PR:AA
THREE SMART GIRLS GROW UP *** (1939) PR:A
THREE SONS * (1939) PR:A
THREE SONS O'GUNS ** (1941) PR:A
THREE SPARE WIVES * (1962, Brit.) PR:A
THREE STEPS IN THE DARK * (1953, Brit.) PR:A
THREE STEPS NORTH * (1951) PR:A
THREE STOOGES GO AROUND THE WORLD IN A DAZE, THE * (1963) PR:AA
THREE STOOGES IN ORBIT, THE * (1962) PR:AA
THREE STOOGES MEET HERCULES, THE * (1962) PR:AA
THREE STOOGES VS. THE WONDER WOMEN * (1975, It./Chi.) PR:C
THREE STRANGERS ***½ (1946) PR:A-C
THREE STRIPES IN THE SUN ** (1955) PR:A
THREE SUNDAYS TO LIVE * (1957, Brit.) PR:A
THREE TALES OF CHEKHOV ** (1961, USSR) PR:A
3:10 TO YUMA ***½ (1957) PR:O
THREE TEXAS STEERS *½ (1939) PR:A
THREE THE HARD WAY **½ (1974) PR:O
3,000 A.D. (SEE:CAPTIVE WOMEN)
THREE TO GO **½ (1971, Aus.) PR:A-C
THREE TOUGH GUYS ** (1974, US/It.) PR:C
THREE VIOLENT PEOPLE **½ (1956) PR:A
THREE WARRIORS ** (1977) PR:A
THREE-WAY SPLIT * (1970) PR:O
THREE WEEKS OF LOVE * (1965) PR:A
THREE WEIRD SISTERS, THE ** (1948, Brit.) PR:A
THREE WHO LOVED *½ (1931) PR:A
THREE WISE FOOLS ** (1946) PR:A
THREE WISE GIRLS ** (1932) PR:A
THREE WISE GUYS, THE * (1936) PR:A
THREE WITNESSES * (1935, Brit.) PR:A
THREE WOMEN *** (1977) PR:C
THREE WORLDS OF GULLIVER, THE **½ (1960, Brit.) PR:AA
THREE YOUNG TEXANS ** (1954) PR:A
THREEPENNY OPERA, THE * (1931, Ger./US) PR:O**
THREE'S A CROWD *½ (1945) PR:A
THREE'S COMPANY * (1953, Brit.) PR:A
THREES, MENAGE A TROIS * (1968) PR:O
THRESHOLD **½ (1983, Can.) PR:C
THRILL HUNTER, THE ** (1933) PR:A
THRILL KILLERS, THE * (1965) PR:O
THRILL OF A LIFETIME ** (1937) PR:A
THRILL OF A ROMANCE **½ (1945) PR:A
THRILL OF BRAZIL, THE ** (1946) PR:A
THRILL OF IT ALL, THE * (1963) PR:A**
THRILL OF YOUTH zero (1932) PR:C
THRILL SEEKERS (SEE:GUTTER GIRLS)
THRONE OF BLOOD ** (1961, Jap.) PR:O**
THROUGH A GLASS DARKLY * (1962, Swed.) PR:O**
THROUGH DAYS AND MONTHS **½ (1969, Jap.) PR:A-C
THROUGH DIFFERENT EYES (SEE:THRU DIFFERENT EYES)
THROUGH HELL TO GLORY (SEE:JET ATTACK)
THROUGH THE STORM (SEE:PRAIRIE SCHOONERS)
THROW MOMMA FROM THE TRAIN **½ (1987) PR:C-O
THROWBACK, THE ** (1935) PR:A
THRU DIFFERENT EYES ** (1929) PR:A
THRU DIFFERENT EYES ** (1942) PR:A
THUMB TRIPPING ** (1972) PR:O
THUMBELINA * (1970) PR:AA**
THUMBS UP ** (1943) PR:A
THUNDER ACROSS THE PACIFIC (SEE:WILD BLUE YONDER, THE)
THUNDER AFLOAT **½ (1939) PR:A
THUNDER ALLEY *½ (1967) PR:A
THUNDER AND LIGHTNING **½ (1977) PR:C
THUNDER AT THE BORDER ** (1966, Ger./Yugo.) PR:A
THUNDER BAY * (1953) PR:A**
THUNDER BELOW *½ (1932) PR:A
THUNDER BIRDS **½ (1942) PR:A
THUNDER IN CAROLINA *½ (1960) PR:A
THUNDER IN DIXIE * (1965) PR:A
THUNDER IN GOD'S COUNTRY ** (1951) PR:A
THUNDER IN THE BLOOD ** (1962, Fr.) PR:C
THUNDER IN THE CITY * (1937, Brit.) PR:A**
THUNDER IN THE DESERT ** (1938) PR:A
THUNDER IN THE DUST (SEE:SUNDOWNERS, THE)
THUNDER IN THE EAST (SEE:BATTLE, THE)
THUNDER IN THE EAST *** (1953) PR:A
THUNDER IN THE NIGHT *½ (1935) PR:A
THUNDER IN THE PINES ** (1949) PR:A
THUNDER IN THE SUN *½ (1959) PR:A
THUNDER IN THE VALLEY (SEE:BOB, SON OF BATTLE)
THUNDER ISLAND ** (1963) PR:A-C
THUNDER MOUNTAIN **½ (1935) PR:A
THUNDER MOUNTAIN ** (1947) PR:A
THUNDER MOUNTAIN (SEE:SHEPHERD OF THE HILLS, THE)
THUNDER OF DRUMS, A **½ (1961) PR:A-C
THUNDER ON THE HILL *** (1951) PR:A
THUNDER ON THE TRAIL (SEE:THUNDERING TRAIL, THE)
THUNDER OVER ARIZONA ** (1956) PR:A
THUNDER OVER HAWAII (SEE:NAKED PARADISE)
THUNDER OVER SANGOLAND ** (1955) PR:A
THUNDER OVER TANGIER * (1957, Brit.) PR:A
THUNDER OVER TEXAS ** (1934) PR:A
THUNDER OVER THE PLAINS **½ (1953) PR:A
THUNDER OVER THE PRAIRIE ** (1941) PR:A
THUNDER PASS (SEE:THUNDER TRAIL)
THUNDER PASS ** (1954) PR:A

THUNDER RIVER FEUD *½ (1942) PR:A
THUNDER ROAD * (1958) PR:C**
THUNDER ROCK ***½ (1944, Brit.) PR:A
THUNDER RUN * (1986) PR:C
THUNDER TOWN *½ (1946) PR:A
THUNDER TRAIL **½ (1937) PR:A
THUNDER WARRIOR ** (1986, It.) PR:O
THUNDERBALL **½ (1965, Brit.) PR:A-C
THUNDERBIRD 6 ** (1968, Brit.) PR:A
THUNDERBIRDS **½ (1952) PR:A
THUNDERBIRDS ARE GO **½ (1968, Brit.) PR:A
THUNDERBOLT zero (1936) PR:A-C
THUNDERBOLT *** (1929) PR:A
**THUNDERBOLT AND LIGHTFOOT ***½
(1974) PR:O**
THUNDERCLOUD
(SEE:COLT .45)
THUNDERHEAD-SON OF FLICKA ****
(1945) PR:AA
THUNDERHOOF *** (1948) PR:A
THUNDERING CARAVANS ** (1952) PR:A
THUNDERING FRONTIER * (1940) PR:A
THUNDERING GUN SLINGERS *½ (1944) PR:A
THUNDERING HERD, THE **½ (1934) PR:A
THUNDERING HOOFS *½ (1941) PR:A
THUNDERING JETS * (1958) PR:A
THUNDERING TRAIL, THE * (1951) PR:A
THUNDERING TRAILS ** (1943) PR:A
THUNDERING WEST, THE ** (1939) PR:A
THUNDERING WHEELS
(SEE:THUNDER IN DIXIE)
THUNDERSTORM ** (1934, USSR) PR:A
THUNDERSTORM ** (1956) PR:A
THURSDAY'S CHILD ** (1943, Brit.) PR:A
THX 1138 * (1971) PR:C**
THY NEIGHBOR'S WIFE *½ (1953) PR:C
TI-CUL TOUGAS ** (1977, Can.) PR:C
TIARA TAHITI **½ (1962, Brit.) PR:A
...TICK...TICK...TICK... **½ (1970) PR:A
TICKET * (1987, S.K.) PR:O
TICKET OF LEAVE * (1936, Brit.) PR:A
TICKET OF LEAVE MAN, THE * (1937, Brit.) PR:A
TICKET TO CRIME *½ (1934) PR:A
TICKET TO HEAVEN * (1981) PR:C**
TICKET TO PARADISE *½ (1936) PR:A
TICKET TO PARADISE * (1961, Brit.) PR:A
TICKET TO TOMAHAWK **½ (1950) PR:A
TICKLE ME ** (1965) PR:A
TICKLED PINK
(SEE:MAGIC SPECTACLES)
TICKLISH AFFAIR, A ** (1963) PR:A
TIDAL WAVE
(SEE:S.O.S. TIDAL WAVE)
TIDAL WAVE * (1975, US/Jap.) PR:A-C
TIERRA BRUTAL
(SEE:SAVAGE GUNS, THE)
TIFFANY JONES ** (1976) PR:O
TIGER AMONG US, THE
(SEE:13 WEST STREET)
TIGER AND THE FLAME, THE **½
(1955, India) PR:A-C
TIGER AND THE PUSSYCAT, THE **½
(1967, U.S./It.) PR:A-C
TIGER BAY * (1933, Brit.) PR:A
TIGER BAY ***½ (1959, Brit.) PR:A
TIGER BY THE TAIL
(SEE:CROSSUP)
TIGER BY THE TAIL ** (1970) PR:C
TIGER FANGS *½ (1943) PR:A
TIGER FLIGHT * (1965, Jap.) PR:A
TIGER GIRL ** (1955, USSR) PR:A
TIGER IN THE SKY
(SEE:MCCONNELL STORY, THE)
TIGER IN THE SMOKE **½ (1956, Brit.) PR:A
TIGER MAKES OUT, THE ** (1967) PR:A-C
TIGER MAN
(SEE:LADY AND THE MONSTER, THE)
TIGER OF BENGAL
(SEE:JOURNEY TO THE LOST CITY)
TIGER OF ESCHNAPUR, THE
(SEE:JOURNEY TO THE LOST CITY)
TIGER OF THE SEVEN SEAS ** (1964, Fr./It.) PR:A
TIGER ROSE ** (1930) PR:A
TIGER SHARK ***½ (1932) PR:A-C
TIGER WALKS, A ** (1964) PR:C
TIGER WOMAN, THE *½ (1945) PR:A
TIGER'S TALE, A ** (1988) PR:C-O

TIGHT LITTLE ISLAND * (1949, Brit.) PR:A**
TIGHT SHOES **½ (1941) PR:A
TIGHT SKIRTS
(SEE:TIGHT SKIRTS, LOOSE PLEASURES)
TIGHT SKIRTS, LOOSE PLEASURES **
(1966, Fr.) PR:O
TIGHT SPOT ***½ (1955) PR:O
TIGHTROPE **½ (1984) PR:C-O
TIJUANA STORY, THE * (1957) PR:A
TIKI TIKI ***½ (1971, Can.) PR:AA
TIKO AND THE SHARK **½ (1966, US/It./Fr.) PR:A
TIKOYO AND HIS SHARK
(SEE:TIKO AND HIS SHARK)
'TIL WE MEET AGAIN *** (1940) PR:A
TILL DEATH * (1978) PR:C-O
TILL DEATH DO US PART
(SEE:ALF 'N' FAMILY)
TILL MARRIAGE DO US PART ** (1979, It.) PR:O
TILL THE CLOUDS ROLL BY * (1946) PR:AA**
TILL THE END OF TIME * (1946) PR:A-C**
TILL TOMORROW COMES **½ (1962, Jap.) PR:C
TILL WE MEET AGAIN **½ (1936) PR:A
TILL WE MEET AGAIN ** (1944) PR:A
TILLIE AND GUS *** (1933) PR:A
TILLIE THE TOILER *½ (1941) PR:A
TILLY OF BLOOMSBURY ** (1931, Brit.) PR:A
TILLY OF BLOOMSBURY *½ (1940, Brit.) PR:A
TILT ** (1979) PR:C
TIM **½ (1981, Aus.) PR:C
TIM DRISCOLL'S DONKEY ** (1955, Brit.) PR:AA
**TIN DRUM, THE ***½
(1979, Ger./Fr./Yugo./Pol.) PR:O**
TIMBER ** (1942) PR:A
TIMBER FURY *½ (1950) PR:A
TIMBER QUEEN *½ (1944) PR:A
TIMBER STAMPEDE ** (1939) PR:A
TIMBER TERRORS *½ (1935) PR:A
TIMBER TRAIL, THE ** (1948) PR:A
TIMBER WAR *½ (1936) PR:A
TIMBERJACK * (1955) PR:A
TIMBUCTOO ** (1933, Brit.) PR:A
TIMBUKTU ** (1959) PR:A
TIME AFTER TIME * (1979, Brit.) PR:O**
TIME AFTER TIME *½ (1985, Brit.) PR:A-C
TIME AND THE TOUCH, THE *½ (1962) PR:C
TIME BANDITS * (1981, Brit.) PR:A-C**
TIME BOMB
(SEE:TERROR ON A TRAIN)
TIME BOMB **½ (1961, Fr./It.) PR:A
TIME FLIES ** (1944, Brit.) PR:A
TIME FOR ACTION
(SEE:TIP ON A DEAD JOCKEY)
TIME FOR DYING, A *** (1971) PR:C
TIME FOR GIVING, A
(SEE:GENERATION)
TIME FOR HEROS, A
(SEE:HELL WITH HEROS, THE)
TIME FOR KILLING, A **½ (1967) PR:A
TIME FOR LOVING, A ** (1971, Brit.) PR:A-C
TIME GENTLEMEN PLEASE? **½ (1953, Brit.) PR:A
TIME IN THE SUN, A *½ (1970, Swed.) PR:O
TIME IS MY ENEMY ** (1957, Brit.) PR:A
TIME LIMIT **** (1957) PR:C
TIME LOCK ** (1959, Brit.) PR:A
TIME LOST AND TIME REMEMBERED **½
(1966, Brit.) PR:A
TIME MACHINE, THE ** (1963, Brit./US) PR:A**
TIME OF DESIRE, THE * (1957, Swed.) PR:O
TIME OF DESTINY, A * (1988) PR:C
TIME OF HIS LIFE, THE ** (1955, Brit.) PR:A
TIME OF INDIFFERENCE ** (1965, Fr./It.) PR:A
TIME OF RETURN, THE
(SEE:MURIEL)
TIME OF ROSES *** (1970, Fin.) PR:C
TIME OF THE HEATHEN *½ (1962) PR:C
TIME OF THE WOLVES **½ (1970, Fr.) PR:O
TIME OF THEIR LIVES, THE ***½ (1946) PR:AA
TIME OF YOUR LIFE, THE ***½ (1948) PR:A-C
TIME OUT FOR LOVE ** (1963, It./Fr.) PR:A
TIME OUT FOR MURDER *½ (1938) PR:A
TIME OUT FOR RHYTHM * (1941) PR:A
TIME OUT FOR ROMANCE ** (1937) PR:A
TIME OUT OF MIND *½ (1947) PR:A
TIME SLIP **½ (1981, Jap.) PR:C
TIME, THE PLACE AND THE GIRL, THE **
(1929) PR:A

TIME, THE PLACE AND THE GIRL, THE **
(1946) PR:A
TIME TO DIE, A ** (1983) PR:O
TIME TO DIE, A ***½ (1985, Colombia/Cuba) PR:C
TIME TO KILL ** (1942) PR:A
TIME TO KILL, A ** (1955, Brit.) PR:A
**TIME TO LOVE AND A TIME TO DIE, A **½
(1958) PR:A-C**
TIME TO REMEMBER *½ (1962, Brit.) PR:A
TIME TO SING, A *½ (1968) PR:A
TIME TRAP
(SEE:TIME TRAVELERS, THE)
TIME TRAVELERS, THE **½ (1964) PR:A
TIME WALKER *½ (1982) PR:A
TIME WITHOUT PITY **½ (1957, Brit.) PR:C
TIMERIDER **½ (1983) PR:C
TIMES GONE BY **½ (1953, It.) PR:C
TIMES SQUARE ** (1929) PR:A
TIMES SQUARE *½ (1980) PR:O
TIMES SQUARE LADY ** (1935) PR:A
TIMES SQUARE PLAYBOY *½ (1936) PR:A
TIMES TO COME ** (1988, Arg.) PR:O
TIMESLIP
(SEE:ATOMIC MAN, THE)
TIMETABLE **½ (1956) PR:A
TIMOTHY'S QUEST *½ (1936) PR:A
TIN GIRL, THE ** (1970, It.) PR:A
TIN GODS *½ (1932, Brit.) PR:A
TIN MAN ** (1983) PR:A
TIN MEN * (1987) PR:C-O**
TIN PAN ALLEY **½ (1940) PR:A
TIN STAR, THE * (1957) PR:A**
TINDER BOX, THE **½ (1968, E. Ger.) PR:AA
TINGLER, THE **½ (1959) PR:C
TINKER *½ (1949, Brit.) PR:A
**TINTORERA...BLOODY WATERS *
(1977, Brit./Mex.) PR:O**
TIOGA KID, THE *½ (1948) PR:A
TIP-OFF, THE ** (1931) PR:A
TIP-OFF GIRLS **½ (1938) PR:A
TIP ON A DEAD JOCKEY **½ (1957) PR:A-C
TIRE AU FLANC
(SEE:ARMY GAME, THE)
TIREZ SUR LE PIANISTE
(SEE:SHOOT THE PIANO PLAYER)
'TIS A PITY SHE'S A WHORE *½ (1973, It.) PR:O
TISH **½ (1942) PR:A
TITANIC ***½ (1953) PR:A-C
TITFIELD THUNDERBOLT, THE **½
(1953, Brit.) PR:A
TITLE SHOT * (1982, Can.) PR:C
TNT JACKSON zero (1975) PR:O
TO ALL A GOODNIGHT zero (1980) PR:O
TO BE A CROOK **½ (1967, Fr.) PR:A
TO BE A LADY *½ (1934, Brit.) PR:A
TO BE A MAN
(SEE:CRY OF BATTLE)
TO BE FREE *½ (1972) PR:O
TO BE OR NOT TO BE *** (1942) PR:A**
TO BE OR NOT TO BE **½ (1983) PR:C
TO BEAT THE BAND *½ (1935) PR:A
TO BED OR NOT TO BED
(SEE:DEVIL, THE)
TO BEGIN AGAIN ** (1982, Sp.) PR:C
TO CATCH A COP zero (1984, Fr.) PR:A
TO CATCH A SPY
(SEE:CATCH ME A SPY)
TO CATCH A THIEF * (1936, Brit.) PR:A
TO CATCH A THIEF ** (1955) PR:C**
TO COMMIT A MURDER ** (1970, Fr./It./Ger.) PR:C
TO DENDRO POU PLIGONAME
(SEE:TREE WE HURT, THE)
TO DOROTHY, A SON
(SEE:CASH ON DELIVERY)
TO EACH HIS OWN **** (1946) PR:A-C
TO ELVIS WITH LOVE
(SEE:TOUCHED BY LOVE)
TO FIND A MAN ** (1972) PR:A
TO HAVE AND HAVE NOT ** (1944) PR:A-C**
TO HAVE AND TO HOLD ** (1951, Brit.) PR:A
TO HAVE AND TO HOLD *½ (1963, Brit.) PR:A
TO HELL AND BACK * (1955) PR:A-C**
TO KILL A CLOWN ** (1972) PR:C-O
TO KILL A MOCKINGBIRD ** (1962) PR:C**
TO KILL A STRANGER **½ (1985) PR:O
TO KILL OR TO DIE * (1973, It.) PR:C

Finding entries in **THE MOTION PICTURE GUIDE** ™

Years 1929-83	Volumes I-IX
1984	Volume IX
1985	1986 ANNUAL
1986	1987 ANNUAL
1987	1988 ANNUAL
1988	1989 ANNUAL

STAR RATINGS

★★★★★ Masterpiece
★★★★ Excellent
★★★ Good
★★ Fair
★ Poor
zero Without Merit

PARENTAL RECOMMENDATION (PR:)

AA Good for Children
A Acceptable for Children
C Cautionary, some objectionable scenes
O Objectionable for Children

BOLD: Films on Videocassette

TO LIVE
(SEE:IKIRU)
TO LIVE AND DIE IN L.A. * (1985) PR:O
TO LIVE IN PEACE *** (1947, It.) PR:A
TO LOVE *** (1964, Swed.) PR:O
TO MARY—WITH LOVE ** (1936) PR:A
TO OBLIGE A LADY * (1931, Brit.) PR:A
TO OUR LOVES
(SEE:A NOS AMOURS)
TO PARIS WITH LOVE **½ (1955, Brit.) PR:A
TO PLEASE A LADY **½ (1950) PR:A
TO SIR, WITH LOVE * (1967, Brit.) PR:A**
TO THE DEVIL A DAUGHTER **
(1976, Brit./Ger.) PR:O
TO THE ENDS OF THE EARTH *** (1948) PR:A-C
TO THE LAST MAN ** (1933) PR:A
TO THE SHORES OF HELL ** (1966) PR:A
TO THE SHORES OF TRIPOLI *** (1942) PR:A
TO THE VICTOR **½ (1938, Brit.) PR:A
TO THE VICTOR ** (1948) PR:A
TO TRAP A SPY *½ (1966) PR:A
TO WHAT RED HELL ** (1929, Brit.) PR:A
TOAST OF NEW ORLEANS ** (1950) PR:A
TOAST OF NEW YORK, THE ***½ (1937) PR:A
TOAST OF THE LEGION
(SEE:KISS ME AGAIN)
TOAST TO LOVE * (1951, Mex.) PR:A
TOBACCO ROAD **** (1941) PR:A
TOBOR THE GREAT ** (1954) PR:AA
TOBRUK **½ (1966) PR:A
TOBY MCTEAGUE ** (1986, Can.) PR:A
TOBY TYLER * (1960) PR:AA**
TODAY * (1930) PR:A
TODAY I HANG ** (1942) PR:A
TODAY IT'S ME. . .TOMORROW YOU? **½
(1968, It.) PR:C
TODAY WE LIVE **½ (1933) PR:C
TODAY WE LIVE
(SEE:DAY AND THE HOUR, THE)
TODD KILLINGS, THE * (1971) PR:O
TOGETHER **½ (1956, Brit.) PR:A
TOGETHER AGAIN *** (1944) PR:A
TOGETHER BROTHERS *** (1974) PR:C
TOGETHER FOR DAYS *½ (1972) PR:C
TOGETHER IN PARIS
(SEE:PARIS WHEN IT SIZZLES)
TOGETHER WE LIVE *½ (1935) PR:A
TOILERS OF THE SEA *½ (1936, Brit.) PR:A
TOKYO AFTER DARK ** (1959) PR:A
TOKYO FILE 212 *½ (1951) PR:A
TOKYO JOE * (1949) PR:A**
TOKYO POP * (1988, Jap.) PR:O**
TOKYO ROSE ** (1945) PR:A
TOKYO STORY **** (1972, Jap.) PR:A
TOL'ABLE DAVID ** (1930) PR:A
TOLL OF THE DESERT * (1936) PR:A
TOM * (1973) PR:O
TOM BROWN OF CULVER **½ (1932) PR:AA
TOM BROWN'S SCHOOL DAYS ** (1940) PR:AA
TOM BROWN'S SCHOOLDAYS **
(1951, Brit.) PR:AA
TOM, DICK AND HARRY ***½ (1941) PR:A
TOM HORN ***½ (1980) PR:O
TOM JONES *** (1963, Brit.) PR:O**
TOM SAWYER *** (1930) PR:AA
TOM SAWYER
(SEE:ADVENTURES OF TOM SAWYER, THE)
TOM SAWYER **½ (1973) PR:AA
TOM SAWYER, DETECTIVE *½ (1939) PR:A
TOM THUMB **½ (1958, Brit./US) PR:AA
TOM THUMB * (1967, Mex.) PR:A
TOMAHAWK ** (1951) PR:A
TOMAHAWK AND THE CROSS, THE
(SEE:PILLARS OF THE SKY)
TOMAHAWK TRAIL ** (1957) PR:A
TOMAHAWK TRAIL, THE
(SEE:IROQUOIS TRAIL, THE)
TOMB OF LIGEIA, THE ** (1965, Brit.) PR:C
TOMB OF THE CAT
(SEE:TOMB OF LIGEIA, THE)
TOMB OF THE LIVING DEAD
(SEE:MAD DOCTOR OF BLOOD ISLAND, THE)
TOMB OF THE UNDEAD * (1972) PR:O
TOMB OF TORTURE * (1966, It.) PR:O
TOMBOY * (1985) PR:O
TOMBOY ** (1940) PR:A
TOMBOY AND THE CHAMP *½ (1961) PR:A
TOMBS OF HORROR
(SEE:CASTLE OF BLOOD)
TOMBSTONE CANYON **½ (1932) PR:A
TOMBSTONE TERROR *½ (1935) PR:A
TOMBSTONE, THE TOWN TOO TOUGH TO DIE **½
(1942) PR:A
TOMCAT, THE * (1968, Brit.) PR:O
TOMMY *½ (1975, Brit.) PR:C
TOMMY STEELE STORY, THE
(SEE:ROCK AROUND THE WORLD)
TOMMY THE TOREADOR ** (1960, Brit.) PR:A

TOMORROW ***½ (1972) PR:C
TOMORROW AND TOMORROW **½ (1932) PR:A
TOMORROW AT MIDNIGHT
(SEE:FOR LOVE OR MONEY)
TOMORROW AT SEVEN ** (1933) PR:A
TOMORROW AT TEN **½ (1964, Brit.) PR:A
TOMORROW IS ANOTHER DAY ** (1951) PR:A
TOMORROW IS FOREVER ** (1946) PR:A
TOMORROW IS MY TURN **
(1962, Fr./It./Ger.) PR:C
TOMORROW NEVER COMES *½
(1978, Brit./Can.) PR:O
TOMORROW THE WORLD ***½ (1944) PR:A
TOMORROW WE LIVE * (1936, Brit.) PR:C
TOMORROW WE LIVE **½ (1942) PR:A
TOMORROW WE LIVE
(SEE:AT DAWN WE DIE)
TOMORROW'S YOUTH * (1935) PR:A
TONI ***½ (1968, Fr.) PR:C
TONIGHT A TOWN DIES ** (1961, Pol.) PR:C
TONIGHT AND EVERY NIGHT * (1945) PR:A**
TONIGHT AT 8:30 *** (1953, Brit.) PR:A
TONIGHT AT TWELVE ** (1929) PR:A
TONIGHT FOR SURE zero (1962) PR:O
TONIGHT IS OURS ** (1933) PR:A
TONIGHT OR NEVER ** (1931) PR:A-C
TONIGHT THE SKIRTS FLY *½ (1956, Fr.) PR:C
TONIGHT WE RAID CALAIS **½ (1943) PR:A
TONIGHT WE SING **½ (1953) PR:A
TONIGHT'S THE NIGHT ** (1932, Brit.) PR:A
TONIGHT'S THE NIGHT ** (1954, Brit.) PR:A
TONIO KROGER * (1968, Fr./Ger.) PR:C
TONKA **½ (1958) PR:AA
TONS OF MONEY *½ (1931, Brit.) PR:A
TONS OF TROUBLE **½ (1956, Brit.) PR:AA
TONTO BASIN OUTLAWS ** (1941) PR:A
TONY DRAWS A HORSE **½ (1951, Brit.) PR:A-C
TONY ROME * (1967) PR:C**
TOO BAD SHE'S BAD ** (1954, It.) PR:C
TOO BUSY TO WORK *½ (1932) PR:A
TOO BUSY TO WORK ** (1939) PR:A
TOO DANGEROUS TO LIVE ** (1939, Brit.) PR:A
TOO DANGEROUS TO LOVE
(SEE:PERFECT STRANGERS)
TOO HOT TO HANDLE *** (1938) PR:A-C
TOO HOT TO HANDLE * (1961, Brit.) PR:C
TOO LATE BLUES **½ (1962) PR:C
TOO LATE FOR TEARS *** (1949) PR:O
TOO LATE THE HERO ** (1970) PR:C
TOO MANY BLONDES * (1941) PR:A
TOO MANY CHEFS
(SEE:WHO IS KILLING THE GREAT CHEFS OF
EUROPE)
TOO MANY COOKS *½ (1931) PR:A
TOO MANY CROOKS **½ (1959, Brit.) PR:A
TOO MANY GIRLS **½ (1940) PR:A
TOO MANY HUSBANDS *½ (1938, Brit.) PR:AA
TOO MANY HUSBANDS *** (1940) PR:A
TOO MANY MILLIONS ** (1934, Brit.) PR:A
TOO MANY PARENTS **½ (1936) PR:A
TOO MANY THIEVES ** (1968) PR:A
TOO MANY WINNERS ** (1947) PR:A
TOO MANY WIVES ** (1933, Brit.) PR:A
TOO MANY WIVES * (1937) PR:A
TOO MANY WOMEN
(SEE:GOD'S GIFT TO WOMEN)
TOO MANY WOMEN * (1942) PR:A
TOO MUCH BEEF *½ (1936) PR:A
TOO MUCH FOR ONE MAN
(SEE:CLIMAX, THE)
TOO MUCH HARMONY ** (1933) PR:A
TOO MUCH, TOO SOON ** (1958) PR:C
TOO SCARED TO SCREAM ** (1985) PR:O
TOO SOON TO LOVE ** (1960) PR:C
TOO TOUGH TO KILL *½ (1935) PR:A
TOO YOUNG TO KISS ** (1951) PR:A
TOO YOUNG TO KNOW ** (1945) PR:A
TOO YOUNG TO LOVE *½ (1960, Brit.) PR:C
TOO YOUNG TO MARRY *½ (1931) PR:A
TOO YOUNG, TOO IMMORAL! zero (1962) PR:O
TOOLBOX MURDERS, THE zero (1978) PR:O
TOOMORROW * (1970, Brit.) PR:A
TOOTSIE ** (1982) PR:C**
TOP BANANA ***½ (1954) PR:A
TOP FLOOR GIRL *½ (1959, Brit.) PR:A
TOP GUN **½ (1955) PR:A-C
TOP GUN ** (1986) PR:A-C
TOP HAT ** (1935) PR:A**
TOP JOB
(SEE:GRAND SLAM)
TOP MAN ** (1943) PR:A
TOP O' THE MORNING ** (1949) PR:A
TOP OF THE BILL
(SEE:FANNY FOLEY HERSELF)
TOP OF THE FORM ** (1953, Brit.) PR:A
TOP OF THE HEAP * (1972) PR:O
TOP OF THE TOWN ** (1937) PR:A
TOP OF THE WORLD ** (1955) PR:A

TOP SECRET
(SEE:MR. POTTS GOES TO MOSCOW)
TOP SECRET! * (1984) PR:C**
TOP SECRET AFFAIR **½ (1957) PR:A
TOP SENSATION
(SEE:SEDUCERS, THE)
TOP SERGEANT ** (1942) PR:A
TOP SERGEANT MULLIGAN * (1941) PR:A
TOP SPEED *** (1930) PR:A
TOPAZ ***½ (1969, Brit.) PR:C
TOPAZE **½ (1933) PR:C
TOPAZE ** (1935, Fr.) PR:A
TOPEKA **½ (1953) PR:A
TOPEKA TERROR, THE ** (1945) PR:A
TOPKAPI ** (1964) PR:A-C**
TOPPER ** (1937) PR:A**
TOPPER RETURNS *** (1941) PR:A
TOPPER TAKES A TRIP ***½ (1939) PR:A
TOPS IS THE LIMIT
(SEE:ANYTHING GOES)
TOPSY-TURVY JOURNEY ** (1970, Jap.) PR:A
TORA-SAN PART 2 *½ (1970, Jap.) PR:C
TORA-SAN'S CHERISHED MOTHER
(SEE:TORA-SAN PART 2)
TORA! TORA! TORA! **½ (1970, US/Jap.) PR:C
TORCH, THE ** (1950) PR:A
TORCH SINGER ** (1933) PR:A
TORCH SONG **½ (1953) PR:A
TORCH SONG TRILOGY **½ (1988) PR:O
TORCHLIGHT *½ (1984) PR:O
TORCHY BLANE IN CHINATOWN *½ (1938) PR:A
TORCHY BLANE IN PANAMA ** (1938) PR:A
TORCHY BLANE RUNS FOR MAYOR
(SEE:TORCHY RUNS FOR MAYOR)
TORCHY BLANE, THE ADVENTUROUS BLONDE
(SEE:ADVENTUROUS BLONDE)
TORCHY GETS HER MAN ** (1938) PR:A
TORCHY PLAYS WITH DYNAMITE ** (1939) PR:A
TORCHY RUNS FOR MAYOR ** (1939) PR:A
TORMENT ***½ (1947, Swed.) PR:A-C
TORMENT
(SEE:PAPER GALLOWS)
TORMENT * (1986) PR:O
TORMENTED * (1960) PR:C
TORMENTED, THE zero (1978, It.) PR:O
TORN CURTAIN * (1966) PR:C**
TORNADO ** (1943) PR:A
TORNADO RANGE ** (1948) PR:A
TORPEDO ALLEY **½ (1953) PR:A
TORPEDO BAY ** (1964, It./Fr.) PR:C
TORPEDO BOAT * (1942) PR:A
TORPEDO RUN **½ (1958) PR:A-C
TORPEDOED ** (1939) PR:C
TORRID ZONE **** (1940) PR:A
TORSO * (1974, It.) PR:O
TORSO MURDER MYSTERY, THE **½
(1940, Brit.) PR:C
TORTILLA FLAT ***** (1942) PR:A
TORTURE CHAMBER OF DR. SADISM, THE
(SEE:BLOOD DEMON, THE)
TORTURE DUNGEON zero (1970) PR:O
TORTURE GARDEN **½ (1968, Brit.) PR:O
TORTURE ME KISS ME * (1970) PR:O
TORTURE SHIP *½ (1939) PR:A
TOTO AND THE POACHERS *½ (1958, Brit.) PR:AA
TOTO IN THE MOON *½ (1957, It./Sp.) PR:A
TOTO, VITTORIO E LA DOTTORESSA
(SEE:LADY DOCTOR, THE)
TOUCH AND GO
(SEE:LIGHT TOUCH, THE)
TOUCH AND GO *½ (1980, Aus.) PR:C
TOUCH AND GO * (1986) PR:C-O**
TOUCH ME NOT ** (1974, Brit.) PR:C
TOUCH OF CLASS, A ** (1973, Brit.) PR:C**
TOUCH OF DEATH *½ (1962, Brit.) PR:A
TOUCH OF EVIL *** (1958) PR:C**
TOUCH OF FLESH, THE ** (1960) PR:C
TOUCH OF HELL, A
(SEE:IMMORAL CHARGE)
TOUCH OF HER FLESH, THE zero (1967) PR:O
TOUCH OF HER LIFE, THE
(SEE:TOUCH OF HER FLESH, THE)
TOUCH OF LARCENY, A ***½ (1960, Brit.) PR:A
TOUCH OF LOVE, A
(SEE:THANK YOU ALL VERY MUCH)
TOUCH OF SATAN, THE * (1971) PR:O
TOUCH OF THE MOON, A * (1936, Brit.) PR:A
TOUCH OF THE OTHER, A * (1970, Brit.) PR:O
TOUCH OF THE SUN, A * (1956, Brit.) PR:A
TOUCH WHITE, TOUCH BLACK
(SEE:VIOLENT ONES, THE)
TOUCH, THE * (1971, US/Swed.) PR:O
TOUCHDOWN **½ (1931) PR:A
TOUCHDOWN, ARMY ** (1938) PR:A
TOUCHE PAS A LA FEMME BLANCHE
(SEE:DON'T TOUCH WHITE WOMEN)
TOUCHED ** (1983) PR:C
TOUCHED BY LOVE **½ (1980) PR:A

TOUGH AS THEY COME *½ (1942) PR:A
TOUGH ASSIGNMENT * (1949) PR:A
TOUGH ENOUGH * (1983) PR:C
TOUGH GUY *** (1936) PR:A
TOUGH GUYS ** (1986, US) PR:C
TOUGH GUYS DON'T DANCE **½ (1987) PR:O
TOUGH KID * (1939) PR:A
TOUGH TO HANDLE * (1937) PR:A
TOUGHER THAN LEATHER *½ (1988) PR:O
TOUGHER THEY COME, THE * (1950) PR:A
TOUGHEST GUN IN TOMBSTONE * (1958) PR:A
TOUGHEST MAN ALIVE ** (1955) PR:A
TOUGHEST MAN IN ARIZONA ** (1952) PR:A
TOURIST TRAP, THE zero (1979) PR:C
TOUT VA BIEN **½ (1973, Fr.) PR:C
TOVARICH *** (1937) PR:AA
TOWARD THE UNKNOWN *** (1956) PR:A
TOWER OF EVIL (SEE:BEYOND THE FOG)
TOWER OF EVIL, 1972 (SEE:HORROR ON SNAPE ISLAND)
TOWER OF LONDON *** (1939) PR:A
TOWER OF LONDON ** (1962) PR:A
TOWER OF TERROR (SEE:ASSAULT)
TOWER OF TERROR, THE * (1942, Brit.) PR:A
TOWERING INFERNO, THE ** (1974) PR:C
TOWING * (1978) PR:C
TOWN CALLED BASTARD, A (SEE:TOWN CALLED HELL, A)
TOWN CALLED HELL, A * (1971, Sp./Brit.) PR:O
TOWN LIKE ALICE, A **½ (1958, Brit.) PR:A
TOWN ON TRIAL *** (1957, Brit.) PR:C
TOWN TAMER ** (1965) PR:A
TOWN THAT CRIED TERROR, THE (SEE:MANIAC?)
TOWN THAT DREADED SUNDOWN, THE * (1977) PR:O
TOWN WENT WILD, THE * (1945) PR:A
TOWN WITHOUT PITY **½ (1961, Ger./Switz./US) PR:C-O
TOXI ** (1952, Ger.) PR:A
TOXIC AVENGER, THE * (1985) PR:O
TOY SOLDIERS * (1984) PR:O
TOY TIGER ** (1956) PR:AA
TOY WIFE, THE ** (1938) PR:A-C
TOY, THE * (1982) PR:C
TOYGRABBERS, THE (SEE:UP YOUR TEDDY BEAR)
TOYS ARE NOT FOR CHILDREN * (1972) PR:O
TOYS IN THE ATTIC **½ (1963) PR:C
T.R. BASKIN *½ (1971) PR:C
TRACK OF THE CAT *** (1954) PR:C
TRACK OF THE MOONBEAST zero (1976) PR:C-O
TRACK OF THE VAMPIRE, (SEE:BLOOD BATH)
TRACK OF THUNDER * (1967) PR:A
TRACK THE MAN DOWN ** (1956, Brit.) PR:A
TRACK 29 ** (1988, Brit.) PR:O
TRACKDOWN zero (1976) PR:O
TRACKS * (1977) PR:O**
TRADE WINDS *** (1938) PR:A
TRADER HORN * (1973) PR:A
TRADER HORN * (1931) PR:C**
TRADER HORNEE zero (1970) PR:O
TRADING HEARTS ** (1988) PR:A-C
TRADING PLACES ***½ (1983) PR:C-O
TRAFFIC **** (1972, Fr.) PR:AA
TRAFFIC IN CRIME ** (1946) PR:A
TRAGEDY AT MIDNIGHT, A ** (1942) PR:A
TRAGEDY OF A RIDICULOUS MAN, THE **½ (1982, It.) PR:A
TRAIL BEYOND, THE ** (1934) PR:A
TRAIL BLAZERS, THE ** (1940) PR:A
TRAIL DRIVE, THE ** (1934) PR:A
TRAIL DUST ** (1936) PR:A
TRAIL GUIDE *½ (1952) PR:A
TRAIL OF KIT CARSON ** (1945) PR:A
TRAIL OF ROBIN HOOD **½ (1950) PR:A
TRAIL OF TERROR ** (1935) PR:AA
TRAIL OF TERROR ** (1944) PR:A
TRAIL OF THE LONESOME PINE, THE ***½ (1936) PR:A-C
TRAIL OF THE PINK PANTHER, THE * (1982) PR:C
TRAIL OF THE SILVER SPURS * (1941) PR:A
TRAIL OF THE VIGILANTES ** (1940) PR:A
TRAIL OF THE YUKON * (1949) PR:A
TRAIL OF VENGEANCE ** (1937) PR:A
TRAIL RIDERS * (1942) PR:AA**
TRAIL STREET * (1947) PR:A**
TRAIL TO GUNSIGHT ** (1944) PR:AA
TRAIL TO SAN ANTONE ** (1947) PR:A
TRAIL TO VENGEANCE ** (1945) PR:A
TRAILIN' TROUBLE (SEE:TRAILING TROUBLE)
TRAILIN' TROUBLE, 1930 (SEE:TRAILING TROUBLE)
TRAILIN' WEST * (1936) PR:A
TRAILING DOUBLE TROUBLE * (1940) PR:A
TRAILING THE KILLER *** (1932) PR:A
TRAILING TROUBLE * (1930) PR:A
TRAILING TROUBLE * (1937) PR:A
TRAIL'S END * (1949) PR:A
TRAILS OF DANGER * (1930) PR:A
TRAILS OF PERIL (SEE:TRAILS OF DANGER)
TRAILS OF THE WILD * (1935) PR:A
TRAIN, THE ** (1965, Fr./It./US) PR:C**
TRAIN GOES EAST, THE *** (1949, USSR) PR:A
TRAIN GOES TO KIEV, THE ** (1961, USSR) PR:A
TRAIN 2419 (SEE:RETURN OF CASEY JONES)
TRAIN OF DREAMS ***½ (1987, Can.) PR:C-O
TRAIN OF EVENTS *** (1952, Brit.) PR:A
TRAIN RIDE TO HOLLYWOOD *½ (1975) PR:A
TRAIN ROBBERS, THE **½ (1973) PR:A
TRAIN ROBBERY CONFIDENTIAL ** (1965, Braz.) PR:A
TRAIN TO ALCATRAZ ** (1948) PR:A
TRAIN TO TOMBSTONE zero (1950) PR:A
TRAINED TO KILL (SEE:NO MERCY MAN, THE)
TRAITOR SPY (SEE:TORSO MURDER MYSTERY, THE)
TRAITOR, THE, 1957 (SEE:ACCURSED, THE)
TRAITOR WITHIN, THE *½ (1942) PR:A
TRAITOR'S GATE ** (1966, Brit./Ger.) PR:A
TRAITOR, THE * (1936) PR:A
TRAITORS * (1957, Jap.) PR:A
TRAITORS, THE * (1963, Brit.) PR:A
TRAITORS, THE, 1958, Brit. (SEE:ACCURSED, THE)
TRAMP, TRAMP, TRAMP ** (1942) PR:A
TRAMPLERS, THE zero (1966, It.) PR:C
TRANCERS * (1985) PR:O
TRANS-EUROP-EXPRESS *** (1968, Fr.) PR:O
TRANSATLANTIC **½ (1931) PR:A
TRANSATLANTIC *½ (1961, Brit.) PR:A
TRANSATLANTIC MERRY-GO-ROUND **½ (1934) PR:A
TRANSATLANTIC TROUBLE (SEE:TAKE IT FROM ME)
TRANSATLANTIC TUNNEL * (1935, Brit.) PR:A**
TRANSCONTINENT EXPRESS (SEE:ROCK ISLAND TRAIL)
TRANSFORMERS: THE MOVIE, THE * (1986) PR:A-C
TRANSGRESSION ** (1931) PR:A
TRANSIENT LADY ** (1935) PR:A
TRANSPORT FROM PARADISE ** (1967, Czech.) PR:A
TRANSYLVANIA 6-5000 * (1985) PR:C
TRAP, THE * (1959) PR:A
TRAP, THE ** (1967, Can./Brit.) PR:A
TRAP DOOR, THE ** (1980) PR:O
TRAP, THE ** (1947) PR:A
TRAPEZE * (1932, Ger.) PR:A
TRAPEZE ***½ (1956) PR:A-C
TRAPP FAMILY, THE * (1961, Ger.) PR:A
TRAPPED * (1931) PR:A
TRAPPED *** (1937) PR:A
TRAPPED ** (1949) PR:A
TRAPPED BY BOSTON BLACKIE ** (1948) PR:A
TRAPPED BY G-MEN *½ (1937) PR:A
TRAPPED BY TELEVISION *½ (1936) PR:A
TRAPPED BY THE TERROR * (1949, Brit.) PR:AA
TRAPPED BY WIRELESS (SEE:YOU MAY BE NEXT)
TRAPPED IN A SUBMARINE **½ (1931, Brit.) PR:A
TRAPPED IN TANGIERS * (1960, It./Sp.) PR:A
TRAPPED IN THE SKY ** (1939 61m COL bw) PR:A
TRAQUENARDS (SEE:EROTIQUE)
TRAUMA *½ (1962) PR:C
TRAUMSTADT (SEE:DREAM TOWN)
TRAVELING EXECUTIONER, THE *** (1970) PR:O
TRAVELING HUSBANDS * (1931) PR:O
TRAVELING LADY (SEE:BABY THE RAIN MUST FALL)
TRAVELING SALESLADY, THE **½ (1935) PR:A
TRAVELING SALESWOMAN ** (1950) PR:A
TRAVELLER'S JOY ** (1951, Brit.) PR:A
TRAVELLING AVANT *** (1988, Fr.) PR:C
TRAVELLING NORTH * (1988, Aus.) PR:C**
TRAVELS WITH ANITA (SEE:LOVERS AND LIARS)
TRAVELS WITH MY AUNT *** (1972, Brit.) PR:C
TRAXX *½ (1988) PR:O
TRE NOTTI D'AMORE (SEE:THREE NIGHTS OF LOVE)
TRE NOTTI VIOLENTE (SEE:WEB OF VIOLENCE)
TRE PASSI NEL DELIRIO (SEE:SPIRITS OF THE DEAD)
TREACHERY ON THE HIGH SEAS ** (1939, Brit.) PR:A
TREACHERY RIDES THE RANGE **½ (1936) PR:A
TREAD SOFTLY *½ (1952, Brit.) PR:A
TREAD SOFTLY STRANGER ** (1959, Brit.) PR:A
TREASON (SEE:GUILTY OF TREASON)
TREASON, 1937 (SEE:OLD LOUISIANA)
TREASURE AT THE MILL **½ (1957, Brit.) PR:AA
TREASURE HUNT ** (1952, Brit.) PR:A
TREASURE ISLAND ***½ (1934) PR:A
TREASURE ISLAND ** (1950, Brit.) PR:A-C**
TREASURE ISLAND * (1972, Brit./Sp./Fr./Ger.) PR:A
TREASURE OF FEAR (SEE:SCARED STIFF)
TREASURE OF JAMAICA REEF, THE zero (1976) PR:C
TREASURE OF KALIFA (SEE:STEEL LADY, THE)
TREASURE OF LOST CANYON, THE **½ (1952) PR:A
TREASURE OF MAKUBA, THE ** (1967, US/Sp.) PR:A
TREASURE OF MATECUMBE *½ (1976) PR:AA
TREASURE OF MONTE CRISTO ** (1949) PR:A
TREASURE OF MONTE CRISTO, THE (SEE:SECRET OF MONTE CRISTO, THE)
TREASURE OF PANCHO VILLA, THE ** (1955) PR:A
TREASURE OF RUBY HILLS * (1955) PR:A
TREASURE OF SAN GENNARO **½ (1968, Fr./It./Ger.) PR:A
TREASURE OF SAN TERESA, THE (SEE:HOT MONEY GIRL)
TREASURE OF SILVER LAKE *½ (1965, Fr./Ger./Yugo.) PR:A
TREASURE OF THE AMAZON, THE *½ (1985, Mex.) PR:O
TREASURE OF THE FOUR CROWNS * (1983, Sp./US) PR:A
TREASURE OF THE GOLDEN CONDOR *** (1953) PR:A
TREASURE OF THE PIRANHA (SEE:KILLER FISH)
TREASURE OF THE SIERRA MADRE, THE *** (1948) PR:C**
TREASURE OF THE YANKEE ZEPHYR ** (1984) PR:A-C
TREAT EM' ROUGH *½ (1942) PR:A
TREATMENT, THE (SEE:STOP ME BEFORE I KILL?)
TREE GROWS IN BROOKLYN, A ** (1945) PR:C**
TREE OF LIBERTY (SEE:HOWARDS OF VIRGINIA, THE)
TREE OF WOODEN CLOGS, THE ***½ (1979, It.) PR:A-C
TREE WE HURT, THE **½ (1986, Gr.) PR:A
TREE, THE *½ (1969) PR:O
TREMENDOUSLY RICH MAN, A *½ (1932, Ger.) PR:A
TRENCHCOAT *½ (1983) PR:A
TRENT'S LAST CASE ** (1953, Brit.) PR:A

Finding entries in **THE MOTION PICTURE GUIDE ™**

Years 1929-83	Volumes I-IX
1984	Volume IX
1985	1986 ANNUAL
1986	1987 ANNUAL
1987	1988 ANNUAL
1988	1989 ANNUAL

STAR RATINGS

★★★★★	Masterpiece
★★★★	Excellent
★★★	Good
★★	Fair
★	Poor
zero	Without Merit

PARENTAL RECOMMENDATION (PR:)

AA	Good for Children
A	Acceptable for Children
C	Cautionary, some objectionable scenes
O	Objectionable for Children

BOLD: Films on Videocassette

TRES NOCHES VIOLENTAS
(SEE:WEB OF VIOLENCE)
TRESPASSER, THE **½ (1929) PR:A
TRESPASSER, THE
(SEE:NIGHT EDITOR)
TRESPASSER, THE ** (1947) PR:A
TRESPASSERS, THE **½ (1976, Aus.) PR:O
TRI
(SEE:THREE)
TRI SESTRY
(SEE:THREE SISTERS, THE)
TRIAL ***½ (1955) PR:A
TRIAL, THE **½ (1948, Aust.) PR:A
TRIAL AND ERROR **½ (1962, Brit.) PR:A
TRIAL BY COMBAT
(SEE:DIRTY KNIGHT'S WORK)
TRIAL OF BILLY JACK, THE zero (1974) PR:C
TRIAL OF JOAN OF ARC *** (1965, Fr.) PR:C
TRIAL OF LEE HARVEY OSWALD, THE ** (1964) PR:A
TRIAL OF MADAM X, THE *½ (1948, Brit.) PR:A
TRIAL OF MARY DUGAN, THE *** (1929) PR:C
TRIAL OF MARY DUGAN, THE ** (1941) PR:A
TRIAL OF PORTIA MERRIMAN, THE
(SEE:PORTIA ON TRIAL)
TRIAL OF SERGEANT RUTLEDGE, THE
(SEE:SERGEANT RUTLEDGE)
TRIAL OF THE CATONSVILLE NINE, THE **½ (1972) PR:A
TRIAL OF VIVIENNE WARE, THE ** (1932) PR:A
TRIAL WITHOUT JURY *½ (1950) PR:A
TRIAL, THE * (1963, Fr./It./Ger.) PR:C**
TRIALS OF OSCAR WILDE, THE
(SEE:MAN WITH THE GREEN CARNATION, THE)
TRIBES ** (1970) PR:A
TRIBUTE ***½ (1980, Can.) PR:C
TRIBUTE TO A BADMAN *** (1956) PR:C
TRICET JEDNA VE STINU
(SEE:90 DEGREES IN THE SHADE)
TRICK BABY * (1973) PR:O
TRICK FOR TRICK * (1933) PR:A
TRICK OR TREAT ** (1986) PR:O
TRICK OR TREATS ** (1982) PR:O
TRICKED
(SEE:BANDITS OF EL DORADO)
TRIGGER FINGERS *½ (1939) PR:A
TRIGGER HAPPY
(SEE:DEADLY COMPANIONS, THE)
TRIGGER PALS * (1939) PR:A
TRIGGER SMITH *½ (1939) PR:A
TRIGGER TRAIL ** (1944) PR:A
TRIGGER TRICKS *½ (1930) PR:A
TRIGGER TRIO, THE *½ (1937) PR:A
TRIGGER, JR. ** (1950) PR:A
TRILOGY
(SEE:TRUMAN CAPOTE'S TRILOGY)
TRINITY IS STILL MY NAME ** (1971, It.) PR:A
TRIO ***½ (1950, Brit.) PR:A
TRIP, THE *½ (1967) PR:O
TRIP, THE
(SEE:CHELSEA GIRLS, THE)
TRIP TO AMERICA, A
(SEE:VOYAGE TO AMERICA)
TRIP TO BOUNTIFUL, THE ** (1985) PR:C**
TRIP TO ITALY, A
(SEE:STRANGERS, THE)
TRIP TO PARIS, A ** (1938) PR:A
TRIP TO TERROR
(SEE:IS THIS TRIP REALLY NECESSARY?)
TRIP WITH ANITA, A
(SEE:LOVERS AND LIARS)
TRIP, THE
(SEE:VOYAGE, THE)
TRIPLE CROSS *** (1967, Fr./Brit.) PR:C-O
TRIPLE CROSS, THE
(SEE:JOE PALOOKA IN TRIPLE CROSS)
TRIPLE DECEPTION ** (1957, Brit.) PR:A
TRIPLE ECHO, THE ** (1973, Brit.) PR:O
TRIPLE IRONS * (1973, Hong Kong) PR:O
TRIPLE JUSTICE ** (1940) PR:A
TRIPLE THREAT * (1948) PR:A
TRIPLE TROUBLE
(SEE:KENTUCKY KERNELS)
TRIPLE TROUBLE *½ (1950) PR:A
TRIPOLI **½ (1950) PR:A
TRISTANA **** (1970, Sp./It./Fr.) PR:C
TRITIY TAYM
(SEE:LAST GAME, THE)
TRIUMPH OF SHERLOCK HOLMES, THE * (1935, Brit.) PR:A**
TRIUMPHS OF A MAN CALLED HORSE * (1983, US/Mex.) PR:O
TROCADERO ** (1944) PR:A
TROG zero (1970, Brit.) PR:A
TROIKA *** (1969) PR:O
TROIS HOMMES A ABATTRE
(SEE:THREE MEN TO DESTROY)
TROIS VERITES
(SEE:THREE FACES OF SIN)
TROJAN BROTHERS, THE *½ (1946) PR:A
TROJAN HORSE, THE **½ (1962, Fr./It.) PR:AA
TROJAN WAR, THE
(SEE:TROJAN HORSE, THE)
TROJAN WOMEN, THE ** (1971, Gr./US) PR:C
TROLL *½ (1986) PR:C
TROLLENBERG TERROR, THE
(SEE:CRAWLING EYE, THE)
TROMBA, THE TIGER MAN *½ (1952, Ger.) PR:C
TRON * (1982) PR:A**
TROOPER HOOK **½ (1957) PR:C
TROOPER, THE
(SEE:FIGHTING TROOPER, THE)
TROOPERS THREE ** (1930) PR:AA
TROOPSHIP ** (1938, Brit.) PR:C
TROPIC FURY * (1939) PR:A
TROPIC HOLIDAY ** (1938) PR:A
TROPIC ZONE *½ (1953) PR:A
TROPICAL HEAT WAVE *½ (1952) PR:A
TROPICAL TROUBLE * (1936, Brit.) PR:A
TROPICANA
(SEE:HEAT'S ON, THE)
TROPICS **½ (1969, It.) PR:O
TROTTIE TRUE
(SEE:GAY LADY, THE)
TROUBLE ** (1933, Brit.) PR:A
TROUBLE AHEAD *½ (1936, Brit.) PR:A
TROUBLE ALONG THE WAY * (1953) PR:O**
TROUBLE AT MIDNIGHT * (1937) PR:A
TROUBLE AT 16
(SEE:PLATINUM HIGH SCHOOL)
TROUBLE BREWING *** (1939, Brit.) PR:A
TROUBLE CHASER
(SEE:LI'L ABNER)
TROUBLE-FETE *** (1964, Can.) PR:O
TROUBLE FOR TWO ** (1936) PR:A
TROUBLE IN MIND ** (1985) PR:O
TROUBLE IN MOROCCO ** (1937) PR:A
TROUBLE IN PANAMA
(SEE:TORCHY BLANE IN PANAMA)
TROUBLE IN PARADISE **** (1932) PR:C
TROUBLE IN STORE **½ (1955, Brit.) PR:A
TROUBLE IN SUNDOWN **½ (1939) PR:A
TROUBLE IN TEXAS **½ (1937) PR:A
TROUBLE IN THE AIR * (1948, Brit.) PR:A
TROUBLE IN THE GLEN ** (1954, Brit.) PR:A
TROUBLE IN THE SKY ** (1961, Brit.) PR:C
TROUBLE MAKERS **½ (1948) PR:AA
TROUBLE MAN * (1972) PR:O
TROUBLE PREFERRED *** (1949) PR:A
TROUBLE WITH ANGELS, THE **½ (1966) PR:AA
TROUBLE WITH DICK, THE **½ (1987) PR:O
TROUBLE WITH EVE
(SEE:IN TROUBLE WITH EVE)
TROUBLE WITH GIRLS (AND HOW TO GET INTO IT), THE *½ (1969) PR:A
TROUBLE WITH HARRY, THE ***½ (1955) PR:A-C
TROUBLE WITH WOMEN, THE ** (1947) PR:A
TROUBLED WATERS **½ (1936, Brit.) PR:A
TROUBLEMAKER, THE *** (1964) PR:O
TROUBLES THROUGH BILLETS
(SEE:BLONDIE FOR VICTORY)
TROUBLESOME DOUBLE, THE ** (1971, Brit.) PR:AA
TROUT, THE ** (1982, Fr.) PR:O
TRUANT, THE
(SEE:TERROR IN THE CITY)
TRUCK BUSTERS ** (1943) PR:A
TRUCK STOP WOMEN ** (1974) PR:O
TRUCK TURNER *½ (1974) PR:O
TRUE AND THE FALSE, THE *½ (1955, Swed.) PR:O
TRUE AS A TURTLE *½ (1957, Brit.) PR:A
TRUE CONFESSION *** (1937) PR:A
TRUE CONFESSIONS ** (1981) PR:O**
TRUE DIARY OF A WAHINE
(SEE:MAEVA)
TRUE GRIT *** (1969) PR:A**
TRUE STORIES **½ (1986) PR:A
TRUE STORY OF A WAHINE
(SEE:MAEVA)
TRUE STORY OF ESKIMO NELL, THE *** (1975, Aus.) PR:O
TRUE STORY OF JESSE JAMES, THE *** (1957) PR:A
TRUE STORY OF LYNN STUART, THE *** (1958) PR:A
TRUE TO LIFE ***½ (1943) PR:A
TRUE TO THE ARMY ** (1942) PR:AA
TRUE TO THE NAVY *½ (1930) PR:A
TRUMAN CAPOTE'S TRILOGY *** (1969) PR:A
TRUMPET BLOWS, THE ** (1934) PR:A
TRUNK CRIME
(SEE:DESIGN FOR MURDER)
TRUNK MYSTERY, THE
(SEE:ONE NEW YORK NIGHT)
TRUNK TO CAIRO ** (1966, Israel/Ger.) PR:C
TRUNK, THE *½ (1961, Brit.) PR:C
TRUNKS OF MR. O.F., THE **** (1932, Ger.) PR:A
TRUST THE NAVY ** (1935, Brit.) PR:A
TRUST YOUR WIFE
(SEE:THE FALL GUY)
TRUSTED OUTLAW, THE ** (1937) PR:A
TRUTH ABOUT MURDER, THE ** (1946) PR:A
TRUTH ABOUT SPRING, THE *** (1965, Brit.) PR:AA
TRUTH ABOUT WOMEN, THE ** (1958, Brit.) PR:A
TRUTH ABOUT YOUTH, THE **½ (1930) PR:A
TRUTH IS STRANGER
(SEE:WHEN LADIES MEET)
TRUTH, THE ** (1961, Fr./It.) PR:O
TRY AND FIND IT
(SEE:HI DIDDLE DIDDLE)
TRY AND GET ME
(SEE:SOUND OF FURY, THE)
TRYGON FACTOR, THE ** (1969, Brit.) PR:C
TSAR'S BRIDE, THE *** (1966, USSR) PR:C
TSARSKAYA NEVESTA
(SEE:TSAR'S BRIDE, THE)
TSUBAKI SANJURO
(SEE:SANJURO)
TU PERDONAS..YO NO
(SEE:GOD FORGIVES-I DON'T)
TU SERAS TERRIBLEMENT GENTILLE
(SEE:YOU ONLY LOVE ONCE)
TUCKER: THE MAN AND HIS DREAM ** (1988) PR:A**
TUCSON *½ (1949) PR:A
TUCSON RAIDERS **½ (1944) PR:A
TUDOR ROSE
(SEE:NINE DAYS A QUEEN)
TUFF TURF zero (1985) PR:O
TUGBOAT ANNIE ***½ (1933) PR:A
TUGBOAT ANNIE SAILS AGAIN ** (1940) PR:AA
TULIPS * (1981, Can.) PR:C
TULSA ***½ (1949) PR:A
TULSA KID, THE ** (1940) PR:A
TUMBLEDOWN RANCH IN ARIZONA **½ (1941) PR:A
TUMBLEWEED ** (1953) PR:A
TUMBLEWEED TRAIL ** (1946) PR:A
TUMBLING TUMBLEWEEDS *½ (1935) PR:AA
TUNA CLIPPER **½ (1949) PR:A
TUNDRA * (1936) PR:A
TUNES OF GLORY ***½ (1960, Brit.) PR:C
TUNNEL OF LOVE, THE **½ (1958) PR:C
TUNNEL TO THE SUN ** (1968, Jap.) PR:C
TUNNEL 28
(SEE:ESCAPE FROM EAST BERLIN)
TUNNEL, THE
(SEE:TRANSATLANTIC TUNNEL)
TUNNELVISION zero (1976) PR:O
TURK 182! * (1985) PR:C
TURKEY SHOOT
(SEE:ESCAPE 2000)
TURKEY TIME **½ (1933, Brit.) PR:A
TURKISH CUCUMBER, THE * (1963, Ger.) PR:C
TURLIS ABENTEUER
(SEE:PINOCCHIO)
TURN BACK THE CLOCK **½ (1933) PR:A
TURN OF THE SCREW **½ (1985, Sp.) PR:O
TURN OF THE TIDE ** (1935, Brit.) PR:A
TURN OFF THE MOON ** (1937) PR:A
TURN ON TO LOVE zero (1969) PR:O
TURN THE KEY SOFTLY ** (1954, Brit.) PR:C
TURNABOUT ** (1940) PR:A
TURNED OUT NICE AGAIN *½ (1941, Brit.) PR:A
TURNERS OF PROSPECT ROAD, THE ** (1947, Brit.) PR:A
TURNING POINT, THE *** (1952) PR:C-O
TURNING POINT, THE * (1977) PR:C**
TURTLE DIARY ***½ (1985, Brit.) PR:C
TUSK * (1980, Fr.) PR:A
TUTTE LE ALTRE RAGAZZE LO FANNO
(SEE:ALL THE OTHER GIRLS DO)
TUTTI A CASA
(SEE:EVERYBODY GO HOME!)
TUTTI FRUTTI
(SEE:CATCH AS CATCH CAN)
TUTTI PAZZI MENO IO
(SEE:KING OF HEARTS)
TUTTLES OF TAHITI **½ (1942) PR:A
TUXEDO JUNCTION ** (1941) PR:A
TVA LEVANDE OCH EN DOD
(SEE:TWO LIVING, ONE DEAD)
TWELFTH NIGHT ***½ (1956, USSR) PR:A
12 ANGRY MEN ** (1957) PR:A**
TWELVE CHAIRS, THE ***½ (1970) PR:A-C
TWELVE CROWDED HOURS **½ (1939) PR:A
TWELVE GOOD MEN ** (1936, Brit.) PR:A
TWELVE-HANDED MEN OF MARS, THE *** (1964, It./Sp.) PR:A
TWELVE HOURS TO KILL * (1960) PR:A
TWELVE O'CLOCK HIGH *** (1949) PR:C**
TWELVE PLUS ONE ** (1970, Fr./It.) PR:A

TWELVE TO THE MOON *½ (1960) PR:A
TWENTIETH CENTURY ***½ (1934) PR:A
20TH CENTURY OZ *** (1977, Aus.) PR:A
25TH HOUR, THE ** (1967, Fr./It./Yugo.) PR:C
24-HOUR LOVER *½ (1970, Ger.) PR:O
24 HOURS *** (1931) PR:A
24 HOURS IN A WOMAN'S LIFE **½
  (1968, Fr./Ger.) PR:C
24 HOURS OF A WOMAN'S LIFE
  (SEE:AFFAIR IN MONTE CARLO)
24 HOURS OF THE REBEL
  (SEE:9-30-55)
24 HOURS TO KILL **½ (1966, Brit.) PR:C
20 MILLION MILES TO EARTH ** (1957) PR:A
TWENTY MILLION SWEETHEARTS *** (1934) PR:A
TWENTY MULE TEAM *** (1940) PR:A
29 OCACIA AVENUE
  (SEE:FACTS OF LOVE)
2019, I NUOVI BARBARI
  (SEE:WARRIORS OF THE WASTELAND)
TWENTY-ONE DAYS
  (SEE:TWENTY-ONE DAYS TOGETHER)
TWENTY-ONE DAYS TOGETHER *½
  (1940, Brit.) PR:A
TWENTY PLUS TWO **½ (1961) PR:C-O
TWENTY QUESTIONS MURDER MYSTERY, THE **
  (1950, Brit.) PR:A
27A * (1974, Aus.) PR:O
27TH DAY, THE **½ (1957) PR:A-C
20,000 EYES ** (1961) PR:C
20,000 LEAGUES UNDER THE SEA **** (1954) PR:A
20,000 MEN A YEAR ** (1939) PR:A
20,000 POUNDS KISS, THE **½ (1964, Brit.) PR:C
20,000 YEARS IN SING SING **** (1933) PR:A
23 1/2 HOURS LEAVE ** (1937) PR:A
23 PACES TO BAKER STREET *** (1956) PR:C
TWICE A MAN ** (1964) PR:O
TWICE AROUND THE DAFFODILS ***
  (1962, Brit.) PR:A
TWICE BLESSED *½ (1945) PR:A
TWICE BRANDED ** (1936, Brit.) PR:A
TWICE IN A LIFETIME *** (1985) PR:C
TWICE TOLD TALES *** (1963) PR:C
TWICE UPON A TIME *½ (1953, Brit.) PR:A
TWICE UPON A TIME *½ (1983) PR:A
TWILIGHT FOR THE GODS ** (1958) PR:A
TWILIGHT HOUR *½ (1944, Brit.) PR:A
TWILIGHT IN THE SIERRAS **½ (1950) PR:A
TWILIGHT OF HONOR **½ (1963) PR:C
TWILIGHT OF THE DEAD
  (SEE:GATES OF HELL, THE)
TWILIGHT ON THE PRAIRIE ** (1944) PR:A
TWILIGHT ON THE RIO GRANDE * (1947) PR:A
TWILIGHT ON THE TRAIL ** (1941) PR:A
TWILIGHT PATH *** (1965, Jap.) PR:C
TWILIGHT PEOPLE zero (1972, Phil.) PR:O
TWILIGHT STORY, THE **½ (1962, Jap.) PR:O
TWILIGHT TIME *½ (1983, US/Yugo.) PR:C
TWILIGHT WOMEN *** (1953, Brit.) PR:C
TWILIGHT ZONE—THE MOVIE ** (1983) PR:C-O
TWILIGHT'S LAST GLEAMING ***½
  (1977, US/Ger.) PR:O
TWIN BEDS *½ (1929) PR:A
TWIN BEDS ** (1942) PR:A
TWIN FACES * (1937, Brit.) PR:A
TWIN HUSBANDS ** (1934) PR:A
TWIN SISTERS OF KYOTO *** (1964, Jap.) PR:C
TWINKLE AND SHINE
  (SEE:IT HAPPENED TO JANE)
TWINKLE IN GOD'S EYE, THE *** (1955) PR:A
TWINKLE, TWINKLE, KILLER KANE
  (SEE:NINTH CONFIGURATION, THE)
TWINKY
  (SEE:LOLA)
TWINS ** (1988) PR:A
TWINS OF EVIL ** (1971, Brit.) PR:O
TWIST ALL NIGHT * (1961) PR:A
TWIST & SHOUT **½ (1986, Den.) PR:O
TWIST AROUND THE CLOCK ** (1961) PR:A
TWIST OF FATE
  (SEE:BEAUTIFUL STRANGER, THE)
TWIST OF SAND, A **½ (1968, Brit.) PR:A
TWIST, THE ** (1976, Fr.) PR:C-O
TWISTED BRAIN
  (SEE:HORROR HIGH)
TWISTED LIVES
  (SEE:LIARS, THE)

TWISTED NERVE ** (1969, Brit.) PR:O
TWISTED ROAD, THE
  (SEE:THEY LIVE BY NIGHT)
TWITCH OF THE DEATH NERVE * (1973, It.) PR:O
TWO **½ (1975) PR:O
TWO A PENNY * (1968, Brit.) PR:A
TWO AGAINST THE WORLD * (1932) PR:A
TWO AGAINST THE WORLD ** (1936) PR:A
TWO ALONE *½ (1934) PR:A
TWO AND ONE TWO ** (1934) PR:A
TWO AND TWO MAKE SIX ** (1962, Brit.) PR:C
TWO ARE GUILTY ** (1964, Fr.) PR:C
TWO BLACK SHEEP
  (SEE:TWO SINNERS)
TWO BLONDES AND A REDHEAD ** (1947) PR:A
TWO BRIGHT BOYS **½ (1939) PR:A
TWO COLONELS, THE **½ (1963, It.) PR:A
TWO DAUGHTERS *** (1963, India) PR:A
TWO DOLLAR BETTOR *½ (1951) PR:A
TWO ENEMIES
  (SEE:BEST OF ENEMIES, THE)
TWO ENGLISH GIRLS ***½ (1972, Fr.) PR:O
TWO EYES, TWELVE HANDS *** (1958, India) PR:C
TWO-FACED WOMAN ** (1941) PR:A
TWO FACES OF DR. JEKYLL
  (SEE:HOUSE OF FRIGHT)
TWO FISTED ** (1935) PR:A
TWO FISTED AGENT
  (SEE:BONANZA TOWN)
TWO-FISTED GENTLEMAN *½ (1936) PR:A
TWO-FISTED JUSTICE *½ (1931) PR:A
TWO FISTED JUSTICE * (1943) PR:A
TWO-FISTED LAW ** (1932) PR:AA
TWO-FISTED RANGERS ** (1940) PR:A
TWO-FISTED SHERIFF *** (1937) PR:A
TWO FLAGS WEST *** (1950) PR:A
TWO FOR DANGER ** (1940, Brit.) PR:A
TWO FOR THE ROAD ***½ (1967, Brit.) PR:C
TWO FOR THE SEESAW ** (1962) PR:C
TWO FOR TONIGHT *½ (1935) PR:A
TWO GALS AND A GUY ** (1951) PR:A
TWO GENTLEMEN SHARING ** (1969, Brit.) PR:O
TWO GIRLS AND A SAILOR *** (1944) PR:A
TWO GIRLS ON BROADWAY **½ (1940) PR:A
TWO GROOMS FOR A BRIDE *½ (1957) PR:A
TWO-GUN CUPID
  (SEE:BAD MAN, THE)
TWO-GUN JUSTICE ** (1938) PR:A
TWO-GUN LADY **½ (1956) PR:A
TWO GUN LAW **½ (1937) PR:A
TWO GUN MAN, THE ** (1931) PR:A
TWO GUN SHERIFF *½ (1941) PR:A
TWO-GUN TROUBADOR ** (1939) PR:A
TWO GUNS AND A BADGE ** (1954) PR:A
TWO GUYS FROM MILWAUKEE **½ (1946) PR:A
TWO GUYS FROM TEXAS ** (1948) PR:A
TWO-HEADED SPY, THE *** (1959, Brit.) PR:C
TWO HEADS ON A PILLOW *½ (1934) PR:A
TWO HEARTS IN HARMONY ** (1935, Brit.) PR:A
TWO HEARTS IN WALTZ TIME ** (1934, Brit.) PR:A
TWO HUNDRED MOTELS *** (1971, Brit.) PR:O
TWO IN A CROWD * (1936) PR:A
TWO IN A MILLION
  (SEE:EAST OF FIFTH AVENUE)
TWO IN A SLEEPING BAG ** (1964, Ger.) PR:C
TWO IN A TAXI *½ (1941) PR:A
TWO IN REVOLT **½ (1936) PR:AA
TWO IN THE DARK *½ (1936) PR:A
TWO IN THE SHADOW **½ (1968, Jap.) PR:C
TWO IS A HAPPY NUMBER
  (SEE:ONE IS A LONELY NUMBER)
TWO KINDS OF WOMEN * (1932) PR:C
TWO KOUNEY LEMELS *** (1966, Israel) PR:A
TWO-LANE BLACKTOP **** (1971) PR:O
TWO LATINS FROM MANHATTAN * (1941) PR:A
TWO LEFT FEET ** (1965, Brit.) PR:O
TWO LETTER ALIBI *½ (1962, Brit.) PR:A
TWO LITTLE BEARS, THE **½ (1961) PR:AA
TWO LIVES OF MATTIA PASCAL, THE **½
  (1985, It./Fr./Gr./Brit.) PR:O
TWO LIVING, ONE DEAD **½
  (1964, Brit./Swed.) PR:C
TWO LOST WORLDS *½ (1950) PR:A
TWO LOVES * (1961) PR:C
TWO-MAN SUBMARINE ** (1944) PR:A
TWO MEN AND A GIRL
  (SEE:HONEYMOON)

TWO MEN AND A MAID *½ (1929) PR:A
TWO MEN IN TOWN *** (1973, Fr.) PR:O
TWO-MINUTE WARNING * (1976) PR:O
TWO MINUTES' SILENCE * (1934, Brit.) PR:A
TWO MINUTES TO PLAY * (1937) PR:A
TWO MOON JUNCTION *½ (1988) PR:O
TWO MRS. CARROLLS, THE ***½ (1947) PR:A-C
TWO MULES FOR SISTER SARA **½ (1970) PR:C
TWO NIGHTS WITH CLEOPATRA *½
  (1953, It.) PR:C
TWO O'CLOCK COURAGE ** (1945) PR:C
TWO OF A KIND ** (1951) PR:C
TWO OF A KIND zero (1983) PR:C
TWO OF US, THE ** (1938, Brit.) PR:A
TWO OF US, THE **** (1968, Fr.) PR:A
TWO ON A DOORSTEP * (1936, Brit.) PR:A
TWO ON A GUILLOTINE ** (1965) PR:C
TWO ON THE TILES
  (SEE:SCHOOL FOR BRIDES)
TWO OR THREE THINGS I KNOW ABOUT HER ***
  (1970, Fr.) PR:O
TWO PEOPLE * (1973) PR:O
2 + 5 MISSIONE HYDRA
  (SEE:STAR PILOT)
TWO ROADS
  (SEE:TEXAS STAGECOACH)
TWO RODE TOGETHER **½ (1961) PR:C
TWO SECONDS ** (1932) PR:C
TWO SENORITAS
  (SEE:TWO SENORITAS FROM CHICAGO)
TWO SENORITAS FROM CHICAGO * (1943) PR:A
TWO SINNERS *½ (1935) PR:A
TWO SISTERS * (1938) PR:A
TWO SISTERS FROM BOSTON *** (1946) PR:A
TWO SMART MEN * (1940, Brit.) PR:A
TWO SMART PEOPLE ** (1946) PR:A
TWO SOLITUDES ** (1978, Can.) PR:A
TWO SUPER COPS *½ (1978, It.) PR:C
TWO TEXAS KNIGHTS
  (SEE:TWO GUYS FROM TEXAS)
TWO THOROUGHBREDS ** (1939) PR:A
TWO THOUSAND MANIACS zero (1964) PR:O
2001: A SPACE ODYSSEY ***½
  (1968, US/Brit.) PR:A
2010 **½ (1984) PR:C
2020 TEXAS GLADIATORS zero (1985, It.) PR:O
2,000 WEEKS **½ (1970, Aus.) PR:C
2,000 WOMEN ** (1944, Brit.) PR:A
2000 YEARS LATER * (1969) PR:O
TWO TICKETS TO BROADWAY *** (1951) PR:A
TWO TICKETS TO LONDON *** (1943) PR:A
TWO TICKETS TO PARIS * (1962) PR:A
TWO TIMES TWO
  (SEE:START THE REVOLUTION WITHOUT ME)
TWO VOICES *½ (1966) PR:C
TWO-WAY STRETCH ***½ (1961, Brit.) PR:A-C
TWO WEEKS IN ANOTHER TOWN ** (1962) PR:O
TWO WEEKS IN SEPTEMBER *½
  (1967, Fr./Brit.) PR:A
TWO WEEKS OFF * (1929) PR:A
TWO WEEKS TO LIVE ** (1943) PR:A
TWO WEEKS WITH LOVE **½ (1950) PR:A
TWO WHITE ARMS
  (SEE:WIVES BEWARE)
TWO WHO DARED ** (1937, Brit.) PR:A
TWO WISE MAIDS ** (1937) PR:A
TWO WIVES AT ONE WEDDING **
  (1961, Brit.) PR:A
TWO WOMEN **½ (1940, Fr.) PR:A
TWO WOMEN **** (1960, It./Fr.) PR:C-O
TWO WORLD ** (1930, Brit.) PR:A
TWO WORLDS OF CHARLY GORDON, THE
  (SEE:CHARLY)
TWO YANKS IN TRINIDAD ** (1942) PR:A
TWO YEARS BEFORE THE MAST ***½ (1946) PR:C
TWO YEARS HOLIDAY
  (SEE:STOLEN DIRIGIBLE, THE)
TWO'S COMPANY ** (1939, Brit.) PR:A
TWONKY, THE * (1953) PR:A
TYCOON ** (1947) PR:A
TYPHOON **½ (1940) PR:A
TYPHOON TREASURE * (1939, Brit.) PR:A
TYRANT OF SYRACUSE, THE
  (SEE:DAMON AND PYTHIAS)
TYRANT OF THE SEA ** (1950) PR:A
TYSTNADEN
  (SEE:SILENCE, THE)

Finding entries in **THE MOTION PICTURE GUIDE** ™

Years 1929-83	Volumes I-IX
1984	Volume IX
1985	1986 ANNUAL
1986	1987 ANNUAL
1987	1988 ANNUAL
1988	1989 ANNUAL

STAR RATINGS

★★★★★ Masterpiece
★★★★ Excellent
★★★ Good
★★ Fair
★ Poor
zero Without Merit

PARENTAL RECOMMENDATION (PR:)

AA Good for Children
A   Acceptable for Children
C   Cautionary, some objectionable scenes
O   Objectionable for Children

BOLD: Films on Videocassette

U

U-BOAT PRISONER * (1944) PR:A
U-47 LT. COMMANDER PRIEN *½ (1967, Ger.) PR:A
U KRUTOGO YARA (SEE:SHE-WOLF, THE)
U.S.S. TEAKETTLE (SEE:YOU'RE IN THE NAVY NOW)
U-TURN *½ (1973, Can.) PR:C
U-BOAT 29 (SEE:SPY IN BLACK, THE)
UCCELLACCI E UCCELLINI (SEE:HAWKS AND THE SPARROWS, THE)
UCCIDERO UN UOMO (SEE:THIS MAN MUST DIE)
UCHUJIN TOKYO NI ARAWARU (SEE:MYSTERIOUS SATELLITE, THE)
UFO (SEE:UNIDENTIFIED FLYING ODDBALL)
UFO: TARGET EARTH * (1974) PR:A
UFORIA ***½ (1985) PR:C
UGETSU *** (1954, Jap.) PR:A**
UGLY AMERICAN, THE **½ (1963) PR:A-C
UGLY DACHSHUND, THE ** (1966) PR:AA
UGLY DUCKLING, THE ** (1959, Brit.) PR:A
UGLY ONES, THE *½ (1968, It./Sp.) PR:O
UKIGUSA (SEE:FLOATING WEEDS)
ULTIMATE CHASE, THE (SEE:ULTIMATE THRILL, THE)
ULTIMATE SOLUTION OF GRACE QUIGLEY, THE **½ (1984) PR:C
ULTIMATE THRILL, THE *½ (1974) PR:A-C
ULTIMATE WARRIOR, THE **½ (1975) PR:O
ULTIMATUM ** (1940, Fr.) PR:A
ULYSSES * (1955, It.) PR:C**
ULYSSES * (1967, US/Brit.) PR:C**
ULZANA'S RAID * (1972) PR:O**
UMBERTO D *** (1955, It.) PR:C**
UMBRELLA WOMAN, THE (SEE:GOOD WIFE, THE)
UMBRELLA, THE ** (1933, Brit.) PR:A
UMBRELLAS OF CHERBOURG, THE ***½ (1964, Fr./Ger.) PR:A-C
UN AMOUR DE POCHE (SEE:NUDE IN HIS POCKET)
UN AMOUR DE SWANN (SEE:SWANN IN LOVE)
UN AMOUR EN ALLEMAGNE (SEE:LOVE IN GERMANY, A)
UN CARNET DE BAL **½ (1938, Fr.) PR:A
UN, DEUX, TROIS, QUATRE? (SEE:BLACK TIGHTS)
UN DIMANCHE A LA CAMPAGNE (SEE:SUNDAY IN THE COUNTRY, A)
UN FILE (SEE:COP, A)
UN HOMBRE DE EXITO (SEE:SUCCESSFUL MAN, A)
UN HOMBRE VIOLENTE ** (1986, Mex.) PR:O
UN HOMME AMOUREUX (SEE:MAN IN LOVE, A)
UN HOMME ET UNE FEMME (SEE:MAN AND A WOMAN, A)
UN SEUL AMOUR (SEE:MAGNIFICENT SINNER)
UN TAXI MAUVE (SEE:PURPLE TAXI, THE)
UN UOMO, UN CAVALLO, UNA PISTOLA (SEE:STRANGER RETURNS, THE)
UN ZOO LA NUIT (SEE:NIGHT ZOO)
UNA MOGLIE AMERICANA (SEE:RUN FOR YOUR WIFE)
UNA SIGNORA DELL'OVEST *½ (1942, It.) PR:A
UNAKRSNA VATRA (SEE:OPERATION CROSS EAGLES)
UNASHAMED *½ (1932) PR:A
UNASHAMED zero (1938) PR:O
UNBEARABLE LIGHTNESS OF BEING, THE **½ (1988) PR:O
UNCANNY, THE ** (1977, Brit./Can.) PR:C
UNCENSORED *½ (1944, Brit.) PR:A
UNCERTAIN GLORY *** (1944) PR:A
UNCERTAIN LADY * (1934) PR:A
UNCHAINED ** (1955) PR:A
UNCHAINED (SEE:ANGEL UNCHAINED)
UNCIVILISED ** (1937, Aus.) PR:A
UNCLE HARRY **½ (1945) PR:C
UNCLE JOE SHANNON * (1978) PR:C
UNCLE SCAM zero (1981) PR:O
UNCLE SILAS (SEE:INHERITANCE, THE)
UNCLE TOM'S CABIN *½ (1969, Fr./It./Ger./Yugo.) PR:C
UNCLE VANYA ** (1958) PR:A
UNCLE VANYA **½ (1972, USSR) PR:A
UNCLE VANYA ** (1977, Brit.) PR:A
UNCLE, THE *** (1966, Brit.) PR:A
UNCOMMON THIEF, AN ** (1967, USSR) PR:A
UNCOMMON VALOR ** (1983) PR:O
UNCONQUERED ***½ (1947) PR:A
UNCONSCIOUS (SEE:FEAR)
UND IMMER RUFT DAS HERZ (SEE:MOONWOLF)
...UND MORGEN FAHRT IHR ZUR HOLIE (SEE:DIRTY HEROES)
UNDEAD, THE ** (1957) PR:A
UNDEFEATED, THE ** (1969) PR:A
UNDER A CLOUD * (1937, Brit.) PR:A
UNDER A TEXAS MOON ** (1930) PR:A
UNDER AGE *½ (1941) PR:A-C
UNDER AGE * (1964) PR:O
UNDER ARIZONA SKIES ** (1946) PR:A
UNDER CALIFORNIA SKIES (SEE:UNDER CALIFORNIA STARS)
UNDER CALIFORNIA STARS *½ (1948) PR:A
UNDER CAPRICORN ** (1949) PR:C
UNDER COLORADO SKIES **½ (1947) PR:A
UNDER COVER **½ (1987) PR:O
UNDER-COVER MAN ** (1932) PR:A
UNDER COVER OF NIGHT ** (1937) PR:A
UNDER COVER ROGUE (SEE:WHITE VOICES)
UNDER EIGHTEEN *½ (1932) PR:A
UNDER FIESTA STARS ** (1941) PR:A
UNDER FIRE ** (1957) PR:A
UNDER FIRE * (1983) PR:O**
UNDER MEXICALI SKIES (SEE:UNDER MEXICALI STARS)
UNDER MEXICALI STARS **½ (1950) PR:A
UNDER MILK WOOD * (1973, Brit.) PR:C**
UNDER MONTANA SKIES *½ (1930) PR:A
UNDER MY SKIN * (1950) PR:A**
UNDER NEVADA SKIES **½ (1946) PR:A
UNDER NEW MANAGEMENT (SEE:HONEYMOON HOTEL)
UNDER PRESSURE **½ (1935) PR:A
UNDER PROOF * (1936, Brit.) PR:A
UNDER-PUP, THE **½ (1939) PR:A
UNDER SATAN'S SUN *** (1988, Fr.) PR:C-O
UNDER SECRET ORDERS *½ (1933) PR:A
UNDER SECRET ORDERS ** (1943, Brit.) PR:A-C
UNDER STRANGE FLAGS ** (1937) PR:A
UNDER SUSPICION * (1931) PR:A
UNDER SUSPICION ** (1937) PR:A
UNDER TEN FLAGS ***½ (1960, US/It.) PR:C
UNDER TEXAS SKIES ** (1931) PR:A
UNDER TEXAS SKIES * (1940) PR:A
UNDER THE BANNER OF SAMURAI **½ (1969, Jap.) PR:C
UNDER THE BIG TOP *½ (1938) PR:A
UNDER THE CHERRY MOON zero (1986) PR:O
UNDER THE CLOCK (SEE:CLOCK, THE)
UNDER THE GREENWOOD TREE ** (1930, Brit.) PR:A
UNDER THE GUN **½ (1951) PR:A
UNDER THE PAMPAS MOON **½ (1935) PR:A
UNDER THE RAINBOW zero (1981) PR:C
UNDER THE RED ROBE ***½ (1937, Brit.) PR:A
UNDER THE ROOFS OF PARIS ** (1930, Fr.) PR:A**
UNDER THE SUN OF ROME *** (1949, It.) PR:A
UNDER THE TONTO RIM *½ (1933) PR:A
UNDER THE TONTO RIM **½ (1947) PR:A
UNDER THE VOLCANO ***½ (1984) PR:O
UNDER THE YUM-YUM TREE **½ (1963) PR:C-O
UNDER TWO FLAGS ***½ (1936) PR:A-C
UNDER WESTERN SKIES *½ (1945) PR:A
UNDER WESTERN STARS **½ (1938) PR:A
UNDER YOUR HAT ** (1940, Brit.) PR:A
UNDER YOUR SPELL *½ (1936) PR:A
UNDERCOVER (SEE:UNDERGROUND GUERRILLAS)
UNDERCOVER AGENT ** (1939) PR:A
UNDERCOVER AGENT ** (1935, Brit.) PR:A
UNDERCOVER DOCTOR ** (1939) PR:A
UNDERCOVER GIRL (SEE:UNDERCOVER MAISIE)
UNDERCOVER GIRL ** (1950) PR:A
UNDERCOVER GIRL * (1957, Brit.) PR:A
UNDERCOVER MAISIE ** (1947) PR:A
UNDERCOVER MAN ** (1936) PR:A
UNDERCOVER MAN *½ (1942) PR:A
UNDERCOVER MAN, THE **½ (1949) PR:C
UNDERCOVER WOMAN, THE ** (1946) PR:A
UNDERCOVERS HERO * (1975, Brit.) PR:O
UNDERCURRENT **½ (1946) PR:A-C
UNDERDOG, THE ** (1943) PR:A
UNDERGROUND **½ (1941) PR:A
UNDERGROUND *½ (1970, Brit.) PR:C
UNDERGROUND AGENT **½ (1942) PR:A
UNDERGROUND GUERRILLAS ** (1944, Brit.) PR:A
UNDERGROUND RUSTLERS ** (1941) PR:A
UNDERGROUND U.S.A. ** (1980) PR:O
UNDERNEATH THE ARCHES ** (1937, Brit.) PR:A
UNDERSEA GIRL zero (1957) PR:A
UNDERSEA ODYSSEY, AN (SEE:NEPTUNE FACTOR, THE)
UNDERTAKER AND HIS PALS, THE zero (1966) PR:O
UNDERTOW * (1930) PR:A
UNDERTOW **½ (1949) PR:A
UNDERWATER! ** (1955) PR:C-O
UNDERWATER CITY, THE zero (1962) PR:A
UNDERWATER ODYSSEY, AN (SEE:NEPTURE FACTOR, THE)
UNDERWATER WARRIOR ** (1958) PR:A
UNDERWORLD ** (1937) PR:A-C
UNDERWORLD AFTER DARK (SEE:BIG TOWN AFTER DARK)
UNDERWORLD INFORMERS ** (1965, Brit.) PR:A
UNDERWORLD STORY, THE (SEE:WHIPPED, THE)
UNDERWORLD U.S.A. ***½ (1961) PR:C
UNDYING MONSTER, THE ** (1942) PR:A
UNE FEMME DEUCE (SEE:GENTLE CREATURE, A)
UNE FEMME EST UNE FEMME (SEE:WOMAN IS A WOMAN, A)
UNE HISTOIRE IMMORTELLE (SEE:IMMORTAL STORY, THE)
UNE JEUNE FILLE (SEE:MAGNIFICENT SINNER)
UNE MERE, UNE FILLE (SEE:ANNA)
UNE PARISIENNE (SEE:LA PARISIENNE)
UNEARTHLY, THE * (1957) PR:O
UNEARTHLY STRANGER, THE *** (1964, Brit.) PR:A
UNEASY TERMS * (1948, Brit.) PR:A
UNEASY VIRTUE ** (1931, Brit.) PR:A
UNEXPECTED FATHER *½ (1932) PR:A
UNEXPECTED FATHER ** (1939) PR:A
UNEXPECTED GUEST **½ (1946) PR:A
UNEXPECTED UNCLE * (1941) PR:A
UNFAITHFUL **½ (1931) PR:A
UNFAITHFUL WIFE, THE (SEE:LA FEMME INFIDELE)
UNFAITHFUL, THE **½ (1947) PR:A
UNFAITHFULLY YOURS *** (1948) PR:A-C**
UNFAITHFULLY YOURS ** (1984) PR:C
UNFAITHFULS, THE ** (1960, It.) PR:A
UNFINISHED BUSINESS * (1985, Aus.) PR:O**
UNFINISHED BUSINESS ** (1941) PR:A
UNFINISHED BUSINESS... * (1987) PR:C-O
UNFINISHED DANCE, THE ** (1947) PR:A
UNFINISHED SYMPHONY, THE *** (1953, Aust./Brit.) PR:A
UNFORGIVEN, THE * (1960) PR:C**
UNGUARDED HOUR, THE **½ (1936) PR:A
UNGUARDED MOMENT, THE **½ (1956) PR:A
UNHINGED zero (1982) PR:O
UNHOLY, THE * (1988) PR:O
UNHOLY DESIRE **½ (1964, Jap.) PR:O
UNHOLY FOUR, THE ** (1954, Brit.) PR:A
UNHOLY FOUR, THE * (1969, It.) PR:C
UNHOLY GARDEN, THE * (1931) PR:A
UNHOLY LOVE * (1932) PR:A
UNHOLY NIGHT, THE ** (1929) PR:A
UNHOLY PARTNERS **½ (1941) PR:A
UNHOLY QUEST, THE *½ (1934, Brit.) PR:A
UNHOLY ROLLERS ** (1972) PR:O
UNHOLY THREE, THE * (1930) PR:C**
UNHOLY WIFE, THE **½ (1957) PR:A
UNIDENTIFIED FLYING ODDBALL, THE **½ (1979, Brit.) PR:A
UNIFORM LOVERS (SEE:HOLD 'EM YALE)
UNINHIBITED, THE *½ (1968, Fr./It./Sp.) PR:C
UNINVITED, THE **** (1944) PR:C
UNINVITED, THE zero (1988) PR:O
UNION CITY ** (1980) PR:A
UNION DEPOT ***½ (1932) PR:A
UNION PACIFIC **** (1939) PR:A
UNION STATION ***½ (1950) PR:C
UNIVERSAL SOLDIER **½ (1971, Brit.) PR:C
UNIVERSITY OF LIFE *** (1941, USSR) PR:C
UNKILLABLES, THE (SEE:DARING GAME)
UNKISSED BRIDE, THE (SEE:MOTHER GOOSE A GO-GO)
UNKNOWN BATTLE, THE (SEE:HEROES OF TELEMARK)

UNKNOWN BLONDE * (1934) PR:A
UNKNOWN GUEST, THE ** (1943) PR:A
UNKNOWN ISLAND * (1948) PR:A
UNKNOWN MAN OF SHANDIGOR, THE *½
(1967, Switz.) PR:A
UNKNOWN MAN, THE *½ (1951) PR:C
UNKNOWN RANGER, THE ** (1936) PR:A
UNKNOWN SATELLITE OVER TOKYO
(SEE:MYSTERIOUS SATELLITE, THE)
UNKNOWN TERROR, THE * (1957) PR:A
UNKNOWN VALLEY ** (1933) PR:A
UNKNOWN WOMAN ** (1935) PR:A
UNKNOWN WORLD *½ (1951) PR:A
UNKNOWN, THE ** (1946) PR:A
UNMAN, WITTERING AND ZIGO **½
(1971, Brit.) PR:C
UNMARRIED ** (1939) PR:A
UNMARRIED WOMAN, AN **** (1978) PR:C-O
UNMASKED ** (1929) PR:A
UNMASKED ** (1950) PR:A
UNO DEI TRE
(SEE:TWO ARE GUILTY)
UNPUBLISHED STORY ** (1942, Brit.) PR:A
UNRECONCILED
(SEE:NOT RECONCILED, OR "ONLY VIOLENCE
HELPS WHERE IT RULES")
UNRUHIGE NACHT
(SEE:RESTLESS NIGHT, THE)
UNSATISFIED, THE *½ (1964, Sp.) PR:A
UNSEEN, THE **½ (1945) PR:A
UNSEEN, THE * (1981) PR:O
UNSEEN ENEMY *½ (1942) PR:A
UNSEEN HEROES
(SEE:MISSILE FROM HELL)
UNSENT LETTER, THE
(SEE:LETTER THAT WAS NEVER SENT, THE)
UNSER BOSS IST EINE DAME
(SEE:TREASURE OF SAN GENNARO)
UNSINKABLE MOLLY BROWN, THE ***
(1964) PR:A
UNSTOPPABLE MAN, THE *½ (1961, Brit.) PR:A
UNSTRAP ME * (1968) PR:O
UNSUITABLE JOB FOR A WOMAN, AN ***
(1982, Brit.) PR:C-O
UNSUSPECTED, THE **½ (1947) PR:A
UNTAMED **½ (1955) PR:C-O
UNTAMED **½ (1940) PR:A
UNTAMED ** (1929) PR:A-C
UNTAMED BREED, THE *½ (1948) PR:A
UNTAMED FRONTIER *½ (1952) PR:A
UNTAMED FURY ** (1947) PR:A
UNTAMED HEIRESS * (1954) PR:A
UNTAMED MISTRESS zero (1960) PR:O
UNTAMED WEST, THE
(SEE:FAR HORIZONS, THE)
UNTAMED WOMEN zero (1952) PR:A
UNTAMED YOUTH * (1957) PR:A
UNTER GEIERN
(SEE:FRONTIER HELLCAT)
UNTIL SEPTEMBER *½ (1984) PR:O
UNTIL THEY SAIL **½ (1957) PR:C
UNTITLED
(SEE:HEAD)
UNTOUCHABLES, THE
(SEE:SCARFACE MOB, THE)
UNTOUCHABLES, THE ** (1987) PR:O
UNTOUCHED *½ (1956) PR:A
UNVANQUISHED, THE
(SEE:APARAJITO)
UNWED MOTHER * (1958) PR:C-O
UNWELCOME STRANGER ** (1935) PR:A
UNWELCOME VISITORS
(SEE:LONE STAR PIONEERS)
UNWILLING AGENT ** (1968, Ger.) PR:A
UNWRITTEN CODE, THE * (1944) PR:A
UNWRITTEN LAW, THE *½ (1932) PR:A
UP FOR MURDER ** (1931) PR:A
UP FOR THE CUP ** (1931, Brit.) PR:A
UP FOR THE CUP **½ (1950, Brit.) PR:A
UP FOR THE DERBY ** (1933, Brit.) PR:A
UP FROM THE BEACH **½ (1965) PR:A
UP FROM THE DEPTHS zero (1979, Phil.) PR:O
UP FRONT *** (1951) PR:A
UP GOES MAISIE ** (1946) PR:A
UP IN ARMS **** (1944) PR:AA
UP IN CENTRAL PARK ** (1948) PR:A
UP IN MABEL'S ROOM **½ (1944) PR:A

UP IN SMOKE * (1957) PR:A
UP IN SMOKE zero (1978) PR:O
UP IN THE AIR ** (1940) PR:A
UP IN THE AIR **½ (1969, Brit.) PR:AA
UP IN THE CELLAR **½ (1970) PR:C
UP IN THE WORLD ** (1957, Brit.) PR:A
UP JUMPED A SWAGMAN ** (1965, Brit.) PR:A
UP PERISCOPE **½ (1959) PR:A
UP POMPEII ** (1971, Brit.) PR:O
UP POPS THE DEVIL ** (1931) PR:A
UP SHE GOES
(SEE:UP GOES MAISIE)
UP THE ACADEMY * (1980) PR:O
UP THE CHASTITY BELT *½ (1971, Brit.) PR:O
UP THE CREEK *** (1958, Brit.) PR:A
UP THE CREEK *** (1984) PR:O
UP THE DOWN STAIRCASE **½ (1967) PR:A-C
UP THE FRONT * (1972, Brit.) PR:C
UP THE JUNCTION ** (1968, Brit.) PR:O
UP THE MACGREGORS ** (1967, It./Sp.) PR:A
UP THE RIVER *** (1930) PR:A
UP THE RIVER **½ (1938) PR:A
UP THE SANDBOX ** (1972) PR:C-O
UP TIGHT
(SEE:UPTIGHT)
UP TO HIS EARS *** (1966, Fr./It.) PR:C
UP TO HIS NECK ** (1954, Brit.) PR:A
UP TO THE NECK **½ (1933, Brit.) PR:A
UP WITH THE LARK * (1943, Brit.) PR:A
UP YOUR TEDDY BEAR zero (1970) PR:O
UPHILL ALL THE WAY * (1986) PR:C
UPPER HAND, THE ** (1967, Fr./It./Ger.) PR:C
UPPER UNDERWORLD
(SEE:RULING VOICE, THE)
UPPER WORLD **½ (1934) PR:A
UPSTAIRS AND DOWNSTAIRS ** (1961, Brit.) PR:A
UPSTATE MURDERS, THE
(SEE:SAVAGE WEEKEND)
UPTIGHT ** (1968) PR:O
UPTOWN NEW YORK ** (1932) PR:A
UPTOWN SATURDAY NIGHT *** (1974) PR:C
UPTURNED GLASS, THE ** (1947, Brit.) PR:A-C
URANIUM BOOM *½ (1956) PR:A
URBAN COWBOY ** (1980) PR:C
URGE TO KILL ** (1960, Brit.) PR:C
URGENT CALL
(SEE:AGAINST THE LAW)
URSUS
(SEE:MIGHTY URSUS)
URSUS, IL GLADIATORE RIBELLE
(SEE:REBEL GLADIATORS, THE)
USCHI DAI SENSO
(SEE:BATTLE IN OUTER SPACE)
USED CARS ***½ (1980) PR:O
UTAH **½ (1945) PR:A
UTAH BLAINE ** (1957) PR:A
UTAH KID, THE ** (1930) PR:A
UTAH TRAIL ** (1938) PR:A
UTAH WAGON TRAIN ** (1951) PR:A
UTILITIES ** (1983, Can.) PR:C-O
UTOPIA **½ (1952, Fr./It.) PR:A
UTU ***½ (1984, New Zealand) PR:O

V

V.D. zero (1961) PR:O
V.I.P.s, THE ***½ (1963, Brit.) PR:A
VACATION DAYS * (1947) PR:A
VACATION FROM LOVE ** (1938) PR:A
VACATION FROM MARRIAGE ***
(1945, Brit.) PR:A
VACATION IN RENO ** (1946) PR:A
VACATION, THE zero (1971, It.) PR:C
VADO...L'AMMAZZO E TORNO
(SEE:ANY GUN CAN PLAY)
VAGABOND ***½ (1985, Fr.) PR:O
VAGABOND KING, THE *** (1930) PR:A
VAGABOND KING, THE *** (1956) PR:A
VAGABOND LADY *½ (1935) PR:A
VAGABOND LOVER ** (1929) PR:A
VAGABOND QUEEN, THE ** (1931, Brit.) PR:A

VAGABOND VIOLINIST
(SEE:BROKEN MELODY, THE)
VAGHE STELLE DELL'ORSA
(SEE:SANDRA)
VALACHI PAPERS, THE *** (1972, It./Fr.) PR:O
VALDEZ IS COMING **½ (1971) PR:O
VALENTINO ** (1951) PR:C
VALENTINO *½ (1977, Brit.) PR:C-O
VALERIE ** (1957) PR:C
VALET GIRLS * (1987) PR:O
VALHALLA *½ (1987, Den.) PR:AA
VALIANT HOMBRE THE ** (1948) PR:A
VALIANT IS THE WORD FOR CARRIE **
(1936) PR:A-C
VALIANT, THE *** (1929) PR:A-C
VALIANT, THE **½ (1962, Brit./It.) PR:A
VALLEY GIRL ***½ (1983) PR:C
VALLEY OF DEATH, THE
(SEE:TANK BATTALION)
VALLEY OF DECISION, THE *** (1945) PR:A
VALLEY OF EAGLES *½ (1952, Brit.) PR:A
VALLEY OF FEAR
(SEE:SHERLOCK HOLMES AND THE DEADLY
NECKLACE)
VALLEY OF FIRE ** (1951) PR:A
VALLEY OF FURY
(SEE:CHIEF CRAZY HORSE)
VALLEY OF GWANGI, THE ***½ (1969) PR:A
VALLEY OF HUNTED MEN **½ (1942) PR:A
VALLEY OF MYSTERY ** (1967) PR:A
VALLEY OF SONG
(SEE:MEN ARE CHILDREN TWICE)
VALLEY OF THE DOLLS zero (1967) PR:O
VALLEY OF THE DRAGONS *½ (1961) PR:A
VALLEY OF THE GIANTS ** (1938) PR:A
VALLEY OF THE HEADHUNTERS *½ (1953) PR:A
VALLEY OF THE KINGS ** (1954) PR:A-C
VALLEY OF THE LAWLESS ** (1936) PR:A
VALLEY OF THE REDWOODS ** (1960) PR:A
VALLEY OF THE SUN ** (1942) PR:A
VALLEY OF THE SWORDS
(SEE:CASTILIAN, THE)
VALLEY OF THE WHITE WOLVES
(SEE:MARA OF THE WILDERNESS)
VALLEY OF THE ZOMBIES *½ (1946) PR:C
VALLEY OF VENGEANCE *½ (1944) PR:A
VALS, THE zero (1985) PR:O
VALUE FOR MONEY **½ (1957, Brit.) PR:A
VAMP ** (1986) PR:O
VAMPING *½ (1984) PR:O
VAMPIRA
(SEE:OLD DRACULA)
VAMPIRE, THE *½ (1968, Mex.) PR:C
VAMPIRE AND THE BALLERINA, THE zero
(1962, It.) PR:C
VAMPIRE AND THE ROBOT, THE
(SEE:MY SON, THE VAMPIRE)
VAMPIRE BAT, THE *** (1933) PR:C
VAMPIRE BEAST CRAVES BLOOD, THE
(SEE:BLOOD BEAST TERROR)
VAMPIRE CIRCUS **½ (1972, Brit.) PR:C-O
VAMPIRE GIRLS, THE
(SEE:THE VAMPIRES)
VAMPIRE HOOKERS, THE zero (1979, Phil.) PR:O
VAMPIRE LOVERS, THE **½ (1970, Brit.) PR:O
VAMPIRE MEN OF THE LOST PLANET
(SEE:HORROR OF THE BLOOD MONSTERS)
VAMPIRE OVER LONDON
(SEE:MY SON, THE VAMPIRE)
VAMPIRE PEOPLE, THE
(SEE:BLOOD DRINKERS, THE)
VAMPIRE'S COFFIN, THE *½ (1958, Mex.) PR:O
VAMPIRE'S NIGHT ORGY, THE *½
(1973, Sp./It.) PR:O
VAMPIRE, THE
(SEE:VAMPYR)
VAMPIRE, THE * (1957) PR:C
VAMPIRES
(SEE:DEVIL'S COMMANDMENT, THE)
VAMPIRES, THE * (1969, Mex.) PR:O
VAMPIRE'S GHOST, THE *½ (1945) PR:C
VAMPIRES IN HAVANA *** (1987, Cuba) PR:C-O
VAMPYR ***** (1932, Fr./Ger.) PR:O
VAMPYRES, DAUGHTERS OF DRACULA **½
(1977, Brit.) PR:O
VAN, THE *½ (1977) PR:O
VAN NUYS BLVD. ** (1979) PR:O

VANDERGILT DIAMOND MYSTERY, THE *
  (1936) PR:A
VANESSA, HER LOVE STORY ** (1935) PR:A
VANISHING AMERICAN, THE ** (1955) PR:A
VANISHING FRONTIER, 1962
  (SEE:BROKEN LAND, THE)
VANISHING FRONTIER, THE ** (1932) PR:A
VANISHING OUTPOST, THE ** (1951) PR:A
VANISHING POINT **½ (1971) PR:C
VANISHING VIRGINIAN, THE ** (1941) PR:A
VANISHING WESTERNER, THE **½ (1950) PR:A
VANITY ** (1935) PR:A
VANITY FAIR * (1932) PR:C
VANITY STREET *½ (1932) PR:A
VANQUISHED, THE *½ (1953) PR:A
VARAN THE UNBELIEVABLE *½
  (1962, US/Jap.) PR:A
VARELSERNA
  (SEE:LES CREATURES)
VARIETY *½ (1935, Brit.) PR:A
VARIETY *½ (1984) PR:O
VARIETY GIRL *** (1947) PR:AA
VARIETY HOUR *½ (1937, Brit.) PR:A
VARIETY JUBILEE ** (1945, Brit.) PR:A
VARIETY LIGHTS **½ (1965, It.) PR:A
VARIETY PARADE ** (1936, Brit.) PR:A
VARSITY *½ (1928) PR:A
VARSITY SHOW **½ (1937) PR:A
VASECTOMY: A DELICATE MATTER zero
  (1986) PR:O
VAULT OF HORROR, THE **½ (1973, Brit.) PR:C-O
VAXDOCKAN
  (SEE:DOLL, THE)
VECHERA NA KHUTORE BLIZ DIKANKI
  (SEE:NIGHT BEFORE CHRISTMAS)
VEIL, THE
  (SEE:HAUNTS)
VEILED WOMAN, THE ** (1929) PR:C
VEILS OF BAGDAD, THE ** (1953) PR:A
VELVET HOUSE
  (SEE:CRUCIBLE OF HORROR)
VELVET TOUCH, THE *** (1948) PR:A
VELVET TRAP, THE zero (1966) PR:O
VELVET VAMPIRE, THE *½ (1971) PR:O
VENDETTA * (1950) PR:A
VENDETTA ** (1986) PR:O
VENDETTA DELLA MASCHERA DI FERRO
  (SEE:PRISONER OF THE IRON MASK)
VENDETTA, 1965
  (SEE:MURIETA)
VENDREDI 13 HEURES
  (SEE:WORLD IN MY POCKET, THE)
VENETIAN AFFAIR, THE ** (1967) PR:C
VENETIAN BIRD
  (SEE:ASSASSIN)
VENETIAN NIGHTS
  (SEE:CARNIVAL)
VENGEANCE *½ (1930) PR:A
VENGEANCE
  (SEE:TRAIL TO VENGEANCE)
VENGEANCE *½ (1964) PR:A
VENGEANCE ** (1968, It./Ger.) PR:C
VENGEANCE IS MINE *½ (1948, Brit.) PR:A
VENGEANCE IS MINE * (1969, It./Sp.) PR:A
VENGEANCE IS MINE *** (1980, Jap.) PR:O
VENGEANCE, 1944
  (SEE:VALLEY OF VENGEANCE)
VENGEANCE, 1965
  (SEE:BRAIN, THE)
VENGEANCE OF FU MANCHU, THE *½
  (1968, Brit./Ger./Hong Kong/Ireland) PR:A
VENGEANCE OF GREGORY
  (SEE:FEUD OF THE WEST)
VENGEANCE OF SHE, THE * (1968, Brit.) PR:A
VENGEANCE OF THE DEEP * (1940, Aus.) PR:A
VENGEANCE OF THE VAMPIRE WOMEN, THE zero
  (1969, Mex.) PR:O
VENGEANCE VALLEY ** (1951) PR:A
VENOM * (1968, Den.) PR:O
VENOM * (1982, Brit.) PR:O
VENOM, 1976
  (SEE:LEGEND OF SPIDER FOREST, THE)
VENTO DELL'EST
  (SEE:WIND FROM THE EAST)
VENUS DER PIRATEN
  (SEE:QUEEN OF THE PIRATES)
VENUS IN FURS *½ (1970, It./Brit./Ger.) PR:O
VENUS MAKES TROUBLE * (1937) PR:A
VENUSIAN, THE
  (SEE:STRANGER FROM VENUS, THE)
VERA *** (1987, Braz.) PR:O
VERA CRUZ *** (1954) PR:C-O
VERBOTEN? *** (1959) PR:C
VERBRECHEN NACH SCHULSCHLUSS
  (SEE:YOUNG GO WILD, THE)
VERDICT ** (1975, Fr./It.) PR:C
VERDICT OF THE SEA *½ (1932, Brit.) PR:A
VERDICT, THE ***½ (1946) PR:C

VERDICT, THE ** (1964, Brit.) PR:A
VERDICT, THE **** (1982) PR:C-O
VERFUHRUNG AM MEER
  (SEE:SEDUCTION BY THE SEA)
VERGELTUNG IN CATANO
  (SEE:SUNSCORCHED)
VERGINITA ** (1953, It.) PR:A-C
VERKLUGENE MELODIE
  (SEE:DEAD MELODY)
VERMILION DOOR ** (1969, Hong Kong) PR:A
VERNE MILLER * (1988) PR:O
VERONA TRIAL, THE **½ (1963, It.) PR:A
VERONIKA VOSS ***½ (1982, Ger.) PR:O
VERSPATUNG IN MARIENBORN
  (SEE:STOP TRAIN 349)
VERTIGO ***** (1958) PR:C
VERY BIG WITHDRAWAL, A
  (SEE:MAN, A WOMAN, AND A BANK, A)
VERY CLOSE QUARTERS * (1986) PR:O
VERY CURIOUS GIRL, A ** (1970, Fr.) PR:O
VERY EDGE, THE ** (1963, Brit.) PR:C
VERY HANDY MAN, A ** (1966, Fr./It.) PR:C
VERY HAPPY ALEXANDER *** (1969, Fr.) PR:A
VERY HONORABLE GUY, A ** (1934) PR:A
VERY IDEA, THE *½ (1929) PR:A
VERY IMPORTANT PERSON, A
  (SEE:COMING-OUT PARTY, A)
VERY NATURAL THING, A **½ (1974) PR:O
VERY PRIVATE AFFAIR, A ** (1962, Fr./It.) PR:C
VERY SPECIAL FAVOR, A ** (1965) PR:A
VERY THOUGHT OF YOU, THE * (1944) PR:A
VERY YOUNG LADY, A ** (1941) PR:A
VESSEL OF WRATH
  (SEE:BEACHCOMBER, THE)
VET IN THE DOGHOUSE
  (SEE:IN THE DOGHOUSE)
VETERAN, THE
  (SEE:DEATHDREAM)
VIA MARGUTTA
  (SEE:RUN WITH THE DEVIL)
VIA PONY EXPRESS * (1933) PR:A
VIAGGIO IN ITALIA
  (SEE:STRANGERS, THE)
VIBRATION *½ (1969, Swed.) PR:O
VICAR OF BRAY, THE ** (1937, Brit.) PR:A
VICE AND VIRTUE *½ (1965, Fr./It.) PR:O
VICE DOLLS *½ (1961, Fr.) PR:C
VICE GIRLS, LTD. * (1964) PR:O
VICE RACKET * (1937) PR:A
VICE RAID ** (1959) PR:C
VICE SQUAD ** (1953) PR:A
VICE SQUAD *½ (1982) PR:O
VICE SQUAD, THE **½ (1931) PR:A
VICE VERSA **½ (1948, Brit.) PR:A
VICE VERSA **½ (1988) PR:A-C
VICIOUS CIRCLE, THE
  (SEE:CIRCLE, THE)
VICIOUS CIRCLE, THE * (1948) PR:A
VICIOUS YEARS, THE ** (1950) PR:A
VICKI **½ (1953) PR:C
VISCOUNT, THE *½ (1967, Fr./Sp./It./Ger.) PR:C
VICTIM *** (1961, Brit.) PR:C-O
VICTIM FIVE
  (SEE:CODE 7, VICTIM 4!)
VICTIMS OF PERSECUTION *½ (1933) PR:A
VICTIMS OF THE BEYOND
  (SEE:SUCKER MONEY)
VICTOR FRANKENSTEIN **½
  (1975, Swed./Ireland) PR:C
VICTORIA THE GREAT **** (1937, Brit.) PR:A
VICTORS, THE ***½ (1963) PR:O
VICTOR/VICTORIA *** (1982) PR:O
VICTORY ** (1940) PR:A-C
VICTORY ** (1981) PR:A-C
VIDEO DEAD ** (1987) PR:C-O
VIDEO MADNESS
  (SEE:JOYSTICKS)
VIDEODROME * (1983, Can.) PR:O
VIENNA WALTZES **½ (1961, Aust.) PR:A
VIENNA, CITY OF SONGS * (1931, Ger.) PR:A
VIENNESE NIGHTS **½ (1930) PR:A
VIEW FROM POMPEY'S HEAD, THE **½
  (1955) PR:C-O
VIEW FROM THE BRIDGE, A **½
  (1962, Fr./It.) PR:C
VIEW TO A KILL, A ** (1985) PR:C
VIGIL *** (1984, New Zealand) PR:C
VIGIL IN THE NIGHT ** (1940) PR:C
VIGILANTE *½ (1983) PR:O
VIGILANTE FORCE ** (1976) PR:C
VIGILANTE HIDEOUT ** (1950) PR:A
VIGILANTE TERROR ** (1953) PR:A
VIGILANTES OF BOOMTOWN ** (1947) PR:A
VIGILANTES OF DODGE CITY ** (1944) PR:AA
VIGILANTES RETURN, THE ** (1947) PR:A
VIGOUR OF YOUTH
  (SEE:SPIRIT OF NOTRE DAME)
VIKING QUEEN, THE ** (1967, Brit.) PR:A

VIKING WOMEN AND THE SEA SERPENT
  (SEE:SAGA OF THE VIKING WOMEN AND THEIR
  VOYAGE TO THE WATERS OF THE GREAT SEA
  SERPENT, THE)
VIKING, THE *½ (1931) PR:A
VIKINGS, THE *** (1958) PR:C
VILLA! ** (1958) PR:A
VILLA RIDES ** (1968) PR:O
VILLAGE, THE ** (1953, Brit./Switz.) PR:A
VILLAGE BARN DANCE ** (1940) PR:A
VILLAGE OF DAUGHTERS *½ (1962, Brit.) PR:A
VILLAGE OF THE DAMNED *** (1960, Brit.) PR:C
VILLAGE OF THE GIANTS *½ (1965) PR:A
VILLAGE SQUIRE, THE * (1935, Brit.) PR:A
VILLAGE TALE *½ (1935) PR:A
VILLAIN zero (1971, Brit.) PR:O
VILLAIN STILL PURSUED HER, THE * (1940) PR:A
VILLAIN, THE * (1979) PR:A
VILLE SANS PITTE
  (SEE:TOWN WITHOUT PITY)
VILLIERS DIAMOND, THE * (1938, Brit.) PR:A
VILNA LEGEND, A * (1949, US/Pol.) PR:A
VINETU
  (SEE:APACHE GOLD)
VINETU II
  (SEE:LAST OF THE RENEGADES)
VINETU III
  (SEE:DESPERADO TRAIL, THE)
VINTAGE, THE *½ (1957) PR:A
VINTAGE WINE ** (1935, Brit.) PR:A
VIOLATED * (1953) PR:C
VIOLATED * (1986) PR:O
VIOLATED LOVE ** (1966, Arg.) PR:C
VIOLATED PARADISE *½ (1963, It./Jap.) PR:O
VIOLATORS, THE * (1957) PR:A
VIOLENCE ** (1947) PR:A
VIOLENT AND THE DAMNED, THE **
  (1962, Braz.) PR:C
VIOLENT ANGELS, THE
  (SEE:ANGELS DIE HARD)
VIOLENT BREED, THE * (1986, It.) PR:O
VIOLENT CITY
  (SEE:FAMILY, THE)
VIOLENT ENEMY, THE *½ (1969, Brit.) PR:A
VIOLENT FOUR, THE ** (1968, It.) PR:A
VIOLENT HOUR, THE
  (SEE:DIAL 1119)
VIOLENT JOURNEY
  (SEE:FOOL KILLER, THE)
VIOLENT LOVE
  (SEE:TAKE HER BY SURPRISE)
VIOLENT MEN, THE *** (1955) PR:A
VIOLENT MIDNIGHT
  (SEE:PSYCHOMANIA)
VIOLENT MOMENT *½ (1966, Brit.) PR:C
VIOLENT ONES, THE *½ (1967) PR:C
VIOLENT PLAYGROUND **½ (1958, Brit.) PR:A
VIOLENT ROAD ** (1958) PR:A
VIOLENT SATURDAY ***½ (1955) PR:O
VIOLENT STRANGER *½ (1957, Brit.) PR:A
VIOLENT STREETS
  (SEE:THIEF)
VIOLENT SUMMER **½ (1961, Fr./It.) PR:C
VIOLENT WOMEN ** (1960) PR:O
VIOLENT YEARS, THE zero (1956) PR:C-O
VIOLENZA PER UNA MONACA
  (SEE:NUN AT THE CROSSROADS, A)
VIOLETS ARE BLUE ** (1986) PR:C-O
VIOLETTE *** (1978, Fr.) PR:O
VIOLIN AND ROLLER **½ (1962, USSR) PR:A
VIPER, THE *½ (1938, Brit.) PR:A
VIRGIN AND THE GYPSY, THE **½
  (1970, Brit.) PR:O
VIRGIN AQUA SEX
  (SEE:MERMAIDS OF TIBURON)
VIRGIN COCOTTE, THE
  (SEE:COQUETTE)
VIRGIN FOR THE PRINCE, A
  (SEE:MAIDEN FOR A PRINCE, A)
VIRGIN ISLAND ** (1960, Brit.) PR:C
VIRGIN OF NUREMBURG, THE
  (SEE:HORROR CASTLE)
VIRGIN PRESIDENT, THE * (1968) PR:A
VIRGIN QUEEN OF ST. FRANCIS HIGH, THE *
  (1987, Can.) PR:A
VIRGIN QUEEN, THE *** (1955) PR:A-C
VIRGIN SACRIFICE *½ (1959) PR:C
VIRGIN SOLDIERS, THE **½ (1970, Brit.) PR:O
VIRGIN SPRING, THE *** (1960, Swed.) PR:C
VIRGIN WITCH, THE * (1973, Brit.) PR:O
VIRGINIA *½ (1941) PR:A
VIRGINIA CITY ***½ (1940) PR:A
VIRGINIA JUDGE, THE ** (1935) PR:A
VIRGINIA'S HUSBAND ** (1934, Brit.) PR:AA
VIRGINIAN, THE ***½ (1929) PR:A
VIRGINIAN, THE **½ (1946) PR:A-C
VIRIDIANA ***** (1962, Mex./Sp.) PR:C-O
VIRTUE *** (1932) PR:C

VIRTUOUS HUSBAND ** (1931) PR:A
VIRTUOUS SIN, THE ** (1930) PR:A
VIRTUOUS TRAMPS, THE
  (SEE:DEVIL'S BROTHER, THE)
VIRTUOUS WIFE, THE
  (SEE:MEN ARE LIKE THAT)
VIRUS **½ (1980, Jap.) PR:C
VIRUS HAS NO MORALS, A *** (1986, Ger.) PR:O
VISA TO CANTON
  (SEE:PASSPORT TO CHINA)
VISA U.S.A. *** (1987, Columbia/Cuba) PR:C
VISION QUEST ** (1985) PR:O
VISIT, THE **½ (1964, Ger./Fr./It./US) PR:C
VISIT TO A CHIEF'S SON **½ (1974) PR:AA
VISIT TO A SMALL PLANET ** (1960) PR:A
VISITING HOURS * (1982, Can.) PR:O
VISITOR, THE ***½ (1973, Can.) PR:C-O
VISITOR, THE * (1980, It./US) PR:O
VISITORS, THE ** (1972) PR:O
VISITORS FROM THE GALAXY **½
  (1981, Yugo.) PR:AA
VISKINGAR OCH ROP
  (SEE:CRIES AND WHISPERS)
VITA PRIVATA
  (SEE:VERY PRIVATE AFFAIR, A)
VITE PERDUTE
  (SEE:LOST SOULS)
VITELLONI ** (1956, It./Fr.) PR:C**
VIVA CISCO KID * (1940) PR:A
VIVA ITALIA *½ (1978, It.) PR:O
VIVA KNIEVEL? * (1977) PR:A
VIVA LAS VEGAS
  (SEE:MEET ME IN LAS VEGAS)
VIVA LAS VEGAS ** (1964) PR:A
VIVA MARIA **½ (1965, Fr./It.) PR:C
VIVA MAX? **½ (1969) PR:A
VIVA VILLA! **** (1934) PR:A-C
VIVA ZAPATA! *** (1952) PR:C**
VIVACIOUS LADY ***½ (1938) PR:A
VIVEMENT DIMANCHE?
  (SEE:CONFIDENTIALLY YOURS)
VIVERE PER VIVERE
  (SEE:LIVE FOR LIFE)
VIVIAMO OGGI
  (SEE:DAY AND THE HOUR, THE)
VIVIR DESVIVIENDOSE
  (SEE:MOMENT OF TRUTH)
VIVO PER LA TUA MORTE
  (SEE:LONG RIDE FROM HELL, A)
VIVRE POUR VIVRE
  (SEE:LIVE FOR LIFE)
VIVRE SA VIE
  (SEE:MY LIFE TO LIVE)
VIXEN ** (1970, Jap.) PR:O
VIXENS, THE * (1969) PR:O
VOGUES
  (SEE:VOGUES OF 1938)
VOGUES OF 1938 **½ (1937) PR:A
VOICE IN THE MIRROR **½ (1958) PR:A
VOICE IN THE NIGHT * (1934) PR:A
VOICE IN THE NIGHT
  (SEE:WANTED FOR MURDER)
VOICE IN THE NIGHT, A ** (1941, Brit.) PR:A
VOICE IN THE WIND * (1944) PR:A
VOICE IN YOUR HEART, A *½ (1952, It.) PR:C
VOICE OF BUGLE ANN ** (1936) PR:A
VOICE OF MERRILL, THE
  (SEE:MURDER WILL OUT)
VOICE OF TERROR
  (SEE:SHERLOCK HOLMES AND THE VOICE OF
  TERROR)
VOICE OF THE CITY ** (1929) PR:A
VOICE OF THE HURRICANE **½ (1964) PR:A
VOICE OF THE TURTLE, THE *** (1947) PR:A
VOICE OF THE WHISTLER **½ (1945) PR:C
VOICE WITHIN, THE *½ (1945, Brit.) PR:A
VOICES **½ (1973, Brit.) PR:O
VOICES ** (1979) PR:C
VOLCANO **½ (1953, It.) PR:A
VOLCANO, 1969
  (SEE:KRAKATOA, EAST OF JAVA)
VOLPONE **½ (1947, Fr.) PR:A
VOLTAIRE ** (1933) PR:A
VOLUNTEERS * (1985) PR:O**
VON RICHTHOFEN AND BROWN ** (1970) PR:C
VON RYAN'S EXPRESS ***½ (1965) PR:C

V1
  (SEE:MISSILE FROM HELL)
VOODOO BLOOD BATH
  (SEE:I EAT YOUR SKIN)
VOODOO GIRL
  (SEE:SUGAR HILL)
VOODOO HEARTBEAT zero (1972) PR:O
VOODOO ISLAND * (1957) PR:A
VOODOO MAN *½ (1944) PR:A
VOODOO TIGER *½ (1952) PR:A
VOODOO WOMAN * (1957) PR:A
VOR SONNENUNTERGANG ** (1961, Ger.) PR:A
VORTEX
  (SEE:DAY TIME ENDED, THE)
VORTEX *½ (1982) PR:O
VOSKRESENIYE
  (SEE:RESURRECTION)
VOTE FOR HUGGETT ** (1948, Brit.) PR:A
VOULEZ-VOUS DANSER AVEC MOI
  (SEE:COME DANCE WITH ME)
VOW, THE ** (1947, USSR) PR:A
VOYAGE, THE * (1974, It.) PR:O
VOYAGE BEYOND THE SUN
  (SEE:SPACE MONSTER)
VOYAGE IN A BALLOON
  (SEE:STOWAWAY IN THE SKY)
VOYAGE OF SILENCE **½ (1968, Fr.) PR:A
VOYAGE OF THE DAMNED *½ (1976, Brit.) PR:A-C
VOYAGE TO AMERICA **½ (1952, Fr.) PR:A
VOYAGE TO PREHISTORY
  (SEE:JOURNEY TO THE BEGINNING OF TIME)
**VOYAGE TO THE BOTTOM OF THE SEA **
  (1961) PR:A**
VOYAGE TO THE END OF THE UNIVERSE **½
  (1963, Czech.) PR:A
VOYAGE TO THE PLANET OF PREHISTORIC
  WOMEN * (1966) PR:A
**VOYAGE TO THE PREHISTORIC PLANET *
  (1965) PR:A**
VOYNA I MIR
  (SEE:WAR AND PEACE)
VRAZDA PO CESKU
  (SEE:MURDER CZECH STYLE)
VRAZDA PO NASEM
  (SEE:MURDER CZECH STYLE)
VREDENS DAG
  (SEE:DAY OF WRATH)
VROODER'S HOOCH
  (SEE:CRAZY WORLD OF JULIUS VROODER, THE)
VU DU PONT
  (SEE:VIEW FROM THE BRIDGE, A)
VULCAN AFFAIR, THE
  (SEE:TO TRAP A SPY)
VULCANO
  (SEE:VOLCANO)
VULTURE, THE ** (1937, Brit.) PR:A
VULTURE, THE *½ (1967, US/Brit./Can.) PR:C
VULTURES OF THE LAW
  (SEE:SON OF THE PLAINS)
VYNALEZ ZKAZY
  (SEE:FABULOUS WORLD OF JULES VERNE)
VZROSLYYE DETI
  (SEE:GROWN-UP CHILDREN)

W zero (1974) PR:C
W.C. FIELDS AND ME *** (1976) PR:C
W.I.A. (WOUNDED IN ACTION) *½ (1966) PR:A
"W" PLAN, THE ** (1931, Brit.) PR:A
W. W. AND THE DIXIE DANCEKINGS **½
  (1975) PR:A
WABASH AVENUE ***½ (1950) PR:A
WAC FROM WALLA WALLA, THE ** (1952) PR:A
**WACKIEST SHIP IN THE ARMY, THE **½
  (1961) PR:A**
WACKIEST WAGON TRAIN IN THE WEST, THE *½
  (1976) PR:A
WACKO zero (1983) PR:C
WACKY WORLD OF DR. MORGUS, THE *
  (1962) PR:A

WACKY WORLD OF MOTHER GOOSE, THE **½
  (1967) PR:AA
WACO **½ (1952) PR:A
WACO ** (1966) PR:C
WAGA KOI WAGA UTA
  (SEE:SONG FROM MY HEART, THE)
WAGES OF FEAR, 1977
  (SEE:SORCERER)
WAGES OF FEAR, THE ** (1955, Fr./It.) PR:O**
WAGNER * (1983, Brit./Hung./Aust.) PR:C-O**
WAGON MASTER, THE *½ (1929) PR:A
WAGON TEAM *½ (1952) PR:A
WAGON TRACKS WEST *½ (1943) PR:A
WAGON TRAIL **½ (1935) PR:A
WAGON TRAIN * (1940) PR:A
WAGON TRAIN, 1952
  (SEE:WAGON TEAM)
WAGON WHEELS ** (1934) PR:A
WAGON WHEELS WESTWARD ** (1956) PR:AA
WAGONMASTER *** (1950) PR:A**
WAGONS ROLL AT NIGHT, THE *** (1941) PR:A
WAGONS WEST ** (1952) PR:A
WAGONS WESTWARD ** (1940) PR:A
WAHINE
  (SEE:MAEVA)
WAIKIKI WEDDING *** (1937) PR:A
WAIT 'TIL THE SUN SHINES, NELLIE **½
  (1952) PR:A
WAIT FOR ME IN HEAVEN ** (1988, Sp.) PR:C
WAIT UNTIL DARK ***½ (1967) PR:O
WAITING AT THE CHURCH
  (SEE:RUNAROUND, THE)
WAITING FOR CAROLINE ** (1969, Can.) PR:C
WAITING FOR THE BRIDE
  (SEE:RUNAROUND, THE)
WAITING FOR THE MOON * (1987) PR:A**
WAITING WOMEN
  (SEE:SECRETS OF WOMEN)
WAITRESS * (1982) PR:O
WAJAN * (1938, Bali) PR:A
WAKAMBA? ** (1955) PR:AA
WAKAMONO TACHI
  (SEE:LIVE YOUR OWN WAY)
WAKARE
  (SEE:FAREWELL, MY BELOVED)
WAKARETE IKURU TOKI MO
  (SEE:ETERNITY OF LOVE)
WAKE ISLAND ** (1942) PR:A**
WAKE ME WHEN IT'S OVER *** (1960) PR:A
WAKE OF THE RED WITCH ***½ (1949) PR:A-C
WAKE UP AND DIE **½ (1967, Fr./It.) PR:C
WAKE UP AND DREAM ** (1934) PR:A
WAKE UP AND DREAM ** (1946) PR:A
WAKE UP AND DREAM, 1942
  (SEE:WHAT'S COOKIN')
WAKE UP AND LIVE *** (1937) PR:AA
WAKE UP FAMOUS ** (1937, Brit.) PR:A
WALK A CROOKED MILE **½ (1948) PR:A
WALK A CROOKED PATH *½ (1969, Brit.) PR:O
WALK A TIGHTROPE ** (1964, US/Brit.) PR:A-C
WALK, DON'T RUN *** (1966) PR:A
WALK EAST ON BEACON *** (1952) PR:A
WALK IN THE SHADOW ** (1966, Brit.) PR:A
WALK IN THE SPRING RAIN, A ** (1970) PR:C
WALK IN THE SUN, A *** (1945) PR:C**
WALK INTO HELL **½ (1957, Aus.) PR:A
WALK LIKE A DRAGON ** (1960) PR:O
WALK LIKE A MAN zero (1987) PR:A-C
WALK ON THE MOON, A *** (1987) PR:O
WALK ON THE WILD SIDE **½ (1962) PR:O
WALK PROUD ** (1979) PR:C
WALK SOFTLY, STRANGER **½ (1950) PR:C
WALK TALL ** (1960) PR:A
WALK THE ANGRY BEACH *½ (1961) PR:C
WALK THE DARK STREET ** (1956) PR:C
WALK THE PROUD LAND **½ (1956) PR:A
WALK THE WALK * (1970) PR:O
WALK WITH LOVE AND DEATH, A ** (1969) PR:C
WALKABOUT ***½ (1971, Aus./US) PR:C
WALKER * (1987) PR:O**
WALKING DEAD, THE ***½ (1936) PR:A
WALKING DOWN BROADWAY ** (1938) PR:A
WALKING DOWN BROADWAY, 1935
  (SEE:HELLO SISTER)
WALKING HILLS, THE *** (1949) PR:A
WALKING MY BABY BACK HOME ** (1953) PR:A
WALKING ON AIR *** (1936) PR:A

WALKING ON AIR * (1946, Brit.) PR:AA
WALKING ON WATER
(SEE:STAND AND DELIVER)
WALKING STICK, THE **½ (1970, Brit.) PR:C
WALKING TALL **½ (1973) PR:O
WALKING TALL, PART II * (1975) PR:O
WALKING TARGET, THE ** (1960) PR:C
WALKING THE EDGE * (1985) PR:O
WALKOVER * (1969, Pol.) PR:C**
WALKOWER
(SEE:WALKOVER)
WALL-EYED NIPPON **½ (1963, Jap.) PR:A
WALL FOR SAN SEBASTIAN
(SEE:GUNS FOR SAN SEBASTIAN)
WALL OF NOISE **½ (1963) PR:A
WALL STREET ** (1929) PR:A
WALL STREET * (1987) PR:O**
WALL STREET COWBOY *½ (1939) PR:A
WALL, THE
(SEE:PINK FLOYD-THE WALL)
WALL, THE * (1985, Fr.) PR:O**
WALLABY JIM OF THE ISLANDS ** (1937) PR:A
WALLET, THE ** (1952, Brit.) PR:A
WALLFLOWER **½ (1948) PR:A
WALLS CAME TUMBLING DOWN, THE **
(1946) PR:A
WALLS OF GOLD * (1933) PR:C
WALLS OF HELL, THE ** (1964, US/Phil.) PR:A
WALLS OF JERICHO **½ (1948) PR:C
WALLS OF MALAPAGA, THE ***
(1950, Fr./It.) PR:A
WALPURGIS NIGHT **½ (1941, Swed.) PR:A-C
WALTZ ACROSS TEXAS ** (1982) PR:A-C
WALTZ OF THE TOREADORS *
(1962, Brit.) PR:A-C**
WALTZ TIME ** (1933, Brit.) PR:A
WALTZ TIME *½ (1946, Brit.) PR:A
WALTZES FROM VIENNA
(SEE:STRAUSS' GREAT WALTZ)
WANDA ***½ (1971) PR:C
WANDA NEVADA * (1979) PR:A-C
WANDER LOVE STORY
(SEE:WANDERLOVE)
WANDERER OF THE WASTELAND *½ (1935) PR:A
WANDERER OF THE WASTELAND ** (1945) PR:A
WANDERER, THE **½ (1969, Fr.) PR:A
WANDERERS OF THE WEST ** (1941) PR:A
WANDERERS, THE ** (1979) PR:O**
WANDERING JEW, THE ***½ (1933) PR:A
WANDERING JEW, THE **½ (1935, Brit.) PR:A
WANDERING JEW, THE *** (1948, It.) PR:O
WANDERLOVE * (1970) PR:O
WANDERLUST
(SEE:MARY JANE'S PA)
WANNSEE CONFERENCE, THE *
(1987, Ger./Aust.) PR:A-C**
WANT A RIDE LITTLE GIRL?
(SEE:IMPULSE)
WANTED
(SEE:HIGH VOLTAGE)
WANTED
(SEE:POLICE CALL)
WANTED **½ (1937, Brit.) PR:A
WANTED BY SCOTLAND YARD **
(1939, Brit.) PR:A
WANTED BY THE POLICE *½ (1938) PR:A
WANTED: DEAD OR ALIVE *½ (1987) PR:O
WANTED FOR MURDER ** (1946, Brit.) PR:C
WANTED MEN
(SEE:WOLVES)
WANTED MEN, 1931
(SEE:LAW OF THE RIO GRANDE)
WANTED WOMEN
(SEE:JESSIE'S GIRLS)
WANTED: JANE TURNER ** (1936) PR:A
WANTON CONTESSA, THE
(SEE:SENSO)
WAR
(SEE:RAT)
WAR AGAINST MRS. HADLEY, THE ***
(1942) PR:A
WAR AND LOVE *½ (1985) PR:O
WAR AND PEACE ** (1956, It./US) PR:A-C**
WAR AND PEACE **½ (1968, USSR) PR:A-C
WAR AND PEACE ** (1983, Ger.) PR:C
WAR AND PIECE
(SEE:HAREM BUNCH, OR WAR AND PIECE, THE)
WAR ARROW **½ (1953) PR:A
WAR BETWEEN MEN AND WOMEN, THE **½
(1972) PR:A-C
**WAR BETWEEN THE PLANETS zero
(1971, It.) PR:A**
WAR CORRESPONDENT ** (1932) PR:A
WAR DOGS ** (1942) PR:A
WAR DRUMS *½ (1957) PR:A
WAR GAMES, 1970
(SEE:SUPPOSE THEY GAVE A WAR AND NO ONE
CAME?)

WAR GAMES, 1983
(SEE:WARGAMES)
WAR GODS OF THE DEEP
(SEE:CITY UNDER THE SEA)
WAR HEAD
(SEE:OPERATION SNAFU)
WAR HERO, WAR MADNESS
(SEE:WAR IS HELL)
WAR HUNT ***½ (1962) PR:C
WAR IS A RACKET * (1934) PR:A-C
WAR IS HELL ** (1964) PR:A-C
WAR IS OVER, THE
(SEE:LA GUERRE EST FINIE)
WAR ITALIAN STYLE ** (1967, It.) PR:A
WAR LORD, THE *** (1965) PR:O
WAR LORD, THE, 1937
(SEE:WEST OF SHANGHAI)
WAR LOVER, THE * (1962, US/Brit.) PR:C-O**
WAR MADNESS
(SEE:WAR IS HELL)
WAR NURSE *½ (1930) PR:A
WAR OF THE ALIENS
(SEE:STARSHIP INVASIONS)
WAR OF THE BUTTONS *** (1963, Fr.) PR:A
WAR OF THE COLOSSAL BEAST *½ (1958) PR:A
WAR OF THE GARGANTUAS, THE zero
(1970, Jap.) PR:A
WAR OF THE MONSTERS ** (1972, Jap.) PR:A
WAR OF THE PLANETS ** (1977, Jap.) PR:A
WAR OF THE RANGE * (1933) PR:A
WAR OF THE SATELLITES * (1958) PR:A
WAR OF THE WILDCATS
(SEE:IN OLD OKLAHOMA)
WAR OF THE WIZARDS *½ (1983, Taiwan) PR:C
WAR OF THE WORLDS—NEXT CENTURY, THE ***
(1981, Pol.) PR:C
WAR OF THE WORLDS, THE ** (1953) PR:C**
WAR OF THE ZOMBIES, THE ** (1965, It.) PR:C-O
WAR PAINT **½ (1953) PR:A
WAR PARTY ** (1965) PR:A
WAR SHOCK
(SEE:WOMAN'S DEVOTION, A)
WAR WAGON, THE ***½ (1967) PR:A
WAR ZONE
(SEE:DEADLINE, Ger./Brit.)
WARD 13
(SEE:HOSPITAL MASSACRE)
WARDOGS * (1987, Swed.) PR:O
WARE CASE, THE *½ (1939, Brit.) PR:A
WARGAMES * (1983) PR:A**
WARKILL **½ (1968, US/Phil.) PR:O
WARLOCK ** (1959) PR:C**
WARLORD OF CRETE, THE
(SEE:MINOTAUR, THE)
WARLORDS OF ATLANTIS ** (1978, Brit.) PR:AA
WARLORDS OF THE DEEP
(SEE:CITY UNDER THE SEA)
WARLORDS OF THE 21ST CENTURY
(SEE:BATTLETRUCK)
WARM BODY, THE
(SEE:THUNDER IN THE BLOOD)
WARM CORNER, A ** (1930, Brit.) PR:AA
WARM DECEMBER, A ** (1973, Brit.) PR:C
WARM IN THE BUD * (1970) PR:A
WARM NIGHTS ON A SLOW MOVING TRAIN **
(1987, Aus.) PR:C
WARN LONDON! **½ (1934, Brit.) PR:A
WARN THAT MAN ** (1943, Brit.) PR:A
WARNING FORM SPACE
(SEE:MYSTERIOUS SATELLITE, THE)
WARNING SHOT ***½ (1967) PR:A-C
WARNING SIGN ** (1985) PR:O
WARNING TO WANTONS, A **½ (1949, Brit.) PR:A
WARPATH **½ (1951) PR:A
WARREN CASE, THE * (1934, Brit.) PR:A
WARRING CLANS **½ (1963, Jap.) PR:C
WARRIOR AND THE SLAVE GIRL, THE **½
(1959, It.) PR:A
**WARRIOR AND THE SORCERESS, THE *
(1984) PR:O**
WARRIOR EMPRESS, THE * (1961, It./Fr.) PR:O
WARRIOR QUEEN * (1987) PR:O
WARRIOR'S HUSBAND THE *** (1933) PR:C
WARRIORS, THE *** (1955) PR:A-C
WARRIORS, THE
(SEE:KELLY'S HEROES)
WARRIORS, THE ***½ (1979) PR:O
WARRIORS FIVE * (1962, Fr./It.) PR:A
**WARRIORS OF THE WASTELAND *
(1984, It.) PR:O**
WARRIORS OF THE WIND ** (1984, Jap.) PR:A
WASHINGTON B.C.
(SEE:HAIL)
WASHINGTON COWBOY
(SEE:ROVIN' TUMBLEWEEDS)
WASHINGTON MASQUERADE *½ (1932) PR:A
WASHINGTON MELODRAMA ** (1941) PR:A
WASHINGTON MERRY-GO-ROUND * (1932) PR:A

WASHINGTON STORY **½ (1952) PR:A
WASP WOMAN, THE * (1959) PR:A
WASTREL, THE *½ (1963, It.) PR:C
WASTRELS, THE
(SEE:VITELLONI)
WATASHI GA SUTETA ONNA
(SEE:GIRL I ABANDONED, THE)
WATCH BEVERLY *½ (1932, Brit.) PR:A
WATCH IT, SAILOR! *½ (1961, Brit.) PR:A
WATCH ON THE RHINE ** (1943) PR:A**
WATCH THE BIRDIE **½ (1950) PR:A
WATCH YOUR STERN ** (1961, Brit.) PR:A
WATCHED ** (1974) PR:O
WATCHER IN THE WOODS, THE *½
(1980, Brit.) PR:C
WATER ** (1985, Brit.) PR:C-O
WATER BABIES, THE **½ (1979, Brit.) PR:AA
WATER CYBORGS
(SEE:TERROR BENEATH THE SEA)
WATER FOR CANITOGA * (1939, Ger.) PR:A
WATER GIPSIES, THE
(SEE:WATER GYPSIES, THE)
WATER GYPSIES, THE ** (1932, Brit.) PR:A
WATER RUSTLERS *½ (1939) PR:A
WATERFRONT * (1939) PR:A
WATERFRONT ** (1944) PR:A
WATERFRONT AT MIDNIGHT **½ (1948) PR:A
WATERFRONT LADY *½ (1935) PR:A
WATERFRONT, 1952
(SEE:WATERFRONT WOMEN)
WATERFRONT WOMEN ** (1952, Brit.) PR:A
WATERHOLE NO. 3 * (1967) PR:C**
WATERLOO ** (1970, It./USSR) PR:C
WATERLOO BRIDGE ***½ (1931) PR:C
WATERLOO BRIDGE ** (1940) PR:C**
WATERLOO ROAD ** (1949, Brit.) PR:A
WATERMELON MAN **½ (1970) PR:C
WATERSHIP DOWN * (1978, Brit.) PR:C-O**
WATTS MONSTER, THE
(SEE:DR. BLACK, MR. HYDE)
WATUSI *½ (1959) PR:A
WATUSI A GO-GO
(SEE:GET YOURSELF A COLLEGE GIRL)
WAVE, A WAC AND A MARINE, A *½ (1944) PR:A
WAVELENGTH ** (1983) PR:C
WAY AHEAD, THE
(SEE:IMMORTAL BATALLION, THE)
WAY BACK HOME ** (1932) PR:A
WAY DOWN EAST ** (1935) PR:A
WAY DOWN SOUTH *½ (1939) PR:A
WAY FOR A SAILOR * (1930) PR:A
WAY OF A GAUCHO **½ (1952) PR:A
WAY OF ALL FLESH, THE * (1940) PR:A
WAY OF ALL MEN, THE *½ (1930) PR:A
WAY OF LIFE, THE
(SEE:THEY CALL IT SIN)
WAY OF LOST SOULS, THE ** (1929, Brit.) PR:C
WAY OF THE WEST, THE *½ (1934) PR:A
WAY OF YOUTH, THE * (1934, Brit.) PR:A
WAY OUT * (1966) PR:O
WAY OUT LOVE
(SEE:TOUCH OF HER FLESH, THE)
WAY OUT WEST ** (1930) PR:A
WAY OUT WEST ** (1937) PR:AA**
WAY OUT, THE *½ (1956, Brit.) PR:A
WAY OUT, WAY IN *½ (1970, Jap.) PR:O
WAY TO LOVE, THE *½ (1933) PR:A
WAY TO THE GOLD, THE **½ (1957) PR:A
WAY TO THE STARS, THE
(SEE:JOHNNY IN THE CLOUDS)
WAY...WAY OUT * (1966) PR:C-O
WAY WE LIVE NOW, THE * (1970) PR:O
WAY WE LIVE, THE *** (1946, Brit.) PR:A
WAY WE WERE, THE * (1973) PR:C**
WAY WEST, THE **½ (1967) PR:A
WAYLAID WOMEN
(SEE:INDECENT)
WAYS OF LOVE ***** (1950, It./Fr.) PR:C-O
WAYSIDE PEBBLE, THE ** (1962, Jap.) PR:A
WAYWARD *½ (1932) PR:A
WAYWARD BUS, THE ** (1957) PR:C
WAYWARD GIRL, THE * (1957) PR:A
WE ACCUSE
(SEE:J'ACCUSE)
WE ARE ALL MURDERERS **½ (1957, Fr.) PR:C
WE ARE ALL NAKED * (1970, Can./Fr.) PR:O
WE ARE IN THE NAVY NOW
(SEE:WE JOINED THE NAVY)
WE ARE NOT ALONE ***½ (1939) PR:A-C
WE DIVE AT DAWN ***½ (1943, Brit.) PR:A
WE GO FAST * (1941) PR:A
WE HAVE ONLY ONE LIFE ** (1963, Gr.) PR:A
WE HAVE OUR MOMENTS ** (1937) PR:A
WE HUMANS
(SEE:YOUNG AMERICA)
WE JOINED THE NAVY *½ (1962, Brit.) PR:A
WE LIVE AGAIN **** (1934) PR:C
WE OF THE NEVER NEVER **½ (1983, Aus.) PR:C

WE SHALL RETURN ** (1963) PR:A
WE SHALL SEE * (1964, Brit.) PR:C
WE STILL KILL THE OLD WAY **½ (1967, It.) PR:C
WE THREE
  (SEE:COMPROMISED)
WE THREE *** (1985, It.) PR:C
WE WANT TO LIVE ALONE
  (SEE:FATHER CAME TOO)
WE WENT TO COLLEGE ** (1936) PR:A
WE WERE DANCING **½ (1942) PR:A
WE WERE STRANGERS ***½ (1949) PR:C
WE WHO ARE ABOUT TO DIE ** (1937) PR:A
WE WHO ARE YOUNG **½ (1940) PR:A-C
WE WILL REMEMBER ** (1966, Jap.) PR:A-C
WEAK AND THE WICKED, THE **
  (1954, Brit.) PR:A
WEAKER SEX, THE ** (1949, Brit.) PR:A
WEAPON, THE **½ (1957, Brit.) PR:C
WEARY RIVER *½ (1929) PR:A
WEATHER IN THE STREETS, THE *½
  (1983, Brit.) PR:C
WEB OF DANGER, THE ** (1947) PR:A
WEB OF EVIDENCE **½ (1959, Brit.) PR:C
WEB OF FEAR **½ (1966, Fr./Sp.) PR:C
WEB OF PASSION ** (1961, Fr.) PR:C
WEB OF SUSPICION *½ (1959, Brit.) PR:A
WEB OF THE SPIDER ** (1972, It./Fr./Ger.) PR:O
WEB OF VIOLENCE ** (1966, It./Sp.) PR:C
WEB, THE *** (1947) PR:A
WEBSTER BOY, THE ** (1962, Brit.) PR:A
WEDDING BELLS
  (SEE:ROYAL WEDDING)
WEDDING BREAKFAST
  (SEE:CATERED AFFAIR, THE)
WEDDING GROUP
  (SEE:WRATH OF JEALOUSY)
WEDDING IN GALILEE **** (1988, Bel./Fr.) PR:O
WEDDING IN WHITE **½ (1972, Can.) PR:O
WEDDING NIGHT * (1970, Ireland) PR:O
WEDDING NIGHT, THE *** (1935) PR:A
WEDDING OF LILLI MARLENE, THE *
  (1953, Brit.) PR:A
WEDDING PARTY, THE * (1969) PR:O
WEDDING PRESENT ** (1936) PR:A
WEDDING PRESENT, 1963
  (SEE:TURKISH CUCUMBER, THE)
WEDDING REHEARSAL **½ (1932, Brit.) PR:A
WEDDING RINGS *½ (1930) PR:A
WEDDING, A * (1978) PR:C
WEDDINGS AND BABIES *** (1960) PR:A
WEDDINGS ARE WONDERFUL ** (1938, Brit.) PR:A
WEDNESDAY CHILDREN, THE *½ (1973) PR:C
WEDNESDAY'S CHILD ** (1934) PR:A
WEDNESDAY'S CHILD
  (SEE:FAMILY LIFE)
WEDNESDAY'S LUCK * (1936, Brit.) PR:A
WEE GEORDIE * (1956, Brit.) PR:A**
WEE WILLIE WINKIE * (1937) PR:AA**
WEEDS ***½ (1987) PR:O
WEEK-END MADNESS
  (SEE:AUGUST WEEK-END)
WEEK-END MARRIAGE ** (1932) PR:A
WEEK-ENDS ONLY ** (1932) PR:A
WEEKEND ** (1964, Den.) PR:C
WEEKEND *** (1968, Fr./It.) PR:O
WEEKEND A ZUYDCOOTE
  (SEE:WEEKEND AT DUNKIRK)
WEEKEND AT DUNKIRK ** (1966, Fr./It.) PR:A
WEEKEND AT THE WALDORF *** (1945) PR:A
WEEKEND BABYSITTER
  (SEE:WEEKEND WITH THE BABYSITTER)
WEEKEND FOR THREE ** (1941) PR:A
WEEKEND IN HAVANA **½ (1941) PR:A
WEEKEND MILLIONAIRE ** (1937, Brit.) PR:A
WEEKEND MURDERS, THE *** (1972, It.) PR:O
WEEKEND OF FEAR * (1966) PR:C
WEEKEND OF SHADOWS * (1978, Aus.) PR:C**
WEEKEND PASS ** (1944) PR:A
WEEKEND PASS * (1984) PR:O
WEEKEND WARRIORS zero (1986) PR:O
WEEKEND WITH FATHER ***½ (1951) PR:A
WEEKEND WITH LULU, A **½ (1961, Brit.) PR:A
WEEKEND WITH THE BABYSITTER * (1970) PR:O
WEEKEND WIVES
  (SEE:WEEKEND, ITALIAN STYLE)
WEEKEND, ITALIAN STYLE **
  (1967, Fr./It./Sp.) PR:A

WEIRD LOVE MAKERS, THE * (1963, Jap.) PR:O
WEIRD ONES, THE zero (1962) PR:C
WEIRD SCIENCE *½ (1985) PR:O
WEIRD WOMAN **½ (1944) PR:A
WELCOME DANGER **½ (1929) PR:A
WELCOME HOME *½ (1935) PR:A
WELCOME HOME
  (SEE:SNAFU)
WELCOME HOME, SOLDIER BOYS * (1972) PR:O
WELCOME IN VIENNA ****
  (1988, Aust./W. Ger.) PR:O
WELCOME KOSTYA? ** (1965, USSR) PR:AA
WELCOME, MR. WASHINGTON **½
  (1944, Brit.) PR:A
WELCOME STRANGER *** (1947) PR:A
WELCOME STRANGER
  (SEE:ACROSS THE SIERRAS)
WELCOME TO ARROW BEACH
  (SEE:TENDER FLESH)
**WELCOME TO BLOOD CITY zero
  (1977, Brit./Can.) PR:O**
WELCOME TO 18 * (1986) PR:O
WELCOME TO GERMANY ***
  (1988, W. Ger./Brit./Switz.) PR:C
WELCOME TO HARD TIMES ** (1967) PR:O
WELCOME TO L.A. **½ (1976) PR:O
WELCOME TO THE CLUB *½ (1971) PR:O
WELCOME, MR. BEDDOES
  (SEE:MAN COULD GET KILLED, A)
WELL, THE *** (1951) PR:A
**WELL-DIGGER'S DAUGHTER, THE **½
  (1946, Fr.) PR:C**
WELL DONE, HENRY * (1936, Brit.) PR:A
WELL-GROOMED BRIDE, THE ** (1946) PR:A
WE'LL GROW THIN TOGETHER * (1979, Fr.) PR:C
WE'LL MEET AGAIN **½ (1942, Brit.) PR:A
WE'LL SMILE AGAIN **½ (1942, Brit.) PR:A
WELLS FARGO **** (1937) PR:A
WELLS FARGO GUNMASTER ** (1951) PR:A
WENT THE DAY WELL?
  (SEE:48 HOURS)
WE'RE GOING TO BE RICH ** (1938, Brit.) PR:A
WE'RE IN THE ARMY NOW
  (SEE:PACK UP YOUR TROUBLES)
WE'RE IN THE LEGION NOW *½ (1937) PR:A
WE'RE IN THE MONEY **½ (1935) PR:A
WE'RE NO ANGELS * (1955) PR:A-C**
WE'RE NOT DRESSING *** (1934) PR:A
WE'RE NOT MARRIED ** (1952) PR:A
WE'RE ON THE JURY ** (1937) PR:A
WE'RE ONLY HUMAN ** (1936) PR:A
WE'RE RICH AGAIN * (1934) PR:A
WEREWOLF IN A GIRL'S DORMITORY zero
  (1961, It./Aust.) PR:C-O
WEREWOLF OF LONDON, THE ***½ (1935) PR:C
WEREWOLF OF WASHINGTON * (1973) PR:C
WEREWOLF VS. THE VAMPIRE WOMAN, THE *½
  (1970, Sp./Ger.) PR:O
WEREWOLF, THE *½ (1956) PR:C-O
WEREWOLVES ON WHEELS * (1971) PR:O
WEST 11 *½ (1963, Brit.) PR:C
WEST OF ABILENE ** (1940) PR:A
WEST OF BROADWAY * (1931) PR:A
WEST OF CARSON CITY ** (1940) PR:A
WEST OF CHEYENNE *½ (1931) PR:A
WEST OF CHEYENNE *½ (1938) PR:A
WEST OF CIMARRON ** (1941) PR:A
WEST OF EL DORADO ** (1949) PR:A
WEST OF MONTANA
  (SEE:MAIL ORDER BRIDE)
WEST OF NEVADA ** (1936) PR:A
WEST OF PINTO BASIN ** (1940) PR:A
WEST OF RAINBOW'S END ** (1938) PR:A
WEST OF SANTA FE ** (1938) PR:A
WEST OF SHANGHAI **½ (1937) PR:A
WEST OF SINGAPORE ** (1933) PR:A
WEST OF SONORA ** (1948) PR:A
WEST OF SUEZ
  (SEE:FIGHTING WILDCATS, THE)
WEST OF TEXAS ** (1943) PR:A
WEST OF THE ALAMO *½ (1946) PR:A
WEST OF THE BRAZOS ** (1950) PR:A
WEST OF THE DIVIDE **½ (1934) PR:A
WEST OF THE GREAT DIVIDE
  (SEE:NORTH OF THE GREAT DIVIDE)
WEST OF THE LAW **½ (1942) PR:A
WEST OF THE PECOS *** (1935) PR:A-C

WEST OF THE PECOS *** (1945) PR:A
WEST OF THE ROCKIES zero (1929) PR:A
WEST OF THE ROCKIES zero (1931) PR:A
WEST OF THE SUEZ
  (SEE:FIGHTING WILDCATS)
WEST OF TOMBSTONE ** (1942) PR:A
WEST OF WYOMING *½ (1950) PR:A
WEST OF ZANZIBAR ** (1954, Brit.) PR:A
WEST POINT OF THE AIR ** (1935) PR:A
WEST POINT STORY, THE ***½ (1950) PR:A
WEST POINT WIDOW ** (1941) PR:A
WEST SIDE KID ** (1943) PR:A
WEST SIDE STORY ** (1961) PR:A-C**
WEST TO GLORY *½ (1947) PR:A
WESTBOUND ** (1959) PR:A
WESTBOUND LIMITED ** (1937) PR:A
WESTBOUND MAIL ** (1937) PR:A
WESTBOUND STAGE ** (1940) PR:A
WESTERN CARAVANS ** (1939) PR:A
WESTERN COURAGE **½ (1935) PR:A
WESTERN CYCLONE ** (1943) PR:A
WESTERN FRONTIER ** (1935) PR:A
WESTERN GOLD * (1937) PR:A
WESTERN HERITAGE ** (1948) PR:A
WESTERN JAMBOREE ** (1938) PR:A
WESTERN JUSTICE ** (1935) PR:A
WESTERN LIMITED * (1932) PR:A
WESTERN MAIL *½ (1942) PR:A
WESTERN PACIFIC AGENT ** (1950) PR:A
WESTERN RENEGADES ** (1949) PR:A
WESTERN TRAILS *½ (1938) PR:A
WESTERN UNION **** (1941) PR:A
WESTERNER, THE *** (1940) PR:A**
WESTERNER, THE ** (1936) PR:A
WESTLAND CASE, THE ** (1937) PR:A
WESTMINSTER PASSION PLAY—BEHOLD THE
  MAN, THE ** (1951, Brit.) PR:A
WESTWARD BOUND **½ (1931) PR:A
WESTWARD BOUND * (1944) PR:A
WESTWARD DESPERADO ** (1961, Jap.) PR:C
WESTWARD HO *½ (1936) PR:A
WESTWARD HO ** (1942) PR:A
WESTWARD HO THE WAGONS? ** (1956) PR:A
WESTWARD PASSAGE **½ (1932) PR:A
WESTWARD THE WOMEN *** (1951) PR:A
WESTWARD TRAIL, THE * (1948) PR:A
WESTWORLD ****½ (1973) PR:C
WET PARADE, THE **½ (1932) PR:C
WETBACKS ** (1956) PR:A
WETHERBY ***½ (1985, Brit.) PR:O
WE'VE NEVER BEEN LICKED *** (1943) PR:A
WHALE OF A TALE, A ** (1977) PR:AA
WHALERS, THE **½ (1942:,, Swed.) PR:A
WHALES OF AUGUST, THE * (1987) PR:A-C**
WHARF ANGEL *½ (1934) PR:A
WHAT! ** (1965:,, Fr./Brit./It.) PR:O
WHAT?
  (SEE:CHE?)
WHAT A BLONDE *½ (1945) PR:A
WHAT A CARRY ON * (1949, Brit.) PR:A
WHAT A CARVE UP! ** (1962, Brit.) PR:A
WHAT A CHASSIS!
  (SEE:LA BELLE AMERICAINE)
WHAT A CRAZY WORLD *½ (1963, Brit.) PR:A
WHAT A LIFE ** (1939) PR:A
WHAT A MAN *½ (1930) PR:A
WHAT A MAN! ** (1937, Brit.) PR:A
WHAT A MAN
  (SEE:NEVER GIVE A SUCKER AN EVEN BREAK)
WHAT A MAN! ** (1944) PR:A
WHAT A NIGHT! * (1931, Brit.) PR:A
WHAT A WAY TO GO *½ (1964) PR:A-C
WHAT A WHOPPER * (1961, Brit.) PR:A
WHAT A WIDOW *½ (1930) PR:A
WHAT A WOMAN
  (SEE:THERE'S THAT WOMAN AGAIN)
WHAT A WOMAN! *½ (1943) PR:A
WHAT A WOMAN!
  (SEE:BEAUTIFUL CHEAT, THE)
WHAT AM I BID? ** (1967) PR:A
WHAT BECAME OF JACK AND JILL? *½
  (1972, Brit.) PR:C-O
WHAT CHANGED CHARLEY FARTHING? *
  (1976, Brit.) PR:C
WHAT COMES AROUND zero (1986) PR:C
WHAT DID YOU DO IN THE WAR, DADDY? *
  (1966) PR:A-C

Finding entries in **THE MOTION PICTURE GUIDE** ™

Years 1929-83	Volumes I-IX
1984	Volume IX
1985	1986 ANNUAL
1986	1987 ANNUAL
1987	1988 ANNUAL
1988	1989 ANNUAL

STAR RATINGS

★★★★★ Masterpiece
★★★★ Excellent
★★★ Good
★★ Fair
★ Poor
zero Without Merit

PARENTAL RECOMMENDATION (PR:)

AA Good for Children
A   Acceptable for Children
C   Cautionary, some objectionable scenes
O   Objectionable for Children

BOLD: Films on Videocassette

WHAT DO WE DO NOW? ** (1945, Brit.) PR:A
WHAT EVER HAPPENED TO AUNT ALICE? * (1969) PR:C**
WHAT EVERY WOMAN KNOWS ** (1934) PR:A
WHAT EVERY WOMAN WANTS **
(1954, Brit.) PR:A
WHAT EVERY WOMAN WANTS **½
(1962, Brit.) PR:A
WHAT HAPPENED THEN? ** (1934, Brit.) PR:A
WHAT HAPPENED TO HARKNESS **
(1934, Brit.) PR:AA
WHAT LOLA WANTS
(SEE:DAMN YANKEES)
WHAT MEN WANT ** (1930) PR:A
WHAT NEXT, CORPORAL HARGROVE? ***
(1945) PR:A
WHAT! NO BEER? ** (1933) PR:A
WHAT PRICE BEAUTY?
(SEE:FALSE FACES)
WHAT PRICE CRIME? * (1935) PR:A
WHAT PRICE DECENCY? *½ (1933) PR:O
WHAT PRICE GLORY? ** (1952) PR:C**
WHAT PRICE HOLLYWOOD? * (1932) PR:C**
WHAT PRICE INNOCENCE? * (1933) PR:A
WHAT PRICE MELODY?
(SEE:LORD BYRON OF BROADWAY)
WHAT PRICE VENGEANCE? *½ (1937) PR:A
WHAT SHALL IT PROFIT
(SEE:HARD STEEL)
WHAT THE BUTLER SAW ** (1950, Brit.) PR:A
WHAT THE PEEPER SAW
(SEE:NIGHT HAIR CHILD)
WHAT WAITS BELOW * (1986) PR:C
WHAT WIVES DON'T WANT
(SEE:VIRTUOUS HUSBAND)
WHAT WOMEN DREAM **½ (1933, Ger.) PR:A
WHAT WOULD YOU DO, CHUMS? **½
(1939, Brit.) PR:A
WHAT WOULD YOU SAY TO SOME SPINACH ***
(1976, Czech.) PR:A
WHAT YOU TAKE FOR GRANTED ** (1984) PR:O
WHATEVER HAPPENED TO BABY JANE? **
(1962) PR:C**
WHATEVER IT TAKES ** (1986) PR:O
WHAT'S BUZZIN COUSIN? *½ (1943) PR:A
WHAT'S COOKIN'? *½ (1942) PR:A
WHAT'S GOOD FOR THE GANDER
(SEE:WHAT'S GOOD FOR THE GOOSE)
WHAT'S GOOD FOR THE GOOSE *
(1969, Brit.) PR:O
**WHAT'S NEW, PUSSYCAT? ***½
(1965, US/Fr.) PR:C**
WHAT'S NEXT? ** (1975, Brit.) PR:AA
WHAT'S SO BAD ABOUT FEELING GOOD? **
(1968) PR:A
WHAT'S THE MATTER WITH HELEN? **
(1971) PR:O
WHAT'S THE TIME, MR. CLOCK? **
(1985, Hung.) PR:A
WHAT'S UP, DOC? * (1972) PR:AA**
WHAT'S UP FRONT * (1964) PR:C
WHAT'S UP, TIGER LILY? **½ (1966) PR:C
WHAT'S YOUR RACKET? * (1934) PR:A
WHEEL OF ASHES *½ (1970, Fr.) PR:C
WHEEL OF FATE * (1953, Brit.) PR:A
WHEEL OF LIFE, THE * (1929) PR:A
WHEELER DEALERS, THE **½ (1963) PR:A
WHEELS OF DESTINY *½ (1934) PR:A
WHEELS OF TERROR
(SEE:MISFIT BRIGADE, THE)
WHEN A GIRL'S BEAUTIFUL * (1947) PR:A
WHEN A MAN RIDES ALONE *½ (1933) PR:A
WHEN A MAN SEES RED *½ (1934) PR:A
WHEN A MAN'S A MAN * (1935) PR:A
WHEN A STRANGER CALLS * (1979) PR:O**
WHEN A WOMAN ASCENDS THE STAIRS ***
(1963, Jap.) PR:C
WHEN ANGELS DON'T FLY
(SEE:AWAKENING, THE)
WHEN BLONDE MEETS BLONDE
(SEE:ANYBODY'S BLONDE)
WHEN DINOSAURS RULED THE EARTH **
(1971, Brit.) PR:A
WHEN EIGHT BELLS TOLL ** (1971, Brit.) PR:C
**WHEN FATHER WAS AWAY ON BUSINESS ***½
(1985, Yugo.) PR:O**
WHEN G-MEN STEP IN *½ (1938) PR:A
WHEN GANGLAND STRIKES *½ (1956) PR:A
WHEN GIRLS LEAVE HOME
(SEE:MISSING GIRLS)
WHEN HELL BROKE LOOSE * (1958) PR:A
WHEN I GROW UP **½ (1951) PR:AA
WHEN IN ROME **½ (1952) PR:A
WHEN JOHNNY COMES MARCHING HOME *½
(1943) PR:A
WHEN KNIGHTHOOD WAS IN FLOWER
(SEE:SWORD AND THE ROSE, THE)
WHEN KNIGHTS WERE BOLD ** (1942, Brit.) PR:A

WHEN LADIES MEET ** (1933) PR:A
WHEN LADIES MEET **½ (1941) PR:A-C
WHEN LONDON SLEEPS ** (1932, Brit.) PR:A
WHEN LONDON SLEEPS *½ (1934, Brit.) PR:A
WHEN LOVE IS YOUNG **½ (1937) PR:A
WHEN LOVERS MEET
(SEE:LOVER COME BACK)
WHEN MEN ARE BEASTS
(SEE:WOMEN IN THE NIGHT)
WHEN MY BABY SMILES AT ME *** (1948) PR:A-C
WHEN NATURE CALLS * (1985) PR:O**
WHEN STRANGERS MARRY *½ (1933) PR:A
WHEN STRANGERS MARRY ***½ (1944) PR:C
WHEN STRANGERS MEET *½ (1934) PR:A
WHEN THE BOUGH BREAKS **½ (1947, Brit.) PR:A
WHEN THE BOYS MEET THE GIRLS *½
(1965) PR:A
WHEN THE CLOCK STRIKES *½ (1961) PR:A
WHEN THE DALTONS RODE ***½ (1940) PR:A
WHEN THE DEVIL WAS WELL *½
(1937, Brit.) PR:A
WHEN THE DOOR OPENED
(SEE:ESCAPE)
WHEN THE GIRLS MEET THE BOYS
(SEE:GIRL CRAZY)
WHEN THE GIRLS TAKE OVER * (1962) PR:C
WHEN THE LEGENDS DIE * (1972) PR:C**
WHEN THE LIGHTS GO ON AGAIN ** (1944) PR:A
WHEN THE RAVEN FLIES *
(1985, Iceland/Swed.) PR:O
WHEN THE REDSKINS RODE *½ (1951) PR:A
WHEN THE TREES WERE TALL **½
(1965, USSR) PR:A
WHEN THE WIND BLOWS ** (1988, Brit.) PR:C**
WHEN THIEF MEETS THIEF *½ (1937, Brit.) PR:A
WHEN TIME RAN OUT zero (1980) PR:C
WHEN TOMORROW COMES ** (1939) PR:A
WHEN TOMORROW DIES * (1966, Can.) PR:C
WHEN WE ARE MARRIED ** (1943, Brit.) PR:A
WHEN WE LOOK BACK
(SEE:FRISCO WATERFRONT)
WHEN WERE YOU BORN? * (1938) PR:A
WHEN WILLIE COMES MARCHING HOME ***½
(1950) PR:A
WHEN WOMEN HAD TAILS zero (1970, It.) PR:O
WHEN WORLDS COLLIDE **½ (1951) PR:A
WHEN YOU COME HOME * (1947, Brit.) PR:A
WHEN YOU COMIN' BACK, RED RYDER? zero
(1979) PR:O
WHEN YOU'RE IN LOVE *** (1937) PR:A
WHEN YOU'RE SMILING *½ (1950) PR:A
WHEN YOUTH CONSPIRES
(SEE:OLD SWIMMIN' HOLE, THE)
WHEN'S YOUR BIRTHDAY? **½ (1937) PR:AA
WHERE ANGELS GO...TROUBLE FOLLOWS *½
(1968) PR:C
WHERE ARE THE CHILDREN? zero (1986) PR:O
WHERE ARE YOUR CHILDREN? ** (1943) PR:A
WHERE DANGER LIVES *** (1950) PR:A
WHERE DID YOU GET THAT GIRL? *½ (1941) PR:A
WHERE DO WE GO FROM HERE? **½
(1945) PR:AA
WHERE DOES IT HURT? * (1972) PR:C-O
WHERE EAGLES DARE ***½ (1968, Brit.) PR:C
WHERE HAS POOR MICKEY GONE? *
(1964, Brit.) PR:A
WHERE IS MY CHILD? * (1937) PR:A
WHERE IS PARSIFAL? zero (1984, Brit.) PR:C
WHERE IS THIS LADY? ** (1932, Brit.) PR:A
WHERE IT'S AT ** (1969) PR:O
WHERE LOVE HAS GONE ** (1964) PR:C
WHERE NO VULTURES FLY
(SEE:IVORY HUNTER)
WHERE SINNERS MEET *½ (1934) PR:A
WHERE THE BLOOD FLOWS
(SEE:HORROR CASTLE)
WHERE THE BOYS ARE **½ (1960) PR:A-C
WHERE THE BOYS ARE '84 * (1984) PR:O
WHERE THE BUFFALO ROAM * (1938) PR:A
WHERE THE BUFFALO ROAM ** (1980) PR:O
WHERE THE BULLETS FLY ** (1966, Brit.) PR:A
WHERE THE GREEN ANTS DREAM *
(1985, Ger.) PR:O**
**WHERE THE HOT WIND BLOWS **½
(1960, Fr./It.) PR:O**
WHERE THE LILIES BLOOM **½ (1974) PR:A
WHERE THE RED FERN GROWS * (1974) PR:A
WHERE THE RIVER BENDS
(SEE:BEND OF THE RIVER)
**WHERE THE RIVER RUNS BLACK **½
(1986) PR:A**
WHERE THE SIDEWALK ENDS ***½ (1950) PR:C
WHERE THE SPIES ARE **½ (1965, Brit.) PR:A
WHERE THE TRUTH LIES * (1962, Fr.) PR:A-C
WHERE THE WEST BEGINS *½ (1938) PR:A
WHERE THERE'S A WILL *** (1936, Brit.) PR:A
WHERE THERE'S A WILL ** (1937, Brit.) PR:A
WHERE THERE'S A WILL ** (1955, Brit.) PR:A

WHERE THERE'S LIFE **½ (1947) PR:A
WHERE TRAILS DIVIDE * (1937) PR:A
WHERE WERE YOU WHEN THE LIGHTS WENT OUT?
** (1968) PR:A-C
WHERE'S CHARLEY? ***½ (1952, Brit.) PR:AA
WHERE'S GEORGE?
(SEE:HOPE OF HIS SIDE, THE)
WHERE'S JACK? ** (1969, Brit.) PR:A
WHERE'S PICONE? **½ (1985, It.) PR:O
WHERE'S POPPA? ***½ (1970) PR:C-O
WHERE'S SALLY? * (1936, Brit.) PR:A
WHERE'S THAT FIRE? ** (1939, Brit.) PR:A
WHEREVER SHE GOES ** (1953, Aus.) PR:A
WHEREVER YOU ARE *
(1988, Brit./Pol./W. Ger.) PR:O
WHICH WAY IS UP? * (1977) PR:O
WHICH WAY TO THE FRONT? *½ (1970) PR:A
WHICH WILL YOU HAVE?
(SEE:BARABBAS THE ROBBER)
WHIFFS * (1975) PR:A
WHILE I LIVE *½ (1947, Brit.) PR:A
WHILE LONDON SLEEPS
(SEE:WHEN LONDON SLEEPS)
WHILE NEW YORK SLEEPS
(SEE:NOW I'LL TELL)
WHILE NEW YORK SLEEPS ** (1938) PR:A
WHILE PARENTS SLEEP *½ (1935, Brit.) PR:A
WHILE PARIS SLEEPS **½ (1932) PR:A
WHILE PLUCKING THE DAISIES
(SEE:PLEASE? MR. BALZAC)
WHILE THE ATTORNEY IS ASLEEP *½
(1945, Den.) PR:A
WHILE THE CITY SLEEPS ** (1956) PR:C**
WHILE THE PATIENT SLEPT * (1935) PR:A
WHILE THE SUN SHINES *½ (1950, Brit.) PR:A
WHIP HAND, THE ** (1951) PR:A
WHIPLASH ** (1948) PR:A
WHIPPED, THE ** (1950) PR:A
WHIP'S WOMEN *½ (1968) PR:O
WHIPSAW *** (1936) PR:A
WHIRLPOOL **½ (1934) PR:A
WHIRLPOOL *** (1949) PR:A
WHIRLPOOL * (1959, Brit.) PR:A
WHIRLPOOL OF FLESH
(SEE:WHIRLPOOL OF WOMAN)
WHIRLPOOL OF WOMAN ** (1966, Jap.) PR:O
WHIRLWIND *½ (1951) PR:A
WHIRLWIND **½ (1968, Jap.) PR:C
WHIRLWIND HORSEMAN * (1938) PR:A
WHIRLWIND OF PARIS * (1946, Fr.) PR:A
WHIRLWIND RAIDERS *½ (1948) PR:A
WHISKY GALORE
(SEE:TIGHT LITTLE ISLAND)
WHISPERERS, THE ***½ (1967, Brit.) PR:C
WHISPERING CITY *** (1947, Can.) PR:A
WHISPERING DEATH
(SEE:NIGHT OF ASKARI)
WHISPERING ENEMIES ** (1939) PR:A
WHISPERING FOOTSTEPS ** (1943) PR:A
WHISPERING GHOSTS *½ (1942) PR:A
WHISPERING JOE ** (1969, Jap.) PR:O
WHISPERING SKULL, THE ** (1944) PR:A
WHISPERING SMITH ***½ (1948) PR:A
WHISPERING SMITH HITS LONDON
(SEE:WHISPERING SMITH VERSUS SCOTLAND
YARD)
WHISPERING SMITH SPEAKS *½ (1935) PR:A
WHISPERING SMITH VERSUS SCOTLAND YARD *½
(1952, Brit.) PR:A
WHISPERING TONGUES * (1934, Brit.) PR:A
WHISPERING WINDS * (1929) PR:A
WHISTLE AT EATON FALLS **½ (1951) PR:A
WHISTLE BLOWER, THE **½ (1987, Brit.) PR:A
**WHISTLE DOWN THE WIND ***½
(1961, Brit.) PR:A**
WHISTLE STOP *½ (1946) PR:A-C
WHISTLER, THE *** (1944) PR:A
WHISTLIN' DAN ** (1932) PR:A
WHISTLING BULLETS ** (1937) PR:A
WHISTLING HILLS *½ (1951) PR:A
WHISTLING IN BROOKLYN ** (1943) PR:A
WHISTLING IN DIXIE ** (1942) PR:A
WHISTLING IN THE DARK ** (1933) PR:A
WHISTLING IN THE DARK ** (1941) PR:A
WHITE ANGEL, THE *½ (1936) PR:A
WHITE BANNERS ** (1938) PR:A
WHITE BONDAGE * (1937) PR:A
WHITE BUFFALO, THE * (1977) PR:C-O
WHITE CAPTIVE
(SEE:WHITE SAVAGE)
WHITE CARGO *½ (1930, Brit.) PR:C
WHITE CARGO *** (1942) PR:C
WHITE CHRISTMAS * (1954) PR:AA**
WHITE CLIFFS OF DOVER, THE ***½
(1944) PR:A-C
WHITE COCKATOO * (1935) PR:A
WHITE CORRIDORS ** (1952, Brit.) PR:A

WHITE CRADLE INN
(SEE:HIGH FURY)
WHITE DAWN, THE **½ (1974) PR:O
WHITE DEATH * (1936, Aus.) PR:A
WHITE DEMON, THE ***½ (1932, Ger.) PR:C
WHITE DEVIL, THE ** (1948, It.) PR:C
WHITE DOG ***½ (1982) PR:O
WHITE EAGLE ** (1932) PR:A
WHITE ELEPHANT ** (1984, Brit.) PR:C
WHITE ENSIGN ** (1934, Brit.) PR:A
WHITE FACE *** (1933, Brit.) PR:A
WHITE FANG ** (1936) PR:A
WHITE FEATHER *** (1955) PR:A
WHITE FIRE ** (1953, Brit.) PR:A
WHITE GHOST ** (1988) PR:C
WHITE GODDESS * (1953) PR:A
WHITE GORILLA zero (1947) PR:A
WHITE HEAT *½ (1934) PR:O
WHITE HEAT *** (1949) PR:C**
WHITE HORSE INN, THE **½ (1959, Ger.) PR:A
WHITE HUNTER ** (1936) PR:A
WHITE HUNTER ** (1965) PR:A
WHITE HUNTRESS *½ (1957, Brit.) PR:A
WHITE LEGION, THE *½ (1936) PR:A
WHITE LIES * (1935) PR:A
WHITE LIGHTNIN' ROAD * (1967) PR:A
WHITE LIGHTNING ** (1953) PR:A
WHITE LIGHTNING * (1973) PR:C**
WHITE LILAC ** (1935, Brit.) PR:A
WHITE LINE, THE ** (1952, It.) PR:C
WHITE LINE FEVER **½ (1975, Can.) PR:C
WHITE MAN, THE
(SEE:SQUAW MAN, THE)
WHITE MISCHIEF **½ (1988, Brit.) PR:O
WHITE NIGHTS *** (1961, It./Fr.) PR:O
WHITE NIGHTS **½ (1985) PR:C
WHITE OF THE EYE * (1988) PR:O**
WHITE ORCHID, THE ** (1954) PR:A
WHITE PARADE, THE **½ (1934) PR:A
WHITE PONGO * (1945) PR:AA
WHITE RAT zero (1972) PR:O
WHITE, RED, YELLOW, PINK * (1966, It.) PR:O
WHITE ROSE OF HONG KONG ** (1965, Jap.) PR:O
WHITE SAVAGE
(SEE:SOUTH OF TAHITI)
WHITE SAVAGE ** (1943) PR:A
WHITE SHADOWS IN THE SOUTH SEAS **½
(1928) PR:A
WHITE SHEIK, THE **½ (1956, It.) PR:C
WHITE SHOULDERS *½ (1931) PR:A
WHITE SISTER, THE *** (1933) PR:A
WHITE SISTER * (1973, It./Span./Fr.) PR:O
WHITE SLAVE *½ (1986, It.) PR:O
WHITE SLAVE SHIP *½ (1962, Fr./It.) PR:C
WHITE SQUAW, THE * (1956) PR:A
WHITE STALLION ** (1947) PR:A
WHITE TIE AND TAILS **½ (1946) PR:A
WHITE TOWER, THE ***½ (1950) PR:A
WHITE TRAP, THE ** (1959, Brit.) PR:C
WHITE TRASH ON MOONSHINE MOUNTAIN
(SEE:MOONSHINE MOUNTAIN)
WHITE UNICORN, THE
(SEE:BAD SISTER)
WHITE VOICES *** (1965, Fr./It.) PR:O
WHITE WARRIOR, THE * (1961, It./Yugo.) PR:A
WHITE WATER SUMMER ** (1987) PR:C
WHITE WITCH DOCTOR *** (1953) PR:A
WHITE WOMAN *½ (1933) PR:C
WHITE ZOMBIE * (1932) PR:O**
WHITEFACE
(SEE:WHITE FACE)
WHO? **½ (1975, Brit./Ger.) PR:C
WHO CAN KILL A CHILD
(SEE:ISLAND OF THE DAMNED)
WHO DARES WIN
(SEE:FINAL OPTION, THE)
WHO DONE IT? **½ (1942) PR:A
WHO DONE IT? ** (1956, Brit.) PR:C
WHO FEARS THE DEVIL *** (1972) PR:A
WHO FRAMED ROGER RABBIT ***** (1988) PR:A
WHO GOES NEXT? **½ (1938, Brit.) PR:C
WHO GOES THERE?
(SEE:PASSIONATE SENTRY, THE)
WHO HAS SEEN THE WIND **½ (1980, Can.) PR:A
WHO IS GUILTY? ** (1940, Brit.) PR:A

WHO IS HARRY KELLERMAN AND WHY IS HE
SAYING THOSE TERRIBLE THINGS ABOUT ME?
** (1971) PR:C
WHO IS HOPE SCHUYLER? * (1942) PR:A
**WHO IS KILLING THE GREAT CHEFS OF EUROPE?
*** (1978, US/Ger.) PR:C**
WHO IS KILLING THE STUNTMEN?
(SEE:STUNTS)
WHO KILLED AUNT MAGGIE? **½ (1940) PR:A
WHO KILLED "DOC" ROBBIN? **½ (1948) PR:AA
WHO KILLED FEN MARKHAM? *½
(1937, Brit.) PR:A
WHO KILLED GAIL PRESTON? ** (1938) PR:A
WHO KILLED JESSIE? *** (1965, Czech.) PR:C
WHO KILLED JOHN SAVAGE? **½
(1937, Brit.) PR:A
**WHO KILLED MARY WHAT'SER NAME? **
(1971) PR:O**
WHO KILLED TEDDY BEAR? * (1965) PR:O
WHO KILLED THE CAT? ** (1966, Brit.) PR:A-C
WHO KILLED VAN LOON? **½ (1984, Brit.) PR:A
WHO RIDES WITH KANE?
(SEE:YOUNG BILLY YOUNG)
WHO SAYS I CAN'T RIDE A RAINBOW? **½
(1971) PR:AA
**WHO SLEW AUNTIE ROO? **½
(1971, US/Brit.) PR:O**
WHO WANTS TO KILL JESSIE?
(SEE:WHO KILLED JESSIE?)
WHO WAS MADDOX? ** (1964, Brit.) PR:A
WHO WAS THAT LADY? *** (1960) PR:A
WHO WOULD KILL A CHILD
(SEE:ISLAND OF THE DAMNED)
WHOEVER SLEW AUNTIE ROO?
(SEE:WHO SLEW AUNTIE ROO?)
WHOLE SHOOTIN' MATCH, THE *** (1979) PR:C
WHOLE TOWN'S TALKING, THE ***** (1935) PR:A
WHOLE TRUTH, THE **½ (1958, Brit.) PR:A
WHO'LL STOP THE RAIN? ***½ (1978) PR:C
WHOLLY MOSES zero (1980) PR:C
WHOM THE GODS DESTROY **½ (1934) PR:A
WHOM THE GODS LOVE
(SEE:MOZART)
WHOOPEE ***½ (1930) **PR:AA**
WHOOPEE BOYS, THE * (1986) PR:O
WHOOPING COUGH **** (1987, Hung.) PR:O
WHO'S AFRAID OF VIRGINIA WOOLF? **
(1966) PR:O**
WHO'S BEEN SLEEPING IN MY BED? **
(1963) PR:C
WHO'S GOT THE ACTION? ** (1962) PR:A
WHO'S GOT THE BLACK BOX? **½
(1970, Fr./Gr./It.) PR:O
WHO'S MINDING THE MINT? ***½ (1967) PR:A
WHO'S MINDING THE STORE? ** (1963) PR:A
WHO'S THAT GIRL **½ (1987) PR:A
WHO'S THAT KNOCKING AT MY DOOR? ***
(1968) PR:O
WHO'S YOUR FATHER? * (1935, Brit.) PR:A
WHO'S YOUR LADY FRIEND? **½
(1937, Brit.) PR:A
WHOSE LIFE IS IT ANYWAY? *** (1981) PR:C-O
WHY ANNA?
(SEE:DIARY OF A SCHIZOPHRENIC GIRL)
WHY BOTHER TO KNOCK *½ (1964, Brit.) PR:O
WHY BRING THAT UP? **½ (1929) PR:A
WHY CHANGE YOUR HUSBAND?
(SEE:GOLD DUST GERTIE)
WHY DOES HERR R. RUN AMOK? ***½
(1977, Ger.) PR:O
WHY GIRLS LEAVE HOME *½ (1945) PR:C
WHY LEAVE HOME? **½ (1929) PR:A
WHY MUST I DIE? **½ (1960) PR:C
WHY NOT?
(SEE:POURQUOI PAS)
WHY PICK ON ME? ** (1937, Brit.) PR:A
WHY ROCK THE BOAT? ***½ (1974, Can.) PR:O
WHY RUSSIANS ARE REVOLTING * (1970) PR:O
WHY SAILORS LEAVE HOME *½ (1930, Brit.) PR:A
WHY SAPS LEAVE HOME *½ (1932, Brit.) PR:A
WHY SHOOT THE TEACHER * (1977, Can.) PR:C**
WHY SPY
(SEE:MAN CALLED DAGGER, A)
WHY WOULD ANYONE WANT TO KILL A NICE
GIRL LIKE YOU?
(SEE:TASTE OF EXCITEMENT)
WHY WOULD I LIE *½ (1980) PR:C

WICHITA ***½ (1955) PR:A
WICKED ** (1931) PR:A
WICKED AS THEY COME
(SEE:PORTRAIT IN SMOKE)
WICKED DIE SLOW, THE * (1968) PR:O
WICKED DREAMS OF PAULA SCHULTZ, THE *½
(1968) PR:C
WICKED GO TO HELL, THE *** (1961, Fr.) PR:O
WICKED LADY, THE *½ (1946, Brit.) PR:A
WICKED LADY, THE * (1983, Brit.) PR:O
WICKED, WICKED * (1973) PR:O
WICKED WIFE ** (1955, Brit.) PR:O
WICKED WOMAN ** (1953) PR:O
WICKED WOMAN, A **½ (1934) PR:C
WICKER MAN, THE ***½ (1974, Brit.) PR:O
WICKHAM MYSTERY, THE *½ (1931, Brit.) PR:A
WIDE BOY *½ (1952, Brit.) PR:A
WIDE OPEN **½ (1930) PR:A
WIDE OPEN FACES ** (1938) PR:A
WIDE OPEN TOWN *** (1941) PR:A
WIDOW AND THE GIGOLO, THE
(SEE:ROMAN SPRING OF MRS. STONE, THE)
WIDOW FROM CHICAGO, THE * (1930) PR:A-C
WIDOW FROM MONTE CARLO, THE *½
(1936) PR:A
WIDOW IN SCARLET * (1932) PR:A
WIDOW IS WILLING, THE
(SEE:VIOLENT SUMMER)
WIDOW'S MIGHT ** (1934, Brit.) PR:A
WIDOWS' NEST ** (1977, US/Sp.) PR:O
WIEN, DU STADT DER LIEDER
(SEE:VIENNA, CITY OF SONGS)
WIEN TANZT
(SEE:VIENNA WALTZES)
WIFE, DOCTOR AND NURSE **½ (1937) PR:A
WIFE, HUSBAND AND FRIEND *** (1939) PR:A
WIFE OF GENERAL LING, THE **½
(1938, Brit.) PR:A
WIFE OF MONTE CRISTO, THE ** (1946) PR:A
WIFE OR TWO, A ** (1935, Brit.) PR:A
WIFE SWAPPERS, THE
(SEE:SWAPPERS, THE)
WIFE TAKES A FLYER, THE ** (1942) PR:A
WIFE VERSUS SECRETARY ***½ (1936) PR:A
WIFE WANTED * (1946) PR:A
WIFEMISTRESS **½ (1979, It.) PR:O
WIFE'S FAMILY, THE
(SEE:MY WIFE'S FAMILY)
WILBY CONSPIRACY, THE **½ (1975, Brit.) PR:C
WILD AFFAIR, THE **½ (1966, Brit.) PR:O
WILD AND THE INNOCENT, THE **½ (1959) PR:C
WILD AND THE SWEET, THE
(SEE:LOVIN' MOLLY)
WILD AND THE WILLING, THE
(SEE:YOUNG AND WILLING)
WILD AND WILLING
(SEE:RAT FINK)
WILD AND WONDERFUL **½ (1964) PR:A
WILD AND WOOLLY **½ (1937) PR:A
WILD ANGELS, THE ** (1966) PR:O
WILD ARCTIC
(SEE:SAVAGE WILD, THE)
WILD BEAUTY ** (1946) PR:A
WILD BILL HICKOK RIDES ** (1942) PR:A
WILD BLUE YONDER, THE *** (1952) PR:A
WILD BOY ** (1934, Brit.) PR:A
WILD BOYS OF THE ROAD ***** (1933) PR:A-C
WILD BRIAN KENT *½ (1936) PR:A
WILD BUNCH, THE *** (1969) PR:O**
WILD CARGO
(SEE:WHITE SLAVE SHIP)
WILD CHILD, THE *** (1970, Fr.) PR:C-O
WILD COMPANY *½ (1930) PR:A
WILD COUNTRY * (1947) PR:A
WILD COUNTRY, THE **½ (1971) PR:AA
WILD DAKOTAS, THE * (1956) PR:A
WILD DRIFTER
(SEE:BORN TO KILL)
WILD DUCK, THE **½ (1977, Ger./Aust.) PR:A
WILD DUCK, THE *½ (1983, Aus.) PR:C
WILD EYE, THE *½ (1968, It.) PR:O
WILD FOR KICKS
(SEE:BEAT GIRL)
WILD, FREE AND HUNGRY * (1970) PR:C
WILD FRONTIER, THE **½ (1947) PR:A
WILD GAME
(SEE:JAIL BAIT)

Years 1929-83	Volumes I-IX
1984	Volume IX
1985	1986 ANNUAL
1986	1987 ANNUAL
1987	1988 ANNUAL
1988	1989 ANNUAL

STAR RATINGS

★★★★★ Masterpiece
★★★★ Excellent
★★★ Good
★★ Fair
★ Poor
zero Without Merit

PARENTAL RECOMMENDATION (PR:)

AA Good for Children
A Acceptable for Children
C Cautionary, some objectionable scenes
O Objectionable for Children

BOLD: Films on Videocassette

WILD GEESE, THE ** (1978, Brit.) PR:O
WILD GEESE CALLING ** (1941) PR:A-C
WILD GEESE II *½ (1985, Brit.) PR:O
WILD GIRL **½ (1932) PR:A
WILD GOLD ** (1934) PR:A
WILD GUITAR * (1962) PR:A
WILD GYPSIES * (1969) PR:O
WILD HARVEST **½ (1947) PR:A
WILD HARVEST * (1962) PR:O
WILD HEART, THE ** (1952, Brit.) PR:C
WILD HERITAGE ** (1958) PR:A
WILD HORSE * (1931) PR:A
WILD HORSE AMBUSH * (1952) PR:A
WILD HORSE CANYON *½ (1939) PR:A
WILD HORSE HANK ** (1979, Can.) PR:A
WILD HORSE MESA **½ (1932) PR:A
WILD HORSE MESA ** (1947) PR:A
WILD HORSE PHANTOM *½ (1944) PR:A
WILD HORSE RODEO *½ (1938) PR:A
WILD HORSE ROUND-UP ** (1937) PR:A
WILD HORSE RUSTLERS *½ (1943) PR:A
WILD HORSE STAMPEDE * (1943) PR:A
WILD HORSE VALLEY *½ (1940) PR:A
WILD HORSES ** (1984, New Zealand) PR:C
WILD IN THE COUNTRY ** (1961) PR:A
WILD IN THE SKY
(SEE:BLACK JACK)
WILD IN THE STREETS **½ (1968) PR:C
WILD INNOCENCE ** (1937, Aus.) PR:A
WILD IS MY LOVE * (1963) PR:O
WILD IS THE WIND *** (1957) PR:A
WILD JUNGLE CAPTIVE
(SEE:JUNGLE CAPTIVE)
WILD LIFE, THE zero (1984) PR:C-O
WILD LOVE-MAKERS
(SEE:WEIRD LOVE-MAKERS)
WILD MAN OF BORNEO, THE **½ (1941) PR:A
WILD McCULLOCHS, THE ** (1975) PR:O
WILD MONEY ** (1937) PR:A
WILD MUSTANG ** (1935) PR:A
WILD 90 * (1968) PR:O
WILD NORTH, THE ** (1952) PR:A
WILD ON THE BEACH * (1965) PR:A
WILD ONE, THE **** (1953) PR:C
WILD ONES ON WHEELS zero (1967) PR:C-O
WILD PACK, THE **½ (1972) PR:O
WILD PAIR, THE * (1987) PR:O
WILD PARTY, THE **½ (1929) PR:A
WILD PARTY, THE * (1956) PR:C-O
WILD PARTY, THE zero (1975) PR:O
WILD RACERS, THE * (1968) PR:A-C
WILD REBELS, THE * (1967) PR:O
WILD RIDE, THE * (1960) PR:C
WILD RIDERS zero (1971) PR:O
WILD RIVER **** (1960) PR:A-C
WILD ROVERS ** (1971) PR:C-O
WILD SCENE, THE zero (1970) PR:O
WILD SEASON **½ (1968, South Africa) PR:A
WILD SEED **½ (1965) PR:A
WILD SIDE, THE
(SEE:SUBURBIA)
WILD STALLION **½ (1952) PR:A
WILD STRAWBERRIES ***** (1959, Swed.) PR:O
WILD THING * (1987, US/Can.) PR:C-O
WILD WEED * (1949) PR:A-C
WILD WEST *½ (1946) PR:A
WILD WEST WHOOPEE zero (1931) PR:A
WILD WESTERNERS, THE *½ (1962) PR:A
WILD WHEELS zero (1969) PR:O
WILD WOMEN OF WONGO, THE zero (1959) PR:C
WILD WORLD OF BATWOMAN, THE zero (1966) PR:C
WILD YOUTH * (1961) PR:C
WILD, WILD PLANET, THE *½ (1967, It.) PR:A-C
WILD, WILD WINTER ** (1966) PR:A
WILD, WILD WOMEN, THE
(SEE:...AND THE WILD, WILD WOMEN)
WILDCAT ** (1942) PR:A
WILDCAT
(SEE:GREAT SCOUT AND CATHOUSE THURSDAY, THE)
WILDCAT BUS * (1940) PR:A
WILDCAT OF TUCSON *½ (1941) PR:A
WILDCAT TROOPER **½ (1936) PR:A
WILDCATS * (1986) PR:C-O
WILDCATS OF ST. TRINIAN'S, THE * (1980, Brit.) PR:A
WILDCATTER, THE * (1937) PR:A
WILDE SEISON
(SEE:WILD SEASON)
WILDERNESS FAMILY PART 2
(SEE:FURTHER ADVENTURES OF THE WILDERNESS FAMILY-PART TWO)
WILDERNESS MAIL *½ (1935) PR:A
WILDFIRE *½ (1945) PR:A
WILDFIRE; THE STORY OF A HORSE
(SEE:WILDFIRE)
WILDROSE ***½ (1985) PR:C
WILDWECHSEL
(SEE:JAIL BAIT)
WILL ANY GENTLEMAN? **½ (1955, Brit.) PR:A
WILL JAMES' SAND
(SEE:SAND)
WILL PENNY ***½ (1968) PR:A-C
WILL SUCCESS SPOIL ROCK HUNTER? *** (1957) PR:A-C
WILL TOMORROW EVER COME
(SEE:THAT'S MY MAN)
WILLARD **½ (1971) PR:O
WILLIAM COMES TO TOWN ** (1948, Brit.) PR:A
WILLIAM FOX MOVIETONE FOLLIES OF 1929
(SEE:FOX MOVIETONE FOLLIES)
WILLIE AND JOE BACK AT THE FRONT
(SEE:BACK AT THE FRONT))
WILLIE AND PHIL **½ (1980) PR:O
WILLIE DYNAMITE **½ (1973) PR:O
WILLIE MCBEAN AND HIS MAGIC MACHINE **½ (1965, US/Jap.) PR:AA
WILLOW ** (1988) PR:AA
WILLS AND BURKE *½ (1985, Aus.) PR:C
WILLY ** (1963, US/Ger.) PR:A
WILLY DYNAMITE
(SEE:WILLIE DYNAMITE)
WILLY WONKA AND THE CHOCOLATE FACTORY **½ (1971) PR:A
WILSON *** (1944) PR:A
WIN, PLACE AND SHOW
(SEE:CRAZY OVER HORSES)
WIN, PLACE, OR STEAL * (1975) PR:A
WINCHESTER '73 **** (1950) PR:C
WIND ACROSS THE EVERGLADES **½ (1958) PR:C
WIND AND THE LION, THE ***½ (1975) PR:C
WIND BLOWETH WHERE IT LISTETH, THE
(SEE:MAN ESCAPED, A)
WIND CANNOT READ, THE **½ (1958, Brit.) PR:A
WIND FROM THE EAST * (1970, Fr./It./Ger.) PR:C
WIND OF CHANGE, THE ** (1961, Brit.) PR:A
WIND, THE **** (1928) PR:C
WIND, THE ***½ (1987) PR:O
WINDBAG THE SAILOR ** (1937, Brit.) PR:A
WINDFALL ** (1935, Brit.) PR:A
WINDFALL ** (1955, Brit.) PR:A
WINDFLOWERS zero (1968) PR:C
WINDJAMMER ** (1937) PR:A
WINDJAMMER, THE *½ (1931, Brit.) PR:A
WINDMILL, THE *½ (1937, Brit.) PR:A
WINDOM'S WAY *** (1958, Brit.) PR:A-C
WINDOW, THE **** (1949) PR:C
WINDOW IN LONDON, A
(SEE:LADY IN DISTRESS)
WINDOW TO THE SKY, A
(SEE:OTHER SIDE OF THE MOUNTAIN, THE)
WINDOWS * (1980) PR:O
WINDOWS OF TIME, THE * (1969, Hung.) PR:A
WINDS OF THE WASTELAND **½ (1936) PR:A
WINDSPLITTER, THE zero (1971) PR:C
WINDWALKER **½ (1980) PR:C
WINDY CITY **½ (1984) PR:C
WINE AND THE MUSIC, THE
(SEE:PIECES OF DREAMS)
WINE, WOMEN AND HORSES * (1937) PR:A
WINE, WOMEN, AND SONG ** (1934) PR:A
WING AND A PRAYER *** (1944) PR:A
WINGED DEVILS
(SEE:ABOVE THE CLOUDS)
WINGED SERPENT
(SEE:STARSHIP INVASIONS)
WINGED SERPENT, THE
(SEE:Q)
WINGED VICTORY **** (1944) PR:A
WINGS AND THE WOMAN **½ (1942, Brit.) PR:A
WINGS FOR THE EAGLE ** (1942) PR:A
WINGS IN THE DARK **½ (1935) PR:A
WINGS OF ADVENTURE * (1930) PR:A
WINGS OF CHANCE ** (1961, Can.) PR:A
WINGS OF DANGER
(SEE:DEAD ON COURSE)
WINGS OF DESIRE ***** (1988, Fr./W. Ger.) PR:C
WINGS OF EAGLES, THE ***½ (1957) PR:A
WINGS OF MYSTERY ** (1963, Brit.) PR:AA
WINGS OF THE HAWK ** (1953) PR:A
WINGS OF THE MORNING *** (1937, Brit.) PR:A
WINGS OF THE NAVY ** (1939) PR:A
WINGS OF VICTORY ** (1941, USSR) PR:A
WINGS OVER AFRICA *½ (1939) PR:A
WINGS OVER HONOLULU ** (1937) PR:A
WINGS OVER THE PACIFIC * (1943) PR:A
WINGS OVER WYOMING
(SEE:HOLLYWOOD COWBOY)
WINK OF AN EYE * (1958) PR:A
WINNER TAKE ALL ***½ (1932) PR:A
WINNER TAKE ALL ** (1939) PR:A
WINNER TAKE ALL
(SEE:JOE PALOOKA IN WINNER TAKE ALL)
WINNER, THE
(SEE:PIT STOP)
WINNERS, THE
(SEE:MY WAY)
WINNER'S CIRCLE, THE ** (1948) PR:A
WINNERS TAKE ALL ** (1987) PR:C
WINNETOU, PART III
(SEE:DESPERADO TRAIL, THE)
WINNETOU, PART I
(SEE:APACHE GOLD)
WINNETOU, PART II
(SEE:LAST OF THE RENEGADES)
WINNING *** (1969) PR:A-C
WINNING OF THE WEST ** (1953) PR:A
WINNING POSITION
(SEE:NOBODY'S PERFECT)
WINNING TEAM, THE ***½ (1952) PR:A
WINNING TICKET, THE *½ (1935) PR:A
WINNING WAY, THE
(SEE:ALL-AMERICAN, THE)
WINSLOW BOY, THE ***½ (1950) PR:A
WINSTANLEY **½ (1979, Brit.) PR:C
WINSTON AFFAIR, THE
(SEE:MAN IN THE MIDDLE)
WINTER A GO-GO * (1965) PR:A
WINTER CARNIVAL * (1939) PR:A
WINTER FLIGHT **½ (1984, Brit.) PR:C
WINTER KEPT US WARM *½ (1968, Can.) PR:C
WINTER KILLS ***½ (1979) PR:O
WINTER LIGHT, THE ** (1963, Swed.) PR:C
WINTER MEETING ** (1948) PR:A
WINTER OF OUR DREAMS **½ (1982, Aus.) PR:O
WINTER RATES
(SEE:OUT OF SEASON)
WINTER WIND *** (1970, Fr./Hung.) PR:C
WINTER WONDERLAND ** (1947) PR:A
WINTERHAWK *½ (1976) PR:C
WINTER'S TALE, THE ** (1968, Brit.) PR:A
WINTERSET ***½ (1936) PR:A-C
WINTERTIME *½ (1943) PR:A
WIRE SERVICE ** (1942) PR:A
WIRED TO KILL * (1986) PR:O
WIRETAPPERS * (1956) PR:A
WISDOM ** (1986) PR:O
WISE BLOOD *** (1979, US/Ger.) PR:O
WISE GIRL *½ (1937) PR:A
WISE GIRLS ** (1930) PR:A
WISE GUYS ** (1937, Brit.) PR:A
WISE GUYS ** (1969, Fr./It.) PR:A
WISE GUYS ** (1986) PR:C-O
WISER AGE **½ (1962, Jap.) PR:C
WISER SEX, THE * (1932) PR:A
WISH YOU WERE HERE **½ (1987, Brit.) PR:C-O
WISHBONE CUTTER *½ (1978) PR:C
WISHBONE, THE *½ (1933, Brit.) PR:A
WISHING MACHINE *** (1971, Czech.) PR:AA
WISTFUL WIDOW, THE
(SEE:WISTFUL WIDOW OF WAGON GAP, THE)
WISTFUL WIDOW OF WAGON GAP, THE ** (1947) PR:A
WITCH, THE * (1969, It.) PR:C
WITCH BENEATH THE SEA, THE
(SEE:MARIZINIA)
WITCH DOCTOR
(SEE:KISENGA, MAN OF AFRICA)
WITCH WITHOUT A BROOM, A *½ (1967, US/Sp.) PR:C
WITCHBOARD ** (1987) PR:O
WITCHCRAFT ** (1964, Brit.) PR:A
WITCHES, THE
(SEE:DEVIL'S OWN, THE)
WITCHES, THE *½ (1969, Fr./It.) PR:C
WITCHES CURSE, THE
(SEE:WITCH'S CURSE, THE)
WITCHES OF EASTWICK, THE ** (1987) PR:O
WITCHES—VIOLATED AND TORTURED TO DEATH
(SEE:MARK OF THE DEVIL II)
WITCHFINDER GENERAL
(SEE:CONQUEROR WORM, THE)
WITCHFIRE * (1986) PR:O
WITCHING, THE
(SEE:NECROMANCY)
WITCHING HOUR, THE ** (1934) PR:A
WITCHMAKER, THE *½ (1969) PR:C
WITCH'S CURSE, THE *½ (1963, It.) PR:A
WITCH'S MIRROR, THE * (1960, Mex.) PR:C
WITH A SMILE *** (1939, Fr.) PR:A
WITH A SONG IN MY HEART ***½ (1952) PR:A
WITH FIRE AND SWORD
(SEE:INVASION 1700)
WITH GUNILLA MONDAY EVENING AND TUESDAY
(SEE:GUILT)
WITH JOYOUS HEART
(SEE:TWO WEEKS IN SEPTEMBER)
WITH LOVE AND KISSES * (1937) PR:A
WITH LOVE AND TENDERNESS **½ (1978, Bulgaria) PR:A
WITH SIX YOU GET EGGROLL *** (1968) PR:A

WITHIN THE LAW
  (SEE:PAID)
WITHIN THE LAW ** (1939) PR:A
WITHIN THESE WALLS ** (1945) PR:A
WITHNAIL AND I * (1987, Brit.) PR:O**
WITHOUT A CLUE **½ (1988) PR:A-C
WITHOUT A HOME **½ (1939, Pol.) PR:A
WITHOUT A TRACE ** (1983) PR:A
WITHOUT APPARENT MOTIVE *** (1972, Fr.) PR:O
WITHOUT CHILDREN
  (SEE:PENTHOUSE PARTY)
WITHOUT EACH OTHER **½ (1962) PR:A
WITHOUT HONOR *½ (1949) PR:A
WITHOUT HONORS ** (1932) PR:A
WITHOUT LOVE **½ (1945) PR:A
WITHOUT ORDERS *½ (1936) PR:A
WITHOUT PITY *½ (1949, It.) PR:C
WITHOUT REGRET **½ (1935) PR:A
WITHOUT RESERVATIONS **½ (1946) PR:A
WITHOUT RISK
  (SEE:PECOS RIVER)
WITHOUT WARNING ** (1952) PR:C
WITHOUT WARNING zero (1980) PR:O
WITHOUT YOU *½ (1934, Brit.) PR:A
WITNESS ** (1985) PR:C-O**
WITNESS CHAIR, THE * (1936) PR:A
**WITNESS FOR THE PROSECUTION ***½
  (1957) PR:A**
WITNESS IN THE DARK ** (1959, Brit.) PR:A
WITNESS OUT OF HELL *** (1967, Ger./Yugo.) PR:O
WITNESS TO MURDER *** (1954) PR:C
WITNESS VANISHES, THE *½ (1939) PR:A
WITNESS, THE ** (1959, Brit.) PR:AA
WITNESS, THE **½ (1982, Hung.) PR:C
WIVES AND LOVERS ** (1963) PR:A
WIVES BEWARE * (1933, Brit.) PR:A
WIVES NEVER KNOW ** (1936) PR:A
WIVES—TEN YEARS AFTER * (1985, Norway) PR:O
WIVES UNDER SUSPICION ** (1938) PR:A
WIZ, THE *½ (1978) PR:C
WIZARD OF BAGHDAD, THE *½ (1960) PR:A
WIZARD OF GORE, THE zero (1970) PR:O
WIZARD OF LONELINESS, THE ** (1988) PR:C
WIZARD OF MARS * (1964) PR:A
WIZARD OF OZ, THE *** (1939) PR:AA**
WIZARDS **½ (1977) PR:C
WIZARDS OF THE LOST KINGDOM zero
  (1985, US/Arg.) PR:A
**WOLF AT THE DOOR, THE **½
  (1987, Fr./Den.) PR:C-O**
WOLF CALL *½ (1939) PR:A
WOLF DOG * (1958, Can.) PR:AA
WOLF HUNTERS, THE *½ (1949) PR:A
WOLF LARSEN ** (1958) PR:A
WOLF LARSEN ** (1978, It.) PR:A
WOLF MAN, THE ** (1941) PR:C**
WOLF OF NEW YORK *½ (1940) PR:A
WOLF OF WALL STREET THE ** (1929) PR:C
WOLF SONG *** (1929) PR:A-C
WOLF'S CLOTHING ** (1936, Brit.) PR:A
WOLF'S HOLE ** (1987, Czech.) PR:C
WOLFEN ***½ (1981) PR:O
WOLFMAN *½ (1979) PR:O
WOLFPACK
  (SEE:McKENZIE BREAK, THE)
WOLFPEN PRINCIPLE, THE ***½
  (1974, Can.) PR:AA
WOLVES zero (1930, Brit.) PR:A
WOLVES OF THE RANGE *½ (1943) PR:A
WOLVES OF THE SEA * (1938) PR:A
WOLVES OF THE UNDERWORLD *
  (1935, Brit.) PR:A
WOMAN ACCUSED **½ (1933) PR:A-C
WOMAN AGAINST THE WORLD * (1938) PR:A
WOMAN AGAINST WOMAN **½ (1938) PR:A
WOMAN ALONE, A
  (SEE:TWO WHO DARED)
WOMAN ALONE, THE
  (SEE:SECRET AGENT, THE)
WOMAN AND THE HUNTER, THE * (1957) PR:A
WOMAN AT HER WINDOW, A **½
  (1978, Fr./It./Ger.) PR:O
WOMAN BETWEEN * (1931) PR:C
WOMAN BETWEEN, THE, 1931
  (SEE:WOMAN DECIDES, THE)
WOMAN BETWEEN, THE, 1937
  (SEE:WOMAN I LOVE, THE)

WOMAN CHASES MAN *½ (1937) PR:A
WOMAN COMMANDS, A ** (1932) PR:A
WOMAN DECIDES, THE *½ (1932, Brit.) PR:A
WOMAN DESTROYED, A
  (SEE:SMASH-UP, THE STORY OF A WOMAN)
WOMAN DOCTOR *½ (1939) PR:A
WOMAN EATER, THE * (1959, Brit.) PR:C
WOMAN FLAMBEE, A
  (SEE:WOMAN IN FLAMES, A)
WOMAN FOR CHARLEY, A
  (SEE:COCKEYED COWBOYS OF CALICO COUNTY)
WOMAN FOR JOE, THE *½ (1955, Brit.) PR:A
WOMAN FROM HEADQUARTERS * (1950) PR:A
WOMAN FROM MONTE CARLO, THE **
  (1932) PR:A
WOMAN FROM TANGIER, THE ** (1948) PR:A
WOMAN HATER *½ (1949, Brit.) PR:A
WOMAN HE SCORNED, THE * (1930, Brit.) PR:A
WOMAN HUNGRY *½ (1931) PR:C
WOMAN HUNT ** (1962) PR:C
WOMAN HUNT, THE zero (1975, US/Phil.) PR:O
WOMAN I LOVE, THE **½ (1937) PR:A
WOMAN I STOLE, THE ** (1933) PR:A
WOMAN IN BONDAGE
  (SEE:WOMAN IN CHAINS)
WOMAN IN BONDAGE
  (SEE:WOMEN IN BONDAGE)
WOMAN IN BROWN
  (SEE:VICIOUS CIRCLE, THE)
WOMAN IN CHAINS **½ (1932, Brit.) PR:A
WOMAN IN COMMAND, THE * (1934, Brit.) PR:A
WOMAN IN DISTRESS *½ (1937) PR:A
WOMAN IN FLAMES, A * (1984, Ger.) PR:O**
WOMAN IN GREEN, THE ** (1945) PR:A
WOMAN IN HER THIRTIES, A
  (SEE:SIDE STREETS)
WOMAN IN HIDING *** (1949) PR:A-C
WOMAN IN HIDING *½ (1953, Brit.) PR:A
WOMAN IN HIS HOUSE, THE
  (SEE:ANIMAL KINGDOM, THE)
WOMAN IN QUESTION, THE
  (SEE:FIVE ANGLES ON MURDER)
WOMAN IN RED, THE *** (1935) PR:A
WOMAN IN RED, THE * (1984) PR:C
WOMAN IN ROOM 13, THE * (1932) PR:A
WOMAN IN THE CASE
  (SEE:HEADLINE WOMAN, THE)
WOMAN IN THE CASE, THE
  (SEE:ALLOTMENT WIVES)
WOMAN IN THE DARK ** (1934) PR:A
WOMAN IN THE DARK * (1952) PR:A
WOMAN IN THE DUNES *** (1964, Jap.) PR:O**
WOMAN IN THE HALL, THE ** (1949, Brit.) PR:A
WOMAN IN THE WINDOW, THE ***½ (1945) PR:C
WOMAN IN WHITE, THE *** (1948) PR:A
WOMAN INSIDE, THE *½ (1981) PR:O
WOMAN IS A WOMAN, A ***½ (1961, Fr./It.) PR:A
WOMAN IS THE JUDGE, A ** (1939) PR:A
WOMAN NEXT DOOR, THE * (1981, Fr.) PR:O**
WOMAN OBSESSED **½ (1959) PR:A-C
WOMAN OF ANTWERP
  (SEE:DEDEE)
WOMAN OF DARKNESS ** (1968, Swed.) PR:O
WOMAN OF DISTINCTION, A ** (1950) PR:A
WOMAN OF DOLWYN
  (SEE:LAST DAYS OF DOLWYN, THE)
WOMAN OF EXPERIENCE, A *½ (1931) PR:A
WOMAN OF MYSTERY, A *½ (1957, Brit.) PR:A
WOMAN OF ROME *½ (1956, It.) PR:O
WOMAN OF SIN ** (1961, Fr.) PR:A
WOMAN OF STRAW **½ (1964, Brit.) PR:C
WOMAN OF THE DUNES
  (SEE:WOMAN IN THE DUNES)
WOMAN OF THE NORTH COUNTRY ** (1952) PR:A
WOMAN OF THE RIVER ** (1954, Fr./It.) PR:O
WOMAN OF THE TOWN, THE **½ (1943) PR:A
WOMAN OF THE WORLD, A
  (SEE:OUTCAST LADY)
WOMAN OF THE YEAR ** (1942) PR:AA**
WOMAN ON FIRE, A *½ (1970, It.) PR:O
WOMAN ON PIER 13, THE *½ (1950) PR:A
WOMAN ON THE BEACH, THE *** (1947) PR:A
WOMAN ON THE RUN ***½ (1950) PR:A
WOMAN POSSESSED ** (1958, Brit.) PR:A
WOMAN RACKET, THE *½ (1930) PR:A
WOMAN REBELS, A ** (1936) PR:A-C

WOMAN TAMER
  (SEE:SHE COULDN'T TAKE IT)
WOMAN THEY ALMOST LYNCHED, THE **
  (1953) PR:A
**WOMAN TIMES SEVEN **
  (1967, US/Fr./It.) PR:C-O**
WOMAN TO WOMAN ** (1929) PR:A
WOMAN TO WOMAN ** (1946, Brit.) PR:A
WOMAN TRAP *½ (1929) PR:A
WOMAN TRAP *½ (1936) PR:A
WOMAN UNAFRAID * (1934) PR:A
WOMAN UNDER THE INFLUENCE, A ***½
  (1974) PR:C
WOMAN WANTED *½ (1935) PR:A
WOMAN WHO CAME BACK ** (1945) PR:A
WOMAN WHO DARED * (1949, Fr.) PR:A
WOMAN WHO WOULDN'T DIE, THE **
  (1965, Brit.) PR:A
WOMAN-WISE ** (1937) PR:A
WOMAN WITH NO NAME, THE
  (SEE:HER PANELLED DOOR)
WOMAN WITH RED BOOTS, THE **
  (1977, Fr./Sp.) PR:O
WOMAN WITHOUT A FACE
  (SEE:MISTER BUDDWING)
WOMAN WITHOUT CAMELLIAS, THE
  (SEE:LADY WITHOUT CAMELIAS)
WOMANEATER
  (SEE:WOMAN EATER, THE)
WOMANHOOD ** (1934, Brit.) PR:A
WOMANLIGHT ** (1979, Fr./Ger./It.) PR:C
WOMAN'S ANGLE, THE * (1954, Brit.) PR:A
WOMAN'S DEVOTION, A ** (1956) PR:A
WOMAN'S FACE, A *** (1939, Swed.) PR:A
WOMAN'S FACE, A ***½ (1941) PR:A-C
WOMAN'S LIFE, A ** (1964, Jap.) PR:A
WOMAN'S PLACE, A
  (SEE:WISER AGE)
WOMAN'S REVENGE, A
  (SEE:MAN FROM SUNDOWN, THE)
WOMAN'S SECRET, A ** (1949) PR:A
WOMAN'S TEMPTATION, A ** (1959, Brit.) PR:A
WOMAN'S VENGEANCE, A
  (SEE:MAN FROM SUNDOWN, THE)
WOMAN'S VENGEANCE, A **½ (1947) PR:A
WOMAN'S WORLD ** (1954) PR:A-C
WOMBLING FREE * (1977, Brit.) PR:AA
WOMEN, THE ** (1939) PR:C**
WOMEN AND BLOODY TERROR zero (1970) PR:O
WOMEN AND WAR ** (1965, Fr.) PR:C
WOMEN ARE LIKE THAT * (1938) PR:A
WOMEN ARE TROUBLE ** (1936) PR:A
WOMEN AREN'T ANGELS **½ (1942, Brit.) PR:A
WOMEN EVERYWHERE ** (1930) PR:A
WOMEN FROM HEADQUARTERS
  (SEE:WOMAN FROM HEADQUARTERS)
WOMEN GO ON FOREVER * (1931) PR:A
WOMEN IN A DRESSING GOWN ***
  (1957, Brit.) PR:A
WOMEN IN BONDAGE ** (1943) PR:A
WOMEN IN CELL BLOCK 7 zero (1977, It./US) PR:O
WOMEN IN HIS LIFE, THE * (1934) PR:A
WOMEN IN LIMBO
  (SEE:LIMBO)
WOMEN IN LOVE ** (1969, Brit.) PR:O
WOMEN IN PRISON
  (SEE:LADIES THEY TALK ABOUT)
WOMEN IN PRISON ** (1938) PR:A
WOMEN IN PRISON ** (1957, Jap.) PR:O
WOMEN IN THE NIGHT *½ (1948) PR:A
WOMEN IN THE WIND **½ (1939) PR:A
WOMEN IN WAR **½ (1940) PR:A
WOMEN IN WAR, 1965
  (SEE:WOMEN AND WAR)
WOMEN LOVE ONCE *½ (1931) PR:A
WOMEN MEN MARRY zero (1931) PR:A
WOMEN MEN MARRY, THE ** (1937) PR:A
WOMEN MUST DRESS * (1935) PR:A
WOMEN OF ALL NATIONS **½ (1931) PR:A-C
WOMEN OF DESIRE zero (1968) PR:O
WOMEN OF GLAMOUR ** (1937) PR:A
WOMEN OF NAZI GERMANY
  (SEE:HITLER)
WOMEN OF PITCAIRN ISLAND, THE * (1957) PR:A
WOMEN OF THE NORTH COUNTRY
  (SEE:WOMAN OF THE NORTH COUNTRY)

WOMEN OF THE PREHISTORIC PLANET *
(1966) PR:A
WOMEN OF TWILIGHT
(SEE:TWILIGHT WOMEN)
WOMEN ON THE VERGE OF A NERVOUS
BREAKDOWN **** (1988, Sp.) PR:C
WOMEN, THE
(SEE:VIXENS, THE)
WOMEN THEY TALK ABOUT ** (1928) PR:A
WOMEN WHO PLAY **½ (1932, Brit.) PR:A
WOMEN WITHOUT MEN
(SEE:BLOND BAIT)
WOMEN WITHOUT NAMES ** (1940) PR:A
WOMEN WON'T TELL * (1933) PR:A
WOMEN'S PRISON ** (1955) PR:A-C
WOMEN'S PRISON MASSACRE zero
(1986, It./Fr.) PR:O
WON TON TON, THE DOG WHO SAVED
HOLLYWOOD * (1976) PR:A
WONDER BAR *** (1934) PR:A
WONDER BOY ** (1951, Brit./Aust.) PR:A
WONDER CHILD
(SEE:WONDER BOY)
WONDER KID
(SEE:WONDER BOY)
WONDER MAN *** (1945) PR:AA
WONDER OF WOMEN * (1929) PR:A
WONDER PLANE
(SEE:MERCY PLANE)
WONDER WOMEN zero (1973, Phil.) PR:C
WONDERFUL COUNTRY, THE *** (1959) PR:A
WONDERFUL DAY
(SEE:I'VE GOTTA HORSE)
WONDERFUL LAND OF OZ, THE ** (1969) PR:AA
WONDERFUL LIFE
(SEE:SWINGER'S PARADISE)
WONDERFUL STORY, THE ** (1932, Brit.) PR:A
WONDERFUL THINGS! **½ (1958, Brit.) PR:A
WONDERFUL TO BE YOUNG! ** (1962, Brit.) PR:A
WONDERFUL WORLD OF THE BROTHERS GRIMM,
THE ** (1962) PR:A-C
WONDERFUL YEARS, THE
(SEE:RESTLESS YEARS, THE)
WONDERS OF ALADDIN, THE *½
(1961, Fr./It.) PR:AA
WONDERWALL *½ (1969, Brit.) PR:O
WOODEN HORSE, THE ***½ (1951, Brit.) PR:A
WOORUZHYON I OCHEN OPASEN
(SEE:ARMED AND DANGEROUS)
WORD, THE
(SEE:ORDET)
WORDS AND MUSIC ** (1929) PR:A
WORDS AND MUSIC **½ (1948) PR:A
WORK IS A FOUR LETTER WORD **
(1968, Brit.) PR:C
WORKING GIRL ***½ (1988) PR:O
WORKING GIRLS ** (1931) PR:A
WORKING GIRLS *** (1986) PR:O
WORKING GIRLS, THE ** (1973) PR:O
WORKING MAN, THE **½ (1933) PR:A
WORKING WIVES
(SEE:WEEK-END MARRIAGE)
WORLD ACCORDING TO GARP, THE ***½
(1982) PR:C-O
WORLD ACCUSES, THE *½ (1935) PR:A
WORLD AND HIS WIFE, THE
(SEE:STATE OF THE UNION)
WORLD AND THE FLESH, THE *½ (1932) PR:A
WORLD APART, A **** (1988, Brit.) PR:C-O
WORLD CHANGES, THE *** (1933) PR:A
WORLD FOR RANSOM *** (1954) PR:C-O
WORLD GONE MAD, THE ** (1933) PR:A
WORLD GONE WILD ** (1988) PR:O
WORLD IN HIS ARMS, THE *** (1952) PR:A-C
WORLD IN MY CORNER **½ (1956) PR:A
WORLD IN MY POCKET, THE **
(1962, Fr./It./Ger.) PR:A
WORLD IS FULL OF MARRIED MEN, THE *
(1980, Brit.) PR:O
WORLD IS JUST A 'B' MOVIE, THE zero (1971) PR:O
WORLD MOVES ON, THE ** (1934) PR:A
WORLD OF APU, THE ***½ (1960, India) PR:A
WORLD OF HANS CHRISTIAN ANDERSEN, THE
**½ (1971, Jap.) PR:AA
WORLD OF HENRY ORIENT, THE *** (1964) PR:C
WORLD OF SPACE, THE
(SEE:BATTLE IN OUTER SPACE)
WORLD OF SUZIE WONG, THE ** (1960) PR:O
WORLD OWES ME A LIVING, THE **
(1944, Brit.) PR:A
WORLD PREMIERE **½ (1941) PR:A
WORLD TEN TIMES OVER, THE
(SEE:PUSSYCAT ALLEY)
WORLD, THE FLESH, AND THE DEVIL, THE **½
(1959) PR:A
WORLD WAR III BREAKS OUT
(SEE:FINAL WAR, THE)
WORLD WAS HIS JURY, THE ** (1958) PR:A

WORLD WITHOUT A MASK, THE **
(1934, Ger.) PR:A
WORLD WITHOUT END ** (1956) PR:A
WORLD, THE FLESH, AND THE DEVIL, THE **
(1932, Brit.) PR:A
WORLDLY GOODS *½ (1930) PR:A
WORLDS APART ** (1980, US/Israel) PR:C
WORLD'S GREATEST ATHLETE, THE ***
(1973) PR:AA
WORLD'S GREATEST LOVER, THE **
(1977) PR:A-C
WORLD'S GREATEST SINNER, THE * (1962) PR:O
WORLD'S GREATEST SWINDLES
(SEE:BEAUTIFUL SWINDLERS)
WORLDS OF GULLIVER, THE
(SEE:THREE WORLDS OF GULLIVER, THE)
WORM EATERS, THE zero (1981) PR:O
WORM'S EYE VIEW ** (1951, Brit.) PR:A
WORST SECRET AGENTS
(SEE:OO-2 MOST SECRET AGENTS)
WORST WOMAN IN PARIS **½ (1933) PR:A
WORTHY DECEIVER
(SEE:BIG BLUFF, THE)
WOULD-BE GENTLEMAN, THE *½ (1960, Fr.) PR:A
WOULD YOU BELIEVE IT! ** (1930, Brit.) PR:AA
WOZZECK *½ (1962, E. Ger.) PR:A
WRAITH, THE * (1986) PR:C
WRANGLER'S ROOST ** (1941) PR:A
WRATH OF GOD, THE **½ (1972) PR:C-O
WRATH OF JEALOUSY ** (1936, Brit.) PR:A
WRECK OF THE MARY DEARE, THE ***½
(1959) PR:A
WRECKER, THE * (1933) PR:A
WRECKERS, THE
(SEE:FURY AT SMUGGLER'S BAY)
WRECKING CREW ** (1942) PR:A
WRECKING CREW ** (1968) PR:C
WRECKING YARD, THE
(SEE:ROTTEN APPLE)
WRESTLER, THE * (1974) PR:C
WRITTEN LAW, THE *½ (1931, Brit.) PR:A
WRITTEN ON THE SAND
(SEE:PLAY DIRTY)
WRITTEN ON THE WIND ***** (1956) PR:C
WRONG ARM OF THE LAW, THE ***
(1963, Brit.) PR:A
WRONG BOX, THE *** (1966, Brit.) PR:A
WRONG DAMN FILM, THE zero (1975) PR:C-O
WRONG GUYS, THE *½ (1988) PR:O
WRONG IS RIGHT ** (1982) PR:O
WRONG KIND OF GIRL, THE
(SEE:BUS STOP)
WRONG MAN, THE **** (1956) PR:A
WRONG NUMBER ** (1959, Brit.) PR:A
WRONG ROAD, THE *½ (1937) PR:A
WRONGLY ACCUSED
(SEE:BAD MEN OF THE HILLS)
WU-HOU
(SEE:EMPRESS WU)
WUSA ** (1970) PR:C
WUTHERING HEIGHTS ***** (1939) PR:C
WUTHERING HEIGHTS ** (1970, Brit.) PR:A
WYLIE
(SEE:EYE OF THE CAT)
WYOMING **½ (1940) PR:A
WYOMING **½ (1947) PR:A
WYOMING BANDIT, THE ** (1949) PR:A
WYOMING KID, THE
(SEE:CHEYENNE)
WYOMING MAIL ** (1950) PR:A
WYOMING OUTLAW ** (1939) PR:A
WYOMING RENEGADES **½ (1955) PR:A
WYOMING WILDCAT ** (1941) PR:A

X

X
(SEE:"X"—THE MAN WITH X-RAY EYES)
"X'—THE MAN WITH THE X-RAY EYES ***½
(1963) PR:C
X-15 ** (1961) PR:A
X MARKS THE SPOT ** (1931) PR:A
X MARKS THE SPOT ** (1942) PR:A
X-RAY
(SEE:HOSPITAL MASSACRE)
X THE UNKNOWN **½ (1957, Brit.) PR:A-C
X Y & ZEE **½ (1972, Brit.) PR:O
XANADU * (1980) PR:C
XICA *** (1982, Braz.) PR:O
XICA DA SILVA
(SEE:XICA)
XOCHIMILCO
(SEE:PORTRAIT OF MARIA)

XTRO zero (1983, Brit.) PR:O
...Y EL DEMONIO CREO A LOS HOMBRES
(SEE:HEAT)

Y

YA KUPIL PAPU
(SEE:DIMKA)
YA SHAGAYU PO MOSKVE
(SEE:MEET ME IN MOSCOW)
YABU NO NAKA NO KURONEKO
(SEE:KURONEKO)
YABUNIRAMI NIPPON
(SEE:WALL-EYED NIPPON)
YAGYU BUGEICHO
(SEE:SECRET SCROLLS, PART I)
YAGYU SECRET SCROLLS
(SEE:SECRET SCROLLS, PART II)
YAKUZA, THE ***½ (1975, US/Jap.) PR:O
YAMANEKO SAKUSEN
(SEE:OPERATION ENEMY FORT)
YAMBAO
(SEE:YOUNG AND EVIL)
YANCO **½ (1964, Mex.) PR:A
YANG KWEI FEI
(SEE:MAGNIFICENT CONCUBINE, THE)
YANGTSE INCIDENT
(SEE:BATTLE HELL)
YANK AT ETON, A ** (1942) PR:A
YANK AT OXFORD, A *** (1938) PR:A
YANK IN DUTCH, A
(SEE:WIFE TAKES A FLYER, THE)
YANK IN ERMINE, A ** (1955, Brit.) PR:A
YANK IN INDO-CHINA, A * (1952) PR:A
YANK IN KOREA, A *½ (1951) PR:A
YANK IN LIBYA, A * (1942) PR:A
YANK IN LONDON, A ** (1946, Brit.) PR:A
YANK IN THE R.A.F., A *** (1941) PR:A
YANK IN VIET-NAM, A ** (1964) PR:A
YANK ON THE BURMA ROAD, A ** (1942) PR:A
YANKEE AT KING ARTHUR'S COURT, THE
(SEE:CONNECTICUT YANKEE, A)
YANKEE BUCCANEER ** (1952) PR:A
YANKEE DON ** (1931) PR:A
YANKEE DOODLE DANDY ***** (1942) PR:AA
YANKEE FAKIR *½ (1947) PR:A
YANKEE IN KING ARTHUR'S COURT, A
(SEE:CONNECTICUT YANKEE IN KING ARTHUR'S
COURT, A)
YANKEE PASHA **½ (1954) PR:A
YANKS **½ (1979) PR:C-O
YANKS AHOY *½ (1943) PR:A
YANKS ARE COMING, THE *½ (1942) PR:A
YAQUI DRUMS *½ (1956) PR:AA
YASEMIN *** (1988, W. Ger.) PR:C
YASHA **½ (1985, Jap.) PR:O
YATO KAZE NO NAKA O HASHIRU
(SEE:BANDITS ON THE WIND)
YAWARA SEMPU DOTO NO TAIKETSU
(SEE:JUDO SHOWDOWN)
YEAR MY VOICE BROKE, THE **½
(1988, Aus.) PR:C
YEAR OF AWAKENING, THE **½ (1987, Sp.) PR:O
YEAR OF LIVING DANGEROUSLY, THE ***½
(1982, Aus.) PR:C
YEAR OF THE CRICKET
(SEE:KENNER)
YEAR OF THE DRAGON *½ (1985) PR:O
YEAR OF THE HORSE
(SEE:HORSE IN THE GRAY FLANNEL SUIT, THE)
YEAR OF THE HORSE, THE ** (1966) PR:AA
YEAR OF THE TIGER, THE
(SEE:YANK IN VIET-NAM, A)
YEAR OF THE YAHOO zero (1971) PR:O
YEAR ONE * (1974, It.) PR:A
YEAR 2889
(SEE:IN THE YEAR 2889)
YEARLING, THE **** (1946) PR:AA
YEARNING ** (1964, Jap.) PR:C
YEARS BETWEEN, THE *½ (1947, Brit.) PR:A
YEARS WITHOUT DAYS
(SEE:CASTLE ON THE HUDSON)
YELLOW BALLOON, THE **½ (1953, Brit.) PR:A
YELLOW CAB MAN, THE **½ (1950) PR:A
YELLOW CANARY, THE ** (1944, Brit.) PR:A
YELLOW CANARY, THE * (1963) PR:A
YELLOW CARGO **½ (1936) PR:A
YELLOW DOG * (1973, Brit.) PR:A-C
YELLOW DUST * (1936) PR:A
YELLOW EARTH *** (1986, Chi.) PR:A
YELLOW FIN **½ (1951) PR:A
YELLOW GOLLIWOG, THE
(SEE:GUTTER GIRLS)

YELLOW HAIR AND THE FORTRESS OF GOLD *½ (1984) PR:O
YELLOW HAT, THE ** (1966, Brit.) PR:A
YELLOW JACK ***½ (1938) PR:A
YELLOW MASK, THE * (1930, Brit.) PR:A
YELLOW MOUNTAIN, THE * (1954) PR:A
YELLOW PASSPORT, THE (SEE:YELLOW TICKET, THE)
YELLOW ROBE, THE ** (1954, Brit.) PR:A
YELLOW ROLLS-ROYCE, THE **½ (1965, Brit.) PR:C
YELLOW ROSE OF TEXAS, THE ** (1944) PR:A
YELLOW SANDS *** (1938, Brit.) PR:A
YELLOW SKY *** (1948) PR:A**
YELLOW SLIPPERS, THE ** (1965, Pol.) PR:A
YELLOW STOCKINGS * (1930, Brit.) PR:AA
YELLOW SUBMARINE ** (1958, Brit.) PR:A**
YELLOW TEDDYBEARS, THE (SEE:GUTTER GIRLS)
YELLOW TICKET, THE ** (1931) PR:A
YELLOW TOMAHAWK, THE ** (1954) PR:A
YELLOWBEARD ** (1983) PR:C-O
YELLOWNECK ** (1955) PR:A
YELLOWSTONE * (1936) PR:A
YELLOWSTONE KELLY ** (1959) PR:A
YENTL * (1983) PR:C
YES, GIORGIO *½ (1982) PR:C
YES, MADAM? ** (1938, Brit.) PR:A
YES, MR. BROWN *½ (1933, Brit.) PR:A
YES, MY DARLING DAUGHTER **½ (1939) PR:A
YES SIR, MR. BONES *½ (1951) PR:A
YES SIR, THAT'S MY BABY ** (1949) PR:A
YESTERDAY * (1980, Can.) PR:C
YESTERDAY, TODAY, AND TOMORROW * (1963, It./Fr.) PR:O**
YESTERDAY'S ENEMY **** (1959, Brit.) PR:O
YESTERDAY'S HERO *½ (1979, Brit.) PR:C-O
YESTERDAY'S HERO, 1937 (SEE:HOOSIER SCHOOLBOY, THE)
YESTERDAY'S HEROES ** (1940) PR:A
YETI zero (1977, It.) PR:A
YIDDLE WITH HIS FIDDLE * (1937, Pol.) PR:A
YIELD TO THE NIGHT (SEE:BLONDE SINNER)
YINGXIONG BENSE (SEE:BETTER TOMORROW)
YNGSJOMORDET (SEE:WOMAN OF DARKNESS)
YO YO *** (1967, Fr.) PR:A
YODELIN' KID FROM PINE RIDGE *½ (1937) PR:A
YOG-MONSTER FROM SPACE * (1970, Jap.) PR:A
YOJIMBO ***½ (1961, Jap.) PR:O
YOKEL BOY ** (1942) PR:A
YOL ***½ (1982, Turk.) PR:O
YOLANDA AND THE THIEF * (1945) PR:A**
YOLANTA ** (1964, USSR) PR:A
YONGKARI MONSTER FROM THE DEEP * (1967, S.K.) PR:A
YOR, THE HUNTER FROM THE FUTURE zero (1983, It.) PR:A
YOSAKOI JOURNEY *½ (1970, Jap.) PR:C
YOSAKOI RYOKO (SEE:YOSAKOI JOURNEY)
YOSEI GORASU (SEE:GORATH)
YOSIE GORATH (SEE:GORATH)
YOTSUYA KAIDAN (SEE:ILLUSION OF BLOOD)
YOU AND ME *** (1938) PR:A-C
YOU ARE THE WORLD FOR ME ** (1964, Aust.) PR:A
YOU BELONG TO ME ** (1934) PR:A
YOU BELONG TO ME *** (1941) PR:A
YOU BELONG TO MY HEART (SEE:MR. IMPERIUM)
YOU BETTER WATCH OUT ** (1980) PR:O
YOU CAME ALONG **½ (1945) PR:A
YOU CAME TOO LATE *½ (1962, Gr.) PR:A
YOU CAN'T BEAT LOVE *½ (1937) PR:A
YOU CAN'T BEAT THE IRISH ** (1952, Brit.) PR:A
YOU CAN'T BEAT THE LAW (SEE:SMART GUY)
YOU CAN'T BUY EVERYTHING ** (1934) PR:A
YOU CAN'T BUY LUCK *½ (1937) PR:A
YOU CAN'T CHEAT AN HONEST MAN ***½ (1939) PR:A
YOU CAN'T DO THAT TO ME (SEE:MAISIE GOES TO RENO)
YOU CAN'T DO WITHOUT LOVE ** (1946, Brit.) PR:A
YOU CAN'T ESCAPE * (1955, Brit.) PR:A
YOU CAN'T ESCAPE FOREVER *½ (1942) PR:A
YOU CAN'T FOOL AN IRISHMAN * (1950, Ireland) PR:A
YOU CAN'T FOOL YOUR WIFE *½ (1940) PR:A
YOU CAN'T GET AWAY WITH MURDER *** (1939) PR:A-C
YOU CAN'T HAVE EVERYTHING * (1937) PR:A**
YOU CAN'T HAVE EVERYTHING (SEE:CACTUS IN THE SNOW)
YOU CAN'T HURRY LOVE * (1988) PR:O
YOU CAN'T RATION LOVE * (1944) PR:A
YOU CAN'T RUN AWAY FROM IT ** (1956) PR:A
YOU CAN'T RUN FAR (SEE:WHEN THE CLOCK STRIKES)
YOU CAN'T SEE 'ROUND CORNERS ** (1969, Aus.) PR:A
YOU CAN'T SLEEP HERE (SEE:I WAS A MALE WAR BRIDE)
YOU CAN'T STEAL LOVE (SEE:MURPH THE SURF)
YOU CAN'T TAKE IT WITH YOU **** (1938) PR:A
YOU CAN'T TAKE MONEY (SEE:INTERNES CAN'T TAKE MONEY)
YOU CAN'T WIN 'EM ALL (SEE:ONCE YOU KISS A STRANGER)
YOU CAN'T WIN 'EM ALL *½ (1970, Brit.) PR:C
YOU DON'T NEED PAJAMAS AT ROSIE'S (SEE:FIRST TIME, THE)
YOU FOR ME **½ (1952) PR:A
YOU GOTTA STAY HAPPY *** (1948) PR:A
YOU HAVE TO RUN FAST ** (1961) PR:A
YOU JUST KILL ME (SEE:ARRIVEDERCI, BABY!)
YOU KNOW WHAT SAILORS ARE ** (1954, Brit.) PR:A
YOU LIGHT UP MY LIFE * (1977) PR:C
YOU LIVE AND LEARN ** (1937, Brit.) PR:A
YOU LUCKY PEOPLE *½ (1955, Brit.) PR:A
YOU MADE ME LOVE YOU *½ (1934, Brit.) PR:A
YOU MAY BE NEXT *½ (1936) PR:A
YOU MUST BE JOKING! **½ (1965, Brit.) PR:A
YOU MUST GET MARRIED *½ (1936, Brit.) PR:A
YOU NEVER CAN TELL ** (1951) PR:A
YOU NEVER KNOW (SEE:YOU NEVER CAN TELL)
YOU ONLY LIVE ONCE ** (1937) PR:C**
YOU ONLY LIVE ONCE ** (1969, Fr.) PR:A
YOU ONLY LIVE TWICE **½ (1967, Brit.) PR:C
YOU PAY YOUR MONEY *½ (1957, Brit.) PR:A
YOU SAID A MOUTHFUL *½ (1932) PR:A
YOU WERE MEANT FOR ME ** (1948) PR:A
YOU WERE NEVER LOVELIER ***½ (1942) PR:A
YOU WILL REMEMBER *½ (1941, Brit.) PR:A
YOU'D BE SURPRISED! *½ (1930, Brit.) PR:A
YOU'LL FIND OUT ** (1940) PR:A
YOU'LL LIKE MY MOTHER *** (1972) PR:C
YOU'LL NEVER GET RICH * (1941) PR:A**
YOUNG AMERICA **½ (1932) PR:AA
YOUNG AMERICA ** (1942) PR:AA
YOUNG AND BEAUTIFUL *½ (1934) PR:A
YOUNG AND DANGEROUS **½ (1957) PR:A
YOUNG AND EAGER (SEE:CLAUDELLE INGLISH)
YOUNG AND EVIL ** (1962, Mex.) PR:C
YOUNG AND IMMORAL, THE (SEE:SINISTER URGE, THE)
YOUNG AND INNOCENT ***½ (1938, Brit.) PR:A
YOUNG AND THE BRAVE, THE ** (1963) PR:A
YOUNG AND THE COOL, THE (SEE:TWIST ALL NIGHT)
YOUNG AND THE DAMNED, THE (SEE:LOS OLVIDADOS)
YOUNG AND THE GUILTY, THE ** (1958, Brit.) PR:A
YOUNG AND THE IMMORAL, THE (SEE:THE SINISTER URGE)
YOUNG AND THE PASSIONATE, THE (SEE:VITELLONI)
YOUNG AND WILD ** (1958) PR:A
YOUNG AND WILLING **½ (1943) PR:A
YOUNG AND WILLING **½ (1964, Brit.) PR:C
YOUNG ANIMALS, THE (SEE:BORN WILD)
YOUNG APHRODITES ** (1966, Gr.) PR:C
YOUNG AS YOU FEEL **½ (1931) PR:AA
YOUNG AS YOU FEEL **½ (1940) PR:AA
YOUNG AT HEART * (1955) PR:A**
YOUNG BESS ***½ (1953) PR:A
YOUNG BILL HICKOK ** (1940) PR:A
YOUNG BILLY YOUNG **½ (1969) PR:A
YOUNG BLOOD *½ (1932) PR:A
YOUNG BRIDE *½ (1932) PR:C
YOUNG BUFFALO BILL **½ (1940) PR:AA
YOUNG CAPTIVES, THE **½ (1959) PR:O
YOUNG CASSIDY *** (1965, US/Brit.) PR:C
YOUNG COMPOSER'S ODYSSEY, A ** (1986, USSR) PR:O
YOUNG CYCLE GIRLS, THE zero (1979) PR:O
YOUNG DANIEL BOONE **½ (1950) PR:AA
YOUNG DESIRE ** (1930) PR:C
YOUNG DILLINGER **½ (1965) PR:O
YOUNG DR. KILDARE ***½ (1938) PR:A
YOUNG DOCTORS, THE **½ (1961) PR:A-C
YOUNG DOCTORS IN LOVE * (1982) PR:O
YOUNG DONOVAN'S KID ** (1931) PR:A
YOUNG DON'T CRY, THE ** (1957) PR:C
YOUNG DRACULA (SEE:SON OF DRACULA)
YOUNG DYNAMITE ** (1937) PR:A
YOUNG EAGLES **½ (1930) PR:AA
YOUNG FRANKENSTEIN ** (1974) PR:C**
YOUNG FUGITIVES **½ (1938) PR:A
YOUNG FURY ** (1965) PR:C
YOUNG GIANTS *½ (1983) PR:A
YOUNG GIRLS OF ROCHEFORT, THE **½ (1968, Fr.) PR:A
YOUNG GIRLS OF WILKO, THE ***½ (1979, Pol./Fr.) PR:C
YOUNG GO WILD, THE **½ (1962, Ger.) PR:C
YOUNG GRADUATES, THE zero (1971) PR:O
YOUNG GUNS, THE ** (1956) PR:A-C
YOUNG GUNS ** (1988) PR:O
YOUNG GUNS OF TEXAS ** (1963) PR:C
YOUNG GUY GRADUATES **½ (1969, Jap.) PR:C
YOUNG GUY ON MT. COOK **½ (1969, Jap.) PR:A
YOUNG HELLIONS (SEE:HIGH SCHOOL CONFIDENTIAL)
YOUNG HUSBANDS *** (1958, It./Fr.) PR:A
YOUNG IDEAS **½ (1943) PR:A
YOUNG IN HEART, THE ***½ (1938) PR:A
YOUNG INVADERS (SEE:DARBY'S RANGERS)
YOUNG JESSE JAMES *½ (1960) PR:C
YOUNG LAND, THE ** (1959) PR:A
YOUNG LIONS, THE ** (1958) PR:C**
YOUNG LORD, THE *** (1970, Ger.) PR:A
YOUNG LOVERS, THE (SEE:NEVER FEAR)
YOUNG LOVERS, THE (SEE:CHANCE MEETING)
YOUNG LOVERS, THE **½ (1964) PR:C-O
YOUNG MAN OF MANHATTAN **½ (1930) PR:A
YOUNG MAN OF MUSIC (SEE:YOUNG MAN WITH A HORN)
YOUNG MAN WITH A HORN ** (1950) PR:C**
YOUNG MAN WITH IDEAS *** (1952) PR:A
YOUNG MAN'S FANCY *** (1943, Brit.) PR:A
YOUNG MR. LINCOLN ** (1939) PR:A**
YOUNG MR. PITT, THE ***½ (1942, Brit.) PR:A
YOUNG MONK, THE ** (1978, Ger.) PR:O
YOUNG NOWHERES *** (1929) PR:A
YOUNG NURSES, THE ** (1973) PR:O
YOUNG ONE, THE **½ (1961, Mex.) PR:O
YOUNG ONES, THE (SEE:WONDERFUL TO BE YOUNG)
YOUNG PAUL BARONI (SEE:KID MONK BARONI)
YOUNG PEOPLE *** (1940) PR:AA
YOUNG PHILADELPHIANS, THE * (1959) PR:C**
YOUNG RACERS, THE ** (1963) PR:C
YOUNG REBEL, THE ** (1969, Fr./It./Sp.) PR:C
YOUNG REBELS, THE (SEE:TEENAGE DOLL)
YOUNG RUNAWAYS, THE ** (1968) PR:O
YOUNG SAVAGES, THE *** (1961) PR:C
YOUNG SCARFACE (SEE:BRIGHTON ROCK)
YOUNG SHERLOCK HOLMES * (1985) PR:C**

Finding entries in **THE MOTION PICTURE GUIDE ™**

Years	Volumes
1929-83	Volumes I-IX
1984	Volume IX
1985	1986 ANNUAL
1986	1987 ANNUAL
1987	1988 ANNUAL
1988	1989 ANNUAL

STAR RATINGS

★★★★★	Masterpiece
★★★★	Excellent
★★★	Good
★★	Fair
★	Poor
zero	Without Merit

PARENTAL RECOMMENDATION (PR:)

AA	Good for Children
A	Acceptable for Children
C	Cautionary, some objectionable scenes
O	Objectionable for Children

BOLD: Films on Videocassette

Z

YOUNG SINNER, THE **½ (1965) PR:C
YOUNG SINNERS ** (1931) PR:A
YOUNG STRANGER, THE *** (1957) PR:C
YOUNG SWINGERS, THE * (1963) PR:AA
YOUNG SWORDSMAN **½ (1964, Jap.) PR:C
YOUNG, THE EVIL AND THE SAVAGE, THE *½
  (1968, It.) PR:O
YOUNG TOM EDISON *** (1940) PR:AA
YOUNG TORLESS ***½ (1968, Fr./Ger.) PR:C
YOUNG WARRIORS, THE ** (1967) PR:C
YOUNG WARRIORS ** (1983) PR:O
YOUNG WIDOW ** (1946) PR:A
YOUNG, WILLING AND EAGER **½
  (1962, Brit.) PR:C
YOUNG WINSTON ***½ (1972, Brit.) PR:A-C
YOUNG WIVES' TALE *** (1954, Brit.) PR:A
YOUNG WOODLEY **½ (1930, Brit.) PR:C
YOUNG WORLD, A * (1966, Fr./It.) PR:C
YOUNGBLOOD * (1978) PR:O**
YOUNGBLOOD ** (1986) PR:O
YOUNGBLOOD HAWKE **½ (1964) PR:O
YOUNGER BROTHERS, THE **½ (1949) PR:A
YOUNGER GENERATION * (1929) PR:A
YOUNGEST PROFESSION, THE **½ (1943) PR:A
YOUNGEST SPY, THE
  (SEE:MY NAME IS IVAN)
YOUR CHEATIN' HEART *** (1964) PR:A
YOUR MONEY OR YOUR WIFE *½
  (1965, Brit.) PR:A
YOUR PAST IS SHOWING * (1958, Brit.) PR:A**
YOUR SHADOW IS MINE **½ (1963, Fr./It.) PR:O
YOUR TEETH IN MY NECK
  (SEE:FEARLESS VAMPIRE KILLERS, OR PARDON
  ME BUT YOUR TEETH ARE IN MY NECK, THE)
YOUR THREE MINUTES ARE UP ***½ (1973) PR:O
YOUR TURN, DARLING **½ (1963, Fr.) PR:C
YOUR UNCLE DUDLEY **½ (1935) PR:A
YOUR WITNESS
  (SEE:EYE WITNESS)
YOU'RE A BIG BOY NOW * (1966) PR:C**
YOU'RE A LUCKY FELLOW, MR. SMITH *½
  (1943) PR:A
YOU'RE A SWEETHEART **½ (1937) PR:A
YOU'RE DEAD RIGHT
  (SEE:ARRIVEDERCI, BABY!)
YOU'RE IN THE ARMY NOW ** (1937, Brit.) PR:A
YOU'RE IN THE ARMY NOW **½ (1941) PR:A
YOU'RE IN THE NAVY NOW *** (1951) PR:A
YOU'RE MY EVERYTHING **½ (1949) PR:A
YOU'RE NEVER TOO YOUNG **½ (1955) PR:A
YOU'RE NOT SO TOUGH ** (1940) PR:A
YOU'RE ONLY YOUNG ONCE **½ (1938) PR:A
YOU'RE ONLY YOUNG TWICE * (1952, Brit.) PR:A
YOU'RE OUT OF LUCK * (1941) PR:A
YOU'RE TELLING ME **** (1934) PR:A
YOU'RE TELLING ME ** (1942) PR:A
YOU'RE THE DOCTOR *½ (1938, Brit.) PR:A
YOU'RE THE ONE * (1941) PR:A
YOURS FOR THE ASKING **½ (1936) PR:A
YOURS, MINE AND OURS *** (1968) PR:AA
YOUTH AFLAME zero (1945) PR:A
YOUTH AND HIS AMULET, THE **½
  (1963, Jap.) PR:C
YOUTH IN FURY ** (1961, Jap.) PR:O
YOUTH ON PARADE **½ (1943) PR:AA
YOUTH ON PAROLE *½ (1937) PR:A
YOUTH ON TRIAL ** (1945) PR:A
YOUTH RUNS WILD *½ (1944) PR:C
YOUTH TAKES A FLING ** (1938) PR:AA
YOUTH TAKES A HAND
  (SEE:BEHIND PRISON WALLS)
YOUTH WILL BE SERVED ** (1940) PR:A
YOUTHFUL FOLLY ** (1934, Brit.) PR:A
YOU'VE GOT TO BE SMART * (1967) PR:A
YOU'VE GOT TO WALK IT LIKE YOU TALK IT OR
  YOU'LL LOSE THAT BEAT *½ (1971) PR:O
YOYO
  (SEE:YO YO)
YR ALCOHOLIG LION ** (1984, Brit.) PR:C
YUKIGUMI
  (SEE:SNOW COUNTRY)
YUKON FLIGHT **½ (1940) PR:A
YUKON GOLD ** (1952) PR:A
YUKON MANHUNT ** (1951) PR:A
YUKON VENGEANCE *½ (1954) PR:A
YUSHA NOMI
  (SEE:NONE BUT THE BRAVE)
YUSHU HEIYA
  (SEE:MADAME AKI)

Z **** (1969, Fr./Algeria) PR:C-O
ZA DVUNMYA ZAYTSAMI
  (SEE:KIEV COMEDY)
ZABRISKIE POINT ** (1970) PR:O
ZACHARIAH ** (1971) PR:C
ZAMBA *½ (1949) PR:A
ZAMBA THE GORILLA
  (SEE:ZAMBA)
ZANDY'S BRIDE **½ (1974) PR:A
ZANZIBAR **½ (1940) PR:A
ZAPPA *** (1984, Den.) PR:O
ZAPPED! * (1982) PR:O
ZARAK **½ (1956, Brit.) PR:C
ZARDOZ * (1974, Brit.) PR:O
ZARTE HAUT IN SCHWARZER SEIDE
  (SEE:DANIELLA BY NIGHT)
ZATO ICHI CHIKEMURI KAIDO
  (SEE:ZATOICHI CHALLENGED)
ZATO ICHI KENKATABI
  (SEE:ZATOICHI)
ZATO ICHI TO YONJINBO
  (SEE:ZATOICHI MEETS YOJIMBO)
ZATOICHI **½ (1968, Jap.) PR:A
ZATOICHI CHALLENGED ** (1970, Jap.) PR:A
ZATOICHI JOGKUTABI
  (SEE:SHOWDOWN FOR ZATOICHI)
ZATOICHI MEETS YOJIMBO **½
  (1970, Jap.) PR:C
ZATOICHI'S CONSPIRACY **½ (1974, Jap.) PR:A
ZAZA ** (1939) PR:C
ZAZIE ***½ (1961, Fr.) PR:A
ZAZIE DANS LE METRO
  (SEE:ZAZIE)
ZBEHOVIA A PUTNICI
  (SEE:DESERTER AND THE NOMADS, THE)
ZEBRA IN THE KITCHEN **½ (1965) PR:AA
ZED & TWO NOUGHTS, A *
  (1985, Brit./Neth.) PR:O
ZEE & CO.
  (SEE:X, Y & ZEE)
ZELIG ** (1983) PR:A
ZELLY AND ME ***½ (1988) PR:A
ZENOBIA ** (1939) PR:A
ZEPPELIN **½ (1971, Brit.) PR:A
ZERO BOYS, THE *½ (1987) PR:C-O
ZERO HOUR, THE * (1939) PR:C
ZERO HOUR! *** (1957) PR:A
ZERO IN THE UNIVERSE zero (1966) PR:O
ZERO POPULATION GROWTH
  (SEE:Z.P.G.)
ZERO TO SIXTY * (1978) PR:C
00-2 MOST SECRET AGENTS *½ (1965, It.) PR:A
ZHENITBA BALZAMINOVA
  (SEE:MARRIAGE OF BALZAMINOV, THE)
ZHENITBA BALZAMINOVA
  (SEE:MARRIAGE OF BALZAMINOVA, THE)
ZHILI-BYLI STARIK SO STARUKHOY
  (SEE:THERE WAS AN OLD COUPLE)
ZIEGFELD FOLLIES *** (1945) PR:AA**
ZIEGFELD GIRL ***½ (1941) PR:A
ZIG-ZAG **½ (1975, Fr/It.) PR:O
ZIGZAG *** (1970) PR:C
ZINA **½ (1985, Brit.) PR:C
ZIS BOOM BAH ** (1941) PR:A
ZITA **½ (1968, Fr.) PR:O
ZOEKEN NAAR EILEEN
  (SEE:LOOKING FOR EILEEN)
ZOKU MIYAMOTO MUSHASHI
  (SEE:SAMURAI PART II)
ZOKU NINGEN NO JOKEN
  (SEE:ROAD TO ETERNITY)
ZOLTAN, HOUND OF DRACULA
  (SEE:DRACULA'S DOG)
ZOMBIE
  (SEE:I EAT YOUR SKIN)
ZOMBIE zero (1980, It.) PR:O
ZOMBIE CREEPING FLESH * (1981, It./Sp.) PR:O
ZOMBIES OF SUGAR HILL
  (SEE:SUGAR HILL)
ZOMBIES OF MORA TAU ** (1957) PR:O
ZOMBIES OF THE STRATOSPHERE
  (SEE:SATAN'S SATELLITES)
ZOMBIES ON BROADWAY **½ (1945) PR:A
ZONING * (1986, Ger.) PR:C
ZONTAR, THE THING FROM VENUS *½
  (1966) PR:A
ZOO BABY ** (1957, Brit.) PR:AA
ZOO GANG, THE ** (1985) PR:C
ZOO IN BUDAPEST ***½ (1933) PR:A
ZOOT SUIT ** (1981) PR:O
ZORBA THE GREEK ***½ (1964, US/Gr.) PR:A

ZORRO CONTRO MACISTE
  (SEE:SAMSON AND THE SLAVE QUEEN)
ZORRO, THE GAY BLADE *½ (1981) PR:A-C
ZOTZ! ** (1962) PR:A
Z.P.G. *½ (1972) PR:C
ZULU *** (1964, Brit.) PR:C**
ZULU DAWN * (1980, Brit.) PR:C-O**
ZVEROLOVY
  (SEE:HUNTING IN SIBERIA)
ZVONYAT, OTKROYTE DVER
  (SEE:GIRL AND THE BUGLER, THE)
ZVYODY I SOLDATY
  (SEE:RED AND THE WHITE, THE)
ZWEI SARGE AUF BESTELLUNG
  (SEE:WE STILL KILL THE OLD WAY)

FILMS BY GENRE

Listed below are the films included in THE MOTION PICTURE GUIDE and its Annuals by the genre or category best suited to the film. Films which can be classeified by more than one genre are listed under each of the genres in which they fit. The War/Drama CASABLANCA for example is listed under both of those genres. The genres utilized by CineBooks are:

Action, Adventure, Animated, Biography, Children's, Comedy, Crime, Dance, Docu-Drama, Drama, Fantasy, Historical, Horror, Musical, Musical Comedy, Mystery, Opera, Political, Religious, Romance, Science Fiction, Sports, Spy, Thriller, War, Western

Action

ABOVE THE LAW, 1988
ACTION JACKSON, 1988
AMATEUR, THE, 1982
AMAZONS, 1987
AMERICAN COMMANDOS, 1986
AMERICAN JUSTICE, 1986
AMERICAN NINJA, 1985
AMERICAN NINJA 2: THE CONFRONTATION, 1987
ANGEL 3: THE FINAL CHAPTER, 1988
ANGEL UNCHAINED, 1970
ANGELS BRIGADE, 1980
ANGELS DIE HARD, 1970
ANGELS FROM HELL, 1968
ANGELS HARD AS THEY COME, 1971
ANNIHILATORS, THE, 1985
ANTONIO DAS MORTES, 1970
ASSASSINATION, 1987
ASSAULT ON PRECINCT 13, 1976
AVENGING FORCE, 1986
BANZAI RUNNER, 1987
BATMAN, 1966
BATTLE OF THE AMAZONS, 1973
BIG BRAWL, THE, 1980
BLACK ANGELS, THE, 1970
BLACK BELT JONES, 1974
BLACK EYE, 1974
BLACK GESTAPO, THE, 1975
BLACK GUNN, 1972
BLACK MAMA, WHITE MAMA, 1973
BLACK MOON RISING, 1986
BLACK SIX, THE, 1974
BLACK SUNDAY, 1977
BLASTFIGHTER, 1985
BLOODSPORT, 1988
BLUE THUNDER, 1983
BORN LOSERS, 1967
BRADDOCK: MISSING IN ACTION III, 1988
BREAKER! BREAKER!, 1977
BRUSHFIRE, 1962
BULLETPROOF, 1988
BULLIES, 1986
BURY ME AN ANGEL, 1972
CALL HIM MR. SHATTER, 1976
CANNONBALL, 1976
CANNONBALL RUN II, 1984
CANNONBALL RUN, THE, 1981
CATCH THE HEAT, 1987
CHAIN GANG, 1985
CHOKE CANYON, 1986
CHROME AND HOT LEATHER, 1971
CIRCLE OF IRON, 1979
CITY LIMITS, 1985
CLAY PIGEON, 1971
CLEOPATRA JONES, 1973
CLEOPATRA JONES AND THE CASINO OF GOLD, 1975
COBRA, THE, 1968
COCAINE WARS, 1986
CODE OF SILENCE, 1985
CODE 7, VICTIM 5, 1964
COLD SWEAT, 1974
COMMANDO, 1985
COMMANDO SQUAD, 1987
CONSPIRACY, 1939
CRY WILDERNESS, 1987
CUT AND RUN, 1986
CYCLE SAVAGES, 1969
CYCLONE, 1987
DANGEROUS CARGO, 1939
DANGEROUS CHARTER, 1962

DANGEROUS WATERS, 1936
DAREDEVIL, THE, 1971
DAREDEVIL DRIVERS, 1938
DAREDEVIL IN THE CASTLE, 1969

DEAD-END DRIVE-IN, 1986
DEAD MAN WALKING, 1988
DEADLY CHINA DOLL, 1973
DEADLY FEMALES, THE, 1976
DEATH BEFORE DISHONOR, 1987
DEATH MACHINES, 1976
DEATH RACE 2000, 1975
DEATH WISH 3, 1985
DEATHCHEATERS, 1976
DEEP THRUST—THE HAND OF DEATH, 1973
DELOS ADVENTURE, THE, 1987
DELTA FORCE, THE, 1986
DESERT WARRIOR, 1985
DEVIL'S EXPRESS, 1975
DIE HARD, 1988
DIRT GANG, THE, 1972
DIRTY MARY, CRAZY LARRY, 1974
DIXIE DYNAMITE, 1976
DOBERMAN GANG, THE, 1972
DOC SAVAGE... THE MAN OF BRONZE, 1975
DOLEMITE, 1975
DOUBLE NICKELS, 1977
DRAGON INN, 1968
DRIFTER, THE, 1932
DUEL AT EZO, 1970
DUEL OF CHAMPIONS, 1964
DUEL OF THE TITANS, 1963
EAT MY DUST!, 1976
EDDIE MACON'S RUN, 1983
EMPEROR OF THE NORTH POLE, 1973
EMPIRE OF THE SUN, 1987
ENTER THE DRAGON, 1973
ENTER THE NINJA, 1982
EQUALIZER 2000, 1987
ESCAPE FROM NEW YORK, 1981
ESCAPE FROM THE BRONX, 1985
ESCAPE FROM ZAHRAIN, 1962
ESCAPE 2000, 1983
EVERY WHICH WAY BUT LOOSE, 1978
EVIL THAT MEN DO, THE, 1984
EXCALIBUR, 1981
EXIT THE DRAGON, ENTER THE TIGER, 1977
EXTERMINATOR, THE, 1980
EXTERMINATORS OF THE YEAR 3000, THE, 1985
EXTREME PREJUDICE, 1987
EYE FOR AN EYE, AN, 1981
EYE OF THE TIGER, 1986
FAIR GAME, 1985
FAIR GAME, 1986
FARMER, THE, 1977
FAST CHARLIE... THE MOONBEAM RIDER, 1979
FATAL BEAUTY, 1987
FEVER HEAT, 1968
FIGHTING MAD, 1976
FINAL CHAPTER—WALKING TALL, 1977
FINAL OPTION, THE, 1982
FIRE IN THE NIGHT, 1986
FIREBIRD 2015 AD, 1981
FIRECRACKER, 1981
FIREFOX, 1982
FIREWALKER, 1986
FIRST BLOOD, 1982
FIST OF FEAR, TOUCH OF DEATH, 1980
FISTS OF FURY, 1973
FIVE FINGERS OF DEATH, 1973
FIVE GOLDEN DRAGONS, 1967
FIVE THE HARD WAY, 1969
FLASH AND THE FIRECAT, 1976
FLASHPOINT, 1984
FLYING GUILLOTINE, THE, 1975
FORCE: FIVE, 1981
FORCE OF ONE, A, 1979
FORCED VENGEANCE, 1982
FOUR DEUCES, THE, 1976
FOXY BROWN, 1974

FUNERAL FOR AN ASSASSIN, 1977
GAME OF DEATH, THE, 1979
GATOR, 1976
GETTING EVEN, 1986
GIRLS FROM THUNDER STRIP, THE, 1966
GLORY STOMPERS, THE, 1967
GLOVE, THE, 1980
GOLDEN BOX, THE, 1970
GOLDEN NEEDLES, 1974
GONE IN 60 SECONDS, 1974
GOOD GUYS WEAR BLACK, 1978
GORDON'S WAR, 1973
GOYOKIN, 1969
GRAND THEFT AUTO, 1977
GREAT SMOKEY ROADBLOCK, THE, 1978
GREAT TEXAS DYNAMITE CHASE, THE, 1976
GREED IN THE SUN, 1965
GROUND ZERO, 1973
GUMBALL RALLY, THE, 1976
GUNPOWDER, 1987
GYMKATA, 1985
HARD RIDE, THE, 1971
HELL SQUAD, 1986
HELLHOLE, 1985
HELL'S ANGELS ON WHEELS, 1967
HELL'S ANGELS '69, 1969
HELL'S BELLES, 1969
HELL'S CHOSEN FEW, 1968
HERO'S ISLAND, 1962
HIDING OUT, 1987
HIGH-BALLIN', 1978
HIGH VELOCITY, 1977
HIGHLANDER, 1986
HIKEN YABURI, 1969
HIT, 1973
HITCHHIKERS, THE, 1972
HOLLYWOOD VICE SQUAD, 1986
HOOPER, 1978
HOSTAGE, 1987
HOT POTATO, 1976
HUMAN FACTOR, THE, 1975
HUMAN TORNADO, THE, 1976
HUNTER'S BLOOD, 1987
IN THE SHADOW OF KILIMANJARO, 1986
INSTANT JUSTICE, 1986
INVASION U.S.A., 1985
IRON EAGLE II, 1988
JAGUAR LIVES, 1979
JESUS TRIP, THE, 1971
JUDO SAGA, 1965
JUDO SHOWDOWN, 1966
JUNGLE RAIDERS, 1986
JUNGLE WARRIORS, 1984
JUNKMAN, THE, 1982
KARATE, THE HAND OF DEATH, 1961
KID FROM KANSAS, THE, 1941
KILL, 1968
KILL A DRAGON, 1967
KILL AND KILL AGAIN, 1981
KILL OR BE KILLED, 1980
KILL SQUAD, 1982
KILL ZONE, 1985
KILLER FORCE, 1975
KILLPOINT, 1984
KNIGHTS OF THE CITY, 1985
LADY ICE, 1973
LAST DRAGON, THE, 1985
LAST MERCENARY, THE, 1969
LAST RUN, THE, 1971
LET'S GET HARRY, 1987
LIGHTNING BOLT, 1967
LIMIT, THE, 1972
LITTLE DRAGONS, THE, 1980
LIVELY SET, THE, 1964
LONE WOLF McQUADE, 1983

LUCKY DEVILS, 1933
MAD MAX, 1979
MAGOICHI SAGA, THE, 1970
MALONE, 1987
MAN FROM HONG KONG, 1975
MANCHURIAN AVENGER, 1985
MANHUNT, THE, 1986
MANKILLERS, 1987
MAN'S GAME, A, 1934
MASTERBLASTER, 1987
MC Q, 1974
MECHANIC, THE, 1972
MELINDA, 1972
MEN AGAINST THE SKY, 1940
MEN WITH WINGS, 1938
MERCENARY FIGHTERS, 1988
MERCY PLANE, 1940
MIGHTY CRUSADERS, THE, 1961
MINOTAUR, THE, 1961
MISSING IN ACTION 2—THE BEGINNING, 1985
MISSION KILL, 1987
MR. MAJESTYK, 1974
MOONRUNNERS, 1975
MOONSHINE COUNTY EXPRESS, 1977
MORO WITCH DOCTOR, 1964
MOTOR PSYCHO, 1965
MOVING TARGETS, 1987
MOVING VIOLATION, 1976
MURPHY'S LAW, 1986
NAKED ANGELS, 1969
NAKED VENGEANCE, 1986
NEVER TOO YOUNG TO DIE, 1986
NIGHTFORCE, 1987
9 DEATHS OF THE NINJA, 1985
NINJA III—THE DOMINATION, 1984
NINJA TURF, 1986
NO RETREAT, NO SURRENDER, 1986
NO MERCY MAN, THE, 1975
NORTH SHORE, 1987
NORTHVILLE CEMETERY MASSACRE, THE, 1976
NOWHERE TO HIDE, 1987
OCTAGON, THE, 1980
OKEFENOKEE, 1960
OMEGA SYNDROME, 1987
ONE DOWN TWO TO GO, 1982
OPEN SEASON, 1974
OPPOSING FORCE, 1987
OSA, 1985
OUTLAW MOTORCYCLES, 1967
OVER THE TOP, 1987
PANTHER SQUAD, 1986
PATRIOT, THE, 1986
PEACE KILLERS, THE, 1971
PEKING OPERA BLUES, 1986
POWERFORCE, 1983
PRAY FOR DEATH, 1986
PRESIDIO, THE, 1988
PROTECTOR, THE, 1985
PROUD RIDER, THE, 1971
QUIET COOL, 1986
RAD, 1986
RAGE OF HONOR, 1987
RAMBO III, 1988
RAVAGER, THE, 1970
RAW DEAL, 1986
REBEL ROUSERS, 1970
REBELLION IN CUBA, 1961
RED HEAT, 1988
RED HEAT, 1988
RENT-A-COP, 1988
RESCUE, THE, 1988
RETURN OF THE DRAGON, 1974
REVENGE OF THE NINJA, 1983
REVENGE OF THE SHOGUN WOMEN, 1982
ROAD WARRIOR, THE, 1982
ROLLER BLADE, 1986
RUCKUS, 1981
RUN, ANGEL, RUN, 1969
RUNNING SCARED, 1986
SACRED KNIVES OF VENGEANCE, THE, 1974
SAVAGE ISLAND, 1985
SAVAGE SISTERS, 1974
SEARCH AND DESTROY, 1981
SHAKEDOWN, 1988
SHOGUN ASSASSIN, 1980
SHOWDOWN FOR ZATOICHI, 1968

SIEGE, 1983
SILENT ASSASSINS, 1988
SILENT RAGE, 1982
SILK, 1986
SITTING TARGET, 1972
SLAUGHTER IN SAN FRANCISCO, 1981
SPEEDTRAP, 1978
SPOOK WHO SAT BY THE DOOR, THE, 1973
STEEL ARENA, 1973
STEELE JUSTICE, 1987
STONE, 1974
STONE KILLER, THE, 1973
SUDDEN DEATH, 1985
SUGAR HILL, 1974
SUPER COPS, THE, 1974
SUPER VAN, 1977
SUPERCHICK, 1973
SUPERFLY, 1972
SUPERFLY T.N.T., 1973
SUPERSPEED, 1935
SWAMP COUNTRY, 1966
SWEET REVENGE, 1987
SWORD OF HEAVEN, 1985
TAFFIN, 1988
TAKE, THE, 1974
THAT MAN BOLT, 1973
THEY CALL HER ONE EYE, 1974
THEY CALL ME BRUCE, 1982
3:15, THE MOMENT OF TRUTH, 1986
THREE TOUGH GUYS, 1974
THUNDER RUN, 1986
THUNDER WARRIOR, 1986
TNT JACKSON, 1975
TO KILL OR TO DIE, 1973
TOUGHER THAN LEATHER, 1988
TRAITORS, 1957
TRAXX, 1988
TRIPLE IRONS, 1973
TRUCK STOP WOMEN, 1974
TRUCK TURNER, 1974
2020 TEXAS GLADIATORS, 1985
UN HOMBRE VIOLENTE, 1986
VENDETTA, 1986
VIOLENT BREED, THE, 1986
WANTED: DEAD OR ALIVE, 1987
WARDOGS, 1987
WARRIORS, THE, 1979
WEREWOLVES ON WHEELS, 1971
WHAT WAITS BELOW, 1986
WHITE GHOST, 1988
WHITE LIGHTNIN' ROAD, 1967
WHITE LIGHTNING, 1973
WHITE LINE FEVER, 1975
WILBY CONSPIRACY, THE, 1975
WILD ANGELS, THE, 1966
WILD, FREE AND HUNGRY, 1970
WILD GEESE II, 1985
WILD WHEELS, 1969
WORLD GONE WILD, 1988
WRESTLER, THE, 1974
YOJIMBO, 1961
YOUNG AND WILD, 1958
YOUNG CYCLE GIRLS, THE, 1979
YOUNG SWORDSMAN, 1964
YOUNGBLOOD, 1978
ZATOICHI, 1968
ZATOICHI CHALLENGED, 1970
ZATOICHI MEETS YOJIMBO, 1970
ZATOICHI'S CONSPIRACY, 1974
ZERO BOYS, THE, 1987

Adventure
ABANDON SHIP, 1957
ACROSS THE WIDE MISSOURI, 1951
ACTION OF THE TIGER, 1957
ADVENTURE, 1945
ADVENTURE IN ODESSA, 1954
ADVENTURE IN SAHARA, 1938
ADVENTURE ISLAND, 1947
ADVENTURE OF SALVATOR ROSA, AN, 1940
ADVENTURERS, THE, 1951
ADVENTURERS, THE, 1970
ADVENTURE'S END, 1937
ADVENTURES IN IRAQ, 1943
ADVENTURES OF A YOUNG MAN, 1962
ADVENTURES OF BULLWHIP GRIFFIN, THE, 1967

ADVENTURES OF CAPTAIN FABIAN, 1951
ADVENTURES OF CASANOVA, 1948
ADVENTURES OF DON JUAN, 1949
ADVENTURES OF FRONTIER FREMONT, THE, 1976
ADVENTURES OF GERARD, THE, 1970
ADVENTURES OF HAJJI BABA, 1954
ADVENTURES OF HAL 5, THE, 1958
ADVENTURES OF HUCKLEBERRY FINN, THE, 1960
ADVENTURES OF MARCO POLO, THE, 1938
ADVENTURES OF MARTIN EDEN, THE, 1942
ADVENTURES OF ROBIN HOOD, THE, 1938
ADVENTURES OF ROBINSON CRUSOE, THE, 1954
ADVENTURES OF SCARAMOUCHE, THE, 1964
ADVENTURES OF THE WILDERNESS FAMILY, THE, 1975
ADVENTURES OF TOM SAWYER, THE, 1938
AFRICA—TEXAS STYLE!, 1967
AFRICAN MANHUNT, 1955
AFRICAN QUEEN, THE, 1951
AFRICAN TREASURE, 1952
AFRICAN, THE, 1983
AGAINST ALL FLAGS, 1952
AIR CIRCUS, THE, 1928
AIR MAIL, 1932
AIR STRIKE, 1955
ALASKA, 1944
ALASKA PASSAGE, 1959
ALASKA SEAS, 1954
ALERT IN THE SOUTH, 1954
ALI BABA AND THE FORTY THIEVES, 1944
ALIEN THUNDER, 1975
ALL THE BROTHERS WERE VALIANT, 1953
ALLAN QUATERMAIN AND THE LOST CITY OF GOLD, 1987
ALLEGHENY UPRISING, 1939
ALOMA OF THE SOUTH SEAS, 1941
ALONE AGAINST ROME, 1963
ALONE ON THE PACIFIC, 1964
AMAZON QUEST, 1949
ANGEL ON THE AMAZON, 1948
ANNE OF THE INDIES, 1951
ANTARCTICA, 1984
APPOINTMENT IN HONDURAS, 1953
ARCTIC FLIGHT, 1952
ARCTIC FURY, 1949
AROUND THE WORLD IN 80 DAYS, 1956
AROUND THE WORLD UNDER THE SEA, 1966
ARTURO'S ISLAND, 1963
ASHANTI, 1979
ASSAULT OF THE REBEL GIRLS, 1960
AT SWORD'S POINT, 1951
AT THE EARTH'S CORE, 1976
ATLANTIS, THE LOST CONTINENT, 1961
ATLAS, 1960
ATLAS AGAINST THE CYCLOPS, 1963
ATLAS AGAINST THE CZAR, 1964
AVENGERS, THE, 1950
AVIATOR, THE, 1985
BABY: SECRET OF A LOST LEGEND, 1985
BACK FROM ETERNITY, 1956
BACK TO GOD'S COUNTRY, 1953
BAGDAD, 1949
BANDIDO, 1956
BANDIT OF SHERWOOD FOREST, THE, 1946
BANDITS OF CORSICA, THE, 1953
BARBARIAN QUEEN, 1985
BARBARIANS, THE, 1987
BARBARY PIRATE, 1949
BAREFOOT MAILMAN, THE, 1951
BARRICADE, 1939
BARRY MC KENZIE HOLDS HIS OWN, 1975
BAY OF SAINT MICHEL, THE, 1963
BEAR ISLAND, 1980
BEAU GESTE, 1939
BEAU GESTE, 1966
BEAU IDEAL, 1931
BEHIND THE IRON MASK, 1977
BELOW THE SEA, 1933
BENEATH THE 12-MILE REEF, 1953
BENGAL BRIGADE, 1954
BENGAZI, 1955
BEYOND EVIL, 1980
BEYOND MOMBASA, 1957
BEYOND THE LAW, 1934
BEYOND THE REEF, 1981
BIG BLUE, THE, 1988

BIG CAT, THE, 1949
BIG GAMBLE, THE, 1961
BIG GAME, THE, 1972
BIG GUSHER, THE, 1951
BIG TROUBLE IN LITTLE CHINA, 1986
BIRD OF PARADISE, 1951
BLACK ARROW, 1948
BLACK BOOK, THE, 1949
BLACK GOLD, 1963
BLACK ICE, THE, 1957
BLACK JACK, 1979
BLACK KNIGHT, THE, 1954
BLACK PIRATES, THE, 1954
BLACK ROSE, THE, 1950
BLACK SHIELD OF FALWORTH, THE, 1954
BLACK STALLION, THE, 1979
BLACK STALLION RETURNS, THE, 1983
BLACK SWAN, THE, 1942
BLACK WATCH, THE, 1929
BLACKBEARD THE PIRATE, 1952
BLADES OF THE MUSKETEERS, 1953
BLAZE OF NOON, 1947
BLAZING FOREST, THE, 1952
BLONDE FROM SINGAPORE, THE, 1941
BLONDE SAVAGE, 1947
BLOOD ALLEY, 1955
BLOWING WILD, 1953
BLUE FIN, 1978
BLUE LAGOON, THE, 1949
BLUE LAGOON, THE, 1980
BMX BANDITS, 1983
BOMBA AND THE HIDDEN CITY, 1950
BOMBA AND THE JUNGLE GIRL, 1952
BOMBA ON PANTHER ISLAND, 1949
BOMBA THE JUNGLE BOY, 1949
BONNIE PRINCE CHARLIE, 1948
BOOLOO, 1938
BORDER FLIGHT, 1936
BORN TO BE WILD, 1938
BOTANY BAY, 1953
BOUNTY, THE, 1984
BOY AND THE PIRATES, THE, 1960
BOY ON A DOLPHIN, 1957
BOY TEN FEET TALL, A, 1965
BOY WHO CAUGHT A CROOK, 1961
BREAKOUT, 1975
BRIGAND OF KANDAHAR, THE, 1965
BRIGAND, THE, 1952
BUCCANEER'S GIRL, 1950
BUDDIES, 1983
BULLET FOR STEFANO, 1950
BULLETPROOF, 1988
BURKE & WILLS, 1985
BUSH CHRISTMAS, 1947
BUSH CHRISTMAS, 1983
BUSHBABY, THE, 1970
BWANA DEVIL, 1953
C. C. AND COMPANY, 1971
CADET-ROUSSELLE, 1954
CALCUTTA, 1947
CALL OF THE JUNGLE, 1944
CALL OF THE KLONDIKE, 1950
CALL OF THE SEA, THE, 1930
CALL OF THE SOUTH SEAS, 1944
CALL OF THE WILD, 1935
CALL OF THE WILD, 1972
CALL OF THE YUKON, 1938
CAMPBELL'S KINGDOM, 1957
CANNIBAL ATTACK, 1954
CAPTAIN BLOOD, 1935
CAPTAIN CALAMITY, 1936
CAPTAIN CAUTION, 1940
CAPTAIN CHINA, 1949
CAPTAIN FROM CASTILE, 1947
CAPTAIN FURY, 1939
CAPTAIN GRANT'S CHILDREN, 1939
CAPTAIN HORATIO HORNBLOWER, 1951
CAPTAIN KIDD, 1945
CAPTAIN KIDD AND THE SLAVE GIRL, 1954
CAPTAIN LIGHTFOOT, 1955
CAPTAIN NEMO AND THE UNDERWATER CITY, 1969
CAPTAIN PIRATE, 1952
CAPTAIN SCARLETT, 1953
CAPTAINS COURAGEOUS, 1937
CAPTIVE GIRL, 1950

CARAVAN TO VACCARES, 1974
CARAVANS, 1978
CARIBBEAN, 1952
CARRY ON JACK, 1963
CARRY ON, UP THE KHYBER, 1968
CARS THAT ATE PARIS, THE, 1974
CARTOUCHE, 1957
CARTOUCHE, 1962
CARYL OF THE MOUNTAINS, 1936
CASINO ROYALE, 1967
CASSANDRA CROSSING, THE, 1977
CASTILIAN, THE, 1963
CAT, THE, 1966
CENTRAL AIRPORT, 1933
CHAIN REACTION, 1980
CHALLENGE, THE, 1939
CHALLENGE FOR ROBIN HOOD, A, 1968
CHALLENGE THE WILD, 1954
CHALLENGE TO BE FREE, 1976
CHARGE OF THE LIGHT BRIGADE, THE, 1936
CHARLIE, THE LONESOME COUGAR, 1967
CHASING DANGER, 1939
CHEATING CHEATERS, 1934
CHECKERED FLAG OR CRASH, 1978
CHEECH AND CHONG'S THE CORSICAN
  BROTHERS, 1984
CHINA CORSAIR, 1951
CHINA PASSAGE, 1937
CHINA SEAS, 1935
CHOKE CANYON, 1986
CHRISTIAN THE LION, 1976
CITY BENEATH THE SEA, 1953
CLARENCE, THE CROSS-EYED LION, 1965
CLEOPATRA'S DAUGHTER, 1963
CLOAK AND DAGGER, 1984
COAST OF SKELETONS, 1965
COLD RIVER, 1982
CONAN THE BARBARIAN, 1982
CONAN THE DESTROYER, 1984
CONQUEROR, THE, 1956
CONQUEST, 1984
CORSICAN BROTHERS, THE, 1941
COUNT OF MONTE CRISTO, THE, 1934
COUNT OF MONTE-CRISTO, 1955
COUNT OF MONTE CRISTO, 1976
COURAGE OF BLACK BEAUTY, 1957
COURT JESTER, THE, 1956
CRIMSON PIRATE, THE, 1952
"CROCODILE" DUNDEE II, 1988
CROSSED SWORDS, 1954
CROSSED SWORDS, 1978
CROSSWINDS, 1951
CRY OF THE PENGUINS, 1972
CUBA, 1979
CURUCU, BEAST OF THE AMAZON, 1956
CUT AND RUN, 1986
DAMN THE DEFIANT!, 1962
DANGER AHEAD, 1940
DANGER IN THE PACIFIC, 1942
DANGEROUS EXILE, 1958
DANGEROUS PARADISE, 1930
DANIEL BOONE, 1936
DANIEL BOONE, TRAIL BLAZER, 1957
DARK VENTURE, 1956
DARKEST AFRICA, 1936
DAUGHTER OF THE JUNGLE, 1949
DAUGHTER OF THE SUN GOD, 1962
DAVY CROCKETT AND THE RIVER PIRATES, 1956
DEATH HUNT, 1981
DEATHSTALKER, THE, 1984
DECEIVERS, THE, 1988
DEEP, THE, 1977
DEERSLAYER, 1943
DEERSLAYER, THE, 1957
DEFEAT OF HANNIBAL, THE, 1937
DELIGHTFUL ROGUE, 1929
DELIVERANCE, 1972
DELTA FACTOR, THE, 1970
DERELICT, 1930
DERSU UZALA, 1976
DESCENDANT OF THE SNOW LEOPARD, THE, 1986
DESERT HAWK, THE, 1950
DESERT HELL, 1958
DESERT LEGION, 1953
DESERT SANDS, 1955
DESERT WARRIOR, 1961

DESPERATE CARGO, 1941
DESPERATE ONES, THE, 1968
DESPERATE SEARCH, 1952
DESTRUCTORS, THE, 1968
DEVIL AT FOUR O'CLOCK, THE, 1961
DEVIL GODDESS, 1955
DEVIL TIGER, 1934
DEVIL WITH WOMEN, A, 1930
DEVIL'S BRIGADE, THE, 1968
DEVIL'S PIPELINE, THE, 1940
DIAMOND CITY, 1949
DIAMOND FRONTIER, 1940
DIAMOND QUEEN, THE, 1953
DIRIGIBLE, 1931
DISTANT DRUMS, 1951
DOCTOR SYN, 1937
DR. SYN, ALIAS THE SCARECROW, 1975
DOGS OF WAR, THE, 1980
DOVE, THE, 1974
DOWN TO THE SEA IN SHIPS, 1949
DRAGONSLAYER, 1981
DRAKE THE PIRATE, 1935
DRUMS, 1938
DRUMS ALONG THE MOHAWK, 1939
DRUMS OF AFRICA, 1963
DRUMS OF DESTINY, 1937
DRUMS OF FU MANCHU, 1943
DRUMS OF JEOPARDY, 1931
DRUMS OF TABU, THE, 1967
DRUMS OF TAHITI, 1954
DRUMS OF THE CONGO, 1942
DRUMS OF THE DESERT, 1940
DUEL IN THE JUNGLE, 1954
DUNGEONMASTER, 1985
EAST OF BORNEO, 1931
EAST OF KILIMANJARO, 1962
EAST OF SUDAN, 1964
EAST OF SUMATRA, 1953
EBB TIDE, 1937
ELEPHANT BOY, 1937
ELEPHANT CALLED SLOWLY, AN, 1970
ELEPHANT GUN, 1959
ELEPHANT STAMPEDE, 1951
ELEPHANT WALK, 1954
ELIMINATORS, 1986
EMERALD FOREST, THE, 1985
EQUALIZER 2000, 1987
ERNEST GOES TO CAMP, 1987
ESCAPADE IN JAPAN, 1957
ESCAPE FROM YESTERDAY, 1939
ESCAPE IN THE SUN, 1956
ESCAPE TO BURMA, 1955
EVE, 1968
FAIR WIND TO JAVA, 1953
FANFAN THE TULIP, 1952
FANGS OF THE ARCTIC, 1953
FANGS OF THE WILD, 1954
FAR HORIZONS, THE, 1955
FERRY TO HONG KONG, 1959
FFOLKES, 1980
FIERCEST HEART, THE, 1961
FIFTY FATHOMS DEEP, 1931
FIGHTING KENTUCKIAN, THE, 1949
FIGHTING MAD, 1939
FIGHTING O'FLYNN, THE, 1949
FIGHTING PIMPERNEL, THE, 1950
FIRE DOWN BELOW, 1957
FIRE OVER AFRICA, 1954
FIRE OVER ENGLAND, 1937
FIRES OF FATE, 1932
FIVE CAME BACK, 1939
FIVE WEEKS IN A BALLOON, 1962
FLAME AND THE ARROW, THE, 1950
FLAME OF ARABY, 1951
FLAME OF CALCUTTA, 1953
FLAME OVER INDIA, 1960
FLAMING SIGNAL, 1933
FLASHPOINT, 1984
FLIGHT FOR FREEDOM, 1943
FLIGHT FROM ASHIYA, 1964
FLIGHT FROM GLORY, 1937
FLIGHT FROM SINGAPORE, 1962
FLIGHT INTO NOWHERE, 1938
FLIGHT OF THE EAGLE, 1983
FLIGHT OF THE LOST BALLOON, 1961
FLIGHT OF THE PHOENIX, THE, 1965

BOLD: Films on Videocassette

FLIGHT TO FURY, 1966
FLYING DOCTOR, THE, 1936
FOR WHOM THE BELL TOLLS, 1943
FOR YOUR EYES ONLY, 1981
FORBIDDEN ISLAND, 1959
FORBIDDEN JUNGLE, 1950
FORCED LANDING, 1941
FOREST RANGERS, THE, 1942
FORTUNES OF CAPTAIN BLOOD, 1950
FOUR FEATHERS, THE, 1939
FOUR FRIGHTENED PEOPLE, 1934
FOUR MUSKETEERS, THE, 1975
FRISCO KID, 1935
FROM HEADQUARTERS, 1929
FROZEN JUSTICE, 1929
FROZEN RIVER, 1929
**FURTHER ADVENTURES OF TENNESSEE BUCK,
THE, 1988**
FURTHER ADVENTURES OF THE WILDERNESS
FAMILY—PART II, 1978
FURY AT SMUGGLERS BAY, 1963
FURY OF HERCULES, THE, 1961
FURY OF THE CONGO, 1951
FURY OF THE PAGANS, 1963
GALLANT BLADE, THE, 1948
GAME OF DEATH, A, 1945
GARDEN OF EVIL, 1954
GENERAL DIED AT DAWN, THE, 1936
GENGHIS KHAN, 1965
GHOST DIVER, 1957
GIANT OF MARATHON, THE, 1960
GIANT OF METROPOLIS, THE, 1963
GIRL FEVER, 1961
GIRL OF THE PORT, 1930
GLADIATOR OF ROME, 1963
GLADIATORS 7, 1964
GLASS SPHINX, THE, 1968
GOIN' COCONUTS, 1978
GOIN' HOME, 1976
GOLDEN ARROW, THE, 1964
GOLDEN BLADE, THE, 1953
GOLDEN CHILD, THE, 1986
GOLDEN HAWK, THE, 1952
GOLDEN IDOL, THE, 1954
GOLDEN MISTRESS, THE, 1954
GOLDEN SALAMANDER, 1950
GOLDEN SEAL, THE, 1983
GOLDEN VOYAGE OF SINBAD, THE, 1974
GOLDFINGER, 1964
GOLIATH AGAINST THE GIANTS, 1963
GOLIATH AND THE BARBARIANS, 1960
GOLIATH AND THE DRAGON, 1961
GOLIATH AND THE SINS OF BABYLON, 1964
GOLIATH AND THE VAMPIRES, 1964
GOLIATHON, 1979
GOODBYE, MY LADY, 1956
GOODBYE PORK PIE, 1981
GOONIES, THE, 1985
GORILLA, 1964
GREAT ADVENTURE, THE, 1955
GREAT ADVENTURE, THE, 1976
GREAT LOCOMOTIVE CHASE, THE, 1956
GREAT WALDO PEPPER, THE, 1975
GREEN DOLPHIN STREET, 1947
GREEN GODDESS, THE, 1930
GREEN HELL, 1940
GREEN ICE, 1981
GREEN MANSIONS, 1959
**GREYSTOKE: THE LEGEND OF TARZAN, LORD OF
THE APES, 1984**
GUARDIAN OF THE WILDERNESS, 1977
GUN RUNNERS, THE, 1958
GUNGA DIN, 1939
GUNS AND THE FURY, THE, 1983
GUNS OF NAVARONE, THE, 1961
GUNS OF THE BLACK WITCH, 1961
GYPSY WILDCAT, 1944
HARRY BLACK AND THE TIGER, 1958
HAWAII CALLS, 1938
HEART OF THE NORTH, 1938
HELL BELOW ZERO, 1954
HELL DIVERS, 1932
HELL HARBOR, 1930
HELL SHIP MUTINY, 1957
HELL SQUAD, 1986
HELLFIGHTERS, 1968

HELL'S CARGO, 1935
HELL'S HEADQUARTERS, 1932
HELL'S ISLAND, 1930
HELL'S ISLAND, 1955
HER JUNGLE LOVE, 1938
HERCULES II, 1985
HERE COMES THE NAVY, 1934
HIDDEN FORTRESS, THE, 1959
HIGH CONQUEST, 1947
HIGH COUNTRY, THE, 1981
HIGH EXPLOSIVE, 1943
HIGH HELL, 1958
HIGH ROAD TO CHINA, 1983
HIGH SEAS, 1929
HIGH WIND IN JAMAICA, A, 1965
HIGHWAYMAN, THE, 1951
HINDU, THE, 1953
HIS MAJESTY O'KEEFE, 1953
HONG KONG, 1951
HONG KONG NIGHTS, 1935
HONOR OF THE FAMILY, 1931
HONOR OF THE MOUNTED, 1932
HUDSON'S BAY, 1940
HUNCH, THE, 1967
HUNDRA, 1984
HUNTERS OF THE GOLDEN COBRA, THE, 1984
HUNTING IN SIBERIA, 1962
HURRICANE, 1929
HURRICANE ISLAND, 1951
HURRICANE SMITH, 1952
I COVER THE WAR, 1937
IF I WERE KING, 1938
IMPASSE, 1969
IN SEARCH OF THE CASTAWAYS, 1962
IN THE LINE OF DUTY, 1931
IN THE WAKE OF THE BOUNTY, 1933
INCREDIBLE JOURNEY, THE, 1963
**INDIANA JONES AND THE TEMPLE OF DOOM,
1984**
INGAGI, 1931
INSULT, 1932
INTRIGUE, 1947
INVINCIBLE GLADIATOR, THE, 1963
INVINCIBLE SIX, THE, 1970
IRON GLOVE, THE, 1954
IRON MASK, THE, 1929
ISLAND, THE, 1980
ISLAND AT THE TOP OF THE WORLD, THE, 1974
ISLAND CAPTIVES, 1937
ISLAND IN THE SKY, 1953
ISLAND OF LOST WOMEN, 1959
ISLE OF DESTINY, 1940
ISLE OF ESCAPE, 1930
ISLE OF FURY, 1936
ISLE OF LOST SHIPS, 1929
ISLE OF MISSING MEN, 1942
IT AIN'T EASY, 1972
IVORY HUNTER, 1952
JACK OF DIAMONDS, THE, 1949
JACKALS, THE, 1967
JAGUAR, 1956
JAKE SPEED, 1986
JAMAICA RUN, 1953
JASON AND THE ARGONAUTS, 1963
JAWS OF THE JUNGLE, 1936
JEREMIAH JOHNSON, 1972
JEWEL OF THE NILE, THE, 1985
JIVARO, 1954
JONIKO AND THE KUSH TA KA, 1969
JOURNEY OF NATTY GANN, THE, 1985
JOURNEY TO THE LOST CITY, 1960
JUNGLE, THE, 1952
JUNGLE BOOK, 1942
JUNGLE BRIDE, 1933
JUNGLE GENTS, 1954
JUNGLE GODDESS, 1948
JUNGLE HEAT, 1957
JUNGLE JIM, 1948
JUNGLE JIM IN THE FORBIDDEN LAND, 1952
JUNGLE MAN, 1941
JUNGLE MAN-EATERS, 1954
JUNGLE MANHUNT, 1951
JUNGLE MOON MEN, 1955
JUNGLE PRINCESS, THE, 1936
JUNGLE RAIDERS, 1986
JUNGLE SIREN, 1942

KAREN, THE LOVEMAKER, 1970
KAZAN, 1949
KHYBER PATROL, 1954
KIDNAPPED, 1938
KIDNAPPED, 1948
KIDNAPPED, 1960
KIDNAPPED, 1971
KILLER APE, 1953
KILLER LEOPARD, 1954
KILLER SHARK, 1950
KILLERS OF KILIMANJARO, 1960
KILLERS OF THE WILD, 1940
KIM, 1950
KING KONG, 1933
KING KONG, 1976
KING KONG LIVES, 1986
KING OF THE GRIZZLIES, 1970
KING OF THE JUNGLE, 1933
KING OF THE KHYBER RIFLES, 1953
KING OF THE WILD HORSES, 1947
KING SOLOMON'S MINES, 1937
KING SOLOMON'S MINES, 1950
KING SOLOMON'S MINES, 1985
KING SOLOMON'S TREASURE, 1978
KING'S PIRATE, 1967
KING'S THIEF, THE, 1955
KLONDIKE FEVER, 1980
KNIGHT WITHOUT ARMOR, 1937
LADY IN THE IRON MASK, 1952
LADYHAWKE, 1985
LAND OF DOOM, 1986
LAND OF FURY, 1955
LAND OF NO RETURN, THE, 1981
LAND OF THE SILVER FOX, 1928
LAND THAT TIME FORGOT, THE, 1975
LAND UNKNOWN, THE, 1957
LASSIE, COME HOME, 1943
LASSIE'S GREAT ADVENTURE, 1963
LASSITER, 1984
LAST ADVENTURE, THE, 1968
LAST ADVENTURERS, THE, 1937
LAST OF THE BUCCANEERS, 1950
LAST OF THE LONE WOLF, 1930
LAST OF THE MOHICANS, THE, 1936
LAST OF THE PAGANS, 1936
LAST OF THE REDMEN, 1947
LAST OF THE VIKINGS, THE, 1962
LAST OUTPOST, THE, 1935
LAST SAFARI, THE, 1967
LAST TRAIN FROM BOMBAY, 1952
LAST VALLEY, THE, 1971
LAST WOMAN OF SHANG, THE, 1964
LAUGHING ANNE, 1954
LAW OF THE JUNGLE, 1942
LAWRENCE OF ARABIA, 1962
LE LEOPARD, 1985
LEATHERNECKS HAVE LANDED, THE, 1936
LEFT HAND OF GOD, THE, 1955
LEGACY OF THE 500,000, THE, 1964
LEGEND OF COUGAR CANYON, 1974
LEGEND OF LOBO, THE, 1962
LEGEND OF THE LOST, 1957
LEGION OF LOST FLYERS, 1939
LEGION OF MISSING MEN, 1937
LEGION OF THE DOOMED, 1958
LET'S GET HARRY, 1987
LETTER THAT WAS NEVER SENT, THE, 1962
LIEUTENANT DARING, RN, 1935
LIFE AND TIMES OF GRIZZLY ADAMS, THE, 1974
LIGHT AT THE EDGE OF THE WORLD, THE, 1971
LION HUNTERS, THE, 1951
LION OF ST. MARK, 1967
LION OF THE DESERT, 1981
LITTLE ARK, THE, 1972
LITTLE JUNGLE BOY, 1969
LITTLE SAVAGE, THE, 1959
LITTLE TREASURE, 1985
LIVE AND LET DIE, 1973
LIVES OF A BENGAL LANCER, 1935
LIVING FREE, 1972
LIVING IDOL, THE, 1957
LONE CLIMBER, THE, 1950
LONG DUEL, THE, 1967
LONG JOHN SILVER, 1954
LONG SHIPS, THE, 1964
LOOTERS, THE, 1955

LORD JIM, 1965
LORD OF THE JUNGLE, 1955
LOST COMMAND, THE, 1966
LOST EMPIRE, THE, 1985
LOST HORIZON, 1937
LOST JUNGLE, THE, 1934
LOST TRIBE, THE, 1949
LOST VOLCANO, THE, 1950_
LOST WORLD, THE, 1960
LOST ZEPPELIN, 1930
LYDIA BAILEY, 1952
MACOMBER AFFAIR, THE, 1947
MAD MAX BEYOND THUNDERDOME, 1985
MADDEST CAR IN THE WORLD, THE, 1974
MAGIC CARPET, THE, 1951
MAID OF THE MOUNTAINS, THE, 1932
MALAYA, 1950
MAMBA, 1930
MAN BEAST, 1956
MAN-EATER OF KUMAON, 1948
MAN FROM COCODY, 1966
MAN FROM MONTREAL, THE, 1940
MAN FROM SNOWY RIVER, THE, 1983
MAN HUNTER, THE, 1930
MAN HUNTERS OF THE CARIBBEAN, 1938
MAN IN THE IRON MASK, THE, 1939
MAN IN THE WILDERNESS, 1971
MAN INSIDE, THE, 1958
MAN WHO WOULD BE KING, THE, 1975
MAN WITH THE GOLDEN GUN, THE, 1974
MANFISH, 1956
MANGANINNIE, 1982
MANHUNT IN THE JUNGLE, 1958
MARA MARU, 1952
MARA OF THE WILDERNESS, 1966
MARCH OR DIE, 1977
MARCO, 1973
MARCO POLO, 1962
MARCO THE MAGNIFICENT, 1966
MARIE OF THE ISLES, 1960
MARIZINIA, 1962
MARK OF THE GORILLA, 1950
MARK OF THE RENEGADE, 1951
MARK OF ZORRO, THE, 1940
MARKETA LAZAROVA, 1968
MAROONED, 1969
MASK OF FU MANCHU, THE, 1932
MASK OF THE AVENGER, 1951
MASQUERADE, 1965
MASTER OF BALLANTRAE, THE, 1953
MASTER OF THE WORLD, 1961
MAYA, 1966
MC GUIRE, GO HOME!, 1966
MEN OF SHERWOOD FOREST, 1957
MEN OF THE SEA, 1951
MERCY ISLAND, 1941
MESSAGE TO GARCIA, A, 1936
**METALSTORM: THE DESTRUCTION OF
    JARED-SYN, 1983**
MICHAEL STROGOFF, 1960
MIGHTY GORGA, THE, 1969
MIGHTY JOE YOUNG, 1949
MIGHTY JUNGLE, THE, 1965
MIGHTY URSUS, 1962
MILLION EYES OF SU-MURU, THE, 1967
MIRACULOUS JOURNEY, 1948
MISS ROBIN CRUSOE, 1954
MISSION BLOODY MARY, 1967
MISSISSIPPI GAMBLER, THE, 1953
MISTER MOSES, 1965
MR. ROBINSON CRUSOE, 1932
MOBY DICK, 1956
MOBY DICK, 1930
MODESTY BLAISE, 1966
MOGAMBO, 1953
MONGOLS, THE, 1966
MONSTER ISLAND, 1981
MOON OVER BURMA, 1940
MOONFLEET, 1955
MOONRAKER, THE, 1958
MOONRAKER, 1979
MOONSTONE, THE, 1934
MOONWOLF, 1966
MORGAN THE PIRATE, 1961
MOSQUITO COAST, THE, 1986
MOST DANGEROUS GAME, THE, 1932

MOTHER LODE, 1982
MOUNTAIN, THE, 1956
MOUNTAIN FAMILY ROBINSON, 1979
MUTINEERS, THE, 1949
MUTINY, 1952
MUTINY AHEAD, 1935
MUTINY IN THE ARCTIC, 1941
MUTINY OF THE ELSINORE, THE, 1939
MUTINY ON THE BLACKHAWK, 1939
MUTINY ON THE BOUNTY, 1935
MUTINY ON THE BOUNTY, 1962
MY DOG, BUDDY, 1960
MY PAL, WOLF, 1944
MY SIDE OF THE MOUNTAIN, 1969
MYSTERY LAKE, 1953
MYSTERY OF THE BLACK JUNGLE, 1955
MYSTERY OF THUG ISLAND, THE, 1966
NABONGA, 1944
NAGANA, 1933
NAKED JUNGLE, THE, 1953
NAKED PREY, THE, 1966
NAPOLEON AND SAMANTHA, 1972
NARROW CORNER, THE, 1933
NATE AND HAYES, 1983
NEVER CRY WOLF, 1983
NEW ADVENTURES OF TARZAN, 1935
NIGHT CREATURE, 1979
NIGHT CROSSING, 1982
NIGHT FLIGHT, 1933
NIGHT TRAIN TO MUNDO FINE, 1966
NORSEMAN, THE, 1978
NORTHERN PURSUIT, 1943
NORTHWEST MOUNTED POLICE, 1940
NORTHWEST PASSAGE, 1940
NOWHERE TO HIDE, 1987
OLD LOUISIANA, 1938
OLLY, OLLY, OXEN FREE, 1978
O'MALLEY OF THE MOUNTED, 1936
OMAR KHAYYAM, 1957
OMOO OMOO, THE SHARK GOD, 1949
ON THE GREAT WHITE TRAIL, 1938
ON THE ISLE OF SAMOA, 1950
ONE MILLION B.C., 1940
ONE MILLION YEARS B.C., 1967
ONE OF OUR DINOSAURS IS MISSING, 1975
ONE STEP TO HELL, 1969
ONE STOLEN NIGHT, 1929
ORCA, 1977
ORPHANS OF THE NORTH, 1940
OUT OF CONTROL, 1985
OUTPOST IN MOROCCO, 1949
PAGAN ISLAND, 1961
PAINTED HILLS, THE, 1951
PANTHER SQUAD, 1986
PEARL OF THE SOUTH PACIFIC, 1955
PEER GYNT, 1965
PEOPLE THAT TIME FORGOT, THE, 1977
PERILS OF GWENDOLINE, THE, 1984
PERILS OF PAULINE, THE, 1967
PHANTOM OF THE JUNGLE, 1955
PHANTOM PATROL, 1936
PHANTOM STOCKMAN, THE, 1953
PHANTOM SUBMARINE, THE, 1941
PICTURE BRIDES, 1934
PIER 5, HAVANA, 1959
PIMPERNEL SVENSSON, 1953
PINK JUNGLE, THE, 1968
PIPER'S TUNE, THE, 1962
PIPPI IN THE SOUTH SEAS, 1974
PIPPI ON THE RUN, 1977
PIRATE AND THE SLAVE GIRL, THE, 1961
PIRATE OF THE BLACK HAWK, THE, 1961
PIRATES, 1986
PIRATES OF BLOOD RIVER, THE, 1962
PIRATES OF CAPRI, THE, 1949
PIRATES OF THE SEVEN SEAS, 1941
PIRATES OF TORTUGA, 1961
PIRATES OF TRIPOLI, 1955
PLUNDER OF THE SUN, 1953
PLYMOUTH ADVENTURE, 1952
POCOLITTLE DOG LOST, 1977
PORT SINISTER, 1953
PREHISTORIC WOMEN, 1950
PREHISTORIC WOMEN, 1967
PRESTIGE, 1932
PRIDE AND THE PASSION, THE, 1957

PRINCE AND THE PAUPER, THE, 1937
PRINCE AND THE PAUPER, THE, 1969
PRINCE OF FOXES, 1949
PRINCE OF PIRATES, 1953
PRINCE OF THIEVES, THE, 1948
PRINCE VALIANT, 1954
PRINCE WHO WAS A THIEF, THE, 1951
PRINCESS AND THE PIRATE, THE, 1944
PRINCESS OF THE NILE, 1954
PRISONER OF THE IRON MASK, 1962
PRISONER OF ZENDA, THE, 1937
PRISONER OF ZENDA, THE, 1952
PRISONER OF ZENDA, THE, 1979
PRISONERS OF THE CASBAH, 1953
PRIVATE LIFE OF DON JUAN, THE, 1934
PROFESSIONAL SOLDIER, 1936
PROUD AND THE DAMNED, THE, 1972
PURPLE MASK, THE, 1955
PYGMY ISLAND, 1950
QUEBEC, 1951
QUEEN OF THE AMAZONS, 1947
QUEEN OF THE PIRATES, 1961
QUENTIN DURWARD, 1955
QUEST FOR FIRE, 1982
RAGE OF THE BUCCANEERS, 1963
RAIDERS OF THE DESERT, 1941
RAIDERS OF THE LOST ARK, 1981
RAIDERS OF THE SEVEN SEAS, 1953
RAINBOW BOYS, THE, 1973
RAISE THE TITANIC, 1980
RAMBO: FIRST BLOOD, PART II, 1985
RAMPAGE, 1963
RANGO, 1931
RED CLOAK, THE, 1961
RED MORNING, 1935
RED SHEIK, THE, 1963
RED SKIES OF MONTANA, 1952
RED TENT, THE, 1971
RENEGADES, 1930
RESCUE, THE, 1988
RETURN OF MONTE CRISTO, THE, 1946
RETURN OF RIN TIN TIN, THE, 1947
RETURN OF THE BLACK EAGLE, 1949
RETURN OF THE SCARLET PIMPERNEL, 1938
RETURN TO SNOWY RIVER: PART II, 1988
RETURN TO TREASURE ISLAND, 1954
REVENGE OF THE GLADIATORS, 1965
RHINO, 1964
RIDE THE HIGH WIND, 1967
RING OF FIRE, 1961
RIVER RAT, THE, 1984
RIVER'S EDGE, THE, 1957
ROAMING LADY, 1936
ROAR, 1981
ROBBERY UNDER ARMS, 1958
ROBBY, 1968
ROBIN AND MARIAN, 1976
ROGUES OF SHERWOOD FOREST, 1950
ROMANCING THE STONE, 1984
ROMMEL'S TREASURE, 1962
ROPE OF SAND, 1949
ROSE OF THE YUKON, 1949
ROUGH WATERS, 1930
ROUNDUP TIME IN TEXAS, 1937
ROYAL AFRICAN RIFLES, THE, 1953
ROYAL FLASH, 1975
ROYAL HUNT OF THE SUN, THE, 1969
RULERS OF THE SEA, 1939
RUN FOR THE SUN, 1956
RUSH, 1984
SABU AND THE MAGIC RING, 1957
SAFARI, 1940
SAFARI, 1956
SAFARI DRUMS, 1953
SAFARI 3000, 1982
SAGA OF THE VIKING WOMEN AND THEIR
    VOYAGE TO THE WATERS OF THE GREAT SEA
    SERPENT, THE, 1957
SAHARA, 1984
SAIGON, 1948
SAMAR, 1962
SAMSON, 1961
SAMSON AND THE SEVEN MIRACLES OF THE
    WORLD, 1963
SAMSON AND THE SLAVE QUEEN, 1963
SAMURAI ASSASSIN, 1965

BOLD: Films on Videocassette

SAN DEMETRIO, LONDON, 1947
SAND PEBBLES, THE, 1966
SANDERS, 1963
SANDERS OF THE RIVER, 1935
SANDOKAN THE GREAT, 1964
SANDS OF THE KALAHARI, 1965
SANJURO, 1962
SANTA FE TRAIL, 1940
SANTIAGO, 1956
SARACEN BLADE, THE, 1954
SASQUATCH, 1978
SAVAGE?, 1962
SAVAGE DRUMS, 1951
SAVAGE GIRL, THE, 1932
SAVAGE GOLD, 1933
SAVAGE HARVEST, 1981
SAVAGE INNOCENTS, THE, 1960
SAVAGE IS LOOSE, THE, 1974
SAVAGE MUTINY, 1953
SAVAGE, THE, 1975
SCALAWAG, 1973
SCARAMOUCHE, 1952
SCARLET PIMPERNEL, THE, 1935
SCARLET SPEAR, THE, 1954
SCAVENGERS, 1988
SCHEHERAZADE, 1965
SCOTT OF THE ANTARCTIC, 1949
SEA BAT, THE, 1930
SEA CHASE, THE, 1955
SEA DEVILS, 1931
SEA DEVILS, 1937
SEA DEVILS, 1953
SEA FURY, 1929
SEA FURY, 1959
SEA GOD, THE, 1930
SEA GYPSIES, THE, 1978
SEA HAWK, THE, 1940
SEA HORNET, THE, 1951
SEA OF LOST SHIPS, 1953
SEA PIRATE, THE, 1967
SEA SHALL NOT HAVE THEM, THE, 1955
SEA SPOILERS, THE, 1936
SEA TIGER, 1952
SEA WIFE, 1957
SEA WOLF, THE, 1930
SECRET MARK OF D'ARTAGNAN, THE, 1963
SECRET OF MONTE CRISTO, THE, 1961
SECRET OF ST. IVES, THE, 1949
SECRET OF STAMBOUL, THE, 1936
SECRET OF THE INCAS, 1954
SECRET OF THE SACRED FOREST, THE, 1970
SECRET SCROLLS (PART I), 1968
SECRET SCROLLS (PART II), 1968
SECRET SEVEN, THE, 1966
SEPTEMBER STORM, 1960
SEQUOIA, 1934
SERPENT ISLAND, 1954
SEVEN BRAVE MEN, 1936
SEVEN CITIES OF GOLD, 1955
SEVEN DARING GIRLS, 1962
SEVEN REVENGES, THE, 1967
SEVEN SLAVES AGAINST THE WORLD, 1965
SEVEN TASKS OF ALI BABA, THE, 1963
SEVENTH DAWN, THE, 1964
SHADOW OF EVIL, 1967
SHADOW OF THE EAGLE, 1955
SHADOW OF THE HAWK, 1976
SHAGGY, 1948
SHAME OF THE SABINE WOMEN, THE, 1962
SHANGHAI MADNESS, 1933
SHANGHAI SURPRISE, 1986
SHARK, 1970
SHARK RIVER, 1953
SHARK WOMAN, THE, 1941
SHARKFIGHTERS, THE, 1956
SHARK'S TREASURE, 1975
SHARPSHOOTERS, 1938
SHE, 1935
SHE, 1965
SHE, 1985
SHE-DEVIL ISLAND, 1936
SHE-DEVILS ON WHEELS, 1968
SHE-WOLF, THE, 1963
SHEENA, 1984
SHEPHERD OF THE HILLS, THE, 1941
SHIP FROM SHANGHAI, THE, 1930

SHIP THAT DIED OF SHAME, THE, 1956
SHIPMATES, 1931
SHIPS OF HATE, 1931
SIAVASH IN PERSEPOLIS, 1966
SIEGE OF THE SAXONS, 1963
SIGN OF THE WOLF, 1941
SIGN OF ZORRO, THE, 1960
SILENT BARRIERS, 1937
SILENT CALL, THE, 1961
SILVER HORDE, THE, 1930
SILVER STALLION, 1941
SINBAD THE SAILOR, 1947
SIREN OF ATLANTIS, 1948
SIXTEEN FATHOMS DEEP, 1934
SIXTEEN FATHOMS DEEP, 1948
SKULL AND CROWN, 1938
SKULLDUGGERY, 1970
SKY BANDITS, 1986
SKY BANDITS, THE, 1940
SKY BIKE, THE, 1967
SKY GIANT, 1938
SKY PARADE, 1936
SKY PATROL, 1939
SKY RAIDERS, 1931
SKY RIDERS, 1976
SLATTERY'S HURRICANE, 1949
SLAVE GIRL, 1947
SLAVE OF THE CANNIBAL GOD, 1979
SLAVE SHIP, 1937
SLAVE, THE, 1963
SLAVERS, 1977
SMALL TOWN IN TEXAS, A, 1976
SMOKEY BITES THE DUST, 1981
SMUGGLERS, THE, 1948
SNOW DOG, 1950
SNOW TREASURE, 1968
SNOWBOUND, 1949
SNOWS OF KILIMANJARO, THE, 1952
SO THIS IS AFRICA, 1933
SOLDIER AND THE LADY, THE, 1937
SOLDIER OF FORTUNE, 1955
SOLDIERS OF THE STORM, 1933
SOLDIERS THREE, 1951
SOLOMON KING, 1974
SOMETIMES A GREAT NOTION, 1971
SON OF ALI BABA, 1952
SON OF CAPTAIN BLOOD, THE, 1964
SON OF FURY, 1942
SON OF KONG, 1933
SON OF MONTE CRISTO, 1940
SON OF ROBIN HOOD, 1959
SON OF SAMSON, 1962
SON OF THE RED CORSAIR, 1963
SONG OF INDIA, 1949
SORCERER, 1977
S.O.S. ICEBERG, 1933
S.O.S. PACIFIC, 1960
SOURDOUGH, 1977
SOUTH OF PAGO PAGO, 1940
SOUTH TO KARANGA, 1940
SOUTHERN STAR, THE, 1969
SPANISH MAIN, THE, 1945
SPANISH SWORD, THE, 1962
SPAWN OF THE NORTH, 1938
SPESSART INN, THE, 1961
SPHINX, 1981
SPIES OF THE AIR, 1940
SPIRAL ROAD, THE, 1962
S.T.A.B., 1976
STANLEY AND LIVINGSTONE, 1939
STAR OF INDIA, 1956
STARK MAD, 1929
STORM OVER BENGAL, 1938
STORM OVER THE ANDES, 1935
STORM OVER THE NILE, 1955
STORM OVER TIBET, 1952
STORM, THE, 1938
STORY OF ROBIN HOOD, THE, 1952
STORY OF THE COUNT OF MONTE CRISTO, THE, 1962
STRANGE HOLIDAY, 1969
STRANGE JOURNEY, 1946
STRANGE VOYAGE, 1945
STRANGE WORLD, 1952
STREET OF DARKNESS, 1958
STUNT PILOT, 1939

SUBMARINE PATROL, 1938
SUDAN, 1945
SUGARLAND EXPRESS, THE, 1974
SULEIMAN THE CONQUEROR, 1963
SULLIVAN'S EMPIRE, 1967
SUN NEVER SETS, THE, 1939
SUNDOWN, 1941
SUPERGIRL, 1984
SUPERMAN IV: THE QUEST FOR PEACE, 1987
SUSANNAH OF THE MOUNTIES, 1939
SWAMP FIRE, 1946
SWASHBUCKLER, 1976
SWEET REVENGE, 1987
SWEET SUGAR, 1972
SWEET SUZY, 1973
SWORD OF ALI BABA, THE, 1965
SWORD OF EL CID, THE, 1965
SWORD OF LANCELOT, 1963
SWORD OF MONTE CRISTO, THE, 1951
SWORD OF SHERWOOD FOREST, 1961
SWORD OF THE AVENGER, 1948
SWORD OF THE CONQUEROR, 1962
SWORD OF THE VALIANT, 1984
SWORD OF VENUS, 1953
SWORDSMAN OF SIENA, THE, 1962
SYNDICATE, THE, 1968
TAFFY AND THE JUNGLE HUNTER, 1965
TAKE ME TO TOWN, 1953
TALES OF ROBIN HOOD, 1951
TANGANYIKA, 1954
TANGIER ASSIGNMENT, 1954
TARGET HONG KONG, 1952
TARTARS, THE, 1962
TARZAN AND HIS MATE, 1934
TARZAN AND THE AMAZONS, 1945
TARZAN AND THE GREAT RIVER, 1967
TARZAN AND THE GREEN GODDESS, 1938
TARZAN AND THE HUNTRESS, 1947
TARZAN AND THE JUNGLE BOY, 1968
TARZAN AND THE LEOPARD WOMAN, 1946
TARZAN AND THE LOST SAFARI, 1957
TARZAN AND THE MERMAIDS, 1948
TARZAN AND THE SHE-DEVIL, 1953
TARZAN AND THE SLAVE GIRL, 1950
TARZAN AND THE VALLEY OF GOLD, 1966
TARZAN ESCAPES, 1936
TARZAN FINDS A SON, 1939
TARZAN GOES TO INDIA, 1962
TARZAN, THE APE MAN, 1932
TARZAN, THE APE MAN, 1959
TARZAN, THE APE MAN, 1981
TARZAN THE FEARLESS, 1933
TARZAN THE MAGNIFICENT, 1960
TARZAN TRIUMPHS, 1943
TARZANA, THE WILD GIRL, 1973
TARZAN'S DEADLY SILENCE, 1970
TARZAN'S DESERT MYSTERY, 1943
TARZAN'S FIGHT FOR LIFE, 1958
TARZAN'S GREATEST ADVENTURE, 1959
TARZAN'S HIDDEN JUNGLE, 1955
TARZAN'S JUNGLE REBELLION, 1970
TARZAN'S MAGIC FOUNTAIN, 1949
TARZAN'S NEW YORK ADVENTURE, 1942
TARZAN'S PERIL, 1951
TARZAN'S REVENGE, 1938
TARZAN'S SAVAGE FURY, 1952
TARZAN'S SECRET TREASURE, 1941
TARZAN'S THREE CHALLENGES, 1963
TATSU, 1962
TEN DAYS TO TULARA, 1958
TEN TALL MEN, 1951
TEN WHO DARED, 1960
TENDER WARRIOR, THE, 1971
TERROR IN THE JUNGLE, 1968
TERROR OF THE BLACK MASK, 1967
TERROR OF THE BLOODHUNTERS, 1962
THAT MAN FROM RIO, 1964
THEY MET IN BOMBAY, 1941
THIEF OF DAMASCUS, 1952
THIEF OF VENICE, THE, 1952
THIRD MAN ON THE MOUNTAIN, 1959
THREE MUSKETEERS, THE, 1935
THREE MUSKETEERS, THE, 1939
THREE MUSKETEERS, THE, 1948
THREE MUSKETEERS, THE, 1974

THREE STOOGES GO AROUND THE WORLD IN A DAZE, THE, 1963
THREE WARRIORS, 1977
THREE WORLDS OF GULLIVER, THE, 1960
THUNDER AND LIGHTNING, 1977
THUNDER BAY, 1953
THUNDER IN THE EAST, 1953
THUNDER IN THE PINES, 1949
THUNDER OVER SANGOLAND, 1955
TIGER FANGS, 1943
TIGER OF THE SEVEN SEAS, 1964
TIGER ROSE, 1930
TIMBER FURY, 1950
TIMBER TERRORS, 1935
TIMBUKTU, 1959
TIME SLIP, 1981
TOILERS OF THE SEA, 1936
TOM SAWYER, 1930
TOM SAWYER, 1973
TONKA, 1958
TOO HOT TO HANDLE, 1938
TOP OF THE WORLD, 1955
TORPEDOED, 1939
TORRID ZONE, 1940
TOY SOLDIERS, 1984
TRADER HORN, 1973
TRADER HORN, 1931
TRAIL OF THE YUKON, 1949
TRAILING THE KILLER, 1932
TRAILS OF THE WILD, 1935
TREASURE ISLAND, 1934
TREASURE ISLAND, 1950
TREASURE ISLAND, 1972
TREASURE OF JAMAICA REEF, THE, 1976
TREASURE OF MAKUBA, THE, 1967
TREASURE OF MATECUMBE, 1976
TREASURE OF THE AMAZON, THE, 1985
TREASURE OF THE FOUR CROWNS, 1983
TREASURE OF THE GOLDEN CONDOR, 1953
TREASURE OF THE SIERRA MADRE, THE, 1948
TREASURE OF THE YANKEE ZEPHYR, 1984
TROJAN HORSE, THE, 1962
TROPIC FURY, 1939
TROUBLE IN MOROCCO, 1937
TRUTH ABOUT SPRING, THE, 1965
TUNDRA, 1936
20,000 MEN A YEAR, 1939
TWILIGHT FOR THE GODS, 1958
TWIST OF SAND, A, 1968
TWO LOST WORLDS, 1950
TYCOON, 1947
TYPHOON, 1940
TYPHOON TREASURE, 1939
TYRANT OF THE SEA, 1950
ULTIMATE WARRIOR, THE, 1975
ULYSSES, 1955
UNCIVILISED, 1937
UNCOMMON VALOR, 1983
UNCONQUERED, 1947
UNDER SUSPICION, 1931
UNDER THE RED ROBE, 1937
UNDER TWO FLAGS, 1936
UNDERSEA GIRL, 1957
UNDERWATER!, 1955
UNDERWATER WARRIOR, 1958
UNKNOWN ISLAND, 1948
UNTAMED, 1955
UNTAMED, 1940
UNTOUCHED, 1956
UP TO HIS NECK, 1954
UTOPIA, 1952
VALLEY OF EAGLES, 1952
VALLEY OF MYSTERY, 1967
VALLEY OF THE GIANTS, 1938
VALLEY OF THE HEADHUNTERS, 1953
VALLEY OF THE KINGS, 1954
VANISHING POINT, 1971
VEILS OF BAGDAD, THE, 1953
VENGEANCE, 1930
VENGEANCE OF SHE, THE, 1968
VENGEANCE OF THE DEEP, 1940
VERDICT OF THE SEA, 1932
VICTORY, 1940
VIKING QUEEN, THE, 1967
VIKING, THE, 1931
VIKINGS, THE, 1958

VIOLENT AND THE DAMNED, THE, 1962
VIRGIN SACRIFICE, 1959
VISIT TO A CHIEF'S SON, 1974
VIVA KNIEVEL?, 1977
VIVA MARIA, 1965
VOICE IN THE NIGHT, 1934
VOODOO TIGER, 1952
WAGES OF FEAR, THE, 1955
WAKE OF THE RED WITCH, 1949
WAKE UP AND DREAM, 1946
WALK INTO HELL, 1957
WALLABY JIM OF THE ISLANDS, 1937
WAR OF THE ZOMBIES, THE, 1965
WARRIOR AND THE SORCERESS, THE, 1984
WATER BABIES, THE, 1979
WATUSI, 1959
WAY TO THE GOLD, THE, 1957
WE OF THE NEVER NEVER, 1983
WE WERE STRANGERS, 1949
WE'RE IN THE LEGION NOW, 1937
WEST OF ZANZIBAR, 1954
WHALERS, THE, 1942:,
WHAT CHANGED CHARLEY FARTHING?, 1976
WHAT WAITS BELOW, 1986
WHEN THE RAVEN FLIES, 1985
WHERE THE RIVER RUNS BLACK, 1986
WHERE'S JACK?, 1969
WHIRLWIND, 1968
WHITE DEVIL, THE, 1948
WHITE FANG, 1936
WHITE GODDESS, 1953
WHITE GORILLA, 1947
WHITE HUNTER, 1936
WHITE HUNTER, 1965
WHITE HUNTRESS, 1957
WHITE ORCHID, THE, 1954
WHITE PONGO, 1945
WHITE SAVAGE, 1943
WHITE SLAVE, 1986
WHITE SLAVE SHIP, 1962
WHITE TOWER, THE, 1950
WHITE WITCH DOCTOR, 1953
WHITE WOMAN, 1933
WICKED LADY, THE, 1946
WICKED LADY, THE, 1983
WIFE OF MONTE CRISTO, THE, 1946
WILD COUNTRY, THE, 1971
WILD GEESE, THE, 1978
WILD GEESE CALLING, 1941
WILD GEESE II, 1985
WIND AND THE LION, THE, 1975
WINDJAMMER, 1937
WINDJAMMER, THE, 1931
WINGS IN THE DARK, 1935
WINGS OF ADVENTURE, 1930
WINGS OF CHANCE, 1961
WINGS OF MYSTERY, 1963
WINGS OVER AFRICA, 1939
WITHOUT REGRET, 1935
WOLF CALL, 1939
WOLF LARSEN, 1958
WOLF LARSEN, 1978
WOLVES OF THE SEA, 1938
WOMAN AND THE HUNTER, THE, 1957
WOMAN HUNT, THE, 1975
WOMAN I STOLE, THE, 1933
WOMAN OBSESSED, 1959
WOMEN OF ALL NATIONS, 1931
WOMEN OF PITCAIRN ISLAND, THE, 1957
WONDERS OF ALADDIN, THE, 1961
WORLD IN HIS ARMS, THE, 1952
WRECK OF THE MARY DEARE, THE, 1959
YANK IN INDO-CHINA, A, 1952
YANKEE BUCCANEER, 1952
YANKEE PASHA, 1954
YEAR OF LIVING DANGEROUSLY, THE, 1982
YELLOW FIN, 1951
YELLOW HAIR AND THE FORTRESS OF GOLD, 1984
YELLOWBEARD, 1983
YELLOWNECK, 1955
YETI, 1977
YOR, THE HUNTER FROM THE FUTURE, 1983
YOU CAN'T WIN 'EM ALL, 1970
YOU ONLY LIVE TWICE, 1967
YOUNG SHERLOCK HOLMES, 1985
YOUNG WINSTON, 1972

YUKON FLIGHT, 1940
YUKON GOLD, 1952
YUKON MANHUNT, 1951
ZAMBA, 1949
ZANZIBAR, 1940
ZARAK, 1956
ZEPPELIN, 1971
ZORRO, THE GAY BLADE, 1981

Animated
ADVENTURES OF ICHABOD AND MR. TOAD, 1949
ADVENTURES OF MARK TWAIN, THE, 1985
ADVENTURES OF THE AMERICAN RABBIT, THE, 1986
ALAKAZAM THE GREAT!, 1961
ALLEGRO NON TROPPO, 1977
AMERICAN POP, 1981
AMERICAN TAIL, AN, 1986
ANIMAL FARM, 1955
ARISTOCATS, THE, 1970
BAMBI, 1942
BLACK CAULDRON, THE, 1985
BON VOYAGE, CHARLIE BROWN (AND DON'T COME BACK), 1980
BOY NAMED CHARLIE BROWN, A, 1969
BUGS BUNNY, SUPERSTAR, 1975
BUGS BUNNY'S THIRD MOVIE—1001 RABBIT TALES, 1982
CAMEL BOY, THE, 1984
CARE BEARS ADVENTURE IN WONDERLAND, THE, 1987
CARE BEARS MOVIE II: A NEW GENERATION, 1986
CARE BEARS MOVIE, THE, 1985
CHARLOTTE'S WEB, 1973
CHIPMUNK ADVENTURE, THE, 1987
CHRONOPOLIS, 1982
CINDERELLA, 1950
COONSKIN, 1975
COSMIC EYE, THE, 1986
DAFFY DUCK'S MOVIE: FANTASTIC ISLAND, 1983
DOT AND THE BUNNY, 1983
DOT AND THE KOALA, 1985
DUMBO, 1941
FANTASIA, 1940
FANTASTIC PLANET, 1973
FIRE AND ICE, 1983
FOX AND THE HOUND, THE, 1981
FOX WITH NINE TAILS, THE, 1969
FUN AND FANCY FREE, 1947
GALAXY EXPRESS, 1982
GAY PURR-EE, 1962
GOBOTS: BATTLE OF THE ROCKLORDS, 1986
GREAT AMERICAN BUGS BUNNY-ROAD RUNNER CHASE, 1979
GREAT MOUSE DETECTIVE, THE, 1986
GRENDEL GRENDEL GRENDEL, 1981
GULLIVER'S TRAVELS, 1939
GULLIVER'S TRAVELS BEYOND THE MOON, 1966
HEATHCLIFF: THE MOVIE, 1986
HEAVY METAL, 1981
HEIDI'S SONG, 1982
HERE COME THE LITTLES, 1985
HEY, GOOD LOOKIN', 1982
HEY THERE, IT'S YOGI BEAR, 1964
HUGO THE HIPPO, 1976
INCREDIBLE MR. LIMPET, THE, 1964
JOHNNY THE GIANT KILLER, 1953
JOURNEY BACK TO OZ, 1974
JUNGLE BOOK, THE, 1967
LADY AND THE TRAMP, 1955
LAND BEFORE TIME, THE, 1988
LAST UNICORN, THE, 1982
LES MAITRES DU TEMPS, 1982
LIGHT YEARS, 1988
LORD OF THE RINGS, THE, 1978
LUCKY LUKE, 1971
MAD MONSTER PARTY, 1967
MAGIC BOY, 1960
MAGIC WORLD OF TOPO GIGIO, THE, 1961
MAKE MINE MUSIC, 1946
MAN CALLED FLINTSTONE, THE, 1966
MELODY TIME, 1948
METAMORPHOSES, 1978
MIDSUMMERS NIGHT'S DREAM, A, 1961
MIGHTY MOUSE IN THE GREAT SPACE CHASE, 1983
MR. BUG GOES TO TOWN, 1941

MR. MAGOO'S HOLIDAY FESTIVAL, 1970
MOUSE AND HIS CHILD, THE, 1977
MY LITTLE PONY, 1986
NUTCRACKER FANTASY, 1979
OF STARS AND MEN, 1961
OLIVER & COMPANY, 1988
ONE HUNDRED AND ONE DALMATIANS, 1961
1001 ARABIAN NIGHTS, 1959
PANDA AND THE MAGIC SERPENT, 1961
PETER PAN, 1953
PETE'S DRAGON, 1977
PHANTOM TOLLBOOTH, THE, 1970
PINOCCHIO, 1940
PINOCCHIO AND THE EMPEROR OF THE NIGHT, 1987
PINOCCHIO IN OUTER SPACE, 1965
POUND PUPPIES AND THE LEGEND OF BIG PAW, 1988
RACE FOR YOUR LIFE, CHARLIE BROWN, 1977
RAGGEDY ANN AND ANDY, 1977
RAINBOW BRITE AND THE STAR STEALER, 1985
RELUCTANT DRAGON, THE, 1941
RESCUERS, THE, 1977
ROBIN HOOD, 1973
SANTA AND THE THREE BEARS, 1970
SECRET OF NIMH, THE, 1982
SECRET OF THE SWORD, THE, 1985
SEVENTH CONTINENT, THE, 1968
SHINBONE ALLEY, 1971
SINGING PRINCESS, THE, 1967
SLEEPING BEAUTY, 1959
SMURFS AND THE MAGIC FLUTE, THE, 1984
SNOOPY, COME HOME, 1972
SNOW QUEEN, THE, 1959
SNOW WHITE AND THE SEVEN DWARFS, 1937
SONG OF THE SOUTH, 1946
SPACE CRUISER, 1977
STARCHASER: THE LEGEND OF ORIN, 1985
SWORD IN THE STONE, THE, 1963
THREE CABALLEROS, THE, 1944
THUNDERBIRD 6, 1968
THUNDERBIRDS ARE GO, 1968
TIKI TIKI, 1971
TRANSFORMERS: THE MOVIE, THE, 1986
TRON, 1982
TWICE UPON A TIME, 1983
VALHALLA, 1987
VAMPIRES IN HAVANA, 1987
VISITORS FROM THE GALAXY, 1981
WACKY WORLD OF MOTHER GOOSE, THE, 1967
WARRIORS OF THE WIND, 1984
WATER BABIES, THE, 1979
WATERSHIP DOWN, 1978
WHEN THE WIND BLOWS, 1988
WHO FRAMED ROGER RABBIT, 1988
WIZARDS, 1977
WORLD OF HANS CHRISTIAN ANDERSEN, THE, 1971
YELLOW SUBMARINE, 1958

Biography
ABE LINCOLN IN ILLINOIS, 1940
ABRAHAM LINCOLN, 1930
ACT ONE, 1964
ADVENTURES OF MARK TWAIN, THE, 1944
AFTER THE BALL, 1957
AGE OF THE MEDICI, THE, 1979
AGONY AND THE ECSTASY, THE, 1965
AL CAPONE, 1959
ALEXANDER HAMILTON, 1931
ALEXANDER THE GREAT, 1956
AMADEUS, 1984
AMAZING MONSIEUR FABRE, THE, 1952
AND THERE CAME A MAN, 1968
ANITA—DANCES OF VICE, 1987
ANNE DEVLIN, 1984
ANNIE'S COMING OUT, 1985
ARCTIC FURY, 1949
AULD LANG SYNE, 1937
BABE RUTH STORY, THE, 1948
BAD LORD BYRON, THE, 1949
BARRETTS OF WIMPOLE STREET, THE, 1934
BARRETTS OF WIMPOLE STREET, THE, 1957
BEAR, THE, 1984
BEAU JAMES, 1957
BELL JAR, THE, 1979

BELOVED INFIDEL, 1959
BENNY GOODMAN STORY, THE, 1956
BERNADETTE OF LOURDES, 1962
BEST THINGS IN LIFE ARE FREE, THE, 1956
BIRD, 1988
BIRDMAN OF ALCATRAZ, 1962
BLACK MAGIC, 1949
BLOSSOMS IN THE DUST, 1941
BOB MATHIAS STORY, THE, 1954
BOHEMIAN RAPTURE, 1948
BOUND FOR GLORY, 1976
BOY IN BLUE, THE, 1986
BRIGHAM YOUNG—FRONTIERSMAN, 1940
BRONTE SISTERS, THE, 1979
BRUCE LEE AND I, 1976
BRUCE LEE—TRUE STORY, 1976
BUDDY HOLLY STORY, THE, 1978
BUFFALO BILL, 1944
BUSTER KEATON STORY, THE, 1957
CAESAR AND CLEOPATRA, 1946
CALAMITY JANE, 1953
CALL, THE, 1938
CALL NORTHSIDE 777, 1948
CANARIS, 1955
CAPONE, 1975
CAPTAIN EDDIE, 1945
CAPTAIN FROM KOEPENICK, 1933
CAPTAIN FROM KOEPENICK, THE, 1956
CARAVAGGIO, 1986
CARDINAL RICHELIEU, 1935
CASANOVA, 1976
CAST A GIANT SHADOW, 1966
CATHERINE THE GREAT, 1934
CELESTE, 1982
CELL 2455, DEATH ROW, 1955
CHAMPIONS, 1984
CHANEL SOLITAIRE, 1981
CHARIOTS OF FIRE, 1981
CHE!, 1969
CHIEF CRAZY HORSE, 1955
CHILDHOOD OF MAXIM GORKY, 1938
CHRISTINE JORGENSEN STORY, THE, 1970
CHRISTINE KEELER AFFAIR, THE, 1964
CHRISTOPHER COLUMBUS, 1949
CHRONICLE OF ANNA MAGDALENA BACH, 1968
CLIVE OF INDIA, 1935
COAL MINER'S DAUGHTER, 1980
COLONEL REDL, 1985
COLOR OF POMEGRANATES, THE, 1980
COMIN' THRU' THE RYE, 1947
CONVICTS FOUR, 1962
COURAGEOUS MR. PENN, THE, 1941
COURT-MARTIAL OF BILLY MITCHELL, THE, 1955
CRAZYLEGS, ALL AMERICAN, 1953
CROMWELL, 1970
CRY FREEDOM, 1987
CUSTER OF THE WEST, 1968
DALTONS RIDE AGAIN, THE, 1945
DANCE WITH A STRANGER, 1985
DANTON, 1931
DANTON, 1983
DARBY'S RANGERS, 1958
DARWIN ADVENTURE, THE, 1972
DAVID LIVINGSTONE, 1936
DAWN, 1979
DE SADE, 1969
DEEP IN MY HEART, 1954
DEFEAT OF HANNIBAL, THE, 1937
DESERT FOX, THE, 1951
DESIREE, 1954
DEVOTION, 1946
DIAMOND JIM, 1935
DIAMOND STUD, 1970
DICK TURPIN, 1933
DILLINGER, 1945
DILLINGER, 1973
DIRTYMOUTH, 1970
DISPATCH FROM REUTERS, A, 1940
DISRAELI, 1929
DIVINE EMMA, THE, 1983
DOC, 1971
DR. CRIPPEN, 1963
DR. EHRLICH'S MAGIC BULLET, 1940
DOLLY SISTERS, THE, 1945
DON'T TOUCH WHITE WOMEN!, 1974
DOOLINS OF OKLAHOMA, THE, 1949

DOVE, THE, 1974
DRAKE THE PIRATE, 1935
DREAMCHILD, 1985
DREYFUS CASE, THE, 1931
DREYFUS CASE, THE, 1940
DU BARRY, WOMAN OF PASSION, 1930
EBOLI, 1980
EDDIE CANTOR STORY, THE, 1953
EDDY DUCHIN STORY, THE, 1956
EDISON, THE MAN, 1940
EDITH AND MARCEL, 1984
EDUCATION OF SONNY CARSON, THE, 1974
EDVARD MUNCH, 1976
EGON SCHIELE—EXCESS AND PUNISHMENT, 1981
1812, 1944
EL CID, 1961
EL GRECO, 1966
ELEPHANT MAN, THE, 1980
ELISABETH OF AUSTRIA, 1931
EMPRESS WU, 1965
ENEMY OF WOMEN, 1944
ETERNAL MELODIES, 1948
ETERNAL SEA, THE, 1955
ETERNAL WALTZ, THE, 1959
EVEL KNIEVEL, 1971
EVERY MAN FOR HIMSELF AND GOD AGAINST ALL, 1975
FABULOUS DORSEYS, THE, 1947
FAR HORIZONS, THE, 1955
FEAR STRIKES OUT, 1957
FEW BULLETS MORE, A, 1968
FIGHTING FATHER DUNNE, 1948
FIREBRAND, THE, 1962
FIVE PENNIES, THE, 1959
FLIGHT OF THE EAGLE, 1983
FLYING IRISHMAN, THE, 1939
FOLLOW THE SUN, 1951
FOREVER MY LOVE, 1962
FRANCES, 1982
FRANCIS OF ASSISI, 1961
FREUD, 1962
FRONTIER MARSHAL, 1939
FRONTIER SCOUT, 1939
FUNNY GIRL, 1968
FUNNY LADY, 1975
GABLE AND LOMBARD, 1976
GALILEO, 1968
GALILEO, 1975
GALLANT HOURS, THE, 1960
GALLANT JOURNEY, 1946
GANDHI, 1982
GENE KRUPA STORY, THE, 1959
GENERAL SUVOROV, 1941
GENGHIS KHAN, 1965
GEORGE RAFT STORY, THE, 1961
GEORGE WASHINGTON CARVER, 1940
GERONIMO, 1939
GERONIMO, 1962
GIRL IN THE RED VELVET SWING, THE, 1955
GIRL IN WHITE, THE, 1952
GIVE 'EM HELL, HARRY!, 1975
GLENN MILLER STORY, THE, 1953
GLENROWAN AFFAIR, THE, 1951
GOOD DISSONANCE LIKE A MAN, A, 1977
GOODBYE, NORMA JEAN, 1976
GOTHIC, 1987
GREASED LIGHTNING, 1977
GREAT CARUSO, THE, 1951
GREAT DAN PATCH, THE, 1949
GREAT GILBERT AND SULLIVAN, THE, 1953
GREAT IMPOSTOR, THE, 1960
GREAT JEWEL ROBBER, THE, 1950
GREAT JOHN L, THE, 1945
GREAT MISSOURI RAID, THE, 1950
GREAT MR. HANDEL, THE, 1942
GREAT MOMENT, THE, 1944
GREAT NORTHFIELD, MINNESOTA RAID, THE, 1972
GREAT VICTOR HERBERT, THE, 1939
GREAT WALTZ, THE, 1938
GREAT WALTZ, THE, 1972
GREAT YEARNING, THE, 1930
GREAT ZIEGFELD, THE, 1936
GREATEST, THE, 1977
GREED OF WILLIAM HART, THE, 1948
GREY FOX, THE, 1983

GUARDIAN OF THE WILDERNESS, 1977
GYPSY, 1962
HANS CHRISTIAN ANDERSEN, 1952
HARLOW, 1965
HARLOW, 1965
HARMON OF MICHIGAN, 1941
HARMONY LANE, 1935
HEART BEAT, 1979
HEART LIKE A WHEEL, 1983
HELEN MORGAN STORY, THE, 1959
HENRY VIII AND HIS SIX WIVES, 1972
HITLER, 1962
HITLER GANG, THE, 1944
HITLER: THE LAST TEN DAYS, 1973
HOUDINI, 1953
HOUNDS. . . OF NOTRE DAME, THE, 1980
HOUSE IS NOT A HOME, A, 1964
HOUSE OF DEATH, 1932
HOUSE OF ROTHSCHILD, THE, 1934
HOUSE OF THE THREE GIRLS, THE, 1961
I DON'T CARE GIRL, THE, 1952
I DREAM OF JEANIE, 1952
I WANT TO LIVE!, 1958
I WAS A CAPTIVE IN NAZI GERMANY, 1936
I'LL CRY TOMORROW, 1955
I'LL SEE YOU IN MY DREAMS, 1951
IN COLD BLOOD, 1967
IN THE MOOD, 1987
INCREDIBLE SARAH, THE, 1976
INTERVISTA, 1987
IRON DUKE, THE, 1935
IRON MAJOR, THE, 1943
IRON MISTRESS, THE, 1952
IVAN THE TERRIBLE, PARTS I & II, 1947
JACK LONDON, 1943
JACKIE ROBINSON STORY, THE, 1950
JEANNE EAGELS, 1957
JESSE AND LESTER, TWO BROTHERS IN A PLACE
    CALLED TRINITY, 1972
JESUS, 1979
JIM THORPE—ALL AMERICAN, 1951
JOAN OF ARC, 1948
JOE HILL, 1971
JOE LOUIS STORY, THE, 1953
JOHN PAUL JONES, 1959
JOHN WESLEY, 1954
JOKER IS WILD, THE, 1957
JOLSON SINGS AGAIN, 1949
JOLSON STORY, THE, 1946
JONI, 1980
JUAREZ, 1939
JULIA, 1977
KING OF KINGS, 1961
KING OF THE ROARING TWENTIES—THE STORY
    OF ARNOLD ROTHSTEIN, 1961
KLONDIKE FEVER, 1980
KNUTE ROCKNE—ALL AMERICAN, 1940
LA BAMBA, 1987
LADY AND THE BANDIT, THE, 1951
LADY JANE, 1986
LADY JANE GREY, 1936
LADY SINGS THE BLUES, 1972
LADY WITH A LAMP, THE, 1951
LADY WITH RED HAIR, 1940
LADY'S MORALS, A, 1930
LAFAYETTE, 1963
LANDRU, 1963
LAST COMMAND, THE, 1955
LAST DAYS OF MUSSOLINI, 1974
LAST EMPEROR, THE, 1987
LAST OF THE DESPERADOES, 1956
LAST ROSE OF SUMMER, THE, 1937
LAST TEN DAYS, THE, 1956
LAW AND ORDER, 1942
LAW OF THE GOLDEN WEST, 1949
LAW VS. BILLY THE KID, THE, 1954
LAWLESS BREED, THE, 1952
LAWRENCE OF ARABIA, 1962
LEADBELLY, 1976
LEFT-HANDED GUN, THE, 1958
LEGIONS OF THE NILE, 1960
LENNY, 1974
LEPKE, 1975
LIFE AND LOVES OF BEETHOVEN, THE, 1937
LIFE AND LOVES OF MOZART, THE, 1959
LIFE OF EMILE ZOLA, THE, 1937

LILLIAN RUSSELL, 1940
LISZTOMANIA, 1975
LITTLE EGYPT, 1951
LOOK FOR THE SILVER LINING, 1949
LOUISIANA, 1947
LOVE ME OR LEAVE ME, 1955
LOVE TIME, 1934
LOVES OF EDGAR ALLAN POE, THE, 1942
LOVES OF ROBERT BURNS, THE, 1930
LUDWIG, 1973
LUST FOR LIFE, 1956
LUTHER, 1974
MAC ARTHUR, 1977
MACHINE GUN KELLY, 1958
MAD DOG COLL, 1961
MAD DOG MORGAN, 1976,Aus.
MADAME CURIE, 1943
MAGIC BOW, THE, 1947
MAGIC BOX, THE, 1952
MAGIC FIRE, 1956
MAGNIFICENT DOLL, 1946
MAGNIFICENT YANKEE, THE, 1950
MAHLER, 1974
MAN CALLED PETER, THE, 1955
MAN LIKE EVA, A, 1985
MAN OF A THOUSAND FACES, 1957
MAN OF CONQUEST, 1939
MAN OF MUSIC, 1953
MAN WHO DARED, THE, 1933
MAN WITH THE GREEN CARNATION, THE, 1960
MANOLETE, 1950
MARCO, 1973
MARCO POLO, 1962
MARCO THE MAGNIFICENT, 1966
MARIE, 1985
MARIE ANTOINETTE, 1938
MARTIN LUTHER, 1953
MARY OF SCOTLAND, 1936
MARY, QUEEN OF SCOTS, 1971
MASK, 1985
MATA HARI, 1931
MATA HARI, 1965
MATA HARI, 1985
MATCH KING, THE, 1932
MAURIE, 1973
MC CONNELL STORY, THE, 1955
MC VICAR, 1982
MEETINGS WITH REMARKABLE MEN, 1979
MELBA, 1953
MELVIN AND HOWARD, 1980
MEXICO IN FLAMES, 1982
MIDNIGHT EXPRESS, 1978
MIGHTY BARNUM, THE, 1934
MILLION DOLLAR MERMAID, 1952
MIRACLE WORKER, THE, 1962
MISHIMA, 1985
MR. H.C. ANDERSEN, 1950
MODIGLIANI OF MONTPARNASSE, 1961
MOMMIE DEAREST, 1981
MONKEY ON MY BACK, 1957
MONSIEUR VINCENT, 1949
MOULIN ROUGE, 1952
MOZART, 1940
MOZART STORY, THE, 1948
MUSIC LOVERS, THE, 1971
MY GAL SAL, 1942
MY WILD IRISH ROSE, 1947
MYSTERY OF ALEXINA, THE, 1985
NAKED GENERAL, THE, 1964
NAKED MAJA, THE, 1959
NAPOLEON, 1955
NED KELLY, 1970
NICHOLAS AND ALEXANDRA, 1971
NIGHT AND DAY, 1946
NIGHT THEY KILLED RASPUTIN, THE, 1962
NIJINSKY, 1980
NUN'S STORY, THE, 1959
OH, YOU BEAUTIFUL DOLL, 1949
ON HIS OWN, 1939
OSCAR WILDE, 1960
OTHER SIDE OF BONNIE AND CLYDE, THE, 1968
OTHER SIDE OF THE MOUNTAIN—PART 2, THE,
    1978
OTHER SIDE OF THE MOUNTAIN, THE, 1975
OUTSIDER, THE, 1962
PACIFIC ADVENTURE, 1947

PARNELL, 1937
PATTON, 1970
PATTY HEARST, 1988
PAVLOVA—A WOMAN FOR ALL TIME, 1985
PERILS OF PAULINE, THE, 1947
PIAF—THE EARLY YEARS, 1982
PICTURES, 1982
PORTRAIT OF A MOBSTER, 1961
PORTRAIT OF CHIEKO, 1968
PORTRAIT OF LENIN, 1967
PRESIDENT'S LADY, THE, 1953
PRICK UP YOUR EARS, 1987
PRIDE OF ST. LOUIS, THE, 1952
PRIDE OF THE YANKEES, THE, 1942
PRIEST OF LOVE, 1981
PRIME MINISTER, THE, 1941
PRISONER OF SHARK ISLAND, THE, 1936
PRIVATE FILES OF J. EDGAR HOOVER, THE, 1978
PRIVATE LIFE OF DON JUAN, THE, 1934
PRIVATE LIFE OF HENRY VIII, THE, 1933
PRIVATE LIVES OF ELIZABETH AND ESSEX, THE,
    1939
PT 109, 1963
RAGING BULL, 1980
RASPUTIN, 1932
RASPUTIN, 1939
RASPUTIN, 1985
RASPUTIN—THE MAD MONK, 1966
REDS, 1981
REMBETIKO, 1985
REMBRANDT, 1936
RHAPSODY IN BLUE, 1945
RHODES, 1936
RIGHT STUFF, THE, 1983
RISE AND FALL OF LEGS DIAMOND, THE, 1960
RISE OF LOUIS XIV, THE, 1970
ROBIN HOOD OF EL DORADO, 1936
ROCK AROUND THE WORLD, 1957
ROGER TOUHY, GANGSTER!, 1944
ROSEMARY, 1960
ROSSINI, 1948
ROUGHLY SPEAKING, 1945
ROYAL BOX, THE, 1930
ROYAL DIVORCE, A, 1938
ROYAL SCANDAL, A, 1945
RUNNING BRAVE, 1983
SAINT JOAN, 1957
ST. LOUIS BLUES, 1958
SALVATORE GIULIANO, 1966
SAM'S SON, 1984
SAVAGE MESSIAH, 1972
SCANDAL IN PARIS, A, 1946
SCARFACE, 1932
SCARLET EMPRESS, THE, 1934
SCOTT JOPLIN, 1977
SCOTT OF THE ANTARCTIC, 1949
SEATED AT HIS RIGHT, 1968
SECRET DIARY OF SIGMUND FREUD, THE, 1984
SECRET HONOR, 1984
SECRET OF NIKOLA TESLA, THE, 1985
SENSE OF FREEDOM, A, 1985
SERGEANT YORK, 1941
SERPICO, 1973
SEVEN ANGRY MEN, 1955
SEVEN LITTLE FOYS, THE, 1955
SEVEN SEAS TO CALAIS, 1963
SHINE ON, HARVEST MOON, 1944
SHOWTIME, 1948
SICILIAN, THE, 1987
SID AND NANCY, 1986
SILENCE OF THE NORTH, 1981
SILKWOOD, 1983
SILVER CITY, 1985
SILVER DOLLAR, 1932
SINFUL DAVEY, 1969
SINGING NUN, THE, 1966
SISTER KENNY, 1946
SMITHY, 1946
SO GOES MY LOVE, 1946
SO THIS IS LOVE, 1953
SOMEBODY LOVES ME, 1952
SOMEBODY UP THERE LIKES ME, 1956
SONG FROM MY HEART, THE, 1970
SONG OF BERNADETTE, THE, 1943
SONG OF LOVE, 1947

SONG OF MY HEART, 1947
SONG OF NORWAY, 1970
SONG OF SCHEHERAZADE, 1947
SONG TO REMEMBER, A, 1945
SONG WITHOUT END, 1960
SONS AND MOTHERS, 1967
SOUND OF MUSIC, THE, 1965
SPIRIT OF ST. LOUIS, THE, 1957
SPIRIT OF WEST POINT, THE, 1947
SPITFIRE, 1943
SPRING SYMPHONY, 1986
SPY IN BLACK, THE, 1939
STANLEY AND LIVINGSTONE, 1939
STAR!, 1968
STAR 80, 1983
STAR MAKER, THE, 1939
STARS AND STRIPES FOREVER, 1952
STAVISKY, 1974
STEVIE, 1978
STORY OF ADELE H., THE, 1975
STORY OF ALEXANDER GRAHAM BELL, THE, 1939
STORY OF DR. WASSELL, THE, 1944
STORY OF G.I. JOE, THE, 1945
STORY OF LOUIS PASTEUR, THE, 1936
STORY OF VERNON AND IRENE CASTLE, THE, 1939
STORY OF VICKIE, THE, 1958
STORY OF WILL ROGERS, THE, 1952
STRATTON STORY, THE, 1949
STRAUSS' GREAT WALTZ, 1934
SUEZ, 1938
SUNRISE AT CAMPOBELLO, 1960
SUTTER'S GOLD, 1936
SWANEE RIVER, 1939
SWEET DREAMS, 1985
SWIMMER, THE, 1988
SYLVIA, 1985
SYMPHONIE FANTASTIQUE, 1947
TENNESSEE JOHNSON, 1942
THAT HAMILTON WOMAN, 1941
THERESE, 1986
THEY DIED WITH THEIR BOOTS ON, 1942
THIS IS ELVIS, 1982
THREE LITTLE WORDS, 1950
TILL THE CLOUDS ROLL BY, 1946
TO HELL AND BACK, 1955
TOAST OF NEW YORK, THE, 1937
TOM HORN, 1980
TONIGHT WE SING, 1953
TOO MUCH, TOO SOON, 1958
TRIPLE CROSS, 1967
TUCKER: THE MAN AND HIS DREAM, 1988
UNFINISHED SYMPHONY, THE, 1953
UNIVERSITY OF LIFE, 1941
VALENTINO, 1951
VALENTINO, 1977
VERNE MILLER, 1988
VICTORIA THE GREAT, 1937
VIENNA WALTZES, 1961
VIOLETTE, 1978
VIVA VILLA!, 1934
VIVA ZAPATA!, 1952
VOLTAIRE, 1933
W.C. FIELDS AND ME, 1976
WAGNER, 1983
WAITING FOR THE MOON, 1987
WALK THE PROUD LAND, 1956
WALKING TALL, 1973
WALKING TALL, PART II, 1975
WATERLOO, 1970
WE OF THE NEVER NEVER, 1983
WE THREE, 1985
WE'LL MEET AGAIN, 1942
WHERE THE BUFFALO ROAM, 1980
WHERE'S JACK?, 1969
WHEREVER SHE GOES, 1953
WHITE ANGEL, THE, 1936
WILSON, 1944
WINGS AND THE WOMAN, 1942
WINGS OF EAGLES, THE, 1957
WINGS OF VICTORY, 1941
WINNING TEAM, THE, 1952
WITH A SONG IN MY HEART, 1952
WOLF AT THE DOOR, THE, 1987
WONDERFUL WORLD OF THE BROTHERS GRIMM, THE, 1962
WORDS AND MUSIC, 1948

WORLD APART, A, 1988
YEAR ONE, 1974
YOU ARE THE WORLD FOR ME, 1964
YOU WILL REMEMBER, 1941
YOUNG BESS, 1953
YOUNG BILL HICKOK, 1940
YOUNG CASSIDY, 1965
YOUNG DANIEL BOONE, 1950
YOUNG DILLINGER, 1965
YOUNG JESSE JAMES, 1960
YOUNG MR. LINCOLN, 1939
YOUNG MR. PITT, THE, 1942
YOUNG REBEL, THE, 1969
YOUNG TOM EDISON, 1940
YOUNG WINSTON, 1972
YOUNGER BROTHERS, THE, 1949
YOUR CHEATIN' HEART, 1964
ZINA, 1985

Children's

ADVENTURE IN THE HOPFIELDS, 1954
ADVENTURES OF HAL 5, THE, 1958
ADVENTURES OF RUSTY, 1945
ALADDIN, 1987
ALL AT SEA, 1970
ALL CREATURES GREAT AND SMALL, 1975
ALL THINGS BRIGHT AND BEAUTIFUL, 1979
ALMOST A GENTLEMAN, 1939
ALMOST ANGELS, 1962
ALONE ON THE PACIFIC, 1964
AMERICAN TAIL, AN, 1986
ARISTOCATS, THE, 1970
BAMBI, 1942
BASHFUL ELEPHANT, THE, 1962
BENJI, 1974
BENJI THE HUNTED, 1987
BIG CATCH, THE, 1968
BIG CHIEF, THE, 1960
BIG RED, 1962
BILL AND COO, 1947
BLOW YOUR OWN TRUMPET, 1958
BLUE BIRD, THE, 1976
BLUE BIRD, THE, 1940
BLUE BLOOD, 1951
BLUE SIERRA, 1946
BON VOYAGE, CHARLIE BROWN (AND DON'T COME BACK), 1980
BOY, A GIRL, AND A DOG, A, 1946
BOY NAMED CHARLIE BROWN, A, 1969
BOY WHO CAUGHT A CROOK, 1961
BRAVE ONE, THE, 1956
BUGSY MALONE, 1976
BUSH CHRISTMAS, 1947
C.H.O.M.P.S., 1979
CALAMITY THE COW, 1967
CAMEL BOY, THE, 1984
CANDLESHOE, 1978
CARE BEARS ADVENTURE IN WONDERLAND, THE, 1987
CARE BEARS MOVIE, THE, 1985
CAT GANG, THE, 1959
CAUGHT IN THE NET, 1960
CHIPMUNK ADVENTURE, THE, 1987
CHRISTMAS TREE, THE, 1966
CIRCUS BOY, 1947
CIRCUS FRIENDS, 1962
CLOWN AND THE KIDS, THE, 1968
CLUE OF THE MISSING APE, THE, 1953
COUNTDOWN TO DANGER, 1967
CRY WOLF, 1968
CUP FEVER, 1965
DANGER FLIGHT, 1939
DANNY BOY, 1946
DARBY O'GILL AND THE LITTLE PEOPLE, 1959
DARK CRYSTAL, THE, 1982
DARK ENEMY, 1984
DAVY CROCKETT AND THE RIVER PIRATES, 1956
DAVY CROCKETT, KING OF THE WILD FRONTIER, 1955
DAYLIGHT ROBBERY, 1964
DEVIL'S PASS, THE, 1957
DIGBY, THE BIGGEST DOG IN THE WORLD, 1974
DIMKA, 1964
DR. COPPELIUS, 1968
DOG AND THE DIAMONDS, THE, 1962
DOG'S BEST FRIEND, A, 1960

DONDI, 1961
DOT AND THE KOALA, 1985
DRAGON OF PENDRAGON CASTLE, THE, 1950
EAGLE ROCK, 1964
ELECTRIC BLUE, 1988
EMIL, 1938
EMIL AND THE DETECTIVE, 1931
EMIL AND THE DETECTIVES, 1964
EMPEROR AND THE NIGHTINGALE, THE, 1949
ENCHANTED FOREST, THE, 1945
ERNEST SAVES CHRISTMAS, 1988
ESCAPE FROM THE SEA, 1968
ESCAPE TO WITCH MOUNTAIN, 1975
FATTY FINN, 1980
FEROCIOUS PAL, 1934
FIGHTING PRINCE OF DONEGAL, THE, 1966
FIRE IN THE STONE, THE, 1983
FISH HAWK, 1981
5,000 FINGERS OF DR. T. THE, 1953
FLASH THE SHEEPDOG, 1967
FLIGHT OF THE DOVES, 1971
FLIPPER, 1963
FLIPPER'S NEW ADVENTURE, 1964
FLOOD, THE, 1963
FLORIAN, 1940
FLOWERS FOR THE MAN IN THE MOON, 1975
FLUFFY, 1965
FLYING EYE, THE, 1955
FLYING SORCERER, THE, 1974
FOR THE LOVE OF BENJI, 1977
FOR THE LOVE OF MIKE, 1960
FOR THE LOVE OF RUSTY, 1947
FOREVER YOUNG, FOREVER FREE, 1976
FORTUNE LANE, 1947
FOUR DAYS WONDER, 1936
FROM THE MIXED-UP FILES OF MRS. BASIL E. FRANKWEILER, 1973
GARBAGE PAIL KIDS MOVIE, THE, 1987
GENTLE GIANT, 1967
GIGANTES PLANETARIOS, 1965
GIRL AND THE BURGLAR, THE, 1967
GIT!, 1965
GIVE A DOG A BONE, 1967
GLITTERBALL, THE, 1977
GNOME-MOBILE, THE, 1967
GO KART GO, 1964
GOLDEN GOOSE, THE, 1966
GOLDEN SEAL, THE, 1983
GOODBYE, MY LADY, 1956
GOOSE GIRL, THE, 1967
GRAND ESCAPADE, THE, 1946
GREAT MIKE, THE, 1944
GREAT MUPPET CAPER, THE, 1981
GREAT PONY RAID, THE, 1968
GREYFRIARS BOBBY, 1961
GUNS IN THE HEATHER, 1968
GYPSY COLT, 1954
HALF PINT, THE, 1960
HANSEL AND GRETEL, 1954
HANSEL AND GRETEL, 1965
HEADLINE HUNTERS, 1968
HEATHCLIFF: THE MOVIE, 1986
HEIDI, 1937
HEIDI AND PETER, 1955
HEIDI, 1954
HEIDI, 1968
HEIDI'S SONG, 1982
HERE COME THE LITTLES, 1985
HERE COMES SANTA CLAUS, 1984
HEY THERE, IT'S YOGI BEAR, 1964
HINDU, THE, 1953
HITCH IN TIME, A, 1978
HOVERBUG, 1970
HUGO THE HIPPO, 1976
HUNCH, THE, 1967
HUNTED IN HOLLAND, 1961
INCREDIBLE JOURNEY, THE, 1963
JACK AND THE BEANSTALK, 1952
JACK AND THE BEANSTALK, 1970
JACK FROST, 1966
JACOB TWO-TWO MEETS THE HOODED FANG, 1979
JOHN AND JULIE, 1957
JOHN OF THE FAIR, 1962
JOHNNY ON THE RUN, 1953
JONIKO AND THE KUSH TA KA, 1969
JUNGLE BOOK, THE, 1967

JUNKET 89, 1970
KADOYNG, 1974
KID FROM CANADA, THE, 1957
KIDCO, 1984
KIND STEPMOTHER, 1936
LABYRINTH, 1986
LAD: A DOG, 1962
LAND BEFORE TIME, THE, 1988
LASSIE, COME HOME, 1943
LASSIE'S GREAT ADVENTURE, 1963
LAST FLIGHT OF NOAH'S ARK, THE, 1980
LAST LOAD, THE, 1948
LAST RHINO, THE, 1961
LEGEND OF COUGAR CANYON, 1974
LET THE BALLOON GO, 1977
LT. ROBIN CRUSOE, U.S.N., 1966
LIONHEART, 1968
LITTLE ARK, THE, 1972
LITTLE BALLERINA, THE, 1951
LITTLE BIG SHOT, 1935
LITTLE CONVICT, THE, 1980
LITTLE KIDNAPPERS, THE, 1954
LITTLE ONES, THE, 1965
LITTLE ORPHAN ANNIE, 1932
LITTLE ORPHAN ANNIE, 1938
LITTLE ORVIE, 1940
LITTLEST HOBO, THE, 1958
LITTLEST OUTLAW, THE, 1955
LONE CLIMBER, THE, 1950
LURE OF THE JUNGLE, THE, 1970
MALACHI'S COVE, 1973
MARCO POLO JUNIOR, 1973
MELODY, 1971
MISCHIEF, 1969
MISSING NOTE, THE, 1961
MR. SUPERINVISIBLE, 1974
MISTY, 1961
MONKEYS, GO HOME!, 1967
MONKEY'S UNCLE, THE, 1965
MOON PILOT, 1962
MOON-SPINNERS, THE. 1964
MOSCOW—CASSIOPEIA, 1974
MUPPET MOVIE, THE, 1979
MUPPETS TAKE MANHATTAN, THE, 1984
MY DOG, BUDDY, 1960
MY DOG RUSTY, 1948
MY FRIEND FLICKA, 1943
MY LITTLE PONY, 1986
MYSTERY MANSION, 1984
MYSTERY ON BIRD ISLAND, 1954
MYSTERY PLANE, 1939
NAVY HEROES, 1959
NEW ADVENTURES OF PIPPI LONGSTOCKING, THE, 1988
NIKKI, WILD DOG OF THE NORTH, 1961
NOTHING VENTURE, 1948
ODONGO, 1956
ODYSSEY OF THE PACIFIC, 1983
OLD YELLER, 1957
OLIVER & COMPANY, 1988
OLLY, OLLY, OXEN FREE, 1978
ON THE RUN, 1969
ONE FAMILY, 1930
ONE HUNDRED AND ONE DALMATIANS, 1961
ONE OF OUR DINOSAURS IS MISSING, 1975
1001 ARABIAN NIGHTS, 1959
OPERATION THIRD FORM, 1966
PAINTED HILLS, THE, 1951
PANDA AND THE MAGIC SERPENT, 1961
PERIL FOR THE GUY, 1956
PERSONALITY KID, 1946
PETER PAN, 1953
PETER RABBIT AND TALES OF BEATRIX POTTER, 1971
PETE'S DRAGON, 1977
PHANTOM TOLLBOOTH, THE, 1970
PINOCCHIO, 1940
PINOCCHIO, 1969
PINOCCHIO AND THE EMPEROR OF THE NIGHT, 1987
PINOCCHIO IN OUTER SPACE, 1965
PIPER'S TUNE, THE, 1962
PIPPI IN THE SOUTH SEAS, 1974
PIPPI ON THE RUN, 1977
POCOLITTLE DOG LOST, 1977
PORTRAIT OF INNOCENCE, 1948

POUND PUPPIES AND THE LEGEND OF BIG PAW, 1988
PRINCESS AND THE MAGIC FROG, THE, 1965
PRINCESS BRIDE, THE, 1987
PUFNSTUF, 1970
PUSS "N' BOOTS, 1964
PUSS "N' BOOTS, 1967
QUEEN'S SWORDSMEN, THE, 1963
RACE FOR YOUR LIFE, CHARLIE BROWN, 1977
RAGGEDY ANN AND ANDY, 1977
RAILWAY CHILDREN, THE, 1971
RAINBOW BRITE AND THE STAR STEALER, 1985
RELUCTANT DRAGON, THE, 1941
RESCUE SQUAD, THE, 1963
RESCUERS, THE, 1977
RETURN FROM WITCH MOUNTAIN, 1978
RETURN TO BOGGY CREEK, 1977
RIDE A WILD PONY, 1976
ROBBY, 1968
ROBIN HOOD, 1973
ROCKET TO NOWHERE, 1962
ROCKETS IN THE DUNES, 1960
RODEO RHYTHM, 1941
RUMPELSTILTSKIN, 1965
RUMPELSTILTSKIN, 1987
RUNAWAY RAILWAY, 1965
RUSTY LEADS THE WAY, 1948
RUSTY SAVES A LIFE, 1949
RUSTY'S BIRTHDAY, 1949
SAD HORSE, THE, 1959
SALTY, 1975
SALVAGE GANG, THE, 1958
SAND CASTLE, THE, 1961
SANDU FOLLOWS THE SUN, 1965
SANDY THE SEAL, 1969
SANTA AND THE THREE BEARS, 1970
SANTA CLAUS, 1960
SANTA'S CHRISTMAS CIRCUS, 1966
SCRAMBLE, 1970
SCRUFFY, 1938
SEA GYPSIES, THE, 1978
SECRET CAVE, THE, 1953
SECRET GARDEN, THE, 1949
SECRET OF MAGIC ISLAND, THE, 1964
SECRET OF NIMH, THE, 1982
SECRET OF THE FOREST, THE, 1955
SESAME STREET PRESENTS: FOLLOW THE BIRD, 1985
SEVEN ALONE, 1975
SEVEN DWARFS TO THE RESCUE, THE, 1965
SEVENTY DEADLY PILLS, 1964
SHAGGY, 1948
SHAMUS, 1959
SHOEMAKER AND THE ELVES, THE, 1967
SIGN OF THE WOLF, 1941
SILENCE, 1974
SILENT CALL, THE, 1961
SKATEBOARD, 1978
SKID KIDS, 1953
SKIPPY, 1931
SKULL AND CROWN, 1938
SKY BIKE, THE, 1967
SLEEPING BEAUTY, 1959
SLEEPING BEAUTY, 1965
SLIPPER AND THE ROSE, THE, 1976
SMURFS AND THE MAGIC FLUTE, THE, 1984
SNOOPY, COME HOME, 1972
SNOW DOG, 1950
SNOW QUEEN, THE, 1959
SNOW WHITE, 1965
SNOW WHITE AND ROSE RED, 1966
SNOW WHITE AND THE SEVEN DWARFS, 1937
SNOWFIRE, 1958
SO DEAR TO MY HEART, 1949
SOAPBOX DERBY, 1958
SON OF LASSIE, 1945
SONG OF THE SOUTH, 1946
SPOTS ON MY LEOPARD, THE, 1974
STARCHASER: THE LEGEND OF ORIN, 1985
STEPS TO THE MOON, 1963
STOLEN AIRLINER, THE, 1962
STOLEN DIRIGIBLE, THE, 1966
STOLEN PLANS, THE, 1962
STORIES FROM A FLYING TRUNK, 1979
STORM BOY, 1976
STORY OF ROBIN HOOD, THE, 1952

STOWAWAY IN THE SKY, 1962
SUMMERDOG, 1977
SUPERBUG, SUPER AGENT, 1976
SUPERZAN AND THE SPACE BOY, 1972
SWALLOWS AND AMAZONS, 1977
SWISS FAMILY ROBINSON, 1940
SWISS FAMILY ROBINSON, 1960
SWORD IN THE STONE, THE, 1963
TAIL OF THE TIGER, 1984
TEENAGERS IN SPACE, 1975
THREE LIVES OF THOMASINA, THE, 1963
THUMBELINA, 1970
TIM DRISCOLL'S DONKEY, 1955
TOBY TYLER, 1960
TOM THUMB, 1958
TOM THUMB, 1967
TOMBOY AND THE CHAMP, 1961
TONKA, 1958
TOTO AND THE POACHERS, 1958
TRAPPED BY THE TERROR, 1949
TREASURE AT THE MILL, 1957
TREASURE OF MATECUMBE, 1976
TROUBLESOME DOUBLE, THE, 1971
TWO IN REVOLT, 1936
TWO LITTLE BEARS, THE, 1961
UGLY DACHSHUND, THE, 1966
UP IN THE AIR, 1969
VISITORS FROM THE GALAXY, 1981
WACKY WORLD OF MOTHER GOOSE, THE, 1967
WAR DOGS, 1942
WATER BABIES, THE, 1979
WHALE OF A TALE, A, 1977
WHO SAYS I CAN'T RIDE A RAINBOW?, 1971
WILD COUNTRY, THE, 1971
WILD INNOCENCE, 1937
WILLIE MCBEAN AND HIS MAGIC MACHINE, 1965
WILLY WONKA AND THE CHOCOLATE FACTORY, 1971
WINGS OF MYSTERY, 1963
WISHING MACHINE, 1971
WOMBLING FREE, 1977
WONDERFUL LAND OF OZ, THE, 1969
WORLD OF HANS CHRISTIAN ANDERSEN, THE, 1971
YEAR OF THE HORSE, THE, 1966
ZEBRA IN THE KITCHEN, 1965
ZOO BABY, 1957

Comedy

A NOUS LA LIBERTE, 1931
ABBOTT AND COSTELLO GO TO MARS, 1953
ABBOTT AND COSTELLO IN HOLLYWOOD, 1945
ABBOTT AND COSTELLO IN THE FOREIGN LEGION, 1950
ABBOTT AND COSTELLO MEET CAPTAIN KIDD, 1952
ABBOTT AND COSTELLO MEET DR. JEKYLL AND MR. HYDE, 1954
ABBOTT AND COSTELLO MEET FRANKENSTEIN, 1948
ABBOTT AND COSTELLO MEET THE INVISIBLE MAN, 1951
ABBOTT AND COSTELLO MEET THE KEYSTONE KOPS, 1955
ABBOTT AND COSTELLO MEET THE KILLER, BORIS KARLOFF, 1949
ABBOTT AND COSTELLO MEET THE MUMMY, 1955
ABDULLAH'S HAREM, 1956
ABIE'S IRISH ROSE, 1928
ABIE'S IRISH ROSE, 1946
ABOUT LAST NIGHT, 1986
ABROAD WITH TWO YANKS, 1944
ABSENT-MINDED PROFESSOR, THE, 1961
ACCIDENTAL TOURIST, THE, 1988
ACQUA E SAPONE, 1985
ACTORS AND SIN, 1952
ADAM'S RIB, 1949
ADELE HASN'T HAD HER SUPPER YET, 1978
ADERYN PAPUR, 1984
ADIOS AMIGO, 1975
ADMIRABLE CRICHTON, THE, 1957
ADMIRAL WAS A LADY, THE, 1950
ADMIRALS ALL, 1935
ADMIRAL'S SECRET, THE, 1934
ADOLF HITLER—MY PART IN HIS DOWNFALL, 1973
ADORABLE CREATURES, 1956
ADORABLE JULIA, 1964

ADORABLE LIAR, 1962
ADVANCE TO THE REAR, 1964
ADVENTURE IN BALTIMORE, 1949
ADVENTURE LIMITED, 1934
ADVENTURE OF SHERLOCK HOLMES' SMARTER BROTHER, THE, 1975
ADVENTURES IN BABYSITTING, 1987
ADVENTURES OF A ROOKIE, 1943
ADVENTURES OF BARRY McKENZIE, 1972
ADVENTURES OF BUCKAROO BANZAI: ACROSS THE 8TH DIMENSION, THE, 1984
ADVENTURES OF BULLWHIP GRIFFIN, THE, 1967
ADVENTURES OF JANE, THE, 1949
ADVENTURES OF PICASSO, THE, 1980
ADVENTURES OF RABBI JACOB, THE, 1973
ADVENTURES OF SADIE, THE, 1955
AFFAIR OF SUSAN, 1935
AFFAIRS OF ANNABEL, 1938
AFFAIRS OF CAPPY RICKS, 1937
AFFAIRS OF CELLINI, THE, 1934
AFFAIRS OF GERALDINE, 1946
AFFAIRS OF JULIE, THE, 1958
AFFAIRS OF MARTHA, THE, 1942
AFFAIRS OF SUSAN, 1945
AFFECTIONATELY YOURS, 1941
AFRICA SCREAMS, 1949
AFTER HOURS, 1985
AFTER OFFICE HOURS, 1935
AFTER THE BALL, 1932
AFTER THE FOX, 1966
AFTER THE THIN MAN, 1936
AFTER YOU, COMRADE, 1967
AGENT 8 3/4, 1963
AGENT FOR H.A.R.M., 1966
AGGIE APPLEBY, MAKER OF MEN, 1933
AH, WILDERNESS!, 1935
A-HAUNTING WE WILL GO, 1942
AIR RAID WARDENS, 1943
AIRPLANE!, 1980
AIRPLANE II: THE SEQUEL, 1982
ALEX IN WONDERLAND, 1970
ALF 'N' FAMILY, 1968
ALFREDO, ALFREDO, 1973
ALF'S BABY, 1953
ALF'S BUTTON, 1930
ALF'S BUTTON AFLOAT, 1938
ALF'S CARPET, 1929
ALI BABA, 1954
ALIAS A GENTLEMAN, 1948
ALIAS JESSE JAMES, 1959
ALIAS THE DEACON, 1940
ALIBI IKE, 1935
ALICE ADAMS, 1935
ALIVE AND KICKING, 1962
ALIVE ON SATURDAY, 1957
ALL-AMERICAN CHUMP, 1936
ALL-AMERICAN CO-ED, 1941
ALL AT SEA, 1935
ALL AT SEA, 1939
ALL AT SEA, 1958
ALL FOR MARY, 1956
ALL HANDS ON DECK, 1961
ALL IN, 1936
ALL IN A NIGHT'S WORK, 1961
ALL NIGHT LONG, 1981
ALL NUDITY SHALL BE PUNISHED, 1974
ALL OF ME, 1984
ALL OVER THE TOWN, 1949
ALL OVER TOWN, 1937
ALL SCREWED UP, 1976
ALL THAT GLITTERS, 1936
...ALL THE MARBLES, 1981
ALL THE WAY, BOYS, 1973
ALL THE WAY UP, 1970
ALL THESE WOMEN, 1964
ALLERGIC TO LOVE, 1943
ALLIGATOR NAMED DAISY, AN, 1957
ALLNIGHTER, THE, 1987
ALLONSANFAN, 1985
ALMOST A DIVORCE, 1931
ALMOST A GENTLEMAN, 1938
ALMOST A HONEYMOON, 1930
ALMOST A HONEYMOON, 1938
ALOHA SUMMER, 1988
ALONG CAME LOVE, 1937
ALONG CAME YOUTH, 1931

ALPHABET MURDERS, THE, 1966
ALVIN PURPLE, 1974
ALVIN RIDES AGAIN, 1974
ALWAYS, 1985
ALWAYS A BRIDE, 1940
ALWAYS A BRIDE, 1954
ALWAYS IN TROUBLE, 1938
ALWAYS LEAVE THEM LAUGHING, 1949
ALWAYS TOGETHER, 1947
ALWAYS VICTORIOUS, 1960
AMARCORD, 1974
AMAZING GRACE, 1974
AMAZING MR. BEECHAM, THE, 1949
AMAZING MR. FORREST, THE, 1943
AMAZON WOMEN ON THE MOON, 1987
AMBASSADOR BILL, 1931
AMBASSADOR'S DAUGHTER, THE, 1956
AMERICAN DREAMER, 1984
AMERICAN GRAFFITI, 1973
AMERICAN LOVE, 1932
AMERICAN SUCCESS COMPANY, THE, 1980
AMERICAN WEREWOLF IN LONDON, AN, 1981
AMERICAN WIFE, AN, 1965
AMERICANIZATION OF EMILY, THE, 1964
AMERICATHON, 1979
AMOROUS ADVENTURES OF MOLL FLANDERS, THE, 1965
AMOROUS MR. PRAWN, THE, 1965
AMOS 'N' ANDY, 1930
AMOUR, AMOUR, 1937
ANATOMIST, THE, 1961
AND BABY MAKES THREE, 1949
AND NOW FOR SOMETHING COMPLETELY DIFFERENT, 1972
AND SO THEY WERE MARRIED, 1936
AND SO TO BED, 1965
AND SUDDENLY IT'S MURDER!, 1964
AND THE SAME TO YOU, 1960
AND THE SHIP SAILS ON, 1983
ANDROCLES AND THE LION, 1952
ANDY HARDY COMES HOME, 1958
ANDY HARDY GETS SPRING FEVER, 1939
ANDY HARDY MEETS DEBUTANTE, 1940
ANDY HARDY'S BLONDE TROUBLE, 1944
ANDY HARDY'S DOUBLE LIFE, 1942
ANDY HARDY'S PRIVATE SECRETARY, 1941
ANGEL FROM TEXAS, AN, 1940
ANGEL IN MY POCKET, 1969
ANGELS ALLEY, 1948
ANGELS IN DISGUISE, 1949
ANGELS IN THE OUTFIELD, 1951
ANGELS WITH BROKEN WINGS, 1941
ANIMAL CRACKERS, 1930
ANNABEL TAKES A TOUR, 1938
ANNABELLE'S AFFAIRS, 1931
ANNIE HALL, 1977
ANNIE LAURIE, 1936
ANNIE, LEAVE THE ROOM, 1935
ANNIVERSARY, THE, 1968
ANOTHER FACE, 1935
ANOTHER SHORE, 1948
ANOTHER THIN MAN, 1939
ANTOINE ET ANTOINETTE, 1947
ANY WEDNESDAY, 1966
ANY WHICH WAY YOU CAN, 1980
ANYBODY'S WOMAN, 1930
ANYBODY'S WAR, 1930
ANYONE CAN PLAY, 1968
ANYTHING CAN HAPPEN, 1952
ANYTHING TO DECLARE?, 1939
APARTMENT, THE, 1960
APPLE DUMPLING GANG, THE, 1975
APPLE DUMPLING GANG RIDES AGAIN, THE, 1979
APPOINTMENT FOR LOVE, 1941
APPRENTICESHIP OF DUDDY KRAVITZ, THE, 1974
APRIL FOOL'S DAY, 1986
APRIL 1, 2000, 1953
ARABELLA, 1969
ARE HUSBANDS NECESSARY?, 1942
ARE YOU A MASON?, 1934
AREN'T MEN BEASTS?, 1937
AREN'T WE ALL?, 1932
AREN'T WE WONDERFUL?, 1959
ARISE, MY LOVE, 1940
ARIZONA WILDCAT, 1938
ARMED AND DANGEROUS, 1986

ARMS AND THE MAN, 1932
ARMS AND THE MAN, 1962
ARMY GAME, THE, 1963
ARNOLD, 1973
AROUND THE WORLD IN EIGHTY WAYS, 1987
ARRIVEDERCI, BABY!, 1966
ARSENIC AND OLD LACE, 1944
ART OF LOVE, THE, 1965
ARTHUR, 1981
ARTHUR TAKES OVER, 1948
ARTHUR 2 ON THE ROCKS, 1988
AS GOOD AS MARRIED, 1937
AS HUSBANDS GO, 1934
AS LONG AS THEY'RE HAPPY, 1957
AS YOU WERE, 1951
AS YOUNG AS YOU FEEL, 1951
ASK A POLICEMAN, 1939
ASK ANY GIRL, 1959
ASK BECCLES, 1933
ASKING FOR TROUBLE, 1942
ASSASSINATION BUREAU, THE, 1969
ASSAULT OF THE KILLER BIMBOS, 1988
ASSOCIATE, THE, 1982
AT THE CIRCUS, 1939
AT WAR WITH THE ARMY, 1950
ATOMIC KID, THE, 1954
ATTACK OF THE KILLER TOMATOES, 1978
AUGUST WEEK-END, 1936
AULD LANG SYNE, 1929
AUNT CLARA, 1954
AUNT FROM CHICAGO, 1960
AUNTIE MAME, 1958
AUTHOR! AUTHOR!, 1982
AUTUMN MARATHON, 1982
AVANTI!, 1972
AVIATOR, THE, 1929
AWFUL TRUTH, THE, 1937
AWFUL TRUTH, THE, 1929
AZAIS, 1931
AZURE EXPRESS, 1938
B.S. I LOVE YOU, 1971
BABES IN BAGDAD, 1952
BABETTE GOES TO WAR, 1960
BABY AND THE BATTLESHIP, THE, 1957
BABY BOOM, 1987
BABY FACE HARRINGTON, 1935
BABY FACE MORGAN, 1942
BABY, IT'S YOU, 1983
BACHELOR AND THE BOBBY-SOXER, THE, 1947
BACHELOR BAIT, 1934
BACHELOR DADDY, 1941
BACHELOR FATHER, 1931
BACHELOR FLAT, 1962
BACHELOR IN PARADISE, 1961
BACHELOR IN PARIS, 1953
BACHELOR MOTHER, 1939
BACHELOR OF HEARTS, 1958
BACHELOR PARTY, 1984
BACHELOR'S AFFAIRS, 1932
BACHELOR'S BABY, 1932
BACHELOR'S DAUGHTERS, THE, 1946
BACK AT THE FRONT, 1952
BACK ROADS, 1981
BACK ROOM BOY, 1942
BACK TO NATURE, 1936
BACK TO SCHOOL, 1986
BACK TO THE BEACH, 1987
BACK TO THE FUTURE, 1985
BAD BOY, 1935
BAD CHARLESTON CHARLIE, 1973
BAD COMPANY, 1986
BAD GUYS, 1986
BAD MANNERS, 1984
BAD MEDICINE, 1985
BAD NEWS BEARS, THE, 1976
BAD NEWS BEARS GO TO JAPAN, THE, 1978
BAD NEWS BEARS IN BREAKING TRAINING, THE, 1977
BADGER'S GREEN, 1934
BADGER'S GREEN, 1949
BAGDAD CAFE, 1988
BAKER'S WIFE, THE, 1940
BALL OF FIRE, 1941
BALLAD OF JOSIE, 1968
BANANA PEEL, 1965
BANANA RIDGE, 1941

BANANAS, 1971
BANG, BANG, YOU'RE DEAD, 1966
BANK DICK, THE, 1940
BANK SHOT, 1974
BANZAI, 1983
BAR ESPERANZA, 1985
BAREFOOT EXECUTIVE, THE, 1971
BAREFOOT IN THE PARK, 1967
BARFLY, 1987
BARGEE, THE, 1964
BARONESS AND THE BUTLER, THE, 1938
BARRANCO, 1932
BARRY MC KENZIE HOLDS HIS OWN, 1975
BASHFUL BACHELOR, THE, 1942
BASIC TRAINING, 1985
BAT WHISPERS, THE, 1930
BATTLE OF BROADWAY, 1938
BATTLE OF LOVE'S RETURN, THE, 1971
BATTLE OF THE SEXES, THE, 1960
BATTLEAXE, THE, 1962
BEACH GIRLS, 1982
BEADS OF ONE ROSARY, THE, 1982
BEAT THE DEVIL, 1953
BEAUTIFUL BLONDE FROM BASHFUL BEND, THE,
    1949
BEAUTIFUL CHEAT, THE, 1946
BEAUTY AND THE BARGE, 1937
BEAUTY AND THE BOSS, 1932
BEAUTY FOR SALE, 1933
BED AND BREAKFAST, 1930
BED SITTING ROOM, THE, 1969
BEDAZZLED, 1967
BEDSIDE MANNER, 1945
BEDTIME FOR BONZO, 1951
BEDTIME STORY, 1942
BEDTIME STORY, 1964
BEER, 1986
BEES IN PARADISE, 1944
BEETLEJUICE, 1988
BEGINNER'S LUCK, 1986
BEHAVE YOURSELF, 1951
BEHIND PRISON WALLS, 1943
BEHIND THE MIKE, 1937
BEING THERE, 1979
BELA LUGOSI MEETS A BROOKLYN GORILLA, 1952
BELL, BOOK AND CANDLE, 1958
BELL-BOTTOM GEORGE, 1943
BELLBOY, THE, 1960
BELLE OF THE NINETIES, 1934
BELLES OF ST. TRINIAN'S, THE, 1954
BELLES ON THEIR TOES, 1952
BELLS GO DOWN, THE, 1943
BELOW THE BELT, 1980
BENJAMIN, 1968
BENJAMIN, 1973
BEST DEFENSE, 1984
BEST HOUSE IN LONDON, THE, 1969
BEST OF ENEMIES, 1933
BEST OF ENEMIES, THE, 1962
BEST OF TIMES, THE, 1986
BETTER A WIDOW, 1969
BETTER LATE THAN NEVER, 1983
BETTER OFF DEAD, 1985
BEVERLY HILLS COP, 1984
BEVERLY HILLS COP II, 1987
BEWARE OF BLONDIE, 1950
BEWARE OF CHILDREN, 1961
BEWARE SPOOKS, 1939
BEYOND THE BLUE HORIZON, 1942
BEYOND THERAPY, 1987
BIG, 1988
BIG BEAT, THE, 1958
BIG BRAIN, THE, 1933
BIG BRAWL, THE, 1980
BIG BUS, THE, 1976
BIG BUSINESS, 1934
BIG BUSINESS, 1988
BIG CHIEF, THE, 1960
BIG DEAL ON MADONNA STREET, THE, 1960
BIG FIX, THE, 1978
BIG GAMBLE, THE, 1931
BIG HAND FOR THE LITTLE LADY, A, 1966
BIG HEARTED HERBERT, 1934
BIG JOB, THE, 1965
BIG MEAT EATER, 1984
BIG MONEY, THE, 1962

BIG MOUTH, THE, 1967
BIG NOISE, THE, 1936
BIG NOISE, THE, 1944
BIG SHOT, THE, 1931
BIG SHOT, THE, 1937
BIG SHOTS, 1987
BIG SHOW, THE, 1937
BIG SPLASH, THE, 1935
BIG STORE, THE, 1941
BIG STREET, THE, 1942
BIG TOP PEE-WEE, 1988
BIG TROUBLE, 1986
BIG TROUBLE IN LITTLE CHINA, 1986
BIGGEST BUNDLE OF THEM ALL, THE, 1968
BIKINI BEACH, 1964
BILL CRACKS DOWN, 1937
BILL OF DIVORCEMENT, A, 1932
BILLION DOLLAR HOBO, THE, 1977
BILL'S LEGACY, 1931
BILOXI BLUES, 1988
BINGO BONGO, 1983
BIOGRAPHY OF A BACHELOR GIRL, 1935
BIRDS AND THE BEES, THE, 1965
BIRDS DO IT, 1966
BIRDS OF A FEATHER, 1935
BIRDS, THE BEES AND THE ITALIANS, THE, 1967
BISHOP MISBEHAVES, THE, 1935
BISHOP'S WIFE, THE, 1947
BIZARRE BIZARRE, 1939
BLACK BIRD, THE, 1975
BLACK DOLL, THE, 1938
BLACK HAND GANG, THE, 1930
BLACK JACK, 1973
BLACK JOY, 1977
BLACK JOY, 1986
BLACK KING, 1932
BLACK SHEEP OF WHITEHALL, THE, 1941
BLACKBEARD'S GHOST, 1968
BLACKMAILER, 1936
BLAME IT ON RIO, 1984
BLAZING SADDLES, 1974
BLESS 'EM ALL, 1949
BLESSED EVENT, 1932
BLIND DATE, 1987
BLIND DIRECTOR, THE, 1986
BLIND FOLLY, 1939
BLINDMAN, 1972
BLISS OF MRS. BLOSSOM, THE, 1968
BLOCK BUSTERS, 1944
BLOCKHEADS, 1938
BLOND CHEAT, 1938
BLONDE DYNAMITE, 1950
BLONDE FROM BROOKLYN, 1945
BLONDE INSPIRATION, 1941
BLONDE RANSOM, 1945
BLONDIE, 1938
BLONDIE BRINGS UP BABY, 1939
BLONDIE FOR VICTORY, 1942
BLONDIE GOES LATIN, 1941
BLONDIE GOES TO COLLEGE, 1942
BLONDIE HAS SERVANT TROUBLE, 1940
BLONDIE HITS THE JACKPOT, 1949
BLONDIE IN SOCIETY, 1941
BLONDIE IN THE DOUGH, 1947
BLONDIE KNOWS BEST, 1946
BLONDIE MEETS THE BOSS, 1939
BLONDIE OF THE FOLLIES, 1932
BLONDIE ON A BUDGET, 1940
BLONDIE PLAYS CUPID, 1940
BLONDIE TAKES A VACATION, 1939
BLONDIE'S ANNIVERSARY, 1947
BLONDIE'S BIG DEAL, 1949
BLONDIE'S BIG MOMENT, 1947
BLONDIE'S BLESSED EVENT, 1942
BLONDIE'S HOLIDAY, 1947
BLONDIE'S HERO, 1950
BLONDIE'S LUCKY DAY, 1946
BLONDIE'S REWARD, 1948
BLONDIE'S SECRET, 1948
BLOODBATH AT THE HOUSE OF DEATH, 1984
BLOODSUCKERS FROM OUTER SPACE, 1987
BLUE IDOL, THE, 1931
BLUE IGUANA, THE, 1988
BLUE MURDER AT ST. TRINIAN'S, 1958
BLUE SKIES AGAIN, 1983
BLUEBEARD'S EIGHTH WIFE, 1938

BLUES BROTHERS, THE, 1980
BLUME IN LOVE, 1973
BOATNIKS, THE, 1970
BOB AND CAROL AND TED AND ALICE, 1969
BOBBIKINS, 1959
BOBO, THE, 1967
BOB'S YOUR UNCLE, 1941
BOCCACCIO '70, 1962
BODY DISAPPEARS, THE, 1941
BODY SAID NO!, THE, 1950
BOEING BOEING, 1965
BOHEMIAN GIRL, THE, 1936
BON VOYAGE, 1962
BONNIE SCOTLAND, 1935
BONZO GOES TO COLLEGE, 1952
BOOGIE MAN WILL GET YOU, THE, 1942
BOOTLEGGERS, 1974
BORN IN EAST L.A., 1987
BORN THAT WAY, 1937
BORN TO BE LOVED, 1959
BORN TO WIN, 1971
BORN YESTERDAY, 1951
BORROW A MILLION, 1934
BORROWED CLOTHES, 1934
BORROWED WIVES, 1930
BORROWING TROUBLE, 1937
BOSS' WIFE, THE, 1986
BOSS'S SON, THE, 1978
BOTTOMS UP, 1960
BOUDOIR DIPLOMAT, 1930
BOUDU SAVED FROM DROWNING, 1967
BOWERY BATTALION, 1951
BOWERY BLITZKRIEG, 1941
BOWERY BOMBSHELL, 1946
BOWERY BOYS MEET THE MONSTERS, THE, 1954
BOWERY BUCKAROOS, 1947
BOWERY CHAMPS, 1944
BOWERY TO BAGDAD, 1955
BOXOFFICE, 1982
BOY, DID I GET A WRONG NUMBER!, 1966
BOY FRIEND, 1939
BOY MEETS GIRL, 1938
BOY WHO STOLE A MILLION, THE, 1960
BOYFRIENDS AND GIRLFRIENDS, 1988
BOYS OF THE CITY, 1940
BOYS WILL BE BOYS, 1936
BOYS WILL BE GIRLS, 1937
BOYS' NIGHT OUT, 1962
BRAIN, THE, 1969
BRANDED MEN, 1931
BRANDY FOR THE PARSON, 1952
BRASS BOTTLE, THE, 1964
BREAD AND CHOCOLATE, 1978
BREAD, LOVE AND DREAMS, 1953
BREAKFAST FOR TWO, 1937
BREAKFAST IN HOLLYWOOD, 1946
BREAKING ALL THE RULES, 1985
BREAKING AWAY, 1979
BREWSTER McCLOUD, 1970
BREWSTER'S MILLIONS, 1935
BREWSTER'S MILLIONS, 1945
BREWSTER'S MILLIONS, 1985
BRIDAL PATH, THE, 1959
BRIDAL SUITE, 1939
BRIDE CAME C.O.D., THE, 1941
BRIDE COMES HOME, 1936
BRIDE FOR SALE, 1949
BRIDE WALKS OUT, THE, 1936
BRIDE WORE BOOTS, THE, 1946
BRIDES ARE LIKE THAT, 1936
BRIGHT EYES, 1934
BRIGHT LIGHTS, 1935
BRIGHTON BEACH MEMOIRS, 1986
BRINGING UP BABY, 1938
BRINGING UP FATHER, 1946
BRINK'S JOB, THE, 1978
BRITTANIA HOSPITAL, 1982
BROADCAST NEWS, 1987
BROADMINDED, 1931
BROADWAY BILL, 1934
BROADWAY DANNY ROSE, 1984
BROADWAY LIMITED, 1941
BRONCO BILLY, 1980
BROOKLYN ORCHID, 1942
BROTH OF A BOY, 1959

BOLD: Films on Videocassette

BROTHER ALFRED, 1932
BROTHER RAT, 1938
BROTHER RAT AND A BABY, 1940
BUCK BENNY RIDES AGAIN, 1940
BUCK PRIVATES, 1941
BUCK PRIVATES COME HOME, 1947
BUDDIES, 1983
BUDDY BUDDY, 1981
BUDDY SYSTEM, THE, 1984
BULL DURHAM, 1988
BULLDOG BREED, THE, 1960
BULLFIGHTERS, THE, 1945
BULLSHOT, 1983
BUNKER BEAN, 1936
BUNNY O'HARE, 1971
BUONA SERA, MRS. CAMPBELL, 1968
BUREAU OF MISSING PERSONS, 1933
BURGLAR, 1987
BUS STOP, 1956
BUSH CHRISTMAS, 1983
BUSINESS AND PLEASURE, 1932
BUSMAN'S HOLIDAY, 1936
BUSTER, 1988
BUSTIN' LOOSE, 1981
BUSYBODY, THE, 1967
BUT NOT FOR ME, 1959
BUTCH MINDS THE BABY, 1942
BUTLER'S DILEMMA, THE, 1943
BUY ME THAT TOWN, 1941
BY CANDLELIGHT, 1934
BY YOUR LEAVE, 1935
BYE BYE BRAVERMAN, 1968
BYE BYE MONKEY, 1978
C.H.O.M.P.S., 1979
CACTUS FLOWER, 1969
CADDY, THE, 1953
CADDYSHACK, 1980
CADDYSHACK II, 1988
CAFE EXPRESS, 1980
CAFE MASCOT, 1936
CAFE METROPOLE, 1937
CAFE SOCIETY, 1939
CALABUCH, 1956
CALIFORNIA GIRLS, 1984
CALIFORNIA SPLIT, 1974
CALIFORNIA SUITE, 1978
CALL IT A DAY, 1937
CALL IT LUCK, 1934
CALL ME BWANA, 1963
CALL ME GENIUS, 1961
CALL ME MAME, 1933
CALLAWAY WENT THATAWAY, 1951
CALLING ALL CROOKS, 1938
CALLING ALL HUSBANDS, 1940
CALM YOURSELF, 1935
CAME A HOT FRIDAY, 1985
CAMELS ARE COMING, THE, 1934
CAMERA BUFF, 1983
CAMPUS CONFESSIONS, 1938
CAMPUS MAN, 1987
CAN SHE BAKE A CHERRY PIE?, 1983
CAN YOU HEAR ME MOTHER?, 1935
CAN'T BUY ME LOVE, 1987
CANARIES SOMETIMES SING, 1930
CANCEL MY RESERVATION, 1972
CANDY, 1968
CANNIBAL GIRLS, 1973
CANNONBALL, 1976
CANNONBALL RUN II, 1984
CANNONBALL RUN, THE, 1981
CANTERVILLE GHOST, THE, 1944
CAPRICE, 1967
CAPRICIOUS SUMMER, 1968
CAPTAIN BILL, 1935
CAPTAIN HATES THE SEA, THE, 1934
CAPTAIN KRONOS: VAMPIRE HUNTER, 1974
CAPTAIN NEWMAN, M.D., 1963
CAPTAIN THUNDER, 1931
CAPTAIN'S PARADISE, THE, 1953
CAPTAIN'S TABLE, THE, 1960
CAR WASH, 1976
CARBON COPY, 1981
CARDBOARD CAVALIER, THE, 1949
CAREER WOMAN, 1936
CARETAKERS DAUGHTER, THE, 1952

CARNABY, M.D., 1967
CARNATION KID, 1929
CARNIVAL, 1935
CARNIVAL, 1953
CAROLINA CANNONBALL, 1955
CARRY ON ADMIRAL, 1957
CARRY ON AGAIN, DOCTOR, 1969
CARRY ON CABBIE, 1963
CARRY ON CAMPING, 1969
CARRY ON CLEO, 1964
CARRY ON CONSTABLE, 1960
CARRY ON COWBOY, 1966
CARRY ON CRUISING, 1962
CARRY ON DOCTOR, 1968
CARRY ON EMANUELLE, 1978
CARRY ON ENGLAND, 1976
CARRY ON HENRY VIII, 1970
CARRY ON JACK, 1963
CARRY ON LOVING, 1970
CARRY ON NURSE, 1959
CARRY ON REGARDLESS, 1961
CARRY ON SCREAMING, 1966
CARRY ON SERGEANT, 1959
CARRY ON SPYING, 1964
CARRY ON TEACHER, 1962
CARRY ON UP THE JUNGLE, 1970
CARRY ON, UP THE KHYBER, 1968
CARS THAT ATE PARIS, THE, 1974
CASANOVA BROWN, 1944
CASANOVA '70, 1965
CASE OF THE 44'S, THE, 1964
CASH ON DELIVERY, 1956
CASINO DE PARIS, 1957
CASINO ROYALE, 1967
CASTAWAY COWBOY, THE, 1974
CASTE, 1930
CASTLE OF THE MONSTERS, 1958
CASUAL SEX?, 1988
CAT AND MOUSE, 1975
CAT AND THE CANARY, THE, 1939
CAT BALLOU, 1965
CAT FROM OUTER SPACE, THE, 1978
CATCH AS CATCH CAN, 1968
CATHERINE & CO., 1976
CAT'S PAW, THE, 1934
CAUGHT IN THE DRAFT, 1941
CAUGHT PLASTERED, 1931
CAUGHT SHORT, 1930
CAVE GIRL, 1985
CAVEMAN, 1981
CAYMAN TRIANGLE, THE, 1977
CENSUS TAKER, THE, 1984
CERTAIN, VERY CERTAIN, AS A MATTER OF
    FACT... PROBABLE, 1970
CESAR AND ROSALIE, 1972
CHAIN, THE, 1985
CHAIN LETTERS, 1985
CHAMPAGNE CHARLIE, 1944
CHAMPAGNE FOR CAESAR, 1950
CHANGE FOR A SOVEREIGN, 1937
CHAPTER TWO, 1979
CHARADE, 1963
CHARGE OF THE MODEL-T'S, 1979
CHARLESTON, 1978
CHARLEY AND THE ANGEL, 1973
CHARLEY'S AUNT, 1930
CHARLEY'S AUNT, 1941
CHARLEY'S (BIG-HEARTED) AUNT, 1940
**CHARLIE CHAN AND THE CURSE OF THE DRAGON
    QUEEN, 1981**
CHARLIE MC CARTHY, DETECTIVE, 1939
CHASTITY BELT, THE, 1968
CHATTANOOGA CHOO CHOO, 1984
CHATTERBOX, 1943
CHEAP DETECTIVE, THE, 1978
CHEAPER BY THE DOZEN, 1950
CHEAPER TO KEEP HER, 1980
CHEATERS, THE, 1945
CHECK IS IN THE MAIL, THE, 1986
CHECKERED FLAG OR CRASH, 1978
CHECKERS, 1937
CHEECH AND CHONG'S NEXT MOVIE, 1980
CHEECH AND CHONG'S NICE DREAMS, 1981
**CHEECH AND CHONG'S THE CORSICAN
    BROTHERS, 1984**
CHEER BOYS CHEER, 1939

CHEER THE BRAVE, 1951
CHESTY ANDERSON, U.S. NAVY, 1976
CHEYENNE SOCIAL CLUB, THE, 1970
CHICAGO 70, 1970
CHICK, 1936
CHICKEN CHRONICLES, THE, 1977
CHICKEN EVERY SUNDAY, 1948
CHICKEN WAGON FAMILY, 1939
CHIEF, THE, 1933
CHILDREN GALORE, 1954
CHILD'S PLAY, 1954
CHINA IS NEAR, 1968
CHIQUTTO PERO PICOSO, 1967
CHOIRBOYS, THE, 1977
CHOOSE ME, 1984
CHRISTMAS IN CONNECTICUT, 1945
CHRISTMAS IN JULY, 1940
CHRISTMAS STORY, A, 1983
CHRISTOPHER BEAN, 1933
CHU CHU AND THE PHILLY FLASH, 1981
CHUMP AT OXFORD, A, 1940
CINDERFELLA, 1960
CIRCUS CLOWN, 1934
CITIZENS BAND, 1977
CITY HEAT, 1984
CITY LIMITS, 1934
CITY NEWS, 1983
CITY PARK, 1934
CLANCY IN WALL STREET, 1930
CLANCY STREET BOYS, 1943
CLARENCE, 1937
CLARETTA AND BEN, 1983
CLASS, 1983
CLASS OF MISS MAC MICHAEL, THE, 1978
CLAUDIA, 1943
CLAUDIA AND DAVID, 1946
CLEANING UP, 1933
CLEAR THE DECKS, 1929
CLIMAX, THE, 1967
CLIMBING HIGH, 1938
CLINIC, THE, 1983
CLIPPED WINGS, 1953
CLOCKWISE, 1986
CLOPORTES, 1966
CLOSELY WATCHED TRAINS, 1967
CLOUDED CRYSTAL, THE, 1948
CLOUDS OVER EUROPE, 1939
CLUB PARADISE, 1986
CLUE, 1985
CLUNY BROWN, 1946
COAST TO COAST, 1980
COCK OF THE AIR, 1932
COCKEYED CAVALIERS, 1934
COCKEYED COWBOYS OF CALICO COUNTY, THE,
    1970
COCKEYED MIRACLE, THE, 1946
COCOANUTS, THE, 1929
COCOON, 1985
COCOON: THE RETURN, 1988
COGNASSE, 1932
COHENS AND KELLYS IN AFRICA, THE, 1930
COHENS AND KELLYS IN ATLANTIC CITY, THE,
    1929
COHENS AND KELLYS IN HOLLYWOOD, THE, 1932
COHENS AND KELLYS IN SCOTLAND, THE, 1930
COHENS AND KELLYS IN TROUBLE, THE, 1933
COLD FEET, 1984
COLD TURKEY, 1971
COLLEGE LOVERS, 1930
COLONEL EFFINGHAM'S RAID, 1945
COME ACROSS, 1929
COME BACK CHARLESTON BLUE, 1972
COME BACK PETER, 1952
COME BLOW YOUR HORN, 1963
COME CLOSER, FOLKS, 1936
COME FLY WITH ME, 1963
COME LIVE WITH ME, 1941
COME ON GEORGE, 1939
COME ON, MARINES, 1934
COME OUT FIGHTING, 1945
COME SEPTEMBER, 1961
COME TO THE STABLE, 1949
COMEBACK TRAIL, THE, 1982
COMEDY!, 1987
COMEDY OF HORRORS, THE, 1964

COMFORT AND JOY, 1984
COMIC MAGAZINE, 1986
COMIN' ROUND THE MOUNTAIN, 1951
COMING OF AGE, 1938
COMING-OUT PARTY, A, 1962
COMING TO AMERICA, 1988
COMING UP ROSES, 1986
COMPROMISING POSITIONS, 1985
COMPULSORY HUSBAND, THE, 1930
COMPULSORY WIFE, THE, 1937
COMPUTER FREE-FOR-ALL, 1969
COMPUTER WORE TENNIS SHOES, THE, 1970
COMRADE X, 1940
CON MEN, THE, 1973
CONDORMAN, 1981
CONFESSIONS FROM A HOLIDAY CAMP, 1977
CONFESSIONS OF A CO-ED, 1931
CONFESSIONS OF A NEWLYWED, 1941
CONFESSIONS OF A POP PERFORMER, 1975
CONFESSIONS OF A ROGUE, 1948
CONFESSIONS OF A WINDOW CLEANER, 1974
CONFIDENTIALLY CONNIE, 1953
CONGO MAISIE, 1940
CONJUGAL BED, THE, 1963
CONNECTICUT YANKEE, A, 1931
CONSOLATION MARRIAGE, 1931
CONSTANT HUSBAND, THE, 1955
CONSUMING PASSIONS, 1988
CONTINENTAL DIVIDE, 1981
CONTRACT, THE, 1982
CONVENTION CITY, 1933
CONVICT 99, 1938
CONVOY, 1978
COOLEY HIGH, 1975
CORKY OF GASOLINE ALLEY, 1951
CORPSE CAME C.O.D., THE, 1947
CORPSE GRINDERS, THE, 1972
CORVETTE SUMMER, 1978
COTTON COMES TO HARLEM, 1970
COTTON QUEEN, 1937
COUCH TRIP, THE, 1988
COUNSEL'S OPINION, 1933
COUNT OF THE MONK'S BRIDGE, THE, 1934
COUNT YOUR BLESSINGS, 1959
COUNTERFEIT CONSTABLE, THE, 1966
COUNTESS FROM HONG KONG, A, 1967
COUNTESS OF MONTE CRISTO, THE, 1934
COUNTRY FAIR, 1941
COUNTRY GENTLEMEN, 1937
COUNTY CHAIRMAN, THE, 1935
COURT JESTER, THE, 1956
COURT OF THE PHARAOH, THE, 1985
COURTSHIP OF ANDY HARDY, THE, 1942
COURTSHIP OF EDDY'S FATHER, THE, 1963
COUSIN, COUSINE, 1976
COVERED TRAILER, THE, 1939
COW AND I, THE, 1961
COWBOY AND THE LADY, THE, 1938
COWBOY QUARTERBACK, 1939
CRACKED NUTS, 1931
CRACKED NUTS, 1941
CRACKERS, 1984
CRACKING UP, 1977
CRACKSMAN, THE, 1963
CRASHING HOLLYWOOD, 1937
CRASHING LAS VEGAS, 1956
CRAZY BOYS, 1987
CRAZY DESIRE, 1964
CRAZY FAMILY, THE, 1986
CRAZY FOR LOVE, 1960
CRAZY KNIGHTS, 1944
CRAZY OVER HORSES, 1951
CRAZY PARADISE, 1965
CRAZY PEOPLE, 1934
CRAZY THAT WAY, 1930
CRAZY WORLD OF JULIUS VROODER, THE, 1974
CREATURE FROM THE HAUNTED SEA, 1961
CREATURE WASN'T NICE, THE, 1981
CRIME AGAINST JOE, 1956
CRIME AND PASSION, 1976
CRIME NOBODY SAW, THE, 1937
CRIME OF MONSIEUR LANGE, THE, 1936
CRIME SCHOOL, 1938
CRIMES OF THE HEART, 1986
CRIMEWAVE, 1985

CRIMINAL LIFE OF ARCHIBALDO DE LA CRUZ,
  THE, 1962
CRIMSON PIRATE, THE, 1952
CRITICAL CONDITION, 1987
CRITIC'S CHOICE, 1963
CRITTERS, 1986
"CROCODILE" DUNDEE, 1986
"CROCODILE" DUNDEE II, 1988
CROOKED CIRCLE, 1932
CROOKS ANONYMOUS, 1963
CROOKS IN CLOISTERS, 1964
CROOKS TOUR, 1940
CROSS MY HEART, 1987
CROSSING DELANCEY, 1988
CROWNING TOUCH, THE, 1959
CRY DR. CHICAGO, 1971
CRY FOR HAPPY, 1961
CRYSTAL BALL, THE, 1943
CUCKOO IN THE NEST, THE, 1933
CUCKOO PATROL, 1965
CUCKOOS, THE, 1930
CUP OF KINDNESS, A, 1934
CUP-TIE HONEYMOON, 1948
CURSE OF THE PINK PANTHER, 1983
CURTAIN CALL AT CACTUS CREEK, 1950
CURTAIN UP, 1952
CYCLE, THE, 1979
CYNTHIA, 1947
CZAR WANTS TO SLEEP, 1934
D.C. CAB, 1983
DAD AND DAVE COME TO TOWN, 1938
DADDY LONG LEGS, 1931
DAD'S ARMY, 1971
DAISIES, 1967
DAMES AHOY, 1930
DANCE WITH ME, HENRY, 1956
DANCE, CHARLIE, DANCE, 1937
DANCING DYNAMITE, 1931
DANCING IN MANHATTAN, 1945
DANCING MASTERS, THE, 1943
DANDY DICK, 1935
DANDY, THE ALL AMERICAN GIRL, 1976
DANGER LIGHTS, 1930
DANGER—LOVE AT WORK, 1937
DANGER! WOMEN AT WORK, 1943
DANGEROUS AFFAIR, A, 1931
DANGEROUS BLONDES, 1943
DANGEROUS CURVES, 1929
DANGEROUS DAVIES—THE LAST DETECTIVE, 1981
DANGEROUS GAME, A, 1941
DANGEROUS KISS, THE, 1961
DANGEROUS NUMBER, 1937
DARING YOUNG MAN, THE, 1942
DARK EYES, 1987
DARK HORSE, THE, 1932
DARKTOWN STRUTTERS, 1975
DARLING, HOW COULD YOU!, 1951
DARTS ARE TRUMPS, 1938
DATE WITH A DREAM, A, 1948
DATE WITH AN ANGEL, 1987
DAUGHTERS OF DESTINY, 1954
DAVID HARUM, 1934
DAVY, 1958
DAY AFTER THE DIVORCE, THE, 1940
DAY AT THE RACES, A, 1937
DAY IN COURT, A, 1965
DAY IN THE DEATH OF JOE EGG, A, 1972
DAY THE BOOKIES WEPT, THE, 1939
DAY THE HOTLINE GOT HOT, THE, 1968
DAY-TIME WIFE, 1939
DAYDREAMER, THE, 1975
DE L'AMOUR, 1968
DEAD END KIDS, 1986
DEAD END KIDS ON DRESS PARADE, 1939
DEAD HEAT, 1988
DEAD HEAT ON A MERRY-GO-ROUND, 1966
DEAD MEN DON'T WEAR PLAID, 1982
DEAD RUN, 1961
DEADHEAD MILES, 1982
DEADLY DECOYS, THE, 1962
DEAL OF THE CENTURY, 1983
DEALING: OR THE BERKELEY TO BOSTON
  FORTY-BRICK LOST-BAG BLUES, 1971
DEAR BRAT, 1951
DEAR BRIGETTE, 1965
DEAR DETECTIVE, 1978

DEAR HEART, 1964
DEAR MR. PROHACK, 1949
DEAR RUTH, 1947
DEAR WIFE, 1949
DEATH OF A BUREAUCRAT, 1979
DEATH OF TARZAN, THE, 1968
DECLINE AND FALL. . .OF A BIRD WATCHER, 1969
DELICATE DELINQUENT, THE, 1957
DELIVERY BOYS, 1984
DELUSIONS OF GRANDEUR, 1971
DEMOBBED, 1944
DENTIST IN THE CHAIR, 1960
DESERT MICE, 1960
DESIGN FOR LIVING, 1933
DESIGN FOR LOVING, 1962
DESIGN FOR SCANDAL, 1941
DESIGNING WOMAN, 1957
DESK SET, 1957
DESPERATE ADVENTURE, A, 1938
DESPERATE MOVES, 1986
DESPERATELY SEEKING SUSAN, 1985
DETECTIVE, THE, 1954
DETECTIVE KITTY O'DAY, 1944
DETECTIVE SCHOOL DROPOUTS, 1986
DEVIL, THE, 1963
DEVIL AND MAX DEVLIN, THE, 1981
DEVIL AND MISS JONES, THE, 1941
DEVIL AND THE TEN COMMANDMENTS, THE, 1962
DEVIL BY THE TAIL, THE, 1969
DEVIL IN LOVE, THE, 1968
DEVIL IS A SISSY, THE, 1936
DEVIL TO PAY, THE, 1930
DEVIL'S BROTHER, THE, 1933
DEVIL'S EYE, THE, 1960
DEVIL'S PIPELINE, THE, 1940
DIAMONDS FOR BREAKFAST, 1968
DIARY OF A BACHELOR, 1964
DIARY OF A MAD HOUSEWIFE, 1970
DID YOU HEAR THE ONE ABOUT THE TRAVELING
  SALESLADY?, 1968
DIE GANS VON SEDAN, 1962
DIE LAUGHING, 1980
DIG THAT URANIUM, 1956
DIM SUM: A LITTLE BIT OF HEART, 1985
DIMBOOLA, 1979
DIME WITH A HALO, 1963
DINER, 1982
DINNER AT EIGHT, 1933
DIPLOMANIACS, 1933
DIRT BIKE KID, THE, 1986
DIRTY DINGUS MAGEE, 1970
DIRTY KNIGHT'S WORK, 1976
DIRTY LAUNDRY, 1987
DIRTY ROTTEN SCOUNDRELS, 1988
DIRTY TRICKS, 1981
DIRTY WORK, 1934
**DISCREET CHARM OF THE BOURGEOISIE, THE,
  1972**
DISHONOR BRIGHT, 1936
DISORDERLIES, 1987
DISORDERLY ORDERLY, THE, 1964
DIVINE MR. J., THE, 1974
DIVORCE AMERICAN STYLE, 1967
DIVORCE OF LADY X, THE, 1938
DIVORCE, ITALIAN STYLE, 1962
DIXIE DUGAN, 1943
DIXIELAND DAIMYO, 1988
DO NOT DISTURB, 1965
DOCKS OF NEW YORK, 1945
DOCTEUR POPAUL, 1972
DOCTOR AT LARGE, 1957
DOCTOR AT SEA, 1955
DOCTOR BEWARE, 1951
DOCTOR DETROIT, 1983
DR. GOLDFOOT AND THE BIKINI MACHINE, 1965
  88m AI c
DR. GOLDFOOT AND THE GIRL BOMBS, 1966
DR. HECKYL AND MR. HYPE, 1980
DOCTOR IN DISTRESS, 1963
DOCTOR IN LOVE, 1960
DOCTOR IN THE HOUSE, 1954
DOCTOR IN TROUBLE, 1970
DR. JOSSER KC, 1931
DR. KNOCK, 1936
**DR. OTTO AND THE RIDDLE OF THE GLOOM
  BEAM, 1986**

BOLD: Films on Videocassette

DR. STRANGELOVE: OR HOW I LEARNED TO STOP
  WORRYING AND LOVE THE BOMB, 1964
DOCTOR TAKES A WIFE, 1940
DOCTOR, YOU'VE GOT TO BE KIDDING, 1967
DOCTOR'S DILEMMA, THE, 1958
DOCTOR'S ORDERS, 1934
DOIN' TIME, 1985
DOING TIME, 1979
DOLL THAT TOOK THE TOWN, THE, 1965
DOLLAR, 1938
$ (DOLLARS), 1971
DOMINANT SEX, THE, 1937
DON CHICAGO, 1945
DON JUAN QUILLIGAN, 1945
DONA FLOR AND HER TWO HUSBANDS, 1977
DONA HERLINDA AND HER SON, 1986
DONATELLA, 1956
DONOVAN AFFAIR, THE, 1929
DONOVAN'S REEF, 1963
DON'S PARTY, 1976
DON'T BE A DUMMY, 1932
DON'T BET ON BLONDES, 1935
DON'T BET ON LOVE, 1933
DON'T BET ON WOMEN, 1931
DON'T BLAME THE STORK, 1954
DON'T CALL ME A CON MAN, 1966
DON'T DRINK THE WATER, 1969
DON'T GET ME WRONG, 1937
DON'T GET PERSONAL, 1936
DON'T GET PERSONAL, 1941
DON'T GIVE UP THE SHIP, 1959
DON'T GO NEAR THE WATER, 1957
DON'T JUST LIE THERE, SAY SOMETHING!, 1973
DON'T JUST STAND THERE, 1968
DON'T LOOK NOW, 1969
DON'T LOSE YOUR HEAD, 1967
DON'T MAKE WAVES, 1967
DON'T RAISE THE BRIDGE, LOWER THE RIVER,
  1968
DON'T RUSH ME, 1936
DON'T SAY DIE, 1950
DON'T TAKE IT TO HEART, 1944
DON'T TELL THE WIFE, 1937
DON'T TRUST YOUR HUSBAND, 1948
DON'T WORRY, WE'LL THINK OF A TITLE, 1966
DOOR TO DOOR, 1984
DOS COSMONAUTAS A LA FUERZA, 1967
DOUBLE-BARRELLED DETECTIVE STORY, THE, 1965
DOUBLE BED, THE, 1965
DOUBLE BUNK, 1961
DOUBLE DANGER, 1938
DOUBLE DATE, 1941
DOUBLE DYNAMITE, 1951
DOUBLE EVENT, THE, 1934
DOUBLE HARNESS, 1933
DOUBLE TROUBLE, 1941
DOUBLE WEDDING, 1937
DOUBTING THOMAS, 1935
DOUGH BOYS, 1930
DOUGHGIRLS, THE, 1944
DOUGHNUTS AND SOCIETY, 1936
DOWN AMONG THE Z MEN, 1952
DOWN AND OUT IN BEVERLY HILLS, 1986
DOWN BY LAW, 1986
DOWN IN ARKANSAW, 1938
DOWN IN SAN DIEGO, 1941
DOWN MEMORY LANE, 1949
DOWN MISSOURI WAY, 1946
DOWN ON THE FARM, 1938
DOWN TO EARTH, 1932
DRACULA AND SON, 1976
DRAG, 1929
DRAGNET, 1987
DRAGONFLY, THE, 1955
DRAUGHTSMAN'S CONTRACT, THE, 1983
DREAM GIRL, 1947
DREAM WIFE, 1953
DREAMBOAT, 1952
DREAMING, 1944
DREAMING OUT LOUD, 1940
DREI GEGEN DREI, 1985
DRIVE-IN, 1976
DROP DEAD, MY LOVE, 1968
DRY ROT, 1956
DUBEAT-E-O, 1984
DUCHESS AND THE DIRTWATER FOX, THE, 1976

DUCK IN ORANGE SAUCE, 1976
DUCK RINGS AT HALF PAST SEVEN, THE, 1969
DUCK SOUP, 1933
DUDE GOES WEST, THE, 1948
DUDE RANCH, 1931
DUDE WRANGLER, THE, 1930
DUFFY, 1968
DULCY, 1940
DUMBBELLS IN ERMINE, 1930
DUTCH TREAT, 1987
DYNAMITE JACK, 1961
EARL OF CHICAGO, THE, 1940
EARL OF PUDDLESTONE, 1940
EARLY BIRD, THE, 1936
EARLY BIRD, THE, 1965
EARLY TO BED, 1936
EARTHWORM TRACTORS, 1936
EAST LYNNE ON THE WESTERN FRONT, 1931
EASY LIVING, 1937
EASY MILLIONS, 1933
EASY MONEY, 1934
EASY MONEY, 1983
EASY RICHES, 1938
EASY TO LOVE, 1934
EASY TO TAKE, 1936
EAT AND RUN, 1986
EATING RAOUL, 1982
ECHO PARK, 1986
EDUCATED EVANS, 1936
EDUCATING FATHER, 1936
EGG AND I, THE, 1947
EIGHT ON THE LAM, 1967
18 AGAIN!, 1988
EIGHTEEN IN THE SUN, 1964
ELECTRIC HORSEMAN, THE, 1979
ELIZA COMES TO STAY, 1936
ELIZA FRASER, 1976
ELLERY QUEEN AND THE MURDER RING, 1941
ELLERY QUEEN AND THE PERFECT CRIME, 1941
ELLERY QUEEN, MASTER DETECTIVE, 1940
ELLERY QUEEN'S PENTHOUSE MYSTERY, 1941
ELLIE, 1984
ELMER AND ELSIE, 1934
ELMER THE GREAT, 1933
ELOPEMENT, 1951
ELVIRA: MISTRESS OF THE DARK, 1988
EMBARRASSING MOMENTS, 1930
EMBARRASSING MOMENTS, 1934
ENCHANTED APRIL, 1935
ENCORE, 1951
END, THE, 1978
END OF A PRIEST, 1970
END OF MRS. CHENEY, 1963
END OF THE ROAD, THE, 1936
ENEMY OF THE POLICE, 1933
ENGAGEMENT ITALIANO, 1966
ENSIGN PULVER, 1964
ENTER LAUGHING, 1967
ENTER MADAME, 1935
ENTERTAINING MR. SLOANE, 1970
EPISODE, 1937
ERIC SOYA'S "17", 1967
ERNEST GOES TO CAMP, 1987
ERNEST SAVES CHRISTMAS, 1988
ERRAND BOY, THE, 1961
ESCAPADE, 1935
ESCAPADE, 1955
ESCAPE TO PARADISE, 1939
ETERNAL FEMININE, THE, 1931
EVE WANTS TO SLEEP, 1961
EVENINGS FOR SALE, 1932
EVER SINCE EVE, 1934
EVER SINCE EVE, 1937
EVERY BASTARD A KING, 1968
EVERY DAY IS A HOLIDAY, 1966
EVERY DAY'S A HOLIDAY, 1938
EVERY GIRL SHOULD BE MARRIED, 1948
EVERY LITTLE CROOK AND NANNY, 1972
EVERY NIGHT AT EIGHT, 1935
EVERY SATURDAY NIGHT, 1936
EVERY WHICH WAY BUT LOOSE, 1978
EVERYBODY DOES IT, 1949
EVERYBODY GO HOME!, 1962
EVERYBODY'S BABY, 1939
EVERYBODY'S DOING IT, 1938
EVERYBODY'S HOBBY, 1939

EVERYBODY'S OLD MAN, 1936
EVERYTHING BUT THE TRUTH, 1956
EVERYTHING HAPPENS TO ME, 1938
EVERYTHING OKAY, 1936
EVERYTHING YOU ALWAYS WANTED TO KNOW
  ABOUT SEX BUT WERE AFRAID TO ASK, 1972
EVERYTHING'S DUCKY, 1961
EVERYTHING'S ROSIE, 1931
EX-BAD BOY, 1931
EX-CHAMP, 1939
EX-MRS. BRADFORD, THE, 1936
EXCESS BAGGAGE, 1933
EXCUSE MY DUST, 1951
EXPENSIVE HUSBANDS, 1937
EXPERT, THE, 1932
EXTERMINATING ANGEL, THE, 1967
EXTORTION, 1938
EXTRAORDINARY SEAMAN, THE, 1969
EYE OF THE NEEDLE, THE, 1965
F MAN, 1936
FABULOUS SENORITA, THE, 1952
FABULOUS SUZANNE, THE, 1946
FACING THE MUSIC, 1941
FACTS OF LIFE, THE, 1960
FACTS OF LOVE, 1949
FAIR EXCHANGE, 1936
FAITHFUL IN MY FASHION, 1946
FAKE'S PROGRESS, 1950
FALL GUY, 1985
FALL GUY, THE, 1930
FALL OF EVE, THE, 1929
FALLING FOR YOU, 1933
FALLING IN LOVE AGAIN, 1980
FALSE PRETENSES, 1935
FAME, 1936
FAMILY, THE, 1987
FAMILY AFFAIR, 1954
FAMILY AFFAIR, A, 1937
FAMILY BUSINESS, 1987
FAMILY GAME, THE, 1984
FAMILY HONEYMOON, 1948
FAMILY JEWELS, THE, 1965
FAMILY NEXT DOOR, THE, 1939
FAMILY PLOT, 1976
FAMILY WAY, THE, 1966
FANCY PANTS, 1950
FANDANGO, 1985
FANFAN THE TULIP, 1952
FANNY FOLEY HERSELF, 1931
FAN'S NOTES, A, 1972
FANTASTIC COMEDY, A, 1975
FANTASTIC THREE, THE, 1967
FAR NORTH, 1988
FARMER IN THE DELL, THE, 1936
FARMER'S DAUGHTER, THE, 1940
FARMER'S DAUGHTER, THE, 1947
FARMER'S OTHER DAUGHTER, THE, 1965
FARMER'S WIFE, THE, 1941
FASCIST, THE, 1965
FASHION MODEL, 1945
FASHIONS IN LOVE, 1929
FAST AND FURIOUS, 1939
FAST AND LOOSE, 1930
FAST AND LOOSE, 1939
FAST AND LOOSE, 1954
FAST AND SEXY, 1960
FAST BREAK, 1979
FAST COMPANIONS, 1932
FAST COMPANY, 1929
FAST COMPANY, 1938
FAST COMPANY, 1953
FAST LADY, THE, 1963
FAST TIMES AT RIDGEMONT HIGH, 1982
FASTEST GUITAR ALIVE, THE, 1967
FAT ANGELS, 1980
FAT GUY GOES NUTZOID!!, 1986
FAT SPY, 1966
FATHER BROWN, DETECTIVE, 1935
FATHER CAME TOO, 1964
FATHER GOOSE, 1964
FATHER MAKES GOOD, 1950
FATHER OF THE BRIDE, 1950
FATHER STEPS OUT, 1937
FATHER TAKES A WIFE, 1941
FATHER TAKES THE AIR, 1951
FATHER WAS A FULLBACK, 1949

BOLD: Films on Videocassette

GENEVIEVE, 1953
GENIUS AT WORK, 1946
GENTLE TERROR, THE, 1962
GENTLEMAN AT HEART, A, 1942
GENTLEMAN MISBEHAVES, THE, 1946
GENTLEMAN'S AGREEMENT, 1935
GENTLEMAN'S GENTLEMAN, A, 1939
GENTLEMEN MARRY BRUNETTES, 1955
GEORGE, 1973
GEORGE AND MARGARET, 1940
GEORGE AND MILDRED, 1980
GEORGE IN CIVVY STREET, 1946
GEORGE WASHINGTON SLEPT HERE, 1942
GEORGY GIRL, 1966
GERT AND DAISY CLEAN UP, 1942
GERT AND DAISY'S WEEKEND, 1941
GET CHARLIE TULLY, 1976
GET CRACKING, 1943
GET CRAZY, 1983
GET GOING, 1943
GET OFF MY FOOT, 1935
GET ON WITH IT, 1963
GET OUT YOUR HANDKERCHIEFS, 1978
GET YOUR MAN, 1934
GET YOURSELF A COLLEGE GIRL, 1964
GETTING EVEN, 1981
GETTING GERTIE'S GARTER, 1945
GHOST AND MR. CHICKEN, THE, 1966
GHOST AND THE GUEST, 1943
GHOST BREAKERS, THE, 1940
GHOST CATCHERS, 1944
GHOST CHASERS, 1951
GHOST FEVER, 1987
GHOST GOES WEST, THE, 1936
GHOST GOES WILD, THE, 1947
GHOST IN THE INVISIBLE BIKINI, 1966
GHOST OF ST. MICHAEL'S, THE, 1941
GHOST TALKS, THE, 1929
GHOST THAT WALKS ALONE, THE, 1944
GHOST TRAIN, THE, 1933
GHOST TRAIN, THE, 1941
GHOSTBUSTERS, 1984
GHOSTS, ITALIAN STYLE, 1969
GHOSTS OF BERKELEY SQUARE, 1947
GHOSTS ON THE LOOSE, 1943
G.I. HONEYMOON, 1945
GIDGET, 1959
GIDGET GOES HAWAIIAN, 1961
GIDGET GOES TO ROME, 1963
GIFT, THE, 1983
GIG, THE, 1985
GIGOT, 1962
GILDED LILY, THE, 1935
GILDERSLEEVE ON BROADWAY, 1943
GILDERSLEEVE'S BAD DAY, 1943
GILDERSLEEVE'S GHOST, 1944
GIMME AN 'F', 1984
GINGER & FRED, 1986
GIRDLE OF GOLD, 1952
GIRL, A GUY AND A GOB, A, 1941
GIRL CAN'T HELP IT, THE, 1956
GIRL CRAZY, 1932
GIRL CRAZY, 1943
GIRL FEVER, 1961
GIRL FROM AVENUE A, 1940
GIRL FROM JONES BEACH, THE, 1949
GIRL FROM MAXIM'S THE, 1936
GIRL FROM MEXICO, THE, 1939
GIRL FROM MISSOURI, THE, 1934
GIRL FROM PETROVKA, THE, 1974
GIRL FROM VALLADOLIO, 1958
GIRL HABIT, 1931
GIRL HE LEFT BEHIND, THE, 1956
GIRL IN A MILLION, A, 1946
GIRL IN EVERY PORT, A, 1952
GIRL IN POSSESSION, 1934
GIRL IN THE CASE, 1944
GIRL IN THE CROWD, THE, 1934
GIRL IN THE PICTURE, THE, 1985
GIRL MOST LIKELY, THE, 1957
GIRL NEXT DOOR, THE, 1953
GIRL O' MY DREAMS, 1935
GIRL OF THE OZARKS, 1936
GIRL ON THE BOAT, THE, 1962
GIRL ON THE FRONT PAGE, THE, 1936
GIRL RUSH, 1944

GIRL RUSH, THE, 1955
GIRL SAID NO, THE, 1930
GIRL THIEF, THE, 1938
GIRL TROUBLE, 1942
GIRL WHO COULDN'T SAY NO, THE, 1969
GIRL WHO FORGOT, THE, 1939
GIRL WITH A PISTOL, THE, 1968
GIRL WITH IDEAS, A, 1937
GIRL WITH THREE CAMELS, THE, 1968
GIRL WITHOUT A ROOM, 1933
GIRLFRIENDS, 1978
GIRLS ABOUT TOWN, 1931
GIRLS AT SEA, 1958
GIRLS DEMAND EXCITEMENT, 1931
GIRLS OF PLEASURE ISLAND, THE, 1953
GIRLS PLEASE!, 1934
GIRLS' SCHOOL, 1938
GIRLS WILL BE BOYS, 1934
GIVE AND TAKE, 1929
GIVE HER THE MOON, 1970
GIVE ME A SAILOR, 1938
GIVE US THE MOON, 1944
GIVE US WINGS, 1940
GLAD RAG DOLL, THE, 1929
GLADIATOR, THE, 1938
GLAMOUR, 1931
GLAMOUR BOY, 1941
GLAMOUR GIRL, 1938
GLASS BOTTOM BOAT, THE, 1966
GLOBAL AFFAIR, A, 1964
GO CHASE YOURSELF, 1938
GO INTO YOUR DANCE, 1935
GO TO BLAZES, 1962
GO WEST, 1940
GO WEST, YOUNG LADY, 1941
GO WEST, YOUNG MAN, 1936
GOBS AND GALS, 1952
GOD'S COUNTRY, 1946
GOD'S GIFT TO WOMEN, 1931
GODS MUST BE CRAZY, THE, 1984
GOIN' TO TOWN, 1935
GOIN' TO TOWN, 1944
GOING APE!, 1981
GOING BERSERK, 1983
GOING HIGHBROW, 1935
GOING IN STYLE, 1979
GOING PLACES, 1939
GOING PLACES, 1974
GOING STEADY, 1958
GOING STRAIGHT, 1933
GOING WILD, 1931
GOLD DUST GERTIE, 1931
GOLD EXPRESS, THE, 1955
GOLD GUITAR, THE, 1966
GOLD OF NAPLES, 1957
GOLD RAIDERS, THE, 1952
GOLD RUSH MAISIE, 1940
GOLDBERGS, THE, 1950
GOLDEN ARROW, THE, 1936
GOLDEN CHILD, THE, 1986
GOLDEN FLEECING, THE, 1940
GOLDEN HEAD, THE, 1965
GOLDEN MOUNTAINS, 1958
GOLDEN RABBIT, THE, 1962
GOLDIE GETS ALONG, 1933
GOLDWYN FOLLIES, THE, 1938
GONE ARE THE DAYS, 1963
GONE TO THE DOGS, 1939
GONG SHOW MOVIE, THE, 1980
GOOD COMPANIONS, 1933
GOOD COMPANIONS, THE, 1957
GOOD FAIRY, THE, 1935
GOOD FELLOWS, THE, 1943
GOOD GIRLS GO TO PARIS, 1939
GOOD GUYS AND THE BAD GUYS, THE, 1969
GOOD HUMOR MAN, THE, 1950
GOOD MORNING, JUDGE, 1943
GOOD MORNING, VIETNAM, 1987
GOOD NEIGHBOR SAM, 1964
GOOD NEWS, 1930
GOOD NEWS, 1947
GOOD OLD DAYS, THE, 1939
GOOD SAM, 1948
GOOD SOLDIER SCHWEIK, THE, 1963
GOOD SPORT, 1931
GOODBYE AGAIN, 1933

GOODBYE BROADWAY, 1938
GOODBYE CHARLIE, 1964
GOODBYE COLUMBUS, 1969
GOODBYE FRANKLIN HIGH, 1978
GOODBYE GIRL, THE, 1977
GOODBYE LOVE, 1934
GOODBYE NEW YORK, 1985
GOODBYE PEOPLE, THE, 1984
GOODNIGHT, LADIES AND GENTLEMEN, 1977
GOOFBALLS, 1987
GOOSE AND THE GANDER, THE, 1935
GOOSE STEPS OUT, THE, 1942
GORILLA, THE, 1931
GORILLA, THE, 1939
GORP, 1980
GOSPEL ACCORDING TO VIC, THE, 1986
GOVERNMENT GIRL, 1943
GRACIE ALLEN MURDER CASE, 1939
GRADUATE, THE, 1967
GRAND CANYON, 1949
GRAND FINALE, 1936
GRAND OLE OPRY, 1940
GRAND SLAM, 1933
GRAND THEFT AUTO, 1977
GRANDAD RUDD, 1935
GRANDPA GOES TO TOWN, 1940
GRASS IS GREENER, THE, 1960
GREASE, 1978
GREASE 2, 1982
GREAT AMERICAN PASTIME, THE, 1956
GREAT BANK HOAX, THE, 1977
GREAT BANK ROBBERY, THE, 1969
GREAT BRAIN, THE, 1978
GREAT CATHERINE, 1968
GREAT DIAMOND ROBBERY, 1953
GREAT DICTATOR, THE, 1940
GREAT GARRICK, THE, 1937
GREAT GILDERSLEEVE, THE, 1942
GREAT GUNS, 1941
GREAT LOVER, THE, 1949
GREAT McGINTY, THE, 1940
GREAT MCGONAGALL, THE, 1975
GREAT MR. NOBODY, THE, 1941
GREAT OUTDOORS, THE, 1988
GREAT PROFILE, THE, 1940
GREAT RACE, THE, 1965
GREAT RUPERT, THE, 1950
GREAT ST. TRINIAN'S TRAIN ROBBERY, THE, 1966
GREAT SCOUT AND CATHOUSE THURSDAY, THE, 1976
GREAT SPY CHASE, THE, 1966
GREAT STUFF, 1933
GREAT WALL, A, 1986
GREAT WAR, THE, 1961
GREEKS HAD A WORD FOR THEM, 1932
GREEN FIELDS, 1937
GREEN FOR DANGER, 1946
GREEN GROW THE RUSHES, 1951
GREEN MAN, THE, 1957
GREEN MARE, THE, 1961
GREGORY'S GIRL, 1982
GRISSOM GANG, THE, 1971
GROOM WORE SPURS, THE, 1951
GROOVE TUBE, THE, 1974
GROUNDS FOR MARRIAGE, 1950
GROWN-UP CHILDREN, 1963
GUARDSMAN, THE, 1931
GUESS WHAT WE LEARNED IN SCHOOL TODAY?, 1970
GUEST OF HONOR, 1934
GUEST WIFE, 1945
GUESTS ARE COMING, 1965
GUIDE FOR THE MARRIED MAN, A, 1967
GUMBALL RALLY, THE, 1976
GUMSHOE, 1972
GUNG HO, 1986
GUS, 1976
HAIL, 1973
HAIL AND FAREWELL, 1936
HAIL THE CONQUERING HERO, 1944
HAIR OF THE DOG, 1962
HAIRSPRAY, 1988
HALF A HERO, 1953
HALF A SINNER, 1934
HALF ANGEL, 1936
HALF ANGEL, 1951

HALF-MARRIAGE, 1929
HALF-NAKED TRUTH, THE, 1932
HALF PINT, THE, 1960
HALF SHOT AT SUNRISE, 1930
HALLELUJAH, I'M A BUM, 1933
HALLELUJAH THE HILLS, 1963
HALLELUJAH TRAIL, THE, 1965
HAMBONE AND HILLIE, 1984
HAMBURGER, 1986
HAMMERSMITH IS OUT, 1972
HANDLE WITH CARE, 1935
HANDS ACROSS THE TABLE, 1935
HANDY ANDY, 1934
HANKY-PANKY, 1982
HANNAH AND HER SISTERS, 1986
HANNIBAL BROOKS, 1969
HAPPENING, THE, 1967
HAPPIDROME, 1943
HAPPIEST DAYS OF YOUR LIFE, 1950
HAPPINESS AHEAD, 1934
HAPPINESS C.O.D., 1935
HAPPY, 1934
HAPPY ANNIVERSARY, 1959
HAPPY BIRTHDAY, WANDA JUNE, 1971
HAPPY END, 1968
HAPPY FAMILY, THE, 1936
HAPPY GO LUCKY, 1943
HAPPY HOOKER GOES TO HOLLYWOOD, THE, 1980
HAPPY HOOKER GOES TO WASHINGTON, THE, 1977
HAPPY HOOKER, THE, 1975
HAPPY HOUR, 1987
HAPPY IS THE BRIDE, 1958
HAPPY NEW YEAR, 1987
HAPPY ROAD, THE, 1957
HAPPY THIEVES, THE, 1962
HAPPY TIME, THE, 1952
HAPPY YEARS, THE, 1950
HARASSED HERO, THE, 1954
HARD BOILED MAHONEY, 1947
HARD TO GET, 1929
HARD TO GET, 1938
HARD TO HANDLE, 1933
HARDBODIES, 1984
HARDBODIES 2, 1986
HARDLY WORKING, 1981
HARDYS RIDE HIGH, THE, 1939
HAREM BUNCH; OR WAR AND PIECE, THE, 1969
HAREM GIRL, 1952
HARMONY AT HOME, 1930
HARMONY ROW, 1933
HAROLD AND MAUDE, 1971
HAROLD TEEN, 1934
HARPER VALLEY, P.T.A., 1978
HARRY AND THE HENDERSONS, 1987
HARRY AND WALTER GO TO NEW YORK, 1976
HARRY'S WAR, 1981
HARVARD, HERE I COME, 1942
HARVEY, 1950
HAS ANYBODY SEEN MY GAL?, 1952
HAT CHECK GIRL, 1932
HAUNTED HONEYMOON, 1986
HAUNTED HOUSE, THE, 1928
HAVANA ROSE, 1951
HAVANA WIDOWS, 1933
HAVE ROCKET, WILL TRAVEL, 1959
HAVING WONDERFUL CRIME, 1945
HAWKS, 1988
HAWKS AND THE SPARROWS, THE, 1967
HAWLEY'S OF HIGH STREET, 1933
HAWMPS!, 1976
HAZARD, 1948
HE COULDN'T SAY NO, 1938
HE HIRED THE BOSS, 1943
HE LAUGHED LAST, 1956
HE LEARNED ABOUT WOMEN, 1933
HE MARRIED HIS WIFE, 1940
HE SNOOPS TO CONQUER, 1944
HE STAYED FOR BREAKFAST, 1940
HEAD, 1968
HEAD OF THE FAMILY, 1967
HEAD OFFICE, 1986
HEADING FOR HEAVEN, 1947
HEADLEYS AT HOME, THE, 1939
HEALTH, 1980
HEAR ME GOOD, 1957

HEART OF NEW YORK, 1932
HEARTACHES, 1981
HEARTBEAT, 1946
HEARTBEEPS, 1981
HEARTBREAK KID, THE, 1972
HEARTBURN, 1986
HEAVEN CAN WAIT, 1943
HEAVEN CAN WAIT, 1978
HEAVEN HELP US, 1985
HEAVENLY BODY, THE, 1943
HEAVENLY DAYS, 1944
HEAVENLY KID, THE, 1985
HEAVENS ABOVE!, 1963
HELL IS SOLD OUT, 1951
HELLO AGAIN, 1987
HELLO ANNAPOLIS, 1942
HELLO DOWN THERE, 1969
HELLO, ELEPHANT, 1954
HELLO—GOODBYE, 1970
HELLO SUCKER, 1941
HELLO SWEETHEART, 1935
HELLZAPOPPIN', 1941
HELP I'M INVISIBLE, 1952
HELP YOURSELF, 1932
HELTER SKELTER, 1949
HENRY ALDRICH, BOY SCOUT, 1944
HENRY ALDRICH, EDITOR, 1942
HENRY ALDRICH FOR PRESIDENT, 1941
HENRY ALDRICH GETS GLAMOUR, 1942
HENRY ALDRICH HAUNTS A HOUSE, 1943
HENRY ALDRICH PLAYS CUPID, 1944
HENRY ALDRICH SWINGS IT, 1943
HENRY ALDRICH'S LITTLE SECRET, 1944
HENRY AND DIZZY, 1942
HENRY GOES ARIZONA, 1939
HENRY STEPS OUT, 1940
HENRY, THE RAINMAKER, 1949
HER ADVENTUROUS NIGHT, 1946
HER CARDBOARD LOVER, 1942
HER FIRST AFFAIR, 1947
HER FIRST MATE, 1933
HER FIRST ROMANCE, 1940
HER HIGHNESS AND THE BELLBOY, 1945
HER HUSBAND'S AFFAIRS, 1947
HER IMAGINARY LOVER, 1933
HER MAN GILBEY, 1949
HER MASTER'S VOICE, 1936
HER NIGHT OUT, 1932
HER PRIMITIVE MAN, 1944
HER REPUTATION, 1931
HER SPLENDID FOLLY, 1933
HER TWELVE MEN, 1954
HER WEDDING NIGHT, 1930
HERBIE GOES BANANAS, 1980
HERBIE GOES TO MONTE CARLO, 1977
HERBIE RIDES AGAIN, 1974
HERCULES' PILLS, 1960
HERE COME THE HUGGETTS, 1948
HERE COME THE MARINES, 1952
HERE COME THE NELSONS, 1952
HERE COME THE TIGERS, 1978
HERE COMES COOKIE, 1935
HERE COMES KELLY, 1943
HERE COMES THE GROOM, 1934
HERE COMES THE GROOM, 1951
HERE COMES THE NAVY, 1934
HERE COMES TROUBLE, 1936
HERE COMES TROUBLE, 1948
HERE IS MY HEART, 1934
HERE WE GO AGAIN, 1942
HERE WE GO ROUND THE MULBERRY BUSH, 1968
HERE'S GEORGE, 1932
HERO AT LARGE, 1980
HEROES, 1977
HE'S A COCKEYED WONDER, 1950
HE'S MY GIRL, 1987
HEY! HEY! U.S.A., 1938
HI DIDDLE DIDDLE, 1943
HI, GANG!, 1941
HI, MOM!, 1970
HI, NEIGHBOR, 1942
HI, NELLIE!, 1934
HI 'YA, CHUM, 1943
HIDEAWAY, 1937
HIDING OUT, 1987
HIGGINS FAMILY, THE, 1938

HIGH AND DRY, 1954
HIGH ANXIETY, 1977
HIGH COST OF LOVING, THE, 1958
HIGH FLYERS, 1937
HIGH INFIDELITY, 1965
HIGH JINKS IN SOCIETY, 1949
HIGH PRESSURE, 1932
HIGH RISK, 1981
HIGH SEASON, 1988
HIGH SOCIETY, 1932
HIGH SOCIETY, 1955
HIGH SPIRITS, 1988
HIGH STAKES, 1931
HIGH TENSION, 1936
HIGHLAND FLING, 1936
HIGHLY DANGEROUS, 1950
HILLBILLY BLITZKRIEG, 1942
HILLBILLYS IN A HAUNTED HOUSE, 1967
HIRED WIFE, 1940
HIS AND HERS, 1961
HIS DOUBLE LIFE, 1933
HIS EXCITING NIGHT, 1938
HIS FAMILY TREE, 1936
HIS FIRST COMMAND, 1929
HIS GIRL FRIDAY, 1940
HIS LORDSHIP GOES TO PRESS, 1939
HIS LORDSHIP REGRETS, 1938
HIS LUCKY DAY, 1929
HIS MAJESTY, KING BALLYHOO, 1931
HIS NIGHT OUT, 1935
HIS WIFE'S MOTHER, 1932
HISTORY OF THE WORLD, PART 1, 1981
HIT THE ROAD, 1941
HOAX, THE, 1972
HOBSON'S CHOICE, 1931
HOBSON'S CHOICE, 1954
HOFFMAN, 1970
HOG WILD, 1980
HOLD 'EM JAIL, 1932
HOLD 'EM YALE, 1935
HOLD MY HAND, 1938
HOLD THAT BABY!, 1949
HOLD THAT BLONDE, 1945
HOLD THAT GHOST, 1941
HOLD THAT GIRL, 1934
HOLD THAT HYPNOTIST, 1957
HOLD THAT KISS, 1938
HOLD THAT LINE, 1952
HOLE IN THE HEAD, A, 1959
HOLIDAY, 1930
HOLIDAY, 1938
HOLIDAY CAMP, 1947
HOLIDAY FOR HENRIETTA, 1955
HOLIDAY FOR LOVERS, 1959
HOLIDAYS WITH PAY, 1948
HOLLYWOOD AND VINE, 1945
HOLLYWOOD BOULEVARD, 1976
HOLLYWOOD CAVALCADE, 1939
HOLLYWOOD COWBOY, 1937
HOLLYWOOD HIGH, 1977
HOLLYWOOD HIGH PART II, 1984
HOLLYWOOD HOT TUBS, 1984
HOLLYWOOD KNIGHTS, THE, 1980
HOLLYWOOD OR BUST, 1956
HOLLYWOOD SHUFFLE, 1987
HOLLYWOOD ZAP!, 1986
HOLY MATRIMONY, 1943
HOME AND AWAY, 1956
HOME FROM HOME, 1939
HOME IS WHERE THE HART IS, 1987
HOME MOVIES, 1979
HOME SWEET HOMICIDE, 1946
HOME TOWNERS, THE, 1928
HOMETOWN U.S.A., 1979
HOMEWORK, 1982
HONEY POT, THE, 1967
HONEYBABY, HONEYBABY, 1974
HONEYMOON DEFERRED, 1940
HONEYMOON DEFERRED, 1951
HONEYMOON FOR THREE, 1941
HONEYMOON HOTEL, 1964
HONEYMOON IN BALI, 1939
HONEYMOON LANE, 1931
HONEYMOON LODGE, 1943
HONEYMOON MACHINE, THE, 1961
HONEYMOON MERRY-GO-ROUND, 1939

BOLD: Films on Videocassette

HONEYMOON'S OVER, THE, 1939
HONKY TONK FREEWAY, 1981
HOOK, LINE AND SINKER, 1930
HOOK, LINE AND SINKER, 1969
HOOPER, 1978
HOOTS MON!, 1939
HOPE AND GLORY, 1987
HOPE OF HIS SIDE, 1935
HOPSCOTCH, 1980
HORIZONTAL LIEUTENANT, THE, 1962
HORN BLOWS AT MIDNIGHT, THE, 1945
HORNET'S NEST, THE, 1955
HORROR HOSPITAL, 1973
HORROR ISLAND, 1941
HORROR OF FRANKENSTEIN, THE, 1970
HORROR OF IT ALL, THE, 1964
HORSE FEATHERS, 1932
HORSEPLAY, 1933
HORSE'S MOUTH, THE, 1958
HOSPITAL, THE, 1971
HOT CHILI, 1986
HOT DOG...THE MOVIE, 1984
HOT ICE, 1952
HOT MILLIONS, 1968
HOT MONEY, 1936
HOT MOVES, 1984
HOT NEWS, 1936
HOT PEPPER, 1933
HOT PURSUIT, 1987
HOT RESORT, 1985
HOT ROCK, THE, 1972
HOT SATURDAY, 1932
HOT SHOTS, 1956
HOT STUFF, 1979
HOT TIMES, 1974
HOT TIP, 1935
HOT TO TROT, 1988
HOT TOMORROWS, 1978
HOTEL HAYWIRE, 1937
HOTEL PARADISO, 1966
HOTEL SAHARA, 1951
HOTEL SPLENDIDE, 1932
H.O.T.S., 1979
HOTTENTOT, THE, 1929
HOUND OF THE BASKERVILLES, THE, 1980
HOURS OF LOVE, THE, 1965
HOUSE, 1986
HOUSE BROKEN, 1936
HOUSE CALLS, 1978
HOUSE OF ERRORS, 1942
HOUSE OF FEAR, THE, 1939
HOUSE OF GOD, THE, 1984
HOUSE OF HORROR, 1929
HOUSE OF MYSTERY, 1934
HOUSEBOAT, 1958
HOUSEHOLDER, THE, 1963
HOUSEKEEPER'S DAUGHTER, 1939
HOUSEMASTER, 1938
HOW COME NOBODY'S ON OUR SIDE?, 1975
HOW DO I LOVE THEE?, 1970
HOW DO YOU DO?, 1946
HOW I WON THE WAR, 1967
HOW NOT TO ROB A DEPARTMENT STORE, 1965
HOW SWEET IT IS, 1968
HOW TO BEAT THE HIGH COST OF LIVING, 1980
HOW TO COMMIT MARRIAGE, 1969
HOW TO FRAME A FIGG, 1971
HOW TO MARRY A MILLIONAIRE, 1953
HOW TO MURDER A RICH UNCLE, 1957
HOW TO MURDER YOUR WIFE, 1965
HOW TO SAVE A MARRIAGE—AND RUIN YOUR
    LIFE, 1968
HOW TO SEDUCE A PLAYBOY, 1968
HOW TO SEDUCE A WOMAN, 1974
HOW TO STEAL A MILLION, 1966
HOWARD THE DUCK, 1986
HOWLING III, THE, 1987
HUCKLEBERRY FINN, 1931
HUCKLEBERRY FINN, 1939
HUE AND CRY, 1950
HUGGETTS ABROAD, THE, 1949
HUGS AND KISSES, 1968
HULLABALOO OVER GEORGIE AND BONNIE'S
    PICTURES, 1979
HUMAN COMEDY, THE, 1943
HUMAN SIDE, THE, 1934

HUMPHREY TAKES A CHANCE, 1950
HUNK, 1987
HURRY, CHARLIE, HURRY, 1941
HURRY UP OR I'LL BE 30, 1973
HYDE PARK CORNER, 1935
HYPNOTIZED, 1933
HYSTERICAL, 1983
I AM A CAMERA, 1955
I CAN'T GIVE YOU ANYTHING BUT LOVE, BABY,
    1940
I COULD NEVER HAVE SEX WITH ANY MAN WHO
    HAS SO LITTLE REGARD FOR MY HUSBAND, 1973
I DIDN'T DO IT, 1945
I HATE BLONDES, 1981
I KILLED EINSTEIN, GENTLEMEN, 1970
I KNOW WHERE I'M GOING, 1947
I LIKE MONEY, 1962
I LIKE YOUR NERVE, 1931
I LIVE MY LIFE, 1935
I LOVE MY WIFE, 1970
I LOVE YOU AGAIN, 1940
I LOVE YOU, ALICE B. TOKLAS!, 1968
I LOVED YOU WEDNESDAY, 1933
I MARRIED A WITCH, 1942
I MARRIED A WOMAN, 1958
I MET HIM IN PARIS, 1937
I ONLY ASKED!, 1958
I OUGHT TO BE IN PICTURES, 1982
I SAILED TO TAHITI WITH AN ALL GIRL CREW,
    1969
I SEE ICE, 1938
I THANK YOU, 1941
I, TOO, AM ONLY A WOMAN, 1963
I WANNA HOLD YOUR HAND, 1978
I WAS A MALE WAR BRIDE, 1949
I WAS A TEENAGE T.V. TERRORIST, 1987
I WAS A TEENAGE ZOMBIE, 1987
I WAS AN ADVENTURESS, 1940
I WILL...I WILL...FOR NOW, 1976
I D RATHER BE RICH, 1964
IDEAL HUSBAND, AN, 1948
IDIOT'S DELIGHT, 1939
IDLE RICH, THE, 1929
IDOL ON PARADE, 1959
IF A MAN ANSWERS, 1962
IF I HAD A MILLION, 1932
IF I WERE RICH, 1936
IF IT'S TUESDAY, THIS MUST BE BELGIUM, 1969
IF YOU COULD ONLY COOK, 1936
I'LL GIVE A MILLION, 1938
I'LL NEVER FORGET WHAT'S 'IS NAME, 1967
I'LL STICK TO YOU, 1933
I'LL TAKE SWEDEN, 1965
I'LL TELL THE WORLD, 1934
ILLEGALLY YOURS, 1988
I'M A STRANGER, 1952
I'M ALL RIGHT, JACK, 1959
I'M AN EXPLOSIVE, 1933
I'M FROM ARKANSAS, 1944
I'M FROM THE CITY, 1938
I'M GONNA GIT YOU SUCKA, 1988
I'M NO ANGEL, 1933
IMITATION GENERAL, 1958
IMMORTAL BACHELOR, THE, 1980
IMPORTANCE OF BEING EARNEST, THE, 1952
IMPOSSIBLE ON SATURDAY, 1966
IMPOSSIBLE YEARS, THE, 1968
IMPOSTORS, 1979
"'IMP''PROBABLE MR. WEE GEE, THE, 1966
IMPROPER CHANNELS, 1981
IMPROPER DUCHESS, THE, 1936
IN FAST COMPANY, 1946
IN GOD WE TRUST, 1980
IN-LAWS, THE, 1979
IN LIKE FLINT, 1967
IN OLD KENTUCKY, 1935
IN SOCIETY, 1944
IN THE DOGHOUSE, 1964
IN THE MEANTIME, DARLING, 1944
IN THE MONEY, 1934
IN THE MONEY, 1958
IN THE MOOD, 1987
IN THE NICK, 1960
IN THE SOUP, 1936
IN THE WILD MOUNTAINS, 1986
IN TROUBLE WITH EVE, 1964

INCORRIGIBLE, 1980
INCREDIBLE SHRINKING WOMAN, THE, 1981
INDISCREET, 1958
INDISCRETIONS OF EVE, 1932
INN FOR TROUBLE, 1960
INNERSPACE, 1987
INNOCENTS IN PARIS, 1955
INSIDE OUT, 1975
INSIDE STORY, THE, 1948
INSIDE THE LAW, 1942
INSOMNIACS, 1986
INSPECTOR CLOUSEAU, 1968
INSPECTOR GENERAL, THE, 1937
INSPECTOR HORNLEIGH, 1939
INSPECTOR HORNLEIGH ON HOLIDAY, 1939
INTERMEZZO, 1937
INTERNATIONAL HOUSE, 1933
INTERRUPTED HONEYMOON, THE, 1936
INTIMATE RELATIONS, 1937
INTO THE NIGHT, 1985
INVASION OF THE BEE GIRLS, 1973
INVASION OF THE SAUCER MEN, 1957
INVASION OF THE STAR CREATURES, 1962
INVASION QUARTET, 1961
INVISIBLE KID, THE, 1988
INVISIBLE WOMAN, THE, 1941
INVITATION, THE, 1975
IRELAND'S BORDER LINE, 1939
IRISH AND PROUD OF IT, 1938
IRISH FOR LUCK, 1936
IRISH IN US, THE, 1935
IRISH LUCK, 1939
IRMA LA DOUCE, 1963
IRON PETTICOAT, THE, 1956
IRRECONCILABLE DIFFERENCES, 1984
IS YOUR HONEYMOON REALLY NECESSARY?, 1953
ISHTAR, 1987
ISLAND OF LOVE, 1963
ISLAND RESCUE, 1952
ISN'T LIFE WONDERFUL!, 1953
IT AIN'T HAY, 1943
IT CAN BE DONE, 1929
IT CAN'T LAST FOREVER, 1937
IT COULD HAPPEN TO YOU, 1939
IT GROWS ON TREES, 1952
IT HAD TO BE YOU, 1947
IT HAD TO HAPPEN, 1936
IT HAPPENED IN ATHENS, 1962
IT HAPPENED IN NEW YORK, 1935
IT HAPPENED IN PARIS, 1935
IT HAPPENED IN PARIS, 1953
IT HAPPENED IN ROME, 1959
IT HAPPENED ON 5TH AVENUE, 1947
IT HAPPENED ONE NIGHT, 1934
IT HAPPENED TO JANE, 1959
IT HAPPENS EVERY SPRING, 1949
IT HAPPENS EVERY THURSDAY, 1953
IT ISN'T DONE, 1937
IT PAYS TO ADVERTISE, 1931
IT SEEMED LIKE A GOOD IDEA AT THE TIME, 1975
IT SHOULD HAPPEN TO YOU, 1954
IT SHOULDN'T HAPPEN TO A DOG, 1946
IT STARTED IN THE ALPS, 1966
IT STARTED WITH A KISS, 1959
ITALIAN SECRET SERVICE, 1968
IT'S A BET, 1935
IT'S A BIKINI WORLD, 1967
IT'S A BOY, 1934
IT'S A COP, 1934
IT'S A DEAL, 1930
IT'S A GIFT, 1934
IT'S A GRAND LIFE, 1953
IT'S A GRAND OLD WORLD, 1937
IT'S A GREAT DAY, 1956
IT'S A GREAT FEELING, 1949
IT'S A GREAT LIFE, 1943
IT'S A JOKE, SON!, 1947
IT'S A KING, 1933
IT'S A MAD, MAD, MAD, MAD WORLD, 1963
IT'S A SMALL WORLD, 1934
IT'S A 2'6" ABOVE THE GROUND WORLD, 1972
IT'S A WISE CHILD, 1931
IT'S A WONDERFUL WORLD, 1939
IT'S ALL YOURS, 1937
IT'S HARD TO BE GOOD, 1950
IT'S IN THE AIR, 1935

IT'S IN THE AIR, 1940
IT'S IN THE BAG, 1936
IT'S IN THE BAG, 1943
IT'S IN THE BAG, 1945
IT'S IN THE BLOOD, 1938
IT'S LOVE I'M AFTER, 1937
IT'S MY TURN, 1980
IT'S NEVER TOO LATE, 1958
IT'S NOT CRICKET, 1937
IT'S NOT CRICKET, 1949
IT'S NOT THE SIZE THAT COUNTS, 1979
IT'S ONLY MONEY, 1962
IT'S THAT MAN AGAIN, 1943
IT'S YOU I WANT, 1936
I'VE GOT A HORSE, 1938
I'VE GOT YOUR NUMBER, 1934
J-MEN FOREVER, 1980
JABBERWOCKY, 1977
JACK AHOY!, 1935
JACK AND THE BEANSTALK, 1952
JACKPOT, THE, 1950
JACQUES AND NOVEMBER, 1985
JAIL BUSTERS, 1955
JAIL HOUSE BLUES, 1942
JAILBIRDS, 1939
JAKE SPEED, 1986
JALOPY, 1953
JANE AUSTEN IN MANHATTAN, 1980
JANE STEPS OUT, 1938
JANIE, 1944
JANIE GETS MARRIED, 1946
JAZZ HEAVEN, 1929
JAZZMAN, 1984
JEKYLL AND HYDE. . .TOGETHER AGAIN, 1982
JENNIFER ON MY MIND, 1971
JERK, THE, 1979
JEWEL ROBBERY, 1932
JIGGS AND MAGGIE IN SOCIETY, 1948
JIGGS AND MAGGIE OUT WEST, 1950
JIMMY AND SALLY, 1933
JIMMY BOY, 1935
JIMMY THE GENT, 1934
JIMMY THE KID, 1982
JINX MONEY, 1948
JINXED!, 1982
JITTERBUGS, 1943
JO JO DANCER, YOUR LIFE IS CALLING, 1986
JOCKS, 1987
JOE AND ETHEL TURP CALL ON THE PRESIDENT, 1939
JOE BUTTERFLY, 1957
JOE PALOOKA IN THE COUNTERPUNCH, 1949
JOE PALOOKA IN WINNER TAKE ALL, 1948
JOE PALOOKA MEETS HUMPHREY, 1950
JOEY BOY, 1965
JOHN AND JULIE, 1957
JOHN GOLDFARB, PLEASE COME HOME, 1964
JOHN LOVES MARY, 1949
JOHNNY BE GOOD, 1988
JOHNNY COME LATELY, 1943
JOHNNY DANGEROUSLY, 1984
JOHNNY DOESN'T LIVE HERE ANY MORE, 1944
JOHNNY STEALS EUROPE, 1932
JOIN THE MARINES, 1937
JOKE OF DESTINY LYING IN WAIT AROUND THE CORNER LIKE A STREET BANDIT, A, 1984
JOKER, THE, 1961
JOKERS, THE, 1967
JOLLY BAD FELLOW, A, 1964
JONAH—WHO WILL BE 25 IN THE YEAR 2000, 1976
JONES FAMILY IN HOLLYWOOD, THE, 1939
JOSEPH ANDREWS, 1977
JOSEPHINE AND MEN, 1955
JOSETTE, 1938
JOSHUA THEN AND NOW, 1985
JOSSER IN THE ARMY, 1932
JOSSER JOINS THE NAVY, 1932
JOSSER ON THE FARM, 1934
JOSSER ON THE RIVER, 1932
JOUR DE FETE, 1952
JOURNEY TO LOVE, 1953
JOY OF LIVING, 1938
JOY OF SEX, 1984
JOY RIDE, 1935
JOYSTICKS, 1983
JUBILEE, 1978

JUBILEE WINDOW, 1935
JUDGE PRIEST, 1934
JUDGE STEPS OUT, THE, 1949
JULIA MISBEHAVES, 1948
JULIE THE REDHEAD, 1963
JULIETTA, 1957
JUMPIN' JACK FLASH, 1986
JUMPING FOR JOY, 1956
JUMPING JACKS, 1952
JUNE BRIDE, 1948
JUNE MOON, 1931
JUNGLE GENTS, 1954
JUNIOR MISS, 1945
JUPITER, 1952
JUST A BIG, SIMPLE GIRL, 1949
JUST A GIGOLO, 1931
JUST ACROSS THE STREET, 1952
JUST JOE, 1960
JUST LIKE A WOMAN, 1939
JUST LIKE A WOMAN, 1967
JUST LIKE HEAVEN, 1930
JUST ME, 1950
JUST MY LUCK, 1933
JUST MY LUCK, 1957
JUST ONE OF THE GUYS, 1985
JUST TELL ME WHAT YOU WANT, 1980
JUST THE WAY YOU ARE, 1984
JUST THIS ONCE, 1952
JUST WILLIAM, 1939
JUST WILLIAM'S LUCK, 1948
JUST YOU AND ME, KID, 1979
KALEIDOSCOPE, 1966
KANSAS CITY PRINCESS, 1934
KAOS, 1985
KATHLEEN, 1941
KATHY O', 1958
KATIE DID IT, 1951
KEEP 'EM FLYING, 1941
KEEP 'EM ROLLING, 1934
KEEP 'EM SLUGGING, 1943
KEEP FIT, 1937
KEEP IT CLEAN, 1956
KEEP IT QUIET, 1934
KEEP YOUR SEATS PLEASE, 1936
KEEPING COMPANY, 1941
KELLY AND ME, 1957
KELLY THE SECOND, 1936
KELLY'S HEROES, 1970
KENTUCKY FRIED MOVIE, THE, 1977
KENTUCKY KERNELS, 1935
KETTLES IN THE OZARKS, THE, 1956
KETTLES ON OLD MACDONALD'S FARM, THE, 1957
KEY EXCHANGE, 1985
KEY TO THE CITY, 1950
KIBITZER, THE, 1929
KID BLUE, 1973
KID DYNAMITE, 1943
KID FOR TWO FARTHINGS, A, 1956
KID FROM KOKOMO, THE, 1939
KID FROM LEFT FIELD, THE, 1953
KID FROM TEXAS, THE, 1939
KID NIGHTINGALE, 1939
KID SISTER, THE, 1945
KIEV COMEDY, A, 1963
KIKI, 1931
KILL OR CURE, 1962
KILL THE UMPIRE, 1950
KILLING GAME, THE, 1968
KILROY WAS HERE, 1947
KIND HEARTS AND CORONETS, 1949
KING AND FOUR QUEENS, THE, 1956
KING AND HIS MOVIE, A, 1986
KING AND THE CHORUS GIRL, THE, 1937
KING ARTHUR WAS A GENTLEMAN, 1942
KING IN NEW YORK, A, 1957
KING OF ALCATRAZ, 1938
KING OF COMEDY, THE, 1983
KING OF HEARTS, 1967
KING OF THE CASTLE, 1936
KING, QUEEN, KNAVE, 1972
KIPPERBANG, 1984
KISS AND MAKE UP, 1934
KISS AND TELL, 1945
KISS FOR CORLISS, A, 1949
KISS IN THE DARK, A, 1949
KISS ME GOODBYE, 1982

KISS ME, SERGEANT, 1930
KISS ME, STUPID, 1964
KISS OF FIRE, THE, 1940
KISS THE BRIDE GOODBYE, 1944
KISS THE OTHER SHEIK, 1968
KISS THEM FOR ME, 1957
KISSES FOR BREAKFAST, 1941
KISSES FOR MY PRESIDENT, 1964
KITCHEN, THE, 1961
KITTY AND THE BAGMAN, 1983
KNACK . . . AND HOW TO GET IT, THE, 1965
KNIGHTS FOR A DAY, 1937
KNOCK ON WOOD, 1954
KNOWING MEN, 1930
KOTCH, 1971
LA BELLE AMERICAINE, 1961
LA CAGE, 1975
LA CAGE AUX FOLLES, 1979
LA CAGE AUX FOLLES II, 1981
LA CAGE AUX FOLLES 3: THE WEDDING, 1985
LA CHEVRE, 1985
LA CONGA NIGHTS, 1940
LA GRANDE BOUFFE, 1973
LA NUIT DE VARENNES, 1983
LA PARISIENNE, 1958
LA SCARLATINE, 1985
LA VIE DE CHATEAU, 1967
LABURNUM GROVE, 1936
LAD, THE, 1935
LADIES' DAY, 1943
LADIES IN LOVE, 1936
LADIES MAN, THE, 1961
LADIES MUST LOVE, 1933
LADIES MUST PLAY, 1930
LADIES ON THE ROCKS, 1985
LADIES SHOULD LISTEN, 1934
LADIES WHO DO, 1964
LADY AND THE MOB, THE, 1939
LADY BE CAREFUL, 1936
LADY BEHAVE, 1937
LADY BODYGUARD, 1942
LADY BY CHOICE, 1934
LADY CHASER, 1946
LADY CRAVED EXCITEMENT, THE, 1950
LADY DOCTOR, THE, 1963
LADY ESCAPES, THE, 1937
LADY EVE, THE, 1941
LADY FOR A DAY, 1933
LADY FROM LISBON, 1942
LADY GODIVA RIDES AGAIN, 1955
LADY HAS PLANS, THE, 1942
LADY IN A JAM, 1942
LADY IN DANGER, 1934
LADY IS WILLING, THE, 1942
LADY IS WILLING, THE, 1934
LADY KILLER, 1933
LADY L, 1965
LADY LIBERTY, 1972
LADY LIES, THE, 1929
LADY LUCK, 1946
LADY MISLAID, A, 1958
LADY OF BURLESQUE, 1943
LADY OF CHANCE, A, 1928
LADY ON A TRAIN, 1945
LADY PAYS OFF, THE, 1951
LADY SAYS NO, THE, 1951
LADY TAKES A CHANCE, A, 1943
LADY TAKES A SAILOR, THE, 1949
LADY TUBBS, 1935
LADY WANTS MINK, THE, 1953
LADY WITH A PAST, 1932
LADYKILLERS, THE, 1956
LADY'S PROFESSION, A, 1933
LAMBETH WALK, THE, 1940
LAMP IN ASSASSIN MEWS, THE, 1962
LANCASHIRE LUCK, 1937
LANDLORD, THE, 1970
LARCENY, INC., 1942
LARCENY STREET, 1941
LAS VEGAS FREE-FOR-ALL, 1968
LAS VEGAS HILLBILLYS, 1966
LAS VEGAS WEEKEND, 1985
LASER MAN, THE, 1988
LASSIE FROM LANCASHIRE, 1938
LAST AMERICAN VIRGIN, THE, 1982
LAST COUPON, THE, 1932

BOLD: Films on Videocassette

LAST CURTAIN, THE, 1937
LAST DANCE, THE, 1930
LAST GENTLEMAN, THE, 1934
LAST HOLIDAY, 1950
LAST HOUR, THE, 1930
LAST MARRIED COUPLE IN AMERICA, THE, 1980
LAST OF MRS. CHEYNEY, THE, 1929
LAST OF MRS. CHEYNEY, THE, 1937
LAST OF THE RED HOT LOVERS, 1972
LAST OF THE SECRET AGENTS?, THE, 1966
LAST PORNO FLICK, THE, 1974
LAST REMAKE OF BEAU GESTE, THE, 1977
LAST RESORT, THE, 1986
LAST STRAW, THE, 1987
LAST TIME I SAW ARCHIE, THE, 1961
LAST WARNING, THE, 1938
LAST WORD, THE, 1979
LATE GEORGE APLEY, THE, 1947
LATIN LOVERS, 1953
LAUGH AND GET RICH, 1931
LAUGH YOUR BLUES AWAY, 1943
LAUGHING AT DANGER, 1940
LAUGHTER, 1930
LAUGHTER HOUSE, 1984
LAUGHTER IN PARADISE, 1951
LAVENDER HILL MOB, THE, 1951
LAW AND DISORDER, 1940
LAW AND DISORDER, 1958
LAW AND DISORDER, 1974
LAW IN HER HANDS, THE, 1936
LAW IS THE LAW, THE, 1959
LAW OF DESIRE, 1987
LAW WEST OF TOMBSTONE, THE, 1938
LAY THAT RIFLE DOWN, 1955
LAZYBONES, 1935
LE BEAU MARIAGE, 1982
LE BON PLAISIR, 1984
LE DENIER MILLIARDAIRE, 1934
LE GENDARME ET LES EXTRATERRESTRES, 1978
LE JEUNE MARIE, 1985
LEAGUE OF GENTLEMEN, THE, 1961
LEAP INTO THE VOID, 1982
LEAP OF FAITH, 1931
LEAP YEAR, 1932
LEATHER-PUSHERS, THE, 1940
LEAVE IT TO BLANCHE, 1934
LEAVE IT TO BLONDIE, 1945
LEAVE IT TO HENRY, 1949
LEAVE IT TO ME, 1933
LEAVE IT TO ME, 1937
LEAVE IT TO SMITH, 1934
LEAVE IT TO THE IRISH, 1944
LEAVE IT TO THE MARINES, 1951
LEFT, RIGHT AND CENTRE, 1959
LEGAL EAGLES, 1986
LEGEND OF FRENCHIE KING, THE, 1971
LEMON DROP KID, THE, 1951
LEMON GROVE KIDS MEET THE MONSTERS, THE, 1966
LEMONADE JOE, 1966
LEND ME YOUR HUSBAND, 1935
LEND ME YOUR WIFE, 1935
LEONARD PART 6, 1987
LES BELLES-DE-NUIT, 1952
LES COMPERES, 1984
LES GIRLS, 1957
LESSON IN LOVE, A, 1960
LET GEORGE DO IT, 1940
LET ME EXPLAIN, DEAR, 1932
LET THE PEOPLE SING, 1942
LET US BE GAY, 1930
LET'S BE FAMOUS, 1939
LET'S BE HAPPY, 1957
LET'S BE RITZY, 1934
LET'S DANCE, 1950
LET'S DO IT AGAIN, 1953
LET'S DO IT AGAIN, 1975
LET'S FACE IT, 1943
LET'S GET MARRIED, 1937
LET'S GET TOUGH, 1942
LET'S GO COLLEGIATE, 1941
LET'S GO NATIVE, 1930
LET'S GO NAVY, 1951
LET'S GO PLACES, 1930
LET'S GO STEADY, 1945
LET'S GO, YOUNG GUY!, 1967

LET'S LIVE A LITTLE, 1948
LET'S LIVE AGAIN, 1948
LET'S LIVE TONIGHT, 1935
LET'S MAKE A NIGHT OF IT, 1937
LET'S MAKE A MILLION, 1937
LET'S MAKE IT LEGAL, 1951
LET'S TALK ABOUT WOMEN, 1964
LETTER FOR EVIE, A, 1945
LETTER OF INTRODUCTION, 1938
LETTER TO BREZHNEV, 1986
LETTERS FROM MY WINDMILL, 1955
LETTING IN THE SUNSHINE, 1933
LIBELED LADY, 1936
LICENSE TO DRIVE, 1988
LIEUTENANT WORE SKIRTS, THE, 1956
LIFE AND TIMES OF CHESTER-ANGUS RAMSGOOD, THE, 1971
LIFE AND TIMES OF JUDGE ROY BEAN, THE, 1972
LIFE BEGINS AT 8:30, 1942
LIFE BEGINS IN COLLEGE, 1937
LIFE IS A CIRCUS, 1962
LIFE OF RILEY, THE, 1949
LIFE OF THE PARTY, 1934
LIFE OF THE PARTY, THE, 1930
LIFE WITH BLONDIE, 1946
LIFE WITH FATHER, 1947
LIFE WITH HENRY, 1941
LIGHT FINGERS, 1957
LIGHT TOUCH, THE, 1955
LIGHT UP THE SKY, 1960
LIGHTNIN', 1930
LIGHTNING CONDUCTOR, 1938
LIGHTNING STRIKES TWICE, 1935
LIKE FATHER, LIKE SON, 1987
LIKELY LADS, THE, 1976
LIKELY STORY, A, 1947
LI'L ABNER, 1940
LILIES OF THE FIELD, 1934
LILY IN LOVE, 1985
LIMELIGHT, 1952
LINDA BE GOOD, 1947
LIONS LOVE, 1969
LISTEN, DARLING, 1938
LITTLE ACCIDENT, 1930
LITTLE ACCIDENT, 1939
LITTLE BIG SHOT, 1952
LITTLE BIT OF BLUFF, A, 1935
LITTLE CIGARS, 1973
LITTLE DORRIT, 1988
LITTLE GIANT, THE, 1933
LITTLE GIANT, 1934
LITTLE HUT, THE, 1957
LITTLE IODINE, 1946
LITTLE JOHNNY JONES, 1930
LITTLE MALCOLM, 1974
LITTLE MISS MARKER, 1934
LITTLE MISS BIG, 1946
LITTLE MISS MARKER, 1980
LITTLE MISS NOBODY, 1933
LITTLE MISS NOBODY, 1936
LITTLE MISS ROUGHNECK, 1938
LITTLE MURDERS, 1971
LITTLE NUNS, THE, 1965
LITTLE OLD NEW YORK, 1940
LITTLE ROMANCE, A, 1979
LITTLE SEX, A, 1982
LITTLE SHOP OF HORRORS, 1961
LITTLE TOUGH GUYS IN SOCIETY, 1938
LITTLE TREASURE, 1985
LITTLE WILDCAT, THE, 1928
LITTLE WORLD OF DON CAMILLO, THE, 1953
LIVE, LOVE AND LEARN, 1937
LIVE NOW—PAY LATER, 1962
LIVE WIRE, THE, 1937
LIVE WIRES, 1946
LIVING IN A BIG WAY, 1947
LIVING ON LOVE, 1937
LOCAL BOY MAKES GOOD, 1931
LOCAL HERO, 1983
LOCK UP YOUR DAUGHTERS, 1969
LONELY GUY, THE, 1984
LONELY HEARTS, 1983
LONELY WIVES, 1931
LONG, LONG TRAILER, THE, 1954
LONGEST YARD, THE, 1974
LONGSHOT, THE, 1986

LOOK UP AND LAUGH, 1935
LOOK WHO'S LAUGHING, 1941
LOOKIN' TO GET OUT, 1982
LOOKING FOR DANGER, 1957
LOOSE ANKLES, 1930
LOOSE CONNECTIONS, 1984
LOOSE IN LONDON, 1953
LOOSE SCREWS, 1985
LOOSE SHOES, 1980
LOOT, 1971
LORD BABS, 1932
LORD LOVE A DUCK, 1966
LORD OF THE MANOR, 1933
LORD RICHARD IN THE PANTRY, 1930
LOS ASTRONAUTAS, 1960
LOS INVISIBLES, 1961
LOSER TAKES ALL, 1956
LOSIN' IT, 1983
LOST AND FOUND, 1979
LOST FACE, THE, 1965
LOST HONEYMOON, 1947
LOST IN A HAREM, 1944
LOST IN ALASKA, 1952
LOST IN AMERICA, 1985
LOST IN THE LEGION, 1934
LOST IN THE STRATOSPHERE, 1935
LOTTERY LOVER, 1935
LOUDSPEAKER, THE, 1934
LOUISA, 1950
LOUISIANA HAYRIDE, 1944
LOVE AFFAIR, 1939
LOVE AFFAIR; OR THE CASE OF THE MISSING SWITCHBOARD OPERATOR, 1968
LOVE AND DEATH, 1975
LOVE AND KISSES, 1965
LOVE AND LARCENY, 1963
LOVE AND MARRIAGE, 1966
LOVE AND THE FRENCHWOMAN, 1961
LOVE AND THE MIDNIGHT AUTO SUPPLY, 1978
LOVE AT FIRST BITE, 1979
LOVE AT FIRST SIGHT, 1977
LOVE AT SEA, 1936
LOVE BEFORE BREAKFAST, 1936
LOVE BEGINS AT TWENTY, 1936
LOVE BIRDS, 1934
LOVE BUG, THE, 1968
LOVE CRAZY, 1941
LOVE DOCTOR, THE, 1929
LOVE FACTORY, 1969
LOVE GOD?, THE, 1969
LOVE HABIT, THE, 1931
LOVE HAPPY, 1949
LOVE, HONOR AND GOODBYE, 1945
LOVE, HONOR, AND OH BABY!, 1933
LOVE, HONOR AND OH, BABY, 1940
LOVE IN A BUNGALOW, 1937
LOVE IN 4 DIMENSIONS, 1965
LOVE IN THE AFTERNOON, 1957
LOVE IN THE DESERT, 1929
LOVE IN WAITING, 1948
LOVE IS A BALL, 1963
LOVE IS A HEADACHE, 1938
LOVE IS BETTER THAN EVER, 1952
LOVE IS LIKE THAT, 1933
LOVE IS NEWS, 1937
LOVE LAUGHS AT ANDY HARDY, 1946
LOVE LIES, 1931
LOVE, LIFE AND LAUGHTER, 1934
LOVE, LIVE AND LAUGH, 1929
LOVE LOTTERY, THE, 1954
LOVE MATCH, THE, 1955
LOVE MATES, 1967
LOVE ME TONIGHT, 1932
LOVE NEST, THE, 1933
LOVE NEST, 1951
LOVE ON A BET, 1936
LOVE ON A BUDGET, 1938
LOVE ON THE RIVIERA, 1964
LOVE ON THE RUN, 1936
LOVE ON THE RUN, 1980
LOVE ON TOAST, 1937
LOVE PAST THIRTY, 1934
LOVE RACE, THE, 1931
LOVE TEST, THE, 1935
LOVE THAT BRUTE, 1950

LOVE, THE ITALIAN WAY, 1964
LOVE THY NEIGHBOR, 1940
LOVE TILL FIRST BLOOD, 1985
LOVE TRAP, THE, 1929
LOVE UP THE POLE, 1936
LOVE WAGER, THE, 1933
LOVE WALTZ, THE, 1930
LOVE WITH THE PROPER STRANGER, 1963
LOVED ONE, THE, 1965
LOVELINES, 1984
LOVER COME BACK, 1946
LOVER COME BACK, 1961
LOVER COME BACK, 1931
LOVERS AND LIARS, 1981
LOVERS AND OTHER STRANGERS, 1970
LOVERS, THE, 1972
LOVES AND TIMES OF SCARAMOUCHE, THE, 1976
LOVES OF A BLONDE, 1966
LOVESICK, 1983
LOVIN' THE LADIES, 1930
LOVING, 1970
LOVING COUPLES, 1980
LOWER DEPTHS, THE, 1962
LUCK OF THE IRISH, 1948
LUCK OF THE IRISH, THE, 1937
LUCK OF THE TURF, 1936
LUCKIEST GIRL IN THE WORLD, THE, 1936
LUCKY BRIDE, THE, 1948
LUCKY DAYS, 1935
LUCKY DEVILS, 1941
LUCKY DOG, 1933
LUCKY JADE, 1937
LUCKY JIM, 1957
LUCKY LADIES, 1932
LUCKY LADY, 1975
LUCKY LARRIGAN, 1933
LUCKY LEGS, 1942
LUCKY LOSER, 1934
LUCKY LOSERS, 1950
LUCKY MASCOT, THE, 1951
LUCKY NIGHT, 1939
LUCKY NUMBER, THE, 1933
LUCKY PARTNERS, 1940
LUCKY STIFF, THE, 1949
LUCKY SWEEP, A, 1932
LUCKY TO ME, 1939
LUGGAGE OF THE GODS, 1983
LUM AND ABNER ABROAD, 1956
LUNCH HOUR, 1962
LUNCH WAGON, 1981
LUST IN THE DUST, 1985
LUV, 1967
LUXURY GIRLS, 1953
LYONS IN PARIS, THE, 1955
MA AND PA KETTLE, 1949
MA AND PA KETTLE AT HOME, 1954
MA AND PA KETTLE AT THE FAIR, 1952
MA AND PA KETTLE AT WAIKIKI, 1955
MA AND PA KETTLE BACK ON THE FARM, 1951
MA AND PA KETTLE GO TO TOWN, 1950
MA AND PA KETTLE ON VACATION, 1953
MACARONI, 1985
MAD HATTERS, THE, 1935
MAD LITTLE ISLAND, 1958
MAD MISS MANTON, THE, 1938
MAD WEDNESDAY, 1950
MADAME, 1963
MADAME LOUISE, 1951
MADAME RACKETEER, 1932
MADCAP OF THE HOUSE, 1950
MADDEST CAR IN THE WORLD, THE, 1974
MADE FOR EACH OTHER, 1939
MADE FOR EACH OTHER, 1971
MADE IN HEAVEN, 1952
MADE IN ITALY, 1967
MADE IN PARIS, 1966
MADIGAN'S MILLIONS, 1970
MADMAN OF LAB 4, THE, 1967
MADWOMAN OF CHAILLOT, THE, 1969
MAGIC CHRISTIAN, THE, 1970
MAGIC SPECTACLES, 1961
MAGIC TOWN, 1947
MAGNET, THE, 1950
MAGNIFICENT CUCKOLD, THE, 1965
MAGNIFICENT DOPE, THE, 1942
MAGNIFICENT ONE, THE, 1974

MAGNIFICENT ROGUE, THE, 1946
MAGNIFICENT SEVEN DEADLY SINS, THE, 1971
MAGNIFICENT TRAMP, THE, 1962
MAGNIFICENT TWO, THE, 1967
MAID FOR MURDER, 1963
MAID TO ORDER, 1932
MAID TO ORDER, 1987
MAIDEN FOR A PRINCE, A, 1967
MAID'S NIGHT OUT, 1938
MAIN EVENT, THE, 1979
MAIN STREET KID, THE, 1947
MAIN STREET TO BROADWAY, 1953
MAISIE, 1939
MAISIE GETS HER MAN, 1942
MAISIE GOES TO RENO, 1944
MAISIE WAS A LADY, 1941
MAJOR AND THE MINOR, THE, 1942
MAJOR BARBARA, 1941
MAJORITY OF ONE, A, 1961
MAKE A MILLION, 1935
MAKE IT THREE, 1938
MAKE ME A STAR, 1932
MAKE ME AN OFFER, 1954
MAKE MINE A DOUBLE, 1962
MAKE MINE A MILLION, 1965
MAKE MINE MINK, 1960
MAKE WAY FOR A LADY, 1936
MAKE YOUR OWN BED, 1944
MAKING MR. RIGHT, 1987
MAKING THE GRADE, 1984
MALATESTA'S CARNIVAL, 1973
MALCOLM, 1986
MALE ANIMAL, THE, 1942
MALE COMPANION, 1965
MALE HUNT, 1965
MALIBU BEACH, 1978
MALIBU BIKINI SHOP, THE, 1987
MALICIOUS, 1974
MALTESE BIPPY, THE, 1969
MAMA LOVES PAPA, 1933
MAMA LOVES PAPA, 1945
MAMA RUNS WILD, 1938
MAMA STEPS OUT, 1937
MAMMA DRACULA, 1980
MAMMY, 1930
MAN, A WOMAN, AND A BANK, A, 1979
MAN, A WOMAN AND A KILLER, A, 1975
MAN ABOUT TOWN, 1939
MAN ABOUT TOWN, 1947
MAN ALIVE, 1945
MAN CALLED DAGGER, A, 1967
MAN COULD GET KILLED, A, 1966
MAN FROM BLANKLEY'S, THE, 1930
MAN FROM O.R.G.Y., THE, 1970
MAN FROM THE DINERS' CLUB, THE, 1963
MAN FROM THE EAST, A, 1974
MAN FROM THE FIRST CENTURY, THE, 1961
MAN FROM TORONTO, THE, 1933
MAN I WANT, THE, 1934
MAN IN A COCKED HAT, 1960
MAN IN POSSESSION, THE, 1931
MAN IN THE DINGHY, THE, 1951
MAN IN THE MOON, 1961
MAN IN THE WHITE SUIT, THE, 1952
MAN OF MAYFAIR, 1931
MAN OF THE MOMENT, 1955
MAN OF THE MOMENT, 1935
MAN ON THE FLYING TRAPEZE, THE, 1935
MAN-PROOF, 1938
MAN WANTED, 1932
MAN WHO BROKE THE BANK AT MONTE CARLO, THE, 1935
MAN WHO CAME FOR COFFEE, THE, 1970
MAN WHO CAME TO DINNER, THE, 1942
MAN WHO COULD WORK MIRACLES, THE, 1937
MAN WHO HAD POWER OVER WOMEN, THE, 1970
MAN WHO LIKED FUNERALS, THE, 1959
MAN WHO LOST HIMSELF, THE, 1941
MAN WHO LOVED REDHEADS, THE, 1955
MAN WHO LOVED WOMEN, THE, 1977
MAN WHO LOVED WOMEN, THE, 1983
MAN WHO STOLE THE SUN, THE, 1980
MAN WHO UNDERSTOOD WOMEN, THE, 1959
MAN WHO WALKED THROUGH THE WALL, THE, 1964
MAN WHO WAS SHERLOCK HOLMES, THE, 1937

MAN WHO WASN'T THERE, THE, 1983
MAN WITH A MILLION, 1954
MAN WITH BOGART'S FACE, THE, 1980
MAN WITH CONNECTIONS, THE, 1970
MAN WITH ONE RED SHOE, THE, 1985
MAN WITH THE BALLOONS, THE, 1968
MAN WITH TWO BRAINS, THE, 1983
MANCHU EAGLE MURDER CAPER MYSTERY, THE, 1975
MANDABI, 1970
MANDARIN MYSTERY, THE, 1937
MANDRAGOLA, 1966
MANHATTAN, 1979
MANHATTAN LOVE SONG, 1934
MANHATTAN MOON, 1935
MANIFESTO, 1988
MANNEQUIN, 1987
MAN'S AFFAIR, A, 1949
MAN'S FAVORITE SPORT (?), 1964
MANULESCU, 1933
MANY A SLIP, 1931
MANY HAPPY RETURNS, 1934
MANY RIVERS TO CROSS, 1955
MANY TANKS MR. ATKINS, 1938
MARCH OF THE SPRING HARE, 1969
MARCH ON PARIS 1914—OF GENERALOBERST ALEXANDER VON KLUCK—AND HIS MEMORY OF JESSIE HOLLADAY, 1977
MARGIE, 1940
MARGIE, 1946
MARGIN FOR ERROR, 1943
MARIGOLD MAN, 1970
MARRIAGE CAME TUMBLING DOWN, THE, 1968
MARRIAGE-GO-ROUND, THE, 1960
MARRIAGE IS A PRIVATE AFFAIR, 1944
MARRIAGE—ITALIAN STYLE, 1964
MARRIAGE OF A YOUNG STOCKBROKER, THE, 1971
MARRIAGE OF BALZAMINOV, THE, 1966
MARRIAGE OF FIGARO, THE, 1963
MARRIAGE ON APPROVAL, 1934
MARRIAGE ON THE ROCKS, 1965
MARRIED BACHELOR, 1941
MARRIED BEFORE BREAKFAST, 1937
MARRIED TO THE MOB, 1988
MARRY ME, 1932
MARRY ME AGAIN, 1953
MARRY ME!, 1949
MARRY ME! MARRY ME!, 1969
MARRY THE GIRL, 1935
MARRY THE GIRL, 1937
MARRYING KIND, THE, 1952
MARTYRS OF LOVE, 1968
MARY HAD A LITTLE, 1961
MARY, MARY, 1963
MARY POPPINS, 1964
M*A*S*H, 1970
MASK OF THE DRAGON, 1951
MASQUERADE, 1929
MASQUERADE, 1965
MASQUERADE IN MEXICO, 1945
MASS IS ENDED, THE, 1988
MASTER AND MAN, 1934
MASTER MINDS, 1949
MASTERMIND, 1977
MATCHLESS, 1967
MATCHMAKER, THE, 1958
MATILDA, 1978
MATING GAME, THE, 1959
MATING OF MILLIE, THE, 1948
MATING SEASON, THE, 1951
MATRIMONIAL BED, THE, 1930
MATTER OF INNOCENCE, A, 1968
MATTER OF TIME, A, 1976
MATTER OF WHO, A, 1962
MAX DUGAN RETURNS, 1983
MAXIE, 1985
MAYBE IT'S LOVE, 1930
MAYBE IT'S LOVE, 1935
MAYFAIR MELODY, 1937
MAYOR'S NEST, THE, 1932
M'BLIMEY, 1931
MC FADDEN'S FLATS, 1935
MC GUFFIN, THE, 1985
MC HALE'S NAVY, 1964
MC HALE'S NAVY JOINS THE AIR FORCE, 1965
MC LINTOCK!, 1963

BOLD: Films on Videocassette

ME AND MARLBOROUGH, 1935
ME AND MY GAL, 1932
ME AND MY PAL, 1939
ME AND THE COLONEL, 1958
ME, NATALIE, 1969
MEANEST GAL IN TOWN, THE, 1934
MEANEST MAN IN THE WORLD, THE, 1943
MEATBALLS, 1979
MEATBALLS PART II, 1984
MEATBALLS III, 1987
MEDICINE MAN, THE, 1930
MEDICINE MAN, THE, 1933
MEET ME AT DAWN, 1947
MEET ME IN MOSCOW, 1966
MEET MR. LUCIFER, 1953
MEET MR. PENNY, 1938
MEET MY SISTER, 1933
MEET THE BARON, 1933
MEET THE BOY FRIEND, 1937
MEET THE CHUMP, 1941
MEET THE DUKE, 1949
MEET THE GIRLS, 1938
MEET THE MAYOR, 1938
MEET THE MISSUS, 1937
MEET THE MISSUS, 1940
MEET THE MOB, 1942
MEET THE STEWARTS, 1942
MEET THE WIFE, 1931
MEET THE WILDCAT, 1940
MEIER, 1987
MELODY AND ROMANCE, 1937
MELODY CLUB, 1949
MELODY IN THE DARK, 1948
MELODY MAKER, THE, 1933
MELVIN AND HOWARD, 1980
MELVIN, SON OF ALVIN, 1984
MEMORIES OF ME, 1988
MEN ARE CHILDREN TWICE, 1953
MEN ARE LIKE THAT, 1930
MEN ARE SUCH FOOLS, 1938
MEN, 1985
MEN IN HER DIARY, 1945
MEN PREFER FAT GIRLS, 1981
MERELY MR. HAWKINS, 1938
MERRILY WE GO TO HELL, 1932
MERRILY WE LIVE, 1938
MERRY COMES TO STAY, 1937
MERRY FRINKS, THE, 1934
MERRY WIDOW, THE, 1934
MERRY WIDOW, THE, 1952
MERRY WIVES OF RENO, THE, 1934
MERRY WIVES OF TOBIAS ROUKE, THE, 1972
MERRY-GO-ROUND, 1948
MERTON OF THE MOVIES, 1947
MEXICAN HAYRIDE, 1948
MEXICAN SPITFIRE, 1939
MEXICAN SPITFIRE AT SEA, 1942
MEXICAN SPITFIRE OUT WEST, 1940
MEXICAN SPITFIRE SEES A GHOST, 1942
MEXICAN SPITFIRE'S BABY, 1941
MEXICAN SPITFIRE'S BLESSED EVENT, 1943
MEXICAN SPITFIRE'S ELEPHANT, 1942
MICKI AND MAUDE, 1984
MIDDLE AGE CRAZY, 1980
MIDDLE AGE SPREAD, 1979
MIDDLE WATCH, THE, 1930
MIDDLE WATCH, THE, 1939
MIDNIGHT, 1939
MIDNIGHT DADDIES, 1929
MIDNIGHT INTRUDER, 1938
MIDNIGHT MADNESS, 1980
MIDNIGHT PLEASURES, 1975
MIDNIGHT RUN, 1988
MIDSHIPMAID GOB, 1932
MIDSUMMER NIGHT'S SEX COMEDY, A, 1982
MIDSUMMER'S NIGHT'S DREAM, A, 1935
MIDWIFE, THE, 1961
MILAGRO BEANFIELD WAR, THE, 1988
MILKMAN, THE, 1950
MILKY WAY, THE, 1936
MILLER'S WIFE, THE, 1957
MILLION, THE, 1931
MILLION DOLLAR BABY, 1935
MILLION DOLLAR KID, 1944
MILLION DOLLAR LEGS, 1932
MILLION DOLLAR LEGS, 1939

MILLION DOLLAR MYSTERY, 1987
MILLION DOLLAR WEEKEND, 1948
MILLIONAIRE, THE, 1931
MILLIONAIRE FOR CHRISTY, A, 1951
MILLIONAIRE PLAYBOY, 1940
MILLIONAIRES IN PRISON, 1940
MILLIONAIRESS, THE, 1960
MILLIONS, 1936
MILLIONS IN THE AIR, 1935
MIN AND BILL, 1930
MIND YOUR OWN BUSINESS, 1937
MINI-AFFAIR, THE, 1968
MINNIE AND MOSKOWITZ, 1971
MIRACLE OF MORGAN'S CREEK, THE, 1944
MIRACLES, 1987
MIRACLES DO HAPPEN, 1938
MIRANDA, 1949
MISADVENTURES OF MERLIN JONES, THE, 1964
MISBEHAVING HUSBANDS, 1941
MISBEHAVING LADIES, 1931
MISCHIEF, 1931
MISCHIEF, 1985
MISLEADING LADY, THE, 1932
MISS GRANT TAKES RICHMOND, 1949
MISS MINK OF 1949, 1949
MISS PACIFIC FLEET, 1935
MISS PILGRIM'S PROGRESS, 1950
MISS PRESIDENT, 1935
MISS ROBIN HOOD, 1952
MISS TATLOCK'S MILLIONS, 1948
MISSING, BELIEVED MARRIED, 1937
MISSING CORPSE, THE, 1945
MISSION, THE, 1984
MISSIONARY, THE, 1982
MR. AND MRS. NORTH, 1941
MR. AND MRS. SMITH, 1941
MR. BELVEDERE RINGS THE BELL, 1951
MR. BELVEDERE GOES TO COLLEGE, 1949
MR. BLANDINGS BUILDS HIS DREAM HOUSE, 1948
MR. BOGGS STEPS OUT, 1938
MR. CHUMP, 1938
MISTER CINDERELLA, 1936
MR. DEEDS GOES TO TOWN, 1936
MR. DOODLE KICKS OFF, 1938
MR. DRAKE'S DUCK, 1951
MISTER 880, 1950
MR. HEX, 1946
MR. HOBBS TAKES A VACATION, 1962
MISTER HOBO, 1936
MR. HULOT'S HOLIDAY, 1954
MR. LEMON OF ORANGE, 1931
MR. LORD SAYS NO, 1952
MR. LOVE, 1986
MR. MOM, 1983
MR. MUGGS RIDES AGAIN, 1945
MR. MUGGS STEPS OUT, 1943
MR. MUSIC, 1950
MR. NORTH, 1988
MR. PEABODY AND THE MERMAID, 1948
MR. PEEK-A-BOO, 1951
MR. POTTS GOES TO MOSCOW, 1953
MR. QUINCEY OF MONTE CARLO, 1933
MISTER ROBERTS, 1955
MR. ROBINSON CRUSOE, 1932
MR. SCOUTMASTER, 1953
MR. SKITCH, 1933
MR. STRINGFELLOW SAYS NO, 1937
MR. SYCAMORE, 1975
MISTER TEN PERCENT, 1967
MR. UNIVERSE, 1951
MR. WALKIE TALKIE, 1952
MR. WASHINGTON GOES TO TOWN, 1941
MR. WHAT'S-HIS-NAME, 1935
MR. WISE GUY, 1942
MIXED DOUBLES, 1933
MOB TOWN, 1941
MODEL AND THE MARRIAGE BROKER, THE, 1951
MODEL WIFE, 1941
MODERN GIRLS, 1986
MODERN LOVE, 1929
MODERN PROBLEMS, 1981
MODERN ROMANCE, 1981
MODERN TIMES, 1936
MOLLY AND ME, 1945
MONDO TRASHO, 1970
MONEY FOR NOTHING, 1932

MONEY FROM HOME, 1953
MONEY MEANS NOTHING, 1932
MONEY PIT, THE, 1986
MONEY TALKS, 1933
MONEY TO BURN, 1940
MONITORS, THE, 1969
MONKEY BUSINESS, 1931
MONKEY BUSINESS, 1952
MONKEY IN WINTER, A, 1962
MONSIEUR, 1964
MONSIEUR BEAUCAIRE, 1946
MONSTER IN THE CLOSET, 1987
MONSTER ISLAND, 1981
MONSTER SQUAD, THE, 1987
MONTE CARLO, 1930
MONTE CARLO BABY, 1953
MONTE CARLO STORY, THE, 1957
MONTY PYTHON AND THE HOLY GRAIL, 1975
MONTY PYTHON'S LIFE OF BRIAN, 1979
MONTY PYTHON'S THE MEANING OF LIFE, 1983
MOON IS BLUE, THE, 1953
MOON OVER HER SHOULDER, 1941
MOON OVER PARADOR, 1988
MOONRUNNERS, 1975
MOON'S OUR HOME, THE, 1936
MOONSTRUCK, 1987
MORALIST, THE, 1964
MORALS OF MARCUS, THE, 1936
MORE THAN A SECRETARY, 1936
MORE THE MERRIER, THE, 1943
MORGAN!, 1966
MORGAN STEWART'S COMING HOME, 1987
MORGAN'S MARAUDERS, 1929
MORONS FROM OUTER SPACE, 1985
MOSCOW DOES NOT BELIEVE IN TEARS, 1980
MOSCOW ON THE HUDSON, 1984
MOST BEAUTIFUL AGE, THE, 1970
MOST WANTED MAN, THE, 1962
MOST WONDERFUL EVENING OF MY LIFE, THE, 1972
MOTEL HELL, 1980
MOTHER DIDN'T TELL ME, 1950
MOTHER GOOSE A GO-GO, 1966
MOTHER IS A FRESHMAN, 1949
MOTHER, JUGS & SPEED, 1976
MOTHER WORE TIGHTS, 1947
MOUNTAIN MOONLIGHT, 1941
MOUNTAIN MUSIC, 1937
MOUNTAIN RHYTHM, 1942
MOUNTAINS O'MOURNE, 1938
MOUSE ON THE MOON, THE, 1963
MOUSE THAT ROARED, THE, 1959
MOVE, 1970
MOVE OVER, DARLING, 1963
MOVERS AND SHAKERS, 1985
MOVIE CRAZY, 1932
MOVIE MOVIE, 1978
MOVIE STAR, AMERICAN STYLE, OR, LSD I HATE YOU!, 1966
MOVING, 1988
MOVING VIOLATIONS, 1985
MRS. BROWN, YOU'VE GOT A LOVELY DAUGHTER, 1968
MRS. GIBBONS' BOYS, 1962
MRS. O'MALLEY AND MR. MALONE, 1950
MRS. POLLIFAX-SPY, 1971
MRS. WIGGS OF THE CABBAGE PATCH, 1934
MRS. WIGGS OF THE CABBAGE PATCH, 1942
MUCH TOO SHY, 1942
MUG TOWN, 1943
MUMMY'S BOYS, 1936
MUNCHIES, 1987
MUNSTER, GO HOME, 1966
MUPPETS TAKE MANHATTAN, THE, 1984
MURDER AHOY, 1964
MURDER AT DAWN, 1932
MURDER AT THE GALLOP, 1963
MURDER BY DEATH, 1976
MURDER CZECH STYLE, 1968
MURDER GOES TO COLLEGE, 1937
MURDER, HE SAYS, 1945
MURDER IN THE BLUE ROOM, 1944
MURDER IN THE PRIVATE CAR, 1934
MURDER MOST FOUL, 1964
MURDER ON A BRIDLE PATH, 1936
MURDER ON A HONEYMOON, 1935

MURDER ON THE BLACKBOARD, 1934
MURDER REPORTED, 1958
MURDERER LIVES AT NUMBER 21, THE, 1947
MURMUR OF THE HEART, 1971
MY AMERICAN COUSIN, 1985
MY AMERICAN WIFE, 1936
MY BEST FRIEND'S GIRL, 1984
MY BREAKFAST WITH BLASSIE, 1983
MY BROTHER TALKS TO HORSES, 1946
MY CHAUFFEUR, 1986
MY DARK LADY, 1987
MY DEAR MISS ALDRICH, 1937
MY DEAR SECRETARY, 1948
MY DEMON LOVER, 1987
MY FAIR LADY, 1964
MY FAVORITE BLONDE, 1942
MY FAVORITE BRUNETTE, 1947
MY FAVORITE SPY, 1942
MY FAVORITE SPY, 1951
MY FAVORITE WIFE, 1940
MY FAVORITE YEAR, 1982
MY FRIEND IRMA, 1949
MY FRIEND IRMA GOES WEST, 1950
MY FRIEND THE KING, 1931
MY GAL LOVES MUSIC, 1944
MY GEISHA, 1962
MY HOBO, 1963
MY KINGDOM FOR A COOK, 1943
MY LEARNED FRIEND, 1943
MY LIFE AS A DOG, 1987
MY LIFE WITH CAROLINE, 1941
MY LIPS BETRAY, 1933
MY LITTLE CHICKADEE, 1940
MY LOVE CAME BACK, 1940
MY LUCKY STAR, 1933
MY MAN ADAM, 1986
MY MAN GODFREY, 1936
MY MAN GODFREY, 1957
MY NEW PARTNER, 1984
MY OLD DUCHESS, 1933
MY OTHER HUSBAND, 1985
MY PAL GUS, 1952
MY SISTER EILEEN, 1942
MY SIX LOVES, 1963
MY SON, THE HERO, 1943
MY SON, THE HERO, 1963
MY SON, THE VAMPIRE, 1963
MY STEPMOTHER IS AN ALIEN, 1988
MY SWEET LITTLE VILLAGE, 1985
MY THIRD WIFE GEORGE, 1968
MY UNCLE, 1958
MY WIDOW AND I, 1950
MY WIFE'S BEST FRIEND, 1952
MY WIFE'S ENEMY, 1967
MY WIFE'S FAMILY, 1932
MY WIFE'S FAMILY, 1941
MY WIFE'S FAMILY, 1962
MY WIFE'S HUSBAND, 1965
MY WIFE'S LODGER, 1952
MY WIFE'S RELATIVES, 1939
MYSTERIOUS MISS X, THE, 1939
MYSTERIOUS MR. DAVIS, THE, 1936
MYSTERY MAN, THE, 1935
MYSTIC PIZZA, 1988
NADINE, 1987
NAKED APE, THE, 1973
NAKED GUN, THE, 1988
NAKED WORLD OF HARRISON MARKS, THE, 1967
NANCY DREW AND THE HIDDEN STAIRCASE, 1939
NANCY DREW—DETECTIVE, 1938
NANCY DREW—REPORTER, 1939
NANCY DREW, TROUBLE SHOOTER, 1939
NASTY HABITS, 1976
NASTY RABBIT, THE, 1964
NATHALIE, 1958
NATHALIE, AGENT SECRET, 1960
NATIONAL HEALTH, OR NURSE NORTON'S
   AFFAIR, THE, 1973
NATIONAL LAMPOON'S ANIMAL HOUSE, 1978
NATIONAL LAMPOON'S CLASS REUNION, 1982
**NATIONAL LAMPOON'S EUROPEAN VACATION,
   1985**
NATIONAL LAMPOON'S VACATION, 1983
NAUGHTY ARLETTE, 1951
NAUGHTY CINDERELLA, 1933
NAUGHTY NINETIES, THE, 1945

NAVY BLUES, 1941
NAVY LARK, THE, 1959
NAVY WIFE, 1956
'NEATH BROOKLYN BRIDGE, 1942
NECK AND NECK, 1931
NEIGHBORS, 1981
NEON PALACE, THE, 1970
NEPTUNE'S DAUGHTER, 1949
NERO'S MISTRESS, 1962
NEVER A DULL MOMENT, 1943
NEVER A DULL MOMENT, 1950
NEVER A DULL MOMENT, 1968
NEVER GIVE A SUCKER AN EVEN BREAK, 1941
NEVER ON SUNDAY, 1960
NEVER PUT IT IN WRITING, 1964
NEVER SAY DIE, 1939
NEVER SAY GOODBYE, 1946
NEVER THE TWAIN SHALL MEET, 1931
NEVER TOO LATE, 1965
NEVER TROUBLE TROUBLE, 1931
NEVER WAVE AT A WAC, 1952
NEW ADVENTURES OF GET-RICH-QUICK
   WALLINGFORD, THE, 1931
NEW KIND OF LOVE, A, 1963
NEW LEAF, A, 1971
NEW LIFE, A, 1988
NEW TEACHER, THE, 1941
NEW YORK TOWN, 1941
NEW YORK'S FINEST, 1988
NEWLY RICH, 1931
NEWS HOUNDS, 1947
NEXT STOP, GREENWICH VILLAGE, 1976
NEXT TIME I MARRY, 1938
NEXT TO NO TIME, 1960
NICE GIRL?, 1941
NICE GIRL LIKE ME, A, 1969
NICE GIRLS DON'T EXPLODE, 1987
NICE LITTLE BANK THAT SHOULD BE ROBBED, A,
   1958
NICKELODEON, 1976
NIGHT ALONE, 1938
NIGHT AND DAY, 1933
NIGHT AT THE OPERA, A, 1935
NIGHT AT THE RITZ, A, 1935
NIGHT BEFORE CHRISTMAS, A, 1963
NIGHT BEFORE THE DIVORCE, THE, 1942
NIGHT CALL NURSES, 1974
NIGHT IN CASABLANCA, A, 1946
NIGHT IN THE LIFE OF JIMMY REARDON, A, 1988
NIGHT LIFE OF THE GODS, 1935
NIGHT LIKE THIS, A, 1932
NIGHT OF MAGIC, A, 1944
NIGHT OF THE GARTER, 1933
NIGHT OF THE PROWLER, THE, 1979
NIGHT PATROL, 1984
NIGHT SHIFT, 1982
NIGHT SPOT, 1938
NIGHT THEY RAIDED MINSKY'S, THE, 1968
NIGHT THEY ROBBED BIG BERTHA'S, THE, 1975
NIGHT WE GOT THE BIRD, THE, 1961
NIGHT WORK, 1930
NIGHT WORK, 1939
NIGHTMARE IN BLOOD, 1978
NINE GIRLS, 1944
NINE TO FIVE, 1980
1941, 1979
90 DAYS, 1986
99 AND 44/100% DEAD, 1974
NINOTCHKA, 1939
NITWITS, THE, 1935
NO DEPOSIT, NO RETURN, 1976
NO EXIT, 1930
NO FUNNY BUSINESS, 1934
NO HAUNT FOR A GENTLEMAN, 1952
NO HOLDS BARRED, 1952
NO LADY, 1931
NO LEAVE, NO LOVE, 1946
NO LIMIT, 1931
NO LIMIT, 1935
NO LOVE FOR JUDY, 1955
NO MAN OF HER OWN, 1933
NO MINOR VICES, 1948
NO MONKEY BUSINESS, 1935
NO MORE EXCUSES, 1968
NO MORE LADIES, 1935
NO, MY DARLING DAUGHTER, 1964

NO PARKING, 1938
NO PLACE TO GO, 1939
NO RANSOM, 1935
NO ROOM AT THE INN, 1950
NO ROOM FOR THE GROOM, 1952
NO SEX PLEASE—WE'RE BRITISH, 1979
NO SMALL AFFAIR, 1984
NO SMOKING, 1955
NO SURRENDER, 1986
NO TIME FOR COMEDY, 1940
NO TIME FOR FLOWERS, 1952
NO TIME FOR LOVE, 1943
NO TIME FOR SERGEANTS, 1958
NO TIME TO MARRY, 1938
NO WAY TO TREAT A LADY, 1968
NOBODY'S BABY, 1937
NOBODY'S FOOL, 1936
NOBODY'S PERFECT, 1968
NOBODY'S PERFEKT, 1981
NOCTURNA, 1979
NOISY NEIGHBORS, 1929
NOOSE HANGS HIGH, THE, 1948
NORMAN...IS THAT YOU?, 1976
NORMAN LOVES ROSE, 1982
NORTH AVENUE IRREGULARS, THE, 1979
NORWOOD, 1970
NOT A HOPE IN HELL, 1960
NOT DAMAGED, 1930
NOT FOR PUBLICATION, 1984
NOT NOW DARLING, 1975
NOT OF THIS EARTH, 1988
NOT ON YOUR LIFE, 1965
NOT QUITE JERUSALEM, 1985
NOT SINCE CASANOVA, 1988
NOT SO DUMB, 1930
NOT SO DUSTY, 1936
NOT SO DUSTY, 1956
NOT SO QUIET ON THE WESTERN FRONT, 1930
NOT WANTED ON VOYAGE, 1957
NOT WITH MY WIFE, YOU DON'T!, 1966
NOTHING BARRED, 1961
NOTHING BUT THE BEST, 1964
NOTHING BUT THE TRUTH, 1929
NOTHING BUT THE TRUTH, 1941
NOTHING BUT TROUBLE, 1944
NOTHING IN COMMON, 1986
NOTHING LASTS FOREVER, 1984
NOTHING LIKE PUBLICITY, 1936
NOTHING PERSONAL, 1980
NOTHING SACRED, 1937
NOTORIOUS LANDLADY, THE, 1962
NOTORIOUS SOPHIE LANG, THE, 1934
NOUS IRONS A PARIS, 1949
NOVEL AFFAIR, A, 1957
NOW YOU SEE HIM, NOW YOU DON'T, 1972
NUDE BOMB, THE, 1980
NUDE IN HIS POCKET, 1962
NUISANCE, THE, 1933
NUMBER SEVENTEEN, 1932
NURSE ON WHEELS, 1964
NUT FARM, THE, 1935
NUTTY, NAUGHTY CHATEAU, 1964
NUTTY PROFESSOR, THE, 1963
O. HENRY'S FULL HOUSE, 1952
O LUCKY MAN!, 1973
OBLIGING YOUNG LADY, 1941
O.C. AND STIGGS, 1987
OCEAN DRIVE WEEKEND, 1986
OCEAN'S ELEVEN, 1960
ODD COUPLE, THE, 1968
ODD JOB, THE, 1978
ODD JOBS, 1986
OF WAYWARD LOVE, 1964
OFF BEAT, 1986
OFF LIMITS, 1953
OFF THE DOLE, 1935
OFF THE WALL, 1983
OFF TO THE RACES, 1937
OFFICE PICNIC, THE, 1974
OFFICER'S MESS, THE, 1931
OH BOY!, 1938
OH! CALCUTTA!, 1972
**OH DAD, POOR DAD, MAMA'S HUNG YOU IN THE
   CLOSET AND I'M FEELIN' SO SAD, 1967**
OH DADDY!, 1935
OH DOCTOR, 1937

BOLD: Films on Videocassette

OH, FOR A MAN!, 1930
OH, GOD!, 1977
OH GOD! BOOK II, 1980
OH GOD! YOU DEVIL, 1984
OH, HEAVENLY DOG!, 1980
OH JOHNNY, HOW YOU CAN LOVE!, 1940
OH, MEN! OH, WOMEN!, 1957
OH, MR. PORTER!, 1937
OH NO DOCTOR!, 1934
OH! SAILOR, BEHAVE!, 1930
OH, WHAT A NIGHT, 1935
O'HARA'S WIFE, 1983
OHAYO, 1962
OKAY FOR SOUND, 1937
OKLAHOMA CRUDE, 1973
OLD BILL AND SON, 1940
OLD BONES OF THE RIVER, 1938
OLD DARK HOUSE, THE, 1963
OLD DRACULA, 1975
OLD FAITHFUL, 1935
OLD-FASHIONED WAY, THE, 1934
OLD HUTCH, 1936
OLD MOTHER RILEY, 1937
OLD MOTHER RILEY, 1952
OLD MOTHER RILEY AT HOME, 1945
OLD MOTHER RILEY, DETECTIVE, 1943
OLD MOTHER RILEY, HEADMISTRESS, 1950
OLD MOTHER RILEY IN BUSINESS, 1940
OLD MOTHER RILEY IN PARIS, 1938
OLD MOTHER RILEY IN SOCIETY, 1940
OLD MOTHER RILEY JOINS UP, 1939
OLD MOTHER RILEY MP, 1939
OLD MOTHER RILEY OVERSEAS, 1943
OLD MOTHER RILEY'S CIRCUS, 1941
OLD MOTHER RILEY'S GHOSTS, 1941
OLD MOTHER RILEY'S JUNGLE TREASURE, 1951
OLD SOLDIERS NEVER DIE, 1931
OLD SPANISH CUSTOM, AN, 1936
OLD SPANISH CUSTOMERS, 1932
OLDEST PROFESSION, THE, 1968
OLSEN'S BIG MOMENT, 1934
OMICRON, 1963
ON AGAIN—OFF AGAIN, 1937
ON APPROVAL, 1930
ON APPROVAL, 1944
ON GOLDEN POND, 1981
ON MOONLIGHT BAY, 1951
ON OUR MERRY WAY, 1948
ON OUR SELECTION, 1930
ON THE AVENUE, 1937
ON THE BEAT, 1962
ON THE BUSES, 1972
ON THE DOUBLE, 1961
ON THE LEVEL, 1930
ON THE RIGHT TRACK, 1981
ON THE RIVIERA, 1951
ON THEIR OWN, 1940
ON VELVET, 1938
ON YOUR TOES, 1939
ONCE A GENTLEMAN, 1930
ONCE BITTEN, 1985
ONCE IN A BLUE MOON, 1936
ONCE IN A LIFETIME, 1932
ONCE MORE, MY DARLING, 1949
ONCE MORE, WITH FEELING, 1960
ONCE UPON A DREAM, 1949
ONCE UPON A HONEYMOON, 1942
ONCE UPON A HORSE, 1958
ONCE UPON A SCOUNDREL, 1973
ONCE UPON A TIME, 1944
ONE BODY TOO MANY, 1944
ONE CRAZY SUMMER, 1986
ONE DARK NIGHT, 1939
ONE EMBARRASSING NIGHT, 1930
1=2?, 1975
ONE EXCITING ADVENTURE, 1935
ONE EXCITING NIGHT, 1945
ONE EXCITING WEEK, 1946
ONE FRIGHTENED NIGHT, 1935
ONE GOOD TURN, 1936
ONE GOOD TURN, 1955
ONE HOUR LATE, 1935
ONE HYSTERICAL NIGHT, 1930
ONE IN A MILLION, 1936
ONE LAST FLING, 1949
$1,000,000 DUCK, 1971

ONE MILLION DOLLARS, 1965
ONE MORE SATURDAY NIGHT, 1986
ONE MORE SPRING, 1935
ONE MORE TIME, 1970
ONE NEW YORK NIGHT, 1935
ONE NIGHT ONLY, 1986
ONE RAINY AFTERNOON, 1936
ONE ROMANTIC NIGHT, 1930
$1,000 A MINUTE, 1935
$1,000 A TOUCHDOWN, 1939
1,000 SHAPES OF A FEMALE, 1963
ONE THRILLING NIGHT, 1942
ONE TOUCH OF VENUS, 1948
ONE, TWO, THREE, 1961
ONE WAY PENDULUM, 1965
ONE WAY TO LOVE, 1946
ONE WAY WAHINI, 1965
ONE WILD NIGHT, 1938
ONE WILD OAT, 1951
ONE WISH TOO MANY, 1956
ONLY A WOMAN, 1966
ONLY GOD KNOWS, 1974
ONLY SAPS WORK, 1930
ONLY TWO CAN PLAY, 1962
ONLY WHEN I LARF, 1968
ONLY WHEN I LAUGH, 1981
OPEN THE DOOR AND SEE ALL THE PEOPLE, 1964
OPENED BY MISTAKE, 1940
OPERATION BULLSHINE, 1963
OPERATION CAMEL, 1961
OPERATION CUPID, 1960
OPERATION DAMES, 1959
OPERATION DELILAH, 1966
OPERATION KID BROTHER, 1967
OPERATION LOVEBIRDS, 1968
OPERATION MAD BALL, 1957
OPERATION PETTICOAT, 1959
OPERATION ST. PETER'S, 1968
OPERATION SNAFU, 1965
OPERATION SNATCH, 1962
OPPOSITE SEX, THE, 1956
ORDERS ARE ORDERS, 1959
ORDERS IS ORDERS, 1934
OTLEY, 1969
OUR BETTERS, 1933
OUR FATHER, 1985
OUR HEARTS WERE GROWING UP, 1946
OUR HEARTS WERE YOUNG AND GAY, 1944
OUR MAN FLINT, 1966
OUR MAN IN HAVANA, 1960
OUR MISS BROOKS, 1956
OUR MISS FRED, 1972
OUR NEIGHBORS—THE CARTERS, 1939
OUR RELATIONS, 1936
OUR WIFE, 1941
OUT ALL NIGHT, 1933
OUT OF IT, 1969
OUT OF THE BLUE, 1947
OUT OF TOWNERS, THE, 1970
OUT WEST WITH THE HARDYS, 1938
OUT WEST WITH THE PEPPERS, 1940
OUTCAST, THE, 1934
OUTLAWS IS COMING, THE, 1965
OUTRAGEOUS!, 1977
OUTRAGEOUS FORTUNE, 1987
OVER MY DEAD BODY, 1942
OVER SHE GOES, 1937
OVER THE BROOKLYN BRIDGE, 1984
OVER THE GARDEN WALL, 1950
OVER THE MOON, 1940
OVER THE ODDS, 1961
OVER 21, 1945
OVERBOARD, 1987
OWL AND THE PUSSYCAT, THE, 1970
PACK UP YOUR TROUBLES, 1932
PACK UP YOUR TROUBLES, 1939
PACK UP YOUR TROUBLES, 1940
PAD...AND HOW TO USE IT, THE, 1966
PADDY, 1970
PADDY, THE NEXT BEST THING, 1933
PAGE MISS GLORY, 1935
PAID IN ERROR, 1938
PAIR OF BRIEFS, A, 1963
PALEFACE, THE, 1948
PALM BEACH STORY, THE, 1942
PALM SPRINGS WEEKEND, 1963

PALMY DAYS, 1931
PALOOKA, 1934
PANAMA HATTIE, 1942
PANDEMONIUM, 1982
PANIC BUTTON, 1964
PANIC IN THE PARLOUR, 1957
PAPA'S DELICATE CONDITION, 1963
PAPER CHASE, THE, 1973
PAPER LION, 1968
PAPER MOON, 1973
PAR OU T'ES RENTRE? ON T'A PAS VUE SORTIR, 1984
PARADISE ALLEY, 1962
PARADISE ALLEY, 1978
PARADISE FOR THREE, 1938
PARADISE MOTEL, 1985
PARADISIO, 1962
PARDNERS, 1956
PARDON MY BRUSH, 1964
PARDON MY FRENCH, 1951
PARDON MY PAST, 1945
PARDON MY SARONG, 1942
PARDON MY STRIPES, 1942
PARDON OUR NERVE, 1939
PARDON US, 1931
PARENT TRAP, THE, 1961
PARIS HONEYMOON, 1939
PARIS IN THE MONTH OF AUGUST, 1968
PARIS OOH-LA-LA!, 1963
PARIS PLAYBOYS, 1954
PARIS WHEN IT SIZZLES, 1964
PARLOR, BEDROOM AND BATH, 1931
PART TIME WIFE, 1930
PART-TIME WIFE, 1961
PARTNERS, 1982
PARTNERS IN TIME, 1946
PARTY, THE, 1968
PARTY CAMP, 1987
PARTY HUSBAND, 1931
PARTY PARTY, 1983
PARTY WIRE, 1935
PARTY'S OVER, THE, 1934
PASS THE AMMO, 1988
PASSAGE FROM HONG KONG, 1941
PASSION HOLIDAY, 1963
PASSIONATE PLUMBER, 1932
PASSIONATE SENTRY, THE, 1952
PASSIONATE THIEF, THE, 1963
PASSKEY TO DANGER, 1946
PASSPORT HUSBAND, 1938
PASSPORT TO DESTINY, 1944
PASSPORT TO PIMLICO, 1949
PAT AND MIKE, 1952
PATERNITY, 1981
PATH OF GLORY, THE, 1934
PATRICIA GETS HER MAN, 1937
PATSY, THE, 1964
PATTI ROCKS, 1988
PAULINE AT THE BEACH, 1983
P.C. JOSSER, 1931
PEACH O'RENO, 1931
PEARL OF TLAYUCAN, THE, 1964
PEARLS BRING TEARS, 1937
PEE-WEE'S BIG ADVENTURE, 1985
PEEK-A-BOO, 1961
PEEPER, 1975
PEG O' MY HEART, 1933
PEGGY, 1950
PEGGY SUE GOT MARRIED, 1986
PEKING OPERA BLUES, 1986
PENELOPE, 1966
PENNY PARADISE, 1938
PENNY POINTS TO PARADISE, 1951
PENNY POOL, THE, 1937
PENNY PRINCESS, 1953
PENNY SERENADE, 1941
PENROD AND HIS TWIN BROTHER, 1938
PENROD AND SAM, 1931
PENROD AND SAM, 1937
PENROD'S DOUBLE TROUBLE, 1938
PEOPLE MEET AND SWEET MUSIC FILLS THE HEART, 1969
PEOPLE WILL TALK, 1935
PEOPLE WILL TALK, 1951
PEPE, 1960
PEPPER, 1936

PEPPERMINT SODA, 1979
PERCY, 1971
PERFECT CLUE, THE, 1935
PERFECT COUPLE, A, 1979
PERFECT FRIDAY, 1970
PERFECT FURLOUGH, THE, 1958
PERFECT GENTLEMAN, THE, 1935
PERFECT LADY, THE, 1931
PERFECT MARRIAGE, THE, 1946
PERFECT MATCH, THE, 1987
PERFECT SNOB, THE, 1941
PERFECT SPECIMEN, THE, 1937
PERFECT STRANGERS, 1950
PERFECT UNDERSTANDING, 1933
PERFECT WOMAN, THE, 1950
PERILS OF PAULINE, THE, 1947
PERILS OF PAULINE, THE, 1967
PERILS OF P.K., THE, 1986
PERIOD OF ADJUSTMENT, 1962
PERSONAL PROPERTY, 1937
PERSONAL SERVICES, 1987
PERSONALS, THE, 1982
PETE 'N' TILLIE, 1972
PETERVILLE DIAMOND, THE, 1942
PETEY WHEATSTRAW, 1978
PETIT CON, 1985
PETTICOAT FEVER, 1936
PETTICOAT LARCENY, 1943
PETTICOAT PIRATES, 1961
PETTICOAT POLITICS, 1941
PETULIA, 1968
PHANTOM OF THE PARADISE, 1974
PHFFFT!, 1954
PHILADELPHIA STORY, THE, 1940
PHONY AMERICAN, THE, 1964
PHYNX, THE, 1970
PICCADILLY JIM, 1936
PICK A STAR, 1937
PICK-UP SUMMER, 1981
PICKWICK PAPERS, THE, 1952
PIECE OF THE ACTION, A, 1977
PIGEON THAT TOOK ROME, THE, 1962
PIGSKIN PARADE, 1936
PILGRIM LADY, THE, 1947
PILLOW TALK, 1959
PILLOW TO POST, 1945
PIMPERNEL SVENSSON, 1953
PIN UP GIRL, 1944
PINK MOTEL, 1983
PINK NIGHTS, 1985
PINK PANTHER, THE, 1964
PINK PANTHER STRIKES AGAIN, THE, 1976
PIRATE MOVIE, THE, 1982
PIZZA TRIANGLE, THE, 1970
PLANES, TRAINS AND AUTOMOBILES, 1987
PLANK, THE, 1967
PLATINUM BLONDE, 1931
PLAY IT AGAIN, SAM, 1972
PLAY UP THE BAND, 1935
PLAYBOY, THE, 1942
PLAYBOY OF PARIS, 1930
PLAYBOY OF THE WESTERN WORLD, THE, 1963
PLAYGIRLS AND THE BELLBOY, THE, 1962
PLAYGROUND, THE, 1965
PLAYING FOR KEEPS, 1986
PLAYMATES, 1941
PLAYTIME, 1973
PLAZA SUITE, 1971
PLEASE BELIEVE ME, 1950
PLEASE DON'T EAT THE DAISIES, 1960
PLEASE! MR. BALZAC, 1957
PLEASE, NOT NOW!, 1963
PLEASE SIR, 1971
PLEASE STAND BY, 1972
PLEASE TEACHER, 1937
PLEASE TURN OVER, 1960
PLEASURE OF HIS COMPANY, THE, 1961
PLUNDER, 1931
POACHER'S DAUGHTER, THE, 1960
POCKETFUL OF MIRACLES, 1961
POET'S PUB, 1949
POLICE ACADEMY, 1984
POLICE ACADEMY 5: ASSIGNMENT MIAMI BEACH, 1988
POLICE ACADEMY 4: CITIZENS ON PATROL, 1987
POLICE ACADEMY 3: BACK IN TRAINING, 1986

POLICE ACADEMY 2: THEIR FIRST ASSIGNMENT, 1985
POLICEMAN OF THE 16TH PRECINCT, THE, 1963
POLITICAL PARTY, A, 1933
POLITICS, 1931
POLLYANNA, 1960
POLO JOE, 1936
POLYESTER, 1981
POM POM GIRLS, THE, 1976
POOR LITTLE RICH GIRL, 1936
POOR OLD BILL, 1931
POOR RICH, THE, 1934
POP ALWAYS PAYS, 1940
POPEYE, 1980
POPI, 1969
POPPY, 1936
POR MIS PISTOLAS, 1969
PORKY'S, 1982
PORKY'S REVENGE, 1985
PORKY'S II: THE NEXT DAY, 1983
PORTNOY'S COMPLAINT, 1972
POSTMAN DIDN'T RING, THE, 1942
POSTMAN'S KNOCK, 1962
POT CARRIERS, THE, 1962
POT LUCK, 1936
POT O' GOLD, 1941
PRACTICALLY YOURS, 1944
PRAISE MARX AND PASS THE AMMUNITION, 1970
PREACHERMAN, 1971
PREPPIES, 1984
PRESENTING LILY MARS, 1943
PRESIDENT'S ANALYST, THE, 1967
PRESS FOR TIME, 1966
PRETTY BABY, 1950
PRETTY MAIDS ALL IN A ROW, 1971
PRETTY SMART, 1987
PRIDE OF THE BOWERY, 1941
PRIDE OF THE FORCE, THE, 1933
PRIEST'S WIFE, THE, 1971
PRIME OF MISS JEAN BRODIE, THE, 1969
PRIMITIVE LOVE, 1966
PRIMROSE PATH, 1940
PRINCE AND THE SHOWGIRL, THE, 1957
PRINCESS ACADEMY, THE, 1987
PRINCESS AND THE PIRATE, THE, 1944
PRINCESS BRIDE, THE, 1987
PRINCESS CHARMING, 1935
PRINCESS COMES ACROSS, THE, 1936
PRINCESS O'HARA, 1935
PRINCESS O'ROURKE, 1943
PRISONER OF SECOND AVENUE, THE, 1975
PRISONER OF ZENDA, THE, 1979
PRIVATE AFFAIRS, 1940
PRIVATE ANGELO, 1949
PRIVATE BENJAMIN, 1980
PRIVATE EYES, 1953
PRIVATE EYES, THE, 1980
PRIVATE FUNCTION, A, 1985
PRIVATE JONES, 1933
PRIVATE LESSONS, 1981
PRIVATE LIFE OF SHERLOCK HOLMES, THE, 1970
PRIVATE LIVES, 1931
PRIVATE LIVES OF ADAM AND EVE, THE, 1961
PRIVATE NAVY OF SGT. O'FARRELL, THE, 1968
PRIVATE PARTS, 1972
PRIVATE RESORT, 1985
PRIVATE SCANDAL, 1934
PRIVATE SCHOOL, 1983
PRIVATE SECRETARY, THE, 1935
PRIVATE WAR OF MAJOR BENSON, THE, 1955
PRIVATE'S AFFAIR, A, 1959
PRIVATES ON PARADE, 1984
PRIVATE'S PROGRESS, 1956
PRIZE, THE, 1952
PRIZE, THE, 1963
PRIZE FIGHTER, THE, 1979
PRIZZI'S HONOR, 1985
PROBATION, 1932
PRODIGAL, THE, 1931
PRODUCERS, THE, 1967
PROFESSIONAL SWEETHEART, 1933
PROFESSOR BEWARE, 1938
PROFESSOR TIM, 1957
PROJECT X, 1987
PROJECTIONIST, THE, 1970
PROMISE HER ANYTHING, 1966

PROMISES, PROMISES, 1963
PROSPERITY, 1932
PROTECTORS, BOOK 1, THE, 1981
PROTOCOL, 1984
PRUDENCE AND THE PILL, 1968
PSYCHO III, 1986
PSYCHOS IN LOVE, 1987
PSYCOSISSIMO, 1962
PUBLIC DEB NO. 1, 1940
PUBLIC EYE, THE, 1972
PUBLIC LIFE OF HENRY THE NINTH, THE, 1934
PUBLIC MENACE, 1935
PUBLIC NUISANCE NO. 1, 1936
PUBLIC PIGEON NO. 1, 1957
PUBLIC WEDDING, 1937
PUDDIN' HEAD, 1941
PULP, 1972
PUNCH AND JUDY MAN, THE, 1963
PUNCHLINE, 1988
PURE HELL OF ST. TRINIAN'S, THE, 1961
PURPLE ROSE OF CAIRO, THE, 1985
PURSUIT OF HAPPINESS, THE, 1934
PUSSYCAT, PUSSYCAT, I LOVE YOU, 1970
PUTNEY SWOPE, 1969
PYGMALION, 1938
QUACKSER FORTUNE HAS A COUSIN IN THE BRONX, 1970
QUALITY STREET, 1937
QUARTERBACK, THE, 1940
QUARTET, 1949
QUEEN FOR A DAY, 1951
QUEEN HIGH, 1930
QUEEN OF HEARTS, 1936
QUEENS, THE, 1968
QUICK, BEFORE IT MELTS, 1964
QUICK, LET'S GET MARRIED, 1965
QUICK MILLIONS, 1939
QUICK MONEY, 1938
QUIET MAN, THE, 1952
QUIET PLEASE, 1938
QUIET WEDDING, 1941
QUIET WEEKEND, 1948
RABBI AND THE SHIKSE, THE, 1976
RABBIT TEST, 1978
RACHEL AND THE STRANGER, 1948
RACING ROMANCE, 1937
RACING WITH THE MOON, 1984
RACKETY RAX, 1932
RACQUET, 1979
RADIO CITY REVELS, 1938
RADIO DAYS, 1987
RADIO LOVER, 1936
RADIO PIRATES, 1935
RADIO STARS ON PARADE, 1945
RADIOACTIVE DREAMS, 1986
RAFFERTY AND THE GOLD DUST TWINS, 1975
RAFTER ROMANCE, 1934
RAINBOW ISLAND, 1944
RAINMAKER, THE, 1956
RAINMAKERS, THE, 1935
RAISING A RIOT, 1957
RAISING ARIZONA, 1987
RALLY 'ROUND THE FLAG, BOYS!, 1958
RAMSBOTTOM RIDES AGAIN, 1956
RANCHO DELUXE, 1975
RANDOLPH FAMILY, THE, 1945
RASCALS, 1938
RAT PFINK AND BOO BOO, 1966
RAT RACE, THE, 1960
RATATAPLAN, 1979
RATIONING, 1944
RATTLE OF A SIMPLE MAN, 1964
RAVEN, THE, 1963
RAVISHING IDIOT, A, 1966
REACHING FOR THE MOON, 1931
REAL GENIUS, 1985
REAL LIFE, 1979
REBOUND, 1931
RECORD CITY, 1978
RECRUITS, 1986
RED GARTERS, 1954
RED HOT RHYTHM, 1930
RED HOT SPEED, 1929
RED INN, THE, 1954
RED LIGHTS AHEAD, 1937
RED MONARCH, 1983

BOLD: Films on Videocassette

RED SALUTE, 1935
REDHEAD, 1941
REDUCING, 1931
REFORM SCHOOL GIRLS, 1986
REFORMER AND THE REDHEAD, THE, 1950
REG'LAR FELLERS, 1941
REIVERS, THE, 1969
RELUCTANT ASTRONAUT, THE, 1967
RELUCTANT DEBUTANTE, THE, 1958
RELUCTANT HEROES, 1951
RELUCTANT SAINT, THE, 1962
REMAINS TO BE SEEN, 1953
REMARKABLE ANDREW, THE, 1942
REMARKABLE MR. KIPPS, 1942
REMARKABLE MR. PENNYPACKER, THE, 1959
REMEMBER?, 1939
REMEMBER LAST NIGHT, 1935
REMEMBER THE NIGHT, 1940
REMOTE CONTROL, 1930
RENDEZ-VOUS, 1932
RENDEZVOUS, 1935
RENDEZVOUS WITH ANNIE, 1946
RENO AND THE DOC, 1984
RENT CONTROL, 1981
RENTADICK, 1972
RENTED LIPS, 1988
REPO MAN, 1984
RESERVED FOR LADIES, 1932
RETURN OF CAPTAIN INVINCIBLE, THE, 1983
RETURN OF OCTOBER, THE, 1948
RETURN OF THE LIVING DEAD, 1985
RETURN OF THE LIVING DEAD PART II, 1988
RETURN OF THE PINK PANTHER, THE, 1975
RETURN TO HORROR HIGH, 1987
REUBEN, REUBEN, 1983
REUNION IN RENO, 1951
REUNION IN VIENNA, 1933
REVENGE OF THE CHEERLEADERS, 1976
REVENGE OF THE NERDS, 1984
REVENGE OF THE NERDS II: NERDS IN PARADISE, 1987
REVENGE OF THE PINK PANTHER, 1978
REVENGE OF THE TEENAGE VIXENS FROM OUTER SPACE, THE, 1986
RHINESTONE, 1984
RHINOCEROS, 1974
RHUBARB, 1951
RHYTHM IN THE CLOUDS, 1937
RHYTHM OF THE ISLANDS, 1943
RHYTHM ON THE RIVER, 1940
RICH KIDS, 1979
RICH MAN, POOR GIRL, 1938
RICHARD, 1972
RICHEST GIRL IN THE WORLD, THE, 1934
RICHEST MAN IN TOWN, 1941
RICOCHET ROMANCE, 1954
RIDE 'EM COWBOY, 1942
RIDE THE WILD SURF, 1964
RIDERS OF THE STORM, 1988
RIDING HIGH, 1937
RIDING HIGH, 1950
RIDING ON AIR, 1937
RIFFRAFF, 1947
RIGHT AGE TO MARRY, THE, 1935
RIGHT TO THE HEART, 1942
RIKKY AND PETE, 1988
RING-A-DING RHYTHM, 1962
RING AROUND THE CLOCK, 1953
RING OF BRIGHT WATER, 1969
RINGS ON HER FINGERS, 1942
RINGSIDE MAISIE, 1941
RIO RITA, 1929
RIO RITA, 1942
RISE AND RISE OF MICHAEL RIMMER, THE, 1970
RISE AND SHINE, 1941
RISING DAMP, 1980
RISKY BUSINESS, 1983
RITA, SUE AND BOB TOO!, 1987
RITZ, THE, 1976
RIVER HOUSE GHOST, THE, 1932
RIVERBOAT RHYTHM, 1946
ROAD SHOW, 1941
ROAD TO BALI, 1952
ROAD TO HONG KONG, THE, 1962
ROAD TO MOROCCO, 1942
ROAD TO RENO, THE, 1938

ROAD TO RIO, 1947
ROAD TO SINGAPORE, 1940
ROAD TO UTOPIA, 1945
ROAD TO ZANZIBAR, 1941
ROADHOUSE 66, 1984
ROADIE, 1980
ROBERTA, 1935
ROBIN AND THE SEVEN HOODS, 1964
ROCCO PAPALEO, 1974
ROCK-A-BYE BABY, 1958
ROCK 'N' ROLL HIGH SCHOOL, 1979
ROCKABILLY BABY, 1957
ROCKERS, 1980
ROCKIN' IN THE ROCKIES, 1945
ROCKIN' ROAD TRIP, 1986
ROCKY HORROR PICTURE SHOW, THE, 1975
ROCKY MOUNTAIN MYSTERY, 1935
ROGUE SONG, THE, 1930
ROLLING HOME, 1935
ROLLING IN MONEY, 1934
ROMAN HOLIDAY, 1953
ROMAN SCANDALS, 1933
ROMANCE A LA CARTE, 1938
ROMANCE AND RICHES, 1937
ROMANCE IN THE RAIN, 1934
ROMANCE ON THE HIGH SEAS, 1948
ROMANCE ON THE RUN, 1938
ROMANOFF AND JULIET, 1961
ROMANTIC COMEDY, 1983
ROMANTIC ENGLISHWOMAN, THE, 1975
ROOKIE, THE, 1959
ROOKIES IN BURMA, 1943
ROOM FOR ONE MORE, 1952
ROOM FOR TWO, 1940
ROOM IN THE HOUSE, 1955
ROOM SERVICE, 1938
ROOM WITH A VIEW, A, 1986
ROOMMATES, 1962
ROONEY, 1958
ROSALIE, 1937
ROSE BOWL, 1936
ROSE FOR EVERYONE, A, 1967
ROSEBUD BEACH HOTEL, 1984
ROSIE!, 1967
ROSIE THE RIVETER, 1944
ROTHSCHILD, 1938
ROTTEN TO THE CORE, 1956
ROUGH CUT, 1980
ROUGH, TOUGH AND READY, 1945
ROXANNE, 1987
ROXIE HART, 1942
ROYAL AFFAIR, A, 1950
ROYAL BED, THE, 1931
ROYAL FAMILY OF BROADWAY, THE, 1930
ROYAL FLASH, 1975
ROYAL SCANDAL, A, 1945
ROYAL WEDDING, 1951
RUBY, 1971
RUGGLES OF RED GAP, 1935
RULING CLASS, THE, 1972
RUN FOR THE HILLS, 1953
RUN FOR YOUR MONEY, A, 1950
RUN FOR YOUR WIFE, 1966
RUNAROUND, THE, 1931
RUNAROUND, THE, 1946
RUNAWAY BRIDE, 1930
RUNAWAY BUS, THE, 1954
RUNAWAY LADIES, 1935
RUSSIANS ARE COMING, THE RUSSIANS ARE COMING, THE, 1966
RUSTLER'S RHAPSODY, 1985
RUTHLESS PEOPLE, 1986
RYDER, P.I., 1986
SABRINA, 1954
SACRED HEARTS, 1984
SAD SACK, THE, 1957
SAFETY IN NUMBERS, 1938
SAIL A CROOKED SHIP, 1961
SAILOR BE GOOD, 1933
SAILOR TAKES A WIFE, THE, 1946
SAILOR'S DON'T CARE, 1940
SAILORS' HOLIDAY, 1929
SAILOR'S HOLIDAY, 1944
SAILOR'S LADY, 1940
SAILOR'S LUCK, 1933
SAILORS ON LEAVE, 1941

ST. BENNY THE DIP, 1951
SAINTED SISTERS, THE, 1948
SAINTLY SINNERS, 1962
SAINTS AND SINNERS, 1949
SALLAH, 1965
SALLY AND SAINT ANNE, 1952
SALOME'S LAST DANCE, 1988
SALT & PEPPER, 1968
SALTO, 1966
SALUTE TO THE MARINES, 1943
SALVATION!, 1987
SAM SMALL LEAVES TOWN, 1937
SAM WHISKEY, 1969
SAME TIME, NEXT YEAR, 1978
SAME TO YOU, 1987
SAN DIEGO, I LOVE YOU, 1944
SAN FERRY ANN, 1965
SANDS OF THE DESERT, 1960
SANDWICH MAN, THE, 1966
SANDY GETS HER MAN, 1940
SANDY IS A LADY, 1940
SAP FROM SYRACUSE, THE, 1930
SAP, THE, 1929
SAPS AT SEA, 1940
SARATOGA, 1937
SARONG GIRL, 1943
SATURDAY NIGHT AT THE BATHS, 1975
SATURDAY NIGHT IN APPLE VALLEY, 1965
SATURDAY NIGHT KID, THE, 1929
SATURDAY THE 14TH, 1981
SATURDAY'S CHILDREN, 1929
SAVAGE, THE, 1975
SAVAGES, 1972
SAVANNAH SMILES, 1983
SAVING GRACE, 1986
SAY IT IN FRENCH, 1938
SAY IT WITH DIAMONDS, 1935
SAY YES, 1986
SCALPHUNTERS, THE, 1968
SCANDAL IN SORRENTO, 1957
SCANDALOUS, 1984
SCANDALOUS JOHN, 1971
SCANDALS OF PARIS, 1935
SCARECROW IN A GARDEN OF CUCUMBERS, 1972
SCARED STIFF, 1945
SCATTERGOOD BAINES, 1941
SCATTERGOOD MEETS BROADWAY, 1941
SCATTERGOOD PULLS THE STRINGS, 1941
SCATTERGOOD RIDES HIGH, 1942
SCATTERGOOD SURVIVES A MURDER, 1942
SCAVENGER HUNT, 1979
SCENT OF A WOMAN, 1976
SCHLOCK, 1973
SCHOOL DAZE, 1988
SCHOOL FOR BRIDES, 1952
SCHOOL FOR HUSBANDS, 1939
SCHOOL FOR RANDLE, 1949
SCHOOL FOR SCANDAL, THE, 1930
SCHOOL FOR SCOUNDRELS, 1960
SCHOOL FOR SEX, 1969
SCHOOL SPIRIT, 1985
SCHWEIK'S NEW ADVENTURES, 1943
SCIENTIFIC CARDPLAYER, THE, 1972
SCOTCH ON THE ROCKS, 1954
SCOUNDREL, THE, 1935
SCREEN TEST, 1986
SCREWBALLS, 1983
SCROOGED, 1988
SCUDDA-HOO? SCUDDA-HAY?, 1948
SEA LEGS, 1930
SEASON OF PASSION, 1961
SEBASTIAN, 1968
SECOND BEST BED, 1937
SECOND BEST SECRET AGENT IN THE WHOLE WIDE WORLD, THE, 1965
SECOND FIDDLE, 1939
SECOND FIDDLE, 1957
SECOND FLOOR MYSTERY, THE, 1930
SECOND-HAND HEARTS, 1981
SECOND HONEYMOON, 1931
SECOND HONEYMOON, 1937
SECOND MR. BUSH, THE, 1940
SECOND TIME LUCKY, 1984
SECRET ADMIRER, 1985
SECRET DIARY OF SIGMUND FREUD, THE, 1984
SECRET LIFE OF AN AMERICAN WIFE, THE, 1968

SECRET LIFE OF WALTER MITTY, THE, 1947
SECRET OF MY SUCCESS, THE, 1965
SECRET OF MY SUCCESS, THE, 1987
SECRET OF SANTA VITTORIA, THE, 1969
SECRET WAR OF HARRY FRIGG, THE, 1968
SECRETS, 1984
SECRETS D'ALCOVE, 1954
SECRETS OF AN ACTRESS, 1938
SECRETS OF WOMEN, 1961
SEE AMERICA THIRST, 1930
SEE HERE, PRIVATE HARGROVE, 1944
SEE HOW THEY RUN, 1955
SEEING IS BELIEVING, 1934
SEEMS LIKE OLD TIMES, 1980
SEMI-TOUGH, 1977
SENATOR WAS INDISCREET, THE, 1947
SEND ME NO FLOWERS, 1964
SENIORS, THE, 1978
SENORA CASADA NECEISITA MARIDO, 1935
SENTIMENTAL BLOKE, 1932
SEPARATE VACATIONS, 1986
SERAFINO, 1970
SERE CUALQUIER COSA PERO TE QUIERO, 1986
SERENADE FOR TWO SPIES, 1966
SERGEANT BERRY, 1938
SERGEANT WAS A LADY, THE, 1961
SERGEANTS 3, 1962
SERIAL, 1980
SERVANTS' ENTRANCE, 1934
SERVICE DE LUXE, 1938
SEVEN, 1979
SEVEN BEAUTIES, 1976
SEVEN CAPITAL SINS, 1962
SEVEN GUNS FOR THE MACGREGORS, 1968
SEVEN KEYS TO BALDPATE, 1930
SEVEN KEYS TO BALDPATE, 1935
SEVEN KEYS TO BALDPATE, 1947
SEVEN MINUTES IN HEAVEN, 1986
SEVEN YEAR ITCH, THE, 1955
SEVERED HEAD, A, 1971
SEX AND THE SINGLE GIRL, 1964
SEX APPEAL, 1986
SEX KITTENS GO TO COLLEGE, 1960
SEX O'CLOCK NEWS, THE, 1986
SEZ O'REILLY TO MACNAB, 1938
SH! THE OCTOPUS, 1937
SHADEY, 1987
SHADOW OF SUSPICION, 1944
SHAGGY D.A., THE, 1976
SHAGGY DOG, THE, 1959
SHAKE HANDS WITH MURDER, 1944
SHAKIEST GUN IN THE WEST, THE, 1968
SHAMELESS OLD LADY, THE, 1966
SHAMPOO, 1975
SHAMUS, 1973
SHE ALWAYS GETS THEIR MAN, 1962
SHE COULDN'T SAY NO, 1939
SHE COULDN'T SAY NO, 1941
SHE COULDN'T SAY NO, 1954
SHE COULDN'T TAKE IT, 1935
SHE DIDN'T SAY NO?, 1962
SHE DONE HIM WRONG, 1933
SHE GETS HER MAN, 1935
SHE GETS HER MAN, 1945
SHE GOT WHAT SHE WANTED, 1930
SHE HAD TO EAT, 1937
SHE HAD TO SAY YES, 1933
SHE KNEW ALL THE ANSWERS, 1941
SHE KNEW WHAT SHE WANTED, 1936
SHE KNOWS Y'KNOW, 1962
SHE LEARNED ABOUT SAILORS, 1934
SHE MADE HER BED, 1934
SHE MAN, THE, 1967
SHE MARRIED A COP, 1939
SHE MARRIED HER BOSS, 1935
SHE WAS ONLY A VILLAGE MAIDEN, 1933
SHE WENT TO THE RACES, 1945
SHE WOULDN'T SAY YES, 1945
SHE WROTE THE BOOK, 1946
SHEEPMAN, THE, 1958
SHEILA LEVINE IS DEAD AND LIVING IN NEW
    YORK, 1975
SHEPHERD OF THE OZARKS, 1942
SHERIFF OF FRACTURED JAW, THE, 1958
SHERLOCK HOLMES, 1932
SHE'S FOR ME, 1943

SHE'S GOT EVERYTHING, 1938
SHE'S GOTTA HAVE IT, 1986
SHE'S HAVING A BABY, 1988
SHE'S IN THE ARMY, 1942
SHE'S MY WEAKNESS, 1930
SHE'S NO LADY, 1937
SHILLINGBURY BLOWERS, THE, 1980
SHOOTING HIGH, 1940
SHOP AROUND THE CORNER, THE, 1940
SHORT CIRCUIT, 1986
SHORT CIRCUIT 2, 1988
SHOT IN THE DARK, A, 1964
SHOTGUN WEDDING, THE, 1963
SHOULD HUSBANDS WORK?, 1939
SHOULD LADIES BEHAVE?, 1933
SHOW FLAT, 1936
SHOW FOLKS, 1928
SHOW GIRL, 1928
SHOW GIRL IN HOLLYWOOD, 1930
SHOW-OFF, THE, 1934
SHOW-OFF, THE, 1946
SHUT MY BIG MOUTH, 1942
SIDE SHOW, 1931
SIDE STREET ANGEL, 1937
SIDELONG GLANCES OF A PIGEON KICKER, THE,
    1970
SIDEWALKS OF LONDON, 1940
SIDEWALKS OF NEW YORK, 1931
SIGN OF THE VIRGIN, 1969
SIGN OF VENUS, THE, 1955
SILENCERS, THE, 1966
SILENT MOVIE, 1976
SILENT PARTNER, THE, 1979
SILKEN AFFAIR, THE, 1957
SILLY BILLIES, 1936
SILVER BEARS, 1978
SILVER DUST, 1953
SILVER SPOON, THE, 1934
SILVER STREAK, 1976
SIMCHON FAMILY, THE, 1969
SIMON, 1980
SIMON AND LAURA, 1956
SIMPLE CASE OF MONEY, A, 1952
SIMPLY TERRIFIC, 1938
SINCERELY CHARLOTTE, 1986
SINFUL DAVEY, 1969
SING AND LIKE IT, 1934
SING AS WE GO, 1934
SINGING SHERIFF, THE, 1944
SINGING THROUGH, 1935
SINGLE SIN, 1931
SIR HENRY AT RAWLINSON END, 1980
SIR, YOU ARE A WIDOWER, 1971
SIREN OF BAGDAD, 1953
SISTER TO ASSIST'ER, A, 1930
SISTER TO ASSIST'ER, A, 1938
SISTER TO ASSIST'ER, A, 1948
SIT TIGHT, 1931
SITTING DUCKS, 1979
SITTING PRETTY, 1948
SITUATION HOPELESS—BUT NOT SERIOUS, 1965
SIX CYLINDER LOVE, 1931
SIX-DAY BIKE RIDER, 1934
SIX DAYS A WEEK, 1966
SIX IN PARIS, 1968
SIX OF A KIND, 1934
SIX PACK, 1982
SIXTEEN CANDLES, 1984
SIZZLE BEACH, U.S.A., 1986
SKATETOWN, U.S.A., 1979
SKI FEVER, 1969
SKIDOO, 1968
SKIMPY IN THE NAVY, 1949
SKIN GAME, 1971
SKINNER STEPS OUT, 1929
SKIPALONG ROSENBLOOM, 1951
SKIPPER SURPRISED HIS WIFE, THE, 1950
SKY DEVILS, 1932
SKY FULL OF MOON, 1952
SKY HIGH, 1952
SKYLARK, 1941
SKYLARKS, 1936
SKYLINE, 1984
SKY'S THE LIMIT, THE, 1937
SLANDER HOUSE, 1938
SLAPSTICK OF ANOTHER KIND, 1984

SLAVE GIRL, 1947
SLEEPER, 1973
SLEEPING CAR, 1933
SLEEPING PARTNERS, 1930
SLIGHT CASE OF LARCENY, A, 1953
SLIGHT CASE OF MURDER, A, 1938
SLIGHTLY DANGEROUS, 1943
SLIGHTLY SCARLET, 1930
SLIGHTLY TEMPTED, 1940
SLIM CARTER, 1957
SLIPPER EPISODE, THE, 1938
SLITHER, 1973
SLUGGER'S WIFE, THE, 1985
SLUMBER PARTY '57, 1977
SMALL CHANGE, 1976
SMALL HOTEL, 1957
SMALL TOWN DEB, 1941
SMALLEST SHOW ON EARTH, THE, 1957
SMART WOMAN, 1931
SMARTEST GIRL IN TOWN, 1936
SMARTY, 1934
SMASHING TIME, 1967
SMILE, 1975
SMILES OF A SUMMER NIGHT, 1957
SMILEY GETS A GUN, 1959
SMILING GHOST, THE, 1941
SMITH'S WIVES, 1935
SMITHY, 1933
SMOKEY AND THE BANDIT, 1977
SMOKEY AND THE BANDIT—PART 3, 1983
SMOKEY AND THE BANDIT II, 1980
SMORGASBORD, 1983
SMUGGLERS' COVE, 1948
SNAFU, 1945
SNOW WHITE AND THE THREE STOOGES, 1961
SNOWBALL EXPRESS, 1972
SNOWED UNDER, 1936
SNUFFY SMITH, YARD BIRD, 1942
SO FINE, 1981
SO GOES MY LOVE, 1946
SO IT'S SUNDAY, 1932
SO THIS IS AFRICA, 1933
SO THIS IS LONDON, 1930
SO THIS IS LONDON, 1940
SO THIS IS NEW YORK, 1948
SO THIS IS WASHINGTON, 1943
SO YOU WON'T TALK?, 1935
SO YOU WON'T TALK, 1940
SOAK THE RICH, 1936
S.O.B., 1981
SOCIAL LION, THE, 1930
SOCIETY FEVER, 1935
SOGGY BOTTOM U.S.A., 1982
SOLDIER IN THE RAIN, 1963
SOLDIER'S PLAYTHING, A, 1931
SOLID GOLD CADILLAC, THE, 1956
SOME KIND OF A NUT, 1969
SOME KIND OF HERO, 1982
SOME LIKE IT COOL, 1979
SOME LIKE IT HOT, 1959
SOME WILL, SOME WON'T, 1970
SOMEBODY KILLED HER HUSBAND, 1978
SOMEONE AT THE DOOR, 1936
SOMEONE AT THE DOOR, 1950
SOMEONE TO LOVE, 1988
SOMETHING ALWAYS HAPPENS, 1934
SOMETHING FOR EVERYONE, 1970
SOMETHING FOR THE BIRDS, 1952
SOMETHING IN THE CITY, 1950
SOMETHING MONEY CAN'T BUY, 1952
SOMETHING SHORT OF PARADISE, 1979
SOMETHING SPECIAL!, 1987
SOMETHING WILD, 1986
SOMETIMES GOOD, 1934
SOMEWHERE IN CAMP, 1942
SOMEWHERE IN CIVVIES, 1943
SOMEWHERE IN ENGLAND, 1940
SOMEWHERE IN FRANCE, 1943
SOMEWHERE IN POLITICS, 1949
SOMEWHERE ON LEAVE, 1942
SON OF A SAILOR, 1933
SON OF DRACULA, 1974
SON OF FLUBBER, 1963
SON OF PALEFACE, 1952
SONG OF IDAHO, 1948
SONS OF THE DESERT, 1933

BOLD: Films on Videocassette

SOPHIE LANG GOES WEST, 1937
SOPHIE'S PLACE, 1970
SOPHIE'S WAYS, 1970
SOPHOMORE, THE, 1929
SORROWFUL JONES, 1949
SO'S YOUR UNCLE, 1943
SOTTO...SOTTO, 1985
SOUL MAN, 1986
SOUND OFF, 1952
SOUP FOR ONE, 1982
SOUP TO NUTS, 1930
SOUTH AMERICAN GEORGE, 1941
SOUTH OF TAHITI, 1941
SOUTH SEA ROSE, 1929
SOUTH SEA WOMAN, 1953
SOUTHERN STAR, THE, 1969
SOUTHERN YANKEE, A, 1948
SPACEBALLS, 1987
SPACED OUT, 1981
SPANISH FLY, 1975
SPARE A COPPER, 1940
SPEAK EASILY, 1932
SPECIAL DELIVERY, 1955
SPECIAL DELIVERY, 1976
SPECIALIST, THE, 1975
SPECTER OF THE ROSE, 1946
SPENCER'S MOUNTAIN, 1963
SPENDTHRIFT, 1936
SPICE OF LIFE, 1954
SPIES LIKE US, 1985
SPIKE OF BENSONHURST, 1988
SPIRIT IS WILLING, THE, 1967
SPLASH, 1984
SPLINTERS, 1929
SPLINTERS IN THE AIR, 1937
SPLINTERS IN THE NAVY, 1931
SPLITZ, 1984
SPOOK BUSTERS, 1946
SPOOK CHASERS, 1957
SPOOKS RUN WILD, 1941
SPORT OF KINGS, THE, 1931
SPORTING CHANCE, A, 1945
SPORTING LOVE, 1936
SPOT OF BOTHER, A, 1938
SPRING BREAK, 1983
SPRING HANDICAP, 1937
SPRING IN PARK LANE, 1949
SPRING MADNESS, 1938
SPRING MEETING, 1941
SPRING TONIC, 1935
SPRINGTIME FOR HENRY, 1934
SPRINGTIME ON THE VOLGA, 1961
SPUTNIK, 1960
SPY CHASERS, 1956
SPY FOR A DAY, 1939
SPY WITH A COLD NOSE, THE, 1966
SPYLARKS, 1965
S•P•Y•S, 1974
SQUARE PEG, THE, 1958
SQUARE ROOT OF ZERO, THE, 1964
SQUEEZE A FLOWER, 1970
SQUEEZE PLAY, 1981
STAGE DOOR, 1937
STAIRCASE, 1969
STALAG 17, 1953
STAND BY ME, 1986
STAND-IN, 1937
STAND-IN, THE, 1985
STAND UP AND BE COUNTED, 1972
STAND UP VIRGIN SOLDIERS, 1977
STANDING ROOM ONLY, 1944
STAR FELL FROM HEAVEN, A, 1936
STAR OF MIDNIGHT, 1935
STAR SLAMMER: THE ESCAPE, 1988
STAR SPANGLED GIRL, 1971
STARDUST MEMORIES, 1980
STARHOPS, 1978
STARS AND BARS, 1988
START THE REVOLUTION WITHOUT ME, 1970
STARTING OVER, 1979
STATE FAIR, 1933
STATE OF THE UNION, 1948
STATIC, 1985
STATUE, THE, 1971
STAY AWAY, JOE, 1968
STEAGLE, THE, 1971

STEEL TRAP, THE, 1952
STEELYARD BLUES, 1973
STELLA, 1950
STEP LIVELY, JEEVES, 1937
STEPFORD WIVES, THE, 1975
STEPPIN' IN SOCIETY, 1945
STEPPING SISTERS, 1932
STEPTOE AND SON, 1972
STERILE CUCKOO, THE, 1969
STEWARDESS SCHOOL, 1986
STICK 'EM UP, 1950
STICK UP, THE, 1978
STICKY FINGERS, 1988
STILL SMOKIN', 1983
STING II, THE, 1983
STING, THE, 1973
STIR CRAZY, 1980
STITCH IN TIME, A, 1967
STITCHES, 1985
STOKER, THE, 1935
STOLEN ASSIGNMENT, 1955
STOLEN KISSES, 1929
STOLEN KISSES, 1969
STOOGEMANIA, 1986
STOOLIE, THE, 1972
STOP PRESS GIRL, 1949
STOP THAT CAB, 1951
STOP, YOU'RE KILLING ME, 1952
STOP, LOOK, AND LOVE, 1939
STORK, 1971
STORK BITES MAN, 1947
STORK PAYS OFF, THE, 1941
STORK TALK, 1964
STORM IN A TEACUP, 1937
STORM IN A WATER GLASS, 1931
STORMS OF AUGUST, THE, 1988
STORMY WEATHER, 1935
STRAIGHT TO HELL, 1987
STRANGE ADVENTURES OF MR. SMITH, THE, 1937
STRANGE BEDFELLOWS, 1965
STRANGE BREW, 1983
STRANGE FACES, 1938
STRANGE WIVES, 1935
STRANGER FROM ARIZONA, THE, 1938
STRANGER IN TOWN, 1932
STRANGERS IN LOVE, 1932
STRANGERS OF THE EVENING, 1932
STRANGERS ON A HONEYMOON, 1937
STRAWBERRY BLONDE, THE, 1941
STREET TRASH, 1987
STRICTLY CONFIDENTIAL, 1959
STRICTLY DISHONORABLE, 1931
STRICTLY DISHONORABLE, 1951
STRICTLY FOR THE BIRDS, 1963
STRICTLY ILLEGAL, 1935
STRIKE IT RICH, 1933
STRIKE IT RICH, 1948
STRIPES, 1981
STROKER ACE, 1983
STRONGEST MAN IN THE WORLD, THE, 1975
STUCK ON YOU, 1983
STUCKEY'S LAST STAND, 1980
STUDENT BODIES, 1981
STUDENT BODY, THE, 1976
STUFF, THE, 1985
STUNT MAN, THE, 1980
SUBSTITUTION, 1970
SUBURBAN WIVES, 1973
SUCCESSFUL CALAMITY, A, 1932
SUCCESSFUL FAILURE, A, 1934
SUCH A GORGEOUS KID LIKE ME, 1973
SUCH GOOD FRIENDS, 1971
SUCH IS LIFE, 1936
SUCKER, THE, 1966
SUDDEN MONEY, 1939
SUDDENLY IT'S SPRING, 1947
SUGARBABY, 1985
SUITOR, THE, 1963
SULLIVAN'S TRAVELS, 1941
SUMMER CAMP, 1979
SUMMER LIGHTNING, 1933
SUMMER LOVERS, 1982
SUMMER MAGIC, 1963
SUMMER OF SECRETS, 1976
SUMMER RENTAL, 1985
SUMMER SCHOOL, 1987

SUMMER SCHOOL TEACHERS, 1977
SUNBURN, 1979
SUNDAY IN NEW YORK, 1963
SUNDAY LOVERS, 1980
SUNDAY PUNCH, 1942
SUNSHINE BOYS, THE, 1975
SUPER FUZZ, 1981
SUPER SLEUTH, 1937
SUPER SPOOK, 1975
SUPERDAD, 1974
SUPPORT YOUR LOCAL GUNFIGHTER, 1971
SUPPORT YOUR LOCAL SHERIFF, 1969
SUPREME KID, THE, 1976
SURE THING, THE, 1985
SURF NAZIS MUST DIE, 1987
SURF PARTY, 1964
SURF II, 1984
SURFTIDE 77, 1962
SURPRISE PACKAGE, 1960
SURPRISE PARTY, 1985
SURRENDER, 1987
SURVIVORS, THE, 1983
SUSAN SLEPT HERE, 1954
SWAP MEET, 1979
SWASHBUCKLER, 1976
SWEDENHIELMS, 1935
SWEEPSTAKE ANNIE, 1935
SWEEPSTAKES, 1931
SWEEPSTAKES WINNER, 1939
SWEET AND SOUR, 1964
SWEET HEART'S DANCE, 1988
SWEET LIBERTY, 1986
SWEETHEARTS AND WIVES, 1930
SWELL-HEAD, 1935
SWEPT AWAY...BY AN UNUSUAL DESTINY IN THE BLUE SEA OF AUGUST, 1975
SWING IT SAILOR, 1937
SWING SHIFT MAISIE, 1943
SWING THAT CHEER, 1938
SWING YOUR LADY, 1938
SWINGER, THE, 1966
SWINGIN' ALONG, 1962
SWINGIN' MAIDEN, THE, 1963
SWINGIN' ON A RAINBOW, 1945
SWINGING THE LEAD, 1934
SWISS MISS, 1938
SWITCHING CHANNELS, 1988
SYLVIA AND THE PHANTOM, 1950
SYLVIA SCARLETT, 1936
TAKE A CHANCE, 1937
TAKE A GIRL LIKE YOU, 1970
TAKE A LETTER, DARLING, 1942
TAKE A POWDER, 1953
TAKE HER, SHE'S MINE, 1963
TAKE IT FROM ME, 1937
TAKE ME TO PARIS, 1951
TAKE ME TO TOWN, 1953
TAKE MY TIP, 1937
TAKE OFF THAT HAT, 1938
TAKE THE HEIR, 1930
TAKE THE MONEY AND RUN, 1969
TAKE THIS JOB AND SHOVE IT, 1981
TAKING OFF, 1971
TALES OF A SALESMAN, 1965
TALES OF MANHATTAN, 1942
TALES OF PARIS, 1962
TALES OF THE THIRD DIMENSION, 1985
TALK ABOUT JACQUELINE, 1942
TALK OF THE TOWN, 1942
TALKING WALLS, 1987
TALL BLOND MAN WITH ONE BLACK SHOE, THE, 1973
TALL, DARK AND HANDSOME, 1941
TALL STORY, 1960
TAMAHINE, 1964
TAMING OF DOROTHY, THE, 1950
TAMING OF THE SHREW, THE, 1929
TAMING OF THE SHREW, THE, 1967
TAMING SUTTON'S GAL, 1957
TAMMY AND THE BACHELOR, 1957
TAMMY AND THE DOCTOR, 1963
TAMMY AND THE MILLIONAIRE, 1967
TAMMY, TELL ME TRUE, 1961
TAMPOPO, 1986

TANK, 1984
TANKS A MILLION, 1941
TANNED LEGS, 1929
TAPEHEADS, 1988
TASTE FOR WOMEN, A, 1966
TASTE OF MONEY, A, 1960
TAWNY PIPIT, 1947
TAXI, 1953
TAXI FOR TWO, 1929
TAXI 13, 1928
TAXI TO HEAVEN, 1944
TAXING WOMAN, A, 1988
TAXING WOMAN'S RETURN, A, 1988
TE QUIERO CON LOCURA, 1935
TEA FOR TWO, 1950
TEACHER'S PET, 1958
TEACHERS, 1984
TEAHOUSE OF THE AUGUST MOON, THE, 1956
TEEN WOLF, 1985
TEEN WOLF TOO, 1987
TEENAGE MILLIONAIRE, 1961
TEL AVIV TAXI, 1957
TELEPHONE, THE, 1988
TELEVISION TALENT, 1937
TELL IT TO THE JUDGE, 1949
TELL ME THAT YOU LOVE ME, JUNIE MOON, 1970
TEMPEST, 1982
TEMPORARY WIDOW, THE, 1930
TEMPTATION, 1935
10, 1979
TEN CENTS A DANCE, 1945
TEN TALL MEN, 1951
TEN THOUSAND BEDROOMS, 1957
TENDER SCOUNDREL, 1967
TENDER TRAP, THE, 1955
TENDERFOOT, THE, 1932
TERMS OF ENDEARMENT, 1983
TERROR HOUSE, 1972
TERRORVISION, 1986
TEVYA, 1939
TEXAS ACROSS THE RIVER, 1966
TEXAS, BROOKLYN AND HEAVEN, 1948
TEXAS CARNIVAL, 1951
THANK EVANS, 1938
THANK HEAVEN FOR SMALL FAVORS, 1965
THANK YOU, JEEVES, 1936
THANK YOUR LUCKY STARS, 1943
THANKS A MILLION, 1935
THANKS FOR EVERYTHING, 1938
THANKS FOR LISTENING, 1937
THANKS FOR THE MEMORY, 1938
THARK, 1932
THAT CERTAIN AGE, 1938
THAT CERTAIN FEELING, 1956
THAT DARN CAT, 1965
THAT FUNNY FEELING, 1965
THAT GANG OF MINE, 1940
THAT GIRL FROM PARIS, 1937
THAT LADY IN ERMINE, 1948
THAT LUCKY TOUCH, 1975
THAT MAN FROM RIO, 1964
THAT MAN FROM TANGIER, 1953
THAT MAN IN ISTANBUL, 1966
THAT NAZTY NUISANCE, 1943
THAT NIGHT IN RIO, 1941
THAT NIGHT WITH YOU, 1945
THAT OTHER WOMAN, 1942
THAT RIVIERA TOUCH, 1968
THAT SINKING FEELING, 1979
THAT TOUCH OF MINK, 1962
THAT UNCERTAIN FEELING, 1941
THAT WONDERFUL URGE, 1948
THAT'S LIFE, 1986
THAT'S MY WIFE, 1933
THAT'S THE SPIRIT, 1945
THAT'S A GOOD GIRL, 1933
THAT'S GRATITUDE, 1934
THAT'S MY BABY, 1944
THAT'S MY BOY, 1951
THAT'S MY GAL, 1947
THAT'S MY UNCLE, 1935
THAT'S RIGHT—YOU'RE WRONG, 1939
THAT'S THE TICKET, 1940
THEATRE ROYAL, 1943
THEIR BIG MOMENT, 1934
THEIR NIGHT OUT, 1933

THEM NICE AMERICANS, 1958
THEODORA GOES WILD, 1936
THERE GOES MY GIRL, 1937
THERE GOES MY HEART, 1938
THERE GOES THE BRIDE, 1933
THERE GOES THE BRIDE, 1980
THERE GOES THE GROOM, 1937
THERE WAS A CROOKED MAN, 1962
THERE WAS A YOUNG LADY, 1953
THERE WAS A YOUNG MAN, 1937
THERE'S A GIRL IN MY SOUP, 1970
THERE'S ALWAYS A THURSDAY, 1957
THERE'S THAT WOMAN AGAIN, 1938
THERE'S ALWAYS A WOMAN, 1938
THERE'S ONE BORN EVERY MINUTE, 1942
THESE GLAMOUR GIRLS, 1939
THEY ALL KISSED THE BRIDE, 1942
THEY ALL LAUGHED, 1981
THEY CALL ME BRUCE, 1982
THEY CALL ME ROBERT, 1967
THEY CALL ME TRINITY, 1971
THEY DIDN'T KNOW, 1936
THEY GOT ME COVERED, 1943
THEY HAD TO SEE PARIS, 1929
THEY JUST HAD TO GET MARRIED, 1933
THEY LEARNED ABOUT WOMEN, 1930
THEY MET IN A TAXI, 1936
THEY MET IN BOMBAY, 1941
THEY MIGHT BE GIANTS, 1971
THEY STILL CALL ME BRUCE, 1987
THEY WANTED TO MARRY, 1937
THEY WENT THAT-A-WAY AND THAT-A-WAY, 1978
THEY'RE A WEIRD MOB, 1966
THIEF OF PARIS, THE, 1967
THIEF WHO CAME TO DINNER, THE, 1973
THIEVES, 1977
THIEVES FALL OUT, 1941
THIN MAN, THE, 1934
THINGS ARE LOOKING UP, 1934
THINGS ARE TOUGH ALL OVER, 1982
THINGS CHANGE, 1988
THINGS HAPPEN AT NIGHT, 1948
THINK DIRTY, 1970
THIRD FINGER, LEFT HAND, 1940
THIRD STRING, THE, 1932
THIRD TIME LUCKY, 1931
THIRTY-DAY PRINCESS, 1934
THIRTY FOOT BRIDE OF CANDY ROCK, THE, 1959
30 IS A DANGEROUS AGE, CYNTHIA, 1968
THIS ACTING BUSINESS, 1933
THIS GREEN HELL, 1936
THIS HAPPY FEELING, 1958
THIS IS HEAVEN, 1929
THIS IS SPINAL TAP, 1984
THIS IS THE LIFE, 1933
THIS IS THE LIFE, 1935
THIS IS THE NIGHT, 1932
THIS MAN IN PARIS, 1939
THIS MAN IS MINE, 1946
THIS MAN IS NEWS, 1939
THIS MARRIAGE BUSINESS, 1938
THIS OTHER EDEN, 1959
THIS RECKLESS AGE, 1932
THIS THING CALLED LOVE, 1929
THIS THING CALLED LOVE, 1940
THIS TIME FOR KEEPS, 1942
THIS TIME FOR KEEPS, 1947
THIS WAY PLEASE, 1937
THIS WEEK OF GRACE, 1933
THIS, THAT AND THE OTHER, 1970
THIS'LL MAKE YOU WHISTLE, 1938
THOSE DARING YOUNG MEN IN THEIR JAUNTY
 JALOPIES, 1969
THOSE ENDEARING YOUNG CHARMS, 1945
THOSE FANTASTIC FLYING FOOLS, 1967
THOSE KIDS FROM TOWN, 1942
THOSE LIPS, THOSE EYES, 1980
THOSE MAGNIFICENT MEN IN THEIR FLYING
 MACHINES; OR HOW I FLEW FROM LONDON TO
 PARIS IN 25 HOURS AND 11 MINUTES, 1965
THOSE PEOPLE NEXT DOOR, 1952
THOSE THREE FRENCH GIRLS, 1930
THOSE WERE THE DAYS, 1934
THOSE WERE THE DAYS, 1940
THOUSAND AND ONE NIGHTS, A, 1945
THOUSAND CLOWNS, A, 1965

THREE AMIGOS, 1986
THREE BITES OF THE APPLE, 1967
THREE BLIND MICE, 1938
THREE COCKEYED SAILORS, 1940
THREE-CORNERED MOON, 1933
THREE DARING DAUGHTERS, 1948
THREE DOLLS FROM HONG KONG, 1966
THREE FOR BEDROOM C, 1952
THREE GIRLS ABOUT TOWN, 1941
THREE GUYS NAMED MIKE, 1951
THREE HEARTS FOR JULIA, 1943
365 NIGHTS IN HOLLYWOOD, 1934
THREE HUSBANDS, 1950
THREE IN THE ATTIC, 1968
3 IS A FAMILY, 1944
THREE KIDS AND A QUEEN, 1935
THREE LEGIONNAIRES, THE, 1937
THREE LIVE GHOSTS, 1929
THREE LIVE GHOSTS, 1935
THREE LOVES HAS NANCY, 1938
THREE MARRIED MEN, 1936
THREE MEN AND A BABY, 1987
THREE MEN AND A CRADLE, 1985
THREE MEN IN A BOAT, 1933
THREE MEN IN A BOAT, 1958
THREE MEN ON A HORSE, 1936
THREE MUSKETEERS, THE, 1939
THREE MUSKETEERS, THE, 1974
THREE NIGHTS OF LOVE, 1969
THREE NUTS IN SEARCH OF A BOLT, 1964
THREE O'CLOCK HIGH, 1987
THREE OF A KIND, 1936
THREE ON A COUCH, 1966
THREE ON A HONEYMOON, 1934
THREE ON A SPREE, 1961
THREE RING CIRCUS, 1954
THREE SMART GIRLS GROW UP, 1939
THREE SONS O'GUNS, 1941
THREE SPARE WIVES, 1962
THREE STOOGES GO AROUND THE WORLD IN A
 DAZE, THE, 1963
THREE STOOGES IN ORBIT, THE, 1962
THREE STOOGES MEET HERCULES, THE, 1962
THREE STOOGES VS. THE WONDER WOMEN, 1975
THREE WISE GIRLS, 1932
THRILL HUNTER, THE, 1933
THRILL OF IT ALL, THE, 1963
THROW MOMMA FROM THE TRAIN, 1987
THUNDER IN THE CITY, 1937
TICKET OF LEAVE, 1936
TICKET TO PARADISE, 1936
TICKET TO TOMAHAWK, 1950
TICKLISH AFFAIR, A, 1963
TIGER AND THE PUSSYCAT, THE, 1967
TIGER MAKES OUT, THE, 1967
TIGER'S TALE, A, 1988
TIGHT LITTLE ISLAND, 1949
TIGHT SHOES, 1941
TIKI TIKI, 1971
TILL MARRIAGE DO US PART, 1979
TILLIE AND GUS, 1933
TILLIE THE TOILER, 1941
TILLY OF BLOOMSBURY, 1931
TILLY OF BLOOMSBURY, 1940
TIMBUCTOO, 1933
TIME BANDITS, 1981
TIME FLIES, 1944
TIME FOR LOVING, A, 1971
TIME GENTLEMEN PLEASE?, 1953
TIME OF HIS LIFE, THE, 1955
TIME OF THEIR LIVES, THE, 1946
TIME OF YOUR LIFE, THE, 1948
TIME OUT FOR MURDER, 1938
TIME OUT FOR ROMANCE, 1937
TIME, THE PLACE AND THE GIRL, THE, 1929
TIME, THE PLACE AND THE GIRL, THE, 1946
TIMES SQUARE PLAYBOY, 1936
TIN MEN, 1987
TIP-OFF, THE, 1931
TISH, 1942
TITFIELD THUNDERBOLT, THE, 1953
TO BE A CROOK, 1967
TO BE OR NOT TO BE, 1942
TO BE OR NOT TO BE, 1983
TO BEAT THE BAND, 1935

BOLD: Films on Videocassette

TO CATCH A COP, 1984
TO CATCH A THIEF, 1936
TO CATCH A THIEF, 1955
TO FIND A MAN, 1972
TO OBLIGE A LADY, 1931
TO PARIS WITH LOVE, 1955
TOBACCO ROAD, 1941
TOGETHER AGAIN, 1944
TOKYO POP, 1988
TOM, DICK AND HARRY, 1941
TOM JONES, 1963
TOMCAT, THE, 1968
TOMMY THE TOREADOR, 1960
TONIGHT AT 8:30, 1953
TONIGHT AT TWELVE, 1929
TONIGHT FOR SURE, 1962
TONIGHT IS OURS, 1933
TONIGHT OR NEVER, 1931
TONIGHT'S THE NIGHT, 1932
TONIGHT'S THE NIGHT, 1954
TONS OF MONEY, 1931
TONS OF TROUBLE, 1956
TONY DRAWS A HORSE, 1951
TOO BAD SHE'S BAD, 1954
TOO BUSY TO WORK, 1939
TOO HOT TO HANDLE, 1938
TOO MANY CROOKS, 1959
TOO MANY HUSBANDS, 1938
TOO MANY HUSBANDS, 1940
TOO MANY MILLIONS, 1934
TOO MANY WIVES, 1933
TOO MANY WIVES, 1937
TOO MANY WOMEN, 1942
TOO MUCH HARMONY, 1933
TOO YOUNG TO KISS, 1951
TOO YOUNG TO MARRY, 1931
TOOTSIE, 1982
TOP BANANA, 1954
TOP HAT, 1935
TOP O' THE MORNING, 1949
TOP OF THE FORM, 1953
TOP SECRET!, 1984
TOP SECRET AFFAIR, 1957
TOP SERGEANT MULLIGAN, 1941
TOPAZE, 1933
TOPAZE, 1935
TOPKAPI, 1964
TOPPER, 1937
TOPPER RETURNS, 1941
TOPPER TAKES A TRIP, 1939
TOPSY-TURVY JOURNEY, 1970
TORA-SAN PART 2, 1970
TORRID ZONE, 1940
TOTO IN THE MOON, 1957
TOUCH AND GO, 1980
TOUCH AND GO, 1986
TOUCH OF CLASS, A, 1973
TOUCH OF LARCENY, A, 1960
TOUCH OF THE MOON, A, 1936
TOUCH OF THE SUN, A, 1956
TOUGH GUYS, 1986
TOVARICH, 1937
TOWING, 1978
TOWN WENT WILD, THE, 1945
TOXIC AVENGER, THE, 1985
TOY TIGER, 1956
TOY, THE, 1982
TRADE WINDS, 1938
TRADER HORNEE, 1970
TRADING PLACES, 1983
TRAFFIC, 1972
TRAIL OF THE PINK PANTHER, THE, 1982
TRAIL OF THE VIGILANTES, 1940
TRAIN GOES EAST, THE, 1949
TRAIN GOES TO KIEV, THE, 1961
TRAIN RIDE TO HOLLYWOOD, 1975
TRAMP, TRAMP, TRAMP, 1942
TRANSATLANTIC, 1931
TRANSYLVANIA 6-5000, 1985
TRAVELING EXECUTIONER, THE, 1970
TRAVELING HUSBANDS, 1931
TRAVELING SALESLADY, THE, 1935
TRAVELING SALESWOMAN, 1950
TRAVELLER'S JOY, 1951
TRAVELS WITH MY AUNT, 1972

TRAXX, 1988
TREASURE HUNT, 1952
TREASURE OF SAN GENNARO, 1968
TREMENDOUSLY RICH MAN, A, 1932
TRENCHCOAT, 1983
TRIAL AND ERROR, 1962
TRIBUTE, 1980
TRINITY IS STILL MY NAME, 1971
TRIP TO PARIS, A, 1938
TRIPLE TROUBLE, 1950
TROIKA, 1969
TROJAN BROTHERS, THE, 1946
TROOPERS THREE, 1930
TROPICAL TROUBLE, 1936
TROUBLE, 1933
TROUBLE AHEAD, 1936
TROUBLE ALONG THE WAY, 1953
TROUBLE BREWING, 1939
TROUBLE FOR TWO, 1936
TROUBLE IN PARADISE, 1932
TROUBLE IN STORE, 1955
TROUBLE IN THE AIR, 1948
TROUBLE IN THE GLEN, 1954
TROUBLE MAKERS, 1948
TROUBLE WITH ANGELS, THE, 1966
TROUBLE WITH DICK, THE, 1987
TROUBLE WITH GIRLS (AND HOW TO GET INTO IT), THE, 1969
TROUBLE WITH HARRY, THE, 1955
TROUBLE WITH WOMEN, THE, 1947
TROUBLEMAKER, THE, 1964
TRUE AS A TURTLE, 1957
TRUE CONFESSION, 1937
TRUE STORIES, 1986
TRUE STORY OF ESKIMO NELL, THE, 1975
TRUE TO LIFE, 1943
TRUE TO THE NAVY, 1930
TRUNKS OF MR. O.F., THE, 1932
TRUST THE NAVY, 1935
TRUTH ABOUT WOMEN, THE, 1958
TRYGON FACTOR, THE, 1969
TUGBOAT ANNIE, 1933
TUGBOAT ANNIE SAILS AGAIN, 1940
TULIPS, 1981
TUNNEL OF LOVE, THE, 1958
TUNNELVISION, 1976
TURKEY TIME, 1933
TURKISH CUCUMBER, THE, 1963
TURN BACK THE CLOCK, 1933
TURNABOUT, 1940
TURNED OUT NICE AGAIN, 1941
TURNERS OF PROSPECT ROAD, THE, 1947
TURTLE DIARY, 1985
TUTTLES OF TAHITI, 1942
TUXEDO JUNCTION, 1941
TWELFTH NIGHT, 1956
TWELVE CHAIRS, THE, 1970
TWELVE-HANDED MEN OF MARS, THE, 1964
TWELVE PLUS ONE, 1970
TWENTIETH CENTURY, 1934
25TH HOUR, THE, 1967
24-HOUR LOVER, 1970
23 1/2 HOURS LEAVE, 1937
TWICE AROUND THE DAFFODILS, 1962
TWICE BLESSED, 1945
TWICE UPON A TIME, 1953
TWILIGHT PATH, 1965
TWIN BEDS, 1929
TWIN BEDS, 1942
TWINS, 1988
TWIST, THE, 1976
TWO AND ONE TWO, 1934
TWO AND TWO MAKE SIX, 1962
TWO COLONELS, THE, 1963
TWO DAUGHTERS, 1963
TWO-FACED WOMAN, 1941
TWO FISTED, 1935
TWO-FISTED GENTLEMAN, 1936
TWO FOR DANGER, 1940
TWO FOR THE ROAD, 1967
TWO FOR THE SEESAW, 1962
TWO GROOMS FOR A BRIDE, 1957
TWO GUYS FROM MILWAUKEE, 1946
TWO IN A CROWD, 1936
TWO IN A SLEEPING BAG, 1964
TWO IN A TAXI, 1941

TWO LATINS FROM MANHATTAN, 1941
TWO LEFT FEET, 1965
TWO LIVES OF MATTIA PASCAL, THE, 1985
TWO NIGHTS WITH CLEOPATRA, 1953
TWO OF US, THE, 1938
TWO OF US, THE, 1968
TWO ON A DOORSTEP, 1936
TWO SENORITAS FROM CHICAGO, 1943
TWO SISTERS FROM BOSTON, 1946
TWO SMART MEN, 1940
TWO SMART PEOPLE, 1946
TWO SUPER COPS, 1978
2000 YEARS LATER, 1969
TWO-WAY STRETCH, 1961
TWO WEEKS OFF, 1929
TWO WEEKS TO LIVE, 1943
TWO YANKS IN TRINIDAD, 1942
TWO'S COMPANY, 1939
UFORIA, 1985
UGLY DACHSHUND, THE, 1966
UGLY DUCKLING, THE, 1959
ULTIMATE SOLUTION OF GRACE QUIGLEY, THE, 1984
UMBRELLA, THE, 1933
UNCERTAIN LADY, 1934
UNCLE SCAM, 1981
UNCOMMON THIEF, AN, 1967
UNDER A TEXAS MOON, 1930
UNDER MONTANA SKIES, 1930
UNDER PROOF, 1936
UNDER THE RAINBOW, 1981
UNDER THE YUM-YUM TREE, 1963
UNDER YOUR HAT, 1940
UNDERCOVER WOMAN, THE, 1946
UNDERCOVERS HERO, 1975
UNDERNEATH THE ARCHES, 1937
UNEASY VIRTUE, 1931
UNEXPECTED FATHER, 1932
UNEXPECTED FATHER, 1939
UNFAITHFULLY YOURS, 1948
UNFAITHFULLY YOURS, 1984
UNFAITHFULS, THE, 1960
UNFINISHED BUSINESS, 1985
UNFINISHED BUSINESS, 1941
UNIDENTIFIED FLYING ODDBALL, THE, 1979
UNION DEPOT, 1932
UNMARRIED WOMAN, AN, 1978
UP FOR THE CUP, 1931
UP FOR THE CUP, 1950
UP FOR THE DERBY, 1933
UP FROM THE DEPTHS, 1979
UP FRONT, 1951
UP GOES MAISIE, 1946
UP IN ARMS, 1944
UP IN CENTRAL PARK, 1948
UP IN MABEL'S ROOM, 1944
UP IN SMOKE, 1957
UP IN SMOKE, 1978
UP IN THE AIR, 1940
UP IN THE CELLAR, 1970
UP IN THE WORLD, 1957
UP JUMPED A SWAGMAN, 1965
UP POMPEII, 1971
UP THE ACADEMY, 1980
UP THE CHASTITY BELT, 1971
UP THE CREEK, 1958
UP THE CREEK, 1984
UP THE FRONT, 1972
UP THE MACGREGORS, 1967
UP THE RIVER, 1930
UP THE RIVER, 1938
UP THE SANDBOX, 1972
UP TO HIS EARS, 1966
UP TO HIS NECK, 1954
UP TO THE NECK, 1933
UP WITH THE LARK, 1943
UP YOUR TEDDY BEAR, 1970
UPHILL ALL THE WAY, 1986
UPSTAIRS AND DOWNSTAIRS, 1961
UPTOWN SATURDAY NIGHT, 1974
USED CARS, 1980
UTILITIES, 1983
UTOPIA, 1952
V.I.P.s, THE, 1963
VACATION IN RENO, 1946
VAGABOND LADY, 1935

VAGABOND QUEEN, THE, 1931
VALET GIRLS, 1987
VALS, THE, 1985
VALUE FOR MONEY, 1957
VAMP, 1986
VAMPIRES IN HAVANA, 1987
VANDERGILT DIAMOND MYSTERY, THE, 1936
VARIETY HOUR, 1937
VASECTOMY: A DELICATE MATTER, 1986
VERY CLOSE QUARTERS, 1986
VERY HANDY MAN, A, 1966
VERY HAPPY ALEXANDER, 1969
VERY HONORABLE GUY, A, 1934
VERY IDEA, THE, 1929
VERY SPECIAL FAVOR, A, 1965
VICE VERSA, 1948
VICE VERSA, 1988
VIENNA, CITY OF SONGS, 1931
VILLAGE OF DAUGHTERS, 1962
VILLAGE SQUIRE, THE, 1935
VILLAIN STILL PURSUED HER, THE, 1940
VILLAIN, THE, 1979
VINTAGE WINE, 1935
VIPER, THE, 1938
VIRGIN PRESIDENT, THE, 1968
VIRGIN SOLDIERS, THE, 1970
VIRGINIA'S HUSBAND, 1934
VIRTUOUS HUSBAND, 1931
VIRUS HAS NO MORALS, A, 1986
VISIT TO A SMALL PLANET, 1960
VIVA ITALIA, 1978
VIVA MARIA, 1965
VIVA MAX?, 1969
VIVACIOUS LADY, 1938
VOGUES OF 1938, 1937
VOICE OF THE TURTLE, THE, 1947
VOLPONE, 1947
VOLUNTEERS, 1985
VOTE FOR HUGGETT, 1948
VOYAGE TO AMERICA, 1952
VULTURE, THE, 1937
W. W. AND THE DIXIE DANCEKINGS, 1975
WAC FROM WALLA WALLA, THE, 1952
WACKIEST SHIP IN THE ARMY, THE, 1961
WACKIEST WAGON TRAIN IN THE WEST, THE, 1976
WACKO, 1983
WAIT FOR ME IN HEAVEN, 1988
WAITRESS, 1982
WAKE ME WHEN IT'S OVER, 1960
WAKE UP FAMOUS, 1937
WALK, DON'T RUN, 1966
WALK LIKE A MAN, 1987
WALL-EYED NIPPON, 1963
WALLFLOWER, 1948
WALTZ OF THE TOREADORS, 1962
WANTED, 1937
WAR AND PEACE, 1983
WAR BETWEEN MEN AND WOMEN, THE, 1972
WAR ITALIAN STYLE, 1967
WAR OF THE BUTTONS, 1963
WARM CORNER, A, 1930
WARNING TO WANTONS, A, 1949
WARRIOR'S HUSBAND THE, 1933
WATCH BEVERLY, 1932
WATCH IT, SAILOR!, 1961
WATCH THE BIRDIE, 1950
WATCH YOUR STERN, 1961
WATER, 1985
WATERHOLE NO. 3, 1967
WATERMELON MAN, 1970
WAVE, A WAC AND A MARINE, A, 1944
WAY OUT WEST, 1930
WAY OUT WEST, 1937
WAY...WAY OUT, 1966
WE JOINED THE NAVY, 1962
WE WENT TO COLLEGE, 1936
WE WERE DANCING, 1942
WEDDING PARTY, THE, 1969
WEDDING PRESENT, 1936
WEDDING REHEARSAL, 1932
WEDDING, A, 1978
WEDDINGS ARE WONDERFUL, 1938
WEE WILLIE WINKIE, 1937
WEEK-END MARRIAGE, 1932
WEEKEND FOR THREE, 1941
WEEKEND MILLIONAIRE, 1937

WEEKEND MURDERS, THE, 1972
WEEKEND PASS, 1984
WEEKEND WARRIORS, 1986
WEEKEND WITH FATHER, 1951
WEEKEND WITH LULU, A, 1961
WEEKEND, ITALIAN STYLE, 1967
WEIRD ONES, THE, 1962
WEIRD SCIENCE, 1985
WELCOME DANGER, 1929
WELCOME HOME, 1935
WELCOME KOSTYA?, 1965
WELCOME STRANGER, 1947
WELCOME TO 18, 1986
WELCOME TO THE CLUB, 1971
WELL DONE, HENRY, 1936
WELL-GROOMED BRIDE, THE, 1946
WE'LL GROW THIN TOGETHER, 1979
WE'LL SMILE AGAIN, 1942
WE'RE IN THE LEGION NOW, 1937
WE'RE IN THE MONEY, 1935
WE'RE NO ANGELS, 1955
WE'RE NOT MARRIED, 1952
WE'RE ON THE JURY, 1937
WE'RE RICH AGAIN, 1934
WEREWOLF OF WASHINGTON, 1973
WHAT A BLONDE, 1945
WHAT A CARRY ON!, 1949
WHAT A LIFE, 1939
WHAT A MAN!, 1937
WHAT A NIGHT!, 1931
WHAT A WAY TO GO, 1964
WHAT A WHOPPER, 1961
WHAT A WIDOW, 1930
WHAT A WOMAN!, 1943
WHAT CHANGED CHARLEY FARTHING?, 1976
WHAT DID YOU DO IN THE WAR, DADDY?, 1966
WHAT DO WE DO NOW?, 1945
WHAT EVERY WOMAN KNOWS, 1934
WHAT EVERY WOMAN WANTS, 1962
WHAT HAPPENED TO HARKNESS, 1934
WHAT NEXT, CORPORAL HARGROVE?, 1945
WHAT! NO BEER?, 1933
WHAT PRICE GLORY?, 1952
WHAT THE BUTLER SAW, 1950
WHAT WOMEN DREAM, 1933
WHAT WOULD YOU SAY TO SOME SPINACH, 1976
WHAT'S GOOD FOR THE GOOSE, 1969
WHAT'S NEW, PUSSYCAT?, 1965
WHAT'S SO BAD ABOUT FEELING GOOD?, 1968
WHAT'S UP, DOC?, 1972
WHAT'S UP FRONT, 1964
WHAT'S UP, TIGER LILY?, 1966
WHEELER DEALERS, THE, 1963
WHEN FATHER WAS AWAY ON BUSINESS, 1985
WHEN IN ROME, 1952
WHEN KNIGHTS WERE BOLD, 1942
WHEN LADIES MEET, 1933
WHEN LADIES MEET, 1941
WHEN NATURE CALLS, 1985
WHEN THE DEVIL WAS WELL, 1937
WHEN THE GIRLS TAKE OVER, 1962
WHEN WE ARE MARRIED, 1943
WHEN WILLIE COMES MARCHING HOME, 1950
WHEN WOMEN HAD TAILS, 1970
WHEN YOU COME HOME, 1947
WHEN'S YOUR BIRTHDAY?, 1937
WHERE DOES IT HURT?, 1972
WHERE IS PARSIFAL?, 1984
WHERE SINNERS MEET, 1934
WHERE THE BOYS ARE, 1960
WHERE THE BOYS ARE '84, 1984
WHERE THE BUFFALO ROAM, 1980
WHERE THE BULLETS FLY, 1966
WHERE THE SPIES ARE, 1965
WHERE THERE'S A WILL, 1936
WHERE THERE'S A WILL, 1937
WHERE THERE'S A WILL, 1955
WHERE THERE'S LIFE, 1947
WHERE WERE YOU WHEN THE LIGHTS WENT
  OUT?, 1968
WHERE'S PICONE?, 1985
WHERE'S POPPA?, 1970
WHERE'S SALLY?, 1936
WHERE'S THAT FIRE?, 1939
WHICH WAY IS UP?, 1977
WHICH WAY TO THE FRONT?, 1970

WHIFFS, 1975
WHILE PARENTS SLEEP, 1935
WHILE THE SUN SHINES, 1950
WHISPERING GHOSTS, 1942
WHISTLING IN THE DARK, 1933
WHISTLING IN THE DARK, 1941
WHITE, RED, YELLOW, PINK, 1966
WHITE SHEIK, THE, 1956
WHITE TIE AND TAILS, 1946
WHITE VOICES, 1965
WHO DONE IT?, 1942
WHO DONE IT?, 1956
WHO FRAMED ROGER RABBIT, 1988
WHO IS GUILTY?, 1940
WHO IS HARRY KELLERMAN AND WHY IS HE
  SAYING THOSE TERRIBLE THINGS ABOUT ME?,
  1971
**WHO IS KILLING THE GREAT CHEFS OF EUROPE?,
  1978**
WHO KILLED AUNT MAGGIE?, 1940
WHO KILLED "DOC" ROBBIN?, 1948
WHO KILLED JESSIE?, 1965
WHO WAS THAT LADY?, 1960
WHOLE SHOOTIN' MATCH, THE, 1979
WHOLE TOWN'S TALKING, THE, 1935
WHOLLY MOSES, 1980
WHOOPEE BOYS, THE, 1986
WHO'S BEEN SLEEPING IN MY BED?, 1963
WHO'S GOT THE ACTION?, 1962
WHO'S MINDING THE MINT?, 1967
WHO'S MINDING THE STORE?, 1963
WHO'S THAT GIRL, 1987
WHO'S YOUR FATHER?, 1935
WHO'S YOUR LADY FRIEND?, 1937
WHY BOTHER TO KNOCK, 1964
WHY BRING THAT UP?, 1929
WHY LEAVE HOME?, 1929
WHY PICK ON ME?, 1937
WHY ROCK THE BOAT?, 1974
WHY RUSSIANS ARE REVOLTING, 1970
WHY SAILORS LEAVE HOME, 1930
WHY SAPS LEAVE HOME, 1932
WHY WOULD I LIE, 1980
WICKED DREAMS OF PAULA SCHULTZ, THE, 1968
WIDE OPEN, 1930
WIDE OPEN FACES, 1938
WIDOW FROM MONTE CARLO, THE, 1936
WIDOW'S MIGHT, 1934
WIFE, DOCTOR AND NURSE, 1937
WIFE OR TWO, A, 1935
WIFE TAKES A FLYER, THE, 1942
WILD AFFAIR, THE, 1966
WILD AND THE INNOCENT, THE, 1959
WILD AND WONDERFUL, 1964
WILD AND WOOLLY, 1937
WILD IN THE STREETS, 1968
WILD LIFE, THE, 1984
WILD MAN OF BORNEO, THE, 1941
WILD MONEY, 1937
WILD PARTY, THE, 1929
WILD, WILD WINTER, 1966
WILDCATS, 1986
WILDCATS OF ST. TRINIAN'S, THE, 1980
WILL ANY GENTLEMAN?, 1955
WILL SUCCESS SPOIL ROCK HUNTER?, 1957
WILLIAM COMES TO TOWN, 1948
WILLS AND BURKE, 1985
WIN, PLACE, OR STEAL, 1975
WINDBAG THE SAILOR, 1937
WINDFALL, 1955
WINK OF AN EYE, 1958
WINNER TAKE ALL, 1939
WINNING TICKET, THE, 1935
WINTER KILLS, 1979
WISE GIRLS, 1930
WISE GUYS, 1937
WISE GUYS, 1986
WISHBONE, THE, 1933
WISTFUL WIDOW OF WAGON GAP, THE, 1947
WITCHES OF EASTWICK, THE, 1987
WITH A SMILE, 1939
WITH SIX YOU GET EGGROLL, 1968
WITHOUT A CLUE, 1988
WITHOUT LOVE, 1945
WITHOUT RESERVATIONS, 1946
WITHOUT YOU, 1934

BOLD: Films on Videocassette

WITNESS, THE, 1982
WIVES AND LOVERS, 1963
WIVES BEWARE, 1933
WIVES NEVER KNOW, 1936
WIVES—TEN YEARS AFTER, 1985
WIZARD OF BAGHDAD, THE, 1960
WOLF'S CLOTHING, 1936
WOLFPEN PRINCIPLE, THE, 1974
WOMAN AGAINST WOMAN, 1938
WOMAN CHASES MAN, 1937
WOMAN HATER, 1949
WOMAN IN RED, THE, 1984
WOMAN OF DISTINCTION, A, 1950
WOMAN OF THE YEAR, 1942
WOMAN TIMES SEVEN, 1967
WOMEN, THE, 1939
WOMEN AREN'T ANGELS, 1942
WOMEN OF ALL NATIONS, 1931
WOMEN OF GLAMOUR, 1937
WOMEN THEY TALK ABOUT, 1928
WOMEN WHO PLAY, 1932
WON TON TON, THE DOG WHO SAVED
    HOLLYWOOD, 1976
WONDER MAN, 1945
WONDERFUL TO BE YOUNG!, 1962
WORK IS A FOUR LETTER WORD, 1968
WORKING GIRLS, THE, 1973
WORKING MAN, THE, 1933
WORLD ACCORDING TO GARP, THE, 1982
WORLD OF HENRY ORIENT, THE, 1964
WORLD PREMIERE, 1941
WORLD WITHOUT A MASK, THE, 1934
WORLD'S GREATEST ATHLETE, THE, 1973
WORLD'S GREATEST LOVER, THE, 1977
WORM EATERS, THE, 1981
WORM'S EYE VIEW, 1951
WOULD YOU BELIEVE IT!, 1930
WRECKING CREW, THE, 1968
WRONG ARM OF THE LAW, THE, 1963
WRONG BOX, THE, 1966
WRONG DAMN FILM, THE, 1975
WRONG GUYS, THE, 1988
YANK AT OXFORD, A, 1938
YANK IN ERMINE, A, 1955
YANKEE FAKIR, 1947
YANKS AHOY, 1943
YEAR OF AWAKENING, THE, 1987
YELLOW CAB MAN, THE, 1950
YELLOW ROLLS-ROYCE, THE, 1965
YELLOW SANDS, 1938
YELLOWBEARD, 1983
YES, GIORGIO, 1982
YES, MY DARLING DAUGHTER, 1939
YESTERDAY, TODAY, AND TOMORROW, 1963
YO YO, 1967
YOU BELONG TO ME, 1941
YOU CAN'T BEAT LOVE, 1937
YOU CAN'T BEAT THE IRISH, 1952
YOU CAN'T CHEAT AN HONEST MAN, 1939
YOU CAN'T DO WITHOUT LOVE, 1946
YOU CAN'T FOOL AN IRISHMAN, 1950
YOU CAN'T FOOL YOUR WIFE, 1940
YOU CAN'T HURRY LOVE, 1988
YOU CAN'T TAKE IT WITH YOU, 1938
YOU FOR ME, 1952
YOU GOTTA STAY HAPPY, 1948
YOU KNOW WHAT SAILORS ARE, 1954
YOU LIVE AND LEARN, 1937
YOU LUCKY PEOPLE, 1955
YOU MADE ME LOVE YOU, 1934
YOU MUST BE JOKING!, 1965
YOU MUST GET MARRIED, 1936
YOU NEVER CAN TELL, 1951
YOU SAID A MOUTHFUL, 1932
YOU'D BE SURPRISED!, 1930
YOUNG AND BEAUTIFUL, 1934
YOUNG AND WILLING, 1943
YOUNG AS YOU FEEL, 1931
YOUNG AS YOU FEEL, 1940
YOUNG DOCTORS IN LOVE, 1982
YOUNG FRANKENSTEIN, 1974
YOUNG FUGITIVES, 1938
YOUNG IDEAS, 1943
YOUNG IN HEART, THE, 1938
YOUNG MAN WITH IDEAS, 1952
YOUNG MAN'S FANCY, 1943

YOUNG MONK, THE, 1978
YOUNG SWINGERS, THE, 1963
YOUNG WIVES' TALE, 1954
YOUNGEST PROFESSION, THE, 1943
YOUR MONEY OR YOUR WIFE, 1965
YOUR PAST IS SHOWING, 1958
YOUR THREE MINUTES ARE UP, 1973
YOUR UNCLE DUDLEY, 1935
YOU'RE A BIG BOY NOW, 1966
YOU'RE IN THE ARMY NOW, 1937
YOU'RE IN THE ARMY NOW, 1941
YOU'RE IN THE NAVY NOW, 1951
YOU'RE NEVER TOO YOUNG, 1955
YOU'RE ONLY YOUNG ONCE, 1938
YOU'RE ONLY YOUNG TWICE, 1952
YOU'RE TELLING ME, 1934
YOU'RE TELLING ME, 1942
YOU'RE THE DOCTOR, 1938
YOURS FOR THE ASKING, 1936
YOURS, MINE AND OURS, 1968
YOUTH TAKES A FLING, 1938
YOU'VE GOT TO WALK IT LIKE YOU TALK IT OR
    YOU'LL LOSE THAT BEAT, 1971
ZAPPED!, 1982
ZAZIE, 1961
ZELIG, 1983
ZENOBIA, 1939
ZERO TO SIXTY, 1978
00-2 MOST SECRET AGENTS, 1965
ZOMBIES ON BROADWAY, 1945
ZOO GANG, THE, 1985
ZOTZ!, 1962

Crime
ABANDONED, 1949
ABDUCTION, 1975
ABDUCTORS, THE, 1957
ABSOLUTE QUIET, 1936
ACAPULCO GOLD, 1978
ACCIDENTAL DEATH, 1963
ACCIDENTS WILL HAPPEN, 1938
ACCORDING TO MRS. HOYLE, 1951
ACCUSED, 1936
ACCUSED, THE, 1949
ACCUSED—STAND UP, 1930
ACCUSING FINGER, THE, 1936
ACQUITTED, 1929
ACROSS 110TH STREET, 1972
ACROSS THE BRIDGE, 1957
ACT, THE, 1984
ACT OF MURDER, 1965
ACT OF VENGEANCE, 1974
ACT OF VIOLENCE, 1949
ACTION STATIONS, 1959
ADULTERESS, THE, 1959
ADVENTURE IN DIAMONDS, 1940
ADVENTURE IN MANHATTAN, 1936
ADVENTURES OF ARSENE LUPIN, 1956
ADVENTURES OF KITTY O'DAY, 1944
ADVENTURES OF PC 49, THE, 1949
AFFAIR BLUM, THE, 1949
AFFAIR IN HAVANA, 1957
AFFAIR IN RENO, 1957
AFRAID TO TALK, 1932
AGAINST ALL ODDS, 1984
AGAINST THE LAW, 1934
AGE OF INFIDELITY, 1958
AIR PATROL, 1962
AIR POLICE, 1931
AL CAPONE, 1959
ALCATRAZ ISLAND, 1937
ALGIERS, 1938
ALIAS BIG SHOT, 1962
ALIAS FRENCH GERTIE, 1930
ALIAS JIMMY VALENTINE, 1928
ALIAS JOHN PRESTON, 1956
ALIAS THE CHAMP, 1949
ALIBI, 1929
ALIBI FOR MURDER, 1936
ALIBI INN, 1935
ALL-AMERICAN SWEETHEART, 1937
ALLEY CAT, 1984
ALMOST HUMAN, 1974
ALPHABET CITY, 1984
AMATEUR CROOK, 1937
AMAZING DOBERMANS, THE, 1976

AMAZING DR. CLITTERHOUSE, THE, 1938
AMBUSH, 1939
AMBUSH IN LEOPARD STREET, 1962
AMERICAN JUSTICE, 1986
AMERICAN NIGHTMARE, 1984
AMERICAN SOLDIER, THE, 1970
AMONG THE MISSING, 1934
ANATOMY OF A PSYCHO, 1961
AND HOPE TO DIE, 1972
AND MILLIONS WILL DIE, 1973
AND WOMEN SHALL WEEP, 1960
ANDERSON TAPES, THE, 1971
ANGEL, 1982
ANGEL, 1984
ANGEL, ANGEL, DOWN WE GO, 1969
ANGEL FACE, 1953
ANGELS WITH DIRTY FACES, 1938
ANOTHER MAN'S POISON, 1952
ANY NUMBER CAN WIN, 1963
APOLOGY FOR MURDER, 1945
APPOINTMENT WITH A SHADOW, 1958
APPOINTMENT WITH CRIME, 1945
APPOINTMENT WITH DANGER, 1951
APPOINTMENT WITH FEAR, 1985
ARCTIC MANHUNT, 1949
ARIZONA TO BROADWAY, 1933
ARMED RESPONSE, 1986
ARMORED CAR, 1937
ARMORED CAR ROBBERY, 1950
ARNELO AFFAIR, THE, 1947
ARSON FOR HIRE, 1959
ARSON GANG BUSTERS, 1938
ARSON, INC., 1949
ARSON SQUAD, 1945
ASPHALT JUNGLE, THE, 1950
ASSA, 1988
ASSASSIN, THE, 1965
ASSASSIN FOR HIRE, 1951
ASSAULT OF THE KILLER BIMBOS, 1988
ASSAULT ON A QUEEN, 1966
ASSIGNED TO DANGER, 1948
ASSIGNMENT TO KILL, 1968
AT CLOSE RANGE, 1986
AT THE STROKE OF NINE, 1957
ATLANTIC CITY, 1981
ATOMIC CITY, THE, 1952
AVENGING ANGEL, 1985
BABY FACE HARRINGTON, 1935
BABY FACE NELSON, 1957
BACK DOOR TO HEAVEN, 1939
BACK STREETS OF PARIS, 1962
BACK TO THE WALL, 1959
BACKLASH, 1986
BAD BLOOD, 1987
BAD BOY, 1938
BAD BOY, 1939
BAD BOY, 1949
BAD BOYS, 1983
BAD COMPANY, 1931
BADGE 373, 1973
BADLANDS, 1974
BAIT, 1950
BAND OF OUTSIDERS, 1966
BAND OF THE HAND, 1986
BANDITS, 1988
BANK ALARM, 1937
BANK MESSENGER MYSTERY, THE, 1936
BANK RAIDERS, THE, 1958
BANK SHOT, 1974
BARE KNUCKLES, 1978
BARS OF HATE, 1936
BEAST OF THE CITY, THE, 1932
BEAT GENERATION, THE, 1959
BEAUTIFUL SWINDLERS, THE, 1967
BEDEVILLED, 1955
BEDROOM EYES, 1984
BEHIND GREEN LIGHTS, 1935
BEHIND THE HIGH WALL, 1956
BELLS, THE, 1931
BELOW THE DEADLINE, 1936
BELOW THE DEADLINE, 1946
BETRAYAL, 1932
BETRAYAL, THE, 1958
BETTER A WIDOW, 1969
BETTER TOMORROW, A, 1987
BETWEEN MIDNIGHT AND DAWN, 1950

BEVERLY HILLS COP, 1984
BEYOND FEAR, 1977
BEYOND REASONABLE DOUBT, 1980
BEYOND THE LAW, 1968
BIG BAD MAMA, 1974
BIG BOODLE, THE, 1957
BIG CAPER, THE, 1957
BIG CHANCE, THE, 1957
BIG CHASE, THE, 1954
BIG CLOCK, THE, 1948
BIG COMBO, THE, 1955
BIG DEAL ON MADONNA STREET, THE, 1960
BIG EASY, THE, 1987
BIG GUY, THE, 1939
BIG HEAT, THE, 1953
BIG HOUSE, U.S.A., 1955
BIG NIGHT, THE, 1960
BIG OPERATOR, THE, 1959
BIG PAYOFF, THE, 1933
BIG SCORE, THE, 1983
BIG SHAKEDOWN, THE, 1934
BIG SHOT, THE, 1942
BIG SLEEP, THE, 1946
BIG STEAL, THE, 1949
BIG TIP OFF, THE, 1955
BIG TOWN AFTER DARK, 1947
BIG TOWN SCANDAL, 1948
BIGGEST BUNDLE OF THEM ALL, THE, 1968
BILLION DOLLAR SCANDAL, 1932
BIRDS OF PREY, 1987
BLACK ABBOT, THE, 1934
BLACK BELLY OF THE TARANTULA, THE, 1972
BLACK CAESAR, 1973
BLACK GLOVE, 1954
BLACK HAND, THE, 1950
BLACK MAGIC, 1949
BLACK MARBLE, THE, 1980
BLACK MARKET BABIES, 1946
BLACK MASK, 1935
BLACK MEMORY, 1947
BLACK PANTHER, THE, 1977
BLACK RIDER, THE, 1954
BLACK 13, 1954
BLACK TUESDAY, 1955
BLACK VEIL FOR LISA, A, 1969
BLACK WATERS, 1929
BLACK WIDOW, 1951
BLACK WIDOW, 1987
BLACKMAIL, 1947
BLACKMAILED, 1951
BLACKOUT, 1950
BLACKOUT, 1978
BLACKWELL'S ISLAND, 1939
BLAME THE WOMAN, 1932
BLAST OF SILENCE, 1961
BLIND ADVENTURE, 1933
BLIND ALIBI, 1938
BLIND ALLEY, 1939
BLIND DATE, 1984
BLIND JUSTICE, 1934
BLIND MAN'S BLUFF, 1952
BLIND SPOT, 1958
BLOCKADE, 1929
BLONDE CRAZY, 1931
BLONDE PICKUP, 1955
BLONDE SINNER, 1956
BLONDIE JOHNSON, 1933
BLOOD IN THE STREETS, 1975
BLOOD MONEY, 1933
BLOOD OF FU MANCHU, THE, 1968
BLOOD SIMPLE, 1984
BLOOD, SWEAT AND FEAR, 1975
BLOODY BROOD, THE, 1959
BLOODY MAMA, 1970
BLUE CITY, 1986
BLUE IGUANA, THE, 1988
BLUEBEARD, 1944
BLUEBEARD, 1972
BLUEBEARD'S TEN HONEYMOONS, 1960
BLUEPRINT FOR ROBBERY, 1961
BOAT FROM SHANGHAI, 1931
BOBBIE JO AND THE OUTLAW, 1976
BOBBY WARE IS MISSING, 1955
BODY HEAT, 1981
BOEFJE, 1939
BOMB IN THE HIGH STREET, 1961

BOND OF FEAR, 1956
BONNIE AND CLYDE, 1967
BONNIE PARKER STORY, THE, 1958
BOOBY TRAP, 1957
BOOK OF NUMBERS, 1973
BOOMERANG, 1960
BOOTLEGGERS, 1974
BORDER HEAT, 1988
BORDER INCIDENT, 1949
BORDERLINE, 1950
BORN RECKLESS, 1930
BORN RECKLESS, 1937
BORN TO KILL, 1947
BORROWED HERO, 1941
BORSALINO, 1970
BORSALINO AND CO., 1974
BOSS OF BIG TOWN, 1943
BOSTON STRANGLER, THE, 1968
BOWERY BOMBSHELL, 1946
BOXCAR BERTHA, 1972
BOY CRIED MURDER, THE, 1966
BOYS, THE, 1962
BOYS IN BROWN, 1949
BOYS NEXT DOOR, THE, 1985
BOY'S REFORMATORY, 1939
BRACELETS, 1931
BRAIN MACHINE, THE, 1955
BRANNIGAN, 1975
BREAKING POINT, 1976
BREATH OF LIFE, 1962
BREATHLESS, 1959
BREATHLESS, 1983
BRIDES OF FU MANCHU, THE, 1966
BRIDES TO BE, 1934
BRIDGE OF SIGHS, 1936
BRIEF RAPTURE, 1952
BRIGGS FAMILY, THE, 1940
BRIGHTON ROCK, 1947
BRIGHTON STRANGLER, THE, 1945
BRING ME THE HEAD OF ALFREDO GARCIA, 1974
BRINK'S JOB, THE, 1978
BROKEN HORSESHOE, THE, 1953
BROTHER ORCHID, 1940
BROTHERHOOD, THE, 1968
BROTHERS AND SISTERS, 1980
BROTHERS RICO, THE, 1957
BUCKTOWN, 1975
BULLET FOR PRETTY BOY, A, 1970
BULLET SCARS, 1942
BULLETS FOR O'HARA, 1941
BULLETS OR BALLOTS, 1936
BULLITT, 1968
BUNCO SQUAD, 1950
BURGLAR, THE, 1956
BURGLARS, THE, 1972
BUSTER, 1988
BUSTING, 1974
BY WHOSE HAND?, 1932
BY WHOSE HAND?, 1932
C-MAN, 1949
C.O.D., 1932
CAFE HOSTESS, 1940
CAGE OF EVIL, 1960
CAGE OF GOLD, 1950
CAGED FURY, 1948
CAIRO, 1963
CAIRO ROAD, 1950
CALCULATED RISK, 1963
CALL A MESSENGER, 1939
CALL NORTHSIDE 777, 1948
CALLBOX MYSTERY, THE, 1932
CALLING BULLDOG DRUMMOND, 1951
CALLING HOMICIDE, 1956
CALLING PAUL TEMPLE, 1948
CAMORRA, 1986
CANDIDATE FOR MURDER, 1966
CANDY MAN, THE, 1969
CANNABIS, 1970
CANNONBALL EXPRESS, 1932
CAPONE, 1975
CAPTAIN APPLEJACK, 1931
CAPTAIN BLACK JACK, 1952
CAPTAIN'S TABLE, THE, 1936
CAPTIVE CITY, 1952
CAR 99, 1935
CARBINE WILLIAMS, 1952

CARNATION KID, 1929
CASE AGAINST BROOKLYN, THE, 1958
CASE FOR THE CROWN, THE, 1934
CASE OF CHARLES PEACE, THE, 1949
CASE OF GABRIEL PERRY, THE, 1935
CASE OF THE FRIGHTENED LADY, THE, 1940.
CASH ON DEMAND, 1962
CASQUE D'OR, 1956
CAT AND MOUSE, 1958
CAT MURKIL AND THE SILKS, 1976
CATAMOUNT KILLING, THE, 1975
CATCH AS CATCH CAN, 1937
CAUGHT CHEATING, 1931
CAUGHT IN THE ACT, 1941
CAULDRON OF DEATH, THE, 1979
CAVALIER OF THE STREETS, THE, 1937
CELIA, 1949
CELL 2455, DEATH ROW, 1955
CEREMONY, THE, 1963
CERTAIN FURY, 1985
CHAIN OF EVENTS, 1958
CHAIN OF EVIDENCE, 1957
CHALLENGE, 1974
CHALLENGE, THE, 1982
CHAMELEON, 1978
CHAMP FOR A DAY, 1953
CHAMPAGNE MURDERS, THE, 1968
CHAN IS MISSING, 1982
CHANCE OF A LIFETIME, THE, 1943
CHANDLER, 1971
CHANGE PARTNERS, 1965
CHARLEY VARRICK, 1973
CHEAT, THE, 1931
CHECKMATE, 1935
CHELSEA STORY, 1951
CHICAGO CONFIDENTIAL, 1957
CHICAGO DEADLINE, 1949
CHICAGO KID, THE, 1945
CHICAGO SYNDICATE, 1955
CHILD AND THE KILLER, THE, 1959
CHILDREN OF CHANCE, 1930
CHINA GIRL, 1987
CHINATOWN AT MIDNIGHT, 1949
CHINATOWN NIGHTS, 1929
CHINATOWN NIGHTS, 1938
CHINATOWN SQUAD, 1935
CHINESE CAT, THE, 1944
CHINESE PUZZLE, THE, 1932
CHOICE OF ARMS, 1983
CHOPPERS, THE, 1961
CIRCUMSTANTIAL EVIDENCE, 1935
CIRCUMSTANTIAL EVIDENCE, 1945
CIRCUMSTANTIAL EVIDENCE, 1954
CISCO PIKE, 1971
CITADEL OF CRIME, 1941
CITY AFTER MIDNIGHT, 1957
CITY GIRL, 1938
CITY HEAT, 1984
CITY OF CHANCE, 1940
CITY OF SHADOWS, 1955
CITY STREETS, 1931
CITY THAT NEVER SLEEPS, 1953
CLOPORTES, 1966
CLOWN MURDERS, THE, 1976
CLUB LIFE, 1987
CLUE OF THE NEW PIN, THE, 1961
COBRA, 1986
COCAINE WARS, 1986
CODE OF SILENCE, 1960
CODE OF THE SECRET SERVICE, 1939
CODE TWO, 1953
COLONEL MARCH INVESTIGATES, 1952
COLORS, 1988
COMBAT SHOCK, 1986
COME DANCE WITH ME!, 1960
COMMISSIONAIRE, 1933
COMPANY OF KILLERS, 1970
COMPELLED, 1960
COMPULSION, 1959
CON ARTISTS, THE, 1981
CONFIDENCE GIRL, 1952
CONFIDENTIAL, 1935
CONFIDENTIALLY YOURS!, 1983
CONGO CROSSING, 1956
CONTACTO CHICANO, 1986
CONTRABAND LOVE, 1931

BOLD: Films on Videocassette

CONVICTED, 1938
CONVICTS AT LARGE, 1938
COOGAN'S BLUFF, 1968
COOL BREEZE, 1972
COP, A, 1973
COP-OUT, 1967
COPS AND ROBBERS, 1973
CORRUPT ONES, THE, 1967
CORRUPTION, 1933
CORSAIR, 1931
COTTON CLUB, THE, 1984
COTTON COMES TO HARLEM, 1970
COUCH, THE, 1962
COUNT THE HOURS, 1953
COUNTERFEIT, 1936
COUNTERFEIT KILLER, THE, 1968
COUNTERFEIT LADY, 1937
COUNTERFEIT PLAN, THE, 1957
COUNTERFEITERS, THE, 1948
COUNTERFEITERS, THE, 1953
COUNTERFEITERS OF PARIS, THE, 1962
COUNTERPLOT, 1959
COUNTY FAIR, THE, 1932
COUP DE TORCHON, 1981
COVER GIRL KILLER, 1960
CRACK IN THE MIRROR, 1960
CRACKERS, 1984
CRASH DONOVAN, 1936
CRASHING HOLLYWOOD, 1937
CRASHING THRU, 1939
CRASHOUT, 1955
CRAZY JOE, 1974
CRAZY MAMA, 1975
CREEPER, THE, 1980
CRIME AND PUNISHMENT, 1935
CRIME AND PUNISHMENT, 1935
CRIME AND PUNISHMENT, 1948
CRIME AND PUNISHMENT, U.S.A., 1959
CRIME AT BLOSSOMS, THE, 1933
CRIME AT PORTA ROMANA, 1980
CRIME BOSS, 1976
CRIME DOCTOR, THE, 1934
CRIME DOCTOR, 1943
CRIME DOCTOR'S COURAGE, THE, 1945
CRIME DOCTOR'S DIARY, THE, 1949
CRIME DOCTOR'S GAMBLE, 1947
CRIME DOCTOR'S STRANGEST CASE, 1943
CRIME DOCTOR'S WARNING, 1945
CRIME DOCTOR'S MAN HUNT, 1946
CRIME DOES NOT PAY, 1962
CRIME IN THE STREETS, 1956
CRIME, INC., 1945
CRIME OF DR. FORBES, 1936
CRIME OF PASSION, 1957
CRIME OF THE CENTURY, 1946
CRIME ON THE HILL, 1933
CRIME OVER LONDON, 1936
CRIME PATROL, THE, 1936
CRIME RING, 1938
CRIME TAKES A HOLIDAY, 1938
CRIME UNLIMITED, 1935
CRIME WAVE, 1954
CRIME WITHOUT PASSION, 1934
CRIMES AT THE DARK HOUSE, 1940
CRIMES OF STEPHEN HAWKE, THE, 1936
CRIMEWAVE, 1985
CRIMINAL COURT, 1946
CRIMINAL LAWYER, 1937
CRIMINALS OF THE AIR, 1937
CRIMINALS WITHIN, 1941
CRIMSON CANDLE, THE, 1934
CRIMSON KIMONO, THE, 1959
CROOK, THE, 1971
CROOKED CIRCLE, THE, 1958
CROOKED LADY, THE, 1932
CROOKED SKY, THE, 1957
CROOKED WAY, THE, 1949
CROSS CHANNEL, 1955
CROSS COUNTRY, 1983
CROSS CURRENTS, 1935
CROSSFIRE, 1933
CROSSFIRE, 1947
CROSSROADS TO CRIME, 1960
CROSSTRAP, 1962
CROW HOLLOW, 1952
CROWN VS STEVENS, 1936

CRUISING, 1980
CRUSADE AGAINST RACKETS, 1937
CRY BABY KILLER, THE, 1958
CRY DANGER, 1951
CRY OF THE CITY, 1948
CRY VENGEANCE, 1954
CURFEW BREAKERS, 1957
CURSE OF THE WRAYDONS, THE, 1946
CUSTOMS AGENT, 1950
CZAR OF BROADWAY, THE, 1930
DADDY-O, 1959
DADDY'S BOYS, 1988
DAMN CITIZEN, 1958
DAMNED DON'T CRY, THE, 1950
DANCE OF DEATH, THE, 1938
DANCE WITH A STRANGER, 1985
DANCE, FOOLS, DANCE, 1931
DANCING WITH CRIME, 1947
DANDY, THE ALL AMERICAN GIRL, 1976
DANGER BY MY SIDE, 1962
DANGER WOMAN, 1946
DANGER ZONE, THE, 1987
DANGEROUS ASSIGNMENT, 1950
DANGEROUS BUSINESS, 1946
DANGEROUS CARGO, 1954
DANGEROUS PROFESSION, A, 1949
DANGEROUS SEAS, 1931
DANGEROUS TO KNOW, 1938
DANGEROUS YEARS, 1947
DANGEROUS YOUTH, 1958
DANGEROUSLY CLOSE, 1986
DANGEROUSLY YOURS, 1933
DANGEROUSLY YOURS, 1937
DARING DOBERMANS, THE, 1973
DARING YOUNG MAN, THE, 1935
DARK CORNER, THE, 1946
DARK HOUR, THE, 1936
DARK INTERVAL, 1950
DARK LIGHT, THE, 1951
DARK MAN, THE, 1951
DARK MANHATTAN, 1937
DARK MOUNTAIN, 1944
DARK PASSAGE, 1947
DARK PAST, THE, 1948
DARK ROAD, THE, 1948
DARK SECRET, 1949
DARK STREETS, 1929
DARK STREETS OF CAIRO, 1940
DARK TOWER, THE, 1943
DARK WORLD, 1935
DARKENED SKIES, 1930
DATE AT MIDNIGHT, 1960
DATE WITH DEATH, A, 1959
DATE WITH DISASTER, 1957
DATE WITH THE FALCON, A, 1941
DATELINE DIAMONDS, 1966
DAUGHTER OF DARKNESS, 1948
DAUGHTER OF SHANGHAI, 1937
DAUGHTER OF THE DRAGON, 1931
DAUGHTER OF THE TONG, 1939
DAY AFTER HALLOWEEN, THE, 1981
DAY OF THE COBRA, THE, 1985
DAY OF THE OWL, THE, 1968
DAY OF THE WOLVES, 1973
DAY THEY ROBBED THE BANK OF ENGLAND, THE, 1960
DAYTON'S DEVILS, 1968
DEAD END, 1937
DEAD HEAT ON A MERRY-GO-ROUND, 1966
DEAD LUCKY, 1960
DEAD MAN'S CHEST, 1965
DEAD MAN'S FLOAT, 1980
DEAD MAN'S SHOES, 1939
DEAD MEN ARE DANGEROUS, 1939
DEAD MEN DON'T WEAR PLAID, 1982
DEAD MEN TELL NO TALES, 1939
DEAD POOL, THE, 1988
DEADFALL, 1968
DEADLIER THAN THE MALE, 1967
DEADLIEST SIN, THE, 1956
DEADLINE FOR MURDER, 1946
DEADLOCK, 1931
DEADLOCK, 1943
DEADLY FORCE, 1983
DEADLY GAME, THE, 1955
DEADLY PASSION, 1985

DEADLY TWINS, 1988
DEAR MURDERER, 1947
DEATH COLLECTOR, 1976
DEATH CROONS THE BLUES, 1937
DEATH GOES TO SCHOOL, 1953
DEATH OF A SCOUNDREL, 1956
DEATH OF A SOLDIER, 1986
DEATH OF AN ANGEL, 1952
DEATH ON THE DIAMOND, 1934
DEATH OVER MY SHOULDER, 1958
DEATH RACE, 1978
DEATH TOOK PLACE LAST NIGHT, 1970
DEATH TRAP, 1962
DEATH VALLEY, 1982
DEATH VENGEANCE, 1982
DEATH WISH, 1974
DEATH WISH 4: THE CRACKDOWN, 1987
DEATH WISH II, 1982
DECEPTION, 1933
DECEPTION, 1946
DECOY, 1946
DEFENDERS OF THE LAW, 1931
DELAVINE AFFAIR, THE, 1954
DELAYED ACTION, 1954
DELIRIUM, 1979
DELTA FOX, 1979
DEPARTMENT STORE, 1935
DEPORTED, 1950
DEPRAVED, THE, 1957
DESERT RAVEN, THE, 1965
DESPERATE, 1947
DESPERATE HOURS, THE, 1955
DESPERATE MAN, THE, 1959
DESTINATION BIG HOUSE, 1950
DESTINATION MURDER, 1950
DETECTIVE, 1985
DETECTIVE, THE, 1968
DETECTIVE BELLI, 1970
DETECTIVE STORY, 1951
DETOUR, 1945
DETROIT 9000, 1973
DEVIL STRIKES AT NIGHT, THE, 1959
DEVIL THUMBS A RIDE, THE, 1947
DEVIL'S ANGELS, 1967
DEVIL'S CARGO, THE, 1948
DEVIL'S 8, THE, 1969
DEVIL'S HARBOR, 1954
DEVIL'S HENCHMEN, THE, 1949
DEVIL'S PARTY, THE, 1938
DEVIL'S SISTERS, THE, 1966
DEVIL'S SLEEP, THE, 1951
DIAGNOSIS: MURDER, 1974
DIAL RED O, 1955
DIAMOND SAFARI, 1958
DIAMOND WIZARD, THE, 1954
DIAMONDS, 1975
DICK BARTON AT BAY, 1950
DICK BARTON—SPECIAL AGENT, 1948
DICK BARTON STRIKES BACK, 1949
DICK TRACY, 1945
DICK TRACY MEETS GRUESOME, 1947
DICK TRACY VS. CUEBALL, 1946
DICK TRACY'S DILEMMA, 1947
DIE SCREAMING, MARIANNE, 1970
DILLINGER, 1945
DILLINGER, 1973
DILLINGER IS DEAD, 1969
DINNER AT THE RITZ, 1937
DIPLOMATIC PASSPORT, 1954
DIRTY HANDS, 1976
DIRTY HARRY, 1971
DIRTY KNIGHT'S WORK, 1976
DIRTY MONEY, 1977
DIRTY ROTTEN SCOUNDRELS, 1988
DISHONORED LADY, 1947
DISORDERLY CONDUCT, 1932
DIVA, 1982
DOCKS OF NEW YORK, 1945
DOCKS OF SAN FRANCISCO, 1932
DOCTOR AND THE DEVILS, THE, 1985
DR. BROADWAY, 1942
DR. CHRISTIAN MEETS THE WOMEN, 1940
DR. CRIPPEN, 1963
DR. MORELLE—THE CASE OF THE MISSING
   HEIRESS, 1949
DOCTOR OF ST. PAUL, THE, 1969

DR. SIN FANG, 1937
DR. SOCRATES, 1935
DOG DAY, 1984
DOG DAY AFTERNOON, 1975
$ (DOLLARS), 1971
DON IS DEAD, THE, 1973
DON'T CALL ME A CON MAN, 1966
DON'T EVER LEAVE ME, 1949
DON'T GAMBLE WITH STRANGERS, 1946
DON'T TALK TO STRANGE MEN, 1962
DON'T TURN 'EM LOOSE, 1936
DOOMED CARGO, 1936
DOORWAY TO HELL, 1930
DOSS HOUSE, 1933
DOUBLE CONFESSION, 1953
DOUBLE CROSS, 1941
DOUBLE CROSS ROADS, 1930
DOUBLE DECEPTION, 1963
DOUBLE EXPOSURE, 1944
DOUBLE INDEMNITY, 1944
DOUBLE JEOPARDY, 1955
DOUBLE LIFE, A, 1947
DOUBLE OR QUITS, 1938
DOULOS—THE FINGER MAN, 1964
DOWN RIVER, 1931
DOWN THREE DARK STREETS, 1954
DOWNFALL, 1964
DRAGNET, 1954
DRAGNET PATROL, 1932
DRESSED TO KILL, 1941
DRIVE A CROOKED ROAD, 1954
DRIVER, THE, 1978
DRUMS OF FU MANCHU, 1943
DUAL ALIBI, 1947
DUBLIN NIGHTMARE, 1958
DUFFY, 1968
DUFFY OF SAN QUENTIN, 1954
DUKE OF CHICAGO, 1949
DUMMY, THE, 1929
DUMMY TALKS, THE, 1943
DUST BE MY DESTINY, 1939
DUSTY AND SWEETS MCGEE, 1971
DYNAMITE DELANEY, 1938
DYNAMITERS, THE, 1956
EARTHBOUND, 1940
EAST OF THE RIVER, 1940
EAST SIDE KIDS, 1940
EASY MONEY, 1936
ECHO MURDERS, THE, 1945
ECHO OF BARBARA, 1961
EDGE OF DOOM, 1950
EDGE OF FURY, 1958
8 MILLION WAYS TO DIE, 1986
ELECTRA GLIDE IN BLUE, 1973
ELEMENT OF CRIME, THE, 1984
11 HARROWHOUSE, 1974
EMBEZZLER, THE, 1954
EMERGENCY CALL, 1933
EMPIRE OF NIGHT, THE, 1963
END OF THE LINE, THE, 1959
END OF THE ROAD, 1944
ENEMIES OF THE LAW, 1931
ENFORCER, THE, 1951
ENFORCER, THE, 1976
ENTER ARSENE LUPIN, 1944
EROTIQUE, 1969
ESCAPADE, 1932
ESCAPE BY NIGHT, 1954
ESCAPE BY NIGHT, 1965
ESCAPE, THE, 1939
ESCAPE FROM CRIME, 1942
ESCAPE FROM SAN QUENTIN, 1957
ESCAPE FROM SEGOVIA, 1984
ESCAPE IN THE DESERT, 1945
ESCAPE IN THE FOG, 1945
ESCAPED FROM DARTMOOR, 1930
ESCORT FOR HIRE, 1960
EUREKA, 1983
EXECUTIONER PART II, THE, 1984
EXPERIMENT IN TERROR, 1962
EXPOSED, 1932
EXPOSED, 1938
EXPOSED, 1947
EXTERMINATOR 2, 1984
EYE WITNESS, 1950
EYEBALL, 1978

EYES OF LAURA MARS, 1978
EYES OF THE UNDERWORLD, 1943
EYES THAT KILL, 1947
FACE AT THE WINDOW, THE, 1932
FACE AT THE WINDOW, THE, 1939
FACE BEHIND THE SCAR, 1940
FACES IN THE DARK, 1960
FACTS OF MURDER, THE, 1965
FAKE, THE, 1953
FALL GUY, THE, 1930
FALLGUY, 1962
FALSE EVIDENCE, 1937
FAMILY, THE, 1974
FAMILY BUSINESS, 1987
FAMILY HONOR, 1973
FAMILY SECRET, THE, 1951
FAMOUS FERGUSON CASE, THE, 1932
FANTOMAS, 1966
FANTOMAS STRIKES BACK, 1965
FAREWELL, FRIEND, 1968
FAREWELL PERFORMANCE, 1963
FAST AND THE FURIOUS, THE, 1954
FATHER BROWN, DETECTIVE, 1935
FBI CODE 98, 1964
FBI GIRL, 1951
FBI STORY, THE, 1959
FEAR, 1946
FEAR IN THE NIGHT, 1947
FEDERAL AGENT AT LARGE, 1950
FEDERAL BULLETS, 1937
FEDERAL MAN, 1950
FEET OF CLAY, 1960
FEMALE FUGITIVE, 1938
FEMALE JUNGLE, THE, 1955
FEMMINA, 1968
FIASCO IN MILAN, 1963
FIEND OF DOPE ISLAND, 1961
FIFTEEN MAIDEN LANE, 1936
52 PICK-UP, 1986
FIGHTING MAD, 1957
FIGHTING ROOKIE, THE, 1934
FIGHTING WILDCATS, THE, 1957
FILE OF THE GOLDEN GOOSE, THE, 1969
FINAL COLUMN, THE, 1955
FINAL EDITION, 1932
FINAL JUSTICE, 1985
FIND THE BLACKMAILER, 1943
FIND THE LADY, 1936
FIND THE LADY, 1956
FINDERS KEEPERS, LOVERS WEEPERS, 1968
FINE PAIR, A, 1969
FINGER MAN, 1955
FINGER POINTS, THE, 1931
FINGERMAN, THE, 1963
FIRE RAISERS, THE, 1933
FIREBALL JUNGLE, 1968
FIRECHASERS, THE, 1970
FIRETRAP, THE, 1935
FIRST AID, 1931
FIRST OFFENCE, 1936
FISH CALLED WANDA, A, 1988
FIVE MINUTES TO LIVE, 1961
5 SINNERS, 1961
FIVE STAR FINAL, 1931
FIVE TO ONE, 1963
FIX, THE, 1985
FLAME, THE, 1948
FLAME OF THE ISLANDS, 1955
FLAME OF YOUTH, 1949
FLAMING FURY, 1949
FLAMINGO AFFAIR, THE, 1948
FLAT TWO, 1962
FLESH MERCHANT, THE, 1956
FLIGHT TO HONG KONG, 1956
FLOATING DUTCHMAN, THE, 1953
FLY NOW, PAY LATER, 1969
FLYING FIFTY-FIVE, 1939
FLYING SQUAD, THE, 1932
FLYING SQUAD, THE, 1940
FOG OVER FRISCO, 1934
FOLLOW ME QUIETLY, 1949
FOOTSTEPS IN THE NIGHT, 1932
FOR LOVE AND MONEY, 1967
FORBIDDEN CARGO, 1954
FORCE OF EVIL, 1948
FORGED PASSPORT, 1939

FORT APACHE, THE BRONX, 1981
FOUL PLAY, 1978
FOUR BOYS AND A GUN, 1957
FOUR FOR THE MORGUE, 1962
FOUR MASKED MEN, 1934
FOUR WAYS OUT, 1954
48 HOURS, 1982
48 HOURS TO ACAPULCO, 1968
FRAME-UP THE, 1937
FRAMED, 1930
FRAMED, 1947
FRANCHETTE; LES INTRIGUES, 1969
FRANCHISE AFFAIR, THE, 1952
FREEBIE AND THE BEAN, 1974
FREEDOM TO DIE, 1962
FRENCH CONNECTION II, 1975
FRENCH CONNECTION, THE, 1971
FRIENDLY KILLER, THE, 1970
FRIENDS OF EDDIE COYLE, THE, 1973
FRIGHTENED CITY, THE, 1961
FRIGHTENED MAN, THE, 1952
FROM HEADQUARTERS, 1933
FUGITIVE AT LARGE, 1939
FUGITIVE FROM JUSTICE, A, 1940
FULL CIRCLE, 1935
FULL CONFESSION, 1939
FUN WITH DICK AND JANE, 1977
FURY, 1936
G-MEN, 1935
GAMBIT, 1966
GAMBLER AND THE LADY, THE, 1952
GAMBLER'S CHOICE, 1944
GAME OF CHANCE, A, 1932
GANG BULLETS, 1938
GANG BUSTERS, 1955
GANG THAT COULDN'T SHOOT STRAIGHT, THE, 1971
GANG WAR, 1928
GANG WAR, 1940
GANG WAR, 1958
GANG WAR, 1962
GANGS OF CHICAGO, 1940
GANGS OF NEW YORK, 1938
GANGS OF THE WATERFRONT, 1945
GANGSTER STORY, 1959
GANGSTER VIP, THE, 1968
GANGSTER, THE, 1947
GANGWAY, 1937
GAOL BREAK, 1936
GAOLBREAK, 1962
GARMENT JUNGLE, THE, 1957
GAUNTLET, THE, 1977
GAY BRIDE, THE, 1934
GENTLE GANGSTER, A, 1943
GENTLE TRAP, THE, 1960
GENTLEMAN AFTER DARK, A, 1942
GENTLEMAN FROM LOUISIANA, 1936
GENTLEMAN FROM NOWHERE, THE, 1948
GENTLEMAN OF PARIS, A, 1931
GENTLEMAN'S FATE, 1931
GET-AWAY, THE, 1941
GET BACK, 1973
GET CARTER, 1971
GET OUTTA TOWN, 1960
GETAWAY, THE, 1972
GHOST CAMERA, THE, 1933
GHOST CHASERS, 1951
GHOST TALKS, THE, 1929
G.I. EXECUTIONER, THE, 1985
GIDEON OF SCOTLAND YARD, 1959
GILDED CAGE, THE, 1954
GILDERSLEEVE'S BAD DAY, 1943
GIRL CAN'T STOP, THE, 1966
GIRL FROM HAVANA, THE, 1929
GIRL IN DANGER, 1934
GIRL IN 419, 1933
GIRL IN GOLD BOOTS, 1968
GIRL IN ROOM 13, 1961
GIRL IN THE FLAT, THE, 1934
GIRL IN THE NIGHT, THE, 1931
GIRL IN THE PICTURE, THE, 1956
GIRL IN THE RED VELVET SWING, THE, 1955
GIRL IN 313, 1940
GIRL ON THE PIER, THE, 1953
GIRL ON THE SPOT, 1946
GIRL SMUGGLERS, 1967

BOLD: Films on Videocassette

GIRL WHO CAME BACK, THE, 1935
GIRLS CAN PLAY, 1937
GIRLS IN CHAINS, 1943
GIRLS IN THE NIGHT, 1953 83m UNIV bw
GIRLS ON PROBATION, 1938
GIRLS ON THE LOOSE, 1958
GIRLS UNDER TWENTY-ONE, 1940
GLENROWAN AFFAIR, THE, 1951
GLIMPSE OF PARADISE, A, 1934
GLORIA, 1980
GO TO BLAZES, 1962
GOD TOLD ME TO, 1976
GODFATHER, THE, 1972
GODFATHER, THE, PART II, 1974
GODSON, THE, 1972
GOLD EXPRESS, THE, 1955
GOLD RACKET, THE, 1937
GOLDEN HEAD, THE, 1965
GOOD BAD GIRL, THE, 1931
GOOD INTENTIONS, 1930
GOOD TIME GIRL, 1950
GRAND EXIT, 1935
GRAND JURY, 1936
GRAND JURY SECRETS, 1939
GRAND SLAM, 1968
GRAVY TRAIN, THE, 1974
GREAT BRITISH TRAIN ROBBERY, THE, 1967
GREAT DIAMOND ROBBERY, 1953
GREAT JEWEL ROBBER, THE, 1950
GREAT PLANE ROBBERY, THE, 1940
GREAT ST. LOUIS BANK ROBBERY, THE, 1959
GREAT TRAIN ROBBERY, THE, 1979
GREAT TRAIN ROBBERY, THE, 1941
GREAT VAN ROBBERY, THE, 1963
GREED OF WILLIAM HART, THE, 1948
GREEN BUDDHA, THE, 1954
GREEN COCKATOO, THE, 1947
GREEN GLOVE, THE, 1952
GRISSOM GANG, THE, 1971
GUILT IS MY SHADOW, 1950
GUILTY AS HELL, 1932
GUILTY BYSTANDER, 1950
GUILTY GENERATION, THE, 1931
GUILTY HANDS, 1931
GUILTY PARENTS, 1934
GUMSHOE, 1972
GUN CRAZY, 1949
GUN RUNNER, 1969
GUN SMOKE, 1931
GUNMAN HAS ESCAPED, A, 1948
GUNS, GIRLS AND GANGSTERS, 1958
GUY CALLED CAESAR, A, 1962
HAIL MAFIA, 1965
HALF A SINNER, 1940
HALF MOON STREET, 1986
HAMMER, 1972
HAND, THE, 1960
HANDCUFFS, LONDON, 1955
HANGMAN WAITS, THE, 1947
HANGMAN'S WHARF, 1950
HANGOVER SQUARE, 1945
HAPPENING, THE, 1967
HAPPY LANDING, 1934
HARASSED HERO, THE, 1954
HARBOR LIGHT YOKOHAMA, 1970
HARBOR OF MISSING MEN, 1950
HARD CHOICES, 1984
HARD CONTRACT, 1969
HARD GUY, 1941
HARRY IN YOUR POCKET, 1973
HATTER'S GHOST, THE, 1982
HAVING WONDERFUL CRIME, 1945
HE COULDN'T TAKE IT, 1934
HE LAUGHED LAST, 1956
HE RAN ALL THE WAY, 1951
HE WALKED BY NIGHT, 1948
HE WAS HER MAN, 1934
HE WHO RIDES A TIGER, 1966
HEART WITHIN, THE, 1957
HEAT, 1987
HEAT LIGHTNING, 1934
HEAT OF MIDNIGHT, 1966
HEATWAVE, 1954
HEIST, THE, 1979
HELD FOR RANSOM, 1938
HELD IN TRUST, 1949

HELL BENT FOR LOVE, 1934
HELL BOUND, 1931
HELL BOUND, 1957
HELL IS EMPTY, 1967
HELL ON FRISCO BAY, 1956
HELL UP IN HARLEM, 1973
HELLCATS, THE, 1968
HELL'S BLOODY DEVILS, 1970
HELL'S HOUSE, 1932
HENTAI, 1966
HER HUSBAND LIES, 1937
HER KIND OF MAN, 1946
HER MAD NIGHT, 1932
HER PRIVATE AFFAIR, 1930
HERO AND THE TERROR, 1988
HEROES IN BLUE, 1939
HI-JACKED, 1950
HI, NELLIE!, 1934
HIDDEN ENEMY, 1940
HIDDEN FEAR, 1957
HIDEAWAY, 1937
HIDE-OUT, 1934
HIDEOUT, 1949
HIDEOUT IN THE ALPS, 1938
HIGH AND LOW, 1963
HIGH JUMP, 1959
HIGH RISK, 1981
HIGH ROLLING, 1977
HIGH SCHOOL BIG SHOT, 1959
HIGH SCHOOL HELLCATS, 1958
HIGH SIERRA, 1941
HIGH SPEED, 1932
HIGH SPEED, 1986
HIGHWAY DRAGNET, 1954
HIGHWAY PATROL, 1938
HIGHWAY PICKUP, 1965
HIGHWAY 13, 1948
HIGHWAY 301, 1950
HIGHWAY TO HELL, 1984
HIGHWAY WEST, 1941
HIGHWAYS BY NIGHT, 1942
HIRED KILLER, THE, 1967
HIS KIND OF WOMAN, 1951
HIT AND RUN, 1957
HIT MAN, 1972
HITCH-HIKER, THE, 1953
HO, 1968
HOLD THAT BLONDE, 1945
HOLD THAT HYPNOTIST, 1957
HOLD THAT WOMAN, 1940
HOLD THE PRESS, 1933
HOLE IN THE WALL, 1929
HOLLOW TRIUMPH, 1948
HOLLYWOOD HARRY, 1985
HOLLYWOOD VICE SQUAD, 1986
HOMICIDE BUREAU, 1939
HOMICIDE SQUAD, 1931
HONEYMOON KILLERS, THE, 1969
HONOR OF THE PRESS, 1932
HOODLUM, THE, 1951
HOODLUM EMPIRE, 1952
HOODWINK, 1981
HOOKED GENERATION, THE, 1969
HORNET'S NEST, THE, 1955
HOT CARS, 1956
HOT CHILD IN THE CITY, 1987
HOT ICE, 1952
HOT NEWS, 1936
HOT NEWS, 1953
HOT ROCK, THE, 1972
HOT SUMMER NIGHT, 1957
HOT TARGET, 1985
HOTSPRINGS HOLIDAY, 1970
HOURS OF LONELINESS, 1930
HOUSE ACROSS THE BAY, THE, 1940
HOUSE ACROSS THE STREET, THE, 1949
HOUSE BY THE RIVER, 1950
HOUSE OF BAMBOO, 1955
HOUSE OF BLACKMAIL, 1953
HOUSE OF DANGER, 1934
HOUSE OF GAMES, 1987
HOUSE OF THE SPANIARD, THE, 1936
HOUSE OPPOSITE, THE, 1931
HOUSTON STORY, THE, 1956
HOW NOT TO ROB A DEPARTMENT STORE, 1965
HOW TO STEAL A MILLION, 1966

HOWARD CASE, THE, 1936
HUE AND CRY, 1950
HUMAN CARGO, 1936
HUMAN JUNGLE, THE, 1954
HUNDRED POUND WINDOW, THE, 1943
HUNT THE MAN DOWN, 1950
HUNTED MEN, 1938
HUNTER, THE, 1980
HUSH MONEY, 1931
HUSTLE, 1975
I ACCUSE MY PARENTS, 1945
I AM A CRIMINAL, 1939
I AM A THIEF, 1935
I AM NOT AFRAID, 1939
I AM THE LAW, 1938
I BECAME A CRIMINAL, 1947
I CAN'T ESCAPE, 1934
I CHEATED THE LAW, 1949
I COVER CHINATOWN, 1938
I COVER THE UNDERWORLD, 1955
I DEMAND PAYMENT, 1938
I DIED A THOUSAND TIMES, 1955
I LOVE THAT MAN, 1933
I MET A MURDERER, 1939
I MISS YOU, HUGS AND KISSES, 1978
I, MOBSTER, 1959
I PROMISE TO PAY, 1937
I STAND ACCUSED, 1938
I STOLE A MILLION, 1939
I TAKE THIS OATH, 1940
I, THE JURY, 1953
I, THE JURY, 1982
I WALK ALONE, 1948
I WANT TO LIVE!, 1958
I WAS A SHOPLIFTER, 1950
I WAS FRAMED, 1942
IF HE HOLLERS, LET HIM GO, 1968
ILLEGAL, 1955
ILLEGAL ENTRY, 1949
ILLEGAL TRAFFIC, 1938
IMMORAL MOMENT, THE, 1967
IMPACT, 1949
IMPACT, 1963
IMPORTANT WITNESS, THE, 1933
IN COLD BLOOD, 1967
IN FAST COMPANY, 1946
IN THE HEAT OF THE NIGHT, 1967
INCIDENT, 1948
INCIDENT AT MIDNIGHT, 1966
INCIDENT IN AN ALLEY, 1962
INDECENT, 1962
INFORMATION RECEIVED, 1962
INNOCENT MEETING, 1959
INQUISITOR, THE, 1982
INSIDE INFORMATION, 1934
INSIDE JOB, 1946
INSIDE THE MAFIA, 1959
INSIDE THE ROOM, 1935
INSPECTOR HORNLEIGH, 1939
INSPECTOR HORNLEIGH ON HOLIDAY, 1939
INSURANCE INVESTIGATOR, 1951
INTERFERENCE, 1928
INTERNES CAN'T TAKE MONEY, 1937
INTIMATE POWER, 1986
INVESTIGATION OF A CITIZEN ABOVE SUSPICION, 1970
INVISIBLE ENEMY, 1938
INVISIBLE OPPONENT, 1933
INVISIBLE STRIPES, 1940
INVISIBLE WALL, THE, 1947
IRON STAIR, THE, 1933
IS THERE JUSTICE?, 1931
IT ALL CAME TRUE, 1940
IT ALWAYS RAINS ON SUNDAY, 1949
IT CAN'T LAST FOREVER, 1937
IT HAD TO HAPPEN, 1936
IT TAKES A THIEF, 1960
IT TAKES ALL KINDS, 1969
ITALIAN CONNECTION, THE, 1973
ITALIAN JOB, THE, 1969
IT'S A COP, 1934
JACK OF DIAMONDS, 1967
JACKPOT, 1960
JAGUAR, 1980
JAIL BAIT, 1954
JAILBIRDS, 1939

JAILBREAK, 1936
JAILBREAKERS, THE, 1960
JAZZ BOAT, 1960
JENIFER HALE, 1937
JENNIFER, 1953
JEWEL, THE, 1933
JEWEL ROBBERY, 1932
JIGSAW, 1949
JIMMY THE GENT, 1934
JINX MONEY, 1948
JOE MACBETH, 1955
JOE PALOOKA IN THE BIG FIGHT, 1949
JOE PALOOKA IN THE SQUARED CIRCLE, 1950
JOE PALOOKA IN TRIPLE CROSS, 1951
JOHNNY ALLEGRO, 1949
JOHNNY APOLLO, 1940
JOHNNY BANCO, 1969
JOHNNY COOL, 1963
JOHNNY DANGEROUSLY, 1984
JOHNNY EAGER, 1942
JOHNNY O'CLOCK, 1947
JOHNNY ON THE SPOT, 1954
JOHNNY ONE-EYE, 1950
JOHNNY ROCCO, 1958
JOHNNY STOOL PIGEON, 1949
JOURNAL OF A CRIME, 1934
JOURNEY INTO NOWHERE, 1963
JOY HOUSE, 1964
JOY RIDE, 1958
JOYRIDE, 1977
JUDEX, 1966
JUDGE, THE, 1949
JUDGMENT DEFERRED, 1952
JUDY'S LITTLE NO-NO, 1969
JUKE GIRL, 1942
JUNGLE BRIDE, 1933
JUNGLE STREET GIRLS, 1963
JURY'S SECRET, THE, 1938
JUST BEFORE NIGHTFALL, 1975
JUST FOR THE HELL OF IT, 1968
JUSTICE TAKES A HOLIDAY, 1933
JUVENILE JUNGLE, 1958
KALEIDOSCOPE, 1966
KANSAS, 1988
KANSAS CITY CONFIDENTIAL, 1952
KATE PLUS TEN, 1938
KELLY OF THE SECRET SERVICE, 1936
KENTUCKY BLUE STREAK, 1935
KEY LARGO, 1948
KEY MAN, THE, 1957
KEY WITNESS, 1947
KICK IN, 1931
KID GLOVES, 1929
KILL, THE, 1968
KILL! KILL! KILL!, 1972
KILL ME TOMORROW, 1958
KILLER DILL, 1947
KILLER INSIDE ME, THE, 1976
KILLER IS LOOSE, THE, 1956
KILLER WALKS, A, 1952
KILLERS, THE, 1946
KILLERS, THE, 1964
KILLERS, THE, 1984
KILLERS THREE, 1968
KILLING, THE, 1956
KILLING OF A CHINESE BOOKIE, THE, 1976
KING FOR A NIGHT, 1933
KING OF CHINATOWN, 1939
KING OF GAMBLERS, 1937
KING OF THE CORAL SEA, 1956
KING OF THE GAMBLERS, 1948
KING OF THE ROARING TWENTIES—THE STORY
   OF ARNOLD ROTHSTEIN, 1961
KING OF THE ROYAL MOUNTED, 1936
KING OF THE STREETS, 1986
KING OF THE UNDERWORLD, 1939
KING SOLOMON OF BROADWAY, 1935
KISS ME DEADLY, 1955
KISS OF DEATH, 1947
KISS THE BLOOD OFF MY HANDS, 1948
KISS TOMORROW GOODBYE, 1950
KITTY AND THE BAGMAN, 1983
KLUTE, 1971
KNOCK ON ANY DOOR, 1949
LA BALANCE, 1983
LA GRANDE BOURGEOISE, 1977

LADY AND THE MOB, THE, 1939
LADY FROM NOWHERE, 1936
LADY FROM NOWHERE, 1931
LADY FROM SHANGHAI, THE, 1948
LADY GANGSTER, 1942
LADY ICE, 1973
LADY IN RED, THE, 1979
LADY SCARFACE, 1941
LADYKILLERS, THE, 1956
LANDSCAPE SUICIDE, 1986
LANDSLIDE, 1937
LARCENY, 1948
LARCENY, INC., 1942
LARCENY ON THE AIR, 1937
LARCENY STREET, 1941
LARGE ROPE, THE, 1953
L'ARGENT, 1984
LAS RATAS NO DUERMEN DE NOCHE, 1974
LAS VEGAS FREE-FOR-ALL, 1968
LAST ADVENTURE, THE, 1968
LAST CROOKED MILE, THE, 1946
LAST CURTAIN, THE, 1937
LAST EXPRESS, THE, 1938
LAST GANGSTER, THE, 1937
LAST HOUSE ON THE LEFT, 1972
LAST PARADE, THE, 1931
LAST PERFORMANCE, THE, 1929
LAST RIDE, THE, 1944
LAST RIDE, THE, 1932
LAST SHOT YOU HEAR, THE, 1969
LATE AT NIGHT, 1946
LATE EXTRA, 1935
LATE SHOW, THE, 1977
LAUGHTER IN HELL, 1933
LAVENDER HILL MOB, THE, 1951
LAW AND DISORDER, 1940
LAW AND THE LADY, THE, 1951
LAW OF THE BARBARY COAST, 1949
LAW OF THE TONG, 1931
LAW OF THE UNDERWORLD, 1938
LAWLESS BREED, THE, 1946
LAWLESS WOMAN, THE, 1931
LE PETIT SOLDAT, 1965
LEAGUE OF GENTLEMEN, THE, 1961
LEATHER AND NYLON, 1969
LEAVE HER TO HEAVEN, 1946
LEGION OF TERROR, 1936
L'ENIGMATIQUE MONSIEUR PARKES, 1930
LEPKE, 1975
LET 'EM HAVE IT, 1935
LET US LIVE, 1939
LETHAL OBSESSION, 1988
LETHAL WEAPON, 1987
L'ETOILE DU NORD, 1983
LIFE GOES ON, 1932
LIGHT FINGERS, 1929
LIGHT TOUCH, THE, 1951
LIGHTNIN' IN THE FOREST, 1948
LIGHTS OF NEW YORK, 1928
LIMEHOUSE BLUES, 1934
LIMPING MAN, THE, 1931
LIMPING MAN, THE, 1936
LIMPING MAN, THE, 1953
LINE ENGAGED, 1935
LINEUP, THE, 1934
LINEUP, THE, 1958
LINKS OF JUSTICE, 1958
LION AND THE LAMB, 1931
LITTLE BIG SHOT, 1952
LITTLE CAESAR, 1931
LITTLE CIGARS, 1973
LITTLE GIANT, THE, 1933
LITTLE LAURA AND BIG JOHN, 1973
LITTLE TOUGH GUY, 1938
LIVE FAST, DIE YOUNG, 1958
LOAN SHARK, 1952
LONELY HEARTS BANDITS, 1950
LONG GOOD FRIDAY, THE, 1982
LONG GOODBYE, THE, 1973
LONG WAIT, THE, 1954
LOOPHOLE, 1981
LOOPHOLE, 1954
LOOT, 1971
LORD JEFF, 1938
LOSERS, THE, 1968
LOST HAPPINESS, 1948

LOST SOULS, 1961
LOVE AND BULLETS, 1979
LOVE HUNGER, 1965
LOVE ME FOREVER, 1935
LOVE NOW...PAY LATER, 1966
LOVE NOW ... PAY LATER, 1966
LOVE ROBOTS, THE, 1965
LOVE THAT BRUTE, 1950
LOVELY WAY TO DIE, A, 1968
LOW BLOW, 1986
LUCKY JADE, 1937
LUCKY JORDAN, 1942
LUCKY NICK CAIN, 1951
LUCKY STIFF, THE, 1949
LURE OF THE ISLANDS, 1942
LURED, 1947
M, 1933
M, 1951
MA BARKER'S KILLER BROOD, 1960
MACAO, 1952
MACHINE GUN KELLY, 1958
MACHINE GUN McCAIN, 1970
MACK, THE, 1973
MACON COUNTY LINE, 1974
MAD BOMBER, THE, 1973
MAD DOCTOR, THE, 1941
MAD DOG COLL, 1961
MAD GAME, THE, 1933
MAD MISS MANTON, THE, 1938
MADAME RACKETEER, 1932
MADE IN U.S.A., 1966
MADIGAN, 1968
MADIGAN'S MILLIONS, 1970
MADONNA OF THE SEVEN MOONS, 1945
MAFIA, 1969
MAFIA, THE, 1972
MAFIA GIRLS, THE, 1969
MAFIOSO, 1962
MAGNUM FORCE, 1973
MAILBAG ROBBERY, 1957
MAIN EVENT, THE, 1938
MAIN STREET AFTER DARK, 1944
MAKE LIKE A THIEF, 1966
MAKE MINE MINK, 1960
MALAGA, 1962
MALIBU HIGH, 1979
MAN, A WOMAN, AND A BANK, A, 1979
MAN ACCUSED, 1959
MAN AGAINST MAN, 1961
MAN AGAINST WOMAN, 1932
MAN BAIT, 1952
MAN BEHIND THE MASK, THE, 1936
MAN BETRAYED, A, 1937
MAN DETAINED, 1961
MAN FROM CAIRO, THE, 1953
MAN FROM CHICAGO, THE, 1931
MAN FROM HEADQUARTERS, 1942
MAN FROM O.R.G.Y., THE, 1970
MAN HUNT, 1936
MAN IN BLACK, THE, 1950
MAN IN THE BACK SEAT, THE, 1961
MAN IN THE DARK, 1953
MAN IN THE DARK, 1963
MAN IN THE TRUNK, THE, 1942
MAN IN THE VAULT, 1956
MAN IS ARMED, THE, 1956
MAN OF COURAGE, 1943
MAN OF VIOLENCE, 1970
MAN ON THE PROWL, 1957
MAN ON THE RUN, 1949
MAN OUTSIDE, THE, 1933
MAN THEY COULDN'T ARREST, THE, 1933
MAN WHO CHANGED HIS NAME, THE, 1934
MAN WHO CHEATED HIMSELF, THE, 1951
MAN WHO COULDN'T WALK, THE, 1964
MAN WHO CRIED WOLF, THE, 1937
MAN WHO DARED, THE, 1939
MAN WHO DARED, THE, 1946
MAN WHO DIED TWICE, THE, 1958
MAN WHO LIVED TWICE, 1936
MAN WHO MADE DIAMONDS, THE, 1937
MAN WHO TALKED TOO MUCH, THE, 1940
MAN WHO WAS NOBODY, THE, 1960
MAN WHO WOULDN'T TALK, THE, 1940
MAN WITH A GUN, 1958

BOLD: Films on Videocassette

MAN WITH MY FACE, THE, 1951
MAN WITH 100 FACES, THE, 1938
MAN WITH THE MAGNETIC EYES, THE, 1945
MAN WITHOUT A FACE, THE, 1935
MANHANDLED, 1949
MANHATTAN MELODRAMA, 1934
MANHUNTER, 1986
MANULESCU, 1933
MARILYN, 1953
MARINES ARE HERE, THE, 1938
MARK OF THE VAMPIRE, 1935
MARKED MEN, 1940
MARKED ONE, THE, 1963
MARKED WOMAN, 1937
MAROC 7, 1967
MARRIED TO THE MOB, 1988
MARTIN'S DAY, 1985
MARY BURNS, FUGITIVE, 1935
MARY RYAN, DETECTIVE, 1949
MASK OF DIMITRIOS, THE, 1944
MASQUERADE, 1929
MASTER TOUCH, THE, 1974
MATCH KING, THE, 1932
MATTER OF MURDER, A, 1949
MAYFAIR GIRL, 1933
MAYOR OF HELL, THE, 1933
MC Q, 1974
MC VICAR, 1982
MEAN FRANK AND CRAZY TONY, 1976
MEAN JOHNNY BARROWS, 1976
MEAN STREETS, 1973
MEET BOSTON BLACKIE, 1941
MEET DANNY WILSON, 1952
MEET THE DUKE, 1949
MEET THE GIRLS, 1938
MEET THE MOB, 1942
MEET THE WILDCAT, 1940
MELINDA, 1972
MELODY CLUB, 1949
MEMBER OF THE JURY, 1937
MEN OF THE NIGHT, 1934
MEN WITHOUT HONOUR, 1939
MEN WITHOUT NAMES, 1935
MENACE IN THE NIGHT, 1958
MERCY PLANE, 1940
MIAMI EXPOSE, 1956
MIAMI STORY, THE, 1954
MICKEY ONE, 1965
MIDAS RUN, 1969
MIDNIGHT ALIBI, 1934
MIDNIGHT CLUB, 1933
MIDNIGHT COURT, 1937
MIDNIGHT LIMITED, 1940
MIDNIGHT MARY, 1933
MIDNIGHT MORALS, 1932
MIDNIGHT PATROL, THE, 1932
MIDNIGHT RUN, 1988
MIDNIGHT TAXI, THE, 1928
MIDNIGHT TAXI, 1937
MILE A MINUTE LOVE, 1937
MILLION DOLLAR COLLAR, THE, 1929
MILLION DOLLAR MANHUNT, 1962
MILLION DOLLAR PURSUIT, 1951
MILLION DOLLAR RANSOM, 1934
MILLION DOLLAR WEEKEND, 1948
MINI-SKIRT MOB, THE, 1968
MIRACLE IN HARLEM, 1948
MIRACLE MAN, THE, 1932
MIRRORS, 1984
MISS GRANT TAKES RICHMOND, 1949
MISS TULIP STAYS THE NIGHT, 1955
MISSING DAUGHTERS, 1939
MISSING EVIDENCE, 1939
MISSING GIRLS, 1936
MISSING WITNESSES, 1937
MISSING WOMEN, 1951
MISSISSIPPI GAMBLER, 1942
MR. CHEDWORTH STEPS OUT, 1939
MR. DENNING DRIVES NORTH, 1953
MR. DISTRICT ATTORNEY, 1941
MR. DISTRICT ATTORNEY, 1946
MR. DYNAMITE, 1935
MR. LEMON OF ORANGE, 1931
MR. LUCKY, 1943
MR. MUGGS RIDES AGAIN, 1945
MR. RICCO, 1975

MR. SATAN, 1938
MR. SMITH CARRIES ON, 1937
MR. WISE GUY, 1942
MR. WONG, DETECTIVE, 1938
MITCHELL, 1975
MOB, THE, 1951
MOBS INC, 1956
MODELS, INC., 1952
MONA LISA, 1986
MONEY, THE, 1975
MONEY AND THE WOMAN, 1940
MONEY MADNESS, 1948
MONEY MOVERS, 1978
MONEY TRAP, THE, 1966
MONSIEUR VERDOUX, 1947
MONSTER OF THE ISLAND, 1953
MONTE CARLO NIGHTS, 1934
MOONFIRE, 1970
MOONSHINE COUNTY EXPRESS, 1977
MOONSHINE MOUNTAIN, 1964
MORE DEADLY THAN THE MALE, 1961
MORNING AFTER, THE, 1986
MOST WANTED MAN, THE, 1962
MOTOR MADNESS, 1937
MOTOR PATROL, 1950
MOUTHPIECE, THE, 1932
MOVING FINGER, THE, 1963
MOVING VIOLATION, 1976
MUG TOWN, 1943
MUGGER, THE, 1958
MUMSY, NANNY, SONNY, AND GIRLY, 1970
MURDER A LA MOD, 1968
MURDER AT COVENT GARDEN, 1932
MURDER AT MONTE CARLO, 1935
MURDER AT THE CABARET, 1936
MURDER AT 3 A.M., 1953
MURDER BY ROPE, 1936
MURDER BY TELEVISION, 1935
MURDER CAN BE DEADLY, 1963
MURDER IN REVERSE, 1946
MURDER IN THE BIG HOUSE, 1942
MURDER IN THE NIGHT, 1940
MURDER, INC., 1960
MURDER MAN, 1935
MURDER ONE, 1988
MURDER TOMORROW, 1938
MURDER WITH PICTURES, 1936
MURDER WITHOUT CRIME, 1951
MURDER WITHOUT TEARS, 1953
MURPH THE SURF, 1974
MUSEUM MYSTERY, 1937
MUSIC BOX KID, THE, 1960
MUSS 'EM UP, 1936
MY BODY HUNGERS, 1967
MY BOYS ARE GOOD BOYS, 1978
MY BUDDY, 1944
MY DEATH IS A MOCKERY, 1952
MY LEARNED FRIEND, 1943
MY NEW PARTNER, 1984
MY SON IS A CRIMINAL, 1939
MY SON IS GUILTY, 1940
MY TRUE STORY, 1951
MYSTERIOUS MR. NICHOLSON, THE, 1947
MYSTERIOUS MR. VALENTINE, THE, 1946
MYSTERY IN MEXICO, 1948
MYSTERY JUNCTION, 1951
MYSTERY OF MR. X, THE, 1934
MYSTIC CIRCLE MURDER, 1939
MYSTIC HOUR, THE, 1934
NAKED CITY, THE, 1948
NAKED DAWN, THE, 1955
NAKED FURY, 1959
NAKED STREET, THE, 1955
NAKED VENGEANCE, 1986
NANCY STEELE IS MISSING, 1937
NARCO MEN, THE, 1969
NEVER A DULL MOMENT, 1968
NEVER LET GO, 1960
NEVER LOVE A STRANGER, 1958
NEVER STEAL ANYTHING SMALL, 1959
NEVER TRUST A GAMBLER, 1951
NEW CENTURIONS, THE, 1972
NEW ORLEANS AFTER DARK, 1958
NEW ORLEANS UNCENSORED, 1955
NEW YORK CONFIDENTIAL, 1955
NEWMAN'S LAW, 1974

NEWS HOUNDS, 1947
NICKEL RIDE, THE, 1974
NIGHT AND THE CITY, 1950
NIGHT BEAT, 1932
NIGHT BEAT, 1948
NIGHT CARGO, 1936
NIGHT COURT, 1932
NIGHT EDITOR, 1946
NIGHT HEAVEN FELL, THE, 1958
NIGHT HOLDS TERROR, THE, 1955
NIGHT IN NEW ORLEANS, A, 1942
NIGHT JOURNEY, 1938
NIGHT KEY, 1937
NIGHT OF LUST, 1965
NIGHT OF THE FOLLOWING DAY, THE, 1969
NIGHT OF THE GENERALS, THE, 1967
NIGHT OF THE JUGGLER, 1980
NIGHT OF THE PROWLER, 1962
NIGHT OF THE WITCHES, 1970
NIGHT RIDE, 1930
NIGHT SPOT, 1938
NIGHT STALKER, THE, 1987
NIGHT WAITRESS, 1936
NIGHT WITHOUT PITY, 1962
NIGHT WITHOUT STARS, 1953
NIGHT WORLD, 1932
NIGHT ZOO, 1988
NIGHTFALL, 1956
NIGHTHAWKS, 1981
NIGHTMARE, 1956
NIGHTMARE ALLEY, 1947
NIGHTMARE HONEYMOON, 1973
NIGHTMARE IN THE SUN, 1964
NIGHTS OF SHAME, 1961
NIGHT HAWK, THE, 1938
NINE LIVES ARE NOT ENOUGH, 1941
1990: THE BRONX WARRIORS, 1983
99 AND 44/100% DEAD, 1974
99 RIVER STREET, 1953
NO ESCAPE, 1934
NO ESCAPE, 1953
NO MAN'S LAND, 1987
NO MERCY, 1986
NO ORCHIDS FOR MISS BLANDISH, 1948
NO PARKING, 1938
NO PLACE TO HIDE, 1975
NO ROAD BACK, 1957
NO SAFETY AHEAD, 1959
NO TRACE, 1950
NO WAY BACK, 1949
NO WAY BACK, 1976
NO WAY OUT, 1975
NO WAY OUT, 1987
NOOSE FOR A LADY, 1953
NORMAN CONQUEST, 1953
NOTORIOUS GENTLEMAN, A, 1935
NOW I'LL TELL, 1934
NOWHERE TO GO, 1959
NUMBER ONE WITH A BULLET, 1987
NUMBER SEVENTEEN, 1928
NUMBER SEVENTEEN, 1932
NUMBER SIX, 1962
NURSE FROM BROOKLYN, 1938
OBJECTIVE 500 MILLION, 1966
OCEAN'S ELEVEN, 1960
ODDS AGAINST TOMORROW, 1959
OFFBEAT, 1961
OFFICER AND THE LADY, THE, 1941
OFFICER O'BRIEN, 1930
OFFICER 13, 1933
OH DOCTOR, 1937
OH, WHAT A NIGHT, 1944
OKAY AMERICA, 1932
OLGA'S GIRLS, 1964
ON DANGEROUS GROUND, 1951
ON SUCH A NIGHT, 1937
ON THE RUN, 1958
ON THE RUN, 1967
ON THE RUN, 1983
ON THE SPOT, 1940
ON THIN ICE, 1933
ONCE A CROOK, 1941
ONCE A THIEF, 1935
ONCE A THIEF, 1950
ONCE A THIEF, 1965
ONCE UPON A TIME IN AMERICA, 1984

ONE DANGEROUS NIGHT, 1943
ONE EXCITING NIGHT, 1945
ONE-EYED SOLDIERS, 1967
ONE HOUR TO LIVE, 1939
$100 A NIGHT, 1968
ONE JUST MAN, 1955
ONE MAN JURY, 1978
ONE WAY OUT, 1955
ONE WAY STREET, 1950
ONE-WAY TICKET, 1935
ONION FIELD, THE, 1979
ONLY WHEN I LARF, 1968
OPERATION MURDER, 1957
OPERATION ST. PETER'S, 1968
ORGANIZATION, THE, 1971
OTHER PEOPLE'S SINS, 1931
OTHER WOMAN, THE, 1954
OUT OF BOUNDS, 1986
OUT OF SINGAPORE, 1932
OUT OF THE FOG, 1941
OUT OF THE FOG, 1962
OUT OF THE STORM, 1948
OUTFIT, THE, 1973
OUTSIDE THE LAW, 1930
OUTSIDE THE LAW, 1956
OUTSIDE THE 3-MILE LIMIT, 1940
OUTSIDER IN AMSTERDAM, 1983
OVERKILL, 1987
OVERNIGHT, 1933
PAID, 1930
PAID TO KILL, 1954
PALLET ON THE FLOOR, 1984
PANIC, 1966
PANIQUE, 1947
PARIS PICK-UP, 1963
PARIS PLANE, 1933
PAROLE, 1936
PAROLE FIXER, 1940
PAROLE GIRL, 1933
PAROLE, INC., 1949
PAROLE RACKET, 1937
PAROLED FROM THE BIG HOUSE, 1938
PAROLED—TO DIE, 1938
PARTY GIRL, 1958
PASSING STRANGER, THE, 1954
PASSING THROUGH, 1977
PASSION HOLIDAY, 1963
PASSIONATE THIEF, THE, 1963
PAY BOX ADVENTURE, 1936
PAY OFF, THE, 1930
PAY OR DIE, 1960
PAYROLL, 1962
PENAL CODE, THE, 1933
PENALTY, THE, 1941
PENELOPE, 1966
PENNY POINTS TO PARADISE, 1951
PENROD AND HIS TWIN BROTHER, 1938
PENROD AND SAM, 1937
PENROD'S DOUBLE TROUBLE, 1938
PENTHOUSE, 1933
PEOPLE AGAINST O'HARA, THE, 1951
PEOPLE'S ENEMY, THE, 1935
PEPE LE MOKO, 1937
PERFECT CLUE, THE, 1935
PERFECT CRIME, THE, 1928
PERFECT FLAW, THE, 1934
PERFECT FRIDAY, 1970
PERFECT STRANGERS, 1984
PERIL, 1985
PERILOUS HOLIDAY, 1946
PERILOUS WATERS, 1948
PERSONS IN HIDING, 1939
PETE KELLY'S BLUES, 1955
PETRIFIED FOREST, THE, 1936
PETTICOAT LARCENY, 1943
PHANTOM RANGER, 1938
PHANTOM SPEAKS, THE, 1945
PHENIX CITY STORY, THE, 1955
PICCADILLY THIRD STOP, 1960
PICK-UP, 1933
PICK-UP ARTIST, THE, 1987
PICKPOCKET, 1963
PICKUP ON SOUTH STREET, 1953
PIERROT LE FOU, 1968
PINK STRING AND SEALING WAX, 1950
PISTOL PACKIN' MAMA, 1943

PITFALL, 1948
PLACE TO GO, A, 1964
PLAYBACK, 1962
PLAYING AROUND, 1930
PLAYMATES, 1969
PLEASURE LOVERS, THE, 1964
PLUCKED, 1969
PLUNDER ROAD, 1957
POCKETFUL OF MIRACLES, 1961
POINT BLANK, 1967
POLICE, 1986
POLICE ACADEMY 2: THEIR FIRST ASSIGNMENT, 1985
POLICE BULLETS, 1942
POLICE CAR 17, 1933
POLICE DOG, 1955
POLICE DOG STORY, THE, 1961
POLICEWOMAN, 1974
POOL OF LONDON, 1951
POPSY POP, 1971
PORT OF ESCAPE, 1955
PORT OF 40 THIEVES, THE, 1944
PORT OF LOST DREAMS, 1935
PORT OF NEW YORK, 1949
PORTLAND EXPOSE, 1957
PORTRAIT IN TERROR, 1965
PORTRAIT OF A MOBSTER, 1961
POST OFFICE INVESTIGATOR, 1949
POSTAL INSPECTOR, 1936
POSTMAN ALWAYS RINGS TWICE, THE, 1946
POSTMAN ALWAYS RINGS TWICE, THE, 1981
POSTMARK FOR DANGER, 1956
POT LUCK, 1936
POWER OF THE PRESS, 1943
PRAYER FOR THE DYING, A, 1987
PRECIOUS JEWELS, 1969
PRESCRIPTION FOR ROMANCE, 1937
PRESSURE OF GUILT, 1964
PRETENDER, THE, 1947
PRETTY BOY FLOYD, 1960
PRETTY MAIDS ALL IN A ROW, 1971
PRETTYKILL, 1987
PRICE OF A SONG, THE, 1935
PRICE OF FOLLY, THE, 1937
PRICE OF SILENCE, THE, 1960
PRIDE OF THE LEGION, THE, 1932
PRIME CUT, 1972
PRIME RISK, 1985
PRIMITIVES, THE, 1962
PRINCE OF THE CITY, 1981
PRINCESS O'HARA, 1935
PRISON TRAIN, 1938
PRISONERS IN PETTICOATS, 1950
PRIVATE HELL 36, 1954
PRIVATE SCANDAL, A, 1932
PRIZE OF ARMS, A, 1962
PRIZE OF GOLD, A, 1955
PRIZZI'S HONOR, 1985
PROFESSIONALS, THE, 1960
PROTECTOR, THE, 1985
PROWL GIRLS, 1968
PSYCHO FROM TEXAS, 1982
PUBLIC ENEMIES, 1941
PUBLIC ENEMY, THE, 1931
PUBLIC ENEMY'S WIFE, 1936
PUBLIC HERO NO. 1, 1935
PUBLIC MENACE, 1935
PULP, 1972
PURPLE GANG, THE, 1960
PURSUIT OF D.B. COOPER, THE, 1981
PUSHOVER, 1954
QUEEN OF THE MOB, 1940
QUEEN OF THE NIGHTCLUBS, 1929
QUESTION OF SILENCE, 1984
QUICK MILLIONS, 1931
QUICK MILLIONS, 1939
QUICKSAND, 1950
QUIET COOL, 1986
QUIET PLEASE, 1938
QUIET PLEASE, MURDER, 1942
QUIET WOMAN, THE, 1951
RACE STREET, 1948
RACKET, THE, 1951
RACKET BUSTERS, 1938
RACKET MAN, THE, 1944
RACKETEER, THE, 1929

RACKETEERS IN EXILE, 1937
RACKETY RAX, 1932
RADIO CAB MURDER, 1954
RADIO PATROL, 1932
RAFFLES, 1930
RAFFLES, 1939
RAGE, THE, 1963
RAGE OF HONOR, 1987
RAGING TIDE, THE, 1951
RAGS TO RICHES, 1941
RAIDERS FROM BENEATH THE SEA, 1964
RAILROADED, 1947
RAT, THE, 1938
RAW DEAL, 1948
RE: LUCKY LUCIANO, 1974
READY FOR THE PEOPLE, 1964
REAL LIFE, 1984
REBEL SET, THE, 1959
RECKLESS LIVING, 1931
RED HOT TIRES, 1935
RED LIGHT, 1949
REDEEMING SIN, THE, 1929
REDNECK, 1975
REFORM GIRL, 1933
REG'LAR FELLERS, 1941
REMOTE CONTROL, 1930
RENTADICK, 1972
REPORT TO THE COMMISSIONER, 1975
RETURN OF A STRANGER, 1962
RETURN OF DR. FU MANCHU, THE, 1930
RETURN OF DR. MABUSE, THE, 1961
RETURN OF JIMMY VALENTINE, THE, 1936
RETURN OF RAFFLES, THE, 1932
RETURN OF SOPHIE LANG, THE, 1936
RETURN OF THE RAT, THE, 1929
RETURN TO SENDER, 1963
REVENGE AT MONTE CARLO, 1933
REVENUE AGENT, 1950
RHYTHM RACKETEER, 1937
RICOCHET, 1966
RIDE, KELLY, RIDE, 1941
RIDE THE PINK HORSE, 1947
RIFF RAFF GIRLS, 1962
RIFIFI, 1956
RIFIFI IN TOKYO, 1963
RIGHT HAND OF THE DEVIL, THE, 1963
RIGHT TO LIVE, THE, 1933
RING OF FIRE, 1961
RIO GRANDE ROMANCE, 1936
RIOT SQUAD, 1941
RISE AND FALL OF LEGS DIAMOND, THE, 1960
RISKY BUSINESS, 1939
RITZ, THE, 1976
RIVALS, THE, 1963
RIVER BEAT, 1954
RIVER HOUSE GHOST, THE, 1932
RIVER'S EDGE, THE, 1957
ROAD TO SHAME, THE, 1962
ROADBLOCK, 1951
ROADHOUSE NIGHTS, 1930
ROARING TWENTIES, THE, 1939
ROBBERY, 1967
ROBBERY WITH VIOLENCE, 1958
ROBIN AND THE SEVEN HOODS, 1964
ROBOCOP, 1987
ROCK ALL NIGHT, 1957
ROCK BABY, ROCK IT, 1957
ROCKERS, 1980
ROGER TOUHY, GANGSTER!, 1944
ROGUE COP, 1954
ROGUE RIVER, 1951
ROSE OF WASHINGTON SQUARE, 1939
ROSES ARE RED, 1947
ROSSITER CASE, THE, 1950
ROTTEN TO THE CORE, 1956
ROUGH CUT, 1980
ROXIE HART, 1942
RUBBER RACKETEERS, 1942
RULING VOICE, THE, 1931
RUMBLE ON THE DOCKS, 1956
RUN ACROSS THE RIVER, 1961
RUN LIKE A THIEF, 1968
RUNAWAY, 1984
RUNAWAY BRIDE, 1930
RUNNING HOT, 1984
RUNNING SCARED, 1986

BOLD: Films on Videocassette

RUNNING TARGET, 1956
RUNNING WILD, 1955
RYDER, P.I., 1986
SAFE AFFAIR, A, 1931
SAFE IN HELL, 1931
SAFECRACKER, THE, 1958
SAIL INTO DANGER, 1957
ST. IVES, 1976
SAINT JACK, 1979
ST. VALENTINE'S DAY MASSACRE, THE, 1967
SAINTLY SINNERS, 1962
SALLY OF THE SUBWAY, 1932
SALVATORE GIULIANO, 1966
SAN FRANCISCO DOCKS, 1941
SATAN IN HIGH HEELS, 1962
SATAN'S BED, 1965
SAVAGE DAWN, 1984
SAVAGE STREETS, 1984
SAVAGES FROM HELL, 1968
SAY IT WITH DIAMONDS, 1935
SCANDAL IN PARIS, A, 1946
SCANDAL INCORPORATED, 1956
SCANDAL SHEET, 1931
SCANDAL SHEET, 1940
SCANDAL SHEET, 1952
SCAREHEADS, 1931
SCARFACE, 1932
SCARFACE, 1983
SCARFACE MOB, THE, 1962
SCARLET ANGEL, 1952
SCARLET CAMELLIA, THE, 1965
SCARLET HOUR, THE, 1956
SCARLET STREET, 1945
SCARLET THREAD, 1951
SCAVENGERS, THE, 1959
SCENE OF THE CRIME, 1949
SCHOONER GANG, THE, 1937
SCOOP, THE, 1934
SCORCHY, 1976
SCOTLAND YARD, 1930
SCOTLAND YARD, 1941
SCOTLAND YARD COMMANDS, 1937
SCOTLAND YARD DRAGNET, 1957
SCOTLAND YARD HUNTS DR. MABUSE, 1963
SCOTLAND YARD INVESTIGATOR, 1945
SCREAM IN THE NIGHT, 1943
SCREAM OF THE BUTTERFLY, 1965
SCUM OF THE EARTH, 1963
SEA SPOILERS, THE, 1936
SEA TIGER, 1952
SEALED LIPS, 1941
SEANCE ON A WET AFTERNOON, 1964
SEARCH FOR BEAUTY, 1934
SECOND CHANCE, 1947
SECOND MATE, THE, 1950
SECRET BRIDE, THE, 1935
SECRET EVIDENCE, 1941
SECRET FILE: HOLLYWOOD, 1962
SECRET OF DEEP HARBOR, 1961
SECRET OF THE PURPLE REEF, THE, 1960
SECRET OF THE WHISTLER, 1946
SECRET PARTNER, THE, 1961
SECRET PEOPLE, 1952
SECRET PLACE, THE, 1958
SECRET SERVICE INVESTIGATOR, 1948
SECRET SERVICE OF THE AIR, 1939
SECRET SEVEN, THE, 1940
SECRET SIX, THE, 1931
SECRET TENT, THE, 1956
SECRET, THE, 1955
SECRETS OF A CO-ED, 1942
SECRETS OF A NURSE, 1938
SECRETS OF A SORORITY GIRL, 1946
SECRETS OF A WINDMILL GIRL, 1966
SECRETS OF A WOMAN'S TEMPLE, 1969
SECRETS OF CHINATOWN, 1935
SECRETS OF MONTE CARLO, 1951
SECRETS OF THE FRENCH POLICE, 1932
SEEING IS BELIEVING, 1934
SELLERS OF GIRLS, 1967
SELLOUT, THE, 1951
SENSATION, 1936
SENSATION HUNTERS, 1945
SENSE OF FREEDOM, A, 1985
SENTENCED FOR LIFE, 1960
SERENA, 1962

SERGEANT MADDEN, 1939
SERPICO, 1973
SET-UP, THE, 1963
SEVEN, 1979
SEVEN DARING GIRLS, 1962
SEVEN GOLDEN MEN, 1969
711 OCEAN DRIVE, 1950
SEVEN KEYS, 1962
SEVEN THIEVES, 1960
SEVEN UPS, THE, 1973
7TH COMMANDMENT, THE, 1961
SEVENTH JUROR, THE, 1964
SHADOW MAN, 1953
SHADOW OF A MAN, 1955
SHADOW OF A WOMAN, 1946
SHADOW OF MIKE EMERALD, THE, 1935
SHADOW OF SUSPICION, 1944
SHADOW OF THE LAW, 1930
SHADOW ON THE WINDOW, THE, 1957
SHADOW, THE, 1936
SHADOWED, 1946
SHADOWED EYES, 1939
SHADOWS, 1931
SHADOWS OF SING SING, 1934
SHADOWS OF THE ORIENT, 1937
SHADOWS RUN BLACK, 1986
SHADY LADY, 1945
SHADY LADY, THE, 1929
SHAFT, 1971
SHAFT IN AFRICA, 1973
SHAFT'S BIG SCORE, 1972
SHAKEDOWN, 1936
SHAKEDOWN, 1950
SHAKEDOWN, 1988
SHAKEDOWN, THE, 1960
SHAMUS, 1973
SHANGHAI GESTURE, THE, 1941
SHARE OUT, THE, 1966
SHARK, 1970
SHARKY'S MACHINE, 1981
SHE PLAYED WITH FIRE, 1957
SHE SHALL HAVE MURDER, 1950
SHEBA BABY, 1975
SHED NO TEARS, 1948
SHE'S DANGEROUS, 1937
SHE'S NO LADY, 1937
SHIELD FOR MURDER, 1954
SHIP THAT DIED OF SHAME, THE, 1956
SHOCKPROOF, 1949
SHOOT FOR THE SUN, 1986
SHOOT IT: BLACK, SHOOT IT: BLUE, 1974
**SHOOT LOUD, LOUDER. . . I DON'T UNDERSTAND,
1966**
SHOOT THE PIANO PLAYER, 1962
SHOOT TO KILL, 1947
SHOOT TO KILL, 1988
SHORT CUT TO HELL, 1957
SHOT AT DAWN, A, 1934
SHOULD A GIRL MARRY?, 1929
SHOW THEM NO MERCY, 1935
SHRIEK IN THE NIGHT, A, 1933
SICILIAN CLAN, THE, 1970
SICILIAN CONNECTION, THE, 1977
SICILIANS, THE, 1964
SIDE STREET, 1929
SIDE STREET, 1950
SIDE STREET ANGEL, 1937
SIDESHOW, 1950
SILENCE, 1931
SILENT PARTNER, 1944
SILENT PARTNER, THE, 1979
SILENT PASSENGER, THE, 1935
SILENT WITNESS, THE, 1962
SILK, 1986
SILK NOOSE, THE, 1950
SILVER BEARS, 1978
SIN OF NORA MORAN, 1933
SIN SHIP, 1931
SIN YOU SINNERS, 1963
SINNER'S HOLIDAY, 1930
SINS PAYDAY, 1932
SIROCCO, 1951
SISTER-IN-LAW, THE, 1975
SITTING DUCKS, 1979
SIX BRIDGES TO CROSS, 1955
SIX MEN, THE, 1951

SKIDOO, 1968
SKIN DEEP, 1929
SKIN GAME, THE, 1965
SKY RAIDERS, THE, 1938
SKYWAY, 1933
SLASHER, THE, 1953
SLAUGHTER, 1972
SLAUGHTER ON TENTH AVENUE, 1957
SLAUGHTER'S BIG RIP-OFF, 1973
SLAYGROUND, 1984
SLEEPERS EAST, 1934
SLEEPERS WEST, 1941
SLEEPING TIGER, THE, 1954
SLIGHT CASE OF LARCENY, A, 1953
SLIGHT CASE OF MURDER, A, 1938
SLIGHTLY DANGEROUS, 1943
SLIGHTLY SCARLET, 1930
SLIGHTLY SCARLET, 1956
SLIPPY MCGEE, 1948
SLITHER, 1973
SMALL WORLD OF SAMMY LEE, THE, 1963
SMART ALEC, 1951
SMART ALECKS, 1942
SMART BLONDE, 1937
SMART GIRLS DON'T TALK, 1948
SMART GUY, 1943
SMART MONEY, 1931
SMASHING THE MONEY RING, 1939
SMASHING THE RACKETS, 1938
SMOKESCREEN, 1964
SMOOTH AS SILK, 1946
SMUGGLERS' COVE, 1948
SMUGGLER'S GOLD, 1951
SMUGGLER'S ISLAND, 1951
SMUGGLERS, THE, 1969
SNIPER, THE, 1952
SNO-LINE, 1986
SNORKEL, THE, 1958
SNOW JOB, 1972
SNOWBALL, 1960
SO DARK THE NIGHT, 1946
SO EVIL MY LOVE, 1948
SO YOU WON'T TALK, 1940
SOCIETY LAWYER, 1939
SOCIETY SMUGGLERS, 1939
SOD SISTERS, 1969
SOL MADRID, 1968
SOLDIERS OF THE STORM, 1933
SOLITAIRE MAN, THE, 1933
SOLO, 1970
SOLO FOR SPARROW, 1966
SOLUTION BY PHONE, 1954
SOME GIRLS DO, 1969
SOME LIKE IT HOT, 1959
SOMEONE AT THE DOOR, 1936
SOMEONE AT THE DOOR, 1950
SOMEONE BEHIND THE DOOR, 1971
SOMETHING FOR EVERYONE, 1970
SOMEWHERE IN THE NIGHT, 1946
SON COMES HOME, A, 1936
SON OF A STRANGER, 1957
SONG AT EVENTIDE, 1934
SOPHIE LANG GOES WEST, 1937
SOPHIE'S PLACE, 1970
SOUL OF THE SLUMS, 1931
SOUND OF FURY, THE, 1950
SOUTH OF SANTA FE, 1942
SOUTH OF SUEZ, 1940
SPECIAL AGENT, 1935
SPECIAL AGENT, 1949
SPECIAL DELIVERY, 1976
SPECIAL INSPECTOR, 1939
SPECIAL INVESTIGATOR, 1936
SPECIALIST, THE, 1975
SPEED CRAZY, 1959
SPEED DEVILS, 1935
SPEED LIMITED, 1940
SPEED REPORTER, 1936
SPEED TO BURN, 1938
SPELLBINDER, THE, 1939
SPIDER, THE, 1940
SPIELER, THE, 1929
SPIN A DARK WEB, 1956
SPLIT, THE, 1968
SPORTING BLOOD, 1931
SQUAD CAR, 1961

SQUADRON OF HONOR, 1938
SQUARE SHOULDERS, 1929
SQUEAKER, THE, 1930
SQUEALER, THE, 1930
SQUEEZE, THE, 1977
SQUEEZE, THE, 1980
SQUIZZY TAYLOR, 1984
STACEY!, 1973
STAGE STRUCK, 1948
STAKEOUT, 1987
STAKEOUT ON DOPE STREET, 1958
STAND ALONE, 1985
STAR REPORTER, 1939
STAR WITNESS, 1931
STATE POLICE, 1938
STATE STREET SADIE, 1928
STATE TROOPER, 1933
STEEL JUNGLE, THE, 1956
STEEL TRAP, THE, 1952
STEELE JUSTICE, 1987
STEELYARD BLUES, 1973
STEP BY STEP, 1946
STEP LIVELY, JEEVES, 1937
STEPPIN' IN SOCIETY, 1945
STICK, 1985
STILETTO, 1969
STING II, THE, 1983
STING, THE, 1973
STINGAREE, 1934
STINGRAY, 1978
STOLEN ASSIGNMENT, 1955
STOLEN HARMONY, 1935
STOLEN HEAVEN, 1931
STOLEN HEAVEN, 1938
STONE COLD DEAD, 1980
STONE KILLER, THE, 1973
STOOLIE, THE, 1972
STOP THAT CAB, 1951
STOP, YOU'RE KILLING ME, 1952
STORK PAYS OFF, THE, 1941
STORM FEAR, 1956
STORMY CROSSING, 1958
STORMY MONDAY, 1988
STORY OF MOLLY X, THE, 1949
STORY OF SHIRLEY YORKE, THE, 1948
STORY OF TEMPLE DRAKE, THE, 1933
STRAIGHT FROM THE SHOULDER, 1936
STRAIGHT IS THE WAY, 1934
STRAIGHT TIME, 1978
STRAIGHT TO HEAVEN, 1939
STRAIGHTAWAY, 1934
STRANGE ADVENTURE, A, 1956
STRANGE AFFAIR, THE, 1968
STRANGE ALIBI, 1941
STRANGE BARGAIN, 1949
STRANGE CARGO, 1936
STRANGE EVIDENCE, 1933
STRANGE EXPERIMENT, 1937
STRANGE FACES, 1938
STRANGE ILLUSION, 1945
STRANGE JUSTICE, 1932
STRANGE LOVE OF MARTHA IVERS, THE, 1946
STRANGE MRS. CRANE, THE, 1948
STRANGE TRIANGLE, 1946
STRANGER AT MY DOOR, 1950
STRANGER IN BETWEEN, THE, 1952
STRANGER ON THE THIRD FLOOR, 1940
STRANGER'S MEETING, 1957
STRANGER, THE, 1987
STRANGERS IN THE HOUSE, 1949
STRANGLEHOLD, 1962
STRANGLER'S WEB, 1966
STRAW DOGS, 1971
STRAW MAN, THE, 1953
STRAY DOG, 1963
STREET BANDITS, 1951
STREET OF MISSING MEN, 1939
STREET PEOPLE, 1976
STREET SMART, 1987
STREET WITH NO NAME, THE, 1948
STREETS OF NEW YORK, 1939
STREETS OF SAN FRANCISCO, 1949
STRICTLY PERSONAL, 1933
STRIP TEASE MURDER, 1961
STRIP, THE, 1951
STRONGER THAN DESIRE, 1939

STRONGROOM, 1962
SUBWAY, 1985
SUBWAY IN THE SKY, 1959
SUBWAY RIDERS, 1981
SUCH WOMEN ARE DANGEROUS, 1934
SUCKER MONEY, 1933
SUDDEN DANGER, 1955
SUDDEN DEATH, 1985
SUDDEN IMPACT, 1983
SUMMERTIME KILLER, 1973
SUN ABOVE, DEATH BELOW, 1969
SUN SETS AT DAWN, THE, 1950
SUNDAY IN THE COUNTRY, 1975
SUNSET MURDER CASE, 1941
SUNSET STRIP, 1985
SUPER COPS, THE, 1974
SUPER FUZZ, 1981
SUPER SPOOK, 1975
SUPERFLY, 1972
SURGEON'S KNIFE, THE, 1957
SURVIVAL RUN, 1980
SUSPECT, 1987
SUSPECT, THE, 1944
SUSPENDED ALIBI, 1957
SWAMP WOMEN, 1956
SWEENEY, 1977
SWEENEY 2, 1978
SWEET JESUS, PREACHER MAN, 1973
SWEET MAMA, 1930
SWEET SMELL OF LOVE, 1966
SWEET TRASH, 1970
SWEETHEARTS AND WIVES, 1930
SWINGING BARMAIDS, THE, 1976
SWINGING THE LEAD, 1934
SWISS CONSPIRACY, THE, 1976
SWITCH, THE, 1963
SWITCHBLADE SISTERS, 1975
SWORN ENEMY, 1936
SYMPHONY FOR A MASSACRE, 1965
SYSTEM, THE, 1953
T-BIRD GANG, 1959
T-MEN, 1947
TAKE ME AWAY, MY LOVE, 1962
TAKE ME TO PARIS, 1951
TAKE ONE FALSE STEP, 1949
TAKE THE MONEY AND RUN, 1969
TAKING OF PELHAM ONE, TWO, THREE, THE, 1974
TALE OF THREE WOMEN, A, 1954
TALL, DARK AND HANDSOME, 1941
TAMING OF DOROTHY, THE, 1950
TANGLED EVIDENCE, 1934
TARGETS, 1968
TASTE OF EXCITEMENT, 1969
TASTE OF FLESH, A, 1967
TASTE OF SIN, A, 1983
TATTOOED STRANGER, THE, 1950
TAXI!, 1932
TAXI 13, 1928
TEAR GAS SQUAD, 1940
TEEN-AGE CRIME WAVE, 1955
TEENAGE DOLL, 1957
TEENAGE GANG DEBS, 1966
TELL NO TALES, 1939
TEMPTATION HARBOR, 1949
TEMPTRESS, THE, 1949
TEN MINUTE ALIBI, 1935
10 RILLINGTON PLACE, 1971
10 TO MIDNIGHT, 1983
10 VIOLENT WOMEN, 1982
TENDERLOIN, 1928
TENTH AVENUE KID, 1938
TERROR AFTER MIDNIGHT, 1965
TERROR AT MIDNIGHT, 1956
TERROR OF DR. MABUSE, THE, 1965
TERROR OF THE TONGS, THE, 1961
TERROR ON TIPTOE, 1936
TERROR SHIP, 1954
TERROR STREET, 1953
TESTAMENT OF DR. MABUSE, THE, 1943
TEXAS TORNADO, 1934
THAT DARN CAT, 1965
THAT I MAY LIVE, 1937
THAT MAN GEORGE, 1967
THAT RIVIERA TOUCH, 1968
THAT SINKING FEELING, 1979
THAT'S MY UNCLE, 1935

THEIR NIGHT OUT, 1933
THERE IS STILL ROOM IN HELL, 1963
THERE WAS A CROOKED MAN, 1962
THEY ALL COME OUT, 1939
THEY ASKED FOR IT, 1939
THEY CAME BY NIGHT, 1940
THEY CAME TO ROB LAS VEGAS, 1969
THEY LIVE BY NIGHT, 1949
THEY MADE ME A CRIMINAL, 1939
THEY MADE ME A KILLER, 1946
THEY RAN FOR THEIR LIVES, 1968
THEY WON'T BELIEVE ME, 1947
THEY'RE PLAYING WITH FIRE, 1984
THIEF, 1981
THIEF OF HEARTS, 1984
THIEVES' HIGHWAY, 1949
THIEVES LIKE US, 1974
THINGS CHANGE, 1988
THIRD CLUE, THE, 1934
THIRD VISITOR, THE, 1951
13 EAST STREET, 1952
THIRTEEN LEAD SOLDIERS, 1948
THIRTY SIX HOURS TO KILL, 1936
THIS DAY AND AGE, 1933
THIS GUN FOR HIRE, 1942
THIS IS MY AFFAIR, 1937
THIS IS THE LIFE, 1933
THIS STUFF'LL KILL YA!, 1971
THIS WOMAN IS DANGEROUS, 1952
THOMAS CROWN AFFAIR, THE, 1968
THOROUGHBRED, 1936
THOSE WHO DANCE, 1930
THOUSAND EYES OF DR. MABUSE, THE, 1960
THREAT, THE, 1949
THREAT, THE, 1960
THREE CROOKED MEN, 1958
THREE DESPERATE MEN, 1951
THREE FOR JAMIE DAWN, 1956
THREE MEN TO DESTROY, 1980
THREE ON A TICKET, 1947
THREE SILENT MEN, 1940
THREE STEPS IN THE DARK, 1953
THREE SUNDAYS TO LIVE, 1957
THREE THE HARD WAY, 1974
THREE-WAY SPLIT, 1970
THREE WEIRD SISTERS, THE, 1948
THREE WITNESSES, 1935
THUNDER IN THE BLOOD, 1962
THUNDER OVER TANGIER, 1957
THUNDER ROAD, 1958
THUNDERBOLT, 1936
THUNDERBOLT, 1929
THUNDERBOLT AND LIGHTFOOT, 1974
TICKET OF LEAVE, 1936
TICKET OF LEAVE MAN, THE, 1937
TIGER BAY, 1933
TIGER BAY, 1959
TIGER BY THE TAIL, 1970
TIGER IN THE SMOKE, 1956
TIGER WOMAN, THE, 1945
TIGHT SKIRTS, LOOSE PLEASURES, 1966
TIGHT SPOT, 1955
TIJUANA STORY, THE, 1957
TIME IS MY ENEMY, 1957
TIME OF THE WOLVES, 1970
TIME TO DIE, A, 1983
TIME TO KILL, A, 1955
TIME TO REMEMBER, 1962
TIME WITHOUT PITY, 1957
TIMETABLE, 1956
TIP-OFF GIRLS, 1938
TIP ON A DEAD JOCKEY, 1957
TITLE SHOT, 1982
TO BE A CROOK, 1967
TO CATCH A THIEF, 1955
TO HAVE AND TO HOLD, 1963
TO KILL A STRANGER, 1985
TO LIVE AND DIE IN L.A., 1985
TO WHAT RED HELL, 1929
TODAY I HANG, 1942
TODD KILLINGS, THE, 1971
TOMORROW IS ANOTHER DAY, 1951
TOMORROW NEVER COMES, 1978
TOMORROW WE LIVE, 1942
TOO BAD SHE'S BAD, 1954
TOO DANGEROUS TO LIVE, 1939

BOLD: Films on Videocassette

TOO HOT TO HANDLE, 1961
TOO LATE FOR TEARS, 1949
TOO MANY CROOKS, 1959
TOO MANY THIEVES, 1968
TOO MANY WINNERS, 1947
TOO SCARED TO SCREAM, 1985
TOP OF THE FORM, 1953
TOP OF THE HEAP, 1972
TOP SERGEANT, 1942
TOPKAPI, 1964
TORCHY BLANE IN CHINATOWN, 1938
TORCHY BLANE IN PANAMA, 1938
TORCHY GETS HER MAN, 1938
TORCHY PLAYS WITH DYNAMITE, 1939
TORCHY RUNS FOR MAYOR, 1939
TOUCH AND GO, 1980
TOUCH OF DEATH, 1962
TOUCH OF EVIL, 1958
TOUCH OF THE OTHER, A, 1970
TOUGH AS THEY COME, 1942
TOUGH ASSIGNMENT, 1949
TOUGH GUYS, 1986
TOUGH GUYS DON'T DANCE, 1987
TOUGH TO HANDLE, 1937
TOUGHEST MAN ALIVE, 1955
TRACK THE MAN DOWN, 1956
TRACKDOWN, 1976
TRAFFIC IN CRIME, 1946
TRAIN ROBBERY CONFIDENTIAL, 1965
TRAITOR'S GATE, 1966
TRANCERS, 1985
TRANS-EUROP-EXPRESS, 1968
TRANSATLANTIC, 1961
TRAPPED, 1931
TRAPPED, 1949
TRAPPED BY G-MEN, 1937
TRAPPED IN TANGIERS, 1960
TRAVELING HUSBANDS, 1931
TREACHERY ON THE HIGH SEAS, 1939
TREAD SOFTLY, 1952
TREAD SOFTLY STRANGER, 1959
TREASURE OF MAKUBA, THE, 1967
TREASURE OF SAN GENNARO, 1968
TRIAL OF VIVIENNE WARE, THE, 1932
TRICK BABY, 1973
TRIPLE DECEPTION, 1957
TRIPLE TROUBLE, 1950
TROPICAL HEAT WAVE, 1952
TROUBLE, 1933
TROUBLE AT MIDNIGHT, 1937
TROUBLE BREWING, 1939
TROUBLE IN MIND, 1985
TROUBLE MAKERS, 1948
TROUBLE MAN, 1972
TROUBLED WATERS, 1936
TROUBLEMAKER, THE, 1964
TRUCK BUSTERS, 1943
TRUE CONFESSIONS, 1981
TRUE STORY OF LYNN STUART, THE, 1958
TRUNK, THE, 1961
TRYGON FACTOR, THE, 1969
TURNING POINT, THE, 1952
TWELVE CROWDED HOURS, 1939
TWELVE HOURS TO KILL, 1960
20,000 EYES, 1961
TWILIGHT WOMEN, 1953
TWIN FACES, 1937
TWIN HUSBANDS, 1934
TWO ARE GUILTY, 1964
TWO FOR DANGER, 1940
TWO LETTER ALIBI, 1962
TWO SECONDS, 1932
TWO SMART PEOPLE, 1946
TWO SUPER COPS, 1978
TWO-WAY STRETCH, 1961
TWO WIVES AT ONE WEDDING, 1961
UGLY DUCKLING, THE, 1959
ULTIMATE SOLUTION OF GRACE QUIGLEY, THE, 1984
ULTIMATE THRILL, THE, 1974
UMBRELLA, THE, 1933
UNCOMMON THIEF, AN, 1967
UNDER A CLOUD, 1937
UNDER AGE, 1941
UNDER COVER, 1987
UNDER-COVER MAN, 1932

UNDERCOVER AGENT, 1939
UNDERCOVER DOCTOR, 1939
UNDERCOVER GIRL, 1950
UNDERCOVER GIRL, 1957
UNDERCOVER MAISIE, 1947
UNDERCOVER MAN, THE, 1949
UNDERSEA GIRL, 1957
UNDERTOW, 1949
UNDERWORLD, 1937
UNDERWORLD INFORMERS, 1965
UNDERWORLD U.S.A., 1961
UNHOLY GARDEN, THE, 1931
UNHOLY PARTNERS, 1941
UNHOLY THREE, THE, 1930
UNHOLY WIFE, THE, 1957
UNION STATION, 1950
UNKNOWN MAN, THE, 1951
UNKNOWN WOMAN, 1935
UNMASKED, 1950
UNSATISFIED, THE, 1964
UNSTOPPABLE MAN, THE, 1961
UNSUSPECTED, THE, 1947
UNTOUCHABLES, THE, 1987
UP IN SMOKE, 1957
UPPER HAND, THE, 1967
UPPER WORLD, 1934
UPTURNED GLASS, THE, 1947
URGE TO KILL, 1960
VACATION IN RENO, 1946
VALACHI PAPERS, THE, 1972
VALIANT, THE, 1929
VALLEY OF THE REDWOODS, 1960
VELVET TOUCH, THE, 1948
VENGEANCE IS MINE, 1948
VENGEANCE IS MINE, 1980
VENGEANCE OF FU MANCHU, THE, 1968
VERDICT OF THE SEA, 1932
VERDICT, THE, 1964
VERNE MILLER, 1988
VICE DOLLS, 1961
VICE GIRLS, LTD., 1964
VICE RACKET, 1937
VICE RAID, 1959
VICE SQUAD, 1953
VICE SQUAD, 1982
VICE SQUAD, THE, 1931
VICIOUS YEARS, THE, 1950
VICKI, 1953
VISCOUNT, THE, 1967
VICTIM, 1961
VICTORY, 1940
VILLAIN, 1971
VILLIERS DIAMOND, THE, 1938
VINTAGE, THE, 1957
VIOLATED, 1953
VIOLATED, 1986
VIOLATED LOVE, 1966
VIOLENCE, 1947
VIOLENT AND THE DAMNED, THE, 1962
VIOLENT ENEMY, THE, 1969
VIOLENT FOUR, THE, 1968
VIOLENT ONES, THE, 1967
VIOLENT PLAYGROUND, 1958
VIOLENT SATURDAY, 1955
VIOLENT STRANGER, 1957
VIOLENT WOMEN, 1960
VIOLENT YEARS, THE, 1956
VIOLETTE, 1978
VIPER, THE, 1938
VIRTUE, 1932
VOICE OF THE CITY, 1929
VOICE WITHIN, THE, 1945
VORTEX, 1982
VULTURE, THE, 1937
W. W. AND THE DIXIE DANCEKINGS, 1975
WAKE UP AND DIE, 1967
WAKE UP FAMOUS, 1937
WALK THE ANGRY BEACH, 1961
WALKING STICK, THE, 1970
WALKING TALL, 1973
WALKING TALL, PART II, 1975
WALKING TARGET, THE, 1960
WALKING THE EDGE, 1985
WALLET, THE, 1952
WANDA, 1971
WANTED, 1937

WANTED BY SCOTLAND YARD, 1939
WANTED BY THE POLICE, 1938
WANTED FOR MURDER, 1946
WANTED: JANE TURNER, 1936
WARN LONDON!, 1934
WATCH THE BIRDIE, 1950
WATCHED, 1974
WATERFRONT AT MIDNIGHT, 1948
WATERFRONT LADY, 1935
WAY OF YOUTH, THE, 1934
WAY OUT, THE, 1956
WE SHALL SEE, 1964
WE STILL KILL THE OLD WAY, 1967
WEB, THE, 1947
WEDNESDAY'S LUCK, 1936
WELCOME DANGER, 1929
WELL DONE, HENRY, 1936
WE'RE NO ANGELS, 1955
WE'RE ONLY HUMAN, 1936
WEST 11, 1963
WHAT A NIGHT!, 1931
WHAT PRICE CRIME?, 1935
WHAT PRICE VENGEANCE?, 1937
WHAT WOULD YOU DO, CHUMS?, 1939
WHAT'S THE MATTER WITH HELEN?, 1971
WHAT'S YOUR RACKET?, 1934
WHEEL OF FATE, 1953
WHEN G-MEN STEP IN, 1938
WHEN GANGLAND STRIKES, 1956
WHEN LONDON SLEEPS, 1932
WHEN THE CLOCK STRIKES, 1961
WHERE DANGER LIVES, 1950
WHERE THE SIDEWALK ENDS, 1950
WHERE THERE'S A WILL, 1936
WHERE THERE'S A WILL, 1937
WHERE'S THAT FIRE?, 1939
WHIFFS, 1975
WHILE PARIS SLEEPS, 1932
WHILE THE ATTORNEY IS ASLEEP, 1945
WHILE THE CITY SLEEPS, 1956
WHIPSAW, 1936
WHISPERING TONGUES, 1934
WHISTLE STOP, 1946
WHISTLING IN THE DARK, 1933
WHITE HEAT, 1949
WHITE LIES, 1935
WHITE LIGHTNING, 1953
WHITE RAT, 1972
WHITE ROSE OF HONG KONG, 1965
WHITE TRAP, THE, 1959
WHO KILLED FEN MARKHAM?, 1937
WHO KILLED THE CAT?, 1966
WHO KILLED VAN LOON?, 1984
WHO WAS MADDOX?, 1964
WHOLE TOWN'S TALKING, THE, 1935
WHO'LL STOP THE RAIN?, 1978
WHY DOES HERR R. RUN AMOK?, 1977
WHY GIRLS LEAVE HOME, 1945
WHY MUST I DIE?, 1960
WHY SAPS LEAVE HOME, 1932
WICKED WIFE, 1955
WIDE BOY, 1952
WIDE OPEN FACES, 1938
WIDOW FROM CHICAGO, THE, 1930
WIDOW IN SCARLET, 1932
WIDOW'S MIGHT, 1934
WIFE WANTED, 1946
WILD BOY, 1934
WILD MONEY, 1937
WILD ONES ON WHEELS, 1967
WILD PAIR, THE, 1987
WILD PARTY, THE, 1956
WILD REBELS, THE, 1967
WILD RIDE, THE, 1960
WILD RIDERS, 1971
WILD THING, 1987
WILD YOUTH, 1961
WILDCAT BUS, 1940
WILLIE DYNAMITE, 1973
WIND OF CHANGE, THE, 1961
WINDJAMMER, 1937
WIRETAPPERS, 1956
WISDOM, 1986
WITHIN THE LAW, 1939
WITHOUT WARNING, 1952
WITNESS, 1985

WITNESS, THE, 1959
WOLF OF NEW YORK, 1940
WOLVES OF THE UNDERWORLD, 1935
WOMAN FROM HEADQUARTERS, 1950
WOMAN IN DISTRESS, 1937
WOMAN IN THE DARK, 1952
WOMAN OF MYSTERY, A, 1957
WOMAN OF STRAW, 1964
WOMAN ON THE RUN, 1950
WOMAN RACKET, THE, 1930
WOMAN TRAP, 1929
WOMAN TRAP, 1936
WOMAN UNAFRAID, 1934
WOMAN WANTED, 1935
WOMANHOOD, 1934
WOMAN'S FACE, A, 1941
WOMAN'S TEMPTATION, A, 1959
WOMEN ARE TROUBLE, 1936
WOMEN IN HIS LIFE, THE, 1934
WORKING GIRL, 1988
WORLD FOR RANSOM, 1954
WORLD GONE MAD, THE, 1933
WRESTLER, THE, 1974
WRONG ARM OF THE LAW, THE, 1963
WRONG MAN, THE, 1956
WRONG NUMBER, 1959
WRONG ROAD, THE, 1937
X MARKS THE SPOT, 1931
X MARKS THE SPOT, 1942
YAKUZA, THE, 1975
YASHA, 1985
YEAR OF THE DRAGON, 1985
YELLOW CANARY, THE, 1963
YELLOW CARGO, 1936
YELLOW MASK, THE, 1930
YELLOW ROBE, THE, 1954
YELLOWSTONE, 1936
YOU CAN'T BUY LUCK, 1937
YOU CAN'T ESCAPE FOREVER, 1942
YOU CAN'T GET AWAY WITH MURDER, 1939
YOU HAVE TO RUN FAST, 1961
YOU MAY BE NEXT, 1936
YOU ONLY LIVE ONCE, 1937
YOU PAY YOUR MONEY, 1957
YOUNG AND INNOCENT, 1938
YOUNG AND WILD, 1958
YOUNG DILLINGER, 1965
YOUNG DONOVAN'S KID, 1931
YOUNG DYNAMITE, 1937
YOUNG NURSES, THE, 1973
YOUNG WARRIORS, 1983
YOU'RE OUT OF LUCK, 1941
YOURS FOR THE ASKING, 1936
YOUTH ON PAROLE, 1937
ZONING, 1986

Dance
BALLERINA, 1950
BLACK TIGHTS, 1962
BLOOD WEDDING, 1981
COURT OF THE PHARAOH, THE, 1985
DARK RED ROSES, 1930
DIRTY DANCING, 1987
DON QUIXOTE, 1973
EL AMOR BRUJO, 1986
FOUETTE, 1986
LADY OF THE CAMELIAS, 1987
LITTLE BALLERINA, THE, 1951
LITTLE HUMPBACKED HORSE, THE, 1962
MORNING STAR, 1962
MYSTERIOUS HOUSE OF DR. C., THE, 1976
NUTCRACKER: THE MOTION PICTURE, 1986
PAVLOVA—A WOMAN FOR ALL TIME, 1985
PETER RABBIT AND TALES OF BEATRIX POTTER, 1971
RED SHOES, THE, 1948
ROMEO AND JULIET, 1955
ROMEO AND JULIET, 1966
SLEEPING BEAUTY, THE, 1966
SOLDIER'S TALE, THE, 1964
SPECTER OF THE ROSE, 1946
SWAN LAKE, THE, 1967
TURNING POINT, THE, 1977
UNFINISHED DANCE, THE, 1947
WHITE NIGHTS, 1985

Disaster
AIRPORT, 1970
AIRPORT 1975, 1974
AIRPORT '77, 1977
AVALANCHE, 1978
BEYOND THE POSEIDON ADVENTURE, 1979
BIG BUS, THE, 1976
BRAVE DON'T CRY, THE, 1952
BROKEN JOURNEY, 1948
CONCORDE, THE—AIRPORT '79, 1979
CRASH LANDING, 1958
CROWDED SKY, THE, 1960
DELUGE, 1933
DISASTER, 1948
DRAEGERMAN COURAGE, 1937
EARTHQUAKE, 1974
FATE IS THE HUNTER, 1964
FLYING HOSTESS, 1936
FRIDAY THE 13TH, 1934
GRAY LADY DOWN, 1978
HIGH AND THE MIGHTY, THE, 1954
HINDENBURG, THE, 1975
HURRICANE, THE, 1937
IN OLD CHICAGO, 1938
JET OVER THE ATLANTIC, 1960
JET STORM, 1961
KRAKATOA, EAST OF JAVA, 1969
LAST VOYAGE, THE, 1960
MEDUSA TOUCH, THE, 1978
MEN WITHOUT WOMEN, 1930
METEOR, 1979
NIGHT TO REMEMBER, A, 1958
POSEIDON ADVENTURE, THE, 1972
PROPHECIES OF NOSTRADAMUS, 1974
ST. HELENS, 1981
SAN FRANCISCO, 1936
SURVIVE!, 1977
SWARM, THE, 1978
THIRTEEN HOURS BY AIR, 1936
TIDAL WAVE, 1975
TITANIC, 1953
TOWERING INFERNO, THE, 1974
TRANSATLANTIC TUNNEL, 1935
TWO-MINUTE WARNING, 1976
WAY OF ALL MEN, THE, 1930
WHEN TIME RAN OUT, 1980

Docu-drama
BEYOND AND BACK, 1978
BIRTH OF A BABY, 1938
CITY OF PAIN, 1951
CRY IN THE DARK, A, 1988
FAR FROM POLAND, 1984
KEROUAC, 1985
LEGEND OF BOGGY CREEK, THE, 1973
MAN OF AFRICA, 1956
MARRIED COUPLE, A, 1969
MEIN KAMPF—MY CRIMES, 1940
MONTREAL MAIN, 1974
PHENIX CITY STORY, THE, 1955
PRINCE JACK, 1985
PURE S, 1976
RAMPARTS WE WATCH, THE, 1940
SALT OF THE EARTH, 1954
SARDINIA: RANSOM, 1968
SAVAGE GOLD, 1933
SAVAGE WILD, THE, 1970
SCHOOL FOR DANGER, 1947
SILENT ENEMY, THE, 1930
SILVER DARLINGS, THE, 1947
STAMMHEIM, 1986
STRIPPER, 1986
TRAIN OF DREAMS, 1987
TRIAL OF LEE HARVEY OSWALD, THE, 1964
TROPICS, 1969
WAJAN, 1938
WAKAMBA?, 1955

Drama
A NOS AMOURS, 1984
ABOVE THE CLOUDS, 1934
ABSENCE OF MALICE, 1981
ABSOLUTION, 1981
ABUSED CONFIDENCE, 1938
ACCATTONE!, 1961
ACCEPTABLE LEVELS, 1983

ACCIDENT, 1967
ACCUSED, THE, 1988
ACE ELI AND RODGER OF THE SKIES, 1973
ACE OF ACES, 1982
ACROSS THE RIVER, 1965
ACT OF LOVE, 1953
ACT OF MURDER, AN, 1948
ACT OF THE HEART, 1970
ACTION FOR SLANDER, 1937
ACTORS AND SIN, 1952
ACTOR'S REVENGE, AN, 1963
ACTRESS, THE, 1953
ADA, 1961
ADAM AT 6 A.M., 1970
ADAM HAD FOUR SONS, 1941
ADDING MACHINE, THE, 1969
ADERYN PAPUR, 1984
ADIEU PHILLIPINE, 1962
ADOLESCENT, THE, 1978
ADOLESCENTS, THE, 1967
ADOPTION, THE, 1978
ADRIFT, 1971
ADUEFUE, 1988
ADULTEROUS AFFAIR, 1966
ADVENTURE FOR TWO, 1945
ADVERSARY, THE, 1973
ADVICE TO THE LOVELORN, 1933
AFFAIR AT AKITSU, 1980
AFFAIR LAFONT, THE, 1939
AFFAIR OF THE SKIN, AN, 1964
AFFAIRS OF A MODEL, 1952
AFFAIRS OF ADELAIDE, 1949
AFFAIRS OF DR. HOLL, 1954
AFTER THE FOG, 1930
AFTER THE REHEARSAL, 1984
AGAINST THE TIDE, 1937
AGE FOR LOVE, THE, 1931
AGE OF CONSENT, 1969
AGE OF INDISCRETION, 1935
AGE OF INNOCENCE, 1934
AGE OF INNOCENCE, 1977
AGENCY, 1981
AGITATOR, THE, 1949
AGOSTINO, 1962
AH YING, 1984
AIR CADET, 1951
AIR DEVILS, 1938
AIR EAGLES, 1932
AIR HAWKS, 1935
AIR HOSTESS, 1933
AIR HOSTESS, 1949
AIRBORNE, 1962
AKE AND HIS WORLD, 1985
ALAMBRISTA!, 1977
ALAMO BAY, 1985
ALASKA HIGHWAY, 1943
ALEX AND THE GYPSY, 1976
ALFIE, 1966
ALFIE DARLING, 1975
ALIAS MARY DOW, 1935
ALIAS NICK BEAL, 1949
ALIAS THE DOCTOR, 1932
ALICE ADAMS, 1935
ALICE DOESN'T LIVE HERE ANYMORE, 1975
ALICE IN THE CITIES, 1974
ALICE, OR THE LAST ESCAPADE, 1977
ALICE'S RESTAURANT, 1969
ALIMONY, 1949
ALIMONY MADNESS, 1933
ALL ABOUT EVE, 1950
ALL-AROUND REDUCED PERSONALITY—OUTTAKES, THE, 1978
ALL FALL DOWN, 1962
ALL I DESIRE, 1953
ALL MEN ARE ENEMIES, 1934
ALL MINE TO GIVE, 1957
ALL MY SONS, 1948
ALL NEAT IN BLACK STOCKINGS, 1969
ALL NIGHT LONG, 1961
ALL OF ME, 1934
ALL SCREWED UP, 1976
ALL THAT HEAVEN ALLOWS, 1955
ALL THE FINE YOUNG CANNIBALS, 1960
ALL THE RIGHT NOISES, 1973
ALL THE WAY HOME, 1963
ALL THESE WOMEN, 1964

BOLD: Films on Videocassette

ALL WOMAN, 1967
ALL WOMEN HAVE SECRETS, 1939
ALLONSANFAN, 1985
ALLOTMENT WIVES, INC., 1945
ALLURING GOAL, THE, 1930
ALMOST TRANSPARENT BLUE, 1980
ALMOST YOU, 1984
ALOHA, 1931
ALOHA, BOBBY AND ROSE, 1975
ALONE IN THE STREETS, 1956
ALPHA BETA, 1973
ALSINO AND THE CONDOR, 1983
ALWAYS, 1985
ALWAYS GOODBYE, 1931
ALWAYS GOODBYE, 1938
ALWAYS IN MY HEART, 1942
AM I GUILTY?, 1940
AMATEUR DADDY, 1932
AMATEUR GENTLEMAN, 1936
AMAZING GRACE AND CHUCK, 1987
AMAZING MRS. HOLLIDAY, 1943
AMBASSADOR, THE, 1984
AMELIE OR THE TIME TO LOVE, 1961
AMERICA, AMERICA, 1963
AMERICAN DREAM, AN, 1966
AMERICAN GIGOLO, 1980
AMERICAN MADNESS, 1932
AMERICAN PRISONER, THE, 1929
AMERICAN ROMANCE, AN, 1944
AMERICAN SUCCESS COMPANY, THE, 1980
AMERICAN TABOO, 1984
AMERICAN TRAGEDY, AN, 1931
AMERICANA, 1981
AMERICANIZATION OF EMILY, THE, 1964
AMIGOS, 1986
AMONG THE CINDERS, 1985
AMY, 1981
ANA, 1985
ANASTASIA, 1956
ANATAHAN, 1953
ANATOMY OF A MARRIAGE (MY DAYS WITH
    JEAN-MARC AND MY NIGHTS WITH FRANCOISE),
    1964
ANATOMY OF A MURDER, 1959
ANATOMY OF LOVE, 1959
AND GOD CREATED WOMAN, 1957
AND GOD CREATED WOMAN, 1988
...AND JUSTICE FOR ALL, 1979
AND NOW MIGUEL, 1966
AND NOW MY LOVE, 1975
AND NOW TOMORROW, 1944
AND ONE WAS BEAUTIFUL, 1940
AND QUIET FLOWS THE DON, 1960
AND SUDDEN DEATH, 1936
AND THE WILD, WILD WOMEN, 1961
ANDY, 1965
ANGEL, 1937
ANGEL AND SINNER, 1947
ANGEL BABY, 1961
ANGEL IN EXILE, 1948
ANGEL LEVINE, THE, 1970
ANGEL WITH THE TRUMPET, THE, 1950
ANGELA, 1955
ANGELA, 1977
ANGELE, 1934
ANGELINA, 1948
ANGELO, 1951
ANGELO IN THE CROWD, 1952
ANGELO MY LOVE, 1983
ANGEL'S HOLIDAY, 1937
ANGELS OF DARKNESS, 1956
ANGELS OF THE STREETS, 1950
ANGELS OVER BROADWAY, 1940
ANGELS WASH THEIR FACES, 1939
ANGI VERA, 1980
ANGKOR-CAMBODIA EXPRESS, 1986
ANGRY BREED, THE, 1969
ANGRY ISLAND, 1960
ANGRY SILENCE, THE, 1960
ANIMAL KINGDOM, THE, 1932
ANN CARVER'S PROFESSION, 1933
ANN VICKERS, 1933
ANNA, 1951
ANNA, 1981
ANNA AND THE KING OF SIAM, 1946
ANNA CHRISTIE, 1930

ANNA CROSS, THE, 1954
ANNA KARENINA, 1935
ANNA KARENINA, 1948
ANNA LUCASTA, 1949
ANNA LUCASTA, 1958
ANNAPOLIS FAREWELL, 1935
ANNAPOLIS SALUTE, 1937
ANNE-MARIE, 1936
ANNE OF GREEN GABLES, 1934
ANNE OF WINDY POPLARS, 1940
ANNE ONE HUNDRED, 1933
ANNE TRISTER, 1986
ANONYMOUS VENETIAN, THE, 1971
ANOTHER COUNTRY, 1984
ANOTHER LOVE STORY, 1986
ANOTHER PART OF THE FOREST, 1948
ANOTHER TIME, ANOTHER PLACE, 1958
ANOTHER TIME, ANOTHER PLACE, 1984
ANOTHER WOMAN, 1988
ANTI-CLOCK, 1980
ANTIGONE, 1962
ANTS IN HIS PANTS, 1940
ANY MAN'S WIFE, 1936
ANY NUMBER CAN PLAY, 1949
ANYTHING FOR A THRILL, 1937
APARAJITO, 1959
APARTMENT, THE, 1960
APARTMENT FOR PEGGY, 1948
APE WOMAN, THE, 1964
APPASSIONATA, 1946
APPLAUSE, 1929
APPOINTMENT, THE, 1969
APPRENTICESHIP OF DUDDY KRAVITZ, THE, 1974
APRES L'AMOUR, 1948
ARCH OF TRIUMPH, 1948
ARE THESE OUR CHILDREN?, 1931
ARE THESE OUR PARENTS?, 1944
ARE WE CIVILIZED?, 1934
ARE YOU LISTENING?, 1932
ARIA, 1988
ARIANE, 1931
ARIANE, RUSSIAN MAID, 1932
ARKANSAS JUDGE, 1941
ARKANSAS TRAVELER, THE, 1938
ARMY BOUND, 1952
ARMY GIRL, 1938
ARRANGEMENT, THE, 1969
ARROWSMITH, 1931
ARTHUR'S HALLOWED GROUND, 1986
AS LONG AS YOU'RE NEAR ME, 1956
AS THE EARTH TURNS, 1934
AS THE SEA RAGES, 1960
AS YOU DESIRE ME, 1932
AS YOU LIKE IT, 1936
AS YOUNG AS WE ARE, 1958
ASCENDANCY, 1983
ASH WEDNESDAY, 1973
ASSAM GARDEN, THE, 1985
ASSAULT, THE, 1986
ASSISTANT, THE, 1982
ASTERO, 1960
ASTONISHED HEART, THE, 1950
ASYA'S HAPPINESS, 1988
AT MIDDLE AGE, 1985
ATALIA, 1985
ATLANTIC, 1929
ATLANTIC FLIGHT, 1937
ATTENTION, THE KIDS ARE WATCHING, 1978
ATTORNEY FOR THE DEFENSE, 1932
AU HASARD, BALTHAZAR, 1970
AU REVOIR LES ENFANTS, 1988
AUTUMN LEAVES, 1956
AUTUMN SONATA, 1978
AVIATOR'S WIFE, THE, 1981
AWAKENING, THE, 1958
AWAKENING OF JIM BURKE, 1935
B. F.'S DAUGHTER, 1948
BABBITT, 1934
BABETTE'S FEAST, 1988
BABIES FOR SALE, 1940
BABY BLUE MARINE, 1976
BABY DOLL, 1956
BABY FACE, 1933
BABY, IT'S YOU, 1983
BABY LOVE, 1969
BABY MAKER, THE, 1970

BABY, THE RAIN MUST FALL, 1965
BABYLON, 1980
BACCHANTES, THE, 1963
BACHELOR GIRL, THE, 1929
BACHELOR MOTHER, 1933
BACHELOR PARTY, THE, 1957
BACK IN CIRCULATION, 1937
BACK PAY, 1930
BACK STREET, 1932
BACK STREET, 1941
BACK STREET, 1961
BACKGROUND, 1953
BAD AND THE BEAUTIFUL, THE, 1952
BAD BLONDE, 1953
BAD COMPANY, 1986
BAD DAY AT BLACK ROCK, 1955
BAD FOR EACH OTHER, 1954
BAD GIRL, 1931
BAD GUY, 1937
BAD LITTLE ANGEL, 1939
BAD ONE, THE, 1930
BAD SEED, THE, 1956
BAD SISTER, 1931
BAD SISTER, 1947
BADGE OF HONOR, 1934
BAILOUT AT 43,000, 1957
BAIT, 1954
BAL TABARIN, 1952
BALBOA, 1986
BALCONY, THE, 1963
BALLAD OF A SOLDIER, 1960
BALLAD OF COSSACK GLOOTA, 1938
BALLAD OF NARAYAMA, 1961
BALLAD OF NARAYAMA, THE, 1984
BALTIC DEPUTY, 1937
BALTIMORE BULLET, THE, 1980
BAMBOLE!, 1965
BAND OF ANGELS, 1957
BAND OF ASSASSINS, 1971
BANDIT, THE, 1949
BANDITS OF ORGOSOLO, 1964
BANDITS ON THE WIND, 1964
BANISHED, 1978
BANJO, 1947
BANK HOLIDAY, 1938
BANNERLINE, 1951
BANNING, 1967
BAR 51—SISTER OF LOVE, 1986
BAR SINISTER, THE, 1955
BARBARY COAST, 1935
BARBER OF SEVILLE, THE, 1973
BARBER OF STAMFORD HILL, THE, 1963
BARCAROLE, 1935
BAREFOOT BOY, 1938
BAREFOOT CONTESSA, THE, 1954
BARGAIN, THE, 1931
BARKER, THE, 1928
BARNACLE BILL, 1935
BARNACLE BILL, 1941
BARNUM WAS RIGHT, 1929
BAROCCO, 1976
BARRIER, 1966
BARTLEBY, 1970
BASILEUS QUARTET, 1984
BASTILLE, 1985
BATTLE FOR MUSIC, 1943
BAXTER, 1973
BAY BOY, 1984
BAY OF ANGELS, 1964
BAYOU, 1957
BE MY GUEST, 1965
BEACHCOMBER, 1938
BEACHCOMBER, 1955
BEACHES, 1988
BEARS AND I, THE, 1974
BEAST OF BUDAPEST, THE, 1958
BEASTS OF BERLIN, 1939
BEASTS OF MARSEILLES, THE, 1959
BEAT, THE, 1988
BEAT THE DEVIL, 1953
BEATNIKS, THE, 1960
BEAU PERE, 1981
BEAUTIFUL STRANGER, 1954
BEAUTY AND THE BOSS, 1932
BEAUTY AND THE DEVIL, 1952
BEAUTY FOR THE ASKING, 1939

BEAUTY JUNGLE, THE, 1966
BEAUTY ON PARADE, 1950
BEAUTY PARLOR, 1932
BEBO'S GIRL, 1964
BECAUSE I LOVED YOU, 1930
BECAUSE OF EVE, 1948
BECKY SHARP, 1935
BECAUSE THEY'RE YOUNG, 1960
BED AND BOARD, 1971
BED AND BREAKFAST, 1936
BED OF ROSES, 1933
BEDELIA, 1946
BEDFORD INCIDENT, THE, 1965
BEDSIDE, 1934
BEDTIME STORY, 1938
BEEN DOWN SO LONG IT LOOKS LIKE UP TO ME, 1977
BEFORE AND AFTER, 1985
BEFORE HIM ALL ROME TREMBLED, 1947
BEFORE THE REVOLUTION, 1964
BEFORE WINTER COMES, 1969
BEG, BORROW OR STEAL, 1937
BEGGARS IN ERMINE, 1934
BEGGARS OF LIFE, 1928
BEGINNING OR THE END, THE, 1947
BEGUILED, THE, 1971
BEHIND CLOSED SHUTTERS, 1952
BEHIND OFFICE DOORS, 1931
BEHIND STONE WALLS, 1932
BEHIND THE EVIDENCE, 1935
BEHIND THE HEADLINES, 1937
BEHIND THE MAKEUP, 1930
BEHIND THE MASK, 1958
BEHIND THE NEWS, 1941
BEHIND YOUR BACK, 1937
BEHOLD MY WIFE, 1935
BELIEVE IN ME, 1971
BELL' ANTONIO, 1962
BELL DIAMOND, 1987
BELL FOR ADANO, A, 1945
BELLA DONNA, 1934
BELLA DONNA, 1983
BELLE DE JOUR, 1968
BELLES OF ST. CLEMENTS, THE, 1936
BELLISSIMA, 1952
BELLS OF ST. MARY'S, THE, 1945
BELLS OF SAN FERNANDO, 1947
BELLY OF AN ARCHITECT, THE, 1987
BELOVED, 1934
BELOVED BACHELOR, THE, 1931
BELOVED BRAT, 1938
BELOVED ENEMY, 1936
BELSTONE FOX, THE, 1976
BENGAL TIGER, 1936
BERLIN AFFAIR, THE, 1985
BERLIN ALEXANDERPLATZ, 1933
BERLIN EXPRESS, 1948
BERMONDSEY KID, THE, 1933
BERMUDA AFFAIR, 1956
BEST FRIENDS, 1982
BEST FRIENDS, 1975
BEST MAN, THE, 1964
BEST MAN WINS, 1948
BEST OF EVERYTHING, THE, 1959
BEST OF TIMES, THE, 1986
BEST WAY, THE, 1978
BEST YEARS OF OUR LIVES, THE, 1946
BETRAYAL, 1939
BETRAYAL, THE, 1948
BETRAYAL, 1983
BETSY, THE, 1978
BETTER TOMORROW, A, 1987
BETTY BLUE, 1986
BETTY CO-ED, 1946
BETWEEN THE LINES, 1977
BETWEEN TWO WOMEN, 1937
BETWEEN TWO WOMEN, 1944
BETWEEN TWO WORLDS, 1944
BETWEEN US GIRLS, 1942
BEWARE OF LADIES, 1937
BEYOND GLORY, 1948
BEYOND GOOD AND EVIL, 1984
BEYOND THE CITIES, 1930
BEYOND THE CURTAIN, 1960
BEYOND VICTORY, 1931
BHOWANI JUNCTION, 1956

BICYCLE THIEF, THE, 1949
BIDDY, 1983
BIG BLUFF, THE, 1933
BIG BLUFF, THE, 1955
BIG BONANZA, THE, 1944
BIG BOSS, THE, 1941
BIG BOUNCE, THE, 1969
BIG BUSINESS, 1937
BIG BUSINESS GIRL, 1931
BIG CAGE, THE, 1933
BIG CARNIVAL, THE, 1951
BIG CHANCE, THE, 1933
BIG CHILL, THE, 1983
BIG CIRCUS, THE, 1959
BIG CITY, 1937
BIG CITY BLUES, 1932
BIG CITY, THE, 1963
BIG CUBE, THE, 1969
BIG DADDY, 1969
BIG DAY, THE, 1960
BIG EXECUTIVE, 1933
BIG FELLA, 1937
BIG HANGOVER, THE, 1950
BIG JIM McLAIN, 1952
BIG KNIFE, THE, 1955
BIG LIFT, THE, 1950
BIG MONEY, 1930
BIG NEWS, 1929
BIG NIGHT, THE, 1951
BIG NOISE, THE, 1936
BIG PARADE, THE, 1987
BIG PUNCH, THE, 1948
BIG SHOTS, 1987
BIG SHOW, THE, 1961
BIG SHOW-OFF, THE, 1945
BIG TIMBER, 1950
BIG TIME, 1929
BIG TIME OR BUST, 1934
BIG TOWN, 1932
BIG TOWN, 1947
BIG TOWN, THE, 1987
BIG TOWN GIRL, 1937
BIG WEDNESDAY, 1978
BIGAMIST, THE, 1953
BIGGER SPLASH, A, 1984
BIGGER THAN LIFE, 1956
BILL OF DIVORCEMENT, 1940
BILLIE, 1965
BILLY BUDD, 1962
BILLY IN THE LOWLANDS, 1979
BILLY JACK, 1971
BILLY JACK GOES TO WASHINGTON, 1977
BILLY LIAR, 1963
BIMBO THE GREAT, 1961
BIQUEFARRE, 1983
BIRCH INTERVAL, 1976
BIRDS COME TO DIE IN PERU, 1968
BIRDS OF PREY, 1988
BIRDY, 1984
BIRTHDAY PARTY, THE, 1968
BIRTHDAY PRESENT, THE, 1957
BISCUIT EATER, THE, 1940
BISCUIT EATER, THE, 1972
BITTER HARVEST, 1963
BITTER RICE, 1950
BITTER SPRINGS, 1950
BITTER TEA OF GENERAL YEN, THE, 1933
BITTER TEARS OF PETRA VON KANT, THE, 1972
BITTERSWEET LOVE, 1976
BLACK AND WHITE, 1986
BLACK AND WHITE IN COLOR, 1976
BLACK BEAUTY, 1933
BLACK BEAUTY, 1946
BLACK BEAUTY, 1971
BLACK DIAMONDS, 1932
BLACK DIAMONDS, 1940
BLACK EYES, 1939
BLACK FURY, 1935
BLACK GIRL, 1972
BLACK GOLD, 1947
BLACK JOY, 1977
BLACK JOY, 1986
BLACK KING, 1932
BLACK KLANSMAN, THE, 1966
BLACK LEGION, THE, 1937
BLACK LIKE ME, 1964

BLACK MIDNIGHT, 1949
BLACK MOON, 1934
BLACK NARCISSUS, 1947
BLACK OAK CONSPIRACY, 1977
BLACK ORCHID, 1959
BLACK ORPHEUS, 1959
BLACK ROSES, 1936
BLACK SAMSON, 1974
BLACK SHAMPOO, 1976
BLACK SHEEP, 1935
BLACK SUN, THE, 1979
BLACK TULIP, THE, 1937
BLACKBOARD JUNGLE, THE, 1955
BLACKMAIL, 1939
BLACKOUT, 1940
BLAME IT ON THE NIGHT, 1984
BLARNEY KISS, 1933
BLAZING BARRIERS, 1937
BLEAK MOMENTS, 1972
BLESS THE BEASTS AND CHILDREN, 1971
BLESS THEIR LITTLE HEARTS, 1984
BLIND CHANCE, 1987
BLIND DATE, 1934
BLIND GODDESS, THE, 1948
BLIND MAN'S BLUFF, 1936
BLIND SPOT, 1932
BLISS, 1985
BLOCKHOUSE, THE, 1974
BLONDE BANDIT, THE, 1950
BLONDE FEVER, 1944
BLONDE VENUS, 1932
BLONDES AT WORK, 1938
BLOOD AND SAND, 1941
BLOOD FEUD, 1979
BLOOD OF A POET, THE, 1930
BLOOD ON THE SUN, 1945
BLOODBROTHERS, 1978
BLOODY KIDS, 1983
BLOOMFIELD, 1971
BLOW TO THE HEART, 1983
BLOW-UP, 1966
BLUE ANGEL, THE, 1930
BLUE ANGEL, THE, 1959
BLUE BLOOD, 1973
BLUE COLLAR, 1978
BLUE COUNTRY, THE, 1977
BLUE DENIM, 1959
BLUE HEAVEN, 1985
BLUE LIGHT, THE, 1932
BLUE SCAR, 1949
BLUE VEIL, THE, 1947
BLUE VEIL, THE, 1951
BLUES FOR LOVERS, 1966
BOARDWALK, 1979
BOFORS GUN, THE, 1968
BOLERO, 1984
BOMBARDMENT OF MONTE CARLO, THE, 1931
BOMBERS B-52, 1957
BONA, 1984
BOND STREET, 1948
BONDAGE, 1933
BONJOUR TRISTESSE, 1958
BONNE CHANCE, 1935
BOOM!, 1968
BOOM TOWN, 1940
BOOST, THE, 1988
BORDER, THE, 1982
BORDERLINE, 1980
BORDERTOWN, 1935
BORN AGAIN, 1978
BORN AMERICAN, 1986
BORN FREE, 1966
BORN RECKLESS, 1959
BORN TO BE BAD, 1934
BORN TO BE BAD, 1950
BORN TO GAMBLE, 1935
BORN TO KILL, 1975
BORN TO LOVE, 1931
BORN WILD, 1968
BOSS, THE, 1956
BOTH SIDES OF THE LAW, 1953
BOTTOM OF THE BOTTLE, THE, 1956
BOUGHT, 1931
BOULDER DAM, 1936
BOULEVARD NIGHTS, 1979
BOWERY, THE, 1933

BOLD: Films on Videocassette

BOWERY BOY, 1940
BOY...A GIRL, A, 1969
BOY, A GIRL AND A BIKE, A, 1949
BOY AND THE BRIDGE, THE, 1959
BOY MEETS GIRL, 1985
BOY OF THE STREETS, 1937
BOY SLAVES, 1938
BOY SOLDIER, 1987
BOY TROUBLE, 1939
BOY WITH THE GREEN HAIR, THE, 1949
BOYS IN THE BAND, THE, 1970
BOYS OF PAUL STREET, THE, 1969
BOYS TOWN, 1938
BRAINWASHED, 1961
BRAMBLE BUSH, THE, 1960
BRASIL ANNO 2,000, 1968
BRAT, THE, 1931
BRAVE BULLS, THE, 1951
BREAD OF LOVE, THE, 1954
BREAK IN THE CIRCLE, THE, 1957
BREAK OF DAY, 1977
BREAK OF HEARTS, 1935
BREAKDOWN, 1953
BREAKER MORANT, 1980
BREAKERS AHEAD, 1935
BREAKERS AHEAD, 1938
BREAKFAST AT TIFFANY'S, 1961
BREAKFAST CLUB, THE, 1985
BREAKFAST IN BED, 1978
BREAKING POINT, THE, 1950
BREAKING THE SOUND BARRIER, 1952
BREAKTHROUGH, 1978
BREATH OF SCANDAL, A, 1960
BREED APART, A, 1984
BREEZING HOME, 1937
BRIDE BY MISTAKE, 1944
BRIDE FOR HENRY, A, 1937
BRIDE OF VENGEANCE, 1949
BRIDE WORE RED, THE, 1937
BRIDGE OF SAN LUIS REY, THE, 1929
BRIDGE OF SAN LUIS REY, THE, 1944
BRIDGE TO THE SUN, 1961
BRIEF MOMENT, 1933
BRIEF VACATION, A, 1975
BRIGHT LEAF, 1950
BRIGHT LIGHTS, BIG CITY, 1988
BRIGHT ROAD, 1953
BRIGHT VICTORY, 1951
BRIGHTY OF THE GRAND CANYON, 1967
BRILLIANT MARRIAGE, 1936
BRINK OF LIFE, 1960
BRITTANIA HOSPITAL, 1982
BROADWAY BAD, 1933
BROADWAY BIG SHOT, 1942
BROADWAY MUSKETEERS, 1938
BROKEN BLOSSOMS, 1936
BROKEN DREAMS, 1933
BROKEN ENGLISH, 1981
BROKEN LOVE, 1946
BROKEN LULLABY, 1932
BROKEN MELODY, 1938
BROKEN MIRRORS, 1985
BRONCO BULLFROG, 1972
BROTHER JOHN, 1971
BROTHERLY LOVE, 1970
BROTHERS, 1930
BROTHERS, 1984
BROTHERS KARAMAZOV, THE, 1958
BROTHERS, THE, 1948
BROWN WALLET, THE, 1936
BROWNING VERSION, THE, 1951
BRUTE, THE, 1952
BUDDHA, 1965
BUDDIES, 1985
BUDDY SYSTEM, THE, 1984
BUGLE SOUNDS, THE, 1941
BULLDOG EDITION, 1936
BULLET IS WAITING, A, 1954
BULLFIGHTER AND THE LADY, 1951
BURG THEATRE, 1936
BURIED ALIVE, 1939
BURIED ALIVE, 1951
BURNING AN ILLUSION, 1982
BURNING CROSS, THE, 1947
BURNING GOLD, 1936
BURNING YEARS, THE, 1979

BUS IS COMING, THE, 1971
BUS RILEY'S BACK IN TOWN, 1965
BUT THE FLESH IS WEAK, 1932
BUTLEY, 1974
BUTTERCUP CHAIN, THE, 1971
BUTTERFIELD 8, 1960
BUTTERFLIES ARE FREE, 1972
BUTTERFLY, 1982
BY APPOINTMENT ONLY, 1933
BY DESIGN, 1982
BY LOVE POSSESSED, 1961
BYE-BYE BRAZIL, 1980
BYGONES, 1988
CABIN IN THE COTTON, 1932
CABOBLANCO, 1981
CACTUS IN THE SNOW, 1972
CADDIE, 1976
CAGLIOSTRO, 1975
CAINE MUTINY, THE, 1954
CAL, 1984
CALENDAR, THE, 1931
CALENDAR, THE, 1948
CALIFORNIA DREAMING, 1979
CALIFORNIA STRAIGHT AHEAD, 1937
CALL HER SAVAGE, 1932
CALL OF THE BLOOD, 1948
CALL OF THE CIRCUS, 1930
CALLED BACK, 1933
CALLING DR. GILLESPIE, 1942
CALLING DR. KILDARE, 1939
CAMILLE 2000, 1969
CANAL ZONE, 1942
CANDIDATE, THE, 1964
CANDIDE, 1962
CANDY MOUNTAIN, 1988
CANNERY ROW, 1982
CANNIBALS, THE, 1970
CANNON AND THE NIGHTINGALE, THE, 1969
CANTERBURY TALE, A, 1944
CAPPY RICKS RETURNS, 1935
CAPTAIN BOYCOTT, 1947
CAPTAIN HURRICANE, 1935
CAPTAIN IS A LADY, THE, 1940
CAPTAIN MILKSHAKE, 1971
CAPTAIN MOONLIGHT, 1940
CAPTAIN NEWMAN, M.D., 1963
CAPTAIN TUGBOAT ANNIE, 1945
CAPTAIN'S KID, THE, 1937
CAPTAIN'S ORDERS, 1937
CAPTIVATION, 1931
CARAVAN, 1946
CAREER, 1939
CAREER, 1959
CAREER GIRL, 1960
CAREER WOMAN, 1936
CAREERS, 1929
CARELESS AGE, 1929
CARELESS YEARS, THE, 1957
CARETAKERS, THE, 1963
CARGO TO CAPETOWN, 1950
CARMELA, 1949
CARMEN, BABY, 1967
CARNAL KNOWLEDGE, 1971
CARNIVAL, 1931
CARNIVAL, 1935
CARNIVAL, 1946
CARNIVAL BOAT, 1932
CARNIVAL IN FLANDERS, 1936
CARNIVAL LADY, 1933
CARNIVAL QUEEN, 1937
CARNIVAL STORY, 1954
CARNY, 1980
CAROLINA, 1934
CAROLINE CHERIE, 1968
CAROLLIE CHERIE, 1951
CARPETBAGGERS, THE, 1964
CARRIE, 1952
CARTER CASE, THE, 1947
CASABLANCA, 1942
CASE AGAINST MRS. AMES, THE, 1936
CASE OF CLARA DEANE, THE, 1932
CASE OF DR. LAURENT, 1958
CASE OF PATTY SMITH, THE, 1962
CASE OF SERGEANT GRISCHA, THE, 1930
CASTLE, THE, 1969
CASTLE IN THE AIR, 1952

CASTLE OF PURITY, 1974
CAT ATE THE PARAKEET, THE, 1972
CAT, THE, 1975
CAT IN THE SACK, THE, 1967
CAT ON A HOT TIN ROOF, 1958
CATERED AFFAIR, THE, 1956
CATHY'S CHILD, 1979
CAUGHT, 1949
CAVALCADE, 1933
CEASE FIRE, 1985
CEDDO, 1978
CEILNG ZERO, 1935
CELINE AND JULIE GO BOATING, 1974
CENTO ANNI D'AMORE, 1954
CENTRAL PARK, 1932
CESAR, 1936
CHAD HANNA, 1940
CHAFED ELBOWS, 1967
CHAIN LIGHTNING, 1950
CHAIN OF CIRCUMSTANCE, 1951
CHAINED HEAT, 1983
CHALK GARDEN, THE, 1964
CHALLENGE TO LASSIE, 1949
CHAMPAGNE CHARLIE, 1944
CHAMPAGNE FOR BREAKFAST, 1935
CHANCE AT HEAVEN, 1933
CHANCE MEETING, 1954
CHANCE OF A LIFETIME, 1950
CHANCE OF A NIGHT-TIME, THE, 1931
CHANCES, 1931
CHANGE OF HEART, 1938
CHANGE OF MIND, 1969
CHANGES, 1969
CHANT OF JIMMIE BLACKSMITH, THE, 1980
CHAPMAN REPORT, THE, 1962
CHAPPAQUA, 1967
CHARADE, 1953
CHARING CROSS ROAD, 1935
CHARLES AND LUCIE, 1982
CHARLES, DEAD OR ALIVE, 1972
CHARLIE BUBBLES, 1968
CHARLY, 1968
CHARMING SINNERS, 1929
CHARTER PILOT, 1940
CHARTROOSE CABOOSE, 1960
CHASE, THE, 1966
CHASER, THE, 1938
CHASING YESTERDAY, 1935
CHASTITY, 1969
CHATTERBOX, 1936
CHEAT, THE, 1950
CHEATERS, 1934
CHEATERS, THE, 1961
CHECKERBOARD, 1969
CHECKERED FLAG, THE, 1963
CHECKPOINT, 1957
CHEERS FOR MISS BISHOP, 1941
CHELSEA GIRLS, THE, 1967
CHELSEA LIFE, 1933
CHESS PLAYERS, THE, 1978
CHICAGO CALLING, 1951
CHIDAMBARAM, 1986
CHILD IN THE HOUSE, 1956
CHILD IS A WILD THING, A, 1976
CHILD IS BORN, A, 1940
CHILD IS WAITING, A, 1963
CHILD OF DIVORCE, 1946
CHILD OF MANHATTAN, 1933
CHILD UNDER A LEAF, 1975
CHILDISH THINGS, 1969
CHILDREN, THE, 1949
CHILDREN OF BABYLON, 1980
CHILDREN OF CHANCE, 1949
CHILDREN OF CHANCE, 1950
CHILDREN OF CHAOS, 1950
CHILDREN OF GOD'S EARTH, 1983
CHILDREN OF HIROSHIMA, 1952
CHILDREN OF RAGE, 1975
CHILDREN OF SANCHEZ, THE, 1978
CHILDREN OF THE FOG, 1935
CHILDRENS GAMES, 1969
CHILDREN'S HOUR, THE, 1961
CHILD'S PLAY, 1972
CHILLY SCENES OF WINTER, 1982
CHIMES AT MIDNIGHT, 1967
CHINA CLIPPER, 1936

CHINA GIRL, 1942
CHINA SYNDROME, THE, 1979
CHINATOWN AFTER DARK, 1931
CHINESE BUNGALOW, THE, 1930
CHINESE DEN, THE, 1940
CHINESE ROULETTE, 1977
CHIVATO, 1961
CHLOE IN THE AFTERNOON, 1972
CHOCOLATE WAR, THE, 1988
CHOIRBOYS, THE, 1977
CHOOSE ME, 1984
CHOSEN, THE, 1982
CHRISTIAN LICORICE STORE, THE, 1971
CHRISTINA, 1929
CHRISTINE, 1959
CHRISTMAS EVE, 1947
CHRISTMAS TREE, THE, 1969
CHUBASCO, 1968
CHUSHINGURA, 1963
CIAO MANHATTAN, 1973
CINCINNATI KID, THE, 1965
CINDERELLA LIBERTY, 1973
CIRCLE OF DANGER, 1951
CIRCLE OF DECEIT, 1982
CIRCLE OF TWO, 1980
CIRCUS KID, THE, 1928
CIRCUS OF LOVE, 1958
CIRCUS WORLD, 1964
CITADEL, THE, 1938
CITIZEN KANE, 1941
CITY ACROSS THE RIVER, 1949
CITY AND THE DOGS, THE, 1987
CITY GIRL, 1930
CITY GIRL, THE, 1984
CITY LOVERS, 1982
CITY NEWS, 1983
CITY OF BEAUTIFUL NONSENSE, THE, 1935
CITY OF PLAY, 1929
CITY OF SECRETS, 1963
CITY OF SILENT MEN, 1942
CITY OF TORMENT, 1950
CITY OF WOMEN, 1980
CITY OF YOUTH, 1938
CITY ON FIRE, 1979
CITY PARK, 1934
CITY STORY, 1954
CITY STREETS, 1938
CITY WITHOUT MEN, 1943
CLAIR DE FEMME, 1980
CLAIRE'S KNEE, 1971
CLAIRVOYANT, THE, 1935
CLAN OF THE CAVE BEAR, THE, 1986
CLARA'S HEART, 1988
CLARENCE AND ANGEL, 1981
CLASH BY NIGHT, 1952
CLASS, 1983
CLASS ENEMY, 1984
CLASS OF '44, 1973
CLASS OF MISS MAC MICHAEL, THE, 1978
CLASS OF 1984, 1982
CLASS RELATIONS, 1986
CLAUDELLE INGLISH, 1961
CLAUDIA, 1943
CLAUDIA AND DAVID, 1946
CLAUDINE, 1974
CLAY, 1964
CLEAN AND SOBER, 1988
CLEAR ALL WIRES, 1933
CLEAR SKIES, 1963
CLEO FROM 5 TO 7, 1961
CLIPPED WINGS, 1938
CLOCKMAKER, THE, 1976
CLOSE TO MY HEART, 1951
CLOSELY WATCHED TRAINS, 1967
CLOTHES AND THE WOMAN, 1937
CLOUD DANCER, 1980
CLOUDED YELLOW, THE, 1950
CLOUDS OVER ISRAEL, 1966
CLOWN, THE, 1953
CLOWN AND THE KID, THE, 1961
CLUB, THE, 1980
CLUB HAVANA, 1946
CLUNY BROWN, 1946
COAST GUARD, 1939
COBWEB, THE, 1955
COCAINE COWBOYS, 1979

COCKTAIL, 1988
COCKTAIL HOUR, 1933
COCKTAIL MOLOTOV, 1980
CODE OF SCOTLAND YARD, 1948
CODE OF THE STREETS, 1939
COFFY, 1973
COLD JOURNEY, 1975
COLD WIND IN AUGUST, 1961
COLLECTOR, THE, 1965
COLLEGE CONFIDENTIAL, 1960
COLLEGE COQUETTE, THE, 1929
COLLEGE SWEETHEARTS, 1942
COLONEL BLOOD, 1934
COLONEL CHABERT, 1947
COLOR OF DESTINY, THE, 1988
COLOR OF MONEY, THE, 1986
COLOR PURPLE, THE, 1985
COME AND GET IT, 1936
COME BACK BABY, 1968
COME BACK LITTLE SHEBA, 1952
COME BACK PETER, 1971
COME BACK TO THE 5 & DIME, JIMMY DEAN,
  JIMMY DEAN, 1982
COME FILL THE CUP, 1951
COME NEXT SPRING, 1956
COME ON, THE, 1956
COME ON, LEATHERNECKS, 1938
COME ON, MARINES, 1934
COME TO THE STABLE, 1949
COMEDIANS, THE, 1967
COMEDY!, 1987
COMEDY MAN, THE, 1964
COMET OVER BROADWAY, 1938
COMETOGETHER, 1971
COMIC, THE, 1969
COMING HOME, 1978
COMING OUT PARTY, 1934
COMMAND PERFORMANCE, 1931
COMMAND PERFORMANCE, 1937
COMMITMENT, THE, 1976
COMMON CLAY, 1930
COMMON LAW, THE, 1931
COMMON LAW WIFE, 1963
COMMON TOUCH, THE, 1941
COMPANY SHE KEEPS, THE, 1950
COMPETITION, THE, 1980
COMPLIMENTS OF MR. FLOW, 1941
COMPROMISED, 1931
COMPROMISED!, 1931
CONCENTRATION CAMP, 1939
CONCRETE ANGELS, 1987
CONCRETE JUNGLE, THE, 1982
CONDEMNED OF ALTONA, THE, 1963
CONDEMNED WOMEN, 1938
CONDUCT UNBECOMING, 1975
CONDUCTOR, THE, 1981
CONFESS DR. CORDA, 1960
CONFESSION, 1937
CONFESSIONS OF A POLICE CAPTAIN, 1971
CONFESSIONS OF AMANS, THE, 1977
CONFESSIONS OF AN OPIUM EATER, 1962
CONFESSIONS OF FELIX KRULL, THE, 1957
CONFESSOR, 1973
CONFIDENCE, 1980
CONFLICT, 1937
CONFLICT, 1939
CONNECTION, THE, 1962
CONQUERORS, THE, 1932
CONQUEST, 1929
CONQUEST OF MYCENE, 1965
CONRACK, 1974
CONSCIENCE BAY, 1960
CONSPIRACY OF HEARTS, 1960
CONSTANCE, 1984
CONSTANT FACTOR, THE, 1980
CONSTANT NYMPH, THE, 1943
CONSTANT NYMPH, THE, 1933
CONSTANTINE AND THE CROSS, 1962
CONSUELO, AN ILLUSION, 1988
CONTAR HASTA TEN, 1986
CONTEMPT, 1963
CONVENTION GIRL, 1935
CONVERSATION, THE, 1974
CONVERSATION PIECE, 1976
CONVICTED, 1950
CONVICT'S CODE, 1930

CONVICT'S CODE, 1939
CONVOY, 1940
COOL AND THE CRAZY, THE, 1958
COOL IT, CAROL!, 1970
COOL WORLD, THE, 1963
COOLEY HIGH, 1975
COPPER CANYON, 1950
COQUETTE, 1929
CORDELIA, 1980
CORKY, 1972
CORN IS GREEN, THE, 1945
CORNBREAD, EARL AND ME, 1975
CORRIDOR OF MIRRORS, 1948
CORRIDORS OF BLOOD, 1962
CORRUPTION OF CHRIS MILLER, THE, 1979
CORVETTE SUMMER, 1978
COSSACKS OF THE DON, 1932
COUNSEL FOR CRIME, 1937
COUNSELLOR-AT-LAW, 1933
COUNT OF TWELVE, 1955
COUNT THREE AND PRAY, 1955
COUNTDOWN AT KUSINI, 1976
COUNTDOWN, 1985
COUNTRY, 1984
COUNTRY DOCTOR, THE, 1936
COUNTRY DOCTOR, THE, 1963
COUNTRY GIRL, THE, 1954
COUNTY FAIR, 1933
COUNTY FAIR, 1937
COUNTY FAIR, 1950
COURAGE, 1930
COURAGE OF LASSIE, 1946
COURAGEOUS DR. CHRISTIAN, THE, 1940
COURIER OF LYONS, 1938
COURRIER SUD, 1937
COURT MARTIAL, 1954
COURT MARTIAL OF MAJOR KELLER, THE, 1961
COURTNEY AFFAIR, THE, 1947
COURTSHIP OF EDDY'S FATHER, THE, 1963
COUSINS, THE, 1959
COUSINS IN LOVE, 1982
COVENANT WITH DEATH, A, 1966
COVER ME BABE, 1970
COVERGIRL, 1984
COWARDS, 1970
CRADLE SONG, 1933
CRAIG'S WIFE, 1936
CRASH, THE, 1932
CRASH DRIVE, 1959
CRASH OF SILENCE, 1952
CRASHIN' THRU DANGER, 1938
CRAZY DESIRE, 1964
CRAZY QUILT, THE, 1966
CRAZY WORLD OF JULIUS VROODER, THE, 1974
CREATURE CALLED MAN, THE, 1970
CREMATOR, THE, 1973
CRIES AND WHISPERS, 1972
CRIME AFLOAT, 1937
CRIME AGAINST JOE, 1956
CRIME AND PASSION, 1976
CRIME AND PUNISHMENT, 1975
CRIME OF DR. HALLET, 1938
CRIME OF HONOR, 1987
CRIME OF MONSIEUR LANGE, THE, 1936
CRIME OF PETER FRAME, THE, 1938
CRIME SCHOOL, 1938
CRIMES OF PASSION, 1984
CRIMES OF THE HEART, 1986
CRIMINAL CONVERSATION, 1980
CRIMINAL LAWYER, 1951
CRIMINAL LIFE OF ARCHIBALDO DE LA CRUZ,
  THE, 1962
CRISIS, 1950
CROOKED ROAD, THE, 1940
CROOKED ROAD, THE, 1965
CROOKED WEB, THE, 1955
CROSS AND THE SWITCHBLADE, THE, 1970
CROSS COUNTRY CRUISE, 1934
CROSS CREEK, 1983
CROSS-EXAMINATION, 1932
CROSS MY HEART, 1937
CROSS OF THE LIVING, 1963
CROSS ROADS, 1930
CROSS STREETS, 1934
CROSSROADS, 1938
CROSSROADS, 1986

BOLD: Films on Videocassette

CROWD INSIDE, THE, 1971
CROWDED DAY, THE, 1954
CROWDED PARADISE, 1956
CROWNING EXPERIENCE, THE, 1960
CRUCIFIX, THE, 1934
CRUEL TOWER, THE, 1956
CRUSADER, THE, 1932
CRY FROM THE STREET, A, 1959
CRY HAVOC, 1943
CRY IN THE NIGHT, A, 1956
CRY OF THE HUNTED, 1953
CRY, THE BELOVED COUNTRY, 1952
CRY TOUGH, 1959
CRYSTAL HEART, 1987
CURE FOR LOVE, THE, 1950
CURTAIN CALL, 1940
CURTAIN FALLS, THE, 1935
CURTAIN RISES, THE, 1939
CYNARA, 1932
CYRANO DE BERGERAC, 1950
DAISIES, 1967
DAISY KENYON, 1947
DAISY MILLER, 1974
DAMAGED GOODS, 1937
DAMAGED LIVES, 1937
DAMAGED LOVE, 1931
DAMNATION, 1988
DAMNED, THE, 1969
DAMNED, THE, 1948
DAMON AND PYTHIAS, 1962
DAN MATTHEWS, 1936
DAN'S MOTEL, 1982
DANCE HALL, 1929
DANCE HALL, 1950
DANCE LITTLE LADY, 1954
DANCE MALL HOSTESS, 1933
DANCE OF DEATH, THE, 1971
DANCE PRETTY LADY, 1932
DANCERS, 1987
DANCING IN THE DARK, 1986
DANGER AHEAD, 1935
DANGER IS A WOMAN, 1952
DANGER LIGHTS, 1930
DANGEROUS, 1936
DANGEROUS ADVENTURE, A, 1937
DANGEROUS AGE, A, 1960
DANGEROUS CURVES, 1929
DANGEROUS HOLIDAY, 1937
DANGEROUS INTRIGUE, 1936
DANGEROUS SECRETS, 1938
DANGEROUS WOMAN, 1929
DANIEL, 1983
DANNY BOY, 1941
DANTE'S INFERNO, 1935
DAPHNE, THE, 1967
DARBY AND JOAN, 1937
DAREDEVILS OF THE CLOUDS, 1948
DARING DAUGHTERS, 1933
DARK AT THE TOP OF THE STAIRS, THE, 1960
DARK DELUSION, 1947
DARK END OF THE STREET, THE, 1981
DARK EYES, 1938
DARK HAZARD, 1934
DARK IS THE NIGHT, 1946
DARK ODYSSEY, 1961
DARK OF THE SUN, 1968
DARK RIVER, 1956
DARK SIDE OF TOMORROW, THE, 1970
DARK VICTORY, 1939
DARLING, 1965
DAS HAUS AM FLUSS, 1986
DATE BAIT, 1960
DAUGHTER OF DECEIT, 1977
DAUGHTER OF THE NILE, 1988
DAUGHTER OF THE SANDS, 1952
DAUGHTERS COURAGEOUS, 1939
DAUGHTERS OF DESTINY, 1954
DAUGHTERS OF TODAY, 1933
DAVID, 1979
DAVID AND LISA, 1962
DAVID COPPERFIELD, 1935
DAVID COPPERFIELD, 1970
DAVID GOLDER, 1932
DAVID HOLZMAN'S DIARY, 1968
DAVY, 1958
DAWN OVER IRELAND, 1938

DAY AT THE BEACH, A, 1970
DAY FOR NIGHT, 1973
DAY IN COURT, A, 1965
DAY OF THE DOLPHIN, THE, 1973
DAY OF THE LOCUST, THE, 1975
DAY OF WRATH, 1948
DAY THE FISH CAME OUT, THE, 1967.
DAY TO REMEMBER, A, 1953
DAY WILL COME, A, 1960
DAYBREAK, 1931
DAYBREAK, 1940
DAYBREAK, 1948
DAYS OF HEAVEN, 1978
DAYS OF 36, 1972
DAYS OF WINE AND ROSES, 1962
DAYTONA BEACH WEEKEND, 1965
DOCTORS, THE, 1956
DEAD, THE, 1987
DEAD END KIDS, 1986
DEAD MELODY, 1938
DEAD OF SUMMER, 1970
DEAD ON COURSE, 1952
DEAD TO THE WORLD, 1961
DEAD WOMAN'S KISS, A, 1951
DEADLIER THAN THE MALE, 1957
DEADLINE, 1987
DEADLINE—U.S.A., 1952
DEAR MR. WONDERFUL, 1983
DEATH DRIVES THROUGH, 1935
DEATH IN SMALL DOSES, 1957
DEATH IN VENICE, 1971
DEATH IS A NUMBER, 1951
DEATH IS CALLED ENGELCHEN, 1963
DEATH OF A SALESMAN, 1952
DEATH OF EMPEDOCLES, THE, 1988
DEATH OF MARIO RICCI, THE, 1985
DEATH OF MICHAEL TURBIN, THE, 1954
DEATH ON THE MOUNTAIN, 1961
DEATH PLAY, 1976
DEBT, THE, 1988
DEBT OF HONOR, 1936
DECAMERON NIGHTS, 1953
DECISION AGAINST TIME, 1957
DECISION OF CHRISTOPHER BLAKE, THE, 1948
DECLINE OF THE AMERICAN EMPIRE, THE, 1986
DEDEE, 1949
DEEP BLUE SEA, THE, 1955
DEEP END, 1970
DEEP IN THE HEART, 1983
DEEP VALLEY, 1947
DEEP WATERS, 1948
DEFEND MY LOVE, 1956
DEFENSE RESTS, THE, 1934
DEFIANCE, 1980
DEGREE OF MURDER, A, 1969
DELICATE BALANCE, A, 1973
DELINQUENT DAUGHTERS, 1944
DELINQUENT PARENTS, 1938
DELINQUENTS, THE, 1957
DEMONIAQUE, 1958
DEMONS, 1987
DEMONS IN THE GARDEN, 1984
DEMONS OF THE MIND, 1972
DEMONSTRATOR, 1971
DEPTH CHARGE, 1960
DERELICT, THE, 1937
DESERT ATTACK, 1958
DESERT BLOOM, 1986
DESERT HEARTS, 1985
DESERTER, 1934
DESERTER AND THE NOMADS, THE, 1969
DESERTERS, 1983
DESIGNING WOMEN, 1934
DESIRABLE, 1934
DESIRE IN THE DUST, 1960
DESIRE ME, 1947
DESIRE, THE INTERIOR LIFE, 1980
DESIRE UNDER THE ELMS, 1958
DESIREE, 1984
DESPAIR, 1978
DESPERATE CHARACTERS, 1971
DESPERATE DECISION, 1954
DESPERATE WOMEN, THE, 1954
DESTINATION MILAN, 1954
DESTINATION 60,000, 1957
DESTINATION UNKNOWN, 1933

DESTINY, 1938
DESTINY, 1944
DESTINY OF A MAN, 1961
DESTROY, SHE SAID, 1969
DESTRUCTORS, THE, 1974
DETOUR, THE, 1968
DEVIL AND THE DEEP, 1932
DEVIL AND THE TEN COMMANDMENTS, THE, 1962
DEVIL DOGS OF THE AIR, 1935
DEVIL IN SILK, 1968
DEVIL IN THE FLESH, 1986
DEVIL IS A WOMAN, THE, 1975
DEVIL IS AN EMPRESS, THE, 1939
DEVIL IS DRIVING, THE, 1932
DEVIL IS DRIVING, THE, 1937
DEVIL MADE A WOMAN, THE, 1962
DEVIL MAKES THREE, THE, 1952
DEVIL ON HORSEBACK, 1954
DEVIL ON WHEELS, THE, 1947
DEVIL PAYS OFF, THE, 1941
DEVIL PROBABLY, THE, 1977
DEVIL SHIP, 1947
DEVIL'S BAIT, 1959
DEVIL'S BEDROOM, THE, 1964
DEVIL'S DAUGHTER, 1949
DEVIL'S GENERAL, THE, 1957
DEVIL'S HOLIDAY, THE, 1930
DEVIL'S IN LOVE, THE, 1933
DEVIL'S ISLAND, 1940
DEVIL'S LOTTERY, 1932
DEVIL'S MAZE, THE, 1929
DEVIL'S PLAYGROUND, 1937
DEVIL'S PLAYGROUND, THE, 1976
DEVIL'S SQUADRON, 1936
DEVIL'S TEMPLE, 1969
DEVIL'S TRAP, THE, 1964
DEVIL'S WANTON, THE, 1962
DEVOTION, 1931
DEVOTION, 1953
DEVOTION, 1955
D.I., THE, 1957
DIALOGUE, 1967
DIAMOND HEAD, 1962
DIAMONDS OF THE NIGHT, 1964
DIANE'S BODY, 1969
DIARY FOR MY CHILDREN, 1984
DIARY OF A BAD GIRL, 1958
DIARY OF A CHAMBERMAID, 1946
DIARY OF A CHAMBERMAID, 1964
DIARY OF A CLOISTERED NUN, 1973
DIARY OF A HIGH SCHOOL BRIDE, 1959
DIARY OF A MAD HOUSEWIFE, 1970
DIARY OF A SCHIZOPHRENIC GIRL, 1970
DIARY OF A SHINJUKU BURGLAR, 1969
DIARY OF ANNE FRANK, THE, 1959
DIE MANNER UM LUCIE, 1931
DIFFERENT SONS, 1962
DIFFERENT STORY, A, 1978
DINER, 1982
DINGAKA, 1965
DINKY, 1935
DINNER AT EIGHT, 1933
DINO, 1957
DIPLOMAT'S MANSION, THE, 1961
DIRTY O'NEIL, 1974
DISBARRED, 1939
DISCORD, 1933
DISCREET CHARM OF THE BOURGEOISIE, THE, 1972
DISHONORED, 1950
DISILLUSION, 1949
DISOBEDIENT, 1953
DISORDER, 1964
DISORDER AND EARLY TORMENT, 1977
DISPUTED PASSAGE, 1939
DISTANCE, 1975
DISTANT JOURNEY, 1950
DISTANT THUNDER, 1988
DISTANT TRUMPET, 1952
DIVIDED HEART, THE, 1955
DIVINE NYMPH, THE, 1979
DIVORCE, 1945
DIVORCE IN THE FAMILY, 1932
DIVORCEE, THE, 1930
DO NOT THROW CUSHIONS INTO THE RING, 1970
DO YOU REMEMBER DOLLY BELL?, 1986

DOCTEUR LAENNEC, 1949
DOCTEUR POPAUL, 1972
DOCTOR AND THE GIRL, THE, 1949
DR. BULL, 1933
DR. GILLESPIE'S CRIMINAL CASE, 1943
DR. GILLESPIE'S NEW ASSISTANT, 1942
DR. KILDARE GOES HOME, 1940
DR. KILDARE'S CRISIS, 1940
DR. KILDARE'S STRANGE CASE, 1940
DR. KILDARE'S VICTORY, 1941
DR. KILDARE'S WEDDING DAY, 1941
DR. MINX, 1975
DOCTOR MONICA, 1934
DR. O'DOWD, 1940
DOCTOR ZHIVAGO, 1965
DOCTOR'S DIARY, A, 1937
DOCTORS DON'T TELL, 1941
DOCTOR'S SECRET, 1929
DOCTORS' WIVES, 1931
DOCTORS' WIVES, 1971
DODES 'KA-DEN, 1970
DOG OF FLANDERS, A, 1935
DOG OF FLANDERS, A, 1959
DOGPOUND SHUFFLE, 1975
DOLL, THE, 1964
DOLL SQUAD, THE, 1973
DOLL'S HOUSE, A, 1973
DOLL'S HOUSE, A, 1973
DOLORES, 1949
DOMINICK AND EUGENE, 1988
DON QUIXOTE, 1961
DON'T CRY, IT'S ONLY THUNDER, 1982
DON'T CRY WITH YOUR MOUTH FULL, 1974
DON'T GAMBLE WITH LOVE, 1936
DON'T LET THE ANGELS FALL, 1969
DON'T TEMPT THE DEVIL, 1964
DOOMSDAY VOYAGE, 1972
DORMIRE, 1985
DOUBLE DEAL, 1950
DOUBLE DOOR, 1934
DOUBLE STOP, 1968
DOUBLE SUICIDE, 1970
DOWN OUR STREET, 1932
DOWN THE ANCIENT STAIRCASE, 1975
DOWN THE STRETCH, 1936
DOWN TO THE SEA, 1936
DOWNSTAIRS, 1932
DOZENS, THE, 1981
DRAGNET NIGHT, 1931
DRAGON CHOW, 1988
DRAGON SEED, 1944
DRAGON SKY, 1964
DRAGON'S GOLD, 1954
DRAKE CASE, THE, 1929
DRAMATIC SCHOOL, 1938
DRANGO, 1957
DREAM LOVER, 1986
DREAM NO MORE, 1950
DREAM OF A COSSACK, 1982
DREAM OF KINGS, A, 1969
DREAM OF PASSION, A, 1978
DREAM ON, 1981
DREAMER, THE, 1936
DREAMER, THE, 1970
DREAMING LIPS, 1937
DREAMING LIPS, 1958
DREAMS, 1960
DREAMS IN A DRAWER, 1957
DREAMS OF GLASS, 1969
DRESSER, THE, 1983
DRIFTER, 1975
DRIFTER, THE, 1966
DRIFTING, 1932
DRIFTING, 1984
DRIFTWOOD, 1947
DRIVER'S SEAT, THE, 1975
DROWNING BY NUMBERS, 1988
DRUM, 1976
DRUMS O' VOODOO, 1934
DRUNKEN ANGEL, 1948
DRY SUMMER, 1967
DRYLANDERS, 1963
DUEL, THE, 1964
DUEL ON THE MISSISSIPPI, 1955
DUEL WITHOUT HONOR, 1953
DUET FOR CANNIBALS, 1969

DUET FOR FOUR, 1982
DUET FOR ONE, 1986
DUKE COMES BACK, THE, 1937
DUKE OF THE NAVY, 1942
DUKE OF WEST POINT, THE, 1938
DULCIMA, 1971
DULCIMER STREET, 1948
DURANT AFFAIR, THE, 1962
DURING ONE NIGHT, 1962
DUST, 1985
DUTCHMAN, 1966
DYNAMITE, 1930
DYNAMITE, 1948
DYNAMITE DENNY, 1932
EAGLE IN A CAGE, 1971
EAGLE WITH TWO HEADS, 1948
EARL OF CHICAGO, THE, 1940
EARLY AUTUMN, 1962
EARRINGS OF MADAME DE..., THE, 1954
EARTH CRIES OUT, THE, 1949
EARTH ENTRANCED, 1970
EARTHLING, THE, 1980
EASIEST WAY, THE, 1931
EAST CHINA SEA, 1969
EAST IS WEST, 1930
EAST LYNNE, 1931
EAST MEETS WEST, 1936
EAST OF EDEN, 1955
EAST OF ELEPHANT ROCK, 1976
EAST OF FIFTH AVE., 1933
EAST OF JAVA, 1935
EAST OF THE WALL, 1986
EAST SIDE SADIE, 1929
EAST SIDE, WEST SIDE, 1949
EASY COME, EASY GO, 1947
EASY LIFE, THE, 1963
EASY LIFE, THE, 1971
EASY LIVING, 1949
EASY MONEY, 1948
EASY RIDER, 1969
EAT THE PEACH, 1987
EAVESDROPPER, THE, 1966
EBB TIDE, 1932
ECHO, THE, 1964
ECHO PARK, 1986
ECHOES OF A SUMMER, 1976
ECHOES OF SILENCE, 1966
ECLIPSE, 1962
ECSTACY OF YOUNG LOVE, 1936
ECSTASY, 1940
EDDIE AND THE CRUISERS, 1983
EDEN CRIED, 1967
EDGE, THE, 1968
EDGE OF HELL, 1956
EDGE OF THE CITY, 1957
EDGE OF THE WORLD, THE, 1937
EDUCATING FATHER, 1936
EDUCATING RITA, 1983
EDWARD, MY SON, 1949
EFFECT OF GAMMA RAYS ON MAN-IN-THE-MOON
   MARIGOLDS, THE, 1972
EFFI BRIEST, 1974
EGLANTINE, 1972
EGYPT BY THREE, 1953
8 1/2, 1963
EIGHT BELLS, 1935
EIGHT GIRLS IN A BOAT, 1934
EIGHT O'CLOCK WALK, 1954
EIGHTEEN AND ANXIOUS, 1957
18 MINUTES, 1935
EIGHTH DAY OF THE WEEK, THE, 1959
84 CHARING CROSS ROAD, 1987
80 STEPS TO JONAH, 1969
80,000 SUSPECTS, 1963
EIN BLICK-UND DIE LIEBE BRICHT AUS, 1987
EL, 1955
EL DIPUTADO, 1985
EL NORTE, 1984
ELDER BROTHER, THE, 1937
ELECTRA, 1962
ELENI, 1985
ELEVENTH COMMANDMENT, 1933
ELI ELI, 1940
ELINOR NORTON, 1935
ELIZA FRASER, 1976
ELIZABETH OF LADYMEAD, 1949

ELIZA'S HOROSCOPE, 1975
ELMER GANTRY, 1960
ELUSIVE CORPORAL, THE, 1963
ELVIS! ELVIS!, 1977
EMANON, 1987
EMBEZZLED HEAVEN, 1959
EMBRACEABLE YOU, 1948
EMBRACERS, THE, 1966
EMBRYOS, 1985
EMERGENCY, 1962
EMERGENCY HOSPITAL, 1956
EMERGENCY LANDING, 1941
EMERGENCY SQUAD, 1940
EMERGENCY WEDDING, 1950
EMIGRANTS, THE, 1972
EMILY, 1976
EMMA, 1932
EMMA MAE, 1976
EMPEROR JONES, THE, 1933
EMPLOYEE'S ENTRANCE, 1933
EMPTY CANVAS, THE, 1964
EMPTY STAR, THE, 1962
ENCHANTED APRIL, 1935
ENCHANTED ISLAND, 1958
ENCHANTED VALLEY, THE, 1948
ENCORE, 1951
ENCOUNTERS IN SALZBURG, 1964
END OF A DAY, THE, 1939
END OF A PRIEST, 1970
END OF AUGUST, THE, 1982
END OF DESIRE, 1962
END OF INNOCENCE, 1960
END OF THE AFFAIR, THE, 1955
END OF THE LINE, 1988
END OF THE RIVER, THE, 1947
END OF THE ROAD, THE, 1954
END OF THE WORLD (IN OUR USUAL BED IN A
   NIGHT FULL OF RAIN), THE, 1978
ENDLESS LOVE, 1981
ENDLESS NIGHT, THE, 1963
ENEMIES OF PROGRESS, 1934
ENEMY OF THE PEOPLE, AN, 1978
ENGAGEMENT ITALIANO, 1966
ENGLAND MADE ME, 1973
ENJO, 1959
ENLIGHTEN THY DAUGHTER, 1934
ENORMOUS CHANGES AT THE LAST MINUTE, 1985
ENTERTAINER, THE, 1960
ENTERTAINER, THE, 1975
ENTRE NOUS, 1983
EPILOGUE, 1967
EQUUS, 1977
ERIC SOYA'S "17", 1967
ERNESTO, 1979
EROICA, 1966
ESCAPE, 1930
ESCAPE ARTIST, THE, 1982
ESCAPE BY NIGHT, 1937
ESCAPE DANGEROUS, 1947
ESCAPE FROM EAST BERLIN, 1962
ESCAPE ME NEVER, 1935
ESCAPE ME NEVER, 1947
ESCAPE TO BERLIN, 1962
ESCAPE TO GLORY, 1940
ESCAPE TO THE SUN, 1972
ESPIONAGE, 1937
ESTHER AND THE KING, 1960
ESTHER WATERS, 1948
ETERNAL HUSBAND, THE, 1946
ETERNAL LOVE, 1960
ETERNAL MASK, THE, 1937
ETERNAL SUMMER, 1961
ETERNALLY YOURS, 1939
ETERNITY OF LOVE, 1961
EUROPEANS, THE, 1979
EVA, 1962
EVENT, AN, 1970
EVENTS, 1970
EVER IN MY HEART, 1933
EVERY DAY IS A HOLIDAY, 1966
EVERY MAN FOR HIMSELF, 1980
EVERY PICTURE TELLS A STORY, 1984
EVERY SPARROW MUST FALL, 1964
EVERYTHING HAPPENS AT NIGHT, 1939
EVERYTHING IS THUNDER, 1936
EVIDENCE, 1929

BOLD: Films on Videocassette

EX-FLAME, 1931
EX-LADY, 1933
EXCLUSIVE, 1937
EXCLUSIVE STORY, 1936
EXCUSE MY GLOVE, 1936
EXECUTIVE SUITE, 1954
EXILE, THE, 1947
EXILE EXPRESS, 1939
EXILED TO SHANGHAI, 1937
EXILES, THE, 1966
EXPENSIVE WOMEN, 1931
**EXPERIENCE PREFERRED... BUT NOT ESSENTIAL,
   1983**
EXPERIMENT ALCATRAZ, 1950
EXPERIMENT PERILOUS, 1944
EXPLOSION, 1969
EXPLOSIVE GENERATION, THE, 1961
EXTERMINATING ANGEL, THE, 1967
EXTRA DAY, THE, 1956
EXTRAVAGANCE, 1930
EXTREMITIES, 1986
EYES OF THE AMARYLLIS, THE, 1982
EYES OF THE WORLD, THE, 1930
EYES, THE MOUTH, THE, 1982
EYES, THE SEA AND A BALL, 1968
FABLE, A, 1971
FACE IN THE CROWD, A, 1957
FACE OF ANOTHER, THE, 1967
FACE OF FIRE, 1959
FACE ON THE BARROOM FLOOR, THE, 1932
FACE TO FACE, 1952
FACE TO FACE, 1976
FACES, 1934
FACES, 1968
FACES IN THE FOG, 1944
FAIL SAFE, 1964
FAILURE, THE, 1986
FAITHFUL CITY, 1952
FAITHFUL HEART, 1933
FAITHLESS, 1932
FALSE FACES, 1932
FALSE MADONNA, 1932
FALSE RAPTURE, 1941
FAME IS THE SPUR, 1947
FAME STREET, 1932
FAMILY DIARY, 1963
FAMILY GAME, THE, 1984
FAMILY LIFE, 1971
FAN, THE, 1949
FANCY BAGGAGE, 1929
FANDANGO, 1985
FANNY, 1948
FANNY, 1961
FANNY AND ALEXANDER, 1983
FANNY HILL: MEMOIRS OF A WOMAN OF
   PLEASURE, 1965
FANTASIES, 1981
FANTASM, 1976
FANTASTICA, 1980
FANTASY MAN, 1984
FAR FROM THE MADDING CROWD, 1967
FAR SHORE, THE, 1976
FAREWELL, DOVES, 1962
FAREWELL, MY BELOVED, 1969
FARMER TAKES A WIFE, THE, 1935
FASCINATION, 1931
FAST LIFE, 1929
FAST-WALKING, 1982
FAST WORKERS, 1933
FATAL NIGHT, THE, 1948
FATE TAKES A HAND, 1962
FATHER, 1967
FATHER AND SON, 1929
FATHER IS A PRINCE, 1940
FATHERS AND SONS, 1960
FATHER'S SON, 1931
FATHER'S SON, 1941
FAUST, 1963
FAUST, 1964
FAVORITES OF THE MOON, 1985
FEAR, 1956
FEAR, THE, 1967
FEAR IN THE NIGHT, 1972
FEAR SHIP, THE, 1933
FEATHER IN HER HAT, A, 1935
FEDORA, 1946

FEDORA, 1978
FELLER NEEDS A FRIEND, 1932
FEMALE, 1933
FEMALE, THE, 1960
FEMALE ANIMAL, THE, 1958
FEMALE BUNCH, THE, 1969
FEMALE FIENDS, 1958
FEMALE RESPONSE, THE, 1972
FEMMES DE PERSONNE, 1986
FEVER PITCH, 1985
FEW DAYS WITH ME, A, 1988
FIFTH HORSEMAN IS FEAR, THE, 1968
FIGHT FOR THE GLORY, 1970
FIGHT FOR YOUR LIFE, 1977
FIGHT TO THE FINISH, A, 1937
FIGHTER, THE, 1952
FIGHTING BACK, 1948
FIGHTING BACK, 1983
FIGHTING CHANCE, THE, 1955
FIGURES IN A LANDSCAPE, 1970
FINAL ASSIGNMENT, 1980
FINAL CHORD, THE, 1936
FINAL COMEDOWN, THE, 1972
FINAL CUT, THE, 1980
FINAL HOUR, THE, 1936
FINAL RECKONING, THE, 1932
FINAL TAKE: THE GOLDEN AGE OF MOVIES, 1986
FINAL WAR, THE, 1960
FINE MADNESS, A, 1966
FINGER OF GUILT, 1956
FINGERS, 1940
FINGERS, 1978
FINISHING SCHOOL, 1934
FINNEGANS WAKE, 1965
FINO A FARTI MALE, 1969
FIRE IN THE FLESH, 1964
FIRE IN THE STRAW, 1943
FIRE WITHIN, THE, 1964
FIRM MAN, THE, 1975
FIRST BABY, 1936
FIRST LEGION, THE, 1951
FIRST MONDAY IN OCTOBER, 1981
FIRST NAME: CARMEN, 1984
FIRST NIGHT, 1937
FIRST OFFENDERS, 1939
FIRST START, 1953
FIRST TASTE OF LOVE, 1962
FIRST YEAR, THE, 1932
FIRSTBORN, 1984
FISHERMAN'S WHARF, 1939
F.I.S.T., 1978
FIST IN HIS POCKET, 1968
FITZCARRALDO, 1982
FIVE AND TEN, 1931
FIVE BRANDED WOMEN, 1960
FIVE DAYS FROM HOME, 1978
FIVE EASY PIECES, 1970
FIVE FINGER EXERCISE, 1962
FIVE LITTLE PEPPERS AND HOW THEY GREW, 1939
FIVE LITTLE PEPPERS AT HOME, 1940
FIVE LITTLE PEPPERS IN TROUBLE, 1940
FIVE MILES TO MIDNIGHT, 1963
FIVE WILD GIRLS, 1966
FIXER, THE, 1968
FIXER DUGAN, 1939
F.J. HOLDEN, THE, 1977
FLAG LIEUTENANT, THE, 1932
FLAME, 1975
FLAME AND THE FLESH, 1954
FLAME IN THE STREETS, 1961
FLAME OF LOVE, THE, 1930
FLAME WITHIN, THE, 1935
FLAMES, 1932
FLAMING GOLD, 1934
FLAMING TEEN-AGE, THE, 1956
FLAMINGO KID, THE, 1984
FLANAGAN, 1985
FLASH OF GREEN, A, 1984
FLASHDANCE, 1983
FLAXFIELD, THE, 1985
FLEDGLINGS, 1965
FLESH AND BLOOD, 1951
FLESH AND FANTASY, 1943
FLESH AND THE WOMAN, 1954
FLESH IS WEAK, THE, 1957
FLESHBURN, 1984

FLIGHT, 1960
FLIGHT AT MIDNIGHT, 1939
FLIGHT FROM DESTINY, 1941
FLIGHT FROM VIENNA, 1956
FLIGHT LIEUTENANT, 1942
FLIGHT TO TANGIER, 1953
FLOATING WEEDS, 1970
FLOOD, THE, 1931
FLOOD TIDE, 1958
FLOWER THIEF, THE, 1962
FLOWING GOLD, 1940
FLY AWAY PETER, 1948
FLYER, THE, 1987
FLYING CADETS, 1941
FLYING DEVILS, 1933
FLYING FONTAINES, THE, 1959
FLYING FOOL, THE, 1931
FLYING MARINE, THE, 1929
FLYING MISSILE, 1950
FLYING SCOTSMAN, THE, 1929
FOLLOW ME, BOYS!, 1966
FOND MEMORIES, 1982
FOOL FOR LOVE, 1985
FOOL KILLER, THE, 1965
FOOLS, 1970
FOOLS OF DESIRE, 1941
FOOTLOOSE HEIRESS, THE, 1937
FOOTSTEPS IN THE FOG, 1955
FOR FREEDOM, 1940
FOR MEN ONLY, 1952
FOR THE DEFENSE, 1930
FOR THE LOVE OF MIKE, 1933
FOR THE LOVE O'LIL, 1930
FOR THEM THAT TRESPASS, 1949
FORBIDDEN, 1932
FORBIDDEN, 1953
FORBIDDEN GAMES, 1953
FORBIDDEN RELATIONS, 1983
FOREIGN CITY, A, 1988
FOREIGNER, THE, 1978
FOREVER MY HEART, 1954
FOREVER YOUNG, 1984
FOREVER YOURS, 1945
FORGET MOZART!, 1985
FORGOTTEN, 1933
FORGOTTEN COMMANDMENTS, 1932
FORGOTTEN FACES, 1936
FORGOTTEN WOMEN, 1932
FORGOTTEN WOMEN, 1949
FORTRESS, THE, 1979
FORTY DEUCE, 1982
FORTY LITTLE MOTHERS, 1940
FORTY-NINE DAYS, 1964
FORTY SQUARE METERS OF GERMANY, 1986
FOUND ALIVE, 1934
FOUNTAIN, THE, 1934
FOUNTAINHEAD, THE, 1949
FOUR DAYS, 1951
FOUR DAYS IN JULY, 1984
FOUR DEVILS, 1929
FOUR FRIENDS, 1981
FOUR GIRLS IN TOWN, 1956
FOUR GIRLS IN WHITE, 1939
**FOUR HORSEMEN OF THE APOCALYPSE, THE,
   1962**
FOUR HOURS TO KILL, 1935
FOUR HUNDRED BLOWS, THE, 1959
FOUR IN A JEEP, 1951
FOUR IN THE MORNING, 1965
FOUR MOTHERS, 1941
FOUR NIGHTS OF A DREAMER, 1972
FOUR POSTER, THE, 1952
FOUR SEASONS, THE, 1981
FOUR SONS, 1940
FOUR WIVES, 1939
FOURTEEN, THE, 1973
FOX AND HIS FRIENDS, 1976
FOX, THE, 1967
FOXES, 1980
FOXFIRE, 1955
FOXTROT, 1977
F.P. 1, 1933
F.P. 1 DOESN'T ANSWER, 1933
FRAGRANCE OF WILD FLOWERS, THE, 1979
FRAIL WOMEN, 1932
FRANKIE AND JOHNNY, 1936

FRATERNITY ROW, 1977
FRECKLES, 1935
FRECKLES, 1960
FRECKLES COMES HOME, 1942
FREE, BLONDE AND 21, 1940
FREE SOUL, A, 1931
FREE, WHITE AND 21, 1963
FREEWHEELIN', 1976
FRENCH POSTCARDS, 1979
FRENCH QUARTER, 1978
FRENCH WAY, THE, 1952
FRENCH WAY, THE, 1975
FRIEDA, 1947
FRIENDLY ENEMIES, 1942
FRIENDLY NEIGHBORS, 1940
FRIENDLY PERSUASION, 1956
FRIENDS, 1971
FRIENDS AND HUSBANDS, 1983
FRIENDS AND LOVERS, 1931
FRIENDS FOR LIFE, 1964
FRIGHTENED BRIDE, THE, 1952
FRINGE DWELLERS, THE, 1986
FRISCO JENNY, 1933
FRISCO LILL, 1942
FROM A ROMAN BALCONY, 1961
FROM HERE TO ETERNITY, 1953
FROM THE LIFE OF THE MARIONETTES, 1980
FROM THE MIXED-UP FILES OF MRS. BASIL E.
    FRANKWEILER, 1973
FROM THE TERRACE, 1960
FRONT PAGE STORY, 1954
FRONT PAGE WOMAN, 1935
FRONT PAGE, THE, 1931
FRONT PAGE, THE, 1974
FRONT, THE, 1976
FROU-FROU, 1955
FRUIT IS RIPE, THE, 1961
FRUSTRATIONS, 1967
FUGITIVE IN THE SKY, 1937
FUGITIVE KIND, THE, 1960
FUGITIVE LADY, 1934
FUGITIVE ROAD, 1934
FUGITIVE, THE, 1947
FULL MOON IN PARIS, 1984
FULL OF LIFE, 1956
FULL SPEED AHEAD, 1936
FULL SPEED AHEAD, 1939
FUNNY FARM, THE, 1982
FUNNY MONEY, 1983
FUNNYMAN, 1967
FURIA, 1947
FURY AND THE WOMAN, 1937
FURY OF THE JUNGLE, 1934
FUSS OVER FEATHERS, 1954
GABRIELA, 1984
GABY, 1956
GAL YOUNG UN, 1979
GALIA, 1966
GALLANT BESS, 1946
GALLANT LADY, 1934
GALLANT LADY, 1942
GALLANT ONE, THE, 1964
GAMBLER, THE, 1958
GAMBLER, THE, 1974
GAMBLERS, THE, 1929
GAMBLERS, THE, 1969
GAMBLING HOUSE, 1950
GAMBLING LADY, 1934
GAMBLING ON THE HIGH SEAS, 1940
GAMBLING SAMURAI, THE, 1966
GAMBLING SEX, 1932
GAMBLING SHIP, 1933
GAMBLING SHIP, 1939
GAME FOR SIX LOVERS, A, 1962
GAME FOR VULTURES, A, 1980
GAME IS OVER, THE, 1967
GAME OF LOVE, THE, 1954
GAMEKEEPER, THE, 1980
GAMES MEN PLAY, THE, 1968
GANG'S ALL HERE, 1941
GANGSTER VIP, THE, 1968
GANGSTER'S BOY, 1938
GANGWAY FOR TOMORROW, 1943
GARBO TALKS, 1984
GARCON!, 1985
GARDEN OF EDEN, 1954

GARDEN OF THE FINZI-CONTINIS, THE, 1971
GARDENS OF STONE, 1987
GARNET BRACELET, THE, 1966
GAS-S-S-S!, 1970
GATE OF FLESH, 1964
GATES OF PARIS, 1958
GATES OF THE NIGHT, 1950
GATEWAY, 1938
GATEWAY TO GLORY, 1970
GATHERING OF EAGLES, A, 1963
GATOR BAIT, 1974
GAY INTRUDERS, THE, 1946
GAY SISTERS, THE, 1942
GEISHA GIRL, 1952
GEISHA, A, 1978
GENERAL DELLA ROVERE, 1960
GENERAL MASSACRE, 1973
GENERALS WITHOUT BUTTONS, 1938
GENTLE CREATURE, A, 1971
GENTLE GUNMAN, THE, 1952
GENTLE PEOPLE AND THE QUIET LAND, THE, 1972
GENTLE RAIN, THE, 1966
GENTLE TOUCH, THE, 1956
GENTLEMAN FROM DIXIE, 1941
GENTLEMAN'S AGREEMENT, 1947
GENTLEMEN ARE BORN, 1934
GENTLEMEN OF THE PRESS, 1929
GEORG, 1964
GEORGIA, GEORGIA, 1972
GEORGY GIRL, 1966
GERMAN SISTERS, THE, 1982
GERMANY IN AUTUMN, 1978
GERMANY PALE MOTHER, 1984
GERMANY, YEAR ZERO, 1949
GERMINAL, 1963
GERTRUD, 1966
GERVAISE, 1956
GET THAT MAN, 1935
GET TO KNOW YOUR RABBIT, 1972
GETTING OF WISDOM, THE, 1977
GETTING OVER, 1981
GETTING STRAIGHT, 1970
GETTING TOGETHER, 1976
GHOST COMES HOME, THE, 1940
GIANT, 1956
GIFT OF LOVE, THE, 1958
GIG, THE, 1985
GIGOLETTE, 1935
GIGOLETTES OF PARIS, 1933
GIGOT, 1962
GILDA, 1946
GILSODOM, 1986
GINGER, 1935
GINGER, 1947
GINGER & FRED, 1986
GIRL AND THE GENERAL, THE, 1967
GIRL AND THE LEGEND, THE, 1966
GIRL FROM CALGARY, 1932
GIRL FROM GOD'S COUNTRY, 1940
GIRL FROM HAVANA, 1940
GIRL FROM LORRAINE, A, 1982
GIRL FROM MANDALAY, 1936
GIRL FROM MANHATTAN, 1948
GIRL FROM TENTH AVENUE, THE, 1935
GIRL FROM THE MARSH CROFT, THE, 1935
GIRL FROM TRIESTE, THE, 1983
GIRL GAME, 1968
GIRL GETTERS, THE, 1966
GIRL GRABBERS, THE, 1968
GIRL I ABANDONED, THE, 1970
GIRL IN DISTRESS, 1941
GIRL IN LOVER'S LANE, THE, 1960
GIRL IN THE BIKINI, THE, 1958
GIRL IN THE GLASS CAGE, THE, 1929
GIRL IN THE PAINTING, THE, 1948
GIRL IN THE SHOW, THE, 1929
GIRL IN THE WOODS, 1958
GIRL IN TROUBLE, 1963
GIRL IS MINE, THE, 1950
GIRL MUST LIVE, A, 1941
GIRL NAMED TAMIKO, A, 1962
GIRL OF THE LIMBERLOST, 1934
GIRL OF THE LIMBERLOST, THE, 1945
GIRL OF THE MOORS, THE, 1961
GIRL OF THE MOUNTAINS, 1958
GIRL OF THE NIGHT, 1960

GIRL OF THE OZARKS, 1936
GIRL OF THE RIO, 1932
GIRL ON APPROVAL, 1962
GIRL ON THE BRIDGE, THE, 1951
GIRL ON THE CANAL, THE, 1947
GIRL OVERBOARD, 1929
GIRL STROKE BOY, 1971
GIRL, THE BODY, AND THE PILL, THE, 1967
GIRL WHO COULDN'T QUITE, THE, 1949
GIRL WHO FORGOT, THE, 1939
GIRL WHO HAD EVERYTHING, THE, 1953
GIRL WITH A SUITCASE, 1961
GIRL WITH GREEN EYES, 1964
GIRL WITH THE GOLDEN EYES, THE, 1962
GIRL WITH THE RED HAIR, THE, 1983
GIRL WITH THREE CAMELS, THE, 1968
GIRLFRIENDS, 1978
GIRLS' DORMITORY, 1936
GIRLS OF THE ROAD, 1940
GIRLS' SCHOOL, 1950
GIRLS' TOWN, 1942
GIRLS' TOWN, 1959
GIRLS, THE, 1972
GIVE ME MY CHANCE, 1958
GIVE ME THE STARS, 1944
GIVE ME YOUR HEART, 1936
GLAD TIDINGS, 1953
GLAMOROUS NIGHT, 1937
GLAMOUR, 1934
GLAMOUR BOY, 1941
GLAMOUR FOR SALE, 1940
GLASS HOUSES, 1972
GLASS MENAGERIE, THE, 1950
GLASS MENAGERIE, THE, 1987
GLASS MOUNTAIN, THE, 1950
GLASS TOWER, THE, 1959
GLASS WALL, THE, 1953
GLEN OR GLENDA, 1953
GLORY BOY, 1971
GLOWING AUTUMN, 1981
GO-BETWEEN, THE, 1971
GO-GETTER, THE, 1937
GO MASTERS, THE, 1985
GO NAKED IN THE WORLD, 1961
GOD IS MY CO-PILOT, 1945
GOD IS MY PARTNER, 1957
GODDESS, THE, 1962
GODDESS, THE, 1958
GOD'S COUNTRY AND THE WOMAN, 1937
GOD'S LITTLE ACRE, 1958
GOHA, 1958
GOIN' DOWN THE ROAD, 1970
GOING AND COMING BACK, 1985
GOING HOME, 1971
GOING PLACES, 1974
GOLD, 1934
GOLD, 1974
GOLD OF NAPLES, 1957
GOLD RUSH MAISIE, 1940
GOLDEN APPLES OF THE SUN, 1971
GOLDEN COACH, THE, 1953
GOLDEN DEMON, 1956
GOLDEN EARRINGS, 1947
GOLDEN GATE GIRL, 1941
GOLDEN HARVEST, 1933
GOLDEN HOOFS, 1941
GOLDEN MADONNA, THE, 1949
GOLDEN MASK, THE, 1954
GOLDEN PLAGUE, THE, 1963
GOLDIE, 1931
GOLDSTEIN, 1964
GONE ARE THE DAYS, 1963
GOOD BEGINNING, THE, 1953
GOOD DAME, 1934
GOOD EARTH, THE, 1937
GOOD FATHER, THE, 1986
GOOD LUCK, MISS WYCKOFF, 1979
GOOD LUCK, MR. YATES, 1943
GOOD MORNING... AND GOODBYE, 1967
GOOD MORNING, MISS DOVE, 1955
GOOD MORNING, VIETNAM, 1987
GOOD MOTHER, THE, 1988
GOOD OLD SOAK, THE, 1937
GOOD WIFE, THE, 1987
GOODBYE BROADWAY, 1938
GOODBYE EMMANUELLE, 1980

GOODBYE FRANKLIN HIGH, 1978
GOODBYE MR. CHIPS, 1939
GOODBYE, MOSCOW, 1968
GOODNIGHT, LADIES AND GENTLEMEN, 1977
GOODNIGHT SWEETHEART, 1944
GORBALS STORY, THE, 1950
GORDEYEV FAMILY, THE, 1961
GORILLA SHIP, THE, 1932
GORILLAS IN THE MIST, 1988
GOT IT MADE, 1974
GOT WHAT SHE WANTED, 1930
GRADUATE, THE, 1967
GRAN VARIETA, 1955
GRAND CANARY, 1934
GRAND HIGHWAY, THE, 1988
GRAND HOTEL, 1932
GRAND OLD GIRL, 1935
GRANDVIEW, U.S.A., 1984
GRAPES OF WRATH, 1940
GRASS EATER, THE, 1961
GRASS IS SINGING, THE, 1982
GRASSHOPPER, THE, 1970
GREASER'S PALACE, 1972
GREAT BIG THING, A, 1968
GREAT CITIZEN, THE, 1939
GREAT DAWN, THE, 1947
GREAT DAY, 1945
GREAT EXPECTATIONS, 1934
GREAT EXPECTATIONS, 1946
GREAT EXPECTATIONS, 1975
GREAT FLAMARION, THE, 1945
GREAT FLIRTATION, THE, 1934
GREAT GAME, THE, 1953
GREAT GATSBY, THE, 1949
GREAT GATSBY, THE, 1974
GREAT GAY ROAD, THE, 1931
GREAT GENERATION, THE, 1986
GREAT GOD GOLD, 1935
GREAT GUY, 1936
GREAT JASPER, THE, 1933
GREAT LIE, THE, 1941
GREAT MAN, THE, 1957
GREAT MAN VOTES, THE, 1939
GREAT O'MALLEY, THE, 1937
GREAT PLANE ROBBERY, 1950
GREAT POWER, THE, 1929
GREAT SANTINI, THE, 1979
GREAT SINNER, THE, 1949
GREAT WALL, A, 1986
GREAT WALL OF CHINA, THE, 1970
GREATEST LOVE, THE, 1954
GREATEST SHOW ON EARTH, THE, 1952
GREEK TYCOON, THE, 1978
GREEN FINGERS, 1947
GREEN GRASS OF WYOMING, 1948
GREEN LIGHT, 1937
GREEN MARE, THE, 1961
GREEN PACK, THE, 1934
GREEN PROMISE, THE, 1949
GREEN ROOM, THE, 1979
GREEN YEARS, THE, 1946
GREENWICH VILLAGE STORY, 1963
GREH, 1962
GREYHOUND LIMITED, THE, 1929
GROUCH, THE, 1961
GROUP, THE, 1966
GRUMPY, 1930
GUESS WHO'S COMING TO DINNER, 1967
GUEST, THE, 1963
GUEST IN THE HOUSE, 1944
GUEST, THE, 1984
GUIDE, THE, 1965
GUILT, 1967
GUILT IS NOT MINE, 1968
GUILT OF JANET AMES, THE, 1947
GUILTY?, 1930
GUINGUETTE, 1959
GUN, THE, 1978
GUNS, 1980
GUNS AT BATASI, 1964
GUNS OF DARKNESS, 1962
GUNS OF THE TREES, 1964
GURU, THE, 1969
GUTS IN THE SUN, 1959
GUTTER GIRLS, 1964
GUY COULD CHANGE, A, 1946

GUYANA, CULT OF THE DAMNED, 1980
GYPSY AND THE GENTLEMAN, THE, 1958
GYPSY FURY, 1950
GYPSY GIRL, 1966
GYPSY MELODY, 1936
GYPSY MOTHS, THE, 1969
HA' PENNY BREEZE, 1950
HADLEY'S REBELLION, 1984
HAIL AND FAREWELL, 1936
HAIL, HERO!, 1969
HAIRY APE, THE, 1944
HALF WAY TO HEAVEN, 1929
HALLELUJAH, 1929
HALLS OF ANGER, 1970
HALLUCINATION GENERATION, 1966
HAMBONE AND HILLIE, 1984
HAMILE, 1965
HAMLET, 1948
HAMLET, 1962
HAMLET, 1964
HAMLET, 1966
HAMLET, 1969
HAMLET, 1976
HAMMERSMITH IS OUT, 1972
HAND IN HAND, 1960
HAND IN THE TRAP, THE, 1963
HANDCUFFED, 1929
HANDFUL OF DUST, A, 1988
HANDLE WITH CARE, 1932
HANDLE WITH CARE, 1958
HANDS OF DESTINY, 1954
HANGUP, 1974
HANK WILLIAMS: THE SHOW HE NEVER GAVE, 1982
HANNAH AND HER SISTERS, 1986
HANNAH K., 1983
HANOI HILTON, THE, 1987
HAPPINESS CAGE, THE, 1972
HAPPINESS OF THREE WOMEN, THE, 1954
HAPPINESS OF US ALONE, 1962
HAPPY AS THE GRASS WAS GREEN, 1973
HAPPY BIRTHDAY, DAVY, 1970
HAPPY BIRTHDAY, GEMINI, 1980
HAPPY DEATHDAY, 1969
HAPPY END, 1968
HAPPY ENDING, THE, 1931
HAPPY ENDING, THE, 1969
HAPPY LAND, 1943
HAPPY ROAD, THE, 1957
HAPPY THIEVES, THE, 1962
HARAKIRI, 1963
HARD COUNTRY, 1981
HARD, FAST, AND BEAUTIFUL, 1951
HARD KNOCKS, 1980
HARD PART BEGINS, THE, 1973
HARD ROAD, THE, 1970
HARD ROCK HARRIGAN, 1935
HARD STEEL, 1941
HARD TIMES, 1988
HARD WAY, THE, 1942
HARDBOILED ROSE, 1929
HARDCORE, 1979
HARDER THEY COME, THE, 1973
HARLEM IS HEAVEN, 1932
HARLEQUIN, 1980
HARPOON, 1948
HARRAD EXPERIMENT, THE, 1973
HARRAD SUMMER, THE, 1974
HARRIET CRAIG, 1950
HARRY AND SON, 1984
HARRY AND TONTO, 1974
HARRY TRACY—DESPERADO, 1982
HARVEST, 1939
HARVESTER, THE, 1936
HARVEY MIDDLEMAN, FIREMAN, 1965
HASSAN, TERRORIST, 1968
HASTY HEART, THE, 1949
HAT, COAT AND GLOVE, 1934
HATARI!, 1962
HATCHET MAN, THE, 1932
HATE IN PARADISE, 1938
HATFUL OF RAIN, A, 1957
HATRED, 1941
HATTER'S CASTLE, 1948
HAVE A HEART, 1934
HAZEL'S PEOPLE, 1978

HAZING, THE, 1978
HEAD OF THE FAMILY, 1933
HEAD OFFICE, 1936
HEAD ON, 1971
HEAD ON, 1981
HEADIN' FOR BROADWAY, 1980
HEADLINE HUNTERS, 1955
HEADLINE SHOOTER, 1933
HEADLINE WOMAN, THE, 1935
HEALER, THE, 1935
HEART AND SOUL, 1950
HEART IS A LONELY HUNTER, THE, 1968
HEART OF A CHILD, 1958
HEART OF A NATION, THE, 1943
HEART OF PARIS, 1939
HEART OF THE MATTER, THE, 1954
HEART OF THE STAG, 1984
HEART SONG, 1933
HEARTBREAK RIDGE, 1986
HEARTBURN, 1986
HEARTS IN DIXIE, 1929
HEARTS OF HUMANITY, 1932
HEARTS OF HUMANITY, 1936
HEAT, 1970
HEAT AND DUST, 1983
HEAT AND SUNLIGHT, 1988
HEAT OF DESIRE, 1984
HEATWAVE, 1983
HEAVEN KNOWS, MR. ALLISON, 1957
HEAVEN ON EARTH, 1931
HEAVEN WITH A BARBED WIRE FENCE, 1939
HEAVENLY BODIES, 1985
HEDDA, 1975
HEIGHTS OF DANGER, 1962
HEIMAT, 1985
HEIRESS, THE, 1949
HEIRLOOM MYSTERY, THE, 1936
HELL AND HIGH WATER, 1933
HELL AND HIGH WATER, 1954
HELL BENT FOR 'FRISCO, 1931
HELL CAT, THE, 1934
HELL DRIVERS, 1958
HELL ON DEVIL'S ISLAND, 1957
HELL ON WHEELS, 1967
HELL WITH HEROES, THE, 1968
HELLDORADO, 1935
HELLFIRE CLUB, THE, 1963
HELLIONS, THE, 1962
HELLO GOD, 1951
HELLO SISTER!, 1933
HELL'S KITCHEN, 1939
HELL'S OUTPOST, 1955
HELL'S PLAYGROUND, 1967
HENNESSY, 1975
HENRY V, 1944
HENRY IV, 1985
HER BODYGUARD, 1933
HER FIRST AFFAIRE, 1932
HER HUSBAND'S SECRETARY, 1937
HER LAST AFFAIRE, 1935
HER PANELLED DOOR, 1951
HER RESALE VALUE, 1933
HER SISTER'S SECRET, 1946
HERE COME THE JETS, 1959
HERE COMES CARTER, 1936
HERE I AM A STRANGER, 1939
HERE'S FLASH CASEY, 1937
HERE'S YOUR LIFE, 1968
HERO AIN'T NOTHIN' BUT A SANDWICH, A, 1977
HERO FOR A DAY, 1939
HEROES ARE MADE, 1944
HEROES, 1977
HEROES FOR SALE, 1933
HEROES OF THE SEA, 1941
HEROINA, 1965
HEROSTRATUS, 1968
HESTER STREET, 1975
HEX, 1973
HEY BABU RIBA, 1987
HI-JACKERS, THE, 1963
HIAWATHA, 1952
HICKEY AND BOGGS, 1972
HIDDEN POWER, 1939
HIDE IN PLAIN SIGHT, 1980
HIDE-OUT, THE, 1930
HIGH, 1968

HIGH BARBAREE, 1947
HIGH COMMAND, 1938
HIGH FINANCE, 1933
HIGH FLIGHT, 1957
HIGH FURY, 1947
HIGH INFIDELITY, 1965
HIGH POWERED, 1945
HIGH SCHOOL, 1940
HIGH SCHOOL CAESAR, 1960
HIGH SCHOOL CONFIDENTIAL, 1958
HIGH SCHOOL GIRL, 1935
HIGH TIDE, 1987
HIGH TIDE AT NOON, 1957
HIGH VOLTAGE, 1929
HIGH YELLOW, 1965
HILDA CRANE, 1956
HILLS OF DONEGAL, THE, 1947
HILLS OF HOME, 1948
HIMATSURI, 1985
HIMMO, KING OF JERUSALEM, 1988
HIPPODROME, 1961
HIPPOLYT, THE LACKEY, 1932
HIRED WIFE, 1934
HIRELING, THE, 1973
HIROSHIMA, MON AMOUR, 1959
HIS BROTHER'S KEEPER, 1939
HIS BROTHER'S WIFE, 1936
HIS CAPTIVE WOMAN, 1929
HIS EXCELLENCY, 1952
HIS FAMILY TREE, 1936
HIS GRACE GIVES NOTICE, 1933
HIS GREATEST GAMBLE, 1934
HIS PRIVATE SECRETARY, 1933
HIS WOMAN, 1931
HISTORY IS MADE AT NIGHT, 1937
HISTORY OF MR. POLLY, THE, 1949
HIT, THE, 1985
HITCH HIKE LADY, 1936
HITCH HIKE TO HEAVEN, 1936
HITLER'S CHILDREN, 1942
H.M. PULHAM, ESQ., 1941
HOA-BINH, 1971
HOLD ME TIGHT, 1933
HOLD YOUR MAN, 1929
HOLIDAY CAMP, 1947
HOLIDAY FOR SINNERS, 1952
HOLIDAY WEEK, 1952
HOLLY AND THE IVY, THE, 1954
HOLLYWOOD BOULEVARD, 1936
HOLLYWOOD CAVALCADE, 1939
HOLLYWOOD MYSTERY, 1934
HOLLYWOOD SPEAKS, 1932
HOLY INNOCENTS, THE, 1984
HOLY MOUNTAIN, THE, 1973
HOME AND THE WORLD, THE, 1984
HOME BEFORE DARK, 1958
HOME FOR TANYA, A, 1961
HOME FREE ALL, 1983
HOME FREE ALL, 1984
HOME FROM THE HILL, 1960
HOME IS THE HERO, 1959
HOME OF THE BRAVE, 1949
HOME, SWEET HOME, 1933
HOME TOWN STORY, 1951
HOMECOMING, THE, 1973
HOMER, 1970
HOMESTRETCH, THE, 1947
HONEYMOON LIMITED, 1936
HONEYSUCKLE ROSE, 1980
HONKY, 1971
HONKYTONK MAN, 1982
HONOR AMONG LOVERS, 1931
HONOURABLE MURDER, AN, 1959
HONOURS EASY, 1935
HOODLUM PRIEST, THE, 1961
HOODLUM SAINT, THE, 1946
HOOSIER SCHOOLBOY, 1937
HOOSIER SCHOOLMASTER, 1935
HOPE AND GLORY, 1987
HOROSCOPE, 1950
HORSE, THE, 1984
HORSE IN THE GRAY FLANNEL SUIT, THE, 1968
HORSE OF PRIDE, 1980
HORSEMEN, THE, 1971
HOSPITAL, THE, 1971
HOSTILE WITNESS, 1968

HOT ANGEL, THE, 1958
HOT BOX, THE, 1972
HOT CAR GIRL, 1958
HOT CARGO, 1946
HOT HOURS, 1963
HOT MONEY GIRL, 1962
HOT MONTH OF AUGUST, THE, 1969
HOT ROD, 1950
HOT ROD GIRL, 1956
HOT ROD HULLABALOO, 1966
HOT ROD RUMBLE, 1957
HOT RODS TO HELL, 1967
HOT SHOT, 1987
HOT SPELL, 1958
HOT STUFF, 1929
HOT WATER, 1937
HOTEL, 1967
HOTEL COLONIAL, 1987
HOTEL CONTINENTAL, 1932
HOTEL FOR WOMEN, 1939
HOTEL IMPERIAL, 1939
HOTEL NEW HAMPSHIRE, THE, 1984
HOTEL NEW YORK, 1985
HOTEL VARIETY, 1933
HOTHEAD, 1963
HOUR OF GLORY, 1949
HOUR OF THE STAR, THE, 1986
HOUR OF THE WOLF, THE, 1968
HOUSE DIVIDED, A, 1932
HOUSE OF GOD, THE, 1984
HOUSE OF GREED, 1934
HOUSE OF LIFE, 1953
HOUSE OF NUMBERS, 1957
HOUSE OF 1,000 DOLLS, 1967
HOUSE OF STRANGERS, 1949
HOUSE OF THE SEVEN GABLES, THE, 1940
HOUSE OF TRENT, THE, 1933
HOUSE ON 56TH STREET, THE, 1933
HOUSE ON THE EDGE OF THE PARK, 1985
HOUSE ON THE SAND, 1967
HOUSE WITH AN ATTIC, THE, 1964
HOUSEKEEPING, 1987
HOUSEWIFE, 1934
HOW DO I LOVE THEE?, 1970
HOW GREEN WAS MY VALLEY, 1941
HOW TO COMMIT MARRIAGE, 1969
HOW WILLINGLY YOU SING, 1975
HOWZER, 1973
HUCKLEBERRY FINN, 1931
HUCKLEBERRY FINN, 1939
HUCKSTERS, THE, 1947
HUK, 1956
HUMAN CONDITION, THE, 1959
HUMAN DESIRE, 1954
HUMAN HIGHWAY, 1982
HUMANITY, 1933
HUMORESQUE, 1946
HUNCHBACK OF ROME, THE, 1963
HUNDRED HOUR HUNT, 1953
HUNGER, 1968
HUNGRY HILL, 1947
HUNT, THE, 1967
HURRY SUNDOWN, 1967
HUSBANDS, 1970
HUSBAND'S HOLIDAY, 1931
I ACCUSE!, 1958
I AIM AT THE STARS, 1960
I AM A CAMERA, 1955
I AM A GROUPIE, 1970
I AM SUZANNE, 1934
I AM THE CHEESE, 1983
I BELIEVE IN YOU, 1953
I BELIEVED IN YOU, 1934
I CAN GET IT FOR YOU WHOLESALE, 1951
I CONFESS, 1953
I CONQUER THE SEA, 1936
I COVER THE WATERFRONT, 1933
I COVER BIG TOWN, 1947
I EVEN MET HAPPY GYPSIES, 1968
I FOUND STELLA PARISH, 1935
I GIVE MY LOVE, 1934
I HAVE LIVED, 1933
I, JANE DOE, 1948
I LIVE IN FEAR, 1967
I LIVE MY LIFE, 1935
I LOVE A SOLDIER, 1944

I LOVE YOU, I KILL YOU, 1972
I LOVED A WOMAN, 1933
I MARRIED A DOCTOR, 1936
I, MAUREEN, 1978
I NEVER PROMISED YOU A ROSE GARDEN, 1977
I NEVER SANG FOR MY FATHER, 1970
I PASSED FOR WHITE, 1960
I REMEMBER MAMA, 1948
I SELL ANYTHING, 1934
I SENT A LETTER TO MY LOVE, 1981
I SPIT ON YOUR GRAVE, 1962
I STAND CONDEMNED, 1936
I START COUNTING, 1970
I TAKE THIS WOMAN, 1931
I TAKE THIS WOMAN, 1940
I THANK A FOOL, 1962
I WALK THE LINE, 1970
I WANT A DIVORCE, 1940
I WANT WHAT I WANT, 1972
I WANT YOU, 1951
I WANTED WINGS, 1941
I WAS A COMMUNIST FOR THE F.B.I., 1951
I WAS A CONVICT, 1939
I WAS A PRISONER ON DEVIL'S ISLAND, 1941
I WAS AN ADVENTURESS, 1940
ICE, 1970
ICE-CAPADES, 1941
ICE CASTLES, 1978
ICE PALACE, 1960
ICE PALACE, THE, 1988
ICEMAN COMETH, THE, 1973
I'D CLIMB THE HIGHEST MOUNTAIN, 1951
I'D GIVE MY LIFE, 1936
IDEAL HUSBAND, AN, 1948
IDENTIFICATION MARKS: NONE, 1969
IDENTIFICATION OF A WOMAN, 1983
IDENTITY UNKNOWN, 1945
IDENTITY UNKNOWN, 1960
IDIOT, THE, 1948
IDIOT, THE, 1960
IDIOT, THE, 1963
IDOL, THE, 1966
IDOL OF PARIS, 1948
IDOL OF THE CROWDS, 1937
IDOLMAKER, THE, 1980
IF . . ., 1968
IF I HAD A MILLION, 1932
IF I WERE BOSS, 1938
IF WINTER COMES, 1947
IF YOU COULD SEE WHAT I HEAR, 1982
IGOROTA, THE LEGEND OF THE TREE OF LIFE,
  1970
IKIRU, 1960
IL GRIDO, 1962
I'LL FIX IT, 1934
I'LL GIVE A MILLION, 1938
I'LL GIVE MY LIFE, 1959
I'LL LOVE YOU ALWAYS, 1935
I'LL NEVER FORGET WHAT'S 'IS NAME, 1967
I'LL NEVER FORGET YOU, 1951
I'LL SELL MY LIFE, 1941
I'LL WAIT FOR YOU, 1941
I'LL WALK BESIDE YOU, 1943
ILLEGAL, 1932
ILLIAC PASSION, THE, 1968
ILLICIT, 1931
ILLICIT INTERLUDE, 1954
ILLUMINATIONS, 1976
ILLUSION TRAVELS BY STREETCAR, THE, 1977
ILLUSIONIST, THE, 1985
ILLUSIONIST, THE, l985
ILLUSTRIOUS ENERGY, 1988
I'M DANCING AS FAST AS I CAN, 1982
I'M FROM MISSOURI, 1939
I'M GOING TO GET YOU . . . ELLIOT BOY, 1971
IMAGES, 1972
IMITATION OF LIFE, 1934
IMITATION OF LIFE, 1959
IMMORAL CHARGE, 1962
IMMORTAL GENTLEMAN, 1935
IMMORTAL STORY, THE, 1969
IMMORTAL VAGABOND, 1931
IMPATIENT MAIDEN, 1932
IMPERFECT LADY, THE, 1947
IMPORTANT MAN, THE, 1961
IMPOSSIBLE OBJECT, 1973

IN A LONELY PLACE, 1950
IN A MONASTERY GARDEN, 1935
IN A YEAR OF THIRTEEN MOONS, 1980
IN CELEBRATION, 1975
IN LOVE WITH LIFE, 1934
IN MACARTHUR PARK, 1977
IN NAME ONLY, 1939
IN OLD CALIFORNIA, 1929
IN OLD MISSOURI, 1940
IN OUR TIME, 1944
IN PRAISE OF OLDER WOMEN, 1978
IN SEARCH OF ANNA, 1978
IN SEARCH OF GREGORY, 1970
IN SPITE OF DANGER, 1935
IN THE COOL OF THE DAY, 1963
IN THE COUNTRY, 1967
IN THE NAME OF LIFE, 1947
IN THE WHITE CITY, 1983
IN THE WILD MOUNTAINS, 1986
IN THIS OUR LIFE, 1942
INADMISSIBLE EVIDENCE, 1968
INBREAKER, THE, 1974
INCIDENT, THE, 1967
INCIDENT IN SHANGHAI, 1937
INDECENT OBSESSION, AN, 1985
INDEPENDENCE DAY, 1976
INDEPENDENCE DAY, 1983
INDISCRETION OF AN AMERICAN WIFE, 1954
INFERNO, 1953
INFORMER, THE, 1929
INFORMER, THE, 1935
INHERIT THE WIND, 1960
INHERITANCE, THE, 1951
INHERITANCE, THE, 1964
INHERITANCE, THE, 1978
INHERITANCE IN PRETORIA, 1936
INHERITORS, THE, 1985
INJUN FENDER, 1973
INN OF THE SIXTH HAPPINESS, THE, 1958
INNERVIEW, THE, 1974
INNOCENCE UNPROTECTED, 1971
INNOCENT, THE, 1979
INNOCENT, THE, 1988
INNOCENT SINNERS, 1958
INSECT WOMAN, THE, 1964
INSIDE AMY, 1975
INSIDE DAISY CLOVER, 1965
INSIDE DETROIT, 1955
INSIDE LOOKING OUT, 1977
INSIDE MOVES, 1980
INSIDE OUT, 1986
INSIDE STORY, 1939
INSIGNIFICANCE, 1985
INSPECTOR CALLS, AN, 1954
INSPIRATION, 1931
INTERIORS, 1978
INTERLUDE, 1968
INTERMEZZO, 1937
INTERNATIONAL SETTLEMENT, 1938
INTERNATIONAL VELVET, 1978
INTERNS, THE, 1962
INTERRUPTED MELODY, 1955
INTIMACY, 1966
INTIMATE LIGHTING, 1969
INTO THE STRAIGHT, 1950
INTRUDER, THE, 1932
INTRUDER, THE, 1955
INTRUDER, THE, 1962
INTRUDER IN THE DUST, 1949
INVASION U.S.A., 1952
INVITATION, THE, 1975
INVITATION TO HAPPINESS, 1939
IO ... TU ... Y ... ELLA, 1933
IPHIGENIA, 1977
IRISH WHISKEY REBELLION, 1973
IRISHMAN, THE, 1978
IRON EAGLE, 1986
IRON MAN, THE, 1931
IRON MAN, THE, 1951
IRON MASTER, THE, 1933
IRONWEED, 1987
IRRECONCILABLE DIFFERENCES, 1984
IS MY FACE RED?, 1932
ISAAC LITTLEFEATHERS, 1984
ISABEL, 1968
ISADORA, 1968

ISLAND, THE, 1962
ISLAND IN THE SUN, 1957
ISLAND OF DOOM, 1933
ISLAND OF DOOMED MEN, 1940
ISLAND OF LOST MEN, 1939
ISLAND OF PROCIDA, THE, 1952
ISLAND OF THE BLUE DOLPHINS, 1964
ISLAND WOMEN, 1958
ISLANDS IN THE STREAM, 1977
ISLE OF FORGOTTEN SINS, 1943
ISLE OF SIN, 1963
ISTANBUL, 1957
IT COULD HAPPEN TO YOU, 1937
IT DON'T PAY TO BE AN HONEST CITIZEN, 1985
IT HAPPENED AT THE INN, 1945
IT HAPPENED HERE, 1966
IT HAPPENED IN CANADA, 1962
IT HAPPENED IN HOLLYWOOD, 1937
IT HAPPENED TO ONE MAN, 1941
IT ONLY HAPPENS TO OTHERS, 1971
IT STARTED IN PARADISE, 1952
IT'S A BIG COUNTRY, 1951
IT'S A GREAT LIFE, 1936
IT'S A PLEASURE, 1945
IT'S A SMALL WORLD, 1950
IT'S A WONDERFUL LIFE, 1946
IT'S NEVER TOO LATE, 1984
IT'S NEVER TOO LATE TO MEND, 1937
IT'S TOUGH TO BE FAMOUS, 1932
I'VE LIVED BEFORE, 1956
IVY, 1947
JACKSON COUNTY JAIL, 1976
JACKTOWN, 1962
JACQUELINE, 1956
JACQUES AND NOVEMBER, 1985
JAIL BAIT, 1977
JALNA, 1935
JAMES JOYCE'S WOMEN, 1985
JAPANESE WAR BRIDE, 1952
JASSY, 1948
JAZZ AGE, THE, 1929
JAZZ HEAVEN, 1929
JAZZBAND FIVE, THE, 1932
JAZZMAN, 1984
JE T'AIME, 1974
JEALOUSY, 1929
JEALOUSY, 1931
JEALOUSY, 1934
JEAN DE FLORETTE, 1987
JEDDA, THE UNCIVILIZED, 1956
JENATSCH, 1987
JENNIE, 1941
JENNIE GERHARDT, 1933
JENNY, 1969
JENNY KISSED ME, 1985
JEOPARDY, 1953
JERUSALEM FILE, THE, 1972
JESSICA, 1962
JET JOB, 1952
JETLAG, 1981
JEZEBEL, 1938
JIM, THE WORLD'S GREATEST, 1976
JIMMY ORPHEUS, 1966
JO JO DANCER, YOUR LIFE IS CALLING, 1986
JOANNA, 1968
JOE, 1970
JOE PANTHER, 1976
JOHANSSON GETS SCOLDED, 1945
JOHN AND MARY, 1969
JOHN HALIFAX—GENTLEMAN, 1938
JOHN MEADE'S WOMAN, 1937
JOHNNY BELINDA, 1948
JOHNNY COME LATELY, 1943
JOHNNY COMES FLYING HOME, 1946
JOHNNY FRENCHMAN, 1946
JOHNNY GOT HIS GUN, 1971
JOHNNY HOLIDAY, 1949
JOHNNY TIGER, 1966
JOHNNY TROUBLE, 1957
JOHNNY VIK, 1973
JONATHAN LIVINGSTON SEAGULL, 1973
JOSHUA, 1976
JOSHUA THEN AND NOW, 1985
JOURNEY, 1977
JOURNEY, THE, 1959
JOURNEY, THE, 1986

JOURNEY AHEAD, 1947
JOURNEY AMONG WOMEN, 1977
JOURNEY INTO LIGHT, 1951
JOURNEY THROUGH ROSEBUD, 1972
JOURNEY TO SPIRIT ISLAND, 1988
JOURNEYS FROM BERLIN—1971, 1980
JOVITA, 1970
JOY, 1983
JOY IN THE MORNING, 1965
JUD, 1971
JUDGE AND THE ASSASSIN, THE, 1979
JUDGE AND THE SINNER, THE, 1964
JUDGE HARDY AND SON, 1939
JUDGE HARDY'S CHILDREN, 1938
JUDGMENT IN BERLIN, 1988
JUGGLER, THE, 1953
JUKE BOX RACKET, 1960
JULES AND JIM, 1962
JULIA AND JULIA, 1988
JULIET OF THE SPIRITS, 1965
JUNGLE FLIGHT, 1947
JUNGLE OF CHANG, 1951
JUNIOR ARMY, 1943
JUNO AND THE PAYCOCK, 1930
JUPITER, 1952
JUST A GIGOLO, 1979
JUST BETWEEN FRIENDS, 1986
JUST ONCE MORE, 1963
JUST OUT OF REACH, 1979
JUSTINE, 1969
JUSTINE, 1969
JUVENILE COURT, 1938
KAGEMUSHA, 1980
KAMERADSCHAFT, 1931
KAMILLA, 1984
KAMOURASKA, 1973
KANCHENJUNGHA, 1966
KANDYLAND, 1988
KANGAROO, 1986
KAOS, 1985
KARAMAZOV, 1931
KARATE KID PART II, THE, 1986
KARMA, 1933
KATHLEEN, 1941
KATHLEEN MAVOURNEEN, 1930
KEEP 'EM ROLLING, 1934
KEEP 'EM SLUGGING, 1943
KEEP SMILING, 1938
KEEPER OF THE BEES, 1935
KEEPER OF THE BEES, 1947
KEEPER OF THE FLAME, 1942
KEEPERS OF YOUTH, 1931
KENNY AND CO., 1976
KEPT HUSBANDS, 1931
KES, 1970
KEY, THE, 1934
KEY, THE, 1958
KEY TO HARMONY, 1935
KEY WITNESS, 1960
KEYHOLE, THE, 1933
KIDNAPPERS, THE, 1964
KILLER THAT STALKED NEW YORK, THE, 1950
KILLING FIELDS, THE, 1984
KILLING GAME, THE, 1968
KILLING HEAT, 1984
KILLING OF ANGEL STREET, THE, 1983
KIND OF LOVING, A, 1962
KINEMA NO TENCHI, 1986
KINFOLK, 1970
KING BLANK, 1983
KING IN NEW YORK, A, 1957
KING LEAR, 1971
KING LEAR, 1988
KING, MURRAY, 1969
KING OF ALCATRAZ, 1938
KING OF COMEDY, THE, 1983
KING OF HEARTS, 1967
KING OF MARVIN GARDENS, THE, 1972
KING OF PARIS, THE, 1934
KING OF THE GYPSIES, 1978
KING OF THE MOUNTAIN, 1981
KING OF THE NEWSBOYS, 1938
KINGFISH CAPER, THE, 1976
KINGS AND DESPERATE MEN, 1984
KING'S CUP, THE, 1933
KING'S JESTER, THE, 1947

KINGS OF THE ROAD, 1976
KINGS ROW, 1942
KISENGA, MAN OF AFRICA, 1952
KISS THEM FOR ME, 1957
KISSING CUP'S RACE, 1930
KITCHEN, THE, 1961
KITTEN WITH A WHIP, 1964
KITTY, 1929
KITTY FOYLE, 1940
KLANSMAN, THE, 1974
KLONDIKE, 1932
KLONDIKE FURY, 1942
KNIFE IN THE WATER, 1963
KNIGHT IN LONDON, A, 1930
KNIGHTRIDERS, 1981
KNOCK, 1955
KOJIRO, 1967
KONA COAST, 1968
KONGI'S HARVEST, 1971
KOTCH, 1971
KRAMER VS. KRAMER, 1979
KURAGEJIMA—LEGENDS FROM A SOUTHERN
  ISLAND, 1970
L-SHAPED ROOM, THE, 1962
LA BABY SITTER, 1975
LA BETE HUMAINE, 1938
LA BONNE SOUPE, 1964
LA BOUM, 1983
LA CAGE, 1975
LA CHIENNE, 1975
LA COLLECTIONNEUSE, 1971
LA CUCARACHA, 1961
LA DOLCE VITA, 1961
LA FERME DU PENDU, 1946
LA FUGA, 1966
LA GUERRE EST FINIE, 1967
LA HABANERA, 1937
LA MARIE DU PORT, 1951
LA MATERNELLE, 1933
LA NOTTE, 1961
LA NOTTE BRAVA, 1962
LA PASSANTE, 1983
LA PRISONNIERE, 1969
LA RONDE, 1954
LA STRADA, 1956
LA TERRA TREMA, 1947
LA VIACCIA, 1962
LA VIE CONTINUE, 1982
LA VISITA, 1966
LACOMBE, LUCIEN, 1974
LADDIE, 1940
LADDIE, 1935
LADIES AND GENTLEMEN, THE FABULOUS
  STAINS, 1982
LADIES CLUB, THE, 1986
LADIES IN DISTRESS, 1938
LADIES LOVE BRUTES, 1930
LADIES' MAN, 1931
LADIES MUST LIVE, 1940
LADIES OF LEISURE, 1930
LADIES OF THE JURY, 1932
LADIES OF THE LOTUS, 1987
LADIES OF THE PARK, 1964
LADIES OF WASHINGTON, 1944
LADY AND GENT, 1932
LADY BY CHOICE, 1934
LADY CHATTERLEY'S LOVER, 1959
LADY CHATTERLEY'S LOVER, 1981
LADY FIGHTS BACK, 1937
LADY FOR A DAY, 1933
LADY FOR A NIGHT, 1941
LADY FROM LOUISIANA, 1941
LADY GAMBLES, THE, 1949
LADY GODIVA, 1955
LADY GREY, 1980
LADY HAMILTON, 1969
LADY IN QUESTION, THE, 1940
LADY IN THE CAR WITH GLASSES AND A GUN,
  THE, 1970
LADY IN THE DEATH HOUSE, 1944
LADY LUCK, 1936
LADY OBJECTS, THE, 1938
LADY OF CHANCE, A, 1928
LADY OF SECRETS, 1936
LADY OF THE TROPICS, 1939
LADY OF VENGEANCE, 1957

LADY PAYS OFF, THE, 1951
LADY REFUSES, THE, 1931
LADY TAKES A FLYER, THE, 1958
LADY TO LOVE, A, 1930
LADY WHO DARED, THE, 1931
LADY WITHOUT CAMELLIAS, THE, 1981
LADY WITHOUT PASSPORT, A, 1950
LADYBUG, LADYBUG, 1963
L'AGE D'OR, 1979
LAKE, THE, 1970
L'AMOUR, 1973
LAMP STILL BURNS, THE, 1943
LANDFALL, 1953
LANDLORD, THE, 1970
LANDSCAPE IN THE MIST, 1988
L'ANNEE DES MEDUSES, 1987
LARGE ROPE, THE, 1953
L'ARMEE DES OMBRES, 1969
LAS VEGAS LADY, 1976
LAS VEGAS SHAKEDOWN, 1955
LAS VEGAS STORY, THE, 1952
LASH, THE, 1934
LAST ACT OF MARTIN WESTON, THE, 1970
LAST AFFAIR, THE, 1976
LAST ANGRY MAN, THE, 1959
LAST CHANCE, THE, 1937
LAST DAYS OF DOLWYN, THE, 1949
LAST DETAIL, THE, 1973
LAST FLIGHT, THE, 1931
LAST JOURNEY, THE, 1936
LAST MAN TO HANG, THE, 1956
LAST MOMENT, THE, 1954
LAST MOMENT, THE, 1966
LAST MOVIE, THE, 1971
LAST NIGHT AT THE ALAMO, 1984
LAST OF MRS. CHEYNEY, THE, 1929
LAST OF MRS. CHEYNEY, THE, 1937
LAST OF THE KNUCKLEMEN, THE, 1981
LAST PICTURE SHOW, THE, 1971
LAST POST, THE, 1929
LAST STOP, THE, 1949
LAST SUMMER, 1969
LAST TRAIN FROM MADRID, THE, 1937
LAST TYCOON, THE, 1976
LAST WORD, THE, 1979
LAST YEAR AT MARIENBAD, 1962
LATE AUTUMN, 1973
LATE SUMMER BLUES, 1988
LAUGHING AT LIFE, 1933
LAUGHING BOY, 1934
LAUGHING LADY, THE, 1930
LAUGHING SINNERS, 1931
LAUGHTER, 1930
L'AVVENTURA, 1960
LAW AND DISORDER, 1974
LAW OF THE SEA, 1932
LAW OF THE TIMBER, 1941
LAW OF THE TROPICS, 1941
LAWFUL LARCENY, 1930
LAWLESS, THE, 1950
LAWYER, THE, 1969
LAWYER MAN, 1933
LAWYER'S SECRET, THE, 1931
LAZARILLO, 1963
LAZY RIVER, 1934
LE AMICHE, 1962
LE BEAU MARIAGE, 1982
LE BEAU SERGE, 1959
LE BONHEUR, 1966
LE CIEL EST A VOUS, 1957
LE CRABE TAMBOUR, 1984
LE GAI SAVOIR, 1968
LE JEUNE MARIE, 1985
LE PETIT THEATRE DE JEAN RENOIR, 1974
LE PLAISIR, 1954
LE VIOL, 1968
LEARNING TREE, THE, 1969
LEASE OF LIFE, 1954
LEATHER BOYS, THE, 1965
LEATHER GLOVES, 1948
LEATHERNECK, THE, 1929
LEFT-HANDED WOMAN, THE, 1980
LEGACY, 1976
LEGEND OF BILLIE JEAN, THE, 1985
LEGEND OF LYLAH CLARE, THE, 1968
LEGEND OF SURAM FORTRESS, 1985

LEMON DROP KID, THE, 1934
LENA RIVERS, 1932
LEO THE LAST, 1970
LEONOR, 1977
LES ABYSSES, 1964
LES BICHES, 1968
LES CARABINIERS, 1968
LES COMPERES, 1984
LES CREATURES, 1969
LES DERNIERES VACANCES, 1947
LES ENFANTS TERRIBLES, 1952
LES GAULOISES BLEUES, 1969
LES JEUX SONT FAITS, 1947
LES LIAISONS DANGEREUSES, 1961
LES MAINS SALES, 1954
LES PARENTS TERRIBLES, 1950
LES PLOUFFE, 1985
LESS THAN ZERO, 1987
LEST WE FORGET, 1934
LET NO MAN WRITE MY EPITAPH, 1960
LET THEM LIVE, 1937
LET'S GET MARRIED, 1960
LET'S TALK IT OVER, 1934
LET'S TRY AGAIN, 1934
LETTER, THE, 1929
LETTER, THE, 1940
LETTER FOR EVIE, A, 1945
LETTER FROM AN UNKNOWN WOMAN, 1948
LETTER OF INTRODUCTION, 1938
LETTER TO THREE WIVES, A, 1948
LETTERS FROM MY WINDMILL, 1955
LETTY LYNTON, 1932
LEVIATHAN, 1961
L'HOMME BLESSE, 1985
LIANNA, 1983
LIARS, THE, 1964
LIAR'S DICE, 1980
LIBEL, 1959
LIBERATION OF L.B. JONES, THE, 1970
LIBIDO, 1973
LIES, 1984
LIES MY FATHER TOLD ME, 1975
LIES MY FATHER TOLD ME, 1960
LIFE AND DEATH OF COLONEL BLIMP, THE, 1945
LIFE AT THE TOP, 1965
LIFE BEGINS, 1932
LIFE BEGINS ANEW, 1938
LIFE BEGINS AT 8:30, 1942
LIFE BEGINS AT 40, 1935
LIFE BEGINS AT 17, 1958
LIFE BEGINS FOR ANDY HARDY, 1941
LIFE BEGINS TOMORROW, 1952
LIFE IN DANGER, 1964
LIFE IN EMERGENCY WARD 10, 1959
LIFE IN HER HANDS, 1951
LIFE LOVE DEATH, 1969
LIFE OF A COUNTRY DOCTOR, 1961
LIFE OF HER OWN, A, 1950
LIFE OF OHARU, 1964
LIFE OF VERGIE WINTERS, THE, 1934
LIFE RETURNS, 1939
LIFE STUDY, 1973
LIFE UPSIDE DOWN, 1965
LIFEBOAT, 1944
LIFEGUARD, 1976
LIFT, THE, 1965
LIGHT ACROSSS THE STREET, THE, 1957
LIGHT IN THE FOREST, THE, 1958
LIGHT IN THE PIAZZA, 1962
LIGHT OF DAY, 1987
LIGHT THAT FAILED, THE, 1939
LIGHT UP THE SKY, 1960
LIGHTHOUSE, 1947
LIGHTNING FLYER, 1931
LIGHTNING—THE WHITE STALLION, 1986
LIGHTSHIP, THE, 1986
LIKE A CROW ON A JUNE BUG, 1972
LIKE A TURTLE ON ITS BACK, 1981
LIKE FATHER LIKE SON, 1961
LILI, 1953
LILI MARLEEN, 1981
LILIES OF THE FIELD, 1930
LILIES OF THE FIELD, 1963
LILITH, 1964
LILLI MARLENE, 1951
LILLY TURNER, 1933

BOLD: Films on Videocassette

LILY CHRISTINE, 1932
LILY OF LAGUNA, 1938
LIMBO, 1972
LIMELIGHT, 1952
L'IMMORTELLE, 1969
LINDA, 1960
LION, THE, 1962
LION AND THE MOUSE, THE, 1928
LION IS IN THE STREETS, A, 1953
LIPSTICK, 1976
LISA, 1962
LISA, TOSCA OF ATHENS, 1961
LISBON, 1956
LISETTE, 1961
LISTEN, LET'S MAKE LOVE, 1969
LISTEN TO THE CITY, 1984
LITTLE ADVENTURESS, THE, 1938
LITTLE ANGEL, 1961
LITTLE AUSTRALIANS, 1940
LITTLE BOY LOST, 1953
LITTLE COLONEL, THE, 1935
LITTLE DARLINGS, 1980
LITTLE FAUSS AND BIG HALSY, 1970
LITTLE FOXES, THE, 1941
LITTLE FRIEND, 1934
LITTLE FUGITIVE, THE, 1953
LITTLE LORD FAUNTLEROY, 1936
LITTLE MALCOLM, 1974
LITTLE MARTYR, THE, 1947
LITTLE MEN, 1935
LITTLE MEN, 1940
LITTLE MINISTER, THE, 1934
LITTLE MISS MOLLY, 1940
LITTLE MISS SOMEBODY, 1937
LITTLE MISS THOROUGHBRED, 1938
LITTLE MISTER JIM, 1946
LITTLE MOTHER, 1973
LITTLE PRINCESS, THE, 1939
LITTLE RED SCHOOLHOUSE, 1936
LITTLE SHEPHERD OF KINGDOM COME, 1961
LITTLE SISTER, THE, 1985
LITTLE STRANGER, 1934
LITTLE VERA, 1988
LITTLE WOMEN, 1933
LITTLE WOMEN, 1949
LITTLEST HORSE THIEVES, THE, 1977
LITTLEST REBEL, THE, 1935
LIVE FOR LIFE, 1967
LIVE YOUR OWN WAY, 1970
LIVING BETWEEN TWO WORLDS, 1963
LIVING CORPSE, THE, 1940
LIVING LEGEND, 1980
LIVING ON TOKYO TIME, 1987
LIVING ON VELVET, 1935
LIVING VENUS, 1961
LIZA, 1976
LIZZIE, 1957
LOCAL COLOR, 1978
LOCKED DOOR, THE, 1929
LOCKET, THE, 1946
LOLA, 1961
LOLA, 1971
LOLA, 1982
LOLA MONTES, 1955
LOLITA, 1962
LOLLIPOP, 1966
LOLLIPOP COVER, THE, 1965
LOLLY-MADONNA XXX, 1973
LONELINESS OF THE LONG DISTANCE RUNNER,
  THE, 1962
LONELY LADY, THE, 1983
LONELY LANE, 1963
LONELYHEARTS, 1958
LONESOME, 1928
LONG ABSENCE, THE, 1962
LONG AGO, TOMORROW, 1971
LONG DARK HALL, THE, 1951
LONG DAY'S JOURNEY INTO NIGHT, 1962
LONG GRAY LINE, THE, 1955
LONG HAUL, THE, 1957
LONG, HOT SUMMER, THE, 1958
LONG IS THE ROAD, 1948
LONG LOST FATHER, 1934
LONG NIGHT, THE, 1947
LONG NIGHT, THE, 1976
LONG SHOT, THE, 1939

LONG SHOT, 1981
LONG VOYAGE HOME, THE, 1940
LONG WEEKEND, 1978
LONGEST NIGHT, THE, 1936
LONGING FOR LOVE, 1966
LONNIE, 1963
LOOK BACK IN ANGER, 1959
LOOK BEFORE YOU LOVE, 1948
LOOK IN ANY WINDOW, 1961
LOOKING FOR MR. GOODBAR, 1977
LOOKING FOR TROUBLE, 1934
LOOKING FORWARD, 1933
LOOKING UP, 1977
LOOKS AND SMILES, 1982
LOOSE ENDS, 1930
LOOSE ENDS, 1975
LORD CAMBER'S LADIES, 1932
LORD OF THE FLIES, 1963
LORDS OF DISCIPLINE, THE, 1983
LORDS OF FLATBUSH, THE, 1974
LORNA DOONE, 1935
LORNA DOONE, 1951
LOS OLVIDADOS, 1950
LOSER, THE HERO, THE, 1985
LOSS OF INNOCENCE, 1961
LOST ANGEL, 1944
LOST BOUNDARIES, 1949
LOST CHORD, THE, 1937
LOST HONOR OF KATHARINA BLUM, THE, 1975
LOST LADY, A, 1934
LOST LAGOON, 1958
LOST, LONELY AND VICIOUS, 1958
LOST MAN, THE, 1969
LOST MOMENT, THE, 1947
LOST ON THE WESTERN FRONT, 1940
LOST ONE, THE, 1951
LOST PEOPLE, THE, 1950
LOST SEX, 1968
LOST SQUADRON, THE, 1932
LOST WEEKEND, THE, 1945
LOTUS LADY, 1930
LOUISIANA HUSSY, 1960
LOULOU, 1980
LOVABLE CHEAT, THE, 1949
LOVE A LA CARTE, 1965
LOVE, 1972
LOVE AND ANARCHY, 1974
LOVE AND MONEY, 1982
LOVE AND PAIN AND THE WHOLE DAMN THING,
  1973
LOVE AT NIGHT, 1961
LOVE AT TWENTY, 1963
LOVE, 1982
LOVE BOUND, 1932
LOVE CAPTIVE, THE, 1934
LOVE CYCLES, 1969
LOVE FEAST, THE, 1966
LOVE HAS MANY FACES, 1965
LOVE, HONOR AND BEHAVE, 1938
LOVE IN A FOUR LETTER WORLD, 1970
LOVE IN A GOLDFISH BOWL, 1961
LOVE IN A HOT CLIMATE, 1958
LOVE IN MOROCCO, 1933
LOVE-INS, THE, 1967
LOVE IS A CAROUSEL, 1970
LOVE IS A RACKET, 1932
LOVE IS A SPLENDID ILLUSION, 1970
LOVE IS MY PROFESSION, 1959
LOVE IS ON THE AIR, 1937
LOVE ISLAND, 1952
LOVE LETTERS, 1945
LOVE LETTERS, 1983
LOVE, LIFE AND LAUGHTER, 1934
LOVE MACHINE, THE, 1971
LOVE MERCHANT, THE, 1966
LOVE ON THE DOLE, 1945
LOVE ON THE GROUND, 1984,Fr.
LOVE ON THE RUN, 1980
LOVE PROBLEMS, 1970
LOVE RACKET, THE, 1929
LOVE STORM, THE, 1931
LOVE STREAMS, 1984
LOVE TAKES FLIGHT, 1937
LOVE TILL FIRST BLOOD, 1985
LOVE TRADER, 1930
LOVE UNDER FIRE, 1937

LOVE WITH THE PROPER STRANGER, 1963
LOVELESS, THE, 1982
LOVERS, THE, 1959
LOVERS AND LOLLIPOPS, 1956
LOVERS AND LUGGERS, 1938
LOVERS COURAGEOUS, 1932
LOVERS, HAPPY LOVERS!, 1955
LOVERS ON A TIGHTROPE, 1962
LOVERS' ROCK, 1966
LOVES OF CARMEN, THE, 1948
LOVES OF JOANNA GODDEN, THE, 1947
LOVE'S OLD SWEET SONG, 1933
LOVIN' MOLLY, 1974
LOVING, 1970
LOVING COUPLES, 1966
LOVING MEMORY, 1970
LOWER DEPTHS, THE, 1937
LOWER DEPTHS, THE, 1962
LOYAL HEART, 1946
LOYALTIES, 1934
LOYALTIES, 1986
LOYALTY OF LOVE, 1937
LUCIANO, 1963
LUCK OF GINGER COFFEY, THE, 1964
LUCKY LADY, 1975
LUCKY STAR, 1929
LUCKY STAR, THE, 1980
LUCKY TO BE A WOMAN, 1955
LUCY GALLANT, 1955
LULLABY, 1961
LULU, 1978
LULU, 1962
LUMIERE, 1976
LUMIERE D'ETE, 1943
LUMMOX, 1930
LUNA, 1979
LUNATICS, THE, 1986
LUXURY GIRLS, 1953
LUXURY LINER, 1933
LYDIA, 1964
MACARONI, 1985
MACARTHUR'S CHILDREN, 1985
MACBETH, 1948
MACBETH, 1963
MACBETH, 1971
MACHETE, 1958
MACHINE GUN MAMA, 1944
MACUSHLA, 1937
MAD ABOUT MUSIC, 1938
MAD AT THE WORLD, 1955
MAD ATLANTIC, THE, 1967
MAD DOCTOR OF MARKET STREET, THE, 1942
MAD GENIUS, THE, 1931
MAD MARTINDALES, THE, 1942
MAD ROOM, THE, 1969
MAD YOUTH, 1940
MADAME AKI, 1963
MADAME BOVARY, 1949
MADAME BUTTERFLY, 1932
MADAME ROSA, 1977
MADAME SOUSATZKA, 1988
MADAME X, 1929
MADAME X, 1937
MADAME X, 1966
MADE, 1972
MADE FOR EACH OTHER, 1939
MADE ON BROADWAY, 1933
MADELEINE IS, 1971
MADEMOISELLE, 1966
MADEMOISELLE FIFI, 1944
MADISON AVENUE, 1962
MADNESS OF THE HEART, 1949
MADONNA OF AVENUE A, 1929
MADONNA OF THE STREETS, 1930
MAEDCHEN IN UNIFORM, 1932
MAEDCHEN IN UNIFORM, 1965
MAEVA, 1961
MAFU CAGE, THE, 1978
MAGIC FACE, THE, 1951
MAGIC GARDEN OF STANLEY SWEETHART, THE,
  1970
MAGIC OF LASSIE, THE, 1978
MAGIC TOWN, 1947
MAGICIAN, THE, 1959
MAGICIAN OF LUBLIN, THE, 1979
MAGNIFICENT AMBERSONS, THE, 1942

MAGNIFICENT BRUTE, THE, 1936
MAGNIFICENT CONCUBINE, THE, 1964
MAGNIFICENT DOPE, THE, 1942
MAGNIFICENT FRAUD, THE, 1939
MAGNIFICENT LIE, 1931
MAGNIFICENT OBSESSION, 1935
MAGNIFICENT OBSESSION, 1954
MAGNIFICENT ROGUE, THE, 1946
MAGNIFICENT SINNER, 1963
MAGNIFICENT TRAMP, THE, 1962
MAHOGANY, 1975
MAIDEN, THE, 1961
MAIDS, THE, 1975
MAIDSTONE, 1970
MAIN ATTRACTION, THE, 1962
MAIN STREET, 1956
MAIN STREET KID, THE, 1947
MAIN STREET LAWYER, 1939
MAIN THING IS TO LOVE, THE, 1975
MAIS OU ET DONC ORNICAR, 1979
MAJDHAR, 1984
MAJORITY OF ONE, A, 1961
MAKE A FACE, 1971
MAKE HASTE TO LIVE, 1954
MAKE-UP, 1937
MAKE WAY FOR LILA, 1962
MAKE WAY FOR TOMORROW, 1937
MAKER OF MEN, 1931
MAKING IT, 1971
MAKING LOVE, 1982
MAKING THE GRADE, 1929
MAKIOKA SISTERS, THE, 1985
MALAY NIGHTS, 1933
MALE AND FEMALE SINCE ADAM AND EVE, 1961
MALOU, 1983
MAMBO, 1955
MAMMA ROMA, 1962
MAN, THE, 1972
MAN, A WOMAN AND A KILLER, A, 1975
MAN AFRAID, 1957
MAN AND A WOMAN, A, 1966
MAN AT THE TOP, 1973
MAN BETRAYED, A, 1941
MAN CALLED ADAM, A, 1966
MAN CALLED BACK, THE, 1932
MAN CRAZY, 1953
MAN ESCAPED, A, 1957
MAN FACING SOUTHEAST, 1986
MAN FOR ALL SEASONS, A, 1966
MAN FRIDAY, 1975
MAN FROM DOWN UNDER, THE, 1943
MAN FROM FRISCO, 1944
MAN FROM THE EAST, THE, 1961
MAN FROM WYOMING, A, 1930
MAN I MARRIED, THE, 1940
MAN I MARRY, THE, 1936
MAN IN BLUE, THE, 1937
MAN IN THE GLASS BOOTH, THE, 1975
MAN IN THE GREY FLANNEL SUIT, THE, 1956
MAN IN THE MIDDLE, 1964
MAN IN THE STORM, THE, 1969
MAN IN THE WATER, THE, 1963
MAN OF CONFLICT, 1953
MAN OF EVIL, 1948
MAN OF FLOWERS, 1984
MAN OF IRON, 1935
MAN OF MARBLE, 1979
MAN OF THE PEOPLE, 1937
MAN OF THE WORLD, 1931
MAN OF TWO WORLDS, 1934
MAN ON A TIGHTROPE, 1953
MAN ON FIRE, 1957
MAN OUTSIDE, 1988
MAN-PROOF, 1938
MAN STOLEN, 1934
MAN TO MAN, 1931
MAN TO REMEMBER, A, 1938
MAN-TRAP, 1961
MAN UPSTAIRS, THE, 1959
MAN WHO CAME BACK, THE, 1931
MAN WHO ENVIED WOMEN, THE, 1985
MAN WHO FINALLY DIED, THE, 1967
MAN WHO FOUND HIMSELF, THE, 1937
MAN WHO LAUGHS, THE, 1966
MAN WHO LIES, THE, 1970
MAN WHO LOVED WOMEN, THE, 1977

MAN WHO PLAYED GOD, THE, 1932
MAN WHO RECLAIMED HIS HEAD, THE, 1935
MAN WHO RETURNED TO LIFE, THE, 1942
MAN WHO WALKED ALONE, THE, 1945
MAN WITH A CLOAK, THE, 1951
MAN WITH THE GOLDEN ARM, THE, 1955
MAN, WOMAN AND CHILD, 1983
MANDINGO, 1975
MANGO TREE, THE, 1981
MANHATTAN COCKTAIL, 1928
MANHATTAN PROJECT, THE, 1986
MANHATTAN SHAKEDOWN, 1939
MANHATTAN TOWER, 1932
MANIAC!, 1977
MANNEQUIN, 1937
MANOLIS, 1962
MANON, 1950
MANON OF THE SPRING, 1987
MANON 70, 1968
MANPOWER, 1941
MAN'S CASTLE, A, 1933
MAN'S WORLD, A, 1942
MANSLAUGHTER, 1930
MANUELA'S LOVES, 1987
MARACAIBO, 1958
MARCH HARE, THE, 1956
MARCH OF THE SPRING HARE, 1969
MARGIN, THE, 1969
MARIA'S LOVERS, 1985
MARIGOLD, 1938
MARIGOLDS IN AUGUST, 1984
MARINE BATTLEGROUND, 1966
MARIUS, 1933
MARJORIE MORNINGSTAR, 1958
MARK, THE, 1961
MARK OF CAIN, THE, 1948
MARK OF THE HAWK, THE, 1958
MARK OF THE WHISTLER, THE, 1944
MARKED GIRLS, 1949
MAROONED, 1933
MARRIAGE, A, 1983
MARRIAGE BOND, THE, 1932
MARRIAGE BY CONTRACT, 1928
MARRIAGE IN THE SHADOWS, 1948
MARRIAGE OF MARIA BRAUN, THE, 1979
MARRIAGE PLAYGROUND, THE, 1929
MARRIED TOO YOUNG, 1962
MARRIED WOMAN, THE, 1965
MARRY ME! MARRY ME!, 1969
MARRY THE BOSS' DAUGHTER, 1941
MARRYING KIND, THE, 1952
MARRYING WIDOWS, 1934
MARTHA JELLNECK, 1988
MARTY, 1955
MARTYR, THE, 1976
MARVIN AND TIGE, 1983
MARY JANE'S PA, 1935
MARY STEVENS, M.D., 1933
MARYJANE, 1968
MARYLAND, 1940
MASCULINE FEMININE, 1966
MASK OF DIIJON, THE, 1946
MASK OF KOREA, 1950
MASOCH, 1980
MASQUERADER, THE, 1933
MASSACRE AT CENTRAL HIGH, 1976
MASSIVE RETALIATION, 1984
MASTER OF BANKDAM, THE, 1947
MASTER OF MEN, 1933
MASTER RACE, THE, 1944
MATCHLESS, 1974
MATEWAN, 1987
MATHIAS SANDORF, 1963
MATTER OF CHOICE, A, 1963
MATTER OF DAYS, A, 1969
MATTER OF HONOR, A, 1988
MATTER OF INNOCENCE, A, 1968
MATTER OF TIME, A, 1976
MAURICE, 1987
MAXIME, 1962
MAYA, 1982
ME, 1970
ME AND MY BROTHER, 1969
ME, NATALIE, 1969
MEAL, THE, 1975
MEDAL FOR BENNY, A, 1945

MEDEA, 1971
MEET DR. CHRISTIAN, 1939
MELANIE, 1982
MELODY FOR THREE, 1941
MEMBER OF THE WEDDING, THE, 1952
MEMED MY HAWK, 1984
MEMOIRS, 1984
MEMORY OF US, 1974
MEN, THE, 1950
MEN AGAINST THE SUN, 1953
MEN ARE LIKE THAT, 1931
MEN ARE NOT GODS, 1937
MEN ARE SUCH FOOLS, 1933
MEN ARE SUCH FOOLS, 1938
MEN IN EXILE, 1937
MEN IN HER LIFE, 1931
MEN IN HER LIFE, THE, 1941
MEN IN WHITE, 1934
MEN MUST FIGHT, 1933
MEN OF BOYS TOWN, 1941
MEN OF CHANCE, 1932
MEN OF IRELAND, 1938
MEN OF SAN QUENTIN, 1942
MEN OF STEEL, 1932
MEN OF TEXAS, 1942
MEN OF THE HOUR, 1935
MEN OF THE NORTH, 1930
MEN OF TOMORROW, 1935
MEN OF YESTERDAY, 1936
MEN'S CLUB, THE, 1986
MEPHISTO, 1981
MERCHANT OF SLAVES, 1949
MERRY WIVES, THE, 1940
MEXICALI ROSE, 1929
MICHAEL AND MARY, 1932
MICHAEL O'HALLORAN, 1937
MICHAEL O'HALLORAN, 1948
MICHELLE, 1970
MICKEY, 1948
MICKEY, THE KID, 1939
MID-DAY MISTRESS, 1968
MIDDLE AGE CRAZY, 1980
MIDDLE AGE SPREAD, 1979
MIDDLE OF THE NIGHT, 1959
MIDDLETON FAMILY AT THE N.Y. WORLD'S FAIR, 1939
MIDNIGHT, 1934
MIDNIGHT COWBOY, 1969
MIDNIGHT FOLLY, 1962
MIDNIGHT LADY, 1932
MIDNIGHT MADONNA, 1937
MIDNIGHT MEETING, 1962
MIDNIGHT SPECIAL, 1931
MIDSHIPMAN JACK, 1933
MIDSTREAM, 1929
MIDSUMMER NIGHT'S DREAM, A, 1984
MIDWIFE, THE, 1961
MIGHTY, THE, 1929
MIGHTY TREVE, THE, 1937
MIKEY AND NICKY, 1976
MILDRED PIERCE, 1945
MILES FROM HOME, 1988
MILESTONES, 1975
MILITARY ACADEMY, 1940
MILITARY ACADEMY WITH THAT TENTH AVENUE GANG, 1950
MILL ON THE FLOSS, 1939
MILLIE, 1931
MILLIE'S DAUGHTER, 1947
MILLION DOLLAR BABY, 1941
MILLIONAIRE, THE, 1931
MILLIONAIRE KID, 1936
MILLIONS LIKE US, 1943
MILLS OF THE GODS, 1935
MIN AND BILL, 1930
MIND READER, THE, 1933
MINE OWN EXECUTIONER, 1948
MINIVER STORY, THE, 1950
MINNIE AND MOSKOWITZ, 1971
MINX, THE, 1969
MIRACLE IN SOHO, 1957
MIRACLE IN THE RAIN, 1956
MIRACLE OF THE WHITE STALLIONS, 1963
MIRACLE ON MAIN STREET, A, 1940
MIRAGE, 1972
MIRROR HAS TWO FACES, THE, 1959

BOLD: Films on Videocassette

MISS ANNIE ROONEY, 1942
MISS FANE'S BABY IS STOLEN, 1934
MISS JESSICA IS PREGNANT, 1970
MISS MARY, 1987
MISS MONA, 1987
MISS SADIE THOMPSON, 1953
MISS SUSIE SLAGLE'S, 1945
MISSING, 1982
MISSION TO MOSCOW, 1943
MISSISSIPPI BURNING, 1988
MISSISSIPPI GAMBLER, 1929
MISSISSIPPI RHYTHM, 1949
MISSISSIPPI SUMMER, 1971
MISSOURI TRAVELER, THE, 1958
MR. ACE, 1946
MISTER ANTONIO, 1929
MR. BILLION, 1977
MISTER BROWN, 1972
MISTER BUDDWING, 1966
MR. COHEN TAKES A WALK, 1936
MISTER CORY, 1957
MISTER 880, 1950
MR. EMMANUEL, 1945
MR. IMPERIUM, 1951
MR. KLEIN, 1976
MR. ORCHID, 1948
MR. PATMAN, 1980
MR. PERRIN AND MR. TRAILL, 1948
MR. RECKLESS, 1948
MISTER ROBERTS, 1955
MR. SCOUTMASTER, 1953
MR. SKEFFINGTON, 1944
MR. SOFT TOUCH, 1949
MR. SYCAMORE, 1975
MISTRESS FOR THE SUMMER, A, 1964
MISUNDERSTOOD, 1984
MIXED BLOOD, 1984
MODEL SHOP, THE, 1969
MODERATO CANTABILE, 1964
MODERN HERO, A, 1934
MODERN MARRIAGE, A, 1950
MODERNS, THE, 1988
MOHAN JOSHI HAAZIR HO, 1984
MOKEY, 1942
MOM AND DAD, 1948
MOMENT OF TERROR, 1969
MOMENTS, 1974
MON ONCLE D'AMERIQUE, 1980
MONDAY'S CHILD, 1967
MONEY MAD, 1934
MONKEY GRIP, 1983
MONKEY HUSTLE, THE, 1976
MONKEY IN WINTER, A, 1962
MOON IS DOWN, THE, 1943
MONSEIGNEUR, 1950
MONSOON, 1953
MONTE CARLO STORY, THE, 1957
MONTENEGRO, 1981
MOON AND SIXPENCE, THE, 1942
MOON IN THE GUTTER, THE, 1983
MOONLIGHT MASQUERADE, 1942
MOONLIGHTING, 1982
MOONLIGHTING WIVES, 1966
MOONRISE, 1948
MOONSHINE WAR, THE, 1970
MOONSHINER'S WOMAN, 1968
MORALS FOR WOMEN, 1931
MORE, 1969
MORE AMERICAN GRAFFITI, 1979
MORGAN!, 1966
MORNING GLORY, 1933
MORTAL STORM, THE, 1940
MOSCOW ON THE HUDSON, 1984
MOSCOW SHANGHAI, 1936
MOST IMMORAL LADY, A, 1929
MOST PRECIOUS THING IN LIFE, 1934
MOST WONDERFUL EVENING OF MY LIFE, THE, 1972
MOTEL, THE OPERATOR, 1940
MOTH, THE, 1934
MOTHER AND DAUGHTER, 1965
MOTHER AND SON, 1931
MOTHER AND THE WHORE, THE, 1973
MOTHER CAREY'S CHICKENS, 1938
MOTHER KNOWS BEST, 1928
MOTHER KUSTERS GOES TO HEAVEN, 1976

MOTHER'S BOY, 1929
MOTHERS CRY, 1930
MOTHERS OF TODAY, 1939
MOTIVE FOR REVENGE, 1935
MOTIVE WAS JEALOUSY, THE, 1970
MOTORCYCLE GANG, 1957
MOUCHETTE, 1970
MOUNTAIN, THE, 1935
MOUNTAIN JUSTICE, 1937
MOUNTED FURY, 1931
MOURNING BECOMES ELECTRA, 1947
MOURNING SUIT, THE, 1975
MOUSE AND THE WOMAN, THE, 1981
MOUTH TO MOUTH, 1978
MOVIE STUNTMEN, 1953
MOZAMBIQUE, 1966
MRS. MIKE, 1949
MRS. MINIVER, 1942
MRS. PARKINGTON, 1944
MRS. SOFFEL, 1984
MRS. WARREN'S PROFESSION, 1960
MRS. WIGGS OF THE CABBAGE PATCH, 1934
MRS. WIGGS OF THE CABBAGE PATCH, 1942
MUDDY RIVER, 1982
MUDLARK, THE, 1950
MUMU, 1961
MURDER CZECH STYLE, 1968
MURDER IN MISSISSIPPI, 1965
MURDER IN THE OLD RED BARN, 1936
MURDERERS AMONG US, 1948
MURIEL, 1963
MURMUR OF THE HEART, 1971
MUSHROOM EATER, THE, 1976
MUSIC MAKER, THE, 1936
MUSIC ROOM, THE, 1963
MY AIN FOLK, 1974
MY AMERICAN COUSIN, 1985
MY BABY IS BLACK!, 1965
MY BEAUTIFUL LAUNDRETTE, 1986
MY BILL, 1938
MY BLOOD RUNS COLD, 1965
MY BODYGUARD, 1980
MY BRILLIANT CAREER, 1980
MY BROTHER JONATHAN, 1949
MY BROTHER'S KEEPER, 1949
MY BROTHER'S WEDDING, 1983
MY CHILDHOOD, 1972
MY DINNER WITH ANDRE, 1981
MY FATHER'S HOUSE, 1947
MY FATHER'S MISTRESS, 1970
MY FIRST LOVE, 1978
MY FIRST WIFE, 1985
MY GEISHA, 1962
MY GIRL TISA, 1948
MY HANDS ARE CLAY, 1948
MY HEART BELONGS TO DADDY, 1942
MY KIND OF TOWN, 1984
MY LIFE AS A DOG, 1987
MY LIFE TO LIVE, 1963
MY LOVER, MY SON, 1970
MY MAN AND I, 1952
MY MARGO, 1969
MY MARRIAGE, 1936
MY MOTHER, 1933
MY NAME IS IVAN, 1963
MY NIGHT AT MAUD'S, 1970
MY OLD DUTCH, 1934
MY OTHER HUSBAND, 1985
MY OWN TRUE LOVE, 1948
MY PAL GUS, 1952
MY PAST, 1931
MY SIN, 1931
MY SISTER AND I, 1948
MY SON, JOHN, 1952
MY SON, MY SON!, 1940
MY SWEET LITTLE VILLAGE, 1985
MY TUTOR, 1983
MY UNCLE ANTOINE, 1971
MY WAY HOME, 1978
MY WOMAN, 1933
MYSTERIES, 1979
MYSTERY SEA RAIDER, 1940
MYSTERY SUBMARINE, 1950
MYSTIQUE, 1981
MYTH, THE, 1965

NAKED AUTUMN, 1963
NAKED EARTH, THE, 1958
NAKED FLAME, THE, 1970
NAKED HEART, THE, 1955
NAKED HEARTS, 1970
NAKED HOURS, THE, 1964
NAKED KISS, THE, 1964
NAKED NIGHT, THE, 1956
NAKED PARADISE, 1957
NAKED WOMAN, THE, 1950
NAKED YOUTH, 1961
NAKED ZOO, THE, 1970
NAMU, THE KILLER WHALE, 1966
NANA, 1934
NANA, 1957
NANA, 1983
NARCOTICS STORY, THE, 1958
NASHVILLE, 1975
NATHALIE GRANGER, 1972
NATION AFLAME, 1937
NATIONAL VELVET, 1944
NATIVE LAND, 1942
NATIVE SON, 1951
NATIVE SON, 1986
NATURAL ENEMIES, 1979
NAUGHTY FLIRT, THE, 1931
NAVAL ACADEMY, 1941
NAVY BLUE AND GOLD, 1937
NAVY BLUES, 1930
NAVY BORN, 1936
NEGATIVES, 1968
NEIGHBORS' WIVES, 1933
NEITHER BY DAY NOR BY NIGHT, 1972
NELLY'S VERSION, 1983
NEST, THE, 1982
NEST OF VIPERS, 1979
NETWORK, 1976
NEVER FEAR, 1950
NEVER LET ME GO, 1953
NEVER LOOK BACK, 1952
NEVER NEVER LAND, 1982
NEVER ON SUNDAY, 1960
NEVER SAY GOODBYE, 1956
NEVER TAKE CANDY FROM A STRANGER, 1961
NEVER TAKE NO FOR AN ANSWER, 1952
NEW EARTH, THE, 1937
NEW GIRL IN TOWN, 1977
NEW HORIZONS, 1939
NEW INTERNS, THE, 1964
NEW LAND, THE, 1973
NEW LIFE STYLE, THE, 1970
NEW LOVE, 1968
NEW MORALS FOR OLD, 1932
NEW ORLEANS, 1929
NEW WINE, 1941
NEW YORK NIGHTS, 1929
NEW YORK NIGHTS, 1984
NEWS IS MADE AT NIGHT, 1939
NEWSBOY'S HOME, 1939
NEWSFRONT, 1979
NEXT TIME WE LOVE, 1936
NEXT VOICE YOU HEAR, THE, 1950
NGATI, 1987
NICE GIRL?, 1941
NICHOLAS NICKLEBY, 1947
NICKEL MOUNTAIN, 1985
NICKEL QUEEN, THE, 1971
NIGHT AFTER NIGHT, 1932
NIGHT ALARM, 1935
NIGHT ANGEL, THE, 1931
NIGHT ANGELS, 1987
NIGHT BEFORE THE DIVORCE, THE, 1942
NIGHT CLUB QUEEN, 1934
NIGHT COMERS, THE, 1971
NIGHT CREATURES, 1962
NIGHT FLOWERS, 1979
NIGHT FREIGHT, 1955
NIGHT GAMES, 1966
NIGHT GAMES, 1980
NIGHT HAIR CHILD, 1971
NIGHT IN HEAVEN, A, 1983
NIGHT IN JUNE, A, 1940
NIGHT INTO MORNING, 1951
NIGHT IS MY FUTURE, 1962
NIGHT IS OURS, 1930
NIGHT LIFE IN RENO, 1931

NIGHT MAYOR, THE, 1932
'NIGHT, MOTHER, 1986
NIGHT MY NUMBER CAME UP, THE, 1955
NIGHT OF EVIL, 1962
NIGHT OF JUNE 13, 1932
NIGHT OF NIGHTS, THE, 1939
NIGHT OF THE ASKARI, 1978
NIGHT OF THE IGUANA, THE, 1964
NIGHT OF THE PROWLER, THE, 1979
NIGHT OF THE QUARTER MOON, 1959
NIGHT OF THE SEAGULL, THE, 1970
NIGHT OF THE SHOOTING STARS, THE, 1982
NIGHT PARADE, 1929
NIGHT PEOPLE, 1954
NIGHT PORTER, THE, 1974
NIGHT RIDE, 1937
NIGHT SONG, 1947
NIGHT THE LIGHTS WENT OUT IN GEORGIA, THE, 1981
NIGHT TIDE, 1963
NIGHT TRAIN FOR INVERNESS, 1960
NIGHT TRAIN TO MEMPHIS, 1946
NIGHT WAS OUR FRIEND, 1951
NIGHT WIND, 1948
NIGHT WORK, 1930
NIGHTHAWKS, 1978
NIGHTMARE'S PASSENGERS, 1986
NIGHTS OF CABIRIA, 1957
NIGHTS OF PRAGUE, THE, 1968
NIGHTSONGS, 1984
9 1/2 WEEKS, 1986
NINE DAYS OF ONE YEAR, 1964
NINE MILES TO NOON, 1963
9/30/55, 1977
1918, 1985
1984, 1956
1984, 1984
1900, 1976
1919, 1984
1969, 1988
90 DEGREES IN THE SHADE, 1966
92 IN THE SHADE, 1975
NINTH CIRCLE, THE, 1961
NINTH CONFIGURATION, THE, 1980
NO DOWN PAYMENT, 1957
NO DRUMS, NO BUGLES, 1971
NO EXIT, 1962
NO GREATER GLORY, 1934
NO GREATER LOVE, 1932
NO GREATER LOVE THAN THIS, 1969
NO GREATER SIN, 1941
NO HIGHWAY IN THE SKY, 1951
NO LIVING WITNESS, 1932
NO LONGER ALONE, 1978
NO LOVE FOR JOHNNIE, 1961
NO MAN OF HER OWN, 1933
NO MAN OF HER OWN, 1950
NO MARRIAGE TIES, 1933
NO MORE ORCHIDS, 1933
NO MORE WOMEN, 1934
NO ONE MAN, 1932
NO OTHER WOMAN, 1933
NO PLACE FOR JENNIFER, 1950
NO PLACE TO HIDE, 1956
NO PLACE TO LAND, 1958
NO RESTING PLACE, 1952
NO RETURN ADDRESS, 1961
NO SAD SONGS FOR ME, 1950
NO TIME FOR BREAKFAST, 1978
NO TIME FOR ECSTASY, 1963
NO TIME FOR TEARS, 1957
NO TIME TO BE YOUNG, 1957
NO TIME TO KILL, 1963
NO TREE IN THE STREET, 1964
NO WAY OUT, 1950
NOBODY LIVES FOREVER, 1946
NOBODY WAVED GOODBYE, 1965
NOBODY'S CHILDREN, 1940
NOMADIC LIVES, 1977
NON-STOP NEW YORK, 1937
NONE BUT THE LONELY HEART, 1944
NONE SHALL ESCAPE, 1944
NORA PRENTISS, 1947
NORAH O'NEALE, 1934
NORMA RAE, 1979
NORTH STAR, THE, 1982

NORTHERN LIGHTS, 1978
NORWOOD, 1970
NOSTALGHIA, 1984
NOT AS A STRANGER, 1955
NOT MINE TO LOVE, 1969
NOT QUITE DECENT, 1929
NOT QUITE JERUSALEM, 1985
NOT RECONCILED, OR ""ONLY VIOLENCE HELPS WHERE IT RULES", 1969
NOT WANTED, 1949
NOTHING BUT A MAN, 1964
NOTHING IN COMMON, 1986
NOTORIOUS AFFAIR, A, 1930
NOTORIOUS BUT NICE, 1934
NOTORIOUS CLEOPATRA, THE, 1970
NOTORIOUS GENTLEMAN, 1945
NOTORIOUS MR. MONKS, THE, 1958
NOW AND FOREVER, 1934
NOW AND FOREVER, 1956
NOW AND FOREVER, 1983
NOW THAT APRIL'S HERE, 1958
NOW, VOYAGER, 1942
NUDE ODYSSEY, 1962
NO. 96, 1974
NUMBER ONE, 1984
NUMBER TWO, 1975
NUNZIO, 1978
NUTCRACKER, 1982
NUTS, 1987
O. HENRY'S FULL HOUSE, 1952
OASIS, THE, 1984
OBEY THE LAW, 1933
OBSESSED, 1988
OBSESSION, 1968
OCEAN BREAKERS, 1949
OCTOBER MOTH, 1960
ODD MAN OUT, 1947
ODD OBSESSION, 1961
ODDO, 1967
ODE TO BILLY JOE, 1976
ODONGO, 1956
OEDIPUS REX, 1957
OEDIPUS THE KING, 1968
OF FLESH AND BLOOD, 1964
OF HUMAN BONDAGE, 1934
OF HUMAN BONDAGE, 1946
OF HUMAN BONDAGE, 1964
OF HUMAN HEARTS, 1938
OF LOVE AND DESIRE, 1963
OF MICE AND MEN, 1939
OFF THE RECORD, 1939
OFF THE WALL, 1977
OFFENDERS, THE, 1980
OFFENSE, THE, 1973
OFFICE GIRLS, 1974
OFFICE PICNIC, THE, 1974
OFFICE SCANDAL, THE, 1929
OFFICE WIFE, THE, 1930
OFFICIAL STORY, THE, 1985
OH, YEAH!, 1929
O'HARA'S WIFE, 1983
OHAYO, 1962
OIL FOR THE LAMPS OF CHINA, 1935
OKAY BILL, 1971
OKLAHOMA CRUDE, 1973
OLD ACQUAINTANCE, 1943
OLD BOYFRIENDS, 1979
OLD CURIOSITY SHOP, THE, 1935
OLD ENGLISH, 1930
OLD ENOUGH, 1984
OLD FAITHFUL, 1935
OLD-FASHIONED GIRL, AN, 1948
OLD HOMESTEAD, THE, 1942
OLD IRON, 1938
OLD MAC, 1961
OLD MAID, THE, 1939
OLD MAN AND THE SEA, THE, 1958
OLD ROSES, 1935
OLD SWIMMIN' HOLE, THE, 1941
OLD YELLER, 1957
OLDEST PROFESSION, THE, 1968
OLIVE TREES OF JUSTICE, THE, 1967
OLIVER TWIST, 1933
OLIVER TWIST, 1951
ON BORROWED TIME, 1939
ON GOLDEN POND, 1981

ON HER BED OF ROSES, 1966
ON OUR MERRY WAY, 1948
ON OUR SELECTION, 1930
ON PROBATION, 1935
ON THE AIR LIVE WITH CAPTAIN MIDNIGHT, 1979
ON THE BEACH, 1959
ON THE LINE, 1984
ON THE LOOSE, 1951
ON THE NICKEL, 1980
ON THE SUNNY SIDE, 1942
ON THE SUNNYSIDE, 1936
ON THE THRESHOLD OF SPACE, 1956
ON THE WATERFRONT, 1954
ON TRIAL, 1928
ON TRIAL, 1939
ON VALENTINE'S DAY, 1986
ON YOUR BACK, 1930
ONCE, 1974
ONCE A DOCTOR, 1937
ONCE A LADY, 1931
ONCE A RAINY DAY, 1968
ONCE A SINNER, 1931
ONCE A SINNER, 1952
ONCE IN PARIS, 1978
ONCE IS NOT ENOUGH, 1975
ONCE TO EVERY BACHELOR, 1934
ONCE TO EVERY WOMAN, 1934
ONCE UPON A COFFEE HOUSE, 1965
ONCE UPON A HONEYMOON, 1942
ONE AND ONLY, THE, 1978
ONE AND ONLY GENUINE ORIGINAL FAMILY BAND, THE, 1968
ONE APRIL 2000, 1952
ONE BIG AFFAIR, 1952
ONE BRIEF SUMMER, 1971
ONE CROWDED NIGHT, 1940
ONE DAY IN THE LIFE OF IVAN DENISOVICH, 1971
ONE DESIRE, 1955
ONE FLEW OVER THE CUCKOO'S NEST, 1975
ONE FOOT IN HEAVEN, 1941
ONE GIRL'S CONFESSION, 1953
125 ROOMS OF COMFORT, 1974
ONE IN A MILLION, 1935
ONE IS A LONELY NUMBER, 1972
ONE MAN, 1979
ONE MAN'S JOURNEY, 1933
ONE MILE FROM HEAVEN, 1937
$1,000,000 RACKET, 1937
ONE MORE RIVER, 1934
ONE MORE TOMORROW, 1946
ONE NIGHT. . .A TRAIN, 1968
ONE NIGHT AT SUSIE'S, 1930
ONE NIGHT STAND, 1976
ONE PLUS ONE, 1961
ONE PLUS ONE, 1969
ONE POTATO, TWO POTATO, 1964
ONE PRECIOUS YEAR, 1933
ONE SINGS, THE OTHER DOESN'T, 1977
ONE SUMMER LOVE, 1976
ONE SUNDAY AFTERNOON, 1933
ONE THIRD OF A NATION, 1939
1,000 CONVICTS AND A WOMAN, 1971
ONE TOO MANY, 1950
ONE-TRICK PONY, 1980
1 2 3 MONSTER EXPRESS, 1977
ONE WAY PASSAGE, 1932
ONE-WAY TICKET, A, 1988
ONE WAY TICKET TO HELL, 1955
ONE WOMAN'S STORY, 1949
ONE YEAR LATER, 1933
ONIMASA, 1983
ONIONHEAD, 1958
ONLY ANGELS HAVE WINGS, 1939
ONLY GAME IN TOWN, THE, 1970
ONLY ONCE IN A LIFETIME, 1979
ONLY ONE NIGHT, 1942
ONLY THING YOU KNOW, THE, 1971
ONLY WAY, THE, 1970
ONLY WAY HOME, THE, 1972
ONLY WHEN I LAUGH, 1981
ONLY YESTERDAY, 1933
ONE MAN'S WAY, 1964
OPEN ALL NIGHT, 1934
OPEN CITY, 1945
OPEN ROAD, THE, 1940
OPEN SECRET, 1948

BOLD: Films on Videocassette

OPENING NIGHT, 1977
OPERATION DISASTER, 1951
OPERATION EICHMANN, 1961
OPERATION ENEMY FORT, 1964
OPERATION HAYLIFT, 1950
OPERATION MANHUNT, 1954
OPERATION THUNDERBOLT, 1978
OPERATION X, 1951
OPERATOR 13, 1934
OPHELIA, 1964
OPIATE '67, 1967
OPTIMISTIC TRAGEDY, THE, 1964
OPTIMISTS, THE, 1973
ORCHIDS TO YOU, 1935
ORDERED TO LOVE, 1963
ORDERS, THE, 1977
ORDET, 1957
ORDINARY PEOPLE, 1980
ORGANIZER, THE, 1964
ORIANE, 1985
ORIENT EXPRESS, 1934
ORPHAN OF THE WILDERNESS, 1937
ORPHANS, 1987
OSCAR, THE, 1966
O'SHAUGHNESSY'S BOY, 1935
OSSESSIONE, 1959
OTHELLO, 1955
OTHELLO, 1960
OTHELLO, 1965
OTHER LOVE, THE, 1947
OTHER MEN'S WOMEN, 1931
OTHER ONE, THE, 1967
OTHER SIDE OF MIDNIGHT, THE, 1977
OTHER SIDE OF THE UNDERNEATH, THE, 1972
OTHER TOMORROW, THE, 1930
OTHER WOMAN, THE, 1931
OUANGA, 1936
OUR BLUSHING BRIDES, 1930
OUR DAILY BREAD, 1934
OUR DAILY BREAD, 1950
OUR HITLER, A FILM FROM GERMANY, 1980
OUR LEADING CITIZEN, 1939
OUR LITTLE GIRL, 1935
OUR MOTHER'S HOUSE, 1967
OUR NEIGHBORS—THE CARTERS, 1939
OUR SILENT LOVE, 1969
OUR TIME, 1974
OUR TOWN, 1940
OUR VERY OWN, 1950
OUR VINES HAVE TENDER GRAPES, 1945
OUR WINNING SEASON, 1978
OUT, 1982
OUT OF IT, 1969
OUT OF ORDER, 1985
OUT OF SEASON, 1975
OUT OF THE BLUE, 1982
OUT OF THE CLOUDS, 1957
OUT OF THE PAST, 1933
OUT OF THE TIGER'S MOUTH, 1962
OUT WEST WITH THE HARDYS, 1938
OUT WEST WITH THE PEPPERS, 1940
OUTBACK, 1971
OUTCAST, 1937
OUTCAST LADY, 1934
OUTCAST OF THE ISLANDS, 1952
OUTCRY, 1949
OUTER GATE, THE, 1937
OUTLAW BLUES, 1977
OUTLAW: THE SAGE OF GISLI, 1982
OUTPOST IN MALAYA, 1952
OUTRAGE, 1950
OUTRAGEOUS!, 1977
OUTSIDE IN, 1972
OUTSIDE THE WALL, 1950
OUTSIDE THESE WALLS, 1939
OUTSIDER, THE, 1933
OUTSIDER, THE, 1940
OUTSIDER, THE, 1949
OUTSIDER, THE, 1980
OUTSIDERS, THE, 1983
OUTSIDERS, THE, 1987
OUTWARD BOUND, 1930
OVER-EXPOSED, 1956
OVER THE EDGE, 1979
OVER THE HILL, 1931
OVER THE SUMMER, 1986

OVER-UNDER, SIDEWAYS-DOWN, 1977
OVERCOAT, THE, 1965
OVERTURE TO GLORY, 1940
OXFORD BLUES, 1984
PACIFIC DESTINY, 1956
PACIFIC LINER, 1939
PADRE PADRONE, 1977
PAGAN LADY, 1931
PAID IN FULL, 1950
PAID TO DANCE, 1937
PAINTED FACES, 1929
PAINTED VEIL, THE, 1934
PAINTED WOMAN, 1932
PALM BEACH, 1979
PALM SPRINGS WEEKEND, 1963
PANAMA FLO, 1932
PANAMA LADY, 1939
PANAMA SAL, 1957
PANDORA AND THE FLYING DUTCHMAN, 1951
PANIC IN NEEDLE PARK, 1971
PANIC IN THE STREETS, 1950
PAPER CHASE, THE, 1973
PAPER MOON, 1973
PAPER TIGER, 1975
PAPERBACK HERO, 1973
PARACHUTE JUMPER, 1933
PARACHUTE NURSE, 1942
PARADES, 1972
PARADINE CASE, THE, 1947
PARADISE, 1982
PARADISE ALLEY, 1962
PARADISE EXPRESS, 1937
PARADISE ISLE, 1937
PARALLELS, 1980
PARENTS ON TRIAL, 1939
PARIS BLUES, 1961
PARIS DOES STRANGE THINGS, 1957
PARIS INTERLUDE, 1934
PARIS MODEL, 1953
PARIS, TEXAS, 1984
PARIS UNDERGROUND, 1945
PARISIAN, THE, 1931
PARISIAN ROMANCE, A, 1932
PARK AVENUE LOGGER, 1937
PARK ROW, 1952
PARRISH, 1961
PARTING GLANCES, 1986
PARTINGS, 1962
PARTNERS, 1976
PARTY CRASHERS, THE, 1958
PARTY GIRL, 1930
PARTY HUSBAND, 1931
PARTY WIRE, 1935
PARTY'S OVER, THE, 1966
PARTY'S OVER, THE, 1934
PASCALI'S ISLAND, 1988
PASSAGE, THE, 1979
PASSAGE HOME, 1955
PASSAGE TO INDIA, A, 1984
PASSAGE TO MARSEILLE, 1944
PASSENGER, THE, 1970
PASSENGER, THE, 1975
PASSING OF THE THIRD FLOOR BACK, THE, 1936
PASSION, 1968
PASSION, 1983
PASSION FLOWER, 1930
PASSION FOR LIFE, 1951
PASSION OF ANNA, THE, 1970
PASSION OF LOVE, 1982
PASSION STREET, U.S.A., 1964
PASSIONATE DEMONS, THE, 1962
PASSIONATE STRANGERS, THE, 1968
PASSIONATE SUMMER, 1959
PASSOVER PLOT, THE, 1976
PASSPORT TO DESTINY, 1944
PASSPORT TO HELL, 1932
PAST OF MARY HOLMES, THE, 1933
PASTEUR, 1936
PATCH OF BLUE, A, 1965
PATHER PANCHALI, 1958
PATTERNS, 1956
PAUL AND MICHELLE, 1974
PAULA, 1952
PAULINE AT THE BEACH, 1983
PAWNBROKER, THE, 1965
PAYDAY, 1972

PAYMENT DEFERRED, 1932
PAYMENT ON DEMAND, 1951
PAYOFF, THE, 1935
PEARL, THE, 1948
PECK'S BAD BOY, 1934
PECK'S BAD BOY WITH THE CIRCUS, 1938
PEDDLIN' IN SOCIETY, 1949
PEDESTRIAN, THE, 1974
PEKING EXPRESS, 1951
PENDULUM, 1969
PENITENT, THE, 1988
PENITENTE MURDER CASE, THE, 1936
PENNY SERENADE, 1941
PENNYWHISTLE BLUES, THE, 1952
PENTHOUSE PARTY, 1936
PEOPLE MEET AND SWEET MUSIC FILLS THE
   HEART, 1969
PEOPLE NEXT DOOR, THE, 1970
PEOPLE VS. DR. KILDARE, THE, 1941
PEPPERMINT SODA, 1979
PERFECT, 1985
PERFECT UNDERSTANDING, 1933
PERFECTIONIST, THE, 1952
PERFORMERS, THE, 1970
PERIOD OF ADJUSTMENT, 1962
PERMANENT RECORD, 1988
PERMANENT VACATION, 1982
PERSONA, 1967
PERSONAL AFFAIR, 1954
PERSONAL FOUL, 1987
PERSONAL MAID, 1931
PERSONAL MAID'S SECRET, 1935
PERSONAL SECRETARY, 1938
PERSONALITY, 1930
PERSONALITY KID, THE, 1934
PETE 'N' TILLIE, 1972
PETERSEN, 1974
PETULIA, 1968
PEYTON PLACE, 1957
PHAEDRA, 1962
PHANTOM IN THE HOUSE, THE, 1929
PHANTOM OF LIBERTY, THE, 1974
PHILADELPHIA ATTRACTION, THE, 1985
PHONE CALL FROM A STRANGER, 1952
PHONY AMERICAN, THE, 1964
PHOTOGRAPH, THE, 1987
PICCADILLY, 1932
PICCADILLY INCIDENT, 1948
PICKUP, 1951
PICKUP ON 101, 1972
PICNIC, 1955
PICNIC AT HANGING ROCK, 1975
PICNIC ON THE GRASS, 1960
PICTURE SHOW MAN, THE, 1980
PICTURE SNATCHER, 1933
PIE IN THE SKY, 1964
PIECE OF THE ACTION, A, 1977
PIECES OF DREAMS, 1970
PIED PIPER, THE, 1972
PIGS, 1984
PILGRIM, FAREWELL, 1980
PILGRIMAGE, 1933
PILGRIMAGE, 1972
PILLARS OF SOCIETY, 1936
PILOT, THE, 1979
PINKY, 1949
PIPE DREAMS, 1976
PIRATES OF THE SKIES, 1939
PITTSBURGH, 1942
PIXOTE, 1981
PIZZA TRIANGLE, THE, 1970
P.K. & THE KID, 1987
PLACE IN THE SUN, A, 1951
PLACE OF WEEPING, 1986
PLACES IN THE HEART, 1984
PLAGUE DOGS, THE, 1984
PLASTIC DOME OF NORMA JEAN, THE, 1966
PLATINUM HIGH SCHOOL, 1960
PLAY DEAD, 1981
PLAY GIRL, 1932
PLAY GIRL, 1940
PLAY IT AS IT LAYS, 1972
PLAY IT COOL, 1963
PLAY IT COOL, 1970
PLAYGIRL, 1954
PLAYING FOR KEEPS, 1986

PLAYTIME, 1963
PLEASANTVILLE, 1976
PLEASE STAND BY, 1972
PLEASURE, 1933
PLEASURE CRAZED, 1929
PLEASURE GIRLS, THE, 1966
PLEASURE PLANTATION, 1970
PLEASURES AND VICES, 1962
PLEASURES OF THE FLESH, THE, 1965
PLEDGEMASTERS, THE, 1971
PLENTY, 1985
PLOUGHMAN'S LUNCH, THE, 1984
POCOMANIA, 1939
POET'S SILENCE, THE, 1987
POIL DE CAROTTE, 1932
POINTING FINGER, THE, 1934
POISON PEN, 1941
POISONED DIAMOND, THE, 1934
POITIN, 1979
POLLY OF THE CIRCUS, 1932
POLYESTER, 1981
POM POM GIRLS, THE, 1976
POOR COW, 1968
POPE OF GREENWICH VILLAGE, THE, 1984
POPPY, 1936
PORT OF CALL, 1963
PORT OF DESIRE, 1960
PORT OF HATE, 1939
PORT OF HELL, 1955
PORT OF MISSING GIRLS, 1938
PORT OF SEVEN SEAS, 1938
PORT OF SHADOWS, 1938
PORT SAID, 1948
PORTIA ON TRIAL, 1937
PORTRAIT IN SMOKE, 1957
PORTRAIT OF A SINNER, 1961
PORTRAIT OF A WOMAN, 1946
PORTRAIT OF CLARE, 1951
PORTRAIT OF HELL, 1969
PORTRAIT OF MARIA, 1946
PORTRAIT OF THE ARTIST AS A YOUNG MAN, A,
   1979
POSSESSED, 1931
POSSESSED, 1947
POSTMAN DIDN'T RING, THE, 1942
POURQUOI PAS!, 1979
P.O.W., THE, 1973
POWER, 1986
POWER AND THE GLORY, THE, 1933
POWER AND THE PRIZE, THE, 1956
POWER DIVE, 1941
POWER OF EVIL, THE, 1985
PRAYING MANTIS, 1982
PREACHERMAN, 1971
PREJUDICE, 1949
PRELUDE TO ECSTASY, 1963
PRELUDE TO FAME, 1950
PRESIDENT VANISHES, THE, 1934
PRESSURE, 1976
PRESSURE POINT, 1962
PRETTY BABY, 1978
PRETTY BUT WICKED, 1965
PRETTY IN PINK, 1986
PRICE OF FLESH, THE, 1962
PRICE OF THINGS, THE, 1930
PRICE OF WISDOM, THE, 1935
PRIDE AND PREJUDICE, 1940
PRIDE OF THE MARINES, 1936
PRIDE OF THE NAVY, 1939
PRIEST OF ST. PAULI, THE, 1970
PRIME OF MISS JEAN BRODIE, THE, 1969
PRIME TIME, THE, 1960
PRIMROSE PATH, 1940
PRINCE OF PLAYERS, 1955
PRINCIPAL, THE, 1987
PRISM, 1971
PRISONER, THE, 1955
PRISONERS, 1929
PRIVATE ACCESS, 1988
PRIVATE AFFAIRS OF BEL AMI, THE, 1947
PRIVATE DUTY NURSES, 1972
PRIVATE ENTERPRISE, A, 1975
PRIVATE INFORMATION, 1952
PRIVATE NURSE, 1941
PRIVATE PROPERTY, 1960
PRIVATE RIGHT, THE, 1967

PRIVATE ROAD, 1971
PRIVATE SHOW, 1985
PRIVATE WORLDS, 1935
PRIVILEGED, 1982
PROBLEM GIRLS, 1953
PRODIGAL, THE, 1931
PRODIGAL, THE, 1984
PRODIGAL SON, THE, 1935
PRODIGAL SON, THE, 1964
PROJECTIONIST, THE, 1970
PROLOGUE, 1970
PROMISE AT DAWN, 1970
PROMISED LAND, 1988
PROMISES IN THE DARK, 1979
PROMOTER, THE, 1952
PROPER TIME, THE, 1959
PROPERTY, 1979
PROSTITUTE, 1980
PROSTITUTION, 1965
PROUD VALLEY, THE, 1941
PROVIDENCE, 1977
PSYCH-OUT, 1968
PSYCHE 59, 1964
PSYCHOUT FOR MURDER, 1971
PUBLIC OPINION, 1935
PUBLIC STENOGRAPHER, 1935
PULSEBEAT, 1986
PUMPKIN EATER, THE, 1964
PUNISHMENT PARK, 1971
PURCHASE PRICE, THE, 1932
PURPLE HAZE, 1982
PURPLE TAXI, THE, 1977
PURSE STRINGS, 1933
PURSUED, 1934
PURSUIT OF HAPPINESS, THE, 1971
PUSHER, THE, 1960
PUSSYCAT ALLEY, 1965
PUT UP OR SHUT UP, 1968
PUZZLE OF A DOWNFALL CHILD, 1970
**QUACKSER FORTUNE HAS A COUSIN IN THE
   BRONX, 1970**
QUADROON, 1972
QUADROPHENIA, 1979
QUALCOSA DI BIONDO, 1985
QUALITY STREET, 1937
QUARTET, 1949
QUARTET, 1981
QUARTIERE, 1987
QUEEN BEE, 1955
QUEEN FOR A DAY, 1951
QUEEN OF BROADWAY, 1942
QUEEN OF SPADES, 1948
QUEEN OF SPADES, 1961
QUEENS, THE, 1968
QUEEN'S GUARDS, THE, 1963
QUERELLE, 1983
QUESTION, THE, 1977
QUESTION OF ADULTERY, A, 1959
QUESTION 7, 1961
QUICK MONEY, 1938
QUICKSILVER, 1986
QUIET AMERICAN, THE, 1958
QUIET DAY IN BELFAST, A, 1974
QUITTERS, THE, 1934
RABBIT, RUN, 1970
RABBIT TRAP, THE, 1959
RABBLE, THE, 1965
RACHEL, RACHEL, 1968
RACING WITH THE MOON, 1984
RACK, THE, 1956
RAGE, 1966
RAGE, 1972
RAGE TO LIVE, A, 1965
RAGGEDY MAN, 1981
RAILROAD MAN, THE, 1965
RAIN, 1932
RAIN FOR A DUSTY SUMMER, 1971
RAIN MAN, 1988
RAIN OR SHINE, 1930
RAIN PEOPLE, THE, 1969
RAINBOW MAN, 1929
RAINS CAME, THE, 1939
RAINS OF RANCHIPUR, THE, 1955
RAISIN IN THE SUN, A, 1961
RAMPANT AGE, THE, 1930
RANDOM HARVEST, 1942

RANSOM, 1956
RAPE, THE, 1965
RAPTURE, 1950
RAPTURE, 1965
RARE BREED, 1984
RASCAL, 1969
RASCALS, 1938
RASHOMON, 1951
RAT FINK, 1965
RATBOY, 1986
RATS, THE, 1955
RATTLE OF A SIMPLE MAN, 1964
RAVEN'S END, 1970
RAW COURAGE, 1984
RAW WEEKEND, 1964
RAW WIND IN EDEN, 1958
RAYMIE, 1960
RAZOR'S EDGE, THE, 1946
RAZOR'S EDGE, THE, 1984
REACH FOR GLORY, 1963
REACHING FOR THE SUN, 1941
REACHING OUT, 1983
READY FOR LOVE, 1934
REAL BLOKE, A, 1935
REALM OF FORTUNE, THE, 1986
REAP THE WILD WIND, 1942
REASONABLE DOUBT, 1936
REBECCA OF SUNNYBROOK FARM, 1932
REBEL, THE, 1933
REBEL ANGEL, 1962
REBEL WITHOUT A CAUSE, 1955
REBELLION, 1967
REBELLION OF THE HANGED, THE, 1954
REBELLIOUS DAUGHTERS, 1938
REBOUND, 1931
RECAPTURED LOVE, 1930
RECESS, 1967
RECKLESS, 1984
RECKLESS HOUR, THE, 1931
RECKLESS LIVING, 1938
RED, 1970
RED AND THE BLACK, THE, 1954
RED DESERT, 1965
RED DUST, 1932
RED-HAIRED ALIBI, THE, 1932
RED HEAD, 1934
RED HEADED WOMAN, 1932
RED KISS, 1985
RED LANTERNS, 1965
RED LIPS, 1964
RED MENACE, THE, 1949
RED SKY AT MORNING, 1971
RED SORGHUM, 1988
RED WAGON, 1936
REDEMPTION, 1930
REEFER MADNESS, 1936
REFLECTIONS, 1984
REFLECTIONS IN A GOLDEN EYE, 1967
REFORM SCHOOL, 1939
REFORM SCHOOL GIRL, 1957
REFUGE, 1981
REGISTERED NURSE, 1934
REIVERS, THE, 1969
RELUCTANT SAINT, THE, 1962
REMEDY FOR RICHES, 1941
REMEMBER THE DAY, 1941
REMEMBRANCE, 1982
REMOVALISTS, THE, 1975
RENALDO AND CLARA, 1978
RENDEZVOUS, 1985
RENO, 1930
RENO, 1939
"'RENT-A-GIRL", 1965
REPEAT PERFORMANCE, 1947
REPENT AT LEISURE, 1941
REPORT ON THE PARTY AND THE GUESTS, A, 1968
RESCUE SQUAD, 1935
REST IS SILENCE, THE, 1960
RESTLESS YEARS, THE, 1958
RESURRECTION, 1980
RETURN OF CAROL DEANE, THE, 1938
RETURN OF CASEY JONES, 1933
RETURN OF THE SECAUCUS SEVEN, 1980
RETURN OF THE SOLDIER, THE, 1983
RETURN TO MACON COUNTY, 1975
RETURN TO PEYTON PLACE, 1961

BOLD: Films on Videocassette

RETURN TO YESTERDAY, 1940
REUNION, 1932
REUNION, 1936
REVERSE BE MY LOT, THE, 1938
REVOLT OF JOB, THE, 1984
REVOLT OF MAMIE STOVER, THE, 1956
REVOLT OF THE MERCENARIES, 1964
REVOLVING DOORS, THE, 1988
REWARD, THE, 1965
RHINOCEROS, 1974
RICE GIRL, 1963
RICH AND FAMOUS, 1981
RICH AND STRANGE, 1932
RICH ARE ALWAYS WITH US, THE, 1932
RICH KIDS, 1979
RICH MAN'S FOLLY, 1931
RICHARD'S THINGS, 1981
RICKSHAW MAN, THE, 1960
RIDE A CROOKED MILE, 1938
RIDE IN A PINK CAR, 1974
RIDE THE HIGH IRON, 1956
RIFF-RAFF, 1936
RIFFRAFF, 1947
RIGHT APPROACH, THE, 1961
RIGHT OF WAY, THE, 1931
RIGHT TO LIVE, THE, 1935
RIGHT TO LOVE, THE, 1931
RIGHT TO ROMANCE, 1933
RING OF BRIGHT WATER, 1969
RINGSIDE, 1949
RIO, 1939
RIOT ON SUNSET STRIP, 1967
RIP-OFF, 1971
RIP TIDE, 1934
RISING OF THE MOON, THE, 1957
RITUAL, THE, 1970
RIVALS, 1972
RIVER, THE, 1951
RIVER, THE, 1961
RIVER, THE, 1984
RIVER CHANGES, THE, 1956
RIVER NIGER, THE, 1976
RIVER OF FOREVER, 1967
RIVER OF ROMANCE, 1929
RIVER OF UNREST, 1937
RIVER WOMAN, THE, 1928
RIVERRUN, 1968
RIVER'S EDGE, 1987
ROAD BACK, THE, 1937
ROAD HOUSE, 1934
ROAD HUSTLERS, THE, 1968
ROAD MOVIE, 1974
ROAD TO FORTUNE, THE, 1930
ROAD TO HAPPINESS, 1942
ROAD TO LIFE, 1932
ROAD TO PARADISE, 1930
ROAD TO RENO, 1931
ROAD TO RUIN, 1934
ROAD TO SALINA, 1971
ROAD TO SINGAPORE, 1931
ROADHOUSE 66, 1984
ROBINSON'S GARDEN, 1988
ROCCO AND HIS BROTHERS, 1961
ROCCO PAPALEO, 1974
ROCKABYE, 1932
ROCKING HORSE WINNER, THE, 1950
ROCKY, 1948
ROLLER BOOGIE, 1979
ROLLING THUNDER, 1977
ROLLOVER, 1981
ROMA, 1972
ROMAN SPRING OF MRS. STONE, THE, 1961
ROMANCE OF A HORSE THIEF, 1971
ROMANCE OF ROSY RIDGE, THE, 1947
ROOKIE COP, THE, 1939
ROOKIE FIREMAN, 1950
ROOM AT THE TOP, 1959
ROOM FOR ONE MORE, 1952
ROOM 43, 1959
ROOM IN THE HOUSE, 1955
ROOM UPSTAIRS, THE, 1948
ROOMMATES, 1962
ROOMMATES, 1971
ROOT OF ALL EVIL, THE, 1947
ROOTS OF HEAVEN, THE, 1958
ROPE OF FLESH, 1965

ROSARY, THE, 1931
ROSE TATTOO, THE, 1955
ROSELAND, 1977
ROSES FOR THE PROSECUTOR, 1961
ROSIE!, 1967
ROTTEN APPLE, THE, 1963
ROUGE OF THE NORTH, 1988
'ROUND MIDNIGHT, 1986
ROUND TRIP, 1967
ROWDYMAN, THE, 1973
ROYAL FAMILY OF BROADWAY, THE, 1930
R.P.M., 1970
RUBBER GUN, THE, 1977
RUBY GENTRY, 1952
RUDE BOY, 1980
RUGGED O'RIORDANS, THE, 1949
RULES OF THE GAME, THE, 1939
RUMBA, 1935
RUMBLE FISH, 1983
RUN FOR THE HILLS, 1953
RUN WILD, RUN FREE, 1969
RUN WITH THE DEVIL, 1963
RUN WITH THE WIND, 1966
RUNAROUND, THE, 1931
RUNAWAY DAUGHTERS, 1957
RUNAWAY GIRL, 1966
RUNNER STUMBLES, THE, 1979
RUNNERS, 1983
RUNNING ON EMPTY, 1988
RUNNING OUT OF LUCK, 1986
RUNNING SCARED, 1972
RUSSKIES, 1987
RUTHLESS, 1948
SAADIA, 1953
SABINA, THE, 1979
SABRE JET, 1953
SACRED FLAME, THE, 1929
SACRED GROUND, 1984
SACRED HEARTS, 1984
SACRIFICE, THE, 1986
SAD HORSE, THE, 1959
SADIE MCKEE, 1934
SAFE PLACE, A, 1971
SAGA OF THE VAGABONDS, 1964
SAILOR FROM GIBRALTAR, THE, 1967
SAILOR WHO FELL FROM GRACE WITH THE SEA, THE, 1976
SAILOR'S RETURN, THE, 1978
ST. ELMO'S FIRE, 1985
ST. LOUIS KID, THE, 1934
SAL OF SINGAPORE, 1929
SALAAM BOMBAY, 1988
SALLY'S HOUNDS, 1968
SALOME, WHERE SHE DANCED, 1945
SALT TO THE DEVIL, 1949
SALTO, 1966
SALUTE JOHN CITIZEN, 1942
SALUTE TO THE MARINES, 1943
SALVADOR, 1986
SALVATION NELL, 1931
SAME TIME, NEXT YEAR, 1978
SAME TO YOU, 1987
SAMMY AND ROSIE GET LAID, 1987
SAM'S SONG, 1971
SAMURAI, 1955
SAMURAI FROM NOWHERE, 1964
SAMURAI (PART II), 1967
SAMURAI (PART III), 1967
SANCTUARY, 1961
SANDPIPER, THE, 1965
SANDRA, 1966
SANDS OF BEERSHEBA, 1966
SANDWICH MAN, THE, 1966
SANGAREE, 1953
SANSHO THE BAILIFF, 1969
SANTA, 1932
SARAH AND SON, 1930
SATAN NEVER SLEEPS, 1962
SATIN MUSHROOM, THE, 1969
SATURDAY NIGHT AND SUNDAY MORNING, 1961
SATURDAY NIGHT AT THE BATHS, 1975
SATURDAY NIGHT AT THE PALACE, 1988
SATURDAY NIGHT FEVER, 1977
SATURDAY NIGHT OUT, 1964
SATURDAY NIGHT REVUE, 1937
SAVAGE BRIGADE, 1948

SAVAGE EYE, THE, 1960
SAVAGE SEVEN, THE, 1968
SAVANNAH SMILES, 1983
SAVE THE TIGER, 1973
SAVING GRACE, 1986
SAXO, 1988
SAXON CHARM, THE, 1948
SAY HELLO TO YESTERDAY, 1971
SAYONARA, 1957
SCALPEL, 1976
SCANDAL, 1929
SCANDAL, 1964
SCANDAL AT SCOURIE, 1953
SCANDAL IN DENMARK, 1970
SCANDAL STREET, 1938
SCANDALOUS ADVENTURES OF BURAIKAN, THE, 1970
SCARECROW, 1973
SCARLET LETTER, THE, 1934
SCARLET PAGES, 1930
SCARRED, 1984
SCATTERGOOD BAINES, 1941
SCATTERGOOD MEETS BROADWAY, 1941
SCATTERGOOD PULLS THE STRINGS, 1941
SCATTERGOOD RIDES HIGH, 1942
SCENES FROM A MARRIAGE, 1974
SCENIC ROUTE, THE, 1978
SCENT OF A WOMAN, 1976
SCHOOL FOR SECRETS, 1946
SCHOOL FOR SEX, 1966
SCHOOLGIRL DIARY, 1947
SCOUNDREL, THE, 1935
SCRAMBLE, 1970
SCRATCH HARRY, 1969
SCRUBBERS, 1984
SCRUFFY, 1938
SCUDDA-HOO? SCUDDA-HAY?, 1948
SEA GHOST, THE, 1931
SEA WOLF, THE, 1941
SEABO, 1978
SEALED VERDICT, 1948
SEARCH, THE, 1948
SEARCHING WIND, THE, 1946
SEASON FOR LOVE, THE, 1963
SEASON OF PASSION, 1961
SECOND CHOICE, 1930
SECOND COMING OF SUZANNE, THE, 1974
SECOND FACE, THE, 1950
SECOND HAND WIFE, 1933
SECOND MRS. TANQUERAY, THE, 1952
SECOND THOUGHTS, 1983
SECOND WIFE, 1930
SECOND WIFE, 1936
SECOND WIND, A, 1978
SECRET CALL, THE, 1931
SECRET CEREMONY, 1968
SECRET GARDEN, THE, 1949
SECRET HEART, THE, 1946
SECRET OF DR. KILDARE, THE, 1939
SECRET OF MADAME BLANCHE, THE, 1933
SECRET PLACES, 1984
SECRET WITNESS, THE, 1931
SECRET WORLD, 1969
SECRETS, 1971
SECRETS, 1984
SECRETS D'ALCOVE, 1954
SECRETS OF A MODEL, 1940
SECRETS OF A SECRETARY, 1931
SECRETS OF SEX, 1970
SECRETS OF WOMEN, 1961
SECRETS SECRETS, 1985
SEDUCED AND ABANDONED, 1964
SEED, 1931
SEED OF INNOCENCE, 1980
SELF-MADE LADY, 1932
SELF-PORTRAIT, 1973
SENSATION HUNTERS, 1934
SENSO, 1968
SENSUALITA, 1954
SENTIMENTAL JOURNEY, 1946
SEPARATE PEACE, A, 1972
SEPARATE TABLES, 1958
SEPARATION, 1968
SEPIA CINDERELLA, 1947
SEPTEMBER, 1987
SERAFINO, 1970

SERENITY, 1962
SERGEANT JIM, 1962
SERGEANT MIKE, 1945
SERGEANT RYKER, 1968
SERGEANT, THE, 1968
SERPENT'S EGG, THE, 1977
SERPENTS OF THE PIRATE MOON, THE, 1973
SERPENT'S WAY, THE, 1987
SERVANT, THE, 1964
SERVANTS' ENTRANCE, 1934
SERVICE DE LUXE, 1938
SET, THE, 1970
SEVEN AGAINST THE SUN, 1968
SEVEN BEAUTIES, 1976
SEVEN DAYS LEAVE, 1930
SEVEN DEADLY SINS, THE, 1953
SEVEN MINUTES IN HEAVEN, 1986
SEVEN MINUTES, THE, 1971
SEVEN NIGHTS IN JAPAN, 1976
SEVEN SAMURAI, THE, 1956
SEVEN SINNERS, 1940
7254, 1971
SEVENTEEN, 1940
SEVENTH SEAL, THE, 1958
SEVENTH SIN, THE, 1957
SEVENTH VEIL, THE, 1946
77 PARK LANE, 1931
SHADES OF SILK, 1979
SHADOW IN THE SKY, 1951
SHADOW OF VICTORY, 1986
SHADOWS, 1960
SHADOWS GROW LONGER, THE, 1962
SHADOWS OF FORGOTTEN ANCESTORS, 1967
SHAKE HANDS WITH THE DEVIL, 1959
SHAKESPEARE WALLAH, 1966
SHAME, 1968
SHAME, 1988
SHAME, SHAME, EVERYBODY KNOWS HER NAME, 1969
SHAMELESS OLD LADY, THE, 1966
SHAMPOO, 1975
SHANGHAI EXPRESS, 1932
SHANGHAI LADY, 1929
SHANGHAIED LOVE, 1931
SHANGRI-LA, 1961
SHANTY TRAMP, 1967
SHANTYTOWN, 1943
SHE AND HE, 1967
SHE AND HE, 1969
SHE COULDN'T SAY NO, 1930
SHE COULDN'T SAY NO, 1954
SHE DANCES ALONE, 1981
SHE GOT WHAT SHE WANTED, 1930
SHE HAD TO CHOOSE, 1934
SHE LEARNED ABOUT SAILORS, 1934
SHE LOVED A FIREMAN, 1937
SHE MADE HER BED, 1934
SHE MARRIED AN ARTIST, 1938
SHE WANTED A MILLIONAIRE, 1932
SHE WAS A LADY, 1934
SHE-WOLF, THE, 1931
SHEEPDOG OF THE HILLS, 1941
SHEP COMES HOME, 1949
SHEPHERD OF THE HILLS, THE, 1964
SHERLOCK HOLMES, 1932
SHE'S A SOLDIER TOO, 1944
SHE'S GOTTA HAVE IT, 1986
SHE'S IN THE ARMY, 1942
SHILLINGBURY BLOWERS, THE, 1980
SHINING HOUR, THE, 1938
SHINING VICTORY, 1941
SHIP OF CONDEMNED WOMEN, THE, 1963
SHIP OF FOOLS, 1965
SHIP OF WANTED MEN, 1933
SHIPBUILDERS, THE, 1943
SHIRALEE, THE, 1957
SHIVERS, 1984
SHOCK, 1934
SHOCK CORRIDOR, 1963
SHOES OF THE FISHERMAN, THE, 1968
SHOOT, 1976
SHOOT THE MOON, 1982
SHOOTING PARTY, THE, 1985
SHOOTING STRAIGHT, 1930
SHOP ANGEL, 1932
SHOP ON MAIN STREET, THE, 1966

SHOPWORN ANGEL, 1938
SHORT IS THE SUMMER, 1968
SHOULD A DOCTOR TELL?, 1931
SHOULD A GIRL MARRY?, 1939
SHOUT AT THE DEVIL, 1976
SHOW GOES ON, THE, 1938
SHRIKE, THE, 1955
SHY PEOPLE, 1988
SIDE STREETS, 1934
SIGN OF THE RAM, THE, 1948
SIGNAL 7, 1984
SIGNS OF LIFE, 1981
SILENCE HAS NO WINGS, 1971
SILENCE OF DEAN MAITLAND, THE, 1934
SILENCE, THE, 1964
SILENT INVASION, THE, 1962
SILK EXPRESS, THE, 1933
SILK HAT KID, 1935
SILVER CORD, 1933
SILVER DUST, 1953
SILVER LINING, 1932
SILVER TOP, 1938
SIMBA, 1955
SIN OF MADELON CLAUDET, THE, 1931
SIN OF MONA KENT, THE, 1961
SIN ON THE BEACH, 1964
SINCE YOU WENT AWAY, 1944
SINCERELY CHARLOTTE, 1986
SINGAPORE, 1947
SINGAPORE WOMAN, 1941
SINGER AND THE DANCER, THE, 1977
SINGING BLACKSMITH, 1938
SINGING IN THE DARK, 1956
SINGLE ROOM FURNISHED, 1968
SINISTER URGE, THE, 1961
SINNERS IN PARADISE, 1938
SINS OF MAN, 1936
SINS OF ROSE BERND, THE, 1959
SINS OF THE CHILDREN, 1930
SINS OF THE FATHERS, 1928
SINS OF THE FATHERS, 1948
SISTERS, 1930
SISTERS, OR THE BALANCE OF HAPPINESS, 1982
SISTERS UNDER THE SKIN, 1934
SISTERS, THE, 1969
SIX IN PARIS, 1968
SIX PACK ANNIE, 1975
SIX WEEKS, 1982
SIXTH AND MAIN, 1977
'68, 1988
SKI BUM, THE, 1971
SKIN DEEP, 1978
SKIN GAME, THE, 1931
SKIP TRACER, THE, 1979
SKY BRIDE, 1932
SKY IS RED, THE, 1952
SKY PIRATE, THE, 1970
SKY SPIDER, THE, 1931
SKYDIVERS, THE, 1963
SKYLINE, 1931
SKYSCRAPER SOULS, 1932
SLANDER, 1956
SLAVES, 1969
SLENDER THREAD, THE, 1965
SLIGHTLY MARRIED, 1933
SLIM, 1937
SLIPSTREAM, 1974
SLOGAN, 1970
SLOW DANCING IN THE BIG CITY, 1978
SLOW MOVES, 1984
SLOW RUN, 1968
SLUMBER PARTY '57, 1977
SMALL CHANGE, 1976
SMALL CIRCLE OF FRIENDS, A, 1980
SMALL HOURS, THE, 1962
SMALL MAN, THE, 1935
SMALL TOWN BOY, 1937
SMART GIRL, 1935
SMART WOMAN, 1931
SMART WOMAN, 1948
SMASH PALACE, 1982
SMASH-UP, THE STORY OF A WOMAN, 1947
SMELL OF HONEY, A SWALLOW OF BRINE? A, 1966
SMILE OF THE LAMB, THE, 1986
SMILE ORANGE, 1976
SMILEY, 1957

SMILEY GETS A GUN, 1959
SMILIN' THROUGH, 1932
SMITHEREENS, 1982
SMITHY, 1933
SMOOTH TALK, 1985
SMUGGLED CARGO, 1939
SNAKE PIT, THE, 1948
SNOW, 1983
SNOW COUNTRY, 1969
SNOWFIRE, 1958
SO BIG, 1932
SO BIG, 1953
SO LITTLE TIME, 1953
SO LONG, BLUE BOY, 1973
SO PROUDLY WE HAIL, 1943
SO WELL REMEMBERED, 1947
SOAK THE RICH, 1936
SOAPBOX DERBY, 1958
SOCIAL REGISTER, 1934
SOCIETY DOCTOR, 1935
SOFI, 1967
SOFT SKIN ON BLACK SILK, 1964
SOFT SKIN, THE, 1964
SOLDIER IN THE RAIN, 1963
SOLDIER OF ORANGE, 1979
SOLDIER'S PLAYTHING, A, 1931
SOLDIER'S REVENGE, 1986
SOLO, 1978
SOME CAME RUNNING, 1959
SOME KIND OF HERO, 1982
SOME OF MY BEST FRIENDS ARE..., 1971
SOME PEOPLE, 1964
SOMEONE, 1968
SOMEONE TO REMEMBER, 1943
SOMETHING MONEY CAN'T BUY, 1952
SOMETHING OF VALUE, 1957
SOMETHING TO LIVE FOR, 1952
SOMETHING WILD, 1961
SOMETHING WILD, 1986
SOMEWHERE IN BERLIN, 1949
SON-DAUGHTER, THE, 1932
SON OF INDIA, 1931
SON OF LASSIE, 1945
SON OF MONGOLIA, 1936
SON OF THE GODS, 1930
SON OF THE NAVY, 1940
SONG AND THE SILENCE, THE, 1969
SONG FOR TOMORROW, A, 1948
SONG OF FREEDOM, 1938
SONG OF KENTUCKY, 1929
SONG OF LIFE, THE, 1931
SONG OF SONGS, 1933
SONG OF SURRENDER, 1949
SONG OF THE CITY, 1937
SONG OF THE EAGLE, 1933
SONG OF THE LOON, 1970
SONG OF THE ROAD, 1937
SONNY BOY, 1929
SONS AND LOVERS, 1960
SONS OF SATAN, 1969
SONS OF STEEL, 1935
SONS OF THE LEGION, 1938
SOOKY, 1931
SOPHIE'S CHOICE, 1982
SOPHIE'S WAYS, 1970
SORORITY GIRL, 1957
SORORITY HOUSE, 1939
SORRELL AND SON, 1934
S.O.S. TIDAL WAVE, 1939
SOTTO...SOTTO, 1985
SOULS AT SEA, 1937
SOUND AND FURY, 1988
SOUND AND THE FURY, THE, 1959
SOUND OF LIFE, THE, 1962
SOUND OF TRUMPETS, THE, 1963
SOUNDER, 1972
SOUNDER, PART 2, 1976
SOURSWEET, 1988
SOUTH BRONX HEROES, 1985
SOUTH RIDING, 1938
SOUTH SEA ROSE, 1929
SOUTH SEA SINNER, 1950
SOUTHERN COMFORT, 1981
SOUTHERNER, THE, 1945
SPACECAMP, 1986
SPANISH GARDENER, THE, 1957

BOLD: Films on Videocassette

SPARE THE ROD, 1961
SPARROWS CAN'T SING, 1963
SPECIAL DAY, A, 1977
SPEED MADNESS, 1932
SPEED TO SPARE, 1937
SPEED TO SPARE, 1948
SPELL OF AMY NUGENT, THE, 1945
SPELL OF THE HYPNOTIST, 1956
SPENCER'S MOUNTAIN, 1963
SPETTERS, 1983
SPIRIT OF CULVER, THE, 1939
SPIRIT OF THE BEEHIVE, THE, 1976
SPIRIT OF THE WIND, 1979
SPITFIRE, 1934
SPLENDID FELLOWS, 1934
SPLENDOR, 1935
SPLENDOR IN THE GRASS, 1961
SPLIT IMAGE, 1982
SPLITTING UP, 1981
SPOILED ROTTEN, 1968
SPOILERS OF THE FOREST, 1957
SPOILERS OF THE NORTH, 1947
SPOILS OF THE NIGHT, 1969
SPORTING CLUB, THE, 1971
SPRING AFFAIR, 1960
SPRING AND PORT WINE, 1970
SPRING FOR THE THIRSTY, A, 1988
SPRING MADNESS, 1938
SPRING REUNION, 1957
SPRING SHOWER, 1932
SPRINGTIME ON THE VOLGA, 1961
SQUALL, THE, 1929
SQUAMISH FIVE, THE, 1988
SQUARE DANCE, 1987
SQUATTER'S DAUGHTER, 1933
STABLEMATES, 1938
STACKING, 1987
STACY'S KNIGHTS, 1983
STAGE DOOR, 1937
STAGE MOTHER, 1933
STAGE STRUCK, 1958
STAIRCASE, 1969
STAKEOUT!, 1962
STALLION ROAD, 1947
STAMBOUL, 1931
STAND AND DELIVER, 1988
STAND UP AND BE COUNTED, 1972
STAR, THE, 1953
STAR DUST, 1940
STAR FOR A NIGHT, 1936
STAR IS BORN, A, 1937
STAR OF HONG KONG, 1962
STAR OF MY NIGHT, 1954
STARDUST, 1974
STARK FEAR, 1963
STARLIGHT HOTEL, 1987
STARS IN MY CROWN, 1950
STARS LOOK DOWN, THE, 1940
STATE OF THINGS, THE, 1983
STATELINE MOTEL, 1976
STATE'S ATTORNEY, 1932
STATION SIX-SAHARA, 1964
STAY AWAY, JOE, 1968
STAY HUNGRY, 1976
STAYING ALIVE, 1983
STEAMBOAT ROUND THE BEND, 1935
STEAMING, 1985
STEEL, 1980
STEEL AGAINST THE SKY, 1941
STEEL FIST, THE, 1952
STEEL TOWN, 1952
STELLA DALLAS, 1937
STEPCHILD, 1947
STEPCHILDREN, 1962
STEPPE, THE, 1963
STEPPENWOLF, 1974
STIGMA, 1972
STOKER, THE, 1932
STOLEN FACE, 1952
STOLEN HOLIDAY, 1937
STOLEN HOURS, 1963
STOLEN IDENTITY, 1953
STOLEN LIFE, 1939
STOLEN LIFE, A, 1946
STONE BOY, THE, 1984
STONY ISLAND, 1978

STOP TRAIN 349, 1964
STORM AT DAYBREAK, 1933
STORM CENTER, 1956
STORM WARNING, 1950
STORM, THE, 1930
STORMBOUND, 1951
STORMY, 1935
STORY OF A CHEAT, THE, 1938
STORY OF A THREE DAY PASS, THE, 1968
STORY OF A WOMAN, 1970
STORY OF ESTHER COSTELLO, THE, 1957
STORY OF FAUSTA, THE, 1988
STORY OF THREE LOVES, THE, 1953
STORY ON PAGE ONE, THE, 1959
STOWAWAY, 1932
STRAIGHT THROUGH THE HEART, 1985
STRAIGHT TO THE HEART, 1988
STRANDED, 1965
STRANGE AFFECTION, 1959
STRANGE CARGO, 1940
STRANGE CASE OF CLARA DEANE, THE, 1932
STRANGE CASE OF DR. MEADE, 1939
STRANGE CONQUEST, 1946
STRANGE DEATH OF ADOLF HITLER, THE, 1943
STRANGE DECEPTION, 1953
STRANGE FASCINATION, 1952
STRANGE INTERLUDE, 1932
STRANGE INTRUDER, 1956
STRANGE LOVE OF MOLLY LOUVAIN, THE, 1932
STRANGE LOVERS, 1963
STRANGE ONE, THE, 1957
STRANGE VENGEANCE OF ROSALIE, THE, 1972
STRANGE WOMAN, THE, 1946
STRANGER, THE, 1967
STRANGER IN HOLLYWOOD, 1968
STRANGER IN MY ARMS, 1959
STRANGER IN TOWN, 1932
STRANGER IN TOWN, A, 1943
STRANGER KNOCKS, A, 1963
STRANGER ON THE PROWL, 1953
STRANGER THAN PARADISE, 1984
STRANGER'S RETURN, 1933
STRANGERS ALL, 1935
STRANGERS IN THE CITY, 1962
STRANGERS IN THE NIGHT, 1944
STRANGERS MAY KISS, 1931
STRANGERS WHEN WE MEET, 1960
STRANGLEHOLD, 1931
STRATEGIC AIR COMMAND, 1955
STRAWBERRY ROAN, 1945
STREAMERS, 1983
STREAMLINE EXPRESS, 1935
STREET ANGEL, 1928
STREET CORNER, 1948
STREET FIGHTER, 1959
STREET IS MY BEAT, THE, 1966
STREET MUSIC, 1982
STREET OF CHANCE, 1930
STREET OF MEMORIES, 1940
STREET OF SINNERS, 1957
STREET OF WOMEN, 1932
STREET SCENE, 1931
STREET STORY, 1988
STREETCAR NAMED DESIRE, A, 1951
STREETWALKIN', 1985
STRICTLY UNCONVENTIONAL, 1930
STRIKE!, 1934
STRIKEBOUND, 1984
STRIPPER, THE, 1963
STROMBOLI, 1950
STRONGER SEX, THE, 1931
STRONGER THAN THE SUN, 1980
STRUGGLE, THE, 1931
STUD, THE, 1979
STUDENT NURSES, THE, 1970
STUDENT TEACHERS, THE, 1973
STUDS LONIGAN, 1960
STUNT MAN, THE, 1980
STUNTS, 1977
SUBJECT WAS ROSES, THE, 1968
SUBMARINE COMMAND, 1951
SUBMARINE D-1, 1937
SUBTERRANEANS, THE, 1960
SUBURBIA, 1984
SUCCESS AT ANY PRICE, 1934
SUCCESS IS THE BEST REVENGE, 1984

SUCCESSFUL MAN, A, 1987
SUCH A GORGEOUS KID LIKE ME, 1973
SUCH IS THE LAW, 1930
SUCH MEN ARE DANGEROUS, 1930
SUDDEN MONEY, 1939
SUDDENLY, A WOMAN!, 1967
SUDDENLY, LAST SUMMER, 1959
SUGAR CANE ALLEY, 1984
SUGARBABY, 1985
SUICIDE CLUB, THE, 1988
SUICIDE LEGION, 1940
SUITOR, THE, 1963
SULLIVANS, THE, 1944
SULLIVAN'S TRAVELS, 1941
SUMMER, 1986
SUMMER, 1988
SUMMER AND SMOKE, 1961
SUMMER CAMP NIGHTMARE, 1987
SUMMER HEAT, 1987
SUMMER LOVERS, 1982
SUMMER OF '42, 1971
SUMMER PLACE, A, 1959
SUMMER SOLDIERS, 1972
SUMMER STORM, 1944
SUMMER TO REMEMBER, A, 1961
SUMMER WISHES, WINTER DREAMS, 1973
SUMMER'S CHILDREN, 1979
SUMMERSKIN, 1962
SUMMERSPELL, 1983
SUMMERTREE, 1971
SUN ALSO RISES, THE, 1957
SUN COMES UP, THE, 1949
SUN SHINES BRIGHT, THE, 1953
SUN SHINES FOR ALL, THE, 1961
SUNDAY BLOODY SUNDAY, 1971
SUNDAY DINNER FOR A SOLDIER, 1944
SUNDAY IN THE COUNTRY, A, 1984
SUNDAY TOO FAR AWAY, 1975
SUNDAYS AND CYBELE, 1962
SUNDOWNERS, THE, 1960
SUNFLOWER, 1970
SUNNYSIDE, 1979
SUNSET BOULEVARD, 1950
SUNSET COVE, 1978
SUNSTRUCK, 1973
SUPPOSE THEY GAVE A WAR AND NOBODY CAME?, 1970
SURF PARTY, 1964
SURPRISE PARTY, 1985
SURVIVAL, 1976
SUSAN AND GOD, 1940
SUSAN SLADE, 1961
SUZY, 1936
SVENGALI, 1931
SVENGALI, 1955
SWAMP WATER, 1941
SWAMP WOMAN, 1941
SWANN IN LOVE, 1984
SWAPPERS, THE, 1970
SWEDENHIELMS, 1935
SWEDISH MISTRESS, THE, 1964
SWEDISH WEDDING NIGHT, 1965
SWEEPINGS, 1933
SWEET BIRD OF YOUTH, 1962
SWEET COUNTRY, 1987
SWEET ECSTASY, 1962
SWEET HUNTERS, 1969
SWEET LIGHT IN A DARK ROOM, 1966
SWEET LORRAINE, 1987
SWEET LOVE, BITTER, 1967
SWEET NOVEMBER, 1968
SWEET RIDE, THE, 1968
SWEET SKIN, 1965
SWEET SMELL OF SUCCESS, 1957
SWEET SUBSTITUTE, 1964
SWEET WILLIAM, 1980
SWEETHEART OF THE NAVY, 1937
SWELL GUY, 1946
SWEPT AWAY...BY AN UNUSUAL DESTINY IN THE BLUE SEA OF AUGUST, 1975
SWIMMER, THE, 1968
SWINDLE, THE, 1962
SWING SHIFT, 1984
SWISS HONEYMOON, 1947
SWORD OF DOOM, THE, 1967
SWORD OF HONOUR, 1938

SWORDKILL, 1984
SYLVESTER, 1985
SYLVIA, 1965
SYLVIA AND THE PHANTOM, 1950
SYLVIA SCARLETT, 1936
SYMPHONIE PASTORALE, 1948
SYMPHONY IN TWO FLATS, 1930
SYMPHONY OF LIFE, 1949
SYMPHONY OF LIVING, 1935
SYMPHONY OF SIX MILLION, 1932
SYNANON, 1965
TABLE FOR FIVE, 1983
TAHITIAN, THE, 1956
TAIL SPIN, 1939
TAILOR MADE MAN, A, 1931
TAKE A GIANT STEP, 1959
TAKE ALL OF ME, 1978
TAKE CARE OF MY LITTLE GIRL, 1951
TAKE HER BY SURPRISE, 1967
TAKE IT ALL, 1966
TAKE IT OR LEAVE IT, 1944
TAKE MY LIFE, 1942
TAKE THIS JOB AND SHOVE IT, 1981
TAKING OFF, 1971
TALE OF FIVE WOMEN, A, 1951
TALE OF RUBY ROSE, THE, 1987
TALES OF ORDINARY MADNESS, 1983
TALK ABOUT A STRANGER, 1952
TALK OF HOLLYWOOD, THE, 1929
TALK OF THE DEVIL, 1937
TALK RADIO, 1988
TALKING TO STRANGERS, 1988
TALKING WALLS, 1987
TALL TIMBERS, 1937
TAMANGO, 1959
TAMING SUTTON'S GAL, 1957
TAMING THE WILD, 1937
TANGA-TIKA, 1953
TANGO, 1936
TANK, 1984
TAP ROOTS, 1948
TAPS, 1981
TARNISHED, 1950
TARNISHED ANGELS, THE, 1957
TARNISHED LADY, 1931
TAROT, 1987
TASTE OF HONEY, A, 1962
TATTERED DRESS, THE, 1957
TATTOO, 1981
TAXI, 1953
TAXI DRIVER, 1976
TEA AND RICE, 1964
TEA AND SYMPATHY, 1956
TEA IN THE HAREM OF ARCHIMEDE, 1985
TEACHER AND THE MIRACLE, THE, 1961
TEACHER, THE, 1974
TEACHERS, 1984
TEARS OF HAPPINESS, 1974
TEENAGE BAD GIRL, 1959
TEENAGE MOTHER, 1967
TEENAGE REBEL, 1956
TEENAGE THUNDER, 1957
TELEPHONE OPERATOR, 1938
TELL ME A RIDDLE, 1980
TELL ME LIES, 1968
TELL ME THAT YOU LOVE ME, JUNIE MOON, 1970
TEMPEST, 1932
TEMPEST, 1982
TEMPTATION, 1936
TEMPTATION, 1946
TEMPTATION, 1962
TEN CENTS A DANCE, 1931
TEN GENTLEMEN FROM WEST POINT, 1942
TEN NIGHTS IN A BARROOM, 1931
10 NORTH FREDERICK, 1958
$10 RAISE, 1935
10:30 P.M. SUMMER, 1966
TENDER COMRADE, 1943
TENDER HEARTS, 1955
TENDER IS THE NIGHT, 1961
TENDER MERCIES, 1982
TENDER YEARS, THE, 1947
TENTH AVENUE ANGEL, 1948
TENTH MAN, THE, 1937
TEOREMA, 1969
TERESA, 1951

TERM OF TRIAL, 1962
TERMS OF ENDEARMENT, 1983
TERRACE, THE, 1964
TERRORISTS, THE, 1975
TERRORIZERS, THE, 1987
TESHA, 1929
TESS, 1980
TESS OF THE STORM COUNTRY, 1932
TESS OF THE STORM COUNTRY, 1961
TEST PILOT, 1938
TESTAMENT, 1983
TESTAMENT, 1988
TESTAMENT OF ORPHEUS, THE, 1962
TEVYA, 1939
TEX, 1982
TEXAS LIGHTNING, 1981
THANK YOU ALL VERY MUCH, 1969
THANK YOU, AUNT, 1969
THANOS AND DESPINA, 1970
THAT BRENNAN GIRL, 1946
THAT CERTAIN SOMETHING, 1941
THAT CERTAIN WOMAN, 1937
THAT COLD DAY IN THE PARK, 1969
THAT FORSYTE WOMAN, 1949
THAT HAGEN GIRL, 1947
THAT KIND OF GIRL, 1963
THAT KIND OF WOMAN, 1959
THAT NIGHT, 1957
THAT OBSCURE OBJECT OF DESIRE, 1977
THAT SPLENDID NOVEMBER, 1971
THAT SUMMER, 1979
THAT TENDER TOUCH, 1969
THAT TENNESSEE BEAT, 1966
THAT WAS THEN...THIS IS NOW, 1985
THAT WAY WITH WOMEN, 1947
THAT WOMAN, 1968
THAT'S MY STORY, 1937
THAT'S THE WAY OF THE WORLD, 1975
THAT'LL BE THE DAY, 1974
THAT'S MY BABY, 1944
THEIR OWN DESIRE, 1929
THERE WAS AN OLD COUPLE, 1967
THERE'S ALWAYS TOMORROW, 1956
THERE'S ALWAYS VANILLA, 1972
THERE'S SOMETHING ABOUT A SOLDIER, 1943
THERESE, 1963
THERESE AND ISABELLE, 1968
THESE CHARMING PEOPLE, 1931
THESE GLAMOUR GIRLS, 1939
THESE THIRTY YEARS, 1934
THESE THREE, 1936
THESE WILDER YEARS, 1956
THEY CALL IT SIN, 1932
THEY CAME TO A CITY, 1944
THEY CAME TO CORDURA, 1959
THEY DRIVE BY NIGHT, 1940
THEY GAVE HIM A GUN, 1937
THEY KNEW MR. KNIGHT, 1945
THEY KNEW WHAT THEY WANTED, 1940
THEY LIVE IN FEAR, 1944
THEY MEET AGAIN, 1941
THEY SHOOT HORSES, DON'T THEY?, 1969
THEY WERE FIVE, 1938
THEY WERE SISTERS, 1945
THEY WERE SO YOUNG, 1955
THEY WERE TEN, 1961
THEY WON'T FORGET, 1937
THIEF OF PARIS, THE, 1967
THIN LINE, THE, 1967
THINGS OF LIFE, THE, 1970
THIRD ALARM, THE, 1930
THIRD DAY, THE, 1965
THIRD LOVER, THE, 1963
THIRD OF A MAN, 1962
THIRD TIME LUCKY, 1950
THIRD WALKER, THE, 1978
THIRTEEN WEST STREET, 1962
—30—, 1959
36 FILLETTE, 1988
THIS ANGRY AGE, 1958
THIS EARTH IS MINE, 1959
THIS HAPPY BREED, 1944
THIS IS A HIJACK, 1973
THIS IS MY LOVE, 1954
THIS IS MY STREET, 1964
THIS LOVE OF OURS, 1945

THIS MADDING CROWD, 1964
THIS MAN IS MINE, 1934
THIS MODERN AGE, 1931
THIS PROPERTY IS CONDEMNED, 1966
THIS REBEL BREED, 1960
THIS SIDE OF HEAVEN, 1934
THIS SIDE OF THE LAW, 1950
THIS SPECIAL FRIENDSHIP, 1967
THIS WAS A WOMAN, 1949
THIS WOMAN IS MINE, 1941
THOROUGHBRED, 1932
THOROUGHBRED, THE, 1930
THOSE CALLOWAYS, 1964
THOSE WE LOVE, 1932
THOSE WHO LOVE, 1929
THOU SHALT NOT KILL, 1939
THOUSAND CRANES, 1969
THREADS, 1932
THREE, 1969
THREE BAD SISTERS, 1956
THREE BRAVE MEN, 1957
THREE BROTHERS, 1982
THREE CARD MONTE, 1978
THREE CHEERS FOR THE IRISH, 1940
THREE COMRADES, 1938
THREE CORNERED FATE, 1954
THREE DAYS OF VIKTOR TSCHERNIKOFF, 1968
THREE FACES OF A WOMAN, 1965
THREE FACES OF EVE, THE, 1957
THREE FACES OF SIN, 1963
THREE FACES WEST, 1940
THREE FOR THE ROAD, 1987
THREE GIRLS LOST, 1931
300 YEAR WEEKEND, 1971
THREE IN ONE, 1956
THREE IN THE ATTIC, 1968
THREE INTO TWO WON'T GO, 1969
THREE MEN IN WHITE, 1944
THREE MOVES TO FREEDOM, 1960
THREE NIGHTS OF LOVE, 1969
THREE ON A MATCH, 1932
THREE SECRETS, 1950
THREE SISTERS, THE, 1930
THREE SISTERS, THE, 1969
THREE SISTERS, 1974
THREE SISTERS, THE, 1977
THREE SONS, 1939
THREE STEPS NORTH, 1951
THREE STRANGERS, 1946
THREE TALES OF CHEKHOV, 1961
THREE TO GO, 1971
THREE WHO LOVED, 1931
THREE WISE GIRLS, 1932
THREE WISE GUYS, THE, 1936
THREE WOMEN, 1977
THREE'S COMPANY, 1953
THREES, MENAGE A TROIS, 1968
THRESHOLD, 1983
THRILL OF YOUTH, 1932
THRONE OF BLOOD, 1961
THROUGH A GLASS DARKLY, 1962
THROUGH DAYS AND MONTHS, 1969
THRU DIFFERENT EYES, 1929
THRU DIFFERENT EYES, 1942
THUMB TRIPPING, 1972
THUNDER BELOW, 1932
THUNDER BIRDS, 1942
THUNDER IN THE CITY, 1937
THUNDER ISLAND, 1963
THUNDER ON THE HILL, 1951
THUNDER ROCK, 1944
THUNDERHEAD-SON OF FLICKA, 1945
THUNDERING JETS, 1958
THUNDERSTORM, 1934
THUNDERSTORM, 1956
THURSDAY'S CHILD, 1943
THY NEIGHBOR'S WIFE, 1953
TI-CUL TOUGAS, 1977
TIARA TAHITI, 1962
...TICK...TICK...TICK..., 1970
TICKET, 1987
TICKET TO HEAVEN, 1981
TIGER AND THE FLAME, THE, 1955
TIGER FLIGHT, 1965
TIGER GIRL, 1955
TIGER SHARK, 1932

BOLD: Films on Videocassette

TIGER WALKS, A, 1964
TIKO AND THE SHARK, 1966
TILL THE END OF TIME, 1946
TILL TOMORROW COMES, 1962
TILT, 1979
TIM, 1981
TIN DRUM, THE, 1979
TIMBER QUEEN, 1944
TIME AFTER TIME, 1985
TIME AND THE TOUCH, THE, 1962
TIME BOMB, 1961
TIME IN THE SUN, A, 1970
TIME LIMIT, 1957
TIME LOCK, 1959
TIME LOST AND TIME REMEMBERED, 1966
TIME OF DESIRE, THE, 1957
TIME OF DESTINY, A, 1988
TIME OF INDIFFERENCE, 1965
TIME OF THE HEATHEN, 1962
TIME OF YOUR LIFE, THE, 1948
TIME OUT FOR LOVE, 1963
TIME OUT OF MIND, 1947
TIME TO DIE, A, 1985
TIME TO SING, A, 1968
TIMES GONE BY, 1953
TIMES SQUARE, 1929
TIMES SQUARE, 1980
TIMES SQUARE LADY, 1935
TIMOTHY'S QUEST, 1936
TIN GODS, 1932
TIN MAN, 1983
TINKER, 1949
TINTORERA...BLOODY WATERS, 1977
'TIS A PITY SHE'S A WHORE, 1973
TO BE A LADY, 1934
TO BE FREE, 1972
TO BE OR NOT TO BE, 1942
TO EACH HIS OWN, 1946
TO FIND A MAN, 1972
TO HAVE AND HAVE NOT, 1944
TO HAVE AND TO HOLD, 1951
TO KILL A CLOWN, 1972
TO KILL A MOCKINGBIRD, 1962
TO LIVE IN PEACE, 1947
TO LOVE, 1964
TO SIR, WITH LOVE, 1967
TO THE SHORES OF TRIPOLI, 1942
TO THE VICTOR, 1938
TO THE VICTOR, 1948
TOAST TO LOVE, 1951
TOBACCO ROAD, 1941
TOBY MCTEAGUE, 1986
TOBY TYLER, 1960
TODAY, 1930
TOGETHER, 1956
TOGETHER FOR DAYS, 1972
TOGETHER WE LIVE, 1935
TOKYO AFTER DARK, 1959
TOKYO JOE, 1949
TOKYO STORY, 1972
TOL'ABLE DAVID, 1930
TOM, 1973
TOM BROWN OF CULVER, 1932
TOM BROWN'S SCHOOL DAYS, 1940
TOM BROWN'S SCHOOLDAYS, 1951
TOMBOY AND THE CHAMP, 1961
TOMORROW, 1972
TOMORROW AND TOMORROW, 1932
TOMORROW IS FOREVER, 1946
TOMORROW IS MY TURN, 1962
TOMORROW THE WORLD, 1944
TOMORROW WE LIVE, 1936
TOMORROW'S YOUTH, 1935
TONI, 1968
TONIGHT AT TWELVE, 1929
TONIGHT THE SKIRTS FLY, 1956
TONIO KROGER, 1968
TOO BUSY TO WORK, 1932
TOO MANY PARENTS, 1936
TOO SOON TO LOVE, 1960
TOO TOUGH TO KILL, 1935
TOO YOUNG TO LOVE, 1960
TOO YOUNG TO MARRY, 1931
TOO YOUNG, TOO IMMORAL!, 1962
TOP GUN, 1986
TOPAZE, 1933

TOPAZE, 1935
TORCH SONG TRILOGY, 1988
TORCHLIGHT, 1984
TORMENT, 1947
TORNADO, 1943
TORPEDO ALLEY, 1953
TORTILLA FLAT, 1942
TORTURE ME KISS ME, 1970
TOUCH OF FLESH, THE, 1960
TOUCH, THE, 1971
TOUCHED BY LOVE, 1980
TOUGH GUY, 1936
TOUGH KID, 1939
TOUGHER THEY COME, THE, 1950
TOUT VA BIEN, 1973
TOWARD THE UNKNOWN, 1956
TOWN WITHOUT PITY, 1961
TOXI, 1952
TOYS ARE NOT FOR CHILDREN, 1972
TOYS IN THE ATTIC, 1963
T.R. BASKIN, 1971
TRACK OF THE CAT, 1954
TRACKS, 1977
TRAGEDY OF A RIDICULOUS MAN, THE, 1982
TRAIL OF THE LONESOME PINE, THE, 1936
TRAIN OF EVENTS, 1952
TRAITOR WITHIN, THE, 1942
TRANSATLANTIC, 1931
TRANSGRESSION, 1931
TRANSIENT LADY, 1935
TRANSPORT FROM PARADISE, 1967
TRAP, THE, 1959
TRAP, THE, 1967
TRAP DOOR, THE, 1980
TRAPEZE, 1932
TRAPEZE, 1956
TRAPP FAMILY, THE, 1961
TRAPPED BY TELEVISION, 1936
TRAVELLING AVANT, 1988
TRAVELLING NORTH, 1988
TREASURE OF MONTE CRISTO, 1949
TREAT EM' ROUGH, 1942
TREE GROWS IN BROOKLYN, A, 1945
TREE OF WOODEN CLOGS, THE, 1979
TREE WE HURT, THE, 1986
TREE, THE, 1969
TRESPASSER, THE, 1929
TRESPASSERS, THE, 1976
TRIAL, 1955
TRIAL, THE, 1948
TRIAL OF BILLY JACK, THE, 1974
TRIAL OF MADAM X, THE, 1948
TRIAL OF MARY DUGAN, THE, 1929
TRIAL OF MARY DUGAN, THE, 1941
TRIAL OF THE CATONSVILLE NINE, THE, 1972
TRIAL, THE, 1963
TRIBES, 1970
TRIBUTE, 1980
TRIO, 1950
TRIP TO BOUNTIFUL, THE, 1985
TRIPLE ECHO, THE, 1973
TRISTANA, 1970
TROJAN BROTHERS, THE, 1946
TROMBA, THE TIGER MAN, 1952
TROOPSHIP, 1938
TROPIC ZONE, 1953
TROUBLE ALONG THE WAY, 1953
TROUBLE-FETE, 1964
TROUBLE IN THE SKY, 1961
TROUBLE PREFERRED, 1949
TROUBLE WITH GIRLS (AND HOW TO GET INTO IT), THE, 1969
TROUT, THE, 1982
TRUE AND THE FALSE, THE, 1955
TRUMAN CAPOTE'S TRILOGY, 1969
TRUMPET BLOWS, THE, 1934
TRUTH ABOUT MURDER, THE, 1946
TRUTH ABOUT YOUTH, THE, 1930
TRUTH, THE, 1961
TUFF TURF, 1985
TUGBOAT ANNIE, 1933
TUGBOAT ANNIE SAILS AGAIN, 1940
TULSA, 1949
TUNA CLIPPER, 1949
TUNES OF GLORY, 1960
TUNNEL TO THE SUN, 1968

TURK 182!, 1985
TURN OF THE SCREW, 1985
TURN ON TO LOVE, 1969
TURN THE KEY SOFTLY, 1954
TURNERS OF PROSPECT ROAD, THE, 1947
TURTLE DIARY, 1985
TUSK, 1980
12 ANGRY MEN, 1957
25TH HOUR, THE, 1967
24 HOURS IN A WOMAN'S LIFE, 1968
TWENTY-ONE DAYS TOGETHER, 1940
27A, 1974
TWICE A MAN, 1964
TWICE BRANDED, 1936
TWICE IN A LIFETIME, 1985
TWILIGHT HOUR, 1944
TWILIGHT OF HONOR, 1963
TWILIGHT PATH, 1965
TWILIGHT STORY, THE, 1962
TWILIGHT TIME, 1983
TWIN SISTERS OF KYOTO, 1964
TWIST & SHOUT, 1986
TWO, 1975
TWO AGAINST THE WORLD, 1932
TWO AGAINST THE WORLD, 1936
TWO ALONE, 1934
TWO BRIGHT BOYS, 1939
TWO DAUGHTERS, 1963
TWO DOLLAR BETTOR, 1951
TWO ENGLISH GIRLS, 1972
TWO FOR THE ROAD, 1967
TWO FOR THE SEESAW, 1962
TWO GENTLEMEN SHARING, 1969
TWO IN A TAXI, 1941
TWO-LANE BLACKTOP, 1971
TWO LIVING, ONE DEAD, 1964
TWO LOVES, 1961
TWO-MAN SUBMARINE, 1944
TWO MEN IN TOWN, 1973
TWO MINUTES' SILENCE, 1934
TWO MOON JUNCTION, 1988
TWO OF US, THE, 1968
TWO OR THREE THINGS I KNOW ABOUT HER, 1970
TWO SISTERS, 1938
TWO SOLITUDES, 1978
TWO THOROUGHBREDS, 1939
2,000 WEEKS, 1970
TWO TICKETS TO LONDON, 1943
TWO VOICES, 1966
TWO WEEKS IN ANOTHER TOWN, 1962
TWO WHO DARED, 1937
TWO WISE MAIDS, 1937
TWO WOMEN, 1940
TWO WOMEN, 1960
TWO YEARS BEFORE THE MAST, 1946
UGETSU, 1954
UGLY AMERICAN, THE, 1963
ULTIMATUM, 1940
ULYSSES, 1967
UMBERTO D, 1955
UN CARNET DE BAL, 1938
UNASHAMED, 1932
UNASHAMED, 1938
UNCENSORED, 1944
UNCERTAIN GLORY, 1944
UNCLE JOE SHANNON, 1978
UNCLE TOM'S CABIN, 1969
UNCLE VANYA, 1958
UNCLE VANYA, 1972
UNCLE VANYA, 1977
UNCLE, THE, 1966
UNDER AGE, 1964
UNDER CAPRICORN, 1949
UNDER FIRE, 1957
UNDER FIRE, 1983
UNDER MILK WOOD, 1973
UNDER PRESSURE, 1935
UNDER SECRET ORDERS, 1933
UNDER THE BANNER OF SAMURAI, 1969
UNDER THE BIG TOP, 1938
UNDER THE GREENWOOD TREE, 1930
UNDER THE ROOFS OF PARIS, 1930
UNDER THE SUN OF ROME, 1949
UNDER THE VOLCANO, 1984
UNDERDOG, THE, 1943
UNDERGROUND, 1941

UNDERGROUND GUERRILLAS, 1944
UNDERGROUND U.S.A., 1980
UNDERTOW, 1930
UNEXPECTED FATHER, 1939
UNEXPECTED UNCLE, 1941
UNFAITHFUL, 1931
UNFAITHFUL, THE, 1947
UNFINISHED BUSINESS, 1985
UNFINISHED BUSINESS..., 1987
UNGUARDED HOUR, THE, 1936
UNGUARDED MOMENT, THE, 1956
UNHOLY DESIRE, 1964
UNHOLY LOVE, 1932
UNINHIBITED, THE, 1968
UNION CITY, 1980
UNION DEPOT, 1932
UNIVERSAL SOLDIER, 1971
UNKNOWN BLONDE, 1934
UNMARRIED, 1939
UNMARRIED WOMAN, AN, 1978
UNSTRAP ME, 1968
UNTAMED FURY, 1947
UNTIL THEY SAIL, 1957
UNWED MOTHER, 1958
UP FOR MURDER, 1931
UP THE DOWN STAIRCASE, 1967
UP THE JUNCTION, 1968
UPTIGHT, 1968
URANIUM BOOM, 1956
URBAN COWBOY, 1980
UTU, 1984
V.D., 1961
V.I.P.s, THE, 1963
VACATION, THE, 1971
VAGABOND, 1985
VALIANT IS THE WORD FOR CARRIE, 1936
VALLEY OF THE DOLLS, 1967
VAMPING, 1984
VAN, THE, 1977
VAN NUYS BLVD., 1979
VANISHING VIRGINIAN, THE, 1941
VANITY, 1935
VANITY FAIR, 1932
VANITY STREET, 1932
VARIETY, 1984
VARIETY LIGHTS, 1965
VARSITY, 1928
VEILED WOMAN, THE, 1929
VELVET TRAP, THE, 1966
VENDETTA, 1950
VENOM, 1968
VENUS IN FURS, 1970
VENUS MAKES TROUBLE, 1937
VERA, 1987
VERBOTEN?, 1959
VERDICT, 1975
VERDICT, THE, 1982
VERGINITA, 1953
VERMILION DOOR, 1969
VERONIKA VOSS, 1982
VERY CURIOUS GIRL, A, 1970
VERY EDGE, THE, 1963
VERY NATURAL THING, A, 1974
VERY PRIVATE AFFAIR, A, 1962
VERY YOUNG LADY, A, 1941
VIBRATION, 1969
VICE AND VIRTUE, 1965
VICIOUS CIRCLE, THE, 1948
VICTIMS OF PERSECUTION, 1933
VIEW FROM POMPEY'S HEAD, THE, 1955
VIEW FROM THE BRIDGE, A, 1962
VIGIL, 1984
VIGIL IN THE NIGHT, 1940
VIGILANTE, 1983
VIGILANTE FORCE, 1976
VILLAGE, THE, 1953
VILLAGE TALE, 1935
VIOLATED PARADISE, 1963
VIOLATORS, THE, 1957
VIOLENT MOMENT, 1966
VIOLENT ROAD, 1958
VIOLENT SUMMER, 1961
VIOLIN AND ROLLER, 1962
VIRGIN AND THE GYPSY, THE, 1970
VIRGIN ISLAND, 1960
VIRGIN SOLDIERS, THE, 1970

VIRGIN SPRING, THE, 1960
VIRGINIA, 1941
VIRGINIA JUDGE, THE, 1935
VIRIDIANA, 1962
VIRTUOUS SIN, THE, 1930
VISA U.S.A., 1987
VISIT, THE, 1964
VISITORS, THE, 1972
VITELLONI, 1956
VIXEN, 1970
VIXENS, THE, 1969
VOICE IN THE MIRROR, 1958
VOICE IN THE NIGHT, A, 1941
VOICE IN THE WIND, 1944
VOICE IN YOUR HEART, A, 1952
VOICE OF BUGLE ANN, 1936
VOICE OF THE HURRICANE, 1964
VOICE OF THE WHISTLER, 1945
VOLCANO, 1953
VOR SONNENUNTERGANG, 1961
VOYAGE, THE, 1974
VOYAGE OF SILENCE, 1968
VOYAGE OF THE DAMNED, 1976
WAGONS ROLL AT NIGHT, THE, 1941
WAIT 'TIL THE SUN SHINES, NELLIE, 1952
WAITING FOR CAROLINE, 1969
WALK IN THE SHADOW, 1966
WALK ON THE MOON, A, 1987
WALK ON THE WILD SIDE, 1962
WALK PROUD, 1979
WALK SOFTLY, STRANGER, 1950
WALK THE WALK, 1970
WALKABOUT, 1971
WALKING DOWN BROADWAY, 1938
WALKING ON AIR, 1946
WALL STREET, 1929
WALL STREET, 1987
WALLS OF GOLD, 1933
WALLS OF JERICHO, 1948
WALLS OF MALAPAGA, THE, 1950
WALPURGIS NIGHT, 1941
WANDERER, THE, 1969
WANDERERS, THE, 1979
WANDERING JEW, THE, 1933
WANDERLOVE, 1970
WAR AGAINST MRS. HADLEY, THE, 1942
WAR AND LOVE, 1985
WAR AND PEACE, 1956
WAR AND PEACE, 1968
WAR BETWEEN MEN AND WOMEN, THE, 1972
WAR IS A RACKET, 1934
WARE CASE, THE, 1939
WARGAMES, 1983
WARM DECEMBER, A, 1973
WARM NIGHTS ON A SLOW MOVING TRAIN, 1987
WARRIOR QUEEN, 1987
WASHINGTON MASQUERADE, 1932
WASTREL, THE, 1963
WATCH ON THE RHINE, 1943
WATER GYPSIES, THE, 1932
WATERFRONT, 1939
WATERFRONT WOMEN, 1952
WATERLOO BRIDGE, 1931
WATERLOO BRIDGE, 1940
WATERLOO ROAD, 1949
WATERMELON MAN, 1970
WAY BACK HOME, 1932
WAY OF ALL FLESH, THE, 1940
WAY OF LOST SOULS, THE, 1929
WAY OUT, 1966
WAY OUT, WAY IN, 1970
WAY WE LIVE NOW, THE, 1970
WAY WE LIVE, THE, 1946
WAYS OF LOVE, 1950
WAYSIDE PEBBLE, THE, 1962
WAYWARD, 1932
WAYWARD BUS, THE, 1957
WAYWARD GIRL, THE, 1957
WE ARE ALL MURDERERS, 1957
WE ARE ALL NAKED, 1970
WE ARE NOT ALONE, 1939
WE GO FAST, 1941
WE HAVE ONLY ONE LIFE, 1963
WEAKER SEX, THE, 1949
WEATHER IN THE STREETS, THE, 1983
WEB OF DANGER, THE, 1947

WEBSTER BOY, THE, 1962
WEDDING IN GALILEE, 1988
WEDDING IN WHITE, 1972
WEDDING NIGHT, 1970
WEDDING NIGHT, THE, 1935
WEDDING, A, 1978
WEDDINGS AND BABIES, 1960
WEDNESDAY'S CHILD, 1934
WEE GEORDIE, 1956
WEE WILLIE WINKIE, 1937
WEEDS, 1987
WEEKEND, 1964
WEEKEND, 1968
WEEKEND OF SHADOWS, 1978
WEEKEND WITH THE BABYSITTER, 1970
WEIRD LOVE MAKERS, THE, 1963
WELCOME HOME, SOLDIER BOYS, 1972
WELCOME KOSTYA?, 1965
WELCOME, MR. WASHINGTON, 1944
WELCOME STRANGER, 1947
WELCOME TO 18, 1986
WELCOME TO GERMANY, 1988
WELCOME TO L.A., 1976
WELL, THE, 1951
WELL-DIGGER'S DAUGHTER, THE, 1946
WE'RE ON THE JURY, 1937
WEST OF BROADWAY, 1931
WEST OF SHANGHAI, 1937
WEST OF SINGAPORE, 1933
WEST POINT OF THE AIR, 1935
WEST SIDE KID, 1943
WET PARADE, THE, 1932
WETBACKS, 1956
WETHERBY, 1985
WHALES OF AUGUST, THE, 1987
WHAT A CRAZY WORLD, 1963
WHAT A LIFE, 1939
WHAT A MAN!, 1944
WHAT COMES AROUND, 1986
WHAT EVERY WOMAN WANTS, 1954
WHAT MEN WANT, 1930
WHAT PRICE DECENCY?, 1933
WHAT PRICE HOLLYWOOD?, 1932
WHAT PRICE INNOCENCE?, 1933
WHAT YOU TAKE FOR GRANTED, 1984
WHATEVER IT TAKES, 1986
WHAT'S NEXT?, 1975
WHEEL OF ASHES, 1970
WHEEL OF LIFE, THE, 1929
WHEN A WOMAN ASCENDS THE STAIRS, 1963
WHEN FATHER WAS AWAY ON BUSINESS, 1985
WHEN I GROW UP, 1951
WHEN IN ROME, 1952
WHEN LONDON SLEEPS, 1934
WHEN LOVE IS YOUNG, 1937
WHEN STRANGERS MARRY, 1933
WHEN STRANGERS MEET, 1934
WHEN THE BOUGH BREAKS, 1947
WHEN THE LEGENDS DIE, 1972
WHEN THE LIGHTS GO ON AGAIN, 1944
WHEN THE TREES WERE TALL, 1965
WHEN THIEF MEETS THIEF, 1937
WHEN TOMORROW COMES, 1939
WHEN TOMORROW DIES, 1966
WHEN YOU COMIN' BACK, RED RYDER?, 1979
WHERE ANGELS GO...TROUBLE FOLLOWS, 1968
WHERE ARE THE CHILDREN?, 1986
WHERE ARE YOUR CHILDREN?, 1943
WHERE IS MY CHILD?, 1937
WHERE IT'S AT, 1969
WHERE LOVE HAS GONE, 1964
WHERE THE GREEN ANTS DREAM, 1985
WHERE THE HOT WIND BLOWS, 1960
WHERE THE LILIES BLOOM, 1974
WHERE THE RED FERN GROWS, 1974
WHEREVER YOU ARE, 1988
WHICH WAY IS UP?, 1977
WHILE I LIVE, 1947
WHIRLPOOL, 1934
WHIRLPOOL, 1959
WHIRLPOOL OF WOMAN, 1966
WHISPERERS, THE, 1967
WHISPERING ENEMIES, 1939
WHISPERING JOE, 1969
WHISPERING WINDS, 1929
WHISTLE AT EATON FALLS, 1951

BOLD: Films on Videocassette

WHISTLE DOWN THE WIND, 1961
WHITE BANNERS, 1938
WHITE BONDAGE, 1937
WHITE CARGO, 1930
WHITE CARGO, 1942
WHITE CORRIDORS, 1952
WHITE DAWN, THE, 1974
WHITE DEATH, 1936
WHITE DEMON, THE, 1932
WHITE DOG, 1982
WHITE ELEPHANT, 1984
WHITE ENSIGN, 1934
WHITE HEAT, 1934
WHITE LEGION, THE, 1936
WHITE LINE, THE, 1952
WHITE NIGHTS, 1961
WHITE PARADE, THE, 1934
WHITE SHADOWS IN THE SOUTH SEAS, 1928
WHITE SHOULDERS, 1931
WHITE SISTER, 1973
WHITE WATER SUMMER, 1987
WHO HAS SEEN THE WIND, 1980
WHO KILLED TEDDY BEAR?, 1965
WHOLE SHOOTIN' MATCH, THE, 1979
WHOM THE GODS DESTROY, 1934
WHO'S AFRAID OF VIRGINIA WOOLF?, 1966
WHO'S THAT KNOCKING AT MY DOOR?, 1968
WHOSE LIFE IS IT ANYWAY?, 1981
WHY SHOOT THE TEACHER, 1977
WHY WOULD I LIE, 1980
WICKED, 1931
WICKED GO TO HELL, THE, 1961
WICKED WOMAN, 1953
WICKED WOMAN, A, 1934
WIDOWS' NEST, 1977
WIFE VERSUS SECRETARY, 1936
WIFEMISTRESS, 1979
WILD BOYS OF THE ROAD, 1933
WILD CHILD, THE, 1970
WILD COMPANY, 1930
WILD DUCK, THE, 1977
WILD DUCK, THE, 1983
WILD EYE, THE, 1968
WILD GUITAR, 1962
WILD GYPSIES, 1969
WILD HARVEST, 1947
WILD HARVEST, 1962
WILD HORSE HANK, 1979
WILD IN THE COUNTRY, 1961
WILD INNOCENCE, 1937
WILD IS MY LOVE, 1963
WILD IS THE WIND, 1957
WILD McCULLOCHS, THE, 1975
WILD 90, 1968
WILD ONE, THE, 1953
WILD PACK, THE, 1972
WILD PARTY, THE, 1975
WILD RIVER, 1960
WILD SCENE, THE, 1970
WILD SEASON, 1968
WILD SEED, 1965
WILD STRAWBERRIES, 1959
WILD WEED, 1949
WILDCAT, 1942
WILDCATTER, THE, 1937
WILDROSE, 1985
WILLIE AND PHIL, 1980
WILLY, 1963
WIND ACROSS THE EVERGLADES, 1958
WIND CANNOT READ, THE, 1958
WIND FROM THE EAST, 1970
WIND, THE, 1928
WINDFALL, 1935
WINDFLOWERS, 1968
WINDMILL, THE, 1937
WINDOM'S WAY, 1958
WINDSPLITTER, THE, 1971
WINDY CITY, 1984
WINE, WOMEN AND HORSES, 1937
WINE, WOMEN, AND SONG, 1934
WINGS FOR THE EAGLE, 1942
WINGS OVER HONOLULU, 1937
WINNERS TAKE ALL, 1987
WINSLOW BOY, THE, 1950
WINTER CARNIVAL, 1939
WINTER FLIGHT, 1984

WINTER KEPT US WARM, 1968
WINTER LIGHT, THE, 1963
WINTER MEETING, 1948
WINTER OF OUR DREAMS, 1982
WINTERSET, 1936
WIRE SERVICE, 1942
WISE BLOOD, 1979
WISE GIRL, 1937
WISE GUYS, 1969
WISER AGE, 1962
WISER SEX, THE, 1932
WISH YOU WERE HERE, 1987
WITCHES, THE, 1969
WITH A SMILE, 1939
WITH LOVE AND TENDERNESS, 1978
WITHNAIL AND I, 1987
WITHOUT A HOME, 1939
WITHOUT A TRACE, 1983
WITHOUT EACH OTHER, 1962
WITHOUT HONOR, 1949
WITHOUT ORDERS, 1936
WITHOUT PITY, 1949
WITNESS OUT OF HELL, 1967
WIVES UNDER SUSPICION, 1938
WIZARD OF LONELINESS, THE, 1988
WOLFPEN PRINCIPLE, THE, 1974
WOLVES, 1930
WOMAN AGAINST THE WORLD, 1938
WOMAN AT HER WINDOW, A, 1978
WOMAN BETWEEN, 1931
WOMAN COMMANDS, A, 1932
WOMAN DOCTOR, 1939
WOMAN FROM MONTE CARLO, THE, 1932
WOMAN HE SCORNED, THE, 1930
WOMAN I LOVE, THE, 1937
WOMAN IN CHAINS, 1932
WOMAN IN FLAMES, A, 1984
WOMAN IN THE DARK, 1934
WOMAN IN THE DUNES, 1964
WOMAN IN THE HALL, THE, 1949
WOMAN INSIDE, THE, 1981
WOMAN IS A WOMAN, A, 1961
WOMAN IS THE JUDGE, A, 1939
WOMAN NEXT DOOR, THE, 1981
WOMAN OF DARKNESS, 1968
WOMAN OF EXPERIENCE, A, 1931
WOMAN OF ROME, 1956
WOMAN OF THE NORTH COUNTRY, 1952
WOMAN OF THE RIVER, 1954
WOMAN ON FIRE, A, 1970
WOMAN ON PIER 13, THE, 1950
WOMAN ON THE BEACH, THE, 1947
WOMAN POSSESSED, A, 1958
WOMAN REBELS, A, 1936
WOMAN TIMES SEVEN, 1967
WOMAN TO WOMAN, 1929
WOMAN TO WOMAN, 1946
WOMAN UNDER THE INFLUENCE, A, 1974
WOMAN WHO DARED, 1949
WOMAN WITH RED BOOTS, THE, 1977
WOMANLIGHT, 1979
WOMAN'S FACE, A, 1939
WOMAN'S LIFE, A, 1964
WOMAN'S SECRET, A, 1949
WOMAN'S VENGEANCE, A, 1947
WOMAN'S WORLD, 1954
WOMEN AND BLOODY TERROR, 1970
WOMEN AND WAR, 1965
WOMEN ARE LIKE THAT, 1938
WOMEN GO ON FOREVER, 1931
WOMEN IN A DRESSING GOWN, 1957
WOMEN IN BONDAGE, 1943
WOMEN IN LOVE, 1969
WOMEN IN THE NIGHT, 1948
WOMEN IN THE WIND, 1939
WOMEN IN WAR, 1940
WOMEN LOVE ONCE, 1931
WOMEN MEN MARRY, 1931
WOMEN MEN MARRY, THE, 1937
WOMEN MUST DRESS, 1935
WOMEN OF DESIRE, 1968
WOMEN OF GLAMOUR, 1937
WOMEN ON THE VERGE OF A NERVOUS
  BREAKDOWN, 1988
WOMEN WITHOUT NAMES, 1940
WOMEN WON'T TELL, 1933

WONDER BOY, 1951
WONDER OF WOMEN, 1929
WONDERWALL, 1969
WORKING GIRLS, 1931
WORKING GIRLS, 1986
WORKING MAN, THE, 1933
WORLD ACCORDING TO GARP, THE, 1982
WORLD ACCUSES, THE, 1935
WORLD AND THE FLESH, THE, 1932
WORLD CHANGES, THE, 1933
WORLD IS FULL OF MARRIED MEN, THE, 1980
WORLD IS JUST A 'B' MOVIE, THE, 1971
WORLD MOVES ON, THE, 1934
WORLD OF APU, THE, 1960
WORLD OF SUZIE WONG, THE, 1960
WORLD WAS HIS JURY, THE, 1958
WORLD, THE FLESH, AND THE DEVIL, THE, 1932
WORLDLY GOODS, 1930
WORLDS APART, 1980
WORLD'S GREATEST SINNER, THE, 1962
WOULD-BE GENTLEMAN, THE, 1960
WOZZECK, 1962
WRECKER, THE, 1933
WRECKING CREW, 1942
WRITTEN LAW, THE, 1931
WRITTEN ON THE WIND, 1956
WRONG IS RIGHT, 1982
WUSA, 1970
X-15, 1961
X Y & ZEE, 1972
XICA, 1982
YANCO, 1964
YANK AT ETON, A, 1942
YANK IN LIBYA, A, 1942
YANK ON THE BURMA ROAD, A, 1942
YEAR MY VOICE BROKE, THE, 1988
YEARLING, THE, 1946
YEARNING, 1964
YEARS BETWEEN, THE, 1947
YELLOW EARTH, 1986
YELLOW JACK, 1938
YELLOW SLIPPERS, THE, 1965
YELLOW TICKET, THE, 1931
YESTERDAY, TODAY, AND TOMORROW, 1963
YOL, 1982
YOSAKOI JOURNEY, 1970
YOU AND ME, 1938
YOU BELONG TO ME, 1934
YOU CAME ALONG, 1945
YOU CAME TOO LATE, 1962
YOU CAN'T BUY EVERYTHING, 1934
YOU CAN'T SEE 'ROUND CORNERS, 1969
YOU ONLY LIVE ONCE, 1969
YOUNG AMERICA, 1932
YOUNG AMERICA, 1942
YOUNG AND DANGEROUS, 1957
YOUNG AND EVIL, 1962
YOUNG AND WILLING, 1964
YOUNG APHRODITES, 1966
YOUNG BRIDE, 1932
YOUNG CAPTIVES, THE, 1959
YOUNG COMPOSER'S ODYSSEY, A, 1986
YOUNG DESIRE, 1930
YOUNG DR. KILDARE, 1938
YOUNG DOCTORS, THE, 1961
YOUNG DON'T CRY, THE, 1957
YOUNG FUGITIVES, 1938
YOUNG GIANTS, 1983
YOUNG GIRLS OF WILKO, THE, 1979
YOUNG GO WILD, THE, 1962
YOUNG GRADUATES, THE, 1971
YOUNG GUY GRADUATES, 1969
YOUNG GUY ON MT. COOK, 1969
YOUNG HUSBANDS, 1958
YOUNG IN HEART, THE, 1938
YOUNG LOVERS, THE, 1964
YOUNG NOWHERES, 1929
YOUNG ONE, THE, 1961
YOUNG PHILADELPHIANS, THE, 1959
YOUNG RUNAWAYS, THE, 1968
YOUNG SAVAGES, THE, 1961
YOUNG SINNER, THE, 1965
YOUNG SINNERS, 1931
YOUNG STRANGER, THE, 1957
YOUNG SWINGERS, THE, 1963
YOUNG TORLESS, 1968

YOUNG WIDOW, 1946
YOUNG, WILLING AND EAGER, 1962
YOUNG WOODLEY, 1930
YOUNG WORLD, A, 1966
YOUNGBLOOD HAWKE, 1964
YOUNGER GENERATION, 1929
YOUR SHADOW IS MINE, 1963
YOUR THREE MINUTES ARE UP, 1973
YOU'RE A BIG BOY NOW, 1966
YOU'RE NOT SO TOUGH, 1940
YOU'RE ONLY YOUNG ONCE, 1938
YOURS, MINE AND OURS, 1968
YOUTH AFLAME, 1945
YOUTH AND HIS AMULET, THE, 1963
YOUTH IN FURY, 1961
YOUTH ON TRIAL, 1945
YOUTH RUNS WILD, 1944
YOU'VE GOT TO BE SMART, 1967
YOU'VE GOT TO WALK IT LIKE YOU TALK IT OR
    YOU'LL LOSE THAT BEAT, 1971
YR ALCOHOLIG LION, 1984
ZABRISKIE POINT, 1970
ZAPPA, 1984
ZAZA, 1939
ZED & TWO NOUGHTS, A, 1985
ZELLY AND ME, 1988
ZERO HOUR, THE, 1939
ZERO HOUR!, 1957
ZERO IN THE UNIVERSE, 1966
ZIG-ZAG, 1975
ZITA, 1968
ZOO GANG, THE, 1985
ZOOT SUIT, 1981
ZORBA THE GREEK, 1964

Fantasy
ABSENT-MINDED PROFESSOR, THE, 1961
ADAM AND EVE, 1958
ADVENTURES OF MARK TWAIN, THE, 1985
ALADDIN AND HIS LAMP, 1952
ALF'S BUTTON, 1930
ALF'S BUTTON AFLOAT, 1938
ALF'S CARPET, 1929
ALICE, 1988
ALICE IN WONDERLAND, 1933
ALICE IN WONDERLAND, 1951
ALICE IN WONDERLAND, 1951
ALICE'S ADVENTURES IN WONDERLAND, 1972
AMAZONS, 1987
ANGEL ON MY SHOULDER, 1946
ANGEL WHO PAWNED HER HARP, THE, 1956
ARABIAN ADVENTURE, 1979
ARABIAN NIGHTS, 1942
ARABIAN NIGHTS, 1980
ATLANTIS, THE LOST CONTINENT, 1961
ATLAS, 1960
ATLAS AGAINST THE CYCLOPS, 1963
ATLAS AGAINST THE CZAR, 1964
AVENGER, THE, 1964
BABES IN TOYLAND, 1934
BABES IN TOYLAND, 1961
BARBARIANS, THE, 1987
BARON MUNCHAUSEN, 1962
BATTERIES NOT INCLUDED, 1987
BEAR, THE, 1963
BEAST, THE, 1975
BEASTMASTER, THE, 1982
BEAUTIFUL PRISONER, THE, 1983
BEAUTY AND THE BEAST, 1947
BEAUTY AND THE BEAST, 1963
BEDKNOBS AND BROOMSTICKS, 1971
BERKELEY SQUARE, 1933
BEYOND TOMORROW, 1940
BISHOP'S WIFE, THE, 1947
BLACK MOON, 1975
BLITHE SPIRIT, 1945
BLUE BIRD, THE, 1976
BLUE BIRD, THE, 1940
BOCCACCIO '70, 1962
BOWERY TO BAGDAD, 1955
BOY AND THE PIRATES, THE, 1960
BOY WHO COULD FLY, THE, 1986
BOY WHO TURNED YELLOW, THE, 1972
BRAZIL, 1985
BRIGHTNESS, 1988
BROTHER FROM ANOTHER PLANET, THE, 1984

CAPTAIN SINDBAD, 1963
CHARLEY AND THE ANGEL, 1973
CHE?, 1973
CHITTY CHITTY BANG BANG, 1968
CHRISTMAS CAROL, A, 1938
CHRISTMAS CAROL, A, 1951
CHU CHIN CHOW, 1934
CLASH OF THE TITANS, 1981
COBRA WOMAN, 1944
COCKEYED MIRACLE, THE, 1946
COLONEL BOGEY, 1948
COMMITTEE, THE, 1968
COMPANY OF WOLVES, THE, 1985
CONAN THE BARBARIAN, 1982
CONAN THE DESTROYER, 1984
CONNECTICUT YANKEE, A, 1931
**CONNECTICUT YANKEE IN KING ARTHUR'S
    COURT, A, 1949**
CONQUEST, 1984
CRATER LAKE MONSTER, THE, 1977
CURSE OF THE CAT PEOPLE, THE, 1944
DA, 1988
DANCE OF THE DWARFS, 1983
DARBY O'GILL AND THE LITTLE PEOPLE, 1959
DARK CRYSTAL, THE, 1982
DATE WITH AN ANGEL, 1987
DAY THE EARTH FROZE, THE, 1959
DAYDREAMER, THE, 1966
DEATH TAKES A HOLIDAY, 1934
DEATHSTALKER, 1983
DEATHSTALKER, THE, 1984
DEJA VU, 1985
DEMON POND, 1980
DER ROSENKONIG, 1986
DEVIL AND DANIEL WEBSTER, THE, 1941
DEVIL DOLL, THE, 1936
DEVIL'S ENVOYS, THE, 1947
DIGBY, THE BIGGEST DOG IN THE WORLD, 1974
DINOSAURUS, 1960
DO YOU KEEP A LION AT HOME?, 1966
DOCTOR FAUSTUS, 1967
DONKEY SKIN, 1975
DOWN TO EARTH, 1947
DRAGONSLAYER, 1981
DREAM ONE, 1984
DREAMCHILD, 1985
DREAMS THAT MONEY CAN BUY, 1948
DUNGEONMASTER, 1985
DYBBUK, THE, 1938
EARTHBOUND, 1940
ECHOES, 1983
ELECTRIC BLUE, 1988
EMPEROR AND THE GOLEM, THE, 1955
ENCHANTING SHADOW, THE, 1965
ERENDIRA, 1984
ERNEST SAVES CHRISTMAS, 1988
E.T. THE EXTRA-TERRESTRIAL, 1982
ETERNAL RETURN, THE, 1943
EXCALIBUR, 1981
EYES OF FATE, 1933
FABULOUS WORLD OF JULES VERNE, THE, 1961
FIDDLERS THREE, 1944
FINAL COUNTDOWN, THE, 1980
FINIAN'S RAINBOW, 1968
FIRE AND ICE, 1983
5,000 FINGERS OF DR. T. THE, 1953
FLIGHT OF THE NAVIGATOR, 1986
FOOD OF THE GODS, THE, 1976
FOR HEAVEN'S SAKE, 1950
GAWAIN AND THE GREEN KNIGHT, 1973
GENIE, THE, 1953
GHOST AND MRS. MUIR, THE, 1942
GHOST DANCE, 1984
GHOST FEVER, 1987
GHOST GOES WEST, THE, 1936
GILDERSLEEVE'S GHOST, 1944
GLASS SLIPPER, THE, 1955
GNOME-MOBILE, THE, 1967
GOLDEN ARROW, THE, 1964
GOLDEN VOYAGE OF SINBAD, THE, 1974
GOLIATH AGAINST THE GIANTS, 1963
GOLIATH AND THE DRAGON, 1961
GOOSE GIRL, THE, 1967
GULLIVER'S TRAVELS, 1939
GULLIVER'S TRAVELS, 1977
GUY NAMED JOE, A, 1943

HAWK THE SLAYER, 1980
HEARTBREAK HOTEL, 1988
HEAVEN CAN WAIT, 1978
HEAVEN ONLY KNOWS, 1947
HERCULES, 1959
HERCULES AGAINST THE MOON MEN, 1965
HERCULES AGAINST THE SONS OF THE SUN, 1964
HERCULES AND THE CAPTIVE WOMEN, 1963
HERCULES, 1983
HERCULES IN NEW YORK, 1970
HERCULES IN THE HAUNTED WORLD, 1964
HERCULES, SAMSON & ULYSSES, 1964
HERCULES II, 1985
HERCULES UNCHAINED, 1960
HERCULES VS-THE GIANT WARRIORS, 1965
HERE COMES MR. JORDAN, 1941
HERO, 1982
HERO OF BABYLON, 1963
HIGHLANDER, 1986
HILDUR AND THE MAGICIAN, 1969
HINOTORI, 1980
HIS LAST TWELVE HOURS, 1953
HITCH IN TIME, A, 1978
HORN BLOWS AT MIDNIGHT, THE, 1945
HORSE'S MOUTH, THE, 1953
HOWARD THE DUCK, 1986
HUNDRA, 1984
ICEMAN, 1984
INCREDIBLE MR. LIMPET, THE, 1964
INNERSPACE, 1987
IT HAPPENED TOMORROW, 1944
JABBERWOCKY, 1977
JACK AND THE BEANSTALK, 1952
JACK AND THE BEANSTALK, 1970
JACK FROST, 1966
JACK THE GIANT KILLER, 1962
JACOB TWO-TWO MEETS THE HOODED FANG, 1979
JASON AND THE ARGONAUTS, 1963
JOHNNY THE GIANT KILLER, 1953
JOURNEY BACK TO OZ, 1974
KID FOR TWO FARTHINGS, A, 1956
KING KONG, 1933
KING KONG, 1976
KING KONG LIVES, 1986
KISMET, 1930
KISMET, 1944
KISMET, 1955
KRULL, 1983
LABYRINTH, 1986
LADYHAWKE, 1985
LAND THAT TIME FORGOT, THE, 1975
LAND UNKNOWN, THE, 1957
LAST DAYS OF POMPEII, THE, 1960
LEGEND, 1985
LET'S MAKE UP, 1955
LIFE IS A BED OF ROSES, 1984
LILIOM, 1930
LILIOM, 1935
LITTLE BOY BLUE, 1963
LITTLE FLAMES, 1985
LITTLE RED RIDING HOOD, 1963
LITTLE RED RIDING HOOD AND HER FRIENDS,
    1964
LITTLE RED RIDING HOOD AND THE MONSTERS,
    1965
LOST CONTINENT, THE, 1968
LOST EMPIRE, THE, 1985
LOST HORIZON, 1937
LOST HORIZON, 1973
LOST WORLD, THE, 1960
LOST WORLD OF SINBAD, THE, 1965
LOUISIANA TERRITORY, 1953
LOVE BUG, THE, 1968
LOVE SLAVES OF THE AMAZONS, 1957
LOVES OF HERCULES, THE, 1960
LUCK OF THE IRISH, 1948
MACARIO, 1961
MAD ABOUT MEN, 1954
MADAME WHITE SNAKE, 1963
MADE IN HEAVEN, 1987
MAGIC CHRISTMAS TREE, 1964
MAGIC FOUNTAIN, THE, 1961
MAGIC SPECTACLES, 1961
MAGIC SWORD, THE, 1962
MAGIC VOYAGE OF SINBAD, THE, 1962
MAGIC WEAVER, THE, 1965

BOLD: Films on Videocassette

MAGUS, THE, 1968
MAJIN, 1968
MAN IN THE MIRROR, THE, 1936
MAN IN THE MOONLIGHT MASK, THE, 1958
MAN WHO COULD WORK MIRACLES, THE, 1937
MAN WHO HAUNTED HIMSELF, THE, 1970
MAN WHO WAGGED HIS TAIL, THE, 1961
MAN WHO WASN'T THERE, THE, 1983
MAN WITH TWO BRAINS, THE, 1983
MARCH ON PARIS 1914—OF GENERALOBERST
    ALEXANDER VON KLUCK—AND HIS MEMORY
    OF JESSIE HOLLADAY, 1977
MASTER OF THE WORLD, 1961
MASTERS OF THE UNIVERSE, 1987
MEET MR. LUCIFER, 1953
MEMENTO MEI, 1963
MEMOIRS OF A SURVIVOR, 1981
MERMAID, THE, 1966
MERMAIDS OF TIBURON, THE, 1962
METAMORPHOSES, 1978
MIDSUMMER NIGHT'S DREAM, A, 1969
MIDSUMMER'S NIGHT'S DREAM, A, 1935
MIDSUMMERS NIGHT'S DREAM, A, 1961
MIDSUMMER NIGHT'S DREAM, A, 1966
MIGHTY GORGA, THE, 1969
MIGHTY JOE YOUNG, 1949
MINOTAUR, THE, 1961
MIRACLE IN MILAN, 1951
MIRACLE OF SANTA'S WHITE REINDEER, THE, 1963
MIRACLE ON 34TH STREET, THE, 1947
MISTER FREEDOM, 1970
MR. PEABODY AND THE MERMAID, 1948
MR. SUPERINVISIBLE, 1974
MISTRESS OF ATLANTIS, THE, 1932
MONSTER OF HIGHGATE PONDS, THE, 1961
MORE THAN A MIRACLE, 1967
MY WEAKNESS, 1933
NAKED WORLD OF HARRISON MARKS, THE, 1967
NEITHER THE SEA NOR THE SAND, 1974
NEVERENDING STORY, THE, 1984
NIGHT IN PARADISE, A, 1946
NIGHT LIFE OF THE GODS, 1935
NIGHT OF MAGIC, A, 1944
NINTH HEART, THE, 1980
NO HAUNT FOR A GENTLEMAN, 1952
NOBODY IN TOYLAND, 1958
NUTCRACKER FANTASY, 1979
ODYSSEY OF THE PACIFIC, 1983
OF STARS AND MEN, 1961
ONE FAMILY, 1930
ONE MAGIC CHRISTMAS, 1985
ORPHEUS, 1950
PARKING, 1985
PEER GYNT, 1965
PEGGY SUE GOT MARRIED, 1986
PEOPLE THAT TIME FORGOT, THE, 1977
PETER IBBETSON, 1935
PHANTOM SPEAKS, THE, 1945
PHANTOM TOLLBOOTH, THE, 1970
PINOCCHIO, 1940
PINOCCHIO, 1969
PINOCCHIO IN OUTER SPACE, 1965
PRINCESS AND THE MAGIC FROG, THE, 1965
PUFNSTUF, 1970
PURPLE ROSE OF CAIRO, THE, 1985
PUSS "N' BOOTS, 1964
PUSS "N' BOOTS, 1967
QUEEN'S SWORDSMEN, THE, 1963
RAT, 1960
RAT SAVIOUR, THE, 1977
RAVAGERS, THE, 1979
RED SONJA, 1985
REMARKABLE ANDREW, THE, 1942
REPENTANCE, 1988
RETURN OF PETER GRIMM, THE, 1935
RETURN TO BOGGY CREEK, 1977
RETURN TO OZ, 1985
RETURN TO WATERLOO, 1985
ROOGIE'S BUMP, 1954
RUMPELSTILTSKIN, 1965
RUMPELSTILTSKIN, 1987
SABU AND THE MAGIC RING, 1957
SAND CASTLE, THE, 1961
SANTA CLAUS: THE MOVIE, 1985
SCROOGE, 1935
SCROOGE, 1970

SEARCH FOR BRIDEY MURPHY, THE, 1956
SECRET LIFE OF WALTER MITTY, THE, 1947
SECRET OF MAGIC ISLAND, THE, 1964
SECRET OF THE LOCH, THE, 1934
SEVEN DWARFS TO THE RESCUE, THE, 1965
SEVEN FACES, 1929
SEVEN FACES OF DR. LAO, 1964
SEVEN TASKS OF ALI BABA, THE, 1963
SEVENTH VOYAGE OF SINBAD, THE, 1958
SHADOW OF THE HAWK, 1976
SHAGGY D.A., THE, 1976
SHAGGY DOG, THE, 1959
SHAMUS, 1959
SHANKS, 1974
SHE, 1935
SHE, 1965
SHE, 1985
SHE-GODS OF SHARK REEF, 1958
SHIRLEY THOMPSON VERSUS THE ALIENS, 1968
SHOEMAKER AND THE ELVES, THE, 1967
SHOOT LOUD, LOUDER. . . I DON'T UNDERSTAND,
    1966
SILENT ONE, THE, 1984
SINBAD AND THE EYE OF THE TIGER, 1977
SKY BIKE, THE, 1967
SLEEPING BEAUTY, 1965
SNOW WHITE AND THE THREE STOOGES, 1961
SOME CALL IT LOVING, 1973
SOMEWHERE IN TIME, 1980
SON OF FLUBBER, 1963
SON OF SINBAD, 1955
SONG OF THE FOREST, 1963
SORCERESS, 1983
SOUTH, 1988
SPLASH, 1984
STAIRWAY TO HEAVEN, 1946
STAR TREK IV: THE VOYAGE HOME, 1986
STORY OF MANKIND, THE, 1957
STREETS OF FIRE, 1984
SUPERGIRL, 1984
SUPERMAN IV: THE QUEST FOR PEACE, 1987
SWORD AND THE DRAGON, THE, 1960
SWORD AND THE SORCERER, THE, 1982
SWORD OF HEAVEN, 1985
TANYA'S ISLAND, 1981
THIEF OF BAGHDAD, THE, 1940
THIEF OF BAGHDAD, THE, 1961
THREE CROWNS OF THE SAILOR, 1984
THREE WISE FOOLS, 1946
THREE WORLDS OF GULLIVER, THE, 1960
TIME BANDITS, 1981
TINDER BOX, THE, 1968
TOM THUMB, 1958
TOM THUMB, 1967
TRIP, THE, 1967
20TH CENTURY OZ, 1977
TWO HUNDRED MOTELS, 1971
TWO LITTLE BEARS, THE, 1961
TWO OF A KIND, 1983
VALLEY OF GWANGI, THE, 1969
VENGEANCE OF SHE, THE, 1968
VISITOR, THE, 1973
WACKY WORLD OF MOTHER GOOSE, THE, 1967
WANDERING JEW, THE, 1935
WHEN DINOSAURS RULED THE EARTH, 1971
WHEN WOMEN HAD TAILS, 1970
WHERE HAS POOR MICKEY GONE?, 1964
WHO FEARS THE DEVIL, 1972
WHO IS HARRY KELLERMAN AND WHY IS HE
    SAYING THOSE TERRIBLE THINGS ABOUT ME?,
    1971
WHY RUSSIANS ARE REVOLTING, 1970
WILLOW, 1988
WILLY WONKA AND THE CHOCOLATE FACTORY,
    1971
WINGS OF DESIRE, 1988
WISHING MACHINE, 1971
WITCH WITHOUT A BROOM, A, 1967
WIZARD OF BAGHDAD, THE, 1960
WIZARD OF OZ, THE, 1939
WIZARDS OF THE LOST KINGDOM, 1985
WOMBLING FREE, 1977
WONDERFUL WORLD OF THE BROTHERS GRIMM,
    THE, 1962
WONDERS OF ALADDIN, THE, 1961
WORK IS A FOUR LETTER WORD, 1968
YETI, 1977

YOU MUST GET MARRIED, 1936

Historical
ABDICATION, THE, 1974
ABDUL THE DAMNED, 1935
ABDULLAH'S HAREM, 1956
ADALEN 31, 1969
ADAM'S WOMAN, 1972
ADVENTURES OF GERARD, THE, 1970
AFFAIRS OF A ROGUE, THE, 1949
AFFAIRS OF MESSALINA, THE, 1954
AGUIRRE, THE WRATH OF GOD, 1977
ALEXANDER NEVSKY, 1939
ALFRED THE GREAT, 1969
ALLEGHENY UPRISING, 1939
AMIN—THE RISE AND FALL, 1982
ANDREI ROUBLOV, 1973
ANNE DEVLIN, 1984
ANNE OF THE THOUSAND DAYS, 1969
ANTHONY ADVERSE, 1936
ANTHONY OF PADUA, 1952
ANTONY AND CLEOPATRA, 1973
ARENA, THE, 1973
ASSASSINATION OF TROTSKY, THE, 1972
ASSISI UNDERGROUND, THE, 1985
ATLANTIC FERRY, 1941
ATTILA, 1958
AUGUSTINE OF HIPPO, 1973
AUSTERLITZ, 1960
BARBARIAN AND THE GEISHA, THE, 1958
BARBERINA, 1932
BARRY LYNDON, 1975
BEATRICE, 1988
BEAU BRUMMELL, 1954
BECKET, 1964
BELIZAIRE THE CAJUN, 1986
BEN HUR, 1959
BLANCHE, 1971
BOSTONIANS, THE, 1984
BOUNTY, THE, 1984
BROTHER SUN, SISTER MOON, 1973
BUCCANEER, THE, 1958
BUCCANEER, THE, 1938
BURKE & WILLS, 1985
BURN, 1970
BUSHIDO BLADE, THE, 1982
CAESAR AND CLEOPATRA, 1946
CAESAR THE CONQUEROR, 1963
CAFFE ITALIA, 1985
CAMELOT, 1967
CAMILA, 1985
CAPTAIN BLOOD, 1935
CAPTAIN FROM CASTILE, 1947
CAPTAIN JOHN SMITH AND POCAHONTAS, 1953
CAPTAIN OF THE GUARD, 1930
CAPTAIN THUNDER, 1931
CARDINAL, THE, 1936
CARRY ON HENRY VIII, 1970
CARTHAGE IN FLAMES, 1961
CASTILIAN, THE, 1963
CATHERINE THE GREAT, 1934
CENTURION, THE, 1962
CHARGE OF THE LIGHT BRIGADE, THE, 1968
CHRISTOPHER COLUMBUS, 1949
CLEOPATRA, 1934
CLEOPATRA, 1963
COLONEL REDL, 1985
COLOSSUS OF RHODES, THE, 1961
COMRADES, 1987
CONQUEROR, THE, 1956
CONQUEST, 1937
CONQUEST OF THE AIR, 1940
COUP DE GRACE, 1978
CRIME DOES NOT PAY, 1962
CRIMSON BLADE, THE, 1964
CRUSADES, THE, 1935
DAMN THE DEFIANT!, 1962
DANGEROUS EXILE, 1958
DANGEROUS LIAISONS, 1988
DANTON, 1983
DEVIL-SHIP PIRATES, THE, 1964
DEVIL'S DISCIPLE, THE, 1959
DIANE, 1955
DIXIELAND DAIMYO, 1988
DOCTOR AND THE DEVILS, THE, 1985
DRAUGHTSMAN'S CONTRACT, THE, 1983

DRUMS ALONG THE MOHAWK, 1939
DRUMS OF DESTINY, 1937
DU BARRY, WOMAN OF PASSION, 1930
DUEL OF CHAMPIONS, 1964
DUEL OF THE TITANS, 1963
DUELLISTS, THE, 1977
DULCINEA, 1962
EGYPTIAN, THE, 1954
ENTENTE CORDIALE, 1939
ERIK THE CONQUEROR, 1963
EXODUS, 1960
FABIOLA, 1951
FALL OF ROME, THE, 1963
FALL OF THE ROMAN EMPIRE, THE, 1964
FELDMANN CASE, THE, 1987
FELLINI SATYRICON, 1969
FEMALE PRINCE, THE, 1966
55 DAYS AT PEKING, 1963
FIGHT FOR ROME, 1969
FIGHTING GUARDSMAN, THE, 1945
FIGHTING PRINCE OF DONEGAL, THE, 1966
FIRE OVER ENGLAND, 1937
FLAME IN THE HEATHER, 1935
FLAME OF CALCUTTA, 1953
FLESH AND BLOOD, 1985
FOLLOWING THE FUHRER, 1986
FOREVER AMBER, 1947
FOREVER AND A DAY, 1943
FOUR MUSKETEERS, THE, 1975
FOXES OF HARROW, THE, 1947
FRENCHMAN'S CREEK, 1944
FURY OF THE PAGANS, 1963
GALLANT BLADE, THE, 1948
GATE OF HELL, 1954
GATES TO PARADISE, 1968
GENERAL CRACK, 1929
GIORDANO BRUNO, 1973
GLASS OF WATER, A, 1962
GO TELL IT ON THE MOUNTAIN, 1984
GODDESS OF LOVE, THE, 1960
GOLD FOR THE CAESARS, 1964
GOLDEN HORDE, THE, 1951
GOLIATH AND THE BARBARIANS, 1960
GONE WITH THE WIND, 1939
GOOD MORNING BABYLON, 1987
GORGEOUS HUSSY, THE, 1936
GREAT MEADOW, THE, 1931
GREAT SIOUX MASSACRE, THE, 1965
GREAT WALL, THE, 1965
GUILTY OF TREASON, 1950
HAGBARD AND SIGNE, 1968
HANNIBAL, 1960
HAWAII, 1966
HAWAIIANS, THE, 1970
HELEN OF TROY, 1956
HERITAGE, 1935
HEROD THE GREAT, 1960
HOWARDS OF VIRGINIA, THE, 1940
HUNS, THE, 1962
IF PARIS WERE TOLD TO US, 1956
IMPERIAL VENUS, 1963
IN OLD CHICAGO, 1938
INVASION 1700, 1965
ISLAND OF ALLAH, 1956
IVANHOE, 1952
JAMAICA INN, 1939
JESTER, THE, 1987
JOHNNY TREMAIN, 1957
JUDGMENT AT NUREMBERG, 1961
JULIUS CAESAR, 1952
JULIUS CAESAR, 1953
JULIUS CAESAR, 1970
KHARTOUM, 1966
KING IN SHADOW, 1961
KING RICHARD AND THE CRUSADERS, 1954
KINGS OF THE SUN, 1963
KNIGHTS OF THE ROUND TABLE, 1953
KNIGHTS OF THE TEUTONIC ORDER, THE, 1962
KNIVES OF THE AVENGER, 1967
KOENIGSMARK, 1935
LA MARSEILLAISE, 1938
LA NUIT DE VARENNES, 1983
LADY CAROLINE LAMB, 1972
LADY OF MONZA, THE, 1970
LADY OSCAR, 1979
LAFAYETTE, 1963

LANCELOT OF THE LAKE, 1975
LAND OF THE PHARAOHS, 1955
LAST DAYS OF POMPEII, THE, 1935
LAST EMPEROR, THE, 1987
LAST OF THE MOHICANS, THE, 1936
LAST WOMAN OF SHANG, THE, 1964
LAUGHING LADY, THE, 1950
LEOPARD, THE, 1963
LES MISERABLES, 1935
LES MISERABLES, 1936
LES MISERABLES, 1952
LES MISERABLES, 1982
LET JOY REIGN SUPREME, 1977
LINCOLN CONSPIRACY, THE, 1977
LION IN WINTER, THE, 1968
LITTLE BIG HORN, 1951
LLOYDS OF LONDON, 1936
LOCK UP YOUR DAUGHTERS, 1969
LOUISIANE, 1984
LOVE UNDER THE CRUCIFIX, 1965
LOVES OF SALAMMBO, THE, 1962
LOVES OF THREE QUEENS, THE, 1954
LUCRECE BORGIA, 1953
LUCREZIA BORGIA, 1937
LYDIA BAILEY, 1952
MAD EMPRESS, THE, 1940
MAD QUEEN, THE, 1950
MADAME, 1963
MADAME DU BARRY, 1934
MADAME DU BARRY, 1954
MADAME GUILLOTINE, 1931
MAID OF SALEM, 1937
MAN FROM THE ALAMO, THE, 1953
MAN IN THE IRON MASK, THE, 1939
MAN OF IRON, 1981
MARIE ANTOINETTE, 1938
MARY OF SCOTLAND, 1936
MARY, QUEEN OF SCOTS, 1971
MASSACRE HILL, 1949
MAYERLING, 1937
MAYERLING, 1968
MESSAGE TO GARCIA, A, 1936
MESSALINE, 1952
MEXICO IN FLAMES, 1982
MICHAEL STROGOFF, 1960
MIGHTY CRUSADERS, THE, 1961
MISSION, THE, 1986
MOLLY MAGUIRES, THE, 1970
MONGOLS, THE, 1966
MONTY PYTHON AND THE HOLY GRAIL, 1975
MORO AFFAIR, THE, 1986
MY UNCLE'S LEGACY, 1988
NELL GWYN, 1935
NELSON AFFAIR, THE, 1973
NERO'S MISTRESS, 1962
NIGHTS OF LUCRETIA BORGIA, THE, 1960
NINE HOURS TO RAMA, 1963
1914, 1932
PATRIOT, THE, 1928
PEARLS OF THE CROWN, 1938
PEG OF OLD DRURY, 1936
PERSECUTION AND ASSASSINATION OF
  JEAN-PAUL MARAT AS PERFORMED BY THE
  INMATES OF THE ASYLUM OF CHARENTON
  UNDER THE DIRECTION OF THE MARQUIS DE
  SADE, THE, 1967
PHAROAH'S WOMAN, THE, 1961
PICKWICK PAPERS, THE, 1952
PLOUGH AND THE STARS, THE, 1936
PLYMOUTH ADVENTURE, 1952
POWER, 1934
PRINCE OF FOXES, 1949
PRISONER OF CORBAL, 1939
PRISONER OF THE VOLGA, 1960
PRIVATE LIFE OF LOUIS XIV, 1936
PURSUIT OF HAPPINESS, THE, 1934
QUEBEC, 1951
QUEEN CHRISTINA, 1933
QUEEN OF SHEBA, 1953
QUEEN OF THE NILE, 1964
QUEEN OF THE PIRATES, 1961
QUENTIN DURWARD, 1955
QUEST FOR FIRE, 1982
QUILOMBO, 1986
QUO VADIS, 1951
RAGTIME, 1981

RAILROAD WORKERS, 1948
RAILWAY CHILDREN, THE, 1971
RAINTREE COUNTY, 1957
RAN, 1985
RASPOUTINE, 1954
RASPUTIN AND THE EMPRESS, 1932
REBEL GLADIATORS, THE, 1963
REBEL LOVE, 1986
REBEL SON, THE, 1939
RED BEARD, 1966
RED CLOAK, THE, 1961
RED LION, 1971
RED SHEIK, THE, 1963
REDS, 1981
REGAL CAVALCADE, 1935
RELUCTANT WIDOW, THE, 1951
RESURRECTION, 1931
RESURRECTION, 1963
RETURN OF MARTIN GUERRE, THE, 1983
RETURN OF MONTE CRISTO, THE, 1946
RETURN OF THE BLACK EAGLE, 1949
RETURN OF THE SCARLET PIMPERNEL, 1938
REVENGE OF THE GLADIATORS, 1965
REVOLT OF THE SLAVES, THE, 1961
REVOLUTION, 1985
RICHARD III, 1956
RISE AGAINST THE SWORD, 1966
ROB ROY, THE HIGHLAND ROGUE, 1954
ROGUES OF SHERWOOD FOREST, 1950
ROME WANTS ANOTHER CAESAR, 1974
ROMEO AND JULIET, 1936
ROMEO AND JULIET, 1954
ROMEO AND JULIET, 1968
ROMEO AND JULIET, 1968
ROUND UP, THE, 1969
ROYAL AFFAIRS IN VERSAILLES, 1957
ROYAL FLASH, 1975
ROYAL HUNT OF THE SUN, THE, 1969
ROYAL WALTZ, THE, 1936
RULERS OF THE SEA, 1939
RUY BLAS, 1948
SACCO AND VANZETTI, 1971
SAINT JOAN, 1957
ST. VALENTINE'S DAY MASSACRE, THE, 1967
SAMSON AND THE SEVEN MIRACLES OF THE
  WORLD, 1963
SAMSON AND THE SLAVE QUEEN, 1963
SANTA FE TRAIL, 1940
SARABAND, 1949
SCARLET COAT, THE, 1955
SCARLET EMPRESS, THE, 1934
SCOTT OF THE ANTARCTIC, 1949
SEA GULL, THE, 1968
SERPENT OF THE NILE, 1953
SEVEN ANGRY MEN, 1955
SEVEN CITIES OF GOLD, 1955
SEVEN SEAS TO CALAIS, 1963
SEVEN WOMEN, 1966
1776, 1972
SHADOW OF THE EAGLE, 1955
SHAME OF THE SABINE WOMEN, THE, 1962
SIAVASH IN PERSEPOLIS, 1966
SIEGE OF SIDNEY STREET, THE, 1960
SIEGE OF SYRACUSE, 1962
SIEGE OF THE SAXONS, 1963
SIGN OF THE CROSS, 1932
SIGN OF THE GLADIATOR, 1959
SIGN OF THE PAGAN, 1954
SINK THE BISMARCK, 1960
SITTING BULL, 1954
SIXTY GLORIOUS YEARS, 1938
SPARTACUS, 1960
SPY OF NAPOLEON, 1939
STORY OF MANKIND, THE, 1957
STRONGHOLD, 1952
SWEET KITTY BELLAIRS, 1930
SWORD AND THE ROSE, THE, 1953
SWORD IN THE DESERT, 1949
SWORD OF MONTE CRISTO, THE, 1951
TAI-PAN, 1986
TALE OF TWO CITIES, A, 1935
TALE OF TWO CITIES, A, 1958
TARAS BULBA, 1962
TARTARS, THE, 1962
TEMPEST, 1958
TEN DAYS THAT SHOOK THE WORLD, THE, 1977

BOLD: Films on Videocassette

TEN WHO DARED, 1960
TENCHU, 1970
THAT LADY, 1955
THEY WANTED PEACE, 1940
THIS ENGLAND, 1941
THIS IS MY AFFAIR, 1937
300 SPARTANS, THE, 1962
TITANIC, 1953
TOY WIFE, THE, 1938
TRAPPED BY THE TERROR, 1949
TRAPPED IN A SUBMARINE, 1931
TRIAL OF JOAN OF ARC, 1965
TRIPOLI, 1950
TROJAN HORSE, THE, 1962
TROJAN WOMEN, THE, 1971
TWILIGHT'S LAST GLEAMING, 1977
VAGABOND KING, THE, 1930
VAGABOND KING, THE, 1956
VALACHI PAPERS, THE, 1972
VERONA TRIAL, THE, 1963
VICAR OF BRAY, THE, 1937
VICTORIA THE GREAT, 1937
VIKING QUEEN, THE, 1967
VIKINGS, THE, 1958
VILLA!, 1958
VILLA RIDES, 1968
VIRGIN QUEEN, THE, 1955
VON RICHTHOFEN AND BROWN, 1970
VOW, THE, 1947
WALK WITH LOVE AND DEATH, A, 1969
WALKER, 1987
WANDERING JEW, THE, 1935
WANNSEE CONFERENCE, THE, 1987
WAR LORD, THE, 1965
WARM IN THE BUD, 1970
WARRING CLANS, 1963
WARRIOR AND THE SLAVE GIRL, THE, 1959
WARRIOR EMPRESS, THE, 1961
WARRIORS, THE, 1955
WE LIVE AGAIN, 1934
WE'RE GOING TO BE RICH, 1938
WHIRLWIND, 1968
WHITE DEVIL, THE, 1948
WHITE WARRIOR, THE, 1961
WICKED LADY, THE, 1946
WICKED LADY, THE, 1983
WIFE OF MONTE CRISTO, THE, 1946
WILD GEESE CALLING, 1941
WILD GIRL, 1932
WILD HEART, THE, 1952
WILLIE MCBEAN AND HIS MAGIC MACHINE, 1965
WIND AND THE LION, THE, 1975
WINSTANLEY, 1979
WINTER'S TALE, THE, 1968
WITCH WITHOUT A BROOM, A, 1967
YOUNG BESS, 1953
ZULU, 1964
ZULU DAWN, 1980

Horror

ABBY, 1974
ABOMINABLE DR. PHIBES, THE, 1971
ALICE, SWEET ALICE, 1978
ALIEN, 1979
ALONE IN THE DARK, 1982
ALRAUNE, 1952
AMERICAN GOTHIC, 1988
AMERICAN WEREWOLF IN LONDON, AN, 1981
AMITYVILLE HORROR, THE, 1979
AMITYVILLE 3-D, 1983
AMITYVILLE II: THE POSSESSION, 1982
ANATOMIST, THE, 1961
AND NOW THE SCREAMING STARTS, 1973
ANDY WARHOL'S DRACULA, 1974
ANDY WARHOL'S FRANKENSTEIN, 1974
ANGUISH, 1988
APE, THE, 1940
APE MAN, THE, 1943
APRIL FOOL'S DAY, 1986
AROUSERS, THE, 1973
ASPHYX, THE, 1972
ASSIGNMENT TERROR, 1970
ASYLUM, 1972
ATOM AGE VAMPIRE, 1961
ATOMIC BRAIN, THE, 1964
ATTACK OF THE GIANT LEECHES, 1959

ATTACK OF THE KILLER TOMATOES, 1978
ATTACK OF THE MAYAN MUMMY, 1963
AUDREY ROSE, 1977
AWAKENING, THE, 1980
AWFUL DR. ORLOFF, THE, 1964
AZTEC MUMMY, THE, 1957
BABY, THE, 1973
BACK FROM THE DEAD, 1957
BAD DREAMS, 1988
BARN OF THE NAKED DEAD, 1976
BARON BLOOD, 1972
BARRACUDA, 1978
BASKET CASE, 1982
BAT PEOPLE, THE, 1974
BEACH GIRLS AND THE MONSTER, THE, 1965
BEAST FROM THE HAUNTED CAVE, 1960
BEAST IN THE CELLAR, THE, 1971
BEAST MUST DIE, THE, 1974
BEAST OF BLOOD, 1970
BEAST WITH FIVE FINGERS, THE, 1946
BEAST WITHIN, THE, 1982
BEDLAM, 1946
BEETLEJUICE, 1988
BEFORE I HANG, 1940
BEHIND LOCKED DOORS, 1976
BEING, THE, 1983
BELIEVERS, THE, 1987
BELLMAN, THE, 1947
BEN, 1972
BERSERK, 1967
BERSERKER, 1988
BEYOND ATLANTIS, 1973
BEYOND THE DOOR, 1975
BEYOND THE DOOR II, 1979
BEYOND THE FOG, 1981
BIG FOOT, 1973
BILLY THE KID VS. DRACULA, 1966
BIRD WITH THE CRYSTAL PLUMAGE, THE, 1970
BIRDS, THE, 1963
BLACK CASTLE, THE, 1952
BLACK CAT, THE, 1934
BLACK CAT, THE, 1941
BLACK CAT, THE, 1966
BLACK CAT, THE, 1984
BLACK CHRISTMAS, 1974
BLACK DRAGONS, 1942
BLACK FRIDAY, 1940
BLACK PIT OF DOCTOR M, 1958
BLACK ROOM, THE, 1935
BLACK ROOM, THE, 1984
BLACK SABBATH, 1963
BLACK SLEEP, THE, 1956
BLACK SPIDER, THE, 1983
BLACK SUNDAY, 1961
BLACK TORMENT, THE, 1965
BLACK ZOO, 1963
BLACKENSTEIN, 1973
BLACULA, 1972
BLADE IN THE DARK, A, 1986
BLIND DEAD, THE, 1972
BLOOD, 1974
BLOOD AND BLACK LACE, 1965
BLOOD AND LACE, 1971
BLOOD AND ROSES, 1961
BLOOD BATH, 1966
BLOOD BATH, 1976
BLOOD BEACH, 1981
BLOOD BEAST TERROR, THE, 1967
BLOOD DEMON, 1967
BLOOD DINER, 1987
BLOOD DRINKERS, THE, 1966
BLOOD FEAST, 1963
BLOOD FROM THE MUMMY'S TOMB, 1972
BLOOD MANIA, 1971
BLOOD OF DRACULA, 1957
BLOOD OF DRACULA'S CASTLE, 1967
BLOOD OF FRANKENSTEIN, 1970
BLOOD OF THE VAMPIRE, 1958
BLOOD ON SATAN'S CLAW, THE, 1970
BLOOD ORGY OF THE SHE-DEVILS, 1973
BLOOD ROSE, THE, 1970
BLOOD SISTERS, 1987
BLOOD SPATTERED BRIDE, THE, 1974
BLOOD TIDE, 1982
BLOOD WATERS OF DOCTOR Z, 1982
BLOODEATERS, 1980

BLOODLUST, 1959
BLOODSUCKING FREAKS, 1982
BLOODTHIRSTY BUTCHERS, 1970
BLOODY BIRTHDAY, 1986
BLOODY PIT OF HORROR, THE, 1965
BLUE MONKEY, 1988
BODY SNATCHER, THE, 1945
BOGGY CREEK II, 1985
BOOGENS, THE, 1982
BOOGEY MAN, THE, 1980
BOOGEYMAN II, 1983
BORN OF FIRE, 1987
BOWERY AT MIDNIGHT, 1942
BOWERY BOYS MEET THE MONSTERS, THE, 1954
BOY WHO CRIED WEREWOLF, THE, 1973
BRAIN DAMAGE, 1988
BRAIN OF BLOOD, 1971
BRAIN THAT WOULDN'T DIE, THE, 1959
BRIDE, THE, 1985
BRIDE AND THE BEAST, THE, 1958
BRIDE OF FRANKENSTEIN, THE, 1935
BRIDE OF THE GORILLA, 1951
BRIDES OF DRACULA, THE, 1960
BROOD, THE, 1979
BROTHERHOOD OF SATAN, THE, 1971
BRUTE MAN, THE, 1946
BUCKET OF BLOOD, 1934
BUCKET OF BLOOD, A, 1959
BURIED ALIVE, 1984
BURKE AND HARE, 1972
BURN WITCH BURN, 1962
BURNING, THE, 1981
BURNT OFFERINGS, 1976
BUTCHER BAKER (NIGHTMARE MAKER), 1982
C.H.U.D., 1984
CABINET OF CALIGARI, THE, 1962
CALTIKI, THE IMMORTAL MONSTER, 1959
CANNIBAL GIRLS, 1973
CANNIBALS IN THE STREETS, 1982
CAPTAIN KRONOS: VAMPIRE HUNTER, 1974
CAPTIVE WILD WOMAN, 1943
CAR, THE, 1977
CARDIAC ARREST, 1980
CARNAGE, 1986
CARNIVAL OF BLOOD, 1976
CARNIVAL OF SINNERS, 1947
CARNIVAL OF SOULS, 1962
CARRIE, 1976
CASTLE OF BLOOD, 1964
CASTLE OF EVIL, 1967
CASTLE OF FU MANCHU, THE, 1968
CASTLE OF THE LIVING DEAD, 1964
CASTLE OF THE MONSTERS, 1958
CASTLE SINISTER, 1932
CAT GIRL, 1957
CAT PEOPLE, 1942
CAT PEOPLE, 1982
CATHY'S CURSE, 1977
CAT'S EYE, 1985
CAULDRON OF BLOOD, 1971
CAVE OF THE LIVING DEAD, 1966
CELLAR DWELLER, 1988
CEMENTERIO DEL TERROR, 1985
CHAMBER OF HORRORS, 1941
CHAMBER OF HORRORS, 1966
CHANGELING, THE, 1980
CHILD, THE, 1977
CHILDREN, THE, 1980
CHILDREN OF THE CORN, 1984
CHILDREN OF THE DAMNED, 1963
CHILDREN SHOULDN'T PLAY WITH DEAD THINGS, 1972
CHILD'S PLAY, 1988
CHOPPING MALL, 1986
CHOSEN, THE, 1978
CHRISTINE, 1983
CIRCUS OF HORRORS, 1960
CITY OF THE WALKING DEAD, 1983
CLASS OF NUKE 'EM HIGH, 1986
CLIMAX, THE, 1944
CLONUS HORROR, THE, 1979
COLOR ME BLOOD RED, 1965
COLOSSUS OF NEW YORK, THE, 1958
COMEBACK, THE, 1982
COMEDY OF HORRORS, THE, 1964
COMPANY OF WOLVES, THE, 1985

CONDEMNED TO LIVE, 1935
CONFESSIONAL, THE, 1977
CONQUEROR WORM, THE, 1968
CORPSE GRINDERS, THE, 1972
CORPSE VANISHES, THE, 1942
CORRUPTION, 1968
COUNT DRACULA, 1971
COUNT DRACULA AND HIS VAMPIRE BRIDE, 1978
COUNT YORGA, VAMPIRE, 1970
COUNTESS DRACULA, 1972
CRASH, 1977
CRAWLING EYE, THE, 1958
CRAWLING HAND, THE, 1963
CRAWLSPACE, 1986
CRAZE, 1974
CRAZIES, THE, 1973
CREATURE, 1985
CREATURE FROM BLACK LAKE, THE, 1976
CREATURE FROM THE BLACK LAGOON, 1954
CREATURE FROM THE HAUNTED SEA, 1961
CREATURE OF THE WALKING DEAD, 1960
CREATURE WALKS AMONG US, THE, 1956
CREATURE WITH THE ATOM BRAIN, 1955
CREATURE WITH THE BLUE HAND, 1971
CREATURES THE WORLD FORGOT, 1971
CREEPER, THE, 1948
CREEPERS, 1985
CREEPING FLESH, THE, 1973
CREEPING TERROR, THE, 1964
CREEPING UNKNOWN, THE, 1956
CREEPSHOW, 1982
CREEPSHOW 2, 1987
CRESCENDO, 1972
CRIME OF DR. CRESPI, THE, 1936
CRIMES OF THE FUTURE, 1969
CRIMSON CULT, THE, 1970
CRITTERS II: THE MAIN COURSE, 1988
CROCODILE, 1979
CRUCIBLE OF HORROR, 1971
CRUCIBLE OF TERROR, 1971
CRY OF THE BANSHEE, 1970
CRY OF THE WEREWOLF, 1944
CRYPT OF THE LIVING DEAD, 1973
CUJO, 1983
CULT OF THE COBRA, 1955
CURIOUS DR. HUMPP, 1967
CURSE OF BIGFOOT, THE, 1972
CURSE OF FRANKENSTEIN, THE, 1957
CURSE OF THE AZTEC MUMMY, THE, 1965
CURSE OF THE BLOOD GHOULS, 1969
CURSE OF THE CAT PEOPLE, THE, 1944
CURSE OF THE CRYING WOMAN, THE, 1969
CURSE OF THE DEMON, 1958
CURSE OF THE DEVIL, 1973
CURSE OF THE DOLL PEOPLE, THE, 1968
CURSE OF THE FACELESS MAN, 1958
CURSE OF THE FLY, 1965
CURSE OF THE LIVING CORPSE, THE, 1964
CURSE OF THE MUMMY'S TOMB, THE, 1965
CURSE OF THE STONE HAND, 1965
CURSE OF THE SWAMP CREATURE, 1966
CURSE OF THE UNDEAD, 1959
CURSE OF THE VAMPIRES, 1970
CURSE OF THE VOODOO, 1965
CURSE OF THE WEREWOLF, THE, 1961
CURSE, THE, 1987
CURTAINS, 1983
DADDY'S DEADLY DARLING, 1984
DAMIEN—OMEN II, 1978
DARK, THE, 1979
DARK INTRUDER, 1965
DARK PLACES, 1974
DAS LETZTE GEHEIMNIS, 1959
DAUGHTER OF DR. JEKYLL, 1957
DAUGHTER OF EVIL, 1930
DAUGHTERS OF DARKNESS, 1971
DAUGHTERS OF SATAN, 1972
DAWN OF THE DEAD, 1979
DAY OF THE ANIMALS, 1977
DAY OF THE DEAD, 1985
DAY OF THE TRIFFIDS, THE, 1963
DEAD AND BURIED, 1981
DEAD ARE ALIVE, THE, 1972
DEAD HEAT, 1988
DEAD KIDS, 1981
DEAD MEN WALK, 1943

DEAD OF NIGHT, 1946
DEAD ONE, THE, 1961
DEAD PEOPLE, 1974
DEAD RINGERS, 1988
DEAD ZONE, THE, 1983
DEADLY BEES, THE, 1967
DEADLY BLESSING, 1981
DEADLY DREAMS, 1988
DEADLY EYES, 1982
DEADLY FRIEND, 1986
DEADTIME STORIES, 1987
DEAR, DEAD DELILAH, 1972
DEATH CURSE OF TARTU, 1967
DEATH SHIP, 1980
DEATHDREAM, 1972
DEATHLINE, 1973
DEATHMASTER, THE, 1972
DEATHROW GAMESHOW, 1987
DECOY FOR TERROR, 1970
DEMENTED, 1980
DEMENTIA, 1955
DEMENTIA 13, 1963
DEMON BARBER OF FLEET STREET, THE, 1939
DEMON LOVER, THE, 1977
DEMON WITCH CHILD, 1974
DEMON, THE, 1981
DEMONOID, 1981
DEMONS, 1985
DEMONS OF LUDLOW, THE, 1983
DERANGED, 1974
DEVIL BAT, THE, 1941
DEVIL COMMANDS, THE, 1941
DEVIL DOLL, THE, 1936
DEVIL DOLL, 1964
DEVIL TIMES FIVE, 1974
DEVIL WITHIN HER, THE, 1976
DEVIL WOMAN, 1976
DEVIL'S BRIDE, THE, 1968
DEVIL'S COMMANDMENT, THE, 1956
DEVIL'S EXPRESS, 1975
DEVIL'S HAND, THE, 1961
DEVIL'S MESSENGER, THE, 1962
DEVIL'S MISTRESS, THE, 1968
DEVIL'S NIGHTMARE, THE, 1971
DEVILS OF DARKNESS, THE, 1965
DEVIL'S OWN, THE, 1967
DEVIL'S PARTNER, THE, 1958
DEVIL'S RAIN, THE, 1975
DEVIL'S WEDDING NIGHT, THE, 1973
DEVIL'S WIDOW, THE, 1972
DEVONSVILLE TERROR, THE, 1983
DIABOLICAL DR. Z, THE, 1966
DIARY OF A MADMAN, 1963
DIE, DIE, MY DARLING, 1965
DIE, MONSTER, DIE, 1965
DISCIPLE OF DEATH, 1972
DISEMBODIED, THE, 1957
DR. BUTCHER, M.D., 1982
DOCTOR CRIMEN, 1953
DOCTOR DEATH: SEEKER OF SOULS, 1973
DR. FRANKENSTEIN ON CAMPUS, 1970
DR. HECKYL AND MR. HYPE, 1980
DR. JEKYLL, 1985
DR. JEKYLL AND MR. HYDE, 1932
DR. JEKYLL AND MR. HYDE, 1941
DR. JEKYLL AND SISTER HYDE, 1971
DR. JEKYLL AND THE WOLFMAN, 1971
DR. JEKYLL'S DUNGEON OF DEATH, 1982
DOCTOR OF DOOM, 1962
DOCTOR PHIBES RISES AGAIN, 1972
DR. RENAULT'S SECRET, 1942
DR. TARR'S TORTURE DUNGEON, 1972
DR. TERROR'S GALLERY OF HORRORS, 1967
DR. TERROR'S HOUSE OF HORRORS, 1965
DOCTOR X, 1932
DOGS, 1976
DOLLS, 1987
DON'T ANSWER THE PHONE, 1980
DON'T GO IN THE HOUSE, 1980
DON'T LOOK IN THE BASEMENT, 1973
DON'T OPEN THE WINDOW, 1974
DON'T OPEN TILL CHRISTMAS, 1984
DOOMED TO DIE, 1985
DORIAN GRAY, 1970
DORM THAT DRIPPED BLOOD, THE, 1983
DR. BLACK AND MR. HYDE, 1976

DR. BLOOD'S COFFIN, 1961
DRACULA, 1931
DRACULA, 1979
DRACULA A.D. 1972, 1972
DRACULA AND THE SEVEN GOLDEN VAMPIRES, 1978
DRACULA HAS RISEN FROM HIS GRAVE, 1968
DRACULA—PRINCE OF DARKNESS, 1966
DRACULA (THE DIRTY OLD MAN), 1969
DRACULA VERSUS FRANKENSTEIN, 1972
DRACULA'S DAUGHTER, 1936
DRACULA'S DOG, 1978
DRACULA'S GREAT LOVE, 1972
DRACULA'S WIDOW, 1988
DREAMANIAC, 1987
DRILLER KILLER, 1979
DRIVE-IN MASSACRE, 1976
DUNGEONS OF HARROW, 1964
DUNWICH HORROR, THE, 1970
EARTH VS. THE SPIDER, 1958
EATEN ALIVE, 1976
EEGAH!, 1962
EFFECTS, 1980
ELVIRA: MISTRESS OF THE DARK, 1988
EMBALMER, THE, 1966
ENCOUNTER WITH THE UNKNOWN, 1973
ENTITY, THE, 1982
EQUINOX, 1970
ERASERHEAD, 1978
ESCAPES, 1987
EVICTORS, THE, 1979
EVIL, THE, 1978
EVIL DEAD, THE, 1983
EVIL DEAD 2: DEAD BY DAWN, 1987
EVIL OF FRANKENSTEIN, THE, 1964
EVILS OF THE NIGHT, 1985
EVILSPEAK, 1982
EXORCISM AT MIDNIGHT, 1966
EXORCISM'S DAUGHTER, 1974
EXORCIST, THE, 1973
EXORCIST II: THE HERETIC, 1977
EXOTIC ONES, THE, 1968
EYE OF THE CAT, 1969
EYE OF THE DEVIL, 1967
EYES OF A STRANGER, 1980
EYES OF FIRE, 1984
FACE BEHIND THE MASK, THE, 1941
FACE OF FU MANCHU, THE, 1965
FACE OF MARBLE, THE, 1946
FACE OF TERROR, 1964
FACE OF THE SCREAMING WEREWOLF, 1959
FADE TO BLACK, 1980
FALL OF THE HOUSE OF USHER, THE, 1952
FALL OF THE HOUSE OF USHER, THE, 1980
FEAR CHAMBER, THE, 1968
FEAR NO EVIL, 1981
FEARLESS VAMPIRE KILLERS, OR PARDON ME BUT YOUR TEETH ARE IN MY NECK, THE, 1967
FEMALE BUTCHER, THE, 1972
FIEND, 1980
FIEND WITHOUT A FACE, 1958
FINAL CONFLICT, THE, 1981
FINAL EXAM, 1981
FINAL TERROR, THE, 1983
FLESH AND BLOOD SHOW, THE, 1974
FLESH EATERS, THE, 1964
FLESH FEAST, 1970
FLYING SERPENT, THE, 1946
FOG, THE, 1980
FORBIDDEN WORLD, 1982
FORCED ENTRY, 1975
FOREST, THE, 1983
FOUR SKULLS OF JONATHAN DRAKE, THE, 1959
FRANKENSTEIN, 1931
FRANKENSTEIN AND THE MONSTER FROM HELL, 1974
FRANKENSTEIN CONQUERS THE WORLD, 1964
FRANKENSTEIN CREATED WOMAN, 1965
FRANKENSTEIN GENERAL HOSPITAL, 1988
FRANKENSTEIN-ITALIAN STYLE, 1977
FRANKENSTEIN MEETS THE WOLF MAN, 1943
FRANKENSTEIN MUST BE DESTROYED!, 1969
FRANKENSTEIN 1970, 1958
FRANKENSTEIN'S BLOODY TERROR, 1968
FRANKENSTEIN'S DAUGHTER, 1958
FRANKENSTEIN, THE VAMPIRE AND CO., 1961

FREAKS, 1932
FRIDAY THE 13TH, 1980
FRIDAY THE 13TH, PART V—A NEW BEGINNING, 1985
FRIDAY THE 13TH PART VI: JASON LIVES, 1986
FRIDAY THE 13TH PART VII—THE NEW BLOOD, 1988
FRIDAY THE 13TH PART III, 1982
FRIDAY THE 13TH PART II, 1981
FRIDAY THE 13TH—THE FINAL CHAPTER, 1984
FRIDAY THE 13TH. . . THE ORPHAN, 1979
FRIGHT NIGHT, 1985
FRIGHTMARE, 1974
FRIGHTMARE, 1983
FROGS, 1972
FROM BEYOND, 1986
FROM BEYOND THE GRAVE, 1974
FROM HELL IT CAME, 1957
FROZEN DEAD, THE, 1967
FULL MOON HIGH, 1982
FUNERAL HOME, 1982
FUNHOUSE, THE, 1981
FUTURE-KILL, 1985
GANJA AND HESS, 1973
GARDEN OF THE DEAD, 1972
GATE, THE, 1987
GATES OF HELL, THE, 1983
GEEK MAGGOT BINGO, 1983
GHASTLY ONES, THE, 1968
GHOST, THE, 1965
GHOST OF DRAGSTRIP HOLLOW, 1959
GHOST OF FRANKENSTEIN, THE, 1942
GHOST SHIP, 1953
GHOST SHIP, THE, 1943
GHOST STORY, 1974
GHOST STORY, 1981
GHOST TOWN, 1988
GHOSTS ON THE LOOSE, 1943
GHOUL, THE, 1934
GHOUL, THE, 1975
GHOULIES, 1985
GHOULIES II, 1988
GIANT FROM THE UNKNOWN, 1958
GIRLS NIGHT OUT, 1984
GIRLS SCHOOL SCREAMERS, 1986
GODSEND, THE, 1980
GOLEM, THE, 1937
GOLIATH AND THE VAMPIRES, 1964
GORGON, THE, 1964
GOTHIC, 1987
GRADUATION DAY, 1981
GRAVE OF THE VAMPIRE, 1972
GRAVEYARD OF HORROR, 1971
GRAVEYARD SHIFT, 1987
GREAT ALLIGATOR, 1980
GREAT GABBO, THE, 1929
GREAT WHITE, THE, 1982
GREMLINS, 1984
GRIM REAPER, THE, 1981
GRIZZLY, 1976
GRUESOME TWOSOME, 1968
GUARDIAN OF HELL, 1985
GUESS WHAT HAPPENED TO COUNT DRACULA, 1970
GURU, THE MAD MONK, 1971
HALLOWEEN, 1978
HALLOWEEN IV: THE RETURN OF MICHAEL MYERS, 1988
HALLOWEEN III: SEASON OF THE WITCH, 1982
HALLOWEEN II, 1981
HAND, THE, 1981
HAND OF NIGHT, THE, 1968
HAND, THE, 1960
HANDS OF A STRANGER, 1962
HANDS OF ORLAC, THE, 1964
HANDS OF THE RIPPER, 1971
HAPPY BIRTHDAY TO ME, 1981
HATCHET FOR A HONEYMOON, 1969
HAUNTED, 1976
HAUNTED HONEYMOON, 1986
HAUNTED PALACE, THE, 1963
HAUNTED STRANGLER, THE, 1958
HAUNTING, THE, 1963
HAUNTING OF JULIA, THE, 1981
HAUNTING OF M, THE, 1979
HAUNTS, 1977

HAVE A NICE WEEKEND, 1975
HE KNOWS YOU'RE ALONE, 1980
HEAD, THE, 1961
HEADLESS GHOST, THE, 1959
HEARSE, THE, 1980
HELL NIGHT, 1981
HELLBOUND: HELLRAISER II, 1988
HELLO MARY LOU, PROM NIGHT II, 1987
HELLRAISER, 1987
HILLBILLYS IN A HAUNTED HOUSE, 1967
HILLS HAVE EYES, THE, 1978
HILLS HAVE EYES II, THE, 1985
HITCHER, THE, 1986
HOME SWEET HOME, 1981
HOMEBODIES, 1974
HOMICIDAL, 1961
HORRIBLE DR. HICHCOCK, THE, 1964
HORROR CASTLE, 1965
HORROR CHAMBER OF DR. FAUSTUS, THE, 1962
HORROR EXPRESS, 1972
HORROR HIGH, 1974
HORROR HOSPITAL, 1973
HORROR HOTEL, 1960
HORROR HOUSE, 1970
HORROR ISLAND, 1941
HORROR OF DRACULA, THE, 1958
HORROR OF FRANKENSTEIN, THE, 1970
HORROR OF PARTY BEACH, THE, 1964
HORROR OF THE ZOMBIES, 1974
HORRORS OF THE BLACK MUSEUM, 1959
HOSPITAL MASSACRE, 1982
HOSPITAL MASSACRE, 1984
HOUSE, 1986
HOUSE II: THE SECOND STORY, 1987
HOUSE BY THE CEMETERY, THE, 1984
HOUSE IN MARSH ROAD, THE, 1960
HOUSE OF DARK SHADOWS, 1970
HOUSE OF DRACULA, 1945
HOUSE OF EVIL, 1968
HOUSE OF EXORCISM, THE, 1976
HOUSE OF FRANKENSTEIN, 1944
HOUSE OF FREAKS, 1973
HOUSE OF FRIGHT, 1961
HOUSE OF HORRORS, 1946
HOUSE OF LONG SHADOWS, THE, 1983
HOUSE OF MYSTERY, 1934
HOUSE OF MYSTERY, 1961
HOUSE OF PSYCHOTIC WOMEN, THE, 1973
HOUSE OF SEVEN CORPSES, THE, 1974
HOUSE OF THE BLACK DEATH, 1965
HOUSE OF THE DAMNED, 1963
HOUSE OF THE LIVING DEAD, 1973
HOUSE OF USHER, 1960
HOUSE OF WAX, 1953
HOUSE OF WHIPCORD, 1974
HOUSE ON HAUNTED HILL, 1958
HOUSE ON SKULL MOUNTAIN, THE, 1974
HOUSE ON SORORITY ROW, THE, 1983
HOUSE THAT DRIPPED BLOOD, THE, 1971
HOUSE THAT SCREAMED, THE, 1970
HOUSE THAT VANISHED, THE, 1974
HOUSE WHERE DEATH LIVES, THE, 1984
HOUSE WHERE EVIL DWELLS, THE, 1982
HOW TO MAKE A MONSTER, 1958
HOWLING, THE, 1981
HOWLING TWO: YOUR SISTER IS A WEREWOLF, 1985
HOWLING III, THE, 1987
HOWLING IV: THE ORIGINAL NIGHTMARE, 1988
HUMAN EXPERIMENTS, 1980
HUMAN MONSTER, THE, 1940
HUMANOIDS FROM THE DEEP, 1980
HUMONGOUS, 1982
HUNCHBACK OF NOTRE DAME, THE, 1939
HUNCHBACK OF NOTRE DAME, THE, 1957
HUNCHBACK OF THE MORGUE, THE, 1972
HUNGER, THE, 1983
HUNGRY WIVES, 1973
HYPNOTIC EYE, THE, 1960
HYSTERICAL, 1983
I DISMEMBER MAMA, 1974
I DRINK YOUR BLOOD, 1971
I EAT YOUR SKIN, 1971
I, MONSTER, 1971
I SPIT ON YOUR GRAVE, 1983
I WALKED WITH A ZOMBIE, 1943

I WAS A TEENAGE FRANKENSTEIN, 1958
I WAS A TEENAGE WEREWOLF, 1957
I WAS A TEENAGE ZOMBIE, 1987
ICE HOUSE, THE, 1969
ILLUSION OF BLOOD, 1966
IMPULSE, 1975
IN THE SHADOW OF KILIMANJARO, 1986
INCENSE FOR THE DAMNED, 1970
INCREDIBLY STRANGE CREATURES WHO STOPPED LIVING AND BECAME CRAZY MIXED-UP ZOMBIES, THE, 1965
INCUBUS, 1966
INCUBUS, THE, 1982
INFERNO, 1980
INITIATION, THE, 1984
INN OF THE DAMNED, 1974
INNOCENTS, THE, 1961
INVASION OF THE BLOOD FARMERS, 1972
INVASION OF THE VAMPIRES, THE, 1961
INVISIBLE GHOST, THE, 1941
INVISIBLE RAY, THE, 1936
INVISIBLE STRANGLER, 1984
IS THIS TRIP REALLY NECESSARY?, 1970
ISLAND OF DR. MOREAU, THE, 1977
ISLAND OF LOST SOULS, 1933
ISLAND OF THE DAMNED, 1976
ISLAND OF THE DOOMED, 1968
ISLE OF THE DEAD, 1945
IT!, 1967
IT LIVES AGAIN, 1978
IT'S ALIVE, 1974
IT'S ALIVE III: ISLAND OF THE ALIVE, 1988
IT'S HOT IN PARADISE, 1962
J.D.'S REVENGE, 1976
JAWS, 1975
JAWS II, 1978
JAWS 3-D, 1983
JAWS OF SATAN, 1980
JAWS: THE REVENGE, 1987
JEKYLL AND HYDE. . .TOGETHER AGAIN, 1982
JENNIFER, 1978
JESSE JAMES MEETS FRANKENSTEIN'S DAUGHTER, 1966
JONATHAN, 1973
JOURNEY INTO DARKNESS, 1968
JOURNEY INTO MIDNIGHT, 1968
JUNGLE CAPTIVE, 1945
JUNGLE WOMAN, 1944
JUST BEFORE DAWN, 1980
KEEP, THE, 1983
KEEP MY GRAVE OPEN, 1980
KEEPER, THE, 1976
KILL BABY KILL, 1966
KILLER KLOWNS FROM OUTER SPACE, 1988
KILLER PARTY, 1986
KILLER WORKOUT, 1987
KILLING HOUR, THE, 1982
KING OF THE ZOMBIES, 1941
KINGDOM OF THE SPIDERS, 1977
KISS OF EVIL, 1963
KISS OF THE TARANTULA, 1975
KONGO, 1932
KUROENKO, 1968
KWAIDAN, 1965
LADY AND THE MONSTER, THE, 1944
LADY DRACULA, THE, 1974
LADY FRANKENSTEIN, 1971
LADY, STAY DEAD, 1982
LAIR OF THE WHITE WORM, THE, 1988
LAKE OF DRACULA, 1973
LAND OF THE MINOTAUR, 1976
LAS RATAS NO DUERMEN DE NOCHE, 1974
LAST HORROR FILM, THE, 1984
LAST HOUSE ON DEAD END STREET, 1977
LAST MAN ON EARTH, THE, 1964
LAST RITES, 1980
LEECH WOMAN, THE, 1960
LEGACY, THE, 1979
LEGACY OF BLOOD, 1973
LEGACY OF BLOOD, 1978
LEGEND OF BLOOD MOUNTAIN, THE, 1965
LEGEND OF BOGGY CREEK, THE, 1973
LEGEND OF HELL HOUSE, THE, 1973
LEGEND OF SPIDER FOREST, THE, 1976
LEGEND OF THE WOLF WOMAN, THE, 1977

LEMON GROVE KIDS MEET THE MONSTERS, THE, 1966
LET'S SCARE JESSICA TO DEATH, 1971
LIFEFORCE, 1985
LITTLE SHOP OF HORRORS, 1961
LIVING COFFIN, THE, 1965
LIVING GHOST, THE, 1942
LIVING HEAD, THE, 1969
LORD SHANGO, 1975
LOST BOYS, THE, 1987
LOVE BUTCHER, THE, 1982
LOVE ME DEADLY, 1972
LUST FOR A VAMPIRE, 1971
M, 1933
MACABRE, 1958
MAD DOCTOR OF BLOOD ISLAND, THE, 1969
MAD GHOUL, THE, 1943
MAD LOVE, 1935
MAD MAGICIAN, THE, 1954
MAD MONSTER, THE, 1942
MADAME DEATH, 1968
MADHOUSE, 1974
MADMAN, 1982
MAKO: THE JAWS OF DEATH, 1976
MALATESTA'S CARNIVAL, 1973
MALENKA, THE VAMPIRE, 1972
MALPERTIUS, 1972
MAMMA DRACULA, 1980
MAN AND THE BEAST, THE, 1951
MAN AND THE MONSTER, THE, 1965
MAN IN HALF-MOON STREET, THE, 1944
MAN IN THE ATTIC, 1953
MAN THEY COULD NOT HANG, THE, 1939
MAN WHO COULD CHEAT DEATH, THE, 1959
MAN WHO TURNED TO STONE, THE, 1957
MAN WITH TWO HEADS, THE, 1972
MAN WITH TWO LIVES, THE, 1942
MANHATTAN BABY, 1986
MANIA, 1961
MANIAC, 1934
MANIAC COP, 1988
MANIAC, 1980
MANITOU, THE, 1978
MANOS, THE HANDS OF FATE, 1966
MANSION OF THE DOOMED, 1976
MANTIS IN LACE, 1968
MARDI GRAS MASSACRE, 1978
MARK OF THE DEVIL, 1970
MARK OF THE DEVIL II, 1975
MARK OF THE VAMPIRE, 1935
MARK OF THE WITCH, 1970
MARTIN, 1979
MARY, MARY, BLOODY MARY, 1975
MASK, THE, 1961
MASK OF FU MANCHU, THE, 1932
MASQUE OF THE RED DEATH, THE, 1964
MASTER MINDS, 1949
MASTER OF HORROR, 1965
MAUSOLEUM, 1983
MAXIMUM OVERDRIVE, 1986
MAZE, THE, 1953
MEAT CLEAVER MASSACRE, 1977
MELODY IN THE DARK, 1948
MEPHISTO WALTZ, THE, 1971
MICROWAVE MASSACRE, 1983
MIDNIGHT, 1983
MILL OF THE STONE WOMEN, 1963
MIRRORS, 1984
MR. SARDONICUS, 1961
MISTRESS OF THE APES, 1981
MONGREL, 1982
MONKEY SHINES: AN EXPERIMENT IN FEAR, 1988
MONKEY'S PAW, THE, 1933
MONSTER, 1979
MONSTER AND THE GIRL, THE, 1941
MONSTER CLUB, THE, 1981
MONSTER DOG, 1986
MONSTER FROM THE OCEAN FLOOR, THE, 1954
MONSTER ISLAND, 1981
MONSTER MAKER, THE, 1944
MONSTER OF LONDON CITY, THE, 1967
MONSTER OF PIEDRAS BLANCAS, THE, 1959
MONSTER ON THE CAMPUS, 1958
MONSTER SHARK, 1986
MONSTER SQUAD, THE, 1987
MONSTER WALKS, THE, 1932

MOONCHILD, 1972
MORTUARY, 1983
MOTEL HELL, 1980
MOTHER'S DAY, 1980
MOUNTAINTOP MOTEL MASSACRE, 1986
MOVIE HOUSE MASSACRE, 1986
MUMMY, THE, 1932
MUMMY, THE, 1959
MUMMY'S CURSE, THE, 1944
MUMMY'S GHOST, THE, 1944
MUMMY'S HAND, THE, 1940
MUMMY'S SHROUD, THE, 1967
MUMMY'S TOMB, THE, 1942
MUMSY, NANNY, SONNY, AND GIRLY, 1970
MUNCHIES, 1987
MURDER BY THE CLOCK, 1931
MURDER CLINIC, THE, 1967
MURDERS IN THE RUE MORGUE, 1971
MURDERS IN THE RUE MORGUE, 1932
MURDERS IN THE ZOO, 1933
MUTATIONS, THE, 1974
MUTILATOR, THE, 1985
MY BLOODY VALENTINE, 1981
MY BODY HUNGERS, 1967
MY BROTHER HAS BAD DREAMS, 1977
MY DEMON LOVER, 1987
MY SON, THE VAMPIRE, 1963
MY WORLD DIES SCREAMING, 1958
MYSTERIOUS DOCTOR, THE, 1943
MYSTERY OF EDWIN DROOD, THE, 1935
MYSTERY OF THE WAX MUSEUM, THE, 1933
NAIL GUN MASSACRE, 1987
NAKED WITCH, THE, 1964
NAME FOR EVIL, A, 1970
NANNY, THE, 1965
NEAR DARK, 1987
NECROMANCY, 1972
NECROPOLIS, 1987
NEON MANIACS, 1986
NEST OF THE CUCKOO BIRDS, THE, 1965
NESTING, THE, 1981
NEW HOUSE ON THE LEFT, THE, 1978
NEW KIDS, THE, 1985
NEW YEAR'S EVIL, 1980
NEXT OF KIN, 1983
NIGHT CHILD, 1975
NIGHT COMES TOO SOON, 1948
NIGHT DIGGER, THE, 1971
NIGHT EVELYN CAME OUT OF THE GRAVE, THE, 1973
NIGHT GOD SCREAMED, THE, 1975
NIGHT OF A THOUSAND CATS, 1974
NIGHT OF BLOODY HORROR, 1969
NIGHT OF DARK SHADOWS, 1971
NIGHT OF TERROR, 1933
NIGHT OF THE COBRA WOMAN, 1974
NIGHT OF THE GHOULS, 1959
NIGHT OF THE LIVING DEAD, 1968
NIGHT OF THE ZOMBIES, 1981
NIGHT OF THE ZOMBIES, 1983
NIGHT SCHOOL, 1981
NIGHT SHADOWS, 1984
NIGHT WALKER, THE, 1964
NIGHTMARE, 1981
NIGHTMARE CASTLE, 1966
NIGHTMARE IN BLOOD, 1978
NIGHTMARE IN WAX, 1969
NIGHTMARE ON ELM STREET 4: THE DREAM MASTER, A, 1988
NIGHTMARE ON ELM STREET PART 2: FREDDY'S REVENGE, A, 1985
NIGHTMARE ON ELM STREET 3: DREAM WARRIORS, A, 1987
NIGHTMARE ON ELM STREET, A, 1984
NIGHTMARE WEEKEND, 1986
NIGHTMARES, 1983
NIGHTWARS, 1988
NIGHTWING, 1979
NOCTURNA, 1979
NOMADS, 1985
NOSFERATU, THE VAMPIRE, 1979
NOTHING BUT THE NIGHT, 1975
NURSE SHERRI, 1978
OBLONG BOX, THE, 1969
OCTAMAN, 1971
OF UNKNOWN ORIGIN, 1983

OFFSPRING, THE, 1987
OLD DARK HOUSE, THE, 1932
OLD DARK HOUSE, THE, 1963
OLD DRACULA, 1975
OLD MOTHER RILEY'S GHOSTS, 1941
OMEN, THE, 1976
ONCE BITTEN, 1985
ONE DARK NIGHT, 1983
ONIBABA, 1965
OPEN HOUSE, 1987
ORGY OF THE DEAD, 1965
ORLAK, THE HELL OF FRANKENSTEIN, 1960
OTHER, THE, 1972
OUTING, THE, 1987
PACK, THE, 1977
PANDEMONIUM, 1982
PAPERHOUSE, 1988
PARANOIAC, 1963
PATRICK, 1979
PEOPLE WHO OWN THE DARK, 1975
PERSECUTION, 1974
PETS, 1974
PHANTASM, 1979
PHANTASM II, 1988
PHANTOM OF THE OPERA, THE, 1929
PHANTOM OF THE OPERA, 1943
PHANTOM OF THE OPERA, THE, 1962
PHANTOM OF THE PARADISE, 1974
PHANTOM OF THE RUE MORGUE, 1954
PHARAOH'S CURSE, 1957
PHOBIA, 1980
PICTURE MOMMY DEAD, 1966
PICTURE OF DORIAN GRAY, THE, 1945
PIECES, 1983
PIT AND THE PENDULUM, THE, 1961
PLACE OF ONE'S OWN, A, 1945
PLAGUE OF THE ZOMBIES, THE, 1966
PLAYGIRLS AND THE VAMPIRE, 1964
POINT OF TERROR, 1971
POLTERGEIST, 1982
POLTERGEIST III, 1988
POLTERGEIST II, 1986
POSSESSION, 1981
POSSESSION OF JOEL DELANEY, THE, 1972
POWER, THE, 1984
PREMATURE BURIAL, THE, 1962
PREMONITION, THE, 1976
PREY, THE, 1984
PRINCE OF DARKNESS, 1987
PRISON, 1988
PRIVATE COLLECTION, 1972
PROM NIGHT, 1980
PROWLER, THE, 1981
PSYCHIC, THE, 1979
PSYCHIC KILLER, 1975
PSYCHO, 1960
PSYCHO A GO-GO!, 1965
PSYCHO III, 1986
PSYCHO II, 1983
PSYCHOMANIA, 1964
PSYCHOMANIA, 1974
PSYCHOPATH, THE, 1966
PSYCHOS IN LOVE, 1987
PUMPKINHEAD, 1988
PYX, THE, 1973
Q, 1982
QUEEN OF BLOOD, 1966
QUIET PLACE IN THE COUNTRY, A, 1970
RABID, 1976
RACE WITH THE DEVIL, 1975
RASPUTIN—THE MAD MONK, 1966
RATS ARE COMING! THE WEREWOLVES ARE HERE!, THE, 1972
RATTLERS, 1976
RAVEN, THE, 1935
RAVEN, THE, 1963
RAW FORCE, 1982
RAWHEAD REX, 1987
RAZORBACK, 1984
RE-ANIMATOR, 1985
REDEEMER, THE, 1978
REFLECTION OF FEAR, A, 1973
REINCARNATE, THE, 1971
REPTILE, THE, 1966
REPULSION, 1965
RETRIBUTION, 1988

BOLD: Films on Videocassette

RETURN OF COUNT YORGA, THE, 1971
RETURN OF DR. X, THE, 1939
RETURN OF DRACULA, THE, 1958
RETURN OF THE APE MAN, 1944
RETURN OF THE LIVING DEAD, 1985
RETURN OF THE LIVING DEAD PART II, 1988
RETURN OF THE VAMPIRE, THE, 1944
RETURN TO HORROR HIGH, 1987
RETURN TO SALEM'S LOT, A, 1988
RETURNING, THE, 1983
REVENGE, 1986
REVENGE OF FRANKENSTEIN, THE, 1958
REVENGE OF THE CREATURE, 1955
REVENGE OF THE ZOMBIES, 1943
REVOLT OF THE ZOMBIES, 1936
RING OF TERROR, 1962
ROBOT VS. THE AZTEC MUMMY, THE, 1965
ROCK 'N' ROLL NIGHTMARE, 1987
ROCKY HORROR PICTURE SHOW, THE, 1975
ROSEMARY'S BABY, 1968
R.O.T.O.R., 1988
ROTWEILER: DOGS OF HELL, 1984
ROWING WITH THE WIND, 1988
RUBY, 1977
SADIST, THE, 1963
SAGA OF DRACULA, THE, 1975
SANTO CONTRA BLUE DEMON EN LA ATLANTIDA,
    1968
SANTO CONTRA EL CEREBRO DIABOLICO, 1962
SANTO CONTRA EL DOCTOR MUERTE, 1974
SANTO CONTRA LA HIJA DE FRANKENSTEIN, 1971
SANTO CONTRA LA INVASION DE LOS
    MARCIANOS, 1966
SANTO EN EL MUSEO DE CERA, 1963
SANTO Y BLUE DEMON CONTRA LOS MONSTRUOS,
    1968
SATAN'S CHEERLEADERS, 1977
SATAN'S MISTRESS, 1982
SATAN'S SADIST, 1969
SATAN'S SLAVE, 1976
SATURDAY THE 14TH, 1981
SAVAGE ABDUCTION, 1975
SAVAGE WEEKEND, 1983
SCALPS, 1983
SCANNERS, 1981
SCARAB, 1982
SCARECROW, THE, 1982
SCARECROWS, 1988
SCARED TO DEATH, 1947
SCARED TO DEATH, 1981
SCARS OF DRACULA, THE, 1970
SCHIZO, 1977
SCHIZOID, 1980
SCHLOCK, 1973
SCOTLAND YARD HUNTS DR. MABUSE, 1963
SCREAM AND SCREAM AGAIN, 1970
SCREAM, BABY, SCREAM, 1969
SCREAM BLACULA SCREAM, 1973
SCREAM BLOODY MURDER, 1972
SCREAMING SKULL, THE, 1958
SCREAMPLAY, 1986
SCREAMS OF A WINTER NIGHT, 1979
SCREAMTIME, 1986
SCUM OF THE EARTH, 1963
SCUM OF THE EARTH, 1976
SEA SERPENT, THE, 1937
SEEDS OF EVIL, 1981
SEIZURE, 1974
SENDER, THE, 1982
SENTINEL, THE, 1977
SERPENT AND THE RAINBOW, THE, 1988
SEVENTH SIGN, THE, 1988
SEVENTH VICTIM, THE, 1943
SHE BEAST, THE, 1966
SHE-CREATURE, THE, 1956
SHE DEMONS, 1958
SHE DEVIL, 1957
SHE FREAK, 1967
SHINING, THE, 1980
SHOCK TREATMENT, 1973
SHOCK TREATMENT, 1981
SHOCK WAVES, 1977
SHOUT, THE, 1978
SHRIEK OF THE MUTILATED, 1974
SHUTTERED ROOM, THE, 1968
SILENT MADNESS, 1984

SILENT NIGHT, BLOODY NIGHT, 1974
SILENT NIGHT, DEADLY NIGHT, 1984
SILENT NIGHT, DEADLY NIGHT PART II, 1987
SILENT SCREAM, 1980
SILIP, 1985
SIMON, KING OF THE WITCHES, 1971
SISTER SISTER, 1988
SISTERS, 1973
SKULL, THE, 1965
SLASHER, THE, 1975
SLAUGHTER HIGH, 1987
SLAUGHTER HOTEL, 1971
SLAUGHTERHOUSE, 1988
SLAUGHTERHOUSE ROCK, 1988
SLAYER, THE, 1982
SLEEPAWAY CAMP, 1983
SLEEPAWAY CAMP 2: UNHAPPY CAMPERS, 1988
SLITHIS, 1978
SLUMBER PARTY MASSACRE II, 1987
SLUMBER PARTY MASSACRE, THE, 1982
SNAKE PEOPLE, THE, 1968
SNAKE WOMAN, THE, 1961
SO SAD ABOUT GLORIA, 1973
SOLE SURVIVOR, 1984
SOMETHING WEIRD, 1967
SOMETHING WICKED THIS WAY COMES, 1983
SON OF DR. JEKYLL, THE, 1951
SON OF DRACULA, 1943
SON OF DRACULA, 1974
SON OF FRANKENSTEIN, 1939
SON OF GODZILLA, 1967
SON OF KONG, 1933
SORCERERS, THE, 1967
SORORITY HOUSE MASSACRE, 1986
SOUL OF A MONSTER, THE, 1944
SOUND OF HORROR, 1966
SPASMS, 1983
SPECTRE OF EDGAR ALLAN POE, THE, 1974
SPIDER, THE, 1958
SPIDER BABY, 1968
SPIDER WOMAN STRIKES BACK, THE, 1946
SPIRIT IS WILLING, THE, 1967
SPIRITISM, 1965
SPIRITS OF THE DEAD, 1969
SPLATTER UNIVERSITY, 1984
SPOOK BUSTERS, 1946
SPOOK CHASERS, 1957
SPOOKS RUN WILD, 1941
SQUIRM, 1976
SSSSSSSS, 1973
STANLEY, 1973
STEPHEN KING'S SILVER BULLET, 1985
STRAIT-JACKET, 1964
STRANGE DOOR, THE, 1951
STRANGE FETISHES, THE, 1967
STRANGER IS WATCHING, A, 1982
STRANGLER OF THE SWAMP, 1945
STRANGLER, THE, 1964
STRANGLERS OF BOMBAY, THE, 1960
STREET TRASH, 1987
STUDENT BODIES, 1981
STUFF, THE, 1985
SUPERBEAST, 1972
SUPERSTITION, 1985
SURVIVOR, 1980
SUSPIRIA, 1977
SWAMP THING, 1982
SWEET SIXTEEN, 1983
SYMPTOMS, 1976
TALES FROM THE CRYPT, 1972
TALES OF TERROR, 1962
TALES OF THE THIRD DIMENSION, 1985
TALES OF THE UNCANNY, 1932
TALES THAT WITNESS MADNESS, 1973
TARGETS, 1968
TASTE OF BLOOD, A, 1967
TASTE THE BLOOD OF DRACULA, 1970
TEEN-AGE STRANGLER, 1967
TEENAGE MONSTER, 1958
TEENAGE ZOMBIES, 1960
TELL-TALE HEART, THE, 1962
TEMPTER, THE, 1978
TEMPTRESS AND THE MONK, THE, 1963
TENANT, THE, 1976
TENDER FLESH, 1976
TENTACLES, 1977

TERRIFIED, 1963
TERROR, THE, 1963
TERROR, 1979
TERROR-CREATURES FROM THE GRAVE, 1967
TERROR HOUSE, 1972
TERROR IN THE WAX MUSEUM, 1973
TERROR IS A MAN, 1959
TERROR ON TOUR, 1980
TERROR TRAIN, 1980
TEXAS CHAIN SAW MASSACRE, THE, 1974
TEXAS CHAINSAW MASSACRE PART 2, THE, 1986
THARK, 1932
THEATRE OF BLOOD, 1973
THEATRE OF DEATH, 1967
THEY CAME FROM WITHIN, 1976
THING THAT COULDN'T DIE, THE, 1958
THING WITH TWO HEADS, THE, 1972
THIRST, 1979
THIRSTY DEAD, THE, 1975
THIRTEEN, THE, 1937
THIRTEEN GHOSTS, 1960
THRILL KILLERS, THE, 1965
TILL DEATH, 1978
TIME WALKER, 1982
TINGLER, THE, 1959
TO ALL A GOODNIGHT, 1980
TO THE DEVIL A DAUGHTER, 1976
TOMB OF LIGEIA, THE, 1965
TOMB OF THE UNDEAD, 1972
TOMB OF TORTURE, 1966
TOOLBOX MURDERS, THE, 1978
TORMENTED, 1960
TORMENTED, THE, 1978
TORSO, 1974
TORTURE DUNGEON, 1970
TORTURE GARDEN, 1968
TORTURE SHIP, 1939
TOUCH OF HER FLESH, THE, 1967
TOUCH OF SATAN, THE, 1971
TOURIST TRAP, THE, 1979
TOWER OF LONDON, 1939
TOWER OF LONDON, 1962
TOWN THAT DREADED SUNDOWN, THE, 1977
TOXIC AVENGER, THE, 1985
TRACK OF THE MOONBEAST, 1976
TRANSYLVANIA 6-5000, 1985
TRAUMA, 1962
TRICK OR TREAT, 1986
TRICK OR TREATS, 1982
TROLL, 1986
TWICE TOLD TALES, 1963
TWILIGHT PEOPLE, 1972
TWILIGHT ZONE—THE MOVIE, 1983
TWINS OF EVIL, 1971
TWITCH OF THE DEATH NERVE, 1973
TWO THOUSAND MANIACS, 1964
UNCANNY, THE, 1977
UNDEAD, THE, 1957
UNDERTAKER AND HIS PALS, THE, 1966
UNDYING MONSTER, THE, 1942
UNEARTHLY, THE, 1957
UNHINGED, 1982
UNHOLY, THE, 1988
UNHOLY QUEST, THE, 1934
UNINVITED, THE, 1944
UNINVITED, THE, 1988
UNKNOWN TERROR, THE, 1957
UNSEEN, THE, 1981
UNTAMED MISTRESS, 1960
UP FROM THE DEPTHS, 1979
VALLEY OF THE ZOMBIES, 1946
VAMP, 1986
VAMPIRE, THE, 1968
VAMPIRE AND THE BALLERINA, THE, 1962
VAMPIRE BAT, THE, 1933
VAMPIRE CIRCUS, 1972
VAMPIRE HOOKERS, THE, 1979
VAMPIRE LOVERS, THE, 1970
VAMPIRE'S COFFIN, THE, 1958
VAMPIRE'S NIGHT ORGY, THE, 1973
VAMPIRE, THE, 1957
VAMPIRES, THE, 1969
VAMPIRE'S GHOST, THE, 1945
VAMPYR, 1932
VAMPYRES, DAUGHTERS OF DRACULA, 1977
VARAN THE UNBELIEVABLE, 1962

VAULT OF HORROR, THE, 1973
VELVET VAMPIRE, THE, 1971
VENGEANCE OF THE VAMPIRE WOMEN, THE, 1969
VICTOR FRANKENSTEIN, 1975
VIDEO DEAD, 1987
VIDEODROME, 1983
VILLAGE OF THE DAMNED, 1960
VIRGIN WITCH, THE, 1973
VISITING HOURS, 1982
VISITOR, THE, 1980
VOICES, 1973
VOODOO HEARTBEAT, 1972
VOODOO ISLAND, 1957
VOODOO MAN, 1944
VOODOO WOMAN, 1957
VULTURE, THE, 1967
WACKO, 1983
WALKING DEAD, THE, 1936
WAR OF THE ZOMBIES, THE, 1965
WARNING SIGN, 1985
WATCHER IN THE WOODS, THE, 1980
WEB OF THE SPIDER, 1972
WEDNESDAY CHILDREN, THE, 1973
WEEKEND OF FEAR, 1966
WEIRD WOMAN, 1944
WEREWOLF IN A GIRL'S DORMITORY, 1961
WEREWOLF OF LONDON, THE, 1935
WEREWOLF OF WASHINGTON, 1973
WEREWOLF VS. THE VAMPIRE WOMAN, THE, 1970
WEREWOLF, THE, 1956
WEREWOLVES ON WHEELS, 1971
WHAT!, 1965:,
WHAT A CARVE UP!, 1962
WHEN A STRANGER CALLS, 1979
WHITE ZOMBIE, 1932
WHO SLEW AUNTIE ROO?, 1971
WICKER MAN, THE, 1974
WILLARD, 1971
WITCH, THE, 1969
WITCHBOARD, 1987
WITCHCRAFT, 1964
WITCHES OF EASTWICK, THE, 1987
WITCHMAKER, THE, 1969
WITCH'S CURSE, THE, 1963
WITCH'S MIRROR, THE, 1960
WIZARD OF GORE, THE, 1970
WOLF MAN, THE, 1941
WOLFEN, 1981
WOLFMAN, 1979
WOMAN EATER, THE, 1959
WOMAN IN WHITE, THE, 1948
WOMAN WHO CAME BACK, 1945
WONDER WOMEN, 1973
WORM EATERS, THE, 1981
WRAITH, THE, 1986
YOU BETTER WATCH OUT, 1980
YOUNG FRANKENSTEIN, 1974
YOUNG, THE EVIL AND THE SAVAGE, THE, 1968
ZOMBIE, 1980
ZOMBIE CREEPING FLESH, 1981
ZOMBIES OF MORA TAU, 1957
ZOMBIES ON BROADWAY, 1945

Musical

AARON SLICK FROM PUNKIN CRICK, 1952
ABOUT FACE, 1952
ABSOLUTE BEGINNERS, 1986
ADORABLE, 1933
AFTER THE BALL, 1957
AFTER THE DANCE, 1935
AIDA, 1954
AIN'T MISBEHAVIN', 1955
ALEXANDER'S RAGTIME BAND, 1938
ALI BABA GOES TO TOWN, 1937
ALL BY MYSELF, 1943
ALL THAT JAZZ, 1979
ALWAYS A BRIDESMAID, 1943
AMADEUS, 1984
AMERICAN HOT WAX, 1978
AMERICAN IN PARIS, AN, 1951
AMERICAN POP, 1981
AMPHYTRYON, 1937
ANCHORS AWEIGH, 1945
ANNIE, 1982
ANNIE GET YOUR GUN, 1950
ANYTHING GOES, 1936

ANYTHING GOES, 1956
APPLE, THE, 1980
APRIL BLOSSOMS, 1937
APRIL LOVE, 1957
APRIL SHOWERS, 1948
ARE YOU THERE?, 1930
AROUND THE TOWN, 1938
AROUND THE WORLD, 1943
ARTISTS AND MODELS, 1937
ARTISTS AND MODELS, 1955
ARTISTS AND MODELS ABROAD, 1938
AT LONG LAST LOVE, 1975
ATHENA, 1954
ATLANTIC CITY, 1944
BABES IN ARMS, 1939
BABES IN TOYLAND, 1934
BABES IN TOYLAND, 1961
BABES ON BROADWAY, 1941
BABES ON SWING STREET, 1944
BACKSTAGE, 1937
BALALAIKA, 1939
BALL AT SAVOY, 1936
BALLAD OF A HUSSAR, 1963
BALLOON GOES UP, THE, 1942
BAND OF THIEVES, 1962
BAND WAGGON, 1940
BAND WAGON, THE, 1953
BANJO ON MY KNEE, 1936
BARBER OF SEVILLE, THE, 1947
BARBER OF SEVILLE, 1949
BARKLEYS OF BROADWAY, THE, 1949
BARNYARD FOLLIES, 1940
BATHING BEAUTY, 1944
BATTLE OF PARIS, THE, 1929
BAWDY ADVENTURES OF TOM JONES, THE, 1976
BE MINE TONIGHT, 1933
BE YOURSELF, 1930
BEACH BALL, 1965
BEAT STREET, 1984
BEAT THE BAND, 1947
BEGGAR STUDENT, THE, 1931
BEGGAR STUDENT, THE, 1958
BEGGAR'S OPERA, THE, 1953
BEHIND CITY LIGHTS, 1945
BELLE OF NEW YORK, THE, 1952
BELLE OF OLD MEXICO, 1950
BELLE OF THE YUKON, 1944
BELOVED IMPOSTER, 1936
BERNARDINE, 1957
BEST FOOT FORWARD, 1943
BEST THINGS IN LIFE ARE FREE, THE, 1956
BEWARE, 1946
BIG BUSINESS, 1930
BIG CITY, 1948
BIG PARTY, THE, 1930
BIG POND, THE, 1930
BIRTH OF THE BLUES, 1941
BITTER SWEET, 1933
BITTER SWEET, 1940
BIZET'S CARMEN, 1984
BLAZE O' GLORY, 1930
BLONDE NIGHTINGALE, 1931
BLOODHOUNDS OF BROADWAY, 1952
BLOSSOMS ON BROADWAY, 1937
BLUE DANUBE, 1932
BLUE HAWAII, 1961
BLUE SKIES, 1946
BLUES IN THE NIGHT, 1941
BOCCACCIO, 1936
BODY ROCK, 1984
BOLERO, 1982
BOOTS! BOOTS!, 1934
BOP GIRL GOES CALYPSO, 1957
BORIS GODUNOV, 1959
BORN LUCKY, 1932
BORN TO SING, 1942
BOUNTIFUL SUMMER, 1951
BOY FRIEND, THE, 1971
BOY! WHAT A GIRL!, 1947
BRAT, THE, 1930
BREAKIN'2: ELECTRIC BOOGALOO, 1984
BREAKIN', 1984
BREAKING GLASS, 1980
BREAKING THE ICE, 1938
BRIDE OF THE LAKE, 1934
BRIDE WITH A DOWRY, 1954

BRIGADOON, 1954
BRIGHT LIGHTS, 1931
BRITANNIA OF BILLINGSGATE, 1933
BROADWAY, 1929
BROADWAY, 1942
BROADWAY BABIES, 1929
BROADWAY HOOFER, THE, 1929
BROADWAY HOSTESS, 1935
BROADWAY MELODY OF 1940, 1940
BROADWAY MELODY, THE, 1929
BROADWAY RHYTHM, 1944
BROADWAY SCANDALS, 1929
BROADWAY SERENADE, 1939
BROADWAY THROUGH A KEYHOLE, 1933
BROADWAY TO HOLLYWOOD, 1933
BROKEN MELODY, THE, 1934
BROKEN ROSARY, THE, 1934
BUGSY MALONE, 1976
CABARET, 1972
CABIN IN THE SKY, 1943
CADET GIRL, 1941
CAGE OF NIGHTINGALES, A, 1947
CAIRO, 1942
CALAMITY JANE, 1953
CALENDAR GIRL, 1947
CALL ME MISTER, 1951
CALL OF THE FLESH, 1930
CALLING THE TUNE, 1936
CALYPSO, 1959
CALYPSO HEAT WAVE, 1957
CALYPSO JOE, 1957
CAMELOT, 1967
CAMEO KIRBY, 1930
CAN-CAN, 1960
CAN'T STOP THE MUSIC, 1980
CAN'T HELP SINGING, 1944
CANTOR'S SON, THE, 1937
CAPTAIN JANUARY, 1935
CAPTAIN OF THE GUARD, 1930
CAREER GIRL, 1944
CARMEN JONES, 1954
CARNEGIE HALL, 1947
CARNIVAL IN COSTA RICA, 1947
CARNIVAL ROCK, 1957
CAROLINA BLUES, 1944
CAROUSEL, 1956
CASA MANANA, 1951
CASBAH, 1948
CAT AND THE FIDDLE, 1934
CATALINA CAPER, THE, 1967
CATCH MY SOUL, 1974
CATSKILL HONEYMOON, 1950
CENTENNIAL SUMMER, 1946
CHA-CHA-CHA BOOM, 1956
CHAMPAGNE WALTZ, 1937
CHANGE OF HABIT, 1969
CHARLEY MOON, 1956
CHARLOTTE'S WEB, 1973
CHEER UP!, 1936
CHEER UP AND SMILE, 1930
CHILDREN OF DREAMS, 1931
CHIP OFF THE OLD BLOCK, 1944
CHIPS, 1938.
CHITTY CHITTY BANG BANG, 1968
CHOCOLATE SOLDIER, THE, 1941
CHORUS LINE, A, 1985
CHRISTMAS THAT ALMOST WASN'T, THE, 1966
CHU CHIN CHOW, 1934
CIGARETTE GIRL, 1947
CINDERELLA, 1937
CLAMBAKE, 1967
CLIMAX, THE, 1930
CLOSE HARMONY, 1929
CLOWN AND THE KIDS, THE, 1968
CLOWN MUST LAUGH, A, 1936
C'MON, LET'S LIVE A LITTLE, 1967
COAL MINER'S DAUGHTER, 1980
COCK O' THE NORTH, 1935
COCOANUT GROVE, 1938
COLLEGE HUMOR, 1933
COLLEGE RHYTHM, 1934
COME DANCE WITH ME, 1950
CONGRESS DANCES, 1932
CONGRESS DANCES, 1957
CONNECTICUT YANKEE IN KING ARTHUR'S
   COURT, A, 1949

BOLD: Films on Videocassette

COOL MIKADO, THE, 1963
CORONADO, 1935
COSSACKS IN EXILE, 1939
COTTON CLUB, THE, 1984
COUNTESS OF MONTE CRISTO, THE, 1948
COUNTRY BRIDE, 1938
COUNTRY MUSIC HOLIDAY, 1958
COUNTRYMAN, 1982
COURT CONCERT, THE, 1936
COWBOY IN MANHATTTAN, 1943
COWBOY SERENADE, 1942
CROONER, 1932
CROSSOVER DREAMS, 1985
CRUISIN' DOWN THE RIVER, 1953
CUBAN FIREBALL, 1951
CUBAN LOVE SONG, THE, 1931
CUBAN PETE, 1946
CURLY TOP, 1935
CYCLONE ON HORSEBACK, 1941
DADDY LONG LEGS, 1955
DANCE BAND, 1935
DANCE OF LIFE, THE, 1929
DANCE, GIRL, DANCE, 1940
DANCERS IN THE DARK, 1932
DANCING FEET, 1936
DANCING HEART, THE, 1959
DANCING IN MANHATTAN, 1945
DANCING LADY, 1933
DANCING ON A DIME, 1940
DANCING PIRATE, 1936
DANCING SWEETIES, 1930
DANCING YEARS, THE, 1950
DANNY BOY, 1934
DARK SANDS, 1938
DARLING LILI, 1970
DAY AT THE RACES, A, 1937
DAY YOU LOVE ME, THE, 1988
DEEP IN MY HEART, 1954
DELICIOUS, 1931
DELIGHTFULLY DANGEROUS, 1945
DEPUTY DRUMMER, THE, 1935
DESERT SONG, THE, 1929
DESERT SONG, THE, 1943
DESERT SONG, THE, 1953
DEVIL MAY CARE, 1929
DEVIL ON HORSEBACK, THE, 1936
DEVIL'S ROCK, 1938
DIAMOND HORSESHOE, 1945
DIMPLES, 1936
DIPLOMATIC LOVER, THE, 1934
DISC JOCKEY, 1951
DISCOVERIES, 1939
DIVINE SPARK, THE, 1935
DIXIE, 1943
DIZZY DAMES, 1936
DO YOU LOVE ME?, 1946
DOCTOR DOLITTLE, 1967
DODGING THE DOLE, 1936
DOLL FACE, 1945
DOLLY GETS AHEAD, 1931
DOLLY SISTERS, THE, 1945
DON QUIXOTE, 1935
DON'T FENCE ME IN, 1945
DON'T KNOCK THE ROCK, 1956
DON'T KNOCK THE TWIST, 1962
DOUBLE TROUBLE, 1967
DOUGHBOYS IN IRELAND, 1943
DOWN AMONG THE SHELTERING PALMS, 1953
DOWN ARGENTINE WAY, 1940
DOWN OUR ALLEY, 1939
DOWN TO THEIR LAST YACHT, 1934
DREAM MAKER, THE, 1963
DREAM OF BUTTERFLY, THE, 1941
DREAM OF SCHONBRUNN, 1933
DREAM OF THE RED CHAMBER, THE, 1966
DRESSED TO THRILL, 1935
DUBEAT-E-O, 1984
DUKE IS THE TOPS, THE, 1938
DUKE WORE JEANS, THE, 1958
EADIE WAS A LADY, 1945
EARL CARROLL SKETCHBOOK, 1946
EARL CARROLL'S VANITIES, 1945
EARLY TO BED, 1933
EASY COME, EASY GO, 1967
EASY TO LOOK AT, 1945
EASY TO LOVE, 1953

EASY TO WED, 1946
ECHO OF A DREAM, 1930
EDDIE CANTOR STORY, THE, 1953
EDDY DUCHIN STORY, THE, 1956
EIGHT GIRLS IN A BOAT, 1932
EMPRESS AND I, THE, 1933
END OF THE ROAD, THE, 1936
ESCAPE TO PARADISE, 1939
EVANGELINE, 1929
EVE KNEW HER APPLES, 1945
EVENSONG, 1934
EVER SINCE VENUS, 1944
EVERGREEN, 1934
EVERY NIGHT AT EIGHT, 1935
EVERYBODY DANCE, 1936
EVERYBODY SING, 1938
EVERYBODY'S DANCIN', 1950
EVERYTHING I HAVE IS YOURS, 1952
EVERYTHING IN LIFE, 1936
EVERYTHING IS RHYTHM, 1940
EVERYTHING'S ON ICE, 1939
EXCUSE MY DUST, 1951
EXILE, THE, 1931
EXPRESSO BONGO, 1959
FABULOUS DORSEYS, THE, 1947
FACING THE MUSIC, 1933
FAITHFUL, 1936
FAME, 1980
FANCY PANTS, 1950
FAREWELL PERFORMANCE, 1963
FARMER TAKES A WIFE, THE, 1953
FAST FORWARD, 1985
FATHER IS A BACHELOR, 1950
FATHER O'FLYNN, 1938
FEELIN' GOOD, 1966
FERRY ACROSS THE MERSEY, 1964
FEUDIN', FUSSIN' AND A-FIGHTIN', 1948
FIDDLER ON THE ROOF, 1971
FIDELIO, 1961
FIDELIO, 1970
FIESTA, 1947
52ND STREET, 1937
FIGHT FOR YOUR LADY, 1937
FINDERS KEEPERS, 1966
FINE FEATHERS, 1937
FINIAN'S RAINBOW, 1968
FIREFLY, THE, 1937
FIRST MRS. FRASER, THE, 1932
FIVE PENNIES, THE, 1959
5,000 FINGERS OF DR. T. THE, 1953
FLEET'S IN, THE, 1942
FLIGHT FROM FOLLY, 1945
FLIRTATION WALK, 1934
FLORODORA GIRL, THE, 1930
FLYING DOWN TO RIO, 1933
FLYING HIGH, 1931
FLYING WITH MUSIC, 1942
FOLIES BERGERE, 1935
FOLIES BERGERE, 1958
FOLLIES GIRL, 1943
FOLLOW THAT DREAM, 1962
FOLLOW THE BAND, 1943
FOLLOW THE BOYS, 1944
FOLLOW THE FLEET, 1936
FOLLOW THE LEADER, 1930
FOLLOW THRU, 1930
FOLLOW YOUR STAR, 1938
FOOTLIGHT PARADE, 1933
FOOTLIGHT SERENADE, 1942
FOOTLIGHTS AND FOOLS, 1929
FOOTLOOSE, 1984
FOR LOVE OF YOU, 1933
FOR ME AND MY GAL, 1942
FOR YOU ALONE, 1945
FORBIDDEN ZONE, 1980
42ND STREET, 1933
FORWARD PASS, THE, 1929
FOUR JACKS AND A JILL, 1941
FOUR JILLS IN A JEEP, 1944
FOX MOVIETONE FOLLIES, 1929
FOX MOVIETONE FOLLIES OF 1930, 1930
FRANKIE AND JOHNNY, 1966
FREDDIE STEPS OUT, 1946
FREDDY UNTER FREMDEN STERNEN, 1962
FREE AND EASY, 1930

FRENCH CANCAN, 1956
FRENCH LINE, THE, 1954
FRESH FROM PARIS, 1955
FROM NASHVILLE WITH MUSIC, 1969
FUN IN ACAPULCO, 1963
FUNNY FACE, 1957
FUNNY GIRL, 1968
FUNNY LADY, 1975
G.I. BLUES, 1960
GAIETY GIRLS, THE, 1938
GANG, THE, 1938
GANG'S ALL HERE, THE, 1943
GANGWAY, 1937
GARDEN OF THE MOON, 1938
GAY DESPERADO, THE, 1936
GAY DIVORCEE, THE, 1934
GAY LOVE, 1936
GENTLEMAN MISBEHAVES, THE, 1946
GENTLEMEN MARRY BRUNETTES, 1955
GENTLEMEN PREFER BLONDES, 1953
GEORGE WHITE'S 1935 SCANDALS, 1935
GEORGE WHITE'S SCANDALS, 1934
GEORGE WHITE'S SCANDALS, 1945
GERALDINE, 1953
GET HEP TO LOVE, 1942
GHOST CATCHERS, 1944
G.I. JANE, 1951
GIFT OF GAB, 1934
GIGI, 1958
GIRL CAN'T HELP IT, THE, 1956
GIRL CRAZY, 1932
GIRL CRAZY, 1943
GIRL FRIEND, THE, 1935
GIRL FROM POLTAVA, 1937
GIRL FROM RIO, THE, 1939
GIRL FROM WOOLWORTH'S, THE, 1929
GIRL HAPPY, 1965
GIRL IN THE STREET, 1938
GIRL IN THE TAXI, 1937
GIRL MOST LIKELY, THE, 1957
GIRL NEXT DOOR, THE, 1953
GIRL OF THE GOLDEN WEST, THE, 1938
GIRL ON THE SPOT, 1946
GIRL RUSH, 1944
GIRL RUSH, THE, 1955
GIRL SAID NO, THE, 1937
GIRLS! GIRLS! GIRLS!, 1962
GIRLS IN THE STREET, 1937
GIRLS OF LATIN QUARTER, 1960
GIRLS ON THE BEACH, 1965
GIVE A GIRL A BREAK, 1953
GIVE HER A RING, 1936
GIVE ME A SAILOR, 1938
GIVE MY REGARDS TO BROAD STREET, 1984
GIVE MY REGARDS TO BROADWAY, 1948
GIVE OUT, SISTERS, 1942
GIVE US THIS NIGHT, 1936
GLAMOUR GIRL, 1947
GLENN MILLER STORY, THE, 1953
GLORIFYING THE AMERICAN GIRL, 1930
GO INTO YOUR DANCE, 1935
GO, JOHNNY, GO!, 1959
GO WEST, YOUNG LADY, 1941
GODSPELL, 1973
GOIN' TO TOWN, 1935
GOING HOLLYWOOD, 1933
GOING MY WAY, 1944
GOING PLACES, 1939
GOLD DIGGERS IN PARIS, 1938
GOLD DIGGERS OF 1933, 1933
GOLD DIGGERS OF 1935, 1935
GOLD DIGGERS OF 1937, 1936
GOLD DIGGERS OF BROADWAY, 1929
GOLDEN CALF, THE, 1930
GOLDEN DAWN, 1930
GOLDEN EIGHTIES, 1986
GOLDEN GIRL, 1951
GOLDWYN FOLLIES, THE, 1938
GONKS GO BEAT, 1965
GOOD COMPANIONS, 1933
GOOD COMPANIONS, THE, 1957
GOOD NEWS, 1930
GOOD NEWS, 1947
GOOD TIMES, 1967
GOODBYE MR. CHIPS, 1969
GRAND OLE OPRY, 1940

GRAND PARADE, THE, 1930
GREASE, 1978
GREASE 2, 1982
GREAT AMERICAN BROADCAST, THE, 1941
GREAT CARUSO, THE, 1951
GREAT GABBO, THE, 1929
GREAT GILBERT AND SULLIVAN, THE, 1953
GREAT LOVER, THE, 1931
GREAT MUPPET CAPER, THE, 1981
GREAT VICTOR HERBERT, THE, 1939
GREAT WALTZ, THE, 1938
GREAT WALTZ, THE, 1972
GREAT ZIEGFELD, THE, 1936
GREENWICH VILLAGE, 1944
GROUNDS FOR MARRIAGE, 1950
GUADALAJARA, 1943
GUILTY MELODY, 1936
GUYS AND DOLLS, 1955
GYPSY, 1962
HAIR, 1979
HALF A SIXPENCE, 1967
HALLELUJAH, I'M A BUM, 1933
HAPPIEST MILLIONAIRE, THE, 1967
HAPPINESS AHEAD, 1934
HAPPY, 1934
HAPPY DAYS, 1930
HAPPY DAYS ARE HERE AGAIN, 1936
HAPPY EVER AFTER, 1932
HAPPY GO LOVELY, 1951
HAPPY-GO-LUCKY, 1937
HAPPY GO LUCKY, 1943
HAPPY LANDING, 1938
HARD TO HOLD, 1984
HARMONY HEAVEN, 1930
HARUM SCARUM, 1965
HARVEST MELODY, 1943
HAT CHECK HONEY, 1944
HATS OFF, 1937
HAVANA ROSE, 1951
HAWAII CALLS, 1938
HAWAIIAN NIGHTS, 1939
HE FOUND A STAR, 1941
HE LOVED AN ACTRESS, 1938
HEAD, 1968
HEAD OVER HEELS IN LOVE, 1937
HEADS UP, 1930
HEART OF A MAN, THE, 1959
HEART'S DESIRE, 1937
HEAVEN IS ROUND THE CORNER, 1944
HELEN MORGAN STORY, THE, 1959
HELLO, FRISCO, HELLO, 1943
HELLO LONDON, 1958
HER LUCKY NIGHT, 1945
HERE COMES THE BAND, 1935
HERE COMES THE SUN, 1945
HERE'S TO ROMANCE, 1935
HE'S MY GUY, 1943
HEY BABE?, 1984
HEY BOY! HEY GIRL!, 1959
HEY, LET'S TWIST!, 1961
HEY, ROOKIE, 1944
HI, BUDDY, 1943
HI-DE-HO, 1947
HI, GOOD-LOOKIN', 1944
HI' YA, SAILOR, 1943
HIDEAWAY GIRL, 1937
HIGH HAT, 1937
HIGH SCHOOL HERO, 1946
HIGH SOCIETY BLUES, 1930
HIGH, WIDE AND HANDSOME, 1937
HIGHER AND HIGHER, 1943
HIT PARADE, THE, 1937
HIT PARADE OF 1951, 1950
HIT PARADE OF 1947, 1947
HIT PARADE OF 1943, 1943
HIT PARADE OF 1941, 1940
HIT THE DECK, 1930
HIT THE DECK, 1955
HITCHHIKE TO HAPPINESS, 1945
HITTING A NEW HIGH, 1937
HOEDOWN, 1950
HOLD THAT CO-ED, 1938
HOLIDAY IN HAVANA, 1949
HOLIDAY IN MEXICO, 1946
HOLIDAY RHYTHM, 1950
HOLLYWOOD BARN DANCE, 1947

HOLY TERROR, THE, 1937
HONEYMOON LODGE, 1943
HONKY TONK, 1929
HONOLULU, 1939
HOORAY FOR LOVE, 1935
HOOSIER HOLIDAY, 1943
HOOTENANNY HOOT, 1963
HOT BLOOD, 1956
HOT FOR PARIS, 1930
HOT HEIRESS, 1931
HOT RHYTHM, 1944
HOT ROD GANG, 1958
HOUND-DOG MAN, 1959
HOW'S ABOUT IT?, 1943
HUCKLEBERRY FINN, 1974
I CAN'T GIVE YOU ANYTHING BUT LOVE, BABY, 1940
I COULD GO ON SINGING, 1963
I DON'T CARE GIRL, THE, 1952
I LIKE IT THAT WAY, 1934
I LIVE FOR LOVE, 1935
I LOVE MELVIN, 1953
I MARRIED AN ANGEL, 1942
I SURRENDER DEAR, 1948
I WONDER WHO'S KISSING HER NOW, 1947
ICE-CAPADES REVUE, 1942
ICE FOLLIES OF 1939, 1939
ICELAND, 1942
IF I HAD MY WAY, 1940
IF I'M LUCKY, 1946
I'LL BE YOUR SWEETHEART, 1945
I'LL BE YOURS, 1947
I'LL GET BY, 1950
I'LL SEE YOU IN MY DREAMS, 1951
I'LL TAKE ROMANCE, 1937
I'LL TURN TO YOU, 1946
I'M NOBODY'S SWEETHEART NOW, 1940
IN CALIENTE, 1935
IN GAY MADRID, 1930
INBETWEEN AGE, THE, 1958
INCENDIARY BLONDE, 1945
INNOCENTS OF PARIS, 1929
INVITATION TO THE DANCE, 1956
INVITATION TO THE WALTZ, 1935
IRISH EYES ARE SMILING, 1944
IS EVERYBODY HAPPY?, 1929
IS EVERYBODY HAPPY?, 1943
ISN'T IT ROMANTIC?, 1948
IT COMES UP LOVE, 1943
IT COULDN'T HAPPEN HERE, 1988
IT HAPPENED AT THE WORLD'S FAIR, 1963
IT'S A BIKINI WORLD, 1967
IT'S A GREAT LIFE, 1930
IT'S A WONDERFUL DAY, 1949
IT'S ALL OVER TOWN, 1963
IT'S GREAT TO BE ALIVE, 1933
IT'S GREAT TO BE YOUNG, 1946
IT'S LOVE AGAIN, 1936
I'VE ALWAYS LOVED YOU, 1946
JACQUES BREL IS ALIVE AND WELL AND LIVING IN PARIS, 1975
JAILBIRD ROCK, 1988
JAILHOUSE ROCK, 1957
JAM SESSION, 1944
JAMBOREE, 1944
JAMBOREE, 1957
JAZZ SINGER, THE, 1927
JAZZ SINGER, THE, 1953
JAZZ SINGER, THE, 1980
JESUS CHRIST, SUPERSTAR, 1973
JIVE JUNCTION, 1944
JOAN AT THE STAKE, 1954
JOHNNY DOUGHBOY, 1943
JOLSON SINGS AGAIN, 1949
JOLSON STORY, THE, 1946
JUKE BOX JENNY, 1942
JUKE BOX RHYTHM, 1959
JUMBO, 1962
JUNIOR PROM, 1946
JUST AROUND THE CORNER, 1938
JUST FOR A SONG, 1930
JUST FOR FUN, 1963
JUST IMAGINE, 1930
KANSAS CITY KITTY, 1944
KATHLEEN, 1938
KAZABLAN, 1974

KEEP 'EM FLYING, 1941
KENTUCKY MINSTRELS, 1934
KID GALAHAD, 1937
KID GALAHAD, 1962
KING AND I, THE, 1956
KING CREOLE, 1958
KING OF HEARTS, 1936
KING STEPS OUT, THE, 1936
KISMET, 1955
KISS ME AGAIN, 1931
KISS THE BOYS GOODBYE, 1941
KISSIN' COUSINS, 1964
KISSING BANDIT, THE, 1948
KNIGHTS OF THE CITY, 1985
KRUSH GROOVE, 1985
LA BOHEME, 1965
LA TRAVIATA, 1968
LA TRAVIATA, 1982
LADIES' MAN, 1947
LADIES OF THE CHORUS, 1948
LADY BE GOOD, 1941
LADY IN THE DARK, 1944
LADY IS A SQUARE, THE, 1959
LADY IS FICKLE, THE, 1948
LADY, LET'S DANCE, 1944
LADY SINGS THE BLUES, 1972
LADY'S MORALS, A, 1930
LAKE PLACID SERENADE, 1944
LARCENY WITH MUSIC, 1943
LAS VEGAS HILLBILLYS, 1966
LAS VEGAS NIGHTS, 1941
LAST ROSE OF SUMMER, THE, 1937
LATIN LOVE, 1930
LATIN LOVERS, 1953
LAUGH IT OFF, 1940
LAUGH IT OFF, 1939
LAUGH PAGLIACCI, 1948
LAUGHING IRISH EYES, 1936
LAUGHING LADY, THE, 1950
LE BAL, 1984
LEADBELLY, 1976
LEATHERNECKING, 1930
LEMON DROP KID, THE, 1951
LES GIRLS, 1957
LET FREEDOM RING, 1939
LET'S BE HAPPY, 1957
LET'S DANCE, 1950
LET'S DO IT AGAIN, 1953
LET'S FACE IT, 1943
LET'S FALL IN LOVE, 1934
LET'S GO COLLEGIATE, 1941
LET'S GO NATIVE, 1930
LET'S GO PLACES, 1930
LET'S GO STEADY, 1945
LET'S MAKE A NIGHT OF IT, 1937
LET'S MAKE MUSIC, 1940
LET'S ROCK, 1958
LET'S SING AGAIN, 1936
LILLIAN RUSSELL, 1940
LISBON STORY, THE, 1946
LISTEN, DARLING, 1938
LITTLE BIT OF HEAVEN, A, 1940
LITTLE DAMOZEL, THE, 1933
LITTLE DOLLY DAYDREAM, 1938
LITTLE JOHNNY JONES, 1930
LITTLE MISS BROADWAY, 1938
LITTLE MISS DEVIL, 1951
LITTLE NELLIE KELLY, 1940
LITTLE NIGHT MUSIC, A, 1977
LITTLE OF WHAT YOU FANCY, A, 1968
LITTLE PRINCE, THE, 1974
LITTLE SHOP OF HORRORS, 1986
LIVE A LITTLE, LOVE A LITTLE, 1968
LIVE AGAIN, 1936
LONDON MELODY, 1930
LOOK FOR THE SILVER LINING, 1949
LOOKING FOR LOVE, 1964
LOOKING ON THE BRIGHT SIDE, 1932
LORD BABS, 1932
LORD BYRON OF BROADWAY, 1930
LOS PLATILLOS VOLADORES, 1955
LOST HORIZON, 1973
LOST IN THE STARS, 1974
LOTTERY BRIDE, THE, 1930
LOUISE, 1940
LOVE AND HISSES, 1937

BOLD: Films on Videocassette

LOVE AND LEARN, 1947
LOVE AT FIRST SIGHT, 1930
LOVE IN THE ROUGH, 1930
LOVE ME FOREVER, 1935
LOVE ME OR LEAVE ME, 1955
LOVE ME TONIGHT, 1932
LOVE ON THE SPOT, 1932
LOVE ON WHEELS, 1932
LOVE SONGS, 1986
LOVING YOU, 1957
LUCKY BOY, 1929
LUCKY BRIDE, THE, 1948
LUCKY GIRL, 1932
LUCKY IN LOVE, 1929
LUCKY ME, 1954
LULU BELLE, 1948
LUPE, 1967
MADAME SATAN, 1930
MAGIC NIGHT, 1932
MAID HAPPY, 1933
MAID OF THE MOUNTAINS, THE, 1932
MAKE BELIEVE BALLROOM, 1949
MALANDRO, 1986
MAMMY, 1930
MAN ABOUT TOWN, 1939
MAN I LOVE, THE, 1946
MAN OF LA MANCHA, 1972
MAN OF THE HOUR, THE, 1940
MAN TROUBLE, 1930
MANHATTAN ANGEL, 1948
MANHATTAN MERRY-GO-ROUND, 1937
MANHATTAN PARADE, 1931
MARCO, 1973
MARDI GRAS, 1958
MARGIE, 1946
MARIANNE, 1929
MARRIED IN HOLLYWOOD, 1929
MARY LOU, 1948
MARY POPPINS, 1964
MASQUERADE IN MEXICO, 1945
MAYFAIR MELODY, 1937
MAYOR OF 44TH STREET, THE, 1942
MAYTIME, 1937
MAYTIME IN MAYFAIR, 1952
MEDIUM, THE, 1951
MEET DANNY WILSON, 1952
MEET ME AFTER THE SHOW, 1951
MEET ME AT THE FAIR, 1952
MEET ME IN LAS VEGAS, 1956
MEET ME IN ST. LOUIS, 1944
MEET ME ON BROADWAY, 1946
MEET MISS BOBBY SOCKS, 1944
MEET THE NAVY, 1946
MEET THE PEOPLE, 1944
MELBA, 1953
MELODY AND MOONLIGHT, 1940
MELODY AND ROMANCE, 1937
MELODY CRUISE, 1933
MELODY FOR TWO, 1937
MELODY IN SPRING, 1934
MELODY IN THE DARK, 1948
MELODY LANE, 1929
MELODY LANE, 1941
MELODY LINGERS ON, THE, 1935
MELODY MAN, 1930
MELODY OF LOVE, THE, 1928
MELODY OF LOVE, 1954
MELODY OF MY HEART, 1936
MELODY PARADE, 1943
MELODY RANCH, 1940
MELODY TIME, 1948
MELODY TRAIL, 1935
MEN OF THE SKY, 1931
MEN ON HER MIND, 1944
MERRY-GO-ROUND OF 1938, 1937
MERRY MONAHANS, THE, 1944
MERRY WIDOW, THE, 1934
MERRY WIDOW, THE, 1952
MERRY WIVES OF WINDSOR, THE, 1952
MERRY WIVES OF WINDSOR, THE, 1966
METROPOLITAN, 1935
MEXICANA, 1945
MIKADO, THE, 1939
MIKADO, THE, 1967
MILLIONS IN THE AIR, 1935
MINSTREL BOY, THE, 1937

MINSTREL MAN, 1944
MR. BIG, 1943
MISTER CINDERS, 1934
MR. DODD TAKES THE AIR, 1937
MR. MUSIC, 1950
MR. QUILP, 1975
MISTER ROCK AND ROLL, 1957
MOLLY AND ME, 1929
MOLLY AND ME, 1945
MONTANA MOON, 1930
MONTE CARLO, 1930
MONTE CARLO BABY, 1953
MOON OVER LAS VEGAS, 1944
MOON OVER MIAMI, 1941
MOON OVER THE ALLEY, 1980
MOONLIGHT AND CACTUS, 1944
MOONLIGHT AND PRETZELS, 1933
MOONLIGHT IN HAVANA, 1942
MOONLIGHT IN HAWAII, 1941
MOONLIGHT IN VERMONT, 1943
MOTHER WORE TIGHTS, 1947
MOULIN ROUGE, 1934
MOULIN ROUGE, 1944
MOUNTAIN MUSIC, 1937
MOUNTAINS O'MOURNE, 1938
MOZART, 1940
MOZART STORY, THE, 1948
MRS. BROWN, YOU'VE GOT A LOVELY DAUGHTER,
  1968
MUPPET MOVIE, THE, 1979
MURDER AT THE CABARET, 1936
MURDER AT THE VANITIES, 1934
MUSCLE BEACH PARTY, 1964
MUSIC FOR MADAME, 1937
MUSIC FOR MILLIONS, 1944
MUSIC GOES 'ROUND, THE, 1936
MUSIC HALL, 1934
MUSIC HALL PARADE, 1939
MUSIC HATH CHARMS, 1935
MUSIC IN MANHATTAN, 1944
MUSIC IN MY HEART, 1940
MUSIC IN THE AIR, 1934
MUSIC IS MAGIC, 1935
MUSIC LOVERS, THE, 1971
MUSIC MACHINE, THE, 1979
MUSIC MAN, 1948
MUSIC MAN, THE, 1962
MUSICAL MUTINY, 1970
MY AIN FOLK, 1944
MY BEST GAL, 1944
MY DREAM IS YOURS, 1949
MY FAIR LADY, 1964
MY FAVORITE SPY, 1942
MY GAL SAL, 1942
MY HEART GOES CRAZY, 1953
MY HEART IS CALLING, 1935
MY LIPS BETRAY, 1933
MY LUCKY STAR, 1938
MY OLD KENTUCKY HOME, 1938
MY SEVEN LITTLE SINS, 1956
MY SONG FOR YOU, 1935
MY SONG GOES ROUND THE WORLD, 1934
MY WEAKNESS, 1933
MY WILD IRISH ROSE, 1947
MYSTERY AT THE BURLESQUE, 1950
NADA MAS QUE UNA MUJER, 1934
NANCY GOES TO RIO, 1950
NASHVILLE REBEL, 1966
NATIONAL BARN DANCE, 1944
NAUGHTY BUT NICE, 1939
NAUGHTY MARIETTA, 1935
NAUGHTY NINETIES, THE, 1945
NAVY BLUES, 1941
NEPTUNE'S DAUGHTER, 1949
NEVER A DULL MOMENT, 1943
NEVER STEAL ANYTHING SMALL, 1959
NEW FACES, 1954
NEW FACES OF 1937, 1937
NEW HOTEL, THE, 1932
NEW MOON, 1930
NEW MOON, 1940
NEW ORLEANS, 1947
NEW YORK, NEW YORK, 1977
NIGHT AND DAY, 1946
NIGHT AT EARL CARROLL'S, A, 1940
NIGHT CLUB GIRL, 1944

NIGHT IS YOUNG, THE, 1935
NIX ON DAMES, 1929
NO LEAVE, NO LOVE, 1946
NO, NO NANETTE, 1930
NO, NO NANETTE, 1940
NOB HILL, 1945
NOBODY'S DARLING, 1943
NORTHWEST OUTPOST, 1947
NOT SO QUIET ON THE WESTERN FRONT, 1930
O, MY DARLING CLEMENTINE, 1943
OFFICE GIRL, THE, 1932
OH! CALCUTTA!, 1972
OH JOHNNY, HOW YOU CAN LOVE!, 1940
OH ROSALINDA, 1956
OH! SAILOR, BEHAVE!, 1930
OH! WHAT A LOVELY WAR, 1969
OH, YOU BEAUTIFUL DOLL, 1949
OKLAHOMA, 1955
OKLAHOMA ANNIE, 1952
OLD HOMESTEAD, THE, 1935
OLD MAN RHYTHM, 1935
OLIVER!, 1968
ON A CLEAR DAY YOU CAN SEE FOREVER, 1970
ON AN ISLAND WITH YOU, 1948
ON MOONLIGHT BAY, 1951
ON STAGE EVERYBODY, 1945
ON THE AIR, 1934
ON THE AVENUE, 1937
ON THE RIVIERA, 1951
ON THE TOWN, 1949
ON VELVET, 1938
ON WITH THE SHOW, 1929
ON YOUR TOES, 1939
ONE DARK NIGHT, 1939
ONE HEAVENLY NIGHT, 1931
100 MEN AND A GIRL, 1937
ONE IN A MILLION, 1936
ONE MAD KISS, 1930
ONE NIGHT OF LOVE, 1934
ONE NIGHT WITH YOU, 1948
ONE SUNDAY AFTERNOON, 1948
ONE TOUCH OF VENUS, 1948
OPERETTA, 1949
OPPOSITE SEX, THE, 1956
ORCHESTRA WIVES, 1942
OTELLO, 1986
OUT OF SIGHT, 1966
OUT OF THE BLUE, 1931
OUT OF THIS WORLD, 1945
OUTSIDE OF PARADISE, 1938
OVER SHE GOES, 1937
OVER THE WALL, 1938
PAGAN LOVE SONG, 1950
PAINT YOUR WAGON, 1969
PAINTED ANGEL, THE, 1929
PAINTING THE CLOUDS WITH SUNSHINE, 1951
PAJAMA GAME, THE, 1957
PAJAMA PARTY, 1964
PALMY DAYS, 1931
PAN-AMERICANA, 1945
PANAMA HATTIE, 1942
PARADISE, HAWAIIAN STYLE, 1966
PARADISE ISLAND, 1930
PARDNERS, 1956
PARDON MY RHYTHM, 1944
PARIS, 1929
PARIS FOLLIES OF 1956, 1955
PARIS HONEYMOON, 1939
PARIS IN SPRING, 1935
PARSIFAL, 1983
PATRICK THE GREAT, 1945
PEG O' MY HEART, 1933
PENNIES FROM HEAVEN, 1936
PENNIES FROM HEAVEN, 1981
PENTHOUSE RHYTHM, 1945
PEOPLE ARE FUNNY, 1945
PEPE, 1960
PERILS OF PAULINE, THE, 1947
PETTY GIRL, THE, 1950
PHANTOM OF THE PARADISE, 1974
PHANTOM PRESIDENT, 1932
PIAF—THE EARLY YEARS, 1982
PICCADILLY NIGHTS, 1930
PIGSKIN PARADE, 1936
PIN UP GIRL, 1944
PINK FLOYD—THE WALL, 1982

PIRATE, THE, 1948
PIRATE MOVIE, THE, 1982
PISTOL PACKIN' MAMA, 1943
PLAYBOY, THE, 1942
PLAYBOY OF PARIS, 1930
PLAYMATES, 1941
PLEASURE SEEKERS, THE, 1964
POINTED HEELS, 1930
POOR LITTLE RICH GIRL, 1936
POPEYE, 1980
PORGY AND BESS, 1959
POT O' GOLD, 1941
POWERS GIRL, THE, 1942
PRESENTING LILY MARS, 1943
PRINCE OF ARCADIA, 1933
PRINCESS CHARMING, 1935
PRIORITIES ON PARADE, 1942
PRIVATE BUCKAROO, 1942
PURPLE HEART DIARY, 1951
PURPLE RAIN, 1984
PUTTIN' ON THE RITZ, 1930
QUEEN HIGH, 1930
RADIO CITY REVELS, 1938
RADIO FOLLIES, 1935
RADIO PIRATES, 1935
RADIO STARS ON PARADE, 1945
RAINBOW ISLAND, 1944
RAINBOW ON THE RIVER, 1936
RAINBOW OVER BROADWAY, 1933
RAINBOW 'ROUND MY SHOULDER, 1952
RAISE THE ROOF, 1930
RANCHO GRANDE, 1938
RAPPIN', 1985
READY, WILLING AND ABLE, 1937
REBECCA OF SUNNYBROOK FARM, 1938
REBEL, 1985
RECKLESS, 1935
RECKLESS AGE, 1944
RED GARTERS, 1954
RED, HOT AND BLUE, 1949
RED HOT RHYTHM, 1930
REDHEAD FROM MANHATTAN, 1954
REDHEADS ON PARADE, 1935
RENDEZ-VOUS, 1932
RETURN TO WATERLOO, 1985
REVEILLE WITH BEVERLY, 1943
RHAPSODY, 1954
RHAPSODY IN BLUE, 1945
RHINESTONE, 1984
RHYTHM IN THE AIR, 1936
RHYTHM IN THE CLOUDS, 1937
RHYTHM INN, 1951
RHYTHM OF THE ISLANDS, 1943
RHYTHM ON THE RANGE, 1936
RHYTHM ON THE RIVER, 1940
RHYTHM PARADE, 1943
RHYTHM RACKETEER, 1937
RHYTHM SERENADE, 1943
RICH, YOUNG AND PRETTY, 1951
RIDE 'EM COWBOY, 1942
RIDING HIGH, 1943
RIDING HIGH, 1950
RIGOLETTO, 1949
RING-A-DING RHYTHM, 1962
RIO RITA, 1929
ROAD IS FINE, THE, 1930
ROAD TO BALI, 1952
ROAD TO HONG KONG, THE, 1962
ROAD TO MOROCCO, 1942
ROAD TO RIO, 1947
ROAD TO SINGAPORE, 1940
ROAD TO UTOPIA, 1945
ROAD TO ZANZIBAR, 1941
ROBBER SYMPHONY, THE, 1937
ROBERTA, 1935
ROCK ALL NIGHT, 1957
ROCK AROUND THE CLOCK, 1956
ROCK AROUND THE WORLD, 1957
ROCK BABY, ROCK IT, 1957
ROCK 'N' ROLL HIGH SCHOOL, 1979
ROCK, PRETTY BABY, 1956
ROCK, ROCK, ROCK!, 1956
ROCK YOU SINNERS, 1957
ROCKABILLY BABY, 1957
ROCKERS, 1980
ROCKIN' IN THE ROCKIES, 1945

ROCKY HORROR PICTURE SHOW, THE, 1975
ROGUE OF THE RIO GRANDE, 1930
ROGUE SONG, THE, 1930
ROMAN SCANDALS, 1933
ROMANCE IN THE DARK, 1938
ROMANCE ON THE HIGH SEAS, 1948
ROMANY LOVE, 1931
ROOKIES ON PARADE, 1941
ROSALIE, 1937
ROSE, THE, 1979
ROSE OF THE RANCHO, 1936
ROSE OF TRALEE, 1938
ROSE OF TRALEE, 1942
ROSE OF WASHINGTON SQUARE, 1939
ROSSINI, 1948
ROUSTABOUT, 1964
ROYAL WALTZ, THE, 1936
ROYAL WEDDING, 1951
RUNAWAY QUEEN, THE, 1935
SAILING ALONG, 1938
ST. LOUIS BLUES, 1939
ST. LOUIS BLUES, 1958
SALSA, 1988
SAMMY STOPS THE WORLD, 1978
SAN ANTONIO ROSE, 1941
SARGE GOES TO COLLEGE, 1947
SATISFACTION, 1988
SAY IT WITH FLOWERS, 1934
SAY IT WITH MUSIC, 1932
SAY IT WITH SONGS, 1929
SCHLAGER-PARADE, 1953
SCHOOL DAZE, 1988
SCOTT JOPLIN, 1977
SCROOGE, 1970
SECOND GREATEST SEX, THE, 1955
SENIOR PROM, 1958
SENORITA FROM THE WEST, 1945
SENSATIONS OF 1945, 1944
SERENADE, 1956
SGT. PEPPER'S LONELY HEARTS CLUB BAND, 1978
SEVEN BRIDES FOR SEVEN BROTHERS, 1954
SEVEN DAYS ASHORE, 1944
SEVEN HILLS OF ROME, THE, 1958
SEVEN LITTLE FOYS, THE, 1955
SEVEN SWEETHEARTS, 1942
1776, 1972
SHAMROCK HILL, 1949
SHE HAS WHAT IT TAKES, 1943
SHEIK STEPS OUT, THE, 1937
SHEPHERD GIRL, THE, 1965
SHE'S A SWEETHEART, 1944
SHE'S BACK ON BROADWAY, 1953
SHINE ON, HARVEST MOON, 1944
SHIP CAFE, 1935
SHIPMATES FOREVER, 1935
SHIPMATES O' MINE, 1936
SHOCK TREATMENT, 1981
SHOCKING MISS PILGRIM, THE, 1947
SHOOT THE WORKS, 1934
SHOW BOAT, 1929
SHOW BOAT, 1936
SHOW BOAT, 1951
SHOW BUSINESS, 1944
SHOW GOES ON, THE, 1937
SHOWTIME, 1948
SIGN OF AQUARIUS, 1970
SILVER SKATES, 1943
SINCERELY YOURS, 1955
SING A JINGLE, 1943
SING AND BE HAPPY, 1937
SING ANOTHER CHORUS, 1941
SING, BOY, SING, 1958
SING, DANCE, PLENTY HOT, 1940
SING FOR YOUR SUPPER, 1941
SING ME A LOVE SONG, 1936
SING, NEIGHBOR, SING, 1944
SING SINNER, SING, 1933
SING WHILE YOU'RE ABLE, 1937
SING YOU SINNERS, 1938
SING YOUR WAY HOME, 1945
SINGIN' IN THE CORN, 1946
SINGIN' IN THE RAIN, 1952
SINGING FOOL, THE, 1928
SINGING KID, THE, 1936
SINGING MARINE, THE, 1937

SINGING NUN, THE, 1966
SITTING ON THE MOON, 1936
6.5 SPECIAL, 1958
SIX LESSONS FROM MADAME LA ZONGA, 1941
SIX P.M., 1946
SKIRTS AHOY!, 1952
SLIGHTLY SCANDALOUS, 1946
SLIGHTLY TERRIFIC, 1944
SLIPPER AND THE ROSE, THE, 1976
SMALL TOWN GIRL, 1953
SMILIN' THROUGH, 1941
SMILING IRISH EYES, 1929
SO DEAR TO MY HEART, 1949
SO THIS IS COLLEGE, 1929
SO THIS IS LOVE, 1953
SO THIS IS PARIS, 1954
SOHO CONSPIRACY, 1951
SOMBRERO, 1953
SOMEBODY LOVES ME, 1952
SOMETHING FOR THE BOYS, 1944
SOMETHING IN THE WIND, 1947
SOMETHING TO SHOUT ABOUT, 1943
SONG AND DANCE MAN, THE, 1936
SONG FOR MISS JULIE, A, 1945
SONG O' MY HEART, 1930
SONG OF LOVE, 1947
SONG OF LOVE, THE, 1929
SONG OF MEXICO, 1945
SONG OF MY HEART, 1947
SONG OF NORWAY, 1970
SONG OF SCHEHERAZADE, 1947
SONG OF SOHO, 1930
SONG OF THE FLAME, 1930
SONG OF THE FORGE, 1937
SONG OF THE ISLANDS, 1942
SONG OF THE SARONG, 1945
SONG OF THE WEST, 1930
SONG OVER MOSCOW, 1964
SONG TO REMEMBER, A, 1945
SONG WITHOUT END, 1960
SONG YOU GAVE ME, THE, 1934
SONGWRITER, 1984
SONS O' GUNS, 1936
SOUND OF MUSIC, THE, 1965
SOUTH OF DIXIE, 1944
SOUTH PACIFIC, 1958
SOUTHERN MAID, A, 1933
SPANISH EYES, 1930
SPARKLE, 1976
SPEEDWAY, 1968
SPINOUT, 1966
SPRING IS HERE, 1930
SPRING PARADE, 1940
SPRING SYMPHONY, 1986
SPRINGTIME IN THE ROCKIES, 1942
SQUARE DANCE JUBILEE, 1949
SQUARE DANCE KATY, 1950
STAGE DOOR CANTEEN, 1943
STAND UP AND CHEER, 1934 80m FOX bw
STAR!, 1968
STAR IS BORN, A, 1954
STAR IS BORN, A, 1976
STAR MAKER, THE, 1939
STARLIFT, 1951
STARS ARE SINGING, THE, 1953
STARS IN YOUR EYES, 1956
STARS ON PARADE, 1944
STARS OVER BROADWAY, 1935
STATE FAIR, 1945
STATE FAIR, 1962
STEPPING TOES, 1938
STOLEN HARMONY, 1935
STOP THE WORLD—I WANT TO GET OFF, 1966
STORMY WEATHER, 1943
STORY OF VERNON AND IRENE CASTLE, THE, 1939
STOWAWAY, 1936
STRAUSS' GREAT WALTZ, 1934
STREET GIRL, 1929
STREET SINGER, THE, 1937
STREET SONG, 1935
STRICTLY IN THE GROOVE, 1942
STRIKE ME PINK, 1936
STRIP, THE, 1951
STUDENT PRINCE, THE, 1954
STUDENT'S ROMANCE, THE, 1936
SULTAN'S DAUGHTER, THE, 1943

BOLD: Films on Videocassette

SUMMER STOCK, 1950
SUN VALLEY SERENADE, 1941
SUNNY, 1941
SUNNY SIDE OF THE STREET, 1951
SUNSHINE AHEAD, 1936
SUSIE STEPS OUT, 1946
SUSPENSE, 1946
SWANEE RIVER, 1939
SWEET ADELINE, 1935
SWEET AND LOWDOWN, 1944
SWEET BEAT, 1962
SWEET DEVIL, 1937
SWEET DREAMS, 1985
SWEET KITTY BELLAIRS, 1930
SWEET MUSIC, 1935
SWEET SURRENDER, 1935
SWEETHEART OF SIGMA CHI, 1933
SWEETHEART OF SIGMA CHI, 1946
SWEETHEART OF THE CAMPUS, 1941
SWEETHEARTS ON PARADE, 1930
SWEETHEARTS ON PARADE, 1953
SWEETIE, 1929
SWING HIGH, 1930
SWING HOSTESS, 1944
SWING OUT, SISTER, 1945
SWING PARADE OF 1946, 1946
SWING TIME, 1936
SWING YOUR PARTNER, 1943
SWINGTIME JOHNNY, 1944
SYNCOPATION, 1929
SYNCOPATION, 1942
TAHITI HONEY, 1943
TAHITI NIGHTS, 1945
TAKE A CHANCE, 1933
TAKE IT BIG, 1944
TAKE ME HIGH, 1973
TAKE ME OUT TO THE BALL GAME, 1949
TAKE ME OVER, 1963
TAKE MY TIP, 1937
TALENT SCOUT, 1937
TALES OF HOFFMANN, THE, 1951
TALK ABOUT A LADY, 1946
TALKING FEET, 1937
TANGO BAR, 1935
TANNED LEGS, 1929
TARS AND SPARS, 1946
TAXI TO HEAVEN, 1944
TE QUIERO CON LOCURA, 1935
TEA FOR TWO, 1950
TEENAGE MILLIONAIRE, 1961
TELL IT TO A STAR, 1945
TEMPTATION, 1935
TEN THOUSAND BEDROOMS, 1957
TEXAS CARNIVAL, 1951
THANK GOD IT'S FRIDAY, 1978
THANK YOUR LUCKY STARS, 1943
THANKS A MILLION, 1935
THANKS FOR EVERYTHING, 1938
THAT CERTAIN AGE, 1938
THAT GIRL FROM PARIS, 1937
THAT LADY IN ERMINE, 1948
THAT MIDNIGHT KISS, 1949
THAT NIGHT IN RIO, 1941
THAT NIGHT WITH YOU, 1945
THAT'S THE SPIRIT, 1945
THAT'S A GOOD GIRL, 1933
THAT'S MY GAL, 1947
THAT'S RIGHT—YOU'RE WRONG, 1939
THERE'S A GIRL IN MY HEART, 1949
THERE'S MAGIC IN MUSIC, 1941
**THERE'S NO BUSINESS LIKE SHOW BUSINESS,
  1954**
THEY LEARNED ABOUT WOMEN, 1930
THEY MET IN ARGENTINA, 1941
THEY SHALL HAVE MUSIC, 1939
THIS IS THE ARMY, 1943
THIS TIME FOR KEEPS, 1947
THIS WAY PLEASE, 1937
THIS WINE OF LOVE, 1948
THIS'LL MAKE YOU WHISTLE, 1938
THISTLEDOWN, 1938
THOSE REDHEADS FROM SEATTLE, 1953
THOSE THREE FRENCH GIRLS, 1930
THOUSANDS CHEER, 1943
THREE CABALLEROS, THE, 1944
THREE CHEERS FOR LOVE, 1936

THREE DARING DAUGHTERS, 1948
THREE FOR THE SHOW, 1955
THREE HATS FOR LISA, 1965
THREE LITTLE GIRLS IN BLUE, 1946
THREE LITTLE WORDS, 1950
THREE PENNY OPERA, 1963
THREE SAILORS AND A GIRL, 1953
THREEPENNY OPERA, THE, 1931
THRILL OF A LIFETIME, 1937
THRILL OF A ROMANCE, 1945
THRILL OF BRAZIL, THE, 1946
THUMBS UP, 1943
TICKLE ME, 1965
TILL THE CLOUDS ROLL BY, 1946
TIME OUT FOR RHYTHM, 1941
TIME, THE PLACE AND THE GIRL, THE, 1929
TIME, THE PLACE AND THE GIRL, THE, 1946
TIN PAN ALLEY, 1940
TOAST OF NEW ORLEANS, THE, 1950
TOM THUMB, 1958
TOMMY, 1975
TOMMY THE TOREADOR, 1960
TONIGHT AND EVERY NIGHT, 1945
TONIGHT WE SING, 1953
TOO LATE BLUES, 1962
TOO MANY BLONDES, 1941
TOO MUCH HARMONY, 1933
TOOMORROW, 1970
TOP BANANA, 1954
TOP HAT, 1935
TOP MAN, 1943
TOP O' THE MORNING, 1949
TOP OF THE TOWN, 1937
TOP SECRET!, 1984
TORCH SINGER, 1933
TORCH SONG, 1953
TRAIN GOES TO KIEV, THE, 1961
TRANSATLANTIC MERRY-GO-ROUND, 1934
TROCADERO, 1944
TROPIC HOLIDAY, 1938
TSAR'S BRIDE, THE, 1966
TURN OFF THE MOON, 1937
20TH CENTURY OZ, 1977
TWILIGHT ON THE PRAIRIE, 1944
TWIST AROUND THE CLOCK, 1961
TWO BLONDES AND A REDHEAD, 1947
TWO GIRLS AND A SAILOR, 1944
TWO GIRLS ON BROADWAY, 1940
TWO HEARTS IN HARMONY, 1935
TWO HEARTS IN WALTZ TIME, 1934
TWO HUNDRED MOTELS, 1971
TWO KOUNEY LEMELS, 1966
TWO LATINS FROM MANHATTAN, 1941
TWO SENORITAS FROM CHICAGO, 1943
TWO SISTERS FROM BOSTON, 1946
UMBRELLAS OF CHERBOURG, THE, 1964
UNDER THE PAMPAS MOON, 1935
UNDER WESTERN SKIES, 1945
UNDER YOUR SPELL, 1936
UNFINISHED DANCE, THE, 1947
UNSINKABLE MOLLY BROWN, THE, 1964
UNTAMED YOUTH, 1957
UP IN ARMS, 1944
UP IN CENTRAL PARK, 1948
UP JUMPED A SWAGMAN, 1965
VAGABOND KING, THE, 1930
VAGABOND KING, THE, 1956
VAGABOND LOVER, 1929
VARIETY, 1935
VARIETY GIRL, 1947
VARIETY JUBILEE, 1945
VARSITY SHOW, 1937
VIENNESE NIGHTS, 1930
VILLAGE BARN DANCE, 1940
VIVA LAS VEGAS, 1964
VOGUES OF 1938, 1937
WABASH AVENUE, 1950
WAKE UP AND DREAM, 1934
WALTZ TIME, 1933
WALTZ TIME, 1946
WAY DOWN SOUTH, 1939
WAY TO LOVE, THE, 1933
WEARY RIVER, 1929
WEDDING OF LILLI MARLENE, THE, 1953
WEEKEND AT THE WALDORF, 1945

WEEKEND IN HAVANA, 1941
WE'LL MEET AGAIN, 1942
WEST SIDE STORY, 1961
WHAT AM I BID?, 1967
WHAT DO WE DO NOW?, 1945
WHAT'S BUZZIN COUSIN?, 1943
WHAT'S COOKIN'?, 1942
WHEN A GIRL'S BEAUTIFUL, 1947
WHEN JOHNNY COMES MARCHING HOME, 1943
WHEN MY BABY SMILES AT ME, 1948
WHEN YOU'RE IN LOVE, 1937
WHEN YOU'RE SMILING, 1950
WHERE DO WE GO FROM HERE?, 1945
WHERE IS THIS LADY?, 1932
WHEREVER SHE GOES, 1953
WHIRLWIND OF PARIS, 1946
WHITE HORSE INN, THE, 1959
WILD, WILD WINTER, 1966
**WILLY WONKA AND THE CHOCOLATE FACTORY,
  1971**
WINTER A GO-GO, 1965
WINTERTIME, 1943
WITH A SONG IN MY HEART, 1952
WITH LOVE AND KISSES, 1937
WIZ, THE, 1978
WIZARD OF OZ, THE, 1939
WOMAN IN COMMAND, THE, 1934
WOMEN EVERYWHERE, 1930
WONDER MAN, 1945
WONDERFUL TO BE YOUNG!, 1962
WONDERFUL WORLD OF THE BROTHERS GRIMM,
  THE, 1962
WORDS AND MUSIC, 1929
WORDS AND MUSIC, 1948
XANADU, 1980
YANKEE DOODLE DANDY, 1942
YANKS ARE COMING, THE, 1942
YELLOW HAT, THE, 1966
YELLOW MASK, THE, 1930
YELLOW SUBMARINE, 1958
YENTL, 1983
YES SIR, MR. BONES, 1951
YIDDLE WITH HIS FIDDLE, 1937
YOKEL BOY, 1942
YOLANDA AND THE THIEF, 1945
YOLANTA, 1964
YOU ARE THE WORLD FOR ME, 1964
YOU CAN'T DO WITHOUT LOVE, 1946
YOU CAN'T HAVE EVERYTHING, 1937
YOU CAN'T RATION LOVE, 1944
YOU CAN'T RUN AWAY FROM IT, 1956
YOU LIGHT UP MY LIFE, 1977
YOU WERE MEANT FOR ME, 1948
YOU WERE NEVER LOVELIER, 1942
YOU WILL REMEMBER, 1941
YOU'LL FIND OUT, 1940
YOU'LL NEVER GET RICH, 1941
YOUNG AT HEART, 1955
YOUNG GIRLS OF ROCHEFORT, THE, 1968
YOUNG LORD, THE, 1970
YOUNG MAN WITH A HORN, 1950
YOUNG PEOPLE, 1940
YOUR CHEATIN' HEART, 1964
YOU'RE A LUCKY FELLOW, MR. SMITH, 1943
YOU'RE A SWEETHEART, 1937
YOU'RE MY EVERYTHING, 1949
YOU'RE THE ONE, 1941
YOUTH ON PARADE, 1943
YOUTH WILL BE SERVED, 1940
ZIEGFELD FOLLIES, 1945
ZIEGFELD GIRL, 1941
ZIS BOOM BAH, 1941

Musical Comedy
AFFAIRS OF DOBIE GILLIS, THE, 1953
ALL ASHORE, 1953
ALL THE KING'S HORSES, 1935
ALONG CAME SALLY, 1934
AND THE ANGELS SING, 1944
ANGEL COMES TO BROOKLYN, AN, 1945
ANYTHING FOR A SONG, 1947
APRIL IN PARIS, 1953
ARE YOU WITH IT?, 1948
ARGENTINE NIGHTS, 1940
ARTHUR, 1931
BABY, TAKE A BOW, 1934

BEACH BLANKET BINGO, 1965
BEACH PARTY, 1963
BEAUTIFUL BUT BROKE, 1944
BECAUSE YOU'RE MINE, 1952
BEDTIME STORY, A, 1933
BEHIND THE EIGHT BALL, 1942
BELLS ARE RINGING, 1960
BEST LITTLE WHOREHOUSE IN TEXAS, THE, 1982
BIG BOY, 1930
BIG BROADCAST, THE, 1932
BIG BROADCAST OF 1936, THE, 1935
BIG BROADCAST OF 1937, THE, 1936
BIG BROADCAST OF 1938, THE, 1937
BLONDE TROUBLE, 1937
BLUES BUSTERS, 1950
BORN TO DANCE, 1936
BOTTOMS UP, 1934
BOWERY TO BROADWAY, 1944
BOYS FROM SYRACUSE, 1940
BRAZIL, 1944
BREAK THE NEWS, 1938
BRIDE OF THE REGIMENT, 1930
BRIDEGROOM FOR TWO, 1932
BRING ON THE GIRLS, 1945
BRING YOUR SMILE ALONG, 1955
BROADWAY GONDOLIER, 1935
BROADWAY MELODY OF 1936, 1935
BROADWAY MELODY OF '38, 1937
BUNDLE OF JOY, 1956
BY THE LIGHT OF THE SILVERY MOON, 1953
BYE BYE BIRDIE, 1963
CAIN AND MABEL, 1936
CALL ME MADAM, 1953
CALL OUT THE MARINES, 1942
CAMPUS HONEYMOON, 1948
CAMPUS RHYTHM, 1943
CAMPUS SLEUTH, 1948
CAN THIS BE DIXIE?, 1936
CAREFREE, 1938
CASANOVA IN BURLESQUE, 1944
CASANOVA'S BIG NIGHT, 1954
CHARMING DECEIVER, THE, 1933
CHASING RAINBOWS, 1930
CHILDREN OF PLEASURE, 1930
CINDERELLA JONES, 1946
CINDERELLA SWINGS IT, 1942
COCK-EYED WORLD, THE, 1929
COLLEEN, 1936
COLLEGE HOLIDAY, 1936
COLLEGE SWING, 1938
COLLEGIATE, 1936
COME OUT OF THE PANTRY, 1935
COMIN' ROUND THE MOUNTAIN, 1940
CONEY ISLAND, 1943
COOL ONES, THE, 1967
COPACABANA, 1947
COTTONPICKIN' CHICKENPICKERS, 1967
COUNSEL FOR ROMANCE, 1938
COUNTRY BOY, 1966
COVER GIRL, 1944
COWBOY FROM BROOKLYN, 1938
CRAZY HOUSE, 1943
CROSS MY HEART, 1946
DAMES, 1934
DAMN YANKEES, 1958
DAMSEL IN DISTRESS, A, 1937
DANCE HALL, 1941
DANCE TEAM, 1932
DANCE, GIRL, DANCE, 1933
DANCING CO-ED, 1939
DANCING IN THE DARK, 1949
DANGEROUS DAN McGREW, 1930
DANGEROUS WHEN WET, 1953
DANGEROUS YOUTH, 1958
DATE WITH JUDY, A, 1948
DAUGHTER OF ROSIE O'GRADY, THE, 1950
DIE FLEDERMAUS, 1964
DING DONG WILLIAMS, 1946
DIXIANA, 1930
DIXIE JAMBOREE, 1945
DR. RHYTHM, 1938
DOUBLE CROSSBONES, 1950
DOUBLE OR NOTHING, 1937
DOWN TO EARTH, 1947
DU BARRY WAS A LADY, 1943
DUCHESS OF IDAHO, THE, 1950

DUFFY'S TAVERN, 1945
EAST SIDE OF HEAVEN, 1939
EASTER PARADE, 1948
EMPEROR WALTZ, THE, 1948
FIRST NUDIE MUSICAL, THE, 1976
FLOWER DRUM SONG, 1961
FLYING MATCHMAKER, THE, 1970
GIRLS JUST WANT TO HAVE FUN, 1985
HANDLE WITH CARE, 1964
HARD DAY'S NIGHT, A, 1964
HARVEY GIRLS, THE, 1946
HAVING A WILD WEEKEND, 1965
HEAT WAVE, 1935
HEAT'S ON, THE, 1943
HELDINNEN, 1962
HELLO, DOLLY!, 1969
HELLO, EVERYBODY, 1933
HELP!, 1965
HER MAJESTY'S LOVE, 1931
HERE COME THE CO-EDS, 1945
HERE COME THE GIRLS, 1953
HERE COME THE WAVES, 1944
HERE COMES ELMER, 1943
HIGH SOCIETY, 1956
HIGH TIME, 1960
HIPS, HIPS, HOORAY, 1934
HIS BUTLER'S SISTER, 1943
HIS LORDSHIP, 1932
HIS MAJESTY AND CO, 1935
HIS ROYAL HIGHNESS, 1932
HIT THE HAY, 1945
HIT THE ICE, 1943
HOLD EVERYTHING, 1930
HOLD ON, 1966
HOLIDAY INN, 1942
HOLLYWOOD CANTEEN, 1944
HOLLYWOOD HOTEL, 1937
HOLLYWOOD PARTY, 1934
HOME SWEET HOME, 1945
HONEY, 1930
HONEYCHILE, 1951
HONEYMOON, 1947
HONEYMOON AHEAD, 1945
HONEYMOON FOR THREE, 1935
HONEYMOON HOTEL, 1946
HONOLULU LU, 1941
HOW TO BE VERY, VERY, POPULAR, 1955
HOW TO STUFF A WILD BIKINI, 1965
HOW TO SUCCEED IN BUSINESS WITHOUT REALLY
   TRYING, 1967
HULLABALOO, 1940
I ADORE YOU, 1933
I DOOD IT, 1943
I DREAM TOO MUCH, 1935
I LOVE A BANDLEADER, 1945
IDEA GIRL, 1946
IF YOU KNEW SUSIE, 1948
I'LL TELL THE WORLD, 1945
IN PERSON, 1935
IN THE GOOD OLD SUMMERTIME, 1949
IN THE NAVY, 1941
INSPECTOR GENERAL, THE, 1949
IRENE, 1940
IT ALL CAME TRUE, 1940
IT HAPPENED IN BROOKLYN, 1947
IT STARTED WITH EVE, 1941
IT'S A DATE, 1940
IT'S A WONDERFUL WORLD, 1956
IT'S ALWAYS FAIR WEATHER, 1955
IT'S GREAT TO BE YOUNG, 1956
I'VE GOTTA HORSE, 1965
JOAN OF OZARK, 1942
JUPITER'S DARLING, 1955
JUST FOR YOU, 1952
KENTUCKY JUBILEE, 1951
KENTUCKY MOONSHINE, 1938
KID FROM BROOKLYN, THE, 1946
KID FROM SPAIN, THE, 1932
KID MILLIONS, 1934
KIMBERLEY JIM, 1965
KING OF BURLESQUE, 1936
KING OF THE RITZ, 1933
KISS ME GOODBYE, 1935
KISS ME KATE, 1953
KLONDIKE ANNIE, 1936
KNICKERBOCKER HOLIDAY, 1944

LADY ON THE TRACKS, THE, 1968
LET'S MAKE LOVE, 1960
LIFE OF THE PARTY, THE, 1937
LI'L ABNER, 1959
LITTLE MISS BROADWAY, 1947
LIVING IT UP, 1954
LOOK OUT SISTER, 1948
LOUISIANA PURCHASE, 1941
LOVE PARADE, THE, 1929
LOVELY TO LOOK AT, 1952
LULLABY OF BROADWAY, THE, 1951
LUXURY LINER, 1948
MA, HE'S MAKING EYES AT ME, 1940
MAKE A WISH, 1937
MAME, 1974
MERRY ANDREW, 1958
MISS LONDON LTD., 1943
MISSISSIPPI, 1935
MY BLUE HEAVEN, 1950
MY MAN, 1928
MY SISTER EILEEN, 1955
MYRT AND MARGE, 1934
ONE HOUR WITH YOU, 1932
ONE NIGHT IN THE TROPICS, 1940
OVER THE GARDEN WALL, 1934
PADDY O'DAY, 1935
PAL JOEY, 1957
PALM SPRINGS, 1936
PATAKIN, 1985
PIRATES OF PENZANCE, THE, 1983
ROSE MARIE, 1936
ROSE MARIE, 1954
SAFETY IN NUMBERS, 1930
SAILOR BEWARE, 1951
SALLY, 1929
SALLY, IRENE AND MARY, 1938
SALUTE FOR THREE, 1943
SAVE A LITTLE SUNSHINE, 1938
SAY ONE FOR ME, 1959
SCARED STIFF, 1953
SCATTERBRAIN, 1940
SEASIDE SWINGERS, 1965
SECOND CHORUS, 1940
SECOND FIDDLE TO A STEEL GUITAR, 1965
SEE MY LAWYER, 1945
SERGEANT DEADHEAD, 1965
SEVEN DAYS LEAVE, 1942
SEXTETTE, 1978
SHAKE, RATTLE, AND ROCK?, 1957
SHALL WE DANCE, 1937
SHANNONS OF BROADWAY, THE, 1929
SHE LOVES ME NOT, 1934
SHE SHALL HAVE MUSIC, 1935
SHE'S WORKING HER WAY THROUGH COLLEGE,
   1952
SHIP AHOY, 1942
SHIPYARD SALLY, 1940
SILK STOCKINGS, 1957
SING AND SWING, 1964
SING AS YOU SWING, 1937
SING, BABY, SING, 1936
SING WHILE YOU DANCE, 1946
SING YOUR WORRIES AWAY, 1942
SINGING TAXI DRIVER, 1953
SIS HOPKINS, 1941
SITTING PRETTY, 1933
SKI PARTY, 1965
SKY'S THE LIMIT, THE, 1943
SLEEPLESS NIGHTS, 1933
SLEEPY LAGOON, 1943
SLEEPYTIME GAL, 1942
SLIGHTLY FRENCH, 1949
SMART POLITICS, 1948
SMILING ALONG, 1938
SMILING LIEUTENANT, THE, 1931
SO LONG LETTY, 1929
SOME LIKE IT HOT, 1939
SOMETHING TO SING ABOUT, 1937
SONG IS BORN, A, 1948
SONG OF THE OPEN ROAD, 1944
SOUTHERN ROSES, 1936
SPOTLIGHT SCANDALS, 1943
SPRING, 1948
SPRING IN THE AIR, 1934
SQUIBS, 1935
STAGE STRUCK, 1936

BOLD: Films on Videocassette

STAR SPANGLED RHYTHM, 1942
STARSTRUCK, 1982
START CHEERING, 1938
STEP LIVELY, 1944
STOOGE, THE, 1952
STORK CLUB, THE, 1945
STRAIGHT, PLACE AND SHOW, 1938
STRICTLY DYNAMITE, 1934
STRIKE UP THE BAND, 1940
STUDENT TOUR, 1934
SUMMER HOLIDAY, 1948
SUMMER HOLIDAY, 1963
SUMMER LOVE, 1958
SUNBONNET SUE, 1945
SUNNY, 1930
SUNNY SIDE UP, 1929
SUNNY SKIES, 1930
SWEATER GIRL, 1942
SWEET CHARITY, 1969
SWEET ROSIE O'GRADY, 1943
SWEETHEART OF THE FLEET, 1942
SWEETHEARTS, 1938
SWEETHEARTS OF THE U.S.A., 1944
SWING FEVER, 1943
SWING HIGH, SWING LOW, 1937
SWING IT, PROFESSOR, 1937
SWING IT SOLDIER, 1941
SWING OUT THE BLUES, 1943
SWING, SISTER, SWING, 1938
SWINGER'S PARADISE, 1965
SWINGIN' SUMMER, A, 1965
THIN ICE, 1937
THIS COULD BE THE NIGHT, 1957
THIS IS THE LIFE, 1944
THOROUGHLY MODERN MILLIE, 1967
THREE SMART GIRLS, 1937
TOO MANY GIRLS, 1940
TOP SPEED, 1930
TRUE TO THE ARMY, 1942
TWENTY MILLION SWEETHEARTS, 1934
TWIST ALL NIGHT, 1961
TWO FOR TONIGHT, 1935
TWO GALS AND A GUY, 1951
TWO GUYS FROM TEXAS, 1948
TWO TICKETS TO BROADWAY, 1951
TWO TICKETS TO PARIS, 1962
TWO WEEKS WITH LOVE, 1950
UNDER-PUP, THE, 1939
UNTAMED HEIRESS, 1954
VARIETY PARADE, 1936
VICTOR/VICTORIA, 1982
WAIKIKI WEDDING, 1937
WAKE UP AND LIVE, 1937
WALKING MY BABY BACK HOME, 1953
WALKING ON AIR, 1936
WEEKEND PASS, 1944
WE'RE NOT DRESSING, 1934
WEST POINT STORY, THE, 1950
WHEN THE BOYS MEET THE GIRLS, 1965
WHERE DID YOU GET THAT GIRL?, 1941
WHERE'S CHARLEY?, 1952
WHITE CHRISTMAS, 1954
WHOOPEE, 1930
WIFE, HUSBAND AND FRIEND, 1939
WILD ON THE BEACH, 1965
WONDER BAR, 1934
YES, MADAM?, 1938
YES, MR. BROWN, 1933
YES SIR, THAT'S MY BABY, 1949

Mystery
ACCOMPLICE, 1946
ACCOUNT RENDERED, 1957
ACCUSED OF MURDER, 1956
ACE OF SPADES, THE, 1935
ADELE HASN'T HAD HER SUPPER YET, 1978
ADVENTURE OF SHERLOCK HOLMES' SMARTER BROTHER, THE, 1975
ADVENTURES OF JANE ARDEN, 1939
ADVENTURES OF KITTY O'DAY, 1944
ADVENTURES OF SHERLOCK HOLMES, THE, 1939
ADVENTUROUS BLONDE, 1937
AFFAIRS OF A GENTLEMAN, 1934
AFTER MIDNIGHT WITH BOSTON BLACKIE, 1943
AFTER THE THIN MAN, 1936
AGNES OF GOD, 1985

ALIAS BOSTON BLACKIE, 1942
ALIAS BULLDOG DRUMMOND, 1935
ALIAS MARY SMITH, 1932
ALIBI, 1931
ALIBI, THE, 1939
ALIBI, THE, 1943
ALIBI FOR MURDER, 1936
ALPHABET MURDERS, THE, 1966
AMAZING MR. BLUNDEN, THE, 1973
AMAZING MR. WILLIAMS, 1939
AMERICAN FRIEND, THE, 1977
AMSTERDAM AFFAIR, THE, 1968
AMSTERDAM KILL, THE, 1978
AND THEN THERE WERE NONE, 1945
ANGEL HEART, 1987
ANGRY MAN, THE, 1979
ANOTHER THIN MAN, 1939
ANYBODY'S BLONDE, 1931
ANYTHING MIGHT HAPPEN, 1935
APPOINTMENT FOR MURDER, 1954
APPOINTMENT WITH DEATH, 1988
APPOINTMENT WITH MURDER, 1948
APPRENTICE TO MURDER, 1988
ARGYLE CASE, THE, 1929
ARGYLE SECRETS, THE, 1948
ARM OF THE LAW, 1932
ARMCHAIR DETECTIVE, THE, 1952
ARREST BULLDOG DRUMMOND, 1939
ARSENAL STADIUM MYSTERY, THE, 1939
ARSENE LUPIN, 1932
ARSENE LUPIN RETURNS, 1938
AS THE DEVIL COMMANDS, 1933
ASSASSIN, THE, 1953
ASSAULT, 1971
ATLANTIC ADVENTURE, 1935
ATTEMPT TO KILL, 1961
AVALANCHE, 1946
AVENGER, THE, 1933
AVENGING HAND, THE, 1936
BACKFIRE, 1950
BACKFIRE!, 1961
BACKLASH, 1947
BANG! YOU'RE DEAD, 1954
BARTON MYSTERY, THE, 1932
BAT, THE, 1959
BEFORE DAWN, 1933
BEFORE MIDNIGHT, 1934
BEFORE MORNING, 1933
BEHIND GREEN LIGHTS, 1946
BEHIND JURY DOORS, 1933
BEHIND THAT CURTAIN, 1929
BEHIND THE HEADLINES, 1956
BEHIND THE MASK, 1932
BEHIND THE MASK, 1946
BELLAMY TRIAL, THE, 1929
BENSON MURDER CASE, THE, 1930
BERMUDA MYSTERY, 1944
BEYOND A REASONABLE DOUBT, 1956
BIG BROWN EYES, 1936
BIG FIX, THE, 1978
BIG FRAME, THE, 1953
BIG SLEEP, THE, 1946
BIG SLEEP, THE, 1978
BIG SWITCH, THE, 1950
BIG TOWN CZAR, 1939
BISHOP MISBEHAVES, THE, 1933
BISHOP MURDER CASE, THE, 1930
BLACK ANGEL, 1946
BLACK BIRD, THE, 1975
BLACK CAMEL, THE, 1931
BLACK COFFEE, 1931
BLACK DOLL, THE, 1938
BLACK EYE, 1974
BLACK LIMELIGHT, 1938
BLACK RAVEN, THE, 1943
BLACK WIDOW, 1954
BLACK WIDOW, 1987
BLACKMAIL, 1929
BLACKMAILER, 1936
BLACKOUT, 1954
BLADE, 1973
BLANCHE FURY, 1948
BLONDE ALIBI, 1946
BLONDE BAIT, 1956
BLONDE BLACKMAILER, 1955
BLONDE FOR A DAY, 1946

BLOOD FEAST, 1976
BLOOD ORANGE, 1953
BLOOD RELATIVES, 1978
BLOODLINE, 1979
BLOW OUT, 1981
BLUE DAHLIA, THE, 1946
BLUE GARDENIA, THE, 1953
BLUE LAMP, THE, 1950
BLUE PARROT, THE, 1953
BLUE VELVET, 1986
BLUE, WHITE, AND PERFECT, 1941
BLUEPRINT FOR MURDER, A, 1953
BODYGUARD, 1948
BOMBAY MAIL, 1934
BOOMERANG, 1934
BOOMERANG, 1947
BOSTON BLACKIE AND THE LAW, 1946
BOSTON BLACKIE BOOKED ON SUSPICION, 1945
BOSTON BLACKIE GOES HOLLYWOOD, 1942
BOSTON BLACKIE'S CHINESE VENTURE, 1949
BOSTON BLACKIE'S RENDEZVOUS, 1945
BOWERY CHAMPS, 1944
BOYS OF THE CITY, 1940
BRASHER DOUBLOON, THE, 1947
BRASS TARGET, 1978
BREAK, THE, 1962
BREAKAWAY, 1956
BRIBE, THE, 1949
BRIDE WORE BLACK, THE, 1968
BRIDE WORE CRUTCHES, THE, 1940
BULLDOG DRUMMOND, 1929
BULLDOG DRUMMOND AT BAY, 1937
BULLDOG DRUMMOND COMES BACK, 1937
BULLDOG DRUMMOND ESCAPES, 1937
BULLDOG DRUMMOND IN AFRICA, 1938
BULLDOG DRUMMOND STRIKES BACK, 1934
BULLDOG DRUMMOND'S BRIDE, 1939
BULLDOG DRUMMOND'S PERIL, 1938
BULLDOG DRUMMOND'S REVENGE, 1937
BULLDOG DRUMMOND'S SECRET POLICE, 1939
BULLDOG SEES IT THROUGH, 1940
BUNNY LAKE IS MISSING, 1965
BURMA CONVOY, 1941
BURY ME DEAD, 1947
BUSMAN'S HONEYMOON, 1940
BYE BYE BARBARA, 1969
CAFE DE PARIS, 1938
CALLING DR. DEATH, 1943
CANARY MURDER CASE, THE, 1929
CANDLES AT NINE, 1944
CAREY TREATMENT, THE, 1972
CARIBBEAN MYSTERY, THE, 1945
CARRY ON SCREAMING, 1966
CASE FOR PC 49, A, 1951
CASE OF THE BLACK CAT, THE, 1936
CASE OF THE BLACK PARROT, THE, 1941
CASE OF THE CURIOUS BRIDE, THE, 1935
CASE OF THE HOWLING DOG, THE, 1934
CASE OF THE LUCKY LEGS, THE, 1935
CASE OF THE MISSING MAN, THE, 1935
CASE OF THE STUTTERING BISHOP, THE, 1937
CASE OF THE VELVET CLAWS, THE, 1936
CASINO MURDER CASE, THE, 1935
CASTLE IN THE DESERT, 1942
CASTLE OF CRIMES, 1940
CAT AND MOUSE, 1975
CAT AND THE CANARY, THE, 1939
CAT AND THE CANARY, THE, 1979
CAT CREEPS, THE, 1930
CAT CREEPS, THE, 1946
CATALINA CAPER, THE, 1967
CATMAN OF PARIS, THE, 1946
CAUGHT IN THE FOG, 1928
CHALLENGE, THE, 1948
CHAMPAGNE CHARLIE, 1936
CHANCE MEETING, 1960
CHANDU THE MAGICIAN, 1932
CHANNEL CROSSING, 1934
CHARLATAN, THE, 1929
CHARLIE CHAN AT MONTE CARLO, 1937
CHARLIE CHAN AT THE CIRCUS, 1936
CHARLIE CHAN AT THE OLYMPICS, 1937
CHARLIE CHAN AT THE OPERA, 1936
CHARLIE CHAN AT THE RACE TRACK, 1936

CHARLIE CHAN AT THE WAX MUSEUM, 1940
CHARLIE CHAN AT TREASURE ISLAND, 1939
CHARLIE CHAN CARRIES ON, 1931
CHARLIE CHAN IN BLACK MAGIC, 1944
CHARLIE CHAN IN EGYPT, 1935
CHARLIE CHAN IN HONOLULU, 1938
CHARLIE CHAN IN LONDON, 1934
CHARLIE CHAN IN PANAMA, 1940
CHARLIE CHAN IN PARIS, 1935
CHARLIE CHAN IN RENO, 1939
CHARLIE CHAN IN RIO, 1941
CHARLIE CHAN IN SHANGHAI, 1935
CHARLIE CHAN IN THE CITY OF DARKNESS, 1939
CHARLIE CHAN IN THE SECRET SERVICE, 1944
CHARLIE CHAN ON BROADWAY, 1937
CHARLIE CHAN'S CHANCE, 1932
CHARLIE CHAN'S COURAGE, 1934
CHARLIE CHAN'S GREATEST CASE, 1933
CHARLIE CHAN'S MURDER CRUISE, 1940
CHARLIE CHAN'S SECRET, 1936
CHARLIE MC CARTHY, DETECTIVE, 1939
CHASE, THE, 1946
CHASING TROUBLE, 1940
CHEAP DETECTIVE, THE, 1978
CHEATERS AT PLAY, 1932
CHEATING BLONDES, 1933
CHECKERED COAT, THE, 1948
CHEERS OF THE CROWD, 1936
CHINATOWN, 1974
CHINESE RING, THE, 1947
CHRISTINA, 1974
CHRISTMAS HOLIDAY, 1944
CIRCLE, THE, 1959
CIRCUS QUEEN MURDER, THE, 1933
CITY OF MISSING GIRLS, 1941
CLAYDON TREASURE MYSTERY, THE, 1938
CLEGG, 1969
CLOSE CALL FOR BOSTON BLACKIE, A, 1946
CLOSE CALL FOR ELLERY QUEEN, A, 1942
CLOUDBURST, 1952
CLUE, 1985
CLUE OF THE NEW PIN, THE, 1929
CLUE OF THE SILVER KEY, THE, 1961
CLUE OF THE TWISTED CANDLE, 1968
COBRA STRIKES, THE, 1948
COLLEGE SCANDAL, 1935
COLLISION, 1932
COMPANIONS IN CRIME, 1954
COMPROMISING POSITIONS, 1985
CONDEMNED TO DEATH, 1932
CONFESSIONS OF BOSTON BLACKIE, 1941
CONFLICT, 1945
CONSPIRACY, 1930
CONTRABAND SPAIN, 1955
CONVICTED, 1931
COP, 1988
COP HATER, 1958
COPPER, THE, 1930
CORPSE OF BEVERLY HILLS, THE, 1965
COSTELLO CASE, THE, 1930
COVER-UP, 1949
CRACK-UP, 1946
CRIME BY NIGHT, 1944
CRIME DOCTOR, 1943
CRIME DOCTOR'S COURAGE, THE, 1945
CRIME DOCTOR'S DIARY, THE, 1949
CRIME DOCTOR'S GAMBLE, 1947
CRIME DOCTOR'S STRANGEST CASE, 1943
CRIME DOCTOR'S WARNING, 1945
CRIME DOCTOR'S MAN HUNT, 1946
CRIME NOBODY SAW, THE, 1937
CRIME OF HELEN STANLEY, 1934
CRIME OF THE CENTURY, THE, 1933
CRIMINAL AT LARGE, 1932
CRIMSON CIRCLE, THE, 1930
CRIMSON CIRCLE, THE, 1936
CRIMSON KEY, THE, 1947
CROOKS TOUR, 1940
CROSBY CASE, THE, 1934
CROSSROADS, 1942
CRY DANGER, 1951
CRY MURDER, 1936
CRY WOLF, 1947
CUCKOO CLOCK, THE, 1938
CURTAIN AT EIGHT, 1934
CUTTER AND BONE, 1981

DANCING MAN, 1934
DANGER ON THE AIR, 1938
DANGER STREET, 1947
DANGER ZONE, 1951
DANGEROUS AFFAIR, A, 1931
DANGEROUS CHARTER, 1962 76m Crown International
  c
DANGEROUS CORNER, 1935
DANGEROUS DAVIES—THE LAST DETECTIVE, 1981
DANGEROUS GAME, A, 1941
DANGEROUS GROUND, 1934
DANGEROUS LADY, 1941
DANGEROUS MEDICINE, 1938
DANGEROUS MILLIONS, 1946
DANGEROUS MONEY, 1946
DANGEROUS PARTNERS, 1945
DANGEROUS PASSAGE, 1944
DARK ALIBI, 1946
DARK EYES OF LONDON, 1961
DARK PURPOSE, 1964
DARKENED ROOMS, 1929
DARKER THAN AMBER, 1970
DAY OF THE NIGHTMARE, 1965
DEAD KIDS, 1981
DEAD MAN'S EYES, 1944
DEAD MEN TELL, 1941
DEAD PIGEON ON BEETHOVEN STREET, 1972
DEAD RECKONING, 1947
DEAD RINGER, 1964
DEADLINE AT DAWN, 1946
DEADLY DUO, 1962
DEADLY GAME, THE, 1941
DEADLY RECORD, 1959
DEATH AT A BROADCAST, 1934
DEATH FLIES EAST, 1935
DEATH FROM A DISTANCE, 1936
DEATH GOES NORTH, 1939
DEATH IN THE SKY, 1937
DEATH KISS, THE, 1933
DEATH OF A CHAMPION, 1939
DEATH ON THE NILE, 1978
DEATHTRAP, 1982
DECEIVER, THE, 1931
DESPERATE CHANCE FOR ELLERY QUEEN, A, 1942
DETECTIVE KITTY O'DAY, 1944
DEVIL BAT'S DAUGHTER, THE, 1946
DEVIL PAYS, THE, 1932
DEVIL'S DAFFODIL, THE, 1961
DEVIL'S MASK, THE, 1946
DEVIL'S MATE, 1933
DIE FASTNACHTSBEICHTE, 1962
DISCARDED LOVERS, 1932
DISGRACED, 1933
D.O.A., 1950
D.O.A., 1988
DOCKS OF NEW ORLEANS, 1948
DONOVAN AFFAIR, THE, 1929
DON'T LOOK NOW, 1973
DOOMED TO DIE, 1940
DOUBLE, THE, 1963
DOUBLE ALIBI, 1940
DOUBLE DANGER, 1938
DOUBLE EXPOSURE, 1954
DOUBLE EXPOSURE, 1982
DOUBLE EXPOSURES, 1937
DOUBLE McGUFFIN, THE, 1979
DRAGNET, 1974
DRAGON MURDER CASE, THE, 1934
DRAMA OF THE RICH, 1975
DRESSED TO KILL, 1946
DROWNING POOL, THE, 1975
ELLERY QUEEN AND THE MURDER RING, 1941
ELLERY QUEEN AND THE PERFECT CRIME, 1941
ELLERY QUEEN, MASTER DETECTIVE, 1940
ELLERY QUEEN'S PENTHOUSE MYSTERY, 1941
END OF THE GAME, 1976
ENDLESS NIGHT, 1971
ENEMY AGENTS MEET ELLERY QUEEN, 1942
ENOUGH ROPE, 1966
ENTER INSPECTOR DUVAL, 1961
EVELYN PRENTICE, 1934
EVIL EYE, 1964
EVIL UNDER THE SUN, 1982
EX-MRS. BRADFORD, THE, 1936
EXTORTION, 1938
EYES IN THE NIGHT, 1942

EYES OF ANNIE JONES, THE, 1963
FABIAN OF THE YARD, 1954
FACE IN THE FOG, A, 1936
FACE OF A STRANGER, 1964
FAIR WARNING, 1937
FALCON AND THE CO-EDS, THE, 1943
FALCON IN DANGER, THE, 1943
FALCON IN HOLLYWOOD, THE, 1944
FALCON IN MEXICO, THE, 1944
FALCON IN SAN FRANCISCO, THE, 1945
FALCON OUT WEST, THE, 1944
FALCON STRIKES BACK, THE, 1943
FALCON TAKES OVER, THE, 1942
FALCON'S ADVENTURE, THE, 1946
FALCON'S ALIBI, THE, 1946
FALCON'S BROTHER, THE, 1942
FALL GUY, 1947
FALLEN ANGEL, 1945
FALSE FACES, 1943
FAREWELL, MY LOVELY, 1975
FASHION MODEL, 1945
FAST AND FURIOUS, 1939
FAST AND LOOSE, 1939
FAST COMPANY, 1938
FAT MAN, THE, 1951
FATAL LADY, 1936
FATAL WITNESS, THE, 1945
FEAR CITY, 1984
FEAR NO MORE, 1961
FEATHERED SERPENT, THE, 1934
FEATHERED SERPENT, THE, 1948
FEMALE ON THE BEACH, 1955
FIFTEEN WIVES, 1934
FILE 113, 1932
FILES FROM SCOTLAND YARD, 1951
FIND THE WITNESS, 1937
FINGERPRINTS DON'T LIE, 1951
FIREBIRD, THE, 1934
FIVE ANGLES ON MURDER, 1950
FLANNELFOOT, 1953
FLETCH, 1984
FLORENTINE DAGGER, THE, 1935
FLY-AWAY BABY, 1937
FOG, 1934
FOG ISLAND, 1945
FOLLOW THAT WOMAN, 1945
FOOTSTEPS IN THE DARK, 1941
FOOTSTEPS IN THE NIGHT, 1957
FORCED LANDING, 1935
FORGOTTEN GIRLS, 1940
FORTY NAUGHTY GIRLS, 1937
FOUR DAYS WONDER, 1936
FOUR FLIES ON GREY VELVET, 1972
FOUR MEN AND A PRAYER, 1938
FOURTH SQUARE, THE, 1961
FRAGMENT OF FEAR, 1971
FRAMED, 1940
FRENCH KEY, THE, 1946
FRISCO SAL, 1945
FROG, THE, 1937
FROZEN GHOST, THE, 1945
FUGITIVE LADY, 1951
FUGITIVES FOR A NIGHT, 1938
FURIES, THE, 1930
GABLES MYSTERY, THE, 1931
GABLES MYSTERY, THE, 1938
GALLANT SONS, 1940
GAMBLING, 1934
GAMBLING DAUGHTERS, 1941
GAME OF TRUTH, THE, 1961
GAME THAT KILLS, THE, 1937
GARDEN MURDER CASE, THE, 1936
GAY FALCON, THE, 1941
GHOST GOES WILD, THE, 1947
GHOST THAT WALKS ALONE, THE, 1944
GHOST TOWN LAW, 1942
GHOST WALKS, THE, 1935
GIRL FROM RIO, THE, 1939
GIRL FROM SCOTLAND YARD, THE, 1937
GIRL HUNTERS, THE, 1963
GIRL IN BLACK STOCKINGS, 1957
GIRL IN THE CASE, 1944
GIRL IN THE KREMLIN, THE, 1957
GIRL IN THE NEWS, THE, 1941
GIRL MISSING, 1933
GIRL ON THE RUN, 1961

BOLD: Films on Videocassette

GIRL OVERBOARD, 1937
GIRL WHO DARED, THE, 1944
GLASS CAGE, THE, 1964
GLASS KEY, THE, 1935
GLASS KEY, THE, 1942
GLASS TOMB, THE, 1955
GLASS WEB, THE, 1953
GOLDEN LINK, THE, 1954
GORILLA, THE, 1931
GORILLA, THE, 1939
GORILLA AT LARGE, 1954
GORKY PARK, 1983
GRACIE ALLEN MURDER CASE, 1939
GRAND CENTRAL MURDER, 1942
GRANNY GET YOUR GUN, 1940
GREAT DEFENDER, THE, 1934
GREAT HOSPITAL MYSTERY, THE, 1937
GREAT HOTEL MURDER, 1935
GREAT MOUSE DETECTIVE, THE, 1986
GREAT SWINDLE, THE, 1941
GREEN EYES, 1934
GREEN FOR DANGER, 1946
GREEN SCARF, THE, 1954
GREENE MURDER CASE, THE, 1929
GRIEF STREET, 1931
GRISSLY'S MILLIONS, 1945
GUARD THAT GIRL, 1935
GUILTY?, 1956
GUILTY, THE, 1947
GUNN, 1967
HALF ANGEL, 1936
HALF PAST MIDNIGHT, 1948
HALF-WAY HOUSE, THE, 1945
HALF WAY TO SHANGHAI, 1942
HAMMER THE TOFF, 1952
HAMMETT, 1982
HAPPY MOTHER'S DAY ... LOVE, GEORGE, 1973
HARBOR LIGHTS, 1963
HARD BOILED MAHONEY, 1947
HARPER, 1966
HATE SHIP, THE, 1930
HAUNTED HOUSE, THE, 1940
HEADLINE, 1943
HEARTACHES, 1947
HELL IS A CITY, 1960
HELL'S HALF ACRE, 1954
HER ADVENTUROUS NIGHT, 1946
HER FORGOTTEN PAST, 1933
HERE COME THE MARINES, 1952
HIDDEN EYE, THE, 1945
HIDDEN HAND, THE, 1942
HIDDEN HOMICIDE, 1959
HIGH JINKS IN SOCIETY, 1949
HIGH-POWERED RIFLE, THE, 1960
HIGH TERRACE, 1957
HIGH TIDE, 1947
HIT AND RUN, 1982
HOLIDAY'S END, 1937
HOLLYWOOD STADIUM MYSTERY, 1938
HOLLYWOOD STORY, 1951
HOME SWEET HOMICIDE, 1946
HOME TO DANGER, 1951
HOMICIDE, 1949
HONEYMOON DEFERRED, 1940
HONEYMOON OF HORROR, 1964
HONG KONG AFFAIR, 1958
HORROR OF IT ALL, THE, 1964
HOT STEEL, 1940
HOUND OF THE BASKERVILLES, 1932
HOUND OF THE BASKERVILLES, THE, 1939
HOUND OF THE BASKERVILLES, THE, 1959
HOUND OF THE BASKERVILLES, THE, 1980
HOUND OF THE BASKERVILLES, THE, 1983
HOUR OF DECISION, 1957
HOUSE OF CARDS, 1969
HOUSE OF FEAR, THE, 1939
HOUSE OF FEAR, THE, 1945
HOUSE OF HORROR, 1929
HOUSE OF MYSTERY, 1941
HOUSE OF SECRETS, 1929
HOUSE OF SECRETS, THE, 1937
HOUSE OF THE ARROW, THE, 1930
HOUSE OF THE ARROW, THE, 1953
HOUSE OF THE SEVEN HAWKS, THE, 1959
HOUSE OF UNREST, THE, 1931
HOW DO YOU DO?, 1946

HUNTED, THE, 1948
HUSTLE, 1975
I AM A THIEF, 1935
I KILLED THAT MAN, 1942
I LOVE A MYSTERY, 1945
I LOVE TROUBLE, 1947
I RING DOORBELLS, 1946
I WAKE UP SCREAMING, 1942
I WOULDN'T BE IN YOUR SHOES, 1948
I'LL REMEMBER APRIL, 1945
IMPERSONATOR, THE, 1962
IN THE HEADLINES, 1929
IN THE NEXT ROOM, 1930
IN THE WAKE OF A STRANGER, 1960
INNER CIRCLE, THE, 1946
INNER SANCTUM, 1948
INQUEST, 1931
INQUEST, 1939
INQUISITOR, THE, 1982
INSIDE INFORMATION, 1939
INTERNATIONAL CRIME, 1938
INVISIBLE AVENGER, THE, 1958
INVISIBLE INFORMER, 1946
INVISIBLE KILLER, THE, 1940
INVISIBLE MENACE, THE, 1938
INVITATION TO MURDER, 1962
IRISH LUCK, 1939
ISLAND IN THE SKY, 1938
IT COULD HAPPEN TO YOU, 1939
IT COULDN'T HAVE HAPPENED—BUT IT DID, 1936
IT HAPPENED IN BROAD DAYLIGHT, 1960
IT HAPPENED IN SOHO, 1948
IT SHOULDN'T HAPPEN TO A DOG, 1946
JACK THE RIPPER, 1959
JACK'S BACK, 1988
JADE MASK, THE, 1945
JAGGED EDGE, THE, 1985
JAGUAR, 1956
JEALOUSY, 1945
JENNY LAMOUR, 1948
JIG SAW, 1965
JIGSAW, 1968
JIM HANVEY, DETECTIVE, 1937
JOE PALOOKA IN THE COUNTERPUNCH, 1949
JOHNNY ANGEL, 1945
JOHNNY NOBODY, 1965
JURY'S EVIDENCE, 1936
JUST BEFORE DAWN, 1946
JUST OFF BROADWAY, 1942
KENNEL MURDER CASE, THE, 1933
KENNER, 1969
KID GLOVE KILLER, 1942
KILL OR BE KILLED, 1950
KILL OR CURE, 1962
KILLER AT LARGE, 1936
KILLER AT LARGE, 1947
KING MURDER, THE, 1932
KING OF THE UNDERWORLD, 1952
KIRLIAN WITNESS, THE, 1978
KISS BEFORE DYING, A, 1956
KISS BEFORE THE MIRROR, THE, 1933
LADIES LOVE DANGER, 1935
LADY AT MIDNIGHT, 1948
LADY CHASER, 1946
LADY CONFESSES, THE, 1945
LADY IN CEMENT, 1968
LADY IN SCARLET, THE, 1935
LADY IN THE LAKE, 1947
LADY IN THE MORGUE, 1938
LADY OF BURLESQUE, 1943
LADY ON A TRAIN, 1945
LADY VANISHES, THE, 1938
LADY VANISHES, THE, 1980
LARCENY IN HER HEART, 1946
LAST MAN, 1932
LAST OF SHEILA, THE, 1973
LAST WARNING, THE, 1929
LAST WARNING, THE, 1938
LAUGHING AT DANGER, 1940
LAUGHING AT TROUBLE, 1937
LAURA, 1944
LEAGUE OF FRIGHTENED MEN, 1937
LEAVENWORTH CASE, THE, 1936
LIGHTNING STRIKES TWICE, 1935
LIGHTNING STRIKES TWICE, 1951
LIPSTICK, 1965

LIST OF ADRIAN MESSENGER, THE, 1963
LIVING DEAD, THE, 1936
LOCKER 69, 1962
LONE WOLF AND HIS LADY, THE, 1949
LONE WOLF IN LONDON, 1947
LONE WOLF IN MEXICO, THE, 1947
LONE WOLF IN PARIS, THE, 1938
LONE WOLF KEEPS A DATE, THE, 1940
LONE WOLF MEETS A LADY, THE, 1940
LONE WOLF RETURNS, THE, 1936
LONE WOLF SPY HUNT, THE, 1939
LONE WOLF STRIKES, THE, 1940
LONE WOLF TAKES A CHANCE, THE, 1941
LONE WOLF'S DAUGHTER, THE, 1929
LORD EDGEWARE DIES, 1934
LOVE IS A WOMAN, 1967
LOVE LETTERS OF A STAR, 1936
LYONS MAIL, THE, 1931
MACUMBA LOVE, 1960
MAD EXECUTIONERS, THE, 1965
MAD HOLIDAY, 1936
MADONNA'S SECRET, THE, 1946
MAID TO ORDER, 1932
MAIGRET LAYS A TRAP, 1958
MAKING THE HEADLINES, 1938
MALPAS MYSTERY, THE, 1967
MALTESE FALCON, THE, 1941
MALTESE FALCON, THE, 1931
MAN AT THE CARLTON TOWER, 1961
MAN HUNT, 1933
MAN IN THE NET, THE, 1959
MAN OF AFFAIRS, 1937
MAN ON A SWING, 1974
MAN ON THE EIFFEL TOWER, THE, 1949
MAN WHO KNEW TOO MUCH, THE, 1935
MAN WHO KNEW TOO MUCH, THE, 1956
MAN WHO WOULD NOT DIE, THE, 1975
MAN WHO WOULDN'T DIE, THE, 1942
MAN WITH BOGART'S FACE, THE, 1980
MAN WITH NINE LIVES, THE, 1940
MAN WITH TWO FACES, THE, 1934
MANCHU EAGLE MURDER CAPER MYSTERY, THE, 1975
MANDARIN MYSTERY, THE, 1937
MANTRAP, THE, 1943
MARLOWE, 1969
MARRIAGE OF CONVENIENCE, 1970
MASK OF THE DRAGON, 1951
MATINEE IDOL, 1933
MATTER OF WHO, A, 1962
MAXWELL ARCHER, DETECTIVE, 1942
MC GUFFIN, THE, 1985
MEET MR. CALLAGHAN, 1954
MEET MR. MALCOLM, 1954
MEET NERO WOLFE, 1936
MEET SEXTON BLAKE, 1944
MEET SIMON CHERRY, 1949
MENACE, THE, 1932
MEXICAN MANHUNT, 1953
MICHAEL SHAYNE, PRIVATE DETECTIVE, 1940
MIDNIGHT CROSSING, 1988
MIDNIGHT EPISODE, 1951
MIDNIGHT MAN, THE, 1974
MIDNIGHT MYSTERY, 1930
MIDNIGHT STORY, THE, 1957
MIDNIGHT WARNING, THE, 1932
MIKE'S MURDER, 1984
MILLERSON CASE, THE, 1947
MILLION DOLLAR MYSTERY, 1987
MINISTRY OF FEAR, 1945
MIRACLES FOR SALE, 1939
MIRAGE, 1965
MIRROR CRACK'D, THE, 1980
MISS PINKERTON, 1932
MISSING CORPSE, THE, 1945
MISSING GUEST, THE, 1938
MISSING JUROR, THE, 1944
MISSING LADY, THE, 1946
MISSING MILLION, THE, 1942
MISSING PEOPLE, THE, 1940
MISSING REMBRANDT, THE, 1932
MISSISSIPPI MERMAID, 1970
MR. AND MRS. NORTH, 1941
MR. ARKADIN, 1962
MR. MOTO IN DANGER ISLAND, 1939
MR. MOTO TAKES A CHANCE, 1938

MR. MOTO TAKES A VACATION, 1938
MR. MOTO'S GAMBLE, 1938
MR. MOTO'S LAST WARNING, 1939
MR. WONG, DETECTIVE, 1938
MR. WONG IN CHINATOWN, 1939
MIX ME A PERSON, 1962
MODEL MURDER CASE, THE, 1964
MONSTER OF LONDON CITY, THE, 1967
MONSTER WALKS, THE, 1932
MOON IN SCORPIO, 1987
MOON-SPINNERS, THE, 1964
MOONLIGHT MURDER, 1936
MOSS ROSE, 1947
MRS. O'MALLEY AND MR. MALONE, 1950
MRS. PYM OF SCOTLAND YARD, 1939
MUMMY'S BOYS, 1936
MURDER, 1930
MURDER AHOY, 1964
MURDER AMONG FRIENDS, 1941
MURDER AT COVENT GARDEN, 1932
MURDER AT DAWN, 1932
MURDER AT GLEN ATHOL, 1936
MURDER AT MIDNIGHT, 1931
MURDER AT MONTE CARLO, 1935
MURDER AT THE BASKERVILLES, 1941
MURDER AT THE GALLOP, 1963
MURDER AT THE VANITIES, 1934
MURDER AT 3 A.M., 1953
MURDER BY AN ARISTOCRAT, 1936
MURDER BY DEATH, 1976
MURDER BY DECREE, 1979
MURDER BY INVITATION, 1941
MURDER BY TELEVISION, 1935
MURDER GOES TO COLLEGE, 1937
MURDER IN EDEN, 1962
MURDER IN GREENWICH VILLAGE, 1937
MURDER IN THE BLUE ROOM, 1944
MURDER IN THE FAMILY, 1938
MURDER IN THE FAMILY, 1938
MURDER IN THE MUSIC HALL, 1946
MURDER IN THE PRIVATE CAR, 1934
MURDER IN TIMES SQUARE, 1943
MURDER IN TRINIDAD, 1934
MURDER IS MY BEAT, 1955
MURDER IS MY BUSINESS, 1946
MURDER IS NEWS, 1939
MURDER MOST FOUL, 1964
MURDER, MY SWEET, 1945
MURDER OF DR. HARRIGAN, THE, 1936
MURDER ON A BRIDLE PATH, 1936
MURDER ON A HONEYMOON, 1935
MURDER ON APPROVAL, 1956
MURDER ON DIAMOND ROW, 1937
MURDER ON THE BLACKBOARD, 1934
MURDER ON THE CAMPUS, 1934
MURDER ON THE CAMPUS, 1963
MURDER ON THE ORIENT EXPRESS, 1974
MURDER ON THE ROOF, 1930
MURDER ON THE SECOND FLOOR, 1932
MURDER ON THE SET, 1936
MURDER ON THE WATERFRONT, 1943
MURDER ON THE YUKON, 1940
MURDER OVER NEW YORK, 1940
MURDER REPORTED, 1958
MURDER WILL OUT, 1930
MURDER WILL OUT, 1939
MURDER WILL OUT, 1953
MURDERER LIVES AT NUMBER 21, THE, 1947
MY COUSIN RACHEL, 1952
MY FAVORITE BRUNETTE, 1947
MY GUN IS QUICK, 1957
MY NAME IS JULIA ROSS, 1945
MYSTERIOUS CROSSING, 1937
MYSTERIOUS DR. FU MANCHU, THE, 1929
MYSTERIOUS INTRUDER, 1946
MYSTERIOUS MISS X, THE, 1939
MYSTERIOUS MR. MOTO, 1938
MYSTERIOUS MR. REEDER, THE, 1940
MYSTERIOUS MR. WONG, 1935
MYSTERY AT THE BURLESQUE, 1950
MYSTERY AT THE VILLA ROSE, 1930
MYSTERY BROADCAST, 1943
MYSTERY HOUSE, 1938
MYSTERY LINER, 1934
MYSTERY MAN, THE, 1935
MYSTERY OF MARIE ROGET, THE, 1942

MYSTERY OF MR. WONG, THE, 1939
MYSTERY OF ROOM 13, 1941
MYSTERY OF THE GOLDEN EYE, THE, 1948
MYSTERY OF THE 13TH GUEST, THE, 1943
MYSTERY OF THE WHITE ROOM, 1939
NAKED ALIBI, 1954
NAKED FACE, THE, 1984
NAKED GUN, THE, 1956
NAME OF THE ROSE, THE, 1986
NAME THE WOMAN, 1934
NANCY DREW AND THE HIDDEN STAIRCASE, 1939
NANCY DREW—DETECTIVE, 1938
NANCY DREW—REPORTER, 1939
NANCY DREW, TROUBLE SHOOTER, 1939
NARROWING CIRCLE, THE, 1956
'NEATH BROOKLYN BRIDGE, 1942
NEVER BACK LOSERS, 1967
NEXT!, 1971
NICK CARTER, MASTER DETECTIVE, 1939
NIGHT AFFAIR, 1961
NIGHT AFTER NIGHT AFTER NIGHT, 1970
NIGHT BIRDS, 1931
NIGHT CLUB LADY, 1932
NIGHT CLUB SCANDAL, 1937
NIGHT FOR CRIME, A, 1942
NIGHT HAS A THOUSAND EYES, 1948
NIGHT IN MONTMARTE, A, 1931
NIGHT MONSTER, 1942
NIGHT MOVES, 1975
NIGHT OF ADVENTURE, A, 1944
NIGHT OF JANUARY 16TH, 1941
NIGHT OF MYSTERY, 1937
NIGHT OF TERROR, 1933
NIGHT OF THE PARTY, THE, 1934
NIGHT OF THE STRANGLER, 1975
NIGHT STALKER, THE, 1987
NIGHT TO REMEMBER, A, 1942
NIGHT WATCH, 1973
NIGHT WITHOUT SLEEP, 1952
NIGHT WON'T TALK, THE, 1952
NINE FORTY-FIVE, 1934
NINTH GUEST, THE, 1934
NO ESCAPE, 1936
NO HANDS ON THE CLOCK, 1941
NO MAN'S WOMAN, 1955
NO PLACE FOR A LADY, 1943
NO WAY TO TREAT A LADY, 1968
NOCTURNE, 1946
NOTORIOUS LANDLADY, THE, 1962
NOTORIOUS LONE WOLF, THE, 1946
NUDE IN A WHITE CAR, 1960
NURSEMAID WHO DISAPPEARED, THE, 1939
NURSE'S SECRET, THE, 1941
OBSESSED, 1951
OCTOBER MAN, THE, 1948
OFF LIMITS, 1988
OLD MAN, THE, 1932
ONE BODY TOO MANY, 1944
ONE FRIGHTENED NIGHT, 1935
ONE IS GUILTY, 1934
ONE JUMP AHEAD, 1955
ONE MYSTERIOUS NIGHT, 1944
ONE NEW YORK NIGHT, 1935
ONE NIGHT IN PARIS, 1940
OPENED BY MISTAKE, 1940
OPERATION DIPLOMAT, 1953
ORDEAL BY INNOCENCE, 1984
ORPHANS OF THE STREET, 1939
OUT OF THE PAST, 1947
OVER MY DEAD BODY, 1942
PALACE OF NUDES, 1961
PANTHER'S CLAW, THE, 1942
PAPER ORCHID, 1949
PARIS BELONGS TO US, 1962
PARIS EXPRESS, THE, 1953
PARIS HOLIDAY, 1958
PARIS PICK-UP, 1963
PARTNER, THE, 1966
PARTNERS IN CRIME, 1937
PASSAGE FROM HONG KONG, 1941
PASSING SHADOWS, 1934
PASSION OF SLOW FIRE, THE, 1962
PASSKEY TO DANGER, 1946
PASSPORT TO TREASON, 1956
PATIENT IN ROOM 18, THE, 1938
PATIENT VANISHES, THE, 1947

PAUL TEMPLE RETURNS, 1952
PAYOFF, THE, 1943
PEARL OF DEATH, THE, 1944
PEEPER, 1975
PENGUIN POOL MURDER, THE, 1932
PERFECT ALIBI, THE, 1931
PERSONAL COLUMN, 1939
PHANTOM BROADCAST, THE, 1933
PHANTOM EXPRESS, THE, 1932
PHANTOM FIEND, THE, 1935
PHANTOM KILLER, 1942
PHANTOM LADY, 1944
PHANTOM LIGHT, THE, 1935
PHANTOM OF CHINATOWN, 1940
PHANTOM OF CRESTWOOD, THE, 1932
PHANTOM OF 42ND STREET, THE, 1945
PHANTOM OF PARIS, THE, 1931
PHANTOM OF SOHO, THE, 1967
PHANTOM RAIDERS, 1940
PHANTOM SHIP, 1937
PHANTOM STRIKES, THE, 1939
PHANTOM THIEF, THE, 1946
PHILO VANCE RETURNS, 1947
PHILO VANCE'S GAMBLE, 1947
PHILO VANCE'S SECRET MISSION, 1947
PHOBIA, 1980
PIER 5, HAVANA, 1959
PIER 13, 1940
PIER 23, 1951
PILLOW OF DEATH, 1945
P.J., 1968
PLOT THICKENS, THE, 1936
POLICE NURSE, 1963
POLICE PYTHON 357, 1976
POPPY IS ALSO A FLOWER, THE, 1966
PORT AFRIQUE, 1956
PORTRAIT IN BLACK, 1960
POWER OF THE WHISTLER, THE, 1945
PRESIDENT'S MYSTERY, THE, 1936
PREVIEW MURDER MYSTERY, 1936
PRICE OF FEAR, THE, 1956
PRINCESS COMES ACROSS, THE, 1936
PRISON BREAK, 1938
PRIVATE DETECTIVE, 1939
PRIVATE DETECTIVE 62, 1933
PRIVATE EYES, 1953
PRIVATE EYES, THE, 1980
PRIVATE LIFE OF SHERLOCK HOLMES, THE, 1970
PRIVATE SCANDAL, 1934
PROFILE, 1954
PSYCHIC, THE, 1979
PSYCHO-CIRCUS, 1967
PSYCHOPATH, THE, 1966
PUBLIC DEFENDER, THE, 1931
PURSUED, 1947
PURSUERS, THE, 1961
PURSUIT TO ALGIERS, 1945
PUT ON THE SPOT, 1936
PYX, THE, 1973
QUEEN OF BURLESQUE, 1946
QUIET PLACE IN THE COUNTRY, A, 1970
RACING LUCK, 1935
RADIO ON, 1980
RAVEN, THE, 1948
RED DRAGON, THE, 1946
REMAINS TO BE SEEN, 1953
REMEMBER LAST NIGHT, 1935
RENDEZVOUS AT MIDNIGHT, 1935
RETURN, 1986
RETURN OF BULLDOG DRUMMOND, THE, 1934
RETURN OF MR. MOTO, THE, 1965
RETURN OF SHERLOCK HOLMES, THE, 1929
RETURN OF THE FROG, THE, 1938
RETURN OF THE PINK PANTHER, THE, 1975
RETURN OF THE TERROR, 1934
RETURN OF THE WHISTLER, THE, 1948
REVENGE OF THE PINK PANTHER, 1978
RING OF FEAR, 1954
RINGER, THE, 1932
RINGER, THE, 1953
RIPPED-OFF, 1971
RIVER HOUSE MYSTERY, THE, 1935
RIVERSIDE MURDER, THE, 1935
ROAD TO ALCATRAZ, 1945
ROADHOUSE MURDER, THE, 1932
ROAR OF THE PRESS, 1941

BOLD: Films on Videocassette

ROARING CITY, 1951
ROCKY MOUNTAIN MYSTERY, 1935
ROGUES GALLERY, 1945
ROGUES' TAVERN, THE, 1936
ROGUE'S YARN, 1956
ROMANCE IN RHYTHM, 1934
ROMANCE ON THE RUN, 1938
ROME EXPRESS, 1933
ROOF, THE, 1933
ROSARY MURDERS, THE, 1987
ROSEMARY, 1960
ROYAL EAGLE, 1936
RUNAROUND, THE, 1946
RX MURDER, 1958
SAINT IN LONDON, THE, 1939
SAINT IN NEW YORK, THE, 1938
SAINT IN PALM SPRINGS, THE, 1941
SAINT MEETS THE TIGER, THE, 1943
SAINT STRIKES BACK, THE, 1939
SAINT TAKES OVER, THE, 1940
SAINT'S DOUBLE TROUBLE, THE, 1940
SAINT'S GIRL FRIDAY, THE, 1954
SAINT'S VACATION, THE, 1941
SALOON BAR, 1940
SALUTE THE TOFF, 1952
SANDERS, 1963
SAPPHIRE, 1959
SARAGOSSA MANUSCRIPT, THE, 1972
SATAN MET A LADY, 1936
SCANDALOUS, 1984
SCAPEGOAT, THE, 1959
SCARAB MURDER CASE, THE, 1936
SCARECROW, THE, 1982
SCARED STIFF, 1945
SCARED TO DEATH, 1947
SCARLET CLAW, THE, 1944
SCARLET CLUE, THE, 1945
SCARLET WEB, THE, 1954
SCARLET WEEKEND, A, 1932
SCATTERGOOD SURVIVES A MURDER, 1942
SCENT OF MYSTERY, 1960
SCOBIE MALONE, 1975
SCOTLAND YARD INSPECTOR, 1952
SCREAM IN THE DARK, A, 1943
SCREAM OF FEAR, 1961
SCREAMING MIMI, 1958
SEARCH FOR DANGER, 1949
SECOND FLOOR MYSTERY, THE, 1930
SECONDS, 1966
SECRET FURY, THE, 1950
SECRET OF THE BLUE ROOM, 1933
SECRET OF THE CHATEAU, 1935
SECRET, THE, 1979
SECRETS OF CHINATOWN, 1935
SECRETS OF THE LONE WOLF, 1941
SECRETS OF WU SIN, 1932
SEDUCERS, THE, 1962
SEND FOR PAUL TEMPLE, 1946
SEVEN DOORS TO DEATH, 1944
SEVEN FOOTPRINTS TO SATAN, 1929
SEVEN KEYS TO BALDPATE, 1930
SEVEN KEYS TO BALDPATE, 1935
SEVEN KEYS TO BALDPATE, 1947
SEVEN-PER-CENT SOLUTION, THE, 1977
70,000 WITNESSES, 1932
SEXTON BLAKE AND THE BEARDED DOCTOR, 1935
SEXTON BLAKE AND THE HOODED TERROR, 1938
SEXTON BLAKE AND THE MADEMOISELLE, 1935
SH! THE OCTOPUS, 1937
SHADOW OF FEAR, 1956
SHADOW OF THE PAST, 1950
SHADOW OF THE THIN MAN, 1941
SHADOW ON THE WALL, 1950
SHADOW PLAY, 1986
SHADOW RETURNS, THE, 1946
SHADOW STRIKES, THE, 1937
SHADOW, THE, 1937
SHADOWMAN, 1974
SHADOWS IN THE NIGHT, 1944
SHADOWS ON THE STAIRS, 1941
SHADOWS OVER CHINATOWN, 1946
SHAKE HANDS WITH MURDER, 1944
SHANGHAI CHEST, THE, 1948
SHANGHAI COBRA, THE, 1945
SHE ASKED FOR IT, 1937
SHE-WOLF OF LONDON, 1946

SHERLOCK HOLMES AND THE DEADLY
  NECKLACE, 1962
**SHERLOCK HOLMES AND THE SECRET WEAPON,
1942**
SHERLOCK HOLMES AND THE SPIDER WOMAN,
  1944
**SHERLOCK HOLMES AND THE VOICE OF TERROR,
1942**
SHERLOCK HOLMES FACES DEATH, 1943
SHERLOCK HOLMES' FATAL HOUR, 1931
SHERLOCK HOLMES IN WASHINGTON, 1943
SHOT IN THE DARK, A, 1933
SHOT IN THE DARK, A, 1935
SHOT IN THE DARK, A, 1964
SHOT IN THE DARK, THE, 1941
SIGN OF FOUR, THE, 1932
SIGN OF FOUR, THE, 1983
SILENT WITNESS, THE, 1932
SINISTER HANDS, 1932
SINISTER MAN, THE, 1965
SINNER TAKE ALL, 1936
SKY DRAGON, 1949
SKY MURDER, 1940
SLAMDANCE, 1987
SLEEP, MY LOVE, 1948
SLEEPING CAR MURDER, THE, 1966
SLEEPING CITY, THE, 1950
SLEUTH, 1972
SLIGHTLY HONORABLE, 1940
SMILING GHOST, THE, 1941
SO LONG AT THE FAIR, 1951
SOLDIERS AND WOMEN, 1930
SOLDIER'S STORY, A, 1984
SOLITARY CHILD, THE, 1958
SOMEBODY KILLED HER HUSBAND, 1978
SOMETHING'S ROTTEN, 1979
SON OF INGAGI, 1940
SONG OF THE THIN MAN, 1947
SOYLENT GREEN, 1973
SPANIARD'S CURSE, THE, 1958
SPANISH CAPE MYSTERY, 1935
SPECIAL AGENT K-7, 1937
SPECKLED BAND, THE, 1931
SPHINX, THE, 1933
SPIDER, THE, 1931
SPIDER, THE, 1945
SPIDER'S WEB, THE, 1960
SPIRITUALIST, THE, 1948
STAR OF MIDNIGHT, 1935
STICK 'EM UP, 1950
STOP ME BEFORE I KILL!, 1961
STOPOVER FOREVER, 1964
STORY WITHOUT WORDS, 1981
STRANGE ADVENTURE, 1932
STRANGE AFFAIR, 1944
STRANGE BOARDERS, 1938
STRANGE CARGO, 1929
STRANGE CASE OF DR. MANNING, THE, 1958
STRANGE CASE OF DR. RX, THE, 1942
STRANGE CONFESSION, 1945
STRANGE IMPERSONATION, 1946
STRANGE MR. GREGORY, THE, 1945
STRANGE PEOPLE, 1933
STRANGE SHADOWS IN AN EMPTY ROOM, 1977
STRANGER IN TOWN, 1957
STRANGERS OF THE EVENING, 1932
STRANGLER, THE, 1941
STRANGLERS OF BOMBAY, THE, 1960
STREET OF CHANCE, 1942
STUDIO MURDER MYSTERY, THE, 1929
STUDY IN SCARLET, A, 1933
STUDY IN TERROR, A, 1966
SUBWAY EXPRESS, 1931
SUED FOR LIBEL, 1940
SUMMERFIELD, 1977
SUNSET, 1988
SUPER SLEUTH, 1937
SUPERNATURAL, 1933
SUSPENSE, 1946
SWEATER GIRL, 1942
T.A.G.: THE ASSASSINATION GAME, 1982
TAKE MY LIFE, 1948
TAKE ONE FALSE STEP, 1949
TAKE THE STAND, 1934
**TALL BLOND MAN WITH ONE BLACK SHOE, THE,
1973**
TANGLED DESTINIES, 1932

TARGET: HARRY, 1980
TASTE FOR WOMEN, A, 1966
TEARS FOR SIMON, 1957
TECKMAN MYSTERY, THE, 1955
TEMPLE TOWER, 1930
TEMPORARY WIDOW, THE, 1930
TEN DAYS' WONDER, 1972
TEN LITTLE INDIANS, 1965
TEN LITTLE INDIANS, 1975
TERROR, THE, 1928
TERROR, THE, 1941
TERROR ABOARD, 1933
TERROR BY NIGHT, 1946
THANK YOU, JEEVES, 1936
THANK YOU, MR. MOTO, 1937
THEIR BIG MOMENT, 1934
THERE GOES KELLY, 1945
THERE'S THAT WOMAN AGAIN, 1938
THERE'S ALWAYS A WOMAN, 1938
THEY CALL ME MISTER TIBBS, 1970
THEY ONLY KILL THEIR MASTERS, 1972
THIN MAN, THE, 1934
THIN MAN GOES HOME, THE, 1944
THINK FAST, MR. MOTO, 1937
THIRD KEY, THE, 1957
THIRD SECRET, THE, 1964
THIRTEENTH CANDLE, THE, 1933
THIRTEENTH CHAIR, THE, 1930
THIRTEENTH CHAIR, THE, 1937
THIRTEENTH GUEST, THE, 1932
13TH HOUR, THE, 1947
THIRTEENTH LETTER, THE, 1951
THIRTEENTH MAN, THE, 1937
THIS MAN IN PARIS, 1939
THIS MAN IS NEWS, 1939
THREE BLONDES IN HIS LIFE, 1961
THREE CASES OF MURDER, 1955
THREE'S A CROWD, 1945
THUNDER IN THE NIGHT, 1935
TICKET TO CRIME, 1934
TIME OUT FOR MURDER, 1938
TIME TO KILL, 1942
TOM SAWYER, DETECTIVE, 1939
TOMORROW AT SEVEN, 1933
TONY ROME, 1967
TOPPER RETURNS, 1941
TOWN ON TRIAL, 1957
TRAGEDY AT MIDNIGHT, A, 1942
TRAP, THE, 1947
TRAPPED BY BOSTON BLACKIE, 1948
TRENCHCOAT, 1983
TRENT'S LAST CASE, 1953
TRESPASSER, THE, 1947
TRIAL WITHOUT JURY, 1950
TRICK FOR TRICK, 1933
TRIUMPH OF SHERLOCK HOLMES, THE, 1935
TROUBLE FOR TWO, 1936
TWENTY PLUS TWO, 1961
TWENTY QUESTIONS MURDER MYSTERY, THE,
  1950
20,000 POUNDS KISS, THE, 1964
TWO IN THE DARK, 1936
TWO O'CLOCK COURAGE, 1945
TWO ON A GUILLOTINE, 1965
UNCLE HARRY, 1945
UNDER COVER OF NIGHT, 1937
UNDER SUSPICION, 1937
UNDERCOVER WOMAN, THE, 1946
UNEASY TERMS, 1948
UNEXPECTED GUEST, 1946
UNHOLY FOUR, THE, 1954
UNHOLY NIGHT, THE, 1929
UNKNOWN GUEST, THE, 1943
UNKNOWN, THE, 1946
UNMAN, WITTERING AND ZIGO, 1971
UNMASKED, 1929
UNSEEN, THE, 1945
UNSUITABLE JOB FOR A WOMAN, AN, 1982
UNWRITTEN LAW, THE, 1932
UP IN THE AIR, 1940
VERDICT, THE, 1946
WALK A TIGHTROPE, 1964
WALLS CAME TUMBLING DOWN, THE, 1946
WARNING SHOT, 1967
WARREN CASE, THE, 1934
WASHINGTON MELODRAMA, 1941

WE HAVE OUR MOMENTS, 1937
WEB OF EVIDENCE, 1959
WEB OF FEAR, 1966
WEB OF PASSION, 1961
WEB OF SUSPICION, 1959
WEB OF VIOLENCE, 1966
WEEKEND MURDERS, THE, 1972
WEIRD WOMAN, 1944
WESTBOUND LIMITED, 1937
WESTERN LIMITED, 1932
WESTLAND CASE, THE, 1937
WHAT DO WE DO NOW?, 1945
WHAT HAPPENED THEN?, 1934
WHAT HAPPENED TO HARKNESS, 1934
WHAT WOMEN DREAM, 1933
WHEN EIGHT BELLS TOLL, 1971
WHEN STRANGERS MARRY, 1944
WHEN WERE YOU BORN?, 1938
WHILE NEW YORK SLEEPS, 1938
WHILE THE PATIENT SLEPT, 1935
WHIPPED, THE, 1950
WHIP'S WOMEN, 1968
WHISPERING GHOSTS, 1942
WHISPERING SMITH VERSUS SCOTLAND YARD,
   1952
WHISTLING IN BROOKLYN, 1943
WHISTLING IN DIXIE, 1942
WHISTLING IN THE DARK, 1941
WHITE COCKATOO, 1935
WHITE FACE, 1933
WHITE FIRE, 1953
WHITE LILAC, 1935
WHITE MISCHIEF, 1988
WHO FRAMED ROGER RABBIT, 1988
WHO IS GUILTY?, 1940
WHO IS HOPE SCHUYLER?, 1942
**WHO IS KILLING THE GREAT CHEFS OF EUROPE?,
   1978**
WHO KILLED AUNT MAGGIE?, 1940
WHO KILLED GAIL PRESTON?, 1938
WHO KILLED JOHN SAVAGE?, 1937
WHO KILLED MARY WHAT'SER NAME?, 1971
WICKED, WICKED, 1973
WICKER MAN, THE, 1974
WICKHAM MYSTERY, THE, 1931
WINK OF AN EYE, 1958
WINTER KILLS, 1979
WITHOUT APPARENT MOTIVE, 1972
WITNESS CHAIR, THE, 1936
WITNESS FOR THE PROSECUTION, 1957
WITNESS VANISHES, THE, 1939
WOMAN FROM TANGIER, THE, 1948
WOMAN HUNT, 1962
WOMAN IN GREEN, THE, 1945
WOMAN IN ROOM 13, THE, 1932
WOMAN IN WHITE, THE, 1948
YELLOWSTONE, 1936
YOUNG SHERLOCK HOLMES, 1985

Prison
BAD BOYS, 1983
BEHIND PRISON GATES, 1939
BETRAYED WOMEN, 1955
BEYOND THE WALLS, 1985
BIG BIRD CAGE, THE, 1972
BIG DOLL HOUSE, THE, 1971
BIG HOUSE, THE, 1930
BIRDMAN OF ALCATRAZ, 1962
BROTHERS, 1977
BRUBAKER, 1980
BRUTE FORCE, 1947
CAGED, 1950
CAGED FURY, 1984
CAGED WOMEN, 1984
CANON CITY, 1948
CASTLE ON THE HUDSON, 1940
CHAIN GANG, 1950
CHAIN GANG, 1985
CONCRETE JUNGLE, THE, 1962
CONDEMNED, 1929
CONVICTED WOMAN, 1940
CONVICTS FOUR, 1962
COOL HAND LUKE, 1967
CRIMINAL CODE, 1931
DAY OF RECKONING, 1933
DEATHWATCH, 1966

DEFIANT ONES, THE, 1958
DOIN' TIME, 1985
EACH DAWN I DIE, 1939
ESCAPE FROM ALCATRAZ, 1979
ESCAPE FROM DEVIL'S ISLAND, 1935
FEDERAL MAN-HUNT, 1939
FORTUNE AND MEN'S EYES, 1971
FUGITIVE FROM A PRISON CAMP, 1940
GIRL ON A CHAIN GANG, 1966
GIRLS IN PRISON, 1956
GIRLS OF THE BIG HOUSE, 1945
GRAND ILLUSION, 1938
GREAT ESCAPE, THE, 1963
GREEN-EYED BLONDE, THE, 1957
HELL'S HIGHWAY, 1932
HILL, THE, 1965
HOLD BACK TOMORROW, 1955
HOLD 'EM JAIL, 1932
HOUSE OF WOMEN, 1962
I AM A FUGITIVE FROM A CHAIN GANG, 1932
I ESCAPED FROM DEVIL'S ISLAND, 1973
INSIDE THE WALLS OF FOLSOM PRISON, 1951
ISLE OF MISSING MEN, 1942
JAIL BUSTERS, 1955
JAIL HOUSE BLUES, 1942
JAILBIRD ROCK, 1988
KING OF THE DAMNED, 1936
KISS OF THE SPIDER WOMAN, 1985
L'ADDITION, 1985
LADIES OF THE BIG HOUSE, 1932
LADIES THEY TALK ABOUT, 1933
LAST MILE, THE, 1932
LAST MILE, THE, 1959
LINE, THE, 1982
LOVE CHILD, 1982
MAYOR OF HELL, THE, 1933
MEAN DOG BLUES, 1978
MEMOIRS OF PRISON, 1984
MEN WITHOUT SOULS, 1940
MERRY CHRISTMAS, MR. LAWRENCE, 1983
MIDNIGHT EXPRESS, 1978
MILLIONAIRES IN PRISON, 1940
MURDER IN THE BIG HOUSE, 1942
MUTINY IN THE BIG HOUSE, 1939
MY SIX CONVICTS, 1952
NAKED CAGE, THE, 1986
NIGHT WATCH, THE, 1964
NOW BARABBAS WAS A ROBBER, 1949
NUMBERED MEN, 1930
ON THE YARD, 1978
OVER THE WALL, 1938
PAPILLON, 1973
PEACH THIEF, THE, 1969
PENITENTIARY, 1938
PENITENTIARY, 1979
PENITENTIARY II, 1982
PENITENTIARY III, 1987
POT CARRIERS, THE, 1962
PRISON, 1988
PRISON BREAK, 1938
PRISON BREAKER, 1936
PRISON FARM, 1938
PRISON GIRL, 1942
PRISON NURSE, 1938
PRISON SHADOWS, 1936
PRISON WARDEN, 1949
PRISON WITHOUT BARS, 1939
PRISONER OF SHARK ISLAND, THE, 1936
QUARE FELLOW, THE, 1962
REFORM SCHOOL GIRLS, 1986
REFORMATORY, 1938
RENEGADE GIRLS, 1974
REVOLT IN THE BIG HOUSE, 1958
RIOT, 1969
RIOT IN CELL BLOCK 11, 1954
RIOT IN JUVENILE PRISON, 1959
ROAD GANG, 1936
ROAD TO THE BIG HOUSE, 1947
RUNAWAY TRAIN, 1985
SAN QUENTIN, 1937
SAN QUENTIN, 1946
SCHOOL FOR GIRLS, 1935
SCHOOL FOR UNCLAIMED GIRLS, 1973
SCUM, 1979
SECRET WAR OF HARRY FRIGG, THE, 1968
SHADOW BETWEEN, THE, 1932

SHOESHINE, 1947
SHORT EYES, 1977
SING SING NIGHTS, 1935
6000 ENEMIES, 1939
SLAMS, THE, 1973
SO EVIL SO YOUNG, 1961
SO YOUNG, SO BAD, 1950
SOUTHSIDE 1-1000, 1950
STAR SLAMMER: THE ESCAPE, 1988
STATE PENITENTIARY, 1950
STEEL CAGE, THE, 1954
STEFANIA, 1968
STIR, 1980
STIR CRAZY, 1980
TAKE THE MONEY AND RUN, 1969
TERMINAL ISLAND, 1973
THOSE HIGH GREY WALLS, 1939
TRAIN TO ALCATRAZ, 1948
20,000 YEARS IN SING SING, 1933
TWO EYES, TWELVE HANDS, 1958
UNCHAINED, 1955
UNDER THE GUN, 1951
UNTAMED YOUTH, 1957
UP THE RIVER, 1930
UP THE RIVER, 1938
VENDETTA, 1986
WALL, THE, 1985
WE WHO ARE ABOUT TO DIE, 1937
WEAK AND THE WICKED, THE, 1954
WEARY RIVER, 1929
WITHIN THESE WALLS, 1945
WOMEN IN CELL BLOCK 7, 1977
WOMEN IN PRISON, 1938
WOMEN IN PRISON, 1957
WOMEN'S PRISON, 1955
WOMEN'S PRISON MASSACRE, 1986
WOODEN HORSE, THE, 1951

Religious
ADAM AND EVE, 1958
AND THERE CAME A MAN, 1968
AVE MARIA, 1984
BARABBAS, 1962
BEN HUR, 1959
BIBLE...IN THE BEGINNING, THE, 1966
BIG FISHERMAN, THE, 1959
CAMMINA CAMMINA, 1983
CARDINAL, THE, 1963
CARDINAL, THE, 1936
CARDINAL RICHELIEU, 1935
CITIZEN SAINT, 1947
CROWNING GIFT, THE, 1967
CRUSADES, THE, 1935
DAVID AND BATHSHEBA, 1951
DAVID AND GOLIATH, 1961
DAY OF TRIUMPH, 1954
DEATH OF AN ANGEL, 1985
DEMETRIUS AND THE GLADIATORS, 1954
DESERT DESPERADOES, 1959
DIARY OF A COUNTRY PRIEST, 1954
DIVINE MR. J., THE, 1974
FOR PETE'S SAKE!, 1966
FRANCIS OF ASSISI, 1961
GIORDANO BRUNO, 1973
GIVEN WORD, THE, 1964
GLORY OF FAITH, THE, 1938
GODLESS GIRL, THE, 1929
GODSPELL, 1973
GOING MY WAY, 1944
GOLGOTHA, 1937
GOSPEL ACCORDING TO ST. MATTHEW, THE, 1966
GOSPEL ROAD, THE, 1973
GREAT COMMANDMENT, THE, 1941
GREATEST STORY EVER TOLD, THE, 1965
GREEN PASTURES, 1936
GREEN TREE, THE, 1965
HAIL, MARY, 1985
HEAD OF A TYRANT, 1960
IN SEARCH OF HISTORIC JESUS, 1980
JESUS, 1979
JESUS CHRIST, SUPERSTAR, 1973
JOAN OF ARC, 1948
JOAN OF THE ANGELS, 1962
JOHN WESLEY, 1954
KEYS OF THE KINGDOM, THE, 1944
KING DAVID, 1985

BOLD: Films on Videocassette

KING OF KINGS, 1961
LADY OF MONZA, THE, 1970
LAST TEMPTATION OF CHRIST, THE, 1988
LATE LIZ, THE, 1971
LAWTON STORY, THE, 1949
LEAP OF FAITH, 1931
LEATHER SAINT, THE, 1956
LOVE UNDER THE CRUCIFIX, 1965
MAN CALLED PETER, THE, 1955
MARTIN LUTHER, 1953
MASS APPEAL, 1984
MESSENGER OF PEACE, 1950
MIGHTY CRUSADERS, THE, 1961
MILKY WAY, THE, 1969
MIRACLE, THE, 1959
MIRACLE OF OUR LADY OF FATIMA, THE, 1952
MIRACLE OF THE BELLS, THE, 1948
MIRACLE OF THE HILLS, THE, 1959
MIRACLE WOMAN, THE, 1931
MR. BROWN COMES DOWN THE HILL, 1966
MOHAMMAD, MESSENGER OF GOD, 1976
MONSIEUR VINCENT, 1949
MONSIGNOR, 1982
MONTY PYTHON'S LIFE OF BRIAN, 1979
MOSES, 1976
MOSES AND AARON, 1975
MURDER IN THE CATHEDRAL, 1952
NAZARIN, 1968
NOAH'S ARK, 1928
NUN, THE, 1971
NUN AT THE CROSSROADS, A, 1970
NUN'S STORY, THE, 1959
OH GOD! YOU DEVIL, 1984
PONTIUS PILATE, 1967
POPE JOAN, 1972
PRINCE OF PEACE, THE, 1951
PRIVATE POTTER, 1963
PRODIGAL, THE, 1955
QUEEN OF BABYLON, THE, 1956
REDEEMER, THE, 1965
RESTLESS ONES, THE, 1965
REVOLT OF THE SLAVES, THE, 1961
RITA, 1963
ROBE, THE, 1953
SAINT JOAN, 1957
SALOME, 1953
SALOME, 1986
SALOME'S LAST DANCE, 1988
SAMSON, 1961
SAMSON AND DELILAH, 1949
SAUL AND DAVID, 1968
SHIELD OF FAITH, THE, 1956
SIDDHARTHA, 1972
SILVER CHALICE, THE, 1954
SINGING NUN, THE, 1966
SINS OF JEZEBEL, 1953
SLAVES OF BABYLON, 1953
SODOM AND GOMORRAH, 1962
SOLOMON AND SHEBA, 1959
SONG OF BERNADETTE, THE, 1943
SOULS IN CONFLICT, 1955
STORY OF DAVID, A, 1960
STORY OF JOSEPH AND HIS BRETHREN THE, 1962
STORY OF RUTH, THE, 1960
SUPREME SECRET, THE, 1958
TARNISHED ANGEL, 1938
TEN COMMANDMENTS, THE, 1956
TWO A PENNY, 1968
UNDER SATAN'S SUN, 1988
WESTMINSTER PASSION PLAY—BEHOLD THE
    MAN, THE, 1951

Romance
AARON LOVES ANGELA, 1975
ABOUT LAST NIGHT, 1986
ABOUT MRS. LESLIE, 1954
ACCENT ON LOVE, 1941
ACCENT ON YOUTH, 1935
ADAM AND EVELYNE, 1950
ADVENTURE IN BLACKMAIL, 1943
ADVENTURES OF CASANOVA, 1948
ADVENTURES OF DON JUAN, 1949
AFFAIR IN MONTE CARLO, 1953
AFFAIR TO REMEMBER, AN, 1957
AFFAIR WITH A STRANGER, 1953
AFFAIRS OF JULIE, THE, 1958

AFFAIRS OF MAUPASSANT, 1938
AFRICAN QUEEN, THE, 1951
AFRICAN, THE, 1983
AFTER OFFICE HOURS, 1932
AFTER OFFICE HOURS, 1935
AFTER TOMORROW, 1932
AFTER TONIGHT, 1933
AGATHA, 1979
AGE OF CONSENT, 1932
AGE OF ILLUSIONS, 1967
ALL THE OTHER GIRLS DO!, 1967
ALL THIS AND HEAVEN TOO, 1940
ALMOST MARRIED, 1942
ALMOST PERFECT AFFAIR, AN, 1979
ALMOST SUMMER, 1978
ALOMA OF THE SOUTH SEAS, 1941
AMAZING MR. WILLIAMS, 1939
ANGEL RIVER, 1986
ANGEL WORE RED, THE, 1960
ANNA OF BROOKLYN, 1958
ANOTHER DAWN, 1937
ANOTHER LANGUAGE, 1933
ANOTHER MAN, ANOTHER CHANCE, 1977
ANOTHER SKY, 1960
ANTHONY ADVERSE, 1936
ANYBODY'S WOMAN, 1930
APOLLO GOES ON HOLIDAY, 1968
APPOINTMENT FOR LOVE, 1941
APRIL BLOSSOMS, 1937
APRIL FOOLS, THE, 1969
APRIL LOVE, 1957
ARISE, MY LOVE, 1940
ARIZONA TO BROADWAY, 1933
ARMY WIVES, 1944
ARNELO AFFAIR, THE, 1947
ARTHUR 2 ON THE ROCKS, 1988
ASSA, 1988
AUTUMN, 1988
AUTUMN CROCUS, 1934
AWAKENING, THE, 1938
BACHELOR APARTMENT, 1931
BACHELOR BAIT, 1934
BACHELOR OF ARTS, 1935
BACHELOR'S DAUGHTERS, THE, 1946
BACK ROADS, 1981
BAD BLOOD, 1987
BAHAMA PASSAGE, 1941
BALL AT THE CASTLE, 1939
BAMBOO BLONDE, THE, 1946
BARBARIAN, THE, 1933
BARFLY, 1987
BARRETTS OF WIMPOLE STREET, THE, 1934
BARRETTS OF WIMPOLE STREET, THE, 1957
BARRICADE, 1939
BATTLE, THE, 1934
BATTLE OF THE VILLA FIORITA, THE, 1965
BEAUTIFUL ADVENTURE, 1932
BECAUSE OF HIM, 1946
BECAUSE OF YOU, 1952
BELOVED VAGABOND, THE, 1936
BENVENUTA, 1983
BERKELEY SQUARE, 1933
BEST OF ENEMIES, 1933
BETWEEN TIME AND ETERNITY, 1960
BEWARE OF PITY, 1946
BEYOND THE FOREST, 1949
BEYOND TOMORROW, 1940
BIG POND, THE, 1930
BIRD OF PARADISE, 1932
BIRD OF PARADISE, 1951
BIRD WATCH, THE, 1983
BIRDS OF A FEATHER, 1931
BLAZE OF NOON, 1947
BLIND DESIRE, 1948
BLONDE CRAZY, 1931
BLUE LAGOON, THE, 1949
BLUE LAGOON, THE, 1980
BLUE SQUADRON, THE, 1934
BOBBY DEERFIELD, 1977
BOLERO, 1934
BOMBAY TALKIE, 1970
BORN TO BE LOVED, 1959
BOYD'S SHOP, 1960
BREEZY, 1973
BRIDE IS MUCH TOO BEAUTIFUL, THE, 1958
BRIEF ECSTASY, 1937

BRIEF ENCOUNTER, 1945
BROADCAST NEWS, 1987
BROWN SUGAR, 1931
BUCCANEER'S GIRL, 1950
BUSTER, 1988
BUT NOT FOR ME, 1959
BYPASS TO HAPPINESS, 1934
CACTUS, 1986
CAMILA, 1985
CAMILLE, 1937
CAR OF DREAMS, 1935
CARELESS LADY, 1932
CASH McCALL, 1960
CASQUE D'OR, 1956
CASS TIMBERLANE, 1947
CAT, THE, 1959
CERTAIN SMILE, A, 1958
CESAR AND ROSALIE, 1972
CHAINED, 1934
CHANGE OF HEART, 1934
CHANGE OF SEASONS, A, 1980
CHILDREN OF A LESSER GOD, 1986
CHILDREN OF PARADISE, 1945
CHINA GIRL, 1987
CHRISTOPHER STRONG, 1933
CHURCH MOUSE, THE, 1934
CIRCLE OF LOVE, 1965
CIRCUS GIRL, 1937
CITY GIRL, 1938
CLEAR THE DECKS, 1929
CLOCK, THE, 1945
COCK O' THE WALK, 1930
COMING TO AMERICA, 1988
CONDEMNED, 1929
CONFIDENTIAL LADY, 1939
CONFIDENTIALLY YOURS!, 1983
CONNECTING ROOMS, 1971
CONQUEST, 1937
CONTINENTAL DIVIDE, 1981
COUNTESS FROM HONG KONG, A, 1967
COURT CONCERT, THE, 1936
CRANES ARE FLYING, THE, 1960
CREATOR, 1985
CROSS COUNTRY ROMANCE, 1940
CROSSING DELANCEY, 1988
CRY FOR HAPPY, 1961
CRY FREEDOM, 1961
CZAR OF BROADWAY, THE, 1930
D-DAY, THE SIXTH OF JUNE, 1956
DADDY LONG LEGS, 1931
DADDY LONG LEGS, 1955
DANCERS, THE, 1930
DAREDEVIL DRIVERS, 1938
DARK ANGEL, THE, 1935
DARK EYES, 1987
DARKENED SKIES, 1930
DAY AND THE HOUR, THE, 1963
DAYS OF GLORY, 1944
DEAR JOHN, 1966
DEATH TAKES A HOLIDAY, 1934
DECEPTION, 1946
DELIGHTFUL ROGUE, 1929
DESIGN FOR LIVING, 1933
DESIGN FOR SCANDAL, 1941
DESIRE, 1936
DESIREE, 1954
DESK SET, 1957
DESPERATE ADVENTURE, A, 1938
DESPERATE CARGO, 1941
DESPERATE MOVES, 1986
DESPERATELY SEEKING SUSAN, 1985
DEVIL IN THE FLESH, THE, 1949
DEVIL IS A WOMAN, THE, 1935
DEVIL MAY CARE, 1929
DEVIL'S ENVOYS, THE, 1947
DIAMOND QUEEN, THE, 1953
DICTATOR, THE, 1935
DISGRACED, 1933
DIVA, 1982
DIVORCE AMONG FRIENDS, 1931
DODSWORTH, 1936
DON'T BET ON LOVE, 1933
DON'T GET PERSONAL, 1936
DREAM OF BUTTERFLY, THE, 1941
EDITH AND MARCEL, 1984
EDWARD AND CAROLINE, 1952

ELECTRIC DREAMS, 1984
ELEPHANT WALK, 1954
ELVIRA MADIGAN, 1967
EMMANUELLE 5, 1987
ENCHANTED COTTAGE, THE, 1945
ENCHANTMENT, 1948
ETERNAL RETURN, THE, 1943
EVENSONG, 1934
EVERY TIME WE SAY GOODBYE, 1986
FACE IN THE SKY, 1933
FACING THE MUSIC, 1933
FAITHFUL IN MY FASHION, 1946
FALL GUY, 1985
FALLING IN LOVE, 1984
FALLING IN LOVE AGAIN, 1980
FAREWELL TO ARMS, A, 1957
FAREWELL TO CINDERELLA, 1937
FAREWELL TO LOVE, 1931
FAREWELL TO ARMS, A, 1932
FASHIONS IN LOVE, 1929
FATAL ATTRACTION, 1987
FATAL DESIRE, 1953
FEAR EATS THE SOUL, 1974
FEATHER, THE, 1929
FIANCES, THE, 1964
FIRE AND ICE, 1987
FIRE WITH FIRE, 1986
FIRST LOVE, 1939
FIRST LOVE, 1970
FIRST LOVE, 1977
FISH CALLED WANDA, A, 1988
FIVE DAYS ONE SUMMER, 1982
FLIGHT, 1929
FLIGHT ANGELS, 1940
FLIGHT COMMAND, 1940
FLOOD TIDE, 1935
FLOODTIDE, 1949
FLYING HOSTESS, 1936
FOLLOW THE BOYS, 1963
FOOL AND THE PRINCESS, THE, 1948
FOOLIN' AROUND, 1980
FOR BETTER FOR WORSE, 1954
FOR LOVE OF IVY, 1968
FOR THE LOVE OF MARY, 1948
FOR YOU I DIE, 1947
FORBIDDEN COMPANY, 1932
FORBIDDEN FRUIT, 1959
FORCE OF ARMS, 1951
FORCE OF IMPULSE, 1961
FOREIGN AFFAIR, A, 1948
FOREVER YOURS, 1937
FOUR COMPANIONS, THE, 1938
FOUR DAUGHTERS, 1938
FOURTH ALARM, THE, 1930
FRAULEIN, 1958
FRENCH GAME, THE, 1963
FRENCH LESSON, 1986
FRENCH LIEUTENANT'S WOMAN, THE, 1981
FRENCHMAN'S CREEK, 1944
FRESH HORSES, 1988
FROM THIS DAY FORWARD, 1946
FUZZY PINK NIGHTGOWN, THE, 1957
GABLE AND LOMBARD, 1976
GARDEN OF ALLAH, THE, 1936
GAY LADY, THE, 1949
GAY SENORITA, THE, 1945
GENTLE JULIA, 1936
GERALDINE, 1929
GHOST AND MRS. MUIR, THE, 1942
GINGER IN THE MORNING, 1973
GIRL DOWNSTAIRS, THE, 1938
GIRL FROM HONG KONG, 1966
GIRL FROM MONTEREY, THE, 1943
GIRL IN THE PICTURE, THE, 1985
GIRL LOVES BOY, 1937
GIRL ON A MOTORCYCLE, THE, 1968
GIRL ON THE BARGE, THE, 1929
GIRL SAID NO, THE, 1930
GIRL THIEF, THE, 1938
GLASS SLIPPER, THE, 1955
GLORY, 1955
GOLDEN CAGE, THE, 1933
GOOD FAIRY, THE, 1935
GOOD SPORT, 1931
GOODBYE AGAIN, 1933
GOODBYE AGAIN, 1961

GOODBYE COLUMBUS, 1969
GOODBYE GIRL, THE, 1977
GOODBYE LOVE, 1934
GOODBYE, MY FANCY, 1951
GOTCHA!, 1985
GRAND MANEUVER, THE, 1956
GRAND PRIX, 1934
GREAT HOPE, THE, 1954
GREEN DOLPHIN STREET, 1947
GREEN FIRE, 1955
GREEN MANSIONS, 1959
GREGORY'S GIRL, 1982
GUILT, 1930
GUY, A GAL AND A PAL, A, 1945
GUY NAMED JOE, A, 1943
GYPSY, 1937
HANOVER STREET, 1979
HARD TO HOLD, 1984
HARD TRAVELING, 1985
HAREM, 1985
HAVING WONDERFUL TIME, 1938
HE KNEW WOMEN, 1930
HEARTBEAT, 1946
HEARTBREAK, 1931
HEARTBREAKER, 1983
HEARTBREAKERS, 1984
HEARTS DIVIDED, 1936
HEARTS IN EXILE, 1929
HEAT OF THE SUMMER, 1961
HEAVEN ON EARTH, 1960
HELL-SHIP MORGAN, 1936
HELLO SISTER, 1930
HER CARDBOARD LOVER, 1942
HER FIRST BEAU, 1941
HER FIRST ROMANCE, 1951
HER HIGHNESS AND THE BELLBOY, 1945
HER IMAGINARY LOVER, 1933
HER MAN, 1930
HER MAN GILBEY, 1949
HER PRIVATE LIFE, 1929
HER STRANGE DESIRE, 1931
HERE COMES HAPPINESS, 1941
HERE IS MY HEART, 1934
HERE'S TO ROMANCE, 1935
HERS TO HOLD, 1943
HE'S MY GIRL, 1987
HI BEAUTIFUL, 1944
HIDDEN MENACE, THE, 1940
HIDE-OUT, 1934
HIGH COUNTRY, THE, 1981
HIGH SPIRITS, 1988
HINDLE WAKES, 1931
HIS GLORIOUS NIGHT, 1929
HOLD BACK THE DAWN, 1941
HOLD YOUR MAN, 1933
HOLIDAY AFFAIR, 1949
HOMECOMING, 1948
HONKY TONK, 1941
HONOLULU-TOKYO-HONG KONG, 1963
HOOPLA, 1933
HORIZONTAL LIEUTENANT, THE, 1962
HOT BLOOD, 1956
HOT SATURDAY, 1932
HOURS OF LOVE, THE, 1965
HU-MAN, 1975
HURRICANE, 1979
I KNOW WHERE I'M GOING, 1947
I LIVED WITH YOU, 1933
I LOVE N.Y., 1987
I MET MY LOVE AGAIN, 1938
I'D RATHER BE RICH, 1964
IF A MAN ANSWERS, 1962
IF EVER I SEE YOU AGAIN, 1978
IF I WERE FREE, 1933
IF THIS BE SIN, 1950
IF YOU COULD ONLY COOK, 1936
I'LL BE SEEING YOU, 1944
ILLEGALLY YOURS, 1988
ILLUSION, 1929
I'M STILL ALIVE, 1940
IMPATIENT YEARS, THE, 1944
IN HIS STEPS, 1936
IN LOVE AND WAR, 1958
IN THE FRENCH STYLE, 1963
INDISCREET, 1931
INDISCREET, 1958

INFERNAL MACHINE, 1933
INTERLUDE, 1957
INTERMEZZO: A LOVE STORY, 1939
INTERVAL, 1973
INVITATION, 1952
ISLAND OF DESIRE, 1952
IT HAPPENED IN PARIS, 1935
IT HAPPENED ONE NIGHT, 1934
IT HAPPENED ONE SUNDAY, 1944
IT STARTED IN NAPLES, 1960
IT STARTED IN THE ALPS, 1966
IT'S MY TURN, 1980
I'VE BEEN AROUND, 1935
JANE EYRE, 1935
JANE EYRE, 1944
JANE EYRE, 1971
JAVA HEAD, 1935
JAZZ CINDERELLA, 1930
JEREMY, 1973
JIVARO, 1954
JOY HOUSE, 1964
JUST ACROSS THE STREET, 1952
JUST THE WAY YOU ARE, 1984
KANSAS, 1988
KENTUCKY, 1938
KEY EXCHANGE, 1985
KING KELLY OF THE U.S.A, 1934
KING OF THE LUMBERJACKS, 1940
KING'S RHAPSODY, 1955
KING'S VACATION, THE, 1933
KIPPERBANG, 1984
KISS OF FIRE, THE, 1940
KISS OF FIRE, 1955
KITTY, 1945
KNIGHT WITHOUT ARMOR, 1937
KNOWING MEN, 1930
LA PETIT SIRENE, 1984
LA SEGUA, 1985
LACEMAKER, THE, 1977
LAD FROM OUR TOWN, 1941
LADIES CRAVE EXCITEMENT, 1935
LADIES' DAY, 1943
LADIES IN LOVE, 1930
LADIES OF THE CHORUS, 1948
LADY BODYGUARD, 1942
LADY CONSENTS, THE, 1936
LADY EVE, THE, 1941
LADY FROM THE SEA, THE, 1929
LADY IN SCARLET, THE, 1935
LADY IS WILLING, THE, 1942
LADY OF SCANDAL, THE, 1930
LADY OF THE PAVEMENTS, 1929
LADY SURRENDERS, A, 1947
LADY SURRENDERS, A, 1930
LADY TAKES A CHANCE, A, 1943
LADY TAKES A SAILOR, THE, 1949
LADY WITH A PAST, 1932
LADY WITH THE DOG, THE, 1962
LAFAYETTE ESCADRILLE, 1958
LARCENY WITH MUSIC, 1943
LASSIE FROM LANCASHIRE, 1938
LAST BARRICADE, THE, 1938
LAST DANCE, THE, 1930
LAST DRAGON, THE, 1985
LAST METRO, THE, 1981
LAST OF THE PAGANS, 1936
LAST TIME I SAW PARIS, THE, 1954
L'ATALANTE, 1947
LATIN LOVE, 1930
LAUGHING IN THE SUNSHINE, 1953
LAW IN HER HANDS, THE, 1936
LE BON PLAISIR, 1984
LEAVE HER TO HEAVEN, 1946
LEFT HAND OF GOD, THE, 1955
LEFTOVER LADIES, 1931
LEO AND LOREE, 1980
LEOPARD IN THE SNOW, 1979
LET US BE GAY, 1930
LET'S LIVE TONIGHT, 1935
LETTER TO BREZHNEV, 1986
LIAR'S MOON, 1982
LIFE BEGINS WITH LOVE, 1937
LIGHT FANTASTIC, 1964
LIGHT FINGERS, 1929
LILIES OF THE FIELD, 1934
LITTLE DAMOZEL, THE, 1933

BOLD: Films on Videocassette

LITTLE HUT, THE, 1957
LITTLE MAN, WHAT NOW?, 1934
LITTLE MELODY FROM VIENNA, 1948
LITTLE ROMANCE, A, 1979
LIVING DANGEROUSLY, 1988
LONELY PASSION OF JUDITH HEARNE, THE, 1988
LOOKING FOR EILEEN, 1987
LOOKING FOR LOVE, 1964
LOVE AFFAIR, 1932
LOVE AFFAIR, 1939
LOVE AMONG THE MILLIONAIRES, 1930
LOVE COMES ALONG, 1930
LOVE CONTRACT, THE, 1932
LOVE ETERNE, THE, 1964
LOVE FINDS ANDY HARDY, 1938
LOVE IN A TAXI, 1980
LOVE IN BLOOM, 1935
LOVE IN EXILE, 1936
LOVE IN GERMANY, A, 1984
LOVE IN THE AFTERNOON, 1957
LOVE IS A BALL, 1963
LOVE IS A FUNNY THING, 1970
LOVE IS A MANY-SPLENDORED THING, 1955
LOVE IS BETTER THAN EVER, 1952
LOVE KISS, THE, 1930
LOVE MATES, 1967
LOVE ON A PILLOW, 1963
LOVE ON SKIS, 1933
LOVE ON THE RIVIERA, 1964
LOVE SPECIALIST, THE, 1959
LOVE STORY, 1949
LOVE STORY, 1970
LOVE, THE ITALIAN WAY, 1964
LOVE TIME, 1934
LOVER'S NET, 1957
LOVERS OF TERUEL, THE, 1962
LOVERS OF TOLEDO, THE, 1954
LOVERS OF VERONA, THE, 1951
LOVES OF MADAME DUBARRY, THE, 1938
LUCAS, 1986
LUCK OF A SAILOR, THE, 1934
LYDIA, 1941
MADALENA, 1965
MADE IN HEAVEN, 1987
MADLY, 1970
MADONNA OF THE SEVEN MOONS, 1945
MAGNIFICENT ROUGHNECKS, 1956
MAIN STREET TO BROADWAY, 1953
MAN ABOUT TOWN, 1932
MAN AND A WOMAN: 20 YEARS LATER, A, 1986
MAN AND THE MOMENT, THE, 1929
MAN FROM YESTERDAY, THE, 1932
MAN IN GREY, THE, 1943
MAN IN HALF-MOON STREET, THE, 1944
MAN IN LOVE, A, 1987
MAN OF SENTIMENT, A, 1933
MAN WANTED, 1932
MAN WHO WON, THE, 1933
MANDALAY, 1934
MANDRAGOLA, 1966
MANHATTAN, 1979
MANHATTAN HEARTBEAT, 1940
MANNEQUIN, 1987
MANON, 1987
MANY A SLIP, 1931
MANY WATERS, 1931
MARIE ANTOINETTE, 1938
MARNIE, 1964
MARRIAGE CAME TUMBLING DOWN, THE, 1968
MARRIAGE-GO-ROUND, THE, 1960
MARRIAGE—ITALIAN STYLE, 1964
MARRIED AND IN LOVE, 1940
MARRY ME, 1932
MARRY ME!, 1949
MARTYRS OF LOVE, 1968
MATA HARI, 1931
MATCHMAKING OF ANNA, THE, 1972
MAXIE, 1985
MAYERLING, 1937
MAYERLING, 1968
MAYTIME, 1937
MAYTIME IN MAYFAIR, 1952
ME AND MARLBOROUGH, 1935
ME AND MY GAL, 1932
MEET ME AT DAWN, 1947
MEET THE BOY FRIEND, 1937

MEET THE STEWARTS, 1942
MELO, 1988
MELODY, 1971
MEN CALL IT LOVE, 1931
MEN ON CALL, 1931
MERELY MARY ANN, 1931
MILLIONAIRE FOR CHRISTY, A, 1951
MIMI, 1935
MISS PRESIDENT, 1935
M'LISS, 1936
MODERN LOVE, 1929
MOGAMBO, 1953
MOMENT BY MOMENT, 1978
MONEY FOR NOTHING, 1932
MONEY MEANS NOTHING, 1934
MONEY ON THE STREET, 1930
MOON OVER LAS VEGAS, 1944
MOONLIGHT SONATA, 1938
MOONSTRUCK, 1987
MOROCCO, 1930
MRS. DANE'S DEFENCE, 1933
MRS. FITZHERBERT, 1950
MURDER IN GREENWICH VILLAGE, 1937
MURPHY'S ROMANCE, 1985
MY COUSIN RACHEL, 1952
MY FOOLISH HEART, 1949
MY REPUTATION, 1946
MYSTIC PIZZA, 1988
NAVY WIFE, 1936
NEITHER THE SEA NOR THE SAND, 1974
NELL GWYN, 1935
NELSON AFFAIR, THE, 1973
NEW LIFE, A, 1988
NEW TEACHER, THE, 1941
NICE WOMAN, 1932
NIGHT IN BANGKOK, 1966
NIGHT IN HONG KONG, A, 1961
NIGHT UNTO NIGHT, 1949
NINE TILL SIX, 1932
90 DAYS, 1986
NO DEFENSE, 1929
NO EXIT, 1930
NO SMALL AFFAIR, 1984
NO TIME FOR LOVE, 1943
NOBODY'S FOOL, 1986
NOT WITH MY WIFE, YOU DON'T!, 1966
OFFERING, THE, 1966
OFFICER AND A GENTLEMAN, AN, 1982
OLIVER'S STORY, 1978
ONE FROM THE HEART, 1982
ONE NIGHT IN LISBON, 1941
ONE ROMANTIC NIGHT, 1930
OUR MODERN MAIDENS, 1929
OUT OF AFRICA, 1985
OUTCASTS OF THE CITY, 1958
OVER THE BROOKLYN BRIDGE, 1984
PAGAN, THE, 1929
PARADISE ISLAND, 1930
PARIS BOUND, 1929
PARIS IN THE MONTH OF AUGUST, 1968
PARIS WHEN IT SIZZLES, 1964
PATRICIA GETS HER MAN, 1937
PEACH THIEF, THE, 1969
PEACOCK ALLEY, 1930
PEG OF OLD DRURY, 1936
PEPE LE MOKO, 1937
PERFECT COUPLE, A, 1979
PERSONAL COLUMN, 1939
PERSONALS, THE, 1982
PETER IBBETSON, 1935
PETTICOAT FEVER, 1936
PHARAOH'S WOMAN, THE, 1961
PICK-UP, 1933
PICK-UP ARTIST, THE, 1987
PIERROT LE FOU, 1968
PILGRIM LADY, THE, 1947
PLACE FOR LOVERS, A, 1969
PLAYERS, 1979
PLAYTHING, THE, 1929
PLEASE BELIEVE ME, 1950
PLEASE, NOT NOW!, 1963
PLEASURE CRUISE, 1933
PLEASURE SEEKERS, THE, 1964
PORT OF LOST DREAMS, 1935
PORTRAIT OF JENNIE, 1949
PRESCRIPTION FOR ROMANCE, 1937

PRESTIGE, 1932
PRIMROSE PATH, THE, 1934
PRINCE OF DIAMONDS, 1930
PRINCESS AND THE PLUMBER, THE, 1930
PRISONER OF CORBAL, 1939
PRISONER OF ZENDA, THE, 1937
PRISONER OF ZENDA, THE, 1952
PRISONERS OF THE CASBAH, 1953
PRIVATE DETECTIVE, 1939
PRIVATE DETECTIVE 62, 1933
PRIVATE LIFE OF DON JUAN, THE, 1934
PRIVATE LIVES OF ELIZABETH AND ESSEX, THE, 1939
PRIVATE NUMBER, 1936
PRIZE, THE, 1963
PRIZZI'S HONOR, 1985
PROMISE, THE, 1969
PROMISE, THE, 1979
PROUD AND THE PROFANE, THE, 1956
PURPLE HEARTS, 1984
QUEEN CHRISTINA, 1933
QUIET MAN, THE, 1952
RAFFLES, 1930
RAFFLES, 1939
RAFTER ROMANCE, 1934
RAGE OF PARIS, THE, 1938
RAGMAN'S DAUGHTER, THE, 1974
REBEL LOVE, 1986
RECKLESS, 1935
RED SALUTE, 1935
REDHEAD, 1941
REFORMER AND THE REDHEAD, THE, 1950
REMEMBER THE NIGHT, 1940
RESERVED FOR LADIES, 1932
RESURRECTION, 1931
RESURRECTION, 1963
RETURN FROM THE SEA, 1954
RETURN OF THE RAT, THE, 1929
RETURN TO PARADISE, 1953
RETURN TO SNOWY RIVER: PART II, 1988
REUNION IN FRANCE, 1942
REUNION IN VIENNA, 1933
RHAPSODY, 1954
RHYTHM IN THE AIR, 1936
RHYTHM SERENADE, 1943
RICH PEOPLE, 1929
RING AROUND THE MOON, 1936
RINGS ON HER FINGERS, 1942
RISING DAMP, 1980
RIVER, THE, 1928
ROAD TO RENO, THE, 1938
ROAMING LADY, 1936
ROBIN AND MARIAN, 1976
ROMAN HOLIDAY, 1953
ROMANCE, 1930
ROMANCE AND RICHES, 1937
ROMANCE IN MANHATTAN, 1935
ROMANCE IN THE DARK, 1938
ROMANCE IN THE RAIN, 1934
ROMANCE OF SEVILLE, A, 1929
ROMANCE OF THE LIMBERLOST, 1938
ROMANCING THE STONE, 1984
ROMANOFF AND JULIET, 1961
ROMANTIC COMEDY, 1983
ROMANTIC ENGLISHWOMAN, THE, 1975
ROMANY LOVE, 1931
ROME ADVENTURE, 1962
ROMEO AND JULIET, 1936
ROMEO AND JULIET, 1954
ROMEO AND JULIET, 1955
ROMEO AND JULIET, 1966
ROMEO AND JULIET, 1968
ROMEO AND JULIET, 1968
ROSE BOWL, 1936
ROSE BOWL STORY, THE, 1952
ROSEANNA McCOY, 1949
ROUGH CUT, 1980
ROYAL DIVORCE, A, 1938
ROYAL ROMANCE, A, 1930
ROYAL WALTZ, THE, 1936
RYAN'S DAUGHTER, 1970
SABRINA, 1954
SALESLADY, 1938
SALLY BISHOP, 1932
SALLY IN OUR ALLEY, 1931
SALSA, 1988

SAN FRANCISCO, 1936
SANTIAGO, 1956
SAP FROM SYRACUSE, THE, 1930
SARABAND, 1949
SARACEN BLADE, THE, 1954
SARATOGA TRUNK, 1945
SARUMBA, 1950
SATURDAY'S CHILDREN, 1940
SCANDAL FOR SALE, 1932
SCANDAL IN SORRENTO, 1957
SCARLET DAWN, 1932
SCHOOL FOR STARS, 1935
SCOTLAND YARD, 1930
SCOTLAND YARD, 1941
SEA DEVILS, 1937
SEA FURY, 1959
SEA HAWK, THE, 1940
SECOND BEST BED, 1937
SECOND BUREAU, 1936
SECOND BUREAU, 1937
SECOND CHANCE, 1947
SECOND FIDDLE, 1957
SECOND-HAND HEARTS, 1981
SECOND HONEYMOON, 1931
SECOND HONEYMOON, 1937
SECRET AGENT, 1933
SECRET OF MONTE CRISTO, THE, 1961
SECRET SINNERS, 1933
SECRETS, 1933
SECRETS OF AN ACTRESS, 1938
SEDUCTION BY THE SEA, 1967
SEEING IS BELIEVING, 1934
SEND ME NO FLOWERS, 1964
SENORA CASADA NECEISITA MARIDO, 1935
SENTIMENTAL BLOKE, 1932
SENTIMIENTOS: MIRTA DE LINIERS A ESTAMBUL, 1987
SEPARATE WAYS, 1981
SEPTEMBER AFFAIR, 1950
SEPTEMBER STORM, 1960
SEVENTH HEAVEN, 1937
SHAKEDOWN, 1936
SHALL WE DANCE, 1937
SHANGHAI, 1935
SHE WAS ONLY A VILLAGE MAIDEN, 1933
SHE'S MY WEAKNESS, 1930
SHOP AROUND THE CORNER, THE, 1940
SHOPWORN, 1932
SHOPWORN ANGEL, THE, 1928
SHOW FOLKS, 1928
SILHOUETTES, 1982
SILVER CITY, 1985
SIN TAKES A HOLIDAY, 1930
SINNERS IN THE SUN, 1932
SINS OF RACHEL CADE, THE, 1960
SISTERS, THE, 1938
SMALL TOWN GIRL, 1936
SO IT'S SUNDAY, 1932
SO RED THE ROSE, 1935
SOB SISTER, 1931
SOCIETY GIRL, 1932
SOFIA, 1987
SOME DAY, 1935
SOME KIND OF WONDERFUL, 1987
SOMEONE TO WATCH OVER ME, 1987
SOMETIMES GOOD, 1934
SOMEWHERE I'LL FIND YOU, 1942
SOMEWHERE IN TIME, 1980
SPIRIT AND THE FLESH, THE, 1948
SPLASH, 1984
SPRINGTIME, 1948
SPRINGTIME FOR HENRY, 1934
STAIRWAY TO HEAVEN, 1946
STAMBOUL QUEST, 1934
STARMAN, 1984
STARTING OVER, 1979
STEADY COMPANY, 1932
STERILE CUCKOO, THE, 1969
STICK UP, THE, 1978
STINGAREE, 1934
STOLEN HEAVEN, 1931
STOLEN KISSES, 1969
STOLEN SWEETS, 1934
STORMY MONDAY, 1988
STORMY WATERS, 1946
STORY OF VICKIE, THE, 1958

STOWAWAY GIRL, 1957
STRANDED, 1935
STRANGE BEDFELLOWS, 1965
STRANGE WIVES, 1935
STRANGERS KISS, 1984
STRANGERS ON A HONEYMOON, 1937
STRANGERS, THE, 1955
STRAWBERRY BLONDE, THE, 1941
STRICTLY MODERN, 1930
SUMMER RUN, 1974
SUMMER STORY, A, 1988
SUMMERTIME, 1955
SUN SHINES, THE, 1939
SUSAN LENOX—HER FALL AND RISE, 1931
SUZANNE, 1980
SWAN, THE, 1956
SWEET ADELINE, 1935
SWEET DEVIL, 1937
SWEET INNISCARRA, 1934
SWEET MUSIC, 1935
SWELLHEAD, THE, 1930
SWING PARADE OF 1946, 1946
SWING TIME, 1936
SWORD AND THE ROSE, THE, 1953
SWORDSMAN, THE, 1947
TAHITI HONEY, 1943
TAKE A LETTER, DARLING, 1942
TALES OF PARIS, 1962
TARZAN AND HIS MATE, 1934
TARZAN, THE APE MAN, 1932
TAXI FOR TWO, 1929
TEAR GAS SQUAD, 1940
TELL IT TO THE JUDGE, 1949
TELL ME IN THE SUNLIGHT, 1967
THAT FUNNY FEELING, 1965
THAT MAN FROM TANGIER, 1953
THAT MAN'S HERE AGAIN, 1937
THAT MIDNIGHT KISS, 1949
THAT OTHER WOMAN, 1942
THAT TOUCH OF MINK, 1962
THAT WONDERFUL URGE, 1948
THERE GOES MY HEART, 1938
THEY MET ON SKIS, 1940
THIEF OF HEARTS, 1984
THIS ABOVE ALL, 1942
THIS ACTING BUSINESS, 1933
THIS IS THE NIGHT, 1932
THIS WOMAN IS DANGEROUS, 1952
THOSE ENDEARING YOUNG CHARMS, 1945
THOSE LIPS, THOSE EYES, 1980
THOSE WERE THE DAYS, 1940
THRASHIN', 1986
THREE COINS IN THE FOUNTAIN, 1954
THREE FABLES OF LOVE, 1963
THREE GUYS NAMED MIKE, 1951
THREE HEARTS FOR JULIA, 1943
THREE HOURS, 1944
THREE LITTLE SISTERS, 1944
THREE LOVES HAS NANCY, 1938
THREE OF A KIND, 1936
THREE ON A HONEYMOON, 1934
THREE RUSSIAN GIRLS, 1943
THREE SMART GIRLS GROW UP, 1939
THREE STRIPES IN THE SUN, 1955
THREE WEEKS OF LOVE, 1965
THUNDERBOLT, 1929
TICKET TO PARADISE, 1961
TICKLISH AFFAIR, A, 1963
TIGER'S TALE, A, 1988
'TIL WE MEET AGAIN, 1940
TILL WE MEET AGAIN, 1936
TIME OUT FOR ROMANCE, 1937
TIME TO LOVE AND A TIME TO DIE, A, 1958
TO BEGIN AGAIN, 1982
TO CATCH A THIEF, 1955
TO MARY—WITH LOVE, 1936
TO PARIS WITH LOVE, 1955
TO PLEASE A LADY, 1950
TOAST OF NEW ORLEANS, THE, 1950
TODAY WE LIVE, 1933
TOMBOY, 1940
TONIGHT IS OURS, 1933
TONIGHT OR NEVER, 1931
TOO MANY BLONDES, 1941
TOO MANY COOKS, 1931
TOO MANY MILLIONS, 1934

TOO YOUNG TO KISS, 1951
TOO YOUNG TO KNOW, 1945
TOOTSIE, 1982
TOP FLOOR GIRL, 1959
TOP HAT, 1935
TOP OF THE WORLD, 1955
TOP SECRET AFFAIR, 1957
TOPSY-TURVY JOURNEY, 1970
TORCH SONG, 1953
TORCH, THE, 1950
TORPEDO BOAT, 1942
TORRID ZONE, 1940
TOUCH AND GO, 1986
TOUCH OF CLASS, A, 1973
TOUCHED, 1983
TOWN WENT WILD, THE, 1945
TRADE WINDS, 1938
TRAIN GOES EAST, THE, 1949
TROUBLE AHEAD, 1936
TROUBLE IN MIND, 1985
TRUE TO THE NAVY, 1930
TRUTH ABOUT SPRING, THE, 1965
TURN OF THE TIDE, 1935
24 HOURS, 1931
TWO AND ONE TWO, 1934
TWO AND TWO MAKE SIX, 1962
TWO-FACED WOMAN, 1941
TWO GROOMS FOR A BRIDE, 1957
TWO HEADS ON A PILLOW, 1934
TWO HEARTS IN WALTZ TIME, 1934
TWO IN A SLEEPING BAG, 1964
TWO IN THE SHADOW, 1968
TWO KINDS OF WOMEN, 1932
TWO MEN AND A MAID, 1929
TWO OF A KIND, 1983
TWO PEOPLE, 1973
TWO SINNERS, 1935
TWO WEEKS IN SEPTEMBER, 1967
TWO WORLD, 1930
TWO'S COMPANY, 1939
TYPHOON, 1940
U-TURN, 1973
UNBEARABLE LIGHTNESS OF BEING, THE, 1988
UNDER EIGHTEEN, 1932
UNDER THE CHERRY MOON, 1986
UNFINISHED BUSINESS, 1941
UNTAMED, 1955
UNTAMED, 1940
UNTAMED, 1929
UNTIL SEPTEMBER, 1984
UP POPS THE DEVIL, 1931
UPTOWN NEW YORK, 1932
UTILITIES, 1983
VACATION DAYS, 1947
VACATION FROM LOVE, 1938
VACATION FROM MARRIAGE, 1945
VAGABOND LADY, 1935
VALLEY GIRL, 1983
VALLEY OF DECISION, THE, 1945
VANESSA, HER LOVE STORY, 1935
VERY THOUGHT OF YOU, THE, 1944
VILLAGE BARN DANCE, 1940
VILNA LEGEND, A, 1949
VINTAGE, THE, 1957
VINTAGE WINE, 1935
VIOLETS ARE BLUE, 1986
VIRGIN QUEEN OF ST. FRANCIS HIGH, THE, 1987
VIRTUE, 1932
VOICES, 1979
WALK IN THE SPRING RAIN, A, 1970
WALK WITH LOVE AND DEATH, A, 1969
WALL-EYED NIPPON, 1963
WALTZ ACROSS TEXAS, 1982
WARNING TO WANTONS, A, 1949
WASHINGTON STORY, 1952
WAY DOWN EAST, 1935
WAY FOR A SAILOR, 1930
WAY TO LOVE, THE, 1933
WAY WE WERE, THE, 1973
WE HAVE OUR MOMENTS, 1937
WE WHO ARE YOUNG, 1940
WEDDING RINGS, 1930
WEEK-ENDS ONLY, 1932
WEEKEND WITH FATHER, 1951
WELL-GROOMED BRIDE, THE, 1946
WEST POINT WIDOW, 1941

BOLD: Films on Videocassette

WESTWARD PASSAGE, 1932
WHARF ANGEL, 1934
WHAT A MAN, 1930
WHEN THE DEVIL WAS WELL, 1937
WHERE IS THIS LADY?, 1932
WHIPSAW, 1936
WHITE MISCHIEF, 1988
WHITE SISTER, THE, 1933
WICKED DREAMS OF PAULA SCHULTZ, THE, 1968
WIDOW FROM MONTE CARLO, THE, 1936
WILD GOLD, 1934
WILD PARTY, THE, 1929
WINGS IN THE DARK, 1935
WINGS OF THE MORNING, 1937
WINGS OF THE NAVY, 1939
WINNING, 1969
WINTER WONDERLAND, 1947
WINTER'S TALE, THE, 1968
WITHOUT RESERVATIONS, 1946
WOLF SONG, 1929
WOMAN AND THE HUNTER, THE, 1957
WOMAN DECIDES, THE, 1932
WOMAN FOR JOE, THE, 1955
WOMAN IN RED, THE, 1935
WOMAN OBSESSED, 1959
WOMAN WANTED, 1935
WOMAN-WISE, 1937
WOMAN'S ANGLE, THE, 1954
WONDERFUL STORY, THE, 1932
WONDERFUL THINGS!, 1958
WORKING GIRL, 1988
WORLD OWES ME A LIVING, THE, 1944
WORST WOMAN IN PARIS, 1933
WRATH OF JEALOUSY, 1936
WUTHERING HEIGHTS, 1939
WUTHERING HEIGHTS, 1970
YANK IN LONDON, A, 1946
YANKEE PASHA, 1954
YANKS, 1979
YASEMIN, 1988
YEAR OF AWAKENING, THE, 1987
YEAR OF LIVING DANGEROUSLY, THE, 1982
YELLOW ROLLS-ROYCE, THE, 1965
YELLOW STOCKINGS, 1930
YES, GIORGIO, 1982
YESTERDAY, 1980
YIDDLE WITH HIS FIDDLE, 1937
YOU BELONG TO ME, 1941
YOU GOTTA STAY HAPPY, 1948
YOUNG AND THE GUILTY, THE, 1958
YOUNG MAN OF MANHATTAN, 1930
YOUTH ON PAROLE, 1937
YOUTHFUL FOLLY, 1934
ZOO IN BUDAPEST, 1933

Science Fiction

ABOMINABLE SNOWMAN OF THE HIMALAYAS,
   THE, 1957
**ADVENTURES OF BUCKAROO BANZAI: ACROSS
   THE 8TH DIMENSION, THE, 1984**
AFTER THE FALL OF NEW YORK, 1984
ALIEN, 1979
ALIEN CONTAMINATION, 1982
ALIEN FACTOR, THE, 1984
ALIEN NATION, 1988
ALIEN PREDATOR, 1987
ALIENS, 1986
ALL RIGHT, MY FRIEND, 1983
ALLIGATOR, 1980
ALLIGATOR PEOPLE, THE, 1959
**ALPHAVILLE, A STRANGE CASE OF LEMMY
   CAUTION, 1965**
ALRAUNE, 1952
ALTERED STATES, 1980
AMAZING COLOSSAL MAN, THE, 1957
AMAZING TRANSPARENT MAN, THE, 1960
AMERICA 3000, 1986
AMPHIBIOUS MAN, THE, 1961
ANDROID, 1982
ANDROMEDA STRAIN, THE, 1971
ANGRY RED PLANET, THE, 1959
APPLE, THE, 1980
APRIL 1, 2000, 1953
ASSIGNMENT OUTER SPACE, 1960
ASSIGNMENT TERROR, 1970
ASTOUNDING SHE-MONSTER, THE, 1958

ASTRO-ZOMBIES, THE, 1969
AT THE EARTH'S CORE, 1976
ATOM AGE VAMPIRE, 1961
ATOMIC BRAIN, THE, 1964
ATOMIC MAN, THE, 1955
ATOMIC SUBMARINE, THE, 1960
ATRAGON, 1965
ATTACK OF THE CRAB MONSTERS, 1957
ATTACK OF THE 50 FOOT WOMAN, 1958
ATTACK OF THE MUSHROOM PEOPLE, 1964
ATTACK OF THE PUPPET PEOPLE, 1958
ATTACK OF THE ROBOTS, 1967
AURORA ENCOUNTER, THE, 1985
BABY: SECRET OF A LOST LEGEND, 1985
BACK TO THE FUTURE, 1985
BAMBOO SAUCER, THE, 1968
BARBARELLA, 1968
BARON MUNCHAUSEN, 1962
BATTERIES NOT INCLUDED, 1987
BATTLE BENEATH THE EARTH, 1968
BATTLE BEYOND THE STARS, 1980
BATTLE BEYOND THE SUN, 1963
BATTLE FOR THE PLANET OF THE APES, 1973
BATTLE IN OUTER SPACE, 1960
BATTLE OF THE WORLDS, 1961
BATTLESTAR GALACTICA, 1979
BATTLETRUCK, 1982
BEAST FROM 20,000 FATHOMS, THE, 1953
BEAST OF HOLLOW MOUNTAIN, THE, 1956
BEAST OF YUCCA FLATS, THE, 1961
BEAST WITH A MILLION EYES, THE, 1956
BEES, THE, 1978
BEGINNING OF THE END, 1957
BEHEMOTH, THE SEA MONSTER, 1959
BELA LUGOSI MEETS A BROOKLYN GORILLA, 1952
BENEATH THE PLANET OF THE APES, 1970
BEWARE! THE BLOB, 1972
BEYOND THE TIME BARRIER, 1960
BIG MEAT EATER, 1984
BLACK HOLE, THE, 1979
BLACK SCORPION, THE, 1957
BLADE RUNNER, 1982
BLOB, THE, 1958
BLOB, THE, 1988
BLOOD BEAST FROM OUTER SPACE, 1965
BLOODSUCKERS FROM OUTER SPACE, 1987
BLUE DEMON VERSUS THE INFERNAL BRAINS,
   1967
BLUE SUNSHINE, 1978
BODY STEALERS, THE, 1969
BOOGIE MAN WILL GET YOU, THE, 1942
BORN IN FLAMES, 1983
BOY AND HIS DOG, A, 1975
BOY WHO TURNED YELLOW, THE, 1972
BRAIN, THE, 1965
BRAIN EATERS, THE, 1958
BRAIN FROM THE PLANET AROUS, THE, 1958
BRAINSTORM, 1983
BRAINWAVES, 1983
BRAZIL, 1985
BREEDERS, 1986
BRIDE OF THE MONSTER, 1955
BRIDES OF BLOOD, 1968
BROTHER FROM ANOTHER PLANET, THE, 1984
BUBBLE, THE, 1967
BUCK ROGERS IN THE 25TH CENTURY, 1979
BUG, 1975
CAPE CANAVERAL MONSTERS, 1960
CAPTIVE WOMEN, 1952
CASTLE OF FU MANCHU, THE, 1968
CAT WOMEN OF THE MOON, 1953
CAVE GIRL, 1985
CEREBROS DIABOLICOS, 1966
CHEREZ TERNII K SVEZDAM, 1981
CHIQUTTO PERO PICOSO, 1967
CHOSEN, THE, 1978
CHOSEN SURVIVORS, 1974
CHRONOPOLIS, 1982
CITY LIMITS, 1985
CITY UNDER THE SEA, 1965
CLOCKWORK ORANGE, A, 1971
CLONES, THE, 1973
CLOSE ENCOUNTERS OF THE THIRD KIND, 1977
COCOON, 1985
COCOON: THE RETURN, 1988
COLOSSUS OF NEW YORK, THE, 1958

COLOSSUS: THE FORBIN PROJECT, 1969
CONQUEST OF SPACE, 1955
CONQUEST OF THE EARTH, 1980
CONQUEST OF THE PLANET OF THE APES, 1972
COSMIC MAN, THE, 1959
COSMIC MONSTERS, 1958
COUNTDOWN, 1968
CRACK IN THE WORLD, 1965
CRAZIES, THE, 1973
CREATION OF THE HUMANOIDS, 1962
CREATURE, 1985
CREEPING UNKNOWN, THE, 1956
CREMATORS, THE, 1972
CRIMES OF THE FUTURE, 1969
CRITTERS, 1986
CROISIERES SIDERALES, 1941
CROSSTALK, 1982
CURIOUS FEMALE, THE, 1969
CYBORG 2087, 1966
CYCLOPS, 1957
CYCLOTRODE X, 1946
DAGORA THE SPACE MONSTER, 1964
DALEKS—INVASION EARTH 2155 A.D., 1966
DAMNATION ALLEY, 1977
DANGER: DIABOLIK, 1968
DARK, THE, 1979
DARK STAR, 1975
D.A.R.Y.L., 1985
DAY MARS INVADED EARTH, THE, 1963
DAY OF THE TRIFFIDS, THE, 1963
DAY THE EARTH CAUGHT FIRE, THE, 1961
DAY THE EARTH STOOD STILL, THE, 1951
DAY THE SKY EXPLODED, THE, 1958
DAY THE WORLD ENDED, THE, 1956
DAY TIME ENDED, THE, 1980
DEAD-END DRIVE-IN, 1986
DEAD MAN WALKING, 1988
DEAD MOUNTAINEER HOTEL, THE, 1979
DEADLY MANTIS, THE, 1957
DEADLY SPAWN, THE, 1983
DEATH RACE 2000, 1975
DEATH WATCH, 1980
DEATHSPORT, 1978
DEF-CON 4, 1985
DEMON FROM DEVIL'S LAKE, THE, 1964
DEMON SEED, 1977
DESTINATION INNER SPACE, 1966
DESTINATION MOON, 1950
DESTROY ALL MONSTERS, 1969
DEVIL GIRL FROM MARS, 1954
DEVIL'S MAN, THE, 1967
DIMENSION 5, 1966
DOCTOR CRIMEN, 1953
DR. CYCLOPS, 1940
DR. MABUSE'S RAYS OF DEATH, 1964
**DR. OTTO AND THE RIDDLE OF THE GLOOM
   BEAM, 1986**
**DR. STRANGELOVE: OR HOW I LEARNED TO STOP
   WORRYING AND LOVE THE BOMB, 1964**
DR. WHO AND THE DALEKS, 1965
DOLL, THE, 1962
DONOVAN'S BRAIN, 1953
DON'T PLAY WITH MARTIANS, 1967
DOOMSDAY MACHINE, 1967
DOOMWATCH, 1972
DOS COSMONAUTAS A LA FUERZA, 1967
DREAM COME TRUE, A, 1963
DREAM TOWN, 1973
DREAMSCAPE, 1984
DUNE, 1984
DYNAMITE JOHNSON, 1978
EARTH DIES SCREAMING, THE, 1964
EARTH VS. THE FLYING SAUCERS, 1956
EARTHBOUND, 1981
EAT AND RUN, 1986
EGGHEAD'S ROBOT, 1970
ELECTRONIC MONSTER, THE, 1960
ELEMENT OF CRIME, THE, 1984
ELIMINATORS, 1986
EMBRYO, 1976
EMPIRE OF THE ANTS, 1977
EMPIRE STRIKES BACK, THE, 1980
END OF AUGUST AT THE HOTEL OZONE, THE, 1967
END OF THE WORLD, THE, 1930
END OF THE WORLD, 1977
ENEMY FROM SPACE, 1957

ENEMY MINE, 1985
ESCAPE FROM NEW YORK, 1981
ESCAPE FROM THE BRONX, 1985
ESCAPE FROM THE PLANET OF THE APES, 1971
ESCAPE TO WITCH MOUNTAIN, 1975
EVILS OF THE NIGHT, 1985
EXPLORERS, 1985
EXTERMINATORS OF THE YEAR 3000, THE, 1985
EYE CREATURES, THE, 1965
FAHRENHEIT 451, 1966
FANTASTIC COMEDY, A, 1975
FANTASTIC PLANET, 1973
FANTASTIC VOYAGE, 1966
FIEND WITHOUT A FACE, 1958
FINAL EXECUTIONER, THE, 1986
FIRE MAIDENS FROM OUTER SPACE, 1956
FIREBIRD 2015 AD, 1981
FIRST MAN INTO SPACE, 1959
FIRST MEN IN THE MOON, 1964
FIRST SPACESHIP ON VENUS, 1960
FIVE MILLION YEARS TO EARTH, 1968
FLAME BARRIER, THE, 1958
FLASH GORDON, 1936
FLASH GORDON, 1980
FLIGHT THAT DISAPPEARED, THE, 1961
FLIGHT TO FAME, 1938
FLIGHT TO MARS, 1951
FLY, THE, 1958
FLY, THE, 1986
FLYING SAUCER, THE, 1950
FOES, 1977
FORBIDDEN PLANET, 1956
FORBIDDEN WORLD, 1982
FORBIDDEN ZONE, 1980
FORCE BEYOND, THE, 1978
FOUR SIDED TRIANGLE, 1953
4D MAN, 1959
FRANKENSTEIN CONQUERS THE WORLD, 1964
FRANKENSTEIN MEETS THE SPACE MONSTER, 1965
FRIENDSHIP'S DEATH, 1988
FROM THE EARTH TO THE MOON, 1958
FUTURE-KILL, 1985
FUTUREWORLD, 1976
GALACTIC GIGOLO, 1988
GALAXINA, 1980
GALAXY EXPRESS, 1982
GALAXY OF TERROR, 1981
GAMERA THE INVINCIBLE, 1966
GAMERA VERSUS BARUGON, 1966
GAMERA VERSUS GAOS, 1967
GAMERA VERSUS GUIRON, 1969
GAMERA VERSUS MONSTER K, 1970
GAMERA VERSUS VIRAS, 1968
GAMERA VERSUS ZIGRA, 1971
GAMMA PEOPLE, THE, 1956
GAPPA THE TRIFIBIAN MONSTER, 1967
GHIDRAH, THE THREE-HEADED MONSTER, 1965
GHOST PATROL, 1936
GHOSTBUSTERS, 1984
GIANT CLAW, THE, 1957
GIANT GILA MONSTER, THE, 1959
GIANT SPIDER INVASION, THE, 1975
GIGANTES PLANETARIOS, 1965
GIGANTIS, 1959
GIRARA, 1967
GIRL FROM STARSHIP VENUS, THE, 1975
GLADIATORS, THE, 1970
GLITTERBALL, THE, 1977
GODZILLA 1985, 1985
GODZILLA, RING OF THE MONSTERS, 1956
GODZILLA VERSUS THE COSMIC MONSTER, 1974
GODZILLA VERSUS THE SEA MONSTER, 1966
GODZILLA VERSUS THE SMOG MONSTER, 1972
GODZILLA VS. MEGALON, 1976
GODZILLA VS. THE THING, 1964
GODZILLA'S REVENGE, 1969
GOG, 1954
GOKE, BODYSNATCHER FROM HELL, 1968
GOLEM, 1980
GORATH, 1964
GORGO, 1961
GREAT BIG WORLD AND LITTLE CHILDREN, THE, 1962
GREEN SLIME, THE, 1969
GULLIVER'S TRAVELS BEYOND THE MOON, 1966

H-MAN, THE, 1959
HALF HUMAN, 1955
HAND OF DEATH, 1962
HANDS OF STEEL, 1986
HANGAR 18, 1980
HAVE ROCKET, WILL TRAVEL, 1959
HEARTBEEPS, 1981
HEAVY METAL, 1981
HELL COMES TO FROGTOWN, 1988
HELP I'M INVISIBLE, 1952
HIDDEN, THE, 1987
HIDEOUS SUN DEMON, THE, 1959
HIGH TREASON, 1929
HORROR OF THE BLOOD MONSTERS, 1970
HORROR PLANET, 1982
HU-MAN, 1975
HUMAN DUPLICATORS, THE, 1965
HUMAN VAPOR, THE, 1964
HUMANOID, THE, 1979
HYPERBOLOID OF ENGINEER GARIN, THE, 1965
I HATE MY BODY, 1975
I KILLED EINSTEIN, GENTLEMEN, 1970
I MARRIED A MONSTER FROM OUTER SPACE, 1958
ICE PIRATES, THE, 1984
IDAHO TRANSFER, 1975
IDEAL LODGER, THE, 1957
ILLUSTRATED MAN, THE, 1969
IN THE YEAR 2889, 1966
INCREDIBLE INVASION, THE, 1971
INCREDIBLE MELTING MAN, THE, 1978
INCREDIBLE PETRIFIED WORLD, THE, 1959
INCREDIBLE SHRINKING MAN, THE, 1957
INCREDIBLE SHRINKING WOMAN, THE, 1981
INCREDIBLE TWO-HEADED TRANSPLANT, THE, 1971
INDESTRUCTIBLE MAN, THE, 1956
INFRA-MAN, 1975
INVADERS FROM MARS, 1953
INVADERS FROM MARS, 1986
INVASION, 1965
INVASION OF THE ANIMAL PEOPLE, 1962
INVASION OF THE BEE GIRLS, 1973
INVASION OF THE BODY SNATCHERS, 1956
INVASION OF THE BODY SNATCHERS, 1978
INVASION OF THE SAUCER MEN, 1957
INVASION OF THE STAR CREATURES, 1962
INVISIBLE AGENT, 1942
INVISIBLE BOY, THE, 1957
INVISIBLE DR. MABUSE, THE, 1965
INVISIBLE INVADERS, 1959
INVISIBLE KID, THE, 1988
INVISIBLE MAN, THE, 1933
INVISIBLE MAN, THE, 1958
INVISIBLE MAN, THE, 1963
INVISIBLE MAN RETURNS, THE, 1940
INVISIBLE MAN'S REVENGE, 1944
INVISIBLE RAY, THE, 1936
INVISIBLE WOMAN, THE, 1941
ISLAND CLAWS, 1981
ISLAND OF DR. MOREAU, THE, 1977
ISLAND OF LOST SOULS, 1933
ISLAND OF TERROR, 1967
ISLAND OF THE BURNING DAMNED, 1971
IT CAME FROM BENEATH THE SEA, 1955
IT CAME FROM OUTER SPACE, 1953
IT CONQUERED THE WORLD, 1956
IT FELL FROM THE SKY, 1980
IT! THE TERROR FROM BEYOND SPACE, 1958
IT'S ALIVE, 1968
IT'S GREAT TO BE ALIVE, 1933
JE T'AIME, JE T'AIME, 1972
JOURNEY BENEATH THE DESERT, 1967
JOURNEY TO THE BEGINNING OF TIME, 1966
JOURNEY TO THE CENTER OF THE EARTH, 1959
JOURNEY TO THE CENTER OF TIME, 1967
JOURNEY TO THE FAR SIDE OF THE SUN, 1969
JOURNEY TO THE SEVENTH PLANET, 1962
JUST IMAGINE, 1930
KADOYNG, 1974
KAMIKAZE '89, 1983
KILLER KLOWNS FROM OUTER SPACE, 1988
KILLER SHREWS, THE, 1959
KILLERS FROM SPACE, 1954
KINDRED, THE, 1987
KING DINOSAUR, 1955

KING KONG ESCAPES, 1968
KING KONG VERSUS GODZILLA, 1963
KING OF THE STREETS, 1986
KONGA, 1961
KRAKATIT, 1948
KRONOS, 1957
LA NAVE DE LOS MONSTRUOS, 1959
LAND OF DOOM, 1986
LASERBLAST, 1978
LAST CHASE, THE, 1981
LAST DAYS OF MAN ON EARTH, THE, 1975
LAST MAN, THE, 1968
LAST STARFIGHTER, THE, 1984
LAST WAR, THE, 1962
LAST WOMAN ON EARTH, THE, 1960
LATITUDE ZERO, 1969
LE DERNIER COMBAT, 1984
LE GENDARME ET LES EXTRATERRESTRES, 1978
LE MONDE TREMBLERA, 1939
LES MAITRES DU TEMPS, 1982
LIFEFORCE, 1985
LIFESPAN, 1975
LIFT, THE, 1983
LIGHT YEARS, 1988
LIGHT YEARS AWAY, 1982
LIQUID SKY, 1982
LOGAN'S RUN, 1976
LOOKER, 1981
LOS ASTRONAUTAS, 1960
LOS AUTOMATAS DE LA MUERTE, 1960
LOS INVISIBLES, 1961
LOS PLATILLOS VOLADORES, 1955
LOSS OF FEELING, 1935
LOST CONTINENT, 1951
LOST FACE, THE, 1965
LOST MISSILE, THE, 1958
MAD MAX BEYOND THUNDERDOME, 1985
MAGNETIC MONSTER, THE, 1953
MALEVIL, 1981
MAN FROM PLANET X, THE, 1951
MAN FROM THE FIRST CENTURY, THE, 1961
MAN MADE MONSTER, 1941
MAN WHO FELL TO EARTH, THE, 1976
MAN WHO LIVED AGAIN, THE, 1936
MAN WHO THOUGHT LIFE, THE, 1969
MAN WITH NINE LIVES, THE, 1940
MAN WITH THE TRANSPLANTED BRAIN, THE, 1972
MAN WITHOUT A BODY, THE, 1957
MANSTER, THE, 1962
MAROONED, 1969
MARS NEEDS WOMEN, 1966
MARTIAN IN PARIS, A, 1961
MASTER OF THE WORLD, 1935
MEGAFORCE, 1982
MEMOIRS OF A SURVIVOR, 1981
MESA OF LOST WOMEN, THE, 1956
MESSAGE FROM SPACE, 1978
METALSTORM: THE DESTRUCTION OF JARED-SYN, 1983
METEOR, 1979
MIND BENDERS, THE, 1963
MIND OF MR. SOAMES, THE, 1970
MISSILE TO THE MOON, 1959
MISSION GALACTICA: THE CYLON ATTACK, 1979
MISSION MARS, 1968
MISSION STARDUST, 1968
MISTRESS OF THE WORLD, 1959
MOLE PEOPLE, THE, 1956
MONITORS, THE, 1969
MONOLITH MONSTERS, THE, 1957
MONSTER A GO-GO, 1965
MONSTER FROM THE GREEN HELL, 1958
MONSTER FROM THE OCEAN FLOOR, THE, 1954
MONSTER IN THE CLOSET, 1987
MONSTER ON THE CAMPUS, 1958
MONSTER SHARK, 1986
MONSTER THAT CHALLENGED THE WORLD, THE, 1957
MONSTER WANGMAGWI, 1967
MONSTER ZERO, 1970
MONSTERS FROM THE UNKNOWN PLANET, 1975
MOON PILOT, 1962
MOON ZERO TWO, 1970
MOONCHILD, 1972
MORONS FROM OUTER SPACE, 1985
MOSCOW—CASSIOPEIA, 1974

BOLD: Films on Videocassette

MOST DANGEROUS MAN ALIVE, THE, 1961
MOTHRA, 1962
MUTANT HUNT, 1987
MUTINY IN OUTER SPACE, 1965
MY SCIENCE PROJECT, 1985
MY STEPMOTHER IS AN ALIEN, 1988
MYSTERIANS, THE, 1959
MYSTERIOUS ISLAND, 1929
MYSTERIOUS ISLAND, 1941
MYSTERIOUS ISLAND, 1961
MYSTERIOUS ISLAND OF CAPTAIN NEMO, THE, 1973
MYSTERIOUS SATELLITE, THE, 1956
N. P., 1971
NAVY VS. THE NIGHT MONSTERS, THE, 1966
NEON MANIACS, 1986
NEPTUNE FACTOR, THE, 1973
NEUTRON CONTRA EL DR. CARONTE, 1962
NEUTRON EL ENMASCARADO NEGRO, 1962
NEW BARBARIANS, THE, 1983
NEXT ONE, THE, 1982
NIGHT OF THE BLOOD BEAST, 1958
NIGHT OF THE BLOODY APES, 1968
NIGHT OF THE COMET, 1984
NIGHT OF THE CREEPS, 1986
NIGHT OF THE LEPUS, 1972
NIGHT THE WORLD EXPLODED, THE, 1957
NIGHTBEAST, 1982
NIGHTMARE CASTLE, 1966
NIGHTMARES, 1983
NO BLADE OF GRASS, 1970
NO SURVIVORS, PLEASE, 1963
NOT OF THIS EARTH, 1957
NOT OF THIS EARTH, 1988
NOW YOU SEE HIM, NOW YOU DON'T, 1972
OMEGA MAN, THE, 1971
OMICRON, 1963
ON THE COMET, 1970
ONCE IN A NEW MOON, 1935
OPERATION GANYMED, 1977
OSA, 1985
OUTLAND, 1981
PANIC IN YEAR ZERO!, 1962
PARADISE POUR TOUS, 1982
PARASITE, 1982
PERFECT WOMAN, THE, 1950
PHANTOM FROM SPACE, 1953
PHANTOM FROM 10,000 LEAGUES, THE, 1956
PHANTOM PLANET, THE, 1961
PHASE IV, 1974
PHILADELPHIA EXPERIMENT, THE, 1984
PIRANHA, 1978
PIRANHA II: THE SPAWNING, 1981
PLAGUE, 1978
PLAN 9 FROM OUTER SPACE, 1959
PLANET OF DINOSAURS, 1978
PLANET OF THE APES, 1968
PLANET OF THE VAMPIRES, 1965
PLANETS AGAINST US, THE, 1961
POPDOWN, 1968
POWER, THE, 1968
PRIMAL SCREAM, 1988
PRIVILEGE, 1967
PROJECT MOONBASE, 1953
PROJECT X, 1968
PROJECTED MAN, THE, 1967
PROPHECIES OF NOSTRADAMUS, 1974
PROPHECY, 1979
PSYCHOTRONIC MAN, THE, 1980
QUATERMASS CONCLUSION, 1980
QUEEN OF BLOOD, 1966
QUEEN OF OUTER SPACE, 1958
QUEST FOR LOVE, 1971
QUIET EARTH, THE, 1985
QUINTET, 1979
RABID, 1976
RADIOACTIVE DREAMS, 1986
RED PLANET MARS, 1952
RELUCTANT ASTRONAUT, THE, 1967
REMOTE CONTROL, 1988
REPO MAN, 1984
REPTILICUS, 1962
RESURRECTION OF ZACHARY WHEELER, THE, 1971
RETURN, THE, 1980
RETURN FROM WITCH MOUNTAIN, 1978

RETURN OF CAPTAIN INVINCIBLE, THE, 1983
RETURN OF THE FLY, 1959
RETURN OF THE JEDI, 1983
REVENGE OF THE CREATURE, 1955
REVENGE OF THE TEENAGE VIXENS FROM OUTER SPACE, THE, 1986
RIDERS OF THE STORM, 1988
RIDERS TO THE STARS, 1954
RIO 70, 1970
ROAD WARRIOR, THE, 1982
ROBINSON CRUSOE ON MARS, 1964
ROBOCOP, 1987
ROBOT HOLOCAUST, 1987
ROBOT MONSTER, 1953
ROBOT VS. THE AZTEC MUMMY, THE, 1965
ROCKET MAN, THE, 1954
ROCKET TO NOWHERE, 1962
ROCKETSHIP X-M, 1950
RODAN, 1958
ROLLER BLADE, 1986
ROLLERBALL, 1975
RUNAWAY, 1984
RUNNING MAN, THE, 1987
RUSH, 1984
SAGA OF THE VIKING WOMEN AND THEIR VOYAGE TO THE WATERS OF THE GREAT SEA SERPENT, THE, 1957
SANTA CLAUS CONQUERS THE MARTIANS, 1964
SANTO CONTRA LA INVASION DE LOS MARCIANOS, 1966
SATAN BUG, THE, 1965
SATAN'S SATELLITES, 1958
SATELLITE IN THE SKY, 1956
SATURN 3, 1980
SCARED TO DEATH, 1981
SCHLOCK, 1973
SCREAMERS, 1978
SECRET OF THE TELEGIAN, THE, 1961
SEED OF MAN, THE, 1970
SHAPE OF THINGS TO COME, THE, 1979
SHIRLEY THOMPSON VERSUS THE ALIENS, 1968
SIGNALS-AN ADVENTURE IN SPACE, 1970
SILENCE OF DR. EVANS, THE, 1973
SILENT RUNNING, 1972
SIX HOURS TO LIVE, 1932
SKY CALLS, THE, 1959
SLAPSTICK OF ANOTHER KIND, 1984
SLAUGHTERHOUSE-FIVE, 1972
SLEEPER, 1973
SLIME PEOPLE, THE, 1963
SLITHIS, 1978
SNOW CREATURE, THE, 1954
SNOW DEVILS, THE, 1965
SOLARBABIES, 1986
SOLARIS, 1972
SOYLENT GREEN, 1973
SPACE AMOEBA, THE, 1970
SPACE CHILDREN, THE, 1958
SPACE CRUISER, 1977
SPACE FIREBIRD 2772, 1979
SPACE MASTER X-7, 1958
SPACE MONSTER, 1965
SPACE RAGE, 1987
SPACE RAIDERS, 1983
SPACE SHIP, THE, 1935
SPACED OUT, 1981
SPACEFLIGHT IC-1, 1965
SPACEHUNTER: ADVENTURES IN THE FORBIDDEN ZONE, 1983
SPACEWAYS, 1953
SPIDER, THE, 1958
STALKER, 1982
STAR CRYSTAL, 1986
STAR INSPECTOR, THE, 1980
STAR PILOT, 1977
STAR SLAMMER: THE ESCAPE, 1988
STAR TREK IV: THE VOYAGE HOME, 1986
STAR TREK: THE MOTION PICTURE, 1979
STAR TREK III: THE SEARCH FOR SPOCK, 1984
STAR TREK II: THE WRATH OF KHAN, 1982
STAR WARS, 1977
STARCHASER: THE LEGEND OF ORIN, 1985
STARCRASH, 1979
STARMAN, 1984
STARSHIP INVASIONS, 1978
STEPFORD WIVES, THE, 1975
STEREO, 1969

STING OF DEATH, 1966
STORM PLANET, 1962
STORY OF MANKIND, THE, 1957
STRANDED, 1987
STRANGE INVADERS, 1983
STRANGER FROM VENUS, THE, 1954
STRYKER, 1983
STUFF, THE, 1985
SUPERARGO, 1968
SUPERARGO VERSUS DIABOLICUS, 1966
SUPERBEAST, 1972
SUPERMAN, 1978
SUPERMAN AND THE MOLE MEN, 1951
SUPERMAN II, 1980
SUPERMAN III, 1983
SUPERNATURALS, THE, 1987
SUPERSONIC MAN, 1979
TAKING TIGER MOUNTAIN, 1983
TARANTULA, 1955
TARGET EARTH, 1954
TEENAGE CAVEMAN, 1958
TEENAGERS FROM OUTER SPACE, 1959
TEENAGERS IN SPACE, 1975
TENTH VICTIM, THE, 1965
TERMINAL MAN, THE, 1974
TERMINATOR, THE, 1984
TERROR BENEATH THE SEA, 1966
TERROR FROM THE YEAR 5,000, 1958
TERRORNAUTS, THE, 1967
TERRORVISION, 1986
TEST OF PILOT PIRX, THE, 1978
THEM!, 1954
THESE ARE THE DAMNED, 1965
THEY CALL ME ROBERT, 1967
THEY CAME FROM BEYOND SPACE, 1967
THEY LIVE, 1988
THEY SAVED HITLER'S BRAIN, 1964
THING, THE, 1951
THING, THE, 1982
THINGS TO COME, 1936
THIRTY FOOT BRIDE OF CANDY ROCK, THE, 1959
THIS IS NOT A TEST, 1962
THIS ISLAND EARTH, 1955
THOSE FANTASTIC FLYING FOOLS, 1967
THOUSAND EYES OF DR. MABUSE, THE, 1960
THREE STOOGES IN ORBIT, THE, 1962
THUNDERBIRD 6, 1968
THUNDERBIRDS ARE GO, 1968
THX 1138, 1971
TIME AFTER TIME, 1979
TIME FLIES, 1944
TIME MACHINE, THE, 1963
TIME OF ROSES, 1970
TIME SLIP, 1981
TIME TRAVELERS, THE, 1964
TIME WALKER, 1982
TIMERIDER, 1983
TIMES TO COME, 1988
TIN GIRL, THE, 1970
TOBOR THE GREAT, 1954
TOOMORROW, 1970
TOTO IN THE MOON, 1957
TRACK OF THE MOONBEAST, 1976
TRANCERS, 1985
TRANSATLANTIC TUNNEL, 1935
TRANSFORMERS: THE MOVIE, THE, 1986
TROG, 1970
TRON, 1982
TWELVE-HANDED MEN OF MARS, THE, 1964
TWELVE TO THE MOON, 1960
20 MILLION MILES TO EARTH, 1957
27TH DAY, THE, 1957
20,000 LEAGUES UNDER THE SEA, 1954
TWILIGHT ZONE—THE MOVIE, 1983
2001: A SPACE ODYSSEY, 1968
2010, 1984
2020 TEXAS GLADIATORS, 1985
TWONKY, THE, 1953
UFO: TARGET EARTH, 1974
UFORIA, 1985
ULTIMATE WARRIOR, THE, 1975
UNDERWATER CITY, THE, 1962
UNEARTHLY STRANGER, THE, 1964
UNIDENTIFIED FLYING ODDBALL, THE, 1979
UNKNOWN WORLD, 1951
UNTAMED WOMEN, 1952

VALLEY OF THE DRAGONS, 1961
VILLAGE OF THE DAMNED, 1960
VILLAGE OF THE GIANTS, 1965
VIRUS, 1980
VISIT TO A SMALL PLANET, 1960
VOYAGE TO THE BOTTOM OF THE SEA, 1961
VOYAGE TO THE END OF THE UNIVERSE, 1963
VOYAGE TO THE PLANET OF PREHISTORIC
   WOMEN, 1966
VOYAGE TO THE PREHISTORIC PLANET, 1965
WACKY WORLD OF DR. MORGUS, THE, 1962
WALKING DEAD, THE, 1936
WAR BETWEEN THE PLANETS, 1971
WAR OF THE COLOSSAL BEAST, 1958
WAR OF THE GARGANTUAS, THE, 1970
WAR OF THE MONSTERS, 1972
WAR OF THE PLANETS, 1977
WAR OF THE SATELLITES, 1958
WAR OF THE WIZARDS, 1983
WAR OF THE WORLDS—NEXT CENTURY, THE, 1981
WAR OF THE WORLDS, THE, 1953
WARLORDS OF ATLANTIS, 1978
WARRIORS OF THE WASTELAND, 1984
WARRIORS OF THE WIND, 1984
WASP WOMAN, THE, 1959
WATCHER IN THE WOODS, THE, 1980
WAVELENGTH, 1983
WAY…WAY OUT, 1966
WEIRD ONES, THE, 1962
WEIRD SCIENCE, 1985
WELCOME TO BLOOD CITY, 1977
WESTWORLD, 1973
WHAT WOULD YOU SAY TO SOME SPINACH, 1976
WHEN WORLDS COLLIDE, 1951
WHO?, 1975
WILD WOMEN OF WONGO, THE, 1959
WILD WORLD OF BATWOMAN, THE, 1966
WILD, WILD PLANET, THE, 1967
WILLIE MCBEAN AND HIS MAGIC MACHINE, 1965
WINDOWS OF TIME, THE, 1969
WIRED TO KILL, 1986
WITHOUT WARNING, 1980
WIZARD OF MARS, 1964
WIZARDS, 1977
WOLF'S HOLE, 1987
WOMEN OF THE PREHISTORIC PLANET, 1966
WORLD, THE FLESH, AND THE DEVIL, THE, 1959
WORLD WITHOUT A MASK, THE, 1934
WORLD WITHOUT END, 1956
"X"—THE MAN WITH THE X-RAY EYES, 1963
X THE UNKNOWN, 1957
XTRO, 1983
YOG-MONSTER FROM SPACE, 1970
YONGKARI MONSTER FROM THE DEEP, 1967
YOR, THE HUNTER FROM THE FUTURE, 1983
ZARDOZ, 1974
ZONTAR, THE THING FROM VENUS, 1966
Z.P.G., 1972

Spy

ABOVE SUSPICION, 1943
ACCURSED, THE, 1958
ACROSS THE PACIFIC, 1942
ACTION IN ARABIA, 1944
ADVENTURES OF TARTU, THE, 1943
ADVENTURESS, THE, 1946
AFFAIR IN TRINIDAD, 1952
AFTER TONIGHT, 1933
AGAINST THE WIND, 1948
AGENT 8 3/4, 1963
AGENT FOR H.A.R.M., 1966
ALASKA PATROL, 1949
ALL THROUGH THE NIGHT, 1942
AMBUSHERS, THE, 1967
AMONG HUMAN WOLVES, 1940
ANGRY HILLS, THE, 1959
ARABESQUE, 1966
ARMORED COMMAND, 1961
ASSASSIN, 1973
ASSAULT ON AGATHON, 1976
ASSIGNMENT IN BRITTANY, 1943
ASSIGNMENT K, 1968
ASSIGNMENT—PARIS, 1952
AT DAWN WE DIE, 1943
AVALANCHE EXPRESS, 1979
BACK DOOR TO HELL, 1964

BACK ROOM BOY, 1942
BACKGROUND TO DANGER, 1943
BALLOON GOES UP, THE, 1942
BANG, BANG, YOU'RE DEAD, 1966
BERLIN CORRESPONDENT, 1942
BILLION DOLLAR BRAIN, 1967
BIONIC BOY, THE, 1977
BLACK DRAGONS, 1942
BLACK PARACHUTE, THE, 1944
BLACK WINDMILL, THE, 1974
BLINDFOLD, 1966
BLONDE FROM PEKING, THE, 1968
BODY AND SOUL, 1931
BOMBAY CLIPPER, 1942
BOWERY BATTALION, 1951
BREAKING POINT, THE, 1961
BRITISH AGENT, 1934
BRITISH INTELLIGENCE, 1940
BULLET FOR JOEY, A, 1955
BUSSES ROAR, 1942
CAFE COLETTE, 1937
CAIRO, 1942
CALLAN, 1975
CALLING ALL MARINES, 1939
CALLING PHILO VANCE, 1940
CANDLELIGHT IN ALGERIA, 1944
CAPETOWN AFFAIR, 1967
CAPTAIN CAREY, U.S.A, 1950
CAPTURE THAT CAPSULE, 1961
CAREFUL, SOFT SHOULDERS, 1942
CARRY ON SPYING, 1964
CARVE HER NAME WITH PRIDE, 1958
CASE OF THE 44'S, THE, 1964
CASE OF THE RED MONKEY, 1955
CASINO ROYALE, 1967
CAT BURGLAR, THE, 1961
CATCH ME A SPY, 1971
CHARGE OF THE LANCERS, 1953
CIPHER BUREAU, 1938
CIRCLE OF DECEPTON, 1961
CITY OF FEAR, 1965
CLOAK AND DAGGER, 1946
CLOSE-UP, 1948
CLOUDS OVER EUROPE, 1939
CODE NAME: EMERALD, 1985
COME SPY WITH ME, 1967
CONFESSIONS OF A NAZI SPY, 1939
CONFIDENTIAL AGENT, 1945
CONSPIRACY IN TEHERAN, 1948
CONSPIRATOR, 1949
CONSPIRATORS, THE, 1944
CONTINENTAL EXPRESS, 1939
COUNTER BLAST, 1948
COUNTER-ESPIONAGE, 1942
COUNTERFEIT TRAITOR, THE, 1962
COUNTERSPY MEETS SCOTLAND YARD, 1950
COVERT ACTION, 1980
CRACK-UP, THE, 1937
CROOKED BILLET, THE, 1930
CROSS-UP, 1958
CROSSPLOT, 1969
CROSSROADS OF PASSION, 1951
CROUCHING BEAST, THE, 1936
CUBA CROSSING, 1980
DANDY IN ASPIC, A, 1968
DANGER IN THE PACIFIC, 1942
DANGER ROUTE, 1968
DANGEROUSLY THEY LIVE, 1942
DANIELLA BY NIGHT, 1962
DARK JOURNEY, 1937
DARLING LILI, 1970
DAVID HARDING, COUNTERSPY, 1950
DAWN EXPRESS, THE, 1942
DAY THE HOTLINE GOT HOT, THE, 1968
DEAD MAN'S EVIDENCE, 1962
DEAD RUN, 1961
DEADLY AFFAIR, THE, 1967
DEADLY DECOYS, THE, 1962
DEADLY NIGHTSHADE, 1953
DEADLY TRAP, THE, 1972
DECISION BEFORE DAWN, 1951
DEFECTOR, THE, 1966
DESERT OF THE TARTARS, THE, 1976
DESTRUCTORS, THE, 1968
DEVIL'S AGENT, THE, 1962
DEVIL'S JEST, THE, 1954

DIAMONDS ARE FOREVER, 1971
DIPLOMATIC CORPSE, THE, 1958
DIPLOMATIC COURIER, 1952
DIRTY GAME, THE, 1966
DISHONORED, 1931
DR. NO, 1962
**DON'T RAISE THE BRIDGE, LOWER THE RIVER,
1968**
DON'T WORRY, WE'LL THINK OF A TITLE, 1966
DOUBLE CRIME IN THE MAGINOT LINE, 1939
DOUBLE CROSS, 1956
DOUBLE MAN, THE, 1967
EAGLE OVER LONDON, 1973
ECHO OF DIANA, 1963
EMBASSY, 1972
EMPEROR'S CANDLESTICKS, THE, 1937
ENEMY AGENT, 1940
ENIGMA, 1983
ESCAPE FROM HONG KONG, 1942
ESCAPE FROM TERROR, 1960
ESCAPE TO DANGER, 1943
ESPIONAGE AGENT, 1939
EXECUTIONER, THE, 1970
EXTERMINATORS, THE, 1965
EYE OF THE NEEDLE, 1981
FACE IN THE RAIN, A, 1963
FALCON AND THE SNOWMAN, THE, 1985
FALCON'S BROTHER, THE, 1942
FALLEN SPARROW, THE, 1943
FATAL HOUR, THE, 1937
FATHOM, 1967
FEDERAL AGENT, 1936
FEDERAL FUGITIVES, 1941
FIVE FINGERS, 1952
FIVE GRAVES TO CAIRO, 1943
FIVE STEPS TO DANGER, 1957
FLAME OF STAMBOUL, 1957
FLIGHT TO NOWHERE, 1946
FLYING BLIND, 1941
FOR YOUR EYES ONLY, 1981
FORBIDDEN JOURNEY, 1950
FOREIGN AGENT, 1942
FOREIGN CORRESPONDENT, 1940
FOREIGN INTRIGUE, 1956
FORT ALGIERS, 1953
48 HOURS TO LIVE, 1960
FORTY-NINTH MAN, THE, 1953
FOURTH PROTOCOL, THE, 1987
FOXHOLE IN CAIRO, 1960
FRAULEIN DOKTOR, 1969
FRIEND WILL COME TONIGHT, A, 1948
FROM RUSSIA WITH LOVE, 1963
FUNERAL IN BERLIN, 1966
FUR COLLAR, THE, 1962
GAY DIPLOMAT, THE, 1931
GIRL WHO KNEW TOO MUCH, THE, 1969
GOLDEN LADY, THE, 1979
GOLDFINGER, 1964
GOOSE STEPS OUT, THE, 1942
GORILLA GREETS YOU, THE, 1958
GORILLA MAN, 1942
GOTCHA!, 1985
GREAT ARMORED CAR SWINDLE, THE, 1964
GREAT IMPERSONATION, THE, 1935
GREAT IMPERSONATION, THE, 1942
GREAT SPY CHASE, THE, 1966
GROUNDSTAR CONSPIRACY, THE, 1972
GUILTY MELODY, 1936
GUNS IN THE HEATHER, 1968
HAMMERHEAD, 1968
HELICOPTER SPIES, THE, 1968
HIGH COMMISSIONER, THE, 1968
HIGH TREASON, 1937
HIGH TREASON, 1951
HIGHLY DANGEROUS, 1950
HIGHWAY TO BATTLE, 1961
HILLBILLY BLITZKRIEG, 1942
HITLER—DEAD OR ALIVE, 1942
HOLCROFT COVENANT, THE, 1985
HOPSCOTCH, 1980
HOTEL BERLIN, 1945
HOTEL RESERVE, 1946
HOUR BEFORE THE DAWN, THE, 1944
HOUR OF THE ASSASSIN, 1987
HOUSE OF A THOUSAND CANDLES, THE, 1936
HOUSE OF INTRIGUE, THE, 1959

BOLD: Films on Videocassette

HOUSE OF STRANGE LOVES, THE, 1969
HOUSE ON 92ND STREET, THE, 1945
HUMAN FACTOR, THE, 1979
I ESCAPED FROM THE GESTAPO, 1943
I MARRIED A SPY, 1938
I SPY, 1933
I WAS A SPY, 1934
I WAS AN AMERICAN SPY, 1951
ICE STATION ZEBRA, 1968
I'LL GET YOU, 1953
IN LIKE FLINT, 1967
INNOCENT BYSTANDERS, 1973
INSIDE THE LINES, 1930
INTERNATIONAL LADY, 1941
INVISIBLE AGENT, 1942
IPCRESS FILE, THE, 1965
IRON CURTAIN, THE, 1948
IT HAPPENED IN GIBRALTAR, 1943
ITALIAN SECRET SERVICE, 1968
JET PILOT, 1957
JEWELS OF BRANDENBURG, 1947
JIGSAW MAN, THE, 1984
JOE SMITH, AMERICAN, 1942
JOURNEY INTO FEAR, 1942
JOURNEY INTO FEAR, 1976
JOURNEY TO FREEDOM, 1957
KARATE KILLERS, THE, 1967
KISS THE GIRLS AND MAKE THEM DIE, 1967
KNOCK ON WOOD, 1954
KREMLIN LETTER, THE, 1970
LADY FROM LISBON, 1942
LADY HAS PLANS, THE, 1942
LADY VANISHES, THE, 1938
LADY VANISHES, THE, 1980
LANCER SPY, 1937
LASSITER, 1984
LIGHTNING CONDUCTOR, 1938
LIMBO LINE, THE, 1969
LIQUIDATOR, THE, 1966
LISBON STORY, THE, 1946
LITTLE DRUMMER GIRL, THE, 1984
LITTLE NIKITA, 1988
LITTLE TOKYO, U.S.A., 1942
LIVE AND LET DIE, 1973
LIVING DAYLIGHTS, THE, 1987
LONG SHADOW, THE, 1961
LOOKING GLASS WAR, THE, 1970
LUCKY DEVILS, 1941
MACKINTOSH MAN, THE, 1973
MAD MEN OF EUROPE, 1940
MADAME SPY, 1934
MADAME SPY, 1942
MAIL TRAIN, 1941
MAN ABOUT TOWN, 1932
MAN AT LARGE, 1941
MAN BETWEEN, THE, 1953
MAN CALLED DAGGER, A, 1967
MAN COULD GET KILLED, A, 1966
MAN HUNT, 1941
MAN ON A STRING, 1960
MAN OUTSIDE, THE, 1968
MAN WHO NEVER WAS, THE, 1956
MAN WHO WASN'T THERE, THE, 1983
MAN WHO WOULDN'T TALK, THE, 1958
MAN WITH ONE RED SHOE, THE, 1985
MAN WITH THE GOLDEN GUN, THE, 1974
MANY TANKS MR. ATKINS, 1938
MARATHON MAN, 1976
MARIE GALANTE, 1934
MASK OF DIMITRIOS, THE, 1944
MASTER PLAN, THE, 1955
MASTER SPY, 1964
MASTERMIND, 1977
MATA HARI, 1931
MATA HARI, 1965
MATA HARI, 1985
MATA HARI'S DAUGHTER, 1954
MATCHLESS, 1967
MC GUIRE, GO HOME!, 1966
MEET BOSTON BLACKIE, 1941
MEN OF THE SKY, 1931
MEXICAN SPITFIRE SEES A GHOST, 1942
MILITARY SECRET, 1945
MILLION DOLLAR MANHUNT, 1962
MILLION EYES OF SU-MURU, THE, 1967
MIND BENDERS, THE, 1963

MINISTRY OF FEAR, 1945
MISS V FROM MOSCOW, 1942
MISSING TEN DAYS, 1941
MISSION BLOODY MARY, 1967
MISSION STARDUST, 1968
MR. DYNAMITE, 1941
MR. POTTS GOES TO MOSCOW, 1953
MR. WONG IN CHINATOWN, 1939
MISTRESS OF THE WORLD, 1959
MODESTY BLAISE, 1966
MOONRAKER, 1979
MORITURI, 1965
MRS. POLLIFAX-SPY, 1971
MURDER AT SITE THREE, 1959
MURDER IN THE AIR, 1940
MURDER IN THE CLOUDS, 1934
MY FAVORITE BLONDE, 1942
MY FAVORITE SPY, 1942
MY FAVORITE SPY, 1951
NAKED RUNNER, THE, 1967
NATHALIE, AGENT SECRET, 1960
NAVY BLUES, 1937
NAVY SECRETS, 1939
NAVY SPY, 1937
NEVER SAY NEVER AGAIN, 1983
NEVER TOO YOUNG TO DIE, 1986
NEXT MAN, THE, 1976
NIGHT BOAT TO DUBLIN, 1946
NIGHT ENCOUNTER, 1963
NIGHT INVADER, THE, 1943
NIGHT OF THE FULL MOON, THE, 1954
NIGHT TRAIN, 1940
NIGHT TRAIN TO PARIS, 1964
NIGHTMARE, 1942
NO ROSES FOR OSS 117, 1968
NORTH BY NORTHWEST, 1959
NORTH SEA PATROL, 1939
NORTHERN PURSUIT, 1943
NOTORIOUS, 1946
NUDE BOMB, THE, 1980
OCTOPUSSY, 1983
ODETTE, 1951
ON HER MAJESTY'S SECRET SERVICE, 1969
ONE NIGHT IN LISBON, 1941
ONE OF OUR SPIES IS MISSING, 1966
ONE SPY TOO MANY, 1966
OPERATION CIA, 1965
OPERATION CONSPIRACY, 1957
OPERATION KID BROTHER, 1967
O.S.S., 1946
OSS 117—MISSION FOR A KILLER, 1966
OTLEY, 1969
OUR MAN FLINT, 1966
OUT OF SIGHT, 1966
PANAMA PATROL, 1939
PARADISIO, 1962
PASSENGER TO LONDON, 1937
PASSPORT TO ALCATRAZ, 1940
PASSPORT TO CHINA, 1961
PASSPORT TO SUEZ, 1943
PAUL TEMPLE'S TRIUMPH, 1951
PERIL FOR THE GUY, 1956
PERMISSION TO KILL, 1975
PHANTOM PLAINSMEN, THE, 1942
PHYNX, THE, 1970
PICKUP ON SOUTH STREET, 1953
PIMPERNEL SMITH, 1942
PINK JUNGLE, THE, 1968
POWDER TOWN, 1942
PRESIDENT'S ANALYST, THE, 1967
PRIDE OF THE ARMY, 1942
PRISON BREAKER, 1936
PRISONER OF JAPAN, 1942
PRIZE, THE, 1963
PROJECT: KILL, 1976
PROJECT M7, 1953
PROJECT X, 1949
PROTECTORS, BOOK 1, THE, 1981
QUILLER MEMORANDUM, THE, 1966
RADAR SECRET SERVICE, 1950
RECORD 413, 1936
RED-DRAGON, 1967
RED SNOW, 1952
REDHEAD AND THE COWBOY, THE, 1950
REMO WILLIAMS: THE ADVENTURE BEGINS, 1985
RENDEZVOUS, 1935

RENDEZVOUS 24, 1946
RENEGADES, 1930
REQUIEM FOR A SECRET AGENT, 1966
RIDDLE OF THE SANDS, THE, 1984
RING OF SPIES, 1964
RIP ROARING RILEY, 1935
ROCKET ATTACK, U.S.A., 1961
ROGUES' REGIMENT, 1948
RUNAWAY, THE, 1964
SABOTAGE, 1937
SABOTAGE, 1939
SABOTAGE AT SEA, 1942
SABOTAGE SQUAD, 1942
SABOTEUR, 1942
SABRA, 1970
SALT & PEPPER, 1968
SALZBURG CONNECTION, THE, 1972
SCARLET COAT, THE, 1955
SCHOOL FOR DANGER, 1947
SCORPIO, 1973
SEBASTIAN, 1968
**SECOND BEST SECRET AGENT IN THE WHOLE
WIDE WORLD, THE, 1965**
SECOND BUREAU, 1936
SECOND BUREAU, 1937
SECRET AGENT, 1933
SECRET AGENT FIREBALL, 1965
SECRET AGENT OF JAPAN, 1942
SECRET AGENT SUPER DRAGON, 1966
SECRET AGENT, THE, 1936
SECRET COMMAND, 1944
SECRET DOCUMENT—VIENNA, 1954
SECRET DOOR, THE, 1964
SECRET ENEMIES, 1942
SECRET MAN, THE, 1958
SECRET MISSION, 1944
SECRET MISSION, 1949
SECRET OF BLOOD ISLAND, THE, 1965
SECRET VENTURE, 1955
SECRET VOICE, THE, 1936
SECRET WAYS, THE, 1961
SECRETS OF SCOTLAND YARD, 1944
SECRETS OF THE UNDERGROUND, 1943
SECURITY RISK, 1954
SEEDS OF DESTRUCTION, 1952
SELL OUT, THE, 1976
SENTENCED FOR LIFE, 1960
SERENADE FOR TWO SPIES, 1966
SERPENT, THE, 1973
SEVEN MILES FROM ALCATRAZ, 1942
SEVENTH SURVIVOR, THE, 1941
SHACK OUT ON 101, 1955
SHADOW OF FEAR, 1963
SHADOWS OVER SHANGHAI, 1938
SHANGHAI DRAMA, THE, 1945
SHANGHAI STORY, THE, 1954
SHARPSHOOTERS, 1938
SHIP AHOY, 1942
SHOOT FIRST, 1953
SHOOT TO KILL, 1961
SILENCERS, THE, 1966
SINGAPORE, SINGAPORE, 1969
SINGING COP, THE, 1938
SIROCCO, 1951
SKY HIGH, 1952
SKY LINER, 1949
SKY MURDER, 1940
SKY PARADE, 1936
SLEEPING CAR TO TRIESTE, 1949
SMASHING THE SPY RING, 1939
SOFIA, 1948
SOLDIER, THE, 1982
SOME GIRLS DO, 1969
SON OF A SAILOR, 1933
SONS OF THE SEA, 1939
SOUTH OF PANAMA, 1941
SOUTH OF THE BORDER, 1939
SPIDER AND THE FLY, THE, 1952
SPIES LIKE US, 1985
SPIES OF THE AIR, 1940
SPY FOR A DAY, 1939
SPY HUNT, 1950
SPY IN BLACK, THE, 1939
SPY IN THE GREEN HAT, THE, 1966
SPY IN THE SKY, 1958
SPY IN YOUR EYE, 1966

SPY OF NAPOLEON, 1939
SPY RING, THE, 1938
SPY SHIP, 1942
SPY TRAIN, 1943
SPY WHO CAME IN FROM THE COLD, THE, 1965
SPY WHO LOVED ME, THE, 1977
SPY WITH A COLD NOSE, THE, 1966
SPY WITH MY FACE, THE, 1966
SPYLARKS, 1965
S*P*Y*S, 1974
SQUADRON LEADER X, 1943
STAMBOUL QUEST, 1934
STATE DEPARTMENT—FILE 649, 1949
STEEL KEY, THE, 1953
STOPOVER TOKYO, 1957
STORM OVER LISBON, 1944
SUBMARINE ALERT, 1943
SUBTERFUGE, 1969
TAMARIND SEED, THE, 1974
TAMPICO, 1944
TANGIER, 1946
TANGIER INCIDENT, 1953
TELEFON, 1977
TELEVISION SPY, 1939
TEXAS MAN HUNT, 1942
THAT MAN IN ISTANBUL, 1966
THAT'S THE TICKET, 1940
THEY CAME TO BLOW UP AMERICA, 1943
THEY CAN'T HANG ME, 1955
THEY GOT ME COVERED, 1943
THEY MADE HER A SPY, 1939
THEY MET IN THE DARK, 1945
THEY SAVED HITLER'S BRAIN, 1964
THIEF, THE, 1952
THIRTEEN FRIGHTENED GIRLS, 1963
13 RUE MADELEINE, 1946
39 STEPS, THE, 1935
THIRTY NINE STEPS, THE, 1960
THIRTY NINE STEPS, THE, 1978
THIS GUN FOR HIRE, 1942
THIS MAD WORLD, 1930
THREE FACES EAST, 1930
THUNDERBALL, 1965
TIFFANY JONES, 1976
TILL WE MEET AGAIN, 1936
TIMBER, 1942
TO COMMIT A MURDER, 1970
TO TRAP A SPY, 1966
TOKYO FILE 212, 1951
TONIGHT WE RAID CALAIS, 1943
TOP SECRET!, 1984
TOPAZ, 1969
TORN CURTAIN, 1966
TORSO MURDER MYSTERY, THE, 1940
TRAITORS, THE, 1963
TRAPPED IN THE SKY, 1939 61m COL bw
TRIPLE CROSS, 1967
TRUNK TO CAIRO, 1966
TWO-HEADED SPY, THE, 1959
UNDER SECRET ORDERS, 1943
UNDER YOUR HAT, 1940
UNDERCOVER AGENT, 1935
UNDERGROUND, 1970
UNDERGROUND AGENT, 1942
UNKNOWN MAN OF SHANDIGOR, THE, 1967
UNSEEN ENEMY, 1942
UNWILLING AGENT, 1968
UNWRITTEN CODE, THE, 1944
VENETIAN AFFAIR, THE, 1967
VIEW TO A KILL, A, 1985
WACKY WORLD OF DR. MORGUS, THE, 1962
WALK A CROOKED MILE, 1948
WALK EAST ON BEACON, 1952
WARN THAT MAN, 1943
WATERFRONT, 1944
WHERE THE BULLETS FLY, 1966
WHERE THE SPIES ARE, 1965
WHIP HAND, THE, 1951
WHISTLE BLOWER, THE, 1987
WHITE NIGHTS, 1985
WHO?, 1975
WIFE OF GENERAL LING, THE, 1938
WRECKING CREW, THE, 1968
YELLOW CANARY, THE, 1944
YELLOW DOG, 1973
YOU ONLY LIVE TWICE, 1967

YOUR TURN, DARLING, 1963

Sports
ALIBI IKE, 1935
ALL-AMERICAN, THE, 1932
ALL-AMERICAN, THE, 1953
ALL-AMERICAN BOY, THE, 1973
...ALL THE MARBLES, 1981
ALL THE RIGHT MOVES, 1983
AMERICAN ANTHEM, 1986
AMERICAN FLYERS, 1985
ANGELS IN THE OUTFIELD, 1951
ARSENAL STADIUM MYSTERY, THE, 1939
BABE RUTH STORY, THE, 1948
BAND PLAYS ON, THE, 1934
BANG THE DRUM SLOWLY, 1973
BASKETBALL FIX, THE, 1951
BEAR, THE, 1984
BIG FIX, THE, 1947
BIG GAME, THE, 1936
BIG LEAGUER, 1953
BIG RACE, THE, 1934
BIG WHEEL, THE, 1949
BINGO LONG TRAVELING ALL-STARS AND MOTOR KINGS, THE, 1976
BLONDE COMET, 1941
BLOOD AND GUTS, 1978
BLUE BLOOD, 1951
BLUE GRASS OF KENTUCKY, 1950
BLUE SMOKE, 1935
BOB MATHIAS STORY, THE, 1954
BOBBY DEERFIELD, 1977
BODY AND SOUL, 1947
BODY AND SOUL, 1981
BODYHOLD, 1950
BOOTS MALONE, 1952
BORN TO FIGHT, 1938
BORN TO SPEED, 1947
BOWERY BLITZKRIEG, 1941
BOXER, 1971
BOY FROM INDIANA, 1950
BOY IN BLUE, THE, 1986
BREAKING AWAY, 1979
BURN 'EM UP O'CONNER, 1939
BURNING UP, 1930
BUSTED UP, 1986
CANNONBALL RUN II, 1984
CASEY'S SHADOW, 1978
CHAMP, 1931
CHAMP, THE, 1979
CHAMPION, 1949
CHAMPIONS, 1984
CHARIOTS OF FIRE, 1981
CITY, FOR CONQUEST, 1941
COACH, 1978
COLLEGE COACH, 1933
COLLEGE LOVE, 1929
COLLEGE LOVERS, 1930
COLLEGE RHYTHM, 1934
CONTENDER, THE, 1944
COUNTY FAIR, THE, 1932
COWBOY AND THE PRIZEFIGHTER, 1950
COWBOY QUARTERBACK, 1939
CRAZYLEGS, ALL AMERICAN, 1953
CROOKED CIRCLE, THE, 1958
CROWD ROARS, THE, 1932
CROWD ROARS, THE, 1938
CUP-TIE HONEYMOON, 1948
DAMN YANKEES, 1958
DANGER ON WHEELS, 1940
DAREDEVILS OF EARTH, 1936
DEATH ON THE DIAMOND, 1934
DECEPTION, 1933
DEVIL'S HAIRPIN, THE, 1957
DOWNHILL RACER, 1969
DRAGSTRIP GIRL, 1957
DRAGSTRIP RIOT, 1958
DREAMER, 1979
DRIVE, HE SAID, 1971
DUKE OF CHICAGO, 1949
EIGHT MEN OUT, 1988
ELMER THE GREAT, 1933
EVERYBODY'S ALL-AMERICAN, 1988
FAST BREAK, 1979
FAST COMPANIONS, 1932
FAST COMPANY, 1929

FAST COMPANY, 1953
FAST LIFE, 1932
FAT CITY, 1972
FEAR STRIKES OUT, 1957
FIFTY-SHILLING BOXER, 1937
FIGHTING CHAMP, 1933
FIGHTING FOOLS, 1949
FIGHTING GENTLEMAN, THE, 1932
FIGHTING MAD, 1948
FIGHTING THOROUGHBREDS, 1939
FIGHTING YOUTH, 1935
FINAL TEST, THE, 1953
FINNEY, 1969
FIREBALL, THE, 1950
FIREBALL 590, 1966
FIREBALL JUNGLE, 1968
FISH THAT SAVED PITTSBURGH, THE, 1979
FLESH, 1932
FLESH AND FURY, 1952
FLYING FIFTY-FIVE, 1939
FLYING FISTS, THE, 1938
FOLLOW THE SUN, 1951
FOLLOW THRU, 1930
FORTUNE COOKIE, THE, 1966
FOUR AGAINST FATE, 1952
FROM HELL TO HEAVEN, 1933
GAME THAT KILLS, THE, 1937
GAMES, THE, 1970
GENTLEMAN JIM, 1942
GIRL FROM MONTEREY, THE, 1943
GLORY, 1955
GLORY ALLEY, 1952
GO, MAN, GO!, 1954
GOLDEN BOY, 1939
GOLDEN GLOVES, 1940
GOLDEN GLOVES STORY, THE, 1950
GOLDENGIRL, 1979
GRAND PRIX, 1934
GRAND PRIX, 1966
GREASED LIGHTNING, 1977
GREAT AMERICAN PASTIME, THE, 1956
GREAT DAN PATCH, THE, 1949
GREAT GAME, THE, 1930
GREAT JOHN L. THE, 1945
GREAT MACARTHY, THE, 1975
GREAT WHITE HOPE, THE, 1970
GREATEST, THE, 1977
GREEN HELMET, THE, 1961
GRIDIRON FLASH, 1935
GRUNT! THE WRESTLING MOVIE, 1985
GUS, 1976
GUY WHO CAME BACK, THE, 1951
HARD TIMES, 1975
HARDER THEY FALL, THE, 1956
HARLEM GLOBETROTTERS, THE, 1951
HARMON OF MICHIGAN, 1941
HARRIGAN'S KID, 1943
HEART OF VIRGINIA, 1948
HEART PUNCH, 1932
HI-RIDERS, 1978
HIGH GEAR, 1933
HIGH SPEED, 1932
HOLD 'EM JAIL, 1932
HOLD 'EM NAVY!, 1937
HOLD 'EM YALE, 1935
HOLD EVERYTHING, 1930
HOLD THAT CO-ED, 1938
HOLD THAT LINE, 1952
HOME IN INDIANA, 1944
HOME ON THE RANGE, 1935
HOOSIERS, 1986
HOPE OF HIS SIDE, 1935
HOT CURVES, 1930
HUDDLE, 1932
HUMPHREY TAKES A CHANCE, 1950
HUSTLER, THE, 1961
IN THIS CORNER, 1948
INDIANAPOLIS SPEEDWAY, 1939
IRON MAJOR, THE, 1943
IRON MAN, THE, 1951
IT HAPPENED IN FLATBUSH, 1942
IT HAPPENS EVERY SPRING, 1949
J.W. COOP, 1971
JACKIE ROBINSON STORY, THE, 1950
JIM THORPE—ALL AMERICAN, 1951
JOE LOUIS STORY, THE, 1953

BOLD: Films on Videocassette

JOE PALOOKA, CHAMP, 1946
JOE PALOOKA IN THE BIG FIGHT, 1949
JOE PALOOKA IN THE COUNTERPUNCH, 1949
JOE PALOOKA IN THE SQUARED CIRCLE, 1950
JOE PALOOKA IN TRIPLE CROSS, 1951
JOE PALOOKA IN WINNER TAKE ALL, 1948
JOE PALOOKA MEETS HUMPHREY, 1950
JOHN GOLDFARB, PLEASE COME HOME, 1964
JOHNNY BE GOOD, 1988
JOHNNY DARK, 1954
JUMP, 1971
JUNIOR BONNER, 1972
KANSAS CITY BOMBER, 1972
KARATE KID, THE, 1984
KENTUCKY, 1938
KENTUCKY BLUE STREAK, 1935
KID COMES BACK, THE, 1937
KID FROM BROOKLYN, THE, 1946
KID FROM CLEVELAND, THE, 1949
KID FROM KOKOMO, THE, 1939
KID FROM LEFT FIELD, THE, 1953
KID FROM SPAIN, THE, 1932
KID GALAHAD, 1937
KID GALAHAD, 1962
KID MONK BARONI, 1952
KID NIGHTINGALE, 1939
KILL THE UMPIRE, 1950
KILLER McCOY, 1947
KING FOR A NIGHT, 1933
KING OF HOCKEY, 1936
KING OF THE GAMBLERS, 1948
KING OF THE TURF, 1939
KNOCKOUT, 1941
KNUTE ROCKNE—ALL AMERICAN, 1940
LADY'S FROM KENTUCKY, THE, 1939
LAST AMERICAN HERO, THE, 1973
LAST CHASE, THE, 1981
LAST FIGHT, THE, 1983
LAST GAME, THE, 1964
LAUGHING IRISH EYES, 1936
LAWLESS COWBOYS, 1952
LAWLESS EIGHTIES, THE, 1957
LE MANS, 1971
LEATHER-PUSHERS, THE, 1940
LET'S DO IT AGAIN, 1975
LIFE BEGINS IN COLLEGE, 1937
LIFE OF JIMMY DOLAN, THE, 1933
LONGEST YARD, THE, 1974
LOVE ON SKIS, 1933
LUSTY MEN, THE, 1952
MADISON SQUARE GARDEN, 1932
MAGNIFICENT MATADOR, THE, 1955
MAIN EVENT, THE, 1979
MAN I LOVE, THE, 1929
MANIACS ON WHEELS, 1951
MANNEQUIN, 1933
MANOLETE, 1950
MARK IT PAID, 1933
MATILDA, 1978
MAURIE, 1973
MAYBE IT'S LOVE, 1930
MIGHTY MCGURK, THE, 1946
MILKY WAY, THE, 1936
MILLION DOLLAR LEGS, 1932
MILLION DOLLAR LEGS, 1939
MILLION DOLLAR MERMAID, 1952
MILLION TO ONE, A, 1938
MIRACLE KID, 1942
MR. CELEBRITY, 1942
MR. HEX, 1946
MR. UNIVERSE, 1951
MIXED COMPANY, 1974
MOMENT OF TRUTH, THE, 1965
MONEY FOR SPEED, 1933
MONEY FROM HOME, 1953
MONKEY ON MY BACK, 1957
MOONLIGHT IN HAVANA, 1942
MOTOR MADNESS, 1937
MY WAY, 1974
NADIA, 1984
NATURAL, THE, 1984
NAVY BOUND, 1951
NAVY WAY, THE, 1944
NORTH DALLAS FORTY, 1979
NUMBER ONE, 1969
ON THE EDGE, 1985

ONE ON ONE, 1977
$1,000 A TOUCHDOWN, 1939
OVER THE GOAL, 1937
PACE THAT THRILLS, THE, 1952
PAPER LION, 1968
PARADISE ALLEY, 1978
PERSONAL BEST, 1982
PHAR LAP, 1984
PIT STOP, 1969
PITTSBURGH KID, THE, 1941
PLAYERS, 1979
POLICE CALL, 1933
POLO JOE, 1936
PRIDE OF MARYLAND, 1951
PRIDE OF ST. LOUIS, THE, 1952
PRIDE OF THE BLUE GRASS, 1954
PRIDE OF THE BLUEGRASS, 1939
PRIDE OF THE YANKEES, THE, 1942
PRISON SHADOWS, 1936
PRIZE FIGHTER, THE, 1979
PRIZEFIGHTER AND THE LADY, THE, 1933
PUBERTY BLUES, 1983
QUARTERBACK, THE, 1940
RACE FOR LIFE, A, 1955
RACERS, THE, 1955
RACETRACK, 1933
RACING BLOOD, 1938
RACING BLOOD, 1954
RACING FEVER, 1964
RACING LADY, 1937
RACING LUCK, 1935
RACING LUCK, 1948
RACING ROMANCE, 1937
RACING STRAIN, THE, 1933
RACING YOUTH, 1932
RACKETY RAX, 1932
RACQUET, 1979
RAD, 1986
RAGING BULL, 1980
RAINBOW JACKET, THE, 1954
RED HOT TIRES, 1935
RED LINE 7000, 1965
RENO AND THE DOC, 1984
REQUIEM FOR A HEAVYWEIGHT, 1962
RETURN OF OCTOBER, THE, 1948
RETURN TO CAMPUS, 1975
RHUBARB, 1951
RIDE, KELLY, RIDE, 1941
RIDE THE WILD SURF, 1964
RIDING HIGH, 1937
RIDING HIGH, 1950
RIGHT CROSS, 1950
RIGHT TO THE HEART, 1942
RING, THE, 1952
RINGSIDE MAISIE, 1941
RIPPED-OFF, 1971
RISE AND SHINE, 1941
ROAD DEMON, 1938
ROADRACERS, THE, 1959
ROAR OF THE CROWD, 1953
ROARING ROADS, 1935
ROCKY, 1976
ROCKY II, 1979
ROCKY III, 1982
ROCKY IV, 1985
ROLLERBALL, 1975
ROOGIE'S BUMP, 1954
ROSE BOWL, 1936
ROSE BOWL STORY, THE, 1952
RUN FOR THE ROSES, 1978
RUNNING, 1979
RUNNING BRAVE, 1983
SAFE AT HOME, 1962
SALTY O'ROURKE, 1945
SALUTE, 1929
SAM'S SON, 1984
SAND, 1949
SATURDAY'S HERO, 1951
SATURDAY'S HEROES, 1937
SATURDAY'S MILLIONS, 1933
SECOND WIND, 1976
SECRETS OF A NURSE, 1938
SEMI-TOUGH, 1977
SEPARATE WAYS, 1981
SERGEANT MURPHY, 1938
SET-UP, THE, 1949

SHAKEDOWN, THE, 1929
SIDECAR RACERS, 1975
SIDEWINDER ONE, 1977
SILVER DREAM RACER, 1982
SILVER SKATES, 1943
SIX PACK, 1982
SKATEBOARD, 1978
SKATETOWN, U.S.A., 1979
SKI FEVER, 1969
SKI PATROL, 1940
SLAP SHOT, 1977
SMALL TOWN STORY, 1953
SO THIS IS COLLEGE, 1929
SOCIAL LION, THE, 1930
SOCIETY GIRL, 1932
SOME BLONDES ARE DANGEROUS, 1937
SOMEBODY UP THERE LIKES ME, 1956
SPEAKEASY, 1929
SPEED, 1936
SPEED CRAZY, 1959
SPEED LOVERS, 1968
SPEED TO BURN, 1938
SPEEDWAY, 1968
SPIKE OF BENSONHURST, 1988
SPIKER, 1986
SPINOUT, 1966
SPIRIT OF NOTRE DAME, THE, 1931
SPIRIT OF STANFORD, THE, 1942
SPIRIT OF WEST POINT, THE, 1947
SPIRIT OF YOUTH, 1937
SPLIT DECISIONS, 1988
SPORT OF KINGS, THE, 1931
SPORT OF KINGS, 1947
SPORT PARADE, THE, 1932
SPORTING BLOOD, 1931
SPORTING BLOOD, 1940
SPORTING CHANCE, 1931
SPORTING LOVE, 1936
SPRING FEVER, 1983
SQUARE JUNGLE, THE, 1955
SQUARE RING, THE, 1955
SQUEEZE PLAY, 1981
STEADY COMPANY, 1932
STEALING HOME, 1988
STEEL ARENA, 1973
STING II, THE, 1983
STOCK CAR, 1955
STORY OF SEABISCUIT, THE, 1949
STRAIGHTAWAY, 1934
STRATTON STORY, THE, 1949
STREETS OF GOLD, 1986
STROKER ACE, 1983
SUNDAY PUNCH, 1942
SUNNY SKIES, 1930
SWEEPSTAKES, 1931
SWELL-HEAD, 1935
SWELLHEAD, THE, 1930
SWING FEVER, 1943
SWING THAT CHEER, 1938
SWING YOUR LADY, 1938
SWINGIN' AFFAIR, A, 1963
TAKE DOWN, 1979
TAKE IT FROM ME, 1937
TAKE ME OUT TO THE BALL GAME, 1949
TAKE ME TO PARIS, 1951
TALL STORY, 1960
TEN LAPS TO GO, 1938
TENNESSEE CHAMP, 1954
THAT CHAMPIONSHIP SEASON, 1982
THAT GANG OF MINE, 1940
THAT'S MY BOY, 1932
THAT'S MY BOY, 1951
THAT'S MY MAN, 1947
THERE AIN'T NO JUSTICE, 1939
THEY LEARNED ABOUT WOMEN, 1930
THEY MADE ME A CRIMINAL, 1939
THEY NEVER COME BACK, 1932
THIRD STRING, THE, 1932
THIS SPORTING AGE, 1932
THIS SPORTING LIFE, 1963
THOROUGHBRED, 1936
THOROUGHBREDS, 1945
THOROUGHBREDS DON'T CRY, 1937
THRASHIN', 1986
THUNDER ALLEY, 1967
THUNDER IN CAROLINA, 1960

THUNDER IN DIXIE, 1965
TO PLEASE A LADY, 1950
TOMBOY, 1985
TOUCHDOWN, 1931
TOUCHDOWN, ARMY, 1938
TOUGH ENOUGH, 1983
TRACK OF THUNDER, 1967
TRADING HEARTS, 1988
TRIPLE THREAT, 1948
TWO MINUTES TO PLAY, 1937
UNDER MY SKIN, 1950
UNHOLY ROLLERS, 1972
UNWELCOME STRANGER, 1935
VICTORY, 1981
VISION QUEST, 1985
WALK, DON'T RUN, 1966
WALKOVER, 1969
WALL OF NOISE, 1963
WE WENT TO COLLEGE, 1936
WHIPLASH, 1948
WHITE LIGHTNING, 1953
WILD BOY, 1934
WILD RACERS, THE, 1968
WILDCATS, 1986
WINNER TAKE ALL, 1932
WINNER TAKE ALL, 1939
WINNER'S CIRCLE, THE, 1948
WINNING, 1969
WINNING TEAM, THE, 1952
WINTER WONDERLAND, 1947
WOMAN-WISE, 1937
WORLD IN MY CORNER, 1956
WORLD'S GREATEST ATHLETE, THE, 1973
YESTERDAY'S HERO, 1979
YESTERDAY'S HEROES, 1940
YOUNG MAN OF MANHATTAN, 1930
YOUNG RACERS, THE, 1963
YOUNGBLOOD, 1986

Thriller
AGENT ON ICE, 1986
ALMOST MARRIED, 1932
AMONG THE LIVING, 1941
AND SOON THE DARKNESS, 1970
ANGEL HEART, 1987
ARNOLD, 1973
ATTIC, THE, 1979
BACKFIRE, 1965
BEDROOM WINDOW, THE, 1987
BEHIND LOCKED DOORS, 1948
BELLS, 1981
BEST SELLER, 1987
BETRAYED, 1988
BEWARE, MY LOVELY, 1952
BEWITCHED, 1945
BEYOND THE LIMIT, 1983
BIG EASY, THE, 1987
BLACKOUT, 1988
BLONDE ICE, 1949
BLONDES FOR DANGER, 1938
BODY DOUBLE, 1984
BOYS FROM BRAZIL, THE, 1978
BRAINSTORM, 1965
BREAKING ALL THE RULES, 1985
BRIDE, THE, 1973
BRIMSTONE AND TREACLE, 1982
BURNT EVIDENCE, 1954
BUTTERFLY ON THE SHOULDER, A, 1978
CALL ME, 1988
CAPE FEAR, 1962
CAPER OF THE GOLDEN BULLS, THE, 1967
CAPRICORN ONE, 1978
CAPTIVE CITY, THE, 1963
CAREFUL, HE MIGHT HEAR YOU, 1984
CASE AGAINST FERRO, THE, 1980
CASE VAN GELDERN, 1932
CAST A DARK SHADOW, 1958
CAT O'NINE TAILS, 1971
CAUSE FOR ALARM, 1951
CHAIRMAN, THE, 1969
CHARADE, 1963
CHASE A CROOKED SHADOW, 1958
CHECKMATE, 1973
CHINESE BOXES, 1984
CITY OF BLOOD, 1988
CITY OF FEAR, 1959

CLAY PIGEON, THE, 1949
CLOAK AND DAGGER, 1984
CLONES, THE, 1973
COLOR ME DEAD, 1969
COMA, 1978
CONCERNING MR. MARTIN, 1937
CORNERED, 1945
CORRUPT, 1984
COUNTDOWN, 1968
CRIMSON CANARY, 1945
CRISS CROSS, 1949
CROSSTALK, 1982
CRY TERROR, 1958
CUL-DE-SAC, 1966
DADDY'S GONE A-HUNTING, 1969
DANGER: DIABOLIK, 1968
DANGER PATROL, 1937
DANGER SIGNAL, 1945
DANGER TOMORROW, 1960
DANGEROUS AFTERNOON, 1961
DANGEROUS CROSSING, 1953
DANGEROUS INTRUDER, 1945
DANGEROUS MISSION, 1954
DANGEROUS MOVES, 1985
DARK CITY, 1950
DARK MIRROR, THE, 1946
DARK STAIRWAY, THE, 1938
DARK WATERS, 1944
DAY OF THE COBRA, THE, 1985
DAY OF THE JACKAL, THE, 1973
DEAD OF WINTER, 1987
DEADLY HERO, 1976
DEADLY STRANGERS, 1974
DEATH GAME, 1977
DEATH IN THE GARDEN, 1961
DECKS RAN RED, THE, 1958
DEEP RED, 1976
DEFENCE OF THE REALM, 1985
DESIGN FOR MURDER, 1940
DESPERATE MOMENT, 1953
DEVIL'S PLOT, THE, 1948
DIABOLICALLY YOURS, 1968
DIABOLIQUE, 1955
DIAL M FOR MURDER, 1954
DIAL 1119, 1950
DIE HAMBURGER KRANKHEIT, 1979
DISAPPEARANCE, THE, 1981
DR. MABUSE'S RAYS OF DEATH, 1964
DOG EAT DOG, 1963
DOMINIQUE, 1978
DOMINO PRINCIPLE, THE, 1977
DON'T BOTHER TO KNOCK, 1952
DOOMSDAY AT ELEVEN, 1963
DOUBLE NEGATIVE, 1980
DOUBLES, 1978
DRAGONWYCH, 1946
DRESSED TO KILL, 1980
DRIFTER, THE, 1988
EIGER SANCTION, THE, 1975
END PLAY, 1975
ENDANGERED SPECIES, 1982
ESCAPE, 1940
ESCAPE, 1948
EXPERT'S OPINION, 1935
EXPOSED, 1983
EYEWITNESS, 1956
EYEWITNESS, 1981
FALLEN IDOL, THE, 1949
FAMILY PLOT, 1976
FAN, THE, 1981
FAR FROM DALLAS, 1972
FATAL ATTRACTION, 1987
FEAR IS THE KEY, 1973
FEARMAKERS, THE, 1958
FEEDBACK, 1979
FICKLE FINGER OF FATE, THE, 1967
FIFTH FLOOR, THE, 1980
52 PICK-UP, 1986
FILE ON THELMA JORDAN, THE, 1950
FINAL APPOINTMENT, 1954
FINGERS AT THE WINDOW, 1942
FIREPOWER, 1979
FIRESTARTER, 1984
FIRST DEADLY SIN, THE, 1980
FIVE FINGERS, 1952
FLAREUP, 1969

FLAW, THE, 1933
FLAW, THE, 1955
FLAXY MARTIN, 1949
FLIGHT TO BERLIN, 1984
FLOODS OF FEAR, 1958
FLOWERS IN THE ATTIC, 1987
FLY BY NIGHT, 1942
FORBIDDEN, 1949
FORBIDDEN TERRITORY, 1938
FORMULA, THE, 1980
FOUR DESPERATE MEN, 1960
FOURTEEN HOURS, 1951
FOURTH MAN, THE, 1984
FOURTH PROTOCOL, THE, 1987
FRANTIC, 1961
FRANTIC, 1988
FRENZY, 1946
FRENZY, 1972
FRIEND WILL COME TONIGHT, A, 1948
FRIGHT, 1971
FROZEN ALIVE, 1966
FUGITIVE, THE, 1940
FURY, THE, 1978
FUTUREWORLD, 1976
F/X, 1986
GAMES, 1967
GASLIGHT, 1940
GASLIGHT, 1944
GIRL IN BLACK STOCKINGS, 1957
GIRL, THE, 1987
GIRO CITY, 1982
GLASS ALIBI, THE, 1946
GOLDEN RENDEZVOUS, 1977
GOLDENGIRL, 1979
GOOD DIE YOUNG, THE, 1954
GOODBYE GEMINI, 1970
GRAFT, 1931
GREAT GAMBINI, THE, 1937
GREAT MANHUNT, THE, 1951
HELL'S FIVE HOURS, 1958
HIDDEN, THE, 1987
HIDDEN ROOM, THE, 1949
HIDE AND SEEK, 1964
HIDEOUT, 1948
HIDEOUT, THE, 1956
HIGH COMMISSIONER, THE, 1968
HIGH SPEED, 1986
HIGH WALL, THE, 1947
HIGHPOINT, 1984
HITCHER, THE, 1986
HOLCROFT COVENANT, THE, 1985
HOMICIDE FOR THREE, 1948
HONEYMOON OF TERROR, 1961
HONG KONG CONFIDENTIAL, 1958
HOSTAGE, THE, 1956
HOSTAGE, THE, 1966
HOT SUMMER WEEK, 1973
HOUR OF THIRTEEN, THE, 1952
HOUSE BY THE LAKE, THE, 1977
HOUSE IN THE WOODS, THE, 1957
HOUSE OF DARKNESS, 1948
HOUSE ON CARROLL STREET, THE, 1988
HOUSE ON TELEGRAPH HILL, 1951
HOUSEKEEPER, THE, 1987
HUSH... HUSH, SWEET CHARLOTTE, 1964
HYPNOSIS, 1966
HYSTERIA, 1965
I BURY THE LIVING, 1958
I LIVE ON DANGER, 1942
I SAW WHAT YOU DID, 1965
IMAGEMAKER, THE, 1986
IMPULSE, 1955
IMPULSE, 1984
INTENT TO KILL, 1958
INTERNECINE PROJECT, THE, 1974
INTERRUPTED JOURNEY, THE, 1949
INTO THE NIGHT, 1985
JAGGED EDGE, THE, 1985
JOHNNY, YOU'RE WANTED, 1956
JUGGERNAUT, 1937
JUGGERNAUT, 1974
JULIE, 1956
JULIE DARLING, 1982
KIDNAPPING OF THE PRESIDENT, THE, 1980
KILL HER GENTLY, 1958
KILLER ELITE, THE, 1975

BOLD: Films on Videocassette

THREE CAME TO KILL, 1960
THREE DAYS OF THE CONDOR, 1975
TIGHTROPE, 1984
TIME AFTER TIME, 1979
TO THE ENDS OF THE EARTH, 1948
TOGETHER BROTHERS, 1974
TOMORROW AT TEN, 1964
TORMENT, 1986
TOUCH ME NOT, 1974
TOWER OF TERROR, THE, 1942
TRACK 29, 1988
TRAIN, THE, 1965
TWELVE GOOD MEN, 1936
24 HOURS TO KILL, 1966
23 PACES TO BAKER STREET, 1956
TWILIGHT'S LAST GLEAMING, 1977
TWISTED NERVE, 1969
TWO MRS. CARROLLS, THE, 1947
TWO OF A KIND, 1951
UNDERCURRENT, 1946
VENOM, 1982
VERTIGO, 1958
VISITING HOURS, 1982
W, 1974
WAIT UNTIL DARK, 1967
WALK A CROOKED PATH, 1969
WALK THE DARK STREET, 1956
WANTED FOR MURDER, 1946
WARNING SIGN, 1985
WEAPON, THE, 1957
WHAT BECAME OF JACK AND JILL?, 1972
WHAT EVER HAPPENED TO AUNT ALICE?, 1969
WHATEVER HAPPENED TO BABY JANE?, 1962
WHERE THE TRUTH LIES, 1962
WHIP HAND, THE, 1951
WHIRLPOOL, 1949
WHISPERING CITY, 1947
WHISPERING FOOTSTEPS, 1943
WHISTLER, THE, 1944
WHITE OF THE EYE, 1988
WHOLE TRUTH, THE, 1958
WHO'S GOT THE BLACK BOX?, 1970
WICKED, WICKED, 1973
WIND, THE, 1987
WINDOW, THE, 1949
WINDOWS, 1980
WITCHFIRE, 1986
WITCHING HOUR, THE, 1934
WITNESS IN THE DARK, 1959
WITNESS TO MURDER, 1954
WOLF OF WALL STREET THE, 1929
WOMAN ACCUSED, 1933
WOMAN IN HIDING, 1949
WOMAN IN HIDING, 1953
WOMAN IN THE WINDOW, THE, 1945
WOMAN OF SIN, 1961
WOMAN WHO WOULDN'T DIE, THE, 1965
WOMAN'S DEVOTION, A, 1956
WORLD IN MY POCKET, THE, 1962
YELLOW BALLOON, THE, 1953
YOU CAN'T ESCAPE, 1955
YOU'LL FIND OUT, 1940
YOU'LL LIKE MY MOTHER, 1972
ZIGZAG, 1970

War
ABOVE AND BEYOND, 1953
ABOVE US THE WAVES, 1956
ACE OF ACES, 1933
ACES HIGH, 1977
ACTION IN ARABIA, 1944
ACTION IN THE NORTH ATLANTIC, 1943
ADDRESS UNKNOWN, 1944
ADMIRAL NAKHIMOV, 1948
ADVENTURES OF TARTU, THE, 1943
AERIAL GUNNER, 1943
AFRICAN QUEEN, THE, 1951
AGAINST ALL FLAGS, 1952
AIR FORCE, 1943
ALAMO, THE, 1960
ALBERT, R.N., 1953
ALEXANDER NEVSKY, 1939
ALEXANDER THE GREAT, 1956
ALL QUIET ON THE WESTERN FRONT, 1930
ALL THE YOUNG MEN, 1960
ALVAREZ KELLY, 1966

ALWAYS ANOTHER DAWN, 1948
AMBUSH BAY, 1966
AMERICAN GUERRILLA IN THE PHILIPPINES, AN, 1950
ANGEL WORE RED, THE, 1960
ANGELS ONE FIVE, 1954
ANGKOR-CAMBODIA EXPRESS, 1986
ANITA GARIBALDI, 1954
ANNA OF RHODES, 1950
ANNAPOLIS STORY, AN, 1955
ANZIO, 1968
APOCALYPSE NOW, 1979
APPOINTMENT IN BERLIN, 1943
APPOINTMENT IN LONDON, 1953
ARMY SURGEON, 1942
ASHES AND DIAMONDS, 1961
ASSAULT, THE, 1986
ASSAULT OF THE REBEL GIRLS, 1960
ASSISI UNDERGROUND, THE, 1985
ATLANTIC CONVOY, 1942
ATTACK!, 1956
ATTACK ON THE IRON COAST, 1968
AU REVOIR LES ENFANTS, 1988
AUSTERLITZ, 1960
AVENGERS, THE, 1942
AWAY ALL BOATS, 1956
BACK DOOR TO HELL, 1964
BACK TO BATAAN, 1945
BALLAD OF A SOLDIER, 1960
BAMBOO BLONDE, THE, 1946
BAMBOO PRISON, THE, 1955
BANANAS, 1971
BAREFOOT BATTALION, THE, 1954
BAT 21, 1988
BATAAN, 1943
BATTLE AT BLOODY BEACH, 1961
BATTLE CIRCUS, 1953
BATTLE CRY, 1955
BATTLE CRY, 1959
BATTLE FLAME, 1959
BATTLE FOR MUSIC, 1943
BATTLE HELL, 1957
BATTLE HYMN, 1957
BATTLE OF ALGIERS, THE, 1967
BATTLE OF BLOOD ISLAND, 1960
BATTLE OF BRITAIN, THE, 1969
BATTLE OF GALLIPOLI, 1931
BATTLE OF NERETVA, 1969
BATTLE OF THE BULGE, 1965
BATTLE OF THE CORAL SEA, 1959
BATTLE OF THE RAILS, 1949
BATTLE STATIONS, 1956
BATTLE TAXI, 1955
BATTLE ZONE, 1952
BATTLEGROUND, 1949
BEACH RED, 1967
BEACHHEAD, 1954
BEAST, THE, 1988
BEASTS OF MARSEILLES, THE, 1959
BEAU GESTE, 1939
BEFORE HIM ALL ROME TREMBLED, 1947
BEHIND THE RISING SUN, 1943
BEHOLD A PALE HORSE, 1964
BELL FOR ADANO, A, 1945
BELLS GO DOWN, THE, 1943
BERLIN EXPRESS, 1948
BEST OF ENEMIES, THE, 1962
BEST YEARS OF OUR LIVES, THE, 1946
BETRAYAL FROM THE EAST, 1945
BETRAYED, 1954
BETWEEN HEAVEN AND HELL, 1956
BIG BLOCKADE, THE, 1942
BIG RED ONE, THE, 1980
BILOXI BLUES, 1988
BIRDY, 1984
BITTER VICTORY, 1958
BLACK AND WHITE IN COLOR, 1976
BLACK PARACHUTE, THE, 1944
BLACK TENT, THE, 1956
BLAZE OF GLORY, 1963
BLOCKADE, 1928
BLOCKADE, 1938
BLOOD AND STEEL, 1959
BLOOD ON THE SUN, 1945
BLUE MAX, THE, 1966
BOAT, THE, 1982

BODY AND SOUL, 1931
BOLD AND THE BRAVE, THE, 1956
BOMBARDIER, 1943
BOMBER'S MOON, 1943
BOMBS OVER BURMA, 1942
BOMBS OVER LONDON, 1937
BOMBSIGHT STOLEN, 1941
BORDER STREET, 1950
BORN FOR GLORY, 1935
BOY, A GIRL, AND A DOG, A, 1946
BOYS FROM BRAZIL, THE, 1978
BOYS IN COMPANY C, THE, 1978
BRADDOCK: MISSING IN ACTION III, 1988
BRADY'S ESCAPE, 1984
BRASS TARGET, 1978
BREAKER MORANT, 1980
BREAKOUT, 1960
BREAKTHROUGH, 1950
BREAKTHROUGH, 1978
BRIDGE AT REMAGEN, THE, 1969
BRIDGE ON THE RIVER KWAI, THE, 1957
BRIDGE TOO FAR, A, 1977
BRIDGE, THE, 1961
BRIDGES AT TOKO-RI, THE, 1954
BUCCANEER, THE, 1958
BUCK PRIVATES, 1941
BURMESE HARP, THE, 1985
BURN, 1970
BUT NOT IN VAIN, 1948
CABARET, 1972
CALL OUT THE MARINES, 1942
CAMP ON BLOOD ISLAND, THE, 1958
CANARIS, 1955
CAPTAIN EDDIE, 1945
CAPTAINS OF THE CLOUDS, 1942
CAPTIVE HEART, THE, 1948
CAPTIVE HEARTS, 1988
CAPTURED, 1933
CARNIVAL IN FLANDERS, 1936
CARRY ON ENGLAND, 1976
CASABLANCA, 1942
CASE OF SERGEANT GRISCHA, THE, 1930
CAST A GIANT SHADOW, 1966
CASTLE KEEP, 1969
CAT, THE, 1959
CATCH-22, 1970
CAVALRY COMMAND, 1963
CAVERN, THE, 1965
CHARGE OF THE LIGHT BRIGADE, THE, 1936
CHETNIKS, 1943
CHIMES AT MIDNIGHT, 1967
CHINA, 1943
CHINA DOLL, 1958
CHINA GATE, 1957
CHINA GIRL, 1942
CHINA SKY, 1945
CHINA VENTURE, 1953
CHINA'S LITTLE DEVILS, 1945
CLANDESTINE, 1948
CLAY PIGEON, THE, 1949
CLOAK AND DAGGER, 1946
CLOUDS OVER ISRAEL, 1966
COCKLESHELL HEROES, THE, 1955
CODE NAME: EMERALD, 1985
COLDITZ STORY, THE, 1955
COLONEL REDL, 1985
COMBAT SQUAD, 1953
COME AND SEE, 1986
COMING HOME, 1978
COMMAND DECISION, 1948
COMMANDO, 1962
COMMANDOS STRIKE AT DAWN, THE, 1942
CONFIRM OR DENY, 1941
CONQUERED CITY, 1966
CONQUEROR, THE, 1956
CONSPIRACY OF HEARTS, 1960
CORNERED, 1945
CORREGIDOR, 1943
CORVETTE K-225, 1943
COSSACKS, THE, 1960
COUNT FIVE AND DIE, 1958
COUNTER-ATTACK, 1945
COUNTERFEIT COMMANDOS, 1981
COUNTERPOINT, 1967
COUP DE GRACE, 1978
COURT MARTIAL, 1954

BOLD: Films on Videocassette

COURT MARTIAL, 1962
COURT-MARTIAL OF BILLY MITCHELL, THE, 1955
COURT MARTIAL OF MAJOR KELLER, THE, 1961
CRANES ARE FLYING, THE, 1960
CRASH DIVE, 1943
CREST OF THE WAVE, 1954
CRIMSON ROMANCE, 1934
CROMWELL, 1970
CROSS OF IRON, 1977
CROSS OF LORRAINE, THE, 1943
CROWNING GIFT, THE, 1967
CRUEL SEA, THE, 1953
CRUISER EMDEN, 1932
CRY FREEDOM, 1961
CRY HAVOC, 1943
CRY OF BATTLE, 1963
CUBA, 1979
D-DAY, THE SIXTH OF JUNE, 1956
DAM BUSTERS, THE, 1955
DAMN THE DEFIANT!, 1962
DANTON, 1983
DARBY'S RANGERS, 1958
DARK IS THE NIGHT, 1946
DARK JOURNEY, 1937
DAVID, 1979
DAWN PATROL, THE, 1930
DAWN PATROL, THE, 1938
DAY AND THE HOUR, THE, 1963
DAY THE WAR ENDED, THE, 1961
DAYS AND NIGHTS, 1946
DAYS OF GLORY, 1944
DEAD MARCH, THE, 1937
DEADLINE, 1987
DEATH BEFORE DISHONOR, 1987
DEATH IS CALLED ENGELCHEN, 1963
DEATH SENTENCE, 1986
DEEP SIX, THE, 1958
DEER HUNTER, THE, 1978
DEF-CON 4, 1985
DEFENSE OF VOLOTCHAYEVSK, THE, 1938
DELTA FORCE, THE, 1986
DESERT ATTACK, 1958
DESERT FOX, THE, 1951
DESERT PATROL, 1962
DESERT RATS, THE, 1953
DESERTER AND THE NOMADS, THE, 1969
DESIREE, 1954
DESPERATE JOURNEY, 1942
DESTINATION GOBI, 1953
DESTINATION TOKYO, 1944
DESTINATION UNKNOWN, 1942
DESTROYER, 1943
DEVIL'S BRIGADE, THE, 1968
D.I., THE, 1957
DIAMONDS OF THE NIGHT, 1964
DIARY OF A NAZI, 1943
DIARY OF AN ITALIAN, 1972
DIARY OF ANNE FRANK, THE, 1959
DIRTY DOZEN, THE, 1967
DIRTY HEROES, 1971
DISTANT DRUMS, 1951
DISTANT THUNDER, 1988
DIVE BOMBER, 1941
DR. STRANGELOVE: OR HOW I LEARNED TO STOP WORRYING AND LOVE THE BOMB, 1964
DOCTOR ZHIVAGO, 1965
DOGS OF WAR, THE, 1980
DON'T CRY, IT'S ONLY THUNDER, 1982
DON'T PANIC CHAPS!, 1959
DOOMED BATTALION, THE, 1932
DRAGON SEED, 1944
DRAGONFLY SQUADRON, 1953
DRUMS, 1938
DRUMS ALONG THE MOHAWK, 1939
DRUMS IN THE DEEP SOUTH, 1951
DUCK SOUP, 1933
DUELLISTS, THE, 1977
DUNKIRK, 1958
EAGLE AND THE HAWK, THE, 1933
EAGLE HAS LANDED, THE, 1976
EAGLE SQUADRON, 1942
EDGE OF DARKNESS, 1943
EIGHT IRON MEN, 1952
EL ALAMEIN, 1954
EL CID, 1961
ELENI, 1985

ELUSIVE CORPORAL, THE, 1963
EMPEROR AND A GENERAL, THE, 1968
EMPIRE OF THE SUN, 1987
ENEMY BELOW, THE, 1957
ENEMY GENERAL, THE, 1960
ENEMY OF WOMEN, 1944
ENSIGN PULVER, 1964
EROICA, 1966
ESCAPE TO ATHENA, 1979
ESCAPE TO GLORY, 1940
ETERNAL SEA, THE, 1955
EVE OF ST. MARK, THE, 1944
EVERY BASTARD A KING, 1968
EVERY TIME WE SAY GOODBYE, 1986
EVERYBODY GO HOME!, 1962
EXTRAORDINARY SEAMAN, THE, 1969
EYE OF THE NEEDLE, 1981
FACING THE MUSIC, 1941
FAIL SAFE, 1964
FALCON FIGHTERS, THE, 1970
FAREWELL TO ARMS, A, 1957
FAREWELL TO ARMS, A, 1932
FATHER GOOSE, 1964
FATHER OF A SOLDIER, 1966
FEAR AND DESIRE, 1953
FIFTH HORSEMAN IS FEAR, THE, 1968
55 DAYS AT PEKING, 1963
FIGHT TO THE LAST, 1938
FIGHTER ATTACK, 1953
FIGHTER SQUADRON, 1948
FIGHTING COAST GUARD, 1951
FIGHTING SEABEES, THE, 1944
FIGHTING 69TH, THE, 1940
FINAL COUNTDOWN, THE, 1980
FINAL OPTION, THE, 1982
FIRE OVER ENGLAND, 1937
FIREFOX, 1982
FIRES ON THE PLAIN, 1962
FIRST BLOOD, 1982
FIRST COMES COURAGE, 1943
FIRST TO FIGHT, 1967
FIRST YANK INTO TOKYO, 1945
FIVE BRANDED WOMEN, 1960
FIVE GATES TO HELL, 1959
FIXED BAYONETS, 1951
FLAG LIEUTENANT, THE, 1932
FLAME OVER VIETNAM, 1967
FLAT TOP, 1952
FLEMISH FARM, THE, 1943
FLESH AND BLOOD, 1985
FLIGHT, 1929
FLIGHT COMMAND, 1940
FLIGHT NURSE, 1953
FLYING DEUCES, THE, 1939
FLYING FORTRESS, 1942
FLYING LEATHERNECKS, 1951
FLYING MISSILE, 1950
FLYING TIGERS, 1942
FOR THOSE IN PERIL, 1944
FOR WHOM THE BELL TOLLS, 1943
FORBIDDEN GAMES, 1953
FORCE OF ARMS, 1951
FORCE 10 FROM NAVARONE, 1978
FOREIGN CORRESPONDENT, 1940
FORT APACHE, 1948
FORT GRAVEYARD, 1966
FORTY THOUSAND HORSEMEN, 1941
FOUR DAYS OF NAPLES, THE, 1963
FOUR FEATHERS, THE, 1939
FOUR HORSEMEN OF THE APOCALYPSE, THE, 1962
FOUR IN A JEEP, 1951
FOUR SONS, 1940
48 HOURS, 1944
FRANCIS IN THE NAVY, 1955
FRAULEIN, 1958
FRENCH LEAVE, 1931
FRENCH LEAVE, 1937
FRIEDA, 1947
FRISCO KID, THE, 1979
FROGMEN, THE, 1951
FROM HELL TO VICTORY, 1979
FROM HERE TO ETERNITY, 1953
FULL METAL JACKET, 1987
GABY, 1956
GALLANT BESS, 1946

GALLANT HOURS, THE, 1960
GALLIPOLI, 1981
GARDEN OF THE FINZI-CONTINIS, THE, 1971
GARDENS OF STONE, 1987
GASBAGS, 1940
GATE OF HELL, 1954
GATEWAY TO GLORY, 1970
GATHERING OF EAGLES, A, 1963
GAY INTRUDERS, THE, 1946
GENERAL DELLA ROVERE, 1960
GENERAL MASSACRE, 1973
GENTLE SEX, THE, 1943
GEORG, 1964
GERMANY, YEAR ZERO, 1949
GHOST OF THE CHINA SEA, 1958
GIRL AND THE GENERAL, THE, 1967
GIRL WITH THE RED HAIR, THE, 1983
GIRLS OF PLEASURE ISLAND, THE, 1953
GLORY AT SEA, 1952
GLORY BOY, 1971
GLORY BRIGADE, THE, 1953
GO FOR BROKE, 1951
GO TELL THE SPARTANS, 1978
GOD IS MY CO-PILOT, 1945
GOING HOME, 1988
GOOD LUCK, MR. YATES, 1943
GOOD MORNING, VIETNAM, 1987
GOOD SOLDIER SCHWEIK, THE, 1963
GRAND ILLUSION, 1938
GREAT DICTATOR, THE, 1940
GREAT ESCAPE, THE, 1963
GREAT GUNS, 1941
GREAT HOPE, THE, 1954
GREAT SANTINI, THE, 1979
GREAT WAR, THE, 1961
GREEN BERETS, THE, 1968
GREEN ROOM, THE, 1979
GUADALCANAL DIARY, 1943
GUERRILLA GIRL, 1953
GUNG HO!, 1943
GUNGA DIN, 1939
GUNS OF NAVARONE, THE, 1961
GUY NAMED JOE, A, 1943
HALLS OF MONTEZUMA, 1951
HAMBURGER HILL, 1987
HANGMEN ALSO DIE, 1943
HANNA'S WAR, 1988
HANNIBAL BROOKS, 1969
HANOI HILTON, THE, 1987
HARP OF BURMA, 1967
HEADIN' FOR GOD'S COUNTRY, 1943
HEARTBREAK, 1931
HEARTBREAK RIDGE, 1986
HEARTS IN BONDAGE, 1936
HEAVEN KNOWS, MR. ALLISON, 1957
HELL BELOW, 1933
HELL BOATS, 1970
HELL, HEAVEN OR HOBOKEN, 1958
HELL IN KOREA, 1956
HELL IN THE HEAVENS, 1934
HELL IN THE PACIFIC, 1968
HELL IS FOR HEROES, 1962
HELL ON EARTH, 1934
HELL RAIDERS, 1968
HELL RAIDERS OF THE DEEP, 1954
HELL SQUAD, 1958
HELL TO ETERNITY, 1960
HELLCATS OF THE NAVY, 1957
HELLO GOD, 1951
HELL'S ANGELS, 1930
HELL'S HORIZON, 1955
HENRY V, 1944
HEROES, 1977
HEROES DIE YOUNG, 1960
HEROES OF TELEMARK, THE, 1965
HEROES OF THE ALAMO, 1938
HIDING PLACE, THE, 1975
HILL, THE, 1965
HILL 24 DOESN'T ANSWER, 1955
HINDENBURG, THE, 1975
HIROSHIMA, MON AMOUR, 1959
HISTORY, 1988
HITLER, 1962
HITLER GANG, THE, 1944
HITLER: THE LAST TEN DAYS, 1973
HITLER'S CHILDREN, 1942

HITLER'S MADMAN, 1943
HOA-BINH, 1971
HOLD BACK THE NIGHT, 1956
HOME OF THE BRAVE, 1949
HOMECOMING, 1948
HOOK, THE, 1962
HOPE AND GLORY, 1987
HORNET'S NEST, 1970
HORSE SOLDIERS, THE, 1959
HOSTAGES, 1943
HOT BOX, THE, 1972
HOTEL SAHARA, 1951
HOUSE ON THE FRONT LINE, THE, 1963
HOW I WON THE WAR, 1967
HUMAN CONDITION, THE, 1959
HUNTERS, THE, 1958
I BOMBED PEARL HARBOR, 1961
I DEAL IN DANGER, 1966
I WAS A CAPTIVE IN NAZI GERMANY, 1936
IMITATION GENERAL, 1958
IMMORTAL BATTALION, THE, 1944
IMMORTAL GARRISON, THE, 1957
IMMORTAL SERGEANT, THE, 1943
IMPOSTER, THE, 1944
IN ENEMY COUNTRY, 1968
IN HARM'S WAY, 1965
IN LOVE AND WAR, 1958
IN THE MEANTIME, DARLING, 1944
IN THE MOUTH OF THE WOLF, 1988
IN WHICH WE SERVE, 1942
INCHON, 1981
INN OF THE SIXTH HAPPINESS, THE, 1958
INTERNATIONAL SQUADRON, 1941
INVADERS, THE, 1941
INVASION QUARTET, 1961
INVASION U.S.A., 1985
IRON ANGEL, 1964
IRON EAGLE, 1986
IRON EAGLE II, 1988
IS PARIS BURNING?, 1966
IT HAPPENED IN GIBRALTAR, 1943
ITALIANO BRAVA GENTE, 1965
IVAN THE TERRIBLE, PARTS I & II, 1947
J'ACCUSE, 1939
JET ATTACK, 1958
JOAN OF PARIS, 1942
JOHNNY GOT HIS GUN, 1971
JOHNNY IN THE CLOUDS, 1945
JOURNEY FOR MARGARET, 1942
JOURNEY TO SHILOH, 1968
JOURNEY TOGETHER, 1946
JOURNEY'S END, 1930
JUDGMENT AT NUREMBERG, 1961
JUDITH, 1965
JUMP INTO HELL, 1955
JUNGLE PATROL, 1948
KAGEMUSHA, 1980
KANAL, 1961
KAPO, 1964
KARMA, 1986
KAYA, I'LL KILL YOU, 1969
KEEP, THE, 1983
KEEP YOUR POWDER DRY, 1945
KELLY'S HEROES, 1970
KILLING FIELDS, THE, 1984
KIM, 1950
KING AND COUNTRY, 1964
KING OF HEARTS, 1967
KING RAT, 1965
KINGS GO FORTH, 1958
KOLBERG, 1945
KOREA PATROL, 1951
LA CUCARACHA, 1961
LA MARSEILLAISE, 1938
LACOMBE, LUCIEN, 1974
LAD FROM OUR TOWN, 1941
LADIES COURAGEOUS, 1944
LADY FROM CHUNGKING, 1943
LADY GENERAL, THE, 1965
LAFAYETTE ESCADRILLE, 1958
LAMP STILL BURNS, THE, 1943
LAST BARRICADE, THE, 1938
LAST BLITZKRIEG, THE, 1958
LAST BRIDGE, THE, 1957
LAST CHANCE, THE, 1945
LAST DAY OF THE WAR, THE, 1969

LAST ESCAPE, THE, 1970
LAST GAME, THE, 1964
LAST GRENADE, THE, 1970
LAST HILL, THE, 1945
LAST HUNTER, THE, 1984
LAST METRO, THE, 1981
LAST OF THE MOHICANS, THE, 1936
LAST STOP, THE, 1949
LAST TRAIN FROM MADRID, THE, 1937
LATINO, 1985
LAWRENCE OF ARABIA, 1962
LE CRABE TAMBOUR, 1984
LES CARABINIERS, 1968
LIFE AND DEATH OF COLONEL BLIMP, THE, 1945
LIFEBOAT, 1944
LIGHTHORSEMEN, THE, 1988
LILI MARLEEN, 1981
LION HAS WINGS, THE, 1940
LION OF THE DESERT, 1981
LITTLE BIG MAN, 1970
LITTLE DRUMMER GIRL, THE, 1984
LIVES OF A BENGAL LANCER, 1935
LOLA, 1982
LONG AND THE SHORT AND THE TALL, THE, 1961
LONG DAY'S DYING, THE, 1968
LONGEST DAY, THE, 1962
LORDS OF DISCIPLINE, THE, 1983
LOST BATTALION, 1961
LOST COMMAND, THE, 1966
LOST PATROL, THE, 1934
LOST PEOPLE, THE, 1950
LOTNA, 1966
LOVE AND ANARCHY, 1974
LOVE AND DEATH, 1975
LOVE IN GERMANY, A, 1984
MAC ARTHUR, 1977
MACARTHUR'S CHILDREN, 1985
MAD PARADE, THE, 1931
MAGIC FACE, THE, 1951
MALAYA, 1950
MALTA STORY, 1954
MAN FROM MOROCCO, THE, 1946
MAN FROM WYOMING, A, 1930
MAN FROM YESTERDAY, THE, 1932
MAN I MARRIED, THE, 1940
MANILA CALLING, 1942
MAN'S HOPE, 1947
MARATHON MAN, 1976
MARCH ON PARIS 1914—OF GENERALOBERST
    ALEXANDER VON KLUCK—AND HIS MEMORY
    OF JESSIE HOLLADAY, 1977
MARCH OR DIE, 1977
MARINE BATTLEGROUND, 1966
MARINE RAIDERS, 1944
MARINES ARE COMING, THE, 1935
MARINES ARE HERE, THE, 1938
MARINES COME THROUGH, THE, 1943
MARINES FLY HIGH, THE, 1940
MARINES, LET'S GO, 1961
MARRIAGE IS A PRIVATE AFFAIR, 1944
MARRIAGE OF MARIA BRAUN, THE, 1979
M*A*S*H, 1970
MASSACRE IN ROME, 1973
MASTER RACE, THE, 1944
MC HALE'S NAVY, 1964
MC HALE'S NAVY JOINS THE AIR FORCE, 1965
MC KENZIE BREAK, THE, 1970
ME AND THE COLONEL, 1958
MEIN KAMPF—MY CRIMES, 1940
MEN, THE, 1950
MEN IN WAR, 1957
MEN MUST FIGHT, 1933
MEN OF THE FIGHTING LADY, 1954
MEN OF THE SEA, 1938
MEN OF YESTERDAY, 1936
MEN WITHOUT WOMEN, 1930
MEPHISTO, 1981
MERRILL'S MARAUDERS, 1962
MERRY CHRISTMAS, MR. LAWRENCE, 1983
MIDDLE COURSE, THE, 1961
MIDWAY, 1976
MINESWEEPER, 1943
MIRACLE OF THE WHITE STALLIONS, 1963
MISFIT BRIGADE, THE, 1988
MISSILE FROM HELL, 1960
MISSING, 1982

MISSING IN ACTION, 1984
MISSING IN ACTION 2—THE BEGINNING, 1985
MISSION BATANGAS, 1968
MISSION OVER KOREA, 1953
MR. ORCHID, 1948
MISTER ROBERTS, 1955
MR. WINKLE GOES TO WAR, 1944
MOON IS DOWN, THE, 1943
MONTE CASSINO, 1948
MORITURI, 1965
MOROCCO, 1930
MOSQUITO SQUADRON, 1970
MOUNTAIN ROAD, THE, 1960
MOUSE THAT ROARED, THE, 1959
MRS. MINIVER, 1942
MURPHY'S WAR, 1971
MY NAME IS IVAN, 1963
MYSTERIOUS DOCTOR, THE, 1943
MYSTERY SEA RAIDER, 1940
MYSTERY SUBMARINE, 1950
MYSTERY SUBMARINE, 1963
NAKED AMONG THE WOLVES, 1967
NAKED AND THE DEAD, THE, 1958
NAKED BRIGADE, THE, 1965
NAPOLEON, 1955
NAVY WAY, THE, 1944
NEUTRAL PORT, 1941
NEVER SO FEW, 1959
NEXT OF KIN, 1942
NICHOLAS AND ALEXANDRA, 1971
NIGHT AMBUSH, 1958
NIGHT FIGHTERS, THE, 1960
NIGHT OF THE GENERALS, THE, 1967
NIGHT OF THE SHOOTING STARS, THE, 1982
NIGHT PLANE FROM CHUNGKING, 1942
NIGHT PORTER, THE, 1974
NIGHT TRAIN, 1940
NIGHTWARS, 1988
NINE MEN, 1943
1941, 1979
NO DEAD HEROES, 1987
NO DRUMS, NO BUGLES, 1971
NO GREATER LOVE, 1944
NO MAN IS AN ISLAND, 1962
NO MAN'S LAND, 1964
NONE BUT THE BRAVE, 1963
NONE BUT THE BRAVE, 1965
NORTH OF SHANGHAI, 1939
NORTH STAR, THE, 1943
NORTHERN PURSUIT, 1943
NUN AND THE SERGEANT, THE, 1962
NUREMBERG, 1961
NURSE EDITH CAVELL, 1939
OBJECTIVE, BURMA!, 1945
ODD ANGRY SHOT, THE, 1979
ODESSA FILE, THE, 1974
OFF LIMITS, 1988
OFFICER AND A GENTLEMAN, AN, 1982
OH! WHAT A LOVELY WAR, 1969
OKINAWA, 1952
ON THE BEACH, 1959
ONCE BEFORE I DIE, 1967
ONCE THERE WAS A GIRL, 1945
ONE MINUTE TO ZERO, 1952
ONE OF OUR AIRCRAFT IS MISSING, 1942
ONE THAT GOT AWAY, THE, 1958
1,000 PLANE RAID, THE, 1969
ONLY THE BRAVE, 1930
ONLY WAY, THE, 1970
OPEN CITY, 1945
OPERATION AMSTERDAM, 1960
OPERATION BIKINI, 1963
OPERATION BOTTLENECK, 1961
OPERATION CIA, 1965
OPERATION CROSS EAGLES, 1969
OPERATION CROSSBOW, 1965
OPERATION DAMES, 1959
OPERATION DAYBREAK, 1976
OPERATION DIAMOND, 1948
OPERATION MAD BALL, 1957
OPERATION PACIFIC, 1951
OPERATION PETTICOAT, 1959
OPERATION SECRET, 1952
OPERATION SNAFU, 1965
OPERATION SNATCH, 1962
OPERATION X, 1963

BOLD: Films on Videocassette

ORDERS TO KILL, 1958
OUT OF THE DEPTHS, 1946
OUTPOST IN MOROCCO, 1949
OUTPOST OF HELL, 1966
OVERLANDERS, THE, 1946
OVERLORD, 1975
PACIFIC BLACKOUT, 1942
PACIFIC RENDEZVOUS, 1942
PACK UP YOUR TROUBLES, 1939
PACK UP YOUR TROUBLES, 1940
PAISAN, 1948
PARACHUTE BATTALION, 1941
PARATROOP COMMAND, 1959
PARATROOPER, 1954
PARIS AFTER DARK, 1943
PARIS CALLING, 1941
PARIS UNDERGROUND, 1945
PASSAGE, THE, 1979
PASSAGE TO MARSEILLE, 1944
PASSION ISLAND, 1943
PASSWORD IS COURAGE, THE, 1962
PASTOR HALL, 1940
PATHS OF GLORY, 1957
PATTON, 1970
PAWNBROKER, THE, 1965
PEACE TO HIM WHO ENTERS, 1963
PEDESTRIAN, THE, 1974
PIED PIPER, THE, 1942
PIGEON THAT TOOK ROME, THE, 1962
PILLAR OF FIRE, THE, 1963
PILOT NO. 5, 1943
PIMPERNEL SMITH, 1942
PLATOON, 1986
PLATOON LEADER, 1988
PLAY DIRTY, 1969
PLENTY, 1985
PORK CHOP HILL, 1959
POSTMAN GOES TO WAR, THE, 1968
P.O.W. THE ESCAPE, 1986
POWER PLAY, 1978
PRIDE OF THE MARINES, 1945
PRISON SHIP, 1945
PRISONER OF JAPAN, 1942
PRISONER OF WAR, 1954
PRIVATE BENJAMIN, 1980
PRIVATE JONES, 1933
PRIVATE NAVY OF SGT. O'FARRELL, THE, 1968
PRIVATE POOLEY, 1962
PRIVATE POTTER, 1963
PRIVATES ON PARADE, 1984
PROMISE, THE, 1969
PROUD AND THE PROFANE, THE, 1956
PT 109, 1963
PURPLE HEART, THE, 1944
PURPLE HEART DIARY, 1951
PURPLE HEARTS, 1984
PURPLE PLAIN, THE, 1954
PURPLE V, THE, 1943
PURSUIT OF THE GRAF SPEE, 1957
QUICK AND THE DEAD, THE, 1963
RAID, THE, 1954
RAID ON ROMMEL, 1971
RAIDERS OF LEYTE GULF, 1963
RAINBOW, THE, 1944
RAMBO: FIRST BLOOD, PART II, 1985
RAMBO III, 1988
RAN, 1985
RATS OF TOBRUK, 1951
RAVAGERS, THE, 1965
RAZOR'S EDGE, THE, 1946
RAZOR'S EDGE, THE, 1984
REACH FOR THE SKY, 1957
REAL GLORY, THE, 1939
REASON TO LIVE, A REASON TO DIE, A, 1974
REBEL, 1985
REBEL, THE, 1933
REBELS AGAINST THE LIGHT, 1964
RED AND THE WHITE, THE, 1969
RED BADGE OF COURAGE, THE, 1951
RED BALL EXPRESS, 1952
RED DANUBE, THE, 1949
RED DAWN, 1984
RED RUNS THE RIVER, 1963
REDHEAD AND THE COWBOY, THE, 1950
REDS, 1981
REMEMBER PEARL HARBOR, 1942

RESTLESS NIGHT, THE, 1964
RETURN FROM THE SEA, 1954
RETURN OF THE SOLDIER, THE, 1983
REUNION IN FRANCE, 1942
REVOLT OF JOB, THE, 1984
REVOLUTION, 1985
RICHARD III, 1956
RIDDLE OF THE SANDS, THE, 1984
RIDER IN THE NIGHT, THE, 1968
RIO GRANDE, 1950
ROAD HOME, THE, 1947
ROAD TO ETERNITY, 1962
ROAD TO GLORY, THE, 1936
ROAR OF THE DRAGON, 1932
ROGUE'S MARCH, 1952
ROLLING THUNDER, 1977
ROOKIES IN BURMA, 1943
ROSIE THE RIVETER, 1944
ROUGH, TOUGH AND READY, 1945
ROVER, THE, 1967
ROYAL DEMAND, A, 1933
RUN SILENT, RUN DEEP, 1958
RYAN'S DAUGHTER, 1970
SABOTAGE AT SEA, 1942
SABOTEUR, 1942
SABRE JET, 1953
SACRIFICE OF HONOR, 1938
SAFECRACKER, THE, 1958
SAHARA, 1943
SAILOR OF THE KING, 1953
SALUTE JOHN CITIZEN, 1942
SALUTE TO THE MARINES, 1943
SALVADOR, 1986
SALZBURG CONNECTION, THE, 1972
SAMURAI, 1945
SAN DEMETRIO, LONDON, 1947
SAND PEBBLES, THE, 1966
SANDS OF IWO JIMA, 1949
SAVAGE BRIGADE, 1948
SAYONARA, 1957
SCHOOL FOR DANGER, 1947
SCHOOL FOR SECRETS, 1946
SCHWEIK'S NEW ADVENTURES, 1943
SCREAMING EAGLES, 1956
SEA CHASE, THE, 1955
SEA GHOST, THE, 1931
SEA HAWK, THE, 1940
SEA SHALL NOT HAVE THEM, THE, 1955
SEA WOLVES, THE, 1981
SEALED CARGO, 1951
SEALED VERDICT, 1948
SEARCHING WIND, THE, 1946
SEAS BENEATH, THE, 1931
SECRET AGENT, 1933
SECRET AGENT OF JAPAN, 1942
SECRET BRIGADE, THE, 1951
SECRET DOCUMENT—VIENNA, 1954
SECRET DOOR, THE, 1964
SECRET INVASION, THE, 1964
SECRET MISSION, 1944
SECRET MISSION, 1949
SECRET OF BLOOD ISLAND, THE, 1965
SECRET OF SANTA VITTORIA, THE, 1969
SECRET SERVICE, 1931
SECRET WAR OF HARRY FRIGG, THE, 1968
SEE HERE, PRIVATE HARGROVE, 1944
SEEDS OF FREEDOM, 1943
SENSO, 1968
SERGEANT JIM, 1962
SERGEANT MIKE, 1945
SERGEANT YORK, 1941
SEVEN AGAINST THE SUN, 1968
SEVEN DAYS IN MAY, 1964
SEVEN WERE SAVED, 1947
SEVEN WOMEN FROM HELL, 1961
SEVENTH CROSS, THE, 1944
SEVENTH SURVIVOR, THE, 1941
SHADOW OF VICTORY, 1986
SHE GOES TO WAR, 1929
SHE WORE A YELLOW RIBBON, 1949
SHELL SHOCK, 1964
SHENANDOAH, 1965
SHERLOCK HOLMES AND THE SECRET WEAPON, 1942
SHIPS WITH WINGS, 1942
SHOCK, 1934

SHOCK TROOPS, 1968
SHOP ON MAIN STREET, THE, 1966
SHOPWORN ANGEL, 1938
SHOPWORN ANGEL, THE, 1928
SHOUT AT THE DEVIL, 1976
SIEGE OF FORT BISMARK, 1968
SILENT ENEMY, THE, 1959
SILENT INVASION, THE, 1962
SILENT RAIDERS, 1954
SILVER FLEET, THE, 1945
SINAI COMMANDOS: THE STORY OF THE SIX DAY WAR, 1968
SINCE YOU WENT AWAY, 1944
SINK THE BISMARCK, 1960
SITUATION HOPELESS—BUT NOT SERIOUS, 1965
SKI BATTALION, 1938
SKI PATROL, 1940
SKI TROOP ATTACK, 1960
SKY ABOVE HEAVEN, 1964
SKY BANDITS, 1986
SKY COMMANDO, 1953
SKY DEVILS, 1932
SKY HAWK, 1929
SLAUGHTERHOUSE-FIVE, 1972
SNIPER'S RIDGE, 1961
SNOW IN THE SOUTH SEAS, 1963
SNOW TREASURE, 1968
SO ENDS OUR NIGHT, 1941
SO LITTLE TIME, 1953
SO PROUDLY WE HAIL, 1943
SOLDIER BLUE, 1970
SOLDIER OF ORANGE, 1979
SOLDIER, SAILOR, 1944
SOLDIER'S PRAYER, A, 1970
SOLDIER'S REVENGE, 1986
SOME KIND OF HERO, 1982
SOME MAY LIVE, 1967
SOMEWHERE I'LL FIND YOU, 1942
SOMEWHERE IN FRANCE, 1943
SON OF THE REGIMENT, 1948
SONG OF RUSSIA, 1943
SONS OF GOOD EARTH, 1967
SONS OF THE SEA, 1939
SOUTH SEA WOMAN, 1953
SOUTHERN COMFORT, 1981
SPARE A COPPER, 1940
SPARTACUS, 1960
SPIDER AND THE FLY, THE, 1952
SPITFIRE, 1943
SPY FOR A DAY, 1939
SPY IN BLACK, THE, 1939
SPY TRAIN, 1943
SQUADRON LEADER X, 1943
SQUADRON 633, 1964
SQUARE OF VIOLENCE, 1963
SQUARE PEG, THE, 1958
STAGE DOOR CANTEEN, 1943
STALAG 17, 1953
STAND BY FOR ACTION, 1942
STARFIGHTERS, THE, 1964
START THE REVOLUTION WITHOUT ME, 1970
STEEL BAYONET, THE, 1958
STEEL CLAW, THE, 1961
STEEL HELMET, THE, 1951
STEEL LADY, THE, 1953
STORM OVER BENGAL, 1938
STORY OF DR. WASSELL, THE, 1944
STORY OF G.I. JOE, THE, 1945
STRANGE DEATH OF ADOLF HITLER, THE, 1943
STRANGER, THE, 1946
STREAMERS, 1983
SUBMARINE BASE, 1943
SUBMARINE COMMAND, 1951
SUBMARINE RAIDER, 1942
SUBMARINE SEAHAWK, 1959
SUBMARINE X-1, 1969
SUICIDE BATTALION, 1958
SUICIDE FLEET, 1931
SUICIDE MISSION, 1956
SUICIDE SQUADRON, 1942
SULLIVANS, THE, 1944
SUNDOWN, 1941
SUNDOWN VALLEY, 1944
SUPERNATURALS, THE, 1987
SURRENDER, 1931
SURRENDER—HELL!, 1959

SUSPENSE, 1930
SUZY, 1936
SWEET LIGHT IN A DARK ROOM, 1966
SWING SHIFT, 1984
TAKE THE HIGH GROUND, 1953
TANK BATTALION, 1958
TANK COMMANDOS, 1959
TANK FORCE, 1958
TANKS ARE COMING, THE, 1951
TARAS BULBA, 1962
TARAS FAMILY, THE, 1946
TARAWA BEACHHEAD, 1958
TARGET UNKNOWN, 1951
TARGET ZERO, 1955
TARNISHED HEROES, 1961
TASK FORCE, 1949
TASTE OF HELL, A, 1973
TAXI FOR TOBRUK, 1965
TEN SECONDS TO HELL, 1959
TESTAMENT, 1983
TEXAS TO BATAAN, 1942
THAT HAMILTON WOMAN, 1941
THAT NAZTY NUISANCE, 1943
THEN THERE WERE THREE, 1961
THERE IS NO 13, 1977
THEY ARE NOT ANGELS, 1948
THEY DARE NOT LOVE, 1941
THEY DIED WITH THEIR BOOTS ON, 1942
THEY RAID BY NIGHT, 1942
THEY WERE EXPENDABLE, 1945
THEY WERE NOT DIVIDED, 1951
THEY WHO DARE, 1954
THIN RED LINE, THE, 1964
13 MEN AND A GUN, 1938
THIRTY SECONDS OVER TOKYO, 1944
36 HOURS, 1965
THIS ABOVE ALL, 1942
THIS IS THE ARMY, 1943
THIS LAND IS MINE, 1943
THIS MAN'S NAVY, 1945
THIS WAS PARIS, 1942
THREE, 1967
THREE CAME HOME, 1950
THREE COCKEYED SAILORS, 1940
THREE HOURS, 1944
THREE RUSSIAN GIRLS, 1943
THRONE OF BLOOD, 1961
THUNDER AFLOAT, 1939
THUNDERBIRDS, 1952
TIGER FANGS, 1943
TILL WE MEET AGAIN, 1944
TIN DRUM, THE, 1979
TIME OF DESTINY, A, 1988
TIME TO LOVE AND A TIME TO DIE, A, 1958
TO BE OR NOT TO BE, 1942
TO BE OR NOT TO BE, 1983
TO HELL AND BACK, 1955
TO LIVE IN PEACE, 1947
TO THE SHORES OF HELL, 1966
TO THE SHORES OF TRIPOLI, 1942
TOBRUK, 1966
TODAY WE LIVE, 1933
TOKYO ROSE, 1945
TOMORROW IS FOREVER, 1946
TOMORROW IS MY TURN, 1962
TOMORROW THE WORLD, 1944
TONIGHT A TOWN DIES, 1961
TONIGHT WE RAID CALAIS, 1943
TOO LATE THE HERO, 1970
TOO YOUNG TO KNOW, 1945
TOP GUN, 1986
TORA! TORA! TORA!, 1970
TORPEDO ALLEY, 1953
TORPEDO BAY, 1964
TORPEDO RUN, 1958
TORPEDOED, 1939
TORTURE ME KISS ME, 1970
TOWN LIKE ALICE, A, 1958
TRACKS, 1977
TRAIN, THE, 1965
TRANSPORT FROM PARADISE, 1967
TUNES OF GLORY, 1960
TWELVE O'CLOCK HIGH, 1949
TWILIGHT'S LAST GLEAMING, 1977
TWO COLONELS, THE, 1963
TWO MINUTES' SILENCE, 1934

2,000 WOMEN, 1944
TWO WOMEN, 1960
TWO WORLD, 1930
U-BOAT PRISONER, 1944
U-47 LT. COMMANDER PRIEN, 1967
UGLY AMERICAN, THE, 1963
ULTIMATUM, 1940
ULZANA'S RAID, 1972
UNBEARABLE LIGHTNESS OF BEING, THE, 1988
UNCENSORED, 1944
UNCERTAIN GLORY, 1944
UNCOMMON VALOR, 1983
UNDER FIRE, 1957
UNDER FIRE, 1983
UNDER TEN FLAGS, 1960
UNDERGROUND, 1941
UNDERGROUND, 1970
UNDERGROUND GUERRILLAS, 1944
UNDERWATER WARRIOR, 1958
UNPUBLISHED STORY, 1942
UNTIL THEY SAIL, 1957
UP FROM THE BEACH, 1965
UP FRONT, 1951
UP IN ARMS, 1944
UP PERISCOPE, 1959
VALIANT, THE, 1962
VERBOTEN?, 1959
VICTORS, THE, 1963
VICTORY, 1981
VIOLENT SUMMER, 1961
VOICE IN THE NIGHT, A, 1941
VOICE IN THE WIND, 1944
VON RICHTHOFEN AND BROWN, 1970
VON RYAN'S EXPRESS, 1965
VOYAGE OF THE DAMNED, 1976
W.I.A. (WOUNDED IN ACTION), 1966
"W" PLAN, THE, 1931
WACKIEST SHIP IN THE ARMY, THE, 1961
WAKE ISLAND, 1942
WALK IN THE SUN, A, 1945
WALKER, 1987
WALLS OF HELL, THE, 1964
WANDERING JEW, THE, 1948
WANNSEE CONFERENCE, THE, 1987
WAR AGAINST MRS. HADLEY, THE, 1942
WAR AND PEACE, 1956
WAR AND PEACE, 1968
WAR AND PEACE, 1983
WAR CORRESPONDENT, 1932
WAR DOGS, 1942
WAR HUNT, 1962
WAR IS HELL, 1964
WAR ITALIAN STYLE, 1967
WAR LORD, THE, 1965
WAR LOVER, THE, 1962
WAR NURSE, 1930
WARGAMES, 1983
WARKILL, 1968
WARN THAT MAN, 1943
WARRIORS FIVE, 1962
WATCH ON THE RHINE, 1943
WATERFRONT, 1944
WATERLOO, 1970
WAY WE LIVE, THE, 1946
WE DIVE AT DAWN, 1943
WE WILL REMEMBER, 1966
WEAKER SEX, THE, 1949
WEEKEND AT DUNKIRK, 1966
WELCOME IN VIENNA, 1988
WELCOME, MR. WASHINGTON, 1944
WESTWARD DESPERADO, 1961
WE'VE NEVER BEEN LICKED, 1943
WHAT DID YOU DO IN THE WAR, DADDY?, 1966
WHAT NEXT, CORPORAL HARGROVE?, 1945
WHAT PRICE GLORY?, 1952
WHAT'S THE TIME, MR. CLOCK?, 1985
WHEN HELL BROKE LOOSE, 1958
WHEN WILLIE COMES MARCHING HOME, 1950
WHERE EAGLES DARE, 1968
WHICH WAY TO THE FRONT?, 1970
WHITE CLIFFS OF DOVER, THE, 1944
WHITE GHOST, 1988
WHO GOES NEXT?, 1938
WHO'LL STOP THE RAIN?, 1978
WHOOPING COUGH, 1987
WIFE TAKES A FLYER, THE, 1942

WILD BLUE YONDER, THE, 1952
WILD GEESE, THE, 1978
WILD GEESE II, 1985
WIND AND THE LION, THE, 1975
WIND CANNOT READ, THE, 1958
WINDMILL, THE, 1937
WING AND A PRAYER, 1944
WINGED VICTORY, 1944
WINGS AND THE WOMAN, 1942
WINGS FOR THE EAGLE, 1942
WINGS OF THE NAVY, 1939
WINGS OVER HONOLULU, 1937
WINGS OVER THE PACIFIC, 1943
WITHOUT PITY, 1949
WOMAN I LOVE, THE, 1937
WOMEN AND WAR, 1965
WOMEN AREN'T ANGELS, 1942
WOMEN IN BONDAGE, 1943
WOMEN IN THE NIGHT, 1948
WOMEN IN WAR, 1940
WOODEN HORSE, THE, 1951
YANK IN INDO-CHINA, A, 1952
YANK IN KOREA, A, 1951
YANK IN LIBYA, A, 1942
YANK IN THE R.A.F., A, 1941
YANK IN VIET-NAM, A, 1964
YANK ON THE BURMA ROAD, A, 1942
YANKS, 1979
YEAR OF LIVING DANGEROUSLY, THE, 1982
YELLOW TOMAHAWK, THE, 1954
YESTERDAY'S ENEMY, 1959
YOUNG AND THE BRAVE, THE, 1963
YOUNG EAGLES, 1930
YOUNG LIONS, THE, 1958
YOUNG WARRIORS, THE, 1967
YOU'RE IN THE ARMY NOW, 1937
YOU'RE IN THE NAVY NOW, 1951
ZEPPELIN, 1971
ZULU, 1964
ZULU DAWN, 1980

Western
ABILENE TOWN, 1946
ABILENE TRAIL, 1951
ACE HIGH, 1969
ACES AND EIGHTS, 1936
ACES WILD, 1937
ACROSS THE BADLANDS, 1950
ACROSS THE GREAT DIVIDE, 1976
ACROSS THE PLAINS, 1939
ACROSS THE RIO GRANDE, 1949
ACROSS THE SIERRAS, 1941
ADIOS AMIGO, 1975
ADIOS GRINGO, 1967
ADIOS SABATA, 1971
ADVENTURES IN SILVERADO, 1948
ADVENTURES OF DON COYOTE, 1947
ADVENTURES OF GALLANT BESS, 1948
AGAINST A CROOKED SKY, 1975
AL JENNINGS OF OKLAHOMA, 1951
ALBUQUERQUE, 1948
ALIAS BILLY THE KID, 1946
ALIAS JESSE JAMES, 1959
ALIAS JOHN LAW, 1935
ALIAS THE BAD MAN, 1931
ALONG CAME JONES, 1945
ALONG THE GREAT DIVIDE, 1951
ALONG THE NAVAJO TRAIL, 1945
ALONG THE OREGON TRAIL, 1947
ALONG THE RIO GRANDE, 1941
ALVAREZ KELLY, 1966
AMBUSH, 1950
AMBUSH AT CIMARRON PASS, 1958
AMBUSH AT TOMAHAWK GAP, 1953
AMBUSH TRAIL, 1946
AMBUSH VALLEY, 1936
AMERICAN EMPIRE, 1942
AMERICANO, THE, 1955
AMONG VULTURES, 1964
ANGEL AND THE BADMAN, 1947
ANIMALS, THE, 1971
ANNIE GET YOUR GUN, 1950
ANNIE OAKLEY, 1935
ANY GUN CAN PLAY, 1968
APACHE, 1954
APACHE AMBUSH, 1955

BOLD: Films on Videocassette

APACHE CHIEF, 1949
APACHE COUNTRY, 1952
APACHE DRUMS, 1951
APACHE GOLD, 1965
APACHE KID, THE, 1941
APACHE RIFLES, 1964
APACHE ROSE, 1947
APACHE TERRITORY, 1958
APACHE TRAIL, 1942
APACHE UPRISING, 1966
APACHE WAR SMOKE, 1952
APACHE WARRIOR, 1957
APACHE WOMAN, 1955
APPALOOSA, THE, 1966
APPLE DUMPLING GANG, THE, 1975
APPLE DUMPLING GANG RIDES AGAIN, THE, 1979
ARENA, 1953
ARIZONA, 1940
ARIZONA BADMAN, 1935
ARIZONA BOUND, 1941
ARIZONA BUSHWHACKERS, 1968
ARIZONA COLT, 1965
ARIZONA COWBOY, THE, 1950
ARIZONA CYCLONE, 1934
ARIZONA CYCLONE, 1941
ARIZONA DAYS, 1937
ARIZONA FRONTIER, 1940
ARIZONA GANGBUSTERS, 1940
ARIZONA GUNFIGHTER, 1937
ARIZONA KID, THE, 1930
ARIZONA KID, THE, 1939
ARIZONA LEGION, 1939
ARIZONA MAHONEY, 1936
ARIZONA MANHUNT, 1951
ARIZONA NIGHTS, 1934
ARIZONA RAIDERS, 1965
ARIZONA RAIDERS, THE, 1936
ARIZONA RANGER, THE, 1948
ARIZONA ROUNDUP, 1942
ARIZONA STAGECOACH, 1942
ARIZONA TERRITORY, 1950
ARIZONA TERROR, 1931
ARIZONA TERRORS, 1942
ARIZONA TRAIL, 1943
ARIZONA TRAILS, 1935
ARIZONA WHIRLWIND, 1944
ARIZONA WILDCAT, 1938
ARIZONIAN, THE, 1935
ARMED AND DANGEROUS, 1977
ARROW IN THE DUST, 1954
ARROWHEAD, 1953
AT GUNPOINT, 1955
AT THE RIDGE, 1931
AVENGER, THE, 1931
AVENGER, THE, 1966
AVENGING RIDER, THE, 1943
AVENGING WATERS, 1936
BACK IN THE SADDLE, 1941
BACK TRAIL, 1948
BACKLASH, 1956
BACKTRACK, 1969
BAD BASCOMB, 1946
BAD COMPANY, 1972
BAD LANDS, 1939
BAD MAN, THE, 1930
BAD MAN, THE, 1941
BAD MAN FROM RED BUTTE, 1940
BAD MAN OF BRIMSTONE, 1938
BAD MAN OF DEADWOOD, 1941
BAD MAN'S RIVER, 1972
BAD MEN OF MISSOURI, 1941
BAD MEN OF THE BORDER, 1945
BAD MEN OF THE HILLS, 1942
BAD MEN OF THUNDER GAP, 1943
BAD MEN OF TOMBSTONE, 1949
BADGE OF MARSHAL BRENNAN, THE, 1957
BADLANDERS, THE, 1958
BADLANDS OF DAKOTA, 1941
BADLANDS OF MONTANA, 1957
BADMAN'S COUNTRY, 1958
BADMAN'S GOLD, 1951
BADMAN'S TERRITORY, 1946
BAKER'S HAWK, 1976
BALLAD OF A GUNFIGHTER, 1964
BALLAD OF CABLE HOGUE, THE, 1970
BALLAD OF GREGORIO CORTEZ, THE, 1983

BALLAD OF JOSIE, 1968
BANDIDO, 1956
BANDIDOS, 1967
BANDIT KING OF TEXAS, 1949
BANDIT OF ZHOBE, THE, 1959
BANDIT QUEEN, 1950
BANDIT RANGER, 1942
BANDIT TRAIL, THE, 1941
BANDITS OF DARK CANYON, 1947
BANDITS OF EL DORADO, 1951
BANDITS OF THE BADLANDS, 1945
BANDITS OF THE WEST, 1953
BANDOLERO!, 1968
BANG BANG KID, THE, 1968
BAR L RANCH, 1930
BAR 20, 1943
BAR 20 JUSTICE, 1938
BAR 20 RIDES AGAIN, 1936
BAR Z BAD MEN, 1937
BARBAROSA, 1982
BARBARY COAST GENT, 1944
BARBED WIRE, 1952
BARON OF ARIZONA, THE, 1950
BARQUERO, 1970
BARRICADE, 1950
BARRIER, THE, 1937
BATTLE AT APACHE PASS, THE, 1952
BATTLE OF GREED, 1934
BATTLE OF ROGUE RIVER, 1954
BATTLES OF CHIEF PONTIAC, 1952
BATTLING BUCKAROO, 1932
BATTLING MARSHAL, 1950
BEAST OF HOLLOW MOUNTAIN, THE, 1956
BEAU BANDIT, 1930
BEAUTY AND THE BANDIT, 1946
BELLE LE GRAND, 1951
BELLE STARR, 1941
BELLE STARR'S DAUGHTER, 1947
BELLS OF CAPISTRANO, 1942
BELLS OF CORONADO, 1950
BELLS OF ROSARITA, 1945
BELLS OF SAN ANGELO, 1947
BELOW THE BORDER, 1942
BEND OF THE RIVER, 1952
BENEATH WESTERN SKIES, 1944
BEST OF THE BADMEN, 1951
BETWEEN FIGHTING MEN, 1932
BETWEEN MEN, 1935
BEYOND THE LAST FRONTIER, 1943
BEYOND THE LAW, 1967
BEYOND THE PECOS, 1945
BEYOND THE PURPLE HILLS, 1950
BEYOND THE RIO GRANDE, 1930
BEYOND THE ROCKIES, 1932
BEYOND THE SACRAMENTO, 1941
BIG AND THE BAD, THE, 1971
BIG COUNTRY, THE, 1958
BIG GUNDOWN, THE, 1968
BIG HAND FOR THE LITTLE LADY, A, 1966
BIG JACK, 1949
BIG JAKE, 1971
BIG LAND, THE, 1957
BIG SHOW, THE, 1937
BIG SKY, THE, 1952
BIG SOMBRERO, THE, 1949
BIG STAMPEDE, THE, 1932
BIG TRAIL, THE, 1930
BIG TREES, THE, 1952
BILLY THE KID, 1930
BILLY THE KID, 1941
BILLY THE KID IN SANTA FE, 1941
BILLY THE KID RETURNS, 1938
BILLY THE KID TRAPPED, 1942
BILLY THE KID VS. DRACULA, 1966
BILLY THE KID WANTED, 1941
BILLY THE KID'S FIGHTING PALS, 1941
BILLY THE KID'S RANGE WAR, 1941
BILLY THE KID'S ROUNDUP, 1941
BILLY TWO HATS, 1973
BITE THE BULLET, 1975
BITTER CREEK, 1954
BLACK ACES, 1937
BLACK BANDIT, 1938
BLACK BART, 1948
BLACK DAKOTAS, THE, 1954
BLACK EAGLE, 1948

BLACK HILLS, 1948
BLACK HILLS AMBUSH, 1952
BLACK HILLS EXPRESS, 1943
BLACK HORSE CANYON, 1954
BLACK LASH, THE, 1952
BLACK MARKET RUSTLERS, 1943
BLACK PATCH, 1957
BLACK RODEO, 1972
BLACK SPURS, 1965
BLACK WHIP, THE, 1956
BLACKJACK KETCHUM, DESPERADO, 1956
BLAZING FRONTIER, 1944
BLAZING GUNS, 1943
BLAZING SADDLES, 1974
BLAZING SIX SHOOTERS, 1940
BLAZING SIXES, 1937
BLAZING SUN, THE, 1950
BLAZING TRAIL, THE, 1949
BLINDMAN, 1972
BLOOD ARROW, 1958
BLOOD MONEY, 1974
BLOOD ON THE ARROW, 1964
BLOOD ON THE MOON, 1948
BLUE, 1968
BLUE CANADIAN ROCKIES, 1952
BLUE MONTANA SKIES, 1939
BLUE STEEL, 1934
BOILING POINT, THE, 1932
BOLD CABALLERO, 1936
BOLD FRONTIERSMAN, THE, 1948
BOLDEST JOB IN THE WEST, THE, 1971
BONANZA TOWN, 1951
BOOT HILL, 1969
BOOTHILL BRIGADE, 1937
BOOTS AND SADDLES, 1937
BOOTS OF DESTINY, 1937
BORDER BADMEN, 1945
BORDER BANDITS, 1946
BORDER BRIGANDS, 1935
BORDER BUCKAROOS, 1943
BORDER CABALLERO, 1936
BORDER CAFE, 1937
BORDER DEVILS, 1932
BORDER FEUD, 1947
BORDER G-MAN, 1938
BORDER LAW, 1931
BORDER LEGION, THE, 1930
BORDER LEGION, THE, 1940
BORDER OUTLAWS, 1950
BORDER PATROL, 1943
BORDER PATROLMAN, THE, 1936
BORDER PHANTOM, 1937
BORDER RANGERS, 1950
BORDER RIVER, 1954
BORDER ROMANCE, 1930
BORDER SADDLEMATES, 1952
BORDER TREASURE, 1950
BORDER VIGILANTES, 1941
BORDER WOLVES, 1938
BORDERLAND, 1937
BORDERTOWN GUNFIGHTERS, 1943
BORN TO THE SADDLE, 1953
BORN TO THE WEST, 1937
BORROWED TROUBLE, 1948
BOSS NIGGER, 1974
BOSS OF BULLION CITY, 1941
BOSS OF HANGTOWN MESA, 1942
BOSS OF LONELY VALLEY, 1937
BOSS OF THE RAWHIDE, 1944
BOSS RIDER OF GUN CREEK, 1936
BOUNTY HUNTER, THE, 1954
BOUNTY HUNTERS, THE, 1970
BOUNTY KILLER, THE, 1965
BOWERY BUCKAROOS, 1947
BOY FROM OKLAHOMA, THE, 1954
BOYS' RANCH, 1946
BRAND OF FEAR, 1949
BRAND OF THE DEVIL, 1944
BRANDED, 1931
BRANDED, 1951
BRANDED A COWARD, 1935
BRASS LEGEND, THE, 1956
BRAVADOS, THE, 1958
BRAVE WARRIOR, 1952
BREAKHEART PASS, 1976
BREED OF THE BORDER, 1933

BRIDE OF THE DESERT, 1929
BRIMSTONE, 1949
BROADWAY TO CHEYENNE, 1932
BROKEN ARROW, 1950
BROKEN LANCE, 1954
BROKEN LAND, THE, 1962
BROKEN STAR, THE, 1956
BROKEN WING, THE, 1932
BRONCO BILLY, 1980
BRONCO BUSTER, 1952
BRONZE BUCKAROO, THE, 1939
BROTHERS IN THE SADDLE, 1949
BROTHERS OF THE WEST, 1938
BROTHERS O'TOOLE, THE, 1973
BRUTE AND THE BEAST, THE, 1968
BUCHANAN RIDES ALONE, 1958
BUCK AND THE PREACHER, 1972
BUCK BENNY RIDES AGAIN, 1940
BUCKAROO FROM POWDER RIVER, 1948
BUCKAROO SHERIFF OF TEXAS, 1951
BUCKSKIN, 1968
BUCKSKIN FRONTIER, 1943
BUCKSKIN LADY, THE, 1957
BUFFALO BILL, 1944
BUFFALO BILL AND THE INDIANS, OR SITTING BULL'S HISTORY LESSON, 1976
BUFFALO BILL, HERO OF THE FAR WEST, 1962
BUFFALO BILL IN TOMAHAWK TERRITORY, 1952
BUFFALO BILL RIDES AGAIN, 1947
BUFFALO GUN, 1961
BUGLES IN THE AFTERNOON, 1952
BULLET CODE, 1940
BULLET FOR A BADMAN, 1964
BULLET FOR SANDOVAL, A, 1970
BULLET FOR THE GENERAL, A, 1967
BULLETS FOR RUSTLERS, 1940
BULLWHIP, 1958
BURNING HILLS, THE, 1956
BURY ME NOT ON THE LONE PRAIRIE, 1941
BUSHWHACKERS, THE, 1952
BUTCH AND SUNDANCE: THE EARLY DAYS, 1979
BUTCH CASSIDY AND THE SUNDANCE KID, 1969
CAHILL, UNITED STATES MARSHAL, 1973
CAIN'S WAY, 1969
CALAMITY JANE AND SAM BASS, 1949
CALIFORNIA, 1946
CALIFORNIA, 1963
CALIFORNIA CONQUEST, 1952
CALIFORNIA FIREBRAND, 1948
CALIFORNIA FRONTIER, 1938
CALIFORNIA JOE, 1944
CALIFORNIA MAIL, THE, 1937
CALIFORNIA PASSAGE, 1950
CALIFORNIA TRAIL, THE, 1933
CALIFORNIAN, THE, 1937
CALL OF THE CANYON, 1942
CALL OF THE PRAIRIE, 1936
CALL OF THE ROCKIES, 1938
CALL THE MESQUITEERS, 1938
CALLAWAY WENT THATAWAY, 1951
CALLING WILD BILL ELLIOTT, 1943
CANADIAN PACIFIC, 1949
CANADIANS, THE, 1961
CANNON FOR CORDOBA, 1970
CANYON AMBUSH, 1952
CANYON CITY, 1943
CANYON CROSSROADS, 1955
CANYON HAWKS, 1930
CANYON OF MISSING MEN, THE, 1930
CANYON PASSAGE, 1946
CANYON RAIDERS, 1951
CANYON RIVER, 1956
CAPTAIN APACHE, 1971
CAPTIVE OF BILLY THE KID, 1952
CAPTURE, THE, 1950
CARAVAN TRAIL, THE, 1946
CARIBOO TRAIL, THE, 1950
CAROLINA MOON, 1940
CARRY ON COWBOY, 1966
CARSON CITY, 1952
CARSON CITY CYCLONE, 1943
CARSON CITY KID, 1940
CARSON CITY RAIDERS, 1948
CASSIDY OF BAR 20, 1938
CAST A LONG SHADOW, 1959
CAT BALLOU, 1965

CATLOW, 1971
CATTLE ANNIE AND LITTLE BRITCHES, 1981
CATTLE DRIVE, 1951
CATTLE EMPIRE, 1958
CATTLE KING, 1963
CATTLE QUEEN, 1951
CATTLE QUEEN OF MONTANA, 1954
CATTLE RAIDERS, 1938
CATTLE STAMPEDE, 1943
CATTLE THIEF, THE, 1936
CATTLE TOWN, 1952
CAUGHT, 1931
CAVALCADE OF THE WEST, 1936
CAVALIER, THE, 1928
CAVALIER OF THE WEST, 1931
CAVALRY, 1936
CAVALRY SCOUT, 1951
CAVE OF OUTLAWS, 1951
CHALLENGE OF THE RANGE, 1949
CHARGE AT FEATHER RIVER, THE, 1953
CHARLEY-ONE-EYE, 1973
CHARRO, 1969
CHATO'S LAND, 1972
CHECK YOUR GUNS, 1948
CHEROKEE FLASH, THE, 1945
CHEROKEE STRIP, 1937
CHEROKEE STRIP, 1940
CHEROKEE UPRISING, 1950
CHEYENNE, 1947
CHEYENNE AUTUMN, 1964
CHEYENNE CYCLONE, THE, 1932
CHEYENNE KID, THE, 1930
CHEYENNE KID, THE, 1933
CHEYENNE KID, THE, 1940
CHEYENNE RIDES AGAIN, 1937
CHEYENNE ROUNDUP, 1943
CHEYENNE SOCIAL CLUB, THE, 1970
CHEYENNE TAKES OVER, 1947
CHEYENNE TORNADO, 1935
CHEYENNE WILDCAT, 1944
CHIEF CRAZY HORSE, 1955
CHINA 9, LIBERTY 37, 1978
CHINO, 1976
CHIP OF THE FLYING U, 1940
CHISUM, 1970
CHRISTMAS KID, THE, 1968
CHUKA, 1967
CIMARRON, 1931
CIMARRON, 1960
CIMARRON KID, THE, 1951
CIRCLE CANYON, 1934
CIRCLE OF DEATH, 1935
CISCO KID, 1931
CISCO KID AND THE LADY, THE, 1939
CISCO KID RETURNS, THE, 1945
CITY OF BAD MEN, 1953
CLEARING THE RANGE, 1931
COCKEYED COWBOYS OF CALICO COUNTY, THE, 1970
CODE OF HONOR, 1930
CODE OF THE CACTUS, 1939
CODE OF THE FEARLESS, 1939
CODE OF THE LAWLESS, 1945
CODE OF THE MOUNTED, 1935
CODE OF THE OUTLAW, 1942
CODE OF THE PRAIRIE, 1944
CODE OF THE RANGE, 1937
CODE OF THE RANGERS, 1938
CODE OF THE SADDLE, 1947
CODE OF THE SILVER SAGE, 1950
CODE OF THE WEST, 1947
COLE YOUNGER, GUNFIGHTER, 1958
COLORADO, 1940
COLORADO AMBUSH, 1951
COLORADO KID, 1938
COLORADO PIONEERS, 1945
COLORADO RANGER, 1950
COLORADO SERENADE, 1946
COLORADO SUNDOWN, 1952
COLORADO SUNSET, 1939
COLORADO TERRITORY, 1949
COLORADO TRAIL, 1938
COLT COMRADES, 1943
COLT .45, 1950
COLUMN SOUTH, 1953
COMANCHE, 1956

COMANCHE STATION, 1960
COMANCHE TERRITORY, 1950
COMANCHEROS, THE, 1961
COME ON, COWBOYS, 1937
COME ON DANGER!, 1932
COME ON DANGER, 1942
COME ON RANGERS, 1939
COME ON TARZAN, 1933
COMES A HORSEMAN, 1978
COMIN' AT YA!, 1981
COMIN' ROUND THE MOUNTAIN, 1936
COMMAND, THE, 1954
COMPANEROS, 1970
CON MEN, THE, 1973
CONCENTRATIN' KID, THE, 1930
CONQUERING HORDE, THE, 1931
CONQUEST OF CHEYENNE, 1946
CONQUEST OF COCHISE, 1953
CONVICT STAGE, 1965
COOGAN'S BLUFF, 1968
COPPER SKY, 1957
CORNERED, 1932
CORONER CREEK, 1948
CORPUS CHRISTI BANDITS, 1945
COUNT YOUR BULLETS, 1972
COUNTRY BEYOND, THE, 1936
COURAGE OF THE WEST, 1937
COURAGEOUS AVENGER, THE, 1935
COURTIN' TROUBLE, 1948
COURTIN' WILDCATS, 1929
COVERED WAGON DAYS, 1940
COVERED WAGON RAID, 1950
COVERED WAGON TRAILS, 1930
COVERED WAGON TRAILS, 1940
COW COUNTRY, 1953
COW TOWN, 1950
COWBOY, 1958
COWBOY AND THE BANDIT, THE, 1935
COWBOY AND THE BLONDE, THE, 1941
COWBOY AND THE INDIANS, THE, 1949
COWBOY AND THE KID, THE, 1936
COWBOY AND THE PRIZEFIGHTER, 1950
COWBOY AND THE SENORITA, 1944
COWBOY BLUES, 1946
COWBOY CANTEEN, 1944
COWBOY CAVALIER, 1948
COWBOY COMMANDOS, 1943
COWBOY COUNSELOR, 1933
COWBOY FROM LONESOME RIVER, 1944
COWBOY FROM SUNDOWN, 1940
COWBOY HOLIDAY, 1934
COWBOY IN MANHATTTAN, 1943
COWBOY IN THE CLOUDS, 1943
COWBOY MILLIONAIRE, 1935
COWBOY SERENADE, 1942
COWBOY STAR, THE, 1936
COWBOYS, THE, 1972
COWBOYS FROM TEXAS, 1939
COYOTE TRAILS, 1935
CRASHING BROADWAY, 1933
CRASHING THRU, 1949
CRIMSON TRAIL, THE, 1935
CRIPPLE CREEK, 1952
CROOKED RIVER, 1950
CROOKED TRAIL, THE, 1936
CROSSED TRAILS, 1948
CROSSFIRE, 1933
CRY BLOOD, APACHE, 1970
CULPEPPER CATTLE COMPANY, THE, 1972
CURSE OF THE UNDEAD, 1959
CURTAIN CALL AT CACTUS CREEK, 1950
CUSTER OF THE WEST, 1968
CYCLONE FURY, 1951
CYCLONE KID, 1931
CYCLONE KID, THE, 1942
CYCLONE OF THE SADDLE, 1935
CYCLONE ON HORSEBACK, 1941
CYCLONE PRAIRIE RANGERS, 1944
CYCLONE RANGER, 1935
DAKOTA, 1945
DAKOTA INCIDENT, 1956
DAKOTA KID, THE, 1951
DAKOTA LIL, 1950
DALLAS, 1950
DALTON GANG, THE, 1949
DALTON GIRLS, THE, 1957

BOLD: Films on Videocassette

DALTON THAT GOT AWAY, 1960
DALTONS RIDE AGAIN, THE, 1945
DALTONS' WOMEN, THE, 1950
DANGER TRAILS, 1935
DANGER VALLEY, 1938
DANGEROUS VENTURE, 1947
DARING CABALLERO, THE, 1949
DARING DANGER, 1932
DARK COMMAND, THE, 1940
DAUGHTER OF THE WEST, 1949
DAVY CROCKETT, INDIAN SCOUT, 1950
DAVY CROCKETT, KING OF THE WILD FRONTIER, 1955
DAWN AT SOCORRO, 1954
DAWN ON THE GREAT DIVIDE, 1942
DAWN RIDER, 1935
DAWN TRAIL, THE, 1931
DAY OF ANGER, 1970
DAY OF FURY, A, 1956
DAY OF THE BAD MAN, 1958
DAY OF THE EVIL GUN, 1968
DAY OF THE OUTLAW, 1959
DAYS OF BUFFALO BILL, 1946
DAYS OF JESSE JAMES, 1939
DAYS OF OLD CHEYENNE, 1943
DEAD DON'T DREAM, THE, 1948
DEAD MAN'S GOLD, 1948
DEAD MAN'S GULCH, 1943
DEAD MAN'S TRAIL, 1952
DEAD OR ALIVE, 1944
DEADLINE, THE, 1932
DEADLINE, 1948
DEADLY COMPANIONS, THE, 1961
DEADLY TRACKERS, 1973
DEADWOOD PASS, 1933
DEADWOOD '76, 1965
DEAF SMITH AND JOHNNY EARS, 1973
DEATH OF A GUNFIGHTER, 1969
DEATH RIDES A HORSE, 1969
DEATH RIDES THE PLAINS, 1944
DEATH RIDES THE RANGE, 1940
DEATH SENTENCE, 1967
DEATH VALLEY, 1946
DEATH VALLEY GUNFIGHTER, 1949
DEATH VALLEY MANHUNT, 1943
DEATH VALLEY OUTLAWS, 1941
DEATH VALLEY RANGERS, 1944
DECISION AT SUNDOWN, 1957
DEEP IN THE HEART OF TEXAS, 1942
DEMON FOR TROUBLE, A, 1934
DENVER AND RIO GRANDE, 1952
DENVER KID, THE, 1948
DEPUTY MARSHAL, 1949
DESERT BANDIT, 1941
DESERT FURY, 1947
DESERT GOLD, 1936
DESERT GUNS, 1936
DESERT HORSEMAN, THE, 1946
DESERT JUSTICE, 1936
DESERT MESA, 1935
DESERT OF LOST MEN, 1951
DESERT PASSAGE, 1952
DESERT PATROL, 1938
DESERT PHANTOM, 1937
DESERT PURSUIT, 1952
DESERT TRAIL, 1935
DESERT VENGEANCE, 1931
DESERT VIGILANTE, 1949
DESERTER, THE, 1971
DESPERADO, THE, 1954
DESPERADO TRAIL, THE, 1965
DESPERADOES, THE, 1943
DESPERADOES ARE IN TOWN, THE, 1956
DESPERADOES OF DODGE CITY, 1948
DESPERADOES OUTPOST, 1952
DESPERADOS, THE, 1969
DESPERATE TRAILS, 1939
DESTRY, 1954
DESTRY RIDES AGAIN, 1932
DESTRY RIDES AGAIN, 1939
DEVIL RIDERS, 1944
DEVIL'S CANYON, 1953
DEVIL'S DOORWAY, 1950
DEVIL'S GODMOTHER, THE, 1938
DEVIL'S MISTRESS, THE, 1968
DEVIL'S PLAYGROUND, THE, 1946

DEVIL'S SADDLE LEGION, THE, 1937
DEVIL'S TRAIL, THE, 1942
DIAMOND TRAIL, 1933
DIRTY DINGUS MAGEE, 1970
DIRTY LITTLE BILLY, 1972
DIRTY OUTLAWS, THE, 1971
DISTANT TRUMPET, A, 1964
DJANGO, 1966
DJANGO KILL, 1967
DOC, 1971
DODGE CITY, 1939
DODGE CITY TRAIL, 1937
DOLLARS FOR A FAST GUN, 1969
DOMINO KID, 1957
DON RICARDO RETURNS, 1946
DON'T FENCE ME IN, 1945
DON'T TOUCH WHITE WOMEN!, 1974
DON'T TURN THE OTHER CHEEK, 1974
DOOLINS OF OKLAHOMA, THE, 1949
DOOMED AT SUNDOWN, 1937
DOOMED CARAVAN, 1941
DOUBLE-BARRELLED DETECTIVE STORY, THE, 1965
DOWN DAKOTA WAY, 1949
DOWN LAREDO WAY, 1953
DOWN MEXICO WAY, 1941
DOWN RIO GRANDE WAY, 1942
DOWN TEXAS WAY, 1942
DOWN THE WYOMING TRAIL, 1939
DRAGON WELLS MASSACRE, 1957
DRIFT FENCE, 1936
DRIFTER, THE, 1944
DRIFTIN' KID, THE, 1941
DRIFTIN' RIVER, 1946
DRIFTING ALONG, 1946
DRIFTING WESTWARD, 1939
DROP THEM OR I'LL SHOOT, 1969
DRUM BEAT, 1954
DRUM TAPS, 1933
DRUMMER OF VENGEANCE, 1974
DRUMS ACROSS THE RIVER, 1954
DUCHESS AND THE DIRTWATER FOX, THE, 1976
DUCK, YOU SUCKER!, 1972
DUDE BANDIT, THE, 1933
DUDE COWBOY, 1941
DUDE GOES WEST, THE, 1948
DUDE RANGER, THE, 1934
DUDES, 1988
DUEL AT APACHE WELLS, 1957
DUEL AT DIABLO, 1966
DUEL AT SILVER CREEK, THE, 1952
DUEL IN THE SUN, 1946
DUGAN OF THE BAD LANDS, 1931
DURANGO KID, THE, 1940
DURANGO VALLEY RAIDERS, 1938
DYNAMITE CANYON, 1941
DYNAMITE PASS, 1950
DYNAMITE RANCH, 1932
EAGLE AND THE HAWK, THE, 1950
EAGLE'S BROOD, THE, 1936
EAGLE'S WING, 1979
EDGE OF ETERNITY, 1959
EL CONDOR, 1970
EL DIABLO RIDES, 1939
EL DORADO, 1967
EL DORADO PASS, 1949
EL PASO, 1949
EL PASO KID, THE, 1946
EL PASO STAMPEDE, 1953
EL TOPO, 1971
ELECTRIC HORSEMAN, THE, 1979
EMPTY HOLSTERS, 1937
EMPTY SADDLES, 1937
END OF THE TRAIL, 1932
END OF THE TRAIL, 1936
ENEMY OF THE LAW, 1945
ESCAPE FROM FORT BRAVO, 1953
ESCAPE FROM RED ROCK, 1958
ESCORT WEST, 1959
EVERYMAN'S LAW, 1936
EYE FOR AN EYE, AN, 1966
EYES OF TEXAS, 1948
FABULOUS TEXAN, THE, 1947
FACE OF A FUGITIVE, 1959
FACE TO FACE, 1967
FAIR WARNING, 1931
FAIR WARNING, 1937

FALCON OUT WEST, THE, 1944
FALSE COLORS, 1943
FALSE PARADISE, 1948
FANDANGO, 1970
FAR COUNTRY, THE, 1955
FAR FRONTIER, THE, 1949
FARGO, 1952
FARGO EXPRESS, 1933
FARGO KID, THE, 1941
FAST BULLETS, 1936
FAST ON THE DRAW, 1950
FASTEST GUITAR ALIVE, THE, 1967
FASTEST GUN ALIVE, 1956
FENCE RIDERS, 1950
FEUD MAKER, 1938
FEUD OF THE RANGE, 1939
FEUD OF THE TRAIL, 1938
FEUD OF THE WEST, 1936
FEW BULLETS MORE, A, 1968
FIDDLIN' BUCKAROO, THE, 1934
FIEND WHO WALKED THE WEST, THE, 1958
FIGHTING BILL CARSON, 1945
FIGHTING BILL FARGO, 1941
FIGHTING BUCKAROO, THE, 1943
FIGHTING CABALLERO, 1935
FIGHTING CARAVANS, 1931
FIGHTING CHAMP, 1933
FIGHTING CODE, THE, 1934
FIGHTING COWBOY, 1933
FIGHTING DEPUTY, THE, 1937
FIGHTING FOOL, THE, 1932
FIGHTING FRONTIER, 1943
FIGHTING GRINGO, THE, 1939
FIGHTING HERO, 1934
FIGHTING KENTUCKIAN, THE, 1949
FIGHTING LAWMAN, THE, 1953
FIGHTING LEGION, THE, 1930
FIGHTING MAN OF THE PLAINS, 1949
FIGHTING MARSHAL, THE, 1932
FIGHTING PARSON, THE, 1933
FIGHTING PIONEERS, 1935
FIGHTING PLAYBOY, 1937
FIGHTING RANGER, THE, 1934
FIGHTING RANGER, THE, 1948
FIGHTING REDHEAD, THE, 1950
FIGHTING RENEGADE, 1939
FIGHTING SHADOWS, 1935
FIGHTING SHERIFF, THE, 1931
FIGHTING STALLION, THE, 1950
FIGHTING TEXAN, 1937
FIGHTING TEXANS, 1933
FIGHTING THRU, 1931
FIGHTING TROOPER, THE, 1935
FIGHTING VALLEY, 1943
FIGHTING VIGILANTES, THE, 1947
FINGER ON THE TRIGGER, 1965
FIREBRAND, THE, 1962
FIREBRAND JORDAN, 1930
FIREBRANDS OF ARIZONA, 1944
FIRECREEK, 1968
FIRST TEXAN, THE, 1956
FISTFUL OF DOLLARS, A, 1964
FIVE BOLD WOMEN, 1960
FIVE CARD STUD, 1968
FIVE GIANTS FROM TEXAS, 1966
FIVE GUNS TO TOMBSTONE, 1961
FIVE GUNS WEST, 1955
FIVE MAN ARMY, THE, 1970
FLAME OF THE BARBARY COAST, 1945
FLAME OF THE WEST, 1945
FLAMING BULLETS, 1945
FLAMING FEATHER, 1951
FLAMING FRONTIER, 1958
FLAMING FRONTIER, 1968
FLAMING GUNS, 1933
FLAMING LEAD, 1939
FLAMING STAR, 1960
FLASHING GUNS, 1947
FLESH AND THE SPUR, 1957
FLIGHT TO NOWHERE, 1946
FOOL'S GOLD, 1946
FOOLS' PARADE, 1971
FOR A FEW DOLLARS MORE, 1967
FOR THE LOVE OF MIKE, 1960
FOR THE SERVICE, 1936
FORBIDDEN TRAIL, 1936

FORBIDDEN TRAILS, 1941
FORBIDDEN VALLEY, 1938
FORLORN RIVER, 1937
FORT APACHE, 1948
FORT BOWIE, 1958
FORT COURAGEOUS, 1965
FORT DEFIANCE, 1951
FORT DOBBS, 1958
FORT DODGE STAMPEDE, 1951
FORT MASSACRE, 1958
FORT OSAGE, 1952
FORT SAVAGE RAIDERS, 1951
FORT TI, 1953
FORT UTAH, 1967
FORT VENGEANCE, 1953
FORT WORTH, 1951
FORT YUMA, 1955
FORTY GUNS, 1957
FORTY-NINERS, THE, 1932
FORTY THIEVES, 1944
FORTYNINERS, THE, 1954
FOUR FACES WEST, 1948
FOUR FAST GUNS, 1959
FOUR FOR TEXAS, 1963
FOUR GUNS TO THE BORDER, 1954
FOUR RODE OUT, 1969
FOURTH HORSEMAN, THE, 1933
40 GUNS TO APACHE PASS, 1967
FREIGHTERS OF DESTINY, 1932
FRENCHIE, 1950
FRISCO TORNADO, 1950
FROM HELL TO TEXAS, 1958
FROM NOON TO THREE, 1976
FRONTIER AGENT, 1948
FRONTIER BADMEN, 1943
FRONTIER CRUSADER, 1940
FRONTIER DAYS, 1934
FRONTIER FEUD, 1945
FRONTIER FUGITIVES, 1945
FRONTIER FURY, 1943
FRONTIER GAL, 1945
FRONTIER GAMBLER, 1956
FRONTIER GUN, 1958
FRONTIER HELLCAT, 1966
FRONTIER INVESTIGATOR, 1949
FRONTIER JUSTICE, 1936
FRONTIER LAW, 1943
FRONTIER MARSHAL, 1934
FRONTIER MARSHAL, 1939
FRONTIER OUTLAWS, 1944
FRONTIER OUTPOST, 1950
FRONTIER PHANTOM, THE, 1952
FRONTIER PONY EXPRESS, 1939
FRONTIER REVENGE, 1948
FRONTIER SCOUT, 1939
FRONTIER TOWN, 1938
FRONTIER UPRISING, 1961
FRONTIER VENGEANCE, 1939
FRONTIERS OF '49, 1939
FRONTIERSMAN, THE, 1938
FUGITIVE FROM SONORA, 1943
FUGITIVE SHERIFF, THE, 1936
FUGITIVE VALLEY, 1941
FUGITIVE, THE, 1933
FURIES, THE, 1950
FURY AT FURNACE CREEK, 1948
FURY AT GUNSIGHT PASS, 1956
FURY AT SHOWDOWN, 1957
FURY IN PARADISE, 1955
FUZZY SETTLES DOWN, 1944
GAL WHO TOOK THE WEST, THE, 1949
GALLANT DEFENDER, 1935
GALLANT FOOL, THE, 1933
GALLANT LEGION, THE, 1948
GALLOPING DYNAMITE, 1937
GALLOPING ROMEO, 1933
GALLOPING THRU, 1932
GAMBLER FROM NATCHEZ, THE, 1954
GAMBLER WORE A GUN, THE, 1961
GAMBLING TERROR, THE, 1937
GANGS OF SONORA, 1941
GANGSTERS OF THE FRONTIER, 1944
GATLING GUN, THE, 1972
GAUCHO SERENADE, 1940
GAUCHOS OF EL DORADO, 1941
GAVILAN, 1968

GAY AMIGO, THE, 1949
GAY BUCKAROO, THE, 1932
GAY CABALLERO, THE, 1932
GAY CABALLERO, THE, 1940
GAY RANCHERO, THE, 1948
GENE AUTRY AND THE MOUNTIES, 1951
GENIUS, THE, 1976
GENTLE ANNIE, 1944
GENTLEMAN FROM ARIZONA, THE, 1940
GENTLEMAN FROM TEXAS, 1946
GENTLEMEN WITH GUNS, 1946
GERONIMO, 1939
GERONIMO, 1962
GET MEAN, 1976
GET THAT GIRL, 1932
GHOST CITY, 1932
GHOST GUNS, 1944
GHOST OF HIDDEN VALLEY, 1946
GHOST OF ZORRO, 1959
GHOST PATROL, 1936
GHOST RIDER, THE, 1935
GHOST TOWN, 1937
GHOST TOWN, 1956
GHOST TOWN, 1988
GHOST TOWN GOLD, 1937
GHOST TOWN LAW, 1942
GHOST TOWN RENEGADES, 1947
GHOST TOWN RIDERS, 1938
GHOST VALLEY, 1932
GHOST VALLEY RAIDERS, 1940
GIRL AND THE GAMBLER, THE, 1939
GIRL FROM ALASKA, 1942
GIRL FROM SAN LORENZO, THE, 1950
GIRL OF THE GOLDEN WEST, 1930
GIRL RUSH, 1944
GIT ALONG, LITTLE DOGIES, 1937
GLORY GUYS, THE, 1965
GLORY TRAIL, THE, 1937
GO WEST, YOUNG LADY, 1941
GOD FORGIVES—I DON'T!, 1969
GOD'S COUNTRY, 1946
GOD'S COUNTRY AND THE MAN, 1931
GOD'S COUNTRY AND THE MAN, 1937
GOD'S GUN, 1977
GOIN' SOUTH, 1978
GOLD, 1932
GOLD FEVER, 1952
GOLD IS WHERE YOU FIND IT, 1938
GOLD MINE IN THE SKY, 1938
GOLD OF THE SEVEN SAINTS, 1961
GOLDEN STALLION, THE, 1949
GOLDEN TRAIL, THE, 1940
GOLDEN WEST, THE, 1932
GOLDTOWN GHOST RIDERS, 1953
GOOD DAY FOR A HANGING, 1958
GOOD GUYS AND THE BAD GUYS, THE, 1969
GOOD, THE BAD, AND THE UGLY, THE, 1967
GRAND CANYON, 1949
GRAND CANYON TRAIL, 1948
GRAYEAGLE, 1977
GREAT BANK ROBBERY, THE, 1969
GREAT DAY IN THE MORNING, 1956
GREAT DIVIDE, THE, 1930
GREAT GUNDOWN, THE, 1977
GREAT JESSE JAMES RAID, THE, 1953
GREAT MAN'S LADY, THE, 1942
GREAT MISSOURI RAID, THE, 1950
GREAT NORTHFIELD, MINNESOTA RAID, THE, 1972
GREAT SCOUT AND CATHOUSE THURSDAY, THE, 1976
GREAT SIOUX MASSACRE, THE, 1965
GREAT SIOUX UPRISING, THE, 1953
GREAT STAGECOACH ROBBERY, 1945
GREY FOX, THE, 1983
GRINGO, 1963
GUILTY TRAILS, 1938
GUN BATTLE AT MONTEREY, 1957
GUN BELT, 1953
GUN BROTHERS, 1956
GUN CODE, 1940
GUN DUEL IN DURANGO, 1957
GUN FEVER, 1958
GUN FIGHT, 1961
GUN FOR A COWARD, 1957
GUN FURY, 1953

GUN GLORY, 1957
GUN HAWK, THE, 1963
GUN JUSTICE, 1934
GUN LAW, 1933
GUN LAW, 1938
GUN LAW JUSTICE, 1949
GUN LORDS OF STIRRUP BASIN, 1937
GUN MAN FROM BODIE, THE, 1941
GUN PACKER, 1938
GUN PLAY, 1936
GUN RANGER, THE, 1937
GUN RIDERS, THE, 1969
GUN RUNNER, 1949
GUN SMOKE, 1931
GUN SMOKE, 1936
GUN SMUGGLERS, 1948
GUN STREET, 1962
GUN TALK, 1948
GUN THAT WON THE WEST, THE, 1955
GUN THE MAN DOWN, 1957
GUN TOWN, 1946
GUNFIGHT AT COMANCHE CREEK, 1964
GUNFIGHT AT DODGE CITY, THE, 1959
GUNFIGHT AT THE O.K. CORRAL, 1957
GUNFIGHT IN ABILENE, 1967
GUNFIGHT, A, 1971
GUNFIGHTER, THE, 1950
GUNFIGHTERS OF ABILENE, 1960
GUNFIGHTERS OF CASA GRANDE, 1965
GUNFIGHTERS, THE, 1947
GUNFIRE, 1950
GUNFIRE AT INDIAN GAP, 1957
GUNMAN'S CODE, 1946
GUNMAN'S WALK, 1958
GUNMEN FROM LAREDO, 1959
GUNMEN OF ABILENE, 1950
GUNMEN OF THE RIO GRANDE, 1965
GUNNING FOR JUSTICE, 1948
GUNPLAY, 1951
GUNPOINT, 1966
GUNS AND GUITARS, 1936
GUNS FOR SAN SEBASTIAN, 1968
GUNS IN THE DARK, 1937
GUNS OF A STRANGER, 1973
GUNS OF DIABLO, 1964
GUNS OF FORT PETTICOAT, THE, 1957
GUNS OF HATE, 1948
GUNS OF THE LAW, 1944
GUNS OF THE MAGNIFICENT SEVEN, 1969
GUNS OF THE PECOS, 1937
GUNS OF THE TIMBERLAND, 1960
GUNSIGHT RIDGE, 1957
GUNSLINGER, 1956
GUNSLINGERS, 1950
GUNSMOKE, 1953
GUNSMOKE IN TUCSON, 1958
GUNSMOKE MESA, 1944
GUNSMOKE RANCH, 1937
GUNSMOKE TRAIL, 1938
HAIL TO THE RANGERS, 1943
HALF-BREED, THE, 1952
HALLELUJAH TRAIL, THE, 1965
HALLIDAY BRAND, THE, 1957
HANDS ACROSS THE BORDER, 1943
HANG 'EM HIGH, 1968
HANGING TREE, THE, 1959
HANGMAN, THE, 1959
HANGMAN'S KNOT, 1952
HANNAH LEE, 1953
HANNIE CALDER, 1971
HARD HOMBRE, 1931
HARD MAN, THE, 1957
HARD TRAIL, 1969
HARLEM ON THE PRAIRIE, 1938
HARLEM RIDES THE RANGE, 1939
HATE FOR HATE, 1967
HAUNTED GOLD, 1932
HAUNTED RANCH, THE, 1943
HAWAIIAN BUCKAROO, 1938
HAWK OF POWDER RIVER, THE, 1948
HAWK OF WILD RIVER, THE, 1952
HE RIDES TALL, 1964
HE WHO SHOOTS FIRST, 1966
HEADIN' EAST, 1937
HEADIN' FOR THE RIO GRANDE, 1937
HEADIN' FOR TROUBLE, 1931

BOLD: Films on Videocassette

HEADIN' NORTH, 1930
HEART OF ARIZONA, 1938
HEART OF THE GOLDEN WEST, 1942
HEART OF THE RIO GRANDE, 1942
HEART OF THE ROCKIES, 1937
HEART OF THE ROCKIES, 1951
HEART OF THE WEST, 1937
HEARTLAND, 1980
HEARTS OF THE WEST, 1975
HEAVEN ONLY KNOWS, 1947
HEAVEN WITH A GUN, 1969
HEAVEN'S GATE, 1980
HEIR TO TROUBLE, 1936
HELL BENT FOR LEATHER, 1960
HELL CANYON OUTLAWS, 1957
HELL FIRE AUSTIN, 1932
HELLBENDERS, THE, 1967
HELLDORADO, 1946
HELLER IN PINK TIGHTS, 1960
HELLFIRE, 1949
HELLGATE, 1952
HELLO TROUBLE, 1932
HELL'S CROSSROADS, 1957
HELL'S HEROES, 1930
HENRY GOES ARIZONA, 1939
HERITAGE OF THE DESERT, 1933
HERITAGE OF THE DESERT, 1939
HEROES OF THE ALAMO, 1938
HEROES OF THE HILLS, 1938
HEROES OF THE RANGE, 1936
HEROES OF THE SADDLE, 1940
HI GAUCHO!, 1936
HI-YO SILVER, 1940
HIDDEN DANGER, 1949
HIDDEN GOLD, 1933
HIDDEN GOLD, 1940
HIDDEN GUNS, 1956
HIDDEN VALLEY, 1932
HIDDEN VALLEY OUTLAWS, 1944
HIGH LONESOME, 1950
HIGH NOON, 1952
HIGH PLAINS DRIFTER, 1973
HIGH, WIDE AND HANDSOME, 1937
HILLS OF OKLAHOMA, 1950
HILLS OF OLD WYOMING, 1937
HILLS OF UTAH, 1951
HILLS RUN RED, THE, 1967
HIRED GUN, THE, 1957
HIRED HAND, THE, 1971
HIS BROTHER'S GHOST, 1945
HIS FIGHTING BLOOD, 1935
HIT THE SADDLE, 1937
HITTIN' THE TRAIL, 1937
HOEDOWN, 1950
HOLLYWOOD COWBOY, 1937
HOLLYWOOD ROUNDUP, 1938
HOLY TERROR, A, 1931
HOMBRE, 1967
HOME IN OKLAHOMA, 1946
HOME IN WYOMIN', 1942
HOME ON THE PRAIRIE, 1939
HOME ON THE RANGE, 1935
HOME ON THE RANGE, 1946
HOMESTEADERS, THE, 1953
HOMESTEADERS OF PARADISE VALLEY, 1947
HONDO, 1953
HONKERS, THE, 1972
HONOR OF THE RANGE, 1934
HONOR OF THE WEST, 1939
HOPALONG CASSIDY, 1935
HOPALONG CASSIDY RETURNS, 1936
HOPALONG RIDES AGAIN, 1937
HOPPY'S HOLIDAY, 1947
HOPPY SERVES A WRIT, 1943
HORIZONS WEST, 1952
HORSE SOLDIERS, THE, 1959
HORSEMEN OF THE SIERRAS, 1950
HOSTILE COUNTRY, 1950
HOSTILE GUNS, 1967
HOT LEAD, 1951
HOT LEAD AND COLD FEET, 1978
HOT SPUR, 1968
HOUR OF THE GUN, 1967
HOW THE WEST WAS WON, 1962
HUD, 1963
HUMAN TARGETS, 1932

HUNTING PARTY, THE, 1977
HURRICANE HORSEMAN, 1931
HURRICANE SMITH, 1942
I KILLED GERONIMO, 1950
I KILLED WILD BILL HICKOK, 1956
I SHOT BILLY THE KID, 1950
I SHOT JESSE JAMES, 1949
IDAHO, 1943
IDAHO KID, THE, 1937
I'M FROM THE CITY, 1938
IN EARLY ARIZONA, 1938
IN OLD AMARILLO, 1951
IN OLD ARIZONA, 1929
IN OLD CALIENTE, 1939
IN OLD CALIFORNIA, 1942
IN OLD CHEYENNE, 1931
IN OLD CHEYENNE, 1941
IN OLD COLORADO, 1941
IN OLD MEXICO, 1938
IN OLD MONTANA, 1939
IN OLD MONTEREY, 1939
IN OLD NEW MEXICO, 1945
IN OLD OKLAHOMA, 1943
IN OLD SACRAMENTO, 1946
IN OLD SANTA FE, 1935
INCIDENT AT PHANTOM HILL, 1966
INDIAN AGENT, 1948
INDIAN FIGHTER, THE, 1955
INDIAN PAINT, 1965
INDIAN TERRITORY, 1950
INDIAN UPRISING, 1951
INSIDE STRAIGHT, 1951
INVITATION TO A GUNFIGHTER, 1964
IRON MISTRESS, THE, 1952
IRON MOUNTAIN TRAIL, 1953
IRON SHERIFF, THE, 1957
IROQUOIS TRAIL, THE, 1950
IT HAPPENED OUT WEST, 1937
IVORY-HANDLED GUN, 1935
J.W. COOP, 1971
JACK MCCALL, DESPERADO, 1953
JACK SLADE, 1953
JACKASS MAIL, 1942
JAWS OF JUSTICE, 1933
JAYHAWKERS, THE, 1959
JEEPERS CREEPERS, 1939
JEREMIAH JOHNSON, 1972
JESSE AND LESTER, TWO BROTHERS IN A PLACE
  CALLED TRINITY, 1972
JESSE JAMES, 1939
JESSE JAMES AT BAY, 1941
JESSE JAMES, JR., 1942
JESSE JAMES MEETS FRANKENSTEIN'S
  DAUGHTER, 1966
JESSE JAMES VERSUS THE DALTONS, 1954
JESSE JAMES' WOMEN, 1954
JESSIE'S GIRLS, 1976
JOE DAKOTA, 1957
JOE KIDD, 1972
JOHNNY CONCHO, 1956
JOHNNY GUITAR, 1954
JOHNNY HAMLET, 1972
JOHNNY RENO, 1966
JOHNNY YUMA, 1967
JORY, 1972
JOURNEY TO SHILOH, 1968
JUBAL, 1956
JUBILEE TRAIL, 1954
JUNCTION CITY, 1952
JUNIOR BONNER, 1972
JUSTICE OF THE RANGE, 1935
KANGAROO, 1952
KANGAROO KID, THE, 1950
KANSAN, THE, 1943
KANSAS CYCLONE, 1941
KANSAS PACIFIC, 1953
KANSAS RAIDERS, 1950
KANSAS TERRITORY, 1952
KANSAS TERRORS, THE, 1939
KENTUCKIAN, THE, 1955
KENTUCKY RIFLE, 1956
KID BLUE, 1973
KID COURAGEOUS, 1935
KID FROM AMARILLO, THE, 1951
KID FROM ARIZONA, THE, 1931
KID FROM BROKEN GUN, THE, 1952

KID FROM GOWER GULCH, THE, 1949
KID FROM SANTA FE, THE, 1940
KID FROM TEXAS, THE, 1939
KID FROM TEXAS, THE, 1950
KID RANGER, THE, 1936
KID RIDES AGAIN, THE, 1943
KID RODELO, 1966
KID VENGEANCE, 1977
KID'S LAST RIDE, THE, 1941
KILL OR BE KILLED, 1967
KILL THEM ALL AND COME BACK ALONE, 1970
KING AND FOUR QUEENS, THE, 1956
KING OF DODGE CITY, 1941
KING OF THE ARENA, 1933
KING OF THE BANDITS, 1948
KING OF THE BULLWHIP, 1950
KING OF THE COWBOYS, 1943
KING OF THE PECOS, 1936
KING OF THE SIERRAS, 1938
KING OF THE STALLIONS, 1942
KING OF THE WILD HORSES, THE, 1934
KING OF THE WILD STALLIONS, 1959
KIT CARSON, 1940
KLONDIKE KATE, 1944
KNIGHT OF THE PLAINS, 1939
KNIGHTS OF THE RANGE, 1940
KONGA, THE WILD STALLION, 1939
LADY FROM CHEYENNE, 1941
LADY FROM TEXAS, THE, 1951
LAND BEYOND THE LAW, 1937
LAND OF FIGHTING MEN, 1938
LAND OF HUNTED MEN, 1943
LAND OF MISSING MEN, THE, 1930
LAND OF THE LAWLESS, 1947
LAND OF THE OPEN RANGE, 1941
LAND OF THE OUTLAWS, 1944
LAND OF THE SIX GUNS, 1940
LAND OF WANTED MEN, 1932
LAND RAIDERS, 1969
LANDRUSH, 1946
LARAMIE, 1949
LARAMIE MOUNTAINS, 1952
LARAMIE TRAIL, THE, 1944
LASCA OF THE RIO GRANDE, 1931
LASH, THE, 1930
LAST BANDIT, THE, 1949
LAST CHALLENGE, THE, 1967
LAST COMMAND, THE, 1955
LAST DAYS OF BOOT HILL, 1947
LAST FRONTIER, THE, 1955
LAST FRONTIER UPRISING, 1947
LAST GUNFIGHTER, THE, 1961
LAST HARD MEN, THE, 1976
LAST HORSEMAN, THE, 1944
LAST HUNT, THE, 1956
LAST MUSKETEER, THE, 1952
LAST OF THE BADMEN, 1957
LAST OF THE CLINTONS, THE, 1935
LAST OF THE COMANCHES, 1952
LAST OF THE DESPERADOES, 1956
LAST OF THE DUANES, 1930
LAST OF THE DUANES, 1941
LAST OF THE FAST GUNS, THE, 1958
LAST OF THE PONY RIDERS, 1953
LAST OF THE RENEGADES, 1966
LAST OF THE WARRENS, THE, 1936
LAST OF THE WILD HORSES, 1948
LAST OUTLAW, THE, 1936
LAST OUTPOST, THE, 1951
LAST POSSE, THE, 1953
LAST REBEL, THE, 1971
LAST REBEL, THE, 1961
LAST ROUND-UP, THE, 1934
LAST ROUND-UP, THE, 1947
LAST STAGECOACH WEST, THE, 1957
LAST STAND, THE, 1938
LAST SUNSET, THE, 1961
LAST TOMAHAWK, THE, 1965
LAST TRAIL, THE, 1934
LAST TRAIN FROM GUN HILL, 1959
LAST WAGON, THE, 1956
LAW AND JAKE WADE, THE, 1958
LAW AND LAWLESS, 1932
LAW AND LEAD, 1937
LAW AND ORDER, 1932
LAW AND ORDER, 1940

LAW AND ORDER, 1942
LAW AND ORDER, 1953
LAW BEYOND THE RANGE, 1935
LAW COMES TO TEXAS, THE, 1939
LAW COMMANDS, THE, 1938
LAW FOR TOMBSTONE, 1937
LAW MEN, 1944
LAW OF THE BADLANDS, 1950
LAW OF THE GOLDEN WEST, 1949
LAW OF THE LASH, 1947
LAW OF THE LAWLESS, 1964
LAW OF THE NORTH, 1932
LAW OF THE NORTHWEST, 1943
LAW OF THE PAMPAS, 1939
LAW OF THE PANHANDLE, 1950
LAW OF THE PLAINS, 1938
LAW OF THE RANGE, 1941
LAW OF THE RANGER, 1937
LAW OF THE RIO GRANDE, 1931
LAW OF THE SADDLE, 1944
LAW OF THE TEXAN, 1938
LAW OF THE VALLEY, 1944
LAW OF THE WEST, 1949
LAW RIDES, THE, 1936
LAW RIDES AGAIN, THE, 1943
LAW VS. BILLY THE KID, THE, 1954
LAW WEST OF TOMBSTONE, THE, 1938
LAWLESS BORDER, 1935
LAWLESS BREED, THE, 1946
LAWLESS BREED, THE, 1952
LAWLESS CODE, 1949
LAWLESS COWBOYS, 1952
LAWLESS EIGHTIES, THE, 1957
LAWLESS EMPIRE, 1946
LAWLESS FRONTIER, THE, 1935
LAWLESS LAND, 1937
LAWLESS NINETIES, THE, 1936
LAWLESS PLAINSMEN, 1942
LAWLESS RANGE, 1935
LAWLESS RIDER, THE, 1954
LAWLESS RIDERS, 1936
LAWLESS STREET, A, 1955
LAWLESS VALLEY, 1938
LAWMAN, 1971
LAWMAN IS BORN, A, 1937
LEADVILLE GUNSLINGER, 1952
LEATHER BURNERS, THE, 1943
LEFT-HANDED GUN, THE, 1958
LEFT-HANDED LAW, 1937
LEGEND OF A BANDIT, THE, 1945
LEGEND OF FRENCHIE KING, THE, 1971
LEGEND OF NIGGER CHARLEY, THE, 1972
LEGEND OF THE LONE RANGER, THE, 1981
LEGEND OF TOM DOOLEY, THE, 1959
LEGION OF THE LAWLESS, 1940
LEMONADE JOE, 1966
LIFE AND TIMES OF JUDGE ROY BEAN, THE, 1972
LIFE IN THE RAW, 1933
LIGHT OF WESTERN STARS, THE, 1930
LIGHT OF WESTERN STARS, THE, 1940
LIGHTNIN' CRANDALL, 1937
LIGHTNING BILL CARSON, 1936
LIGHTNING GUNS, 1950
LIGHTNING RAIDERS, 1945
LIGHTNING RANGE, 1934
LIGHTNING STRIKES WEST, 1940
LIGHTS OF OLD SANTA FE, 1944
LION AND THE HORSE, THE, 1952
LION'S DEN, THE, 1936
LITTLE BIG HORN, 1951
LITTLE BIG MAN, 1970
LITTLE JOE, THE WRANGLER, 1942
LLANO KID, THE, 1940
LOADED PISTOLS, 1948
LOCAL BAD MAN, 1932
LONG ROPE, THE, 1961
LONE AVENGER, THE, 1933
LONE COWBOY, 1934
LONE GUN, THE, 1954
LONE HAND, THE, 1953
LONE HAND TEXAN, THE, 1947
LONE PRAIRIE, THE, 1942
LONE RANGER, THE, 1955
LONE RANGER AND THE LOST CITY OF GOLD, THE, 1958
LONE RIDER, THE, 1930

LONE RIDER AMBUSHED, THE, 1941
LONE RIDER AND THE BANDIT, THE, 1942
LONE RIDER CROSSES THE RIO, THE, 1941
LONE RIDER FIGHTS BACK, THE, 1941
LONE RIDER IN CHEYENNE, THE, 1942
LONE RIDER IN GHOST TOWN, THE, 1941
LONE STAR, 1952
LONE STAR LAW MEN, 1942
LONE STAR PIONEERS, 1939
LONE STAR RAIDERS, 1940
LONE STAR RANGER, THE, 1930
LONE STAR RANGER, 1942
LONE STAR TRAIL, THE, 1943
LONE STAR VIGILANTES, THE, 1942
LONE TEXAN, 1959
LONE TEXAS RANGER, 1945
LONE TRAIL, THE, 1932
LONELY ARE THE BRAVE, 1962
LONELY MAN, THE, 1957
LONELY TRAIL, THE, 1936
LONESOME COWBOYS, 1968
LONESOME TRAIL, THE, 1930
LONESOME TRAIL, THE, 1955
LONG, LONG TRAIL, THE, 1929
LONG RIDE FROM HELL, A, 1970
LONG RIDERS, THE, 1980
LONGHORN, THE, 1951
LOST CANYON, 1943
LOST RANCH, 1937
LOST TRAIL, THE, 1945
LOVE ME TENDER, 1956
LUCK OF ROARING CAMP, THE, 1937
LUCKY CISCO KID, 1940
LUCKY LARRIGAN, 1933
LUCKY LUKE, 1971
LUCKY TERROR, 1936
LUCKY TEXAN, THE, 1934
LUMBERJACK, 1944
LURE OF THE WASTELAND, 1939
LUST FOR GOLD, 1949
LUST IN THE DUST, 1985
LUSTY MEN, THE, 1952
MACHISMO—40 GRAVES FOR 40 GUNS, 1970
MACHO CALLAHAN, 1970
MACKENNA'S GOLD, 1969
MACKINTOSH & T.J., 1975
MAD DOG MORGAN, 1976, Aus.
MADONNA OF THE DESERT, 1948
MADRON, 1970
MAGNIFICENT BANDITS, THE, 1969
MAGNIFICENT SEVEN, THE, 1960
MAGNIFICENT SEVEN RIDE, THE, 1972
MAIL ORDER BRIDE, 1964
MAJOR DUNDEE, 1965
MAN ALONE, A, 1955
MAN AND BOY, 1972
MAN BEHIND THE GUN, THE, 1952
MAN CALLED GANNON, A, 1969
MAN CALLED HORSE, A, 1970
MAN CALLED NOON, THE, 1973
MAN CALLED SLEDGE, A, 1971
MAN FROM BITTER RIDGE, THE, 1955
MAN FROM BLACK HILLS, THE, 1952
MAN FROM BUTTON WILLOW, THE, 1965
MAN FROM CHEYENNE, 1942
MAN FROM COLORADO, THE, 1948
MAN FROM DAKOTA, THE, 1940
MAN FROM DEATH VALLEY, THE, 1931
MAN FROM DEL RIO, 1956
MAN FROM GALVESTON, THE, 1964
MAN FROM GOD'S COUNTRY, 1958
MAN FROM GUN TOWN, THE, 1936
MAN FROM HELL, THE, 1934
MAN FROM HELL'S EDGES, 1932
MAN FROM LARAMIE, THE, 1955
MAN FROM MONTANA, 1941
MAN FROM MONTEREY, THE, 1933
MAN FROM MUSIC MOUNTAIN, 1938
MAN FROM MUSIC MOUNTAIN, 1943
MAN FROM NEW MEXICO, THE, 1932
MAN FROM OKLAHOMA, THE, 1945
MAN FROM RAINBOW VALLEY, THE, 1946
MAN FROM SNOWY RIVER, THE, 1983
MAN FROM SUNDOWN, THE, 1939
MAN FROM TEXAS, THE, 1939
MAN FROM TEXAS, THE, 1948

MAN FROM THE ALAMO, THE, 1953
MAN FROM THE EAST, A, 1974
MAN FROM THE RIO GRANDE, THE, 1943
MAN FROM THUNDER RIVER, THE, 1943
MAN FROM TUMBLEWEEDS, THE, 1940
MAN FROM UTAH, THE, 1934
MAN IN THE SADDLE, 1951
MAN IN THE SHADOW, 1957
MAN OF CONQUEST, 1939
MAN OF THE FOREST, 1933
MAN OF THE WEST, 1958
MAN OR GUN, 1958
MAN TRAILER, THE, 1934
MAN WHO KILLED BILLY THE KID, THE, 1967
MAN WHO LOVED CAT DANCING, THE, 1973
MAN WHO SHOT LIBERTY VALANCE, THE, 1962
MAN WITH THE GUN, 1955
MAN WITHOUT A STAR, 1955
MANCHURIAN AVENGER, 1985
MAN'S COUNTRY, 1938
MAN'S LAND, A, 1932
MARAUDERS, THE, 1947
MARAUDERS, THE, 1955
MARIE-ANN, 1978
MARK OF THE LASH, 1948
MARKED FOR MURDER, 1945
MARKED TRAILS, 1944
MARKSMAN, THE, 1953
MARSHAL OF AMARILLO, 1948
MARSHAL OF CEDAR ROCK, 1953
MARSHAL OF CRIPPLE CREEK, THE, 1947
MARSHAL OF GUNSMOKE, 1944
MARSHAL OF HELDORADO, 1950
MARSHAL OF LAREDO, 1945
MARSHAL OF MESA CITY, THE, 1939
MARSHAL OF RENO, 1944
MARSHAL'S DAUGHTER, THE, 1953
MASKED RAIDERS, 1949
MASKED RIDER, THE, 1941
MASON OF THE MOUNTED, 1932
MASSACRE, 1934
MASSACRE, 1956
MASSACRE CANYON, 1954
MASSACRE RIVER, 1949
MASTER GUNFIGHTER, THE, 1975
MASTERSON OF KANSAS, 1954
MAVERICK, THE, 1952
MAVERICK QUEEN, THE, 1956
MC CABE AND MRS. MILLER, 1971
MC KENNA OF THE MOUNTED, 1932
MC LINTOCK!, 1963
MC MASTERS, THE, 1970
MEDICO OF PAINTED SPRINGS, THE, 1941
MELODY OF THE PLAINS, 1937
MELODY RANCH, 1940
MELODY TRAIL, 1935
MEN OF AMERICA, 1933
MEN OF THE PLAINS, 1936
MEN OF THE TIMBERLAND, 1941
MEN WITHOUT LAW, 1930
MERCENARY, THE, 1970
MESQUITE BUCKAROO, 1939
MEXICALI KID, THE, 1938
MEXICALI ROSE, 1939
MICHIGAN KID, THE, 1947
MINE WITH THE IRON DOOR, THE, 1936
MINNESOTA CLAY, 1966
MINUTE TO PRAY, A SECOND TO DIE, A, 1968
MIRACLE OF THE HILLS, THE, 1959
MISFITS, THE, 1961
MISSOURI BREAKS, THE, 1976
MISSOURI OUTLAW, A, 1942
MISSOURIANS, THE, 1950
MOHAWK, 1956
MOJAVE FIREBRAND, 1944
MOLLY AND LAWLESS JOHN, 1972
MONEY, WOMEN AND GUNS, 1958
MONTANA, 1950
MONTANA BELLE, 1952
MONTANA DESPERADO, 1951
MONTANA KID, THE, 1931
MONTANA MOON, 1930
MONTANA TERRITORY, 1952
MONTE WALSH, 1970
MOONLIGHT ON THE PRAIRIE, 1936
MOONLIGHT ON THE RANGE, 1937

BOLD: Films on Videocassette

MOONLIGHTER, THE, 1953
MORE DEAD THAN ALIVE, 1968
MOUNTAIN JUSTICE, 1930
MOUNTAIN MEN, THE, 1980
MOUNTAIN RHYTHM, 1939
MOUNTED STRANGER, THE, 1930
MULE TRAIN, 1950
MURIETA, 1965
MUSTANG, 1959
MUSTANG COUNTRY, 1976
MY BROTHER, THE OUTLAW, 1951
MY DARLING CLEMENTINE, 1946
MY LITTLE CHICKADEE, 1940
MY NAME IS NOBODY, 1974
MY NAME IS PECOS, 1966
MY PAL, THE KING, 1932
MY PAL TRIGGER, 1946
MYSTERIOUS AVENGER, THE, 1936
MYSTERIOUS DESPERADO, THE, 1949
MYSTERIOUS RIDER, THE, 1933
MYSTERIOUS RIDER, THE, 1938
MYSTERIOUS RIDER, THE, 1942
MYSTERY MAN, 1944
MYSTERY OF THE HOODED HORSEMEN, THE, 1937
MYSTERY RANCH, 1932
MYSTERY RANGE, 1937
NAKED HILLS, THE, 1956
NAKED IN THE SUN, 1957
NAKED SPUR, THE, 1953
NATCHEZ TRACE, 1960
NAVAJO, 1952
NAVAJO JOE, 1967
NAVAJO KID, THE, 1946
NAVAJO RUN, 1966
NAVAJO TRAIL RAIDERS, 1949
NAVAJO TRAIL, THE, 1945
'NEATH THE ARIZONA SKIES, 1934
NEBRASKAN, THE, 1953
NED KELLY, 1970
NEVADA, 1936
NEVADA, 1944
NEVADA BADMEN, 1951
NEVADA CITY, 1941
NEVADA SMITH, 1966
NEVADAN, THE, 1950
NEW FRONTIER, THE, 1935
NEW FRONTIER, 1939
NEW MEXICO, 1951
NIGHT OF THE GRIZZLY, THE, 1966
NIGHT PASSAGE, 1957
NIGHT RAIDERS, 1952
NIGHT RIDER, THE, 1932
NIGHT RIDERS, THE, 1939
NIGHT RIDERS OF MONTANA, 1951
NIGHT STAGE TO GALVESTON, 1952
NIGHT TIME IN NEVADA, 1948
99 WOUNDS, 1931
NO MAN'S RANGE, 1935
NO NAME ON THE BULLET, 1959
NO ROOM TO DIE, 1969
NOOSE FOR A GUNMAN, 1960
NORTH FROM LONE STAR, 1941
NORTH OF NOME, 1937
NORTH OF THE GREAT DIVIDE, 1950
NORTH OF THE RIO GRANDE, 1937
NORTH OF THE YUKON, 1939
NORTH TO ALASKA, 1960
NORTH TO THE KLONDIKE, 1942
NORTHERN FRONTIER, 1935
NORTHERN PATROL, 1953
NORTHWEST OUTPOST, 1947
NORTHWEST RANGERS, 1942
NORTHWEST STAMPEDE, 1948
NORTHWEST TERRITORY, 1952
NORTHWEST TRAIL, 1945
OH, SUSANNA, 1937
OH! SUSANNA, 1951
OKLAHOMA, 1955
OKLAHOMA ANNIE, 1952
OKLAHOMA BADLANDS, 1948
OKLAHOMA BLUES, 1948
OKLAHOMA CYCLONE, 1930
OKLAHOMA FRONTIER, 1939
OKLAHOMA JIM, 1931
OKLAHOMA JUSTICE, 1951
OKLAHOMA KID, THE, 1939

OKLAHOMA RAIDERS, 1944
OKLAHOMA RENEGADES, 1940
OKLAHOMA TERRITORY, 1960
OKLAHOMA TERROR, 1939
OKLAHOMA WOMAN, THE, 1956
OKLAHOMAN, THE, 1957
OLD BARN DANCE, THE, 1938
OLD CHISHOLM TRAIL, 1943
OLD CORRAL, THE, 1937
OLD FRONTIER, THE, 1950
OLD LOS ANGELES, 1948
OLD OKLAHOMA PLAINS, 1952
OLD OVERLAND TRAIL, 1953
OLD SHATTERHAND, 1968
OLD TEXAS TRAIL, THE, 1944
OLD WEST, THE, 1952
OLD WYOMING TRAIL, THE, 1937
OMAHA TRAIL, THE, 1942
ON THE OLD SPANISH TRAIL, 1947
ON TOP OF OLD SMOKY, 1953
ONCE UPON A HORSE, 1958
ONCE UPON A TIME IN THE WEST, 1969
ONE-EYED JACKS, 1961
ONE FOOT IN HELL, 1960
100 RIFLES, 1969
ONE LITTLE INDIAN, 1973
ONE MAN JUSTICE, 1937
ONE-MAN LAW, 1932
ONE MAN'S LAW, 1940
ONE MORE TRAIN TO ROB, 1971
ONE WAY TRAIL, THE, 1931
ONLY THE VALIANT, 1951
OREGON PASSAGE, 1958
OREGON TRAIL, THE, 1936
OREGON TRAIL, 1945
OREGON TRAIL, THE, 1959
OREGON TRAIL SCOUTS, 1947
ORPHAN OF THE PECOS, 1938
OUT CALIFORNIA WAY, 1946
OUTCAST, THE, 1954
OUTCAST OF BLACK MESA, 1950
OUTCASTS OF POKER FLAT, THE, 1937
OUTCASTS OF POKER FLAT, THE, 1952
OUTCASTS OF THE TRAIL, 1949
OUTLAW, THE, 1943
OUTLAW BRAND, 1948
OUTLAW COUNTRY, 1949
OUTLAW DEPUTY, THE, 1935
OUTLAW EXPRESS, 1938
OUTLAW GOLD, 1950
OUTLAW JOSEY WALES, THE, 1976
OUTLAW JUSTICE, 1933
OUTLAW OF THE PLAINS, 1946
OUTLAW STALLION, THE, 1954
OUTLAW TRAIL, 1944
OUTLAW TREASURE, 1955
OUTLAW WOMEN, 1952
OUTLAWED GUNS, 1935
OUTLAW'S DAUGHTER, THE, 1954
OUTLAWS IS COMING, THE, 1965
OUTLAWS OF PINE RIDGE, 1942
OUTLAWS OF SANTA FE, 1944
OUTLAWS OF SONORA, 1938
OUTLAWS OF STAMPEDE PASS, 1943
OUTLAWS OF TEXAS, 1950
OUTLAWS OF THE CHEROKEE TRAIL, 1941
OUTLAWS OF THE DESERT, 1941
OUTLAWS OF THE ORIENT, 1937
OUTLAWS OF THE PANHANDLE, 1941
OUTLAWS OF THE PRAIRIE, 1938
OUTLAWS OF THE RIO GRANDE, 1941
OUTLAWS OF THE ROCKIES, 1945
OUTLAW'S PARADISE, 1939
OUTLAW'S SON, 1957
OUTPOST OF THE MOUNTIES, 1939
OUTRAGE, THE, 1964
OUTRIDERS, THE, 1950
OVER THE BORDER, 1950
OVERLAND BOUND, 1929
OVERLAND EXPRESS, THE, 1938
OVERLAND MAIL, 1939
OVERLAND MAIL ROBBERY, 1943
OVERLAND PACIFIC, 1954
OVERLAND RIDERS, 1946
OVERLAND STAGE RAIDERS, 1938
OVERLAND STAGECOACH, 1942

OVERLAND TELEGRAPH, 1951
OX-BOW INCIDENT, THE, 1943
PACK TRAIN, 1953
PAINT YOUR WAGON, 1969
PAINTED DESERT, THE, 1931
PAINTED DESERT, THE, 1938
PAINTED TRAIL, THE, 1938
PAL FROM TEXAS, THE, 1939
PALE RIDER, 1985
PALOMINO, THE, 1950
PALS OF THE GOLDEN WEST, 1952
PALS OF THE PECOS, 1941
PALS OF THE RANGE, 1935
PALS OF THE SADDLE, 1938
PALS OF THE SILVER SAGE, 1940
PANAMINT'S BAD MAN, 1938
PANCHO VILLA, 1975
PANCHO VILLA RETURNS, 1950
PANHANDLE, 1948
PARADE OF THE WEST, 1930
PARADISE CANYON, 1935
PARDNERS, 1956
PARDON MY GUN, 1930
PARDON MY GUN, 1942
PARSON AND THE OUTLAW, THE, 1957
PARSON OF PANAMINT, THE, 1941
PARTNERS, 1932
PARTNERS OF THE PLAINS, 1938
PARTNERS OF THE SUNSET, 1948
PARTNERS OF THE TRAIL, 1931
PARTNERS OF THE TRAIL, 1944
PASSAGE WEST, 1951
PASSION, 1954
PAT GARRETT AND BILLY THE KID, 1973
PATHFINDER, THE, 1952
PAWNEE, 1957
PAYMENT IN BLOOD, 1968
PEACE FOR A GUNFIGHTER, 1967
PEACEMAKER, THE, 1956
PECOS RIVER, 1951
PERILOUS JOURNEY, A, 1953
PERSUADER, THE, 1957
PHANTOM COWBOY, THE, 1941
PHANTOM GOLD, 1938
PHANTOM OF SANTA FE, 1937
PHANTOM OF THE DESERT, 1930
PHANTOM OF THE PLAINS, 1945
PHANTOM OF THE RANGE, THE, 1938
PHANTOM PLAINSMEN, THE, 1942
PHANTOM RANCHER, 1940
PHANTOM RANGER, 1938
PHANTOM STAGE, THE, 1939
PHANTOM STAGECOACH, THE, 1957
PHANTOM STALLION, THE, 1954
PHANTOM THUNDERBOLT, THE, 1933
PHANTOM VALLEY, 1948
PIERRE OF THE PLAINS, 1942
PILLARS OF THE SKY, 1956
PINTO BANDIT, THE, 1944
PINTO CANYON, 1940
PINTO KID, THE, 1941
PINTO RUSTLERS, 1937
PIONEER DAYS, 1940
PIONEER JUSTICE, 1947
PIONEER MARSHAL, 1950
PIONEER TRAIL, 1938
PIONEERS, THE, 1941
PIONEERS OF THE FRONTIER, 1940
PIONEERS OF THE WEST, 1940
PIRATES OF MONTEREY, 1947
PIRATES OF THE PRAIRIE, 1942
PIRATES ON HORSEBACK, 1941
PISTOL FOR RINGO, A, 1966
PISTOL HARVEST, 1951
PLACE CALLED GLORY, A, 1966
PLAINSMAN, THE, 1937
PLAINSMAN, THE, 1966
PLAINSMAN AND THE LADY, 1946
PLAINSONG, 1982
PLUNDERERS, THE, 1948
PLUNDERERS, THE, 1960
PLUNDERERS OF PAINTED FLATS, 1959
POCATELLO KID, 1932
POCKET MONEY, 1972
PONY EXPRESS, 1953
PONY EXPRESS RIDER, 1976

PONY POST, 1940
PONY SOLDIER, 1952
POR MIS PISTOLAS, 1969
POSSE, 1975
POSSE FROM HELL, 1961
POWDER RIVER, 1953
POWDER RIVER RUSTLERS, 1949
POWDERSMOKE RANGE, 1935
PRAIRIE, THE, 1948
PRAIRIE BADMEN, 1946
PRAIRIE EXPRESS, 1947
PRAIRIE JUSTICE, 1938
PRAIRIE LAW, 1940
PRAIRIE MOON, 1938
PRAIRIE OUTLAWS, 1948
PRAIRIE PALS, 1942
PRAIRIE PIONEERS, 1941
PRAIRIE ROUNDUP, 1951
PRAIRIE RUSTLERS, 1945
PRAIRIE SCHOONERS, 1940
PRAIRIE STRANGER, 1941
PRAIRIE THUNDER, 1937
PRESCOTT KID, THE, 1936
PRICE OF POWER, THE, 1969
PRIDE OF THE PLAINS, 1944
PRIDE OF THE WEST, 1938
PRINCE OF THE PLAINS, 1949
PROFESSIONALS, THE, 1966
PROUD ONES, THE, 1956
PROUD REBEL, THE, 1958
PUBLIC COWBOY NO. 1, 1937
PURPLE HILLS, THE, 1961
PURPLE VIGILANTES, THE, 1938
PURSUED, 1947
PURSUIT, 1975
QUANDO EL AMOR RIE, 1933
QUANTEZ, 1957
QUANTRILL'S RAIDERS, 1958
QUEEN OF THE YUKON, 1940
QUICK GUN, THE, 1964
QUICK ON THE TRIGGER, 1949
QUIET GUN, THE, 1957
QUINCANNON, FRONTIER SCOUT, 1956
RACHEL AND THE STRANGER, 1948
RACKETEERS OF THE RANGE, 1939
RAGE AT DAWN, 1955
RAGTIME COWBOY JOE, 1940
RAIDERS, THE, 1952
RAIDERS, THE, 1964
RAIDERS OF OLD CALIFORNIA, 1957
RAIDERS OF RED GAP, 1944
RAIDERS OF SAN JOAQUIN, 1943
RAIDERS OF SUNSET PASS, 1943
RAIDERS OF THE BORDER, 1944
RAIDERS OF THE RANGE, 1942
RAIDERS OF THE SOUTH, 1947
RAIDERS OF THE WEST, 1942
RAIDERS OF TOMAHAWK CREEK, 1950
RAILS INTO LARAMIE, 1954
RAINBOW OVER TEXAS, 1946
RAINBOW OVER THE RANGE, 1940
RAINBOW OVER THE ROCKIES, 1947
RAINBOW RANCH, 1933
RAINBOW TRAIL, 1932
RAINBOW VALLEY, 1935
RAINBOW'S END, 1935
RAMONA, 1936
RAMPAGE AT APACHE WELLS, 1966
RAMROD, 1947
RAMRODDER, THE, 1969
RAMSBOTTOM RIDES AGAIN, 1956
RANCHO DELUXE, 1975
RANCHO GRANDE, 1938
RANCHO GRANDE, 1940
RANCHO NOTORIOUS, 1952
RANDY RIDES ALONE, 1934
RANGE BEYOND THE BLUE, 1947
RANGE BUSTERS, THE, 1940
RANGE DEFENDERS, 1937
RANGE FEUD, THE, 1931
RANGE JUSTICE, 1949
RANGE LAND, 1949
RANGE LAW, 1931
RANGE LAW, 1944
RANGE RENEGADES, 1948
RANGE WAR, 1939

RANGER AND THE LADY, THE, 1940
RANGER COURAGE, 1937
RANGER OF CHEROKEE STRIP, 1949
RANGER'S CODE, THE, 1933
RANGERS OF FORTUNE, 1940
RANGERS RIDE, THE, 1948
RANGER'S ROUNDUP, THE, 1938
RANGERS STEP IN, THE, 1937
RANGERS TAKE OVER, THE, 1942
RANGLE RIVER, 1939
RARE BREED, THE, 1966
RATON PASS, 1951
RAW DEAL, 1977
RAW EDGE, 1956
RAW TIMBER, 1937
RAWHIDE, 1938
RAWHIDE, 1951
RAWHIDE RANGERS, 1941
RAWHIDE TRAIL, THE, 1958
RAWHIDE YEARS, THE, 1956
REASON TO LIVE, A REASON TO DIE, A, 1974
REBEL CITY, 1953
REBEL IN TOWN, 1956
REBELLION, 1938
RED BADGE OF COURAGE, THE, 1951
RED BLOOD OF COURAGE, 1935
RED CANYON, 1949
RED DESERT, 1949
RED FORK RANGE, 1931
RED GARTERS, 1954
RED HEADED STRANGER, 1987
RED MOUNTAIN, 1951
RED PONY, THE, 1949
RED RIVER, 1948
RED RIVER RANGE, 1938
RED RIVER RENEGADES, 1946
RED RIVER ROBIN HOOD, 1943
RED RIVER SHORE, 1953
RED RIVER VALLEY, 1936
RED RIVER VALLEY, 1941
RED ROCK OUTLAW, 1950
RED ROPE, THE, 1937
RED RUNS THE RIVER, 1963
RED STALLION, THE, 1947
RED STALLION IN THE ROCKIES, 1949
RED SUN, 1972
RED SUNDOWN, 1956
RED TOMAHAWK, 1967
RED, WHITE AND BLACK, THE, 1970
REDHEAD AND THE COWBOY, THE, 1950
REDHEAD FROM WYOMING, THE, 1953
REDWOOD FOREST TRAIL, 1950
RELENTLESS, 1948
RENEGADE GIRL, 1946
RENEGADE RANGER, 1938
RENEGADE TRAIL, 1939
RENEGADES, 1946
RENEGADES OF SONORA, 1948
RENEGADES OF THE RIO GRANDE, 1945
RENEGADES OF THE SAGE, 1949
RENEGADES OF THE WEST, 1932
RENFREW OF THE ROYAL MOUNTED, 1937
REPRISAL, 1956
REQUIEM FOR A GUNFIGHTER, 1965
RESTLESS BREED, THE, 1957
RETURN OF A MAN CALLED HORSE, THE, 1976
RETURN OF DANIEL BOONE, THE, 1941
RETURN OF FRANK JAMES, THE, 1940
RETURN OF JACK SLADE, THE, 1955
RETURN OF JESSE JAMES, THE, 1950
RETURN OF JOSEY WALES, THE, 1987
RETURN OF RINGO, THE, 1966
RETURN OF SABATA, 1972
RETURN OF THE BADMEN, 1948
RETURN OF THE CISCO KID, 1939
RETURN OF THE FRONTIERSMAN, 1950
RETURN OF THE LASH, 1947
RETURN OF THE RANGERS, THE, 1943
RETURN OF THE SEVEN, 1966
RETURN OF THE TEXAN, 1952
RETURN OF WILD BILL, THE, 1940
RETURN OF WILDFIRE, THE, 1948
RETURN TO SNOWY RIVER: PART II, 1988
RETURN TO WARBOW, 1958
REVENGE AT EL PASO, 1968
REVENGE RIDER, THE, 1935

REVENGERS, THE, 1972
REVOLT AT FORT LARAMIE, 1957
RHYTHM OF THE RIO GRANDE, 1940
RHYTHM OF THE SADDLE, 1938
RHYTHM ON THE RANGE, 1936
RIDE A CROOKED TRAIL, 1958
RIDE A NORTHBOUND HORSE, 1969
RIDE A VIOLENT MILE, 1957
RIDE BACK, THE, 1957
RIDE BEYOND VENGEANCE, 1966
RIDE CLEAR OF DIABLO, 1954
RIDE 'EM COWBOY, 1936
RIDE 'EM COWBOY, 1942
RIDE 'EM COWGIRL, 1939
RIDE HIM, COWBOY, 1932
RIDE IN THE WHIRLWIND, 1966
RIDE LONESOME, 1959
RIDE ON VAQUERO, 1941
RIDE OUT FOR REVENGE, 1957
RIDE, RANGER, RIDE, 1936
RIDE, RYDER, RIDE!, 1949
RIDE, TENDERFOOT, RIDE, 1940
RIDE THE HIGH COUNTRY, 1962
RIDE THE MAN DOWN, 1952
RIDE TO HANGMAN'S TREE, THE, 1967
RIDE, VAQUERO!, 1953
RIDER FROM TUCSON, 1950
RIDER OF DEATH VALLEY, 1932
RIDER OF THE LAW, THE, 1935
RIDER OF THE PLAINS, 1931
RIDER ON A DEAD HORSE, 1962
RIDERS FROM NOWHERE, 1940
RIDERS IN THE SKY, 1949
RIDERS OF BLACK MOUNTAIN, 1941
RIDERS OF BLACK RIVER, 1939
RIDERS OF DESTINY, 1933
RIDERS OF PASCO BASIN, 1940
RIDERS OF THE BADLANDS, 1941
RIDERS OF THE BLACK HILLS, 1938
RIDERS OF THE CACTUS, 1931
RIDERS OF THE DAWN, 1937
RIDERS OF THE DAWN, 1945
RIDERS OF THE DEADLINE, 1943
RIDERS OF THE DESERT, 1932
RIDERS OF THE DUSK, 1949
RIDERS OF THE FRONTIER, 1939
RIDERS OF THE GOLDEN GULCH, 1932
RIDERS OF THE NORTH, 1931
RIDERS OF THE NORTHLAND, 1942
RIDERS OF THE NORTHWEST MOUNTED, 1943
RIDERS OF THE PURPLE SAGE, 1931
RIDERS OF THE PURPLE SAGE, 1941
RIDERS OF THE RANGE, 1949
RIDERS OF THE RIO GRANDE, 1943
RIDERS OF THE ROCKIES, 1937
RIDERS OF THE SANTA FE, 1944
RIDERS OF THE WEST, 1942
RIDERS OF THE WHISTLING PINES, 1949
RIDERS OF THE WHISTLING SKULL, 1937
RIDIN' DOWN THE CANYON, 1942
RIDIN' DOWN THE TRAIL, 1947
RIDIN' FOR JUSTICE, 1932
RIDIN' LAW, 1930
RIDIN' ON A RAINBOW, 1941
RIDIN' THE LONE TRAIL, 1937
RIDIN' THE OUTLAW TRAIL, 1951
RIDING AVENGER, THE, 1936
RIDING HIGH, 1943
RIDING ON, 1937
RIDING SHOTGUN, 1954
RIDING SPEED, 1934
RIDING THE CHEROKEE TRAIL, 1941
RIDING THE SUNSET TRAIL, 1941
RIDING THE WIND, 1942
RIDING TORNADO, THE, 1932
RIDING WEST, 1944
RIM OF THE CANYON, 1949
RIMFIRE, 1949
RINGO AND HIS GOLDEN PISTOL, 1966
RIO BRAVO, 1959
RIO CONCHOS, 1964
RIO GRANDE, 1939
RIO GRANDE, 1950
RIO GRANDE PATROL, 1950
RIO GRANDE RAIDERS, 1946
RIO GRANDE RANGER, 1937

RIO LOBO, 1970
RIP ROARIN' BUCKAROO, 1936
RIVER LADY, 1948
RIVER OF NO RETURN, 1954
RIVER'S END, 1931
RIVER'S END, 1940
ROAD AGENT, 1941
ROAD AGENT, 1952
ROAD TO DENVER, THE, 1955
ROAD TO FORT ALAMO, THE, 1966
ROAD TO RENO, THE, 1938
ROAMING COWBOY, THE, 1937
ROARIN' GUNS, 1936
ROARIN' LEAD, 1937
ROARING RANCH, 1930
ROARING SIX GUNS, 1937
ROARING TIMBER, 1937
ROARING WESTWARD, 1949
ROBBERS OF THE RANGE, 1941
ROBBERS' ROOST, 1933
ROBIN HOOD OF EL DORADO, 1936
ROBIN HOOD OF THE PECOS, 1941
ROBIN HOOD OF THE RANGE, 1943
ROBIN OF TEXAS, 1947
ROCK ISLAND TRAIL, 1950
ROCK RIVER RENEGADES, 1942
ROCKIN' IN THE ROCKIES, 1945
ROCKY MOUNTAIN, 1950
ROCKY MOUNTAIN MYSTERY, 1935
ROCKY MOUNTAIN RANGERS, 1940
ROCKY RHODES, 1934
RODEO, 1952
RODEO KING AND THE SENORITA, 1951
RODEO RHYTHM, 1941
ROGUE OF THE RANGE, 1937
ROGUE OF THE RIO GRANDE, 1930
ROGUE RIVER, 1951
ROLL ALONG, COWBOY, 1938
ROLL ON TEXAS MOON, 1946
ROLL, THUNDER, ROLL, 1949
ROLL, WAGONS, ROLL, 1939
ROLLIN' HOME TO TEXAS, 1941
ROLLIN' PLAINS, 1938
ROLLIN' WESTWARD, 1939
ROLLING CARAVANS, 1938
ROLLING DOWN THE GREAT DIVIDE, 1942
ROMANCE OF THE REDWOODS, 1939
ROMANCE OF THE RIO GRANDE, 1929
ROMANCE OF THE RIO GRANDE, 1941
ROMANCE OF THE ROCKIES, 1938
ROMANCE OF THE WEST, 1946
ROMANCE ON THE RANGE, 1942
ROMANCE RIDES THE RANGE, 1936
ROOSTER COGBURN, 1975
ROOTIN' TOOTIN' RHYTHM, 1937
ROSE OF CIMARRON, 1952
ROSE OF THE RANCHO, 1936
ROSE OF THE RIO GRANDE, 1938
ROUGH NIGHT IN JERICHO, 1967
ROUGH RIDERS OF CHEYENNE, 1945
ROUGH RIDERS OF DURANGO, 1951
ROUGH RIDERS' ROUNDUP, 1939
ROUGH RIDIN' RHYTHM, 1937
ROUGH RIDING RANGER, 1935
ROUGH ROMANCE, 1930
ROUGH, TOUGH WEST, THE, 1952
ROUGHSHOD, 1949
ROUNDERS, THE, 1965
ROUNDUP, THE, 1941
ROUNDUP TIME IN TEXAS, 1937
ROVIN' TUMBLEWEEDS, 1939
ROYAL MOUNTED PATROL, THE, 1941
RUN FOR COVER, 1955
RUN HOME SLOW, 1965
RUN OF THE ARROW, 1957
RUNNING WILD, 1973
RUSTLERS, 1949
RUSTLER'S HIDEOUT, 1944
RUSTLERS OF DEVIL'S CANYON, 1947
RUSTLERS ON HORSEBACK, 1950
RUSTLER'S PARADISE, 1935
RUSTLER'S RHAPSODY, 1985
RUSTLERS' ROUNDUP, 1933
RUSTLER'S ROUNDUP, 1946
RUSTLER'S VALLEY, 1937
RUSTY RIDES ALONE, 1933

RUTHLESS FOUR, THE, 1969
SABATA, 1969
SADDLE BUSTER, THE, 1932
SADDLE LEGION, 1951
SADDLE MOUNTAIN ROUNDUP, 1941
SADDLE PALS, 1947
SADDLE THE WIND, 1958
SADDLE TRAMP, 1950
SADDLEMATES, 1941
SAGA OF DEATH VALLEY, 1939
SAGA OF HEMP BROWN, THE, 1958
SAGEBRUSH FAMILY TRAILS WEST, THE, 1940
SAGEBRUSH LAW, 1943
SAGEBRUSH POLITICS, 1930
SAGEBRUSH TRAIL, 1934
SAGEBRUSH TROUBADOR, 1935
SAGINAW TRAIL, 1953
SALLY FIELDGOOD & CO., 1975
SALT LAKE RAIDERS, 1950
SAM WHISKEY, 1969
SAN ANTONE, 1953
SAN ANTONE AMBUSH, 1949
SAN ANTONIO, 1945
SAN ANTONIO KID, THE, 1944
SAN FERNANDO VALLEY, 1944
SAN FRANCISCO STORY, THE, 1952
SANDFLOW, 1937
SANTA FE, 1951
SANTA FE BOUND, 1937
SANTA FE MARSHAL, 1940
SANTA FE PASSAGE, 1955
SANTA FE SADDLEMATES, 1945
SANTA FE SCOUTS, 1943
SANTA FE STAMPEDE, 1938
SANTA FE TRAIL, THE, 1930
SANTA FE UPRISING, 1946
SANTEE, 1973
SASKATCHEWAN, 1954
SATAN'S CRADLE, 1949
SAVAGE FRONTIER, 1953
SAVAGE GUNS, THE, 1962
SAVAGE HORDE, THE, 1950
SAVAGE PAMPAS, 1967
SAVAGE SAM, 1963
SAVAGE, THE, 1953
SCALPHUNTERS, THE, 1968
SCANDALOUS JOHN, 1971
SCARLET BRAND, 1932
SCARLET RIVER, 1933
SCAVENGERS, THE, 1969
SEA OF GRASS, THE, 1947
SEARCHERS, THE, 1956
SECOND TIME AROUND, THE, 1961
SECRET MENACE, 1931
SECRET OF CONVICT LAKE, THE, 1951
SECRET OF TREASURE MOUNTAIN, 1956
SECRET PATROL, 1936
SECRET VALLEY, 1937
SECRETS, 1933
SECRETS OF THE WASTELANDS, 1941
SEMINOLE, 1953
SEMINOLE UPRISING, 1955
SENOR AMERICANO, 1929
SERGEANT BERRY, 1938
SERGEANT RUTLEDGE, 1960
SERGEANTS 3, 1962
SEVEN ALONE, 1975
SEVEN GUNS FOR THE MACGREGORS, 1968
SEVEN GUNS TO MESA, 1958
SEVEN MEN FROM NOW, 1956
SEVEN WAYS FROM SUNDOWN, 1960
SEVENTH CAVALRY, 1956
SHADOW RANCH, 1930
SHADOW VALLEY, 1947
SHADOWS OF DEATH, 1945
SHADOWS OF THE WEST, 1949
SHADOWS OF TOMBSTONE, 1953
SHADOWS ON THE SAGE, 1942
SHAKIEST GUN IN THE WEST, THE, 1968
SHALAKO, 1968
SHANE, 1953
SHE WORE A YELLOW RIBBON, 1949
SHEEPMAN, THE, 1958
SHERIFF OF CIMARRON, 1945
SHERIFF OF FRACTURED JAW, THE, 1958
SHERIFF OF LAS VEGAS, 1944

SHERIFF OF REDWOOD VALLEY, 1946
SHERIFF OF SAGE VALLEY, 1942
SHERIFF OF SUNDOWN, 1944
SHERIFF OF TOMBSTONE, 1941
SHERIFF OF WICHITA, 1949
SHINE ON, HARVEST MOON, 1938
SHOOT FIRST, LAUGH LAST, 1967
SHOOT OUT, 1971
SHOOT OUT AT BIG SAG, 1962
SHOOT-OUT AT MEDICINE BEND, 1957
SHOOTING HIGH, 1940
SHOOTING, THE, 1971
SHOOTIST, THE, 1976
SHORT GRASS, 1950
SHOTGUN, 1955
SHOTGUN PASS, 1932
SHOWDOWN, THE, 1950
SHOWDOWN, 1963
SHOWDOWN, 1973
SHOWDOWN AT ABILENE, 1956
SHOWDOWN AT BOOT HILL, 1958
SHOWDOWN, THE, 1940
SIEGE AT RED RIVER, THE, 1954
SIERRA, 1950
SIERRA BARON, 1958
SIERRA PASSAGE, 1951
SIERRA STRANGER, 1957
SIERRA SUE, 1941
SILENT CONFLICT, 1948
SILVER BANDIT, THE, 1950
SILVER BULLET, THE, 1942
SILVER CANYON, 1951
SILVER CITY, 1951
SILVER CITY BONANZA, 1951
SILVER CITY KID, 1944
SILVER CITY RAIDERS, 1943
SILVER LODE, 1954
SILVER ON THE SAGE, 1939
SILVER QUEEN, 1942
SILVER RAIDERS, 1950
SILVER RIVER, 1948
SILVER SPURS, 1936
SILVER SPURS, 1943
SILVER STALLION, 1941
SILVER STAR, THE, 1955
SILVER TRAIL, THE, 1937
SILVER TRAILS, 1948
SILVER WHIP, THE, 1953
SILVERADO, 1985
SIN TOWN, 1942
SING, COWBOY, SING, 1937
SINGER NOT THE SONG, THE, 1961
SINGING BUCKAROO, THE, 1937
SINGING COWBOY, THE, 1936
SINGING COWGIRL, THE, 1939
SINGING GUNS, 1950
SINGING HILL, THE, 1941
SINGING OUTLAW, 1937
SINGING SHERIFF, THE, 1944
SINGING VAGABOND, THE, 1935
SINGLE-HANDED SANDERS, 1932
SINISTER JOURNEY, 1948
SIOUX CITY SUE, 1946
SITTING BULL, 1954
SIX BLACK HORSES, 1962
SIX GUN GOLD, 1941
SIX GUN GOSPEL, 1943
SIX-GUN LAW, 1948
SIX GUN MAN, 1946
SIX-GUN RHYTHM, 1939
SIX GUN SERENADE, 1947
SIX SHOOTIN' SHERIFF, 1938
SKIPALONG ROSENBLOOM, 1951
SLAUGHTER TRAIL, 1951
SLIM CARTER, 1957
SMITH, 1969
SMOKE IN THE WIND, 1975
SMOKE SIGNAL, 1955
SMOKE TREE RANGE, 1937
SMOKEY SMITH, 1935
SMOKING GUNS, 1934
SMOKY, 1933
SMOKY, 1946
SMOKY, 1966
SMOKY CANYON, 1952
SMOKY MOUNTAIN MELODY, 1949

SMOKY TRAILS, 1939
SNAKE RIVER DESPERADOES, 1951
SOLDIER BLUE, 1970
SOMBRERO KID, THE, 1942
SOMETHING BIG, 1971
SOMEWHERE IN SONORA, 1933
SON OF A BADMAN, 1949
SON OF A GUNFIGHTER, 1966
SON OF BELLE STARR, 1953
SON OF BILLY THE KID, 1949
SON OF DAVY CROCKETT, THE, 1941
SON OF GOD'S COUNTRY, 1948
SON OF OKLAHOMA, 1932
SON OF PALEFACE, 1952
SON OF ROARING DAN, 1940
SON OF THE BORDER, 1933
SON OF THE PLAINS, 1931
SON OF THE RENEGADE, 1953
SONG OF ARIZONA, 1946
SONG OF NEVADA, 1944
SONG OF OLD WYOMING, 1945
SONG OF TEXAS, 1943
SONG OF THE BUCKAROO, 1939
SONG OF THE CABELLERO, 1930
SONG OF THE DRIFTER, 1948
SONG OF THE GRINGO, 1936
SONG OF THE SADDLE, 1936
SONG OF THE SIERRAS, 1946
SONG OF THE TRAIL, 1936
SONG OF THE WASTELAND, 1947
SONGS AND BULLETS, 1938
SONNY AND JED, 1974
SONORA STAGECOACH, 1944
SONS OF ADVENTURE, 1948
SONS OF KATIE ELDER, THE, 1965
SONS OF NEW MEXICO, 1949
SONS OF THE PIONEERS, 1942
SONS OF THE SADDLE, 1930
SOUL OF NIGGER CHARLEY, THE, 1973
SOUTH OF ARIZONA, 1938
SOUTH OF CALIENTE, 1951
SOUTH OF DEATH VALLEY, 1949
SOUTH OF RIO, 1949
SOUTH OF ST. LOUIS, 1949
SOUTH OF SANTA FE, 1932
SOUTH OF SANTA FE, 1942
SOUTH OF SONORA, 1930
SOUTH OF THE BORDER, 1939
SOUTH OF THE RIO GRANDE, 1932
SOUTH OF THE RIO GRANDE, 1945
SOUTH PACIFIC TRAIL, 1952
SOUTHWARD HO?, 1939
SOUTHWEST PASSAGE, 1954
SPEED WINGS, 1934
SPIKES GANG, THE, 1974
SPIRIT OF THE WEST, 1932
SPOILERS, THE, 1942
SPOILERS OF THE PLAINS, 1951
SPOILERS OF THE RANGE, 1939
SPOILERS, THE, 1930
SPOILERS, THE, 1955
SPOOK TOWN, 1944
SPRINGFIELD RIFLE, 1952
SPRINGTIME IN THE ROCKIES, 1937
SPRINGTIME IN THE SIERRAS, 1947
SPURS, 1930
SQUARE DANCE JUBILEE, 1949
SQUARES, 1972
SQUAW MAN, THE, 1931
STAGE TO BLUE RIVER, 1951
STAGE TO CHINO, 1940
STAGE TO MESA CITY, 1947
STAGE TO THUNDER ROCK, 1964
STAGE TO TUCSON, 1950
STAGECOACH, 1939
STAGECOACH, 1966
STAGECOACH BUCKAROO, 1942
STAGECOACH DAYS, 1938
STAGECOACH EXPRESS, 1942
STAGECOACH KID, 1949
STAGECOACH OUTLAWS, 1945
STAGECOACH TO DANCER'S PARK, 1962
STAGECOACH TO DENVER, 1946
STAGECOACH TO FURY, 1956
STAGECOACH TO MONTEREY, 1944
STAGECOACH WAR, 1940

STALKING MOON, THE, 1969
STALLION CANYON, 1949
STAMPEDE, 1936
STAMPEDE, 1949
STAND AT APACHE RIVER, THE, 1953
STAND UP AND FIGHT, 1939
STAR IN THE DUST, 1956
STAR OF TEXAS, 1953
STAR PACKER, THE, 1934
STARDUST ON THE SAGE, 1942
STARLIGHT OVER TEXAS, 1938
STARS OVER ARIZONA, 1937
STARS OVER TEXAS, 1946
STATION WEST, 1948
STICK TO YOUR GUNS, 1941
STONE OF SILVER CREEK, 1935
STORM OVER WYOMING, 1950
STORM RIDER, THE, 1957
STORMY TRAILS, 1936
STRAIGHT SHOOTER, 1940
STRAIGHT TO HELL, 1987
STRANGE GAMBLE, 1948
STRANGE LADY IN TOWN, 1955
STRANGER AT MY DOOR, 1956
STRANGER FROM ARIZONA, THE, 1938
STRANGER FROM PECOS, THE, 1943
STRANGER FROM TEXAS, THE, 1940
STRANGER IN TOWN, A, 1968
STRANGER ON HORSEBACK, 1955
STRANGER RETURNS, THE, 1968
STRANGER WORE A GUN, THE, 1953
STRANGER'S GUNDOWN, THE, 1974
STRAWBERRY ROAN, 1933
STRAWBERRY ROAN, THE, 1948
STREETS OF GHOST TOWN, 1950
STREETS OF LAREDO, 1949
SUDDEN BILL DORN, 1938
SUGARFOOT, 1951
SUN VALLEY CYCLONE, 1946
SUNDOWN IN SANTA FE, 1948
SUNDOWN JIM, 1942
SUNDOWN KID, THE, 1942
SUNDOWN ON THE PRAIRIE, 1939
SUNDOWN RIDER, THE, 1933
SUNDOWN RIDERS, 1948
SUNDOWN SAUNDERS, 1937
SUNDOWN TRAIL, 1931
SUNDOWN VALLEY, 1944
SUNDOWNERS, THE, 1950
SUNRISE TRAIL, 1931
SUNSCORCHED, 1966
SUNSET, 1988
SUNSET IN EL DORADO, 1945
SUNSET IN THE WEST, 1950
SUNSET IN WYOMING, 1941
SUNSET OF POWER, 1936
SUNSET ON THE DESERT, 1942
SUNSET PASS, 1933
SUNSET PASS, 1946
SUNSET RANGE, 1935
SUNSET SERENADE, 1942
SUNSET TRAIL, 1932
SUNSET TRAIL, 1938
SUPPORT YOUR LOCAL GUNFIGHTER, 1971
SUPPORT YOUR LOCAL SHERIFF, 1969
SURRENDER, 1950
SUSANNA PASS, 1949
SUTTER'S GOLD, 1936
SWEET CREEK COUNTY WAR, THE, 1979
SWIFTY, 1936
SWING IN THE SADDLE, 1944
TAGGART, 1964
TAKE A HARD RIDE, 1975
TALISMAN, THE, 1966
TALL IN THE SADDLE, 1944
TALL MAN RIDING, 1955
TALL MEN, THE, 1955
TALL STRANGER, THE, 1957
TALL T, THE, 1957
TALL TEXAN, THE, 1953
TALL WOMEN, THE, 1967
TAMING OF THE WEST, THE, 1939
TARGET, 1952
TAZA, SON OF COCHISE, 1954
TELEGRAPH TRAIL, THE, 1933
TELL THEM WILLIE BOY IS HERE, 1969

10,000 DOLLARS BLOOD MONEY, 1966
TEN WANTED MEN, 1955
TENDERFOOT GOES WEST, A, 1937
TENNESSEE'S PARTNER, 1955
TENSION AT TABLE ROCK, 1956
TENTING TONIGHT ON THE OLD CAMP GROUND, 1943
TERROR AT BLACK FALLS, 1962
TERROR IN A TEXAS TOWN, 1958
TERROR OF TINY TOWN, THE, 1938
TERROR TRAIL, 1933
TERRORS ON HORSEBACK, 1946
TEX RIDES WITH THE BOY SCOUTS, 1937
TEX TAKES A HOLIDAY, 1932
TEXAN MEETS CALAMITY JANE, THE, 1950
TEXAN, THE, 1930
TEXANS NEVER CRY, 1951
TEXANS, THE, 1938
TEXAS, 1941
TEXAS ACROSS THE RIVER, 1966
TEXAS BAD MAN, 1932
TEXAS BAD MAN, 1953
TEXAS BUDDIES, 1932
TEXAS CITY, 1952
TEXAS CYCLONE, 1932
TEXAS DYNAMO, 1950
TEXAS GUN FIGHTER, 1932
TEXAS KID, THE, 1944
TEXAS LADY, 1955
TEXAS LAWMEN, 1951
TEXAS MAN HUNT, 1942
TEXAS MARSHAL, THE, 1941
TEXAS MASQUERADE, 1944
TEXAS PIONEERS, 1932
TEXAS RANGER, THE, 1931
TEXAS RANGERS RIDE AGAIN, 1940
TEXAS RANGERS, THE, 1936
TEXAS RANGERS, THE, 1951
TEXAS STAGECOACH, 1940
TEXAS STAMPEDE, 1939
TEXAS TERROR, 1935
TEXAS TERRORS, 1940
TEXAS TO BATAAN, 1942
TEXAS TORNADO, 1934
TEXAS TRAIL, 1937
TEXAS WILDCATS, 1939
TEXICAN, THE, 1966
THERE WAS A CROOKED MAN, 1970
THESE THOUSAND HILLS, 1959
THEY CALL ME TRINITY, 1971
THEY DIED WITH THEIR BOOTS ON, 1942
THEY RODE WEST, 1954
THIRTEEN FIGHTING MEN, 1960
THIS MAN CAN'T DIE, 1970
THIS SAVAGE LAND, 1969
THOMASINE AND BUSHROD, 1974
THOSE DIRTY DOGS, 1974
THREE GODFATHERS, 1936
THREE GODFATHERS, THE, 1948
THREE GUNS FOR TEXAS, 1968
THREE HOURS TO KILL, 1954
THREE IN THE SADDLE, 1945
THREE MEN FROM TEXAS, 1940
THREE MESQUITEERS, THE, 1936
THREE ON THE TRAIL, 1936
THREE OUTLAWS, THE, 1956
THREE ROGUES, 1931
3:10 TO YUMA, 1957
THREE TEXAS STEERS, 1939
THREE VIOLENT PEOPLE, 1956
THREE YOUNG TEXANS, 1954
THRILL HUNTER, THE, 1933
THROWBACK, THE, 1935
THUNDER AT THE BORDER, 1966
THUNDER IN GOD'S COUNTRY, 1951
THUNDER IN THE DESERT, 1938
THUNDER IN THE SUN, 1959
THUNDER MOUNTAIN, 1935
THUNDER MOUNTAIN, 1947
THUNDER OF DRUMS, A, 1961
THUNDER OVER ARIZONA, 1956
THUNDER OVER TEXAS, 1934
THUNDER OVER THE PLAINS, 1953
THUNDER OVER THE PRAIRIE, 1941
THUNDER PASS, 1954
THUNDER RIVER FEUD, 1942

BOLD: Films on Videocassette

THUNDER TOWN, 1946
THUNDER TRAIL, 1937
THUNDERHOOF, 1948
THUNDERING CARAVANS, 1952
THUNDERING FRONTIER, 1940
THUNDERING GUN SLINGERS, 1944
THUNDERING HERD, THE, 1934
THUNDERING HOOFS, 1941
THUNDERING TRAIL, THE, 1951
THUNDERING TRAILS, 1943
THUNDERING WEST, THE, 1939
TICKET TO TOMAHAWK, 1950
TIMBER STAMPEDE, 1939
TIMBER TRAIL, THE, 1948
TIMBER WAR, 1936
TIMBERJACK, 1955
TIME FOR DYING, A, 1971
TIME FOR KILLING, A, 1967
TIMERIDER, 1983
TIN STAR, THE, 1957
TIOGA KID, THE, 1948
TO THE LAST MAN, 1933
TODAY IT'S ME...TOMORROW YOU?, 1968
TOLL OF THE DESERT, 1936
TOM HORN, 1980
TOMAHAWK, 1951
TOMAHAWK TRAIL, 1957
TOMBSTONE CANYON, 1932
TOMBSTONE TERROR, 1935
TOMBSTONE, THE TOWN TOO TOUGH TO DIE, 1942
TONTO BASIN OUTLAWS, 1941
TOO MUCH BEEF, 1936
TOP GUN, 1955
TOPEKA, 1953
TOPEKA TERROR, THE, 1945
TORNADO RANGE, 1948
TOUGHEST GUN IN TOMBSTONE, 1958
TOUGHEST MAN IN ARIZONA, 1952
TOWN CALLED HELL, A, 1971
TOWN TAMER, 1965
TRAIL BEYOND, THE, 1934
TRAIL BLAZERS, THE, 1940
TRAIL DRIVE, THE, 1934
TRAIL DUST, 1936
TRAIL GUIDE, 1952
TRAIL OF KIT CARSON, 1945
TRAIL OF ROBIN HOOD, 1950
TRAIL OF TERROR, 1935
TRAIL OF TERROR, 1944
TRAIL OF THE SILVER SPURS, 1941
TRAIL OF THE VIGILANTES, 1940
TRAIL OF VENGEANCE, 1937
TRAIL RIDERS, 1942
TRAIL STREET, 1947
TRAIL TO GUNSIGHT, 1944
TRAIL TO SAN ANTONE, 1947
TRAIL TO VENGEANCE, 1945
TRAILIN' WEST, 1936
TRAILING DOUBLE TROUBLE, 1940
TRAILING TROUBLE, 1930
TRAILING TROUBLE, 1937
TRAIL'S END, 1949
TRAILS OF DANGER, 1930
TRAIN ROBBERS, THE, 1973
TRAIN TO TOMBSTONE, 1950
TRAITOR, THE, 1936
TRAMPLERS, THE, 1966
TRAPPED, 1937
TREACHERY RIDES THE RANGE, 1936
TREASURE OF LOST CANYON, THE, 1952
TREASURE OF PANCHO VILLA, THE, 1955
TREASURE OF RUBY HILLS, 1955
TREASURE OF SILVER LAKE, 1965
TRIBUTE TO A BADMAN, 1956
TRIGGER FINGERS, 1939
TRIGGER PALS, 1939
TRIGGER SMITH, 1939
TRIGGER TRAIL, 1944
TRIGGER TRICKS, 1930
TRIGGER TRIO, THE, 1937
TRIGGER, JR., 1950
TRINITY IS STILL MY NAME, 1971
TRIPLE JUSTICE, 1940
TRIUMPHS OF A MAN CALLED HORSE, 1983
TROOPER HOOK, 1957
TROUBLE AT MIDNIGHT, 1937

TROUBLE IN SUNDOWN, 1939
TROUBLE IN TEXAS, 1937
TRUE GRIT, 1969
TRUE STORY OF JESSE JAMES, THE, 1957
TRUSTED OUTLAW, THE, 1937
TUCSON, 1949
TUCSON RAIDERS, 1944
TULSA KID, THE, 1940
TUMBLEDOWN RANCH IN ARIZONA, 1941
TUMBLEWEED, 1953
TUMBLEWEED TRAIL, 1946
TUMBLING TUMBLEWEEDS, 1935
TWENTY MULE TEAM, 1940
TWILIGHT IN THE SIERRAS, 1950
TWILIGHT ON THE PRAIRIE, 1944
TWILIGHT ON THE RIO GRANDE, 1947
TWILIGHT ON THE TRAIL, 1941
TWINKLE IN GOD'S EYE, THE, 1955
TWO-FISTED JUSTICE, 1931
TWO FISTED JUSTICE, 1943
TWO-FISTED LAW, 1932
TWO-FISTED RANGERS, 1940
TWO-FISTED SHERIFF, 1937
TWO FLAGS WEST, 1950
TWO-GUN JUSTICE, 1938
TWO-GUN LADY, 1956
TWO GUN LAW, 1937
TWO GUN MAN, THE, 1931
TWO GUN SHERIFF, 1941
TWO-GUN TROUBADOR, 1939
TWO GUNS AND A BADGE, 1954
TWO GUYS FROM TEXAS, 1948
TWO MULES FOR SISTER SARA, 1970
TWO RODE TOGETHER, 1961
UGLY ONES, THE, 1968
ULZANA'S RAID, 1972
UNA SIGNORA DELL'OVEST, 1942
UNDEFEATED, THE, 1969
UNDER A TEXAS MOON, 1930
UNDER ARIZONA SKIES, 1946
UNDER CALIFORNIA STARS, 1948
UNDER COLORADO SKIES, 1947
UNDER FIESTA STARS, 1941
UNDER MEXICALI STARS, 1950
UNDER MONTANA SKIES, 1930
UNDER NEVADA SKIES, 1946
UNDER STRANGE FLAGS, 1937
UNDER TEXAS SKIES, 1931
UNDER TEXAS SKIES, 1940
UNDER THE PAMPAS MOON, 1935
UNDER THE TONTO RIM, 1933
UNDER THE TONTO RIM, 1947
UNDER WESTERN SKIES, 1945
UNDER WESTERN STARS, 1938
UNDERCOVER MAN, 1936
UNDERCOVER MAN, 1942
UNDERGROUND RUSTLERS, 1941
UNEXPECTED GUEST, 1946
UNFORGIVEN, THE, 1960
UNHOLY FOUR, THE, 1969
UNION PACIFIC, 1939
UNKNOWN RANGER, THE, 1936
UNKNOWN VALLEY, 1933
UNTAMED BREED, THE, 1948
UNTAMED FRONTIER, 1952
UP THE MACGREGORS, 1967
UTAH, 1945
UTAH BLAINE, 1957
UTAH KID, THE, 1930
UTAH TRAIL, 1938
UTAH WAGON TRAIN, 1951
VALDEZ IS COMING, 1971
VALERIE, 1957
VALIANT HOMBRE THE, 1948
VALLEY OF FIRE, 1951
VALLEY OF GWANGI, THE, 1969
VALLEY OF HUNTED MEN, 1942
VALLEY OF THE LAWLESS, 1936
VALLEY OF THE SUN, 1942
VALLEY OF VENGEANCE, 1944
VANISHING AMERICAN, THE, 1955
VANISHING FRONTIER, THE, 1932
VANISHING OUTPOST, THE, 1951
VANISHING WESTERNER, THE, 1950
VANQUISHED, THE, 1953
VENGEANCE, 1964

VENGEANCE, 1968
VENGEANCE IS MINE, 1969
VENGEANCE VALLEY, 1951
VERA CRUZ, 1954
VIA PONY EXPRESS, 1933
VIGILANTE HIDEOUT, 1950
VIGILANTE TERROR, 1953
VIGILANTES OF BOOMTOWN, 1947
VIGILANTES OF DODGE CITY, 1944
VIGILANTES RETURN, THE, 1947
VILLA!, 1958
VILLA RIDES, 1968
VILLAIN, THE, 1979
VIOLENT MEN, THE, 1955
VIRGINIA CITY, 1940
VIRGINIAN, THE, 1929
VIRGINIAN, THE, 1946
VIVA CISCO KID, 1940
WACKIEST WAGON TRAIN IN THE WEST, THE, 1976
WACO, 1952
WACO, 1966
WAGON MASTER, THE, 1929
WAGON TEAM, 1952
WAGON TRACKS WEST, 1943
WAGON TRAIL, 1935
WAGON TRAIN, 1940
WAGON WHEELS, 1934
WAGON WHEELS WESTWARD, 1956
WAGONMASTER, 1950
WAGONS WEST, 1952
WAGONS WESTWARD, 1940
WALK LIKE A DRAGON, 1960
WALK TALL, 1960
WALK THE PROUD LAND, 1956
WALKING HILLS, THE, 1949
WALL STREET COWBOY, 1939
WANDA NEVADA, 1979
WANDERER OF THE WASTELAND, 1935
WANDERER OF THE WASTELAND, 1945
WANDERERS OF THE WEST, 1941
WAR ARROW, 1953
WAR DRUMS, 1957
WAR OF THE RANGE, 1933
WAR PAINT, 1953
WAR PARTY, 1965
WAR WAGON, THE, 1967
WARLOCK, 1959
WARPATH, 1951
WATER FOR CANITOGA, 1939
WATER RUSTLERS, 1939
WATERHOLE NO. 3, 1967
WAY OF A GAUCHO, 1952
WAY OF THE WEST, THE, 1934
WAY OUT WEST, 1930
WAY OUT WEST, 1937
WAY WEST, THE, 1967
WELCOME TO BLOOD CITY, 1977
WELCOME TO HARD TIMES, 1967
WELLS FARGO, 1937
WELLS FARGO GUNMASTER, 1951
WEST OF ABILENE, 1940
WEST OF CARSON CITY, 1940
WEST OF CHEYENNE, 1931
WEST OF CHEYENNE, 1938
WEST OF CIMARRON, 1941
WEST OF EL DORADO, 1949
WEST OF NEVADA, 1936
WEST OF PINTO BASIN, 1940
WEST OF RAINBOW'S END, 1938
WEST OF SANTA FE, 1938
WEST OF SONORA, 1948
WEST OF TEXAS, 1943
WEST OF THE ALAMO, 1946
WEST OF THE BRAZOS, 1950
WEST OF THE DIVIDE, 1934
WEST OF THE LAW, 1942
WEST OF THE PECOS, 1935
WEST OF THE PECOS, 1945
WEST OF THE ROCKIES, 1929
WEST OF THE ROCKIES, 1931
WEST OF TOMBSTONE, 1942
WEST OF WYOMING, 1950
WEST TO GLORY, 1947
WESTBOUND, 1959
WESTBOUND MAIL, 1937
WESTBOUND STAGE, 1940

WESTERN CARAVANS, 1939
WESTERN COURAGE, 1935
WESTERN CYCLONE, 1943
WESTERN FRONTIER, 1935
WESTERN GOLD, 1937
WESTERN HERITAGE, 1948
WESTERN JAMBOREE, 1938
WESTERN JUSTICE, 1935
WESTERN MAIL, 1942
WESTERN PACIFIC AGENT, 1950
WESTERN RENEGADES, 1949
WESTERN TRAILS, 1938
WESTERN UNION, 1941
WESTERNER, THE, 1940
WESTERNER, THE, 1936
WESTWARD BOUND, 1931
WESTWARD BOUND, 1944
WESTWARD HO, 1936
WESTWARD HO, 1942
WESTWARD HO THE WAGONS?, 1956
WESTWARD THE WOMEN, 1951
WESTWARD TRAIL, THE, 1948
WESTWORLD, 1973
WHEELS OF DESTINY, 1934
WHEN A MAN RIDES ALONE, 1933
WHEN A MAN SEES RED, 1934
WHEN A MAN'S A MAN, 1935
WHEN THE DALTONS RODE, 1940
WHEN THE REDSKINS RODE, 1951
WHERE THE BUFFALO ROAM, 1938
WHERE THE WEST BEGINS, 1938
WHERE TRAILS DIVIDE, 1937
WHIRLWIND, 1951
WHIRLWIND HORSEMAN, 1938
WHIRLWIND RAIDERS, 1948
WHISPERING SKULL, THE, 1944
WHISPERING SMITH, 1948
WHISPERING SMITH SPEAKS, 1935
WHISTLIN' DAN, 1932
WHISTLING BULLETS, 1937
WHISTLING HILLS, 1951
WHITE BUFFALO, THE, 1977
WHITE EAGLE, 1932
WHITE FEATHER, 1955
WHITE SQUAW, THE, 1956
WHITE STALLION, 1947
WICHITA, 1955
WICKED DIE SLOW, THE, 1968
WIDE OPEN TOWN, 1941
WILD AND THE INNOCENT, THE, 1959
WILD AND WOOLLY, 1937
WILD BEAUTY, 1946
WILD BILL HICKOK RIDES, 1942
WILD BRIAN KENT, 1936
WILD BUNCH, THE, 1969
WILD COUNTRY, 1947
WILD DAKOTAS, THE, 1956
WILD FRONTIER, THE, 1947
WILD HERITAGE, 1958
WILD HORSE, 1931
WILD HORSE AMBUSH, 1952
WILD HORSE CANYON, 1939
WILD HORSE MESA, 1932
WILD HORSE MESA, 1947
WILD HORSE PHANTOM, 1944
WILD HORSE RODEO, 1938
WILD HORSE ROUND-UP, 1937
WILD HORSE RUSTLERS, 1943
WILD HORSE STAMPEDE, 1943
WILD HORSE VALLEY, 1940
WILD HORSES, 1984
WILD MUSTANG, 1935
WILD NORTH, THE, 1952
WILD ROVERS, 1971
WILD STALLION, 1952
WILD WEST, 1946
WILD WEST WHOOPEE, 1931
WILD WESTERNERS, THE, 1962
WILDCAT OF TUCSON, 1941
WILDCAT TROOPER, 1936
WILDERNESS MAIL, 1935
WILDFIRE, 1945
WILL PENNY, 1968
WINCHESTER '73, 1950
WINDS OF THE WASTELAND, 1936
WINDWALKER, 1980

WINGS OF THE HAWK, 1953
WINNING OF THE WEST, 1953
WINTERHAWK, 1976
WISHBONE CUTTER, 1978
WITHOUT HONORS, 1932
WOLF CALL, 1939
WOLF DOG, 1958
WOLF HUNTERS, THE, 1949
WOLVES OF THE RANGE, 1943
WOMAN HUNGRY, 1931
WOMAN OF THE TOWN, THE, 1943
WOMAN THEY ALMOST LYNCHED, THE, 1953
WONDERFUL COUNTRY, THE, 1959
WRANGLER'S ROOST, 1941
WRATH OF GOD, THE, 1972
WYOMING, 1940
WYOMING, 1947
WYOMING BANDIT, THE, 1949
WYOMING MAIL, 1950
WYOMING OUTLAW, 1939
WYOMING RENEGADES, 1955
WYOMING WILDCAT, 1941
YANKEE DON, 1931
YANKEE FAKIR, 1947
YAQUI DRUMS, 1956
YELLOW DUST, 1936
YELLOW MOUNTAIN, THE, 1954
YELLOW ROSE OF TEXAS, THE, 1944
YELLOW SKY, 1948
YELLOWSTONE KELLY, 1959
YODELIN' KID FROM PINE RIDGE, 1937
YOUNG BILL HICKOK, 1940
YOUNG BILLY YOUNG, 1969
YOUNG BLOOD, 1932
YOUNG BUFFALO BILL, 1940
YOUNG DANIEL BOONE, 1950
YOUNG FURY, 1965
YOUNG GUNS, THE, 1956
YOUNG GUNS, 1988
YOUNG GUNS OF TEXAS, 1963
YOUNG JESSE JAMES, 1960
YOUNG LAND, THE, 1959
YOUNGER BROTHERS, THE, 1949
YUKON VENGEANCE, 1954
ZACHARIAH, 1971
ZANDY'S BRIDE, 1974

BOLD: Films on Videocassette

FILMS BY STAR RATING

Listed below are films included in THE MOTION PICTURE GUIDE and its Annuals by Star Rating. The ratings indicate:

5 stars: Masterpiece; 4 Stars: Excellent; 3 Stars: Good; 2 Stars: Fair; 1 Star: Poor; Zero Stars: Without Merit

Bold indicates films available on videocassette.

5 Stars

A NOUS LA LIBERTE, 1931
ABSOLUTE BEGINNERS, 1986
ADVENTURES OF ROBIN HOOD, THE, 1938
AFRICAN QUEEN, THE, 1951
ALGIERS, 1938
ALL ABOUT EVE, 1950
ALL QUIET ON THE WESTERN FRONT, 1930
ALL THE KING'S MEN, 1949
AMADEUS, 1984
AMERICAN IN PARIS, AN, 1951
ANGELS WITH DIRTY FACES, 1938
ASPHALT JUNGLE, THE, 1950
ASYA'S HAPPINESS, 1988
AU HASARD, BALTHAZAR, 1970
AWFUL TRUTH, THE, 1937
BAD AND THE BEAUTIFUL, THE, 1952
BAD DAY AT BLACK ROCK, 1955
BEAU GESTE, 1939
BEAUTY AND THE BEAST, 1947
BEING THERE, 1979
BEN HUR, 1959
BEST YEARS OF OUR LIVES, THE, 1946
BICYCLE THIEF, THE, 1949
BIG SLEEP, THE, 1946
BLITHE SPIRIT, 1945
BLUE ANGEL, THE, 1930
BODY AND SOUL, 1947
BORIS GODUNOV, 1959
BORN YESTERDAY, 1951
BOYFRIENDS AND GIRLFRIENDS, 1988
BOYS TOWN, 1938
BRIDE OF FRANKENSTEIN, THE, 1935
BRIDGE ON THE RIVER KWAI, THE, 1957
BRIEF ENCOUNTER, 1945
BRINGING UP BABY, 1938
BROWNING VERSION, THE, 1951
BUTCH CASSIDY AND THE SUNDANCE KID, 1969
CABARET, 1972
CAMILLE, 1937
CAPTAINS COURAGEOUS, 1937
CASABLANCA, 1942
CHAMPAGNE FOR CAESAR, 1950
CHAMPION, 1949
CHARGE OF THE LIGHT BRIGADE, THE, 1936
CHILDREN OF PARADISE, 1945
CHINATOWN, 1974
CITIZEN KANE, 1941
CRANES ARE FLYING, THE, 1960
DARBY O'GILL AND THE LITTLE PEOPLE, 1959
DAVID COPPERFIELD, 1935
DAY FOR NIGHT, 1973
DAY OF THE LOCUST, THE, 1975
DAYBREAK, 1940
DAYS OF HEAVEN, 1978
DEAD, THE, 1987
DEAD END, 1937
DEATH OF A SALESMAN, 1952
DECISION BEFORE DAWN, 1951
DEER HUNTER, THE, 1978
DETECTIVE STORY, 1951
DINNER AT EIGHT, 1933
DODSWORTH, 1936
DOUBLE INDEMNITY, 1944
DOUBLE LIFE, A, 1947
DRUMS ALONG THE MOHAWK, 1939
DUMBO, 1941
EAST OF EDEN, 1955
ENCHANTED COTTAGE, THE, 1945
EXECUTIVE SUITE, 1954
FALLEN IDOL, THE, 1949
FANTASIA, 1940
FIGHTING 69TH, THE, 1940
FIVE EASY PIECES, 1970
FOREIGN CORRESPONDENT, 1940
FORT APACHE, 1948
42ND STREET, 1933
FOUR FEATHERS, THE, 1939

FOUR HUNDRED BLOWS, THE, 1959
FRENCH CONNECTION, THE, 1971
FROM HERE TO ETERNITY, 1953
FRONT PAGE, THE, 1931
FUGITIVE, THE, 1947
FURY, 1936
GANDHI, 1982
GASLIGHT, 1940
GASLIGHT, 1944
GIGI, 1958
GODFATHER, THE, 1972
GODFATHER, THE, PART II, 1974
GOING MY WAY, 1944
GONE WITH THE WIND, 1939
GOOD EARTH, THE, 1937
GRADUATE, THE, 1967
GRAND HOTEL, 1932
GRAND ILLUSION, 1938
GRAPES OF WRATH, 1940
GREAT EXPECTATIONS, 1946
GREAT ZIEGFELD, THE, 1936
GUNFIGHT AT THE O.K. CORRAL, 1957
GUNFIGHTER, THE, 1950
GUNGA DIN, 1939
HANNAH AND HER SISTERS, 1986
HEIRESS, THE, 1949
HENRY V, 1944
HIGH NOON, 1952
HIS GIRL FRIDAY, 1940
HOPE AND GLORY, 1987
HOW GREEN WAS MY VALLEY, 1941
HUNCHBACK OF NOTRE DAME, THE, 1939
HUSTLER, THE, 1961
I AM A FUGITIVE FROM A CHAIN GANG, 1932
IN A LONELY PLACE, 1950
INFORMER, THE, 1935
INHERIT THE WIND, 1960
INTERMEZZO: A LOVE STORY, 1939
INVADERS, THE, 1941
IT HAPPENED ONE NIGHT, 1934
IT'S A GIFT, 1934
IT'S A WONDERFUL LIFE, 1946
IT'S LOVE I'M AFTER, 1937
JESSE JAMES, 1939
JOHNNY BELINDA, 1948
JUAREZ, 1939
JULES AND JIM, 1962
JULIUS CAESAR, 1953
KEY LARGO, 1948
KIND HEARTS AND CORONETS, 1949
KING AND I, THE, 1956
KING KONG, 1933
KNIGHT WITHOUT ARMOR, 1937
LA DOLCE VITA, 1961
LA STRADA, 1956
LADY EVE, THE, 1941
LADY VANISHES, THE, 1938
L'ARGENT, 1984
LAST PICTURE SHOW, THE, 1971
L'ATALANTE, 1947
LAUGHTER, 1930
LAURA, 1944
L'AVVENTURA, 1960
LAWRENCE OF ARABIA, 1962
LES MISERABLES, 1935
LIFE OF EMILE ZOLA, THE, 1937
LIFEBOAT, 1944
LITTLE FOXES, THE, 1941
LITTLE WOMEN, 1933
LOLA MONTES, 1955
LONG DAY'S JOURNEY INTO NIGHT, 1962
LONG RIDERS, THE, 1980
LONG VOYAGE HOME, THE, 1940
LOST HORIZON, 1937
LOST WEEKEND, THE, 1945
LOVE ME TONIGHT, 1932
LUST FOR LIFE, 1956
LUSTY MEN, THE, 1952

M, 1933
MAEDCHEN IN UNIFORM, 1932
MAGNIFICENT AMBERSONS, THE, 1942
MAJOR BARBARA, 1941
MALTESE FALCON, THE, 1941
MAN FOR ALL SEASONS, A, 1966
MAN OF THE WEST, 1958
MAN WHO WOULD BE KING, THE, 1975
MANHATTAN, 1979
MARY POPPINS, 1964
MASK OF DIMITRIOS, THE, 1944
MAYERLING, 1937
MEET JOHN DOE, 1941
MEET ME IN ST. LOUIS, 1944
MELO, 1988
MERRY WIDOW, THE, 1934
MILDRED PIERCE, 1945
MIRACLE OF MORGAN'S CREEK, THE, 1944
MIRACLE ON 34TH STREET, THE, 1947
MIRACLE WORKER, THE, 1962
MR. DEEDS GOES TO TOWN, 1936
MR. HULOT'S HOLIDAY, 1954
MR. SMITH GOES TO WASHINGTON, 1939
MOBY DICK, 1956
MRS. MINIVER, 1942
MURDER, MY SWEET, 1945
MUSIC MAN, THE, 1962
MUTINY ON THE BOUNTY, 1935
MY DARLING CLEMENTINE, 1946
MY MAN GODFREY, 1936
NASHVILLE, 1975
NETWORK, 1976
NIGHT OF THE HUNTER, THE, 1955
NIGHT TRAIN, 1940
NINOTCHKA, 1939
NORTH BY NORTHWEST, 1959
NORTHWEST PASSAGE, 1940
NOTHING SACRED, 1937
NOTORIOUS, 1946
NUN'S STORY, THE, 1959
ODD MAN OUT, 1947
OF MICE AND MEN, 1939
OLIVER!, 1968
ON THE TOWN, 1949
ON THE WATERFRONT, 1954
ONCE UPON A TIME IN THE WEST, 1969
ORPHEUS, 1950
OUT OF THE PAST, 1947
OUTLAW JOSEY WALES, THE, 1976
OX-BOW INCIDENT, THE, 1943
PATHS OF GLORY, 1957
PATTON, 1970
PEPE LE MOKO, 1937
PHILADELPHIA STORY, THE, 1940
PINOCCHIO, 1940
PLACE IN THE SUN, A, 1951
POSTMAN ALWAYS RINGS TWICE, THE, 1946
PRIDE OF THE YANKEES, THE, 1942
PRISONER OF ZENDA, THE, 1937
PSYCHO, 1960
PUBLIC ENEMY, THE, 1931
PYGMALION, 1938
QUEEN CHRISTINA, 1933
QUIET MAN, THE, 1952
RAGING BULL, 1980
RAIDERS OF THE LOST ARK, 1981
RAN, 1985
RASHOMON, 1951
REAL LIFE, 1979
REAR WINDOW, 1954
RED BADGE OF COURAGE, THE, 1951
RED RIVER, 1948
RED SHOES, THE, 1948
REPULSION, 1965
RICHARD III, 1956
RIDE THE HIGH COUNTRY, 1962
RIFIFI, 1956
RIGHT STUFF, THE, 1983

BOLD: Films on Videocassette

'ROUND MIDNIGHT, 1986
RULES OF THE GAME, THE, 1939
SAHARA, 1943
SALT OF THE EARTH, 1954
SAN FRANCISCO, 1936
SANSHO THE BAILIFF, 1969
SATURDAY NIGHT AND SUNDAY MORNING, 1961
SCARFACE, 1932
SEA HAWK, THE, 1940
SEARCHERS, THE, 1956
SERGEANT YORK, 1941
SEVEN BRIDES FOR SEVEN BROTHERS, 1954
SEVEN SAMURAI, THE, 1956
SHADOW OF A DOUBT, 1943
SHANE, 1953
SHOOT THE PIANO PLAYER, 1962
SHOP AROUND THE CORNER, THE, 1940
SINGIN' IN THE RAIN, 1952
SNOW WHITE AND THE SEVEN DWARFS, 1937
SOME LIKE IT HOT, 1959
STAGE DOOR, 1937
STAGECOACH, 1939
STALAG 17, 1953
STAR IS BORN, A, 1937
STAR WARS, 1977
STING, THE, 1973
STRANGERS ON A TRAIN, 1951
STREETCAR NAMED DESIRE, A, 1951
SULLIVAN'S TRAVELS, 1941
SUNSET BOULEVARD, 1950
TESTAMENT OF ORPHEUS, THE, 1962
THEY WERE EXPENDABLE, 1945
THIEF OF BAGHDAD, THE, 1940
THING, THE, 1951
THIRD MAN, THE, 1950
39 STEPS, THE, 1935
THREE GODFATHERS, THE, 1948
TO BE OR NOT TO BE, 1942
TOM JONES, 1963
TORTILLA FLAT, 1942
TOUCH OF EVIL, 1958
TREASURE OF THE SIERRA MADRE, THE, 1948
TRUE GRIT, 1969
TWELVE O'CLOCK HIGH, 1949
UGETSU, 1954
UMBERTO D, 1955
UNFAITHFULLY YOURS, 1948
VAMPYR, 1932
VERTIGO, 1958
VIRIDIANA, 1962
VIVA ZAPATA!, 1952
WAGONMASTER, 1950
WALK IN THE SUN, A, 1945
WAYS OF LOVE, 1950
WESTERNER, THE, 1940
WHITE HEAT, 1949
WHO FRAMED ROGER RABBIT, 1988
WHOLE TOWN'S TALKING, THE, 1935
WILD BOYS OF THE ROAD, 1933
WILD BUNCH, THE, 1969
WILD STRAWBERRIES, 1959
WINGS OF DESIRE, 1988
WIZARD OF OZ, THE, 1939
WOMAN IN THE DUNES, 1964
WRITTEN ON THE WIND, 1956
WUTHERING HEIGHTS, 1939
YANKEE DOODLE DANDY, 1942
YELLOW SKY, 1948
ZIEGFELD FOLLIES, 1945
ZULU, 1964

4 Stars

ABBOTT AND COSTELLO MEET FRANKENSTEIN,
1948
ACTION IN THE NORTH ATLANTIC, 1943
ADVENTURE OF SHERLOCK HOLMES' SMARTER
BROTHER, THE, 1975
ADVENTURES OF DON JUAN, 1949
ADVENTURES OF ICHABOD AND MR. TOAD, 1949
ADVENTURES OF MARK TWAIN, THE, 1944
ADVENTURES OF SHERLOCK HOLMES, THE, 1939
ADVENTURESS, THE, 1946
ADVISE AND CONSENT, 1962
AFTER HOURS, 1985
AH, WILDERNESS!, 1935
AIR FORCE, 1943

AL CAPONE, 1959
ALAMO, THE, 1960
ALEXANDER NEVSKY, 1939
ALIENS, 1986
ALL MY SONS, 1948
ALL THAT HEAVEN ALLOWS, 1955
ALL THROUGH THE NIGHT, 1942
AMERICAN GRAFFITI, 1973
AMERICAN MADNESS, 1932
ANASTASIA, 1956
ANATOMY OF A MURDER, 1959
ANCHORS AWEIGH, 1945
AND THEN THERE WERE NONE, 1945
ANGELS OVER BROADWAY, 1940
ANNA AND THE KING OF SIAM, 1946
ANNA KARENINA, 1935
ANNE OF THE THOUSAND DAYS, 1969
ANNIE HALL, 1977
ANOTHER WOMAN, 1988
APARTMENT, THE, 1960
AROUND THE WORLD IN 80 DAYS, 1956
AROUND THE WORLD IN EIGHTY WAYS, 1987
ARROWSMITH, 1931
ARSENIC AND OLD LACE, 1944
ASSAULT, THE, 1986
ATLANTIC CITY, 1981
AUNTIE MAME, 1958
B. F.'S DAUGHTER, 1948
BACHELOR AND THE BOBBY-SOXER, THE, 1947
BACHELOR MOTHER, 1939
BACK STREET, 1941
BACK TO BATAAN, 1945
BAD BLOOD, 1987
BAKER'S WIFE, THE, 1940
BALLAD OF A SOLDIER, 1960
BALLAD OF NARAYAMA, THE, 1984
BAMBI, 1942
BAND OF ANGELS, 1957
BAND WAGON, THE, 1953
BANK DICK, THE, 1940
BARFLY, 1987
BARRETTS OF WIMPOLE STREET, THE, 1934
BARRETTS OF WIMPOLE STREET, THE, 1957
BATAAN, 1943
BATTLE OF BRITAIN, THE, 1969
BATTLEGROUND, 1949
BEAT THE DEVIL, 1953
BECKET, 1964
BEGGARS OF LIFE, 1928
BELLS OF ST. MARY'S, THE, 1945
BETTY BLUE, 1986
BIG CLOCK, THE, 1948
BIG HEAT, THE, 1953
BIG KNIFE, THE, 1955
BILL OF DIVORCEMENT, A, 1932
BIRD, 1988
BIRD WITH THE CRYSTAL PLUMAGE, THE, 1970
BIRDMAN OF ALCATRAZ, 1962
BIRDY, 1984
BIZET'S CARMEN, 1984
BLACK NARCISSUS, 1947
BLACK ROSE, THE, 1950
BLACK STALLION, THE, 1979
BLACK SWAN, THE, 1942
BLACK TIGHTS, 1962
BLACKBOARD JUNGLE, THE, 1955
BLADE RUNNER, 1982
BLONDE VENUS, 1932
BLOOD AND SAND, 1941
BLUE DAHLIA, THE, 1946
BLUE SKIES, 1946
BLUE VELVET, 1986
BOAT, THE, 1982
BODY HEAT, 1981
BONNIE AND CLYDE, 1967
BOOM TOWN, 1940
BOOMERANG, 1947
BOWERY, THE, 1933
BOY WHO COULD FLY, THE, 1986
BRAVE BULLS, THE, 1951
BREAK THE NEWS, 1938
BREAKER MORANT, 1980
BREAKFAST AT TIFFANY'S, 1961
BREATHLESS, 1959
BREWSTER'S MILLIONS, 1945
BRIDE FOR SALE, 1949

BRIDGE AT REMAGEN, THE, 1969
BRIDGE OF SAN LUIS REY, THE, 1929
BRIDGES AT TOKO-RI, THE, 1954
BRIGHT VICTORY, 1951
BRIGHTNESS, 1988
BRING ME THE HEAD OF ALFREDO GARCIA, 1974
BROADCAST NEWS, 1987
BROADWAY DANNY ROSE, 1984
BRUTE FORCE, 1947
BULLDOG DRUMMOND STRIKES BACK, 1934
BULLITT, 1968
CAESAR AND CLEOPATRA, 1946
CAINE MUTINY, THE, 1954
CALL NORTHSIDE 777, 1948
CANDY MOUNTAIN, 1988
CAPTAIN BLOOD, 1935
CAPTAIN FROM CASTILE, 1947
CAPTAIN'S PARADISE, THE, 1953
CAROUSEL, 1956
CASQUE D'OR, 1956
CAT BALLOU, 1965
CAT ON A HOT TIN ROOF, 1958
CATERED AFFAIR, THE, 1956
CHARADE, 1963
CHARIOTS OF FIRE, 1981
CHEYENNE AUTUMN, 1964
CHILDREN OF A LESSER GOD, 1986
CHINA SYNDROME, THE, 1979
CHRISTMAS STORY, A, 1983
CIMARRON, 1931
CINCINNATI KID, THE, 1965
CINDERELLA, 1950
CIRCLE OF DECEIT, 1982
CITADEL, THE, 1938
CLASH BY NIGHT, 1952
CLOSE ENCOUNTERS OF THE THIRD KIND, 1977
CLUNY BROWN, 1946
COAL MINER'S DAUGHTER, 1980
COCOANUTS, THE, 1929
COMANCHE STATION, 1960
COME BACK LITTLE SHEBA, 1952
COMING HOME, 1978
COMPULSION, 1959
CONFESSION, THE, 1970
CONFESSIONS OF A NAZI SPY, 1939
CONNECTICUT YANKEE, A, 1931
CONNECTICUT YANKEE IN KING ARTHUR'S
COURT, A, 1949
CONTEMPT, 1963
CONVERSATION, THE, 1974
COOL HAND LUKE, 1967
CORSICAN BROTHERS, THE, 1941
CORVETTE K-225, 1943
COUNSELLOR-AT-LAW, 1933
COUNT OF MONTE CRISTO, THE, 1934
COUNTRY, 1984
COUNTRY GIRL, THE, 1954
COURT-MARTIAL OF BILLY MITCHELL, THE, 1955
COVER GIRL, 1944
CRAIG'S WIFE, 1936
CRASH DIVE, 1943
CRIES AND WHISPERS, 1972
CRIME OF MONSIEUR LANGE, THE, 1936
CRIME WITHOUT PASSION, 1934
CRIMSON PIRATE, THE, 1952
CROSSFIRE, 1947
CRUEL SEA, THE, 1953
CURLY TOP, 1935
CUTTER AND BONE, 1981
CYRANO DE BERGERAC, 1950
DADDY LONG LEGS, 1931
DADDY LONG LEGS, 1955
DAMN YANKEES, 1958
DAMNATION, 1988
DAMNED, THE, 1969
DARK VICTORY, 1939
DARLING, 1965
DAVID AND LISA, 1962
DAWN PATROL, THE, 1938
DAY OF THE JACKAL, THE, 1973
DAY OF WRATH, 1948
DAY THE EARTH STOOD STILL, THE, 1951
DAYS OF 36, 1972
DAYS OF WINE AND ROSES, 1962
DEAD OF NIGHT, 1946
DEAD RINGERS, 1988

DEADLY AFFAIR, THE, 1967
DEATH IN VENICE, 1971
DEATH OF TARZAN, THE, 1968
DEATH ON THE NILE, 1978
DEATH TAKES A HOLIDAY, 1934
DEBT, THE, 1988
DEEP IN MY HEART, 1954
DEFIANT ONES, THE, 1958
DESCENDANT OF THE SNOW LEOPARD, THE, 1986
DESERT FOX, THE, 1951
DESIRE, 1936
DESPERATE CHARACTERS, 1971
DESPERATE HOURS, THE, 1955
DESTINATION TOKYO, 1944
DETOUR, 1945
DEVIL AND DANIEL WEBSTER, THE, 1941
DIABOLIQUE, 1955
DIARY OF A CHAMBERMAID, 1964
DIARY OF A COUNTRY PRIEST, 1954
DIARY OF ANNE FRANK, THE, 1959
DINER, 1982
DIVA, 1982
DIVORCE, ITALIAN STYLE, 1962
DR. EHRLICH'S MAGIC BULLET, 1940
DR. JEKYLL AND MR. HYDE, 1932
DOCTOR X, 1932
DOCTOR ZHIVAGO, 1965
DODGE CITY, 1939
DOG DAY AFTERNOON, 1975
DON QUIXOTE, 1935
DON QUIXOTE, 1961
DONA HERLINDA AND HER SON, 1986
DON'S PARTY, 1976
DOUGH BOYS, 1930
DOWN AND OUT IN BEVERLY HILLS, 1986
DRACULA, 1931
DREYFUS CASE, THE, 1931
DRIVER, THE, 1978
DRUMS, 1938
DRUNKEN ANGEL, 1948
DUCK SOUP, 1933
EASTER PARADE, 1948
EASY RIDER, 1969
EDISON, THE MAN, 1940
EFFI BRIEST, 1974
EGG AND I, THE, 1947
8 1/2, 1963
EL, 1955
EL NORTE, 1984
ELEPHANT MAN, THE, 1980
ELMER GANTRY, 1960
ELVIRA MADIGAN, 1967
EMERALD FOREST, THE, 1985
EMIGRANTS, THE, 1972
EMPEROR JONES, THE, 1933
EMPIRE OF THE SUN, 1987
END OF INNOCENCE, 1960
ENEMY BELOW, THE, 1957
ENFORCER, THE, 1951
ENTERTAINER, THE, 1960
EQUUS, 1977
E.T. THE EXTRA-TERRESTRIAL, 1982
ETERNAL MASK, THE, 1937
EXCALIBUR, 1981
EXODUS, 1960
EXORCIST, THE, 1973
EXTERMINATING ANGEL, THE, 1967
FACE IN THE CROWD, A, 1957
FACE TO FACE, 1976
FACES, 1968
FAIL SAFE, 1964
FANFAN THE TULIP, 1952
FANNY AND ALEXANDER, 1983
FAR COUNTRY, THE, 1955
FAREWELL TO ARMS, A, 1932
FAT CITY, 1972
FEAR STRIKES OUT, 1957
FELLINI SATYRICON, 1969
FIRE OVER ENGLAND, 1937
FITZCARRALDO, 1982
FIVE FINGERS, 1952
FIVE GRAVES TO CAIRO, 1943
5,000 FINGERS OF DR. T. THE, 1953
FLASH GORDON, 1936
FLIGHT OF THE PHOENIX, THE, 1965
FLY, THE, 1986

FLYING DOWN TO RIO, 1933
FOOTLIGHT PARADE, 1933
FOR WHOM THE BELL TOLLS, 1943
FORBIDDEN GAMES, 1953
FORBIDDEN PLANET, 1956
FOREVER AND A DAY, 1943
FORTUNE, THE, 1975
FOUL PLAY, 1978
FOUR DAUGHTERS, 1938
FOX AND THE HOUND, THE, 1981
FRANKENSTEIN, 1931
FRANTIC, 1988
FREAKS, 1932
FRENCH CANCAN, 1956
FROM RUSSIA WITH LOVE, 1963
FULL METAL JACKET, 1987
FUNNY GIRL, 1968
G-MEN, 1935
GALLIPOLI, 1981
GARDEN OF ALLAH, THE, 1936
GARDEN OF THE FINZI-CONTINIS, THE, 1971
GATE OF HELL, 1954
GAY DIVORCEE, THE, 1934
GENTLE CREATURE, A, 1971
GENTLEMAN JIM, 1942
GENTLEMAN'S AGREEMENT, 1947
GEORGE WASHINGTON SLEPT HERE, 1942
GEORGY GIRL, 1966
GHOST AND MRS. MUIR, THE, 1942
GHOST GOES WEST, THE, 1936
GIANT, 1956
GIG, THE, 1985
GILDA, 1946
GIRL CRAZY, 1943
GIRL FROM HAVANA, THE, 1929
GIRL IN WHITE, THE, 1952
GLENN MILLER STORY, THE, 1953
GNOME-MOBILE, THE, 1967
GO-BETWEEN, THE, 1971
GODS MUST BE CRAZY, THE, 1984
GOING IN STYLE, 1979
GOLD DIGGERS OF 1933, 1933
GOLDEN BOY, 1939
GOLDFINGER, 1964
GOOD NEWS, 1947
GOOD, THE BAD, AND THE UGLY, THE, 1967
GOODBYE GIRL, THE, 1977
GOODBYE MR. CHIPS, 1939
GRAND MANEUVER, THE, 1956
GREAT DICTATOR, THE, 1940
GREAT ESCAPE, THE, 1963
GREAT GATSBY, THE, 1949
GREAT McGINTY, THE, 1940
GREAT MOUSE DETECTIVE, THE, 1986
GREAT NORTHFIELD, MINNESOTA RAID, THE, 1972
GREAT SANTINI, THE, 1979
GREATEST SHOW ON EARTH, THE, 1952
GREEN MAN, THE, 1957
GREY FOX, THE, 1983
GREYSTOKE: THE LEGEND OF TARZAN, LORD OF THE APES, 1984
GUADALCANAL DIARY, 1943
GUARDSMAN, THE, 1931
GUY NAMED JOE, A, 1943
GYPSY, 1962
HAIL, MARY, 1985
HAIL THE CONQUERING HERO, 1944
HAIR, 1979
HALLELUJAH, 1929
HALLOWEEN, 1978
HAMLET, 1948
HAMLET, 1964
HARD DAY'S NIGHT, A, 1964
HARDER THEY FALL, THE, 1956
HARVEY, 1950
HASTY HEART, THE, 1949
HE WALKED BY NIGHT, 1948
HEARTBREAK RIDGE, 1986
HEARTLAND, 1980
HEAT AND SUNLIGHT, 1988
HELL'S HEROES, 1930
HERE COMES MR. JORDAN, 1941
HERE COMES THE GROOM, 1951
HERE I AM A STRANGER, 1939
HIDDEN FORTRESS, THE, 1959

HIGH AND LOW, 1963
HIGH SIERRA, 1941
HIMATSURI, 1985
HIROSHIMA, MON AMOUR, 1959
HISTORY IS MADE AT NIGHT, 1937
HIT, THE, 1985
HOBSON'S CHOICE, 1954
HOLD BACK THE DAWN, 1941
HOLIDAY FOR HENRIETTA, 1955
HOLIDAY INN, 1942
HOLLYWOOD CANTEEN, 1944
HOMECOMING, THE, 1973
HOOSIERS, 1986
HORROR OF DRACULA, THE, 1958
HORSE FEATHERS, 1932
HORSE SOLDIERS, THE, 1959
HORSE'S MOUTH, THE, 1958
HOUND OF THE BASKERVILLES, THE, 1939
HOUSE OF GAMES, 1987
HOUSE OF ROTHSCHILD, THE, 1934
HOUSE ON 92ND STREET, THE, 1945
HOW THE WEST WAS WON, 1962
HOW TO SUCCEED IN BUSINESS WITHOUT REALLY TRYING, 1967
HUCKSTERS, THE, 1947
HUNT, THE, 1967
HURRICANE, THE, 1937
I LOVE YOU, ALICE B. TOKLAS!, 1968
I REMEMBER MAMA, 1948
I'LL CRY TOMORROW, 1955
I'M ALL RIGHT, JACK, 1959
I'M NO ANGEL, 1933
IMPORTANCE OF BEING EARNEST, THE, 1952
IN OLD CHICAGO, 1938
IN THE HEAT OF THE NIGHT, 1967
IN WHICH WE SERVE, 1942
INCIDENT, 1948
INCREDIBLE SHRINKING MAN, THE, 1957
INNOCENCE UNPROTECTED, 1971
INNOCENTS, THE, 1961
INTERIORS, 1978
INTERNATIONAL HOUSE, 1933
INTERVISTA, 1987
INTRUDER IN THE DUST, 1949
INVASION OF THE BODY SNATCHERS, 1956
ISLAND OF LOST SOULS, 1933
IT HAPPENS EVERY SPRING, 1949
IT SHOULD HAPPEN TO YOU, 1954
IT'S A MAD, MAD, MAD, MAD WORLD, 1963
IT'S ALWAYS FAIR WEATHER, 1955
IVAN THE TERRIBLE, PARTS I & II, 1947
IVANHOE, 1952
JANE EYRE, 1944
JASON AND THE ARGONAUTS, 1963
JAWS, 1975
JEZEBEL, 1938
JIM THORPE—ALL AMERICAN, 1951
JOUR DE FETE, 1952
JOURNEY INTO FEAR, 1942
JUGGLER, THE, 1953
JULIA, 1977
JULIET OF THE SPIRITS, 1965
JUNGLE BOOK, 1942
KAGEMUSHA, 1980
KAMERADSCHAFT, 1931
KHARTOUM, 1966
KID FOR TWO FARTHINGS, A, 1956
KILLERS, THE, 1946
KILLING, THE, 1956
KING AND COUNTRY, 1964
KING LEAR, 1988
KING OF COMEDY, THE, 1983
KING SOLOMON'S MINES, 1950
KINGS ROW, 1942
KISS ME DEADLY, 1955
KISS ME KATE, 1953
KISS OF DEATH, 1947
KISS OF THE SPIDER WOMAN, 1985
KNACK . . . AND HOW TO GET IT, THE, 1965
KNIFE IN THE WATER, 1963
KNUTE ROCKNE—ALL AMERICAN, 1940
KRAMER VS. KRAMER, 1979
KWAIDAN, 1965
L-SHAPED ROOM, THE, 1962
LA BAMBA, 1987
LA CAGE AUX FOLLES, 1979

BOLD: Films on Videocassette

LA RONDE, 1954
LA TERRA TREMA, 1947
LA TRAVIATA, 1982
LADY IN THE LAKE, 1947
LADYKILLERS, THE, 1956
L'AGE D'OR, 1979
LASSIE, COME HOME, 1943
LAST DETAIL, THE, 1973
LAST EMPEROR, THE, 1987
LAST OF THE MOHICANS, THE, 1936
LAST STOP, THE, 1949
LAST TEMPTATION OF CHRIST, THE, 1988
LAST WAVE, THE, 1978
LAST YEAR AT MARIENBAD, 1962
LATE GEORGE APLEY, THE, 1947
LAVENDER HILL MOB, THE, 1951
LE BEAU MARIAGE, 1982
LE GAI SAVOIR, 1968
LE PETIT THEATRE DE JEAN RENOIR, 1974
LES PARENTS TERRIBLES, 1950
LETTER, THE, 1940
LETTER TO THREE WIVES, A, 1948
LIBELED LADY, 1936
LIFE AND DEATH OF COLONEL BLIMP, THE, 1945
LIFE WITH FATHER, 1947
LIGHT THAT FAILED, THE, 1939
LIMELIGHT, 1952
LION IN WINTER, THE, 1968
LITTLE CAESAR, 1931
LITTLE DORRIT, 1988
LITTLE ROMANCE, A, 1979
LIVES OF A BENGAL LANCER, 1935
LOCAL HERO, 1983
LODGER, THE, 1944
LONELINESS OF THE LONG DISTANCE RUNNER,
   THE, 1962
LONELY ARE THE BRAVE, 1962
LONG, HOT SUMMER, THE, 1958
LONGEST DAY, THE, 1962
LORD JIM, 1965
LOS OLVIDADOS, 1950
LOVE AFFAIR, 1939
LOVE CRAZY, 1941
LOVE FROM A STRANGER, 1937
LOVE ME OR LEAVE ME, 1955
MAD LOVE, 1935
MADAME CURIE, 1943
MAGIC BOX, THE, 1952
MAGNIFICENT SEVEN, THE, 1960
MAGNIFICENT YANKEE, THE, 1950
MAJOR AND THE MINOR, THE, 1942
MALE ANIMAL, THE, 1942
MAMMA ROMA, 1962
MAN ESCAPED, A, 1957
MAN FACING SOUTHEAST, 1986
MAN FROM LARAMIE, THE, 1955
MAN HUNT, 1941
MAN IN THE WHITE SUIT, THE, 1952
MAN OF IRON, 1981
MAN ON A TIGHTROPE, 1953
MAN ON THE EIFFEL TOWER, THE, 1949
MAN ON THE FLYING TRAPEZE, THE, 1935
MAN WHO CAME TO DINNER, THE, 1942
MAN WHO KNEW TOO MUCH, THE, 1935
MAN WHO KNEW TOO MUCH, THE, 1956
MANHATTAN MELODRAMA, 1934
MAN'S HOPE, 1947
MARATHON MAN, 1976
MARGIE, 1946
MARIE ANTOINETTE, 1938
MARK OF ZORRO, THE, 1940
MARKETA LAZAROVA, 1968
MARRIAGE OF MARIA BRAUN, THE, 1979
MARTY, 1955
MASCULINE FEMININE, 1966
M*A*S*H, 1970
MATCHMAKING OF ANNA, THE, 1972
MATEWAN, 1987
MAYTIME, 1937
MEAN STREETS, 1973
MEDIUM COOL, 1969
MEN, THE, 1950
MEN OF THE FIGHTING LADY, 1954
MEPHISTO, 1981
MERRY CHRISTMAS, MR. LAWRENCE, 1983
MIDNIGHT COWBOY, 1969

MIDNIGHT EXPRESS, 1978
MIDSUMMERS NIGHT'S DREAM, A, 1961
MIN AND BILL, 1930
MINISTRY OF FEAR, 1945
MIRACLE IN MILAN, 1951
MIRAGE, 1972
MISSING, 1982
MISTER ROBERTS, 1955
MODERN TIMES, 1936
MODERNS, THE, 1988
MOGAMBO, 1953
MON ONCLE D'AMERIQUE, 1980
MONKEY SHINES: AN EXPERIMENT IN FEAR, 1988
MOON AND SIXPENCE, THE, 1942
MOONLIGHTING, 1982
MOROCCO, 1930
MOUSE THAT ROARED, THE, 1959
MUMMY, THE, 1932
MURDER, 1930
MURDER BY DEATH, 1976
MURDER, HE SAYS, 1945
MURIEL, 1963
MURMUR OF THE HEART, 1971
MY BRILLIANT CAREER, 1980
MY FAIR LADY, 1964
MY FAVORITE BRUNETTE, 1947
MY FAVORITE YEAR, 1982
MY FIRST WIFE, 1985
MY FRIEND FLICKA, 1943
MY LIFE TO LIVE, 1963
MY NIGHT AT MAUD'S, 1970
MY SON, MY SON!, 1940
MY UNCLE, 1958
MYSTERY OF THE WAX MUSEUM, THE, 1933
NAKED CITY, THE, 1948
NAKED SPUR, THE, 1953
NATIONAL VELVET, 1944
NEXT STOP, GREENWICH VILLAGE, 1976
NIGHT AT THE OPERA, A, 1935
NIGHT MUST FALL, 1937
NIGHT TO REMEMBER, A, 1958
NIGHT WATCH, THE, 1964
NIGHTMARE ALLEY, 1947
NO GREATER GLORY, 1934
NONE BUT THE LONELY HEART, 1944
NORMA RAE, 1979
NOSTALGHIA, 1984
O LUCKY MAN!, 1973
OBJECTIVE, BURMA!, 1945
ODD COUPLE, THE, 1968
OF HUMAN BONDAGE, 1934
OF STARS AND MEN, 1961
OKLAHOMA, 1955
OLD MAN AND THE SEA, THE, 1958
OLIVER TWIST, 1951
ON GOLDEN POND, 1981
ONCE UPON A TIME IN AMERICA, 1984
ONE FLEW OVER THE CUCKOO'S NEST, 1975
ONLY ANGELS HAVE WINGS, 1939
OPEN CITY, 1945
ORCHESTRA WIVES, 1942
ORPHANS, 1987
OUR RELATIONS, 1936
OUR TOWN, 1940
OUR VINES HAVE TENDER GRAPES, 1945
OUT OF TOWNERS, THE, 1970
PAISAN, 1948
PAJAMA GAME, THE, 1957
PAL JOEY, 1957
PALM BEACH STORY, THE, 1942
PAPILLON, 1973
PARADISE ALLEY, 1978
PARIS, TEXAS, 1984
PASSENGER, THE, 1975
PAT AND MIKE, 1952
PATTERNS, 1956
PAWNBROKER, THE, 1965
PAYDAY, 1972
PEOPLE WILL TALK, 1951
PERSONA, 1967
PETER PAN, 1953
PETRIFIED FOREST, THE, 1936
PHANTOM OF LIBERTY, THE, 1974
PHANTOM OF THE OPERA, THE, 1929
PICKPOCKET, 1963
PICNIC, 1955

PIERROT LE FOU, 1968
PINKY, 1949
PIXOTE, 1981
PLANET OF THE APES, 1968
PLATOON, 1986
PLAZA SUITE, 1971
PLOUGHMAN'S LUNCH, THE, 1984
POIL DE CAROTTE, 1932
POLLYANNA, 1960
PORK CHOP HILL, 1959
PORT OF SHADOWS, 1938
PORTRAIT OF JENNIE, 1949
PRIDE AND PREJUDICE, 1940
PRIDE OF THE MARINES, 1945
PRINCE OF FOXES, 1949
PRISONER OF SHARK ISLAND, THE, 1936
PRIVATE LIFE OF HENRY VIII, THE, 1933
PRIVATE LIVES, 1931
PRODUCERS, THE, 1967
PROVIDENCE, 1977
PUMPKIN EATER, THE, 1964
PURPLE HEART, THE, 1944
QUADROPHENIA, 1979
QUARTET, 1949
RACKET, THE, 1951
RANCHO NOTORIOUS, 1952
RASPUTIN AND THE EMPRESS, 1932
RAZOR'S EDGE, THE, 1946
REBECCA, 1940
REBEL WITHOUT A CAUSE, 1955
RED SORGHUM, 1988
REMBRANDT, 1936
REPENTANCE, 1988
RIO BRAVO, 1959
RIO GRANDE, 1950
ROAD TO MOROCCO, 1942
ROARING TWENTIES, THE, 1939
ROBERTA, 1935
ROCK 'N' ROLL HIGH SCHOOL, 1979
ROCKY, 1976
ROMAN HOLIDAY, 1953
ROMEO AND JULIET, 1936
ROMEO AND JULIET, 1954
ROOM AT THE TOP, 1959
ROOM WITH A VIEW, A, 1986
ROSE MARIE, 1936
ROSE TATTOO, THE, 1955
ROSEMARY'S BABY, 1968
ROYAL FAMILY OF BROADWAY, THE, 1930
ROYAL WEDDING, 1951
RUGGLES OF RED GAP, 1935
RUMBLE FISH, 1983
SABOTEUR, 1942
SABRINA, 1954
SACRIFICE, THE, 1986
SALVADOR, 1986
SAND PEBBLES, THE, 1966
SANDS OF IWO JIMA, 1949
SAVE THE TIGER, 1973
SAYONARA, 1957
SCARLET EMPRESS, THE, 1934
SCARLET PIMPERNEL, THE, 1935
SCHOOL FOR SCOUNDRELS, 1960
SEA WOLF, THE, 1941
SEANCE ON A WET AFTERNOON, 1964
SEARCH, THE, 1948
SECRET LIFE OF WALTER MITTY, THE, 1947
SEPARATE TABLES, 1958
SEPTEMBER, 1987
SERPICO, 1973
SET-UP, THE, 1949
SEVEN DAYS IN MAY, 1964
SEVEN THIEVES, 1960
SEVEN YEAR ITCH, THE, 1955
SEVENTH SEAL, THE, 1958
SEVENTH VEIL, THE, 1946
SHADOWS, 1960
SHANGHAI EXPRESS, 1932
SHE DONE HIM WRONG, 1933
SHE WORE A YELLOW RIBBON, 1949
SHIP OF FOOLS, 1965
SHOOTING, THE, 1971
SHOOTIST, THE, 1976
SHOT IN THE DARK, A, 1964
SHOW BOAT, 1936
SID AND NANCY, 1986

SILK STOCKINGS, 1957
SILKWOOD, 1983
SIN OF MADELON CLAUDET, THE, 1931
SINCE YOU WENT AWAY, 1944
SINK THE BISMARCK, 1960
SITTING PRETTY, 1948
SLEUTH, 1972
SLIGHT CASE OF MURDER, A, 1938
SMALL CHANGE, 1976
SMILING LIEUTENANT, THE, 1931
SO DEAR TO MY HEART, 1949
SO PROUDLY WE HAIL, 1943
SOLID GOLD CADILLAC, THE, 1956
SOMEONE TO LOVE, 1988
SON OF FRANKENSTEIN, 1939
SONG OF BERNADETTE, THE, 1943
SONG OF THE SOUTH, 1946
SORRY, WRONG NUMBER, 1948
SOUND OF MUSIC, THE, 1965
SOUTH PACIFIC, 1958
SOUTHERNER, THE, 1945
SPARTACUS, 1960
SPELLBOUND, 1945
SPIRAL STAIRCASE, THE, 1946
SPIRIT OF ST. LOUIS, THE, 1957
SPY WHO CAME IN FROM THE COLD, THE, 1965
STAGE DOOR CANTEEN, 1943
STAIRWAY TO HEAVEN, 1946
STAMMHEIM, 1986
STAR IS BORN, A, 1954
STAR TREK IV: THE VOYAGE HOME, 1986
STARS LOOK DOWN, THE, 1940
STATE FAIR, 1945
STATE OF THE UNION, 1948
STATE'S ATTORNEY, 1932
STEEL HELMET, THE, 1951
STELLA DALLAS, 1937
STOLEN KISSES, 1969
STORY OF A CHEAT, THE, 1938
STORY OF ADELE H., THE, 1975
STORY OF ESTHER COSTELLO, THE, 1957
STORY OF G.I. JOE, THE, 1945
STORY OF LOUIS PASTEUR, THE, 1936
STRAIGHT TIME, 1978
STRANGER, THE, 1946
STRANGERS KISS, 1984
STREET SCENE, 1931
STUNT MAN, THE, 1980
SUBJECT WAS ROSES, THE, 1968
SULLIVANS, THE, 1944
SUMMER OF '42, 1971
SUMMERTIME, 1955
SUN ALSO RISES, THE, 1957
SUNDAY IN THE COUNTRY, A, 1984
SUNDOWNERS, THE, 1960
SUNRISE AT CAMPOBELLO, 1960
SUNSHINE BOYS, THE, 1975
SWAN LAKE, THE, 1967
SWEET SMELL OF SUCCESS, 1957
SWIMMER, THE, 1988
T-MEN, 1947
TAKE ME OUT TO THE BALL GAME, 1949
TAKING OFF, 1971
TALE OF TWO CITIES, A, 1935
TALES OF MANHATTAN, 1942
TALK OF THE TOWN, 1942
TALL T, THE, 1957
TARNISHED ANGELS, THE, 1957
TASTE OF HONEY, A, 1962
TEAHOUSE OF THE AUGUST MOON, THE, 1956
TEN COMMANDMENTS, THE, 1956
TENSION, 1949
TEST PILOT, 1938
THERESE, 1986
THESE THREE, 1936
THEY DIED WITH THEIR BOOTS ON, 1942
THEY DRIVE BY NIGHT, 1940
THEY LIVE BY NIGHT, 1949
THEY WON'T FORGET, 1937
THIN MAN, THE, 1934
THINGS TO COME, 1936
THIRD MAN ON THE MOUNTAIN, 1959
THIRTY SECONDS OVER TOKYO, 1944
THIS GUN FOR HIRE, 1942
THIS IS THE NIGHT, 1932
THOUSAND CLOWNS, A, 1965

THREAT, THE, 1949
THREE CABALLEROS, THE, 1944
THREE CAME HOME, 1950
THREE COMRADES, 1938
THREE INTO TWO WON'T GO, 1969
THREE LITTLE WORDS, 1950
THREE MUSKETEERS, THE, 1948
THREE MUSKETEERS, THE, 1974
THRONE OF BLOOD, 1961
THUNDERHEAD-SON OF FLICKA, 1945
TIME LIMIT, 1957
TIME MACHINE, THE, 1963
TO CATCH A THIEF, 1955
TO EACH HIS OWN, 1946
TO HAVE AND HAVE NOT, 1944
TO KILL A MOCKINGBIRD, 1962
TOBACCO ROAD, 1941
TOKYO STORY, 1972
TOOTSIE, 1982
TOP HAT, 1935
TOPKAPI, 1964
TOPPER, 1937
TORRID ZONE, 1940
TOUCH OF CLASS, A, 1973
TRAFFIC, 1972
TRAIN, THE, 1965
TREASURE ISLAND, 1950
TREE GROWS IN BROOKLYN, A, 1945
TRIP TO BOUNTIFUL, THE, 1985
TRISTANA, 1970
TRUE CONFESSIONS, 1981
TRUNKS OF MR. O.F., THE, 1932
TUCKER: THE MAN AND HIS DREAM, 1988
12 ANGRY MEN, 1957
20,000 LEAGUES UNDER THE SEA, 1954
20,000 YEARS IN SING SING, 1933
TWO-LANE BLACKTOP, 1971
TWO OF US, THE, 1968
TWO WOMEN, 1960
UNDER THE ROOFS OF PARIS, 1930
UNINVITED, THE, 1944
UNION PACIFIC, 1939
UNMARRIED WOMAN, AN, 1978
UP IN ARMS, 1944
VERDICT, THE, 1982
VICTORIA THE GREAT, 1937
VITELLONI, 1956
VIVA VILLA!, 1934
WAGES OF FEAR, THE, 1955
WAKE ISLAND, 1942
WANDERERS, THE, 1979
WAR AND PEACE, 1956
WAR OF THE WORLDS, THE, 1953
WARLOCK, 1959
WATCH ON THE RHINE, 1943
WATERLOO BRIDGE, 1940
WAY OUT WEST, 1937
WE LIVE AGAIN, 1934
WEDDING IN GALILEE, 1988
WELCOME IN VIENNA, 1988
WELLS FARGO, 1937
WEST SIDE STORY, 1961
WESTERN UNION, 1941
WHAT PRICE GLORY?, 1952
WHATEVER HAPPENED TO BABY JANE?, 1962
WHEN THE WIND BLOWS, 1988
WHILE THE CITY SLEEPS, 1956
WHOOPING COUGH, 1987
WHO'S AFRAID OF VIRGINIA WOOLF?, 1966
WILD ONE, THE, 1953
WILD RIVER, 1960
WINCHESTER "73, 1950
WIND, THE, 1928
WINDOW, THE, 1949
WINGED VICTORY, 1944
WITNESS, 1985
WOLF MAN, THE, 1941
WOMAN OF THE YEAR, 1942
WOMEN, THE, 1939
WOMEN ON THE VERGE OF A NERVOUS
   BREAKDOWN, 1988
WORLD APART, A, 1988
WRONG MAN, THE, 1956
YEARLING, THE, 1946
YELLOW SUBMARINE, 1958

YESTERDAY'S ENEMY, 1959
YOU CAN'T TAKE IT WITH YOU, 1938
YOU ONLY LIVE ONCE, 1937
YOUNG FRANKENSTEIN, 1974
YOUNG LIONS, THE, 1958
YOUNG MAN WITH A HORN, 1950
YOUNG MR. LINCOLN, 1939
YOU'RE TELLING ME, 1934
Z, 1969

3.5 Stars

ABRAHAM LINCOLN, 1930
ACROSS THE PACIFIC, 1942
ACT OF MURDER, AN, 1948
ADAM'S RIB, 1949
ADVENTURES OF MARTIN EDEN, THE, 1942
ADVENTURES OF ROBINSON CRUSOE, THE, 1954
ADVENTURES OF TOM SAWYER, THE, 1938
AFTER THE THIN MAN, 1936
ALAMO BAY, 1985
ALEXANDER'S RAGTIME BAND, 1938
ALI BABA AND THE FORTY THIEVES, 1944
ALICE, 1988
ALL THE PRESIDENT'S MEN, 1976
ANGEL AND THE BADMAN, 1947
ANGEL ON MY SHOULDER, 1946
ANGELS IN THE OUTFIELD, 1951
ANGUISH, 1988
ANITA—DANCES OF VICE, 1987
ANNA CHRISTIE, 1930
ANNIE GET YOUR GUN, 1950
ANOTHER LANGUAGE, 1933
APOCALYPSE NOW, 1979
ARTHUR, 1981
ARTISTS AND MODELS, 1937
ASSA, 1988
AT CLOSE RANGE, 1986
BABES IN ARMS, 1939
BABES ON BROADWAY, 1941
BACHELOR PARTY, THE, 1957
BACK TO SCHOOL, 1986
BACK TO THE FUTURE, 1985
BAD NEWS BEARS, THE, 1976
BAGDAD CAFE, 1988
BALLAD OF CABLE HOGUE, THE, 1970
BAREFOOT CONTESSA, THE, 1954
BATTLE OF THE BULGE, 1965
BAYAN KO, 1985
BEAST, THE, 1988
BED SITTING ROOM, THE, 1969
BEDAZZLED, 1967
BEDFORD INCIDENT, THE, 1965
BEDKNOBS AND BROOMSTICKS, 1971
BEETLEJUICE, 1988
BEHOLD A PALE HORSE, 1964
BELL FOR ADANO, A, 1945
BELLE DE JOUR, 1968
BELLS ARE RINGING, 1960
BENJAMIN, 1968
BENJI, 1974
BEST MAN, THE, 1964
BEST SELLER, 1987
BEST THINGS IN LIFE ARE FREE, THE, 1956
BETRAYAL, 1983
BETTER TOMORROW, A, 1987
BEYOND THE WALLS, 1985
BIG, 1988
BIG CARNIVAL, THE, 1951
BIG COUNTRY, THE, 1958
BIG HOUSE, THE, 1930
BIG SKY, THE, 1952
BILLY LIAR, 1963
BILOXI BLUES, 1988
BLACK CAT, THE, 1934
BLACK CAULDRON, THE, 1985
BLACK FURY, 1935
BLACK SUNDAY, 1977
BLESSED EVENT, 1932
BLIND ALLEY, 1939
BLIND CHANCE, 1987
BLISS OF MRS. BLOSSOM, THE, 1968
BLOCKHEADS, 1938
BLOOD MONEY, 1933
BLOOD ON THE SUN, 1945
BLUE LAMP, THE, 1950
BLUEPRINT FOR MURDER, A, 1953

BOLD: Films on Videocassette

BLUME IN LOVE, 1973
BOB AND CAROL AND TED AND ALICE, 1969
BOFORS GUN, THE, 1968
BOMBSHELL, 1933
BONA, 1984
BOOTS MALONE, 1952
BORDERLINE, 1980
BORN TO BE BAD, 1950
BOUDU SAVED FROM DROWNING, 1967
BOUND FOR GLORY, 1976
BOY FRIEND, THE, 1971
BOY MEETS GIRL, 1938
BOY SOLDIER, 1987
BOYS FROM BRAZIL, THE, 1978
BRAZIL, 1985
BREAKIN'2: ELECTRIC BOOGALOO, 1984
BREWSTER'S MILLIONS, 1935
BRIDE COMES HOME, 1936
BRIDGE OF SAN LUIS REY, THE, 1944
BRIEF VACATION, A, 1975
BRIGHTON BEACH MEMOIRS, 1986
BRITISH AGENT, 1934
BROADWAY BILL, 1934
BROADWAY MELODY OF 1936, 1935
BROKEN ARROW, 1950
BROKEN LANCE, 1954
BROTHER ORCHID, 1940
BROTHER RAT, 1938
BROTHERHOOD, THE, 1968
BROTHERS KARAMAZOV, THE, 1958
BRUBAKER, 1980
BUDDY HOLLY STORY, THE, 1978
BUFFALO BILL, 1944
BUGSY MALONE, 1976
BULL DURHAM, 1988
BULLETS OR BALLOTS, 1936
BUNNY LAKE IS MISSING, 1965
BUS STOP, 1956
CABIN IN THE SKY, 1943
CADDYSHACK, 1980
CALIFORNIA SUITE, 1978
CALL OF THE WILD, 1935
CALLAWAY WENT THATAWAY, 1951
CANDIDATE, THE, 1972
CAPE FEAR, 1962
CAPTAIN HORATIO HORNBLOWER, 1951
CARAVAN, 1946
CARMEN, 1983
CARS THAT ATE PARIS, THE, 1974
CASANOVA BROWN, 1944
CASBAH, 1948
CAST A GIANT SHADOW, 1966
CEILNG ZERO, 1935
CESAR, 1936
CHAIN, THE, 1985
CHAMP, 1931
CHARLEY VARRICK, 1973
CHARLEY'S AUNT, 1941
CHARLIE CHAN AT THE OPERA, 1936
CHARLOTTE'S WEB, 1973
CHASE A CROOKED SHADOW, 1958
CHEAPER BY THE DOZEN, 1950
CHEATERS, THE, 1945
CHILDREN'S HOUR, THE, 1961
CHIMES AT MIDNIGHT, 1967
CHINA SEAS, 1935
CHRISTMAS CAROL, A, 1938
CHRISTMAS IN CONNECTICUT, 1945
CHRISTMAS IN JULY, 1940
CHRONOPOLIS, 1982
CHUSHINGURA, 1963
CITY AND THE DOGS, THE, 1987
CITY, FOR CONQUEST, 1941
CITY STREETS, 1931
CLAIRE'S KNEE, 1971
CLAUDIA, 1943
CLAUDIA AND DAVID, 1946
CLEOPATRA, 1934
CLEOPATRA, 1963
CLOCK, THE, 1945
CLOSELY WATCHED TRAINS, 1967
COCA-COLA KID, THE, 1985
COLOR OF DESTINY, THE, 1988
COLOR OF MONEY, THE, 1986
COLOSSUS: THE FORBIN PROJECT, 1969
COME AND SEE, 1986

COME FILL THE CUP, 1951
COME LIVE WITH ME, 1941
COME TO THE STABLE, 1949
COMIC MAGAZINE, 1986
COMING UP ROSES, 1986
COMMAND DECISION, 1948
COMMANDOS STRIKE AT DAWN, THE, 1942
COMPANY OF WOLVES, THE, 1985
CONEY ISLAND, 1943
CONFIDENTIALLY YOURS!, 1983
CONFLICT, 1945
CONRACK, 1974
CONSTANT HUSBAND, THE, 1955
COOGAN'S BLUFF, 1968
COP, 1988
CORN IS GREEN, THE, 1945
CORNERED, 1945
COTTON CLUB, THE, 1984
COUNTDOWN, 1968
COUNTERFEIT TRAITOR, THE, 1962
COURT JESTER, THE, 1956
COURT MARTIAL, 1954
COURTSHIP OF EDDY'S FATHER, THE, 1963
COWBOY, 1958
CRACK-UP, 1946
CRIME AND PUNISHMENT, 1935
CRIME AND PUNISHMENT, 1935
CRIMINAL LIFE OF ARCHIBALDO DE LA CRUZ,
  THE, 1962
CRISS CROSS, 1949
"CROCODILE" DUNDEE, 1986
CROSSROADS, 1938
CROSSROADS, 1942
CROWD ROARS, THE, 1932
CRUSADES, THE, 1935
CRY FROM THE STREET, A, 1959
CRY IN THE DARK, A, 1988
CRY OF THE CITY, 1948
CRY, THE BELOVED COUNTRY, 1952
CUCKOOS, THE, 1930
CURSE OF THE DEMON, 1958
CYNARA, 1932
DA, 1988
DAISY KENYON, 1947
DAM BUSTERS, THE, 1955
DAMES, 1934
DANCE, GIRL, DANCE, 1940
DANGEROUS LIAISONS, 1988
DANGEROUS MOVES, 1985
DARK ANGEL, THE, 1935
DARK AT THE TOP OF THE STAIRS, THE, 1960
DARK COMMAND, THE, 1940
DARK CORNER, THE, 1946
DARK EYES, 1987
DARK JOURNEY, 1937
DARK MIRROR, THE, 1946
DARK PASSAGE, 1947
DATE WITH JUDY, A, 1948
DAUGHTER OF THE NILE, 1988
DAVID AND BATHSHEBA, 1951
DAY AT THE RACES, A, 1937
DEAD-END DRIVE-IN, 1986
DEAD RECKONING, 1947
DEADLINE—U.S.A., 1952
DEAR BRIGETTE, 1965
DEATH OF A SOLDIER, 1986
DEATH WATCH, 1980
DEATHWATCH, 1966
DECISION AT SUNDOWN, 1957
DECLINE OF THE AMERICAN EMPIRE, THE, 1986
DEEP BLUE SEA, THE, 1955
DEEP VALLEY, 1947
DEFENCE OF THE REALM, 1985
DELIVERANCE, 1972
DEMETRIUS AND THE GLADIATORS, 1954
DEMON POND, 1980
DESERT RATS, THE, 1953
DESIGNING WOMAN, 1957
DESPERATE, 1947
DESTRY RIDES AGAIN, 1939
DETECTIVE, 1985
DETECTIVE, THE, 1968
DEVIL AND MISS JONES, THE, 1941
DEVIL AT FOUR O'CLOCK, THE, 1961
DEVIL DOLL, THE, 1936
DEVIL IS A SISSY, THE, 1936

DEVIL'S ENVOYS, THE, 1947
DIAL M FOR MURDER, 1954
DIARY OF A CHAMBERMAID, 1946
DIARY OF A MAD HOUSEWIFE, 1970
DIMBOOLA, 1979
DIRTY DANCING, 1987
DIRTY HARRY, 1971
DISRAELI, 1929
DISTANT DRUMS, 1951
DIVORCEE, THE, 1930
D.O.A., 1950
D.O.A., 1988
DR. BULL, 1933
DR. NO, 1962
DR. STRANGELOVE: OR HOW I LEARNED TO STOP
  WORRYING AND LOVE THE BOMB, 1964
DOG OF FLANDERS, A, 1959
DON'T GO NEAR THE WATER, 1957
DON'T LOOK NOW, 1973
DOORWAY TO HELL, 1930
DOWN ARGENTINE WAY, 1940
DOWNHILL RACER, 1969
DRAGON CHOW, 1988
DRAGONSLAYER, 1981
DREAMBOAT, 1952
DRIVE-IN, 1976
DUEL IN THE SUN, 1946
EACH DAWN I DIE, 1939
EAGLE AND THE HAWK, THE, 1933
EAGLE SQUADRON, 1942
EAGLE WITH TWO HEADS, 1948
EASY LIFE, THE, 1963
EASY MONEY, 1983
EDGE OF DARKNESS, 1943
EIGHT O'CLOCK WALK, 1954
EIGHTH DAY OF THE WEEK, THE, 1959
ELECTRONIC MONSTER, THE, 1960
ELIZA FRASER, 1976
EMIL AND THE DETECTIVE, 1931
EMMA, 1932
EMPIRE STRIKES BACK, THE, 1980
EMPLOYEE'S ENTRANCE, 1933
ENCHANTED FOREST, THE, 1945
END OF THE TRAIL, 1932
ENEMY FROM SPACE, 1957
ENGLAND MADE ME, 1973
ENTERTAINER, THE, 1975
ENTERTAINING MR. SLOANE, 1970
ESCAPADE, 1935
ESCAPE FROM ALCATRAZ, 1979
ETERNAL RETURN, THE, 1943
EVERY MAN FOR HIMSELF AND GOD AGAINST
  ALL, 1975
EVIL DEAD, THE, 1983
EX-MRS. BRADFORD, THE, 1936
EXCUSE MY DUST, 1951
EXPERIENCE PREFERRED. . . BUT NOT ESSENTIAL,
  1983
EXPERIMENT PERILOUS, 1944
EYE OF THE NEEDLE, 1981
FALLEN ANGEL, 1945
FALLEN SPARROW, THE, 1943
FAMILY, THE, 1987
FAMILY PLOT, 1976
FAMILY WAY, THE, 1966
FANNY, 1948
FAR HORIZONS, THE, 1955
FARMER'S DAUGHTER, THE, 1947
FASHIONS OF 1934, 1934
FATHER GOOSE, 1964
FATHER OF THE BRIDE, 1950
FAVORITES OF THE MOON, 1985
FEARLESS VAMPIRE KILLERS, OR PARDON ME BUT
  YOUR TEETH ARE IN MY NECK, THE, 1967
FELDMANN CASE, THE, 1987
FEW DAYS WITH ME, A, 1988
FIDDLER ON THE ROOF, 1971
FIGHTER SQUADRON, 1948
FILE ON THELMA JORDAN, THE, 1950
FIREFOX, 1982
FIREMAN'S BALL, THE, 1968
FIRST NAME: CARMEN, 1984
FISH CALLED WANDA, A, 1988
FIVE BRANDED WOMEN, 1960
FIVE MILLION YEARS TO EARTH, 1968
FIVE ON THE BLACK HAND SIDE, 1973

FIXER, THE, 1968
FLAME AND THE ARROW, THE, 1950
FLAMING STAR, 1960
FLAMINGO KID, THE, 1984
FLASH OF GREEN, A, 1984
FLIGHT FROM DESTINY, 1941
FLIGHT FROM GLORY, 1937
FLIPPER, 1963
FLY, THE, 1958
FOG OVER FRISCO, 1934
FOLLOW ME QUIETLY, 1949
FOLLOW THE BOYS, 1944
FOLLOW THE FLEET, 1936
FOOTSTEPS IN THE FOG, 1955
FOR A FEW DOLLARS MORE, 1967
FOR ME AND MY GAL, 1942
FOR THE DEFENSE, 1930
FORCE OF ARMS, 1951
FORCE OF EVIL, 1948
FORCE 10 FROM NAVARONE, 1978
FORSAKING ALL OTHERS, 1935
FOUR FRIENDS, 1981
FOUR MUSKETEERS, THE, 1975
FOUR NIGHTS OF A DREAMER, 1972
FOURTEEN HOURS, 1951
FOXES OF HARROW, THE, 1947
FRANCESCA, 1987
FRATERNITY ROW, 1977
FREAKY FRIDAY, 1976
FREE AND EASY, 1930
FREE SOUL, A, 1931
FRENCH CONNECTION II, 1975
FRENZY, 1972
FRIENDLY PERSUASION, 1956
FRIENDS OF EDDIE COYLE, THE, 1973
FRIGHT NIGHT, 1985
FROM HELL TO TEXAS, 1958
FULL MOON IN BLUE WATER, 1988
FULL MOON IN PARIS, 1984
FULLER BRUSH MAN, 1948
FUNERAL IN BERLIN, 1966
FUNNY FACE, 1957
FUNNY LADY, 1975
F/X, 1986
GAY DESPERADO, THE, 1936
GENERAL DELLA ROVERE, 1960
GENERAL DIED AT DAWN, THE, 1936
GENEVIEVE, 1953
GERMANY PALE MOTHER, 1984
GETAWAY, THE, 1972
GETTING STRAIGHT, 1970
GHOST BREAKERS, THE, 1940
GHOST SHIP, THE, 1943
GHOST WALKS, THE, 1935
GHOSTBUSTERS, 1984
GIGOT, 1962
GILDED LILY, THE, 1935
GILSODOM, 1986
GIRL WITH A SUITCASE, 1961
GIRL WITH GREEN EYES, 1964
GIRLFRIENDS, 1978
GLADIATOR, THE, 1938
GLAMOUR BOY, 1941
GLASS KEY, THE, 1942
GLASS MENAGERIE, THE, 1987
GLORIA, 1980
GO TELL THE SPARTANS, 1978
GOD IS MY CO-PILOT, 1945
GOIN' DOWN THE ROAD, 1970
GOLDEN EIGHTIES, 1986
GOLDEN VOYAGE OF SINBAD, THE, 1974
GOOD DISSONANCE LIKE A MAN, A, 1977
GOOD FAIRY, THE, 1935
GOOD MORNING, VIETNAM, 1987
GOOD NEIGHBOR SAM, 1964
GREASE, 1978
GREAT CARUSO, THE, 1951
GREAT GENERATION, THE, 1986
GREAT MANHUNT, THE, 1951
GREAT SINNER, THE, 1949
GREAT WHITE HOPE, THE, 1970
GREATEST STORY EVER TOLD, THE, 1965
GREEN PASTURES, 1936
GREEN ROOM, THE, 1979
GUNS OF NAVARONE, THE, 1961
GUYS AND DOLLS, 1955

HAIRSPRAY, 1988
HALLS OF MONTEZUMA, 1951
HAMBURGER HILL, 1987
HAMLET, 1962
HAMLET, 1969
HAMMETT, 1982
HANDS ACROSS THE TABLE, 1935
HANGMEN ALSO DIE, 1943
HANK WILLIAMS: THE SHOW HE NEVER GAVE, 1982
HAPPIEST DAYS OF YOUR LIFE, 1950
HAPPY BIRTHDAY, WANDA JUNE, 1971
HAPPY TIME, THE, 1952
HARD KNOCKS, 1980
HARD WAY, THE, 1942
HAROLD AND MAUDE, 1971
HARP OF BURMA, 1967
HARRIET CRAIG, 1950
HARVEST, 1939
HATTER'S CASTLE, 1948
HAUNTING, THE, 1963
HE RAN ALL THE WAY, 1951
HEART AND SOUL, 1950
HEARTS OF THE WEST, 1975
HEAVEN CAN WAIT, 1943
HEAVEN HELP US, 1985
HEIDI, 1937
HEIDI, 1968
HEIMAT, 1985
HELL IN KOREA, 1956
HELL IS FOR HEROES, 1962
HELL'S ANGELS, 1930
HER HUSBAND'S AFFAIRS, 1947
HER PRIMITIVE MAN, 1944
HERBIE RIDES AGAIN, 1974
HERE COME THE CO-EDS, 1945
HERE COME THE WAVES, 1944
HESTER STREET, 1975
HIDDEN, THE, 1987
HIDE IN PLAIN SIGHT, 1980
HIGH PLAINS DRIFTER, 1973
HIGH SEASON, 1988
HIGH WALL, THE, 1947
HIGH, WIDE AND HANDSOME, 1937
HIRELING, THE, 1973
H.M. PULHAM, ESQ., 1941
HOLIDAY, 1938
HOLLOW TRIUMPH, 1948
HOLLY AND THE IVY, THE, 1954
HOLLYWOOD HOTEL, 1937
HOLY MATRIMONY, 1943
HOPSCOTCH, 1980
HORROR CHAMBER OF DR. FAUSTUS, THE, 1962
HOT MILLIONS, 1968
HOUR OF THE GUN, 1967
HOUSE OF BAMBOO, 1955
HOUSE OF USHER, 1960
HOUSEKEEPING, 1987
HOW I WON THE WAR, 1967
HOW TO MURDER YOUR WIFE, 1965
HOW TO STEAL A MILLION, 1966
HOWLING, THE, 1981
HUCKLEBERRY FINN, 1939
HUGO THE HIPPO, 1976
HUMAN COMEDY, THE, 1943
HUMORESQUE, 1946
HUSH... HUSH, SWEET CHARLOTTE, 1964
HUSTLE, 1975
I ACCUSE!, 1958
I CAN GET IT FOR YOU WHOLESALE, 1951
I LIVE IN FEAR, 1967
I LOVE YOU AGAIN, 1940
I MARRIED A WITCH, 1942
I NEVER PROMISED YOU A ROSE GARDEN, 1977
I NEVER SANG FOR MY FATHER, 1970
I OUGHT TO BE IN PICTURES, 1982
IDIOT, THE, 1948
IDIOT'S DELIGHT, 1939
IDOLMAKER, THE, 1980
IF I HAD A MILLION, 1932
IF I WERE KING, 1938
I'LL BE SEEING YOU, 1944
IMITATION OF LIFE, 1934
IMMORTAL STORY, THE, 1969
IMPOSSIBLE YEARS, THE, 1968
IN THE GOOD OLD SUMMERTIME, 1949

IN THE WHITE CITY, 1983
IN THE WILD MOUNTAINS, 1986
INDIAN FIGHTER, THE, 1955
INDIANA JONES AND THE TEMPLE OF DOOM, 1984
INDISCREET, 1958
INN OF THE SIXTH HAPPINESS, THE, 1958
INTERRUPTED MELODY, 1955
INTIMATE LIGHTING, 1969
INTRUDER, THE, 1962
INVESTIGATION OF A CITIZEN ABOVE SUSPICION, 1970
INVISIBLE MAN, THE, 1933
INVITATION, THE, 1975
INVITATION TO THE DANCE, 1956
IPCRESS FILE, THE, 1965
IS PARIS BURNING?, 1966
IT CAME FROM OUTER SPACE, 1953
IT HAPPENED AT THE INN, 1945
IT HAPPENED HERE, 1966
IT HAPPENED TOMORROW, 1944
IT'S A WONDERFUL WORLD, 1939
J'ACCUSE, 1939
JAZZBAND FIVE, THE, 1932
JEAN DE FLORETTE, 1987
JEREMIAH JOHNSON, 1972
JESTER, THE, 1987
JOAN OF ARC, 1948
JOE LOUIS STORY, THE, 1953
JOE SMITH, AMERICAN, 1942
JOHN AND MARY, 1969
JOHNNY APOLLO, 1940
JOHNNY EAGER, 1942
JOHNNY IN THE CLOUDS, 1945
JOHNNY O'CLOCK, 1947
JOHNNY TREMAIN, 1957
JOKER IS WILD, THE, 1957
JOKERS, THE, 1967
JOLSON SINGS AGAIN, 1949
JOLSON STORY, THE, 1946
JONAH—WHO WILL BE 25 IN THE YEAR 2000, 1976
JOURNEY FOR MARGARET, 1942
JOURNEY TO THE CENTER OF THE EARTH, 1959
JOURNEY TOGETHER, 1946
JUBAL, 1956
JUBILEE, 1978
JUDEX, 1966
JUDGE HARDY'S CHILDREN, 1938
JUDGMENT AT NUREMBERG, 1961
JULIA MISBEHAVES, 1948
JUNGLE BOOK, THE, 1967
KAMILLA, 1984
KANAL, 1961
KARATE KID, THE, 1984
KATERINA IZMAILOVA, 1969
KENNEL MURDER CASE, THE, 1933
KENTUCKY, 1938
KID FROM SPAIN, THE, 1932
KID GALAHAD, 1937
KIDNAPPED, 1971
KILLING FIELDS, THE, 1984
KIND OF LOVING, A, 1962
KING AND HIS MOVIE, A, 1986
KING OF ALCATRAZ, 1938
KING OF KINGS, 1961
KING OF THE GYPSIES, 1978
KING OF THE KHYBER RIFLES, 1953
KING'S JESTER, THE, 1947
KINGS OF THE ROAD, 1976
KIT CARSON, 1940
KNOCK ON ANY DOOR, 1949
LA BETE HUMAINE, 1938
LA BOHEME, 1965
LA CHIENNE, 1975
LA MARSEILLAISE, 1938
LA NOTTE, 1961
LABYRINTH, 1986
LACEMAKER, THE, 1977
LADIES IN RETIREMENT, 1941
LADY AND THE TRAMP, 1955
LADY FOR A DAY, 1933
LADY FROM SHANGHAI, THE, 1948
LADY IN THE DARK, 1944
LADY IN WHITE, 1988
LADY JANE, 1986
LADY KILLER, 1933

BOLD: Films on Videocassette

LADY ON A TRAIN, 1945
LADY SINGS THE BLUES, 1972
LAND BEFORE TIME, THE, 1988
LANDSCAPE IN THE MIST, 1988
L'ARMEE DES OMBRES, 1969
LAST ANGRY MAN, THE, 1959
LAST BRIDGE, THE, 1957
LAST CHANCE, THE, 1945
LAST COMMAND, THE, 1955
LAST HUNT, THE, 1956
LAST HURRAH, THE, 1958
LAST METRO, THE, 1981
LAST MILE, THE, 1932
LAST ROUND-UP, THE, 1947
LAST STARFIGHTER, THE, 1984
LAST TIME I SAW PARIS, THE, 1954
LAST TRAIN FROM GUN HILL, 1959
LATE SHOW, THE, 1977
LAW AND ORDER, 1932
LE BEAU SERGE, 1959
LE PLAISIR, 1954
LEADBELLY, 1976
LEAGUE OF GENTLEMEN, THE, 1961
LEFT HAND OF GOD, THE, 1955
LEFT-HANDED GUN, THE, 1958
LEOPARD MAN, THE, 1943
LES BICHES, 1968
LES COMPERES, 1984
LETTER FROM AN UNKNOWN WOMAN, 1948
LETTER TO BREZHNEV, 1986
LETTERS FROM MY WINDMILL, 1955
LIES MY FATHER TOLD ME, 1975
LIFE AND LOVES OF BEETHOVEN, THE, 1937
LIFE AT THE TOP, 1965
LIFE BEGINS FOR ANDY HARDY, 1941
LIFE OF OHARU, 1964
LIGHT IN THE PIAZZA, 1962
LILI, 1953
LILIES OF THE FIELD, 1963
LION IS IN THE STREETS, A, 1953
LIQUID SKY, 1982
LIST OF ADRIAN MESSENGER, THE, 1963
LITTLE COLONEL, THE, 1935
LITTLE FUGITIVE, THE, 1953
LITTLE GIRL WHO LIVES DOWN THE LANE, THE,
   1977
LITTLE KIDNAPPERS, THE, 1954
LITTLE MAN, WHAT NOW?, 1934
LITTLE MISS MARKER, 1934
LITTLE MURDERS, 1971
LITTLE PRINCESS, THE, 1939
LITTLE VERA, 1988
LITTLEST REBEL, THE, 1935
LIVING DAYLIGHTS, THE, 1987
LIVING IT UP, 1954
LLOYDS OF LONDON, 1936
LOLA, 1982
LOLITA, 1962
LONELYHEARTS, 1958
LONG GOOD FRIDAY, THE, 1982
LONG GRAY LINE, THE, 1955
LONGEST YARD, THE, 1974
LOOKING FOR MR. GOODBAR, 1977
LOST ONE, THE, 1951
LOST PATROL, THE, 1934
LOVE AND DEATH, 1975
LOVE ON THE RUN, 1980
LOVE PARADE, THE, 1929
LOVE STREAMS, 1984
LOVER COME BACK, 1961
LOVERS AND OTHER STRANGERS, 1970
LOVES OF A BLONDE, 1966
MAC ARTHUR, 1977
MACBETH, 1971
MACOMBER AFFAIR, THE, 1947
MAD MAX, 1979
MADAME ROSA, 1977
MADE FOR EACH OTHER, 1939
MADELEINE, 1950
MADIGAN, 1968
MAGIC CHRISTIAN, THE, 1970
MAGICIAN, THE, 1959
MAKE WAY FOR TOMORROW, 1937
MAKIOKA SISTERS, THE, 1985
MAN AND A WOMAN, A, 1966
MAN CALLED PETER, THE, 1955

MAN IN LOVE, A, 1987
MAN IN THE GLASS BOOTH, THE, 1975
MAN IN THE GREY FLANNEL SUIT, THE, 1956
MAN OF A THOUSAND FACES, 1957
MAN OF FLOWERS, 1984
MAN OF MARBLE, 1979
MAN WHO COULD WORK MIRACLES, THE, 1937
MAN WHO FELL TO EARTH, THE, 1976
MAN WITH BOGART'S FACE, THE, 1980
MAN WITHOUT A STAR, 1955
MANCHURIAN CANDIDATE, THE, 1962
MANON OF THE SPRING, 1987
MARCH ON PARIS 1914—OF GENERALOBERST
   ALEXANDER VON KLUCK—AND HIS MEMORY
   OF JESSIE HOLLADAY, 1977
MARIE, 1985
MARIGOLDS IN AUGUST, 1984
MARIUS, 1933
MARK, THE, 1961
MARKED WOMAN, 1937
MARRIAGE OF A YOUNG STOCKBROKER, THE, 1971
MARRIED WOMAN, THE, 1965
MARTIN, 1979
MASCARA, 1987
MASOCH, 1980
MASQUE OF THE RED DEATH, THE, 1964
MASS IS ENDED, THE, 1988
MATA HARI, 1931
MATCH KING, THE, 1932
MATCHMAKER, THE, 1958
MATILDA, 1978
MC KENZIE BREAK, THE, 1970
MELODY TIME, 1948
MELVIN AND HOWARD, 1980
MEN, 1985
MEN IN WAR, 1957
MERRILL'S MARAUDERS, 1962
MICKI AND MAUDE, 1984
MIDDLE OF THE NIGHT, 1959
MIDNIGHT, 1939
MIDNIGHT RUN, 1988
MIDSUMMER'S NIGHT'S DREAM, A, 1935
MILKY WAY, THE, 1936
MILKY WAY, THE, 1969
MIRACLE OF THE BELLS, THE, 1948
MIRACLE WOMAN, THE, 1931
MISHIMA, 1985
MISS GRANT TAKES RICHMOND, 1949
MISS MONA, 1987
MISSISSIPPI MERMAID, 1970
MISTER 880, 1950
MIXED BLOOD, 1984
MOBY DICK, 1930
MODERN ROMANCE, 1981
MOHAN JOSHI HAAZIR HO, 1984
MONA LISA, 1986
MOON IS DOWN, THE, 1943
MONTE CARLO, 1930
MOONRISE, 1948
MOONSTRUCK, 1987
MORE THE MERRIER, THE, 1943
MORO AFFAIR, THE, 1986
MORTAL STORM, THE, 1940
MOUCHETTE, 1970
MOULIN ROUGE, 1952
MOVIE CRAZY, 1932
MUDDY RIVER, 1982
MURDER AT THE GALLOP, 1963
MURDER ON THE ORIENT EXPRESS, 1974
MUSHROOM EATER, THE, 1976
MY BEAUTIFUL LAUNDRETTE, 1986
MY BODYGUARD, 1980
MY BROTHER'S WEDDING, 1983
MY NAME IS JULIA ROSS, 1945
MY PAL TRIGGER, 1946
MY SISTER EILEEN, 1955
MY UNCLE ANTOINE, 1971
MYSTERIOUS HOUSE OF DR. C., THE, 1976
MYSTERY STREET, 1950
NAKED JUNGLE, THE, 1953
NAKED PREY, THE, 1966
NAKED YOUTH, 1961
NATIONAL LAMPOON'S ANIMAL HOUSE, 1978
NAUGHTY MARIETTA, 1935
NEAR DARK, 1987
NEVADA SMITH, 1966

NEVER CRY WOLF, 1983
NEVERENDING STORY, THE, 1984
NEW YORK, NEW YORK, 1977
NIAGARA, 1953
NICHOLAS AND ALEXANDRA, 1971
NIGHT AND THE CITY, 1950
'NIGHT, MOTHER, 1986
NIGHT OF JUNE 13, 1932
NIGHT OF THE COMET, 1984
NIGHT PEOPLE, 1954
NIGHTFALL, 1956
NIGHTHAWKS, 1981
NIGHTMARE ON ELM STREET, A, 1984
NIGHTMARE'S PASSENGERS, 1986
NIKKI, WILD DOG OF THE NORTH, 1961
NINE MEN, 1943
9/30/55, 1977
1918, 1985
NO DRUMS, NO BUGLES, 1971
NO HIGHWAY IN THE SKY, 1951
NO LIMIT, 1935
NO LOVE FOR JOHNNIE, 1961
NO NAME ON THE BULLET, 1959
NO SURRENDER, 1986
NO TIME FOR COMEDY, 1940
NO TIME FOR SERGEANTS, 1958
NO TIME FOR TEARS, 1957
NO WAY TO TREAT A LADY, 1968
NONE SHALL ESCAPE, 1944
NORTH DALLAS FORTY, 1979
NORTH TO ALASKA, 1960
NOTORIOUS GENTLEMAN, 1945
NUN, THE, 1971
NUTTY PROFESSOR, THE, 1963
O. HENRY'S FULL HOUSE, 1952
ODESSA FILE, THE, 1974
OF HUMAN HEARTS, 1938
OFFICER AND A GENTLEMAN, AN, 1982
OFFICIAL STORY, THE, 1985
OH! WHAT A LOVELY WAR, 1969
OLD DARK HOUSE, THE, 1932
OLD-FASHIONED WAY, THE, 1934
OLD MAID, THE, 1939
OLD YELLER, 1957
ON HER MAJESTY'S SECRET SERVICE, 1969
ON VALENTINE'S DAY, 1986
ONCE IN PARIS, 1978
ONE-EYED JACKS, 1961
ONE FOOT IN HEAVEN, 1941
ONE HUNDRED AND ONE DALMATIANS, 1961
ONE OF OUR AIRCRAFT IS MISSING, 1942
ONE, TWO, THREE, 1961
ONLY TWO CAN PLAY, 1962
ONLY WHEN I LAUGH, 1981
OPERATION PETTICOAT, 1959
ORDINARY PEOPLE, 1980
OSCAR WILDE, 1960
O.S.S., 1946
OTELLO, 1986
OTHELLO, 1965
OUR BETTERS, 1933
OUR MOTHER'S HOUSE, 1967
OUT OF THE FOG, 1941
OUT WEST WITH THE HARDYS, 1938
OUTCAST OF THE ISLANDS, 1952
OUTCRY, 1949
OUTRAGEOUS!, 1977
OUTSIDER, THE, 1980
OVER THE HILL, 1931
OVERLANDERS, THE, 1946
OVERLORD, 1975
PADRE PADRONE, 1977
PALE RIDER, 1985
PALEFACE, THE, 1948
PAPER MOON, 1973
PARALLAX VIEW, THE, 1974
PARANOIAC, 1963
PARIS DOES STRANGE THINGS, 1957
PARTY GIRL, 1958
PASSAGE TO INDIA, A, 1984
PASSAGE TO MARSEILLE, 1944
PASSENGER, THE, 1970
PASSION, 1983
PATHER PANCHALI, 1958
PATRIOT, THE, 1928
PAULINE AT THE BEACH, 1983

PEARL, THE, 1948
PEARLS OF THE CROWN, 1938
PEDESTRIAN, THE, 1974
PEE-WEE'S BIG ADVENTURE, 1985
PEGGY SUE GOT MARRIED, 1986
PEKING OPERA BLUES, 1986
PEPPERMINT SODA, 1979
PERILS OF PAULINE, THE, 1947
PETE 'N' TILLIE, 1972
PETER IBBETSON, 1935
PEYTON PLACE, 1957
PHANTASM, 1979
PHANTOM LADY, 1944
PHANTOM TOLLBOOTH, THE, 1970
PHAR LAP, 1984
PHOBIA, 1988
PICKUP ON SOUTH STREET, 1953
PICTURE OF DORIAN GRAY, THE, 1945
PIED PIPER, THE, 1942
PILGRIMAGE, 1933
PILLOW TALK, 1959
PIMPERNEL SMITH, 1942
PINK PANTHER, THE, 1964
PIRATE, THE, 1948
PIT AND THE PENDULUM, THE, 1961
PITFALL, 1948
PLACES IN THE HEART, 1984
PLAINSMAN, THE, 1937
PLAY IT AGAIN, SAM, 1972
PLAY MISTY FOR ME, 1971
PLAYTIME, 1973
PLUMBER, THE, 1980
POCKETFUL OF MIRACLES, 1961
PORGY AND BESS, 1959
PORTRAIT OF CHIEKO, 1968
POSSESSED, 1947
PRESIDENT'S ANALYST, THE, 1967
PRESSURE POINT, 1962
PRETTY BABY, 1978
PRETTY POISON, 1968
PRICK UP YOUR EARS, 1987
PRIDE OF ST. LOUIS, THE, 1952
PRIME OF MISS JEAN BRODIE, THE, 1969
PRINCE AND THE PAUPER, THE, 1937
PRINCE AND THE SHOWGIRL, THE, 1957
PRINCE OF PLAYERS, 1955
PRINCE OF THE CITY, 1981
PRINCESS BRIDE, THE, 1987
PRISONER, THE, 1955
PRIVATE LIFE OF SHERLOCK HOLMES, THE, 1970
**PRIVATE LIVES OF ELIZABETH AND ESSEX, THE,
    1939**
PROFESSIONALS, THE, 1966
PROJECTIONIST, THE, 1970
PROUD REBEL, THE, 1958
PUBLIC HERO NO. 1, 1935
PULP, 1972
PUNCHLINE, 1988
PURSUED, 1947
PUSHOVER, 1954
Q, 1982
QUEEN OF SPADES, 1948
QUESTION, THE, 1977
QUESTION OF SILENCE, 1984
QUO VADIS, 1951
RACHEL, RACHEL, 1968
RADIO DAYS, 1987
RAFFLES, 1930
RAIN MAN, 1988
RAINS CAME, THE, 1939
RAISIN IN THE SUN, A, 1961
RANDOM HARVEST, 1942
RAVEN, THE, 1963
REAL GLORY, THE, 1939
REAP THE WILD WIND, 1942
RED DESERT, 1965
RED DUST, 1932
RED KISS, 1985
REDS, 1981
RELUCTANT DEBUTANTE, THE, 1958
REMEMBER THE NIGHT, 1940
REPO MAN, 1984
REQUIEM FOR A HEAVYWEIGHT, 1962
RETURN OF FRANK JAMES, THE, 1940
RETURN OF MARTIN GUERRE, THE, 1983
RETURN OF THE JEDI, 1983

RETURN OF THE PINK PANTHER, THE, 1975
RETURN OF THE SECAUCUS SEVEN, 1980
REUNION, 1932
REVENGE OF THE NERDS, 1984
REVOLT OF JOB, THE, 1984
REVOLUTIONARY, THE, 1970
RHAPSODY IN BLUE, 1945
RHODES, 1936
RHYTHM ON THE RIVER, 1940
RICHEST GIRL IN THE WORLD, THE, 1934
RICKSHAW MAN, THE, 1960
RIDE A CROOKED MILE, 1938
RIDE BACK, THE, 1957
RIDE THE PINK HORSE, 1947
RIDER OF DEATH VALLEY, 1932
RIDER ON THE RAIN, 1970
RIDING HIGH, 1950
RIO RITA, 1929
RIOT IN CELL BLOCK 11, 1954
RISE AND FALL OF LEGS DIAMOND, THE, 1960
RITZ, THE, 1976
RIVER, THE, 1951
RIVER OF NO RETURN, 1954
RIVER'S EDGE, 1987
ROAD TO LIFE, 1932
ROAD TO RIO, 1947
ROAD TO UTOPIA, 1945
ROAD TO ZANZIBAR, 1941
ROAD WARRIOR, THE, 1982
ROBE, THE, 1953
ROBINSON'S GARDEN, 1988
ROBOCOP, 1987
ROCCO AND HIS BROTHERS, 1961
ROCKING HORSE WINNER, THE, 1950
ROCKY II, 1979
ROMA, 1972
ROMAN SCANDALS, 1933
ROMAN SPRING OF MRS. STONE, THE, 1961
ROMANCING THE STONE, 1984
ROMANOFF AND JULIET, 1961
ROMANTIC ENGLISHWOMAN, THE, 1975
ROMEO AND JULIET, 1968
ROMEO AND JULIET, 1968
ROOM FOR ONE MORE, 1952
ROSEMARY, 1960
ROUND UP, THE, 1969
ROUNDERS, THE, 1965
ROXANNE, 1987
RULING CLASS, THE, 1972
RUN FOR COVER, 1955
RUNAWAY TRAIN, 1985
**RUSSIANS ARE COMING, THE RUSSIANS ARE
    COMING, THE, 1966**
RUTHLESS PEOPLE, 1986
SABOTAGE, 1937
SAINT IN LONDON, THE, 1939
SAINT STRIKES BACK, THE, 1939
ST. VALENTINE'S DAY MASSACRE, THE, 1967
SAINT'S GIRL FRIDAY, THE, 1954
SALOME'S LAST DANCE, 1988
SAME TIME, NEXT YEAR, 1978
SAMMY AND ROSIE GET LAID, 1987
SAMSON AND DELILAH, 1949
SAN DIEGO, I LOVE YOU, 1944
SANTA FE TRAIL, 1940
SARATOGA, 1937
SATURDAY NIGHT FEVER, 1977
SCANDAL SHEET, 1952
SCARAMOUCHE, 1952
SCOTT OF THE ANTARCTIC, 1949
SCOUNDREL, THE, 1935
SCREAM OF FEAR, 1961
SCROOGE, 1970
SCUDDA-HOO? SCUDDA-HAY?, 1948
SEA GULL, THE, 1968
SEARCHING WIND, THE, 1946
SECONDS, 1966
SECRET AGENT, THE, 1936
SECRET SIX, THE, 1931
SECRETS OF WOMEN, 1961
SEDUCTION OF JOE TYNAN, THE, 1979
SENATOR WAS INDISCREET, THE, 1947
SENSO, 1968
SENTIMIENTOS: MIRTA DE LINIERS A ESTAMBUL,
    1987
SERGEANT RUTLEDGE, 1960

SERPENT, THE, 1973
SERPENT'S WAY, THE, 1987
SEVEN BEAUTIES, 1976
SEVEN DAYS TO NOON, 1950
SEVEN FACES OF DR. LAO, 1964
SEVEN LITTLE FOYS, THE, 1955
SEVEN MEN FROM NOW, 1956
SEVEN SINNERS, 1940
SEVENTH CROSS, THE, 1944
SEVENTH VOYAGE OF SINBAD, THE, 1958
SHAKE HANDS WITH THE DEVIL, 1959
SHAKEDOWN, 1950
SHALL WE DANCE, 1937
SHAME, 1968
SHAME, 1988
SHANGHAI GESTURE, THE, 1941
SHENANDOAH, 1965
SHIP THAT DIED OF SHAME, THE, 1956
SHIVERS, 1984
SHOESHINE, 1947
SHOP ON MAIN STREET, THE, 1966
SHOPWORN ANGEL, 1938
SHORT EYES, 1977
SHOW BOAT, 1951
SHOWDOWN AT BOOT HILL, 1958
SHY PEOPLE, 1988
SICILIAN CLAN, THE, 1970
SIGN OF THE CROSS, 1932
SILENT DUST, 1949
SILENT MOVIE, 1976
SILENT PARTNER, THE, 1979
SILVER BULLET, THE, 1942
SILVER DOLLAR, 1932
SING YOU SINNERS, 1938
SIR, YOU ARE A WIDOWER, 1971
SISTER KENNY, 1946
SISTERS, THE, 1938
SKIN DEEP, 1978
SKIN GAME, 1971
SKIPPY, 1931
SLEEPER, 1973
SLEEPING BEAUTY, 1959
SLEEPING CAR MURDER, THE, 1966
SMART MONEY, 1931
SMILE, 1975
SMILEY, 1957
SMILIN' THROUGH, 1932
SNAKE PIT, THE, 1948
SNOOPY, COME HOME, 1972
SNOWS OF KILIMANJARO, THE, 1952
SO DARK THE NIGHT, 1946
SO EVIL MY LOVE, 1948
SO LONG AT THE FAIR, 1951
SOFIA, 1987
SOLARIS, 1972
SOLDIER OF ORANGE, 1979
SOLDIER'S STORY, A, 1984
SOME CAME RUNNING, 1959
SOMEBODY UP THERE LIKES ME, 1956
SOMETHING OF VALUE, 1957
SOMETHING TO SING ABOUT, 1937
SOMETHING WILD, 1986
SOMETIMES A GREAT NOTION, 1971
SON OF PALEFACE, 1952
SONG IS BORN, A, 1948
SONG TO REMEMBER, A, 1945
SONG WITHOUT END, 1960
SONS AND LOVERS, 1960
SONS OF THE DESERT, 1933
SOPHIE'S CHOICE, 1982
SORCERER, 1977
SOULS AT SEA, 1937
SOUND AND FURY, 1988
SOUND AND THE FURY, THE, 1959
SOUNDER, 1972
SOUTH, 1988
SOUTH OF ST. LOUIS, 1949
SOUTHERN COMFORT, 1981
SPAWN OF THE NORTH, 1938
SPIRIT OF THE BEEHIVE, THE, 1976
SPITFIRE, 1943
SPLASH, 1984
SPOILERS, THE, 1942
SPRING FOR THE THIRSTY, A, 1988
SPRING IN PARK LANE, 1949
STAKEOUT, 1987

BOLD: Films on Videocassette

STALKER, 1982
STAMBOUL QUEST, 1934
STAND AND DELIVER, 1988
STAND BY ME, 1986
STAND-IN, 1937
STAR!, 1968
STAR SPANGLED RHYTHM, 1942
STARTING OVER, 1979
STATE OF SIEGE, 1973
STATE OF THINGS, THE, 1983
STAVISKY, 1974
STEEL TRAP, THE, 1952
STEPFATHER, THE, 1987
STERILE CUCKOO, THE, 1969
STOLEN FACE, 1952
STONE BOY, THE, 1984
STORMY MONDAY, 1988
STORMY WEATHER, 1943
STORY OF A THREE DAY PASS, THE, 1968
STORY OF ALEXANDER GRAHAM BELL, THE, 1939
STORY OF ROBIN HOOD, THE, 1952
STORY OF TEMPLE DRAKE, THE, 1933
STORY OF VERNON AND IRENE CASTLE, THE, 1939
STRAIGHT THROUGH THE HEART, 1985
STRANGE DECEPTION, 1953
STRANGE LOVE OF MARTHA IVERS, THE, 1946
STRANGER ON THE THIRD FLOOR, 1940
STRANGERS MAY KISS, 1931
STRATTON STORY, THE, 1949
STRAWBERRY BLONDE, THE, 1941
STRAY DOG, 1963
STREAMERS, 1983
STREET WITH NO NAME, THE, 1948
STRICTLY DISHONORABLE, 1931
STRIKE UP THE BAND, 1940
SUDDEN FEAR, 1952
SUDDEN IMPACT, 1983
SUDDENLY, 1954
SUEZ, 1938
SUGARBABY, 1985
SUMMER, 1986
SUMMER HOLIDAY, 1948
SUMMER STOCK, 1950
SUN VALLEY SERENADE, 1941
SUNDAY BLOODY SUNDAY, 1971
SUPERMAN II, 1980
SUPPORT YOUR LOCAL SHERIFF, 1969
SUSAN LENOX—HER FALL AND RISE, 1931
SUSPICION, 1941
SWEDENHIELMS, 1935
SWEENEY 2, 1978
SWEET BIRD OF YOUTH, 1962
SWEET CHARITY, 1969
SWEETHEARTS, 1938
SWEPT AWAY...BY AN UNUSUAL DESTINY IN THE
  BLUE SEA OF AUGUST, 1975
SWINDLE, THE, 1962
SWING TIME, 1936
SWISS FAMILY ROBINSON, 1960
SWORD IN THE DESERT, 1949
SYMPHONIE PASTORALE, 1948
TAKE THE MONEY AND RUN, 1969
TAKING OF PELHAM ONE, TWO, THREE, THE, 1974
TALES OF TERROR, 1962
TALK RADIO, 1988
TALL MEN, THE, 1955
TALL TIMBERS, 1937
TAMING OF THE SHREW, THE, 1967
TAMPOPO, 1986
TAP ROOTS, 1948
TAPS, 1981
TARGETS, 1968
TARZAN AND HIS MATE, 1934
TARZAN, THE APE MAN, 1932
TASK FORCE, 1949
TAXI!, 1932
TAXING WOMAN, A, 1988
TEA AND SYMPATHY, 1956
TEA FOR TWO, 1950
TEA IN THE HAREM OF ARCHIMEDE, 1985
TELL THEM WILLIE BOY IS HERE, 1969
TEMPEST, 1958
TENDER IS THE NIGHT, 1961
TERMS OF ENDEARMENT, 1983
TERROR HOUSE, 1942
TESTAMENT OF DR. MABUSE, THE, 1943

TEXAS, 1941
THANK YOUR LUCKY STARS, 1943
THAT OBSCURE OBJECT OF DESIRE, 1977
THAT TOUCH OF MINK, 1962
THEM!, 1954
THERE'S ALWAYS TOMORROW, 1956
THERE'S NO BUSINESS LIKE SHOW BUSINESS,
  1954
THEY ALL KISSED THE BRIDE, 1942
THEY CAME TO CORDURA, 1959
THEY DRIVE BY NIGHT, 1938
THEY KNEW WHAT THEY WANTED, 1940
THEY LIVE, 1988
THEY SHOOT HORSES, DON'T THEY?, 1969
THEY WON'T BELIEVE ME, 1947
THIEF, 1981
THIEVES LIKE US, 1974
THIN ICE, 1937
THINGS CHANGE, 1988
13 RUE MADELEINE, 1946
30 IS A DANGEROUS AGE, CYNTHIA, 1968
THIS ABOVE ALL, 1942
THIS HAPPY BREED, 1944
THIS IS SPINAL TAP, 1984
THIS LAND IS MINE, 1943
THIS MAN MUST DIE, 1970
THIS SPORTING LIFE, 1963
THOSE MAGNIFICENT MEN IN THEIR FLYING
  MACHINES; OR HOW I FLEW FROM LONDON TO
  PARIS IN 25 HOURS AND 11 MINUTES, 1965
THOUSAND EYES OF DR. MABUSE, THE, 1960
THOUSANDS CHEER, 1943
THREE DAYS OF THE CONDOR, 1975
THREE FACES OF EVE, THE, 1957
THREE SISTERS, 1974
THREE STRANGERS, 1946
3:10 TO YUMA, l957
THUNDER ROCK, 1944
THUNDERBOLT AND LIGHTFOOT, 1974
TIGER BAY, 1959
TIGER SHARK, 1932
TIGHT SPOT, 1955
TIKI TIKI, 1971
TIN DRUM, THE, 1979
TIME OF THEIR LIVES, THE, 1946
TIME OF YOUR LIFE, THE, 1948
TIME TO DIE, A, 1985
TITANIC, 1953
TOAST OF NEW YORK, THE, 1937
TOM, DICK AND HARRY, 1941
TOM HORN, 1980
TOMORROW, 1972
TOMORROW THE WORLD, 1944
TONI, 1968
TOP BANANA, 1954
TOPAZ, 1969
TOPAZE, 1933
TOPPER TAKES A TRIP, 1939
TORMENT, 1947
TOUCH OF LARCENY, A, 1960
TRADING PLACES, 1983
TRAIL OF THE LONESOME PINE, THE, 1936
TRAIN OF DREAMS, 1987
TRAPEZE, 1956
TREASURE ISLAND, 1934
TREE OF WOODEN CLOGS, THE, 1979
TRIAL, 1955
TRIBUTE, 1980
TRIO, 1950
TROUBLE WITH HARRY, THE, 1955
TRUE TO LIFE, 1943
TUGBOAT ANNIE, 1933
TULSA, 1949
TUNES OF GLORY, 1960
TURTLE DIARY, 1985
TWELFTH NIGHT, 1956
TWELVE CHAIRS, THE, 1970
TWENTIETH CENTURY, 1934
TWILIGHT'S LAST GLEAMING, 1977
TWO ENGLISH GIRLS, 1972
TWO FOR THE ROAD, 1967
TWO MRS. CARROLLS, THE, 1947
2001: A SPACE ODYSSEY, 1968
TWO-WAY STRETCH, 1961
TWO YEARS BEFORE THE MAST, 1946
UFORIA, 1985

UMBRELLAS OF CHERBOURG, THE, 1964
UNCONQUERED, 1947
UNDER TEN FLAGS, 1960
UNDER THE RED ROBE, 1937
UNDER THE VOLCANO, 1984
UNDER TWO FLAGS, 1936
UNDERWORLD U.S.A., 1961
UNION DEPOT, 1932
UNION STATION, 1950
USED CARS, 1980
UTU, 1984
V.I.P.s, THE, 1963
VAGABOND, 1985
VALLEY GIRL, 1983
VALLEY OF GWANGI, THE, 1969
VERDICT, THE, 1946
VERONIKA VOSS, 1982
VICTORS, THE, 1963
VIOLENT SATURDAY, 1955
VIRGINIA CITY, 1940
VIRGINIAN, THE, 1929
VISITOR, THE, 1973
VIVACIOUS LADY, 1938
VON RYAN'S EXPRESS, 1965
WABASH AVENUE, 1950
WAIT UNTIL DARK, 1967
WAKE OF THE RED WITCH, 1949
WALKABOUT, 1971
WALKING DEAD, THE, 1936
WANDA, 1971
WANDERING JEW, THE, 1933
WAR HUNT, 1962
WAR WAGON, THE, 1967
WARNING SHOT, 1967
WARRIORS, THE, 1979
WATERLOO BRIDGE, 1931
WE ARE NOT ALONE, 1939
WE DIVE AT DAWN, 1943
WE WERE STRANGERS, 1949
WEEDS, 1987
WEEKEND WITH FATHER, 1951
WEREWOLF OF LONDON, THE, 1935
WEST POINT STORY, THE, 1950
WESTWORLD, 1973
WETHERBY, 1985
WHAT'S NEW, PUSSYCAT?, 1965
WHEN FATHER WAS AWAY ON BUSINESS, 1985
WHEN STRANGERS MARRY, 1944
WHEN THE DALTONS RODE, 1940
WHEN WILLIE COMES MARCHING HOME, 1950
WHERE EAGLES DARE, 1968
WHERE THE SIDEWALK ENDS, 1950
WHERE'S CHARLEY?, 1952
WHERE'S POPPA?, 1970
WHISPERERS, THE, 1967
WHISPERING SMITH, 1948
WHISTLE DOWN THE WIND, 1961
WHITE CLIFFS OF DOVER, THE, 1944
WHITE DEMON, THE, 1932
WHITE DOG, 1982
WHITE TOWER, THE, 1950
WHO'LL STOP THE RAIN?, 1978
WHOOPEE, 1930
WHO'S MINDING THE MINT?, 1967
WHY DOES HERR R. RUN AMOK?, 1977
WHY ROCK THE BOAT?, 1974
WICHITA, 1955
WICKER MAN, THE, 1974
WIFE VERSUS SECRETARY, 1936
WILDROSE, 1985
WILL PENNY, 1968
WIND AND THE LION, THE, 1975
WIND, THE, 1987
WINGS OF EAGLES, THE, 1957
WINNER TAKE ALL, 1932
WINNING TEAM, THE, 1952
WINSLOW BOY, THE, 1950
WINTER KILLS, 1979
WINTERSET, 1936
WITH A SONG IN MY HEART, 1952
WITNESS FOR THE PROSECUTION, 1957
WOLFEN, 1981
WOLFPEN PRINCIPLE, THE, 1974
WOMAN IN THE WINDOW, THE, 1945
WOMAN IS A WOMAN, A, 1961
WOMAN ON THE RUN, 1950

WOMAN UNDER THE INFLUENCE, A, 1974
WOMAN'S FACE, A, 1941
WOODEN HORSE, THE, 1951
WORKING GIRL, 1988
WORLD ACCORDING TO GARP, THE, 1982
WORLD OF APU, THE, 1960
WRECK OF THE MARY DEARE, THE, 1959
"X'—THE MAN WITH THE X-RAY EYES, 1963
YAKUZA, THE, 1975
YEAR OF LIVING DANGEROUSLY, THE, 1982
YELLOW JACK, 1938
YOJIMBO, 1961
YOL, 1982
YOU CAN'T CHEAT AN HONEST MAN, 1939
YOU WERE NEVER LOVELIER, 1942
YOUNG AND INNOCENT, 1938
YOUNG BESS, 1953
YOUNG DR. KILDARE, 1938
YOUNG GIRLS OF WILKO, THE, 1979
YOUNG IN HEART, THE, 1938
YOUNG MR. PITT, THE, 1942
YOUNG TORLESS, 1968
YOUNG WINSTON, 1972
YOUR THREE MINUTES ARE UP, 1973
ZAZIE, 1961
ZELLY AND ME, 1988
ZIEGFELD GIRL, 1941
ZOO IN BUDAPEST, 1933
ZORBA THE GREEK, 1964

3 Stars
ACCIDENTAL TOURIST, THE, 1988
ADUEFUE, 1988
BABETTE'S FEAST, 1988
BAT 21, 1988
BEATRICE, 1988
BLOB, THE, 1988
BYGONES, 1988
CHOCOLATE WAR, THE, 1988
CITY OF BLOOD, 1988
CLEAN AND SOBER, 1988
COLORS, 1988
CROSSING DELANCEY, 1988
DEAD POOL, THE, 1988
DEATH OF EMPEDOCLES, THE, 1988
DIE HARD, 1988
DIXIELAND DAIMYO, 1988
DOMINICK AND EUGENE, 1988
DROWNING BY NUMBERS, 1988
EIGHT MEN OUT, 1988
END OF THE LINE, 1988
FINAL TAKE: THE GOLDEN AGE OF MOVIES, 1986
FRIENDSHIP'S DEATH, 1988
GORILLAS IN THE MIST, 1988
HALLOWEEN IV: THE RETURN OF MICHAEL MYERS, 1988
HARD TIMES, 1988
HIDING OUT, 1987
HOUSE ON CARROLL STREET, THE, 1988
ILLUSTRIOUS ENERGY, 1988
I'M GONNA GIT YOU SUCKA, 1988
JACK'S BACK, 1988
LATE SUMMER BLUES, 1988
ABANDON SHIP, 1957
ABANDONED, 1949
ABBOTT AND COSTELLO IN HOLLYWOOD, 1945
ABE LINCOLN IN ILLINOIS, 1940
ABILENE TOWN, 1946
ABOVE AND BEYOND, 1953
ABOVE SUSPICION, 1943
ABOVE US THE WAVES, 1956
ABSENT-MINDED PROFESSOR, THE, 1961
ABSOLUTE QUIET, 1936
ACCIDENTAL TOURIST, THE, 1988
ACCUSED, THE, 1949
ACE OF ACES, 1933
ACES HIGH, 1977
ACROSS THE BRIDGE, 1957
ACROSS THE GREAT DIVIDE, 1976
ACROSS THE WIDE MISSOURI, 1951
ACT OF VIOLENCE, 1949
ADALEN 31, 1969
ADAM HAD FOUR SONS, 1941
ADDING MACHINE, THE, 1969
ADUEFUE, 1988
ADVENTURE, 1945

ADVENTURE FOR TWO, 1945
ADVENTURES OF A YOUNG MAN, 1962
ADVENTURES OF BUCKAROO BANZAI: ACROSS THE 8TH DIMENSION, THE, 1984
ADVENTURES OF BULLWHIP GRIFFIN, THE, 1967
ADVENTURES OF FRONTIER FREMONT, THE, 1976
ADVENTURES OF MARCO POLO, THE, 1938
ADVENTURES OF MARK TWAIN, THE, 1985
ADVENTURES OF TARTU, THE, 1943
ADVENTURES OF THE WILDERNESS FAMILY, THE, 1975
ADVICE TO THE LOVELORN, 1933
AFFAIR TO REMEMBER, AN, 1957
AFFAIRS OF ANNABEL, 1938
AFFAIRS OF CELLINI, THE, 1934
AFFAIRS OF MAUPASSANT, 1938
AFFAIRS OF SUSAN, 1945
AFRICA SCREAMS, 1949
AFRICA—TEXAS STYLE!, 1967
AFTER THE FOX, 1966
AGNES OF GOD, 1985
AGONY AND THE ECSTASY, THE, 1965
AGUIRRE, THE WRATH OF GOD, 1977
AH YING, 1984
AIR MAIL, 1932
ALAMBRISTA!, 1977
ALEXANDER THE GREAT, 1956
ALFIE, 1966
ALIAS NICK BEAL, 1949
ALICE ADAMS, 1935
ALICE IN THE CITIES, 1974
ALICE IN WONDERLAND, 1933
ALICE IN WONDERLAND, 1951
ALIEN, 1979
ALIVE AND KICKING, 1962
ALL AT SEA, 1958
ALL CREATURES GREAT AND SMALL, 1975
ALL OF ME, 1984
ALL THE BROTHERS WERE VALIANT, 1953
ALL THE WAY HOME, 1963
ALL THINGS BRIGHT AND BEAUTIFUL, 1979
ALL THIS AND HEAVEN TOO, 1940
ALLEGRO NON TROPPO, 1977
ALLIGATOR, 1980
ALLIGATOR NAMED DAISY, AN, 1957
ALOMA OF THE SOUTH SEAS, 1941
ALONE ON THE PACIFIC, 1964
ALONG CAME JONES, 1945
ALPHAVILLE, A STRANGE CASE OF LEMMY CAUTION, 1965
AMARCORD, 1974
AMATEUR GENTLEMAN, 1936
AMAZING DR. CLITTERHOUSE, THE, 1938
AMAZING MRS. HOLLIDAY, 1943
AMBASSADOR, THE, 1984
AMBUSH BAY, 1966
AMERICAN EMPIRE, 1942
AMERICAN FRIEND, THE, 1977
AMERICAN GUERRILLA IN THE PHILIPPINES, AN, 1950
AMERICAN HOT WAX, 1978
AMERICAN ROMANCE, AN, 1944
AMERICAN SOLDIER, THE, 1970
AMERICAN SUCCESS COMPANY, THE, 1980
AMERICAN TRAGEDY, AN, 1931
AMERICANA, 1981
AMIGOS, 1986
AMONG THE LIVING, 1941
ANA, 1985
AND HOPE TO DIE, 1972
AND NOW MY LOVE, 1975
AND SO THEY WERE MARRIED, 1936
AND THE ANGELS SING, 1944
AND THE SHIP SAILS ON, 1983
ANDREI ROUBLOV, 1973
ANDROID, 1982
ANDY HARDY GETS SPRING FEVER, 1939
ANDY HARDY'S BLONDE TROUBLE, 1944
ANDY WARHOL'S DRACULA, 1974
ANGEL, 1982
ANGEL AND SINNER, 1947
ANGEL FACE, 1953
ANGI VERA, 1980
ANIMAL CRACKERS, 1930
ANIMAL KINGDOM, THE, 1932
ANNA KARENINA, 1948

ANNE TRISTER, 1986
ANNIE, 1982
ANNIE OAKLEY, 1935
ANNIE'S COMING OUT, 1985
ANNIVERSARY, THE, 1968
ANOTHER MAN, ANOTHER CHANCE, 1977
ANOTHER MAN'S POISON, 1952
ANOTHER PART OF THE FOREST, 1948
ANOTHER THIN MAN, 1939
ANTARCTICA, 1984
ANTHONY ADVERSE, 1936
ANTIGONE, 1962
ANTONIO DAS MORTES, 1970
ANY NUMBER CAN WIN, 1963
ANYTHING GOES, 1936
APACHE, 1954
APACHE DRUMS, 1951
APARAJITO, 1959
APARTMENT FOR PEGGY, 1948
APPLAUSE, 1929
APPOINTMENT FOR LOVE, 1941
APPOINTMENT WITH DANGER, 1951
APPOINTMENT WITH DEATH, 1988
APPRENTICESHIP OF DUDDY KRAVITZ, THE, 1974
APRES L'AMOUR, 1948
ARABESQUE, 1966
ARABIAN NIGHTS, 1942
ARCH OF TRIUMPH, 1948
ARISE, MY LOVE, 1940
ARISTOCATS, THE, 1970
ARIZONA, 1940
ARMORED CAR ROBBERY, 1950
ARNELO AFFAIR, THE, 1947
ARSENE LUPIN, 1932
AS LONG AS THEY'RE HAPPY, 1957
AS YOU DESIRE ME, 1932
AS YOU LIKE IT, 1936
AS YOUNG AS YOU FEEL, 1951
ASHES AND DIAMONDS, 1961
ASK ANY GIRL, 1959
ASSASSINATION BUREAU, THE, 1969
ASSAULT ON PRECINCT 13, 1976
ASSIGNMENT—PARIS, 1952
ASSISI UNDERGROUND, THE, 1985
ASSOCIATE, THE, 1982
ASTONISHED HEART, THE, 1950
ASYLUM, 1972
AT THE CIRCUS, 1939
ATTACK!, 1956
AUTUMN LEAVES, 1956
AVENGERS, THE, 1942
BABE RUTH STORY, THE, 1948
BABES IN TOYLAND, 1934
BABETTE'S FEAST, 1988
BABY AND THE BATTLESHIP, THE, 1957
BABY BOOM, 1987
BABYLON, 1980
BACK IN CIRCULATION, 1937
BACKFIRE, 1965
BACKGROUND TO DANGER, 1943
BACKLASH, 1986
BAD BOYS, 1983
BAD COMPANY, 1972
BAD COMPANY, 1986
BAD MAN OF BRIMSTONE, 1938
BAD SEED, THE, 1956
BADLANDERS, THE, 1958
BAKER'S HAWK, 1976
BALCONY, THE, 1963
BALL OF FIRE, 1941
BALLAD OF GREGORIO CORTEZ, THE, 1983
BANANAS, 1971
BANDITS OF ORGOSOLO, 1964
BANG THE DRUM SLOWLY, 1973
BANJO ON MY KNEE, 1936
BARABBAS, 1962
BARBAROSA, 1982
BARBARY COAST, 1935
BARBER OF SEVILLE, THE, 1973
BAREFOOT EXECUTIVE, THE, 1971
BAREFOOT IN THE PARK, 1967
BARKLEYS OF BROADWAY, THE, 1949
BARON OF ARIZONA, THE, 1950
BARQUERO, 1970
BARRY LYNDON, 1975
BASILEUS QUARTET, 1984

BOLD: Films on Videocassette

BASKETBALL FIX, THE, 1951
BASTILLE, 1985
BAT 21, 1988
BAT WHISPERS, THE, 1930
BATTLE FOR MUSIC, 1943
BATTLE OF ALGIERS, THE, 1967
BATTLE OF NERETVA, 1969
BATTLE OF THE SEXES, THE, 1960
BEACH BLANKET BINGO, 1965
BEACHCOMBER, 1938
BEACHHEAD, 1954
BEAST OF THE CITY, THE, 1932
BEAST WITH FIVE FINGERS, THE, 1946
BEATRICE, 1988
BEAU BRUMMELL, 1954
BEAU GESTE, 1966
BEAUTIFUL BLONDE FROM BASHFUL BEND, THE,
   1949
BEDLAM, 1946
BEDROOM WINDOW, THE, 1987
BEDTIME STORY, 1942
BEGGAR'S OPERA, THE, 1953
BEGINNING OR THE END, THE, 1947
BEHIND THAT CURTAIN, 1929
BEHIND THE RISING SUN, 1943
BELIEVE IN ME, 1971
BELIZAIRE THE CAJUN, 1986
BELL, BOOK AND CANDLE, 1958
BELL DIAMOND, 1987
BELLE STARR, 1941
BELLES OF ST. TRINIAN'S, THE, 1954
BELLISSIMA, 1952
BELLS OF ROSARITA, 1945
BELLS OF SAN ANGELO, 1947
BELLY OF AN ARCHITECT, THE, 1987
BELOVED ENEMY, 1936
BELOVED INFIDEL, 1959
BELOW THE SEA, 1933
BELSTONE FOX, THE, 1976
BENJAMIN, 1973
BENJI THE HUNTED, 1987
BERKELEY SQUARE, 1933
BEST FOOT FORWARD, 1943
BEST OF ENEMIES, THE, 1962
BEST OF THE BADMEN, 1951
BETRAYED, 1954
BETWEEN THE LINES, 1977
BEVERLY HILLS COP, 1984
BEWARE OF PITY, 1946
BEWITCHED, 1945
BEYOND THE ROCKIES, 1932
BEYOND THE SACRAMENTO, 1941
BIBLE...IN THE BEGINNING, THE, 1966
BIG BOSS, THE, 1941
BIG BROADCAST OF 1937, THE, 1936
BIG BROADCAST OF 1938, THE, 1937
BIG CHILL, THE, 1983
BIG CITY BLUES, 1932
BIG DEAL ON MADONNA STREET, THE, 1960
BIG EASY, THE, 1987
BIG GUY, THE, 1939
BIG HAND FOR THE LITTLE LADY, A, 1966
BIG HEARTED HERBERT, 1934
BIG HOUSE, U.S.A., 1955
BIG JOB, THE, 1965
BIG LIFT, THE, 1950
BIG PARADE, THE, 1987
BIG RED ONE, THE, 1980
BIG SHOTS, 1987
BIG SHOW, THE, 1937
BIG STEAL, THE, 1949
BIG TRAIL, THE, 1930
BIG TROUBLE IN LITTLE CHINA, 1986
BILLY THE KID RETURNS, 1938
BIRCH INTERVAL, 1976
BIRDS, THE, 1963
BIRTH OF THE BLUES, 1941
BISHOP MURDER CASE, THE, 1930
BISHOP'S WIFE, THE, 1947
BITE THE BULLET, 1975
BITTER RICE, 1950
BITTER SWEET, 1940
BITTER TEA OF GENERAL YEN, THE, 1933
BLACK AND WHITE IN COLOR, 1976
BLACK ANGEL, 1946
BLACK ARROW, 1948

BLACK BIRD, THE, 1975
BLACK HAND, THE, 1950
BLACK HOLE, THE, 1979
BLACK LEGION, THE, 1937
BLACK ORCHID, 1959
BLACK ORPHEUS, 1959
BLACK ROOM, THE, 1935
BLACK SABBATH, 1963
BLACK WATCH, THE, 1929
BLACK WIDOW, 1954
BLACKBEARD'S GHOST, 1968
BLACKMAIL, 1929
BLACULA, 1972
BLAZING SADDLES, 1974
BLESS THE BEASTS AND CHILDREN, 1971
BLESS THEIR LITTLE HEARTS, 1984
BLOB, THE, 1988
BLOCKADE, 1938
BLONDE CRAZY, 1931
BLOOD OF A POET, THE, 1930
BLOOD ON THE MOON, 1948
BLOOD WEDDING, 1981
BLOODHOUNDS OF BROADWAY, 1952
BLUE COLLAR, 1978
BLUE DENIM, 1959
BLUE GARDENIA, THE, 1953
BLUE MAX, THE, 1966
BLUE THUNDER, 1983
BLUES IN THE NIGHT, 1941
BODY AND SOUL, 1931
BODY SNATCHER, THE, 1945
BOEING BOEING, 1965
BOMBARDIER, 1943
**BON VOYAGE, CHARLIE BROWN (AND DON'T
   COME BACK), 1980**
BONJOUR TRISTESSE, 1958
BONNIE PRINCE CHARLIE, 1948
BOOGIE MAN WILL GET YOU, THE, 1942
BORDER INCIDENT, 1949
BORDER STREET, 1950
BORDERTOWN, 1935
BORN FREE, 1966
BORN TO DANCE, 1936
BORSALINO, 1970
BOSS, THE, 1956
BOSTON STRANGLER, THE, 1968
BOTTOM OF THE BOTTLE, THE, 1956
BOTTOMS UP, 1934
BOUNTY, THE, 1984
BOUNTY KILLER, THE, 1965
BOWERY TO BROADWAY, 1944
BOY MEETS GIRL, 1985
BOY ON A DOLPHIN, 1957
BOY TEN FEET TALL, A, 1965
BOY WHO STOLE A MILLION, THE, 1960
BOY WITH THE GREEN HAIR, THE, 1949
BOYS FROM SYRACUSE, 1940
BOYS IN COMPANY C, THE, 1978
BOYS IN THE BAND, THE, 1970
BOYS NEXT DOOR, THE, 1985
BOYS' NIGHT OUT, 1962
BRAINSTORM, 1965
BRAINSTORM, 1983
BRANDED, 1951
BRASHER DOUBLOON, THE, 1947
BRAVADOS, THE, 1958
BREAD OF LOVE, THE, 1954
BREAK OF DAY, 1977
BREAKHEART PASS, 1976
BREAKING POINT, THE, 1950
BREAKING THE SOUND BARRIER, 1952
BREAKOUT, 1960
BREEZY, 1973
BRIBE, THE, 1949
BRIDE CAME C.O.D., THE, 1941
BRIDE WORE BOOTS, THE, 1946
BRIDE WORE RED, THE, 1937
BRIDGE TOO FAR, A, 1977
BRIDGE, THE, 1961
BRIGADOON, 1954
BRIGAND, THE, 1952
BRIGHAM YOUNG—FRONTIERSMAN, 1940
BRIGHT EYES, 1934
BRIGHT LEAF, 1950
BRIGHT ROAD, 1953
BRIGHTON ROCK, 1947

BRIMSTONE, 1949
BRIMSTONE AND TREACLE, 1982
BRING ON THE GIRLS, 1945
BRING YOUR SMILE ALONG, 1955
BRITTANIA HOSPITAL, 1982
BROADWAY, 1929
BROADWAY, 1942
BROADWAY MELODY OF 1940, 1940
BROADWAY MELODY OF '38, 1937
BROADWAY MELODY, THE, 1929
BROKEN JOURNEY, 1948
BROKEN LULLABY, 1932
BRONCO BILLY, 1980
BROTHER SUN, SISTER MOON, 1973
BUCCANEER, THE, 1938
BUDDY SYSTEM, THE, 1984
BUGS BUNNY, SUPERSTAR, 1975
BULLDOG DRUMMOND, 1929
BULLDOG DRUMMOND'S PERIL, 1938
BULLFIGHTER AND THE LADY, 1951
BUREAU OF MISSING PERSONS, 1933
BURKE & WILLS, 1985
BURMESE HARP, THE, 1985
BURN, 1970
BURY ME DEAD, 1947
BUSHWHACKERS, THE, 1952
BUSTING, 1974
BUTTERFIELD 8, 1960
BY THE LIGHT OF THE SILVERY MOON, 1953
BY WHOSE HAND?, 1932
BY WHOSE HAND?, 1932
BY YOUR LEAVE, 1935
BYE BYE BIRDIE, 1963
BYE-BYE BRAZIL, 1980
BYGONES, 1988
CABIN IN THE COTTON, 1932
CAFE METROPOLE, 1937
CAFFE ITALIA, 1985
CAGE OF NIGHTINGALES, A, 1947
CAGED, 1950
CAL, 1984
CALCUTTA, 1947
CALL ME MADAM, 1953
CALL ME MISTER, 1951
CAMEL BOY, THE, 1984
CAMELOT, 1967
CAMERA BUFF, 1983
CANARIS, 1955
CANNERY ROW, 1982
CANTERVILLE GHOST, THE, 1944
CANYON PASSAGE, 1946
CAPRICIOUS SUMMER, 1968
CAPRICORN ONE, 1978
CAPTAIN FROM KOEPENICK, 1933
CAPTAIN FROM KOEPENICK, THE, 1956
CAPTAIN FURY, 1939
CAPTAIN HATES THE SEA, THE, 1934
CAPTAIN JANUARY, 1935
CAPTAIN KRONOS: VAMPIRE HUNTER, 1974
CAPTAIN SINDBAD, 1963
CAPTIVE CITY, 1952
CAPTIVE HEART, THE, 1948
CAPTIVE WILD WOMAN, 1943
CAPTURE, THE, 1950
CAR WASH, 1976
CARBINE WILLIAMS, 1952
CARDINAL, THE, 1963
CAREFREE, 1938
CARIBOO TRAIL, THE, 1950
CARMEN JONES, 1954
CARNIVAL IN FLANDERS, 1936
CARNIVAL OF SINNERS, 1947
CARNIVAL OF SOULS, 1962
CARNY, 1980
CARRIE, 1952
CARTOUCHE, 1962
CARVE HER NAME WITH PRIDE, 1958
CASANOVA '70, 1965
CASE OF THE BLACK CAT, THE, 1936
CASEY'S SHADOW, 1978
CASH McCALL, 1960
CASS TIMBERLANE, 1947
CAST A DARK SHADOW, 1958
CASTLE, THE, 1969
CASTLE KEEP, 1969
CASTLE OF PURITY, 1974

CAT AND THE CANARY, THE, 1939
CAT AND THE FIDDLE, 1934
CAT CREEPS, THE, 1930
CAT FROM OUTER SPACE, THE, 1978
CAT PEOPLE, 1942
CATCH-22, 1970
CATHERINE THE GREAT, 1934
CAT'S PAW, THE, 1934
CATTLE DRIVE, 1951
CAUGHT IN THE DRAFT, 1941
CAUSE FOR ALARM, 1951
CAVALCADE, 1933
CELINE AND JULIE GO BOATING, 1974
CESAR AND ROSALIE, 1972
CHAD HANNA, 1940
CHAIN LIGHTNING, 1950
CHAIN REACTION, 1980
CHAIRMAN, THE, 1969
CHAMPIONS, 1984
CHAN IS MISSING, 1982
CHANCE MEETING, 1954
CHANCES, 1931
CHANGELING, THE, 1980
CHAPTER TWO, 1979
CHARGE OF THE LIGHT BRIGADE, THE, 1968
CHARING CROSS ROAD, 1935
CHARLIE CHAN AT THE RACE TRACK, 1936
CHARLIE CHAN CARRIES ON, 1931
CHARLIE CHAN IN EGYPT, 1935
CHARLIE CHAN'S SECRET, 1936
CHARLY, 1968
CHASE, THE, 1946
CHEAP DETECTIVE, THE, 1978
CHEYENNE SOCIAL CLUB, THE, 1970
CHICAGO DEADLINE, 1949
CHILD IS WAITING, A, 1963
CHINA, 1943
CHINA GIRL, 1942
CHINESE BOXES, 1984
CHINESE ROULETTE, 1977
CHIP OFF THE OLD BLOCK, 1944
CHISUM, 1970
CHLOE IN THE AFTERNOON, 1972
CHOCOLATE SOLDIER, THE, 1941
CHOCOLATE WAR, THE, 1988
CHOOSE ME, 1984
CHORUS LINE, A, 1985
CHOSEN, THE, 1982
CHRISTMAS HOLIDAY, 1944
CHRISTOPHER STRONG, 1933
CIRCUS WORLD, 1964
CITIZENS BAND, 1977
CITY OF BLOOD, 1988
CITY OF TORMENT, 1950
CITY OF WOMEN, 1980
CITY THAT NEVER SLEEPS, 1953
CLAIRVOYANT, THE, 1935
CLARENCE, THE CROSS-EYED LION, 1965
CLAUDINE, 1974
CLEAN AND SOBER, 1988
CLEAR SKIES, 1963
CLIVE OF INDIA, 1935
CLOAK AND DAGGER, 1946
CLOAK AND DAGGER, 1984
CLOCKMAKER, THE, 1976
CLOCKWISE, 1986
CLOPORTES, 1966
CLOUDED YELLOW, THE, 1950
CLOUDS OVER EUROPE, 1939
CLOWN, THE, 1953
COCKLESHELL HEROES, THE, 1955
COCKTAIL MOLOTOV, 1980
COCOON, 1985
CODE OF SILENCE, 1985
COLD FEET, 1984
COLD TURKEY, 1971
COLDITZ STORY, THE, 1955
COLLEEN, 1936
COLONEL REDL, 1985
COLOR OF POMEGRANATES, THE, 1980
COLORADO TERRITORY, 1949
COLORS, 1988
COME AND GET IT, 1936
COME BLOW YOUR HORN, 1963
COMEDY!, 1987
COMFORT AND JOY, 1984

COMMAND, THE, 1954
COMPROMISING POSITIONS, 1985
COMPUTER WORE TENNIS SHOES, THE, 1970
COMRADE X, 1940
COMRADES, 1987
CONAN THE DESTROYER, 1984
CONCENTRATION CAMP, 1939
CONCRETE JUNGLE, THE, 1962
CONDUCT UNBECOMING, 1975
CONDUCTOR, THE, 1981
CONFESSIONS OF A POLICE CAPTAIN, 1971
CONFESSIONS OF A ROGUE, 1948
CONFESSIONS OF AMANS, THE, 1977
CONFESSIONS OF BOSTON BLACKIE, 1941
CONFORMIST, THE, 1971
CONQUEROR WORM, THE, 1968
CONQUEST, 1937
CONSTANCE, 1984
CONSTANT NYMPH, THE, 1943
CONTRACT, THE, 1982
CONVENTION CITY, 1933
CONVICTED, 1950
CONVICTS FOUR, 1962
COOLEY HIGH, 1975
COP HATER, 1958
COPPER CANYON, 1950
CORONER CREEK, 1948
CORRIDORS OF BLOOD, 1962
CORRUPT, 1984
CORSAIR, 1931
CORVETTE SUMMER, 1978
COSMIC EYE, THE, 1986
COTTON COMES TO HARLEM, 1970
COUNT OF MONTE CRISTO, 1976
COUNT YOUR BULLETS, 1972
COUNTDOWN, 1985
COUNTER-ATTACK, 1945
COUNTESS DRACULA, 1972
COUNTRYMAN, 1982
COUNTY CHAIRMAN, THE, 1935
COUP DE TORCHON, 1981
COURAGE OF LASSIE, 1946
COURT CONCERT, THE, 1936
COUSIN, COUSINE, 1976
COUSINS, THE, 1959
COW AND I, THE, 1961
COWBOY AND THE LADY, THE, 1938
COWBOYS, THE, 1972
CRACK IN THE MIRROR, 1960
CRACK-UP, THE, 1937
CRAZIES, THE, 1973
CRAZY FAMILY, THE, 1986
CRAZY THAT WAY, 1930
CREATOR, 1985
CREATURE FROM THE BLACK LAGOON, 1954
CREEPSHOW, 1982
CREMATOR, THE, 1973
CRIME OF PASSION, 1957
CRIMINAL COURT, 1946
CRIMSON CANARY, 1945
CRIMSON KIMONO, THE, 1959
CRIMSON ROMANCE, 1934
CRISIS, 1950
CROOK, THE, 1971
CROOKS IN CLOISTERS, 1964
CROONER, 1932
CROSS COUNTRY ROMANCE, 1940
CROSS OF IRON, 1977
CROSS OF LORRAINE, THE, 1943
CROSSED TRAILS, 1948
CROSSING DELANCEY, 1988
CROSSOVER DREAMS, 1985
CROSSROADS, 1986
CROWD ROARS, THE, 1938
CRUEL TOWER, THE, 1956
CRUISER EMDEN, 1932
CRY BABY KILLER, THE, 1958
CRY DANGER, 1951
CRY FREEDOM, 1961
CRY OF THE HUNTED, 1953
CRY TERROR, 1958
CRY VENGEANCE, 1954
CUBA, 1979
CUBAN LOVE SONG, THE, 1931
CUL-DE-SAC, 1966
CULPEPPER CATTLE COMPANY, THE, 1972

CURSE OF FRANKENSTEIN, THE, 1957
CURSE OF THE VAMPIRES, 1970
CURSE OF THE WEREWOLF, THE, 1961
CYCLE, THE, 1979
D-DAY, THE SIXTH OF JUNE, 1956
DALLAS, 1950
DAMN THE DEFIANT!, 1962
DAMNED DON'T CRY, THE, 1950
DAMNED, THE, 1948
DAMSEL IN DISTRESS, A, 1937
DANCE, FOOLS, DANCE, 1931
DANCING CO-ED, 1939
DANCING IN THE DARK, 1949
DANCING LADY, 1933
DANGER SIGNAL, 1945
DANGEROUS, 1936
DANTE'S INFERNO, 1935
DANTON, 1931
DAREDEVIL IN THE CASTLE, 1969
DARK CITY, 1950
DARK CRYSTAL, THE, 1982
DARK HAZARD, 1934
DARK IS THE NIGHT, 1946
DARK PAST, THE, 1948
DATE WITH AN ANGEL, 1987
DAUGHTER OF THE SANDS, 1952
DAUGHTERS COURAGEOUS, 1939
DAUGHTERS OF DARKNESS, 1971
DAUGHTERS OF DESTINY, 1954
DAVID, 1979
DAVID HOLZMAN'S DIARY, 1968
DAVY CROCKETT, INDIAN SCOUT, 1950
DAVY CROCKETT, KING OF THE WILD FRONTIER, 1955
DAWN AT SOCORRO, 1954
DAWN OF THE DEAD, 1979
DAWN PATROL, THE, 1930
DAY OF FURY, A, 1956
DAY OF THE BAD MAN, 1958
DAY OF THE DEAD, 1985
DAY OF THE OUTLAW, 1959
DAY OF THE OWL, THE, 1968
DAY OF THE TRIFFIDS, THE, 1963
DAY OF TRIUMPH, 1954
DAY THE EARTH CAUGHT FIRE, THE, 1961
DAY-TIME WIFE, 1939
DAY TO REMEMBER, A, 1953
DAYDREAMER, THE, 1966
DAYTON'S DEVILS, 1968
DEAD MOUNTAINEER HOTEL, THE, 1979
DEAD OF SUMMER, 1970
DEAD PIGEON ON BEETHOVEN STREET, 1972
DEAD POOL, THE, 1988
DEADHEAD MILES, 1982
DEADLIER THAN THE MALE, 1957
DEADLY COMPANIONS, THE, 1961
DEADLY HERO, 1976
DEAR HEART, 1964
DEAR RUTH, 1947
DEAR WIFE, 1949
DEATH IN THE GARDEN, 1961
DEATH IS CALLED ENGELCHEN, 1963
DEATH OF A BUREAUCRAT, 1979
DEATH OF A SCOUNDREL, 1956
DEATH OF EMPEDOCLES, THE, 1988
DEATH OF MARIO RICCI, THE, 1985
DEATH RACE 2000, 1975
DECAMERON NIGHTS, 1953
DECEPTION, 1946
DECOY, 1946
DEEP END, 1970
DEF-CON 4, 1985
DEFIANCE, 1980
DELUSIONS OF GRANDEUR, 1971
DEMON SEED, 1977
DEMONS IN THE GARDEN, 1984
DER ROSENKONIG, 1986
DERSU UZALA, 1976
DESERT ATTACK, 1958
DESERT HEARTS, 1985
DESERT SONG, THE, 1943
DESERTER, 1934
DESIGN FOR LIVING, 1933
DESIGN FOR SCANDAL, 1941
DESIREE, 1954

BOLD: Films on Videocassette

DESK SET, 1957
DESPERADOES, THE, 1943
DESPERATE MOMENT, 1953
DESTINATION GOBI, 1953
DESTINATION MOON, 1950
DESTROYER, 1943
DETECTIVE, THE, 1954
DETECTIVE SCHOOL DROPOUTS, 1986
DEVIL BY THE TAIL, THE, 1969
DEVIL COMMANDS, THE, 1941
DEVIL DOGS OF THE AIR, 1935
DEVIL DOLL, 1964
DEVIL IS A WOMAN, THE, 1935
DEVIL ON HORSEBACK, 1954
DEVIL PAYS OFF, THE, 1941
DEVIL PROBABLY, THE, 1977
DEVIL STRIKES AT NIGHT, THE, 1959
DEVIL TO PAY, THE, 1930
DEVIL'S DAUGHTER, 1949
DEVIL'S DISCIPLE, THE, 1959
DEVIL'S EYE, THE, 1960
DEVIL'S ISLAND, 1940
DEVIL'S PLAYGROUND, THE, 1976
DEVIL'S PLOT, THE, 1948
D.I., THE, 1957
DIAMOND HORSESHOE, 1945
DIAMOND JIM, 1935
DIAMONDS ARE FOREVER, 1971
DIARY FOR MY CHILDREN, 1984
DIE, DIE, MY DARLING, 1965
DIE HARD, 1988
DIE, MONSTER, DIE, 1965
DIM SUM: A LITTLE BIT OF HEART, 1985
DIMPLES, 1936
DINO, 1957
DIPLOMATIC COURIER, 1952
DIRIGIBLE, 1931
DIRTY DOZEN, THE, 1967
DIRTY HANDS, 1976
DISHONORED, 1931
DISORDER AND EARLY TORMENT, 1977
DISORDERLY ORDERLY, THE, 1964
DISPATCH FROM REUTERS, A, 1940
DISTANCE, 1975
DISTANT JOURNEY, 1950
DIVE BOMBER, 1941
DIVIDED HEART, THE, 1955
DIVORCE AMERICAN STYLE, 1967
DIVORCE OF LADY X, THE, 1938
DIXIE, 1943
DIXIELAND DAIMYO, 1988
DO YOU KEEP A LION AT HOME?, 1966
DO YOU LOVE ME?, 1946
DO YOU REMEMBER DOLLY BELL?, 1986
DOCTEUR POPAUL, 1972
DOCTOR BEWARE, 1951
DR. COPPELIUS, 1968
DOCTOR DOLITTLE, 1967
DOCTOR IN THE HOUSE, 1954
DR. JEKYLL AND MR. HYDE, 1941
DOCTOR PHIBES RISES AGAIN, 1972
DODES 'KA-DEN, 1970
DOG AND THE DIAMONDS, THE, 1962
DOLL'S HOUSE, A, 1973
DOMINICK AND EUGENE, 1988
DON QUIXOTE, 1973
DONA FLOR AND HER TWO HUSBANDS, 1977
DONKEY SKIN, 1975
DONOVAN'S BRAIN, 1953
DONOVAN'S REEF, 1963
DON'T BOTHER TO KNOCK, 1952
DON'T CRY, IT'S ONLY THUNDER, 1982
DON'T TAKE IT TO HEART, 1944
DOOLINS OF OKLAHOMA, THE, 1949
DOOMED CARAVAN, 1941
DOSS HOUSE, 1933
DOUBLE HARNESS, 1933
DOUBLE SUICIDE, 1970
DOVE, THE, 1974
DOWN MEMORY LANE, 1949
DOWN TO THE SEA IN SHIPS, 1949
DRAEGERMAN COURAGE, 1937
DRAGNET, 1954
DRAGON SEED, 1944
DRAGONWYCH, 1946

DRAKE THE PIRATE, 1935
DRAMA OF THE RICH, 1975
DRANGO, 1957
DRAUGHTSMAN'S CONTRACT, THE, 1983
DREAM OF KINGS, A, 1969
DREAMING LIPS, 1937
DREAMSCAPE, 1984
DRESSED TO KILL, 1941
DRESSED TO KILL, 1980
DRIFTER, 1975
DRIFTING, 1984
DRIFTWOOD, 1947
DRIVE A CROOKED ROAD, 1954
DROWNING BY NUMBERS, 1988
DROWNING POOL, THE, 1975
DRUM BEAT, 1954
DRUMS IN THE DEEP SOUTH, 1951
DUCK, YOU SUCKER!, 1972
DUDE GOES WEST, THE, 1948
DUELLISTS, THE, 1977
DUET FOR ONE, 1986
DUFFY'S TAVERN, 1945
DULCY, 1940
DUNKIRK, 1958
DUST, 1985
DUST BE MY DESTINY, 1939
DUTCHMAN, 1966
DYBBUK, THE, 1938
DYNAMITE, 1930
EAGLE HAS LANDED, THE, 1976
EAGLE IN A CAGE, 1971
EARL OF CHICAGO, THE, 1940
EARTH ENTRANCED, 1970
EARTH VS. THE FLYING SAUCERS, 1956
EAST OF SUMATRA, 1953
EASY LIFE, THE, 1971
EASY LIVING, 1937
EASY TO LOVE, 1953
EASY TO WED, 1946
EAT THE PEACH, 1987
EBB TIDE, 1937
ECLIPSE, 1962
ECSTACY OF YOUNG LOVE, 1936
ECSTASY, 1940
EDGE, THE, 1968
EDGE OF DOOM, 1950
EDGE OF ETERNITY, 1959
EDGE OF THE CITY, 1957
EDGE OF THE WORLD, THE, 1937
EDVARD MUNCH, 1976
EDWARD, MY SON, 1949
EFFECT OF GAMMA RAYS ON MAN-IN-THE-MOON
   MARIGOLDS, THE, 1972
EGLANTINE, 1972
EIGHT GIRLS IN A BOAT, 1934
EIGHT MEN OUT, 1988
1812, 1944
18 MINUTES, 1935
84 CHARING CROSS ROAD, 1987
80,000 SUSPECTS, 1963
EIN BLICK-UND DIE LIEBE BRICHT AUS, 1987
EL AMOR BRUJO, 1986
EL CID, 1961
EL DORADO, 1967
ELECTRIC DREAMS, 1984
ELEPHANT BOY, 1937
ELMER THE GREAT, 1933
ELUSIVE CORPORAL, THE, 1963
EMIL, 1938
EMPEROR AND THE NIGHTINGALE, THE, 1949
EMPEROR OF THE NORTH POLE, 1973
EMPEROR WALTZ, THE, 1948
EMPIRE OF NIGHT, THE, 1963
EMPRESS AND I, THE, 1933
ENCHANTMENT, 1948
ENCORE, 1951
END OF A DAY, THE, 1939
END OF THE LINE, 1988
END OF THE ROAD, THE, 1954
END OF THE TRAIL, 1936
END PLAY, 1975
ENJO, 1959
ENTENTE CORDIALE, 1939
ENTER THE DRAGON, 1973
ENTRE NOUS, 1983
EQUINOX, 1970

ERASERHEAD, 1978
EROICA, 1966
ESCAPE, 1940
ESCAPE, 1948
ESCAPE FROM FORT BRAVO, 1953
ESCAPE FROM HONG KONG, 1942
ESCAPE FROM SEGOVIA, 1984
ETERNAL HUSBAND, THE, 1946
ETERNITY OF LOVE, 1961
EVA, 1962
EVE OF ST. MARK, THE, 1944
EVE WANTS TO SLEEP, 1961
EVENT, AN, 1970
EVER SINCE VENUS, 1944
EVERGREEN, 1934
EVERY MAN FOR HIMSELF, 1980
EVERYBODY DOES IT, 1949
EVERYTHING IS THUNDER, 1936
EVIL DEAD 2: DEAD BY DAWN, 1987
EXPERIMENT IN TERROR, 1962
EXPOSED, 1983
EXTREME PREJUDICE, 1987
EXTREMITIES, 1986
EYES IN THE NIGHT, 1942
EYES OF TEXAS, 1948
EYEWITNESS, 1981
FABULOUS WORLD OF JULES VERNE, THE, 1961
FACE TO FACE, 1952
FAHRENHEIT 451, 1966
FAITHFUL IN MY FASHION, 1946
FALCON AND THE CO-EDS, THE, 1943
FALCON AND THE SNOWMAN, THE, 1985
FALCON IN MEXICO, THE, 1944
FALCON TAKES OVER, THE, 1942
FALCON'S ALIBI, THE, 1946
FALCON'S BROTHER, THE, 1942
FALL GUY, 1985
FAMILY AFFAIR, A, 1937
FAMILY GAME, THE, 1984
FAMILY SECRET, THE, 1951
FANNY, 1961
FANTASTIC PLANET, 1973
FANTASTIC THREE, THE, 1967
FANTASTIC VOYAGE, 1966
FANTOMAS, 1966
FAR SHORE, THE, 1976
FAREWELL, FRIEND, 1968
FAREWELL, MY LOVELY, 1975
FARMER TAKES A WIFE, THE, 1935
FASCIST, THE, 1965
FAST AND LOOSE, 1939
FATE IS THE HUNTER, 1964
FATHER, 1967
FATHER'S DILEMMA, 1952
FATHER'S LITTLE DIVIDEND, 1951
FBI STORY, THE, 1959
FEAR, 1946
FEAR, 1956
FEAR AND DESIRE, 1953
FEAR EATS THE SOUL, 1974
FEAR IN THE NIGHT, 1947
FEARLESS FAGAN, 1952
FEARMAKERS, THE, 1958
FEDORA, 1946
FEET FIRST, 1930
FEMININE TOUCH, THE, 1941
FIEND WITHOUT A FACE, 1958
FIFTH HORSEMAN IS FEAR, THE, 1968
55 DAYS AT PEKING, 1963
FIFTY ROADS TO TOWN, 1937
FIGHTING KENTUCKIAN, THE, 1949
FIGHTING O'FLYNN, THE, 1949
FIGHTING SEABEES, THE, 1944
FINAL TAKE: THE GOLDEN AGE OF MOVIES, 1986
FINAL TEST, THE, 1953
FINAL WAR, THE, 1960
FINGER POINTS, THE, 1931
FINGERMAN, THE, 1963
FINGERS, 1978
FINGERS AT THE WINDOW, 1942
FINNEGANS WAKE, 1965
FIRE IN THE STRAW, 1943
FIRE WITHIN, THE, 1964
FIREMAN, SAVE MY CHILD, 1932
FIREMAN SAVE MY CHILD, 1954
FIRES ON THE PLAIN, 1962

FIRST LADY, 1937
FIRST LEGION, THE, 1951
FIRST SPACESHIP ON VENUS, 1960
FIRST TIME, THE, 1978
FIRST TO FIGHT, 1967
FIRSTBORN, 1984
F.I.S.T., 1978
FISTFUL OF DOLLARS, A, 1964
FIVE GATES TO HELL, 1959
FIVE PENNIES, THE, 1959
FIVE STAR FINAL, 1931
FIXED BAYONETS, 1951
FLAME IN THE STREETS, 1961
FLAME OF THE WEST, 1945
FLAME OVER INDIA, 1960
FLAMINGO ROAD, 1949
FLAT TOP, 1952
FLEET'S IN, THE, 1942
FLESH, 1932
FLESH AND BLOOD, 1951
FLESH AND BLOOD, 1985
FLESH AND FANTASY, 1943
FLESH AND FURY, 1952
FLETCH, 1984
FLIGHT, 1929
FLIGHT COMMAND, 1940
FLIGHT FOR FREEDOM, 1943
FLIGHT OF THE DOVES, 1971
FLIGHT OF THE NAVIGATOR, 1986
FLIGHT TO TANGIER, 1953
FLIM-FLAM MAN, THE, 1967
FLIPPER'S NEW ADVENTURE, 1964
FLIRTATION WALK, 1934
FLOODS OF FEAR, 1958
FLORENTINE DAGGER, THE, 1935
FLY BY NIGHT, 1942
FLYING HIGH, 1931
FLYING LEATHERNECKS, 1951
FLYING TIGERS, 1942
FOLIES BERGERE, 1935
FOLLOW ME, BOYS!, 1966
FOLLY TO BE WISE, 1953
FOND MEMORIES, 1982
FOOLS' PARADE, 1971
FOR BETTER FOR WORSE, 1954
FOR FREEDOM, 1940
FOR LOVE OR MONEY, 1939
FOR MEN ONLY, 1952
FOR THE FIRST TIME, 1959
FOR VALOR, 1937
FOR YOUR EYES ONLY, 1981
FORBIDDEN, 1932
FORBIDDEN FRUIT, 1959
FORBIDDEN MUSIC, 1936
FOREIGN AFFAIR, A, 1948
FOREVER FEMALE, 1953
FOREVER MY LOVE, 1962
FORT MASSACRE, 1958
FORTUNE COOKIE, THE, 1966
FORTY SQUARE METERS OF GERMANY, 1986
FOUETTE, 1986
FOUR BAGS FULL, 1957
FOUR FACES WEST, 1948
FOUR FRIGHTENED PEOPLE, 1934
FOUR POSTER, THE, 1952
FOUR SEASONS, THE, 1981
4D MAN, 1959
FOURTEEN, THE, 1973
48 HOURS, 1982
FOX AND HIS FRIENDS, 1976
FOX, THE, 1967
F.P. 1 DOESN'T ANSWER, 1933
FRAGMENT OF FEAR, 1971
FRAGRANCE OF WILD FLOWERS, THE, 1979
FRANCIS, 1949
FRANKENSTEIN CREATED WOMAN, 1965
FRANKENSTEIN MEETS THE WOLF MAN, 1943
FRANKENSTEIN MUST BE DESTROYED!, 1969
FRANTIC, 1961
FRENCHMAN'S CREEK, 1944
FRIDAY THE 13TH, 1934
FRIEDA, 1947
FRIEND WILL COME TONIGHT, A, 1948
FRIENDS AND HUSBANDS, 1983
FRIENDS OF MR. SWEENEY, 1934
FRIENDSHIP'S DEATH, 1988

FRIGHTENED CITY, THE, 1961
FRINGE DWELLERS, THE, 1986
FRISCO KID, 1935
FROGMEN, THE, 1951
FRONT PAGE, THE, 1974
FRONTIER GAL, 1945
FRONTIER MARSHAL, 1939
FROZEN LIMITS, THE, 1939
FUGITIVE FROM JUSTICE, A, 1940
FULL CONFESSION, 1939
FULL OF LIFE, 1956
FULLER BRUSH GIRL, THE, 1950
FUN AT ST. FANNY'S, 1956
FUN ON A WEEKEND, 1979
FUNNY THING HAPPENED ON THE WAY TO THE FORUM, A, 1966
FURIA, 1947
FURIES, THE, 1950
FURTHER UP THE CREEK!, 1958
FURY AT FURNACE CREEK, 1948
FURY AT SHOWDOWN, 1957
FUSS OVER FEATHERS, 1954
FUTUREWORLD, 1976
FUZZ, 1972
GABRIEL OVER THE WHITE HOUSE, 1933
GAILY, GAILY, 1969
GALILEO, 1975
GALLANT HOURS, THE, 1960
GAMBIT, 1966
GAMBLER, THE, 1974
GAMBLING SAMURAI, THE, 1966
GAME IS OVER, THE, 1967
GANG WAR, 1958
GANG'S ALL HERE, THE, 1943
GANGSTER, THE, 1947
GARBO TALKS, 1984
GARMENT JUNGLE, THE, 1957
GARNET BRACELET, THE, 1966
GAS-S-S-S!, 1970
GATES OF PARIS, 1958
GATES OF THE NIGHT, 1950
GATEWAY, 1938
GAY INTRUDERS, THE, 1946
GAZEBO, THE, 1959
GEISHA BOY, THE, 1958
GEISHA, A, 1978
GENERAL SUVOROV, 1941
GENTLE GIANT, 1967
GENTLE GUNMAN, THE, 1952
GENTLE JULIA, 1936
GENTLEMAN AT HEART, A, 1942
GENTLEMAN FROM LOUISIANA, 1936
GENTLEMEN PREFER BLONDES, 1953
GEORGE AND MARGARET, 1940
GERMANY, YEAR ZERO, 1949
GERONIMO, 1939
GERVAISE, 1956
GET CARTER, 1971
GET GOING, 1943
GETTING GERTIE'S GARTER, 1945
GETTING OF WISDOM, THE, 1977
GHOST AND MR. CHICKEN, THE, 1966
GHOST AND THE GUEST, 1943
GHOST CATCHERS, 1944
GHOST OF FRANKENSTEIN, THE, 1942
GHOST TOWN LAW, 1942
GHOUL, THE, 1934
GIDEON OF SCOTLAND YARD, 1959
GIDGET, 1959
GINGER & FRED, 1986
GIORDANO BRUNO, 1973
GIRL, A GUY AND A GOB, A, 1941
GIRL AND THE BURGLER, 1967
GIRL FROM LORRAINE, A, 1982
GIRL FROM MISSOURI, THE, 1934
GIRL IN THE PAINTING, THE, 1948
GIRL IN THE PICTURE, THE, 1985
GIRL MUST LIVE, A, 1941
GIRL WITH IDEAS, A, 1937
GIRLS' DORMITORY, 1936
GIVE HER THE MOON, 1970
GIVE MY REGARDS TO BROADWAY, 1948
GIVE'EM HELL, HARRY!, 1975
GLASS ALIBI, THE, 1946
GLASS BOTTOM BOAT, THE, 1966
GLASS KEY, THE, 1935

GLASS MENAGERIE, THE, 1950
GLITTERBALL, THE, 1977
GLORY BRIGADE, THE, 1953
GO CHASE YOURSELF, 1938
GO FOR BROKE, 1951
GO, MAN, GO!, 1954
GO TELL IT ON THE MOUNTAIN, 1984
GOD TOLD ME TO, 1976
GODDESS, THE, 1962
GOD'S LITTLE ACRE, 1958
GODSON, THE, 1972
GOING HOLLYWOOD, 1933
GOLD DIGGERS OF 1935, 1935
GOLD DIGGERS OF 1937, 1936
GOLD IS WHERE YOU FIND IT, 1938
GOLDEN GIRL, 1951
GOLDEN LINK, THE, 1954
GOLDEN SALAMANDER, 1950
GOLEM, THE, 1937
GONE ARE THE DAYS, 1963
GOOD FATHER, THE, 1986
GOOD HUMOR MAN, THE, 1950
GOOD MORNING, MISS DOVE, 1955
GOOD SOLDIER SCHWEIK, THE, 1963
GOODBYE AGAIN, 1961
GOODBYE, MY LADY, 1956
GOODBYE NEW YORK, 1985
GOODBYE PEOPLE, THE, 1984
GORILLAS IN THE MIST, 1988
GORKY PARK, 1983
GOSPEL ACCORDING TO ST. MATTHEW, THE, 1966
GOSPEL ACCORDING TO VIC, THE, 1986
GRAN VARIETA, 1955
GRAND CENTRAL MURDER, 1942
GRAND SLAM, 1968
GRASSHOPPER, THE, 1970
GRAVY TRAIN, THE, 1974
GREASED LIGHTNING, 1977
GREAT ADVENTURE, THE, 1955
GREAT AMERICAN BROADCAST, THE, 1941
GREAT AMERICAN BUGS BUNNY-ROAD RUNNER CHASE, 1979
GREAT BIG WORLD AND LITTLE CHILDREN, THE, 1962
GREAT BRITISH TRAIN ROBBERY, THE, 1967
GREAT EXPECTATIONS, 1975
GREAT FLAMARION, THE, 1945
GREAT GABBO, THE, 1929
GREAT GARRICK, THE, 1937
GREAT IMPERSONATION, THE, 1942
GREAT JEWEL ROBBER, THE, 1950
GREAT JOHN L. THE, 1945
GREAT LIE, THE, 1941
GREAT LOCOMOTIVE CHASE, THE, 1956
GREAT MAN, THE, 1957
GREAT MAN VOTES, THE, 1939
GREAT MOMENT, THE, 1944
GREAT MUPPET CAPER, THE, 1981
GREAT O'MALLEY, THE, 1937
GREAT PROFILE, THE, 1940
GREAT RACE, THE, 1965
GREAT RUPERT, THE, 1950
GREAT TRAIN ROBBERY, THE, 1979
GREAT VICTOR HERBERT, THE, 1939
GREAT WALDO PEPPER, THE, 1975
GREAT WALTZ, THE, 1938
GREATEST LOVE, THE, 1954
GREEKS HAD A WORD FOR THEM, 1932
GREEN BERETS, THE, 1968
GREEN DOLPHIN STREET, 1947
GREENE MURDER CASE, THE, 1929
GREGORY'S GIRL, 1982
GROOVE TUBE, THE, 1974
GROUNDS FOR MARRIAGE, 1950
GROUP, THE, 1966
GUEST, THE, 1963
GUEST, THE, 1984
GUIDE FOR THE MARRIED MAN, A, 1967
GUILTY?, 1956
GUILTY GENERATION, THE, 1931
GUMSHOE, 1972
GUN LAW, 1938
GUN THE MAN DOWN, 1957
GUNFIGHT, A, 1971
GUNG HO!, 1943
GUNMAN'S WALK, 1958

BOLD: Films on Videocassette

GUNS AT BATASI, 1964
GYPSY MOTHS, THE, 1969
H-MAN, THE, 1959
HAGBARD AND SIGNE, 1968
HAIRY APE, THE, 1944
HALF A SIXPENCE, 1967
HALF-NAKED TRUTH, THE, 1932
HALF SHOT AT SUNRISE, 1930
HALF-WAY HOUSE, THE, 1945
HALLELUJAH, I'M A BUM, 1933
HALLIDAY BRAND, THE, 1957
HALLOWEEN IV: THE RETURN OF MICHAEL MYERS, 1988
HALLS OF ANGER, 1970
HAND IN HAND, 1960
HANDS OF THE RIPPER, 1971
HANGING TREE, THE, 1959
HANGMAN, THE, 1959
HANGMAN'S KNOT, 1952
HANGOVER SQUARE, 1945
HANS CHRISTIAN ANDERSEN, 1952
HAPPINESS AHEAD, 1934
HAPPY ANNIVERSARY, 1959
HAPPY DAYS, 1930
HAPPY GO LOVELY, 1951
HAPPY LAND, 1943
HAPPY ROAD, THE, 1957
HARAKIRI, 1963
HARD CHOICES, 1984
HARD CONTRACT, 1969
HARD COUNTRY, 1981
HARD HOMBRE, 1931
HARD PART BEGINS, THE, 1973
HARD TIMES, 1975
HARD TIMES, 1988
HARD TO HANDLE, 1933
HARDER THEY COME, THE, 1973
HARDYS RIDE HIGH, THE, 1939
HARLEM IS HEAVEN, 1932
HARMONY LANE, 1935
HARRY AND TONTO, 1974
HARRY BLACK AND THE TIGER, 1958
HARVEY GIRLS, THE, 1946
HAS ANYBODY SEEN MY GAL?, 1952
HATFUL OF RAIN, A, 1957
HAUNTED STRANGLER, THE, 1958
HAUNTING OF JULIA, THE, 1981
HAUNTING OF M, THE, 1979
HAVING A WILD WEEKEND, 1965
HAVING WONDERFUL CRIME, 1945
HAVING WONDERFUL TIME, 1938
HAWAII, 1966
HAWKS AND THE SPARROWS, THE, 1967
HEAD, 1968
HEAD OF THE FAMILY, 1967
HEADLINE SHOOTER, 1933
HEART OF A NATION, THE, 1943
HEART OF PARIS, 1939
HEART OF THE NORTH, 1938
HEARTACHES, 1981
HEARTBREAKERS, 1984
HEAT AND DUST, 1983
HEAVEN CAN WAIT, 1978
HEAVEN KNOWS, MR. ALLISON, 1957
HEAVEN ONLY KNOWS, 1947
HEAVENS ABOVE!, 1963
HEDDA, 1975
HELEN MORGAN STORY, THE, 1959
HELL AND HIGH WATER, 1954
HELL BELOW, 1933
HELL BELOW ZERO, 1954
HELL DRIVERS, 1958
HELL, HEAVEN OR HOBOKEN, 1958
HELL ON FRISCO BAY, 1956
HELLO, DOLLY!, 1969
HELLO, FRISCO, HELLO, 1943
HELLZAPOPPIN', 1941
HENRY ALDRICH GETS GLAMOUR, 1942
HENRY VIII AND HIS SIX WIVES, 1972
HER FIRST AFFAIR, 1947
HER SISTER'S SECRET, 1946
HERCULES' PILLS, 1960
HERE COMES COOKIE, 1935
HERE COMES THE NAVY, 1934
HERE WE GO ROUND THE MULBERRY BUSH, 1968
HERITAGE OF THE DESERT, 1939

HEROES DIE YOUNG, 1960
HEROES OF TELEMARK, THE, 1965
HEY BABU RIBA, 1987
HI DIDDLE DIDDLE, 1943
HICKEY AND BOGGS, 1972
HIDDEN EYE, THE, 1945
HIDDEN GUNS, 1956
HIDDEN ROOM, THE, 1949
HIDEOUT, 1948
HIDING OUT, 1987
HIDING PLACE, THE, 1975
HIGH AND THE MIGHTY, THE, 1954
HIGH ANXIETY, 1977
HIGH COST OF LOVING, THE, 1958
HIGH PRESSURE, 1932
HIGH SOCIETY, 1956
HIGH WIND IN JAMAICA, A, 1965
HILDUR AND THE MAGICIAN, 1969
HILL, THE, 1965
HILL 24 DOESN'T ANSWER, 1955
HILLS HAVE EYES, THE, 1978
HILLS OF HOME, 1948
HINOTORI, 1980
HIS KIND OF WOMAN, 1951
HIS MAJESTY O'KEEFE, 1953
HIT THE DECK, 1955
HIT THE ICE, 1943
HITCH-HIKER, THE, 1953
HITCH IN TIME, A, 1978
HITLER'S MADMAN, 1943
HOA-BINH, 1971
HOLD BACK THE NIGHT, 1956
HOLD EVERYTHING, 1930
HOLD THAT GHOST, 1941
HOLD YOUR MAN, 1933
HOLIDAY, 1930
HOLLYWOOD BOULEVARD, 1976
HOLLYWOOD CAVALCADE, 1939
HOLLYWOOD COWBOY, 1937
HOLLYWOOD ROUNDUP, 1938
HOLY INNOCENTS, THE, 1984
HOMBRE, 1967
HOME AND THE WORLD, THE, 1984
HOME BEFORE DARK, 1958
HOME FROM THE HILL, 1960
HOME IN INDIANA, 1944
HOME IS THE HERO, 1959
HOME OF THE BRAVE, 1949
HOME SWEET HOMICIDE, 1946
HONDO, 1953
HONEYMOON KILLERS, THE, 1969
HONEYSUCKLE ROSE, 1980
HONKY TONK, 1941
HONOR AMONG LOVERS, 1931
HOODLUM PRIEST, THE, 1961
HOODWINK, 1981
HOPALONG CASSIDY, 1935
HORN BLOWS AT MIDNIGHT, THE, 1945
HORROR EXPRESS, 1972
HORSE, THE, 1984
HOSPITAL, THE, 1971
HOT BLOOD, 1956
HOT ROCK, THE, 1972
HOT TOMORROWS, 1978
HOTEL, 1967
HOTEL BERLIN, 1945
HOTEL NEW YORK, 1985
HOTEL RESERVE, 1946
HOUDINI, 1953
HOUND-DOG MAN, 1959
HOUND OF THE BASKERVILLES, THE, 1959
HOUR OF THE STAR, THE, 1986
HOUR OF THIRTEEN, THE, 1952
HOUSE OF CARDS, 1969
HOUSE OF STRANGERS, 1949
HOUSE OF THE ARROW, THE, 1953
HOUSE OF WAX, 1953
HOUSE ON CARROLL STREET, THE, 1988
HOUSE ON HAUNTED HILL, 1958
HOUSE ON TELEGRAPH HILL, 1951
HOUSE ON THE FRONT LINE, THE, 1963
HOUSEBOAT, 1958
HOW NOT TO ROB A DEPARTMENT STORE, 1965
HOW TO MARRY A MILLIONAIRE, 1953
HOWARDS OF VIRGINIA, THE, 1940
HU-MAN, 1975

HUCKLEBERRY FINN, 1931
HUMAN CONDITION, THE, 1959
HUMAN MONSTER, THE, 1940
HUMAN SIDE, THE, 1934
HUNGER, 1968
HUNT THE MAN DOWN, 1950
HUNTERS, THE, 1958
HYSTERIA, 1965
I AM THE LAW, 1938
I BELIEVE IN YOU, 1953
I CONFESS, 1953
I KNOW WHERE I'M GOING, 1947
I LIVE MY LIFE, 1935
I MARRIED A MONSTER FROM OUTER SPACE, 1958
I MET HIM IN PARIS, 1937
I, MOBSTER, 1959
I ONLY ASKED!, 1958
I SAW WHAT YOU DID, 1965
I SENT A LETTER TO MY LOVE, 1981
I SHOT JESSE JAMES, 1949
I STOLE A MILLION, 1939
I, THE JURY, 1953
I WAKE UP SCREAMING, 1942
I WALK ALONE, 1948
I WALK THE LINE, 1970
I WALKED WITH A ZOMBIE, 1943
I WANNA HOLD YOUR HAND, 1978
I WANT TO LIVE!, 1958
I WANT YOU, 1951
I WANTED WINGS, 1941
I WAS A MALE WAR BRIDE, 1949
I WAS A TEENAGE WEREWOLF, 1957
I WAS AN ADVENTURESS, 1940
ICEMAN COMETH, THE, 1973
I'D CLIMB THE HIGHEST MOUNTAIN, 1951
IDENTIFICATION OF A WOMAN, 1983
IDENTITY UNKNOWN, 1945
IDIOT, THE, 1960
IF . . ., 1968
IF IT'S TUESDAY, THIS MUST BE BELGIUM, 1969
IF YOU COULD ONLY COOK, 1936
IKIRU, 1960
I'LL NEVER FORGET YOU, 1951
ILLEGAL, 1955
ILLICIT INTERLUDE, 1954
ILLUSION TRAVELS BY STREETCAR, THE, 1977
ILLUSTRIOUS ENERGY, 1988
I'M GONNA GIT YOU SUCKA, 1988
I'M NOBODY'S SWEETHEART NOW, 1940
IMITATION GENERAL, 1958
IMITATION OF LIFE, 1959
IMMORAL CHARGE, 1962
IMPACT, 1949
IMPORTANT MAN, THE, 1961
IMPOSSIBLE OBJECT, 1973
IN HARM'S WAY, 1965
IN-LAWS, THE, 1979
IN NAME ONLY, 1939
IN OLD ARIZONA, 1929
IN OLD KENTUCKY, 1935
IN OLD SANTA FE, 1935
IN THE FRENCH STYLE, 1963
IN THE MOOD, 1987
IN THE SOUP, 1936
INADMISSIBLE EVIDENCE, 1968
INCENDIARY BLONDE, 1945
INCREDIBLE JOURNEY, THE, 1963
INDIAN AGENT, 1948
INFERNO, 1953
INFRA-MAN, 1975
INHERITANCE, THE, 1978
INNERSPACE, 1987
INNOCENT, THE, 1979
INQUISITOR, THE, 1982
INSECT WOMAN, THE, 1964
INSIDE THE WALLS OF FOLSOM PRISON, 1951
INSPECTOR CALLS, AN, 1954
INSPECTOR CLOUSEAU, 1968
INSPECTOR GENERAL, THE, 1937
INSPECTOR GENERAL, THE, 1949
INSPECTOR HORNLEIGH ON HOLIDAY, 1939
INTENT TO KILL, 1958
INTERNATIONAL SQUADRON, 1941
INTERRUPTED HONEYMOON, THE, 1936
INTIMATE POWER, 1986

INVADERS FROM MARS, 1953
INVASION OF THE BEE GIRLS, 1973
INVISIBLE BOY, THE, 1957
INVISIBLE DR. MABUSE, THE, 1965
INVISIBLE MAN RETURNS, THE, 1940
INVISIBLE STRIPES, 1940
INVITATION, 1952
INVITATION TO A GUNFIGHTER, 1964
INVITATION TO HAPPINESS, 1939
IRENE, 1940
IRISH EYES ARE SMILING, 1944
IRISH IN US, THE, 1935
IRISHMAN, THE, 1978
IRMA LA DOUCE, 1963
IRON CURTAIN, THE, 1948
IRON MAJOR, THE, 1943
IRON MAN, THE, 1931
IRON MASK, THE, 1929
IRRECONCILABLE DIFFERENCES, 1984
ISHTAR, 1987
ISLAND AT THE TOP OF THE WORLD, THE, 1974
ISLAND IN THE SKY, 1953
ISLAND OF DESIRE, 1952
ISLAND OF PROCIDA, THE, 1952
ISLANDS IN THE STREAM, 1977
ISLE OF THE DEAD, 1945
IT HAD TO HAPPEN, 1936
IT HAPPENED IN BROOKLYN, 1947
IT HAPPENED IN GIBRALTAR, 1943
IT HAPPENS EVERY THURSDAY, 1953
IT LIVES AGAIN, 1978
IT'S A DEAL, 1930
IT'S A GREAT FEELING, 1949
IT'S GREAT TO BE YOUNG, 1956
IT'S IN THE BLOOD, 1938
IT'S MY TURN, 1980
IT'S NEVER TOO LATE, 1984
IT'S ONLY MONEY, 1962
J.W. COOP, 1971
JACK FROST, 1966
JACK THE GIANT KILLER, 1962
JACKPOT, THE, 1950
JACK'S BACK, 1988
JACQUES AND NOVEMBER, 1985
JAGGED EDGE, THE, 1985
JAGUAR, 1980
JAIL BAIT, 1977
JALOPY, 1953
JAMES JOYCE'S WOMEN, 1985
JAPANESE WAR BRIDE, 1952
JAWS II, 1978
JAZZ SINGER, THE, 1927
JE T'AIME, JE T'AIME, 1972
JENATSCH, 1987
JENNIE GERHARDT, 1933
JENNY LAMOUR, 1948
JEWEL OF THE NILE, THE, 1985
JEWEL ROBBERY, 1932
JOAN OF PARIS, 1942
JOE, 1970
JOE AND ETHEL TURP CALL ON THE PRESIDENT, 1939
JOHN AND JULIE, 1957
JOHN PAUL JONES, 1959
JOHN WESLEY, 1954
JOHNNY GUITAR, 1954
JOHNNY HOLIDAY, 1949
JOHNNY ON THE RUN, 1953
JOHNNY STEALS EUROPE, 1932
JOHNNY TROUBLE, 1957
JOIN THE MARINES, 1937
JONATHAN, 1973
JOSHUA THEN AND NOW, 1985
JOURNEY, THE, 1986
JOURNEY OF NATTY GANN, THE, 1985
JOURNEY TO SHILOH, 1968
JOURNEY'S END, 1930
JUDGE AND THE ASSASSIN, THE, 1979
JUDGE HARDY AND SON, 1939
JUGGERNAUT, 1974
JUNE BRIDE, 1948
JUNIOR BONNER, 1972
JUNIOR MISS, 1945
JUST A GIGOLO, 1979
KADOYNG, 1974
KANCHENJUNGHA, 1966

KANSAS CITY CONFIDENTIAL, 1952
KAOS, 1985
KAPO, 1964
KARMA, 1986
KAZABLAN, 1974
KEEPER OF THE FLAME, 1942
KEY, THE, 1934
KEYS OF THE KINGDOM, THE, 1944
KID BLUE, 1973
KID FROM BROOKLYN, THE, 1946
KID GLOVE KILLER, 1942
KIDNAPPED, 1938
KIEV COMEDY, A, 1963
KILL BABY KILL, 1966
KILLERS, THE, 1964
KIM, 1950
KIND LADY, 1951
KINEMA NO TENCHI, 1986
KING CREOLE, 1958
KING IN SHADOW, 1961
KING LEAR, 1971
KING OF BURLESQUE, 1936
KING OF THE COWBOYS, 1943
KING OF THE PECOS, 1936
KING OF THE TURF, 1939
KING SOLOMON'S MINES, 1937
KING STEPS OUT, THE, 1936
KINGDOM OF THE SPIDERS, 1977
KINGS GO FORTH, 1958
KIPPERBANG, 1984
KIRLIAN WITNESS, THE, 1978
KISMET, 1930
KISMET, 1944
KISS BEFORE DYING, A, 1956
KISS OF EVIL, 1963
KISS OF FIRE, THE, 1940
KISS THE BLOOD OFF MY HANDS, 1948
KISS TOMORROW GOODBYE, 1950
KITCHEN, THE, 1961
KITTY, 1945
KNIGHTRIDERS, 1981
KNIGHTS OF THE ROUND TABLE, 1953
KNIGHTS OF THE TEUTONIC ORDER, THE, 1962
KNIVES OF THE AVENGER, 1967
KNOCK ON WOOD, 1954
KOENIGSMARK, 1935
KOJIRO, 1967
KONGA, THE WILD STALLION, 1939
KONGO, 1932
KOTCH, 1971
KREMLIN LETTER, THE, 1970
KRONOS, 1957
LA BELLE AMERICAINE, 1961
LA CHEVRE, 1985
LA CHINOISE, 1967
LA COLLECTIONNEUSE, 1971
LA FEMME INFIDELE, 1969
LA MARIE DU PORT, 1951
LA NUIT DE VARENNES, 1983
LA PARISIENNE, 1958
LA PASSANTE, 1983
LA PETIT SIRENE, 1984
LACOMBE, LUCIEN, 1974
LADDIE, 1935
L'ADDITION, 1985
LADIES OF THE PARK, 1964
LADIES ON THE ROCKS, 1985
LADY AND THE MOB, THE, 1939
LADY BE GOOD, 1941
LADY BY CHOICE, 1934
LADY IN A CAGE, 1964
LADY IN QUESTION, THE, 1940
LADY IN RED, THE, 1979
LADY IS WILLING, THE, 1942
LADY JANE GREY, 1936
LADY LIES, THE, 1929
LADY OF THE CAMELIAS, 1987
LADY WITH A LAMP, THE, 1951
LADY WITHOUT CAMELLIAS, THE, 1981
LADYHAWKE, 1985
LADY'S MORALS, A, 1930
LAMP STILL BURNS, THE, 1943
LANCELOT OF THE LAKE, 1975
LANCER SPY, 1937
LANDLORD, THE, 1970
LARCENY, 1948

LARCENY, INC., 1942
LAST ADVENTURERS, THE, 1937
LAST AMERICAN HERO, THE, 1973
LAST DAYS OF MUSSOLINI, 1974
LAST DAYS OF POMPEII, THE, 1935
LAST FLIGHT, THE, 1931
LAST GAME, THE, 1964
LAST GANGSTER, THE, 1937
LAST HOLIDAY, 1950
LAST MILE, THE, 1959
LAST NIGHT AT THE ALAMO, 1984
LAST OF THE KNUCKLEMEN, THE, 1981
LAST OUTLAW, THE, 1936
LAST OUTPOST, THE, 1951
LAST PERFORMANCE, THE, 1929
LAST STRAW, THE, 1987
LAST SUMMER, 1969
LAST SUNSET, THE, 1961
LAST TEN DAYS, THE, 1956
LAST TRAIN FROM MADRID, THE, 1937
LAST VOYAGE, THE, 1960
LAST WAGON, THE, 1956
LAST WAR, THE, 1962
LATE AUTUMN, 1973
LATE SUMMER BLUES, 1988
LATENT IMAGE, 1988
LATIN LOVERS, 1953
LAW AND DISORDER, 1958
LAW AND DISORDER, 1974
LAW AND JAKE WADE, THE, 1958
LAW OF THE PLAINS, 1938
LAWLESS, THE, 1950
LAWLESS BREED, THE, 1952
LAWLESS STREET, A, 1955
LAWMAN, 1971
LAWMAN IS BORN, A, 1937
LE AMICHE, 1962
LE CIEL EST A VOUS, 1957
LE CRABE TAMBOUR, 1984
LE DERNIER COMBAT, 1984
LE MANS, 1971
LE VIOL, 1968
LEAP INTO THE VOID, 1982
LEAP OF FAITH, 1931
LEASE OF LIFE, 1954
LEATHER BOYS, THE, 1965
LEAVE HER TO HEAVEN, 1946
LEFT-HANDED WOMAN, THE, 1980
LEGEND, 1985
LEGEND OF TOM DOOLEY, THE, 1959
LEMON DROP KID, THE, 1934
LEMON DROP KID, THE, 1951
LEMONADE JOE, 1966
LENNY, 1974
LES CREATURES, 1969
LES DERNIERES VACANCES, 1947
LES ENFANTS TERRIBLES, 1952
LES GIRLS, 1957
LES MISERABLES, 1936
LES MISERABLES, 1952
LESSON IN LOVE, A, 1960
LET 'EM HAVE IT, 1935
LET FREEDOM RING, 1939
LET JOY REIGN SUPREME, 1977
LET US LIVE, 1939
LET'S DO IT AGAIN, 1975
LET'S GO NAVY, 1951
LET'S KILL UNCLE, 1966
LET'S TALK ABOUT WOMEN, 1964
LEVIATHAN, 1961
LIANNA, 1983
LIEUTENANT DARING, RN, 1935
LIEUTENANT WORE SKIRTS, THE, 1956
LIFE AND LOVES OF MOZART, THE, 1959
LIFE BEGINS, 1932
LIFE BEGINS AT 40, 1935
LIFE IN EMERGENCY WARD 10, 1959
LIFE IS A BED OF ROSES, 1984
LIFE OF RILEY, THE, 1949
LIFEGUARD, 1976
LIGHT IN THE FOREST, THE, 1958
LIGHT OF WESTERN STARS, THE, 1930
LIGHTNIN', 1930
LIGHTSHIP, THE, 1986
LIKE A CROW ON A JUNE BUG, 1972
LI'L ABNER, 1959

BOLD: Films on Videocassette

LILIES OF THE FIELD, 1930
LILIOM, 1935
LIMBO, 1972
L'IMMORTELLE, 1969
LINEUP, THE, 1958
LION, THE, 1962
LIONS LOVE, 1969
LISTEN, DARLING, 1938
LITTLE ARK, THE, 1972
LITTLE BIG HORN, 1951
LITTLE BOY LOST, 1953
LITTLE FRIEND, 1934
LITTLE GIANT, THE, 1933
LITTLE LORD FAUNTLEROY, 1936
LITTLE MALCOLM, 1974
LITTLE MARTYR, THE, 1947
LITTLE MINISTER, THE, 1934
LITTLE SHOP OF HORRORS, 1961
LITTLE SHOP OF HORRORS, 1986
LITTLE WORLD OF DON CAMILLO, THE, 1953
LITTLEST HORSE THIEVES, THE, 1977
LITTLEST OUTLAW, THE, 1955
LOLA, 1961
LONE WOLF SPY HUNT, THE, 1939
LONELY LANE, 1963
LONELY PASSION OF JUDITH HEARNE, THE, 1988
LONG ABSENCE, THE, 1962
LONG AGO, TOMORROW, 1971
LONG AND THE SHORT AND THE TALL, THE, 1961
LONG IS THE ROAD, 1948
LONG, LONG TRAILER, THE, 1954
LONG NIGHT, THE, 1947
LONG SHOT, 1981
LOOK BACK IN ANGER, 1959
LOOK OUT SISTER, 1948
LOOKS AND SMILES, 1982
LOOT, 1971
LORD LOVE A DUCK, 1966
LORDS OF FLATBUSH, THE, 1974
LOST ANGEL, 1944
LOST BOUNDARIES, 1949
LOST SQUADRON, THE, 1932
LOTNA, 1966
LOUISA, 1950
LOULOU, 1980
LOVE, 1972
LOVE AFFAIR; OR THE CASE OF THE MISSING
  SWITCHBOARD OPERATOR, 1968
LOVE AND LARCENY, 1963
LOVE AND MONEY, 1982
LOVE AND PAIN AND THE WHOLE DAMN THING,
  1973
LOVE AND THE FRENCHWOMAN, 1961
LOVE AT TWENTY, 1963
LOVE BUG, THE, 1968
LOVE FINDS ANDY HARDY, 1938
LOVE IN A TAXI, 1980
LOVE IN THE AFTERNOON, 1957
LOVE IS A FAT WOMAN, 1988
LOVE IS A RACKET, 1932
LOVE IS NEWS, 1937
LOVE LETTERS, 1983
LOVE ON THE DOLE, 1945
LOVE ON THE RUN, 1936
LOVE STORY, 1949
LOVE STORY, 1970
LOVE WITH THE PROPER STRANGER, 1963
LOVED ONE, THE, 1965
LOVELY TO LOOK AT, 1952
LOVERS AND LUGGERS, 1938
LOVER'S NET, 1957
LOVERS OF TERUEL, THE, 1962
LOVERS OF VERONA, THE, 1951
LOVING YOU, 1957
LOWER DEPTHS, THE, 1937
LOWER DEPTHS, THE, 1962
LOYALTIES, 1986
LUCAS, 1986
LUCK OF GINGER COFFEY, THE, 1964
LUCK OF THE IRISH, 1948
LUCK OF THE IRISH, THE, 1937
LUCKY DEVILS, 1933
LUCKY JORDAN, 1942
LUCKY STAR, THE, 1980
LUMIERE D'ETE, 1943
LUNATICS, THE, 1986

LURED, 1947
M, 1951
MACAO, 1952
MACARTHUR'S CHILDREN, 1985
MAD ABOUT MUSIC, 1938
MAD DOG MORGAN, 1976,Aus.
MAD MAX BEYOND THUNDERDOME, 1985
MAD WEDNESDAY, 1950
MADAME AKI, 1963
MADAME BOVARY, 1949
MADAME BUTTERFLY, 1955
MADAME SOUSATZKA, 1988
MADAME X, 1966
MADE FOR EACH OTHER, 1971
MADE IN HEAVEN, 1987
MADE IN ITALY, 1967
MAGIC, 1978
MAGIC SWORD, THE, 1962
MAGNETIC MONSTER, THE, 1953
MAGNIFICENT OBSESSION, 1935
MAGNUM FORCE, 1973
MAILBAG ROBBERY, 1957
MAJOR DUNDEE, 1965
MAJORITY OF ONE, A, 1961
MAKE ME A STAR, 1932
MAKE MINE MINK, 1960
MAKE MINE MUSIC, 1946
MALAYA, 1950
MALCOLM, 1986
MALICIOUS, 1974
MALOU, 1983
MALTA STORY, 1954
MALTESE FALCON, THE, 1931
MAN ALONE, A, 1955
MAN AND A WOMAN: 20 YEARS LATER, A, 1986
MAN BETWEEN, THE, 1953
MAN-EATER OF KUMAON, 1948
MAN FROM BLANKLEY'S, THE, 1930
MAN FROM DEL RIO, 1956
MAN FROM SNOWY RIVER, THE, 1983
MAN FROM THE ALAMO, THE, 1953
MAN FROM THE DINERS' CLUB, THE, 1963
MAN FROM THE EAST, A, 1974
MAN FROM YESTERDAY, THE, 1932
MAN I LOVE, THE, 1946
MAN I MARRIED, THE, 1940
MAN IN GREY, THE, 1943
MAN IN HALF-MOON STREET, THE, 1944
MAN IN THE IRON MASK, THE, 1939
MAN IN THE MIDDLE, 1964
MAN IN THE MOON, 1961
MAN MADE MONSTER, 1941
MAN OF CONQUEST, 1939
MAN OF THE HOUR, THE, 1940
MAN ON A SWING, 1974
MAN ON FIRE, 1957
MAN TO REMEMBER, A, 1938
MAN UNDER SUSPICION, 1985
MAN UPSTAIRS, THE, 1959
MAN WHO CAME FOR COFFEE, THE, 1970
MAN WHO LIVED AGAIN, THE, 1936
MAN WHO LOVED REDHEADS, THE, 1955
MAN WHO LOVED WOMEN, THE, 1977
MAN WHO NEVER WAS, THE, 1956
MAN WHO RECLAIMED HIS HEAD, THE, 1935
MAN WHO SHOT LIBERTY VALANCE, THE, 1962
MAN WHO WAS SHERLOCK HOLMES, THE, 1937
MAN WITH A CLOAK, THE, 1951
MAN WITH A MILLION, 1954
MAN WITH NINE LIVES, THE, 1940
MAN WITH THE GREEN CARNATION, THE, 1960
MAN WITH THE GUN, 1955
MAN WITH TWO FACES, THE, 1934
MANHUNTER, 1986
MANIFESTO, 1988
MANILA CALLING, 1942
MANPOWER, 1941
MAN'S CASTLE, A, 1933
MARAUDERS, THE, 1947
MARCH HARE, THE, 1956
MARCH OR DIE, 1977
MARCO, 1973
MARCO THE MAGNIFICENT, 1966
MARIE GALANTE, 1934
MARK OF THE HAWK, THE, 1958
MARK OF THE VAMPIRE, 1935

MARLOWE, 1969
MAROC 7, 1967
MAROONED, 1969
MARRIAGE, A, 1983
MARRIAGE BY CONTRACT, 1928
MARRIAGE—ITALIAN STYLE, 1964
MARRIAGE PLAYGROUND, THE, 1929
MARRIED BACHELOR, 1941
MARRIED COUPLE, A, 1969
MARRIED TO THE MOB, 1988
MARSHAL OF MESA CITY, THE, 1939
MARSHAL OF RENO, 1944
MARTYR, THE, 1976
MARY BURNS, FUGITIVE, 1935
MASK, 1985
MASK OF FU MANCHU, THE, 1932
MASQUERADE, 1965
MASS APPEAL, 1984
MASSACRE AT CENTRAL HIGH, 1976
MASSACRE IN ROME, 1973
MASTER OF BALLANTRAE, THE, 1953
MASTER OF BANKDAM, THE, 1947
MATA HARI, 1965
MATING GAME, THE, 1959
MATTER OF DAYS, A, 1969
MAVERICK QUEEN, THE, 1956
MAYOR OF HELL, THE, 1933
MEAL, THE, 1975
MEDEA, 1971
MEDIUM, THE, 1951
MEET DANNY WILSON, 1952
MEET ME AFTER THE SHOW, 1951
MEET ME IN LAS VEGAS, 1956
MEET NERO WOLFE, 1936
MEIER, 1987
MELODY, 1971
MEMBER OF THE WEDDING, THE, 1952
MEN ARE CHILDREN TWICE, 1953
MEN IN HER LIFE, THE, 1941
MEN IN WHITE, 1934
MEN OF THE SEA, 1951
MEN WITHOUT WOMEN, 1930
MEPHISTO WALTZ, THE, 1971
MERRILY WE LIVE, 1938
MERTON OF THE MOVIES, 1947
MIDDLE AGE SPREAD, 1979
MIDNIGHT LACE, 1960
MIDNIGHT STORY, THE, 1957
MIDSUMMER NIGHT'S DREAM, A, 1966
MIGHTY MOUSE IN THE GREAT SPACE CHASE,
  1983
MILES FROM HOME, 1988
MILESTONES, 1975
MILLION, THE, 1931
MILLION DOLLAR LEGS, 1932
MILLION DOLLAR MERMAID, 1952
MILLIONAIRE, THE, 1931
MILLIONAIRESS, THE, 1960
MILLIONS LIKE US, 1943
MIND BENDERS, THE, 1963
MIND OF MR. SOAMES, THE, 1970
MINE OWN EXECUTIONER, 1948
MIRACLE OF OUR LADY OF FATIMA, THE, 1952
MIRACLES FOR SALE, 1939
MIRANDA, 1949
MIRROR CRACK'D, THE, 1980
MISCHIEF, 1931
MISFITS, THE, 1961
MISS FANE'S BABY IS STOLEN, 1934
MISS SADIE THOMPSON, 1953
MISS TATLOCK'S MILLIONS, 1948
MISSING CORPSE, THE, 1945
MISSING JUROR, THE, 1944
MISSING WITNESSES, 1937
MISSION, THE, 1984
MISSION, THE, 1986
MISSION TO MOSCOW, 1943
MISSISSIPPI GAMBLER, THE, 1953
MISSOURI BREAKS, THE, 1976
MISSOURI TRAVELER, THE, 1958
MR. AND MRS. SMITH, 1941
MR. BELVEDERE RINGS THE BELL, 1951
MR. BELVEDERE GOES TO COLLEGE, 1949
MR. BLANDINGS BUILDS HIS DREAM HOUSE, 1948
MR. BUG GOES TO TOWN, 1941
MISTER CORY, 1957

MR. DENNING DRIVES NORTH, 1953
MR. HOBBS TAKES A VACATION, 1962
MISTER HOBO, 1936
MR. LUCKY, 1943
MR. MAGOO'S HOLIDAY FESTIVAL, 1970
MR. MAJESTYK, 1974
MR. PERRIN AND MR. TRAILL, 1948
MR. POTTS GOES TO MOSCOW, 1953
MISTER ROCK AND ROLL, 1957
MR. SARDONICUS, 1961
MR. SKEFFINGTON, 1944
MISTY, 1961
MOB, THE, 1951
MODEL AND THE MARRIAGE BROKER, THE, 1951
MODEL SHOP, THE, 1969
MODIGLIANI OF MONTPARNASSE, 1961
MOLLY AND ME, 1945
MOLLY MAGUIRES, THE, 1970
MOMENT OF TERROR, 1969
MONKEY BUSINESS, 1931
MONKEY BUSINESS, 1952
MONKEY IN WINTER, A, 1962
MONSIEUR BEAUCAIRE, 1946
MONSIEUR VINCENT, 1949
MONTE WALSH, 1970
MONTENEGRO, 1981
MOON IN THE GUTTER, THE, 1983
MOONLIGHT SONATA, 1938
MOONRAKER, 1979
MOON'S OUR HOME, THE, 1936
MORGAN!, 1966
MORITURI, 1965
MORNING GLORY, 1933
MOSCOW ON THE HUDSON, 1984
MOSES AND AARON, 1975
MOSS ROSE, 1947
MOST DANGEROUS GAME, THE, 1932
MOTHER AND THE WHORE, THE, 1973
MOTHER WORE TIGHTS, 1947
MOUTH TO MOUTH, 1978
MOUTHPIECE, THE, 1932
MOVING TARGETS, 1987
MRS. PYM OF SCOTLAND YARD, 1939
MRS. WIGGS OF THE CABBAGE PATCH, 1934
MUMMY, THE, 1959
MUMMY'S HAND, THE, 1940
MUPPET MOVIE, THE, 1979
MURDER AHOY, 1964
MURDER BY DECREE, 1979
MURDER CZECH STYLE, 1968
MURDER IN REVERSE, 1946
MURDER, INC., 1960
MURDER IS MY BEAT, 1955
MURDER MAN, 1935
MURDER MOST FOUL, 1964
MURDER ON A HONEYMOON, 1935
MURDER ON MONDAY, 1953
MURDER ON THE BLACKBOARD, 1934
MURDER ON THE CAMPUS, 1934
MURDER ONE, 1988
MURDERER LIVES AT NUMBER 21, THE, 1947
MURDERERS AMONG US, 1948
MURPH THE SURF, 1974
MUSIC HATH CHARMS, 1935
MUSIC ROOM, THE, 1963
MUSS 'EM UP, 1936
MY AMERICAN COUSIN, 1985
MY BROTHER TALKS TO HORSES, 1946
MY COUSIN RACHEL, 1952
MY DEAR MISS ALDRICH, 1937
MY FAVORITE BLONDE, 1942
MY FAVORITE SPY, 1951
MY FAVORITE WIFE, 1940
MY GAL LOVES MUSIC, 1944
MY GAL SAL, 1942
MY HOBO, 1963
MY KINGDOM FOR A COOK, 1943
MY LEARNED FRIEND, 1943
MY LIFE AS A DOG, 1987
MY LOVE CAME BACK, 1940
MY NAME IS NOBODY, 1974
MY PAL, THE KING, 1932
MY PAL, WOLF, 1944
MY PAST, 1931
MY SIDE OF THE MOUNTAIN, 1969
MY SISTER EILEEN, 1942

MY SIX CONVICTS, 1952
MY SONG FOR YOU, 1935
MY SWEET LITTLE VILLAGE, 1985
MY UNCLE'S LEGACY, 1988
MY WEAKNESS, 1933
MY WIDOW AND I, 1950
MYSTERIOUS AVENGER, THE, 1936
MYSTERIOUS DESPERADO, THE, 1949
MYSTERIOUS DR. FU MANCHU, THE, 1929
MYSTERIOUS INTRUDER, 1946
MYSTERIOUS ISLAND, 1941
MYSTERIOUS ISLAND, 1961
MYSTERIOUS MR. MOTO, 1938
MYSTERIOUS MR. WONG, 1935
MYSTERY LINER, 1934
MYSTERY OF EDWIN DROOD, THE, 1935
MYSTERY OF MR. WONG, THE, 1939
MYSTERY OF MR. X, THE, 1934
MYSTERY ON BIRD ISLAND, 1954
MYSTERY RANCH, 1932
NAKED ALIBI, 1954
NAKED AMONG THE WOLVES, 1967
NAKED HOURS, THE, 1964
NAKED NIGHT, THE, 1956
NAKED STREET, THE, 1955
NANCY STEELE IS MISSING, 1937
NANNY, THE, 1965
NARROW CORNER, THE, 1933
NARROW MARGIN, THE, 1952
NASTY HABITS, 1976
NATIONAL HEALTH, OR NURSE NORTON'S
    AFFAIR, THE, 1973
**NATIONAL LAMPOON'S EUROPEAN VACATION,
1985**
NATURAL, THE, 1984
NAVAJO, 1952
NEITHER BY DAY NOR BY NIGHT, 1972
NELL GWYN, 1935
NEVER A DULL MOMENT, 1968
NEVER FEAR, 1950
NEVER GIVE A SUCKER AN EVEN BREAK, 1941
NEVER ON SUNDAY, 1960
NEVER SO FEW, 1959
NEVER TAKE CANDY FROM A STRANGER, 1961
NEVER WAVE AT A WAC, 1952
NEW LAND, THE, 1973
NEW LEAF, A, 1971
NEWSFRONT, 1979
NEXT VOICE YOU HEAR, THE, 1950
NGATI, 1987
NICK CARTER, MASTER DETECTIVE, 1939
NICKEL RIDE, THE, 1974
NIGHT AFTER NIGHT, 1932
NIGHT AMBUSH, 1958
NIGHT AND DAY, 1946
NIGHT ANGELS, 1987
NIGHT COURT, 1932
NIGHT FIGHTERS, THE, 1960
NIGHT FLIGHT, 1933
NIGHT HAS A THOUSAND EYES, 1948
NIGHT HOLDS TERROR, THE, 1955
NIGHT IN CASABLANCA, A, 1946
NIGHT IN THE LIFE OF JIMMY REARDON, A, 1988
NIGHT LIKE THIS, A, 1932
NIGHT MUST FALL, 1964
NIGHT NURSE, 1931
NIGHT OF THE GENERALS, THE, 1967
NIGHT OF THE LIVING DEAD, 1968
NIGHT OF THE SHOOTING STARS, THE, 1982
NIGHT RUNNER, THE, 1957
NIGHT SHIFT, 1982
NIGHT THEY RAIDED MINSKY'S, THE, 1968
NIGHTMARE, 1942
NIGHTMARE, 1956
NIGHTS OF CABIRIA, 1957
NIGHTS OF PRAGUE, THE, 1968
NINE DAYS OF ONE YEAR, 1964
NINE HOURS TO RAMA, 1963
NINE TO FIVE, 1980
1984, 1984
1900, 1976
1919, 1984
90 DAYS, 1986
NINTH CIRCLE, THE, 1961
NINTH CONFIGURATION, THE, 1980
NINTH HEART, THE, 1980

NO EXIT, 1962
NO GREATER LOVE, 1944
NO LONGER ALONE, 1978
NO MAN IS AN ISLAND, 1962
NO MINOR VICES, 1948
NO MORE ORCHIDS, 1933
NO, NO NANETTE, 1930
NO PLACE TO GO, 1939
NO ROOM AT THE INN, 1950
NO TIME FOR BREAKFAST, 1978
NO TIME FOR LOVE, 1943
NO TRACE, 1950
NO WAY OUT, 1950
NOAH'S ARK, 1928
NOBODY LIVES FOREVER, 1946
NOBODY'S FOOL, 1936
NOISY NEIGHBORS, 1929
NOOSE HANGS HIGH, THE, 1948
NORA PRENTISS, 1947
NORTHERN PURSUIT, 1943
NORTHWEST MOUNTED POLICE, 1940
NOSFERATU, THE VAMPIRE, 1979
NOTHING BUT A MAN, 1964
NOTHING BUT THE TRUTH, 1941
NOTHING IN COMMON, 1986
NOTORIOUS LANDLADY, THE, 1962
NOW, VOYAGER, 1942
NOW YOU SEE HIM, NOW YOU DON'T, 1972
NUMBER SEVENTEEN, 1932
NURSE EDITH CAVELL, 1939
NUTCRACKER: THE MOTION PICTURE, 1986
NUTS, 1987
ODDS AGAINST TOMORROW, 1959
ODE TO BILLY JOE, 1976
ODETTE, 1951
OEDIPUS THE KING, 1968
OFFENSE, THE, 1973
OFFICE PICNIC, THE, 1974
OH GOD! YOU DEVIL, 1984
OH, MEN! OH, WOMEN!, 1957
OHAYO, 1962
OIL FOR THE LAMPS OF CHINA, 1935
OKLAHOMA KID, THE, 1939
OLD BONES OF THE RIVER, 1938
OLD ENOUGH, 1984
ON AN ISLAND WITH YOU, 1948
ON BORROWED TIME, 1939
ON DANGEROUS GROUND, 1951
ON MOONLIGHT BAY, 1951
ON PROBATION, 1935
ON THE AVENUE, 1937
ON THE DOUBLE, 1961
ON THE LINE, 1984
ON THE THRESHOLD OF SPACE, 1956
ON THE YARD, 1978
ONCE MORE, WITH FEELING, 1960
ONCE THERE WAS A GIRL, 1945
ONE AND ONLY, THE, 1978
ONE HOUR WITH YOU, 1932
ONE IS A LONELY NUMBER, 1972
ONE MAN JUSTICE, 1937
ONE MILLION B.C., 1940
ONE MORE RIVER, 1934
ONE MORE SPRING, 1935
ONE MORE TRAIN TO ROB, 1971
ONE POTATO, TWO POTATO, 1964
ONE SUNDAY AFTERNOON, 1933
1001 ARABIAN NIGHTS, 1959
ONE-TRICK PONY, 1980
ONE WAY PASSAGE, 1932
ONE WAY PENDULUM, 1965
ONE WOMAN'S STORY, 1949
ONION FIELD, THE, 1979
ONLY WAY, THE, 1970
OPERATION MAD BALL, 1957
OPERATION PACIFIC, 1951
OPTIMISTS, THE, 1973
ORDERS, THE, 1977
ORDERS IS ORDERS, 1934
ORGANIZER, THE, 1964
OSSESSIONE, 1959
OTHER, THE, 1972
OUR DAILY BREAD, 1934
OUR HITLER, A FILM FROM GERMANY, 1980
OUR MAN FLINT, 1966
OUR MAN IN HAVANA, 1960

BOLD: Films on Videocassette

OUR WIFE, 1941
OUT OF SEASON, 1975
OUT OF THE BLUE, 1947
OUTSIDERS, THE, 1983
OUTSIDERS, THE, 1987
OVER MY DEAD BODY, 1942
OVER SHE GOES, 1937
OVER THE ODDS, 1961
OVER 21, 1945
OVERLAND STAGE RAIDERS, 1938
OVERTURE TO GLORY, 1940
PACK UP YOUR TROUBLES, 1939
PADDY, 1970
PADDY O'DAY, 1935
PADDY, THE NEXT BEST THING, 1933
PAID, 1930
PAINTED HILLS, THE, 1951
PAINTED TRAIL, THE, 1938
PAINTED VEIL, THE, 1934
PALM BEACH, 1979
PALMY DAYS, 1931
PALOOKA, 1934
PANHANDLE, 1948
PANIC IN THE STREETS, 1950
PANIC IN YEAR ZERO!, 1962
PAPA'S DELICATE CONDITION, 1963
PAPER BULLETS, 1941
PAPER GALLOWS, 1950
PAPER LION, 1968
PARADINE CASE, THE, 1947
PARADISE FOR THREE, 1938
PARADISE ISLE, 1937
PARENT TRAP, THE, 1961
PARIS BELONGS TO US, 1962
PARTING GLANCES, 1986
PASSING OF THE THIRD FLOOR BACK, THE, 1936
PASSION OF ANNA, THE, 1970
PASSIONATE SENTRY, THE, 1952
PASSIONATE THIEF, THE, 1963
PASSPORT TO PIMLICO, 1949
PATAKIN, 1985
PATCH OF BLUE, A, 1965
PATRICK, 1979
PATTI ROCKS, 1988
PAY OR DIE, 1960
PAYMENT ON DEMAND, 1951
PEACE TO HIM WHO ENTERS, 1963
PEACH THIEF, THE, 1969
PEARL OF DEATH, THE, 1944
PEG OF OLD DRURY, 1936
PENGUIN POOL MURDER, THE, 1932
PENNIES FROM HEAVEN, 1936
PENNY PRINCESS, 1953
PENTHOUSE, 1933
PEOPLE AGAINST O'HARA, THE, 1951
PERFECT FRIDAY, 1970
PERFECT SPECIMEN, THE, 1937
PERIOD OF ADJUSTMENT, 1962
PERSONAL COLUMN, 1939
PERSONAL SERVICES, 1987
PERSONALS, THE, 1982
PETE KELLY'S BLUES, 1955
PETER RABBIT AND TALES OF BEATRIX POTTER, 1971
PETTY GIRL, THE, 1950
PETULIA, 1968
PHANTOM LIGHT, THE, 1935
PHANTOM OF THE OPERA, 1943
PHANTOM OF THE OPERA, THE, 1962
PHANTOM RAIDERS, 1940
PHFFFT!, 1954
PHONE CALL FROM A STRANGER, 1952
PHOTOGRAPH, THE, 1987
PIAF—THE EARLY YEARS, 1982
PICKWICK PAPERS, THE, 1952
PICNIC AT HANGING ROCK, 1975
PICNIC ON THE GRASS, 1960
PICTURE SHOW MAN, THE, 1980
PIE IN THE SKY, 1964
PIED PIPER, THE, 1972
PIGSKIN PARADE, 1936
PINK PANTHER STRIKES AGAIN, THE, 1976
PINOCCHIO AND THE EMPEROR OF THE NIGHT, 1987
PIRATES, 1986
PIRATES OF PENZANCE, THE, 1983

PITTSBURGH, 1942
PLACE OF ONE'S OWN, A, 1945
PLACE OF WEEPING, 1986
PLAGUE OF THE ZOMBIES, THE, 1966
PLANES, TRAINS AND AUTOMOBILES, 1987
PLANET OF THE VAMPIRES, 1965
PLATINUM BLONDE, 1931
PLAY DIRTY, 1969
PLAYBOY, THE, 1942
PLAYBOY OF THE WESTERN WORLD, THE, 1963
PLAYTIME, 1963
PLEASE DON'T EAT THE DAISIES, 1960
PLEASE TURN OVER, 1960
PLEASURE OF HIS COMPANY, THE, 1961
PLENTY, 1985
PLOUGH AND THE STARS, THE, 1936
PLUNDER ROAD, 1957
PLUNDERERS, THE, 1948
PLUNDERERS, THE, 1960
POET'S SILENCE, THE, 1987
POISON PEN, 1941
POLICE, 1986
POLICE PYTHON 357, 1976
PONY EXPRESS, 1953
PONY SOLDIER, 1952
POOR COW, 1968
POPI, 1969
POPPY, 1936
POPPY IS ALSO A FLOWER, THE, 1966
PORT OF 40 THIEVES, THE, 1944
PORT OF NEW YORK, 1949
PORT OF SEVEN SEAS, 1938
PORTRAIT OF A WOMAN, 1946
PORTRAIT OF HELL, 1969
POSSE, 1975
POSSE FROM HELL, 1961
POT CARRIERS, THE, 1962
POURQUOI PAS!, 1979
POWDER RIVER, 1953
POWER, 1986
POWER AND THE GLORY, THE, 1933
PRELUDE TO FAME, 1950
PRESIDENT'S LADY, THE, 1953
PRESSURE OF GUILT, 1964
PRETENDER, THE, 1947
PRETTY IN PINK, 1986
PRIME CUT, 1972
PRIMROSE PATH, 1940
PRINCE OF DARKNESS, 1987
PRINCESS AND THE PIRATE, THE, 1944
PRINCESS COMES ACROSS, THE, 1936
PRINCESS O'ROURKE, 1943
PRISONER OF SECOND AVENUE, THE, 1975
PRISONER OF ZENDA, THE, 1952
PRIVATE ACCESS, 1988
PRIVATE AFFAIRS OF BEL AMI, THE, 1947
PRIVATE FUNCTION, A, 1985
PRIVATE PROPERTY, 1960
PRIVATE WORLDS, 1935
PRIZE, THE, 1952
PRIZE OF ARMS, A, 1962
PRIZE OF GOLD, A, 1955
PRIZEFIGHTER AND THE LADY, THE, 1933
PRIZZI'S HONOR, 1985
PROFESSIONAL SWEETHEART, 1933
PROJECT M7, 1953
PROJECT X, 1987
PROLOGUE, 1970
PROMISED LAND, 1988
PROMOTER, THE, 1952
PROUD ONES, THE, 1956
PROUD RIDER, THE, 1971
PROWLER, THE, 1951
PSYCHO III, 1986
PSYCHOPATH, THE, 1966
PT 109, 1963
PUBLIC AFFAIR, A, 1962
PUBLIC COWBOY NO. 1, 1937
PUBLIC DEFENDER, THE, 1931
PUBLIC ENEMIES, 1941
PUBLIC ENEMY'S WIFE, 1936
PULSE, 1988
PURE HELL OF ST. TRINIAN'S, THE, 1961
PURPLE NOON, 1961
PURPLE PLAIN, THE, 1954
PURPLE ROSE OF CAIRO, THE, 1985

PURPLE VIGILANTES, THE, 1938
PURSUIT OF HAPPINESS, THE, 1934
PYX, THE, 1973
QUARE FELLOW, THE, 1962
QUEEN BEE, 1955
QUEEN OF BLOOD, 1966
QUEEN OF SPADES, 1961
QUENTIN DURWARD, 1955
QUERY, 1945
QUEST FOR FIRE, 1982
QUEST FOR LOVE, 1971
QUICK MILLIONS, 1931
QUICKSAND, 1950
QUIET WEDDING, 1941
QUILLER MEMORANDUM, THE, 1966
QUILOMBO, 1986
RACERS, THE, 1955
RACHEL AND THE STRANGER, 1948
RACKET BUSTERS, 1938
RAFFLES, 1939
RAGGEDY MAN, 1981
RAGTIME, 1981
RAID, THE, 1954
RAILROADED, 1947
RAILWAY CHILDREN, THE, 1971
RAIN PEOPLE, THE, 1969
RAINMAKER, THE, 1956
RAINS OF RANCHIPUR, THE, 1955
RAINTREE COUNTY, 1957
RAISING ARIZONA, 1987
RAMROD, 1947
RANSOM, 1956
RARE BREED, THE, 1966
RASCAL, 1969
RASPUTIN, 1985
RAT, 1960
RAT FINK, 1965
RAT SAVIOUR, THE, 1977
RATS, THE, 1955
RAVEN, THE, 1935
RAVEN, THE, 1948
RAW DEAL, 1948
RAWHIDE, 1951
RE: LUCKY LUCIANO, 1974
REACH FOR THE SKY, 1957
REALM OF FORTUNE, THE, 1986
REBEL IN TOWN, 1956
REBELLION, 1967
RED, 1970
RED BEARD, 1966
RED HEADED WOMAN, 1932
RED HEAT, 1988
RED HOUSE, THE, 1947
RED INN, THE, 1954
RED LANTERNS, 1965
RED MOUNTAIN, 1951
RED TENT, THE, 1971
REFORMER AND THE REDHEAD, THE, 1950
RELENTLESS, 1948
REMEMBER THE DAY, 1941
REMO WILLIAMS: THE ADVENTURE BEGINS, 1985
RENDEZVOUS, 1935
RENDEZVOUS, 1985
RENT CONTROL, 1981
RESCUERS, THE, 1977
RESERVED FOR LADIES, 1932
RESURRECTION, 1963
RETURN OF PETER GRIMM, THE, 1935
RETURN OF THE BADMEN, 1948
RETURN OF THE SOLDIER, THE, 1983
RETURN OF THE TEXAN, 1952
RETURN OF WILDFIRE, 1948
RETURN TO SNOWY RIVER: PART II, 1988
REVENGE OF THE PINK PANTHER, 1978
REVENUE AGENT, 1950
REVOLT IN THE BIG HOUSE, 1958
RHAPSODY, 1954
RHINO, 1964
RHYTHM ON THE RANGE, 1936
RICE GIRL, 1963
RICH AND STRANGE, 1932
RICH KIDS, 1979
RICH MAN'S FOLLY, 1931
RICH, YOUNG AND PRETTY, 1951
RICHARD, 1972
RIDE CLEAR OF DIABLO, 1954

RIDE 'EM COWBOY, 1942
RIDE HIM, COWBOY, 1932
RIDE LONESOME, 1959
RIDE ON VAQUERO, 1941
RIDE, RANGER, RIDE, 1936
RIDE, TENDERFOOT, RIDE, 1940
RIDER FROM TUCSON, 1950
RIDERS OF DESTINY, 1933
RIDERS OF THE RANGE, 1949
RIDERS OF THE ROCKIES, 1937
RIDERS OF THE WHISTLING SKULL, 1937
RIDIN' THE OUTLAW TRAIL, 1951
RIDING THE SUNSET TRAIL, 1941
RIFF-RAFF, 1936
RIGHT CROSS, 1950
RIGHT TO LOVE, THE, 1931
RING, THE, 1952
RING OF BRIGHT WATER, 1969
RING OF FIRE, 1961
RIO CONCHOS, 1964
RIOT ON SUNSET STRIP, 1967
RIP-OFF, 1971
RIP TIDE, 1934
RISE OF LOUIS XIV, THE, 1970
RISING DAMP, 1980
RISING OF THE MOON, THE, 1957
RISKY BUSINESS, 1983
RITA, SUE AND BOB TOO!, 1987
RIVER, THE, 1984
RIVER CHANGES, THE, 1956
ROAD BACK, THE, 1937
ROAD HOUSE, 1948
ROAD MOVIE, 1974
ROAD TO ETERNITY, 1962
ROADBLOCK, 1951
ROBBER SYMPHONY, THE, 1937
ROBBERS' ROOST, 1933
ROBBERY, 1967
ROBIN AND MARIAN, 1976
ROBIN AND THE SEVEN HOODS, 1964
ROBIN HOOD, 1973
ROBIN OF TEXAS, 1947
ROBINSON CRUSOE ON MARS, 1964
ROCK-A-BYE BABY, 1958
ROCK AROUND THE CLOCK, 1956
ROCKERS, 1980
ROCKETSHIP X-M, 1950
ROCKY III, 1982
ROCKY MOUNTAIN, 1950
ROGUE COP, 1954
ROGUE SONG, THE, 1930
ROLLERBALL, 1975
ROLLERCOASTER, 1977
ROLLING THUNDER, 1977
ROMANCE, 1930
ROMANCE OF ROSY RIDGE, THE, 1947
ROMANCE ON THE HIGH SEAS, 1948
ROME EXPRESS, 1933
ROME WANTS ANOTHER CAESAR, 1974
ROMEO AND JULIET, 1966
ROOM SERVICE, 1938
ROONEY, 1958
ROOTIN' TOOTIN' RHYTHM, 1937
ROOTS OF HEAVEN, THE, 1958
ROPE, 1948
ROPE OF SAND, 1949
ROSALIE, 1937
ROSE, THE, 1979
ROSE MARIE, 1954
ROSE OF WASHINGTON SQUARE, 1939
ROSEANNA McCOY, 1949
ROSELAND, 1977
ROSES FOR THE PROSECUTOR, 1961
ROUGE OF THE NORTH, 1988
ROUGHSHOD, 1949
ROWING WITH THE WIND, 1988
ROXIE HART, 1942
ROYAL AFFAIR, A, 1950
ROYAL AFFAIRS IN VERSAILLES, 1957
ROYAL FLASH, 1975
ROYAL MOUNTED PATROL, THE, 1941
ROYAL SCANDAL, A, 1945
RUDE BOY, 1980
RUN FOR YOUR MONEY, A, 1950
RUN OF THE ARROW, 1957
RUN SILENT, RUN DEEP, 1958

RUNNING MAN, THE, 1963
RUNNING ON EMPTY, 1988
RUNNING TARGET, 1956
SACCO AND VANZETTI, 1971
SAD SACK, THE, 1957
SADDLE THE WIND, 1958
SADDLE TRAMP, 1950
SADIE McKEE, 1934
SAGA OF THE VAGABONDS, 1964
SAIGON, 1948
SAINT IN NEW YORK, THE, 1938
SAINT IN PALM SPRINGS, THE, 1941
ST. LOUIS KID, THE, 1934
SAINT TAKES OVER, THE, 1940
SAINT'S VACATION, THE, 1941
SALAAM BOMBAY, 1988
SALLY AND SAINT ANNE, 1952
SALLY BISHOP, 1932
SALLY, IRENE AND MARY, 1938
SALOME, 1953
SALOON BAR, 1940
SALSA, 1988
SALT LAKE RAIDERS, 1950
SALT TO THE DEVIL, 1949
SALTO, 1966
SALTY O'ROURKE, 1945
SALVATORE GIULIANO, 1966
SAMURAI, 1955
SAN ANTONIO, 1945
SAN QUENTIN, 1937
SAND CASTLE, THE, 1961
SANDERS OF THE RIVER, 1935
SANDFLOW, 1937
SANTA FE PASSAGE, 1955
SANTIAGO, 1956
SAPPHIRE, 1959
SARABAND, 1949
SARATOGA TRUNK, 1945
SARDINIA: RANSOM, 1968
SASKATCHEWAN, 1954
SATURDAY'S CHILDREN, 1929
SATURDAY'S CHILDREN, 1940
SATURDAY'S HERO, 1951
SAVAGE EYE, THE, 1960
SAVAGE INNOCENTS, THE, 1960
SAVAGE MESSIAH, 1972
SAVAGE PAMPAS, 1967
SAVAGES, 1972
SAVING GRACE, 1986
SCALPHUNTERS, THE, 1968
SCANDAL, 1964
SCANDAL IN PARIS, A, 1946
SCANNERS, 1981
SCARECROW, 1973
SCARLET CLAW, THE, 1944
SCARLET STREET, 1945
SCENE OF THE CRIME, 1949
SCENE OF THE CRIME, 1986
SCENES FROM A MARRIAGE, 1974
SCOTLAND YARD INVESTIGATOR, 1945
SCOTT JOPLIN, 1977
SCREAM AND SCREAM AGAIN, 1970
SCROOGE, 1935
SCUM, 1979
SEA GYPSIES, THE, 1978
SEA SHALL NOT HAVE THEM, THE, 1955
SEA WOLVES, THE, 1981
SEALED CARGO, 1951
SEASON OF PASSION, 1961
SECOND CHANCE, 1953
SECOND CHORUS, 1940
SECOND FIDDLE, 1939
SECRET BEYOND THE DOOR, THE, 1948
SECRET GARDEN, THE, 1949
SECRET HEART, THE, 1946
SECRET LIFE OF AN AMERICAN WIFE, THE, 1968
SECRET OF NIMH, THE, 1982
SECRET OF THE WHISTLER, 1946
SECRETS OF THE LONE WOLF, 1941
SEE NO EVIL, 1971
SEEMS LIKE OLD TIMES, 1980
SEMI-TOUGH, 1977
SENDER, THE, 1982
SENTIMENTAL JOURNEY, 1946
SEPARATE PEACE, A, 1972
SEPTEMBER AFFAIR, 1950

SEQUOIA, 1934
SERENADE, 1956
SERGEANT JIM, 1962
SERGEANT RYKER, 1968
SERIAL, 1980
SERPENT AND THE RAINBOW, THE, 1988
SERVANT, THE, 1964
SEVEN ANGRY MEN, 1955
SEVEN CAPITAL SINS, 1962
SEVEN CITIES OF GOLD, 1955
SEVEN DEADLY SINS, THE, 1953
711 OCEAN DRIVE, 1950
SEVEN MILES FROM ALCATRAZ, 1942
SEVEN-PER-CENT SOLUTION, THE, 1977
SEVEN UPS, THE, 1973
SEVEN WOMEN, 1966
SEVENTH CONTINENT, THE, 1968
SEVENTH VICTIM, THE, 1943
SEX AND THE SINGLE GIRL, 1964
SEZ O'REILLY TO MACNAB, 1938
SHADOW OF THE LAW, 1930
SHADOW OF THE THIN MAN, 1941
SHADOW OF VICTORY, 1986
SHADOWMAN, 1974
SHADOWS OF FORGOTTEN ANCESTORS, 1967
SHAFT, 1971
SHAGGY D.A., THE, 1976
SHAGGY DOG, THE, 1959
SHAKESPEARE WALLAH, 1966
SHAMELESS OLD LADY, THE, 1966
SHAMPOO, 1975
SHANGHAI DRAMA, THE, 1945
SHARK, 1970
SHARKY'S MACHINE, 1981
SHE, 1935
SHE DIDN'T SAY NO?, 1962
SHE GOES TO WAR, 1929
SHE MARRIED HER BOSS, 1935
SHEEPMAN, THE, 1958
SHEPHERD OF THE HILLS, THE, 1941
SHERIFF OF FRACTURED JAW, THE, 1958
SHERLOCK HOLMES, 1932
**SHERLOCK HOLMES AND THE SECRET WEAPON,
1942**
SHERLOCK HOLMES FACES DEATH, 1943
SHE'S GOTTA HAVE IT, 1986
SHE'S WORKING HER WAY THROUGH COLLEGE,
1952
SHINING, THE, 1980
SHIRLEY THOMPSON VERSUS THE ALIENS, 1968
SHOCK TROOPS, 1968
SHOCKPROOF, 1949
SHOES OF THE FISHERMAN, THE, 1968
SHOGUN ASSASSIN, 1980
SHOOT FIRST, 1953
SHOOT TO KILL, 1947
SHOOT TO KILL, 1988
SHORT CUT TO HELL, 1957
SHORT GRASS, 1950
SHOT AT DAWN, A, 1934
SHOTGUN, 1955
SHOUT, THE, 1978
SHOW BUSINESS, 1944
SHOW-OFF, THE, 1934
SHOW THEM NO MERCY, 1935
SHOWDOWN, THE, 1950
SHOWDOWN AT ABILENE, 1956
SHUT MY BIG MOUTH, 1942
SHUTTERED ROOM, THE, 1968
SIDDHARTHA, 1972
SIDEWALKS OF LONDON, 1940
SIEGE, 1983
SIEGE AT RED RIVER, THE, 1954
SIGNAL 7, 1984
SIGNPOST TO MURDER, 1964
SIGNS OF LIFE, 1981
SILENCE, THE, 1964
SILENT PLAYGROUND, THE, 1964
SILENT RUNNING, 1972
SILENT WITNESS, THE, 1932
SILVER CITY RAIDERS, 1943
SILVER DUST, 1953
SILVER LODE, 1954
SILVER SPURS, 1943
SIMON, 1980
SIMON AND LAURA, 1956

BOLD: Films on Videocassette

SINBAD THE SAILOR, 1947
SINCERELY CHARLOTTE, 1986
SING AS WE GO, 1934
SING, BABY, SING, 1936
SING, COWBOY, SING, 1937
SINGER AND THE DANCER, THE, 1977
SINGER NOT THE SONG, THE, 1961
SINGING BLACKSMITH, 1938
SINGING FOOL, THE, 1928
SINNER TAKE ALL, 1936
SINNER'S HOLIDAY, 1930
SINS OF THE CHILDREN, 1930
SIR HENRY AT RAWLINSON END, 1980
SIROCCO, 1951
SISTERS, 1973
SITTING DUCKS, 1979
SITTING ON THE MOON, 1936
SITTING PRETTY, 1933
SIX GUN GOLD, 1941
SIX IN PARIS, 1968
SIX OF A KIND, 1934
SIX PACK ANNIE, 1975
6000 ENEMIES, 1939
SIXTEEN CANDLES, 1984
SIXTY GLORIOUS YEARS, 1938
SKIP TRACER, THE, 1979
SKIPALONG ROSENBLOOM, 1951
SKY GIANT, 1938
SKYLINE, 1984
SLAMDANCE, 1987
SLAP SHOT, 1977
SLAUGHTER ON TENTH AVENUE, 1957
SLAVERS, 1977
SLEEP, MY LOVE, 1948
SLEEPING CITY, THE, 1950
SLENDER THREAD, THE, 1965
SLIGHTLY DANGEROUS, 1943
SLIGHTLY SCARLET, 1956
SLIPPER AND THE ROSE, THE, 1976
SLITHER, 1973
SMALL WORLD OF SAMMY LEE, THE, 1963
SMALLEST SHOW ON EARTH, THE, 1957
SMASH PALACE, 1982
SMASH-UP, THE STORY OF A WOMAN, 1947
SMILE OF THE LAMB, THE, 1986
SMILES OF A SUMMER NIGHT, 1957
SMILIN' THROUGH, 1941
SMOKY, 1946
SMUGGLERS' COVE, 1948
SNIPER, THE, 1952
SNORKEL, THE, 1958
SO BIG, 1953
SO ENDS OUR NIGHT, 1941
SO FINE, 1981
SO THIS IS NEW YORK, 1948
SOLDIER'S PRAYER, A, 1970
SOME KIND OF HERO, 1982
SOME KIND OF WONDERFUL, 1987
SOMEBODY LOVES ME, 1952
SOMEONE TO REMEMBER, 1943
SOMEONE TO WATCH OVER ME, 1987
SOMETHING FOR EVERYONE, 1970
SOMEWHERE I'LL FIND YOU, 1942
SOMEWHERE IN THE NIGHT, 1946
SON OF FURY, 1942
SON OF KONG, 1933
SONG O' MY HEART, 1930
SONG OF FREEDOM, 1938
SONG OF THE BUCKAROO, 1939
SONG OF THE THIN MAN, 1947
SONGWRITER, 1984
SONS AND MOTHERS, 1967
SONS OF KATIE ELDER, THE, 1965
SORROWFUL JONES, 1949
SORCERERS, THE, 1967
SOUND OF FURY, THE, 1950
SOUND OF LIFE, THE, 1962
SOUND OF TRUMPETS, THE, 1963
SOUNDER, PART 2, 1976
SOUTH RIDING, 1938
SOUTHERN YANKEE, A, 1948
SPANISH GARDENER, THE, 1957
SPECIAL AGENT, 1935
SPECIAL EFFECTS, 1984
SPECKLED BAND, THE, 1931
SPECTER OF THE ROSE, 1946

SPENCER'S MOUNTAIN, 1963
SPETTERS, 1983
SPIRITS OF THE DEAD, 1969
SPITFIRE, 1934
SPLENDOR IN THE GRASS, 1961
SPLIT IMAGE, 1982
SPLIT SECOND, 1953
SPOILERS, THE, 1930
SPORTING BLOOD, 1931
SPRING PARADE, 1940
SPRING SHOWER, 1932
SPRINGFIELD RIFLE, 1952
SPY IN BLACK, THE, 1939
SQUARE OF VIOLENCE, 1963
STABLEMATES, 1938
STAGE FRIGHT, 1950
STAND BY FOR ACTION, 1942
STAND UP AND FIGHT, 1939
STANDING ROOM ONLY, 1944
STANLEY AND LIVINGSTONE, 1939
STAR, THE, 1953
STAR CHAMBER, THE, 1983
STAR DUST, 1940
STAR 80, 1983
STAR IS BORN, A, 1976
STAR MAKER, THE, 1939
STAR OF MIDNIGHT, 1935
STAR TREK III: THE SEARCH FOR SPOCK, 1984
STAR TREK II: THE WRATH OF KHAN, 1982
STAR WITNESS, 1931
STARLIGHT HOTEL, 1987
STARMAN, 1984
STARS AND STRIPES FOREVER, 1952
START THE REVOLUTION WITHOUT ME, 1970
STATE FAIR, 1933
STATION WEST, 1948
STEP LIVELY, 1944
STEPCHILDREN, 1962
STIR, 1980
STIR CRAZY, 1980
STITCH IN TIME, A, 1967
STOLEN DIRIGIBLE, THE, 1966
STOLEN HOURS, 1963
STOLEN LIFE, A, 1946
STONY ISLAND, 1978
STORM BOY, 1976
STORM IN A TEACUP, 1937
STORM PLANET, 1962
STORM WARNING, 1950
STORMS OF AUGUST, THE, 1988
STORMY WATERS, 1946
STORMY WEATHER, 1935
STORY OF DR. WASSELL, THE, 1944
STORY OF FAUSTA, THE, 1988
STORY OF THREE LOVES, THE, 1953
STORY OF WILL ROGERS, THE, 1952
STOWAWAY, 1936
STOWAWAY GIRL, 1957
STRANGE BREW, 1983
STRANGE CARGO, 1940
STRANGE INTERLUDE, 1932
STRANGE INVADERS, 1983
STRANGE ONE, THE, 1957
STRANGE WOMAN, THE, 1946
STRANGER AT MY DOOR, 1956
STRANGERS IN THE HOUSE, 1949
STRANGERS IN THE NIGHT, 1944
STRATEGIC AIR COMMAND, 1955
STREET OF CHANCE, 1942
STREET OF SINNERS, 1957
STREETWALKIN', 1985
STRICTLY DISHONORABLE, 1951
STRIKE ME PINK, 1936
STRIP, THE, 1951
STRIPES, 1981
STRONGEST MAN IN THE WORLD, THE, 1975
SUBURBIA, 1984
SUBVERSIVES, THE, 1967
SUCCESS IS THE BEST REVENGE, 1984
SUCH A GORGEOUS KID LIKE ME, 1973
SUCKER, THE, 1966
SUDDEN FURY, 1975
SUGAR CANE ALLEY, 1984
SUGARLAND EXPRESS, THE, 1974
SUMMER AND SMOKE, 1961
SUMMER STORM, 1944

SUMMER TO REMEMBER, A, 1961
SUMMERSKIN, 1962
SUMMERSPELL, 1983
SUNDAY IN NEW YORK, 1963
SUNDAY TOO FAR AWAY, 1975
SUNDAYS AND CYBELE, 1962
SUNNY SIDE UP, 1929
SUNSET SERENADE, 1942
SUNSET TRAIL, 1938
SUPER COPS, THE, 1974
SUPER SLEUTH, 1937
SUPERFLY, 1972
SUPERMAN, 1978
SUPERZAN AND THE SPACE BOY, 1972
SUPPORT YOUR LOCAL GUNFIGHTER, 1971
SURE THING, THE, 1985
SURVIVOR, 1980
SUSAN AND GOD, 1940
SUSPECT, THE, 1944
SUSPIRIA, 1977
SUZY, 1936
SWALLOWS AND AMAZONS, 1977
SWAN, THE, 1956
SWANEE RIVER, 1939
SWEDISH MISTRESS, THE, 1964
SWEET DREAMS, 1985
SWEET LIGHT IN A DARK ROOM, 1966
SWEET LORRAINE, 1987
SWEET ROSIE O'GRADY, 1943
SWING HIGH, SWING LOW, 1937
SWORD AND THE DRAGON, THE, 1960
SWORD AND THE ROSE, THE, 1953
SYLVESTER, 1985
SYLVIA, 1965
SYLVIA, 1985
SYNANON, 1965
TABLE FOR FIVE, 1983
TAKE IT ALL, 1966
TAKE ONE FALSE STEP, 1949
TAKE THE HIGH GROUND, 1953
TALE OF RUBY ROSE, THE, 1987
TALE OF TWO CITIES, A, 1958
TALES FROM THE CRYPT, 1972
TALES OF THE UNCANNY, 1932
TALL, DARK AND HANDSOME, 1941
TALL IN THE SADDLE, 1944
TAMMY AND THE BACHELOR, 1957
TANGLED DESTINIES, 1932
TARANTULA, 1955
TARAWA BEACHHEAD, 1958
TAROT, 1987
TARZAN AND THE MERMAIDS, 1948
TARZAN ESCAPES, 1936
TARZAN FINDS A SON, 1939
TARZAN'S GREATEST ADVENTURE, 1959
TARZAN'S THREE CHALLENGES, 1963
TASTE OF SIN, A, 1983
TATTOOED STRANGER, THE, 1950
TEA AND RICE, 1964
TEACHER'S PET, 1958
TEARS FOR SIMON, 1957
TELEFON, 1977
10, 1979
10 RILLINGTON PLACE, 1971
TENANT, THE, 1976
TENNESSEE JOHNSON, 1942
TENNESSEE'S PARTNER, 1955
TENTH VICTIM, THE, 1965
TEOREMA, 1969
TERESA, 1951
TERMINATOR, THE, 1984
TERRACE, THE, 1964
TESS, 1980
TEX, 1982
TEXAN, THE, 1930
TEXAS CHAIN SAW MASSACRE, THE, 1974
THANK YOU ALL VERY MUCH, 1969
THANK YOU, AUNT, 1969
THANKS A MILLION, 1935
THARK, 1932
THAT DARN CAT, 1965
THAT FORSYTE WOMAN, 1949
THAT GIRL FROM PARIS, 1937
THAT MAN FROM RIO, 1964
THAT MIDNIGHT KISS, 1949
THAT NIGHT, 1957

THAT NIGHT IN RIO, 1941
THAT SINKING FEELING, 1979
THAT WONDERFUL URGE, 1948
THAT'LL BE THE DAY, 1974
THEATRE OF BLOOD, 1973
THEATRE ROYAL, 1943
THERE WAS A CROOKED MAN, 1962
THERE WAS A CROOKED MAN, 1970
THERE WAS AN OLD COUPLE, 1967
THERE'S ALWAYS A WOMAN, 1938
THERESE, 1963
THESE ARE THE DAMNED, 1965
THESE THOUSAND HILLS, 1959
THESE WILDER YEARS, 1956
THEY ALL LAUGHED, 1981
THEY GAVE HIM A GUN, 1937
THEY MADE ME A CRIMINAL, 1939
THEY MET IN BOMBAY, 1941
THEY WERE FIVE, 1938
THIEF, THE, 1952
THIEF OF HEARTS, 1984
THIEF OF PARIS, THE, 1967
THIEVES' HIGHWAY, 1949
THIN LINE, THE, 1967
THINGS OF LIFE, THE, 1970
THINK FAST, MR. MOTO, 1937
THIRD KEY, THE, 1957
THIRD LOVER, THE, 1963
THIRD VOICE, THE, 1960
THIRTEEN, THE, 1937
13 MEN AND A GUN, 1938
THIRTEENTH LETTER, THE, 1951
—30—, 1959
36 HOURS, 1965
THIS GREEN HELL, 1936
THIS IS THE ARMY, 1943
THIS IS THE LIFE, 1933
THIS ISLAND EARTH, 1955
THIS SPECIAL FRIENDSHIP, 1967
THIS THING CALLED LOVE, 1940
THIS WINE OF LOVE, 1948
THOMAS CROWN AFFAIR, THE, 1968
THOROUGHLY MODERN MILLIE, 1967
THOSE CALLOWAYS, 1964
THOSE HIGH GREY WALLS, 1939
THOSE LIPS, THOSE EYES, 1980
THOSE WERE THE DAYS, 1934
THOSE WERE THE DAYS, 1940
THOUSAND AND ONE NIGHTS, A, 1945
THOUSAND CRANES, 1969
THREE, 1967
THREE, 1969
THREE BLIND MICE, 1938
THREE BROTHERS, 1982
THREE CASES OF MURDER, 1955
THREE COINS IN THE FOUNTAIN, 1954
THREE-CORNERED MOON, 1933
THREE CROWNS OF THE SAILOR, 1984
THREE HOURS TO KILL, 1954
THREE LITTLE GIRLS IN BLUE, 1946
THREE LIVES OF THOMASINA, THE, 1963
THREE MEN FROM TEXAS, 1940
THREE MEN ON A HORSE, 1936
THREE ON A MATCH, 1932
THREE SMART GIRLS, 1937
THREE SMART GIRLS GROW UP, 1939
THREE WOMEN, 1977
THREEPENNY OPERA, THE, 1931
THRILL OF IT ALL, THE, 1963
THROUGH A GLASS DARKLY, 1962
THUMBELINA, 1970
THUNDER BAY, 1953
THUNDER IN THE CITY, 1937
THUNDER IN THE EAST, 1953
THUNDER ON THE HILL, 1951
THUNDER ROAD, 1958
THUNDERBOLT, 1929
THUNDERHOOF, 1948
THX 1138, 1971
TICKET TO HEAVEN, 1981
TIGHT LITTLE ISLAND, 1949
'TIL WE MEET AGAIN, 1940
TILL THE CLOUDS ROLL BY, 1946
TILL THE END OF TIME, 1946
TILLIE AND GUS, 1933
TIME AFTER TIME, 1979

TIME BANDITS, 1981
TIME FOR DYING, A, 1971
TIME OF ROSES, 1970
TIN MEN, 1987
TIN STAR, THE, 1957
TO HELL AND BACK, 1955
TO LIVE IN PEACE, 1947
TO LOVE, 1964
TO SIR, WITH LOVE, 1967
TO THE ENDS OF THE EARTH, 1948
TO THE SHORES OF TRIPOLI, 1942
TOAST OF NEW ORLEANS, THE, 1950
TOBY TYLER, 1960
TOGETHER AGAIN, 1944
TOGETHER BROTHERS, 1974
TOKYO JOE, 1949
TOKYO POP, 1988
TOM SAWYER, 1930
TONIGHT AND EVERY NIGHT, 1945
TONIGHT AT 8:30, 1953
TONY ROME, 1967
TOO HOT TO HANDLE, 1938
TOO LATE FOR TEARS, 1949
TOO LATE THE HERO, 1970
TOO MANY HUSBANDS, 1940
TOP SECRET!, 1984
TOP SPEED, 1930
TOPPER RETURNS, 1941
TORN CURTAIN, 1966
TOUCH AND GO, 1986
TOUGH GUY, 1936
TOVARICH, 1937
TOWARD THE UNKNOWN, 1956
TOWER OF LONDON, 1939
TOWN ON TRIAL, 1957
TRACK OF THE CAT, 1954
TRACKS, 1977
TRADE WINDS, 1938
TRADER HORN, 1931
TRAIL RIDERS, 1942
TRAIL STREET, 1947
TRAILING THE KILLER, 1932
TRAIN GOES EAST, THE, 1949
TRAIN OF EVENTS, 1952
TRANS-EUROP-EXPRESS, 1968
TRANSATLANTIC TUNNEL, 1935
TRAPPED, 1937
TRAVELING EXECUTIONER, THE, 1970
TRAVELLING AVANT, 1988
TRAVELLING NORTH, 1988
TRAVELS WITH MY AUNT, 1972
TREASURE OF THE GOLDEN CONDOR, 1953
TRIAL OF JOAN OF ARC, 1965
TRIAL OF MARY DUGAN, THE, 1929
TRIAL, THE, 1963
TRIBUTE TO A BADMAN, 1956
TRIPLE CROSS, 1967
TRIUMPH OF SHERLOCK HOLMES, THE, 1935
TROIKA, 1969
TRON, 1982
TROUBLE ALONG THE WAY, 1953
TROUBLE BREWING, 1939
TROUBLE-FETE, 1964
TROUBLE PREFERRED, 1949
TROUBLEMAKER, THE, 1964
TRUE CONFESSION, 1937
TRUE STORY OF ESKIMO NELL, THE, 1975
TRUE STORY OF JESSE JAMES, THE, 1957
TRUE STORY OF LYNN STUART, THE, 1958
TRUMAN CAPOTE'S TRILOGY, 1969
TRUTH ABOUT SPRING, THE, 1965
TSAR'S BRIDE, THE, 1966
TURNING POINT, THE, 1952
TURNING POINT, THE, 1977
TWELVE-HANDED MEN OF MARS, THE, 1964
20TH CENTURY OZ, 1977
24 HOURS, 1931
TWENTY MILLION SWEETHEARTS, 1934
TWENTY MULE TEAM, 1940
23 PACES TO BAKER STREET, 1956
TWICE AROUND THE DAFFODILS, 1962
TWICE IN A LIFETIME, 1985
TWICE TOLD TALES, 1963
TWILIGHT PATH, 1965
TWILIGHT WOMEN, 1953
TWIN SISTERS OF KYOTO, 1964

TWINKLE IN GOD'S EYE, THE, 1955
TWO DAUGHTERS, 1963
TWO EYES, TWELVE HANDS, 1958
TWO-FISTED SHERIFF, 1937
TWO FLAGS WEST, 1950
TWO GIRLS AND A SAILOR, 1944
TWO GUYS FROM TEXAS, 1948
TWO-HEADED SPY, THE, 1959
TWO HUNDRED MOTELS, 1971
TWO KOUNEY LEMELS, 1966
TWO MEN IN TOWN, 1973
TWO OR THREE THINGS I KNOW ABOUT HER, 1970
TWO SISTERS FROM BOSTON, 1946
TWO TICKETS TO BROADWAY, 1951
ULYSSES, 1955
ULYSSES, 1967
ULZANA'S RAID, 1972
UNCERTAIN GLORY, 1944
UNCLE, THE, 1966
UNDER FIRE, 1983
UNDER MILK WOOD, 1973
UNDER MY SKIN, 1950
UNDER SATAN'S SUN, 1988
UNDER THE SUN OF ROME, 1949
UNEARTHLY STRANGER, THE, 1964
UNFINISHED BUSINESS, 1985
UNFINISHED SYMPHONY, THE, 1953
UNFORGIVEN, THE, 1960
UNHOLY THREE, THE, 1930
UNIVERSITY OF LIFE, 1941
UNSINKABLE MOLLY BROWN, THE, 1964
UNSUITABLE JOB FOR A WOMAN, AN, 1982
UP FRONT, 1951
UP THE CREEK, 1958
UP THE CREEK, 1984
UP THE RIVER, 1930
UP TO HIS EARS, 1966
UPTOWN SATURDAY NIGHT, 1974
VACATION FROM MARRIAGE, 1945
VAGABOND KING, THE, 1930
VAGABOND KING, THE, 1956
VALACHI PAPERS, THE, 1972
VALIANT, THE, 1929
VALLEY OF DECISION, THE, 1945
VAMPIRE BAT, THE, 1933
VAMPIRES IN HAVANA, 1987
VARIETY GIRL, 1947
VELVET TOUCH, THE, 1948
VENGEANCE IS MINE, 1980
VERA, 1987
VERA CRUZ, 1954
VERBOTEN?, 1959
VERY HAPPY ALEXANDER, 1969
VICTIM, 1961
VICTOR/VICTORIA, 1982
VIGIL, 1984
VIKINGS, THE, 1958
VILLAGE OF THE DAMNED, 1960
VIOLENT MEN, THE, 1955
VIOLETTE, 1978
VIRGIN QUEEN, THE, 1955
VIRGIN SPRING, THE, 1960
VIRTUE, 1932
VIRUS HAS NO MORALS, A, 1986
VISA U.S.A., 1987
VOICE OF THE TURTLE, THE, 1947
VOLUNTEERS, 1985
W.C. FIELDS AND ME, 1976
WAGNER, 1983
WAGONS ROLL AT NIGHT, THE, 1941
WAIKIKI WEDDING, 1937
WAITING FOR THE MOON, 1987
WAKE ME WHEN IT'S OVER, 1960
WAKE UP AND LIVE, 1937
WALK, DON'T RUN, 1966
WALK EAST ON BEACON, 1952
WALK IN THE SHADOW, 1966
WALK ON THE MOON, A, 1987
WALKER, 1987
WALKING HILLS, THE, 1949
WALKING ON AIR, 1936
WALKOVER, 1969
WALL STREET, 1987
WALL, THE, 1985
WALLS OF MALAPAGA, THE, 1950
WALTZ OF THE TOREADORS, 1962

BOLD: Films on Videocassette

WANDERING JEW, THE, 1948
WANNSEE CONFERENCE, THE, 1987
WAR AGAINST MRS. HADLEY, THE, 1942
WAR LORD, THE, 1965
WAR LOVER, THE, 1962
WAR OF THE BUTTONS, 1963
WAR OF THE WORLDS—NEXT CENTURY, THE, 1981
WARGAMES, 1983
WARRIOR'S HUSBAND THE, 1933
WARRIORS, THE, 1955
WATERHOLE NO. 3, 1967
WATERSHIP DOWN, 1978
WAY WE LIVE, THE, 1946
WAY WE WERE, THE, 1973
WE THREE, 1985
WEB, THE, 1947
WEDDING NIGHT, THE, 1935
WEDDINGS AND BABIES, 1960
WEE GEORDIE, 1956
WEE WILLIE WINKIE, 1937
WEEKEND, 1968
WEEKEND AT THE WALDORF, 1945
WEEKEND MURDERS, THE, 1972
WEEKEND OF SHADOWS, 1978
WELCOME STRANGER, 1947
WELCOME TO GERMANY, 1988
WELL, THE, 1951
WE'RE NO ANGELS, 1955
WE'RE NOT DRESSING, 1934
WEST OF THE PECOS, 1935
WEST OF THE PECOS, 1945
WESTWARD THE WOMEN, 1951
WE'VE NEVER BEEN LICKED, 1943
WHALES OF AUGUST, THE, 1987
WHAT EVER HAPPENED TO AUNT ALICE?, 1969
WHAT NEXT, CORPORAL HARGROVE?, 1945
WHAT PRICE HOLLYWOOD?, 1932
WHAT WOULD YOU SAY TO SOME SPINACH, 1976
WHAT'S UP, DOC?, 1972
WHEN A STRANGER CALLS, 1979
WHEN A WOMAN ASCENDS THE STAIRS, 1963
WHEN MY BABY SMILES AT ME, 1948
WHEN NATURE CALLS, 1985
WHEN THE LEGENDS DIE, 1972
WHEN YOU'RE IN LOVE, 1937
WHERE DANGER LIVES, 1950
WHERE THE GREEN ANTS DREAM, 1985
WHERE THERE'S A WILL, 1936
WHIPSAW, 1936
WHIRLPOOL, 1949
WHISPERING CITY, 1947
WHISTLER, THE, 1944
WHISTLING IN THE DARK, 1941
WHITE CARGO, 1942
WHITE CHRISTMAS, 1954
WHITE FACE, 1933
WHITE FEATHER, 1955
WHITE LIGHTNING, 1973
WHITE NIGHTS, 1961
WHITE OF THE EYE, 1988
WHITE SISTER, THE, 1933
WHITE VOICES, 1965
WHITE WITCH DOCTOR, 1953
WHITE ZOMBIE, 1932
WHO FEARS THE DEVIL, 1972
WHO IS KILLING THE GREAT CHEFS OF EUROPE?, 1978
WHO KILLED JESSIE?, 1965
WHO WAS THAT LADY?, 1960
WHOLE SHOOTIN' MATCH, THE, 1979
WHO'S THAT KNOCKING AT MY DOOR?, 1968
WHOSE LIFE IS IT ANYWAY?, 1981
WHY SHOOT THE TEACHER, 1977
WICKED GO TO HELL, THE, 1961
WIDE OPEN TOWN, 1941
WIFE, HUSBAND AND FRIEND, 1939
WILD BLUE YONDER, THE, 1952
WILD CHILD, THE, 1970
WILD IS THE WIND, 1957
WILL SUCCESS SPOIL ROCK HUNTER?, 1957
WILSON, 1944
WINDOM'S WAY, 1958
WING AND A PRAYER, 1944
WINGS OF THE MORNING, 1937
WINNING, 1969
WINTER WIND, 1970

WISE BLOOD, 1979
WISHING MACHINE, 1971
WITH A SMILE, 1939
WITH SIX YOU GET EGGROLL, 1968
WITHNAIL AND I, 1987
WITHOUT APPARENT MOTIVE, 1972
WITNESS OUT OF HELL, 1967
WITNESS TO MURDER, 1954
WOLF SONG, 1929
WOMAN IN FLAMES, A, 1984
WOMAN IN HIDING, 1949
WOMAN IN RED, THE, 1935
WOMAN IN WHITE, THE, 1948
WOMAN NEXT DOOR, THE, 1981
WOMAN ON THE BEACH, THE, 1947
WOMAN'S FACE, A, 1939
WOMAN'S WORLD, 1954
WOMEN IN A DRESSING GOWN, 1957
WONDER BAR, 1934
WONDER MAN, 1945
WONDERFUL COUNTRY, THE, 1959
WORKING GIRLS, 1986
WORLD CHANGES, THE, 1933
WORLD FOR RANSOM, 1954
WORLD IN HIS ARMS, THE, 1952
WORLD OF HENRY ORIENT, THE, 1964
WORLD'S GREATEST ATHLETE, THE, 1973
WRONG ARM OF THE LAW, THE, 1963
WRONG BOX, THE, 1966
XICA, 1982
YANK AT OXFORD, A, 1938
YANK IN THE R.A.F., A, 1941
YASEMIN, 1988
YELLOW EARTH, 1986
YELLOW SANDS, 1938
YESTERDAY, TODAY, AND TOMORROW, 1963
YO YO, 1967
YOLANDA AND THE THIEF, 1945
YOU AND ME, 1938
YOU BELONG TO ME, 1941
YOU CAN'T GET AWAY WITH MURDER, 1939
YOU CAN'T HAVE EVERYTHING, 1937
YOU GOTTA STAY HAPPY, 1948
YOU'LL LIKE MY MOTHER, 1972
YOU'LL NEVER GET RICH, 1941
YOUNG AT HEART, 1955
YOUNG CASSIDY, 1965
YOUNG HUSBANDS, 1958
YOUNG LORD, THE, 1970
YOUNG MAN WITH IDEAS, 1952
YOUNG MAN'S FANCY, 1943
YOUNG NOWHERES, 1929
YOUNG PEOPLE, 1940
YOUNG PHILADELPHIANS, THE, 1959
YOUNG SAVAGES, THE, 1961
YOUNG SHERLOCK HOLMES, 1985
YOUNG STRANGER, THE, 1957
YOUNG TOM EDISON, 1940
YOUNG WIVES' TALE, 1954
YOUNGBLOOD, 1978
YOUR CHEATIN' HEART, 1964
YOUR PAST IS SHOWING, 1958
YOU'RE A BIG BOY NOW, 1966
YOU'RE IN THE NAVY NOW, 1951
YOURS, MINE AND OURS, 1968
ZAPPA, 1984
ZERO HOUR!, 1957
ZIGZAG, 1970
ZULU DAWN, 1980

2.5 Stars
A NOS AMOURS, 1984
ABBOTT AND COSTELLO MEET THE INVISIBLE MAN, 1951
ABOVE THE LAW, 1988
ABSENCE OF MALICE, 1981
ABUSED CONFIDENCE, 1938
ACCENT ON YOUTH, 1935
ACCEPTABLE LEVELS, 1983
ACCUSED, THE, 1988
ACCUSED, 1936
ACCUSED OF MURDER, 1956
ACCUSING FINGER, THE, 1936
ACT OF LOVE, 1953
ACT ONE, 1964
ACTION FOR SLANDER, 1937

ACTORS AND SIN, 1952
ACTRESS, THE, 1953
ADAM'S WOMAN, 1972
ADERYN PAPUR, 1984
ADORABLE, 1933
ADVANCE TO THE REAR, 1964
ADVENTURE IN BALTIMORE, 1949
ADVENTURE IN DIAMONDS, 1940
ADVENTURE IN MANHATTAN, 1936
ADVENTURE IN THE HOPFIELDS, 1954
ADVENTURE OF SALVATOR ROSA, AN, 1940
ADVENTURERS, THE, 1951
ADVENTURES IN BABYSITTING, 1987
ADVENTURES OF ARSENE LUPIN, 1956
ADVENTURES OF GALLANT BESS, 1948
ADVENTURES OF HUCKLEBERRY FINN, THE, 1960
ADVENTURES OF KITTY O'DAY, 1944
ADVENTUROUS BLONDE, 1937
ADVERSARY, THE, 1973
AERIAL GUNNER, 1943
AFFAIR LAFONT, THE, 1939
AFFAIRS OF MARTHA, THE, 1942
AFFECTIONATELY YOURS, 1941
AFTER THE BALL, 1957
AGAINST ALL FLAGS, 1952
AGAINST THE WIND, 1948
A-HAUNTING WE WILL GO, 1942
AIN'T MISBEHAVIN', 1955
AIR HAWKS, 1935
AIR RAID WARDENS, 1943
AIRPLANE!, 1980
AKE AND HIS WORLD, 1985
ALAKAZAM THE GREAT!, 1961
ALEXANDER HAMILTON, 1931
ALF 'N' FAMILY, 1968
ALI BABA GOES TO TOWN, 1937
ALIAS BIG SHOT, 1962
ALIAS JESSE JAMES, 1959
ALIBI, THE, 1943
ALICE DOESN'T LIVE HERE ANYMORE, 1975
ALICE IN WONDERLAND, 1951
ALICE, OR THE LAST ESCAPADE, 1977
ALL FALL DOWN, 1962
ALL I DESIRE, 1953
ALL IN A NIGHT'S WORK, 1961
ALL NIGHT LONG, 1981
ALL OF ME, 1934
ALL THAT JAZZ, 1979
ALL THE YOUNG MEN, 1960
ALMOST TRANSPARENT BLUE, 1980
ALMOST YOU, 1984
ALOHA SUMMER, 1988
ALONG THE GREAT DIVIDE, 1951
ALSINO AND THE CONDOR, 1983
ALVAREZ KELLY, 1966
ALVIN PURPLE, 1974
ALWAYS TOGETHER, 1947
AMAZING MR. WILLIAMS, 1939
AMAZING MONSIEUR FABRE, THE, 1952
AMELIE OR THE TIME TO LOVE, 1961
AMERICAN NINJA 2: THE CONFRONTATION, 1987
AMERICAN WEREWOLF IN LONDON, AN, 1981
AMONG THE CINDERS, 1985
AMOROUS ADVENTURES OF MOLL FLANDERS, THE, 1965
AMSTERDAM AFFAIR, THE, 1968
AMY, 1981
ANATOMY OF A MARRIAGE (MY DAYS WITH JEAN-MARC AND MY NIGHTS WITH FRANCOISE), 1964
AND NOW TOMORROW, 1944
AND QUIET FLOWS THE DON, 1960
AND SUDDENLY IT'S MURDER!, 1964
ANDERSON TAPES, THE, 1971
ANDROMEDA STRAIN, THE, 1971
ANDY, 1965
ANDY HARDY MEETS DEBUTANTE, 1940
ANDY HARDY'S DOUBLE LIFE, 1942
ANDY WARHOL'S FRANKENSTEIN, 1974
ANGEL, 1937
ANGEL HEART, 1987
ANGELS WASH THEIR FACES, 1939
ANGRY ISLAND, 1960
ANGRY SILENCE, THE, 1960
ANNA, 1951

ANNA, 1981
ANNA LUCASTA, 1958
ANOTHER FACE, 1935
ANOTHER LOVE STORY, 1986
ANY NUMBER CAN PLAY, 1949
ANY WHICH WAY YOU CAN, 1980
ANYTHING GOES, 1956
APACHE WARRIOR, 1957
APPOINTMENT WITH CRIME, 1945
APRIL FOOLS, THE, 1969
APRIL SHOWERS, 1948
ARABIAN NIGHTS, 1980
ARE HUSBANDS NECESSARY?, 1942
ARE YOU WITH IT?, 1948
AREN'T WE WONDERFUL?, 1959
ARIZONA RAIDERS, 1965
ARIZONA RANGER, THE, 1948
ARIZONA TO BROADWAY, 1933
ARMORED CAR, 1937
ARMORED COMMAND, 1961
AROUND THE WORLD, 1943
ARROWHEAD, 1953
ARSENE LUPIN RETURNS, 1938
ART OF LOVE, THE, 1965
ARTHUR'S HALLOWED GROUND, 1986
ARTISTS AND MODELS, 1955
ARTISTS AND MODELS ABROAD, 1938
AS HUSBANDS GO, 1934
ASHANTI, 1979
AT GUNPOINT, 1955
AT SWORD'S POINT, 1951
AT WAR WITH THE ARMY, 1950
ATHENA, 1954
ATRAGON, 1965
AU REVOIR LES ENFANTS, 1988
AUNT CLARA, 1954
AUNT FROM CHICAGO, 1960
AUSTERLITZ, 1960
AUTUMN, 1988
AVENGING FORCE, 1986
AWFUL TRUTH, THE, 1929
BABY BLUE MARINE, 1976
BABY MAKER, THE, 1970
BABY: SECRET OF A LOST LEGEND, 1985
BACHELOR'S DAUGHTERS, THE, 1946
BACK AT THE FRONT, 1952
BACK STREET, 1932
BACK STREETS OF PARIS, 1962
BACK TO THE BEACH, 1987
BACKFIRE, 1950
BAD BASCOMB, 1946
BAD LANDS, 1939
BAD MAN, THE, 1941
BAD MEN OF MISSOURI, 1941
BAD MEN OF TOMBSTONE, 1949
BADLANDS OF DAKOTA, 1941
BADMAN'S COUNTRY, 1958
BALALAIKA, 1939
BALLAD OF JOSIE, 1968
BALTIMORE BULLET, THE, 1980
BAMBOO BLONDE, THE, 1946
BANANA PEEL, 1965
BANG! YOU'RE DEAD, 1954
BAR SINISTER, THE, 1955
BATHING BEAUTY, 1944
BATMAN, 1966
BATTLE, THE, 1934
BATTLE CRY, 1955
BATTLE CRY, 1959
BATTLE FLAME, 1959
BATTLE OF THE RAILS, 1949
BATTLETRUCK, 1982
BAWDY ADVENTURES OF TOM JONES, THE, 1976
BAY BOY, 1984
BAY OF ANGELS, 1964
BEACH BALL, 1965
BEACHCOMBER, 1955
BEAR, THE, 1984
BEAT STREET, 1984
BEAU JAMES, 1957
BEAUTY AND THE DEVIL, 1952
BEBO'S GIRL, 1964
BECAUSE OF HIM, 1946
BEDTIME FOR BONZO, 1951
BEFORE DAWN, 1933
BEHAVE YOURSELF, 1951

BEHIND THE EIGHT BALL, 1942
BEHIND THE MASK, 1958
BELLE OF THE NINETIES, 1934
BELLES ON THEIR TOES, 1952
BELLMAN, THE, 1947
BELLS GO DOWN, THE, 1943
BELOW THE BELT, 1980
BEN, 1972
BENNY GOODMAN STORY, THE, 1956
BERLIN CORRESPONDENT, 1942
BERLIN EXPRESS, 1948
BERNADETTE OF LOURDES, 1962
BEST HOUSE IN LONDON, THE, 1969
BETRAYAL, 1939
BETRAYED, 1988
BETTER OFF DEAD, 1985
BETWEEN HEAVEN AND HELL, 1956
BETWEEN TWO WORLDS, 1944
BEYOND GLORY, 1948
BIG BRAWL, THE, 1980
BIG BROADCAST OF 1936, THE, 1935
BIG BROWN EYES, 1936
BIG BUS, THE, 1976
BIG CHIEF, THE, 1960
BIG CIRCUS, THE, 1959
BIG CITY, 1937
BIG CITY, 1948
BIG FIX, THE, 1978
BIG MEAT EATER, 1984
BIG NOISE, THE, 1944
BIG OPERATOR, THE, 1959
BIG POND, THE, 1930
BIG SHOT, THE, 1942
BIG STORE, THE, 1941
BIG STREET, THE, 1942
BIG TOP PEE-WEE, 1988
BIG TOWN GIRL, 1937
BIG TROUBLE, 1986
BILL OF DIVORCEMENT, 1940
BILLY BUDD, 1962
BILLY THE KID, 1941
BILLY TWO HATS, 1973
BINGO BONGO, 1983
**BINGO LONG TRAVELING ALL-STARS AND MOTOR
     KINGS, THE, 1976**
BIOGRAPHY OF A BACHELOR GIRL, 1935
BIRD OF PARADISE, 1932
BIRDS AND THE BEES, THE, 1965
BISCUIT EATER, THE, 1972
BITTER SWEET, 1933
BITTER TEARS OF PETRA VON KANT, THE, 1972
BITTER VICTORY, 1958
BLACK BART, 1948
BLACK BEAUTY, 1946
BLACK CAESAR, 1973
BLACK CAMEL, THE, 1931
BLACK JACK, 1979
BLACK JOY, 1977
BLACK JOY, 1986
BLACK KNIGHT, THE, 1954
BLACK MARBLE, THE, 1980
BLACK MOON, 1975
BLACK MOON RISING, 1986
BLACK SHIELD OF FALWORTH, THE, 1954
BLACK WIDOW, 1987
BLACK WINDMILL, THE, 1974
BLACKBEARD THE PIRATE, 1952
BLACKMAIL, 1939
BLACKOUT, 1940
BLACKWELL'S ISLAND, 1939
BLANCHE FURY, 1948
BLAST OF SILENCE, 1961
BLAZE O' GLORY, 1930
BLONDIE, 1938
BLONDIE OF THE FOLLIES, 1932
BLOOD AND GUTS, 1978
BLOOD BEAST FROM OUTER SPACE, 1965
BLOODBROTHERS, 1978
BLOODY KIDS, 1983
BLOSSOMS IN THE DUST, 1941
BLUE ANGEL, THE, 1959
BLUE FIN, 1978
BLUE GRASS OF KENTUCKY, 1950
BLUE LAGOON, THE, 1949
BLUE MURDER AT ST. TRINIAN'S, 1958
BLUE SUNSHINE, 1978

BLUE VEIL, THE, 1951
BLUE, WHITE, AND PERFECT, 1941
BLUEBEARD, 1944
BMX BANDITS, 1983
BOARDWALK, 1979
BOATNIKS, THE, 1970
BOB MATHIAS STORY, THE, 1954
BODY DISAPPEARS, THE, 1941
BODYGUARD, 1948
BOLD CABALLERO, 1936
BOLERO, 1934
BOND STREET, 1948
BONNE CHANCE, 1935
BONNIE PARKER STORY, THE, 1958
BOOK OF NUMBERS, 1973
BOOTHILL BRIGADE, 1937
BORDER HEAT, 1988
BORDER LAW, 1931
BORDER PHANTOM, 1937
BORDER RIVER, 1954
BORDER, THE, 1982
BORDERLINE, 1950
BORN AGAIN, 1978
BORN FOR GLORY, 1935
BORN IN EAST L.A., 1987
BORN IN FLAMES, 1983
BORN RECKLESS, 1930
BORN TO THE WEST, 1937
BORN TO WIN, 1971
BORSALINO AND CO., 1974
BOSS'S SON, THE, 1978
BOSTON BLACKIE AND THE LAW, 1946
BOSTON BLACKIE'S RENDEZVOUS, 1945
BOTANY BAY, 1953
BOULEVARD NIGHTS, 1979
BOUNTY HUNTER, THE, 1954
BOXCAR BERTHA, 1972
BOY AND THE PIRATES, THE, 1960
BOY, DID I GET A WRONG NUMBER!, 1966
BOY FROM OKLAHOMA, THE, 1954
BOY NAMED CHARLIE BROWN, A, 1969
BRADY'S ESCAPE, 1984
BRAIN DAMAGE, 1988
BRAIN, THE, 1969
BRAINWASHED, 1961
BRAINWAVES, 1983
BRANNIGAN, 1975
BREAD AND CHOCOLATE, 1978
BREAD, LOVE AND DREAMS, 1953
BREAK OF HEARTS, 1935
BREAKFAST CLUB, THE, 1985
BREAKFAST FOR TWO, 1937
BREAKIN', 1984
BREAKING AWAY, 1979
BREAKING GLASS, 1980
BREAKTHROUGH, 1950
BREAKTHROUGH, 1978
BREWSTER McCLOUD, 1970
BRIDAL PATH, THE, 1959
BRIDE, THE, 1985
BRIDE OF THE LAKE, 1934
BRIDE OF THE REGIMENT, 1930
BRIDE OF VENGEANCE, 1949
BRIDE WALKS OUT, THE, 1936
BRIDES ARE LIKE THAT, 1936
BRIDES OF DRACULA, THE, 1960
BRIDGE TO THE SUN, 1961
BRIEF MOMENT, 1933
BRIGHT LIGHTS, 1935
BRIGHT LIGHTS, BIG CITY, 1988
BRIGHTON STRANGLER, THE, 1945
BRINK'S JOB, THE, 1978
BROADWAY BAD, 1933
BROADWAY GONDOLIER, 1935
BROADWAY MUSKETEERS, 1938
BROADWAY SERENADE, 1939
BROADWAY THROUGH A KEYHOLE, 1933
BROADWAY TO HOLLYWOOD, 1933
BROKEN MIRRORS, 1985
BRONCO BUSTER, 1952
BROTHER FROM ANOTHER PLANET, THE, 1984
BROTHER RAT AND A BABY, 1940
BROTHERLY LOVE, 1970
BROTHERS IN LAW, 1957
BROTHERS RICO, THE, 1957
BUCK PRIVATES, 1941

BOLD: Films on Videocassette

BUCK PRIVATES COME HOME, 1947
BUDDIES, 1983
BUDDIES, 1985
BULLET CODE, 1940
BULLET FOR A BADMAN, 1964
BULLET FOR JOEY, A, 1955
BULLET FOR THE GENERAL, A, 1967
BULLSHOT, 1983
BURNING AN ILLUSION, 1982
BUS RILEY'S BACK IN TOWN, 1965
BUSH CHRISTMAS, 1947
BUSHBABY, THE, 1970
BUSMAN'S HONEYMOON, 1940
BUSSES ROAR, 1942
BUSTER, 1988
BUSYBODY, THE, 1967
BUT NOT FOR ME, 1959
BUTCH MINDS THE BABY, 1942
BUTTERFLIES ARE FREE, 1972
BUY ME THAT TOWN, 1941
BY CANDLELIGHT, 1934
C-MAN, 1949
CACTUS, 1986
CADDIE, 1976
CAFE EXPRESS, 1980
CAIRO, 1942
CALABUCH, 1956
CALAMITY JANE, 1953
CALL ME GENIUS, 1961
CALLAN, 1975
CALTIKI, THE IMMORTAL MONSTER, 1959
CAME A HOT FRIDAY, 1985
CAMILA, 1985
CAMORRA, 1986
CAMP ON BLOOD ISLAND, THE, 1958
CAMPBELL'S KINGDOM, 1957
CAMPUS MAN, 1987
CANARY MURDER CASE, THE, 1929
CANDLELIGHT IN ALGERIA, 1944
CANDLESHOE, 1978
CANNON AND THE NIGHTINGALE, THE, 1969
CANON CITY, 1948
CAN'T HELP SINGING, 1944
CANTERBURY TALE, A, 1944
CANYON CROSSROADS, 1955
CAPTAIN CAREY, U.S.A., 1950
CAPTAIN EDDIE, 1945
CAPTAIN KIDD, 1945
CAPTAIN NEMO AND THE UNDERWATER CITY, 1969
CAPTAIN NEWMAN, M.D., 1963
CAPTAIN PIRATE, 1952
CAPTAINS OF THE CLOUDS, 1942
CAPTAIN'S TABLE, THE, 1960
CAPTIVE OF BILLY THE KID, 1952
CAR 99, 1935
CARAVAGGIO, 1986
CARBON COPY, 1981
CARDINAL RICHELIEU, 1935
CARE BEARS MOVIE, THE, 1985
CAREER, 1959
CAREFUL, HE MIGHT HEAR YOU, 1984
CARELESS YEARS, THE, 1957
CARETAKERS, THE, 1963
CARGO TO CAPETOWN, 1950
CARIBBEAN MYSTERY, THE, 1945
CARMEN, 1946
CARNEGIE HALL, 1947
CARNIVAL, 1953
CARNIVAL STORY, 1954
CAROLLIE CHERIE, 1951
CARRIE, 1976
CARRY ON ADMIRAL, 1957
CARRY ON CABBIE, 1963
CARRY ON CAMPING, 1969
CARRY ON CONSTABLE, 1960
CARRY ON NURSE, 1959
CARRY ON SERGEANT, 1959
CARRY ON SPYING, 1964
CARRY ON, UP THE KHYBER, 1968
CARSON CITY, 1952
CASANOVA IN BURLESQUE, 1944
CASE AGAINST BROOKLYN, THE, 1958
CASE OF DR. LAURENT, 1958
CASE OF THE LUCKY LEGS, THE, 1935
CASH ON DELIVERY, 1956

CASTLE OF BLOOD, 1964
CASTLE ON THE HUDSON, 1940
CASUAL SEX?, 1988
CAT, THE, 1975
CAT PEOPLE, 1982
CATCH ME A SPY, 1971
CATCH MY SOUL, 1974
CATHY'S CHILD, 1979
CATMAN OF PARIS, THE, 1946
CATTLE ANNIE AND LITTLE BRITCHES, 1981
CATTLE EMPIRE, 1958
CAVERN, THE, 1965
CEASE FIRE, 1985
CELESTE, 1982
CENTENNIAL SUMMER, 1946
CHAIN LETTERS, 1985
CHAINED, 1934
CHALK GARDEN, THE, 1964
CHALLENGE, THE, 1939
CHALLENGE TO LASSIE, 1949
CHAMP, THE, 1979
CHAMP FOR A DAY, 1953
CHAMPAGNE CHARLIE, 1944
CHAMPAGNE WALTZ, 1937
CHANCE MEETING, 1960
CHANCE OF A LIFETIME, THE, 1943
CHANDU THE MAGICIAN, 1932
CHARGE AT FEATHER RIVER, THE, 1953
CHARLES AND LUCIE, 1982
CHARLES, DEAD OR ALIVE, 1972
CHARLEY AND THE ANGEL, 1973
CHARLIE BUBBLES, 1968
CHARLIE CHAN AT THE CIRCUS, 1936
CHARLIE CHAN AT THE OLYMPICS, 1937
CHARLIE CHAN IN HONOLULU, 1938
CHARLIE CHAN IN LONDON, 1934
CHARLIE CHAN IN PANAMA, 1940
CHARLIE CHAN IN RENO, 1939
CHARLIE CHAN ON BROADWAY, 1937
CHARLIE CHAN'S GREATEST CASE, 1933
CHARLIE, THE LONESOME COUGAR, 1967
CHASER, THE, 1938
CHATTERBOX, 1936
CHEATERS, THE, 1961
CHEATING BLONDES, 1933
CHECKERS, 1937
CHECKPOINT, 1957
CHEERS FOR MISS BISHOP, 1941
CHEREZ TERNII K SVEZDAM, 1981
CHEYENNE, 1947
CHICAGO CONFIDENTIAL, 1957
CHICKEN EVERY SUNDAY, 1948
CHIEF CRAZY HORSE, 1955
CHILD IN THE HOUSE, 1956
CHILD OF DIVORCE, 1946
CHILDREN, THE, 1949
CHILDREN OF HIROSHIMA, 1952
CHILDREN SHOULDN'T PLAY WITH DEAD THINGS, 1972
CHILD'S PLAY, 1988
CHILLY SCENES OF WINTER, 1982
CHINA DOLL, 1958
CHINA GIRL, 1987
CHINA IS NEAR, 1968
CHINA 9, LIBERTY 37, 1978
CHINA SKY, 1945
CHIPMUNK ADVENTURE, THE, 1987
CHITTY CHITTY BANG BANG, 1968
CHOIRBOYS, THE, 1977
CHRISTMAS EVE, 1947
CHRISTMAS KID, THE, 1968
CHRISTOPHER COLUMBUS, 1949
CHRONICLE OF ANNA MAGDALENA BACH, 1968
CHUMP AT OXFORD, A, 1940
CIRCLE, THE, 1959
CIRCUS QUEEN MURDER, THE, 1933
CISCO KID AND THE LADY, THE, 1939
CITY ACROSS THE RIVER, 1949
CITY GIRL, THE, 1984
CITY LIMITS, 1985
CITY NEWS, 1983
CITY OF FEAR, 1959
CITY OF SECRETS, 1963
CITY OF YOUTH, 1938
CLARENCE AND ANGEL, 1981
CLARETTA AND BEN, 1983

CLASH OF THE TITANS, 1981
CLASS RELATIONS, 1986
CLAY PIGEON, THE, 1949
CLIMAX, THE, 1944
CLIMAX, THE, 1967
CLIMBING HIGH, 1938
CLOSE CALL FOR BOSTON BLACKIE, A, 1946
CLOSE HARMONY, 1929
CLOSE TO MY HEART, 1951
CLOUDBURST, 1952
CLOUDS OVER ISRAEL, 1966
CLUB, THE, 1980
CLUE OF THE NEW PIN, THE, 1961
CLUE OF THE SILVER KEY, THE, 1961
COBWEB, THE, 1955
COCK O' THE WALK, 1930
COCKEYED MIRACLE, THE, 1946
COCOANUT GROVE, 1938
COCOON: THE RETURN, 1988
CODE NAME: EMERALD, 1985
CODE OF SCOTLAND YARD, 1948
CODE TWO, 1953
COHENS AND KELLYS IN SCOTLAND, THE, 1930
COLLEGE HOLIDAY, 1936
COLORADO SUNSET, 1939
COLT .45, 1950
COMANCHE, 1956
COMANCHEROS, THE, 1961
COME BACK TO THE 5 & DIME, JIMMY DEAN, JIMMY DEAN, 1982
COME NEXT SPRING, 1956
COME ON, THE, 1956
COME ON DANGER!, 1932
COME OUT OF THE PANTRY, 1935
COME SEPTEMBER, 1961
COMEDIANS, THE, 1967
COMEDY MAN, THE, 1964
COMING-OUT PARTY, A, 1962
COMING TO AMERICA, 1988
COMMANDO, 1962
COMMANDO, 1985
COMMON TOUCH, THE, 1941
COMPANY SHE KEEPS, THE, 1950
COMPLIMENTS OF MR. FLOW, 1941
CONCERNING MR. MARTIN, 1937
CONDEMNED, 1929
CONDORMAN, 1981
CONFESS DR. CORDA, 1960
CONFESSION, 1937
CONFESSIONS OF A NEWLYWED, 1941
CONFESSIONS OF FELIX KRULL, THE, 1957
CONFESSOR, 1973
CONFIDENCE, 1980
CONFIDENTIAL AGENT, 1945
CONFIDENTIALLY CONNIE, 1953
CONFLICT, 1939
CONGRESS DANCES, 1932
CONJUGAL BED, THE, 1963
CONNECTION, THE, 1962
CONQUERED CITY, 1966
CONQUERING HORDE, THE, 1931
CONQUEST OF THE PLANET OF THE APES, 1972
CONSOLATION MARRIAGE, 1931
CONSPIRACY OF HEARTS, 1960
CONSPIRATORS, THE, 1944
CONSTANT FACTOR, THE, 1980
CONSTANT NYMPH, THE, 1933
CONSTANTINE AND THE CROSS, 1962
CONSUELO, AN ILLUSION, 1988
CONVICT 99, 1938
CONVICTED, 1931
CONVOY, 1940
COOL WORLD, THE, 1963
COONSKIN, 1975
COPS AND ROBBERS, 1973
COQUETTE, 1929
CORDELIA, 1980
CORNBREAD, EARL AND ME, 1975
CORPSE CAME C.O.D., THE, 1947
CORRIDOR OF MIRRORS, 1948
COSMIC MAN, THE, 1959
COUCH TRIP, THE, 1988
COUNT FIVE AND DIE, 1958
COUNT THREE AND PRAY, 1955
COUNTDOWN AT KUSINI, 1976
COUNTERFEIT PLAN, THE, 1957

COUNTERFEITERS OF PARIS, THE, 1962
COUNTERPOINT, 1967
COUNTRY DOCTOR, THE, 1936
COUNTY FAIR, 1933
COUP DE GRACE, 1978
COURAGE OF THE WEST, 1937
COURT MARTIAL OF MAJOR KELLER, THE, 1961
COURT OF THE PHARAOH, 1985
COURTNEY AFFAIR, THE, 1947
COURTSHIP OF ANDY HARDY, THE, 1942
COVER GIRL KILLER, 1960
COWBOY CANTEEN, 1944
COWBOY FROM BROOKLYN, 1938
CRASH OF SILENCE, 1952
CRASHING HOLLYWOOD, 1937
CRAZY BOYS, 1987
CRAZY DESIRE, 1964
CRAZYLEGS, ALL AMERICAN, 1953
CREATURE FROM THE HAUNTED SEA, 1961
CREMATORS, THE, 1972
CREST OF THE WAVE, 1954
CRIME AGAINST JOE, 1956
CRIME AND PUNISHMENT, U.S.A., 1959
CRIME DOCTOR, 1943
CRIME DOES NOT PAY, 1962
CRIME IN THE STREETS, 1956
CRIME OF DR. FORBES, 1936
CRIME WAVE, 1954
CRIMES AT THE DARK HOUSE, 1940
CRIMINAL CONVERSATION, 1980
CRIMINAL LAWYER, 1951
CRIMSON KEY, THE, 1947
CRIMSON TRAIL, THE, 1935
CRIPPLE CREEK, 1952
CRITTERS, 1986
CROOKS ANONYMOUS, 1963
CROSS COUNTRY, 1983
CROSS MY HEART, 1987
CROSSED SWORDS, 1978
CROSSROADS OF PASSION, 1951
CROSSTALK, 1982
CROSSWINDS, 1951
CROWDED DAY, THE, 1954
CROWDED PARADISE, 1956
CROWDED SKY, THE, 1960
CRUCIFIX, THE, 1934
CRUISIN' DOWN THE RIVER, 1953
CRUSADE AGAINST RACKETS, 1937
CRY BLOOD, APACHE, 1970
CRY FOR HAPPY, 1961
CRY FREEDOM, 1987
CRY HAVOC, 1943
CRY IN THE NIGHT, A, 1956
CRY TOUGH, 1959
CRY WOLF, 1947
CRYSTAL BALL, THE, 1943
CUBAN PETE, 1946
CURE FOR LOVE, THE, 1950
CYNTHIA, 1947
DAD AND DAVE COME TO TOWN, 1938
DAD'S ARMY, 1971
DAFFY DUCK'S MOVIE: FANTASTIC ISLAND, 1983
DAKOTA, 1945
DAKOTA INCIDENT, 1956
DANCE OF DEATH, THE, 1971
DANCE OF LIFE, THE, 1929
DANGER FLIGHT, 1939
DANGER—LOVE AT WORK, 1937
DANGER PATROL, 1937
DANGEROUS CROSSING, 1953
DANGEROUS CURVES, 1929
DANGEROUS EXILE, 1958
DANGEROUS MEDICINE, 1938
DANGEROUS SECRETS, 1938
DANGEROUS WHEN WET, 1953
DANGEROUSLY CLOSE, 1986
DANGEROUSLY THEY LIVE, 1942
DANTON, 1983
DARBY'S RANGERS, 1958
DARK EYES OF LONDON, 1961
DARK SANDS, 1938
DARK STAR, 1975
DARK WATERS, 1944
DARTS ARE TRUMPS, 1938
DAS HAUS AM FLUSS, 1986
DAUGHTER OF DARKNESS, 1948

DAUGHTER OF DECEIT, 1977
DAUGHTER OF ROSIE O'GRADY, THE, 1950
DAUGHTER OF SHANGHAI, 1937
DAUGHTER OF THE WEST, 1949
DAVID HARUM, 1934
DAVY CROCKETT AND THE RIVER PIRATES, 1956
DAWN ON THE GREAT DIVIDE, 1942
DAY AND THE HOUR, THE, 1963
DAY THE BOOKIES WEPT, THE, 1939
DAY THE SUN ROSE, THE, 1969
DAY THE WAR ENDED, THE, 1961
DAY THEY ROBBED THE BANK OF ENGLAND, THE, 1960
DAYS AND NIGHTS, 1946
DAYS OF GLORY, 1944
DEAD END KIDS, 1986
DEAD HEAT ON A MERRY-GO-ROUND, 1966
DEAD MAN'S EVIDENCE, 1962
DEAD MAN'S GULCH, 1943
DEAD OF WINTER, 1987
DEAD ZONE, THE, 1983
DEADLIER THAN THE MALE, 1967
DEADLIEST SIN, THE, 1956
DEADLINE AT DAWN, 1946
DEADLINE FOR MURDER, 1946
DEADLY BLESSING, 1981
DEAR JOHN, 1966
DEAR MR. WONDERFUL, 1983
DEATH BEFORE DISHONOR, 1987
DEATH HUNT, 1981
DEATH OF A GUNFIGHTER, 1969
DEATH SENTENCE, 1986
DEATH VALLEY RANGERS, 1944
DEATHSPORT, 1978
DEATHTRAP, 1982
DECISION AGAINST TIME, 1957
DECKS RAN RED, THE, 1958
DEEP SIX, THE, 1958
DEEP WATERS, 1948
DEFEND MY LOVE, 1956
DEGREE OF MURDER, A, 1969
DELICATE DELINQUENT, THE, 1957
DEMENTIA 13, 1963
DEMONS, 1987
DEMONSTRATOR, 1971
DENVER AND RIO GRANDE, 1952
DEPORTED, 1950
DESERT BLOOM, 1986
DESERT MICE, 1960
DESERT OF THE TARTARS, THE, 1976
DESERT SANDS, 1955
DESERT SONG, THE, 1929
DESIRABLE, 1934
DESIRE IN THE DUST, 1960
DESIREE, 1984
DESPAIR, 1978
DESPERATE JOURNEY, 1942
DESPERATE SEARCH, 1952
DESPERATELY SEEKING SUSAN, 1985
DESTINATION BIG HOUSE, 1950
DESTINATION MURDER, 1950
DESTINY, 1944
DESTROY ALL MONSTERS, 1969
DESTRY, 1954
DETOUR, THE, 1968
DETROIT 9000, 1973
DEVIL, THE, 1963
DEVIL AND MAX DEVLIN, THE, 1981
DEVIL AND THE DEEP, 1932
DEVIL AND THE TEN COMMANDMENTS, THE, 1962
DEVIL IN SILK, 1968
DEVIL IN THE FLESH, 1986
DEVIL IS AN EMPRESS, THE, 1939
DEVIL MAKES THREE, THE, 1952
DEVIL MAY CARE, 1929
DEVIL-SHIP PIRATES, THE, 1964
DEVIL WITHIN HER, THE, 1976
DEVIL'S AGENT, THE, 1962
DEVIL'S BRIDE, THE, 1968
DEVIL'S DOORWAY, 1950
DEVIL'S GENERAL, THE, 1957
DEVIL'S HAIRPIN, THE, 1957
DEVIL'S HOLIDAY, THE, 1930
DEVIL'S IN LOVE, THE, 1933
DEVIL'S MASK, THE, 1946
DEVIL'S PLAYGROUND, 1937

DEVONSVILLE TERROR, THE, 1983
DEVOTION, 1931
DIABOLICALLY YOURS, 1968
DIAGNOSIS: MURDER, 1974
DIAL 1119, 1950
DIAL RED O, 1955
DIAMONDS, 1975
DIAMONDS FOR BREAKFAST, 1968
DIANE, 1955
DIANE'S BODY, 1969
DIARY OF A SCHIZOPHRENIC GIRL, 1970
DIARY OF A SHINJUKU BURGLAR, 1969
DIARY OF AN ITALIAN, 1972
DICK BARTON STRIKES BACK, 1949
DICK TRACY, 1945
DICK TRACY MEETS GRUESOME, 1947
DICTATOR, THE, 1935
DIE FLEDERMAUS, 1964
DIFFICULT YEARS, 1950
DIME WITH A HALO, 1963
DIMKA, 1964
DIPLOMANIACS, 1933
DIRTY GAME, THE, 1966
DIRTY KNIGHT'S WORK, 1976
DIRTY LITTLE BILLY, 1972
DIRTY ROTTEN SCOUNDRELS, 1988
DISCARDED LOVERS, 1932
DISCOVERIES, 1939
DISORDERLY CONDUCT, 1932
DIVORCE IN THE FAMILY, 1932
DJANGO, 1966
DO NOT DISTURB, 1965
DO NOT THROW CUSHIONS INTO THE RING, 1970
DOCTEUR LAENNEC, 1949
DOCTOR AT LARGE, 1957
DOCTOR AT SEA, 1955
DR. CYCLOPS, 1940
DR. HECKYL AND MR. HYPE, 1980
DOCTOR IN LOVE, 1960
DR. JEKYLL AND SISTER HYDE, 1971
DR. KNOCK, 1936
DOCTOR TAKES A WIFE, 1940
DR. TERROR'S HOUSE OF HORRORS, 1965
DR. WHO AND THE DALEKS, 1965
DOCTOR'S DILEMMA, THE, 1958
DOING TIME, 1979
DOLL, THE, 1962
DOLL FACE, 1945
DOLLAR, 1938
$ (DOLLARS), 1971
DOLORES, 1949
DOMINO KID, 1957
DON GIOVANNI, 1955
DON GIOVANNI, 1979
DONDI, 1961
DONOVAN AFFAIR, THE, 1929
DON'T CRY WITH YOUR MOUTH FULL, 1974
DON'T FENCE ME IN, 1945
DON'T KNOCK THE ROCK, 1956
DON'T LET THE ANGELS FALL, 1969
DON'T TOUCH WHITE WOMEN!, 1974
DOOMED AT SUNDOWN, 1937
DOT AND THE BUNNY, 1983
DOUBLE CROSS ROADS, 1930
DOUBLE TROUBLE, 1941
DOUBLE WEDDING, 1937
DOUBTING THOMAS, 1935
DOUGHGIRLS, THE, 1944
DOWN AMONG THE SHELTERING PALMS, 1953
DOWN BY LAW, 1986
DOWN DAKOTA WAY, 1949
DOWN MEXICO WAY, 1941
DOWN MISSOURI WAY, 1946
DOWN RIO GRANDE WAY, 1942
DR. BLACK AND MR. HYDE, 1976
DRACULA AND SON, 1976
DRACULA HAS RISEN FROM HIS GRAVE, 1968
DRACULA—PRINCE OF DARKNESS, 1966
DRAGNET, 1974
DRAGNET, 1987
DRAGON WELLS MASSACRE, 1957
DRAMATIC SCHOOL, 1938
DREAM GIRL, 1947
DREAM OF PASSION, A, 1978
DREAM ONE, 1984
DREAM WIFE, 1953

BOLD: Films on Videocassette

DREAMCHILD, 1985
DREAMS COME TRUE, 1936
DREAMS IN A DRAWER, 1957
DRIFT FENCE, 1936
DRIFTING ALONG, 1946
DRUMS OF THE CONGO, 1942
DRYLANDERS, 1963
DUCHESS OF IDAHO, THE, 1950
DUDE COWBOY, 1941
DUDE RANGER, THE, 1934
DUDES, 1988
DUEL, THE, 1964
DUEL AT APACHE WELLS, 1957
DUEL AT DIABLO, 1966
DUEL AT SILVER CREEK, THE, 1952
DUEL IN THE JUNGLE, 1954
DUKE OF WEST POINT, THE, 1938
DULCINEA, 1962
DUNWICH HORROR, THE, 1970
DURANGO KID, THE, 1940
EAGLE AND THE HAWK, THE, 1950
EAGLE'S BROOD, THE, 1936
EARLY TO BED, 1936
EARLY WORKS, 1970
EARTHBOUND, 1940
EARTHWORM TRACTORS, 1936
EASIEST WAY, THE, 1931
EAST SIDE OF HEAVEN, 1939
EAST SIDE, WEST SIDE, 1949
EASY LIVING, 1949
EASY TO TAKE, 1936
EBOLI, 1980
ECHO OF BARBARA, 1961
EDDY DUCHIN STORY, THE, 1956
EDITH AND MARCEL, 1984
EDUCATING RITA, 1983
EDUCATION OF SONNY CARSON, THE, 1974
EDWARD AND CAROLINE, 1952
EGON SCHIELE—EXCESS AND PUNISHMENT, 1981
EIGHT BELLS, 1935
EIGHT IRON MEN, 1952
EL DIPUTADO, 1985
ELECTRIC HORSEMAN, THE, 1979
ELEPHANT WALK, 1954
ELISABETH OF AUSTRIA, 1931
EMBARRASSING MOMENTS, 1930
EMBASSY, 1972
EMBRACEABLE YOU, 1948
EMERGENCY HOSPITAL, 1956
EMPEROR AND A GENERAL, THE, 1968
ENCOUNTERS IN SALZBURG, 1964
END OF MRS. CHENEY, 1963
END OF THE GAME, 1976
END OF THE ROAD, THE, 1936
ENDLESS NIGHT, THE, 1963
ENEMIES OF PROGRESS, 1934
ENEMY AGENT, 1940
ENORMOUS CHANGES AT THE LAST MINUTE, 1985
ENSIGN PULVER, 1964
ENTER LAUGHING, 1967
ENTER MADAME, 1935
ENTITY, THE, 1982
ERENDIRA, 1984
ERNEST SAVES CHRISTMAS, 1988
ERRAND BOY, THE, 1961
ESCAPADE, 1955
ESCAPE ARTIST, THE, 1982
ESCAPE, THE, 1939
ESCAPE FROM EAST BERLIN, 1962
ESCAPE FROM NEW YORK, 1981
ESCAPE FROM RED ROCK, 1958
ESCAPE FROM THE PLANET OF THE APES, 1971
ESCAPE FROM YESTERDAY, 1939
ESCAPE IN THE DESERT, 1945
ESCAPE IN THE SUN, 1956
ESCAPE ME NEVER, 1947
ESCAPE TO WITCH MOUNTAIN, 1975
ESCORT WEST, 1959
ESPIONAGE AGENT, 1939
ESTHER WATERS, 1948
ETERNAL SEA, THE, 1955
EVEL KNIEVEL, 1971
EVELYN PRENTICE, 1934
EVENSONG, 1934
EVENTS, 1970
EVER IN MY HEART, 1933

EVERY BASTARD A KING, 1968
EVERY GIRL SHOULD BE MARRIED, 1948
EVERY NIGHT AT EIGHT, 1935
EVERY PICTURE TELLS A STORY, 1984
EVERY TIME WE SAY GOODBYE, 1986
EVERY WHICH WAY BUT LOOSE, 1978
EVERYBODY'S ALL-AMERICAN, 1988
EVERYTHING HAPPENS AT NIGHT, 1939
EVERYTHING I HAVE IS YOURS, 1952
EVERYTHING YOU ALWAYS WANTED TO KNOW
    ABOUT SEX BUT WERE AFRAID TO ASK, 1972
EXCLUSIVE, 1937
EXECUTIVE ACTION, 1973
EXILE EXPRESS, 1939
EXILED TO SHANGHAI, 1937
EXILES, THE, 1966
EXPENSIVE HUSBANDS, 1937
EYE FOR AN EYE, AN, 1966
EYES, THE MOUTH, THE, 1982
EYES, THE SEA AND A BALL, 1968
FABIOLA, 1951
FABLE, A, 1971
FABULOUS DORSEYS, THE, 1947
FACE BEHIND THE MASK, THE, 1941
FACE IN THE RAIN, A, 1963
FACE OF FU MANCHU, THE, 1965
FACES IN THE DARK, 1960
FACTS OF LIFE, THE, 1960
FACTS OF MURDER, THE, 1965
FAIR EXCHANGE, 1936
FAIR WARNING, 1931
FAIR WIND TO JAVA, 1953
FAITHFUL CITY, 1952
FALCON IN DANGER, THE, 1943
FALCON IN HOLLYWOOD, THE, 1944
FALCON OUT WEST, THE, 1944
FALCON STRIKES BACK, THE, 1943
FALCON'S ADVENTURE, THE, 1946
FALL GUY, 1947
FALL OF THE ROMAN EMPIRE, THE, 1964
FAME, 1980
FAME IS THE SPUR, 1947
FAMILY HONEYMOON, 1948
FAMILY JEWELS, THE, 1965
FAMILY LIFE, 1971
FANCY PANTS, 1950
FANTASTIC COMEDY, A, 1975
FAR FROM THE MADDING CROWD, 1967
FAREWELL TO ARMS, A, 1957
FAREWELL TO LOVE, 1931
FARMER'S DAUGHTER, THE, 1940
FASHION MODEL, 1945
FAST AND FURIOUS, 1939
FAST TIMES AT RIDGEMONT HIGH, 1982
FASTEST GUN ALIVE, 1956
FATAL ATTRACTION, 1987
FATE TAKES A HAND, 1962
FATHER OF A SOLDIER, 1966
FATHER TAKES THE AIR, 1951
FATHER WAS A FULLBACK, 1949
FAUST, 1963
FEAR CITY, 1984
FEARLESS FRANK, 1967
FEDERAL MAN-HUNT, 1939
FEMALE FIENDS, 1958
FEMMES DE PERSONNE, 1986
FERNANDEL THE DRESSMAKER, 1957
FEUDIN', FUSSIN' AND A-FIGHTIN', 1948
FICKLE FINGER OF FATE, THE, 1967
FIDELIO, 1961
FIDELIO, 1970
FIFTH AVENUE GIRL, 1939
52 PICK-UP, 1986
FIGHT FOR ROME, 1969
FIGHTER, THE, 1952
FIGHTER ATTACK, 1953
FIGHTING BACK, 1983
FIGHTING FRONTIER, 1943
FIGHTING GRINGO, THE, 1939
FIGHTING MAD, 1948
FIGHTING MAD, 1976
FIGHTING PIMPERNEL, THE, 1950
FIGHTING RANGER, THE, 1934
FIGHTING THOROUGHBREDS, 1939
FILE OF THE GOLDEN GOOSE, THE, 1969
FINDERS KEEPERS, 1984

FINE MADNESS, A, 1966
FINGER OF GUILT, 1956
FINIAN'S RAINBOW, 1968
FINNEY, 1969
FIRE DOWN BELOW, 1957
FIRE IN THE STONE, THE, 1983
FIRESTARTER, 1984
FIRST A GIRL, 1935
FIRST COMES COURAGE, 1943
FIRST LOVE, 1939
FIRST LOVE, 1970
FIRST MAN INTO SPACE, 1959
FIRST MONDAY IN OCTOBER, 1981
FIRST 100 YEARS, THE, 1938
FIRST YEAR, THE, 1932
FIVE AND TEN, 1931
FIVE ANGLES ON MURDER, 1950
FIVE CAME BACK, 1939
FIVE CORNERS, 1988
FIVE GOLDEN DRAGONS, 1967
FIVE GOLDEN HOURS, 1961
F.J. HOLDEN, THE, 1977
FLAME BARRIER, THE, 1958
FLAME OF NEW ORLEANS, THE, 1941
FLAME OVER VIETNAM, 1967
FLAMING FEATHER, 1951
FLAXY MARTIN, 1949
FLEA IN HER EAR, A, 1968
FLEMISH FARM, THE, 1943
FLESH EATERS, THE, 1964
FLIGHT INTO NOWHERE, 1938
FLIGHT OF THE EAGLE, 1983
FLIGHT THAT DISAPPEARED, THE, 1961
FLIGHT TO BERLIN, 1984
FLIGHT TO FURY, 1966
FLIGHT TO HONG KONG, 1956
FLIRTING WITH DANGER, 1935
FLOATING WEEDS, 1970
FLORIDA SPECIAL, 1936
FLORODORA GIRL, THE, 1930
FLOWING GOLD, 1940
FLUFFY, 1965
FLY-AWAY BABY, 1937
FLY AWAY PETER, 1948
FLYER, THE, 1987
FLYING EYE, THE, 1955
FLYING FONTAINES, THE, 1959
FLYING FOOL, THE, 1931
FLYING HOSTESS, 1936
FLYING MISSILE, 1950
FLYING SAUCER, THE, 1950
FLYING SAUCER, THE, 1964
FOLIES BERGERE, 1958
FOLLOW THAT DREAM, 1962
FOLLOW THAT HORSE!, 1960
FOLLOW THE LEADER, 1930
FOLLOW THE SUN, 1951
FOLLOW THRU, 1930
FOLLOW YOUR STAR, 1938
FOLLOWING THE FUHRER, 1986
FOOL AND THE PRINCESS, THE, 1948
FOOTLIGHT SERENADE, 1942
FOOTLOOSE, 1984
FOOTSTEPS IN THE DARK, 1941
FOR HEAVEN'S SAKE, 1950
FOR LOVE OF IVY, 1968
FOR LOVE OR MONEY, 1934
FOR THE LOVE OF BENJI, 1977
FOR THE LOVE OF MARY, 1948
FOR THEM THAT TRESPASS, 1949
FOR THOSE IN PERIL, 1944
FORBIDDEN, 1949
FORBIDDEN, 1953
FORBIDDEN ISLAND, 1959
FORBIDDEN TERRITORY, 1938
FOREIGN AFFAIRES, 1935
FOREIGN AGENT, 1942
FOREIGN INTRIGUE, 1956
FOREST RANGERS, THE, 1942
FOREVER AMBER, 1947
FORT APACHE, THE BRONX, 1981
FORT BOWIE, 1958
FORT COURAGEOUS, 1965
FORT DEFIANCE, 1951
FORT GRAVEYARD, 1966
FORT SAVAGE RAIDERS, 1951

FORTY CARATS, 1973
FORTY GUNS, 1957
FORTY LITTLE MOTHERS, 1940
FORTY POUNDS OF TROUBLE, 1962
FORTY THOUSAND HORSEMEN, 1941
FORWARD PASS, THE, 1929
FOUNTAINHEAD, THE, 1949
FOUR AGAINST FATE, 1952
FOUR DAYS IN JULY, 1984
FOUR DAYS WONDER, 1936
FOUR FLIES ON GREY VELVET, 1972
FOUR JACKS AND A JILL, 1941
FOUR JILLS IN A JEEP, 1944
FOUR MEN AND A PRAYER, 1938
FOUR MOTHERS, 1941
FOUR SKULLS OF JONATHAN DRAKE, THE, 1959
FOUR SONS, 1940
FOUR'S A CROWD, 1938
FOURTH ALARM, THE, 1930
FOURTH HORSEMAN, THE, 1933
FOURTH MAN, THE, 1984
FOX MOVIETONE FOLLIES, 1929
FOX WITH NINE TAILS, THE, 1969
FOXES, 1980
F.P. 1, 1933
FRAIL WOMEN, 1932
FRAME-UP THE, 1937
FRAMED, 1947
FRANCES, 1982
FRAULEIN, 1958
FRAULEIN DOKTOR, 1969
FREE FOR ALL, 1949
FREEBIE AND THE BEAN, 1974
FRENCH LESSON, 1986
FRENCH MISTRESS, 1960
FRENCH QUARTER, 1978
FRENCH TOUCH, THE, 1954
FRENZY, 1946
FRESHMAN LOVE, 1936
FREUD, 1962
FRIC FRAC, 1939
FRIGHT, 1971
FRISCO JENNY, 1933
FROGS, 1972
FROM BEYOND, 1986
FROM HELL TO HEAVEN, 1933
FROM NOON TO THREE, 1976
FROM THE LIFE OF THE MARIONETTES, 1980
FROM THE MIXED-UP FILES OF MRS. BASIL E.
   FRANKWEILER, 1973
FROM THIS DAY FORWARD, 1946
FROM TOP TO BOTTOM, 1933
FRONT PAGE STORY, 1954
FRONT PAGE WOMAN, 1935
FRONTIER BADMEN, 1943
FRONTIER MARSHAL, 1934
FRONTIER OUTPOST, 1950
FUGITIVE, THE, 1940
FUGITIVE FROM SONORA, 1943
FUGITIVE LADY, 1934
FUGITIVE LADY, 1951
FUNNYMAN, 1967
FURTHER ADVENTURES OF THE WILDERNESS
   FAMILY—PART II, 1978
FURY AT GUNSIGHT PASS, 1956
FURY OF THE CONGO, 1951
GAL YOUNG UN, 1979
GALAXY EXPRESS, 1982
GALILEO, 1968
GALLOPING THRU, 1932
GAMBLER FROM NATCHEZ, THE, 1954
GAMBLING HOUSE, 1950
GAMBLING LADY, 1934
GAMBLING SHIP, 1933
GAME OF DEATH, A, 1945
GAMEKEEPER, THE, 1980
GAMES, 1967
GANG BUSTER, THE, 1931
GANGS OF NEW YORK, 1938
GANGSTER STORY, 1959
GANGWAY FOR TOMORROW, 1943
GAOL BREAK, 1936
GARCON!, 1985
GARDEN OF EVIL, 1954
GASBAGS, 1940
GASOLINE ALLEY, 1951

GATE, THE, 1987
GAWAIN AND THE GREEN KNIGHT, 1973
GAY DECEPTION, THE, 1935
GAY FALCON, THE, 1941
GAY LOVE, 1936
GAY PURR-EE, 1962
GAY RANCHERO, THE, 1948
GENE AUTRY AND THE MOUNTIES, 1951
GENE KRUPA STORY, THE, 1959
GENERAL SPANKY, 1937
GENERALS WITHOUT BUTTONS, 1938
GENGHIS KHAN, 1965
GENIUS, THE, 1976
GENTLE SEX, THE, 1943
GENTLEMAN FROM NOWHERE, THE, 1948
GENTLEMAN'S FATE, 1931
GENTLEMEN MARRY BRUNETTES, 1955
GENTLEMEN OF THE PRESS, 1929
GEORG, 1964
GEORGE RAFT STORY, THE, 1961
GEORGE WHITE'S SCANDALS, 1934
GERONIMO, 1962
GERTRUD, 1966
GET CRACKING, 1943
GET CRAZY, 1983
GET HEP TO LOVE, 1942
GET OUT YOUR HANDKERCHIEFS, 1978
GHIDRAH, THE THREE-HEADED MONSTER, 1965
GHOST CAMERA, THE, 1933
GHOST COMES HOME, THE, 1940
GHOST OF ST. MICHAEL'S. THE, 1941
GHOST STORY, 1981
GHOST VALLEY, 1932
GHOSTS OF BERKELEY SQUARE, 1947
GHOUL, THE, 1975
GIANT GILA MONSTER, THE, 1959
GIFT OF GAB, 1934
GILDERSLEEVE ON BROADWAY, 1943
GIRL CRAZY, 1932
GIRL DOWNSTAIRS, THE, 1938
GIRL FRIEND, THE, 1935
GIRL FROM JONES BEACH, THE, 1949
GIRL FROM MEXICO, THE, 1939
GIRL FROM POLTAVA, 1937
GIRL FROM TENTH AVENUE, THE, 1935
GIRL GETTERS, THE, 1966
GIRL HE LEFT BEHIND, THE, 1956
GIRL HUNTERS, THE, 1963
GIRL IN DISTRESS, 1941
GIRL IN EVERY PORT, A, 1952
GIRL IN 419, 1933
GIRL IN THE NEWS, THE, 1941
GIRL IN THE RED VELVET SWING, THE, 1955
GIRL MOST LIKELY, THE, 1957
GIRL NAMED TAMIKO, A, 1962
GIRL NEXT DOOR, THE, 1953
GIRL OF THE GOLDEN WEST, 1930
GIRL OF THE GOLDEN WEST, THE, 1938
GIRL OF THE OZARKS, 1936
GIRL RUSH, THE, 1955
GIRL STROKE BOY, 1971
GIRL TROUBLE, 1942
GIRL WHO HAD EVERYTHING, THE, 1953
GIRL WITH A PISTOL, THE, 1968
GIRLS ABOUT TOWN, 1931
GIRLS! GIRLS! GIRLS!, 1962
GIRLS OF PLEASURE ISLAND, THE, 1953
GIRLS ON THE LOOSE, 1958
GIRLS' SCHOOL, 1938
GIRLS UNDER TWENTY-ONE, 1940
GIRLS WILL BE BOYS, 1934
GIT!, 1965
GIVE A GIRL A BREAK, 1953
GIVE ME A SAILOR, 1938
GIVE ME YOUR HEART, 1936
GIVEN WORD, THE, 1964
GLAMOROUS NIGHT, 1937
GLAMOUR GIRL, 1947
GLASS HOUSES, 1972
GLASS WALL, THE, 1953
GLASS WEB, THE, 1953
GLORIFYING THE AMERICAN GIRL, 1930
GLORY, 1955
GLORY AT SEA, 1952
GLORY OF FAITH, THE, 1938
GO INTO YOUR DANCE, 1935

GO, JOHNNY, GO!, 1959
GO TO BLAZES, 1962
GO WEST, 1940
GODDESS, THE, 1958
GODZILLA, RING OF THE MONSTERS, 1956
GOHA, 1958
GOIN' COCONUTS, 1978
GOIN' HOME, 1976
GOIN' TO TOWN, 1944
GOING PLACES, 1974
GOLD DIGGERS IN PARIS, 1938
GOLD DIGGERS OF BROADWAY, 1929
GOLDBERGS, THE, 1950
GOLDEN ARROW, THE, 1936
GOLDEN BLADE, THE, 1953
GOLDEN COACH, THE, 1953
GOLDEN DEMON, 1956
GOLDEN EARRINGS, 1947
GOLDEN GOOSE, THE, 1966
GOLDEN HARVEST, 1933
GOLDEN HAWK, THE, 1952
GOLDEN HOOFS, 1941
GOLDEN HORDE, THE, 1951
GOLDEN MADONNA, THE, 1949
GOLDEN MASK, THE, 1954
GOLDEN MOUNTAINS, 1958
GOLDEN STALLION, THE, 1949
GOLDSTEIN, 1964
GOLGOTHA, 1937
GOOD COMPANIONS, THE, 1957
GOOD DAY FOR A HANGING, 1958
GOOD DIE YOUNG, THE, 1954
GOOD GIRLS GO TO PARIS, 1939
GOOD GUYS WEAR BLACK, 1978
GOOD MORNING BABYLON, 1987
GOOD MORNING, JUDGE, 1943
GOOD SAM, 1948
GOOD SPORT, 1931
GOOD TIME GIRL, 1950
GOODBYE AGAIN, 1933
GOODBYE CHARLIE, 1964
GOODBYE FRANKLIN HIGH, 1978
GOODBYE MR. CHIPS, 1969
GOODBYE PORK PIE, 1981
GOODNIGHT, LADIES AND GENTLEMEN, 1977
GOOSE GIRL, THE, 1967
GORDEYEV FAMILY, THE, 1961
GORGEOUS HUSSY, THE, 1936
GORGO, 1961
GORGON, THE, 1964
GORILLA AT LARGE, 1954
GORILLA GREETS YOU, THE, 1958
GRAND CANYON TRAIL, 1948
GRAND HIGHWAY, THE, 1988
GRAND SLAM, 1933
GRAND SUBSTITUTION, THE, 1965
GRAND THEFT AUTO, 1977
GRANDAD RUDD, 1935
GRANDVIEW, U.S.A., 1984
GREASE 2, 1982
GREASER'S PALACE, 1972
GREAT AMERICAN PASTIME, THE, 1956
GREAT BANK HOAX, THE, 1977
GREAT DAN PATCH, THE, 1949
GREAT DAY IN THE MORNING, 1956
GREAT EXPECTATIONS, 1934
GREAT GAY ROAD, THE, 1931
GREAT GILBERT AND SULLIVAN, THE, 1953
GREAT GUNS, 1941
GREAT GUY, 1936
GREAT HOPE, THE, 1954
GREAT IMPOSTOR, THE, 1960
GREAT JASPER, THE, 1933
GREAT LOVER, THE, 1931
GREAT LOVER, THE, 1949
GREAT MACARTHY, THE, 1975
GREAT MAN'S LADY, THE, 1942
GREAT MIKE, THE, 1944
GREAT MISSOURI RAID, THE, 1950
GREAT MR. NOBODY, THE, 1941
GREAT PONY RAID, THE, 1968
GREAT ST. TRINIAN'S TRAIN ROBBERY, THE, 1966
GREAT SIOUX MASSACRE, THE, 1965
GREAT SMOKEY ROADBLOCK, THE, 1978
GREAT SPY CHASE, THE, 1966
GREAT TEXAS DYNAMITE CHASE, THE, 1976

BOLD: Films on Videocassette

GREAT VAN ROBBERY, THE, 1963
GREAT WALL, A, 1986
GREAT WALL, THE, 1965
GREED IN THE SUN, 1965
GREED OF WILLIAM HART, THE, 1948
GREEN GODDESS, THE, 1930
GREEN GRASS OF WYOMING, 1948
GREEN GROW THE RUSHES, 1951
GREEN LIGHT, 1937
GREEN MARE, THE, 1961
GREEN PACK, THE, 1934
GREEN TREE, THE, 1965
GREENWICH VILLAGE STORY, 1963
GREYFRIARS BOBBY, 1961
GROUNDSTAR CONSPIRACY, THE, 1972
GROWN-UP CHILDREN, 1963
GRUMPY, 1930
GUESS WHO'S COMING TO DINNER, 1967
GUEST WIFE, 1945
GUIDE, THE, 1965
GUILT, 1967
GUILT IS NOT MINE, 1968
GUILT OF JANET AMES, THE, 1947
GUILTY AS HELL, 1932
GUILTY HANDS, 1931
GUILTY OF TREASON, 1950
GULLIVER'S TRAVELS, 1939
GUN BELT, 1953
GUN BROTHERS, 1956
GUN DUEL IN DURANGO, 1957
GUN FIGHT, 1961
GUN FOR A COWARD, 1957
GUN FURY, 1953
GUN GLORY, 1957
GUN JUSTICE, 1934
GUN PACKER, 1938
GUN RUNNERS, THE, 1958
GUNFIGHT AT DODGE CITY, THE, 1959
GUNFIGHT IN ABILENE, 1967
GUNG HO, 1986
GUNN, 1967
GUNSMOKE, 1953
GURU, THE, 1969
GUTTER GIRLS, 1964
GUY WHO CAME BACK, THE, 1951
GYPSY, 1937
GYPSY COLT, 1954
GYPSY GIRL, 1966
GYPSY MELODY, 1936
HAIL AND FAREWELL, 1936
HAIL, HERO!, 1969
HAIL MAFIA, 1965
HALF A HERO, 1953
HALF ANGEL, 1951
HALLELUJAH THE HILLS, 1963
HALLELUJAH TRAIL, THE, 1965
HAND IN THE TRAP, THE, 1963
HAND OF NIGHT, THE, 1968
HANDFUL OF DUST, A, 1988
HANDS ACROSS THE BORDER, 1943
HANDS OF A STRANGER, 1962
HANDY ANDY, 1934
HANG'EM HIGH, 1968
HANNAH LEE, 1953
HANNA'S WAR, 1988
HANNIBAL BROOKS, 1969
HANOI HILTON, THE, 1987
HANOVER STREET, 1979
HANSEL AND GRETEL, 1965
HAPPENING, THE, 1967
HAPPINESS OF THREE WOMEN, THE, 1954
HAPPINESS OF US ALONE, 1962
HAPPY EVER AFTER, 1932
HAPPY-GO-LUCKY, 1937
HAPPY LANDING, 1938
HAPPY NEW YEAR, 1987
HAPPY THIEVES, THE, 1962
HAPPY YEARS, THE, 1950
HARBOR OF MISSING MEN, 1950
HARD, FAST, AND BEAUTIFUL, 1951
HARD RIDE, THE, 1971
HARD ROCK HARRIGAN, 1935
HARD TO GET, 1929
HARD TO GET, 1938
HARD TRAVELING, 1985
HARLEM GLOBETROTTERS, THE, 1951

HARLEQUIN, 1980
HARPER, 1966
HARRY AND SON, 1984
HARRY'S WAR, 1981
HASSAN, TERRORIST, 1968
HAT CHECK GIRL, 1932
HATARI!, 1962
HATCHET MAN, THE, 1932
HATRED, 1941
HATTER'S GHOST, THE, 1982
HAUNTED PALACE, THE, 1963
HAWK OF WILD RIVER, THE, 1952
HE COULDN'T SAY NO, 1938
HE KNEW WOMEN, 1930
HE LAUGHED LAST, 1956
HE MARRIED HIS WIFE, 1940
HE WAS HER MAN, 1934
HE WHO RIDES A TIGER, 1966
HEAD OF A TYRANT, 1960
HEAD ON, 1981
HEADIN' FOR THE RIO GRANDE, 1937
HEADLINE WOMAN, THE, 1935
HEART IS A LONELY HUNTER, THE, 1968
HEART LIKE A WHEEL, 1983
HEART OF ARIZONA, 1938
HEART OF THE GOLDEN WEST, 1942
HEART OF THE MATTER, THE, 1954
HEART OF THE ROCKIES, 1951
HEART OF THE STAG, 1984
HEART OF THE WEST, 1937
HEART WITHIN, THE, 1957
HEARTBEAT, 1946
HEARTBREAKER, 1983
HEARTS IN DIXIE, 1929
HEAT'S ON, THE, 1943
HEAVENLY BODY, THE, 1943
HEIDI, 1954
HELL DIVERS, 1932
HELL IS A CITY, 1960
HELL IS SOLD OUT, 1951
HELL ON EARTH, 1934
HELLDORADO, 1946
HELLO SISTER!, 1933
HELLRAISER, 1987
HELL'S HIGHWAY, 1932
HELP!, 1965
HENNESSY, 1975
HENRY ALDRICH FOR PRESIDENT, 1941
HENRY ALDRICH HAUNTS A HOUSE, 1943
HENRY IV, 1985
HER CARDBOARD LOVER, 1942
HER FIRST ROMANCE, 1940
HER MAN GILBEY, 1949
HERE COME THE JETS, 1959
HERE COME THE NELSONS, 1952
HERE COMES ELMER, 1943
HERE COMES KELLY, 1943
HERE COMES SANTA CLAUS, 1984
HERE IS MY HEART, 1934
HERE WE GO AGAIN, 1942
HERE'S GEORGE, 1932
HERE'S YOUR LIFE, 1968
HERITAGE OF THE DESERT, 1933
HERO AT LARGE, 1980
HEROES OF THE HILLS, 1938
HERO'S ISLAND, 1962
HERS TO HOLD, 1943
HE'S A COCKEYED WONDER, 1950
HEY BOY! HEY GIRL!, 1959
HI-DE-HO, 1947
HI-YO SILVER, 1940
HIDDEN GOLD, 1940
HIDDEN HAND, THE, 1942
HIDEOUT IN THE ALPS, 1938
HIGH CONQUEST, 1947
HIGH EXPLOSIVE, 1943
HIGH LONESOME, 1950
HIGH-POWERED RIFLE, THE, 1960
HIGH SCHOOL CONFIDENTIAL, 1958
HIGH TENSION, 1936
HIGH TERRACE, 1957
HIGH TIDE, 1987
HIGH TIDE AT NOON, 1957
HIGHWAY PICKUP, 1965
HIGHWAYMAN, THE, 1951
HIKEN YABURI, 1969

HIMMO, KING OF JERUSALEM, 1988
HINDENBURG, THE, 1975
HINDU, THE, 1953
HIRED GUN, THE, 1957
HIRED HAND, THE, 1971
HIRED WIFE, 1940
HIS DOUBLE LIFE, 1933
HIS EXCELLENCY, 1952
HISTORY OF MR. POLLY, THE, 1949
HIT PARADE OF 1943, 1943
HITCHHIKE TO HAPPINESS, 1945
HITLER GANG, THE, 1944
HITLER'S CHILDREN, 1942
HOLD BACK TOMORROW, 1955
HOLD 'EM YALE, 1935
HOLD THAT GIRL, 1934
HOLE IN THE HEAD, A, 1959
HOLE IN THE WALL, 1929
HOLIDAY AFFAIR, 1949
HOLIDAY CAMP, 1947
HOLIDAY IN HAVANA, 1949
HOLLYWOOD AND VINE, 1945
HOLLYWOOD SHUFFLE, 1987
HOLY TERROR, THE, 1937
HOME IN OKLAHOMA, 1946
HOME MOVIES, 1979
HOME TOWNERS, THE, 1928
HOMEBODIES, 1974
HOMESTRETCH, THE, 1947
HOMICIDAL, 1961
HONEY, 1930
HONEYMOON, 1947
HONEYMOON AHEAD, 1945
HONEYMOON FOR THREE, 1935
HONEYMOON IN BALI, 1939
HONEYMOON MACHINE, THE, 1961
HONEYMOON MERRY-GO-ROUND, 1939
HONG KONG, 1951
HONG KONG CONFIDENTIAL, 1958
HONG KONG NIGHTS, 1935
HONKERS, THE, 1972
HONKYTONK MAN, 1982
HONOLULU, 1939
HOODLUM EMPIRE, 1952
HOODLUM SAINT, THE, 1946
HOOTS MON!, 1939
HOPALONG CASSIDY RETURNS, 1936
HORIZONS WEST, 1952
HORROR HOTEL, 1960
HORSE OF PRIDE, 1980
HOSTAGE, THE, 1966
HOSTILE GUNS, 1967
HOT BOX, THE, 1972
HOT HOURS, 1963
HOT ICE, 1952
HOT LEAD AND COLD FEET, 1978
HOT ROD GANG, 1958
HOT RODS TO HELL, 1967
HOT TIP, 1935
HOTEL IMPERIAL, 1939
HOTEL NEW HAMPSHIRE, THE, 1984
HOTEL PARADISO, 1966
HOTEL SAHARA, 1951
HOTSPRINGS HOLIDAY, 1970
HOUND OF THE BASKERVILLES, 1932
HOUNDS... OF NOTRE DAME, THE, 1980
HOUR OF GLORY, 1949
HOURS OF LOVE, THE, 1965
HOUSE ACROSS THE BAY, THE, 1940
HOUSE BY THE RIVER, 1950
HOUSE CALLS, 1978
HOUSE DIVIDED, A, 1932
HOUSE IN THE WOODS, THE, 1957
HOUSE OF DARK SHADOWS, 1970
HOUSE OF DRACULA, 1945
HOUSE OF FEAR, THE, 1945
HOUSE OF FRANKENSTEIN, 1944
HOUSE OF HORRORS, 1946
HOUSE OF NUMBERS, 1957
HOUSE OF THE ARROW, THE, 1930
HOUSE OF THE SEVEN GABLES, THE, 1940
HOUSE ON 56TH STREET, THE, 1933
HOUSE THAT DRIPPED BLOOD, THE, 1971
HOUSE THAT SCREAMED, THE, 1970
HOUSE WITH AN ATTIC, THE, 1964
HOUSEKEEPER'S DAUGHTER, 1939

HOUSEMASTER, 1938
HOUSTON STORY, THE, 1956
HOW SWEET IT IS, 1968
HOW TO BE VERY, VERY, POPULAR, 1955
HOW TO COMMIT MARRIAGE, 1969
HOW TO MAKE A MONSTER, 1958
HOW TO MURDER A RICH UNCLE, 1957
HOW WILLINGLY YOU SING, 1975
HUD, 1963
HUDSON'S BAY, 1940
HUGS AND KISSES, 1968
HULLABALOO, 1940
HUMAN DESIRE, 1954
HUMAN JUNGLE, THE, 1954
HUMANOIDS FROM THE DEEP, 1980
HUNCHBACK OF ROME, THE, 1963
HUNDRED HOUR HUNT, 1953
HUNTED MEN, 1938
HUNTER'S BLOOD, 1987
HURRY UP OR I'LL BE 30, 1973
HUSBANDS, 1970
HYDE PARK CORNER, 1935
I AIM AT THE STARS, 1960
I COVER THE WAR, 1937
I DIDN'T DO IT, 1945
I KILLED THAT MAN, 1942
I LIKE MONEY, 1962
I LIVE ON DANGER, 1942
I LIVED WITH YOU, 1933
I LOVE MELVIN, 1953
I LOVED A WOMAN, 1933
I MARRIED A DOCTOR, 1936
I MET A MURDERER, 1939
I MET MY LOVE AGAIN, 1938
I, MONSTER, 1971
I PROMISE TO PAY, 1937
I SEE ICE, 1938
I WAS A SPY, 1934
I WONDER WHO'S KISSING HER NOW, 1947
ICE-CAPADES REVUE, 1942
ICE FOLLIES OF 1939, 1939
ICE PALACE, 1960
ICE PALACE, THE, 1988
ICE STATION ZEBRA, 1968
ICEMAN, 1984
I'D RATHER BE RICH, 1964
IDAHO, 1943
IDENTIFICATION MARKS: NONE, 1969
IDLE RICH, THE, 1929
IDOL OF THE CROWDS, 1937
IDOL ON PARADE, 1959
IF PARIS WERE TOLD TO US, 1956
IF WINTER COMES, 1947
IF YOU KNEW SUSIE, 1948
I'LL BE YOURS, 1947
I'LL GET BY, 1950
I'LL GIVE A MILLION, 1938
I'LL SEE YOU IN MY DREAMS, 1951
I'LL TAKE ROMANCE, 1937
I'LL TAKE SWEDEN, 1965
I'LL TURN TO YOU, 1946
ILLEGAL ENTRY, 1949
ILLEGALLY YOURS, 1988
ILLICIT, 1931
I'M STILL ALIVE, 1940
IMMORTAL BACHELOR, THE, 1980
IMMORTAL BATTALION, THE, 1944
IMMORTAL GENTLEMAN, 1935
IMMORTAL SERGEANT, THE, 1943
IMMORTAL VAGABOND, 1931
IMPASSE, 1969
IMPATIENT MAIDEN, 1932
IMPATIENT YEARS, THE, 1944
IMPOSTER, THE, 1944
IMPULSE, 1955
IMPULSE, 1984
IN CALIENTE, 1935
IN CELEBRATION, 1975
IN LOVE AND WAR, 1958
IN OLD AMARILLO, 1951
IN OLD COLORADO, 1941
IN OLD MEXICO, 1938
IN OLD NEW MEXICO, 1945
IN SEARCH OF THE CASTAWAYS, 1962
IN SOCIETY, 1944

IN THE MONEY, 1958
IN THE MOUTH OF THE WOLF, 1988
IN THE NAME OF LIFE, 1947
IN THE NAVY, 1941
IN THIS OUR LIFE, 1942
INCIDENT, THE, 1967
INCREDIBLE MR. LIMPET, THE, 1964
**INCREDIBLY STRANGE CREATURES WHO
   STOPPED LIVING AND BECAME CRAZY
   MIXED-UP ZOMBIES, THE, 1965**
INDEPENDENCE DAY, 1976
INDIAN PAINT, 1965
INDIAN TERRITORY, 1950
INDISCRETION OF AN AMERICAN WIFE, 1954
INN FOR TROUBLE, 1960
INNOCENT BYSTANDERS, 1973
INNOCENT MEETING, 1959
INNOCENTS IN PARIS, 1955
INQUEST, 1939
INSIDE MOVES, 1980
INSIDE OUT, 1975
INSIDE STORY, 1939
INSIDE THE MAFIA, 1959
INSIDE THE ROOM, 1935
INSPECTOR HORNLEIGH, 1939
INSULT, 1932
INTERLUDE, 1968
INTERMEZZO, 1937
INTERNATIONAL CRIME, 1938
INTERNATIONAL LADY, 1941
INTERNATIONAL SETTLEMENT, 1938
INTERNATIONAL VELVET, 1978
INTERNES CAN'T TAKE MONEY, 1937
INTERNS, THE, 1962
INTO THE NIGHT, 1985
INTRUDER, THE, 1955
INVASION, 1965
INVASION OF THE BODY SNATCHERS, 1978
INVISIBLE AGENT, 1942
INVISIBLE AVENGER, THE, 1958
INVISIBLE RAY, THE, 1936
INVISIBLE WOMAN, THE, 1941
IPHIGENIA, 1977
IRON DUKE, THE, 1935
IRON GLOVE, THE, 1954
IRON MAN, THE, 1951
IRON MISTRESS, THE, 1952
IRON SHERIFF, THE, 1957
IS MY FACE RED?, 1932
ISABEL, 1968
ISLAND, THE, 1962
ISLAND OF DOOM, 1933
ISLAND OF DOOMED MEN, 1940
ISLAND OF LOVE, 1963
ISLAND OF TERROR, 1967
ISLAND OF THE BLUE DOLPHINS, 1964
ISLAND RESCUE, 1952
ISLE OF LOST SHIPS, 1929
ISN'T LIFE WONDERFUL!, 1953
IT AIN'T HAY, 1943
IT CAME FROM BENEATH THE SEA, 1955
IT COMES UP LOVE, 1943
IT CONQUERED THE WORLD, 1956
IT COULD HAPPEN TO YOU, 1939
IT GROWS ON TREES, 1952
IT HAPPENED AT THE WORLD'S FAIR, 1963
IT HAPPENED IN FLATBUSH, 1942
IT HAPPENED TO JANE, 1959
IT ONLY HAPPENS TO OTHERS, 1971
IT PAYS TO ADVERTISE, 1931
IT SHOULDN'T HAPPEN TO A DOG, 1946
IT STARTED WITH A KISS, 1959
IT STARTED WITH EVE, 1941
IT! THE TERROR FROM BEYOND SPACE, 1958
ITALIAN JOB, THE, 1969
IT'S A BET, 1935
IT'S A BOY, 1934
IT'S ALIVE III: ISLAND OF THE ALIVE, 1988
IT'S GREAT TO BE ALIVE, 1933
IT'S IN THE BAG, 1945
IT'S LOVE AGAIN, 1936
IT'S NEVER TOO LATE TO MEND, 1937
IT'S NOT CRICKET, 1937
IT'S NOT CRICKET, 1949
I'VE LIVED BEFORE, 1956
IVORY HUNTER, 1952

IVY, 1947
J.D.'S REVENGE, 1976
J-MEN FOREVER, 1980
JACK AND THE BEANSTALK, 1952
JACK LONDON, 1943
JACKASS MAIL, 1942
JACKSON COUNTY JAIL, 1976
JACOB TWO-TWO MEETS THE HOODED FANG, 1979
JACQUELINE, 1956
JAIL BUSTERS, 1955
JAILBIRDS, 1939
JAILHOUSE ROCK, 1957
JAKE SPEED, 1986
JAM SESSION, 1944
JAMBOREE, 1957
JANIE, 1944
JASSY, 1948
JAZZ AGE, THE, 1929
JAZZ HEAVEN, 1929
JAZZ SINGER, THE, 1953
JEANNE EAGELS, 1957
JEOPARDY, 1953
JESSE JAMES AT BAY, 1941
JIG SAW, 1965
JIGSAW, 1949
JIMMY THE GENT, 1934
JINX MONEY, 1948
JIVARO, 1954
JOAN OF OZARK, 1942
JOAN OF THE ANGELS, 1962
JOANNA, 1968
JOE HILL, 1971
JOE MACBETH, 1955
JOE PALOOKA, CHAMP, 1946
JOE PALOOKA IN THE BIG FIGHT, 1949
JOE PALOOKA IN THE COUNTERPUNCH, 1949
JOE PALOOKA IN THE SQUARED CIRCLE, 1950
JOE PALOOKA IN WINNER TAKE ALL, 1948
JOE PALOOKA MEETS HUMPHREY, 1950
JOE PANTHER, 1976
JOHN LOVES MARY, 1949
JOHN OF THE FAIR, 1962
JOHNNY DANGEROUSLY, 1984
JOHNNY DARK, 1954
JOHNNY DOESN'T LIVE HERE ANY MORE, 1944
JOHNNY ONE-EYE, 1950
JOHNNY RENO, 1966
JOHNNY STOOL PIGEON, 1949
JOHNNY TIGER, 1966
JOHNNY VIK, 1973
JOKER, THE, 1961
JOLLY BAD FELLOW, A, 1964
JONI, 1980
JONIKO AND THE KUSH TA KA, 1969
JOSETTE, 1938
JOURNEY, THE, 1959
JOURNEY INTO LIGHT, 1951
JOURNEY INTO NOWHERE, 1963
JOURNEY TO SPIRIT ISLAND, 1988
JOURNEY TO THE BEGINNING OF TIME, 1966
JOURNEYS FROM BERLIN—1971, 1980
JOVITA, 1970
JUBILEE TRAIL, 1954
JUDGE AND THE SINNER, THE, 1964
JUDGE PRIEST, 1934
JUDGE STEPS OUT, THE, 1949
JUDGMENT DEFERRED, 1952
JUDO SAGA, 1965
JUDO SHOWDOWN, 1966
JUKE BOX JENNY, 1942
JUKE BOX RHYTHM, 1959
JULIE THE REDHEAD, 1963
JUNGLE PATROL, 1948
JUNGLE PRINCESS, THE, 1936
JUNO AND THE PAYCOCK, 1930
JUST FOR YOU, 1952
JUST IMAGINE, 1930
JUST OFF BROADWAY, 1942
JUST ONE OF THE GUYS, 1985
JUST THIS ONCE, 1952
KAMOURASKA, 1973
KANGAROO, 1952
KANSAS CITY KITTY, 1944
KANSAS CYCLONE, 1941
KANSAS RAIDERS, 1950
KANSAS TERRITORY, 1952

BOLD: Films on Videocassette

KARAMAZOV, 1931
KARATE KID PART II, THE, 1986
KATHLEEN, 1938
KATHY O', 1958
KAYA, I'LL KILL YOU, 1969
KEEP YOUR SEATS PLEASE, 1936
KELLY'S HEROES, 1970
KENNY AND CO., 1976
KENTUCKIAN, THE, 1955
KENTUCKY MOONSHINE, 1938
KES, 1970
KETTLES IN THE OZARKS, THE, 1956
KETTLES ON OLD MACDONALD'S FARM, THE, 1957
KEY, THE, 1958
KEY TO THE CITY, 1950
KEY WITNESS, 1960
KHYBER PATROL, 1954
KID COMES BACK, THE, 1937
KID FROM LEFT FIELD, THE, 1953
KID MILLIONS, 1934
KID NIGHTINGALE, 1939
KID SISTER, THE, 1945
KIDCO, 1984
KIDNAPPING OF THE PRESIDENT, THE, 1980
KILL, 1968
KILL THE UMPIRE, 1950
KILL THEM ALL AND COME BACK ALONE, 1970
KILLER AT LARGE, 1947
KILLER INSIDE ME, THE, 1976
KILLER IS LOOSE, THE, 1956
KILLER McCOY, 1947
KILLER THAT STALKED NEW YORK, THE, 1950
KILLERS, THE, 1984
KILLER'S KISS, 1955
KILLING GAME, THE, 1968
KILLING KIND, THE, 1973
KILLING OF ANGEL STREET, THE, 1983
KING AND THE CHORUS GIRL, THE, 1937
KING FOR A NIGHT, 1933
KING IN NEW YORK, A, 1957
KING OF CHINATOWN, 1939
KING OF HEARTS, 1967
KING OF MARVIN GARDENS, THE, 1972
KING OF THE BANDITS, 1948
KING OF THE ROARING TWENTIES—THE STORY
   OF ARNOLD ROTHSTEIN, 1961
KING OF THE ROYAL MOUNTED, 1936
KING OF THE UNDERWORLD, 1939
KING OF THE WILD STALLIONS, 1959
KING RAT, 1965
KING SOLOMON'S MINES, 1985
KING'S RHAPSODY, 1955
KING'S THIEF, THE, 1955
KING'S VACATION, THE, 1933
KISMET, 1955
KISS AND TELL, 1945
KISS IN THE DARK, A, 1949
KISS THE BOYS GOODBYE, 1941
KISSES FOR MY PRESIDENT, 1964
KITTY FOYLE, 1940
KLONDIKE ANNIE, 1936
KNIGHTS OF THE RANGE, 1940
KNOCKOUT, 1941
KRAKATIT, 1948
KRAKATOA, EAST OF JAVA, 1969
KURAGEJIMA—LEGENDS FROM A SOUTHERN
   ISLAND, 1970
LA BALANCE, 1983
LA BOUM, 1983
LA MATERNELLE, 1933
LA NOTTE BRAVA, 1962
LA VIACCIA, 1962
LA VIE DE CHATEAU, 1967
LAD: A DOG, 1962
LADDIE, 1940
LADIES AND GENTLEMEN, THE FABULOUS
   STAINS, 1982
LADIES CLUB, THE, 1986
LADIES IN LOVE, 1936
LADIES' MAN, 1931
LADIES MAN, THE, 1961
LADIES OF LEISURE, 1930
LADIES OF THE BIG HOUSE, 1932
LADY AND THE MONSTER, THE, 1944
LADY CONSENTS, THE, 1936
LADY FROM CHEYENNE, 1941

LADY FROM LISBON, 1942
LADY FROM LOUISIANA, 1941
LADY FROM TEXAS, THE, 1951
LADY GAMBLES, THE, 1949
LADY HAS PLANS, THE, 1942
LADY IN A JAM, 1942
LADY IN DISTRESS, 1942
LADY IN THE CAR WITH GLASSES AND A GUN,
   THE, 1970
LADY IN THE IRON MASK, 1952
LADY IN THE MORGUE, 1938
LADY IS WILLING, THE, 1934
LADY, LET'S DANCE, 1944
LADY OF BURLESQUE, 1943
LADY TAKES A CHANCE, A, 1943
LADY TO LOVE, A, 1930
LADY WITH THE DOG, THE, 1962
LADYBUG, LADYBUG, 1963
LAFAYETTE ESCADRILLE, 1958
LAIR OF THE WHITE WORM, THE, 1988
LAND BEYOND THE LAW, 1937
LAND UNKNOWN, THE, 1957
LANDRU, 1963
LARAMIE TRAIL, THE, 1944
LAS VEGAS SHAKEDOWN, 1955
LASCA OF THE RIO GRANDE, 1931
LASH, THE, 1934
LASSIE FROM LANCASHIRE, 1938
LASSITER, 1984
LAST BANDIT, THE, 1949
LAST BLITZKRIEG, THE, 1958
LAST CHALLENGE, THE, 1967
LAST CHANCE, THE, 1937
LAST COUPON, THE, 1932
LAST CROOKED MILE, THE, 1946
LAST DAYS OF DOLWYN, THE, 1949
LAST DAYS OF POMPEII, THE, 1960
LAST DRAGON, THE, 1985
LAST EMBRACE, 1979
LAST GENTLEMAN, THE, 1934
LAST HARD MEN, THE, 1976
LAST HOUR, THE, 1930
LAST HOUSE ON THE LEFT, 1972
LAST MAN, THE, 1968
LAST OF MRS. CHEYNEY, THE, 1929
LAST OF THE BUCCANEERS, 1950
LAST OF THE DESPERADOES, 1956
LAST OF THE REDMEN, 1947
LAST OUTPOST, THE, 1935
LAST POSSE, THE, 1953
LAST TIME I SAW ARCHIE, THE, 1961
LAST TYCOON, THE, 1976
LAST UNICORN, THE, 1982
LAST WORD, THE, 1979
LATIN LOVE, 1930
LAUGH IT OFF, 1940
LAUGHING POLICEMAN, THE, 1973
LAUGHTER IN PARADISE, 1951
LAW AND DISORDER, 1940
LAW COMES TO TEXAS, THE, 1939
LAW IS THE LAW, THE, 1959
LAW OF DESIRE, 1987
LAW OF THE GOLDEN WEST, 1949
LAW OF THE LAWLESS, 1964
LAW WEST OF TOMBSTONE, THE, 1938
LAWLESS EIGHTIES, THE, 1957
LAWLESS VALLEY, 1938
LAZYBONES, 1935
LE BAL, 1984
LE BON PLAISIR, 1984
LE BONHEUR, 1966
LE BOUCHER, 1971
LE DENIER MILLIARDAIRE, 1934
LE PETIT SOLDAT, 1965
LEARNING TREE, THE, 1969
LEAVE IT TO ME, 1933
LEFT, RIGHT AND CENTRE, 1959
LEGACY, 1976
LEGACY OF THE 500,000, THE, 1964
LEGEND OF LOBO, THE, 1962
LEGEND OF LYLAH CLARE, THE, 1968
LEMON GROVE KIDS MEET THE MONSTERS, THE,
   1966
LEOPARD, THE, 1963
LEOPARD IN THE SNOW, 1979
LEPKE, 1975

LES BELLES-DE-NUIT, 1952
LES CARABINIERS, 1968
LES MAITRES DU TEMPS, 1982
LET ME EXPLAIN, DEAR, 1932
LETHAL WEAPON, 1987
LET'S BE FAMOUS, 1939
LET'S DANCE, 1950
LET'S FACE IT, 1943
LET'S MAKE IT LEGAL, 1951
LET'S MAKE LOVE, 1960
LETTER OF INTRODUCTION, 1938
LETTY LYNTON, 1932
LIAR'S DICE, 1980
LIBEL, 1959
LIBIDO, 1973
LIFE BEGINS ANEW, 1938
LIFE BEGINS AT 17, 1958
LIFE BEGINS IN COLLEGE, 1937
LIFE IN HER HANDS, 1951
LIFE IN THE BALANCE, A, 1955
LIFE IN THE RAW, 1933
LIFE IS A CIRCUS, 1962
LIFE OF JIMMY DOLAN, THE, 1933
LIFE OF THE PARTY, THE, 1930
LIFE OF VERGIE WINTERS, THE, 1934
LIFE WITH BLONDIE, 1946
LIGHT ACROSSS THE STREET, THE, 1957
LIGHTHORSEMEN, THE, 1988
LIGHTNING CONDUCTOR, 1938
LIGHTNING GUNS, 1950
LIGHTS OF OLD SANTA FE, 1944
LIKE A TURTLE ON ITS BACK, 1981
LILLIAN RUSSELL, 1940
LIQUIDATOR, THE, 1966
LISA, 1962
LISBON STORY, THE, 1946
LITTLE BIG MAN, 1970
LITTLE CIGARS, 1973
LITTLE EGYPT, 1951
LITTLE FLAMES, 1985
LITTLE HUMPBACKED HORSE, THE, 1962
LITTLE MISS BROADWAY, 1938
LITTLE NELLIE KELLY, 1940
LITTLE NIKITA, 1988
LITTLE NUNS, THE, 1965
LITTLE OLD NEW YORK, 1940
LITTLE RED RIDING HOOD, 1963
LITTLE SHEPHERD OF KINGDOM COME, 1961
LITTLE WOMEN, 1949
LITTLEST HOBO, THE, 1958
LIVE AND LET DIE, 1973
LIVE WIRES, 1946
LIVING FREE, 1972
LIVING ON VELVET, 1935
LIZZIE, 1957
LOADED PISTOLS, 1948
LOGAN'S RUN, 1976
LOLLIPOP COVER, THE, 1965
LONE CLIMBER, THE, 1950
LONE HAND, THE, 1953
LONE RANGER, THE, 1955
LONE STAR, 1952
LONE STAR TRAIL, THE, 1943
LONE TEXAN, 1959
LONE WOLF RETURNS, THE, 1936
LONELY HEARTS, 1983
LONELY MAN, THE, 1957
LONG JOHN SILVER, 1954
LONG LOST FATHER, 1934
LONG NIGHT, THE, 1976
LONG WAIT, THE, 1954
LONG WEEKEND, 1978
LOOK WHO'S LAUGHING, 1941
LOOKING FOR EILEEN, 1987
LOOSE ANKLES, 1930
LOOSE IN LONDON, 1953
LORD JEFF, 1938
LORD OF THE MANOR, 1933
LORD OF THE RINGS, THE, 1978
LORDS OF DISCIPLINE, THE, 1983
LOSS OF FEELING, 1935
LOST AND FOUND, 1979
LOST BOYS, THE, 1987
LOST COMMAND, THE, 1966
LOST HONEYMOON, 1947
LOST HONOR OF KATHARINA BLUM, THE, 1975

LOST IN AMERICA, 1985
LOST MAN, THE, 1969
LOST MOMENT, THE, 1947
LOST ON THE WESTERN FRONT, 1940
LOST PEOPLE, THE, 1950
LOST SEX, 1968
LOUISIANA PURCHASE, 1941
LOVE A LA CARTE, 1965
LOVE AND ANARCHY, 1974
LOVE AND MARRIAGE, 1966
LOVE AT FIRST BITE, 1979
LOVE, 1982
LOVE BEFORE BREAKFAST, 1936
LOVE CAPTIVE, THE, 1934
LOVE CHILD, 1982
LOVE ETERNE, THE, 1964
LOVE FROM A STRANGER, 1947
LOVE HABIT, THE, 1931
LOVE HAPPY, 1949
LOVE, HONOR AND BEHAVE, 1938
LOVE IN A GOLDFISH BOWL, 1961
LOVE IN 4 DIMENSIONS, 1965
LOVE IN GERMANY, A, 1984
LOVE IN PAWN, 1953
LOVE IS BETTER THAN EVER, 1952
LOVE IS MY PROFESSION, 1959
LOVE LETTERS, 1945
LOVE LETTERS OF A STAR, 1936
LOVE LOTTERY, THE, 1954
LOVE MATCH, THE, 1955
LOVE ME FOREVER, 1935
LOVE THAT BRUTE, 1950
LOVELESS, THE, 1982
LOVER COME BACK, 1946
LOVERS AND LOLLIPOPS, 1956
LOVES OF CARMEN, THE, 1948
LOVES OF THREE QUEENS, THE, 1954
LOYALTIES, 1934
LUCK OF THE TURF, 1936
LUCKY BRIDE, THE, 1948
LUCKY CISCO KID, 1940
LUCKY DOG, 1933
LUCKY JIM, 1957
LUCKY NICK CAIN, 1951
LUCKY TEXAN, THE, 1934
LUCRECE BORGIA, 1953
LUCREZIA BORGIA, 1937
LUGGAGE OF THE GODS, 1983
LULLABY OF BROADWAY, THE, 1951
LUMIERE, 1976
LURE OF THE JUNGLE, THE, 1970
LUTHER, 1974
LYDIA, 1941
LYDIA BAILEY, 1952
LYONS IN PARIS, THE, 1955
MA AND PA KETTLE, 1949
MACBETH, 1963
MACHINE GUN KELLY, 1958
MACHISMO—40 GRAVES FOR 40 GUNS, 1970
MACKENNA'S GOLD, 1969
MACKINTOSH MAN, THE, 1973
MAD ATLANTIC, THE, 1967
MAD GAME, THE, 1933
MAD GENIUS, THE, 1931
MAD GHOUL, THE, 1943
MAD LITTLE ISLAND, 1958
MAD MISS MANTON, THE, 1938
MAD MONSTER PARTY, 1967
MADALENA, 1965
MADAME, 1963
MADAME BUTTERFLY, 1932
MADAME SATAN, 1930
MADAME WHITE SNAKE, 1963
MADAME X, 1937
MADE IN U.S.A., 1966
MADEMOISELLE, 1966
MADEMOISELLE FIFI, 1944
MADONNA OF THE SEVEN MOONS, 1945
MAFIOSO, 1962
MAGIC TOWN, 1947
MAGIC WORLD OF TOPO GIGIO, THE, 1961
MAGICIAN OF LUBLIN, THE, 1979
MAGNIFICENT CUCKOLD, THE, 1965
MAGNIFICENT OBSESSION, 1954
MAGNIFICENT ONE, THE, 1974
MAGNIFICENT SEVEN DEADLY SINS, THE, 1971

MAGNIFICENT SINNER, 1963
MAHLER, 1974
MAID TO ORDER, 1987
MAID'S NIGHT OUT, 1938
MAIN THING IS TO LOVE, THE, 1975
MAIS OU ET DONC ORNICAR, 1979
MAISIE WAS A LADY, 1941
MAJDHAR, 1984
MAKE MINE A MILLION, 1965
MALACHI'S COVE, 1973
MALANDRO, 1986
MALONE, 1987
MAMBO, 1955
MAME, 1974
MAMMY, 1930
MAN, A WOMAN, AND A BANK, A, 1979
MAN, A WOMAN AND A KILLER, A, 1975
MAN ABOUT TOWN, 1939
MAN AND THE BEAST, THE, 1951
MAN BEHIND THE MASK, THE, 1936
MAN CALLED FLINTSTONE, THE, 1966
MAN CALLED HORSE, A, 1970
MAN CALLED SLEDGE, A, 1971
MAN DETAINED, 1961
MAN FRIDAY, 1975
MAN FROM BITTER RIDGE, THE, 1955
MAN FROM MUSIC MOUNTAIN, 1938
MAN FROM MUSIC MOUNTAIN, 1943
MAN FROM PLANET X, THE, 1951
MAN FROM RAINBOW VALLEY, THE, 1946
MAN FROM TEXAS, THE, 1939
MAN FROM THUNDER RIVER, THE, 1943
MAN FROM TUMBLEWEEDS, THE, 1940
MAN IN BLUE, THE, 1937
MAN IN THE ATTIC, 1953
MAN IN THE DARK, 1953
MAN IN THE SADDLE, 1951
MAN IN THE SHADOW, 1957
MAN IN THE WILDERNESS, 1971
MAN INSIDE, THE, 1958
MAN OF EVIL, 1948
MAN OF THE FOREST, 1933
MAN OF THE MOMENT, 1955
MAN OF THE MOMENT, 1935
MAN STOLEN, 1934
MAN THEY COULD NOT HANG, THE, 1939
MAN TO MAN, 1931
MAN TRAILER, THE, 1934
MAN WHO CHEATED HIMSELF, THE, 1951
MAN WHO COULD CHEAT DEATH, THE, 1959
MAN WHO COULDN'T WALK, THE, 1964
MAN WHO CRIED WOLF, THE, 1937
MAN WHO DARED, THE, 1946
MAN WHO ENVIED WOMEN, THE, 1985
MAN WHO LIES, THE, 1970
MAN WHO LIVED TWICE, 1936
MAN WHO MADE DIAMONDS, THE, 1937
MAN WHO PLAYED GOD, THE, 1932
MAN WHO UNDERSTOOD WOMEN, THE, 1959
MAN WHO WAGGED HIS TAIL, THE, 1961
MAN WHO WOULDN'T TALK, THE, 1958
MAN WITH THE GOLDEN ARM, THE, 1955
MAN WITH THE TRANSPLANTED BRAIN, THE, 1972
MANGANINNIE, 1982
MANGO TREE, THE, 1981
MANNEQUIN, 1937
MAN'S FAVORITE SPORT (?), 1964
MANULESCU, 1933
MANY RIVERS TO CROSS, 1955
MANY TANKS MR. ATKINS, 1938
MARA MARU, 1952
MARA OF THE WILDERNESS, 1966
MARACAIBO, 1958
MARDI GRAS, 1958
MARIA'S LOVERS, 1985
MARIGOLD, 1938
MARINE RAIDERS, 1944
MARINES, LET'S GO, 1961
MARJORIE MORNINGSTAR, 1958
MARK OF THE WHISTLER, THE, 1944
MARNIE, 1964
MARRIAGE OF BALZAMINOV, THE, 1966
MARRY ME AGAIN, 1953
MARRYING KIND, THE, 1952
MARSHAL OF AMARILLO, 1948
MARSHAL OF CEDAR ROCK, 1953

MARSHAL OF GUNSMOKE, 1944
MARTHA JELLNECK, 1988
MARTIN LUTHER, 1953
MARY JANE'S PA, 1935
MARY, MARY, 1963
MARY OF SCOTLAND, 1936
MASK OF THE AVENGER, 1951
MASKED RAIDERS, 1949
MASKED RIDER, THE, 1941
MASQUERADER, THE, 1933
MASTERMIND, 1977
MASTERS OF THE UNIVERSE, 1987
MASTERSON OF KANSAS, 1954
MATCHLESS, 1974
MATING OF MILLIE, THE, 1948
MATING SEASON, THE, 1951
MATTER OF HONOR, A, 1988
MATTER OF MORALS, A, 1961
MAURICE, 1987
MAZE, THE, 1953
MC CONNELL STORY, THE, 1955
MC HALE'S NAVY, 1964
MC HALE'S NAVY JOINS THE AIR FORCE, 1965
MC LINTOCK!, 1963
MC VICAR, 1982
ME, 1970
ME AND MARLBOROUGH, 1935
MEAN SEASON, THE, 1985
MEDAL FOR BENNY, A, 1945
MEET BOSTON BLACKIE, 1941
MEET DR. CHRISTIAN, 1939
MEET ME AT THE FAIR, 1952
MEET MY SISTER, 1933
MEET THE BARON, 1933
MEET THE MISSUS, 1940
MEET THE NAVY, 1946
MEET THE STEWARTS, 1942
MELBA, 1953
MELODY FOR THREE, 1941
MEN AGAINST THE SUN, 1953
MEN IN HER DIARY, 1945
MEN OF BOYS TOWN, 1941
MEN OF SHERWOOD FOREST, 1957
MEN OF TEXAS, 1942
MEN OF YESTERDAY, 1936
MEN WITH WINGS, 1938
MERCENARY, THE, 1970
MERELY MARY ANN, 1931
MERRY ANDREW, 1958
MERRY MONAHANS, THE, 1944
MERRY WIVES OF WINDSOR, THE, 1966
MESSAGE FROM SPACE, 1978
MESSALINE, 1952
MEXICALI ROSE, 1939
MEXICAN SPITFIRE, 1939
MICHAEL SHAYNE, PRIVATE DETECTIVE, 1940
MICKEY ONE, 1965
MIDDLE AGE CRAZY, 1980
MIDNIGHT ANGEL, 1941
MIDNIGHT MAN, THE, 1974
MIDNIGHT WARNING, THE, 1932
MIDSUMMER NIGHT'S DREAM, A, 1969
MIDSUMMER NIGHT'S DREAM, A, 1984
MIDSUMMER NIGHT'S SEX COMEDY, A, 1982
MIGHTY BARNUM, THE, 1934
MIGHTY TREVE, THE, 1937
MIKADO, THE, 1939
MIKADO, THE, 1967
MIKEY AND NICKY, 1976
MILAGRO BEANFIELD WAR, THE, 1988
MILITARY SECRET, 1945
MILL ON THE FLOSS, 1939
MILLION DOLLAR LEGS, 1939
MINNESOTA CLAY, 1966
MIRACLE IN SOHO, 1957
MIRACLE MAN, THE, 1932
MIRACLE OF THE HILLS, THE, 1959
MIRACLES, 1987
MIRAGE, 1965
MIRROR HAS TWO FACES, THE, 1959
MISADVENTURES OF MERLIN JONES, THE, 1964
MISS PRESIDENT, 1935
MISS SUSIE SLAGLE'S, 1945
MISSILE FROM HELL, 1960
MISSING EVIDENCE, 1939
MISSING IN ACTION 2—THE BEGINNING, 1985

MISSING TEN DAYS, 1941
MISSIONARY, THE, 1982
MISSISSIPPI, 1935
MISSOURIANS, THE, 1950
MR. AND MRS. NORTH, 1941
MR. ARKADIN, 1962
MISTER BROWN, 1972
MR. CHEDWORTH STEPS OUT, 1939
MR. COHEN TAKES A WALK, 1936
MR. DRAKE'S DUCK, 1951
MR. KLEIN, 1976
MR. LORD SAYS NO, 1952
MR. LOVE, 1986
MR. MOM, 1983
MISTER MOSES, 1965
MR. MOTO IN DANGER ISLAND, 1939
MR. MOTO'S GAMBLE, 1938
MR. MOTO'S LAST WARNING, 1939
MR. MUGGS STEPS OUT, 1943
MR. MUSIC, 1950
MR. ORCHID, 1948
MR. PEABODY AND THE MERMAID, 1948
MR. QUINCEY OF MONTE CARLO, 1933
MR. SCOUTMASTER, 1953
MR. WHAT'S-HIS-NAME, 1935
MISTRESS OF ATLANTIS, THE, 1932
MIXED COMPANY, 1974
MODEL WIFE, 1941
MODERATO CANTABILE, 1964
MODERN LOVE, 1929
MODESTY BLAISE, 1966
MOHAMMAD, MESSENGER OF GOD, 1976
MOHAWK, 1956
MOMENTS, 1974
MONEY MOVERS, 1978
MONEY TALKS, 1933
MONKEY GRIP, 1983
MONKEY ON MY BACK, 1957
MONKEY'S PAW, THE, 1953
MONSIEUR VERDOUX, 1947
MONSTER AND THE GIRL, THE, 1941
MONSTER THAT CHALLENGED THE WORLD, THE, 1957
MONTANA MOON, 1930
MONTY PYTHON AND THE HOLY GRAIL, 1975
MOON IS BLUE, THE, 1953
MOON OVER MIAMI, 1941
MOON PILOT, 1962
MOON-SPINNERS, THE, 1964
MOONFLEET, 1955
MOONLIGHT AND PRETZELS, 1933
MOONRAKER, THE, 1958
MOONTIDE, 1942
MORE, 1969
MORE DEAD THAN ALIVE, 1968
MORGAN'S MARAUDERS, 1929
MORNING AFTER, THE, 1986
MOSCOW—CASSIOPEIA, 1974
MOSCOW DOES NOT BELIEVE IN TEARS, 1980
MOST BEAUTIFUL AGE, THE, 1970
MOST DANGEROUS MAN ALIVE, THE, 1961
MOST WONDERFUL EVENING OF MY LIFE, THE, 1972
MOTHER CAREY'S CHICKENS, 1938
MOTHER DIDN'T TELL ME, 1950
MOTHER IS A FRESHMAN, 1949
MOTHER KUSTERS GOES TO HEAVEN, 1976
MOTHRA, 1962
MOULIN ROUGE, 1934
MOUNTAIN JUSTICE, 1937
MOUNTAIN ROAD, THE, 1960
MOUNTAINS O'MOURNE, 1938
MOUSE AND THE WOMAN, THE, 1981
MOUSE ON THE MOON, THE, 1963
MOVIE MOVIE, 1978
MRS. MIKE, 1949
MRS. PARKINGTON, 1944
MRS. SOFFEL, 1984
MUDLARK, THE, 1950
MUMMY'S TOMB, THE, 1942
MUMU, 1961
MUPPETS TAKE MANHATTAN, THE, 1984
MURDER AT THE BASKERVILLES, 1941
MURDER AT THE VANITIES, 1934
MURDER BY THE CLOCK, 1931
MURDER IN THE CLOUDS, 1934

MURDER IN THE MUSIC HALL, 1946
MURDER IN TIMES SQUARE, 1943
MURDER OVER NEW YORK, 1940
MURDER REPORTED, 1958
MURDERS IN THE RUE MORGUE, 1932
MURPHY'S ROMANCE, 1985
MURPHY'S WAR, 1971
MUSCLE BEACH PARTY, 1964
MUSIC IN THE AIR, 1934
MUTINY IN THE ARCTIC, 1941
MUTINY ON THE BOUNTY, 1962
MY BLUE HEAVEN, 1950
MY BROTHER'S KEEPER, 1949
MY BUDDY, 1944
MY CHILDHOOD, 1972
MY DARK LADY, 1987
MY DEAR SECRETARY, 1948
MY DREAM IS YOURS, 1949
MY FOOLISH HEART, 1949
MY FORBIDDEN PAST, 1951
MY FRIEND IRMA GOES WEST, 1950
MY GIRL TISA, 1948
MY KIND OF TOWN, 1984
MY LITTLE CHICKADEE, 1940
MY LUCKY STAR, 1938
MY MAN, 1928
MY MAN AND I, 1952
MY MARGO, 1969
MY NEW PARTNER, 1984
MY SEVEN LITTLE SINS, 1956
MY SON IS A CRIMINAL, 1939
MY SON, JOHN, 1952
MY SON, THE HERO, 1963
MY WILD IRISH ROSE, 1947
MYSTERIOUS RIDER, THE, 1933
MYSTERIOUS RIDER, THE, 1938
MYSTERIOUS SATELLITE, THE, 1956
MYSTERY IN MEXICO, 1948
MYSTERY LAKE, 1953
MYSTERY MAN, THE, 1935
MYSTERY OF ALEXINA, THE, 1985
MYSTERY OF THE HOODED HORSEMEN, THE, 1937
MYSTIC HOUR, THE, 1934
MYSTIC PIZZA, 1988
NAKED DAWN, THE, 1955
NAKED FACE, THE, 1984
NAKED FURY, 1959
NAKED GENERAL, THE, 1964
NAKED GUN, THE, 1988
NAKED KISS, THE, 1964
NAME OF THE GAME IS KILL, THE, 1968
NAMU, THE KILLER WHALE, 1966
NANA, 1934
NANCY DREW AND THE HIDDEN STAIRCASE, 1939
NANCY DREW, TROUBLE SHOOTER, 1939
NANCY GOES TO RIO, 1950
NAPOLEON AND SAMANTHA, 1972
NARROWING CIRCLE, THE, 1956
NATE AND HAYES, 1983
NATHALIE, 1958
NATIVE LAND, 1942
NATIVE SON, 1951
NATIVE SON, 1986
NAVY BLUES, 1941
NAZARIN, 1968
'NEATH BROOKLYN BRIDGE, 1942
NED KELLY, 1970
NEIGHBORS, 1981
NEPTUNE'S DAUGHTER, 1949
NEST, THE, 1982
NEUTRAL PORT, 1941
NEVADA, 1944
NEVADAN, THE, 1950
NEVER LET GO, 1960
NEVER NEVER LAND, 1982
NEVER SAY NEVER AGAIN, 1983
NEVER STEAL ANYTHING SMALL, 1959
NEVER TAKE NO FOR AN ANSWER, 1952
NEVER TOO YOUNG TO DIE, 1986
NEW INTERNS, THE, 1964
NEW YORK TOWN, 1941
NEXT MAN, THE, 1976
NEXT TO NO TIME, 1960
NICE GIRL LIKE ME, A, 1969
NICE GIRLS DON'T EXPLODE, 1987
NIGHT ALONE, 1938

NIGHT CLUB SCANDAL, 1937
NIGHT CREATURES, 1962
NIGHT EDITOR, 1946
NIGHT ENCOUNTER, 1963
NIGHT IN BANGKOK, 1966
NIGHT IN HONG KONG, A, 1961
NIGHT IN JUNE, A, 1940
NIGHT INTO MORNING, 1951
NIGHT INVADER, THE, 1943
NIGHT IS MY FUTURE, 1962
NIGHT KEY, 1937
NIGHT LIFE OF THE GODS, 1935
NIGHT MAIL, 1935
NIGHT MAYOR, THE, 1932
NIGHT MOVES, 1975
NIGHT MY NUMBER CAME UP, THE, 1955
NIGHT OF NIGHTS, THE, 1939
NIGHT OF THE IGUANA, THE, 1964
NIGHT OF THE SEAGULL, THE, 1970
NIGHT PASSAGE, 1957
NIGHT PLANE FROM CHUNGKING, 1942
NIGHT PORTER, THE, 1974
NIGHT TIDE, 1963
NIGHT TIME IN NEVADA, 1948
NIGHT TO REMEMBER, A, 1942
NIGHT TRAIN FOR INVERNESS, 1960
NIGHT WON'T TALK, THE, 1952
NIGHT WORK, 1930
NIGHT WORLD, 1932
NIGHTMARE CASTLE, 1966
NIGHTMARE ON ELM STREET 4: THE DREAM MASTER, A, 1988
NIGHTMARE ON ELM STREET PART 2: FREDDY'S REVENGE, A, 1985
NIGHTS OF SHAME, 1961
NIGHTSONGS, 1984
NINE FORTY-FIVE, 1934
NINE GIRLS, 1944
NINE LIVES ARE NOT ENOUGH, 1941
NINE MILES TO NOON, 1963
1984, 1956
1941, 1979
90 DEGREES IN THE SHADE, 1966
NINTH GUEST, THE, 1934
NITWITS, THE, 1935
NO DOWN PAYMENT, 1957
NO ESCAPE, 1934
NO ESCAPE, 1936
NO GREATER LOVE THAN THIS, 1969
NO HANDS ON THE CLOCK, 1941
NO HOLDS BARRED, 1952
NO MAN OF HER OWN, 1933
NO MAN OF HER OWN, 1950
NO MERCY, 1986
NO, MY DARLING DAUGHTER, 1964
NO QUESTIONS ASKED, 1951
NO RETURN ADDRESS, 1961
NO SEX PLEASE—WE'RE BRITISH, 1979
NO TIME FOR ECSTASY, 1963
NO TIME TO KILL, 1963
NO TIME TO MARRY, 1938
NOB HILL, 1945
NOBODY'S BABY, 1937
NOCTURNE, 1946
NOMADS, 1985
NON-STOP NEW YORK, 1937
NOOSE FOR A GUNMAN, 1960
NORTH AVENUE IRREGULARS, THE, 1979
NORTH STAR, THE, 1943
NORTHERN LIGHTS, 1978
NORTHWEST OUTPOST, 1947
NOT AS A STRANGER, 1955
NOT FOR PUBLICATION, 1984
NOT MINE TO LOVE, 1969
NOT OF THIS EARTH, 1957
NOT SO DUSTY, 1936
NOT SO QUIET ON THE WESTERN FRONT, 1930
NOT WANTED, 1949
NOT WITH MY WIFE, YOU DON'T!, 1966
NOTHING BARRED, 1961
NOTHING BUT THE TRUTH, 1929
NOTHING BUT TROUBLE, 1944
NOTHING LIKE PUBLICITY, 1936
NOTHING VENTURE, 1948
NOVEL AFFAIR, A, 1957
NOW BARABBAS WAS A ROBBER, 1949

NOW I'LL TELL, 1934
NOWHERE TO GO, 1959
NUDE IN A WHITE CAR, 1960
NUISANCE, THE, 1933
NUMBER ONE, 1984
NUNZIO, 1978
NURSE ON WHEELS, 1964
NURSEMAID WHO DISAPPEARED, THE, 1939
NURSE'S SECRET, THE, 1941
NUTCRACKER FANTASY, 1979
OCEAN'S ELEVEN, 1960
OCTOBER MAN, THE, 1948
ODD JOBS, 1986
OF HUMAN BONDAGE, 1946
OF UNKNOWN ORIGIN, 1983
OFF LIMITS, 1953
OFF THE DOLE, 1935
OFF THE WALL, 1983
OFFBEAT, 1961
OFFERING, THE, 1966
OFFICER'S MESS, THE, 1931
OH, FOR A MAN!, 1930
OH, GOD!, 1977
OH ROSALINDA, 1956
OH! SAILOR, BEHAVE!, 1930
OH, YOU BEAUTIFUL DOLL, 1949
OKLAHOMA CRUDE, 1973
OKLAHOMA TERRITORY, 1960
OKLAHOMAN, THE, 1957
OLD ACQUAINTANCE, 1943
OLD CURIOSITY SHOP, THE, 1935
OLD DARK HOUSE, THE, 1963
OLD ENGLISH, 1930
OLD FAITHFUL, 1935
OLD HUTCH, 1936
OLD MOTHER RILEY IN PARIS, 1938
OLIVE TREES OF JUSTICE, THE, 1967
OLIVER & COMPANY, 1988
ON A CLEAR DAY YOU CAN SEE FOREVER, 1970
ON APPROVAL, 1944
ON OUR SELECTION, 1930
ON THE BEACH, 1959
ON THE COMET, 1970
ON TRIAL, 1939
ON WITH THE SHOW, 1929
ONCE A CROOK, 1941
ONCE A RAINY DAY, 1968
ONCE A THIEF, 1965
ONCE IN A LIFETIME, 1932
ONCE MORE, MY DARLING, 1949
ONCE UPON A SCOUNDREL, 1973
ONE BODY TOO MANY, 1944
ONE CRAZY SUMMER, 1986
ONE DARK NIGHT, 1983
ONE DESIRE, 1955
ONE EMBARRASSING NIGHT, 1930
ONE EXCITING ADVENTURE, 1935
$100 A NIGHT, 1968
100 MEN AND A GIRL, 1937
ONE LITTLE INDIAN, 1973
ONE MAN, 1979
ONE MAN'S JOURNEY, 1933
$1,000,000 DUCK, 1971
ONE NEW YORK NIGHT, 1935
ONE NIGHT AT SUSIE'S, 1930
ONE NIGHT IN LISBON, 1941
ONE NIGHT IN THE TROPICS, 1940
ONE THAT GOT AWAY, THE, 1958
$1,000 A MINUTE, 1935
ONE TOUCH OF VENUS, 1948
ONE-WAY TICKET, A, 1988
ONE WAY TRAIL, THE, 1931
ONE WISH TOO MANY, 1956
ONLY THE VALIANT, 1951
ONLY WHEN I LARF, 1968
ONLY YESTERDAY, 1933
OPEN THE DOOR AND SEE ALL THE PEOPLE, 1964
OPERATION GANYMED, 1977
OPERATION MANHUNT, 1954
OPERATION SECRET, 1952
OPERATION SNATCH, 1962
OPERATION THUNDERBOLT, 1978
OPERETTA, 1949
OPPOSING FORCE, 1987
ORDET, 1957
OREGON TRAIL, THE, 1936

ORIANE, 1985
ORPHAN OF THE WILDERNESS, 1937
ORPHANS OF THE STREET, 1939
O'SHAUGHNESSY'S BOY, 1935
OSS 117—MISSION FOR A KILLER, 1966
OTHELLO, 1960
OTHER ONE, THE, 1967
OTHER TOMORROW, THE, 1930
OTLEY, 1969
OUR BLUSHING BRIDES, 1930
OUR DAILY BREAD, 1950
OUR FATHER, 1985
OUR HEARTS WERE GROWING UP, 1946
OUR HEARTS WERE YOUNG AND GAY, 1944
OUR LITTLE GIRL, 1935
OUR MISS BROOKS, 1956
OUR MODERN MAIDENS, 1929
OUR SILENT LOVE, 1969
OUT, 1982
OUT OF AFRICA, 1985
OUT OF IT, 1969
OUT OF SINGAPORE, 1932
OUT OF THE BLUE, 1982
OUT OF THIS WORLD, 1945
OUTBACK, 1971
OUTCAST, 1937
OUTCAST, THE, 1954
OUTCASTS OF POKER FLAT, THE, 1952
OUTLAW BLUES, 1977
OUTLAW COUNTRY, 1949
OUTLAW DEPUTY, THE, 1935
OUTLAWS IS COMING, THE, 1965
OUTLAWS OF PINE RIDGE, 1942
OUTLAWS OF TEXAS, 1950
OUTLAWS OF THE PRAIRIE, 1938
OUTPOST IN MALAYA, 1952
OUTRAGE, 1950
OUTSIDE MAN, THE, 1973
OUTSIDE OF PARADISE, 1938
OUTSIDE THE WALL, 1950
OUTSIDE THESE WALLS, 1939
OUTSIDER, THE, 1949
OUTWARD BOUND, 1930
OVER THE BROOKLYN BRIDGE, 1984
OVER THE EDGE, 1979
OVER THE SUMMER, 1986
OVERCOAT, THE, 1965
OVERLAND MAIL, 1939
OVERLAND PACIFIC, 1954
OVERLAND TELEGRAPH, 1951
OVERNIGHT, 1933
OWL AND THE PUSSYCAT, THE, 1970
PACK, THE, 1977
PACK UP YOUR TROUBLES, 1932
PAGAN, THE, 1929
PAGE MISS GLORY, 1935
PAID IN FULL, 1950
PAINTED ANGEL, THE, 1929
PAINTED DESERT, THE, 1931
PAJAMA PARTY, 1964
PALM SPRINGS WEEKEND, 1963
PALOMINO, THE, 1950
PALS OF THE PECOS, 1941
PALS OF THE SADDLE, 1938
PAN-AMERICANA, 1945
PANAMA PATROL, 1939
PANIC BUTTON, 1964
PANTHER'S CLAW, THE, 1942
PAPER CHASE, THE, 1973
PAPER ORCHID, 1949
PAPERBACK HERO, 1973
PARACHUTE JUMPER, 1933
PARADISE CANYON, 1935
PARADISE EXPRESS, 1937
PARATROOPER, 1954
PARDON MY PAST, 1945
PARDON MY SARONG, 1942
PARDON US, 1931
PARIS AFTER DARK, 1943
PARIS BLUES, 1961
PARIS EXPRESS, THE, 1953
PARIS HOLIDAY, 1958
PARIS HONEYMOON, 1939
PARIS IN THE MONTH OF AUGUST, 1968
PARISIAN, THE, 1931
PARKING, 1985

PARLOR, BEDROOM AND BATH, 1931
PART TIME WIFE, 1930
PARTNERS OF THE PLAINS, 1938
PASS THE AMMO, 1988
PASSAGE HOME, 1955
PASSAGE WEST, 1951
PASSING THROUGH, 1977
PASSION FOR LIFE, 1951
PASSION ISLAND, 1943
PASSION OF SLOW FIRE, THE, 1962
PASSIONATE PLUMBER, 1932
PASSWORD IS COURAGE, THE, 1962
PASTOR HALL, 1940
PATTY HEARST, 1988
PAYMENT DEFERRED, 1932
P.C. JOSSER, 1931
PEARLS BRING TEARS, 1937
PECK'S BAD BOY, 1934
PEEPING TOM, 1960
PEG O' MY HEART, 1933
PEGGY, 1950
PEKING EXPRESS, 1951
PENDULUM, 1969
PENITENT, THE, 1988
PENITENTIARY, 1979
PENITENTIARY III, 1987
PENNIES FROM HEAVEN, 1981
PENNY POOL, THE, 1937
PENNY SERENADE, 1941
PEOPLE WILL TALK, 1935
PEPE, 1960
PERFECT CRIME, THE, 1937
PERFECT FURLOUGH, THE, 1958
PERFECT WOMAN, THE, 1950
PERFORMERS, THE, 1970
PERIL, 1985
PERILOUS HOLIDAY, 1946
PERILOUS JOURNEY, A, 1953
PERMANENT RECORD, 1988
PERMANENT VACATION, 1982
PERSONAL AFFAIR, 1954
PERSONAL FOUL, 1987
PERSONAL MAID, 1931
PERSONAL PROPERTY, 1937
PERSONS IN HIDING, 1939
PETERSEN, 1974
PETERVILLE DIAMOND, THE, 1942
PETIT CON, 1985
PHAEDRA, 1962
PHANTOM OF PARIS, THE, 1931
PHANTOM OF THE PARADISE, 1974
PHANTOM PRESIDENT, THE, 1932
PHANTOM STRIKES, THE, 1939
PHANTOM THIEF, THE, 1946
PHASE IV, 1974
PHENIX CITY STORY, THE, 1955
PHILADELPHIA ATTRACTION, THE, 1985
PHILADELPHIA EXPERIMENT, THE, 1984
PHILO VANCE'S SECRET MISSION, 1947
PICCADILLY JIM, 1936
PICKUP ON 101, 1972
PICTURE MOMMY DEAD, 1966
PICTURE SNATCHER, 1933
PIECE OF THE ACTION, A, 1977
PILLARS OF SOCIETY, 1936
PILLARS OF THE SKY, 1956
PILLOW TO POST, 1945
PINK JUNGLE, THE, 1968
PINK NIGHTS, 1985
PIONEER JUSTICE, 1947
PIPE DREAMS, 1976
PIPER'S TUNE, THE, 1962
PIPPI IN THE SOUTH SEAS, 1974
PIPPI ON THE RUN, 1977
PIRANHA, 1978
PIRATES OF BLOOD RIVER, THE, 1962
PIRATES OF CAPRI, THE, 1949
PISTOL FOR RINGO, A, 1966
PIT OF DARKNESS, 1961
PIZZA TRIANGLE, THE, 1970
P.K. & THE KID, 1987
PLACE CALLED GLORY, A, 1966
PLANK, THE, 1967
PLAY GIRL, 1940
PLAY IT COOL, 1970
PLAYBOY OF PARIS, 1930

PLAYGIRL, 1954
PLAYMATES, 1969
PLEASE BELIEVE ME, 1950
PLEASURE SEEKERS, THE, 1964
PLEASURES OF THE FLESH, THE, 1965
PLUCKED, 1969
PLUNDER OF THE SUN, 1953
PLYMOUTH ADVENTURE, 1952
POACHER'S DAUGHTER, THE, 1960
POINT BLANK, 1967
POINTED HEELS, 1930
POLICE NURSE, 1963
POLITICAL PARTY, A, 1933
POLTERGEIST II, 1986
PONY EXPRESS RIDER, 1976
POOL OF LONDON, 1951
POPE OF GREENWICH VILLAGE, THE, 1984
POR MIS PISTOLAS, 1969
PORT OF CALL, 1963
PORTIA ON TRIAL, 1937
PORTLAND EXPOSE, 1957
PORTRAIT OF THE ARTIST AS A YOUNG MAN, A, 1979
POSEIDON ADVENTURE, THE, 1972
POSSESSED, 1931
POSTMARK FOR DANGER, 1956
POT LUCK, 1936
P.O.W., THE, 1973
POWDER RIVER RUSTLERS, 1949
POWDERSMOKE RANGE, 1935
POWER, 1934
POWER, THE, 1968
POWER AND THE PRIZE, THE, 1956
POWER DIVE, 1941
PRACTICALLY YOURS, 1944
PRAIRIE MOON, 1938
PRAIRIE ROUNDUP, 1951
PRAY FOR DEATH, 1986
PREMATURE BURIAL, THE, 1962
PRESENTING LILY MARS, 1943
PRESS FOR TIME, 1966
PRESSURE, 1976
PRETTY BOY FLOYD, 1960
PRETTY MAIDS ALL IN A ROW, 1971
PREVIEW MURDER MYSTERY, 1936
PRICE OF FEAR, THE, 1956
PRIDE AND THE PASSION, THE, 1957
PRIDE OF THE WEST, 1938
PRIEST OF LOVE, 1981
PRIME RISK, 1985
PRINCE OF ARCADIA, 1933
PRINCE OF PIRATES, 1953
PRINCE VALIANT, 1954
PRINCE WHO WAS A THIEF, THE, 1951
PRINCESS OF THE NILE, 1954
PRISON, 1988
PRIVATE ANGELO, 1949
PRIVATE BENJAMIN, 1980
PRIVATE COLLECTION, 1972
PRIVATE EYES, 1953
PRIVATE EYES, THE, 1980
PRIVATE FILES OF J. EDGAR HOOVER, THE, 1978
PRIVATE HELL 36, 1954
PRIVATE WAR OF MAJOR BENSON, THE, 1955
PRIZE, THE, 1963
PROFESSIONAL SOLDIER, 1936
PROFESSOR BEWARE, 1938
PROFESSOR TIM, 1957
PROJECT X, 1968
PROMISE AT DAWN, 1970
PROPHECIES OF NOSTRADAMUS, 1974
PROSTITUTE, 1980
PROSTITUTION, 1965
PRUDENCE AND THE PILL, 1968
PSYCH-OUT, 1968
PSYCHO II, 1983
PUBERTY BLUES, 1983
PUBLIC MENACE, 1935
PUBLIC PIGEON NO. 1, 1957
PUNISHMENT PARK, 1971
PURE S, 1976
PURPLE GANG, THE, 1960
PURPLE HAZE, 1982
PURPLE HEART DIARY, 1951
PURPLE MASK, THE, 1955
PURSUED, 1934

PURSUIT OF HAPPINESS, THE, 1971
PURSUIT TO ALGIERS, 1945
PUSSYCAT ALLEY, 1965
PUZZLE OF A DOWNFALL CHILD, 1970
QUANTRILL'S RAIDERS, 1958
QUATERMASS CONCLUSION, 1980
QUEBEC, 1951
QUEEN FOR A DAY, 1951
QUEEN HIGH, 1930
QUEEN OF HEARTS, 1936
QUEEN OF THE MOB, 1940
QUEEN OF THE NIGHTCLUBS, 1929
QUEEN'S SWORDSMEN, THE, 1963
QUESTION 7, 1961
QUICK, BEFORE IT MELTS, 1964
QUICK GUN, THE, 1964
QUICK MILLIONS, 1939
QUIET AMERICAN, THE, 1958
QUIET COOL, 1986
QUIET DAY IN BELFAST, A, 1974
QUIET EARTH, THE, 1985
QUIET GUN, THE, 1957
QUIET PLACE IN THE COUNTRY, A, 1970
QUIET PLEASE, MURDER, 1942
QUIET WEEKEND, 1948
RABBLE, THE, 1965
RACE FOR YOUR LIFE, CHARLIE BROWN, 1977
RACE STREET, 1948
RACE WITH THE DEVIL, 1975
RACING WITH THE MOON, 1984
RACK, THE, 1956
RACKETEERS OF THE RANGE, 1939
RACKETY RAX, 1932
RADIO FOLLIES, 1935
RADIO ON, 1980
RAGE, 1966
RAGE AT DAWN, 1955
RAGE OF PARIS, THE, 1938
RAGMAN'S DAUGHTER, THE, 1974
RAIDERS, THE, 1952
RAIDERS, THE, 1964
RAIDERS OF TOMAHAWK CREEK, 1950
RAILROAD MAN, THE, 1965
RAILROAD WORKERS, 1948
RAILS INTO LARAMIE, 1954
RAIN, 1932
RAIN OR SHINE, 1930
RAINBOW BOYS, THE, 1973
RAINBOW ISLAND, 1944
RANCHO DELUXE, 1975
RANDY RIDES ALONE, 1934
RANGERS OF FORTUNE, 1940
RAPE, THE, 1965
RAPTURE, 1950
RAPTURE, 1965
RASPUTIN, 1939
RASPUTIN—THE MAD MONK, 1966
RAT RACE, THE, 1960
RATATAPLAN, 1979
RATBOY, 1986
RATON PASS, 1951
RATTLE OF A SIMPLE MAN, 1964
RAVEN'S END, 1970
RAW DEAL, 1977
RAWHIDE, 1938
RAYMIE, 1960
RAZORBACK, 1984
RAZOR'S EDGE, THE, 1984
RE-ANIMATOR, 1985
REACH FOR GLORY, 1963
REACHING FOR THE SUN, 1941
READY FOR LOVE, 1934
REBEL ROUSERS, 1970
REBEL SET, THE, 1959
REBELLION OF THE HANGED, THE, 1954
REBELS AGAINST THE LIGHT, 1964
REBOUND, 1931
RECESS, 1967
RECKLESS, 1935
RECKLESS AGE, 1944
RED AND THE BLACK, THE, 1954
RED AND THE WHITE, THE, 1969
RED BALL EXPRESS, 1952
RED CANYON, 1949
RED DESERT, 1949
RED-DRAGON, 1967

RED GARTERS, 1954
RED, HOT AND BLUE, 1949
RED LINE 7000, 1965
RED PONY, THE, 1949
RED RIVER VALLEY, 1941
RED SKIES OF MONTANA, 1952
RED STALLION IN THE ROCKIES, 1949
RED, WHITE AND BLACK, THE, 1970
REDHEAD AND THE COWBOY, THE, 1950
REDHEAD FROM WYOMING, THE, 1953
REFORM SCHOOL GIRL, 1957
REGAL CAVALCADE, 1935
REINCARNATION OF PETER PROUD, THE, 1975
RELUCTANT ASTRONAUT, THE, 1967
RELUCTANT DRAGON, THE, 1941
REMARKABLE MR. PENNYPACKER, THE, 1959
REMEDY FOR RICHES, 1941
REMEMBER MY NAME, 1978
REMEMBRANCE, 1982
REMOVALISTS, THE, 1975
RENDEZ-VOUS, 1932
RENDEZVOUS WITH ANNIE, 1946
RENEGADE RANGER, 1938
RENEGADES, 1946
RENO, 1939
REPEAT PERFORMANCE, 1947
REPORT TO THE COMMISSIONER, 1975
REQUIEM FOR A GUNFIGHTER, 1965
REST IS SILENCE, THE, 1960
RESURRECTION OF ZACHARY WHEELER, THE, 1971
RETURN FROM THE SEA, 1954
RETURN FROM WITCH MOUNTAIN, 1978
RETURN OF A STRANGER, 1962
RETURN OF DR. MABUSE, THE, 1961
RETURN OF DR. X, THE, 1939
RETURN OF JESSE JAMES, THE, 1950
RETURN OF JIMMY VALENTINE, THE, 1936
RETURN OF MR. MOTO, THE, 1965
RETURN OF MONTE CRISTO, THE, 1946
RETURN OF RIN TIN TIN, THE, 1947
RETURN OF SHERLOCK HOLMES, THE, 1929
RETURN OF THE BLACK EAGLE, 1949
RETURN OF THE DRAGON, 1974
RETURN OF THE RAT, THE, 1929
RETURN OF THE VAMPIRE, THE, 1944
RETURN TO OZ, 1985
RETURN TO PEYTON PLACE, 1961
RETURN TO SALEM'S LOT, A, 1988
REUNION, 1936
REUNION IN FRANCE, 1942
REUNION IN RENO, 1951
REVENGE OF FRANKENSTEIN, THE, 1958
REVENGERS, THE, 1972
REVOLT AT FORT LARAMIE, 1957
REVOLT OF MAMIE STOVER, THE, 1956
REVOLT OF THE MERCENARIES, 1964
REVOLVING DOORS, THE, 1988
REWARD, THE, 1965
RHUBARB, 1951
RICH ARE ALWAYS WITH US, THE, 1932
RICH MAN, POOR GIRL, 1938
RICH PEOPLE, 1929
RICOCHET, 1966
RICOCHET ROMANCE, 1954
RIDE A WILD PONY, 1976
RIDE 'EM COWBOY, 1936
RIDE THE HIGH WIND, 1967
RIDE THE WILD SURF, 1964
RIDE TO HANGMAN'S TREE, THE, 1967
RIDERS IN THE SKY, 1949
RIDERS OF THE BADLANDS, 1941
RIDERS OF THE BLACK HILLS, 1938
RIDERS OF THE DEADLINE, 1943
RIDERS OF THE NORTHLAND, 1942
RIDERS OF THE PURPLE SAGE, 1931
RIDERS OF THE RIO GRANDE, 1943
RIDIN' DOWN THE CANYON, 1942
RIDIN' FOR JUSTICE, 1932
RIDING ON AIR, 1937
RIDING THE WIND, 1942
RIDING TORNADO, THE, 1932
RIDING WEST, 1944
RIFF RAFF GIRLS, 1962
RIFFRAFF, 1947
RIFIFI IN TOKYO, 1963

RIGHT TO THE HEART, 1942
RIGOLETTO, 1949
RIKKY AND PETE, 1988
RIM OF THE CANYON, 1949
RING-A-DING RHYTHM, 1962
RING AROUND THE CLOCK, 1953
RING OF SPIES, 1964
RING OF TERROR, 1962
RINGSIDE, 1949
RIO, 1939
RIO GRANDE RAIDERS, 1946
RIO RITA, 1942
RIOT, 1969
RISE AGAINST THE SWORD, 1966
RISE AND RISE OF MICHAEL RIMMER, THE, 1970
RISE AND SHINE, 1941
RISK, THE, 1961
RISKY BUSINESS, 1939
RIVER, THE, 1928
RIVER, THE, 1961
RIVER LADY, 1948
RIVER OF UNREST, 1937
RIVER RAT, THE, 1984
RIVER'S EDGE, THE, 1957
RIVER'S END, 1931
RIVER'S END, 1940
ROAD GAMES, 1981
ROAD SHOW, 1941
ROAD TO BALI, 1952
ROAD TO DENVER, THE, 1955
ROAD TO GLORY, THE, 1936
ROAD TO RENO, THE, 1938
ROAD TO SALINA, 1971
ROAD TO SINGAPORE, 1931
ROAD TO SINGAPORE, 1940
ROADHOUSE MURDER, THE, 1932
ROADHOUSE NIGHTS, 1930
ROAMING LADY, 1936
ROBBERS OF THE RANGE, 1941
ROBIN HOOD OF EL DORADO, 1936
ROCK ISLAND TRAIL, 1950
ROCK, ROCK, ROCK!, 1956
ROCKET TO NOWHERE, 1962
ROCKY MOUNTAIN MYSTERY, 1935
ROGUE RIVER, 1951
ROLL ON TEXAS MOON, 1946
ROLL, WAGONS, ROLL, 1939
ROMANCE AND RICHES, 1937
ROMANCE OF THE RIO GRANDE, 1929
ROMANTIC COMEDY, 1983
ROOM UPSTAIRS, THE, 1948
ROSE FOR EVERYONE, A, 1967
ROSE OF CIMARRON, 1952
ROTTEN TO THE CORE, 1956
ROUGH CUT, 1980
ROUGH RIDERS' ROUNDUP, 1939
ROUGH WATERS, 1930
ROUNDUP TIME IN TEXAS, 1937
ROUSTABOUT, 1964
ROWDYMAN, THE, 1973
ROYAL HUNT OF THE SUN, THE, 1969
RUBY, 1971
RUCKUS, 1981
RUMPELSTILTSKIN, 1987
RUN FOR YOUR WIFE, 1966
RUN WILD, RUN FREE, 1969
RUNAWAY, 1984
RUNAWAY BUS, THE, 1954
RUNNING SCARED, 1972
RUNNING SCARED, 1986
RUNNING WILD, 1973
RUSTLERS OF DEVIL'S CANYON, 1947
RUSTLER'S RHAPSODY, 1985
RUY BLAS, 1948
RYAN'S DAUGHTER, 1970
SABATA, 1969
SABRA, 1970
SACRED GROUND, 1984
SACRED HEARTS, 1984
SAD HORSE, THE, 1959
SAFECRACKER, THE, 1958
ST. BENNY THE DIP, 1951
SAINT JACK, 1979
SAINT JOAN, 1957
ST. LOUIS BLUES, 1939
SAINTLY SINNERS, 1962

SAINT'S DOUBLE TROUBLE, THE, 1940
SAL OF SINGAPORE, 1929
SALESLADY, 1938
SALLAH, 1965
SALLY, 1929
SALLY IN OUR ALLEY, 1931
SALUTE, 1929
SALUTE JOHN CITIZEN, 1942
SALUTE TO THE MARINES, 1943
SALVAGE GANG, THE, 1958
SALVATION!, 1987
SALVATION NELL, 1931
SAM WHISKEY, 1969
SAMAR, 1962
SAM'S SON, 1984
SAMURAI ASSASSIN, 1965
SAMURAI FROM NOWHERE, 1964
SAN ANTONIO KID, THE, 1944
SAN ANTONIO ROSE, 1941
SAN DEMETRIO, LONDON, 1947
SAN FRANCISCO STORY, THE, 1952
SAN QUENTIN, 1946
SAND, 1949
SANDRA, 1966
SANDS OF BEERSHEBA, 1966
SANDS OF THE KALAHARI, 1965
SANDU FOLLOWS THE SUN, 1965
SANDWICH MAN, THE, 1966
SANDY GETS HER MAN, 1940
SANJURO, 1962
SANTA FE, 1951
SANTA FE STAMPEDE, 1938
SANTEE, 1973
SAP FROM SYRACUSE, THE, 1930
SAPS AT SEA, 1940
SARACEN BLADE, THE, 1954
SARAGOSSA MANUSCRIPT, THE, 1972
SARAH AND SON, 1930
SATAN BUG, THE, 1965
SATAN MET A LADY, 1936
SATURDAY'S MILLIONS, 1933
SAUL AND DAVID, 1968
SAVAGE GOLD, 1933
SAVAGE GUNS, THE, 1962
SAVAGE IS LOOSE, THE, 1974
SAVAGE SEVEN, THE, 1968
SAVAGE, THE, 1953
SAVANNAH SMILES, 1983
SAXON CHARM, THE, 1948
SAY IT WITH MUSIC, 1932
SAY IT WITH SONGS, 1929
SCANDALOUS JOHN, 1971
SCAPEGOAT, THE, 1959
SCARECROW IN A GARDEN OF CUCUMBERS, 1972
SCARED STIFF, 1953
SCARF, THE, 1951
SCARFACE MOB, THE, 1962
SCARLET CAMELLIA, THE, 1965
SCARLET CLUE, THE, 1945
SCARLET COAT, THE, 1955
SCARLET DAWN, 1932
SCARLET PAGES, 1930
SCARLET RIVER, 1933
SCARRED, 1984
SCATTERGOOD BAINES, 1941
SCENT OF A WOMAN, 1976
SCENT OF MYSTERY, 1960
SCHOOL FOR SECRETS, 1946
SCHOOL FOR SEX, 1966
SCHOOLGIRL DIARY, 1947
SCOTCH ON THE ROCKS, 1954
SCOTLAND YARD HUNTS DR. MABUSE, 1963
SCREAMING MIMI, 1958
SCRUBBERS, 1984
SEA BAT, THE, 1930
SEA DEVILS, 1937
SEA FURY, 1959
SEA OF GRASS, THE, 1947
SEA OF LOST SHIPS, 1953
SEA WOLF, THE, 1930
SEAS BENEATH, THE, 1931
SEBASTIAN, 1968
SECOND BEST BED, 1937
SECOND HONEYMOON, 1937
SECOND MRS. TANQUERAY, THE, 1952
SECOND TIME AROUND, THE, 1961

SECOND WOMAN, THE, 1951
SECRET AGENT, 1933
SECRET BRIDE, THE, 1935
SECRET COMMAND, 1944
SECRET DOCUMENT—VIENNA, 1954
SECRET FOUR, THE, 1940
SECRET FURY, THE, 1950
SECRET INVASION, THE, 1964
SECRET MISSION, 1944
SECRET OF BLOOD ISLAND, THE, 1965
SECRET OF CONVICT LAKE, THE, 1951
SECRET OF DR. KILDARE, THE, 1939
SECRET OF MADAME BLANCHE, THE, 1933
SECRET OF NIKOLA TESLA, THE, 1985
SECRET OF SANTA VITTORIA, THE, 1969
SECRET OF THE BLUE ROOM, 1933
SECRET OF THE INCAS, 1954
SECRET OF THE TELEGIAN, THE, 1961
SECRET PLACES, 1984
SECRET SCROLLS (PART I), 1968
SECRET SCROLLS (PART II), 1968
SECRET SERVICE OF THE AIR, 1939
SECRET WAR OF HARRY FRIGG, THE, 1968
SECRET WORLD, 1969
SECRET, THE, 1979
SECRETS, 1984
SECRETS D'ALCOVE, 1954
SECRETS SECRETS, 1985
SEE HERE, PRIVATE HARGROVE, 1944
SEMINOLE, 1953
SEND ME NO FLOWERS, 1964
SENSE OF FREEDOM, A, 1985
SENSUALITA, 1954
SEPARATE WAYS, 1981
SERAFINO, 1970
SERENADE FOR TWO SPIES, 1966
SERENITY, 1962
SERGEANT MADDEN, 1939
SERPENTS OF THE PIRATE MOON, THE, 1973
SERVICE DE LUXE, 1938
SESAME STREET PRESENTS: FOLLOW THE BIRD, 1985
SEVEN AGAINST THE SUN, 1968
SEVEN DARING GIRLS, 1962
SEVEN DWARFS TO THE RESCUE, THE, 1965
SEVEN GUNS FOR THE MACGREGORS, 1968
SEVEN KEYS TO BALDPATE, 1935
SEVEN MINUTES IN HEAVEN, 1986
SEVENTEEN, 1940
SEVENTH CAVALRY, 1956
SEVENTH HEAVEN, 1937
SEVENTH SURVIVOR, THE, 1941
SEXTON BLAKE AND THE HOODED TERROR, 1938
SHADES OF SILK, 1979
SHADOW BETWEEN, THE, 1932
SHADOW IN THE SKY, 1951
SHADOW OF FEAR, 1963
SHADOW OF THE EAGLE, 1955
SHADOW ON THE WALL, 1950
SHADOW ON THE WINDOW, THE, 1957
SHADOW, THE, 1937
SHADOWS GROW LONGER, THE, 1962
SHADY LADY, 1945
SHAFT'S BIG SCORE, 1972
SHAGGY, 1948
SHAKE, RATTLE, AND ROCK?, 1957
SHAKEDOWN, 1988
SHAKEDOWN, THE, 1960
SHAMROCK HILL, 1949
SHARE OUT, THE, 1966
SHARPSHOOTERS, 1938
SHE, 1965
SHE AND HE, 1967
SHE BEAST, THE, 1966
SHE DANCES ALONE, 1981
SHE LOVES ME NOT, 1934
SHE WOULDN'T SAY YES, 1945
SHE WROTE THE BOOK, 1946
SHEENA, 1984
SHEPHERD GIRL, THE, 1965
SHEPHERD OF THE OZARKS, 1942
SHERIFF OF CIMARRON, 1945
SHERIFF OF WICHITA, 1949
SHERLOCK HOLMES AND THE DEADLY NECKLACE, 1962

BOLD: Films on Videocassette

SHERLOCK HOLMES AND THE SPIDER WOMAN, 1944
SHERLOCK HOLMES AND THE VOICE OF TERROR, 1942
SHERLOCK HOLMES' FATAL HOUR, 1931
SHE'S IN THE ARMY, 1942
SHIELD FOR MURDER, 1954
SHILLINGBURY BLOWERS, THE, 1980
SHINING HOUR, THE, 1938
SHIP OF CONDEMNED WOMEN, THE, 1963
SHIPBUILDERS, THE, 1943
SHIPMATES FOREVER, 1935
SHIRALEE, THE, 1957
SHOCK CORRIDOR, 1963
SHOCK WAVES, 1977
SHOEMAKER AND THE ELVES, THE, 1967
SHOOT-OUT AT MEDICINE BEND, 1957
SHOOTING PARTY, THE, 1985
SHOOTING STRAIGHT, 1930
SHOPWORN ANGEL, THE, 1928
SHORT IS THE SUMMER, 1968
SHOT IN THE DARK, THE, 1941
SHOUT AT THE DEVIL, 1976
SHOW GOES ON, THE, 1937
SHOWDOWN, 1973
SHOWDOWN FOR ZATOICHI, 1968
SHOWDOWN, THE, 1940
SHOWTIME, 1948
SIAVASH IN PERSEPOLIS, 1966
SIDE STREET, 1929
SIDE STREET, 1950
SIDE STREET ANGEL, 1937
SIEGE OF FORT BISMARK, 1968
SIEGE OF SIDNEY STREET, THE, 1960
SIEGE OF THE SAXONS, 1963
SIERRA BARON, 1958
SIERRA SUE, 1941
SIGN OF FOUR, THE, 1932
SIGN OF THE VIRGIN, 1969
SILENCE, 1931
SILENCE, 1974
SILENCE HAS NO WINGS, 1971
SILENCE OF DEAN MAITLAND, THE, 1934
SILENCE OF DR. EVANS, THE, 1973
SILENT CALL, THE, 1961
SILENT ENEMY, THE, 1959
SILENT ONE, THE, 1984
SILENT PASSENGER, THE, 1935
SILK NOOSE, THE, 1950
SILVER CANYON, 1951
SILVER CITY, 1951
SILVER CITY, 1985
SILVER CITY BONANZA, 1951
SILVER CORD, 1933
SILVER FLEET, THE, 1945
SILVER HORDE, THE, 1930
SILVER ON THE SAGE, 1939
SILVER SKATES, 1943
SILVER STREAK, 1976
SILVER TRAILS, 1948
SILVER WHIP, THE, 1953
SIMBA, 1955
SIMCHON FAMILY, THE, 1969
SIMPLE CASE OF MONEY, A, 1952
SIN TAKES A HOLIDAY, 1930
SINAI COMMANDOS: THE STORY OF THE SIX DAY WAR, 1968
SINFUL DAVEY, 1969
SINGING COWBOY, THE, 1936
SINGING OUTLAW, 1937
SINGING PRINCESS, THE, 1967
SINISTER MAN, THE, 1965
SINS OF RACHEL CADE, THE, 1960
SINS OF THE FATHERS, 1928
SINS OF THE FATHERS, 1948
SIOUX CITY SUE, 1946
SIREN OF BAGDAD, 1953
SISTERS, OR THE BALANCE OF HAPPINESS, 1982
SITTING BULL, 1954
SITUATION HOPELESS—BUT NOT SERIOUS, 1965
SIX BRIDGES TO CROSS, 1955
SIX-GUN LAW, 1948
SIX SHOOTIN' SHERIFF, 1938
SIXTH AND MAIN, 1977
SKELETON ON HORSEBACK, 1940
SKI BATTALION, 1938

SKULL, THE, 1965
SKY ABOVE HEAVEN, 1964
SKY CALLS, THE, 1959
SKY DRAGON, 1949
SKY FULL OF MOON, 1952
SKY HAWK, 1929
SKYLARK, 1941
SKY'S THE LIMIT, THE, 1937
SKY'S THE LIMIT, THE, 1943
SLANDER, 1956
SLATTERY'S HURRICANE, 1949
SLAUGHTER HIGH, 1987
SLAUGHTERHOUSE-FIVE, 1972
SLEEPING BEAUTY, 1965
SLEEPING BEAUTY, THE, 1966
SLEEPING DOGS, 1977
SLEEPING TIGER, THE, 1954
SLEEPLESS NIGHTS, 1933
SLIGHTLY HONORABLE, 1940
SLIM, 1937
SLIM CARTER, 1957
SLIPSTREAM, 1974
SLOW DANCING IN THE BIG CITY, 1978
SLOW MOVES, 1984
SLUMBER PARTY MASSACRE II, 1987
SMALL MAN, THE, 1935
SMALL TOWN GIRL, 1936
SMALL TOWN GIRL, 1953
SMALL TOWN IN TEXAS, A, 1976
SMART POLITICS, 1948
SMASHING THE MONEY RING, 1939
SMILEY GETS A GUN, 1959
SMILING ALONG, 1938
SMILING IRISH EYES, 1929
SMITH, 1969
SMITHEREENS, 1982
SMITHY, 1946
SMOKE TREE RANGE, 1937
SMOOTH AS SILK, 1946
SMUGGLERS, THE, 1948
SNIPER'S RIDGE, 1961
SNOW, 1983
SNOW QUEEN, THE, 1959
SO GOES MY LOVE, 1946
SO IT'S SUNDAY, 1932
SO LITTLE TIME, 1953
SO RED THE ROSE, 1935
SO THIS IS LONDON, 1930
SO THIS IS LONDON, 1940
SO THIS IS LOVE, 1953
SO THIS IS PARIS, 1954
SO THIS IS WASHINGTON, 1943
SO WELL REMEMBERED, 1947
SO YOUNG, SO BAD, 1950
SOAPBOX DERBY, 1958
SODOM AND GOMORRAH, 1962
SOFT SKIN, THE, 1964
SOL MADRID, 1968
SOLDIER AND THE LADY, THE, 1937
SOLDIER IN THE RAIN, 1963
SOLDIER OF FORTUNE, 1955
SOLDIERS THREE, 1951
SOLITARY CHILD, THE, 1958
SOMBRERO, 1953
SOME CALL IT LOVING, 1973
SOME LIKE IT HOT, 1939
SOMETHING BIG, 1971
SOMETHING FOR THE BIRDS, 1952
SOMETHING FOR THE BOYS, 1944
SOMETHING IN THE WIND, 1947
SOMETHING SPECIAL!, 1987
SOMETHING TO LIVE FOR, 1952
SOMETHING WICKED THIS WAY COMES, 1983
SOMEWHERE IN CAMP, 1942
SOMEWHERE IN TIME, 1980
SON OF A BADMAN, 1949
SON OF BELLE STARR, 1953
SON OF DRACULA, 1943
SON OF FLUBBER, 1963
SON OF LASSIE, 1945
SON OF ROARING DAN, 1940
SON OF THE PLAINS, 1931
SONG FROM MY HEART, THE, 1970
SONG OF LOVE, 1947
SONG OF NEVADA, 1944
SONG OF NORWAY, 1970

SONG OF SONGS, 1933
SONG OF TEXAS, 1943
SONS OF ADVENTURE, 1948
SOPHIE'S PLACE, 1970
SOPHIE'S WAYS, 1970
SORORITY HOUSE, 1939
S.O.S. ICEBERG, 1933
SOTTO...SOTTO, 1985
SOUL MAN, 1986
SOUND OFF, 1952
SOURSWEET, 1988
SOUTH OF PAGO PAGO, 1940
SOUTH OF SUEZ, 1940
SOUTH OF TAHITI, 1941
SOUTH SEA WOMAN, 1953
SOUTHSIDE 1-1000, 1950
SOYLENT GREEN, 1973
SPACE CHILDREN, THE, 1958
SPACE SHIP, THE, 1935
SPANIARD'S CURSE, THE, 1958
SPANISH AFFAIR, 1958
SPANISH MAIN, THE, 1945
SPEAK EASILY, 1932
SPECIAL DELIVERY, 1955
SPECIAL DELIVERY, 1976
SPECIAL INVESTIGATOR, 1936
SPENDTHRIFT, 1936
SPHINX, THE, 1933
SPIDER AND THE FLY, THE, 1952
SPIES OF THE AIR, 1940
SPIKE OF BENSONHURST, 1988
SPIKES GANG, THE, 1974
SPIRITUALIST, THE, 1948
SPLIT, THE, 1968
SPOILERS, THE, 1955
SPOILS OF THE NIGHT, 1969
SPOOK BUSTERS, 1946
SPOOKS RUN WILD, 1941
SPOTLIGHT SCANDALS, 1943
SPOTS ON MY LEOPARD, THE, 1974
SPRING AND PORT WINE, 1970
SPRING MEETING, 1941
SPRING SYMPHONY, 1986
SPRINGTIME IN THE ROCKIES, 1942
SPRINGTIME IN THE SIERRAS, 1947
SPY FOR A DAY, 1939
SPY WITH A COLD NOSE, THE, 1966
SQUADRON 633, 1964
SQUAMISH FIVE, THE, 1988
SQUARE JUNGLE, THE, 1955
SQUARE RING, THE, 1955
SQUARE SHOULDERS, 1929
SQUARES, 1972
SSSSSSSS, 1973
STACKING, 1987
STAGE STRUCK, 1958
STAGE TO THUNDER ROCK, 1964
STAGECOACH BUCKAROO, 1942
STAGECOACH TO DANCER'S PARK, 1962
STAIRCASE, 1969
STAKEOUT ON DOPE STREET, 1958
STAND-IN, THE, 1985
STAND UP AND CHEER, 1934 80m FOX bw
STAR FOR A NIGHT, 1936
STAR IN THE DUST, 1956
STAR TREK: THE MOTION PICTURE, 1979
STARDUST, 1974
STARDUST MEMORIES, 1980
STARLIFT, 1951
STARS ARE SINGING, THE, 1953
STARS IN MY CROWN, 1950
STARSTRUCK, 1982
START CHEERING, 1938
STATE FAIR, 1962
STATIC, 1985
STEAMING, 1985
STEEL, 1980
STELLA, 1950
STEPFORD WIVES, THE, 1975
STEPS TO THE MOON, 1963
STOLEN HARMONY, 1935
STOLEN HEAVEN, 1938
STOLEN HOLIDAY, 1937
STONE, 1974
STONE KILLER, THE, 1973
STONE OF SILVER CREEK, 1935

STOOLIE, THE, 1972
STOP ME BEFORE I KILL!, 1961
STOPOVER TOKYO, 1957
STORK, 1971
STORK CLUB, THE, 1945
STORM FEAR, 1956
STORM OVER LISBON, 1944
STORM OVER THE ANDES, 1935
STORM, THE, 1930
STORM, THE, 1938
STORY OF SEABISCUIT, THE, 1949
STORY OF VICKIE, THE, 1958
STORY WITHOUT WORDS, 1981
STRAIT-JACKET, 1964
STRANDED, 1965
STRANDED, 1987
STRANGE AFFECTION, 1959
STRANGE BARGAIN, 1949
STRANGE BEDFELLOWS, 1965
STRANGE LADY IN TOWN, 1955
STRANGE TRIANGLE, 1946
STRANGER FROM ARIZONA, THE, 1938
STRANGER IN BETWEEN, THE, 1952
STRANGER IN MY ARMS, 1959
STRANGER ON THE PROWL, 1953
STRANGER THAN PARADISE, 1984
STRANGER WORE A GUN, THE, 1953
STRANGER'S HAND, THE, 1955
STRANGERS IN THE CITY, 1962
STRANGERS ON A HONEYMOON, 1937
STRANGERS WHEN WE MEET, 1960
STRAWBERRY ROAN, THE, 1948
STREET MUSIC, 1982
STREETS OF FIRE, 1984
STREETS OF GOLD, 1986
STREETS OF LAREDO, 1949
STUDENT PRINCE, THE, 1954
STUNTS, 1977
SUBMARINE COMMAND, 1951
SUBMARINE SEAHAWK, 1959
SUBMARINE X-1, 1969
SUBWAY IN THE SKY, 1959
SUCCESSFUL CALAMITY, A, 1932
SUCCESSFUL MAN, A, 1987
SUCH IS LIFE, 1936
SUDAN, 1945
SUDDEN DANGER, 1955
SUDDEN TERROR, 1970
SUDDENLY IT'S SPRING, 1947
SUDDENLY, LAST SUMMER, 1959
SUGARFOOT, 1951
SUICIDE BATTALION, 1958
SUICIDE LEGION, 1940
SUICIDE MISSION, 1956
SUITOR, THE, 1963
SUMMER HOLIDAY, 1963
SUMMER LOVE, 1958
SUMMER MAGIC, 1963
SUMMER RUN, 1974
SUMMER SOLDIERS, 1972
SUMMERFIELD, 1977
SUN ABOVE, DEATH BELOW, 1969
SUN SHINES FOR ALL, THE, 1961
SUNBONNET SUE, 1945
SUNDAY DINNER FOR A SOLDIER, 1944
SUNDAY PUNCH, 1942
SUNDOWN, 1941
SUNDOWN JIM, 1942
SUNDOWN RIDER, THE, 1933
SUNDOWNERS, THE, 1950
SUNNY, 1930
SUNRISE TRAIL, 1931
SUNSET IN THE WEST, 1950
SUNSET OF POWER, 1936
SUNSET PASS, 1933
SUNSTRUCK, 1973
SUPERNATURAL, 1933
SUPERSPEED, 1935
SUPREME KID, THE, 1976
SURRENDER, 1950
SURRENDER, 1987
SUSAN SLADE, 1961
SUSANNAH OF THE MOUNTIES, 1939
SUSPECT, 1987
SUSPECTED PERSON, 1943
SUSPENSE, 1946

SVENGALI, 1931
SWAMP WATER, 1941
SWANN IN LOVE, 1984
SWEDISH WEDDING NIGHT, 1965
SWEEPSTAKES WINNER, 1939
SWEET ADELINE, 1935
SWEET AND SOUR, 1964
SWEET DEVIL, 1937
SWEET LIBERTY, 1986
SWEET REVENGE, 1987
SWEET WILLIAM, 1980
SWIMMER, THE, 1968
SWING IT, PROFESSOR, 1937
SWINGER, THE, 1966
SWISS FAMILY ROBINSON, 1940
SWITCHING CHANNELS, 1988
SWORD IN THE STONE, THE, 1963
SWORD OF MONTE CRISTO, THE, 1951
SWORD OF SHERWOOD FOREST, 1961
SWORDKILL, 1984
SWORN ENEMY, 1936
SYLVIA AND THE PHANTOM, 1950
SYLVIA SCARLETT, 1936
SYMPHONY FOR A MASSACRE, 1965
SYMPHONY OF LIFE, 1949
SYMPHONY OF LIVING, 1935
TAIL OF THE TIGER, 1984
TAKE A LETTER, DARLING, 1942
TAKE DOWN, 1979
TAKE HER BY SURPRISE, 1967
TAKE HER, SHE'S MINE, 1963
TALES OF HOFFMANN, THE, 1951
TALES OF PARIS, 1962
TALES OF ROBIN HOOD, 1951
TALES THAT WITNESS MADNESS, 1973
TALISMAN, THE, 1966
TALL BLOND MAN WITH ONE BLACK SHOE, THE, 1973
TAMANGO, 1959
TAMING OF THE SHREW, THE, 1929
TANK, 1984
TANYA'S ISLAND, 1981
TARGET, 1985
TARGET HONG KONG, 1952
TARZAN AND THE AMAZONS, 1945
TARZAN AND THE HUNTRESS, 1947
TARZAN AND THE LEOPARD WOMAN, 1946
TARZAN AND THE LOST SAFARI, 1957
TARZAN TRIUMPHS, 1943
TARZAN'S FIGHT FOR LIFE, 1958
TARZAN'S NEW YORK ADVENTURE, 1942
TARZAN'S PERIL, 1951
TARZAN'S SECRET TREASURE, 1941
TASTE THE BLOOD OF DRACULA, 1970
TATSU, 1962
TATTERED DRESS, THE, 1957
TAWNY PIPIT, 1947
TAXI 13, 1928
TAXING WOMAN'S RETURN, A, 1988
TAZA, SON OF COCHISE, 1954
TEACHER AND THE MIRACLE, THE, 1961
TEACHERS, 1984
TECKMAN MYSTERY, THE, 1955
TEEN WOLF, 1985
TEENAGE BAD GIRL, 1959
TEENAGERS IN SPACE, 1975
TELL IT TO THE JUDGE, 1949
TELL ME A RIDDLE, 1980
TELL-TALE HEART, THE, 1962
TEMPEST, 1932
10 NORTH FREDERICK, 1958
TEN SECONDS TO HELL, 1959
TEN TALL MEN, 1951
TENDER MERCIES, 1982
TENDER TRAP, THE, 1955
TENDERFOOT, THE, 1932
TENNESSEE CHAMP, 1954
TENSION AT TABLE ROCK, 1956
TENTING TONIGHT ON THE OLD CAMP GROUND, 1943
TEQUILA SUNRISE, 1988
TERM OF TRIAL, 1962
TERROR, THE, 1928
TERROR IN A TEXAS TOWN, 1958
TERROR OF THE TONGS, THE, 1961
TERRORIZERS, THE, 1987

TERRORVISION, 1986
TESS OF THE STORM COUNTRY, 1932
TESTAMENT, 1983
TESTAMENT, 1988
TEVYA, 1939
TEXANS, THE, 1938
TEXAS BAD MAN, 1932
TEXAS MASQUERADE, 1944
TEXAS RANGER, THE, 1931
TEXAS RANGERS RIDE AGAIN, 1940
TEXAS RANGERS, THE, 1936
TEXAS RANGERS, THE, 1951
TEXAS STAGECOACH, 1940
TEXAS TERROR, 1935
THANK HEAVEN FOR SMALL FAVORS, 1965
THANK YOU, MR. MOTO, 1937
THANKS FOR EVERYTHING, 1938
THAT CERTAIN AGE, 1938
THAT CERTAIN WOMAN, 1937
THAT HAMILTON WOMAN, 1941
THAT HOUSE IN THE OUTSKIRTS, 1980
THAT LADY IN ERMINE, 1948
THAT UNCERTAIN FEELING, 1941
THAT WAS THEN...THIS IS NOW, 1985
THAT'S LIFE, 1986
THAT'S MY WIFE, 1933
THAT'S THE SPIRIT, 1945
THEIR OWN DESIRE, 1929
THEODORA GOES WILD, 1936
THERE GOES MY HEART, 1938
THERE'S A GIRL IN MY SOUP, 1970
THERE'S ALWAYS A THURSDAY, 1957
THERE'S ONE BORN EVERY MINUTE, 1942
THEY ALL COME OUT, 1939
THEY ARE NOT ANGELS, 1948
THEY CALL ME MISTER TIBBS, 1970
THEY CALL ME ROBERT, 1967
THEY CAME TO A CITY, 1944
THEY CAME TO BLOW UP AMERICA, 1943
THEY HAD TO SEE PARIS, 1929
THEY MIGHT BE GIANTS, 1971
THEY STILL CALL ME BRUCE, 1987
THEY WERE SISTERS, 1945
THEY WHO DARE, 1954
THEY'RE A WEIRD MOB, 1966
THIEF OF VENICE, THE, 1952
THIEVES FALL OUT, 1941
THIN MAN GOES HOME, THE, 1944
THIN RED LINE, THE, 1964
THINGS ARE LOOKING UP, 1934
THIRD ALIBI, THE, 1961
THIRD DAY, THE, 1965
THIRD SECRET, THE, 1964
THIRD TIME LUCKY, 1931
13 EAST STREET, 1952
THIRTEEN GHOSTS, 1960
THIRTEEN HOURS BY AIR, 1936
THIRTEEN LEAD SOLDIERS, 1948
THIRTEENTH GUEST, THE, 1932
THIRTY-DAY PRINCESS, 1934
THIRTY NINE STEPS, THE, 1978
THIRTY SIX HOURS TO KILL, 1936
THIS COULD BE THE NIGHT, 1957
THIS DAY AND AGE, 1933
THIS HAPPY FEELING, 1958
THIS IS ELVIS, 1982
THIS IS MY AFFAIR, 1937
THIS IS MY STREET, 1964
THIS IS THE LIFE, 1935
THIS IS THE LIFE, 1944
THIS LOVE OF OURS, 1945
THIS MADDING CROWD, 1964
THIS MAN IN PARIS, 1939
THIS MAN IS MINE, 1934
THIS MAN IS MINE, 1946
THIS MAN IS NEWS, 1939
THIS MAN'S NAVY, 1945
THIS MODERN AGE, 1931
THIS PROPERTY IS CONDEMNED, 1966
THIS SAVAGE LAND, 1969
THIS SIDE OF HEAVEN, 1934
THIS WEEK OF GRACE, 1933
THIS WOMAN IS DANGEROUS, 1952
THOMASINE AND BUSHROD, 1974
THOROUGHBREDS DON'T CRY, 1937
THOSE REDHEADS FROM SEATTLE, 1953

BOLD: Films on Videocassette

THOSE WE LOVE, 1932
THRASHIN', 1986
THREE BRAVE MEN, 1957
THREE CHEERS FOR THE IRISH, 1940
THREE COCKEYED SAILORS, 1940
THREE DARING DAUGHTERS, 1948
THREE FACES EAST, 1930
THREE FACES WEST, 1940
THREE FOR THE SHOW, 1955
THREE GODFATHERS, 1936
THREE GUYS NAMED MIKE, 1951
THREE HATS FOR LISA, 1965
THREE HOURS, 1944
365 NIGHTS IN HOLLYWOOD, 1934
THREE HUSBANDS, 1950
THREE IN ONE, 1956
3 IS A FAMILY, 1944
THREE LITTLE SISTERS, 1944
THREE LOVES HAS NANCY, 1938
THREE MEN AND A BABY, 1987
THREE MESQUITEERS, THE, 1936
THREE MOVES TO FREEDOM, 1960
THREE MUSKETEERS, THE, 1935
THREE MUSKETEERS, THE, 1939
THREE NIGHTS OF LOVE, 1969
THREE ON A TICKET, 1947
THREE SECRETS, 1950
THREE THE HARD WAY, 1974
THREE TO GO, 1971
THREE VIOLENT PEOPLE, 1956
THREE WORLDS OF GULLIVER, THE, 1960
THRESHOLD, 1983
THRILL OF A ROMANCE, 1945
THROUGH DAYS AND MONTHS, 1969
THROW MOMMA FROM THE TRAIN, 1987
THUNDER AFLOAT, 1939
THUNDER AND LIGHTNING, 1977
THUNDER BIRDS, 1942
THUNDER MOUNTAIN, 1935
THUNDER OF DRUMS, A, 1961
THUNDER OVER THE PLAINS, 1953
THUNDER TRAIL, 1937
THUNDERBALL, 1965
THUNDERBIRDS, 1952
THUNDERBIRDS ARE GO, 1968
THUNDERING HERD, THE, 1934
TIARA TAHITI, 1962
...TICK...TICK...TICK..., 1970
TICKET TO TOMAHAWK, 1950
TIGER AND THE FLAME, THE, 1955
TIGER AND THE PUSSYCAT, THE, 1967
TIGER IN THE SMOKE, 1956
TIGHT SHOES, 1941
TIGHTROPE, 1984
TIKO AND THE SHARK, 1966
TILL TOMORROW COMES, 1962
TILL WE MEET AGAIN, 1936
TIM, 1981
TIME BOMB, 1961
TIME FOR KILLING, A, 1967
TIME GENTLEMEN PLEASE?, 1953
TIME LOST AND TIME REMEMBERED, 1966
TIME OF THE WOLVES, 1970
TIME OUT FOR LOVE, 1963
TIME SLIP, 1981
TIME TO LOVE AND A TIME TO DIE, A, 1958
TIME TRAVELERS, THE, 1964
TIME WITHOUT PITY, 1957
TIMERIDER, 1983
TIMES GONE BY, 1953
TIMETABLE, 1956
TIN PAN ALLEY, 1940
TINDER BOX, THE, 1968
TINGLER, THE, 1959
TIP-OFF GIRLS, 1938
TIP ON A DEAD JOCKEY, 1957
TISH, 1942
TITFIELD THUNDERBOLT, THE, 1953
TO BE A CROOK, 1967
TO BE OR NOT TO BE, 1983
TO KILL A STRANGER, 1985
TO PARIS WITH LOVE, 1955
TO PLEASE A LADY, 1950
TO THE VICTOR, 1938
TOBRUK, 1966
TODAY IT'S ME...TOMORROW YOU?, 1968

TODAY WE LIVE, 1933
TOGETHER, 1956
TOM BROWN OF CULVER, 1932
TOM SAWYER, 1973
TOM THUMB, 1958
TOMBSTONE CANYON, 1932
TOMBSTONE, THE TOWN TOO TOUGH TO DIE, 1942
TOMORROW AND TOMORROW, 1932
TOMORROW AT TEN, 1964
TOMORROW WE LIVE, 1942
TONIGHT WE RAID CALAIS, 1943
TONIGHT WE SING, 1953
TONKA, 1958
TONS OF TROUBLE, 1956
TONY DRAWS A HORSE, 1951
TOO BUSY TO WORK, 1932
TOO LATE BLUES, 1962
TOO MANY CROOKS, 1959
TOO MANY GIRLS, 1940
TOO MANY PARENTS, 1936
TOP GUN, 1955
TOP SECRET AFFAIR, 1957
TOPEKA, 1953
TORA! TORA! TORA!, 1970
TORCH SONG, 1953
TORCH SONG TRILOGY, 1988
TORPEDO ALLEY, 1953
TORPEDO RUN, 1958
TORSO MURDER MYSTERY, THE, 1940
TORTURE GARDEN, 1968
TOUCHDOWN, 1931
TOUCHED BY LOVE, 1980
TOUGH GUYS DON'T DANCE, 1987
TOUT VA BIEN, 1973
TOWN LIKE ALICE, A, 1958
TOWN WITHOUT PITY, 1961
TOYS IN THE ATTIC, 1963
TRAGEDY OF A RIDICULOUS MAN, THE, 1982
TRAIL OF ROBIN HOOD, 1950
TRAIN ROBBERS, THE, 1973
TRANSATLANTIC, 1931
TRANSATLANTIC MERRY-GO-ROUND, 1934
TRAPPED IN A SUBMARINE, 1931
TRAVELING SALESLADY, THE, 1935
TREACHERY RIDES THE RANGE, 1936
TREASURE AT THE MILL, 1957
TREASURE OF LOST CANYON, THE, 1952
TREASURE OF SAN GENNARO, 1968
TREE WE HURT, THE, 1986
TRESPASSER, THE, 1929
TRESPASSERS, THE, 1976
TRIAL, THE, 1948
TRIAL AND ERROR, 1962
TRIAL OF THE CATONSVILLE NINE, THE, 1972
TRIPOLI, 1950
TROJAN HORSE, THE, 1962
TROOPER HOOK, 1957
TROPICS, 1969
TROUBLE IN STORE, 1955
TROUBLE IN SUNDOWN, 1939
TROUBLE IN TEXAS, 1937
TROUBLE MAKERS, 1948
TROUBLE WITH ANGELS, THE, 1966
TROUBLE WITH DICK, THE, 1987
TROUBLED WATERS, 1936
TRUE STORIES, 1986
TRUTH ABOUT YOUTH, THE, 1930
TUCSON RAIDERS, 1944
TUMBLEDOWN RANCH IN ARIZONA, 1941
TUNA CLIPPER, 1949
TUNNEL OF LOVE, THE, 1958
TURKEY TIME, 1933
TURN BACK THE CLOCK, 1933
TURN OF THE SCREW, 1985
TUTTLES OF TAHITI, 1942
TWELVE CROWDED HOURS, 1939
24 HOURS IN A WOMAN'S LIFE, 1968
24 HOURS TO KILL, 1966
TWENTY PLUS TWO, 1961
27TH DAY, THE, 1957
20,000 POUNDS KISS, THE, 1964
TWILIGHT IN THE SIERRAS, 1950
TWILIGHT OF HONOR, 1963
TWILIGHT STORY, THE, 1962
TWIST & SHOUT, 1986
TWIST OF SAND, A, 1968

TWO, 1975
TWO BRIGHT BOYS, 1939
TWO COLONELS, THE, 1963
TWO GIRLS ON BROADWAY, 1940
TWO-GUN LADY, 1956
TWO GUN LAW, 1937
TWO GUYS FROM MILWAUKEE, 1946
TWO IN REVOLT, 1936
TWO IN THE SHADOW, 1968
TWO LITTLE BEARS, THE, 1961
TWO LIVES OF MATTIA PASCAL, THE, 1985
TWO LIVING, ONE DEAD, 1964
TWO MULES FOR SISTER SARA, 1970
TWO RODE TOGETHER, 1961
2010, 1984
2,000 WEEKS, 1970
TWO WEEKS WITH LOVE, 1950
TWO WOMEN, 1940
TYPHOON, 1940
UGLY AMERICAN, THE, 1963
ULTIMATE SOLUTION OF GRACE QUIGLEY, THE, 1984
ULTIMATE WARRIOR, THE, 1975
UN CARNET DE BAL, 1938
UNBEARABLE LIGHTNESS OF BEING, THE, 1988
UNCLE HARRY, 1945
UNCLE VANYA, 1972
UNDER COLORADO SKIES, 1947
UNDER COVER, 1987
UNDER MEXICALI STARS, 1950
UNDER NEVADA SKIES, 1946
UNDER PRESSURE, 1935
UNDER-PUP, THE, 1939
UNDER THE BANNER OF SAMURAI, 1969
UNDER THE GUN, 1951
UNDER THE PAMPAS MOON, 1935
UNDER THE TONTO RIM, 1947
UNDER THE YUM-YUM TREE, 1963
UNDER WESTERN STARS, 1938
UNDERCOVER MAN, THE, 1949
UNDERCURRENT, 1946
UNDERGROUND, 1941
UNDERGROUND AGENT, 1942
UNDERTOW, 1949
UNEXPECTED GUEST, 1946
UNFAITHFUL, 1931
UNFAITHFUL, THE, 1947
UNGUARDED HOUR, THE, 1936
UNGUARDED MOMENT, THE, 1956
UNHOLY DESIRE, 1964
UNHOLY PARTNERS, 1941
UNHOLY WIFE, THE, 1957
UNIDENTIFIED FLYING ODDBALL, THE, 1979
UNIVERSAL SOLDIER, 1971
UNMAN, WITTERING AND ZIGO, 1971
UNSEEN, THE, 1945
UNSUSPECTED, THE, 1947
UNTAMED, 1955
UNTAMED, 1940
UNTIL THEY SAIL, 1957
UP FOR THE CUP, 1950
UP FROM THE BEACH, 1965
UP IN MABEL'S ROOM, 1944
UP IN THE AIR, 1969
UP IN THE CELLAR, 1970
UP PERISCOPE, 1959
UP THE DOWN STAIRCASE, 1967
UP THE RIVER, 1938
UP TO THE NECK, 1933
UPPER WORLD, 1934
UTAH, 1945
UTOPIA, 1952
VALDEZ IS COMING, 1971
VALENTINO, 1977
VALHALLA, 1987
VALIANT, THE, 1962
VALLEY OF HUNTED MEN, 1942
VALUE FOR MONEY, 1957
VAMPIRE CIRCUS, 1972
VAMPIRE LOVERS, THE, 1970
VAMPYRES, DAUGHTERS OF DRACULA, 1977
VANISHING POINT, 1971
VANISHING WESTERNER, THE, 1950
VARIETY LIGHTS, 1965
VARSITY SHOW, 1937
VAULT OF HORROR, THE, 1973

VERONA TRIAL, THE, 1963
VERY NATURAL THING, A, 1974
VICE SQUAD, THE, 1931
VICE VERSA, 1948
VICE VERSA, 1988
VICKI, 1953
VICTOR FRANKENSTEIN, 1975
VIENNA WALTZES, 1961
VIENNESE NIGHTS, 1930
VIEW FROM POMPEY'S HEAD, THE, 1955
VIEW FROM THE BRIDGE, A, 1962
VIOLENT PLAYGROUND, 1958
VIOLENT SUMMER, 1961
VIOLIN AND ROLLER, 1962
VIRGIN AND THE GYPSY, THE, 1970
VIRGIN SOLDIERS, THE, 1970
VIRGINIAN, THE, 1946
VIRUS, 1980
VISIT, THE, 1964
VISIT TO A CHIEF'S SON, 1974
VISITORS FROM THE GALAXY, 1981
VIVA MARIA, 1965
VIVA MAX?, 1969
VOGUES OF 1938, 1937
VOICE IN THE MIRROR, 1958
VOICE OF THE HURRICANE, 1964
VOICE OF THE WHISTLER, 1945
VOICES, 1973
VOLCANO, 1953
VOLPONE, 1947
VOYAGE OF SILENCE, 1968
VOYAGE TO AMERICA, 1952
VOYAGE TO THE END OF THE UNIVERSE, 1963
W. W. AND THE DIXIE DANCEKINGS, 1975
WACKIEST SHIP IN THE ARMY, THE, 1961
WACKY WORLD OF MOTHER GOOSE, THE, 1967
WACO, 1952
WAGON TRAIL, 1935
WAIT 'TIL THE SUN SHINES, NELLIE, 1952
WAKE UP AND DIE, 1967
WALK A CROOKED MILE, 1948
WALK INTO HELL, 1957
WALK ON THE WILD SIDE, 1962
WALK SOFTLY, STRANGER, 1950
WALK THE PROUD LAND, 1956
WALKING STICK, THE, 1970
WALKING TALL, 1973
WALL-EYED NIPPON, 1963
WALL OF NOISE, 1963
WALLFLOWER, 1948
WALLS OF JERICHO, 1948
WALPURGIS NIGHT, 1941
WANDERER, THE, 1969
WANDERING JEW, THE, 1935
WANTED, 1937
WAR AND PEACE, 1968
WAR ARROW, 1953
WAR BETWEEN MEN AND WOMEN, THE, 1972
WAR PAINT, 1953
WARE CASE, THE, 1939
WARKILL, 1968
WARN LONDON!, 1934
WARNING TO WANTONS, A, 1949
WARPATH, 1951
WARRING CLANS, 1963
WARRIOR AND THE SLAVE GIRL, THE, 1959
WASHINGTON STORY, 1952
WATCH THE BIRDIE, 1950
WATER BABIES, THE, 1979
WATERFRONT AT MIDNIGHT, 1948
WATERMELON MAN, 1970
WAY OF A GAUCHO, 1952
WAY TO THE GOLD, THE, 1957
WAY WEST, THE, 1967
WE ARE ALL MURDERERS, 1957
WE OF THE NEVER NEVER, 1983
WE STILL KILL THE OLD WAY, 1967
WE WERE DANCING, 1942
WE WHO ARE YOUNG, 1940
WEAPON, THE, 1957
WEB OF EVIDENCE, 1959
WEB OF FEAR, 1966
WEDDING IN WHITE, 1972
WEDDING REHEARSAL, 1932
WEEKEND IN HAVANA, 1941
WEEKEND WITH LULU, A, 1961

WEIRD WOMAN, 1944
WELCOME DANGER, 1929
WELCOME, MR. WASHINGTON, 1944
WELCOME TO L.A., 1976
WELL-DIGGER'S DAUGHTER, THE, 1946
WE'LL MEET AGAIN, 1942
WE'LL SMILE AGAIN, 1942
WE'RE IN THE MONEY, 1935
WE'RE NOT MARRIED, 1952
WEST OF SHANGHAI, 1937
WEST OF THE DIVIDE, 1934
WEST OF THE LAW, 1942
WESTERN COURAGE, 1935
WESTWARD BOUND, 1931
WESTWARD PASSAGE, 1932
WET PARADE, THE, 1932
WHALERS, THE, 1942:,
WHAT EVERY WOMAN WANTS, 1962
WHAT WOMEN DREAM, 1933
WHAT WOULD YOU DO, CHUMS?, 1939
WHAT'S UP, TIGER LILY?, 1966
WHEELER DEALERS, THE, 1963
WHEN I GROW UP, 1951
WHEN IN ROME, 1952
WHEN LADIES MEET, 1941
WHEN LOVE IS YOUNG, 1937
WHEN THE BOUGH BREAKS, 1947
WHEN THE TREES WERE TALL, 1965
WHEN WORLDS COLLIDE, 1951
WHEN'S YOUR BIRTHDAY?, 1937
WHERE DO WE GO FROM HERE?, 1945
WHERE THE BOYS ARE, 1960
WHERE THE HOT WIND BLOWS, 1960
WHERE THE LILIES BLOOM, 1974
WHERE THE RIVER RUNS BLACK, 1986
WHERE THE SPIES ARE, 1965
WHERE THERE'S LIFE, 1947
WHERE'S PICONE?, 1985
WHILE PARIS SLEEPS, 1932
WHIRLPOOL, 1934
WHIRLWIND, 1968
WHISTLE AT EATON FALLS, 1951
WHISTLE BLOWER, THE, 1987
WHITE DAWN, THE, 1974
WHITE HORSE INN, THE, 1959
WHITE LINE FEVER, 1975
WHITE MISCHIEF, 1988
WHITE NIGHTS, 1985
WHITE PARADE, THE, 1934
WHITE SHADOWS IN THE SOUTH SEAS, 1928
WHITE SHEIK, THE, 1956
WHITE TIE AND TAILS, 1946
WHO?, 1975
WHO DONE IT?, 1942
WHO GOES NEXT?, 1938
WHO HAS SEEN THE WIND, 1980
WHO KILLED AUNT MAGGIE?, 1940
WHO KILLED "DOC" ROBBIN?, 1948
WHO KILLED JOHN SAVAGE?, 1937
WHO KILLED VAN LOON?, 1984
WHO SAYS I CAN'T RIDE A RAINBOW?, 1971
WHO SLEW AUNTIE ROO?, 1971
WHOLE TRUTH, THE, 1958
WHOM THE GODS DESTROY, 1934
WHO'S GOT THE BLACK BOX?, 1970
WHO'S THAT GIRL, 1987
WHO'S YOUR LADY FRIEND?, 1937
WHY BRING THAT UP?, 1929
WHY LEAVE HOME?, 1929
WHY MUST I DIE?, 1960
WICKED WOMAN, A, 1934
WIDE OPEN, 1930
WIFE, DOCTOR AND NURSE, 1937
WIFE OF GENERAL LING, THE, 1938
WIFEMISTRESS, 1979
WILBY CONSPIRACY, THE, 1975
WILD AFFAIR, THE, 1966
WILD AND THE INNOCENT, THE, 1959
WILD AND WONDERFUL, 1964
WILD AND WOOLLY, 1937
WILD COUNTRY, THE, 1971
WILD DUCK, THE, 1977
WILD FRONTIER, THE, 1947
WILD GIRL, 1932
WILD HARVEST, 1947
WILD HORSE MESA, 1932

WILD IN THE STREETS, 1968
WILD MAN OF BORNEO, THE, 1941
WILD PACK, THE, 1972
WILD PARTY, THE, 1929
WILD SEASON, 1968
WILD SEED, 1965
WILD STALLION, 1952
WILDCAT TROOPER, 1936
WILL ANY GENTLEMAN?, 1955
WILLARD, 1971
WILLIE AND PHIL, 1980
WILLIE DYNAMITE, 1973
WILLIE MCBEAN AND HIS MAGIC MACHINE, 1965
WILLY WONKA AND THE CHOCOLATE FACTORY, 1971
WIND ACROSS THE EVERGLADES, 1958
WIND CANNOT READ, THE, 1958
WINDS OF THE WASTELAND, 1936
WINDWALKER, 1980
WINDY CITY, 1984
WINGS AND THE WOMAN, 1942
WINGS IN THE DARK, 1935
WINSTANLEY, 1979
WINTER FLIGHT, 1984
WINTER OF OUR DREAMS, 1982
WISER AGE, 1962
WISH YOU WERE HERE, 1987
WITH LOVE AND TENDERNESS, 1978
WITHOUT A CLUE, 1988
WITHOUT A HOME, 1939
WITHOUT EACH OTHER, 1962
WITHOUT LOVE, 1945
WITHOUT REGRET, 1935
WITHOUT RESERVATIONS, 1946
WITNESS, THE, 1982
WIZARDS, 1977
WOLF AT THE DOOR, THE, 1987
WOMAN ACCUSED, 1933
WOMAN AGAINST WOMAN, 1938
WOMAN AT HER WINDOW, A, 1978
WOMAN I LOVE, THE, 1937
WOMAN IN CHAINS, 1932
WOMAN OBSESSED, 1959
WOMAN OF STRAW, 1964
WOMAN OF THE TOWN, THE, 1943
WOMAN'S VENGEANCE, A, 1947
WOMEN AREN'T ANGELS, 1942
WOMEN IN THE WIND, 1939
WOMEN IN WAR, 1940
WOMEN OF ALL NATIONS, 1931
WOMEN WHO PLAY, 1932
WONDERFUL THINGS!, 1958
WORDS AND MUSIC, 1948
WORKING MAN, THE, 1933
WORLD IN MY CORNER, 1956
WORLD OF HANS CHRISTIAN ANDERSEN, THE, 1971
WORLD PREMIERE, 1941
WORLD, THE FLESH, AND THE DEVIL, THE, 1959
WORST WOMAN IN PARIS, 1933
WRATH OF GOD, THE, 1972
WYOMING, 1940
WYOMING, 1947
WYOMING RENEGADES, 1955
X THE UNKNOWN, 1957
X Y & ZEE, 1972
YANCO, 1964
YANKEE PASHA, 1954
YANKS, 1979
YASHA, 1985
YEAR MY VOICE BROKE, THE, 1988
YEAR OF AWAKENING, THE, 1987
YELLOW BALLOON, THE, 1953
YELLOW CAB MAN, THE, 1950
YELLOW CARGO, 1936
YELLOW FIN, 1951
YELLOW ROLLS-ROYCE, THE, 1965
YES, MY DARLING DAUGHTER, 1939
YOU CAME ALONG, 1945
YOU FOR ME, 1952
YOU MUST BE JOKING!, 1965
YOU ONLY LIVE TWICE, 1967
YOUNG AMERICA, 1932
YOUNG AND DANGEROUS, 1957
YOUNG AND WILLING, 1943
YOUNG AND WILLING, 1964

BOLD: Films on Videocassette

YOUNG AS YOU FEEL, 1931
YOUNG AS YOU FEEL, 1940
YOUNG BILLY YOUNG, 1969
YOUNG BUFFALO BILL, 1940
YOUNG CAPTIVES, THE, 1959
YOUNG DANIEL BOONE, 1950
YOUNG DILLINGER, 1965
YOUNG DOCTORS, THE, 1961
YOUNG EAGLES, 1930
YOUNG FUGITIVES, 1938
YOUNG GIRLS OF ROCHEFORT, THE, 1968
YOUNG GO WILD, THE, 1962
YOUNG GUY GRADUATES, 1969
YOUNG GUY ON MT. COOK, 1969
YOUNG IDEAS, 1943
YOUNG LOVERS, THE, 1964
YOUNG MAN OF MANHATTAN, 1930
YOUNG ONE, THE, 1961
YOUNG SINNER, THE, 1965
YOUNG SWORDSMAN, 1964
YOUNG, WILLING AND EAGER, 1962
YOUNG WOODLEY, 1930
YOUNGBLOOD HAWKE, 1964
YOUNGER BROTHERS, THE, 1949
YOUNGEST PROFESSION, THE, 1943
YOUR SHADOW IS MINE, 1963
YOUR TURN, DARLING, 1963
YOUR UNCLE DUDLEY, 1935
YOU'RE A SWEETHEART, 1937
YOU'RE IN THE ARMY NOW, 1941
YOU'RE MY EVERYTHING, 1949
YOU'RE NEVER TOO YOUNG, 1955
YOU'RE ONLY YOUNG ONCE, 1938
YOURS FOR THE ASKING, 1936
YOUTH AND HIS AMULET, THE, 1963
YOUTH ON PARADE, 1943
YUKON FLIGHT, 1940
ZANDY'S BRIDE, 1974
ZANZIBAR, 1940
ZARAK, 1956
ZATOICHI, 1968
ZATOICHI MEETS YOJIMBO, 1970
ZATOICHI'S CONSPIRACY, 1974
ZEBRA IN THE KITCHEN, 1965
ZEPPELIN, 1971
ZIG-ZAG, 1975
ZINA, 1985
ZITA, 1968
ZOMBIES ON BROADWAY, 1945

2 Stars
AARON LOVES ANGELA, 1975
AARON SLICK FROM PUNKIN CRICK, 1952
ABBOTT AND COSTELLO IN THE FOREIGN
  LEGION, 1950
**ABBOTT AND COSTELLO MEET CAPTAIN KIDD,
  1952**
ABBOTT AND COSTELLO MEET THE KEYSTONE
  KOPS, 1955
**ABBOTT AND COSTELLO MEET THE KILLER,
  BORIS KARLOFF, 1949**
ABBOTT AND COSTELLO MEET THE MUMMY, 1955
ABBY, 1974
ABDICATION, THE, 1974
ABDUCTORS, THE, 1957
ABIE'S IRISH ROSE, 1928
ABILENE TRAIL, 1951
ABOMINABLE SNOWMAN OF THE HIMALAYAS,
  THE, 1957
ABOUT FACE, 1952
ABOUT LAST NIGHT, 1986
ABOUT MRS. LESLIE, 1954
ABOVE THE CLOUDS, 1934
ABROAD WITH TWO YANKS, 1944
ACCATTONE!, 1961
ACCIDENT, 1967
ACCIDENTAL DEATH, 1963
ACCIDENTS WILL HAPPEN, 1938
ACCOUNT RENDERED, 1957
ACCURSED, THE, 1958
ACCUSED—STAND UP, 1930
ACE ELI AND RODGER OF THE SKIES, 1973
ACE HIGH, 1969
ACE OF ACES, 1982
ACE OF SPADES, THE, 1935
ACES AND EIGHTS, 1936
ACQUA E SAPONE, 1985

ACROSS 110TH STREET, 1972
ACROSS THE BADLANDS, 1950
ACROSS THE RIO GRANDE, 1949
ACROSS THE SIERRAS, 1941
ACT, THE, 1984
ACT OF MURDER, 1965
ACTION IN ARABIA, 1944
ACTION OF THE TIGER, 1957
ADA, 1961
ADAM AND EVELYNE, 1950
ADDRESS UNKNOWN, 1944
ADIOS AMIGO, 1975
ADIOS SABATA, 1971
ADMIRAL NAKHIMOV, 1948
ADMIRAL WAS A LADY, THE, 1950
ADMIRALS ALL, 1935
ADOLESCENT, THE, 1978
ADOLESCENTS, THE, 1967
ADORABLE JULIA, 1964
ADULTERESS, THE, 1959
ADVENTURE IN BLACKMAIL, 1943
ADVENTURE IN ODESSA, 1954
ADVENTURE IN SAHARA, 1938
ADVENTURE IN WASHINGTON, 1941
ADVENTURES IN SILVERADO, 1948
ADVENTURES OF A ROOKIE, 1943
ADVENTURES OF CAPTAIN FABIAN, 1951
ADVENTURES OF CASANOVA, 1948
ADVENTURES OF DON COYOTE, 1947
ADVENTURES OF GERARD, THE, 1970
ADVENTURES OF HAJJI BABA, 1954
ADVENTURES OF JANE ARDEN, 1939
ADVENTURES OF PC 49, THE, 1949
ADVENTURES OF RABBI JACOB, THE, 1973
ADVENTURES OF RUSTY, 1945
ADVENTURES OF SADIE, THE, 1955
ADVENTURES OF SCARAMOUCHE, THE, 1964
**ADVENTURES OF THE AMERICAN RABBIT, THE,
  1986**
AFFAIR AT AKITSU, 1980
AFFAIR BLUM, THE, 1949
AFFAIR IN MONTE CARLO, 1953
AFFAIR IN RENO, 1957
AFFAIR IN TRINIDAD, 1952
AFFAIR WITH A STRANGER, 1953
AFFAIRS OF A GENTLEMAN, 1934
AFFAIRS OF A MODEL, 1952
AFFAIRS OF A ROGUE, THE, 1949
AFFAIRS OF ADELAIDE, 1949
AFFAIRS OF DOBIE GILLIS, THE, 1953
AFFAIRS OF DR. HOLL, 1954
AFFAIRS OF GERALDINE, 1946
AFRAID TO TALK, 1932
AFRICAN, THE, 1983
AFTER MIDNIGHT WITH BOSTON BLACKIE, 1943
AFTER OFFICE HOURS, 1935
AFTER THE BALL, 1932
AFTER THE DANCE, 1935
AFTER THE REHEARSAL, 1984
AFTER TOMORROW, 1932
AFTER YOU, COMRADE, 1967
AGAINST A CROOKED SKY, 1975
AGAINST THE LAW, 1934
AGE OF CONSENT, 1932
AGE OF CONSENT, 1969
AGE OF ILLUSIONS, 1967
AGE OF INDISCRETION, 1935
AGE OF INFIDELITY, 1958
AGE OF INNOCENCE, 1934
AGENT 8 3/4, 1963
AGENT FOR H.A.R.M., 1966
AGOSTINO, 1962
AIDA, 1954
AIR CADET, 1951
AIR CIRCUS, THE, 1928
AIR HOSTESS, 1949
AIRBORNE, 1962
AIRPLANE II: THE SEQUEL, 1982
AIRPORT, 1970
AIRPORT 1975, 1974
AIRPORT '77, 1977
AL JENNINGS OF OKLAHOMA, 1951
ALADDIN AND HIS LAMP, 1952
ALASKA PATROL, 1949
ALBERT, R.N., 1953
ALBUQUERQUE, 1948

ALERT IN THE SOUTH, 1954
ALEX IN WONDERLAND, 1970
ALFRED THE GREAT, 1969
ALIAS A GENTLEMAN, 1948
ALIAS BOSTON BLACKIE, 1942
ALIAS BULLDOG DRUMMOND, 1935
ALIAS MARY DOW, 1935
ALIAS THE DEACON, 1940
ALIBI, 1929
ALIBI, THE, 1939
ALIBI IKE, 1935
ALICE, SWEET ALICE, 1978
ALICE'S RESTAURANT, 1969
ALIEN FACTOR, THE, 1984
ALIEN NATION, 1988
ALIEN THUNDER, 1975
ALL-AMERICAN, THE, 1932
ALL-AMERICAN, THE, 1953
ALL-AROUND REDUCED
  PERSONALITY—OUTTAKES, THE, 1978
ALL ASHORE, 1953
ALL BY MYSELF, 1943
ALL FOR MARY, 1956
ALL IN, 1936
ALL MINE TO GIVE, 1957
ALL NEAT IN BLACK STOCKINGS, 1969
ALL NIGHT LONG, 1961
ALL NUDITY SHALL BE PUNISHED, 1974
ALL OVER THE TOWN, 1949
ALL SCREWED UP, 1976
...ALL THE MARBLES, 1981
ALL THE OTHER GIRLS DO!, 1967
ALL THE RIGHT MOVES, 1983
ALL THE RIGHT NOISES, 1973
ALL THE WAY UP, 1970
ALL THESE WOMEN, 1964
ALLEGHENY UPRISING, 1939
ALLERGIC TO LOVE, 1943
ALLIGATOR PEOPLE, THE, 1959
ALMOST ANGELS, 1962
ALMOST MARRIED, 1932
ALMOST MARRIED, 1942
ALOHA, BOBBY AND ROSE, 1975
ALONE IN THE DARK, 1982
ALONE IN THE STREETS, 1956
ALONG THE NAVAJO TRAIL, 1945
ALPHA BETA, 1973
ALRAUNE, 1952
ALTERED STATES, 1980
ALVIN RIDES AGAIN, 1974
ALWAYS A BRIDE, 1954
ALWAYS GOODBYE, 1938
ALWAYS IN MY HEART, 1942
ALWAYS IN TROUBLE, 1938
ALWAYS LEAVE THEM LAUGHING, 1949
ALWAYS VICTORIOUS, 1960
AM I GUILTY?, 1940
AMATEUR, THE, 1982
AMAZING COLOSSAL MAN, THE, 1957
AMAZING GRACE AND CHUCK, 1987
AMAZING MR. BLUNDEN, THE, 1973
AMAZON WOMEN ON THE MOON, 1987
AMBASSADOR BILL, 1931
AMBASSADOR'S DAUGHTER, THE, 1956
AMBUSH, 1950
AMBUSH AT CIMARRON PASS, 1958
AMBUSH AT TOMAHAWK GAP, 1953
AMBUSH IN LEOPARD STREET, 1962
AMBUSHERS, THE, 1967
AMERICA, AMERICA, 1963
AMERICAN DREAMER, 1984
AMERICAN FLYERS, 1985
AMERICAN GOTHIC, 1988
AMERICAN JUSTICE, 1986
AMERICAN NINJA, 1985
AMERICAN PRISONER, THE, 1929
AMERICAN TABOO, 1984
AMERICAN TAIL, AN, 1986
AMERICAN WIFE, AN, 1965
AMERICANIZATION OF EMILY, THE, 1964
AMERICANO, THE, 1955
AMITYVILLE HORROR, THE, 1979
AMONG HUMAN WOLVES, 1940
AMOROUS MR. PRAWN, THE, 1965
AMPHIBIOUS MAN, THE, 1961
AMPHYTRYON, 1937

AMSTERDAM KILL, THE, 1978
AND BABY MAKES THREE, 1949
AND GOD CREATED WOMAN, 1957
...AND JUSTICE FOR ALL, 1979
**AND NOW FOR SOMETHING COMPLETELY
    DIFFERENT, 1972**
AND NOW MIGUEL, 1966
AND NOW THE SCREAMING STARTS, 1973
AND THERE CAME A MAN, 1968
ANDROCLES AND THE LION, 1952
ANDY HARDY COMES HOME, 1958
ANDY HARDY'S PRIVATE SECRETARY, 1941
ANGEL, 1984
ANGEL BABY, 1961
ANGEL COMES TO BROOKLYN, AN, 1945
ANGEL FROM TEXAS, AN, 1940
ANGEL IN EXILE, 1948
ANGEL IN MY POCKET, 1969
ANGEL LEVINE, THE, 1970
ANGEL ON THE AMAZON, 1948
ANGEL RIVER, 1986
ANGEL WHO PAWNED HER HARP, THE, 1956
ANGEL WITH THE TRUMPET, THE, 1950
ANGEL WORE RED, THE, 1960
ANGELA, 1955
ANGELE, 1934
ANGELINA, 1948
ANGELO, 1951
ANGELO IN THE CROWD, 1952
ANGELO MY LOVE, 1983
ANGEL'S HOLIDAY, 1937
ANGELS OF THE STREETS, 1950
ANGELS ONE FIVE, 1954
ANGELS WITH BROKEN WINGS, 1941
ANGRY HILLS, THE, 1959
ANGRY MAN, THE, 1979
ANIMAL FARM, 1955
ANITA GARIBALDI, 1954
ANNA CROSS, THE, 1954
ANNA LUCASTA, 1949
ANNA OF BROOKLYN, 1958
ANNA OF RHODES, 1950
ANNABEL TAKES A TOUR, 1938
ANNABELLE'S AFFAIRS, 1931
ANNAPOLIS FAREWELL, 1935
ANNAPOLIS STORY, AN, 1955
ANNE DEVLIN, 1984
ANNE OF GREEN GABLES, 1934
ANNE OF THE INDIES, 1951
ANNE ONE HUNDRED, 1933
ANNIE LAURIE, 1936
ANNIHILATORS, THE, 1985
ANOTHER COUNTRY, 1984
ANOTHER DAWN, 1937
ANOTHER TIME, ANOTHER PLACE, 1958
ANTOINE ET ANTOINETTE, 1947
ANTONY AND CLEOPATRA, 1973
ANY GUN CAN PLAY, 1968
ANY WEDNESDAY, 1966
ANYBODY'S WOMAN, 1930
ANYONE CAN PLAY, 1968
ANYTHING CAN HAPPEN, 1952
ANYTHING MIGHT HAPPEN, 1935
ANZIO, 1968
APACHE AMBUSH, 1955
APACHE GOLD, 1965
APACHE RIFLES, 1964
APACHE TERRITORY, 1958
APACHE TRAIL, 1942
APACHE UPRISING, 1966
APACHE WAR SMOKE, 1952
APACHE WOMAN, 1955
APE WOMAN, THE, 1964
APOLLO GOES ON HOLIDAY, 1968
APPALOOSA, THE, 1966
APPLE DUMPLING GANG, THE, 1975
APPOINTMENT IN BERLIN, 1943
APPOINTMENT IN HONDURAS, 1953
APPOINTMENT IN LONDON, 1953
APRIL BLOSSOMS, 1937
APRIL FOOL'S DAY, 1986
APRIL IN PARIS, 1953
APRIL LOVE, 1957
ARABELLA, 1969
ARENA, 1953
AREN'T MEN BEASTS?, 1937

AREN'T WE ALL?, 1932
ARGYLE CASE, THE, 1929
ARIA, 1988
ARIANE, 1931
ARIZONA BOUND, 1941
ARIZONA BUSHWHACKERS, 1968
ARIZONA COWBOY, THE, 1950
ARIZONA CYCLONE, 1941
ARIZONA KID, THE, 1939
ARIZONA LEGION, 1939
ARIZONA RAIDERS, THE, 1936
ARIZONA TERRORS, 1942
ARIZONA TRAIL, 1943
ARIZONA WILDCAT, 1938
ARIZONIAN, THE, 1935
ARMS AND THE MAN, 1932
ARMS AND THE MAN, 1962
ARMY GAME, THE, 1963
ARMY GIRL, 1938
AROUND THE WORLD UNDER THE SEA, 1966
ARREST BULLDOG DRUMMOND, 1939
ARROW IN THE DUST, 1954
ARSON, INC., 1949
ARTHUR TAKES OVER, 1948
AS GOOD AS MARRIED, 1937
AS LONG AS YOU'RE NEAR ME, 1956
AS THE EARTH TURNS, 1934
ASCENDANCY, 1983
ASK A POLICEMAN, 1939
ASPHYX, THE, 1972
ASSASSIN FOR HIRE, 1951
ASSASSINATION OF TROTSKY, THE, 1972
ASSAULT OF THE KILLER BIMBOS, 1988
ASSAULT ON A QUEEN, 1966
ASSIGNMENT IN BRITTANY, 1943
ASSISTANT, THE, 1982
AT LONG LAST LOVE, 1975
AT MIDDLE AGE, 1985
AT THE RIDGE, 1931
AT THE STROKE OF NINE, 1957
ATALIA, 1985
ATLANTIC, 1929
ATLANTIC CONVOY, 1942
ATOMIC CITY, THE, 1952
ATOMIC SUBMARINE, THE, 1960
ATTACK ON THE IRON COAST, 1968
ATTEMPT TO KILL, 1961
ATTENTION, THE KIDS ARE WATCHING, 1978
ATTIC, THE, 1979
AUDREY ROSE, 1977
AUGUSTINE OF HIPPO, 1973
AURORA ENCOUNTER, THE, 1985
AUTHOR! AUTHOR!, 1982
AUTUMN MARATHON, 1982
AVANTI!, 1972
AVE MARIA, 1984
AVENGING HAND, THE, 1936
AVIATOR'S WIFE, THE, 1981
AWAKENING, THE, 1958
AWAY ALL BOATS, 1956
AZURE EXPRESS, 1938
BABBITT, 1934
BABES IN TOYLAND, 1961
BABETTE GOES TO WAR, 1960
BABIES FOR SALE, 1940
BABY DOLL, 1956
BABY FACE, 1933
BABY FACE HARRINGTON, 1935
BABY FACE MORGAN, 1942
BABY FACE NELSON, 1957
BABY, IT'S YOU, 1983
BABY, TAKE A BOW, 1934
BABY, THE RAIN MUST FALL, 1965
BACHELOR DADDY, 1941
BACHELOR FATHER, 1931
BACHELOR FLAT, 1962
BACHELOR IN PARADISE, 1961
BACHELOR IN PARIS, 1953
BACHELOR'S AFFAIRS, 1932
BACK DOOR TO HEAVEN, 1939
BACK ROADS, 1981
BACK STREET, 1961
BACKLASH, 1956
BACKTRACK, 1969
BAD DREAMS, 1988
BAD LITTLE ANGEL, 1939

BAD LORD BYRON, THE, 1949
BAD MEDICINE, 1985
BADGER'S GREEN, 1949
BADLANDS OF MONTANA, 1957
BADMAN'S TERRITORY, 1946
BAGDAD, 1949
BAIT, 1954
BALLAD OF A HUSSAR, 1963
BALLAD OF COSSACK GLOOTA, 1938
BALLAD OF NARAYAMA, 1961
BALLERINA, 1950
BAMBOLE!, 1965
BAMBOO PRISON, THE, 1955
BAND OF ASSASSINS, 1971
BAND OF OUTSIDERS, 1966
BAND OF THE HAND, 1986
BAND OF THIEVES, 1962
BAND WAGGON, 1940
BANDIDO, 1956
BANDIT, THE, 1949
BANDIT KING OF TEXAS, 1949
BANDIT OF SHERWOOD FOREST, THE, 1946
BANDITS, 1988
BANDITS OF CORSICA, THE, 1953
BANDITS ON THE WIND, 1964
BANISHED, 1978
BANK SHOT, 1974
BANNERLINE, 1951
BAR ESPERANZA, 1985
BARBARIAN, THE, 1933
BARBARIAN AND THE GEISHA, THE, 1958
BARBARIAN QUEEN, 1985
BARBARY COAST GENT, 1944
BARBED WIRE, 1952
BAREFOOT BATTALION, THE, 1954
BAREFOOT BOY, 1938
BARGEE, THE, 1964
BARNACLE BILL, 1935
BARNACLE BILL, 1941
BARONESS AND THE BUTLER, THE, 1938
BARRICADE, 1939
BARRIER, 1966
BAT, THE, 1959
BAT PEOPLE, THE, 1974
BATTERIES NOT INCLUDED, 1987
BATTLE AT APACHE PASS, THE, 1952
BATTLE BEYOND THE STARS, 1980
BATTLE CIRCUS, 1953
BATTLE FOR THE PLANET OF THE APES, 1973
BATTLE HELL, 1957
BATTLE HYMN, 1957
BATTLE OF BROADWAY, 1938
BATTLE OF GALLIPOLI, 1931
BATTLE OF THE CORAL SEA, 1959
BATTLE OF THE WORLDS, 1961
BATTLE ZONE, 1952
BATTLEAXE, THE, 1962
BAXTER, 1973
BAY OF SAINT MICHEL, THE, 1963
BE MINE TONIGHT, 1933
BE YOURSELF, 1930
BEACH GIRLS, 1982
BEACH PARTY, 1963
BEACH RED, 1967
BEADS OF ONE ROSARY, THE, 1982
BEAR, THE, 1963
BEARS AND I, THE, 1974
BEAST, THE, 1975
BEAST FROM 20,000 FATHOMS, THE, 1953
BEAST OF HOLLOW MOUNTAIN, THE, 1956
BEASTS OF MARSEILLES, THE, 1959
BEAUTIFUL STRANGER, 1954
BEAUTIFUL SWINDLERS, THE, 1967
BEAUTY JUNGLE, THE, 1966
BECKY SHARP, 1935
BECAUSE THEY'RE YOUNG, 1960
BED AND BOARD, 1971
BEDELIA, 1946
BEDEVILLED, 1955
BEDSIDE MANNER, 1945
BEDTIME STORY, A, 1933
BEES IN PARADISE, 1944
BEFORE I HANG, 1940
BEFORE WINTER COMES, 1969
BEGGARS IN ERMINE, 1934
BEGINNER'S LUCK, 1986

BOLD: Films on Videocassette

BEGUILED, THE, 1971
BEHIND CITY LIGHTS, 1945
BEHIND CLOSED SHUTTERS, 1952
BEHIND GREEN LIGHTS, 1935
BEHIND GREEN LIGHTS, 1946
BEHIND LOCKED DOORS, 1948
BEHIND OFFICE DOORS, 1931
BEHIND PRISON GATES, 1939
BEHIND PRISON WALLS, 1943
BEHIND THE HEADLINES, 1937
BEHIND THE MAKEUP, 1930
BEHIND THE MASK, 1932
BEHIND YOUR BACK, 1937
BELL' ANTONIO, 1962
BELLAMY TRIAL, THE, 1929
BELLBOY, THE, 1960
BELLE OF NEW YORK, THE, 1952
BELLES OF ST. CLEMENTS, THE, 1936
BELLS, THE, 1931
BELLS OF CORONADO, 1950
BELOVED, 1934
BELOVED BACHELOR, THE, 1931
BELOVED BRAT, 1938
BELOW THE BORDER, 1942
BELOW THE DEADLINE, 1946
BEND OF THE RIVER, 1952
BENEATH THE PLANET OF THE APES, 1970
BENEATH THE 12-MILE REEF, 1953
BENGAL TIGER, 1936
BENGAZI, 1955
BENSON MURDER CASE, THE, 1930
BENVENUTA, 1983
BERLIN AFFAIR, THE, 1985
BERSERK, 1967
BEST FRIENDS, 1982
BEST MAN WINS, 1948
BEST OF EVERYTHING, THE, 1959
BEST WAY, THE, 1978
BETRAYAL FROM THE EAST, 1945
BETTER LATE THAN NEVER, 1983
BETWEEN MEN, 1935
BETWEEN MIDNIGHT AND DAWN, 1950
BETWEEN TWO WOMEN, 1944
BEWARE OF BLONDIE, 1950
BEWARE OF LADIES, 1937
BEWARE SPOOKS, 1939
BEYOND A REASONABLE DOUBT, 1956
BEYOND MOMBASA, 1957
BEYOND REASONABLE DOUBT, 1980
BEYOND THE BLUE HORIZON, 1942
BEYOND THE LAST FRONTIER, 1943
BEYOND THE LAW, 1934
BEYOND THE LAW, 1968
BEYOND THE PECOS, 1945
BEYOND TOMORROW, 1940
BEYOND VICTORY, 1931
BHOWANI JUNCTION, 1956
BIG AND THE BAD, THE, 1971
BIG BEAT, THE, 1958
BIG BONANZA, THE, 1944
BIG BOODLE, THE, 1957
BIG BOY, 1930
BIG BRAIN, THE, 1933
BIG BROADCAST, THE, 1932
BIG BUSINESS, 1988
BIG CAGE, THE, 1933
BIG CHASE, THE, 1954
BIG CITY, THE, 1963
BIG COMBO, THE, 1955
BIG CUBE, THE, 1969
BIG DAY, THE, 1960
BIG EXECUTIVE, 1933
BIG FELLA, 1937
BIG FISHERMAN, THE, 1959
BIG GAMBLE, THE, 1961
BIG GAME, THE, 1936
BIG GUNDOWN, THE, 1968
BIG HANGOVER, THE, 1950
BIG JAKE, 1971
BIG JIM McLAIN, 1952
BIG LAND, THE, 1957
BIG MONEY, 1930
BIG MONEY, THE, 1962
BIG MOUTH, THE, 1967
BIG NEWS, 1929
BIG NIGHT, THE, 1960

BIG NOISE, THE, 1936
BIG PARTY, THE, 1930
BIG PAYOFF, THE, 1933
BIG PUNCH, THE, 1948
BIG RACE, THE, 1934
BIG SHOT, THE, 1937
BIG SHOW-OFF, THE, 1945
BIG STAMPEDE, THE, 1932
BIG TIME, 1929
BIG TIME OR BUST, 1934
BIG TOWN, 1932
BIG TOWN, THE, 1987
BIG TOWN AFTER DARK, 1947
BIG TOWN SCANDAL, 1948
BIG WHEEL, THE, 1949
BIGGER SPLASH, A, 1984
BIGGER THAN LIFE, 1956
BIGGEST BUNDLE OF THEM ALL, THE, 1968
BIKINI BEACH, 1964
BILL AND COO, 1947
BILLIE, 1965
BILLY JACK GOES TO WASHINGTON, 1977
BILLY THE KID, 1930
BILLY THE KID TRAPPED, 1942
BILLY THE KID VS. DRACULA, 1966
BILLY THE KID WANTED, 1941
BILLY THE KID'S ROUNDUP, 1941
BIQUEFARRE, 1983
BIRDS COME TO DIE IN PERU, 1968
BIRDS OF A FEATHER, 1935
BIRDS OF PREY, 1988
BIRDS, THE BEES AND THE ITALIANS, THE, 1967
BIRTH OF A BABY, 1938
BIRTHDAY PARTY, THE, 1968
BIRTHDAY PRESENT, THE, 1957
BISCUIT EATER, THE, 1940
BISHOP MISBEHAVES, THE, 1933
BITTER CREEK, 1954
BITTER HARVEST, 1963
BITTER SPRINGS, 1950
BITTERSWEET LOVE, 1976
BIZARRE BIZARRE, 1939
BLACK ACES, 1937
BLACK AND WHITE, 1986
BLACK BANDIT, 1938
BLACK BEAUTY, 1933
BLACK BEAUTY, 1971
BLACK BELT JONES, 1974
BLACK CASTLE, THE, 1952
BLACK CAT, THE, 1941
BLACK DAKOTAS, THE, 1954
BLACK DIAMONDS, 1940
BLACK DRAGONS, 1942
BLACK EAGLE, 1948
BLACK EYES, 1939
BLACK FRIDAY, 1940
BLACK GIRL, 1972
BLACK GOLD, 1947
BLACK HILLS EXPRESS, 1943
BLACK HORSE CANYON, 1954
BLACK LIKE ME, 1964
BLACK MAGIC, 1949
BLACK PARACHUTE, THE, 1944
BLACK RODEO, 1972
BLACK SAMSON, 1974
BLACK SHEEP, 1935
BLACK SPURS, 1965
BLACK TENT, THE, 1956
BLACK 13, 1954
BLACK TORMENT, THE, 1965
BLACK TUESDAY, 1955
BLACK WATERS, 1929
BLACK WHIP, THE, 1956
BLACKJACK KETCHUM, DESPERADO, 1956
BLACKOUT, 1978
BLADE, 1973
BLANCHE, 1971
BLAZE OF NOON, 1947
BLAZING FOREST, THE, 1952
BLAZING SIX SHOOTERS, 1940
BLAZING SUN, THE, 1950
BLEAK MOMENTS, 1972
BLIND ALIBI, 1938
BLIND DATE, 1987
BLIND DEAD, THE, 1972
BLIND GODDESS, THE, 1948

BLIND JUSTICE, 1934
BLIND MAN'S BLUFF, 1936
BLOCKADE, 1928
BLOCKHOUSE, THE, 1974
BLONDE FEVER, 1944
BLONDE FROM BROOKLYN, 1945
BLONDE RANSOM, 1945
BLONDE TROUBLE, 1937
BLONDES FOR DANGER, 1938
BLONDIE GOES LATIN, 1941
BLONDIE PLAYS CUPID, 1940
BLONDIE TAKES A VACATION, 1939
BLONDIE'S ANNIVERSARY, 1947
BLONDIE'S BIG DEAL, 1949
BLONDIE'S BIG MOMENT, 1947
BLONDIE'S BLESSED EVENT, 1942
BLONDIE'S HERO, 1950
BLOOD AND BLACK LACE, 1965
BLOOD AND LACE, 1971
BLOOD AND ROSES, 1961
BLOOD AND STEEL, 1959
BLOOD DEMON, 1967
BLOOD FROM THE MUMMY'S TOMB, 1972
BLOOD IN THE STREETS, 1975
BLOOD OF FRANKENSTEIN, 1970
BLOOD ON SATAN'S CLAW, THE, 1970
BLOOD ON THE ARROW, 1964
BLOOD ROSE, THE, 1970
BLOOD SIMPLE, 1984
BLOODLINE, 1979
BLOODSPORT, 1988
BLOSSOMS ON BROADWAY, 1937
BLOW TO THE HEART, 1983
BLOWING WILD, 1953
BLUE BIRD, THE, 1940
BLUE COUNTRY, THE, 1977
BLUE HAWAII, 1961
BLUE HEAVEN, 1985
BLUE SIERRA, 1946
BLUE SKIES AGAIN, 1983
BLUE VEIL, THE, 1947
BLUES BUSTERS, 1950
BLUES FOR LOVERS, 1966
BOBBIKINS, 1959
BOBBY DEERFIELD, 1977
BOBO, THE, 1967
BOCCACCIO, 1936
BOLD AND THE BRAVE, THE, 1956
BOLD FRONTIERSMAN, THE, 1948
BOMBARDMENT OF MONTE CARLO, THE, 1931
BOMBAY CLIPPER, 1942
BOMBAY MAIL, 1934
BOMBERS B-52, 1957
BOMBER'S MOON, 1943
BONNIE SCOTLAND, 1935
BONZO GOES TO COLLEGE, 1952
BOOMERANG, 1960
BOP GIRL GOES CALYPSO, 1957
BORDER DEVILS, 1932
BORDER FLIGHT, 1936
BORDER PATROLMAN, THE, 1936
BORDER VIGILANTES, 1941
BORN LOSERS, 1967
BORN RECKLESS, 1937
BORN TO BE LOVED, 1959
BORN TO BE WILD, 1938
BORN TO KILL, 1947
BORN TO KILL, 1975
BOSS OF BIG TOWN, 1943
BOSTON BLACKIE BOOKED ON SUSPICION, 1945
BOSTON BLACKIE GOES HOLLYWOOD, 1942
BOSTON BLACKIE'S CHINESE VENTURE, 1949
BOSTONIANS, THE, 1984
BOULDER DAM, 1936
BOUNTIFUL SUMMER, 1951
BOUNTY HUNTERS, THE, 1970
BOWERY TO BAGDAD, 1955
BOXER, 1971
BOY AND THE BRIDGE, THE, 1959
BOY OF THE STREETS, 1937
BOY WHO CRIED WEREWOLF, THE, 1973
BOYD'S SHOP, 1960
BOYS, THE, 1962
BOYS OF PAUL STREET, THE, 1969
BRAIN MACHINE, THE, 1955
BRAIN THAT WOULDN'T DIE, THE, 1959

BRAMBLE BUSH, THE, 1960
BRANDED A COWARD, 1935
BRANDED MEN, 1931
BRANDY FOR THE PARSON, 1952
BRASS BOTTLE, THE, 1964
BRASS LEGEND, THE, 1956
BRASS TARGET, 1978
BRAT, THE, 1931
BRAVE DON'T CRY, THE, 1952
BRAVE ONE, THE, 1956
BRAVE WARRIOR, 1952
BRAZIL, 1944
BREAKFAST IN BED, 1978
BREAKFAST IN HOLLYWOOD, 1946
BREAKING ALL THE RULES, 1985
BREAKING POINT, 1976
BREAKING THE ICE, 1938
BREATHLESS, 1983
BREEZING HOME, 1937
BREWSTER'S MILLIONS, 1985
BRIDAL SUITE, 1939
BRIDE IS MUCH TOO BEAUTIFUL, THE, 1958
BRIDE WITH A DOWRY, 1954
BRIDE WORE BLACK, THE, 1968
BRIDE, THE, 1973
BRIDES OF FU MANCHU, THE, 1966
BRIGAND OF KANDAHAR, THE, 1965
BRIGHTY OF THE GRAND CANYON, 1967
BRINK OF LIFE, 1960
BRITISH INTELLIGENCE, 1940
BROADMINDED, 1931
BROADWAY BABIES, 1929
BROADWAY BIG SHOT, 1942
BROADWAY HOOFER, THE, 1929
BROADWAY HOSTESS, 1935
BROADWAY LIMITED, 1941
BROADWAY RHYTHM, 1944
BROADWAY SCANDALS, 1929
BROADWAY TO CHEYENNE, 1932
BROKEN DREAMS, 1933
BROKEN LAND, THE, 1962
BROKEN LOVE, 1946
BROKEN STAR, THE, 1956
BRONTE SISTERS, THE, 1979
BRONZE BUCKAROO, THE, 1939
BROTHER JOHN, 1971
BROTHERS, 1930
BROTHERS, 1977
BROTHERS, 1984
BROTHERS AND SISTERS, 1980
BROTHERS IN THE SADDLE, 1949
BROTHERS, THE, 1948
BROWN WALLET, THE, 1936
BRUTE, THE, 1952
BRUTE MAN, THE, 1946
BUBBLE, THE, 1967
BUCCANEER, THE, 1958
BUCCANEER'S GIRL, 1950
BUCHANAN RIDES ALONE, 1958
BUCK BENNY RIDES AGAIN, 1940
BUCKAROO FROM POWDER RIVER, 1948
BUCKET OF BLOOD, 1934
BUCKET OF BLOOD, A, 1959
BUCKSKIN, 1968
BUCKSKIN FRONTIER, 1943
BUDDHA, 1965
BUDDY BUDDY, 1981
BUFFALO BILL, HERO OF THE FAR WEST, 1962
BUFFALO BILL IN TOMAHAWK TERRITORY, 1952
BUGLE SOUNDS, THE, 1941
BUGLES IN THE AFTERNOON, 1952
BUGS BUNNY'S THIRD MOVIE—1001 RABBIT TALES, 1982
BULLDOG DRUMMOND ESCAPES, 1937
BULLDOG DRUMMOND IN AFRICA, 1938
BULLDOG EDITION, 1936
BULLET FOR SANDOVAL, A, 1970
BULLFIGHTERS, THE, 1945
BULLWHIP, 1958
BUNDLE OF JOY, 1956
BUNKER BEAN, 1936
BUNNY O'HARE, 1971
BUONA SERA, MRS. CAMPBELL, 1968
BURGLAR, THE, 1956
BURGLARS, THE, 1972
BURMA CONVOY, 1941

BURN 'EM UP O'CONNER, 1939
BURN WITCH BURN, 1962
BURNING HILLS, THE, 1956
BURNING YEARS, THE, 1979
BURNT EVIDENCE, 1954
BURY ME NOT ON THE LONE PRAIRIE, 1941
BUS IS COMING, THE, 1971
BUSH CHRISTMAS, 1983
BUSHIDO BLADE, THE, 1982
BUSINESS AND PLEASURE, 1932
BUSTIN' LOOSE, 1981
BUTLER'S DILEMMA, THE, 1943
BUTTERFLY, 1982
BUTTERFLY ON THE SHOULDER, A, 1978
BWANA DEVIL, 1953
BY DESIGN, 1982
BY LOVE POSSESSED, 1961
BYE BYE BARBARA, 1969
BYE BYE MONKEY, 1978
C.H.O.M.P.S., 1979
C.H.U.D., 1984
CABINET OF CALIGARI, THE, 1962
CABOBLANCO, 1981
CACTUS FLOWER, 1969
CADDY, THE, 1953
CADET-ROUSSELLE, 1954
CAFE DE PARIS, 1938
CAFE SOCIETY, 1939
CAGE OF EVIL, 1960
CAGE OF GOLD, 1950
CAGED FURY, 1948
CAGLIOSTRO, 1975
CAHILL, UNITED STATES MARSHAL, 1973
CAIN AND MABEL, 1936
CAIRO, 1963
CAIRO ROAD, 1950
CALAMITY JANE AND SAM BASS, 1949
CALIFORNIA, 1946
CALIFORNIA CONQUEST, 1952
CALIFORNIA DREAMING, 1979
CALIFORNIA FRONTIER, 1938
CALIFORNIA PASSAGE, 1950
CALIFORNIA SPLIT, 1974
CALL HER SAVAGE, 1932
CALL ME, 1988
CALL ME BWANA, 1963
CALL OF THE CANYON, 1942
CALL OF THE FLESH, 1930
CALL OUT THE MARINES, 1942
CALLING BULLDOG DRUMMOND, 1951
CALLING DR. DEATH, 1943
CALLING DR. GILLESPIE, 1942
CALLING DR. KILDARE, 1939
CALLING HOMICIDE, 1956
CALLING WILD BILL ELLIOTT, 1943
CALYPSO, 1959
CALYPSO HEAT WAVE, 1957
CAMELS ARE COMING, THE, 1934
CAMMINA CAMMINA, 1983
CAMPUS CONFESSIONS, 1938
CAN-CAN, 1960
CAN SHE BAKE A CHERRY PIE?, 1983
CAN YOU HEAR ME MOTHER?, 1935
CAN'T BUY ME LOVE, 1987
CANADIAN PACIFIC, 1949
CANADIANS, THE, 1961
CANDIDATE FOR MURDER, 1966
CANNON FOR CORDOBA, 1970
CANNONBALL, 1976
CANYON RIVER, 1956
CAPTAIN CHINA, 1949
CAPTAIN JOHN SMITH AND POCAHONTAS, 1953
CAPTAIN LIGHTFOOT, 1955
CAPTAIN OF THE GUARD, 1930
CAPTAIN TUGBOAT ANNIE, 1945
CAPTAIN'S KID, THE, 1937
CAPTIVE HEARTS, 1988
CAPTURED, 1933
CAR OF DREAMS, 1935
CARAVAN, 1934
CARAVAN TO VACCARES, 1974
CARAVANS, 1978
CARDBOARD CAVALIER, THE, 1949
CARE BEARS MOVIE II: A NEW GENERATION, 1986
CAREER WOMAN, 1936
CAREY TREATMENT, THE, 1972

CARIBBEAN, 1952
CARMELA, 1949
CARMEN, 1949
CARNATION KID, 1929
CARNIVAL, 1935
CARNIVAL IN COSTA RICA, 1947
CARNIVAL ROCK, 1957
CAROLINA BLUES, 1944
CAROLINE CHERIE, 1968
CARPETBAGGERS, THE, 1964
CARRY ON AGAIN, DOCTOR, 1969
CARRY ON COWBOY, 1966
CARRY ON CRUISING, 1962
CARRY ON DOCTOR, 1968
CARRY ON HENRY VIII, 1970
CARRY ON JACK, 1963
CARRY ON REGARDLESS, 1961
CARRY ON SCREAMING, 1966
CARRY ON TEACHER, 1962
CARRY ON UP THE JUNGLE, 1970
CARSON CITY CYCLONE, 1943
CARSON CITY RAIDERS, 1948
CASANOVA, 1976
CASANOVA'S BIG NIGHT, 1954
CASE AGAINST FERRO, THE, 1980
CASE OF THE BLACK PARROT, THE, 1941
CASE OF THE CURIOUS BRIDE, THE, 1935
CASE OF THE HOWLING DOG, THE, 1934
CASE OF THE VELVET CLAWS, THE, 1936
CASE VAN GELDERN, 1932
CASH ON DEMAND, 1962
CASINO DE PARIS, 1957
CASINO ROYALE, 1967
CASSANDRA CROSSING, THE, 1977
CASSIDY OF BAR 20, 1938
CASTAWAY COWBOY, THE, 1974
CASTILIAN, THE, 1963
CASTLE OF THE LIVING DEAD, 1964
CAT, THE, 1959
CAT AND MOUSE, 1975
CAT AND THE CANARY, THE, 1979
CAT CREEPS, THE, 1946
CAT GIRL, 1957
CATAMOUNT KILLING, THE, 1975
CATCH AS CATCH CAN, 1937
CATCH AS CATCH CAN, 1968
CATHERINE & CO., 1976
CATLOW, 1971
CAT'S EYE, 1985
CATTLE QUEEN OF MONTANA, 1954
CATTLE TOWN, 1952
CAUGHT, 1949
CAUGHT SHORT, 1930
CAULDRON OF BLOOD, 1971
CAVALIER OF THE WEST, 1931
CAVALRY COMMAND, 1963
CAVALRY SCOUT, 1951
CAVE OF OUTLAWS, 1951
CAVEMAN, 1981
CEDDO, 1978
CELL 2455, DEATH ROW, 1955
CEMENTERIO DEL TERROR, 1985
CENSUS TAKER, THE, 1984
CENTO ANNI D'AMORE, 1954
CENTRAL AIRPORT, 1933
CENTRAL PARK, 1932
CEREMONY, THE, 1963
CERTAIN SMILE, A, 1958
CERTAIN, VERY CERTAIN, AS A MATTER OF FACT... PROBABLE, 1970
CHAFED ELBOWS, 1967
CHALLENGE, THE, 1948
CHALLENGE, THE, 1982
CHALLENGE OF THE RANGE, 1949
CHALLENGE TO BE FREE, 1976
CHAMBER OF HORRORS, 1941
CHAMPAGNE CHARLIE, 1936
CHAMPAGNE MURDERS, THE, 1968
CHANCE AT HEAVEN, 1933
CHANGE OF HEART, 1934
CHANGE OF HEART, 1938
CHANNEL CROSSING, 1934
CHARADE, 1953
CHARGE OF THE LANCERS, 1953
CHARLIE CHAN AT MONTE CARLO, 1937
CHARLIE CHAN AT TREASURE ISLAND, 1939

BOLD: Films on Videocassette

CHARLIE CHAN IN PARIS, 1935
CHARLIE CHAN IN SHANGHAI, 1935
CHARLIE CHAN'S CHANCE, 1932
CHARLIE CHAN'S MURDER CRUISE, 1940
CHARLIE MC CARTHY, DETECTIVE, 1939
CHARTER PILOT, 1940
CHASING DANGER, 1939
CHASING RAINBOWS, 1930
CHASTITY, 1969
CHATO'S LAND, 1972
CHE?, 1973
CHEAT, THE, 1931
CHEAT, THE, 1950
CHEATERS, 1934
CHEATERS AT PLAY, 1932
CHEATING CHEATERS, 1934
CHECK IS IN THE MAIL, THE, 1986
CHECK YOUR GUNS, 1948
CHECKERED COAT, THE, 1948
CHEER BOYS CHEER, 1939
CHELSEA GIRLS, THE, 1967
CHEROKEE FLASH, THE, 1945
CHEROKEE STRIP, 1940
CHEROKEE UPRISING, 1950
CHESS PLAYERS, THE, 1978
CHEYENNE WILDCAT, 1944
CHICAGO KID, THE, 1945
CHICAGO 70, 1970
CHICAGO SYNDICATE, 1955
CHIDAMBARAM, 1986
CHILD IS A WILD THING, A, 1976
CHILD IS BORN, A, 1940
CHILD UNDER A LEAF, 1975
CHILDREN OF CHANCE, 1950
CHILDREN OF CHAOS, 1950
CHILDREN OF GOD'S EARTH, 1983
CHILDREN OF THE DAMNED, 1963
CHILD'S PLAY, 1954
CHILD'S PLAY, 1972
CHINA CLIPPER, 1936
CHINA GATE, 1957
CHINA PASSAGE, 1937
CHINA VENTURE, 1953
CHINATOWN AT MIDNIGHT, 1949
CHINATOWN NIGHTS, 1929
CHINATOWN SQUAD, 1935
CHINESE DEN, THE, 1940
CHINO, 1976
CHIP OF THE FLYING U, 1940
CHIPS, 1938.
CHOICE OF ARMS, 1983
CHOKE CANYON, 1986
CHOPPING MALL, 1986
CHRISTIAN THE LION, 1976
CHRISTINA, 1974
CHRISTMAS CAROL, A, 1951
CHRISTMAS TREE, THE, 1966
CHRISTMAS TREE, THE, 1969
CHROME AND HOT LEATHER, 1971
CHU CHIN CHOW, 1934
CHU CHU AND THE PHILLY FLASH, 1981
CHUKA, 1967
CHURCH MOUSE, THE, 1934
CIGARETTE GIRL, 1947
CIMARRON, 1960
CINDERELLA JONES, 1946
CINDERELLA LIBERTY, 1973
CINDERFELLA, 1960
CIRCLE OF DANGER, 1951
CIRCLE OF DECEPTON, 1961
CIRCLE OF TWO, 1980
CIRCUMSTANTIAL EVIDENCE, 1935
CIRCUS BOY, 1947
CIRCUS CLOWN, 1934
CIRCUS FRIENDS, 1962
CIRCUS KID, THE, 1928
CIRCUS OF LOVE, 1958
CISCO PIKE, 1971
CITIZEN SAINT, 1947
CITY AFTER MIDNIGHT, 1957
CITY BENEATH THE SEA, 1953
CITY OF BAD MEN, 1953
CITY OF BEAUTIFUL NONSENSE, THE, 1935
CITY OF PAIN, 1951
CLAMBAKE, 1967
CLANCY STREET BOYS, 1943

CLASS ENEMY, 1984
CLASS OF '44, 1973
CLAY, 1964
CLAYDON TREASURE MYSTERY, THE, 1938
CLEANING UP, 1933
CLEAR THE DECKS, 1929
CLEGG, 1969
CLEO FROM 5 TO 7, 1961
CLEOPATRA'S DAUGHTER, 1963
CLINIC, THE, 1983
CLONUS HORROR, THE, 1979
CLOSE CALL FOR ELLERY QUEEN, A, 1942
CLOSE-UP, 1948
CLOTHES AND THE WOMAN, 1937
CLOUD DANCER, 1980
CLOUDED CRYSTAL, THE, 1948
CLOWN MURDERS, THE, 1976
CLUB LIFE, 1987
CLUB PARADISE, 1986
CLUE OF THE MISSING APE, THE, 1953
CLUE OF THE NEW PIN, THE, 1929
CLUE OF THE TWISTED CANDLE, 1968
COAST GUARD, 1939
COAST OF SKELETONS, 1965
COBRA WOMAN, 1944
COCK-EYED WORLD, THE, 1929
COCK OF THE AIR, 1932
COCKEYED CAVALIERS, 1934
COCKEYED COWBOYS OF CALICO COUNTY, THE, 1970
CODE OF SILENCE, 1960
CODE OF THE PRAIRIE, 1944
CODE OF THE WEST, 1947
COGNASSE, 1932
COHENS AND KELLYS IN ATLANTIC CITY, THE, 1929
COHENS AND KELLYS IN HOLLYWOOD, THE, 1932
COHENS AND KELLYS IN TROUBLE, THE, 1933
COLD SWEAT, 1974
COLD WIND IN AUGUST, 1961
COLE YOUNGER, GUNFIGHTER, 1958
COLLECTOR, THE, 1965
COLLEGE COACH, 1933
COLLEGE CONFIDENTIAL, 1960
COLLEGE HUMOR, 1933
COLLEGE RHYTHM, 1934
COLLEGE SCANDAL, 1935
COLONEL BLOOD, 1934
COLONEL BOGEY, 1948
COLONEL EFFINGHAM'S RAID, 1945
COLONEL MARCH INVESTIGATES, 1952
COLOR PURPLE, THE, 1985
COLORADO PIONEERS, 1945
COLORADO SERENADE, 1946
COLORADO SUNDOWN, 1952
COLORADO TRAIL, 1938
COLOSSUS OF RHODES, THE, 1961
COLUMN SOUTH, 1953
COMA, 1978
COMANCHE TERRITORY, 1950
COME BACK CHARLESTON BLUE, 1972
COME DANCE WITH ME, 1950
COME FLY WITH ME, 1963
COME ON GEORGE, 1939
COME ON RANGERS, 1939
COME ON TARZAN, 1933
COME OUT FIGHTING, 1945
COMEBACK, THE, 1982
COMEDY OF HORRORS, THE, 1964
COMET OVER BROADWAY, 1938
COMIN' ROUND THE MOUNTAIN, 1951
COMIN' ROUND THE MOUNTAIN, 1936
COMING OF AGE, 1938
COMMAND PERFORMANCE, 1931
COMMANDO SQUAD, 1987
COMMITTEE, THE, 1968
COMPANEROS, 1970
COMPANY OF KILLERS, 1970
COMPELLED, 1960
COMPULSORY HUSBAND, THE, 1930
COMPULSORY WIFE, THE, 1937
COMPUTER FREE-FOR-ALL, 1969
CONAN THE BARBARIAN, 1982
CONCORDE, THE—AIRPORT '79, 1979
CONCRETE JUNGLE, THE, 1982
CONDEMNED OF ALTONA, THE, 1963

CONDEMNED TO DEATH, 1932
CONDEMNED TO LIVE, 1935
CONFESSIONS OF A CO-ED, 1931
CONFESSIONS OF AN OPIUM EATER, 1962
CONFIDENTIAL, 1935
CONFIDENTIAL LADY, 1939
CONFIRM OR DENY, 1941
CONGO CROSSING, 1956
CONGRESS DANCES, 1957
CONNECTING ROOMS, 1971
CONQUERORS, THE, 1932
CONQUEST OF CHEYENNE, 1946
CONSPIRACY, 1939
CONSPIRATOR, 1949
CONSUMING PASSIONS, 1988
CONTAR HASTA TEN, 1986
CONTENDER, THE, 1944
CONTINENTAL DIVIDE, 1981
CONTINENTAL EXPRESS, 1939
CONTRABAND SPAIN, 1955
CONVERSATION PIECE, 1976
CONVICTED WOMAN, 1940
COOL AND THE CRAZY, THE, 1958
COOL BREEZE, 1972
COOL MIKADO, THE, 1963
COP, A, 1973
COP-OUT, 1967
COPACABANA, 1947
COPPER, THE, 1930
CORKY, 1972
CORKY OF GASOLINE ALLEY, 1951
CORONADO, 1935
CORPSE OF BEVERLY HILLS, THE, 1965
CORPUS CHRISTI BANDITS, 1945
CORREGIDOR, 1943
CORRUPT ONES, THE, 1967
CORRUPTION, 1968
CORRUPTION OF CHRIS MILLER, THE, 1979
COUNSEL FOR CRIME, 1937
COUNSEL FOR ROMANCE, 1938
COUNSEL'S OPINION, 1933
COUNT DRACULA, 1971
COUNT DRACULA AND HIS VAMPIRE BRIDE, 1978
COUNT OF MONTE-CRISTO, 1955
COUNT OF THE MONK'S BRIDGE, THE, 1934
COUNT THE HOURS, 1953
COUNT YORGA, VAMPIRE, 1970
COUNTER BLAST, 1948
COUNTER-ESPIONAGE, 1942
COUNTERFEIT, 1936
COUNTERFEIT COMMANDOS, 1981
COUNTERFEIT KILLER, THE, 1968
COUNTERFEITERS, THE, 1948
COUNTERSPY MEETS SCOTLAND YARD, 1950
COUNTESS OF MONTE CRISTO, THE, 1934
COUNTRY GENTLEMEN, 1937
COURAGE, 1930
COURAGE OF BLACK BEAUTY, 1957
COURIER OF LYONS, 1938
COURRIER SUD, 1937
COURT MARTIAL, 1962
COVENANT WITH DEATH, A, 1966
COVER-UP, 1949
COWBOY AND THE BLONDE, THE, 1941
COWBOY AND THE INDIANS, THE, 1949
COWBOY AND THE PRIZEFIGHTER, 1950
COWBOY AND THE SENORITA, 1944
COWBOY COUNSELOR, 1933
COWBOY IN THE CLOUDS, 1943
COWBOY MILLIONAIRE, 1935
COWBOY SERENADE, 1942
COWBOY STAR, THE, 1936
CRACKSMAN, THE, 1963
CRASH DONOVAN, 1936
CRASHOUT, 1955
CRAZY HOUSE, 1943
CRAZY JOE, 1974
CRAZY OVER HORSES, 1951
CRAZY PEOPLE, 1934
CRAZY QUILT, THE, 1966
CREATURE, 1985
CREATURE WITH THE BLUE HAND, 1971
CREEPER, THE, 1948
CREEPERS, 1985
CREEPING FLESH, THE, 1973
CREEPING UNKNOWN, THE, 1956

CRIME AND PUNISHMENT, 1975
CRIME AT BLOSSOMS, THE, 1933
CRIME AT PORTA ROMANA, 1980
CRIME BY NIGHT, 1944
CRIME DOCTOR, THE, 1934
CRIME DOCTOR'S DIARY, THE, 1949
CRIME DOCTOR'S GAMBLE, 1947
CRIME DOCTOR'S WARNING, 1945
CRIME OF DR. CRESPI, THE, 1936
CRIME OF DR. HALLET, 1938
CRIME OF PETER FRAME, THE, 1938
CRIME OF THE CENTURY, THE, 1933
CRIME ON THE HILL, 1933
CRIME OVER LONDON, 1936
CRIME SCHOOL, 1938
CRIME TAKES A HOLIDAY, 1938
CRIMES OF STEPHEN HAWKE, THE, 1936
CRIMEWAVE, 1985
CRIMINAL CODE, 1931
CRIMINAL LAWYER, 1937
CRIMINALS OF THE AIR, 1937
CRIMSON BLADE, THE, 1964
CRIMSON CIRCLE, THE, 1936
CRITIC'S CHOICE, 1963
CRITTERS II: THE MAIN COURSE, 1988
"CROCODILE" DUNDEE II, 1988
CROMWELL, 1970
CROOKED BILLET, THE, 1930
CROOKED CIRCLE, THE, 1958
CROOKED LADY, THE, 1932
CROOKED ROAD, THE, 1965
CROOKED SKY, THE, 1957
CROOKED WAY, THE, 1949
CROOKED WEB, THE, 1955
CROSS AND THE SWITCHBLADE, THE, 1970
CROSS CREEK, 1983
CROSS CURRENTS, 1935
CROSS MY HEART, 1937
CROSS MY HEART, 1946
CROSSED SWORDS, 1954
CROSSFIRE, 1933
CROSSPLOT, 1969
CROSSROADS TO CRIME, 1960
CROW HOLLOW, 1952
CROWN VS STEVENS, 1936
CROWNING EXPERIENCE, THE, 1960
CROWNING TOUCH, THE, 1959
CRY OF BATTLE, 1963
CRY OF THE PENGUINS, 1972
CRY OF THE WEREWOLF, 1944
CRY WOLF, 1968
CRYSTAL HEART, 1987
CUBAN FIREBALL, 1951
CUCKOO CLOCK, THE, 1938
CUCKOO IN THE NEST, THE, 1933
CUJO, 1983
CULT OF THE COBRA, 1955
CURSE OF THE CAT PEOPLE, THE, 1944
CURSE OF THE DOLL PEOPLE, THE, 1968
CURSE OF THE LIVING CORPSE, THE, 1964
CURSE OF THE MUMMY'S TOMB, THE, 1965
CURTAIN CALL AT CACTUS CREEK, 1950
CURTAIN FALLS, THE, 1935
CURTAIN RISES, THE, 1939
CUSTER OF THE WEST, 1968
CUSTOMS AGENT, 1950
CUT AND RUN, 1986
CYCLONE, 1987
CYCLONE FURY, 1951
CYCLONE PRAIRIE RANGERS, 1944
CYCLONE RANGER, 1935
CYCLOTRODE X, 1946
CZAR OF BROADWAY, THE, 1930
CZAR WANTS TO SLEEP, 1934
D.C. CAB, 1983
DADDY'S BOYS, 1988
DADDY'S GONE A-HUNTING, 1969
DAKOTA LIL, 1950
DALEKS—INVASION EARTH 2155 A.D., 1966
DALTON GIRLS, THE, 1957
DALTONS RIDE AGAIN, THE, 1945
DAMN CITIZEN, 1958
DAMON AND PYTHIAS, 1962
DANCE HALL, 1929
DANCE HALL, 1941
DANCE OF THE DWARFS, 1983

DANCE TEAM, 1932
DANCE WITH A STRANGER, 1985
DANCE WITH ME, HENRY, 1956
DANCE, CHARLIE, DANCE, 1937
DANCERS, 1987
DANCING IN THE DARK, 1986
DANCING MASTERS, THE, 1943
DANCING PIRATE, 1936
DANDY, THE ALL AMERICAN GIRL, 1976
DANGER BY MY SIDE, 1962
DANGER: DIABOLIK, 1968
DANGER IN THE PACIFIC, 1942
DANGER IS A WOMAN, 1952
DANGER ON THE AIR, 1938
DANGER ON WHEELS, 1940
DANGER ROUTE, 1968
DANGER TOMORROW, 1960
DANGER! WOMEN AT WORK, 1943
DANGEROUS ADVENTURE, A, 1937
DANGEROUS ASSIGNMENT, 1950
DANGEROUS BUSINESS, 1946
DANGEROUS CARGO, 1939
DANGEROUS DAN McGREW, 1930
DANGEROUS DAVIES—THE LAST DETECTIVE, 1981
DANGEROUS INTRIGUE, 1936
DANGEROUS INTRUDER, 1945
DANGEROUS MILLIONS, 1946
DANGEROUS MONEY, 1946
DANGEROUS NUMBER, 1937
DANGEROUS PASSAGE, 1944
DANGEROUS PROFESSION, A, 1949
DANGEROUS SEAS, 1931
DANGEROUS VENTURE, 1947
DANGEROUS YOUTH, 1958
DANGEROUSLY YOURS, 1933
DANIEL, 1983
DANIEL BOONE, 1936
DANIELLA BY NIGHT, 1962
DANNY BOY, 1934
DANNY BOY, 1946
DARING DAUGHTERS, 1933
DARING DOBERMANS, THE, 1973
DARING YOUNG MAN, THE, 1942
DARK DELUSION, 1947
DARK ENEMY, 1984
DARK EYES, 1938
DARK HORSE, THE, 1932
DARK INTRUDER, 1965
DARK ODYSSEY, 1961
DARK OF THE SUN, 1968
DARK RED ROSES, 1930
DARK STAIRWAY, THE, 1938
DARWIN ADVENTURE, THE, 1972
DATE AT MIDNIGHT, 1960
DATE WITH A DREAM, A, 1948
DATE WITH THE FALCON, A, 1941
DAUGHTER OF DR. JEKYLL, 1957
DAUGHTER OF EVIL, 1930
DAUGHTER OF THE DRAGON, 1931
DAUGHTER OF THE SUN GOD, 1962
DAVID COPPERFIELD, 1970
DAVID GOLDER, 1932
DAVID HARDING, COUNTERSPY, 1950
DAVY, 1958
DAWN OVER IRELAND, 1938
DAWN RIDER, 1935
DAWN TRAIL, THE, 1931
DAY IN THE DEATH OF JOE EGG, A, 1972
DAY MARS INVADED EARTH, THE, 1963
DAY OF RECKONING, 1933
DAY OF THE COBRA, THE, 1985
DAY OF THE DOLPHIN, THE, 1973
DAY OF THE EVIL GUN, 1968
DAY OF THE WOLVES, 1973
DAY THE EARTH FROZE, THE, 1959
DAY THE WORLD ENDED, THE, 1956
DAY WILL COME, A, 1960
DAY YOU LOVE ME, THE, 1988
DAYBREAK, 1948
DAYDREAMER, THE, 1975
DAYLIGHT ROBBERY, 1964
DAYS OF BUFFALO BILL, 1946
DAYS OF JESSE JAMES, 1939
DOCTORS, THE, 1956
DE L'AMOUR, 1968
DEAD END KIDS ON DRESS PARADE, 1939

DEAD KIDS, 1981
DEAD MAN'S FLOAT, 1980
DEAD MAN'S GOLD, 1948
DEAD MAN'S SHOES, 1939
DEAD MAN'S TRAIL, 1952
DEAD MEN ARE DANGEROUS, 1939
DEAD MEN DON'T WEAR PLAID, 1982
DEAD MEN TELL, 1941
DEAD MEN TELL NO TALES, 1939
DEAD MEN WALK, 1943
DEAD OR ALIVE, 1944
DEAD RINGER, 1964
DEAD RUN, 1961
DEADLINE, 1987
DEADLY BEES, THE, 1967
DEADLY EYES, 1982
DEADLY FRIEND, 1986
DEADLY GAME, THE, 1955
DEADLY PASSION, 1985
DEADLY STRANGERS, 1974
DEAR BRAT, 1951
DEAR DETECTIVE, 1978
DEAR MR. PROHACK, 1949
DEAR MURDERER, 1947
DEATH AT A BROADCAST, 1934
DEATH COLLECTOR, 1976
DEATH DRIVES THROUGH, 1935
DEATH FLIES EAST, 1935
DEATH GOES TO SCHOOL, 1953
DEATH IN SMALL DOSES, 1957
DEATH IS A NUMBER, 1951
DEATH OF A CHAMPION, 1939
DEATH OF AN ANGEL, 1952
DEATH OF AN ANGEL, 1985
DEATH OVER MY SHOULDER, 1958
DEATH RIDES A HORSE, 1969
DEATH TOOK PLACE LAST NIGHT, 1970
DEATH VALLEY GUNFIGHTER, 1949
DEATH VENGEANCE, 1982
DEATH WISH, 1974
DEATHCHEATERS, 1976
DEATHDREAM, 1972
DEBT OF HONOR, 1936
DECEIVER, THE, 1931
DECEIVERS, THE, 1988
DECLINE AND FALL...OF A BIRD WATCHER, 1969
DEDEE, 1949
DEEP, THE, 1977
DEEP IN THE HEART, 1983
DEEP IN THE HEART OF TEXAS, 1942
DEEP RED, 1976
DEERSLAYER, THE, 1957
DEFECTOR, THE, 1966
DEFENSE OF VOLOTCHAYEVSK, THE, 1938
DEFENSE RESTS, THE, 1934
DEJA VU, 1985
DELAVINE AFFAIR, THE, 1954
DELAYED ACTION, 1954
DELICATE BALANCE, A, 1973
DELICIOUS, 1931
DELIGHTFULLY DANGEROUS, 1945
DELINQUENTS, THE, 1957
DELTA FACTOR, THE, 1970
DELTA FORCE, THE, 1986
DELUGE, 1933
DEMENTED, 1980
DEMOBBED, 1944
DEMON FOR TROUBLE, A, 1934
DEMON, THE, 1981
DEMONIAQUE, 1958
DEMONS OF LUDLOW, THE, 1983
DEMONS OF THE MIND, 1972
DENTIST IN THE CHAIR, 1960
DEPTH CHARGE, 1960
DEPUTY MARSHAL, 1949
DER FREISCHUTZ, 1970
DERELICT, 1930
DESERT FURY, 1947
DESERT HAWK, THE, 1950
DESERT HELL, 1958
DESERT HORSEMAN, THE, 1946
DESERT LEGION, 1953
DESERT PASSAGE, 1952
DESERT PATROL, 1962
DESERT PHANTOM, 1937
DESERT TRAIL, 1935

EAST CHINA SEA, 1969
EAST LYNNE, 1931
EAST LYNNE ON THE WESTERN FRONT, 1931
EAST MEETS WEST, 1936
EAST OF BORNEO, 1931
EAST OF JAVA, 1935
EAST OF KILIMANJARO, 1962
EAST OF SUDAN, 1964
EAST OF THE RIVER, 1940
EAST OF THE WALL, 1986
EAST SIDE SADIE, 1929
EASY COME, EASY GO, 1947
EASY COME, EASY GO, 1967
EASY MONEY, 1934
EASY MONEY, 1936
EASY MONEY, 1948
EASY TO LOOK AT, 1945
EASY TO LOVE, 1934
EAT MY DUST!, 1976
EATEN ALIVE, 1976
EAVESDROPPER, THE, 1966
EBB TIDE, 1932
ECHO, THE, 1964
ECHOES, 1983
ECHOES OF A SUMMER, 1976
ECHOES OF SILENCE, 1966
EDGE OF HELL, 1956
EDUCATED EVANS, 1936
EDUCATING FATHER, 1936
EGGHEAD'S ROBOT, 1970
EGYPT BY THREE, 1953
EGYPTIAN, THE, 1954
EIGER SANCTION, THE, 1975
EIGHT GIRLS IN A BOAT, 1932
80 STEPS TO JONAH, 1969
EL ALAMEIN, 1954
EL GRECO, 1966
EL PASO, 1949
EL PASO KID, THE, 1946
ELECTRA, 1962
ELECTRA GLIDE IN BLUE, 1973
ELECTRIC BLUE, 1988
ELEMENT OF CRIME, THE, 1984
ELEPHANT CALLED SLOWLY, AN, 1970
ELEPHANT GUN, 1959
11 HARROWHOUSE, 1974
ELIMINATORS, 1986
ELIZA'S HOROSCOPE, 1975
ELLERY QUEEN AND THE MURDER RING, 1941
ELLERY QUEEN, MASTER DETECTIVE, 1940
ELLERY QUEEN'S PENTHOUSE MYSTERY, 1941
ELMER AND ELSIE, 1934
ELOPEMENT, 1951
ELVIRA: MISTRESS OF THE DARK, 1988
ELVIS! ELVIS!, 1977
EMBEZZLED HEAVEN, 1959
EMBRYOS, 1985
EMERGENCY, 1962
EMERGENCY CALL, 1933
EMERGENCY SQUAD, 1940
EMERGENCY WEDDING, 1950
EMIL AND THE DETECTIVES, 1964
EMMA MAE, 1976
EMPEROR AND THE GOLEM, THE, 1955
EMPEROR'S CANDLESTICKS, THE, 1937
EMPRESS WU, 1965
EMPTY SADDLES, 1937
EMPTY STAR, THE, 1962
ENCHANTED ISLAND, 1958
ENCHANTED VALLEY, THE, 1948
ENCHANTING SHADOW, THE, 1965
END, THE, 1978
END OF A PRIEST, 1970
END OF AUGUST AT THE HOTEL OZONE, THE, 1967
END OF DESIRE, 1962
END OF THE AFFAIR, THE, 1955
END OF THE RIVER, THE, 1947
END OF THE ROAD, 1944
ENDLESS NIGHT, 1971
ENEMY GENERAL, THE, 1960
ENEMY OF THE LAW, 1945
ENEMY OF THE PEOPLE, AN, 1978
ENEMY OF WOMEN, 1944
ENFORCER, THE, 1976
ENGAGEMENT ITALIANO, 1966
ENOUGH ROPE, 1966

ENTER ARSENE LUPIN, 1944
ENTER INSPECTOR DUVAL, 1961
EPILOGUE, 1967
EPISODE, 1937
ERIC SOYA'S "17", 1967
ESCAPADE IN JAPAN, 1957
ESCAPE, 1930
ESCAPE BY NIGHT, 1954
ESCAPE BY NIGHT, 1965
ESCAPE FROM CRIME, 1942
ESCAPE FROM DEVIL'S ISLAND, 1935
ESCAPE FROM SAN QUENTIN, 1957
ESCAPE FROM TERROR, 1960
ESCAPE FROM ZAHRAIN, 1962
ESCAPE IN THE FOG, 1945
ESCAPE TO ATHENA, 1979
ESCAPE TO BERLIN, 1962
ESCAPE TO BURMA, 1955
ESCAPE TO THE SUN, 1972
ESCAPED FROM DARTMOOR, 1930
ESPIONAGE, 1937
ETERNAL WALTZ, THE, 1959
ETERNALLY YOURS, 1939
EUREKA, 1983
EUROPEANS, THE, 1979
EVANGELINE, 1929
EVE KNEW HER APPLES, 1945
EVENINGS FOR SALE, 1932
EVER SINCE EVE, 1934
EVER SINCE EVE, 1937
EVERY DAY IS A HOLIDAY, 1966
EVERY DAY'S A HOLIDAY, 1938
EVERY SATURDAY NIGHT, 1936
EVERYBODY DANCE, 1936
EVERYBODY GO HOME!, 1962
EVERYBODY SING, 1938
EVERYBODY'S BABY, 1939
EVERYBODY'S DANCIN', 1950
EVERYBODY'S DOING IT, 1938
EVERYBODY'S OLD MAN, 1936
EVERYTHING BUT THE TRUTH, 1956
EVERYTHING HAPPENS TO ME, 1938
EVERYTHING IS RHYTHM, 1940
EVERYTHING'S ON ICE, 1939
EVERYTHING'S ROSIE, 1931
EVIDENCE, 1929
EVIL, THE, 1978
EVIL EYE, 1964
EVIL UNDER THE SUN, 1982
EX-BAD BOY, 1931
EX-CHAMP, 1939
EXCESS BAGGAGE, 1933
EXCLUSIVE STORY, 1936
EXILE, THE, 1947
EXPERIMENT ALCATRAZ, 1950
EXPERT, THE, 1932
EXPLORERS, 1985
EXPLOSION, 1969
EXPLOSIVE GENERATION, THE, 1961
EXPOSED, 1947
EYE OF THE DEVIL, 1967
EYE OF THE NEEDLE, THE, 1965
EYE WITNESS, 1950
EYES OF ANNIE JONES, THE, 1963
EYES OF FATE, 1933
EYES OF LAURA MARS, 1978
EYEWITNESS, 1956
F MAN, 1936
FABIAN OF THE YARD, 1954
FABULOUS SUZANNE, THE, 1946
FABULOUS TEXAN, THE, 1947
FACE AT THE WINDOW, THE, 1932
FACE AT THE WINDOW, THE, 1939
FACE BEHIND THE SCAR, 1940
FACE IN THE FOG, A, 1936
FACE IN THE SKY, 1933
FACE OF A FUGITIVE, 1959
FACE OF A STRANGER, 1964
FACE OF FIRE, 1959
FACE TO FACE, 1967
FACES IN THE FOG, 1944
FACTS OF LOVE, 1949
FAILURE, THE, 1986
FAIR GAME, 1986
FAIR WARNING, 1937
FAITHFUL, 1936

FAITHLESS, 1932
FAKE, THE, 1953
FALCON FIGHTERS, THE, 1970
FALCON IN SAN FRANCISCO, THE, 1945
FALL GUY, THE, 1930
FALL OF EVE, THE, 1929
FALL OF ROME, THE, 1963
FALLING FOR YOU, 1933
FALLING IN LOVE, 1984
FALSE COLORS, 1943
FALSE EVIDENCE, 1937
FALSE PARADISE, 1948
FAME, 1936
FAMILY, THE, 1974
FAMILY AFFAIR, 1954
FAMILY BUSINESS, 1987
FAMILY DIARY, 1963
FAN, THE, 1949
FAN, THE, 1981
FANCY BAGGAGE, 1929
FANDANGO, 1970
FANDANGO, 1985
FANGS OF THE ARCTIC, 1953
FANGS OF THE WILD, 1954
FAN'S NOTES, A, 1972
FANTOMAS STRIKES BACK, 1965
FAR FROM DALLAS, 1972
FAR FROM POLAND, 1984
FAR FRONTIER, THE, 1949
FAREWELL, MY BELOVED, 1969
FAREWELL TO CINDERELLA, 1937
FARGO, 1952
FARGO KID, THE, 1941
FARMER IN THE DELL, THE, 1936
FARMER TAKES A WIFE, THE, 1953
FARMER'S OTHER DAUGHTER, THE, 1965
FASHIONS IN LOVE, 1929
FAST AND SEXY, 1960
FAST AND THE FURIOUS, THE, 1954
FAST BULLETS, 1936
FAST COMPANIONS, 1932
FAST COMPANY, 1929
FAST COMPANY, 1938
FAST COMPANY, 1953
FAST FORWARD, 1985
FAST LADY, THE, 1963
FAT MAN, THE, 1951
FATAL DESIRE, 1953
FATAL HOUR, THE, 1937
FATAL NIGHT, THE, 1948
FATHER AND SON, 1929
FATHER BROWN, DETECTIVE, 1935
FATHER CAME TOO, 1964
FATHER IS A PRINCE, 1940
FATHER MAKES GOOD, 1950
FATHER STEPS OUT, 1937
FATHERS AND SONS, 1960
FATHER'S DOING FINE, 1952
FATHER'S SON, 1931
FATTY FINN, 1980
FEAR, THE, 1967
FEAR IS THE KEY, 1973
FEAR NO EVIL, 1981
FEAR NO MORE, 1961
FEATHER YOUR NEST, 1937
FEDERAL BULLETS, 1937
FEDERAL MAN, 1950
FEDORA, 1978
FEMALE, 1933
FEMALE, THE, 1960
FEMALE FUGITIVE, 1938
FEMALE ON THE BEACH, 1955
FEMMINA, 1968
FERRIS BUELLER'S DAY OFF, 1986
FERRY ACROSS THE MERSEY, 1964
FERRY TO HONG KONG, 1959
FEVER IN THE BLOOD, A, 1961
FEW BULLETS MORE, A, 1968
FIANCES, THE, 1964
FIASCO IN MILAN, 1963
FIEND WHO WALKED THE WEST, THE, 1958
FIERCEST HEART, THE, 1961
FIESTA, 1947
FIFTY MILLION FRENCHMEN, 1931
FIFTY-SHILLING BOXER, 1937
FIGHT TO THE FINISH, A, 1937

BOLD: Films on Videocassette

FIGHT TO THE LAST, 1938
FIGHTING BACK, 1948
FIGHTING BILL FARGO, 1942
FIGHTING CARAVANS, 1931
FIGHTING COAST GUARD, 1951
FIGHTING FATHER DUNNE, 1948
FIGHTING FOOLS, 1949
FIGHTING GUARDSMAN, THE, 1945
FIGHTING LAWMAN, THE, 1953
FIGHTING MAN OF THE PLAINS, 1949
FIGHTING MARSHAL, THE, 1932
FIGHTING PIONEERS, 1935
FIGHTING PRINCE OF DONEGAL, THE, 1966
FIGHTING REDHEAD, THE, 1950
FIGHTING RENEGADE, 1939
FIGHTING STOCK, 1935
FIGHTING THRU, 1931
FIGHTING TROUBLE, 1956
FIGHTING VALLEY, 1943
FIGHTING VIGILANTES, THE, 1947
FIGHTING WILDCATS, THE, 1957
FIGHTING YOUTH, 1935
FIGURES IN A LANDSCAPE, 1970
FILM WITHOUT A NAME, 1950
FINAL CHORD, THE, 1936
FINAL COMEDOWN, THE, 1972
FINAL COUNTDOWN, THE, 1980
FINAL CUT, THE, 1980
FINAL EDITION, 1932
FINAL JUSTICE, 1985
FIND THE LADY, 1956
FINDERS KEEPERS, 1951
FINDERS KEEPERS, 1966
FINE PAIR, A, 1969
FINGER ON THE TRIGGER, 1965
FINGERS, 1940
FINN AND HATTIE, 1931
FINO A FARTI MALE, 1969
FIRE AND ICE, 1987
FIRE HAS BEEN ARRANGED, A, 1935
FIRE IN THE FLESH, 1964
FIRE MAIDENS FROM OUTER SPACE, 1956
FIRE OVER AFRICA, 1954
FIRE RAISERS, THE, 1933
FIREBALL, THE, 1950
FIREBALL 590, 1966
FIREBALL JUNGLE, 1968
FIREBRAND, THE, 1962
FIREBRANDS OF ARIZONA, 1944
FIRECREEK, 1968
FIREFLY, THE, 1937
FIRM MAN, THE, 1975
FIRST BABY, 1936
FIRST MEN IN THE MOON, 1964
FIRST MRS. FRASER, THE, 1932
FIRST OFFENCE, 1936
FIRST START, 1953
FIRST TASTE OF LOVE, 1962
FIRST TEXAN, THE, 1956
FIRST TIME, THE, 1952
FIRST TIME, THE, 1983
FIRST YANK INTO TOKYO, 1945
FIST IN HIS POCKET, 1968
FISTS OF FURY, 1973
FIT FOR A KING, 1937
FIVE BOLD WOMEN, 1960
FIVE CARD STUD, 1968
FIVE GIANTS FROM TEXAS, 1966
FIVE GUNS WEST, 1955
FIVE LITTLE PEPPERS AND HOW THEY GREW, 1939
FIVE MAN ARMY, THE, 1970
FIVE MINUTES TO LIVE, 1961
5 SINNERS, 1961
FIVE STEPS TO DANGER, 1957
FIVE THE HARD WAY, 1969
FIVE WEEKS IN A BALLOON, 1962
FIX, THE, 1985
FLAG LIEUTENANT, THE, 1932
FLAME, 1975
FLAME AND THE FLESH, 1954
FLAME OF ARABY, 1951
FLAME OF CALCUTTA, 1953
FLAME OF THE BARBARY COAST, 1945
FLAME WITHIN, THE, 1935
FLAMING BULLETS, 1945
FLAMING FURY, 1949

FLAMING SIGNAL, 1933
FLANAGAN, 1985
FLAREUP, 1969
FLASH GORDON, 1980
FLASHING GUNS, 1947
FLAW, THE, 1933
FLAXFIELD, THE, 1985
FLESH AND THE WOMAN, 1954
FLESH FEAST, 1970
FLIGHT AT MIDNIGHT, 1939
FLIGHT FROM ASHIYA, 1964
FLIGHT FROM VIENNA, 1956
FLIGHT LIEUTENANT, 1942
FLIGHT TO FAME, 1938
FLIGHT TO MARS, 1951
FLIRTING WIDOW, THE, 1930
FLOATING DUTCHMAN, THE, 1953
FLOOD TIDE, 1935
FLOOD TIDE, 1958
FLORIAN, 1940
FLOWER DRUM SONG, 1961
FLOWERS FOR THE MAN IN THE MOON, 1975
FLYING BLIND, 1941
FLYING DEVILS, 1933
FLYING FOOL, 1929
FLYING GUILLOTINE, THE, 1975
FLYING IRISHMAN, THE, 1939
FLYING MATCHMAKER, THE, 1970
FLYING SCOTSMAN, THE, 1929
FLYING SQUAD, THE, 1932
FLYING WILD, 1941
FM, 1978
FOG, 1934
FOG, THE, 1980
FOLLIES GIRL, 1943
FOLLOW A STAR, 1959
FOLLOW THAT CAMEL, 1967
FOLLOW THAT WOMAN, 1945
FOLLOW THE BAND, 1943
FOLLOW THE LEADER, 1944
FOLLOW YOUR HEART, 1936
FOOL FOR LOVE, 1985
FOOL KILLER, THE, 1965
FOOLIN' AROUND, 1980
FOOLS FOR SCANDAL, 1938
FOOL'S GOLD, 1946
FOOTLIGHT GLAMOUR, 1943
FOOTSTEPS IN THE NIGHT, 1957
FOR LOVE OR MONEY, 1963
FOR PETE'S SAKE, 1977
FOR THE LOVE OF MIKE, 1933
FOR THE LOVE OF MIKE, 1960
FOR THE LOVE OF RUSTY, 1947
FOR THE SERVICE, 1936
FOR THOSE WHO THINK YOUNG, 1964
FORBIDDEN CARGO, 1954
FORBIDDEN COMPANY, 1932
FORBIDDEN RELATIONS, 1983
FORBIDDEN TRAIL, 1936
FORBIDDEN TRAILS, 1941
FORCE OF ONE, A, 1979
FORCED LANDING, 1941
FOREIGN BODY, 1986
FOREIGN CITY, A, 1988
FOREVER YOUNG, FOREVER FREE, 1976
FOREVER YOURS, 1937
FOREVER YOURS, 1945
FORGED PASSPORT, 1939
FORGET MOZART!, 1985
FORGOTTEN WOMAN, THE, 1939
FORGOTTEN WOMEN, 1932
FORT ALGIERS, 1953
FORT DOBBS, 1958
FORT DODGE STAMPEDE, 1951
FORT VENGEANCE, 1953
FORT WORTH, 1951
FORT YUMA, 1955
FORTRESS, THE, 1979
FORTUNE LANE, 1947
FORTY DEUCE, 1982
48 HOURS TO LIVE, 1960
45 FATHERS, 1937
FORTY-NINE DAYS, 1964
FORTY-NINTH MAN, THE, 1953
FORTY THIEVES, 1944
FOUNTAIN OF LOVE, THE, 1968

FOUR BOYS AND A GUN, 1957
FOUR COMPANIONS, THE, 1938
FOUR DAYS, 1951
FOUR DAYS LEAVE, 1950
FOUR DAYS OF NAPLES, THE, 1963
FOUR DESPERATE MEN, 1960
FOUR DEUCES, THE, 1976
FOUR DEVILS, 1929
FOUR FAST GUNS, 1959
FOUR GIRLS IN WHITE, 1939
FOUR GUNS TO THE BORDER, 1954
FOUR HORSEMEN OF THE APOCALYPSE, THE, 1962
FOUR HOURS TO KILL, 1935
FOUR IN A JEEP, 1951
FOUR IN THE MORNING, 1965
FOUR MASKED MEN, 1934
FOUR WAYS OUT, 1954
FOUR WIVES, 1939
FOURTH PROTOCOL, THE, 1987
FOURTH SQUARE, THE, 1961
48 HOURS TO ACAPULCO, 1968
FOX MOVIETONE FOLLIES OF 1930, 1930
FOXFIRE, 1955
FOXHOLE IN CAIRO, 1960
FOXTROT, 1977
FRAMED, 1930
FRAMED, 1975
FRANCHISE AFFAIR, THE, 1952
FRANCIS COVERS THE BIG TOWN, 1953
FRANCIS GOES TO THE RACES, 1951
FRANCIS GOES TO WEST POINT, 1952
FRANCIS IN THE NAVY, 1955
FRANCIS JOINS THE WACS, 1954
FRANCIS OF ASSISI, 1961
FRANKENSTEIN AND THE MONSTER FROM HELL, 1974
FRANKENSTEIN 1970, 1958
FRANKIE AND JOHNNY, 1966
FRECKLES, 1935
FRECKLES, 1960
FRECKLES COMES HOME, 1942
FREDDIE STEPS OUT, 1946
FREE, BLONDE AND 21, 1940
FREEDOM OF THE SEAS, 1934
FREEDOM TO DIE, 1962
FREIGHTERS OF DESTINY, 1932
FRENCH DRESSING, 1964
FRENCH GAME, THE, 1963
FRENCH KEY, THE, 1946
FRENCH LEAVE, 1937
FRENCH LEAVE, 1948
FRENCH LINE, THE, 1954
FRENCH POSTCARDS, 1979
FRENCH, THEY ARE A FUNNY RACE, THE, 1956
FRENCH WAY, THE, 1952
FRENCH WAY, THE, 1975
FRENCH WITHOUT TEARS, 1939
FRENCHIE, 1950
FRESHMAN YEAR, 1938
FRIDAY FOSTER, 1975
FRIEND OF THE FAMILY, 1965
FRIENDLY KILLER, THE, 1970
FRIENDLY NEIGHBORS, 1940
FRIENDS AND NEIGHBORS, 1963
FRIENDS FOR LIFE, 1964
FRIGHTENED BRIDE, THE, 1952
FRIGHTENED MAN, THE, 1952
FRIGHTMARE, 1974
FRISCO KID, THE, 1979
FRISCO SAL, 1945
FRISCO WATERFRONT, 1935
FROG, THE, 1937
FROM BEYOND THE GRAVE, 1974
FROM HEADQUARTERS, 1933
FROM HELL IT CAME, 1957
FROM HELL TO VICTORY, 1979
FROM THE TERRACE, 1960
FRONT LINE KIDS, 1942
FRONTIER DAYS, 1934
FRONTIER FEUD, 1945
FRONTIER FURY, 1943
FRONTIER GUN, 1958
FRONTIER HELLCAT, 1966
FRONTIER INVESTIGATOR, 1949
FRONTIER OUTLAWS, 1944

FRONTIER PHANTOM, THE, 1952
FRONTIER PONY EXPRESS, 1939
FRONTIER REVENGE, 1948
FRONTIERSMAN, THE, 1938
FROU-FROU, 1955
FROZEN GHOST, THE, 1945
FROZEN JUSTICE, 1929
FRUIT IS RIPE, THE, 1961
FUGITIVE AT LARGE, 1939
FUGITIVE IN THE SKY, 1937
FUGITIVE KIND, THE, 1960
FUGITIVE LOVERS, 1934
FUGITIVE ROAD, 1934
FUGITIVE SHERIFF, THE, 1936
FUGITIVE, THE, 1933
FUGITIVES FOR A NIGHT, 1938
FULL SPEED AHEAD, 1939
FUN AND FANCY FREE, 1947
FUN IN ACAPULCO, 1963
FUN WITH DICK AND JANE, 1977
FUNHOUSE, THE, 1981
FUNNY FARM, THE, 1982
FURTHER ADVENTURES OF TENNESSEE BUCK, THE, 1988
FURY AND THE WOMAN, 1937
FURY AT SMUGGLERS BAY, 1963
FUTURE-KILL, 1985
FUZZY PINK NIGHTGOWN, THE, 1957
G.I. BLUES, 1960
GABRIELA, 1984
GABY, 1956
GAIETY GIRLS, THE, 1938
GAL WHO TOOK THE WEST, THE, 1949
GALIA, 1966
GALLANT BESS, 1946
GALLANT BLADE, THE, 1948
GALLANT LADY, 1934
GALLANT LEGION, THE, 1948
GALLANT ONE, THE, 1964
GALLANT SONS, 1940
GALLOPING MAJOR, THE, 1951
GAMBLER'S CHOICE, 1944
GAMBLERS, THE, 1929
GAMBLERS, THE, 1969
GAMBLING ON THE HIGH SEAS, 1940
GAMBLING TERROR, THE, 1937
GAME FOR SIX LOVERS, A, 1962
GAME FOR THREE LOSERS, 1965
GAME OF LOVE, THE, 1954
GAME OF TRUTH, THE, 1961
GAMES, THE, 1970
GAMMA PEOPLE, THE, 1956
GANG, THE, 1938
GANGS OF CHICAGO, 1940
GANGS OF SONORA, 1941
GARBAGE MAN, THE, 1963
GARDEN OF THE MOON, 1938
GARDENS OF STONE, 1987
GARRISON FOLLIES, 1940
GATES TO PARADISE, 1968
GATHERING OF EAGLES, A, 1963
GATOR, 1976
GAUCHO SERENADE, 1940
GAUNTLET, THE, 1977
GAVILAN, 1968
GAY AMIGO, THE, 1949
GAY BLADES, 1946
GAY BRIDE, THE, 1934
GAY CABALLERO, THE, 1932
GAY CABALLERO, THE, 1940
GAY LADY, THE, 1949
GAY SENORITA, THE, 1945
GENERAL CRACK, 1929
GENERAL JOHN REGAN, 1933
GENERAL MASSACRE, 1973
GENIE, THE, 1953
GENTLE ANNIE, 1944
GENTLE GANGSTER, A, 1943
GENTLE TOUCH, THE, 1956
GENTLEMAN AFTER DARK, A, 1942
GENTLEMAN FROM ARIZONA, THE, 1940
GENTLEMAN FROM DIXIE, 1941
GENTLEMEN ARE BORN, 1934
GEORGE, 1973
GEORGE WASHINGTON CARVER, 1940
GEORGE WHITE'S 1935 SCANDALS, 1935

GEORGE WHITE'S SCANDALS, 1945
GERALDINE, 1929
GERALDINE, 1953
GERMAN SISTERS, THE, 1982
GERMANY IN AUTUMN, 1978
GERMINAL, 1963
GERT AND DAISY CLEAN UP, 1942
GERT AND DAISY'S WEEKEND, 1941
GET-AWAY, THE, 1941
GET BACK, 1973
GET CHARLIE TULLY, 1976
GET ON WITH IT, 1963
GET TO KNOW YOUR RABBIT, 1972
GHOST CHASERS, 1951
GHOST DIVER, 1957
GHOST GOES WILD, THE, 1947
GHOST GUNS, 1944
GHOST OF THE CHINA SEA, 1958
GHOST OF ZORRO, 1959
GHOST PATROL, 1936
GHOST SHIP, 1953
GHOST STORY, 1974
GHOST TALKS, THE, 1929
GHOST TOWN, 1956
GHOST TOWN, 1988
GHOST TOWN GOLD, 1937
GHOST TOWN RENEGADES, 1947
GHOST TRAIN, THE, 1933
GHOST TRAIN, THE, 1941
GHOST VALLEY RAIDERS, 1940
GHOSTS, ITALIAN STYLE, 1969
GHOSTS ON THE LOOSE, 1943
G.I. EXECUTIONER, THE, 1985
G.I. HONEYMOON, 1945
G.I. JANE, 1951
GIANT OF MARATHON, THE, 1960
GIDGET GOES HAWAIIAN, 1961
GIFT OF LOVE, THE, 1958
GIFT, THE, 1983
GIGANTES PLANETARIOS, 1965
GILDED CAGE, THE, 1954
GILDERSLEEVE'S BAD DAY, 1943
GILDERSLEEVE'S GHOST, 1944
GINGER, 1935
GINGER, 1947
GINGER IN THE MORNING, 1973
GIRL AND THE GAMBLER, THE, 1939
GIRL AND THE GENERAL, THE, 1967
GIRL CAN'T HELP IT, THE, 1956
GIRL FROM ALASKA, 1942
GIRL FROM AVENUE A, 1940
GIRL FROM CALGARY, 1932
GIRL FROM GOD'S COUNTRY, 1940
GIRL FROM HAVANA, 1940
GIRL FROM HONG KONG, 1966
GIRL FROM MANHATTAN, 1948
GIRL FROM MAXIM'S THE, 1936
GIRL FROM MONTEREY, THE, 1943
GIRL FROM RIO, THE, 1939
GIRL FROM SAN LORENZO, THE, 1950
GIRL FROM SCOTLAND YARD, THE, 1937
GIRL FROM THE MARSH CROFT, THE, 1935
GIRL HAPPY, 1965
GIRL IN A MILLION, A, 1946
GIRL IN BLACK STOCKINGS, 1957
GIRL IN DANGER, 1934
GIRL IN POSSESSION, 1934
GIRL IN THE CASE, 1944
GIRL IN THE NIGHT, THE, 1931
GIRL IN THE PICTURE, THE, 1956
GIRL IN THE STREET, 1938
GIRL IN THE WOODS, 1958
GIRL IN 313, 1940
GIRL IS MINE, THE, 1950
GIRL LOVES BOY, 1937
GIRL O' MY DREAMS, 1935
GIRL OF THE LIMBERLOST, 1934
GIRL OF THE LIMBERLOST, THE, 1945
GIRL OF THE MOORS, THE, 1961
GIRL OF THE MOUNTAINS, 1958
GIRL OF THE NIGHT, 1960
GIRL OF THE RIO, 1932
GIRL ON A MOTORCYCLE, THE, 1968
GIRL ON THE BOAT, THE, 1962
GIRL ON THE CANAL, THE, 1947
GIRL ON THE FRONT PAGE, THE, 1936

GIRL ON THE SPOT, 1946
GIRL RUSH, 1944
GIRL WHO COULDN'T QUITE, THE, 1949
GIRL WHO COULDN'T SAY NO, THE, 1969
GIRL WITH THE RED HAIR, THE, 1983
GIRL WITH THREE CAMELS, THE, 1968
GIRL WITHOUT A ROOM, 1933
GIRLS AT SEA, 1958
GIRLS CAN PLAY, 1937
GIRLS JUST WANT TO HAVE FUN, 1985
GIRLS OF THE BIG HOUSE, 1945
GIRLS ON THE BEACH, 1965
GIRLS' TOWN, 1942
GIRLS, THE, 1972
GIVE ME MY CHANCE, 1958
GIVE ME THE STARS, 1944
GIVE MY REGARDS TO BROAD STREET, 1984
GIVE OUT, SISTERS, 1942
GIVE US THE MOON, 1944
GIVE US THIS NIGHT, 1936
GIVE US WINGS, 1940
GLAD RAG DOLL, THE, 1929
GLAMOUR FOR SALE, 1940
GLAMOUR GIRL, 1938
GLASS CAGE, THE, 1964
GLASS MOUNTAIN, THE, 1950
GLASS SLIPPER, THE, 1955
GLASS TOWER, THE, 1959
GLOBAL AFFAIR, A, 1964
GLORY ALLEY, 1952
GLORY GUYS, THE, 1965
GLOWING AUTUMN, 1981
GO-GETTER, THE, 1937
GO KART GO, 1964
GO NAKED IN THE WORLD, 1961
GO WEST, YOUNG LADY, 1941
GO WEST, YOUNG MAN, 1936
GOBS AND GALS, 1952
GODDESS OF LOVE, THE, 1960
GODLESS GIRL, THE, 1929
GOD'S COUNTRY AND THE MAN, 1937
GOD'S COUNTRY AND THE WOMAN, 1937
GOD'S GIFT TO WOMEN, 1931
GODSPELL, 1973
GOG, 1954
GOIN' SOUTH, 1978
GOIN' TO TOWN, 1935
GOING AND COMING BACK, 1985
GOING HIGHBROW, 1935
GOING HOME, 1971
GOING HOME, 1988
GOING PLACES, 1939
GOING STEADY, 1958
GOING WILD, 1931
GOLD, 1932
GOLD, 1934
GOLD, 1974
GOLD FEVER, 1952
GOLD MINE IN THE SKY, 1938
GOLD OF NAPLES, 1957
GOLD OF THE SEVEN SAINTS, 1961
GOLD RUSH MAISIE, 1940
GOLDEN BOX, THE, 1970
GOLDEN CAGE, THE, 1933
GOLDEN CALF, THE, 1930
GOLDEN DAWN, 1930
GOLDEN FLEECING, THE, 1940
GOLDEN GATE GIRL, 1941
GOLDEN GLOVES, 1940
GOLDEN GLOVES STORY, THE, 1950
GOLDEN HEAD, THE, 1965
GOLDEN IDOL, THE, 1954
GOLDEN MISTRESS, THE, 1954
GOLDEN SEAL, THE, 1983
GOLDEN TRAIL, THE, 1940
GOLDEN WEST, THE, 1932
GOLDIE GETS ALONG, 1933
GOLDTOWN GHOST RIDERS, 1953
GOLDWYN FOLLIES, THE, 1938
GOLEM, 1980
GOLIATH AND THE BARBARIANS, 1960
GOLIATH AND THE SINS OF BABYLON, 1964
GONE IN 60 SECONDS, 1974
GOOD BAD GIRL, THE, 1931
GOOD COMPANIONS, 1933
GOOD FELLOWS, THE, 1943

BOLD: Films on Videocassette

GOOD INTENTIONS, 1930
GOOD LUCK, MR. YATES, 1943
GOOD MOTHER, THE, 1988
GOOD NEWS, 1930
GOOD OLD DAYS, THE, 1939
GOOD OLD SOAK, THE, 1937
GOOD WIFE, THE, 1987
GOODBYE BROADWAY, 1938
GOODBYE, MOSCOW, 1968
GOODBYE, MY FANCY, 1951
GOOSE AND THE GANDER, THE, 1935
GOOSE STEPS OUT, THE, 1942
GORILLA, THE, 1939
GORILLA, 1964
GORILLA MAN, 1942
GOSPEL ROAD, THE, 1973
GOT IT MADE, 1974
GOTCHA!, 1985
GOVERNMENT GIRL, 1943
GOYOKIN, 1969
GRACIE ALLEN MURDER CASE, 1939
GRAFT, 1931
GRAND CANYON, 1949
GRAND ESCAPADE, THE, 1946
GRAND EXIT, 1935
GRAND OLE OPRY, 1940
GRAND PRIX, 1934
GRANDPA GOES TO TOWN, 1940
GRASS IS GREENER, THE, 1960
GRASS IS SINGING, THE, 1982
GRAYEAGLE, 1977
GREAT ARMORED CAR SWINDLE, THE, 1964
GREAT BANK ROBBERY, THE, 1969
GREAT BRAIN, THE, 1978
GREAT DAWN, THE, 1947
GREAT DIAMOND ROBBERY, 1953
GREAT GAMBINI, THE, 1937
GREAT GAME, THE, 1953
GREAT GILDERSLEEVE, THE, 1942
GREAT GOD GOLD, 1935
GREAT HOSPITAL MYSTERY, THE, 1937
GREAT HOTEL MURDER, 1935
GREAT IMPERSONATION, THE, 1935
GREAT PLANE ROBBERY, THE, 1940
GREAT SIOUX UPRISING, THE, 1953
GREAT STAGECOACH ROBBERY, 1945
GREAT WALTZ, THE, 1972
GREAT WAR, THE, 1961
GREAT YEARNING, THE, 1930
GREEN FIELDS, 1937
GREEN FINGERS, 1947
GREEN FIRE, 1955
GREEN FOR DANGER, 1946
GREEN GLOVE, THE, 1952
GREEN HELL, 1940
GREEN MANSIONS, 1959
GREEN PROMISE, THE, 1949
GREEN SCARF, THE, 1954
GREEN YEARS, THE, 1946
GREENWICH VILLAGE, 1944
GREH, 1962
GRENDEL GRENDEL GRENDEL, 1981
GREYHOUND LIMITED, THE, 1929
GRINGO, 1963
GRISSLY'S MILLIONS, 1945
GROOM WORE SPURS, THE, 1951
GUARDIAN OF THE WILDERNESS, 1977
GUEST IN THE HOUSE, 1944
GUILT IS MY SHADOW, 1950
GUILTY BYSTANDER, 1950
GUILTY TRAILS, 1938
GUILTY, THE, 1947
GUINGUETTE, 1959
GULLIVER'S TRAVELS BEYOND THE MOON, 1966
GUN CRAZY, 1949
GUN LORDS OF STIRRUP BASIN, 1937
GUN MAN FROM BODIE, THE, 1941
GUN PLAY, 1936
GUN RANGER, THE, 1937
GUN RIDERS, THE, 1969
GUN RUNNER, 1969
GUN SMUGGLERS, 1948
GUN TALK, 1948
GUN THAT WON THE WEST, THE, 1955
GUNFIGHT AT COMANCHE CREEK, 1964
GUNFIGHTERS OF CASA GRANDE, 1965

GUNMAN HAS ESCAPED, A, 1948
GUNMEN OF ABILENE, 1950
GUNMEN OF THE RIO GRANDE, 1965
GUNPOINT, 1966
GUNPOWDER, 1987
GUNS, 1980
GUNS FOR SAN SEBASTIAN, 1968
GUNS IN THE DARK, 1937
GUNS IN THE HEATHER, 1968
GUNS OF DARKNESS, 1962
GUNS OF FORT PETTICOAT, THE, 1957
GUNS OF HATE, 1948
GUNS OF THE BLACK WITCH, 1961
GUNS OF THE MAGNIFICENT SEVEN, 1969
GUNS OF THE TIMBERLAND, 1960
GUNSIGHT RIDGE, 1957
GUNSLINGER, 1956
GUNSMOKE IN TUCSON, 1958
GUNSMOKE MESA, 1944
GUNSMOKE TRAIL, 1938
GUS, 1976
GYPSY FURY, 1950
GYPSY WILDCAT, 1944
HA' PENNY BREEZE, 1950
HADLEY'S REBELLION, 1984
HAIL, 1973
HALF A SINNER, 1934
HALF ANGEL, 1936
HALF-BREED, THE, 1952
HALF-MARRIAGE, 1929
HALF PAST MIDNIGHT, 1948
HALF PINT, THE, 1960
HALLOWEEN III: SEASON OF THE WITCH, 1982
HAMBONE AND HILLIE, 1984
HAMLET, 1966
HAMLET, 1976
HAMMER, 1972
HAMMER THE TOFF, 1952
HAMMERHEAD, 1968
HAND, THE, 1981
HAND, THE, 1960
HANDCUFFED, 1929
HANDCUFFS, LONDON, 1955
HANDLE WITH CARE, 1958
HANDLE WITH CARE, 1964
HANDS OF ORLAC, THE, 1964
HANGMAN WAITS, THE, 1947
HANNAH K., 1983
HANNIE CALDER, 1971
HANSEL AND GRETEL, 1954
HAPPINESS CAGE, THE, 1972
HAPPINESS C.O.D., 1935
HAPPY, 1934
HAPPY END, 1968
HAPPY ENDING, THE, 1969
HAPPY GO LUCKY, 1943
HAPPY IS THE BRIDE, 1958
HAPPY LANDING, 1938
HAPPY MOTHER'S DAY . . . LOVE, GEORGE, 1973
HARBOR LIGHT YOKOHAMA, 1970
HARBOR LIGHTS, 1963
HARD BOILED MAHONEY, 1947
HARD GUY, 1941
HARD MAN, THE, 1957
HAREM, 1985
HAREM GIRL, 1952
HARMON OF MICHIGAN, 1941
HAROLD TEEN, 1934
HARPOON, 1948
HARRIGAN'S KID, 1943
HARRY AND THE HENDERSONS, 1987
HARRY AND WALTER GO TO NEW YORK, 1976
HARRY IN YOUR POCKET, 1973
HARRY TRACY—DESPERADO, 1982
HARVARD, HERE I COME, 1942
HARVEST MELODY, 1943
HARVEY MIDDLEMAN, FIREMAN, 1965
HAT, COAT AND GLOVE, 1934
HATE FOR HATE, 1967
HAUNTED GOLD, 1932
HAUNTED HOUSE, THE, 1940
HAUNTED RANCH, THE, 1943
HAVANA WIDOWS, 1933
HAVE ROCKET, WILL TRAVEL, 1959
HAWAII CALLS, 1938
HAWAIIAN BUCKAROO, 1938

HAWAIIAN NIGHTS, 1939
HAWAIIANS, THE, 1970
HAWK THE SLAYER, 1980
HAWLEY'S OF HIGH STREET, 1933
HAZARD, 1948
HAZING, THE, 1978
HE FOUND A STAR, 1941
HE HIRED THE BOSS, 1943
HE LOVED AN ACTRESS, 1938
HE RIDES TALL, 1964
HE STAYED FOR BREAKFAST, 1940
HEAD OF THE FAMILY, 1933
HEAD OFFICE, 1936
HEAD OVER HEELS IN LOVE, 1937
HEADIN' EAST, 1937
HEADIN' FOR GOD'S COUNTRY, 1943
HEADIN' NORTH, 1930
HEADING FOR HEAVEN, 1947
HEADLESS GHOST, THE, 1959
HEADLEYS AT HOME, THE, 1939
HEADLINE, 1943
HEADLINE HUNTERS, 1955
HEADLINE HUNTERS, 1968
HEADS UP, 1930
HEART BEAT, 1979
HEART OF A MAN, THE, 1959
HEART OF NEW YORK, 1932
HEART OF THE ROCKIES, 1937
HEART OF VIRGINIA, 1948
HEART PUNCH, 1932
HEART SONG, 1933
HEARTACHES, 1947
HEARTBEEPS, 1981
HEARTBREAK, 1931
HEARTBREAK KID, THE, 1972
HEARTBURN, 1986
HEART'S DESIRE, 1937
HEARTS IN BONDAGE, 1936
HEARTS IN EXILE, 1929
HEARTS OF HUMANITY, 1932
HEARTS OF HUMANITY, 1936
HEAT, 1987
HEAT LIGHTNING, 1934
HEAT OF DESIRE, 1984
HEAT OF THE SUMMER, 1961
HEAT WAVE, 1935
HEATHCLIFF: THE MOVIE, 1986
HEATWAVE, 1954
HEATWAVE, 1983
HEAVEN ON EARTH, 1931
HEAVEN WITH A BARBED WIRE FENCE, 1939
HEAVEN WITH A GUN, 1969
HEAVENLY DAYS, 1944
HEIDI AND PETER, 1955
HEIDI'S SONG, 1982
HEIR TO TROUBLE, 1936
HEIRLOOM MYSTERY, THE, 1936
HELDINNEN, 1962
HELL BENT FOR LOVE, 1934
HELL BOATS, 1970
HELL BOUND, 1957
HELL CANYON OUTLAWS, 1957
HELL COMES TO FROGTOWN, 1988
HELL FIRE AUSTIN, 1932
HELL HARBOR, 1930
HELL IN THE PACIFIC, 1968
HELL ON DEVIL'S ISLAND, 1957
HELL RAIDERS OF THE DEEP, 1954
HELL TO ETERNITY, 1960
HELLBENDERS, THE, 1967
HELLBOUND: HELLRAISER II, 1988
HELLCATS OF THE NAVY, 1957
HELLDORADO, 1935
HELLER IN PINK TIGHTS, 1960
HELLFIGHTERS, 1968
HELLFIRE, 1949
HELLFIRE CLUB, THE, 1963
HELLGATE, 1952
HELLIONS, THE, 1962
HELLO DOWN THERE, 1969
HELLO, EVERYBODY, 1933
HELLO—GOODBYE, 1970
HELLO TROUBLE, 1932
HELL'S CARGO, 1935
HELL'S FIVE HOURS, 1958
HELL'S HOUSE, 1932

HELL'S ISLAND, 1930
HELL'S ISLAND, 1955
HELL'S KITCHEN, 1939
HELL'S OUTPOST, 1955
HENRY ALDRICH, BOY SCOUT, 1944
HENRY ALDRICH PLAYS CUPID, 1944
HENRY ALDRICH SWINGS IT, 1943
HENRY ALDRICH'S LITTLE SECRET, 1944
HENRY GOES ARIZONA, 1939
HENRY, THE RAINMAKER, 1949
HENTAI, 1966
HER FIRST BEAU, 1941
HER FIRST MATE, 1933
HER HIGHNESS AND THE BELLBOY, 1945
HER HUSBAND LIES, 1937
HER IMAGINARY LOVER, 1933
HER JUNGLE LOVE, 1938
HER KIND OF MAN, 1946
HER LUCKY NIGHT, 1945
HER MAN, 1930
HER MASTER'S VOICE, 1936
HER PANELLED DOOR, 1951
HER PRIVATE AFFAIR, 1930
HER PRIVATE LIFE, 1929
HER STRANGE DESIRE, 1931
HER WEDDING NIGHT, 1930
HERBIE GOES BANANAS, 1980
HERBIE GOES TO MONTE CARLO, 1977
HERCULES, 1959
HERCULES IN THE HAUNTED WORLD, 1964
HERE COME THE GIRLS, 1953
HERE COME THE LITTLES, 1985
HERE COME THE MARINES, 1952
HERE COMES CARTER, 1936
HERE COMES HAPPINESS, 1941
HERE COMES THE SUN, 1945
HERITAGE, 1935
HERO, 1982
HERO AIN'T NOTHIN' BUT A SANDWICH, A, 1977
HERO AND THE TERROR, 1988
HEROES ARE MADE, 1944
HEROES IN BLUE, 1939
HEROES OF THE RANGE, 1936
HEROES OF THE SEA, 1941
HEROINA, 1965
HE'S MY GUY, 1943
HEY, LET'S TWIST!, 1961
HEY, ROOKIE, 1944
HEY THERE, IT'S YOGI BEAR, 1964
HI BEAUTIFUL, 1944
HI, BUDDY, 1943
HI, GANG!, 1941
HI, GOOD-LOOKIN', 1944
HI, MOM!, 1970
HI, NELLIE!, 1934
HI' YA, SAILOR, 1943
HIAWATHA, 1952
HIDDEN DANGER, 1949
HIDDEN GOLD, 1933
HIDDEN HOMICIDE, 1959
HIDDEN MENACE, THE, 1940
HIDDEN VALLEY, 1932
HIDDEN VALLEY OUTLAWS, 1944
HIDEAWAY GIRL, 1937
HIDE-OUT, 1934
HIDE-OUT, THE, 1930
HIDEOUT, 1949
HIDEOUT, THE, 1956
HIGGINS FAMILY, THE, 1938
HIGH AND DRY, 1954
HIGH COMMISSIONER, THE, 1968
HIGH FLIGHT, 1957
HIGH FURY, 1947
HIGH HELL, 1958
HIGH INFIDELITY, 1965
HIGH JINKS IN SOCIETY, 1949
HIGH ROAD TO CHINA, 1983
HIGH ROLLING, 1977
HIGH SCHOOL, 1940
HIGH SCHOOL BIG SHOT, 1959
HIGH SCHOOL CAESAR, 1960
HIGH SOCIETY BLUES, 1930
HIGH SPEED, 1986
HIGH SPIRITS, 1988
HIGH STAKES, 1931
HIGH TIDE, 1947

HIGH TIME, 1960
HIGH TREASON, 1951
HIGH VELOCITY, 1977
HIGHER AND HIGHER, 1943
HIGHLANDER, 1986
HIGHPOINT, 1984
HIGHWAY 301, 1950
HIGHWAY TO BATTLE, 1961
HILDA CRANE, 1956
HILLS OF OKLAHOMA, 1950
HILLS OF OLD WYOMING, 1937
HILLS OF UTAH, 1951
HILLS RUN RED, THE, 1967
HINDLE WAKES, 1931
HIPPODROME, 1961
HIPPOLYT, THE LACKEY, 1932
HIPS, HIPS, HOORAY, 1934
HIRED KILLER, THE, 1967
HIRED WIFE, 1934
HIS AND HERS, 1961
HIS BROTHER'S GHOST, 1945
HIS BROTHER'S WIFE, 1936
HIS BUTLER'S SISTER, 1943
HIS EXCITING NIGHT, 1938
HIS FAMILY TREE, 1936
HIS GLORIOUS NIGHT, 1929
HIS LAST TWELVE HOURS, 1953
HIS MAJESTY, KING BALLYHOO, 1931
HIS NIGHT OUT, 1935
HIS WOMAN, 1931
HISTORY, 1988
HISTORY OF THE WORLD, PART 1, 1981
HIT, 1973
HIT AND RUN, 1982
HIT PARADE, THE, 1937
HIT PARADE OF 1951, 1950
HIT PARADE OF 1947, 1947
HIT PARADE OF 1941, 1940
HIT THE DECK, 1930
HIT THE SADDLE, 1937
HITCH HIKE LADY, 1936
HITLER—DEAD OR ALIVE, 1942
HITLER: THE LAST TEN DAYS, 1973
HOAX, THE, 1972
HOLCROFT COVENANT, THE, 1985
HOLD 'EM JAIL, 1932
HOLD 'EM NAVY!, 1937
HOLD MY HAND, 1938
HOLD ON, 1966
HOLD THAT BABY!, 1949
HOLD THAT BLONDE, 1945
HOLD THAT CO-ED, 1938
HOLD THAT HYPNOTIST, 1957
HOLD THAT KISS, 1938
HOLD THAT LINE, 1952
HOLD THE PRESS, 1933
HOLIDAY FOR LOVERS, 1959
HOLIDAY FOR SINNERS, 1952
HOLIDAY IN MEXICO, 1946
HOLIDAY RHYTHM, 1950
HOLIDAY'S END, 1937
HOLLYWOOD BOULEVARD, 1936
HOLLYWOOD PARTY, 1934
HOLLYWOOD SPEAKS, 1932
HOLLYWOOD STADIUM MYSTERY, 1938
HOLLYWOOD STORY, 1951
HOLLYWOOD VICE SQUAD, 1986
HOLY MOUNTAIN, THE, 1973
HOLY TERROR, A, 1931
HOME FOR TANYA, A, 1961
HOME FREE ALL, 1983
HOME FROM HOME, 1939
HOME IN WYOMIN', 1942
HOME ON THE PRAIRIE, 1939
HOME ON THE RANGE, 1946
HOME, SWEET HOME, 1933
HOMECOMING, 1948
HOMER, 1970
HOMESTEADERS, THE, 1953
HOMETOWN U.S.A., 1979
HOMICIDE, 1949
HOMICIDE FOR THREE, 1948
HOMICIDE SQUAD, 1931
HONEY POT, THE, 1967
HONEYCHILE, 1951
HONEYMOON DEFERRED, 1951

HONEYMOON HOTEL, 1946
HONEYMOON LODGE, 1943
HONEYMOON'S OVER, THE, 1939
HONG KONG AFFAIR, 1958
HONKY, 1971
HONKY TONK, 1929
HONKY TONK FREEWAY, 1981
HONOR OF THE RANGE, 1934
HONOR OF THE WEST, 1939
HONOURS EASY, 1935
HOODLUM, THE, 1951
HOOK, THE, 1962
HOOK, LINE AND SINKER, 1930
HOOPLA, 1933
HOORAY FOR LOVE, 1935
HOOSIER HOLIDAY, 1943
HOOSIER SCHOOLBOY, 1937
HOOSIER SCHOOLMASTER, 1935
HOOTENANNY HOOT, 1963
HOPALONG RIDES AGAIN, 1937
HOPE OF HIS SIDE, 1935
HOPPY SERVES A WRIT, 1943
HORIZONTAL LIEUTENANT, THE, 1962
HORNET'S NEST, 1970
HORRIBLE DR. HICHCOCK, THE, 1964
HORROR CASTLE, 1965
HORROR OF IT ALL, THE, 1964
HORRORS OF THE BLACK MUSEUM, 1959
HORSEMEN, THE, 1971
HORSEMEN OF THE SIERRAS, 1950
HOSTAGES, 1943
HOSTILE COUNTRY, 1950
HOT CARGO, 1946
HOT CARS, 1956
HOT CURVES, 1930
HOT FOR PARIS, 1930
HOT HEIRESS, 1931
HOT LEAD, 1951
HOT MONEY GIRL, 1962
HOT NEWS, 1953
HOT PEPPER, 1933
HOT PURSUIT, 1987
HOT RHYTHM, 1944
HOT SATURDAY, 1932
HOT SPELL, 1958
HOT SUMMER NIGHT, 1957
HOT TARGET, 1985
HOT WATER, 1937
HOTEL CONTINENTAL, 1932
HOTEL FOR WOMEN, 1939
HOTEL HAYWIRE, 1937
HOTTENTOT, THE, 1929
HOUND OF THE BASKERVILLES, THE, 1983
HOUR OF THE ASSASSIN, 1987
HOUR OF THE WOLF, THE, 1968
HOUSE BROKEN, 1936
HOUSE BY THE LAKE, THE, 1977
HOUSE IN MARSH ROAD, THE, 1960
HOUSE OF A THOUSAND CANDLES, THE, 1936
HOUSE OF BLACKMAIL, 1953
HOUSE OF DARKNESS, 1948
HOUSE OF DEATH, 1932
HOUSE OF FRIGHT, 1961
HOUSE OF GOD, THE, 1984
HOUSE OF INTRIGUE, THE, 1959
HOUSE OF LONG SHADOWS, THE, 1983
HOUSE OF MYSTERY, 1934
HOUSE OF MYSTERY, 1941
HOUSE OF MYSTERY, 1961
HOUSE OF SECRETS, THE, 1937
HOUSE OF SEVEN CORPSES, THE, 1974
HOUSE OF THE BLACK DEATH, 1965
HOUSE OF THE SEVEN HAWKS, THE, 1959
HOUSE OF THE SPANIARD, THE, 1936
HOUSE OF THE THREE GIRLS, THE, 1961
HOUSE OF TRENT, THE, 1933
HOUSE OF WOMEN, 1962
HOUSE ON SORORITY ROW, THE, 1983
HOUSEWIFE, 1934
HOVERBUG, 1970
HOW TO FRAME A FIGG, 1971
HOW TO SAVE A MARRIAGE—AND RUIN YOUR
   LIFE, 1968
HOW TO SEDUCE A WOMAN, 1974
HOW TO STUFF A WILD BIKINI, 1965
HOWLING IV: THE ORIGINAL NIGHTMARE, 1988

BOLD: Films on Videocassette

HOW'S ABOUT IT?, 1943
HOWZER, 1973
HUE AND CRY, 1950
HULLABALOO OVER GEORGIE AND BONNIE'S PICTURES, 1979
HUMAN FACTOR, THE, 1979
HUMAN TARGETS, 1932
HUMANOID, THE, 1979
HUNCH, THE, 1967
HUNCHBACK OF NOTRE DAME, THE, 1957
HUNDRA, 1984
HUNGRY HILL, 1947
HUNTED IN HOLLAND, 1961
HUNTERS OF THE GOLDEN COBRA, THE, 1984
HUNTING IN SIBERIA, 1962
HURRICANE ISLAND, 1951
HURRICANE SMITH, 1942
HURRY, CHARLIE, HURRY, 1941
HYPERBOLOID OF ENGINEER GARIN, THE, 1965
I ADORE YOU, 1933
I AM A CAMERA, 1955
I AM A CRIMINAL, 1939
I AM A THIEF, 1935
I AM SUZANNE, 1934
I BECAME A CRIMINAL, 1947
I BOMBED PEARL HARBOR, 1961
I BURY THE LIVING, 1958
I COULD GO ON SINGING, 1963
I COVER BIG TOWN, 1947
I COVER THE UNDERWORLD, 1955
I COVER THE WATERFRONT, 1933
I DIED A THOUSAND TIMES, 1955
I DON'T CARE GIRL, THE, 1952
I DOOD IT, 1943
I DREAM TOO MUCH, 1935
I ESCAPED FROM THE GESTAPO, 1943
I EVEN MET HAPPY GYPSIES, 1968
I FOUND STELLA PARISH, 1935
I GIVE MY LOVE, 1934
I HATE BLONDES, 1981
I, JANE DOE, 1948
I KILLED EINSTEIN, GENTLEMEN, 1970
I LIKE IT THAT WAY, 1934
I LIVE FOR LOVE, 1935
I LOVE A BANDLEADER, 1945
I LOVE A MYSTERY, 1945
I LOVE A SOLDIER, 1944
I LOVE TROUBLE, 1947
I LOVE YOU, I KILL YOU, 1972
I MARRIED A SPY, 1938
I MARRIED AN ANGEL, 1942
I MISS YOU, HUGS AND KISSES, 1978
I PASSED FOR WHITE, 1960
I STAND ACCUSED, 1938
I STAND CONDEMNED, 1936
I START COUNTING, 1970
I TAKE THIS WOMAN, 1931
I THANK A FOOL, 1962
I THANK YOU, 1941
I WANT A DIVORCE, 1940
I WANT WHAT I WANT, 1972
I WAS A COMMUNIST FOR THE F.B.I., 1951
I WAS AN AMERICAN SPY, 1951
I WAS FRAMED, 1942
I WOULDN'T BE IN YOUR SHOES, 1948
ICE-CAPADES, 1941
ICE CASTLES, 1978
ICE HOUSE, THE, 1969
ICE PIRATES, THE, 1984
ICELAND, 1942
IDEA GIRL, 1946
IDEAL HUSBAND, AN, 1948
IDIOT, THE, 1963
IDOL, THE, 1966
IF A MAN ANSWERS, 1962
IF I HAD MY WAY, 1940
IF I WERE RICH, 1936
IF I'M LUCKY, 1946
IF THIS BE SIN, 1950
IGOROTA, THE LEGEND OF THE TREE OF LIFE, 1970
I'LL GET YOU, 1953
I'LL NEVER FORGET WHAT'S 'IS NAME, 1967
I'LL WALK BESIDE YOU, 1943
ILLEGAL TRAFFIC, 1938
ILLUMINATIONS, 1976

ILLUSION, 1929
ILLUSION OF BLOOD, 1966
ILLUSIONIST, THE, 1985
ILLUSIONIST, THE, l985
ILLUSTRATED MAN, THE, 1969
I'M AN EXPLOSIVE, 1933
I'M DANCING AS FAST AS I CAN, 1982
I'M FROM THE CITY, 1938
IMMORAL MOMENT, THE, 1967
IMMORTAL GARRISON, THE, 1957
IMPACT, 1963
IMPERFECT LADY, THE, 1947
IMPERIAL VENUS, 1963
IMPERSONATOR, THE, 1962
IMPORTANT WITNESS, THE, 1933
IMPOSSIBLE ON SATURDAY, 1966
IMPROPER CHANNELS, 1981
IN A MONASTERY GARDEN, 1935
IN A YEAR OF THIRTEEN MOONS, 1980
IN EARLY ARIZONA, 1938
IN ENEMY COUNTRY, 1968
IN FAST COMPANY, 1946
IN GAY MADRID, 1930
IN HIS STEPS, 1936
IN LOVE WITH LIFE, 1934
IN OLD CALIENTE, 1939
IN OLD CALIFORNIA, 1942
IN OLD CHEYENNE, 1931
IN OLD CHEYENNE, 1941
IN OLD MISSOURI, 1940
IN OLD MONTEREY, 1939
IN OLD OKLAHOMA, 1943
IN OLD SACRAMENTO, 1946
IN OUR TIME, 1944
IN PERSON, 1935
IN SEARCH OF GREGORY, 1970
IN THE COUNTRY, 1967
IN THE DOGHOUSE, 1964
IN THE HEADLINES, 1929
IN THE LINE OF DUTY, 1931
IN THE MEANTIME, DARLING, 1944
IN THE NICK, 1960
IN THE SHADOW OF KILIMANJARO, 1986
IN THE WAKE OF A STRANGER, 1960
IN THIS CORNER, 1948
INBETWEEN AGE, THE, 1958
INCENSE FOR THE DAMNED, 1970
INCIDENT AT MIDNIGHT, 1966
INCIDENT AT PHANTOM HILL, 1966
INCIDENT IN AN ALLEY, 1962
INCORRIGIBLE, 1980
INCREDIBLE MELTING MAN, THE, 1978
INCREDIBLE SHRINKING WOMAN, THE, 1981
INDECENT, 1962
INDECENT OBSESSION, AN, 1985
INDEPENDENCE DAY, 1983
INDIAN UPRISING, 1951
INDIANAPOLIS SPEEDWAY, 1939
INDISCREET, 1931
INDISCRETIONS OF EVE, 1932
INFERNO, 1980
INFORMATION RECEIVED, 1962
INHERITANCE, THE, 1951
INHERITANCE, THE, 1964
INHERITORS, THE, 1985
INJUN FENDER, 1973
INN OF THE DAMNED, 1974
INNOCENT, THE, 1988
INNOCENTS OF PARIS, 1929
INQUEST, 1931
INSIDE DETROIT, 1955
INSIDE INFORMATION, 1939
INSIDE LOOKING OUT, 1977
INSIDE OUT, 1986
INSIDE STORY, THE, 1948
INSIDE STRAIGHT, 1951
INSIDE THE LAW, 1942
INSOMNIACS, 1986
INSPIRATION, 1931
INSURANCE INVESTIGATOR, 1951
INTERFERENCE, 1928
INTERMEZZO, 1937
INTERNECINE PROJECT, THE, 1974
INTERRUPTED JOURNEY, THE, 1949
INTERVAL, 1973
INTIMACY, 1966

INTIMATE RELATIONS, 1937
INTO THE STRAIGHT, 1950
INVASION QUARTET, 1961
INVASION U.S.A., 1952
INVASION U.S.A., 1985
INVISIBLE MAN, THE, 1963
INVISIBLE MAN'S REVENGE, 1944
INVISIBLE MENACE, THE, 1938
INVISIBLE OPPONENT, 1933
INVITATION TO MURDER, 1962
IRELAND'S BORDER LINE, 1939
IRISH LUCK, 1939
IRISH WHISKEY REBELLION, 1973
IRON MASTER, THE, 1933
IRON MOUNTAIN TRAIL, 1953
IROQUOIS TRAIL, THE, 1950
IS EVERYBODY HAPPY?, 1943
IS YOUR HONEYMOON REALLY NECESSARY?, 1953
ISLAND IN THE SKY, 1938
ISLAND OF LOST MEN, 1939
ISLAND OF THE BURNING DAMNED, 1971
ISLE OF FORGOTTEN SINS, 1943
ISLE OF FURY, 1936
ISTANBUL, 1957
IT ALL CAME TRUE, 1940
IT ALWAYS RAINS ON SUNDAY, 1949
IT CAN BE DONE, 1929
IT DON'T PAY TO BE AN HONEST CITIZEN, 1985
IT HAD TO BE YOU, 1947
IT HAPPENED IN CANADA, 1962
IT HAPPENED IN HOLLYWOOD, 1937
IT HAPPENED IN NEW YORK, 1935
IT HAPPENED IN PARIS, 1953
IT HAPPENED IN ROME, 1959
IT HAPPENED ON 5TH AVENUE, 1947
IT HAPPENED OUT WEST, 1937
IT HAPPENED TO ONE MAN, 1941
IT ISN'T DONE, 1937
IT STARTED IN NAPLES, 1960
IT STARTED IN PARADISE, 1952
IT TAKES A THIEF, 1960
IT TAKES ALL KINDS, 1969
ITALIAN CONNECTION, THE, 1973
ITALIAN SECRET SERVICE, 1968
ITALIANO BRAVA GENTE, 1965
IT'S A BIG COUNTRY, 1951
IT'S A DATE, 1940
IT'S A GREAT LIFE, 1943
IT'S A PLEASURE, 1945
IT'S A SMALL WORLD, 1950
IT'S A WISE CHILD, 1931
IT'S A WONDERFUL WORLD, 1956
IT'S ALIVE, 1974
IT'S ALL OVER TOWN, 1963
IT'S ALL YOURS, 1937
IT'S HARD TO BE GOOD, 1950
IT'S IN THE BAG, 1943
IT'S NEVER TOO LATE, 1958
IT'S THAT MAN AGAIN, 1943
IT'S TOUGH TO BE FAMOUS, 1932
IT'S YOU I WANT, 1936
I'VE ALWAYS LOVED YOU, 1946
I'VE GOT A HORSE, 1938
I'VE GOT YOUR NUMBER, 1934
I'VE GOTTA HORSE, 1965
IVORY-HANDLED GUN, 1935
JABBERWOCKY, 1977
JACK McCALL, DESPERADO, 1953
JACK OF DIAMONDS, THE, 1949
JACKALS, THE, 1967
JACKIE ROBINSON STORY, THE, 1950
JACKTOWN, 1962
JACQUES BREL IS ALIVE AND WELL AND LIVING IN PARIS, 1975
JADE MASK, THE, 1945
JAGUAR, 1956
JAIL HOUSE BLUES, 1942
JAILBIRD ROCK, 1988
JALNA, 1935
JAMAICA INN, 1939
JAMAICA RUN, 1953
JAMBOREE, 1944
JANE AUSTEN IN MANHATTAN, 1980
JANE EYRE, 1971
JANE STEPS OUT, 1938
JAWS 3-D, 1983

JAWS OF JUSTICE, 1933
JAWS OF THE JUNGLE, 1936
JAYHAWKERS, THE, 1959
JAZZ BOAT, 1960
JEALOUSY, 1945
JEDDA, THE UNCIVILIZED, 1956
JEEPERS CREEPERS, 1939
JENIFER HALE, 1937
JENNY KISSED ME, 1985
JEREMY, 1973
JERK, THE, 1979
JESSE AND LESTER, TWO BROTHERS IN A PLACE
 CALLED TRINITY, 1972
JESUS CHRIST, SUPERSTAR, 1973
JET OVER THE ATLANTIC, 1960
JET PILOT, 1957
JET STORM, 1961
JETLAG, 1981
JIGSAW MAN, THE, 1984
JIM, THE WORLD'S GREATEST, 1976
JITTERBUGS, 1943
JIVE JUNCTION, 1944
JO JO DANCER, YOUR LIFE IS CALLING, 1986
JOE BUTTERFLY, 1957
JOE DAKOTA, 1957
JOE KIDD, 1972
JOE PALOOKA IN TRIPLE CROSS, 1951
JOHN GOLDFARB, PLEASE COME HOME, 1964
JOHN MEADE'S WOMAN, 1937
JOHNNY ALLEGRO, 1949
JOHNNY ANGEL, 1945
JOHNNY COME LATELY, 1943
JOHNNY COMES FLYING HOME, 1946
JOHNNY DOUGHBOY, 1943
JOHNNY FRENCHMAN, 1946
JOHNNY GOT HIS GUN, 1971
JOHNNY NOBODY, 1965
JOHNNY ROCCO, 1958
JOHNNY THE GIANT KILLER, 1953
JOHNNY, YOU'RE WANTED, 1956
JONES FAMILY IN HOLLYWOOD, THE, 1939
JOSEPH ANDREWS, 1977
JOSEPHINE AND MEN, 1955
JOSSER IN THE ARMY, 1932
JOSSER JOINS THE NAVY, 1932
JOURNAL OF A CRIME, 1934
JOURNEY AHEAD, 1947
JOURNEY AMONG WOMEN, 1977
JOURNEY BACK TO OZ, 1974
JOURNEY BENEATH THE DESERT, 1967
JOURNEY INTO DARKNESS, 1968
JOURNEY INTO FEAR, 1976
JOURNEY INTO MIDNIGHT, 1968
JOURNEY THROUGH ROSEBUD, 1972
JOURNEY TO FREEDOM, 1957
JOURNEY TO LOVE, 1953
JOURNEY TO THE CENTER OF TIME, 1967
JOURNEY TO THE FAR SIDE OF THE SUN, 1969
JOURNEY TO THE SEVENTH PLANET, 1962
JOY HOUSE, 1964
JOY IN THE MORNING, 1965
JOY RIDE, 1958
JOYRIDE, 1977
JUDGE, THE, 1949
JUGGERNAUT, 1937
JUKE GIRL, 1942
JULIE, 1956
JULIUS CAESAR, 1952
JULIUS CAESAR, 1970
JUMBO, 1962
JUMPIN' JACK FLASH, 1986
JUMPING FOR JOY, 1956
JUMPING JACKS, 1952
JUNGLE CAPTIVE, 1945
JUNGLE FLIGHT, 1947
JUNGLE JIM, 1948
JUNGLE JIM IN THE FORBIDDEN LAND, 1952
JUNGLE MAN-EATERS, 1954
JUNGLE MANHUNT, 1951
JUNGLE MOON MEN, 1955
JUNGLE SIREN, 1942
JUNGLE WARRIORS, 1984
JUNIOR PROM, 1946
JUNKET 89, 1970
JUPITER, 1952
JURY'S SECRET, THE, 1938

JUST ACROSS THE STREET, 1952
JUST AROUND THE CORNER, 1938
JUST BEFORE DAWN, 1946
JUST BEFORE NIGHTFALL, 1975
JUST BETWEEN FRIENDS, 1986
JUST LIKE A WOMAN, 1939
JUST LIKE A WOMAN, 1967
JUST MY LUCK, 1933
JUST MY LUCK, 1957
JUST ONCE MORE, 1963
JUST TELL ME WHAT YOU WANT, 1980
JUST WILLIAM, 1939
JUSTICE OF THE RANGE, 1935
JUSTINE, 1969
JUSTINE, 1969
JUVENILE COURT, 1938
KALEIDOSCOPE, 1966
KAMIKAZE '89, 1983
KANGAROO, 1986
KANGAROO KID, THE, 1950
KANSAN, THE, 1943
KANSAS CITY PRINCESS, 1934
KANSAS PACIFIC, 1953
KANSAS TERRORS, THE, 1939
KARATE KILLERS, THE, 1967
KARATE, THE HAND OF DEATH, 1961
KARMA, 1933
KATE PLUS TEN, 1938
KATHLEEN, 1941
KATHLEEN MAVOURNEEN, 1930
KATIE DID IT, 1951
KEEP, THE, 1983
KEEP 'EM FLYING, 1941
KEEP 'EM SLUGGING, 1943
KEEP FIT, 1937
KEEP SMILING, 1938
KEEP YOUR POWDER DRY, 1945
KEEPERS OF YOUTH, 1931
KELLY AND ME, 1957
KELLY OF THE SECRET SERVICE, 1936
KENTUCKY FRIED MOVIE, THE, 1977
KENTUCKY JUBILEE, 1951
KENTUCKY KERNELS, 1935
KENTUCKY RIFLE, 1956
KEPT HUSBANDS, 1931
KEROUAC, 1985
KEYHOLE, THE, 1933
KIBITZER, THE, 1929
KID FROM CANADA, THE, 1957
KID FROM CLEVELAND, THE, 1949
KID FROM KOKOMO, THE, 1939
KID FROM TEXAS, THE, 1939
KID GALAHAD, 1962
KID GLOVES, 1929
KID MONK BARONI, 1952
KIDNAPPED, 1948
KIDNAPPED, 1960
KIDNAPPERS, THE, 1964
KILL, THE, 1968
KILL AND KILL AGAIN, 1981
KILL! KILL! KILL!, 1972
KILL ME TOMORROW, 1958
KILL OR BE KILLED, 1950
KILL OR BE KILLED, 1967
KILL OR BE KILLED, 1980
KILL OR CURE, 1962
KILLER APE, 1953
KILLER ELITE, THE, 1975
KILLER FORCE, 1975
KILLER LEOPARD, 1954
KILLERS OF KILIMANJARO, 1960
KILLING HEAT, 1984
KILROY WAS HERE, 1947
KIMBERLEY JIM, 1965
KING AND FOUR QUEENS, THE, 1956
KING ARTHUR WAS A GENTLEMAN, 1942
KING DAVID, 1985
KING MURDER, THE, 1932
KING, MURRAY, 1969
KING OF DODGE CITY, 1941
KING OF GAMBLERS, 1937
KING OF HEARTS, 1936
KING OF PARIS, THE, 1934
KING OF THE ARENA, 1933
KING OF THE BULLWHIP, 1950
KING OF THE GRIZZLIES, 1970

KING OF THE JUNGLE, 1933
KING OF THE MOUNTAIN, 1981
KING OF THE NEWSBOYS, 1938
KING OF THE SIERRAS, 1938
KING OF THE WILD HORSES, 1947
KING, QUEEN, KNAVE, 1972
KING RICHARD AND THE CRUSADERS, 1954
KING SOLOMON OF BROADWAY, 1935
KINGS AND DESPERATE MEN, 1984
KINGS OF THE SUN, 1963
KING'S PIRATE, 1967
KISENGA, MAN OF AFRICA, 1952
KISS AND MAKE UP, 1934
KISS BEFORE THE MIRROR, THE, 1933
KISS ME AGAIN, 1931
KISS ME GOODBYE, 1935
KISS OF FIRE, 1955
KISS THE BRIDE GOODBYE, 1944
KISS THEM FOR ME, 1957
KISSES FOR BREAKFAST, 1941
KISSIN' COUSINS, 1964
KITTY AND THE BAGMAN, 1983
KLONDIKE, 1932
KLONDIKE FURY, 1942
KLUTE, 1971
KNICKERBOCKER HOLIDAY, 1944
KNIGHT IN LONDON, A, 1930
KNIGHT OF THE PLAINS, 1939
KNOWING MEN, 1930
KONA COAST, 1968
KONGA, 1961
KONGI'S HARVEST, 1971
KOREA PATROL, 1951
KRUSH GROOVE, 1985
KUROENKO, 1968
LA BABY SITTER, 1975
LA BONNE SOUPE, 1964
LA CAGE, 1975
LA CAGE AUX FOLLES II, 1981
LA CAGE AUX FOLLES 3: THE WEDDING, 1985
LA FUGA, 1966
LA GRANDE BOUFFE, 1973
LA GRANDE BOURGEOISE, 1977
LA GUERRE EST FINIE, 1967
LA HABANERA, 1937
LA PRISONNIERE, 1969
LA SCARLATINE, 1985
LA TRAVIATA, 1968
LA VIE CONTINUE, 1982
LA VISITA, 1966
LABURNUM GROVE, 1936
LAD FROM OUR TOWN, 1941
LADIES COURAGEOUS, 1944
LADIES CRAVE EXCITEMENT, 1935
LADIES' DAY, 1943
LADIES IN LOVE, 1930
LADIES LOVE BRUTES, 1930
LADIES LOVE DANGER, 1935
LADIES' MAN, 1947
LADIES MUST LIVE, 1940
LADIES OF THE CHORUS, 1948
LADIES OF THE JURY, 1932
LADIES OF WASHINGTON, 1944
LADIES SHOULD LISTEN, 1934
LADIES THEY TALK ABOUT, 1933
LADIES WHO DO, 1964
LADY AND GENT, 1932
LADY AND THE BANDIT, THE, 1951
LADY AT MIDNIGHT, 1948
LADY BODYGUARD, 1942
LADY CHATTERLEY'S LOVER, 1959
LADY CONFESSES, THE, 1945
LADY DOCTOR, THE, 1963
LADY ESCAPES, THE, 1937
LADY FIGHTS BACK, 1937
LADY FOR A NIGHT, 1941
LADY FROM CHUNGKING, 1943
LADY FROM NOWHERE, 1936
LADY FROM THE SEA, THE, 1929
LADY GENERAL, THE, 1965
LADY GODIVA RIDES AGAIN, 1955
LADY IN CEMENT, 1968
LADY IS A SQUARE, THE, 1959
LADY IS FICKLE, THE, 1948
LADY LUCK, 1936
LADY LUCK, 1946

BOLD: Films on Videocassette

LIVE, LOVE AND LEARN, 1937
LIVE NOW—PAY LATER, 1962
LIVE WIRE, THE, 1937
LIVE YOUR OWN WAY, 1970
LIVELY SET, THE, 1964
LIVING BETWEEN TWO WORLDS, 1963
LIVING CORPSE, THE, 1940
LIVING DANGEROUSLY, 1936
LIVING DANGEROUSLY, 1988
LIVING IN A BIG WAY, 1947
LIVING ON LOVE, 1937
LIVING ON TOKYO TIME, 1987
LOAN SHARK, 1952
LOCAL BOY MAKES GOOD, 1931
LOCKET, THE, 1946
LONG ROPE, THE, 1961
LOLLIPOP, 1966
LOLLY-MADONNA XXX, 1973
LONDON BLACKOUT MURDERS, 1942
LONE AVENGER, THE, 1933
LONE HAND TEXAN, THE, 1947
**LONE RANGER AND THE LOST CITY OF GOLD,
THE, 1958**
LONE STAR PIONEERS, 1939
LONE STAR VIGILANTES, THE, 1942
LONE WOLF AND HIS LADY, THE, 1949
LONE WOLF IN PARIS, THE, 1938
LONE WOLF McQUADE, 1983
LONE WOLF MEETS A LADY, THE, 1940
LONE WOLF STRIKES, THE, 1940
LONE WOLF TAKES A CHANCE, THE, 1941
LONELY HEARTS BANDITS, 1950
LONELY TRAIL, THE, 1936
LONESOME, 1928
LONESOME TRAIL, THE, 1955
LONG DARK HALL, THE, 1951
LONG DUEL, THE, 1967
LONG HAUL, THE, 1957
LONG KNIFE, THE, 1958
LONG MEMORY, THE, 1953
LONG SHADOW, THE, 1961
LONG SHOT, THE, 1939
LONGHORN, THE, 1951
LONGING FOR LOVE, 1966
LOOK BEFORE YOU LOVE, 1948
LOOK IN ANY WINDOW, 1961
LOOKIN' TO GET OUT, 1982
LOOKING FOR DANGER, 1957
LOOKING FOR LOVE, 1964
LOOKING FORWARD, 1933
LOOKING GLASS WAR, THE, 1970
LOOKING ON THE BRIGHT SIDE, 1932
LOOKING UP, 1977
LOOSE CONNECTIONS, 1984
LOOSE SHOES, 1980
LOOTERS, THE, 1955
LORD BABS, 1932
LORD BYRON OF BROADWAY, 1930
LORD CAMBER'S LADIES, 1932
LORD EDGEWARE DIES, 1934
LORD OF THE FLIES, 1963
LORD SHANGO, 1975
LORNA DOONE, 1935
LORNA DOONE, 1951
LOS ASTRONAUTAS, 1960
LOSER TAKES ALL, 1956
LOSS OF INNOCENCE, 1961
LOST CANYON, 1943
LOST CONTINENT, THE, 1968
LOST FACE, THE, 1965
LOST IN A HAREM, 1944
LOST IN ALASKA, 1952
LOST IN THE STARS, 1974
LOST LADY, A, 1934
LOST MISSILE, THE, 1958
LOST TRIBE, THE, 1949
LOST VOLCANO, THE, 1950
LOST WORLD OF SINBAD, THE, 1965
LOST ZEPPELIN, 1930
LOUDSPEAKER, THE, 1934
LOUISIANA, 1947
LOUISIANE, 1984
LOVABLE CHEAT, THE, 1949
LOVE AFFAIR, 1932
LOVE AND HISSES, 1937
LOVE AND KISSES, 1965

LOVE AT FIRST SIGHT, 1930
LOVE AT NIGHT, 1961
LOVE BEGINS AT TWENTY, 1936
LOVE CONTRACT, THE, 1932
LOVE CYCLES, 1969
LOVE FACTORY, 1969
LOVE HAS MANY FACES, 1965
LOVE IN A HOT CLIMATE, 1958
LOVE IN EXILE, 1936
LOVE-INS, THE, 1967
LOVE IS A BALL, 1963
LOVE IS A FUNNY THING, 1970
LOVE IS A HEADACHE, 1938
LOVE IS A MANY-SPLENDORED THING, 1955
LOVE IS ON THE AIR, 1937
LOVE LIES, 1931
LOVE, LIFE AND LAUGHTER, 1934
LOVE NEST, THE, 1933
LOVE NEST, 1951
LOVE NOW . . . PAY LATER, 1966
LOVE ON A BET, 1936
LOVE ON A BUDGET, 1938
LOVE ON A PILLOW, 1963
LOVE ON THE RIVIERA, 1964
LOVE ON THE SPOT, 1932
LOVE PROBLEMS, 1970
LOVE RACE, THE, 1931
LOVE TEST, THE, 1935
LOVE, THE ITALIAN WAY, 1964
LOVE THY NEIGHBOR, 1940
LOVE TILL FIRST BLOOD, 1985
LOVE TRAP, THE, 1929
LOVE UNDER THE CRUCIFIX, 1965
LOVE WAGER, THE, 1933
LOVE WALTZ, THE, 1930
LOVELY WAY TO DIE, A, 1968
LOVERS, THE, 1959
LOVERS COURAGEOUS, 1932
LOVERS, HAPPY LOVERS!, 1955
LOVERS ON A TIGHTROPE, 1962
LOVERS' ROCK, 1966
LOVES OF EDGAR ALLAN POE, THE, 1942
LOVES OF MADAME DUBARRY, THE, 1938
LOVES OF ROBERT BURNS, THE, 1930
LOVE'S OLD SWEET SONG, 1933
LOVESICK, 1983
LOVIN' MOLLY, 1974
LOVIN' THE LADIES, 1930
LOVING, 1970
LOVING COUPLES, 1980
LOVING COUPLES, 1966
LOYAL HEART, 1946
LOYALTY OF LOVE, 1937
LUCIANO, 1963
LUCK OF A SAILOR, THE, 1934
LUCKIEST GIRL IN THE WORLD, THE, 1936
LUCKY BOY, 1929
LUCKY DEVILS, 1941
LUCKY JADE, 1937
LUCKY LOSER, 1934
LUCKY LOSERS, 1950
LUCKY LUKE, 1971
LUCKY ME, 1954
LUCKY NUMBER, THE, 1933
LUCKY STAR, 1929
LUCKY STIFF, THE, 1949
LUCY GALLANT, 1955
LUDWIG, 1973
LULLABY, 1961
LULU, 1962
LUMBERJACK, 1944
LUMMOX, 1930
LUNCH HOUR, 1962
LUNCH WAGON, 1981
LURE, THE, 1933
LURE OF THE SWAMP, 1957
LURE OF THE WASTELAND, 1939
LURE OF THE WILDERNESS, 1952
LUST FOR A VAMPIRE, 1971
LUST FOR GOLD, 1949
LUXURY GIRLS, 1953
LUXURY LINER, 1948
LYDIA, 1964
LYONS MAIL, THE, 1931
MA AND PA KETTLE AT HOME, 1954
MA AND PA KETTLE AT THE FAIR, 1952

MA AND PA KETTLE AT WAIKIKI, 1955
MA AND PA KETTLE BACK ON THE FARM, 1951
MA AND PA KETTLE GO TO TOWN, 1950
MA AND PA KETTLE ON VACATION, 1953
MA BARKER'S KILLER BROOD, 1960
MACABRE, 1958
MACARIO, 1961
MACARONI, 1985
MACBETH, 1948
MACHINE GUN McCAIN, 1970
MACKINTOSH & T.J., 1975
MACON COUNTY LINE, 1974
MACUSHLA, 1937
MAD ABOUT MEN, 1954
MAD AT THE WORLD, 1955
MAD BOMBER, THE, 1973
MAD DOCTOR, THE, 1941
MAD DOG COLL, 1961
MAD EMPRESS, THE, 1940
MAD EXECUTIONERS, THE, 1965
MAD HATTERS, THE, 1935
MAD MAGICIAN, THE, 1954
MAD MARTINDALES, THE, 1942
MAD MEN OF EUROPE, 1940
MAD PARADE, THE, 1931
MAD QUEEN, THE, 1950
MAD ROOM, THE, 1969
MADAME DU BARRY, 1954
MADAME RACKETEER, 1932
MADAME SPY, 1934
MADAME X, 1929
MADE IN HEAVEN, 1952
MADE IN PARIS, 1966
MADE ON BROADWAY, 1933
MADISON AVENUE, 1962
MADISON SQUARE GARDEN, 1932
MADMAN OF LAB 4, THE, 1967
MADNESS OF THE HEART, 1949
MADONNA OF THE DESERT, 1948
MADONNA'S SECRET, THE, 1946
MAEDCHEN IN UNIFORM, 1965
MAEVA, 1961
MAFIA, 1969
MAFIA, THE, 1972
MAFU CAGE, THE, 1978
MAGIC BOY, 1960
MAGIC CARPET, THE, 1951
MAGIC CHRISTMAS TREE, 1964
MAGIC FACE, THE, 1951
MAGIC FIRE, 1956
MAGIC FOUNTAIN, THE, 1961
MAGIC NIGHT, 1932
MAGIC VOYAGE OF SINBAD, THE, 1962
MAGIC WEAVER, THE, 1965
MAGNET, THE, 1950
MAGNIFICENT BRUTE, THE, 1936
MAGNIFICENT CONCUBINE, THE, 1964
MAGNIFICENT DOLL, 1946
MAGNIFICENT DOPE, THE, 1942
MAGNIFICENT LIE, 1931
MAGNIFICENT MATADOR, THE, 1955
MAGNIFICENT SEVEN RIDE, THE, 1972
MAGNIFICENT TRAMP, THE, 1962
MAGNIFICENT TWO, THE, 1967
MAGOICHI SAGA, THE, 1970
MAID FOR MURDER, 1963
MAID HAPPY, 1933
MAID OF SALEM, 1937
MAIDEN, THE, 1961
MAIDEN FOR A PRINCE, A, 1967
MAIDS, THE, 1975
MAIGRET LAYS A TRAP, 1958
MAIL ORDER BRIDE, 1964
MAIL TRAIN, 1941
MAIN EVENT, THE, 1979
MAIN STREET AFTER DARK, 1944
MAIN STREET, 1956
MAIN STREET KID, THE, 1947
MAISIE, 1939
MAISIE GETS HER MAN, 1942
MAISIE GOES TO RENO, 1944
MAJIN, 1968
MAKE A FACE, 1971
MAKE A WISH, 1937
MAKE BELIEVE BALLROOM, 1949
MAKE HASTE TO LIVE, 1954

BOLD: Films on Videocassette

MAKE LIKE A THIEF, 1966
MAKE MINE A DOUBLE, 1962
MAKE WAY FOR A LADY, 1936
MAKE WAY FOR LILA, 1962
MAKE YOUR OWN BED, 1944
MAKING THE GRADE, 1984
MALE AND FEMALE SINCE ADAM AND EVE, 1961
MALE COMPANION, 1965
MALE HUNT, 1965
MALEVIL, 1981
MALPAS MYSTERY, THE, 1967
MAMA LOVES PAPA, 1933
MAMA STEPS OUT, 1937
MAN, THE, 1972
MAN ABOUT THE HOUSE, A, 1947
MAN ABOUT TOWN, 1947
MAN AFRAID, 1957
MAN AGAINST MAN, 1961
MAN AND THE MOMENT, THE, 1929
MAN AT THE CARLTON TOWER, 1961
MAN AT THE TOP, 1973
MAN BAIT, 1952
MAN BEHIND THE GUN, THE, 1952
MAN CALLED ADAM, A, 1966
MAN CALLED GANNON, A, 1969
MAN CALLED NOON, THE, 1973
MAN COULD GET KILLED, A, 1966
MAN CRAZY, 1953
MAN FROM BLACK HILLS, THE, 1952
MAN FROM BUTTON WILLOW, THE, 1965
MAN FROM CHEYENNE, 1942
MAN FROM COLORADO, THE, 1948
MAN FROM DAKOTA, THE, 1940
MAN FROM DOWN UNDER, THE, 1943
MAN FROM FRISCO, 1944
MAN FROM GOD'S COUNTRY, 1958
MAN FROM GUN TOWN, THE, 1936
MAN FROM HEADQUARTERS, 1942
MAN FROM MONTEREY, THE, 1933
MAN FROM MONTREAL, THE, 1940
MAN FROM NEW MEXICO, THE, 1932
MAN FROM OKLAHOMA, THE, 1945
MAN FROM THE EAST, THE, 1961
MAN FROM TORONTO, THE, 1933
MAN HUNT, 1933
MAN HUNT, 1936
MAN I LOVE, THE, 1929
MAN I MARRY, THE, 1936
MAN IN A COCKED HAT, 1960
MAN IN POSSESSION, THE, 1931
MAN IN THE BACK SEAT, THE, 1961
MAN IN THE DINGHY, THE, 1951
MAN IN THE MIRROR, THE, 1936
MAN IN THE ROAD, THE, 1957
MAN IN THE STORM, THE, 1969
MAN LIKE EVA, A, 1985
MAN OF AFRICA, 1956
MAN OF CONFLICT, 1953
MAN OF MUSIC, 1953
MAN OF THE PEOPLE, 1937
MAN OF THE WORLD, 1931
MAN ON A STRING, 1960
MAN ON FIRE, 1987
MAN OUTSIDE, THE, 1968
MAN-TRAP, 1961
MAN TROUBLE, 1930
MAN WHO BROKE THE BANK AT MONTE CARLO,
   THE, 1935
MAN WHO DARED, THE, 1939
MAN WHO DARED, THE, 1933
MAN WHO FOUND HIMSELF, THE, 1937
MAN WHO HAD POWER OVER WOMEN, THE, 1970
MAN WHO HAUNTED HIMSELF, THE, 1970
MAN WHO LOST HIMSELF, THE, 1941
MAN WHO LOVED CAT DANCING, THE, 1973
MAN WHO RETURNED TO LIFE, THE, 1942
MAN WHO STOLE THE SUN, THE, 1980
MAN WHO WALKED THROUGH THE WALL, THE,
   1964
MAN WHO WAS NOBODY, THE, 1960
MAN WHO WOULDN'T DIE, THE, 1942
MAN WHO WOULDN'T TALK, THE, 1940
MAN WITH A GUN, 1958
MAN WITH CONNECTIONS, THE, 1970
MAN WITH MY FACE, THE, 1951
MAN WITH 100 FACES, THE, 1938

MAN WITH THE BALLOONS, THE, 1968
MAN WITH THE GOLDEN GUN, THE, 1974
MAN WITH TWO BRAINS, THE, 1983
MAN, WOMAN AND CHILD, 1983
MANDABI, 1970
MANDINGO, 1975
MANDRAGOLA, 1966
MANHANDLED, 1949
MANHATTAN COCKTAIL, 1928
MANHATTAN HEARTBEAT, 1940
MANHATTAN LOVE SONG, 1934
MANHATTAN MOON, 1935
MANHATTAN PROJECT, THE, 1986
MANHUNT IN THE JUNGLE, 1958
MANIA, 1961
MANIAC, 1963
MANIACS ON WHEELS, 1951
MANITOU, THE, 1978
MANOLETE, 1950
MANOLIS, 1962
MANON, 1950
MANON, 1987
MANON 70, 1968
MAN'S AFFAIR, A, 1949
MAN'S COUNTRY, 1938
MAN'S LAND, A, 1932
MAN'S WORLD, A, 1942
MANSLAUGHTER, 1930
MANUELA'S LOVES, 1987
MANY WATERS, 1931
MARAUDERS, THE, 1955
MARCO POLO, 1962
MARGIE, 1940
MARGIN, THE, 1969
MARGIN FOR ERROR, 1943
MARIANNE, 1929
MARIE-ANN, 1978
MARIE OF THE ISLES, 1960
MARINES ARE COMING, THE, 1935
MARINES ARE HERE, THE, 1938
MARK IT PAID, 1933
MARK OF CAIN, THE, 1948
MARK OF THE GORILLA, 1950
MARK OF THE RENEGADE, 1951
MARKED FOR MURDER, 1945
MARKED TRAILS, 1944
MARKSMAN, THE, 1953
MARRIAGE BOND, THE, 1932
MARRIAGE CAME TUMBLING DOWN, THE, 1968
MARRIAGE IN THE SHADOWS, 1948
MARRIAGE IS A PRIVATE AFFAIR, 1944
MARRIAGE OF CONVENIENCE, 1970
MARRIAGE OF FIGARO, THE, 1963
MARRIAGE OF FIGARO, THE, 1970
MARRIAGE ON THE ROCKS, 1965
MARRIED AND IN LOVE, 1940
MARRIED BEFORE BREAKFAST, 1937
MARRIED IN HOLLYWOOD, 1929
MARRIED TOO YOUNG, 1962
MARRY ME!, 1949
MARRY ME! MARRY ME!, 1969
MARSHAL OF CRIPPLE CREEK, THE, 1947
MARSHAL OF HELDORADO, 1950
MARSHAL OF LAREDO, 1945
MARTYRS OF LOVE, 1968
MARVIN AND TIGE, 1983
MARY HAD A LITTLE, 1961
MARY LOU, 1948
MARY, QUEEN OF SCOTS, 1971
MARY RYAN, DETECTIVE, 1949
MARY STEVENS, M.D., 1933
MARYLAND, 1940
MASON OF THE MOUNTED, 1932
MASQUERADE IN MEXICO, 1945
MASSACRE, 1934
MASSACRE HILL, 1949
MASTER OF THE WORLD, 1961
MASTER PLAN, THE, 1955
MASTER RACE, THE, 1944
MASTER SPY, 1964
MATA HARI'S DAUGHTER, 1954
MATCHLESS, 1967
MATHIAS SANDORF, 1963
MATTER OF CHOICE, A, 1963
MATTER OF INNOCENCE, A, 1968
MATTER OF WHO, A, 1962

MAX DUGAN RETURNS, 1983
MAXIE, 1985
MAXIME, 1962
MAYBE IT'S LOVE, 1930
MAYERLING, 1968
MAYFAIR MELODY, 1937
MAYTIME IN MAYFAIR, 1952
MC GUIRE, GO HOME!, 1966
MC MASTERS, THE, 1970
MC Q, 1974
ME AND MY GAL, 1932
ME AND MY PAL, 1939
ME AND THE COLONEL, 1958
ME, NATALIE, 1969
MEAN FRANK AND CRAZY TONY, 1976
MEAN JOHNNY BARROWS, 1976
MEANEST MAN IN THE WORLD, THE, 1943
MECHANIC, THE, 1972
MEDICO OF PAINTED SPRINGS, THE, 1941
MEET ME AT DAWN, 1947
MEET ME IN MOSCOW, 1966
MEET ME ON BROADWAY, 1946
MEET MR. CALLAGHAN, 1954
MEET MR. LUCIFER, 1953
MEET SEXTON BLAKE, 1944
MEET SIMON CHERRY, 1949
MEET THE CHUMP, 1941
MEET THE MISSUS, 1937
MEET THE MOB, 1942
MEET THE PEOPLE, 1944
MEET THE WIFE, 1931
MEETINGS WITH REMARKABLE MEN, 1979
MEIN KAMPF—MY CRIMES, 1940
MELANIE, 1982
MELODY AND ROMANCE, 1937
MELODY CRUISE, 1933
MELODY IN SPRING, 1934
MELODY LINGERS ON, THE, 1935
MELODY MAN, 1930
MELODY OF LOVE, THE, 1928
MELODY PARADE, 1943
MELODY RANCH, 1940
MELODY TRAIL, 1935
MEMED MY HAWK, 1984
MEMOIRS OF PRISON, 1984
MEMORIES OF ME, 1988
MEMORY OF US, 1974
MEN AGAINST THE SKY, 1940
MEN ARE SUCH FOOLS, 1938
MEN IN EXILE, 1937
MEN IN HER LIFE, 1931
MEN OF IRELAND, 1938
MEN OF THE NIGHT, 1934
MEN OF THE NORTH, 1930
MEN OF THE SKY, 1931
MEN OF TOMORROW, 1935
MEN ON HER MIND, 1944
MEN PREFER FAT GIRLS, 1981
MEN WITHOUT LAW, 1930
MEN WITHOUT NAMES, 1935
MEN WITHOUT SOULS, 1940
MENACE, 1934
MENACE IN THE NIGHT, 1958
MERCY ISLAND, 1941
MERCY PLANE, 1940
MERMAID, THE, 1966
MERRY COMES TO STAY, 1937
MERRY FRINKS, THE, 1934
MERRY-GO-ROUND OF 1938, 1937
MERRY WIDOW, THE, 1952
MERRY WIVES OF WINDSOR, THE, 1952
MERRY WIVES, THE, 1940
METROPOLITAN, 1935
MEXICAN SPITFIRE OUT WEST, 1940
MEXICAN SPITFIRE'S ELEPHANT, 1942
MEXICANA, 1945
MIAMI EXPOSE, 1956
MIAMI STORY, THE, 1954
MICHAEL AND MARY, 1932
MICHAEL O'HALLORAN, 1937
MICHAEL O'HALLORAN, 1948
MICHIGAN KID, THE, 1947
MIDAS RUN, 1969
MIDDLE WATCH, THE, 1930
MIDNIGHT, 1983
MIDNIGHT CROSSING, 1988

MIDNIGHT EPISODE, 1951
MIDNIGHT FOLLY, 1962
MIDNIGHT INTRUDER, 1938
MIDNIGHT LIMITED, 1940
MIDNIGHT MARY, 1933
MIDNIGHT MEETING, 1962
MIDNIGHT MYSTERY, 1930
MIDNIGHT PLEASURES, 1975
MIDWAY, 1976
MIGHTY JOE YOUNG, 1949
MIGHTY MCGURK, THE, 1946
MIKE'S MURDER, 1984
MILITARY ACADEMY, 1940
MILKMAN, THE, 1950
MILL OF THE STONE WOMEN, 1963
MILLION DOLLAR BABY, 1941
MILLION DOLLAR COLLAR, THE, 1929
MILLION DOLLAR KID, 1944
MILLION DOLLAR PURSUIT, 1951
MILLIONAIRE FOR CHRISTY, A, 1951
MILLIONAIRE PLAYBOY, 1940
MILLIONS IN THE AIR, 1935
MIMI, 1935
MINE WITH THE IRON DOOR, THE, 1936
MINESWEEPER, 1943
MINIVER STORY, THE, 1950
MINNIE AND MOSKOWITZ, 1971
MINSTREL MAN, 1944
MINUTE TO PRAY, A SECOND TO DIE, A, 1968
MIRACLE, THE, 1959
MIRACLE IN HARLEM, 1948
MIRACLE IN THE RAIN, 1956
MIRACLE OF THE WHITE STALLIONS, 1963
MIRACLE ON MAIN STREET, A, 1940
MIRACULOUS JOURNEY, 1948
MISCHIEF, 1985
MISFIT BRIGADE, THE, 1988
MISLEADING LADY, THE, 1932
MISS ANNIE ROONEY, 1942
MISS JESSICA IS PREGNANT, 1970
MISS LONDON LTD., 1943
MISS MARY, 1987
MISS MINK OF 1949, 1949
MISS PILGRIM'S PROGRESS, 1950
MISS ROBIN CRUSOE, 1954
MISSING GIRLS, 1936
MISSING IN ACTION, 1984
MISSING LADY, THE, 1946
MISSING PEOPLE, THE, 1940
MISSION BLOODY MARY, 1967
MISSION KILL, 1987
MISSION OVER KOREA, 1953
MISSISSIPPI BURNING, 1988
MISSISSIPPI GAMBLER, 1929
MISSOURI OUTLAW, A, 1942
MR. ACE, 1946
MISTER ANTONIO, 1929
MR. BIG, 1943
MR. BILLION, 1977
MR. BROWN COMES DOWN THE HILL, 1966
MISTER BUDDWING, 1966
MR. CELEBRITY, 1942
MR. CHUMP, 1938
MISTER CINDERS, 1934
MR. DISTRICT ATTORNEY, 1946
MR. DODD TAKES THE AIR, 1937
MR. DYNAMITE, 1935
MR. DYNAMITE, 1941
MR. EMMANUEL, 1945
MISTER FREEDOM, 1970
MR. HEX, 1946
MR. IMPERIUM, 1951
MR. MOTO TAKES A CHANCE, 1938
MR. MOTO TAKES A VACATION, 1938
MR. MUGGS RIDES AGAIN, 1945
MR. NORTH, 1988
MR. PEEK-A-BOO, 1951
MR. SATAN, 1938
MR. SMITH CARRIES ON, 1937
MR. SOFT TOUCH, 1949
MR. STRINGFELLOW SAYS NO, 1937
MR. SUPERINVISIBLE, 1974
MR. UNIVERSE, 1951
MR. WALKIE TALKIE, 1952
MR. WASHINGTON GOES TO TOWN, 1941
MR. WINKLE GOES TO WAR, 1944

MR. WISE GUY, 1942
MR. WONG, DETECTIVE, 1938
MR. WONG IN CHINATOWN, 1939
MISTRESS FOR THE SUMMER, A, 1964
MISTRESS OF THE WORLD, 1959
MISUNDERSTOOD, 1984
MITCHELL, 1975
M'LISS, 1936
MODEL MURDER CASE, THE, 1964
MODERN HERO, A, 1934
MOLLY AND LAWLESS JOHN, 1972
MOLLY AND ME, 1929
MOMENT OF TRUTH, THE, 1965
MOMENT TO MOMENT, 1966
MONEY, THE, 1975
MONEY FOR NOTHING, 1932
MONEY FOR SPEED, 1933
MONEY FROM HOME, 1953
MONEY JUNGLE, THE, 1968
MONEY ON THE STREET, 1930
MONEY PIT, THE, 1986
MONEY, WOMEN AND GUNS, 1958
MONGOLS, THE, 1966
MONITORS, THE, 1969
MONKEYS, GO HOME!, 1967
MONKEY'S UNCLE, THE, 1965
MONOLITH MONSTERS, THE, 1957
MONSEIGNEUR, 1950
MONSIEUR, 1964
MONSTER IN THE CLOSET, 1987
MONSTER OF HIGHGATE PONDS, THE, 1961
MONSTER ON THE CAMPUS, 1958
MONSTER SQUAD, THE, 1987
MONSTER WALKS, THE, 1932
MONSTER ZERO, 1970
MONSTERS FROM THE UNKNOWN PLANET, 1975
MONTANA, 1950
MONTANA DESPERADO, 1951
MONTE CARLO STORY, THE, 1957
MONTE CASSINO, 1948
MONTY PYTHON'S LIFE OF BRIAN, 1979
MOON OVER BURMA, 1940
MOON OVER HER SHOULDER, 1941
MOON OVER PARADOR, 1988
MOONCHILD, 1972
MOONLIGHT AND CACTUS, 1944
MOONLIGHT IN HAVANA, 1942
MOONLIGHT ON THE PRAIRIE, 1936
MOONLIGHT ON THE RANGE, 1937
MOONSHINE COUNTY EXPRESS, 1977
MOONSHINE WAR, THE, 1970
MOONSTONE, THE, 1934
MORALIST, THE, 1964
MORALS OF MARCUS, THE, 1936
MORE AMERICAN GRAFFITI, 1979
MORE THAN A SECRETARY, 1936
MORGAN STEWART'S COMING HOME, 1987
MORGAN THE PIRATE, 1961
MORNING STAR, 1962
MORONS FROM OUTER SPACE, 1985
MOSCOW SHANGHAI, 1936
MOSES, 1976
MOSQUITO SQUADRON, 1970
MOST PRECIOUS THING IN LIFE, 1934
MOST WANTED MAN, THE, 1962
MOTEL, THE OPERATOR, 1940
MOTHER AND DAUGHTER, 1965
MOTHER KNOWS BEST, 1928
MOTHERS OF TODAY, 1939
MOTIVE WAS JEALOUSY, THE, 1970
MOULIN ROUGE, 1944
MOUNTAIN FAMILY ROBINSON, 1979
MOUNTAIN JUSTICE, 1930
MOUNTAIN MOONLIGHT, 1941
MOUNTAIN MUSIC, 1937
MOUNTAIN RHYTHM, 1942
MOURNING BECOMES ELECTRA, 1947
MOURNING SUIT, THE, 1975
MOVE OVER, DARLING, 1963
MOVING FINGER, THE, 1963
MOVING VIOLATION, 1976
MOZART STORY, THE, 1948
MRS. FITZHERBERT, 1950
MRS. GIBBONS' BOYS, 1962
MRS. O'MALLEY AND MR. MALONE, 1950
MRS. WARREN'S PROFESSION, 1960

MS. 45, 1981
MUGGER, THE, 1958
MULE TRAIN, 1950
MUMMY'S GHOST, THE, 1944
MUNSTER, GO HOME, 1966
MURDER AMONG FRIENDS, 1941
MURDER AT 45 R.P.M., 1965
MURDER BY CONTRACT, 1958
MURDER GAME, THE, 1966
MURDER GOES TO COLLEGE, 1937
MURDER IN EDEN, 1962
MURDER IN THE AIR, 1940
MURDER IN THE CATHEDRAL, 1952
MURDER IN TRINIDAD, 1934
MURDER IS MY BUSINESS, 1946
MURDER OF DR. HARRIGAN, THE, 1936
MURDER ON A BRIDLE PATH, 1936
MURDER ON DIAMOND ROW, 1937
MURDER ON THE ROOF, 1930
MURDER ON THE YUKON, 1940
MURDER WILL OUT, 1953
MURDER WITH PICTURES, 1936
MURDERS IN THE RUE MORGUE, 1971
MURDERS IN THE ZOO, 1933
MURPHY'S LAW, 1986
MUSIC BOX KID, THE, 1960
MUSIC FOR MILLIONS, 1944
MUSIC HALL, 1934
MUSIC HALL PARADE, 1939
MUSIC IN MANHATTAN, 1944
MUSIC IS MAGIC, 1935
MUSIC MAN, 1948
MUSTANG COUNTRY, 1976
MUTINY AHEAD, 1935
MUTINY IN OUTER SPACE, 1965
MUTINY IN THE BIG HOUSE, 1939
MUTINY ON THE BLACKHAWK, 1939
MY AIN FOLK, 1974
MY AMERICAN WIFE, 1936
MY BABY IS BLACK!, 1965
MY BEST FRIEND'S GIRL, 1984
MY BILL, 1938
MY BREAKFAST WITH BLASSIE, 1983
MY BROTHER JONATHAN, 1949
MY CHAUFFEUR, 1986
MY DEATH IS A MOCKERY, 1952
MY DOG, BUDDY, 1960
MY DOG RUSTY, 1948
MY FIRST LOVE, 1978
MY FRIEND IRMA, 1949
MY FRIEND THE KING, 1931
MY GEISHA, 1962
MY LITTLE PONY, 1986
MY LUCKY STAR, 1933
MY MAN GODFREY, 1957
MY MARRIAGE, 1936
MY MOTHER, 1933
MY NAME IS IVAN, 1963
MY OLD DUCHESS, 1933
MY OLD DUTCH, 1934
MY OLD KENTUCKY HOME, 1938
MY OTHER HUSBAND, 1985
MY OWN TRUE LOVE, 1948
MY PAL GUS, 1952
MY REPUTATION, 1946
MY SIX LOVES, 1963
MY SON IS GUILTY, 1940
MY SON, THE HERO, 1943
MY THIRD WIFE GEORGE, 1968
MY TUTOR, 1983
MY WAY, 1974
MY WIFE'S BEST FRIEND, 1952
MY WIFE'S ENEMY, 1967
MY WIFE'S FAMILY, 1932
MY WIFE'S FAMILY, 1941
MY WIFE'S HUSBAND, 1965
MY WIFE'S LODGER, 1952
MY WOMAN, 1933
MY WORLD DIES SCREAMING, 1958
MYSTERIANS, THE, 1959
MYSTERIOUS CROSSING, 1937
MYSTERIOUS MISS X, THE, 1939
MYSTERIOUS MR. REEDER, THE, 1940
MYSTERIOUS MR. VALENTINE, THE, 1946
MYSTERIOUS RIDER, THE, 1942
MYSTERY AT THE BURLESQUE, 1950

BOLD: Films on Videocassette

MYSTERY AT THE VILLA ROSE, 1930
MYSTERY BROADCAST, 1943
MYSTERY MANSION, 1984
MYSTERY OF MARIE ROGET, THE, 1942
MYSTERY OF ROOM 13, 1941
MYSTERY PLANE, 1939
MYSTERY RANGE, 1937
MYSTERY SEA RAIDER, 1940
MYSTERY SHIP, 1941
MYSTERY SUBMARINE, 1963
MYSTERY WOMAN, 1935
MYTH, THE, 1965
N. P., 1971
NADA GANG, THE, 1974
NADIA, 1984
NADINE, 1987
NAGANA, 1933
NAKED AUTUMN, 1963
NAKED BRIGADE, THE, 1965
NAKED EDGE, THE, 1961
NAKED FLAME, THE, 1970
NAKED HILLS, THE, 1956
NAKED IN THE SUN, 1957
NAKED PARADISE, 1957
NAME OF THE ROSE, THE, 1986
NANCY DREW—DETECTIVE, 1938
NANCY DREW—REPORTER, 1939
NAPOLEON, 1955
NARCO MEN, THE, 1969
NASHVILLE REBEL, 1966
NASTY RABBIT, THE, 1964
NATCHEZ TRACE, 1960
NATHALIE, AGENT SECRET, 1960
NATIONAL BARN DANCE, 1944
NATIONAL LAMPOON'S VACATION, 1983
NAUGHTY ARLETTE, 1951
NAUGHTY BUT NICE, 1939
NAUGHTY CINDERELLA, 1933
NAUGHTY NINETIES, THE, 1945
NAVAJO JOE, 1967
NAVAJO RUN, 1966
NAVAJO TRAIL RAIDERS, 1949
NAVAJO TRAIL, THE, 1945
NAVY BLUE AND GOLD, 1937
NAVY BLUES, 1930
NAVY HEROES, 1959
NAVY LARK, THE, 1959
NAVY SECRETS, 1939
NAVY VS. THE NIGHT MONSTERS, THE, 1966
NAVY WIFE, 1936
'NEATH THE ARIZONA SKIES, 1934
NEGATIVES, 1968
NELSON AFFAIR, THE, 1973
NEON PALACE, THE, 1970
NEVADA, 1936
NEVADA CITY, 1941
NEVER A DULL MOMENT, 1943
NEVER A DULL MOMENT, 1950
NEVER BACK LOSERS, 1967
NEVER LET ME GO, 1953
NEVER LOOK BACK, 1952
NEVER PUT IT IN WRITING, 1964
NEVER SAY GOODBYE, 1956
NEW ADVENTURES OF GET-RICH-QUICK
   WALLINGFORD, THE, 1931
**NEW ADVENTURES OF PIPPI LONGSTOCKING,
   THE, 1988**
NEW CENTURIONS, THE, 1972
NEW EARTH, THE, 1937
NEW FACES, 1954
NEW GIRL IN TOWN, 1977
NEW LIFE, A, 1988
NEW MEXICO, 1951
NEW MOON, 1940
NEW MORALS FOR OLD, 1932
NEW ORLEANS, 1929
NEW ORLEANS, 1947
NEW ORLEANS AFTER DARK, 1958
NEW ORLEANS UNCENSORED, 1955
NEW WINE, 1941
NEW YORK CONFIDENTIAL, 1955
NEW YORK NIGHTS, 1929
NEWMAN'S LAW, 1974
NEWS HOUNDS, 1947
NEWS IS MADE AT NIGHT, 1939
NICE GIRL?, 1941

NICHOLAS NICKLEBY, 1947
NICKEL MOUNTAIN, 1985
NICKEL QUEEN, THE, 1971
NICKELODEON, 1976
NIGHT AFFAIR, 1961
NIGHT ANGEL, THE, 1931
NIGHT AT EARL CARROLL'S, A, 1940
NIGHT AT THE RITZ, A, 1935
NIGHT BEFORE CHRISTMAS, A, 1963
NIGHT BEFORE THE DIVORCE, THE, 1942
NIGHT BOAT TO DUBLIN, 1946
NIGHT CALL NURSES, 1974
NIGHT CLUB GIRL, 1944
NIGHT CLUB LADY, 1932
NIGHT CLUB QUEEN, 1934
NIGHT COMES TOO SOON, 1948
NIGHT DIGGER, THE, 1971
NIGHT GAMES, 1966
NIGHT GAMES, 1980
NIGHT HEAVEN FELL, THE, 1958
NIGHT IN NEW ORLEANS, A, 1942
NIGHT IN PARADISE, A, 1946
NIGHT IS YOUNG, THE, 1935
NIGHT JOURNEY, 1938
NIGHT MONSTER, 1942
NIGHT OF A THOUSAND CATS, 1974
NIGHT OF ADVENTURE, A, 1944
NIGHT OF MAGIC, A, 1944
NIGHT OF THE ASKARI, 1978
NIGHT OF THE CREEPS, 1986
NIGHT OF THE PROWLER, 1962
NIGHT PARADE, 1929
NIGHT RIDE, 1930
NIGHT RIDE, 1937
NIGHT RIDERS, THE, 1939
NIGHT STAGE TO GALVESTON, 1952
**NIGHT THE LIGHTS WENT OUT IN GEORGIA, THE,
   1981**
NIGHT THEY KILLED RASPUTIN, THE, 1962
NIGHT TRAIN TO PARIS, 1964
NIGHT UNTO NIGHT, 1949
NIGHT WATCH, 1973
NIGHT WITHOUT PITY, 1962
NIGHT WITHOUT SLEEP, 1952
NIGHT WORK, 1939
NIGHT ZOO, 1988
NIGHTHAWKS, 1978
NIGHTMARE, 1963
**NIGHTMARE ON ELM STREET 3: DREAM
   WARRIORS, A, 1987**
NIGHTMARES, 1983
NIGHTWARS, 1988
NIJINSKY, 1980
9 1/2 WEEKS, 1986
9 DEATHS OF THE NINJA, 1985
NINE TILL SIX, 1932
1914, 1932
1990: THE BRONX WARRIORS, 1983
1969, 1988
99 AND 44/100% DEAD, 1974
99 RIVER STREET, 1953
NIX ON DAMES, 1929
NO BLADE OF GRASS, 1970
NO DEPOSIT, NO RETURN, 1976
NO ESCAPE, 1953
NO EXIT, 1930
NO GREATER LOVE, 1932
NO GREATER SIN, 1941
NO HAUNT FOR A GENTLEMAN, 1952
NO LIMIT, 1931
NO LIVING WITNESS, 1932
NO LOVE FOR JUDY, 1955
NO MAN'S LAND, 1964
NO MAN'S LAND, 1987
NO MAN'S RANGE, 1935
NO MAN'S WOMAN, 1955
NO MARRIAGE TIES, 1933
NO MORE EXCUSES, 1968
NO MORE LADIES, 1935
NO PARKING, 1938
NO PLACE FOR A LADY, 1943
NO PLACE FOR JENNIFER, 1950
NO PLACE TO HIDE, 1956
NO RANSOM, 1935
NO RESTING PLACE, 1952
NO ROOM TO DIE, 1969

NO ROSES FOR OSS 117, 1968
NO SAD SONGS FOR ME, 1950
NO SMALL AFFAIR, 1984
NO TIME TO BE YOUNG, 1957
NO TREE IN THE STREET, 1964
NO WAY BACK, 1949
NOBODY IN TOYLAND, 1958
NOBODY WAVED GOODBYE, 1965
NOBODY'S CHILDREN, 1940
NOBODY'S DARLING, 1943
NOBODY'S FOOL, 1986
NOBODY'S PERFECT, 1968
NOMADIC LIVES, 1977
NONE BUT THE BRAVE, 1963
NONE BUT THE BRAVE, 1965
NOOSE FOR A LADY, 1953
NORMAN...IS THAT YOU?, 1976
NORMAN LOVES ROSE, 1982
NORSEMAN, THE, 1978
NORTH FROM LONE STAR, 1941
NORTH OF THE RIO GRANDE, 1937
NORTH OF THE YUKON, 1939
NORTH SHORE, 1987
NORTH STAR, THE, 1982
NORTH TO THE KLONDIKE, 1942
NORTHERN FRONTIER, 1935
NORTHWEST RANGERS, 1942
NORTHWEST STAMPEDE, 1948
NORWOOD, 1970
NOT ON YOUR LIFE, 1965
NOT QUITE DECENT, 1929
NOT QUITE JERUSALEM, 1985
NOT RECONCILED, OR "'ONLY VIOLENCE HELPS
   WHERE IT RULES", 1969
NOT SINCE CASANOVA, 1988
NOT WANTED ON VOYAGE, 1957
NOTHING BUT THE BEST, 1964
NOTHING BUT THE NIGHT, 1975
NOTHING LASTS FOREVER, 1984
NOTORIOUS GENTLEMAN, A, 1935
NOTORIOUS LONE WOLF, THE, 1946
NOTORIOUS MR. MONKS, THE, 1958
NOUS IRONS A PARIS, 1949
NOW AND FOREVER, 1934
NOW AND FOREVER, 1956
NOW AND FOREVER, 1983
NOWHERE TO HIDE, 1987
NUDE IN HIS POCKET, 1962
NUDE ODYSSEY, 1962
NUMBER SIX, 1962
NUMBER TWO, 1975
NUMBERED MEN, 1930
NUN AND THE SERGEANT, THE, 1962
NUN AT THE CROSSROADS, A, 1970
NURSE FROM BROOKLYN, 1938
NURSE SHERRI, 1978
NUT FARM, THE, 1935
NUTTY, NAUGHTY CHATEAU, 1964
OBJECTIVE 500 MILLION, 1966
OBSESSED, 1951
OBSESSION, 1968
OBSESSION, 1976
OCEAN BREAKERS, 1949
OCTAGON, THE, 1980
OCTOBER MOTH, 1960
OCTOPUSSY, 1983
ODD ANGRY SHOT, THE, 1979
ODD JOB, THE, 1978
ODD OBSESSION, 1961
ODONGO, 1956
ODYSSEY OF THE PACIFIC, 1983
OEDIPUS REX, 1957
OF FLESH AND BLOOD, 1964
OF HUMAN BONDAGE, 1964
OF WAYWARD LOVE, 1964
OFF BEAT, 1986
OFF LIMITS, 1988
OFF THE RECORD, 1939
OFF TO THE RACES, 1937
OFFICE WIFE, THE, 1930
OFFSPRING, THE, 1987
OH BOY!, 1938
OH DOCTOR, 1937
OH GOD! BOOK II, 1980
OH, HEAVENLY DOG!, 1980
OH, MR. PORTER!, 1937

OH NO DOCTOR!, 1934
OH! SUSANNA, 1951
OH, YEAH!, 1929
O'HARA'S WIFE, 1983
OKAY BILL, 1971
OKAY FOR SOUND, 1937
OKINAWA, 1952
OKLAHOMA ANNIE, 1952
OKLAHOMA BADLANDS, 1948
OKLAHOMA BLUES, 1948
OKLAHOMA CYCLONE, 1930
OKLAHOMA FRONTIER, 1939
OKLAHOMA JUSTICE, 1951
OKLAHOMA RAIDERS, 1944
OKLAHOMA RENEGADES, 1940
OLD BARN DANCE, THE, 1938
OLD BILL AND SON, 1940
OLD BOYFRIENDS, 1979
OLD CHISHOLM TRAIL, 1943
OLD-FASHIONED GIRL, AN, 1948
OLD HOMESTEAD, THE, 1935
OLD IRON, 1938
OLD MAC, 1961
OLD MAN, THE, 1932
OLD MAN RHYTHM, 1935
OLD MOTHER RILEY, 1952
OLD MOTHER RILEY IN BUSINESS, 1940
OLD MOTHER RILEY MP, 1939
OLD MOTHER RILEY OVERSEAS, 1943
OLD MOTHER RILEY'S CIRCUS, 1941
OLD MOTHER RILEY'S GHOSTS, 1941
OLD MOTHER RILEY'S JUNGLE TREASURE, 1951
OLD SHATTERHAND, 1968
OLD SPANISH CUSTOMERS, 1932
OLD TEXAS TRAIL, THE, 1944
OLD WYOMING TRAIL, THE, 1937
OLIVER TWIST, 1933
OMAHA TRAIL, THE, 1942
OMAR KHAYYAM, 1957
OMEGA MAN, THE, 1971
OMEGA SYNDROME, 1987
OMEN, THE, 1976
OMICRON, 1963
ON AGAIN—OFF AGAIN, 1937
ON HIS OWN, 1939
ON OUR MERRY WAY, 1948
ON STAGE EVERYBODY, 1945
ON SUCH A NIGHT, 1937
ON THE AIR, 1934
ON THE BEAT, 1962
ON THE EDGE, 1985
ON THE ISLE OF SAMOA, 1950
ON THE LOOSE, 1951
ON THE OLD SPANISH TRAIL, 1947
ON THE RIVIERA, 1951
ON THE RUN, 1958
ON THE RUN, 1967
ON THE RUN, 1969
ON THE RUN, 1983
ON THE SUNNY SIDE, 1942
ON THE SUNNYSIDE, 1936
ON THEIR OWN, 1940
ON TRIAL, 1928
ONCE A DOCTOR, 1937
ONCE A GENTLEMAN, 1930
ONCE A LADY, 1931
ONCE A THIEF, 1935
ONCE IN A NEW MOON, 1935
ONCE TO EVERY BACHELOR, 1934
ONCE TO EVERY WOMAN, 1934
ONCE UPON A DREAM, 1949
ONCE UPON A HORSE, 1958
ONE BIG AFFAIR, 1952
ONE DANGEROUS NIGHT, 1943
ONE DARK NIGHT, 1939
ONE DAY IN THE LIFE OF IVAN DENISOVICH, 1971
ONE DEADLY SUMMER, 1984
ONE EXCITING NIGHT, 1945
ONE EXCITING WEEK, 1946
ONE-EYED SOLDIERS, 1967
ONE FOOT IN HELL, 1960
ONE FRIGHTENED NIGHT, 1935
ONE FROM THE HEART, 1982
ONE GOOD TURN, 1955
ONE HEAVENLY NIGHT, 1931
100 RIFLES, 1969

ONE HYSTERICAL NIGHT, 1930
ONE IN A MILLION, 1936
ONE IS GUILTY, 1934
ONE JUMP AHEAD, 1955
ONE-MAN LAW, 1932
ONE MAN'S LAW, 1940
ONE MILE FROM HEAVEN, 1937
ONE MILLION DOLLARS, 1965
ONE MILLION YEARS B.C., 1967
ONE MINUTE TO ZERO, 1952
ONE MORE TOMORROW, 1946
ONE MYSTERIOUS NIGHT, 1944
ONE NIGHT...A TRAIN, 1968
ONE NIGHT IN PARIS, 1940
ONE NIGHT OF LOVE, 1934
ONE NIGHT STAND, 1976
ONE OF OUR DINOSAURS IS MISSING, 1975
ONE OF OUR SPIES IS MISSING, 1966
ONE ON ONE, 1977
ONE PLUS ONE, 1969
ONE PRECIOUS YEAR, 1933
ONE RAINY AFTERNOON, 1936
ONE SINGS, THE OTHER DOESN'T, 1977
ONE SPY TOO MANY, 1966
ONE SUNDAY AFTERNOON, 1948
ONE THIRD OF A NATION, 1939
$1,000 A TOUCHDOWN, 1939
ONE THRILLING NIGHT, 1942
1 2 3 MONSTER EXPRESS, 1977
ONE WILD OAT, 1951
ONE YEAR LATER, 1933
ONIMASA, 1983
ONIONHEAD, 1958
ONLY ONE NIGHT, 1942
ONLY SAPS WORK, 1930
ONLY THING YOU KNOW, THE, 1971
ONLY WAY HOME, THE, 1972
ONE MAN'S WAY, 1964
OPEN ALL NIGHT, 1934
OPEN SECRET, 1948
OPENING NIGHT, 1977
OPERATION AMSTERDAM, 1960
OPERATION BIKINI, 1963
OPERATION BULLSHINE, 1963
OPERATION CAMEL, 1961
OPERATION CROSS EAGLES, 1969
OPERATION CROSSBOW, 1965
OPERATION DAYBREAK, 1976
OPERATION DIAMOND, 1948
OPERATION DIPLOMAT, 1953
OPERATION DISASTER, 1951
OPERATION EICHMANN, 1961
OPERATION HAYLIFT, 1950
OPERATION SNAFU, 1965
OPERATION THIRD FORM, 1966
OPERATION X, 1963
OPERATOR 13, 1934
OPIATE '67, 1967
OPPOSITE SEX, THE, 1956
ORCHIDS TO YOU, 1935
ORDEAL BY INNOCENCE, 1984
ORDERED TO LOVE, 1963
ORDERS TO KILL, 1958
OREGON PASSAGE, 1958
OREGON TRAIL, THE, 1959
OREGON TRAIL SCOUTS, 1947
ORGANIZATION, THE, 1971
ORPHAN OF THE PECOS, 1938
OSTERMAN WEEKEND, THE, 1983
OTHELLO, 1955
OTHER PEOPLE'S SINS, 1931
OUR NEIGHBORS—THE CARTERS, 1939
OUR VERY OWN, 1950
OUT ALL NIGHT, 1933
OUT CALIFORNIA WAY, 1946
OUT OF ORDER, 1985
OUT OF THE BLUE, 1931
OUT OF THE CLOUDS, 1957
OUT OF THE PAST, 1933
OUT OF THE STORM, 1948
OUT OF THE TIGER'S MOUTH, 1962
OUTCAST, THE, 1934
OUTCAST OF BLACK MESA, 1950
OUTCASTS OF POKER FLAT, THE, 1937
OUTCASTS OF THE CITY, 1958
OUTCASTS OF THE TRAIL, 1949

OUTER GATE, THE, 1937
OUTFIT, THE, 1973
OUTLAND, 1981
OUTLAW JUSTICE, 1933
OUTLAW STALLION, THE, 1954
OUTLAW: THE SAGE OF GISLI, 1982
OUTLAW TRAIL, 1944
OUTLAW WOMEN, 1952
OUTLAWED GUNS, 1935
OUTLAW'S DAUGHTER, THE, 1954
OUTLAWS OF SANTA FE, 1944
OUTLAWS OF SONORA, 1938
OUTLAWS OF THE ORIENT, 1937
OUTLAWS OF THE PANHANDLE, 1941
OUTLAWS OF THE RIO GRANDE, 1941
OUTLAW'S PARADISE, 1939
OUTLAW'S SON, 1957
OUTPOST IN MOROCCO, 1949
OUTPOST OF HELL, 1966
OUTRAGEOUS FORTUNE, 1987
OUTRIDERS, THE, 1950
OUTSIDER, THE, 1933
OUTSIDER, THE, 1940
OUTSIDER, THE, 1962
OUTSIDER IN AMSTERDAM, 1983
OVER THE GARDEN WALL, 1934
OVER THE GOAL, 1937
OVER THE MOON, 1940
OVER THE WALL, 1938
OVERBOARD, 1987
OVERLAND BOUND, 1929
OVERLAND RIDERS, 1946
OVERLAND STAGECOACH, 1942
PACE THAT THRILLS, THE, 1952
PACIFIC DESTINY, 1956
PACIFIC LINER, 1939
PACIFIC RENDEZVOUS, 1942
PACK TRAIN, 1953
PACK UP YOUR TROUBLES, 1940
PAGAN ISLAND, 1961
PAGAN LOVE SONG, 1950
PAID IN ERROR, 1938
PAID TO KILL, 1954
PAINT YOUR WAGON, 1969
PAINTED FACES, 1929
PAINTING THE CLOUDS WITH SUNSHINE, 1951
PAIR OF BRIEFS, A, 1963
PAL FROM TEXAS, THE, 1939
PALM SPRINGS, 1936
PALS OF THE GOLDEN WEST, 1952
PALS OF THE RANGE, 1935
PALS OF THE SILVER SAGE, 1940
PANAMA HATTIE, 1942
PANCHO VILLA RETURNS, 1950
PANDA AND THE MAGIC SERPENT, 1961
PANDORA AND THE FLYING DUTCHMAN, 1951
PANIC IN THE PARLOUR, 1957
PANIQUE, 1947
PAPERHOUSE, 1988
PARACHUTE BATTALION, 1941
PARACHUTE NURSE, 1942
PARADES, 1972
PARADISE ALLEY, 1962
PARADISE, HAWAIIAN STYLE, 1966
PARADISE POUR TOUS, 1982
PARALLELS, 1980
PARATROOP COMMAND, 1959
PARDNERS, 1956
PARDON MY RHYTHM, 1944
PARDON OUR NERVE, 1939
PARIS, 1929
PARIS BOUND, 1929
PARIS CALLING, 1941
PARIS FOLLIES OF 1956, 1955
PARIS MODEL, 1953
PARIS OOH-LA-LA!, 1963
PARIS PICK-UP, 1963
PARIS PLANE, 1933
PARIS PLAYBOYS, 1954
PARIS UNDERGROUND, 1945
PARIS WHEN IT SIZZLES, 1964
PARK AVENUE LOGGER, 1937
PARK ROW, 1952
PAROLE FIXER, 1940
PARSIFAL, 1983
PARSON AND THE OUTLAW, THE, 1957

PARSON OF PANAMINT, THE, 1941
PARTINGS, 1962
PARTNERS, 1976
PARTNERS OF THE TRAIL, 1944
PARTY, THE, 1968
PARTY WIRE, 1935
PASSAGE FROM HONG KONG, 1941
PASSING SHADOWS, 1934
PASSING STRANGER, THE, 1954
PASSION, 1954
PASSION, 1968
PASSION OF LOVE, 1982
PASSIONATE DEMONS, THE, 1962
PASSIONATE SUMMER, 1959
PASSKEY TO DANGER, 1946
PASSPORT TO CHINA, 1961
PASSPORT TO DESTINY, 1944
PASSPORT TO SUEZ, 1943
PAT GARRETT AND BILLY THE KID, 1973
PATERNITY, 1981
PATH OF GLORY, THE, 1934
PATHFINDER, THE, 1952
PATIENT IN ROOM 18, THE, 1938
PATRICK THE GREAT, 1945
PAUL TEMPLE RETURNS, 1952
PAULA, 1952
PAVLOVA—A WOMAN FOR ALL TIME, 1985
PAYROLL, 1962
PEACEMAKER, THE, 1956
PEACH O'RENO, 1931
PEARL OF TLAYUCAN, THE, 1964
PECK'S BAD BOY WITH THE CIRCUS, 1938
PECOS RIVER, 1951
PEDDLIN' IN SOCIETY, 1949
PENALTY, THE, 1941
PENELOPE, 1966
PENITENTE MURDER CASE, THE, 1936
PENITENTIARY, 1938
PENNY PARADISE, 1938
PENNYWHISTLE BLUES, THE, 1952
PENROD AND HIS TWIN BROTHER, 1938
PENROD AND SAM, 1931
PENROD AND SAM, 1937
PENROD'S DOUBLE TROUBLE, 1938
PENTHOUSE PARTY, 1936
PEOPLE MEET AND SWEET MUSIC FILLS THE
  HEART, 1969
PEOPLE VS. DR. KILDARE, THE, 1941
PEOPLE'S ENEMY, THE, 1935
PEPPER, 1936
PERFECT ALIBI, THE, 1931
PERFECT CLUE, THE, 1935
PERFECT CRIME, THE, 1928
PERFECT GENTLEMAN, THE, 1935
PERFECT LADY, THE, 1931
PERFECT MATCH, THE, 1987
PERFECT SNOB, THE, 1941
PERFECT STRANGERS, 1950
PERFECT STRANGERS, 1984
PERFECTIONIST, THE, 1952
PERIL FOR THE GUY, 1956
PERILOUS WATERS, 1948
PERILS OF PAULINE, THE, 1967
PERSECUTION AND ASSASSINATION OF
  JEAN-PAUL MARAT AS PERFORMED BY THE
  INMATES OF THE ASYLUM OF CHARENTON
  UNDER THE DIRECTION OF THE MARQUIS DE
  SADE, THE, 1967
PERSONAL BEST, 1982
PERSONAL MAID'S SECRET, 1935
PERSONAL SECRETARY, 1938
PERSONALITY, 1930
PERSONALITY KID, THE, 1934
PERSUADER, THE, 1957
PETE'S DRAGON, 1977
PETTICOAT FEVER, 1936
PETTICOAT PIRATES, 1961
PETTICOAT POLITICS, 1941
PHANTASM II, 1988
PHANTOM COWBOY, THE, 1941
PHANTOM GOLD, 1938
PHANTOM IN THE HOUSE, THE, 1929
PHANTOM KILLER, 1942
PHANTOM OF CHINATOWN, 1940
PHANTOM OF CRESTWOOD, THE, 1932
PHANTOM OF 42ND STREET, THE, 1945
PHANTOM OF SANTA FE, 1937

PHANTOM OF SOHO, THE, 1967
PHANTOM OF THE JUNGLE, 1955
PHANTOM OF THE PLAINS, 1945
PHANTOM OF THE RANGE, THE, 1938
PHANTOM PLAINSMEN, THE, 1942
PHANTOM PLANET, THE, 1961
PHANTOM RANCHER, 1940
PHANTOM SHIP, 1937
PHANTOM STAGE, THE, 1939
PHANTOM STALLION, THE, 1954
PHANTOM STOCKMAN, THE, 1953
PHILO VANCE RETURNS, 1947
PHILO VANCE'S GAMBLE, 1947
PHONY AMERICAN, THE, 1964
PICCADILLY INCIDENT, 1948
PICCADILLY NIGHTS, 1930
PICCADILLY THIRD STOP, 1960
PICK A STAR, 1937
PICK-UP ARTIST, THE, 1987
PICKUP ALLEY, 1957
PICTURES, 1982
PIECES OF DREAMS, 1970
PIER 13, 1940
PIERRE OF THE PLAINS, 1942
PIGEON THAT TOOK ROME, THE, 1962
PIGS, 1984
PILGRIM, FAREWELL, 1980
PILGRIM LADY, THE, 1947
PILGRIMAGE, 1972
PILLAR OF FIRE, THE, 1963
PILLOW OF DEATH, 1945
PILOT, THE, 1979
PILOT NO. 5, 1943
PIN UP GIRL, 1944
PINK FLOYD—THE WALL, 1982
PINK STRING AND SEALING WAX, 1950
PINOCCHIO, 1969
PINOCCHIO IN OUTER SPACE, 1965
PINTO BANDIT, THE, 1944
PINTO CANYON, 1940
PIONEER TRAIL, 1938
PIONEERS OF THE FRONTIER, 1940
PIONEERS OF THE WEST, 1940
PIRATE OF THE BLACK HAWK, THE, 1961
PIRATES OF THE PRAIRIE, 1942
PIRATES OF THE SEVEN SEAS, 1941
PIRATES OF THE SKIES, 1939
PIRATES OF TORTUGA, 1961
PIRATES OF TRIPOLI, 1955
PISTOL HARVEST, 1951
PLACE TO GO, A, 1964
PLAGUE DOGS, THE, 1984
PLAINSMAN, THE, 1966
PLAINSMAN AND THE LADY, 1946
PLAINSONG, 1982
PLANET OF DINOSAURS, 1978
PLANETS AGAINST US, THE, 1961
PLATOON LEADER, 1988
PLAY UP THE BAND, 1935
PLAYBACK, 1962
PLAYMATES, 1941
PLEASANTVILLE, 1976
PLEASE, NOT NOW!, 1963
PLEASE TEACHER, 1937
PLEASURE LOVERS, THE, 1964
PLEASURES AND VICES, 1962
PLUNDER, 1931
PLUNDERERS OF PAINTED FLATS, 1959
POCKET MONEY, 1972
POCOLITTLE DOG LOST, 1977
POCOMANIA, 1939
POET'S PUB, 1949
POINTING FINGER, THE, 1934
POISONED DIAMOND, THE, 1934
POITIN, 1979
POLICE BULLETS, 1942
POLICE CAR 17, 1933
POLICE DOG, 1955
POLICE DOG STORY, THE, 1961
POLITICAL ASYLUM, 1975
POLITICS, 1931
POLTERGEIST, 1982
POLYESTER, 1981
PONTIUS PILATE, 1967
POOR LITTLE RICH GIRL, 1936
POP ALWAYS PAYS, 1940

POPDOWN, 1968
POPEYE, 1980
POPSY POP, 1971
PORT OF ESCAPE, 1955
PORT OF HELL, 1955
PORT OF LOST DREAMS, 1935
PORT SAID, 1948
PORTRAIT IN BLACK, 1960
PORTRAIT IN SMOKE, 1957
PORTRAIT OF A MOBSTER, 1961
PORTRAIT OF A SINNER, 1961
PORTRAIT OF CLARE, 1951
PORTRAIT OF INNOCENCE, 1948
PORTRAIT OF LENIN, 1967
PORTRAIT OF MARIA, 1946
POST OFFICE INVESTIGATOR, 1949
POSTMAN DIDN'T RING, THE, 1942
POSTMAN GOES TO WAR, THE, 1968
POSTMAN'S KNOCK, 1962
**POUND PUPPIES AND THE LEGEND OF BIG PAW,
  1988**
P.O.W. THE ESCAPE, 1986
POWER OF EVIL, THE, 1985
POWER OF THE WHISTLER, THE, 1945
POWER PLAY, 1978
PRAIRIE, THE, 1948
PRAIRIE BADMEN, 1946
PRAIRIE JUSTICE, 1938
PRAIRIE LAW, 1940
PRAIRIE OUTLAWS, 1948
PRAIRIE PIONEERS, 1941
PRAIRIE RUSTLERS, 1945
PRAISE MARX AND PASS THE AMMUNITION, 1970
PRAYER FOR THE DYING, A, 1987
PRAYING MANTIS, 1982
PREDATOR, 1987
PRELUDE TO ECSTASY, 1963
PREMONITION, THE, 1976
PREPPIES, 1984
PRESCOTT KID, THE, 1936
PRESCRIPTION FOR ROMANCE, 1937
PRESIDENT VANISHES, THE, 1934
PRESTIGE, 1932
PRETTY BABY, 1950
PRICE OF A SONG, THE, 1935
PRICE OF POWER, THE, 1969
PRIDE OF MARYLAND, 1951
PRIDE OF THE ARMY, 1942
PRIDE OF THE BLUE GRASS, 1954
PRIDE OF THE BLUEGRASS, 1936
PRIDE OF THE FORCE, THE, 1933
PRIDE OF THE LEGION, THE, 1932
PRIDE OF THE MARINES, 1936
PRIDE OF THE PLAINS, 1944
PRIEST OF ST. PAULI, THE, 1970
PRIME MINISTER, THE, 1941
PRIMITIVES, THE, 1962
PRIMROSE PATH, THE, 1934
PRINCE JACK, 1985
PRINCE OF DIAMONDS, 1930
PRINCE OF THE PLAINS, 1949
PRINCE OF THIEVES, THE, 1948
PRINCESS AND THE MAGIC FROG, THE, 1965
PRINCESS AND THE PLUMBER, THE, 1930
PRINCESS CHARMING, 1935
PRINCESS O'HARA, 1935
PRISM, 1971
PRISON BREAK, 1938
PRISON BREAKER, 1936
PRISON FARM, 1938
PRISON NURSE, 1938
PRISON SHIP, 1945
PRISON WARDEN, 1949
PRISON WITHOUT BARS, 1939
PRISONER OF CORBAL, 1939
PRISONER OF THE IRON MASK, 1962
PRISONER OF WAR, 1954
PRISONER OF ZENDA, THE, 1979
PRIVATE AFFAIRS, 1940
PRIVATE BUCKAROO, 1942
PRIVATE DETECTIVE, 1939
PRIVATE DETECTIVE 62, 1933
PRIVATE DUTY NURSES, 1972
PRIVATE JONES, 1933
PRIVATE LIFE OF DON JUAN, THE, 1934
PRIVATE LIFE OF LOUIS XIV, 1936

PRIVATE NUMBER, 1936
PRIVATE POOLEY, 1962
PRIVATE POTTER, 1963
PRIVATE RIGHT, THE, 1967
PRIVATE SCANDAL, 1934
PRIVATE SECRETARY, THE, 1935
PRIVATE'S AFFAIR, A, 1959
PRIVATE'S PROGRESS, 1956
PROBATION, 1932
PROBLEM GIRLS, 1953
PRODIGAL, THE, 1984
PRODIGAL SON, THE, 1935
PRODIGAL SON, THE, 1964
PROJECTED MAN, THE, 1967
PROMISE HER ANYTHING, 1966
PROMISES IN THE DARK, 1979
PROPERTY, 1979
PROSPERITY, 1932
PROTECTOR, THE, 1985
PROTOCOL, 1984
PROUD VALLEY, THE, 1941
PSYCHO-CIRCUS, 1967
PSYCHOMANIA, 1974
PSYCHOUT FOR MURDER, 1971
PSYCOSISSIMO, 1962
PUBLIC LIFE OF HENRY THE NINTH, THE, 1934
PUBLIC OPINION, 1935
PUBLIC WEDDING, 1937
PUDDIN' HEAD, 1941
PUFNSTUF, 1970
PUMPKINHEAD, 1988
PUNCH AND JUDY MAN, THE, 1963
PURPLE HEARTS, 1984
PURPLE HILLS, THE, 1961
PURPLE RAIN, 1984
PURPLE V, THE, 1943
PURSUERS, THE, 1961
PURSUIT, 1935
PUSHER, THE, 1960
PUSS "N' BOOTS, 1964
PUSS "N' BOOTS, 1967
PUT ON THE SPOT, 1936
PUTNEY SWOPE, 1969
PUTTIN' ON THE RITZ, 1930
PYGMY ISLAND, 1950
PYRO, 1964
**QUACKSER FORTUNE HAS A COUSIN IN THE
  BRONX, 1970**
QUALCOSA DI BIONDO, 1985
QUANTEZ, 1957
QUARTERBACK, THE, 1940
QUARTET, 1981
QUARTIERE, 1987
QUEEN OF BABYLON, THE, 1956
QUEEN OF BURLESQUE, 1946
QUEEN OF OUTER SPACE, 1958
QUEEN OF THE AMAZONS, 1947
QUEEN OF THE NILE, 1964
QUEEN OF THE PIRATES, 1961
QUEEN OF THE YUKON, 1940
QUEEN'S GUARDS, THE, 1963
QUERELLE, 1983
QUESTION OF ADULTERY, A, 1959
QUESTION OF SUSPENSE, A, 1961
QUICK AND THE DEAD, THE, 1963
QUICK MONEY, 1938
QUICK ON THE TRIGGER, 1949
QUIET PLEASE, 1938
QUIET WOMAN, THE, 1951
RABBI AND THE SHIKSE, THE, 1976
RABBIT TRAP, THE, 1959
RACETRACK, 1933
RACING ROMANCE, 1937
RACKET MAN, THE, 1944
RACKETEER, THE, 1929
RADIO CAB MURDER, 1954
RADIO CITY REVELS, 1938
RADIO LOVER, 1936
RADIO PIRATES, 1935
RAFFERTY AND THE GOLD DUST TWINS, 1975
RAFTER ROMANCE, 1934
RAGE IN HEAVEN, 1941
RAGE OF HONOR, 1987
RAGGEDY ANN AND ANDY, 1977
RAGING TIDE, THE, 1951
RAGTIME COWBOY JOE, 1940

RAIDERS FROM BENEATH THE SEA, 1964
RAIDERS OF RED GAP, 1944
RAIDERS OF SAN JOAQUIN, 1943
RAIDERS OF SUNSET PASS, 1943
RAIDERS OF THE BORDER, 1944
RAIDERS OF THE DESERT, 1941
RAIDERS OF THE RANGE, 1942
RAIDERS OF THE SEVEN SEAS, 1953
RAINBOW, THE, 1944
RAINBOW JACKET, THE, 1954
RAINBOW ON THE RIVER, 1936
RAINBOW OVER BROADWAY, 1933
RAINBOW OVER TEXAS, 1946
RAINBOW 'ROUND MY SHOULDER, 1952
RAINBOW TRAIL, 1932
RAINBOW VALLEY, 1935
RAINBOW'S END, 1935
RAISE THE ROOF, 1930
RAISING A RIOT, 1957
RALLY 'ROUND THE FLAG, BOYS!, 1958
RAMONA, 1936
RAMPAGE, 1963
RAMPAGE AT APACHE WELLS, 1966
RAMPARTS WE WATCH, THE, 1940
RANDOLPH FAMILY, THE, 1945
RANGE BUSTERS, THE, 1940
RANGE DEFENDERS, 1937
RANGE FEUD, THE, 1931
RANGE JUSTICE, 1949
RANGE LAND, 1949
RANGE LAW, 1931
RANGER AND THE LADY, THE, 1940
RANGER OF CHEROKEE STRIP, 1949
RANGLE RIVER, 1939
RAPPIN', 1985
RARE BREED, 1984
RASCALS, 1938
RASPOUTINE, 1954
RASPUTIN, 1932
RAT PFINK AND BOO BOO, 1966
RATIONING, 1944
RAVAGERS, THE, 1965
RAVISHING IDIOT, A, 1966
RAW DEAL, 1986
RAW EDGE, 1956
RAWHIDE RANGERS, 1941
RAWHIDE YEARS, THE, 1956
REACHING FOR THE MOON, 1931
READY FOR THE PEOPLE, 1964
REAL BLOKE, A, 1935
REAL GENIUS, 1985
REAL LIFE, 1984
REBECCA OF SUNNYBROOK FARM, 1932
REBECCA OF SUNNYBROOK FARM, 1938
REBEL, THE, 1933
REBEL GLADIATORS, THE, 1963
REBELLION, 1938
RECAPTURED LOVE, 1930
RECKLESS, 1984
RECKLESS HOUR, THE, 1931
RECKLESS LIVING, 1931
RED BLOOD OF COURAGE, 1935
RED CLOAK, THE, 1961
RED DANUBE, THE, 1949
RED DRESS, THE, 1954
RED-HAIRED ALIBI, THE, 1932
RED HEAD, 1934
RED HEADED STRANGER, 1987
RED HOT TIRES, 1935
RED LIGHT, 1949
RED LION, 1971
RED RIVER RANGE, 1938
RED RIVER ROBIN HOOD, 1943
RED RIVER VALLEY, 1936
RED ROPE, THE, 1937
RED SALUTE, 1935
RED SHEIK, THE, 1963
RED SNOW, 1952
RED STALLION, THE, 1947
RED SUN, 1972
RED SUNDOWN, 1956
RED TOMAHAWK, 1967
RED WAGON, 1936
REDEEMER, THE, 1965
REDUCING, 1931
REDWOOD FOREST TRAIL, 1950

REFLECTION OF FEAR, A, 1973
REFLECTIONS, 1984
REFORM SCHOOL, 1939
RELUCTANT HEROES, 1951
RELUCTANT SAINT, THE, 1962
REMAINS TO BE SEEN, 1953
REMARKABLE ANDREW, THE, 1942
REMARKABLE MR. KIPPS, 1942
REMBETIKO, 1985
REMEMBER PEARL HARBOR, 1942
REMOTE CONTROL, 1930
RENDEZVOUS 24, 1946
RENEGADE GIRL, 1946
RENEGADE TRAIL, 1939
RENEGADES, 1930
RENEGADES OF SONORA, 1948
RENEGADES OF THE RIO GRANDE, 1945
RENEGADES OF THE SAGE, 1949
RENT-A-COP, 1988
RENTADICK, 1972
REPORT ON THE PARTY AND THE GUESTS, A, 1968
REPRISAL, 1956
RESCUE SQUAD, THE, 1963
RESTLESS BREED, THE, 1957
RESTLESS NIGHT, THE, 1964
RESTLESS ONES, THE, 1965
RESURRECTION, 1931
RESURRECTION, 1980
RETURN, 1986
RETURN FROM THE ASHES, 1965
RETURN OF A MAN CALLED HORSE, THE, 1976
RETURN OF BULLDOG DRUMMOND, THE, 1934
RETURN OF CAPTAIN INVINCIBLE, THE, 1983
RETURN OF CAROL DEANE, THE, 1938
RETURN OF CASEY JONES, 1933
RETURN OF COUNT YORGA, THE, 1971
RETURN OF DANIEL BOONE, THE, 1941
RETURN OF DR. FU MANCHU, THE, 1930
RETURN OF DRACULA, THE, 1958
RETURN OF OCTOBER, THE, 1948
RETURN OF RAFFLES, THE, 1932
RETURN OF SOPHIE LANG, THE, 1936
RETURN OF THE FRONTIERSMAN, 1950
RETURN OF THE LIVING DEAD, 1985
RETURN OF THE LIVING DEAD PART II, 1988
RETURN OF THE SCARLET PIMPERNEL, 1938
RETURN OF THE WHISTLER, THE, 1948
RETURN OF WILD BILL, THE, 1940
RETURN TO PARADISE, 1953
RETURN TO SENDER, 1963
RETURN TO TREASURE ISLAND, 1954
RETURN TO WATERLOO, 1985
RETURN TO YESTERDAY, 1940
REUBEN, REUBEN, 1983
REUNION IN VIENNA, 1933
REVEILLE WITH BEVERLY, 1943
REVENGE AT EL PASO, 1968
REVENGE OF THE CREATURE, 1955
REVENGE RIDER, THE, 1935
REVOLT OF THE SLAVES, THE, 1961
REVOLUTION, 1985
RHINOCEROS, 1974
RHYTHM IN THE AIR, 1936
RHYTHM IN THE CLOUDS, 1937
RHYTHM OF THE ISLANDS, 1943
RHYTHM OF THE RIO GRANDE, 1940
RHYTHM PARADE, 1943
RHYTHM SERENADE, 1943
RICHARD'S THINGS, 1981
RIDDLE OF THE SANDS, THE, 1984
RIDE A CROOKED TRAIL, 1958
RIDE A NORTHBOUND HORSE, 1969
RIDE 'EM COWGIRL, 1939
RIDE OUT FOR REVENGE, 1957
RIDE, RYDER, RIDE!, 1949
RIDE THE HIGH IRON, 1956
RIDE THE MAN DOWN, 1952
RIDE, VAQUERO!, 1953
RIDER OF THE LAW, THE, 1935
RIDER OF THE PLAINS, 1931
RIDER ON A DEAD HORSE, 1962
RIDERS FROM NOWHERE, 1940
RIDERS OF BLACK RIVER, 1939
RIDERS OF PASCO BASIN, 1940
RIDERS OF THE DAWN, 1937
RIDERS OF THE DESERT, 1932

BOLD: Films on Videocassette

RIDERS OF THE DUSK, 1949
RIDERS OF THE GOLDEN GULCH, 1932
RIDERS OF THE NORTH, 1931
RIDERS OF THE PURPLE SAGE, 1941
RIDERS OF THE STORM, 1988
RIDERS TO THE STARS, 1954
RIDIN' ON A RAINBOW, 1941
RIDING AVENGER, THE, 1936
RIDING HIGH, 1937
RIDING SHOTGUN, 1954
RIDING THE CHEROKEE TRAIL, 1941
RIGHT AGE TO MARRY, THE, 1935
RIGHT APPROACH, THE, 1961
RIGHT TO LIVE, THE, 1935
RIGHT TO ROMANCE, 1933
RIMFIRE, 1949
RING OF FEAR, 1954
RINGER, THE, 1953
RINGO AND HIS GOLDEN PISTOL, 1966
RINGS ON HER FINGERS, 1942
RINGSIDE MAISIE, 1941
RIO GRANDE, 1939
RIOT IN JUVENILE PRISON, 1959
RIOT SQUAD, 1941
RIPPED-OFF, 1971
RITA, 1963
RITUAL, THE, 1970
RIVALS, THE, 1963
RIVALS, 1972
RIVER BEAT, 1954
RIVER NIGER, THE, 1976
RIVER OF ROMANCE, 1929
RIVER WOMAN, THE, 1928
RIVERRUN, 1968
RIVERSIDE MURDER, THE, 1935
ROAD AGENT, 1941
ROAD AGENT, 1952
ROAD DEMON, 1938
ROAD GANG, 1936
ROAD HOME, THE, 1947
ROAD HOUSE, 1934
ROAD IS FINE, THE, 1930
ROAD TO ALCATRAZ, 1945
ROAD TO HONG KONG, THE, 1962
ROAD TO PARADISE, 1930
ROAD TO RENO, 1931
ROAD TO SHAME, THE, 1962
ROAMING COWBOY, THE, 1937
ROAR OF THE DRAGON, 1932
ROARIN' LEAD, 1937
ROARING TIMBER, 1937
ROBBERY UNDER ARMS, 1958
ROBIN HOOD OF THE PECOS, 1941
ROBIN HOOD OF THE RANGE, 1943
ROCCO PAPALEO, 1974
ROCK ALL NIGHT, 1957
ROCKABILLY BABY, 1957
ROCKABYE, 1932
ROCKIN' ROAD TRIP, 1986
ROCKY MOUNTAIN RANGERS, 1940
ROCKY RHODES, 1934
RODEO, 1952
RODEO KING AND THE SENORITA, 1951
ROGER TOUHY, GANGSTER!, 1944
ROGUE OF THE RIO GRANDE, 1930
ROGUES GALLERY, 1945
ROGUE'S MARCH, 1952
ROGUES OF SHERWOOD FOREST, 1950
ROGUES' REGIMENT, 1948
ROGUES' TAVERN, THE, 1936
ROGUE'S YARN, 1956
ROLLIN' HOME TO TEXAS, 1941
ROLLING DOWN THE GREAT DIVIDE, 1942
ROLLOVER, 1981
ROMANCE IN MANHATTAN, 1935
ROMANCE IN RHYTHM, 1934
ROMANCE IN THE RAIN, 1934
ROMANCE OF A HORSE THIEF, 1971
ROMANCE OF THE LIMBERLOST, 1938
ROMANCE OF THE RIO GRANDE, 1941
ROMANCE OF THE ROCKIES, 1938
ROMANCE ON THE RANGE, 1942
ROME ADVENTURE, 1962
ROMEO AND JULIET, 1955
ROOF, THE, 1933
ROOKIE COP, THE, 1939

ROOKIE FIREMAN, 1950
ROOKIES IN BURMA, 1943
ROOKIES ON PARADE, 1941
ROOM 43, 1959
ROOM IN THE HOUSE, 1955
ROOM TO LET, 1949
ROOMMATES, 1962
ROSARY MURDERS, THE, 1987
ROSE BOWL STORY, THE, 1952
ROSE OF THE YUKON, 1949
ROSEBUD BEACH HOTEL, 1984
ROSES ARE RED, 1947
ROSIE THE RIVETER, 1944
ROSSINI, 1948
ROTHSCHILD, 1938
ROUGH RIDERS OF CHEYENNE, 1945
ROUGH RIDERS OF DURANGO, 1951
ROUGH, TOUGH AND READY, 1945
ROUGH, TOUGH WEST, THE, 1952
ROUGHLY SPEAKING, 1945
ROYAL AFRICAN RIFLES, THE, 1953
ROYAL BED, THE, 1931
ROYAL DIVORCE, A, 1938
ROYAL EAGLE, 1936
ROYAL WALTZ, THE, 1936
RUBBER GUN, THE, 1977
RUBY GENTRY, 1952
RUGGED O'RIORDANS, THE, 1949
RULERS OF THE SEA, 1939
RUMBA, 1935
RUMBLE ON THE DOCKS, 1956
RUMPELSTILTSKIN, 1965
RUN, ANGEL, RUN, 1969
RUN FOR THE SUN, 1956
RUN HOME SLOW, 1965
RUNAROUND, THE, 1946
RUNAWAY DAUGHTERS, 1957
RUNAWAY GIRL, 1966
RUNAWAY LADIES, 1935
RUNAWAY QUEEN, THE, 1935
RUNAWAY RAILWAY, 1965
RUNNER STUMBLES, THE, 1979
RUNNING MAN, THE, 1987
RUSSIAN ROULETTE, 1975
RUSTLERS, 1949
RUSTLERS ON HORSEBACK, 1950
RUSTLER'S PARADISE, 1935
RUSTLERS' ROUNDUP, 1933
RUTHLESS FOUR, THE, 1969
RX MURDER, 1958
SABOTAGE, 1939
SACRIFICE OF HONOR, 1938
SADDLE LEGION, 1951
SADDLE MOUNTAIN ROUNDUP, 1941
SADDLE PALS, 1947
SADDLEMATES, 1941
SAFARI, 1956
SAFARI DRUMS, 1953
SAFARI 3000, 1982
SAFE AT HOME, 1962
SAFE IN HELL, 1931
SAFE PLACE, A, 1971
SAFETY IN NUMBERS, 1930
SAFETY IN NUMBERS, 1938
SAGA OF DEATH VALLEY, 1939
SAGA OF HEMP BROWN, THE, 1958
SAGEBRUSH TRAIL, 1934
SAGEBRUSH TROUBADOR, 1935
SAGINAW TRAIL, 1953
SAIL A CROOKED SHIP, 1961
SAIL INTO DANGER, 1957
SAILING ALONG, 1938
SAILOR BEWARE, 1951
SAILOR OF THE KING, 1953
SAILOR TAKES A WIFE, THE, 1946
SAILOR WHO FELL FROM GRACE WITH THE SEA, THE, 1976
SAILOR'S DON'T CARE, 1940
SAILOR'S HOLIDAY, 1944
SAILOR'S LADY, 1940
SAILOR'S LUCK, 1933
SAILORS ON LEAVE, 1941
ST. HELENS, 1981
ST. IVES, 1976
ST. LOUIS BLUES, 1958
SAINT MEETS THE TIGER, THE, 1943

SAINTED SISTERS, THE, 1948
SAINTS AND SINNERS, 1949
SALT & PEPPER, 1968
SALUTE FOR THREE, 1943
SALUTE THE TOFF, 1952
SAM SMALL LEAVES TOWN, 1937
SAME TO YOU, 1987
SAMSON AND THE SEVEN MIRACLES OF THE
    WORLD, 1963
SAMSON AND THE SLAVE QUEEN, 1963
SAMURAI (PART II), 1967
SAMURAI (PART III), 1967
SAN ANTONE, 1953
SAN ANTONE AMBUSH, 1949
SAN FERNANDO VALLEY, 1944
SAN FERRY ANN, 1965
SAN FRANCISCO DOCKS, 1941
SANDERS, 1963
SANDOKAN THE GREAT, 1964
SANDY IS A LADY, 1940
SANDY THE SEAL, 1969
SANGAREE, 1953
SANTA AND THE THREE BEARS, 1970
SANTA FE BOUND, 1937
SANTA FE MARSHAL, 1940
SANTA FE SADDLEMATES, 1945
SANTA FE SCOUTS, 1943
SANTA FE TRAIL, THE, 1930
SANTA FE UPRISING, 1946
SARONG GIRL, 1943
SATAN NEVER SLEEPS, 1962
SATAN'S CRADLE, 1949
SATURDAY NIGHT AT THE BATHS, 1975
SATURDAY NIGHT AT THE PALACE, 1988
SATURDAY NIGHT KID, THE, 1929
SATURDAY NIGHT OUT, 1964
SATURDAY NIGHT REVUE, 1937
SATURDAY'S HEROES, 1937
SAVAGE?, 1962
SAVAGE HORDE, THE, 1950
SAVAGE SAM, 1963
SAVAGE, THE, 1975
SAY IT IN FRENCH, 1938
SAY IT WITH FLOWERS, 1934
SCALPEL, 1976
SCANDAL, 1929
SCANDAL AT SCOURIE, 1953
SCANDAL FOR SALE, 1932
SCANDAL IN SORRENTO, 1957
SCANDAL STREET, 1938
SCANDALOUS, 1984
SCANDALOUS ADVENTURES OF BURAIKAN, THE,
    1970
SCANDALS OF PARIS, 1935
SCARECROW, THE, 1982
SCARECROWS, 1988
SCARED STIFF, 1945
SCARLET ANGEL, 1952
SCARLET HOUR, THE, 1956
SCARLET LETTER, THE, 1934
SCARLET THREAD, 1951
SCARLET WEB, THE, 1954
SCATTERBRAIN, 1940
SCATTERGOOD MEETS BROADWAY, 1941
SCATTERGOOD PULLS THE STRINGS, 1941
SCATTERGOOD RIDES HIGH, 1942
SCATTERGOOD SURVIVES A MURDER, 1942
SCAVENGERS, THE, 1959
SCENIC ROUTE, THE, 1978
SCHIZOID, 1980
SCHLAGER-PARADE, 1953
SCHLOCK, 1973
SCHOOL FOR BRIDES, 1952
SCHOOL FOR HUSBANDS, 1939
SCHOOL FOR RANDLE, 1949
SCHOOL FOR UNCLAIMED GIRLS, 1973
SCIENTIFIC CARDPLAYER, THE, 1972
SCOBIE MALONE, 1975
SCOTLAND YARD, 1930
SCOTLAND YARD, 1941
SCRAMBLE, 1970
SCRATCH HARRY, 1969
SCREAM BLACULA SCREAM, 1973
SCREAM IN THE DARK, A, 1943
SCREAMING EAGLES, 1956
SCREAMING SKULL, THE, 1958

SCREAMTIME, 1986
SCRUFFY, 1938
SEA CHASE, THE, 1955
SEA DEVILS, 1953
SEA GHOST, THE, 1931
SEA GOD, THE, 1930
SEA LEGS, 1930
SEA TIGER, 1952
SEA WIFE, 1957
SEALED LIPS, 1941
SEALED VERDICT, 1948
SEARCH FOR BRIDEY MURPHY, THE, 1956
SEASON FOR LOVE, THE, 1963
SEATED AT HIS RIGHT, 1968
SECOND BUREAU, 1936
SECOND BUREAU, 1937
SECOND CHANCE, 1947
SECOND CHOICE, 1930
SECOND FIDDLE, 1957
SECOND FIDDLE TO A STEEL GUITAR, 1965
SECOND FLOOR MYSTERY, THE, 1930
SECOND GREATEST SEX, THE, 1955
SECOND HONEYMOON, 1931
SECOND WIFE, 1930
SECOND WIND, 1976
SECOND WIND, A, 1978
SECRET AGENT FIREBALL, 1965
SECRET AGENT OF JAPAN, 1942
SECRET BRIGADE, THE, 1951
SECRET CALL, THE, 1931
SECRET DOOR, THE, 1964
SECRET ENEMIES, 1942
SECRET EVIDENCE, 1941
SECRET HONOR, 1984
SECRET MAN, THE, 1958
SECRET MARK OF D'ARTAGNAN, THE, 1963
SECRET MISSION, 1949
SECRET OF MAGIC ISLAND, THE, 1964
SECRET OF MONTE CRISTO, THE, 1961
SECRET OF STAMBOUL, THE, 1936
SECRET OF THE FOREST, THE, 1955
SECRET OF THE PURPLE REEF, THE, 1960
SECRET PARTNER, THE, 1961
SECRET PLACE, THE, 1958
SECRET SERVICE, 1931
SECRET SERVICE INVESTIGATOR, 1948
SECRET SEVEN, THE, 1940
SECRET VALLEY, 1937
SECRET WAYS, THE, 1961
SECRET, THE, 1955
SECRETS, 1933
SECRETS OF A SECRETARY, 1931
SECRETS OF A WOMAN'S TEMPLE, 1969
SECRETS OF MONTE CARLO, 1951
SECRETS OF SCOTLAND YARD, 1944
SECRETS OF THE UNDERGROUND, 1943
SECRETS OF THE WASTELANDS, 1941
SECURITY RISK, 1954
SEDUCED AND ABANDONED, 1964
SEDUCTION BY THE SEA, 1967
SEE AMERICA THIRST, 1930
SEE HOW THEY RUN, 1955
SEE MY LAWYER, 1945
SEED OF MAN, THE, 1970
SEEDS OF FREEDOM, 1943
SELL OUT, THE, 1976
SELLERS OF GIRLS, 1967
SELLOUT, THE, 1951
SEND FOR PAUL TEMPLE, 1946
SENIORS, THE, 1978
SENOR AMERICANO, 1929
SENORA CASADA NECEISITA MARIDO, 1935
SENORITA FROM THE WEST, 1945
SENSATION HUNTERS, 1934
SENSATIONS OF 1945, 1944
SENTIMENTAL BLOKE, 1932
SEPIA CINDERELLA, 1947
SEPTEMBER STORM, 1960
SERE CUALQUIER COSA PERO TE QUIERO, 1986
SERENA, 1962
SERGEANT BERRY, 1938
SERGEANT MIKE, 1945
SERGEANT WAS A LADY, THE, 1961
SERGEANTS 3, 1962
SERPENT OF THE NILE, 1953
SERPENT'S EGG, THE, 1977

SERVANTS' ENTRANCE, 1934
SET-UP, THE, 1963
SEVEN, 1979
SEVEN ALONE, 1975
SEVEN BRAVE MEN, 1936
SEVEN DAYS LEAVE, 1930
SEVEN DAYS LEAVE, 1942
SEVEN HILLS OF ROME, THE, 1958
SEVEN KEYS TO BALDPATE, 1930
SEVEN KEYS TO BALDPATE, 1947
SEVEN NIGHTS IN JAPAN, 1976
SEVEN SEAS TO CALAIS, 1963
SEVEN SLAVES AGAINST THE WORLD, 1965
SEVEN SWEETHEARTS, 1942
SEVEN TASKS OF ALI BABA, THE, 1963
1776, 1972
SEVENTH DAWN, THE, 1964
SEVENTH JUROR, THE, 1964
SEVENTY DEADLY PILLS, 1964
77 PARK LANE, 1931
70,000 WITNESSES, 1932
SEX APPEAL, 1986
SEXTON BLAKE AND THE MADEMOISELLE, 1935
SHADEY, 1987
SHADOW MAN, 1953
SHADOW OF A DOUBT, 1935
SHADOW OF A MAN, 1955
SHADOW OF A WOMAN, 1946
SHADOW OF EVIL, 1967
SHADOW OF FEAR, 1956
SHADOW OF MIKE EMERALD, THE, 1935
SHADOW OF SUSPICION, 1944
SHADOW OF TERROR, 1945
SHADOW OF THE CAT, THE, 1961
SHADOW OF THE PAST, 1950
SHADOW RANCH, 1930
SHADOW RETURNS, THE, 1946
SHADOWS IN THE NIGHT, 1944
SHADOWS OF THE WEST, 1949
SHADOWS ON THE SAGE, 1942
SHADOWS ON THE STAIRS, 1941
SHADOWS OVER CHINATOWN, 1946
SHADY LADY, THE, 1929
SHAFT IN AFRICA, 1973
SHAKE HANDS WITH MURDER, 1944
SHAKEDOWN, THE, 1929
SHALAKO, 1968
SHAMUS, 1959
SHAMUS, 1973
SHANGHAI, 1935
SHANGHAI LADY, 1929
SHANGHAI MADNESS, 1933
SHANGHAI STORY, THE, 1954
SHANGHAI SURPRISE, 1986
SHANGHAIED LOVE, 1931
SHANKS, 1974
SHANNONS OF BROADWAY, THE, 1929
SHANTYTOWN, 1943
SHARK RIVER, 1953
SHARK WOMAN, THE, 1941
SHE AND HE, 1969
SHE COULDN'T SAY NO, 1930
SHE COULDN'T SAY NO, 1939
SHE COULDN'T SAY NO, 1941
SHE COULDN'T TAKE IT, 1935
SHE GETS HER MAN, 1945
SHE GOT WHAT SHE WANTED, 1930
SHE HAD TO SAY YES, 1933
SHE KNEW ALL THE ANSWERS, 1941
SHE KNOWS Y'KNOW, 1962
SHE LEARNED ABOUT SAILORS, 1934
SHE LOVED A FIREMAN, 1937
SHE MARRIED A COP, 1939
SHE SHALL HAVE MUSIC, 1935
SHE WAS ONLY A VILLAGE MAIDEN, 1933
SHE-WOLF, THE, 1931
SHE-WOLF, THE, 1963
SHEEPDOG OF THE HILLS, 1941
SHEILA LEVINE IS DEAD AND LIVING IN NEW
    YORK, 1975
SHEP COMES HOME, 1949
SHEPHERD OF THE HILLS, THE, 1964
SHERIFF OF LAS VEGAS, 1944
SHERIFF OF REDWOOD VALLEY, 1946
SHERIFF OF SAGE VALLEY, 1942
SHERIFF OF SUNDOWN, 1944

SHERIFF OF TOMBSTONE, 1941
SHERLOCK HOLMES IN WASHINGTON, 1943
SHE'S A SOLDIER TOO, 1944
SHE'S A SWEETHEART, 1944
SHE'S BACK ON BROADWAY, 1953
SHE'S FOR ME, 1943
SHE'S HAVING A BABY, 1988
SHIELD OF FAITH, THE, 1956
SHINBONE ALLEY, 1971
SHINE ON, HARVEST MOON, 1944
SHINING VICTORY, 1941
SHIP AHOY, 1942
SHIP FROM SHANGHAI, THE, 1930
SHIP OF WANTED MEN, 1933
SHIPMATES, 1931
SHIPMATES O' MINE, 1936
SHIPS WITH WINGS, 1942
SHIPYARD SALLY, 1940
SHOCK, 1934
SHOCK, 1946
SHOCK TREATMENT, 1964
SHOCK TREATMENT, 1973
SHOCKING MISS PILGRIM, THE, 1947
SHOOT FIRST, LAUGH LAST, 1967
SHOOT FOR THE SUN, 1986
**SHOOT LOUD, LOUDER... I DON'T UNDERSTAND,
    1966**
SHOOT OUT, 1971
SHOOT OUT AT BIG SAG, 1962
SHOOT THE MOON, 1982
SHOOT THE WORKS, 1934
SHOOT TO KILL, 1961
SHOP ANGEL, 1932
SHOPWORN, 1932
SHOT IN THE DARK, A, 1935
SHOTGUN WEDDING, THE, 1963
SHOULD HUSBANDS WORK?, 1939
SHOULD LADIES BEHAVE?, 1933
SHOW BOAT, 1929
SHOW FOLKS, 1928
SHOW GIRL, 1928
SHOW GIRL IN HOLLYWOOD, 1930
SHOW GOES ON, THE, 1938
SHOW-OFF, THE, 1946
SHOWDOWN, 1963
SHRIKE, THE, 1955
SICILIAN, THE, 1987
SICILIANS, THE, 1964
SIDE SHOW, 1931
SIDE STREETS, 1934
SIDELONG GLANCES OF A PIGEON KICKER, THE,
    1970
SIDESHOW, 1950
SIDEWALKS OF NEW YORK, 1931
SIEGE OF SYRACUSE, 1962
SIERRA PASSAGE, 1951
SIGN OF AQUARIUS, 1970
SIGN OF THE RAM, THE, 1948
SIGN OF THE WOLF, 1941
SIGNALS-AN ADVENTURE IN SPACE, 1970
SILENCE OF THE NORTH, 1981
SILENCERS, THE, 1966
SILENT ASSASSINS, 1988
SILENT BARRIERS, 1937
SILENT INVASION, THE, 1962
SILENT NIGHT, BLOODY NIGHT, 1974
SILENT PARTNER, 1944
SILENT RAIDERS, 1954
SILENT WITNESS, THE, 1962
SILK EXPRESS, THE, 1933
SILKEN AFFAIR, THE, 1957
SILVER BEARS, 1978
SILVER CITY KID, 1944
SILVER DARLINGS, THE, 1947
SILVER LINING, 1932
SILVER QUEEN, 1942
SILVER RAIDERS, 1950
SILVER RIVER, 1948
SILVER SPURS, 1936
SILVER STREAK, THE, 1935
SILVERADO, 1985
SIN OF MONA KENT, THE, 1961
SIN ON THE BEACH, 1964
SIN TOWN, 1942
SINBAD AND THE EYE OF THE TIGER, 1977
SING A JINGLE, 1943

BOLD: Films on Videocassette

SING AND BE HAPPY, 1937
SING AND LIKE IT, 1934
SING AND SWING, 1964
SING ANOTHER CHORUS, 1941
SING AS YOU SWING, 1937
SING, BOY, SING, 1958
SING, DANCE, PLENTY HOT, 1940
SING FOR YOUR SUPPER, 1941
SING WHILE YOU DANCE, 1946
SING YOUR WORRIES AWAY, 1942
SINGAPORE, SINGAPORE, 1969
SINGAPORE WOMAN, 1941
SINGING BUCKAROO, THE, 1937
SINGING COP, THE, 1938
SINGING GUNS, 1950
SINGING HILL, THE, 1941
SINGING KID, THE, 1936
SINGING MARINE, THE, 1937
SINGING NUN, THE, 1966
SINGING SHERIFF, THE, 1944
SINGING THROUGH, 1935
SINGING VAGABOND, THE, 1935
SINISTER JOURNEY, 1948
SINNERS IN THE SUN, 1932
SINS OF JEZEBEL, 1953
SINS OF ROSE BERND, THE, 1959
SIS HOPKINS, 1941
SISTER-IN-LAW, THE, 1975
SISTER SISTER, 1988
SISTERS, 1930
SISTERS UNDER THE SKIN, 1934
SISTERS, THE, 1969
SITTING TARGET, 1972
SIX BLACK HORSES, 1962
SIX CYLINDER LOVE, 1931
SIX DAYS A WEEK, 1966
6.5 SPECIAL, 1958
SIX GUN GOSPEL, 1943
SIX-GUN RHYTHM, 1939
SIX GUN SERENADE, 1947
SIX PACK, 1982
SIX P.M., 1946
SIXTEEN FATHOMS DEEP, 1934
SIXTEEN FATHOMS DEEP, 1948
SKI PARTY, 1965
SKI PATROL, 1940
SKI TROOP ATTACK, 1960
SKID KIDS, 1953
SKIN GAME, THE, 1931
SKIN GAME, THE, 1965
SKIPPER SURPRISED HIS WIFE, THE, 1950
SKIRTS AHOY!, 1952
SKULLDUGGERY, 1970
SKY BANDITS, 1986
SKY BANDITS, THE, 1940
SKY BIKE, THE, 1967
SKY BRIDE, 1932
SKY DEVILS, 1932
SKY LINER, 1949
SKY PIRATE, THE, 1970
SKY RIDERS, 1976
SKY SPIDER, THE, 1931
SKYJACKED, 1972
SKYLINE, 1931
SLASHER, THE, 1953
SLAVE SHIP, 1937
SLAVES, 1969
SLEEPING CAR, 1933
SLEEPING CAR TO TRIESTE, 1949
SLIGHT CASE OF LARCENY, A, 1953
SLIGHTLY FRENCH, 1949
SLIGHTLY SCARLET, 1930
SLIPPER EPISODE, THE, 1938
SLIPPY MCGEE, 1948
SLOGAN, 1970
SMALL CIRCLE OF FRIENDS, A, 1980
SMALL HOTEL, 1957
SMALL TOWN DEB, 1941
SMART GIRL, 1935
SMART WOMAN, 1931
SMART WOMAN, 1948
SMARTEST GIRL IN TOWN, 1936
SMARTY, 1934
SMASHING THE RACKETS, 1938
SMASHING TIME, 1967
SMILE ORANGE, 1976

SMITHY, 1933
SMOKE SIGNAL, 1955
SMOKY, 1933
SMOKY, 1966
SMOKY CANYON, 1952
SMOKY MOUNTAIN MELODY, 1949
SMOOTH TALK, 1985
SMUGGLED CARGO, 1939
SMUGGLER'S GOLD, 1951
SMUGGLER'S ISLAND, 1951
SNAFU, 1945
SNAKE RIVER DESPERADOES, 1951
SNOW COUNTRY, 1969
SNOW DOG, 1950
SNOW IN THE SOUTH SEAS, 1963
SNOW WHITE, 1965
SNOW WHITE AND ROSE RED, 1966
SNOWBALL, 1960
SNOWBALL EXPRESS, 1972
SNOWBOUND, 1949
SNOWFIRE, 1958
SO BIG, 1932
SO EVIL SO YOUNG, 1961
SO LONG, BLUE BOY, 1973
SO LONG LETTY, 1929
SO THIS IS COLLEGE, 1929
SO YOU WON'T TALK?, 1935
SO YOU WON'T TALK, 1940
SOAK THE RICH, 1936
S.O.B., 1981
SOB SISTER, 1931
SOCIETY DOCTOR, 1935
SOCIETY GIRL, 1932
SOCIETY LAWYER, 1939
SOFI, 1967
SOFIA, 1948
SOGGY BOTTOM U.S.A., 1982
SOLDIER, SAILOR, 1944
SOLDIERS AND WOMEN, 1930
SOLDIER'S TALE, THE, 1964
SOLITAIRE MAN, THE, 1933
SOLO, 1970
SOLO, 1978
SOLO FOR SPARROW, 1966
SOLOMON AND SHEBA, 1959
SOMBRERO KID, THE, 1942
SOME DAY, 1935
SOME GIRLS DO, 1969
SOMEONE AT THE DOOR, 1950
SOMETHING ALWAYS HAPPENS, 1934
SOMETHING IN THE CITY, 1950
SOMETHING MONEY CAN'T BUY, 1952
SOMETHING TO HIDE, 1972
SOMETHING WILD, 1961
SOMEWHERE IN BERLIN, 1949
SOMEWHERE IN ENGLAND, 1940
SOMEWHERE IN FRANCE, 1943
SOMEWHERE IN POLITICS, 1949
SOMEWHERE IN SONORA, 1933
SON COMES HOME, A, 1936
SON OF A GUNFIGHTER, 1966
SON OF ALI BABA, 1952
SON OF BILLY THE KID, 1949
SON OF INDIA, 1931
SON OF MONGOLIA, 1936
SON OF MONTE CRISTO, 1940
SON OF OKLAHOMA, 1932
SON OF ROBIN HOOD, 1959
SON OF THE NAVY, 1940
SON OF THE RED CORSAIR, 1963
SONG AND DANCE MAN, THE, 1936
SONG AT EVENTIDE, 1934
SONG OF ARIZONA, 1946
SONG OF IDAHO, 1948
SONG OF INDIA, 1949
SONG OF LIFE, THE, 1931
SONG OF LOVE, THE, 1929
SONG OF MY HEART, 1947
SONG OF RUSSIA, 1943
SONG OF SCHEHERAZADE, 1947
SONG OF SURRENDER, 1949
SONG OF THE CABELLERO, 1930
SONG OF THE DRIFTER, 1948
SONG OF THE EAGLE, 1933
SONG OF THE FOREST, 1963

SONG OF THE FORGE, 1937
SONG OF THE GRINGO, 1936
SONG OF THE ISLANDS, 1942
SONG OF THE LOON, 1970
SONG OF THE OPEN ROAD, 1944
SONG OF THE SADDLE, 1936
SONG OF THE WEST, 1930
SONG OVER MOSCOW, 1964
SONNY BOY, 1929
SONORA STAGECOACH, 1944
SONS OF NEW MEXICO, 1949
SONS OF STEEL, 1935
SONS OF THE PIONEERS, 1942
SONS OF THE SADDLE, 1930
SONS OF THE SEA, 1939
SOOKY, 1931
SOPHOMORE, THE, 1929
SORRELL AND SON, 1934
S.O.S. PACIFIC, 1960
S.O.S. TIDAL WAVE, 1939
SO'S YOUR UNCLE, 1943
SOUL OF NIGGER CHARLEY, THE, 1973
SOUP FOR ONE, 1982
SOUTH AMERICAN GEORGE, 1941
SOUTH BRONX HEROES, 1985
SOUTH OF SANTA FE, 1932
SOUTH OF SANTA FE, 1942
SOUTH OF THE RIO GRANDE, 1932
SOUTH PACIFIC TRAIL, 1952
SOUTH SEA ROSE, 1929
SOUTHERN MAID, A, 1933
SOUTHERN STAR, THE, 1969
SOUTHWARD HO?, 1939
SOUTHWEST PASSAGE, 1954
SPACE CRUISER, 1977
SPACE FIREBIRD 2772, 1979
SPACE MASTER X-7, 1958
SPACE RAGE, 1987
SPACEBALLS, 1987
SPACECAMP, 1986
SPACEFLIGHT IC-1, 1965
SPACEHUNTER: ADVENTURES IN THE FORBIDDEN ZONE, 1983
SPACEWAYS, 1953
SPANISH CAPE MYSTERY, 1935
SPARE A COPPER, 1940
SPARE THE ROD, 1961
SPARKLE, 1976
SPARROWS CAN'T SING, 1963
SPECIAL AGENT, 1949
SPECIAL EDITION, 1938
SPEED, 1936
SPEED TO BURN, 1938
SPEED WINGS, 1934
SPEEDTRAP, 1978
SPEEDWAY, 1968
SPELL OF AMY NUGENT, THE, 1945
SPESSART INN, THE, 1961
SPICE OF LIFE, 1954
SPIDER WOMAN STRIKES BACK, THE, 1946
SPIDER, THE, 1945
SPIDER'S WEB, THE, 1960
SPIN A DARK WEB, 1956
SPINOUT, 1966
SPIRIT AND THE FLESH, THE, 1948
SPIRIT IS WILLING, THE, 1967
SPIRIT OF NOTRE DAME, THE, 1931
SPIRIT OF THE WIND, 1979
SPIRITISM, 1965
SPLENDOR, 1935
SPLINTERS IN THE NAVY, 1931
SPLIT DECISIONS, 1988
SPLITTING UP, 1981
SPOILERS OF THE PLAINS, 1951
SPOOK TOWN, 1944
SPORT PARADE, THE, 1932
SPORTING BLOOD, 1940
SPORTING CHANCE, A, 1945
SPORTING LOVE, 1936
SPOT OF BOTHER, A, 1938
SPRING AFFAIR, 1960
SPRING IS HERE, 1930
SPRING MADNESS, 1938
SPRINGTIME, 1948
SPRINGTIME ON THE VOLGA, 1961
SPURS, 1930

SPY CHASERS, 1956
SPY HUNT, 1950
SPY IN YOUR EYE, 1966
SPY OF NAPOLEON, 1939
SPY TRAIN, 1943
SPY WHO LOVED ME, THE, 1977
SPYLARKS, 1965
SQUAD CAR, 1961
SQUADRON LEADER X, 1943
SQUARE DANCE, 1987
SQUARE PEG, THE, 1958
SQUATTER'S DAUGHTER, 1933
SQUAW MAN, THE, 1931
SQUEAKER, THE, 1930
SQUEALER, THE, 1930
SQUEEZE, THE, 1977
SQUEEZE A FLOWER, 1970
SQUEEZE, THE, 1987
SQUIZZY TAYLOR, 1984
STAGE MOTHER, 1933
STAGE STRUCK, 1936
STAGE TO CHINO, 1940
STAGE TO TUCSON, 1950
STAGECOACH, 1966
STAGECOACH TO FURY, 1956
STAGECOACH TO MONTEREY, 1944
STAKEOUT!, 1962
STALLION CANYON, 1949
STALLION ROAD, 1947
STAMBOUL, 1931
STAMPEDE, 1949
STAR FELL FROM HEAVEN, A, 1936
STAR OF HONG KONG, 1962
STAR OF MY NIGHT, 1954
STAR OF TEXAS, 1953
STAR SLAMMER: THE ESCAPE, 1988
STARCHASER: THE LEGEND OF ORIN, 1985
STARHOPS, 1978
STARLIGHT OVER TEXAS, 1938
STARS ON PARADE, 1944
STARS OVER ARIZONA, 1937
STARS OVER BROADWAY, 1935
STARS OVER TEXAS, 1946
STARSHIP INVASIONS, 1978
STATE DEPARTMENT—FILE 649, 1949
STATE PENITENTIARY, 1950
STATE STREET SADIE, 1928
STATE TROOPER, 1933
STATION SIX-SAHARA, 1964
STAY HUNGRY, 1976
STEADY COMPANY, 1932
STEAMBOAT ROUND THE BEND, 1935
STEEL CAGE, THE, 1954
STEEL FIST, THE, 1952
STEEL KEY, THE, 1953
STEEL TOWN, 1952
STEELYARD BLUES, 1973
STEFANIA, 1968
STEP BY STEP, 1946
STEP DOWN TO TERROR, 1958
STEPPE, THE, 1963
STEPPENWOLF, 1974
STICK, 1985
STICK 'EM UP, 1950
STICK TO YOUR GUNS, 1941
STILL OF THE NIGHT, 1982
STINGAREE, 1934
STINGRAY, 1978
STOCK CAR, 1955
STOKER, THE, 1932
STOKER, THE, 1935
STOLEN AIRLINER, THE, 1962
STOLEN IDENTITY, 1953
STOLEN KISSES, 1929
STOLEN LIFE, 1939
STOLEN PLANS, THE, 1962
STOOGE, THE, 1952
STOP THE WORLD—I WANT TO GET OFF, 1966
STOP TRAIN 349, 1964
STOP, YOU'RE KILLING ME, 1952
STOP, LOOK, AND LOVE, 1939
STOPOVER FOREVER, 1964
STORIES FROM A FLYING TRUNK, 1979
STORK BITES MAN, 1947
STORK PAYS OFF, THE, 1941
STORK TALK, 1964

STORM CENTER, 1956
STORM IN A WATER GLASS, 1931
STORM OVER BENGAL, 1938
STORM OVER THE NILE, 1955
STORM OVER WYOMING, 1950
STORM RIDER, THE, 1957
STORMY, 1935
STORMY CROSSING, 1958
STORMY TRAILS, 1936
STORY OF DAVID, A, 1960
STORY OF MOLLY X, THE, 1949
STORY OF RUTH, THE, 1960
STORY OF SHIRLEY YORKE, THE, 1948
STORY ON PAGE ONE, THE, 1959
STOWAWAY, 1932
STOWAWAY IN THE SKY, 1962
STRAIGHT FROM THE HEART, 1935
STRAIGHT FROM THE SHOULDER, 1936
STRAIGHT ON TILL MORNING, 1974
STRAIGHT, PLACE AND SHOW, 1938
STRAIGHT TO HEAVEN, 1939
STRAIGHT TO THE HEART, 1988
STRANDED, 1935
STRANGE AFFAIR, 1944
STRANGE AFFAIR, THE, 1968
STRANGE ALIBI, 1941
STRANGE CARGO, 1929
STRANGE CASE OF DR. MEADE, 1939
STRANGE CONFESSION, 1945
STRANGE CONQUEST, 1946
STRANGE GAMBLE, 1948
STRANGE HOLIDAY, 1945
STRANGE ILLUSION, 1945
STRANGE IMPERSONATION, 1946
STRANGE INTRUDER, 1956
STRANGE MR. GREGORY, THE, 1945
STRANGE VENGEANCE OF ROSALIE, THE, 1972
STRANGE VOYAGE, 1945
STRANGER AT MY DOOR, 1950
STRANGER FROM PECOS, THE, 1943
STRANGER FROM TEXAS, THE, 1940
STRANGER IN TOWN, 1932
STRANGER IN TOWN, 1957
STRANGER IN TOWN, A, 1943
STRANGER IS WATCHING, A, 1982
STRANGER KNOCKS, A, 1963
STRANGER ON HORSEBACK, 1955
STRANGER RETURNS, THE, 1968
STRANGER'S RETURN, 1933
STRANGERS IN LOVE, 1932
STRANGERS OF THE EVENING, 1932
STRANGERS, THE, 1955
STRANGLEHOLD, 1931
STRANGLEHOLD, 1962
STRANGLER OF THE SWAMP, 1945
STRANGLERS OF BOMBAY, THE, 1960
STRAW MAN, THE, 1953
STRAWBERRY ROAN, 1933
STRAWBERRY STATEMENT, THE, 1970
STREAMLINE EXPRESS, 1935
STREET ANGEL, 1928
STREET BANDITS, 1951
STREET FIGHTER, 1959
STREET GIRL, 1929
STREET OF CHANCE, 1930
STREET OF MEMORIES, 1940
STREET OF MISSING MEN, 1939
STREET SINGER, THE, 1937
STREET TRASH, 1987
STREETS OF SAN FRANCISCO, 1949
STRICTLY FOR THE BIRDS, 1963
STRICTLY ILLEGAL, 1935
STRICTLY MODERN, 1930
STRIKE!, 1934
STRIKE IT RICH, 1948
STRIKEBOUND, 1984
STRIPPED TO KILL, 1987
STRIPPER, THE, 1963
STROMBOLI, 1950
STRONGER SEX, THE, 1931
STRONGER THAN THE SUN, 1980
STRONGHOLD, 1952
STRONGROOM, 1962
STUD, THE, 1979
STUDENT TEACHERS, THE, 1973
STUDENT TOUR, 1934

STUDY IN SCARLET, A, 1933
STUDY IN TERROR, A, 1966
STUFF, THE, 1985
STUNT PILOT, 1939
SUBMARINE D-1, 1937
SUBMARINE PATROL, 1938
SUBWAY, 1985
SUBWAY RIDERS, 1981
SUCCESS AT ANY PRICE, 1934
SUCH IS THE LAW, 1930
SUCH MEN ARE DANGEROUS, 1930
SUDDENLY, A WOMAN!, 1967
SUED FOR LIBEL, 1940
SUGAR HILL, 1974
SUICIDE FLEET, 1931
SUMMER, 1988
SUMMER CAMP NIGHTMARE, 1987
SUMMER HEAT, 1987
SUMMER LIGHTNING, 1933
SUMMER OF SECRETS, 1976
SUMMER PLACE, A, 1959
SUMMER RENTAL, 1985
SUMMER SCHOOL TEACHERS, 1977
SUMMER WISHES, WINTER DREAMS, 1973
SUMMERDOG, 1977
SUMMERTIME KILLER, 1973
SUMMERTREE, 1971
SUN COMES UP, THE, 1949
SUN SHINES BRIGHT, THE, 1953
SUNBURN, 1979
SUNDAY LOVERS, 1980
SUNDOWN KID, THE, 1942
SUNDOWN RIDERS, 1948
SUNDOWN SAUNDERS, 1937
SUNDOWN TRAIL, 1931
SUNDOWN VALLEY, 1944
SUNNY, 1941
SUNNY SIDE OF THE STREET, 1951
SUNSCORCHED, 1966
SUNSET ON THE DESERT, 1942
SUNSET PASS, 1946
SUNSET RANGE, 1935
SUNSET TRAIL, 1932
SUNSHINE AHEAD, 1936
SUPER SPOOK, 1975
SUPERARGO, 1968
SUPERARGO VERSUS DIABOLICUS, 1966
SUPERMAN AND THE MOLE MEN, 1951
SUPERMAN III, 1983
SUPERNATURALS, THE, 1987
SUPPOSE THEY GAVE A WAR AND NOBODY CAME?, 1970
SUPREME SECRET, THE, 1958
SURF NAZIS MUST DIE, 1987
SURGEON'S KNIFE, THE, 1957
SURPRISE PACKAGE, 1960
SURPRISE PARTY, 1985
SURRENDER—HELL!, 1959
SURVIVORS, THE, 1983
SUSAN SLEPT HERE, 1954
SUSIE STEPS OUT, 1946
SUSPENDED ALIBI, 1957
SUSPENSE, 1930
SUTTER'S GOLD, 1936
SVENGALI, 1955
SWAMP COUNTRY, 1966
SWAMP THING, 1982
SWEENEY, 1977
SWEEPSTAKE ANNIE, 1935
SWEEPSTAKES, 1931
SWEET COUNTRY, 1987
SWEET ECSTASY, 1962
SWEET HEART'S DANCE, 1988
SWEET HUNTERS, 1969
SWEET KITTY BELLAIRS, 1930
SWEET LOVE, BITTER, 1967
SWEET NOVEMBER, 1968
SWEET SKIN, 1965
SWEET SMELL OF LOVE, 1966
SWEET SUBSTITUTE, 1964
SWEETHEART OF SIGMA CHI, 1933
SWEETHEART OF SIGMA CHI, 1946
SWEETHEART OF THE FLEET, 1942
SWEETIE, 1929
SWELL GUY, 1946
SWELLHEAD, THE, 1930

BOLD: Films on Videocassette

SWING IN THE SADDLE, 1944
SWING OUT, SISTER, 1945
SWING OUT THE BLUES, 1943
SWING PARADE OF 1946, 1946
SWING SHIFT, 1984
SWING, SISTER, SWING, 1938
SWINGER'S PARADISE, 1965
SWINGIN' SUMMER, A, 1965
SWINGIN' MAIDEN, THE, 1963
SWINGING THE LEAD, 1934
SWISS MISS, 1938
SWITCHBLADE SISTERS, 1975
SWORD OF DOOM, THE, 1967
SWORD OF EL CID, THE, 1965
SWORD OF LANCELOT, 1963
SWORDSMAN OF SIENA, THE, 1962
SYMPHONY OF SIX MILLION, 1932
SYNCOPATION, 1942
SYNDICATE, THE, 1968
SYSTEM, THE, 1953
TAFFY AND THE JUNGLE HUNTER, 1965
TAGGART, 1964
TAHITI HONEY, 1943
TAHITI NIGHTS, 1945
TAIL SPIN, 1939
TAKE A CHANCE, 1937
TAKE A GIANT STEP, 1959
TAKE A GIRL LIKE YOU, 1970
TAKE A HARD RIDE, 1975
TAKE CARE OF MY LITTLE GIRL, 1951
TAKE IT BIG, 1944
TAKE IT OR LEAVE IT, 1944
TAKE ME HIGH, 1973
TAKE ME OVER, 1963
TAKE ME TO PARIS, 1951
TAKE ME TO TOWN, 1953
TAKE MY TIP, 1937
TAKE OFF THAT HAT, 1938
TAKE THE HEIR, 1930
TAKE THIS JOB AND SHOVE IT, 1981
TAKE, THE, 1974
TAKING TIGER MOUNTAIN, 1983
TALE OF FIVE WOMEN, A, 1951
TALENT SCOUT, 1937
TALES OF ORDINARY MADNESS, 1983
TALES OF THE THIRD DIMENSION, 1985
TALK ABOUT A STRANGER, 1952
TALK ABOUT JACQUELINE, 1942
TALK OF THE DEVIL, 1937
TALKING TO STRANGERS, 1988
TALKING WALLS, 1987
TALL MAN RIDING, 1955
TALL STRANGER, THE, 1957
TALL TARGET, THE, 1951
TALL TEXAN, THE, 1953
TALL WOMEN, THE, 1967
TAMAHINE, 1964
TAMING OF THE WEST, THE, 1939
TAMMY AND THE DOCTOR, 1963
TAMMY AND THE MILLIONAIRE, 1967
TAMMY, TELL ME TRUE, 1961
TANGA-TIKA, 1953
TANGANYIKA, 1954
TANGIER INCIDENT, 1953
TANGO BAR, 1935
TANK BATTALION, 1958
TANK COMMANDOS, 1959
TANK FORCE, 1958
TANKS A MILLION, 1941
TANKS ARE COMING, THE, 1951
TANNED LEGS, 1929
TARAS FAMILY, THE, 1946
TARGET, 1952
TARGET UNKNOWN, 1951
TARGET ZERO, 1955
TARNISHED, 1950
TARNISHED ANGEL, 1938
TARNISHED HEROES, 1961
TARNISHED LADY, 1931
TARS AND SPARS, 1946
TARZAN AND THE SLAVE GIRL, 1950
TARZAN AND THE VALLEY OF GOLD, 1966
TARZAN GOES TO INDIA, 1962
TARZAN THE FEARLESS, 1933
TARZAN'S DESERT MYSTERY, 1943
TARZAN'S HIDDEN JUNGLE, 1955

TARZAN'S MAGIC FOUNTAIN, 1949
TASTE FOR WOMEN, A, 1966
TASTE OF EXCITEMENT, 1969
TASTE OF MONEY, A, 1960
TAXI, 1953
TAXI FOR TOBRUK, 1965
TAXI FOR TWO, 1929
TAXI TO HEAVEN, 1944
TE QUIERO CON LOCURA, 1935
TEACHER, THE, 1974
TEENAGE CAVEMAN, 1958
TEENAGE DOLL, 1957
TEENAGE MILLIONAIRE, 1961
TEENAGE REBEL, 1956
TELEVISION TALENT, 1937
TELL IT TO A STAR, 1945
TELL ME IN THE SUNLIGHT, 1967
TELL ME LIES, 1968
TELL ME THAT YOU LOVE ME, JUNIE MOON, 1970
TELL NO TALES, 1939
TEMPEST, 1982
TEMPORARY WIDOW, THE, 1930
TEMPTATION, 1936
TEMPTATION, 1946
TEMPTATION HARBOR, 1949
TEMPTRESS AND THE MONK, THE, 1963
TEMPTRESS, THE, 1949
TEN CENTS A DANCE, 1931
TEN CENTS A DANCE, 1945
TEN GENTLEMEN FROM WEST POINT, 1942
TEN MINUTE ALIBI, 1935
TEN THOUSAND BEDROOMS, 1957
10 VIOLENT WOMEN, 1982
TEN WANTED MEN, 1955
TENCHU, 1970
TENDER COMRADE, 1943
TENDER HEARTS, 1955
TENDER SCOUNDREL, 1967
TENDER WARRIOR, THE, 1971
TENDER YEARS, THE, 1947
TENDERFOOT GOES WEST, A, 1937
TENDERLOIN, 1928
TENTH AVENUE KID, 1938
TENTH MAN, THE, 1937
TERMINAL ISLAND, 1973
TERMINAL MAN, THE, 1974
TERROR, THE, 1941
TERROR, THE, 1963
TERROR ABOARD, 1933
TERROR AFTER MIDNIGHT, 1965
TERROR BY NIGHT, 1946
TERROR FROM UNDER THE HOUSE, 1971
TERROR IS A MAN, 1959
TERROR OF DR. MABUSE, THE, 1965
TERROR SHIP, 1954
TERROR TRAIL, 1933
TERROR TRAIN, 1980
TERRORS ON HORSEBACK, 1946
TESHA, 1929
TESS OF THE STORM COUNTRY, 1961
TEST OF PILOT PIRX, THE, 1978
TEXANS NEVER CRY, 1951
TEXAS ACROSS THE RIVER, 1966
TEXAS BAD MAN, 1953
TEXAS, BROOKLYN AND HEAVEN, 1948
TEXAS CARNIVAL, 1951
TEXAS CYCLONE, 1932
TEXAS KID, THE, 1944
TEXAS LADY, 1955
TEXAS LAWMEN, 1951
TEXAS LIGHTNING, 1981
TEXAS MAN HUNT, 1942
TEXAS MARSHAL, THE, 1941
TEXAS PIONEERS, 1932
TEXAS STAMPEDE, 1939
TEXAS TORNADO, 1934
TEXAS TRAIL, 1937
TEXAS WILDCATS, 1939
THANK YOU, JEEVES, 1936
THANKS FOR THE MEMORY, 1938
THANOS AND DESPINA, 1970
THAT CERTAIN SOMETHING, 1941
THAT CHAMPIONSHIP SEASON, 1982
THAT COLD DAY IN THE PARK, 1969
THAT FUNNY FEELING, 1965
THAT I MAY LIVE, 1937

THAT KIND OF WOMAN, 1959
THAT LADY, 1955
THAT MAN FROM TANGIER, 1953
THAT MAN GEORGE, 1967
THAT MAN IN ISTANBUL, 1966
THAT NIGHT WITH YOU, 1945
THAT OTHER WOMAN, 1942
THAT RIVIERA TOUCH, 1968
THAT SUMMER, 1979
THAT WAY WITH WOMEN, 1947
THAT WOMAN, 1968
THAT'S THE WAY OF THE WORLD, 1975
THAT'S MY BOY, 1951
THAT'S MY MAN, 1947
THAT'S RIGHT—YOU'RE WRONG, 1939
THEATRE OF DEATH, 1967
THEIR NIGHT OUT, 1933
THEM NICE AMERICANS, 1958
THERE GOES MY GIRL, 1937
THERE GOES THE GROOM, 1937
THERE IS NO 13, 1977
THERE WAS A YOUNG LADY, 1953
THERE'S A GIRL IN MY HEART, 1949
THERE'S MAGIC IN MUSIC, 1941
THERE'S THAT WOMAN AGAIN, 1938
THERESE AND ISABELLE, 1968
THESE GLAMOUR GIRLS, 1939
THESE THIRTY YEARS, 1934
THEY CALL ME TRINITY, 1971
THEY CAN'T HANG ME, 1955
THEY GOT ME COVERED, 1943
THEY LEARNED ABOUT WOMEN, 1930
THEY LIVE IN FEAR, 1944
THEY MADE HER A SPY, 1939
THEY MET IN A TAXI, 1936
THEY MET IN THE DARK, 1945
THEY RODE WEST, 1954
THEY SHALL HAVE MUSIC, 1939
THEY WANTED TO MARRY, 1937
THEY WERE NOT DIVIDED, 1951
THEY WERE SO YOUNG, 1955
THEY WERE TEN, 1961
THIEF OF BAGHDAD, THE, 1961
THIEF WHO CAME TO DINNER, THE, 1973
THING, THE, 1982
THING WITH TWO HEADS, THE, 1972
THIRD ALARM, THE, 1930
THIRD FINGER, LEFT HAND, 1940
THIRD OF A MAN, 1962
THIRD TIME LUCKY, 1950
THIRD WALKER, THE, 1978
THIRST, 1979
THIRTEEN FIGHTING MEN, 1960
THIRTEEN WEST STREET, 1962
THIRTEEN WOMEN, 1932
THIRTEENTH CHAIR, THE, 1930
THIRTEENTH CHAIR, THE, 1937
THIRTEENTH MAN, THE, 1937
THIRTY FOOT BRIDE OF CANDY ROCK, THE, 1959
THIRTY NINE STEPS, THE, 1960
THIS ANGRY AGE, 1958
THIS EARTH IS MINE, 1959
THIS IS HEAVEN, 1929
THIS MAD WORLD, 1930
THIS MAN CAN'T DIE, 1970
THIS MARRIAGE BUSINESS, 1938
THIS OTHER EDEN, 1959
THIS SIDE OF THE LAW, 1950
THIS THING CALLED LOVE, 1929
THIS TIME FOR KEEPS, 1947
THIS WAS A WOMAN, 1949
THIS WAS PARIS, 1942
THIS WAY PLEASE, 1937
THIS'LL MAKE YOU WHISTLE, 1938
THOROUGHBRED, THE, 1930
THOROUGHBREDS, 1945
THOSE ENDEARING YOUNG CHARMS, 1945
THOSE FANTASTIC FLYING FOOLS, 1967
THOSE KIDS FROM TOWN, 1942
THOSE WHO DANCE, 1930
THREAT, THE, 1960
THREE CARD MONTE, 1978
THREE CROOKED MEN, 1958
THREE DAYS OF VIKTOR TSCHERNIKOFF, 1968
THREE DESPERATE MEN, 1951
THREE FABLES OF LOVE, 1963

THREE FACES OF A WOMAN, 1965
3:15, THE MOMENT OF TRUTH, 1986
THREE FOR JAMIE DAWN, 1956
THREE GIRLS ABOUT TOWN, 1941
THREE IN THE SADDLE, 1945
THREE KIDS AND A QUEEN, 1935
THREE MARRIED MEN, 1936
THREE MEN IN A BOAT, 1958
THREE MEN TO DESTROY, 1980
THREE O'CLOCK HIGH, 1987
THREE OF A KIND, 1936
THREE ON THE TRAIL, 1936
THREE OUTLAWS, THE, 1956
THREE PENNY OPERA, 1963
THREE RING CIRCUS, 1954
THREE ROGUES, 1931
THREE SAILORS AND A GIRL, 1953
THREE SILENT MEN, 1940
THREE SISTERS, THE, 1930
THREE SISTERS, THE, 1969
THREE SISTERS, THE, 1977
THREE SONS O'GUNS, 1941
THREE STRIPES IN THE SUN, 1955
THREE TALES OF CHEKHOV, 1961
THREE TOUGH GUYS, 1974
THREE WARRIORS, 1977
THREE WEIRD SISTERS, THE, 1948
THREE WISE FOOLS, 1946
THREE WISE GIRLS, 1932
THREE YOUNG TEXANS, 1954
THRILL HUNTER, THE, 1933
THRILL OF A LIFETIME, 1937
THRILL OF BRAZIL, THE, 1946
THROWBACK, THE, 1935
THRU DIFFERENT EYES, 1929
THRU DIFFERENT EYES, 1942
THUMB TRIPPING, 1972
THUMBS UP, 1943
THUNDER AT THE BORDER, 1966
THUNDER IN GOD'S COUNTRY, 1951
THUNDER IN THE BLOOD, 1962
THUNDER IN THE DESERT, 1938
THUNDER IN THE PINES, 1949
THUNDER ISLAND, 1963
THUNDER MOUNTAIN, 1947
THUNDER OVER ARIZONA, 1956
THUNDER OVER SANGOLAND, 1955
THUNDER OVER TEXAS, 1934
THUNDER OVER THE PRAIRIE, 1941
THUNDER PASS, 1954
THUNDER WARRIOR, 1986
THUNDERBIRD 6, 1968
THUNDERING CARAVANS, 1952
THUNDERING TRAILS, 1943
THUNDERING WEST, THE, 1939
THUNDERSTORM, 1934
THUNDERSTORM, 1956
THURSDAY'S CHILD, 1943
TI-CUL TOUGAS, 1977
TICKLE ME, 1965
TICKLISH AFFAIR, A, 1963
TIFFANY JONES, 1976
TIGER BY THE TAIL, 1970
TIGER GIRL, 1955
TIGER MAKES OUT, THE, 1967
TIGER OF THE SEVEN SEAS, 1964
TIGER ROSE, 1930
TIGER WALKS, A, 1964
TIGER'S TALE, A, 1988
TIGHT SKIRTS, LOOSE PLEASURES, 1966
TILL MARRIAGE DO US PART, 1979
TILL WE MEET AGAIN, 1944
TILLY OF BLOOMSBURY, 1931
TILT, 1979
TIM DRISCOLL'S DONKEY, 1955
TIMBER, 1942
TIMBER STAMPEDE, 1939
TIMBER TRAIL, THE, 1948
TIMBUCTOO, 1933
TIMBUKTU, 1959
TIME FLIES, 1944
TIME FOR LOVING, A, 1971
TIME IS MY ENEMY, 1957
TIME LOCK, 1959
TIME OF HIS LIFE, THE, 1955
TIME OF INDIFFERENCE, 1965

TIME OUT FOR ROMANCE, 1937
TIME, THE PLACE AND THE GIRL, THE, 1929
TIME, THE PLACE AND THE GIRL, THE, 1946
TIME TO DIE, A, 1983
TIME TO KILL, 1942
TIME TO KILL, A, 1955
TIMES SQUARE, 1929
TIMES SQUARE LADY, 1935
TIMES TO COME, 1988
TIN GIRL, THE, 1970
TIN MAN, 1983
TIP-OFF, THE, 1931
TO BEGIN AGAIN, 1982
TO COMMIT A MURDER, 1970
TO FIND A MAN, 1972
TO HAVE AND TO HOLD, 1951
TO KILL A CLOWN, 1972
TO MARY—WITH LOVE, 1936
TO THE DEVIL A DAUGHTER, 1976
TO THE LAST MAN, 1933
TO THE SHORES OF HELL, 1966
TO THE VICTOR, 1948
TO WHAT RED HELL, 1929
TOBOR THE GREAT, 1954
TOBY MCTEAGUE, 1986
TODAY I HANG, 1942
TOKYO AFTER DARK, 1959
TOKYO ROSE, 1945
TOL'ABLE DAVID, 1930
TOM BROWN'S SCHOOL DAYS, 1940
TOM BROWN'S SCHOOLDAYS, 1951
TOMAHAWK, 1951
TOMAHAWK TRAIL, 1957
TOMB OF LIGEIA, THE, 1965
TOMBOY, 1940
TOMMY THE TOREADOR, 1960
TOMORROW AT SEVEN, 1933
TOMORROW IS ANOTHER DAY, 1951
TOMORROW IS FOREVER, 1946
TOMORROW IS MY TURN, 1962
TONIGHT A TOWN DIES, 1961
TONIGHT AT TWELVE, 1929
TONIGHT IS OURS, 1933
TONIGHT OR NEVER, 1931
TONIGHT'S THE NIGHT, 1932
TONIGHT'S THE NIGHT, 1954
TONTO BASIN OUTLAWS, 1941
TOO BAD SHE'S BAD, 1954
TOO BUSY TO WORK, 1939
TOO DANGEROUS TO LIVE, 1939
TOO MANY MILLIONS, 1934
TOO MANY THIEVES, 1968
TOO MANY WINNERS, 1947
TOO MANY WIVES, 1943
TOO MUCH HARMONY, 1933
TOO MUCH, TOO SOON, 1958
TOO SCARED TO SCREAM, 1985
TOO SOON TO LOVE, 1960
TOO YOUNG TO KISS, 1951
TOO YOUNG TO KNOW, 1945
TOP GUN, 1986
TOP MAN, 1943
TOP O' THE MORNING, 1949
TOP OF THE FORM, 1953
TOP OF THE TOWN, 1937
TOP OF THE WORLD, 1955
TOP SERGEANT, 1942
TOPAZE, 1935
TOPEKA TERROR, THE, 1945
TOPSY-TURVY JOURNEY, 1970
TORCH SINGER, 1933
TORCH, THE, 1950
TORCHY BLANE IN PANAMA, 1938
TORCHY GETS HER MAN, 1938
TORCHY PLAYS WITH DYNAMITE, 1939
TORCHY RUNS FOR MAYOR, 1939
TORNADO, 1943
TORNADO RANGE, 1948
TORPEDO BAY, 1964
TORPEDOED, 1939
TOUCH ME NOT, 1974
TOUCH OF FLESH, THE, 1960
TOUCHDOWN, ARMY, 1938
TOUCHED, 1983
TOUGH GUYS, 1986
TOUGHEST MAN ALIVE, 1955

TOUGHEST MAN IN ARIZONA, 1952
TOWER OF LONDON, 1962
TOWERING INFERNO, THE, 1974
TOWN TAMER, 1965
TOXI, 1952
TOY TIGER, 1956
TOY WIFE, THE, 1938
TRACK THE MAN DOWN, 1956
TRACK 29, 1988
TRADING HEARTS, 1988
TRAFFIC IN CRIME, 1946
TRAGEDY AT MIDNIGHT, A, 1942
TRAIL BEYOND, THE, 1934
TRAIL BLAZERS, THE, 1940
TRAIL DRIVE, THE, 1934
TRAIL DUST, 1936
TRAIL OF KIT CARSON, 1945
TRAIL OF TERROR, 1935
TRAIL OF TERROR, 1944
TRAIL OF THE VIGILANTES, 1940
TRAIL OF VENGEANCE, 1937
TRAIL TO GUNSIGHT, 1944
TRAIL TO SAN ANTONE, 1947
TRAIL TO VENGEANCE, 1945
TRAIN GOES TO KIEV, THE, 1961
TRAIN ROBBERY CONFIDENTIAL, 1965
TRAIN TO ALCATRAZ, 1948
TRAITOR'S GATE, 1966
TRAMP, TRAMP, TRAMP, 1942
TRANSGRESSION, 1931
TRANSIENT LADY, 1935
TRANSPORT FROM PARADISE, 1967
TRAP, THE, 1967
TRAP DOOR, THE, 1980
TRAP, THE, 1947
TRAPPED, 1949
TRAPPED BY BOSTON BLACKIE, 1948
TRAPPED IN THE SKY, 1939 61m COL bw
TRAVELING SALESWOMAN, 1950
TRAVELLER'S JOY, 1951
TREACHERY ON THE HIGH SEAS, 1939
TREAD SOFTLY STRANGER, 1959
TREASURE HUNT, 1952
TREASURE OF MAKUBA, THE, 1967
TREASURE OF MONTE CRISTO, 1949
TREASURE OF PANCHO VILLA, THE, 1955
TREASURE OF THE YANKEE ZEPHYR, 1984
TRENT'S LAST CASE, 1953
TRESPASSER, THE, 1947
TRIAL OF LEE HARVEY OSWALD, THE, 1964
TRIAL OF MARY DUGAN, THE, 1941
TRIAL OF VIVIENNE WARE, THE, 1932
TRIBES, 1970
TRICK OR TREAT, 1986
TRICK OR TREATS, 1982
TRIGGER TRAIL, 1944
TRIGGER, JR., 1950
TRINITY IS STILL MY NAME, 1971
TRIP TO PARIS, A, 1938
TRIPLE DECEPTION, 1957
TRIPLE ECHO, THE, 1973
TRIPLE JUSTICE, 1940
TROCADERO, 1944
TROJAN WOMEN, THE, 1971
TROOPERS THREE, 1930
TROOPSHIP, 1938
TROPIC HOLIDAY, 1938
TROUBLE, 1933
TROUBLE FOR TWO, 1936
TROUBLE IN MIND, 1985
TROUBLE IN MOROCCO, 1937
TROUBLE IN THE GLEN, 1954
TROUBLE IN THE SKY, 1961
TROUBLE WITH WOMEN, THE, 1947
TROUBLESOME DOUBLE, THE, 1971
TROUT, THE, 1982
TRUCK BUSTERS, 1943
TRUCK STOP WOMEN, 1974
TRUE TO THE ARMY, 1942
TRUMPET BLOWS, THE, 1934
TRUNK TO CAIRO, 1966
TRUST THE NAVY, 1935
TRUSTED OUTLAW, THE, 1937
TRUTH ABOUT MURDER, THE, 1946
TRUTH ABOUT WOMEN, THE, 1958
TRUTH, THE, 1961

BOLD: Films on Videocassette

TRYGON FACTOR, THE, 1969
TUGBOAT ANNIE SAILS AGAIN, 1940
TULSA KID, THE, 1940
TUMBLEWEED, 1953
TUMBLEWEED TRAIL, 1946
TUNNEL TO THE SUN, 1968
TURN OF THE TIDE, 1935
TURN OFF THE MOON, 1937
TURN THE KEY SOFTLY, 1954
TURNABOUT, 1940
TURNERS OF PROSPECT ROAD, THE, 1947
TUXEDO JUNCTION, 1941
TWELVE GOOD MEN, 1936
TWELVE PLUS ONE, 1970
25TH HOUR, THE, 1967
20 MILLION MILES TO EARTH, 1957
TWENTY QUESTIONS MURDER MYSTERY, THE, 1950
20,000 EYES, 1961
20,000 MEN A YEAR, 1939
23 1/2 HOURS LEAVE, 1937
TWICE A MAN, 1964
TWICE BRANDED, 1936
TWILIGHT FOR THE GODS, 1958
TWILIGHT ON THE PRAIRIE, 1944
TWILIGHT ON THE TRAIL, 1941
TWILIGHT ZONE—THE MOVIE, 1983
TWIN BEDS, 1942
TWIN HUSBANDS, 1934
TWINS, 1988
TWINS OF EVIL, 1971
TWIST AROUND THE CLOCK, 1961
TWIST, THE, 1976
TWISTED NERVE, 1969
TWO AGAINST THE WORLD, 1936
TWO AND ONE TWO, 1934
TWO AND TWO MAKE SIX, 1962
TWO ARE GUILTY, 1964
TWO BLONDES AND A REDHEAD, 1947
TWO-FACED WOMAN, 1941
TWO FISTED, 1935
TWO-FISTED LAW, 1932
TWO-FISTED RANGERS, 1940
TWO FOR DANGER, 1940
TWO FOR THE SEESAW, 1962
TWO GALS AND A GUY, 1951
TWO GENTLEMEN SHARING, 1969
TWO-GUN JUSTICE, 1938
TWO GUN MAN, THE, 1931
TWO-GUN TROUBADOR, 1939
TWO GUNS AND A BADGE, 1954
TWO HEARTS IN HARMONY, 1935
TWO HEARTS IN WALTZ TIME, 1934
TWO IN A SLEEPING BAG, 1964
TWO LEFT FEET, 1965
TWO-MAN SUBMARINE, 1944
TWO O'CLOCK COURAGE, 1945
TWO OF A KIND, 1951
TWO OF US, THE, 1938
TWO ON A GUILLOTINE, 1965
TWO SECONDS, 1932
TWO SMART PEOPLE, 1946
TWO SOLITUDES, 1978
TWO THOROUGHBREDS, 1939
2,000 WOMEN, 1944
TWO TICKETS TO LONDON, 1943
TWO WEEKS IN ANOTHER TOWN, 1962
TWO WEEKS TO LIVE, 1943
TWO WHO DARED, 1937
TWO WISE MAIDS, 1937
TWO WIVES AT ONE WEDDING, 1961
TWO WORLD, 1930
TWO YANKS IN TRINIDAD, 1942
TWO'S COMPANY, 1939
TYCOON, 1947
TYRANT OF THE SEA, 1950
UGLY DACHSHUND, THE, 1966
UGLY DUCKLING, THE, 1959
ULTIMATUM, 1940
UMBRELLA, THE, 1933
UN HOMBRE VIOLENTE, 1986
UNCANNY, THE, 1977
UNCHAINED, 1955
UNCIVILISED, 1937
UNCLE VANYA, 1958
UNCLE VANYA, 1977

UNCOMMON THIEF, AN, 1967
UNCOMMON VALOR, 1983
UNDEAD, THE, 1957
UNDEFEATED, THE, 1969
UNDER A TEXAS MOON, 1930
UNDER ARIZONA SKIES, 1946
UNDER CAPRICORN, 1949
UNDER-COVER MAN, 1932
UNDER COVER OF NIGHT, 1937
UNDER FIESTA STARS, 1941
UNDER FIRE, 1957
UNDER SECRET ORDERS, 1943
UNDER STRANGE FLAGS, 1937
UNDER SUSPICION, 1937
UNDER TEXAS SKIES, 1931
UNDER THE GREENWOOD TREE, 1930
UNDER YOUR HAT, 1940
UNDERCOVER AGENT, 1939
UNDERCOVER AGENT, 1935
UNDERCOVER DOCTOR, 1939
UNDERCOVER GIRL, 1950
UNDERCOVER MAISIE, 1947
UNDERCOVER MAN, 1936
UNDERCOVER WOMAN, THE, 1946
UNDERDOG, THE, 1943
UNDERGROUND GUERRILLAS, 1944
UNDERGROUND RUSTLERS, 1941
UNDERGROUND U.S.A., 1980
UNDERNEATH THE ARCHES, 1937
UNDERWATER!, 1955
UNDERWATER WARRIOR, 1958
UNDERWORLD, 1937
UNDERWORLD INFORMERS, 1965
UNDYING MONSTER, THE, 1942
UNEASY VIRTUE, 1931
UNEXPECTED FATHER, 1939
UNFAITHFULLY YOURS, 1984
UNFAITHFULS, THE, 1960
UNFINISHED BUSINESS, 1941
UNFINISHED DANCE, THE, 1947
UNHOLY FOUR, THE, 1954
UNHOLY NIGHT, THE, 1929
UNHOLY ROLLERS, 1972
UNION CITY, 1980
UNKNOWN GUEST, THE, 1943
UNKNOWN RANGER, THE, 1936
UNKNOWN VALLEY, 1933
UNKNOWN WOMAN, 1935
UNKNOWN, THE, 1946
UNMARRIED, 1939
UNMASKED, 1929
UNMASKED, 1950
UNPUBLISHED STORY, 1942
UNTAMED, 1929
UNTAMED FURY, 1947
UNTOUCHABLES, THE, 1987
UNWELCOME STRANGER, 1935
UNWILLING AGENT, 1968
UP FOR MURDER, 1931
UP FOR THE CUP, 1931
UP FOR THE DERBY, 1933
UP GOES MAISIE, 1946
UP IN CENTRAL PARK, 1948
UP IN THE AIR, 1940
UP IN THE WORLD, 1957
UP JUMPED A SWAGMAN, 1965
UP POMPEII, 1971
UP POPS THE DEVIL, 1931
UP THE JUNCTION, 1968
UP THE MACGREGORS, 1967
UP THE SANDBOX, 1972
UP TO HIS NECK, 1954
UPPER HAND, THE, 1967
UPSTAIRS AND DOWNSTAIRS, 1961
UPTIGHT, 1968
UPTURNED GLASS, THE, 1947
UPTOWN NEW YORK, 1932
URBAN COWBOY, 1980
URGE TO KILL, 1960
UTAH BLAINE, 1957
UTAH KID, THE, 1930
UTAH TRAIL, 1938
UTAH WAGON TRAIN, 1951
UTILITIES, 1983
VACATION FROM LOVE, 1938
VACATION IN RENO, 1946

VAGABOND LOVER, 1929
VAGABOND QUEEN, THE, 1931
VALENTINO, 1951
VALERIE, 1957
VALIANT HOMBRE THE, 1948
VALIANT IS THE WORD FOR CARRIE, 1936
VALLEY OF FIRE, 1951
VALLEY OF MYSTERY, 1967
VALLEY OF THE GIANTS, 1938
VALLEY OF THE KINGS, 1954
VALLEY OF THE LAWLESS, 1936
VALLEY OF THE REDWOODS, 1960
VALLEY OF THE SUN, 1942
VAMP, 1986
VAN NUYS BLVD., 1979
VANESSA, HER LOVE STORY, 1935
VANISHING AMERICAN, THE, 1955
VANISHING FRONTIER, THE, 1932
VANISHING OUTPOST, THE, 1951
VANISHING VIRGINIAN, THE, 1941
VANITY, 1935
VARIETY JUBILEE, 1945
VARIETY PARADE, 1936
VEILED WOMAN, THE, 1929
VEILS OF BAGDAD, THE, 1953
VENDETTA, 1986
VENETIAN AFFAIR, THE, 1967
VENGEANCE, 1968
VENGEANCE VALLEY, 1951
VERDICT, 1975
VERDICT, THE, 1964
VERGINITA, 1953
VERMILION DOOR, 1969
VERY CURIOUS GIRL, A, 1970
VERY EDGE, THE, 1963
VERY HANDY MAN, A, 1966
VERY HONORABLE GUY, A, 1934
VERY PRIVATE AFFAIR, A, 1962
VERY SPECIAL FAVOR, A, 1965
VERY YOUNG LADY, A, 1941
VICAR OF BRAY, THE, 1937
VICE RAID, 1959
VICE SQUAD, 1953
VICIOUS YEARS, THE, 1950
VICTORY, 1940
VICTORY, 1981
VIDEO DEAD, 1987
VIEW TO A KILL, A, 1985
VIGIL IN THE NIGHT, 1940
VIGILANTE FORCE, 1976
VIGILANTE HIDEOUT, 1950
VIGILANTE TERROR, 1953
VIGILANTES OF BOOMTOWN, 1947
VIGILANTES OF DODGE CITY, 1944
VIGILANTES RETURN, THE, 1947
VIKING QUEEN, THE, 1967
VILLA!, 1958
VILLA RIDES, 1968
VILLAGE, THE, 1953
VILLAGE BARN DANCE, 1940
VINTAGE WINE, 1935
VIOLATED LOVE, 1966
VIOLENCE, 1947
VIOLENT AND THE DAMNED, THE, 1962
VIOLENT FOUR, THE, 1968
VIOLENT ROAD, 1958
VIOLENT WOMEN, 1960
VIOLETS ARE BLUE, 1986
VIRGIN ISLAND, 1960
VIRGINIA JUDGE, THE, 1935
VIRGINIA'S HUSBAND, 1934
VIRTUOUS HUSBAND, 1931
VIRTUOUS SIN, THE, 1930
VISION QUEST, 1985
VISIT TO A SMALL PLANET, 1960
VISITORS, THE, 1972
VIVA LAS VEGAS, 1964
VIXEN, 1970
VOICE IN THE NIGHT, A, 1941
VOICE OF BUGLE ANN, 1936
VOICE OF THE CITY, 1929
VOICES, 1979
VOLTAIRE, 1933
VON RICHTHOFEN AND BROWN, 1970
VOR SONNENUNTERGANG, 1961
VOTE FOR HUGGETT, 1948

VOW, THE, 1947
VOYAGE TO THE BOTTOM OF THE SEA, 1961
VULTURE, THE, 1937
"W" PLAN, THE, 1931
WAC FROM WALLA WALLA, THE, 1952
WACO, 1966
WAGON WHEELS, 1934
WAGON WHEELS WESTWARD, 1956
WAGONS WEST, 1952
WAGONS WESTWARD, 1940
WAIT FOR ME IN HEAVEN, 1988
WAITING FOR CAROLINE, 1969
WAKAMBA?, 1955
WAKE UP AND DREAM, 1934
WAKE UP AND DREAM, 1946
WAKE UP FAMOUS, 1937
WALK A TIGHTROPE, 1964
WALK IN THE SPRING RAIN, A, 1970
WALK LIKE A DRAGON, 1960
WALK PROUD, 1979
WALK TALL, 1960
WALK THE DARK STREET, 1956
WALK WITH LOVE AND DEATH, A, 1969
WALKING DOWN BROADWAY, 1938
WALKING MY BABY BACK HOME, 1953
WALKING TARGET, THE, 1960
WALL STREET, 1929
WALLABY JIM OF THE ISLANDS, 1937
WALLET, THE, 1952
WALLS CAME TUMBLING DOWN, THE, 1946
WALLS OF HELL, THE, 1964
WALTZ ACROSS TEXAS, 1982
WALTZ TIME, 1933
WANDERER OF THE WASTELAND, 1945
WANDERERS OF THE WEST, 1941
WANTED BY SCOTLAND YARD, 1939
WANTED FOR MURDER, 1946
WANTED: JANE TURNER, 1936
WAR AND PEACE, 1983
WAR CORRESPONDENT, 1932
WAR DOGS, 1942
WAR IS HELL, 1964
WAR ITALIAN STYLE, 1967
WAR OF THE MONSTERS, 1972
WAR OF THE ZOMBIES, THE, 1965
WAR PARTY, 1965
WARLORDS OF ATLANTIS, 1978
WARM CORNER, A, 1930
WARM DECEMBER, A, 1973
WARM NIGHTS ON A SLOW MOVING TRAIN, 1987
WARN THAT MAN, 1943
WARNING SIGN, 1985
WARRIORS FIVE, 1962
WARRIORS OF THE WIND, 1984
WASHINGTON MELODRAMA, 1941
WATCH YOUR STERN, 1961
WATCHED, 1974
WATER, 1985
WATER GYPSIES, THE, 1932
WATERFRONT, 1944
WATERFRONT WOMEN, 1952
WATERLOO, 1970
WATERLOO ROAD, 1949
WAVELENGTH, 1983
WAY BACK HOME, 1932
WAY DOWN EAST, 1935
WAY OF LOST SOULS, THE, 1929
WAY OUT WEST, 1930
WAYSIDE PEBBLE, THE, 1962
WAYWARD BUS, THE, 1957
WE HAVE ONLY ONE LIFE, 1963
WE HAVE OUR MOMENTS, 1937
WE SHALL RETURN, 1963
WE WENT TO COLLEGE, 1936
WE WHO ARE ABOUT TO DIE, 1937
WE WILL REMEMBER, 1966
WEAK AND THE WICKED, THE, 1954
WEAKER SEX, THE, 1949
WEB OF DANGER, THE, 1947
WEB OF PASSION, 1961
WEB OF THE SPIDER, 1972
WEB OF VIOLENCE, 1966
WEBSTER BOY, THE, 1962
WEDDING PRESENT, 1936
WEDDINGS ARE WONDERFUL, 1938
WEDNESDAY'S CHILD, 1934

WEEK-END MARRIAGE, 1932
WEEK-ENDS ONLY, 1932
WEEKEND, 1964
WEEKEND AT DUNKIRK, 1966
WEEKEND FOR THREE, 1941
WEEKEND MILLIONAIRE, 1937
WEEKEND PASS, 1944
WEEKEND, ITALIAN STYLE, 1967
WELCOME KOSTYA?, 1965
WELCOME TO HARD TIMES, 1967
WELL-GROOMED BRIDE, THE, 1946
WELLS FARGO GUNMASTER, 1951
WE'RE GOING TO BE RICH, 1938
WE'RE ON THE JURY, 1937
WE'RE ONLY HUMAN, 1936
WEST OF ABILENE, 1940
WEST OF CARSON CITY, 1940
WEST OF CIMARRON, 1941
WEST OF EL DORADO, 1949
WEST OF NEVADA, 1936
WEST OF PINTO BASIN, 1940
WEST OF RAINBOW'S END, 1938
WEST OF SANTA FE, 1938
WEST OF SINGAPORE, 1933
WEST OF SONORA, 1948
WEST OF TEXAS, 1943
WEST OF THE BRAZOS, 1950
WEST OF TOMBSTONE, 1942
WEST OF ZANZIBAR, 1954
WEST POINT OF THE AIR, 1935
WEST POINT WIDOW, 1941
WEST SIDE KID, 1943
WESTBOUND, 1959
WESTBOUND LIMITED, 1937
WESTBOUND MAIL, 1937
WESTBOUND STAGE, 1939
WESTERN CARAVANS, 1939
WESTERN CYCLONE, 1943
WESTERN FRONTIER, 1935
WESTERN HERITAGE, 1948
WESTERN JAMBOREE, 1938
WESTERN JUSTICE, 1935
WESTERN PACIFIC AGENT, 1950
WESTERN RENEGADES, 1949
WESTERNER, THE, 1936
WESTLAND CASE, THE, 1937
WESTMINSTER PASSION PLAY—BEHOLD THE
   MAN, THE, 1951
WESTWARD DESPERADO, 1961
WESTWARD HO, 1942
WESTWARD HO THE WAGONS?, 1956
WETBACKS, 1956
WHALE OF A TALE, A, 1977
WHAT!, 1965:,
WHAT A CARVE UP!, 1962
WHAT A LIFE, 1939
WHAT A MAN!, 1937
WHAT A MAN!, 1944
WHAT AM I BID?, 1967
WHAT DO WE DO NOW?, 1945
WHAT EVERY WOMAN KNOWS, 1934
WHAT EVERY WOMAN WANTS, 1954
WHAT HAPPENED THEN?, 1934
WHAT HAPPENED TO HARKNESS, 1934
WHAT MEN WANT, 1930
WHAT! NO BEER?, 1933
WHAT THE BUTLER SAW, 1950
WHAT YOU TAKE FOR GRANTED, 1984
WHATEVER IT TAKES, 1986
WHAT'S NEXT?, 1975
WHAT'S SO BAD ABOUT FEELING GOOD?, 1968
WHAT'S THE MATTER WITH HELEN?, 1971
WHAT'S THE TIME, MR. CLOCK?, 1985
WHEN DINOSAURS RULED THE EARTH, 1971
WHEN EIGHT BELLS TOLL, 1971
WHEN KNIGHTS WERE BOLD, 1942
WHEN LADIES MEET, 1933
WHEN LONDON SLEEPS, 1932
WHEN THE LIGHTS GO ON AGAIN, 1944
WHEN TOMORROW COMES, 1939
WHEN WE ARE MARRIED, 1943
WHERE ARE YOUR CHILDREN?, 1943
WHERE IS THIS LADY?, 1932
WHERE IT'S AT, 1969
WHERE LOVE HAS GONE, 1964
WHERE THE BUFFALO ROAM, 1980

WHERE THE BULLETS FLY, 1966
WHERE THE TRUTH LIES, 1962
WHERE THERE'S A WILL, 1937
WHERE THERE'S A WILL, 1955
WHERE WERE YOU WHEN THE LIGHTS WENT
   OUT?, 1968
WHERE'S JACK?, 1969
WHERE'S SALLY?, 1936
WHERE'S THAT FIRE?, 1939
WHEREVER SHE GOES, 1953
WHEREVER YOU ARE, 1988
WHILE NEW YORK SLEEPS, 1938
WHIP HAND, THE, 1951
WHIPLASH, 1948
WHIPPED, THE, 1950
WHIRLPOOL OF WOMAN, 1966
WHISPERING ENEMIES, 1939
WHISPERING FOOTSTEPS, 1943
WHISPERING JOE, 1969
WHISPERING SKULL, THE, 1944
WHISTLIN' DAN, 1932
WHISTLING BULLETS, 1937
WHISTLING IN BROOKLYN, 1943
WHISTLING IN DIXIE, 1942
WHISTLING IN THE DARK, 1933
WHITE BANNERS, 1938
WHITE CORRIDORS, 1952
WHITE DEVIL, THE, 1948
WHITE EAGLE, 1932
WHITE ELEPHANT, 1984
WHITE ENSIGN, 1934
WHITE FANG, 1936
WHITE FIRE, 1953
WHITE GHOST, 1988
WHITE HUNTER, 1936
WHITE HUNTER, 1965
WHITE LIGHTNING, 1953
WHITE LILAC, 1935
WHITE LINE, THE, 1952
WHITE ORCHID, THE, 1954
WHITE ROSE OF HONG KONG, 1965
WHITE SAVAGE, 1943
WHITE STALLION, 1947
WHITE TRAP, THE, 1959
WHITE WATER SUMMER, 1987
WHO DONE IT?, 1956
WHO IS GUILTY?, 1940
WHO IS HARRY KELLERMAN AND WHY IS HE
   SAYING THOSE TERRIBLE THINGS ABOUT ME?,
   1971
WHO KILLED GAIL PRESTON?, 1938
WHO KILLED MARY WHAT'SER NAME?, 1971
WHO KILLED THE CAT?, 1966
WHO WAS MADDOX?, 1964
WHO'S BEEN SLEEPING IN MY BED?, 1963
WHO'S GOT THE ACTION?, 1962
WHO'S MINDING THE STORE?, 1963
WHY PICK ON ME?, 1937
WICKED, 1931
WICKED WIFE, 1955
WICKED WOMAN, 1953
WIDE OPEN FACES, 1938
WIDOW'S MIGHT, 1934
WIDOWS' NEST, 1977
WIFE OF MONTE CRISTO, THE, 1946
WIFE OR TWO, A, 1935
WIFE TAKES A FLYER, THE, 1942
WILD ANGELS, THE, 1966
WILD BEAUTY, 1946
WILD BILL HICKOK RIDES, 1942
WILD BOY, 1934
WILD GEESE, THE, 1978
WILD GEESE CALLING, 1941
WILD GOLD, 1934
WILD HEART, THE, 1952
WILD HERITAGE, 1958
WILD HORSE HANK, 1979
WILD HORSE MESA, 1947
WILD HORSE ROUND-UP, 1937
WILD HORSES, 1984
WILD IN THE COUNTRY, 1961
WILD INNOCENCE, 1937
WILD McCULLOCHS, THE, 1975
WILD MONEY, 1937
WILD MUSTANG, 1935
WILD NORTH, THE, 1952

BOLD: Films on Videocassette

WILD ROVERS, 1971
WILD, WILD WINTER, 1966
WILDCAT, 1942
WILLIAM COMES TO TOWN, 1948
WILLOW, 1988
WILLY, 1963
WIND OF CHANGE, THE, 1961
WINDBAG THE SAILOR, 1937
WINDFALL, 1935
WINDFALL, 1955
WINDJAMMER, 1937
WINE, WOMEN, AND SONG, 1934
WINGS FOR THE EAGLE, 1942
WINGS OF CHANCE, 1961
WINGS OF MYSTERY, 1963
WINGS OF THE HAWK, 1953
WINGS OF THE NAVY, 1939
WINGS OF VICTORY, 1941
WINGS OVER HONOLULU, 1937
WINNER TAKE ALL, 1939
WINNER'S CIRCLE, THE, 1948
WINNERS TAKE ALL, 1987
WINNING OF THE WEST, 1953
WINTER LIGHT, THE, 1963
WINTER MEETING, 1948
WINTER WONDERLAND, 1947
WINTER'S TALE, THE, 1968
WIRE SERVICE, 1942
WISDOM, 1986
WISE GIRLS, 1930
WISE GUYS, 1937
WISE GUYS, 1969
WISE GUYS, 1986
WISTFUL WIDOW OF WAGON GAP, THE, 1947
WITCHBOARD, 1987
WITCHCRAFT, 1964
WITCHES OF EASTWICK, THE, 1987
WITCHING HOUR, THE, 1934
WITHIN THE LAW, 1939
WITHIN THESE WALLS, 1945
WITHOUT A TRACE, 1983
WITHOUT HONORS, 1932
WITHOUT WARNING, 1952
WITNESS IN THE DARK, 1959
WITNESS, THE, 1959
WIVES AND LOVERS, 1963
WIVES NEVER KNOW, 1936
WIVES UNDER SUSPICION, 1938
WIZARD OF LONELINESS, THE, 1988
WOLF LARSEN, 1958
WOLF LARSEN, 1978
WOLF OF WALL STREET THE, 1929
WOLF'S CLOTHING, 1936
WOLF'S HOLE, 1987
WOMAN COMMANDS, A, 1932
WOMAN FROM MONTE CARLO, THE, 1932
WOMAN FROM TANGIER, THE, 1948
WOMAN HUNT, 1962
WOMAN I STOLE, THE, 1933
WOMAN IN GREEN, THE, 1945
WOMAN IN THE DARK, 1934
WOMAN IN THE HALL, THE, 1949
WOMAN IS THE JUDGE, A, 1939
WOMAN OF DARKNESS, 1968
WOMAN OF DISTINCTION, A, 1950
WOMAN OF SIN, 1961
WOMAN OF THE NORTH COUNTRY, 1952
WOMAN OF THE RIVER, 1954
WOMAN POSSESSED, A, 1958
WOMAN REBELS, A, 1936
WOMAN THEY ALMOST LYNCHED, THE, 1953
WOMAN TIMES SEVEN, 1967
WOMAN TO WOMAN, 1929
WOMAN TO WOMAN, 1946
WOMAN WHO CAME BACK, 1945
WOMAN WHO WOULDN'T DIE, THE, 1965
WOMAN-WISE, 1937
WOMAN WITH RED BOOTS, THE, 1977
WOMANHOOD, 1934
WOMANLIGHT, 1979
WOMAN'S DEVOTION, A, 1956
WOMAN'S LIFE, A, 1964
WOMAN'S SECRET, A, 1949
WOMAN'S TEMPTATION, A, 1959
WOMEN AND WAR, 1965
WOMEN ARE TROUBLE, 1936

WOMEN EVERYWHERE, 1930
WOMEN IN BONDAGE, 1943
WOMEN IN LOVE, 1969
WOMEN IN PRISON, 1938
WOMEN IN PRISON, 1957
WOMEN MEN MARRY, THE, 1937
WOMEN OF GLAMOUR, 1937
WOMEN THEY TALK ABOUT, 1928
WOMEN WITHOUT NAMES, 1940
WOMEN'S PRISON, 1955
WONDER BOY, 1951
WONDERFUL LAND OF OZ, THE, 1969
WONDERFUL STORY, THE, 1932
WONDERFUL TO BE YOUNG!, 1962
WONDERFUL WORLD OF THE BROTHERS GRIMM,
   THE, 1962
WORDS AND MUSIC, 1929
WORK IS A FOUR LETTER WORD, 1968
WORKING GIRLS, 1931
WORKING GIRLS, THE, 1973
WORLD GONE MAD, THE, 1933
WORLD GONE WILD, 1988
WORLD IN MY POCKET, THE, 1962
WORLD MOVES ON, THE, 1934
WORLD OF SUZIE WONG, THE, 1960
WORLD OWES ME A LIVING, THE, 1944
WORLD WAS HIS JURY, THE, 1958
WORLD WITHOUT A MASK, THE, 1934
WORLD WITHOUT END, 1956
WORLD, THE FLESH, AND THE DEVIL, THE, 1932
WORLDS APART, 1980
WORLD'S GREATEST LOVER, THE, 1977
WORM'S EYE VIEW, 1951
WOULD YOU BELIEVE IT!, 1930
WRANGLER'S ROOST, 1941
WRATH OF JEALOUSY, 1936
WRECKING CREW, 1942
WRECKING CREW, THE, 1968
WRONG IS RIGHT, 1982
WRONG NUMBER, 1959
WUSA, 1970
WUTHERING HEIGHTS, 1970
WYOMING BANDIT, THE, 1949
WYOMING MAIL, 1950
WYOMING OUTLAW, 1939
WYOMING WILDCAT, 1941
X-15, 1961
X MARKS THE SPOT, 1931
X MARKS THE SPOT, 1942
YANK AT ETON, A, 1942
YANK IN ERMINE, A, 1955
YANK IN LONDON, A, 1946
YANK IN VIET-NAM, A, 1964
YANK ON THE BURMA ROAD, A, 1942
YANKEE BUCCANEER, 1952
YANKEE DON, 1931
YEAR OF THE HORSE, THE, 1966
YEARNING, 1964
YELLOW CANARY, THE, 1944
YELLOW HAT, THE, 1966
YELLOW ROBE, THE, 1954
YELLOW ROSE OF TEXAS, THE, 1944
YELLOW SLIPPERS, THE, 1965
YELLOW TICKET, THE, 1931
YELLOW TOMAHAWK, THE, 1954
YELLOWBEARD, 1983
YELLOWNECK, 1955
YELLOWSTONE KELLY, 1959
YES, MADAM?, 1938
YES SIR, THAT'S MY BABY, 1949
YESTERDAY'S HEROES, 1940
YOKEL BOY, 1942
YOLANTA, 1964
YOU ARE THE WORLD FOR ME, 1964
YOU BELONG TO ME, 1934
YOU BETTER WATCH OUT, 1980
YOU CAN'T BEAT THE IRISH, 1952
YOU CAN'T BUY EVERYTHING, 1934
YOU CAN'T DO WITHOUT LOVE, 1946
YOU CAN'T RUN AWAY FROM IT, 1956
YOU CAN'T SEE 'ROUND CORNERS, 1969
YOU HAVE TO RUN FAST, 1961
YOU KNOW WHAT SAILORS ARE, 1954
YOU LIVE AND LEARN, 1937
YOU NEVER CAN TELL, 1951
YOU ONLY LIVE ONCE, 1969

YOU WERE MEANT FOR ME, 1948
YOU'LL FIND OUT, 1940
YOUNG AMERICA, 1942
YOUNG AND EVIL, 1962
YOUNG AND THE BRAVE, THE, 1963
YOUNG AND THE GUILTY, THE, 1958
YOUNG AND WILD, 1958
YOUNG APHRODITES, 1966
YOUNG BILL HICKOK, 1940
YOUNG COMPOSER'S ODYSSEY, A, 1986
YOUNG DESIRE, 1930
YOUNG DONOVAN'S KID, 1931
YOUNG DON'T CRY, THE, 1957
YOUNG DYNAMITE, 1937
YOUNG FURY, 1965
YOUNG GUNS, THE, 1956
YOUNG GUNS, 1988
YOUNG GUNS OF TEXAS, 1963
YOUNG LAND, THE, 1959
YOUNG MONK, THE, 1978
YOUNG NURSES, THE, 1973
YOUNG RACERS, THE, 1963
YOUNG REBEL, THE, 1969
YOUNG RUNAWAYS, THE, 1968
YOUNG SINNERS, 1931
YOUNG WARRIORS, THE, 1967
YOUNG WARRIORS, 1983
YOUNG WIDOW, 1946
YOUNGBLOOD, 1986
YOU'RE IN THE ARMY NOW, 1937
YOU'RE NOT SO TOUGH, 1940
YOU'RE TELLING ME, 1942
YOUTH IN FURY, 1961
YOUTH ON TRIAL, 1945
YOUTH TAKES A FLING, 1938
YOUTH WILL BE SERVED, 1940
YOUTHFUL FOLLY, 1934
YR ALCOHOLIG LION, 1984
YUKON GOLD, 1952
YUKON MANHUNT, 1951
ZABRISKIE POINT, 1970
ZACHARIAH, 1971
ZATOICHI CHALLENGED, 1970
ZAZA, 1939
ZED & TWO NOUGHTS, A, 1985
ZELIG, 1983
ZENOBIA, 1939
ZIS BOOM BAH, 1941
ZOMBIES OF MORA TAU, 1957
ZOO BABY, 1957
ZOO GANG, THE, 1985
ZOOT SUIT, 1981
ZOTZ!, 1962

1.5 Stars
**ABBOTT AND COSTELLO MEET DR. JEKYLL AND
   MR. HYDE, 1954**
ABDULLAH'S HAREM, 1956
ACCENT ON LOVE, 1941
ACCOMPLICE, 1946
ACCORDING TO MRS. HOYLE, 1951
ACROSS THE PLAINS, 1939
ACTION JACKSON, 1988
ACTOR'S REVENGE, AN, 1963
ADIOS GRINGO, 1967
ADORABLE CREATURES, 1956
ADORABLE LIAR, 1962
ADRIFT, 1971
ADVENTURE ISLAND, 1947
ADVENTURE'S END, 1937
ADVENTURES IN IRAQ, 1943
ADVENTURES OF JANE, THE, 1949
AFTER OFFICE HOURS, 1932
AFTER TONIGHT, 1933
AGE OF INNOCENCE, 1977
ALASKA SEAS, 1954
ALCATRAZ ISLAND, 1937
ALEX AND THE GYPSY, 1976
ALF'S BUTTON, 1930
ALF'S BUTTON AFLOAT, 1938
ALIAS BILLY THE KID, 1946
ALIAS FRENCH GERTIE, 1930
ALIAS JIMMY VALENTINE, 1928
ALIAS JOHN PRESTON, 1956
ALIAS THE BAD MAN, 1931
ALIAS THE DOCTOR, 1932

ALIVE ON SATURDAY, 1957
ALL-AMERICAN CO-ED, 1941
ALL AT SEA, 1935
ALL AT SEA, 1939
ALL AT SEA, 1970
ALL RIGHT, MY FRIEND, 1983
ALL THAT GLITTERS, 1936
ALLEY CAT, 1984
ALLONSANFAN, 1985
ALLOTMENT WIVES, INC., 1945
ALMOST A GENTLEMAN, 1938
ALMOST SUMMER, 1978
ALPHABET MURDERS, THE, 1966
ALWAYS A BRIDESMAID, 1943
AMAZING DOBERMANS, THE, 1976
AMERICAN ANTHEM, 1986
AMERICAN LOVE, 1932
AMOS 'N' ANDY, 1930
ANATOMIST, THE, 1961
AND ONE WAS BEAUTIFUL, 1940
AND SO TO BED, 1965
AND THE WILD, WILD WOMEN, 1961
AND WOMEN SHALL WEEP, 1960
ANGELS ALLEY, 1948
ANGELS IN DISGUISE, 1949
ANIMALS, THE, 1971
ANN VICKERS, 1933
ANNE OF WINDY POPLARS, 1940
ANNIE, LEAVE THE ROOM, 1935
ANOTHER TIME, ANOTHER PLACE, 1984
ANYTHING TO DECLARE?, 1939
APPASSIONATA, 1946
APPLE DUMPLING GANG RIDES AGAIN, THE, 1979
APPOINTMENT WITH A SHADOW, 1958
APPOINTMENT WITH MURDER, 1948
ARABIAN ADVENTURE, 1979
ARCTIC FLIGHT, 1952
ARE YOU A MASON?, 1934
ARGENTINE NIGHTS, 1940
ARGYLE SECRETS, THE, 1948
ARIZONA DAYS, 1937
ARIZONA FRONTIER, 1940
ARIZONA KID, THE, 1930
ARIZONA MANHUNT, 1951
ARIZONA STAGECOACH, 1942
ARIZONA TERRITORY, 1950
ARKANSAS JUDGE, 1941
ARKANSAS TRAVELER, THE, 1938
ARMCHAIR DETECTIVE, THE, 1952
ARMED AND DANGEROUS, 1977
ARMED AND DANGEROUS, 1986
ARMED RESPONSE, 1986
ARSON GANG BUSTERS, 1938
ARSON SQUAD, 1945
ARTHUR, 1931
ARTURO'S ISLAND, 1963
AS YOUNG AS WE ARE, 1958
ASKING FOR TROUBLE, 1942
ASSAM GARDEN, THE, 1985
ASSASSINATION, 1987
ASSAULT, 1971
ASSIGNED TO DANGER, 1948
ATLANTIC ADVENTURE, 1935
ATLANTIC CITY, 1944
ATLANTIS, THE LOST CONTINENT, 1961
ATTACK OF THE CRAB MONSTERS, 1957
ATTACK OF THE PUPPET PEOPLE, 1958
AULD LANG SYNE, 1929
AULD LANG SYNE, 1937
AVALANCHE, 1946
AVALANCHE EXPRESS, 1979
AVENGING ANGEL, 1985
AVIATOR, THE, 1985
AWAKENING, THE, 1980
AWAKENING OF JIM BURKE, 1935
B.S. I LOVE YOU, 1971
BABES IN BAGDAD, 1952
BACCHANTES, THE, 1963
BACHELOR OF HEARTS, 1958
BACK FROM ETERNITY, 1956
BACK ROOM BOY, 1942
BACK TO THE WALL, 1959
BACKFIRE!, 1961
BAD BLONDE, 1953
BAD BOY, 1938
BAD BOY, 1949

BAD GUY, 1937
BAD MAN, THE, 1930
BAD MAN FROM RED BUTTE, 1940
BAD MANNERS, 1984
BAD MEN OF THE BORDER, 1945
BAD NEWS BEARS GO TO JAPAN, THE, 1978
BAD SISTER, 1931
BADGER'S GREEN, 1934
BADMAN'S GOLD, 1951
BAIT, 1950
BALLAD OF A GUNFIGHTER, 1964
BALTIC DEPUTY, 1937
BANANA RIDGE, 1941
BANDIT TRAIL, THE, 1941
BANDITS OF THE BADLANDS, 1945
BANDOLERO!, 1968
BANG BANG KID, THE, 1968
BANG, BANG, YOU'RE DEAD, 1966
BANK RAIDERS, THE, 1958
BAR 51—SISTER OF LOVE, 1986
BARBER OF STAMFORD HILL, THE, 1963
BARBERINA, 1932
BARCAROLE, 1935
BAREFOOT MAILMAN, THE, 1951
BARNYARD FOLLIES, 1940
BAROCCO, 1976
BARON BLOOD, 1972
BARRICADE, 1950
BARRY MC KENZIE HOLDS HIS OWN, 1975
BARTLEBY, 1970
BASHFUL BACHELOR, THE, 1942
BASHFUL ELEPHANT, THE, 1962
BATTLE AT BLOODY BEACH, 1961
BATTLE IN OUTER SPACE, 1960
BATTLE OF ROGUE RIVER, 1954
BAYOU, 1957
BE MY GUEST, 1965
BEAR ISLAND, 1980
BEAST FROM THE HAUNTED CAVE, 1960
BEAST IN THE CELLAR, THE, 1971
BEAST OF BLOOD, 1970
BEAST OF BUDAPEST, THE, 1958
BEAST OF YUCCA FLATS, THE, 1961
BEASTMASTER, THE, 1982
BEASTS OF BERLIN, 1939
BEAT, THE, 1988
BEAU IDEAL, 1931
BEAUTIFUL BUT BROKE, 1944
BEAUTIFUL CHEAT, THE, 1946
BEAUTY AND THE BARGE, 1937
BEAUTY FOR SALE, 1933
BEAUTY ON PARADE, 1950
BECAUSE OF EVE, 1948
BECAUSE OF YOU, 1952
BECAUSE YOU'RE MINE, 1952
BED OF ROSES, 1933
BEDROOM EYES, 1984
BEDTIME STORY, 1964
BEER, 1986
BEFORE HIM ALL ROME TREMBLED, 1947
BEFORE THE REVOLUTION, 1964
BEGINNING OF THE END, 1957
BEHIND THE HEADLINES, 1956
BEHIND THE HIGH WALL, 1956
BEHIND THE IRON MASK, 1977
BEHIND THE MIKE, 1937
BEING, THE, 1983
BELL-BOTTOM GEORGE, 1943
BELL JAR, THE, 1979
BELLA DONNA, 1934
BELLE LE GRAND, 1951
BELLE OF THE YUKON, 1944
BELLS OF CAPISTRANO, 1942
BELOVED VAGABOND, THE, 1936
BELOW THE DEADLINE, 1936
BERMONDSEY KID, THE, 1933
BERNARDINE, 1957
BEST OF TIMES, THE, 1986
BETRAYAL, 1932
BETRAYAL, THE, 1958
BETRAYED WOMEN, 1955
BETWEEN TIME AND ETERNITY, 1960
BEWARE, MY LOVELY, 1952
BEYOND EVIL, 1980
BEYOND FEAR, 1977
BEYOND THE CURTAIN, 1960

BEYOND THE LAW, 1967
BEYOND THE LIMIT, 1983
BEYOND THE PURPLE HILLS, 1950
BIG BLOCKADE, THE, 1942
BIG BLUE, THE, 1988
BIG BLUFF, THE, 1955
BIG BUSINESS GIRL, 1931
BIG CAPER, THE, 1957
BIG CAT, THE, 1949
BIG FIX, THE, 1947
BIG GUSHER, THE, 1951
BIG JACK, 1949
BIG LEAGUER, 1953
BIG RED, 1962
BIG SHAKEDOWN, THE, 1934
BIG SHOW, THE, 1961
BIG SLEEP, THE, 1978
BIG SOMBRERO, THE, 1949
BIG TIMBER, 1950
BIG TIP OFF, THE, 1955
BIG WEDNESDAY, 1978
BILL'S LEGACY, 1931
BIRD OF PARADISE, 1951
BIRD WATCH, THE, 1983
BLACK BOOK, THE, 1949
BLACK CAT, THE, 1966
BLACK CAT, THE, 1984
BLACK COFFEE, 1931
BLACK DOLL, THE, 1938
BLACK EYE, 1974
BLACK GOLD, 1963
BLACK HILLS AMBUSH, 1952
BLACK KING, 1932
BLACK LASH, THE, 1952
BLACK LIMELIGHT, 1938
BLACK MARKET BABIES, 1946
BLACK MIDNIGHT, 1949
BLACK MOON, 1934
BLACK OAK CONSPIRACY, 1977
BLACK PANTHER, THE, 1977
BLACK RAVEN, THE, 1943
BLACK ROSES, 1936
BLACK SCORPION, THE, 1957
BLACK SHEEP OF WHITEHALL, THE, 1941
BLACK SLEEP, THE, 1956
BLACK SPIDER, THE, 1983
BLACK STALLION RETURNS, THE, 1983
BLACK SUN, THE, 1979
BLACK SUNDAY, 1961
BLACK TULIP, THE, 1937
BLACK VEIL FOR LISA, A, 1969
BLACK WIDOW, 1951
BLACK ZOO, 1963
BLACKMAIL, 1947
BLACKMAILED, 1951
BLACKMAILER, 1936
BLACKOUT, 1950
BLACKOUT, 1954
BLADE IN THE DARK, A, 1986
BLADES OF THE MUSKETEERS, 1953
BLAME THE WOMAN, 1932
BLARNEY KISS, 1933
BLASTFIGHTER, 1985
BLAZING FRONTIER, 1944
BLAZING GUNS, 1943
BLAZING TRAIL, THE, 1949
BLIND DESIRE, 1948
BLIND DIRECTOR, THE, 1986
BLIND SPOT, 1958
BLINDFOLD, 1966
BLISS, 1985
BLOB, THE, 1958
BLONDE BANDIT, THE, 1950
BLONDE DYNAMITE, 1950
BLONDE FROM PEKING, THE, 1968
BLONDE FROM SINGAPORE, THE, 1941
BLONDE INSPIRATION, 1941
BLONDE NIGHTINGALE, 1931
BLONDE PICKUP, 1955
BLONDIE BRINGS UP BABY, 1939
BLONDIE FOR VICTORY, 1942
BLONDIE GOES TO COLLEGE, 1942
BLONDIE HAS SERVANT TROUBLE, 1940
BLONDIE HITS THE JACKPOT, 1949
BLONDIE IN SOCIETY, 1941
BLONDIE JOHNSON, 1933

BOLD: Films on Videocassette

BLONDIE KNOWS BEST, 1946
BLONDIE MEETS THE BOSS, 1939
BLONDIE ON A BUDGET, 1940
BLONDIE'S HOLIDAY, 1947
BLONDIE'S LUCKY DAY, 1946
BLONDIE'S REWARD, 1948
BLOOD ALLEY, 1955
BLOOD ARROW, 1958
BLOOD BEACH, 1981
BLOOD DRINKERS, THE, 1966
BLOOD OF DRACULA, 1957
BLOOD OF THE VAMPIRE, 1958
BLOODTHIRSTY BUTCHERS, 1970
BLOOMFIELD, 1971
BLUE, 1968
BLUE BIRD, THE, 1976
BLUE BLOOD, 1951
BLUE CITY, 1986
BLUE LIGHT, THE, 1932
BLUE MONTANA SKIES, 1939
BLUE STEEL, 1934
BLUEBEARD, 1972
BLUEBEARD'S EIGHTH WIFE, 1938
BLUEBEARD'S TEN HONEYMOONS, 1960
BLUEPRINT FOR ROBBERY, 1961
BLUES BROTHERS, THE, 1980
BODY ROCK, 1984
BODY STEALERS, THE, 1969
BODYHOLD, 1950
BOGGY CREEK II, 1985
BOHEMIAN GIRL, THE, 1936
BOILING POINT, THE, 1932
BOMB IN THE HIGH STREET, 1961
BOMBA AND THE JUNGLE GIRL, 1952
BOMBA THE JUNGLE BOY, 1949
BOMBS OVER LONDON, 1937
BOMBSIGHT STOLEN, 1941
BON VOYAGE, 1962
BONDAGE, 1933
BOOGEYMAN II, 1983
BOOLOO, 1938
BOOST, THE, 1988
BOOTLEGGERS, 1974
BORDER BRIGANDS, 1935
BORDER CABALLERO, 1936
BORDER CAFE, 1937
BORDER G-MAN, 1938
BORDER LEGION, THE, 1930
BORDER LEGION, THE, 1940
BORDER OUTLAWS, 1950
BORDER PATROL, 1943
BORDER RANGERS, 1950
BORDERLAND, 1937
BORDERTOWN GUNFIGHTERS, 1943
BORN TO FIGHT, 1938
BORN TO LOVE, 1931
BORN TO SPEED, 1947
BORN TO THE SADDLE, 1953
BORROWED HERO, 1941
BORROWED TROUBLE, 1948
BOSS NIGGER, 1974
BOSS OF BULLION CITY, 1941
BOSS OF HANGTOWN MESA, 1942
BOSS OF THE RAWHIDE, 1944
BOUGHT, 1931
BOWERY AT MIDNIGHT, 1942
BOWERY BUCKAROOS, 1947
BOWERY CHAMPS, 1944
BOXOFFICE, 1982
BOY FRIEND, 1939
BOY FROM INDIANA, 1950
BOY IN BLUE, THE, 1986
BOY SLAVES, 1938
BOY TROUBLE, 1939
BOY! WHAT A GIRL, 1947
BOY WHO CAUGHT A CROOK, 1961
BOYS IN BROWN, 1949
BOYS OF THE CITY, 1940
BOYS' RANCH, 1946
BRAIN EATERS, THE, 1958
BRAIN FROM THE PLANET AROUS, THE, 1958
BRAIN OF BLOOD, 1971
BRAND OF THE DEVIL, 1944
BREAK IN THE CIRCLE, THE, 1957
BREAK, THE, 1962
BREAKDOWN, 1953

BREAKER! BREAKER!, 1977
BREAKOUT, 1975
BREATH OF SCANDAL, A, 1960
BREED APART, A, 1984
BRIDE OF THE DESERT, 1929
BRIDGE OF SIGHS, 1936
BRIEF RAPTURE, 1952
BRIGGS FAMILY, THE, 1940
BRINGING UP FATHER, 1946
BRITANNIA OF BILLINGSGATE, 1933
BROKEN BLOSSOMS, 1936
BROKEN ENGLISH, 1981
BROKEN MELODY, 1938
BROKEN MELODY, THE, 1934
BROOD, THE, 1979
BROTH OF A BOY, 1959
BRUCE LEE—TRUE STORY, 1976
BUCKSKIN LADY, THE, 1957
BULLDOG BREED, THE, 1960
BULLDOG DRUMMOND COMES BACK, 1937
BULLDOG DRUMMOND'S BRIDE, 1939
BULLDOG DRUMMOND'S REVENGE, 1937
BULLDOG DRUMMOND'S SECRET POLICE, 1939
BULLET FOR STEFANO, 1950
BULLET IS WAITING, A, 1954
BUNCO SQUAD, 1950
BURG THEATRE, 1936
BURNING CROSS, THE, 1947
BUSTER KEATON STORY, THE, 1957
BY APPOINTMENT ONLY, 1933
BYE BYE BRAVERMAN, 1968
CACTUS IN THE SNOW, 1972
CADET GIRL, 1941
CAESAR THE CONQUEROR, 1963
CAFE COLETTE, 1937
CAFE HOSTESS, 1940
CAFE MASCOT, 1936
CALAMITY THE COW, 1967
CALCULATED RISK, 1963
CALENDAR GIRL, 1947
CALIFORNIA FIREBRAND, 1948
CALIFORNIA STRAIGHT AHEAD, 1937
CALIFORNIAN, THE, 1937
CALL A MESSENGER, 1939
CALL IT A DAY, 1937
CALL ME MAME, 1933
CALL OF THE CIRCUS, 1930
CALL OF THE KLONDIKE, 1950
CALL OF THE SEA, THE, 1930
CALL OF THE SOUTH SEAS, 1944
CALL OF THE WILD, 1972
CALL THE MESQUITEERS, 1938
CALLED BACK, 1933
CALLING ALL CROOKS, 1938
CALLING ALL MARINES, 1939
CALLING PAUL TEMPLE, 1948
CALLING PHILO VANCE, 1940
CALYPSO JOE, 1957
CAMPUS HONEYMOON, 1948
CAMPUS RHYTHM, 1943
CAN THIS BE DIXIE?, 1936
CANDIDE, 1962
CANDLES AT NINE, 1944
CANNABIS, 1970
CANNIBAL GIRLS, 1973
CANNIBALS, THE, 1970
CANTOR'S SON, THE, 1937
CANYON RAIDERS, 1951
CAPER OF THE GOLDEN BULLS, THE, 1967
CAPETOWN AFFAIR, 1967
CAPTAIN APPLEJACK, 1931
CAPTAIN BOYCOTT, 1947
CAPTAIN CAUTION, 1940
CAPTAIN IS A LADY, THE, 1940
CAPTAIN KIDD AND THE SLAVE GIRL, 1954
CAPTAIN MILKSHAKE, 1971
CAPTAIN SCARLETT, 1953
CAPTAIN'S ORDERS, 1937
CAPTIVE CITY, THE, 1963
CAPTIVE GIRL, 1950
CAPTIVE WOMEN, 1952
CARAVAN TRAIL, THE, 1946
CAREER, 1939
CAREER GIRL, 1944
CAREERS, 1929
CAREFUL, SOFT SHOULDERS, 1942

CARMEN, 1931
CARNIVAL, 1931
CARNIVAL BOAT, 1932
CARNIVAL QUEEN, 1937
CAROLINA, 1934
CARRY ON CLEO, 1964
CARRY ON LOVING, 1970
CARSON CITY KID, 1940
CARTHAGE IN FLAMES, 1961
CASE AGAINST MRS. AMES, THE, 1936
CASE FOR PC 49, A, 1951
CASE OF CHARLES PEACE, THE, 1949
CASE OF PATTY SMITH, THE, 1962
CASE OF THE RED MONKEY, 1955
CASE OF THE STUTTERING BISHOP, THE, 1937
CASINO MURDER CASE, THE, 1935
CAST A LONG SHADOW, 1959
CASTLE IN THE DESERT, 1942
CASTLE OF CRIMES, 1940
CASTLE OF THE MONSTERS, 1958
CAT AND MOUSE, 1958
CAT, THE, 1966
CAT BURGLAR, THE, 1961
CAT GANG, THE, 1959
CATTLE KING, 1963
CATTLE RAIDERS, 1938
CATTLE THIEF, THE, 1936
CAUGHT IN THE NET, 1960
CAVALIER OF THE STREETS, THE, 1937
CELIA, 1949
CELLAR DWELLER, 1988
CHAIN GANG, 1950
CHAIN OF EVENTS, 1958
CHAIN OF EVIDENCE, 1957
CHAINED FOR LIFE, 1950
CHALLENGE FOR ROBIN HOOD, A, 1968
CHANDLER, 1971
CHANEL SOLITAIRE, 1981
CHANGE FOR A SOVEREIGN, 1937
CHANGE OF HABIT, 1969
CHANGE OF MIND, 1969
CHANGE PARTNERS, 1965
CHANGES, 1969
CHARLEY MOON, 1956
CHARLEY-ONE-EYE, 1973
CHARLEY'S AUNT, 1930
CHARLEY'S (BIG-HEARTED) AUNT, 1940
CHARLIE CHAN AT THE WAX MUSEUM, 1940
CHARLIE CHAN IN BLACK MAGIC, 1944
CHARLIE CHAN'S COURAGE, 1934
CHARMING SINNERS, 1929
CHARTROOSE CABOOSE, 1960
CHASING YESTERDAY, 1935
CHECKERBOARD, 1969
CHECKERED FLAG OR CRASH, 1978
CHEER UP!, 1936
CHEER UP AND SMILE, 1930
CHELSEA STORY, 1951
CHEROKEE STRIP, 1937
CHETNIKS, 1943
CHEYENNE KID, THE, 1933
CHEYENNE RIDES AGAIN, 1937
CHEYENNE ROUNDUP, 1943
CHEYENNE TAKES OVER, 1947
CHICAGO CALLING, 1951
CHICK, 1936
CHILDREN OF THE CORN, 1984
CHINA'S LITTLE DEVILS, 1945
CHINATOWN NIGHTS, 1938
CHINESE PUZZLE, THE, 1932
CHIQUTTO PERO PICOSO, 1967
CHOSEN, THE, 1978
CHOSEN SURVIVORS, 1974
CHRISTIAN LICORICE STORE, THE, 1971
CHRISTINE KEELER AFFAIR, THE, 1964
CHUBASCO, 1968
CIMARRON KID, THE, 1951
CIPHER BUREAU, 1938
CIRCLE OF DEATH, 1935
CIRCLE OF IRON, 1979
CIRCUMSTANTIAL EVIDENCE, 1945
CIRCUS GIRL, 1937
CISCO KID RETURNS, THE, 1945
CITY GIRL, 1930
CITY GIRL, 1938
CITY HEAT, 1984

CITY LIMITS, 1934
CITY OF CHANCE, 1940
CITY OF FEAR, 1965
CITY OF PLAY, 1929
CITY PARK, 1934
CITY STREETS, 1938
CITY UNDER THE SEA, 1965
CLAN OF THE CAVE BEAR, THE, 1986
CLANDESTINE, 1948
CLARA'S HEART, 1988
CLASS OF MISS MAC MICHAEL, THE, 1978
CLAUDELLE INGLISH, 1961
CLAY PIGEON, 1971
CLEAR ALL WIRES, 1933
CLIPPED WINGS, 1953
CLONES, THE, 1973
CLOWN AND THE KIDS, THE, 1968
CLOWN MUST LAUGH, A, 1936
CLUE, 1985
C'MON, LET'S LIVE A LITTLE, 1967
COACH, 1978
COAST TO COAST, 1980
COCAINE WARS, 1986
COCK O' THE NORTH, 1935
COCKTAIL HOUR, 1933
CODE OF THE LAWLESS, 1945
CODE OF THE OUTLAW, 1942
CODE OF THE RANGE, 1937
CODE OF THE RANGERS, 1938
CODE OF THE SADDLE, 1947
CODE OF THE SECRET SERVICE, 1939
CODE OF THE SILVER SAGE, 1950
CODE OF THE STREETS, 1939
CODE 7, VICTIM 5, 1964
COHENS AND KELLYS IN AFRICA, THE, 1930
COLD JOURNEY, 1975
COLD RIVER, 1982
COLLEGE LOVE, 1929
COLLEGE LOVERS, 1930
COLONEL CHABERT, 1947
COLOR ME DEAD, 1969
COLORADO, 1940
COLORADO AMBUSH, 1951
COLOSSUS OF NEW YORK, THE, 1958
COMBAT SQUAD, 1953
COME DANCE WITH ME!, 1960
COME ON, COWBOYS, 1937
COME ON, LEATHERNECKS, 1938
COME ON, MARINES, 1934
COMEBACK TRAIL, THE, 1982
COMES A HORSEMAN, 1978
COMIN' ROUND THE MOUNTAIN, 1951
COMMAND PERFORMANCE, 1937
COMMISSIONAIRE, 1933
COMMON CLAY, 1930
COMMON LAW, THE, 1931
COMPANIONS IN CRIME, 1954
COMPETITION, THE, 1980
COMPROMISED, 1931
CONCENTRATIN' KID, THE, 1930
CONCRETE ANGELS, 1987
CONFIDENCE GIRL, 1952
CONFLICT, 1937
CONGO MAISIE, 1940
CONQUEROR, THE, 1956
CONQUEST OF COCHISE, 1953
CONQUEST OF MYCENE, 1965
CONQUEST OF SPACE, 1955
CONQUEST OF THE AIR, 1940
CONQUEST OF THE EARTH, 1980
CONSCIENCE BAY, 1960
CONTRABAND LOVE, 1931
CONVICT STAGE, 1965
CONVICTED, 1938
CONVICT'S CODE, 1930
COOL IT, CAROL!, 1970
CORNERED, 1932
CORPSE VANISHES, THE, 1942
COSMIC MONSTERS, 1958
COSSACKS, THE, 1960
COTTON QUEEN, 1937
COUNTDOWN TO DANGER, 1967
COUNTERFEIT CONSTABLE, THE, 1966
COUNTERFEIT LADY, 1937
COUNTERFEITERS, THE, 1953
COUNTRY FAIR, 1941

COUNTY FAIR, 1937
COUNTY FAIR, 1950
COURAGEOUS DR. CHRISTIAN, THE, 1940
COURAGEOUS MR. PENN, THE, 1941
COURTIN' TROUBLE, 1948
COURTIN' WILDCATS, 1929
COVERED TRAILER, THE, 1939
COVERED WAGON DAYS, 1940
COVERED WAGON RAID, 1950
COW COUNTRY, 1953
COW TOWN, 1950
COWBOY COMMANDOS, 1943
COWBOY FROM LONESOME RIVER, 1944
COWBOY HOLIDAY, 1934
COWBOY IN MANHATTTAN, 1943
COWBOY QUARTERBACK, 1939
CRACK IN THE WORLD, 1965
CRACKED NUTS, 1931
CRASHING LAS VEGAS, 1956
CREATURE FROM BLACK LAKE, THE, 1976
CREATURE OF THE WALKING DEAD, 1960
CREATURES THE WORLD FORGOT, 1971
CRIME AND PASSION, 1976
CRIME BOSS, 1976
CRIME DOCTOR'S COURAGE, THE, 1945
CRIME DOCTOR'S STRANGEST CASE, 1943
CRIME DOCTOR'S MAN HUNT, 1946
CRIMES OF THE FUTURE, 1969
CRIMES OF THE HEART, 1986
CRIMSON CANDLE, THE, 1934
CRITICAL CONDITION, 1987
CROOKED CIRCLE, 1932
CROOKED ROAD, THE, 1940
CROSS CHANNEL, 1955
CROSS OF THE LIVING, 1963
CROSS ROADS, 1930
CROSS-UP, 1958
CROSSTRAP, 1962
CROWNING GIFT, THE, 1967
CRUCIBLE OF HORROR, 1971
CRY OF THE BANSHEE, 1970
CUP FEVER, 1965
CUP OF KINDNESS, A, 1934
CUP-TIE HONEYMOON, 1948
CURFEW BREAKERS, 1957
CURSE OF THE FLY, 1965
CURSE OF THE UNDEAD, 1959
CURSE OF THE VOODOO, 1965
CURSE OF THE WRAYDONS, THE, 1946
CURSE, THE, 1987
CURTAIN AT EIGHT, 1934
CURTAIN CALL, 1940
CURTAIN UP, 1952
CYBORG 2087, 1966
CYCLE SAVAGES, 1969
CYCLONE KID, 1931
CYCLONE KID, THE, 1942
CYCLOPS, 1957
DAISIES, 1967
DALTON GANG, THE, 1949
DANCE BAND, 1935
DANCE LITTLE LADY, 1954
DANCE OF DEATH, THE, 1938
DANCE PRETTY LADY, 1932
DANCING HEART, THE, 1959
DANDY DICK, 1935
DANDY IN ASPIC, A, 1968
DANGEROUS AFTERNOON, 1961
DANGEROUS AGE, A, 1960
DANGEROUS BLONDES, 1943
DANGEROUS CARGO, 1954
DANGEROUS CORNER, 1935
DANGEROUS GROUND, 1934
DANGEROUS MISSION, 1954
DANGEROUS PARADISE, 1930
DANGEROUS WATERS, 1936
DANGEROUS WOMAN, 1929
DANGEROUSLY YOURS, 1937
DANIEL BOONE, TRAIL BLAZER, 1957
DANNY BOY, 1941
DARBY AND JOAN, 1937
DAREDEVILS OF THE CLOUDS, 1948
DARK ALIBI, 1946
DARK END OF THE STREET, THE, 1981
DARK HORSE, THE, 1946
DARK LIGHT, THE, 1951

DARK MOUNTAIN, 1944
DARK SECRET, 1949
DARK STREETS, 1929
DARK WORLD, 1935
DARKENED ROOMS, 1929
DARKENED SKIES, 1930
DARKER THAN AMBER, 1970
DARKEST AFRICA, 1936
DARLING, HOW COULD YOU!, 1951
D.A.R.Y.L., 1985
DATE WITH DISASTER, 1957
DAUGHTER OF THE JUNGLE, 1949
DAVID AND GOLIATH, 1961
DAWN, 1979
DAWN EXPRESS, THE, 1942
DAY AFTER THE DIVORCE, THE, 1940
DAY AT THE BEACH, A, 1970
DAY THE HOTLINE GOT HOT, THE, 1968
DAY THE SKY EXPLODED, THE, 1958
DAY TIME ENDED, THE, 1980
DAYBREAK, 1931
DAYS OF OLD CHEYENNE, 1943
DEAD DON'T DREAM, THE, 1948
DEAD LUCKY, 1960
DEAD MAN WALKING, 1988
DEAD MAN'S EYES, 1944
DEAD ON COURSE, 1952
DEAD TO THE WORLD, 1961
DEADFALL, 1968
DEADLINE, THE, 1932
DEADLINE, 1948
DEADLOCK, 1931
DEADLOCK, 1943
DEADLY MANTIS, THE, 1957
DEADLY NIGHTSHADE, 1953
DEADLY RECORD, 1959
DEADLY TRACKERS, 1973
DEADLY TRAP, THE, 1972
DEAL OF THE CENTURY, 1983
DEALING: OR THE BERKELEY TO BOSTON
      FORTY-BRICK LOST-BAG BLUES, 1971
DEATH CROONS THE BLUES, 1937
DEATH FROM A DISTANCE, 1936
DEATH GOES NORTH, 1939
DEATH ON THE DIAMOND, 1934
DEATH RACE, 1978
DEATH TRAP, 1962
DEATH VALLEY, 1946
DEATH VALLEY, 1982
DEATH VALLEY MANHUNT, 1943
DEATH VALLEY OUTLAWS, 1941
DEATHLINE, 1973
DEATHSTALKER, THE, 1984
DEFENDERS OF THE LAW, 1931
DELIGHTFUL ROGUE, 1929
DELTA FOX, 1979
DEMENTIA, 1955
DEMON BARBER OF FLEET STREET, THE, 1939
DEMONOID, 1981
DEPRAVED, THE, 1957
DEPUTY DRUMMER, THE, 1935
DESERT BANDIT, 1941
DESERT DESPERADOES, 1959
DESERT GOLD, 1936
DESERT JUSTICE, 1936
DESERT RAVEN, THE, 1965
DESERT SONG, THE, 1953
DESERT VENGEANCE, 1931
DESERT WARRIOR, 1961
DESIGNING WOMEN, 1934
DESPERATE DECISION, 1954
DESPERATE MAN, THE, 1959
DESPERATE TRAILS, 1939
DESTINATION INNER SPACE, 1966
DESTINATION UNKNOWN, 1942
DESTROY, SHE SAID, 1969
DESTRUCTORS, THE, 1968
DESTRUCTORS, THE, 1974
DEVIL BAT'S DAUGHTER, THE, 1946
DEVIL IS A WOMAN, THE, 1975
DEVIL IS DRIVING, THE, 1932
DEVIL IS DRIVING, THE, 1937
DEVIL PAYS, THE, 1932
DEVIL RIDERS, 1944
DEVIL TIMES FIVE, 1974
DEVIL WITH WOMEN, A, 1930

BOLD: Films on Videocassette

DEVIL'S CARGO, THE, 1948
DEVIL'S GODMOTHER, THE, 1938
DEVIL'S MATE, 1933
DEVIL'S MAZE, THE, 1929
DEVILS OF DARKNESS, THE, 1965
DEVIL'S PASS, THE, 1957
DEVIL'S PLAYGROUND, THE, 1946
DEVIL'S SADDLE LEGION, THE, 1937
DEVIL'S TEMPLE, 1969
DEVOTION, 1955
DIABOLICAL DR. Z, THE, 1966
DIALOGUE, 1967
DIARY OF A BAD GIRL, 1958
DICK BARTON—SPECIAL AGENT, 1948
DIE HAMBURGER KRANKHEIT, 1979
DIMENSION 5, 1966
DINKY, 1935
DIPLOMATIC LOVER, THE, 1934
DIRTY TRICKS, 1981
DISHONORED, 1950
DISORDER, 1964
DIVINE SPARK, THE, 1935
DIVORCE, 1945
DIVORCE AMONG FRIENDS, 1931
DIXIE DUGAN, 1943
DIXIE JAMBOREE, 1945
DIZZY DAMES, 1936
DOC SAVAGE. . . THE MAN OF BRONZE, 1975
DOCKS OF SAN FRANCISCO, 1932
DOCTOR DEATH: SEEKER OF SOULS, 1973
DR. GOLDFOOT AND THE BIKINI MACHINE, 1965
   88m AI c
DOCTOR IN TROUBLE, 1970
DR. KILDARE GOES HOME, 1940
DR. MABUSE'S RAYS OF DEATH, 1964
DOCTOR MONICA, 1934
DR. MORELLE—THE CASE OF THE MISSING
   HEIRESS, 1949
DOCTOR OF ST. PAUL, THE, 1969
DOCTORS DON'T TELL, 1941
DOG EAT DOG, 1963
DOLLS, 1987
DOMINO PRINCIPLE, THE, 1977
DON'T BET ON BLONDES, 1935
DON'T BET ON WOMEN, 1931
DON'T EVER LEAVE ME, 1949
DON'T GET PERSONAL, 1936
DON'T GET PERSONAL, 1941
DON'T JUST STAND THERE, 1968
DON'T LOSE YOUR HEAD, 1967
DON'T SAY DIE, 1950
DOOMED TO DIE, 1940
DOOMSDAY AT ELEVEN, 1963
DORIAN GRAY, 1970
DOUBLE, THE, 1963
DOUBLE CRIME IN THE MAGINOT LINE, 1939
DOUBLE EXPOSURE, 1954
DOUBLE EXPOSURES, 1937
DOUBLE NEGATIVE, 1980
DOUBLE NICKELS, 1977
DOUGHBOYS IN IRELAND, 1943
DOWN LAREDO WAY, 1953
DOWNSTAIRS, 1932
DRACULA AND THE SEVEN GOLDEN VAMPIRES,
   1978
DRAGON INN, 1968
DRAGONFLY SQUADRON, 1953
DRAGON'S GOLD, 1954
DREAMER, 1979
DREAMING, 1944
DREAMING LIPS, 1958
DREAMS THAT MONEY CAN BUY, 1948
DRIFTER, THE, 1932
DRILLER KILLER, 1979
DROP THEM OR I'LL SHOOT, 1969
DRUMMER OF VENGEANCE, 1974
DUBEAT-E-O, 1984
DUFFY, 1968
DUGAN OF THE BAD LANDS, 1931
DUKE COMES BACK, THE, 1937
DUKE OF THE NAVY, 1942
DYNAMITE DELANEY, 1938
DYNAMITE RANCH, 1932
EAGLE'S WING, 1979
EARLY BIRD, THE, 1936
EARTH CRIES OUT, THE, 1949

EARTHLING, THE, 1980
EAST IS WEST, 1930
EAST OF FIFTH AVE., 1933
EASY MILLIONS, 1933
EASY RICHES, 1938
ECHO MURDERS, THE, 1945
ECHO OF DIANA, 1963
EDDIE AND THE CRUISERS, 1983
EDDIE CANTOR STORY, THE, 1953
EDEN CRIED, 1967
EFFECTS, 1980
EIGHTEEN AND ANXIOUS, 1957
EL DORADO PASS, 1949
ELEPHANT STAMPEDE, 1951
ELEVENTH COMMANDMENT, 1933
ELI ELI, 1940
ELINOR NORTON, 1935
ELIZA COMES TO STAY, 1936
ELIZABETH OF LADYMEAD, 1949
EMBARRASSING MOMENTS, 1934
EMBEZZLER, THE, 1954
EMPTY HOLSTERS, 1937
ENCOUNTER WITH THE UNKNOWN, 1973
END OF THE WORLD (IN OUR USUAL BED IN A
   NIGHT FULL OF RAIN), THE, 1978
ENEMY MINE, 1985
ENIGMA, 1983
ERIK THE CONQUEROR, 1963
EROTIQUE, 1969
ESCAPADE, 1932
ESCAPE BY NIGHT, 1937
ESCAPE DANGEROUS, 1947
ESCAPE ME NEVER, 1935
ESCAPE TO DANGER, 1943
ESCAPE TO GLORY, 1940
ESCAPE TO PARADISE, 1939
ESCORT FOR HIRE, 1960
ETERNAL FEMININE, THE, 1931
EVERY LITTLE CROOK AND NANNY, 1972
EVERYBODY'S HOBBY, 1939
EVERYMAN'S LAW, 1936
EVERYTHING IN LIFE, 1936
EVIL OF FRANKENSTEIN, THE, 1964
EVILSPEAK, 1982
EX-LADY, 1933
EXCUSE MY GLOVE, 1936
EXECUTIONER, THE, 1970
EXPERT'S OPINION, 1935
EXPOSED, 1932
EXPRESSO BONGO, 1959
EXTRA DAY, THE, 1956
EYE FOR AN EYE, AN, 1981
EYE OF THE CAT, 1969
EYE OF THE TIGER, 1986
EYES OF FIRE, 1984
EYES OF THE AMARYLLIS, THE, 1982
EYES OF THE WORLD, THE, 1930
EYES THAT KILL, 1947
FABULOUS SENORITA, THE, 1952
FACE OF ANOTHER, THE, 1967
FACE OF MARBLE, THE, 1946
FACING THE MUSIC, 1933
FALLGUY, 1962
FALLING IN LOVE AGAIN, 1980
FALSE FACES, 1932
FALSE PRETENSES, 1935
FALSE RAPTURE, 1941
FAME STREET, 1932
FAMILY HONOR, 1973
FANNY FOLEY HERSELF, 1931
FANTASTICA, 1980
FAR NORTH, 1988
FAREWELL, DOVES, 1962
FARGO EXPRESS, 1933
FARMER'S WIFE, THE, 1941
FASCINATION, 1931
FAST BREAK, 1979
FAST LIFE, 1929
FAST LIFE, 1932
FAST-WALKING, 1982
FAT ANGELS, 1980
FATAL BEAUTY, 1987
FATHER IS A BACHELOR, 1950
FATHER O'FLYNN, 1938
FATHER TAKES A WIFE, 1941
FATHER'S WILD GAME, 1950

FBI GIRL, 1951
FEATHER IN HER HAT, A, 1935
FEATHERED SERPENT, THE, 1934
FEATHERED SERPENT, THE, 1948
FEDERAL AGENT, 1936
FEDERAL AGENT AT LARGE, 1950
FEDERAL FUGITIVES, 1941
FELLER NEEDS A FRIEND, 1932
FEMALE ANIMAL, THE, 1958
FEUD MAKER, 1938
FEUD OF THE RANGE, 1939
FFOLKES, 1980
FIDDLERS THREE, 1944
FIDDLIN' BUCKAROO, THE, 1934
FIEND OF DOPE ISLAND, 1961
FIFTY FATHOMS DEEP, 1931
FIGHT FOR THE GLORY, 1970
FIGHTING BILL CARSON, 1945
FIGHTING BUCKAROO, THE, 1943
FIGHTING CABALLERO, 1935
FIGHTING CODE, THE, 1934
FIGHTING COWBOY, 1933
FIGHTING LEGION, THE, 1930
FIGHTING RANGER, THE, 1948
FIGHTING SHADOWS, 1935
FILES FROM SCOTLAND YARD, 1951
FINAL APPOINTMENT, 1954
FINE MESS, A, 1986
FINISHING SCHOOL, 1934
FIRE AND ICE, 1983
FIREBIRD, THE, 1934
FIREBIRD 2015 AD, 1981
FIREPOWER, 1979
FIRETRAP, THE, 1935
FIREWALKER, 1986
FIRST DEADLY SIN, THE, 1980
FIRST OFFENDERS, 1939
FISHERMAN'S WHARF, 1939
FIVE DAYS FROM HOME, 1978
FIVE FINGER EXERCISE, 1962
FIVE GUNS TO TOMBSTONE, 1961
FIVE LITTLE PEPPERS AT HOME, 1940
FIVE OF A KIND, 1938
FIVE POUND MAN, THE, 1937
FIVE TO ONE, 1963
FIVE WILD GIRLS, 1966
FLAME, THE, 1948
FLAME OF STAMBOUL, 1957
FLAME OF THE ISLANDS, 1955
FLAMES, 1932
FLAMING FRONTIER, 1968
FLAMING GUNS, 1933
FLAMING LEAD, 1939
FLASHPOINT, 1984
FLAW, THE, 1955
FLIGHT, 1960
FLIGHT FROM FOLLY, 1945
FLIGHT FROM SINGAPORE, 1962
FLIGHT NURSE, 1953
FLIRTING WITH FATE, 1938
FLOODTIDE, 1949
FLOWERS IN THE ATTIC, 1987
FLYING CADETS, 1941
FLYING FISTS, THE, 1938
FLYING FORTRESS, 1942
FLYING MARINE, THE, 1929
FLYING WITH MUSIC, 1942
FOG ISLAND, 1945
FOLLOW THAT MAN, 1961
FOLLOW THE BOYS, 1963
FOOLISH HUSBANDS, 1948
FOOTLIGHT FEVER, 1941
FOOTLIGHTS AND FOOLS, 1929
FOOTLOOSE HEIRESS, THE, 1937
FOOTSTEPS IN THE NIGHT, 1932
FOR BEAUTY'S SAKE, 1941
FOR YOU ALONE, 1945
FORBIDDEN VALLEY, 1938
FORBIDDEN ZONE, 1980
FOREIGNER, THE, 1978
FOREVER YOUNG, 1984
FORLORN RIVER, 1937
FORMULA, THE, 1980
FORT TI, 1953
FORTUNES OF CAPTAIN BLOOD, 1950
FORTY ACRE FEUD, 1965

FORTYNINERS, THE, 1954
FOUNTAIN, THE, 1934
FOUR FOR THE MORGUE, 1962
FOUR SIDED TRIANGLE, 1953
48 HOURS, 1944
40 GUNS TO APACHE PASS, 1967
FOXY LADY, 1971
FRAMED, 1940
FRANCHETTE; LES INTRIGUES, 1969
FRANCIS IN THE HAUNTED HOUSE, 1956
FRATERNITY VACATION, 1985
FREDDY UNTER FREMDEN STERNEN, 1962
FREE LOVE, 1930
FREEWHEELIN', 1976
FRENCH CONSPIRACY, THE, 1973
FRESH FROM PARIS, 1955
FRIENDLY ENEMIES, 1942
FRIENDS AND LOVERS, 1931
FRISCO LILL, 1942
FRISCO TORNADO, 1950
FRISKY, 1955
FROM A ROMAN BALCONY, 1961
FROM THE EARTH TO THE MOON, 1958
FRONT, THE, 1976
FRONTIER AGENT, 1948
FRONTIER CRUSADER, 1940
FRONTIER JUSTICE, 1936
FRONTIER LAW, 1943
FRONTIER UPRISING, 1961
FRONTIERS OF '49, 1939
FROZEN DEAD, THE, 1967
FUGITIVE VALLEY, 1941
FUNERAL FOR AN ASSASSIN, 1977
FUNNY FARM, 1988
FURIES, THE, 1930
FURY, THE, 1978
FURY BELOW, 1938
FURY OF HERCULES, THE, 1961
FURY OF THE PAGANS, 1963
G.I. WAR BRIDES, 1946
GABLES MYSTERY, THE, 1931
GALLANT DEFENDER, 1935
GALLANT FOOL, THE, 1933
GALLANT JOURNEY, 1946
GALLANT LADY, 1942
GALLOPING DYNAMITE, 1937
GALLOPING ROMEO, 1933
GALS, INCORPORATED, 1943
GAMBLER AND THE LADY, THE, 1952
GAMBLER WORE A GUN, THE, 1961
GAMBLER, THE, 1958
GAMBLING, 1934
GAMBLING DAUGHTERS, 1941
GAMBLING SEX, 1932
GAMBLING SHIP, 1939
GAME THAT KILLS, THE, 1937
GAMERA VERSUS BARUGON, 1966
GAMERA VERSUS GAOS, 1967
GAMERA VERSUS GUIRON, 1969
GAMERA VERSUS MONSTER K, 1970
GAMERA VERSUS VIRAS, 1968
GAMERA VERSUS ZIGRA, 1971
GAMES THAT LOVERS PLAY, 1971
GANG WAR, 1928
GANG WAR, 1962
GANG'S ALL HERE, 1941
GANGS OF THE WATERFRONT, 1945
GANGSTER'S BOY, 1938
GANGSTERS OF THE FRONTIER, 1944
GANGWAY, 1937
GAOLBREAK, 1962
GAPPA THE TRIFIBIAN MONSTER, 1967
GARDEN MURDER CASE, THE, 1936
GARDEN OF EDEN, 1954
GAS HOUSE KIDS, 1946
GATLING GUN, THE, 1972
GAUCHOS OF EL DORADO, 1941
GAY BUCKAROO, THE, 1932
GAY DECEIVERS, THE, 1969
GAY DOG, THE, 1954
GAY INTRUDERS, THE, 1948
GAY OLD DOG, 1936
GAY SISTERS, THE, 1942
GAY VAGABOND, THE, 1941
GEISHA GIRL, 1952
GENERATION, 1969

GENIUS AT WORK, 1946
GENTLE PEOPLE AND THE QUIET LAND, THE, 1972
GENTLE RAIN, THE, 1966
GENTLE TERROR, THE, 1962
GENTLEMAN OF PARIS, A, 1931
GENTLEMAN'S GENTLEMAN, A, 1939
GENTLEMEN WITH GUNS, 1946
GEORGE IN CIVVY STREET, 1946
GET MEAN, 1976
GET OUTTA TOWN, 1960
GET THAT MAN, 1935
GETTING EVEN, 1986
GHOST DANCE, 1984
GHOST IN THE INVISIBLE BIKINI, 1966
GHOST OF HIDDEN VALLEY, 1946
GHOST TOWN, 1937
GHOST TOWN RIDERS, 1938
GHOULIES, 1985
GIANT OF METROPOLIS, THE, 1963
GIDGET GOES TO ROME, 1963
GIGANTIS, 1959
GIGOLETTE, 1935
GIRARA, 1967
GIRDLE OF GOLD, 1952
GIRL AND THE LEGEND, THE, 1966
GIRL CAN'T STOP, THE, 1966
GIRL FROM PETROVKA, THE, 1974
GIRL FROM VALLADOLIO, 1958
GIRL FROM WOOLWORTH'S, THE, 1929
GIRL HABIT, 1931
GIRL I ABANDONED, THE, 1970
GIRL IN THE BIKINI, THE, 1958
GIRL IN THE CROWD, THE, 1934
GIRL IN THE GLASS CAGE, THE, 1929
GIRL IN THE SHOW, THE, 1929
GIRL ON APPROVAL, 1962
GIRL ON THE BARGE, THE, 1929
GIRL OVERBOARD, 1929
GIRL SAID NO, THE, 1937
GIRL WHO CAME BACK, THE, 1935
GIRL WHO DARED, THE, 1944
GIRL WITH THE GOLDEN EYES, THE, 1962
GIRL, THE, 1987
GIRLS IN CHAINS, 1943
GIRLS IN PRISON, 1956
GIRLS IN THE NIGHT, 1953 83m UNIV bw
GIRLS IN THE STREET, 1937
GIRLS OF THE ROAD, 1940
GIRLS PLEASE!, 1934
GIRLS SCHOOL SCREAMERS, 1986
GIVE AND TAKE, 1929
GLAD TIDINGS, 1953
GLADIATORS 7, 1964
GLADIATORS, THE, 1970
GLAMOUR, 1931
GLAMOUR, 1934
GLASS OF WATER, A, 1962
GLENROWAN AFFAIR, THE, 1951
GLIMPSE OF PARADISE, A, 1934
GLORY BOY, 1971
GLORY TRAIL, THE, 1937
GLOVE, THE, 1980
GOD FORGIVES—I DON'T!, 1969
GOD IS MY PARTNER, 1957
GOD'S COUNTRY, 1946
GOD'S COUNTRY AND THE MAN, 1931
GOD'S GUN, 1977
GODZILLA 1985, 1985
GODZILLA VERSUS THE COSMIC MONSTER, 1974
GODZILLA VERSUS THE SEA MONSTER, 1966
GODZILLA VS. MEGALON, 1976
GODZILLA VS. THE THING, 1964
GOING APE!, 1981
GOLD DUST GERTIE, 1931
GOLD FOR THE CAESARS, 1964
GOLD GUITAR, THE, 1966
GOLDEN ARROW, THE, 1964
GOLDEN NEEDLES, 1974
GOLDEN PLAGUE, THE, 1963
GOLIATH AND THE DRAGON, 1961
GONE TO THE DOGS, 1939
GONKS GO BEAT, 1965
GOOD GUYS AND THE BAD GUYS, THE, 1969
GOOD TIMES, 1967
GOODBYE LOVE, 1934
GOODNIGHT SWEETHEART, 1944

GORATH, 1964
GORBALS STORY, THE, 1950
GORILLA, THE, 1931
GOTHIC, 1987
GRAND CANARY, 1934
GRAND JURY, 1936
GRAND JURY SECRETS, 1939
GRAND PARADE, THE, 1930
GRAND PRIX, 1966
GRAVEYARD SHIFT, 1987
GREAT ADVENTURE, THE, 1976
GREAT CITIZEN, THE, 1939
GREAT COMMANDMENT, THE, 1941
GREAT DAY, 1945
GREAT DIVIDE, THE, 1930
GREAT FLIRTATION, THE, 1934
GREAT GUNDOWN, THE, 1977
GREAT JESSE JAMES RAID, THE, 1953
GREAT MEADOW, THE, 1931
GREAT MR. HANDEL, THE, 1942
GREAT PLANE ROBBERY, 1950
GREAT ST. LOUIS BANK ROBBERY, THE, 1959
GREAT SWINDLE, THE, 1941
GREAT TRAIN ROBBERY, THE, 1941
GREEN-EYED BLONDE, THE, 1957
GREEN EYES, 1934
GREEN HELMET, THE, 1961
GREEN ICE, 1981
GRIDIRON FLASH, 1935
GRIEF STREET, 1931
GRIM REAPER, THE, 1981
GRIZZLY, 1976
GROUCH, THE, 1961
GUADALAJARA, 1943
GUARD THAT GIRL, 1935
GUILTY?, 1930
GUILTY MELODY, 1936
GUILTY PARENTS, 1934
GULLIVER'S TRAVELS, 1977
GUMBALL RALLY, THE, 1976
GUN CODE, 1940
GUN HAWK, THE, 1963
GUN LAW, 1933
GUN LAW JUSTICE, 1949
GUN RUNNER, 1949
GUN SMOKE, 1931
GUN TOWN, 1946
GUN, THE, 1978
GUNFIGHTERS OF ABILENE, 1960
GUNFIGHTERS, THE, 1947
GUNFIRE, 1950
GUNFIRE AT INDIAN GAP, 1957
GUNMEN FROM LAREDO, 1959
GUNNING FOR JUSTICE, 1948
GUNS AND GUITARS, 1936
GUNS AND THE FURY, THE, 1983
GUNS, GIRLS AND GANGSTERS, 1958
GUNS OF DIABLO, 1964
GUNS OF THE LAW, 1944
GUNS OF THE PECOS, 1937
GUNSLINGERS, 1950
GUY, A GAL AND A PAL, A, 1945
GUY CALLED CAESAR, A, 1962
GUY COULD CHANGE, A, 1946
GYMKATA, 1985
GYPSY AND THE GENTLEMAN, THE, 1958
HAIL TO THE RANGERS, 1943
HAIR OF THE DOG, 1962
HALF A SINNER, 1940
HALF HUMAN, 1955
HALF WAY TO HEAVEN, 1929
HALF WAY TO SHANGHAI, 1942
HALLOWEEN II, 1981
HALLUCINATION GENERATION, 1966
HAMMERSMITH IS OUT, 1972
HAND OF DEATH, 1962
HANDLE WITH CARE, 1932
HANDS OF DESTINY, 1954
HANGMAN'S WHARF, 1950
HAPPY BIRTHDAY, GEMINI, 1980
HAPPY BIRTHDAY TO ME, 1981
HAPPY DAYS ARE HERE AGAIN, 1936
HAPPY DEATHDAY, 1969
HARASSED HERO, THE, 1954
HARD STEEL, 1941
HARDBOILED ROSE, 1929

BOLD: Films on Videocassette

HAREM BUNCH; OR WAR AND PIECE, THE, 1969
HARLEM RIDES THE RANGE, 1939
HARLOW, 1965
HARMONY AT HOME, 1930
HARMONY ROW, 1933
HARRAD EXPERIMENT, THE, 1973
HAT CHECK HONEY, 1944
HATE IN PARADISE, 1938
HATE SHIP, THE, 1930
HAUNTED HONEYMOON, 1986
HAUNTED HOUSE, THE, 1928
HAVANA ROSE, 1951
HAVE A HEART, 1934
HAVE A NICE WEEKEND, 1975
HAWMPS!, 1976
HE LEARNED ABOUT WOMEN, 1933
HE SNOOPS TO CONQUER, 1944
HE WHO SHOOTS FIRST, 1966
HEALER, THE, 1935
HEAR ME GOOD, 1957
HEARSE, THE, 1980
HEART OF A CHILD, 1958
HEART OF THE RIO GRANDE, 1942
HEARTS DIVIDED, 1936
HEAT, 1970
HEAVEN ON EARTH, 1960
HEIGHTS OF DANGER, 1962
HELD IN TRUST, 1949
HELICOPTER SPIES, THE, 1968
HELL BENT FOR LEATHER, 1960
HELL IS EMPTY, 1967
HELL ON WHEELS, 1967
HELL-SHIP MORGAN, 1936
HELL SQUAD, 1958
HELLO, ELEPHANT, 1954
HELLO SISTER, 1930
HELLO SWEETHEART, 1935
HELL'S BELLES, 1969
HELL'S CROSSROADS, 1957
HELL'S HALF ACRE, 1954
HELL'S HORIZON, 1955
HELP YOURSELF, 1932
HER ADVENTUROUS NIGHT, 1946
HER BODYGUARD, 1933
HER FIRST AFFAIRE, 1932
HER FIRST ROMANCE, 1951
HER LAST AFFAIRE, 1935
HER MAJESTY LOVE, 1931
HER NIGHT OUT, 1932
HER SPLENDID FOLLY, 1933
HER TWELVE MEN, 1954
HERCULES AGAINST THE MOON MEN, 1965
HERE COMES THE BAND, 1935
HERE COMES THE GROOM, 1934
HERE COMES TROUBLE, 1936
HERE COMES TROUBLE, 1948
HERO OF BABYLON, 1963
HEROD THE GREAT, 1960
HEROES, 1977
HEROES OF THE SADDLE, 1940
HEX, 1973
HEY, GOOD LOOKIN', 1982
HEY! HEY! U.S.A., 1938
HI-JACKED, 1950
HI-JACKERS, THE, 1963
HI, NEIGHBOR, 1942
HIDDEN ENEMY, 1940
HIDE AND SEEK, 1964
HIDEOUS SUN DEMON, THE, 1959
HIGH, 1968
HIGH COMMAND, 1938
HIGH FLYERS, 1937
HIGH JUMP, 1959
HIGH POWERED, 1945
HIGH RISK, 1981
HIGH SCHOOL GIRL, 1935
HIGH SEAS, 1929
HIGH SOCIETY, 1932
HIGH SPEED, 1932
HIGH TREASON, 1937
HIGH VOLTAGE, 1929
HIGHLY DANGEROUS, 1950
HIGHWAY DRAGNET, 1954
HIGHWAY PATROL, 1938
HIGHWAY WEST, 1941
HIGHWAYS BY NIGHT, 1942

HILLBILLYS IN A HAUNTED HOUSE, 1967
HILLS HAVE EYES II, THE, 1985
HIS BROTHER'S KEEPER, 1939
HIS FIRST COMMAND, 1929
HIS GRACE GIVES NOTICE, 1933
HIS LUCKY DAY, 1929
HIS MAJESTY AND CO, 1935
HIS PRIVATE SECRETARY, 1933
HIT THE HAY, 1945
HIT THE ROAD, 1941
HITLER, 1962
HITTING A NEW HIGH, 1937
HO, 1968
HOBSON'S CHOICE, 1931
HOEDOWN, 1950
HOFFMAN, 1970
HOLD ME TIGHT, 1933
HOLIDAY WEEK, 1952
HOLLYWOOD BARN DANCE, 1947
HOLLYWOOD MYSTERY, 1934
HOLLYWOOD OR BUST, 1956
HOME AND AWAY, 1956
HOME FREE ALL, 1984
HOME ON THE RANGE, 1935
HOME SWEET HOME, 1945
HOME SWEET HOME, 1981
HOME TO DANGER, 1951
HOME TOWN STORY, 1951
HOMESTEADERS OF PARADISE VALLEY, 1947
HONEYMOON DEFERRED, 1940
HONEYMOON FOR THREE, 1941
HONEYMOON HOTEL, 1964
HONOLULU LU, 1941
HONOLULU-TOKYO-HONG KONG, 1963
HONOR OF THE FAMILY, 1931
HONOR OF THE MOUNTED, 1932
HONOR OF THE PRESS, 1932
HOPPY'S HOLIDAY, 1947
HORNET'S NEST, THE, 1955
HOROSCOPE, 1950
HORROR HOSPITAL, 1973
HORROR HOUSE, 1970
HORSE IN THE GRAY FLANNEL SUIT, THE, 1968
HORSEPLAY, 1933
HORSE'S MOUTH, THE, 1953
HOSTAGE, 1987
HOSTILE WITNESS, 1968
HOT ANGEL, THE, 1958
HOT CAR GIRL, 1958
HOT MONEY, 1936
HOT NEWS, 1936
HOT POTATO, 1976
HOT RESORT, 1985
HOT ROD, 1950
HOT ROD GIRL, 1956
HOT ROD RUMBLE, 1957
HOT STUFF, 1929
HOT TIMES, 1974
HOTEL SPLENDIDE, 1932
HOTEL VARIETY, 1933
HOUR BEFORE THE DAWN, THE, 1944
HOUR OF DECISION, 1957
HOUSE ACROSS THE STREET, THE, 1949
HOUSE IS NOT A HOME, A, 1964
HOUSE OF ERRORS, 1942
HOUSE OF EVIL, 1968
HOUSE OF FEAR, THE, 1939
HOUSE OF LIFE, 1953
HOUSE OF STRANGE LOVES, THE, 1969
HOUSE OF UNREST, THE, 1931
HOUSE ON THE SAND, 1967
HOUSE OPPOSITE, THE, 1931
HOUSE WHERE EVIL DWELLS, THE, 1982
HOW DO I LOVE THEE?, 1970
HOW DO YOU DO?, 1946
HOWARD CASE, THE, 1936
HOWARD THE DUCK, 1986
HOWLING TWO: YOUR SISTER IS A WEREWOLF, 1985
HOWLING III, THE, 1987
HUCKLEBERRY FINN, 1974
HUDDLE, 1932
HUGGETTS ABROAD, THE, 1949
HUK, 1956
HUMAN CARGO, 1936
HUMAN EXPERIMENTS, 1980

HUMAN TORNADO, THE, 1976
HUMAN VAPOR, THE, 1964
HUNDRED POUND WINDOW, THE, 1943
HUNK, 1987
HUNTED, THE, 1948
HURRICANE HORSEMAN, 1931
HURRICANE SMITH, 1952
HUSBAND'S HOLIDAY, 1931
HUSH MONEY, 1931
HYPNOTIC EYE, THE, 1960
I AM NOT AFRAID, 1939
I CAN'T ESCAPE, 1934
I CHEATED THE LAW, 1949
I COVER CHINATOWN, 1938
I DEAL IN DANGER, 1966
I DEMAND PAYMENT, 1938
I HATE MY BODY, 1975
I KILLED GERONIMO, 1950
I KILLED WILD BILL HICKOK, 1956
I LIKE YOUR NERVE, 1931
I LOVE MY WIFE, 1970
I LOVE THAT MAN, 1933
I LOVED YOU WEDNESDAY, 1933
I, MAUREEN, 1978
I RING DOORBELLS, 1946
I SELL ANYTHING, 1934
I SHOT BILLY THE KID, 1950
I SPY, 1933
I SURRENDER DEAR, 1948
I TAKE THIS WOMAN, 1940
I, THE JURY, 1982
I, TOO, AM ONLY A WOMAN, 1963
I WAS A CAPTIVE IN NAZI GERMANY, 1936
I WAS A CONVICT, 1939
I WAS A SHOPLIFTER, 1950
I WAS A TEENAGE FRANKENSTEIN, 1958
I WAS A TEENAGE ZOMBIE, 1987
I WILL . . .I WILL . . .FOR NOW, 1976
I'D GIVE MY LIFE, 1936
IDOL OF PARIS, 1948
IF I WERE FREE, 1933
IF YOU COULD SEE WHAT I HEAR, 1982
I'LL BE YOUR SWEETHEART, 1945
I'LL LOVE YOU ALWAYS, 1935
I'LL REMEMBER APRIL, 1945
I'LL SELL MY LIFE, 1941
I'LL STICK TO YOU, 1933
I'LL TELL THE WORLD, 1945
ILLEGAL, 1932
I'M A STRANGER, 1952
I'M FROM MISSOURI, 1939
IMPROPER DUCHESS, THE, 1936
IN LIKE FLINT, 1967
IN MACARTHUR PARK, 1977
IN OLD CALIFORNIA, 1929
IN OLD MONTANA, 1939
IN SEARCH OF ANNA, 1978
IN SPITE OF DANGER, 1935
IN THE COOL OF THE DAY, 1963
IN THE NEXT ROOM, 1930
IN THE YEAR 2889, 1966
IN TROUBLE WITH EVE, 1964
INBREAKER, THE, 1974
INCREDIBLE PETRIFIED WORLD, THE, 1959
INCREDIBLE SARAH, THE, 1976
INCUBUS, 1966
INFERNAL MACHINE, 1933
INFORMER, THE, 1929
INITIATION, THE, 1984
INNER CIRCLE, THE, 1946
INNOCENT SINNERS, 1958
INSIDE DAISY CLOVER, 1965
INSIDE INFORMATION, 1934
INSIDE JOB, 1946
INSIDE THE LINES, 1930
INSIGNIFICANCE, 1985
INTERLUDE, 1957
INTRIGUE, 1947
INTRUDER, THE, 1932
INVADERS FROM MARS, 1986
INVASION OF THE ANIMAL PEOPLE, 1962
INVASION OF THE SAUCER MEN, 1957
INVASION 1700, 1965
INVINCIBLE GLADIATOR, THE, 1963
INVISIBLE ENEMY, 1938
INVISIBLE INFORMER, 1946

INVISIBLE INVADERS, 1959
INVISIBLE KILLER, THE, 1940
INVISIBLE MAN, THE, 1958
INVISIBLE STRANGLER, 1984
INVISIBLE WALL, THE, 1947
INVITATION TO THE WALTZ, 1935
IO . . . TU . . . Y . . . ELLA, 1933
IRISH AND PROUD OF IT, 1938
IRISH FOR LUCK, 1936
IRON ANGEL, 1964
IRON EAGLE, 1986
IRON PETTICOAT, THE, 1956
IRONWEED, 1987
IS THERE JUSTICE?, 1931
ISAAC LITTLEFEATHERS, 1984
ISLAND IN THE SUN, 1957
ISLAND OF LOST WOMEN, 1959
ISLAND OF THE DAMNED, 1976
ISLAND OF THE DOOMED, 1968
ISLE OF DESTINY, 1940
ISLE OF ESCAPE, 1930
ISLE OF MISSING MEN, 1942
ISLE OF SIN, 1963
ISN'T IT ROMANTIC?, 1948
IT AIN'T EASY, 1972
IT CAN'T LAST FOREVER, 1937
IT COULD HAPPEN TO YOU, 1937
IT HAPPENED IN BROAD DAYLIGHT, 1960
IT HAPPENED IN PARIS, 1935
IT STARTED IN THE ALPS, 1966
IT'S A BIKINI WORLD, 1967
IT'S A GRAND OLD WORLD, 1937
IT'S A JOKE, SON!, 1947
IT'S A SMALL WORLD, 1935
IT'S A WONDERFUL DAY, 1949
IT'S ALIVE, 1968
IT'S GREAT TO BE YOUNG, 1946
IT'S IN THE AIR, 1935
IT'S NOT THE SIZE THAT COUNTS, 1979
JACK AHOY!, 1935
JACK OF DIAMONDS, 1967
JACK SLADE, 1953
JACK THE RIPPER, 1959
JACKPOT, 1960
JANIE GETS MARRIED, 1946
JAVA HEAD, 1935
JAZZ CINDERELLA, 1930
JAZZMAN, 1984
JEALOUSY, 1931
JEALOUSY, 1934
JEKYLL AND HYDE. . .TOGETHER AGAIN, 1982
JENNIE, 1941
JENNIFER, 1953
JERUSALEM FILE, THE, 1972
JESSE JAMES MEETS FRANKENSTEIN'S
 DAUGHTER, 1966
JESSE JAMES VERSUS THE DALTONS, 1954
JESSICA, 1962
JET JOB, 1952
JEWELS OF BRANDENBURG, 1947
JIGGS AND MAGGIE IN SOCIETY, 1948
JIGGS AND MAGGIE OUT WEST, 1950
JIGSAW, 1968
JIM HANVEY, DETECTIVE, 1937
JIMMY AND SALLY, 1933
JIMMY ORPHEUS, 1966
JOEY BOY, 1965
JOHANSSON GETS SCOLDED, 1945
JOHNNY BANCO, 1969
JOHNNY CONCHO, 1956
JOHNNY HAMLET, 1972
JOHNNY YUMA, 1967
JOSSER ON THE FARM, 1934
JOY OF LIVING, 1938
JOY RIDE, 1935
JUDGMENT IN BERLIN, 1988
JUDY'S LITTLE NO-NO, 1969
JUKE BOX RACKET, 1960
JULIA AND JULIA, 1988
JULIETTA, 1957
JUMP, 1971
JUMP INTO HELL, 1955
JUNGLE GENTS, 1954
JUNGLE GODDESS, 1948
JUNGLE STREET GIRLS, 1963
JUNIOR ARMY, 1943

JUPITER'S DARLING, 1955
JURY'S EVIDENCE, 1936
JUST BEFORE DAWN, 1980
JUST FOR A SONG, 1930
JUST ME, 1950
JUST OUT OF REACH, 1979
JUVENILE JUNGLE, 1958
KEEP 'EM ROLLING, 1934
KEEP IT CLEAN, 1956
KEEP IT QUIET, 1934
KEEPER OF THE BEES, 1935
KEEPING COMPANY, 1941
KELLY THE SECOND, 1936
KENNER, 1969
KENTUCKY BLUE STREAK, 1935
KEY MAN, THE, 1957
KICK IN, 1931
KID COURAGEOUS, 1935
KID FROM GOWER GULCH, THE, 1949
KID FROM KANSAS, THE, 1941
KID FROM SANTA FE, THE, 1940
KID FROM TEXAS, THE, 1950
KID RANGER, THE, 1936
KID RIDES AGAIN, THE, 1943
KID'S LAST RIDE, THE, 1941
KILL A DRAGON, 1967
KILL HER GENTLY, 1958
KILLER AT LARGE, 1936
KILLER KLOWNS FROM OUTER SPACE, 1988
KILLER PARTY, 1986
KILLER SHARK, 1950
KILLER SHREWS, THE, 1959
KILLERS OF THE WILD, 1940
KILLING OF A CHINESE BOOKIE, THE, 1976
KIND STEPMOTHER, 1936
KINDRED, THE, 1987
KING KONG, 1976
KING KONG ESCAPES, 1968
KING KONG VERSUS GODZILLA, 1963
KING OF THE CASTLE, 1936
KING OF THE DAMNED, 1936
KING OF THE GAMBLERS, 1948
KING OF THE LUMBERJACKS, 1940
KING OF THE RITZ, 1933
KING OF THE STALLIONS, 1942
KING OF THE UNDERWORLD, 1952
KINGFISH CAPER, THE, 1976
KING'S CUP, THE, 1933
KISS FOR CORLISS, A, 1949
KISS ME GOODBYE, 1982
KISS ME, STUPID, 1964
KISSING CUP'S RACE, 1930
KLONDIKE FEVER, 1980
KLONDIKE KATE, 1944
KNIGHTS FOR A DAY, 1937
KNOCK, 1955
KRULL, 1983
LA CONGA NIGHTS, 1940
LA CUCARACHA, 1961
LA FERME DU PENDU, 1946
LA SEGUA, 1985
LADIES IN DISTRESS, 1938
LADY BEHAVE, 1937
LADY CHASER, 1946
LADY GODIVA, 1955
LADY HAMILTON, 1969
LADY ICE, 1973
LADY IN DANGER, 1934
LADY OBJECTS, THE, 1938
LADY OF THE TROPICS, 1939
LADY VANISHES, THE, 1980
LADY WANTS MINK, THE, 1953
LAFAYETTE, 1963
LAMBETH WALK, THE, 1940
LAMP IN ASSASSIN MEWS, THE, 1962
LANCASHIRE LUCK, 1937
LAND OF NO RETURN, THE, 1981
LAND OF THE MINOTAUR, 1976
LAND OF THE SIX GUNS, 1940
LANDSCAPE SUICIDE, 1986
LARAMIE, 1949
LARAMIE MOUNTAINS, 1952
LARCENY STREET, 1941
LAS VEGAS FREE-FOR-ALL, 1968
LAS VEGAS LADY, 1976
LAS VEGAS NIGHTS, 1941

LASERBLAST, 1978
LAST ACT OF MARTIN WESTON, THE, 1970
LAST ADVENTURE, THE, 1968
LAST CURTAIN, THE, 1937
LAST DAYS OF MAN ON EARTH, THE, 1975
LAST FIGHT, THE, 1983
LAST FRONTIER UPRISING, 1947
LAST MAN TO HANG, THE, 1956
LAST OF THE DUANES, 1930
LAST OF THE RED HOT LOVERS, 1972
LAST OF THE VIKINGS, THE, 1962
LAST POST, THE, 1929
LAST REMAKE OF BEAU GESTE, THE, 1977
LAST ROSE OF SUMMER, THE, 1937
LAST ROUND-UP, THE, 1934
LAST TRAIL, THE, 1934
LAST TRAIN FROM BOMBAY, 1952
LAST WARNING, THE, 1929
LAST WARNING, THE, 1938
LAST WOMAN ON EARTH, THE, 1960
LATE EXTRA, 1935
LAUGHING AT DANGER, 1940
LAUGHING AT LIFE, 1933
LAUGHING IN THE SUNSHINE, 1953
LAW AND ORDER, 1942
LAW AND ORDER, 1953
LAW AND THE LADY, THE, 1951
LAW FOR TOMBSTONE, 1937
LAW OF THE BARBARY COAST, 1949
LAW OF THE JUNGLE, 1942
LAW OF THE NORTHWEST, 1943
LAW OF THE PANHANDLE, 1950
LAW OF THE TIMBER, 1941
LAW OF THE TROPICS, 1941
LAW OF THE UNDERWORLD, 1938
LAW RIDES AGAIN, THE, 1943
LAWLESS LAND, 1937
LAWLESS PLAINSMEN, 1942
LAWLESS WOMAN, THE, 1931
LAWYER'S SECRET, THE, 1931
LAY THAT RIFLE DOWN, 1955
LAZY RIVER, 1934
LEADVILLE GUNSLINGER, 1952
LEAP YEAR, 1932
LEATHER-PUSHERS, THE, 1940
LEATHERNECK, THE, 1929
LEATHERNECKING, 1930
LEATHERNECKS HAVE LANDED, THE, 1936
LEAVE IT TO SMITH, 1934
LEAVE IT TO THE IRISH, 1944
LEFT-HANDED LAW, 1937
LEGACY, THE, 1979
LEGION OF LOST FLYERS, 1939
LENA RIVERS, 1932
LEND ME YOUR HUSBAND, 1935
LEO THE LAST, 1970
LES ABYSSES, 1964
LESS THAN ZERO, 1987
LET'S GO COLLEGIATE, 1941
LET'S GO NATIVE, 1930
LET'S LIVE TONIGHT, 1935
LET'S MAKE A NIGHT OF IT, 1937
LET'S MAKE A MILLION, 1937
LET'S ROCK, 1958
LET'S TALK IT OVER, 1934
LIFE AND TIMES OF GRIZZLY ADAMS, THE, 1974
LIFE RETURNS, 1939
LIFEFORCE, 1985
LIFT, THE, 1965
LIGHT AT THE EDGE OF THE WORLD, THE, 1971
LIGHT FINGERS, 1957
LILLI MARLENE, 1951
LILY OF LAGUNA, 1938
LIMPING MAN, THE, 1931
LIMPING MAN, THE, 1936
LION AND THE HORSE, THE, 1952
LION HUNTERS, THE, 1951
LION OF THE DESERT, 1981
LISA, TOSCA OF ATHENS, 1961
LISETTE, 1961
LISTEN, LET'S MAKE LOVE, 1969
LISTEN TO THE CITY, 1984
LISZTOMANIA, 1975
LITTLE ADVENTURESS, THE, 1938
LITTLE BIG SHOT, 1952
LITTLE BIT OF BLUFF, A, 1935

BOLD: Films on Videocassette

LITTLE DOLLY DAYDREAM, 1938
LITTLE DRAGONS, THE, 1980
LITTLE DRUMMER GIRL, THE, 1984
LITTLE JOE, THE WRANGLER, 1942
LITTLE JUNGLE BOY, 1969
LITTLE MISS BIG, 1946
LITTLE MISS BROADWAY, 1947
LITTLE MISS DEVIL, 1951
LITTLE MISS MARKER, 1980
LITTLE MISS NOBODY, 1936
LITTLE MISS THOROUGHBRED, 1938
LITTLE MISTER JIM, 1946
LITTLE MOTHER, 1973
LITTLE OF WHAT YOU FANCY, A, 1968
LITTLE ORVIE, 1940
LITTLE RED SCHOOLHOUSE, 1936
LITTLE TOUGH GUYS IN SOCIETY, 1938
LITTLE TREASURE, 1985
LIVE A LITTLE, LOVE A LITTLE, 1968
LIVE FAST, DIE YOUNG, 1958
LIVING COFFIN, THE, 1965
LIVING HEAD, THE, 1969
LIVING IDOL, THE, 1957
LLANO KID, THE, 1940
LOCAL BAD MAN, 1932
LOCKED DOOR, THE, 1929
LOCKER 69, 1962
LONDON BY NIGHT, 1937
LONE COWBOY, 1934
LONE GUN, THE, 1954
LONE PRAIRIE, THE, 1942
LONE RIDER, THE, 1930
LONE RIDER AMBUSHED, THE, 1941
LONE RIDER AND THE BANDIT, THE, 1942
LONE RIDER CROSSES THE RIO, THE, 1941
LONE RIDER FIGHTS BACK, THE, 1941
LONE RIDER IN CHEYENNE, THE, 1942
LONE RIDER IN GHOST TOWN, THE, 1941
LONE STAR RANGER, THE, 1930
LONE STAR RANGER, 1942
LONE TEXAS RANGER, 1945
LONE TRAIL, THE, 1932
LONE WOLF IN LONDON, 1947
LONE WOLF IN MEXICO, THE, 1947
LONE WOLF KEEPS A DATE, THE, 1940
LONE WOLF'S DAUGHTER, THE, 1929
LONELY GUY, THE, 1984
LONELY WIVES, 1931
LONERS, THE, 1972
LONESOME TRAIL, THE, 1930
LONG, LONG TRAIL, THE, 1929
LONG RIDE FROM HELL, A, 1970
LONGEST NIGHT, THE, 1936
LOOK FOR THE SILVER LINING, 1949
LOOK UP AND LAUGH, 1935
LOOKER, 1981
LOOKING FOR TROUBLE, 1934
LOOPHOLE, 1954
LOOSE ENDS, 1930
LOOSE ENDS, 1975
LORD RICHARD IN THE PANTRY, 1930
LOST BATTALION, 1961
LOST CHORD, THE, 1937
LOST CONTINENT, 1951
LOST HAPPINESS, 1948
LOST IN THE LEGION, 1934
LOST JUNGLE, THE, 1934
LOST LAGOON, 1958
LOST, LONELY AND VICIOUS, 1958
LOST SOULS, 1961
LOST TRAIL, THE, 1945
LOST WORLD, THE, 1960
LOTTERY LOVER, 1935
LOUISE, 1940
LOUISIANA TERRITORY, 1953
LOVE AMONG THE MILLIONAIRES, 1930
LOVE AND BULLETS, 1979
LOVE AND LEARN, 1947
LOVE AT FIRST SIGHT, 1977
LOVE AT SEA, 1936
LOVE BIRDS, 1934
LOVE BUTCHER, THE, 1982
LOVE COMES ALONG, 1930
LOVE DOCTOR, THE, 1929
LOVE FEAST, THE, 1966
LOVE GOD?, THE, 1969

LOVE, HONOR AND GOODBYE, 1945
LOVE, HONOR, AND OH BABY!, 1933
LOVE, HONOR AND OH, BABY, 1940
LOVE IN BLOOM, 1935
LOVE IN THE DESERT, 1929
LOVE IN THE ROUGH, 1930
LOVE IS A SPLENDID ILLUSION, 1970
LOVE IS A WOMAN, 1967
LOVE ISLAND, 1952
LOVE KISS, THE, 1930
LOVE LAUGHS AT ANDY HARDY, 1946
LOVE MACHINE, THE, 1971
LOVE ME TENDER, 1956
LOVE ON SKIS, 1933
LOVE ON TOAST, 1937
LOVE ON WHEELS, 1932
LOVE PAST THIRTY, 1934
LOVE RACKET, THE, 1929
LOVE SONGS, 1986
LOVE STORM, THE, 1931
LOVE UNDER FIRE, 1937
LOVE UP THE POLE, 1936
LOVER COME BACK, 1931
LOVERS AND LIARS, 1981
LOVERS, THE, 1972
LOVERS OF TOLEDO, THE, 1954
LOVES AND TIMES OF SCARAMOUCHE, THE, 1976
LOVES OF JOANNA GODDEN, THE, 1947
LOVING MEMORY, 1970
LUCK OF ROARING CAMP, THE, 1937
LUCKY DAYS, 1935
LUCKY GIRL, 1932
LUCKY IN LOVE, 1929
LUCKY LADIES, 1932
LUCKY LADY, 1975
LUCKY LARRIGAN, 1933
LUCKY LEGS, 1942
LUCKY MASCOT, THE, 1951
LUCKY PARTNERS, 1940
LUCKY TO ME, 1939
LULU, 1978
LULU BELLE, 1948
LUNA, 1979
MA, HE'S MAKING EYES AT ME, 1940
MACK, THE, 1973
MAD HOLIDAY, 1936
MADAME DU BARRY, 1934
MADAME GUILLOTINE, 1931
MADAME LOUISE, 1951
MADAME SPY, 1942
MADCAP OF THE HOUSE, 1950
MADE, 1972
MADELEINE IS, 1971
MADHOUSE, 1974
MADLY, 1970
MADONNA OF AVENUE A, 1929
MADONNA OF THE STREETS, 1930
MAGIC BOW, THE, 1947
MAGNIFICENT BANDITS, THE, 1969
MAGNIFICENT FRAUD, THE, 1939
MAGNIFICENT ROGUE, THE, 1946
MAGNIFICENT ROUGHNECKS, 1956
MAHOGANY, 1975
MAID OF THE MOUNTAINS, THE, 1932
MAID TO ORDER, 1932
MAIN ATTRACTION, THE, 1962
MAIN STREET TO BROADWAY, 1953
MAKE A MILLION, 1935
MAKE ME AN OFFER, 1954
MAKER OF MEN, 1931
MAKING IT, 1971
MAKING THE GRADE, 1929
MALATESTA'S CARNIVAL, 1973
MALPERTIUS, 1972
MALTESE BIPPY, THE, 1969
MAMA LOVES PAPA, 1945
MAN ABOUT TOWN, 1932
MAN AGAINST WOMAN, 1932
MAN ALIVE, 1945
MAN AND BOY, 1972
MAN AT LARGE, 1941
MAN BEAST, 1956
MAN BETRAYED, A, 1941
MAN FROM CAIRO, THE, 1953
MAN FROM CHICAGO, THE, 1931
MAN FROM COCODY, 1966

MAN FROM DEATH VALLEY, THE, 1931
MAN FROM HONG KONG, 1975
MAN FROM MONTANA, 1941
MAN FROM MOROCCO, THE, 1946
MAN FROM SUNDOWN, THE, 1939
MAN FROM THE RIO GRANDE, THE, 1943
MAN FROM YESTERDAY, THE, 1949
MAN IN THE MOONLIGHT MASK, THE, 1958
MAN IN THE NET, THE, 1959
MAN IN THE VAULT, 1956
MAN IN THE WATER, THE, 1963
MAN OF LA MANCHA, 1972
MAN OF MAYFAIR, 1931
MAN OF SENTIMENT, A, 1933
MAN ON THE RUN, 1949
MAN OR GUN, 1958
MAN OUTSIDE, THE, 1933
MAN-PROOF, 1938
MAN WANTED, 1932
MAN WHO DIED TWICE, THE, 1958
MAN WHO FINALLY DIED, THE, 1967
MAN WHO LIKED FUNERALS, THE, 1959
MAN WHO LOVED WOMEN, THE, 1983
MAN WHO TALKED TOO MUCH, THE, 1940
MAN WHO THOUGHT LIFE, THE, 1969
MAN WHO WOULD NOT DIE, THE, 1975
MAN WITH ONE RED SHOE, THE, 1985
MAN WITH THE MAGNETIC EYES, THE, 1945
MAN WITH TWO LIVES, THE, 1942
MANCHU EAGLE MURDER CAPER MYSTERY, THE, 1975
MANDALAY, 1934
MANDARIN MYSTERY, THE, 1937
MANFISH, 1956
MANHATTAN ANGEL, 1948
MANHATTAN PARADE, 1931
MANHATTAN TOWER, 1932
MANIAC COP, 1988
MAN'S GAME, A, 1934
MANTIS IN LACE, 1968
MANTRAP, THE, 1943
MANY HAPPY RETURNS, 1934
MARCH OF THE SPRING HARE, 1969
MARINE BATTLEGROUND, 1966
MARINES FLY HIGH, THE, 1940
MARIZINIA, 1962
MARK OF THE LASH, 1948
MARK OF THE PHOENIX, 1958
MARK OF THE WITCH, 1970
MARKED GIRLS, 1949
MARKED ONE, THE, 1963
MAROONED, 1933
MARRIAGE-GO-ROUND, THE, 1960
MARRY ME, 1932
MARRY THE BOSS' DAUGHTER, 1941
MARRY THE GIRL, 1935
MARRY THE GIRL, 1937
MARSHAL'S DAUGHTER, THE, 1953
MASK, THE, 1961
MASK OF DIIJON, THE, 1946
MASK OF KOREA, 1950
MASK OF THE DRAGON, 1951
MASQUERADE, 1988
MASSACRE RIVER, 1949
MASTER AND MAN, 1934
MASTER OF HORROR, 1965
MASTER OF THE WORLD, 1935
MATA HARI, 1985
MATINEE IDOL, 1933
MAURIE, 1973
MAVERICK, THE, 1952
MAYA, 1966
MAYOR'S NEST, THE, 1932
MC KENNA OF THE MOUNTED, 1932
MEAN DOG BLUES, 1978
MEATBALLS, 1979
MEATBALLS III, 1987
MEET MR. MALCOLM, 1954
MEET MR. PENNY, 1938
MEET THE DUKE, 1949
MEET THE GIRLS, 1938
MELINDA, 1972
MELODY AND MOONLIGHT, 1940
MELODY FOR TWO, 1937
MELODY LANE, 1929
MELODY MAKER, THE, 1933

MELODY OF MY HEART, 1936
MELVIN, SON OF ALVIN, 1984
MEMOIRS OF A SURVIVOR, 1981
MEN ARE LIKE THAT, 1930
MEN ARE LIKE THAT, 1931
MEN OF CHANCE, 1932
MEN OF STEEL, 1932
MEN OF THE PLAINS, 1936
MEN OF THE SEA, 1938
MEN OF THE TIMBERLAND, 1941
MENACE, THE, 1932
MEN'S CLUB, THE, 1986
MERRILY WE GO TO HELL, 1932
MERRY WIVES OF RENO, THE, 1934
MESSAGE TO GARCIA, A, 1936
MESSENGER OF PEACE, 1950
METAMORPHOSES, 1978
MEXICALI KID, THE, 1938
MEXICALI ROSE, 1929
MEXICAN HAYRIDE, 1948
MEXICAN SPITFIRE AT SEA, 1942
MEXICAN SPITFIRE'S BABY, 1941
MEXICAN SPITFIRE'S BLESSED EVENT, 1943
MEXICO IN FLAMES, 1982
MICHAEL STROGOFF, 1960
MICKEY, THE KID, 1939
MIDAS TOUCH, THE, 1940
MIDDLE COURSE, THE, 1961
MIDDLE WATCH, THE, 1939
MIDDLETON FAMILY AT THE N.Y. WORLD'S FAIR, 1939
MIDNIGHT, 1934
MIDNIGHT ALIBI, 1934
MIDNIGHT CLUB, 1933
MIDNIGHT COURT, 1937
MIDNIGHT MADONNA, 1937
MIDNIGHT PATROL, THE, 1932
MIDNIGHT TAXI, THE, 1928
MIDNIGHT TAXI, 1937
MIDSHIPMAID GOB, 1932
MIDSHIPMAN JACK, 1933
MIDSTREAM, 1929
MIGHTY, THE, 1929
MIGHTY URSUS, 1962
MILLER'S WIFE, THE, 1957
MILLERSON CASE, THE, 1947
MILLIE, 1931
MILLIE'S DAUGHTER, 1947
MILLION DOLLAR BABY, 1935
MILLION DOLLAR RANSOM, 1934
MILLION DOLLAR WEEKEND, 1948
MILLIONAIRE KID, 1936
MILLIONAIRES IN PRISON, 1940
MILLIONS, 1936
MILLS OF THE GODS, 1935
MIND READER, THE, 1933
MIND YOUR OWN BUSINESS, 1937
MINI-SKIRT MOB, THE, 1968
MINX, THE, 1969
MISBEHAVING HUSBANDS, 1941
MISBEHAVING LADIES, 1931
MISS PACIFIC FLEET, 1935
MISS PINKERTON, 1932
MISS V FROM MOSCOW, 1942
MISSING MILLION, THE, 1942
MISSING REMBRANDT, THE, 1932
MISSING WOMEN, 1951
MISSION BATANGAS, 1968
MISSISSIPPI GAMBLER, 1942
MISSISSIPPI RHYTHM, 1949
MR. BOGGS STEPS OUT, 1938
MISTER CINDERELLA, 1936
MR. DISTRICT ATTORNEY, 1941
MR. DOODLE KICKS OFF, 1938
MR. LEMON OF ORANGE, 1931
MR. PATMAN, 1980
MR. QUILP, 1975
MR. RECKLESS, 1948
MR. RICCO, 1975
MR. SKITCH, 1933
MISTER TEN PERCENT, 1967
MIX ME A PERSON, 1962
MODEL FOR MURDER, 1960
MODERN MARRIAGE, A, 1950
MODERN PROBLEMS, 1981
MOJAVE FIREBRAND, 1944

MOKEY, 1942
MONEY MEANS NOTHING, 1934
MONEY TO BURN, 1940
MONEY TRAP, THE, 1966
MONKEY HUSTLE, THE, 1976
MONSOON, 1953
MONSTER CLUB, THE, 1981
MONSTER FROM THE GREEN HELL, 1958
MONSTER OF PIEDRAS BLANCAS, THE, 1959
MONSTER OF THE ISLAND, 1953
MONTREAL MAIN, 1974
MOON OVER LAS VEGAS, 1944
MOONLIGHT IN VERMONT, 1943
MOONLIGHT MASQUERADE, 1942
MOONLIGHT MURDER, 1936
MOONRUNNERS, 1975
MOONWOLF, 1966
MORALS FOR WOMEN, 1931
MORE THAN A MIRACLE, 1967
MOSQUITO COAST, THE, 1986
MOTHERS CRY, 1930
MOTOR MADNESS, 1937
MOTORCYCLE GANG, 1957
MOUNTAIN, THE, 1956
MOVING VIOLATIONS, 1985
MOZAMBIQUE, 1966
MOZART, 1940
MRS. BROWN, YOU'VE GOT A LOVELY DAUGHTER, 1968
MRS. WIGGS OF THE CABBAGE PATCH, 1942
MUCH TOO SHY, 1942
MUG TOWN, 1943
MUMMY'S BOYS, 1936
MUMMY'S CURSE, THE, 1944
MURDER AT COVENT GARDEN, 1932
MURDER AT GLEN ATHOL, 1936
MURDER AT MIDNIGHT, 1931
MURDER BY AN ARISTOCRAT, 1936
MURDER BY INVITATION, 1941
MURDER CAN BE DEADLY, 1963
MURDER CLINIC, THE, 1967
MURDER IN THE BIG HOUSE, 1942
MURDER IN THE BLUE ROOM, 1944
MURDER IN THE FAMILY, 1938
MURDER IN THE FAMILY, 1938
MURDER IN THE MUSEUM, 1934
MURDER IN THE PRIVATE CAR, 1934
MURDER ON THE CAMPUS, 1963
MURDER REPORTED, 1958
MURDER TOMORROW, 1938
MURIETA, 1965
MUSIC GOES 'ROUND, THE, 1936
MUTINY, 1952
MY BLOOD RUNS COLD, 1965
MY DEMON LOVER, 1987
MY FATHER'S MISTRESS, 1970
MY GUN IS QUICK, 1957
MY HEART GOES CRAZY, 1953
MY HEART IS CALLING, 1935
MY LIFE WITH CAROLINE, 1941
MY LIPS BETRAY, 1933
MY NAME IS PECOS, 1966
MY SON, THE VAMPIRE, 1963
MY SONG GOES ROUND THE WORLD, 1934
MY TRUE STORY, 1951
MY WIFE'S FAMILY, 1962
MYSTERIOUS MR. NICHOLSON, THE, 1947
MYSTERY MAN, 1944
MYSTERY OF THUG ISLAND, THE, 1966
MYSTERY SUBMARINE, 1950
NADA MAS QUE UNA MUJER, 1934
NAKED CAGE, THE, 1986
NAKED EARTH, THE, 1958
NAKED HEART, THE, 1955
NAKED HEARTS, 1970
NAKED WITCH, THE, 1964
NAKED WORLD OF HARRISON MARKS, THE, 1967
NANA, 1957
NATURAL ENEMIES, 1979
NAVAJO KID, THE, 1946
NAVAL ACADEMY, 1941
NAVY BOUND, 1951
NAVY WIFE, 1956
NEIGHBORS' WIVES, 1933
NELLY'S VERSION, 1983
NEPTUNE FACTOR, THE, 1973

NEST OF VIPERS, 1979
NESTING, THE, 1981
NEVADA BADMEN, 1951
NEVER LOVE A STRANGER, 1958
NEVER MENTION MURDER, 1964
NEVER SAY DIE, 1939
NEVER SAY GOODBYE, 1946
NEVER THE TWAIN SHALL MEET, 1931
NEVER TOO LATE, 1965
NEVER TROUBLE TROUBLE, 1931
NEVER TRUST A GAMBLER, 1951
NEW ADVENTURES OF TARZAN, 1935
NEW FACES OF 1937, 1937
NEW FRONTIER, THE, 1935
NEW FRONTIER, 1939
NEW HOTEL, THE, 1932
NEW KIND OF LOVE, A, 1963
NEW LIFE STYLE, THE, 1970
NEW LOVE, 1968
NEW MOON, 1930
NEW TEACHER, THE, 1941
NEWLY RICH, 1931
NEWSBOY'S HOME, 1939
NEXT OF KIN, 1942
NEXT TIME I MARRY, 1938
NEXT TIME WE LOVE, 1936
NICE LITTLE BANK THAT SHOULD BE ROBBED, A, 1958
NIGHT AFTER NIGHT AFTER NIGHT, 1970
NIGHT ALARM, 1935
NIGHT AND DAY, 1933
NIGHT BEAT, 1932
NIGHT CROSSING, 1982
NIGHT EVELYN CAME OUT OF THE GRAVE, THE, 1973
NIGHT FOR CRIME, A, 1942
NIGHT FREIGHT, 1955
NIGHT IN MONTMARTE, A, 1931
NIGHT IS OURS, 1930
NIGHT OF LUST, 1965
NIGHT OF THE BLOOD BEAST, 1958
NIGHT OF THE GARTER, 1933
NIGHT OF THE GRIZZLY, THE, 1966
NIGHT RAIDERS, 1952
NIGHT RIDER, THE, 1932
NIGHT RIDERS OF MONTANA, 1951
NIGHT SHADOWS, 1984
NIGHT SONG, 1947
NIGHT SPOT, 1938
NIGHT THE WORLD EXPLODED, THE, 1957
NIGHT TRAIN TO MEMPHIS, 1946
NIGHT VISITOR, THE, 1970
NIGHT WAITRESS, 1936
NIGHT WALKER, THE, 1964
NIGHT WAS OUR FRIEND, 1951
NIGHT WE GOT THE BIRD, THE, 1961
NIGHT WITHOUT STARS, 1953
NIGHTBEAST, 1982
NIGHTMARE IN BLOOD, 1978
NIGHTMARE IN THE SUN, 1964
NIGHTS OF LUCRETIA BORGIA, THE, 1960
NIGHT HAWK, THE, 1938
NINJA III—THE DOMINATION, 1984
NO LEAVE, NO LOVE, 1946
NO MONKEY BUSINESS, 1935
NO, NO NANETTE, 1940
NO OTHER WOMAN, 1933
NO ROAD BACK, 1957
NO SMOKING, 1955
NO TIME FOR FLOWERS, 1952
NO WAY OUT, 1975
NO WAY OUT, 1987
NORAH O'NEALE, 1934
NORTH OF NOME, 1937
NORTH OF SHANGHAI, 1939
NORTH OF THE GREAT DIVIDE, 1950
NORTHWEST TERRITORY, 1952
NOT DAMAGED, 1930
NOT NOW DARLING, 1975
NOT SO DUSTY, 1956
NOTORIOUS AFFAIR, A, 1930
NOTORIOUS CLEOPATRA, THE, 1970
NOTORIOUS SOPHIE LANG, THE, 1934
NOW THAT APRIL'S HERE, 1958
NUDE BOMB, THE, 1980
NO. 96, 1974

BOLD: Films on Videocassette

NUMBER ONE, 1969
NUMBER SEVENTEEN, 1928
OBEY THE LAW, 1933
OBLIGING YOUNG LADY, 1941
OBSESSION, 1954
OFF THE WALL, 1977
OFFICE SCANDAL, THE, 1929
OFFICER AND THE LADY, THE, 1941
OFFICER O'BRIEN, 1930
OH DAD, POOR DAD, MAMA'S HUNG YOU IN THE
　CLOSET AND I'M FEELIN' SO SAD, 1967
OH DADDY!, 1935
OH JOHNNY, HOW YOU CAN LOVE!, 1940
OH, SUSANNA, 1937
OH, WHAT A NIGHT, 1935
OH, WHAT A NIGHT, 1944
OKAY AMERICA, 1932
OKLAHOMA JIM, 1931
OKLAHOMA TERROR, 1939
OLD DRACULA, 1975
OLD FRONTIER, THE, 1950
OLD HOMESTEAD, THE, 1942
OLD LOS ANGELES, 1948
OLD LOUISIANA, 1938
OLD MOTHER RILEY, 1937
OLD MOTHER RILEY AT HOME, 1945
OLD MOTHER RILEY, DETECTIVE, 1943
OLD MOTHER RILEY IN SOCIETY, 1940
OLD MOTHER RILEY JOINS UP, 1939
OLD OKLAHOMA PLAINS, 1952
OLD ROSES, 1935
OLD SOLDIERS NEVER DIE, 1931
OLD SPANISH CUSTOM, AN, 1936
OLD WEST, THE, 1952
OLLY, OLLY, OXEN FREE, 1978
OLSEN'S BIG MOMENT, 1934
O'MALLEY OF THE MOUNTED, 1936
ON APPROVAL, 1930
ON THE AIR LIVE WITH CAPTAIN MIDNIGHT, 1979
ON THE LEVEL, 1930
ON THE NICKEL, 1980
ON THE RIGHT TRACK, 1981
ON THE SPOT, 1940
ON THIN ICE, 1933
ON TOP OF OLD SMOKY, 1953
ON YOUR BACK, 1930
ON YOUR TOES, 1939
ONCE A SINNER, 1931
ONCE A SINNER, 1952
ONCE BEFORE I DIE, 1967
ONCE UPON A COFFEE HOUSE, 1965
ONCE UPON A HONEYMOON, 1942
ONCE UPON A TIME, 1944
ONE AND ONLY GENUINE ORIGINAL FAMILY
　BAND, THE, 1968
ONE APRIL 2000, 1952
ONE CROWDED NIGHT, 1940
ONE DOWN TWO TO GO, 1982
1 = 2?, 1975
ONE FAMILY, 1930
ONE GIRL'S CONFESSION, 1953
ONE GOOD TURN, 1936
ONE HOUR LATE, 1935
ONE HOUR TO LIVE, 1939
ONE MAGIC CHRISTMAS, 1985
ONE MORE TIME, 1970
ONE NIGHT WITH YOU, 1948
ONE ROMANTIC NIGHT, 1930
ONE STEP TO HELL, 1969
ONE STOLEN NIGHT, 1929
1,000 PLANE RAID, THE, 1969
1,000 SHAPES OF A FEMALE, 1963
ONE WAY OUT, 1955
ONE WAY STREET, 1950
ONE-WAY TICKET, 1935
ONE WAY TO LOVE, 1946
ONIBABA, 1965
ONLY A WOMAN, 1966
ONLY GAME IN TOWN, THE, 1970
ONLY THE BRAVE, 1930
OPEN ROAD, THE, 1940
OPENED BY MISTAKE, 1940
OPERATION CIA, 1965
OPERATION DAMES, 1959
OPERATION DELILAH, 1966
OPERATION ENEMY FORT, 1964

OPERATION KID BROTHER, 1967
OPERATION X, 1951
OPTIMISTIC TRAGEDY, THE, 1964
ORDERS ARE ORDERS, 1959
OREGON TRAIL, 1945
ORIENT EXPRESS, 1934
OSA, 1985
OTHER LOVE, THE, 1947
OTHER MEN'S WOMEN, 1931
OTHER SIDE OF THE MOUNTAIN—PART 2, THE,
　1978
OTHER SIDE OF THE MOUNTAIN, THE, 1975
OTHER WOMAN, THE, 1954
OUANGA, 1936
OUR LEADING CITIZEN, 1939
OUR TIME, 1974
OUR WINNING SEASON, 1978
OUT OF CONTROL, 1985
OUT OF SIGHT, 1966
OUT OF THE DEPTHS, 1946
OUT WEST WITH THE PEPPERS, 1940
OUTCAST LADY, 1934
OUTING, THE, 1987
OUTLAW BRAND, 1948
OUTLAW EXPRESS, 1938
OUTLAW GOLD, 1950
OUTLAWS OF STAMPEDE PASS, 1943
OUTLAWS OF THE CHEROKEE TRAIL, 1941
OUTLAWS OF THE DESERT, 1941
OUTLAWS OF THE ROCKIES, 1945
OUTPOST OF THE MOUNTIES, 1939
OUTRAGE, THE, 1964
OUTSIDE IN, 1972
OUTSIDE THE LAW, 1956
OUTSIDE THE 3-MILE LIMIT, 1940
OVER-EXPOSED, 1956
OVER THE BORDER, 1950
OVERLAND EXPRESS, THE, 1938
OVERLAND MAIL ROBBERY, 1943
PACIFIC BLACKOUT, 1942
PAINTED DESERT, THE, 1938
PALACE OF NUDES, 1961
PALLET ON THE FLOOR, 1984
PANAMA LADY, 1939
PANAMA SAL, 1957
PANAMINT'S BAD MAN, 1938
PANCHO VILLA, 1975
PANIC, 1966
PANIC IN NEEDLE PARK, 1971
PANIC IN THE CITY, 1968
PARADE OF THE WEST, 1930
PARDON MY FRENCH, 1951
PARDON MY GUN, 1944
PARDON MY STRIPES, 1942
PARIS INTERLUDE, 1934
PARISIAN ROMANCE, A, 1932
PAROLE, 1936
PAROLE GIRL, 1933
PAROLED—TO DIE, 1938
PARRISH, 1961
PARTNER, THE, 1966
PARTNERS, 1932
PARTNERS IN TIME, 1946
PARTNERS OF THE TRAIL, 1931
PARTY CRASHERS, THE, 1958
PARTY GIRL, 1930
PARTY'S OVER, THE, 1934
PASCALI'S ISLAND, 1988
PASSION FLOWER, 1930
PASSPORT HUSBAND, 1938
PASSPORT TO ALCATRAZ, 1940
PASSPORT TO HELL, 1932
PASSPORT TO TREASON, 1956
PATIENT VANISHES, THE, 1947
PATRICIA GETS HER MAN, 1937
PATSY, THE, 1964
PAUL AND MICHELLE, 1974
PAUL TEMPLE'S TRIUMPH, 1951
PAYOFF, THE, 1935
PAYOFF, THE, 1943
PEACOCK ALLEY, 1930
PEARL OF THE SOUTH PACIFIC, 1955
PEER GYNT, 1965
PENNY POINTS TO PARADISE, 1951
PEOPLE ARE FUNNY, 1945
PERFECT, 1985

PERFECT COUPLE, A, 1979
PERFECT FLAW, THE, 1934
PERFECT MARRIAGE, THE, 1946
PERFECT UNDERSTANDING, 1933
PERILS OF GWENDOLINE, THE, 1984
PERMISSION TO KILL, 1975
PERSECUTION, 1974
PERSONALITY KID, 1946
PETTICOAT LARCENY, 1943
PHANTOM BROADCAST, THE, 1933
PHANTOM EXPRESS, THE, 1932
PHANTOM FIEND, THE, 1935
PHANTOM FROM SPACE, 1953
PHANTOM OF THE RUE MORGUE, 1954
PHANTOM RANGER, 1938
PHANTOM SPEAKS, THE, 1945
PHANTOM STAGECOACH, THE, 1957
PHANTOM THUNDERBOLT, THE, 1933
PHANTOM VALLEY, 1948
PHARAOH'S CURSE, 1957
PHOBIA, 1980
PICCADILLY, 1932
PICK-UP, 1933
PIER 5, HAVANA, 1959
PIER 23, 1951
PIMPERNEL SVENSSON, 1953
PINTO KID, THE, 1941
PINTO RUSTLERS, 1937
PIONEER DAYS, 1940
PIONEERS, THE, 1941
PIRANHA II: THE SPAWNING, 1981
PIRATE AND THE SLAVE GIRL, THE, 1961
PIRATES OF MONTEREY, 1947
PIRATES ON HORSEBACK, 1941
PISTOL PACKIN' MAMA, 1943
PITTSBURGH KID, THE, 1941
PLASTIC DOME OF NORMA JEAN, THE, 1966
PLATINUM HIGH SCHOOL, 1960
PLAY IT COOL, 1963
PLAYING AROUND, 1930
PLAYING FOR KEEPS, 1986
PLAYTHING, THE, 1929
PLEASE! MR. BALZAC, 1957
PLEASE MURDER ME, 1956
PLEASE SIR, 1971
PLEASURE CRAZED, 1929
PLEASURE CRUISE, 1933
PLEASURE GIRLS, THE, 1966
PLOT THICKENS, THE, 1936
POCATELLO KID, 1932
POLICE ACADEMY 3: BACK IN TRAINING, 1986
POLLY OF THE CIRCUS, 1932
POLTERGEIST III, 1988
POM POM GIRLS, THE, 1976
POOR OLD BILL, 1931
POOR RICH, THE, 1934
PORKY'S II: THE NEXT DAY, 1983
PORT AFRIQUE, 1956
PORT OF DESIRE, 1960
PORTRAIT IN TERROR, 1965
POSTAL INSPECTOR, 1936
POSTMAN ALWAYS RINGS TWICE, THE, 1981
POT O' GOLD, 1941
POWDER TOWN, 1942
POWERS GIRL, THE, 1942
PRAIRIE EXPRESS, 1947
PRAIRIE SCHOONERS, 1940
PRAIRIE THUNDER, 1937
PREJUDICE, 1949
PRESIDENT'S MYSTERY, THE, 1936
PRESIDIO, THE, 1988
PRIDE OF THE BOWERY, 1941
PRIDE OF THE NAVY, 1939
PRINCE AND THE PAUPER, THE, 1969
PRINCE OF PEACE, THE, 1951
PRINCIPAL, THE, 1987
PRIORITIES ON PARADE, 1942
PRISON GIRL, 1942
PRISON TRAIN, 1938
PRISONER OF JAPAN, 1942
PRISONER OF THE VOLGA, 1960
PRISONERS, 1929
PRISONERS IN PETTICOATS, 1950
PRIVATE ENTERPRISE, A, 1975
PRIVATE INFORMATION, 1952
PRIVATE LIVES OF ADAM AND EVE, THE, 1961

PRIVATE ROAD, 1971
PRIVATE SCANDAL, A, 1932
PRIVATE SHOW, 1985
PRIVILEGE, 1967
PRIVILEGED, 1982
PRIZE FIGHTER, THE, 1979
PRODIGAL, THE, 1931
PROFESSIONALS, THE, 1960
PROFILE, 1954
PROMISE, THE, 1979
PROPER TIME, THE, 1959
PROUD AND THE DAMNED, THE, 1972
PROUD AND THE PROFANE, THE, 1956
PSYCHE 59, 1964
PSYCHIC KILLER, 1975
PSYCHOMANIA, 1964
PSYCHOS IN LOVE, 1987
PUBLIC DEB NO. 1, 1940
PUBLIC EYE, THE, 1972
PUBLIC NUISANCE NO. 1, 1936
PUPPET ON A CHAIN, 1971
PURSUIT, 1975
PURSUIT OF THE GRAF SPEE, 1957
QUALITY STREET, 1937
QUANDO EL AMOR RIE, 1933
QUEEN OF BROADWAY, 1942
QUEENS, THE, 1968
RACE FOR LIFE, A, 1955
RACING BLOOD, 1954
RACING LADY, 1937
RACING LUCK, 1935
RACKETEERS IN EXILE, 1937
RADIO STARS ON PARADE, 1945
RADIOACTIVE DREAMS, 1986
RAGE, 1972
RAGE TO LIVE, A, 1965
RAGS TO RICHES, 1941
RAIDERS OF LEYTE GULF, 1963
RAIDERS OF OLD CALIFORNIA, 1957
RAIDERS OF THE WEST, 1942
RAIN FOR A DUSTY SUMMER, 1971
RAINBOW BRITE AND THE STAR STEALER, 1985
RAINBOW MAN, 1929
RAINBOW OVER THE RANGE, 1940
RAINBOW OVER THE ROCKIES, 1947
RAINMAKERS, THE, 1935
RAMBO III, 1988
RAMPANT AGE, THE, 1930
RAMSBOTTOM RIDES AGAIN, 1956
RANCHO GRANDE, 1938
RANCHO GRANDE, 1940
RANGE BEYOND THE BLUE, 1947
RANGE RENEGADES, 1948
RANGE WAR, 1939
RANGER COURAGE, 1937
RANGERS RIDE, THE, 1948
RANGER'S ROUNDUP, THE, 1938
RANGERS TAKE OVER, THE, 1942
RAT, THE, 1938
RATS OF TOBRUK, 1951
RAW WIND IN EDEN, 1958
RAWHIDE TRAIL, THE, 1958
REACHING OUT, 1983
READY, WILLING AND ABLE, 1937
REASON TO LIVE, A REASON TO DIE, A, 1974
REASONABLE DOUBT, 1936
REBEL, 1985
REBEL ANGEL, 1962
REBEL CITY, 1953
REBEL LOVE, 1986
REBEL SON, THE, 1939
RECKLESS LIVING, 1938
RECORD 413, 1936
RED DRAGON, THE, 1946
RED HOT RHYTHM, 1930
RED HOT SPEED, 1929
RED LIPS, 1964
RED MONARCH, 1983
RED RIVER RENEGADES, 1946
RED RIVER SHORE, 1953
RED RUNS THE RIVER, 1963
RED SKY AT MORNING, 1971
RED SONJA, 1985
REDEEMING SIN, THE, 1929
REDHEAD FROM MANHATTAN, 1954
REDHEADS ON PARADE, 1935

REFORM GIRL, 1933
REFORMATORY, 1938
REG'LAR FELLERS, 1941
REINCARNATE, THE, 1971
REIVERS, THE, 1969
RELUCTANT WIDOW, THE, 1951
REMEMBER LAST NIGHT, 1935
RENALDO AND CLARA, 1978
RENDEZVOUS AT MIDNIGHT, 1935
RENEGADE GIRLS, 1974
RENFREW OF THE ROYAL MOUNTED, 1937
REPENT AT LEISURE, 1941
REPORTED MISSING, 1937
REPTILE, THE, 1966
RESTLESS YEARS, THE, 1958
RETURN OF JACK SLADE, THE, 1955
RETURN OF JOSEY WALES, THE, 1987
RETURN OF RINGO, THE, 1966
RETURN OF THE APE MAN, 1944
RETURN OF THE CISCO KID, 1939
RETURN OF THE FLY, 1959
RETURN OF THE SEVEN, 1966
RETURN TO BOGGY CREEK, 1977
RETURN TO CAMPUS, 1975
RETURN TO HORROR HIGH, 1987
RETURN TO WARBOW, 1958
REVENGE AT MONTE CARLO, 1933
REVENGE OF THE GLADIATORS, 1965
REVENGE OF THE TEENAGE VIXENS FROM OUTER SPACE, THE, 1986
REVENGE OF THE ZOMBIES, 1943
RHYTHM INN, 1951
RHYTHM OF THE SADDLE, 1938
RICHEST MAN IN TOWN, 1941
RIDE IN A PINK CAR, 1974
RIDE, KELLY, RIDE, 1941
RIDERS OF THE DAWN, 1945
RIDERS OF THE FRONTIER, 1939
RIDERS OF THE NORTHWEST MOUNTED, 1943
RIDERS OF THE SANTA FE, 1944
RIDERS OF THE WHISTLING PINES, 1949
RIDIN' DOWN THE TRAIL, 1947
RIDING HIGH, 1943
RIDING ON, 1937
RINGER, THE, 1932
RIO GRANDE PATROL, 1950
RIO GRANDE ROMANCE, 1936
RIO LOBO, 1970
RIP ROARIN' BUCKAROO, 1936
RIP ROARING RILEY, 1935
RIVER GANG, 1945
RIVER HOUSE GHOST, THE, 1932
RIVERBOAT RHYTHM, 1946
ROAD HUSTLERS, THE, 1968
ROAD TO FORT ALAMO, THE, 1966
ROAD TO RUIN, 1934
ROAD TO THE BIG HOUSE, 1947
ROAR, 1981
ROAR OF THE CROWD, 1953
ROAR OF THE PRESS, 1941
ROARIN' GUNS, 1936
ROARING RANCH, 1930
ROARING SIX GUNS, 1937
ROBBY, 1968
ROCK AROUND THE WORLD, 1957
ROCK RIVER RENEGADES, 1942
ROCKET MAN, THE, 1954
ROCKETS IN THE DUNES, 1960
ROCKY IV, 1985
RODAN, 1958
RODEO RHYTHM, 1941
ROGUE OF THE RANGE, 1937
ROLL, THUNDER, ROLL, 1949
ROLLIN' PLAINS, 1938
ROLLIN' WESTWARD, 1939
ROLLING CARAVANS, 1938
ROMANCE IN THE DARK, 1938
ROMANCE OF SEVILLE, A, 1929
ROMANCE OF THE REDWOODS, 1939
ROMANCE OF THE WEST, 1946
ROMANCE ON THE RUN, 1938
ROMMEL'S TREASURE, 1962
ROOSTER COGBURN, 1975
ROPE OF FLESH, 1965
ROSARY, THE, 1931
ROSE OF THE RANCHO, 1936

ROSE OF TRALEE, 1942
ROSIE!, 1967
ROSSITER CASE, THE, 1950
ROUGH NIGHT IN JERICHO, 1967
ROUGH RIDIN' RHYTHM, 1937
ROUGH ROMANCE, 1930
ROYAL ROMANCE, A, 1930
RUBBER RACKETEERS, 1942
RULING VOICE, THE, 1931
RUN FOR THE ROSES, 1978
RUN LIKE A THIEF, 1968
RUN WITH THE DEVIL, 1963
RUNAWAY, THE, 1964
RUNNING, 1979
RUNNING BRAVE, 1983
RUNNING WILD, 1955
RUSTLER'S ROUNDUP, 1946
RUSTY LEADS THE WAY, 1948
RUSTY RIDES ALONE, 1933
RUSTY SAVES A LIFE, 1949
RUSTY'S BIRTHDAY, 1949
SAADIA, 1953
SABOTAGE AT SEA, 1942
SABRE JET, 1953
SACRED FLAME, THE, 1929
SADDLE BUSTER, THE, 1932
SADIST, THE, 1963
SAFARI, 1940
SAFE AFFAIR, A, 1931
SAGEBRUSH LAW, 1943
SAILOR BE GOOD, 1933
SAILORS' HOLIDAY, 1929
SALLY OF THE SUBWAY, 1932
SANDS OF THE DESERT, 1960
SANTA'S CHRISTMAS CIRCUS, 1966
SAP, THE, 1929
SARGE GOES TO COLLEGE, 1947
SARUMBA, 1950
SASQUATCH, 1978
SATAN'S BED, 1965
SATAN'S SATELLITES, 1958
SATELLITE IN THE SKY, 1956
SATIN MUSHROOM, THE, 1969
SATURDAY NIGHT IN APPLE VALLEY, 1965
SAVAGE BRIGADE, 1948
SAVAGE FRONTIER, 1953
SAVAGE MUTINY, 1953
SAVAGE WILD, THE, 1970
SAVE A LITTLE SUNSHINE, 1938
SAY IT WITH DIAMONDS, 1935
SCALAWAG, 1973
SCANDAL IN DENMARK, 1970
SCANDAL SHEET, 1931
SCANDAL SHEET, 1940
SCARED TO DEATH, 1947
SCARLET BRAND, 1932
SCARS OF DRACULA, THE, 1970
SCHEHERAZADE, 1965
SCHOOL DAZE, 1988
SCHOOL FOR GIRLS, 1935
SCHOOL FOR SCANDAL, THE, 1930
SCHWEIK'S NEW ADVENTURES, 1943
SCOTLAND YARD DRAGNET, 1957
SCOTLAND YARD INSPECTOR, 1952
SCREAM IN THE NIGHT, 1943
SCREAM OF THE BUTTERFLY, 1965
SCREAMERS, 1978
SCREAMPLAY, 1986
SCROOGED, 1988
SEA FURY, 1929
SEA HORNET, THE, 1951
SEA SPOILERS, THE, 1936
SEABO, 1978
SEARCH AND DESTROY, 1981
SEARCH FOR BEAUTY, 1934
SEARCH FOR DANGER, 1949
SEASIDE SWINGERS, 1965
SECOND BEST SECRET AGENT IN THE WHOLE WIDE WORLD, THE, 1965
SECOND COMING OF SUZANNE, THE, 1974
SECOND MATE, THE, 1950
SECOND MR. BUSH, THE, 1940
SECOND TIME LUCKY, 1984
SECRET OF DEEP HARBOR, 1961
SECRET OF ST. IVES, THE, 1949
SECRET OF THE CHATEAU, 1935

BOLD: Films on Videocassette

SECRET OF THE LOCH, THE, 1934
SECRET OF THE SACRED FOREST, THE, 1970
SECRET OF THE SWORD, THE, 1985
SECRET OF TREASURE MOUNTAIN, 1956
SECRET PATROL, 1936
SECRET PEOPLE, 1952
SECRET SEVEN, THE, 1966
SECRET TENT, THE, 1956
SECRET VENTURE, 1955
SECRET VOICE, THE, 1936
SECRETS OF A CO-ED, 1942
SECRETS OF A SORORITY GIRL, 1946
SECRETS OF A WINDMILL GIRL, 1966
SECRETS OF THE FRENCH POLICE, 1932
SECRETS OF WU SIN, 1932
SEDUCERS, THE, 1962
SEED, 1931
SEIZURE, 1974
SELF-MADE LADY, 1932
SEMINOLE UPRISING, 1955
SENSATION, 1936
SENSATION HUNTERS, 1945
SENTENCED FOR LIFE, 1960
SEPARATE VACATIONS, 1986
SEPARATION, 1968
SERGEANT DEADHEAD, 1965
SERGEANT MURPHY, 1938
SERPENT ISLAND, 1954
SEVEN DAYS ASHORE, 1944
SEVEN DOORS TO DEATH, 1944
SEVEN FACES, 1929
SEVEN FOOTPRINTS TO SATAN, 1929
SEVEN GOLDEN MEN, 1969
SEVEN GUNS TO MESA, 1958
SEVEN KEYS, 1962
SEVEN WAYS FROM SUNDOWN, 1960
7TH COMMANDMENT, THE, 1961
SEVENTH SIN, THE, 1957
SEVERED HEAD, A, 1971
SH! THE OCTOPUS, 1937
SHACK OUT ON 101, 1955
SHADOW OF THE HAWK, 1976
SHADOW STRIKES, THE, 1937
SHADOW VALLEY, 1947
SHADOW, THE, 1936
SHADOWED, 1946
SHADOWED EYES, 1939
SHADOWS, 1931
SHADOWS OF DEATH, 1945
SHADOWS OF SING SING, 1934
SHADOWS OF TOMBSTONE, 1953
SHADOWS OVER SHANGHAI, 1938
SHAKEDOWN, 1936
SHAKIEST GUN IN THE WEST, THE, 1968
SHAME OF THE SABINE WOMEN, THE, 1962
SHANGHAI CHEST, THE, 1948
SHANGHAI COBRA, THE, 1945
SHARKFIGHTERS, THE, 1956
SHARK'S TREASURE, 1975
SHE ASKED FOR IT, 1937
SHE COULDN'T SAY NO, 1954
SHE-CREATURE, THE, 1956
SHE DEVIL, 1957
SHE-DEVIL ISLAND, 1936
SHE FREAK, 1967
SHE GETS HER MAN, 1935
SHE-GODS OF SHARK REEF, 1958
SHE HAD TO CHOOSE, 1934
SHE HAS WHAT IT TAKES, 1943
SHE KNEW WHAT SHE WANTED, 1936
SHE MARRIED AN ARTIST, 1938
SHE PLAYED WITH FIRE, 1957
SHE WANTED A MILLIONAIRE, 1932
SHE WAS A LADY, 1934
SHE WENT TO THE RACES, 1945
SHE-WOLF OF LONDON, 1946
SHED NO TEARS, 1948
SHEIK STEPS OUT, THE, 1937
SHE'S DANGEROUS, 1937
SHE'S GOT EVERYTHING, 1938
SHE'S MY WEAKNESS, 1930
SHINE ON, HARVEST MOON, 1938
SHIP CAFE, 1935
SHOOTING HIGH, 1940
SHORT CIRCUIT, 1986
SHOT IN THE DARK, A, 1933

SHOULD A GIRL MARRY?, 1929
SHRIEK IN THE NIGHT, A, 1933
SIERRA, 1950
SIGN OF THE PAGAN, 1954
SIGN OF ZORRO, THE, 1960
SILENT CONFLICT, 1948
SILENT RAGE, 1982
SILENT SCREAM, 1980
SILVER TOP, 1938
SILVER TRAIL, THE, 1937
SIMPLY TERRIFIC, 1938
SIN SHIP, 1931
SING ALONG WITH ME, 1952
SING ME A LOVE SONG, 1936
SING, NEIGHBOR, SING, 1944
SING SING NIGHTS, 1935
SINGING TAXI DRIVER, 1953
SINGLE SIN, 1931
SISTER TO ASSIST'ER, A, 1930
SISTER TO ASSIST'ER, A, 1938
SISTER TO ASSIST'ER, A, 1948
SIT TIGHT, 1931
SIX GUN MAN, 1946
SIX HOURS TO LIVE, 1932
SIX LESSONS FROM MADAME LA ZONGA, 1941
SIX MEN, THE, 1951
SIX WEEKS, 1982
'68, 1988
SKINNER STEPS OUT, 1929
SKY COMMANDO, 1953
SKY MURDER, 1940
SKY PARADE, 1936
SKY PATROL, 1939
SKYSCRAPER SOULS, 1932
SLANDER HOUSE, 1938
SLAUGHTER, 1972
SLAUGHTER TRAIL, 1951
SLAUGHTERHOUSE, 1988
SLAUGHTER'S BIG RIP-OFF, 1973
SLAVE GIRL, 1947
SLAVE, THE, 1963
SLAVES OF BABYLON, 1953
SLAYER, THE, 1982
SLAYGROUND, 1984
SLEEPAWAY CAMP, 1983
SLEEPERS EAST, 1934
SLEEPERS WEST, 1941
SLEEPING PARTNERS, 1930
SLEEPY LAGOON, 1943
SLEEPYTIME GAL, 1942
SLIGHTLY MARRIED, 1933
SLIGHTLY SCANDALOUS, 1946
SLIGHTLY TERRIFIC, 1944
SLUGGER'S WIFE, THE, 1985
SLUMBER PARTY MASSACRE, THE, 1982
SMALL TOWN BOY, 1937
SMART ALECKS, 1942
SMART BLONDE, 1937
SMART GIRLS DON'T TALK, 1948
SMART GUY, 1943
SMASHING THE SPY RING, 1939
SMILING GHOST, THE, 1941
SMOKESCREEN, 1964
SMOKEY AND THE BANDIT, 1977
SMOKEY SMITH, 1935
SMORGASBORD, 1983
SMURFS AND THE MAGIC FLUTE, THE, 1984
SNOWED UNDER, 1936
SNUFFY SMITH, YARD BIRD, 1942
SOCIAL LION, THE, 1930
SOCIAL REGISTER, 1934
SOCIETY FEVER, 1935
SOLDIERS OF THE STORM, 1933
SOLDIER'S PLAYTHING, A, 1931
SOLDIER'S REVENGE, 1986
SOLUTION BY PHONE, 1954
SOME MAY LIVE, 1967
SOME OF MY BEST FRIENDS ARE. . ., 1971
SOME WILL, SOME WON'T, 1970
SOMEONE, 1968
SOMETHING SHORT OF PARADISE, 1979
SOMETHING TO SHOUT ABOUT, 1943
SOMEWHERE ON LEAVE, 1942
SON-DAUGHTER, THE, 1932
SON OF A SAILOR, 1933
SON OF CAPTAIN BLOOD, THE, 1964

SON OF DAVY CROCKETT, THE, 1941
SON OF DR. JEKYLL, THE, 1951
SON OF GOD'S COUNTRY, 1948
SON OF INGAGI, 1940
SON OF SAMSON, 1962
SON OF SINBAD, 1955
SON OF THE BORDER, 1933
SON OF THE REGIMENT, 1948
SON OF THE RENEGADE, 1953
SONG AND THE SILENCE, THE, 1969
SONG FOR MISS JULIE, A, 1945
SONG OF KENTUCKY, 1929
SONG OF OLD WYOMING, 1945
SONG OF THE CITY, 1937
SONG OF THE FLAME, 1930
SONG OF THE ROAD, 1937
SONG OF THE SARONG, 1945
SONG OF THE SIERRAS, 1946
SONG OF THE TRAIL, 1936
SONG YOU GAVE ME, THE, 1934
SONGS AND BULLETS, 1938
SONS O' GUNS, 1936
SONS OF GOOD EARTH, 1967
SONS OF THE LEGION, 1938
SORORITY GIRL, 1957
SOUL OF A MONSTER, THE, 1944
SOULS IN CONFLICT, 1955
SOURDOUGH, 1977
SOUTH OF ARIZONA, 1938
SOUTH OF DEATH VALLEY, 1949
SOUTH OF DIXIE, 1944
SOUTH OF RIO, 1949
SOUTH SEA SINNER, 1950
SOUTHERN ROSES, 1936
SPANISH SWORD, THE, 1962
SPEAKEASY, 1929
SPECIALIST, THE, 1975
SPECTRE OF EDGAR ALLAN POE, THE, 1974
SPEED MADNESS, 1932
SPEED TO SPARE, 1948
SPELLBINDER, THE, 1939
SPIDER, THE, 1958
SPIDER, THE, 1931
SPIDER, THE, 1940
SPIELER, THE, 1929
SPIRIT OF CULVER, THE, 1939
SPIRIT OF THE WEST, 1932
SPIRIT OF WEST POINT, THE, 1947
SPLENDID FELLOWS, 1934
SPLINTERS, 1929
SPLINTERS IN THE AIR, 1937
SPOILERS OF THE FOREST, 1957
SPOILERS OF THE NORTH, 1947
SPOOK CHASERS, 1957
SPORT OF KINGS, THE, 1931
SPORT OF KINGS, 1947
SPORTING CHANCE, 1931
SPRING, 1948
SPRING FEVER, 1983
SPRING REUNION, 1957
SPRINGTIME FOR HENRY, 1934
SPRINGTIME IN THE ROCKIES, 1937
SPUTNIK, 1960
SPY IN THE GREEN HAT, THE, 1966
SPY IN THE SKY, 1958
SPY RING, THE, 1938
SPY SHIP, 1942
SPY WITH MY FACE, THE, 1966
SQUADRON OF HONOR, 1938
SQUARE DANCE JUBILEE, 1949
SQUARE DANCE KATY, 1950
SQUARE ROOT OF ZERO, THE, 1964
SQUEEZE, THE, 1980
SQUIBS, 1935
STACEY!, 1973
STAGE STRUCK, 1948
STAGE TO BLUE RIVER, 1951
STAGE TO MESA CITY, 1947
STAGECOACH EXPRESS, 1942
STAGECOACH OUTLAWS, 1945
STAGECOACH TO DENVER, 1946
STALKING MOON, THE, 1969
STAMPEDE, 1936
STAND AT APACHE RIVER, THE, 1953
STAND UP AND BE COUNTED, 1972
STAND UP VIRGIN SOLDIERS, 1977

STAR CRYSTAL, **1986**
STAR INSPECTOR, THE, 1980
STAR OF INDIA, 1956
STAR REPORTER, 1939
STARCRASH, 1979
STARDUST ON THE SAGE, 1942
STARFIGHTERS, THE, 1964
STARK MAD, 1929
STARS IN YOUR EYES, 1956
STATE POLICE, 1938
STEAGLE, THE, 1971
STEEL AGAINST THE SKY, 1941
STEEL ARENA, 1973
STEEL JUNGLE, THE, 1956
STEEL LADY, THE, 1953
STEP LIVELY, JEEVES, 1937
STEPPIN' IN SOCIETY, 1945
STEPPING TOES, 1938
STEVIE, 1978
STICKY FINGERS, 1988
STOLEN HEAVEN, 1931
STOLEN SWEETS, 1934
STONE COLD DEAD, 1980
STOP THAT CAB, 1951
STORM AT DAYBREAK, 1933
STORM OVER TIBET, 1952
STORY OF JOSEPH AND HIS BRETHREN THE, 1962
STRANGE ADVENTURE, A, 1956
STRANGE ADVENTURES OF MR. SMITH, THE, 1937
STRANGE BOARDERS, 1938
STRANGE CARGO, 1936
STRANGE DEATH OF ADOLF HITLER, THE, 1943
STRANGE DOOR, THE, 1951
STRANGE EXPERIMENT, 1937
STRANGE FASCINATION, 1952
STRANGE HOLIDAY, 1969
STRANGE LOVE OF MOLLY LOUVAIN, THE, 1932
STRANGE WIVES, 1935
STRANGER FROM VENUS, THE, 1954
STRANGER'S GUNDOWN, THE, 1974
STRANGLER'S WEB, 1966
STRANGLER, THE, 1964
STRATEGY OF TERROR, 1969
STRAUSS' GREAT WALTZ, 1934
STRAWBERRY ROAN, 1945
STREET IS MY BEAT, THE, 1966
STREET OF DARKNESS, 1958
STREET OF WOMEN, 1932
STREET SMART, 1987
STREET SONG, 1935
STREETS OF NEW YORK, 1939
STRIPPER, 1986
STRONGER THAN DESIRE, 1939
STUDS LONIGAN, 1960
SUCCESSFUL FAILURE, A, 1934
SUCH WOMEN ARE DANGEROUS, 1934
SUCKER MONEY, 1933
SUDDEN BILL DORN, 1938
SUDDEN MONEY, 1939
SUICIDE SQUADRON, 1942
SULEIMAN THE CONQUEROR, 1963
SULTAN'S DAUGHTER, THE, 1943
SUMMER LOVERS, 1982
SUMMER STORY, A, 1988
SUMMER'S CHILDREN, 1979
SUN SETS AT DAWN, THE, 1950
SUN SHINES, THE, 1939
SUN VALLEY CYCLONE, 1946
SUNDAY IN THE COUNTRY, 1975
SUNDOWN IN SANTA FE, 1948
SUNFLOWER, 1970
SUNSET IN EL DORADO, 1945
SUNSET IN WYOMING, 1941
SUPERDAD, 1974
SURRENDER, 1931
SUSANNA PASS, 1949
SWAMP FIRE, 1946
SWEATER GIRL, 1942
SWEET AND LOWDOWN, 1944
SWEET CREEK COUNTY WAR, THE, 1979
SWEET INNISCARRA, 1934
SWEET MUSIC, 1935
SWEET RIDE, THE, 1968
SWEET TRASH, 1970
SWEETHEART OF THE NAVY, 1937
SWEETHEARTS AND WIVES, 1930

SWEETHEARTS ON PARADE, 1930
SWEETHEARTS ON PARADE, 1953
SWIFTY, 1936
SWING FEVER, 1943
SWING HOSTESS, 1944
SWING IT SOLDIER, 1941
SWING SHIFT MAISIE, 1943
SWING YOUR PARTNER, 1943
SWINGIN' ALONG, 1962
SWINGING BARMAIDS, THE, 1976
SWORD OF HONOUR, 1938
SWORD OF THE CONQUEROR, 1962
SWORDSMAN, THE, 1947
SYMPHONIE FANTASTIQUE, 1947
SYMPHONY IN TWO FLATS, 1930
SYMPTOMS, 1976
SYNCOPATION, 1929
T-BIRD GANG, 1959
T.A.G.: THE ASSASSINATION GAME, 1982
TAILOR MADE MAN, A, 1931
TAKE A CHANCE, 1933
TAKE ALL OF ME, 1978
TAKE IT FROM ME, 1937
TAKE MY LIFE, 1942
TAKE MY LIFE, 1948
TAKE THE STAND, 1934
TALES OF A SALESMAN, 1965
TALK ABOUT A LADY, 1946
TALK OF HOLLYWOOD, THE, 1929
TALKING FEET, 1937
TALL STORY, 1960
TAMARIND SEED, THE, 1974
TAMING OF DOROTHY, THE, 1950
TAMING SUTTON'S GAL, 1957
TAMING THE WILD, 1937
TANGIER, 1946
TANGLED EVIDENCE, 1934
TANGO, 1936
TAPEHEADS, 1988
TARAS BULBA, 1962
TARGET EARTH, 1954
TARGET: HARRY, 1980
TARTARS, THE, 1962
TARZAN AND THE GREAT RIVER, 1967
TARZAN AND THE JUNGLE BOY, 1968
TARZAN THE MAGNIFICENT, 1960
TARZAN'S SAVAGE FURY, 1952
TELEGRAPH TRAIL, THE, 1933
TELEVISION SPY, 1939
TEMPLE TOWER, 1930
TEMPTATION, 1935
TEN DAYS THAT SHOOK THE WORLD, THE, 1977
TEN DAYS' WONDER, 1972
TEN LITTLE INDIANS, 1975
10:30 P.M. SUMMER, 1966
10,000 DOLLARS BLOOD MONEY, 1966
TENDER FLESH, 1976
TERMINAL CHOICE, 1985
TERROR AT MIDNIGHT, 1956
TERROR BENEATH THE SEA, 1966
TERROR HOUSE, 1972
TERROR IN THE WAX MUSEUM, 1973
TERROR OF THE BLACK MASK, 1967
TERROR ON A TRAIN, 1953
TERROR ON TIPTOE, 1936
TERRORNAUTS, THE, 1967
TEXAS BUDDIES, 1932
TEXAS CITY, 1952
TEXAS DYNAMO, 1950
TEXAS GUN FIGHTER, 1932
THANK EVANS, 1938
THAT BRENNAN GIRL, 1946
THAT GANG OF MINE, 1940
THAT MAN'S HERE AGAIN, 1937
THAT NAZTY NUISANCE, 1943
THAT TENNESSEE BEAT, 1966
THAT'S MY BABY, 1944
THAT'S MY BOY, 1932
THAT'S MY GAL, 1947
THAT'S THE TICKET, 1940
THEIR BIG MOMENT, 1934
THEN THERE WERE THREE, 1961
THERE GOES THE BRIDE, 1933
THERE IS STILL ROOM IN HELL, 1963
THERE'S ALWAYS VANILLA, 1972
THERE'S SOMETHING ABOUT A SOLDIER, 1943

THESE CHARMING PEOPLE, 1931
THEY ASKED FOR IT, 1939
THEY CALL IT SIN, 1932
THEY CAME BY NIGHT, 1940
THEY CAME FROM BEYOND SPACE, 1967
THEY CAME FROM WITHIN, 1976
THEY DARE NOT LOVE, 1941
THEY JUST HAD TO GET MARRIED, 1933
THEY MEET AGAIN, 1941
THEY MET IN ARGENTINA, 1941
THEY MET ON SKIS, 1940
THEY NEVER COME BACK, 1932
THEY ONLY KILL THEIR MASTERS, 1972
THEY RAN FOR THEIR LIVES, 1968
THEY WANTED PEACE, 1940
THIEF OF DAMASCUS, 1952
THIEVES, 1977
THIRD CLUE, THE, 1934
THIRD STRING, THE, 1932
THIRD VISITOR, THE, 1951
THIRTEENTH CANDLE, THE, 1933
13TH HOUR, THE, 1947
36 FILLETTE, 1988
THIS ACTING BUSINESS, 1933
THIS IS MY LOVE, 1954
THIS REBEL BREED, 1960
THIS RECKLESS AGE, 1932
THIS SPORTING AGE, 1932
THOROUGHBRED, 1936
THOSE DARING YOUNG MEN IN THEIR JAUNTY
 JALOPIES, 1969
THOSE THREE FRENCH GIRLS, 1930
THOSE WHO LOVE, 1929
THREE BAD SISTERS, 1956
THREE BITES OF THE APPLE, 1967
THREE CHEERS FOR LOVE, 1936
THREE CORNERED FATE, 1954
THREE DOLLS FROM HONG KONG, 1966
THREE FACES OF SIN, 1963
THREE GIRLS LOST, 1931
THREE HEARTS FOR JULIA, 1943
THREE IN THE ATTIC, 1968
THREE LIVE GHOSTS, 1929
THREE LIVE GHOSTS, 1935
THREE MEN IN A BOAT, 1933
THREE MEN IN WHITE, 1944
THREE RUSSIAN GIRLS, 1943
THREE TEXAS STEERS, 1939
THREE WHO LOVED, 1931
THREE'S A CROWD, 1945
THUNDER ALLEY, 1967
THUNDER BELOW, 1932
THUNDER IN CAROLINA, 1960
THUNDER IN THE NIGHT, 1935
THUNDER IN THE SUN, 1959
THUNDER RIVER FEUD, 1942
THUNDER TOWN, 1946
THUNDERING GUN SLINGERS, 1944
THUNDERING HOOFS, 1941
THY NEIGHBOR'S WIFE, 1953
TICKET TO CRIME, 1934
TICKET TO PARADISE, 1936
TIGER FANGS, 1943
TIGER WOMAN, THE, 1945
TILLIE THE TOILER, 1941
TILLY OF BLOOMSBURY, 1940
TIMBER FURY, 1950
TIMBER QUEEN, 1944
TIMBER TERRORS, 1935
TIMBER WAR, 1936
TIME AFTER TIME, 1985
TIME AND THE TOUCH, THE, 1962
TIME IN THE SUN, A, 1970
TIME OF THE HEATHEN, 1962
TIME OUT FOR MURDER, 1938
TIME OUT OF MIND, 1947
TIME TO REMEMBER, 1962
TIME TO SING, A, 1968
TIME WALKER, 1982
TIMES SQUARE, 1980
TIMES SQUARE PLAYBOY, 1936
TIMOTHY'S QUEST, 1936
TIN GODS, 1932
TINKER, 1949
TIOGA KID, THE, 1948
'TIS A PITY SHE'S A WHORE, 1973

BOLD: Films on Videocassette

TO BE A LADY, 1934
TO BE FREE, 1972
TO BEAT THE BAND, 1935
TO HAVE AND TO HOLD, 1963
TO TRAP A SPY, 1966
TOGETHER FOR DAYS, 1972
TOGETHER WE LIVE, 1935
TOILERS OF THE SEA, 1936
TOKYO FILE 212, 1951
TOM SAWYER, DETECTIVE, 1939
TOMBOY AND THE CHAMP, 1961
TOMBSTONE TERROR, 1935
TOMMY, 1975
TOMORROW NEVER COMES, 1978
TONIGHT THE SKIRTS FLY, 1956
TONS OF MONEY, 1931
TOO MANY COOKS, 1931
TOO MANY HUSBANDS, 1938
TOO MUCH BEEF, 1936
TOO TOUGH TO KILL, 1935
TOO YOUNG TO LOVE, 1960
TOO YOUNG TO MARRY, 1931
TOP FLOOR GIRL, 1959
TORA-SAN PART 2, 1970
TORCHLIGHT, 1984
TORCHY BLANE IN CHINATOWN, 1938
TORTURE SHIP, 1939
TOTO AND THE POACHERS, 1958
TOTO IN THE MOON, 1957
TOUCH AND GO, 1980
TOUCH OF DEATH, 1962
TOUGH AS THEY COME, 1942
TOUGHER THAN LEATHER, 1988
T.R. BASKIN, 1971
TRAIL GUIDE, 1952
TRAIN RIDE TO HOLLYWOOD, 1975
TRAITOR WITHIN, THE, 1942
TRANSATLANTIC, 1961
TRAPPED BY G-MEN, 1937
TRAPPED BY TELEVISION, 1936
TRAUMA, 1962
TREAD SOFTLY, 1952
TREASURE OF MATECUMBE, 1976
TREASURE OF SILVER LAKE, 1965
TREASURE OF THE AMAZON, THE, 1985
TREAT EM' ROUGH, 1942
TREE, THE, 1969
TREMENDOUSLY RICH MAN, A, 1932
TRENCHCOAT, 1983
TRIAL OF MADAM X, THE, 1948
TRIAL WITHOUT JURY, 1950
TRIGGER FINGERS, 1939
TRIGGER SMITH, 1939
TRIGGER TRICKS, 1930
TRIGGER TRIO, THE, 1937
TRIP, THE, 1967
TRIPLE TROUBLE, 1950
TROJAN BROTHERS, THE, 1946
TROLL, 1986
TROMBA, THE TIGER MAN, 1952
TROPIC ZONE, 1953
TROPICAL HEAT WAVE, 1952
TROUBLE AHEAD, 1936
TROUBLE WITH GIRLS (AND HOW TO GET INTO IT), THE, 1969
TRUCK TURNER, 1974
TRUE AND THE FALSE, THE, 1955
TRUE AS A TURTLE, 1957
TRUE TO THE NAVY, 1930
TRUNK, THE, 1961
TUCSON, 1949
TUMBLING TUMBLEWEEDS, 1935
TURNED OUT NICE AGAIN, 1941
TWELVE TO THE MOON, 1960
24-HOUR LOVER, 1970
TWENTY-ONE DAYS TOGETHER, 1940
TWICE BLESSED, 1945
TWICE UPON A TIME, 1953
TWICE UPON A TIME, 1983
TWILIGHT HOUR, 1944
TWILIGHT TIME, 1983
TWIN BEDS, 1929
TWO ALONE, 1934
TWO DOLLAR BETTOR, 1951
TWO-FISTED GENTLEMAN, 1936

TWO-FISTED JUSTICE, 1931
TWO FOR TONIGHT, 1935
TWO GROOMS FOR A BRIDE, 1957
TWO GUN SHERIFF, 1941
TWO HEADS ON A PILLOW, 1934
TWO IN A TAXI, 1941
TWO IN THE DARK, 1936
TWO LETTER ALIBI, 1962
TWO LOST WORLDS, 1950
TWO MEN AND A MAID, 1929
TWO MOON JUNCTION, 1988
TWO NIGHTS WITH CLEOPATRA, 1953
TWO SINNERS, 1935
TWO SUPER COPS, 1978
TWO VOICES, 1966
TWO WEEKS IN SEPTEMBER, 1967
U-47 LT. COMMANDER PRIEN, 1967
U-TURN, 1973
UGLY ONES, THE, 1968
ULTIMATE THRILL, THE, 1974
UNA SIGNORA DELL'OVEST, 1942
UNASHAMED, 1932
UNCENSORED, 1944
UNCLE TOM'S CABIN, 1969
UNDER AGE, 1941
UNDER CALIFORNIA STARS, 1948
UNDER EIGHTEEN, 1932
UNDER MONTANA SKIES, 1930
UNDER SECRET ORDERS, 1933
UNDER THE BIG TOP, 1938
UNDER THE TONTO RIM, 1933
UNDER WESTERN SKIES, 1945
UNDER YOUR SPELL, 1936
UNDERCOVER MAN, 1942
UNDERGROUND, 1970
UNEXPECTED FATHER, 1932
UNHOLY QUEST, THE, 1934
UNINHIBITED, THE, 1968
UNKNOWN MAN OF SHANDIGOR, THE, 1967
UNKNOWN MAN, THE, 1951
UNKNOWN WORLD, 1951
UNSATISFIED, THE, 1964
UNSEEN ENEMY, 1942
UNSTOPPABLE MAN, THE, 1961
UNTAMED BREED, THE, 1948
UNTAMED FRONTIER, 1952
UNTIL SEPTEMBER, 1984
UNTOUCHED, 1956
UNWRITTEN LAW, THE, 1932
UP THE CHASTITY BELT, 1971
URANIUM BOOM, 1956
VAGABOND LADY, 1935
VALLEY OF EAGLES, 1952
VALLEY OF THE DRAGONS, 1961
VALLEY OF THE HEADHUNTERS, 1953
VALLEY OF THE ZOMBIES, 1946
VALLEY OF VENGEANCE, 1944
VAMPING, 1984
VAMPIRE, THE, 1968
VAMPIRE'S COFFIN, THE, 1958
VAMPIRE'S NIGHT ORGY, THE, 1973
VAMPIRE'S GHOST, THE, 1945
VAN, THE, 1977
VANITY STREET, 1932
VANQUISHED, THE, 1953
VARAN THE UNBELIEVABLE, 1962
VARIETY, 1935
VARIETY, 1984
VARIETY HOUR, 1937
VARSITY, 1928
VELVET VAMPIRE, THE, 1971
VENGEANCE, 1930
VENGEANCE, 1964
VENGEANCE IS MINE, 1948
VENGEANCE OF FU MANCHU, THE, 1968
VENUS IN FURS, 1970
VERDICT OF THE SEA, 1932
VERY IDEA, THE, 1929
VIBRATION, 1969
VICE AND VIRTUE, 1965
VICE DOLLS, 1961
VICE SQUAD, 1982
VISCOUNT, THE, 1967
VICTIMS OF PERSECUTION, 1933
VIGILANTE, 1983
VIKING, THE, 1931

VILLAGE OF DAUGHTERS, 1962
VILLAGE OF THE GIANTS, 1965
VILLAGE TALE, 1935
VINTAGE, THE, 1957
VIOLATED PARADISE, 1963
VIOLENT ENEMY, THE, 1969
VIOLENT MOMENT, 1966
VIOLENT ONES, THE, 1967
VIOLENT STRANGER, 1957
VIPER, THE, 1938
VIRGIN SACRIFICE, 1959
VIRGINIA, 1941
VIVA ITALIA, 1978
VOICE IN YOUR HEART, A, 1952
VOICE WITHIN, THE, 1945
VOODOO MAN, 1944
VOODOO TIGER, 1952
VORTEX, 1982
VOYAGE OF THE DAMNED, 1976
VULTURE, THE, 1967
W.I.A. (WOUNDED IN ACTION), 1966
WACKIEST WAGON TRAIN IN THE WEST, THE, 1976
WAGON MASTER, THE, 1929
WAGON TEAM, 1952
WAGON TRACKS WEST, 1943
WALK A CROOKED PATH, 1969
WALK THE ANGRY BEACH, 1961
WALL STREET COWBOY, 1939
WALTZ TIME, 1946
WANDERER OF THE WASTELAND, 1935
WANTED BY THE POLICE, 1938
WANTED: DEAD OR ALIVE, 1987
WAR AND LOVE, 1985
WAR DRUMS, 1957
WAR NURSE, 1930
WAR OF THE COLOSSAL BEAST, 1958
WAR OF THE WIZARDS, 1983
WASHINGTON MASQUERADE, 1932
WASTREL, THE, 1963
WATCH BEVERLY, 1932
WATCH IT, SAILOR!, 1961
WATCHER IN THE WOODS, THE, 1980
WATER RUSTLERS, 1939
WATERFRONT LADY, 1935
WAVE, A WAC AND A MARINE, A, 1944
WAY DOWN SOUTH, 1939
WAY OF ALL MEN, THE, 1930
WAY OF THE WEST, THE, 1934
WAY OUT, THE, 1956
WAY OUT, WAY IN, 1970
WAY TO LOVE, THE, 1933
WAYWARD, 1932
WE JOINED THE NAVY, 1962
WEARY RIVER, 1929
WEATHER IN THE STREETS, THE, 1983
WEB OF SUSPICION, 1959
WEDDING RINGS, 1930
WEDNESDAY CHILDREN, THE, 1973
WEIRD SCIENCE, 1985
WELCOME HOME, 1935
WELCOME TO THE CLUB, 1971
WE'RE IN THE LEGION NOW, 1937
WEREWOLF VS. THE VAMPIRE WOMAN, THE, 1970
WEREWOLF, THE, 1956
WEST 11, 1963
WEST OF CHEYENNE, 1931
WEST OF CHEYENNE, 1938
WEST OF THE ALAMO, 1946
WEST OF WYOMING, 1950
WEST TO GLORY, 1947
WESTERN MAIL, 1942
WESTERN TRAILS, 1938
WESTWARD HO, 1936
WHARF ANGEL, 1934
WHAT A BLONDE, 1945
WHAT A CRAZY WORLD, 1963
WHAT A MAN, 1930
WHAT A WAY TO GO, 1964
WHAT A WHOPPER, 1961
WHAT A WIDOW, 1930
WHAT A WOMAN!, 1943
WHAT BECAME OF JACK AND JILL?, 1972
WHAT PRICE DECENCY?, 1933
WHAT PRICE VENGEANCE?, 1937
WHAT'S BUZZIN COUSIN?, 1943

WHAT'S COOKIN'?, 1942
WHEEL OF ASHES, 1970
WHEELS OF DESTINY, 1934
WHEN A MAN RIDES ALONE, 1933
WHEN A MAN SEES RED, 1934
WHEN G-MEN STEP IN, 1938
WHEN GANGLAND STRIKES, 1956
WHEN JOHNNY COMES MARCHING HOME, 1943
WHEN LONDON SLEEPS, 1934
WHEN STRANGERS MARRY, 1933
WHEN STRANGERS MEET, 1934
WHEN THE BOYS MEET THE GIRLS, 1965
WHEN THE CLOCK STRIKES, 1961
WHEN THE DEVIL WAS WELL, 1937
WHEN THE REDSKINS RODE, 1951
WHEN THIEF MEETS THIEF, 1937
WHEN YOU'RE SMILING, 1950
WHERE ANGELS GO...TROUBLE FOLLOWS, 1968
WHERE DID YOU GET THAT GIRL?, 1941
WHERE SINNERS MEET, 1934
WHERE THE WEST BEGINS, 1938
WHICH WAY TO THE FRONT?, 1970
WHILE I LIVE, 1947
WHILE PARENTS SLEEP, 1935
WHILE THE ATTORNEY IS ASLEEP, 1945
WHILE THE SUN SHINES, 1950
WHIP'S WOMEN, 1968
WHIRLWIND, 1951
WHIRLWIND RAIDERS, 1948
WHISPERING GHOSTS, 1942
WHISPERING SMITH SPEAKS, 1935
WHISPERING SMITH VERSUS SCOTLAND YARD, 1952
WHISTLE STOP, 1946
WHISTLING HILLS, 1951
WHITE ANGEL, THE, 1936
WHITE CARGO, 1930
WHITE HEAT, 1934
WHITE HUNTRESS, 1957
WHITE LEGION, THE, 1936
WHITE SHOULDERS, 1931
WHITE SLAVE, 1986
WHITE SLAVE SHIP, 1962
WHITE WOMAN, 1933
WHO KILLED FEN MARKHAM?, 1937
WHY BOTHER TO KNOCK, 1964
WHY GIRLS LEAVE HOME, 1945
WHY SAILORS LEAVE HOME, 1930
WHY SAPS LEAVE HOME, 1932
WHY WOULD I LIE, 1980
WICKED DREAMS OF PAULA SCHULTZ, THE, 1968
WICKED LADY, THE, 1946
WICKHAM MYSTERY, THE, 1931
WIDE BOY, 1952
WIDOW FROM MONTE CARLO, THE, 1936
WILD BRIAN KENT, 1936
WILD COMPANY, 1930
WILD DUCK, THE, 1983
WILD EYE, THE, 1968
WILD GEESE II, 1985
WILD HORSE CANYON, 1939
WILD HORSE PHANTOM, 1944
WILD HORSE RODEO, 1938
WILD HORSE RUSTLERS, 1943
WILD HORSE VALLEY, 1940
WILD WEST, 1946
WILD WESTERNERS, THE, 1962
WILD, WILD PLANET, THE, 1967
WILDCAT OF TUCSON, 1941
WILDERNESS MAIL, 1935
WILDFIRE, 1945
WILLS AND BURKE, 1985
WINDJAMMER, THE, 1931
WINDMILL, THE, 1937
WINGS OVER AFRICA, 1939
WINNING TICKET, THE, 1935
WINTER KEPT US WARM, 1968
WINTERHAWK, 1976
WINTERTIME, 1943
WISE GIRL, 1937
WISHBONE CUTTER, 1978
WISHBONE, THE, 1933
WITCH WITHOUT A BROOM, A, 1967
WITCHES, THE, 1969
WITCHMAKER, THE, 1969
WITCH'S CURSE, THE, 1963

WITHOUT HONOR, 1949
WITHOUT ORDERS, 1936
WITHOUT PITY, 1949
WITHOUT YOU, 1934
WITNESS VANISHES, THE, 1939
WIZ, THE, 1978
WIZARD OF BAGHDAD, THE, 1960
WOLF CALL, 1939
WOLF HUNTERS, THE, 1949
WOLF OF NEW YORK, 1940
WOLFMAN, 1979
WOLVES OF THE RANGE, 1943
WOMAN CHASES MAN, 1937
WOMAN DECIDES, THE, 1932
WOMAN DOCTOR, 1939
WOMAN FOR JOE, THE, 1955
WOMAN HATER, 1949
WOMAN HUNGRY, 1931
WOMAN IN DISTRESS, 1937
WOMAN IN HIDING, 1953
WOMAN INSIDE, THE, 1981
WOMAN OF EXPERIENCE, A, 1931
WOMAN OF MYSTERY, A, 1957
WOMAN OF ROME, 1956
WOMAN ON FIRE, A, 1970
WOMAN ON PIER 13, THE, 1950
WOMAN RACKET, THE, 1930
WOMAN TRAP, 1929
WOMAN TRAP, 1936
WOMAN WANTED, 1935
WOMEN IN THE NIGHT, 1948
WOMEN LOVE ONCE, 1931
WONDERS OF ALADDIN, THE, 1961
WONDERWALL, 1969
WORLD ACCUSES, THE, 1935
WORLD AND THE FLESH, THE, 1932
WORLDLY GOODS, 1930
WOULD-BE GENTLEMAN, THE, 1960
WOZZECK, 1962
WRITTEN LAW, THE, 1931
WRONG GUYS, THE, 1988
WRONG ROAD, THE, 1937
YANK IN KOREA, A, 1951
YANKEE FAKIR, 1947
YANKS AHOY, 1943
YANKS ARE COMING, THE, 1942
YAQUI DRUMS, 1956
YEAR OF THE DRAGON, 1985
YEARS BETWEEN, THE, 1947
YELLOW HAIR AND THE FORTRESS OF GOLD, 1984
YES, GIORGIO, 1982
YES, MR. BROWN, 1933
YES SIR, MR. BONES, 1951
YESTERDAY'S HERO, 1979
YODELIN' KID FROM PINE RIDGE, 1937
YOSAKOI JOURNEY, 1970
YOU CAME TOO LATE, 1962
YOU CAN'T BEAT LOVE, 1937
YOU CAN'T BUY LUCK, 1937
YOU CAN'T ESCAPE FOREVER, 1942
YOU CAN'T FOOL YOUR WIFE, 1940
YOU CAN'T WIN 'EM ALL, 1970
YOU LUCKY PEOPLE, 1955
YOU MADE ME LOVE YOU, 1934
YOU MAY BE NEXT, 1936
YOU MUST GET MARRIED, 1936
YOU PAY YOUR MONEY, 1957
YOU SAID A MOUTHFUL, 1932
YOU WILL REMEMBER, 1941
YOU'D BE SURPRISED!, 1930
YOUNG AND BEAUTIFUL, 1934
YOUNG BLOOD, 1932
YOUNG BRIDE, 1932
YOUNG GIANTS, 1983
YOUNG JESSE JAMES, 1960
YOUNG, THE EVIL AND THE SAVAGE, THE, 1968
YOUR MONEY OR YOUR WIFE, 1972
YOU'RE A LUCKY FELLOW, MR. SMITH, 1943
YOU'RE THE DOCTOR, 1938
YOUTH ON PAROLE, 1937
YOUTH RUNS WILD, 1944
YOU'VE GOT TO WALK IT LIKE YOU TALK IT OR YOU'LL LOSE THAT BEAT, 1971
YUKON VENGEANCE, 1954
ZAMBA, 1949
ZERO BOYS, THE, 1987

00-2 MOST SECRET AGENTS, 1965
ZONTAR, THE THING FROM VENUS, 1966
ZORRO, THE GAY BLADE, 1981
Z.P.G., 1972

1 Star
ABBOTT AND COSTELLO GO TO MARS, 1953
ABDUCTION, 1975
ABDUL THE DAMNED, 1935
ABIE'S IRISH ROSE, 1946
ABOMINABLE DR. PHIBES, THE, 1971
ABSOLUTION, 1981
ACES WILD, 1937
ACQUITTED, 1929
ACROSS THE RIVER, 1965
ACT OF THE HEART, 1970
ACT OF VENGEANCE, 1974
ACTION STATIONS, 1959
ADAM AT 6 A.M., 1970
ADIEU PHILLIPINE, 1962
ADMIRAL'S SECRET, THE, 1934
ADOLF HITLER—MY PART IN HIS DOWNFALL, 1973
ADOPTION, THE, 1978
ADVENTURE LIMITED, 1934
ADVENTURES OF BARRY McKENZIE, 1972
ADVENTURES OF HAL 5, THE, 1958
ADVENTURES OF PICASSO, THE, 1980
AFFAIR IN HAVANA, 1957
AFFAIR OF SUSAN, 1935
AFFAIR OF THE SKIN, AN, 1964
AFFAIRS OF CAPPY RICKS, 1937
AFFAIRS OF JULIE, THE, 1958
AFRICAN TREASURE, 1952
AFTER THE FALL OF NEW YORK, 1984
AFTER THE FOG, 1930
AGAINST ALL ODDS, 1984
AGAINST THE TIDE, 1937
AGATHA, 1979
AGE FOR LOVE, THE, 1931
AGE OF THE MEDICI, THE, 1979
AGENCY, 1981
AGENT ON ICE, 1986
AGGIE APPLEBY, MAKER OF MEN, 1933
AGITATOR, THE, 1949
AIR DEVILS, 1938
AIR EAGLES, 1932
AIR HOSTESS, 1933
AIR PATROL, 1962
AIR POLICE, 1931
AIR STRIKE, 1955
ALASKA, 1944
ALASKA HIGHWAY, 1943
ALASKA PASSAGE, 1959
ALFIE DARLING, 1975
ALFREDO, ALFREDO, 1973
ALF'S BABY, 1953
ALF'S CARPET, 1929
ALI BABA, 1954
ALIAS JOHN LAW, 1935
ALIAS MARY SMITH, 1932
ALIAS THE CHAMP, 1949
ALIBI, 1931
ALIBI FOR MURDER, 1936
ALIBI INN, 1935
ALICE'S ADVENTURES IN WONDERLAND, 1972
ALIEN PREDATOR, 1987
ALIMONY, 1949
ALL-AMERICAN BOY, THE, 1973
ALL-AMERICAN CHUMP, 1936
ALL-AMERICAN SWEETHEART, 1937
ALL HANDS ON DECK, 1961
ALL MEN ARE ENEMIES, 1934
ALL OVER TOWN, 1937
ALL THE FINE YOUNG CANNIBALS, 1960
ALL THE KING'S HORSES, 1935
ALL THE WAY, BOYS, 1973
ALL WOMEN HAVE SECRETS, 1939
ALLAN QUATERMAIN AND THE LOST CITY OF GOLD, 1987
ALLURING GOAL, THE, 1930
ALMOST A DIVORCE, 1931
ALMOST A HONEYMOON, 1930
ALMOST A HONEYMOON, 1938
ALMOST PERFECT AFFAIR, AN, 1979
ALONE AGAINST ROME, 1963
ALONG CAME LOVE, 1937

BOLD: Films on Videocassette

ALONG CAME SALLY, 1934
ALONG CAME YOUTH, 1931
ALONG THE OREGON TRAIL, 1947
ALONG THE RIO GRANDE, 1941
ALPHABET CITY, 1984
ALWAYS, 1985
ALWAYS A BRIDE, 1940
ALWAYS ANOTHER DAWN, 1948
ALWAYS GOODBYE, 1931
AMATEUR DADDY, 1932
AMAZING GRACE, 1974
AMAZING MR. BEECHAM, THE, 1949
AMAZING MR. FORREST, THE, 1943
AMAZON QUEST, 1949
AMAZONS, 1987
AMBUSH, 1939
AMBUSH TRAIL, 1946
AMBUSH VALLEY, 1936
AMERICA 3000, 1986
AMERICAN COMMANDOS, 1986
AMERICAN DREAM, AN, 1966
AMERICAN POP, 1981
AMERICATHON, 1979
AMITYVILLE 3-D, 1983
AMITYVILLE II: THE POSSESSION, 1982
AMONG THE MISSING, 1934
AMONG VULTURES, 1964
AMOUR, AMOUR, 1937
ANATAHAN, 1953
ANATOMY OF A PSYCHO, 1961
ANATOMY OF LOVE, 1959
AND MILLIONS WILL DIE, 1973
AND SOON THE DARKNESS, 1970
AND SUDDEN DEATH, 1936
AND THE SAME TO YOU, 1960
ANGEL 3: THE FINAL CHAPTER, 1988
ANGEL UNCHAINED, 1970
ANGELS BRIGADE, 1980
ANGELS DIE HARD, 1970
ANGELS FROM HELL, 1968
ANGELS HARD AS THEY COME, 1971
ANGELS OF DARKNESS, 1956
ANGKOR-CAMBODIA EXPRESS, 1986
ANGRY BREED, THE, 1969
ANGRY RED PLANET, THE, 1959
ANN CARVER'S PROFESSION, 1933
ANNAPOLIS SALUTE, 1937
ANNE-MARIE, 1936
ANOTHER SHORE, 1948
ANOTHER SKY, 1960
ANTS IN HIS PANTS, 1940
ANY MAN'S WIFE, 1936
ANYBODY'S BLONDE, 1931
ANYTHING FOR A SONG, 1947
ANYTHING FOR A THRILL, 1937
APACHE CHIEF, 1949
APACHE COUNTRY, 1952
APACHE KID, THE, 1941
APACHE ROSE, 1947
APE, THE, 1940
APE MAN, THE, 1943
APOLOGY FOR MURDER, 1945
APPLE, THE, 1980
APPOINTMENT, THE, 1969
APPOINTMENT FOR MURDER, 1954
APPOINTMENT WITH FEAR, 1985
APPRENTICE TO MURDER, 1988
APRIL 1, 2000, 1953
ARCTIC FURY, 1949
ARCTIC MANHUNT, 1949
ARE THESE OUR CHILDREN?, 1931
ARE THESE OUR PARENTS?, 1944
ARE WE CIVILIZED?, 1934
ARE YOU LISTENING?, 1932
ARIANE, RUSSIAN MAID, 1932
ARIZONA BADMAN, 1935
ARIZONA COLT, 1965
ARIZONA CYCLONE, 1934
ARIZONA GANGBUSTERS, 1940
ARIZONA GUNFIGHTER, 1937
ARIZONA MAHONEY, 1936
ARIZONA NIGHTS, 1934
ARIZONA ROUNDUP, 1942
ARIZONA TERROR, 1931
ARIZONA TRAILS, 1935
ARIZONA WHIRLWIND, 1944

ARM OF THE LAW, 1932
ARMY BOUND, 1952
ARMY SURGEON, 1942
ARMY WIVES, 1944
ARNOLD, 1973
AROUND THE TOWN, 1938
AROUSERS, THE, 1973
ARRANGEMENT, THE, 1969
ARRIVEDERCI, BABY!, 1966
ARSENAL STADIUM MYSTERY, THE, 1939
ARSON FOR HIRE, 1959
ARTHUR 2 ON THE ROCKS, 1988
AS THE DEVIL COMMANDS, 1933
AS THE SEA RAGES, 1960
AS YOU WERE, 1951
ASH WEDNESDAY, 1973
ASK BECCLES, 1933
ASSASSIN, 1973
ASSASSIN, THE, 1953
ASSASSIN, THE, 1965
ASSAULT ON AGATHON, 1976
ASSIGNMENT K, 1968
ASSIGNMENT TO KILL, 1968
ASTERO, 1960
AT DAWN WE DIE, 1943
AT THE EARTH'S CORE, 1976
ATLANTIC FERRY, 1941
ATLANTIC FLIGHT, 1937
ATLAS, 1960
ATLAS AGAINST THE CYCLOPS, 1963
ATOM AGE VAMPIRE, 1961
ATOMIC BRAIN, THE, 1964
ATOMIC KID, THE, 1954
ATOMIC MAN, THE, 1955
ATTACK OF THE 50 FOOT WOMAN, 1958
ATTACK OF THE KILLER TOMATOES, 1978
ATTACK OF THE MUSHROOM PEOPLE, 1964
ATTACK OF THE ROBOTS, 1967
ATTILA, 1958
ATTORNEY FOR THE DEFENSE, 1932
AUGUST WEEK-END, 1936
AUTUMN CROCUS, 1934
AVALANCHE, 1978
AVENGER, THE, 1931
AVENGER, THE, 1933
AVENGER, THE, 1964
AVENGER, THE, 1966
AVENGERS, THE, 1950
AVENGING RIDER, THE, 1943
AVENGING WATERS, 1936
AVIATOR, THE, 1929
AWAKENING, THE, 1938
AZAIS, 1931
BABES ON SWING STREET, 1944
BACHELOR APARTMENT, 1931
BACHELOR BAIT, 1934
BACHELOR GIRL, THE, 1929
BACHELOR MOTHER, 1933
BACHELOR OF ARTS, 1935
BACHELOR'S BABY, 1932
BACK DOOR TO HELL, 1964
BACK FROM THE DEAD, 1957
BACK IN THE SADDLE, 1941
BACK PAY, 1930
BACK TO GOD'S COUNTRY, 1953
BACK TO NATURE, 1936
BACK TRAIL, 1948
BACKGROUND, 1953
BACKLASH, 1947
BACKSTAGE, 1937
BAD BOY, 1935
BAD BOY, 1939
BAD COMPANY, 1931
BAD FOR EACH OTHER, 1954
BAD GIRL, 1931
BAD MAN OF DEADWOOD, 1941
BAD MAN'S RIVER, 1972
BAD MEN OF THE HILLS, 1942
BAD MEN OF THUNDER GAP, 1943
BAD NEWS BEARS IN BREAKING TRAINING, THE, 1977
BAD ONE, THE, 1930
BAD SISTER, 1947
BADGE OF HONOR, 1934
BADGE OF MARSHAL BRENNAN, THE, 1957
BADGE 373, 1973

BADLANDS, 1974
BAHAMA PASSAGE, 1941
BAILOUT AT 43,000, 1957
BAL TABARIN, 1952
BALBOA, 1986
BALL AT SAVOY, 1936
BALL AT THE CASTLE, 1939
BALLOON GOES UP, THE, 1942
BAMBOO SAUCER, THE, 1968
BAND PLAYS ON, THE, 1934
BANDIDOS, 1967
BANDIT OF ZHOBE, THE, 1959
BANDIT QUEEN, 1950
BANDIT RANGER, 1942
BANDITS OF DARK CANYON, 1947
BANDITS OF EL DORADO, 1951
BANDITS OF THE WEST, 1953
BANJO, 1947
BANK ALARM, 1937
BANK HOLIDAY, 1938
BANK MESSENGER MYSTERY, THE, 1936
BANNING, 1967
BANZAI, 1983
BANZAI RUNNER, 1987
BAR L RANCH, 1930
BAR 20, 1943
BAR 20 JUSTICE, 1938
BAR 20 RIDES AGAIN, 1936
BAR Z BAD MEN, 1937
BARBARELLA, 1968
BARBARIANS, THE, 1987
BARBARY PIRATE, 1949
BARBER OF SEVILLE, THE, 1947
BARBER OF SEVILLE, 1949
BARGAIN, THE, 1931
BARKER, THE, 1928
BARNUM WAS RIGHT, 1929
BARON MUNCHAUSEN, 1962
BARRACUDA, 1978
BARRANCO, 1932
BARRIER, THE, 1937
BARS OF HATE, 1936
BARTON MYSTERY, THE, 1932
BASKET CASE, 1982
BATTLE BENEATH THE EARTH, 1968
BATTLE OF BLOOD ISLAND, 1960
BATTLE OF GREED, 1934
BATTLE OF LOVE'S RETURN, THE, 1971
BATTLE OF PARIS, THE, 1929
BATTLE OF THE AMAZONS, 1973
BATTLE OF THE VILLA FIORITA, THE, 1965
BATTLE STATIONS, 1956
BATTLE TAXI, 1955
BATTLES OF CHIEF PONTIAC, 1952
BATTLESTAR GALACTICA, 1979
BATTLING BUCKAROO, 1932
BATTLING MARSHAL, 1950
BEACH GIRLS AND THE MONSTER, THE, 1965
BEACHES, 1988
BEAST MUST DIE, THE, 1974
BEAST WITHIN, THE, 1982
BEAT GENERATION, THE, 1959
BEAT THE BAND, 1947
BEATNIKS, THE, 1960
BEAU BANDIT, 1930
BEAU PERE, 1981
BEAUTIFUL ADVENTURE, 1932
BEAUTIFUL PRISONER, THE, 1983
BEAUTY AND THE BANDIT, 1946
BEAUTY AND THE BOSS, 1932
BEAUTY FOR THE ASKING, 1939
BEAUTY PARLOR, 1932
BECAUSE I LOVED YOU, 1930
BED AND BREAKFAST, 1930
BED AND BREAKFAST, 1936
BEDSIDE, 1934
BEDTIME STORY, 1938
BEEN DOWN SO LONG IT LOOKS LIKE UP TO ME, 1977
BEES, THE, 1978
BEFORE MIDNIGHT, 1934
BEFORE MORNING, 1933
BEG, BORROW OR STEAL, 1937
BEGGAR STUDENT, THE, 1931
BEGGAR STUDENT, THE, 1958
BEHEMOTH, THE SEA MONSTER, 1959

BEHIND JURY DOORS, 1933
BEHIND STONE WALLS, 1932
BEHIND THE EVIDENCE, 1935
BEHIND THE MASK, 1946
BEHIND THE NEWS, 1941
BEHOLD MY WIFE, 1935
BELA LUGOSI MEETS A BROOKLYN GORILLA, 1952
BELLA DONNA, 1983
BELLE OF OLD MEXICO, 1950
BELLE STARR'S DAUGHTER, 1947
BELLS OF SAN FERNANDO, 1947
BELOVED IMPOSTER, 1936
BENEATH WESTERN SKIES, 1944
BENGAL BRIGADE, 1954
BERLIN ALEXANDERPLATZ, 1933
BERMUDA AFFAIR, 1956
BERMUDA MYSTERY, 1944
BEST LITTLE WHOREHOUSE IN TEXAS, THE, 1982
BEST OF ENEMIES, 1933
BETRAYAL, THE, 1948
BETSY, THE, 1978
BETTER A WIDOW, 1969
BETTY CO-ED, 1946
BETWEEN FIGHTING MEN, 1932
BETWEEN TWO WOMEN, 1937
BETWEEN US GIRLS, 1942
BEVERLY HILLS COP II, 1987
BEWARE, 1946
BEWARE OF CHILDREN, 1961
BEWARE! THE BLOB, 1972
BEYOND AND BACK, 1978
BEYOND GOOD AND EVIL, 1984
BEYOND THE CITIES, 1930
BEYOND THE FOREST, 1949
BEYOND THE POSEIDON ADVENTURE, 1979
BEYOND THE RIO GRANDE, 1930
BEYOND THE TIME BARRIER, 1960
BEYOND THERAPY, 1987
BIDDY, 1983
BIG BLUFF, THE, 1933
BIG BUSINESS, 1930
BIG BUSINESS, 1934
BIG BUSINESS, 1937
BIG CATCH, THE, 1968
BIG CHANCE, THE, 1933
BIG CHANCE, THE, 1957
BIG DADDY, 1969
BIG DOLL HOUSE, THE, 1971
BIG FOOT, 1973
BIG FRAME, THE, 1953
BIG GAMBLE, THE, 1931
BIG GAME, THE, 1972
BIG NIGHT, THE, 1951
BIG NOISE, THE, 1936
BIG SCORE, THE, 1983
BIG SHOT, THE, 1931
BIG SPLASH, THE, 1935
BIG SWITCH, THE, 1950
BIG TOWN, 1947
BIG TOWN CZAR, 1939
BIG TREES, THE, 1952
BIGAMIST, THE, 1953
BILL CRACKS DOWN, 1937
BILLION DOLLAR BRAIN, 1967
BILLION DOLLAR HOBO, THE, 1977
BILLION DOLLAR SCANDAL, 1932
BILLY IN THE LOWLANDS, 1979
BILLY JACK, 1971
BILLY THE KID IN SANTA FE, 1941
BILLY THE KID'S FIGHTING PALS, 1941
BILLY THE KID'S RANGE WAR, 1941
BIMBO THE GREAT, 1961
BIONIC BOY, THE, 1977
BIRDS DO IT, 1966
BIRDS OF A FEATHER, 1931
BIRDS OF PREY, 1987
BLACK ABBOT, THE, 1934
BLACK BELLY OF THE TARANTULA, THE, 1972
BLACK CHRISTMAS, 1974
BLACK DIAMONDS, 1932
BLACK GESTAPO, THE, 1975
BLACK GLOVE, 1954
BLACK GUNN, 1972
BLACK HAND GANG, THE, 1930
BLACK HILLS, 1948
BLACK ICE, THE, 1957

BLACK JACK, 1973
BLACK KLANSMAN, THE, 1966
BLACK MARKET RUSTLERS, 1943
BLACK MASK, 1935
BLACK MEMORY, 1947
BLACK PATCH, 1957
BLACK PIRATES, THE, 1954
BLACK PIT OF DOCTOR M, 1958
BLACK RIDER, THE, 1954
BLACK SIX, THE, 1974
BLACKENSTEIN, 1973
BLACKOUT, 1988
BLAME IT ON THE NIGHT, 1984
BLAZE OF GLORY, 1963
BLAZING BARRIERS, 1937
BLAZING SIXES, 1937
BLESS 'EM ALL, 1949
BLIND ADVENTURE, 1933
BLIND DATE, 1934
BLIND DATE, 1984
BLIND FOLLY, 1939
BLIND MAN'S BLUFF, 1952
BLIND SPOT, 1932
BLINDMAN, 1972
BLOND CHEAT, 1938
BLONDE ALIBI, 1946
BLONDE BAIT, 1956
BLONDE BLACKMAILER, 1955
BLONDE COMET, 1941
BLONDE FOR A DAY, 1946
BLONDE ICE, 1949
BLONDE SAVAGE, 1947
BLONDE SINNER, 1956
BLONDES AT WORK, 1938
BLONDIE IN THE DOUGH, 1947
BLONDIE'S SECRET, 1948
BLOOD, 1974
BLOOD BATH, 1966
BLOOD BATH, 1976
BLOOD BEAST TERROR, THE, 1967
BLOOD DINER, 1987
BLOOD FEUD, 1979
BLOOD OF FU MANCHU, THE, 1968
BLOOD ORANGE, 1953
BLOOD ORGY OF THE SHE-DEVILS, 1973
BLOOD RELATIVES, 1978
BLOOD SPATTERED BRIDE, THE, 1974
BLOOD, SWEAT AND FEAR, 1975
BLOOD TIDE, 1982
BLOOD WATERS OF DOCTOR Z, 1982
BLOODEATERS, 1980
BLOODLUST, 1959
BLOODSUCKERS FROM OUTER SPACE, 1987
BLOODY BIRTHDAY, 1986
BLOW-UP, 1966
BLOW YOUR OWN TRUMPET, 1958
BLUE BLOOD, 1973
BLUE CANADIAN ROCKIES, 1952
BLUE DANUBE, 1932
BLUE DEMON VERSUS THE INFERNAL BRAINS, 1967
BLUE IDOL, THE, 1931
BLUE IGUANA, THE, 1988
BLUE LAGOON, THE, 1980
BLUE PARROT, THE, 1953
BLUE SCAR, 1949
BLUE SMOKE, 1935
BLUE SQUADRON, THE, 1934
BOAT FROM SHANGHAI, 1931
BOBBY WARE IS MISSING, 1955
BOB'S YOUR UNCLE, 1941
BOCCACCIO '70, 1962
BODY SAID NO!, THE, 1950
BOEFJE, 1939
BOHEMIAN RAPTURE, 1948
BOLDEST JOB IN THE WEST, THE, 1971
BOLERO, 1982
BOMBA AND THE HIDDEN CITY, 1950
BOMBA ON PANTHER ISLAND, 1949
BOMBAY TALKIE, 1970
BOMBS OVER BURMA, 1942
BONANZA TOWN, 1951
BOND OF FEAR, 1956
BOOBY TRAP, 1957
BOOGENS, THE, 1982
BOOM!, 1968

BOOMERANG, 1934
BOOT HILL, 1969
BOOTS AND SADDLES, 1937
BOOTS! BOOTS!, 1934
BOOTS OF DESTINY, 1937
BORDER BADMEN, 1945
BORDER BANDITS, 1946
BORDER BUCKAROOS, 1943
BORDER FEUD, 1947
BORDER ROMANCE, 1930
BORDER TREASURE, 1950
BORDER WOLVES, 1938
BORN AMERICAN, 1986
BORN LUCKY, 1932
BORN RECKLESS, 1959
BORN THAT WAY, 1937
BORN TO BE BAD, 1934
BORN TO SING, 1942
BORN WILD, 1968
BORROW A MILLION, 1934
BORROWED CLOTHES, 1934
BORROWED WIVES, 1930
BORROWING TROUBLE, 1937
BOSS OF LONELY VALLEY, 1937
BOSS RIDER OF GUN CREEK, 1936
BOSS' WIFE, THE, 1986
BOTH SIDES OF THE LAW, 1953
BOTTOMS UP, 1960
BOUDOIR DIPLOMAT, 1930
BOWERY BATTALION, 1951
BOWERY BLITZKRIEG, 1941
BOWERY BOY, 1940
BOWERY BOYS MEET THE MONSTERS, THE, 1954
BOY, A GIRL AND A BIKE, A, 1949
BOY, A GIRL, AND A DOG, A, 1946
BOY CRIED MURDER, THE, 1966
BOY WHO TURNED YELLOW, THE, 1972
BOY'S REFORMATORY, 1939
BOYS WILL BE BOYS, 1936
BOYS WILL BE GIRLS, 1937
BRACELETS, 1931
BRADDOCK: MISSING IN ACTION III, 1988
BRAIN, THE, 1965
BRAND OF FEAR, 1949
BRANDED, 1931
BRASIL ANNO 2,000, 1968
BRAT, THE, 1930
BREAKAWAY, 1956
BREAKERS AHEAD, 1935
BREAKERS AHEAD, 1938
BREAKING POINT, THE, 1961
BREATH OF LIFE, 1962
BREED OF THE BORDER, 1933
BRIDE AND THE BEAST, THE, 1958
BRIDE BY MISTAKE, 1944
BRIDE FOR HENRY, A, 1937
BRIDE OF THE GORILLA, 1951
BRIDE OF THE MONSTER, 1955
BRIDE WORE CRUTCHES, THE, 1940
BRIDEGROOM FOR TWO, 1932
BRIDES TO BE, 1934
BRIEF ECSTASY, 1937
BRIGHT LIGHTS, 1931
BRILLIANT MARRIAGE, 1936
BROKEN HORSESHOE, THE, 1953
BROKEN ROSARY, THE, 1934
BROKEN WING, THE, 1932
BRONCO BULLFROG, 1972
BROOKLYN ORCHID, 1942
BROTHER ALFRED, 1932
BROTHERHOOD OF SATAN, THE, 1971
BROTHERS OF THE WEST, 1938
BROTHERS O'TOOLE, THE, 1973
BROWN SUGAR, 1931
BRUSHFIRE, 1962
BRUTE AND THE BEAST, THE, 1968
BUCK AND THE PREACHER, 1972
BUCK ROGERS IN THE 25TH CENTURY, 1979
BUCKAROO SHERIFF OF TEXAS, 1951
BUFFALO BILL RIDES AGAIN, 1947
BUFFALO GUN, 1961
BUG, 1975
BULLDOG DRUMMOND AT BAY, 1937
BULLDOG SEES IT THROUGH, 1940
BULLET FOR PRETTY BOY, A, 1970
BULLET SCARS, 1942

BOLD: Films on Videocassette

BULLETS FOR O'HARA, 1941
BULLETS FOR RUSTLERS, 1940
BULLIES, 1986
BUNGALOW 13, 1948
BURIED ALIVE, 1939
BURIED ALIVE, 1951
BURKE AND HARE, 1972
BURNING GOLD, 1936
BURNING UP, 1930
BURNT OFFERINGS, 1976
BUSMAN'S HOLIDAY, 1936
BUSTED UP, 1986
BUT NOT IN VAIN, 1948
BUT THE FLESH IS WEAK, 1932
BUTCH AND SUNDANCE: THE EARLY DAYS, 1979
BUTCHER BAKER (NIGHTMARE MAKER), 1982
BUTLEY, 1974
BUTTERCUP CHAIN, THE, 1971
BYPASS TO HAPPINESS, 1934
C.O.D., 1932
C. C. AND COMPANY, 1971
CADDYSHACK II, 1988
CAGED FURY, 1984
CAGED WOMEN, 1984
CAIN'S WAY, 1969
CALENDAR, THE, 1931
CALENDAR, THE, 1948
CALIFORNIA, 1963
CALIFORNIA GIRLS, 1984
CALIFORNIA JOE, 1944
CALIFORNIA MAIL, THE, 1937
CALIFORNIA TRAIL, THE, 1933
CALL, THE, 1938
CALL HIM MR. SHATTER, 1976
CALL IT LUCK, 1934
CALL OF THE BLOOD, 1948
CALL OF THE JUNGLE, 1944
CALL OF THE PRAIRIE, 1936
CALL OF THE ROCKIES, 1938
CALL OF THE YUKON, 1938
CALLBOX MYSTERY, THE, 1932
CALLING ALL HUSBANDS, 1940
CALLING THE TUNE, 1936
CAMEO KIRBY, 1930
CAMPUS SLEUTH, 1948
CANARIES SOMETIMES SING, 1930
CANCEL MY RESERVATION, 1972
CANDY, 1968
CANNIBAL ATTACK, 1954
CANNIBALS IN THE STREETS, 1982
CANNONBALL EXPRESS, 1932
CANYON AMBUSH, 1952
CANYON CITY, 1943
CANYON HAWKS, 1930
CANYON OF MISSING MEN, THE, 1930
CAPE CANAVERAL MONSTERS, 1960
CAPPY RICKS RETURNS, 1935
CAPRICE, 1967
CAPTAIN APACHE, 1971
CAPTAIN BILL, 1935
CAPTAIN BLACK JACK, 1952
CAPTAIN CALAMITY, 1936
CAPTAIN MOONLIGHT, 1940
CAPTAIN'S TABLE, THE, 1936
CAR, THE, 1977
CARE BEARS ADVENTURE IN WONDERLAND, THE, 1987
CARELESS AGE, 1929
CARELESS LADY, 1932
CARETAKERS DAUGHTER, THE, 1952
CARMEN, BABY, 1967
CARNABY, M.D., 1967
CARNAL KNOWLEDGE, 1971
CARNIVAL, 1946
CARNIVAL LADY, 1933
CAROLINA CANNONBALL, 1955
CAROLINA MOON, 1940
CARRY ON EMANUELLE, 1978
CARRY ON ENGLAND, 1976
CARTER CASE, THE, 1947
CARTOUCHE, 1957
CARYL OF THE MOUNTAINS, 1936
CASE FOR THE CROWN, THE, 1934
CASE OF CLARA DEANE, THE, 1932
CASE OF GABRIEL PERRY, THE, 1935
CASE OF SERGEANT GRISCHA, THE, 1930

CASE OF THE 44'S, THE, 1964
CASE OF THE FRIGHTENED LADY, THE, 1940.
CASE OF THE MISSING MAN, THE, 1935
CASTE, 1930
CASTLE IN THE AIR, 1952
CASTLE OF EVIL, 1967
CASTLE OF FU MANCHU, THE, 1968
CAT IN THE SACK, THE, 1967
CAT O'NINE TAILS, 1971
CAT WOMEN OF THE MOON, 1953
CATALINA CAPER, THE, 1967
CATCH THE HEAT, 1987
CATHY'S CURSE, 1977
CATTLE QUEEN, 1951
CATTLE STAMPEDE, 1943
CAUGHT CHEATING, 1931
CAUGHT IN THE FOG, 1928
CAUGHT PLASTERED, 1931
CAULDRON OF DEATH, THE, 1979
CAVALCADE OF THE WEST, 1936
CAVALIER, THE, 1928
CAVALRY, 1936
CAVE OF THE LIVING DEAD, 1966
CAYMAN TRIANGLE, THE, 1977
CENTURION, THE, 1962
CEREBROS DIABOLICOS, 1966
CHA-CHA-CHA BOOM, 1956
CHAIN GANG, 1985
CHAIN OF CIRCUMSTANCE, 1951
CHALLENGE THE WILD, 1954
CHAMBER OF HORRORS, 1966
CHAMPAGNE FOR BREAKFAST, 1935
CHANCE OF A NIGHT-TIME, THE, 1931
CHANGE OF SEASONS, A, 1980
CHANT OF JIMMIE BLACKSMITH, THE, 1980
CHAPPAQUA, 1967
CHARGE OF THE MODEL-T'S, 1979
CHARLATAN, THE, 1929
CHARLIE CHAN IN RIO, 1941
CHARLIE CHAN IN THE CITY OF DARKNESS, 1939
CHARLIE CHAN IN THE SECRET SERVICE, 1944
CHARRO, 1969
CHASE, THE, 1966
CHASTITY BELT, THE, 1968
CHATTANOOGA CHOO CHOO, 1984
CHATTERBOX, 1943
CHE!, 1969
CHECKERED FLAG, THE, 1963
CHECKMATE, 1935
CHEER THE BRAVE, 1951
CHELSEA LIFE, 1933
CHESTY ANDERSON, U.S. NAVY, 1976
CHEYENNE CYCLONE, THE, 1932
CHEYENNE KID, THE, 1930
CHEYENNE KID, THE, 1940
CHEYENNE TORNADO, 1935
CHICKEN CHRONICLES, THE, 1977
CHICKEN WAGON FAMILY, 1939
CHIEF, THE, 1933
CHILD, THE, 1977
CHILD AND THE KILLER, THE, 1959
CHILD OF MANHATTAN, 1933
CHILDHOOD OF MAXIM GORKY, 1938
CHILDREN GALORE, 1954
CHILDREN OF CHANCE, 1930
CHILDREN OF CHANCE, 1949
CHILDREN OF PLEASURE, 1930
CHILDREN OF RAGE, 1975
CHILDREN OF SANCHEZ, THE, 1978
CHILDREN OF THE FOG, 1935
CHILDRENS GAMES, 1969
CHINA CORSAIR, 1951
CHINESE BUNGALOW, THE, 1930
CHINESE CAT, THE, 1944
CHINESE RING, THE, 1947
CHIVATO, 1961
CHOPPERS, THE, 1961
CHRISTINA, 1929
CHRISTINE, 1959
CHRISTINE, 1983
CHRISTINE JORGENSEN STORY, THE, 1970
CHRISTMAS THAT ALMOST WASN'T, THE, 1966
CHRISTOPHER BEAN, 1933
CINDERELLA, 1937
CINDERELLA SWINGS IT, 1942
CIRCLE CANYON, 1934

CIRCLE OF LOVE, 1965
CIRCUMSTANTIAL EVIDENCE, 1954
CIRCUS OF HORRORS, 1960
CISCO KID, 1931
CITADEL OF CRIME, 1941
CITY OF MISSING GIRLS, 1941
CITY OF SHADOWS, 1955
CITY OF SILENT MEN, 1942
CITY OF THE WALKING DEAD, 1983
CITY ON FIRE, 1979
CITY STORY, 1954
CITY WITHOUT MEN, 1943
CLAIR DE FEMME, 1980
CLANCY IN WALL STREET, 1930
CLARENCE, 1937
CLASS, 1983
CLASS OF NUKE 'EM HIGH, 1986
CLEARING THE RANGE, 1931
CLEOPATRA JONES, 1973
CLEOPATRA JONES AND THE CASINO OF GOLD, 1975
CLIMAX, THE, 1930
CLIPPED WINGS, 1938
CLOCKWORK ORANGE, A, 1971
CLOWN AND THE KID, THE, 1961
CLUB HAVANA, 1946
COBRA, THE, 1968
COBRA STRIKES, THE, 1948
COCAINE COWBOYS, 1979
COCKTAIL, 1988
CODE OF HONOR, 1930
CODE OF THE CACTUS, 1939
CODE OF THE FEARLESS, 1939
CODE OF THE MOUNTED, 1935
COFFY, 1973
COLLEGE SWEETHEARTS, 1942
COLLEGE SWING, 1938
COLLEGIATE, 1936
COLLISION, 1932
COLORADO RANGER, 1950
COLT COMRADES, 1943
COME ACROSS, 1929
COME BACK PETER, 1952
COME BACK PETER, 1971
COME CLOSER, FOLKS, 1936
COME ON DANGER, 1942
COME SPY WITH ME, 1967
COMIC, THE, 1969
COMIN' AT YA!, 1981
COMIN' ROUND THE MOUNTAIN, 1940
COMIN' THRU' THE RYE, 1947
COMING OUT PARTY, 1934
COMMITMENT, THE, 1976
COMMON LAW WIFE, 1963
CON ARTISTS, THE, 1981
CON MEN, THE, 1973
CONDEMNED WOMEN, 1938
CONFESSIONS FROM A HOLIDAY CAMP, 1977
CONFESSIONS OF A POP PERFORMER, 1975
CONFESSIONS OF A WINDOW CLEANER, 1974
CONQUEST, 1929
CONQUEST, 1984
CONSPIRACY IN TEHERAN, 1948
CONVENTION GIRL, 1935
CONVICT'S CODE, 1939
CONVOY, 1978
COOL ONES, THE, 1967
COPPER SKY, 1957
CORRUPTION, 1933
COSSACKS IN EXILE, 1939
COSTELLO CASE, THE, 1930
COUCH, THE, 1962
COUNT OF TWELVE, 1955
COUNT YOUR BLESSINGS, 1959
COUNTERPLOT, 1959
COUNTESS FROM HONG KONG, A, 1967
COUNTESS OF MONTE CRISTO, THE, 1948
COUNTRY BEYOND, THE, 1936
COUNTRY MUSIC HOLIDAY, 1958
COUNTY FAIR, THE, 1932
COURAGEOUS AVENGER, THE, 1935
COUSINS IN LOVE, 1982
COVERED WAGON TRAILS, 1930
COVERED WAGON TRAILS, 1940
COVERGIRL, 1984
COVERT ACTION, 1980

COWBOY AND THE BANDIT, THE, 1935
COWBOY AND THE KID, THE, 1936
COWBOY BLUES, 1946
COWBOY CAVALIER, 1948
COWBOY FROM SUNDOWN, 1940
COWBOYS FROM TEXAS, 1939
COYOTE TRAILS, 1935
CRACKED NUTS, 1941
CRACKING UP, 1977
CRADLE SONG, 1933
CRASH, THE, 1932
CRASH, 1977
CRASH DRIVE, 1959
CRASH LANDING, 1958
CRASHIN' THRU DANGER, 1938
CRASHING BROADWAY, 1933
CRASHING THRU, 1939
CRASHING THRU, 1949
CRATER LAKE MONSTER, THE, 1977
CRAWLING EYE, THE, 1958
CRAWLING HAND, THE, 1963
CRAWLSPACE, 1986
CRAZY FOR LOVE, 1960
CRAZY KNIGHTS, 1944
CRAZY PARADISE, 1965
CRAZY WORLD OF JULIUS VROODER, THE, 1974
CREATION OF THE HUMANOIDS, 1962
CREATURE CALLED MAN, THE, 1970
CREATURE WALKS AMONG US, THE, 1956
CREATURE WASN'T NICE, THE, 1981
CREATURE WITH THE ATOM BRAIN, 1955
CREEPER, THE, 1980
CREEPING TERROR, THE, 1964
CREEPSHOW 2, 1987
CRESCENDO, 1972
CRIME AFLOAT, 1937
CRIME AND PUNISHMENT, 1948
CRIME, INC., 1945
CRIME NOBODY SAW, THE, 1937
CRIME OF HELEN STANLEY, 1934
CRIME OF HONOR, 1987
CRIME OF THE CENTURY, 1946
CRIME PATROL, THE, 1936
CRIME RING, 1938
CRIME UNLIMITED, 1935
CRIMINAL AT LARGE, 1932
CRIMSON CIRCLE, THE, 1930
CROISIERES SIDERALES, 1941
CROOKED RIVER, 1950
CROOKED TRAIL, THE, 1936
CROOKS TOUR, 1940
CROSBY CASE, THE, 1934
CROSS COUNTRY CRUISE, 1934
CROSS-EXAMINATION, 1932
CROSS STREETS, 1934
CROUCHING BEAST, THE, 1936
CROWD INSIDE, THE, 1971
CRUCIBLE OF TERROR, 1971
CRUSADER, THE, 1932
CRY MURDER, 1936
CURIOUS DR. HUMPP, 1967
CURSE OF BIGFOOT, 1972
CURSE OF THE AZTEC MUMMY, THE, 1965
CURSE OF THE DEVIL, 1973
CURSE OF THE FACELESS MAN, 1958
CURSE OF THE SWAMP CREATURE, 1966
CURUCU, BEAST OF THE AMAZON, 1956
CYCLONE OF THE SADDLE, 1935
CYCLONE ON HORSEBACK, 1941
DADDY-O, 1959
DAGORA THE SPACE MONSTER, 1964
DAISY MILLER, 1974
DAKOTA KID, THE, 1951
DALTON THAT GOT AWAY, 1960
DALTONS' WOMEN, THE, 1950
DAMAGED GOODS, 1937
DAMAGED LIVES, 1937
DAMAGED LOVE, 1931
DAMES AHOY, 1930
DAMIEN—OMEN II, 1978
DAMNATION ALLEY, 1977
DAN MATTHEWS, 1936
DAN'S MOTEL, 1982
DANCE HALL, 1950
DANCE MALL HOSTESS, 1933
DANCE, GIRL, DANCE, 1933

DANCERS, THE, 1930
DANCERS IN THE DARK, 1932
DANCING DYNAMITE, 1931
DANCING FEET, 1936
DANCING IN MANHATTAN, 1945
DANCING MAN, 1934
DANCING ON A DIME, 1940
DANCING SWEETIES, 1930
DANCING WITH CRIME, 1947
DANCING YEARS, THE, 1950
DANGER AHEAD, 1935
DANGER AHEAD, 1940
DANGER LIGHTS, 1930
DANGER STREET, 1947
DANGER TRAILS, 1935
DANGER VALLEY, 1938
DANGER WOMAN, 1946
DANGER ZONE, 1951
DANGER ZONE, THE, 1987
DANGEROUS AFFAIR, A, 1931
DANGEROUS CHARTER, 1962

DANGEROUS GAME, A, 1941
DANGEROUS HOLIDAY, 1937
DANGEROUS KISS, THE, 1961
DANGEROUS LADY, 1941
DANGEROUS TO KNOW, 1938
DANGEROUS YEARS, 1947
DAPHNE, THE, 1967
DAREDEVIL, THE, 1971
DAREDEVIL DRIVERS, 1938
DAREDEVILS OF EARTH, 1936
DARING CABALLERO, THE, 1949
DARING DANGER, 1932
DARING GAME, 1968
DARING YOUNG MAN, THE, 1935
DARK, THE, 1979
DARK HOUR, THE, 1936
DARK INTERVAL, 1950
DARK MAN, THE, 1951
DARK MANHATTAN, 1937
DARK PLACES, 1974
DARK PURPOSE, 1964
DARK RIVER, 1956
DARK ROAD, THE, 1948
DARK SIDE OF TOMORROW, THE, 1970
DARK STREETS OF CAIRO, 1940
DARK TOWER, THE, 1943
DARLING LILI, 1970
DAS LETZTE GEHEIMNIS, 1959
DATE BAIT, 1960
DATELINE DIAMONDS, 1966
DAUGHTER OF THE TONG, 1939
DAUGHTERS OF SATAN, 1972
DAUGHTERS OF TODAY, 1933
DAVID LIVINGSTONE, 1936
DAY IN COURT, A, 1965
DAY OF ANGER, 1970
DAY OF THE NIGHTMARE, 1965
DAY THE FISH CAME OUT, THE, 1967.
DEAD AND BURIED, 1981
DEAD ARE ALIVE, THE, 1972
DEAD HEAT, 1988
DEAD MAN'S CHEST, 1965
DEAD MARCH, THE, 1937
DEAD MELODY, 1938
DEAD ONE, THE, 1961
DEAD WOMAN'S KISS, A, 1951
DEADLY CHINA DOLL, 1973
DEADLY DECOYS, THE, 1962
DEADLY DREAMS, 1988
DEADLY DUO, 1962
DEADLY FORCE, 1983
DEADLY GAME, THE, 1941
DEADWOOD PASS, 1933
DEAF SMITH AND JOHNNY EARS, 1973
DEATH CURSE OF TARTU, 1967
DEATH IN THE SKY, 1937
DEATH KISS, THE, 1933
DEATH OF MICHAEL TURBIN, THE, 1954
DEATH ON THE MOUNTAIN, 1961
DEATH PLAY, 1976
DEATH RIDES THE PLAINS, 1944
DEATH RIDES THE RANGE, 1940
DEATH SENTENCE, 1967
DEATH SHIP, 1980

DEATH WISH 4: THE CRACKDOWN, 1987
DEATHSTALKER, 1983
DECEPTION, 1933
DECISION OF CHRISTOPHER BLAKE, THE, 1948
DEEP THRUST—THE HAND OF DEATH, 1973
DEERSLAYER, 1943
DELINQUENT DAUGHTERS, 1944
DELINQUENT PARENTS, 1938
DELIRIUM, 1979
DELIVERY BOYS, 1984
DELOS ADVENTURE, THE, 1987
DEMON FROM DEVIL'S LAKE, THE, 1964
DEMON WITCH CHILD, 1974
DENVER KID, THE, 1948
DEPARTMENT STORE, 1935
DERELICT, THE, 1937
DESERT GUNS, 1936
DESERT MESA, 1935
DESERT OF LOST MEN, 1951
DESERT PATROL, 1938
DESERT PURSUIT, 1952
DESERTERS, 1983
DESIRE UNDER THE ELMS, 1958
DESPERATE CHANCE FOR ELLERY QUEEN, A, 1942
DESPERATE MOVES, 1986
DESTINATION MILAN, 1954
DETECTIVE BELLI, 1970
DEVIL BAT, THE, 1941
DEVIL IN LOVE, THE, 1968
DEVIL SHIP, 1947
DEVIL'S ANGELS, 1967
DEVIL'S BAIT, 1959
DEVIL'S BEDROOM, THE, 1964
DEVIL'S HAND, THE, 1961
DEVIL'S LOTTERY, 1932
DEVIL'S MAN, THE, 1967
DEVIL'S MESSENGER, THE, 1962
DEVIL'S MISTRESS, THE, 1968
DEVIL'S RAIN, THE, 1975
DEVIL'S ROCK, 1938
DEVIL'S SISTERS, THE, 1966
DEVIL'S SLEEP, THE, 1951
DEVIL'S TRAIL, THE, 1942
DEVOTION, 1953
DIAMOND HEAD, 1962
DIAMOND STUD, 1970
DIAMOND TRAIL, 1933
DIARY OF A BACHELOR, 1964
DIARY OF A CLOISTERED NUN, 1973
DIARY OF A HIGH SCHOOL BRIDE, 1959
DIARY OF A REVOLUTIONIST, 1932
DIFFERENT SONS, 1962
DIGBY, THE BIGGEST DOG IN THE WORLD, 1974
DIPLOMAT'S MANSION, THE, 1961
DIRT GANG, THE, 1972
DIRTY MARY, CRAZY LARRY, 1974
DISAPPEARANCE, THE, 1981
DISASTER, 1948
DISCIPLE OF DEATH, 1972
DISEMBODIED, THE, 1957
DISGRACED, 1933
DIVINE EMMA, THE, 1983
DIXIANA, 1930
DOCKS OF NEW ORLEANS, 1948
DR. BUTCHER, M.D., 1982
DR. CHRISTIAN MEETS THE WOMEN, 1940
DOCTOR FAUSTUS, 1967
DR. FRANKENSTEIN ON CAMPUS, 1970
DR. GOLDFOOT AND THE GIRL BOMBS, 1966
DR. JEKYLL, 1985
DR. O'DOWD, 1940
DOCTOR'S DIARY, A, 1937
DOCTOR'S SECRET, 1929
DOCTORS' WIVES, 1971
DODGE CITY TRAIL, 1937
DOLEMITE, 1975
DOLLARS FOR A FAST GUN, 1969
DOLLY GETS AHEAD, 1931
DOMINANT SEX, THE, 1937
DON JUAN, 1956
DON JUAN QUILLIGAN, 1945
DON RICARDO RETURNS, 1946
DON'T ANSWER THE PHONE, 1980
DON'T BE A DUMMY, 1932
DON'T BLAME THE STORK, 1954
DON'T GAMBLE WITH STRANGERS, 1946

BOLD: Films on Videocassette

DON'T JUST LIE THERE, SAY SOMETHING!, 1973
DON'T PANIC CHAPS!, 1959
DON'T PLAY WITH MARTIANS, 1967
DON'T RAISE THE BRIDGE, LOWER THE RIVER, 1968
DON'T TALK TO STRANGE MEN, 1962
DON'T TURN 'EM LOOSE, 1936
DON'T WORRY, WE'LL THINK OF A TITLE, 1966
DOOMSDAY VOYAGE, 1972
DORM THAT DRIPPED BLOOD, THE, 1983
DORMIRE, 1985
DOS COSMONAUTAS A LA FUERZA, 1967
DOUBLE BED, THE, 1965
DOUBLE BUNK, 1961
DOUBLE DOOR, 1934
DOUBLE EVENT, THE, 1934
DOUBLE JEOPARDY, 1955
DOUBLE TROUBLE, 1967
DOUGHNUTS AND SOCIETY, 1936
DOWN IN ARKANSAW, 1938
DOWN OUR ALLEY, 1939
DOWN THE WYOMING TRAIL, 1939
DOWN TO THE SEA, 1936
DOWN TO THEIR LAST YACHT, 1934
DRACULA A.D. 1972, 1972
DRACULA'S DOG, 1978
DRACULA'S GREAT LOVE, 1972
DRACULA'S WIDOW, 1988
DRAGNET NIGHT, 1931
DRAGNET PATROL, 1932
DRAGON MURDER CASE, THE, 1934
DRAGON OF PENDRAGON CASTLE, THE, 1950
DREAM LOVER, 1986
DREAM NO MORE, 1950
DREAM ON, 1981
DREAM TOWN, 1973
DRESSED TO THRILL, 1935
DRIFTER, THE, 1988
DRIFTER, THE, 1944
DRIFTIN' KID, THE, 1941
DRIFTING, 1932
DRIVER'S SEAT, THE, 1975
DROP DEAD, MY LOVE, 1968
DRUMS O' VOODOO, 1934
DRUMS OF AFRICA, 1963
DRUMS OF DESTINY, 1937
DRUMS OF JEOPARDY, 1931
DRUMS OF TAHITI, 1954
DRUMS OF THE DESERT, 1940
DU BARRY, WOMAN OF PASSION, 1930
DUDE WRANGLER, THE, 1930
DUEL WITHOUT HONOR, 1953
DUET FOR FOUR, 1982
DUMMY, THE, 1929
DUNGEONMASTER, 1985
DURANGO VALLEY RAIDERS, 1938
DURING ONE NIGHT, 1962
DUSTY AND SWEETS MCGEE, 1971
DYNAMITE DENNY, 1932
DYNAMITERS, THE, 1956
EARTH VS. THE SPIDER, 1958
EARTHBOUND, 1981
EAST OF ELEPHANT ROCK, 1976
EAST SIDE KIDS, 1940
EAT AND RUN, 1986
ECHO OF A DREAM, 1930
ECHO PARK, 1986
EDDIE MACON'S RUN, 1983
EEGAH!, 1962
8 MILLION WAYS TO DIE, 1986
EIGHT ON THE LAM, 1967
18 AGAIN!, 1988
EIGHTEEN IN THE SUN, 1964
EL CONDOR, 1970
EL DIABLO RIDES, 1939
EL PASO STAMPEDE, 1953
EL TOPO, 1971
ELDER BROTHER, THE, 1937
ELENI, 1985
ELLERY QUEEN AND THE PERFECT CRIME, 1941
EMANON, 1987
EMBRACERS, THE, 1966
EMBRYO, 1976
EMERGENCY LANDING, 1941
EMILY, 1976
EMMANUELLE 5, 1987

EMPIRE OF THE ANTS, 1977
EMPTY CANVAS, THE, 1964
ENCHANTED APRIL, 1935
END OF AUGUST, THE, 1982
END OF THE LINE, THE, 1959
END OF THE WORLD, THE, 1930
END OF THE WORLD, 1977
ENEMIES OF THE LAW, 1931
ENEMY AGENTS MEET ELLERY QUEEN, 1942
ENEMY OF THE POLICE, 1933
ENLIGHTEN THY DAUGHTER, 1934
ENTER THE NINJA, 1982
EQUALIZER 2000, 1987
ERNEST GOES TO CAMP, 1987
ERNESTO, 1979
ESCAPE FROM THE BRONX, 1985
ESCAPE FROM THE SEA, 1968
ESCAPE 2000, 1983
ESTHER AND THE KING, 1960
ETERNAL LOVE, 1960
ETERNAL MELODIES, 1948
ETERNAL SUMMER, 1961
EVE, 1968
EVERY SPARROW MUST FALL, 1964
EVERYTHING OKAY, 1936
EVIL THAT MEN DO, THE, 1984
EX-FLAME, 1931
EXILE, THE, 1931
EXIT THE DRAGON, ENTER THE TIGER, 1977
EXORCISM AT MIDNIGHT, 1966
EXORCIST II: THE HERETIC, 1977
EXPENSIVE WOMEN, 1931
EXPOSED, 1938
EXTERMINATORS, THE, 1965
EXTERMINATORS OF THE YEAR 3000, THE, 1985
EXTORTION, 1938
EXTRAVAGANCE, 1930
EYES OF THE UNDERWORLD, 1943
FACE OF TERROR, 1964
FACE OF THE SCREAMING WEREWOLF, 1959
FACE ON THE BARROOM FLOOR, THE, 1932
FACES, 1934
FACING THE MUSIC, 1941
FADE TO BLACK, 1980
FAITHFUL HEART, 1933
FAKE'S PROGRESS, 1950
FALL OF THE HOUSE OF USHER, THE, 1952
FALL OF THE HOUSE OF USHER, THE, 1980
FALSE FACES, 1943
FALSE MADONNA, 1932
FAMILY NEXT DOOR, THE, 1939
FAMOUS FERGUSON CASE, THE, 1932
FANTASY MAN, 1984
FAREWELL PERFORMANCE, 1963
FAST AND LOOSE, 1930
FAST AND LOOSE, 1954
FAST CHARLIE... THE MOONBEAM RIDER, 1979
FAST ON THE DRAW, 1950
FAST WORKERS, 1933
FASTEST GUITAR ALIVE, THE, 1967
FAT GUY GOES NUTZOID!!, 1986
FAT SPY, 1966
FATAL LADY, 1936
FATAL WITNESS, THE, 1945
FATHER'S SON, 1941
FATHOM, 1967
FATSO, 1980
FAUST, 1964
FBI CODE 98, 1964
FEAR CHAMBER, THE, 1968
FEAR IN THE NIGHT, 1972
FEAR SHIP, THE, 1933
FEATHER, THE, 1929
FEEDBACK, 1979
FEELIN' GOOD, 1966
FEET OF CLAY, 1960
FEMALE JUNGLE, THE, 1955
FEMALE PRINCE, THE, 1966
FEMALE RESPONSE, THE, 1972
FEMALE TROUBLE, 1975
FENCE RIDERS, 1950
FEROCIOUS PAL, 1934
FEUD OF THE TRAIL, 1938
FEUD OF THE WEST, 1936
FEUDIN' FOOLS, 1952
FEVER HEAT, 1968

FEVER PITCH, 1985
FIEND, 1980
FIENDISH PLOT OF DR. FU MANCHU, THE, 1980
FIFTEEN MAIDEN LANE, 1936
FIFTEEN WIVES, 1934
FIFTH FLOOR, THE, 1980
52ND STREET, 1937
50,000 B.C. (BEFORE CLOTHING), 1963
FIGHT FOR YOUR LADY, 1937
FIGHTING CHAMP, 1933
FIGHTING CHANCE, THE, 1955
FIGHTING DEPUTY, THE, 1937
FIGHTING FOOL, THE, 1932
FIGHTING GENTLEMAN, THE, 1932
FIGHTING HERO, 1934
FIGHTING MAD, 1939
FIGHTING MAD, 1957
FIGHTING PARSON, THE, 1933
FIGHTING ROOKIE, THE, 1934
FIGHTING SHERIFF, THE, 1931
FIGHTING STALLION, THE, 1950
FIGHTING TEXAN, 1937
FIGHTING TEXANS, 1933
FIGHTING TROOPER, THE, 1935
FILE 113, 1932
FINAL ASSIGNMENT, 1980
FINAL COLUMN, THE, 1955
FINAL CONFLICT, THE, 1981
FINAL EXECUTIONER, THE, 1986
FINAL HOUR, THE, 1936
FINAL OPTION, THE, 1982
FINAL RECKONING, THE, 1932
FINAL TERROR, THE, 1983
FIND THE BLACKMAILER, 1943
FIND THE LADY, 1936
FIND THE WITNESS, 1937
FINDERS KEEPERS, LOVERS WEEPERS, 1968
FINE FEATHERS, 1937
FINGER MAN, 1955
FINGERPRINTS DON'T LIE, 1951
FIRE WITH FIRE, 1986
FIREBRAND JORDAN, 1930
FIRECHASERS, THE, 1970
FIRED WIFE, 1943
FIRES OF FATE, 1932
FIRST AID, 1931
FIRST LOVE, 1977
FIRST NIGHT, 1937
FIRST NUDIE MUSICAL, THE, 1976
FIRST TIME, THE, 1969
FIRST TRAVELING SALESLADY, THE, 1956
FISH HAWK, 1981
FISH THAT SAVED PITTSBURGH, THE, 1979
FIVE DAYS ONE SUMMER, 1982
FIVE FINGERS OF DEATH, 1973
FIVE LITTLE PEPPERS IN TROUBLE, 1940
FIVE MILES TO MIDNIGHT, 1963
FIXER DUGAN, 1939
FLAME IN THE HEATHER, 1935
FLAME OF LOVE, THE, 1930
FLAME OF YOUTH, 1949
FLAMING FRONTIER, 1958
FLAMING GOLD, 1934
FLAMING TEEN-AGE, THE, 1956
FLAMINGO AFFAIR, THE, 1948
FLANNELFOOT, 1953
FLASH AND THE FIRECAT, 1976
FLASH THE SHEEPDOG, 1967
FLASHDANCE, 1983
FLAT TWO, 1962
FLEDGLINGS, 1965
FLESH AND BLOOD SHOW, THE, 1974
FLESH AND THE SPUR, 1957
FLESH IS WEAK, THE, 1957
FLESH MERCHANT, THE, 1956
FLICKS, 1987
FLIGHT ANGELS, 1940
FLOOD, THE, 1931
FLOOD, THE, 1963
FLOWER THIEF, THE, 1962
FLYING DEUCES, THE, 1939
FLYING DOCTOR, THE, 1936
FLYING FIFTY-FIVE, 1939
FLYING SERPENT, THE, 1946
FLYING SORCERER, THE, 1974

FLYING SQUAD, THE, 1940
FOOLS, 1970
FOOLS OF DESIRE, 1941
FOOLS RUSH IN, 1949
FOR KEEPS, 1988
FOR LOVE OF YOU, 1933
FOR PETE'S SAKE!, 1966
FOR THE LOVE O'LIL, 1930
FOR YOU I DIE, 1947
FORBIDDEN HEAVEN, 1936
FORBIDDEN JOURNEY, 1950
FORBIDDEN JUNGLE, 1950
FORBIDDEN WORLD, 1982
FORCE: FIVE, 1981
FORCE OF IMPULSE, 1961
FORCED ENTRY, 1975
FORCED LANDING, 1935
FORCED VENGEANCE, 1982
FORCES' SWEETHEART, 1953
FOREST, THE, 1983
FOREVER DARLING, 1956
FOREVER MY HEART, 1954
FORGOTTEN, 1933
FORGOTTEN FACES, 1936
FORGOTTEN GIRLS, 1940
FORGOTTEN WOMEN, 1949
FORT OSAGE, 1952
FORT UTAH, 1967
FORTUNATE FOOL, THE, 1933
FORTUNE AND MEN'S EYES, 1971
FORTUNE TELLER, THE, 1961
FORTY NAUGHTY GIRLS, 1937
FORTY-NINERS, THE, 1932
FOUND ALIVE, 1934
FOUR FOR TEXAS, 1963
FOUR GIRLS IN TOWN, 1956
FOUR RODE OUT, 1969
FOXY BROWN, 1974
FRANKENSTEIN'S BLOODY TERROR, 1968
FRANKENSTEIN, THE VAMPIRE AND CO., 1961
FRANKIE AND JOHNNY, 1936
FRASIER, THE SENSUOUS LION, 1973
FREE AND EASY, 1941
FREE GRASS, 1969
FREE, WHITE AND 21, 1963
FRENCH LEAVE, 1931
FRENCH LIEUTENANT'S WOMAN, THE, 1981
FRIDAY THE 13TH PART VI: JASON LIVES, 1986
FRIDAY THE 13TH PART III, 1982
FRIDAY THE 13TH. . . THE ORPHAN, 1979
FRIENDS, 1971
FRIGHTMARE, 1983
FROM HEADQUARTERS, 1929
FROM NASHVILLE WITH MUSIC, 1969
FROM THE HIP, 1987
FRONTIER FUGITIVES, 1945
FRONTIER GAMBLER, 1956
FRONTIER SCOUT, 1939
FRONTIER TOWN, 1938
FRONTIER VENGEANCE, 1939
FROZEN ALIVE, 1966
FROZEN RIVER, 1929
FRUSTRATIONS, 1967
FUGITIVE FROM A PRISON CAMP, 1940
FULL MOON HIGH, 1982
FULL SPEED AHEAD, 1936
FUNERAL HOME, 1982
FUR COLLAR, THE, 1962
FURY IN PARADISE, 1955
FURY OF THE JUNGLE, 1934
FUZZY SETTLES DOWN, 1944
GABLE AND LOMBARD, 1976
GABLES MYSTERY, THE, 1938
GALAXINA, 1980
GALAXY OF TERROR, 1981
GAME FOR VULTURES, A, 1980
GAME OF CHANCE, A, 1932
GAME OF DEATH, THE, 1979
GAMES MEN PLAY, THE, 1968
GANG BULLETS, 1938
GANG BUSTERS, 1955
GANG THAT COULDN'T SHOOT STRAIGHT, THE, 1971
GANG WAR, 1940
GANGSTER VIP, THE, 1968
GANJA AND HESS, 1973

GAS HOUSE KIDS GO WEST, 1947
GAS HOUSE KIDS IN HOLLYWOOD, 1947
GATE OF FLESH, 1964
GATEWAY TO GLORY, 1970
GATOR BAIT, 1974
GAY ADVENTURE, THE, 1936
GAY ADVENTURE, THE, 1953
GAY DIPLOMAT, THE, 1931
GENDARME OF ST. TROPEZ, THE, 1966
GENTLE TRAP, THE, 1960
GENTLEMAN FROM TEXAS, 1946
GENTLEMAN MISBEHAVES, THE, 1946
GENTLEMAN'S AGREEMENT, 1935
GEORGE AND MILDRED, 1980
GEORGIA, GEORGIA, 1972
GET OFF MY FOOT, 1935
GET THAT GIRL, 1932
GET YOUR MAN, 1934
GET YOURSELF A COLLEGE GIRL, 1964
GETTING EVEN, 1981
GETTING OVER, 1981
GHOST CITY, 1932
GHOST RIDER, THE, 1935
GHOST THAT WALKS ALONE, THE, 1944
GHOULIES II, 1988
GIANT CLAW, THE, 1957
GIGOLETTES OF PARIS, 1933
GIRL FEVER, 1961
GIRL FROM MANDALAY, 1936
GIRL FROM TRIESTE, THE, 1983
GIRL GAME, 1968
GIRL IN GOLD BOOTS, 1968
GIRL IN ROOM 13, 1961
GIRL IN THE FLAT, THE, 1934
GIRL IN THE TAXI, 1937
GIRL IN TROUBLE, 1963
GIRL MISSING, 1933
GIRL OF THE PORT, 1930
GIRL ON A CHAIN GANG, 1966
GIRL ON THE PIER, THE, 1953
GIRL ON THE RUN, 1961
GIRL OVERBOARD, 1937
GIRL SAID NO, THE, 1930
GIRL SMUGGLERS, 1967
GIRL THIEF, THE, 1938
GIRL WHO FORGOT, THE, 1939
GIRL WHO KNEW TOO MUCH, THE, 1969
GIRLS DEMAND EXCITEMENT, 1931
GIRLS OF LATIN QUARTER, 1960
GIRLS ON PROBATION, 1938
GIRLS' SCHOOL, 1950
GIRLS' TOWN, 1959
GIRO CITY, 1982
GIT ALONG, LITTLE DOGIES, 1937
GIVE A DOG A BONE, 1967
GIVE HER A RING, 1936
GLADIATOR OF ROME, 1963
GLASS SPHINX, THE, 1968
GLASS TOMB, THE, 1955
GOBOTS: BATTLE OF THE ROCKLORDS, 1986
GODSEND, THE, 1980
GODZILLA'S REVENGE, 1969
GOING STRAIGHT, 1933
GOKE, BODYSNATCHER FROM HELL, 1968
GOLD EXPRESS, THE, 1955
GOLD RACKET, THE, 1937
GOLD RAIDERS, THE, 1952
GOLDEN CHILD, THE, 1986
GOLDEN LADY, THE, 1979
GOLDEN RABBIT, THE, 1962
GOLDEN RENDEZVOUS, 1977
GOLDIE, 1931
GOLIATH AGAINST THE GIANTS, 1963
GOLIATH AND THE VAMPIRES, 1964
GOOD BEGINNING, THE, 1953
GOOD DAME, 1934
GOODBYE COLUMBUS, 1969
GOODBYE GEMINI, 1970
GOOFBALLS, 1987
GOONIES, THE, 1985
GORDON'S WAR, 1973
GORILLA SHIP, THE, 1932
GOT WHAT SHE WANTED, 1930
GRADUATION DAY, 1981
GRAND FINALE, 1936
GRAND OLD GIRL, 1935

GRANNY GET YOUR GUN, 1940
GRASS EATER, THE, 1961
GRAY LADY DOWN, 1978
GREAT ALLIGATOR, 1980
GREAT BIG THING, A, 1968
GREAT CATHERINE, 1968
GREAT DEFENDER, THE, 1934
GREAT GAME, THE, 1930
GREAT GATSBY, THE, 1974
GREAT MCGONAGALL, THE, 1975
GREAT OUTDOORS, THE, 1988
GREAT SCOUT AND CATHOUSE THURSDAY, THE, 1976
GREAT STUFF, 1933
GREAT WHITE, THE, 1982
GREEK TYCOON, THE, 1978
GREEN BUDDHA, THE, 1954
GREEN COCKATOO, THE, 1947
GREEN SLIME, THE, 1969
GREMLINS, 1984
GRISSOM GANG, THE, 1971
GUESS WHAT HAPPENED TO COUNT DRACULA, 1970
GUEST OF HONOR, 1934
GUESTS ARE COMING, 1965
GUILT, 1930
GUN BATTLE AT MONTEREY, 1957
GUN FEVER, 1958
GUN SMOKE, 1936
GUN STREET, 1962
GUNMAN'S CODE, 1946
GUNPLAY, 1951
GUNS OF A STRANGER, 1973
GUNS OF THE TREES, 1964
GUNSMOKE RANCH, 1937
GURU, THE MAD MONK, 1971
GUTS IN THE SUN, 1959
HALF MOON STREET, 1986
HAMILE, 1965
HANDLE WITH CARE, 1935
HANDS OF STEEL, 1986
HANGAR 18, 1980
HANGUP, 1974
HANKY-PANKY, 1982
HANNIBAL, 1960
HAPPIDROME, 1943
HAPPIEST MILLIONAIRE, THE, 1967
HAPPY AS THE GRASS WAS GREEN, 1973
HAPPY ENDING, THE, 1931
HAPPY FAMILY, THE, 1936
HAPPY HOOKER GOES TO WASHINGTON, THE, 1977
HAPPY HOOKER, THE, 1975
HARD ROAD, THE, 1970
HARD TO HOLD, 1984
HARDBODIES, 1984
HARDBODIES 2, 1986
HARDLY WORKING, 1981
HARLEM ON THE PRAIRIE, 1938
HARLOW, 1965
HARMONY HEAVEN, 1930
HARRAD SUMMER, THE, 1974
HARUM SCARUM, 1965
HARVESTER, THE, 1936
HATCHET FOR A HONEYMOON, 1969
HATS OFF, 1937
HAUNTED, 1976
HAUNTS, 1977
HAWK OF POWDER RIVER, THE, 1948
HAWKS, 1988
HE COULDN'T TAKE IT, 1934
HE KNOWS YOU'RE ALONE, 1980
HEAD, THE, 1961
HEAD ON, 1971
HEADIN' FOR TROUBLE, 1931
HEADLINE CRASHER, 1937
HEALTH, 1980
HEARTBREAK HOTEL, 1988
HEAT OF MIDNIGHT, 1966
HEAVEN IS ROUND THE CORNER, 1944
HEAVENLY BODIES, 1985
HEAVENLY KID, THE, 1985
HEAVEN'S GATE, 1980
HEAVY METAL, 1981
HEIST, THE, 1979
HELD FOR RANSOM, 1938

BOLD: Films on Videocassette

HELEN OF TROY, 1956
HELL BENT FOR 'FRISCO, 1931
HELL BOUND, 1931
HELL CAT, THE, 1934
HELL IN THE HEAVENS, 1934
HELL RAIDERS, 1968
HELL SHIP MUTINY, 1957
HELL WITH HEROES, THE, 1968
HELLHOLE, 1985
HELLO AGAIN, 1987
HELLO ANNAPOLIS, 1942
HELLO GOD, 1951
HELLO MARY LOU, PROM NIGHT II, 1987
HELL'S BLOODY DEVILS, 1970
HELL'S HEADQUARTERS, 1932
HELL'S PLAYGROUND, 1967
HELP I'M INVISIBLE, 1952
HELTER SKELTER, 1949
HENRY ALDRICH, EDITOR, 1942
HENRY AND DIZZY, 1942
HENRY STEPS OUT, 1940
HER FORGOTTEN PAST, 1933
HER HUSBAND'S SECRETARY, 1937
HER MAD NIGHT, 1932
HER REPUTATION, 1931
HER RESALE VALUE, 1933
HERCULES AGAINST THE SONS OF THE SUN, 1964
HERCULES AND THE CAPTIVE WOMEN, 1963
HERCULES IN NEW YORK, 1970
HERCULES, SAMSON & ULYSSES, 1964
HERCULES UNCHAINED, 1960
HERCULES VS-THE GIANT WARRIORS, 1965
HERE COME THE HUGGETTS, 1948
HERE COME THE TIGERS, 1978
HERE'S FLASH CASEY, 1937
HERE'S TO ROMANCE, 1935
HEROSTRATUS, 1968
HE'S MY GIRL, 1987
HEY BABE?, 1984
HI GAUCHO!, 1936
HI-RIDERS, 1978
HI 'YA, CHUM, 1943
HIDDEN FEAR, 1957
HIDDEN POWER, 1939
HIDEAWAY, 1937
HIGH-BALLIN', 1978
HIGH BARBAREE, 1947
HIGH FINANCE, 1933
HIGH GEAR, 1933
HIGH HAT, 1937
HIGH SCHOOL HELLCATS, 1958
HIGH SCHOOL HERO, 1946
HIGH SOCIETY, 1955
HIGH TREASON, 1929
HIGH YELLOW, 1965
HIGHLAND FLING, 1936
HIGHWAY '13, 1948
HIGHWAY TO HELL, 1984
HILLS OF DONEGAL, THE, 1947
HIS CAPTIVE WOMAN, 1929
HIS FIGHTING BLOOD, 1935
HIS GREATEST GAMBLE, 1934
HIS LORDSHIP, 1932
HIS LORDSHIP GOES TO PRESS, 1939
HIS LORDSHIP REGRETS, 1938
HIS ROYAL HIGHNESS, 1932
HIS WIFE'S MOTHER, 1932
HIT AND RUN, 1957
HITCH HIKE TO HEAVEN, 1936
HITCHER, THE, 1986
HITTIN' THE TRAIL, 1937
HOLD THAT WOMAN, 1940
HOLD YOUR MAN, 1929
HOLIDAYS WITH PAY, 1948
HOLLYWOOD HARRY, 1985
HOLLYWOOD ZAP!, 1986
HONEYBABY, HONEYBABY, 1974
HONEYMOON LANE, 1931
HONEYMOON LIMITED, 1936
HONEYMOON OF HORROR, 1964
HONOURABLE MURDER, AN, 1959
HOOK, LINE AND SINKER, 1969
HOOPER, 1978
HORROR OF FRANKENSTEIN, THE, 1970
HORROR OF PARTY BEACH, THE, 1964

HORROR OF THE ZOMBIES, 1974
HOSTAGE, THE, 1956
HOT CHILD IN THE CITY, 1987
HOT DOG. . .THE MOVIE, 1984
HOT MONTH OF AUGUST, THE, 1969
HOT MOVES, 1984
HOT ROD HULLABALOO, 1966
HOT SHOT, 1987
HOT SHOTS, 1956
HOT STEEL, 1940
HOT STUFF, 1979
HOT SUMMER WEEK, 1973
HOT TO TROT, 1988
HOTEL COLONIAL, 1987
HOTHEAD, 1963
H.O.T.S., 1979
HOUND OF THE BASKERVILLES, THE, 1980
HOURS OF LONELINESS, 1930
HOUSE, 1986
HOUSE II: THE SECOND STORY, 1987
HOUSE OF DANGER, 1934
HOUSE OF GREED, 1934
HOUSE OF HORROR, 1929
HOUSE OF 1,000 DOLLS, 1967
HOUSE OF SECRETS, 1929
HOUSE OF THE DAMNED, 1963
HOUSE OF THE LIVING DEAD, 1973
HOUSE ON SKULL MOUNTAIN, THE, 1974
HOUSE THAT VANISHED, THE, 1974
HOUSE WHERE DEATH LIVES, THE, 1984
HOUSEHOLDER, THE, 1963
HOUSEKEEPER, THE, 1987
HOW COME NOBODY'S ON OUR SIDE?, 1975
HOW TO BEAT THE HIGH COST OF LIVING, 1980
HOW TO SEDUCE A PLAYBOY, 1968
HUMAN DUPLICATORS, THE, 1965
HUMAN FACTOR, THE, 1975
HUMAN HIGHWAY, 1982
HUMANITY, 1933
HUMONGOUS, 1982
HUMPHREY TAKES A CHANCE, 1950
HUNGRY WIVES, 1973
HUNS, THE, 1962
HUNTER, THE, 1980
HUNTING PARTY, THE, 1977
HURRICANE, 1929
HURRY SUNDOWN, 1967
HYPNOSIS, 1966
I ACCUSE MY PARENTS, 1945
I AM A GROUPIE, 1970
I AM THE CHEESE, 1983
I BELIEVED IN YOU, 1934
I CONQUER THE SEA, 1936
I DREAM OF JEANIE, 1952
I DRINK YOUR BLOOD, 1971
I HAVE LIVED, 1933
I LOVE N.Y., 1987
I MARRIED A WOMAN, 1958
I SAILED TO TAHITI WITH AN ALL GIRL CREW, 1969
I SPIT ON YOUR GRAVE, 1962
I TAKE THIS OATH, 1940
I WAS A PRISONER ON DEVIL'S ISLAND, 1941
IDAHO KID, THE, 1937
IDAHO TRANSFER, 1975
IDEAL LODGER, THE, 1957
IDENTITY UNKNOWN, 1960
IF HE HOLLERS, LET HIM GO, 1968
IF I WERE BOSS, 1938
I'LL FIX IT, 1934
I'LL GIVE MY LIFE, 1959
I'LL TELL THE WORLD, 1934
I'LL WAIT FOR YOU, 1941
I'M FROM ARKANSAS, 1944
IMAGEMAKER, THE, 1986
IMAGES, 1972
IMPOSTORS, 1979
"'IMP"PROBABLE MR. WEE GEE, THE, 1966
IN COLD BLOOD, 1967
IN PRAISE OF OLDER WOMEN, 1978
IN SEARCH OF HISTORIC JESUS, 1980
IN THE MONEY, 1934
IN THE WAKE OF THE BOUNTY, 1933
INCIDENT IN SHANGHAI, 1937
INCREDIBLE TWO-HEADED TRANSPLANT, THE, 1971

INCUBUS, THE, 1982
INDESTRUCTIBLE MAN, THE, 1956
INGAGI, 1931
INHERITANCE IN PRETORIA, 1936
INNER SANCTUM, 1948
INVASION OF THE BLOOD FARMERS, 1972
INVASION OF THE STAR CREATURES, 1962
INVASION OF THE VAMPIRES, THE, 1961
INVISIBLE GHOST, THE, 1941
IRON EAGLE II, 1988
IRON STAIR, THE, 1933
IS EVERYBODY HAPPY?, 1929
ISADORA, 1968
ISLAND OF ALLAH, 1956
ISLAND OF DR. MOREAU, THE, 1977
ISLAND WOMEN, 1958
IT!, 1967
IT COULDN'T HAPPEN HERE, 1988
IT COULDN'T HAVE HAPPENED—BUT IT DID, 1936
IT FELL FROM THE SKY, 1980
IT HAPPENED IN ATHENS, 1962
IT HAPPENED IN SOHO, 1948
IT HAPPENED ONE SUNDAY, 1944
IT'S A COP, 1934
IT'S A GRAND LIFE, 1953
IT'S A GREAT DAY, 1956
IT'S A GREAT LIFE, 1930
IT'S A GREAT LIFE, 1936
IT'S A KING, 1933
IT'S A 2'6" ABOVE THE GROUND WORLD, 1972
IT'S IN THE AIR, 1940
IT'S IN THE BAG, 1936
I'VE BEEN AROUND, 1935
JACK AND THE BEANSTALK, 1970
JAIL BAIT, 1954
JAILBREAK, 1936
JANE EYRE, 1935
JAWS OF SATAN, 1980
JAWS: THE REVENGE, 1987
JAZZ SINGER, THE, 1980
JE T'AIME, 1974
JEALOUSY, 1929
JENNY, 1969
JESSE JAMES, JR., 1942
JESSE JAMES' WOMEN, 1954
JESSIE'S GIRLS, 1976
JESUS TRIP, THE, 1971
JEWEL, THE, 1933
JIMMY BOY, 1935
JIMMY THE KID, 1982
JINXED!, 1982
JOAN AT THE STAKE, 1954
JOHN HALIFAX—GENTLEMAN, 1938
JOHNNY COOL, 1963
JOHNNY ON THE SPOT, 1954
JOKE OF DESTINY LYING IN WAIT AROUND THE CORNER LIKE A STREET BANDIT, A, 1984
JONATHAN LIVINGSTON SEAGULL, 1973
JORY, 1972
JOSHUA, 1976
JOSSER ON THE RIVER, 1932
JOURNEY, 1977
JOURNEY TO THE LOST CITY, 1960
JOYSTICKS, 1983
JUBILEE WINDOW, 1935
JUD, 1971
JUDITH, 1965
JULIE DARLING, 1982
JUNCTION CITY, 1952
JUNE MOON, 1931
JUNGLE BRIDE, 1933
JUNGLE HEAT, 1957
JUNGLE MAN, 1941
JUNGLE OF CHANG, 1951
JUNGLE RAIDERS, 1986
JUNGLE WOMAN, 1944
JUNKMAN, THE, 1982
JUST A BIG, SIMPLE GIRL, 1949
JUST A GIGOLO, 1931
JUST FOR FUN, 1963
JUST JOE, 1960
JUST LIKE HEAVEN, 1930
JUST THE WAY YOU ARE, 1984
JUST WILLIAM'S LUCK, 1948
JUST YOU AND ME, KID, 1979
JUSTICE TAKES A HOLIDAY, 1933

KANDYLAND, 1988
KANSAS, 1988
KANSAS CITY BOMBER, 1972
KAREN, THE, LOVEMAKER, 1970
KAZAN, 1949
KEEP MY GRAVE OPEN, 1980
KEEPER, THE, 1976
KEEPER OF THE BEES, 1947
KENTUCKY MINSTRELS, 1934
KEY EXCHANGE, 1985
KEY TO HARMONY, 1935
KEY WITNESS, 1947
KID DYNAMITE, 1943
KID FROM ARIZONA, THE, 1931
KID FROM BROKEN GUN, THE, 1952
KID RODELO, 1966
KID VENGEANCE, 1977
KIKI, 1931
KILLER DILL, 1947
KILLER WALKS, A, 1952
KILLERS FROM SPACE, 1954
KILLERS THREE, 1968
KILLING HOUR, THE, 1982
KIND LADY, 1935
KING BLANK, 1983
KING DINOSAUR, 1955
KING KELLY OF THE U.S.A, 1934
KING KONG LIVES, 1986
KING OF HOCKEY, 1936
KING OF THE CORAL SEA, 1956
KING OF THE STREETS, 1986
KING OF THE WILD HORSES, THE, 1934
KING OF THE ZOMBIES, 1941
KING SOLOMON'S TREASURE, 1978
KISS ME, SERGEANT, 1930
KISS OF THE TARANTULA, 1975
KISS THE GIRLS AND MAKE THEM DIE, 1967
KISS THE OTHER SHEIK, 1968
KISSING BANDIT, THE, 1948
KITTY, 1929
KLANSMAN, THE, 1974
KNIGHTS OF THE CITY, 1985
KOLBERG, 1945
LAD, THE, 1935
LADIES MUST LOVE, 1933
LADIES MUST PLAY, 1930
LADY BE CAREFUL, 1936
LADY CAROLINE LAMB, 1972
LADY CRAVED EXCITEMENT, THE, 1950
LADY DRACULA, THE, 1974
LADY GANGSTER, 1942
LADY IN SCARLET, THE, 1935
LADY IN THE DEATH HOUSE, 1944
LADY L, 1965
LADY LIBERTY, 1972
LADY OF MONZA, THE, 1970
LADY OF VENGEANCE, 1957
LADY POSSESSED, 1952
LADY REFUSES, THE, 1931
LADY SURRENDERS, A, 1930
LADY WHO DARED, THE, 1931
LADY'S PROFESSION, A, 1933
LAKE, THE, 1970
LANDRUSH, 1946
LARGE ROPE, THE, 1953
LAS RATAS NO DUERMEN DE NOCHE, 1974
LAS VEGAS HILLBILLYS, 1966
LAS VEGAS STORY, THE, 1952
LAST AFFAIR, THE, 1976
LAST AMERICAN VIRGIN, THE, 1982
LAST GUNFIGHTER, THE, 1961
LAST HUNTER, THE, 1984
LAST MOMENT, THE, 1954
LAST MOVIE, THE, 1971
LAST OF SHEILA, THE, 1973
LAST OF THE CLINTONS, THE, 1935
LAST OF THE SECRET AGENTS?, THE, 1966
LAST OF THE WARRENS, THE, 1936
LAST REBEL, THE, 1971
LAST RIDE, THE, 1944
LAST RITES, 1988
LAST SHOT YOU HEAR, THE, 1969
LATE AT NIGHT, 1946
LAUGH IT OFF, 1939
LAUGH YOUR BLUES AWAY, 1943
LAUGHING BOY, 1934

LAUGHTER IN HELL, 1933
LAW COMMANDS, THE, 1938
LAW IN HER HANDS, THE, 1936
LAW MEN, 1944
LAW OF THE NORTH, 1932
LAW OF THE RANGE, 1941
LAW OF THE RANGER, 1937
LAW OF THE RIO GRANDE, 1931
LAW OF THE SADDLE, 1944
LAW OF THE TEXAN, 1938
LAWLESS COWBOYS, 1952
LAWLESS EMPIRE, 1946
LAWLESS RIDERS, 1936
LAZARILLO, 1963
LEAGUE OF FRIGHTENED MEN, 1937
LEAVE IT TO BLANCHE, 1934
LEAVE IT TO THE MARINES, 1951
LEAVENWORTH CASE, THE, 1936
LEFTOVER LADIES, 1931
LEGACY OF BLOOD, 1973
LEGEND OF BILLIE JEAN, THE, 1985
LEGEND OF BLOOD MOUNTAIN, THE, 1965
LEGEND OF FRENCHIE KING, THE, 1971
LEGEND OF SPIDER FOREST, THE, 1976
LEGEND OF SURAM FORTRESS, 1985
LEGEND OF THE LOST, 1957
LEGION OF MISSING MEN, 1937
LEGION OF THE DOOMED, 1958
LEONOR, 1977
LES GAULOISES BLEUES, 1969
LET THE BALLOON GO, 1977
L'ETOILE DU NORD, 1983
LET'S GO, YOUNG GUY!, 1967
LETTER, THE, 1929
LIAR'S MOON, 1982
LICENSE TO DRIVE, 1988
LIES, 1984
LT. ROBIN CRUSOE, U.S.N., 1966
LIFE AND TIMES OF JUDGE ROY BEAN, THE, 1972
LIFE IN DANGER, 1964
LIFE LOVE DEATH, 1969
LIFE OF THE PARTY, 1934
LIGHT TOUCH, THE, 1955
LIGHTNING BILL CARSON, 1936
LIGHTNING BOLT, 1967
LIGHTNING STRIKES TWICE, 1935
LIKELY LADS, THE, 1976
LILAC DOMINO, THE, 1940
LILLY TURNER, 1933
LILY CHRISTINE, 1932
LIMEHOUSE BLUES, 1934
LINCOLN CONSPIRACY, THE, 1977
LINE, THE, 1982
LION AND THE LAMB, 1931
LION AND THE MOUSE, THE, 1928
LITTLE BOY BLUE, 1963
LITTLE MEN, 1940
LITTLE MISS ROUGHNECK, 1938
LITTLE MISS SOMEBODY, 1937
LITTLE ORPHAN ANNIE, 1938
LITTLE SEX, A, 1982
LITTLE STRANGER, 1934
LITTLE TOKYO, U.S.A., 1942
LIVE AGAIN, 1936
LIVING DEAD, THE, 1936
LIVING GHOST, THE, 1942
LOLA, 1971
LONDON MELODY, 1930
LONE STAR LAW MEN, 1942
LONE STAR RAIDERS, 1940
LONG DAY'S DYING, THE, 1968
LONG GOODBYE, THE, 1973
LONNIE, 1963
LOOPHOLE, 1981
LORD OF THE JUNGLE, 1955
LOS AUTOMATAS DE LA MUERTE, 1960
LOS INVISIBLES, 1961
LOSER, THE HERO, THE, 1985
LOSIN' IT, 1983
LOST EMPIRE, THE, 1985
LOST IN THE STRATOSPHERE, 1935
LOST RANCH, 1937
LOTUS LADY, 1930
LOUISIANA HAYRIDE, 1944
LOUISIANA HUSSY, 1960
LOVE AND THE MIDNIGHT AUTO SUPPLY, 1978

LOVE BOUND, 1932
LOVE HUNGER, 1965
LOVE IN A BUNGALOW, 1937
LOVE IN A FOUR LETTER WORLD, 1970
LOVE IN MOROCCO, 1933
LOVE IN WAITING, 1948
LOVE IS A CAROUSEL, 1970
LOVE IS LIKE THAT, 1933
LOVE, LIVE AND LAUGH, 1929
LOVE MATES, 1967
LOVE ME DEADLY, 1972
LOVE MERCHANT, THE, 1966
LOVE ON THE GROUND, 1984,Fr.
LOVE ROBOTS, THE, 1965
LOVE SLAVES OF THE AMAZONS, 1957
LOVE SPECIALIST, THE, 1959
LOVE TAKES FLIGHT, 1937
LOVE TIME, 1934
LOVE TRADER, 1930
LOVES OF HERCULES, THE, 1960
LOVES OF SALAMMBO, THE, 1962
LOW BLOW, 1986
LUCKY NIGHT, 1939
LUCKY SWEEP, A, 1932
LUCKY TERROR, 1936
LUCKY TO BE A WOMAN, 1955
LUM AND ABNER ABROAD, 1956
LURE OF THE ISLANDS, 1942
LUV, 1967
MACHETE, 1958
MACHO CALLAHAN, 1970
MACUMBA LOVE, 1960
MAD DOCTOR OF BLOOD ISLAND, THE, 1969
MAD DOCTOR OF MARKET STREET, THE, 1942
MAD MONSTER, THE, 1942
MAD YOUTH, 1940
MADDEST CAR IN THE WORLD, THE, 1974
MADIGAN'S MILLIONS, 1970
MADRON, 1970
MADWOMAN OF CHAILLOT, THE, 1969
MAFIA GIRLS, THE, 1969
MAGIC GARDEN OF STANLEY SWEETHART, THE, 1970
MAGIC OF LASSIE, THE, 1978
MAGUS, THE, 1968
MAIN CHANCE, THE, 1966
MAIN STREET LAWYER, 1939
MAKE IT THREE, 1938
MAKE-UP, 1937
MAKING LOVE, 1982
MAKING MR. RIGHT, 1987
MAKING THE HEADLINES, 1938
MAKO: THE JAWS OF DEATH, 1976
MALAGA, 1962
MALIBU BEACH, 1978
MALIBU BIKINI SHOP, THE, 1987
MAMA RUNS WILD, 1938
MAMBA, 1930
MAMMA DRACULA, 1980
MAN ACCUSED, 1959
MAN AND THE MONSTER, THE, 1965
MAN BETRAYED, A, 1937
MAN CALLED BACK, THE, 1932
MAN CALLED DAGGER, A, 1967
MAN FROM GALVESTON, THE, 1964
MAN FROM HELL, THE, 1934
MAN FROM HELL'S EDGES, 1932
MAN FROM TEXAS, THE, 1948
MAN FROM THE FIRST CENTURY, THE, 1961
MAN FROM UTAH, THE, 1934
MAN FROM WYOMING, A, 1930
MAN HUNTER, THE, 1930
MAN I WANT, THE, 1934
MAN IN BLACK, THE, 1950
MAN IN THE DARK, 1963
MAN IN THE TRUNK, THE, 1942
MAN IS ARMED, THE, 1956
MAN OF AFFAIRS, 1937
MAN OF COURAGE, 1943
MAN OF IRON, 1935
MAN OF TWO WORLDS, 1934
MAN ON THE PROWL, 1957
MAN OUTSIDE, 1988
MAN THEY COULDN'T ARREST, THE, 1933
MAN WHO CAME BACK, THE, 1931
MAN WHO CHANGED HIS NAME, THE, 1934

BOLD: Films on Videocassette

MAN WHO KILLED BILLY THE KID, THE, 1967
MAN WHO LAUGHS, THE, 1966
MAN WHO WALKED ALONE, THE, 1945
MAN WHO WON, THE, 1933
MAN WITHOUT A BODY, THE, 1957
MAN WITHOUT A FACE, THE, 1935
MANCHURIAN AVENGER, 1985
MANHATTAN MERRY-GO-ROUND, 1937
MANHATTAN SHAKEDOWN, 1939
MANHUNT, THE, 1986
MANIAC, 1980
MANNEQUIN, 1933
MANNEQUIN, 1987
MANY A SLIP, 1931
MARCO POLO JUNIOR, 1973
MARILYN, 1953
MARINES COME THROUGH, THE, 1943
MARK OF THE DEVIL, 1970
MARK OF THE DEVIL II, 1975
MARKED MEN, 1940
MARRIAGE ON APPROVAL, 1934
MARRYING WIDOWS, 1934
MARTIAN IN PARIS, A, 1961
MARTIN'S DAY, 1985
MARY, MARY, BLOODY MARY, 1975
MARYJANE, 1968
MASSACRE, 1956
MASSACRE CANYON, 1954
MASSIVE RETALIATION, 1984
MASTER MINDS, 1949
MASTER OF MEN, 1933
MASTER TOUCH, THE, 1974
MASTERBLASTER, 1987
MATRIMONIAL BED, THE, 1930
MATTER OF MURDER, A, 1949
MATTER OF TIME, A, 1976
MAXWELL ARCHER, DETECTIVE, 1942
MAYBE IT'S LOVE, 1935
MAYFAIR GIRL, 1933
MAYOR OF 44TH STREET, THE, 1942
MC CABE AND MRS. MILLER, 1971
MC FADDEN'S FLATS, 1935
MC GUFFIN, THE, 1985
MEANEST GAL IN TOWN, THE, 1934
MEATBALLS PART II, 1984
MEDICINE MAN, THE, 1930
MEDICINE MAN, THE, 1933
MEDUSA TOUCH, THE, 1978
MEET MISS BOBBY SOCKS, 1944
MEET THE BOY FRIEND, 1937
MEET THE MAYOR, 1938
MEET THE WILDCAT, 1940
MELODY CLUB, 1949
MELODY IN THE DARK, 1948
MELODY LANE, 1941
MELODY OF LOVE, 1954
MELODY OF THE PLAINS, 1937
MEMBER OF THE JURY, 1937
MEMENTO MEI, 1963
MEMOIRS, 1984
MEN ARE NOT GODS, 1937
MEN ARE SUCH FOOLS, 1933
MEN CALL IT LOVE, 1931
MEN MUST FIGHT, 1933
MEN OF AMERICA, 1933
MEN OF SAN QUENTIN, 1942
MEN OF THE HOUR, 1935
MEN ON CALL, 1931
MEN WITHOUT HONOUR, 1939
MERCENARY FIGHTERS, 1988
MERCHANT OF SLAVES, 1949
MERELY MR. HAWKINS, 1938
MERMAIDS OF TIBURON, THE, 1962
MERRY WIVES OF TOBIAS ROUKE, THE, 1972
MESQUITE BUCKAROO, 1939
METEOR, 1979
MEXICAN MANHUNT, 1953
MEXICAN SPITFIRE SEES A GHOST, 1942
MICHELLE, 1970
MICKEY, 1948
MIDNIGHT AT THE WAX MUSEUM, 1936
MIDNIGHT DADDIES, 1929
MIDNIGHT LADY, 1932
MIDNIGHT MADNESS, 1980
MIDNIGHT MORALS, 1932
MIDNIGHT SPECIAL, 1931

MIDWIFE, THE, 1961
MIGHTY CRUSADERS, THE, 1961
MIGHTY JUNGLE, THE, 1965
MILE A MINUTE LOVE, 1937
MILITARY ACADEMY WITH THAT TENTH AVENUE
   GANG, 1950
MILLION DOLLAR MANHUNT, 1962
MILLION DOLLAR MYSTERY, 1987
MILLION EYES OF SU-MURU, THE, 1967
MILLION TO ONE, A, 1938
MINI-AFFAIR, THE, 1968
MINOTAUR, THE, 1961
MINSTREL BOY, THE, 1937
MIRACLE KID, 1942
MIRACLE OF SANTA'S WHITE REINDEER, THE, 1963
MIRACLES DO HAPPEN, 1938
MIRRORS, 1984
MISCHIEF, 1969
MISS ROBIN HOOD, 1952
MISS TULIP STAYS THE NIGHT, 1955
MISSILE TO THE MOON, 1959
MISSING, BELIEVED MARRIED, 1937
MISSING DAUGHTERS, 1939
MISSING GUEST, THE, 1938
MISSING NOTE, THE, 1961
MISSION GALACTICA: THE CYLON ATTACK, 1979
MISSION MARS, 1968
MISSION STARDUST, 1968
MISSISSIPPI SUMMER, 1971
MR. H.C. ANDERSEN, 1950
MR. ROBINSON CRUSOE, 1932
MR. SYCAMORE, 1975
MISTRESS OF THE APES, 1981
MIXED DOUBLES, 1933
MOBS INC, 1956
MODELS, INC., 1952
MODERN GIRLS, 1986
MOLE PEOPLE, THE, 1956
MOM AND DAD, 1948
MOMENT OF INDISCRETION, 1958
MONDAY'S CHILD, 1967
MONEY AND THE WOMAN, 1940
MONEY MAD, 1934
MONEY MADNESS, 1948
MONEY MEANS NOTHING, 1932
MONKEY'S PAW, THE, 1948
MONSTER ISLAND, 1981
MONSTER MAKER, THE, 1944
MONSTER OF LONDON CITY, THE, 1967
MONSTER WANGMAGWI, 1967
MONTANA BELLE, 1952
MONTANA TERRITORY, 1952
MONTE CARLO BABY, 1953
MONTE CARLO NIGHTS, 1934
MOON IN SCORPIO, 1987
MOON ZERO TWO, 1970
MOONLIGHT IN HAWAII, 1941
MOONLIGHTER, THE, 1953
MORE DEADLY THAN THE MALE, 1961
MORO WITCH DOCTOR, 1964
MOST IMMORAL LADY, A, 1929
MOTH, THE, 1934
MOTHER AND SON, 1931
MOTHER GOOSE A GO-GO, 1966
MOTHER LODE, 1982
MOTHER'S BOY, 1929
MOTIVE FOR REVENGE, 1935
MOTOR PATROL, 1950
MOUNTAIN, THE, 1935
MOUNTAIN MEN, THE, 1980
MOUNTAIN RHYTHM, 1939
MOUNTED STRANGER, THE, 1930
MOUSE AND HIS CHILD, THE, 1977
MOVERS AND SHAKERS, 1985
MOVIE HOUSE MASSACRE, 1986
MOVIE STAR, AMERICAN STYLE, OR, LSD I HATE
   YOU!, 1966
MOVIE STUNTMEN, 1953
MOVING, 1988
MRS. DANE'S DEFENCE, 1933
MRS. POLLIFAX-SPY, 1971
MUMMY'S SHROUD, THE, 1967
MURDER A LA MOD, 1968
MURDER AT DAWN, 1932
MURDER AT MONTE CARLO, 1935
MURDER AT SITE THREE, 1959

MURDER AT THE CABARET, 1936
MURDER AT THE INN, 1934
MURDER AT 3 A.M., 1953
MURDER BY ROPE, 1936
MURDER BY TELEVISION, 1935
MURDER IN GREENWICH VILLAGE, 1937
MURDER IN THE OLD RED BARN, 1936
MURDER ON APPROVAL, 1956
MURDER ON THE SECOND FLOOR, 1932
MURDER ON THE SET, 1936
MURDER WILL OUT, 1930
MURDER WILL OUT, 1939
MURDER WITHOUT CRIME, 1951
MURDER WITHOUT TEARS, 1953
MUSEUM MYSTERY, 1937
MUSIC FOR MADAME, 1937
MUSIC IN MY HEART, 1940
MUSIC MACHINE, THE, 1979
MUSIC MAKER, THE, 1936
MUTATIONS, THE, 1974
MUTILATOR, THE, 1985
MUTINEERS, THE, 1949
MUTINY OF THE ELSINORE, THE, 1939
MY AIN FOLK, 1944
MY BEST GAL, 1944
MY BODY HUNGERS, 1967
MY BOYS ARE GOOD BOYS, 1978
MY BROTHER HAS BAD DREAMS, 1977
MY BROTHER, THE OUTLAW, 1951
MY DINNER WITH ANDRE, 1981
MY FATHER'S HOUSE, 1947
MY FAVORITE SPY, 1942
MY HANDS ARE CLAY, 1948
MY HEART BELONGS TO DADDY, 1942
MY LOVER, MY SON, 1970
MY SIN, 1931
MY SISTER AND I, 1948
MY STEPMOTHER IS AN ALIEN, 1988
MY WIFE'S RELATIVES, 1939
MYSTERIOUS ISLAND, 1929
MYSTERIOUS ISLAND OF CAPTAIN NEMO, THE,
   1973
MYSTERIOUS MR. DAVIS, THE, 1936
MYSTERY HOUSE, 1938
MYSTERY JUNCTION, 1951
MYSTERY OF THE BLACK JUNGLE, 1955
MYSTERY OF THE GOLDEN EYE, THE, 1948
MYSTERY OF THE 13TH GUEST, THE, 1943
MYSTERY TRAIN, 1931
MYSTIC CIRCLE MURDER, 1939
NAIL GUN MASSACRE, 1987
NAKED AND THE DEAD, THE, 1958
NAKED ANGELS, 1969
NAKED APE, THE, 1973
NAKED GUN, THE, 1956
NAKED MAJA, THE, 1959
NAKED RUNNER, THE, 1967
NAKED VENGEANCE, 1986
NAKED WOMAN, THE, 1950
NAME FOR EVIL, A, 1970
NAME THE WOMAN, 1934
NATHALIE GRANGER, 1972
NAUGHTY FLIRT, THE, 1931
NAVY BLUES, 1937
NAVY BORN, 1936
NAVY WAY, THE, 1944
NEBRASKAN, THE, 1953
NECK AND NECK, 1931
NECROMANCY, 1972
NEITHER THE SEA NOR THE SAND, 1974
NEON MANIACS, 1986
NEST OF THE CUCKOO BIRDS, THE, 1965
NEUTRON CONTRA EL DR. CARONTE, 1962
NEUTRON EL ENMASCARADO NEGRO, 1962
NEW HORIZONS, 1939
NEW YORK NIGHTS, 1984
NEXT!, 1971
NEXT OF KIN, 1983
NEXT ONE, THE, 1982
NICE WOMAN, 1932
NIGHT BEAT, 1948
NIGHT BIRDS, 1931
NIGHT CARGO, 1936
NIGHT CHILD, 1975
NIGHT COMERS, THE, 1971
NIGHT CREATURE, 1979

NIGHT FLOWERS, 1979
NIGHT GOD SCREAMED, THE, 1975
NIGHT HAIR CHILD, 1971
NIGHT IN HEAVEN, A, 1983
NIGHT LIFE IN RENO, 1931
NIGHT OF DARK SHADOWS, 1971
NIGHT OF EVIL, 1962
NIGHT OF JANUARY 16TH, 1941
NIGHT OF MYSTERY, 1937
NIGHT OF TERROR, 1933
NIGHT OF THE COBRA WOMAN, 1974
NIGHT OF THE FOLLOWING DAY, THE, 1969
NIGHT OF THE FULL MOON, THE, 1954
NIGHT OF THE JUGGLER, 1980
NIGHT OF THE LEPUS, 1972
NIGHT OF THE PARTY, THE, 1934
NIGHT OF THE QUARTER MOON, 1959
NIGHT OF THE STRANGLER, 1975
NIGHT SCHOOL, 1981
NIGHT STALKER, THE, 1987
NIGHT TRAIN TO MUNDO FINE, 1966
NIGHT WIND, 1948
NIGHTFORCE, 1987
NIGHTMARE HONEYMOON, 1973
NIGHTWING, 1979
99 WOUNDS, 1931
92 IN THE SHADE, 1975
NO DEFENSE, 1929
NO FUNNY BUSINESS, 1934
NO LADY, 1931
NO MORE WOMEN, 1934
NO ONE MAN, 1932
NO PLACE TO HIDE, 1975
NO PLACE TO LAND, 1958
NO RETREAT, NO SURRENDER, 1986
NO ROOM FOR THE GROOM, 1952
NO SAFETY AHEAD, 1959
NO SURVIVORS, PLEASE, 1963
NO MERCY MAN, THE, 1975
NORMAN CONQUEST, 1953
NORTH SEA PATROL, 1939
NORTHERN PATROL, 1953
NORTHWEST TRAIL, 1945
NOT A HOPE IN HELL, 1960
NOT OF THIS EARTH, 1988
NOT SO DUMB, 1930
NOTHING PERSONAL, 1980
NOTORIOUS BUT NICE, 1934
NUMBER ONE WITH A BULLET, 1987
NUREMBERG, 1961
O, MY DARLING CLEMENTINE, 1943
OASIS, THE, 1984
OBLONG BOX, THE, 1969
OBSESSED, 1988
O.C. AND STIGGS, 1987
OF LOVE AND DESIRE, 1963
OFFICE GIRL, THE, 1932
OFFICER 13, 1933
OKEFENOKEE, 1960
OKLAHOMA WOMAN, THE, 1956
OLD CORRAL, THE, 1937
OLD MOTHER RILEY, HEADMISTRESS, 1950
OLD OVERLAND TRAIL, 1953
OLD SWIMMIN' HOLE, THE, 1941
OLDEST PROFESSION, THE, 1968
OLIVER'S STORY, 1978
OMOO OMOO, THE SHARK GOD, 1949
ON THE BUSES, 1972
ON THE GREAT WHITE TRAIL, 1938
ON VELVET, 1938
ONCE, 1974
ONCE A THIEF, 1950
ONCE BITTEN, 1985
ONCE IN A BLUE MOON, 1936
ONCE IS NOT ENOUGH, 1975
ONCE YOU KISS A STRANGER, 1969
ONE BRIEF SUMMER, 1971
125 ROOMS OF COMFORT, 1974
ONE IN A MILLION, 1935
ONE JUST MAN, 1955
ONE LAST FLING, 1949
ONE MAD KISS, 1930
ONE MAN JURY, 1978
$1,000,000 RACKET, 1937
ONE MORE SATURDAY NIGHT, 1986
ONE SUMMER LOVE, 1976

ONE TOO MANY, 1950
ONE WAY TICKET TO HELL, 1955
ONE WAY WAHINI, 1965
ONE WILD NIGHT, 1938
ONLY GOD KNOWS, 1974
ONLY ONCE IN A LIFETIME, 1979
OPEN HOUSE, 1987
OPEN SEASON, 1974
OPERATION BOTTLENECK, 1961
OPERATION CONSPIRACY, 1957
OPERATION CUPID, 1960
OPERATION LOVEBIRDS, 1968
OPERATION MURDER, 1957
OPERATION ST. PETER'S, 1968
ORCA, 1977
ORLAK, THE HELL OF FRANKENSTEIN, 1960
ORPHANS OF THE NORTH, 1940
OSCAR, THE, 1966
OTHER SIDE OF BONNIE AND CLYDE, THE, 1968
OTHER SIDE OF MIDNIGHT, THE, 1977
OTHER SIDE OF THE UNDERNEATH, THE, 1972
OTHER WOMAN, THE, 1931
OUR MISS FRED, 1972
OUT OF THE FOG, 1962
OUTLAW, THE, 1943
OUTLAW MOTORCYCLES, 1967
OUTLAW OF THE PLAINS, 1946
OUTLAW TREASURE, 1955
OUTSIDE THE LAW, 1930
OVER THE GARDEN WALL, 1950
OVER THE TOP, 1987
OVER-UNDER, SIDEWAYS-DOWN, 1977
OXFORD BLUES, 1984
PACIFIC ADVENTURE, 1947
PAD...AND HOW TO USE IT, THE, 1966
PAGAN LADY, 1931
PAID TO DANCE, 1937
PAINTED WOMAN, 1932
PANAMA FLO, 1932
PAPER TIGER, 1975
PARADISE ISLAND, 1930
PARADISE MOTEL, 1985
PARADISIO, 1962
PARDON MY GUN, 1930
PARENTS ON TRIAL, 1939
PARIS IN SPRING, 1935
PARNELL, 1937
PAROLE, INC., 1949
PAROLE RACKET, 1937
PAROLED FROM THE BIG HOUSE, 1938
PART-TIME WIFE, 1961
PARTNERS, 1982
PARTNERS IN CRIME, 1937
PARTNERS OF THE SUNSET, 1948
PARTY CAMP, 1987
PARTY HUSBAND, 1931
PARTY'S OVER, THE, 1966
PASSENGER TO LONDON, 1937
PASSION HOLIDAY, 1963
PASSION IN THE SUN, 1964
PASSION STREET, U.S.A., 1964
PASSIONATE STRANGERS, THE, 1968
PASSOVER PLOT, THE, 1976
PAST OF MARY HOLMES, THE, 1933
PASTEUR, 1936
PATRIOT, THE, 1986
PAY BOX ADVENTURE, 1936
PAY OFF, THE, 1930
PAYMENT IN BLOOD, 1968
PEACE FOR A GUNFIGHTER, 1967
PEACE KILLERS, THE, 1971
PEEK-A-BOO, 1961
PEEPER, 1975
PENAL CODE, THE, 1933
PENTHOUSE RHYTHM, 1945
PEOPLE NEXT DOOR, THE, 1970
PEOPLE THAT TIME FORGOT, THE, 1977
PEOPLE WHO OWN THE DARK, 1975
PERCY, 1971
PHANTOM FROM 10,000 LEAGUES, THE, 1956
PHANTOM OF THE DESERT, 1930
PHANTOM PATROL, 1936
PHANTOM SUBMARINE, THE, 1941
PHAROAH'S WOMAN, THE, 1961
PICKUP, 1951
PICTURE BRIDES, 1934

PIECES, 1983
PIONEER MARSHAL, 1950
P.J., 1968
PLAGUE, 1978
PLAY DEAD, 1981
PLAY GIRL, 1932
PLAY IT AS IT LAYS, 1972
PLAYGIRLS AND THE VAMPIRE, 1964
PLEASE STAND BY, 1972
POINT OF TERROR, 1971
POLICE ACADEMY, 1984
**POLICE ACADEMY 5: ASSIGNMENT MIAMI BEACH,
   1988**
POLICE ACADEMY 4: CITIZENS ON PATROL, 1987
POLICE CALL, 1933
POLICEWOMAN, 1974
POLO JOE, 1936
PONY POST, 1940
POPE JOAN, 1972
PORKY'S, 1982
PORKY'S REVENGE, 1985
PORT OF HATE, 1939
PORT OF MISSING GIRLS, 1938
PORT SINISTER, 1953
PORTNOY'S COMPLAINT, 1972
POSSESSION, 1981
POSSESSION OF JOEL DELANEY, THE, 1972
POWER, THE, 1984
POWER OF THE PRESS, 1943
POWERFORCE, 1983
PRAIRIE PALS, 1942
PRAIRIE STRANGER, 1941
PRECIOUS JEWELS, 1969
PREHISTORIC WOMEN, 1950
PREHISTORIC WOMEN, 1967
PRETTYKILL, 1987
PREY, THE, 1984
PRICE OF FLESH, THE, 1962
PRICE OF FOLLY, THE, 1937
PRICE OF SILENCE, THE, 1960
PRICE OF THINGS, THE, 1930
PRICE OF WISDOM, THE, 1935
PRIEST'S WIFE, THE, 1971
PRIMAL SCREAM, 1988
PRIMITIVE LOVE, 1966
PRISON SHADOWS, 1936
PRISONERS OF THE CASBAH, 1953
PRIVATE LESSONS, 1981
PRIVATE NAVY OF SGT. O'FARRELL, THE, 1968
PRIVATE NURSE, 1941
PRIVATE PARTS, 1972
PRIVATE RESORT, 1985
PRIVATES ON PARADE, 1984
PRODIGAL, THE, 1955
PROJECT: KILL, 1976
PROJECT MOONBASE, 1953
PROJECT X, 1949
PROM NIGHT, 1980
PROMISE, THE, 1969
PROPHECY, 1979
PROTECTORS, BOOK 1, THE, 1981
PROWLER, THE, 1981
PSYCHIC, THE, 1979
PSYCHO A GO-GO!, 1965
PSYCHOPATH, THE, 1973
PSYCHOTRONIC MAN, THE, 1980
PUBLIC STENOGRAPHER, 1935
PULSEBEAT, 1986
PURCHASE PRICE, THE, 1932
PURPLE TAXI, THE, 1977
PURSE STRINGS, 1933
PURSUIT OF D.B. COOPER, THE, 1981
PUSSYCAT, PUSSYCAT, I LOVE YOU, 1970
PUT UP OR SHUT UP, 1968
QUADROON, 1972
QUEEN OF SHEBA, 1953
QUICKSILVER, 1986
QUINCANNON, FRONTIER SCOUT, 1956
QUITTERS, THE, 1934
RABBIT, RUN, 1970
RABBIT TEST, 1978
RABID, 1976
RACING STRAIN, THE, 1933
RACING YOUTH, 1932
RAD, 1986
RADAR SECRET SERVICE, 1950

BOLD: Films on Videocassette

RADIO PATROL, 1932
RAGE OF THE BUCCANEERS, 1963
RAID ON ROMMEL, 1971
RAIDERS OF THE SOUTH, 1947
RAINBOW RANCH, 1933
RAISE THE TITANIC, 1980
RAMRODDER, THE, 1969
RANGE LAW, 1944
RANGER'S CODE, THE, 1933
RANGERS STEP IN, THE, 1937
RANGO, 1931
RATTLERS, 1976
RAVAGER, THE, 1970
RAVAGERS, THE, 1979
RAW TIMBER, 1937
RAW WEEKEND, 1964
RAWHEAD REX, 1987
REBELLION IN CUBA, 1961
REBELLIOUS DAUGHTERS, 1938
RECORD CITY, 1978
RED DAWN, 1984
RED FORK RANGE, 1931
RED LIGHTS AHEAD, 1937
RED MENACE, THE, 1949
RED MORNING, 1935
RED PLANET MARS, 1952
RED ROCK OUTLAW, 1950
REDEMPTION, 1930
REDHEAD, 1941
REEFER MADNESS, 1936
REFLECTIONS IN A GOLDEN EYE, 1967
REFORM SCHOOL GIRLS, 1986
REFUGE, 1981
REGISTERED NURSE, 1934
REMEMBER?, 1939
REMOTE CONTROL, 1988
RENEGADES OF THE WEST, 1932
RENO, 1930
RENO AND THE DOC, 1984
"'RENT-A-GIRL", 1965
REPTILICUS, 1962
REQUIEM FOR A SECRET AGENT, 1966
RESCUE, THE, 1988
RESCUE SQUAD, 1935
RETRIBUTION, 1988
RETURN, THE, 1980
RETURN OF THE FROG, THE, 1938
RETURN OF THE RANGERS, THE, 1943
RETURN OF THE TERROR, 1934
RETURN TO MACON COUNTY, 1975
REVENGE OF THE NERDS II: NERDS IN PARADISE, 1987
REVENGE OF THE NINJA, 1983
REVERSE BE MY LOT, THE, 1938
REVOLT OF THE ZOMBIES, 1936
RHYTHM RACKETEER, 1937
RICH AND FAMOUS, 1981
RIDE A VIOLENT MILE, 1957
RIDE IN THE WHIRLWIND, 1966
RIDER IN THE NIGHT, THE, 1968
RIDERS OF BLACK MOUNTAIN, 1941
RIDERS OF THE CACTUS, 1931
RIDERS OF THE WEST, 1942
RIDING SPEED, 1934
RIGHT HAND OF THE DEVIL, THE, 1963
RIGHT OF WAY, THE, 1931
RIGHT TO LIVE, THE, 1933
RING AROUND THE MOON, 1936
RIO GRANDE RANGER, 1937
RIO 70, 1970
RIVER HOUSE MYSTERY, THE, 1935
RIVER OF FOREVER, 1967
RIVER WOLVES, THE, 1934
ROAD TO FORTUNE, THE, 1930
ROAD TO HAPPINESS, 1942
ROADHOUSE 66, 1984
ROADIE, 1980
ROADRACERS, THE, 1959
ROARING CITY, 1951
ROARING ROADS, 1935
ROARING WESTWARD, 1949
ROB ROY, THE HIGHLAND ROGUE, 1954
ROBBERY WITH VIOLENCE, 1958
ROCK, PRETTY BABY, 1956
ROCK YOU SINNERS, 1957
ROCKIN' IN THE ROCKIES, 1945

ROCKY, 1948
ROCKY HORROR PICTURE SHOW, THE, 1975
ROLL ALONG, COWBOY, 1938
ROLLING HOME, 1935
ROLLING IN MONEY, 1934
ROMANCE A LA CARTE, 1938
ROMANCE RIDES THE RANGE, 1936
ROMANY LOVE, 1931
ROOGIE'S BUMP, 1954
ROOKIE, THE, 1959
ROOM FOR TWO, 1940
ROOMMATES, THE, 1973
ROOT OF ALL EVIL, THE, 1947
ROSE BOWL, 1936
ROSE OF THE RIO GRANDE, 1938
ROSE OF TRALEE, 1938
ROSEBUD, 1975
ROTTEN APPLE, THE, 1963
ROUGH RIDING RANGER, 1935
ROUND TRIP, 1967
ROUNDUP, THE, 1941
ROVER, THE, 1967
ROVIN' TUMBLEWEEDS, 1939
ROYAL BOX, THE, 1930
ROYAL DEMAND, A, 1933
RUBY, 1977
RUN ACROSS THE RIVER, 1961
RUN WITH THE WIND, 1966
RUNAROUND, THE, 1931
RUNAWAY BRIDE, 1930
RUNNERS, 1983
RUNNING HOT, 1984
RUSH, 1984
RUSSKIES, 1987
RUSTLER'S HIDEOUT, 1944
RUSTLER'S VALLEY, 1937
RUTHLESS, 1948
SABINA, THE, 1979
SABOTAGE SQUAD, 1942
SABU AND THE MAGIC RING, 1957
SACRED KNIVES OF VENGEANCE, THE, 1974
SAGA OF DRACULA, THE, 1975
SAGEBRUSH FAMILY TRAILS WEST, THE, 1940
SAGEBRUSH POLITICS, 1930
SAHARA, 1984
SAILOR FROM GIBRALTAR, THE, 1967
SAILOR'S RETURN, THE, 1978
ST. ELMO'S FIRE, 1985
SALAMANDER, THE, 1983
SALLY FIELDGOOD & CO., 1975
SALLY'S HOUNDS, 1968
SALOME, WHERE SHE DANCED, 1945
SALTY, 1975
SALZBURG CONNECTION, THE, 1972
SAM'S SONG, 1971
SAMSON, 1961
SAMURAI, 1945
SANCTUARY, 1961
SANDPIPER, THE, 1965
SANTA, 1932
SANTA CLAUS, 1960
SANTA CLAUS: THE MOVIE, 1985
SANTO CONTRA BLUE DEMON EN LA ATLANTIDA, 1968
SANTO CONTRA EL DOCTOR MUERTE, 1974
SANTO CONTRA LA HIJA DE FRANKENSTEIN, 1971
SANTO CONTRA LA INVASION DE LOS MARCIANOS, 1966
SANTO EN EL MUSEO DE CERA, 1963
SATISFACTION, 1988
SATURDAY THE 14TH, 1981
SATURN 3, 1980
SAVAGE DAWN, 1984
SAVAGE DRUMS, 1951
SAVAGE GIRL, THE, 1932
SAVAGE HARVEST, 1981
SAVAGE SISTERS, 1974
SAVAGE STREETS, 1984
SAVAGES FROM HELL, 1968
SAXO, 1988
SAY HELLO TO YESTERDAY, 1971
SAY ONE FOR ME, 1959
SAY YES, 1986
SCANDAL INCORPORATED, 1956
SCARAB, 1982
SCARAB MURDER CASE, THE, 1936

SCARED TO DEATH, 1981
SCAREHEADS, 1931
SCARLET SPEAR, THE, 1954
SCARLET WEEKEND, A, 1932
SCAVENGER HUNT, 1979
SCAVENGERS, 1988
SCHIZO, 1977
SCHOOL FOR DANGER, 1947
SCHOOL FOR SEX, 1969
SCHOOL FOR STARS, 1935
SCHOONER GANG, THE, 1937
SCOOP, THE, 1934
SCORPIO, 1973
SCOTLAND YARD COMMANDS, 1937
SCREAM, BABY, SCREAM, 1969
SEA DEVILS, 1931
SEA PIRATE, THE, 1967
SEA SERPENT, THE, 1937
SECOND FACE, THE, 1950
SECOND-HAND HEARTS, 1981
SECOND HAND WIFE, 1933
SECRET ADMIRER, 1985
SECRET CAVE, THE, 1953
SECRET CEREMONY, 1968
SECRET DIARY OF SIGMUND FREUD, THE, 1984
SECRET FILE: HOLLYWOOD, 1962
SECRET MENACE, 1931
SECRET OF MY SUCCESS, THE, 1965
SECRET OF MY SUCCESS, THE, 1987
SECRET SINNERS, 1933
SECRET WITNESS, THE, 1931
SECRETS, 1971
SECRETS OF A MODEL, 1940
SECRETS OF A NURSE, 1938
SECRETS OF AN ACTRESS, 1938
SECRETS OF CHINATOWN, 1935
SEED OF INNOCENCE, 1980
SEEDS OF DESTRUCTION, 1952
SEEING IS BELIEVING, 1934
SENIOR PROM, 1958
SENTINEL, THE, 1977
SET, THE, 1970
SEVEN MINUTES, THE, 1971
SEVEN REVENGES, THE, 1967
SEVEN WERE SAVED, 1947
SEVEN WOMEN FROM HELL, 1961
SEVENTH SIGN, THE, 1988
SEX KITTENS GO TO COLLEGE, 1960
SEXTETTE, 1978
SEXTON BLAKE AND THE BEARDED DOCTOR, 1935
SHADOW PLAY, 1986
SHADOWS OF THE ORIENT, 1937
SHAME, SHAME, EVERYBODY KNOWS HER NAME, 1969
SHANGRI-LA, 1961
SHANTY TRAMP, 1967
SHAPE OF THINGS TO COME, THE, 1979
SHE ALWAYS GETS THEIR MAN, 1962
SHE DEMONS, 1958
SHE HAD TO EAT, 1937
SHE MADE HER BED, 1934
SHE SHALL HAVE MURDER, 1950
SHEBA BABY, 1975
SHELL SHOCK, 1964
SHE'S NO LADY, 1937
SHIPS OF HATE, 1931
SHOOT, 1976
SHOOT IT: BLACK, SHOOT IT: BLUE, 1974
SHORT CIRCUIT 2, 1988
SHOTGUN PASS, 1932
SHOULD A GIRL MARRY?, 1939
SHOW FLAT, 1936
SICILIAN CONNECTION, THE, 1977
SIDECAR RACERS, 1975
SIDEWINDER ONE, 1977
SIERRA STRANGER, 1957
SIGN OF FOUR, THE, 1983
SIGN OF THE GLADIATOR, 1959
SIGN OF VENUS, THE, 1955
SILENT ENEMY, THE, 1930
SILENT MADNESS, 1984
SILENT NIGHT, DEADLY NIGHT, 1984
SILK, 1986
SILK HAT KID, 1935
SILLY BILLIES, 1936
SILVER CHALICE, THE, 1954

SILVER DREAM RACER, 1982
SILVER SPOON, THE, 1934
SILVER STALLION, 1941
SILVER STAR, THE, 1955
SIMON, KING OF THE WITCHES, 1971
SIN OF NORA MORAN, 1933
SIN YOU SINNERS, 1963
SING WHILE YOU'RE ABLE, 1937
SING YOUR WAY HOME, 1945
SINGAPORE, 1947
SINGING COWGIRL, THE, 1939
SINGING IN THE DARK, 1956
SINGLE-HANDED SANDERS, 1932
SINGLE ROOM FURNISHED, 1968
SINISTER HANDS, 1932
SINNERS IN PARADISE, 1938
SINS OF MAN, 1936
SINS PAYDAY, 1932
SIREN OF ATLANTIS, 1948
SIX-DAY BIKE RIDER, 1934
SKATEBOARD, 1978
SKATETOWN, U.S.A., 1979
SKI FEVER, 1969
SKIMPY IN THE NAVY, 1949
SKIN DEEP, 1929
SKULL AND CROWN, 1938
SKY HIGH, 1952
SKY IS RED, THE, 1952
SKY RAIDERS, 1931
SKY RAIDERS, THE, 1938
SKYDIVERS, THE, 1963
SKYLARKS, 1936
SKYWAY, 1933
SLAMS, THE, 1973
SLAPSTICK OF ANOTHER KIND, 1984
SLASHER, THE, 1975
SLAUGHTER HOTEL, 1971
SLAUGHTER IN SAN FRANCISCO, 1981
SLAUGHTERHOUSE ROCK, 1988
SLAVE OF THE CANNIBAL GOD, 1979
SLIGHTLY TEMPTED, 1940
SLIME PEOPLE, THE, 1963
SLITHIS, 1978
SLOW RUN, 1968
SMALL HOURS, THE, 1962
SMALL TOWN STORY, 1953
SMART ALEC, 1951
SMELL OF HONEY, A SWALLOW OF BRINE? A, 1966
SMITH'S WIVES, 1935
SMOKE IN THE WIND, 1975
SMOKEY AND THE BANDIT II, 1980
SMOKY TRAILS, 1939
SMUGGLERS, THE, 1969
SNAKE PEOPLE, THE, 1968
SNAKE WOMAN, THE, 1961
SNO-LINE, 1986
SNOW JOB, 1972
SNOW TREASURE, 1968
SNOW WHITE AND THE THREE STOOGES, 1961
SO THIS IS AFRICA, 1933
SOCIETY SMUGGLERS, 1939
SOFT SKIN ON BLACK SILK, 1964
SOHO CONSPIRACY, 1951
SOLDIER BLUE, 1970
SOLDIER, THE, 1982
SOLE SURVIVOR, 1984
SOME BLONDES ARE DANGEROUS, 1937
SOME LIKE IT COOL, 1979
SOME PEOPLE, 1964
SOMEBODY KILLED HER HUSBAND, 1978
SOMEONE AT THE DOOR, 1936
SOMEONE BEHIND THE DOOR, 1971
SOMETHING WEIRD, 1967
SOMETHING'S ROTTEN, 1979
SOMETIMES GOOD, 1934
SOMEWHERE IN CIVVIES, 1943
SON OF A STRANGER, 1957
SON OF DRACULA, 1974
SON OF GODZILLA, 1967
SONG FOR TOMORROW, A, 1948
SONG OF MEXICO, 1945
SONG OF SOHO, 1930
SONG OF THE WASTELAND, 1947
SONNY AND JED, 1974
SONS OF SATAN, 1969
SOPHIE LANG GOES WEST, 1937

SORCERESS, 1983
SOUL OF THE SLUMS, 1931
SOUND OF HORROR, 1966
SOUP TO NUTS, 1930
SOUTH OF CALIENTE, 1951
SOUTH OF PANAMA, 1941
SOUTH OF SONORA, 1930
SOUTH OF THE BORDER, 1939
SOUTH OF THE RIO GRANDE, 1945
SOUTH TO KARANGA, 1940
SPACE AMOEBA, THE, 1970
SPACE MONSTER, 1965
SPANISH EYES, 1930
SPECIAL AGENT K-7, 1937
SPECIAL DAY, A, 1977
SPECIAL INSPECTOR, 1939
SPEED DEVILS, 1935
SPEED TO SPARE, 1937
SPELL OF THE HYPNOTIST, 1956
SPIES LIKE US, 1985
SPIKER, 1986
SPIRAL ROAD, THE, 1962
SPIRAL STAIRCASE, THE, 1975
SPIRIT OF STANFORD, THE, 1942
SPIRIT OF YOUTH, 1937
SPOILERS OF THE RANGE, 1939
SPRING BREAK, 1983
SPRING HANDICAP, 1937
SPRING IN THE AIR, 1934
SPRING TONIC, 1935
S*P*Y*S, 1974
SQUALL, THE, 1929
SQUEEZE PLAY, 1981
SQUIRM, 1976
S.T.A.B., 1976
STACY'S KNIGHTS, 1983
STAGECOACH DAYS, 1938
STAGECOACH KID, 1949
STAGECOACH WAR, 1940
STAR PACKER, THE, 1934
STAR PILOT, 1977
STAR SPANGLED GIRL, 1971
STARK FEAR, 1963
STARS AND BARS, 1988
STATELINE MOTEL, 1976
STAY AWAY, JOE, 1968
STEALING HOME, 1988
STEEL BAYONET, THE, 1958
STEEL CLAW, THE, 1961
STEELE JUSTICE, 1987
STEPCHILD, 1947
STEPPING SISTERS, 1932
STEPTOE AND SON, 1972
STEREO, 1969
STICK UP, THE, 1978
STILETTO, 1969
STILL SMOKIN', 1983
STING II, THE, 1983
STOLEN ASSIGNMENT, 1955
STOOGEMANIA, 1986
STOP PRESS GIRL, 1949
STORMBOUND, 1951
STORY OF A WOMAN, 1970
STORY OF THE COUNT OF MONTE CRISTO, THE,
  1962
STRAIGHT IS THE WAY, 1934
STRAIGHT SHOOTER, 1940
STRAIGHT TO HELL, 1987
STRAIGHTAWAY, 1934
STRANGE ADVENTURE, 1932
STRANGE CASE OF CLARA DEANE, THE, 1932
STRANGE CASE OF DR. MANNING, THE, 1958
STRANGE CASE OF DR. RX, THE, 1942
STRANGE EVIDENCE, 1933
STRANGE FACES, 1938
STRANGE JOURNEY, 1946
STRANGE JUSTICE, 1932
STRANGE LOVERS, 1963
STRANGE MRS. CRANE, THE, 1948
STRANGE PEOPLE, 1933
STRANGE SHADOWS IN AN EMPTY ROOM, 1977
STRANGE WORLD, 1952
STRANGER, THE, 1967
STRANGER IN HOLLYWOOD, 1968
STRANGER IN TOWN, A, 1968
STRANGER'S MEETING, 1957

STRANGER, THE, 1987
STRANGERS ALL, 1935
STRANGLER, THE, 1941
STREET CORNER, 1948
STREETS OF GHOST TOWN, 1950
STRICTLY PERSONAL, 1933
STRICTLY UNCONVENTIONAL, 1930
STRIKE IT RICH, 1933
STRIP TEASE MURDER, 1961
STRUGGLE, THE, 1931
STRYKER, 1983
STUCKEY'S LAST STAND, 1980
STUDENT BODIES, 1981
STUDENT BODY, THE, 1976
STUDENT NURSES, THE, 1970
STUDENT'S ROMANCE, THE, 1936
STUDIO MURDER MYSTERY, THE, 1929
SUBMARINE ALERT, 1943
SUBMARINE BASE, 1943
SUBMARINE RAIDER, 1942
SUBSTITUTION, 1970
SUBTERFUGE, 1969
SUBTERRANEANS, THE, 1960
SUBURBAN WIVES, 1973
SUBWAY EXPRESS, 1931
SUCH GOOD FRIENDS, 1971
SUDDEN DEATH, 1985
SUICIDE CLUB, THE, 1988
SULLIVAN'S EMPIRE, 1967
SUMMER SCHOOL, 1987
SUN NEVER SETS, THE, 1939
SUNDOWN ON THE PRAIRIE, 1939
SUNNY SKIES, 1930
SUNNYSIDE, 1979
SUNSET, 1988
SUNSET COVE, 1978
SUNSET MURDER CASE, 1941
SUPER FUZZ, 1981
SUPER VAN, 1977
SUPERBUG, SUPER AGENT, 1976
SUPERFLY T.N.T., 1973
SUPERGIRL, 1984
SUPERMAN IV: THE QUEST FOR PEACE, 1987
SUPERSONIC MAN, 1979
SURF PARTY, 1964
SURFTIDE 77, 1962
SURVIVAL RUN, 1980
SUZANNE, 1980
SWAMP WOMEN, 1956
SWARM, THE, 1978
SWASHBUCKLER, 1976
SWEEPINGS, 1933
SWEET BEAT, 1962
SWEET BODY OF DEBORAH, THE, 1969
SWEET JESUS, PREACHER MAN, 1973
SWEET MAMA, 1930
SWEET SIXTEEN, 1983
SWEET SURRENDER, 1935
SWEET SUZY, 1973
SWEETHEART OF THE CAMPUS, 1941
SWEETHEARTS OF THE U.S.A., 1944
SWELL-HEAD, 1935
SWING HIGH, 1930
SWING IT SAILOR, 1937
SWING THAT CHEER, 1938
SWING YOUR LADY, 1938
SWINGIN' AFFAIR, A, 1963
SWINGIN' ON A RAINBOW, 1945
SWINGTIME JOHNNY, 1944
SWISS CONSPIRACY, THE, 1976
SWISS HONEYMOON, 1947
SWITCH, THE, 1963
SWORD AND THE SORCERER, THE, 1982
SWORD OF ALI BABA, THE, 1965
SWORD OF THE AVENGER, 1948
SWORD OF THE VALIANT, 1984
SWORD OF VENUS, 1953
TAFFIN, 1988
TAHITIAN, THE, 1956
TAI-PAN, 1986
TAKE A POWDER, 1953
TAKE ME AWAY, MY LOVE, 1962
TALE OF THREE WOMEN, A, 1954
TAMPICO, 1944
TANGIER ASSIGNMENT, 1954
TARZAN AND THE GREEN GODDESS, 1938

BOLD: Films on Videocassette

TARZAN AND THE SHE-DEVIL, 1953
TARZAN, THE APE MAN, 1959
TARZANA, THE WILD GIRL, 1973
TARZAN'S DEADLY SILENCE, 1970
TARZAN'S JUNGLE REBELLION, 1970
TARZAN'S REVENGE, 1938
TASTE OF HELL, A, 1973
TAXI DRIVER, 1976
TEAR GAS SQUAD, 1940
TEARS OF HAPPINESS, 1974
TEEN-AGE CRIME WAVE, 1955
TEEN WOLF TOO, 1987
TEENAGE GANG DEBS, 1966
TEENAGE THUNDER, 1957
TELEPHONE, THE, 1988
TELEPHONE OPERATOR, 1938
TEMPTATION, 1962
TEN DAYS TO TULARA, 1958
TEN LAPS TO GO, 1938
TEN LITTLE INDIANS, 1965
TEN NIGHTS IN A BARROOM, 1931
$10 RAISE, 1935
10 TO MIDNIGHT, 1983
TENTACLES, 1977
TENTH AVENUE ANGEL, 1948
TERRIFIED, 1963
TERROR, 1979
TERROR AT BLACK FALLS, 1962
TERROR EYES, 1981
TERROR FROM THE YEAR 5,000, 1958
TERROR OF THE BLOODHUNTERS, 1962
TERROR OF TINY TOWN, THE, 1938
TERROR STREET, 1953
TERRORISTS, THE, 1975
TEX RIDES WITH THE BOY SCOUTS, 1937
TEX TAKES A HOLIDAY, 1932
TEXAN MEETS CALAMITY JANE, THE, 1950
TEXAS TERRORS, 1940
TEXAS TO BATAAN, 1942
TEXICAN, THE, 1966
THANKS FOR LISTENING, 1937
THAT CERTAIN FEELING, 1956
THAT LUCKY TOUCH, 1975
THAT SPLENDID NOVEMBER, 1971
THAT TENDER TOUCH, 1969
THAT'S MY STORY, 1937
THAT'S A GOOD GIRL, 1933
THAT'S GRATITUDE, 1934
THAT'S MY UNCLE, 1935
THERE AIN'T NO JUSTICE, 1939
THERE GOES KELLY, 1945
THERE WAS A YOUNG MAN, 1937
THEY CAME TO ROB LAS VEGAS, 1969
THEY DIDN'T KNOW, 1936
THEY KNEW MR. KNIGHT, 1945
THEY MADE ME A KILLER, 1946
THEY RAID BY NIGHT, 1942
THEY WENT THAT-A-WAY AND THAT-A-WAY, 1978
THEY'RE PLAYING WITH FIRE, 1984
THING THAT COULDN'T DIE, THE, 1958
THINGS HAPPEN AT NIGHT, 1948
THIRTEEN FRIGHTENED GIRLS, 1963
THIS ENGLAND, 1941
THIS TIME FOR KEEPS, 1942
THIS WOMAN IS MINE, 1941
THIS, THAT AND THE OTHER, 1970
THISTLEDOWN, 1938
THOROUGHBRED, 1932
THOSE DIRTY DOGS, 1974
THOSE PEOPLE NEXT DOOR, 1952
THOU SHALT NOT KILL, 1939
THREADS, 1932
THREE AMIGOS, 1986
THREE BLONDES IN HIS LIFE, 1961
THREE CAME TO KILL, 1960
THREE FOR BEDROOM C, 1952
THREE FOR THE ROAD, 1987
THREE GUNS FOR TEXAS, 1968
300 SPARTANS, THE, 1962
THREE LEGIONNAIRES, THE, 1937
THREE MEN AND A CRADLE, 1985
THREE NUTS IN SEARCH OF A BOLT, 1964
THREE ON A HONEYMOON, 1934
THREE ON A SPREE, 1961
THREE SONS, 1939
THREE SPARE WIVES, 1962

THREE STEPS IN THE DARK, 1953
THREE STEPS NORTH, 1951
THREE STOOGES GO AROUND THE WORLD IN A DAZE, THE, 1963
THREE STOOGES IN ORBIT, THE, 1962
THREE STOOGES MEET HERCULES, THE, 1962
THREE STOOGES VS. THE WONDER WOMEN, 1975
THREE SUNDAYS TO LIVE, 1957
THREE-WAY SPLIT, 1970
THREE WEEKS OF LOVE, 1965
THREE WISE GUYS, THE, 1936
THREE WITNESSES, 1935
THREE'S COMPANY, 1953
THREES, MENAGE A TROIS, 1968
THRILL KILLERS, THE, 1965
THUNDER IN DIXIE, 1965
THUNDER OVER TANGIER, 1957
THUNDER RUN, 1986
THUNDERING FRONTIER, 1940
THUNDERING JETS, 1958
THUNDERING TRAIL, THE, 1951
TICKET, 1987
TICKET OF LEAVE, 1936
TICKET OF LEAVE MAN, THE, 1937
TICKET TO PARADISE, 1961
TIDAL WAVE, 1975
TIGER BAY, 1933
TIGER FLIGHT, 1965
TIJUANA STORY, THE, 1957
TILL DEATH, 1978
TIMBERJACK, 1955
TIME OF DESIRE, THE, 1957
TIME OF DESTINY, A, 1988
TIME OUT FOR RHYTHM, 1941
TINTORERA...BLOODY WATERS, 1977
TITLE SHOT, 1982
TO CATCH A THIEF, 1936
TO KILL OR TO DIE, 1973
TO LIVE AND DIE IN L.A., 1985
TO OBLIGE A LADY, 1931
TOAST TO LOVE, 1951
TODAY, 1930
TODD KILLINGS, THE, 1971
TOLL OF THE DESERT, 1936
TOM, 1973
TOM THUMB, 1967
TOMB OF THE UNDEAD, 1972
TOMB OF TORTURE, 1966
TOMBOY, 1985
TOMCAT, THE, 1968
TOMORROW WE LIVE, 1936
TOMORROW'S YOUTH, 1935
TONIO KROGER, 1968
TOO HOT TO HANDLE, 1961
TOO MANY BLONDES, 1941
TOO MANY WIVES, 1937
TOO MANY WOMEN, 1942
TOOMORROW, 1970
TOP OF THE HEAP, 1972
TOP SERGEANT MULLIGAN, 1941
TORMENT, 1986
TORMENTED, 1960
TORPEDO BOAT, 1942
TORSO, 1974
TORTURE ME KISS ME, 1970
TOUCH OF SATAN, THE, 1971
TOUCH OF THE MOON, A, 1936
TOUCH OF THE OTHER, A, 1970
TOUCH OF THE SUN, A, 1956
TOUCH, THE, 1971
TOUGH ASSIGNMENT, 1949
TOUGH ENOUGH, 1983
TOUGH KID, 1939
TOUGH TO HANDLE, 1937
TOUGHER THEY COME, THE, 1950
TOUGHEST GUN IN TOMBSTONE, 1958
TOWER OF TERROR, THE, 1942
TOWING, 1978
TOWN CALLED HELL, A, 1971
TOWN THAT DREADED SUNDOWN, THE, 1977
TOWN WENT WILD, THE, 1945
TOXIC AVENGER, THE, 1985
TOY SOLDIERS, 1984
TOY, THE, 1982
TOYS ARE NOT FOR CHILDREN, 1972
TRACK OF THUNDER, 1967

TRADER HORN, 1973
TRAIL OF THE PINK PANTHER, THE, 1982
TRAIL OF THE SILVER SPURS, 1941
TRAIL OF THE YUKON, 1949
TRAILIN' WEST, 1936
TRAILING DOUBLE TROUBLE, 1940
TRAILING TROUBLE, 1930
TRAILING TROUBLE, 1937
TRAIL'S END, 1949
TRAILS OF DANGER, 1930
TRAILS OF THE WILD, 1935
TRAITOR, THE, 1936
TRAITORS, 1957
TRAITORS, THE, 1963
TRANCERS, 1985
TRANSFORMERS: THE MOVIE, THE, 1986
TRANSYLVANIA 6-5000, 1985
TRAP, THE, 1959
TRAPEZE, 1932
TRAPP FAMILY, THE, 1961
TRAPPED, 1931
TRAPPED BY THE TERROR, 1949
TRAPPED IN TANGIERS, 1960
TRAVELING HUSBANDS, 1931
TREASURE ISLAND, 1972
TREASURE OF RUBY HILLS, 1955
TREASURE OF THE FOUR CROWNS, 1983
TRICK BABY, 1973
TRICK FOR TRICK, 1933
TRIGGER PALS, 1939
TRIPLE IRONS, 1973
TRIPLE THREAT, 1948
TRIUMPHS OF A MAN CALLED HORSE, 1983
TROPIC FURY, 1939
TROPICAL TROUBLE, 1936
TROUBLE AT MIDNIGHT, 1937
TROUBLE IN THE AIR, 1948
TROUBLE MAN, 1972
TULIPS, 1981
TUNDRA, 1936
TURK 182!, 1985
TURKISH CUCUMBER, THE, 1963
TUSK, 1980
TWELVE HOURS TO KILL, 1960
27A, 1974
TWILIGHT ON THE RIO GRANDE, 1947
TWIN FACES, 1937
TWIST ALL NIGHT, 1961
TWITCH OF THE DEATH NERVE, 1973
TWO A PENNY, 1968
TWO AGAINST THE WORLD, 1932
TWO FISTED JUSTICE, 1943
TWO IN A CROWD, 1936
TWO KINDS OF WOMEN, 1932
TWO LATINS FROM MANHATTAN, 1941
TWO LOVES, 1961
TWO-MINUTE WARNING, 1976
TWO MINUTES' SILENCE, 1934
TWO MINUTES TO PLAY, 1937
TWO ON A DOORSTEP, 1936
TWO PEOPLE, 1973
TWO SENORITAS FROM CHICAGO, 1943
TWO SISTERS, 1938
TWO SMART MEN, 1940
2000 YEARS LATER, 1969
TWO TICKETS TO PARIS, 1962
TWO WEEKS OFF, 1929
TWONKY, THE, 1953
TYPHOON TREASURE, 1939
U-BOAT PRISONER, 1944
UFO: TARGET EARTH, 1974
UNCERTAIN LADY, 1934
UNCLE JOE SHANNON, 1978
UNDER A CLOUD, 1937
UNDER AGE, 1964
UNDER PROOF, 1936
UNDER SUSPICION, 1931
UNDER TEXAS SKIES, 1940
UNDERCOVER GIRL, 1957
UNDERCOVERS HERO, 1975
UNDERTOW, 1930
UNEARTHLY, THE, 1957
UNEASY TERMS, 1948
UNEXPECTED UNCLE, 1941
UNFINISHED BUSINESS..., 1987
UNHOLY, THE, 1988

UNHOLY FOUR, THE, 1969
UNHOLY GARDEN, THE, 1931
UNHOLY LOVE, 1932
UNKNOWN BLONDE, 1934
UNKNOWN ISLAND, 1948
UNKNOWN TERROR, THE, 1957
UNSEEN, THE, 1981
UNSTRAP ME, 1968
UNTAMED HEIRESS, 1954
UNTAMED YOUTH, 1957
UNWED MOTHER, 1958
UNWRITTEN CODE, THE, 1944
UP IN SMOKE, 1957
UP THE ACADEMY, 1980
UP THE FRONT, 1972
UP WITH THE LARK, 1943
UPHILL ALL THE WAY, 1986
VACATION DAYS, 1947
VALET GIRLS, 1987
VAMPIRE, THE, 1957
VAMPIRES, THE, 1969
VANDERGILT DIAMOND MYSTERY, THE, 1936
VANITY FAIR, 1932
VENDETTA, 1950
VENGEANCE IS MINE, 1969
VENGEANCE OF SHE, THE, 1968
VENGEANCE OF THE DEEP, 1940
VENOM, 1968
VENOM, 1982
VENUS MAKES TROUBLE, 1937
VERNE MILLER, 1988
VERY CLOSE QUARTERS, 1986
VERY THOUGHT OF YOU, THE, 1944
VIA PONY EXPRESS, 1933
VICE GIRLS, LTD., 1964
VICE RACKET, 1937
VICIOUS CIRCLE, THE, 1948
VIDEODROME, 1983
VIENNA, CITY OF SONGS, 1931
VILLAGE SQUIRE, THE, 1935
VILLAIN STILL PURSUED HER, THE, 1940
VILLAIN, THE, 1979
VILLIERS DIAMOND, THE, 1938
VILNA LEGEND, A, 1949
VIOLATED, 1953
VIOLATED, 1986
VIOLATORS, THE, 1957
VIOLENT BREED, THE, 1986
VIRGIN PRESIDENT, THE, 1968
VIRGIN QUEEN OF ST. FRANCIS HIGH, THE, 1987
VIRGIN WITCH, THE, 1973
VISITING HOURS, 1982
VISITOR, THE, 1980
VIVA CISCO KID, 1940
VIVA KNIEVEL?, 1977
VIXENS, THE, 1969
VOICE IN THE NIGHT, 1934
VOICE IN THE WIND, 1944
VOODOO ISLAND, 1957
VOODOO WOMAN, 1957
VOYAGE, THE, 1974
VOYAGE TO THE PLANET OF PREHISTORIC
    WOMEN, 1966
VOYAGE TO THE PREHISTORIC PLANET, 1965
WACKY WORLD OF DR. MORGUS, THE, 1962
WAGON TRAIN, 1940
WAITRESS, 1982
WAJAN, 1938
WALK THE WALK, 1970
WALKING ON AIR, 1946
WALKING TALL, PART II, 1975
WALKING THE EDGE, 1985
WALLS OF GOLD, 1933
WANDA NEVADA, 1979
WANDERLOVE, 1970
WAR IS A RACKET, 1934
WAR OF THE PLANETS, 1977
WAR OF THE RANGE, 1933
WAR OF THE SATELLITES, 1958
WARDOGS, 1987
WARM IN THE BUD, 1970
WARREN CASE, THE, 1934
WARRIOR AND THE SORCERESS, THE, 1984
WARRIOR EMPRESS, THE, 1961
WARRIOR QUEEN, 1987
WARRIORS OF THE WASTELAND, 1984

WASHINGTON MERRY-GO-ROUND, 1932
WASP WOMAN, THE, 1959
WATER FOR CANITOGA, 1939
WATERFRONT, 1939
WAY FOR A SAILOR, 1930
WAY OF ALL FLESH, THE, 1940
WAY OF YOUTH, THE, 1934
WAY OUT, 1966
WAY...WAY OUT, 1966
WAY WE LIVE NOW, THE, 1970
WAYWARD GIRL, THE, 1957
WE ARE ALL NAKED, 1970
WE GO FAST, 1941
WE SHALL SEE, 1964
WEDDING NIGHT, 1970
WEDDING OF LILLI MARLENE, THE, 1953
WEDDING PARTY, THE, 1969
WEDDING, A, 1978
WEDNESDAY'S LUCK, 1936
WEEKEND OF FEAR, 1966
WEEKEND PASS, 1984
WEEKEND WITH THE BABYSITTER, 1970
WEIRD LOVE MAKERS, THE, 1963
WELCOME HOME, SOLDIER BOYS, 1972
WELCOME TO 18, 1986
WELL DONE, HENRY, 1936
WE'LL GROW THIN TOGETHER, 1979
WE'RE RICH AGAIN, 1934
WEREWOLF OF WASHINGTON, 1973
WEREWOLVES ON WHEELS, 1971
WEST OF BROADWAY, 1931
WESTERN GOLD, 1937
WESTERN LIMITED, 1932
WESTWARD BOUND, 1944
WESTWARD TRAIL, THE, 1948
WHAT A CARRY ON!, 1949
WHAT A NIGHT!, 1931
WHAT CHANGED CHARLEY FARTHING?, 1976
WHAT DID YOU DO IN THE WAR, DADDY?, 1966
WHAT PRICE CRIME?, 1935
WHAT PRICE INNOCENCE?, 1933
WHAT WAITS BELOW, 1986
WHAT'S GOOD FOR THE GOOSE, 1969
WHAT'S UP FRONT, 1964
WHAT'S YOUR RACKET?, 1934
WHEEL OF FATE, 1953
WHEEL OF LIFE, THE, 1929
WHEN A GIRL'S BEAUTIFUL, 1947
WHEN A MAN'S A MAN, 1935
WHEN HELL BROKE LOOSE, 1958
WHEN THE GIRLS TAKE OVER, 1962
WHEN THE RAVEN FLIES, 1985
WHEN TOMORROW DIES, 1966
WHEN WERE YOU BORN?, 1938
WHEN YOU COME HOME, 1947
WHERE DOES IT HURT?, 1972
WHERE HAS POOR MICKEY GONE?, 1964
WHERE IS MY CHILD?, 1937
WHERE THE BOYS ARE '84, 1984
WHERE THE BUFFALO ROAM, 1938
WHERE THE RED FERN GROWS, 1974
WHERE TRAILS DIVIDE, 1937
WHICH WAY IS UP?, 1977
WHIFFS, 1975
WHILE THE PATIENT SLEPT, 1935
WHIRLPOOL, 1959
WHIRLWIND HORSEMAN, 1938
WHIRLWIND OF PARIS, 1946
WHISPERING TONGUES, 1934
WHISPERING WINDS, 1929
WHITE BONDAGE, 1937
WHITE BUFFALO, THE, 1977
WHITE COCKATOO, 1935
WHITE DEATH, 1936
WHITE GODDESS, 1953
WHITE LIES, 1935
WHITE LIGHTNIN' ROAD, 1967
WHITE PONGO, 1945
WHITE, RED, YELLOW, PINK, 1966
WHITE SISTER, 1973
WHITE SQUAW, THE, 1956
WHITE WARRIOR, THE, 1961
WHO IS HOPE SCHUYLER?, 1942
WHO KILLED TEDDY BEAR?, 1965
WHOOPEE BOYS, THE, 1986
WHO'S YOUR FATHER?, 1935

WHY RUSSIANS ARE REVOLTING, 1970
WICKED DIE SLOW, THE, 1968
WICKED LADY, THE, 1983
WICKED, WICKED, 1973
WIDOW FROM CHICAGO, THE, 1930
WIDOW IN SCARLET, 1932
WIFE WANTED, 1946
WILD COUNTRY, 1947
WILD DAKOTAS, THE, 1956
WILD, FREE AND HUNGRY, 1970
WILD GUITAR, 1962
WILD GYPSIES, 1969
WILD HARVEST, 1962
WILD HORSE, 1931
WILD HORSE AMBUSH, 1952
WILD HORSE STAMPEDE, 1943
WILD IS MY LOVE, 1963
WILD 90, 1968
WILD ON THE BEACH, 1965
WILD PAIR, THE, 1987
WILD PARTY, THE, 1956
WILD RACERS, THE, 1968
WILD REBELS, THE, 1967
WILD RIDE, THE, 1960
WILD THING, 1987
WILD WEED, 1949
WILD YOUTH, 1961
WILDCAT BUS, 1940
WILDCATS, 1986
WILDCATS OF ST. TRINIAN'S, THE, 1980
WILDCATTER, THE, 1937
WIN, PLACE, OR STEAL, 1975
WIND FROM THE EAST, 1970
WINDOWS, 1980
WINDOWS OF TIME, THE, 1969
WINE, WOMEN AND HORSES, 1937
WINGS OF ADVENTURE, 1930
WINGS OVER THE PACIFIC, 1943
WINK OF AN EYE, 1958
WINTER A GO-GO, 1965
WINTER CARNIVAL, 1939
WIRED TO KILL, 1986
WIRETAPPERS, 1956
WISER SEX, THE, 1932
WITCH, THE, 1969
WITCHFIRE, 1986
WITCH'S MIRROR, THE, 1960
WITH LOVE AND KISSES, 1937
WITNESS CHAIR, THE, 1936
WIVES BEWARE, 1933
WIVES—TEN YEARS AFTER, 1985
WIZARD OF MARS, 1964
WOLF DOG, 1958
WOLVES OF THE SEA, 1938
WOLVES OF THE UNDERWORLD, 1935
WOMAN AGAINST THE WORLD, 1938
WOMAN AND THE HUNTER, THE, 1957
WOMAN BETWEEN, 1931
WOMAN EATER, THE, 1959
WOMAN FROM HEADQUARTERS, 1950
WOMAN HE SCORNED, THE, 1930
WOMAN IN COMMAND, THE, 1934
WOMAN IN RED, THE, 1984
WOMAN IN ROOM 13, THE, 1932
WOMAN IN THE DARK, 1952
WOMAN UNAFRAID, 1934
WOMAN WHO DARED, 1949
WOMAN'S ANGLE, THE, 1954
WOMBLING FREE, 1977
WOMEN ARE LIKE THAT, 1938
WOMEN GO ON FOREVER, 1931
WOMEN IN HIS LIFE, THE, 1934
WOMEN MUST DRESS, 1935
WOMEN OF PITCAIRN ISLAND, THE, 1957
WOMEN OF THE PREHISTORIC PLANET, 1966
WOMEN WON'T TELL, 1933
WON TON TON, THE DOG WHO SAVED
    HOLLYWOOD, 1976
WONDER OF WOMEN, 1929
WORLD IS FULL OF MARRIED MEN, THE, 1980
WORLD'S GREATEST SINNER, THE, 1962
WRAITH, THE, 1986
WRECKER, THE, 1933
WRESTLER, THE, 1974
XANADU, 1980
YANK IN INDO-CHINA, A, 1952

BOLD: Films on Videocassette

YANK IN LIBYA, A, 1942
YEAR ONE, 1974
YELLOW CANARY, THE, 1963
YELLOW DOG, 1973
YELLOW DUST, 1936
YELLOW MASK, THE, 1930
YELLOW MOUNTAIN, THE, 1954
YELLOW STOCKINGS, 1930
YELLOWSTONE, 1936
YENTL, 1983
YESTERDAY, 1980
YIDDLE WITH HIS FIDDLE, 1937
YOG-MONSTER FROM SPACE, 1970
YONGKARI MONSTER FROM THE DEEP, 1967
YOU CAN'T ESCAPE, 1955
YOU CAN'T FOOL AN IRISHMAN, 1950
YOU CAN'T HURRY LOVE, 1988
YOU CAN'T RATION LOVE, 1944
YOU LIGHT UP MY LIFE, 1977
YOUNG DOCTORS IN LOVE, 1982
YOUNG SWINGERS, THE, 1963
YOUNG WORLD, A, 1966
YOUNGER GENERATION, 1929
YOU'RE ONLY YOUNG TWICE, 1952
YOU'RE OUT OF LUCK, 1941
YOU'RE THE ONE, 1941
YOU'VE GOT TO BE SMART, 1967
ZAPPED!, 1982
ZARDOZ, 1974
ZERO HOUR, THE, 1939
ZERO TO SIXTY, 1978
ZOMBIE CREEPING FLESH, 1981
ZONING, 1986

Zero Stars
ACAPULCO GOLD, 1978
ADAM AND EVE, 1958
ADELE HASN'T HAD HER SUPPER YET, 1978
ADULTEROUS AFFAIR, 1966
ADVENTURERS, THE, 1970
AFFAIRS OF MESSALINA, THE, 1954
AFRICAN MANHUNT, 1955
ALADDIN, 1987
ALIEN CONTAMINATION, 1982
ALIMONY MADNESS, 1933
ALL WOMAN, 1967
ALLNIGHTER, THE, 1987
ALMOST A GENTLEMAN, 1939
ALMOST HUMAN, 1974
ALOHA, 1931
AMATEUR CROOK, 1937
AMAZING TRANSPARENT MAN, THE, 1960
AMERICAN GIGOLO, 1980
AMERICAN NIGHTMARE, 1984
AMIN—THE RISE AND FALL, 1982
AND GOD CREATED WOMAN, 1988
ANGEL, ANGEL, DOWN WE GO, 1969
ANGELA, 1977
ANONYMOUS VENETIAN, THE, 1971
ANTHONY OF PADUA, 1952
ANTI-CLOCK, 1980
ANYBODY'S WAR, 1930
ARE YOU THERE?, 1930
ARENA, THE, 1973
ASSAULT OF THE REBEL GIRLS, 1960
ASSIGNMENT OUTER SPACE, 1960
ASSIGNMENT TERROR, 1970
ASTOUNDING SHE-MONSTER, THE, 1958
ASTRO-ZOMBIES, THE, 1969
ATLAS AGAINST THE CZAR, 1964
ATTACK OF THE GIANT LEECHES, 1959
ATTACK OF THE MAYAN MUMMY, 1963
AUTUMN SONATA, 1978
AWFUL DR. ORLOFF, THE, 1964
AZTEC MUMMY, THE, 1957
BABY, THE, 1973
BABY LOVE, 1969
BACHELOR PARTY, 1984
BAD CHARLESTON CHARLIE, 1973
BAD GUYS, 1986
BARE KNUCKLES, 1978
BARN OF THE NAKED DEAD, 1976
BASIC TRAINING, 1985
BATTLE BEYOND THE SUN, 1963
BEAST WITH A MILLION EYES, THE, 1956
BEAUTY AND THE BEAST, 1963

BEFORE AND AFTER, 1985
BEHIND LOCKED DOORS, 1976
BELIEVERS, THE, 1987
BELLS, 1981
BERSERKER, 1988
BEST DEFENSE, 1984
BEST FRIENDS, 1975
BEYOND ATLANTIS, 1973
BEYOND THE DOOR, 1975
BEYOND THE DOOR II, 1979
BEYOND THE FOG, 1981
BEYOND THE REEF, 1981
BIG BAD MAMA, 1974
BIG BIRD CAGE, THE, 1972
BIG BOUNCE, THE, 1969
BLACK ANGELS, THE, 1970
BLACK MAMA, WHITE MAMA, 1973
BLACK ROOM, THE, 1984
BLACK SHAMPOO, 1976
BLAME IT ON RIO, 1984
BLOCK BUSTERS, 1944
BLOCKADE, 1929
BLOOD FEAST, 1963
BLOOD FEAST, 1976
BLOOD MANIA, 1971
BLOOD MONEY, 1974
BLOOD OF DRACULA'S CASTLE, 1967
BLOOD SISTERS, 1987
BLOODBATH AT THE HOUSE OF DEATH, 1984
BLOODSUCKING FREAKS, 1982
BLOODY BROOD, THE, 1959
BLOODY MAMA, 1970
BLOODY PIT OF HORROR, THE, 1965
BLOW OUT, 1981
BOBBIE JO AND THE OUTLAW, 1976
BODY AND SOUL, 1981
BODY DOUBLE, 1984
BOLERO, 1984
BOOGEY MAN, THE, 1980
BORDER SADDLEMATES, 1952
BORN OF FIRE, 1987
BORN TO GAMBLE, 1935
BOWERY BOMBSHELL, 1946
BOY...A GIRL, A, 1969
BOY AND HIS DOG, A, 1975
BREEDERS, 1986
BRIDES OF BLOOD, 1968
BRUCE LEE AND I, 1976
BUCKTOWN, 1975
**BUFFALO BILL AND THE INDIANS, OR SITTING
    BULL'S HISTORY LESSON, 1976**
BULLETPROOF, 1988
BURGLAR, 1987
BURIED ALIVE, 1984
BURNING, THE, 1981
BURY ME AN ANGEL, 1972
CALM YOURSELF, 1935
CAMILLE 2000, 1969
CAN'T STOP THE MUSIC, 1980
CANAL ZONE, 1942
CANDIDATE, THE, 1964
CANDY MAN, THE, 1969
CANNONBALL RUN II, 1984
CANNONBALL RUN, THE, 1981
CAPONE, 1975
CAPTAIN GRANT'S CHILDREN, 1939
CAPTAIN HURRICANE, 1935
CAPTAIN THUNDER, 1931
CAPTIVATION, 1931
CAPTURE THAT CAPSULE, 1961
CARDIAC ARREST, 1980
CARDINAL, THE, 1936
CAREER GIRL, 1960
CARNAGE, 1986
CARNIVAL OF BLOOD, 1976
CASA MANANA, 1951
CASTLE SINISTER, 1932
CAT ATE THE PARAKEET, THE, 1972
CAT MURKIL AND THE SILKS, 1976
CATSKILL HONEYMOON, 1950
CAUGHT, 1931
CAUGHT IN THE ACT, 1941
CAVE GIRL, 1985
CERTAIN FURY, 1985
CHAINED HEAT, 1983
CHALLENGE, 1974

CHAMELEON, 1978
CHANCE OF A LIFETIME, 1950
CHAPMAN REPORT, THE, 1962
CHARLESTON, 1978
**CHARLIE CHAN AND THE CURSE OF THE DRAGON
    QUEEN, 1981**
CHARMING DECEIVER, THE, 1933
CHASING TROUBLE, 1940
CHEAPER TO KEEP HER, 1980
CHECKMATE, 1973
CHEECH AND CHONG'S NEXT MOVIE, 1980
CHEECH AND CHONG'S NICE DREAMS, 1981
**CHEECH AND CHONG'S THE CORSICAN
    BROTHERS, 1984**
CHEERS OF THE CROWD, 1936
CHILDISH THINGS, 1969
CHILDREN, THE, 1980
CHILDREN OF BABYLON, 1980
CHILDREN OF DREAMS, 1931
CHINATOWN AFTER DARK, 1931
CIAO MANHATTAN, 1973
CITY LOVERS, 1982
CLASS OF 1984, 1982
COBRA, 1986
COLLEGE COQUETTE, THE, 1929
COLOR ME BLOOD RED, 1965
COLORADO KID, 1938
COMBAT SHOCK, 1986
COME BACK BABY, 1968
COMETOGETHER, 1971
COMPROMISED!, 1931
CONFESSIONAL, THE, 1977
CONSPIRACY, 1930
CONTACTO CHICANO, 1986
CONVICTS AT LARGE, 1938
CORPSE GRINDERS, THE, 1972
COSSACKS OF THE DON, 1932
COTTONPICKIN' CHICKENPICKERS, 1967
COUNTRY BOY, 1966
COUNTRY BRIDE, 1938
COUNTRY DOCTOR, THE, 1963
COVER ME BABE, 1970
COWARDS, 1970
CRACKERS, 1984
CRAZE, 1974
CRAZY MAMA, 1975
CRIMES OF PASSION, 1984
CRIMINALS WITHIN, 1941
CRIMSON CULT, THE, 1970
CROCODILE, 1979
CRUISING, 1980
CRY DR. CHICAGO, 1971
CRY WILDERNESS, 1987
CRYPT OF THE LIVING DEAD, 1973
CUBA CROSSING, 1980
CUCKOO PATROL, 1965
CURIOUS FEMALE, THE, 1969
CURSE OF THE BLOOD GHOULS, 1969
CURSE OF THE CRYING WOMAN, THE, 1969
CURSE OF THE PINK PANTHER, 1983
CURSE OF THE STONE HAND, 1965
CURTAINS, 1983
DADDY'S DEADLY DARLING, 1984
DANGEROUS PARTNERS, 1945
DARK VENTURE, 1956
DARKTOWN STRUTTERS, 1975
DATE WITH DEATH, A, 1959
DAY AFTER HALLOWEEN, THE, 1981
DAY OF THE ANIMALS, 1977
DAYTONA BEACH WEEKEND, 1965
DE SADE, 1969
DEAD PEOPLE, 1974
DEADLY FEMALES, THE, 1976
DEADLY SPAWN, THE, 1983
DEADLY TWINS, 1988
DEADTIME STORIES, 1987
DEADWOOD '76, 1965
DEAR, DEAD DELILAH, 1972
DEATH GAME, 1977
DEATH MACHINES, 1976
DEATH WISH 3, 1985
DEATH WISH II, 1982
DEATHMASTER, THE, 1972
DEATHROW GAMESHOW, 1987
DECOY FOR TERROR, 1970
DEFEAT OF HANNIBAL, THE, 1937

DEMON LOVER, THE, 1977
DEMONS, 1985
DESERT WARRIOR, 1985
DESPERATE WOMEN, THE, 1954
DEVIL GODDESS, 1955
DEVIL WOMAN, 1976
DEVIL'S COMMANDMENT, THE, 1956
DEVIL'S EXPRESS, 1975
DEVIL'S NIGHTMARE, THE, 1971
DEVIL'S WEDDING NIGHT, THE, 1973
DEVIL'S WIDOW, THE, 1972
DID YOU HEAR THE ONE ABOUT THE TRAVELING
    SALESLADY?, 1968
DIE LAUGHING, 1980
DILLINGER, 1973
DIRTY LAUNDRY, 1987
DIRTY O'NEIL, 1974
DIVINE MR. J., THE, 1974
DOCTOR DETROIT, 1983
DR. JEKYLL AND THE WOLFMAN, 1971
DR. JEKYLL'S DUNGEON OF DEATH, 1982
DR. MINX, 1975
DR. TERROR'S GALLERY OF HORRORS, 1967
DOG DAY, 1984
DOGS, 1976
DOIN' TIME, 1985
DOLL SQUAD, THE, 1973
DON'T GO IN THE HOUSE, 1980
DON'T LOOK IN THE BASEMENT, 1973
DON'T OPEN THE WINDOW, 1974
DON'T OPEN TILL CHRISTMAS, 1984
DOOMED TO DIE, 1985
DOOMSDAY MACHINE, 1967
DOUBLE EXPOSURE, 1982
DRACULA VERSUS FRANKENSTEIN, 1972
DREAMANIAC, 1987
DREI GEGEN DREI, 1985
DRUM, 1976
DRUMS OF TABU, THE, 1967
DUEL OF CHAMPIONS, 1964
DUNGEONS OF HARROW, 1964
DYNAMITE JACK, 1961
DYNAMITE JOHNSON, 1978
EARTHQUAKE, 1974
EATING RAOUL, 1982
EDGE OF FURY, 1958
ELLIE, 1984
EMBALMER, THE, 1966
ENDANGERED SPECIES, 1982
ENDLESS LOVE, 1981
ESCAPES, 1987
EVERYTHING'S DUCKY, 1961
EVICTORS, THE, 1979
EVILS OF THE NIGHT, 1985
EXECUTIONER PART II, THE, 1984
EXORCISM'S DAUGHTER, 1974
EXOTIC ONES, THE, 1968
EXTERMINATOR, THE, 1980
EXTERMINATOR 2, 1984
EXTRAORDINARY SEAMAN, THE, 1969
EYE CREATURES, THE, 1965
EYEBALL, 1978
EYES OF A STRANGER, 1980
FAIR GAME, 1985
FANNY HILL: MEMOIRS OF A WOMAN OF
    PLEASURE, 1965
FANTASIES, 1981
FANTASM, 1976
FARMER, THE, 1977
FEMALE BUNCH, THE, 1969
FEMALE BUTCHER, THE, 1972
FIGHT FOR YOUR LIFE, 1977
FIGHTING PLAYBOY, 1937
FINAL CHAPTER—WALKING TALL, 1977
FINAL EXAM, 1981
FIRE IN THE NIGHT, 1986
FIRECRACKER, 1981
FIREHOUSE, 1987
FIRST BLOOD, 1982
FIRST FAMILY, 1980
FIRST TURN-ON?, THE, 1984
FIST OF FEAR, TOUCH OF DEATH, 1980
FLAP, 1970
FLESHBURN, 1984
FLIGHT OF THE LOST BALLOON, 1961
FLIGHT TO NOWHERE, 1946

FLY NOW, PAY LATER, 1969
FOES, 1977
FOOD OF THE GODS, THE, 1976
FOR LOVE AND MONEY, 1967
FOR SINGLES ONLY, 1968
FORCE BEYOND, THE, 1978
FOREPLAY, 1975
FORGOTTEN COMMANDMENTS, 1932
FRANKENSTEIN CONQUERS THE WORLD, 1964
FRANKENSTEIN GENERAL HOSPITAL, 1988
FRANKENSTEIN-ITALIAN STYLE, 1977
FRANKENSTEIN MEETS THE SPACE MONSTER,
    1965
FRANKENSTEIN'S DAUGHTER, 1958
FREE RIDE, 1986
FRESH HORSES, 1988
FRIDAY THE 13TH, 1980
FRIDAY THE 13TH, PART V—A NEW BEGINNING,
    1985
FRIDAY THE 13TH PART VII—THE NEW BLOOD,
    1988
FRIDAY THE 13TH PART II, 1981
FRIDAY THE 13TH—THE FINAL CHAPTER, 1984
FULL CIRCLE, 1935
FUNNY MONEY, 1983
GALACTIC GIGOLO, 1988
GAMERA THE INVINCIBLE, 1966
GARBAGE PAIL KIDS MOVIE, THE, 1987
GARDEN OF THE DEAD, 1972
GAS, 1981
GATES OF HELL, THE, 1983
GEEK MAGGOT BINGO, 1983
GETTING TOGETHER, 1976
GHASTLY ONES, THE, 1968
GHOST, THE, 1965
GHOST FEVER, 1987
GHOST OF DRAGSTRIP HOLLOW, 1959
GIANT FROM THE UNKNOWN, 1958
GIANT SPIDER INVASION, THE, 1975
GIMME AN 'F', 1984
GIRL FROM STARSHIP VENUS, THE, 1975
GIRL GRABBERS, THE, 1968
GIRL IN LOVER'S LANE, THE, 1960
GIRL IN THE KREMLIN, THE, 1957
GIRL ON THE BRIDGE, THE, 1951
GIRL, THE BODY, AND THE PILL, THE, 1967
GIRLS FROM THUNDER STRIP, THE, 1966
GIRLS NIGHT OUT, 1984
GLEN OR GLENDA, 1953
GLORY STOMPERS, THE, 1967
GODZILLA VERSUS THE SMOG MONSTER, 1972
GOING BERSERK, 1983
GOLDEN APPLES OF THE SUN, 1971
GOLDENGIRL, 1979
GOLIATHON, 1979
GONG SHOW MOVIE, THE, 1980
GOOD LUCK, MISS WYCKOFF, 1979
GOOD MORNING... AND GOODBYE, 1967
GOODBYE EMMANUELLE, 1980
GOODBYE, NORMA JEAN, 1976
GORP, 1980
GRAVE OF THE VAMPIRE, 1972
GRAVEYARD OF HORROR, 1971
GREAT POWER, THE, 1929
GREAT WALL OF CHINA, THE, 1970
GREATEST, THE, 1977
GROUND ZERO, 1973
GRUESOME TWOSOME, 1968
GRUNT! THE WRESTLING MOVIE, 1985
GUARDIAN OF HELL, 1985
GUERRILLA GIRL, 1953
GUESS WHAT WE LEARNED IN SCHOOL TODAY?,
    1970
GUYANA, CULT OF THE DAMNED, 1980
HAMBURGER, 1986
HAPPY BIRTHDAY, DAVY, 1970
HAPPY HOOKER GOES TO HOLLYWOOD, THE, 1980
HAPPY HOUR, 1987
HARD TRAIL, 1969
HARDCORE, 1979
HARPER VALLEY, P.T.A., 1978
HAZEL'S PEOPLE, 1978
HEAD OFFICE, 1986
HEADIN' FOR BROADWAY, 1980
HELL AND HIGH WATER, 1933
HELL NIGHT, 1981

HELL SQUAD, 1986
HELL UP IN HARLEM, 1973
HELLCATS, THE, 1968
HELLO LONDON, 1958
HELLO SUCKER, 1941
HELL'S ANGELS ON WHEELS, 1967
HELL'S ANGELS '69, 1969
HELL'S CHOSEN FEW, 1968
HERCULES, 1983
HERCULES II, 1985
HERO FOR A DAY, 1939
HEROES FOR SALE, 1933
HEROES OF THE ALAMO, 1938
HIGH COUNTRY, THE, 1981
HILLBILLY BLITZKRIEG, 1942
HIT MAN, 1972
HITCHHIKERS, THE, 1972
HOG WILD, 1980
HOLLYWOOD HIGH, 1977
HOLLYWOOD HIGH PART II, 1984
HOLLYWOOD HOT TUBS, 1984
HOLLYWOOD KNIGHTS, THE, 1980
HOME IS WHERE THE HART IS, 1987
HOMEWORK, 1982
HONEYMOON OF TERROR, 1961
HOOKED GENERATION, THE, 1969
HORROR HIGH, 1974
HORROR ISLAND, 1941
HORROR OF THE BLOOD MONSTERS, 1970
HORROR PLANET, 1982
HOSPITAL MASSACRE, 1982
HOSPITAL MASSACRE, 1984
HOT CHILI, 1986
HOT SPUR, 1968
HOUSE BY THE CEMETERY, THE, 1984
HOUSE OF EXORCISM, THE, 1976
HOUSE OF FREAKS, 1973
HOUSE OF PSYCHOTIC WOMEN, THE, 1973
HOUSE OF WHIPCORD, 1974
HOUSE ON THE EDGE OF THE PARK, 1985
HUNCHBACK OF THE MORGUE, THE, 1972
HUNGER, THE, 1983
HURRICANE, 1979
HYPNOTIZED, 1933
HYSTERICAL, 1983
I CAN'T GIVE YOU ANYTHING BUT LOVE, BABY,
    1940
I COULD NEVER HAVE SEX WITH ANY MAN WHO
    HAS SO LITTLE REGARD FOR MY HUSBAND, 1973
I DISMEMBER MAMA, 1974
I EAT YOUR SKIN, 1971
I ESCAPED FROM DEVIL'S ISLAND, 1973
I SPIT ON YOUR GRAVE, 1983
I WAS A TEENAGE T.V. TERRORIST, 1987
ICE, 1970
IF EVER I SEE YOU AGAIN, 1978
ILLIAC PASSION, THE, 1968
I'M GOING TO GET YOU ... ELLIOT BOY, 1971
IMPULSE, 1975
IN GOD WE TRUST, 1980
INCHON, 1981
INCREDIBLE INVASION, THE, 1971
INNERVIEW, THE, 1974
INSIDE AMY, 1975
INSTANT JUSTICE, 1986
INVINCIBLE SIX, THE, 1970
INVISIBLE KID, THE, 1988
IS THIS TRIP REALLY NECESSARY?, 1970
ISLAND, THE, 1980
ISLAND CAPTIVES, 1937
ISLAND CLAWS, 1981
IT SEEMED LIKE A GOOD IDEA AT THE TIME, 1975
IT'S HOT IN PARADISE, 1962
JAGUAR LIVES, 1979
JAILBREAKERS, THE, 1960
JENNIFER, 1978
JENNIFER ON MY MIND, 1971
JESUS, 1979
JET ATTACK, 1958
JOCKS, 1987
JOHNNY BE GOOD, 1988
JOY, 1983
JOY OF SEX, 1984
JUNGLE, THE, 1952
JUST FOR THE HELL OF IT, 1968
KID FROM AMARILLO, THE, 1951

BOLD: Films on Videocassette

KILL SQUAD, 1982
KILL ZONE, 1985
KILLER FISH, 1979
KILLER WORKOUT, 1987
KILLPOINT, 1984
KINFOLK, 1970
KITTEN WITH A WHIP, 1964
LA NAVE DE LOS MONSTRUOS, 1959
LADIES OF THE LOTUS, 1987
LADY CHATTERLEY'S LOVER, 1981
LADY FRANKENSTEIN, 1971
LADY FROM NOWHERE, 1931
LADY GREY, 1980
LADY, STAY DEAD, 1982
L'AMOUR, 1973
LAND OF DOOM, 1986
L'ANNEE DES MEDUSES, 1987
LAS VEGAS WEEKEND, 1985
LAST HORROR FILM, THE, 1984
LAST HOUSE ON DEAD END STREET, 1977
LAST MOMENT, THE, 1966
LAST PORNO FLICK, THE, 1974
LAST RESORT, THE, 1986
LAST RIDE, THE, 1932
LAST RITES, 1980
LATE LIZ, THE, 1971
LAUGHING ANNE, 1954
LAW OF THE SEA, 1932
LAW OF THE TONG, 1931
LAW OF THE WEST, 1949
LE GENDARME ET LES EXTRATERRESTRES, 1978
LEGACY OF BLOOD, 1978
LEGEND OF THE LONE RANGER, THE, 1981
LEGEND OF THE WOLF WOMAN, THE, 1977
LEONARD PART 6, 1987
LIPSTICK, 1976
LITTLE AUSTRALIANS, 1940
LIVING LEGEND, 1980
LIVING VENUS, 1961
LIZA, 1976
LOCAL COLOR, 1978
LOCK UP YOUR DAUGHTERS, 1969
LONELY LADY, THE, 1983
LONESOME COWBOYS, 1968
LONG SHIPS, THE, 1964
LONGSHOT, THE, 1986
LOOSE SCREWS, 1985
LOS PLATILLOS VOLADORES, 1955
LOSERS, THE, 1968
LOSERS, THE, 1970
LOST HORIZON, 1973
LOTTERY BRIDE, THE, 1930
LOVE NOW...PAY LATER, 1966
LOVELINES, 1984
LUPE, 1967
LUST IN THE DUST, 1985
LUXURY LINER, 1933
MACHINE GUN MAMA, 1944
MADAME DEATH, 1968
MADMAN, 1982
MAGIC SPECTACLES, 1961
MAIDSTONE, 1970
MAIN EVENT, THE, 1938
MALAY NIGHTS, 1933
MALE SERVICE, 1966
MALENKA, THE VAMPIRE, 1972
MALIBU HIGH, 1979
MAN FROM O.R.G.Y., THE, 1970
MAN HUNTERS OF THE CARIBBEAN, 1938
MAN OF VIOLENCE, 1970
MAN WHO TURNED TO STONE, THE, 1957
MAN WHO WASN'T THERE, THE, 1983
MAN WITH TWO HEADS, THE, 1972
MANHATTAN BABY, 1986
MANIAC, 1934
MANIAC!, 1977
MANIAC MANSION, 1978
MANKILLERS, 1987
MANOS, THE HANDS OF FATE, 1966
MANSION OF THE DOOMED, 1976
MANSTER, THE, 1962
MARDI GRAS MASSACRE, 1978
MARIGOLD MAN, 1970
MARS NEEDS WOMEN, 1966
MASQUERADE, 1929
MASTER GUNFIGHTER, THE, 1975

MAUSOLEUM, 1983
MAXIMUM OVERDRIVE, 1986
MAYA, 1982
M'BLIMEY, 1931
ME AND MY BROTHER, 1969
MEAT CLEAVER MASSACRE, 1977
MEGAFORCE, 1982
MERRY-G0-ROUND, 1948
MESA OF LOST WOMEN, THE, 1956
METALSTORM: THE DESTRUCTION OF
    JARED-SYN, 1983
MICROWAVE MASSACRE, 1983
MID-DAY MISTRESS, 1968
MIGHTY GORGA, THE, 1969
MOB TOWN, 1941
MOMENT BY MOMENT, 1978
MOMMIE DEAREST, 1981
MONDO TRASHO, 1970
MONGREL, 1982
MONSIGNOR, 1982
MONSTER, 1979
MONSTER A GO-GO, 1965
MONSTER DOG, 1986
MONSTER FROM THE OCEAN FLOOR, THE, 1954
MONSTER SHARK, 1986
MONTANA KID, THE, 1931
MONTY PYTHON'S THE MEANING OF LIFE, 1983
MOON OVER THE ALLEY, 1980
MOONFIRE, 1970
MOONLIGHTING WIVES, 1966
MOONSHINE MOUNTAIN, 1964
MOONSHINER'S WOMAN, 1968
MORTUARY, 1983
MOTEL HELL, 1980
MOTHER, JUGS & SPEED, 1976
MOTHER'S DAY, 1980
MOTOR PSYCHO, 1965
MOUNTAINTOP MOTEL MASSACRE, 1986
MOUNTED FURY, 1931
MOVE, 1970
MUMSY, NANNY, SONNY, AND GIRLY, 1970
MUNCHIES, 1987
MURDER IN MISSISSIPPI, 1965
MURDER IN THE NIGHT, 1940
MURDER IS NEWS, 1939
MURDER ON THE WATERFRONT, 1943
MURDERERS' ROW, 1966
MUSIC LOVERS, THE, 1971
MUSICAL MUTINY, 1970
MUSTANG, 1959
MUTANT HUNT, 1987
MY BLOODY VALENTINE, 1981
MY MAN ADAM, 1986
MY SCIENCE PROJECT, 1985
MY WAY HOME, 1978
MYRT AND MARGE, 1934
MYSTERIES, 1979
MYSTERIOUS DOCTOR, THE, 1943
MYSTERY OF THE WHITE ROOM, 1939
MYSTIQUE, 1981
NABONGA, 1944
NAKED ZOO, THE, 1970
NANA, 1983
NARCOTICS STORY, THE, 1958
NATION AFLAME, 1937
NATIONAL LAMPOON'S CLASS REUNION, 1982
NAVY SPY, 1937
NECROPOLIS, 1987
NERO'S MISTRESS, 1962
NEW BARBARIANS, THE, 1983
NEW HOUSE ON THE LEFT, THE, 1978
NEW KIDS, THE, 1985
NEW YEAR'S EVIL, 1980
NEW YORK'S FINEST, 1988
NIGHT OF BLOODY HORROR, 1969
NIGHT OF THE BLOODY APES, 1968
NIGHT OF THE GHOULS, 1959
NIGHT OF THE PROWLER, THE, 1979
NIGHT OF THE WITCHES, 1970
NIGHT OF THE ZOMBIES, 1981
NIGHT OF THE ZOMBIES, 1983
NIGHT PATROL, 1984
NIGHT THEY ROBBED BIG BERTHA'S, THE, 1975
NIGHTMARE, 1981
NIGHTMARE IN WAX, 1969
NIGHTMARE WEEKEND, 1986

NINJA TURF, 1986
NO DEAD HEROES, 1987
NO ORCHIDS FOR MISS BLANDISH, 1948
NO WAY BACK, 1976
NOBODY'S PERFEKT, 1981
NOCTURNA, 1979
NORTHVILLE CEMETERY MASSACRE, THE, 1976
NUTCRACKER, 1982
OCEAN DRIVE WEEKEND, 1986
OCTAMAN, 1971
ODDO, 1967
OFFENDERS, THE, 1980
OFFICE GIRLS, 1974
OH! CALCUTTA!, 1972
OLGA'S GIRLS, 1964
ON HER BED OF ROSES, 1966
ONE NIGHT ONLY, 1986
ONE PLUS ONE, 1961
1,000 CONVICTS AND A WOMAN, 1971
OPHELIA, 1964
ORGY OF THE DEAD, 1965
OUT OF BOUNDS, 1986
OVERKILL, 1987
PANDEMONIUM, 1982
PANTHER SQUAD, 1986
PAR OU T'ES RENTRE? ON T'A PAS VUE SORTIR,
    1984
PARADISE, 1982
PARASITE, 1982
PARDON MY BRUSH, 1964
PARTY PARTY, 1983
PASSAGE, THE, 1979
PAWNEE, 1957
PENITENTIARY II, 1982
PENTHOUSE, THE, 1967
PERILS OF P.K., THE, 1986
PETEY WHEATSTRAW, 1978
PETS, 1974
PHYNX, THE, 1970
PICK-UP SUMMER, 1981
PINK MOTEL, 1983
PIRATE MOVIE, THE, 1982
PIT STOP, 1969
PLACE FOR LOVERS, A, 1969
PLAN 9 FROM OUTER SPACE, 1959
PLAYERS, 1979
PLAYGIRLS AND THE BELLBOY, THE, 1962
PLAYGROUND, THE, 1965
PLEASURE, 1933
PLEASURE PLANTATION, 1970
PLEDGEMASTERS, THE, 1971
POLICE ACADEMY 2: THEIR FIRST ASSIGNMENT,
    1985
POLICEMAN OF THE 16TH PRECINCT, THE, 1963
PREACHERMAN, 1971
PRETTY BUT WICKED, 1965
PRETTY SMART, 1987
PRIME TIME, THE, 1960
PRINCESS ACADEMY, THE, 1987
PRIVATE SCHOOL, 1983
PROMISES, PROMISES, 1963
PROWL GIRLS, 1968
PSYCHO FROM TEXAS, 1982
QUICK, LET'S GET MARRIED, 1965
QUINTET, 1979
RACING BLOOD, 1938
RACING FEVER, 1964
RACING LUCK, 1948
RACQUET, 1979
RAGE, THE, 1963
RAMBO: FIRST BLOOD, PART II, 1985
RATS ARE COMING! THE WEREWOLVES ARE
    HERE!, THE, 1972
RAW COURAGE, 1984
RAW FORCE, 1982
RECRUITS, 1986
RED HEAT, 1988
REDEEMER, THE, 1978
REDNECK, 1975
RENTED LIPS, 1988
RETURN OF SABATA, 1972
RETURN OF THE LASH, 1947
RETURNING, THE, 1983
REVENGE, 1986
REVENGE OF THE CHEERLEADERS, 1976
REVENGE OF THE SHOGUN WOMEN, 1982

RHINESTONE, 1984
RIDE BEYOND VENGEANCE, 1966
RIDIN' LAW, 1930
RIDIN' THE LONE TRAIL, 1937
ROBOT HOLOCAUST, 1987
ROBOT MONSTER, 1953
ROBOT VS. THE AZTEC MUMMY, THE, 1965
ROCK BABY, ROCK IT, 1957
ROCK 'N' ROLL NIGHTMARE, 1987
ROCKET ATTACK, U.S.A., 1961
ROLLER BLADE, 1986
ROLLER BOOGIE, 1979
ROOMMATES, 1971
R.O.T.O.R., 1988
ROTWEILER: DOGS OF HELL, 1984
R.P.M., 1970
RUN FOR THE HILLS, 1953
RUNNING OUT OF LUCK, 1986
RYDER, P.I., 1986
SAGA OF THE VIKING WOMEN AND THEIR
   VOYAGE TO THE WATERS OF THE GREAT SEA
   SERPENT, THE, 1957
SALOME, 1986
SAMMY STOPS THE WORLD, 1978
SANTA CLAUS CONQUERS THE MARTIANS, 1964
SANTO CONTRA EL CEREBRO DIABOLICO, 1962
SANTO Y BLUE DEMON CONTRA LOS MONSTRUOS,
   1968
SATAN IN HIGH HEELS, 1962
SATAN'S CHEERLEADERS, 1977
SATAN'S MISTRESS, 1982
SATAN'S SADIST, 1969
SATAN'S SLAVE, 1976
SAVAGE ABDUCTION, 1975
SAVAGE ISLAND, 1985
SAVAGE WEEKEND, 1983
SCALPS, 1983
SCARFACE, 1983
SCAVENGERS, THE, 1969
SCHOOL SPIRIT, 1985
SCORCHY, 1976
SCREAM BLOODY MURDER, 1972
SCREAM FOR HELP, 1984
SCREAMS OF A WINTER NIGHT, 1979
SCREEN TEST, 1986
SCREWBALLS, 1983
SCUM OF THE EARTH, 1963
SCUM OF THE EARTH, 1976
SECOND THOUGHTS, 1983
SECOND WIFE, 1936
SECRET AGENT SUPER DRAGON, 1966
SECRETS OF SEX, 1970
SEDUCTION, THE, 1982
SEEDS OF EVIL, 1981
SELF-PORTRAIT, 1973
SGT. PEPPER'S LONELY HEARTS CLUB BAND, 1978
SERGEANT, THE, 1968
SEVEN HOURS TO JUDGEMENT, 1988
7254, 1971
SEX O'CLOCK NEWS, THE, 1986
SHADOWS RUN BLACK, 1986
SHE, 1985
SHE-DEVILS ON WHEELS, 1968
SHE MAN, THE, 1967
SHOCK TREATMENT, 1981
SHOULD A DOCTOR TELL?, 1931
SHRIEK OF THE MUTILATED, 1974
SILENT NIGHT, DEADLY NIGHT PART II, 1987
SILHOUETTES, 1982
SILIP, 1985
SILVER BANDIT, THE, 1950
SINCERELY YOURS, 1955
SING SINNER, SING, 1933
SINGIN' IN THE CORN, 1946
SINISTER URGE, THE, 1961
SIZZLE BEACH, U.S.A., 1986
SKI BUM, THE, 1971
SKIDOO, 1968
SLEEPAWAY CAMP 2: UNHAPPY CAMPERS, 1988
SLUMBER PARTY '57, 1977
SMOKEY AND THE BANDIT—PART 3, 1983
SMOKEY BITES THE DUST, 1981
SMOKING GUNS, 1934
SNOW CREATURE, THE, 1954
SNOW DEVILS, THE, 1965
SO SAD ABOUT GLORIA, 1973

SOD SISTERS, 1969
SOLARBABIES, 1986
SOLOMON KING, 1974
SOME KIND OF A NUT, 1969
SORORITY HOUSE MASSACRE, 1986
SPACE RAIDERS, 1983
SPACED OUT, 1981
SPANISH FLY, 1975
SPASMS, 1983
SPEED CRAZY, 1959
SPEED LIMITED, 1940
SPEED LOVERS, 1968
SPEED REPORTER, 1936
SPHINX, 1981
SPIDER BABY, 1968
SPLATTER UNIVERSITY, 1984
SPLITZ, 1984
SPOILED ROTTEN, 1968
SPOOK WHO SAT BY THE DOOR, THE, 1973
SPORTING CLUB, THE, 1971
STAND ALONE, 1985
STANLEY, 1973
STATUE, THE, 1971
STAYING ALIVE, 1983
STEPHEN KING'S SILVER BULLET, 1985
STEWARDESS SCHOOL, 1986
STIGMA, 1972
STITCHES, 1985
STORY OF MANKIND, THE, 1957
STRANGE FETISHES, THE, 1967
STRAW DOGS, 1971
STREET PEOPLE, 1976
STRICTLY CONFIDENTIAL, 1959
STRICTLY DYNAMITE, 1934
STRICTLY IN THE GROOVE, 1942
STROKER ACE, 1983
STUCK ON YOU, 1983
SUMMER CAMP, 1979
SUNSET STRIP, 1985
SUPERBEAST, 1972
SUPERCHICK, 1973
SUPERSTITION, 1985
SURF II, 1984
SURROGATE, THE, 1984
SURVIVAL, 1976
SURVIVE!, 1977
SWAMP WOMAN, 1941
SWAP MEET, 1979
SWAPPERS, THE, 1970
SWEET SUGAR, 1972
SWORD OF HEAVEN, 1985
TARZAN, THE APE MAN, 1981
TASTE OF BLOOD, A, 1967
TASTE OF FLESH, A, 1967
TATTOO, 1981
TEEN-AGE STRANGLER, 1967
TEENAGE MONSTER, 1958
TEENAGE MOTHER, 1967
TEENAGE ZOMBIES, 1960
TEENAGERS FROM OUTER SPACE, 1959
TEL AVIV TAXI, 1957
TEMPTER, THE, 1978
TEN WHO DARED, 1960
TERROR-CREATURES FROM THE GRAVE, 1967
TERROR IN THE JUNGLE, 1968
TERROR ON TOUR, 1980
TEXAS CHAINSAW MASSACRE PART 2, THE, 1986
THANK GOD IT'S FRIDAY, 1978
THAT HAGEN GIRL, 1947
THAT KIND OF GIRL, 1963
THAT MAN BOLT, 1973
THERE GOES THE BRIDE, 1980
THEY CALL HER ONE EYE, 1974
THEY CALL ME BRUCE?, 1982
THEY SAVED HITLER'S BRAIN, 1964
THINGS ARE TOUGH ALL OVER, 1982
THINK DIRTY, 1970
THIRSTY DEAD, THE, 1975
THIS IS A HIJACK, 1973
THIS IS NOT A TEST, 1962
THIS STUFF'LL KILL YA!, 1971
300 YEAR WEEKEND, 1971
THREE ON A COUCH, 1966
THRILL OF YOUTH, 1932
THUNDERBOLT, 1936

TNT JACKSON, 1975
TO ALL A GOODNIGHT, 1980
TO CATCH A COP, 1984
TONIGHT FOR SURE, 1962
TOO YOUNG, TOO IMMORAL!, 1962
TOOLBOX MURDERS, THE, 1978
TORMENTED, THE, 1978
TORTURE DUNGEON, 1970
TOUCH OF HER FLESH, THE, 1967
TOURIST TRAP, THE, 1979
TRACK OF THE MOONBEAST, 1976
TRACKDOWN, 1976
TRADER HORNEE, 1970
TRAIN TO TOMBSTONE, 1950
TRAMPLERS, THE, 1966
TREASURE OF JAMAICA REEF, THE, 1976
TRIAL OF BILLY JACK, THE, 1974
TROG, 1970
TUFF TURF, 1985
TUNNELVISION, 1976
TURN ON TO LOVE, 1969
TWILIGHT PEOPLE, 1972
TWO OF A KIND, 1983
TWO THOUSAND MANIACS, 1964
2020 TEXAS GLADIATORS, 1985
UNASHAMED, 1938
UNCLE SCAM, 1981
UNDER THE CHERRY MOON, 1986
UNDER THE RAINBOW, 1981
UNDERSEA GIRL, 1957
UNDERTAKER AND HIS PALS, THE, 1966
UNDERWATER CITY, THE, 1962
UNHINGED, 1982
UNINVITED, THE, 1988
UNTAMED MISTRESS, 1960
UNTAMED WOMEN, 1952
UP FROM THE DEPTHS, 1979
UP IN SMOKE, 1978
UP YOUR TEDDY BEAR, 1970
V.D., 1961
VACATION, THE, 1971
VALLEY OF THE DOLLS, 1967
VALS, THE, 1985
VAMPIRE AND THE BALLERINA, THE, 1962
VAMPIRE HOOKERS, THE, 1979
VASECTOMY: A DELICATE MATTER, 1986
VELVET TRAP, THE, 1966
VENGEANCE OF THE VAMPIRE WOMEN, THE, 1969
VILLAIN, 1971
VIOLENT YEARS, THE, 1956
VOODOO HEARTBEAT, 1972
W, 1974
WACKO, 1983
WALK LIKE A MAN, 1987
WAR BETWEEN THE PLANETS, 1971
WAR OF THE GARGANTUAS, THE, 1970
WEEKEND WARRIORS, 1986
WEIRD ONES, THE, 1962
WELCOME TO BLOOD CITY, 1977
WEREWOLF IN A GIRL'S DORMITORY, 1961
WEST OF THE ROCKIES, 1929
WEST OF THE ROCKIES, 1931
WHAT COMES AROUND, 1986
WHEN TIME RAN OUT, 1980
WHEN WOMEN HAD TAILS, 1970
WHEN YOU COMIN' BACK, RED RYDER?, 1979
WHERE ARE THE CHILDREN?, 1986
WHERE IS PARSIFAL?, 1984
WHITE GORILLA, 1947
WHITE RAT, 1972
WHOLLY MOSES, 1980
WILD LIFE, THE, 1984
WILD ONES ON WHEELS, 1967
WILD PARTY, THE, 1975
WILD RIDERS, 1971
WILD SCENE, THE, 1970
WILD WEST WHOOPEE, 1931
WILD WHEELS, 1969
WILD WOMEN OF WONGO, THE, 1959
WILD WORLD OF BATWOMAN, THE, 1966
WINDFLOWERS, 1968
WINDSPLITTER, THE, 1971
WITHOUT WARNING, 1980
WIZARD OF GORE, THE, 1970
WIZARDS OF THE LOST KINGDOM, 1985
WOLVES, 1930

BOLD: Films on Videocassette

WOMAN HUNT, THE, 1975
WOMEN AND BLOODY TERROR, 1970
WOMEN IN CELL BLOCK 7, 1977
WOMEN MEN MARRY, 1931
WOMEN OF DESIRE, 1968
WOMEN'S PRISON MASSACRE, 1986
WONDER WOMEN, 1973
WORLD IS JUST A 'B' MOVIE, THE, 1971
WORM EATERS, THE, 1981
WRONG DAMN FILM, THE, 1975
XTRO, 1983
YEAR OF THE YAHOO, 1971
YETI, 1977
YOR, THE HUNTER FROM THE FUTURE, 1983
YOUNG CYCLE GIRLS, THE, 1979
YOUNG GRADUATES, THE, 1971
YOUTH AFLAME, 1945
ZERO IN THE UNIVERSE, 1966
ZOMBIE, 1980

FILMS BY PARENTAL RECOMMENDATION

Listed below are films included in THE MOTION PICTURE GUIDE and its Annuals by Parental Recommendation (PR), an evaluation of the film with respect to its suitability for children. The Parental Recommendations indicate:

AA: Good for children; A: Acceptable for children; C: Cautionary—some scenes may be objectionable; O: Objectionable for children

AA
AARON SLICK FROM PUNKIN CRICK, 1952
ABBOTT AND COSTELLO IN HOLLYWOOD, 1945
ABE LINCOLN IN ILLINOIS, 1940
ABRAHAM LINCOLN, 1930
ABSENT-MINDED PROFESSOR, THE, 1961
ACROSS THE GREAT DIVIDE, 1976
ADVENTURE IN BALTIMORE, 1949
ADVENTURE IN THE HOPFIELDS, 1954
ADVENTURE OF SHERLOCK HOLMES' SMARTER BROTHER, THE, 1975
ADVENTURES OF BULLWHIP GRIFFIN, THE, 1967
ADVENTURES OF FRONTIER FREMONT, THE, 1976
ADVENTURES OF GALLANT BESS, 1948
ADVENTURES OF HUCKLEBERRY FINN, THE, 1960
ADVENTURES OF ICHABOD AND MR. TOAD, 1949
ADVENTURES OF MARK TWAIN, THE, 1985
ADVENTURES OF MARK TWAIN, THE, 1944
ADVENTURES OF ROBIN HOOD, THE, 1938
ADVENTURES OF ROBINSON CRUSOE, THE, 1954
ADVENTURES OF THE AMERICAN RABBIT, THE, 1986
ADVENTURES OF THE WILDERNESS FAMILY, THE, 1975
ADVENTURES OF TOM SAWYER, THE, 1938
AFRICA SCREAMS, 1949
AFRICA—TEXAS STYLE!, 1967
AFRICAN QUEEN, THE, 1951
AH, WILDERNESS!, 1935
A-HAUNTING WE WILL GO, 1942
AIR RAID WARDENS, 1943
ALADDIN AND HIS LAMP, 1952
ALAKAZAM THE GREAT!, 1961
ALAMO, THE, 1960
ALEXANDER'S RAGTIME BAND, 1938
ALF'S BUTTON, 1930
ALI BABA AND THE FORTY THIEVES, 1944
ALI BABA GOES TO TOWN, 1937
ALIAS BILLY THE KID, 1946
ALIBI IKE, 1935
ALICE IN WONDERLAND, 1933
ALICE IN WONDERLAND, 1951
ALIVE AND KICKING, 1962
ALL ASHORE, 1953
ALL CREATURES GREAT AND SMALL, 1975
ALL MINE TO GIVE, 1957
ALL OVER THE TOWN, 1949
ALL THINGS BRIGHT AND BEAUTIFUL, 1979
ALMOST ANGELS, 1962
ALONE ON THE PACIFIC, 1964
ALWAYS IN MY HEART, 1942
ALWAYS IN TROUBLE, 1938
AMAZING DOBERMANS, THE, 1976
AMAZING MRS. HOLLIDAY, 1943
AMERICAN IN PARIS, AN, 1951
AMERICAN TAIL, AN, 1986
AMPHIBIOUS MAN, THE, 1961
AMY, 1981
ANCHORS AWEIGH, 1945
AND NOW MIGUEL, 1966
AND SO THEY WERE MARRIED, 1936
AND THERE CAME A MAN, 1968
ANDY HARDY COMES HOME, 1958
ANDY HARDY GETS SPRING FEVER, 1939
ANDY HARDY MEETS DEBUTANTE, 1940
ANDY HARDY'S BLONDE TROUBLE, 1944
ANDY HARDY'S DOUBLE LIFE, 1942
ANDY HARDY'S PRIVATE SECRETARY, 1941
ANGEL COMES TO BROOKLYN, AN, 1945
ANGEL IN MY POCKET, 1969
ANGELS IN THE OUTFIELD, 1951
ANIMAL CRACKERS, 1930
ANNIE, 1982
ANNIE GET YOUR GUN, 1950
ANNIE OAKLEY, 1935
ANTS IN HIS PANTS, 1940
APPLE DUMPLING GANG, THE, 1975
APPLE DUMPLING GANG RIDES AGAIN, THE, 1979
APRIL LOVE, 1957

ARABIAN ADVENTURE, 1979
ARABIAN NIGHTS, 1942
ARCTIC FURY, 1949
ARE YOU THERE?, 1930
ARE YOU WITH IT?, 1948
ARGENTINE NIGHTS, 1940
ARISTOCATS, THE, 1970
ARIZONA WILDCAT, 1938
AROUND THE WORLD IN 80 DAYS, 1956
ARTISTS AND MODELS, 1937
AT THE CIRCUS, 1939
AWAKENING, THE, 1958
BABE RUTH STORY, THE, 1948
BABES IN ARMS, 1939
BABES IN TOYLAND, 1934
BABES IN TOYLAND, 1961
BABES ON BROADWAY, 1941
BABY, TAKE A BOW, 1934
BACHELOR AND THE BOBBY-SOXER, THE, 1947
BAD BASCOMB, 1946
BAD LITTLE ANGEL, 1939
BAMBI, 1942
BANDIT OF SHERWOOD FOREST, THE, 1946
BANJO, 1947
BAREFOOT EXECUTIVE, THE, 1971
BATMAN, 1966
BATTERIES NOT INCLUDED, 1987
BEAR, THE, 1963
BECAUSE YOU'RE MINE, 1952
BEDKNOBS AND BROOMSTICKS, 1971
BEDTIME FOR BONZO, 1951
BEDTIME STORY, A, 1933
BEDTIME STORY, 1938
BELLBOY, THE, 1960
BELLES OF ST. TRINIAN'S, THE, 1954
BELLES ON THEIR TOES, 1952
BELLS ARE RINGING, 1960
BELLS OF CORONADO, 1950
BELLS OF ROSARITA, 1945
BELLS OF ST. MARY'S, THE, 1945
BELSTONE FOX, THE, 1976
BENEATH THE PLANET OF THE APES, 1970
BENJAMIN, 1973
BENJI, 1974
BENJI THE HUNTED, 1987
BENNY GOODMAN STORY, THE, 1956
BERNARDINE, 1957
BEST MAN WINS, 1948
BEST THINGS IN LIFE ARE FREE, THE, 1956
BETRAYAL FROM THE EAST, 1945
BEWARE OF BLONDIE, 1950
BIBLE. . .IN THE BEGINNING, THE, 1966
BIG BROADCAST, THE, 1932
BIG BROADCAST OF 1936, THE, 1935
BIG BROADCAST OF 1937, THE, 1936
BIG BROADCAST OF 1938, THE, 1937
BIG CHIEF, THE, 1960
BIG CITY, 1948
BIG MOUTH, THE, 1967
BIG NOISE, THE, 1944
BIG RACE, THE, 1934
BIG RED, 1962
BIG STORE, THE, 1941
BIG TOWN, 1947
BIG TOWN AFTER DARK, 1947
BIG TOWN SCANDAL, 1948
BILL AND COO, 1947
BINGO BONGO, 1983
BIRDS OF A FEATHER, 1931
BISCUIT EATER, THE, 1940
BISCUIT EATER, THE, 1972
BISHOP MISBEHAVES, THE, 1933
BLACK BEAUTY, 1933
BLACK BEAUTY, 1946
BLACK BEAUTY, 1971
BLACK JACK, 1979
BLACK MIDNIGHT, 1949
BLACK STALLION, THE, 1979

BLACKBEARD'S GHOST, 1968
BLIND MAN'S BLUFF, 1936
BLOCKHEADS, 1938
BLONDIE, 1938
BLONDIE BRINGS UP BABY, 1939
BLONDIE GOES LATIN, 1941
BLONDIE GOES TO COLLEGE, 1942
BLONDIE HAS SERVANT TROUBLE, 1940
BLONDIE HITS THE JACKPOT, 1949
BLONDIE IN SOCIETY, 1941
BLONDIE IN THE DOUGH, 1947
BLONDIE KNOWS BEST, 1946
BLONDIE MEETS THE BOSS, 1939
BLONDIE ON A BUDGET, 1940
BLONDIE PLAYS CUPID, 1940
BLONDIE TAKES A VACATION, 1939
BLONDIE'S ANNIVERSARY, 1947
BLONDIE'S BIG DEAL, 1949
BLONDIE'S BIG MOMENT, 1947
BLONDIE'S BLESSED EVENT, 1942
BLONDIE'S HOLIDAY, 1947
BLONDIE'S HERO, 1950
BLONDIE'S LUCKY DAY, 1946
BLONDIE'S REWARD, 1948
BLONDIE'S SECRET, 1948
BLUE BIRD, THE, 1976
BLUE BIRD, THE, 1940
BLUE BLOOD, 1951
BLUE GRASS OF KENTUCKY, 1950
BLUE MONTANA SKIES, 1939
BLUE MURDER AT ST. TRINIAN'S, 1958
BLUE SIERRA, 1946
BLUE SKIES, 1946
BLUES BUSTERS, 1950
BMX BANDITS, 1983
BOATNIKS, THE, 1970
BOB MATHIAS STORY, THE, 1954
BODY SAID NO!, THE, 1950
BOEFJE, 1939
BON VOYAGE, 1962
BON VOYAGE, CHARLIE BROWN (AND DON'T COME BACK), 1980
BONNIE SCOTLAND, 1935
BONZO GOES TO COLLEGE, 1952
BORN FREE, 1966
BOY AND THE PIRATES, THE, 1960
BOY, DID I GET A WRONG NUMBER!, 1966
BOY NAMED CHARLIE BROWN, A, 1969
BOY TEN FEET TALL, A, 1965
BOY WHO CAUGHT A CROOK, 1961
BOY WHO STOLE A MILLION, THE, 1960
BOY WHO TURNED YELLOW, THE, 1972
BOY WITH THE GREEN HAIR, THE, 1949
BOYS IN BROWN, 1949
BOYS TOWN, 1938
BOYS WILL BE GIRLS, 1937
BRAVE ONE, THE, 1956
BRIGHT EYES, 1934
BRIGHTON STRANGLER, THE, 1945
BUCK PRIVATES, 1941
BUCK PRIVATES COME HOME, 1947
BUFFALO BILL, 1944
BUGS BUNNY, SUPERSTAR, 1975
BUGS BUNNY'S THIRD MOVIE—1001 RABBIT TALES, 1982
BUGSY MALONE, 1976
BUSH CHRISTMAS, 1947
BUSH CHRISTMAS, 1983
BUSHBABY, THE, 1970
C.H.O.M.P.S., 1979
CABIN IN THE SKY, 1943
CALAMITY JANE, 1953
CALAMITY THE COW, 1967
CALL OF THE WILD, 1935
CALLAWAY WENT THATAWAY, 1951
CAMEL BOY, THE, 1984
CAMMINA CAMMINA, 1983
CANDLESHOE, 1978
CANTERVILLE GHOST, THE, 1944

BOLD: Films on Videocassette

CAPTAIN EDDIE, 1945
CAPTAIN GRANT'S CHILDREN, 1939
CAPTAIN JANUARY, 1935
CAPTAINS COURAGEOUS, 1937
CARE BEARS ADVENTURE IN WONDERLAND, THE, 1987
CARE BEARS MOVIE II: A NEW GENERATION, 1986
CARE BEARS MOVIE, THE, 1985
CARSON CITY KID, 1940
CARYL OF THE MOUNTAINS, 1936
CASTAWAY COWBOY, THE, 1974
CAT, THE, 1966
CAT CREEPS, THE, 1930
CAT CREEPS, THE, 1946
CAT FROM OUTER SPACE, THE, 1978
CAT GANG, THE, 1959
CATTLE DRIVE, 1951
CAUGHT IN THE DRAFT, 1941
CAUGHT IN THE NET, 1960
CENTENNIAL SUMMER, 1946
CHALLENGE THE WILD, 1954
CHALLENGE TO LASSIE, 1949
CHAMP, 1931
CHAMP, THE, 1979
CHAMPAGNE FOR CAESAR, 1950
CHARGE OF THE MODEL-T'S, 1979
CHARIOTS OF FIRE, 1981
CHARLEY AND THE ANGEL, 1973
CHARLEY'S AUNT, 1941
CHARLIE MC CARTHY, DETECTIVE, 1939
CHARLIE, THE LONESOME COUGAR, 1967
CHARLOTTE'S WEB, 1973
CHEAPER BY THE DOZEN, 1950
CHILDREN, THE, 1949
CHIPMUNK ADVENTURE, THE, 1987
CHITTY CHITTY BANG BANG, 1968
CHRISTIAN THE LION, 1976
CHRISTMAS CAROL, A, 1938
CHRISTMAS CAROL, A, 1951
CHRISTMAS IN CONNECTICUT, 1945
CHRISTMAS TREE, THE, 1966
CINDERELLA, 1950
CINDERELLA JONES, 1946
CIRCUS BOY, 1947
CIRCUS FRIENDS, 1962
CISCO KID, 1931
CITIZEN SAINT, 1947
CITY OF MISSING GIRLS, 1941
CLAMBAKE, 1967
CLARENCE, THE CROSS-EYED LION, 1965
CLASH OF THE TITANS, 1981
CLAUDIA AND DAVID, 1946
CLOWN AND THE KIDS, THE, 1968
CLUE OF THE MISSING APE, THE, 1953
COCKEYED COWBOYS OF CALICO COUNTY, THE, 1970
COCKEYED MIRACLE, THE, 1946
COCOANUT GROVE, 1938
COME NEXT SPRING, 1956
COME OUT OF THE PANTRY, 1935
COME TO THE STABLE, 1949
COMIN' ROUND THE MOUNTAIN, 1951
COMIN' ROUND THE MOUNTAIN, 1936
COMIN' ROUND THE MOUNTAIN, 1940
COMPUTER WORE TENNIS SHOES, THE, 1970
CONDORMAN, 1981
CONNECTICUT YANKEE, A, 1931
CONNECTICUT YANKEE IN KING ARTHUR'S COURT, A, 1949
CONSPIRACY OF HEARTS, 1960
CORKY OF GASOLINE ALLEY, 1951
COSMIC EYE, THE, 1986
COUNT OF MONTE CRISTO, THE, 1934
COUNTDOWN TO DANGER, 1967
COURAGE OF BLACK BEAUTY, 1957
COURAGE OF LASSIE, 1946
COURT JESTER, THE, 1956
COURTSHIP OF EDDY'S FATHER, THE, 1963
COVER GIRL, 1944
COVERED TRAILER, THE, 1939
CRACKED NUTS, 1931
CRAZYLEGS, ALL AMERICAN, 1953
CRIME SCHOOL, 1938
CRIMSON TRAIL, THE, 1935
CRY FROM THE STREET, A, 1959
CRY WOLF, 1968

CUCKOOS, THE, 1930
CUP FEVER, 1965
CURLY TOP, 1935
CURTAIN CALL AT CACTUS CREEK, 1950
CYNTHIA, 1947
CYRANO DE BERGERAC, 1950
DADDY LONG LEGS, 1931
DADDY LONG LEGS, 1955
DAFFY DUCK'S MOVIE: FANTASTIC ISLAND, 1983
DAKOTA KID, THE, 1951
DAMES, 1934
DAMES AHOY, 1930
DANCE HALL, 1941
DANCE TEAM, 1932
DANCING YEARS, THE, 1950
DANGER FLIGHT, 1939
DANGER LIGHTS, 1930
DANGER VALLEY, 1938
DANGEROUS CURVES, 1929
DANGEROUS HOLIDAY, 1937
DANIEL BOONE, 1936
DANIEL BOONE, TRAIL BLAZER, 1957
DANNY BOY, 1946
DARBY O'GILL AND THE LITTLE PEOPLE, 1959
DARING DOBERMANS, THE, 1973
DARK SANDS, 1938
D.A.R.Y.L., 1985
DATE WITH JUDY, A, 1948
DAUGHTER OF ROSIE O'GRADY, THE, 1950
DAVY CROCKETT AND THE RIVER PIRATES, 1956
DAVY CROCKETT, INDIAN SCOUT, 1950
DAVY CROCKETT, KING OF THE WILD FRONTIER, 1955
DAY AT THE RACES, A, 1937
DAY THE EARTH FROZE, THE, 1959
DAYDREAMER, THE, 1966
DAYLIGHT ROBBERY, 1964
DEAR WIFE, 1949
DEEP IN MY HEART, 1954
DESCENDANT OF THE SNOW LEOPARD, THE, 1986
DEVIL'S BROTHER, THE, 1933
DEVIL'S PASS, THE, 1957
DIGBY, THE BIGGEST DOG IN THE WORLD, 1974
DIMKA, 1964
DIMPLES, 1936
DINOSAURUS, 1960
DO YOU KEEP A LION AT HOME?, 1966
DR. COPPELIUS, 1968
DOCTOR DOLITTLE, 1967
DR. RHYTHM, 1938
DR. SYN, ALIAS THE SCARECROW, 1975
DOCTOR TAKES A WIFE, 1940
DOG AND THE DIAMONDS, THE, 1962
DOG OF FLANDERS, A, 1935
DOG OF FLANDERS, A, 1959
DOG'S BEST FRIEND, A, 1960
DOLLY SISTERS, THE, 1945
DONDI, 1961
DOOMED AT SUNDOWN, 1937
DOT AND THE BUNNY, 1983
DOT AND THE KOALA, 1985
DOUBLE CROSSBONES, 1950
DOUBLE DANGER, 1938
DOUBLE DATE, 1941
DOUGH BOYS, 1930
DOVE, THE, 1974
DOWN ARGENTINE WAY, 1940
DOWN TO THE SEA IN SHIPS, 1949
DRAGON OF PENDRAGON CASTLE, THE, 1950
DREAMBOAT, 1952
DRUMS ALONG THE MOHAWK, 1939
DUCK SOUP, 1933
DUMBO, 1941
EASTER PARADE, 1948
EDDIE CANTOR STORY, THE, 1953
EDISON, THE MAN, 1940
EGG AND I, THE, 1947
ELEPHANT BOY, 1937
EMIL, 1938
EMIL AND THE DETECTIVE, 1931
EMIL AND THE DETECTIVES, 1964
EMPEROR AND THE NIGHTINGALE, THE, 1949
EMPEROR WALTZ, THE, 1948
ENCHANTED FOREST, THE, 1945
ESCAPE FROM THE SEA, 1968
ESCAPE TO WITCH MOUNTAIN, 1975

E.T. THE EXTRA-TERRESTRIAL, 1982
EVERYTHING BUT THE TRUTH, 1956
EXCUSE MY DUST, 1951
FABULOUS WORLD OF JULES VERNE, THE, 1961
FAMILY AFFAIR, A, 1937
FANTASIA, 1940
FANTOMAS, 1966
FARMER'S DAUGHTER, THE, 1947
FATHER GOOSE, 1964
FATHER OF THE BRIDE, 1950
FATHER'S LITTLE DIVIDEND, 1951
FEARLESS FAGAN, 1952
FEROCIOUS PAL, 1934
FIDDLER ON THE ROOF, 1971
FIFTY MILLION FRENCHMEN, 1931
FIGHTING FRONTIER, 1943
FIGHTING MARSHAL, THE, 1932
FIGHTING PRINCE OF DONEGAL, THE, 1966
FIGHTING RENEGADE, 1939
FINDERS KEEPERS, 1951
FIRE IN THE STONE, THE, 1983
FISH HAWK, 1981
FISH THAT SAVED PITTSBURGH, THE, 1979
FISHERMAN'S WHARF, 1939
FIVE LITTLE PEPPERS AND HOW THEY GREW, 1939
FIVE LITTLE PEPPERS AT HOME, 1940
FIVE OF A KIND, 1938
5,000 FINGERS OF DR. T. THE, 1953
FLASH GORDON, 1936
FLASH GORDON, 1980
FLASH THE SHEEPDOG, 1967
FLEET'S IN, THE, 1942
FLIGHT OF THE DOVES, 1971
FLIPPER, 1963
FLIPPER'S NEW ADVENTURE, 1964
FLIRTATION WALK, 1934
FLOOD, THE, 1963
FLORIAN, 1940
FLUFFY, 1965
FLYING DEUCES, THE, 1939
FLYING EYE, THE, 1955
FOLLOW ME, BOYS!, 1966
FOLLOW THE BOYS, 1944
FOLLOW THE FLEET, 1936
FOR THE LOVE OF BENJI, 1977
FOR THE LOVE OF MIKE, 1960
FOR THE LOVE OF RUSTY, 1947
FORBIDDEN VALLEY, 1938
FOREVER YOUNG, FOREVER FREE, 1976
FORLORN RIVER, 1937
FORT DODGE STAMPEDE, 1951
FORT TI, 1953
FORTUNE LANE, 1947
45 FATHERS, 1937
FORTY POUNDS OF TROUBLE, 1962
FOUR DAYS WONDER, 1936
FOURTH HORSEMAN, THE, 1933
FOX AND THE HOUND, THE, 1981
FOX WITH NINE TAILS, THE, 1969
FRANCIS, 1949
FRANCIS COVERS THE BIG TOWN, 1953
FRANCIS GOES TO THE RACES, 1951
FRANCIS GOES TO WEST POINT, 1952
FRANCIS IN THE HAUNTED HOUSE, 1956
FRANCIS IN THE NAVY, 1955
FRANCIS JOINS THE WACS, 1954
FRASIER, THE SENSUOUS LION, 1973
FREAKY FRIDAY, 1976
FROM NASHVILLE WITH MUSIC, 1969
FROM THE MIXED-UP FILES OF MRS. BASIL E. FRANKWEILER, 1973
FRONT LINE KIDS, 1942
FULLER BRUSH GIRL, THE, 1950
FULLER BRUSH MAN, 1948
FUN AND FANCY FREE, 1947
FUN AT ST. FANNY'S, 1956
FUN ON A WEEKEND, 1979
FUNNY FACE, 1957
FURTHER ADVENTURES OF THE WILDERNESS FAMILY—PART II, 1978
FURTHER UP THE CREEK!, 1958
FURY OF THE CONGO, 1951
FUSS OVER FEATHERS, 1954
GASOLINE ALLEY, 1951
GAY DIVORCEE, THE, 1934
GAY PURR-EE, 1962

GENERAL SPANKY, 1937
GENTLE GIANT, 1967
GEORGE WHITE'S SCANDALS, 1934
GILDED LILY, THE, 1935
GIRL AND THE BURGLER, THE, 1967
GIRL CRAZY, 1943
GIRL FROM JONES BEACH, THE, 1949
GIRL MOST LIKELY, THE, 1957
GIRL OF THE GOLDEN WEST, THE, 1938
GIRL THIEF, THE, 1938
GIT!, 1965
GLADIATOR, THE, 1938
GLAMOUR BOY, 1941
GLENN MILLER STORY, THE, 1953
GLITTERBALL, THE, 1977
GLORY, 1955
GNOME-MOBILE, THE, 1967
GO KART GO, 1964
GOBOTS: BATTLE OF THE ROCKLORDS, 1986
GOIN' COCONUTS, 1978
GOIN' HOME, 1976
GOING MY WAY, 1944
GOLDEN CALF, THE, 1930
GOLDEN GIRL, 1951
GOLDEN GOOSE, THE, 1966
GOLDEN HOOFS, 1941
GOLDEN IDOL, THE, 1954
GOLDEN SEAL, THE, 1983
GOLDEN VOYAGE OF SINBAD, THE, 1974
GOOD NEWS, 1947
GOODBYE MR. CHIPS, 1939
GOODBYE, MY LADY, 1956
GORGEOUS HUSSY, THE, 1936
GREAT ADVENTURE, THE, 1955
**GREAT AMERICAN BUGS BUNNY-ROAD RUNNER
    CHASE, 1979**
GREAT BRAIN, THE, 1978
GREAT CATHERINE, 1968
GREAT DAN PATCH, THE, 1949
GREAT DICTATOR, THE, 1940
GREAT EXPECTATIONS, 1934
GREAT EXPECTATIONS, 1946
GREAT EXPECTATIONS, 1975
GREAT GILBERT AND SULLIVAN, THE, 1953
GREAT GUNS, 1941
GREAT LOCOMOTIVE CHASE, THE, 1956
GREAT MOUSE DETECTIVE, THE, 1986
GREAT MUPPET CAPER, THE, 1981
GREAT PONY RAID, THE, 1968
GREAT RUPERT, THE, 1950
GREAT ST. TRINIAN'S TRAIN ROBBERY, THE, 1966
GREAT VICTOR HERBERT, THE, 1939
GREAT WALTZ, THE, 1938
GREAT WALTZ, THE, 1972
GREAT ZIEGFELD, THE, 1936
GREATEST SHOW ON EARTH, THE, 1952
GREATEST STORY EVER TOLD, THE, 1965
GREEN GRASS OF WYOMING, 1948
GREEN PASTURES, 1936
GRENDEL GRENDEL GRENDEL, 1981
GREYFRIARS BOBBY, 1961
GUARDIAN OF THE WILDERNESS, 1977
GULLIVER'S TRAVELS, 1939
GULLIVER'S TRAVELS, 1977
GULLIVER'S TRAVELS BEYOND THE MOON, 1966
GUNS IN THE HEATHER, 1968
GUS, 1976
GYPSY COLT, 1954
HALF A HERO, 1953
HALF PINT, THE, 1960
HAND IN HAND, 1960
HANS CHRISTIAN ANDERSEN, 1952
HANSEL AND GRETEL, 1954
HANSEL AND GRETEL, 1965
HAPPIEST MILLIONAIRE, THE, 1967
HAPPY GO LUCKY, 1943
HAPPY TIME, THE, 1952
HARDYS RIDE HIGH, THE, 1939
HARVEY GIRLS, THE, 1946
HEADLINE HUNTERS, 1968
HEATHCLIFF: THE MOVIE, 1986
HEAVENS ABOVE!, 1963
HEIDI, 1937
HEIDI AND PETER, 1955
HEIDI, 1954
HEIDI, 1968

HEIDI'S SONG, 1982
HELLO, DOLLY!, 1969
HERBIE GOES BANANAS, 1980
HERBIE GOES TO MONTE CARLO, 1977
HERBIE RIDES AGAIN, 1974
HERE COME THE CO-EDS, 1945
HERE COME THE LITTLES, 1985
HERE COMES SANTA CLAUS, 1984
HERE WE GO AGAIN, 1942
HEY THERE, IT'S YOGI BEAR, 1964
HI-YO SILVER, 1940
HIAWATHA, 1952
HIGH SOCIETY, 1955
HILDUR AND THE MAGICIAN, 1969
HILLS OF HOME, 1948
HINDU, THE, 1953
HIT THE DECK, 1955
HITCH IN TIME, A, 1978
HOLD EVERYTHING, 1930
HOLD THAT GHOST, 1941
HOLLYWOOD AND VINE, 1945
HOLLYWOOD HOTEL, 1937
HOLLYWOOD PARTY, 1934
HOME IN INDIANA, 1944
HOME SWEET HOMICIDE, 1946
HONEYMOON MERRY-GO-ROUND, 1939
HORN BLOWS AT MIDNIGHT, THE, 1945
HORSE IN THE GRAY FLANNEL SUIT, THE, 1968
HOT LEAD AND COLD FEET, 1978
HOVERBUG, 1970
HOW THE WEST WAS WON, 1962
HOW TO FRAME A FIGG, 1971
HUCKLEBERRY FINN, 1931
HUCKLEBERRY FINN, 1939
HUCKLEBERRY FINN, 1974
HUGO THE HIPPO, 1976
HUNCH, THE, 1967
HUNTED IN HOLLAND, 1961
I REMEMBER MAMA, 1948
I'LL TELL THE WORLD, 1945
IN OLD NEW MEXICO, 1945
IN SEARCH OF HISTORIC JESUS, 1980
IN SEARCH OF THE CASTAWAYS, 1962
IN SOCIETY, 1944
IN THE GOOD OLD SUMMERTIME, 1949
IN THE MONEY, 1958
IN THE NAVY, 1941
INCREDIBLE JOURNEY, THE, 1963
INCREDIBLE MR. LIMPET, THE, 1964
INDIAN PAINT, 1965
INN OF THE SIXTH HAPPINESS, THE, 1958
INNOCENT SINNERS, 1958
INSPECTOR GENERAL, THE, 1949
INTERNATIONAL VELVET, 1978
INVISIBLE BOY, THE, 1957
ISLAND AT THE TOP OF THE WORLD, THE, 1974
ISLAND OF THE BLUE DOLPHINS, 1964
IT AIN'T HAY, 1943
IT HAPPENS EVERY SPRING, 1949
IT'S A BIG COUNTRY, 1951
IT'S A GIFT, 1934
IT'S A GREAT LIFE, 1943
IT'S A MAD, MAD, MAD, MAD WORLD, 1963
IT'S A WONDERFUL LIFE, 1946
JACK AND THE BEANSTALK, 1952
JACK AND THE BEANSTALK, 1970
JACK FROST, 1966
JACK THE GIANT KILLER, 1962
JACKIE ROBINSON STORY, THE, 1950
JACOB TWO-TWO MEETS THE HOODED FANG, 1979
JAIL BUSTERS, 1955
JALOPY, 1953
JANIE, 1944
JASON AND THE ARGONAUTS, 1963
JIGGS AND MAGGIE IN SOCIETY, 1948
JIGGS AND MAGGIE OUT WEST, 1950
JITTERBUGS, 1943
JOE PALOOKA, CHAMP, 1946
JOE PALOOKA IN THE BIG FIGHT, 1949
JOE PALOOKA IN THE COUNTERPUNCH, 1949
JOE PALOOKA IN TRIPLE CROSS, 1951
JOE PALOOKA IN WINNER TAKE ALL, 1948
JOE PALOOKA MEETS HUMPHREY, 1950
JOE PANTHER, 1976
JOHN AND JULIE, 1957
JOHN OF THE FAIR, 1962

JOHN WESLEY, 1954
JOHNNY DOUGHBOY, 1943
JOHNNY ON THE RUN, 1953
JOHNNY THE GIANT KILLER, 1953
JOHNNY TREMAIN, 1957
JONIKO AND THE KUSH TA KA, 1969
JOURNEY BACK TO OZ, 1974
JOURNEY FOR MARGARET, 1942
JOURNEY TO SPIRIT ISLAND, 1988
JOURNEY TO THE BEGINNING OF TIME, 1966
JOURNEY TO THE CENTER OF THE EARTH, 1959
JUDGE HARDY AND SON, 1939
JUDGE HARDY'S CHILDREN, 1938
JUDGE PRIEST, 1934
JUKE BOX JENNY, 1942
JUMBO, 1962
JUNGLE, THE, 1952
JUNGLE BOOK, 1942
JUNGLE BOOK, THE, 1967
JUNGLE GENTS, 1954
JUNGLE JIM, 1948
JUNGLE JIM IN THE FORBIDDEN LAND, 1952
JUNGLE MAN-EATERS, 1954
JUNGLE MANHUNT, 1951
JUNGLE MOON MEN, 1955
JUNIOR ARMY, 1943
JUNIOR MISS, 1945
JUNIOR PROM, 1946
JUNKET 89, 1970
JUST AROUND THE CORNER, 1938
JUST FOR FUN, 1963
JUST WILLIAM, 1939
KADOYNG, 1974
KATHLEEN, 1941
KAZAN, 1949
KEEP 'EM FLYING, 1941
KEEP 'EM SLUGGING, 1943
KELLY AND ME, 1957
KENTUCKY, 1938
KENTUCKY MOONSHINE, 1938
KETTLES IN THE OZARKS, THE, 1956
KETTLES ON OLD MACDONALD'S FARM, THE, 1957
KID DYNAMITE, 1943
KID FROM BROOKLYN, THE, 1946
KID FROM CANADA, THE, 1957
KID FROM LEFT FIELD, THE, 1953
KID FROM SANTA FE, THE, 1940
KID FROM SPAIN, THE, 1932
KID FROM TEXAS, THE, 1939
KID MILLIONS, 1934
KIDNAPPED, 1938
KIDNAPPED, 1948
KIDNAPPED, 1960
KIDNAPPED, 1971
KILL THE UMPIRE, 1950
KILLER APE, 1953
KILLERS OF THE WILD, 1940
KILROY WAS HERE, 1947
KIM, 1950
KIND STEPMOTHER, 1936
KING AND I, THE, 1956
KING AND THE CHORUS GIRL, THE, 1937
KING DINOSAUR, 1955
KING OF HEARTS, 1936
KING OF HOCKEY, 1936
KING OF KINGS, 1961
KING OF THE COWBOYS, 1943
KING OF THE GRIZZLIES, 1970
KING OF THE WILD STALLIONS, 1959
KISS ME KATE, 1953
KNUTE ROCKNE—ALL AMERICAN, 1940
KONGA, THE WILD STALLION, 1939
LABYRINTH, 1986
LAD: A DOG, 1962
LADDIE, 1940
LADDIE, 1935
LADY AND THE TRAMP, 1955
LAFAYETTE, 1963
LAND BEFORE TIME, THE, 1988
LAND OF THE SILVER FOX, 1928
LASSIE, COME HOME, 1943
LASSIE FROM LANCASHIRE, 1938
LASSIE'S GREAT ADVENTURE, 1963
LAST FLIGHT OF NOAH'S ARK, THE, 1980
LAST LOAD, THE, 1948
LAST OF THE REDMEN, 1947

BOLD: Films on Videocassette

LAST RHINO, THE, 1961
LAST ROUND-UP, THE, 1947
LAST UNICORN, THE, 1982
LATITUDE ZERO, 1969
LAUGHTER IN PARADISE, 1951
LAW OF THE NORTH, 1932
LAWLESS BREED, THE, 1946
LEGEND OF LOBO, THE, 1962
LET'S MAKE LOVE, 1960
LT. ROBIN CRUSOE, U.S.N., 1966
LIFE AND TIMES OF GRIZZLY ADAMS, THE, 1974
LIFE BEGINS AT 40, 1935
LIFE BEGINS IN COLLEGE, 1937
LIFE OF EMILE ZOLA, THE, 1937
LIFE WITH BLONDIE, 1946
LIFE WITH FATHER, 1947
LIFE WITH HENRY, 1941
LIGHT IN THE FOREST, THE, 1958
LI'L ABNER, 1940
LI'L ABNER, 1959
LILI, 1953
LION HUNTERS, THE, 1951
LIONHEART, 1968
LISTEN, DARLING, 1938
LITTLE ADVENTURESS, THE, 1938
LITTLE ARK, THE, 1972
LITTLE BALLERINA, THE, 1951
LITTLE BIG SHOT, 1935
LITTLE BIT OF HEAVEN, A, 1940
LITTLE COLONEL, THE, 1935
LITTLE CONVICT, THE, 1980
LITTLE DOLLY DAYDREAM, 1938
LITTLE KIDNAPPERS, THE, 1954
LITTLE LORD FAUNTLEROY, 1936
LITTLE MEN, 1940
LITTLE MISS MARKER, 1934
LITTLE MISS NOBODY, 1936
LITTLE MISS ROUGHNECK, 1938
LITTLE MISS THOROUGHBRED, 1938
LITTLE ONES, THE, 1965
LITTLE ORPHAN ANNIE, 1932
LITTLE ORVIE, 1940
LITTLE PRINCE, THE, 1974
LITTLE PRINCESS, THE, 1939
LITTLE RED SCHOOLHOUSE, 1936
LITTLE WOMEN, 1933
LITTLE WOMEN, 1949
LITTLEST HOBO, THE, 1958
LITTLEST HORSE THIEVES, THE, 1977
LITTLEST OUTLAW, THE, 1955
LITTLEST REBEL, THE, 1935
LONE CLIMBER, THE, 1950
LONE RANGER, THE, 1955
LONE RANGER AND THE LOST CITY OF GOLD, THE, 1958
LORD JEFF, 1938
LOST IN ALASKA, 1952
LOST VOLCANO, THE, 1950
LOVE BUG, THE, 1968
LOVE FINDS ANDY HARDY, 1938
LOYAL HEART, 1946
LUCKY BRIDE, THE, 1948
LUCKY DOG, 1933
LUCKY TO ME, 1939
LUM AND ABNER ABROAD, 1956
LURE OF THE JUNGLE, THE, 1970
MACARIO, 1961
MAD MONSTER PARTY, 1967
MADAME CURIE, 1943
MADDEST CAR IN THE WORLD, THE, 1974
MADE FOR EACH OTHER, 1939
MAGIC BOX, THE, 1952
MAGIC OF LASSIE, THE, 1978
MAGIC TOWN, 1947
MAGNIFICENT YANKEE, THE, 1950
MAKE MINE MUSIC, 1946
MALACHI'S COVE, 1973
MAN ABOUT TOWN, 1939
MAN CALLED FLINTSTONE, THE, 1966
MAN CALLED PETER, THE, 1955
MAN FROM BUTTON WILLOW, THE, 1965
MAN FROM OKLAHOMA, THE, 1945
MAN WHO DARED, THE, 1933
MARGIE, 1946
MARTIN LUTHER, 1953
MARY POPPINS, 1964

MEET ME IN ST. LOUIS, 1944
MELODY, 1971
MELODY TIME, 1948
MELODY TRAIL, 1935
MEN OF BOYS TOWN, 1941
MERRY ANDREW, 1958
MIDSUMMERS NIGHT'S DREAM, A, 1961
MIGHTY MOUSE IN THE GREAT SPACE CHASE, 1983
MIGHTY TREVE, THE, 1937
MIKADO, THE, 1967
MILKY WAY, THE, 1936
MIRACLE OF THE WHITE STALLIONS, 1963
MIRACLE ON 34TH STREET, THE, 1947
MISADVENTURES OF MERLIN JONES, THE, 1964
MISSING NOTE, THE, 1961
MR. BUG GOES TO TOWN, 1941
MISTER 880, 1950
MR. HOBBS TAKES A VACATION, 1962
MR. HULOT'S HOLIDAY, 1954
MR. MAGOO'S HOLIDAY FESTIVAL, 1970
MR. PEABODY AND THE MERMAID, 1948
MR. SMITH GOES TO WASHINGTON, 1939
MR. SUPERINVISIBLE, 1974
MISTY, 1961
MONKEYS, GO HOME!, 1967
MONKEY'S UNCLE, THE, 1965
MONSTER OF HIGHGATE PONDS, THE, 1961
MONTE CARLO, 1930
MOON OVER LAS VEGAS, 1944
MOON PILOT, 1962
MOON-SPINNERS, THE, 1964
MOUNTAIN RHYTHM, 1942
MOUSE ON THE MOON, THE, 1963
MOUSE THAT ROARED, THE, 1959
MRS. WIGGS OF THE CABBAGE PATCH, 1942
MUPPET MOVIE, THE, 1979
MUPPETS TAKE MANHATTAN, THE, 1984
MUSCLE BEACH PARTY, 1964
MUSIC FOR MILLIONS, 1944
MUSIC MAN, 1948
MUSIC MAN, THE, 1962
MY BROTHER TALKS TO HORSES, 1946
MY DOG RUSTY, 1948
MY FAIR LADY, 1964
MY FRIEND FLICKA, 1943
MY LITTLE PONY, 1986
MY PAL TRIGGER, 1946
MY SIDE OF THE MOUNTAIN, 1969
MY SISTER EILEEN, 1942
MY SISTER EILEEN, 1955
MY SIX LOVES, 1963
MY UNCLE, 1958
MY WEAKNESS, 1933
MY WIFE'S RELATIVES, 1939
MYSTERIOUS ISLAND, 1961
MYSTERIOUS ISLAND OF CAPTAIN NEMO, THE, 1973
NANCY DREW AND THE HIDDEN STAIRCASE, 1939
NANCY DREW—DETECTIVE, 1938
NANCY DREW—REPORTER, 1939
NANCY DREW, TROUBLE SHOOTER, 1939
NAPOLEON AND SAMANTHA, 1972
NATIONAL VELVET, 1944
NAUGHTY NINETIES, THE, 1945
NEWLY RICH, 1931
NEXT VOICE YOU HEAR, THE, 1950
NIKKI, WILD DOG OF THE NORTH, 1961
NO DEPOSIT, NO RETURN, 1976
NOBODY'S CHILDREN, 1940
NOOSE HANGS HIGH, THE, 1948
NOTHING BUT TROUBLE, 1944
NOTHING VENTURE, 1948
NOW YOU SEE HIM, NOW YOU DON'T, 1972
NUTCRACKER FANTASY, 1979
NUTCRACKER: THE MOTION PICTURE, 1986
O. HENRY'S FULL HOUSE, 1952
ODYSSEY OF THE PACIFIC, 1983
OF STARS AND MEN, 1961
OH! SAILOR, BEHAVE!, 1930
OKLAHOMA, 1955
OLIVER!, 1968
OLIVER & COMPANY, 1988
OLIVER TWIST, 1951
ON A CLEAR DAY YOU CAN SEE FOREVER, 1970
ON MOONLIGHT BAY, 1951

ON THE AVENUE, 1937
ON THE SUNNY SIDE, 1942
ONE AND ONLY GENUINE ORIGINAL FAMILY BAND, THE, 1968
ONE DESIRE, 1955
ONE FOOT IN HEAVEN, 1941
ONE HUNDRED AND ONE DALMATIANS, 1961
100 MEN AND A GIRL, 1937
ONE IN A MILLION, 1936
ONE LITTLE INDIAN, 1973
ONE MAGIC CHRISTMAS, 1985
$1,000,000 DUCK, 1971
ONE OF OUR DINOSAURS IS MISSING, 1975
1001 ARABIAN NIGHTS, 1959
OPERATION THIRD FORM, 1966
ORPHANS OF THE NORTH, 1940
ORPHANS OF THE STREET, 1939
OUR LITTLE GIRL, 1935
OUR MISS BROOKS, 1956
OUR NEIGHBORS—THE CARTERS, 1939
OUR RELATIONS, 1936
OUT WEST WITH THE HARDYS, 1938
OUT WEST WITH THE PEPPERS, 1940
PACK UP YOUR TROUBLES, 1932
PACK UP YOUR TROUBLES, 1939
PAINTED HILLS, THE, 1951
PAJAMA PARTY, 1964
PALOMINO, THE, 1950
PALOOKA, 1934
PARDON MY SARONG, 1942
PARDON US, 1931
PARENT TRAP, THE, 1961
PECK'S BAD BOY, 1934
PECK'S BAD BOY WITH THE CIRCUS, 1938
PENROD AND HIS TWIN BROTHER, 1938
PENROD AND SAM, 1931
PENROD AND SAM, 1937
PENROD'S DOUBLE TROUBLE, 1938
PEOPLE THAT TIME FORGOT, THE, 1977
PEPE, 1960
PEPPER, 1936
PERSONALITY KID, 1946
PETER PAN, 1953
PETER RABBIT AND TALES OF BEATRIX POTTER, 1971
PETE'S DRAGON, 1977
PHANTOM TOLLBOOTH, THE, 1970
PICK A STAR, 1937
PICKWICK PAPERS, THE, 1952
PINOCCHIO, 1940
PINOCCHIO, 1969
PINOCCHIO AND THE EMPEROR OF THE NIGHT, 1987
PINOCCHIO IN OUTER SPACE, 1965
PINTO CANYON, 1940
PIPER'S TUNE, THE, 1962
PIPPI IN THE SOUTH SEAS, 1974
PIPPI ON THE RUN, 1977
PLAYBOY, THE, 1942
PLAYTIME, 1973
PLYMOUTH ADVENTURE, 1952
POCKETFUL OF MIRACLES, 1961
POCOLITTLE DOG LOST, 1977
POLLYANNA, 1960
POUND PUPPIES AND THE LEGEND OF BIG PAW, 1988
PRIDE OF ST. LOUIS, THE, 1952
PRIDE OF THE ARMY, 1942
PRIDE OF THE BLUEGRASS, 1939
PRIDE OF THE YANKEES, THE, 1942
PRINCE AND THE PAUPER, THE, 1937
PRINCE AND THE PAUPER, THE, 1969
PRINCE OF ARCADIA, 1933
PRINCE OF PEACE, THE, 1951
PRINCE VALIANT, 1954
PRINCESS AND THE MAGIC FROG, THE, 1965
PRINCESS OF THE NILE, 1954
PUDDIN' HEAD, 1941
PUFNSTUF, 1970
PUSS "N' BOOTS, 1964
PUSS "N' BOOTS, 1967
QUEEN'S SWORDSMEN, THE, 1963
RACE FOR YOUR LIFE, CHARLIE BROWN, 1977
RAGGEDY ANN AND ANDY, 1977
RAINBOW BRITE AND THE STAR STEALER, 1985
RANGERS OF FORTUNE, 1940

RASCAL, 1969
RASCALS, 1938
RAYMIE, 1960
REBECCA OF SUNNYBROOK FARM, 1938
RED PONY, THE, 1949
RED STALLION IN THE ROCKIES, 1949
RELUCTANT DRAGON, THE, 1941
RESCUERS, THE, 1977
RESERVED FOR LADIES, 1932
RETURN FROM WITCH MOUNTAIN, 1978
RETURN OF RIN TIN TIN, THE, 1947
RETURN TO BOGGY CREEK, 1977
RHAPSODY IN BLUE, 1945
RICOCHET ROMANCE, 1954
RIDE A NORTHBOUND HORSE, 1969
RIDE A WILD PONY, 1976
RIDE 'EM COWBOY, 1942
RIDING ON AIR, 1937
RIO RITA, 1942
ROAD TO BALI, 1952
ROAD TO HONG KONG, THE, 1962
ROAD TO MOROCCO, 1942
ROAD TO RIO, 1947
ROAD TO SINGAPORE, 1940
ROAD TO UTOPIA, 1945
ROAD TO ZANZIBAR, 1941
ROBBY, 1968
ROBIN HOOD, 1973
ROCKET TO NOWHERE, 1962
ROCKETS IN THE DUNES, 1960
RODEO RHYTHM, 1941
ROOM FOR ONE MORE, 1952
ROOMMATES, 1962
ROSE MARIE, 1936
ROSE MARIE, 1954
ROSEANNA McCOY, 1949
ROUGH WATERS, 1930
RUMPELSTILTSKIN, 1987
RUNAWAY RAILWAY, 1965
RUNNING WILD, 1973
SAD HORSE, THE, 1959
SALVAGE GANG, THE, 1958
SAND CASTLE, THE, 1961
SANDU FOLLOWS THE SUN, 1965
SANDY GETS HER MAN, 1940
SANDY IS A LADY, 1940
SANDY THE SEAL, 1969
SANTA AND THE THREE BEARS, 1970
SANTA CLAUS, 1960
SANTA'S CHRISTMAS CIRCUS, 1966
SATAN'S SATELLITES, 1958
SAVANNAH SMILES, 1983
SCANDALOUS JOHN, 1971
SCHOOL FOR SCOUNDRELS, 1960
SCRAMBLE, 1970
SCROOGE, 1935
SCROOGE, 1970
SCRUFFY, 1938
SEA GYPSIES, THE, 1978
SEASIDE SWINGERS, 1965
SECRET GARDEN, THE, 1949
SECRET OF MAGIC ISLAND, THE, 1964
SECRET OF NIMH, THE, 1982
SECRET OF THE FOREST, THE, 1955
SECRET OF THE SWORD, THE, 1985
**SESAME STREET PRESENTS: FOLLOW THE BIRD,
 1985**
SEVEN ALONE, 1975
SEVEN BRIDES FOR SEVEN BROTHERS, 1954
SEVEN LITTLE FOYS, THE, 1955
SEVENTH VOYAGE OF SINBAD, THE, 1958
SEVENTY DEADLY PILLS, 1964
SHAGGY, 1948
SHAGGY D.A., THE, 1976
SHAGGY DOG, THE, 1959
SHAMROCK HILL, 1949
SHAMUS, 1959
SHEP COMES HOME, 1949
SHOEMAKER AND THE ELVES, THE, 1967
SHOULD HUSBANDS WORK?, 1939
SHOW BUSINESS, 1944
SHUT MY BIG MOUTH, 1942
SIDEWALKS OF LONDON, 1940
SIDEWALKS OF NEW YORK, 1931
SIGN OF THE WOLF, 1941
SIGN OF ZORRO, THE, 1960

SILENCE, 1974
SINBAD AND THE EYE OF THE TIGER, 1977
SING FOR YOUR SUPPER, 1941
SING YOU SINNERS, 1938
SINGING BUCKAROO, THE, 1937
SINGING HILL, THE, 1941
SITTING PRETTY, 1948
SIX-GUN LAW, 1948
SKID KIDS, 1953
SKIPPY, 1931
SKULL AND CROWN, 1938
SKY BIKE, THE, 1967
SLEEPING BEAUTY, 1959
SLEEPING BEAUTY, 1965
SLEEPING BEAUTY, THE, 1966
SLIPPER AND THE ROSE, THE, 1976
SMURFS AND THE MAGIC FLUTE, THE, 1984
SNOOPY, COME HOME, 1972
SNOW DOG, 1950
SNOW QUEEN, THE, 1959
SNOW WHITE, 1965
SNOW WHITE AND ROSE RED, 1966
SNOW WHITE AND THE SEVEN DWARFS, 1937
SNOWBALL EXPRESS, 1972
SNOWFIRE, 1958
SO DEAR TO MY HEART, 1949
SOAPBOX DERBY, 1958
SON OF FLUBBER, 1963
SON OF LASSIE, 1945
SONG OF BERNADETTE, THE, 1943
SONG OF THE SOUTH, 1946
SOUND OF MUSIC, THE, 1965
SOUNDER, 1972
SOUNDER, PART 2, 1976
SOURDOUGH, 1977
SOUTHERN YANKEE, A, 1948
SPIRIT OF ST. LOUIS, THE, 1957
STANLEY AND LIVINGSTONE, 1939
STAR FELL FROM HEAVEN, A, 1936
STAR MAKER, THE, 1939
STARS AND STRIPES FOREVER, 1952
STARSHIP INVASIONS, 1978
STOLEN AIRLINER, THE, 1962
STOLEN DIRIGIBLE, THE, 1966
STOLEN PLANS, THE, 1962
STORIES FROM A FLYING TRUNK, 1979
STORM BOY, 1976
STORY OF ALEXANDER GRAHAM BELL, THE, 1939
STORY OF LOUIS PASTEUR, THE, 1936
STORY OF ROBIN HOOD, THE, 1952
STOWAWAY, 1936
STOWAWAY IN THE SKY, 1962
STRATTON STORY, THE, 1949
STRIKE UP THE BAND, 1940
SUMMER HOLIDAY, 1948
SUMMER MAGIC, 1963
SUMMERDOG, 1977
SUN COMES UP, THE, 1949
SUN VALLEY SERENADE, 1941
SUNDOWN RIDER, THE, 1933
SUNSET ON THE DESERT, 1942
SUPERBUG, SUPER AGENT, 1976
SUPERDAD, 1974
SUPERMAN, 1978
SUPERZAN AND THE SPACE BOY, 1972
SUSANNAH OF THE MOUNTIES, 1939
SWALLOWS AND AMAZONS, 1977
SWAN LAKE, THE, 1967
SWING TIME, 1936
SWISS FAMILY ROBINSON, 1940
SWISS FAMILY ROBINSON, 1960
SWISS MISS, 1938
SWORD IN THE STONE, THE, 1963
TAFFY AND THE JUNGLE HUNTER, 1965
TAIL OF THE TIGER, 1984
TAKE ME OUT TO THE BALL GAME, 1949
TAKE THE HEIR, 1930
TALES OF MANHATTAN, 1942
TALK OF THE TOWN, 1942
TARZAN AND THE GREEN GODDESS, 1938
TARZAN AND THE HUNTRESS, 1947
TARZAN AND THE JUNGLE BOY, 1968
TARZAN AND THE LEOPARD WOMAN, 1946
TARZAN AND THE LOST SAFARI, 1957
TARZAN AND THE MERMAIDS, 1948
TARZAN AND THE SHE-DEVIL, 1953

TARZAN AND THE SLAVE GIRL, 1950
TARZAN AND THE VALLEY OF GOLD, 1966
TARZAN FINDS A SON, 1939
TARZAN GOES TO INDIA, 1962
TARZAN, THE APE MAN, 1932
TARZAN THE FEARLESS, 1933
TARZAN TRIUMPHS, 1943
TARZAN'S DEADLY SILENCE, 1970
TARZAN'S DESERT MYSTERY, 1943
TARZAN'S FIGHT FOR LIFE, 1958
TARZAN'S GREATEST ADVENTURE, 1959
TARZAN'S HIDDEN JUNGLE, 1955
TARZAN'S JUNGLE REBELLION, 1970
TARZAN'S MAGIC FOUNTAIN, 1949
TARZAN'S NEW YORK ADVENTURE, 1942
TARZAN'S REVENGE, 1938
TARZAN'S SAVAGE FURY, 1952
TARZAN'S SECRET TREASURE, 1941
TARZAN'S THREE CHALLENGES, 1963
TAXI 13, 1928
TEAHOUSE OF THE AUGUST MOON, THE, 1956
TEENAGERS IN SPACE, 1975
TEN COMMANDMENTS, THE, 1956
TEN TALL MEN, 1951
TENDER WARRIOR, THE, 1971
THAT DARN CAT, 1965
THERE'S THAT WOMAN AGAIN, 1938
THIEF OF BAGHDAD, THE, 1940
THIRTY FOOT BRIDE OF CANDY ROCK, THE, 1959
THIS COULD BE THE NIGHT, 1957
THIS IS THE ARMY, 1943
THIS MAN'S NAVY, 1945
THIS SIDE OF HEAVEN, 1934
THIS TIME FOR KEEPS, 1947
THIS WAY PLEASE, 1937
THIS WINE OF LOVE, 1948
THOROUGHBREDS, 1945
THOROUGHBREDS DON'T CRY, 1937
THOSE CALLOWAYS, 1964
THOSE FANTASTIC FLYING FOOLS, 1967
THOSE REDHEADS FROM SEATTLE, 1953
THREE CABALLEROS, THE, 1944
THREE LITTLE WORDS, 1950
THREE LIVES OF THOMASINA, THE, 1963
THREE SMART GIRLS, 1937
THREE STOOGES GO AROUND THE WORLD IN A
 DAZE, THE, 1963
THREE STOOGES IN ORBIT, THE, 1962
THREE STOOGES MEET HERCULES, THE, 1962
THREE WORLDS OF GULLIVER, THE, 1960
THUMBELINA, 1970
THUNDERHEAD-SON OF FLICKA, 1945
TIKI TIKI, 1971
TILL THE CLOUDS ROLL BY, 1946
TIM DRISCOLL'S DONKEY, 1955
TIME OF THEIR LIVES, THE, 1946
TINDER BOX, THE, 1968
TINKER, 1949
TOBOR THE GREAT, 1954
TOBY TYLER, 1960
TOM BROWN OF CULVER, 1932
TOM BROWN'S SCHOOL DAYS, 1940
TOM BROWN'S SCHOOLDAYS, 1951
TOM SAWYER, 1930
TOM SAWYER, 1973
TOM THUMB, 1958
TONKA, 1958
TONS OF TROUBLE, 1956
TOO MANY HUSBANDS, 1938
TOTO AND THE POACHERS, 1958
TOVARICH, 1937
TOY TIGER, 1956
TRAFFIC, 1972
TRAIL OF TERROR, 1935
TRAIL RIDERS, 1942
TRAIL TO GUNSIGHT, 1944
TRAPPED BY THE TERROR, 1949
TREASURE AT THE MILL, 1957
TREASURE OF MATECUMBE, 1976
TROJAN HORSE, THE, 1962
TROOPERS THREE, 1930
TROUBLE MAKERS, 1948
TROUBLE WITH ANGELS, THE, 1966
TROUBLESOME DOUBLE, THE, 1971
TRUE TO THE ARMY, 1942
TRUTH ABOUT SPRING, THE, 1965

BOLD: Films on Videocassette

TUGBOAT ANNIE SAILS AGAIN, 1940
TUMBLING TUMBLEWEEDS, 1935
TWO-FISTED LAW, 1932
TWO IN REVOLT, 1936
TWO LITTLE BEARS, THE, 1961
UGLY DACHSHUND, THE, 1966
UP IN ARMS, 1944
UP IN THE AIR, 1969
VALHALLA, 1987
VARIETY GIRL, 1947
VIGILANTES OF DODGE CITY, 1944
VIRGINIA'S HUSBAND, 1934
VISIT TO A CHIEF'S SON, 1974
VISITORS FROM THE GALAXY, 1981
WACKY WORLD OF MOTHER GOOSE, THE, 1967
WAGON WHEELS WESTWARD, 1956
WAKAMBA?, 1955
WAKE UP AND LIVE, 1937
WALKING ON AIR, 1946
WARLORDS OF ATLANTIS, 1978
WARM CORNER, A, 1930
WATER BABIES, THE, 1979
WAY OUT WEST, 1937
WEE WILLIE WINKIE, 1937
WELCOME KOSTYA?, 1965
WHALE OF A TALE, A, 1977
WHAT HAPPENED TO HARKNESS, 1934
WHAT'S NEXT?, 1975
WHAT'S UP, DOC?, 1972
WHEN I GROW UP, 1951
WHEN'S YOUR BIRTHDAY?, 1937
WHERE DO WE GO FROM HERE?, 1945
WHERE'S CHARLEY?, 1952
WHITE CHRISTMAS, 1954
WHITE PONGO, 1945
WHO KILLED "DOC" ROBBIN?, 1948
WHO SAYS I CAN'T RIDE A RAINBOW?, 1971
WHOOPEE, 1930
WILD COUNTRY, THE, 1971
WILLIE MCBEAN AND HIS MAGIC MACHINE, 1965
WILLOW, 1988
WINGS OF MYSTERY, 1963
WISHING MACHINE, 1971
WITNESS, THE, 1959
WIZARD OF OZ, THE, 1939
WOLF DOG, 1958
WOLFPEN PRINCIPLE, THE, 1974
WOMAN OF THE YEAR, 1942
WOMBLING FREE, 1977
WONDER MAN, 1945
WONDERFUL LAND OF OZ, THE, 1969
WONDERS OF ALADDIN, THE, 1961
WORLD OF HANS CHRISTIAN ANDERSEN, THE, 1971
WORLD'S GREATEST ATHLETE, THE, 1973
WOULD YOU BELIEVE IT!, 1930
YANKEE DOODLE DANDY, 1942
YAQUI DRUMS, 1956
YEAR OF THE HORSE, THE, 1966
YEARLING, THE, 1946
YELLOW STOCKINGS, 1930
YOUNG AMERICA, 1932
YOUNG AMERICA, 1942
YOUNG AS YOU FEEL, 1931
YOUNG AS YOU FEEL, 1940
YOUNG BUFFALO BILL, 1940
YOUNG DANIEL BOONE, 1950
YOUNG EAGLES, 1930
YOUNG PEOPLE, 1940
YOUNG SWINGERS, THE, 1963
YOUNG TOM EDISON, 1940
YOURS, MINE AND OURS, 1968
YOUTH ON PARADE, 1943
YOUTH TAKES A FLING, 1938
ZEBRA IN THE KITCHEN, 1965
ZIEGFELD FOLLIES, 1945
ZOO BABY, 1957

A

A NOUS LA LIBERTE, 1931
ABBOTT AND COSTELLO GO TO MARS, 1953
ABBOTT AND COSTELLO IN THE FOREIGN LEGION, 1950
ABBOTT AND COSTELLO MEET CAPTAIN KIDD, 1952

ABBOTT AND COSTELLO MEET DR. JEKYLL AND MR. HYDE, 1954
ABBOTT AND COSTELLO MEET FRANKENSTEIN, 1948
ABBOTT AND COSTELLO MEET THE INVISIBLE MAN, 1951
ABBOTT AND COSTELLO MEET THE KEYSTONE KOPS, 1955
ABBOTT AND COSTELLO MEET THE KILLER, BORIS KARLOFF, 1949
ABBOTT AND COSTELLO MEET THE MUMMY, 1955
ABDUCTORS, THE, 1957
ABIE'S IRISH ROSE, 1928
ABILENE TOWN, 1946
ABILENE TRAIL, 1951
ABOMINABLE SNOWMAN OF THE HIMALAYAS, THE, 1957
ABOUT FACE, 1952
ABOUT MRS. LESLIE, 1954
ABOVE AND BEYOND, 1953
ABOVE SUSPICION, 1943
ABOVE THE CLOUDS, 1934
ABOVE US THE WAVES, 1956
ABROAD WITH TWO YANKS, 1944
ACCENT ON LOVE, 1941
ACCENT ON YOUTH, 1935
ACCIDENTS WILL HAPPEN, 1938
ACCOMPLICE, 1946
ACCORDING TO MRS. HOYLE, 1951
ACCOUNT RENDERED, 1957
ACCURSED, THE, 1958
ACCUSED, 1936
ACCUSED OF MURDER, 1956
ACCUSED—STAND UP, 1930
ACCUSING FINGER, THE, 1936
ACE ELI AND RODGER OF THE SKIES, 1973
ACE OF SPADES, THE, 1935
ACES AND EIGHTS, 1936
ACES WILD, 1937
ACROSS THE BADLANDS, 1950
ACROSS THE PACIFIC, 1942
ACROSS THE PLAINS, 1939
ACROSS THE RIO GRANDE, 1949
ACROSS THE SIERRAS, 1941
ACROSS THE WIDE MISSOURI, 1951
ACT ONE, 1964
ACTION FOR SLANDER, 1937
ACTION IN ARABIA, 1944
ACTION IN THE NORTH ATLANTIC, 1943
ACTION OF THE TIGER, 1957
ACTRESS, THE, 1953
ADAM AND EVELYNE, 1950
ADAM HAD FOUR SONS, 1941
ADAM'S RIB, 1949
ADDRESS UNKNOWN, 1944
ADIOS GRINGO, 1967
ADIOS SABATA, 1971
ADMIRABLE CRICHTON, THE, 1957
ADMIRAL WAS A LADY, THE, 1950
ADMIRALS ALL, 1935
ADMIRAL'S SECRET, THE, 1934
ADOLF HITLER—MY PART IN HIS DOWNFALL, 1973
ADORABLE, 1933
ADULTEROUS AFFAIR, 1966
ADVANCE TO THE REAR, 1964
ADVENTURE, 1945
ADVENTURE FOR TWO, 1945
ADVENTURE IN BLACKMAIL, 1943
ADVENTURE IN DIAMONDS, 1940
ADVENTURE IN MANHATTAN, 1936
ADVENTURE IN SAHARA, 1938
ADVENTURE ISLAND, 1947
ADVENTURE LIMITED, 1934
ADVENTURE OF SALVATOR ROSA, AN, 1940
ADVENTURE'S END, 1937
ADVENTURES IN IRAQ, 1943
ADVENTURES IN SILVERADO, 1948
ADVENTURES OF A ROOKIE, 1943
ADVENTURES OF A YOUNG MAN, 1962
ADVENTURES OF ARSENE LUPIN, 1956
ADVENTURES OF CAPTAIN FABIAN, 1951
ADVENTURES OF CASANOVA, 1948
ADVENTURES OF DON COYOTE, 1947
ADVENTURES OF DON JUAN, 1949
ADVENTURES OF GERARD, THE, 1970
ADVENTURES OF HAL 5, THE, 1958
ADVENTURES OF JANE, THE, 1949

ADVENTURES OF JANE ARDEN, 1939
ADVENTURES OF KITTY O'DAY, 1944
ADVENTURES OF MARCO POLO, THE, 1938
ADVENTURES OF MARTIN EDEN, THE, 1942
ADVENTURES OF PC 49, THE, 1949
ADVENTURES OF RUSTY, 1945
ADVENTURES OF SADIE, THE, 1955
ADVENTURES OF SHERLOCK HOLMES, THE, 1939
ADVENTURES OF TARTU, THE, 1943
ADVENTURESS, THE, 1946
ADVENTUROUS BLONDE, 1937
ADVERSARY, THE, 1973
ADVICE TO THE LOVELORN, 1933
AERIAL GUNNER, 1943
AFFAIR IN MONTE CARLO, 1953
AFFAIR IN RENO, 1957
AFFAIR OF SUSAN, 1935
AFFAIR TO REMEMBER, AN, 1957
AFFAIR WITH A STRANGER, 1953
AFFAIRS OF A GENTLEMAN, 1934
AFFAIRS OF A ROGUE, THE, 1949
AFFAIRS OF ANNABEL, 1938
AFFAIRS OF CAPPY RICKS, 1937
AFFAIRS OF DOBIE GILLIS, THE, 1953
AFFAIRS OF DR. HOLL, 1954
AFFAIRS OF GERALDINE, 1946
AFFAIRS OF MARTHA, THE, 1942
AFFAIRS OF MAUPASSANT, 1938
AFFAIRS OF SUSAN, 1945
AFFECTIONATELY YOURS, 1941
AFRICAN MANHUNT, 1955
AFRICAN TREASURE, 1952
AFTER MIDNIGHT WITH BOSTON BLACKIE, 1943
AFTER OFFICE HOURS, 1932
AFTER OFFICE HOURS, 1935
AFTER THE BALL, 1957
AFTER THE DANCE, 1935
AFTER THE FOX, 1966
AFTER THE THIN MAN, 1936
AFTER TOMORROW, 1932
AFTER TONIGHT, 1933
AFTER YOU, COMRADE, 1967
AGAINST ALL FLAGS, 1952
AGAINST THE TIDE, 1937
AGAINST THE WIND, 1948
AGE FOR LOVE, THE, 1931
AGE OF INNOCENCE, 1977
AGGIE APPLEBY, MAKER OF MEN, 1933
AGITATOR, THE, 1949
AGONY AND THE ECSTASY, THE, 1965
AH YING, 1984
AIDA, 1954
AIN'T MISBEHAVIN', 1955
AIR CADET, 1951
AIR CIRCUS, THE, 1928
AIR DEVILS, 1938
AIR FORCE, 1943
AIR HAWKS, 1935
AIR HOSTESS, 1933
AIR HOSTESS, 1949
AIR MAIL, 1932
AIR POLICE, 1931
AIR STRIKE, 1955
AIRBORNE, 1962
AIRPORT, 1970
AL JENNINGS OF OKLAHOMA, 1951
ALADDIN, 1987
ALASKA, 1944
ALASKA HIGHWAY, 1943
ALASKA PASSAGE, 1959
ALASKA PATROL, 1949
ALASKA SEAS, 1954
ALBERT, R.N., 1953
ALBUQUERQUE, 1948
ALCATRAZ ISLAND, 1937
ALERT IN THE SOUTH, 1954
ALEXANDER HAMILTON, 1931
ALEXANDER THE GREAT, 1956
ALF'S BABY, 1953
ALF'S BUTTON AFLOAT, 1938
ALF'S CARPET, 1929
ALI BABA, 1954
ALIAS A GENTLEMAN, 1948
ALIAS BOSTON BLACKIE, 1942
ALIAS BULLDOG DRUMMOND, 1935
ALIAS FRENCH GERTIE, 1930

ALIAS JESSE JAMES, 1959
ALIAS JIMMY VALENTINE, 1928
ALIAS JOHN LAW, 1935
ALIAS JOHN PRESTON, 1956
ALIAS MARY DOW, 1935
ALIAS MARY SMITH, 1932
ALIAS NICK BEAL, 1949
ALIAS THE BAD MAN, 1931
ALIAS THE CHAMP, 1949
ALIAS THE DEACON, 1940
ALIAS THE DOCTOR, 1932
ALIBI, 1931
ALIBI FOR MURDER, 1936
ALIBI INN, 1935
ALICE ADAMS, 1935
ALICE IN THE CITIES, 1974
ALICE IN WONDERLAND, 1951
ALICE'S ADVENTURES IN WONDERLAND, 1972
ALIVE ON SATURDAY, 1957
ALL ABOUT EVE, 1950
ALL-AMERICAN, THE, 1932
ALL-AMERICAN, THE, 1953
ALL-AMERICAN CHUMP, 1936
ALL-AMERICAN CO-ED, 1941
ALL-AMERICAN SWEETHEART, 1937
ALL-AROUND REDUCED
   PERSONALITY—OUTTAKES, THE, 1978
ALL AT SEA, 1935
ALL AT SEA, 1939
ALL AT SEA, 1958
ALL AT SEA, 1970
ALL BY MYSELF, 1943
ALL FOR MARY, 1956
ALL HANDS ON DECK, 1961
ALL I DESIRE, 1953
ALL IN, 1936
ALL MEN ARE ENEMIES, 1934
ALL OVER TOWN, 1937
ALL RIGHT, MY FRIEND, 1983
ALL THAT GLITTERS, 1936
ALL THAT HEAVEN ALLOWS, 1955
ALL THE BROTHERS WERE VALIANT, 1953
ALL THE KING'S HORSES, 1935
ALL THE WAY HOME, 1963
ALL THE WAY UP, 1970
ALL THE YOUNG MEN, 1960
ALL THIS AND HEAVEN TOO, 1940
ALL THROUGH THE NIGHT, 1942
ALL WOMEN HAVE SECRETS, 1939
ALLEGHENY UPRISING, 1939
ALLEGRO NON TROPPO, 1977
ALLERGIC TO LOVE, 1943
ALLIGATOR NAMED DAISY, AN, 1957
ALLOTMENT WIVES, INC., 1945
ALLURING GOAL, THE, 1930
ALMOST A DIVORCE, 1931
ALMOST A GENTLEMAN, 1938
ALMOST A GENTLEMAN, 1939
ALMOST A HONEYMOON, 1930
ALMOST A HONEYMOON, 1938
ALMOST MARRIED, 1942
ALMOST SUMMER, 1978
ALOHA, 1931
ALOMA OF THE SOUTH SEAS, 1941
ALONG CAME JONES, 1945
ALONG CAME LOVE, 1937
ALONG CAME SALLY, 1934
ALONG CAME YOUTH, 1931
ALONG THE NAVAJO TRAIL, 1945
ALONG THE OREGON TRAIL, 1947
ALONG THE RIO GRANDE, 1941
ALPHABET MURDERS, THE, 1966
**ALPHAVILLE, A STRANGE CASE OF LEMMY
   CAUTION, 1965**
ALVAREZ KELLY, 1966
ALWAYS A BRIDE, 1940
ALWAYS A BRIDE, 1954
ALWAYS A BRIDESMAID, 1943
ALWAYS ANOTHER DAWN, 1948
ALWAYS GOODBYE, 1931
ALWAYS GOODBYE, 1938
ALWAYS LEAVE THEM LAUGHING, 1949
ALWAYS TOGETHER, 1947
ALWAYS VICTORIOUS, 1960
AM I GUILTY?, 1940
AMATEUR CROOK, 1937

AMATEUR DADDY, 1932
AMATEUR GENTLEMAN, 1936
AMAZING COLOSSAL MAN, THE, 1957
AMAZING GRACE, 1974
AMAZING MR. BEECHAM, THE, 1949
AMAZING MR. FORREST, THE, 1943
AMAZING MR. WILLIAMS, 1939
AMAZING MONSIEUR FABRE, THE, 1952
AMAZON QUEST, 1949
AMBASSADOR BILL, 1931
AMBASSADOR'S DAUGHTER, THE, 1956
AMBUSH, 1939
AMBUSH, 1950
AMBUSH AT CIMARRON PASS, 1958
AMBUSH TRAIL, 1946
AMBUSH VALLEY, 1936
AMBUSHERS, THE, 1967
AMELIE OR THE TIME TO LOVE, 1961
AMERICA, AMERICA, 1963
AMERICAN EMPIRE, 1942
AMERICAN GUERRILLA IN THE PHILIPPINES, AN,
   1950
AMERICAN HOT WAX, 1978
AMERICAN LOVE, 1932
AMERICAN MADNESS, 1932
AMERICAN PRISONER, THE, 1929
AMERICAN ROMANCE, AN, 1944
AMERICANO, THE, 1955
AMONG HUMAN WOLVES, 1940
AMONG THE MISSING, 1934
AMONG VULTURES, 1964
AMOROUS MR. PRAWN, THE, 1965
AMOS 'N' ANDY, 1930
AMOUR, AMOUR, 1937
AMPHYTRYON, 1937
ANASTASIA, 1956
AND BABY MAKES THREE, 1949
AND NOW TOMORROW, 1944
AND ONE WAS BEAUTIFUL, 1940
AND QUIET FLOWS THE DON, 1960
AND SUDDEN DEATH, 1936
AND THE ANGELS SING, 1944
AND THE SAME TO YOU, 1960
AND THE SHIP SAILS ON, 1983
AND THEN THERE WERE NONE, 1945
ANDREI ROUBLOV, 1973
ANDROCLES AND THE LION, 1952
ANDROMEDA STRAIN, THE, 1971
ANDY, 1965
ANGEL AND THE BADMAN, 1947
ANGEL FROM TEXAS, AN, 1940
ANGEL IN EXILE, 1948
ANGEL LEVINE, THE, 1970
ANGEL ON MY SHOULDER, 1946
ANGEL ON THE AMAZON, 1948
ANGEL WHO PAWNED HER HARP, THE, 1956
ANGEL WORE RED, THE, 1960
ANGELA, 1955
ANGELO IN THE CROWD, 1952
ANGELS ALLEY, 1948
ANGEL'S HOLIDAY, 1937
ANGELS IN DISGUISE, 1949
ANGELS ONE FIVE, 1954
ANGELS OVER BROADWAY, 1940
ANGELS WASH THEIR FACES, 1939
ANGELS WITH BROKEN WINGS, 1941
ANGRY HILLS, THE, 1959
ANGRY ISLAND, 1960
ANGRY RED PLANET, THE, 1959
ANIMAL FARM, 1955
ANIMAL KINGDOM, THE, 1932
ANN CARVER'S PROFESSION, 1933
ANN VICKERS, 1933
ANNA, 1981
ANNA AND THE KING OF SIAM, 1946
ANNA CROSS, THE, 1954
ANNA KARENINA, 1935
ANNA KARENINA, 1948
ANNA OF RHODES, 1950
ANNABEL TAKES A TOUR, 1938
ANNABELLE'S AFFAIRS, 1931
ANNAPOLIS FAREWELL, 1935
ANNAPOLIS SALUTE, 1937
ANNAPOLIS STORY, AN, 1955
ANNE-MARIE, 1936
ANNE OF GREEN GABLES, 1934

ANNE OF THE INDIES, 1951
ANNE OF WINDY POPLARS, 1940
ANNE ONE HUNDRED, 1933
ANNIE LAURIE, 1936
ANNIE, LEAVE THE ROOM, 1935
ANOTHER DAWN, 1937
ANOTHER FACE, 1935
ANOTHER LANGUAGE, 1933
ANOTHER SHORE, 1948
ANOTHER SKY, 1960
ANOTHER THIN MAN, 1939
ANOTHER TIME, ANOTHER PLACE, 1958
ANTARCTICA, 1984
ANTHONY ADVERSE, 1936
ANTIGONE, 1962
ANTOINE ET ANTOINETTE, 1947
ANTONY AND CLEOPATRA, 1973
ANY MAN'S WIFE, 1936
ANY NUMBER CAN PLAY, 1949
ANY NUMBER CAN WIN, 1963
ANYBODY'S BLONDE, 1931
ANYBODY'S WOMAN, 1930
ANYBODY'S WAR, 1930
ANYTHING CAN HAPPEN, 1952
ANYTHING FOR A SONG, 1947
ANYTHING FOR A THRILL, 1937
ANYTHING GOES, 1936
ANYTHING GOES, 1956
ANYTHING MIGHT HAPPEN, 1935
ANYTHING TO DECLARE?, 1939
ANZIO, 1968
APACHE, 1954
APACHE AMBUSH, 1955
APACHE CHIEF, 1949
APACHE COUNTRY, 1952
APACHE DRUMS, 1951
APACHE GOLD, 1965
APACHE KID, THE, 1941
APACHE RIFLES, 1964
APACHE ROSE, 1947
APACHE TERRITORY, 1958
APACHE TRAIL, 1942
APACHE UPRISING, 1966
APACHE WAR SMOKE, 1952
APACHE WARRIOR, 1957
APACHE WOMAN, 1955
APARAJITO, 1959
APARTMENT FOR PEGGY, 1948
APOLLO GOES ON HOLIDAY, 1968
APOLOGY FOR MURDER, 1945
APPASSIONATA, 1946
APPLAUSE, 1929
APPOINTMENT FOR LOVE, 1941
APPOINTMENT IN BERLIN, 1943
APPOINTMENT IN HONDURAS, 1953
APPOINTMENT IN LONDON, 1953
APPOINTMENT WITH A SHADOW, 1958
APPOINTMENT WITH CRIME, 1945
APPOINTMENT WITH MURDER, 1948
APPRENTICESHIP OF DUDDY KRAVITZ, THE, 1974
APRIL BLOSSOMS, 1937
APRIL IN PARIS, 1953
APRIL 1, 2000, 1953
APRIL SHOWERS, 1948
ARABELLA, 1969
ARCTIC FLIGHT, 1952
ARCTIC MANHUNT, 1949
ARE HUSBANDS NECESSARY?, 1942
ARE THESE OUR CHILDREN?, 1931
ARE THESE OUR PARENTS?, 1944
ARE WE CIVILIZED?, 1934
ARE YOU A MASON?, 1934
ARE YOU LISTENING?, 1932
ARENA, 1953
AREN'T MEN BEASTS?, 1937
AREN'T WE ALL?, 1932
AREN'T WE WONDERFUL?, 1959
ARGYLE CASE, THE, 1929
ARGYLE SECRETS, THE, 1948
ARIANE, 1931
ARIANE, RUSSIAN MAID, 1932
ARISE, MY LOVE, 1940
ARIZONA, 1940
ARIZONA BADMAN, 1935
ARIZONA BOUND, 1941
ARIZONA BUSHWHACKERS, 1968

BOLD: Films on Videocassette

ARIZONA COWBOY, THE, 1950
ARIZONA CYCLONE, 1934
ARIZONA CYCLONE, 1941
ARIZONA DAYS, 1937
ARIZONA FRONTIER, 1940
ARIZONA GANGBUSTERS, 1940
ARIZONA GUNFIGHTER, 1937
ARIZONA KID, THE, 1930
ARIZONA KID, THE, 1939
ARIZONA LEGION, 1939
ARIZONA MAHONEY, 1936
ARIZONA MANHUNT, 1951
ARIZONA NIGHTS, 1934
ARIZONA RAIDERS, 1965
ARIZONA RAIDERS, THE, 1936
ARIZONA RANGER, THE, 1948
ARIZONA ROUNDUP, 1942
ARIZONA STAGECOACH, 1942
ARIZONA TERRITORY, 1950
ARIZONA TERROR, 1931
ARIZONA TERRORS, 1942
ARIZONA TO BROADWAY, 1933
ARIZONA TRAIL, 1943
ARIZONA TRAILS, 1935
ARIZONA WHIRLWIND, 1944
ARIZONIAN, THE, 1935
ARKANSAS JUDGE, 1941
ARKANSAS TRAVELER, THE, 1938
ARM OF THE LAW, 1932
ARMCHAIR DETECTIVE, THE, 1952
ARMED AND DANGEROUS, 1977
ARMORED CAR, 1937
ARMORED CAR ROBBERY, 1950
ARMS AND THE MAN, 1932
ARMS AND THE MAN, 1962
ARMY BOUND, 1952
ARMY GIRL, 1938
ARMY SURGEON, 1942
ARMY WIVES, 1944
ARNELO AFFAIR, THE, 1947
AROUND THE TOWN, 1938
AROUND THE WORLD, 1943
AROUND THE WORLD UNDER THE SEA, 1966
ARREST BULLDOG DRUMMOND, 1939
ARROW IN THE DUST, 1954
ARROWSMITH, 1931
ARSENAL STADIUM MYSTERY, THE, 1939
ARSENE LUPIN, 1932
ARSENE LUPIN RETURNS, 1938
ARSENIC AND OLD LACE, 1944
ARSON FOR HIRE, 1959
ARSON GANG BUSTERS, 1938
ARSON, INC., 1949
ARSON SQUAD, 1945
ART OF LOVE, THE, 1965
ARTHUR TAKES OVER, 1948
ARTISTS AND MODELS, 1955
ARTISTS AND MODELS ABROAD, 1938
AS GOOD AS MARRIED, 1937
AS HUSBANDS GO, 1934
AS LONG AS THEY'RE HAPPY, 1957
AS LONG AS YOU'RE NEAR ME, 1956
AS THE DEVIL COMMANDS, 1933
AS THE EARTH TURNS, 1934
AS THE SEA RAGES, 1960
AS YOU DESIRE ME, 1932
AS YOU LIKE IT, 1936
AS YOU WERE, 1951
AS YOUNG AS YOU FEEL, 1951
ASK A POLICEMAN, 1939
ASK ANY GIRL, 1959
ASK BECCLES, 1933
ASKING FOR TROUBLE, 1942
ASSASSIN, THE, 1953
ASSAULT OF THE REBEL GIRLS, 1960
ASSAULT ON A QUEEN, 1966
ASSIGNED TO DANGER, 1948
ASSIGNMENT IN BRITTANY, 1943
ASSIGNMENT K, 1968
ASSIGNMENT—PARIS, 1952
ASSOCIATE, THE, 1982
ASTERO, 1960
AT DAWN WE DIE, 1943
AT GUNPOINT, 1955
AT LONG LAST LOVE, 1975
AT SWORD'S POINT, 1951

AT THE RIDGE, 1931
AT THE STROKE OF NINE, 1957
AT WAR WITH THE ARMY, 1950
ATHENA, 1954
ATLANTIC, 1929
ATLANTIC ADVENTURE, 1935
ATLANTIC CITY, 1944
ATLANTIC CONVOY, 1942
ATLANTIC FERRY, 1941
ATLANTIC FLIGHT, 1937
ATLANTIS, THE LOST CONTINENT, 1961
ATLAS AGAINST THE CYCLOPS, 1963
ATLAS AGAINST THE CZAR, 1964
ATOMIC CITY, THE, 1952
ATOMIC KID, THE, 1954
ATOMIC MAN, THE, 1955
ATOMIC SUBMARINE, THE, 1960
ATRAGON, 1965
ATTACK OF THE CRAB MONSTERS, 1957
ATTACK OF THE 50 FOOT WOMAN, 1958
ATTACK OF THE MUSHROOM PEOPLE, 1964
ATTACK OF THE PUPPET PEOPLE, 1958
ATTACK ON THE IRON COAST, 1968
ATTEMPT TO KILL, 1961
ATTORNEY FOR THE DEFENSE, 1932
AUGUST WEEK-END, 1936
AUGUSTINE OF HIPPO, 1973
AULD LANG SYNE, 1929
AULD LANG SYNE, 1937
AUNT CLARA, 1954
AUNTIE MAME, 1958
AUSTERLITZ, 1960
AUTHOR! AUTHOR!, 1982
AUTUMN CROCUS, 1934
AUTUMN MARATHON, 1982
AVALANCHE, 1946
AVENGER, THE, 1931
AVENGER, THE, 1933
AVENGERS, THE, 1942
AVENGERS, THE, 1950
AVENGING HAND, THE, 1936
AVENGING RIDER, THE, 1943
AVENGING WATERS, 1936
AVIATOR, THE, 1929
AWAKENING, THE, 1938
AWAKENING OF JIM BURKE, 1935
AWAY ALL BOATS, 1956
AWFUL TRUTH, THE, 1937
AWFUL TRUTH, THE, 1929
AZAIS, 1931
AZURE EXPRESS, 1938
B. F.'S DAUGHTER, 1948
BABBITT, 1934
BABES IN BAGDAD, 1952
BABES ON SWING STREET, 1944
BABETTE'S FEAST, 1988
BABY AND THE BATTLESHIP, THE, 1957
BABY BOOM, 1987
BABY FACE HARRINGTON, 1935
BABY FACE MORGAN, 1942
BACCHANTES, THE, 1963
BACHELOR BAIT, 1934
BACHELOR DADDY, 1941
BACHELOR FATHER, 1931
BACHELOR FLAT, 1962
BACHELOR GIRL, THE, 1929
BACHELOR IN PARADISE, 1961
BACHELOR IN PARIS, 1953
BACHELOR MOTHER, 1939
BACHELOR OF ARTS, 1935
BACHELOR OF HEARTS, 1958
BACHELOR'S AFFAIRS, 1932
BACHELOR'S DAUGHTERS, THE, 1946
BACK AT THE FRONT, 1952
BACK DOOR TO HEAVEN, 1939
BACK DOOR TO HELL, 1964
BACK IN CIRCULATION, 1937
BACK IN THE SADDLE, 1941
BACK PAY, 1930
BACK ROOM BOY, 1942
BACK STREET, 1932
BACK STREET, 1941
BACK STREET, 1961
BACK TO BATAAN, 1945
BACK TO GOD'S COUNTRY, 1953
BACK TO NATURE, 1936

BACK TRAIL, 1948
BACKFIRE, 1950
BACKFIRE!, 1961
BACKGROUND TO DANGER, 1943
BACKLASH, 1947
BACKLASH, 1956
BACKSTAGE, 1937
BACKTRACK, 1969
BAD BOY, 1935
BAD BOY, 1938
BAD BOY, 1939
BAD BOY, 1949
BAD CHARLESTON CHARLIE, 1973
BAD COMPANY, 1931
BAD COMPANY, 1972
BAD DAY AT BLACK ROCK, 1955
BAD FOR EACH OTHER, 1954
BAD GUY, 1937
BAD LANDS, 1939
BAD LORD BYRON, THE, 1949
BAD MAN, THE, 1930
BAD MAN, THE, 1941
BAD MAN FROM RED BUTTE, 1940
BAD MAN OF BRIMSTONE, 1938
BAD MAN OF DEADWOOD, 1941
BAD MAN'S RIVER, 1972
BAD MEN OF MISSOURI, 1941
BAD MEN OF THE BORDER, 1945
BAD MEN OF THE HILLS, 1942
BAD MEN OF THUNDER GAP, 1943
BAD SISTER, 1931
BAD SISTER, 1947
BADGE OF HONOR, 1934
BADGE OF MARSHAL BRENNAN, THE, 1957
BADGER'S GREEN, 1934
BADGER'S GREEN, 1949
BADLANDERS, THE, 1958
BADLANDS OF DAKOTA, 1941
BADLANDS OF MONTANA, 1957
BADMAN'S COUNTRY, 1958
BADMAN'S GOLD, 1951
BADMAN'S TERRITORY, 1946
BAGDAD, 1949
BAHAMA PASSAGE, 1941
BAILOUT AT 43,000, 1957
BAIT, 1950
BAKER'S HAWK, 1976
BAL TABARIN, 1952
BALALAIKA, 1939
BALL AT SAVOY, 1936
BALL AT THE CASTLE, 1939
BALL OF FIRE, 1941
BALLAD OF A GUNFIGHTER, 1964
BALLAD OF A HUSSAR, 1963
BALLAD OF A SOLDIER, 1960
BALLAD OF COSSACK GLOOTA, 1938
BALLAD OF JOSIE, 1968
BALLERINA, 1950
BALLOON GOES UP, THE, 1942
BALTIC DEPUTY, 1937
BAMBOO BLONDE, THE, 1946
BAMBOO PRISON, THE, 1955
BAMBOO SAUCER, THE, 1968
BANANA RIDGE, 1941
BAND OF ANGELS, 1957
BAND OF THIEVES, 1962
BAND PLAYS ON, THE, 1934
BAND WAGGON, 1940
BAND WAGON, THE, 1953
BANDIDO, 1956
BANDIDOS, 1967
BANDIT, THE, 1949
BANDIT KING OF TEXAS, 1949
BANDIT OF ZHOBE, THE, 1959
BANDIT QUEEN, 1950
BANDIT RANGER, 1942
BANDIT TRAIL, THE, 1941
BANDITS OF CORSICA, THE, 1953
BANDITS OF DARK CANYON, 1947
BANDITS OF EL DORADO, 1951
BANDITS OF ORGOSOLO, 1964
BANDITS OF THE BADLANDS, 1945
BANDITS OF THE WEST, 1953
BANDITS ON THE WIND, 1964
BANDOLERO!, 1968
BANG BANG KID, THE, 1968

BANG, BANG, YOU'RE DEAD, 1966
BANG THE DRUM SLOWLY, 1973
BANJO ON MY KNEE, 1936
BANK ALARM, 1937
BANK DICK, THE, 1940
BANK MESSENGER MYSTERY, THE, 1936
BANK RAIDERS, THE, 1958
BANK SHOT, 1974
BANNERLINE, 1951
BAR L RANCH, 1930
BAR SINISTER, THE, 1955
BAR 20, 1943
BAR 20 JUSTICE, 1938
BAR 20 RIDES AGAIN, 1936
BAR Z BAD MEN, 1937
BARBARIAN AND THE GEISHA, THE, 1958
BARBARY COAST, 1935
BARBARY COAST GENT, 1944
BARBARY PIRATE, 1949
BARBED WIRE, 1952
BARBER OF SEVILLE, THE, 1947
BARBER OF SEVILLE, 1949
BARBER OF SEVILLE, THE, 1973
BARBER OF STAMFORD HILL, THE, 1963
BARBERINA, 1932
BARCAROLE, 1935
BAREFOOT BATTALION, THE, 1954
BAREFOOT BOY, 1938
BAREFOOT CONTESSA, THE, 1954
BAREFOOT IN THE PARK, 1967
BAREFOOT MAILMAN, THE, 1951
BARGAIN, THE, 1931
BARKER, THE, 1928
BARKLEYS OF BROADWAY, THE, 1949
BARNACLE BILL, 1935
BARNACLE BILL, 1941
BARNUM WAS RIGHT, 1929
BARNYARD FOLLIES, 1940
BARON MUNCHAUSEN, 1962
BARON OF ARIZONA, THE, 1950
BARONESS AND THE BUTLER, THE, 1938
BARRANCO, 1932
BARRETTS OF WIMPOLE STREET, THE, 1934
BARRETTS OF WIMPOLE STREET, THE, 1957
BARRICADE, 1939
BARRICADE, 1950
BARRIER, THE, 1937
BARRIER, 1966
BARS OF HATE, 1936
BARTLEBY, 1970
BARTON MYSTERY, THE, 1932
BASHFUL BACHELOR, THE, 1942
BASHFUL ELEPHANT, THE, 1962
BASKETBALL FIX, THE, 1951
BAT WHISPERS, THE, 1930
BATHING BEAUTY, 1944
BATTLE, THE, 1934
BATTLE AT APACHE PASS, THE, 1952
BATTLE AT BLOODY BEACH, 1961
BATTLE BENEATH THE EARTH, 1968
BATTLE CIRCUS, 1953
BATTLE CRY, 1955
BATTLE CRY, 1959
BATTLE FLAME, 1959
BATTLE FOR MUSIC, 1943
BATTLE FOR THE PLANET OF THE APES, 1973
BATTLE HELL, 1957
BATTLE HYMN, 1957
BATTLE IN OUTER SPACE, 1960
BATTLE OF BLOOD ISLAND, 1960
BATTLE OF BRITAIN, THE, 1969
BATTLE OF BROADWAY, 1938
BATTLE OF GALLIPOLI, 1931
BATTLE OF GREED, 1934
BATTLE OF LOVE'S RETURN, THE, 1971
BATTLE OF NERETVA, 1969
BATTLE OF PARIS, THE, 1929
BATTLE OF ROGUE RIVER, 1954
BATTLE OF THE AMAZONS, 1973
BATTLE OF THE BULGE, 1965
BATTLE OF THE CORAL SEA, 1959
BATTLE OF THE RAILS, 1949
BATTLE OF THE SEXES, THE, 1960
BATTLE OF THE VILLA FIORITA, THE, 1965
BATTLE OF THE WORLDS, 1961
BATTLE STATIONS, 1956

BATTLE TAXI, 1955
BATTLE ZONE, 1952
BATTLEAXE, THE, 1962
BATTLEGROUND, 1949
BATTLES OF CHIEF PONTIAC, 1952
BATTLESTAR GALACTICA, 1979
BATTLING BUCKAROO, 1932
BATTLING MARSHAL, 1950
BAY OF SAINT MICHEL, THE, 1963
BAYOU, 1957
BE MINE TONIGHT, 1933
BE MY GUEST, 1965
BE YOURSELF, 1930
BEACH BALL, 1965
BEACH BLANKET BINGO, 1965
BEACH PARTY, 1963
BEACH RED, 1967
BEACHCOMBER, 1938
BEACHCOMBER, 1955
BEADS OF ONE ROSARY, THE, 1982
BEAST MUST DIE, THE, 1974
BEAST OF HOLLOW MOUNTAIN, THE, 1956
BEAST WITH A MILLION EYES, THE, 1956
BEAT THE BAND, 1947
BEAT THE DEVIL, 1953
BEAU BANDIT, 1930
BEAU BRUMMELL, 1954
BEAU GESTE, 1939
BEAU GESTE, 1966
BEAU IDEAL, 1931
BEAU JAMES, 1957
BEAUTIFUL ADVENTURE, 1932
BEAUTIFUL BLONDE FROM BASHFUL BEND, THE, 1949
BEAUTIFUL BUT BROKE, 1944
BEAUTIFUL CHEAT, THE, 1946
BEAUTY AND THE BANDIT, 1946
BEAUTY AND THE BARGE, 1937
BEAUTY AND THE BEAST, 1947
BEAUTY AND THE BOSS, 1932
BEAUTY AND THE DEVIL, 1952
BEAUTY FOR SALE, 1933
BEAUTY FOR THE ASKING, 1939
BEAUTY ON PARADE, 1950
BEAUTY PARLOR, 1932
BEBO'S GIRL, 1964
BECAUSE OF HIM, 1946
BECAUSE OF YOU, 1952
BED AND BREAKFAST, 1930
BED AND BREAKFAST, 1936
BED OF ROSES, 1933
BEDELIA, 1946
BEDSIDE, 1934
BEDSIDE MANNER, 1945
BEDTIME STORY, 1942
BEEN DOWN SO LONG IT LOOKS LIKE UP TO ME, 1977
BEES IN PARADISE, 1944
BEFORE DAWN, 1933
BEFORE HIM ALL ROME TREMBLED, 1947
BEFORE I HANG, 1940
BEFORE MIDNIGHT, 1934
BEFORE MORNING, 1933
BEG, BORROW OR STEAL, 1937
BEGGAR STUDENT, THE, 1931
BEGGAR STUDENT, THE, 1958
BEGGARS IN ERMINE, 1934
BEGINNING OR THE END, THE, 1947
BEHEMOTH, THE SEA MONSTER, 1959
BEHIND CITY LIGHTS, 1945
BEHIND GREEN LIGHTS, 1935
BEHIND GREEN LIGHTS, 1946
BEHIND JURY DOORS, 1933
BEHIND LOCKED DOORS, 1948
BEHIND OFFICE DOORS, 1931
BEHIND PRISON GATES, 1939
BEHIND PRISON WALLS, 1943
BEHIND STONE WALLS, 1932
BEHIND THE EIGHT BALL, 1942
BEHIND THE EVIDENCE, 1935
BEHIND THE HEADLINES, 1937
BEHIND THE HEADLINES, 1956
BEHIND THE MASK, 1946
BEHIND THE MIKE, 1937
BEHIND THE NEWS, 1941
BEHIND YOUR BACK, 1937

BELA LUGOSI MEETS A BROOKLYN GORILLA, 1952
BELL, BOOK AND CANDLE, 1958
BELL-BOTTOM GEORGE, 1943
BELL FOR ADANO, A, 1945
BELLA DONNA, 1934
BELLE LE GRAND, 1951
BELLE OF NEW YORK, THE, 1952
BELLE OF OLD MEXICO, 1950
BELLE OF THE YUKON, 1944
BELLE STARR, 1941
BELLE STARR'S DAUGHTER, 1947
BELLES OF ST. CLEMENTS, THE, 1936
BELLS GO DOWN, THE, 1943
BELLS OF CAPISTRANO, 1942
BELLS OF SAN ANGELO, 1947
BELLS OF SAN FERNANDO, 1947
BELOVED, 1934
BELOVED BACHELOR, THE, 1931
BELOVED BRAT, 1938
BELOVED IMPOSTER, 1936
BELOVED INFIDEL, 1959
BELOVED VAGABOND, THE, 1936
BELOW THE BORDER, 1942
BELOW THE DEADLINE, 1936
BELOW THE DEADLINE, 1946
BELOW THE SEA, 1933
BEN, 1972
BEN HUR, 1959
BENEATH THE 12-MILE REEF, 1953
BENEATH WESTERN SKIES, 1944
BENGAL BRIGADE, 1954
BENGAL TIGER, 1936
BENSON MURDER CASE, THE, 1930
BERKELEY SQUARE, 1933
BERLIN ALEXANDERPLATZ, 1933
BERLIN CORRESPONDENT, 1942
BERMONDSEY KID, THE, 1933
BERMUDA AFFAIR, 1956
BERMUDA MYSTERY, 1944
BERNADETTE OF LOURDES, 1962
BEST FOOT FORWARD, 1943
BEST FRIENDS, 1982
BEST HOUSE IN LONDON, THE, 1969
BEST OF ENEMIES, 1933
BEST OF ENEMIES, THE, 1962
BEST OF THE BADMEN, 1951
BEST YEARS OF OUR LIVES, THE, 1946
BETRAYAL, 1932
BETRAYAL, 1939
BETRAYAL, THE, 1948
BETRAYAL, THE, 1958
BETTY CO-ED, 1946
BETWEEN FIGHTING MEN, 1932
BETWEEN HEAVEN AND HELL, 1956
BETWEEN MEN, 1935
BETWEEN TIME AND ETERNITY, 1960
BETWEEN TWO WOMEN, 1944
BETWEEN TWO WORLDS, 1944
BEWARE, 1946
BEWARE OF CHILDREN, 1961
BEWARE OF LADIES, 1937
BEWARE OF PITY, 1946
BEWARE SPOOKS, 1939
BEWARE! THE BLOB, 1972
BEYOND AND BACK, 1978
BEYOND EVIL, 1980
BEYOND GLORY, 1948
BEYOND THE BLUE HORIZON, 1942
BEYOND THE CITIES, 1930
BEYOND THE CURTAIN, 1960
BEYOND THE LAST FRONTIER, 1943
BEYOND THE LAW, 1934
BEYOND THE PECOS, 1945
BEYOND THE PURPLE HILLS, 1950
BEYOND THE RIO GRANDE, 1930
BEYOND THE ROCKIES, 1932
BEYOND THE SACRAMENTO, 1941
BEYOND TOMORROW, 1940
BIDDY, 1983
BIG BEAT, THE, 1958
BIG BLOCKADE, THE, 1942
BIG BLUE, THE, 1988
BIG BLUFF, THE, 1933
BIG BOSS, THE, 1941
BIG BOY, 1930
BIG BRAIN, THE, 1933

BOLD: Films on Videocassette

BIG BROWN EYES, 1936
BIG BUS, THE, 1976
BIG BUSINESS, 1930
BIG BUSINESS, 1934
BIG BUSINESS, 1937
BIG BUSINESS GIRL, 1931
BIG CAGE, THE, 1933
BIG CATCH, THE, 1968
BIG CHANCE, THE, 1933
BIG CHANCE, THE, 1957
BIG CHASE, THE, 1954
BIG CIRCUS, THE, 1959
BIG CITY, 1937
BIG CITY, THE, 1963
BIG COUNTRY, THE, 1958
BIG DAY, THE, 1960
BIG DEAL ON MADONNA STREET, THE, 1960
BIG EXECUTIVE, 1933
BIG FELLA, 1937
BIG FIX, THE, 1947
BIG FRAME, THE, 1953
BIG GAMBLE, THE, 1931
BIG GAMBLE, THE, 1961
BIG GAME, THE, 1936
BIG GUNDOWN, THE, 1968
BIG GUSHER, THE, 1951
BIG GUY, THE, 1939
BIG HAND FOR THE LITTLE LADY, A, 1966
BIG HEARTED HERBERT, 1934
BIG JOB, THE, 1965
BIG LAND, THE, 1957
BIG LEAGUER, 1953
BIG MONEY, 1930
BIG MONEY, THE, 1962
BIG NEWS, 1929
BIG NOISE, THE, 1936
BIG NOISE, THE, 1936
BIG PARTY, THE, 1930
BIG PAYOFF, THE, 1933
BIG POND, THE, 1930
BIG PUNCH, THE, 1948
BIG SHAKEDOWN, THE, 1934
BIG SHOT, THE, 1931
BIG SHOT, THE, 1937
BIG SHOT, THE, 1942
BIG SHOW, THE, 1937
BIG SHOW, THE, 1961
BIG SKY, THE, 1952
BIG SOMBRERO, THE, 1949
BIG SPLASH, THE, 1935
BIG STAMPEDE, THE, 1932
BIG STREET, THE, 1942
BIG TIME, 1929
BIG TIME OR BUST, 1934
BIG TOP PEE-WEE, 1988
BIG TOWN GIRL, 1937
BIG TRAIL, THE, 1930
BIGGEST BUNDLE OF THEM ALL, THE, 1968
BIKINI BEACH, 1964
BILL CRACKS DOWN, 1937
BILLIE, 1965
BILLION DOLLAR HOBO, THE, 1977
BILLION DOLLAR SCANDAL, 1932
BILL'S LEGACY, 1931
BILLY THE KID, 1930
BILLY THE KID, 1941
BILLY THE KID IN SANTA FE, 1941
BILLY THE KID RETURNS, 1938
BILLY THE KID TRAPPED, 1942
BILLY THE KID VS. DRACULA, 1966
BILLY THE KID WANTED, 1941
BILLY THE KID'S FIGHTING PALS, 1941
BILLY THE KID'S RANGE WAR, 1941
BILLY THE KID'S ROUNDUP, 1941
BIMBO THE GREAT, 1961
BIOGRAPHY OF A BACHELOR GIRL, 1935
BIQUEFARRE, 1983
BIRCH INTERVAL, 1976
BIRDS AND THE BEES, THE, 1965
BIRDS DO IT, 1966
BIRDS OF A FEATHER, 1935
BIRTH OF THE BLUES, 1941
BISHOP MURDER CASE, THE, 1930
BISHOP'S WIFE, THE, 1947
BITTER CREEK, 1954
BITTER SPRINGS, 1950

BITTER SWEET, 1933
BITTER SWEET, 1940
BIZARRE BIZARRE, 1939
BLACK ABBOT, THE, 1934
BLACK ACES, 1937
BLACK ANGEL, 1946
BLACK ARROW, 1948
BLACK BANDIT, 1938
BLACK BOOK, THE, 1949
BLACK CAMEL, THE, 1931
BLACK CAT, THE, 1941
BLACK COFFEE, 1931
BLACK DIAMONDS, 1932
BLACK DIAMONDS, 1940
BLACK DOLL, THE, 1938
BLACK DRAGONS, 1942
BLACK EAGLE, 1948
BLACK EYES, 1939
BLACK FRIDAY, 1940
BLACK GIRL, 1972
BLACK GLOVE, 1954
BLACK GOLD, 1947
BLACK HAND GANG, THE, 1930
BLACK HILLS, 1948
BLACK HILLS EXPRESS, 1943
BLACK HORSE CANYON, 1954
BLACK ICE, THE, 1957
BLACK KING, 1932
BLACK LASH, THE, 1952
BLACK LIMELIGHT, 1938
BLACK MARKET RUSTLERS, 1943
BLACK MASK, 1935
BLACK MEMORY, 1947
BLACK PARACHUTE, THE, 1944
BLACK RAVEN, THE, 1943
BLACK RIDER, THE, 1954
BLACK ROSE, THE, 1950
BLACK ROSES, 1936
BLACK SHEEP, 1935
BLACK SHEEP OF WHITEHALL, THE, 1941
BLACK SPURS, 1965
BLACK SUN, THE, 1979
BLACK SWAN, THE, 1942
BLACK TENT, THE, 1956
BLACK 13, 1954
BLACK TIGHTS, 1962
BLACK TORMENT, THE, 1965
BLACK TULIP, THE, 1937
BLACK WATERS, 1929
BLACK WHIP, THE, 1956
BLACK WIDOW, 1951
BLACKJACK KETCHUM, DESPERADO, 1956
BLACKMAIL, 1929
BLACKMAIL, 1939
BLACKMAIL, 1947
BLACKMAILED, 1951
BLACKMAILER, 1936
BLACKOUT, 1940
BLACKOUT, 1950
BLACKWELL'S ISLAND, 1939
BLADES OF THE MUSKETEERS, 1953
BLAME THE WOMAN, 1932
BLARNEY KISS, 1933
BLAZE O' GLORY, 1930
BLAZE OF GLORY, 1963
BLAZING BARRIERS, 1937
BLAZING FRONTIER, 1944
BLAZING GUNS, 1943
BLAZING SIX SHOOTERS, 1940
BLAZING SIXES, 1937
BLAZING SUN, THE, 1950
BLAZING TRAIL, THE, 1949
BLESS 'EM ALL, 1949
BLIND ADVENTURE, 1933
BLIND ALIBI, 1938
BLIND DATE, 1934
BLIND DESIRE, 1948
BLIND FOLLY, 1939
BLIND GODDESS, THE, 1948
BLIND JUSTICE, 1934
BLIND MAN'S BLUFF, 1952
BLIND SPOT, 1932
BLIND SPOT, 1958
BLINDFOLD, 1966
BLITHE SPIRIT, 1945

BLOCK BUSTERS, 1944
BLOCKADE, 1928
BLOCKADE, 1929
BLOCKADE, 1938
BLOCKHOUSE, THE, 1974
BLOND CHEAT, 1938
BLONDE ALIBI, 1946
BLONDE BAIT, 1956
BLONDE BLACKMAILER, 1955
BLONDE COMET, 1941
BLONDE CRAZY, 1931
BLONDE DYNAMITE, 1950
BLONDE FEVER, 1944
BLONDE FOR A DAY, 1946
BLONDE FROM BROOKLYN, 1945
BLONDE FROM PEKING, THE, 1968
BLONDE FROM SINGAPORE, THE, 1941
BLONDE INSPIRATION, 1941
BLONDE NIGHTINGALE, 1931
BLONDE PICKUP, 1955
BLONDE RANSOM, 1945
BLONDE SAVAGE, 1947
BLONDE TROUBLE, 1937
BLONDES AT WORK, 1938
BLONDES FOR DANGER, 1938
BLONDIE FOR VICTORY, 1942
BLONDIE JOHNSON, 1933
BLOOD AND STEEL, 1959
BLOOD ON THE MOON, 1948
BLOOD ORANGE, 1953
BLOOD WEDDING, 1981
BLOODHOUNDS OF BROADWAY, 1952
BLOSSOMS IN THE DUST, 1941
BLOSSOMS ON BROADWAY, 1937
BLOW YOUR OWN TRUMPET, 1958
BLUE CANADIAN ROCKIES, 1952
BLUE DANUBE, 1932
BLUE FIN, 1978
BLUE HAWAII, 1961
BLUE IDOL, THE, 1931
BLUE LIGHT, THE, 1932
BLUE PARROT, THE, 1953
BLUE SCAR, 1949
BLUE SKIES AGAIN, 1983
BLUE SMOKE, 1935
BLUE SQUADRON, THE, 1934
BLUE STEEL, 1934
BLUE SUNSHINE, 1978
BLUE VEIL, THE, 1947
BLUE VEIL, THE, 1951
BLUE, WHITE, AND PERFECT, 1941
BLUEBEARD, 1944
BLUEPRINT FOR ROBBERY, 1961
BLUES FOR LOVERS, 1966
BLUES IN THE NIGHT, 1941
BOAT FROM SHANGHAI, 1931
BOBBIKINS, 1959
BOBBY WARE IS MISSING, 1955
BOB'S YOUR UNCLE, 1941
BOCCACCIO, 1936
BODY AND SOUL, 1931
BODY DISAPPEARS, THE, 1941
BODY SNATCHER, THE, 1945
BODY STEALERS, THE, 1969
BODYGUARD, 1948
BODYHOLD, 1950
BOHEMIAN GIRL, THE, 1936
BOHEMIAN RAPTURE, 1948
BOILING POINT, THE, 1932
BOLD AND THE BRAVE, THE, 1956
BOLD CABALLERO, 1936
BOLD FRONTIERSMAN, THE, 1948
BOLERO, 1982
BOMB IN THE HIGH STREET, 1961
BOMBA AND THE HIDDEN CITY, 1950
BOMBA AND THE JUNGLE GIRL, 1952
BOMBA ON PANTHER ISLAND, 1949
BOMBA THE JUNGLE BOY, 1949
BOMBARDIER, 1943
BOMBARDMENT OF MONTE CARLO, THE, 1931
BOMBAY CLIPPER, 1942
BOMBAY MAIL, 1934
BOMBERS B-52, 1957
BOMBER'S MOON, 1943
BOMBS OVER BURMA, 1942
BOMBS OVER LONDON, 1937

BOMBSIGHT STOLEN, 1941
BONANZA TOWN, 1951
BOND OF FEAR, 1956
BOND STREET, 1948
BONNE CHANCE, 1935
BONNIE PRINCE CHARLIE, 1948
BOOBY TRAP, 1957
BOOGENS, THE, 1982
BOOLOO, 1938
BOOM TOWN, 1940
BOOMERANG, 1934
BOOT HILL, 1969
BOOTHILL BRIGADE, 1937
BOOTS AND SADDLES, 1937
BOOTS! BOOTS!, 1934
BOOTS MALONE, 1952
BOOTS OF DESTINY, 1937
BOP GIRL GOES CALYPSO, 1957
BORDER BADMEN, 1945
BORDER BANDITS, 1946
BORDER BRIGANDS, 1935
BORDER BUCKAROOS, 1943
BORDER CABALLERO, 1936
BORDER CAFE, 1937
BORDER DEVILS, 1932
BORDER FEUD, 1947
BORDER FLIGHT, 1936
BORDER G-MAN, 1938
BORDER LAW, 1931
BORDER LEGION, THE, 1930
BORDER LEGION, THE, 1940
BORDER OUTLAWS, 1950
BORDER PATROL, 1943
BORDER PATROLMAN, THE, 1936
BORDER PHANTOM, 1937
BORDER RANGERS, 1950
BORDER RIVER, 1954
BORDER ROMANCE, 1930
BORDER SADDLEMATES, 1952
BORDER STREET, 1950
BORDER TREASURE, 1950
BORDER VIGILANTES, 1941
BORDER WOLVES, 1938
BORDERLAND, 1937
BORDERLINE, 1950
BORDERTOWN GUNFIGHTERS, 1943
BORIS GODUNOV, 1959
BORN AGAIN, 1978
BORN FOR GLORY, 1935
BORN LUCKY, 1932
BORN RECKLESS, 1937
BORN RECKLESS, 1959
BORN THAT WAY, 1937
BORN TO BE BAD, 1934
BORN TO BE BAD, 1950
BORN TO BE LOVED, 1959
BORN TO BE WILD, 1938
BORN TO DANCE, 1936
BORN TO FIGHT, 1938
BORN TO GAMBLE, 1935
BORN TO KILL, 1947
BORN TO LOVE, 1931
BORN TO SING, 1942
BORN TO SPEED, 1947
BORN TO THE SADDLE, 1953
BORN TO THE WEST, 1937
BORN YESTERDAY, 1951
BORROW A MILLION, 1934
BORROWED CLOTHES, 1934
BORROWED HERO, 1941
BORROWED TROUBLE, 1948
BORROWED WIVES, 1930
BORROWING TROUBLE, 1937
BOSS, THE, 1956
BOSS OF BIG TOWN, 1943
BOSS OF BULLION CITY, 1941
BOSS OF HANGTOWN MESA, 1942
BOSS OF LONELY VALLEY, 1937
BOSS OF THE RAWHIDE, 1944
BOSS RIDER OF GUN CREEK, 1936
BOSS'S SON, THE, 1978
BOSTON BLACKIE AND THE LAW, 1946
BOSTON BLACKIE BOOKED ON SUSPICION, 1945
BOSTON BLACKIE GOES HOLLYWOOD, 1942
BOSTON BLACKIE'S CHINESE VENTURE, 1949
BOSTON BLACKIE'S RENDEZVOUS, 1945

BOTH SIDES OF THE LAW, 1953
BOTTOM OF THE BOTTLE, THE, 1956
BOTTOMS UP, 1934
BOTTOMS UP, 1960
BOULDER DAM, 1936
BOUNTIFUL SUMMER, 1951
BOUNTY HUNTER, THE, 1954
BOWERY, THE, 1933
BOWERY AT MIDNIGHT, 1942
BOWERY BATTALION, 1951
BOWERY BLITZKRIEG, 1941
BOWERY BOMBSHELL, 1946
BOWERY BOY, 1940
BOWERY BOYS MEET THE MONSTERS, THE, 1954
BOWERY BUCKAROOS, 1947
BOWERY CHAMPS, 1944
BOWERY TO BAGDAD, 1955
BOWERY TO BROADWAY, 1944
BOXER, 1971
BOY, A GIRL AND A BIKE, A, 1949
BOY, A GIRL, AND A DOG, A, 1946
BOY AND THE BRIDGE, THE, 1959
BOY FRIEND, 1939
BOY FRIEND, THE, 1971
BOY FROM INDIANA, 1950
BOY FROM OKLAHOMA, THE, 1954
BOY MEETS GIRL, 1938
BOY OF THE STREETS, 1937
BOY SLAVES, 1938
BOY TROUBLE, 1939
BOY! WHAT A GIRL, 1947
BOY WHO COULD FLY, THE, 1986
BOYD'S SHOP, 1960
BOYFRIENDS AND GIRLFRIENDS, 1988
BOYS FROM SYRACUSE, 1940
BOYS OF PAUL STREET, THE, 1969
BOYS OF THE CITY, 1940
BOYS' RANCH, 1946
BOY'S REFORMATORY, 1939
BOYS WILL BE BOYS, 1936
BRACELETS, 1931
BRAIN, THE, 1965
BRAIN MACHINE, THE, 1955
BRAIN, THE, 1969
BRAND OF FEAR, 1949
BRAND OF THE DEVIL, 1944
BRANDED, 1931
BRANDED, 1951
BRANDED A COWARD, 1935
BRANDED MEN, 1931
BRANDY FOR THE PARSON, 1952
BRASHER DOUBLOON, THE, 1947
BRASIL ANNO 2,000, 1968
BRASS BOTTLE, THE, 1964
BRASS LEGEND, THE, 1956
BRAT, THE, 1930
BRAT, THE, 1931
BRAVE BULLS, THE, 1951
BRAVE DON'T CRY, THE, 1952
BRAVE WARRIOR, 1952
BRAZIL, 1944
BREAD AND CHOCOLATE, 1978
BREAD OF LOVE, THE, 1954
BREAK IN THE CIRCLE, THE, 1957
BREAK OF DAY, 1977
BREAK OF HEARTS, 1935
BREAK THE NEWS, 1938
BREAK, THE, 1962
BREAKAWAY, 1956
BREAKDOWN, 1953
BREAKERS AHEAD, 1935
BREAKERS AHEAD, 1938
BREAKFAST AT TIFFANY'S, 1961
BREAKFAST FOR TWO, 1937
BREAKFAST IN HOLLYWOOD, 1946
BREAKING POINT, THE, 1950
BREAKING POINT, THE, 1961
BREAKING THE ICE, 1938
BREAKING THE SOUND BARRIER, 1952
BREAKOUT, 1960
BREAKTHROUGH, 1950
BREATH OF LIFE, 1962
BREATH OF SCANDAL, A, 1960
BREED OF THE BORDER, 1933
BREEZING HOME, 1937
BREWSTER'S MILLIONS, 1935

BREWSTER'S MILLIONS, 1945
BRIDAL PATH, THE, 1959
BRIDAL SUITE, 1939
BRIDE BY MISTAKE, 1944
BRIDE CAME C.O.D., THE, 1941
BRIDE COMES HOME, 1936
BRIDE FOR HENRY, A, 1937
BRIDE FOR SALE, 1949
BRIDE OF THE DESERT, 1929
BRIDE OF THE GORILLA, 1951
BRIDE OF THE LAKE, 1934
BRIDE OF THE MONSTER, 1955
BRIDE OF THE REGIMENT, 1930
BRIDE OF VENGEANCE, 1949
BRIDE WALKS OUT, THE, 1936
BRIDE WITH A DOWRY, 1954
BRIDE WORE BOOTS, THE, 1946
BRIDE WORE CRUTCHES, THE, 1940
BRIDE WORE RED, THE, 1937
BRIDEGROOM FOR TWO, 1932
BRIDES ARE LIKE THAT, 1936
BRIDES OF FU MANCHU, THE, 1966
BRIDES TO BE, 1934
BRIDGE OF SAN LUIS REY, THE, 1929
BRIDGE OF SAN LUIS REY, THE, 1944
BRIDGE OF SIGHS, 1936
BRIDGE TO THE SUN, 1961
BRIDGE, THE, 1961
BRIDGES AT TOKO-RI, THE, 1954
BRIEF ECSTASY, 1937
BRIEF ENCOUNTER, 1945
BRIEF MOMENT, 1933
BRIGADOON, 1954
BRIGAND OF KANDAHAR, THE, 1965
BRIGAND, THE, 1952
BRIGGS FAMILY, THE, 1940
BRIGHAM YOUNG—FRONTIERSMAN, 1940
BRIGHT LEAF, 1950
BRIGHT LIGHTS, 1931
BRIGHT LIGHTS, 1935
BRIGHT ROAD, 1953
BRIGHT VICTORY, 1951
BRIGHTY OF THE GRAND CANYON, 1967
BRILLIANT MARRIAGE, 1936
BRIMSTONE, 1949
BRING ON THE GIRLS, 1945
BRING YOUR SMILE ALONG, 1955
BRINGING UP BABY, 1938
BRINGING UP FATHER, 1946
BRITANNIA OF BILLINGSGATE, 1933
BRITISH AGENT, 1934
BRITISH INTELLIGENCE, 1940
BROADMINDED, 1931
BROADWAY, 1929
BROADWAY, 1942
BROADWAY BABIES, 1929
BROADWAY BAD, 1933
BROADWAY BIG SHOT, 1942
BROADWAY BILL, 1934
BROADWAY GONDOLIER, 1935
BROADWAY HOOFER, THE, 1929
BROADWAY HOSTESS, 1935
BROADWAY LIMITED, 1941
BROADWAY MELODY OF 1936, 1935
BROADWAY MELODY OF 1940, 1940
BROADWAY MELODY OF '38, 1937
BROADWAY MELODY, THE, 1929
BROADWAY MUSKETEERS, 1938
BROADWAY RHYTHM, 1944
BROADWAY SCANDALS, 1929
BROADWAY SERENADE, 1939
BROADWAY THROUGH A KEYHOLE, 1933
BROADWAY TO CHEYENNE, 1932
BROADWAY TO HOLLYWOOD, 1933
BROKEN ARROW, 1950
BROKEN BLOSSOMS, 1936
BROKEN DREAMS, 1933
BROKEN HORSESHOE, THE, 1953
BROKEN JOURNEY, 1948
BROKEN LANCE, 1954
BROKEN LAND, THE, 1962
BROKEN LOVE, 1946
BROKEN LULLABY, 1932
BROKEN MELODY, 1938
BROKEN MELODY, THE, 1934
BROKEN ROSARY, THE, 1934

BOLD: Films on Videocassette

BROKEN STAR, THE, 1956
BROKEN WING, THE, 1932
BRONCO BULLFROG, 1972
BRONCO BUSTER, 1952
BRONTE SISTERS, THE, 1979
BRONZE BUCKAROO, THE, 1939
BROOKLYN ORCHID, 1942
BROTH OF A BOY, 1959
BROTHER ALFRED, 1932
BROTHER JOHN, 1971
BROTHER ORCHID, 1940
BROTHER RAT, 1938
BROTHER RAT AND A BABY, 1940
BROTHER SUN, SISTER MOON, 1973
BROTHERS, 1930
BROTHERS AND SISTERS, 1980
BROTHERS IN LAW, 1957
BROTHERS IN THE SADDLE, 1949
BROTHERS OF THE WEST, 1938
BROTHERS O'TOOLE, THE, 1973
BROTHERS, THE, 1948
BROWN SUGAR, 1931
BROWN WALLET, THE, 1936
BROWNING VERSION, THE, 1951
BRUSHFIRE, 1962
BRUTE MAN, THE, 1946
BUBBLE, THE, 1967
BUCCANEER, THE, 1958
BUCCANEER, THE, 1938
BUCCANEER'S GIRL, 1950
BUCHANAN RIDES ALONE, 1958
BUCK BENNY RIDES AGAIN, 1940
BUCKAROO FROM POWDER RIVER, 1948
BUCKAROO SHERIFF OF TEXAS, 1951
BUCKET OF BLOOD, A, 1959
BUCKSKIN, 1968
BUCKSKIN FRONTIER, 1943
BUCKSKIN LADY, THE, 1957
BUDDIES, 1983
BUFFALO BILL, HERO OF THE FAR WEST, 1962
BUFFALO BILL IN TOMAHAWK TERRITORY, 1952
BUFFALO BILL RIDES AGAIN, 1947
BUFFALO GUN, 1961
BUGLE SOUNDS, THE, 1941
BUGLES IN THE AFTERNOON, 1952
BULLDOG BREED, THE, 1960
BULLDOG DRUMMOND, 1929
BULLDOG DRUMMOND AT BAY, 1937
BULLDOG DRUMMOND COMES BACK, 1937
BULLDOG DRUMMOND ESCAPES, 1937
BULLDOG DRUMMOND IN AFRICA, 1938
BULLDOG DRUMMOND STRIKES BACK, 1934
BULLDOG DRUMMOND'S BRIDE, 1939
BULLDOG DRUMMOND'S PERIL, 1938
BULLDOG DRUMMOND'S REVENGE, 1937
BULLDOG DRUMMOND'S SECRET POLICE, 1939
BULLDOG EDITION, 1936
BULLDOG SEES IT THROUGH, 1940
BULLET CODE, 1940
BULLET FOR A BADMAN, 1964
BULLET FOR JOEY, A, 1955
BULLET FOR STEFANO, 1950
BULLET IS WAITING, A, 1954
BULLET SCARS, 1942
BULLETS FOR O'HARA, 1941
BULLETS FOR RUSTLERS, 1940
BULLETS OR BALLOTS, 1936
BULLFIGHTER AND THE LADY, 1951
BULLFIGHTERS, THE, 1945
BULLWHIP, 1958
BUNCO SQUAD, 1950
BUNDLE OF JOY, 1956
BUNGALOW 13, 1948
BUNKER BEAN, 1936
BUREAU OF MISSING PERSONS, 1933
BURG THEATRE, 1936
BURGLAR, THE, 1956
BURIED ALIVE, 1939
BURMA CONVOY, 1941
BURN 'EM UP O'CONNER, 1939
BURNING GOLD, 1936
BURNING HILLS, THE, 1956
BURNING UP, 1930
BURY ME NOT ON THE LONE PRAIRIE, 1941
BUS RILEY'S BACK IN TOWN, 1965
BUS STOP, 1956

BUSHWHACKERS, THE, 1952
BUSINESS AND PLEASURE, 1932
BUSMAN'S HOLIDAY, 1936
BUSMAN'S HONEYMOON, 1940
BUSSES ROAR, 1942
BUSTER KEATON STORY, THE, 1957
BUSYBODY, THE, 1967
BUT NOT FOR ME, 1959
BUT NOT IN VAIN, 1948
BUT THE FLESH IS WEAK, 1932
BUTCH CASSIDY AND THE SUNDANCE KID, 1969
BUTCH MINDS THE BABY, 1942
BUTLER'S DILEMMA, THE, 1943
BUTTERFLIES ARE FREE, 1972
BUY ME THAT TOWN, 1941
BWANA DEVIL, 1953
BY APPOINTMENT ONLY, 1933
BY CANDLELIGHT, 1934
BY THE LIGHT OF THE SILVERY MOON, 1953
BY WHOSE HAND?, 1932
BY WHOSE HAND?, 1932
BY YOUR LEAVE, 1935
BYE BYE BARBARA, 1969
BYE BYE BIRDIE, 1963
BYE BYE BRAVERMAN, 1968
BYPASS TO HAPPINESS, 1934
C-MAN, 1949
C.O.D., 1932
CABINET OF CALIGARI, THE, 1962
CACTUS IN THE SNOW, 1972
CADDY, THE, 1953
CADET GIRL, 1941
CADET-ROUSSELLE, 1954
CAESAR AND CLEOPATRA, 1946
CAFE COLETTE, 1937
CAFE DE PARIS, 1938
CAFE HOSTESS, 1940
CAFE MASCOT, 1936
CAFE SOCIETY, 1939
CAGE OF GOLD, 1950
CAGE OF NIGHTINGALES, A, 1947
CAGED FURY, 1948
CAIN AND MABEL, 1936
CAINE MUTINY, THE, 1954
CAIRO, 1942
CAIRO, 1963
CAIRO ROAD, 1950
CALABUCH, 1956
CALAMITY JANE AND SAM BASS, 1949
CALCULATED RISK, 1963
CALCUTTA, 1947
CALENDAR, THE, 1931
CALENDAR, THE, 1948
CALENDAR GIRL, 1947
CALIFORNIA, 1946
CALIFORNIA, 1963
CALIFORNIA CONQUEST, 1952
CALIFORNIA FIREBRAND, 1948
CALIFORNIA FRONTIER, 1938
CALIFORNIA JOE, 1944
CALIFORNIA MAIL, THE, 1937
CALIFORNIA PASSAGE, 1950
CALIFORNIA STRAIGHT AHEAD, 1937
CALIFORNIA TRAIL, THE, 1933
CALIFORNIAN, THE, 1937
CALL, THE, 1938
CALL A MESSENGER, 1939
CALL HER SAVAGE, 1932
CALL IT A DAY, 1937
CALL IT LUCK, 1934
CALL ME BWANA, 1963
CALL ME GENIUS, 1961
CALL ME MADAM, 1953
CALL ME MAME, 1933
CALL ME MISTER, 1951
CALL NORTHSIDE 777, 1948
CALL OF THE BLOOD, 1948
CALL OF THE CANYON, 1942
CALL OF THE CIRCUS, 1930
CALL OF THE FLESH, 1930
CALL OF THE JUNGLE, 1944
CALL OF THE KLONDIKE, 1950
CALL OF THE PRAIRIE, 1936
CALL OF THE ROCKIES, 1938
CALL OF THE SEA, THE, 1930
CALL OF THE SOUTH SEAS, 1944

CALL OF THE WILD, 1972
CALL OF THE YUKON, 1938
CALL OUT THE MARINES, 1942
CALL THE MESQUITEERS, 1938
CALLBOX MYSTERY, THE, 1932
CALLED BACK, 1933
CALLING ALL CROOKS, 1938
CALLING ALL HUSBANDS, 1940
CALLING ALL MARINES, 1939
CALLING DR. DEATH, 1943
CALLING DR. GILLESPIE, 1942
CALLING DR. KILDARE, 1939
CALLING PAUL TEMPLE, 1948
CALLING PHILO VANCE, 1940
CALLING THE TUNE, 1936
CALLING WILD BILL ELLIOTT, 1943
CALM YOURSELF, 1935
CALYPSO HEAT WAVE, 1957
CALYPSO JOE, 1957
CAMELS ARE COMING, THE, 1934
CAMEO KIRBY, 1930
CAMERA BUFF, 1983
CAMPBELL'S KINGDOM, 1957
CAMPUS CONFESSIONS, 1938
CAMPUS HONEYMOON, 1948
CAMPUS RHYTHM, 1943
CAMPUS SLEUTH, 1948
CAN THIS BE DIXIE?, 1936
CAN YOU HEAR ME MOTHER?, 1935
CANADIAN PACIFIC, 1949
CANADIANS, THE, 1961
CANAL ZONE, 1942
CANARIES SOMETIMES SING, 1930
CANARY MURDER CASE, THE, 1929
CANCEL MY RESERVATION, 1972
CANDIDATE FOR MURDER, 1966
CANDIDE, 1962
CANDLELIGHT IN ALGERIA, 1944
CANDLES AT NINE, 1944
CANNIBAL ATTACK, 1954
CANNON AND THE NIGHTINGALE, THE, 1969
CANNONBALL EXPRESS, 1932
CANNONBALL RUN, THE, 1981
CANON CITY, 1948
CAN'T HELP SINGING, 1944
CANTERBURY TALE, A, 1944
CANTOR'S SON, THE, 1937
CANYON AMBUSH, 1952
CANYON CITY, 1943
CANYON CROSSROADS, 1955
CANYON HAWKS, 1930
CANYON OF MISSING MEN, THE, 1930
CANYON PASSAGE, 1946
CANYON RAIDERS, 1951
CANYON RIVER, 1956
CAPE CANAVERAL MONSTERS, 1960
CAPER OF THE GOLDEN BULLS, THE, 1967
CAPPY RICKS RETURNS, 1935
CAPRICE, 1967
CAPTAIN APPLEJACK, 1931
CAPTAIN BILL, 1935
CAPTAIN BLACK JACK, 1952
CAPTAIN BLOOD, 1935
CAPTAIN BOYCOTT, 1947
CAPTAIN CALAMITY, 1936
CAPTAIN CAREY, U.S.A, 1950
CAPTAIN CAUTION, 1940
CAPTAIN CHINA, 1949
CAPTAIN FROM KOEPENICK, 1933
CAPTAIN FROM KOEPENICK, THE, 1956
CAPTAIN FURY, 1939
CAPTAIN HATES THE SEA, THE, 1934
CAPTAIN HORATIO HORNBLOWER, 1951
CAPTAIN HURRICANE, 1935
CAPTAIN IS A LADY, THE, 1940
CAPTAIN JOHN SMITH AND POCAHONTAS, 1953
CAPTAIN KIDD, 1945
CAPTAIN KIDD AND THE SLAVE GIRL, 1954
CAPTAIN LIGHTFOOT, 1955
CAPTAIN MOONLIGHT, 1940
CAPTAIN NEMO AND THE UNDERWATER CITY, 1969
CAPTAIN OF THE GUARD, 1930
CAPTAIN PIRATE, 1952
CAPTAIN SCARLETT, 1953
CAPTAIN SINDBAD, 1963

CAPTAIN THUNDER, 1931
CAPTAIN TUGBOAT ANNIE, 1945
CAPTAIN'S KID, THE, 1937
CAPTAIN'S ORDERS, 1937
CAPTAIN'S PARADISE, THE, 1953
CAPTAIN'S TABLE, THE, 1936
CAPTAIN'S TABLE, THE, 1960
CAPTIVATION, 1931
CAPTIVE CITY, 1952
CAPTIVE GIRL, 1950
CAPTIVE OF BILLY THE KID, 1952
CAPTIVE WILD WOMAN, 1943
CAPTIVE WOMEN, 1952
CAPTURE, THE, 1950
CAPTURED, 1933
CAR 99, 1935
CAR OF DREAMS, 1935
CARAVAN, 1934
CARAVAN, 1946
CARAVAN TRAIL, THE, 1946
CARBINE WILLIAMS, 1952
CARDBOARD CAVALIER, THE, 1949
CARDINAL, THE, 1936
CARDINAL RICHELIEU, 1935
CAREER, 1939
CAREER GIRL, 1944
CAREER WOMAN, 1936
CAREERS, 1929
CAREFREE, 1938
CAREFUL, SOFT SHOULDERS, 1942
CARELESS AGE, 1929
CARELESS LADY, 1932
CARELESS YEARS, THE, 1957
CARETAKERS DAUGHTER, THE, 1952
CARGO TO CAPETOWN, 1950
CARIBBEAN, 1952
CARIBBEAN MYSTERY, THE, 1945
CARIBOO TRAIL, THE, 1950
CARMELA, 1949
CARMEN, 1931
CARMEN, 1946
CARMEN, 1949
CARNATION KID, 1929
CARNEGIE HALL, 1947
CARNIVAL, 1931
CARNIVAL, 1935
CARNIVAL, 1946
CARNIVAL, 1953
CARNIVAL BOAT, 1932
CARNIVAL IN COSTA RICA, 1947
CARNIVAL IN FLANDERS, 1936
CARNIVAL LADY, 1933
CARNIVAL OF SINNERS, 1947
CARNIVAL QUEEN, 1937
CARNIVAL ROCK, 1957
CARNIVAL STORY, 1954
CAROLINA, 1934
CAROLINA BLUES, 1944
CAROLINA CANNONBALL, 1955
CAROLINA MOON, 1940
CAROLLIE CHERIE, 1951
CAROUSEL, 1956
CARRY ON ADMIRAL, 1957
CARRY ON COWBOY, 1966
CARRY ON ENGLAND, 1976
CARRY ON JACK, 1963
CARRY ON NURSE, 1959
CARRY ON SCREAMING, 1966
CARRY ON SERGEANT, 1959
CARRY ON SPYING, 1964
CARRY ON TEACHER, 1962
CARRY ON UP THE JUNGLE, 1970
CARRY ON, UP THE KHYBER, 1968
CARSON CITY, 1952
CARSON CITY CYCLONE, 1943
CARSON CITY RAIDERS, 1948
CARTER CASE, THE, 1947
CARTOUCHE, 1957
CARTOUCHE, 1962
CARVE HER NAME WITH PRIDE, 1958
CASA MANANA, 1951
CASABLANCA, 1942
CASANOVA BROWN, 1944
CASANOVA IN BURLESQUE, 1944
CASANOVA'S BIG NIGHT, 1954
CASE AGAINST BROOKLYN, THE, 1958

CASE AGAINST MRS. AMES, THE, 1936
CASE FOR PC 49, A, 1951
CASE FOR THE CROWN, THE, 1934
CASE OF CHARLES PEACE, THE, 1949
CASE OF CLARA DEANE, THE, 1932
CASE OF GABRIEL PERRY, THE, 1935
CASE OF SERGEANT GRISCHA, THE, 1930
CASE OF THE BLACK CAT, THE, 1936
CASE OF THE BLACK PARROT, THE, 1941
CASE OF THE CURIOUS BRIDE, THE, 1935
CASE OF THE HOWLING DOG, THE, 1934
CASE OF THE LUCKY LEGS, THE, 1935
CASE OF THE MISSING MAN, THE, 1935
CASE OF THE RED MONKEY, 1955
CASE OF THE STUTTERING BISHOP, THE, 1937
CASE OF THE VELVET CLAWS, THE, 1936
CASEY'S SHADOW, 1978
CASH ON DELIVERY, 1956
CASINO MURDER CASE, THE, 1935
CASINO ROYALE, 1967
CASSIDY OF BAR 20, 1938
CAST A DARK SHADOW, 1958
CASTE, 1930
CASTLE IN THE AIR, 1952
CASTLE IN THE DESERT, 1942
CASTLE OF CRIMES, 1940
CAT AND THE CANARY, THE, 1939
CAT AND THE CANARY, THE, 1979
CAT AND THE FIDDLE, 1934
CAT ATE THE PARAKEET, THE, 1972
CAT WOMEN OF THE MOON, 1953
CATALINA CAPER, THE, 1967
CATCH AS CATCH CAN, 1937
CATERED AFFAIR, THE, 1956
CATMAN OF PARIS, THE, 1946
CAT'S PAW, THE, 1934
CATSKILL HONEYMOON, 1950
CATTLE EMPIRE, 1958
CATTLE KING, 1963
CATTLE QUEEN, 1951
CATTLE QUEEN OF MONTANA, 1954
CATTLE RAIDERS, 1938
CATTLE STAMPEDE, 1943
CATTLE THIEF, THE, 1936
CATTLE TOWN, 1952
CAUGHT, 1931
CAUGHT CHEATING, 1931
CAUGHT IN THE ACT, 1941
CAUGHT IN THE FOG, 1928
CAUGHT PLASTERED, 1931
CAUGHT SHORT, 1930
CAVALCADE, 1933
CAVALCADE OF THE WEST, 1936
CAVALIER, THE, 1928
CAVALIER OF THE STREETS, THE, 1937
CAVALIER OF THE WEST, 1931
CAVALRY, 1936
CAVALRY COMMAND, 1963
CAVALRY SCOUT, 1951
CAVE OF OUTLAWS, 1951
CAVE OF THE LIVING DEAD, 1966
CAVERN, THE, 1965
CEILNG ZERO, 1935
CELESTE, 1982
CELIA, 1949
CENTRAL AIRPORT, 1933
CENTRAL PARK, 1932
CENTURION, THE, 1962
CEREBROS DIABOLICOS, 1966
CESAR, 1936
CHA-CHA-CHA BOOM, 1956
CHAIN LIGHTNING, 1950
CHAIN OF CIRCUMSTANCE, 1951
CHAIN OF EVIDENCE, 1957
CHALK GARDEN, THE, 1964
CHALLENGE, THE, 1939
CHALLENGE, THE, 1948
CHALLENGE FOR ROBIN HOOD, A, 1968
CHALLENGE OF THE RANGE, 1949
CHALLENGE TO BE FREE, 1976
CHAMBER OF HORRORS, 1941
CHAMP FOR A DAY, 1953
CHAMPAGNE CHARLIE, 1936
CHAMPAGNE CHARLIE, 1944
CHAMPAGNE FOR BREAKFAST, 1935
CHAMPAGNE WALTZ, 1937

CHANCE AT HEAVEN, 1933
CHANCE MEETING, 1954
CHANCE OF A LIFETIME, THE, 1943
CHANCE OF A LIFETIME, 1950
CHANCE OF A NIGHT-TIME, THE, 1931
CHANCES, 1931
CHANDLER, 1971
CHANDU THE MAGICIAN, 1932
CHANGE FOR A SOVEREIGN, 1937
CHANGE OF HEART, 1934
CHANGE OF HEART, 1938
CHANNEL CROSSING, 1934
CHARADE, 1953
CHARGE OF THE LANCERS, 1953
CHARGE OF THE LIGHT BRIGADE, THE, 1936
CHARING CROSS ROAD, 1935
CHARLATAN, THE, 1929
CHARLES AND LUCIE, 1982
CHARLESTON, 1978
CHARLEY MOON, 1956
CHARLEY'S AUNT, 1930
CHARLEY'S (BIG-HEARTED) AUNT, 1940
**CHARLIE CHAN AND THE CURSE OF THE DRAGON
    QUEEN, 1981**
CHARLIE CHAN AT MONTE CARLO, 1937
CHARLIE CHAN AT THE CIRCUS, 1936
CHARLIE CHAN AT THE OLYMPICS, 1937
CHARLIE CHAN AT THE OPERA, 1936
CHARLIE CHAN AT THE RACE TRACK, 1936
CHARLIE CHAN AT THE WAX MUSEUM, 1940
CHARLIE CHAN AT TREASURE ISLAND, 1939
CHARLIE CHAN CARRIES ON, 1931
CHARLIE CHAN IN BLACK MAGIC, 1944
CHARLIE CHAN IN EGYPT, 1935
CHARLIE CHAN IN HONOLULU, 1938
CHARLIE CHAN IN LONDON, 1934
CHARLIE CHAN IN PANAMA, 1940
CHARLIE CHAN IN PARIS, 1935
CHARLIE CHAN IN RENO, 1939
CHARLIE CHAN IN RIO, 1941
CHARLIE CHAN IN SHANGHAI, 1935
CHARLIE CHAN IN THE CITY OF DARKNESS, 1939
CHARLIE CHAN IN THE SECRET SERVICE, 1944
CHARLIE CHAN ON BROADWAY, 1937
CHARLIE CHAN'S CHANCE, 1932
CHARLIE CHAN'S COURAGE, 1934
CHARLIE CHAN'S GREATEST CASE, 1933
CHARLIE CHAN'S MURDER CRUISE, 1940
CHARLIE CHAN'S SECRET, 1936
CHARMING DECEIVER, THE, 1933
CHARMING SINNERS, 1929
CHARRO, 1969
CHARTER PILOT, 1940
CHARTROOSE CABOOSE, 1960
CHASE, THE, 1946
CHASE A CROOKED SHADOW, 1958
CHASER, THE, 1938
CHASING DANGER, 1939
CHASING RAINBOWS, 1930
CHASING TROUBLE, 1940
CHASING YESTERDAY, 1935
CHATTERBOX, 1936
CHATTERBOX, 1943
CHEATERS, 1934
CHEATERS, THE, 1945
CHEATERS AT PLAY, 1932
CHEATING BLONDES, 1933
CHEATING CHEATERS, 1934
CHECK YOUR GUNS, 1948
CHECKERED COAT, THE, 1948
CHECKERS, 1937
CHECKMATE, 1935
CHECKPOINT, 1957
CHEER BOYS CHEER, 1939
CHEER THE BRAVE, 1951
CHEER UP!, 1936
CHEER UP AND SMILE, 1930
CHEERS FOR MISS BISHOP, 1941
CHEERS OF THE CROWD, 1936
CHELSEA LIFE, 1933
CHELSEA STORY, 1951
CHEREZ TERNII K SVEZDAM, 1981
CHEROKEE FLASH, THE, 1945
CHEROKEE STRIP, 1937
CHEROKEE STRIP, 1940
CHEROKEE UPRISING, 1950

BOLD: Films on Videocassette

CHETNIKS, 1943
CHEYENNE, 1947
CHEYENNE AUTUMN, 1964
CHEYENNE CYCLONE, THE, 1932
CHEYENNE KID, THE, 1930
CHEYENNE KID, THE, 1933
CHEYENNE KID, THE, 1940
CHEYENNE RIDES AGAIN, 1937
CHEYENNE ROUNDUP, 1943
CHEYENNE TAKES OVER, 1947
CHEYENNE TORNADO, 1935
CHEYENNE WILDCAT, 1944
CHICAGO CALLING, 1951
CHICAGO CONFIDENTIAL, 1957
CHICAGO DEADLINE, 1949
CHICAGO KID, THE, 1945
CHICAGO SYNDICATE, 1955
CHICK, 1936
CHICKEN EVERY SUNDAY, 1948
CHICKEN WAGON FAMILY, 1939
CHIEF, THE, 1933
CHIEF CRAZY HORSE, 1955
CHILD IN THE HOUSE, 1956
CHILD IS BORN, A, 1940
CHILD IS WAITING, A, 1963
CHILD OF DIVORCE, 1946
CHILDHOOD OF MAXIM GORKY, 1938
CHILDREN GALORE, 1954
CHILDREN OF CHANCE, 1930
CHILDREN OF CHANCE, 1949
CHILDREN OF CHANCE, 1950
CHILDREN OF DREAMS, 1931
CHILDREN OF PLEASURE, 1930
CHILDREN OF THE FOG, 1935
CHILD'S PLAY, 1954
CHINA CLIPPER, 1936
CHINA GIRL, 1942
CHINA PASSAGE, 1937
CHINA SEAS, 1935
CHINA SYNDROME, THE, 1979
CHINATOWN AFTER DARK, 1931
CHINATOWN NIGHTS, 1929
CHINATOWN NIGHTS, 1938
CHINATOWN SQUAD, 1935
CHINESE BUNGALOW, THE, 1930
CHINESE CAT, THE, 1944
CHINESE DEN, THE, 1940
CHINESE PUZZLE, THE, 1932
CHINESE RING, THE, 1947
CHIP OF THE FLYING U, 1940
CHIP OFF THE OLD BLOCK, 1944
CHIPS, 1938.
CHIQUTTO PERO PICOSO, 1967
CHISUM, 1970
CHOCOLATE SOLDIER, THE, 1941
CHOKE CANYON, 1986
CHOSEN, THE, 1982
CHRISTINA, 1929
CHRISTMAS EVE, 1947
CHRISTMAS HOLIDAY, 1944
CHRISTMAS IN JULY, 1940
CHRISTMAS STORY, A, 1983
CHRISTMAS THAT ALMOST WASN'T, THE, 1966
CHRISTMAS TREE, THE, 1969
CHRISTOPHER BEAN, 1933
CHRISTOPHER COLUMBUS, 1949
CHU CHIN CHOW, 1934
CHU CHU AND THE PHILLY FLASH, 1981
CHUBASCO, 1968
CHUMP AT OXFORD, A, 1940
CHURCH MOUSE, THE, 1934
CIGARETTE GIRL, 1947
CIMARRON, 1931
CIMARRON, 1960
CIMARRON KID, THE, 1951
CINDERELLA, 1937
CINDERELLA SWINGS IT, 1942
CINDERFELLA, 1960
CIPHER BUREAU, 1938
CIRCLE CANYON, 1934
CIRCLE OF DEATH, 1935
CIRCUMSTANTIAL EVIDENCE, 1935
CIRCUS CLOWN, 1934
CIRCUS GIRL, 1937
CIRCUS KID, THE, 1928
CIRCUS WORLD, 1964

CISCO KID AND THE LADY, THE, 1939
CISCO KID RETURNS, THE, 1945
CITADEL, THE, 1938
CITIZEN KANE, 1941
CITY, FOR CONQUEST, 1941
CITY GIRL, 1930
CITY LIMITS, 1934
CITY OF BAD MEN, 1953
CITY OF BEAUTIFUL NONSENSE, THE, 1935
CITY OF PLAY, 1929
CITY OF SHADOWS, 1955
CITY PARK, 1934
CITY STREETS, 1931
CITY STREETS, 1938
CITY THAT NEVER SLEEPS, 1953
CITY UNDER THE SEA, 1965
CITY WITHOUT MEN, 1943
CLAIRVOYANT, THE, 1935
CLANCY IN WALL STREET, 1930
CLANCY STREET BOYS, 1943
CLARENCE, 1937
CLAUDIA, 1943
CLAUDINE, 1974
CLAY PIGEON, THE, 1949
CLAYDON TREASURE MYSTERY, THE, 1938
CLEANING UP, 1933
CLEAR ALL WIRES, 1933
CLEAR THE DECKS, 1929
CLEARING THE RANGE, 1931
CLIMAX, THE, 1930
CLIMAX, THE, 1944
CLIMBING HIGH, 1938
CLIPPED WINGS, 1938
CLIPPED WINGS, 1953
CLIVE OF INDIA, 1935
CLOAK AND DAGGER, 1946
CLOCK, THE, 1945
CLOCKWISE, 1986
CLONES, THE, 1973
CLOSE CALL FOR BOSTON BLACKIE, A, 1946
CLOSE CALL FOR ELLERY QUEEN, A, 1942
CLOSE ENCOUNTERS OF THE THIRD KIND, 1977
CLOSE HARMONY, 1929
CLOSE TO MY HEART, 1951
CLOSE-UP, 1948
CLOTHES AND THE WOMAN, 1937
CLOUD DANCER, 1980
CLOUDBURST, 1952
CLOUDED CRYSTAL, THE, 1948
CLOUDED YELLOW, THE, 1950
CLOUDS OVER EUROPE, 1939
CLOWN, THE, 1953
CLOWN AND THE KID, THE, 1961
CLOWN MUST LAUGH, A, 1936
CLUB HAVANA, 1946
CLUE OF THE NEW PIN, THE, 1929
CLUE OF THE TWISTED CANDLE, 1968
CLUNY BROWN, 1946
C'MON, LET'S LIVE A LITTLE, 1967
COAST GUARD, 1939
COAST OF SKELETONS, 1965
COAST TO COAST, 1980
COBRA, THE, 1968
COBRA STRIKES, THE, 1948
COBRA WOMAN, 1944
COBWEB, THE, 1955
COCK O' THE NORTH, 1935
COCK O' THE WALK, 1930
COCK OF THE AIR, 1932
COCKEYED CAVALIERS, 1934
COCKLESHELL HEROES, THE, 1955
COCKTAIL MOLOTOV, 1980
COCOANUTS, THE, 1929
COCOON: THE RETURN, 1988
CODE OF HONOR, 1930
CODE OF THE CACTUS, 1939
CODE OF THE FEARLESS, 1939
CODE OF THE LAWLESS, 1945
CODE OF THE MOUNTED, 1935
CODE OF THE OUTLAW, 1942
CODE OF THE PRAIRIE, 1944
CODE OF THE RANGE, 1937
CODE OF THE RANGERS, 1938
CODE OF THE SADDLE, 1947
CODE OF THE SECRET SERVICE, 1939
CODE OF THE SILVER SAGE, 1950

CODE OF THE STREETS, 1939
CODE OF THE WEST, 1947
CODE 7, VICTIM 5, 1964
CODE TWO, 1953
COGNASSE, 1932
COHENS AND KELLYS IN AFRICA, THE, 1930
COHENS AND KELLYS IN ATLANTIC CITY, THE, 1929
COHENS AND KELLYS IN HOLLYWOOD, THE, 1932
COHENS AND KELLYS IN SCOTLAND, THE, 1930
COHENS AND KELLYS IN TROUBLE, THE, 1933
COLD RIVER, 1982
COLD TURKEY, 1971
COLDITZ STORY, THE, 1955
COLE YOUNGER, GUNFIGHTER, 1958
COLLEEN, 1936
COLLEGE COACH, 1933
COLLEGE COQUETTE, THE, 1929
COLLEGE HOLIDAY, 1936
COLLEGE HUMOR, 1933
COLLEGE LOVE, 1929
COLLEGE LOVERS, 1930
COLLEGE RHYTHM, 1934
COLLEGE SCANDAL, 1935
COLLEGE SWEETHEARTS, 1942
COLLEGE SWING, 1938
COLLEGIATE, 1936
COLLISION, 1932
COLONEL BLOOD, 1934
COLONEL BOGEY, 1948
COLONEL CHABERT, 1947
COLONEL EFFINGHAM'S RAID, 1945
COLONEL MARCH INVESTIGATES, 1952
COLORADO, 1940
COLORADO AMBUSH, 1951
COLORADO KID, 1938
COLORADO PIONEERS, 1945
COLORADO RANGER, 1950
COLORADO SERENADE, 1946
COLORADO SUNDOWN, 1952
COLORADO SUNSET, 1939
COLORADO TERRITORY, 1949
COLORADO TRAIL, 1938
COLOSSUS OF NEW YORK, THE, 1958
COLOSSUS OF RHODES, THE, 1961
COLOSSUS: THE FORBIN PROJECT, 1969
COLT COMRADES, 1943
COLT .45, 1950
COLUMN SOUTH, 1953
COMA, 1978
COMANCHE, 1956
COMANCHE STATION, 1960
COMANCHE TERRITORY, 1950
COMANCHEROS, THE, 1961
COMBAT SQUAD, 1953
COME ACROSS, 1929
COME AND GET IT, 1936
COME BACK PETER, 1952
COME CLOSER, FOLKS, 1936
COME DANCE WITH ME, 1950
COME FLY WITH ME, 1963
COME LIVE WITH ME, 1941
COME ON, THE, 1956
COME ON, COWBOYS, 1937
COME ON DANGER!, 1932
COME ON DANGER, 1942
COME ON GEORGE, 1939
COME ON, LEATHERNECKS, 1938
COME ON, MARINES, 1934
COME ON, RANGERS, 1939
COME ON TARZAN, 1933
COME OUT FIGHTING, 1945
COME SEPTEMBER, 1961
COME SPY WITH ME, 1967
COMEDY MAN, THE, 1964
COMEDY OF HORRORS, THE, 1964
COMET OVER BROADWAY, 1938
COMIC, THE, 1969
COMIN' THRU' THE RYE, 1947
COMING OF AGE, 1938
COMING OUT PARTY, 1934
COMING UP ROSES, 1986
COMMAND, THE, 1954
COMMAND DECISION, 1948
COMMAND PERFORMANCE, 1931
COMMAND PERFORMANCE, 1937

BOLD: Films on Videocassette

CRITIC'S CHOICE, 1963
CROISIERES SIDERALES, 1941
CROMWELL, 1970
CROOK, THE, 1971
CROOKED BILLET, THE, 1930
CROOKED CIRCLE, 1932
CROOKED LADY, THE, 1932
CROOKED RIVER, 1950
CROOKED ROAD, THE, 1940
CROOKED SKY, THE, 1957
CROOKED TRAIL, THE, 1936
CROOKED WEB, THE, 1955
CROOKS IN CLOISTERS, 1964
CROOKS TOUR, 1940
CROONER, 1932
CROSBY CASE, THE, 1934
CROSS AND THE SWITCHBLADE, THE, 1970
CROSS COUNTRY ROMANCE, 1940
CROSS CURRENTS, 1935
CROSS-EXAMINATION, 1932
CROSS MY HEART, 1937
CROSS MY HEART, 1946
CROSS ROADS, 1930
CROSS STREETS, 1934
CROSS-UP, 1958
CROSSED SWORDS, 1954
CROSSED SWORDS, 1978
CROSSED TRAILS, 1948
CROSSFIRE, 1933
CROSSROADS, 1938
CROSSROADS, 1942
CROSSROADS OF PASSION, 1951
CROSSTALK, 1982
CROSSWINDS, 1951
CROUCHING BEAST, THE, 1936
CROWD ROARS, THE, 1938
CROWDED DAY, THE, 1954
CROWDED SKY, THE, 1960
CROWN VS STEVENS, 1936
CROWNING EXPERIENCE, THE, 1960
CROWNING GIFT, THE, 1967
CROWNING TOUCH, THE, 1959
CRUCIFIX, THE, 1934
CRUEL SEA, THE, 1953
CRUEL TOWER, THE, 1956
CRUISER EMDEN, 1932
CRUISIN' DOWN THE RIVER, 1953
CRUSADE AGAINST RACKETS, 1937
CRUSADER, THE, 1932
CRUSADES, THE, 1935
CRY DANGER, 1951
CRY FREEDOM, 1961
CRY HAVOC, 1943
CRY MURDER, 1936
CRY OF BATTLE, 1963
CRY OF THE HUNTED, 1953
CRY OF THE PENGUINS, 1972
CRY, THE BELOVED COUNTRY, 1952
CRY TOUGH, 1959
CRY VENGEANCE, 1954
CRY WOLF, 1947
CRYSTAL BALL, THE, 1943
CUBAN FIREBALL, 1951
CUBAN LOVE SONG, THE, 1931
CUBAN PETE, 1946
CUCKOO CLOCK, THE, 1938
CUCKOO PATROL, 1965
CUP OF KINDNESS, A, 1934
CUP-TIE HONEYMOON, 1948
CURE FOR LOVE, THE, 1950
CURSE OF THE PINK PANTHER, 1983
CURTAIN AT EIGHT, 1934
CURTAIN CALL, 1940
CURTAIN FALLS, THE, 1935
CURTAIN RISES, THE, 1939
CURTAIN UP, 1952
CUSTOMS AGENT, 1950
CYBORG 2087, 1966
CYCLONE FURY, 1951
CYCLONE KID, 1931
CYCLONE KID, THE, 1942
CYCLONE OF THE SADDLE, 1935
CYCLONE ON HORSEBACK, 1941
CYCLONE PRAIRIE RANGERS, 1944
CYCLONE RANGER, 1935
CYCLOTRODE X, 1946

CZAR OF BROADWAY, THE, 1930
CZAR WANTS TO SLEEP, 1934
D-DAY, THE SIXTH OF JUNE, 1956
DAD AND DAVE COME TO TOWN, 1938
DAD'S ARMY, 1971
DAGORA THE SPACE MONSTER, 1964
DAKOTA, 1945
DAKOTA INCIDENT, 1956
DAKOTA LIL, 1950
DALEKS—INVASION EARTH 2155 A.D., 1966
DALLAS, 1950
DALTON GANG, THE, 1949
DALTON GIRLS, THE, 1957
DALTON THAT GOT AWAY, 1960
DALTONS RIDE AGAIN, THE, 1945
DALTONS' WOMEN, THE, 1950
DAM BUSTERS, THE, 1955
DAMN CITIZEN, 1958
DAMN THE DEFIANT!, 1962
DAMN YANKEES, 1958
DAMON AND PYTHIAS, 1962
DAMSEL IN DISTRESS, A, 1937
DAN MATTHEWS, 1936
DANCE BAND, 1935
DANCE HALL, 1929
DANCE HALL, 1950
DANCE LITTLE LADY, 1954
DANCE MALL HOSTESS, 1933
DANCE OF DEATH, THE, 1938
DANCE OF LIFE, THE, 1929
DANCE PRETTY LADY, 1932
DANCE WITH ME, HENRY, 1956
DANCE, CHARLIE, DANCE, 1937
DANCE, GIRL, DANCE, 1933
DANCE, GIRL, DANCE, 1940
DANCERS, 1987
DANCERS, THE, 1930
DANCERS IN THE DARK, 1932
DANCING CO-ED, 1939
DANCING DYNAMITE, 1931
DANCING FEET, 1936
DANCING HEART, THE, 1959
DANCING IN MANHATTAN, 1945
DANCING IN THE DARK, 1949
DANCING LADY, 1933
DANCING MAN, 1934
DANCING MASTERS, THE, 1943
DANCING ON A DIME, 1940
DANCING PIRATE, 1936
DANCING SWEETIES, 1930
DANCING WITH CRIME, 1947
DANDY DICK, 1935
DANDY IN ASPIC, A, 1968
DANDY, THE ALL AMERICAN GIRL, 1976
DANGER AHEAD, 1935
DANGER AHEAD, 1940
DANGER: DIABOLIK, 1968
DANGER IN THE PACIFIC, 1942
DANGER—LOVE AT WORK, 1937
DANGER ON THE AIR, 1938
DANGER ON WHEELS, 1940
DANGER PATROL, 1937
DANGER ROUTE, 1968
DANGER SIGNAL, 1945
DANGER STREET, 1947
DANGER TRAILS, 1935
DANGER WOMAN, 1946
DANGER! WOMEN AT WORK, 1943
DANGEROUS ADVENTURE, A, 1937
DANGEROUS AFFAIR, A, 1931
DANGEROUS AGE, A, 1960
DANGEROUS BLONDES, 1943
DANGEROUS BUSINESS, 1946
DANGEROUS CARGO, 1939
DANGEROUS CHARTER, 1962 76m Crown International
c
DANGEROUS CORNER, 1935
DANGEROUS CROSSING, 1953
DANGEROUS DAN McGREW, 1930
DANGEROUS DAVIES—THE LAST DETECTIVE, 1981
DANGEROUS EXILE, 1958
DANGEROUS GAME, A, 1941
DANGEROUS GROUND, 1934
DANGEROUS INTRIGUE, 1936
DANGEROUS INTRUDER, 1945
DANGEROUS KISS, THE, 1961

DANGEROUS LADY, 1941
DANGEROUS MEDICINE, 1938
DANGEROUS MILLIONS, 1946
DANGEROUS MONEY, 1946
DANGEROUS NUMBER, 1937
DANGEROUS PARADISE, 1930
DANGEROUS PARTNERS, 1945
DANGEROUS PASSAGE, 1944
DANGEROUS PROFESSION, A, 1949
DANGEROUS SEAS, 1931
DANGEROUS SECRETS, 1938
DANGEROUS TO KNOW, 1938
DANGEROUS VENTURE, 1947
DANGEROUS WATERS, 1936
DANGEROUS WHEN WET, 1953
DANGEROUS WOMAN, 1929
DANGEROUS YEARS, 1947
DANGEROUS YOUTH, 1958
DANGEROUSLY THEY LIVE, 1942
DANGEROUSLY YOURS, 1933
DANGEROUSLY YOURS, 1937
DANNY BOY, 1934
DANNY BOY, 1941
DANTE'S INFERNO, 1935
DANTON, 1931
DARBY AND JOAN, 1937
DARBY'S RANGERS, 1958
DAREDEVIL DRIVERS, 1938
DAREDEVIL IN THE CASTLE, 1969
DAREDEVILS OF EARTH, 1936
DAREDEVILS OF THE CLOUDS, 1948
DARING CABALLERO, THE, 1949
DARING DANGER, 1932
DARING DAUGHTERS, 1933
DARING GAME, 1968
DARING YOUNG MAN, THE, 1935
DARING YOUNG MAN, THE, 1942
DARK ALIBI, 1946
DARK ANGEL, THE, 1935
DARK CITY, 1950
DARK COMMAND, THE, 1940
DARK CRYSTAL, THE, 1982
DARK DELUSION, 1947
DARK ENEMY, 1984
DARK EYES OF LONDON, 1961
DARK HAZARD, 1934
DARK HORSE, THE, 1932
DARK HORSE, THE, 1946
DARK HOUR, THE, 1936
DARK JOURNEY, 1937
DARK MAN, THE, 1951
DARK MOUNTAIN, 1944
DARK OF THE SUN, 1968
DARK PASSAGE, 1947
DARK PAST, THE, 1948
DARK PLACES, 1974
DARK RED ROSES, 1930
DARK SECRET, 1949
DARK STAIRWAY, THE, 1938
DARK STREETS, 1929
DARK STREETS OF CAIRO, 1940
DARK TOWER, THE, 1943
DARK VENTURE, 1956
DARK VICTORY, 1939
DARK WATERS, 1944
DARK WORLD, 1935
DARKENED ROOMS, 1929
DARKENED SKIES, 1930
DARKEST AFRICA, 1936
DARLING, HOW COULD YOU!, 1951
DARTS ARE TRUMPS, 1938
DARWIN ADVENTURE, THE, 1972
DATE WITH A DREAM, A, 1948
DATE WITH DEATH, A, 1959
DATE WITH THE FALCON, A, 1941
DATELINE DIAMONDS, 1966
DAUGHTER OF DR. JEKYLL, 1957
DAUGHTER OF SHANGHAI, 1937
DAUGHTER OF THE DRAGON, 1931
DAUGHTER OF THE JUNGLE, 1949
DAUGHTER OF THE SUN GOD, 1962
DAUGHTER OF THE TONG, 1939
DAUGHTER OF THE WEST, 1949
DAUGHTERS COURAGEOUS, 1939
DAUGHTERS OF TODAY, 1933
DAVID AND GOLIATH, 1961

DAVID COPPERFIELD, 1935
DAVID COPPERFIELD, 1970
DAVID GOLDER, 1932
DAVID HARDING, COUNTERSPY, 1950
DAVID HARUM, 1934
DAVID LIVINGSTONE, 1936
DAVY, 1958
DAWN AT SOCORRO, 1954
DAWN EXPRESS, THE, 1942
DAWN ON THE GREAT DIVIDE, 1942
DAWN OVER IRELAND, 1938
DAWN PATROL, THE, 1930
DAWN RIDER, 1935
DAWN TRAIL, THE, 1931
DAY AFTER THE DIVORCE, THE, 1940
DAY AND THE HOUR, THE, 1963
DAY OF FURY, A, 1956
DAY OF THE BAD MAN, 1958
DAY OF THE DOLPHIN, THE, 1973
DAY OF THE EVIL GUN, 1968
DAY OF THE OUTLAW, 1959
DAY OF TRIUMPH, 1954
DAY THE BOOKIES WEPT, THE, 1939
DAY THE EARTH CAUGHT FIRE, THE, 1961
DAY THE EARTH STOOD STILL, THE, 1951
DAY THE HOTLINE GOT HOT, THE, 1968
DAY THE SKY EXPLODED, THE, 1958
DAY THE SUN ROSE, THE, 1969
DAY THE WORLD ENDED, THE, 1956
DAY THEY ROBBED THE BANK OF ENGLAND, THE, 1960
DAY TIME ENDED, THE, 1980
DAY TO REMEMBER, A, 1953
DAY WILL COME, A, 1960
DAY YOU LOVE ME, THE, 1988
DAYBREAK, 1931
DAYBREAK, 1940
DAYDREAMER, THE, 1975
DAYS OF BUFFALO BILL, 1946
DAYS OF GLORY, 1944
DAYS OF HEAVEN, 1978
DAYS OF JESSE JAMES, 1939
DAYS OF OLD CHEYENNE, 1943
DAYTON'S DEVILS, 1968
DOCTORS, THE, 1956
DEAD, THE, 1987
DEAD DON'T DREAM, THE, 1948
DEAD END KIDS ON DRESS PARADE, 1939
DEAD HEAT ON A MERRY-GO-ROUND, 1966
DEAD MAN'S EYES, 1944
DEAD MAN'S GOLD, 1948
DEAD MAN'S GULCH, 1943
DEAD MAN'S SHOES, 1939
DEAD MAN'S TRAIL, 1952
DEAD MEN ARE DANGEROUS, 1939
DEAD MEN TELL, 1941
DEAD MEN TELL NO TALES, 1939
DEAD MEN WALK, 1943
DEAD OR ALIVE, 1944
DEAD TO THE WORLD, 1961
DEAD WOMAN'S KISS, A, 1951
DEADLIEST SIN, THE, 1956
DEADLINE, THE, 1932
DEADLINE, 1948
DEADLINE AT DAWN, 1946
DEADLINE FOR MURDER, 1946
DEADLOCK, 1931
DEADLOCK, 1943
DEADLY DUO, 1962
DEADLY GAME, THE, 1941
DEADLY GAME, THE, 1955
DEADLY MANTIS, THE, 1957
DEADLY NIGHTSHADE, 1953
DEADLY RECORD, 1959
DEADWOOD PASS, 1933
DEAR BRAT, 1951
DEAR BRIGETTE, 1965
DEAR HEART, 1964
DEAR MR. PROHACK, 1949
DEAR RUTH, 1947
DEATH AT A BROADCAST, 1934
DEATH CROONS THE BLUES, 1937
DEATH DRIVES THROUGH, 1935
DEATH FLIES EAST, 1935
DEATH FROM A DISTANCE, 1936
DEATH GOES NORTH, 1939

DEATH GOES TO SCHOOL, 1953
DEATH KISS, THE, 1933
DEATH OF A CHAMPION, 1939
DEATH OF AN ANGEL, 1952
DEATH OF EMPEDOCLES, THE, 1988
DEATH OF MICHAEL TURBIN, THE, 1954
DEATH ON THE DIAMOND, 1934
DEATH RIDES THE PLAINS, 1944
DEATH RIDES THE RANGE, 1940
DEATH VALLEY, 1946
DEATH VALLEY GUNFIGHTER, 1949
DEATH VALLEY MANHUNT, 1943
DEATH VALLEY OUTLAWS, 1941
DEATH VALLEY RANGERS, 1944
DEBT, THE, 1988
DEBT OF HONOR, 1936
DECAMERON NIGHTS, 1953
DECEIVER, THE, 1931
DECEPTION, 1933
DECISION AGAINST TIME, 1957
DECISION BEFORE DAWN, 1951
DECISION OF CHRISTOPHER BLAKE, THE, 1948
DEEP IN THE HEART OF TEXAS, 1942
DEEP SIX, THE, 1958
DEEP WATERS, 1948
DEERSLAYER, 1943
DEERSLAYER, THE, 1957
DEFENDERS OF THE LAW, 1931
DEFENSE OF VOLOTCHAYEVSK, THE, 1938
DEFENSE RESTS, THE, 1934
DELAVINE AFFAIR, THE, 1954
DELAYED ACTION, 1954
DELICATE DELINQUENT, THE, 1957
DELICIOUS, 1931
DELIGHTFUL ROGUE, 1929
DELIGHTFULLY DANGEROUS, 1945
DELINQUENT PARENTS, 1938
DELUGE, 1933
DEMOBBED, 1944
DEMON FOR TROUBLE, A, 1934
DEMON FROM DEVIL'S LAKE, THE, 1964
DENTIST IN THE CHAIR, 1960
DENVER AND RIO GRANDE, 1952
DENVER KID, THE, 1948
DEPARTMENT STORE, 1935
DEPORTED, 1950
DEPUTY DRUMMER, THE, 1935
DEPUTY MARSHAL, 1949
DER FREISCHUTZ, 1970
DERELICT, 1930
DERELICT, THE, 1937
DERSU UZALA, 1976
DESERT ATTACK, 1958
DESERT BANDIT, 1941
DESERT DESPERADOES, 1959
DESERT FOX, THE, 1951
DESERT GOLD, 1936
DESERT GUNS, 1936
DESERT HAWK, THE, 1950
DESERT HELL, 1958
DESERT HORSEMAN, THE, 1946
DESERT JUSTICE, 1936
DESERT LEGION, 1953
DESERT MESA, 1935
DESERT MICE, 1960
DESERT OF LOST MEN, 1951
DESERT PASSAGE, 1952
DESERT PATROL, 1938
DESERT PHANTOM, 1937
DESERT PURSUIT, 1952
DESERT RATS, THE, 1953
DESERT RAVEN, THE, 1965
DESERT SANDS, 1955
DESERT SONG, THE, 1929
DESERT SONG, THE, 1943
DESERT SONG, THE, 1953
DESERT TRAIL, 1935
DESERT VENGEANCE, 1931
DESERT VIGILANTE, 1949
DESERT WARRIOR, 1961
DESERTER, 1934
DESIGN FOR LIVING, 1933
DESIGN FOR LOVING, 1962
DESIGN FOR SCANDAL, 1941
DESIGNING WOMAN, 1957
DESIGNING WOMEN, 1934

DESIRABLE, 1934
DESIRE, 1936
DESIRE ME, 1947
DESIREE, 1954
DESK SET, 1957
DESPERADO, THE, 1954
DESPERADO TRAIL, THE, 1965
DESPERADOES, THE, 1943
DESPERADOES ARE IN TOWN, THE, 1956
DESPERADOES OF DODGE CITY, 1948
DESPERADOES OUTPOST, 1952
DESPERATE ADVENTURE, A, 1938
DESPERATE CARGO, 1941
DESPERATE CHANCE FOR ELLERY QUEEN, A, 1942
DESPERATE JOURNEY, 1942
DESPERATE MOMENT, 1953
DESPERATE SEARCH, 1952
DESPERATE TRAILS, 1939
DESTINATION BIG HOUSE, 1950
DESTINATION GOBI, 1953
DESTINATION INNER SPACE, 1966
DESTINATION MILAN, 1954
DESTINATION MOON, 1950
DESTINATION 60,000, 1957
DESTINATION TOKYO, 1944
DESTINATION UNKNOWN, 1933
DESTINATION UNKNOWN, 1942
DESTINY, 1938
DESTINY, 1944
DESTINY OF A MAN, 1961
DESTROY ALL MONSTERS, 1969
DESTROYER, 1943
DESTRY, 1954
DESTRY RIDES AGAIN, 1932
DESTRY RIDES AGAIN, 1939
DETECTIVE, THE, 1954
DETECTIVE KITTY O'DAY, 1944
DETOUR, THE, 1968
DEVIL, THE, 1963
DEVIL AND DANIEL WEBSTER, THE, 1941
DEVIL AND MAX DEVLIN, THE, 1981
DEVIL AND MISS JONES, THE, 1941
DEVIL AT FOUR O'CLOCK, THE, 1961
DEVIL BAT, THE, 1941
DEVIL BAT'S DAUGHTER, THE, 1946
DEVIL DOGS OF THE AIR, 1935
DEVIL GIRL FROM MARS, 1954
DEVIL GODDESS, 1955
DEVIL IS A SISSY, THE, 1936
DEVIL IS AN EMPRESS, THE, 1939
DEVIL IS DRIVING, THE, 1932
DEVIL IS DRIVING, THE, 1937
DEVIL MADE A WOMAN, THE, 1962
DEVIL MAY CARE, 1929
DEVIL ON HORSEBACK, THE, 1936
DEVIL ON HORSEBACK, 1954
DEVIL ON WHEELS, 1947
DEVIL PAYS OFF, THE, 1941
DEVIL PAYS, THE, 1932
DEVIL RIDERS, 1944
DEVIL SHIP, 1947
DEVIL THUMBS A RIDE, THE, 1947
DEVIL TIGER, 1934
DEVIL TO PAY, THE, 1930
DEVIL WITH WOMEN, A, 1930
DEVIL'S BAIT, 1959
DEVIL'S CANYON, 1953
DEVIL'S CARGO, THE, 1948
DEVIL'S DAFFODIL, THE, 1961
DEVIL'S DAUGHTER, 1949
DEVIL'S DISCIPLE, THE, 1959
DEVIL'S DOORWAY, 1950
DEVIL'S ENVOYS, THE, 1947
DEVIL'S GODMOTHER, THE, 1938
DEVIL'S HAIRPIN, THE, 1957
DEVIL'S HENCHMEN, THE, 1949
DEVIL'S HOLIDAY, THE, 1930
DEVIL'S IN LOVE, THE, 1933
DEVIL'S JEST, THE, 1954
DEVIL'S LOTTERY, 1932
DEVIL'S MASK, THE, 1946
DEVIL'S MATE, 1933
DEVIL'S PARTY, THE, 1938
DEVIL'S PIPELINE, THE, 1940
DEVIL'S PLAYGROUND, 1937
DEVIL'S PLAYGROUND, THE, 1946

BOLD: Films on Videocassette

DEVIL'S PLAYGROUND, THE, 1976
DEVIL'S ROCK, 1938
DEVIL'S SADDLE LEGION, THE, 1937
DEVIL'S SLEEP, THE, 1951
DEVIL'S SQUADRON, 1936
DEVIL'S TRAIL, THE, 1942
DEVOTION, 1931
DEVOTION, 1946
DEVOTION, 1955
D.I., THE, 1957
DIALOGUE, 1967
DIAMOND CITY, 1949
DIAMOND FRONTIER, 1940
DIAMOND HORSESHOE, 1945
DIAMOND JIM, 1935
DIAMOND QUEEN, THE, 1953
DIAMOND SAFARI, 1958
DIAMOND TRAIL, 1933
DIAMOND WIZARD, THE, 1954
DIANE'S BODY, 1969
DIARY OF A CHAMBERMAID, 1946
DIARY OF A COUNTRY PRIEST, 1954
DIARY OF A REVOLUTIONIST, 1932
DIARY OF A SCHIZOPHRENIC GIRL, 1970
DIARY OF ANNE FRANK, THE, 1959
DICK BARTON AT BAY, 1950
DICK BARTON—SPECIAL AGENT, 1948
DICK BARTON STRIKES BACK, 1949
DICK TURPIN, 1933
DICTATOR, THE, 1935
DIE FASTNACHTSBEICHTE, 1962
DIE FLEDERMAUS, 1964
DIE GANS VON SEDAN, 1962
DIE MANNER UM LUCIE, 1931
DIG THAT URANIUM, 1956
DIM SUM: A LITTLE BIT OF HEART, 1985
DIME WITH A HALO, 1963
DIMENSION 5, 1966
DING DONG WILLIAMS, 1946
DINGAKA, 1965
DINKY, 1935
DINNER AT THE RITZ, 1937
DINO, 1957
DIPLOMANIACS, 1933
DIPLOMATIC CORPSE, THE, 1958
DIPLOMATIC COURIER, 1952
DIPLOMATIC LOVER, THE, 1934
DIPLOMATIC PASSPORT, 1954
DIRIGIBLE, 1931
DIRT BIKE KID, THE, 1986
DIRTY HEROES, 1971
DIRTY WORK, 1934
DISASTER, 1948
DISBARRED, 1939
DISC JOCKEY, 1951
DISCARDED LOVERS, 1932
DISCORD, 1933
DISCOVERIES, 1939
DISGRACED, 1933
DISHONOR BRIGHT, 1936
DISHONORED, 1950
DISILLUSION, 1949
DISORDER, 1964
DISORDER AND EARLY TORMENT, 1977
DISORDERLY CONDUCT, 1932
DISORDERLY ORDERLY, THE, 1964
DISPATCH FROM REUTERS, A, 1940
DISPUTED PASSAGE, 1939
DISRAELI, 1929
DISTANT DRUMS, 1951
DISTANT TRUMPET, 1952
DISTANT TRUMPET, A, 1964
DIVIDED HEART, THE, 1955
DIVINE EMMA, THE, 1983
DIVINE SPARK, THE, 1935
DIVORCE, 1945
DIVORCE IN THE FAMILY, 1932
DIVORCE OF LADY X, THE, 1938
DIVORCE, ITALIAN STYLE, 1962
DIXIANA, 1930
DIXIE, 1943
DIXIE DUGAN, 1943
DIXIE JAMBOREE, 1945
DIXIELAND DAIMYO, 1988
DIZZY DAMES, 1936
DO NOT DISTURB, 1965

DO YOU LOVE ME?, 1946
D.O.A., 1950
DOC SAVAGE... THE MAN OF BRONZE, 1975
DOCKS OF NEW ORLEANS, 1948
DOCKS OF NEW YORK, 1945
DOCKS OF SAN FRANCISCO, 1932
DOCTEUR LAENNEC, 1949
DOCTOR AT LARGE, 1957
DOCTOR AT SEA, 1955
DR. BULL, 1933
DR. CHRISTIAN MEETS THE WOMEN, 1940
DR. CYCLOPS, 1940
DR. EHRLICH'S MAGIC BULLET, 1940
DR. GILLESPIE'S CRIMINAL CASE, 1943
DR. GILLESPIE'S NEW ASSISTANT, 1942
DOCTOR IN DISTRESS, 1963
DOCTOR IN LOVE, 1960
DOCTOR IN THE HOUSE, 1954
DOCTOR IN TROUBLE, 1970
DR. JEKYLL AND SISTER HYDE, 1971
DR. JOSSER KC, 1931
DR. KILDARE GOES HOME, 1940
DR. KILDARE'S CRISIS, 1940
DR. KILDARE'S STRANGE CASE, 1940
DR. KILDARE'S VICTORY, 1941
DR. KILDARE'S WEDDING DAY, 1941
DR. KNOCK, 1936
DR. MABUSE'S RAYS OF DEATH, 1964
DOCTOR MONICA, 1934
DR. MORELLE—THE CASE OF THE MISSING
   HEIRESS, 1949
DR. O'DOWD, 1940
DR. OTTO AND THE RIDDLE OF THE GLOOM
   BEAM, 1986
DR. SIN FANG, 1937
DOCTOR SYN, 1937
DR. WHO AND THE DALEKS, 1965
DOCTOR X, 1932
DOCTOR, YOU'VE GOT TO BE KIDDING, 1967
DOCTOR'S DIARY, A, 1937
DOCTOR'S DILEMMA, THE, 1958
DOCTORS DON'T TELL, 1941
DOCTOR'S ORDERS, 1934
DOCTOR'S SECRET, 1929
DODGE CITY, 1939
DODGE CITY TRAIL, 1937
DODGING THE DOLE, 1936
DODSWORTH, 1936
DOG EAT DOG, 1963
DOGPOUND SHUFFLE, 1975
DOING TIME, 1979
DOLL, THE, 1962
DOLL FACE, 1945
DOLL THAT TOOK THE TOWN, THE, 1965
DOLLAR, 1938
DOLLARS FOR A FAST GUN, 1969
DOLL'S HOUSE, A, 1973
DOLL'S HOUSE, A, 1973
DOLLY GETS AHEAD, 1931
DOLORES, 1949
DOMINANT SEX, THE, 1937
DOMINO KID, 1957
DON CHICAGO, 1945
DON GIOVANNI, 1955
DON GIOVANNI, 1979
DON JUAN, 1956
DON JUAN QUILLIGAN, 1945
DON QUIXOTE, 1935
DON QUIXOTE, 1961
DON QUIXOTE, 1973
DON RICARDO RETURNS, 1946
DONATELLA, 1956
DONOVAN AFFAIR, THE, 1929
DONOVAN'S REEF, 1963
DON'T BE A DUMMY, 1932
DON'T BET ON BLONDES, 1935
DON'T BET ON LOVE, 1933
DON'T BET ON WOMEN, 1931
DON'T BLAME THE STORK, 1954
DON'T CALL ME A CON MAN, 1966
DON'T CRY WITH YOUR MOUTH FULL, 1974
DON'T DRINK THE WATER, 1969
DON'T EVER LEAVE ME, 1949
DON'T FENCE ME IN, 1945
DON'T GAMBLE WITH LOVE, 1936
DON'T GAMBLE WITH STRANGERS, 1946

DON'T GET ME WRONG, 1937
DON'T GET PERSONAL, 1936
DON'T GET PERSONAL, 1941
DON'T GIVE UP THE SHIP, 1959
DON'T GO NEAR THE WATER, 1957
DON'T JUST STAND THERE, 1968
DON'T KNOCK THE ROCK, 1956
DON'T KNOCK THE TWIST, 1962
DON'T LET THE ANGELS FALL, 1969
DON'T LOOK NOW, 1969
DON'T MAKE WAVES, 1967
DON'T PANIC CHAPS!, 1959
DON'T PLAY WITH MARTIANS, 1967
DON'T RAISE THE BRIDGE, LOWER THE RIVER,
   1968
DON'T RUSH ME, 1936
DON'T SAY DIE, 1950
DON'T TAKE IT TO HEART, 1944
DON'T TELL THE WIFE, 1937
DON'T TEMPT THE DEVIL, 1964
DON'T TURN 'EM LOOSE, 1936
DON'T WORRY, WE'LL THINK OF A TITLE, 1966
DOOLINS OF OKLAHOMA, THE, 1949
DOOMED BATTALION, THE, 1932
DOOMED CARAVAN, 1941
DOOMED CARGO, 1936
DOOMED TO DIE, 1940
DOOMSDAY MACHINE, 1967
DOS COSMONAUTAS A LA FUERZA, 1967
DOUBLE, THE, 1963
DOUBLE ALIBI, 1940
DOUBLE-BARRELLED DETECTIVE STORY, THE, 1965
DOUBLE BUNK, 1961
DOUBLE CRIME IN THE MAGINOT LINE, 1939
DOUBLE CROSS, 1941
DOUBLE CROSS ROADS, 1930
DOUBLE DEAL, 1950
DOUBLE DYNAMITE, 1951
DOUBLE EVENT, THE, 1934
DOUBLE EXPOSURE, 1944
DOUBLE EXPOSURES, 1937
DOUBLE JEOPARDY, 1955
DOUBLE McGUFFIN, THE, 1979
DOUBLE OR NOTHING, 1937
DOUBLE OR QUITS, 1938
DOUBLE TROUBLE, 1941
DOUBLE TROUBLE, 1967
DOUBLE WEDDING, 1937
DOUBTING THOMAS, 1935
DOUGHBOYS IN IRELAND, 1943
DOUGHGIRLS, THE, 1944
DOUGHNUTS AND SOCIETY, 1936
DOWN AMONG THE SHELTERING PALMS, 1953
DOWN AMONG THE Z MEN, 1952
DOWN DAKOTA WAY, 1949
DOWN IN ARKANSAW, 1938
DOWN IN SAN DIEGO, 1941
DOWN LAREDO WAY, 1953
DOWN MEMORY LANE, 1949
DOWN MEXICO WAY, 1941
DOWN MISSOURI WAY, 1946
DOWN ON THE FARM, 1938
DOWN OUR ALLEY, 1939
DOWN OUR STREET, 1932
DOWN RIO GRANDE WAY, 1942
DOWN RIVER, 1931
DOWN TEXAS WAY, 1942
DOWN THE STRETCH, 1936
DOWN THE WYOMING TRAIL, 1939
DOWN TO EARTH, 1932
DOWN TO EARTH, 1947
DOWN TO THE SEA, 1936
DOWN TO THEIR LAST YACHT, 1934
DOWNSTAIRS, 1932
DRAEGERMAN COURAGE, 1937
DRAG, 1929
DRAGNET, 1954
DRAGNET, 1974
DRAGNET NIGHT, 1931
DRAGNET PATROL, 1932
DRAGON MURDER CASE, THE, 1934
DRAGON SEED, 1944
DRAGON SKY, 1964
DRAGON WELLS MASSACRE, 1957
DRAGONFLY, THE, 1955
DRAGONFLY SQUADRON, 1953

DRAGON'S GOLD, 1954
DRAGONWYCH, 1946
DRAGSTRIP GIRL, 1957
DRAKE CASE, THE, 1929
DRAKE THE PIRATE, 1935
DRANGO, 1957
DREAM COME TRUE, A, 1963
DREAM GIRL, 1947
DREAM MAKER, THE, 1963
DREAM NO MORE, 1950
DREAM OF A COSSACK, 1982
DREAM OF BUTTERFLY, THE, 1941
DREAM OF SCHONBRUNN, 1933
DREAM OF THE RED CHAMBER, THE, 1966
DREAM ONE, 1984
DREAM WIFE, 1953
DREAMCHILD, 1985
DREAMER, THE, 1936
DREAMER, 1979
DREAMING, 1944
DREAMING OUT LOUD, 1940
DREAMS COME TRUE, 1936
DREAMS IN A DRAWER, 1957
DRESSED TO KILL, 1941
DRESSED TO KILL, 1946
DRESSED TO THRILL, 1935
DREYFUS CASE, THE, 1931
DREYFUS CASE, THE, 1940
DRIFT FENCE, 1936
DRIFTER, THE, 1932
DRIFTER, THE, 1944
DRIFTIN' KID, THE, 1941
DRIFTIN' RIVER, 1946
DRIFTING, 1932
DRIFTING ALONG, 1946
DRIFTING WESTWARD, 1939
DRIFTWOOD, 1947
DRUM BEAT, 1954
DRUM TAPS, 1933
DRUMS, 1938
DRUMS ACROSS THE RIVER, 1954
DRUMS IN THE DEEP SOUTH, 1951
DRUMS O' VOODOO, 1934
DRUMS OF AFRICA, 1963
DRUMS OF DESTINY, 1937
DRUMS OF FU MANCHU, 1943
DRUMS OF JEOPARDY, 1931
DRUMS OF TABU, THE, 1967
DRUMS OF TAHITI, 1954
DRUMS OF THE CONGO, 1942
DRUMS OF THE DESERT, 1940
DRY ROT, 1956
DRY SUMMER, 1967
DRYLANDERS, 1963
DU BARRY WAS A LADY, 1943
DUAL ALIBI, 1947
DUCHESS OF IDAHO, THE, 1950
DUDE BANDIT, THE, 1933
DUDE COWBOY, 1941
DUDE GOES WEST, THE, 1948
DUDE RANCH, 1931
DUDE RANGER, THE, 1934
DUDE WRANGLER, THE, 1930
DUEL, THE, 1964
DUEL AT APACHE WELLS, 1957
DUEL AT DIABLO, 1966
DUEL AT SILVER CREEK, THE, 1952
DUEL IN THE JUNGLE, 1954
DUEL OF CHAMPIONS, 1964
DUEL OF THE TITANS, 1963
DUEL ON THE MISSISSIPPI, 1955
DUEL WITHOUT HONOR, 1953
DUFFY OF SAN QUENTIN, 1954
DUFFY'S TAVERN, 1945
DUGAN OF THE BAD LANDS, 1931
DUKE COMES BACK, THE, 1937
DUKE IS THE TOPS, THE, 1938
DUKE OF CHICAGO, 1949
DUKE OF THE NAVY, 1942
DUKE OF WEST POINT, THE, 1938
DUKE WORE JEANS, THE, 1958
DULCIMA, 1971
DULCIMER STREET, 1948
DULCY, 1940
DUMBBELLS IN ERMINE, 1930
DUMMY TALKS, THE, 1943

DUNKIRK, 1958
DURANGO KID, THE, 1940
DURANGO VALLEY RAIDERS, 1938
DURING ONE NIGHT, 1962
DUST BE MY DESTINY, 1939
DYBBUK, THE, 1938
DYNAMITE, 1930
DYNAMITE, 1948
DYNAMITE CANYON, 1941
DYNAMITE DELANEY, 1938
DYNAMITE DENNY, 1932
DYNAMITE JACK, 1961
DYNAMITE JOHNSON, 1978
DYNAMITE PASS, 1950
DYNAMITE RANCH, 1932
DYNAMITERS, THE, 1956
EACH DAWN I DIE, 1939
EADIE WAS A LADY, 1945
EAGLE AND THE HAWK, THE, 1950
EAGLE IN A CAGE, 1971
EAGLE ROCK, 1964
EAGLE SQUADRON, 1942
EAGLE WITH TWO HEADS, 1948
EAGLE'S BROOD, THE, 1936
EAGLE'S WING, 1979
EARL CARROLL SKETCHBOOK, 1946
EARL CARROLL'S VANITIES, 1945
EARL OF CHICAGO, THE, 1940
EARL OF PUDDLESTONE, 1940
EARLY BIRD, THE, 1936
EARLY BIRD, THE, 1965
EARLY TO BED, 1933
EARLY TO BED, 1936
EARRINGS OF MADAME DE..., THE, 1954
EARTH CRIES OUT, THE, 1949
EARTH DIES SCREAMING, THE, 1964
EARTH VS. THE FLYING SAUCERS, 1956
EARTH VS. THE SPIDER, 1958
EARTHBOUND, 1940
EARTHQUAKE, 1974
EARTHWORM TRACTORS, 1936
EAST LYNNE, 1931
EAST LYNNE ON THE WESTERN FRONT, 1931
EAST MEETS WEST, 1936
EAST OF BORNEO, 1931
EAST OF JAVA, 1935
EAST OF KILIMANJARO, 1962
EAST OF SUDAN, 1964
EAST OF SUMATRA, 1953
EAST OF THE RIVER, 1940
EAST SIDE KIDS, 1940
EAST SIDE OF HEAVEN, 1939
EAST SIDE SADIE, 1929
EASY COME, EASY GO, 1947
EASY COME, EASY GO, 1967
EASY LIVING, 1937
EASY LIVING, 1949
EASY MILLIONS, 1933
EASY MONEY, 1934
EASY MONEY, 1936
EASY MONEY, 1948
EASY RICHES, 1938
EASY TO LOOK AT, 1945
EASY TO LOVE, 1934
EASY TO LOVE, 1953
EASY TO TAKE, 1936
EASY TO WED, 1946
EAT MY DUST!, 1976
EBB TIDE, 1932
EBB TIDE, 1937
EBOLI, 1980
ECHO MURDERS, THE, 1945
ECHOES OF A SUMMER, 1976
ECSTACY OF YOUNG LOVE, 1936
EDDY DUCHIN STORY, THE, 1956
EDEN CRIED, 1967
EDGE OF DARKNESS, 1943
EDGE OF ETERNITY, 1959
EDGE OF HELL, 1956
EDGE OF THE CITY, 1957
EDGE OF THE WORLD, THE, 1937
EDITH AND MARCEL, 1984
EDUCATED EVANS, 1936
EDUCATING FATHER, 1936
EDUCATING RITA, 1983
EDWARD AND CAROLINE, 1952

EGGHEAD'S ROBOT, 1970
EGLANTINE, 1972
EGYPT BY THREE, 1953
EIGHT BELLS, 1935
EIGHT GIRLS IN A BOAT, 1932
EIGHT O'CLOCK WALK, 1954
EIGHT ON THE LAM, 1967
1812, 1944
18 MINUTES, 1935
80 STEPS TO JONAH, 1969
EL AMOR BRUJO, 1986
EL CID, 1961
EL DIABLO RIDES, 1939
EL DORADO PASS, 1949
EL GRECO, 1966
EL PASO, 1949
EL PASO KID, THE, 1946
EL PASO STAMPEDE, 1953
ELDER BROTHER, THE, 1937
ELECTRA, 1962
ELEPHANT CALLED SLOWLY, AN, 1970
ELEPHANT GUN, 1959
ELEPHANT STAMPEDE, 1951
ELEPHANT WALK, 1954
ELEVENTH COMMANDMENT, 1933
ELI ELI, 1940
ELINOR NORTON, 1935
ELISABETH OF AUSTRIA, 1931
ELIZA COMES TO STAY, 1936
ELIZABETH OF LADYMEAD, 1949
ELLERY QUEEN AND THE MURDER RING, 1941
ELLERY QUEEN AND THE PERFECT CRIME, 1941
ELLERY QUEEN, MASTER DETECTIVE, 1940
ELLERY QUEEN'S PENTHOUSE MYSTERY, 1941
ELMER AND ELSIE, 1934
ELMER THE GREAT, 1933
ELOPEMENT, 1951
ELUSIVE CORPORAL, THE, 1963
ELVIS! ELVIS!, 1977
EMBARRASSING MOMENTS, 1930
EMBARRASSING MOMENTS, 1934
EMBEZZLED HEAVEN, 1959
EMBEZZLER, THE, 1954
EMBRACEABLE YOU, 1948
EMERGENCY, 1962
EMERGENCY CALL, 1933
EMERGENCY HOSPITAL, 1956
EMERGENCY LANDING, 1941
EMERGENCY SQUAD, 1940
EMERGENCY WEDDING, 1950
EMIGRANTS, THE, 1972
EMMA, 1932
EMPEROR AND THE GOLEM, THE, 1955
EMPEROR'S CANDLESTICKS, THE, 1937
EMPIRE OF THE SUN, 1987
EMPIRE STRIKES BACK, THE, 1980
EMPLOYEE'S ENTRANCE, 1933
EMPRESS AND I, THE, 1933
EMPRESS WU, 1965
EMPTY HOLSTERS, 1937
EMPTY SADDLES, 1937
EMPTY STAR, THE, 1962
ENCHANTED APRIL, 1935
ENCHANTED COTTAGE, THE, 1945
ENCHANTED ISLAND, 1958
ENCHANTED VALLEY, THE, 1948
ENCHANTING SHADOW, THE, 1965
ENCHANTMENT, 1948
ENCORE, 1951
END OF A DAY, THE, 1939
END OF DESIRE, 1962
END OF MRS. CHENEY, 1963
END OF THE AFFAIR, THE, 1955
END OF THE RIVER, THE, 1947
END OF THE ROAD, 1944
END OF THE ROAD, THE, 1954
END OF THE ROAD, THE, 1936
END OF THE TRAIL, 1932
END OF THE TRAIL, 1936
END OF THE WORLD, THE, 1930
ENEMIES OF PROGRESS, 1934
ENEMIES OF THE LAW, 1931
ENEMY AGENT, 1940
ENEMY AGENTS MEET ELLERY QUEEN, 1942
ENEMY BELOW, THE, 1957
ENEMY FROM SPACE, 1957

BOLD: Films on Videocassette

ENEMY GENERAL, THE, 1960
ENEMY OF THE LAW, 1945
ENEMY OF THE PEOPLE, AN, 1978
ENEMY OF THE POLICE, 1933
ENGAGEMENT ITALIANO, 1966
ENLIGHTEN THY DAUGHTER, 1934
ENORMOUS CHANGES AT THE LAST MINUTE, 1985
ENOUGH ROPE, 1966
ENSIGN PULVER, 1964
ENTENTE CORDIALE, 1939
ENTER ARSENE LUPIN, 1944
ENTER LAUGHING, 1967
ENTER MADAME, 1935
ENTERTAINER, THE, 1960
EPILOGUE, 1967
EPISODE, 1937
ERNEST SAVES CHRISTMAS, 1988
ERRAND BOY, THE, 1961
ESCAPADE, 1932
ESCAPADE, 1935
ESCAPADE, 1955
ESCAPADE IN JAPAN, 1957
ESCAPE, 1930
ESCAPE, 1940
ESCAPE BY NIGHT, 1937
ESCAPE, 1948
ESCAPE, THE, 1939
ESCAPE DANGEROUS, 1947
ESCAPE FROM CRIME, 1942
ESCAPE FROM DEVIL'S ISLAND, 1935
ESCAPE FROM EAST BERLIN, 1962
ESCAPE FROM FORT BRAVO, 1953
ESCAPE FROM HONG KONG, 1942
ESCAPE FROM RED ROCK, 1958
ESCAPE FROM SAN QUENTIN, 1957
ESCAPE FROM TERROR, 1960
ESCAPE FROM YESTERDAY, 1939
ESCAPE FROM ZAHRAIN, 1962
ESCAPE IN THE DESERT, 1945
ESCAPE IN THE FOG, 1945
ESCAPE IN THE SUN, 1956
ESCAPE ME NEVER, 1935
ESCAPE ME NEVER, 1947
ESCAPE TO BERLIN, 1962
ESCAPE TO BURMA, 1955
ESCAPE TO DANGER, 1943
ESCAPE TO GLORY, 1940
ESCAPE TO PARADISE, 1939
ESCAPES, 1987
ESCORT WEST, 1959
ESPIONAGE, 1937
ESPIONAGE AGENT, 1939
ESTHER AND THE KING, 1960
ETERNAL FEMININE, THE, 1931
ETERNAL LOVE, 1960
ETERNAL MELODIES, 1948
ETERNAL RETURN, THE, 1943
ETERNAL SEA, THE, 1955
ETERNAL SUMMER, 1961
ETERNAL WALTZ, THE, 1959
ETERNALLY YOURS, 1939
EUROPEANS, THE, 1979
EVANGELINE, 1929
EVE, 1968
EVE KNEW HER APPLES, 1945
EVE WANTS TO SLEEP, 1961
EVEL KNIEVEL, 1971
EVENINGS FOR SALE, 1932
EVENSONG, 1934
EVER SINCE EVE, 1934
EVER SINCE EVE, 1937
EVER SINCE VENUS, 1944
EVERGREEN, 1934
EVERY DAY IS A HOLIDAY, 1966
EVERY DAY'S A HOLIDAY, 1938
EVERY GIRL SHOULD BE MARRIED, 1948
EVERY MAN FOR HIMSELF AND GOD AGAINST ALL, 1975
EVERY NIGHT AT EIGHT, 1935
EVERY SATURDAY NIGHT, 1936
EVERYBODY DANCE, 1936
EVERYBODY DOES IT, 1949
EVERYBODY GO HOME!, 1962
EVERYBODY SING, 1938
EVERYBODY'S BABY, 1939
EVERYBODY'S DANCIN', 1950

EVERYBODY'S DOING IT, 1938
EVERYBODY'S HOBBY, 1939
EVERYBODY'S OLD MAN, 1936
EVERYMAN'S LAW, 1936
EVERYTHING HAPPENS AT NIGHT, 1939
EVERYTHING HAPPENS TO ME, 1938
EVERYTHING I HAVE IS YOURS, 1952
EVERYTHING IN LIFE, 1936
EVERYTHING IS RHYTHM, 1940
EVERYTHING IS THUNDER, 1936
EVERYTHING OKAY, 1936
EVERYTHING'S DUCKY, 1961
EVERYTHING'S ON ICE, 1939
EVERYTHING'S ROSIE, 1931
EVIDENCE, 1929
EVIL EYE, 1964
EVIL OF FRANKENSTEIN, THE, 1964
EVIL UNDER THE SUN, 1982
EX-BAD BOY, 1931
EX-CHAMP, 1939
EX-FLAME, 1931
EX-LADY, 1933
EX-MRS. BRADFORD, THE, 1936
EXCESS BAGGAGE, 1933
EXCLUSIVE, 1937
EXCLUSIVE STORY, 1936
EXCUSE MY GLOVE, 1936
EXECUTIVE SUITE, 1954
EXILE, THE, 1947
EXILE EXPRESS, 1939
EXILED TO SHANGHAI, 1937
EXPENSIVE HUSBANDS, 1937
EXPERIMENT ALCATRAZ, 1950
EXPERIMENT PERILOUS, 1944
EXPERT, THE, 1932
EXPERT'S OPINION, 1935
EXPOSED, 1932
EXPOSED, 1938
EXPOSED, 1947
EXTORTION, 1938
EXTRA DAY, THE, 1956
EXTRAORDINARY SEAMAN, THE, 1969
EXTRAVAGANCE, 1930
EYES IN THE NIGHT, 1942
EYES OF ANNIE JONES, THE, 1963
EYES OF FATE, 1933
EYES OF TEXAS, 1948
EYES OF THE UNDERWORLD, 1943
EYES THAT KILL, 1947
EYES, THE SEA AND A BALL, 1968
EYEWITNESS, 1956
F MAN, 1936
FABIAN OF THE YARD, 1954
FABULOUS DORSEYS, THE, 1947
FABULOUS SENORITA, THE, 1952
FABULOUS SUZANNE, THE, 1946
FABULOUS TEXAN, THE, 1947
FACE BEHIND THE SCAR, 1940
FACE IN THE FOG, A, 1936
FACE IN THE RAIN, A, 1963
FACE IN THE SKY, 1933
FACE OF A FUGITIVE, 1959
FACE OF MARBLE, THE, 1946
FACE OF THE SCREAMING WEREWOLF, 1959
FACE ON THE BARROOM FLOOR, THE, 1932
FACE TO FACE, 1952
FACES, 1934
FACES IN THE DARK, 1960
FACES IN THE FOG, 1944
FACING THE MUSIC, 1933
FACING THE MUSIC, 1941
FACTS OF LIFE, THE, 1960
FACTS OF LOVE, 1949
FAIR EXCHANGE, 1936
FAIR WARNING, 1931
FAIR WARNING, 1937
FAIR WIND TO JAVA, 1953
FAITHFUL, 1936
FAITHFUL CITY, 1952
FAITHFUL HEART, 1933
FAITHFUL IN MY FASHION, 1946
FAITHLESS, 1932
FAKE, THE, 1953
FAKE'S PROGRESS, 1950
FALCON AND THE CO-EDS, THE, 1943
FALCON IN DANGER, THE, 1943

FALCON IN HOLLYWOOD, THE, 1944
FALCON IN MEXICO, THE, 1944
FALCON IN SAN FRANCISCO, THE, 1945
FALCON OUT WEST, THE, 1944
FALCON STRIKES BACK, THE, 1943
FALCON TAKES OVER, THE, 1942
FALCON'S ADVENTURE, THE, 1946
FALCON'S ALIBI, THE, 1946
FALCON'S BROTHER, THE, 1942
FALL GUY, THE, 1930
FALL OF EVE, THE, 1929
FALLEN ANGEL, 1945
FALLEN IDOL, THE, 1949
FALLGUY, 1962
FALLING FOR YOU, 1933
FALSE COLORS, 1943
FALSE FACES, 1932
FALSE FACES, 1943
FALSE MADONNA, 1932
FALSE PARADISE, 1948
FALSE PRETENSES, 1935
FALSE RAPTURE, 1941
FAME, 1936
FAME IS THE SPUR, 1947
FAME STREET, 1932
FAMILY, THE, 1987
FAMILY AFFAIR, 1954
FAMILY DIARY, 1963
FAMILY HONEYMOON, 1948
FAMILY JEWELS, THE, 1965
FAMILY NEXT DOOR, THE, 1939
FAMILY SECRET, THE, 1951
FAMOUS FERGUSON CASE, THE, 1932
FAN, THE, 1949
FANCY BAGGAGE, 1929
FANCY PANTS, 1950
FANFAN THE TULIP, 1952
FANGS OF THE ARCTIC, 1953
FANGS OF THE WILD, 1954
FANNY FOLEY HERSELF, 1931
FANTASTIC PLANET, 1973
FANTASTIC THREE, THE, 1967
FANTASTIC VOYAGE, 1966
FANTOMAS STRIKES BACK, 1965
FAR COUNTRY, THE, 1955
FAR FROM THE MADDING CROWD, 1967
FAR FRONTIER, THE, 1949
FAR HORIZONS, THE, 1955
FAREWELL, DOVES, 1962
FAREWELL TO CINDERELLA, 1937
FAREWELL TO LOVE, 1931
FARGO, 1952
FARGO EXPRESS, 1933
FARGO KID, THE, 1941
FARMER IN THE DELL, THE, 1936
FARMER TAKES A WIFE, THE, 1935
FARMER TAKES A WIFE, THE, 1953
FARMER'S DAUGHTER, THE, 1940
FARMER'S OTHER DAUGHTER, THE, 1965
FARMER'S WIFE, THE, 1941
FAREWELL TO ARMS, A, 1932
FASCINATION, 1931
FASCIST, THE, 1965
FASHION MODEL, 1945
FASHIONS OF 1934, 1934
FAST AND FURIOUS, 1939
FAST AND LOOSE, 1930
FAST AND LOOSE, 1939
FAST AND LOOSE, 1954
FAST AND SEXY, 1960
FAST AND THE FURIOUS, THE, 1954
FAST BREAK, 1979
FAST BULLETS, 1936
FAST COMPANIONS, 1932
FAST COMPANY, 1929
FAST COMPANY, 1938
FAST COMPANY, 1953
FAST LADY, THE, 1963
FAST LIFE, 1929
FAST LIFE, 1932
FAST ON THE DRAW, 1950
FAST WORKERS, 1933
FASTEST GUITAR ALIVE, THE, 1967
FASTEST GUN ALIVE, 1956
FAT MAN, THE, 1951
FAT SPY, 1966

FATAL HOUR, THE, 1937
FATAL LADY, 1936
FATAL NIGHT, THE, 1948
FATAL WITNESS, THE, 1945
FATE IS THE HUNTER, 1964
FATE TAKES A HAND, 1962
FATHER, 1967
FATHER AND SON, 1929
FATHER BROWN, DETECTIVE, 1935
FATHER CAME TOO, 1964
FATHER IS A BACHELOR, 1950
FATHER IS A PRINCE, 1940
FATHER MAKES GOOD, 1950
FATHER O'FLYNN, 1938
FATHER STEPS OUT, 1937
FATHER TAKES A WIFE, 1941
FATHER TAKES THE AIR, 1951
FATHER WAS A FULLBACK, 1949
FATHERS AND SONS, 1960
FATHER'S DILEMMA, 1952
FATHER'S DOING FINE, 1952
FATHER'S SON, 1931
FATHER'S SON, 1941
FATHER'S WILD GAME, 1950
FATHOM, 1967
FATSO, 1980
FAUST, 1963
FAUST, 1964
FBI CODE 98, 1964
FBI GIRL, 1951
FEAR, 1956
FEAR SHIP, THE, 1933
FEARMAKERS, THE, 1958
FEATHER, THE, 1929
FEATHER IN HER HAT, A, 1935
FEATHER YOUR NEST, 1937
FEATHERED SERPENT, THE, 1934
FEATHERED SERPENT, THE, 1948
FEDERAL AGENT, 1936
FEDERAL AGENT AT LARGE, 1950
FEDERAL BULLETS, 1937
FEDERAL FUGITIVES, 1941
FEDERAL MAN, 1950
FEDERAL MAN-HUNT, 1939
FEDORA, 1946
FEELIN' GOOD, 1966
FEET FIRST, 1930
FEET OF CLAY, 1960
FELLER NEEDS A FRIEND, 1932
FEMALE, 1933
FEMALE ANIMAL, THE, 1958
FEMALE FIENDS, 1958
FEMALE FUGITIVE, 1938
FEMININE TOUCH, THE, 1941
FENCE RIDERS, 1950
FERNANDEL THE DRESSMAKER, 1957
FERRY ACROSS THE MERSEY, 1964
FERRY TO HONG KONG, 1959
FEUD MAKER, 1938
FEUD OF THE RANGE, 1939
FEUD OF THE TRAIL, 1938
FEUD OF THE WEST, 1936
FEUDIN' FOOLS, 1952
FEUDIN', FUSSIN' AND A-FIGHTIN', 1948
FEVER HEAT, 1968
FEVER IN THE BLOOD, A, 1961
FEW BULLETS MORE, A, 1968
FIANCES, THE, 1964
FIASCO IN MILAN, 1963
FICKLE FINGER OF FATE, THE, 1967
FIDDLERS THREE, 1944
FIDDLIN' BUCKAROO, THE, 1934
FIDELIO, 1961
FIDELIO, 1970
FIERCEST HEART, THE, 1961
FIESTA, 1947
FIFTEEN MAIDEN LANE, 1936
FIFTEEN WIVES, 1934
FIFTH AVENUE GIRL, 1939
FIFTY FATHOMS DEEP, 1931
55 DAYS AT PEKING, 1963
FIFTY ROADS TO TOWN, 1937
52ND STREET, 1937
FIFTY-SHILLING BOXER, 1937
FIGHT FOR ROME, 1969
FIGHT FOR YOUR LADY, 1937

FIGHT TO THE FINISH, A, 1937
FIGHTER, THE, 1952
FIGHTER ATTACK, 1953
FIGHTER SQUADRON, 1948
FIGHTING BACK, 1948
FIGHTING BILL CARSON, 1945
FIGHTING BILL FARGO, 1942
FIGHTING BUCKAROO, THE, 1943
FIGHTING CABALLERO, 1935
FIGHTING CARAVANS, 1931
FIGHTING CHAMP, 1933
FIGHTING CHANCE, THE, 1955
FIGHTING COAST GUARD, 1951
FIGHTING CODE, THE, 1934
FIGHTING COWBOY, 1933
FIGHTING DEPUTY, THE, 1937
FIGHTING FATHER DUNNE, 1948
FIGHTING FOOL, THE, 1932
FIGHTING FOOLS, 1949
FIGHTING GENTLEMAN, THE, 1932
FIGHTING GRINGO, THE, 1939
FIGHTING GUARDSMAN, THE, 1945
FIGHTING HERO, 1934
FIGHTING KENTUCKIAN, THE, 1949
FIGHTING LAWMAN, THE, 1953
FIGHTING LEGION, THE, 1930
FIGHTING MAD, 1939
FIGHTING MAD, 1948
FIGHTING MAN OF THE PLAINS, 1949
FIGHTING O'FLYNN, THE, 1949
FIGHTING PARSON, THE, 1933
FIGHTING PIMPERNEL, THE, 1950
FIGHTING PIONEERS, 1935
FIGHTING PLAYBOY, 1937
FIGHTING RANGER, THE, 1934
FIGHTING RANGER, THE, 1948
FIGHTING REDHEAD, THE, 1950
FIGHTING ROOKIE, THE, 1934
FIGHTING SHADOWS, 1935
FIGHTING SHERIFF, THE, 1931
FIGHTING 69TH, THE, 1940
FIGHTING STALLION, THE, 1950
FIGHTING STOCK, 1935
FIGHTING TEXAN, 1937
FIGHTING TEXANS, 1933
FIGHTING THOROUGHBREDS, 1939
FIGHTING THRU, 1931
FIGHTING TROOPER, THE, 1935
FIGHTING TROUBLE, 1956
FIGHTING VALLEY, 1943
FIGHTING VIGILANTES, THE, 1947
FIGHTING YOUTH, 1935
FILE 113, 1932
FILES FROM SCOTLAND YARD, 1951
FILM WITHOUT A NAME, 1950
FINAL APPOINTMENT, 1954
FINAL COLUMN, THE, 1955
FINAL EDITION, 1932
FINAL HOUR, THE, 1936
FINAL RECKONING, THE, 1932
FINAL TAKE: THE GOLDEN AGE OF MOVIES, 1986
FINAL TEST, THE, 1953
FIND THE BLACKMAILER, 1943
FIND THE LADY, 1936
FIND THE LADY, 1956
FIND THE WITNESS, 1937
FINDERS KEEPERS, 1966
FINE FEATHERS, 1937
FINGER MAN, 1955
FINGER OF GUILT, 1956
FINGER ON THE TRIGGER, 1965
FINGERPRINTS DON'T LIE, 1951
FINGERS, 1940
FINIAN'S RAINBOW, 1968
FINISHING SCHOOL, 1934
FINN AND HATTIE, 1931
FINNEGANS WAKE, 1965
FINNEY, 1969
FIRE AND ICE, 1987
FIRE HAS BEEN ARRANGED, A, 1935
FIRE IN THE FLESH, 1964
FIRE IN THE STRAW, 1943
FIRE MAIDENS FROM OUTER SPACE, 1956
FIRE OVER AFRICA, 1954
FIRE OVER ENGLAND, 1937
FIRE RAISERS, THE, 1933

FIREBALL, THE, 1950
FIREBALL 590, 1966
FIREBIRD, THE, 1934
FIREBRAND JORDAN, 1930
FIREBRANDS OF ARIZONA, 1944
FIRED WIFE, 1943
FIREFLY, THE, 1937
FIREMAN, SAVE MY CHILD, 1932
FIREMAN SAVE MY CHILD, 1954
FIRES OF FATE, 1932
FIRETRAP, THE, 1935
FIREWALKER, 1986
FIRST A GIRL, 1935
FIRST AID, 1931
FIRST BABY, 1936
FIRST COMES COURAGE, 1943
FIRST LADY, 1937
FIRST LEGION, THE, 1951
FIRST LOVE, 1939
FIRST MAN INTO SPACE, 1959
FIRST MEN IN THE MOON, 1964
FIRST MRS. FRASER, THE, 1932
FIRST NIGHT, 1937
FIRST OFFENCE, 1936
FIRST OFFENDERS, 1939
FIRST 100 YEARS, THE, 1938
FIRST SPACESHIP ON VENUS, 1960
FIRST START, 1953
FIRST TEXAN, THE, 1956
FIRST TIME, THE, 1952
FIRST TRAVELING SALESLADY, THE, 1956
FIRST YEAR, THE, 1932
FIT FOR A KING, 1937
FIVE AND TEN, 1931
FIVE ANGLES ON MURDER, 1950
FIVE BOLD WOMEN, 1960
FIVE CAME BACK, 1939
FIVE DAYS ONE SUMMER, 1982
FIVE FINGER EXERCISE, 1962
FIVE FINGERS, 1952
FIVE GOLDEN HOURS, 1961
FIVE GRAVES TO CAIRO, 1943
FIVE GUNS TO TOMBSTONE, 1961
FIVE GUNS WEST, 1955
FIVE LITTLE PEPPERS IN TROUBLE, 1940
FIVE MILLION YEARS TO EARTH, 1968
FIVE ON THE BLACK HAND SIDE, 1973
FIVE PENNIES, THE, 1959
FIVE STEPS TO DANGER, 1957
FIVE WEEKS IN A BALLOON, 1962
FIXED BAYONETS, 1951
FIXER DUGAN, 1939
FLAG LIEUTENANT, THE, 1932
FLAME, THE, 1948
FLAME AND THE ARROW, THE, 1950
FLAME IN THE HEATHER, 1935
FLAME IN THE STREETS, 1961
FLAME OF ARABY, 1951
FLAME OF CALCUTTA, 1953
FLAME OF LOVE, THE, 1930
FLAME OF STAMBOUL, 1957
FLAME OF THE BARBARY COAST, 1945
FLAME OF THE ISLANDS, 1955
FLAME OF THE WEST, 1945
FLAME OF YOUTH, 1949
FLAME OVER INDIA, 1960
FLAME OVER VIETNAM, 1967
FLAMES, 1932
FLAMING BULLETS, 1945
FLAMING FEATHER, 1951
FLAMING FRONTIER, 1958
FLAMING FRONTIER, 1968
FLAMING FURY, 1949
FLAMING GOLD, 1934
FLAMING GUNS, 1933
FLAMING LEAD, 1939
FLAMING SIGNAL, 1933
FLAMING TEEN-AGE, THE, 1956
FLAMINGO AFFAIR, THE, 1948
FLANNELFOOT, 1953
FLAP, 1970
FLASHING GUNS, 1947
FLAT TOP, 1952
FLAW, THE, 1933
FLAW, THE, 1955
FLAXY MARTIN, 1949

BOLD: Films on Videocassette

FLEMISH FARM, THE, 1943
FLESH AND FURY, 1952
FLIGHT, 1929
FLIGHT ANGELS, 1940
FLIGHT AT MIDNIGHT, 1939
FLIGHT COMMAND, 1940
FLIGHT FOR FREEDOM, 1943
FLIGHT FROM ASHIYA, 1964
FLIGHT FROM DESTINY, 1941
FLIGHT FROM FOLLY, 1945
FLIGHT FROM GLORY, 1937
FLIGHT FROM SINGAPORE, 1962
FLIGHT FROM VIENNA, 1956
FLIGHT INTO NOWHERE, 1938
FLIGHT LIEUTENANT, 1942
FLIGHT NURSE, 1953
FLIGHT OF THE NAVIGATOR, 1986
FLIGHT THAT DISAPPEARED, THE, 1961
FLIGHT TO FAME, 1938
FLIGHT TO MARS, 1951
FLIGHT TO TANGIER, 1953
FLIM-FLAM MAN, THE, 1967
FLIRTING WIDOW, THE, 1930
FLIRTING WITH DANGER, 1935
FLIRTING WITH FATE, 1938
FLOATING DUTCHMAN, THE, 1953
FLOATING WEEDS, 1970
FLOOD, THE, 1931
FLOOD TIDE, 1935
FLOODS OF FEAR, 1958
FLOODTIDE, 1949
FLORENTINE DAGGER, THE, 1935
FLORIDA SPECIAL, 1936
FLORODORA GIRL, THE, 1930
FLOWER DRUM SONG, 1961
FLOWERS FOR THE MAN IN THE MOON, 1975
FLOWING GOLD, 1940
FLY-AWAY BABY, 1937
FLY AWAY PETER, 1948
FLY BY NIGHT, 1942
FLYING BLIND, 1941
FLYING CADETS, 1941
FLYING DEVILS, 1933
FLYING DOCTOR, THE, 1936
FLYING DOWN TO RIO, 1933
FLYING FIFTY-FIVE, 1939
FLYING FISTS, THE, 1938
FLYING FONTAINES, THE, 1959
FLYING FOOL, 1929
FLYING FOOL, THE, 1931
FLYING FORTRESS, 1942
FLYING HIGH, 1931
FLYING HOSTESS, 1936
FLYING IRISHMAN, THE, 1939
FLYING MARINE, THE, 1929
FLYING MATCHMAKER, THE, 1970
FLYING MISSILE, 1950
FLYING SAUCER, THE, 1950
FLYING SAUCER, THE, 1964
FLYING SCOTSMAN, THE, 1929
FLYING SORCERER, THE, 1974
FLYING SQUAD, THE, 1932
FLYING SQUAD, THE, 1940
FLYING WILD, 1941
FLYING WITH MUSIC, 1942
FOG, 1934
FOG ISLAND, 1945
FOG OVER FRISCO, 1934
FOLIES BERGERE, 1935
FOLLIES GIRL, 1943
FOLLOW A STAR, 1959
FOLLOW THAT CAMEL, 1967
FOLLOW THAT DREAM, 1962
FOLLOW THAT HORSE!, 1960
FOLLOW THAT MAN, 1961
FOLLOW THAT WOMAN, 1945
FOLLOW THE BAND, 1943
FOLLOW THE BOYS, 1963
FOLLOW THE LEADER, 1930
FOLLOW THE LEADER, 1944
FOLLOW THE SUN, 1951
FOLLOW THRU, 1930
FOLLOW YOUR HEART, 1936
FOLLOW YOUR STAR, 1938
FOLLY TO BE WISE, 1953
FOOL AND THE PRINCESS, THE, 1948

FOOLS FOR SCANDAL, 1938
FOOL'S GOLD, 1946
FOOLS RUSH IN, 1949
FOOTLIGHT FEVER, 1941
FOOTLIGHT GLAMOUR, 1943
FOOTLIGHT PARADE, 1933
FOOTLIGHT SERENADE, 1942
FOOTLIGHTS AND FOOLS, 1929
FOOTLOOSE HEIRESS, THE, 1937
FOOTSTEPS IN THE DARK, 1941
FOOTSTEPS IN THE FOG, 1955
FOOTSTEPS IN THE NIGHT, 1932
FOOTSTEPS IN THE NIGHT, 1957
FOR BEAUTY'S SAKE, 1941
FOR BETTER FOR WORSE, 1954
FOR FREEDOM, 1940
FOR HEAVEN'S SAKE, 1950
FOR LOVE OF IVY, 1968
FOR LOVE OF YOU, 1933
FOR LOVE OR MONEY, 1934
FOR LOVE OR MONEY, 1939
FOR LOVE OR MONEY, 1963
FOR ME AND MY GAL, 1942
FOR MEN ONLY, 1952
FOR PETE'S SAKE!, 1966
FOR THE FIRST TIME, 1959
FOR THE LOVE OF MARY, 1948
FOR THE LOVE OF MIKE, 1933
FOR THE LOVE O'LIL, 1930
FOR THE SERVICE, 1936
FOR THEM THAT TRESPASS, 1949
FOR THOSE IN PERIL, 1944
FOR THOSE WHO THINK YOUNG, 1964
FOR VALOR, 1937
FOR YOU ALONE, 1945
FOR YOU I DIE, 1947
FOR YOUR EYES ONLY, 1981
FORBIDDEN, 1953
FORBIDDEN CARGO, 1954
FORBIDDEN COMPANY, 1932
FORBIDDEN HEAVEN, 1936
FORBIDDEN JOURNEY, 1950
FORBIDDEN JUNGLE, 1950
FORBIDDEN MUSIC, 1936
FORBIDDEN TERRITORY, 1938
FORBIDDEN TRAIL, 1936
FORBIDDEN TRAILS, 1941
FORCE OF ARMS, 1951
FORCE OF IMPULSE, 1961
FORCED LANDING, 1935
FORCED LANDING, 1941
FORCES' SWEETHEART, 1953
FOREIGN AFFAIRES, 1935
FOREIGN AGENT, 1942
FOREIGN CORRESPONDENT, 1940
FOREST RANGERS, THE, 1942
FOREVER AND A DAY, 1943
FOREVER DARLING, 1956
FOREVER FEMALE, 1953
FOREVER MY LOVE, 1962
FOREVER YOURS, 1937
FOREVER YOURS, 1945
FORGED PASSPORT, 1939
FORGET MOZART!, 1985
FORGOTTEN, 1933
FORGOTTEN COMMANDMENTS, 1932
FORGOTTEN FACES, 1936
FORGOTTEN GIRLS, 1940
FORGOTTEN WOMAN, THE, 1939
FORGOTTEN WOMEN, 1932
FORGOTTEN WOMEN, 1949
FORSAKING ALL OTHERS, 1935
FORT ALGIERS, 1953
FORT APACHE, 1948
FORT BOWIE, 1958
FORT COURAGEOUS, 1965
FORT DEFIANCE, 1951
FORT DOBBS, 1958
FORT OSAGE, 1952
FORT SAVAGE RAIDERS, 1951
FORT UTAH, 1967
FORT VENGEANCE, 1953
FORT WORTH, 1951
FORT YUMA, 1955
FORTUNATE FOOL, THE, 1933
FORTUNES OF CAPTAIN BLOOD, 1950

FORTY ACRE FEUD, 1965
48 HOURS TO LIVE, 1960
FORTY LITTLE MOTHERS, 1940
FORTY NAUGHTY GIRLS, 1937
FORTY-NINE DAYS, 1964
FORTY-NINERS, THE, 1932
FORTY-NINTH MAN, THE, 1953
42ND STREET, 1933
FORTY SQUARE METERS OF GERMANY, 1986
FORTY THIEVES, 1944
FORTY THOUSAND HORSEMEN, 1941
FORTYNINERS, THE, 1954
FORWARD PASS, THE, 1929
FOUND ALIVE, 1934
FOUNTAIN, THE, 1934
FOUNTAINHEAD, THE, 1949
FOUR AGAINST FATE, 1952
FOUR COMPANIONS, THE, 1938
FOUR DAUGHTERS, 1938
FOUR DAYS, 1951
FOUR DAYS LEAVE, 1950
FOUR DAYS OF NAPLES, THE, 1963
FOUR DEVILS, 1929
FOUR FACES WEST, 1948
FOUR FAST GUNS, 1959
FOUR FEATHERS, THE, 1939
FOUR GIRLS IN TOWN, 1956
FOUR GIRLS IN WHITE, 1939
FOUR GUNS TO THE BORDER, 1954
FOUR HORSEMEN OF THE APOCALYPSE, THE, 1962
FOUR HOURS TO KILL, 1935
FOUR IN A JEEP, 1951
FOUR JACKS AND A JILL, 1941
FOUR JILLS IN A JEEP, 1944
FOUR MASKED MEN, 1934
FOUR MEN AND A PRAYER, 1938
FOUR MOTHERS, 1941
FOUR POSTER, THE, 1952
FOUR SONS, 1940
FOUR WIVES, 1939
4D MAN, 1959
FOUR'S A CROWD, 1938
FOURTEEN, THE, 1973
FOURTH ALARM, THE, 1930
48 HOURS, 1944
40 GUNS TO APACHE PASS, 1967
FOX MOVIETONE FOLLIES, 1929
FOX MOVIETONE FOLLIES OF 1930, 1930
FOXES OF HARROW, THE, 1947
FOXHOLE IN CAIRO, 1960
FOXY LADY, 1971
F.P. 1, 1933
F.P. 1 DOESN'T ANSWER, 1933
FRAME-UP THE, 1937
FRAMED, 1930
FRAMED, 1940
FRANCHISE AFFAIR, THE, 1952
FRANCIS OF ASSISI, 1961
FRANKIE AND JOHNNY, 1966
FRECKLES, 1935
FRECKLES, 1960
FRECKLES COMES HOME, 1942
FREDDIE STEPS OUT, 1946
FREDDY UNTER FREMDEN STERNEN, 1962
FREE AND EASY, 1930
FREE AND EASY, 1941
FREE, BLONDE AND 21, 1940
FREE FOR ALL, 1949
FREEDOM OF THE SEAS, 1934
FREEDOM TO DIE, 1962
FREEWHEELIN', 1976
FREIGHTERS OF DESTINY, 1932
FRENCH CANCAN, 1956
FRENCH CONSPIRACY, THE, 1973
FRENCH DRESSING, 1964
FRENCH KEY, THE, 1946
FRENCH LEAVE, 1931
FRENCH LEAVE, 1937
FRENCH LEAVE, 1948
FRENCH MISTRESS, 1960
FRENCH, THEY ARE A FUNNY RACE, THE, 1956
FRENCH TOUCH, THE, 1954
FRENCH WAY, THE, 1952
FRENCH WITHOUT TEARS, 1939
FRENCHIE, 1950

FRENCHMAN'S CREEK, 1944
FRENZY, 1946
FRESH FROM PARIS, 1955
FRESHMAN LOVE, 1936
FRESHMAN YEAR, 1938
FRIC FRAC, 1939
FRIDAY THE 13TH, 1934
FRIEDA, 1947
FRIEND OF THE FAMILY, 1965
FRIEND WILL COME TONIGHT, A, 1948
FRIENDLY ENEMIES, 1942
FRIENDLY NEIGHBORS, 1940
FRIENDLY PERSUASION, 1956
FRIENDS AND LOVERS, 1931
FRIENDS AND NEIGHBORS, 1963
FRIENDS FOR LIFE, 1964
FRIENDS OF MR. SWEENEY, 1934
FRIENDSHIP'S DEATH, 1988
FRIGHTENED BRIDE, THE, 1952
FRIGHTENED CITY, THE, 1961
FRIGHTENED MAN, THE, 1952
FRISCO JENNY, 1933
FRISCO KID, 1935
FRISCO LILL, 1942
FRISCO SAL, 1945
FRISCO TORNADO, 1950
FRISCO WATERFRONT, 1935
FRISKY, 1955
FROG, THE, 1937
FROGMEN, THE, 1951
FROM HEADQUARTERS, 1929
FROM HEADQUARTERS, 1933
FROM RUSSIA WITH LOVE, 1963
FROM THE EARTH TO THE MOON, 1958
FROM THIS DAY FORWARD, 1946
FROM TOP TO BOTTOM, 1933
FRONT PAGE STORY, 1954
FRONT PAGE WOMAN, 1935
FRONT PAGE, THE, 1931
FRONTIER AGENT, 1948
FRONTIER BADMEN, 1943
FRONTIER CRUSADER, 1940
FRONTIER DAYS, 1934
FRONTIER FEUD, 1945
FRONTIER FUGITIVES, 1945
FRONTIER FURY, 1943
FRONTIER GAL, 1945
FRONTIER GAMBLER, 1956
FRONTIER GUN, 1958
FRONTIER HELLCAT, 1966
FRONTIER INVESTIGATOR, 1949
FRONTIER JUSTICE, 1936
FRONTIER LAW, 1943
FRONTIER MARSHAL, 1934
FRONTIER MARSHAL, 1939
FRONTIER OUTLAWS, 1944
FRONTIER OUTPOST, 1950
FRONTIER PHANTOM, THE, 1952
FRONTIER PONY EXPRESS, 1939
FRONTIER REVENGE, 1948
FRONTIER SCOUT, 1939
FRONTIER TOWN, 1938
FRONTIER UPRISING, 1961
FRONTIER VENGEANCE, 1939
FRONTIERS OF '49, 1939
FRONTIERSMAN, THE, 1938
FROU-FROU, 1955
FROZEN ALIVE, 1966
FROZEN JUSTICE, 1929
FROZEN LIMITS, THE, 1939
FROZEN RIVER, 1929
FUGITIVE, THE, 1940
FUGITIVE AT LARGE, 1939
FUGITIVE FROM A PRISON CAMP, 1940
FUGITIVE FROM JUSTICE, A, 1940
FUGITIVE FROM SONORA, 1943
FUGITIVE IN THE SKY, 1937
FUGITIVE LOVERS, 1934
FUGITIVE ROAD, 1934
FUGITIVE SHERIFF, THE, 1936
FUGITIVE VALLEY, 1941
FUGITIVE, THE, 1933
FULL CIRCLE, 1935
FULL OF LIFE, 1956
FULL SPEED AHEAD, 1936
FULL SPEED AHEAD, 1939

FUN IN ACAPULCO, 1963
FUNERAL FOR AN ASSASSIN, 1977
FUNNY GIRL, 1968
FUNNY LADY, 1975
FUR COLLAR, THE, 1962
FURIES, THE, 1930
FURY AND THE WOMAN, 1937
FURY AT FURNACE CREEK, 1948
FURY AT SMUGGLERS BAY, 1963
FURY BELOW, 1938
FURY IN PARADISE, 1955
FURY OF HERCULES, THE, 1961
FUZZY PINK NIGHTGOWN, THE, 1957
FUZZY SETTLES DOWN, 1944
G.I. BLUES, 1960
G.I. WAR BRIDES, 1946
G-MEN, 1935
GABLES MYSTERY, THE, 1931
GABLES MYSTERY, THE, 1938
GABY, 1956
GAIETY GIRLS, THE, 1938
GAL WHO TOOK THE WEST, THE, 1949
GALAXY EXPRESS, 1982
GALILEO, 1968
GALILEO, 1975
GALLANT BESS, 1946
GALLANT BLADE, THE, 1948
GALLANT DEFENDER, 1935
GALLANT FOOL, THE, 1933
GALLANT HOURS, THE, 1960
GALLANT JOURNEY, 1946
GALLANT LADY, 1934
GALLANT LADY, 1942
GALLANT LEGION, THE, 1948
GALLANT ONE, THE, 1964
GALLANT SONS, 1940
GALLOPING DYNAMITE, 1937
GALLOPING MAJOR, THE, 1951
GALLOPING ROMEO, 1933
GALLOPING THRU, 1932
GALS, INCORPORATED, 1943
GAMBLER AND THE LADY, THE, 1952
GAMBLER FROM NATCHEZ, THE, 1954
GAMBLER WORE A GUN, THE, 1961
GAMBLER'S CHOICE, 1944
GAMBLERS, THE, 1929
GAMBLERS, THE, 1969
GAMBLING, 1934
GAMBLING DAUGHTERS, 1941
GAMBLING HOUSE, 1950
GAMBLING LADY, 1934
GAMBLING ON THE HIGH SEAS, 1940
GAMBLING SEX, 1932
GAMBLING SHIP, 1933
GAMBLING SHIP, 1939
GAMBLING TERROR, THE, 1937
GAME FOR SIX LOVERS, A, 1962
GAME FOR THREE LOSERS, 1965
GAME OF CHANCE, A, 1932
GAME OF DEATH, A, 1945
GAME THAT KILLS, THE, 1937
GAMEKEEPER, THE, 1980
GAMERA THE INVINCIBLE, 1966
GAMERA VERSUS BARUGON, 1966
GAMERA VERSUS GAOS, 1967
GAMERA VERSUS GUIRON, 1969
GAMERA VERSUS MONSTER K, 1970
GAMERA VERSUS VIRAS, 1968
GAMERA VERSUS ZIGRA, 1971
GAMES, THE, 1970
GAMMA PEOPLE, THE, 1956
GANDHI, 1982
GANG BULLETS, 1938
GANG BUSTER, THE, 1931
GANG BUSTERS, 1955
GANG WAR, 1928
GANG WAR, 1962
GANG'S ALL HERE, 1941
GANG, THE, 1938
GANG'S ALL HERE, THE, 1943
GANGS OF CHICAGO, 1940
GANGS OF NEW YORK, 1938
GANGS OF SONORA, 1941
GANGS OF THE WATERFRONT, 1945
GANGSTER STORY, 1959
GANGSTER'S BOY, 1938

GANGSTERS OF THE FRONTIER, 1944
GANGWAY, 1937
GANGWAY FOR TOMORROW, 1943
GAOL BREAK, 1936
GAOLBREAK, 1962
GAPPA THE TRIFIBIAN MONSTER, 1967
GARDEN MURDER CASE, THE, 1936
GARDEN OF THE MOON, 1938
GARMENT JUNGLE, THE, 1957
GARNET BRACELET, THE, 1966
GARRISON FOLLIES, 1940
GAS HOUSE KIDS, 1946
GAS HOUSE KIDS GO WEST, 1947
GAS HOUSE KIDS IN HOLLYWOOD, 1947
GASBAGS, 1940
GATEWAY, 1938
GATHERING OF EAGLES, A, 1963
GAUCHO SERENADE, 1940
GAUCHOS OF EL DORADO, 1941
GAY ADVENTURE, THE, 1936
GAY ADVENTURE, THE, 1953
GAY AMIGO, THE, 1949
GAY BLADES, 1946
GAY BUCKAROO, THE, 1932
GAY CABALLERO, THE, 1932
GAY CABALLERO, THE, 1940
GAY DECEPTION, THE, 1935
GAY DESPERADO, THE, 1936
GAY DIPLOMAT, THE, 1931
GAY DOG, THE, 1954
GAY FALCON, THE, 1941
GAY INTRUDERS, THE, 1946
GAY INTRUDERS, THE, 1948
GAY LADY, THE, 1949
GAY LOVE, 1936
GAY OLD DOG, 1936
GAY RANCHERO, THE, 1948
GAY SENORITA, THE, 1945
GAY VAGABOND, THE, 1941
GAZEBO, THE, 1959
GEISHA BOY, THE, 1958
GEISHA GIRL, 1952
GEISHA, A, 1978
GENE AUTRY AND THE MOUNTIES, 1951
GENERAL JOHN REGAN, 1933
GENERAL SUVOROV, 1941
GENERALS WITHOUT BUTTONS, 1938
GENEVIEVE, 1953
GENIE, THE, 1953
GENIUS AT WORK, 1946
GENTLE ANNIE, 1944
GENTLE GANGSTER, A, 1943
GENTLE JULIA, 1936
GENTLE PEOPLE AND THE QUIET LAND, THE, 1972
GENTLE SEX, THE, 1943
GENTLE TERROR, THE, 1962
GENTLE TOUCH, THE, 1956
GENTLE TRAP, THE, 1960
GENTLEMAN AFTER DARK, A, 1942
GENTLEMAN AT HEART, A, 1942
GENTLEMAN FROM ARIZONA, THE, 1940
GENTLEMAN FROM DIXIE, 1941
GENTLEMAN FROM LOUISIANA, 1936
GENTLEMAN FROM NOWHERE, THE, 1948
GENTLEMAN FROM TEXAS, 1946
GENTLEMAN JIM, 1942
GENTLEMAN MISBEHAVES, THE, 1946
GENTLEMAN OF PARIS, A, 1931
GENTLEMAN'S AGREEMENT, 1935
GENTLEMAN'S AGREEMENT, 1947
GENTLEMAN'S GENTLEMAN, A, 1939
GENTLEMEN ARE BORN, 1934
GENTLEMEN MARRY BRUNETTES, 1955
GENTLEMEN OF THE PRESS, 1929
GENTLEMEN PREFER BLONDES, 1953
GENTLEMEN WITH GUNS, 1946
GEORGE, 1973
GEORGE AND MARGARET, 1940
GEORGE IN CIVVY STREET, 1946
GEORGE RAFT STORY, THE, 1961
GEORGE WASHINGTON CARVER, 1940
GEORGE WASHINGTON SLEPT HERE, 1942
GEORGE WHITE'S 1935 SCANDALS, 1935
GEORGE WHITE'S SCANDALS, 1945
GERALDINE, 1929
GERALDINE, 1953

BOLD: Films on Videocassette

GERMINAL, 1963
GERT AND DAISY CLEAN UP, 1942
GERT AND DAISY'S WEEKEND, 1941
GERTRUD, 1966
GET CRACKING, 1943
GET GOING, 1943
GET HEP TO LOVE, 1942
GET OFF MY FOOT, 1935
GET ON WITH IT, 1963
GET THAT MAN, 1935
GET YOUR MAN, 1934
GET YOURSELF A COLLEGE GIRL, 1964
GETTING GERTIE'S GARTER, 1945
GHIDRAH, THE THREE-HEADED MONSTER, 1965
GHOST AND MR. CHICKEN, THE, 1966
GHOST AND MRS. MUIR, THE, 1942
GHOST AND THE GUEST, 1943
GHOST BREAKERS, THE, 1940
GHOST CAMERA, THE, 1933
GHOST CATCHERS, 1944
GHOST CHASERS, 1951
GHOST CITY, 1932
GHOST COMES HOME, THE, 1940
GHOST DIVER, 1957
GHOST GOES WEST, THE, 1936
GHOST GOES WILD, THE, 1947
GHOST GUNS, 1944
GHOST OF HIDDEN VALLEY, 1946
GHOST OF ST. MICHAEL'S, THE, 1941
GHOST OF THE CHINA SEA, 1958
GHOST OF ZORRO, 1959
GHOST PATROL, 1936
GHOST RIDER, THE, 1935
GHOST SHIP, 1953
GHOST TALKS, THE, 1929
GHOST THAT WALKS ALONE, THE, 1944
GHOST TOWN, 1937
GHOST TOWN, 1956
GHOST TOWN GOLD, 1937
GHOST TOWN RENEGADES, 1947
GHOST TOWN RIDERS, 1938
GHOST TRAIN, THE, 1933
GHOST TRAIN, THE, 1941
GHOST VALLEY, 1932
GHOST VALLEY RAIDERS, 1940
GHOST WALKS, THE, 1935
GHOSTS OF BERKELEY SQUARE, 1947
GHOSTS ON THE LOOSE, 1943
G.I. HONEYMOON, 1945
G.I. JANE, 1951
GIANT, 1956
GIANT CLAW, THE, 1957
GIANT GILA MONSTER, THE, 1959
GIANT OF METROPOLIS, THE, 1963
GIANT SPIDER INVASION, THE, 1975
GIDEON OF SCOTLAND YARD, 1959
GIDGET, 1959
GIDGET GOES HAWAIIAN, 1961
GIDGET GOES TO ROME, 1963
GIFT OF GAB, 1934
GIFT OF LOVE, THE, 1958
GIGANTES PLANETARIOS, 1965
GIGANTIS, 1959
GIGI, 1958
GIGOLETTES OF PARIS, 1933
GIGOT, 1962
GILDED CAGE, THE, 1954
GILDERSLEEVE ON BROADWAY, 1943
GILDERSLEEVE'S BAD DAY, 1943
GILDERSLEEVE'S GHOST, 1944
GINGER, 1935
GINGER, 1947
GINGER IN THE MORNING, 1973
GIRARA, 1967
GIRDLE OF GOLD, 1952
GIRL, A GUY AND A GOB, A, 1941
GIRL AND THE GAMBLER, THE, 1939
GIRL AND THE LEGEND, THE, 1966
GIRL CRAZY, 1932
GIRL DOWNSTAIRS, THE, 1938
GIRL FEVER, 1961
GIRL FRIEND, THE, 1935
GIRL FROM ALASKA, 1942
GIRL FROM AVENUE A, 1940
GIRL FROM CALGARY, 1932
GIRL FROM GOD'S COUNTRY, 1940

GIRL FROM HAVANA, 1940
GIRL FROM HAVANA, THE, 1929
GIRL FROM HONG KONG, 1966
GIRL FROM MANDALAY, 1936
GIRL FROM MANHATTAN, 1948
GIRL FROM MAXIM'S THE, 1936
GIRL FROM MEXICO, THE, 1939
GIRL FROM MONTEREY, THE, 1943
GIRL FROM PETROVKA, THE, 1974
GIRL FROM POLTAVA, 1937
GIRL FROM RIO, THE, 1939
GIRL FROM SAN LORENZO, THE, 1950
GIRL FROM SCOTLAND YARD, THE, 1937
GIRL FROM TENTH AVENUE, THE, 1935
GIRL FROM THE MARSH CROFT, THE, 1935
GIRL FROM VALLADOLIO, 1958
GIRL FROM WOOLWORTH'S, THE, 1929
GIRL HABIT, 1931
GIRL HAPPY, 1965
GIRL HE LEFT BEHIND, THE, 1956
GIRL IN A MILLION, A, 1946
GIRL IN DANGER, 1934
GIRL IN DISTRESS, 1941
GIRL IN EVERY PORT, A, 1952
GIRL IN 419, 1933
GIRL IN LOVER'S LANE, THE, 1960
GIRL IN POSSESSION, 1934
GIRL IN ROOM 13, 1961
GIRL IN THE CASE, 1944
GIRL IN THE CROWD, THE, 1934
GIRL IN THE FLAT, THE, 1934
GIRL IN THE GLASS CAGE, THE, 1929
GIRL IN THE KREMLIN, THE, 1957
GIRL IN THE NEWS, THE, 1941
GIRL IN THE NIGHT, THE, 1931
GIRL IN THE PAINTING, THE, 1948
GIRL IN THE PICTURE, THE, 1956
GIRL IN THE SHOW, THE, 1929
GIRL IN THE STREET, 1938
GIRL IN THE TAXI, 1937
GIRL IN THE WOODS, 1958
GIRL IN 313, 1940
GIRL IN WHITE, THE, 1952
GIRL IS MINE, THE, 1950
GIRL LOVES BOY, 1937
GIRL MISSING, 1933
GIRL MUST LIVE, A, 1941
GIRL NAMED TAMIKO, A, 1962
GIRL NEXT DOOR, THE, 1953
GIRL O' MY DREAMS, 1935
GIRL OF THE GOLDEN WEST, 1930
GIRL OF THE LIMBERLOST, 1934
GIRL OF THE LIMBERLOST, THE, 1945
GIRL OF THE OZARKS, 1936
GIRL OF THE PORT, 1930
GIRL OF THE RIO, 1932
GIRL ON APPROVAL, 1962
GIRL ON THE BARGE, THE, 1929
GIRL ON THE BOAT, THE, 1962
GIRL ON THE BRIDGE, THE, 1951
GIRL ON THE CANAL, THE, 1947
GIRL ON THE FRONT PAGE, THE, 1936
GIRL ON THE PIER, THE, 1953
GIRL ON THE RUN, 1961
GIRL ON THE SPOT, 1946
GIRL OVERBOARD, 1929
GIRL OVERBOARD, 1937
GIRL RUSH, 1944
GIRL RUSH, THE, 1955
GIRL SAID NO, THE, 1937
GIRL SAID NO, THE, 1930
GIRL TROUBLE, 1942
GIRL WHO CAME BACK, THE, 1935
GIRL WHO COULDN'T QUITE, THE, 1949
GIRL WHO COULDN'T SAY NO, THE, 1969
GIRL WHO DARED, THE, 1944
GIRL WHO FORGOT, THE, 1939
GIRL WHO HAD EVERYTHING, THE, 1953
GIRL WITH A PISTOL, THE, 1968
GIRL WITH A SUITCASE, 1961
GIRL WITH IDEAS, A, 1937
GIRL WITH THE RED HAIR, THE, 1983
GIRL WITH THREE CAMELS, THE, 1968
GIRL WITHOUT A ROOM, 1933
GIRLS AT SEA, 1958
GIRLS CAN PLAY, 1937

GIRLS DEMAND EXCITEMENT, 1931
GIRLS' DORMITORY, 1936
GIRLS! GIRLS! GIRLS!, 1962
GIRLS IN CHAINS, 1943
GIRLS IN THE STREET, 1937
GIRLS OF LATIN QUARTER, 1960
GIRLS OF PLEASURE ISLAND, THE, 1953
GIRLS OF THE BIG HOUSE, 1945
GIRLS ON PROBATION, 1938
GIRLS ON THE BEACH, 1965
GIRLS PLEASE!, 1934
GIRLS' SCHOOL, 1938
GIRLS' SCHOOL, 1950
GIRLS' TOWN, 1942
GIRLS UNDER TWENTY-ONE, 1940
GIRLS WILL BE BOYS, 1934
GIT ALONG, LITTLE DOGIES, 1937
GIVE A DOG A BONE, 1967
GIVE A GIRL A BREAK, 1953
GIVE AND TAKE, 1929
GIVE HER A RING, 1936
GIVE HER THE MOON, 1970
GIVE ME A SAILOR, 1938
GIVE ME THE STARS, 1944
GIVE ME YOUR HEART, 1936
GIVE MY REGARDS TO BROADWAY, 1948
GIVE OUT, SISTERS, 1942
GIVE US THE MOON, 1944
GIVE US THIS NIGHT, 1936
GIVE US WINGS, 1940
GIVE'EM HELL, HARRY!, 1975
GIVEN WORD, THE, 1964
GLAD TIDINGS, 1953
GLAMOUR, 1931
GLAMOUR FOR SALE, 1940
GLAMOUR GIRL, 1938
GLAMOUR GIRL, 1947
GLASS ALIBI, THE, 1946
GLASS BOTTOM BOAT, THE, 1966
GLASS MENAGERIE, THE, 1950
GLASS MOUNTAIN, THE, 1950
GLASS OF WATER, A, 1962
GLASS SLIPPER, THE, 1955
GLASS SPHINX, THE, 1968
GLASS TOMB, THE, 1955
GLASS TOWER, THE, 1959
GLASS WALL, THE, 1953
GLASS WEB, THE, 1953
GLIMPSE OF PARADISE, A, 1934
GLOBAL AFFAIR, A, 1964
GLORIFYING THE AMERICAN GIRL, 1930
GLORY AT SEA, 1952
GLORY OF FAITH, THE, 1938
GLORY TRAIL, THE, 1937
GO CHASE YOURSELF, 1938
GO FOR BROKE, 1951
GO-GETTER, THE, 1937
GO INTO YOUR DANCE, 1935
GO, JOHNNY, GO!, 1959
GO, MAN, GO!, 1954
GO TELL IT ON THE MOUNTAIN, 1984
GO TO BLAZES, 1962
GO WEST, 1940
GO WEST, YOUNG LADY, 1941
GOBS AND GALS, 1952
GOD IS MY CO-PILOT, 1945
GOD IS MY PARTNER, 1957
GOD'S COUNTRY, 1946
GOD'S COUNTRY AND THE MAN, 1931
GOD'S COUNTRY AND THE MAN, 1937
GOD'S COUNTRY AND THE WOMAN, 1937
GOD'S GIFT TO WOMEN, 1931
GOG, 1954
GOIN' TO TOWN, 1944
GOING APE!, 1981
GOING HIGHBROW, 1935
GOING HOLLYWOOD, 1933
GOING PLACES, 1939
GOING STEADY, 1958
GOING STRAIGHT, 1933
GOING WILD, 1931
GOLD, 1932
GOLD DIGGERS IN PARIS, 1938
GOLD DIGGERS OF 1933, 1933
GOLD DIGGERS OF 1935, 1935
GOLD DIGGERS OF 1937, 1936

GOLD DIGGERS OF BROADWAY, 1929
GOLD DUST GERTIE, 1931
GOLD EXPRESS, THE, 1955
GOLD FEVER, 1952
GOLD GUITAR, THE, 1966
GOLD IS WHERE YOU FIND IT, 1938
GOLD MINE IN THE SKY, 1938
GOLD OF THE SEVEN SAINTS, 1961
GOLD RACKET, THE, 1937
GOLD RAIDERS, THE, 1952
GOLD RUSH MAISIE, 1940
GOLDBERGS, THE, 1950
GOLDEN ARROW, THE, 1936
GOLDEN ARROW, THE, 1964
GOLDEN BLADE, THE, 1953
GOLDEN BOY, 1939
GOLDEN CAGE, THE, 1933
GOLDEN COACH, THE, 1953
GOLDEN DAWN, 1930
GOLDEN EIGHTIES, 1986
GOLDEN FLEECING, THE, 1940
GOLDEN GLOVES, 1940
GOLDEN GLOVES STORY, THE, 1950
GOLDEN HARVEST, 1933
GOLDEN HAWK, THE, 1952
GOLDEN HEAD, THE, 1965
GOLDEN HORDE, THE, 1951
GOLDEN LINK, THE, 1954
GOLDEN MADONNA, THE, 1949
GOLDEN MASK, THE, 1954
GOLDEN MISTRESS, THE, 1954
GOLDEN MOUNTAINS, 1958
GOLDEN PLAGUE, THE, 1963
GOLDEN RABBIT, THE, 1962
GOLDEN SALAMANDER, 1950
GOLDEN STALLION, THE, 1949
GOLDEN TRAIL, THE, 1940
GOLDEN WEST, THE, 1932
GOLDIE, 1931
GOLDIE GETS ALONG, 1933
GOLDTOWN GHOST RIDERS, 1953
GOLDWYN FOLLIES, THE, 1938
GOLGOTHA, 1937
GOLIATH AGAINST THE GIANTS, 1963
GOLIATH AND THE BARBARIANS, 1960
GOLIATH AND THE DRAGON, 1961
GOLIATH AND THE SINS OF BABYLON, 1964
GONE ARE THE DAYS, 1963
GONE TO THE DOGS, 1939
GONE WITH THE WIND, 1939
GONKS GO BEAT, 1965
GOOD BEGINNING, THE, 1953
GOOD COMPANIONS, 1933
GOOD COMPANIONS, THE, 1957
GOOD DAME, 1934
GOOD DAY FOR A HANGING, 1958
GOOD EARTH, THE, 1937
GOOD FAIRY, THE, 1935
GOOD FELLOWS, THE, 1943
GOOD GIRLS GO TO PARIS, 1939
GOOD HUMOR MAN, THE, 1950
GOOD INTENTIONS, 1930
GOOD LUCK, MR. YATES, 1943
GOOD MORNING, JUDGE, 1943
GOOD MORNING, MISS DOVE, 1955
GOOD NEWS, 1930
GOOD OLD DAYS, THE, 1939
GOOD OLD SOAK, THE, 1937
GOOD SAM, 1948
GOOD SPORT, 1931
GOOD TIMES, 1967
GOODBYE AGAIN, 1933
GOODBYE BROADWAY, 1938
GOODBYE FRANKLIN HIGH, 1978
GOODBYE LOVE, 1934
GOODBYE MR. CHIPS, 1969
GOODBYE, MY FANCY, 1951
GOODNIGHT SWEETHEART, 1944
GOOSE AND THE GANDER, THE, 1935
GOOSE STEPS OUT, THE, 1942
GORILLA, THE, 1931
GORILLA, THE, 1939
GORILLA MAN, 1942
GORILLA SHIP, THE, 1932
GOSPEL ACCORDING TO ST. MATTHEW, THE, 1966
GOSPEL ROAD, THE, 1973

GOT WHAT SHE WANTED, 1930
GOVERNMENT GIRL, 1943
GRACIE ALLEN MURDER CASE, 1939
GRADUATE, THE, 1967
GRAN VARIETA, 1955
GRAND CANARY, 1934
GRAND CANYON, 1949
GRAND CANYON TRAIL, 1948
GRAND CENTRAL MURDER, 1942
GRAND ESCAPADE, THE, 1946
GRAND EXIT, 1935
GRAND FINALE, 1936
GRAND HOTEL, 1932
GRAND ILLUSION, 1938
GRAND JURY, 1936
GRAND JURY SECRETS, 1939
GRAND OLD GIRL, 1935
GRAND OLE OPRY, 1940
GRAND PARADE, THE, 1930
GRAND PRIX, 1934
GRAND SLAM, 1933
GRANDAD RUDD, 1935
GRANDPA GOES TO TOWN, 1940
GRANNY GET YOUR GUN, 1940
GRAPES OF WRATH, 1940
GRASS IS GREENER, THE, 1960
GRASS IS SINGING, THE, 1982
GREASE, 1978
GREAT ADVENTURE, THE, 1976
GREAT AMERICAN BROADCAST, THE, 1941
GREAT AMERICAN PASTIME, THE, 1956
GREAT ARMORED CAR SWINDLE, THE, 1964
GREAT BANK ROBBERY, THE, 1969
GREAT BIG WORLD AND LITTLE CHILDREN, THE, 1962
GREAT BRITISH TRAIN ROBBERY, THE, 1967
GREAT CARUSO, THE, 1951
GREAT CITIZEN, THE, 1939
GREAT COMMANDMENT, THE, 1941
GREAT DAWN, THE, 1947
GREAT DAY, 1945
GREAT DAY IN THE MORNING, 1956
GREAT DEFENDER, THE, 1934
GREAT DIAMOND ROBBERY, 1953
GREAT DIVIDE, THE, 1930
GREAT ESCAPE, THE, 1963
GREAT FLIRTATION, THE, 1934
GREAT GAMBINI, THE, 1937
GREAT GAME, THE, 1930
GREAT GAME, THE, 1953
GREAT GARRICK, THE, 1937
GREAT GATSBY, THE, 1949
GREAT GATSBY, THE, 1974
GREAT GAY ROAD, THE, 1931
GREAT GILDERSLEEVE, THE, 1942
GREAT GOD GOLD, 1935
GREAT GUY, 1936
GREAT HOSPITAL MYSTERY, THE, 1937
GREAT HOTEL MURDER, 1935
GREAT IMPERSONATION, THE, 1935
GREAT IMPERSONATION, THE, 1942
GREAT IMPOSTOR, THE, 1960
GREAT JASPER, THE, 1933
GREAT JESSE JAMES RAID, THE, 1953
GREAT JEWEL ROBBER, THE, 1950
GREAT JOHN L. THE, 1945
GREAT LIE, THE, 1941
GREAT LOVER, THE, 1931
GREAT LOVER, THE, 1949
GREAT MAN, THE, 1957
GREAT MAN VOTES, THE, 1939
GREAT MANHUNT, THE, 1951
GREAT MAN'S LADY, THE, 1942
GREAT McGINTY, THE, 1940
GREAT MEADOW, THE, 1931
GREAT MIKE, THE, 1944
GREAT MISSOURI RAID, THE, 1950
GREAT MR. HANDEL, THE, 1942
GREAT MR. NOBODY, THE, 1941
GREAT MOMENT, THE, 1944
GREAT O'MALLEY, THE, 1937
GREAT PLANE ROBBERY, THE, 1940
GREAT PLANE ROBBERY, 1950
GREAT POWER, THE, 1929
GREAT PROFILE, THE, 1940
GREAT SINNER, THE, 1949

GREAT SIOUX MASSACRE, THE, 1965
GREAT SIOUX UPRISING, THE, 1953
GREAT STAGECOACH ROBBERY, 1945
GREAT STUFF, 1933
GREAT SWINDLE, THE, 1941
GREAT TRAIN ROBBERY, THE, 1979
GREAT TRAIN ROBBERY, THE, 1941
GREAT WALL, A, 1986
GREAT YEARNING, THE, 1930
GREEKS HAD A WORD FOR THEM, 1932
GREEN BUDDHA, THE, 1954
GREEN COCKATOO, THE, 1947
GREEN EYES, 1934
GREEN FIELDS, 1937
GREEN FINGERS, 1947
GREEN FOR DANGER, 1946
GREEN GLOVE, THE, 1952
GREEN GODDESS, THE, 1930
GREEN GROW THE RUSHES, 1951
GREEN HELL, 1940
GREEN HELMET, THE, 1961
GREEN LIGHT, 1937
GREEN MAN, THE, 1957
GREEN MANSIONS, 1959
GREEN PROMISE, THE, 1949
GREEN SCARF, THE, 1954
GREEN TREE, THE, 1965
GREEN YEARS, THE, 1946
GREENE MURDER CASE, THE, 1929
GREENWICH VILLAGE, 1944
GREYHOUND LIMITED, THE, 1929
GRIDIRON FLASH, 1935
GRIEF STREET, 1931
GRISSLY'S MILLIONS, 1945
GROOM WORE SPURS, THE, 1951
GROUCH, THE, 1961
GROUNDS FOR MARRIAGE, 1950
GROWN-UP CHILDREN, 1963
GRUMPY, 1930
GUADALAJARA, 1943
GUARD THAT GIRL, 1935
GUARDSMAN, THE, 1931
GUEST IN THE HOUSE, 1944
GUEST OF HONOR, 1934
GUEST WIFE, 1945
GUESTS ARE COMING, 1965
GUIDE, THE, 1965
GUILT, 1930
GUILT IS NOT MINE, 1968
GUILT OF JANET AMES, THE, 1947
GUILTY?, 1930
GUILTY?, 1956
GUILTY AS HELL, 1932
GUILTY GENERATION, THE, 1931
GUILTY MELODY, 1936
GUILTY TRAILS, 1938
GUMBALL RALLY, THE, 1976
GUN BELT, 1953
GUN BROTHERS, 1956
GUN CODE, 1940
GUN DUEL IN DURANGO, 1957
GUN FURY, 1953
GUN GLORY, 1957
GUN JUSTICE, 1934
GUN LAW, 1933
GUN LAW, 1938
GUN LAW JUSTICE, 1949
GUN LORDS OF STIRRUP BASIN, 1937
GUN MAN FROM BODIE, THE, 1941
GUN PACKER, 1938
GUN PLAY, 1936
GUN RANGER, THE, 1937
GUN RUNNER, 1949
GUN RUNNERS, THE, 1958
GUN SMOKE, 1931
GUN SMOKE, 1936
GUN SMUGGLERS, 1948
GUN TALK, 1948
GUN TOWN, 1946
GUNFIGHT AT COMANCHE CREEK, 1964
GUNFIGHT AT DODGE CITY, THE, 1959
GUNFIGHTERS OF ABILENE, 1960
GUNFIGHTERS, THE, 1947
GUNFIRE, 1950
GUNFIRE AT INDIAN GAP, 1957
GUNMAN'S CODE, 1946

BOLD: Films on Videocassette

GUNMEN OF ABILENE, 1950
GUNNING FOR JUSTICE, 1948
GUNPLAY, 1951
GUNPOINT, 1966
GUNS AND GUITARS, 1936
GUNS IN THE DARK, 1937
GUNS OF A STRANGER, 1973
GUNS OF FORT PETTICOAT, THE, 1957
GUNS OF HATE, 1948
GUNS OF THE LAW, 1944
GUNS OF THE PECOS, 1937
GUNS OF THE TIMBERLAND, 1960
GUNSIGHT RIDGE, 1957
GUNSLINGERS, 1950
GUNSMOKE, 1953
GUNSMOKE IN TUCSON, 1958
GUNSMOKE MESA, 1944
GUNSMOKE RANCH, 1937
GUNSMOKE TRAIL, 1938
GUY, A GAL AND A PAL, A, 1945
GUY CALLED CAESAR, A, 1962
GUY COULD CHANGE, A, 1946
GUY NAMED JOE, A, 1943
GUY WHO CAME BACK, THE, 1951
GUYS AND DOLLS, 1955
GYPSY, 1937
GYPSY MELODY, 1936
GYPSY WILDCAT, 1944
HA' PENNY BREEZE, 1950
HAIL AND FAREWELL, 1936
HAIL THE CONQUERING HERO, 1944
HAIL TO THE RANGERS, 1943
HAIR OF THE DOG, 1962
HAIRY APE, THE, 1944
HALF A SINNER, 1934
HALF A SINNER, 1940
HALF A SIXPENCE, 1967
HALF ANGEL, 1951
HALF-BREED, THE, 1952
HALF-MARRIAGE, 1929
HALF-NAKED TRUTH, THE, 1932
HALF PAST MIDNIGHT, 1948
HALF SHOT AT SUNRISE, 1930
HALF WAY TO HEAVEN, 1929
HALLELUJAH, 1929
HALLELUJAH, I'M A BUM, 1933
HALLELUJAH TRAIL, THE, 1965
HAMBONE AND HILLIE, 1984
HAMLET, 1948
HAMLET, 1962
HAMLET, 1964
HAMLET, 1969
HAMMER THE TOFF, 1952
HANDCUFFED, 1929
HANDCUFFS, LONDON, 1955
HANDLE WITH CARE, 1932
HANDLE WITH CARE, 1935
HANDLE WITH CARE, 1958
HANDLE WITH CARE, 1964
HANDS ACROSS THE BORDER, 1943
HANDS ACROSS THE TABLE, 1935
HANDS OF DESTINY, 1954
HANDS OF ORLAC, THE, 1964
HANDY ANDY, 1934
HANGAR 18, 1980
HANGMAN, THE, 1959
HANGMAN'S WHARF, 1950
HANNAH LEE, 1953
HANNIBAL, 1960
HAPPIDROME, 1943
HAPPIEST DAYS OF YOUR LIFE, 1950
HAPPINESS AHEAD, 1934
HAPPINESS C.O.D., 1935
HAPPINESS OF THREE WOMEN, THE, 1954
HAPPINESS OF US ALONE, 1962
HAPPY, 1934
HAPPY AS THE GRASS WAS GREEN, 1973
HAPPY DAYS, 1930
HAPPY DAYS ARE HERE AGAIN, 1936
HAPPY ENDING, THE, 1931
HAPPY EVER AFTER, 1932
HAPPY FAMILY, THE, 1936
HAPPY GO LOVELY, 1951
HAPPY-GO-LUCKY, 1937
HAPPY IS THE BRIDE, 1958
HAPPY LAND, 1943

HAPPY LANDING, 1934
HAPPY LANDING, 1938
HAPPY ROAD, THE, 1957
HAPPY YEARS, THE, 1950
HARASSED HERO, THE, 1954
HARBOR LIGHTS, 1963
HARBOR OF MISSING MEN, 1950
HARD BOILED MAHONEY, 1947
HARD DAY'S NIGHT, A, 1964
HARD, FAST, AND BEAUTIFUL, 1951
HARD GUY, 1941
HARD HOMBRE, 1931
HARD MAN, THE, 1957
HARD ROCK HARRIGAN, 1935
HARD STEEL, 1941
HARD TIMES, 1988
HARD TO GET, 1929
HARD TO GET, 1938
HARD TO HANDLE, 1933
HARD TRAVELING, 1985
HARDBOILED ROSE, 1929
HARDLY WORKING, 1981
HAREM GIRL, 1952
HARLEM GLOBETROTTERS, THE, 1951
HARLEM IS HEAVEN, 1932
HARLEM ON THE PRAIRIE, 1938
HARLEM RIDES THE RANGE, 1939
HARMON OF MICHIGAN, 1941
HARMONY AT HOME, 1930
HARMONY HEAVEN, 1930
HARMONY LANE, 1935
HARMONY ROW, 1933
HAROLD TEEN, 1934
HARPOON, 1948
HARRIGAN'S KID, 1943
HARUM SCARUM, 1965
HARVARD, HERE I COME, 1942
HARVEST MELODY, 1943
HARVESTER, THE, 1936
HARVEY, 1950
HAS ANYBODY SEEN MY GAL?, 1952
HASTY HEART, THE, 1949
HAT CHECK HONEY, 1944
HAT, COAT AND GLOVE, 1934
HATARI!, 1962
HATE IN PARADISE, 1938
HATE SHIP, THE, 1930
HATRED, 1941
HATS OFF, 1937
HAUNTED GOLD, 1932
HAUNTED HONEYMOON, 1986
HAUNTED HOUSE, THE, 1928
HAUNTED HOUSE, THE, 1940
HAUNTED RANCH, THE, 1943
HAVANA ROSE, 1951
HAVANA WIDOWS, 1933
HAVE A HEART, 1934
HAVE ROCKET, WILL TRAVEL, 1959
HAVING A WILD WEEKEND, 1965
HAVING WONDERFUL CRIME, 1945
HAVING WONDERFUL TIME, 1938
HAWAII CALLS, 1938
HAWAIIAN BUCKAROO, 1938
HAWAIIAN NIGHTS, 1939
HAWK OF POWDER RIVER, THE, 1948
HAWK OF WILD RIVER, THE, 1952
HAWK THE SLAYER, 1980
HAWLEY'S OF HIGH STREET, 1933
HAWMPS!, 1976
HAZARD, 1948
HE COULDN'T SAY NO, 1938
HE COULDN'T TAKE IT, 1934
HE FOUND A STAR, 1941
HE HIRED THE BOSS, 1943
HE KNEW WOMEN, 1930
HE LAUGHED LAST, 1956
HE LEARNED ABOUT WOMEN, 1933
HE LOVED AN ACTRESS, 1938
HE MARRIED HIS WIFE, 1940
HE RIDES TALL, 1964
HE SNOOPS TO CONQUER, 1944
HE STAYED FOR BREAKFAST, 1940
HE WHO RIDES A TIGER, 1966
HEAD, 1968
HEAD OF THE FAMILY, 1933
HEAD OFFICE, 1936

HEAD OVER HEELS IN LOVE, 1937
HEADIN' EAST, 1937
HEADIN' FOR GOD'S COUNTRY, 1943
HEADIN' FOR THE RIO GRANDE, 1937
HEADIN' FOR TROUBLE, 1931
HEADIN' NORTH, 1930
HEADING FOR HEAVEN, 1947
HEADLESS GHOST, THE, 1959
HEADLEYS AT HOME, THE, 1939
HEADLINE, 1943
HEADLINE CRASHER, 1937
HEADLINE HUNTERS, 1955
HEADLINE SHOOTER, 1933
HEADLINE WOMAN, THE, 1935
HEADS UP, 1930
HEALER, THE, 1935
HEAR ME GOOD, 1957
HEARSE, THE, 1980
HEART AND SOUL, 1950
HEART OF A MAN, THE, 1959
HEART OF A NATION, THE, 1943
HEART OF ARIZONA, 1938
HEART OF NEW YORK, 1932
HEART OF PARIS, 1939
HEART OF THE GOLDEN WEST, 1942
HEART OF THE NORTH, 1938
HEART OF THE RIO GRANDE, 1942
HEART OF THE ROCKIES, 1937
HEART OF THE ROCKIES, 1951
HEART OF THE WEST, 1937
HEART OF VIRGINIA, 1948
HEART PUNCH, 1932
HEART SONG, 1933
HEART WITHIN, THE, 1957
HEARTACHES, 1947
HEARTBEAT, 1946
HEARTBEEPS, 1981
HEARTBREAK, 1931
HEARTLAND, 1980
HEART'S DESIRE, 1937
HEARTS DIVIDED, 1936
HEARTS IN BONDAGE, 1936
HEARTS IN DIXIE, 1929
HEARTS IN EXILE, 1929
HEARTS OF HUMANITY, 1932
HEARTS OF HUMANITY, 1936
HEARTS OF THE WEST, 1975
HEAT LIGHTNING, 1934
HEAT OF THE SUMMER, 1961
HEAT WAVE, 1935
HEATWAVE, 1954
HEAVEN CAN WAIT, 1943
HEAVEN IS ROUND THE CORNER, 1944
HEAVEN KNOWS, MR. ALLISON, 1957
HEAVEN ON EARTH, 1931
HEAVEN ON EARTH, 1960
HEAVEN ONLY KNOWS, 1947
HEAVEN WITH A BARBED WIRE FENCE, 1939
HEAVENLY BODY, THE, 1943
HEAVENLY DAYS, 1944
HEIGHTS OF DANGER, 1962
HEIR TO TROUBLE, 1936
HEIRESS, THE, 1949
HEIRLOOM MYSTERY, THE, 1936
HEIST, THE, 1979
HELD FOR RANSOM, 1938
HELD IN TRUST, 1949
HELDINNEN, 1962
HELEN MORGAN STORY, THE, 1959
HELEN OF TROY, 1956
HELICOPTER SPIES, THE, 1968
HELL AND HIGH WATER, 1933
HELL AND HIGH WATER, 1954
HELL BELOW, 1933
HELL BELOW ZERO, 1954
HELL BENT FOR 'FRISCO, 1931
HELL BENT FOR LEATHER, 1960
HELL BENT FOR LOVE, 1934
HELL BOATS, 1970
HELL BOUND, 1931
HELL BOUND, 1957
HELL CANYON OUTLAWS, 1957
HELL CAT, THE, 1934
HELL DIVERS, 1932
HELL DRIVERS, 1958
HELL FIRE AUSTIN, 1932

HELL HARBOR, 1930
HELL, HEAVEN OR HOBOKEN, 1958
HELL IN THE HEAVENS, 1934
HELL IS A CITY, 1960
HELL IS SOLD OUT, 1951
HELL ON DEVIL'S ISLAND, 1957
HELL ON EARTH, 1934
HELL ON WHEELS, 1967
HELL RAIDERS OF THE DEEP, 1954
HELL-SHIP MORGAN, 1936
HELL SHIP MUTINY, 1957
HELL SQUAD, 1958
HELL TO ETERNITY, 1960
HELLBENDERS, THE, 1967
HELLCATS OF THE NAVY, 1957
HELLDORADO, 1935
HELLDORADO, 1946
HELLFIGHTERS, 1968
HELLFIRE, 1949
HELLGATE, 1952
HELLO ANNAPOLIS, 1942
HELLO DOWN THERE, 1969
HELLO, ELEPHANT, 1954
HELLO, EVERYBODY, 1933
HELLO, FRISCO, HELLO, 1943
HELLO GOD, 1951
HELLO LONDON, 1958
HELLO SISTER, 1930
HELLO SUCKER, 1941
HELLO SWEETHEART, 1935
HELLO TROUBLE, 1932
HELL'S CARGO, 1935
HELL'S CROSSROADS, 1957
HELL'S FIVE HOURS, 1958
HELL'S HALF ACRE, 1954
HELL'S HEADQUARTERS, 1932
HELL'S HEROES, 1930
HELL'S HIGHWAY, 1932
HELL'S HORIZON, 1955
HELL'S HOUSE, 1932
HELL'S ISLAND, 1930
HELL'S ISLAND, 1955
HELL'S KITCHEN, 1939
HELL'S OUTPOST, 1955
HELL'S PLAYGROUND, 1967
HELLZAPOPPIN', 1941
HELP!, 1965
HELP I'M INVISIBLE, 1952
HELP YOURSELF, 1932
HELTER SKELTER, 1949
HENRY ALDRICH, BOY SCOUT, 1944
HENRY ALDRICH, EDITOR, 1942
HENRY ALDRICH FOR PRESIDENT, 1941
HENRY ALDRICH GETS GLAMOUR, 1942
HENRY ALDRICH HAUNTS A HOUSE, 1943
HENRY ALDRICH PLAYS CUPID, 1944
HENRY ALDRICH SWINGS IT, 1943
HENRY ALDRICH'S LITTLE SECRET, 1944
HENRY AND DIZZY, 1942
HENRY VIII AND HIS SIX WIVES, 1972
HENRY V, 1944
HENRY GOES ARIZONA, 1939
HENRY STEPS OUT, 1940
HENRY, THE RAINMAKER, 1949
HER ADVENTUROUS NIGHT, 1946
HER BODYGUARD, 1933
HER CARDBOARD LOVER, 1942
HER FIRST AFFAIR, 1947
HER FIRST AFFAIRE, 1932
HER FIRST BEAU, 1941
HER FIRST MATE, 1933
HER FIRST ROMANCE, 1940
HER FIRST ROMANCE, 1951
HER FORGOTTEN PAST, 1933
HER HIGHNESS AND THE BELLBOY, 1945
HER HUSBAND LIES, 1937
HER HUSBAND'S AFFAIRS, 1947
HER HUSBAND'S SECRETARY, 1937
HER IMAGINARY LOVER, 1933
HER JUNGLE LOVE, 1938
HER KIND OF MAN, 1946
HER LAST AFFAIRE, 1935
HER LUCKY NIGHT, 1945
HER MAD NIGHT, 1932
HER MAJESTY LOVE, 1931
HER MAN GILBEY, 1949

HER MASTER'S VOICE, 1936
HER NIGHT OUT, 1932
HER PANELLED DOOR, 1951
HER PRIMITIVE MAN, 1944
HER PRIVATE AFFAIR, 1930
HER PRIVATE LIFE, 1929
HER REPUTATION, 1931
HER RESALE VALUE, 1933
HER SISTER'S SECRET, 1946
HER SPLENDID FOLLY, 1933
HER STRANGE DESIRE, 1931
HER TWELVE MEN, 1954
HER WEDDING NIGHT, 1930
HERCULES AGAINST THE MOON MEN, 1965
HERCULES AGAINST THE SONS OF THE SUN, 1964
HERCULES AND THE CAPTIVE WOMEN, 1963
HERCULES, 1983
HERCULES IN NEW YORK, 1970
HERCULES, SAMSON & ULYSSES, 1964
HERCULES UNCHAINED, 1960
HERCULES VS-THE GIANT WARRIORS, 1965
HERE COME THE GIRLS, 1953
HERE COME THE HUGGETTS, 1948
HERE COME THE JETS, 1959
HERE COME THE MARINES, 1952
HERE COME THE NELSONS, 1952
HERE COME THE WAVES, 1944
HERE COMES CARTER, 1936
HERE COMES COOKIE, 1935
HERE COMES ELMER, 1943
HERE COMES HAPPINESS, 1941
HERE COMES KELLY, 1943
HERE COMES MR. JORDAN, 1941
HERE COMES THE BAND, 1935
HERE COMES THE GROOM, 1934
HERE COMES THE GROOM, 1951
HERE COMES THE NAVY, 1934
HERE COMES THE SUN, 1945
HERE COMES TROUBLE, 1936
HERE COMES TROUBLE, 1948
HERE I AM A STRANGER, 1939
HERE IS MY HEART, 1934
HERE'S FLASH CASEY, 1937
HERE'S GEORGE, 1932
HERE'S TO ROMANCE, 1935
HERITAGE, 1935
HERITAGE OF THE DESERT, 1933
HERITAGE OF THE DESERT, 1939
HERO AT LARGE, 1980
HERO FOR A DAY, 1939
HERO OF BABYLON, 1963
HEROES, 1977
HEROES FOR SALE, 1933
HEROES IN BLUE, 1939
HEROES OF THE ALAMO, 1938
HEROES OF THE HILLS, 1938
HEROES OF THE RANGE, 1936
HEROES OF THE SADDLE, 1940
HEROES OF THE SEA, 1941
HERO'S ISLAND, 1962
HERS TO HOLD, 1943
HE'S A COCKEYED WONDER, 1950
HE'S MY GUY, 1943
HEY BABE?, 1984
HEY BOY! HEY GIRL!, 1959
HEY! HEY! U.S.A., 1938
HEY, LET'S TWIST!, 1961
HEY, ROOKIE, 1944
HI BEAUTIFUL, 1944
HI, BUDDY, 1943
HI-DE-HO, 1947
HI DIDDLE DIDDLE, 1943
HI, GANG!, 1941
HI GAUCHO!, 1936
HI, GOOD-LOOKIN', 1944
HI-JACKED, 1950
HI-JACKERS, THE, 1963
HI, NEIGHBOR, 1942
HI, NELLIE!, 1934
HI 'YA, CHUM, 1943
HI' YA, SAILOR, 1943
HIDDEN DANGER, 1949
HIDDEN ENEMY, 1940
HIDDEN EYE, THE, 1945
HIDDEN GOLD, 1933
HIDDEN GOLD, 1940

HIDDEN MENACE, THE, 1940
HIDDEN POWER, 1939
HIDDEN ROOM, THE, 1949
HIDDEN VALLEY, 1932
HIDDEN VALLEY OUTLAWS, 1944
HIDE AND SEEK, 1964
HIDEAWAY, 1937
HIDEAWAY GIRL, 1937
HIDE-OUT, 1934
HIDE-OUT, THE, 1930
HIDEOUT, 1949
HIDEOUT IN THE ALPS, 1938
HIGGINS FAMILY, THE, 1938
HIGH AND DRY, 1954
HIGH AND THE MIGHTY, THE, 1954
HIGH BARBAREE, 1947
HIGH COMMAND, 1938
HIGH CONQUEST, 1947
HIGH COST OF LOVING, THE, 1958
HIGH COUNTRY, THE, 1981
HIGH EXPLOSIVE, 1943
HIGH FINANCE, 1933
HIGH FLIGHT, 1957
HIGH FLYERS, 1937
HIGH FURY, 1947
HIGH GEAR, 1933
HIGH HAT, 1937
HIGH JINKS IN SOCIETY, 1949
HIGH JUMP, 1959
HIGH LONESOME, 1950
HIGH POWERED, 1945
HIGH-POWERED RIFLE, THE, 1960
HIGH PRESSURE, 1932
HIGH SCHOOL, 1940
HIGH SCHOOL GIRL, 1935
HIGH SCHOOL HERO, 1946
HIGH SEAS, 1929
HIGH SOCIETY, 1932
HIGH SOCIETY, 1956
HIGH SOCIETY BLUES, 1930
HIGH SPEED, 1932
HIGH STAKES, 1931
HIGH TENSION, 1936
HIGH TERRACE, 1957
HIGH TIDE, 1947
HIGH TIDE AT NOON, 1957
HIGH TIME, 1960
HIGH TREASON, 1929
HIGH TREASON, 1937
HIGH TREASON, 1951
HIGH VOLTAGE, 1929
HIGH, WIDE AND HANDSOME, 1937
HIGH WIND IN JAMAICA, A, 1965
HIGHER AND HIGHER, 1943
HIGHLAND FLING, 1936
HIGHLY DANGEROUS, 1950
HIGHWAY DRAGNET, 1954
HIGHWAY PATROL, 1938
HIGHWAY 13, 1948
HIGHWAY TO BATTLE, 1961
HIGHWAY WEST, 1941
HIGHWAYS BY NIGHT, 1942
HILDA CRANE, 1956
HILL 24 DOESN'T ANSWER, 1955
HILLBILLY BLITZKRIEG, 1942
HILLBILLYS IN A HAUNTED HOUSE, 1967
HILLS OF DONEGAL, THE, 1947
HILLS OF OKLAHOMA, 1950
HILLS OF OLD WYOMING, 1937
HILLS OF UTAH, 1951
HINDLE WAKES, 1931
HIPPOLYT, THE LACKEY, 1932
HIPS, HIPS, HOORAY, 1934
HIRED GUN, THE, 1957
HIRED HAND, THE, 1971
HIRED WIFE, 1934
HIRED WIFE, 1940
HIS AND HERS, 1961
HIS BROTHER'S GHOST, 1945
HIS BUTLER'S SISTER, 1943
HIS CAPTIVE WOMAN, 1929
HIS DOUBLE LIFE, 1933
HIS EXCELLENCY, 1952
HIS EXCITING NIGHT, 1938
HIS FAMILY TREE, 1936
HIS FIGHTING BLOOD, 1935

BOLD: Films on Videocassette

HIS FIRST COMMAND, 1929
HIS GRACE GIVES NOTICE, 1933
HIS GREATEST GAMBLE, 1934
HIS LAST TWELVE HOURS, 1953
HIS LORDSHIP, 1932
HIS LORDSHIP GOES TO PRESS, 1939
HIS LORDSHIP REGRETS, 1938
HIS LUCKY DAY, 1929
HIS MAJESTY AND CO, 1935
HIS MAJESTY, KING BALLYHOO, 1931
HIS MAJESTY O'KEEFE, 1953
HIS NIGHT OUT, 1935
HIS PRIVATE SECRETARY, 1933
HIS ROYAL HIGHNESS, 1932
HIS WIFE'S MOTHER, 1932
HIS WOMAN, 1931
HISTORY OF MR. POLLY, THE, 1949
HIT PARADE, THE, 1937
HIT PARADE OF 1951, 1950
HIT PARADE OF 1947, 1947
HIT PARADE OF 1943, 1943
HIT PARADE OF 1941, 1940
HIT THE DECK, 1930
HIT THE HAY, 1945
HIT THE ICE, 1943
HIT THE ROAD, 1941
HIT THE SADDLE, 1937
HITCH HIKE LADY, 1936
HITCH HIKE TO HEAVEN, 1936
HITCHHIKE TO HAPPINESS, 1945
HITLER—DEAD OR ALIVE, 1942
HITLER GANG, THE, 1944
HITLER'S MADMAN, 1943
HITTIN' THE TRAIL, 1937
HITTING A NEW HIGH, 1937
H.M. PULHAM, ESQ., 1941
HOBSON'S CHOICE, 1931
HOBSON'S CHOICE, 1954
HOEDOWN, 1950
HOFFMAN, 1970
HOLD BACK THE DAWN, 1941
HOLD BACK THE NIGHT, 1956
HOLD 'EM JAIL, 1932
HOLD 'EM NAVY!, 1937
HOLD 'EM YALE, 1935
HOLD ME TIGHT, 1933
HOLD MY HAND, 1938
HOLD ON, 1966
HOLD THAT BABY!, 1949
HOLD THAT BLONDE, 1945
HOLD THAT CO-ED, 1938
HOLD THAT GIRL, 1934
HOLD THAT HYPNOTIST, 1957
HOLD THAT KISS, 1938
HOLD THAT LINE, 1952
HOLD THAT WOMAN, 1940
HOLE IN THE HEAD, A, 1959
HOLIDAY, 1930
HOLIDAY, 1938
HOLIDAY AFFAIR, 1949
HOLIDAY FOR HENRIETTA, 1955
HOLIDAY FOR LOVERS, 1959
HOLIDAY IN HAVANA, 1949
HOLIDAY IN MEXICO, 1946
HOLIDAY INN, 1942
HOLIDAY RHYTHM, 1950
HOLIDAY WEEK, 1952
HOLIDAY'S END, 1937
HOLIDAYS WITH PAY, 1948
HOLLOW TRIUMPH, 1948
HOLLY AND THE IVY, THE, 1954
HOLLYWOOD BARN DANCE, 1947
HOLLYWOOD BOULEVARD, 1936
HOLLYWOOD CANTEEN, 1944
HOLLYWOOD CAVALCADE, 1939
HOLLYWOOD COWBOY, 1937
HOLLYWOOD OR BUST, 1956
HOLLYWOOD ROUNDUP, 1938
HOLLYWOOD STADIUM MYSTERY, 1938
HOLLYWOOD STORY, 1951
HOLY MATRIMONY, 1943
HOLY TERROR, A, 1931
HOLY TERROR, THE, 1937
HOME AND AWAY, 1956
HOME FOR TANYA, A, 1961
HOME FREE ALL, 1983

HOME FROM HOME, 1939
HOME IN OKLAHOMA, 1946
HOME IN WYOMIN', 1942
HOME ON THE PRAIRIE, 1939
HOME ON THE RANGE, 1935
HOME ON THE RANGE, 1946
HOME, SWEET HOME, 1933
HOME SWEET HOME, 1945
HOME TO DANGER, 1951
HOME TOWNERS, THE, 1928
HOMECOMING, 1948
HOMESTEADERS, THE, 1953
HOMESTEADERS OF PARADISE VALLEY, 1947
HOMESTRETCH, THE, 1947
HOMICIDE SQUAD, 1931
HONEY, 1930
HONEY POT, THE, 1967
HONEYCHILE, 1951
HONEYMOON, 1947
HONEYMOON AHEAD, 1945
HONEYMOON DEFERRED, 1940
HONEYMOON DEFERRED, 1951
HONEYMOON FOR THREE, 1935
HONEYMOON FOR THREE, 1941
HONEYMOON HOTEL, 1946
HONEYMOON IN BALI, 1939
HONEYMOON LANE, 1931
HONEYMOON LIMITED, 1936
HONEYMOON LODGE, 1943
HONEYMOON MACHINE, THE, 1961
HONG KONG, 1951
HONG KONG AFFAIR, 1958
HONG KONG CONFIDENTIAL, 1958
HONG KONG NIGHTS, 1935
HONKY TONK, 1929
HONOLULU, 1939
HONOLULU LU, 1941
HONOLULU-TOKYO-HONG KONG, 1963
HONOR AMONG LOVERS, 1931
HONOR OF THE FAMILY, 1931
HONOR OF THE MOUNTED, 1932
HONOR OF THE PRESS, 1932
HONOR OF THE RANGE, 1934
HONOR OF THE WEST, 1939
HONOURS EASY, 1935
HOODLUM EMPIRE, 1952
HOODLUM SAINT, THE, 1946
HOOK, LINE AND SINKER, 1930
HOOK, LINE AND SINKER, 1969
HOOPER, 1978
HOORAY FOR LOVE, 1935
HOOSIER HOLIDAY, 1943
HOOSIER SCHOOLBOY, 1937
HOOSIER SCHOOLMASTER, 1935
HOOTENANNY HOOT, 1963
HOOTS MON!, 1939
HOPALONG CASSIDY, 1935
HOPALONG RIDES AGAIN, 1937
HOPE OF HIS SIDE, 1935
HOPPY'S HOLIDAY, 1947
HOPPY SERVES A WRIT, 1943
HORIZONS WEST, 1952
HORIZONTAL LIEUTENANT, THE, 1962
HORNET'S NEST, THE, 1955
HORROR ISLAND, 1941
HORROR OF IT ALL, THE, 1964
HORSE FEATHERS, 1932
HORSE OF PRIDE, 1980
HORSEMEN OF THE SIERRAS, 1950
HORSEPLAY, 1933
HORSE'S MOUTH, THE, 1953
HORSE'S MOUTH, THE, 1958
HOSTAGE, THE, 1956
HOSTAGE, THE, 1966
HOSTAGES, 1943
HOSTILE COUNTRY, 1950
HOSTILE GUNS, 1967
HOSTILE WITNESS, 1968
HOT BLOOD, 1956
HOT CARGO, 1946
HOT CARS, 1956
HOT CURVES, 1930
HOT FOR PARIS, 1930
HOT HEIRESS, 1931
HOT ICE, 1952
HOT LEAD, 1951

HOT MONEY, 1936
HOT NEWS, 1936
HOT NEWS, 1953
HOT PEPPER, 1933
HOT RHYTHM, 1944
HOT ROD, 1950
HOT ROD GANG, 1958
HOT ROD GIRL, 1956
HOT SATURDAY, 1932
HOT SHOT, 1987
HOT SHOTS, 1956
HOT STEEL, 1940
HOT STUFF, 1929
HOT SUMMER NIGHT, 1957
HOT TIP, 1935
HOT WATER, 1937
HOTEL, 1967
HOTEL BERLIN, 1945
HOTEL CONTINENTAL, 1932
HOTEL FOR WOMEN, 1939
HOTEL HAYWIRE, 1937
HOTEL IMPERIAL, 1939
HOTEL RESERVE, 1946
HOTEL SAHARA, 1951
HOTEL SPLENDIDE, 1932
HOTEL VARIETY, 1933
HOTSPRINGS HOLIDAY, 1970
HOTTENTOT, THE, 1929
HOUDINI, 1953
HOUND-DOG MAN, 1959
HOUND OF THE BASKERVILLES, 1932
HOUND OF THE BASKERVILLES, THE, 1939
HOUNDS. . . OF NOTRE DAME, THE, 1980
HOUR BEFORE THE DAWN, THE, 1944
HOUR OF DECISION, 1957
HOUR OF GLORY, 1949
HOUR OF THIRTEEN, THE, 1952
HOURS OF LOVE, THE, 1965
HOUSE ACROSS THE BAY, THE, 1940
HOUSE ACROSS THE STREET, THE, 1949
HOUSE BROKEN, 1936
HOUSE IN MARSH ROAD, THE, 1960
HOUSE OF A THOUSAND CANDLES, THE, 1936
HOUSE OF DANGER, 1934
HOUSE OF DRACULA, 1945
HOUSE OF ERRORS, 1942
HOUSE OF FEAR, THE, 1939
HOUSE OF FEAR, THE, 1945
HOUSE OF FRANKENSTEIN, 1944
HOUSE OF GREED, 1934
HOUSE OF HORROR, 1929
HOUSE OF INTRIGUE, THE, 1959
HOUSE OF LIFE, 1953
HOUSE OF MYSTERY, 1934
HOUSE OF MYSTERY, 1941
HOUSE OF NUMBERS, 1957
HOUSE OF ROTHSCHILD, THE, 1934
HOUSE OF SECRETS, THE, 1937
HOUSE OF THE ARROW, THE, 1930
HOUSE OF THE ARROW, THE, 1953
HOUSE OF THE SEVEN GABLES, THE, 1940
HOUSE OF THE SEVEN HAWKS, THE, 1959
HOUSE OF THE SPANIARD, THE, 1936
HOUSE OF THE THREE GIRLS, THE, 1961
HOUSE OF TRENT, THE, 1933
HOUSE OF UNREST, THE, 1931
HOUSE ON 92ND STREET, THE, 1945
HOUSE ON THE FRONT LINE, THE, 1963
HOUSE OPPOSITE, THE, 1931
HOUSE WITH AN ATTIC, THE, 1964
HOUSEBOAT, 1958
HOUSEHOLDER, THE, 1963
HOUSEKEEPER'S DAUGHTER, 1939
HOUSEMASTER, 1938
HOUSEWIFE, 1934
HOUSTON STORY, THE, 1956
HOW COME NOBODY'S ON OUR SIDE?, 1975
HOW DO YOU DO?, 1946
HOW GREEN WAS MY VALLEY, 1941
HOW NOT TO ROB A DEPARTMENT STORE, 1965
HOW TO BE VERY, VERY, POPULAR, 1955
HOW TO BEAT THE HIGH COST OF LIVING, 1980
HOW TO COMMIT MARRIAGE, 1969
HOW TO MARRY A MILLIONAIRE, 1953
HOW TO MURDER A RICH UNCLE, 1957
HOW TO MURDER YOUR WIFE, 1965

HOW TO SAVE A MARRIAGE—AND RUIN YOUR LIFE, 1968
HOW TO STEAL A MILLION, 1966
HOW TO STUFF A WILD BIKINI, 1965
HOW TO SUCCEED IN BUSINESS WITHOUT REALLY TRYING, 1967
HOWARD CASE, THE, 1936
HOWARDS OF VIRGINIA, THE, 1940
HOW'S ABOUT IT?, 1943
HOWZER, 1973
HUCKSTERS, THE, 1947
HUDDLE, 1932
HUDSON'S BAY, 1940
HUE AND CRY, 1950
HUGGETTS ABROAD, THE, 1949
HULLABALOO, 1940
HULLABALOO OVER GEORGIE AND BONNIE'S PICTURES, 1979
HUMAN CARGO, 1936
HUMAN COMEDY, THE, 1943
HUMAN DUPLICATORS, THE, 1965
HUMAN JUNGLE, THE, 1954
HUMAN SIDE, THE, 1934
HUMAN TARGETS, 1932
HUMAN VAPOR, THE, 1964
HUMANITY, 1933
HUMPHREY TAKES A CHANCE, 1950
HUNDRED HOUR HUNT, 1953
HUNDRED POUND WINDOW, THE, 1943
HUNT THE MAN DOWN, 1950
HUNTED, THE, 1948
HUNTED MEN, 1938
HUNTERS OF THE GOLDEN COBRA, THE, 1984
HUNTING IN SIBERIA, 1962
HURRICANE, 1929
HURRICANE, THE, 1937
HURRICANE, 1979
HURRICANE HORSEMAN, 1931
HURRICANE ISLAND, 1951
HURRICANE SMITH, 1942
HURRICANE SMITH, 1952
HURRY, CHARLIE, HURRY, 1941
HUSBAND'S HOLIDAY, 1931
HUSH MONEY, 1931
HYDE PARK CORNER, 1935
HYPERBOLOID OF ENGINEER GARIN, THE, 1965
HYPNOTIZED, 1933
I ACCUSE!, 1958
I ACCUSE MY PARENTS, 1945
I ADORE YOU, 1933
I AIM AT THE STARS, 1960
I AM A CAMERA, 1955
I AM A CRIMINAL, 1939
I AM A THIEF, 1935
I AM NOT AFRAID, 1939
I AM SUZANNE, 1934
I AM THE CHEESE, 1983
I AM THE LAW, 1938
I BECAME A CRIMINAL, 1947
I BELIEVE IN YOU, 1953
I BELIEVED IN YOU, 1934
I BOMBED PEARL HARBOR, 1961
I BURY THE LIVING, 1958
I CAN GET IT FOR YOU WHOLESALE, 1951
I CAN'T ESCAPE, 1934
I CAN'T GIVE YOU ANYTHING BUT LOVE, BABY, 1940
I CHEATED THE LAW, 1949
I CONFESS, 1953
I CONQUER THE SEA, 1936
I COULD GO ON SINGING, 1963
I COVER BIG TOWN, 1947
I COVER CHINATOWN, 1938
I COVER THE UNDERWORLD, 1955
I COVER THE WAR, 1937
I COVER THE WATERFRONT, 1933
I DEAL IN DANGER, 1966
I DEMAND PAYMENT, 1938
I DIDN'T DO IT, 1945
I DON'T CARE GIRL, THE, 1952
I DOOD IT, 1943
I DREAM OF JEANIE, 1952
I DREAM TOO MUCH, 1935
I ESCAPED FROM THE GESTAPO, 1943
I EVEN MET HAPPY GYPSIES, 1968
I FOUND STELLA PARISH, 1935

I GIVE MY LOVE, 1934
I HATE BLONDES, 1981
I HATE MY BODY, 1975
I HAVE LIVED, 1933
I, JANE DOE, 1948
I KILLED EINSTEIN, GENTLEMEN, 1970
I KILLED GERONIMO, 1950
I KILLED THAT MAN, 1942
I KILLED WILD BILL HICKOK, 1956
I KNOW WHERE I'M GOING, 1947
I LIKE IT THAT WAY, 1934
I LIKE MONEY, 1962
I LIKE YOUR NERVE, 1931
I LIVE FOR LOVE, 1935
I LIVE IN FEAR, 1967
I LIVE MY LIFE, 1935
I LIVE ON DANGER, 1942
I LIVED WITH YOU, 1933
I LOVE A BANDLEADER, 1945
I LOVE A MYSTERY, 1945
I LOVE A SOLDIER, 1944
I LOVE MELVIN, 1953
I LOVE THAT MAN, 1933
I LOVE TROUBLE, 1947
I LOVE YOU AGAIN, 1940
I LOVED A WOMAN, 1933
I LOVED YOU WEDNESDAY, 1933
I MARRIED A DOCTOR, 1936
I MARRIED A SPY, 1938
I MARRIED A WITCH, 1942
I MARRIED A WOMAN, 1958
I MARRIED AN ANGEL, 1942
I, MAUREEN, 1978
I MET HIM IN PARIS, 1937
I MET MY LOVE AGAIN, 1938
I ONLY ASKED!, 1958
I PASSED FOR WHITE, 1960
I PROMISE TO PAY, 1937
I RING DOORBELLS, 1946
I SAILED TO TAHITI WITH AN ALL GIRL CREW, 1969
I SEE ICE, 1938
I SELL ANYTHING, 1934
I SENT A LETTER TO MY LOVE, 1981
I SHOT BILLY THE KID, 1950
I SHOT JESSE JAMES, 1949
I SPY, 1933
I STAND ACCUSED, 1938
I STAND CONDEMNED, 1936
I STOLE A MILLION, 1939
I SURRENDER DEAR, 1948
I TAKE THIS OATH, 1940
I TAKE THIS WOMAN, 1931
I TAKE THIS WOMAN, 1940
I THANK YOU, 1941
I WAKE UP SCREAMING, 1942
I WALK THE LINE, 1970
I WANNA HOLD YOUR HAND, 1978
I WANT A DIVORCE, 1940
I WANT YOU, 1951
I WANTED WINGS, 1941
I WAS A CAPTIVE IN NAZI GERMANY, 1936
I WAS A CONVICT, 1939
I WAS A MALE WAR BRIDE, 1949
I WAS A PRISONER ON DEVIL'S ISLAND, 1941
I WAS A SHOPLIFTER, 1950
I WAS A SPY, 1934
I WAS AN ADVENTURESS, 1940
I WAS AN AMERICAN SPY, 1951
I WAS FRAMED, 1942
I WONDER WHO'S KISSING HER NOW, 1947
I WOULDN'T BE IN YOUR SHOES, 1948
ICE-CAPADES, 1941
ICE-CAPADES REVUE, 1942
ICE CASTLES, 1978
ICE FOLLIES OF 1939, 1939
ICE STATION ZEBRA, 1968
ICELAND, 1942
I'D CLIMB THE HIGHEST MOUNTAIN, 1951
I'D GIVE MY LIFE, 1936
I'D RATHER BE RICH, 1964
IDAHO, 1943
IDAHO KID, THE, 1937
IDEA GIRL, 1946
IDEAL HUSBAND, AN, 1948
IDENTIFICATION MARKS: NONE, 1969

IDENTITY UNKNOWN, 1945
IDENTITY UNKNOWN, 1960
IDIOT, THE, 1948
IDIOT'S DELIGHT, 1939
IDLE RICH, THE, 1929
IDOL OF PARIS, 1948
IDOL OF THE CROWDS, 1937
IDOL ON PARADE, 1959
IF A MAN ANSWERS, 1962
IF I HAD A MILLION, 1932
IF I HAD MY WAY, 1940
IF I WERE BOSS, 1938
IF I WERE FREE, 1933
IF I WERE KING, 1938
IF I WERE RICH, 1936
IF I'M LUCKY, 1946
IF IT'S TUESDAY, THIS MUST BE BELGIUM, 1969
IF PARIS WERE TOLD TO US, 1956
IF THIS BE SIN, 1950
IF WINTER COMES, 1947
IF YOU COULD ONLY COOK, 1936
IF YOU COULD SEE WHAT I HEAR, 1982
IF YOU KNEW SUSIE, 1948
IKIRU, 1960
I'LL BE SEEING YOU, 1944
I'LL BE YOUR SWEETHEART, 1945
I'LL BE YOURS, 1947
I'LL FIX IT, 1934
I'LL GET BY, 1950
I'LL GET YOU, 1953
I'LL GIVE A MILLION, 1938
I'LL GIVE MY LIFE, 1959
I'LL LOVE YOU ALWAYS, 1935
I'LL NEVER FORGET YOU, 1951
I'LL REMEMBER APRIL, 1945
I'LL SEE YOU IN MY DREAMS, 1951
I'LL SELL MY LIFE, 1941
I'LL STICK TO YOU, 1933
I'LL TAKE ROMANCE, 1937
I'LL TAKE SWEDEN, 1965
I'LL TELL THE WORLD, 1934
I'LL TURN TO YOU, 1946
I'LL WAIT FOR YOU, 1941
I'LL WALK BESIDE YOU, 1943
ILLEGAL, 1932
ILLEGAL ENTRY, 1949
ILLEGAL TRAFFIC, 1938
ILLEGALLY YOURS, 1988
ILLUSION, 1929
I'M A STRANGER, 1952
I'M ALL RIGHT, JACK, 1959
I'M AN EXPLOSIVE, 1933
I'M FROM ARKANSAS, 1944
I'M FROM MISSOURI, 1939
I'M FROM THE CITY, 1938
I'M NOBODY'S SWEETHEART NOW, 1940
I'M STILL ALIVE, 1940
IMITATION GENERAL, 1958
IMITATION OF LIFE, 1934
IMITATION OF LIFE, 1959
IMMORAL CHARGE, 1962
IMMORTAL BATTALION, THE, 1944
IMMORTAL GARRISON, THE, 1957
IMMORTAL GENTLEMAN, 1935
IMMORTAL SERGEANT, THE, 1943
IMMORTAL VAGABOND, 1931
IMPACT, 1949
IMPATIENT YEARS, THE, 1944
IMPERFECT LADY, THE, 1947
IMPERIAL VENUS, 1963
IMPORTANCE OF BEING EARNEST, THE, 1952
IMPORTANT WITNESS, THE, 1933
IMPOSSIBLE ON SATURDAY, 1966
IMPOSSIBLE YEARS, THE, 1968
IMPOSTER, THE, 1944
""IMP"PROBABLE MR. WEE GEE, THE, 1966
IMPROPER DUCHESS, THE, 1936
IN A MONASTERY GARDEN, 1935
IN CALIENTE, 1935
IN EARLY ARIZONA, 1938
IN FAST COMPANY, 1946
IN GAY MADRID, 1930
IN HARM'S WAY, 1965
IN HIS STEPS, 1936
IN-LAWS, THE, 1979
IN LIKE FLINT, 1967

BOLD: Films on Videocassette

IN LOVE AND WAR, 1958
IN LOVE WITH LIFE, 1934
IN NAME ONLY, 1939
IN OLD AMARILLO, 1951
IN OLD ARIZONA, 1929
IN OLD CALIENTE, 1939
IN OLD CALIFORNIA, 1929
IN OLD CALIFORNIA, 1942
IN OLD CHEYENNE, 1931
IN OLD CHEYENNE, 1941
IN OLD CHICAGO, 1938
IN OLD COLORADO, 1941
IN OLD KENTUCKY, 1935
IN OLD MEXICO, 1938
IN OLD MISSOURI, 1940
IN OLD MONTANA, 1939
IN OLD MONTEREY, 1939
IN OLD OKLAHOMA, 1943
IN OLD SANTA FE, 1935
IN PERSON, 1935
IN SPITE OF DANGER, 1935
IN THE COUNTRY, 1967
IN THE DOGHOUSE, 1964
IN THE HEADLINES, 1929
IN THE LINE OF DUTY, 1931
IN THE MEANTIME, DARLING, 1944
IN THE MONEY, 1934
IN THE NEXT ROOM, 1930
IN THE NICK, 1960
IN THE SOUP, 1936
IN THE WAKE OF THE BOUNTY, 1933
IN THIS CORNER, 1948
IN TROUBLE WITH EVE, 1964
IN WHICH WE SERVE, 1942
INBETWEEN AGE, THE, 1958
INCENDIARY BLONDE, 1945
INCIDENT AT MIDNIGHT, 1966
INCIDENT AT PHANTOM HILL, 1966
INCIDENT IN AN ALLEY, 1962
INCIDENT IN SHANGHAI, 1937
INCREDIBLE PETRIFIED WORLD, THE, 1959
INCREDIBLE SHRINKING MAN, THE, 1957
INDESTRUCTIBLE MAN, THE, 1956
INDIAN AGENT, 1948
INDIAN TERRITORY, 1950
INDIAN UPRISING, 1951
INDIANAPOLIS SPEEDWAY, 1939
INDISCRETIONS OF EVE, 1932
INFERNAL MACHINE, 1933
INFORMER, THE, 1929
INHERIT THE WIND, 1960
INHERITANCE, THE, 1951
INN FOR TROUBLE, 1960
INNER CIRCLE, THE, 1946
INNER SANCTUM, 1948
INNOCENTS IN PARIS, 1955
INNOCENTS OF PARIS, 1929
INSIDE INFORMATION, 1934
INSIDE INFORMATION, 1939
INSIDE JOB, 1946
INSIDE STORY, 1939
INSIDE STORY, THE, 1948
INSIDE THE LAW, 1942
INSIDE THE LINES, 1930
INSPECTOR CLOUSEAU, 1968
INSPECTOR GENERAL, THE, 1937
INSPECTOR HORNLEIGH, 1939
INSPECTOR HORNLEIGH ON HOLIDAY, 1939
INTENT TO KILL, 1958
INTERFERENCE, 1928
INTERLUDE, 1957
INTERMEZZO, 1937
INTERMEZZO, 1937
INTERMEZZO: A LOVE STORY, 1939
INTERNATIONAL CRIME, 1938
INTERNATIONAL HOUSE, 1933
INTERNATIONAL LADY, 1941
INTERNATIONAL SETTLEMENT, 1938
INTERNATIONAL SQUADRON, 1941
INTERNES CAN'T TAKE MONEY, 1937
INTERRUPTED HONEYMOON, THE, 1936
INTERRUPTED MELODY, 1955
INTIMATE LIGHTING, 1969
INTIMATE RELATIONS, 1937
INTRIGUE, 1947
INTRUDER, THE, 1932

INVADERS, THE, 1941
INVADERS FROM MARS, 1953
INVASION, 1965
INVASION OF THE ANIMAL PEOPLE, 1962
INVASION OF THE BODY SNATCHERS, 1956
INVASION OF THE STAR CREATURES, 1962
INVASION QUARTET, 1961
INVASION U.S.A., 1952
INVINCIBLE SIX, THE, 1970
INVISIBLE AGENT, 1942
INVISIBLE AVENGER, THE, 1958
INVISIBLE ENEMY, 1938
INVISIBLE INFORMER, 1946
INVISIBLE KILLER, THE, 1940
INVISIBLE MAN, THE, 1958
INVISIBLE MAN, THE, 1963
INVISIBLE MAN RETURNS, THE, 1940
INVISIBLE MAN'S REVENGE, 1944
INVISIBLE MENACE, THE, 1938
INVISIBLE OPPONENT, 1933
INVISIBLE STRIPES, 1940
INVISIBLE WALL, THE, 1947
INVISIBLE WOMAN, THE, 1941
INVITATION, 1952
INVITATION TO HAPPINESS, 1939
INVITATION TO THE DANCE, 1956
INVITATION TO THE WALTZ, 1935
IO ... TU ... Y ... ELLA, 1933
IPHIGENIA, 1977
IRELAND'S BORDER LINE, 1939
IRENE, 1940
IRISH AND PROUD OF IT, 1938
IRISH EYES ARE SMILING, 1944
IRISH FOR LUCK, 1936
IRISH IN US, THE, 1935
IRISH LUCK, 1939
IRISHMAN, THE, 1978
IRON ANGEL, 1964
IRON CURTAIN, THE, 1948
IRON DUKE, THE, 1935
IRON GLOVE, THE, 1954
IRON MAJOR, THE, 1943
IRON MAN, THE, 1931
IRON MASK, THE, 1929
IRON MASTER, THE, 1933
IRON MOUNTAIN TRAIL, 1953
IRON PETTICOAT, THE, 1956
IRON SHERIFF, THE, 1957
IRON STAIR, THE, 1933
IROQUOIS TRAIL, THE, 1950
IS EVERYBODY HAPPY?, 1929
IS EVERYBODY HAPPY?, 1943
IS MY FACE RED?, 1932
IS PARIS BURNING?, 1966
IS THERE JUSTICE?, 1931
IS YOUR HONEYMOON REALLY NECESSARY?, 1953
ISLAND CAPTIVES, 1937
ISLAND IN THE SKY, 1938
ISLAND IN THE SKY, 1953
ISLAND OF ALLAH, 1956
ISLAND OF DOOM, 1933
ISLAND OF LOST MEN, 1939
ISLAND OF LOST WOMEN, 1959
ISLAND OF LOVE, 1963
ISLAND RESCUE, 1952
ISLAND WOMEN, 1958
ISLE OF DESTINY, 1940
ISLE OF FORGOTTEN SINS, 1943
ISLE OF FURY, 1936
ISLE OF LOST SHIPS, 1929
ISLE OF MISSING MEN, 1942
ISN'T IT ROMANTIC?, 1948
ISN'T LIFE WONDERFUL!, 1953
ISTANBUL, 1957
IT CAME FROM BENEATH THE SEA, 1955
IT CAME FROM OUTER SPACE, 1953
IT CAN BE DONE, 1929
IT CAN'T LAST FOREVER, 1937
IT COMES UP LOVE, 1943
IT CONQUERED THE WORLD, 1956
IT COULD HAPPEN TO YOU, 1937
IT COULD HAPPEN TO YOU, 1939
IT COULDN'T HAVE HAPPENED—BUT IT DID, 1936
IT GROWS ON TREES, 1952
IT HAD TO BE YOU, 1947
IT HAD TO HAPPEN, 1936

IT HAPPENED AT THE INN, 1945
IT HAPPENED AT THE WORLD'S FAIR, 1963
IT HAPPENED IN ATHENS, 1962
IT HAPPENED IN BROAD DAYLIGHT, 1960
IT HAPPENED IN BROOKLYN, 1947
IT HAPPENED IN CANADA, 1962
IT HAPPENED IN FLATBUSH, 1942
IT HAPPENED IN GIBRALTAR, 1943
IT HAPPENED IN HOLLYWOOD, 1937
IT HAPPENED IN NEW YORK, 1935
IT HAPPENED IN PARIS, 1935
IT HAPPENED IN PARIS, 1953
IT HAPPENED IN ROME, 1959
IT HAPPENED ON 5TH AVENUE, 1947
IT HAPPENED ONE NIGHT, 1934
IT HAPPENED ONE SUNDAY, 1944
IT HAPPENED OUT WEST, 1937
IT HAPPENED TO JANE, 1959
IT HAPPENED TO ONE MAN, 1941
IT HAPPENED TOMORROW, 1944
IT HAPPENS EVERY THURSDAY, 1953
IT ISN'T DONE, 1937
IT PAYS TO ADVERTISE, 1931
IT SHOULD HAPPEN TO YOU, 1954
IT SHOULDN'T HAPPEN TO A DOG, 1946
IT STARTED IN PARADISE, 1952
IT STARTED IN THE ALPS, 1966
IT STARTED WITH EVE, 1941
ITALIAN JOB, THE, 1969
ITALIANO BRAVA GENTE, 1965
IT'S A BET, 1935
IT'S A BIKINI WORLD, 1967
IT'S A BOY, 1934
IT'S A COP, 1934
IT'S A DATE, 1940
IT'S A GRAND LIFE, 1953
IT'S A GRAND OLD WORLD, 1937
IT'S A GREAT DAY, 1956
IT'S A GREAT FEELING, 1949
IT'S A GREAT LIFE, 1930
IT'S A GREAT LIFE, 1936
IT'S A JOKE, SON!, 1947
IT'S A KING, 1933
IT'S A PLEASURE, 1945
IT'S A SMALL WORLD, 1935
IT'S A SMALL WORLD, 1950
IT'S A WISE CHILD, 1931
IT'S A WONDERFUL WORLD, 1939
IT'S A WONDERFUL DAY, 1949
IT'S A WONDERFUL WORLD, 1956
IT'S ALL OVER TOWN, 1963
IT'S ALL YOURS, 1937
IT'S ALWAYS FAIR WEATHER, 1955
IT'S GREAT TO BE ALIVE, 1933
IT'S GREAT TO BE YOUNG, 1946
IT'S GREAT TO BE YOUNG, 1956
IT'S HARD TO BE GOOD, 1950
IT'S IN THE AIR, 1935
IT'S IN THE AIR, 1940
IT'S IN THE BAG, 1936
IT'S IN THE BAG, 1943
IT'S IN THE BAG, 1945
IT'S IN THE BLOOD, 1938
IT'S LOVE AGAIN, 1936
IT'S LOVE I'M AFTER, 1937
IT'S NEVER TOO LATE, 1958
IT'S NEVER TOO LATE TO MEND, 1937
IT'S NOT CRICKET, 1937
IT'S NOT CRICKET, 1949
IT'S ONLY MONEY, 1962
IT'S THAT MAN AGAIN, 1943
IT'S TOUGH TO BE FAMOUS, 1932
IT'S YOU I WANT, 1936
IVAN THE TERRIBLE, PARTS I & II, 1947
IVANHOE, 1952
I'VE ALWAYS LOVED YOU, 1946
I'VE BEEN AROUND, 1935
I'VE GOT A HORSE, 1938
I'VE GOT YOUR NUMBER, 1934
I'VE GOTTA HORSE, 1965
I'VE LIVED BEFORE, 1956
IVORY-HANDLED GUN, 1935
IVORY HUNTER, 1952
IVY, 1947
J.W. COOP, 1971
JACK AHOY!, 1935

JACK LONDON, **1943**
JACK MCCALL, DESPERADO, 1953
JACK OF DIAMONDS, THE, 1949
JACK OF DIAMONDS, 1967
JACKALS, THE, 1967
JACKASS MAIL, 1942
JACKPOT, THE, 1950
JACKPOT, 1960
JACKTOWN, 1962
JACQUELINE, 1956
JACQUES BREL IS ALIVE AND WELL AND LIVING IN PARIS, 1975
JADE MASK, THE, 1945
JAGUAR, 1956
JAIL HOUSE BLUES, 1942
JAILBIRDS, 1939
JAILBREAK, 1936
JAILBREAKERS, THE, 1960
JAILHOUSE ROCK, 1957
JALNA, 1935
JAM SESSION, 1944
JAMAICA RUN, 1953
JAMBOREE, 1944
JAMBOREE, 1957
JANE AUSTEN IN MANHATTAN, 1980
JANE EYRE, 1935
JANE EYRE, 1944
JANE EYRE, 1971
JANE STEPS OUT, 1938
JANIE GETS MARRIED, 1946
JAPANESE WAR BRIDE, 1952
JASSY, 1948
JAWS II, 1978
JAWS OF JUSTICE, 1933
JAYHAWKERS, THE, 1959
JAZZ AGE, THE, 1929
JAZZ BOAT, 1960
JAZZ CINDERELLA, 1930
JAZZ HEAVEN, 1929
JAZZ SINGER, THE, 1927
JAZZ SINGER, THE, 1953
JAZZBAND FIVE, THE, 1932
JEALOUSY, 1931
JEALOUSY, 1945
JEAN DE FLORETTE, 1987
JEDDA, THE UNCIVILIZED, 1956
JEEPERS CREEPERS, 1939
JENIFER HALE, 1937
JENNIE, 1941
JENNIE GERHARDT, 1933
JENNIFER, 1953
JENNY, 1969
JENNY LAMOUR, 1948
JEOPARDY, 1953
JEREMY, 1973
JESSE AND LESTER, TWO BROTHERS IN A PLACE CALLED TRINITY, 1972
JESSE JAMES, 1939
JESSE JAMES AT BAY, 1941
JESSE JAMES, JR., 1942
JESSE JAMES MEETS FRANKENSTEIN'S DAUGHTER, 1966
JESSE JAMES VERSUS THE DALTONS, 1954
JESSE JAMES' WOMEN, 1954
JESUS, 1979
JESUS CHRIST, SUPERSTAR, 1973
JET ATTACK, 1958
JET JOB, 1952
JET OVER THE ATLANTIC, 1960
JET STORM, 1961
JEWEL, THE, 1933
JEWEL ROBBERY, 1932
JEWELS OF BRANDENBURG, 1947
JEZEBEL, 1938
JIG SAW, 1965
JIGSAW, 1949
JIM HANVEY, DETECTIVE, 1937
JIM, THE WORLD'S GREATEST, 1976
JIM THORPE—ALL AMERICAN, 1951
JIMMY AND SALLY, 1933
JIMMY BOY, 1935
JIMMY THE GENT, 1934
JIMMY THE KID, 1982
JINX MONEY, 1948
JIVARO, 1954
JIVE JUNCTION, 1944

JOAN AT THE STAKE, 1954
JOAN OF ARC, 1948
JOAN OF OZARK, 1942
JOAN OF PARIS, 1942
JOE AND ETHEL TURP CALL ON THE PRESIDENT, 1939
JOE BUTTERFLY, 1957
JOE LOUIS STORY, THE, 1953
JOE PALOOKA IN THE SQUARED CIRCLE, 1950
JOE SMITH, AMERICAN, 1942
JOHANSSON GETS SCOLDED, 1945
JOHN HALIFAX—GENTLEMAN, 1938
JOHN LOVES MARY, 1949
JOHN PAUL JONES, 1959
JOHNNY ANGEL, 1945
JOHNNY APOLLO, 1940
JOHNNY COME LATELY, 1943
JOHNNY COMES FLYING HOME, 1946
JOHNNY CONCHO, 1956
JOHNNY DARK, 1954
JOHNNY DOESN'T LIVE HERE ANY MORE, 1944
JOHNNY FRENCHMAN, 1946
JOHNNY HOLIDAY, 1949
JOHNNY IN THE CLOUDS, 1945
JOHNNY O'CLOCK, 1947
JOHNNY ON THE SPOT, 1954
JOHNNY ONE-EYE, 1950
JOHNNY ROCCO, 1958
JOHNNY STEALS EUROPE, 1932
JOHNNY TIGER, 1966
JOHNNY TROUBLE, 1957
JOHNNY, YOU'RE WANTED, 1956
JOIN THE MARINES, 1937
JOLSON SINGS AGAIN, 1949
JOLSON STORY, THE, 1946
JONATHAN LIVINGSTON SEAGULL, 1973
JONES FAMILY IN HOLLYWOOD, THE, 1939
JONI, 1980
JORY, 1972
JOSEPHINE AND MEN, 1955
JOSETTE, 1938
JOSSER IN THE ARMY, 1932
JOSSER JOINS THE NAVY, 1932
JOSSER ON THE FARM, 1934
JOSSER ON THE RIVER, 1932
JOUR DE FETE, 1952
JOURNEY AHEAD, 1947
JOURNEY BENEATH THE DESERT, 1967
JOURNEY INTO DARKNESS, 1968
JOURNEY INTO FEAR, 1942
JOURNEY INTO MIDNIGHT, 1968
JOURNEY TO FREEDOM, 1957
JOURNEY TO LOVE, 1953
JOURNEY TO THE CENTER OF TIME, 1967
JOURNEY TO THE FAR SIDE OF THE SUN, 1969
JOURNEY TO THE LOST CITY, 1960
JOURNEY TOGETHER, 1946
JOY OF LIVING, 1938
JOY RIDE, 1935
JUAREZ, 1939
JUBILEE TRAIL, 1954
JUBILEE WINDOW, 1935
JUDGE STEPS OUT, THE, 1949
JUDGMENT DEFERRED, 1952
JUDGMENT IN BERLIN, 1988
JUKE BOX RACKET, 1960
JUKE BOX RHYTHM, 1959
JUKE GIRL, 1942
JULIA MISBEHAVES, 1948
JULIE, 1956
JULIE THE REDHEAD, 1963
JULIETTA, 1957
JULIUS CAESAR, 1952
JULIUS CAESAR, 1970
JUMP, 1971
JUMP INTO HELL, 1955
JUMPING FOR JOY, 1956
JUMPING JACKS, 1952
JUNCTION CITY, 1952
JUNE BRIDE, 1948
JUNE MOON, 1931
JUNGLE BRIDE, 1933
JUNGLE CAPTIVE, 1945
JUNGLE FLIGHT, 1947
JUNGLE GODDESS, 1948
JUNGLE HEAT, 1957

JUNGLE MAN, 1941
JUNGLE OF CHANG, 1951
JUNGLE PATROL, 1948
JUNGLE PRINCESS, THE, 1936
JUNGLE SIREN, 1942
JUNGLE STREET GIRLS, 1963
JUNGLE WOMAN, 1944
JUNO AND THE PAYCOCK, 1930
JUPITER, 1952
JUPITER'S DARLING, 1955
JURY'S EVIDENCE, 1936
JURY'S SECRET, THE, 1938
JUST A BIG, SIMPLE GIRL, 1949
JUST A GIGOLO, 1931
JUST ACROSS THE STREET, 1952
JUST BEFORE DAWN, 1946
JUST FOR A SONG, 1930
JUST FOR YOU, 1952
JUST IMAGINE, 1930
JUST JOE, 1960
JUST LIKE A WOMAN, 1939
JUST LIKE HEAVEN, 1930
JUST ME, 1950
JUST MY LUCK, 1933
JUST MY LUCK, 1957
JUST OFF BROADWAY, 1942
JUST THIS ONCE, 1952
JUST WILLIAM'S LUCK, 1948
JUSTICE OF THE RANGE, 1935
JUSTICE TAKES A HOLIDAY, 1933
JUVENILE COURT, 1938
JUVENILE JUNGLE, 1958
KANCHENJUNGHA, 1966
KANGAROO, 1952
KANGAROO KID, THE, 1950
KANSAN, THE, 1943
KANSAS CITY KITTY, 1944
KANSAS CITY PRINCESS, 1934
KANSAS CYCLONE, 1941
KANSAS PACIFIC, 1953
KANSAS RAIDERS, 1950
KANSAS TERRITORY, 1952
KANSAS TERRORS, THE, 1939
KARATE KILLERS, THE, 1967
KARMA, 1933
KATE PLUS TEN, 1938
KATERINA IZMAILOVA, 1969
KATHLEEN, 1938
KATHLEEN MAVOURNEEN, 1930
KATHY O', 1958
KATIE DID IT, 1951
KAYA, I'LL KILL YOU, 1969
KAZABLAN, 1974
KEEP 'EM ROLLING, 1934
KEEP FIT, 1937
KEEP IT CLEAN, 1956
KEEP IT QUIET, 1934
KEEP SMILING, 1938
KEEP YOUR POWDER DRY, 1945
KEEP YOUR SEATS PLEASE, 1936
KEEPER, THE, 1976
KEEPER OF THE BEES, 1935
KEEPER OF THE BEES, 1947
KEEPER OF THE FLAME, 1942
KEEPERS OF YOUTH, 1931
KEEPING COMPANY, 1941
KELLY OF THE SECRET SERVICE, 1936
KELLY THE SECOND, 1936
KENNEL MURDER CASE, THE, 1933
KENTUCKIAN, THE, 1955
KENTUCKY BLUE STREAK, 1935
KENTUCKY JUBILEE, 1951
KENTUCKY KERNELS, 1935
KENTUCKY MINSTRELS, 1934
KENTUCKY RIFLE, 1956
KEY, THE, 1934
KEY MAN, THE, 1957
KEY TO HARMONY, 1935
KEY TO THE CITY, 1950
KEYHOLE, THE, 1933
KEYS OF THE KINGDOM, THE, 1944
KHYBER PATROL, 1954
KIBITZER, THE, 1929
KID COMES BACK, THE, 1937
KID COURAGEOUS, 1935
KID FOR TWO FARTHINGS, A, 1956

BOLD: Films on Videocassette

KID FROM AMARILLO, THE, 1951
KID FROM ARIZONA, THE, 1931
KID FROM BROKEN GUN, THE, 1952
KID FROM CLEVELAND, THE, 1949
KID FROM GOWER GULCH, THE, 1949
KID FROM KOKOMO, THE, 1939
KID GALAHAD, 1962
KID NIGHTINGALE, 1939
KID RANGER, THE, 1936
KID RIDES AGAIN, THE, 1943
KID SISTER, THE, 1945
KIDNAPPERS, THE, 1964
KID'S LAST RIDE, THE, 1941
KIKI, 1931
KILLER LEOPARD, 1954
KILLER McCOY, 1947
KILLER SHARK, 1950
KILLER WALKS, A, 1952
KILLERS FROM SPACE, 1954
KILLERS OF KILIMANJARO, 1960
KILLING OF ANGEL STREET, THE, 1983
KIMBERLEY JIM, 1965
KIND LADY, 1935
KINEMA NO TENCHI, 1986
KING AND FOUR QUEENS, THE, 1956
KING ARTHUR WAS A GENTLEMAN, 1942
KING CREOLE, 1958
KING IN NEW YORK, A, 1957
KING IN SHADOW, 1961
KING KELLY OF THE U.S.A, 1934
KING OF BURLESQUE, 1936
KING OF DODGE CITY, 1941
KING OF GAMBLERS, 1937
KING OF PARIS, THE, 1934
KING OF THE ARENA, 1933
KING OF THE BANDITS, 1948
KING OF THE CASTLE, 1936
KING OF THE GAMBLERS, 1948
KING OF THE JUNGLE, 1933
KING OF THE KHYBER RIFLES, 1953
KING OF THE LUMBERJACKS, 1940
KING OF THE NEWSBOYS, 1938
KING OF THE PECOS, 1936
KING OF THE RITZ, 1933
KING OF THE ROYAL MOUNTED, 1936
KING OF THE SIERRAS, 1938
KING OF THE STALLIONS, 1942
KING OF THE TURF, 1939
KING OF THE UNDERWORLD, 1952
KING OF THE WILD HORSES, THE, 1934
KING OF THE WILD HORSES, 1947
KING RICHARD AND THE CRUSADERS, 1954
KING SOLOMON OF BROADWAY, 1935
KING SOLOMON'S MINES, 1937
KING SOLOMON'S MINES, 1950
KING SOLOMON'S TREASURE, 1978
KING STEPS OUT, THE, 1936
KINGFISH CAPER, THE, 1976
KING'S CUP, THE, 1933
KINGS GO FORTH, 1958
KING'S PIRATE, 1967
KING'S RHAPSODY, 1955
KING'S THIEF, THE, 1955
KING'S VACATION, THE, 1933
KISMET, 1930
KISMET, 1944
KISMET, 1955
KISS AND MAKE UP, 1934
KISS AND TELL, 1945
KISS BEFORE DYING, A, 1956
KISS BEFORE THE MIRROR, THE, 1933
KISS FOR CORLISS, A, 1949
KISS IN THE DARK, A, 1949
KISS ME AGAIN, 1931
KISS ME GOODBYE, 1935
KISS ME, SERGEANT, 1930
KISS OF FIRE, THE, 1940
KISS OF FIRE, 1955
KISS THE BOYS GOODBYE, 1941
KISS THE BRIDE GOODBYE, 1944
KISS THEM FOR ME, 1957
KISSES FOR BREAKFAST, 1941
KISSES FOR MY PRESIDENT, 1964
KISSIN' COUSINS, 1964
KISSING BANDIT, THE, 1948
KISSING CUP'S RACE, 1930

KIT CARSON, 1940
KITCHEN, THE, 1961
KITTY, 1929
KITTY, 1945
KLONDIKE, 1932
KLONDIKE FEVER, 1980
KLONDIKE FURY, 1942
KLONDIKE KATE, 1944
KNICKERBOCKER HOLIDAY, 1944
KNIGHT IN LONDON, A, 1930
KNIGHT OF THE PLAINS, 1939
KNIGHT WITHOUT ARMOR, 1937
KNIGHTS FOR A DAY, 1937
KNIGHTS OF THE RANGE, 1940
KNIGHTS OF THE ROUND TABLE, 1953
KNIGHTS OF THE TEUTONIC ORDER, THE, 1962
KNIVES OF THE AVENGER, 1967
KNOCK, 1955
KNOCK ON WOOD, 1954
KNOCKOUT, 1941
KNOWING MEN, 1930
KOENIGSMARK, 1935
KOJIRO, 1967
KONGI'S HARVEST, 1971
KRAKATOA, EAST OF JAVA, 1969
KRAMER VS. KRAMER, 1979
KRONOS, 1957
KRULL, 1983
LA BELLE AMERICAINE, 1961
LA BETE HUMAINE, 1938
LA BOHEME, 1965
LA BOUM, 1983
LA CHEVRE, 1985
LA CONGA NIGHTS, 1940
LA CUCARACHA, 1961
LA HABANERA, 1937
LA MARSEILLAISE, 1938
LA MATERNELLE, 1933
LA TERRA TREMA, 1947
LA TRAVIATA, 1968
LA TRAVIATA, 1982
LA VIE CONTINUE, 1982
LA VIE DE CHATEAU, 1967
LABURNUM GROVE, 1936
LAD, THE, 1935
LAD FROM OUR TOWN, 1941
LADIES COURAGEOUS, 1944
LADIES CRAVE EXCITEMENT, 1935
LADIES' DAY, 1943
LADIES IN DISTRESS, 1938
LADIES IN LOVE, 1930
LADIES IN LOVE, 1936
LADIES LOVE BRUTES, 1930
LADIES LOVE DANGER, 1935
LADIES MAN, THE, 1961
LADIES' MAN, 1947
LADIES MUST LIVE, 1940
LADIES MUST LOVE, 1933
LADIES MUST PLAY, 1930
LADIES OF THE BIG HOUSE, 1932
LADIES OF THE CHORUS, 1948
LADIES OF THE JURY, 1932
LADIES OF WASHINGTON, 1944
LADIES SHOULD LISTEN, 1934
LADIES THEY TALK ABOUT, 1933
LADIES WHO DO, 1964
LADY AND GENT, 1932
LADY AND THE BANDIT, THE, 1951
LADY AND THE MOB, THE, 1939
LADY AT MIDNIGHT, 1948
LADY BE CAREFUL, 1936
LADY BE GOOD, 1941
LADY BEHAVE, 1937
LADY BODYGUARD, 1942
LADY BY CHOICE, 1934
LADY CAROLINE LAMB, 1972
LADY CHASER, 1946
LADY CHATTERLEY'S LOVER, 1959
LADY CONFESSES, THE, 1945
LADY CONSENTS, THE, 1936
LADY CRAVED EXCITEMENT, THE, 1950
LADY ESCAPES, THE, 1937
LADY EVE, THE, 1941
LADY FIGHTS BACK, 1937
LADY FOR A DAY, 1933
LADY FOR A NIGHT, 1941

LADY FROM CHEYENNE, 1941
LADY FROM CHUNGKING, 1943
LADY FROM LISBON, 1942
LADY FROM LOUISIANA, 1941
LADY FROM NOWHERE, 1936
LADY FROM NOWHERE, 1931
LADY FROM TEXAS, THE, 1951
LADY FROM THE SEA, THE, 1929
LADY GAMBLES, THE, 1949
LADY GANGSTER, 1942
LADY GENERAL, THE, 1965
LADY GODIVA, 1955
LADY GODIVA RIDES AGAIN, 1955
LADY HAS PLANS, THE, 1942
LADY IN A JAM, 1942
LADY IN DANGER, 1934
LADY IN DISTRESS, 1942
LADY IN QUESTION, THE, 1940
LADY IN SCARLET, THE, 1935
LADY IN THE DARK, 1944
LADY IN THE DEATH HOUSE, 1944
LADY IN THE IRON MASK, 1952
LADY IN THE LAKE, 1947
LADY IN THE MORGUE, 1938
LADY IS A SQUARE, THE, 1959
LADY IS FICKLE, THE, 1948
LADY IS WILLING, THE, 1942
LADY IS WILLING, THE, 1934
LADY JANE GREY, 1936
LADY KILLER, 1933
LADY, LET'S DANCE, 1944
LADY LIES, THE, 1929
LADY LUCK, 1936
LADY LUCK, 1946
LADY MISLAID, A, 1958
LADY OBJECTS, THE, 1938
LADY OF CHANCE, A, 1928
LADY OF SCANDAL, THE, 1930
LADY OF SECRETS, 1936
LADY OF THE PAVEMENTS, 1929
LADY OF VENGEANCE, 1957
LADY ON A TRAIN, 1945
LADY ON THE TRACKS, THE, 1968
LADY PAYS OFF, THE, 1951
LADY POSSESSED, 1952
LADY REFUSES, THE, 1931
LADY SAYS NO, THE, 1951
LADY SCARFACE, 1941
LADY SURRENDERS, A, 1947
LADY SURRENDERS, A, 1930
LADY TAKES A CHANCE, A, 1943
LADY TAKES A FLYER, THE, 1958
LADY TAKES A SAILOR, THE, 1949
LADY TO LOVE, A, 1930
LADY TUBBS, 1935
LADY VANISHES, THE, 1938
LADY WANTS MINK, THE, 1953
LADY WHO DARED, THE, 1931
LADY WITH A LAMP, THE, 1951
LADY WITH A PAST, 1932
LADY WITH RED HAIR, 1940
LADY WITH THE DOG, THE, 1962
LADY WITHOUT PASSPORT, A, 1950
LADY'S FROM KENTUCKY, THE, 1939
LADY'S MORALS, A, 1930
LADY'S PROFESSION, A, 1933
LAFAYETTE ESCADRILLE, 1958
LAKE PLACID SERENADE, 1944
LAMBETH WALK, THE, 1940
LAMP IN ASSASSIN MEWS, THE, 1962
LAMP STILL BURNS, THE, 1943
LANCASHIRE LUCK, 1937
LANCER SPY, 1937
LAND BEYOND THE LAW, 1937
LAND OF FIGHTING MEN, 1938
LAND OF FURY, 1955
LAND OF HUNTED MEN, 1943
LAND OF MISSING MEN, THE, 1930
LAND OF NO RETURN, THE, 1981
LAND OF THE LAWLESS, 1947
LAND OF THE OPEN RANGE, 1941
LAND OF THE OUTLAWS, 1944
LAND OF THE SIX GUNS, 1940
LAND OF WANTED MEN, 1932
LAND THAT TIME FORGOT, THE, 1975
LAND UNKNOWN, THE, 1957

LANDFALL, 1953
LANDRUSH, 1946
LANDSLIDE, 1937
LARAMIE, 1949
LARAMIE MOUNTAINS, 1952
LARAMIE TRAIL, THE, 1944
LARCENY IN HER HEART, 1946
LARCENY, INC., 1942
LARCENY ON THE AIR, 1937
LARCENY STREET, 1941
LARCENY WITH MUSIC, 1943
LARGE ROPE, THE, 1953
LAS VEGAS HILLBILLYS, 1966
LAS VEGAS LADY, 1976
LAS VEGAS NIGHTS, 1941
LAS VEGAS SHAKEDOWN, 1955
LAS VEGAS STORY, THE, 1952
LASCA OF THE RIO GRANDE, 1931
LASH, THE, 1930
LAST ADVENTURE, THE, 1968
LAST ADVENTURERS, THE, 1937
LAST ANGRY MAN, THE, 1959
LAST BANDIT, THE, 1949
LAST BLITZKRIEG, THE, 1958
LAST CHALLENGE, THE, 1967
LAST CHANCE, THE, 1937
LAST CHANCE, THE, 1945
LAST CHASE, THE, 1981
LAST COMMAND, THE, 1955
LAST COUPON, THE, 1932
LAST CROOKED MILE, THE, 1946
LAST CURTAIN, THE, 1937
LAST DANCE, THE, 1930
LAST DAY OF THE WAR, THE, 1969
LAST DAYS OF BOOT HILL, 1947
LAST DAYS OF DOLWYN, THE, 1949
LAST DAYS OF MUSSOLINI, 1974
LAST DAYS OF POMPEII, THE, 1960
LAST DAYS OF POMPEII, THE, 1935
LAST ESCAPE, THE, 1970
LAST EXPRESS, THE, 1938
LAST FLIGHT, THE, 1931
LAST FRONTIER, THE, 1955
LAST FRONTIER UPRISING, 1947
LAST GANGSTER, THE, 1937
LAST GENTLEMAN, THE, 1934
LAST GUNFIGHTER, THE, 1961
LAST HILL, THE, 1945
LAST HOLIDAY, 1950
LAST HORSEMAN, THE, 1944
LAST HOUR, THE, 1930
LAST HURRAH, THE, 1958
LAST JOURNEY, THE, 1936
LAST MAN, 1932
LAST MILE, THE, 1932
LAST MOMENT, THE, 1954
LAST MUSKETEER, THE, 1952
LAST OF MRS. CHEYNEY, THE, 1929
LAST OF MRS. CHEYNEY, THE, 1937
LAST OF THE BADMEN, 1957
LAST OF THE BUCCANEERS, 1950
LAST OF THE CLINTONS, THE, 1935
LAST OF THE COMANCHES, 1952
LAST OF THE DESPERADOES, 1956
LAST OF THE DUANES, 1930
LAST OF THE DUANES, 1941
LAST OF THE FAST GUNS, THE, 1958
LAST OF THE KNUCKLEMEN, THE, 1981
LAST OF THE LONE WOLF, 1930
LAST OF THE MOHICANS, THE, 1936
LAST OF THE PAGANS, 1936
LAST OF THE PONY RIDERS, 1953
LAST OF THE RED HOT LOVERS, 1972
LAST OF THE RENEGADES, 1966
LAST OF THE SECRET AGENTS?, THE, 1966
LAST OF THE VIKINGS, THE, 1962
LAST OF THE WARRENS, THE, 1936
LAST OF THE WILD HORSES, 1948
LAST OUTLAW, THE, 1936
LAST OUTPOST, THE, 1935
LAST OUTPOST, THE, 1951
LAST PARADE, THE, 1931
LAST POSSE, THE, 1953
LAST RIDE, THE, 1944
LAST RIDE, THE, 1932
LAST ROSE OF SUMMER, THE, 1937

LAST ROUND-UP, THE, 1934
LAST RUN, THE, 1971
LAST SAFARI, THE, 1967
LAST STAGECOACH WEST, THE, 1957
LAST STAND, THE, 1938
LAST TEN DAYS, THE, 1956
LAST TIME I SAW ARCHIE, THE, 1961
LAST TIME I SAW PARIS, THE, 1954
LAST TOMAHAWK, THE, 1965
LAST TRAIL, THE, 1934
LAST TRAIN FROM BOMBAY, 1952
LAST TRAIN FROM MADRID, THE, 1937
LAST VALLEY, THE, 1971
LAST VOYAGE, THE, 1960
LAST WALTZ, THE, 1936
LAST WARNING, THE, 1929
LAST WARNING, THE, 1938
LAST WAVE, THE, 1978
LAST WOMAN OF SHANG, THE, 1964
LAST WOMAN ON EARTH, THE, 1960
LAST WORD, THE, 1979
LATE AT NIGHT, 1946
LATE AUTUMN, 1973
LATE EXTRA, 1935
LATE GEORGE APLEY, THE, 1947
LATE LIZ, THE, 1971
LATIN LOVE, 1930
LATIN LOVERS, 1953
LAUGH AND GET RICH, 1931
LAUGH IT OFF, 1940
LAUGH IT OFF, 1939
LAUGH PAGLIACCI, 1948
LAUGH YOUR BLUES AWAY, 1943
LAUGHING ANNE, 1954
LAUGHING AT DANGER, 1940
LAUGHING AT LIFE, 1933
LAUGHING AT TROUBLE, 1937
LAUGHING BOY, 1934
LAUGHING IN THE SUNSHINE, 1953
LAUGHING IRISH EYES, 1936
LAUGHING LADY, THE, 1930
LAUGHING LADY, THE, 1950
LAUGHTER IN HELL, 1933
LAURA, 1944
LAVENDER HILL MOB, THE, 1951
L'AVVENTURA, 1960
LAW AND DISORDER, 1940
LAW AND DISORDER, 1958
LAW AND JAKE WADE, THE, 1958
LAW AND LAWLESS, 1932
LAW AND LEAD, 1937
LAW AND ORDER, 1932
LAW AND ORDER, 1940
LAW AND ORDER, 1942
LAW AND ORDER, 1953
LAW AND THE LADY, THE, 1951
LAW BEYOND THE RANGE, 1935
LAW COMES TO TEXAS, THE, 1939
LAW COMMANDS, THE, 1938
LAW FOR TOMBSTONE, 1937
LAW IN HER HANDS, THE, 1936
LAW IS THE LAW, THE, 1959
LAW MEN, 1944
LAW OF THE BADLANDS, 1950
LAW OF THE BARBARY COAST, 1949
LAW OF THE GOLDEN WEST, 1949
LAW OF THE JUNGLE, 1942
LAW OF THE LASH, 1947
LAW OF THE LAWLESS, 1964
LAW OF THE NORTHWEST, 1943
LAW OF THE PAMPAS, 1939
LAW OF THE PANHANDLE, 1950
LAW OF THE PLAINS, 1938
LAW OF THE RANGE, 1941
LAW OF THE RANGER, 1937
LAW OF THE RIO GRANDE, 1931
LAW OF THE SADDLE, 1944
LAW OF THE SEA, 1932
LAW OF THE TEXAN, 1938
LAW OF THE TIMBER, 1941
LAW OF THE TONG, 1931
LAW OF THE TROPICS, 1941
LAW OF THE UNDERWORLD, 1938
LAW OF THE VALLEY, 1944
LAW OF THE WEST, 1949
LAW RIDES, THE, 1936

LAW RIDES AGAIN, THE, 1943
LAW VS. BILLY THE KID, THE, 1954
LAW WEST OF TOMBSTONE, THE, 1938
LAWFUL LARCENY, 1930
LAWLESS BORDER, 1935
LAWLESS BREED, THE, 1952
LAWLESS CODE, 1949
LAWLESS COWBOYS, 1952
LAWLESS EMPIRE, 1946
LAWLESS FRONTIER, THE, 1935
LAWLESS LAND, 1937
LAWLESS NINETIES, THE, 1936
LAWLESS PLAINSMEN, 1942
LAWLESS RANGE, 1935
LAWLESS RIDER, THE, 1954
LAWLESS RIDERS, 1936
LAWLESS STREET, A, 1955
LAWLESS VALLEY, 1938
LAWLESS WOMAN, THE, 1931
LAWMAN IS BORN, A, 1937
LAWTON STORY, THE, 1949
LAWYER MAN, 1933
LAWYER'S SECRET, THE, 1931
LAY THAT RIFLE DOWN, 1955
LAZARILLO, 1963
LAZY RIVER, 1934
LAZYBONES, 1935
LE BAL, 1984
LE CIEL EST A VOUS, 1957
LE DENIER MILLIARDAIRE, 1934
LE GAI SAVOIR, 1968
LE MANS, 1971
LE MONDE TREMBLERA, 1939
LEADVILLE GUNSLINGER, 1952
LEAGUE OF FRIGHTENED MEN, 1937
LEAP OF FAITH, 1931
LEAP YEAR, 1932
LEASE OF LIFE, 1954
LEATHER BURNERS, THE, 1943
LEATHER GLOVES, 1948
LEATHER-PUSHERS, THE, 1940
LEATHER SAINT, THE, 1956
LEATHERNECK, THE, 1929
LEATHERNECKING, 1930
LEATHERNECKS HAVE LANDED, THE, 1936
LEAVE IT TO BLANCHE, 1934
LEAVE IT TO BLONDIE, 1945
LEAVE IT TO HENRY, 1949
LEAVE IT TO ME, 1933
LEAVE IT TO ME, 1937
LEAVE IT TO SMITH, 1934
LEAVE IT TO THE IRISH, 1944
LEAVE IT TO THE MARINES, 1951
LEAVENWORTH CASE, THE, 1936
LEFT HAND OF GOD, THE, 1955
LEFT-HANDED LAW, 1937
LEFT, RIGHT AND CENTRE, 1959
LEFTOVER LADIES, 1931
LEGACY OF THE 500,000, THE, 1964
LEGEND, 1985
LEGEND OF A BANDIT, THE, 1945
LEGEND OF COUGAR CANYON, 1974
LEGEND OF TOM DOOLEY, THE, 1959
LEGION OF LOST FLYERS, 1939
LEGION OF MISSING MEN, 1937
LEGION OF TERROR, 1936
LEGION OF THE DOOMED, 1958
LEGION OF THE LAWLESS, 1940
LEGIONS OF THE NILE, 1960
LEMON DROP KID, THE, 1934
LEMON DROP KID, THE, 1951
LEMONADE JOE, 1966
LENA RIVERS, 1932
LEND ME YOUR HUSBAND, 1935
LEND ME YOUR WIFE, 1935
L'ENIGMATIQUE MONSIEUR PARKES, 1930
LEO AND LOREE, 1980
LEOPARD IN THE SNOW, 1979
LES COMPERES, 1984
LES CREATURES, 1969
LES GAULOISES BLEUES, 1969
LES GIRLS, 1957
LES MAITRES DU TEMPS, 1982
LES MISERABLES, 1935
LES MISERABLES, 1936
LES MISERABLES, 1952

BOLD: Films on Videocassette

LES MISERABLES, 1982
LES PARENTS TERRIBLES, 1950
LET 'EM HAVE IT, 1935
LET FREEDOM RING, 1939
LET GEORGE DO IT, 1940
LET ME EXPLAIN, DEAR, 1932
LET NO MAN WRITE MY EPITAPH, 1960
LET THE BALLOON GO, 1977
LET THE PEOPLE SING, 1942
LET THEM LIVE, 1937
LET US BE GAY, 1930
LET US LIVE, 1939
LET'S BE FAMOUS, 1939
LET'S BE HAPPY, 1957
LET'S BE RITZY, 1934
LET'S DANCE, 1950
LET'S DO IT AGAIN, 1953
LET'S DO IT AGAIN, 1975
LET'S FACE IT, 1943
LET'S FALL IN LOVE, 1934
LET'S GET MARRIED, 1937
LET'S GET MARRIED, 1960
LET'S GET TOUGH, 1942
LET'S GO COLLEGIATE, 1941
LET'S GO NATIVE, 1930
LET'S GO NAVY, 1951
LET'S GO PLACES, 1930
LET'S GO STEADY, 1945
LET'S GO, YOUNG GUY!, 1967
LET'S LIVE A LITTLE, 1948
LET'S LIVE AGAIN, 1948
LET'S LIVE TONIGHT, 1935
LET'S MAKE A NIGHT OF IT, 1937
LET'S MAKE A MILLION, 1937
LET'S MAKE IT LEGAL, 1951
LET'S MAKE MUSIC, 1940
LET'S MAKE UP, 1955
LET'S ROCK, 1958
LET'S SING AGAIN, 1936
LET'S TALK IT OVER, 1934
LET'S TRY AGAIN, 1934
LETTER, THE, 1929
LETTER, THE, 1940
LETTER FOR EVIE, A, 1945
LETTER FROM AN UNKNOWN WOMAN, 1948
LETTER OF INTRODUCTION, 1938
LETTER THAT WAS NEVER SENT, THE, 1962
LETTER TO THREE WIVES, A, 1948
LETTERS FROM MY WINDMILL, 1955
LETTING IN THE SUNSHINE, 1933
LIARS, THE, 1964
LIBEL, 1959
LIBELED LADY, 1936
LIES MY FATHER TOLD ME, 1975
LIES MY FATHER TOLD ME, 1960
LIEUTENANT DARING, RN, 1935
LIEUTENANT WORE SKIRTS, THE, 1956
LIFE AND DEATH OF COLONEL BLIMP, THE, 1945
LIFE AND LOVES OF BEETHOVEN, THE, 1937
LIFE BEGINS ANEW, 1938
LIFE BEGINS AT 8:30, 1942
LIFE BEGINS FOR ANDY HARDY, 1941
LIFE BEGINS WITH LOVE, 1937
LIFE IN DANGER, 1964
LIFE IN THE RAW, 1933
LIFE IS A CIRCUS, 1962
LIFE OF A COUNTRY DOCTOR, 1961
LIFE OF JIMMY DOLAN, THE, 1933
LIFE OF RILEY, THE, 1949
LIFE OF THE PARTY, 1934
LIFE OF THE PARTY, THE, 1930
LIFE OF THE PARTY, THE, 1937
LIFEBOAT, 1944
LIGHT FANTASTIC, 1964
LIGHT FINGERS, 1929
LIGHT FINGERS, 1957
LIGHT IN THE PIAZZA, 1962
LIGHT OF WESTERN STARS, THE, 1930
LIGHT OF WESTERN STARS, THE, 1940
LIGHT THAT FAILED, THE, 1939
LIGHT TOUCH, THE, 1955
LIGHT UP THE SKY, 1960
LIGHTHOUSE, 1947
LIGHTNIN', 1930
LIGHTNIN' CRANDALL, 1937
LIGHTNING BILL CARSON, 1936

LIGHTNING BOLT, 1967
LIGHTNING CONDUCTOR, 1938
LIGHTNING FLYER, 1931
LIGHTNING GUNS, 1950
LIGHTNING RAIDERS, 1945
LIGHTNING RANGE, 1934
LIGHTNING STRIKES TWICE, 1935
LIGHTNING STRIKES WEST, 1940
LIGHTNING—THE WHITE STALLION, 1986
LIGHTS OF NEW YORK, 1928
LIGHTS OF OLD SANTA FE, 1944
LIKELY LADS, THE, 1976
LIKELY STORY, A, 1947
LILAC DOMINO, THE, 1940
LILIES OF THE FIELD, 1934
LILIES OF THE FIELD, 1963
LILIOM, 1935
LILLIAN RUSSELL, 1940
LIMELIGHT, 1952
LIMPING MAN, THE, 1931
LIMPING MAN, THE, 1936
LIMPING MAN, THE, 1953
LINCOLN CONSPIRACY, THE, 1977
LINDA, 1960
LINDA BE GOOD, 1947
LINE ENGAGED, 1935
LINEUP, THE, 1934
LINKS OF JUSTICE, 1958
LION, THE, 1962
LION AND THE HORSE, THE, 1952
LION AND THE LAMB, 1931
LION AND THE MOUSE, THE, 1928
LION HAS WINGS, THE, 1940
LION IN WINTER, THE, 1968
LION IS IN THE STREETS, A, 1953
LION OF ST. MARK, 1967
LION'S DEN, THE, 1936
LISA, TOSCA OF ATHENS, 1961
LISBON STORY, THE, 1946
LIST OF ADRIAN MESSENGER, THE, 1963
LITTLE ACCIDENT, 1930
LITTLE ACCIDENT, 1939
LITTLE ANGEL, 1961
LITTLE BIG SHOT, 1952
LITTLE BIT OF BLUFF, A, 1935
LITTLE BOY BLUE, 1963
LITTLE BOY LOST, 1953
LITTLE CIGARS, 1973
LITTLE DAMOZEL, THE, 1933
LITTLE DORRIT, 1988
LITTLE EGYPT, 1951
LITTLE FUGITIVE, THE, 1953
LITTLE GIANT, THE, 1933
LITTLE GIANT, 1946
LITTLE HUMPBACKED HORSE, THE, 1962
LITTLE HUT, THE, 1957
LITTLE IODINE, 1946
LITTLE JOE, THE WRANGLER, 1942
LITTLE JOHNNY JONES, 1930
LITTLE JUNGLE BOY, 1969
LITTLE MAN, WHAT NOW?, 1934
LITTLE MARTYR, THE, 1947
LITTLE MELODY FROM VIENNA, 1948
LITTLE MEN, 1935
LITTLE MINISTER, THE, 1934
LITTLE MISS BIG, 1946
LITTLE MISS BROADWAY, 1938
LITTLE MISS BROADWAY, 1947
LITTLE MISS DEVIL, 1951
LITTLE MISS MOLLY, 1940
LITTLE MISS NOBODY, 1933
LITTLE MISS SOMEBODY, 1937
LITTLE MISTER JIM, 1946
LITTLE NELLIE KELLY, 1940
LITTLE NUNS, THE, 1965
LITTLE OF WHAT YOU FANCY, A, 1968
LITTLE OLD NEW YORK, 1940
LITTLE ORPHAN ANNIE, 1938
LITTLE RED RIDING HOOD, 1963
LITTLE RED RIDING HOOD AND HER FRIENDS, 1964
LITTLE ROMANCE, A, 1979
LITTLE SAVAGE, THE, 1959
LITTLE SHEPHERD OF KINGDOM COME, 1961
LITTLE STRANGER, 1934
LITTLE TOKYO, U.S.A., 1942

LITTLE TOUGH GUY, 1938
LITTLE TOUGH GUYS IN SOCIETY, 1938
LITTLE WILDCAT, THE, 1928
LITTLE WORLD OF DON CAMILLO, THE, 1953
LIVE A LITTLE, LOVE A LITTLE, 1968
LIVE AGAIN, 1936
LIVE FAST, DIE YOUNG, 1958
LIVE FOR LIFE, 1967
LIVE, LOVE AND LEARN, 1937
LIVE NOW—PAY LATER, 1962
LIVE WIRE, THE, 1937
LIVE WIRES, 1946
LIVE YOUR OWN WAY, 1970
LIVELY SET, THE, 1964
LIVES OF A BENGAL LANCER, 1935
LIVING BETWEEN TWO WORLDS, 1963
LIVING CORPSE, THE, 1940
LIVING DANGEROUSLY, 1936
LIVING DEAD, THE, 1936
LIVING FREE, 1972
LIVING GHOST, THE, 1942
LIVING IN A BIG WAY, 1947
LIVING IT UP, 1954
LIVING ON LOVE, 1937
LIVING ON VELVET, 1935
LLANO KID, THE, 1940
LLOYDS OF LONDON, 1936
LOADED PISTOLS, 1948
LOAN SHARK, 1952
LOCAL BAD MAN, 1932
LOCAL BOY MAKES GOOD, 1931
LOCKED DOOR, THE, 1929
LOCKER 69, 1962
LONG ROPE, THE, 1961
LOGAN'S RUN, 1976
LOLLIPOP COVER, THE, 1965
LOLLY-MADONNA XXX, 1973
LONDON BLACKOUT MURDERS, 1942
LONDON BY NIGHT, 1937
LONDON MELODY, 1930
LONE AVENGER, THE, 1933
LONE COWBOY, 1934
LONE GUN, THE, 1954
LONE HAND, THE, 1953
LONE HAND TEXAN, THE, 1947
LONE PRAIRIE, THE, 1942
LONE RIDER, THE, 1930
LONE RIDER AMBUSHED, THE, 1941
LONE RIDER AND THE BANDIT, THE, 1942
LONE RIDER CROSSES THE RIO, THE, 1941
LONE RIDER FIGHTS BACK, THE, 1941
LONE RIDER IN CHEYENNE, THE, 1942
LONE RIDER IN GHOST TOWN, THE, 1941
LONE STAR, 1952
LONE STAR LAW MEN, 1942
LONE STAR PIONEERS, 1939
LONE STAR RAIDERS, 1940
LONE STAR RANGER, THE, 1930
LONE STAR RANGER, 1942
LONE STAR TRAIL, THE, 1943
LONE STAR VIGILANTES, THE, 1942
LONE TEXAN, 1959
LONE TEXAS RANGER, 1945
LONE TRAIL, THE, 1932
LONE WOLF AND HIS LADY, THE, 1949
LONE WOLF IN LONDON, 1947
LONE WOLF IN MEXICO, THE, 1947
LONE WOLF IN PARIS, THE, 1938
LONE WOLF KEEPS A DATE, THE, 1940
LONE WOLF MEETS A LADY, THE, 1940
LONE WOLF RETURNS, THE, 1936
LONE WOLF SPY HUNT, THE, 1939
LONE WOLF STRIKES, THE, 1940
LONE WOLF TAKES A CHANCE, THE, 1941
LONE WOLF'S DAUGHTER, THE, 1929
LONELY HEARTS BANDITS, 1950
LONELY MAN, THE, 1957
LONELY TRAIL, THE, 1936
LONELY WIVES, 1931
LONESOME, 1928
LONESOME TRAIL, THE, 1930
LONESOME TRAIL, THE, 1955
LONG ABSENCE, THE, 1962
LONG AND THE SHORT AND THE TALL, THE, 1961
LONG DUEL, THE, 1967
LONG GRAY LINE, THE, 1955

LONG HAUL, THE, 1957
LONG IS THE ROAD, 1948
LONG JOHN SILVER, 1954
LONG, LONG TRAIL, THE, 1929
LONG, LONG TRAILER, THE, 1954
LONG LOST FATHER, 1934
LONG MEMORY, THE, 1953
LONG NIGHT, THE, 1947
LONG NIGHT, THE, 1976
LONG SHADOW, THE, 1961
LONG SHOT, THE, 1939
LONG VOYAGE HOME, THE, 1940
LONG WAIT, THE, 1954
LONGEST NIGHT, THE, 1936
LONGHORN, THE, 1951
LOOK BEFORE YOU LOVE, 1948
LOOK FOR THE SILVER LINING, 1949
LOOK IN ANY WINDOW, 1961
LOOK OUT SISTER, 1948
LOOK UP AND LAUGH, 1935
LOOK WHO'S LAUGHING, 1941
LOOKING FOR DANGER, 1957
LOOKING FOR LOVE, 1964
LOOKING FOR TROUBLE, 1934
LOOKING FORWARD, 1933
LOOKING ON THE BRIGHT SIDE, 1932
LOOPHOLE, 1954
LOOSE ANKLES, 1930
LOOSE ENDS, 1930
LOOSE IN LONDON, 1953
LOOTERS, THE, 1955
LORD BABS, 1932
LORD BYRON OF BROADWAY, 1930
LORD CAMBER'S LADIES, 1932
LORD EDGEWARE DIES, 1934
LORD JIM, 1965
LORD LOVE A DUCK, 1966
LORD OF THE JUNGLE, 1955
LORD OF THE MANOR, 1933
LORD OF THE RINGS, THE, 1978
LORD RICHARD IN THE PANTRY, 1930
LORNA DOONE, 1935
LORNA DOONE, 1951
LOS ASTRONAUTAS, 1960
LOS AUTOMATAS DE LA MUERTE, 1960
LOS INVISIBLES, 1961
LOS PLATILLOS VOLADORES, 1955
LOSER TAKES ALL, 1956
LOSER, THE HERO, THE, 1985
LOSS OF FEELING, 1935
LOST ANGEL, 1944
LOST BATTALION, 1961
LOST BOUNDARIES, 1949
LOST CANYON, 1943
LOST CHORD, THE, 1937
LOST CONTINENT, 1951
LOST CONTINENT, THE, 1968
LOST HAPPINESS, 1948
LOST HONEYMOON, 1947
LOST HORIZON, 1937
LOST HORIZON, 1973
LOST IN A HAREM, 1944
LOST IN THE LEGION, 1934
LOST IN THE STARS, 1974
LOST IN THE STRATOSPHERE, 1935
LOST JUNGLE, THE, 1934
LOST LADY, A, 1934
LOST LAGOON, 1958
LOST, LONELY AND VICIOUS, 1958
LOST MISSILE, THE, 1958
LOST MOMENT, THE, 1947
LOST ON THE WESTERN FRONT, 1940
LOST PEOPLE, THE, 1950
LOST RANCH, 1937
LOST TRAIL, THE, 1945
LOST TRIBE, THE, 1949
LOST WORLD, THE, 1960
LOST WORLD OF SINBAD, THE, 1965
LOST ZEPPELIN, 1930
LOTTERY BRIDE, THE, 1930
LOTTERY LOVER, 1935
LOTUS LADY, 1930
LOUDSPEAKER, THE, 1934
LOUISA, 1950
LOUISE, 1940
LOUISIANA, 1947

LOUISIANA HAYRIDE, 1944
LOUISIANA PURCHASE, 1941
LOUISIANA TERRITORY, 1953
LOVABLE CHEAT, THE, 1949
LOVE AFFAIR, 1932
LOVE AFFAIR, 1939
LOVE AMONG THE MILLIONAIRES, 1930
LOVE AND HISSES, 1937
LOVE AND KISSES, 1965
LOVE AND LARCENY, 1963
LOVE AND LEARN, 1947
LOVE AT FIRST SIGHT, 1930
LOVE AT FIRST SIGHT, 1977
LOVE AT SEA, 1936
LOVE BEFORE BREAKFAST, 1936
LOVE BEGINS AT TWENTY, 1936
LOVE BIRDS, 1934
LOVE BOUND, 1932
LOVE CAPTIVE, THE, 1934
LOVE COMES ALONG, 1930
LOVE CONTRACT, THE, 1932
LOVE CRAZY, 1941
LOVE DOCTOR, THE, 1929
LOVE ETERNE, THE, 1964
LOVE FROM A STRANGER, 1947
LOVE GOD?, THE, 1969
LOVE HABIT, THE, 1931
LOVE HAPPY, 1949
LOVE, HONOR AND BEHAVE, 1938
LOVE, HONOR AND GOODBYE, 1945
LOVE, HONOR, AND OH BABY!, 1933
LOVE, HONOR AND OH, BABY, 1940
LOVE IN A BUNGALOW, 1937
LOVE IN A GOLDFISH BOWL, 1961
LOVE IN A HOT CLIMATE, 1958
LOVE IN A TAXI, 1980
LOVE IN BLOOM, 1935
LOVE IN EXILE, 1936
LOVE IN MOROCCO, 1933
LOVE IN PAWN, 1953
LOVE IN THE AFTERNOON, 1957
LOVE IN THE DESERT, 1929
LOVE IN THE ROUGH, 1930
LOVE IN WAITING, 1948
LOVE IS A BALL, 1963
LOVE IS A HEADACHE, 1938
LOVE IS A MANY-SPLENDORED THING, 1955
LOVE IS A RACKET, 1932
LOVE IS BETTER THAN EVER, 1952
LOVE IS LIKE THAT, 1933
LOVE IS NEWS, 1937
LOVE IS ON THE AIR, 1937
LOVE ISLAND, 1952
LOVE KISS, THE, 1930
LOVE LAUGHS AT ANDY HARDY, 1946
LOVE LETTERS, 1945
LOVE LETTERS OF A STAR, 1936
LOVE LIES, 1931
LOVE, LIFE AND LAUGHTER, 1934
LOVE, LIVE AND LAUGH, 1929
LOVE LOTTERY, THE, 1954
LOVE MATCH, THE, 1955
LOVE MATES, 1967
LOVE ME FOREVER, 1935
LOVE ME OR LEAVE ME, 1955
LOVE ME TENDER, 1956
LOVE ME TONIGHT, 1932
LOVE NEST, THE, 1933
LOVE NEST, 1951
LOVE ON A BET, 1936
LOVE ON A BUDGET, 1938
LOVE ON SKIS, 1933
LOVE ON THE DOLE, 1945
LOVE ON THE RUN, 1936
LOVE ON THE SPOT, 1932
LOVE ON TOAST, 1937
LOVE ON WHEELS, 1932
LOVE PAST THIRTY, 1934
LOVE RACE, THE, 1931
LOVE RACKET, THE, 1929
LOVE SLAVES OF THE AMAZONS, 1957
LOVE SPECIALIST, THE, 1959
LOVE STORM, THE, 1931
LOVE TAKES FLIGHT, 1937
LOVE TEST, THE, 1935
LOVE THAT BRUTE, 1950

LOVE THY NEIGHBOR, 1940
LOVE TIME, 1934
LOVE TRADER, 1930
LOVE TRAP, THE, 1929
LOVE UNDER FIRE, 1937
LOVE UNDER THE CRUCIFIX, 1965
LOVE UP THE POLE, 1936
LOVE WAGER, THE, 1933
LOVE WALTZ, THE, 1930
LOVELY TO LOOK AT, 1952
LOVER COME BACK, 1946
LOVER COME BACK, 1961
LOVER COME BACK, 1931
LOVERS AND LOLLIPOPS, 1956
LOVERS AND LUGGERS, 1938
LOVERS COURAGEOUS, 1932
LOVERS OF TERUEL, THE, 1962
LOVERS OF TOLEDO, THE, 1954
LOVERS OF VERONA, THE, 1951
LOVERS ON A TIGHTROPE, 1962
LOVERS' ROCK, 1966
LOVES OF A BLONDE, 1966
LOVES OF EDGAR ALLAN POE, THE, 1942
LOVES OF HERCULES, THE, 1960
LOVES OF JOANNA GODDEN, THE, 1947
LOVES OF MADAME DUBARRY, THE, 1938
LOVES OF ROBERT BURNS, THE, 1930
LOVES OF SALAMMBO, THE, 1962
LOVES OF THREE QUEENS, THE, 1954
LOVE'S OLD SWEET SONG, 1933
LOVIN' THE LADIES, 1930
LOVING YOU, 1957
LOYALTIES, 1934
LOYALTY OF LOVE, 1937
LUCAS, 1986
LUCK OF A SAILOR, THE, 1934
LUCK OF ROARING CAMP, THE, 1937
LUCK OF THE IRISH, 1948
LUCK OF THE IRISH, THE, 1937
LUCK OF THE TURF, 1936
LUCKIEST GIRL IN THE WORLD, THE, 1936
LUCKY BOY, 1929
LUCKY CISCO KID, 1940
LUCKY DAYS, 1935
LUCKY DEVILS, 1933
LUCKY GIRL, 1932
LUCKY IN LOVE, 1929
LUCKY JADE, 1937
LUCKY JORDAN, 1942
LUCKY LADIES, 1932
LUCKY LARRIGAN, 1933
LUCKY LEGS, 1942
LUCKY LOSER, 1934
LUCKY LUKE, 1971
LUCKY MASCOT, THE, 1951
LUCKY ME, 1954
LUCKY NICK CAIN, 1951
LUCKY NIGHT, 1939
LUCKY NUMBER, THE, 1933
LUCKY PARTNERS, 1940
LUCKY STAR, 1929
LUCKY STAR, THE, 1980
LUCKY STIFF, THE, 1949
LUCKY SWEEP, A, 1932
LUCKY TERROR, 1936
LUCKY TEXAN, THE, 1934
LUCREZIA BORGIA, 1937
LULLABY, 1961
LULLABY OF BROADWAY, THE, 1951
LULU BELLE, 1948
LUMBERJACK, 1944
LUMMOX, 1930
LURE, THE, 1933
LURE OF THE ISLANDS, 1942
LURE OF THE WASTELAND, 1939
LURED, 1947
LUXURY LINER, 1933
LUXURY LINER, 1948
LYDIA, 1941
LYDIA BAILEY, 1952
LYONS IN PARIS, THE, 1955
LYONS MAIL, THE, 1931
MA AND PA KETTLE, 1949
MA AND PA KETTLE AT HOME, 1954
MA AND PA KETTLE AT THE FAIR, 1952
MA AND PA KETTLE AT WAIKIKI, 1955

BOLD: Films on Videocassette

MA AND PA KETTLE BACK ON THE FARM, 1951
MA AND PA KETTLE GO TO TOWN, 1950
MA AND PA KETTLE ON VACATION, 1953
MA, HE'S MAKING EYES AT ME, 1940
MAC ARTHUR, 1977
MACBETH, 1948
MACBETH, 1963
MACHETE, 1958
MACHINE GUN MAMA, 1944
MACUMBA LOVE, 1960
MACUSHLA, 1937
MAD ABOUT MEN, 1954
MAD ABOUT MUSIC, 1938
MAD DOCTOR, THE, 1941
MAD DOCTOR OF MARKET STREET, THE, 1942
MAD EMPRESS, THE, 1940
MAD GAME, THE, 1933
MAD HATTERS, THE, 1935
MAD HOLIDAY, 1936
MAD LITTLE ISLAND, 1958
MAD MARTINDALES, THE, 1942
MAD MEN OF EUROPE, 1940
MAD MONSTER, THE, 1942
MAD PARADE, THE, 1931
MAD QUEEN, THE, 1950
MAD WEDNESDAY, 1950
MAD YOUTH, 1940
MADALENA, 1965
MADAME BOVARY, 1949
MADAME BUTTERFLY, 1932
MADAME BUTTERFLY, 1955
MADAME DU BARRY, 1934
MADAME GUILLOTINE, 1931
MADAME LOUISE, 1951
MADAME RACKETEER, 1932
MADAME SATAN, 1930
MADAME SPY, 1934
MADAME SPY, 1942
MADAME X, 1929
MADAME X, 1937
MADAME X, 1966
MADCAP OF THE HOUSE, 1950
MADE IN HEAVEN, 1952
MADE IN HEAVEN, 1987
MADE IN PARIS, 1966
MADE ON BROADWAY, 1933
MADELEINE, 1950
MADEMOISELLE FIFI, 1944
MADIGAN'S MILLIONS, 1970
MADISON AVENUE, 1962
MADISON SQUARE GARDEN, 1932
MADMAN OF LAB 4, THE, 1967
MADNESS OF THE HEART, 1949
MADONNA OF AVENUE A, 1929
MADONNA OF THE DESERT, 1948
MADONNA OF THE STREETS, 1930
MADONNA'S SECRET, 1946
MADWOMAN OF CHAILLOT, THE, 1969
MAGIC BOW, THE, 1947
MAGIC BOY, 1960
MAGIC CARPET, THE, 1951
MAGIC CHRISTMAS TREE, 1964
MAGIC FACE, THE, 1951
MAGIC FIRE, 1956
MAGIC FOUNTAIN, THE, 1961
MAGIC NIGHT, 1932
MAGIC SWORD, THE, 1962
MAGIC VOYAGE OF SINBAD, THE, 1962
MAGIC WEAVER, THE, 1965
MAGIC WORLD OF TOPO GIGIO, THE, 1961
MAGNET, THE, 1950
MAGNIFICENT AMBERSONS, THE, 1942
MAGNIFICENT BRUTE, THE, 1936
MAGNIFICENT CONCUBINE, THE, 1964
MAGNIFICENT CUCKOLD, THE, 1965
MAGNIFICENT DOLL, 1946
MAGNIFICENT DOPE, THE, 1942
MAGNIFICENT FRAUD, THE, 1939
MAGNIFICENT LIE, 1931
MAGNIFICENT MATADOR, THE, 1955
MAGNIFICENT OBSESSION, 1935
MAGNIFICENT OBSESSION, 1954
MAGNIFICENT ONE, THE, 1974
MAGNIFICENT ROGUE, THE, 1946
MAGNIFICENT ROUGHNECKS, 1956
MAGNIFICENT SEVEN RIDE, THE, 1972

MAGNIFICENT SINNER, 1963
MAGNIFICENT TRAMP, THE, 1962
MAGNIFICENT TWO, THE, 1967
MAID FOR MURDER, 1963
MAID HAPPY, 1933
MAID OF SALEM, 1937
MAID OF THE MOUNTAINS, THE, 1932
MAID TO ORDER, 1932
MAIDEN, THE, 1961
MAIDEN FOR A PRINCE, A, 1967
MAID'S NIGHT OUT, 1938
MAIL ORDER BRIDE, 1964
MAIL TRAIN, 1941
MAIN ATTRACTION, THE, 1962
MAIN CHANCE, THE, 1966
MAIN EVENT, THE, 1938
MAIN STREET AFTER DARK, 1944
MAIN STREET, 1956
MAIN STREET KID, THE, 1947
MAIN STREET LAWYER, 1939
MAIN STREET TO BROADWAY, 1953
MAISIE, 1939
MAISIE GETS HER MAN, 1942
MAISIE GOES TO RENO, 1944
MAISIE WAS A LADY, 1941
MAJIN, 1968
MAJOR AND THE MINOR, THE, 1942
MAJOR BARBARA, 1941
MAJORITY OF ONE, A, 1961
MAKE A MILLION, 1935
MAKE A WISH, 1937
MAKE BELIEVE BALLROOM, 1949
MAKE HASTE TO LIVE, 1954
MAKE IT THREE, 1938
MAKE LIKE A THIEF, 1966
MAKE ME A STAR, 1932
MAKE ME AN OFFER, 1954
MAKE MINE A DOUBLE, 1962
MAKE MINE A MILLION, 1965
MAKE MINE MINK, 1960
MAKE-UP, 1937
MAKE WAY FOR A LADY, 1936
MAKE WAY FOR LILA, 1962
MAKE WAY FOR TOMORROW, 1937
MAKE YOUR OWN BED, 1944
MAKER OF MEN, 1931
MAKING THE GRADE, 1929
MAKING THE HEADLINES, 1938
MALAGA, 1962
MALAY NIGHTS, 1933
MALAYA, 1950
MALE AND FEMALE SINCE ADAM AND EVE, 1961
MALE ANIMAL, THE, 1942
MALE COMPANION, 1965
MALE HUNT, 1965
MALPAS MYSTERY, THE, 1967
MALTESE BIPPY, THE, 1969
MALTESE FALCON, THE, 1941
MALTESE FALCON, THE, 1931
MAMA LOVES PAPA, 1933
MAMA LOVES PAPA, 1945
MAMA RUNS WILD, 1938
MAMA STEPS OUT, 1937
MAMBA, 1930
MAME, 1974
MAMMY, 1930
MAN, THE, 1972
MAN ABOUT THE HOUSE, A, 1947
MAN ABOUT TOWN, 1932
MAN ABOUT TOWN, 1947
MAN AFRAID, 1957
MAN AGAINST WOMAN, 1932
MAN ALIVE, 1945
MAN ALONE, A, 1955
MAN AND BOY, 1972
MAN AND THE BEAST, THE, 1951
MAN AND THE MOMENT, THE, 1929
MAN AND THE MONSTER, THE, 1965
MAN AT LARGE, 1941
MAN AT THE TOP, 1973
MAN BEAST, 1956
MAN BEHIND THE GUN, THE, 1952
MAN BEHIND THE MASK, THE, 1936
MAN BETRAYED, A, 1937
MAN BETRAYED, A, 1941

MAN BETWEEN, THE, 1953
MAN CALLED DAGGER, A, 1967
MAN CALLED GANNON, A, 1969
MAN COULD GET KILLED, A, 1966
MAN CRAZY, 1953
MAN-EATER OF KUMAON, 1948
MAN ESCAPED, A, 1957
MAN FOR ALL SEASONS, A, 1966
MAN FROM BITTER RIDGE, THE, 1955
MAN FROM BLACK HILLS, THE, 1952
MAN FROM BLANKLEY'S, THE, 1930
MAN FROM CAIRO, THE, 1953
MAN FROM CHEYENNE, 1942
MAN FROM CHICAGO, THE, 1931
MAN FROM COCODY, 1966
MAN FROM DAKOTA, THE, 1940
MAN FROM DEATH VALLEY, THE, 1931
MAN FROM DEL RIO, 1956
MAN FROM FRISCO, 1944
MAN FROM GALVESTON, THE, 1964
MAN FROM GOD'S COUNTRY, 1958
MAN FROM GUN TOWN, THE, 1936
MAN FROM HEADQUARTERS, 1942
MAN FROM HELL, THE, 1934
MAN FROM HELL'S EDGES, 1932
MAN FROM MONTANA, 1941
MAN FROM MONTEREY, THE, 1933
MAN FROM MONTREAL, THE, 1940
MAN FROM MOROCCO, THE, 1946
MAN FROM MUSIC MOUNTAIN, 1938
MAN FROM MUSIC MOUNTAIN, 1943
MAN FROM NEW MEXICO, THE, 1932
MAN FROM PLANET X, THE, 1951
MAN FROM RAINBOW VALLEY, THE, 1946
MAN FROM SUNDOWN, THE, 1939
MAN FROM TEXAS, THE, 1939
MAN FROM TEXAS, THE, 1948
MAN FROM THE ALAMO, THE, 1953
MAN FROM THE DINERS' CLUB, THE, 1963
MAN FROM THE EAST, THE, 1961
MAN FROM THE FIRST CENTURY, THE, 1961
MAN FROM THE RIO GRANDE, THE, 1943
MAN FROM THUNDER RIVER, THE, 1943
MAN FROM TORONTO, THE, 1933
MAN FROM TUMBLEWEEDS, THE, 1940
MAN FROM UTAH, THE, 1934
MAN FROM WYOMING, A, 1930
MAN FROM YESTERDAY, THE, 1932
MAN HUNT, 1933
MAN HUNT, 1936
MAN HUNT, 1941
MAN HUNTER, THE, 1930
MAN HUNTERS OF THE CARIBBEAN, 1938
MAN I LOVE, THE, 1929
MAN I LOVE, THE, 1946
MAN I MARRIED, THE, 1940
MAN I MARRY, THE, 1936
MAN I WANT, THE, 1934
MAN IN A COCKED HAT, 1960
MAN IN BLUE, THE, 1937
MAN IN HALF-MOON STREET, THE, 1944
MAN IN THE BACK SEAT, THE, 1961
MAN IN THE DARK, 1953
MAN IN THE DARK, 1963
MAN IN THE DINGHY, THE, 1951
MAN IN THE GLASS BOOTH, THE, 1975
MAN IN THE GREY FLANNEL SUIT, THE, 1956
MAN IN THE IRON MASK, THE, 1939
MAN IN THE MIRROR, THE, 1936
MAN IN THE MOON, 1961
MAN IN THE MOONLIGHT MASK, THE, 1958
MAN IN THE NET, THE, 1959
MAN IN THE ROAD, THE, 1957
MAN IN THE SADDLE, 1951
MAN IN THE SHADOW, 1957
MAN IN THE STORM, THE, 1969
MAN IN THE TRUNK, THE, 1942
MAN IN THE VAULT, 1956
MAN IN THE WATER, THE, 1963
MAN IN THE WHITE SUIT, THE, 1952
MAN IS ARMED, THE, 1956
MAN MADE MONSTER, 1941
MAN OF A THOUSAND FACES, 1957
MAN OF AFFAIRS, 1937
MAN OF AFRICA, 1956
MAN OF CONFLICT, 1953

MAN OF CONQUEST, 1939
MAN OF COURAGE, 1943
MAN OF EVIL, 1948
MAN OF IRON, 1935
MAN OF MAYFAIR, 1931
MAN OF MUSIC, 1953
MAN OF SENTIMENT, A, 1933
MAN OF THE FOREST, 1933
MAN OF THE HOUR, THE, 1940
MAN OF THE MOMENT, 1955
MAN OF THE MOMENT, 1935
MAN OF THE PEOPLE, 1937
MAN OF THE WORLD, 1931
MAN OF TWO WORLDS, 1934
MAN ON A STRING, 1960
MAN ON A TIGHTROPE, 1953
MAN ON FIRE, 1957
MAN ON THE EIFFEL TOWER, THE, 1949
MAN ON THE FLYING TRAPEZE, THE, 1935
MAN ON THE PROWL, 1957
MAN ON THE RUN, 1949
MAN OR GUN, 1958
MAN OUTSIDE, THE, 1933
MAN OUTSIDE, THE, 1968
MAN-PROOF, 1938
MAN STOLEN, 1934
MAN THEY COULDN'T ARREST, THE, 1933
MAN TO MAN, 1931
MAN TO REMEMBER, A, 1938
MAN TRAILER, THE, 1934
MAN-TRAP, 1961
MAN TROUBLE, 1930
MAN UPSTAIRS, THE, 1959
MAN WANTED, 1932
MAN WHO BROKE THE BANK AT MONTE CARLO, THE, 1935
MAN WHO CAME TO DINNER, THE, 1942
MAN WHO CHANGED HIS NAME, THE, 1934
MAN WHO CHEATED HIMSELF, THE, 1951
MAN WHO COULD WORK MIRACLES, THE, 1937
MAN WHO COULDN'T WALK, THE, 1964
MAN WHO CRIED WOLF, THE, 1937
MAN WHO DARED, THE, 1939
MAN WHO DARED, THE, 1946
MAN WHO DIED TWICE, THE, 1958
MAN WHO FINALLY DIED, THE, 1967
MAN WHO FOUND HIMSELF, THE, 1937
MAN WHO HAUNTED HIMSELF, THE, 1970
MAN WHO KILLED BILLY THE KID, THE, 1967
MAN WHO KNEW TOO MUCH, THE, 1956
MAN WHO LIKED FUNERALS, THE, 1959
MAN WHO LIVED AGAIN, THE, 1936
MAN WHO LIVED TWICE, 1936
MAN WHO LOST HIMSELF, THE, 1941
MAN WHO LOVED REDHEADS, THE, 1955
MAN WHO MADE DIAMONDS, THE, 1937
MAN WHO NEVER WAS, THE, 1956
MAN WHO PLAYED GOD, THE, 1932
MAN WHO RECLAIMED HIS HEAD, THE, 1935
MAN WHO RETURNED TO LIFE, THE, 1942
MAN WHO SHOT LIBERTY VALANCE, THE, 1962
MAN WHO TALKED TOO MUCH, THE, 1940
MAN WHO THOUGHT LIFE, THE, 1969
MAN WHO WAGGED HIS TAIL, THE, 1961
MAN WHO WALKED ALONE, THE, 1945
MAN WHO WALKED THROUGH THE WALL, THE, 1964
MAN WHO WAS SHERLOCK HOLMES, THE, 1937
MAN WHO WON, THE, 1933
MAN WHO WOULDN'T DIE, THE, 1942
MAN WHO WOULDN'T TALK, THE, 1940
MAN WHO WOULDN'T TALK, THE, 1958
MAN WITH A CLOAK, THE, 1951
MAN WITH A MILLION, 1954
MAN WITH MY FACE, THE, 1951
MAN WITH NINE LIVES, THE, 1940
MAN WITH 100 FACES, THE, 1938
MAN WITH THE BALLOONS, THE, 1968
MAN WITH THE GOLDEN GUN, THE, 1974
MAN WITH THE GREEN CARNATION, THE, 1960
MAN WITH THE TRANSPLANTED BRAIN, THE, 1972
MAN WITH TWO LIVES, THE, 1942
MAN WITHOUT A BODY, THE, 1957
MAN WITHOUT A FACE, THE, 1935
MAN, WOMAN AND CHILD, 1983

MANCHU EAGLE MURDER CAPER MYSTERY, THE, 1975
MANDABI, 1970
MANDARIN MYSTERY, THE, 1937
MANDRAGOLA, 1966
MANFISH, 1956
MANGANINNIE, 1982
MANHANDLED, 1949
MANHATTAN ANGEL, 1948
MANHATTAN COCKTAIL, 1928
MANHATTAN HEARTBEAT, 1940
MANHATTAN LOVE SONG, 1934
MANHATTAN MELODRAMA, 1934
MANHATTAN MERRY-GO-ROUND, 1937
MANHATTAN MOON, 1935
MANHATTAN PARADE, 1931
MANHATTAN PROJECT, THE, 1986
MANHATTAN SHAKEDOWN, 1939
MANHATTAN TOWER, 1932
MANHUNT IN THE JUNGLE, 1958
MANIACS ON WHEELS, 1951
MANILA CALLING, 1942
MANNEQUIN, 1933
MANNEQUIN, 1937
MANOLETE, 1950
MANOLIS, 1962
MANON, 1950
MANPOWER, 1941
MAN'S AFFAIR, A, 1949
MAN'S CASTLE, A, 1933
MAN'S COUNTRY, 1938
MAN'S FAVORITE SPORT (?), 1964
MAN'S GAME, A, 1934
MAN'S HOPE, 1947
MAN'S LAND, A, 1932
MAN'S WORLD, A, 1942
MANSLAUGHTER, 1930
MANSTER, THE, 1962
MANTRAP, THE, 1943
MANULESCU, 1933
MANY A SLIP, 1931
MANY HAPPY RETURNS, 1934
MANY RIVERS TO CROSS, 1955
MANY TANKS MR. ATKINS, 1938
MANY WATERS, 1931
MARA MARU, 1952
MARA OF THE WILDERNESS, 1966
MARACAIBO, 1958
MARAUDERS, THE, 1947
MARAUDERS, THE, 1955
MARCH HARE, THE, 1956
MARCO, 1973
MARCO POLO, 1962
MARCO POLO JUNIOR, 1973
MARDI GRAS, 1958
MARGIE, 1940
MARGIN, THE, 1969
MARGIN FOR ERROR, 1943
MARIANNE, 1929
MARIE-ANN, 1978
MARIE ANTOINETTE, 1938
MARIE GALANTE, 1934
MARIE OF THE ISLES, 1960
MARIGOLD, 1938
MARINE BATTLEGROUND, 1966
MARINE RAIDERS, 1944
MARINES ARE COMING, THE, 1935
MARINES ARE HERE, THE, 1938
MARINES COME THROUGH, THE, 1943
MARINES FLY HIGH, THE, 1940
MARINES, LET'S GO, 1961
MARIZINIA, 1962
MARK, THE, 1961
MARK IT PAID, 1933
MARK OF CAIN, THE, 1948
MARK OF THE GORILLA, 1950
MARK OF THE HAWK, THE, 1958
MARK OF THE LASH, 1948
MARK OF THE RENEGADE, 1951
MARK OF THE WHISTLER, THE, 1944
MARK OF ZORRO, THE, 1940
MARKED FOR MURDER, 1945
MARKED GIRLS, 1949
MARKED MEN, 1940
MARKED ONE, THE, 1963
MARKED TRAILS, 1944

MARLOWE, 1969
MAROC 7, 1967
MAROONED, 1969
MARRIAGE BOND, THE, 1932
MARRIAGE BY CONTRACT, 1928
MARRIAGE CAME TUMBLING DOWN, THE, 1968
MARRIAGE-GO-ROUND, THE, 1960
MARRIAGE IN THE SHADOWS, 1948
MARRIAGE IS A PRIVATE AFFAIR, 1944
MARRIAGE OF A YOUNG STOCKBROKER, THE, 1971
MARRIAGE OF BALZAMINOV, THE, 1966
MARRIAGE OF CONVENIENCE, 1970
MARRIAGE OF FIGARO, THE, 1963
MARRIAGE OF FIGARO, THE, 1970
MARRIAGE ON APPROVAL, 1934
MARRIAGE PLAYGROUND, THE, 1929
MARRIED AND IN LOVE, 1940
MARRIED BACHELOR, 1941
MARRIED BEFORE BREAKFAST, 1937
MARRIED IN HOLLYWOOD, 1929
MARRIED TOO YOUNG, 1962
MARRY ME, 1932
MARRY ME AGAIN, 1953
MARRY ME!, 1949
MARRY ME! MARRY ME!, 1969
MARRY THE BOSS' DAUGHTER, 1941
MARRY THE GIRL, 1935
MARRY THE GIRL, 1937
MARRYING KIND, THE, 1952
MARS NEEDS WOMEN, 1966
MARSHAL OF AMARILLO, 1948
MARSHAL OF CEDAR ROCK, 1953
MARSHAL OF CRIPPLE CREEK, THE, 1947
MARSHAL OF GUNSMOKE, 1944
MARSHAL OF HELDORADO, 1950
MARSHAL OF LAREDO, 1945
MARSHAL OF MESA CITY, THE, 1939
MARSHAL OF RENO, 1944
MARSHAL'S DAUGHTER, THE, 1953
MARTIAN IN PARIS, A, 1961
MARTY, 1955
MARTYRS OF LOVE, 1968
MARY BURNS, FUGITIVE, 1935
MARY JANE'S PA, 1935
MARY LOU, 1948
MARY OF SCOTLAND, 1936
MARY STEVENS, M.D., 1933
MARYLAND, 1940
MASK OF DIMITRIOS, THE, 1944
MASK OF KOREA, 1950
MASK OF THE AVENGER, 1951
MASK OF THE DRAGON, 1951
MASKED RAIDERS, 1949
MASKED RIDER, THE, 1941
MASON OF THE MOUNTED, 1932
MASQUERADE, 1929
MASQUERADE, 1965
MASQUERADER, THE, 1933
MASSACRE, 1934
MASSACRE, 1956
MASSACRE CANYON, 1954
MASSACRE HILL, 1949
MASSACRE RIVER, 1949
MASTER AND MAN, 1934
MASTER MINDS, 1949
MASTER OF BALLANTRAE, THE, 1953
MASTER OF MEN, 1933
MASTER OF THE WORLD, 1935
MASTER OF THE WORLD, 1961
MASTER PLAN, THE, 1955
MASTER SPY, 1964
MASTERMIND, 1977
MASTERSON OF KANSAS, 1954
MATA HARI, 1931
MATA HARI'S DAUGHTER, 1954
MATCHMAKER, THE, 1958
MATHIAS SANDORF, 1963
MATILDA, 1978
MATINEE IDOL, 1933
MATING GAME, THE, 1959
MATING OF MILLIE, THE, 1948
MATING SEASON, THE, 1951
MATRIMONIAL BED, THE, 1930
MATTER OF CHOICE, A, 1963
MATTER OF INNOCENCE, A, 1968
MATTER OF MURDER, A, 1949

BOLD: Films on Videocassette

MATTER OF WHO, A, 1962
MAURIE, 1973
MAVERICK, THE, 1952
MAVERICK QUEEN, THE, 1956
MAX DUGAN RETURNS, 1983
MAXIME, 1962
MAYA, 1966
MAYBE IT'S LOVE, 1930
MAYBE IT'S LOVE, 1935
MAYFAIR GIRL, 1933
MAYFAIR MELODY, 1937
MAYOR OF 44TH STREET, THE, 1942
MAYOR'S NEST, THE, 1932
MAYTIME, 1937
MAYTIME IN MAYFAIR, 1952
M'BLIMEY, 1931
MC CONNELL STORY, THE, 1955
MC FADDEN'S FLATS, 1935
MC GUIRE, GO HOME!, 1966
MC HALE'S NAVY, 1964
MC HALE'S NAVY JOINS THE AIR FORCE, 1965
MC KENNA OF THE MOUNTED, 1932
MC LINTOCK!, 1963
ME, 1970
ME AND MARLBOROUGH, 1935
ME AND MY GAL, 1932
ME AND MY PAL, 1939
ME AND THE COLONEL, 1958
MEANEST GAL IN TOWN, THE, 1934
MEANEST MAN IN THE WORLD, THE, 1943
MEDAL FOR BENNY, A, 1945
MEDICINE MAN, THE, 1930
MEDICINE MAN, THE, 1933
MEDICO OF PAINTED SPRINGS, THE, 1941
MEDIUM, THE, 1951
MEET BOSTON BLACKIE, 1941
MEET DANNY WILSON, 1952
MEET DR. CHRISTIAN, 1939
MEET JOHN DOE, 1941
MEET ME AFTER THE SHOW, 1951
MEET ME AT DAWN, 1947
MEET ME AT THE FAIR, 1952
MEET ME IN LAS VEGAS, 1956
MEET ME IN MOSCOW, 1966
MEET ME ON BROADWAY, 1946
MEET MISS BOBBY SOCKS, 1944
MEET MR. CALLAGHAN, 1954
MEET MR. LUCIFER, 1953
MEET MR. MALCOLM, 1954
MEET MR. PENNY, 1938
MEET MY SISTER, 1933
MEET NERO WOLFE, 1936
MEET SEXTON BLAKE, 1944
MEET SIMON CHERRY, 1949
MEET THE BARON, 1933
MEET THE BOY FRIEND, 1937
MEET THE CHUMP, 1941
MEET THE DUKE, 1949
MEET THE GIRLS, 1938
MEET THE MAYOR, 1938
MEET THE MISSUS, 1937
MEET THE MISSUS, 1940
MEET THE MOB, 1942
MEET THE NAVY, 1946
MEET THE PEOPLE, 1944
MEET THE STEWARTS, 1942
MEET THE WIFE, 1931
MEET THE WILDCAT, 1940
MEETINGS WITH REMARKABLE MEN, 1979
MELANIE, 1982
MELBA, 1953
MELO, 1988
MELODY AND MOONLIGHT, 1940
MELODY AND ROMANCE, 1937
MELODY CLUB, 1949
MELODY CRUISE, 1933
MELODY FOR THREE, 1941
MELODY FOR TWO, 1937
MELODY IN SPRING, 1934
MELODY IN THE DARK, 1948
MELODY LANE, 1929
MELODY LANE, 1941
MELODY LINGERS ON, THE, 1935
MELODY MAKER, THE, 1933
MELODY MAN, 1930
MELODY OF LOVE, THE, 1928

MELODY OF LOVE, 1954
MELODY OF MY HEART, 1936
MELODY OF THE PLAINS, 1937
MELODY PARADE, 1943
MELODY RANCH, 1940
MEMBER OF THE JURY, 1937
MEMBER OF THE WEDDING, THE, 1952
MEMORY OF US, 1974
MEN AGAINST THE SKY, 1940
MEN AGAINST THE SUN, 1953
MEN ARE CHILDREN TWICE, 1953
MEN ARE LIKE THAT, 1930
MEN ARE LIKE THAT, 1931
MEN ARE SUCH FOOLS, 1933
MEN ARE SUCH FOOLS, 1938
MEN IN EXILE, 1937
MEN IN HER DIARY, 1945
MEN IN HER LIFE, 1931
MEN IN HER LIFE, THE, 1941
MEN IN WHITE, 1934
MEN MUST FIGHT, 1933
MEN OF AMERICA, 1933
MEN OF CHANCE, 1932
MEN OF IRELAND, 1938
MEN OF SAN QUENTIN, 1942
MEN OF SHERWOOD FOREST, 1957
MEN OF STEEL, 1932
MEN OF TEXAS, 1942
MEN OF THE FIGHTING LADY, 1954
MEN OF THE HOUR, 1935
MEN OF THE NIGHT, 1934
MEN OF THE NORTH, 1930
MEN OF THE PLAINS, 1936
MEN OF THE SEA, 1938
MEN OF THE SEA, 1951
MEN OF THE SKY, 1931
MEN OF THE TIMBERLAND, 1941
MEN OF TOMORROW, 1935
MEN OF YESTERDAY, 1936
MEN ON CALL, 1931
MEN ON HER MIND, 1944
MEN WITH WINGS, 1938
MEN WITHOUT HONOUR, 1939
MEN WITHOUT LAW, 1930
MEN WITHOUT NAMES, 1935
MEN WITHOUT SOULS, 1940
MEN WITHOUT WOMEN, 1930
MENACE, 1934
MENACE IN THE NIGHT, 1958
MERCY ISLAND, 1941
MERCY PLANE, 1940
MERELY MARY ANN, 1931
MERELY MR. HAWKINS, 1938
MERMAID, THE, 1966
MERRILY WE LIVE, 1938
MERRY COMES TO STAY, 1937
MERRY FRINKS, THE, 1934
MERRY-GO-ROUND OF 1938, 1937
MERRY MONAHANS, THE, 1944
MERRY WIDOW, THE, 1952
MERRY WIVES OF RENO, THE, 1934
MERRY WIVES OF TOBIAS ROUKE, THE, 1972
MERRY WIVES OF WINDSOR, THE, 1952
MERRY WIVES OF WINDSOR, THE, 1966
MERRY-G0-ROUND, 1948
MERTON OF THE MOVIES, 1947
MESA OF LOST WOMEN, THE, 1956
MESQUITE BUCKAROO, 1939
MESSAGE FROM SPACE, 1978
MESSAGE TO GARCIA, A, 1936
MESSALINE, 1952
MESSENGER OF PEACE, 1950
METAMORPHOSES, 1978
METROPOLITAN, 1935
MEXICALI KID, THE, 1938
MEXICALI ROSE, 1929
MEXICALI ROSE, 1939
MEXICAN HAYRIDE, 1948
MEXICAN MANHUNT, 1953
MEXICAN SPITFIRE, 1939
MEXICAN SPITFIRE AT SEA, 1942
MEXICAN SPITFIRE OUT WEST, 1940
MEXICAN SPITFIRE SEES A GHOST, 1942
MEXICAN SPITFIRE'S BABY, 1941
MEXICAN SPITFIRE'S BLESSED EVENT, 1943
MEXICAN SPITFIRE'S ELEPHANT, 1942

MEXICANA, 1945
MIAMI EXPOSE, 1956
MIAMI STORY, THE, 1954
MICHAEL AND MARY, 1932
MICHAEL O'HALLORAN, 1937
MICHAEL O'HALLORAN, 1948
MICHAEL SHAYNE, PRIVATE DETECTIVE, 1940
MICHAEL STROGOFF, 1960
MICHIGAN KID, THE, 1947
MICKEY, 1948
MICKEY, THE KID, 1939
MIDAS TOUCH, THE, 1940
MIDDLE COURSE, THE, 1961
MIDDLE WATCH, THE, 1930
MIDDLE WATCH, THE, 1939
MIDDLETON FAMILY AT THE N.Y. WORLD'S FAIR, 1939
MIDNIGHT, 1934
MIDNIGHT ALIBI, 1934
MIDNIGHT ANGEL, 1941
MIDNIGHT AT THE WAX MUSEUM, 1936
MIDNIGHT, 1939
MIDNIGHT CLUB, 1933
MIDNIGHT COURT, 1937
MIDNIGHT DADDIES, 1929
MIDNIGHT EPISODE, 1951
MIDNIGHT INTRUDER, 1938
MIDNIGHT LADY, 1932
MIDNIGHT LIMITED, 1940
MIDNIGHT MADONNA, 1937
MIDNIGHT MEETING, 1962
MIDNIGHT MORALS, 1932
MIDNIGHT MYSTERY, 1930
MIDNIGHT PATROL, THE, 1932
MIDNIGHT SPECIAL, 1931
MIDNIGHT STORY, THE, 1957
MIDNIGHT TAXI, THE, 1928
MIDNIGHT TAXI, 1937
MIDNIGHT WARNING, THE, 1932
MIDSHIPMAID GOB, 1932
MIDSHIPMAN JACK, 1933
MIDSTREAM, 1929
MIDSUMMER NIGHT'S DREAM, A, 1969
MIDSUMMER'S NIGHT'S DREAM, A, 1935
MIDSUMMER NIGHT'S DREAM, A, 1966
MIDWAY, 1976
MIDWIFE, THE, 1961
MIGHTY, THE, 1929
MIGHTY BARNUM, THE, 1934
MIGHTY CRUSADERS, THE, 1961
MIGHTY GORGA, THE, 1969
MIGHTY JOE YOUNG, 1949
MIGHTY JUNGLE, THE, 1965
MIGHTY MCGURK, THE, 1946
MIGHTY URSUS, 1962
MIKADO, THE, 1939
MILDRED PIERCE, 1945
MILE A MINUTE LOVE, 1937
MILITARY ACADEMY, 1940
MILITARY ACADEMY WITH THAT TENTH AVENUE GANG, 1950
MILITARY SECRET, 1945
MILKMAN, THE, 1950
MILL ON THE FLOSS, 1939
MILLERSON CASE, THE, 1947
MILLIE, 1931
MILLIE'S DAUGHTER, 1947
MILLION, THE, 1931
MILLION DOLLAR BABY, 1935
MILLION DOLLAR BABY, 1941
MILLION DOLLAR COLLAR, THE, 1929
MILLION DOLLAR KID, 1944
MILLION DOLLAR LEGS, 1932
MILLION DOLLAR LEGS, 1939
MILLION DOLLAR MANHUNT, 1962
MILLION DOLLAR MERMAID, 1952
MILLION DOLLAR PURSUIT, 1951
MILLION DOLLAR RANSOM, 1934
MILLION DOLLAR WEEKEND, 1948
MILLION EYES OF SU-MURU, THE, 1967
MILLION TO ONE, A, 1938
MILLIONAIRE, THE, 1931
MILLIONAIRE FOR CHRISTY, A, 1951
MILLIONAIRE KID, 1936
MILLIONAIRE PLAYBOY, 1940
MILLIONAIRES IN PRISON, 1940

MILLIONAIRESS, THE, 1960
MILLIONS, 1936
MILLIONS IN THE AIR, 1935
MILLIONS LIKE US, 1943
MILLS OF THE GODS, 1935
MIMI, 1935
MIN AND BILL, 1930
MIND OF MR. SOAMES, THE, 1970
MIND READER, THE, 1933
MIND YOUR OWN BUSINESS, 1937
MINE WITH THE IRON DOOR, THE, 1936
MINESWEEPER, 1943
MINI-AFFAIR, THE, 1968
MINIVER STORY, THE, 1950
MINOTAUR, THE, 1961
MINSTREL BOY, THE, 1937
MINSTREL MAN, 1944
MIRACLE, THE, 1959
MIRACLE IN HARLEM, 1948
MIRACLE IN MILAN, 1951
MIRACLE IN SOHO, 1957
MIRACLE IN THE RAIN, 1956
MIRACLE KID, 1942
MIRACLE MAN, THE, 1932
MIRACLE OF OUR LADY OF FATIMA, THE, 1952
MIRACLE OF SANTA'S WHITE REINDEER, THE, 1963
MIRACLE OF THE BELLS, THE, 1948
MIRACLE OF THE HILLS, THE, 1959
MIRACLE ON MAIN STREET, A, 1940
MIRACLE WORKER, THE, 1962
MIRACLES DO HAPPEN, 1938
MIRACLES FOR SALE, 1939
MIRACULOUS JOURNEY, 1948
MIRANDA, 1949
MIRROR HAS TWO FACES, THE, 1959
MISBEHAVING HUSBANDS, 1941
MISBEHAVING LADIES, 1931
MISCHIEF, 1969
MISCHIEF, 1931
MISLEADING LADY, THE, 1932
MISS ANNIE ROONEY, 1942
MISS FANE'S BABY IS STOLEN, 1934
MISS GRANT TAKES RICHMOND, 1949
MISS LONDON LTD., 1943
MISS MINK OF 1949, 1949
MISS PACIFIC FLEET, 1935
MISS PILGRIM'S PROGRESS, 1950
MISS PINKERTON, 1932
MISS PRESIDENT, 1935
MISS ROBIN CRUSOE, 1954
MISS ROBIN HOOD, 1952
MISS SUSIE SLAGLE'S, 1945
MISS TATLOCK'S MILLIONS, 1948
MISS TULIP STAYS THE NIGHT, 1955
MISS V FROM MOSCOW, 1942
MISSILE FROM HELL, 1960
MISSILE TO THE MOON, 1959
MISSING, BELIEVED MARRIED, 1937
MISSING CORPSE, THE, 1945
MISSING DAUGHTERS, 1939
MISSING EVIDENCE, 1939
MISSING GIRLS, 1936
MISSING GUEST, THE, 1938
MISSING JUROR, THE, 1944
MISSING LADY, THE, 1946
MISSING MILLION, THE, 1942
MISSING PEOPLE, THE, 1940
MISSING REMBRANDT, THE, 1932
MISSING TEN DAYS, 1941
MISSING WITNESSES, 1937
MISSING WOMEN, 1951
MISSION BATANGAS, 1968
MISSION BLOODY MARY, 1967
MISSION GALACTICA: THE CYLON ATTACK, 1979
MISSION MARS, 1968
MISSION OVER KOREA, 1953
MISSION STARDUST, 1968
MISSION TO MOSCOW, 1943
MISSISSIPPI, 1935
MISSISSIPPI GAMBLER, 1929
MISSISSIPPI GAMBLER, 1942
MISSISSIPPI MERMAID, 1970
MISSISSIPPI RHYTHM, 1949
MISSOURI OUTLAW, A, 1942
MISSOURI TRAVELER, THE, 1958
MISSOURIANS, THE, 1950

MR. ACE, 1946
MR. AND MRS. NORTH, 1941
MR. AND MRS. SMITH, 1941
MISTER ANTONIO, 1929
MR. BELVEDERE RINGS THE BELL, 1951
MR. BELVEDERE GOES TO COLLEGE, 1949
MR. BIG, 1943
MR. BILLION, 1977
MR. BLANDINGS BUILDS HIS DREAM HOUSE, 1948
MR. BOGGS STEPS OUT, 1938
MR. BROWN COMES DOWN THE HILL, 1966
MR. CELEBRITY, 1942
MR. CHEDWORTH STEPS OUT, 1939
MR. CHUMP, 1938
MISTER CINDERELLA, 1936
MISTER CINDERS, 1934
MR. COHEN TAKES A WALK, 1936
MISTER CORY, 1957
MR. DEEDS GOES TO TOWN, 1936
MR. DENNING DRIVES NORTH, 1953
MR. DISTRICT ATTORNEY, 1941
MR. DISTRICT ATTORNEY, 1946
MR. DODD TAKES THE AIR, 1937
MR. DOODLE KICKS OFF, 1938
MR. DRAKE'S DUCK, 1951
MR. DYNAMITE, 1935
MR. DYNAMITE, 1941
MR. EMMANUEL, 1945
MISTER FREEDOM, 1970
MR. H.C. ANDERSEN, 1950
MR. HEX, 1946
MISTER HOBO, 1936
MR. IMPERIUM, 1951
MR. LEMON OF ORANGE, 1931
MR. LORD SAYS NO, 1952
MR. LOVE, 1986
MR. LUCKY, 1943
MISTER MOSES, 1965
MR. MOTO IN DANGER ISLAND, 1939
MR. MOTO TAKES A CHANCE, 1938
MR. MOTO TAKES A VACATION, 1938
MR. MOTO'S GAMBLE, 1938
MR. MOTO'S LAST WARNING, 1939
MR. MUGGS RIDES AGAIN, 1945
MR. MUGGS STEPS OUT, 1943
MR. MUSIC, 1950
MR. NORTH, 1988
MR. ORCHID, 1948
MR. PEEK-A-BOO, 1951
MR. PERRIN AND MR. TRAILL, 1948
MR. POTTS GOES TO MOSCOW, 1953
MR. QUILP, 1975
MR. QUINCEY OF MONTE CARLO, 1933
MR. RECKLESS, 1948
MISTER ROBERTS, 1955
MR. ROBINSON CRUSOE, 1932
MISTER ROCK AND ROLL, 1957
MR. SATAN, 1938
MR. SCOUTMASTER, 1953
MR. SKITCH, 1933
MR. SMITH CARRIES ON, 1937
MR. SOFT TOUCH, 1949
MR. STRINGFELLOW SAYS NO, 1937
MR. SYCAMORE, 1975
MISTER TEN PERCENT, 1967
MR. UNIVERSE, 1951
MR. WALKIE TALKIE, 1952
MR. WASHINGTON GOES TO TOWN, 1941
MR. WHAT'S-HIS-NAME, 1935
MR. WINKLE GOES TO WAR, 1944
MR. WISE GUY, 1942
MR. WONG, DETECTIVE, 1938
MR. WONG IN CHINATOWN, 1939
MISTRESS OF ATLANTIS, THE, 1932
MISTRESS OF THE WORLD, 1959
MIXED DOUBLES, 1933
M'LISS, 1936
MOB TOWN, 1941
MOBS INC, 1956
MOBY DICK, 1930
MODEL AND THE MARRIAGE BROKER, THE, 1951
MODEL FOR MURDER, 1960
MODEL MURDER CASE, THE, 1964
MODEL WIFE, 1941
MODERN HERO, A, 1934
MODERN LOVE, 1929

MODERN TIMES, 1936
MODESTY BLAISE, 1966
MODIGLIANI OF MONTPARNASSE, 1961
MOGAMBO, 1953
MOHAN JOSHI HAAZIR HO, 1984
MOHAWK, 1956
MOJAVE FIREBRAND, 1944
MOKEY, 1942
MOLE PEOPLE, THE, 1956
MOLLY AND LAWLESS JOHN, 1972
MOLLY AND ME, 1929
MOLLY AND ME, 1945
MOMENT OF INDISCRETION, 1958
MOMENT OF TRUTH, THE, 1965
MOMENT TO MOMENT, 1966
MONEY AND THE WOMAN, 1940
MONEY FOR NOTHING, 1932
MONEY FOR SPEED, 1933
MONEY FROM HOME, 1953
MONEY JUNGLE, THE, 1968
MONEY MAD, 1934
MONEY MADNESS, 1948
MONEY MEANS NOTHING, 1934
MONEY MEANS NOTHING, 1932
MONEY ON THE STREET, 1930
MONEY TALKS, 1933
MONEY TO BURN, 1940
MONEY, WOMEN AND GUNS, 1958
MONGOLS, THE, 1966
MONKEY BUSINESS, 1931
MONKEY BUSINESS, 1952
MONKEY GRIP, 1983
MONKEY IN WINTER, A, 1962
MONKEY'S PAW, THE, 1948
MONOLITH MONSTERS, THE, 1957
MONSEIGNEUR, 1950
MONSIEUR, 1964
MONSIEUR BEAUCAIRE, 1946
MONSIEUR VINCENT, 1949
MONSTER FROM THE GREEN HELL, 1958
MONSTER FROM THE OCEAN FLOOR, THE, 1954
MONSTER OF THE ISLAND, 1953
MONSTER THAT CHALLENGED THE WORLD, THE, 1957
MONSTER WALKS, THE, 1932
MONSTER WANGMAGWI, 1967
MONSTER ZERO, 1970
MONSTERS FROM THE UNKNOWN PLANET, 1975
MONTANA, 1950
MONTANA BELLE, 1952
MONTANA DESPERADO, 1951
MONTANA KID, THE, 1931
MONTANA MOON, 1930
MONTANA TERRITORY, 1952
MONTE CARLO BABY, 1953
MONTE CARLO NIGHTS, 1934
MONTE CARLO STORY, THE, 1957
MONTE CASSINO, 1948
MOON AND SIXPENCE, THE, 1942
MOON OVER BURMA, 1940
MOON OVER HER SHOULDER, 1941
MOON OVER MIAMI, 1941
MOON ZERO TWO, 1970
MOONFLEET, 1955
MOONLIGHT AND CACTUS, 1944
MOONLIGHT AND PRETZELS, 1933
MOONLIGHT IN HAVANA, 1942
MOONLIGHT IN HAWAII, 1941
MOONLIGHT IN VERMONT, 1943
MOONLIGHT MASQUERADE, 1942
MOONLIGHT MURDER, 1936
MOONLIGHT ON THE PRAIRIE, 1936
MOONLIGHT ON THE RANGE, 1937
MOONLIGHT SONATA, 1938
MOONLIGHTER, THE, 1953
MOONRAKER, THE, 1958
MOONRAKER, 1979
MOONRUNNERS, 1975
MOON'S OUR HOME, THE, 1936
MOONSHINE MOUNTAIN, 1964
MOONSTONE, THE, 1934
MOONTIDE, 1942
MOONWOLF, 1966
MORALIST, THE, 1964
MORALS FOR WOMEN, 1931
MORALS OF MARCUS, THE, 1936

MORE THAN A SECRETARY, 1936
MORE THE MERRIER, THE, 1943
MORGAN THE PIRATE, 1961
MORGAN'S MARAUDERS, 1929
MORNING STAR, 1962
MORTAL STORM, THE, 1940
MOSCOW—CASSIOPEIA, 1974
MOSCOW DOES NOT BELIEVE IN TEARS, 1980
MOSCOW SHANGHAI, 1936
MOSES, 1976
MOSQUITO SQUADRON, 1970
MOSS ROSE, 1947
MOST DANGEROUS MAN ALIVE, THE, 1961
MOST IMMORAL LADY, A, 1929
MOST PRECIOUS THING IN LIFE, 1934
MOST WANTED MAN, THE, 1962
MOST WONDERFUL EVENING OF MY LIFE, THE, 1972
MOTH, THE, 1934
MOTHER AND DAUGHTER, 1965
MOTHER AND SON, 1931
MOTHER CAREY'S CHICKENS, 1938
MOTHER DIDN'T TELL ME, 1950
MOTHER GOOSE A GO-GO, 1966
MOTHER IS A FRESHMAN, 1949
MOTHER KNOWS BEST, 1928
MOTHER WORE TIGHTS, 1947
MOTHER'S BOY, 1929
MOTHERS CRY, 1930
MOTHRA, 1962
MOTIVE FOR REVENGE, 1935
MOTOR MADNESS, 1937
MOTOR PATROL, 1950
MOULIN ROUGE, 1934
MOULIN ROUGE, 1944
MOUNTAIN, THE, 1935
MOUNTAIN, THE, 1956
MOUNTAIN FAMILY ROBINSON, 1979
MOUNTAIN JUSTICE, 1930
MOUNTAIN JUSTICE, 1937
MOUNTAIN MOONLIGHT, 1941
MOUNTAIN MUSIC, 1937
MOUNTAIN RHYTHM, 1939
MOUNTAIN ROAD, THE, 1960
MOUNTAINS O'MOURNE, 1938
MOUNTED FURY, 1931
MOUNTED STRANGER, THE, 1930
MOUSE AND HIS CHILD, THE, 1977
MOUTHPIECE, THE, 1932
MOVE OVER, DARLING, 1963
MOVIE CRAZY, 1932
MOVIE STUNTMEN, 1953
MOVING VIOLATIONS, 1985
MOZAMBIQUE, 1966
MOZART, 1940
MOZART STORY, THE, 1948
MRS. BROWN, YOU'VE GOT A LOVELY DAUGHTER, 1968
MRS. DANE'S DEFENCE, 1933
MRS. FITZHERBERT, 1950
MRS. GIBBONS' BOYS, 1962
MRS. MIKE, 1949
MRS. MINIVER, 1942
MRS. O'MALLEY AND MR. MALONE, 1950
MRS. PARKINGTON, 1944
MRS. POLLIFAX-SPY, 1971
MRS. PYM OF SCOTLAND YARD, 1939
MRS. WARREN'S PROFESSION, 1960
MRS. WIGGS OF THE CABBAGE PATCH, 1934
MUCH TOO SHY, 1942
MUDDY RIVER, 1982
MUDLARK, THE, 1950
MUG TOWN, 1943
MUGGER, THE, 1958
MULE TRAIN, 1950
MUMMY'S BOYS, 1936
MUMMY'S CURSE, THE, 1944
MUMMY'S GHOST, THE, 1944
MUMU, 1961
MUNSTER, GO HOME, 1966
MURDER, 1930
MURDER AHOY, 1964
MURDER AMONG FRIENDS, 1941
MURDER AT COVENT GARDEN, 1932
MURDER AT DAWN, 1932
MURDER AT 45 R.P.M., 1965

MURDER AT GLEN ATHOL, 1936
MURDER AT MIDNIGHT, 1931
MURDER AT MONTE CARLO, 1935
MURDER AT SITE THREE, 1959
MURDER AT THE BASKERVILLES, 1941
MURDER AT THE CABARET, 1936
MURDER AT THE GALLOP, 1963
MURDER AT THE INN, 1934
MURDER AT THE VANITIES, 1934
MURDER AT 3 A.M., 1953
MURDER BY AN ARISTOCRAT, 1936
MURDER BY INVITATION, 1941
MURDER BY ROPE, 1936
MURDER BY TELEVISION, 1935
MURDER CAN BE DEADLY, 1963
MURDER CZECH STYLE, 1968
MURDER GAME, THE, 1966
MURDER GOES TO COLLEGE, 1937
MURDER, HE SAYS, 1945
MURDER IN EDEN, 1962
MURDER IN GREENWICH VILLAGE, 1937
MURDER IN REVERSE, 1946
MURDER IN THE AIR, 1940
MURDER IN THE BIG HOUSE, 1942
MURDER IN THE BLUE ROOM, 1944
MURDER IN THE CATHEDRAL, 1952
MURDER IN THE CLOUDS, 1934
MURDER IN THE FAMILY, 1938
MURDER IN THE FAMILY, 1938
MURDER IN THE PRIVATE CAR, 1934
MURDER MOST FOUL, 1964
MURDER ON A HONEYMOON, 1935
MURDER ON THE BLACKBOARD, 1934
MURDER ON THE CAMPUS, 1934
MURDER ON THE CAMPUS, 1963
MURDER ON THE ROOF, 1930
MURDER ON THE SECOND FLOOR, 1932
MURDER ON THE SET, 1936
MURDER ON THE WATERFRONT, 1943
MURDER ON THE YUKON, 1940
MURDER OVER NEW YORK, 1940
MURDER REPORTED, 1958
MURDER TOMORROW, 1938
MURDER WILL OUT, 1930
MURDER WILL OUT, 1939
MURDER WILL OUT, 1953
MURDER WITH PICTURES, 1936
MURDER WITHOUT CRIME, 1951
MURDER WITHOUT TEARS, 1953
MURDERER LIVES AT NUMBER 21, THE, 1947
MURIEL, 1963
MUSEUM MYSTERY, 1937
MUSIC FOR MADAME, 1937
MUSIC GOES 'ROUND, THE, 1936
MUSIC HALL, 1934
MUSIC HALL PARADE, 1939
MUSIC HATH CHARMS, 1935
MUSIC IN MANHATTAN, 1944
MUSIC IN MY HEART, 1940
MUSIC IN THE AIR, 1934
MUSIC IS MAGIC, 1935
MUSIC MAKER, THE, 1936
MUSIC ROOM, THE, 1963
MUSICAL MUTINY, 1970
MUSS 'EM UP, 1936
MUSTANG, 1959
MUSTANG COUNTRY, 1976
MUTINEERS, THE, 1949
MUTINY, 1952
MUTINY AHEAD, 1935
MUTINY IN OUTER SPACE, 1965
MUTINY IN THE ARCTIC, 1941
MUTINY IN THE BIG HOUSE, 1939
MUTINY OF THE ELSINORE, THE, 1939
MUTINY ON THE BLACKHAWK, 1939
MUTINY ON THE BOUNTY, 1935
MY AIN FOLK, 1944
MY AIN FOLK, 1974
MY AMERICAN WIFE, 1936
MY BABY IS BLACK!, 1965
MY BEST GAL, 1944
MY BILL, 1938
MY BLUE HEAVEN, 1950
MY BODYGUARD, 1980
MY BOYS ARE GOOD BOYS, 1978
MY BROTHER JONATHAN, 1949

MY BROTHER, THE OUTLAW, 1951
MY BROTHER'S KEEPER, 1949
MY BROTHER'S WEDDING, 1983
MY BUDDY, 1944
MY CHILDHOOD, 1972
MY COUSIN RACHEL, 1952
MY DARK LADY, 1987
MY DARLING CLEMENTINE, 1946
MY DEAR MISS ALDRICH, 1937
MY DREAM IS YOURS, 1949
MY FATHER'S HOUSE, 1947
MY FAVORITE BLONDE, 1942
MY FAVORITE BRUNETTE, 1947
MY FAVORITE SPY, 1942
MY FAVORITE SPY, 1951
MY FAVORITE WIFE, 1940
MY FRIEND IRMA, 1949
MY FRIEND IRMA GOES WEST, 1950
MY FRIEND THE KING, 1931
MY GAL LOVES MUSIC, 1944
MY GAL SAL, 1942
MY GEISHA, 1962
MY GIRL TISA, 1948
MY HANDS ARE CLAY, 1948
MY HEART BELONGS TO DADDY, 1942
MY HEART GOES CRAZY, 1953
MY HEART IS CALLING, 1935
MY HOBO, 1963
MY KIND OF TOWN, 1984
MY KINGDOM FOR A COOK, 1943
MY LEARNED FRIEND, 1943
MY LIFE TO LIVE, 1963
MY LIPS BETRAY, 1933
MY LITTLE CHICKADEE, 1940
MY LOVE CAME BACK, 1940
MY LUCKY STAR, 1933
MY LUCKY STAR, 1938
MY MAN, 1928
MY MAN AND I, 1952
MY MAN GODFREY, 1936
MY MAN GODFREY, 1957
MY MARRIAGE, 1936
MY MOTHER, 1933
MY NAME IS JULIA ROSS, 1945
MY NIGHT AT MAUD'S, 1970
MY OLD DUCHESS, 1933
MY OLD DUTCH, 1934
MY OLD KENTUCKY HOME, 1938
MY OWN TRUE LOVE, 1948
MY PAL GUS, 1952
MY PAL, THE KING, 1932
MY PAL, WOLF, 1944
MY PAST, 1931
MY SEVEN LITTLE SINS, 1956
MY SON IS A CRIMINAL, 1939
MY SON, MY SON!, 1940
MY SON, THE HERO, 1943
MY SON, THE HERO, 1963
MY SON, THE VAMPIRE, 1963
MY SONG FOR YOU, 1935
MY SONG GOES ROUND THE WORLD, 1934
MY SWEET LITTLE VILLAGE, 1985
MY THIRD WIFE GEORGE, 1968
MY TRUE STORY, 1951
MY WAY, 1974
MY WIFE'S BEST FRIEND, 1952
MY WIFE'S ENEMY, 1967
MY WIFE'S FAMILY, 1932
MY WIFE'S FAMILY, 1941
MY WIFE'S FAMILY, 1962
MY WIFE'S HUSBAND, 1965
MY WIFE'S LODGER, 1952
MY WILD IRISH ROSE, 1947
MY WOMAN, 1933
MYRT AND MARGE, 1934
MYSTERIANS, THE, 1959
MYSTERIOUS AVENGER, THE, 1936
MYSTERIOUS DESPERADO, THE, 1949
MYSTERIOUS DR. FU MANCHU, THE, 1929
MYSTERIOUS HOUSE OF DR. C., THE, 1976
MYSTERIOUS INTRUDER, 1946
MYSTERIOUS ISLAND, 1929
MYSTERIOUS ISLAND, 1941
MYSTERIOUS MISS X, THE, 1939
MYSTERIOUS MR. DAVIS, THE, 1936
MYSTERIOUS MR. MOTO, 1938

MYSTERIOUS MR. NICHOLSON, THE, 1947
MYSTERIOUS MR. VALENTINE, THE, 1946
MYSTERIOUS RIDER, THE, 1933
MYSTERIOUS RIDER, THE, 1938
MYSTERIOUS RIDER, THE, 1942
MYSTERIOUS SATELLITE, THE, 1956
MYSTERY AT THE BURLESQUE, 1950
MYSTERY AT THE VILLA ROSE, 1930
MYSTERY MAN, 1944
MYSTERY BROADCAST, 1943
MYSTERY HOUSE, 1938
MYSTERY IN MEXICO, 1948
MYSTERY JUNCTION, 1951
MYSTERY LAKE, 1953
MYSTERY LINER, 1934
MYSTERY MAN, THE, 1935
MYSTERY OF MARIE ROGET, THE, 1942
MYSTERY OF MR. WONG, THE, 1939
MYSTERY OF ROOM 13, 1941
MYSTERY OF THE BLACK JUNGLE, 1955
MYSTERY OF THE GOLDEN EYE, THE, 1948
MYSTERY OF THE HOODED HORSEMEN, THE, 1937
MYSTERY OF THE 13TH GUEST, THE, 1943
MYSTERY OF THE WHITE ROOM, 1939
MYSTERY OF THUG ISLAND, THE, 1966
MYSTERY ON BIRD ISLAND, 1954
MYSTERY PLANE, 1939
MYSTERY RANCH, 1932
MYSTERY RANGE, 1937
MYSTERY SEA RAIDER, 1940
MYSTERY SHIP, 1941
MYSTERY SUBMARINE, 1950
MYSTERY SUBMARINE, 1963
MYSTERY TRAIN, 1931
MYSTERY WOMAN, 1935
MYSTIC CIRCLE MURDER, 1939
MYSTIC HOUR, THE, 1934
N. P., 1971
NABONGA, 1944
NADA GANG, THE, 1974
NADA MAS QUE UNA MUJER, 1934
NAGANA, 1933
NAKED ALIBI, 1954
NAKED AUTUMN, 1963
NAKED BRIGADE, THE, 1965
NAKED DAWN, THE, 1955
NAKED EARTH, THE, 1958
NAKED GENERAL, THE, 1964
NAKED GUN, THE, 1956
NAKED HEART, THE, 1955
NAKED HEARTS, 1970
NAKED HILLS, THE, 1956
NAKED MAJA, THE, 1959
NAKED PARADISE, 1957
NAKED WOMAN, THE, 1950
NAME THE WOMAN, 1934
NAMU, THE KILLER WHALE, 1966
NANCY GOES TO RIO, 1950
NANCY STEELE IS MISSING, 1937
NAPOLEON, 1955
NARROW MARGIN, THE, 1952
NASHVILLE REBEL, 1966
NASTY RABBIT, THE, 1964
NATHALIE, 1958
NATHALIE, AGENT SECRET, 1960
NATION AFLAME, 1937
NATIONAL BARN DANCE, 1944
NATIVE LAND, 1942
NAUGHTY BUT NICE, 1939
NAUGHTY CINDERELLA, 1933
NAUGHTY FLIRT, THE, 1931
NAUGHTY MARIETTA, 1935
NAVAJO, 1952
NAVAJO KID, THE, 1946
NAVAJO TRAIL RAIDERS, 1949
NAVAJO TRAIL, THE, 1945
NAVAL ACADEMY, 1941
NAVY BLUE AND GOLD, 1937
NAVY BLUES, 1930
NAVY BLUES, 1937
NAVY BLUES, 1941
NAVY BORN, 1936
NAVY BOUND, 1951
NAVY HEROES, 1959
NAVY LARK, THE, 1959
NAVY SECRETS, 1939

NAVY SPY, 1937
NAVY WAY, THE, 1944
NAVY WIFE, 1936
NAVY WIFE, 1956
NAZARIN, 1968
'NEATH BROOKLYN BRIDGE, 1942
'NEATH THE ARIZONA SKIES, 1934
NEBRASKAN, THE, 1953
NECK AND NECK, 1931
NEIGHBORS' WIVES, 1933
NEITHER BY DAY NOR BY NIGHT, 1972
NEITHER THE SEA NOR THE SAND, 1974
NELLY'S VERSION, 1983
NEON PALACE, THE, 1970
NEPTUNE FACTOR, THE, 1973
NEPTUNE'S DAUGHTER, 1949
NEST, THE, 1982
NEUTRAL PORT, 1941
NEUTRON CONTRA EL DR. CARONTE, 1962
NEUTRON EL ENMASCARADO NEGRO, 1962
NEVADA, 1936
NEVADA, 1944
NEVADA BADMEN, 1951
NEVADA CITY, 1941
NEVADAN, THE, 1950
NEVER A DULL MOMENT, 1943
NEVER A DULL MOMENT, 1950
NEVER A DULL MOMENT, 1968
NEVER BACK LOSERS, 1967
NEVER FEAR, 1950
NEVER GIVE A SUCKER AN EVEN BREAK, 1941
NEVER LET ME GO, 1953
NEVER LOOK BACK, 1952
NEVER LOVE A STRANGER, 1958
NEVER MENTION MURDER, 1964
NEVER NEVER LAND, 1982
NEVER PUT IT IN WRITING, 1964
NEVER SAY DIE, 1939
NEVER SAY GOODBYE, 1946
NEVER SAY GOODBYE, 1956
NEVER SAY NEVER AGAIN, 1983
NEVER TAKE NO FOR AN ANSWER, 1952
NEVER THE TWAIN SHALL MEET, 1931
NEVER TOO LATE, 1965
NEVER TROUBLE TROUBLE, 1931
NEVER TRUST A GAMBLER, 1951
NEVER WAVE AT A WAC, 1952
NEW ADVENTURES OF GET-RICH-QUICK
    WALLINGFORD, THE, 1931
**NEW ADVENTURES OF PIPPI LONGSTOCKING,
    THE, 1988**
NEW ADVENTURES OF TARZAN, 1935
NEW EARTH, THE, 1937
NEW FACES, 1954
NEW FACES OF 1937, 1937
NEW FRONTIER, THE, 1935
NEW FRONTIER, 1939
NEW HORIZONS, 1940
NEW LAND, THE, 1973
NEW MEXICO, 1951
NEW MOON, 1930
NEW MOON, 1940
NEW MORALS FOR OLD, 1932
NEW ORLEANS, 1929
NEW ORLEANS, 1947
NEW ORLEANS UNCENSORED, 1955
NEW TEACHER, THE, 1941
NEW WINE, 1941
NEW YORK NIGHTS, 1929
NEW YORK TOWN, 1941
NEWMAN'S LAW, 1974
NEWS HOUNDS, 1947
NEWS IS MADE AT NIGHT, 1939
NEWSBOY'S HOME, 1939
NEXT OF KIN, 1942
NEXT TIME I MARRY, 1938
NEXT TIME WE LOVE, 1936
NEXT TO NO TIME, 1960
NGATI, 1987
NICE GIRL?, 1941
NICE LITTLE BANK THAT SHOULD BE ROBBED, A,
    1958
NICE WOMAN, 1932
NICHOLAS NICKLEBY, 1947
NICK CARTER, MASTER DETECTIVE, 1939
NICKEL QUEEN, THE, 1971

NIGHT AFFAIR, 1961
NIGHT ALARM, 1935
NIGHT ALONE, 1938
NIGHT AMBUSH, 1958
NIGHT AND DAY, 1933
NIGHT AND DAY, 1946
NIGHT ANGEL, THE, 1931
NIGHT AT EARL CARROLL'S, A, 1940
NIGHT AT THE OPERA, A, 1935
NIGHT AT THE RITZ, A, 1935
NIGHT BEAT, 1932
NIGHT BEAT, 1948
NIGHT BEFORE CHRISTMAS, A, 1963
NIGHT BEFORE THE DIVORCE, THE, 1942
NIGHT BIRDS, 1931
NIGHT BOAT TO DUBLIN, 1946
NIGHT CARGO, 1936
NIGHT CLUB GIRL, 1944
NIGHT CLUB LADY, 1932
NIGHT CLUB QUEEN, 1934
NIGHT CLUB SCANDAL, 1937
NIGHT COURT, 1932
NIGHT CREATURE, 1979
NIGHT CREATURES, 1962
NIGHT EDITOR, 1946
NIGHT ENCOUNTER, 1963
NIGHT FIGHTERS, THE, 1960
NIGHT FLIGHT, 1933
NIGHT FOR CRIME, A, 1942
NIGHT FREIGHT, 1955
NIGHT IN BANGKOK, 1966
NIGHT IN CASABLANCA, A, 1946
NIGHT IN HONG KONG, A, 1961
NIGHT IN JUNE, A, 1940
NIGHT IN MONTMARTE, A, 1931
NIGHT IN NEW ORLEANS, A, 1942
NIGHT IN PARADISE, A, 1946
NIGHT INTO MORNING, 1951
NIGHT IS MY FUTURE, 1962
NIGHT IS OURS, 1930
NIGHT IS YOUNG, THE, 1935
NIGHT JOURNEY, 1938
NIGHT KEY, 1937
NIGHT LIFE IN RENO, 1931
NIGHT LIFE OF THE GODS, 1935
NIGHT LIKE THIS, A, 1932
NIGHT MAYOR, THE, 1932
NIGHT MONSTER, 1942
NIGHT OF ADVENTURE, A, 1944
NIGHT OF JANUARY 16TH, 1941
NIGHT OF JUNE 13, 1932
NIGHT OF MAGIC, A, 1944
NIGHT OF MYSTERY, 1937
NIGHT OF NIGHTS, THE, 1939
NIGHT OF TERROR, 1933
NIGHT OF THE BLOOD BEAST, 1958
NIGHT OF THE GARTER, 1933
NIGHT OF THE GRIZZLY, THE, 1966
NIGHT OF THE PARTY, THE, 1934
NIGHT PARADE, 1929
NIGHT PASSAGE, 1957
NIGHT PEOPLE, 1954
NIGHT PLANE FROM CHUNGKING, 1942
NIGHT RAIDERS, 1952
NIGHT RIDE, 1930
NIGHT RIDER, THE, 1932
NIGHT RIDERS, THE, 1939
NIGHT RIDERS OF MONTANA, 1951
NIGHT RUNNER, THE, 1957
NIGHT SONG, 1947
NIGHT SPOT, 1938
NIGHT STAGE TO GALVESTON, 1952
NIGHT THE WORLD EXPLODED, THE, 1957
NIGHT TIME IN NEVADA, 1948
NIGHT TO REMEMBER, A, 1942
NIGHT TO REMEMBER, A, 1958
NIGHT TRAIN, 1940
NIGHT TRAIN TO MEMPHIS, 1946
NIGHT TRAIN TO MUNDO FINE, 1966
NIGHT TRAIN TO PARIS, 1964
NIGHT UNTO NIGHT, 1949
NIGHT WAITRESS, 1936
NIGHT WATCH, THE, 1964
NIGHT WIND, 1948
NIGHT WITHOUT STARS, 1953
NIGHT WORK, 1930

BOLD: Films on Videocassette

NIGHT WORK, 1939
NIGHT WORLD, 1932
NIGHTFALL, 1956
NIGHTS OF LUCRETIA BORGIA, THE, 1960
NIGHT HAWK, THE, 1938
NINE FORTY-FIVE, 1934
NINE LIVES ARE NOT ENOUGH, 1941
NINE MEN, 1943
NINE TILL SIX, 1932
99 WOUNDS, 1931
NINOTCHKA, 1939
NINTH GUEST, THE, 1934
NINTH HEART, THE, 1980
NITWITS, THE, 1935
NIX ON DAMES, 1929
NO DEFENSE, 1929
NO DRUMS, NO BUGLES, 1971
NO EXIT, 1930
NO FUNNY BUSINESS, 1934
NO GREATER GLORY, 1934
NO GREATER LOVE, 1932
NO GREATER SIN, 1941
NO HANDS ON THE CLOCK, 1941
NO HAUNT FOR A GENTLEMAN, 1952
NO HIGHWAY IN THE SKY, 1951
NO HOLDS BARRED, 1952
NO LADY, 1931
NO LEAVE, NO LOVE, 1946
NO LIMIT, 1931
NO LIMIT, 1935
NO LIVING WITNESS, 1932
NO MAN OF HER OWN, 1933
NO MAN OF HER OWN, 1950
NO MAN'S RANGE, 1935
NO MARRIAGE TIES, 1933
NO MINOR VICES, 1948
NO MONKEY BUSINESS, 1935
NO MORE ORCHIDS, 1933
NO MORE WOMEN, 1934
NO, MY DARLING DAUGHTER, 1964
NO NAME ON THE BULLET, 1959
NO, NO NANETTE, 1930
NO, NO NANETTE, 1940
NO ONE MAN, 1932
NO OTHER WOMAN, 1933
NO PARKING, 1938
NO PLACE FOR A LADY, 1943
NO PLACE FOR JENNIFER, 1950
NO PLACE TO GO, 1939
NO PLACE TO HIDE, 1956
NO QUESTIONS ASKED, 1951
NO RANSOM, 1935
NO RESTING PLACE, 1952
NO RETURN ADDRESS, 1961
NO ROAD BACK, 1957
NO ROOM AT THE INN, 1950
NO ROOM FOR THE GROOM, 1952
NO SMOKING, 1955
NO TIME FOR COMEDY, 1940
NO TIME FOR FLOWERS, 1952
NO TIME FOR LOVE, 1943
NO TIME FOR SERGEANTS, 1958
NO TIME FOR TEARS, 1957
NO TIME TO MARRY, 1938
NO TRACE, 1950
NO TREE IN THE STREET, 1964
NO WAY OUT, 1950
NOB HILL, 1945
NOBODY IN TOYLAND, 1958
NOBODY LIVES FOREVER, 1946
NOBODY'S BABY, 1937
NOBODY'S DARLING, 1943
NOBODY'S FOOL, 1936
NOBODY'S PERFECT, 1968
NOISY NEIGHBORS, 1929
NON-STOP NEW YORK, 1937
NONE BUT THE LONELY HEART, 1944
NONE SHALL ESCAPE, 1944
NOOSE FOR A GUNMAN, 1960
NOOSE FOR A LADY, 1953
NORA PRENTISS, 1947
NORAH O'NEALE, 1934
NORMAN CONQUEST, 1953
NORTH AVENUE IRREGULARS, THE, 1979
NORTH BY NORTHWEST, 1959
NORTH FROM LONE STAR, 1941

NORTH OF NOME, 1937
NORTH OF SHANGHAI, 1939
NORTH OF THE GREAT DIVIDE, 1950
NORTH OF THE RIO GRANDE, 1937
NORTH OF THE YUKON, 1939
NORTH SEA PATROL, 1939
NORTH TO ALASKA, 1960
NORTH TO THE KLONDIKE, 1942
NORTHERN FRONTIER, 1935
NORTHERN LIGHTS, 1978
NORTHERN PATROL, 1953
NORTHERN PURSUIT, 1943
NORTHWEST MOUNTED POLICE, 1940
NORTHWEST OUTPOST, 1947
NORTHWEST RANGERS, 1942
NORTHWEST STAMPEDE, 1948
NORTHWEST TERRITORY, 1952
NORTHWEST TRAIL, 1945
NORWOOD, 1970
NOT A HOPE IN HELL, 1960
NOT MINE TO LOVE, 1969
NOT OF THIS EARTH, 1957
NOT QUITE DECENT, 1929
NOT SO DUMB, 1930
NOT SO DUSTY, 1936
NOT SO DUSTY, 1956
NOT SO QUIET ON THE WESTERN FRONT, 1930
NOT WANTED, 1949
NOT WANTED ON VOYAGE, 1957
NOT WITH MY WIFE, YOU DON'T!, 1966
NOTHING BARRED, 1961
NOTHING BUT A MAN, 1964
NOTHING BUT THE NIGHT, 1975
NOTHING BUT THE TRUTH, 1929
NOTHING BUT THE TRUTH, 1941
NOTHING LIKE PUBLICITY, 1936
NOTHING SACRED, 1937
NOTORIOUS, 1946
NOTORIOUS AFFAIR, A, 1930
NOTORIOUS BUT NICE, 1934
NOTORIOUS GENTLEMAN, A, 1935
NOTORIOUS LONE WOLF, THE, 1946
NOTORIOUS SOPHIE LANG, THE, 1934
NOUS IRONS A PARIS, 1949
NOVEL AFFAIR, A, 1957
NOW AND FOREVER, 1934
NOW AND FOREVER, 1956
NOW BARABBAS WAS A ROBBER, 1949
NOW THAT APRIL'S HERE, 1958
NOWHERE TO GO, 1959
NUDE BOMB, THE, 1980
NUDE IN HIS POCKET, 1962
NUDE ODYSSEY, 1962
NUISANCE, THE, 1933
NUMBER SEVENTEEN, 1928
NUMBER SEVENTEEN, 1932
NUMBER SIX, 1962
NUMBERED MEN, 1930
NUN AND THE SERGEANT, THE, 1962
NUN AT THE CROSSROADS, A, 1970
NUN'S STORY, THE, 1959
NUREMBERG, 1961
NURSE EDITH CAVELL, 1939
NURSE FROM BROOKLYN, 1938
NURSEMAID WHO DISAPPEARED, THE, 1939
NURSE'S SECRET, THE, 1941
NUT FARM, THE, 1935
NUTTY PROFESSOR, THE, 1963
O, MY DARLING CLEMENTINE, 1943
OBEY THE LAW, 1933
OBLIGING YOUNG LADY, 1941
OCEAN BREAKERS, 1949
OCEAN'S ELEVEN, 1960
OCTOBER MAN, THE, 1948
ODD COUPLE, THE, 1968
ODONGO, 1956
OEDIPUS REX, 1957
OF HUMAN HEARTS, 1938
OFF LIMITS, 1953
OFF THE DOLE, 1935
OFF THE RECORD, 1939
OFF TO THE RACES, 1937
OFFBEAT, 1961
OFFICE GIRL, THE, 1932
OFFICE SCANDAL, THE, 1929
OFFICE WIFE, THE, 1930

OFFICER AND THE LADY, THE, 1941
OFFICER O'BRIEN, 1930
OFFICER 13, 1933
OFFICER'S MESS, THE, 1931
OH BOY!, 1938
OH DADDY!, 1935
OH DOCTOR, 1937
OH, FOR A MAN!, 1930
OH, HEAVENLY DOG!, 1980
OH JOHNNY, HOW YOU CAN LOVE!, 1940
OH, MR. PORTER!, 1937
OH NO DOCTOR!, 1934
OH ROSALINDA, 1956
OH, SUSANNA, 1937
OH! SUSANNA, 1951
OH, WHAT A NIGHT, 1935
OH, WHAT A NIGHT, 1944
OH, YEAH!, 1929
OH, YOU BEAUTIFUL DOLL, 1949
OHAYO, 1962
OIL FOR THE LAMPS OF CHINA, 1935
OKAY AMERICA, 1932
OKAY FOR SOUND, 1937
OKINAWA, 1952
OKLAHOMA ANNIE, 1952
OKLAHOMA BADLANDS, 1948
OKLAHOMA BLUES, 1948
OKLAHOMA CYCLONE, 1930
OKLAHOMA FRONTIER, 1939
OKLAHOMA JIM, 1931
OKLAHOMA JUSTICE, 1951
OKLAHOMA KID, THE, 1939
OKLAHOMA RAIDERS, 1944
OKLAHOMA RENEGADES, 1940
OKLAHOMA TERRITORY, 1960
OKLAHOMA TERROR, 1939
OKLAHOMAN, THE, 1957
OLD BARN DANCE, THE, 1938
OLD BILL AND SON, 1940
OLD BONES OF THE RIVER, 1938
OLD CHISHOLM TRAIL, 1943
OLD CORRAL, THE, 1937
OLD CURIOSITY SHOP, THE, 1935
OLD DARK HOUSE, THE, 1932
OLD DARK HOUSE, THE, 1963
OLD ENGLISH, 1930
OLD FAITHFUL, 1935
OLD-FASHIONED GIRL, AN, 1948
OLD-FASHIONED WAY, THE, 1934
OLD FRONTIER, THE, 1950
OLD HOMESTEAD, THE, 1935
OLD HOMESTEAD, THE, 1942
OLD HUTCH, 1936
OLD IRON, 1938
OLD LOS ANGELES, 1948
OLD LOUISIANA, 1938
OLD MAC, 1961
OLD MAN, THE, 1932
OLD MAN AND THE SEA, THE, 1958
OLD MAN RHYTHM, 1935
OLD MOTHER RILEY, 1937
OLD MOTHER RILEY, 1952
OLD MOTHER RILEY AT HOME, 1945
OLD MOTHER RILEY, DETECTIVE, 1943
OLD MOTHER RILEY, HEADMISTRESS, 1950
OLD MOTHER RILEY IN BUSINESS, 1940
OLD MOTHER RILEY IN PARIS, 1938
OLD MOTHER RILEY IN SOCIETY, 1940
OLD MOTHER RILEY JOINS UP, 1939
OLD MOTHER RILEY MP, 1939
OLD MOTHER RILEY OVERSEAS, 1943
OLD MOTHER RILEY'S CIRCUS, 1941
OLD MOTHER RILEY'S GHOSTS, 1941
OLD MOTHER RILEY'S JUNGLE TREASURE, 1951
OLD OKLAHOMA PLAINS, 1952
OLD OVERLAND TRAIL, 1953
OLD ROSES, 1935
OLD SHATTERHAND, 1968
OLD SOLDIERS NEVER DIE, 1931
OLD SPANISH CUSTOM, AN, 1936
OLD SPANISH CUSTOMERS, 1932
OLD SWIMMIN' HOLE, THE, 1941
OLD TEXAS TRAIL, THE, 1944
OLD WEST, THE, 1952
OLD WYOMING TRAIL, THE, 1937
OLD YELLER, 1957

OLIVE TREES OF JUSTICE, THE, 1967
OLIVER TWIST, 1933
OLLY, OLLY, OXEN FREE, 1978
OLSEN'S BIG MOMENT, 1934
OMAHA TRAIL, THE, 1942
O'MALLEY OF THE MOUNTED, 1936
OMAR KHAYYAM, 1957
OMICRON, 1963
OMOO OMOO, THE SHARK GOD, 1949
ON AGAIN—OFF AGAIN, 1937
ON AN ISLAND WITH YOU, 1948
ON APPROVAL, 1930
ON APPROVAL, 1944
ON BORROWED TIME, 1939
ON HIS OWN, 1939
ON OUR MERRY WAY, 1948
ON OUR SELECTION, 1930
ON PROBATION, 1935
ON STAGE EVERYBODY, 1945
ON SUCH A NIGHT, 1937
ON THE AIR, 1934
ON THE BEAT, 1962
ON THE COMET, 1970
ON THE DOUBLE, 1961
ON THE GREAT WHITE TRAIL, 1938
ON THE ISLE OF SAMOA, 1950
ON THE LEVEL, 1930
ON THE LOOSE, 1951
ON THE OLD SPANISH TRAIL, 1947
ON THE RIVIERA, 1951
ON THE RUN, 1958
ON THE RUN, 1967
ON THE RUN, 1969
ON THE SPOT, 1940
ON THE SUNNYSIDE, 1936
ON THE THRESHOLD OF SPACE, 1956
ON THE TOWN, 1949
ON THEIR OWN, 1940
ON THIN ICE, 1933
ON TOP OF OLD SMOKY, 1953
ON TRIAL, 1928
ON TRIAL, 1939
ON VELVET, 1938
ON WITH THE SHOW, 1929
ON YOUR BACK, 1930
ON YOUR TOES, 1939
ONCE A CROOK, 1941
ONCE A DOCTOR, 1937
ONCE A GENTLEMAN, 1930
ONCE A LADY, 1931
ONCE A RAINY DAY, 1968
ONCE A SINNER, 1931
ONCE A SINNER, 1952
ONCE A THIEF, 1935
ONCE A THIEF, 1950
ONCE IN A BLUE MOON, 1936
ONCE IN A LIFETIME, 1932
ONCE IN A NEW MOON, 1935
ONCE MORE, MY DARLING, 1949
ONCE TO EVERY BACHELOR, 1934
ONCE TO EVERY WOMAN, 1934
ONCE UPON A COFFEE HOUSE, 1965
ONCE UPON A DREAM, 1949
ONCE UPON A HONEYMOON, 1942
ONCE UPON A HORSE, 1958
ONCE UPON A SCOUNDREL, 1973
ONCE UPON A TIME, 1944
ONE APRIL 2000, 1952
ONE BIG AFFAIR, 1952
ONE BODY TOO MANY, 1944
ONE BRIEF SUMMER, 1971
ONE CROWDED NIGHT, 1940
ONE DANGEROUS NIGHT, 1943
ONE DARK NIGHT, 1939
ONE DAY IN THE LIFE OF IVAN DENISOVICH, 1971
ONE EMBARRASSING NIGHT, 1930
ONE EXCITING ADVENTURE, 1935
ONE EXCITING NIGHT, 1945
ONE EXCITING WEEK, 1946
ONE FAMILY, 1930
ONE FOOT IN HELL, 1960
ONE FRIGHTENED NIGHT, 1935
ONE GOOD TURN, 1936
ONE GOOD TURN, 1955
ONE HEAVENLY NIGHT, 1931
ONE HOUR LATE, 1935

ONE HOUR TO LIVE, 1939
ONE HYSTERICAL NIGHT, 1930
ONE IN A MILLION, 1935
ONE IS GUILTY, 1934
ONE JUMP AHEAD, 1955
ONE JUST MAN, 1955
ONE LAST FLING, 1949
ONE MAD KISS, 1930
ONE MAN JUSTICE, 1937
ONE-MAN LAW, 1932
ONE MAN'S JOURNEY, 1933
ONE MAN'S LAW, 1940
ONE MILE FROM HEAVEN, 1937
$1,000,000 RACKET, 1937
ONE MILLION DOLLARS, 1965
ONE MILLION YEARS B.C., 1967
ONE MINUTE TO ZERO, 1952
ONE MORE RIVER, 1934
ONE MORE SPRING, 1935
ONE MORE TIME, 1970
ONE MORE TOMORROW, 1946
ONE MORE TRAIN TO ROB, 1971
ONE MYSTERIOUS NIGHT, 1944
ONE NEW YORK NIGHT, 1935
ONE NIGHT AT SUSIE'S, 1930
ONE NIGHT IN LISBON, 1941
ONE NIGHT IN PARIS, 1940
ONE NIGHT IN THE TROPICS, 1940
ONE NIGHT OF LOVE, 1934
ONE NIGHT WITH YOU, 1948
ONE OF OUR AIRCRAFT IS MISSING, 1942
ONE OF OUR SPIES IS MISSING, 1966
ONE ON ONE, 1977
ONE PRECIOUS YEAR, 1933
ONE RAINY AFTERNOON, 1936
ONE ROMANTIC NIGHT, 1930
ONE SPY TOO MANY, 1966
ONE STOLEN NIGHT, 1929
ONE SUNDAY AFTERNOON, 1933
ONE SUNDAY AFTERNOON, 1948
ONE THAT GOT AWAY, THE, 1958
ONE THIRD OF A NATION, 1939
$1,000 A MINUTE, 1935
$1,000 A TOUCHDOWN, 1939
1,000 PLANE RAID, THE, 1969
1,000 SHAPES OF A FEMALE, 1963
ONE THRILLING NIGHT, 1942
ONE TOO MANY, 1950
ONE TOUCH OF VENUS, 1948
ONE, TWO, THREE, 1961
ONE WAY OUT, 1955
ONE WAY PASSAGE, 1932
ONE WAY PENDULUM, 1965
ONE WAY STREET, 1950
ONE-WAY TICKET, 1935
ONE WAY TICKET TO HELL, 1955
ONE WAY TO LOVE, 1946
ONE WAY TRAIL, THE, 1931
ONE WILD NIGHT, 1938
ONE WILD OAT, 1951
ONE WISH TOO MANY, 1956
ONE WOMAN'S STORY, 1949
ONE YEAR LATER, 1933
ONIONHEAD, 1958
ONLY A WOMAN, 1966
ONLY ANGELS HAVE WINGS, 1939
ONLY GOD KNOWS, 1974
ONLY SAPS WORK, 1930
ONLY THE BRAVE, 1930
ONLY THE VALIANT, 1951
ONLY WAY, THE, 1970
ONLY WHEN I LARF, 1968
ONE MAN'S WAY, 1964
OPEN ROAD, THE, 1940
OPEN SECRET, 1948
OPEN THE DOOR AND SEE ALL THE PEOPLE, 1964
OPENED BY MISTAKE, 1940
OPERATION AMSTERDAM, 1960
OPERATION BIKINI, 1963
OPERATION BOTTLENECK, 1961
OPERATION BULLSHINE, 1963
OPERATION CAMEL, 1961
OPERATION CIA, 1965
OPERATION CONSPIRACY, 1957
OPERATION CROSS EAGLES, 1969
OPERATION CROSSBOW, 1965

OPERATION CUPID, 1960
OPERATION DAYBREAK, 1976
OPERATION DELILAH, 1966
OPERATION DIAMOND, 1948
OPERATION DIPLOMAT, 1953
OPERATION DISASTER, 1951
OPERATION EICHMANN, 1961
OPERATION ENEMY FORT, 1964
OPERATION HAYLIFT, 1950
OPERATION KID BROTHER, 1967
OPERATION LOVEBIRDS, 1968
OPERATION MAD BALL, 1957
OPERATION MANHUNT, 1954
OPERATION MURDER, 1957
OPERATION PACIFIC, 1951
OPERATION PETTICOAT, 1959
OPERATION ST. PETER'S, 1968
OPERATION SECRET, 1952
OPERATION SNAFU, 1965
OPERATION SNATCH, 1962
OPERATOR 13, 1934
OPERETTA, 1949
OPPOSITE SEX, THE, 1956
OPTIMISTIC TRAGEDY, THE, 1964
OPTIMISTS, THE, 1973
ORCHESTRA WIVES, 1942
ORCHIDS TO YOU, 1935
ORDERS ARE ORDERS, 1959
ORDERS IS ORDERS, 1934
ORDERS TO KILL, 1958
OREGON PASSAGE, 1958
OREGON TRAIL, THE, 1936
OREGON TRAIL, 1945
OREGON TRAIL, THE, 1959
OREGON TRAIL SCOUTS, 1947
ORGANIZER, THE, 1964
ORIENT EXPRESS, 1934
ORPHAN OF THE PECOS, 1938
ORPHAN OF THE WILDERNESS, 1937
ORPHEUS, 1950
OSCAR, THE, 1966
O'SHAUGHNESSY'S BOY, 1935
OTHELLO, 1960
OTHELLO, 1965
OTHER LOVE, THE, 1947
OTHER PEOPLE'S SINS, 1931
OTHER SIDE OF THE MOUNTAIN—PART 2, THE, 1978
OTHER SIDE OF THE MOUNTAIN, THE, 1975
OTHER TOMORROW, THE, 1930
OTHER WOMAN, THE, 1931
OUANGA, 1936
OUR BLUSHING BRIDES, 1930
OUR DAILY BREAD, 1934
OUR HEARTS WERE GROWING UP, 1946
OUR HEARTS WERE YOUNG AND GAY, 1944
OUR LEADING CITIZEN, 1939
OUR MAN FLINT, 1966
OUR MAN IN HAVANA, 1960
OUR MODERN MAIDENS, 1929
OUR SILENT LOVE, 1969
OUR TIME, 1974
OUR TOWN, 1940
OUR VERY OWN, 1950
OUR VINES HAVE TENDER GRAPES, 1945
OUR WIFE, 1941
OUT ALL NIGHT, 1933
OUT CALIFORNIA WAY, 1946
OUT OF IT, 1969
OUT OF SIGHT, 1966
OUT OF THE BLUE, 1931
OUT OF THE BLUE, 1947
OUT OF THE CLOUDS, 1957
OUT OF THE DEPTHS, 1946
OUT OF THE FOG, 1962
OUT OF THE PAST, 1933
OUT OF THE STORM, 1948
OUT OF THE TIGER'S MOUTH, 1962
OUT OF THIS WORLD, 1945
OUT OF TOWNERS, THE, 1970
OUTCAST, THE, 1934
OUTCAST, 1937
OUTCAST, THE, 1954
OUTCAST LADY, 1934
OUTCAST OF BLACK MESA, 1950
OUTCAST OF THE ISLANDS, 1952

BOLD: Films on Videocassette

OUTCASTS OF POKER FLAT, THE, 1937
OUTCASTS OF POKER FLAT, THE, 1952
OUTCASTS OF THE CITY, 1958
OUTCASTS OF THE TRAIL, 1949
OUTER GATE, THE, 1937
OUTLAW BLUES, 1977
OUTLAW BRAND, 1948
OUTLAW COUNTRY, 1949
OUTLAW DEPUTY, THE, 1935
OUTLAW EXPRESS, 1938
OUTLAW GOLD, 1950
OUTLAW JUSTICE, 1933
OUTLAW OF THE PLAINS, 1946
OUTLAW STALLION, THE, 1954
OUTLAW TRAIL, 1944
OUTLAW TREASURE, 1955
OUTLAW WOMEN, 1952
OUTLAWED GUNS, 1935
OUTLAW'S DAUGHTER, THE, 1954
OUTLAWS IS COMING, THE, 1965
OUTLAWS OF PINE RIDGE, 1942
OUTLAWS OF SANTA FE, 1944
OUTLAWS OF SONORA, 1938
OUTLAWS OF STAMPEDE PASS, 1943
OUTLAWS OF TEXAS, 1950
OUTLAWS OF THE CHEROKEE TRAIL, 1941
OUTLAWS OF THE DESERT, 1941
OUTLAWS OF THE ORIENT, 1937
OUTLAWS OF THE PANHANDLE, 1941
OUTLAWS OF THE PRAIRIE, 1938
OUTLAWS OF THE RIO GRANDE, 1941
OUTLAWS OF THE ROCKIES, 1945
OUTLAW'S PARADISE, 1939
OUTLAW'S SON, 1957
OUTPOST IN MALAYA, 1952
OUTPOST IN MOROCCO, 1949
OUTPOST OF HELL, 1966
OUTPOST OF THE MOUNTIES, 1939
OUTRIDERS, THE, 1950
OUTSIDE OF PARADISE, 1938
OUTSIDE THE LAW, 1930
OUTSIDE THE LAW, 1956
OUTSIDE THE 3-MILE LIMIT, 1940
OUTSIDE THE WALL, 1950
OUTSIDE THESE WALLS, 1939
OUTSIDER, THE, 1933
OUTSIDER, THE, 1940
OUTSIDER, THE, 1949
OVER MY DEAD BODY, 1942
OVER SHE GOES, 1937
OVER THE BORDER, 1950
OVER THE GARDEN WALL, 1934
OVER THE GARDEN WALL, 1950
OVER THE GOAL, 1937
OVER THE MOON, 1940
OVER THE ODDS, 1961
OVER THE WALL, 1938
OVERLAND BOUND, 1929
OVERLAND EXPRESS, THE, 1938
OVERLAND MAIL, 1939
OVERLAND MAIL ROBBERY, 1943
OVERLAND PACIFIC, 1954
OVERLAND RIDERS, 1946
OVERLAND STAGE RAIDERS, 1938
OVERLAND STAGECOACH, 1942
OVERLAND TELEGRAPH, 1951
PACIFIC ADVENTURE, 1947
PACIFIC BLACKOUT, 1942
PACIFIC DESTINY, 1956
PACIFIC RENDEZVOUS, 1942
PACK TRAIN, 1953
PACK UP YOUR TROUBLES, 1940
PADDY O'DAY, 1935
PADDY, THE NEXT BEST THING, 1933
PAGAN ISLAND, 1961
PAGAN LADY, 1931
PAGAN LOVE SONG, 1950
PAGE MISS GLORY, 1935
PAID, 1930
PAID IN ERROR, 1938
PAID IN FULL, 1950
PAINTED ANGEL, THE, 1929
PAINTED DESERT, THE, 1931
PAINTED DESERT, THE, 1938
PAINTED FACES, 1929
PAINTED TRAIL, THE, 1938

PAINTED VEIL, THE, 1934
PAINTED WOMAN, 1932
PAINTING THE CLOUDS WITH SUNSHINE, 1951
PAIR OF BRIEFS, A, 1963
PAJAMA GAME, THE, 1957
PAL FROM TEXAS, THE, 1939
PALEFACE, THE, 1948
PALM BEACH STORY, THE, 1942
PALM SPRINGS, 1936
PALMY DAYS, 1931
PALS OF THE GOLDEN WEST, 1952
PALS OF THE PECOS, 1941
PALS OF THE RANGE, 1935
PALS OF THE SADDLE, 1938
PALS OF THE SILVER SAGE, 1940
PAN-AMERICANA, 1945
PANAMA FLO, 1932
PANAMA HATTIE, 1942
PANAMA LADY, 1939
PANAMA PATROL, 1939
PANAMA SAL, 1957
PANAMINT'S BAD MAN, 1938
PANCHO VILLA RETURNS, 1950
PANDA AND THE MAGIC SERPENT, 1961
PANHANDLE, 1948
PANIC, 1966
PANIC BUTTON, 1964
PANIC IN THE PARLOUR, 1957
PANTHER SQUAD, 1986
PANTHER'S CLAW, THE, 1942
PAPA'S DELICATE CONDITION, 1963
PAPER BULLETS, 1941
PAPER GALLOWS, 1950
PAPER LION, 1968
PAR OU T'ES RENTRE? ON T'A PAS VUE SORTIR, 1984
PARACHUTE BATTALION, 1941
PARACHUTE JUMPER, 1933
PARACHUTE NURSE, 1942
PARADE OF THE WEST, 1930
PARADISE ALLEY, 1962
PARADISE CANYON, 1935
PARADISE EXPRESS, 1937
PARADISE FOR THREE, 1938
PARADISE, HAWAIIAN STYLE, 1966
PARADISE ISLAND, 1930
PARADISE ISLE, 1937
PARATROOP COMMAND, 1959
PARATROOPER, 1954
PARDNERS, 1956
PARDON MY FRENCH, 1951
PARDON MY GUN, 1930
PARDON MY GUN, 1942
PARDON MY PAST, 1945
PARDON MY RHYTHM, 1944
PARDON MY STRIPES, 1942
PARDON OUR NERVE, 1939
PARENTS ON TRIAL, 1939
PARIS, 1929
PARIS AFTER DARK, 1943
PARIS BOUND, 1929
PARIS CALLING, 1941
PARIS DOES STRANGE THINGS, 1957
PARIS EXPRESS, THE, 1953
PARIS FOLLIES OF 1956, 1955
PARIS HOLIDAY, 1958
PARIS HONEYMOON, 1939
PARIS IN SPRING, 1935
PARIS IN THE MONTH OF AUGUST, 1968
PARIS INTERLUDE, 1934
PARIS MODEL, 1953
PARIS PLANE, 1933
PARIS PLAYBOYS, 1954
PARIS UNDERGROUND, 1945
PARIS WHEN IT SIZZLES, 1964
PARISIAN, THE, 1931
PARISIAN ROMANCE, A, 1932
PARK AVENUE LOGGER, 1937
PARK ROW, 1952
PARLOR, BEDROOM AND BATH, 1931
PAROLE, 1936
PAROLE FIXER, 1940
PAROLE GIRL, 1933
PAROLE, INC., 1949
PAROLE RACKET, 1937
PAROLED FROM THE BIG HOUSE, 1938

PAROLED—TO DIE, 1938
PARRISH, 1961
PARSIFAL, 1983
PARSON AND THE OUTLAW, THE, 1957
PARSON OF PANAMINT, THE, 1941
PART TIME WIFE, 1930
PART-TIME WIFE, 1961
PARTINGS, 1962
PARTNER, THE, 1966
PARTNERS, 1932
PARTNERS IN CRIME, 1937
PARTNERS IN TIME, 1946
PARTNERS OF THE PLAINS, 1938
PARTNERS OF THE SUNSET, 1948
PARTNERS OF THE TRAIL, 1931
PARTNERS OF THE TRAIL, 1944
PARTY, THE, 1968
PARTY CRASHERS, THE, 1958
PARTY GIRL, 1930
PARTY HUSBAND, 1931
PARTY WIRE, 1935
PARTY'S OVER, THE, 1934
PASSAGE FROM HONG KONG, 1941
PASSAGE HOME, 1955
PASSAGE TO MARSEILLE, 1944
PASSAGE WEST, 1951
PASSENGER TO LONDON, 1937
PASSING OF THE THIRD FLOOR BACK, THE, 1936
PASSING SHADOWS, 1934
PASSING STRANGER, THE, 1954
PASSION, 1954
PASSION FLOWER, 1930
PASSION FOR LIFE, 1951
PASSION ISLAND, 1943
PASSIONATE DEMONS, THE, 1962
PASSIONATE PLUMBER, 1932
PASSIONATE SUMMER, 1959
PASSIONATE THIEF, THE, 1963
PASSKEY TO DANGER, 1946
PASSPORT HUSBAND, 1938
PASSPORT TO ALCATRAZ, 1940
PASSPORT TO CHINA, 1961
PASSPORT TO DESTINY, 1944
PASSPORT TO HELL, 1932
PASSPORT TO PIMLICO, 1949
PASSPORT TO SUEZ, 1943
PASSPORT TO TREASON, 1956
PASSWORD IS COURAGE, THE, 1962
PAST OF MARY HOLMES, THE, 1933
PASTEUR, 1936
PASTOR HALL, 1940
PAT AND MIKE, 1952
PATAKIN, 1985
PATCH OF BLUE, A, 1965
PATH OF GLORY, THE, 1934
PATHER PANCHALI, 1958
PATHFINDER, THE, 1952
PATIENT IN ROOM 18, THE, 1938
PATIENT VANISHES, THE, 1947
PATRICIA GETS HER MAN, 1937
PATRICK THE GREAT, 1945
PATSY, THE, 1964
PATTERNS, 1956
PAUL TEMPLE RETURNS, 1952
PAUL TEMPLE'S TRIUMPH, 1951
PAULA, 1952
PAWNEE, 1957
PAY BOX ADVENTURE, 1936
PAY OFF, THE, 1930
PAYMENT DEFERRED, 1932
PAYOFF, THE, 1935
PAYOFF, THE, 1943
PAYROLL, 1962
P.C. JOSSER, 1931
PEACE TO HIM WHO ENTERS, 1963
PEACEMAKER, THE, 1956
PEACH O'RENO, 1931
PEACOCK ALLEY, 1930
PEARL, THE, 1948
PEARL OF DEATH, THE, 1944
PEARL OF THE SOUTH PACIFIC, 1955
PEARL OF TLAYUCAN, THE, 1964
PEARLS BRING TEARS, 1937
PEARLS OF THE CROWN, 1938
PECOS RIVER, 1951
PEDDLIN' IN SOCIETY, 1949

PEE-WEE'S BIG ADVENTURE, 1985
PEEPER, 1975
PEER GYNT, 1965
PEG O' MY HEART, 1933
PEG OF OLD DRURY, 1936
PEGGY, 1950
PEKING EXPRESS, 1951
PENAL CODE, THE, 1933
PENELOPE, 1966
PENGUIN POOL MURDER, THE, 1932
PENITENTIARY, 1938
PENNIES FROM HEAVEN, 1936
PENNY PARADISE, 1938
PENNY POINTS TO PARADISE, 1951
PENNY POOL, THE, 1937
PENNY PRINCESS, 1953
PENNY SERENADE, 1941
PENNYWHISTLE BLUES, THE, 1952
PENTHOUSE, 1933
PENTHOUSE PARTY, 1936
PENTHOUSE RHYTHM, 1945
PEOPLE ARE FUNNY, 1945
PEOPLE VS. DR. KILDARE, THE, 1941
PEOPLE WILL TALK, 1935
PEOPLE'S ENEMY, THE, 1935
PERFECT ALIBI, THE, 1931
PERFECT CLUE, THE, 1935
PERFECT CRIME, THE, 1937
PERFECT FLAW, THE, 1934
PERFECT FURLOUGH, THE, 1958
PERFECT GENTLEMAN, THE, 1935
PERFECT LADY, THE, 1931
PERFECT MARRIAGE, THE, 1946
PERFECT SNOB, THE, 1941
PERFECT SPECIMEN, THE, 1937
PERFECT STRANGERS, 1950
PERFECT WOMAN, THE, 1950
PERFECTIONIST, THE, 1952
PERIL FOR THE GUY, 1956
PERILOUS HOLIDAY, 1946
PERILOUS JOURNEY, A, 1953
PERILOUS WATERS, 1948
PERILS OF PAULINE, THE, 1947
PERILS OF PAULINE, THE, 1967
PERSONAL MAID, 1931
PERSONAL MAID'S SECRET, 1935
PERSONAL PROPERTY, 1937
PERSONAL SECRETARY, 1938
PERSONALITY, 1930
PERSONALITY KID, THE, 1934
PERSUADER, THE, 1957
PETER IBBETSON, 1935
PETERVILLE DIAMOND, THE, 1942
PETRIFIED FOREST, THE, 1936
PETTICOAT FEVER, 1936
PETTICOAT LARCENY, 1943
PETTICOAT PIRATES, 1961
PETTICOAT POLITICS, 1941
PETTY GIRL, THE, 1950
PHANTOM BROADCAST, THE, 1933
PHANTOM COWBOY, THE, 1941
PHANTOM EXPRESS, THE, 1932
PHANTOM FIEND, THE, 1935
PHANTOM FROM SPACE, 1953
PHANTOM FROM 10,000 LEAGUES, THE, 1956
PHANTOM GOLD, 1938
PHANTOM IN THE HOUSE, THE, 1929
PHANTOM KILLER, 1942
PHANTOM OF CHINATOWN, 1940
PHANTOM OF CRESTWOOD, THE, 1932
PHANTOM OF 42ND STREET, THE, 1945
PHANTOM OF PARIS, THE, 1931
PHANTOM OF SANTA FE, 1937
PHANTOM OF THE DESERT, 1930
PHANTOM OF THE JUNGLE, 1955
PHANTOM OF THE OPERA, THE, 1929
PHANTOM OF THE OPERA, THE, 1943
PHANTOM OF THE PLAINS, 1945
PHANTOM OF THE RANGE, THE, 1938
PHANTOM PATROL, 1936
PHANTOM PLAINSMEN, THE, 1942
PHANTOM PLANET, THE, 1961
PHANTOM PRESIDENT, THE, 1932
PHANTOM RAIDERS, 1940
PHANTOM RANCHER, 1940
PHANTOM RANGER, 1938

PHANTOM SHIP, 1937
PHANTOM SPEAKS, THE, 1945
PHANTOM STAGE, THE, 1939
PHANTOM STAGECOACH, THE, 1957
PHANTOM STALLION, THE, 1954
PHANTOM STOCKMAN, THE, 1953
PHANTOM STRIKES, THE, 1939
PHANTOM SUBMARINE, THE, 1941
PHANTOM THIEF, THE, 1946
PHANTOM THUNDERBOLT, THE, 1933
PHANTOM VALLEY, 1948
PHARAOH'S CURSE, 1957
PHAROAH'S WOMAN, THE, 1961
PHASE IV, 1974
PHFFFT!, 1954
PHILADELPHIA ATTRACTION, THE, 1985
PHILADELPHIA STORY, THE, 1940
PHILO VANCE RETURNS, 1947
PHILO VANCE'S GAMBLE, 1947
PHILO VANCE'S SECRET MISSION, 1947
PHONY AMERICAN, THE, 1964
PICCADILLY INCIDENT, 1948
PICCADILLY JIM, 1936
PICCADILLY NIGHTS, 1930
PICCADILLY THIRD STOP, 1960
PICK-UP, 1933
PICKPOCKET, 1963
PICKUP, 1951
PICKUP ALLEY, 1957
PICNIC, 1955
PICTURE BRIDES, 1934
PICTURE SHOW MAN, THE, 1980
PIE IN THE SKY, 1964
PIER 5, HAVANA, 1959
PIER 13, 1940
PIER 23, 1951
PIERRE OF THE PLAINS, 1942
PIGSKIN PARADE, 1936
PILGRIM LADY, THE, 1947
PILLAR OF FIRE, THE, 1963
PILLARS OF SOCIETY, 1936
PILLARS OF THE SKY, 1956
PILLOW OF DEATH, 1945
PILLOW TALK, 1959
PILLOW TO POST, 1945
PILOT NO. 5, 1943
PIMPERNEL SMITH, 1942
PIMPERNEL SVENSSON, 1953
PIN UP GIRL, 1944
PINK JUNGLE, THE, 1968
PINK NIGHTS, 1985
PINK PANTHER, THE, 1964
PINK PANTHER STRIKES AGAIN, THE, 1976
PINK STRING AND SEALING WAX, 1950
PINKY, 1949
PINTO BANDIT, THE, 1944
PINTO KID, THE, 1941
PINTO RUSTLERS, 1937
PIONEER DAYS, 1940
PIONEER JUSTICE, 1947
PIONEER MARSHAL, 1950
PIONEER TRAIL, 1938
PIONEERS, THE, 1941
PIONEERS OF THE FRONTIER, 1940
PIONEERS OF THE WEST, 1940
PIRATE, THE, 1948
PIRATE AND THE SLAVE GIRL, THE, 1961
PIRATE OF THE BLACK HAWK, THE, 1961
PIRATES OF BLOOD RIVER, THE, 1962
PIRATES OF CAPRI, THE, 1949
PIRATES OF MONTEREY, 1947
PIRATES OF PENZANCE, THE, 1983
PIRATES OF THE PRAIRIE, 1942
PIRATES OF THE SEVEN SEAS, 1941
PIRATES OF THE SKIES, 1939
PIRATES OF TORTUGA, 1961
PIRATES OF TRIPOLI, 1955
PIRATES ON HORSEBACK, 1941
PISTOL HARVEST, 1951
PISTOL PACKIN' MAMA, 1943
PIT OF DARKNESS, 1961
PITTSBURGH, 1942
PITTSBURGH KID, THE, 1941
P.K. & THE KID, 1987
PLACE OF ONE'S OWN, A, 1945
PLACE TO GO, A, 1964

PLAINSMAN, THE, 1966
PLAINSMAN AND THE LADY, 1946
PLAN 9 FROM OUTER SPACE, 1959
PLANET OF DINOSAURS, 1978
PLANK, THE, 1967
PLATINUM BLONDE, 1931
PLATINUM HIGH SCHOOL, 1960
PLAY GIRL, 1932
PLAY GIRL, 1940
PLAY IT COOL, 1963
PLAY UP THE BAND, 1935
PLAYBACK, 1962
PLAYBOY OF PARIS, 1930
PLAYGIRL, 1954
PLAYING AROUND, 1930
PLAYMATES, 1941
PLAYTHING, THE, 1929
PLEASANTVILLE, 1976
PLEASE BELIEVE ME, 1950
PLEASE DON'T EAT THE DAISIES, 1960
PLEASE MURDER ME, 1956
PLEASE SIR, 1971
PLEASE TEACHER, 1937
PLEASURE, 1933
PLEASURE CRAZED, 1929
PLEASURE CRUISE, 1933
PLEASURE OF HIS COMPANY, THE, 1961
PLEASURE SEEKERS, THE, 1964
PLOT THICKENS, THE, 1936
PLOUGH AND THE STARS, THE, 1936
PLUNDER, 1931
PLUNDER OF THE SUN, 1953
PLUNDER ROAD, 1957
PLUNDERERS, THE, 1948
PLUNDERERS, THE, 1960
PLUNDERERS OF PAINTED FLATS, 1959
POACHER'S DAUGHTER, THE, 1960
POCATELLO KID, 1932
POET'S PUB, 1949
POIL DE CAROTTE, 1932
POINTED HEELS, 1930
POINTING FINGER, THE, 1934
POISON PEN, 1941
POISONED DIAMOND, THE, 1934
POITIN, 1979
POLICE BULLETS, 1942
POLICE CALL, 1933
POLICE CAR 17, 1933
POLICE DOG, 1955
POLICE DOG STORY, THE, 1961
POLICE NURSE, 1963
POLICEMAN OF THE 16TH PRECINCT, THE, 1963
POLITICAL ASYLUM, 1975
POLITICAL PARTY, A, 1933
POLITICS, 1931
POLLY OF THE CIRCUS, 1932
POLO JOE, 1936
PONTIUS PILATE, 1967
PONY EXPRESS, 1953
PONY EXPRESS RIDER, 1976
PONY POST, 1940
PONY SOLDIER, 1952
POOL OF LONDON, 1951
POOR LITTLE RICH GIRL, 1936
POOR OLD BILL, 1931
POOR RICH, THE, 1934
POP ALWAYS PAYS, 1940
POPDOWN, 1968
POPEYE, 1980
POPI, 1969
POPPY, 1936
POPSY POP, 1971
POR MIS PISTOLAS, 1969
PORT AFRIQUE, 1956
PORT OF ESCAPE, 1955
PORT OF 40 THIEVES, THE, 1944
PORT OF HATE, 1939
PORT OF HELL, 1955
PORT OF LOST DREAMS, 1935
PORT OF MISSING GIRLS, 1938
PORT OF NEW YORK, 1949
PORT OF SEVEN SEAS, 1938
PORT OF SHADOWS, 1938
PORT SAID, 1948
PORT SINISTER, 1953
PORTIA ON TRIAL, 1937

BOLD: Films on Videocassette

PORTLAND EXPOSE, 1957
PORTRAIT OF A WOMAN, 1946
PORTRAIT OF CHIEKO, 1968
PORTRAIT OF CLARE, 1951
PORTRAIT OF HELL, 1969
PORTRAIT OF INNOCENCE, 1948
PORTRAIT OF JENNIE, 1949
PORTRAIT OF LENIN, 1967
PORTRAIT OF THE ARTIST AS A YOUNG MAN, A, 1979
POSEIDON ADVENTURE, THE, 1972
POSSE FROM HELL, 1961
POST OFFICE INVESTIGATOR, 1949
POSTAL INSPECTOR, 1936
POSTMAN DIDN'T RING, THE, 1942
POSTMAN GOES TO WAR, THE, 1968
POSTMAN'S KNOCK, 1962
POSTMARK FOR DANGER, 1956
POT CARRIERS, THE, 1962
POT LUCK, 1936
POT O' GOLD, 1941
POWDER RIVER, 1953
POWDER RIVER RUSTLERS, 1949
POWDER TOWN, 1942
POWDERSMOKE RANGE, 1935
POWER, 1934
POWER, THE, 1968
POWER AND THE PRIZE, THE, 1956
POWER DIVE, 1941
POWER OF THE PRESS, 1943
POWER OF THE WHISTLER, THE, 1945
POWERS GIRL, THE, 1942
PRACTICALLY YOURS, 1944
PRAIRIE, THE, 1948
PRAIRIE BADMEN, 1946
PRAIRIE EXPRESS, 1947
PRAIRIE JUSTICE, 1938
PRAIRIE LAW, 1940
PRAIRIE MOON, 1938
PRAIRIE OUTLAWS, 1948
PRAIRIE PALS, 1942
PRAIRIE PIONEERS, 1941
PRAIRIE ROUNDUP, 1951
PRAIRIE RUSTLERS, 1945
PRAIRIE SCHOONERS, 1940
PRAIRIE STRANGER, 1941
PRAIRIE THUNDER, 1937
PRAISE MARX AND PASS THE AMMUNITION, 1970
PREJUDICE, 1949
PRELUDE TO FAME, 1950
PRESCOTT KID, THE, 1936
PRESCRIPTION FOR ROMANCE, 1937
PRESENTING LILY MARS, 1943
PRESIDENT VANISHES, THE, 1934
PRESIDENT'S MYSTERY, THE, 1936
PRESS FOR TIME, 1966
PRESTIGE, 1932
PRETENDER, THE, 1947
PRETTY BABY, 1950
PREVIEW MURDER MYSTERY, 1936
PRICE OF A SONG, THE, 1935
PRICE OF FEAR, THE, 1956
PRICE OF FOLLY, THE, 1937
PRICE OF SILENCE, THE, 1960
PRICE OF THINGS, THE, 1930
PRICE OF WISDOM, THE, 1935
PRIDE AND PREJUDICE, 1940
PRIDE OF MARYLAND, 1951
PRIDE OF THE BLUE GRASS, 1954
PRIDE OF THE BOWERY, 1941
PRIDE OF THE FORCE, THE, 1933
PRIDE OF THE LEGION, THE, 1932
PRIDE OF THE MARINES, 1936
PRIDE OF THE NAVY, 1939
PRIDE OF THE PLAINS, 1944
PRIDE OF THE WEST, 1938
PRIME MINISTER, THE, 1941
PRIMITIVES, THE, 1962
PRIMROSE PATH, THE, 1934
PRINCE AND THE SHOWGIRL, THE, 1957
PRINCE JACK, 1985
PRINCE OF DIAMONDS, 1930
PRINCE OF PIRATES, 1953
PRINCE OF THE PLAINS, 1949
PRINCE OF THIEVES, THE, 1948
PRINCE WHO WAS A THIEF, THE, 1951

PRINCESS AND THE PIRATE, THE, 1944
PRINCESS AND THE PLUMBER, THE, 1930
PRINCESS CHARMING, 1935
PRINCESS COMES ACROSS, THE, 1936
PRINCESS O'HARA, 1935
PRINCESS O'ROURKE, 1943
PRIORITIES ON PARADE, 1942
PRISON BREAK, 1938
PRISON BREAKER, 1936
PRISON FARM, 1938
PRISON GIRL, 1942
PRISON NURSE, 1938
PRISON SHADOWS, 1936
PRISON TRAIN, 1938
PRISON WARDEN, 1949
PRISON WITHOUT BARS, 1939
PRISONER OF JAPAN, 1942
PRISONER OF SHARK ISLAND, THE, 1936
PRISONER OF THE IRON MASK, 1962
PRISONER OF ZENDA, THE, 1937
PRISONER OF ZENDA, THE, 1952
PRISONER OF ZENDA, THE, 1979
PRISONERS, 1929
PRISONERS IN PETTICOATS, 1950
PRISONERS OF THE CASBAH, 1953
PRIVATE AFFAIRS, 1940
PRIVATE AFFAIRS OF BEL AMI, THE, 1947
PRIVATE ANGELO, 1949
PRIVATE BUCKAROO, 1942
PRIVATE DETECTIVE, 1939
PRIVATE DETECTIVE 62, 1933
PRIVATE ENTERPRISE, A, 1975
PRIVATE EYES, 1953
PRIVATE EYES, THE, 1980
PRIVATE INFORMATION, 1952
PRIVATE JONES, 1933
PRIVATE LIFE OF DON JUAN, THE, 1934
PRIVATE LIFE OF LOUIS XIV, 1936
PRIVATE LIVES, 1931
PRIVATE LIVES OF ELIZABETH AND ESSEX, THE, 1939
PRIVATE NAVY OF SGT. O'FARRELL, THE, 1968
PRIVATE NUMBER, 1936
PRIVATE NURSE, 1941
PRIVATE RIGHT, THE, 1967
PRIVATE SCANDAL, A, 1932
PRIVATE SCANDAL, 1934
PRIVATE SECRETARY, THE, 1935
PRIVATE WAR OF MAJOR BENSON, THE, 1955
PRIVATE'S AFFAIR, A, 1959
PRIVATE'S PROGRESS, 1956
PRIVILEGE, 1967
PRIZE, THE, 1952
PRIZE OF ARMS, A, 1962
PRIZE OF GOLD, A, 1955
PRIZEFIGHTER AND THE LADY, THE, 1933
PROBATION, 1932
PROBLEM GIRLS, 1953
PRODIGAL, THE, 1931
PRODIGAL, THE, 1984
PRODIGAL SON, THE, 1935
PROFESSIONAL SOLDIER, 1936
PROFESSIONAL SWEETHEART, 1933
PROFESSIONALS, THE, 1960
PROFESSOR BEWARE, 1938
PROFESSOR TIM, 1957
PROFILE, 1954
PROJECT MOONBASE, 1953
PROJECT M7, 1953
PROJECT X, 1949
PROJECT X, 1968
PROJECT X, 1987
PROJECTED MAN, THE, 1967
PROMISE, THE, 1969
PROMISE AT DAWN, 1970
PROMISE HER ANYTHING, 1966
PROMOTER, THE, 1952
PROPER TIME, THE, 1959
PROSPERITY, 1932
PROUD ONES, THE, 1956
PROUD REBEL, THE, 1958
PROUD VALLEY, THE, 1941
PT 109, 1963
PUBLIC COWBOY NO. 1, 1937
PUBLIC DEFENDER, THE, 1931
PUBLIC ENEMIES, 1941

PUBLIC ENEMY'S WIFE, 1936
PUBLIC EYE, THE, 1972
PUBLIC HERO NO. 1, 1935
PUBLIC LIFE OF HENRY THE NINTH, THE, 1934
PUBLIC NUISANCE NO. 1, 1936
PUBLIC OPINION, 1935
PUBLIC PIGEON NO. 1, 1957
PUBLIC WEDDING, 1937
PUNCH AND JUDY MAN, THE, 1963
PURPLE HEART DIARY, 1951
PURPLE MASK, THE, 1955
PURPLE VIGILANTES, THE, 1938
PURSE STRINGS, 1933
PURSUED, 1934
PURSUERS, THE, 1961
PURSUIT, 1935
PURSUIT OF THE GRAF SPEE, 1957
PURSUIT TO ALGIERS, 1945
PUSHOVER, 1954
PUT ON THE SPOT, 1936
PUTTIN' ON THE RITZ, 1930
PYGMALION, 1938
PYGMY ISLAND, 1950
QUALITY STREET, 1937
QUANDO EL AMOR RIE, 1933
QUANTEZ, 1957
QUANTRILL'S RAIDERS, 1958
QUARTERBACK, THE, 1940
QUEBEC, 1951
QUEEN CHRISTINA, 1933
QUEEN FOR A DAY, 1951
QUEEN HIGH, 1930
QUEEN OF BABYLON, THE, 1956
QUEEN OF BROADWAY, 1942
QUEEN OF HEARTS, 1936
QUEEN OF OUTER SPACE, 1958
QUEEN OF THE AMAZONS, 1947
QUEEN OF THE YUKON, 1940
QUENTIN DURWARD, 1955
QUICK, BEFORE IT MELTS, 1964
QUICK GUN, THE, 1964
QUICK MILLIONS, 1939
QUICK MONEY, 1938
QUICK ON THE TRIGGER, 1949
QUIET AMERICAN, THE, 1958
QUIET GUN, THE, 1957
QUIET MAN, THE, 1952
QUIET PLEASE, 1938
QUIET PLEASE, MURDER, 1942
QUIET WEDDING, 1941
QUIET WEEKEND, 1948
QUIET WOMAN, THE, 1951
QUINCANNON, FRONTIER SCOUT, 1956
QUITTERS, THE, 1934
RABBI AND THE SHIKSE, THE, 1976
RABBIT TRAP, THE, 1959
RABBLE, THE, 1965
RACE FOR LIFE, A, 1955
RACERS, THE, 1955
RACETRACK, 1933
RACHEL AND THE STRANGER, 1948
RACING BLOOD, 1938
RACING BLOOD, 1954
RACING LADY, 1937
RACING LUCK, 1935
RACING LUCK, 1948
RACING ROMANCE, 1937
RACING STRAIN, THE, 1933
RACING YOUTH, 1932
RACK, THE, 1956
RACKET BUSTERS, 1938
RACKET MAN, THE, 1944
RACKETEER, THE, 1929
RACKETEERS IN EXILE, 1937
RACKETEERS OF THE RANGE, 1939
RACKETY RAX, 1932
RADAR SECRET SERVICE, 1950
RADIO CAB MURDER, 1954
RADIO CITY REVELS, 1938
RADIO FOLLIES, 1935
RADIO LOVER, 1936
RADIO PATROL, 1932
RADIO PIRATES, 1935
RADIO STARS ON PARADE, 1945
RAFFLES, 1930
RAFFLES, 1939

RAFTER ROMANCE, 1934
RAGE AT DAWN, 1955
RAGE OF PARIS, THE, 1938
RAGE OF THE BUCCANEERS, 1963
RAGING TIDE, THE, 1951
RAGS TO RICHES, 1941
RAGTIME COWBOY JOE, 1940
RAIDERS, THE, 1952
RAIDERS, THE, 1964
RAIDERS FROM BENEATH THE SEA, 1964
RAIDERS OF LEYTE GULF, 1963
RAIDERS OF OLD CALIFORNIA, 1957
RAIDERS OF RED GAP, 1944
RAIDERS OF SAN JOAQUIN, 1943
RAIDERS OF SUNSET PASS, 1943
RAIDERS OF THE BORDER, 1944
RAIDERS OF THE DESERT, 1941
RAIDERS OF THE RANGE, 1942
RAIDERS OF THE SEVEN SEAS, 1953
RAIDERS OF THE SOUTH, 1947
RAIDERS OF THE WEST, 1942
RAIDERS OF TOMAHAWK CREEK, 1950
RAILROAD MAN, THE, 1965
RAILROAD WORKERS, 1948
RAILS INTO LARAMIE, 1954
RAILWAY CHILDREN, THE, 1971
RAIN OR SHINE, 1930
RAINBOW BOYS, THE, 1973
RAINBOW ISLAND, 1944
RAINBOW JACKET, THE, 1954
RAINBOW MAN, 1929
RAINBOW ON THE RIVER, 1936
RAINBOW OVER BROADWAY, 1933
RAINBOW OVER TEXAS, 1946
RAINBOW OVER THE RANGE, 1940
RAINBOW OVER THE ROCKIES, 1947
RAINBOW RANCH, 1933
RAINBOW 'ROUND MY SHOULDER, 1952
RAINBOW TRAIL, 1932
RAINBOW VALLEY, 1935
RAINBOW'S END, 1935
RAINMAKER, THE, 1956
RAINMAKERS, THE, 1935
RAINS CAME, THE, 1939
RAINS OF RANCHIPUR, THE, 1955
RAISE THE ROOF, 1930
RAISIN IN THE SUN, A, 1961
RAISING A RIOT, 1957
RAMONA, 1936
RAMPAGE, 1963
RAMPAGE AT APACHE WELLS, 1966
RAMPANT AGE, THE, 1930
RAMPARTS WE WATCH, THE, 1940
RAMROD, 1947
RAMSBOTTOM RIDES AGAIN, 1956
RANCHO GRANDE, 1938
RANCHO GRANDE, 1940
RANCHO NOTORIOUS, 1952
RANDOLPH FAMILY, THE, 1945
RANDOM HARVEST, 1942
RANDY RIDES ALONE, 1934
RANGE BEYOND THE BLUE, 1947
RANGE BUSTERS, THE, 1940
RANGE DEFENDERS, 1937
RANGE FEUD, THE, 1931
RANGE JUSTICE, 1949
RANGE LAND, 1949
RANGE LAW, 1931
RANGE LAW, 1944
RANGE RENEGADES, 1948
RANGE WAR, 1939
RANGER AND THE LADY, THE, 1940
RANGER COURAGE, 1937
RANGER OF CHEROKEE STRIP, 1949
RANGER'S CODE, THE, 1933
RANGERS RIDE, THE, 1948
RANGER'S ROUNDUP, THE, 1938
RANGERS STEP IN, THE, 1937
RANGERS TAKE OVER, THE, 1942
RANGLE RIVER, 1939
RANGO, 1931
RANSOM, 1956
RAPTURE, 1950
RARE BREED, THE, 1966
RARE BREED, 1984
RASPUTIN, 1932

RASPUTIN, 1939
RAT, THE, 1938
RAT, 1960
RAT PFINK AND BOO BOO, 1966
RAT RACE, THE, 1960
RAT SAVIOUR, THE, 1977
RATATAPLAN, 1979
RATIONING, 1944
RATON PASS, 1951
RATS, THE, 1955
RATS OF TOBRUK, 1951
RAVAGERS, THE, 1965
RAVAGERS, THE, 1979
RAVEN, THE, 1935
RAVEN, THE, 1948
RAVEN'S END, 1970
RAVISHING IDIOT, A, 1966
RAW DEAL, 1977
RAW EDGE, 1956
RAW TIMBER, 1937
RAW WIND IN EDEN, 1958
RAWHIDE, 1938
RAWHIDE, 1951
RAWHIDE RANGERS, 1941
RAWHIDE TRAIL, THE, 1958
RAWHIDE YEARS, THE, 1956
REACH FOR GLORY, 1963
REACH FOR THE SKY, 1957
REACHING FOR THE MOON, 1931
REACHING FOR THE SUN, 1941
READY FOR LOVE, 1934
READY FOR THE PEOPLE, 1964
READY, WILLING AND ABLE, 1937
REAL BLOKE, A, 1935
REAL GLORY, THE, 1939
REAP THE WILD WIND, 1942
REASON TO LIVE, A REASON TO DIE, A, 1974
REASONABLE DOUBT, 1936
REBECCA OF SUNNYBROOK FARM, 1932
REBEL, THE, 1933
REBEL CITY, 1953
REBEL GLADIATORS, THE, 1963
REBEL IN TOWN, 1956
REBEL SET, THE, 1959
REBEL SON, THE, 1939
REBELLION, 1938
REBELLION IN CUBA, 1961
REBELLIOUS DAUGHTERS, 1938
REBELS AGAINST THE LIGHT, 1964
REBOUND, 1931
RECAPTURED LOVE, 1930
RECESS, 1967
RECKLESS, 1935
RECKLESS AGE, 1944
RECKLESS HOUR, THE, 1931
RECKLESS LIVING, 1931
RECKLESS LIVING, 1938
RECORD 413, 1936
RED AND THE BLACK, THE, 1954
RED AND THE WHITE, THE, 1969
RED BALL EXPRESS, 1952
RED BLOOD OF COURAGE, 1935
RED CANYON, 1949
RED CLOAK, THE, 1961
RED DANUBE, THE, 1949
RED DESERT, 1949
RED DRAGON, THE, 1946
RED-DRAGON, 1967
RED DRESS, THE, 1954
RED FORK RANGE, 1931
RED GARTERS, 1954
RED-HAIRED ALIBI, THE, 1932
RED HEAD, 1934
RED HEADED WOMAN, 1932
RED, HOT AND BLUE, 1949
RED HOT RHYTHM, 1930
RED HOT SPEED, 1929
RED HOT TIRES, 1935
RED HOUSE, THE, 1947
RED INN, THE, 1954
RED LIGHTS AHEAD, 1937
RED LION, 1971
RED MENACE, THE, 1949
RED MORNING, 1935
RED PLANET MARS, 1952
RED RIVER, 1948

RED RIVER RANGE, 1938
RED RIVER RENEGADES, 1946
RED RIVER ROBIN HOOD, 1943
RED RIVER SHORE, 1953
RED RIVER VALLEY, 1936
RED RIVER VALLEY, 1941
RED ROCK OUTLAW, 1950
RED ROPE, THE, 1937
RED RUNS THE RIVER, 1963
RED SALUTE, 1935
RED SHEIK, THE, 1963
RED SHOES, THE, 1948
RED SKIES OF MONTANA, 1952
RED SNOW, 1952
RED STALLION, THE, 1947
RED SUN, 1972
RED SUNDOWN, 1956
RED TENT, THE, 1971
RED TOMAHAWK, 1967
RED WAGON, 1936
REDEEMER, THE, 1965
REDEEMING SIN, THE, 1929
REDEMPTION, 1930
REDHEAD, 1941
REDHEAD AND THE COWBOY, THE, 1950
REDHEAD FROM MANHATTAN, 1954
REDHEAD FROM WYOMING, THE, 1953
REDHEADS ON PARADE, 1935
REDUCING, 1931
REDWOOD FOREST TRAIL, 1950
REFORM GIRL, 1933
REFORM SCHOOL, 1939
REFORM SCHOOL GIRL, 1957
REFORMATORY, 1938
REFORMER AND THE REDHEAD, THE, 1950
REGAL CAVALCADE, 1935
REGISTERED NURSE, 1934
REG'LAR FELLERS, 1941
RELENTLESS, 1948
RELUCTANT ASTRONAUT, THE, 1967
RELUCTANT DEBUTANTE, THE, 1958
RELUCTANT HEROES, 1951
RELUCTANT SAINT, THE, 1962
RELUCTANT WIDOW, THE, 1951
REMAINS TO BE SEEN, 1953
REMARKABLE ANDREW, THE, 1942
REMARKABLE MR. KIPPS, 1942
REMARKABLE MR. PENNYPACKER, THE, 1959
REMBRANDT, 1936
REMEDY FOR RICHES, 1941
REMEMBER?, 1939
REMEMBER LAST NIGHT, 1935
REMEMBER PEARL HARBOR, 1942
REMEMBER THE DAY, 1941
REMEMBER THE NIGHT, 1940
REMOTE CONTROL, 1930
RENDEZ-VOUS, 1932
RENDEZVOUS, 1935
RENDEZVOUS AT MIDNIGHT, 1935
RENDEZVOUS 24, 1946
RENDEZVOUS WITH ANNIE, 1946
RENEGADE GIRL, 1946
RENEGADE RANGER, 1938
RENEGADE TRAIL, 1939
RENEGADES, 1930
RENEGADES, 1946
RENEGADES OF SONORA, 1948
RENEGADES OF THE RIO GRANDE, 1945
RENEGADES OF THE SAGE, 1949
RENEGADES OF THE WEST, 1932
RENFREW OF THE ROYAL MOUNTED, 1937
RENO, 1930
RENO, 1939
REPEAT PERFORMANCE, 1947
REPENT AT LEISURE, 1941
REPORT ON THE PARTY AND THE GUESTS, A, 1968
REPORTED MISSING, 1937
REPRISAL, 1956
REPTILICUS, 1962
REQUIEM FOR A GUNFIGHTER, 1965
REQUIEM FOR A SECRET AGENT, 1966
RESCUE SQUAD, 1935
RESCUE SQUAD, THE, 1963
RESTLESS BREED, THE, 1957
RESTLESS ONES, THE, 1965
RESTLESS YEARS, THE, 1958

BOLD: Films on Videocassette

RESURRECTION, 1931
RESURRECTION, 1963
RESURRECTION OF ZACHARY WHEELER, THE, 1971
RETURN FROM THE ASHES, 1965
RETURN FROM THE SEA, 1954
RETURN OF BULLDOG DRUMMOND, THE, 1934
RETURN OF CAROL DEANE, THE, 1938
RETURN OF CASEY JONES, 1933
RETURN OF DANIEL BOONE, THE, 1941
RETURN OF DR. FU MANCHU, THE, 1930
RETURN OF FRANK JAMES, THE, 1940
RETURN OF JACK SLADE, THE, 1955
RETURN OF JESSE JAMES, THE, 1950
RETURN OF JIMMY VALENTINE, THE, 1936
RETURN OF MR. MOTO, THE, 1965
RETURN OF MONTE CRISTO, THE, 1946
RETURN OF OCTOBER, THE, 1948
RETURN OF PETER GRIMM, THE, 1935
RETURN OF RAFFLES, THE, 1932
RETURN OF RINGO, THE, 1966
RETURN OF SHERLOCK HOLMES, THE, 1929
RETURN OF SOPHIE LANG, THE, 1936
RETURN OF THE APE MAN, 1944
RETURN OF THE BLACK EAGLE, 1949
RETURN OF THE CISCO KID, 1939
RETURN OF THE FLY, 1959
RETURN OF THE FROG, THE, 1938
RETURN OF THE FRONTIERSMAN, 1950
RETURN OF THE LASH, 1947
RETURN OF THE RANGERS, THE, 1943
RETURN OF THE RAT, THE, 1929
RETURN OF THE SCARLET PIMPERNEL, 1938
RETURN OF THE SEVEN, 1966
RETURN OF THE TEXAN, 1952
RETURN OF THE VAMPIRE, THE, 1944
RETURN OF THE WHISTLER, THE, 1948
RETURN OF WILD BILL, THE, 1940
RETURN OF WILDFIRE, THE, 1948
RETURN TO PARADISE, 1953
RETURN TO PEYTON PLACE, 1961
RETURN TO SENDER, 1963
RETURN TO SNOWY RIVER: PART II, 1988
RETURN TO TREASURE ISLAND, 1954
RETURN TO WARBOW, 1958
RETURN TO YESTERDAY, 1940
REUNION, 1932
REUNION, 1936
REUNION IN FRANCE, 1942
REUNION IN RENO, 1951
REVEILLE WITH BEVERLY, 1943
REVENGE AT EL PASO, 1968
REVENGE AT MONTE CARLO, 1933
REVENGE OF THE CREATURE, 1955
REVENGE OF THE GLADIATORS, 1965
REVENGE OF THE NINJA, 1983
REVENGE OF THE ZOMBIES, 1943
REVENGE RIDER, THE, 1935
REVENUE AGENT, 1950
REVERSE BE MY LOT, THE, 1938
REVOLT AT FORT LARAMIE, 1957
REVOLT IN THE BIG HOUSE, 1958
REVOLT OF MAMIE STOVER, THE, 1956
REVOLT OF THE MERCENARIES, 1964
REVOLVING DOORS, THE, 1988
REWARD, THE, 1965
RHAPSODY, 1954
RHINO, 1964
RHODES, 1936
RHUBARB, 1951
RHYTHM IN THE AIR, 1936
RHYTHM IN THE CLOUDS, 1937
RHYTHM INN, 1951
RHYTHM OF THE ISLANDS, 1943
RHYTHM OF THE RIO GRANDE, 1940
RHYTHM OF THE SADDLE, 1938
RHYTHM ON THE RANGE, 1936
RHYTHM ON THE RIVER, 1940
RHYTHM PARADE, 1943
RHYTHM RACKETEER, 1937
RHYTHM SERENADE, 1943
RICH ARE ALWAYS WITH US, THE, 1932
RICH MAN, POOR GIRL, 1938
RICH MAN'S FOLLY, 1931
RICH PEOPLE, 1929
RICHEST GIRL IN THE WORLD, THE, 1934

RICHEST MAN IN TOWN, 1941
RIDE 'EM COWBOY, 1936
RIDE 'EM COWGIRL, 1939
RIDE HIM, COWBOY, 1932
RIDE, KELLY, RIDE, 1941
RIDE ON VAQUERO, 1941
RIDE, RANGER, RIDE, 1936
RIDE, RYDER, RIDE!, 1949
RIDE, TENDERFOOT, RIDE, 1940
RIDE THE HIGH IRON, 1956
RIDE THE HIGH WIND, 1967
RIDE THE WILD SURF, 1964
RIDE TO HANGMAN'S TREE, THE, 1967
RIDE, VAQUERO!, 1953
RIDER FROM TUCSON, 1950
RIDER OF DEATH VALLEY, 1932
RIDER OF THE LAW, THE, 1935
RIDER OF THE PLAINS, 1931
RIDERS FROM NOWHERE, 1940
RIDERS IN THE SKY, 1949
RIDERS OF BLACK MOUNTAIN, 1941
RIDERS OF BLACK RIVER, 1939
RIDERS OF DESTINY, 1933
RIDERS OF PASCO BASIN, 1940
RIDERS OF THE BADLANDS, 1941
RIDERS OF THE BLACK HILLS, 1938
RIDERS OF THE CACTUS, 1931
RIDERS OF THE DAWN, 1937
RIDERS OF THE DAWN, 1945
RIDERS OF THE DEADLINE, 1943
RIDERS OF THE DESERT, 1932
RIDERS OF THE DUSK, 1949
RIDERS OF THE FRONTIER, 1939
RIDERS OF THE GOLDEN GULCH, 1932
RIDERS OF THE NORTH, 1931
RIDERS OF THE NORTHLAND, 1942
RIDERS OF THE NORTHWEST MOUNTED, 1943
RIDERS OF THE PURPLE SAGE, 1931
RIDERS OF THE PURPLE SAGE, 1941
RIDERS OF THE RANGE, 1949
RIDERS OF THE RIO GRANDE, 1943
RIDERS OF THE ROCKIES, 1937
RIDERS OF THE SANTA FE, 1944
RIDERS OF THE WEST, 1942
RIDERS OF THE WHISTLING PINES, 1949
RIDERS TO THE STARS, 1954
RIDIN' DOWN THE CANYON, 1942
RIDIN' DOWN THE TRAIL, 1947
RIDIN' FOR JUSTICE, 1932
RIDIN' LAW, 1930
RIDIN' ON A RAINBOW, 1941
RIDIN' THE LONE TRAIL, 1937
RIDIN' THE OUTLAW TRAIL, 1951
RIDING AVENGER, THE, 1936
RIDING HIGH, 1937
RIDING HIGH, 1943
RIDING HIGH, 1950
RIDING ON, 1937
RIDING SHOTGUN, 1954
RIDING SPEED, 1934
RIDING THE CHEROKEE TRAIL, 1941
RIDING THE SUNSET TRAIL, 1941
RIDING THE WIND, 1942
RIDING TORNADO, THE, 1932
RIDING WEST, 1944
RIFF-RAFF, 1936
RIFFRAFF, 1947
RIGHT AGE TO MARRY, THE, 1935
RIGHT APPROACH, THE, 1961
RIGHT OF WAY, THE, 1931
RIGHT TO LIVE, THE, 1933
RIGHT TO LIVE, THE, 1935
RIGHT TO THE HEART, 1942
RIGOLETTO, 1949
RIM OF THE CANYON, 1949
RIMFIRE, 1949
RING, THE, 1952
RING-A-DING RHYTHM, 1962
RING AROUND THE CLOCK, 1953
RING AROUND THE MOON, 1936
RING OF BRIGHT WATER, 1969
RING OF FEAR, 1954
RING OF SPIES, 1964
RING OF TERROR, 1962
RINGER, THE, 1932
RINGER, THE, 1953

RINGO AND HIS GOLDEN PISTOL, 1966
RINGS ON HER FINGERS, 1942
RINGSIDE, 1949
RINGSIDE MAISIE, 1941
RIO, 1939
RIO BRAVO, 1959
RIO CONCHOS, 1964
RIO GRANDE, 1939
RIO GRANDE, 1950
RIO GRANDE PATROL, 1950
RIO GRANDE RAIDERS, 1946
RIO GRANDE RANGER, 1937
RIO GRANDE ROMANCE, 1936
RIO LOBO, 1970
RIO RITA, 1929
RIOT SQUAD, 1941
RIP ROARIN' BUCKAROO, 1936
RIP ROARING RILEY, 1935
RIP TIDE, 1934
RISE AGAINST THE SWORD, 1966
RISE AND SHINE, 1941
RISE OF LOUIS XIV, THE, 1970
RISING OF THE MOON, THE, 1957
RISK, THE, 1961
RISKY BUSINESS, 1939
RIVALS, THE, 1963
RIVER, THE, 1928
RIVER, THE, 1951
RIVER, THE, 1961
RIVER BEAT, 1954
RIVER CHANGES, THE, 1956
RIVER GANG, 1945
RIVER HOUSE GHOST, THE, 1932
RIVER HOUSE MYSTERY, THE, 1935
RIVER LADY, 1948
RIVER OF NO RETURN, 1954
RIVER OF ROMANCE, 1929
RIVER OF UNREST, 1937
RIVER RAT, THE, 1984
RIVER WOLVES, THE, 1934
RIVER WOMAN, THE, 1928
RIVERBOAT RHYTHM, 1946
RIVER'S END, 1931
RIVER'S END, 1940
RIVERSIDE MURDER, THE, 1935
ROAD AGENT, 1941
ROAD AGENT, 1952
ROAD BACK, THE, 1937
ROAD DEMON, 1938
ROAD HOME, THE, 1947
ROAD HOUSE, 1934
ROAD IS FINE, THE, 1930
ROAD SHOW, 1941
ROAD TO ALCATRAZ, 1945
ROAD TO DENVER, THE, 1955
ROAD TO FORTUNE, THE, 1930
ROAD TO HAPPINESS, 1942
ROAD TO LIFE, 1932
ROAD TO PARADISE, 1930
ROAD TO RENO, 1931
ROAD TO RENO, THE, 1938
ROAD TO SINGAPORE, 1931
ROAD TO THE BIG HOUSE, 1947
ROADBLOCK, 1951
ROADHOUSE MURDER, THE, 1932
ROADHOUSE NIGHTS, 1930
ROADRACERS, THE, 1959
ROAMING COWBOY, THE, 1937
ROAMING LADY, 1936
ROAR, 1981
ROAR OF THE CROWD, 1953
ROAR OF THE DRAGON, 1932
ROAR OF THE PRESS, 1941
ROARIN' GUNS, 1936
ROARIN' LEAD, 1937
ROARING CITY, 1951
ROARING RANCH, 1930
ROARING ROADS, 1935
ROARING SIX GUNS, 1937
ROARING TIMBER, 1937
ROARING WESTWARD, 1949
ROB ROY, THE HIGHLAND ROGUE, 1954
ROBBER SYMPHONY, THE, 1937
ROBBERS OF THE RANGE, 1941
ROBBERS' ROOST, 1933
ROBBERY UNDER ARMS, 1958

ROBBERY WITH VIOLENCE, 1958
ROBE, THE, 1953
ROBERTA, 1935
ROBIN HOOD OF THE PECOS, 1941
ROBIN HOOD OF THE RANGE, 1943
ROBIN OF TEXAS, 1947
ROBINSON CRUSOE ON MARS, 1964
ROBOT MONSTER, 1953
ROCK-A-BYE BABY, 1958
ROCK ALL NIGHT, 1957
ROCK AROUND THE CLOCK, 1956
ROCK AROUND THE WORLD, 1957
ROCK BABY, ROCK IT, 1957
ROCK ISLAND TRAIL, 1950
ROCK, PRETTY BABY, 1956
ROCK RIVER RENEGADES, 1942
ROCK, ROCK, ROCK!, 1956
ROCK YOU SINNERS, 1957
ROCKABILLY BABY, 1957
ROCKABYE, 1932
ROCKET ATTACK, U.S.A., 1961
ROCKET MAN, THE, 1954
ROCKETSHIP X-M, 1950
ROCKIN' IN THE ROCKIES, 1945
ROCKY, 1948
ROCKY MOUNTAIN, 1950
ROCKY MOUNTAIN MYSTERY, 1935
ROCKY MOUNTAIN RANGERS, 1940
ROCKY RHODES, 1934
RODAN, 1958
RODEO, 1952
RODEO KING AND THE SENORITA, 1951
ROGER TOUHY, GANGSTER!, 1944
ROGUE OF THE RANGE, 1937
ROGUE OF THE RIO GRANDE, 1930
ROGUE RIVER, 1951
ROGUE SONG, THE, 1930
ROGUES GALLERY, 1945
ROGUE'S MARCH, 1952
ROGUES OF SHERWOOD FOREST, 1950
ROGUES' REGIMENT, 1948
ROGUES' TAVERN, THE, 1936
ROGUE'S YARN, 1956
ROLL ALONG, COWBOY, 1938
ROLL ON TEXAS MOON, 1946
ROLL, THUNDER, ROLL, 1949
ROLL, WAGONS, ROLL, 1939
ROLLIN' HOME TO TEXAS, 1941
ROLLIN' PLAINS, 1938
ROLLIN' WESTWARD, 1939
ROLLING CARAVANS, 1938
ROLLING DOWN THE GREAT DIVIDE, 1942
ROLLING HOME, 1935
ROLLING IN MONEY, 1934
ROMAN HOLIDAY, 1953
ROMANCE, 1930
ROMANCE A LA CARTE, 1938
ROMANCE AND RICHES, 1937
ROMANCE IN MANHATTAN, 1935
ROMANCE IN THE DARK, 1938
ROMANCE IN THE RAIN, 1934
ROMANCE OF A HORSE THIEF, 1971
ROMANCE OF ROSY RIDGE, THE, 1947
ROMANCE OF SEVILLE, A, 1929
ROMANCE OF THE LIMBERLOST, 1938
ROMANCE OF THE REDWOODS, 1939
ROMANCE OF THE RIO GRANDE, 1929
ROMANCE OF THE RIO GRANDE, 1941
ROMANCE OF THE ROCKIES, 1938
ROMANCE OF THE WEST, 1946
ROMANCE ON THE HIGH SEAS, 1948
ROMANCE ON THE RANGE, 1942
ROMANCE ON THE RUN, 1938
ROMANCE RIDES THE RANGE, 1936
ROMANOFF AND JULIET, 1961
ROMANY LOVE, 1931
ROME ADVENTURE, 1962
ROME EXPRESS, 1933
ROME WANTS ANOTHER CAESAR, 1974
ROMEO AND JULIET, 1954
ROMEO AND JULIET, 1955
ROMEO AND JULIET, 1966
ROMMEL'S TREASURE, 1962
ROOF, THE, 1933
ROOGIE'S BUMP, 1954
ROOKIE, THE, 1959

ROOKIE COP, THE, 1939
ROOKIE FIREMAN, 1950
ROOKIES IN BURMA, 1943
ROOKIES ON PARADE, 1941
ROOM FOR TWO, 1940
ROOM 43, 1959
ROOM IN THE HOUSE, 1955
ROOM SERVICE, 1938
ROOM TO LET, 1949
ROONEY, 1958
ROOSTER COGBURN, 1975
ROOT OF ALL EVIL, THE, 1947
ROOTIN' TOOTIN' RHYTHM, 1937
ROPE OF SAND, 1949
ROSALIE, 1937
ROSE BOWL, 1936
ROSE BOWL STORY, THE, 1952
ROSE OF CIMARRON, 1952
ROSE OF THE RANCHO, 1936
ROSE OF THE RIO GRANDE, 1938
ROSE OF THE YUKON, 1949
ROSE OF TRALEE, 1938
ROSE OF TRALEE, 1942
ROSE OF WASHINGTON SQUARE, 1939
ROSES ARE RED, 1947
ROSES FOR THE PROSECUTOR, 1961
ROSIE!, 1967
ROSIE THE RIVETER, 1944
ROSSINI, 1948
ROSSITER CASE, THE, 1950
ROTHSCHILD, 1938
ROUGH RIDERS OF CHEYENNE, 1945
ROUGH RIDERS OF DURANGO, 1951
ROUGH RIDERS' ROUNDUP, 1939
ROUGH RIDIN' RHYTHM, 1937
ROUGH RIDING RANGER, 1935
ROUGH ROMANCE, 1930
ROUGH, TOUGH AND READY, 1945
ROUGH, TOUGH WEST, THE, 1952
ROUGHLY SPEAKING, 1945
ROUGHSHOD, 1949
ROUNDUP, THE, 1941
ROUNDUP TIME IN TEXAS, 1937
ROUSTABOUT, 1964
ROVIN' TUMBLEWEEDS, 1939
ROXIE HART, 1942
ROYAL AFFAIR, A, 1950
ROYAL AFFAIRS IN VERSAILLES, 1957
ROYAL AFRICAN RIFLES, THE, 1953
ROYAL BED, THE, 1931
ROYAL BOX, THE, 1930
ROYAL DEMAND, A, 1933
ROYAL DIVORCE, A, 1938
ROYAL EAGLE, 1936
ROYAL FAMILY OF BROADWAY, THE, 1930
ROYAL HUNT OF THE SUN, THE, 1969
ROYAL MOUNTED PATROL, THE, 1941
ROYAL ROMANCE, A, 1930
ROYAL WALTZ, THE, 1936
ROYAL WEDDING, 1951
RUBBER RACKETEERS, 1942
RUGGED O'RIORDANS, THE, 1949
RUGGLES OF RED GAP, 1935
RULERS OF THE SEA, 1939
RULING VOICE, THE, 1931
RUMBA, 1935
RUMBLE ON THE DOCKS, 1956
RUMPELSTILTSKIN, 1965
RUN ACROSS THE RIVER, 1961
RUN FOR THE HILLS, 1953
RUN FOR THE SUN, 1956
RUN FOR YOUR MONEY, A, 1950
RUN WILD, RUN FREE, 1969
RUN WITH THE DEVIL, 1963
RUNAROUND, THE, 1931
RUNAROUND, THE, 1946
RUNAWAY BRIDE, 1930
RUNAWAY BUS, THE, 1954
RUNAWAY DAUGHTERS, 1957
RUNAWAY LADIES, 1935
RUNAWAY QUEEN, THE, 1935
RUNAWAY, THE, 1964
RUNNERS, 1983
RUNNING TARGET, 1956
RUNNING WILD, 1955

RUSSIANS ARE COMING, THE RUSSIANS ARE
  COMING, THE, 1966
RUSSKIES, 1987
RUSTLERS, 1949
RUSTLER'S HIDEOUT, 1944
RUSTLERS OF DEVIL'S CANYON, 1947
RUSTLERS ON HORSEBACK, 1950
RUSTLER'S PARADISE, 1935
RUSTLERS' ROUNDUP, 1933
RUSTLER'S ROUNDUP, 1946
RUSTLER'S VALLEY, 1937
RUSTY LEADS THE WAY, 1948
RUSTY RIDES ALONE, 1933
RUSTY SAVES A LIFE, 1949
RUSTY'S BIRTHDAY, 1949
RUTHLESS, 1948
RUY BLAS, 1948
RX MURDER, 1958
SAADIA, 1953
SABOTAGE, 1939
SABOTAGE AT SEA, 1942
SABOTAGE SQUAD, 1942
SABOTEUR, 1942
SABRE JET, 1953
SABRINA, 1954
SABU AND THE MAGIC RING, 1957
SACRED FLAME, THE, 1929
SACRED HEARTS, 1984
SACRIFICE OF HONOR, 1938
SAD SACK, THE, 1957
SADDLE BUSTER, THE, 1932
SADDLE LEGION, 1951
SADDLE MOUNTAIN ROUNDUP, 1941
SADDLE PALS, 1947
SADDLE THE WIND, 1958
SADDLE TRAMP, 1950
SADDLEMATES, 1941
SADIE MCKEE, 1934
SADIST, THE, 1963
SAFARI, 1940
SAFARI, 1956
SAFARI DRUMS, 1953
SAFE AFFAIR, A, 1931
SAFE AT HOME, 1962
SAFE IN HELL, 1931
SAFE PLACE, A, 1971
SAFECRACKER, THE, 1958
SAFETY IN NUMBERS, 1930
SAFETY IN NUMBERS, 1938
SAGA OF DEATH VALLEY, 1939
SAGA OF HEMP BROWN, THE, 1958
SAGA OF THE VAGABONDS, 1964
SAGA OF THE VIKING WOMEN AND THEIR
  VOYAGE TO THE WATERS OF THE GREAT SEA
  SERPENT, THE, 1957
SAGEBRUSH FAMILY TRAILS WEST, THE, 1940
SAGEBRUSH LAW, 1943
SAGEBRUSH POLITICS, 1930
SAGEBRUSH TRAIL, 1934
SAGEBRUSH TROUBADOR, 1935
SAGINAW TRAIL, 1953
SAHARA, 1943
SAIGON, 1948
SAIL A CROOKED SHIP, 1961
SAIL INTO DANGER, 1957
SAILING ALONG, 1938
SAILOR BE GOOD, 1933
SAILOR BEWARE, 1951
SAILOR OF THE KING, 1953
SAILOR TAKES A WIFE, THE, 1946
SAILOR'S DON'T CARE, 1940
SAILORS' HOLIDAY, 1929
SAILOR'S HOLIDAY, 1944
SAILOR'S LADY, 1940
SAILOR'S LUCK, 1933
SAILORS ON LEAVE, 1941
ST. BENNY THE DIP, 1951
ST. HELENS, 1981
SAINT IN LONDON, THE, 1939
SAINT IN NEW YORK, THE, 1938
SAINT IN PALM SPRINGS, THE, 1941
ST. LOUIS BLUES, 1939
ST. LOUIS BLUES, 1958
ST. LOUIS KID, THE, 1934
SAINT MEETS THE TIGER, THE, 1943
SAINT STRIKES BACK, THE, 1939

BOLD: Films on Videocassette

SECRET OF THE INCAS, 1954
SECRET OF THE LOCH, THE, 1934
SECRET OF THE PURPLE REEF, THE, 1960
SECRET OF THE SACRED FOREST, THE, 1970
SECRET OF THE TELEGIAN, THE, 1961
SECRET OF THE WHISTLER, 1946
SECRET OF TREASURE MOUNTAIN, 1956
SECRET PARTNER, THE, 1961
SECRET PATROL, 1936
SECRET PEOPLE, 1952
SECRET PLACE, THE, 1958
SECRET SERVICE, 1931
SECRET SERVICE INVESTIGATOR, 1948
SECRET SERVICE OF THE AIR, 1939
SECRET SEVEN, THE, 1940
SECRET SEVEN, THE, 1966
SECRET SINNERS, 1933
SECRET TENT, THE, 1956
SECRET VALLEY, 1937
SECRET VENTURE, 1955
SECRET VOICE, THE, 1936
SECRET WITNESS, THE, 1931
SECRET, THE, 1955
SECRETS OF A CO-ED, 1942
SECRETS OF A NURSE, 1938
SECRETS OF A SECRETARY, 1931
SECRETS OF A SORORITY GIRL, 1946
SECRETS OF CHINATOWN, 1935
SECRETS OF MONTE CARLO, 1951
SECRETS OF SCOTLAND YARD, 1944
SECRETS OF THE FRENCH POLICE, 1932
SECRETS OF THE LONE WOLF, 1941
SECRETS OF THE UNDERGROUND, 1943
SECRETS OF THE WASTELANDS, 1941
SECRETS OF WU SIN, 1932
SECURITY RISK, 1954
SEE AMERICA THIRST, 1930
SEE HERE, PRIVATE HARGROVE, 1944
SEE HOW THEY RUN, 1955
SEE MY LAWYER, 1945
SEED, 1931
SEEDS OF DESTRUCTION, 1952
SEEDS OF FREEDOM, 1943
SEEING IS BELIEVING, 1934
SELF-MADE LADY, 1932
SELLOUT, THE, 1951
SEMINOLE UPRISING, 1955
SENATOR WAS INDISCREET, THE, 1947
SEND FOR PAUL TEMPLE, 1946
SEND ME NO FLOWERS, 1964
SENIOR PROM, 1958
SENOR AMERICANO, 1929
SENORA CASADA NECEISITA MARIDO, 1935
SENORITA FROM THE WEST, 1945
SENSATION, 1936
SENSATION HUNTERS, 1934
SENSATION HUNTERS, 1945
SENSATIONS OF 1945, 1944
SENSO, 1968
SENSUALITA, 1954
SENTENCED FOR LIFE, 1960
SENTIMENTAL BLOKE, 1932
SENTIMENTAL JOURNEY, 1946
SEPARATE PEACE, A, 1972
SEPARATION, 1968
SEPIA CINDERELLA, 1947
SEPTEMBER, 1987
SEPTEMBER AFFAIR, 1950
SEPTEMBER STORM, 1960
SEQUOIA, 1934
SERAFINO, 1970
SERENADE, 1956
SERENADE FOR TWO SPIES, 1966
SERENITY, 1962
SERGEANT BERRY, 1938
SERGEANT DEADHEAD, 1965
SERGEANT JIM, 1962
SERGEANT MADDEN, 1939
SERGEANT MIKE, 1945
SERGEANT MURPHY, 1938
SGT. PEPPER'S LONELY HEARTS CLUB BAND, 1978
SERGEANT RYKER, 1968
SERGEANT WAS A LADY, THE, 1961
SERGEANT YORK, 1941
SERGEANTS 3, 1962
SERPENT ISLAND, 1954

SERPENT OF THE NILE, 1953
SERVANTS' ENTRANCE, 1934
SERVICE DE LUXE, 1938
SET-UP, THE, 1963
SEVEN AGAINST THE SUN, 1968
SEVEN ANGRY MEN, 1955
SEVEN BRAVE MEN, 1936
SEVEN DARING GIRLS, 1962
SEVEN DAYS ASHORE, 1944
SEVEN DAYS LEAVE, 1930
SEVEN DAYS LEAVE, 1942
SEVEN DEADLY SINS, THE, 1953
SEVEN DOORS TO DEATH, 1944
SEVEN DWARFS TO THE RESCUE, THE, 1965
SEVEN FACES, 1929
SEVEN FACES OF DR. LAO, 1964
SEVEN GOLDEN MEN, 1969
SEVEN GUNS FOR THE MACGREGORS, 1968
SEVEN GUNS TO MESA, 1958
SEVEN HILLS OF ROME, THE, 1958
SEVEN KEYS, 1962
SEVEN KEYS TO BALDPATE, 1930
SEVEN KEYS TO BALDPATE, 1935
SEVEN KEYS TO BALDPATE, 1947
SEVEN MEN FROM NOW, 1956
SEVEN MILES FROM ALCATRAZ, 1942
SEVEN SEAS TO CALAIS, 1963
SEVEN SINNERS, 1940
SEVEN SLAVES AGAINST THE WORLD, 1965
SEVEN SWEETHEARTS, 1942
SEVEN TASKS OF ALI BABA, THE, 1963
SEVEN WAYS FROM SUNDOWN, 1960
SEVEN WERE SAVED, 1947
SEVEN WOMEN FROM HELL, 1961
SEVENTEEN, 1940
1776, 1972
SEVENTH CAVALRY, 1956
7TH COMMANDMENT, THE, 1961
SEVENTH CONTINENT, THE, 1968
SEVENTH JUROR, THE, 1964
SEVENTH SIN, THE, 1957
SEVENTH SURVIVOR, THE, 1941
SEVENTH VICTIM, THE, 1943
77 PARK LANE, 1931
70,000 WITNESSES, 1932
SEX KITTENS GO TO COLLEGE, 1960
SEXTON BLAKE AND THE BEARDED DOCTOR, 1935
SEXTON BLAKE AND THE HOODED TERROR, 1938
SEXTON BLAKE AND THE MADEMOISELLE, 1935
SEZ O'REILLY TO MACNAB, 1938
SH! THE OCTOPUS, 1937
SHACK OUT ON 101, 1955
SHADOW BETWEEN, THE, 1932
SHADOW IN THE SKY, 1951
SHADOW MAN, 1953
SHADOW OF A DOUBT, 1935
SHADOW OF A WOMAN, 1946
SHADOW OF EVIL, 1967
SHADOW OF FEAR, 1956
SHADOW OF FEAR, 1963
SHADOW OF MIKE EMERALD, THE, 1935
SHADOW OF SUSPICION, 1944
SHADOW OF TERROR, 1945
SHADOW OF THE CAT, THE, 1961
SHADOW OF THE EAGLE, 1955
SHADOW OF THE HAWK, 1976
SHADOW OF THE LAW, 1930
SHADOW OF THE PAST, 1950
SHADOW OF THE THIN MAN, 1941
SHADOW ON THE WALL, 1950
SHADOW ON THE WINDOW, THE, 1957
SHADOW RANCH, 1930
SHADOW RETURNS, THE, 1946
SHADOW STRIKES, THE, 1937
SHADOW VALLEY, 1947
SHADOW, THE, 1936
SHADOW, THE, 1937
SHADOWED, 1946
SHADOWMAN, 1974
SHADOWS GROW LONGER, THE, 1962
SHADOWS IN THE NIGHT, 1944
SHADOWS OF DEATH, 1945
SHADOWS OF FORGOTTEN ANCESTORS, 1967
SHADOWS OF SING SING, 1934
SHADOWS OF THE ORIENT, 1937
SHADOWS OF THE WEST, 1949

SHADOWS OF TOMBSTONE, 1953
SHADOWS ON THE SAGE, 1942
SHADOWS ON THE STAIRS, 1941
SHADOWS OVER CHINATOWN, 1946
SHADOWS OVER SHANGHAI, 1938
SHADY LADY, 1945
SHADY LADY, THE, 1929
SHAKE HANDS WITH MURDER, 1944
SHAKE, RATTLE, AND ROCK?, 1957
SHAKEDOWN, THE, 1929
SHAKEDOWN, 1936
SHAKESPEARE WALLAH, 1966
SHAKIEST GUN IN THE WEST, THE, 1968
SHALL WE DANCE, 1937
SHAME OF THE SABINE WOMEN, THE, 1962
SHAMELESS OLD LADY, THE, 1966
SHANGHAI, 1935
SHANGHAI CHEST, THE, 1948
SHANGHAI COBRA, THE, 1945
SHANGHAI DRAMA, THE, 1945
SHANGHAI LADY, 1929
SHANGHAI MADNESS, 1933
SHANGHAI STORY, THE, 1954
SHANGHAIED LOVE, 1931
SHANKS, 1974
SHANNONS OF BROADWAY, THE, 1929
SHANTYTOWN, 1943
SHAPE OF THINGS TO COME, THE, 1979
SHARE OUT, THE, 1966
SHARK RIVER, 1953
SHARK WOMAN, THE, 1941
SHARKFIGHTERS, THE, 1956
SHARK'S TREASURE, 1975
SHARPSHOOTERS, 1938
SHE, 1935
SHE ALWAYS GETS THEIR MAN, 1962
SHE AND HE, 1967
SHE ASKED FOR IT, 1937
SHE COULDN'T SAY NO, 1930
SHE COULDN'T SAY NO, 1939
SHE COULDN'T SAY NO, 1941
SHE COULDN'T SAY NO, 1954
SHE COULDN'T TAKE IT, 1935
SHE-CREATURE, THE, 1956
SHE DANCES ALONE, 1981
SHE DEMONS, 1958
SHE DEVIL, 1957
SHE-DEVIL ISLAND, 1936
SHE DIDN'T SAY NO?, 1962
SHE GETS HER MAN, 1935
SHE GETS HER MAN, 1945
SHE-GODS OF SHARK REEF, 1958
SHE GOES TO WAR, 1929
SHE GOT WHAT SHE WANTED, 1930
SHE HAD TO CHOOSE, 1934
SHE HAD TO EAT, 1937
SHE HAD TO SAY YES, 1933
SHE HAS WHAT IT TAKES, 1943
SHE KNEW ALL THE ANSWERS, 1941
SHE KNEW WHAT SHE WANTED, 1936
SHE LEARNED ABOUT SAILORS, 1934
SHE LOVED A FIREMAN, 1937
SHE LOVES ME NOT, 1934
SHE MADE HER BED, 1934
SHE MARRIED A COP, 1939
SHE MARRIED AN ARTIST, 1938
SHE MARRIED HER BOSS, 1935
SHE SHALL HAVE MURDER, 1950
SHE SHALL HAVE MUSIC, 1935
SHE WANTED A MILLIONAIRE, 1932
SHE WAS A LADY, 1934
SHE WAS ONLY A VILLAGE MAIDEN, 1933
SHE WENT TO THE RACES, 1945
SHE-WOLF, THE, 1931
SHE-WOLF, THE, 1963
SHE-WOLF OF LONDON, 1946
SHE WORE A YELLOW RIBBON, 1949
SHE WOULDN'T SAY YES, 1945
SHE WROTE THE BOOK, 1946
SHED NO TEARS, 1948
SHEEPDOG OF THE HILLS, 1941
SHEEPMAN, THE, 1958
SHEIK STEPS OUT, THE, 1937
SHEPHERD GIRL, THE, 1965
SHEPHERD OF THE HILLS, THE, 1941
SHEPHERD OF THE HILLS, THE, 1964

BOLD: Films on Videocassette

SHEPHERD OF THE OZARKS, 1942
SHERIFF OF CIMARRON, 1945
SHERIFF OF FRACTURED JAW, THE, 1958
SHERIFF OF LAS VEGAS, 1944
SHERIFF OF REDWOOD VALLEY, 1946
SHERIFF OF SAGE VALLEY, 1942
SHERIFF OF SUNDOWN, 1944
SHERIFF OF TOMBSTONE, 1941
SHERIFF OF WICHITA, 1949
SHERLOCK HOLMES, 1932
SHERLOCK HOLMES AND THE DEADLY
  NECKLACE, 1962
SHERLOCK HOLMES AND THE SECRET WEAPON,
  1942
SHERLOCK HOLMES AND THE SPIDER WOMAN,
  1944
SHERLOCK HOLMES AND THE VOICE OF TERROR,
  1942
SHERLOCK HOLMES' FATAL HOUR, 1931
SHERLOCK HOLMES IN WASHINGTON, 1943
SHE'S A SOLDIER TOO, 1944
SHE'S A SWEETHEART, 1944
SHE'S BACK ON BROADWAY, 1953
SHE'S DANGEROUS, 1937
SHE'S FOR ME, 1943
SHE'S GOT EVERYTHING, 1938
SHE'S IN THE ARMY, 1942
SHE'S MY WEAKNESS, 1930
SHE'S NO LADY, 1937
SHE'S WORKING HER WAY THROUGH COLLEGE,
  1952
SHIELD FOR MURDER, 1954
SHIELD OF FAITH, THE, 1956
SHILLINGBURY BLOWERS, THE, 1980
SHINBONE ALLEY, 1971
SHINE ON, HARVEST MOON, 1938
SHINE ON, HARVEST MOON, 1944
SHINING VICTORY, 1941
SHIP AHOY, 1942
SHIP CAFE, 1935
SHIP FROM SHANGHAI, THE, 1930
SHIP OF CONDEMNED WOMEN, THE, 1963
SHIP OF WANTED MEN, 1933
SHIP THAT DIED OF SHAME, THE, 1956
SHIPBUILDERS, THE, 1943
SHIPMATES, 1931
SHIPMATES FOREVER, 1935
SHIPMATES O' MINE, 1936
SHIPS OF HATE, 1931
SHIPS WITH WINGS, 1942
SHIPYARD SALLY, 1940
SHOCKING MISS PILGRIM, THE, 1947
SHOES OF THE FISHERMAN, THE, 1968
SHOOT-OUT AT MEDICINE BEND, 1957
SHOOT THE WORKS, 1934
SHOOT TO KILL, 1961
SHOOTING HIGH, 1940
SHOOTING STRAIGHT, 1930
SHOP AROUND THE CORNER, THE, 1940
SHOPWORN, 1932
SHOPWORN ANGEL, 1938
SHOPWORN ANGEL, THE, 1928
SHORT CIRCUIT 2, 1988
SHOT IN THE DARK, A, 1933
SHOTGUN PASS, 1932
SHOULD A GIRL MARRY?, 1929
SHOULD A GIRL MARRY?, 1939
SHOW BOAT, 1929
SHOW BOAT, 1936
SHOW BOAT, 1951
SHOW FLAT, 1936
SHOW FOLKS, 1928
SHOW GIRL, 1928
SHOW GIRL IN HOLLYWOOD, 1930
SHOW GOES ON, THE, 1937
SHOW-OFF, THE, 1934
SHOW-OFF, THE, 1946
SHOWDOWN, THE, 1950
SHOWDOWN, 1963
SHOWDOWN, 1973
SHOWDOWN AT ABILENE, 1956
SHOWDOWN AT BOOT HILL, 1958
SHOWDOWN, THE, 1940
SHOWTIME, 1948
SHRIEK IN THE NIGHT, A, 1933
SICILIANS, THE, 1964
SIDE SHOW, 1931

SIDE STREET, 1929
SIDE STREET ANGEL, 1937
SIDE STREETS, 1934
SIDECAR RACERS, 1975
SIEGE OF THE SAXONS, 1963
SIERRA, 1950
SIERRA BARON, 1958
SIERRA PASSAGE, 1951
SIERRA SUE, 1941
SIGN OF THE RAM, THE, 1948
SIGNALS-AN ADVENTURE IN SPACE, 1970
SILENCE HAS NO WINGS, 1971
SILENT BARRIERS, 1937
SILENT CALL, THE, 1961
SILENT CONFLICT, 1948
SILENT DUST, 1949
SILENT INVASION, THE, 1962
SILENT ONE, THE, 1984
SILENT PASSENGER, THE, 1935
SILK EXPRESS, THE, 1933
SILK HAT KID, 1935
SILK NOOSE, THE, 1950
SILK STOCKINGS, 1957
SILKEN AFFAIR, THE, 1957
SILLY BILLIES, 1936
SILVER BANDIT, THE, 1950
SILVER CANYON, 1951
SILVER CHALICE, THE, 1954
SILVER CITY BONANZA, 1951
SILVER CITY KID, 1944
SILVER CITY RAIDERS, 1943
SILVER CORD, 1933
SILVER DARLINGS, THE, 1947
SILVER DOLLAR, 1932
SILVER FLEET, THE, 1945
SILVER HORDE, THE, 1930
SILVER LINING, 1932
SILVER LODE, 1954
SILVER ON THE SAGE, 1939
SILVER QUEEN, 1942
SILVER RAIDERS, 1950
SILVER RIVER, 1948
SILVER SKATES, 1943
SILVER SPOON, THE, 1934
SILVER SPURS, 1936
SILVER SPURS, 1943
SILVER STALLION, 1941
SILVER STAR, THE, 1955
SILVER STREAK, THE, 1935
SILVER TOP, 1938
SILVER TRAIL, THE, 1937
SILVER TRAILS, 1948
SILVER WHIP, THE, 1953
SIMPLE CASE OF MONEY, A, 1952
SIMPLY TERRIFIC, 1938
SIN OF NORA MORAN, 1933
SIN SHIP, 1931
SIN TAKES A HOLIDAY, 1930
SIN TOWN, 1942
SINBAD THE SAILOR, 1947
SINCE YOU WENT AWAY, 1944
SINCERELY YOURS, 1955
SING A JINGLE, 1943
SING ALONG WITH ME, 1952
SING AND BE HAPPY, 1937
SING AND LIKE IT, 1934
SING ANOTHER CHORUS, 1941
SING AS WE GO, 1934
SING AS YOU SWING, 1937
SING, BABY, SING, 1936
SING, COWBOY, SING, 1937
SING, DANCE, PLENTY HOT, 1940
SING ME A LOVE SONG, 1936
SING, NEIGHBOR, SING, 1944
SING WHILE YOU DANCE, 1946
SING WHILE YOU'RE ABLE, 1937
SING YOUR WAY HOME, 1945
SING YOUR WORRIES AWAY, 1942
SINGAPORE, 1947
SINGAPORE WOMAN, 1941
SINGIN' IN THE RAIN, 1952
SINGING COP, THE, 1938
SINGING COWBOY, THE, 1936
SINGING COWGIRL, THE, 1939
SINGING FOOL, THE, 1928

SINGING GUNS, 1950
SINGING IN THE DARK, 1956
SINGING KID, THE, 1936
SINGING MARINE, THE, 1937
SINGING NUN, THE, 1966
SINGING OUTLAW, 1937
SINGING PRINCESS, THE, 1967
SINGING SHERIFF, THE, 1944
SINGING TAXI DRIVER, 1953
SINGING THROUGH, 1935
SINGING VAGABOND, THE, 1935
SINGLE-HANDED SANDERS, 1932
SINGLE SIN, 1931
SINISTER HANDS, 1932
SINISTER JOURNEY, 1948
SINK THE BISMARCK, 1960
SINNER'S HOLIDAY, 1930
SINS OF MAN, 1936
SINS OF THE CHILDREN, 1930
SINS OF THE FATHERS, 1928
SINS PAYDAY, 1932
SIOUX CITY SUE, 1946
SIREN OF ATLANTIS, 1948
SIREN OF BAGDAD, 1953
SIROCCO, 1951
SIS HOPKINS, 1941
SISTER KENNY, 1946
SISTER TO ASSIST'ER, A, 1930
SISTER TO ASSIST'ER, A, 1938
SISTER TO ASSIST'ER, A, 1948
SISTERS, 1930
SISTERS, THE, 1938
SIT TIGHT, 1931
SITTING ON THE MOON, 1936
SITTING PRETTY, 1933
SITUATION HOPELESS—BUT NOT SERIOUS, 1965
SIX BLACK HORSES, 1962
SIX BRIDGES TO CROSS, 1955
SIX CYLINDER LOVE, 1931
SIX-DAY BIKE RIDER, 1934
6.5 SPECIAL, 1958
SIX GUN GOLD, 1941
SIX GUN GOSPEL, 1943
SIX GUN MAN, 1946
SIX-GUN RHYTHM, 1939
SIX GUN SERENADE, 1947
SIX LESSONS FROM MADAME LA ZONGA, 1941
SIX MEN, THE, 1951
SIX OF A KIND, 1934
SIX P.M., 1946
SIX SHOOTIN' SHERIFF, 1938
SIXTEEN FATHOMS DEEP, 1934
SIXTEEN FATHOMS DEEP, 1948
SIXTY GLORIOUS YEARS, 1938
SKATETOWN, U.S.A., 1979
SKI PARTY, 1965
SKI PATROL, 1940
SKIMPY IN THE NAVY, 1949
SKINNER STEPS OUT, 1929
SKIPALONG ROSENBLOOM, 1951
SKIPPER SURPRISED HIS WIFE, THE, 1950
SKIRTS AHOY!, 1952
SKY BANDITS, THE, 1940
SKY BRIDE, 1932
SKY CALLS, THE, 1959
SKY COMMANDO, 1953
SKY DEVILS, 1932
SKY DRAGON, 1949
SKY FULL OF MOON, 1952
SKY GIANT, 1938
SKY HAWK, 1929
SKY HIGH, 1952
SKY LINER, 1949
SKY MURDER, 1940
SKY PARADE, 1936
SKY PATROL, 1939
SKY RAIDERS, 1931
SKY RAIDERS, THE, 1938
SKY SPIDER, THE, 1931
SKYJACKED, 1972
SKYLARK, 1941
SKYLARKS, 1936
SKYLINE, 1931
SKY'S THE LIMIT, THE, 1937
SKY'S THE LIMIT, THE, 1943
SKYSCRAPER SOULS, 1932

SKYWAY, 1933
SLANDER, 1956
SLANDER HOUSE, 1938
SLAUGHTER TRAIL, 1951
SLAVE GIRL, 1947
SLAVE SHIP, 1937
SLAVE, THE, 1963
SLAVES OF BABYLON, 1953
SLEEP, MY LOVE, 1948
SLEEPERS EAST, 1934
SLEEPERS WEST, 1941
SLEEPING CAR, 1933
SLEEPING CAR TO TRIESTE, 1949
SLEEPING PARTNERS, 1930
SLEEPLESS NIGHTS, 1933
SLEEPY LAGOON, 1943
SLEEPYTIME GAL, 1942
SLIGHT CASE OF LARCENY, A, 1953
SLIGHT CASE OF MURDER, A, 1938
SLIGHTLY DANGEROUS, 1943
SLIGHTLY FRENCH, 1949
SLIGHTLY HONORABLE, 1940
SLIGHTLY MARRIED, 1933
SLIGHTLY SCANDALOUS, 1946
SLIGHTLY SCARLET, 1930
SLIGHTLY TEMPTED, 1940
SLIGHTLY TERRIFIC, 1944
SLIM, 1937
SLIM CARTER, 1957
SLIME PEOPLE, THE, 1963
SLIPPER EPISODE, THE, 1938
SLIPPY MCGEE, 1948
SMALL HOTEL, 1957
SMALL MAN, THE, 1935
SMALL TOWN BOY, 1937
SMALL TOWN DEB, 1941
SMALL TOWN GIRL, 1936
SMALL TOWN GIRL, 1953
SMALL TOWN STORY, 1953
SMALLEST SHOW ON EARTH, THE, 1957
SMART ALEC, 1951
SMART ALECKS, 1942
SMART BLONDE, 1937
SMART GIRL, 1935
SMART GIRLS DON'T TALK, 1948
SMART GUY, 1943
SMART MONEY, 1931
SMART POLITICS, 1948
SMART WOMAN, 1931
SMART WOMAN, 1948
SMARTEST GIRL IN TOWN, 1936
SMARTY, 1934
SMASHING THE MONEY RING, 1939
SMASHING THE RACKETS, 1938
SMASHING THE SPY RING, 1939
SMILES OF A SUMMER NIGHT, 1957
SMILEY, 1957
SMILEY GETS A GUN, 1959
SMILIN' THROUGH, 1932
SMILIN' THROUGH, 1941
SMILING ALONG, 1938
SMILING GHOST, THE, 1941
SMILING IRISH EYES, 1929
SMITH, 1969
SMITH'S WIVES, 1935
SMITHY, 1933
SMITHY, 1946
SMOKE SIGNAL, 1955
SMOKE TREE RANGE, 1937
SMOKESCREEN, 1964
SMOKEY SMITH, 1935
SMOKING GUNS, 1934
SMOKY, 1933
SMOKY, 1946
SMOKY, 1966
SMOKY CANYON, 1952
SMOKY MOUNTAIN MELODY, 1949
SMOKY TRAILS, 1939
SMOOTH AS SILK, 1946
SMUGGLED CARGO, 1939
SMUGGLERS' COVE, 1948
SMUGGLER'S GOLD, 1951
SMUGGLER'S ISLAND, 1951
SMUGGLERS, THE, 1948
SNAFU, 1945
SNAKE RIVER DESPERADOES, 1951

SNIPER'S RIDGE, 1961
SNORKEL, THE, 1958
SNOW CREATURE, THE, 1954
SNOW DEVILS, THE, 1965
SNOW JOB, 1972
SNOW TREASURE, 1968
SNOW WHITE AND THE THREE STOOGES, 1961
SNOWBALL, 1960
SNOWBOUND, 1949
SNOWED UNDER, 1936
SNUFFY SMITH, YARD BIRD, 1942
SO BIG, 1932
SO BIG, 1953
SO ENDS OUR NIGHT, 1941
SO EVIL SO YOUNG, 1961
SO GOES MY LOVE, 1946
SO IT'S SUNDAY, 1932
SO LITTLE TIME, 1953
SO LONG AT THE FAIR, 1951
SO LONG LETTY, 1929
SO PROUDLY WE HAIL, 1943
SO RED THE ROSE, 1935
SO THIS IS AFRICA, 1933
SO THIS IS COLLEGE, 1929
SO THIS IS LONDON, 1930
SO THIS IS LONDON, 1940
SO THIS IS LOVE, 1953
SO THIS IS NEW YORK, 1948
SO THIS IS PARIS, 1954
SO THIS IS WASHINGTON, 1943
SO YOU WON'T TALK?, 1935
SO YOU WON'T TALK, 1940
SO YOUNG, SO BAD, 1950
SOAK THE RICH, 1936
SOB SISTER, 1931
SOCIAL LION, THE, 1930
SOCIAL REGISTER, 1934
SOCIETY DOCTOR, 1935
SOCIETY FEVER, 1935
SOCIETY GIRL, 1932
SOCIETY LAWYER, 1939
SOCIETY SMUGGLERS, 1939
SOFI, 1967
SOFIA, 1948
SOHO CONSPIRACY, 1951
SOLDIER, SAILOR, 1944
SOLDIERS AND WOMEN, 1930
SOLDIERS OF THE STORM, 1933
SOLDIER'S PLAYTHING, A, 1931
SOLDIER'S TALE, THE, 1964
SOLDIERS THREE, 1951
SOLID GOLD CADILLAC, THE, 1956
SOLITAIRE MAN, THE, 1933
SOLITARY CHILD, THE, 1958
SOLO FOR SPARROW, 1966
SOLUTION BY PHONE, 1954
SOMBRERO KID, THE, 1942
SOME BLONDES ARE DANGEROUS, 1937
SOME DAY, 1935
SOME LIKE IT HOT, 1939
SOME MAY LIVE, 1967
SOME PEOPLE, 1964
SOME WILL, SOME WON'T, 1970
SOMEBODY KILLED HER HUSBAND, 1978
SOMEBODY LOVES ME, 1952
SOMEONE AT THE DOOR, 1936
SOMEONE AT THE DOOR, 1950
SOMEONE TO LOVE, 1988
SOMEONE TO REMEMBER, 1943
SOMETHING ALWAYS HAPPENS, 1934
SOMETHING BIG, 1971
SOMETHING FOR THE BIRDS, 1952
SOMETHING FOR THE BOYS, 1944
SOMETHING IN THE CITY, 1950
SOMETHING IN THE WIND, 1947
SOMETHING MONEY CAN'T BUY, 1952
SOMETHING TO LIVE FOR, 1952
SOMETHING TO SHOUT ABOUT, 1943
SOMETHING TO SING ABOUT, 1937
SOMETHING WILD, 1961
SOMETIMES GOOD, 1934
SOMEWHERE I'LL FIND YOU, 1942
SOMEWHERE IN BERLIN, 1949
SOMEWHERE IN CAMP, 1942
SOMEWHERE IN CIVVIES, 1943
SOMEWHERE IN ENGLAND, 1940

SOMEWHERE IN FRANCE, 1943
SOMEWHERE IN POLITICS, 1949
SOMEWHERE IN SONORA, 1933
SOMEWHERE ON LEAVE, 1942
SON COMES HOME, A, 1936
SON-DAUGHTER, THE, 1932
SON OF A BADMAN, 1949
SON OF A GUNFIGHTER, 1966
SON OF A SAILOR, 1933
SON OF ALI BABA, 1952
SON OF BELLE STARR, 1953
SON OF BILLY THE KID, 1949
SON OF CAPTAIN BLOOD, THE, 1964
SON OF DAVY CROCKETT, THE, 1941
SON OF DR. JEKYLL, THE, 1951
SON OF FURY, 1942
SON OF GOD'S COUNTRY, 1948
SON OF INDIA, 1931
SON OF INGAGI, 1940
SON OF KONG, 1933
SON OF MONGOLIA, 1936
SON OF MONTE CRISTO, 1940
SON OF OKLAHOMA, 1932
SON OF PALEFACE, 1952
SON OF ROARING DAN, 1940
SON OF ROBIN HOOD, 1959
SON OF SAMSON, 1962
SON OF SINBAD, 1955
SON OF THE BORDER, 1933
SON OF THE GODS, 1930
SON OF THE NAVY, 1940
SON OF THE PLAINS, 1931
SON OF THE RED CORSAIR, 1963
SON OF THE REGIMENT, 1948
SON OF THE RENEGADE, 1953
SONG AND DANCE MAN, THE, 1936
SONG AND THE SILENCE, THE, 1969
SONG FOR MISS JULIE, A, 1945
SONG FOR TOMORROW, A, 1948
SONG FROM MY HEART, THE, 1970
SONG IS BORN, A, 1948
SONG O' MY HEART, 1930
SONG OF ARIZONA, 1946
SONG OF FREEDOM, 1938
SONG OF IDAHO, 1948
SONG OF INDIA, 1949
SONG OF KENTUCKY, 1929
SONG OF LIFE, THE, 1931
SONG OF LOVE, 1947
SONG OF LOVE, THE, 1929
SONG OF MEXICO, 1945
SONG OF MY HEART, 1947
SONG OF NEVADA, 1944
SONG OF NORWAY, 1970
SONG OF OLD WYOMING, 1945
SONG OF RUSSIA, 1943
SONG OF SCHEHERAZADE, 1947
SONG OF SOHO, 1930
SONG OF SURRENDER, 1949
SONG OF TEXAS, 1943
SONG OF THE BUCKAROO, 1939
SONG OF THE CABELLERO, 1930
SONG OF THE CITY, 1937
SONG OF THE DRIFTER, 1948
SONG OF THE EAGLE, 1933
SONG OF THE FLAME, 1930
SONG OF THE FOREST, 1963
SONG OF THE FORGE, 1937
SONG OF THE GRINGO, 1936
SONG OF THE ISLANDS, 1942
SONG OF THE OPEN ROAD, 1944
SONG OF THE ROAD, 1937
SONG OF THE SADDLE, 1936
SONG OF THE SARONG, 1945
SONG OF THE SIERRAS, 1946
SONG OF THE THIN MAN, 1947
SONG OF THE TRAIL, 1936
SONG OF THE WASTELAND, 1947
SONG OF THE WEST, 1930
SONG OVER MOSCOW, 1964
SONG TO REMEMBER, A, 1945
SONG WITHOUT END, 1960
SONG YOU GAVE ME, THE, 1934
SONGS AND BULLETS, 1938
SONNY BOY, 1929
SONORA STAGECOACH, 1944

BOLD: Films on Videocassette

SONS AND MOTHERS, 1967
SONS O' GUNS, 1936
SONS OF ADVENTURE, 1948
SONS OF KATIE ELDER, THE, 1965
SONS OF NEW MEXICO, 1949
SONS OF STEEL, 1935
SONS OF THE DESERT, 1933
SONS OF THE LEGION, 1938
SONS OF THE PIONEERS, 1942
SONS OF THE SADDLE, 1930
SONS OF THE SEA, 1939
SOOKY, 1931
SOPHIE LANG GOES WEST, 1937
SOPHOMORE, THE, 1929
SORORITY HOUSE, 1939
SORRELL AND SON, 1934
SORROWFUL JONES, 1949
S.O.S. ICEBERG, 1933
S.O.S. PACIFIC, 1960
S.O.S. TIDAL WAVE, 1939
SO'S YOUR UNCLE, 1943
SOUL OF A MONSTER, THE, 1944
SOUL OF THE SLUMS, 1931
SOULS AT SEA, 1937
SOULS IN CONFLICT, 1955
SOUND OF LIFE, THE, 1962
SOUND OF TRUMPETS, THE, 1963
SOUND OFF, 1952
SOUP TO NUTS, 1930
SOUTH AMERICAN GEORGE, 1941
SOUTH OF ARIZONA, 1938
SOUTH OF CALIENTE, 1951
SOUTH OF DEATH VALLEY, 1949
SOUTH OF DIXIE, 1944
SOUTH OF PAGO PAGO, 1940
SOUTH OF PANAMA, 1941
SOUTH OF RIO, 1949
SOUTH OF ST. LOUIS, 1949
SOUTH OF SANTA FE, 1932
SOUTH OF SANTA FE, 1942
SOUTH OF SONORA, 1930
SOUTH OF SUEZ, 1940
SOUTH OF TAHITI, 1941
SOUTH OF THE BORDER, 1939
SOUTH OF THE RIO GRANDE, 1932
SOUTH OF THE RIO GRANDE, 1945
SOUTH PACIFIC, 1958
SOUTH PACIFIC TRAIL, 1952
SOUTH RIDING, 1938
SOUTH SEA ROSE, 1929
SOUTH SEA SINNER, 1950
SOUTH SEA WOMAN, 1953
SOUTH TO KARANGA, 1940
SOUTHERN MAID, A, 1933
SOUTHERN ROSES, 1936
SOUTHERNER, THE, 1945
SOUTHSIDE 1-1000, 1950
SOUTHWARD HO?, 1939
SOUTHWEST PASSAGE, 1954
SPACE AMOEBA, THE, 1970
SPACE CHILDREN, THE, 1958
SPACE CRUISER, 1977
SPACE FIREBIRD 2772, 1979
SPACE MASTER X-7, 1958
SPACE MONSTER, 1965
SPACE SHIP, THE, 1935
SPACECAMP, 1986
SPACEFLIGHT IC-1, 1965
SPACEWAYS, 1953
SPANIARD'S CURSE, THE, 1958
SPANISH AFFAIR, 1958
SPANISH CAPE MYSTERY, 1935
SPANISH EYES, 1930
SPANISH GARDENER, THE, 1957
SPANISH MAIN, THE, 1945
SPANISH SWORD, THE, 1962
SPARE A COPPER, 1940
SPARE THE ROD, 1961
SPARROWS CAN'T SING, 1963
SPAWN OF THE NORTH, 1938
SPEAK EASILY, 1932
SPEAKEASY, 1929
SPECIAL AGENT, 1949
SPECIAL AGENT K-7, 1937
SPECIAL DELIVERY, 1955
SPECIAL EDITION, 1938

SPECIAL INSPECTOR, 1939
SPECIAL INVESTIGATOR, 1936
SPECKLED BAND, THE, 1931
SPEED, 1936
SPEED DEVILS, 1935
SPEED LIMITED, 1940
SPEED LOVERS, 1968
SPEED MADNESS, 1932
SPEED REPORTER, 1936
SPEED TO BURN, 1938
SPEED TO SPARE, 1937
SPEED TO SPARE, 1948
SPEED WINGS, 1934
SPEEDTRAP, 1978
SPEEDWAY, 1968
SPELL OF AMY NUGENT, THE, 1945
SPELL OF THE HYPNOTIST, 1956
SPELLBINDER, THE, 1939
SPENDTHRIFT, 1936
SPESSART INN, THE, 1961
SPHINX, THE, 1933
SPICE OF LIFE, 1954
SPIDER, THE, 1958
SPIDER AND THE FLY, THE, 1952
SPIDER WOMAN STRIKES BACK, THE, 1946
SPIDER, THE, 1931
SPIDER, THE, 1940
SPIDER, THE, 1945
SPIDER'S WEB, THE, 1960
SPIELER, THE, 1929
SPIES OF THE AIR, 1940
SPIN A DARK WEB, 1956
SPINOUT, 1966
SPIRAL ROAD, THE, 1962
SPIRIT AND THE FLESH, THE, 1948
SPIRIT IS WILLING, THE, 1967
SPIRIT OF CULVER, THE, 1939
SPIRIT OF NOTRE DAME, THE, 1931
SPIRIT OF STANFORD, THE, 1942
SPIRIT OF THE WEST, 1932
SPIRIT OF WEST POINT, THE, 1947
SPIRIT OF YOUTH, 1937
SPIRITUALIST, THE, 1948
SPITFIRE, 1934
SPITFIRE, 1943
SPLENDID FELLOWS, 1934
SPLENDOR, 1935
SPLINTERS, 1929
SPLINTERS IN THE AIR, 1937
SPLINTERS IN THE NAVY, 1931
SPLIT SECOND, 1953
SPOILERS, THE, 1942
SPOILERS OF THE FOREST, 1957
SPOILERS OF THE NORTH, 1947
SPOILERS OF THE PLAINS, 1951
SPOILERS OF THE RANGE, 1939
SPOILERS, THE, 1930
SPOOK BUSTERS, 1946
SPOOK CHASERS, 1957
SPOOK TOWN, 1944
SPOOKS RUN WILD, 1941
SPORT OF KINGS, THE, 1931
SPORT OF KINGS, 1947
SPORT PARADE, THE, 1932
SPORTING BLOOD, 1931
SPORTING BLOOD, 1940
SPORTING CHANCE, 1931
SPORTING CHANCE, A, 1945
SPORTING LOVE, 1936
SPOT OF BOTHER, A, 1938
SPOTLIGHT SCANDALS, 1943
SPOTS ON MY LEOPARD, THE, 1974
SPRING, 1948
SPRING AFFAIR, 1960
SPRING HANDICAP, 1937
SPRING IN PARK LANE, 1949
SPRING IN THE AIR, 1934
SPRING IS HERE, 1930
SPRING MADNESS, 1938
SPRING MEETING, 1941
SPRING PARADE, 1940
SPRING REUNION, 1957
SPRING SHOWER, 1932
SPRING TONIC, 1935
SPRINGFIELD RIFLE, 1952
SPRINGTIME, 1948

SPRINGTIME FOR HENRY, 1934
SPRINGTIME IN THE ROCKIES, 1937
SPRINGTIME IN THE ROCKIES, 1942
SPRINGTIME IN THE SIERRAS, 1947
SPRINGTIME ON THE VOLGA, 1961
SPURS, 1930
SPUTNIK, 1960
SPY CHASERS, 1956
SPY FOR A DAY, 1939
SPY HUNT, 1950
SPY IN BLACK, THE, 1939
SPY IN THE GREEN HAT, THE, 1966
SPY IN THE SKY, 1958
SPY IN YOUR EYE, 1966
SPY OF NAPOLEON, 1939
SPY RING, THE, 1938
SPY SHIP, 1942
SPY TRAIN, 1943
SPY WITH A COLD NOSE, THE, 1966
SPY WITH MY FACE, THE, 1966
SPYLARKS, 1965
SQUAD CAR, 1961
SQUADRON LEADER X, 1943
SQUADRON OF HONOR, 1938
SQUALL, THE, 1929
SQUARE DANCE JUBILEE, 1949
SQUARE DANCE KATY, 1950
SQUARE JUNGLE, THE, 1955
SQUARE OF VIOLENCE, 1963
SQUARE PEG, THE, 1958
SQUARE RING, THE, 1955
SQUARE SHOULDERS, 1929
SQUARES, 1972
SQUATTER'S DAUGHTER, 1933
SQUAW MAN, THE, 1931
SQUEAKER, THE, 1930
SQUEALER, THE, 1930
SQUEEZE A FLOWER, 1970
SQUIBS, 1935
STABLEMATES, 1938
STAGE DOOR CANTEEN, 1943
STAGE MOTHER, 1933
STAGE STRUCK, 1936
STAGE TO BLUE RIVER, 1951
STAGE TO CHINO, 1940
STAGE TO MESA CITY, 1947
STAGE TO THUNDER ROCK, 1964
STAGE TO TUCSON, 1950
STAGECOACH BUCKAROO, 1942
STAGECOACH DAYS, 1938
STAGECOACH EXPRESS, 1942
STAGECOACH KID, 1949
STAGECOACH OUTLAWS, 1945
STAGECOACH TO DANCER'S PARK, 1962
STAGECOACH TO DENVER, 1946
STAGECOACH TO FURY, 1956
STAGECOACH TO MONTEREY, 1944
STAGECOACH WAR, 1940
STAIRWAY TO HEAVEN, 1946
STAKEOUT!, 1962
STALKING MOON, THE, 1969
STALLION CANYON, 1949
STALLION ROAD, 1947
STAMBOUL, 1931
STAMBOUL QUEST, 1934
STAMPEDE, 1936
STAMPEDE, 1949
STAND AND DELIVER, 1988
STAND AT APACHE RIVER, THE, 1953
STAND BY FOR ACTION, 1942
STAND-IN, 1937
STAND UP AND CHEER, 1934 80m FOX bw
STANDING ROOM ONLY, 1944
STAR, THE, 1953
STAR DUST, 1940
STAR FOR A NIGHT, 1936
STAR IN THE DUST, 1956
STAR INSPECTOR, THE, 1980
STAR OF HONG KONG, 1962
STAR OF INDIA, 1956
STAR OF MIDNIGHT, 1935
STAR OF TEXAS, 1953
STAR PACKER, THE, 1934
STAR PILOT, 1977
STAR REPORTER, 1939
STAR SPANGLED GIRL, 1971

STAR SPANGLED RHYTHM, 1942
STAR TREK: THE MOTION PICTURE, 1979
STAR TREK II: THE WRATH OF KHAN, 1982
STAR WITNESS, 1931
STARDUST ON THE SAGE, 1942
STARFIGHTERS, THE, 1964
STARK MAD, 1929
STARLIFT, 1951
STARLIGHT HOTEL, 1987
STARLIGHT OVER TEXAS, 1938
STARS ARE SINGING, THE, 1953
STARS IN MY CROWN, 1950
STARS IN YOUR EYES, 1956
STARS ON PARADE, 1944
STARS OVER ARIZONA, 1937
STARS OVER BROADWAY, 1935
STARS OVER TEXAS, 1946
START CHEERING, 1938
STATE DEPARTMENT—FILE 649, 1949
STATE FAIR, 1933
STATE FAIR, 1945
STATE FAIR, 1962
STATE OF THE UNION, 1948
STATE OF THINGS, THE, 1983
STATE PENITENTIARY, 1950
STATE POLICE, 1938
STATE TROOPER, 1933
STATE'S ATTORNEY, 1932
STATION WEST, 1948
STAY AWAY, JOE, 1968
STEADY COMPANY, 1932
STEAMBOAT ROUND THE BEND, 1935
STEEL AGAINST THE SKY, 1941
STEEL BAYONET, THE, 1958
STEEL CAGE, THE, 1954
STEEL CLAW, THE, 1961
STEEL FIST, THE, 1952
STEEL JUNGLE, THE, 1956
STEEL KEY, THE, 1953
STEEL LADY, THE, 1953
STEEL TOWN, 1952
STEEL TRAP, THE, 1952
STELLA, 1950
STELLA DALLAS, 1937
STEP BY STEP, 1946
STEP DOWN TO TERROR, 1958
STEP LIVELY, 1944
STEP LIVELY, JEEVES, 1937
STEPCHILD, 1947
STEPCHILDREN, 1962
STEPPE, THE, 1963
STEPPIN' IN SOCIETY, 1945
STEPPING SISTERS, 1932
STEPPING TOES, 1938
STEPS TO THE MOON, 1963
STEVIE, 1978
STICK 'EM UP, 1950
STICK TO YOUR GUNS, 1941
STICK UP, THE, 1978
STINGAREE, 1934
STITCH IN TIME, A, 1967
STOCK CAR, 1955
STOKER, THE, 1932
STOKER, THE, 1935
STOLEN ASSIGNMENT, 1955
STOLEN FACE, 1952
STOLEN HARMONY, 1935
STOLEN HEAVEN, 1931
STOLEN HEAVEN, 1938
STOLEN HOLIDAY, 1937
STOLEN IDENTITY, 1953
STOLEN KISSES, 1929
STOLEN LIFE, 1939
STOLEN SWEETS, 1934
STONE OF SILVER CREEK, 1935
STOOGE, THE, 1952
STOOGEMANIA, 1986
STOP PRESS GIRL, 1949
STOP THAT CAB, 1951
STOP THE WORLD—I WANT TO GET OFF, 1966
STOP TRAIN 349, 1964
STOP, YOU'RE KILLING ME, 1952
STOP, LOOK, AND LOVE, 1939
STOPOVER FOREVER, 1964
STOPOVER TOKYO, 1957
STORK BITES MAN, 1947

STORK CLUB, THE, 1945
STORK PAYS OFF, THE, 1941
STORM AT DAYBREAK, 1933
STORM CENTER, 1956
STORM FEAR, 1956
STORM IN A TEACUP, 1937
STORM IN A WATER GLASS, 1931
STORM OVER BENGAL, 1938
STORM OVER LISBON, 1944
STORM OVER THE ANDES, 1935
STORM OVER THE NILE, 1955
STORM OVER TIBET, 1952
STORM OVER WYOMING, 1950
STORM PLANET, 1962
STORM RIDER, THE, 1957
STORM, THE, 1930
STORM, THE, 1938
STORMBOUND, 1951
STORMY, 1935
STORMY TRAILS, 1936
STORMY WATERS, 1946
STORMY WEATHER, 1935
STORMY WEATHER, 1943
STORY OF DAVID, A, 1960
STORY OF JOSEPH AND HIS BRETHREN THE, 1962
STORY OF MANKIND, THE, 1957
STORY OF MOLLY X, THE, 1949
STORY OF RUTH, THE, 1960
STORY OF SEABISCUIT, THE, 1949
STORY OF SHIRLEY YORKE, THE, 1948
STORY OF THE COUNT OF MONTE CRISTO, THE, 1962
STORY OF THREE LOVES, THE, 1953
STORY OF VERNON AND IRENE CASTLE, THE, 1939
STORY OF VICKIE, THE, 1958
STORY OF WILL ROGERS, THE, 1952
STORY WITHOUT WORDS, 1981
STOWAWAY, 1932
STOWAWAY GIRL, 1957
STRAIGHT FROM THE HEART, 1935
STRAIGHT FROM THE SHOULDER, 1936
STRAIGHT IS THE WAY, 1934
STRAIGHT, PLACE AND SHOW, 1938
STRAIGHT SHOOTER, 1940
STRAIGHT TO HEAVEN, 1939
STRAIGHTAWAY, 1934
STRANDED, 1935
STRANGE ADVENTURE, 1932
STRANGE ADVENTURE, A, 1956
STRANGE ADVENTURES OF MR. SMITH, THE, 1937
STRANGE AFFAIR, 1944
STRANGE AFFECTION, 1959
STRANGE ALIBI, 1941
STRANGE BARGAIN, 1949
STRANGE BOARDERS, 1938
STRANGE CARGO, 1929
STRANGE CARGO, 1936
STRANGE CASE OF CLARA DEANE, THE, 1932
STRANGE CASE OF DR. MANNING, THE, 1958
STRANGE CASE OF DR. MEADE, 1939
STRANGE CASE OF DR. RX, THE, 1942
STRANGE CONFESSION, 1945
STRANGE CONQUEST, 1946
STRANGE DEATH OF ADOLF HITLER, THE, 1943
STRANGE DOOR, THE, 1951
STRANGE EVIDENCE, 1933
STRANGE EXPERIMENT, 1937
STRANGE FACES, 1938
STRANGE FASCINATION, 1952
STRANGE GAMBLE, 1948
STRANGE HOLIDAY, 1945
STRANGE HOLIDAY, 1969
STRANGE ILLUSION, 1945
STRANGE IMPERSONATION, 1946
STRANGE INTRUDER, 1956
STRANGE JOURNEY, 1946
STRANGE JUSTICE, 1932
STRANGE LADY IN TOWN, 1955
STRANGE LOVE OF MOLLY LOUVAIN, THE, 1932
STRANGE MR. GREGORY, THE, 1945
STRANGE MRS. CRANE, THE, 1948
STRANGE PEOPLE, 1933
STRANGE TRIANGLE, 1946
STRANGE VOYAGE, 1945
STRANGE WIVES, 1935
STRANGE WORLD, 1952

STRANGER AT MY DOOR, 1950
STRANGER AT MY DOOR, 1956
STRANGER FROM ARIZONA, THE, 1938
STRANGER FROM PECOS, THE, 1943
STRANGER FROM TEXAS, THE, 1940
STRANGER FROM VENUS, THE, 1954
STRANGER IN BETWEEN, THE, 1952
STRANGER IN MY ARMS, 1959
STRANGER IN TOWN, 1932
STRANGER IN TOWN, 1957
STRANGER IN TOWN, A, 1943
STRANGER ON HORSEBACK, 1955
STRANGER RETURNS, THE, 1968
STRANGER WORE A GUN, THE, 1953
STRANGER'S MEETING, 1957
STRANGER'S RETURN, 1933
STRANGERS ALL, 1935
STRANGER'S HAND, THE, 1955
STRANGERS IN LOVE, 1932
STRANGERS IN THE CITY, 1962
STRANGERS MAY KISS, 1931
STRANGERS OF THE EVENING, 1932
STRANGERS ON A HONEYMOON, 1937
STRANGERS, THE, 1955
STRANGLEHOLD, 1931
STRANGLEHOLD, 1962
STRANGLER OF THE SWAMP, 1945
STRATEGIC AIR COMMAND, 1955
STRATEGY OF TERROR, 1969
STRAUSS' GREAT WALTZ, 1934
STRAW MAN, THE, 1953
STRAWBERRY BLONDE, THE, 1941
STRAWBERRY ROAN, 1933
STRAWBERRY ROAN, 1945
STRAWBERRY ROAN, THE, 1948
STREAMLINE EXPRESS, 1935
STREET ANGEL, 1928
STREET BANDITS, 1951
STREET FIGHTER, 1959
STREET GIRL, 1929
STREET OF CHANCE, 1930
STREET OF CHANCE, 1942
STREET OF DARKNESS, 1958
STREET OF MEMORIES, 1940
STREET OF MISSING MEN, 1939
STREET OF SINNERS, 1957
STREET OF WOMEN, 1932
STREET SINGER, THE, 1937
STREET SONG, 1935
STREETS OF GHOST TOWN, 1950
STREETS OF NEW YORK, 1939
STREETS OF SAN FRANCISCO, 1949
STRICTLY CONFIDENTIAL, 1959
STRICTLY DISHONORABLE, 1951
STRICTLY DYNAMITE, 1934
STRICTLY ILLEGAL, 1935
STRICTLY IN THE GROOVE, 1942
STRICTLY MODERN, 1930
STRICTLY PERSONAL, 1933
STRICTLY UNCONVENTIONAL, 1930
STRIKE!, 1934
STRIKE IT RICH, 1933
STRIKE IT RICH, 1948
STRIKE ME PINK, 1936
STRONGER SEX, THE, 1931
STRONGER THAN DESIRE, 1939
STRONGER THAN THE SUN, 1980
STRONGEST MAN IN THE WORLD, THE, 1975
STRONGHOLD, 1952
STRONGROOM, 1962
STUDENT PRINCE, THE, 1954
STUDENT TOUR, 1934
STUDENT'S ROMANCE, THE, 1936
STUDIO MURDER MYSTERY, THE, 1929
STUDS LONIGAN, 1960
STUDY IN SCARLET, A, 1933
STUDY IN TERROR, A, 1966
STUNT PILOT, 1939
SUBMARINE ALERT, 1943
SUBMARINE BASE, 1943
SUBMARINE COMMAND, 1951
SUBMARINE D-1, 1937
SUBMARINE PATROL, 1938
SUBMARINE RAIDER, 1942
SUBMARINE SEAHAWK, 1959
SUBMARINE X-1, 1969

BOLD: Films on Videocassette

TANGLED DESTINIES, 1932
TANGLED EVIDENCE, 1934
TANGO, 1936
TANGO BAR, 1935
TANK BATTALION, 1958
TANK COMMANDOS, 1959
TANK FORCE, 1958
TANKS A MILLION, 1941
TANKS ARE COMING, THE, 1951
TANNED LEGS, 1929
TARANTULA, 1955
TARAS BULBA, 1962
TARAS FAMILY, THE, 1946
TARAWA BEACHHEAD, 1958
TARGET, 1952
TARGET EARTH, 1954
TARGET HONG KONG, 1952
TARGET UNKNOWN, 1951
TARGET ZERO, 1955
TARNISHED, 1950
TARNISHED ANGEL, 1938
TARNISHED HEROES, 1961
TARNISHED LADY, 1931
TARS AND SPARS, 1946
TARTARS, THE, 1962
TARZAN AND THE AMAZONS, 1945
TARZAN AND THE GREAT RIVER, 1967
TARZAN ESCAPES, 1936
TARZAN, THE APE MAN, 1959
TARZAN THE MAGNIFICENT, 1960
TARZAN'S PERIL, 1951
TASK FORCE, 1949
TASTE OF MONEY, A, 1960
TAWNY PIPIT, 1947
TAXI, 1953
TAXI!, 1932
TAXI FOR TOBRUK, 1965
TAXI FOR TWO, 1929
TAXI TO HEAVEN, 1944
TAZA, SON OF COCHISE, 1954
TE QUIERO CON LOCURA, 1935
TEA AND RICE, 1964
TEA FOR TWO, 1950
TEACHER AND THE MIRACLE, THE, 1961
TEACHER'S PET, 1958
TEAR GAS SQUAD, 1940
TEARS FOR SIMON, 1957
TEARS OF HAPPINESS, 1974
TECKMAN MYSTERY, THE, 1955
TEENAGE CAVEMAN, 1958
TEENAGE MILLIONAIRE, 1961
TEENAGE MONSTER, 1958
TEENAGE REBEL, 1956
TEENAGE THUNDER, 1957
TEENAGERS FROM OUTER SPACE, 1959
TEL AVIV TAXI, 1957
TELEGRAPH TRAIL, THE, 1933
TELEPHONE OPERATOR, 1938
TELEVISION SPY, 1939
TELEVISION TALENT, 1937
TELL IT TO A STAR, 1945
TELL IT TO THE JUDGE, 1949
TELL ME A RIDDLE, 1980
TELL NO TALES, 1939
TEMPLE TOWER, 1930
TEMPTATION, 1935
TEMPTATION, 1936
TEMPTATION, 1946
TEMPTATION HARBOR, 1949
TEMPTRESS, THE, 1949
TEN CENTS A DANCE, 1931
TEN CENTS A DANCE, 1945
TEN DAYS TO TULARA, 1958
TEN GENTLEMEN FROM WEST POINT, 1942
TEN LAPS TO GO, 1938
TEN LITTLE INDIANS, 1965
TEN MINUTE ALIBI, 1935
TEN NIGHTS IN A BARROOM, 1931
$10 RAISE, 1935
TEN SECONDS TO HELL, 1959
TEN THOUSAND BEDROOMS, 1957
TEN WHO DARED, 1960
TENDER COMRADE, 1943
TENDER HEARTS, 1955
TENDER TRAP, THE, 1955
TENDERFOOT GOES WEST, A, 1937

TENDERFOOT, THE, 1932
TENDERLOIN, 1928
TENNESSEE CHAMP, 1954
TENNESSEE JOHNSON, 1942
TENSION AT TABLE ROCK, 1956
TENTH AVENUE ANGEL, 1948
TENTH AVENUE KID, 1938
TENTH MAN, THE, 1937
TENTING TONIGHT ON THE OLD CAMP GROUND, 1943
TERESA, 1951
TERROR, THE, 1928
TERROR, THE, 1941
TERROR ABOARD, 1933
TERROR AT MIDNIGHT, 1956
TERROR BY NIGHT, 1946
TERROR FROM THE YEAR 5,000, 1958
TERROR IN A TEXAS TOWN, 1958
TERROR IN THE JUNGLE, 1968
TERROR OF THE BLACK MASK, 1967
TERROR OF THE BLOODHUNTERS, 1962
TERROR OF TINY TOWN, THE, 1938
TERROR ON A TRAIN, 1953
TERROR ON TIPTOE, 1936
TERROR SHIP, 1954
TERROR STREET, 1953
TERROR TRAIL, 1933
TERRORNAUTS, THE, 1967
TERRORS ON HORSEBACK, 1946
TESHA, 1929
TESS OF THE STORM COUNTRY, 1932
TESS OF THE STORM COUNTRY, 1961
TEST PILOT, 1938
TESTAMENT, 1983
TEVYA, 1939
TEX, 1982
TEX RIDES WITH THE BOY SCOUTS, 1937
TEX TAKES A HOLIDAY, 1932
TEXAN MEETS CALAMITY JANE, THE, 1950
TEXAN, THE, 1930
TEXANS NEVER CRY, 1951
TEXANS, THE, 1938
TEXAS, 1941
TEXAS ACROSS THE RIVER, 1966
TEXAS BAD MAN, 1932
TEXAS BAD MAN, 1953
TEXAS, BROOKLYN AND HEAVEN, 1948
TEXAS BUDDIES, 1932
TEXAS CARNIVAL, 1951
TEXAS CITY, 1952
TEXAS CYCLONE, 1932
TEXAS DYNAMO, 1950
TEXAS GUN FIGHTER, 1932
TEXAS KID, THE, 1944
TEXAS LADY, 1955
TEXAS LAWMEN, 1951
TEXAS MAN HUNT, 1942
TEXAS MARSHAL, THE, 1941
TEXAS MASQUERADE, 1944
TEXAS PIONEERS, 1932
TEXAS RANGER, THE, 1931
TEXAS RANGERS RIDE AGAIN, 1940
TEXAS RANGERS, THE, 1936
TEXAS RANGERS, THE, 1951
TEXAS STAGECOACH, 1940
TEXAS STAMPEDE, 1939
TEXAS TERROR, 1935
TEXAS TERRORS, 1940
TEXAS TO BATAAN, 1942
TEXAS TORNADO, 1934
TEXAS TRAIL, 1937
TEXAS WILDCATS, 1939
TEXICAN, THE, 1966
THANK EVANS, 1938
THANK HEAVEN FOR SMALL FAVORS, 1965
THANK YOU, JEEVES, 1936
THANK YOU, MR. MOTO, 1937
THANK YOUR LUCKY STARS, 1943
THANKS A MILLION, 1935
THANKS FOR EVERYTHING, 1938
THANKS FOR LISTENING, 1937
THANKS FOR THE MEMORY, 1938
THARK, 1932
THAT BRENNAN GIRL, 1946
THAT CERTAIN AGE, 1938
THAT CERTAIN FEELING, 1956

THAT CERTAIN SOMETHING, 1941
THAT GANG OF MINE, 1940
THAT GIRL FROM PARIS, 1937
THAT HAMILTON WOMAN, 1941
THAT I MAY LIVE, 1937
THAT LADY IN ERMINE, 1948
THAT MAN FROM RIO, 1964
THAT MAN FROM TANGIER, 1953
THAT MAN'S HERE AGAIN, 1937
THAT MIDNIGHT KISS, 1949
THAT NAZTY NUISANCE, 1943
THAT NIGHT, 1957
THAT NIGHT WITH YOU, 1945
THAT OTHER WOMAN, 1942
THAT RIVIERA TOUCH, 1968
THAT SINKING FEELING, 1979
THAT TENNESSEE BEAT, 1966
THAT UNCERTAIN FEELING, 1941
THAT WAY WITH WOMEN, 1947
THAT WONDERFUL URGE, 1948
THAT'S MY STORY, 1937
THAT'S MY WIFE, 1933
THAT'S THE SPIRIT, 1945
THAT'S A GOOD GIRL, 1933
THAT'S GRATITUDE, 1934
THAT'S MY BABY, 1944
THAT'S MY BOY, 1932
THAT'S MY BOY, 1951
THAT'S MY GAL, 1947
THAT'S MY MAN, 1947
THAT'S MY UNCLE, 1935
THAT'S RIGHT—YOU'RE WRONG, 1939
THAT'S THE TICKET, 1940
THEATRE ROYAL, 1943
THEIR BIG MOMENT, 1934
THEIR NIGHT OUT, 1933
THEIR OWN DESIRE, 1929
THEM NICE AMERICANS, 1958
THEODORA GOES WILD, 1936
THERE AIN'T NO JUSTICE, 1939
THERE GOES KELLY, 1945
THERE GOES MY GIRL, 1937
THERE GOES MY HEART, 1938
THERE GOES THE BRIDE, 1933
THERE GOES THE GROOM, 1937
THERE WAS A CROOKED MAN, 1962
THERE WAS A YOUNG LADY, 1953
THERE WAS A YOUNG MAN, 1937
THERE WAS AN OLD COUPLE, 1967
THERE'S A GIRL IN MY HEART, 1949
THERE'S ALWAYS A THURSDAY, 1957
THERE'S ALWAYS TOMORROW, 1956
THERE'S MAGIC IN MUSIC, 1941
THERE'S NO BUSINESS LIKE SHOW BUSINESS, 1954
THERE'S SOMETHING ABOUT A SOLDIER, 1943
THERE'S ALWAYS A WOMAN, 1938
THERE'S ONE BORN EVERY MINUTE, 1942
THESE CHARMING PEOPLE, 1931
THESE GLAMOUR GIRLS, 1939
THESE THIRTY YEARS, 1934
THESE THOUSAND HILLS, 1959
THEY ALL COME OUT, 1939
THEY ALL LAUGHED, 1981
THEY ARE NOT ANGELS, 1948
THEY ASKED FOR IT, 1939
THEY CALL IT SIN, 1932
THEY CALL ME ROBERT, 1967
THEY CALL ME TRINITY, 1971
THEY CAME BY NIGHT, 1940
THEY CAME FROM BEYOND SPACE, 1967
THEY CAME TO A CITY, 1944
THEY CAME TO BLOW UP AMERICA, 1943
THEY CAN'T HANG ME, 1955
THEY DARE NOT LOVE, 1941
THEY DIDN'T KNOW, 1936
THEY DIED WITH THEIR BOOTS ON, 1942
THEY GAVE HIM A GUN, 1937
THEY GOT ME COVERED, 1943
THEY HAD TO SEE PARIS, 1929
THEY JUST HAD TO GET MARRIED, 1933
THEY KNEW MR. KNIGHT, 1945
THEY LEARNED ABOUT WOMEN, 1930
THEY LIVE IN FEAR, 1944
THEY MADE HER A SPY, 1939
THEY MADE ME A CRIMINAL, 1939

BOLD: Films on Videocassette

THEY MADE ME A KILLER, 1946
THEY MEET AGAIN, 1941
THEY MET IN A TAXI, 1936
THEY MET IN ARGENTINA, 1941
THEY MET IN BOMBAY, 1941
THEY MET IN THE DARK, 1945
THEY MET ON SKIS, 1940
THEY MIGHT BE GIANTS, 1971
THEY NEVER COME BACK, 1932
THEY RAID BY NIGHT, 1942
THEY RAN FOR THEIR LIVES, 1968
THEY RODE WEST, 1954
THEY SHALL HAVE MUSIC, 1939
THEY WANTED PEACE, 1940
THEY WANTED TO MARRY, 1937
THEY WERE EXPENDABLE, 1945
THEY WERE FIVE, 1938
THEY WERE NOT DIVIDED, 1951
THEY WERE SISTERS, 1945
THEY WERE SO YOUNG, 1955
THEY WERE TEN, 1961
THEY WHO DARE, 1954
THEY'RE A WEIRD MOB, 1966
THIEF OF BAGHDAD, THE, 1961
THIEF OF DAMASCUS, 1952
THIEF OF PARIS, THE, 1967
THIEF OF VENICE, THE, 1952
THIEF WHO CAME TO DINNER, THE, 1973
THIEVES, 1977
THIEVES FALL OUT, 1941
THIN ICE, 1937
THIN MAN, THE, 1934
THIN MAN GOES HOME, THE, 1944
THINGS ARE LOOKING UP, 1934
THINGS HAPPEN AT NIGHT, 1948
THINK FAST, MR. MOTO, 1937
THIRD ALARM, THE, 1930
THIRD ALIBI, THE, 1961
THIRD CLUE, THE, 1934
THIRD FINGER, LEFT HAND, 1940
THIRD KEY, THE, 1957
THIRD MAN ON THE MOUNTAIN, 1959
THIRD STRING, THE, 1932
THIRD TIME LUCKY, 1931
THIRD TIME LUCKY, 1950
THIRD VISITOR, THE, 1951
THIRTEEN, THE, 1937
13 EAST STREET, 1952
THIRTEEN FRIGHTENED GIRLS, 1963
THIRTEEN GHOSTS, 1960
THIRTEEN HOURS BY AIR, 1936
THIRTEEN LEAD SOLDIERS, 1948
13 MEN AND A GUN, 1938
THIRTEENTH CANDLE, THE, 1933
THIRTEENTH CHAIR, THE, 1930
THIRTEENTH CHAIR, THE, 1937
THIRTEENTH GUEST, THE, 1932
13TH HOUR, THE, 1947
THIRTEENTH MAN, THE, 1937
THIRTY-DAY PRINCESS, 1934
39 STEPS, THE, 1935
THIRTY SECONDS OVER TOKYO, 1944
THIRTY SIX HOURS TO KILL, 1936
THIS ABOVE ALL, 1942
THIS ACTING BUSINESS, 1933
THIS DAY AND AGE, 1933
THIS ENGLAND, 1941
THIS GREEN HELL, 1936
THIS HAPPY BREED, 1944
THIS HAPPY FEELING, 1958
THIS IS ELVIS, 1982
THIS IS HEAVEN, 1929
THIS IS MY AFFAIR, 1937
THIS IS NOT A TEST, 1962
THIS IS THE LIFE, 1933
THIS IS THE LIFE, 1935
THIS IS THE LIFE, 1944
THIS IS THE NIGHT, 1932
THIS ISLAND EARTH, 1955
THIS LAND IS MINE, 1943
THIS MAN IN PARIS, 1939
THIS MAN IS MINE, 1934
THIS MAN IS MINE, 1946
THIS MAN IS NEWS, 1939
THIS MARRIAGE BUSINESS, 1938
THIS OTHER EDEN, 1959

THIS RECKLESS AGE, 1932
THIS SAVAGE LAND, 1969
THIS SPORTING AGE, 1932
THIS TIME FOR KEEPS, 1942
THIS WEEK OF GRACE, 1933
THIS WOMAN IS MINE, 1941
THIS'LL MAKE YOU WHISTLE, 1938
THISTLEDOWN, 1938
THOROUGHBRED, 1932
THOROUGHBRED, THE, 1930
THOROUGHLY MODERN MILLIE, 1967
THOSE DARING YOUNG MEN IN THEIR JAUNTY
    JALOPIES, 1969
THOSE ENDEARING YOUNG CHARMS, 1945
THOSE KIDS FROM TOWN, 1942
**THOSE MAGNIFICENT MEN IN THEIR FLYING
    MACHINES; OR HOW I FLEW FROM LONDON TO
    PARIS IN 25 HOURS AND 11 MINUTES, 1965**
THOSE PEOPLE NEXT DOOR, 1952
THOSE THREE FRENCH GIRLS, 1930
THOSE WERE THE DAYS, 1934
THOSE WERE THE DAYS, 1940
THOSE WHO DANCE, 1930
THOSE WHO LOVE, 1929
THOU SHALT NOT KILL, 1939
THOUSAND AND ONE NIGHTS, A, 1945
THOUSANDS CHEER, 1943
THREADS, 1932
THREE BITES OF THE APPLE, 1967
THREE BLIND MICE, 1938
THREE BRAVE MEN, 1957
THREE CASES OF MURDER, 1955
THREE CHEERS FOR LOVE, 1936
THREE CHEERS FOR THE IRISH, 1940
THREE COCKEYED SAILORS, 1940
THREE COMRADES, 1938
THREE CORNERED FATE, 1954
THREE-CORNERED MOON, 1932
THREE CROOKED MEN, 1958
THREE DARING DAUGHTERS, 1948
THREE DESPERATE MEN, 1951
THREE FACES EAST, 1930
THREE FACES WEST, 1940
THREE FOR BEDROOM C, 1952
THREE FOR JAMIE DAWN, 1956
THREE FOR THE SHOW, 1955
THREE GIRLS ABOUT TOWN, 1941
THREE GIRLS LOST, 1931
THREE GODFATHERS, 1936
THREE GODFATHERS, THE, 1948
THREE GUNS FOR TEXAS, 1968
THREE GUYS NAMED MIKE, 1951
THREE HATS FOR LISA, 1965
THREE HEARTS FOR JULIA, 1943
THREE HOURS, 1944
THREE HOURS TO KILL, 1954
365 NIGHTS IN HOLLYWOOD, 1934
300 SPARTANS, THE, 1962
THREE HUSBANDS, 1950
THREE IN ONE, 1956
THREE IN THE SADDLE, 1945
3 IS A FAMILY, 1944
THREE KIDS AND A QUEEN, 1935
THREE LEGIONNAIRES, THE, 1937
THREE LITTLE GIRLS IN BLUE, 1946
THREE LITTLE SISTERS, 1944
THREE LIVE GHOSTS, 1929
THREE LIVE GHOSTS, 1935
THREE LOVES HAS NANCY, 1938
THREE MARRIED MEN, 1936
THREE MEN FROM TEXAS, 1940
THREE MEN IN A BOAT, 1933
THREE MEN IN A BOAT, 1958
THREE MEN IN WHITE, 1944
THREE MEN ON A HORSE, 1936
THREE MESQUITEERS, THE, 1936
THREE MOVES TO FREEDOM, 1960
THREE MUSKETEERS, THE, 1935
THREE MUSKETEERS, THE, 1939
THREE OF A KIND, 1936
THREE ON A COUCH, 1966
THREE ON A HONEYMOON, 1934
THREE ON A SPREE, 1961
THREE ON A TICKET, 1947
THREE ON THE TRAIL, 1936
THREE OUTLAWS, THE, 1956

THREE PENNY OPERA, 1963
THREE RING CIRCUS, 1954
THREE ROGUES, 1931
THREE RUSSIAN GIRLS, 1943
THREE SAILORS AND A GIRL, 1953
THREE SECRETS, 1950
THREE SILENT MEN, 1940
THREE SISTERS, THE, 1930
THREE SISTERS, THE, 1977
THREE SMART GIRLS GROW UP, 1939
THREE SONS, 1939
THREE SONS O'GUNS, 1941
THREE SPARE WIVES, 1962
THREE STEPS IN THE DARK, 1953
THREE STEPS NORTH, 1951
THREE STRIPES IN THE SUN, 1955
THREE SUNDAYS TO LIVE, 1957
THREE TALES OF CHEKHOV, 1961
THREE TEXAS STEERS, 1939
THREE VIOLENT PEOPLE, 1956
THREE WARRIORS, 1977
THREE WEEKS OF LOVE, 1965
THREE WEIRD SISTERS, THE, 1948
THREE WHO LOVED, 1931
THREE WISE FOOLS, 1946
THREE WISE GIRLS, 1932
THREE WISE GUYS, THE, 1936
THREE WITNESSES, 1935
THREE YOUNG TEXANS, 1954
THREE'S A CROWD, 1945
THREE'S COMPANY, 1953
THRILL HUNTER, THE, 1933
THRILL OF A LIFETIME, 1937
THRILL OF A ROMANCE, 1945
THRILL OF BRAZIL, THE, 1946
THRILL OF IT ALL, THE, 1963
THROWBACK, THE, 1935
THRU DIFFERENT EYES, 1929
THRU DIFFERENT EYES, 1942
THUMBS UP, 1943
THUNDER AFLOAT, 1939
THUNDER ALLEY, 1967
THUNDER AT THE BORDER, 1966
THUNDER BAY, 1953
THUNDER BELOW, 1932
THUNDER BIRDS, 1942
THUNDER IN CAROLINA, 1960
THUNDER IN DIXIE, 1965
THUNDER IN GOD'S COUNTRY, 1951
THUNDER IN THE CITY, 1937
THUNDER IN THE DESERT, 1938
THUNDER IN THE EAST, 1953
THUNDER IN THE NIGHT, 1935
THUNDER IN THE PINES, 1949
THUNDER IN THE SUN, 1959
THUNDER MOUNTAIN, 1935
THUNDER MOUNTAIN, 1947
THUNDER ON THE HILL, 1951
THUNDER OVER ARIZONA, 1956
THUNDER OVER SANGOLAND, 1955
THUNDER OVER TANGIER, 1957
THUNDER OVER TEXAS, 1934
THUNDER OVER THE PLAINS, 1953
THUNDER OVER THE PRAIRIE, 1941
THUNDER PASS, 1954
THUNDER RIVER FEUD, 1942
THUNDER ROCK, 1944
THUNDER TOWN, 1946
THUNDER TRAIL, 1937
THUNDERBIRD 6, 1968
THUNDERBIRDS, 1952
THUNDERBIRDS ARE GO, 1968
THUNDERBOLT, 1929
THUNDERHOOF, 1948
THUNDERING CARAVANS, 1952
THUNDERING FRONTIER, 1940
THUNDERING GUN SLINGERS, 1944
THUNDERING HERD, THE, 1934
THUNDERING HOOFS, 1941
THUNDERING JETS, 1958
THUNDERING TRAIL, THE, 1951
THUNDERING TRAILS, 1943
THUNDERING WEST, THE, 1939
THUNDERSTORM, 1934
THUNDERSTORM, 1956
THURSDAY'S CHILD, 1943

TIARA TAHITI, 1962
...TICK...TICK...TICK..., 1970
TICKET OF LEAVE, 1936
TICKET OF LEAVE MAN, THE, 1937
TICKET TO CRIME, 1934
TICKET TO PARADISE, 1936
TICKET TO PARADISE, 1961
TICKET TO TOMAHAWK, 1950
TICKLE ME, 1965
TICKLISH AFFAIR, A, 1963
TIGER BAY, 1933
TIGER BAY, 1959
TIGER FANGS, 1943
TIGER FLIGHT, 1965
TIGER GIRL, 1955
TIGER IN THE SMOKE, 1956
TIGER OF THE SEVEN SEAS, 1964
TIGER ROSE, 1930
TIGER WOMAN, THE, 1945
TIGHT LITTLE ISLAND, 1949
TIGHT SHOES, 1941
TIJUANA STORY, THE, 1957
TIKO AND THE SHARK, 1966
'TIL WE MEET AGAIN, 1940
TILL WE MEET AGAIN, 1936
TILL WE MEET AGAIN, 1944
TILLIE AND GUS, 1933
TILLIE THE TOILER, 1941
TILLY OF BLOOMSBURY, 1931
TILLY OF BLOOMSBURY, 1940
TIMBER, 1942
TIMBER FURY, 1950
TIMBER QUEEN, 1944
TIMBER STAMPEDE, 1939
TIMBER TERRORS, 1935
TIMBER TRAIL, THE, 1948
TIMBER WAR, 1936
TIMBERJACK, 1955
TIMBUCTOO, 1933
TIMBUKTU, 1959
TIME BOMB, 1961
TIME FLIES, 1944
TIME FOR KILLING, A, 1967
TIME GENTLEMEN PLEASE?, 1953
TIME IS MY ENEMY, 1957
TIME LOCK, 1959
TIME LOST AND TIME REMEMBERED, 1966
TIME MACHINE, THE, 1963
TIME OF HIS LIFE, THE, 1955
TIME OF INDIFFERENCE, 1965
TIME OUT FOR LOVE, 1963
TIME OUT FOR MURDER, 1938
TIME OUT FOR RHYTHM, 1941
TIME OUT FOR ROMANCE, 1937
TIME OUT OF MIND, 1947
TIME, THE PLACE AND THE GIRL, THE, 1929
TIME, THE PLACE AND THE GIRL, THE, 1946
TIME TO KILL, 1942
TIME TO KILL, A, 1955
TIME TO REMEMBER, 1962
TIME TO SING, A, 1968
TIME TRAVELERS, THE, 1964
TIME WALKER, 1982
TIMES SQUARE, 1929
TIMES SQUARE LADY, 1935
TIMES SQUARE PLAYBOY, 1936
TIMETABLE, 1956
TIMOTHY'S QUEST, 1936
TIN GIRL, THE, 1970
TIN GODS, 1932
TIN MAN, 1983
TIN PAN ALLEY, 1940
TIN STAR, THE, 1957
TIOGA KID, THE, 1948
TIP-OFF, THE, 1931
TIP-OFF GIRLS, 1938
TISH, 1942
TITFIELD THUNDERBOLT, THE, 1953
TO BE A CROOK, 1967
TO BE A LADY, 1934
TO BE OR NOT TO BE, 1942
TO BEAT THE BAND, 1935
TO CATCH A COP, 1984
TO CATCH A THIEF, 1936
TO FIND A MAN, 1972
TO HAVE AND TO HOLD, 1951

TO HAVE AND TO HOLD, 1963
TO LIVE IN PEACE, 1947
TO MARY—WITH LOVE, 1936
TO OBLIGE A LADY, 1931
TO PARIS WITH LOVE, 1955
TO PLEASE A LADY, 1950
TO SIR, WITH LOVE, 1967
TO THE LAST MAN, 1933
TO THE SHORES OF HELL, 1966
TO THE SHORES OF TRIPOLI, 1942
TO THE VICTOR, 1938
TO THE VICTOR, 1948
TO TRAP A SPY, 1966
TO WHAT RED HELL, 1929
TOAST OF NEW ORLEANS, THE, 1950
TOAST OF NEW YORK, THE, 1937
TOAST TO LOVE, 1951
TOBACCO ROAD, 1941
TOBRUK, 1966
TOBY MCTEAGUE, 1986
TODAY, 1930
TODAY I HANG, 1942
TOGETHER, 1956
TOGETHER AGAIN, 1944
TOGETHER WE LIVE, 1935
TOILERS OF THE SEA, 1936
TOKYO AFTER DARK, 1959
TOKYO FILE 212, 1951
TOKYO JOE, 1949
TOKYO ROSE, 1945
TOKYO STORY, 1972
TOL'ABLE DAVID, 1930
TOLL OF THE DESERT, 1936
TOM, DICK AND HARRY, 1941
TOM SAWYER, DETECTIVE, 1939
TOM THUMB, 1967
TOMAHAWK, 1951
TOMAHAWK TRAIL, 1957
TOMBOY, 1940
TOMBOY AND THE CHAMP, 1961
TOMBSTONE CANYON, 1932
TOMBSTONE TERROR, 1935
TOMBSTONE, THE TOWN TOO TOUGH TO DIE, 1942
TOMMY THE TOREADOR, 1960
TOMORROW AND TOMORROW, 1932
TOMORROW AT SEVEN, 1933
TOMORROW AT TEN, 1964
TOMORROW IS ANOTHER DAY, 1951
TOMORROW IS FOREVER, 1946
TOMORROW THE WORLD, 1944
TOMORROW WE LIVE, 1942
TOMORROW'S YOUTH, 1935
TONIGHT AND EVERY NIGHT, 1945
TONIGHT AT 8:30, 1953
TONIGHT AT TWELVE, 1929
TONIGHT IS OURS, 1933
TONIGHT WE RAID CALAIS, 1943
TONIGHT WE SING, 1953
TONIGHT'S THE NIGHT, 1932
TONIGHT'S THE NIGHT, 1954
TONS OF MONEY, 1931
TONTO BASIN OUTLAWS, 1941
TOO BUSY TO WORK, 1932
TOO BUSY TO WORK, 1939
TOO DANGEROUS TO LIVE, 1939
TOO MANY BLONDES, 1941
TOO MANY COOKS, 1931
TOO MANY CROOKS, 1959
TOO MANY GIRLS, 1940
TOO MANY HUSBANDS, 1940
TOO MANY MILLIONS, 1934
TOO MANY PARENTS, 1936
TOO MANY THIEVES, 1968
TOO MANY WINNERS, 1947
TOO MANY WIVES, 1933
TOO MANY WIVES, 1937
TOO MANY WOMEN, 1942
TOO MUCH BEEF, 1936
TOO MUCH HARMONY, 1933
TOO TOUGH TO KILL, 1935
TOO YOUNG TO KISS, 1951
TOO YOUNG TO KNOW, 1945
TOO YOUNG TO MARRY, 1931
TOOMORROW, 1970
TOP BANANA, 1954
TOP FLOOR GIRL, 1959

TOP HAT, 1935
TOP MAN, 1943
TOP O' THE MORNING, 1949
TOP OF THE FORM, 1953
TOP OF THE TOWN, 1937
TOP OF THE WORLD, 1955
TOP SECRET AFFAIR, 1957
TOP SERGEANT, 1942
TOP SERGEANT MULLIGAN, 1941
TOP SPEED, 1930
TOPAZE, 1935
TOPEKA, 1953
TOPEKA TERROR, THE, 1945
TOPPER, 1937
TOPPER RETURNS, 1941
TOPPER TAKES A TRIP, 1939
TOPSY-TURVY JOURNEY, 1970
TORCH SINGER, 1933
TORCH SONG, 1953
TORCH, THE, 1950
TORCHY BLANE IN CHINATOWN, 1938
TORCHY BLANE IN PANAMA, 1938
TORCHY GETS HER MAN, 1938
TORCHY PLAYS WITH DYNAMITE, 1939
TORCHY RUNS FOR MAYOR, 1939
TORMENT, 1947
TORNADO, 1943
TORNADO RANGE, 1948
TORPEDO ALLEY, 1953
TORPEDO BOAT, 1942
TORRID ZONE, 1940
TORTILLA FLAT, 1942
TORTURE SHIP, 1939
TOTO IN THE MOON, 1957
TOUCH OF DEATH, 1962
TOUCH OF LARCENY, A, 1960
TOUCH OF THE MOON, A, 1936
TOUCH OF THE SUN, A, 1956
TOUCHDOWN, 1931
TOUCHDOWN, ARMY, 1938
TOUCHED BY LOVE, 1980
TOUGH AS THEY COME, 1942
TOUGH ASSIGNMENT, 1949
TOUGH GUY, 1936
TOUGH KID, 1939
TOUGH TO HANDLE, 1937
TOUGHER THEY COME, THE, 1950
TOUGHEST GUN IN TOMBSTONE, 1958
TOUGHEST MAN ALIVE, 1955
TOUGHEST MAN IN ARIZONA, 1952
TOWARD THE UNKNOWN, 1956
TOWER OF LONDON, 1939
TOWER OF LONDON, 1962
TOWER OF TERROR, THE, 1942
TOWN LIKE ALICE, A, 1958
TOWN TAMER, 1965
TOWN WENT WILD, THE, 1945
TOXI, 1952
TRACK OF THUNDER, 1967
TRACK THE MAN DOWN, 1956
TRADE WINDS, 1938
TRADER HORN, 1973
TRAFFIC IN CRIME, 1946
TRAGEDY AT MIDNIGHT, A, 1942
TRAGEDY OF A RIDICULOUS MAN, THE, 1982
TRAIL BEYOND, THE, 1934
TRAIL BLAZERS, THE, 1940
TRAIL DRIVE, THE, 1934
TRAIL DUST, 1936
TRAIL GUIDE, 1952
TRAIL OF KIT CARSON, 1945
TRAIL OF ROBIN HOOD, 1950
TRAIL OF TERROR, 1944
TRAIL OF THE SILVER SPURS, 1941
TRAIL OF THE VIGILANTES, 1940
TRAIL OF THE YUKON, 1949
TRAIL OF VENGEANCE, 1937
TRAIL STREET, 1947
TRAIL TO SAN ANTONE, 1947
TRAIL TO VENGEANCE, 1945
TRAILIN' WEST, 1936
TRAILING DOUBLE TROUBLE, 1940
TRAILING THE KILLER, 1932
TRAILING TROUBLE, 1930
TRAILING TROUBLE, 1937
TRAIL'S END, 1949

BOLD: Films on Videocassette

TRAILS OF DANGER, 1930
TRAILS OF THE WILD, 1935
TRAIN GOES EAST, THE, 1949
TRAIN GOES TO KIEV, THE, 1961
TRAIN OF EVENTS, 1952
TRAIN RIDE TO HOLLYWOOD, 1975
TRAIN ROBBERS, THE, 1973
TRAIN ROBBERY CONFIDENTIAL, 1965
TRAIN TO ALCATRAZ, 1948
TRAIN TO TOMBSTONE, 1950
TRAITOR WITHIN, THE, 1942
TRAITOR'S GATE, 1966
TRAITOR, THE, 1936
TRAITORS, 1957
TRAITORS, THE, 1963
TRAMP, TRAMP, TRAMP, 1942
TRANSATLANTIC, 1931
TRANSATLANTIC, 1961
TRANSATLANTIC MERRY-GO-ROUND, 1934
TRANSATLANTIC TUNNEL, 1935
TRANSGRESSION, 1931
TRANSIENT LADY, 1935
TRANSPORT FROM PARADISE, 1967
TRAP, THE, 1959
TRAP, THE, 1967
TRAP, THE, 1947
TRAPEZE, 1932
TRAPP FAMILY, THE, 1961
TRAPPED, 1931
TRAPPED, 1937
TRAPPED, 1949
TRAPPED BY BOSTON BLACKIE, 1948
TRAPPED BY G-MEN, 1937
TRAPPED BY TELEVISION, 1936
TRAPPED IN A SUBMARINE, 1931
TRAPPED IN TANGIERS, 1960
TRAPPED IN THE SKY, 1939 61m COL bw
TRAVELING SALESLADY, THE, 1935
TRAVELING SALESWOMAN, 1950
TRAVELLER'S JOY, 1951
TREACHERY ON THE HIGH SEAS, 1939
TREACHERY RIDES THE RANGE, 1936
TREAD SOFTLY, 1952
TREAD SOFTLY STRANGER, 1959
TREASURE HUNT, 1952
TREASURE ISLAND, 1934
TREASURE ISLAND, 1972
TREASURE OF LOST CANYON, THE, 1952
TREASURE OF MAKUBA, THE, 1967
TREASURE OF MONTE CRISTO, 1949
TREASURE OF PANCHO VILLA, THE, 1955
TREASURE OF RUBY HILLS, 1955
TREASURE OF SAN GENNARO, 1968
TREASURE OF SILVER LAKE, 1965
TREASURE OF THE FOUR CROWNS, 1983
TREASURE OF THE GOLDEN CONDOR, 1953
TREAT EM' ROUGH, 1942
TREE WE HURT, THE, 1986
TREMENDOUSLY RICH MAN, A, 1932
TRENCHCOAT, 1983
TRENT'S LAST CASE, 1953
TRESPASSER, THE, 1929
TRESPASSER, THE, 1947
TRIAL, 1955
TRIAL, THE, 1948
TRIAL AND ERROR, 1962
TRIAL OF LEE HARVEY OSWALD, THE, 1964
TRIAL OF MADAM X, THE, 1948
TRIAL OF MARY DUGAN, THE, 1941
TRIAL OF THE CATONSVILLE NINE, THE, 1972
TRIAL OF VIVIENNE WARE, THE, 1932
TRIAL WITHOUT JURY, 1950
TRIBES, 1970
TRICK FOR TRICK, 1933
TRIGGER FINGERS, 1939
TRIGGER PALS, 1939
TRIGGER SMITH, 1939
TRIGGER TRAIL, 1944
TRIGGER TRICKS, 1930
TRIGGER TRIO, THE, 1937
TRIGGER, JR., 1950
TRINITY IS STILL MY NAME, 1971
TRIO, 1950
TRIP TO PARIS, A, 1938
TRIPLE DECEPTION, 1957
TRIPLE JUSTICE, 1940

TRIPLE THREAT, 1948
TRIPLE TROUBLE, 1950
TRIPOLI, 1950
TRIUMPH OF SHERLOCK HOLMES, THE, 1935
TROCADERO, 1944
TROG, 1970
TROJAN BROTHERS, THE, 1946
TRON, 1982
TROPIC FURY, 1939
TROPIC HOLIDAY, 1938
TROPIC ZONE, 1953
TROPICAL HEAT WAVE, 1952
TROPICAL TROUBLE, 1936
TROUBLE, 1933
TROUBLE AHEAD, 1936
TROUBLE AT MIDNIGHT, 1937
TROUBLE BREWING, 1939
TROUBLE FOR TWO, 1936
TROUBLE IN MOROCCO, 1937
TROUBLE IN STORE, 1955
TROUBLE IN SUNDOWN, 1939
TROUBLE IN TEXAS, 1937
TROUBLE IN THE AIR, 1948
TROUBLE IN THE GLEN, 1954
TROUBLE PREFERRED, 1949
TROUBLE WITH GIRLS (AND HOW TO GET INTO IT), THE, 1969
TROUBLE WITH WOMEN, THE, 1947
TROUBLED WATERS, 1936
TRUCK BUSTERS, 1943
TRUE AS A TURTLE, 1957
TRUE CONFESSION, 1937
TRUE GRIT, 1969
TRUE STORIES, 1986
TRUE STORY OF JESSE JAMES, THE, 1957
TRUE STORY OF LYNN STUART, THE, 1958
TRUE TO LIFE, 1943
TRUE TO THE NAVY, 1930
TRUMAN CAPOTE'S TRILOGY, 1969
TRUMPET BLOWS, THE, 1934
TRUNKS OF MR. O.F., THE, 1932
TRUST THE NAVY, 1935
TRUSTED OUTLAW, THE, 1937
TRUTH ABOUT MURDER, THE, 1946
TRUTH ABOUT WOMEN, THE, 1958
TRUTH ABOUT YOUTH, THE, 1930
TUCKER: THE MAN AND HIS DREAM, 1988
TUCSON, 1949
TUCSON RAIDERS, 1944
TUGBOAT ANNIE, 1933
TULSA, 1949
TULSA KID, THE, 1940
TUMBLEDOWN RANCH IN ARIZONA, 1941
TUMBLEWEED, 1953
TUMBLEWEED TRAIL, 1946
TUNA CLIPPER, 1949
TUNDRA, 1936
TURKEY TIME, 1933
TURN BACK THE CLOCK, 1933
TURN OF THE TIDE, 1935
TURN OFF THE MOON, 1937
TURNABOUT, 1940
TURNED OUT NICE AGAIN, 1941
TURNERS OF PROSPECT ROAD, THE, 1947
TUSK, 1980
TUTTLES OF TAHITI, 1942
TUXEDO JUNCTION, 1941
TWELFTH NIGHT, 1956
12 ANGRY MEN, 1957
TWELVE CROWDED HOURS, 1939
TWELVE GOOD MEN, 1936
TWELVE-HANDED MEN OF MARS, THE, 1964
TWELVE HOURS TO KILL, 1960
TWELVE PLUS ONE, 1970
TWELVE TO THE MOON, 1960
TWENTIETH CENTURY, 1934
20TH CENTURY OZ, 1977
24 HOURS, 1931
20 MILLION MILES TO EARTH, 1957
TWENTY MILLION SWEETHEARTS, 1934
TWENTY MULE TEAM, 1940
TWENTY-ONE DAYS TOGETHER, 1940
TWENTY QUESTIONS MURDER MYSTERY, THE, 1950
20,000 LEAGUES UNDER THE SEA, 1954
20,000 MEN A YEAR, 1939

20,000 YEARS IN SING SING, 1933
23 1/2 HOURS LEAVE, 1937
TWICE AROUND THE DAFFODILS, 1962
TWICE BLESSED, 1945
TWICE BRANDED, 1936
TWICE UPON A TIME, 1953
TWICE UPON A TIME, 1983
TWILIGHT FOR THE GODS, 1958
TWILIGHT HOUR, 1944
TWILIGHT IN THE SIERRAS, 1950
TWILIGHT ON THE PRAIRIE, 1944
TWILIGHT ON THE RIO GRANDE, 1947
TWILIGHT ON THE TRAIL, 1941
TWIN BEDS, 1929
TWIN BEDS, 1942
TWIN FACES, 1937
TWIN HUSBANDS, 1934
TWINKLE IN GOD'S EYE, THE, 1955
TWINS, 1988
TWIST ALL NIGHT, 1961
TWIST AROUND THE CLOCK, 1961
TWIST OF SAND, A, 1968
TWO A PENNY, 1968
TWO AGAINST THE WORLD, 1932
TWO AGAINST THE WORLD, 1936
TWO ALONE, 1934
TWO AND ONE TWO, 1934
TWO BLONDES AND A REDHEAD, 1947
TWO BRIGHT BOYS, 1939
TWO COLONELS, THE, 1963
TWO DAUGHTERS, 1963
TWO DOLLAR BETTOR, 1951
TWO-FACED WOMAN, 1941
TWO FISTED, 1935
TWO-FISTED GENTLEMAN, 1936
TWO-FISTED JUSTICE, 1931
TWO FISTED JUSTICE, 1943
TWO-FISTED RANGERS, 1940
TWO-FISTED SHERIFF, 1937
TWO FLAGS WEST, 1950
TWO FOR DANGER, 1940
TWO FOR TONIGHT, 1935
TWO GALS AND A GUY, 1951
TWO GIRLS AND A SAILOR, 1944
TWO GIRLS ON BROADWAY, 1940
TWO GROOMS FOR A BRIDE, 1957
TWO-GUN JUSTICE, 1938
TWO-GUN LADY, 1956
TWO GUN LAW, 1937
TWO GUN MAN, THE, 1931
TWO GUN SHERIFF, 1941
TWO-GUN TROUBADOR, 1939
TWO GUNS AND A BADGE, 1954
TWO GUYS FROM MILWAUKEE, 1946
TWO GUYS FROM TEXAS, 1948
TWO HEADS ON A PILLOW, 1934
TWO HEARTS IN HARMONY, 1935
TWO HEARTS IN WALTZ TIME, 1934
TWO IN A CROWD, 1936
TWO IN A TAXI, 1941
TWO IN THE DARK, 1936
TWO KOUNEY LEMELS, 1966
TWO LATINS FROM MANHATTAN, 1941
TWO LETTER ALIBI, 1962
TWO LOST WORLDS, 1950
TWO-MAN SUBMARINE, 1944
TWO MEN AND A MAID, 1929
TWO MINUTES' SILENCE, 1934
TWO MINUTES TO PLAY, 1937
TWO OF US, THE, 1938
TWO OF US, THE, 1968
TWO ON A DOORSTEP, 1936
TWO SENORITAS FROM CHICAGO, 1943
TWO SINNERS, 1935
TWO SISTERS, 1938
TWO SISTERS FROM BOSTON, 1946
TWO SMART MEN, 1940
TWO SMART PEOPLE, 1946
TWO SOLITUDES, 1978
TWO THOROUGHBREDS, 1939
2001: A SPACE ODYSSEY, 1968
2,000 WOMEN, 1944
TWO TICKETS TO BROADWAY, 1951
TWO TICKETS TO LONDON, 1943
TWO TICKETS TO PARIS, 1962
TWO WEEKS OFF, 1929

TWO WEEKS TO LIVE, 1943
TWO WEEKS WITH LOVE, 1950
TWO WHO DARED, 1937
TWO WISE MAIDS, 1937
TWO WIVES AT ONE WEDDING, 1961
TWO WOMEN, 1940
TWO WORLD, 1930
TWO YANKS IN TRINIDAD, 1942
TWO'S COMPANY, 1939
TWONKY, THE, 1953
TYCOON, 1947
TYPHOON, 1940
TYPHOON TREASURE, 1939
TYRANT OF THE SEA, 1950
U-BOAT PRISONER, 1944
U-47 LT. COMMANDER PRIEN, 1967
UFO: TARGET EARTH, 1974
UGETSU, 1954
UGLY DUCKLING, THE, 1959
ULTIMATUM, 1940
UMBRELLA, THE, 1933
UN CARNET DE BAL, 1938
UNA SIGNORA DELL'OVEST, 1942
UNASHAMED, 1932
UNCENSORED, 1944
UNCERTAIN GLORY, 1944
UNCERTAIN LADY, 1934
UNCHAINED, 1955
UNCIVILISED, 1937
UNCLE VANYA, 1958
UNCLE VANYA, 1972
UNCLE VANYA, 1977
UNCLE, THE, 1966
UNCOMMON THIEF, AN, 1967
UNCONQUERED, 1947
UNDEAD, THE, 1957
UNDEFEATED, THE, 1969
UNDER A CLOUD, 1937
UNDER A TEXAS MOON, 1930
UNDER ARIZONA SKIES, 1946
UNDER CALIFORNIA STARS, 1948
UNDER COLORADO SKIES, 1947
UNDER-COVER MAN, 1932
UNDER COVER OF NIGHT, 1937
UNDER EIGHTEEN, 1932
UNDER FIESTA STARS, 1941
UNDER FIRE, 1957
UNDER MEXICALI STARS, 1950
UNDER MONTANA SKIES, 1930
UNDER MY SKIN, 1950
UNDER NEVADA SKIES, 1946
UNDER PRESSURE, 1935
UNDER PROOF, 1936
UNDER-PUP, THE, 1939
UNDER SECRET ORDERS, 1933
UNDER STRANGE FLAGS, 1937
UNDER SUSPICION, 1931
UNDER SUSPICION, 1937
UNDER TEXAS SKIES, 1931
UNDER TEXAS SKIES, 1940
UNDER THE BIG TOP, 1938
UNDER THE GREENWOOD TREE, 1930
UNDER THE GUN, 1951
UNDER THE PAMPAS MOON, 1935
UNDER THE RED ROBE, 1937
UNDER THE ROOFS OF PARIS, 1930
UNDER THE SUN OF ROME, 1949
UNDER THE TONTO RIM, 1933
UNDER THE TONTO RIM, 1947
UNDER WESTERN SKIES, 1945
UNDER WESTERN STARS, 1938
UNDER YOUR HAT, 1940
UNDER YOUR SPELL, 1936
UNDERCOVER AGENT, 1939
UNDERCOVER AGENT, 1935
UNDERCOVER DOCTOR, 1939
UNDERCOVER GIRL, 1950
UNDERCOVER GIRL, 1957
UNDERCOVER MAISIE, 1947
UNDERCOVER MAN, 1936
UNDERCOVER MAN, 1942
UNDERCOVER WOMAN, THE, 1946
UNDERDOG, THE, 1943
UNDERGROUND, 1941
UNDERGROUND AGENT, 1942
UNDERGROUND GUERRILLAS, 1944

UNDERGROUND RUSTLERS, 1941
UNDERNEATH THE ARCHES, 1937
UNDERSEA GIRL, 1957
UNDERTOW, 1930
UNDERTOW, 1949
UNDERWATER CITY, THE, 1962
UNDERWATER WARRIOR, 1958
UNDERWORLD INFORMERS, 1965
UNDYING MONSTER, THE, 1942
UNEARTHLY STRANGER, THE, 1964
UNEASY TERMS, 1948
UNEASY VIRTUE, 1931
UNEXPECTED FATHER, 1932
UNEXPECTED FATHER, 1939
UNEXPECTED GUEST, 1946
UNEXPECTED UNCLE, 1941
UNFAITHFUL, 1931
UNFAITHFUL, THE, 1947
UNFAITHFULS, THE, 1960
UNFINISHED BUSINESS, 1941
UNFINISHED DANCE, THE, 1947
UNFINISHED SYMPHONY, THE, 1953
UNGUARDED HOUR, THE, 1936
UNGUARDED MOMENT, THE, 1956
UNHOLY FOUR, THE, 1954
UNHOLY GARDEN, THE, 1931
UNHOLY LOVE, 1932
UNHOLY NIGHT, THE, 1929
UNHOLY PARTNERS, 1941
UNHOLY QUEST, THE, 1934
UNHOLY WIFE, THE, 1957
UNIDENTIFIED FLYING ODDBALL, THE, 1979
UNION CITY, 1980
UNION DEPOT, 1932
UNION PACIFIC, 1939
UNKNOWN BLONDE, 1934
UNKNOWN GUEST, THE, 1943
UNKNOWN ISLAND, 1948
UNKNOWN MAN OF SHANDIGOR, THE, 1967
UNKNOWN RANGER, THE, 1936
UNKNOWN TERROR, THE, 1957
UNKNOWN VALLEY, 1933
UNKNOWN WOMAN, 1935
UNKNOWN WORLD, 1951
UNKNOWN, THE, 1946
UNMARRIED, 1939
UNMASKED, 1929
UNMASKED, 1950
UNPUBLISHED STORY, 1942
UNSATISFIED, THE, 1964
UNSEEN, THE, 1945
UNSEEN ENEMY, 1942
UNSINKABLE MOLLY BROWN, THE, 1964
UNSTOPPABLE MAN, THE, 1961
UNSUSPECTED, THE, 1947
UNTAMED, 1940
UNTAMED BREED, THE, 1948
UNTAMED FRONTIER, 1952
UNTAMED FURY, 1947
UNTAMED HEIRESS, 1954
UNTAMED WOMEN, 1952
UNTAMED YOUTH, 1957
UNTOUCHED, 1956
UNWELCOME STRANGER, 1935
UNWILLING AGENT, 1968
UNWRITTEN CODE, THE, 1944
UNWRITTEN LAW, THE, 1932
UP FOR MURDER, 1931
UP FOR THE CUP, 1931
UP FOR THE CUP, 1950
UP FOR THE DERBY, 1933
UP FROM THE BEACH, 1965
UP FRONT, 1951
UP GOES MAISIE, 1946
UP IN CENTRAL PARK, 1948
UP IN MABEL'S ROOM, 1944
UP IN SMOKE, 1957
UP IN THE AIR, 1940
UP IN THE WORLD, 1957
UP JUMPED A SWAGMAN, 1965
UP PERISCOPE, 1959
UP POPS THE DEVIL, 1931
UP THE CREEK, 1958
UP THE MACGREGORS, 1967
UP THE RIVER, 1930
UP THE RIVER, 1938

UP TO HIS NECK, 1954
UP TO THE NECK, 1933
UP WITH THE LARK, 1943
UPPER WORLD, 1934
UPSTAIRS AND DOWNSTAIRS, 1961
UPTOWN NEW YORK, 1932
URANIUM BOOM, 1956
UTAH, 1945
UTAH BLAINE, 1957
UTAH KID, THE, 1930
UTAH TRAIL, 1938
UTAH WAGON TRAIN, 1951
UTOPIA, 1952
V.I.P.s, THE, 1963
VACATION DAYS, 1947
VACATION FROM LOVE, 1938
VACATION FROM MARRIAGE, 1945
VACATION IN RENO, 1946
VAGABOND KING, THE, 1930
VAGABOND KING, THE, 1956
VAGABOND LADY, 1935
VAGABOND LOVER, 1929
VAGABOND QUEEN, THE, 1931
VALIANT HOMBRE THE, 1948
VALIANT, THE, 1962
VALLEY OF DECISION, THE, 1945
VALLEY OF EAGLES, 1952
VALLEY OF FIRE, 1951
VALLEY OF GWANGI, THE, 1969
VALLEY OF HUNTED MEN, 1942
VALLEY OF MYSTERY, 1967
VALLEY OF THE DRAGONS, 1961
VALLEY OF THE GIANTS, 1938
VALLEY OF THE HEADHUNTERS, 1953
VALLEY OF THE LAWLESS, 1936
VALLEY OF THE REDWOODS, 1960
VALLEY OF THE SUN, 1942
VALLEY OF VENGEANCE, 1944
VALUE FOR MONEY, 1957
VANDERGILT DIAMOND MYSTERY, THE, 1936
VANESSA, HER LOVE STORY, 1935
VANISHING AMERICAN, THE, 1955
VANISHING FRONTIER, THE, 1932
VANISHING OUTPOST, THE, 1951
VANISHING VIRGINIAN, THE, 1941
VANISHING WESTERNER, THE, 1950
VANITY, 1935
VANITY STREET, 1932
VANQUISHED, THE, 1953
VARAN THE UNBELIEVABLE, 1962
VARIETY, 1935
VARIETY HOUR, 1937
VARIETY JUBILEE, 1945
VARIETY LIGHTS, 1965
VARIETY PARADE, 1936
VARSITY, 1928
VARSITY SHOW, 1937
VEILS OF BAGDAD, THE, 1953
VELVET TOUCH, THE, 1948
VENDETTA, 1950
VENGEANCE, 1930
VENGEANCE, 1964
VENGEANCE IS MINE, 1948
VENGEANCE IS MINE, 1969
VENGEANCE OF FU MANCHU, THE, 1968
VENGEANCE OF SHE, THE, 1968
VENGEANCE OF THE DEEP, 1940
VENGEANCE VALLEY, 1951
VENUS MAKES TROUBLE, 1937
VERDICT OF THE SEA, 1932
VERDICT, THE, 1964
VERMILION DOOR, 1969
VERONA TRIAL, THE, 1963
VERY HAPPY ALEXANDER, 1969
VERY HONORABLE GUY, A, 1934
VERY IDEA, THE, 1929
VERY SPECIAL FAVOR, A, 1965
VERY THOUGHT OF YOU, THE, 1944
VERY YOUNG LADY, A, 1941
VIA PONY EXPRESS, 1933
VICAR OF BRAY, THE, 1937
VICE RACKET, 1937
VICE SQUAD, 1953
VICE SQUAD, THE, 1931
VICE VERSA, 1948
VICIOUS CIRCLE, THE, 1948

BOLD: Films on Videocassette

VICIOUS YEARS, THE, 1950
VICTIMS OF PERSECUTION, 1933
VICTORIA THE GREAT, 1937
VIENNA WALTZES, 1961
VIENNA, CITY OF SONGS, 1931
VIENNESE NIGHTS, 1930
VIGILANTE HIDEOUT, 1950
VIGILANTE TERROR, 1953
VIGILANTES OF BOOMTOWN, 1947
VIGILANTES RETURN, THE, 1947
VIKING QUEEN, THE, 1967
VIKING, THE, 1931
VILLA!, 1958
VILLAGE, THE, 1953
VILLAGE BARN DANCE, 1940
VILLAGE OF DAUGHTERS, 1962
VILLAGE OF THE GIANTS, 1965
VILLAGE SQUIRE, THE, 1935
VILLAGE TALE, 1935
VILLAIN STILL PURSUED HER, THE, 1940
VILLAIN, THE, 1979
VILLIERS DIAMOND, THE, 1938
VILNA LEGEND, A, 1949
VINTAGE, THE, 1957
VINTAGE WINE, 1935
VIOLATORS, THE, 1957
VIOLENCE, 1947
VIOLENT ENEMY, THE, 1969
VIOLENT FOUR, THE, 1968
VIOLENT MEN, THE, 1955
VIOLENT PLAYGROUND, 1958
VIOLENT ROAD, 1958
VIOLENT STRANGER, 1957
VIOLIN AND ROLLER, 1962
VIPER, THE, 1938
VIRGIN PRESIDENT, THE, 1968
VIRGIN QUEEN OF ST. FRANCIS HIGH, THE, 1987
VIRGINIA, 1941
VIRGINIA CITY, 1940
VIRGINIA JUDGE, THE, 1935
VIRGINIAN, THE, 1929
VIRTUOUS HUSBAND, 1931
VIRTUOUS SIN, THE, 1930
VISIT TO A SMALL PLANET, 1960
VIVA CISCO KID, 1940
VIVA KNIEVEL?, 1977
VIVA LAS VEGAS, 1964
VIVA MAX?, 1969
VIVACIOUS LADY, 1938
VOGUES OF 1938, 1937
VOICE IN THE MIRROR, 1958
VOICE IN THE NIGHT, 1934
VOICE IN THE NIGHT, A, 1941
VOICE IN THE WIND, 1944
VOICE OF BUGLE ANN, 1936
VOICE OF THE CITY, 1929
VOICE OF THE HURRICANE, 1964
VOICE OF THE TURTLE, THE, 1947
VOICE WITHIN, THE, 1945
VOLCANO, 1953
VOLPONE, 1947
VOLTAIRE, 1933
VOODOO ISLAND, 1957
VOODOO MAN, 1944
VOODOO TIGER, 1952
VOODOO WOMAN, 1957
VOR SONNENUNTERGANG, 1961
VOTE FOR HUGGETT, 1948
VOW, THE, 1947
VOYAGE OF SILENCE, 1968
VOYAGE TO AMERICA, 1952
VOYAGE TO THE BOTTOM OF THE SEA, 1961
VOYAGE TO THE END OF THE UNIVERSE, 1963
VOYAGE TO THE PLANET OF PREHISTORIC
 WOMEN, 1966
VOYAGE TO THE PREHISTORIC PLANET, 1965
VULTURE, THE, 1937
W.I.A. (WOUNDED IN ACTION), 1966
"W" PLAN, THE, 1931
W. W. AND THE DIXIE DANCEKINGS, 1975
WABASH AVENUE, 1950
WAC FROM WALLA WALLA, THE, 1952
WACKIEST SHIP IN THE ARMY, THE, 1961
WACKIEST WAGON TRAIN IN THE WEST, THE, 1976
WACKY WORLD OF DR. MORGUS, THE, 1962
WACO, 1952

WAGON MASTER, THE, 1929
WAGON TEAM, 1952
WAGON TRACKS WEST, 1943
WAGON TRAIL, 1935
WAGON TRAIN, 1940
WAGON WHEELS, 1934
WAGONMASTER, 1950
WAGONS ROLL AT NIGHT, THE, 1941
WAGONS WEST, 1952
WAGONS WESTWARD, 1940
WAIKIKI WEDDING, 1937
WAIT 'TIL THE SUN SHINES, NELLIE, 1952
WAITING FOR THE MOON, 1987
WAJAN, 1938
WAKE ISLAND, 1942
WAKE ME WHEN IT'S OVER, 1960
WAKE UP AND DREAM, 1934
WAKE UP AND DREAM, 1946
WAKE UP FAMOUS, 1937
WALK A CROOKED MILE, 1948
WALK, DON'T RUN, 1966
WALK EAST ON BEACON, 1952
WALK IN THE SHADOW, 1966
WALK INTO HELL, 1957
WALK TALL, 1960
WALK THE PROUD LAND, 1956
WALKING DEAD, THE, 1936
WALKING DOWN BROADWAY, 1938
WALKING HILLS, THE, 1949
WALKING MY BABY BACK HOME, 1953
WALKING ON AIR, 1936
WALL-EYED NIPPON, 1963
WALL OF NOISE, 1963
WALL STREET, 1929
WALL STREET COWBOY, 1939
WALLABY JIM OF THE ISLANDS, 1937
WALLET, THE, 1952
WALLFLOWER, 1948
WALLS CAME TUMBLING DOWN, THE, 1946
WALLS OF HELL, THE, 1964
WALLS OF MALAPAGA, THE, 1950
WALTZ TIME, 1933
WALTZ TIME, 1946
WANDERER OF THE WASTELAND, 1935
WANDERER OF THE WASTELAND, 1945
WANDERER, THE, 1969
WANDERERS OF THE WEST, 1941
WANDERING JEW, THE, 1933
WANDERING JEW, THE, 1935
WANTED, 1937
WANTED BY SCOTLAND YARD, 1939
WANTED BY THE POLICE, 1938
WANTED: JANE TURNER, 1936
WAR AGAINST MRS. HADLEY, THE, 1942
WAR ARROW, 1953
WAR BETWEEN THE PLANETS, 1971
WAR CORRESPONDENT, 1932
WAR DOGS, 1942
WAR DRUMS, 1957
WAR ITALIAN STYLE, 1967
WAR NURSE, 1930
WAR OF THE BUTTONS, 1963
WAR OF THE COLOSSAL BEAST, 1958
WAR OF THE GARGANTUAS, THE, 1970
WAR OF THE MONSTERS, 1972
WAR OF THE PLANETS, 1977
WAR OF THE RANGE, 1933
WAR OF THE SATELLITES, 1958
WAR PAINT, 1953
WAR PARTY, 1965
WAR WAGON, THE, 1967
WARE CASE, THE, 1939
WARGAMES, 1983
WARM IN THE BUD, 1970
WARN LONDON!, 1934
WARN THAT MAN, 1943
WARNING TO WANTONS, A, 1949
WARPATH, 1951
WARREN CASE, THE, 1934
WARRIOR AND THE SLAVE GIRL, THE, 1959
WARRIORS FIVE, 1962
WASHINGTON MASQUERADE, 1932
WASHINGTON MELODRAMA, 1941
WASHINGTON MERRY-GO-ROUND, 1932
WASHINGTON STORY, 1952
WASP WOMAN, THE, 1959

WATCH BEVERLY, 1932
WATCH IT, SAILOR!, 1961
WATCH ON THE RHINE, 1943
WATCH THE BIRDIE, 1950
WATCH YOUR STERN, 1961
WATER FOR CANITOGA, 1939
WATER GYPSIES, THE, 1932
WATER RUSTLERS, 1939
WATERFRONT, 1939
WATERFRONT, 1944
WATERFRONT AT MIDNIGHT, 1948
WATERFRONT LADY, 1935
WATERFRONT WOMEN, 1952
WATERLOO ROAD, 1949
WATUSI, 1959
WAVE, A WAC AND A MARINE, A, 1944
WAY BACK HOME, 1932
WAY DOWN EAST, 1935
WAY DOWN SOUTH, 1939
WAY FOR A SAILOR, 1930
WAY OF A GAUCHO, 1952
WAY OF ALL FLESH, THE, 1940
WAY OF ALL MEN, THE, 1930
WAY OF THE WEST, THE, 1934
WAY OF YOUTH, THE, 1934
WAY OUT WEST, 1930
WAY OUT, THE, 1956
WAY TO LOVE, THE, 1933
WAY TO THE GOLD, THE, 1957
WAY WE LIVE, THE, 1946
WAY WEST, THE, 1967
WAYSIDE PEBBLE, THE, 1962
WAYWARD, 1932
WAYWARD GIRL, THE, 1957
WE DIVE AT DAWN, 1943
WE GO FAST, 1941
WE HAVE ONLY ONE LIFE, 1963
WE HAVE OUR MOMENTS, 1937
WE JOINED THE NAVY, 1962
WE SHALL RETURN, 1963
WE WENT TO COLLEGE, 1936
WE WERE DANCING, 1942
WE WHO ARE ABOUT TO DIE, 1937
WEAK AND THE WICKED, THE, 1954
WEAKER SEX, THE, 1949
WEARY RIVER, 1929
WEB OF DANGER, THE, 1947
WEB OF SUSPICION, 1959
WEB, THE, 1947
WEBSTER BOY, THE, 1962
WEDDING NIGHT, THE, 1935
WEDDING OF LILLI MARLENE, THE, 1953
WEDDING PRESENT, 1936
WEDDING REHEARSAL, 1932
WEDDING RINGS, 1930
WEDDINGS AND BABIES, 1960
WEDDINGS ARE WONDERFUL, 1938
WEDNESDAY'S CHILD, 1934
WEDNESDAY'S LUCK, 1936
WEE GEORDIE, 1956
WEEK-END MARRIAGE, 1932
WEEK-ENDS ONLY, 1932
WEEKEND AT DUNKIRK, 1966
WEEKEND AT THE WALDORF, 1945
WEEKEND FOR THREE, 1941
WEEKEND IN HAVANA, 1941
WEEKEND MILLIONAIRE, 1937
WEEKEND PASS, 1944
WEEKEND WITH FATHER, 1951
WEEKEND WITH LULU, A, 1961
WEEKEND, ITALIAN STYLE, 1967
WEIRD WOMAN, 1944
WELCOME DANGER, 1929
WELCOME HOME, 1935
WELCOME, MR. WASHINGTON, 1944
WELCOME STRANGER, 1947
WELL, THE, 1951
WELL DONE, HENRY, 1936
WELL-GROOMED BRIDE, THE, 1946
WE'LL MEET AGAIN, 1942
WE'LL SMILE AGAIN, 1942
WELLS FARGO, 1937
WELLS FARGO GUNMASTER, 1951
WE'RE GOING TO BE RICH, 1938
WE'RE IN THE LEGION NOW, 1937
WE'RE IN THE MONEY, 1935

WE'RE NOT DRESSING, 1934
WE'RE NOT MARRIED, 1952
WE'RE ON THE JURY, 1937
WE'RE ONLY HUMAN, 1936
WE'RE RICH AGAIN, 1934
WEST OF ABILENE, 1940
WEST OF BROADWAY, 1931
WEST OF CARSON CITY, 1940
WEST OF CHEYENNE, 1931
WEST OF CHEYENNE, 1938
WEST OF CIMARRON, 1941
WEST OF EL DORADO, 1949
WEST OF NEVADA, 1936
WEST OF PINTO BASIN, 1940
WEST OF RAINBOW'S END, 1938
WEST OF SANTA FE, 1938
WEST OF SHANGHAI, 1937
WEST OF SINGAPORE, 1933
WEST OF SONORA, 1948
WEST OF TEXAS, 1943
WEST OF THE ALAMO, 1946
WEST OF THE BRAZOS, 1950
WEST OF THE DIVIDE, 1934
WEST OF THE LAW, 1942
WEST OF THE PECOS, 1945
WEST OF THE ROCKIES, 1929
WEST OF THE ROCKIES, 1931
WEST OF TOMBSTONE, 1942
WEST OF WYOMING, 1950
WEST OF ZANZIBAR, 1954
WEST POINT OF THE AIR, 1935
WEST POINT STORY, THE, 1950
WEST POINT WIDOW, 1941
WEST SIDE KID, 1943
WEST TO GLORY, 1947
WESTBOUND, 1959
WESTBOUND LIMITED, 1937
WESTBOUND MAIL, 1937
WESTBOUND STAGE, 1940
WESTERN CARAVANS, 1939
WESTERN COURAGE, 1935
WESTERN CYCLONE, 1943
WESTERN FRONTIER, 1935
WESTERN GOLD, 1937
WESTERN HERITAGE, 1948
WESTERN JAMBOREE, 1938
WESTERN JUSTICE, 1935
WESTERN LIMITED, 1932
WESTERN MAIL, 1942
WESTERN PACIFIC AGENT, 1950
WESTERN RENEGADES, 1949
WESTERN TRAILS, 1938
WESTERN UNION, 1941
WESTERNER, THE, 1940
WESTERNER, THE, 1936
WESTLAND CASE, THE, 1937
WESTMINSTER PASSION PLAY—BEHOLD THE
  MAN, THE, 1951
WESTWARD BOUND, 1931
WESTWARD BOUND, 1944
WESTWARD HO, 1936
WESTWARD HO, 1942
WESTWARD HO THE WAGONS?, 1956
WESTWARD PASSAGE, 1932
WESTWARD THE WOMEN, 1951
WESTWARD TRAIL, THE, 1948
WETBACKS, 1956
WE'VE NEVER BEEN LICKED, 1943
WHALERS, THE, 1942:,
WHARF ANGEL, 1934
WHAT A BLONDE, 1945
WHAT A CARRY ON!, 1949
WHAT A CARVE UP!, 1962
WHAT A CRAZY WORLD, 1963
WHAT A LIFE, 1939
WHAT A MAN, 1930
WHAT A MAN!, 1937
WHAT A MAN!, 1944
WHAT A NIGHT!, 1931
WHAT A WHOPPER, 1961
WHAT A WIDOW, 1930
WHAT A WOMAN!, 1943
WHAT AM I BID?, 1967
WHAT DO WE DO NOW?, 1945
WHAT EVERY WOMAN KNOWS, 1934
WHAT EVERY WOMAN WANTS, 1954

WHAT EVERY WOMAN WANTS, 1962
WHAT HAPPENED THEN?, 1934
WHAT MEN WANT, 1930
WHAT NEXT, CORPORAL HARGROVE?, 1945
WHAT! NO BEER?, 1933
WHAT PRICE CRIME?, 1935
WHAT PRICE INNOCENCE?, 1933
WHAT PRICE VENGEANCE?, 1937
WHAT THE BUTLER SAW, 1950
WHAT WOMEN DREAM, 1933
WHAT WOULD YOU DO, CHUMS?, 1939
WHAT WOULD YOU SAY TO SOME SPINACH, 1976
WHAT'S BUZZIN COUSIN?, 1943
WHAT'S COOKIN'?, 1942
WHAT'S SO BAD ABOUT FEELING GOOD?, 1968
WHAT'S THE TIME, MR. CLOCK?, 1985
WHAT'S YOUR RACKET?, 1934
WHEEL OF FATE, 1953
WHEEL OF LIFE, THE, 1929
WHEELER DEALERS, THE, 1963
WHEELS OF DESTINY, 1934
WHEN A GIRL'S BEAUTIFUL, 1947
WHEN A MAN RIDES ALONE, 1933
WHEN A MAN SEES RED, 1934
WHEN A MAN'S A MAN, 1935
WHEN DINOSAURS RULED THE EARTH, 1971
WHEN G-MEN STEP IN, 1938
WHEN GANGLAND STRIKES, 1956
WHEN HELL BROKE LOOSE, 1958
WHEN IN ROME, 1952
WHEN JOHNNY COMES MARCHING HOME, 1943
WHEN KNIGHTS WERE BOLD, 1942
WHEN LADIES MEET, 1933
WHEN LONDON SLEEPS, 1932
WHEN LONDON SLEEPS, 1934
WHEN LOVE IS YOUNG, 1937
WHEN STRANGERS MARRY, 1933
WHEN STRANGERS MEET, 1934
WHEN THE BOUGH BREAKS, 1947
WHEN THE BOYS MEET THE GIRLS, 1965
WHEN THE CLOCK STRIKES, 1961
WHEN THE DALTONS RODE, 1940
WHEN THE DEVIL WAS WELL, 1937
WHEN THE LIGHTS GO ON AGAIN, 1944
WHEN THE REDSKINS RODE, 1951
WHEN THE TREES WERE TALL, 1965
WHEN THIEF MEETS THIEF, 1937
WHEN TOMORROW COMES, 1939
WHEN WE ARE MARRIED, 1943
WHEN WERE YOU BORN?, 1938
WHEN WILLIE COMES MARCHING HOME, 1950
WHEN WORLDS COLLIDE, 1951
WHEN YOU COME HOME, 1947
WHEN YOU'RE IN LOVE, 1937
WHEN YOU'RE SMILING, 1950
WHERE ARE YOUR CHILDREN?, 1943
WHERE DANGER LIVES, 1950
WHERE DID YOU GET THAT GIRL?, 1941
WHERE HAS POOR MICKEY GONE?, 1964
WHERE IS MY CHILD?, 1937
WHERE IS THIS LADY?, 1932
WHERE SINNERS MEET, 1934
WHERE THE BUFFALO ROAM, 1938
WHERE THE BULLETS FLY, 1966
WHERE THE LILIES BLOOM, 1974
WHERE THE RED FERN GROWS, 1974
WHERE THE RIVER RUNS BLACK, 1986
WHERE THE SPIES ARE, 1965
WHERE THE WEST BEGINS, 1938
WHERE THERE'S A WILL, 1936
WHERE THERE'S A WILL, 1937
WHERE THERE'S A WILL, 1955
WHERE THERE'S LIFE, 1947
WHERE TRAILS DIVIDE, 1937
WHERE'S JACK?, 1969
WHERE'S SALLY?, 1936
WHERE'S THAT FIRE?, 1939
WHEREVER SHE GOES, 1953
WHICH WAY TO THE FRONT?, 1970
WHIFFS, 1975
WHILE I LIVE, 1947
WHILE NEW YORK SLEEPS, 1938
WHILE PARENTS SLEEP, 1935
WHILE PARIS SLEEPS, 1932
WHILE THE ATTORNEY IS ASLEEP, 1945
WHILE THE PATIENT SLEPT, 1935

WHILE THE SUN SHINES, 1950
WHIP HAND, THE, 1951
WHIPLASH, 1948
WHIPPED, THE, 1950
WHIPSAW, 1936
WHIRLPOOL, 1934
WHIRLPOOL, 1949
WHIRLPOOL, 1959
WHIRLWIND, 1951
WHIRLWIND HORSEMAN, 1938
WHIRLWIND OF PARIS, 1946
WHIRLWIND RAIDERS, 1948
WHISPERING CITY, 1947
WHISPERING ENEMIES, 1939
WHISPERING FOOTSTEPS, 1943
WHISPERING GHOSTS, 1942
WHISPERING SKULL, THE, 1944
WHISPERING SMITH, 1948
WHISPERING SMITH SPEAKS, 1935
WHISPERING SMITH VERSUS SCOTLAND YARD,
  1952
WHISPERING TONGUES, 1934
WHISPERING WINDS, 1929
WHISTLE AT EATON FALLS, 1951
WHISTLE BLOWER, THE, 1987
WHISTLE DOWN THE WIND, 1961
WHISTLER, THE, 1944
WHISTLIN' DAN, 1932
WHISTLING BULLETS, 1937
WHISTLING HILLS, 1951
WHISTLING IN BROOKLYN, 1943
WHISTLING IN DIXIE, 1942
WHISTLING IN THE DARK, 1933
WHISTLING IN THE DARK, 1941
WHITE ANGEL, THE, 1936
WHITE BANNERS, 1938
WHITE BONDAGE, 1937
WHITE COCKATOO, 1935
WHITE CORRIDORS, 1952
WHITE DEATH, 1936
WHITE EAGLE, 1932
WHITE ENSIGN, 1934
WHITE FACE, 1933
WHITE FANG, 1936
WHITE FEATHER, 1955
WHITE FIRE, 1953
WHITE GODDESS, 1953
WHITE GORILLA, 1947
WHITE HORSE INN, THE, 1959
WHITE HUNTER, 1936
WHITE HUNTER, 1965
WHITE HUNTRESS, 1957
WHITE LEGION, THE, 1936
WHITE LIES, 1935
WHITE LIGHTNIN' ROAD, 1967
WHITE LIGHTNING, 1953
WHITE LILAC, 1935
WHITE ORCHID, THE, 1954
WHITE PARADE, THE, 1934
WHITE SAVAGE, 1943
WHITE SHADOWS IN THE SOUTH SEAS, 1928
WHITE SHOULDERS, 1931
WHITE SISTER, THE, 1933
WHITE SQUAW, THE, 1956
WHITE STALLION, 1947
WHITE TIE AND TAILS, 1946
WHITE TOWER, THE, 1950
WHITE WITCH DOCTOR, 1953
WHO DONE IT?, 1942
WHO FEARS THE DEVIL, 1972
WHO FRAMED ROGER RABBIT, 1988
WHO HAS SEEN THE WIND, 1980
WHO IS GUILTY?, 1940
WHO IS HOPE SCHUYLER?, 1942
WHO KILLED AUNT MAGGIE?, 1940
WHO KILLED FEN MARKHAM?, 1937
WHO KILLED GAIL PRESTON?, 1938
WHO KILLED JOHN SAVAGE?, 1937
WHO KILLED VAN LOON?, 1984
WHO WAS MADDOX?, 1964
WHO WAS THAT LADY?, 1960
WHOLE TOWN'S TALKING, THE, 1935
WHOLE TRUTH, THE, 1958
WHOM THE GODS DESTROY, 1934
WHO'S GOT THE ACTION?, 1962
WHO'S MINDING THE MINT?, 1967

BOLD: Films on Videocassette

WHO'S MINDING THE STORE?, 1963
WHO'S THAT GIRL, 1987
WHO'S YOUR FATHER?, 1935
WHO'S YOUR LADY FRIEND?, 1937
WHY BRING THAT UP?, 1929
WHY LEAVE HOME?, 1929
WHY PICK ON ME?, 1937
WHY SAILORS LEAVE HOME, 1930
WHY SAPS LEAVE HOME, 1932
WICHITA, 1955
WICKED, 1931
WICKED LADY, THE, 1946
WICKHAM MYSTERY, THE, 1931
WIDE BOY, 1952
WIDE OPEN, 1930
WIDE OPEN FACES, 1938
WIDE OPEN TOWN, 1941
WIDOW FROM MONTE CARLO, THE, 1936
WIDOW IN SCARLET, 1932
WIDOW'S MIGHT, 1934
WIFE, DOCTOR AND NURSE, 1937
WIFE, HUSBAND AND FRIEND, 1939
WIFE OF GENERAL LING, THE, 1938
WIFE OF MONTE CRISTO, THE, 1946
WIFE OR TWO, A, 1935
WIFE TAKES A FLYER, THE, 1942
WIFE VERSUS SECRETARY, 1936
WIFE WANTED, 1946
WILD AND WONDERFUL, 1964
WILD AND WOOLLY, 1937
WILD BEAUTY, 1946
WILD BILL HICKOK RIDES, 1942
WILD BLUE YONDER, THE, 1952
WILD BOY, 1934
WILD BRIAN KENT, 1936
WILD COMPANY, 1930
WILD COUNTRY, 1947
WILD DAKOTAS, THE, 1956
WILD DUCK, THE, 1977
WILD FRONTIER, THE, 1947
WILD GIRL, 1932
WILD GOLD, 1934
WILD GUITAR, 1962
WILD HARVEST, 1947
WILD HERITAGE, 1958
WILD HORSE, 1931
WILD HORSE AMBUSH, 1952
WILD HORSE CANYON, 1939
WILD HORSE HANK, 1979
WILD HORSE MESA, 1932
WILD HORSE MESA, 1947
WILD HORSE PHANTOM, 1944
WILD HORSE RODEO, 1938
WILD HORSE ROUND-UP, 1937
WILD HORSE RUSTLERS, 1943
WILD HORSE STAMPEDE, 1943
WILD HORSE VALLEY, 1940
WILD IN THE COUNTRY, 1961
WILD INNOCENCE, 1937
WILD IS THE WIND, 1957
WILD MAN OF BORNEO, THE, 1941
WILD MONEY, 1937
WILD MUSTANG, 1935
WILD NORTH, THE, 1952
WILD ON THE BEACH, 1965
WILD PARTY, THE, 1929
WILD SEASON, 1968
WILD SEED, 1965
WILD STALLION, 1952
WILD WEST, 1946
WILD WEST WHOOPEE, 1931
WILD WESTERNERS, THE, 1962
WILD, WILD WINTER, 1966
WILDCAT, 1942
WILDCAT BUS, 1940
WILDCAT OF TUCSON, 1941
WILDCAT TROOPER, 1936
WILDCATS OF ST. TRINIAN'S, THE, 1980
WILDCATTER, THE, 1937
WILDERNESS MAIL, 1935
WILDFIRE, 1945
WILL ANY GENTLEMAN?, 1955
WILLIAM COMES TO TOWN, 1948
WILLY, 1963
WILLY WONKA AND THE CHOCOLATE FACTORY, 1971

WILSON, 1944
WIN, PLACE, OR STEAL, 1975
WIND CANNOT READ, THE, 1958
WIND OF CHANGE, THE, 1961
WINDBAG THE SAILOR, 1937
WINDFALL, 1935
WINDFALL, 1955
WINDJAMMER, 1937
WINDJAMMER, THE, 1931
WINDMILL, THE, 1937
WINDOWS OF TIME, THE, 1969
WINDS OF THE WASTELAND, 1936
WINE, WOMEN AND HORSES, 1937
WINE, WOMEN, AND SONG, 1934
WING AND A PRAYER, 1944
WINGED VICTORY, 1944
WINGS AND THE WOMAN, 1942
WINGS FOR THE EAGLE, 1942
WINGS IN THE DARK, 1935
WINGS OF ADVENTURE, 1930
WINGS OF CHANCE, 1961
WINGS OF EAGLES, THE, 1957
WINGS OF THE HAWK, 1953
WINGS OF THE MORNING, 1937
WINGS OF THE NAVY, 1939
WINGS OF VICTORY, 1941
WINGS OVER AFRICA, 1939
WINGS OVER HONOLULU, 1937
WINGS OVER THE PACIFIC, 1943
WINK OF AN EYE, 1958
WINNER TAKE ALL, 1932
WINNER TAKE ALL, 1939
WINNER'S CIRCLE, THE, 1948
WINNING OF THE WEST, 1953
WINNING TEAM, THE, 1952
WINNING TICKET, THE, 1935
WINSLOW BOY, THE, 1950
WINTER A GO-GO, 1965
WINTER CARNIVAL, 1939
WINTER MEETING, 1948
WINTER WONDERLAND, 1947
WINTER'S TALE, THE, 1968
WINTERTIME, 1943
WIRE SERVICE, 1942
WIRETAPPERS, 1956
WISE GIRL, 1937
WISE GIRLS, 1930
WISE GUYS, 1937
WISE GUYS, 1969
WISER SEX, THE, 1932
WISHBONE, THE, 1933
WISTFUL WIDOW OF WAGON GAP, THE, 1947
WITCHCRAFT, 1964
WITCHING HOUR, THE, 1934
WITCH'S CURSE, THE, 1963
WITH A SMILE, 1939
WITH A SONG IN MY HEART, 1952
WITH LOVE AND KISSES, 1937
WITH LOVE AND TENDERNESS, 1978
WITH SIX YOU GET EGGROLL, 1968
WITHIN THE LAW, 1939
WITHIN THESE WALLS, 1945
WITHOUT A HOME, 1939
WITHOUT A TRACE, 1983
WITHOUT EACH OTHER, 1962
WITHOUT HONOR, 1949
WITHOUT HONORS, 1932
WITHOUT LOVE, 1945
WITHOUT ORDERS, 1936
WITHOUT REGRET, 1935
WITHOUT RESERVATIONS, 1946
WITHOUT YOU, 1934
WITNESS CHAIR, THE, 1936
WITNESS FOR THE PROSECUTION, 1957
WITNESS IN THE DARK, 1959
WITNESS VANISHES, THE, 1939
WIVES AND LOVERS, 1963
WIVES BEWARE, 1933
WIVES NEVER KNOW, 1936
WIVES UNDER SUSPICION, 1938
WIZARD OF BAGHDAD, THE, 1960
WIZARD OF MARS, 1964
WIZARDS OF THE LOST KINGDOM, 1985
WOLF CALL, 1939
WOLF HUNTERS, THE, 1949
WOLF LARSEN, 1958

WOLF LARSEN, 1978
WOLF OF NEW YORK, 1940
WOLF'S CLOTHING, 1936
WOLVES, 1930
WOLVES OF THE RANGE, 1943
WOLVES OF THE SEA, 1938
WOLVES OF THE UNDERWORLD, 1935
WOMAN AGAINST THE WORLD, 1938
WOMAN AGAINST WOMAN, 1938
WOMAN AND THE HUNTER, THE, 1957
WOMAN CHASES MAN, 1937
WOMAN COMMANDS, A, 1932
WOMAN DECIDES, THE, 1932
WOMAN DOCTOR, 1939
WOMAN FOR JOE, THE, 1955
WOMAN FROM HEADQUARTERS, 1950
WOMAN FROM MONTE CARLO, THE, 1932
WOMAN FROM TANGIER, THE, 1948
WOMAN HATER, 1949
WOMAN HE SCORNED, THE, 1930
WOMAN I LOVE, THE, 1937
WOMAN I STOLE, THE, 1933
WOMAN IN CHAINS, 1932
WOMAN IN COMMAND, THE, 1934
WOMAN IN DISTRESS, 1937
WOMAN IN GREEN, THE, 1945
WOMAN IN HIDING, 1953
WOMAN IN RED, THE, 1935
WOMAN IN ROOM 13, THE, 1932
WOMAN IN THE DARK, 1934
WOMAN IN THE DARK, 1952
WOMAN IN THE HALL, THE, 1949
WOMAN IS A WOMAN, A, 1961
WOMAN IS THE JUDGE, A, 1939
WOMAN OF DISTINCTION, A, 1950
WOMAN OF EXPERIENCE, A, 1931
WOMAN OF MYSTERY, A, 1957
WOMAN OF SIN, 1961
WOMAN OF THE NORTH COUNTRY, 1952
WOMAN OF THE TOWN, THE, 1943
WOMAN ON PIER 13, THE, 1950
WOMAN ON THE BEACH, THE, 1947
WOMAN ON THE RUN, 1950
WOMAN POSSESSED, A, 1958
WOMAN RACKET, THE, 1930
WOMAN THEY ALMOST LYNCHED, THE, 1953
WOMAN TO WOMAN, 1929
WOMAN TO WOMAN, 1946
WOMAN TRAP, 1929
WOMAN TRAP, 1936
WOMAN UNAFRAID, 1934
WOMAN WANTED, 1935
WOMAN WHO CAME BACK, 1945
WOMAN WHO DARED, 1949
WOMAN WHO WOULDN'T DIE, THE, 1965
WOMAN-WISE, 1937
WOMANHOOD, 1934
WOMAN'S ANGLE, THE, 1954
WOMAN'S DEVOTION, A, 1956
WOMAN'S FACE, A, 1939
WOMAN'S LIFE, A, 1964
WOMAN'S SECRET, A, 1949
WOMAN'S TEMPTATION, A, 1959
WOMAN'S VENGEANCE, A, 1947
WOMEN ARE LIKE THAT, 1938
WOMEN ARE TROUBLE, 1936
WOMEN AREN'T ANGELS, 1942
WOMEN EVERYWHERE, 1930
WOMEN GO ON FOREVER, 1931
WOMEN IN A DRESSING GOWN, 1957
WOMEN IN BONDAGE, 1943
WOMEN IN HIS LIFE, THE, 1934
WOMEN IN PRISON, 1938
WOMEN IN THE NIGHT, 1948
WOMEN IN THE WIND, 1939
WOMEN IN WAR, 1940
WOMEN LOVE ONCE, 1931
WOMEN MEN MARRY, 1931
WOMEN MEN MARRY, THE, 1937
WOMEN MUST DRESS, 1935
WOMEN OF GLAMOUR, 1937
WOMEN OF PITCAIRN ISLAND, THE, 1957
WOMEN OF THE PREHISTORIC PLANET, 1966
WOMEN THEY TALK ABOUT, 1928
WOMEN WHO PLAY, 1932
WOMEN WITHOUT NAMES, 1940

WOMEN WON'T TELL, 1933
WON TON TON, THE DOG WHO SAVED
   HOLLYWOOD, 1976
WONDER BAR, 1934
WONDER BOY, 1951
WONDER OF WOMEN, 1929
WONDERFUL COUNTRY, THE, 1959
WONDERFUL STORY, THE, 1932
WONDERFUL THINGS!, 1958
WONDERFUL TO BE YOUNG!, 1962
WOODEN HORSE, THE, 1951
WORDS AND MUSIC, 1929
WORDS AND MUSIC, 1948
WORKING GIRLS, 1931
WORKING MAN, THE, 1933
WORLD ACCUSES, THE, 1935
WORLD AND THE FLESH, THE, 1932
WORLD CHANGES, THE, 1933
WORLD GONE MAD, THE, 1933
WORLD IN MY CORNER, 1956
WORLD IN MY POCKET, THE, 1962
WORLD MOVES ON, THE, 1934
WORLD OF APU, THE, 1960
WORLD OWES ME A LIVING, THE, 1944
WORLD PREMIERE, 1941
WORLD, THE, FLESH, AND THE DEVIL, THE, 1959
WORLD WAS HIS JURY, THE, 1958
WORLD WITHOUT A MASK, THE, 1934
WORLD WITHOUT END, 1956
WORLD, THE FLESH, AND THE DEVIL, THE, 1932
WORLDLY GOODS, 1930
WORM'S EYE VIEW, 1951
WORST WOMAN IN PARIS, 1933
WOULD-BE GENTLEMAN, THE, 1960
WOZZECK, 1962
WRANGLER'S ROOST, 1941
WRATH OF JEALOUSY, 1936
WRECK OF THE MARY DEARE, THE, 1959
WRECKER, THE, 1933
WRECKING CREW, 1942
WRITTEN LAW, THE, 1931
WRONG ARM OF THE LAW, THE, 1963
WRONG BOX, THE, 1966
WRONG GUYS, THE, 1988
WRONG MAN, THE, 1956
WRONG NUMBER, 1959
WRONG ROAD, THE, 1937
WUTHERING HEIGHTS, 1970
WYOMING, 1940
WYOMING, 1947
WYOMING BANDIT, THE, 1949
WYOMING MAIL, 1950
WYOMING OUTLAW, 1939
WYOMING RENEGADES, 1955
WYOMING WILDCAT, 1941
X-15, 1961
X MARKS THE SPOT, 1931
X MARKS THE SPOT, 1942
YANCO, 1964
YANK AT ETON, A, 1942
YANK AT OXFORD, A, 1938
YANK IN ERMINE, A, 1955
YANK IN INDO-CHINA, A, 1952
YANK IN KOREA, A, 1951
YANK IN LIBYA, A, 1942
YANK IN LONDON, A, 1946
YANK IN THE R.A.F., A, 1941
YANK IN VIET-NAM, A, 1964
YANK ON THE BURMA ROAD, A, 1942
YANKEE BUCCANEER, 1952
YANKEE DON, 1931
YANKEE FAKIR, 1947
YANKEE PASHA, 1954
YANKS AHOY, 1943
YANKS ARE COMING, THE, 1942
YEAR ONE, 1974
YEARS BETWEEN, THE, 1947
YELLOW BALLOON, THE, 1953
YELLOW CAB MAN, THE, 1950
YELLOW CANARY, THE, 1944
YELLOW CANARY, THE, 1963
YELLOW CARGO, 1936
YELLOW DUST, 1936
YELLOW EARTH, 1986
YELLOW FIN, 1951
YELLOW HAT, THE, 1966

YELLOW JACK, 1938
YELLOW MASK, THE, 1930
YELLOW MOUNTAIN, THE, 1954
YELLOW ROBE, THE, 1954
YELLOW ROSE OF TEXAS, THE, 1944
YELLOW SANDS, 1938
YELLOW SKY, 1948
YELLOW SLIPPERS, THE, 1965
YELLOW SUBMARINE, 1958
YELLOW TICKET, THE, 1931
YELLOW TOMAHAWK, THE, 1954
YELLOWNECK, 1955
YELLOWSTONE, 1936
YELLOWSTONE KELLY, 1959
YES, MADAM?, 1938
YES, MR. BROWN, 1933
YES, MY DARLING DAUGHTER, 1939
YES SIR, MR. BONES, 1951
YES SIR, THAT'S MY BABY, 1949
YESTERDAY'S HEROES, 1940
YETI, 1977
YIDDLE WITH HIS FIDDLE, 1937
YO YO, 1967
YODELIN' KID FROM PINE RIDGE, 1937
YOG-MONSTER FROM SPACE, 1970
YOKEL BOY, 1942
YOLANDA AND THE THIEF, 1945
YOLANTA, 1964
YONGKARI MONSTER FROM THE DEEP, 1967
YOR, THE HUNTER FROM THE FUTURE, 1983
YOU ARE THE WORLD FOR ME, 1964
YOU BELONG TO ME, 1934
YOU BELONG TO ME, 1941
YOU CAME ALONG, 1945
YOU CAME TOO LATE, 1962
YOU CAN'T BEAT LOVE, 1937
YOU CAN'T BEAT THE IRISH, 1952
YOU CAN'T BUY EVERYTHING, 1934
YOU CAN'T BUY LUCK, 1937
YOU CAN'T CHEAT AN HONEST MAN, 1939
YOU CAN'T DO WITHOUT LOVE, 1946
YOU CAN'T ESCAPE, 1955
YOU CAN'T ESCAPE FOREVER, 1942
YOU CAN'T FOOL AN IRISHMAN, 1950
YOU CAN'T FOOL YOUR WIFE, 1940
YOU CAN'T HAVE EVERYTHING, 1937
YOU CAN'T RATION LOVE, 1944
YOU CAN'T RUN AWAY FROM IT, 1956
YOU CAN'T SEE 'ROUND CORNERS, 1969
YOU CAN'T TAKE IT WITH YOU, 1938
YOU FOR ME, 1952
YOU GOTTA STAY HAPPY, 1948
YOU HAVE TO RUN FAST, 1961
YOU KNOW WHAT SAILORS ARE, 1954
YOU LIVE AND LEARN, 1937
YOU LUCKY PEOPLE, 1955
YOU MADE ME LOVE YOU, 1934
YOU MAY BE NEXT, 1936
YOU MUST BE JOKING!, 1965
YOU MUST GET MARRIED, 1936
YOU NEVER CAN TELL, 1951
YOU ONLY LIVE ONCE, 1969
YOU PAY YOUR MONEY, 1957
YOU SAID A MOUTHFUL, 1932
YOU WERE MEANT FOR ME, 1948
YOU WERE NEVER LOVELIER, 1942
YOU WILL REMEMBER, 1941
YOU'D BE SURPRISED!, 1930
YOU'LL FIND OUT, 1940
YOU'LL NEVER GET RICH, 1941
YOUNG AND BEAUTIFUL, 1934
YOUNG AND DANGEROUS, 1957
YOUNG AND INNOCENT, 1938
YOUNG AND THE BRAVE, THE, 1963
YOUNG AND THE GUILTY, THE, 1958
YOUNG AND WILD, 1958
YOUNG AND WILLING, 1943
YOUNG AT HEART, 1955
YOUNG BESS, 1953
YOUNG BILL HICKOK, 1940
YOUNG BILLY YOUNG, 1969
YOUNG BLOOD, 1932
YOUNG DR. KILDARE, 1938
YOUNG DONOVAN'S KID, 1931
YOUNG DYNAMITE, 1937
YOUNG FUGITIVES, 1938

YOUNG GIANTS, 1983
YOUNG GIRLS OF ROCHEFORT, THE, 1968
YOUNG GUY ON MT. COOK, 1969
YOUNG HUSBANDS, 1958
YOUNG IDEAS, 1943
YOUNG IN HEART, THE, 1938
YOUNG LAND, THE, 1959
YOUNG LORD, THE, 1970
YOUNG MAN OF MANHATTAN, 1930
YOUNG MAN WITH IDEAS, 1952
YOUNG MAN'S FANCY, 1943
YOUNG MR. LINCOLN, 1939
YOUNG MR. PITT, THE, 1942
YOUNG NOWHERES, 1929
YOUNG SINNERS, 1931
YOUNG WIDOW, 1946
YOUNG WIVES' TALE, 1954
YOUNGER BROTHERS, THE, 1949
YOUNGER GENERATION, 1929
YOUNGEST PROFESSION, THE, 1943
YOUR CHEATIN' HEART, 1964
YOUR MONEY OR YOUR WIFE, 1965
YOUR PAST IS SHOWING, 1958
YOUR UNCLE DUDLEY, 1935
YOU'RE A LUCKY FELLOW, MR. SMITH, 1943
YOU'RE A SWEETHEART, 1937
YOU'RE IN THE ARMY NOW, 1937
YOU'RE IN THE ARMY NOW, 1941
YOU'RE IN THE NAVY NOW, 1951
YOU'RE MY EVERYTHING, 1949
YOU'RE NEVER TOO YOUNG, 1955
YOU'RE NOT SO TOUGH, 1940
YOU'RE ONLY YOUNG ONCE, 1938
YOU'RE ONLY YOUNG TWICE, 1952
YOU'RE OUT OF LUCK, 1941
YOU'RE TELLING ME, 1934
YOU'RE TELLING ME, 1942
YOU'RE THE DOCTOR, 1938
YOU'RE THE ONE, 1941
YOURS FOR THE ASKING, 1936
YOUTH AFLAME, 1945
YOUTH ON PAROLE, 1937
YOUTH ON TRIAL, 1945
YOUTH WILL BE SERVED, 1940
YOUTHFUL FOLLY, 1934
YOU'VE GOT TO BE SMART, 1967
YUKON FLIGHT, 1940
YUKON GOLD, 1952
YUKON MANHUNT, 1951
YUKON VENGEANCE, 1954
ZAMBA, 1949
ZANDY'S BRIDE, 1974
ZANZIBAR, 1940
ZATOICHI, 1968
ZATOICHI CHALLENGED, 1970
ZATOICHI'S CONSPIRACY, 1974
ZAZIE, 1961
ZELIG, 1983
ZELLY AND ME, 1988
ZENOBIA, 1939
ZEPPELIN, 1971
ZERO HOUR!, 1957
00-2 MOST SECRET AGENTS, 1965
ZIEGFELD GIRL, 1941
ZIS BOOM BAH, 1941
ZOMBIES ON BROADWAY, 1945
ZONTAR, THE THING FROM VENUS, 1966
ZOO IN BUDAPEST, 1933
ZORBA THE GREEK, 1964
ZOTZ!, 1962

A-C
ACTION STATIONS, 1959
ADERYN PAPUR, 1984
ALL OF ME, 1984
**ALLAN QUATERMAIN AND THE LOST CITY OF
   GOLD, 1987**
AMAZING GRACE AND CHUCK, 1987
AMERICAN DREAMER, 1984
APPOINTMENT WITH DEATH, 1988
AROUND THE WORLD IN EIGHTY WAYS, 1987
ASSAM GARDEN, THE, 1985
ASSASSINATION, 1987
ASYA'S HAPPINESS, 1988
AU REVOIR LES ENFANTS, 1988
AVIATOR, THE, 1985

BAD BLOOD, 1987
BEAT STREET, 1984
BEGGARS OF LIFE, 1928
BENGAZI, 1955
BEYOND MOMBASA, 1957
BEYOND THE POSEIDON ADVENTURE, 1979
BICYCLE THIEF, THE, 1949
BIG, 1988
BIG FISHERMAN, THE, 1959
BIG HANGOVER, THE, 1950
BIG LIFT, THE, 1950
BIG PARADE, THE, 1987
BIG TIMBER, 1950
BIG TREES, THE, 1952
BIG WEDNESDAY, 1978
BIG WHEEL, THE, 1949
BILL OF DIVORCEMENT, A, 1932
BILLY IN THE LOWLANDS, 1979
BILLY LIAR, 1963
BINGO LONG TRAVELING ALL-STARS AND MOTOR
    KINGS, THE, 1976
BIZET'S CARMEN, 1984
BLACK BIRD, THE, 1975
BLACK CAULDRON, THE, 1985
BLACK DAKOTAS, THE, 1954
BLACK GOLD, 1963
BLACK HILLS AMBUSH, 1952
BLACK HOLE, THE, 1979
BLACK KNIGHT, THE, 1954
BLACK NARCISSUS, 1947
BLACK SHIELD OF FALWORTH, THE, 1954
BLACK STALLION RETURNS, THE, 1983
BLACKBEARD THE PIRATE, 1952
BLACKOUT, 1954
BLACKOUT, 1978
BLANCHE FURY, 1948
BLAZE OF NOON, 1947
BLAZING FOREST, THE, 1952
BLESS THE BEASTS AND CHILDREN, 1971
BLESSED EVENT, 1932
BLOB, THE, 1958
BLONDE BANDIT, THE, 1950
BLONDIE OF THE FOLLIES, 1932
BLOOD ALLEY, 1955
BLOOD ARROW, 1958
BLUE LAGOON, THE, 1949
BLUEBEARD'S EIGHTH WIFE, 1938
BLUEBEARD'S TEN HONEYMOONS, 1960
BLUEPRINT FOR MURDER, A, 1953
BOBO, THE, 1967
BOFORS GUN, THE, 1968
BOLDEST JOB IN THE WEST, THE, 1971
BOLERO, 1934
BOMBSHELL, 1933
BOOMERANG, 1960
BOOTLEGGERS, 1974
BOSTONIANS, THE, 1984
BOUGHT, 1931
BOUND FOR GLORY, 1976
BOUNTY HUNTERS, THE, 1970
BOUNTY KILLER, THE, 1965
BOY WHO CRIED WEREWOLF, THE, 1973
BRAINWASHED, 1961
BRANNIGAN, 1975
BRASS TARGET, 1978
BREAKER MORANT, 1980
BREAKIN'2: ELECTRIC BOOGALOO, 1984
BREAKIN', 1984
BREED APART, A, 1984
BRINK'S JOB, THE, 1978
BROADWAY DANNY ROSE, 1984
BRUTE, THE, 1952
BUCK ROGERS IN THE 25TH CENTURY, 1979
BUDDY HOLLY STORY, THE, 1978
BUDDY SYSTEM, THE, 1984
BUG, 1975
BULLSHOT, 1983
BURKE & WILLS, 1985
CABIN IN THE COTTON, 1932
CAFE METROPOLE, 1937
CAGE OF EVIL, 1960
CALIFORNIA SUITE, 1978
CALLING BULLDOG DRUMMOND, 1951
CALLING HOMICIDE, 1956
CALYPSO, 1959
CAMELOT, 1967

CAMILLE, 1937
CAN-CAN, 1960
CANDIDATE, THE, 1972
CAPTAINS OF THE CLOUDS, 1942
CAREFUL, HE MIGHT HEAR YOU, 1984
CAST A GIANT SHADOW, 1966
CAT AND MOUSE, 1975
CAT BALLOU, 1965
CATCH ME A SPY, 1971
CHAD HANNA, 1940
CHAIN OF EVENTS, 1958
CHAIRMAN, THE, 1969
CHARADE, 1963
CHARLY, 1968
CHATTANOOGA CHOO CHOO, 1984
CHILD'S PLAY, 1972
CHINO, 1976
CHIVATO, 1961
CHRONICLE OF ANNA MAGDALENA BACH, 1968
CHRONOPOLIS, 1982
CINCINNATI KID, THE, 1965
CLASS RELATIONS, 1986
CLEAR SKIES, 1963
CLEOPATRA, 1963
CLUE OF THE NEW PIN, THE, 1961
CLUE OF THE SILVER KEY, THE, 1961
COAL MINER'S DAUGHTER, 1980
COLOR PURPLE, THE, 1985
COME BACK LITTLE SHEBA, 1952
COME BLOW YOUR HORN, 1963
COMES A HORSEMAN, 1978
COMFORT AND JOY, 1984
COMING-OUT PARTY, A, 1962
COMPELLED, 1960
CONCORDE, THE—AIRPORT '79, 1979
CONDUCT UNBECOMING, 1975
CONDUCTOR, THE, 1981
CONFIDENTIALLY YOURS!, 1983
CONQUEST OF MYCENE, 1965
CONSPIRATOR, 1949
CONTINENTAL DIVIDE, 1981
CONVERSATION, THE, 1974
CORKY, 1972
COUNT YOUR BLESSINGS, 1959
COUNTERFEIT CONSTABLE, THE, 1966
COUNTERFEIT TRAITOR, THE, 1962
COUNTERPOINT, 1967
COUNTRY GIRL, THE, 1954
COURT MARTIAL, 1962
COURT MARTIAL OF MAJOR KELLER, THE, 1961
COWBOYS, THE, 1972
CRACKERS, 1984
CRAIG'S WIFE, 1936
CRASH DRIVE, 1959
CRIME WAVE, 1954
CRIMES AT THE DARK HOUSE, 1940
CRIMES OF STEPHEN HAWKE, THE, 1936
CRIMSON CANDLE, THE, 1934
CRIMSON KIMONO, THE, 1959
"CROCODILE" DUNDEE, 1986
CROOKED CIRCLE, THE, 1958
CROOKED WAY, THE, 1949
CROOKS ANONYMOUS, 1963
CROSS CHANNEL, 1955
CROSS COUNTRY CRUISE, 1934
CROW HOLLOW, 1952
CROWD ROARS, THE, 1932
CRY TERROR, 1958
CUCKOO IN THE NEST, THE, 1933
CULT OF THE COBRA, 1955
CURSE OF THE AZTEC MUMMY, THE, 1965
CURSE OF THE WRAYDONS, THE, 1946
CYCLE, THE, 1979
CYNARA, 1932
DA, 1988
DAISY KENYON, 1947
DAMNED DON'T CRY, THE, 1950
DANCE, FOOLS, DANCE, 1931
DANGER BY MY SIDE, 1962
DANGER TOMORROW, 1960
DANGEROUS, 1936
DANGEROUS AFTERNOON, 1961
DANGEROUS ASSIGNMENT, 1950
DANGEROUS MISSION, 1954
DAPHNE, THE, 1967
DARK EYES, 1987

DATE AT MIDNIGHT, 1960
DATE WITH AN ANGEL, 1987
DAUGHTER OF DECEIT, 1977
DAVID AND LISA, 1962
DAY FOR NIGHT, 1973
DAY OF THE WOLVES, 1973
DAY THE WAR ENDED, THE, 1961
DAY-TIME WIFE, 1939
DAYTONA BEACH WEEKEND, 1965
DEAD MAN'S CHEST, 1965
DEAD MAN'S EVIDENCE, 1962
DEAD ON COURSE, 1952
DEADHEAD MILES, 1982
DEADLY AFFAIR, THE, 1967
DEADLY DECOYS, THE, 1962
DEATH IS A NUMBER, 1951
DEATH OF A BUREAUCRAT, 1979
DEATH OVER MY SHOULDER, 1958
DECEPTION, 1946
DECKS RAN RED, THE, 1958
DEFEND MY LOVE, 1956
DEPRAVED, THE, 1957
DEPTH CHARGE, 1960
DESERT BLOOM, 1986
DESPERATE CHARACTERS, 1971
DESPERATE MAN, THE, 1959
DETECTIVE SCHOOL DROPOUTS, 1986
DEVIL MAKES THREE, THE, 1952
DEVIL'S GENERAL, THE, 1957
DEVIL'S MAZE, THE, 1929
DEVIL'S TRAP, THE, 1964
DIAL M FOR MURDER, 1954
DIANE, 1955
DICK TRACY, 1945
DICK TRACY MEETS GRUESOME, 1947
DID YOU HEAR THE ONE ABOUT THE TRAVELING
    SALESLADY?, 1968
DIRTY LAUNDRY, 1987
DISORDERLIES, 1987
DIVE BOMBER, 1941
DR. SOCRATES, 1935
DOCTOR ZHIVAGO, 1965
DOOMSDAY AT ELEVEN, 1963
DOSS HOUSE, 1933
DOUBLE CROSS, 1956
DOUBLE DECEPTION, 1963
DOUBLE EXPOSURE, 1954
DOUBLE HARNESS, 1933
DRAMA OF THE RICH, 1975
DRAMATIC SCHOOL, 1938
DU BARRY, WOMAN OF PASSION, 1930
DUBLIN NIGHTMARE, 1958
DUMMY, THE, 1929
DURANT AFFAIR, THE, 1962
EAST SIDE, WEST SIDE, 1949
EAT THE PEACH, 1987
ECHO OF A DREAM, 1930
ECHO OF DIANA, 1963
EDDIE MACON'S RUN, 1983
EGYPTIAN, THE, 1954
84 CHARING CROSS ROAD, 1987
EL ALAMEIN, 1954
EL DORADO, 1967
ELECTRIC BLUE, 1988
ELECTRIC DREAMS, 1984
ELECTRIC HORSEMAN, THE, 1979
ELENI, 1985
ELEPHANT MAN, THE, 1980
ELIMINATORS, 1986
ELVIRA MADIGAN, 1967
EMANON, 1987
END OF THE LINE, THE, 1959
END OF THE LINE, 1988
ENEMY MINE, 1985
ENTER INSPECTOR DUVAL, 1961
ENTERTAINER, THE, 1975
ERNEST GOES TO CAMP, 1987
ESCAPE BY NIGHT, 1954
ESCORT FOR HIRE, 1960
ETERNAL MASK, THE, 1937
EVE OF ST. MARK, THE, 1944
EXTERMINATORS, THE, 1965
EYE CREATURES, THE, 1965
EYE WITNESS, 1950
EYES OF THE AMARYLLIS, THE, 1982
FABIOLA, 1951

FACE OF A STRANGER, 1964
FALSE EVIDENCE, 1937
FANNY, 1948
FANNY, 1961
FAREWELL PERFORMANCE, 1963
FASHIONS IN LOVE, 1929
FAST FORWARD, 1985
FATTY FINN, 1980
FEARLESS FRANK, 1967
FEMALE ON THE BEACH, 1955
FIGHTING MAD, 1957
FIGHTING WILDCATS, THE, 1957
FILE ON THELMA JORDAN, THE, 1950
FINE MESS, A, 1986
FIRE SALE, 1977
F.I.S.T., 1978
FLAME OF NEW ORLEANS, THE, 1941
FLASH OF GREEN, A, 1984
FLAT TWO, 1962
FLESH AND FANTASY, 1943
FLIGHT OF THE EAGLE, 1983
FOOTLOOSE, 1984
FOR KEEPS, 1988
FOR THE DEFENSE, 1930
FORBIDDEN, 1932
FORBIDDEN, 1949
FORCE 10 FROM NAVARONE, 1978
FORTUNE COOKIE, THE, 1966
FORTUNE TELLER, THE, 1961
FORTY CARATS, 1973
FORTY GUNS, 1957
FOUL PLAY, 1978
FOUR BAGS FULL, 1957
FOUR HUNDRED BLOWS, THE, 1959
FOUR MUSKETEERS, THE, 1975
FOURTH SQUARE, THE, 1961
FRANKIE AND JOHNNY, 1936
FRANTIC, 1988
FRENCH POSTCARDS, 1979
FREUD, 1962
FRINGE DWELLERS, THE, 1986
FULL MOON HIGH, 1982
GALLIPOLI, 1981
GAMBIT, 1966
GANG THAT COULDN'T SHOOT STRAIGHT, THE, 1971
GAY BRIDE, THE, 1934
GAY SISTERS, THE, 1942
GENE KRUPA STORY, THE, 1959
GENERAL CRACK, 1929
GEORGE AND MILDRED, 1980
GEORGY GIRL, 1966
GETTING OVER, 1981
GHOSTBUSTERS, 1984
GIG, THE, 1985
GIGOLETTE, 1935
GINGER & FRED, 1986
GIRL FROM MISSOURI, THE, 1934
GIRL WITH GREEN EYES, 1964
GIRLFRIENDS, 1978
GIVE MY REGARDS TO BROAD STREET, 1984
GLOWING AUTUMN, 1981
GO-BETWEEN, THE, 1971
GOOD GUYS AND THE BAD GUYS, THE, 1969
GOOD NEIGHBOR SAM, 1964
GOODBYE PEOPLE, THE, 1984
GRAND SLAM, 1968
GREAT FLAMARION, THE, 1945
GREAT OUTDOORS, THE, 1988
GREAT RACE, THE, 1965
GREEN DOLPHIN STREET, 1947
HAIRSPRAY, 1988
HANKY-PANKY, 1982
HARD TIMES, 1975
HARD TO HOLD, 1984
HARD WAY, THE, 1942
HAROLD AND MAUDE, 1971
HARRIET CRAIG, 1950
HARRY AND THE HENDERSONS, 1987
HE WAS HER MAN, 1934
HEART OF THE MATTER, THE, 1954
HEAT'S ON, THE, 1943
HEDDA, 1975
HELL RAIDERS, 1968
HELLO AGAIN, 1987
HIGH TIDE, 1987

HIS BROTHER'S KEEPER, 1939
HIS BROTHER'S WIFE, 1936
HOLE IN THE WALL, 1929
HONKYTONK MAN, 1982
HOOSIERS, 1986
HOT ROCK, THE, 1972
HOUSEKEEPING, 1987
HOW WILLINGLY YOU SING, 1975
HOWARD THE DUCK, 1986
HUMORESQUE, 1946
HUNCHBACK OF NOTRE DAME, THE, 1939
HUNCHBACK OF NOTRE DAME, THE, 1957
HUNTERS, THE, 1958
I DIED A THOUSAND TIMES, 1955
I NEVER SANG FOR MY FATHER, 1970
I THANK A FOOL, 1962
ICE PALACE, 1960
ICE PIRATES, THE, 1984
ICEMAN, 1984
IDOLMAKER, THE, 1980
I'LL CRY TOMORROW, 1955
IN ENEMY COUNTRY, 1968
INDISCREET, 1958
INDISCRETION OF AN AMERICAN WIFE, 1954
INTERRUPTED JOURNEY, THE, 1949
IPCRESS FILE, THE, 1965
IRRECONCILABLE DIFFERENCES, 1984
ISHTAR, 1987
IT ALL CAME TRUE, 1940
IT'S A DEAL, 1930
JAKE SPEED, 1986
JOHN GOLDFARB, PLEASE COME HOME, 1964
JOHNNY ALLEGRO, 1949
JOKERS, THE, 1967
JOURNEY, THE, 1959
JUGGERNAUT, 1974
JULIA, 1977
JULIET OF THE SPIRITS, 1965
JUNGLE RAIDERS, 1986
JUNIOR BONNER, 1972
JUST BEFORE NIGHTFALL, 1975
KALEIDOSCOPE, 1966
KAMERADSCHAFT, 1931
KAMILLA, 1984
KARATE KID, THE, 1984
KARATE KID PART II, THE, 1986
KID GALAHAD, 1937
KIND HEARTS AND CORONETS, 1949
KIND OF LOVING, A, 1962
KING KONG, 1933
KING LEAR, 1988
KING OF THE UNDERWORLD, 1939
KIPPERBANG, 1984
KITTY FOYLE, 1940
KLONDIKE ANNIE, 1936
KOTCH, 1971
LA STRADA, 1956
LADIES OF LEISURE, 1930
LADY ICE, 1973
LADYKILLERS, THE, 1956
LAND OF THE PHARAOHS, 1955
LARCENY, 1948
LATE SHOW, THE, 1977
LAUGHTER, 1930
LAWLESS, THE, 1950
LE BON PLAISIR, 1984
LEAGUE OF GENTLEMEN, THE, 1961
LEATHER AND NYLON, 1969
LEGEND OF BOGGY CREEK, THE, 1973
LEGEND OF LYLAH CLARE, THE, 1968
LEONARD PART 6, 1987
LEOPARD, THE, 1963
LES DERNIERES VACANCES, 1947
LES ENFANTS TERRIBLES, 1952
LES JEUX SONT FAITS, 1947
LES MAINS SALES, 1954
LETTY LYNTON, 1932
LIFE GOES ON, 1932
LIFE OF HER OWN, A, 1950
LIGHTHORSEMEN, THE, 1988
LIMEHOUSE BLUES, 1934
LITTLE DRAGONS, THE, 1980
LITTLE FOXES, THE, 1941
LITTLE NIKITA, 1988
LOCAL HERO, 1983
LONG DARK HALL, THE, 1951

LONG, HOT SUMMER, THE, 1958
LORD OF THE FLIES, 1963
LOST AND FOUND, 1979
LOST COMMAND, THE, 1966
LOUISIANE, 1984
LOVE AND DEATH, 1975
LOVE ON THE RUN, 1980
LOVE PARADE, THE, 1929
LOVE STORY, 1970
LUCK OF GINGER COFFEY, THE, 1964
LUV, 1967
MAD GENIUS, THE, 1931
MAD MISS MANTON, THE, 1938
MADAME, 1963
MADAME SOUSATZKA, 1988
MAGNIFICENT SEVEN DEADLY SINS, THE, 1971
MAHLER, 1974
MAILBAG ROBBERY, 1957
MAIN EVENT, THE, 1979
MALTA STORY, 1954
MAN AND A WOMAN, A, 1966
MAN FRIDAY, 1975
MAN FROM COLORADO, THE, 1948
MAN FROM DOWN UNDER, THE, 1943
MAN IN GREY, THE, 1943
MAN IN POSSESSION, THE, 1931
MAN IN THE MIDDLE, 1964
MAN WHO UNDERSTOOD WOMEN, THE, 1959
MAN WHO WOULD BE KING, THE, 1975
MAN WITH BOGART'S FACE, THE, 1980
MAN WITH TWO FACES, THE, 1934
MANDALAY, 1934
MANNEQUIN, 1987
MARJORIE MORNINGSTAR, 1958
MARRIAGE ON THE ROCKS, 1965
MARY, MARY, 1963
MARY, QUEEN OF SCOTS, 1971
MASK OF DIIJON, THE, 1946
MATTER OF TIME, A, 1976
MC GUFFIN, THE, 1985
MEN ARE NOT GODS, 1937
MEN IN WAR, 1957
MENACE, THE, 1932
MERMAIDS OF TIBURON, THE, 1962
MERRILY WE GO TO HELL, 1932
MERRY WIDOW, THE, 1934
MIDDLE OF THE NIGHT, 1959
MIDNIGHT MARY, 1933
MILLION DOLLAR MYSTERY, 1987
MIRACLE WOMAN, THE, 1931
MIRAGE, 1965
MIRROR CRACK'D, THE, 1980
MISSING, 1982
MR. MOM, 1983
MODERN PROBLEMS, 1981
MONDAY'S CHILD, 1967
MONEY PIT, THE, 1986
MONSTER IN THE CLOSET, 1987
MONSTER SQUAD, THE, 1987
MOON IS BLUE, THE, 1953
MORGAN STEWART'S COMING HOME, 1987
MOULIN ROUGE, 1952
MOVIE MOVIE, 1978
MY AMERICAN COUSIN, 1985
MY DEAR SECRETARY, 1948
MY DINNER WITH ANDRE, 1981
MY FOOLISH HEART, 1949
MY LIFE WITH CAROLINE, 1941
MY REPUTATION, 1946
MY SIN, 1931
MY SIX CONVICTS, 1952
MYSTERIOUS CROSSING, 1937
MYSTERIOUS MR. REEDER, THE, 1940
NAKED EDGE, THE, 1961
NAKED JUNGLE, THE, 1953
NAKED RUNNER, THE, 1967
NAKED SPUR, THE, 1953
NANA, 1957
NELL GWYN, 1935
NEW HOTEL, THE, 1932
NEW KIND OF LOVE, A, 1963
NIGHT MY NUMBER CAME UP, THE, 1955
NIGHT NURSE, 1931
1984, 1956
NO PLACE TO LAND, 1958
NO SAD SONGS FOR ME, 1950

BOLD: Films on Videocassette

NOAH'S ARK, 1928
NORMA RAE, 1979
NORTH STAR, THE, 1943
NORTHWEST PASSAGE, 1940
NOT AS A STRANGER, 1955
NOTHING IN COMMON, 1986
NOTHING PERSONAL, 1980
NOTORIOUS LANDLADY, THE, 1962
NOW I'LL TELL, 1934
NOW, VOYAGER, 1942
ODETTE, 1951
OH, GOD!, 1977
OH! GOD BOOK II, 1980
OH GOD! YOU DEVIL, 1984
OH, MEN! OH, WOMEN!, 1957
OH! WHAT A LOVELY WAR, 1969
OLD ACQUAINTANCE, 1943
ON GOLDEN POND, 1981
ON VALENTINE'S DAY, 1986
ONCE MORE, WITH FEELING, 1960
ONE HOUR WITH YOU, 1932
ONE MILLION B.C., 1940
OPERATION X, 1951
ORDET, 1957
ORPHANS, 1987
OTELLO, 1986
OTHER MEN'S WOMEN, 1931
OUTSIDER, THE, 1962
PAGAN, THE, 1929
PANDORA AND THE FLYING DUTCHMAN, 1951
PAPER CHASE, THE, 1973
PAPER TIGER, 1975
PARADINE CASE, THE, 1947
PARALLELS, 1980
PARIS BELONGS TO US, 1962
PARNELL, 1937
PAVLOVA—A WOMAN FOR ALL TIME, 1985
PAYMENT ON DEMAND, 1951
PENDULUM, 1969
PEOPLE WILL TALK, 1951
PERFECT COUPLE, A, 1979
PERFECT CRIME, THE, 1928
PERFECT UNDERSTANDING, 1933
PERIOD OF ADJUSTMENT, 1962
PERMANENT RECORD, 1988
PERSONAL FOUL, 1987
PERSONS IN HIDING, 1939
PETE 'N' TILLIE, 1972
PHONE CALL FROM A STRANGER, 1952
PIAF—THE EARLY YEARS, 1982
PICCADILLY, 1932
PICK-UP ARTIST, THE, 1987
PICTURE SNATCHER, 1933
PICTURES, 1982
PILGRIMAGE, 1933
PLACES IN THE HEART, 1984
PLAZA SUITE, 1971
POCKET MONEY, 1972
PORGY AND BESS, 1959
PORTRAIT IN BLACK, 1960
POSSESSED, 1931
POSSESSED, 1947
POWER AND THE GLORY, THE, 1933
PRESIDENT'S LADY, THE, 1953
PRINCESS BRIDE, THE, 1987
PRISONER OF SECOND AVENUE, THE, 1975
PRIVATE LIFE OF HENRY VIII, THE, 1933
PRIVATE POTTER, 1963
PRIVATE WORLDS, 1935
PRODIGAL, THE, 1955
PROJECTIONIST, THE, 1970
PROMISE, THE, 1979
PROPERTY, 1979
PROTOCOL, 1984
PROUD AND THE PROFANE, THE, 1956
PURPLE PLAIN, THE, 1954
QUACKSER FORTUNE HAS A COUSIN IN THE BRONX, 1970
QUEEN OF SPADES, 1948
QUEEN OF THE NIGHTCLUBS, 1929
QUICKSILVER, 1986
RACHEL, RACHEL, 1968
RAD, 1986
RADIO DAYS, 1987
RAID, THE, 1954
RAISE THE TITANIC, 1980

RASHOMON, 1951
RAW DEAL, 1948
RECORD CITY, 1978
RED LIGHT, 1949
RED MOUNTAIN, 1951
RESCUE, THE, 1988
RETURN OF THE JEDI, 1983
RETURN OF THE PINK PANTHER, THE, 1975
REUNION IN VIENNA, 1933
REVENGE OF THE PINK PANTHER, 1978
REVENGERS, THE, 1972
REVOLUTIONARY, THE, 1970
RHINOCEROS, 1974
RICH, YOUNG AND PRETTY, 1951
RICHARD III, 1956
RIDE A CROOKED TRAIL, 1958
RIDERS OF THE WHISTLING SKULL, 1937
RIFIFI, 1956
RIFIFI IN TOKYO, 1963
RIGHT CROSS, 1950
RIGHT STUFF, THE, 1983
RIGHT TO ROMANCE, 1933
RING OF FIRE, 1961
RIVER, THE, 1984
RIVER OF FOREVER, 1967
ROAD TO GLORY, THE, 1936
ROADIE, 1980
ROBBERY, 1967
ROBIN AND MARIAN, 1976
ROBIN AND THE SEVEN HOODS, 1964
ROCKY, 1976
ROCKY II, 1979
ROCKY III, 1982
ROMAN SCANDALS, 1933
ROMANTIC COMEDY, 1983
ROMEO AND JULIET, 1968
ROUNDERS, THE, 1965
ROXANNE, 1987
ROYAL FLASH, 1975
RUN FOR COVER, 1955
RUN SILENT, RUN DEEP, 1958
RUNNING MAN, THE, 1963
SAFARI 3000, 1982
SAINT JOAN, 1957
SALTY O'ROURKE, 1945
SAME TIME, NEXT YEAR, 1978
SAM'S SON, 1984
SAMURAI, 1945
SAN ANTONIO, 1945
SANDERS OF THE RIVER, 1935
SARATOGA TRUNK, 1945
SASKATCHEWAN, 1954
SEA CHASE, THE, 1955
SEA GULL, THE, 1968
SEA OF GRASS, THE, 1947
SEA SHALL NOT HAVE THEM, THE, 1955
SEARCHING WIND, THE, 1946
SEASON FOR LOVE, THE, 1963
SECOND BEST SECRET AGENT IN THE WHOLE WIDE WORLD, THE, 1965
SECOND CHANCE, 1953
SECOND-HAND HEARTS, 1981
SECOND WOMAN, THE, 1951
SECRET AGENT FIREBALL, 1965
SECRET FILE: HOLLYWOOD, 1962
SECRET OF MY SUCCESS, THE, 1965
SECRET SCROLLS (PART I), 1968
SECRET SCROLLS (PART II), 1968
SECRET WAR OF HARRY FRIGG, THE, 1968
SECRET WAYS, THE, 1961
SECRETS, 1933
SECRETS, 1984
SECRETS OF AN ACTRESS, 1938
SEEMS LIKE OLD TIMES, 1980
SEPARATE TABLES, 1958
SERENA, 1962
SERPENT, THE, 1973
SEVEN CITIES OF GOLD, 1955
SEVEN THIEVES, 1960
SEVEN YEAR ITCH, THE, 1955
SEVENTH DAWN, THE, 1964
SEVENTH HEAVEN, 1937
SEVENTH VEIL, THE, 1946
SHADOW OF A MAN, 1955
SHADOWED EYES, 1939
SHADOWS, 1931

SHE, 1965
SHEILA LEVINE IS DEAD AND LIVING IN NEW YORK, 1975
SHINING HOUR, THE, 1938
SHORT CIRCUIT, 1986
SHOT IN THE DARK, A, 1964
SHOTGUN WEDDING, THE, 1963
SILENT MOVIE, 1976
SIMON, 1980
SIXTEEN CANDLES, 1984
SKY BANDITS, 1986
SLAPSTICK OF ANOTHER KIND, 1984
SLAUGHTER ON TENTH AVENUE, 1957
SLEEPER, 1973
SMILING LIEUTENANT, THE, 1931
SO WELL REMEMBERED, 1947
SOLARBABIES, 1986
SOMBRERO, 1953
SONG OF SONGS, 1933
SONS OF GOOD EARTH, 1967
SPECIAL AGENT, 1935
SPELLBOUND, 1945
SPLASH, 1984
SPRING FOR THE THIRSTY, A, 1988
SPRING SYMPHONY, 1986
SPY WHO CAME IN FROM THE COLD, THE, 1965
STACKING, 1987
STAGE DOOR, 1937
STAGE FRIGHT, 1950
STAGE STRUCK, 1958
STAGECOACH, 1966
STAND UP AND FIGHT, 1939
STAR!, 1968
STAR IS BORN, A, 1954
STAR TREK IV: THE VOYAGE HOME, 1986
STAR TREK III: THE SEARCH FOR SPOCK, 1984
STAR WARS, 1977
STARS LOOK DOWN, THE, 1940
STEPFORD WIVES, THE, 1975
STEPTOE AND SON, 1972
STOLEN HOURS, 1963
STOLEN LIFE, A, 1946
STORMY CROSSING, 1958
STORY OF DR. WASSELL, THE, 1944
STORY OF G.I. JOE, THE, 1945
STRANDED, 1987
STRANGE BEDFELLOWS, 1965
STRANGER IN HOLLYWOOD, 1968
STRANGER ON THE PROWL, 1953
STRANGERS IN THE NIGHT, 1944
STRANGLER'S WEB, 1966
STRAY DOG, 1963
STREET MUSIC, 1982
STREETS OF LAREDO, 1949
STRICTLY DISHONORABLE, 1931
STRUGGLE, THE, 1931
SUDAN, 1945
SUDDEN FEAR, 1952
SUMMERTIME, 1955
SUNSHINE BOYS, THE, 1975
SUPERNATURAL, 1933
SURRENDER, 1987
SUSPENSE, 1946
SUSPICION, 1941
SVENGALI, 1931
SWANEE RIVER, 1939
SWEET LIBERTY, 1986
SWING HIGH, SWING LOW, 1937
SWING SHIFT, 1984
SYLVIA, 1985
SYLVIA SCARLETT, 1936
TAMING OF THE SHREW, THE, 1967
TARZAN AND HIS MATE, 1934
TEEN WOLF, 1985
TEEN WOLF TOO, 1987
TELL ME THAT YOU LOVE ME, JUNIE MOON, 1970
TEN DAYS THAT SHOOK THE WORLD, THE, 1977
10 NORTH FREDERICK, 1958
TEN WANTED MEN, 1955
TENDER MERCIES, 1982
TENDER YEARS, THE, 1947
TERMS OF ENDEARMENT, 1983
TESS, 1980
THAT CERTAIN WOMAN, 1937
THAT FORSYTE WOMAN, 1949
THAT HAGEN GIRL, 1947

THAT LUCKY TOUCH, 1975
THAT MAN GEORGE, 1967
THAT MAN IN ISTANBUL, 1966
THAT NIGHT IN RIO, 1941
THAT SUMMER, 1979
THEN THERE WERE THREE, 1961
THEY ALL KISSED THE BRIDE, 1942
THEY DRIVE BY NIGHT, 1940
THEY STILL CALL ME BRUCE, 1987
13 RUE MADELEINE, 1946
—30—, 1959
30 IS A DANGEROUS AGE, CYNTHIA, 1968
THIS MODERN AGE, 1931
THIS WOMAN IS DANGEROUS, 1952
THOUSAND CLOWNS, A, 1965
THRASHIN', 1986
THREE FACES OF EVE, THE, 1957
THREE MEN AND A BABY, 1987
THREE STRANGERS, 1946
THREE TO GO, 1971
THROUGH DAYS AND MONTHS, 1969
THUNDER ISLAND, 1963
THUNDER OF DRUMS, A, 1961
THUNDERBALL, 1965
THUNDERBOLT, 1936
TIDAL WAVE, 1975
TIGER AND THE FLAME, THE, 1955
TIGER AND THE PUSSYCAT, THE, 1967
TIGER MAKES OUT, THE, 1967
TIGER SHARK, 1932
TILL THE END OF TIME, 1946
TIME AFTER TIME, 1985
TIME BANDITS, 1981
TIME FOR LOVING, A, 1971
TIME OF YOUR LIFE, THE, 1948
TIME TO LOVE AND A TIME TO DIE, A, 1958
TIP ON A DEAD JOCKEY, 1957
TITANIC, 1953
TO EACH HIS OWN, 1946
TO HAVE AND HAVE NOT, 1944
TO HELL AND BACK, 1955
TO THE ENDS OF THE EARTH, 1948
TONIGHT OR NEVER, 1931
TONY DRAWS A HORSE, 1951
TOO HOT TO HANDLE, 1938
TOP GUN, 1955
TOP GUN, 1986
TOPKAPI, 1964
TORPEDO RUN, 1958
TOY WIFE, THE, 1938
TRADING HEARTS, 1988
TRAIL OF THE LONESOME PINE, THE, 1936
TRANSFORMERS: THE MOVIE, THE, 1986
TRAPEZE, 1956
TREASURE ISLAND, 1950
TREASURE OF THE YANKEE ZEPHYR, 1984
TREE OF WOODEN CLOGS, THE, 1979
TROUBLE WITH HARRY, THE, 1955
TWELVE CHAIRS, THE, 1970
27TH DAY, THE, 1957
TWO MRS. CARROLLS, THE, 1947
TWO-WAY STRETCH, 1961
UGLY AMERICAN, THE, 1963
ULTIMATE THRILL, THE, 1974
UMBRELLAS OF CHERBOURG, THE, 1964
UNDER AGE, 1941
UNDER SECRET ORDERS, 1943
UNDER TWO FLAGS, 1936
UNDERCURRENT, 1946
UNDERWORLD, 1937
UNFAITHFULLY YOURS, 1948
UNTAMED, 1929
UP THE DOWN STAIRCASE, 1967
UPTURNED GLASS, THE, 1947
VALIANT IS THE WORD FOR CARRIE, 1936
VALIANT, THE, 1929
VALLEY OF THE KINGS, 1954
VERGINITA, 1953
VICE VERSA, 1988
VICTORY, 1940
VICTORY, 1981
VIRGIN QUEEN, THE, 1955
VIRGINIAN, THE, 1946
VIVA VILLA!, 1934
VOYAGE OF THE DAMNED, 1976
WAKE OF THE RED WITCH, 1949

WALK A TIGHTROPE, 1964
WALK LIKE A MAN, 1987
WALPURGIS NIGHT, 1941
WALTZ ACROSS TEXAS, 1982
WALTZ OF THE TOREADORS, 1962
WANDA NEVADA, 1979
WANNSEE CONFERENCE, THE, 1987
WAR AND PEACE, 1956
WAR AND PEACE, 1968
WAR BETWEEN MEN AND WOMEN, THE, 1972
WAR IS A RACKET, 1934
WAR IS HELL, 1964
WARNING SHOT, 1967
WARRIORS, THE, 1955
WE ARE NOT ALONE, 1939
WE WHO ARE YOUNG, 1940
WE WILL REMEMBER, 1966
WE'RE NO ANGELS, 1955
WEST OF THE PECOS, 1935
WEST SIDE STORY, 1961
WHALES OF AUGUST, THE, 1987
WHAT A WAY TO GO, 1964
WHAT DID YOU DO IN THE WAR, DADDY?, 1966
WHEN LADIES MEET, 1941
WHEN MY BABY SMILES AT ME, 1948
WHERE THE BOYS ARE, 1960
WHERE THE TRUTH LIES, 1962
WHERE WERE YOU WHEN THE LIGHTS WENT
    OUT?, 1968
WHISTLE STOP, 1946
WHITE CLIFFS OF DOVER, THE, 1944
WHO KILLED THE CAT?, 1966
WIDOW FROM CHICAGO, THE, 1930
WILD BOYS OF THE ROAD, 1933
WILD GEESE CALLING, 1941
WILD RACERS, THE, 1968
WILD RIVER, 1960
WILD WEED, 1949
WILD, WILD PLANET, THE, 1967
WILL PENNY, 1968
WILL SUCCESS SPOIL ROCK HUNTER?, 1957
WINDOM'S WAY, 1958
WINNING, 1969
WINTERSET, 1936
WITHOUT A CLUE, 1988
WOLF SONG, 1929
WOMAN ACCUSED, 1933
WOMAN IN HIDING, 1949
WOMAN OBSESSED, 1959
WOMAN REBELS, A, 1936
WOMAN'S FACE, A, 1941
WOMAN'S WORLD, 1954
WOMEN OF ALL NATIONS, 1931
WOMEN'S PRISON, 1955
WONDERFUL WORLD OF THE BROTHERS GRIMM,
    THE, 1962
WORLD IN HIS ARMS, THE, 1952
WORLD'S GREATEST LOVER, THE, 1977
X THE UNKNOWN, 1957
YELLOW DOG, 1973
YOU AND ME, 1938
YOU CAN'T GET AWAY WITH MURDER, 1939
YOUNG DOCTORS, THE, 1961
YOUNG GUNS, THE, 1956
YOUNG WINSTON, 1972
ZORRO, THE GAY BLADE, 1981

C

ABANDONED, 1949
ABDUL THE DAMNED, 1935
ABIE'S IRISH ROSE, 1946
ABSOLUTE BEGINNERS, 1986
ABSOLUTE QUIET, 1936
ACCEPTABLE LEVELS, 1983
ACCIDENTAL DEATH, 1963
ACCUSED, THE, 1949
ACE OF ACES, 1933
ACES HIGH, 1977
ACQUA E SAPONE, 1985
ACQUITTED, 1929
ACROSS THE BRIDGE, 1957
ACROSS THE RIVER, 1965
ACT OF LOVE, 1953
ACT OF MURDER, AN, 1948
ACT OF MURDER, 1965
ACT OF VIOLENCE, 1949

ACTORS AND SIN, 1952
ADA, 1961
ADALEN 31, 1969
ADAM'S WOMAN, 1972
ADDING MACHINE, THE, 1969
ADELE HASN'T HAD HER SUPPER YET, 1978
ADIEU PHILLIPINE, 1962
ADIOS AMIGO, 1975
ADMIRAL NAKHIMOV, 1948
ADOLESCENT, THE, 1978
ADOLESCENTS, THE, 1967
ADORABLE JULIA, 1964
ADORABLE LIAR, 1962
ADUEFUE, 1988
ADVENTURE IN ODESSA, 1954
ADVENTURE IN WASHINGTON, 1941
ADVENTURERS, THE, 1951
ADVENTURES IN BABYSITTING, 1987
ADVENTURES OF HAJJI BABA, 1954
ADVENTURES OF RABBI JACOB, THE, 1973
ADVENTURES OF SCARAMOUCHE, THE, 1964
ADVISE AND CONSENT, 1962
AFFAIR BLUM, THE, 1949
AFFAIR IN TRINIDAD, 1952
AFFAIRS OF ADELAIDE, 1949
AFFAIRS OF CELLINI, THE, 1934
AFFAIRS OF JULIE, THE, 1958
AFRAID TO TALK, 1932
AFRICAN, THE, 1983
AFTER THE BALL, 1932
AFTER THE FOG, 1930
AGAINST A CROOKED SKY, 1975
AGAINST THE LAW, 1934
AGATHA, 1979
AGE OF CONSENT, 1932
AGE OF INDISCRETION, 1935
AGE OF INNOCENCE, 1934
AGE OF THE MEDICI, THE, 1979
AGENT 8 3/4, 1963
AGENT FOR H.A.R.M., 1966
AGNES OF GOD, 1985
AGOSTINO, 1962
AIR EAGLES, 1932
AIR PATROL, 1962
AIRPLANE!, 1980
AIRPLANE II: THE SEQUEL, 1982
AIRPORT 1975, 1974
AIRPORT '77, 1977
ALAMBRISTA!, 1977
ALEX AND THE GYPSY, 1976
ALEX IN WONDERLAND, 1970
ALEXANDER NEVSKY, 1939
ALF 'N' FAMILY, 1968
ALFRED THE GREAT, 1969
ALGIERS, 1938
ALIAS BIG SHOT, 1962
ALIBI, 1929
ALIBI, THE, 1939
ALIBI, THE, 1943
ALICE, OR THE LAST ESCAPADE, 1977
ALIEN FACTOR, THE, 1984
ALIEN THUNDER, 1975
ALIMONY, 1949
ALIMONY MADNESS, 1933
ALL FALL DOWN, 1962
ALL IN A NIGHT'S WORK, 1961
ALL MY SONS, 1948
ALL NEAT IN BLACK STOCKINGS, 1969
ALL NIGHT LONG, 1961
ALL NIGHT LONG, 1981
ALL OF ME, 1934
ALL QUIET ON THE WESTERN FRONT, 1930
ALL THE FINE YOUNG CANNIBALS, 1960
ALL THE KING'S MEN, 1949
...ALL THE MARBLES, 1981
ALL THE OTHER GIRLS DO!, 1967
ALL THE PRESIDENT'S MEN, 1976
ALL THE RIGHT MOVES, 1983
ALL THE WAY, BOYS, 1973
ALLIGATOR PEOPLE, THE, 1959
ALLONSANFAN, 1985
ALMOST MARRIED, 1932
ALMOST PERFECT AFFAIR, AN, 1979
ALMOST YOU, 1984
ALOHA, BOBBY AND ROSE, 1975
ALOHA SUMMER, 1988

BOLD: Films on Videocassette

ALONE AGAINST ROME, 1963
ALONE IN THE STREETS, 1956
ALONG THE GREAT DIVIDE, 1951
ALPHA BETA, 1973
ALSINO AND THE CONDOR, 1983
ALVIN PURPLE, 1974
AMADEUS, 1984
AMATEUR, THE, 1982
AMAZING DR. CLITTERHOUSE, THE, 1938
AMAZING MR. BLUNDEN, THE, 1973
AMAZING TRANSPARENT MAN, THE, 1960
AMBASSADOR, THE, 1984
AMBUSH AT TOMAHAWK GAP, 1953
AMBUSH BAY, 1966
AMBUSH IN LEOPARD STREET, 1962
AMERICA 3000, 1986
AMERICAN ANTHEM, 1986
AMERICAN FLYERS, 1985
AMERICAN FRIEND, THE, 1977
AMERICAN GRAFFITI, 1973
AMERICAN SOLDIER, THE, 1970
AMERICAN SUCCESS COMPANY, THE, 1980
AMERICAN TRAGEDY, AN, 1931
AMERICANA, 1981
AMERICANIZATION OF EMILY, THE, 1964
AMERICATHON, 1979
AMIGOS, 1986
AMONG THE LIVING, 1941
AMOROUS ADVENTURES OF MOLL FLANDERS,
   THE, 1965
AMSTERDAM AFFAIR, THE, 1968
ANA, 1985
ANATAHAN, 1953
ANATOMIST, THE, 1961
ANATOMY OF A MURDER, 1959
ANATOMY OF A PSYCHO, 1961
ANATOMY OF LOVE, 1959
AND HOPE TO DIE, 1972
AND MILLIONS WILL DIE, 1973
AND NOW MY LOVE, 1975
AND SUDDENLY IT'S MURDER!, 1964
AND WOMEN SHALL WEEP, 1960
ANGEL, 1937
ANGEL, 1982
ANGEL AND SINNER, 1947
ANGEL BABY, 1961
ANGEL FACE, 1953
ANGEL UNCHAINED, 1970
ANGEL WITH THE TRUMPET, THE, 1950
ANGELE, 1934
ANGELINA, 1948
ANGELO, 1951
ANGELS OF THE STREETS, 1950
ANGELS WITH DIRTY FACES, 1938
ANGI VERA, 1980
ANGRY MAN, THE, 1979
ANGRY SILENCE, THE, 1960
ANITA GARIBALDI, 1954
ANNA CHRISTIE, 1930
ANNA LUCASTA, 1949
ANNA LUCASTA, 1958
ANNA OF BROOKLYN, 1958
ANNE DEVLIN, 1984
ANNIE'S COMING OUT, 1985
ANONYMOUS VENETIAN, THE, 1971
ANOTHER COUNTRY, 1984
ANOTHER MAN'S POISON, 1952
ANOTHER PART OF THE FOREST, 1948
ANOTHER WOMAN, 1988
ANY GUN CAN PLAY, 1968
ANY WHICH WAY YOU CAN, 1980
APE, THE, 1940
APE MAN, THE, 1943
APE WOMAN, THE, 1964
APPALOOSA, THE, 1966
APPOINTMENT FOR MURDER, 1954
APPOINTMENT WITH DANGER, 1951
APPRENTICE TO MURDER, 1988
APRIL FOOLS, THE, 1969
ARABESQUE, 1966
ARCH OF TRIUMPH, 1948
ARIZONA COLT, 1965
ARMED AND DANGEROUS, 1986
ARMORED COMMAND, 1961
ARNOLD, 1973
ARROWHEAD, 1953

ARTHUR, 1931
ARTHUR, 1981
ARTHUR 2 ON THE ROCKS, 1988
ARTHUR'S HALLOWED GROUND, 1986
ARTURO'S ISLAND, 1963
AS YOUNG AS WE ARE, 1958
ASCENDANCY, 1983
ASH WEDNESDAY, 1973
ASHES AND DIAMONDS, 1961
ASPHALT JUNGLE, THE, 1950
ASPHYX, THE, 1972
ASSA, 1988
ASSASSIN, 1973
ASSASSIN FOR HIRE, 1951
ASSAULT, THE, 1986
ASSIGNMENT OUTER SPACE, 1960
ASSIGNMENT TO KILL, 1968
ASSISI UNDERGROUND, THE, 1985
ASSISTANT, THE, 1982
ASTONISHED HEART, THE, 1950
ASTOUNDING SHE-MONSTER, THE, 1958
ASTRO-ZOMBIES, THE, 1969
AT MIDDLE AGE, 1985
AT THE EARTH'S CORE, 1976
ATALIA, 1985
ATOM AGE VAMPIRE, 1961
ATTACK OF THE KILLER TOMATOES, 1978
ATTACK OF THE MAYAN MUMMY, 1963
ATTACK OF THE ROBOTS, 1967
ATTENTION, THE KIDS ARE WATCHING, 1978
ATTILA, 1958
AUDREY ROSE, 1977
AUNT FROM CHICAGO, 1960
AURORA ENCOUNTER, THE, 1985
AUTUMN, 1988
AUTUMN LEAVES, 1956
AVALANCHE EXPRESS, 1979
AVANTI!, 1972
AVENGER, THE, 1964
AVENGER, THE, 1966
BABETTE GOES TO WAR, 1960
BABIES FOR SALE, 1940
BABY BLUE MARINE, 1976
BABY: SECRET OF A LOST LEGEND, 1985
BABY, THE RAIN MUST FALL, 1965
BACHELOR APARTMENT, 1931
BACHELOR MOTHER, 1933
BACHELOR PARTY, THE, 1957
BACHELOR'S BABY, 1932
BACK FROM ETERNITY, 1956
BACK TO SCHOOL, 1986
BACK TO THE BEACH, 1987
BACK TO THE FUTURE, 1985
BACKFIRE, 1965
BACKGROUND, 1953
BAD AND THE BEAUTIFUL, THE, 1952
BAD BLONDE, 1953
BAD GIRL, 1931
BAD MANNERS, 1984
BAD MEDICINE, 1985
BAD MEN OF TOMBSTONE, 1949
BAD NEWS BEARS, THE, 1976
BAD NEWS BEARS GO TO JAPAN, THE, 1978
BAD NEWS BEARS IN BREAKING TRAINING, THE,
   1977
BAD ONE, THE, 1930
BAD SEED, THE, 1956
BAIT, 1954
BAKER'S WIFE, THE, 1940
BALLAD OF CABLE HOGUE, THE, 1970
BALLAD OF NARAYAMA, 1961
BALLAD OF NARAYAMA, THE, 1984
BALTIMORE BULLET, THE, 1980
BAMBOLE!, 1965
BANANA PEEL, 1965
BANANAS, 1971
BAND OF ASSASSINS, 1971
BANDITS, 1988
BANG! YOU'RE DEAD, 1954
BANISHED, 1978
BANK HOLIDAY, 1938
BANNING, 1967
BANZAI RUNNER, 1987
BARABBAS, 1962
BARBARIAN, THE, 1933
BARBAROSA, 1982

BARGEE, THE, 1964
BARON BLOOD, 1972
BARRACUDA, 1978
BARRY MC KENZIE HOLDS HIS OWN, 1975
BAT, THE, 1959
BAT PEOPLE, THE, 1974
BATAAN, 1943
BATTLE BEYOND THE STARS, 1980
BATTLE OF ALGIERS, THE, 1967
BATTLETRUCK, 1982
BAXTER, 1973
BAY BOY, 1984
BAY OF ANGELS, 1964
BEACH GIRLS AND THE MONSTER, THE, 1965
BEACHES, 1988
BEACHHEAD, 1954
BEAR, THE, 1984
BEAR ISLAND, 1980
BEARS AND I, THE, 1974
BEAST FROM THE HAUNTED CAVE, 1960
BEAST FROM 20,000 FATHOMS, THE, 1953
BEAST IN THE CELLAR, THE, 1971
BEAST OF BUDAPEST, THE, 1958
BEAST OF YUCCA FLATS, THE, 1961
BEAST WITH FIVE FINGERS, THE, 1946
BEASTMASTER, THE, 1982
BEASTS OF BERLIN, 1939
BEASTS OF MARSEILLES, THE, 1959
BEAT GENERATION, THE, 1959
BEAUTIFUL PRISONER, THE, 1983
BEAUTIFUL STRANGER, 1954
BEAUTY AND THE BEAST, 1963
BEAUTY JUNGLE, THE, 1966
BECAUSE I LOVED YOU, 1930
BECKET, 1964
BECKY SHARP, 1935
BECAUSE THEY'RE YOUNG, 1960
BED AND BOARD, 1971
BED SITTING ROOM, THE, 1969
BEDAZZLED, 1967
BEDEVILLED, 1955
BEDFORD INCIDENT, THE, 1965
BEDLAM, 1946
BEDTIME STORY, 1964
BEES, THE, 1978
BEETLEJUICE, 1988
BEFORE AND AFTER, 1985
BEFORE THE REVOLUTION, 1964
BEFORE WINTER COMES, 1969
BEGGAR'S OPERA, THE, 1953
BEGINNING OF THE END, 1957
BEHAVE YOURSELF, 1951
BEHIND THAT CURTAIN, 1929
BEHIND THE HIGH WALL, 1956
BEHIND THE IRON MASK, 1977
BEHIND THE MAKEUP, 1930
BEHIND THE MASK, 1932
BEHIND THE MASK, 1958
BEHIND THE RISING SUN, 1943
BEHOLD A PALE HORSE, 1964
BEHOLD MY WIFE, 1935
BEING, THE, 1983
BEING THERE, 1979
BELIZAIRE THE CAJUN, 1986
BELL DIAMOND, 1987
BELLA DONNA, 1983
BELLAMY TRIAL, THE, 1929
BELLE OF THE NINETIES, 1934
BELLISSIMA, 1952
BELLMAN, THE, 1947
BELLS, THE, 1931
BELOVED ENEMY, 1936
BELOW THE BELT, 1980
BEND OF THE RIVER, 1952
BENVENUTA, 1983
BERLIN EXPRESS, 1948
BEST MAN, THE, 1964
BEST WAY, THE, 1978
BETRAYED, 1954
BETRAYED WOMEN, 1955
BETSY, THE, 1978
BETTER LATE THAN NEVER, 1983
BETTER OFF DEAD, 1985
BETWEEN MIDNIGHT AND DAWN, 1950
BETWEEN THE LINES, 1977
BETWEEN TWO WOMEN, 1937

BETWEEN US GIRLS, 1942
BEWARE, MY LOVELY, 1952
BEWITCHED, 1945
BEYOND A REASONABLE DOUBT, 1956
BEYOND FEAR, 1977
BEYOND REASONABLE DOUBT, 1980
BEYOND THE FOREST, 1949
BEYOND THE LAW, 1967
BEYOND THE LAW, 1968
BEYOND THE LIMIT, 1983
BEYOND THE REEF, 1981
BEYOND THE TIME BARRIER, 1960
BEYOND VICTORY, 1931
BHOWANI JUNCTION, 1956
BIG AND THE BAD, THE, 1971
BIG BLUFF, THE, 1955
BIG BONANZA, THE, 1944
BIG BOODLE, THE, 1957
BIG BRAWL, THE, 1980
BIG BUSINESS, 1988
BIG CAPER, THE, 1957
BIG CAT, THE, 1949
BIG CHILL, THE, 1983
BIG CITY BLUES, 1932
BIG CLOCK, THE, 1948
BIG FIX, THE, 1978
BIG GAME, THE, 1972
BIG HEAT, THE, 1953
BIG HOUSE, THE, 1930
BIG JACK, 1949
BIG JIM McLAIN, 1952
BIG NIGHT, THE, 1951
BIG NIGHT, THE, 1960
BIG RED ONE, THE, 1980
BIG SCORE, THE, 1983
BIG SHOTS, 1987
BIG SHOW-OFF, THE, 1945
BIG SLEEP, THE, 1946
BIG SLEEP, THE, 1978
BIG STEAL, THE, 1949
BIG TIP OFF, THE, 1955
BIG TOWN, 1932
BIG TOWN CZAR, 1939
BIG TROUBLE, 1986
BIGAMIST, THE, 1953
BIGGER THAN LIFE, 1956
BILL OF DIVORCEMENT, 1940
BILLION DOLLAR BRAIN, 1967
BILLY BUDD, 1962
BILLY JACK GOES TO WASHINGTON, 1977
BIRD OF PARADISE, 1932
BIRD OF PARADISE, 1951
BIRD WATCH, THE, 1983
BIRD WITH THE CRYSTAL PLUMAGE, THE, 1970
BIRDMAN OF ALCATRAZ, 1962
BIRDS, THE, 1963
BIRDS COME TO DIE IN PERU, 1968
BIRDS OF PREY, 1988
BIRTH OF A BABY, 1938
BIRTHDAY PARTY, THE, 1968
BIRTHDAY PRESENT, THE, 1957
BITE THE BULLET, 1975
BITTER HARVEST, 1963
BITTER TEA OF GENERAL YEN, THE, 1933
BITTER VICTORY, 1958
BITTERSWEET LOVE, 1976
BLACK AND WHITE IN COLOR, 1976
BLACK BART, 1948
BLACK CASTLE, THE, 1952
BLACK CAT, THE, 1934
BLACK FURY, 1935
BLACK HAND, THE, 1950
BLACK JACK, 1973
BLACK LEGION, THE, 1937
BLACK LIKE ME, 1964
BLACK MAGIC, 1949
BLACK MOON, 1934
BLACK MOON, 1975
BLACK OAK CONSPIRACY, 1977
BLACK ORCHID, 1959
BLACK ORPHEUS, 1959
BLACK PATCH, 1957
BLACK PIRATES, THE, 1954
BLACK RODEO, 1972
BLACK ROOM, THE, 1935
BLACK SCORPION, THE, 1957

BLACK SIX, THE, 1974
BLACK SLEEP, THE, 1956
BLACK SUNDAY, 1977
BLACK TUESDAY, 1955
BLACK VEIL FOR LISA, A, 1969
BLACK WATCH, THE, 1929
BLACK WIDOW, 1954
BLACK WINDMILL, THE, 1974
BLACK ZOO, 1963
BLACKBOARD JUNGLE, THE, 1955
BLAME IT ON THE NIGHT, 1984
BLANCHE, 1971
BLAST OF SILENCE, 1961
BLEAK MOMENTS, 1972
BLIND ALLEY, 1939
BLIND DATE, 1987
BLISS OF MRS. BLOSSOM, THE, 1968
BLONDE ICE, 1949
BLONDE SINNER, 1956
BLOOD, 1974
BLOOD AND SAND, 1941
BLOOD BATH, 1966
BLOOD BEACH, 1981
BLOOD BEAST FROM OUTER SPACE, 1965
BLOOD BEAST TERROR, THE, 1967
BLOOD IN THE STREETS, 1975
BLOOD MONEY, 1933
BLOOD OF A POET, THE, 1930
BLOOD ON THE ARROW, 1964
BLOOD ON THE SUN, 1945
BLOODEATERS, 1980
BLOOMFIELD, 1971
BLOWING WILD, 1953
BLUE, 1968
BLUE BLOOD, 1973
BLUE DAHLIA, THE, 1946
BLUE GARDENIA, THE, 1953
BLUE LAMP, THE, 1950
BLUE MAX, THE, 1966
BLUE THUNDER, 1983
BOBBY DEERFIELD, 1977
BODY AND SOUL, 1947
BODY AND SOUL, 1981
BODY HEAT, 1981
BODY ROCK, 1984
BOEING BOEING, 1965
BOGGY CREEK II, 1985
BOMBAY TALKIE, 1970
BONDAGE, 1933
BOOGIE MAN WILL GET YOU, THE, 1942
BOOMERANG, 1947
BORDER INCIDENT, 1949
BORDERLINE, 1980
BORDERTOWN, 1935
BORN RECKLESS, 1930
BORN TO WIN, 1971
BORN WILD, 1968
BOSS NIGGER, 1974
BOTANY BAY, 1953
BOUDOIR DIPLOMAT, 1930
BOUDU SAVED FROM DROWNING, 1967
BOY ON A DOLPHIN, 1957
BOYS, THE, 1962
BOYS' NIGHT OUT, 1962
BRADY'S ESCAPE, 1984
BRAIN EATERS, THE, 1958
BRAIN FROM THE PLANET AROUS, THE, 1958
BRAIN OF BLOOD, 1971
BRAINSTORM, 1965
BRAVADOS, THE, 1958
BREAKER! BREAKER!, 1977
BREAKFAST IN BED, 1978
BREAKHEART PASS, 1976
BREAKOUT, 1975
BREAKTHROUGH, 1978
BREWSTER McCLOUD, 1970
BRIBE, THE, 1949
BRIDE, THE, 1985
BRIDE AND THE BEAST, THE, 1958
BRIDE OF FRANKENSTEIN, THE, 1935
BRIDE WORE BLACK, THE, 1968
BRIDGE AT REMAGEN, THE, 1969
BRIDGE ON THE RIVER KWAI, THE, 1957
BRIDGE TOO FAR, A, 1977
BRIEF RAPTURE, 1952
BRIEF VACATION, A, 1975

BRIGHTON BEACH MEMOIRS, 1986
BRIGHTON ROCK, 1947
BRIMSTONE AND TREACLE, 1982
BRITTANIA HOSPITAL, 1982
BRONCO BILLY, 1980
BROOD, THE, 1979
BROTHERS, 1977
BROTHERS RICO, THE, 1957
BRUTE AND THE BEAST, THE, 1968
BRUTE FORCE, 1947
BUCK AND THE PREACHER, 1972
BUCKTOWN, 1975
BUDDHA, 1965
BUDDY BUDDY, 1981
**BUFFALO BILL AND THE INDIANS, OR SITTING
    BULL'S HISTORY LESSON, 1976**
BULLET FOR PRETTY BOY, A, 1970
BULLET FOR SANDOVAL, A, 1970
BULLET FOR THE GENERAL, A, 1967
BULLITT, 1968
BUNNY LAKE IS MISSING, 1965
BUNNY O'HARE, 1971
BUONA SERA, MRS. CAMPBELL, 1968
BURGLARS, THE, 1972
BURIED ALIVE, 1951
BURNING AN ILLUSION, 1982
BURNING CROSS, THE, 1947
BURY ME DEAD, 1947
BUSTING, 1974
BUTCH AND SUNDANCE: THE EARLY DAYS, 1979
BYGONES, 1988
CABARET, 1972
CABOBLANCO, 1981
CACTUS, 1986
CACTUS FLOWER, 1969
CADDIE, 1976
CADDYSHACK II, 1988
CAESAR THE CONQUEROR, 1963
CAFE EXPRESS, 1980
CAGLIOSTRO, 1975
CAHILL, UNITED STATES MARSHAL, 1973
CALIFORNIA DREAMING, 1979
CALIFORNIA SPLIT, 1974
CALLAN, 1975
CALTIKI, THE IMMORTAL MONSTER, 1959
CAME A HOT FRIDAY, 1985
CAMPUS MAN, 1987
CAN SHE BAKE A CHERRY PIE?, 1983
CAN'T BUY ME LOVE, 1987
CAN'T STOP THE MUSIC, 1980
CANARIS, 1955
CANDIDATE, THE, 1964
CANDY MOUNTAIN, 1988
CANNIBAL GIRLS, 1973
CANNONBALL, 1976
CAPETOWN AFFAIR, 1967
CAPRICIOUS SUMMER, 1968
CAPRICORN ONE, 1978
CAPTAIN APACHE, 1971
CAPTAIN NEWMAN, M.D., 1963
CAPTIVE CITY, THE, 1963
CAPTIVE HEART, THE, 1948
CAPTIVE HEARTS, 1988
CAPTURE THAT CAPSULE, 1961
CAR, THE, 1977
CAR WASH, 1976
CARAVAN TO VACCARES, 1974
CARAVANS, 1978
CARBON COPY, 1981
CARDINAL, THE, 1963
CAREER, 1959
CAREER GIRL, 1960
CARETAKERS, THE, 1963
CAREY TREATMENT, THE, 1972
CARMEN, 1983
CARMEN JONES, 1954
CARNABY, M.D., 1967
CARNAGE, 1986
CARNIVAL OF BLOOD, 1976
CARNIVAL OF SOULS, 1962
CARPETBAGGERS, THE, 1964
CARRIE, 1952
CARRY ON AGAIN, DOCTOR, 1969
CARRY ON CABBIE, 1963
CARRY ON CAMPING, 1969

BOLD: Films on Videocassette

CARRY ON CLEO, 1964
CARRY ON CONSTABLE, 1960
CARRY ON CRUISING, 1962
CARRY ON DOCTOR, 1968
CARRY ON REGARDLESS, 1961
CASBAH, 1948
CASE AGAINST FERRO, THE, 1980
CASE OF DR. LAURENT, 1958
CASE OF THE 44'S, THE, 1964
CASE OF THE FRIGHTENED LADY, THE, 1940.
CASE VAN GELDERN, 1932
CASH McCALL, 1960
CASH ON DEMAND, 1962
CASINO DE PARIS, 1957
CASQUE D'OR, 1956
CASS TIMBERLANE, 1947
CASSANDRA CROSSING, THE, 1977
CAST A LONG SHADOW, 1959
CASTILIAN, THE, 1963
CASTLE, THE, 1969
CASTLE KEEP, 1969
CASTLE OF EVIL, 1967
CASTLE OF FU MANCHU, THE, 1968
CASTLE OF THE LIVING DEAD, 1964
CASTLE OF THE MONSTERS, 1958
CASTLE ON THE HUDSON, 1940
CASTLE SINISTER, 1932
CAT, THE, 1959
CAT AND MOUSE, 1958
CAT BURGLAR, THE, 1961
CAT, THE, 1975
CAT GIRL, 1957
CAT IN THE SACK, THE, 1967
CAT ON A HOT TIN ROOF, 1958
CAT PEOPLE, 1942
CATAMOUNT KILLING, THE, 1975
CATCH AS CATCH CAN, 1968
CATCH MY SOUL, 1974
CATCH THE HEAT, 1987
CATHERINE THE GREAT, 1934
CATHY'S CHILD, 1979
CATLOW, 1971
CAT'S EYE, 1985
CATTLE ANNIE AND LITTLE BRITCHES, 1981
CAUGHT, 1949
CAULDRON OF BLOOD, 1971
CAUSE FOR ALARM, 1951
CAVEMAN, 1981
CEDDO, 1978
CELINE AND JULIE GO BOATING, 1974
CELL 2455, DEATH ROW, 1955
CENTO ANNI D'AMORE, 1954
CEREMONY, THE, 1963
CESAR AND ROSALIE, 1972
CHAIN, THE, 1985
CHAIN GANG, 1950
CHAIN REACTION, 1980
CHAINED, 1934
CHAINED FOR LIFE, 1950
CHALLENGE, THE, 1982
CHAMELEON, 1978
CHAMP, 1931
CHAMPAGNE MURDERS, THE, 1968
CHAMPION, 1949
CHAMPIONS, 1984
CHAN IS MISSING, 1982
CHANCE MEETING, 1960
CHANEL SOLITAIRE, 1981
CHANGE OF MIND, 1969
CHANGE PARTNERS, 1965
CHAPTER TWO, 1979
CHARGE AT FEATHER RIVER, THE, 1953
CHARGE OF THE LIGHT BRIGADE, THE, 1968
CHARLES, DEAD OR ALIVE, 1972
CHARLEY-ONE-EYE, 1973
CHARLEY VARRICK, 1973
CHARLIE BUBBLES, 1968
CHASTITY, 1969
CHASTITY BELT, THE, 1968
CHE!, 1969
CHEAP DETECTIVE, THE, 1978
CHECKERED FLAG, THE, 1963
CHECKERED FLAG OR CRASH, 1978
CHESS PLAYERS, THE, 1978
CHEYENNE SOCIAL CLUB, THE, 1970
CHICAGO 70, 1970

CHICKEN CHRONICLES, THE, 1977
CHILD AND THE KILLER, THE, 1959
CHILD OF MANHATTAN, 1933
CHILDREN OF CHAOS, 1950
CHILDREN OF GOD'S EARTH, 1983
CHILDREN OF PARADISE, 1945
CHILDREN'S HOUR, THE, 1961
CHILLY SCENES OF WINTER, 1982
CHIMES AT MIDNIGHT, 1967
CHINA, 1943
CHINA CORSAIR, 1951
CHINA DOLL, 1958
CHINA GATE, 1957
CHINA SKY, 1945
CHINA VENTURE, 1953
CHINA'S LITTLE DEVILS, 1945
CHINATOWN AT MIDNIGHT, 1949
CHOCOLATE WAR, THE, 1988
CHOICE OF ARMS, 1983
CHORUS LINE, A, 1985
CHOSEN SURVIVORS, 1974
CHRISTIAN LICORICE STORE, THE, 1971
CHRISTINA, 1974
CHRISTINE, 1959
CHRISTMAS KID, THE, 1968
CHRISTOPHER STRONG, 1933
CHUKA, 1967
CHUSHINGURA, 1963
CIRCLE, THE, 1959
CIRCLE OF DANGER, 1951
CIRCLE OF DECEPTON, 1961
CIRCUMSTANTIAL EVIDENCE, 1945
CIRCUMSTANTIAL EVIDENCE, 1954
CIRCUS OF LOVE, 1958
CIRCUS QUEEN MURDER, THE, 1933
CITADEL OF CRIME, 1941
CITIZENS BAND, 1977
CITY ACROSS THE RIVER, 1949
CITY AFTER MIDNIGHT, 1957
CITY BENEATH THE SEA, 1953
CITY GIRL, 1938
CITY LIMITS, 1985
CITY LOVERS, 1982
CITY NEWS, 1983
CITY OF CHANCE, 1940
CITY OF FEAR, 1959
CITY OF FEAR, 1965
CITY OF PAIN, 1951
CITY OF SILENT MEN, 1942
CITY OF TORMENT, 1950
CITY OF YOUTH, 1938
CITY STORY, 1954
CLANDESTINE, 1948
CLARA'S HEART, 1988
CLARENCE AND ANGEL, 1981
CLASH BY NIGHT, 1952
CLASS OF '44, 1973
CLEO FROM 5 TO 7, 1961
CLEOPATRA, 1934
CLEOPATRA'S DAUGHTER, 1963
CLOAK AND DAGGER, 1984
CLOSELY WATCHED TRAINS, 1967
CLOWN MURDERS, THE, 1976
CLUB, THE, 1980
CLUB PARADISE, 1986
COCK-EYED WORLD, THE, 1929
COCKTAIL HOUR, 1933
COCOON, 1985
CODE NAME: EMERALD, 1985
CODE OF SILENCE, 1960
COLD FEET, 1984
COLD JOURNEY, 1975
COLLECTOR, THE, 1965
COLLEGE CONFIDENTIAL, 1960
COLOR ME DEAD, 1969
COME BACK PETER, 1971
COME FILL THE CUP, 1951
COMEBACK, THE, 1982
COMEDIANS, THE, 1967
COMMANDO, 1962
COMMANDO SQUAD, 1987
COMMITMENT, THE, 1976
COMMITTEE, THE, 1968
COMMON LAW, THE, 1931
COMPANEROS, 1970
COMPANY SHE KEEPS, THE, 1950

COMPETITION, THE, 1980
COMPUTER FREE-FOR-ALL, 1969
COMRADES, 1987
CONAN THE DESTROYER, 1984
CONCRETE JUNGLE, THE, 1962
CONDEMNED, 1929
CONFESS DR. CORDA, 1960
CONFESSION, THE, 1970
CONFESSIONS OF A NAZI SPY, 1939
CONFESSIONS OF AN OPIUM EATER, 1962
CONFIDENTIAL AGENT, 1945
CONFORMIST, THE, 1971
CONQUERED CITY, 1966
CONQUEST, 1929
CONQUEST, 1937
CONSCIENCE BAY, 1960
CONSTANT HUSBAND, THE, 1955
CONSUELO, AN ILLUSION, 1988
CONVERSATION PIECE, 1976
CONVOY, 1978
COOL BREEZE, 1972
COOL HAND LUKE, 1967
COOLEY HIGH, 1975
COONSKIN, 1975
COP HATER, 1958
COQUETTE, 1929
CORNBREAD, EARL AND ME, 1975
CORNERED, 1945
CORONER CREEK, 1948
CORPSE VANISHES, THE, 1942
CORREGIDOR, 1943
CORRUPT ONES, THE, 1967
CORSAIR, 1931
COTTONPICKIN' CHICKENPICKERS, 1967
COUNTDOWN AT KUSINI, 1976
COUNTDOWN, 1985
COUNTERFEITERS OF PARIS, THE, 1962
COUNTESS FROM HONG KONG, A, 1967
COUNTRY, 1984
COUNTRYMAN, 1982
COUP DE GRACE, 1978
COURT OF THE PHARAOH, THE, 1985
COVENANT WITH DEATH, A, 1966
CRACK IN THE MIRROR, 1960
CRASHOUT, 1955
CRAWLING EYE, THE, 1958
CRAZE, 1974
CRAZY DESIRE, 1964
CREATION OF THE HUMANOIDS, 1962
CREATURE CALLED MAN, THE, 1970
CREATURE FROM BLACK LAKE, THE, 1976
CREATURE FROM THE HAUNTED SEA, 1961
CREATURE OF THE WALKING DEAD, 1960
CREEPING TERROR, THE, 1964
CREEPING UNKNOWN, THE, 1956
CREMATORS, THE, 1972
CRIES AND WHISPERS, 1972
CRIME AGAINST JOE, 1956
CRIME AND PUNISHMENT, 1935
CRIME BOSS, 1976
CRIME OF DR. CRESPI, THE, 1936
CRIME OF PASSION, 1957
CRIMEWAVE, 1985
CRIMINAL CONVERSATION, 1980
CRIMSON ROMANCE, 1934
CRISS CROSS, 1949
CRITICAL CONDITION, 1987
CRITTERS II: THE MAIN COURSE, 1988
"CROCODILE" DUNDEE II, 1988
CROOKED ROAD, THE, 1965
CROSS CREEK, 1983
CROSSFIRE, 1947
CROSSING DELANCEY, 1988
CROSSPLOT, 1969
CROSSROADS TO CRIME, 1960
CROSSTRAP, 1962
CROWD INSIDE, THE, 1971
CROWDED PARADISE, 1956
CRUCIBLE OF HORROR, 1971
CRY BABY KILLER, THE, 1958
CRY DR. CHICAGO, 1971
CRY FOR HAPPY, 1961
CRY FREEDOM, 1987
CRY IN THE DARK, A, 1988
CRY IN THE NIGHT, A, 1956
CRY OF THE CITY, 1948

CRY WILDERNESS, 1987
CRYPT OF THE LIVING DEAD, 1973
CUBA, 1979
CULPEPPER CATTLE COMPANY, THE, 1972
CURFEW BREAKERS, 1957
CURSE OF BIGFOOT, THE, 1972
CURSE OF THE CRYING WOMAN, THE, 1969
CURSE OF THE FACELESS MAN, 1958
CURSE OF THE FLY, 1965
CURSE OF THE MUMMY'S TOMB, THE, 1965
CURSE OF THE STONE HAND, 1965
CURSE OF THE SWAMP CREATURE, 1966
CURSE OF THE UNDEAD, 1959
CURUCU, BEAST OF THE AMAZON, 1956
CUSTER OF THE WEST, 1968
CYCLONE, 1987
D.C. CAB, 1983
DADDY-O, 1959
DADDY'S GONE A-HUNTING, 1969
DAMAGED GOODS, 1937
DAMAGED LIVES, 1937
DAMAGED LOVE, 1931
DAMNATION ALLEY, 1977
DAMNED, THE, 1948
DANCE OF DEATH, THE, 1971
DANCE OF THE DWARFS, 1983
DANCING IN THE DARK, 1986
DANGER ZONE, 1951
DANGEROUS CARGO, 1954
DANGEROUS MOVES, 1985
DANIEL, 1983
DANIELLA BY NIGHT, 1962
DAREDEVIL, THE, 1971
DARK AT THE TOP OF THE STAIRS, THE, 1960
DARK CORNER, THE, 1946
DARK INTERVAL, 1950
DARK INTRUDER, 1965
DARK LIGHT, THE, 1951
DARK MANHATTAN, 1937
DARK MIRROR, THE, 1946
DARK ODYSSEY, 1961
DARK PURPOSE, 1964
DARK STAR, 1975
DARKTOWN STRUTTERS, 1975
DARLING LILI, 1970
DAS LETZTE GEHEIMNIS, 1959
DATE WITH DISASTER, 1957
DAUGHTER OF THE NILE, 1988
DAUGHTERS OF DESTINY, 1954
DAUGHTERS OF SATAN, 1972
DAVID, 1979
DAVID AND BATHSHEBA, 1951
DAWN, 1979
DAWN PATROL, THE, 1938
DAY MARS INVADED EARTH, THE, 1963
DAY OF THE ANIMALS, 1977
DAY OF THE JACKAL, THE, 1973
DAY OF THE NIGHTMARE, 1965
DAY OF THE OWL, THE, 1968
DAY OF THE TRIFFIDS, THE, 1963
DAY OF WRATH, 1948
DAY THE FISH CAME OUT, THE, 1967.
DAYS AND NIGHTS, 1946
DAYS OF 36, 1972
DAYS OF WINE AND ROSES, 1962
DE L'AMOUR, 1968
DEAD END, 1937
DEAD LUCKY, 1960
DEAD MAN'S FLOAT, 1980
DEAD MARCH, THE, 1937
DEAD MELODY, 1938
DEAD MEN DON'T WEAR PLAID, 1982
DEAD MOUNTAINEER HOTEL, THE, 1979
DEAD ONE, THE, 1961
DEAD PIGEON ON BEETHOVEN STREET, 1972
DEAD RECKONING, 1947
DEAD RINGER, 1964
DEAD RUN, 1961
DEADFALL, 1968
DEADLIER THAN THE MALE, 1957
DEADLIER THAN THE MALE, 1967
DEADLINE—U.S.A., 1952
DEADLY BEES, THE, 1967
DEADLY COMPANIONS, THE, 1961
DEADLY STRANGERS, 1974
DEADLY TRAP, THE, 1972

DEADWOOD '76, 1965
DEAF SMITH AND JOHNNY EARS, 1973
DEAL OF THE CENTURY, 1983
DEAR DETECTIVE, 1978
DEAR JOHN, 1966
DEAR MR. WONDERFUL, 1983
DEAR MURDERER, 1947
DEATH BEFORE DISHONOR, 1987
DEATH HUNT, 1981
DEATH IN SMALL DOSES, 1957
DEATH IN THE SKY, 1937
DEATH IN VENICE, 1971
DEATH IS CALLED ENGELCHEN, 1963
DEATH OF A GUNFIGHTER, 1969
DEATH OF A SCOUNDREL, 1956
DEATH OF AN ANGEL, 1985
DEATH OF MARIO RICCI, THE, 1985
DEATH OF TARZAN, THE, 1968
DEATH ON THE NILE, 1978
DEATH PLAY, 1976
DEATH TAKES A HOLIDAY, 1934
DEATH TRAP, 1962
DEATHCHEATERS, 1976
DEATHTRAP, 1982
DECISION AT SUNDOWN, 1957
DECLINE AND FALL...OF A BIRD WATCHER, 1969
DEDEE, 1949
DEEP BLUE SEA, THE, 1955
DEEP VALLEY, 1947
DEFEAT OF HANNIBAL, THE, 1937
DEFECTOR, THE, 1966
DEFIANCE, 1980
DEFIANT ONES, THE, 1958
DELICATE BALANCE, A, 1973
DELINQUENT DAUGHTERS, 1944
DELINQUENTS, THE, 1957
DELTA FACTOR, THE, 1970
DELUSIONS OF GRANDEUR, 1971
DEMENTIA 13, 1963
DEMETRIUS AND THE GLADIATORS, 1954
DEMON POND, 1980
DESERT FURY, 1947
DESERT OF THE TARTARS, THE, 1976
DESERT PATROL, 1962
DESERTERS, 1983
DESIGN FOR MURDER, 1940
DESIRE IN THE DUST, 1960
DESPERATE, 1947
DESPERATE HOURS, THE, 1955
DESPERATE ONES, THE, 1968
DESTINATION MURDER, 1950
DESTRUCTORS, THE, 1968
DESTRUCTORS, THE, 1974
DETECTIVE, THE, 1968
DETECTIVE STORY, 1951
DEVIL AND THE DEEP, 1932
DEVIL AND THE TEN COMMANDMENTS, THE, 1962
DEVIL BY THE TAIL, THE, 1969
DEVIL COMMANDS, THE, 1941
DEVIL DOLL, THE, 1936
DEVIL DOLL, 1964
DEVIL IN LOVE, THE, 1968
DEVIL IN SILK, 1968
DEVIL IN THE FLESH, THE, 1949
DEVIL IS A WOMAN, THE, 1935
DEVIL PROBABLY, THE, 1977
DEVIL-SHIP PIRATES, THE, 1964
DEVIL STRIKES AT NIGHT, THE, 1959
DEVIL TIMES FIVE, 1974
DEVIL'S AGENT, THE, 1962
DEVIL'S BRIGADE, THE, 1968
DEVIL'S 8, THE, 1969
DEVIL'S EYE, THE, 1960
DEVIL'S HAND, THE, 1961
DEVIL'S HARBOR, 1954
DEVIL'S ISLAND, 1940
DEVIL'S MAN, THE, 1967
DEVIL'S MESSENGER, THE, 1962
DEVILS OF DARKNESS, THE, 1965
DEVIL'S OWN, THE, 1967
DEVIL'S PLOT, THE, 1948
DEVIL'S WANTON, THE, 1962
DIABOLICALLY YOURS, 1968
DIAGNOSIS: MURDER, 1974
DIAL 1119, 1950
DIAL RED O, 1955

DIAMOND HEAD, 1962
DIAMOND STUD, 1970
DIAMONDS, 1975
DIAMONDS ARE FOREVER, 1971
DIAMONDS FOR BREAKFAST, 1968
DIAMONDS OF THE NIGHT, 1964
DIARY OF A BAD GIRL, 1958
DIARY OF A NAZI, 1943
DIARY OF AN ITALIAN, 1972
DICK TRACY VS. CUEBALL, 1946
DICK TRACY'S DILEMMA, 1947
DIE HAMBURGER KRANKHEIT, 1979
DIE, MONSTER, DIE, 1965
DIFFICULT YEARS, 1950
DINNER AT EIGHT, 1933
DIPLOMAT'S MANSION, THE, 1961
DIRTY DANCING, 1987
DIRTY DINGUS MAGEE, 1970
DIRTY GAME, THE, 1966
DIRTY KNIGHT'S WORK, 1976
DIRTY MONEY, 1977
DIRTY ROTTEN SCOUNDRELS, 1988
DIRTY TRICKS, 1981
DISAPPEARANCE, THE, 1981
DISCREET CHARM OF THE BOURGEOISIE, THE, 1972
DISEMBODIED, THE, 1957
DISHONORED, 1931
DISHONORED LADY, 1947
DISTANT JOURNEY, 1950
DIVA, 1982
DIVORCE AMERICAN STYLE, 1967
DIVORCE AMONG FRIENDS, 1931
DIVORCEE, THE, 1930
DIXIE DYNAMITE, 1976
DOBERMAN GANG, THE, 1972
DOCTOR AND THE GIRL, THE, 1949
DOCTOR BEWARE, 1951
DR. BROADWAY, 1942
DOCTOR CRIMEN, 1953
DR. CRIPPEN, 1963
DOCTOR FAUSTUS, 1967
DR. GOLDFOOT AND THE BIKINI MACHINE, 1965
  88m AI c
DR. NO, 1962
DOCTOR OF ST. PAUL, THE, 1969
DR. RENAULT'S SECRET, 1942
DR. STRANGELOVE: OR HOW I LEARNED TO STOP WORRYING AND LOVE THE BOMB, 1964
DOCTORS' WIVES, 1931
DODES 'KA-DEN, 1970
DOLL, THE, 1964
DOMINICK AND EUGENE, 1988
DOMINIQUE, 1978
DONOVAN'S BRAIN, 1953
DON'T LOSE YOUR HEAD, 1967
DON'T TALK TO STRANGE MEN, 1962
DON'T TOUCH WHITE WOMEN!, 1974
DON'T TRUST YOUR HUSBAND, 1948
DON'T TURN THE OTHER CHEEK, 1974
DOOMWATCH, 1972
DOOR TO DOOR, 1984
DORMIRE, 1985
DOUBLE BED, THE, 1965
DOUBLE CONFESSION, 1953
DOUBLE INDEMNITY, 1944
DOUBLE MAN, THE, 1967
DOUBLE NICKELS, 1977
DOUBLE STOP, 1968
DOUBLES, 1978
DOULOS—THE FINGER MAN, 1964
DOWN THREE DARK STREETS, 1954
DOWNFALL, 1964
DOWNHILL RACER, 1969
DOZENS, THE, 1981
DRACULA, 1979
DRACULA AND SON, 1976
DRAGNET, 1987
DRAGON CHOW, 1988
DRAGON INN, 1968
DRAGSTRIP RIOT, 1958
DREAM LOVER, 1986
DREAM OF KINGS, A, 1969
DREAM OF PASSION, A, 1978
DREAM TOWN, 1973
DREAMING LIPS, 1937

BOLD: Films on Videocassette

DREAMING LIPS, 1958
DREAMS, 1960
DREAMS OF GLASS, 1969
DREAMS THAT MONEY CAN BUY, 1948
DREI GEGEN DREI, 1985
DRESSER, THE, 1983
DRIFTER, THE, 1966
DRIVE A CROOKED ROAD, 1954
DROP DEAD, MY LOVE, 1968
DROWNING POOL, THE, 1975
DRUNKEN ANGEL, 1948
DUCHESS AND THE DIRTWATER FOX, THE, 1976
DUCK IN ORANGE SAUCE, 1976
DUCK, YOU SUCKER!, 1972
DUEL AT EZO, 1970
DUELLISTS, THE, 1977
DUET FOR FOUR, 1982
DUFFY, 1968
DULCINEA, 1962
DUNWICH HORROR, THE, 1970
DUTCHMAN, 1966
EAGLE AND THE HAWK, THE, 1933
EAGLE HAS LANDED, THE, 1976
EAGLE OVER LONDON, 1973
EARLY AUTUMN, 1962
EARTH ENTRANCED, 1970
EARTHBOUND, 1981
EARTHLING, THE, 1980
EASIEST WAY, THE, 1931
EAST CHINA SEA, 1969
EAST IS WEST, 1930
EAST OF FIFTH AVE., 1933
EAST OF THE WALL, 1986
EASY LIFE, THE, 1963
EASY LIFE, THE, 1971
EAVESDROPPER, THE, 1966
ECHO, THE, 1964
ECHO OF BARBARA, 1961
ECHOES OF SILENCE, 1966
ECLIPSE, 1962
EDDIE AND THE CRUISERS, 1983
EDGE, THE, 1968
EDGE OF DOOM, 1950
EDUCATION OF SONNY CARSON, THE, 1974
EDVARD MUNCH, 1976
EDWARD, MY SON, 1949
EEGAH!, 1962
EFFECT OF GAMMA RAYS ON MAN-IN-THE-MOON
    MARIGOLDS, THE, 1972
EIGER SANCTION, THE, 1975
8 1/2, 1963
EIGHT GIRLS IN A BOAT, 1934
EIGHT IRON MEN, 1952
18 AGAIN!, 1988
EIGHTEEN AND ANXIOUS, 1957
EIGHTEEN IN THE SUN, 1964
80,000 SUSPECTS, 1963
ELECTRA GLIDE IN BLUE, 1973
ELECTRONIC MONSTER, THE, 1960
11 HARROWHOUSE, 1974
ELIZA FRASER, 1976
ELMER GANTRY, 1960
ELVIRA: MISTRESS OF THE DARK, 1988
EMBALMER, THE, 1966
EMBASSY, 1972
EMBRACERS, THE, 1966
EMBRYO, 1976
EMPEROR JONES, THE, 1933
EMPEROR OF THE NORTH POLE, 1973
EMPIRE OF THE ANTS, 1977
EMPIRE OF NIGHT, THE, 1963
ENCOUNTER WITH THE UNKNOWN, 1973
ENCOUNTERS IN SALZBURG, 1964
END OF A PRIEST, 1970
END OF AUGUST AT THE HOTEL OZONE, THE, 1967
END OF THE WORLD, 1977
END OF THE WORLD (IN OUR USUAL BED IN A
    NIGHT FULL OF RAIN), THE, 1978
END PLAY, 1975
ENDLESS NIGHT, THE, 1963
ENDLESS NIGHT, 1971
ENEMY OF WOMEN, 1944
ENFORCER, THE, 1951
ENGLAND MADE ME, 1973
ENIGMA, 1983
ENTRE NOUS, 1983

ERIK THE CONQUEROR, 1963
EROICA, 1966
EROTIQUE, 1969
ESCAPE ARTIST, THE, 1982
ESCAPE BY NIGHT, 1965
ESCAPE FROM ALCATRAZ, 1979
ESCAPE FROM SEGOVIA, 1984
ESCAPE FROM THE PLANET OF THE APES, 1971
ESCAPE TO ATHENA, 1979
ESCAPE TO THE SUN, 1972
ESCAPED FROM DARTMOOR, 1930
ESTHER WATERS, 1948
ETERNAL HUSBAND, THE, 1946
ETERNITY OF LOVE, 1961
EVELYN PRENTICE, 1934
EVENT, AN, 1970
EVER IN MY HEART, 1933
EVERY BASTARD A KING, 1968
EVERY LITTLE CROOK AND NANNY, 1972
EVERY PICTURE TELLS A STORY, 1984
EVERY SPARROW MUST FALL, 1964
EVERY TIME WE SAY GOODBYE, 1986
EVERY WHICH WAY BUT LOOSE, 1978
EXECUTIONER, THE, 1970
EXECUTIVE ACTION, 1973
EXILES, THE, 1966
EXODUS, 1960
EXPENSIVE WOMEN, 1931
**EXPERIENCE PREFERRED. . . BUT NOT ESSENTIAL,
    1983**
EXPERIMENT IN TERROR, 1962
EXPLORERS, 1985
EXPLOSIVE GENERATION, THE, 1961
EXPRESSO BONGO, 1959
EYE FOR AN EYE, AN, 1966
EYE OF THE CAT, 1969
EYE OF THE DEVIL, 1967
EYE OF THE NEEDLE, THE, 1965
EYES OF THE WORLD, THE, 1930
FACE AT THE WINDOW, THE, 1932
FACE AT THE WINDOW, THE, 1939
FACE BEHIND THE MASK, THE, 1941
FACE IN THE CROWD, A, 1957
FACE OF FIRE, 1959
FACE OF TERROR, 1964
FAHRENHEIT 451, 1966
FAIL SAFE, 1964
FALCON FIGHTERS, THE, 1970
FALL GUY, 1947
FALL GUY, 1985
FALL OF ROME, THE, 1963
FALL OF THE HOUSE OF USHER, THE, 1952
FALLEN SPARROW, THE, 1943
FALLING IN LOVE, 1984
FALLING IN LOVE AGAIN, 1980
FAME, 1980
FAMILY BUSINESS, 1987
FAMILY GAME, THE, 1984
FAMILY PLOT, 1976
FANDANGO, 1985
FAN'S NOTES, A, 1972
FANTASTIC COMEDY, A, 1975
FANTASY MAN, 1984
FAR FROM DALLAS, 1972
FAR FROM POLAND, 1984
FAR NORTH, 1988
FAREWELL TO ARMS, A, 1957
FAST CHARLIE. . . THE MOONBEAM RIDER, 1979
FAT ANGELS, 1980
FAT CITY, 1972
FATAL DESIRE, 1953
FATHER OF A SOLDIER, 1966
FAVORITES OF THE MOON, 1985
FBI STORY, THE, 1959
FEAR, 1946
FEAR AND DESIRE, 1953
FEAR CHAMBER, THE, 1968
FEAR IN THE NIGHT, 1972
FEAR IS THE KEY, 1973
FEAR NO MORE, 1961
FEAR STRIKES OUT, 1957
FEARLESS VAMPIRE KILLERS, OR PARDON ME BUT
    YOUR TEETH ARE IN MY NECK, THE, 1967
FEDORA, 1978
FEEDBACK, 1979
FEMALE, THE, 1960

FEMALE JUNGLE, THE, 1955
FEMALE PRINCE, THE, 1966
FEMMINA, 1968
FERRIS BUELLER'S DAY OFF, 1986
FEW DAYS WITH ME, A, 1988
FFOLKES, 1980
FIEND OF DOPE ISLAND, 1961
FIENDISH PLOT OF DR. FU MANCHU, THE, 1980
FIFTH HORSEMAN IS FEAR, THE, 1968
FIGHT FOR THE GLORY, 1970
FIGHT TO THE LAST, 1938
FIGHTING BACK, 1983
FIGHTING MAD, 1976
FIGHTING SEABEES, THE, 1944
FIGURES IN A LANDSCAPE, 1970
FILE OF THE GOLDEN GOOSE, THE, 1969
FINAL ASSIGNMENT, 1980
FINAL CHORD, THE, 1936
FINAL COUNTDOWN, THE, 1980
FINAL WAR, THE, 1960
FINE MADNESS, A, 1966
FINE PAIR, A, 1969
FINGER POINTS, THE, 1931
FINGERMAN, THE, 1963
FINGERS AT THE WINDOW, 1942
FIRE AND ICE, 1983
FIRE DOWN BELOW, 1957
FIREBALL JUNGLE, 1968
FIREBRAND, THE, 1962
FIRECHASERS, THE, 1970
FIRECREEK, 1968
FIREFOX, 1982
FIREMAN'S BALL, THE, 1968
FIRM MAN, THE, 1975
FIRST TASTE OF LOVE, 1962
FIRST TIME, THE, 1969
FIRST TO FIGHT, 1967
FIRST YANK INTO TOKYO, 1945
FIRSTBORN, 1984
FISTFUL OF DOLLARS, A, 1964
FITZCARRALDO, 1982
FIVE BRANDED WOMEN, 1960
FIVE CARD STUD, 1968
FIVE DAYS FROM HOME, 1978
FIVE GIANTS FROM TEXAS, 1966
FIVE MAN ARMY, THE, 1970
FIVE MINUTES TO LIVE, 1961
FIVE POUND MAN, THE, 1937
FIVE STAR FINAL, 1931
FIVE TO ONE, 1963
FLAME, 1975
FLAME AND THE FLESH, 1954
FLAME BARRIER, THE, 1958
FLAME WITHIN, THE, 1935
FLAMINGO KID, THE, 1984
FLAMINGO ROAD, 1949
FLASH AND THE FIRECAT, 1976
FLEA IN HER EAR, A, 1968
FLESH, 1932
FLESH AND BLOOD, 1951
FLESH AND THE SPUR, 1957
FLETCH, 1984
FLIGHT, 1960
FLIGHT OF THE LOST BALLOON, 1961
FLIGHT OF THE PHOENIX, THE, 1965
FLIGHT TO FURY, 1966
FLIGHT TO HONG KONG, 1956
FLIGHT TO NOWHERE, 1946
FLOOD TIDE, 1958
FLYING LEATHERNECKS, 1951
FLYING SERPENT, THE, 1946
FLYING TIGERS, 1942
FM, 1978
FOES, 1977
FOLIES BERGERE, 1958
FOLLOW ME QUIETLY, 1949
FOLLOWING THE FUHRER, 1986
FOND MEMORIES, 1982
FOOLIN' AROUND, 1980
FOOLISH HUSBANDS, 1948
FOOLS OF DESIRE, 1941
FOOLS' PARADE, 1971
FOR A FEW DOLLARS MORE, 1967
FOR PETE'S SAKE, 1977
FOR WHOM THE BELL TOLLS, 1943
FORBIDDEN FRUIT, 1959

FORBIDDEN GAMES, 1953
FORBIDDEN ISLAND, 1959
FORBIDDEN PLANET, 1956
FORBIDDEN ZONE, 1980
FORCE BEYOND, THE, 1978
FORCE OF EVIL, 1948
FOREIGN AFFAIR, A, 1948
FOREIGN CITY, A, 1988
FOREIGN INTRIGUE, 1956
FOREIGNER, THE, 1978
FOREVER MY HEART, 1954
FOREVER YOUNG, 1984
FORMULA, THE, 1980
FORT GRAVEYARD, 1966
FORT MASSACRE, 1958
FORTRESS, THE, 1979
FORTUNE, THE, 1975
FOUNTAIN OF LOVE, THE, 1968
FOUR BOYS AND A GUN, 1957
FOUR DESPERATE MEN, 1960
FOUR FLIES ON GREY VELVET, 1972
FOUR FOR TEXAS, 1963
FOUR FOR THE MORGUE, 1962
FOUR FRIGHTENED PEOPLE, 1934
FOUR IN THE MORNING, 1965
FOUR SEASONS, THE, 1981
FOUR SIDED TRIANGLE, 1953
FOUR WAYS OUT, 1954
FOURTEEN HOURS, 1951
FOURTH PROTOCOL, THE, 1987
48 HOURS TO ACAPULCO, 1968
FOXFIRE, 1955
FRAGRANCE OF WILD FLOWERS, THE, 1979
FRAIL WOMEN, 1932
FRAMED, 1947
FRANKENSTEIN CONQUERS THE WORLD, 1964
FRANKENSTEIN MEETS THE SPACE MONSTER, 1965
FRANKENSTEIN MEETS THE WOLF MAN, 1943
FRANKENSTEIN 1970, 1958
FRANKENSTEIN'S BLOODY TERROR, 1968
FRANKENSTEIN, THE VAMPIRE AND CO., 1961
FRANTIC, 1961
FRATERNITY VACATION, 1985
FRAULEIN, 1958
FREE LOVE, 1930
FREE SOUL, A, 1931
FREE, WHITE AND 21, 1963
FRENCH GAME, THE, 1963
FRENCH LESSON, 1986
FRENCH LINE, THE, 1954
FRESH HORSES, 1988
FRIENDS AND HUSBANDS, 1983
FRISCO KID, THE, 1979
FROGS, 1972
FROM A ROMAN BALCONY, 1961
FROM BEYOND THE GRAVE, 1974
FROM HELL IT CAME, 1957
FROM HELL TO HEAVEN, 1933
FROM HELL TO TEXAS, 1958
FROM HELL TO VICTORY, 1979
FROM HERE TO ETERNITY, 1953
FROM NOON TO THREE, 1976
FROM THE HIP, 1987
FROM THE TERRACE, 1960
FRONT, THE, 1976
FROZEN DEAD, THE, 1967
FROZEN GHOST, THE, 1945
FRUIT IS RIPE, THE, 1961
FUGITIVE KIND, THE, 1960
FUGITIVE LADY, 1934
FUGITIVE, THE, 1947
FUGITIVES FOR A NIGHT, 1938
FULL CONFESSION, 1939
FUNERAL IN BERLIN, 1966
FUNNY FARM, 1988
FUNNY FARM, THE, 1982
FUNNY THING HAPPENED ON THE WAY TO THE FORUM, A, 1966
FUNNYMAN, 1967
FURIES, THE, 1950
FURY, 1936
FURY OF THE PAGANS, 1963
FUTUREWORLD, 1976
GABRIEL OVER THE WHITE HOUSE, 1933
GAL YOUNG UN, 1979

GALIA, 1966
GAMBLER, THE, 1958
GAMBLING SAMURAI, THE, 1966
GAME OF LOVE, THE, 1954
GAME OF TRUTH, THE, 1961
GANG WAR, 1940
GANGSTER VIP, THE, 1968
GANGSTER, THE, 1947
GARBAGE MAN, THE, 1963
GARBAGE PAIL KIDS MOVIE, THE, 1987
GARBO TALKS, 1984
GARCON!, 1985
GARDEN OF ALLAH, THE, 1936
GARDEN OF EVIL, 1954
GARDEN OF THE FINZI-CONTINIS, THE, 1971
GASLIGHT, 1940
GASLIGHT, 1944
GATE, THE, 1987
GATES OF PARIS, 1958
GATES TO PARADISE, 1968
GATEWAY TO GLORY, 1970
GATLING GUN, THE, 1972
GATOR, 1976
GAVILAN, 1968
GENERAL DELLA ROVERE, 1960
GENERAL DIED AT DAWN, THE, 1936
GENERATION, 1969
GENGHIS KHAN, 1965
GENIUS, THE, 1976
GENTLE CREATURE, A, 1971
GENTLE GUNMAN, THE, 1952
GENTLEMAN'S FATE, 1931
GEORG, 1964
GERMANY, YEAR ZERO, 1949
GERONIMO, 1939
GERONIMO, 1962
GERVAISE, 1956
GET-AWAY, THE, 1941
GET BACK, 1973
GET CHARLIE TULLY, 1976
GET MEAN, 1976
GET OUTTA TOWN, 1960
GET THAT GIRL, 1932
GETTING EVEN, 1981
GETTING OF WISDOM, THE, 1977
GHOST FEVER, 1987
GHOST IN THE INVISIBLE BIKINI, 1966
GHOST OF DRAGSTRIP HOLLOW, 1959
GHOST OF FRANKENSTEIN, THE, 1942
GHOST SHIP, THE, 1943
GHOST STORY, 1974
GHOST TOWN LAW, 1942
GHOUL, THE, 1934
GIANT FROM THE UNKNOWN, 1958
GILDA, 1946
GIRL AND THE GENERAL, THE, 1967
GIRL CAN'T HELP IT, THE, 1956
GIRL CAN'T STOP, THE, 1966
GIRL FROM TRIESTE, THE, 1983
GIRL GAME, 1968
GIRL GETTERS, THE, 1966
GIRL IN BLACK STOCKINGS, 1957
GIRL IN THE BIKINI, THE, 1958
GIRL IN THE PICTURE, THE, 1985
GIRL IN THE RED VELVET SWING, THE, 1955
GIRL IN TROUBLE, 1963
GIRL STROKE BOY, 1971
GIRL WITH THE GOLDEN EYES, THE, 1962
GIRLS IN PRISON, 1956
GIRLS IN THE NIGHT, 1953 83m UNIV bw
GIRLS JUST WANT TO HAVE FUN, 1985
GIRLS OF THE ROAD, 1940
GIRLS' TOWN, 1959
GIRO CITY, 1982
GIVE ME MY CHANCE, 1958
GLADIATOR OF ROME, 1963
GLAMOROUS NIGHT, 1937
GLAMOUR, 1934
GLASS KEY, THE, 1935
GLASS MENAGERIE, THE, 1987
GLENROWAN AFFAIR, THE, 1951
GLORY ALLEY, 1952
GLORY BRIGADE, THE, 1953
GLORY GUYS, THE, 1965
GO MASTERS, THE, 1985

GO WEST, YOUNG MAN, 1936
GODDESS, THE, 1962
GODLESS GIRL, THE, 1929
GODS MUST BE CRAZY, THE, 1984
GODSPELL, 1973
GODZILLA 1985, 1985
GODZILLA, RING OF THE MONSTERS, 1956
GODZILLA VERSUS THE COSMIC MONSTER, 1974
GODZILLA VERSUS THE SEA MONSTER, 1966
GODZILLA VERSUS THE SMOG MONSTER, 1972
GODZILLA VS. MEGALON, 1976
GODZILLA VS. THE THING, 1964
GODZILLA'S REVENGE, 1969
GOIN' TO TOWN, 1935
GOING HOME, 1988
GOING IN STYLE, 1979
GOLD, 1934
GOLD FOR THE CAESARS, 1964
GOLDEN CHILD, THE, 1986
GOLDEN DEMON, 1956
GOLDEN EARRINGS, 1947
GOLDEN GATE GIRL, 1941
GOLEM, THE, 1937
GOLEM, 1980
GOLIATH AND THE VAMPIRES, 1964
GOLIATHON, 1979
GONE IN 60 SECONDS, 1974
GONG SHOW MOVIE, THE, 1980
GOOD BAD GIRL, THE, 1931
GOOD DIE YOUNG, THE, 1954
GOOD DISSONANCE LIKE A MAN, A, 1977
GOOD SOLDIER SCHWEIK, THE, 1963
GOODBYE AGAIN, 1961
GOODBYE CHARLIE, 1964
GOODBYE GIRL, THE, 1977
GOODBYE PORK PIE, 1981
GOOFBALLS, 1987
GOONIES, THE, 1985
GORATH, 1964
GORBALS STORY, THE, 1950
GORGO, 1961
GORILLA, 1964
GORILLA AT LARGE, 1954
GORILLA GREETS YOU, THE, 1958
GORILLAS IN THE MIST, 1988
GOSPEL ACCORDING TO VIC, THE, 1986
GRAFT, 1931
GRAND MANEUVER, THE, 1956
GRAND SUBSTITUTION, THE, 1965
GRAND THEFT AUTO, 1977
GRASS EATER, THE, 1961
GRAY LADY DOWN, 1978
GRAYEAGLE, 1977
GREASED LIGHTNING, 1977
GREASER'S PALACE, 1972
GREAT BANK HOAX, THE, 1977
GREAT BIG THING, A, 1968
GREAT GABBO, THE, 1929
GREAT HOPE, THE, 1954
GREAT SANTINI, THE, 1979
GREAT SMOKEY ROADBLOCK, THE, 1978
GREAT SPY CHASE, THE, 1966
GREAT WALDO PEPPER, THE, 1975
GREATEST LOVE, THE, 1954
GREEK TYCOON, THE, 1978
GREEN BERETS, THE, 1968
GREEN-EYED BLONDE, THE, 1957
GREEN FIRE, 1955
GREEN ICE, 1981
GREEN PACK, THE, 1934
GREEN SLIME, THE, 1969
GREENWICH VILLAGE STORY, 1963
GREGORY'S GIRL, 1982
GREY FOX, THE, 1983
GREYSTOKE: THE LEGEND OF TARZAN, LORD OF THE APES, 1984
GRIZZLY, 1976
GROUNDSTAR CONSPIRACY, THE, 1972
GUADALCANAL DIARY, 1943
GUERRILLA GIRL, 1953
GUESS WHO'S COMING TO DINNER, 1967
GUEST, THE, 1963
GUIDE FOR THE MARRIED MAN, A, 1967
GUILTY BYSTANDER, 1950
GUILTY HANDS, 1931
GUILTY OF TREASON, 1950

BOLD: Films on Videocassette

GUILTY PARENTS, 1934
GUILTY, THE, 1947
GUINGUETTE, 1959
GUMSHOE, 1972
GUN BATTLE AT MONTEREY, 1957
GUN FIGHT, 1961
GUN HAWK, THE, 1963
GUN STREET, 1962
GUN THAT WON THE WEST, THE, 1955
GUN THE MAN DOWN, 1957
GUNFIGHT AT THE O.K. CORRAL, 1957
GUNFIGHT IN ABILENE, 1967
GUNFIGHTER, THE, 1950
GUNFIGHTERS OF CASA GRANDE, 1965
GUNG HO!, 1943
GUNG HO, 1986
GUNGA DIN, 1939
GUNMAN HAS ESCAPED, A, 1948
GUNMAN'S WALK, 1958
GUNMEN OF THE RIO GRANDE, 1965
GUNN, 1967
GUNPOWDER, 1987
GUNS AT BATASI, 1964
GUNS, GIRLS AND GANGSTERS, 1958
GUNS OF DARKNESS, 1962
GUNS OF DIABLO, 1964
GUNS OF NAVARONE, THE, 1961
GUNS OF THE BLACK WITCH, 1961
GUNS OF THE MAGNIFICENT SEVEN, 1969
GUNSLINGER, 1956
GURU, THE, 1969
GYPSY, 1962
GYPSY FURY, 1950
GYPSY GIRL, 1966
HADLEY'S REBELLION, 1984
HAIL, HERO!, 1969
HALF ANGEL, 1936
HALF-WAY HOUSE, THE, 1945
HALF WAY TO SHANGHAI, 1942
HALLELUJAH THE HILLS, 1963
HALLIDAY BRAND, THE, 1957
HALLS OF MONTEZUMA, 1951
HALLUCINATION GENERATION, 1966
HAMILE, 1965
HAMLET, 1966
HAMMERHEAD, 1968
HAMMERSMITH IS OUT, 1972
HAMMETT, 1982
HAND IN THE TRAP, THE, 1963
HAND OF DEATH, 1962
HAND OF NIGHT, THE, 1968
HAND, THE, 1960
HANDFUL OF DUST, A, 1988
HANDS OF A STRANGER, 1962
HANG'EM HIGH, 1968
HANGING TREE, THE, 1959
HANGMAN WAITS, THE, 1947
HANGMAN'S KNOT, 1952
HANGOVER SQUARE, 1945
HANK WILLIAMS: THE SHOW HE NEVER GAVE, 1982
HANNAH AND HER SISTERS, 1986
HANNAH K., 1983
HANNIBAL BROOKS, 1969
HANOVER STREET, 1979
HAPPENING, THE, 1967
HAPPINESS CAGE, THE, 1972
HAPPY ANNIVERSARY, 1959
HAPPY BIRTHDAY, WANDA JUNE, 1971
HAPPY DEATHDAY, 1969
HAPPY ENDING, THE, 1969
HAPPY MOTHER'S DAY ... LOVE, GEORGE, 1973
HAPPY NEW YEAR, 1987
HAPPY THIEVES, THE, 1962
HARD CONTRACT, 1969
HARD PART BEGINS, THE, 1973
HARD RIDE, THE, 1971
HARD TRAVELING, 1985
HARDER THEY COME, THE, 1973
HARLOW, 1965
HARLOW, 1965
HARPER, 1966
HARPER VALLEY, P.T.A., 1978
HARRY AND SON, 1984
HARRY AND TONTO, 1974
HARRY AND WALTER GO TO NEW YORK, 1976

HARRY BLACK AND THE TIGER, 1958
HARRY IN YOUR POCKET, 1973
HARRY TRACY—DESPERADO, 1982
HARRY'S WAR, 1981
HARVEY MIDDLEMAN, FIREMAN, 1965
HAT CHECK GIRL, 1932
HATE FOR HATE, 1967
HATFUL OF RAIN, A, 1957
HATTER'S CASTLE, 1948
HATTER'S GHOST, THE, 1982
HAUNTING OF M, THE, 1979
HAWAII, 1966
HAWAIIANS, THE, 1970
HAWKS, 1988
HAWKS AND THE SPARROWS, THE, 1967
HAZEL'S PEOPLE, 1978
HAZING, THE, 1978
HE RAN ALL THE WAY, 1951
HE WALKED BY NIGHT, 1948
HE WHO SHOOTS FIRST, 1966
HEAD OF A TYRANT, 1960
HEAD OF THE FAMILY, 1967
HEAD OFFICE, 1986
HEADIN' FOR BROADWAY, 1980
HEART LIKE A WHEEL, 1983
HEART OF A CHILD, 1958
HEARTBREAK HOTEL, 1988
HEARTBREAKER, 1983
HEAT AND DUST, 1983
HEAVEN CAN WAIT, 1978
HEAVEN WITH A GUN, 1969
HELL IN KOREA, 1956
HELL IS EMPTY, 1967
HELL IS FOR HEROES, 1962
HELL ON FRISCO BAY, 1956
HELL WITH HEROES, THE, 1968
HELLER IN PINK TIGHTS, 1960
HELLFIRE CLUB, THE, 1963
HELL'S ANGELS, 1930
HENNESSY, 1975
HENRY IV, 1985
HER MAN, 1930
HERCULES IN THE HAUNTED WORLD, 1964
HERCULES' PILLS, 1960
HERCULES II, 1985
HERE COME THE TIGERS, 1978
HERE WE GO ROUND THE MULBERRY BUSH, 1968
HERO, 1982
HEROD THE GREAT, 1960
HEROES DIE YOUNG, 1960
HEROES OF TELEMARK, THE, 1965
HEROINA, 1965
HEROSTRATUS, 1968
HE'S MY GIRL, 1987
HESTER STREET, 1975
HEY BABU RIBA, 1987
HICKEY AND BOGGS, 1972
HIDDEN FEAR, 1957
HIDDEN FORTRESS, THE, 1959
HIDDEN GUNS, 1956
HIDDEN HAND, THE, 1942
HIDDEN HOMICIDE, 1959
HIDE IN PLAIN SIGHT, 1980
HIDEOUS SUN DEMON, THE, 1959
HIDEOUT, 1948
HIDEOUT, THE, 1956
HIDING OUT, 1987
HIGH ANXIETY, 1977
HIGH-BALLIN', 1978
HIGH HELL, 1958
HIGH NOON, 1952
HIGH ROAD TO CHINA, 1983
HIGH SCHOOL BIG SHOT, 1959
HIGH SCHOOL CAESAR, 1960
HIGH SIERRA, 1941
HIGH SPIRITS, 1988
HIGH VELOCITY, 1977
HIGH WALL, THE, 1947
HIGHPOINT, 1984
HIGHWAY PICKUP, 1965
HIGHWAY 301, 1950
HIGHWAYMAN, THE, 1951
HIKEN YABURI, 1969
HILLS RUN RED, THE, 1967
HINDENBURG, THE, 1975
HIRED KILLER, THE, 1967

HIRELING, THE, 1973
HIS GIRL FRIDAY, 1940
HIS GLORIOUS NIGHT, 1929
HISTORY IS MADE AT NIGHT, 1937
HIT AND RUN, 1957
HITLER, 1962
HITLER: THE LAST TEN DAYS, 1973
HITLER'S CHILDREN, 1942
HOAX, THE, 1972
HOLD THE PRESS, 1933
HOLD YOUR MAN, 1929
HOLD YOUR MAN, 1933
HOLIDAY CAMP, 1947
HOLIDAY FOR SINNERS, 1952
HOLLYWOOD MYSTERY, 1934
HOMBRE, 1967
HOME AND THE WORLD, THE, 1984
HOME BEFORE DARK, 1958
HOME IS THE HERO, 1959
HOME IS WHERE THE HART IS, 1987
HOME MOVIES, 1979
HOME OF THE BRAVE, 1949
HOME TOWN STORY, 1951
HOMECOMING, THE, 1973
HOMER, 1970
HOMETOWN U.S.A., 1979
HOMICIDE, 1949
HOMICIDE FOR THREE, 1948
HONDO, 1953
HONEYBABY, HONEYBABY, 1974
HONEYMOON HOTEL, 1964
HONEYMOON'S OVER, THE, 1939
HONEYSUCKLE ROSE, 1980
HONKERS, THE, 1972
HONKY TONK, 1941
HONKY TONK FREEWAY, 1981
HONOURABLE MURDER, AN, 1959
HOODLUM, THE, 1951
HOODLUM PRIEST, THE, 1961
HOODWINK, 1981
HOOK, THE, 1962
HOOPLA, 1933
HOPALONG CASSIDY RETURNS, 1936
HOPE AND GLORY, 1987
HOPSCOTCH, 1980
HORROR EXPRESS, 1972
HORROR HOTEL, 1960
HORROR OF PARTY BEACH, THE, 1964
HORROR OF THE ZOMBIES, 1974
HORSE SOLDIERS, THE, 1959
HORSEMEN, THE, 1971
HOSPITAL, THE, 1971
HOT ANGEL, THE, 1958
HOT MILLIONS, 1968
HOT MONEY GIRL, 1962
HOT MONTH OF AUGUST, THE, 1969
HOT ROD HULLABALOO, 1966
HOT ROD RUMBLE, 1957
HOT STUFF, 1979
HOT TO TROT, 1988
HOT TOMORROWS, 1978
HOTEL PARADISO, 1966
HOTHEAD, 1963
HOUND OF THE BASKERVILLES, THE, 1959
HOUND OF THE BASKERVILLES, THE, 1980
HOUND OF THE BASKERVILLES, THE, 1983
HOUR OF THE GUN, 1967
HOURS OF LONELINESS, 1930
HOUSE BY THE RIVER, 1950
HOUSE CALLS, 1978
HOUSE DIVIDED, A, 1932
HOUSE IN THE WOODS, THE, 1957
HOUSE OF BAMBOO, 1955
HOUSE OF BLACKMAIL, 1953
HOUSE OF CARDS, 1969
HOUSE OF DEATH, 1932
HOUSE OF FRIGHT, 1961
HOUSE OF HORRORS, 1946
HOUSE OF MYSTERY, 1961
HOUSE OF STRANGE LOVES, THE, 1969
HOUSE OF STRANGERS, 1949
HOUSE OF THE DAMNED, 1963
HOUSE OF THE LIVING DEAD, 1973
HOUSE OF WAX, 1953
HOUSE ON CARROLL STREET, THE, 1988
HOUSE ON 56TH STREET, THE, 1933

HOUSE ON HAUNTED HILL, 1958
HOUSE ON SKULL MOUNTAIN, THE, 1974
HOUSE ON TELEGRAPH HILL, 1951
HOUSE ON THE SAND, 1967
HOUSEKEEPER, THE, 1987
HOW DO I LOVE THEE?, 1970
HOW I WON THE WAR, 1967
HOW TO MAKE A MONSTER, 1958
HOW TO SEDUCE A PLAYBOY, 1968
HU-MAN, 1975
HUMAN DESIRE, 1954
HUMAN FACTOR, THE, 1979
HUMANOID, THE, 1979
HUNCHBACK OF ROME, THE, 1963
HUNDRA, 1984
HUNGRY HILL, 1947
HUNK, 1987
HUNS, THE, 1962
HUNTER, THE, 1980
HURRY UP OR I'LL BE 30, 1973
HUSBANDS, 1970
HUSTLER, THE, 1961
I LOVE N.Y., 1987
I, MONSTER, 1971
I OUGHT TO BE IN PICTURES, 1982
I, TOO, AM ONLY A WOMAN, 1963
I WALK ALONE, 1948
I WAS A COMMUNIST FOR THE F.B.I., 1951
I WAS A TEENAGE T.V. TERRORIST, 1987
I WILL . . . I WILL . . . FOR NOW, 1976
ICE PALACE, THE, 1988
ICEMAN COMETH, THE, 1973
IDAHO TRANSFER, 1975
IF EVER I SEE YOU AGAIN, 1978
IL GRIDO, 1962
ILLEGAL, 1955
ILLICIT, 1931
ILLUSION TRAVELS BY STREETCAR, THE, 1977
ILLUSIONIST, THE, 1985
ILLUSIONIST, THE, 1985
ILLUSTRIOUS ENERGY, 1988
I'M NO ANGEL, 1933
IMMORAL MOMENT, THE, 1967
IMMORTAL STORY, THE, 1969
IMPACT, 1963
IMPATIENT MAIDEN, 1932
IMPERSONATOR, THE, 1962
IMPROPER CHANNELS, 1981
IMPULSE, 1955
IN A LONELY PLACE, 1950
IN OLD SACRAMENTO, 1946
IN OUR TIME, 1944
IN THE COOL OF THE DAY, 1963
IN THE HEAT OF THE NIGHT, 1967
IN THE MOOD, 1987
IN THE WAKE OF A STRANGER, 1960
IN THE WILD MOUNTAINS, 1986
IN THE YEAR 2889, 1966
INADMISSIBLE EVIDENCE, 1968
INCIDENT, 1948
INCORRIGIBLE, 1980
INCREDIBLE SARAH, THE, 1976
INCREDIBLE SHRINKING WOMAN, THE, 1981
INDIAN FIGHTER, THE, 1955
INDISCREET, 1931
INFORMATION RECEIVED, 1962
INFORMER, THE, 1935
INFRA-MAN, 1975
INGAGI, 1931
INHERITANCE, THE, 1964
INHERITANCE IN PRETORIA, 1936
INNERSPACE, 1987
INNOCENCE UNPROTECTED, 1971
INNOCENT MEETING, 1959
INQUEST, 1931
INQUEST, 1939
INSECT WOMAN, THE, 1964
INSIDE LOOKING OUT, 1977
INSIDE MOVES, 1980
INSIDE OUT, 1975
INSIDE THE ROOM, 1935
INSIDE THE WALLS OF FOLSOM PRISON, 1951
INSPIRATION, 1931
INSULT, 1932
INSURANCE INVESTIGATOR, 1951
INTERLUDE, 1968

INTERVAL, 1973
INTERVISTA, 1987
INTO THE STRAIGHT, 1950
INTRUDER, THE, 1955
INTRUDER, THE, 1962
INVADERS FROM MARS, 1986
INVASION OF THE SAUCER MEN, 1957
INVASION 1700, 1965
INVINCIBLE GLADIATOR, THE, 1963
INVISIBLE DR. MABUSE, THE, 1965
INVISIBLE GHOST, THE, 1941
INVISIBLE INVADERS, 1959
INVISIBLE KID, THE, 1988
INVISIBLE MAN, THE, 1933
INVISIBLE RAY, THE, 1936
INVITATION TO A GUNFIGHTER, 1964
INVITATION TO MURDER, 1962
IRISH WHISKEY REBELLION, 1973
IRON EAGLE, 1986
IRON EAGLE II, 1988
IRON MAN, THE, 1951
IRON MISTRESS, THE, 1952
ISAAC LITTLEFEATHERS, 1984
ISLAND, THE, 1962
ISLAND IN THE SUN, 1957
ISLAND OF DESIRE, 1952
ISLAND OF DR. MOREAU, THE, 1977
ISLAND OF DOOMED MEN, 1940
ISLAND OF LOST SOULS, 1933
ISLAND OF PROCIDA, THE, 1952
ISLAND OF TERROR, 1967
ISLAND OF THE BURNING DAMNED, 1971
ISLAND OF THE DOOMED, 1968
ISLANDS IN THE STREAM, 1977
ISLE OF ESCAPE, 1930
ISLE OF THE DEAD, 1945
IT ALWAYS RAINS ON SUNDAY, 1949
IT FELL FROM THE SKY, 1980
IT HAPPENED HERE, 1966
IT HAPPENED IN SOHO, 1948
IT ONLY HAPPENS TO OTHERS, 1971
IT STARTED IN NAPLES, 1960
IT STARTED WITH A KISS, 1959
IT TAKES A THIEF, 1960
IT TAKES ALL KINDS, 1969
IT! THE TERROR FROM BEYOND SPACE, 1958
ITALIAN SECRET SERVICE, 1968
IT'S ALIVE, 1968
IT'S HOT IN PARADISE, 1962
IT'S MY TURN, 1980
J-MEN FOREVER, 1980
JACK SLADE, 1953
JACQUES AND NOVEMBER, 1985
JAGUAR, 1980
JAGUAR LIVES, 1979
JAIL BAIT, 1954
JAMAICA INN, 1939
JAVA HEAD, 1935
JAWS OF THE JUNGLE, 1936
JAZZ SINGER, THE, 1980
JAZZMAN, 1984
JE T'AIME, 1974
JE T'AIME, JE T'AIME, 1972
JEALOUSY, 1929
JEALOUSY, 1934
JEANNE EAGELS, 1957
JENATSCH, 1987
JENNY KISSED ME, 1985
JERUSALEM FILE, THE, 1972
JESSICA, 1962
JESUS TRIP, THE, 1971
JET PILOT, 1957
JETLAG, 1981
JEWEL OF THE NILE, THE, 1985
JIGSAW MAN, THE, 1984
JIMMY ORPHEUS, 1966
JOE DAKOTA, 1957
JOE HILL, 1971
JOE KIDD, 1972
JOE MACBETH, 1955
JOHN MEADE'S WOMAN, 1937
JOHNNY BELINDA, 1948
JOHNNY DANGEROUSLY, 1984
JOHNNY EAGER, 1942
JOHNNY GUITAR, 1954
JOHNNY STOOL PIGEON, 1949

JOHNNY VIK, 1973
JOKE OF DESTINY LYING IN WAIT AROUND THE CORNER LIKE A STREET BANDIT, A, 1984
JOKER IS WILD, THE, 1957
JOLLY BAD FELLOW, A, 1964
JONAH—WHO WILL BE 25 IN THE YEAR 2000, 1976
JOURNAL OF A CRIME, 1934
JOURNEY INTO LIGHT, 1951
JOURNEY OF NATTY GANN, THE, 1985
JOURNEY TO SHILOH, 1968
JOURNEY TO THE SEVENTH PLANET, 1962
JOURNEY'S END, 1930
JOY RIDE, 1958
JUBAL, 1956
JUDEX, 1966
JUDGE AND THE ASSASSIN, THE, 1979
JUDGE AND THE SINNER, THE, 1964
JUDGMENT AT NUREMBERG, 1961
JUDO SAGA, 1965
JUDO SHOWDOWN, 1966
JULIUS CAESAR, 1953
JUST LIKE A WOMAN, 1967
JUST ONE OF THE GUYS, 1985
JUST OUT OF REACH, 1979
JUST TELL ME WHAT YOU WANT, 1980
JUST THE WAY YOU ARE, 1984
JUST YOU AND ME, KID, 1979
JUSTINE, 1969
KAGEMUSHA, 1980
KANAL, 1961
KANGAROO, 1986
KARAMAZOV, 1931
KARATE, THE HAND OF DEATH, 1961
KENNER, 1969
KENNY AND CO., 1976
KEPT HUSBANDS, 1931
KES, 1970
KEY LARGO, 1948
KEY WITNESS, 1947
KHARTOUM, 1966
KICK IN, 1931
KID BLUE, 1973
KID FROM KANSAS, THE, 1941
KID FROM TEXAS, THE, 1950
KID GLOVE KILLER, 1942
KID GLOVES, 1929
KID MONK BARONI, 1952
KID RODELO, 1966
KID VENGEANCE, 1977
KIDCO, 1984
KIEV COMEDY, A, 1963
KILL, 1968
KILL ME TOMORROW, 1958
KILL OR BE KILLED, 1950
KILL OR BE KILLED, 1967
KILL OR BE KILLED, 1980
KILL OR CURE, 1962
KILLER DILL, 1947
KILLER SHREWS, THE, 1959
KILLERS, THE, 1946
KILLER'S KISS, 1955
KILLING, THE, 1956
KILLING GAME, THE, 1968
KILLING OF A CHINESE BOOKIE, THE, 1976
KING AND COUNTRY, 1964
KING AND HIS MOVIE, A, 1986
KING DAVID, 1985
KING FOR A NIGHT, 1933
KING KONG ESCAPES, 1968
KING KONG LIVES, 1986
KING KONG VERSUS GODZILLA, 1963
KING LEAR, 1971
KING OF ALCATRAZ, 1938
KING OF COMEDY, THE, 1983
KING OF HEARTS, 1967
KING OF THE BULLWHIP, 1950
KING OF THE CORAL SEA, 1956
KING OF THE DAMNED, 1936
KING OF THE ROARING TWENTIES—THE STORY OF ARNOLD ROTHSTEIN, 1961
KING OF THE ZOMBIES, 1941
KING SOLOMON'S MINES, 1985
KINGDOM OF THE SPIDERS, 1977
KINGS AND DESPERATE MEN, 1984
KINGS OF THE ROAD, 1976
KISENGA, MAN OF AFRICA, 1952

BOLD: Films on Videocassette

KISS ME GOODBYE, 1982
KISS ME, STUPID, 1964
KISS OF EVIL, 1963
KISS THE OTHER SHEIK, 1968
KLANSMAN, THE, 1974
KNACK ... AND HOW TO GET IT, THE, 1965
KNIGHTRIDERS, 1981
KNOCK ON ANY DOOR, 1949
KONA COAST, 1968
KONGA, 1961
KOREA PATROL, 1951
KRAKATIT, 1948
L-SHAPED ROOM, THE, 1962
LA BAMBA, 1987
LA BONNE SOUPE, 1964
LA CAGE, 1975
LA CAGE AUX FOLLES 3: THE WEDDING, 1985
LA DOLCE VITA, 1961
LA FEMME INFIDELE, 1969
LA FERME DU PENDU, 1946
LA GRANDE BOURGEOISE, 1977
LA MARIE DU PORT, 1951
LA PASSANTE, 1983
LA PETIT SIRENE, 1984
LA SCARLATINE, 1985
LADIES IN RETIREMENT, 1941
LADIES' MAN, 1931
LADIES OF THE PARK, 1964
LADY AND THE MONSTER, THE, 1944
LADY DOCTOR, THE, 1963
LADY FROM SHANGHAI, THE, 1948
LADY IN WHITE, 1988
LADY JANE, 1986
LADY L, 1965
LADY LIBERTY, 1972
LADY OF BURLESQUE, 1943
LADY OF THE CAMELIAS, 1987
LADY OF THE TROPICS, 1939
LADY OSCAR, 1979
LADY VANISHES, THE, 1980
LADYBUG, LADYBUG, 1963
LADYHAWKE, 1985
L'AGE D'OR, 1979
LANCELOT OF THE LAKE, 1975
LAND OF DOOM, 1986
LAND RAIDERS, 1969
LANDLORD, THE, 1970
LANDSCAPE IN THE MIST, 1988
L'ARMEE DES OMBRES, 1969
LAS VEGAS FREE-FOR-ALL, 1968
LASERBLAST, 1978
LASH, THE, 1934
LAST ACT OF MARTIN WESTON, THE, 1970
LAST AMERICAN HERO, THE, 1973
LAST BARRICADE, THE, 1938
LAST DRAGON, THE, 1985
LAST EMPEROR, THE, 1987
LAST GAME, THE, 1964
LAST GRENADE, THE, 1970
LAST HUNT, THE, 1956
LAST MAN, THE, 1968
LAST MAN TO HANG, THE, 1956
LAST MERCENARY, THE, 1969
LAST MILE, THE, 1959
LAST MOMENT, THE, 1966
LAST OF SHEILA, THE, 1973
LAST PERFORMANCE, THE, 1929
LAST POST, THE, 1929
LAST REBEL, THE, 1971
LAST REBEL, THE, 1961
LAST REMAKE OF BEAU GESTE, THE, 1977
LAST SHOT YOU HEAR, THE, 1969
LAST STARFIGHTER, THE, 1984
LAST TRAIN FROM GUN HILL, 1959
LAST TYCOON, THE, 1976
LAST WAGON, THE, 1956
LAST WAR, THE, 1962
LAST YEAR AT MARIENBAD, 1962
L'ATALANTE, 1947
LATE SUMMER BLUES, 1988
LAUGHING SINNERS, 1931
LAUGHTER HOUSE, 1984
LAWLESS EIGHTIES, THE, 1957
LAWMAN, 1971
LAWRENCE OF ARABIA, 1962
LE AMICHE, 1962

LE BONHEUR, 1966
LE GENDARME ET LES EXTRATERRESTRES, 1978
LE JEUNE MARIE, 1985
LE PETIT SOLDAT, 1965
LE PETIT THEATRE DE JEAN RENOIR, 1974
LEECH WOMAN, THE, 1960
LEFT-HANDED GUN, THE, 1958
LEGAL EAGLES, 1986
LEGEND OF FRENCHIE KING, THE, 1971
LEGEND OF HELL HOUSE, THE, 1973
LEGEND OF NIGGER CHARLEY, THE, 1972
LEGEND OF SPIDER FOREST, THE, 1976
LEGEND OF SURAM FORTRESS, 1985
LEGEND OF THE LONE RANGER, THE, 1981
LEGEND OF THE LOST, 1957
LEMON GROVE KIDS MEET THE MONSTERS, THE,
  1966
LES BELLES-DE-NUIT, 1952
LES PLOUFFE, 1985
LESSON IN LOVE, A, 1960
LEST WE FORGET, 1934
LET JOY REIGN SUPREME, 1977
LET'S KILL UNCLE, 1966
LET'S SCARE JESSICA TO DEATH, 1971
LET'S TALK ABOUT WOMEN, 1964
LIES, 1984
LIFE AND LOVES OF MOZART, THE, 1959
LIFE AND TIMES OF CHESTER-ANGUS RAMSGOOD,
  THE, 1971
LIFE AND TIMES OF JUDGE ROY BEAN, THE, 1972
LIFE AT THE TOP, 1965
LIFE BEGINS, 1932
LIFE BEGINS AT 17, 1958
LIFE BEGINS TOMORROW, 1952
LIFE IN EMERGENCY WARD 10, 1959
LIFE IN HER HANDS, 1951
LIFE IS A BED OF ROSES, 1984
LIFE OF OHARU, 1964
LIFE OF VERGIE WINTERS, THE, 1934
LIFE RETURNS, 1939
LIFE UPSIDE DOWN, 1965
LIFEGUARD, 1976
LIFESPAN, 1975
LIFT, THE, 1983
LIGHT OF DAY, 1987
LIGHT TOUCH, THE, 1951
LIGHT YEARS, 1988
LIGHT YEARS AWAY, 1982
LIGHTNIN' IN THE FOREST, 1948
LIGHTNING STRIKES TWICE, 1951
LIGHTSHIP, THE, 1986
LIKE A CROW ON A JUNE BUG, 1972
LIKE FATHER LIKE SON, 1961
LIKE FATHER, LIKE SON, 1987
LILIOM, 1930
LILITH, 1964
LILLI MARLENE, 1951
LILLY TURNER, 1933
LILY CHRISTINE, 1932
LILY IN LOVE, 1985
LILY OF LAGUNA, 1938
LIMIT, THE, 1972
L'IMMORTELLE, 1969
LINE, THE, 1982
LIQUIDATOR, THE, 1966
LISETTE, 1961
LITTLE AUSTRALIANS, 1940
LITTLE BIG HORN, 1951
LITTLE CAESAR, 1931
LITTLE FRIEND, 1934
LITTLE MALCOLM, 1974
LITTLE MISS MARKER, 1980
LITTLE NIGHT MUSIC, A, 1977
LITTLE RED RIDING HOOD AND THE MONSTERS,
  1965
LITTLE SHOP OF HORRORS, 1986
LIVE AND LET DIE, 1973
LIVING COFFIN, THE, 1965
LIVING DANGEROUSLY, 1988
LIVING DAYLIGHTS, THE, 1987
LIVING ON TOKYO TIME, 1987
LIZZIE, 1957
LOCKET, THE, 1946
LOLA, 1961
LOLA MONTES, 1955
LONELY ARE THE BRAVE, 1962

LONELYHEARTS, 1958
LONG AGO, TOMORROW, 1971
LONG DAY'S JOURNEY INTO NIGHT, 1962
LONG KNIFE, THE, 1958
LONG SHIPS, THE, 1964
LONG SHOT, 1981
LONGEST DAY, THE, 1962
LONNIE, 1963
LOOKING GLASS WAR, THE, 1970
LOOKING UP, 1977
LOOKS AND SMILES, 1982
LOOPHOLE, 1981
LOOSE CONNECTIONS, 1984
LOOSE ENDS, 1975
LOOSE SHOES, 1980
LOOT, 1971
LORDS OF FLATBUSH, THE, 1974
LOSS OF INNOCENCE, 1961
LOST FACE, THE, 1965
LOST HONOR OF KATHARINA BLUM, THE, 1975
LOST MAN, THE, 1969
LOST ONE, THE, 1951
LOST PATROL, THE, 1934
LOST SQUADRON, THE, 1932
LOTNA, 1966
LOUISIANA HUSSY, 1960
LOVE, 1972
LOVE AND BULLETS, 1979
LOVE AND MARRIAGE, 1966
LOVE AND PAIN AND THE WHOLE DAMN THING,
  1973
LOVE AT FIRST BITE, 1979
LOVE AT TWENTY, 1963
LOVE, 1982
LOVE CYCLES, 1969
LOVE FROM A STRANGER, 1937
LOVE HAS MANY FACES, 1965
LOVE IN 4 DIMENSIONS, 1965
LOVE-INS, THE, 1967
LOVE IS A FUNNY THING, 1970
LOVE IS A WOMAN, 1967
LOVE LETTERS, 1983
LOVE NOW ... PAY LATER, 1966
LOVE ON THE GROUND, 1984,Fr.
LOVE ON THE RIVIERA, 1964
LOVE PROBLEMS, 1970
LOVE ROBOTS, THE, 1965
LOVE SONGS, 1986
LOVE STORY, 1949
LOVE STREAMS, 1984
LOVE, THE ITALIAN WAY, 1964
LOVE WITH THE PROPER STRANGER, 1963
LOVED ONE, THE, 1965
LOVELY WAY TO DIE, A, 1968
LOVERS AND OTHER STRANGERS, 1970
LOVERS, THE, 1972
LOVERS, HAPPY LOVERS!, 1955
LOVER'S NET, 1957
LOVES AND TIMES OF SCARAMOUCHE, THE, 1976
LOVES OF CARMEN, THE, 1948
LOVESICK, 1983
LOVING, 1970
LOWER DEPTHS, THE, 1937
LOWER DEPTHS, THE, 1962
LUCIANO, 1963
LUCKY DEVILS, 1941
LUCKY JIM, 1957
LUCKY LOSERS, 1950
LUCY GALLANT, 1955
LUGGAGE OF THE GODS, 1983
LUMIERE D'ETE, 1943
LUNCH HOUR, 1962
LURE OF THE SWAMP, 1957
LURE OF THE WILDERNESS, 1952
LUST FOR LIFE, 1956
LUSTY MEN, THE, 1952
LUTHER, 1974
LUXURY GIRLS, 1953
M, 1951
MACABRE, 1958
MACAO, 1952
MACARONI, 1985
MACARTHUR'S CHILDREN, 1985
MACKENNA'S GOLD, 1969
MACKINTOSH MAN, THE, 1973
MACOMBER AFFAIR, THE, 1947

MAD AT THE WORLD, 1955
MAD DOG COLL, 1961
MAD GHOUL, THE, 1943
MAD LOVE, 1935
MAD MAGICIAN, THE, 1954
MADAME DU BARRY, 1954
MADAME WHITE SNAKE, 1963
MADE, 1972
MADE FOR EACH OTHER, 1971
MADE IN ITALY, 1967
MADE IN U.S.A., 1966
MADEMOISELLE, 1966
MADHOUSE, 1974
MADIGAN, 1968
MADONNA OF THE SEVEN MOONS, 1945
MAEDCHEN IN UNIFORM, 1932
MAEDCHEN IN UNIFORM, 1965
MAFIA, 1969
MAFIA, THE, 1972
MAFIOSO, 1962
MAGICIAN, THE, 1959
MAGICIAN OF LUBLIN, THE, 1979
MAGNETIC MONSTER, THE, 1953
MAGNIFICENT BANDITS, THE, 1969
MAGNIFICENT SEVEN, THE, 1960
MAGOICHI SAGA, THE, 1970
MAGUS, THE, 1968
MAHOGANY, 1975
MAID TO ORDER, 1987
MAIDS, THE, 1975
MAIDSTONE, 1970
MAIGRET LAYS A TRAP, 1958
MAIN THING IS TO LOVE, THE, 1975
MAIS OU ET DONC ORNICAR, 1979
MAJDHAR, 1984
MAKE A FACE, 1971
MAKO: THE JAWS OF DEATH, 1976
MALANDRO, 1986
MALCOLM, 1986
MALEVIL, 1981
MALIBU BEACH, 1978
MALOU, 1983
MALPERTIUS, 1972
MAMBO, 1955
MAMMA ROMA, 1962
MAN, A WOMAN, AND A BANK, A, 1979
MAN ACCUSED, 1959
MAN AGAINST MAN, 1961
MAN AND A WOMAN: 20 YEARS LATER, A, 1986
MAN AT THE CARLTON TOWER, 1961
MAN CALLED ADAM, A, 1966
MAN CALLED BACK, THE, 1932
MAN CALLED NOON, THE, 1973
MAN DETAINED, 1961
MAN FROM LARAMIE, THE, 1955
MAN FROM SNOWY RIVER, THE, 1983
MAN IN THE ATTIC, 1953
MAN INSIDE, THE, 1958
MAN OF IRON, 1981
MAN OF LA MANCHA, 1972
MAN ON A SWING, 1974
MAN OUTSIDE, 1988
MAN THEY COULD NOT HANG, THE, 1939
MAN UNDER SUSPICION, 1985
MAN WHO CAME BACK, THE, 1931
MAN WHO COULD CHEAT DEATH, THE, 1959
MAN WHO ENVIED WOMEN, THE, 1985
MAN WHO HAD POWER OVER WOMEN, THE, 1970
MAN WHO KNEW TOO MUCH, THE, 1935
MAN WHO LIES, THE, 1970
MAN WHO STOLE THE SUN, THE, 1980
MAN WHO TURNED TO STONE, THE, 1957
MAN WHO WAS NOBODY, THE, 1960
MAN WHO WASN'T THERE, THE, 1983
MAN WHO WOULD NOT DIE, THE, 1975
MAN WITH A GUN, 1958
MAN WITH CONNECTIONS, THE, 1970
MAN WITH ONE RED SHOE, THE, 1985
MAN WITH THE GUN, 1955
MAN WITH THE MAGNETIC EYES, THE, 1945
MAN WITHOUT A STAR, 1955
MANHATTAN, 1979
MANIAC, 1963
MANIAC!, 1977
MANITOU, THE, 1978
MANON OF THE SPRING, 1987

MANOS, THE HANDS OF FATE, 1966
MARCH ON PARIS 1914—OF GENERALOBERST
   ALEXANDER VON KLUCK—AND HIS MEMORY
   OF JESSIE HOLLADAY, 1977
MARCO THE MAGNIFICENT, 1966
MARIE, 1985
MARIGOLD MAN, 1970
MARIGOLDS IN AUGUST, 1984
MARIUS, 1933
MARK OF THE PHOENIX, 1958
MARK OF THE VAMPIRE, 1935
MARK OF THE WITCH, 1970
MARKED WOMAN, 1937
MARKSMAN, THE, 1953
MARNIE, 1964
MAROONED, 1933
MARRIAGE, A, 1983
MARRIED WOMAN, THE, 1965
MARRYING WIDOWS, 1934
MARTHA JELLNECK, 1988
MARTIN'S DAY, 1985
MARTYR, THE, 1976
MARVIN AND TIGE, 1983
MARY HAD A LITTLE, 1961
MARY RYAN, DETECTIVE, 1949
MASK, 1985
MASK OF FU MANCHU, THE, 1932
MASQUE OF THE RED DEATH, THE, 1964
MASQUERADE IN MEXICO, 1945
MASS APPEAL, 1984
MASS IS ENDED, THE, 1988
MASSACRE IN ROME, 1973
MASTER GUNFIGHTER, THE, 1975
MASTER OF BANKDAM, THE, 1947
MASTER RACE, THE, 1944
MASTER TOUCH, THE, 1974
MATA HARI, 1965
MATCH KING, THE, 1932
MATCHLESS, 1967
MATEWAN, 1987
MATTER OF HONOR, A, 1988
MAXIE, 1985
MAXWELL ARCHER, DETECTIVE, 1942
MAYA, 1982
MAYERLING, 1968
MAYOR OF HELL, THE, 1933
MAZE, THE, 1953
MC KENZIE BREAK, THE, 1970
MC VICAR, 1982
ME, NATALIE, 1969
MEATBALLS, 1979
MEATBALLS PART II, 1984
MEDUSA TOUCH, THE, 1978
MEGAFORCE, 1982
MEIN KAMPF—MY CRIMES, 1940
MEMED MY HAWK, 1984
MEMENTO MEI, 1963
MEMOIRS OF A SURVIVOR, 1981
MEMORIES OF ME, 1988
MEN, THE, 1950
MEN CALL IT LOVE, 1931
MEN PREFER FAT GIRLS, 1981
MERCENARY, THE, 1970
MERCHANT OF SLAVES, 1949
MERRY WIVES, THE, 1940
**METALSTORM: THE DESTRUCTION OF
   JARED-SYN, 1983**
METEOR, 1979
MICHELLE, 1970
MICKI AND MAUDE, 1984
MIDAS RUN, 1969
MIDNiGHT FOLLY, 1962
MIDNIGHT LACE, 1960
MIDNIGHT MADNESS, 1980
MILAGRO BEANFIELD WAR, THE, 1988
MILES FROM HOME, 1988
MILESTONES, 1975
MILKY WAY, THE, 1969
MINISTRY OF FEAR, 1945
MINNESOTA CLAY, 1966
MINNIE AND MOSKOWITZ, 1971
MINUTE TO PRAY, A SECOND TO DIE, A, 1968
MIRACLE OF MORGAN'S CREEK, THE, 1944
MIRACLES, 1987
MIRAGE, 1972
MISFITS, THE, 1961

MISSION, THE, 1986
MISSISSIPPI GAMBLER, THE, 1953
MISSISSIPPI SUMMER, 1971
MR. ARKADIN, 1962
MISTER BROWN, 1972
MISTER BUDDWING, 1966
MR. KLEIN, 1976
MR. MAJESTYK, 1974
MR. PATMAN, 1980
MR. RICCO, 1975
MR. SARDONICUS, 1961
MR. SKEFFINGTON, 1944
MISTRESS FOR THE SUMMER, A, 1964
MISUNDERSTOOD, 1984
MIX ME A PERSON, 1962
MIXED COMPANY, 1974
MOBY DICK, 1956
MODELS, INC., 1952
MODERATO CANTABILE, 1964
MODERN ROMANCE, 1981
MOMENT OF TERROR, 1969
MON ONCLE D'AMERIQUE, 1980
MONEY TRAP, THE, 1966
MONITORS, THE, 1969
MONKEY ON MY BACK, 1957
MONKEY'S PAW, THE, 1933
MOON IS DOWN, THE, 1943
MONSOON, 1953
MONSTER A GO-GO, 1965
MONSTER AND THE GIRL, THE, 1941
MONSTER CLUB, THE, 1981
MONSTER ISLAND, 1981
MONSTER MAKER, THE, 1944
MONSTER OF PIEDRAS BLANCAS, THE, 1959
MONSTER ON THE CAMPUS, 1958
MONTE WALSH, 1970
MOON OVER PARADOR, 1988
MOONLIGHTING, 1982
MOONRISE, 1948
MOONSHINE COUNTY EXPRESS, 1977
MOONSHINE WAR, THE, 1970
MOONSTRUCK, 1987
MORE AMERICAN GRAFFITI, 1979
MORE DEAD THAN ALIVE, 1968
MORE DEADLY THAN THE MALE, 1961
MORGAN!, 1966
MORITURI, 1965
MORNING GLORY, 1933
MORO WITCH DOCTOR, 1964
MOROCCO, 1930
MORONS FROM OUTER SPACE, 1985
MOSES AND AARON, 1975
MOST BEAUTIFUL AGE, THE, 1970
MOTEL, THE OPERATOR, 1940
MOTHER AND THE WHORE, THE, 1973
MOTHER LODE, 1982
MOTHERS OF TODAY, 1939
MOTIVE WAS JEALOUSY, THE, 1970
MOUCHETTE, 1970
MOURNING BECOMES ELECTRA, 1947
MOURNING SUIT, THE, 1975
MOUTH TO MOUTH, 1978
MOVE, 1970
MOVERS AND SHAKERS, 1985
MOVIE STAR, AMERICAN STYLE, OR, LSD I HATE
   YOU!, 1966
MOVING FINGER, THE, 1963
MOVING TARGETS, 1987
MOVING VIOLATION, 1976
MRS. SOFFEL, 1984
MUMMY, THE, 1959
MUMMY'S HAND, THE, 1940
MUMMY'S SHROUD, THE, 1967
MUMMY'S TOMB, THE, 1942
MUNCHIES, 1987
MURDER A LA MOD, 1968
MURDER BY CONTRACT, 1958
MURDER BY DEATH, 1976
MURDER BY DECREE, 1979
MURDER BY THE CLOCK, 1931
MURDER CLINIC, THE, 1967
MURDER IN MISSISSIPPI, 1965
MURDER IN THE MUSEUM, 1934
MURDER MAN, 1935
MURDER ON APPROVAL, 1956
MURDER ON DIAMOND ROW, 1937

BOLD: Films on Videocassette

MURDER ON MONDAY, 1953
MURDER ON THE ORIENT EXPRESS, 1974
MURDERERS' ROW, 1966
MURDERS IN THE RUE MORGUE, 1932
MURPH THE SURF, 1974
MUSIC BOX KID, THE, 1960
MY DEMON LOVER, 1987
MY DOG, BUDDY, 1960
MY FATHER'S MISTRESS, 1970
MY FAVORITE YEAR, 1982
MY FORBIDDEN PAST, 1951
MY LIFE AS A DOG, 1987
MY MARGO, 1969
MY NAME IS PECOS, 1966
MY OTHER HUSBAND, 1985
MY SISTER AND I, 1948
MY SON IS GUILTY, 1940
MY SON, JOHN, 1952
MY STEPMOTHER IS AN ALIEN, 1988
MY UNCLE ANTOINE, 1971
MY UNCLE'S LEGACY, 1988
MY WAY HOME, 1978
MY WIDOW AND I, 1950
MY WORLD DIES SCREAMING, 1958
MYSTERIES, 1979
MYSTERIOUS DOCTOR, THE, 1943
MYSTERIOUS MR. WONG, 1935
MYSTERY MANSION, 1984
MYSTERY OF EDWIN DROOD, THE, 1935
MYSTERY OF MR. X, THE, 1934
MYSTERY OF THE WAX MUSEUM, THE, 1933
MYSTERY STREET, 1950
NADIA, 1984
NADINE, 1987
NAKED AMONG THE WOLVES, 1967
NAKED APE, THE, 1973
NAKED CITY, THE, 1948
NAKED FACE, THE, 1984
NAKED FLAME, THE, 1970
NAKED FURY, 1959
NAKED HOURS, THE, 1964
NAKED IN THE SUN, 1957
NAKED STREET, THE, 1955
NAKED WITCH, THE, 1964
NAKED ZOO, THE, 1970
NAME OF THE GAME IS KILL, THE, 1968
NANA, 1934
NARROW CORNER, THE, 1933
NARROWING CIRCLE, THE, 1956
NASTY HABITS, 1976
NATCHEZ TRACE, 1960
NATE AND HAYES, 1983
NATHALIE GRANGER, 1972
NATIONAL HEALTH, OR NURSE NORTON'S
    AFFAIR, THE, 1973
NATIONAL LAMPOON'S ANIMAL HOUSE, 1978
**NATIONAL LAMPOON'S EUROPEAN VACATION,
    1985**
NATIONAL LAMPOON'S VACATION, 1983
NATIVE SON, 1986
NATURAL, THE, 1984
NAVAJO JOE, 1967
NAVAJO RUN, 1966
NAVY VS. THE NIGHT MONSTERS, THE, 1966
NECROMANCY, 1972
NED KELLY, 1970
NEGATIVES, 1968
NELSON AFFAIR, THE, 1973
NERO'S MISTRESS, 1962
NEST OF THE CUCKOO BIRDS, THE, 1965
NETWORK, 1976
NEVADA SMITH, 1966
NEVER CRY WOLF, 1983
NEVER LET GO, 1960
NEVER SO FEW, 1959
NEVER STEAL ANYTHING SMALL, 1959
NEVERENDING STORY, THE, 1984
NEW INTERNS, THE, 1964
NEW LIFE, A, 1988
NEW ORLEANS AFTER DARK, 1958
NEW YORK CONFIDENTIAL, 1955
NEW YORK, NEW YORK, 1977
NEWSFRONT, 1979
NEXT ONE, THE, 1982
NEXT STOP, GREENWICH VILLAGE, 1976
NIAGARA, 1953

NICE GIRL LIKE ME, A, 1969
NICE GIRLS DON'T EXPLODE, 1987
NICHOLAS AND ALEXANDRA, 1971
NICKEL MOUNTAIN, 1985
NICKEL RIDE, THE, 1974
NICKELODEON, 1976
NIGHT AFTER NIGHT, 1932
NIGHT COMES TOO SOON, 1948
NIGHT CROSSING, 1982
NIGHT HAS A THOUSAND EYES, 1948
NIGHT HOLDS TERROR, THE, 1955
NIGHT INVADER, THE, 1943
NIGHT MAIL, 1935
'NIGHT, MOTHER, 1986
NIGHT MOVES, 1975
NIGHT OF DARK SHADOWS, 1971
NIGHT OF EVIL, 1962
NIGHT OF LUST, 1965
NIGHT OF THE ASKARI, 1978
NIGHT OF THE FULL MOON, THE, 1954
NIGHT OF THE LEPUS, 1972
NIGHT OF THE PROWLER, 1962
NIGHT OF THE QUARTER MOON, 1959
NIGHT OF THE SEAGULL, THE, 1970
NIGHT RIDE, 1937
NIGHT SHIFT, 1982
**NIGHT THE LIGHTS WENT OUT IN GEORGIA, THE,
    1981**
NIGHT THEY KILLED RASPUTIN, THE, 1962
NIGHT TIDE, 1963
NIGHT TRAIN FOR INVERNESS, 1960
NIGHT VISITOR, THE, 1970
NIGHT WALKER, THE, 1964
NIGHT WATCH, 1973
NIGHT WE GOT THE BIRD, THE, 1961
NIGHT WITHOUT PITY, 1962
NIGHT WITHOUT SLEEP, 1952
NIGHT WON'T TALK, THE, 1952
NIGHTMARE, 1942
NIGHTMARE, 1956
NIGHTMARE CASTLE, 1966
NIGHTS OF CABIRIA, 1957
NIGHTS OF PRAGUE, THE, 1968
NIGHTSONGS, 1984
NINE GIRLS, 1944
NINE HOURS TO RAMA, 1963
NINE MILES TO NOON, 1963
9/30/55, 1977
1918, 1985
1914, 1932
1919, 1984
1990: THE BRONX WARRIORS, 1983
1969, 1988
99 RIVER STREET, 1953
92 IN THE SHADE, 1975
NO DOWN PAYMENT, 1957
NO ESCAPE, 1934
NO ESCAPE, 1936
NO GREATER LOVE THAN THIS, 1969
NO LONGER ALONE, 1978
NO LOVE FOR JUDY, 1955
NO MAN IS AN ISLAND, 1962
NO MAN'S WOMAN, 1955
NO MORE LADIES, 1935
NO RETREAT, NO SURRENDER, 1986
NO ROSES FOR OSS 117, 1968
NO SAFETY AHEAD, 1959
NO SEX PLEASE—WE'RE BRITISH, 1979
NO SURVIVORS, PLEASE, 1963
NO TIME TO KILL, 1963
NO WAY BACK, 1949
NOBODY WAVED GOODBYE, 1965
NOBODY'S FOOL, 1986
NOBODY'S PERFEKT, 1981
NOCTURNE, 1946
NOMADIC LIVES, 1977
NONE BUT THE BRAVE, 1963
NORMAN...IS THAT YOU?, 1976
NORSEMAN, THE, 1978
NORTH SHORE, 1987
NORTH STAR, THE, 1982
NOT DAMAGED, 1930
NOT RECONCILED, OR ""ONLY VIOLENCE HELPS
    WHERE IT RULES'', 1969
NOTHING BUT THE BEST, 1964
NOTHING LASTS FOREVER, 1984

NOTORIOUS GENTLEMAN, 1945
NOTORIOUS MR. MONKS, THE, 1958
NUDE IN A WHITE CAR, 1960
NO. 96, 1974
NUMBER ONE, 1969
NUMBER ONE, 1984
NUN, THE, 1971
NUTTY, NAUGHTY CHATEAU, 1964
OBJECTIVE, BURMA!, 1945
OBJECTIVE 500 MILLION, 1966
OBSESSED, 1951
OBSESSED, 1988
OBSESSION, 1954
OBSESSION, 1968
OBSESSION, 1976
OCEAN DRIVE WEEKEND, 1986
OCTOPUSSY, 1983
ODD ANGRY SHOT, THE, 1979
ODDS AGAINST TOMORROW, 1959
ODESSA FILE, THE, 1974
OEDIPUS THE KING, 1968
OF FLESH AND BLOOD, 1964
OFF BEAT, 1986
OFF THE WALL, 1977
OFFERING, THE, 1966
OFFICE PICNIC, THE, 1974
**OH DAD, POOR DAD, MAMA'S HUNG YOU IN THE
    CLOSET AND I'M FEELIN' SO SAD, 1967**
O'HARA'S WIFE, 1983
OKLAHOMA WOMAN, THE, 1956
OLD DRACULA, 1975
OLD ENOUGH, 1984
OLD MAID, THE, 1939
OLIVER'S STORY, 1978
OMEGA MAN, THE, 1971
ON DANGEROUS GROUND, 1951
ON HER BED OF ROSES, 1966
ON HER MAJESTY'S SECRET SERVICE, 1969
ON THE AIR LIVE WITH CAPTAIN MIDNIGHT, 1979
ON THE BUSES, 1972
ON THE RIGHT TRACK, 1981
ON THE RUN, 1983
ONCE, 1974
ONCE A THIEF, 1965
ONCE BEFORE I DIE, 1967
ONCE IN PARIS, 1978
ONCE THERE WAS A GIRL, 1945
ONE AND ONLY, THE, 1978
ONE CRAZY SUMMER, 1986
ONE DARK NIGHT, 1983
1=2?, 1975
ONE-EYED SOLDIERS, 1967
ONE GIRL'S CONFESSION, 1953
$100 A NIGHT, 1968
ONE IS A LONELY NUMBER, 1972
ONE MAN, 1979
ONE NIGHT...A TRAIN, 1968
ONE POTATO, TWO POTATO, 1964
ONE STEP TO HELL, 1969
ONE SUMMER LOVE, 1976
1 2 3 MONSTER EXPRESS, 1977
ONE-WAY TICKET, A, 1988
ONIBABA, 1965
ONLY GAME IN TOWN, THE, 1970
ONLY ONCE IN A LIFETIME, 1979
ONLY ONE NIGHT, 1942
ONLY THING YOU KNOW, THE, 1971
ONLY TWO CAN PLAY, 1962
ONLY WAY HOME, THE, 1972
ONLY WHEN I LAUGH, 1981
ONLY YESTERDAY, 1933
OPENING NIGHT, 1977
OPERATION DAMES, 1959
OPERATION GANYMED, 1977
OPERATION THUNDERBOLT, 1978
OPERATION X, 1963
OPHELIA, 1964
OPIATE '67, 1967
ORCA, 1977
ORDEAL BY INNOCENCE, 1984
ORGANIZATION, THE, 1971
OSCAR WILDE, 1960
O.S.S., 1946
OSS 117—MISSION FOR A KILLER, 1966
OSSESSIONE, 1959
OTHELLO, 1955

OTHER ONE, THE, 1967
OTLEY, 1969
OUR BETTERS, 1933
OUR MISS FRED, 1972
OUR WINNING SEASON, 1978
OUT OF AFRICA, 1985
OUT OF ORDER, 1985
OUT OF SINGAPORE, 1932
OUT OF THE FOG, 1941
OUT OF THE PAST, 1947
OUTLAW: THE SAGE OF GISLI, 1982
OUTRAGE, 1950
OUTRAGE, THE, 1964
OUTSIDE IN, 1972
OUTSIDE MAN, THE, 1973
OUTSIDERS, THE, 1983
OUTWARD BOUND, 1930
OVER-EXPOSED, 1956
OVER THE HILL, 1931
OVER THE TOP, 1987
OVER 21, 1945
OVER-UNDER, SIDEWAYS-DOWN, 1977
OVERBOARD, 1987
OVERLANDERS, THE, 1946
OVERNIGHT, 1933
OVERTURE TO GLORY, 1940
OWL AND THE PUSSYCAT, THE, 1970
PACE THAT THRILLS, THE, 1952
PACIFIC LINER, 1939
PADRE PADRONE, 1977
PAID TO DANCE, 1937
PAID TO KILL, 1954
PAINT YOUR WAGON, 1969
PAISAN, 1948
PAL JOEY, 1957
PALACE OF NUDES, 1961
PALM SPRINGS WEEKEND, 1963
PANCHO VILLA, 1975
PANDEMONIUM, 1982
PANIC IN THE STREETS, 1950
PANIQUE, 1947
PAPER MOON, 1973
PAPER ORCHID, 1949
PAPERHOUSE, 1988
PARIS PICK-UP, 1963
PARKING, 1985
PARTNERS, 1976
PARTY GIRL, 1958
PARTY PARTY, 1983
PASSAGE TO INDIA, A, 1984
PASSENGER, THE, 1975
PASSION HOLIDAY, 1963
PASSION OF ANNA, THE, 1970
PASSION OF SLOW FIRE, THE, 1962
PASSION STREET, U.S.A., 1964
PASSIONATE SENTRY, THE, 1952
PASSIONATE STRANGERS, THE, 1968
PASSOVER PLOT, THE, 1976
PAT GARRETT AND BILLY THE KID, 1973
PATERNITY, 1981
PATHS OF GLORY, 1957
PATRIOT, THE, 1928
PATTON, 1970
PAWNBROKER, THE, 1965
PAY OR DIE, 1960
PEACE FOR A GUNFIGHTER, 1967
PEACH THIEF, THE, 1969
PEDESTRIAN, THE, 1974
PEGGY SUE GOT MARRIED, 1986
PEKING OPERA BLUES, 1986
PENALTY, THE, 1941
PEOPLE AGAINST O'HARA, THE, 1951
PEPE LE MOKO, 1937
PEPPERMINT SODA, 1979
PERFECT FRIDAY, 1970
PERFECT MATCH, THE, 1987
PERFORMERS, THE, 1970
PERMANENT VACATION, 1982
PERMISSION TO KILL, 1975
PERSECUTION, 1974
PERSECUTION AND ASSASSINATION OF
    JEAN-PAUL MARAT AS PERFORMED BY THE
    INMATES OF THE ASYLUM OF CHARENTON
    UNDER THE DIRECTION OF THE MARQUIS DE
    SADE, THE, 1967
PERSONAL AFFAIR, 1954

PERSONAL COLUMN, 1939
PERSONALS, THE, 1982
PETE KELLY'S BLUES, 1955
PETERSEN, 1974
PETULIA, 1968
PEYTON PLACE, 1957
PHAEDRA, 1962
PHANTOM LADY, 1944
PHANTOM LIGHT, THE, 1935
PHANTOM OF SOHO, THE, 1967
PHANTOM OF THE PARADISE, 1974
PHANTOM OF THE RUE MORGUE, 1954
PHAR LAP, 1984
PHENIX CITY STORY, THE, 1955
PHILADELPHIA EXPERIMENT, THE, 1984
PHOTOGRAPH, THE, 1987
PHYNX, THE, 1970
PICKUP ON 101, 1972
PICKUP ON SOUTH STREET, 1953
PICNIC ON THE GRASS, 1960
PICTURE OF DORIAN GRAY, THE, 1945
PIECE OF THE ACTION, A, 1977
PIECES OF DREAMS, 1970
PIED PIPER, THE, 1942
PIED PIPER, THE, 1972
PIGEON THAT TOOK ROME, THE, 1962
PIGS, 1984
PILGRIM, FAREWELL, 1980
PILGRIMAGE, 1972
PILOT, THE, 1979
PIPE DREAMS, 1976
PIRATE MOVIE, THE, 1982
PIRATES, 1986
PISTOL FOR RINGO, A, 1966
PIT AND THE PENDULUM, THE, 1961
PITFALL, 1948
PLACE CALLED GLORY, A, 1966
PLACE IN THE SUN, A, 1951
PLAGUE, 1978
PLAGUE OF THE ZOMBIES, THE, 1966
PLAINSMAN, THE, 1937
PLAINSONG, 1982
PLANET OF THE APES, 1968
PLANET OF THE VAMPIRES, 1965
PLANETS AGAINST US, THE, 1961
PLASTIC DOME OF NORMA JEAN, THE, 1966
PLAY DIRTY, 1969
PLAY IT AGAIN, SAM, 1972
PLAY IT COOL, 1970
PLAYBOY OF THE WESTERN WORLD, THE, 1963
PLAYING FOR KEEPS, 1986
PLAYTIME, 1963
PLEASE! MR. BALZAC, 1957
PLEASE, NOT NOW!, 1963
PLEASE STAND BY, 1972
PLEASE TURN OVER, 1960
PLEASURE GIRLS, THE, 1966
PLEASURE LOVERS, THE, 1964
PLEASURES AND VICES, 1962
PLEASURES OF THE FLESH, THE, 1965
POCOMANIA, 1939
POET'S SILENCE, THE, 1987
**POLICE ACADEMY 5: ASSIGNMENT MIAMI BEACH,
    1988**
POLICE ACADEMY 4: CITIZENS ON PATROL, 1987
POLICE PYTHON 357, 1976
POOR COW, 1968
POPE JOAN, 1972
POPPY IS ALSO A FLOWER, THE, 1966
PORK CHOP HILL, 1959
PORT OF CALL, 1963
PORT OF DESIRE, 1960
PORTRAIT OF A MOBSTER, 1961
PORTRAIT OF A SINNER, 1961
PORTRAIT OF MARIA, 1946
POSSE, 1975
POURQUOI PAS!, 1979
P.O.W., THE, 1973
POWER PLAY, 1978
PRAYING MANTIS, 1982
PRECIOUS JEWELS, 1969
PREHISTORIC WOMEN, 1950
PRELUDE TO ECSTASY, 1963
PREMATURE BURIAL, THE, 1962
PREMONITION, THE, 1976
PRESSURE, 1976

PRESSURE OF GUILT, 1964
PRESSURE POINT, 1962
PRETTY IN PINK, 1986
PRICE OF POWER, THE, 1969
PRIDE AND THE PASSION, THE, 1957
PRIDE OF THE MARINES, 1945
PRIEST OF ST. PAULI, THE, 1970
PRIME OF MISS JEAN BRODIE, THE, 1969
PRIME RISK, 1985
PRIMROSE PATH, 1940
PRINCE OF FOXES, 1949
PRINCE OF PLAYERS, 1955
PRISM, 1971
PRISON SHIP, 1945
PRISONER, THE, 1955
PRISONER OF CORBAL, 1939
PRISONER OF THE VOLGA, 1960
PRISONER OF WAR, 1954
PRIVATE FILES OF J. EDGAR HOOVER, THE, 1978
PRIVATE HELL 36, 1954
PRIVATE LIFE OF SHERLOCK HOLMES, THE, 1970
PRIVATE LIVES OF ADAM AND EVE, THE, 1961
PRIVATE POOLEY, 1962
PRIZE, THE, 1963
PRIZE FIGHTER, THE, 1979
PRODIGAL SON, THE, 1964
PROLOGUE, 1970
PROMISES IN THE DARK, 1979
PROPHECIES OF NOSTRADAMUS, 1974
PROSTITUTION, 1965
PROUD RIDER, THE, 1971
PSYCHE 59, 1964
PUBLIC AFFAIR, A, 1962
PUBLIC DEB NO. 1, 1940
PUBLIC MENACE, 1935
PUBLIC STENOGRAPHER, 1935
PULSE, 1988
PUNCHLINE, 1988
PURE HELL OF ST. TRINIAN'S, THE, 1961
PURPLE ROSE OF CAIRO, THE, 1985
PURSUIT OF D.B. COOPER, THE, 1981
PURSUIT OF HAPPINESS, THE, 1934
QUARTET, 1949
QUARTET, 1981
QUATERMASS CONCLUSION, 1980
QUEEN BEE, 1955
QUEEN OF BURLESQUE, 1946
QUEEN OF SHEBA, 1953
QUEEN OF SPADES, 1961
QUEEN OF THE MOB, 1940
QUEEN OF THE NILE, 1964
QUEEN OF THE PIRATES, 1961
QUEEN'S GUARDS, THE, 1963
QUEST FOR LOVE, 1971
QUESTION OF ADULTERY, A, 1959
QUESTION OF SUSPENSE, A, 1961
QUESTION 7, 1961
QUICK, LET'S GET MARRIED, 1965
QUICK MILLIONS, 1931
QUICKSAND, 1950
QUIET DAY IN BELFAST, A, 1974
QUILLER MEMORANDUM, THE, 1966
QUO VADIS, 1951
RACE STREET, 1948
RACE WITH THE DEVIL, 1975
RACING FEVER, 1964
RACING WITH THE MOON, 1984
RACKET, THE, 1951
RADIO ON, 1980
RAGE, 1966
RAGE, 1972
RAGE IN HEAVEN, 1941
RAGE TO LIVE, A, 1965
RAGGEDY MAN, 1981
RAGMAN'S DAUGHTER, THE, 1974
RAGTIME, 1981
RAID ON ROMMEL, 1971
RAILROADED, 1947
RAIN FOR A DUSTY SUMMER, 1971
RAINBOW, THE, 1944
RAINTREE COUNTY, 1957
RAISING ARIZONA, 1987
RALLY 'ROUND THE FLAG, BOYS!, 1958
RANCHO DELUXE, 1975
RAPTURE, 1965

BOLD: Films on Videocassette

RASPOUTINE, 1954
RASPUTIN AND THE EMPRESS, 1932
RASPUTIN—THE MAD MONK, 1966
RAT FINK, 1965
RATBOY, 1986
RATTLE OF A SIMPLE MAN, 1964
RATTLERS, 1976
RAVEN, THE, 1963
RAZOR'S EDGE, THE, 1946
REAL GENIUS, 1985
REAL LIFE, 1979
REAL LIFE, 1984
REAR WINDOW, 1954
REBECCA, 1940
REBEL ANGEL, 1962
REBELLION, 1967
REBELLION OF THE HANGED, THE, 1954
RED, 1970
RED BADGE OF COURAGE, THE, 1951
RED DUST, 1932
RED LANTERNS, 1965
RED LINE 7000, 1965
RED MONARCH, 1983
RED SKY AT MORNING, 1971
RED, WHITE AND BLACK, THE, 1970
REFLECTION OF FEAR, A, 1973
REFLECTIONS, 1984
REINCARNATE, THE, 1971
REIVERS, THE, 1969
REMBETIKO, 1985
REMO WILLIAMS: THE ADVENTURE BEGINS, 1985
REMOTE CONTROL, 1988
REMOVALISTS, THE, 1975
RENT-A-COP, 1988
RENT CONTROL, 1981
REPENTANCE, 1988
REPORT TO THE COMMISSIONER, 1975
REPTILE, THE, 1966
REQUIEM FOR A HEAVYWEIGHT, 1962
REST IS SILENCE, THE, 1960
RESTLESS NIGHT, THE, 1964
RESURRECTION, 1980
RETURN, THE, 1980
RETURN OF A MAN CALLED HORSE, THE, 1976
RETURN OF A STRANGER, 1962
RETURN OF CAPTAIN INVINCIBLE, THE, 1983
RETURN OF COUNT YORGA, THE, 1971
RETURN OF DR. MABUSE, THE, 1961
RETURN OF DR. X, THE, 1939
RETURN OF DRACULA, THE, 1958
RETURN OF JOSEY WALES, THE, 1987
RETURN OF MARTIN GUERRE, THE, 1983
RETURN OF SABATA, 1972
RETURN OF THE BADMEN, 1948
RETURN OF THE SOLDIER, THE, 1983
RETURN OF THE TERROR, 1934
RETURN TO CAMPUS, 1975
RETURN TO OZ, 1985
RETURN TO WATERLOO, 1985
REVENGE OF FRANKENSTEIN, THE, 1958
REVENGE OF THE NERDS II: NERDS IN PARADISE, 1987
REVENGE OF THE TEENAGE VIXENS FROM OUTER SPACE, THE, 1986
REVOLT OF THE SLAVES, THE, 1961
REVOLT OF THE ZOMBIES, 1936
REVOLUTION, 1985
RHINESTONE, 1984
RICH AND STRANGE, 1932
RICH KIDS, 1979
RICHARD, 1972
RICOCHET, 1966
RIDDLE OF THE SANDS, THE, 1984
RIDE A CROOKED MILE, 1938
RIDE A VIOLENT MILE, 1957
RIDE BACK, THE, 1957
RIDE CLEAR OF DIABLO, 1954
RIDE IN THE WHIRLWIND, 1966
RIDE LONESOME, 1959
RIDE OUT FOR REVENGE, 1957
RIDE THE HIGH COUNTRY, 1962
RIDE THE MAN DOWN, 1952
RIDE THE PINK HORSE, 1947
RIDER IN THE NIGHT, THE, 1968
RIDER ON A DEAD HORSE, 1962
RIDER ON THE RAIN, 1970

RIGHT HAND OF THE DEVIL, THE, 1963
RIGHT TO LOVE, THE, 1931
RIO 70, 1970
RIOT IN CELL BLOCK 11, 1954
RIOT IN JUVENILE PRISON, 1959
RIOT ON SUNSET STRIP, 1967
RISE AND FALL OF LEGS DIAMOND, THE, 1960
RISE AND RISE OF MICHAEL RIMMER, THE, 1970
RISING DAMP, 1980
RITA, 1963
RIVER'S EDGE, THE, 1957
ROAD GANG, 1936
ROAD HOUSE, 1948
ROAD HUSTLERS, THE, 1968
ROAD TO FORT ALAMO, THE, 1966
ROADHOUSE 66, 1984
ROARING TWENTIES, THE, 1939
ROBIN HOOD OF EL DORADO, 1936
ROCCO AND HIS BROTHERS, 1961
ROCK 'N' ROLL HIGH SCHOOL, 1979
ROCKY IV, 1985
ROGUE COP, 1954
ROLLER BOOGIE, 1979
ROMAN SPRING OF MRS. STONE, THE, 1961
ROMANCE IN RHYTHM, 1934
ROMEO AND JULIET, 1936
ROMEO AND JULIET, 1968
ROOM UPSTAIRS, THE, 1948
ROOM WITH A VIEW, A, 1986
ROOTS OF HEAVEN, THE, 1958
ROSEBUD, 1975
ROSELAND, 1977
ROSEMARY, 1960
ROTTEN TO THE CORE, 1956
ROUGE OF THE NORTH, 1988
ROUGH CUT, 1980
'ROUND MIDNIGHT, 1986
ROUND TRIP, 1967
ROVER, THE, 1967
ROWDYMAN, THE, 1973
ROWING WITH THE WIND, 1988
R.P.M., 1970
RUBBER GUN, THE, 1977
RUBY, 1971
RUCKUS, 1981
RULES OF THE GAME, THE, 1939
RUN FOR THE ROSES, 1978
RUN FOR YOUR WIFE, 1966
RUN HOME SLOW, 1965
RUN LIKE A THIEF, 1968
RUNAWAY GIRL, 1966
RUNNER STUMBLES, THE, 1979
RUNNING, 1979
RUNNING BRAVE, 1983
RUNNING ON EMPTY, 1988
RUSSIAN ROULETTE, 1975
RUSTLER'S RHAPSODY, 1985
RUTHLESS FOUR, THE, 1969
SABATA, 1969
SABRA, 1970
SACCO AND VANZETTI, 1971
SACRED GROUND, 1984
SACRIFICE, THE, 1986
SAHARA, 1984
SALLAH, 1965
SALLY OF THE SUBWAY, 1932
SALLY'S HOUNDS, 1968
SALOME, 1953
SALOME, WHERE SHE DANCED, 1945
SALOON BAR, 1940
SALSA, 1988
SALT & PEPPER, 1968
SALT OF THE EARTH, 1954
SALUTE TO THE MARINES, 1943
SALZBURG CONNECTION, THE, 1972
SAMAR, 1962
SAMMY STOPS THE WORLD, 1978
SAMSON AND DELILAH, 1949
SAMURAI FROM NOWHERE, 1964
SAN ANTONE, 1953
SAN DEMETRIO, LONDON, 1947
SAN QUENTIN, 1937
SANDS OF IWO JIMA, 1949
SANGAREE, 1953
SANJURO, 1962
SANTA FE STAMPEDE, 1938

SANTA FE TRAIL, 1940
SANTO CONTRA EL CEREBRO DIABOLICO, 1962
SARDINIA: RANSOM, 1968
SATAN NEVER SLEEPS, 1962
SATIN MUSHROOM, THE, 1969
SATURDAY NIGHT AT THE PALACE, 1988
SATURDAY NIGHT IN APPLE VALLEY, 1965
SATURN 3, 1980
SAVAGE GOLD, 1933
SAVAGE IS LOOSE, THE, 1974
SAVAGE PAMPAS, 1967
SAVAGE, THE, 1975
SAY HELLO TO YESTERDAY, 1971
SAY ONE FOR ME, 1959
SAYONARA, 1957
SCANDAL SHEET, 1952
SCANDALOUS, 1984
SCANDALOUS ADVENTURES OF BURAIKAN, THE, 1970
SCARECROW, THE, 1982
SCARECROW IN A GARDEN OF CUCUMBERS, 1972
SCARLET CAMELLIA, THE, 1965
SCARLET EMPRESS, THE, 1934
SCARLET STREET, 1945
SCAVENGER HUNT, 1979
SCAVENGERS, 1988
SCORPIO, 1973
SCOTT JOPLIN, 1977
SCOUNDREL, THE, 1935
SCREAM OF FEAR, 1961
SCROOGED, 1988
SEA WOLF, THE, 1941
SEANCE ON A WET AFTERNOON, 1964
SEARCH AND DESTROY, 1981
SEARCHERS, THE, 1956
SEASON OF PASSION, 1961
SECOND COMING OF SUZANNE, THE, 1974
SECOND HONEYMOON, 1937
SECOND THOUGHTS, 1983
SECOND TIME LUCKY, 1984
SECOND WIND, A, 1978
SECONDS, 1966
SECRET ADMIRER, 1985
SECRET AGENT, THE, 1936
SECRET BEYOND THE DOOR, THE, 1948
SECRET HEART, THE, 1946
SECRET HONOR, 1984
SECRET OF DEEP HARBOR, 1961
SECRET PLACES, 1984
SECRET SIX, THE, 1931
SECRET WORLD, 1969
SECRETS D'ALCOVE, 1954
SECRETS OF A MODEL, 1940
SECRETS OF WOMEN, 1961
SEDUCED AND ABANDONED, 1964
SEDUCERS, THE, 1962
SEDUCTION BY THE SEA, 1967
SEE NO EVIL, 1971
SEIZURE, 1974
SELL OUT, THE, 1976
SEMINOLE, 1953
SENSE OF FREEDOM, A, 1985
SERGEANT RUTLEDGE, 1960
SERVANT, THE, 1964
SET-UP, THE, 1949
SEVEN DAYS IN MAY, 1964
SEVEN DAYS TO NOON, 1950
SEVEN FOOTPRINTS TO SATAN, 1929
711 OCEAN DRIVE, 1950
SEVEN MINUTES IN HEAVEN, 1986
SEVEN NIGHTS IN JAPAN, 1976
SEVEN-PER-CENT SOLUTION, THE, 1977
SEVEN REVENGES, THE, 1967
SEVEN SAMURAI, THE, 1956
SEVEN UPS, THE, 1973
SEVEN WOMEN, 1966
SEVENTH CROSS, THE, 1944
SEVENTH SEAL, THE, 1958
SEVENTH SIGN, THE, 1988
SEX AND THE SINGLE GIRL, 1964
SEXTETTE, 1978
SHADEY, 1987
SHADOW OF A DOUBT, 1943
SHAKE HANDS WITH THE DEVIL, 1959
SHAKEDOWN, 1950
SHAKEDOWN, THE, 1960

SHAMUS, 1973
SHANE, 1953
SHANGHAI GESTURE, THE, 1941
SHANGHAI SURPRISE, 1986
SHARK, 1970
SHE BEAST, THE, 1966
SHE DONE HIM WRONG, 1933
SHE KNOWS Y'KNOW, 1962
SHE MAN, THE, 1967
SHE PLAYED WITH FIRE, 1957
SHEBA BABY, 1975
SHELL SHOCK, 1964
SHENANDOAH, 1965
SHIP OF FOOLS, 1965
SHIRALEE, THE, 1957
SHIVERS, 1984
SHOCK, 1934
SHOCKPROOF, 1949
SHOESHINE, 1947
SHOOT OUT, 1971
SHOOT OUT AT BIG SAG, 1962
SHOOT THE PIANO PLAYER, 1962
SHOOT TO KILL, 1947
SHOP ANGEL, 1932
SHORT GRASS, 1950
SHOT AT DAWN, A, 1934
SHOT IN THE DARK, A, 1935
SHOT IN THE DARK, THE, 1941
SHOULD A DOCTOR TELL?, 1931
SHOUT AT THE DEVIL, 1976
SHOW GOES ON, THE, 1938
SHOW THEM NO MERCY, 1935
SHRIKE, THE, 1955
SIAVASH IN PERSEPOLIS, 1966
SIDDHARTHA, 1972
SIDE STREET, 1950
SIDESHOW, 1950
SIDEWINDER ONE, 1977
SIEGE AT RED RIVER, THE, 1954
SIEGE OF SYRACUSE, 1962
SIERRA STRANGER, 1957
SIGN OF FOUR, THE, 1932
SIGN OF FOUR, THE, 1983
SIGN OF THE GLADIATOR, 1959
SIGN OF THE PAGAN, 1954
SIGN OF VENUS, THE, 1955
SILENCE OF DR. EVANS, THE, 1973
SILENCE OF THE NORTH, 1981
SILENT ENEMY, THE, 1930
SILENT ENEMY, THE, 1959
SILENT PARTNER, 1944
SILENT RAIDERS, 1954
SILENT RUNNING, 1972
SILENT WITNESS, THE, 1932
SILHOUETTES, 1982
SILVER BEARS, 1978
SILVER BULLET, THE, 1942
SILVER CITY, 1951
SILVER CITY, 1985
SILVER DREAM RACER, 1982
SILVER DUST, 1953
SILVER STREAK, 1976
SILVERADO, 1985
SIMCHON FAMILY, THE, 1969
SIN OF MADELON CLAUDET, THE, 1931
SINAI COMMANDOS: THE STORY OF THE SIX DAY
	WAR, 1968
SING AND SWING, 1964
SING, BOY, SING, 1958
SING SING NIGHTS, 1935
SING SINNER, SING, 1933
SINGAPORE, SINGAPORE, 1969
SINGER AND THE DANCER, THE, 1977
SINGING BLACKSMITH, 1938
SINISTER MAN, THE, 1965
SINNER TAKE ALL, 1936
SINNERS IN PARADISE, 1938
SINNERS IN THE SUN, 1932
SINS OF JEZEBEL, 1953
SINS OF THE FATHERS, 1948
SISTERS UNDER THE SKIN, 1934
SISTERS, THE, 1969
SITTING BULL, 1954
SITTING DUCKS, 1979
SIX HOURS TO LIVE, 1932
SIX PACK, 1982

6000 ENEMIES, 1939
SIX WEEKS, 1982
SIXTH AND MAIN, 1977
SKATEBOARD, 1978
SKELETON ON HORSEBACK, 1940
SKI BATTALION, 1938
SKI FEVER, 1969
SKI TROOP ATTACK, 1960
SKIDOO, 1968
SKIN DEEP, 1929
SKIN GAME, 1971
SKIN GAME, THE, 1931
SKIP TRACER, THE, 1979
SKULLDUGGERY, 1970
SKY ABOVE HEAVEN, 1964
SKY PIRATE, THE, 1970
SKY RIDERS, 1976
SKYDIVERS, THE, 1963
SKYLINE, 1984
SLATTERY'S HURRICANE, 1949
SLEEPING CITY, THE, 1950
SLEEPING DOGS, 1977
SLEEPING TIGER, THE, 1954
SLENDER THREAD, THE, 1965
SLIGHTLY SCARLET, 1956
SLITHER, 1973
SLITHIS, 1978
SLOGAN, 1970
SLOW DANCING IN THE BIG CITY, 1978
SMALL CHANGE, 1976
SMALL TOWN IN TEXAS, A, 1976
SMALL WORLD OF SAMMY LEE, THE, 1963
SMASH-UP, THE STORY OF A WOMAN, 1947
SMASHING TIME, 1967
SMILE ORANGE, 1976
SMOKE IN THE WIND, 1975
SMOKEY BITES THE DUST, 1981
SMORGASBORD, 1983
SMUGGLERS, THE, 1969
SNAKE PIT, THE, 1948
SNAKE WOMAN, THE, 1961
SNOW IN THE SOUTH SEAS, 1963
SNOWS OF KILIMANJARO, THE, 1952
SO DARK THE NIGHT, 1946
SO EVIL MY LOVE, 1948
SODOM AND GOMORRAH, 1962
SOGGY BOTTOM U.S.A., 1982
SOL MADRID, 1968
SOLARIS, 1972
SOLDIER AND THE LADY, THE, 1937
SOLDIER IN THE RAIN, 1963
SOLDIER OF FORTUNE, 1955
SOLDIER'S PRAYER, A, 1970
SOLDIER'S REVENGE, 1986
SOLDIER'S STORY, A, 1984
SOLOMON AND SHEBA, 1959
SOME CAME RUNNING, 1959
SOME GIRLS DO, 1969
SOME KIND OF A NUT, 1969
SOME KIND OF WONDERFUL, 1987
SOME LIKE IT HOT, 1959
SOMEBODY UP THERE LIKES ME, 1956
SOMEONE BEHIND THE DOOR, 1971
SOMETHING SPECIAL!, 1987
SOMETHING WICKED THIS WAY COMES, 1983
SOMETHING'S ROTTEN, 1979
SOMEWHERE IN THE NIGHT, 1946
SOMEWHERE IN TIME, 1980
SON OF DRACULA, 1943
SON OF DRACULA, 1974
SON OF FRANKENSTEIN, 1939
SON OF GODZILLA, 1967
SONG AT EVENTIDE, 1934
SONS AND LOVERS, 1960
SONS OF SATAN, 1969
SOPHIE'S PLACE, 1970
SORCERERS, THE, 1967
SORORITY GIRL, 1957
SORRY, WRONG NUMBER, 1948
SOUL MAN, 1986
SOUND OF FURY, THE, 1950
SOUND OF HORROR, 1966
SOUTHERN STAR, THE, 1969
SOYLENT GREEN, 1973
SPACE RAIDERS, 1983
SPACEBALLS, 1987

SPACEHUNTER: ADVENTURES IN THE
	FORBIDDEN ZONE, 1983
SPARTACUS, 1960
SPECIAL DAY, A, 1977
SPECIAL DELIVERY, 1976
SPECTER OF THE ROSE, 1946
SPEED CRAZY, 1959
SPENCER'S MOUNTAIN, 1963
SPHINX, 1981
SPIES LIKE US, 1985
SPIKE OF BENSONHURST, 1988
SPIKES GANG, THE, 1974
SPIRAL STAIRCASE, THE, 1946
SPIRIT OF THE BEEHIVE, THE, 1976
SPIRIT OF THE WIND, 1979
SPIRITISM, 1965
SPLENDOR IN THE GRASS, 1961
SPLITTING UP, 1981
SPOILERS, THE, 1955
SPRING FEVER, 1983
SPY WHO LOVED ME, THE, 1977
S*P*Y*S, 1974
SQUADRON 633, 1964
SQUAMISH FIVE, THE, 1988
SQUARE DANCE, 1987
SQUARE ROOT OF ZERO, THE, 1964
SQUIRM, 1976
SSSSSSSS, 1973
STACY'S KNIGHTS, 1983
STAGE STRUCK, 1948
STAGECOACH, 1939
STAKEOUT ON DOPE STREET, 1958
STALAG 17, 1953
STALKER, 1982
STAMMHEIM, 1986
STAND BY ME, 1986
STAND UP AND BE COUNTED, 1972
STAR IS BORN, A, 1937
STAR OF MY NIGHT, 1954
STARCHASER: THE LEGEND OF ORIN, 1985
STARCRASH, 1979
STARDUST MEMORIES, 1980
STARK FEAR, 1963
STARMAN, 1984
STARSTRUCK, 1982
STATE OF SIEGE, 1973
STATE STREET SADIE, 1928
STATION SIX-SAHARA, 1964
STAVISKY, 1974
STAYING ALIVE, 1983
STEALING HOME, 1988
STEEL, 1980
STEEL ARENA, 1973
STEEL HELMET, THE, 1951
STEELYARD BLUES, 1973
STERILE CUCKOO, THE, 1969
STICKY FINGERS, 1988
STING OF DEATH, 1966
STING II, THE, 1983
STING, THE, 1973
STINGRAY, 1978
STONE BOY, THE, 1984
STONY ISLAND, 1978
STOOLIE, THE, 1972
STOP ME BEFORE I KILL!, 1961
STORMS OF AUGUST, THE, 1988
STORY OF ESTHER COSTELLO, THE, 1957
STORY OF FAUSTA, THE, 1988
STORY ON PAGE ONE, THE, 1959
STRANGE BREW, 1983
STRANGE CARGO, 1940
STRANGE INTERLUDE, 1932
STRANGE LOVE OF MARTHA IVERS, THE, 1946
STRANGE VENGEANCE OF ROSALIE, THE, 1972
STRANGE WOMAN, THE, 1946
STRANGER IN TOWN, A, 1968
STRANGER KNOCKS, A, 1963
STRANGER ON THE THIRD FLOOR, 1940
STRANGER'S GUNDOWN, THE, 1974
STRANGER, THE, 1946
STRANGERS IN THE HOUSE, 1949
STRANGERS KISS, 1984
STRANGERS WHEN WE MEET, 1960
STRANGLER, THE, 1941
STRANGLER, THE, 1964
STRANGLERS OF BOMBAY, THE, 1960

BOLD: Films on Videocassette

STRAWBERRY STATEMENT, THE, 1970
STREET CORNER, 1948
STREET IS MY BEAT, THE, 1966
STREET SCENE, 1931
STREETS OF FIRE, 1984
STREETS OF GOLD, 1986
STRICTLY FOR THE BIRDS, 1963
STRIP, THE, 1951
STROKER ACE, 1983
STUCKEY'S LAST STAND, 1980
STUFF, THE, 1985
SUBJECT WAS ROSES, THE, 1968
SUBTERRANEANS, THE, 1960
SUBVERSIVES, THE, 1967
SUBWAY IN THE SKY, 1959
SUDDEN FURY, 1975
SUDDENLY, 1954
SUGAR CANE ALLEY, 1984
SUGAR HILL, 1974
SUGARLAND EXPRESS, THE, 1974
SUICIDE CLUB, THE, 1988
SUICIDE LEGION, 1940
SUICIDE MISSION, 1956
SUITOR, THE, 1963
SULLIVAN'S TRAVELS, 1941
SUMMER CAMP NIGHTMARE, 1987
SUMMER PLACE, A, 1959
SUMMER RENTAL, 1985
SUMMER SCHOOL, 1987
SUMMER SCHOOL TEACHERS, 1977
SUMMER SOLDIERS, 1972
SUMMER STORM, 1944
SUMMERSKIN, 1962
SUMMERSPELL, 1983
SUMMERTIME KILLER, 1973
SUN ABOVE, DEATH BELOW, 1969
SUN ALSO RISES, THE, 1957
SUNBURN, 1979
SUNDAY IN NEW YORK, 1963
SUNDAY TOO FAR AWAY, 1975
SUNDAYS AND CYBELE, 1962
SUNDOWN, 1941
SUNSET, 1988
SUNSET MURDER CASE, 1941
SUPER FUZZ, 1981
SUPER VAN, 1977
SUPERGIRL, 1984
SUPERMAN IV: THE QUEST FOR PEACE, 1987
SUPREME KID, THE, 1976
SURE THING, THE, 1985
SURGEON'S KNIFE, THE, 1957
SURPRISE PACKAGE, 1960
SURPRISE PARTY, 1985
SURRENDER, 1950
SURRENDER—HELL!, 1959
SURVIVAL, 1976
SUSAN LENOX—HER FALL AND RISE, 1931
SUSAN SLADE, 1961
SUSAN SLEPT HERE, 1954
SUSPECT, THE, 1944
SUSPENSE, 1930
SUZANNE, 1980
SUZY, 1936
SVENGALI, 1955
SWAMP THING, 1982
SWARM, THE, 1978
SWEDISH WEDDING NIGHT, 1965
SWEET ECSTASY, 1962
SWEET HUNTERS, 1969
SWEET LORRAINE, 1987
SWEET LOVE, BITTER, 1967
SWEET RIDE, THE, 1968
SWEET SUBSTITUTE, 1964
SWIMMER, THE, 1968
SWISS CONSPIRACY, THE, 1976
SWITCH, THE, 1963
SWORD IN THE DESERT, 1949
SWORD OF THE CONQUEROR, 1962
SWORD OF THE VALIANT, 1984
SWORDKILL, 1984
SYMPHONIE PASTORALE, 1948
SYNANON, 1965
T-BIRD GANG, 1959
T-MEN, 1947
TABLE FOR FIVE, 1983
TAFFIN, 1988

T.A.G.: THE ASSASSINATION GAME, 1982
TAGGART, 1964
TAKE A HARD RIDE, 1975
TAKE DOWN, 1979
TAKE ONE FALSE STEP, 1949
TAKE THE MONEY AND RUN, 1969
TAKE, THE, 1974
TALE OF RUBY ROSE, THE, 1987
TALES FROM THE CRYPT, 1972
TALES OF A SALESMAN, 1965
TALES OF TERROR, 1962
TALES OF THE UNCANNY, 1932
TALISMAN, THE, 1966
TALL BLOND MAN WITH ONE BLACK SHOE, THE, 1973
TALL STORY, 1960
TAMAHINE, 1964
TAMANGO, 1959
TAMARIND SEED, THE, 1974
TANK, 1984
TAP ROOTS, 1948
TAPS, 1981
TARGET: HARRY, 1980
TARNISHED ANGELS, THE, 1957
TAROT, 1987
TATSU, 1962
TATTERED DRESS, THE, 1957
TEACHER, THE, 1974
TEEN-AGE CRIME WAVE, 1955
TEENAGE ZOMBIES, 1960
TELEPHONE, THE, 1988
TELL THEM WILLIE BOY IS HERE, 1969
TEMPEST, 1932
TEMPEST, 1958
TEMPORARY WIDOW, THE, 1930
TEMPTATION, 1962
TEMPTRESS AND THE MONK, THE, 1963
TEN LITTLE INDIANS, 1975
TENDER IS THE NIGHT, 1961
TENDER SCOUNDREL, 1967
TENNESSEE'S PARTNER, 1955
TENTACLES, 1977
TERM OF TRIAL, 1962
TERMINAL MAN, THE, 1974
TERROR, THE, 1963
TERROR AFTER MIDNIGHT, 1965
TERROR AT BLACK FALLS, 1962
TERROR BENEATH THE SEA, 1966
TERROR FROM UNDER THE HOUSE, 1971
TERROR HOUSE, 1942
TERROR IN THE WAX MUSEUM, 1973
TERROR IS A MAN, 1959
TERROR OF DR. MABUSE, THE, 1965
TERRORISTS, THE, 1975
TEST OF PILOT PIRX, THE, 1978
TESTAMENT, 1988
TESTAMENT OF DR. MABUSE, THE, 1943
TESTAMENT OF ORPHEUS, THE, 1962
THANK GOD IT'S FRIDAY, 1978
THANK YOU ALL VERY MUCH, 1969
THANOS AND DESPINA, 1970
THAT FUNNY FEELING, 1965
THAT KIND OF WOMAN, 1959
THAT LADY, 1955
THAT TOUCH OF MINK, 1962
THAT'S LIFE, 1986
THAT'S THE WAY OF THE WORLD, 1975
THAT'LL BE THE DAY, 1974
THEM!, 1954
THERE GOES THE BRIDE, 1980
THERE WAS A CROOKED MAN, 1970
THERE'S A GIRL IN MY SOUP, 1970
THERE'S ALWAYS VANILLA, 1972
THERESE, 1986
THESE ARE THE DAMNED, 1965
THESE THREE, 1936
THESE WILDER YEARS, 1956
THEY CALL ME BRUCE, 1982
THEY CALL ME MISTER TIBBS, 1970
THEY DRIVE BY NIGHT, 1938
THEY KNEW WHAT THEY WANTED, 1940
THEY LIVE BY NIGHT, 1949
THEY ONLY KILL THEIR MASTERS, 1972

THEY SAVED HITLER'S BRAIN, 1964
THEY WENT THAT-A-WAY AND THAT-A-WAY, 1978
THEY WON'T BELIEVE ME, l947
THEY WON'T FORGET, 1937
THIEF, THE, 1952
THIEVES' HIGHWAY, 1949
THIEVES LIKE US, 1974
THIN MAN, THE, 1967
THING, THE, 1951
THING THAT COULDN'T DIE, THE, 1958
THING WITH TWO HEADS, THE, 1972
THINGS CHANGE, 1988
THINGS OF LIFE, THE, 1970
THINGS TO COME, 1936
THIRD DAY, THE, 1965
THIRD MAN, THE, 1950
THIRD OF A MAN, 1962
THIRD SECRET, THE, 1964
THIRD WALKER, THE, 1978
THIRTEEN FIGHTING MEN, 1960
THIRTEEN WOMEN, 1932
THIRTEENTH LETTER, THE, 1951
THIRTY NINE STEPS, THE, 1960
THIRTY NINE STEPS, THE, 1978
36 HOURS, 1965
THIS ANGRY AGE, 1958
THIS IS A HIJACK, 1973
THIS LOVE OF OURS, 1945
THIS MAD WORLD, 1930
THIS MADDING CROWD, 1964
THIS SIDE OF THE LAW, 1950
THIS THING CALLED LOVE, 1929
THIS WAS PARIS, 1942
THOMAS CROWN AFFAIR, THE, 1968
THOROUGHBRED, 1936
THOSE DIRTY DOGS, 1974
THOSE HIGH GREY WALLS, 1939
THOSE WE LOVE, 1932
THREE, 1967
THREE AMIGOS, 1986
THREE BAD SISTERS, 1956
THREE BLONDES IN HIS LIFE, 1961
THREE BROTHERS, 1982
THREE CAME TO KILL, 1960
THREE CARD MONTE, 1978
THREE COINS IN THE FOUNTAIN, 1954
THREE DAYS OF VIKTOR TSCHERNIKOFF, 1968
THREE DOLLS FROM HONG KONG, 1966
THREE FABLES OF LOVE, 1963
THREE FACES OF A WOMAN, 1965
THREE FOR THE ROAD, 1987
300 YEAR WEEKEND, 1971
THREE MEN AND A CRADLE, 1985
THREE MUSKETEERS, THE, 1948
THREE MUSKETEERS, THE, 1974
THREE O'CLOCK HIGH, 1987
THREE ON A MATCH, 1932
THREE SISTERS, THE, 1969
THREE SISTERS, 1974
THREE STOOGES VS. THE WONDER WOMEN, 1975
THREE TOUGH GUYS, 1974
THREE WOMEN, 1977
THRESHOLD, 1983
THRILL OF YOUTH, 1932
THUNDER AND LIGHTNING, 1977
THUNDER IN THE BLOOD, 1962
THUNDER ROAD, 1958
THUNDER RUN, 1986
THX 1138, 1971
THY NEIGHBOR'S WIFE, 1953
TI-CUL TOUGAS, 1977
TICKET TO HEAVEN, 1981
TIGER BY THE TAIL, 1970
TIGER WALKS, A, 1964
TILL TOMORROW COMES, 1962
TILT, 1979
TIM, 1981
TIME AND THE TOUCH, THE, 1962
TIME FOR DYING, A, 1971
TIME LIMIT, 1957
TIME OF DESTINY, A, 1988
TIME OF ROSES, 1970
TIME OF THE HEATHEN, 1962
TIME SLIP, 1981
TIME TO DIE, A, 1985
TIME WITHOUT PITY, 1957

TIMERIDER, 1983
TIMES GONE BY, 1953
TINGLER, THE, 1959
TITLE SHOT, 1982
TO BE OR NOT TO BE, 1983
TO BEGIN AGAIN, 1982
TO CATCH A THIEF, 1955
TO COMMIT A MURDER, 1970
TO KILL A MOCKINGBIRD, 1962
TO KILL OR TO DIE, 1973
TODAY IT'S ME...TOMORROW YOU?, 1968
TODAY WE LIVE, 1933
TOGETHER BROTHERS, 1974
TOGETHER FOR DAYS, 1972
TOMB OF LIGEIA, THE, 1965
TOMMY, 1975
TOMORROW, 1972
TOMORROW IS MY TURN, 1962
TOMORROW WE LIVE, 1936
TONI, 1968
TONIGHT A TOWN DIES, 1961
TONIGHT THE SKIRTS FLY, 1956
TONIO KROGER, 1968
TONY ROME, 1967
TOO BAD SHE'S BAD, 1954
TOO HOT TO HANDLE, 1961
TOO LATE BLUES, 1962
TOO LATE THE HERO, 1970
TOO MUCH, TOO SOON, 1958
TOO SOON TO LOVE, 1960
TOO YOUNG TO LOVE, 1960
TOOTSIE, 1982
TOP SECRET!, 1984
TOPAZ, 1969
TOPAZE, 1933
TORA-SAN PART 2, 1970
TORA! TORA! TORA!, 1970
TORMENTED, 1960
TORN CURTAIN, 1966
TORPEDO BAY, 1964
TORPEDOED, 1939
TORSO MURDER MYSTERY, THE, 1940
TOUCH AND GO, 1980
TOUCH ME NOT, 1974
TOUCH OF CLASS, A, 1973
TOUCH OF EVIL, 1958
TOUCH OF FLESH, THE, 1960
TOUCHED, 1983
TOUGH ENOUGH, 1983
TOUGH GUYS, 1986
TOURIST TRAP, THE, 1979
TOUT VA BIEN, 1973
TOWERING INFERNO, THE, 1974
TOWING, 1978
TOWN ON TRIAL, 1957
TOY, THE, 1982
TOYS IN THE ATTIC, 1963
T.R. BASKIN, 1971
TRACK OF THE CAT, 1954
TRADER HORN, 1931
TRAIL OF THE PINK PANTHER, THE, 1982
TRAIN, THE, 1965
TRAMPLERS, THE, 1966
TRANSYLVANIA 6-5000, 1985
TRAUMA, 1962
TRAVELLING AVANT, 1988
TRAVELLING NORTH, 1988
TRAVELS WITH MY AUNT, 1972
TREASURE OF JAMAICA REEF, THE, 1976
TREASURE OF THE SIERRA MADRE, THE, 1948
TREE GROWS IN BROOKLYN, A, 1945
TRIAL OF BILLY JACK, THE, 1974
TRIAL OF JOAN OF ARC, 1965
TRIAL OF MARY DUGAN, THE, 1929
TRIAL, THE, 1963
TRIBUTE, 1980
TRIBUTE TO A BADMAN, 1956
TRIP TO BOUNTIFUL, THE, 1985
TRISTANA, 1970
TROJAN WOMEN, THE, 1971
TROLL, 1986
TROMBA, THE TIGER MAN, 1952
TROOPER HOOK, 1957
TROOPSHIP, 1938
TROUBLE IN PARADISE, 1932
TROUBLE IN THE SKY, 1961

TRUNK TO CAIRO, 1966
TRUNK, THE, 1961
TRYGON FACTOR, THE, 1969
TSAR'S BRIDE, THE, 1966
TULIPS, 1981
TUNES OF GLORY, 1960
TUNNEL OF LOVE, THE, 1958
TUNNEL TO THE SUN, 1968
TURK 182!, 1985
TURKISH CUCUMBER, THE, 1963
TURN THE KEY SOFTLY, 1954
TURNING POINT, THE, 1977
TURTLE DIARY, 1985
TWELVE O'CLOCK HIGH, 1949
25TH HOUR, THE, 1967
24 HOURS IN A WOMAN'S LIFE, 1968
24 HOURS TO KILL, 1966
20,000 EYES, 1961
20,000 POUNDS KISS, THE, 1964
23 PACES TO BAKER STREET, 1956
TWICE TOLD TALES, 1963
TWILIGHT OF HONOR, 1963
TWILIGHT PATH, 1965
TWILIGHT TIME, 1983
TWILIGHT WOMEN, 1953
TWIN SISTERS OF KYOTO, 1964
TWO AND TWO MAKE SIX, 1962
TWO ARE GUILTY, 1964
TWO EYES, TWELVE HANDS, 1958
TWO FOR THE ROAD, 1967
TWO FOR THE SEESAW, 1962
TWO-HEADED SPY, THE, 1959
TWO IN A SLEEPING BAG, 1964
TWO IN THE SHADOW, 1968
TWO KINDS OF WOMEN, 1932
TWO LIVING, ONE DEAD, 1964
TWO LOVES, 1961
TWO MULES FOR SISTER SARA, 1970
TWO NIGHTS WITH CLEOPATRA, 1953
TWO O'CLOCK COURAGE, 1945
TWO OF A KIND, 1951
TWO OF A KIND, 1983
TWO ON A GUILLOTINE, 1965
TWO RODE TOGETHER, 1961
TWO SECONDS, 1932
TWO SUPER COPS, 1978
2010, 1984
2,000 WEEKS, 1970
TWO VOICES, 1966
TWO YEARS BEFORE THE MAST, 1946
U-TURN, 1973
UFORIA, 1985
ULTIMATE SOLUTION OF GRACE QUIGLEY, THE, 1984
ULYSSES, 1955
ULYSSES, 1967
UMBERTO D, 1955
UNCANNY, THE, 1977
UNCLE HARRY, 1945
UNCLE JOE SHANNON, 1978
UNCLE TOM'S CABIN, 1969
UNDER CAPRICORN, 1949
UNDER MILK WOOD, 1973
UNDER TEN FLAGS, 1960
UNDER THE BANNER OF SAMURAI, 1969
UNDER THE RAINBOW, 1981
UNDERCOVER MAN, THE, 1949
UNDERGROUND, 1970
UNDERWORLD U.S.A., 1961
UNFAITHFULLY YOURS, 1984
UNFORGIVEN, THE, 1960
UNHOLY FOUR, THE, 1969
UNHOLY THREE, THE, 1930
UNINHIBITED, THE, 1968
UNINVITED, THE, 1944
UNION STATION, 1950
UNIVERSAL SOLDIER, 1971
UNIVERSITY OF LIFE, 1941
UNKNOWN MAN, THE, 1951
UNMAN, WITTERING AND ZIGO, 1971
UNTIL THEY SAIL, 1957
UP IN THE CELLAR, 1970
UP THE FRONT, 1972
UP TO HIS EARS, 1966
UPHILL ALL THE WAY, 1986
UPPER HAND, THE, 1967

UPTOWN SATURDAY NIGHT, 1974
URBAN COWBOY, 1980
URGE TO KILL, 1960
VACATION, THE, 1971
VALENTINO, 1951
VALERIE, 1957
VALLEY GIRL, 1983
VALLEY OF THE ZOMBIES, 1946
VAMPIRE, THE, 1968
VAMPIRE AND THE BALLERINA, THE, 1962
VAMPIRE BAT, THE, 1933
VAMPIRE, THE, 1957
VAMPIRE'S GHOST, THE, 1945
VANISHING POINT, 1971
VANITY FAIR, 1932
VEILED WOMAN, THE, 1929
VENETIAN AFFAIR, THE, 1967
VENGEANCE, 1968
VERBOTEN?, 1959
VERDICT, 1975
VERDICT, THE, 1946
VERTIGO, 1958
VERY EDGE, THE, 1963
VERY HANDY MAN, A, 1966
VERY PRIVATE AFFAIR, A, 1962
VICE DOLLS, 1961
VICE RAID, 1959
VICKI, 1953
VISCOUNT, THE, 1967
VICTOR FRANKENSTEIN, 1975
VIEW FROM THE BRIDGE, A, 1962
VIEW TO A KILL, A, 1985
VIGIL, 1984
VIGIL IN THE NIGHT, 1940
VIGILANTE FORCE, 1976
VIKINGS, THE, 1958
VILLAGE OF THE DAMNED, 1960
VIOLATED, 1953
VIOLATED LOVE, 1966
VIOLENT AND THE DAMNED, THE, 1962
VIOLENT MOMENT, 1966
VIOLENT ONES, THE, 1967
VIOLENT SUMMER, 1961
VIRGIN ISLAND, 1960
VIRGIN SACRIFICE, 1959
VIRGIN SPRING, THE, 1960
VIRTUE, 1932
VIRUS, 1980
VISA U.S.A., 1987
VISIT, THE, 1964
VITELLONI, 1956
VIVA MARIA, 1965
VIVA ZAPATA!, 1952
VOICE IN YOUR HEART, A, 1952
VOICE OF THE WHISTLER, 1945
VOICES, 1979
VON RICHTHOFEN AND BROWN, 1970
VON RYAN'S EXPRESS, 1965
VULTURE, THE, 1967
W, 1974
W.C. FIELDS AND ME, 1976
WACKO, 1983
WACO, 1966
WAIT FOR ME IN HEAVEN, 1988
WAITING FOR CAROLINE, 1969
WAKE UP AND DIE, 1967
WALK IN THE SPRING RAIN, A, 1970
WALK IN THE SUN, A, 1945
WALK PROUD, 1979
WALK SOFTLY, STRANGER, 1950
WALK THE ANGRY BEACH, 1961
WALK THE DARK STREET, 1956
WALK WITH LOVE AND DEATH, A, 1969
WALKABOUT, 1971
WALKING STICK, THE, 1970
WALKING TARGET, THE, 1960
WALKOVER, 1969
WALLS OF GOLD, 1933
WALLS OF JERICHO, 1948
WANDA, 1971
WANTED FOR MURDER, 1946
WAR AND PEACE, 1983
WAR HUNT, 1962
WAR OF THE WIZARDS, 1983
WAR OF THE WORLDS—NEXT CENTURY, THE, 1981
WAR OF THE WORLDS, THE, 1953

BOLD: Films on Videocassette

WARLOCK, 1959
WARM DECEMBER, A, 1973
WARM NIGHTS ON A SLOW MOVING TRAIN, 1987
WARRING CLANS, 1963
WARRIOR'S HUSBAND THE, 1933
WARRIORS OF THE WIND, 1984
WASTREL, THE, 1963
WATCHER IN THE WOODS, THE, 1980
WATERHOLE NO. 3, 1967
WATERLOO, 1970
WATERLOO BRIDGE, 1931
WATERLOO BRIDGE, 1940
WATERMELON MAN, 1970
WAVELENGTH, 1983
WAY OF LOST SOULS, THE, 1929
WAY WE WERE, THE, 1973
WAYWARD BUS, THE, 1957
WE ARE ALL MURDERERS, 1957
WE LIVE AGAIN, 1934
WE OF THE NEVER NEVER, 1983
WE SHALL SEE, 1964
WE STILL KILL THE OLD WAY, 1967
WE THREE, 1985
WE WERE STRANGERS, 1949
WEAPON, THE, 1957
WEATHER IN THE STREETS, THE, 1983
WEB OF EVIDENCE, 1959
WEB OF FEAR, 1966
WEB OF PASSION, 1961
WEB OF VIOLENCE, 1966
WEDDING, A, 1978
WEDNESDAY CHILDREN, THE, 1973
WEEKEND, 1964
WEEKEND OF FEAR, 1966
WEEKEND OF SHADOWS, 1978
WEIRD ONES, THE, 1962
WELCOME TO GERMANY, 1988
WELL-DIGGER'S DAUGHTER, THE, 1946
WE'LL GROW THIN TOGETHER, 1979
WEREWOLF OF LONDON, THE, 1935
WEREWOLF OF WASHINGTON, 1973
WEST 11, 1963
WESTWARD DESPERADO, 1961
WESTWORLD, 1973
WET PARADE, THE, 1932
WHAT CHANGED CHARLEY FARTHING?, 1976
WHAT COMES AROUND, 1986
WHAT EVER HAPPENED TO AUNT ALICE?, 1969
WHAT PRICE GLORY?, 1952
WHAT PRICE HOLLYWOOD?, 1932
WHAT WAITS BELOW, 1986
WHATEVER HAPPENED TO BABY JANE?, 1962
WHAT'S NEW, PUSSYCAT?, 1965
WHAT'S UP FRONT, 1964
WHAT'S UP, TIGER LILY?, 1966
WHEEL OF ASHES, 1970
WHEN A WOMAN ASCENDS THE STAIRS, 1963
WHEN EIGHT BELLS TOLL, 1971
WHEN STRANGERS MARRY, 1944
WHEN THE GIRLS TAKE OVER, 1962
WHEN THE LEGENDS DIE, 1972
WHEN THE WIND BLOWS, 1988
WHEN TIME RAN OUT, 1980
WHEN TOMORROW DIES, 1966
WHERE ANGELS GO...TROUBLE FOLLOWS, 1968
WHERE EAGLES DARE, 1968
WHERE IS PARSIFAL?, 1984
WHERE LOVE HAS GONE, 1964
WHERE THE SIDEWALK ENDS, 1950
WHILE THE CITY SLEEPS, 1956
WHIRLWIND, 1968
WHISPERERS, THE, 1967
WHITE CARGO, 1930
WHITE CARGO, 1942
WHITE DEMON, THE, 1932
WHITE DEVIL, THE, 1948
WHITE ELEPHANT, 1984
WHITE GHOST, 1988
WHITE HEAT, 1949
WHITE LIGHTNING, 1973
WHITE LINE, THE, 1952
WHITE LINE FEVER, 1975
WHITE NIGHTS, 1985
WHITE SHEIK, THE, 1956
WHITE SLAVE SHIP, 1962
WHITE TRAP, THE, 1959

WHITE WARRIOR, THE, 1961
WHITE WATER SUMMER, 1987
WHITE WOMAN, 1933
WHO?, 1975
WHO DONE IT?, 1956
WHO GOES NEXT?, 1938
WHO IS HARRY KELLERMAN AND WHY IS HE SAYING THOSE TERRIBLE THINGS ABOUT ME?, 1971
WHO IS KILLING THE GREAT CHEFS OF EUROPE?, 1978
WHO KILLED JESSIE?, 1965
WHOLE SHOOTIN' MATCH, THE, 1979
WHO'LL STOP THE RAIN?, 1978
WHOLLY MOSES, 1980
WHO'S BEEN SLEEPING IN MY BED?, 1963
WHY GIRLS LEAVE HOME, 1945
WHY MUST I DIE?, 1960
WHY SHOOT THE TEACHER?, 1977
WHY WOULD I LIE, 1980
WICKED DREAMS OF PAULA SCHULTZ, THE, 1968
WICKED WOMAN, A, 1934
WILBY CONSPIRACY, THE, 1975
WILD AND THE INNOCENT, THE, 1959
WILD DUCK, THE, 1983
WILD, FREE AND HUNGRY, 1970
WILD HEART, THE, 1952
WILD HORSES, 1984
WILD IN THE STREETS, 1968
WILD ONE, THE, 1953
WILD RIDE, THE, 1960
WILD WOMEN OF WONGO, THE, 1959
WILD WORLD OF BATWOMAN, THE, 1966
WILD YOUTH, 1961
WILDROSE, 1985
WILLS AND BURKE, 1985
WINCHESTER "73, 1950
WIND ACROSS THE EVERGLADES, 1958
WIND AND THE LION, THE, 1975
WIND FROM THE EAST, 1970
WIND, THE, 1928
WINDFLOWERS, 1968
WINDOW, THE, 1949
WINDSPLITTER, THE, 1971
WINDWALKER, 1980
WINDY CITY, 1984
WINGS OF DESIRE, 1988
WINNERS TAKE ALL, 1987
WINSTANLEY, 1979
WINTER FLIGHT, 1984
WINTER KEPT US WARM, 1968
WINTER LIGHT, THE, 1963
WINTER WIND, 1970
WINTERHAWK, 1976
WISER AGE, 1962
WISHBONE CUTTER, 1978
WITCH, THE, 1969
WITCH WITHOUT A BROOM, A, 1967
WITCHES, THE, 1969
WITCHMAKER, THE, 1969
WITCH'S MIRROR, THE, 1960
WITHOUT PITY, 1949
WITHOUT WARNING, 1952
WITNESS TO MURDER, 1954
WITNESS, THE, 1982
WIZ, THE, 1978
WIZARD OF LONELINESS, THE, 1988
WIZARDS, 1977
WOLF MAN, THE, 1941
WOLF OF WALL STREET THE, 1929
WOLF'S HOLE, 1987
WOMAN BETWEEN, 1931
WOMAN EATER, THE, 1959
WOMAN HUNGRY, 1931
WOMAN HUNT, 1962
WOMAN IN RED, THE, 1984
WOMAN IN THE WINDOW, THE, 1945
WOMAN IN WHITE, THE, 1948
WOMAN OF STRAW, 1964
WOMAN UNDER THE INFLUENCE, A, 1974
WOMANLIGHT, 1979
WOMEN, THE, 1939
WOMEN AND WAR, 1965
WOMEN ON THE VERGE OF A NERVOUS BREAKDOWN, 1988
WONDER WOMEN, 1973

WORK IS A FOUR LETTER WORD, 1968
WORLD OF HENRY ORIENT, THE, 1964
WORLDS APART, 1980
WRAITH, THE, 1986
WRECKING CREW, THE, 1968
WRESTLER, THE, 1974
WRITTEN ON THE WIND, 1956
WUSA, 1970
WUTHERING HEIGHTS, 1939
"X'—THE MAN WITH THE X-RAY EYES, 1963
XANADU, 1980
YASEMIN, 1988
YEAR MY VOICE BROKE, THE, 1988
YEAR OF LIVING DANGEROUSLY, THE, 1982
YEARNING, 1964
YELLOW ROLLS-ROYCE, THE, 1965
YENTL, 1983
YES, GIORGIO, 1982
YESTERDAY, 1980
YOSAKOI JOURNEY, 1970
YOU CAN'T WIN 'EM ALL, 1970
YOU LIGHT UP MY LIFE, 1977
YOU ONLY LIVE ONCE, 1937
YOU ONLY LIVE TWICE, 1967
YOU'LL LIKE MY MOTHER, 1972
YOUNG AND EVIL, 1962
YOUNG AND WILLING, 1964
YOUNG APHRODITES, 1966
YOUNG BRIDE, 1932
YOUNG CASSIDY, 1965
YOUNG DESIRE, 1930
YOUNG DON'T CRY, THE, 1957
YOUNG FRANKENSTEIN, 1974
YOUNG FURY, 1965
YOUNG GIRLS OF WILKO, THE, 1979
YOUNG GO WILD, THE, 1962
YOUNG GUNS OF TEXAS, 1963
YOUNG GUY GRADUATES, 1969
YOUNG JESSE JAMES, 1960
YOUNG LIONS, THE, 1958
YOUNG MAN WITH A HORN, 1950
YOUNG PHILADELPHIANS, THE, 1959
YOUNG RACERS, THE, 1963
YOUNG REBEL, THE, 1969
YOUNG SAVAGES, THE, 1961
YOUNG SHERLOCK HOLMES, 1985
YOUNG SINNER, THE, 1965
YOUNG STRANGER, THE, 1957
YOUNG SWORDSMAN, 1964
YOUNG TORLESS, 1968
YOUNG WARRIORS, THE, 1967
YOUNG, WILLING AND EAGER, 1962
YOUNG WOODLEY, 1930
YOUNG WORLD, A, 1966
YOUR TURN, DARLING, 1963
YOU'RE A BIG BOY NOW, 1966
YOUTH AND HIS AMULET, THE, 1963
YOUTH RUNS WILD, 1944
YR ALCOHOLIG LION, 1984
ZACHARIAH, 1971
ZARAK, 1956
ZATOICHI MEETS YOJIMBO, 1970
ZAZA, 1939
ZERO HOUR, THE, 1939
ZERO TO SIXTY, 1978
ZIGZAG, 1970
ZINA, 1985
ZONING, 1986
ZOO GANG, THE, 1985
Z.P.G., 1972
ZULU, 1964

C-O
ABANDON SHIP, 1957
ABDICATION, THE, 1974
ABUSED CONFIDENCE, 1938
ACCIDENTAL TOURIST, THE, 1988
ADVENTURES OF BARRY McKENZIE, 1972
ADVENTURES OF BUCKAROO BANZAI: ACROSS THE 8TH DIMENSION, THE, 1984
AFTER THE REHEARSAL, 1984
AGAINST ALL ODDS, 1984
AL CAPONE, 1959
ALLNIGHTER, THE, 1987
AMERICAN NINJA 2: THE CONFRONTATION, 1987
AND THE WILD, WILD WOMEN, 1961

ANDERSON TAPES, THE, 1971
ANNA, 1951
ANNE OF THE THOUSAND DAYS, 1969
ANNIE HALL, 1977
ANOTHER MAN, ANOTHER CHANCE, 1977
ANTI-CLOCK, 1980
ANTONIO DAS MORTES, 1970
ANY WEDNESDAY, 1966
APARTMENT, THE, 1960
APPLE, THE, 1980
ARMY GAME, THE, 1963
ARRIVEDERCI, BABY!, 1966
ASSIGNMENT TERROR, 1970
ATLANTIC CITY, 1981
ATLAS, 1960
ATTACK OF THE GIANT LEECHES, 1959
ATTIC, THE, 1979
AU HASARD, BALTHAZAR, 1970
BABY, THE, 1973
BABY, IT'S YOU, 1983
BACK FROM THE DEAD, 1957
BACK STREETS OF PARIS, 1962
BAD GUYS, 1986
BAGDAD CAFE, 1988
BALLAD OF GREGORIO CORTEZ, THE, 1983
BAND OF OUTSIDERS, 1966
BANZAI, 1983
BARRY LYNDON, 1975
BASTILLE, 1985
BEACH GIRLS, 1982
BEAST OF BLOOD, 1970
BEAST OF THE CITY, THE, 1932
BEAT, THE, 1988
BECAUSE OF EVE, 1948
BELL' ANTONIO, 1962
BEST OF EVERYTHING, THE, 1959
BIG TROUBLE IN LITTLE CHINA, 1986
BILOXI BLUES, 1988
BIRD, 1988
BIRDS OF PREY, 1987
BLACK MARBLE, THE, 1980
BLAZING SADDLES, 1974
BLONDE VENUS, 1932
BLOOD AND ROSES, 1961
BLOOD, SWEAT AND FEAR, 1975
BLOODBATH AT THE HOUSE OF DEATH, 1984
BLUE COUNTRY, THE, 1977
BLUE DENIM, 1959
BLUES BROTHERS, THE, 1980
BOARDWALK, 1979
BOAT, THE, 1982
BOBBIE JO AND THE OUTLAW, 1976
BONJOUR TRISTESSE, 1958
BOSS' WIFE, THE, 1986
BOXOFFICE, 1982
BOY CRIED MURDER, THE, 1966
BOY IN BLUE, THE, 1986
BOY SOLDIER, 1987
BOYS FROM BRAZIL, THE, 1978
BRAINSTORM, 1983
BREAKING AWAY, 1979
BREAKING GLASS, 1980
BREAKING POINT, 1976
BRIDE, THE, 1973
BRINK OF LIFE, 1960
BROADCAST NEWS, 1987
BROTHERHOOD OF SATAN, THE, 1971
BROTHERHOOD, THE, 1968
BROTHERS KARAMAZOV, THE, 1958
BRUBAKER, 1980
BRUCE LEE AND I, 1976
BRUCE LEE—TRUE STORY, 1976
BURNT OFFERINGS, 1976
BUS IS COMING, THE, 1971
BUSTER, 1988
BUTTERFLY ON THE SHOULDER, A, 1978
BYE-BYE BRAZIL, 1980
CADDYSHACK, 1980
CAFFE ITALIA, 1985
CANNERY ROW, 1982
CANNIBALS, THE, 1970
CANNON FOR CORDOBA, 1970
CAPTAIN FROM CASTILE, 1947
CARRY ON LOVING, 1970
CARTHAGE IN FLAMES, 1961
CASE OF PATTY SMITH, THE, 1962

CASTLE OF PURITY, 1974
CAYMAN TRIANGLE, THE, 1977
CERTAIN SMILE, A, 1958
CHAFED ELBOWS, 1967
CHANGE OF HABIT, 1969
CHANGE OF SEASONS, A, 1980
CHEAT, THE, 1931
CHEAT, THE, 1950
CHECK IS IN THE MAIL, THE, 1986
CHILDREN OF A LESSER GOD, 1986
CHILDREN OF HIROSHIMA, 1952
CHILDREN OF THE CORN, 1984
CHILDRENS GAMES, 1969
CHINA IS NEAR, 1968
CHOPPERS, THE, 1961
CHRISTINE, 1983
CINDERELLA LIBERTY, 1973
CIRCLE OF LOVE, 1965
CLAIRE'S KNEE, 1971
CLAUDELLE INGLISH, 1961
CLAY, 1964
CLIMAX, THE, 1967
CLOPORTES, 1966
CLOUDS OVER ISRAEL, 1966
COACH, 1978
CODE OF SCOTLAND YARD, 1948
COLOR OF DESTINY, THE, 1988
COLOR OF MONEY, THE, 1986
COLOR OF POMEGRANATES, THE, 1980
COME DANCE WITH ME!, 1960
COMEDY!, 1987
COMING HOME, 1978
COMPROMISING POSITIONS, 1985
COMPULSION, 1959
CONAN THE BARBARIAN, 1982
CONCRETE ANGELS, 1987
CONFESSIONS OF AMANS, THE, 1977
CONFESSIONS OF FELIX KRULL, THE, 1957
CONFIDENCE, 1980
CONSTANT FACTOR, THE, 1980
CONSTANTINE AND THE CROSS, 1962
CONTEMPT, 1963
COOGAN'S BLUFF, 1968
COOL AND THE CRAZY, THE, 1958
COOL WORLD, THE, 1963
COP-OUT, 1967
CORDELIA, 1980
CORRIDORS OF BLOOD, 1962
CORVETTE SUMMER, 1978
COUCH, THE, 1962
COUNT DRACULA, 1971
COUNT DRACULA AND HIS VAMPIRE BRIDE, 1978
COUSINS, THE, 1959
COVER GIRL KILLER, 1960
COWARDS, 1970
CRASH, 1977
CRAZY FOR LOVE, 1960
CRAZY WORLD OF JULIUS VROODER, THE, 1974
CREEPSHOW 2, 1987
CRIME AND PASSION, 1976
CRIME DOES NOT PAY, 1962
CRIME IN THE STREETS, 1956
CRIME OF MONSIEUR LANGE, THE, 1936
CRIMES OF THE HEART, 1986
CRITTERS, 1986
CROSS OF LORRAINE, THE, 1943
CROSS OF THE LIVING, 1963
CROSSOVER DREAMS, 1985
CROSSROADS, 1986
CRY OF THE WEREWOLF, 1944
CRYSTAL HEART, 1987
CUL-DE-SAC, 1966
CURSE OF THE CAT PEOPLE, THE, 1944
CURSE OF THE DOLL PEOPLE, THE, 1968
CYCLOPS, 1957
DAISIES, 1967
DAISY MILLER, 1974
DANCE WITH A STRANGER, 1985
DANGER IS A WOMAN, 1952
DARK IS THE NIGHT, 1946
DAUGHTER OF THE SANDS, 1952
DAVID HOLZMAN'S DIARY, 1968
DAY OF THE LOCUST, THE, 1975
DAYBREAK, 1948
DEAD END KIDS, 1986
DEAD OF SUMMER, 1970

DEATH CURSE OF TARTU, 1967
DEATH RACE, 1978
DECOY, 1946
DEFENCE OF THE REALM, 1985
DELOS ADVENTURE, THE, 1987
DEMONIAQUE, 1958
DESPERATE MOVES, 1986
DEVIL'S PARTNER, THE, 1958
DEVIL'S TEMPLE, 1969
DEVOTION, 1953
DIARY OF A HIGH SCHOOL BRIDE, 1959
DIARY OF A MAD HOUSEWIFE, 1970
DIARY OF A MADMAN, 1963
DILLINGER, 1945
DINER, 1982
DIRTY DOZEN, THE, 1967
DIRTY LITTLE BILLY, 1972
D.O.A., 1988
DR. JEKYLL AND MR. HYDE, 1941
DOCTOR PHIBES RISES AGAIN, 1972
DONKEY SKIN, 1975
DON'S PARTY, 1976
DOUBLE DOOR, 1934
DOUBLE LIFE, A, 1947
DOWN AND OUT IN BEVERLY HILLS, 1986
DRACULA, 1931
DRAGONSLAYER, 1981
DREAMSCAPE, 1984
DUEL IN THE SUN, 1946
DUNE, 1984
DUNGEONMASTER, 1985
DUTCH TREAT, 1987
EAST OF EDEN, 1955
EASY MONEY, 1983
EIGHT MEN OUT, 1988
EIGHTH DAY OF THE WEEK, THE, 1959
EL, 1955
EMERALD FOREST, THE, 1985
END OF AUGUST, THE, 1982
END OF THE GAME, 1976
EQUINOX, 1970
EQUUS, 1977
EVERYBODY'S ALL-AMERICAN, 1988
EXCALIBUR, 1981
EXILE, THE, 1931
EXORCISM AT MIDNIGHT, 1966
EYE OF THE NEEDLE, 1981
FAN, THE, 1981
FANNY AND ALEXANDER, 1983
FANTASTICA, 1980
FAREWELL, MY LOVELY, 1975
FEAR IN THE NIGHT, 1947
FELLINI SATYRICON, 1969
ƒEVER PITCH, 1985
FIEND WITHOUT A FACE, 1958
FINDERS KEEPERS, 1984
FIRST LOVE, 1970
FISH CALLED WANDA, A, 1988
FIVE EASY PIECES, 1970
5 SINNERS, 1961
FIX, THE, 1985
FLAMING STAR, 1960
FLOWERS IN THE ATTIC, 1987
FOG, THE, 1980
FORCE OF ONE, A, 1979
FOREIGN BODY, 1986
FOREVER AMBER, 1947
FOUR DAYS IN JULY, 1984
FOUR SKULLS OF JONATHAN DRAKE, THE, 1959
FOXTROT, 1977
FRAGMENT OF FEAR, 1971
FRANKENSTEIN, 1931
FRANKENSTEIN MUST BE DESTROYED!, 1969
FRANKENSTEIN'S DAUGHTER, 1958
FRAULEIN DOKTOR, 1969
FRENZY, 1972
FRIENDLY KILLER, THE, 1970
FRONT PAGE, THE, 1974
FUN WITH DICK AND JANE, 1977
F/X, 1986
GAILY, GAILY, 1969
GANG WAR, 1958
GATE OF HELL, 1954
GATES OF THE NIGHT, 1950
GAWAIN AND THE GREEN KNIGHT, 1973
GERMAN SISTERS, THE, 1982

BOLD: Films on Videocassette

GETTING STRAIGHT, 1970
GHOST TOWN, 1988
GHOULIES II, 1988
GIRL HUNTERS, THE, 1963
GIRL I ABANDONED, THE, 1970
GIRL OF THE MOORS, THE, 1961
GIRL OF THE MOUNTAINS, 1958
GIRL OF THE NIGHT, 1960
GLADIATORS, THE, 1970
GODDESS, THE, 1958
GODSON, THE, 1972
GOLD OF NAPLES, 1957
GOLDFINGER, 1964
GOOD MORNING BABYLON, 1987
GOOD WIFE, THE, 1987
GOODNIGHT, LADIES AND GENTLEMEN, 1977
GOOSE GIRL, THE, 1967
GORGON, THE, 1964
GOT IT MADE, 1974
GRAVEYARD SHIFT, 1987
GREASE 2, 1982
GREAT MACARTHY, THE, 1975
GREAT ST. LOUIS BANK ROBBERY, THE, 1959
GREAT WALL OF CHINA, THE, 1970
GREAT WHITE HOPE, THE, 1970
GREATEST, THE, 1977
GREED OF WILLIAM HART, THE, 1948
GREEN ROOM, THE, 1979
GRISSOM GANG, THE, 1971
HAGBARD AND SIGNE, 1968
HAIR, 1979
HALF HUMAN, 1955
HANGMEN ALSO DIE, 1943
HANNA'S WAR, 1988
HAPPY END, 1968
HARBOR LIGHT YOKOHAMA, 1970
HAREM BUNCH; OR WAR AND PIECE, THE, 1969
HARLEQUIN, 1980
HARP OF BURMA, 1967
HATCHET MAN, THE, 1932
HAUNTED PALACE, THE, 1963
HAUNTING, THE, 1963
HEALTH, 1980
HEARTBREAK KID, THE, 1972
HEARTBREAKERS, 1984
HEARTBURN, 1986
HEIMAT, 1985
HELLO SISTER!, 1933
HERCULES, 1959
HERE'S YOUR LIFE, 1968
HERO AIN'T NOTHIN' BUT A SANDWICH, A, 1977
HEROES ARE MADE, 1944
HIDING PLACE, THE, 1975
HIGH AND LOW, 1963
HIGH COMMISSIONER, THE, 1968
HIGH SEASON, 1988
HIGH YELLOW, 1965
HIMMO, KING OF JERUSALEM, 1988
HIPPODROME, 1961
HIROSHIMA, MON AMOUR, 1959
HIS KIND OF WOMAN, 1951
HISTORY OF THE WORLD, PART 1, 1981
HIT AND RUN, 1982
HITCH-HIKER, THE, 1953
HOA-BINH, 1971
HOLLYWOOD SPEAKS, 1932
HOSTAGE, 1987
HOT PURSUIT, 1987
HOT RODS TO HELL, 1967
HOT SPELL, 1958
HOT TARGET, 1985
HOTEL NEW HAMPSHIRE, THE, 1984
HOUSE, 1986
HOUSE II: THE SECOND STORY, 1987
HOUSE OF DARK SHADOWS, 1970
HOUSE OF SEVEN CORPSES, THE, 1974
HOW SWEET IT IS, 1968
HOWLING III, THE, 1987
HYPNOSIS, 1966
I MET A MURDERER, 1939
I MISS YOU, HUGS AND KISSES, 1978
I, MOBSTER, 1959
I SAW WHAT YOU DID, 1965
I, THE JURY, 1953
I WALKED WITH A ZOMBIE, 1943
I WAS A TEENAGE FRANKENSTEIN, 1958

I WAS A TEENAGE WEREWOLF, 1957
IDENTIFICATION OF A WOMAN, 1983
IDIOT, THE, 1963
I'M DANCING AS FAST AS I CAN, 1982
IMAGEMAKER, THE, 1986
IMAGES, 1972
IMPOSSIBLE OBJECT, 1973
IN GOD WE TRUST, 1980
IN MACARTHUR PARK, 1977
IN THE WHITE CITY, 1983
IN THIS OUR LIFE, 1942
INCREDIBLE INVASION, THE, 1971
INDECENT OBSESSION, AN, 1985
INDEPENDENCE DAY, 1976
INDIANA JONES AND THE TEMPLE OF DOOM, 1984
INNOCENTS, THE, 1961
INQUISITOR, THE, 1982
INTERIORS, 1978
INTIMATE POWER, 1986
INTRUDER IN THE DUST, 1949
INVASION OF THE BODY SNATCHERS, 1978
INVISIBLE STRANGLER, 1984
INVITATION, THE, 1975
IRMA LA DOUCE, 1963
IRONWEED, 1987
ISLE OF SIN, 1963
IT AIN'T EASY, 1972
IT COULDN'T HAPPEN HERE, 1988
J'ACCUSE, 1939
JAWS, 1975
JAWS 3-D, 1983
JENNIFER, 1978
JEREMIAH JOHNSON, 1972
JO JO DANCER, YOUR LIFE IS CALLING, 1986
JUDITH, 1965
JUGGLER, THE, 1953
JULES AND JIM, 1962
JULIA AND JULIA, 1988
JUNKMAN, THE, 1982
KANSAS, 1988
KANSAS CITY CONFIDENTIAL, 1952
KELLY'S HEROES, 1970
KILLER KLOWNS FROM OUTER SPACE, 1988
KILLERS, THE, 1964
KING KONG, 1976
KING OF MARVIN GARDENS, THE, 1972
KINGS ROW, 1942
KISS OF DEATH, 1947
KISS THE BLOOD OFF MY HANDS, 1948
KISS TOMORROW GOODBYE, 1950
KITTEN WITH A WHIP, 1964
KREMLIN LETTER, THE, 1970
LA CAGE AUX FOLLES II, 1981
LA CHIENNE, 1975
LA CHINOISE, 1967
LA COLLECTIONNEUSE, 1971
LA GRANDE BOUFFE, 1973
LA GUERRE EST FINIE, 1967
LA NAVE DE LOS MONSTRUOS, 1959
LA NOTTE, 1961
LA PARISIENNE, 1958
LA VIACCIA, 1962
LADIES ON THE ROCKS, 1985
LADY WITHOUT CAMELLIAS, THE, 1981
LAST METRO, THE, 1981
LAST PICTURE SHOW, THE, 1971
LAST SUNSET, THE, 1961
LATINO, 1985
LE BEAU MARIAGE, 1982
LE BEAU SERGE, 1959
LE PLAISIR, 1954
LEADBELLY, 1976
LEFT-HANDED WOMAN, THE, 1980
LENNY, 1974
LETTER TO BREZHNEV, 1986
LIPSTICK, 1965
LITTLE BIG MAN, 1970
LITTLE DRUMMER GIRL, THE, 1984
LITTLE SHOP OF HORRORS, 1961
LIVING IDOL, THE, 1957
LOCK UP YOUR DAUGHTERS, 1969
LODGER, THE, 1944
LOLA, 1971
LOLITA, 1962
LONE WOLF McQUADE, 1983

LONELINESS OF THE LONG DISTANCE RUNNER, THE, 1962
LONG DAY'S DYING, THE, 1968
LONG WEEKEND, 1978
LOOK BACK IN ANGER, 1959
LOOKING FOR MR. GOODBAR, 1977
LOST WEEKEND, THE, 1945
LOVE AND THE FRENCHWOMAN, 1961
LOVE AND THE MIDNIGHT AUTO SUPPLY, 1978
LOVE AT NIGHT, 1961
LOVE FACTORY, 1969
LOVE TILL FIRST BLOOD, 1985
LUCKY LADY, 1975
LUCKY TO BE A WOMAN, 1955
MACHINE GUN KELLY, 1958
MACKINTOSH & T.J., 1975
MAD MAX BEYOND THUNDERDOME, 1985
MAFIA GIRLS, THE, 1969
MAGIC CHRISTIAN, THE, 1970
MAGNUM FORCE, 1973
MAJOR DUNDEE, 1965
MAKING MR. RIGHT, 1987
MAKIOKA SISTERS, THE, 1985
MAN FROM THE EAST, A, 1974
MAN IN BLACK, THE, 1950
MAN OF MARBLE, 1979
MAN OF THE WEST, 1958
MAN WHO FELL TO EARTH, THE, 1976
MAN WHO LOVED CAT DANCING, THE, 1973
MANCHURIAN CANDIDATE, THE, 1962
MANUELA'S LOVES, 1987
MARCH OR DIE, 1977
MASCULINE FEMININE, 1966
M*A*S*H, 1970
MASTER OF HORROR, 1965
MASTERBLASTER, 1987
MASTERS OF THE UNIVERSE, 1987
MAYERLING, 1937
MELVIN AND HOWARD, 1980
MEN'S CLUB, THE, 1986
MEPHISTO WALTZ, THE, 1971
MERRILL'S MARAUDERS, 1962
MICKEY ONE, 1965
MIDSUMMER NIGHT'S SEX COMEDY, A, 1982
MIKEY AND NICKY, 1976
MIND BENDERS, THE, 1963
MINE OWN EXECUTIONER, 1948
MISSION KILL, 1987
MISSOURI BREAKS, THE, 1976
MOB, THE, 1951
MODEL SHOP, THE, 1969
MOHAMMAD, MESSENGER OF GOD, 1976
MOLLY MAGUIRES, THE, 1970
MOMMIE DEAREST, 1981
MORNING AFTER, THE, 1986
MORO AFFAIR, THE, 1986
MOSCOW ON THE HUDSON, 1984
MOST DANGEROUS GAME, THE, 1932
MOTHER KUSTERS GOES TO HEAVEN, 1976
MOTORCYCLE GANG, 1957
MUMMY, THE, 1932
MURDER, MY SWEET, 1945
MURPHY'S ROMANCE, 1985
MURPHY'S WAR, 1971
MUTINY ON THE BOUNTY, 1962
MY DEATH IS A MOCKERY, 1952
MY SCIENCE PROJECT, 1985
NAKED GUN, THE, 1988
NAKED YOUTH, 1961
NAME FOR EVIL, A, 1970
NAME OF THE ROSE, THE, 1986
NASHVILLE, 1975
NATIVE SON, 1951
NAUGHTY ARLETTE, 1951
NEIGHBORS, 1981
NEVER TAKE CANDY FROM A STRANGER, 1961
NEW GIRL IN TOWN, 1977
NEW LEAF, A, 1971
NIGHT AFTER NIGHT AFTER NIGHT, 1970
NIGHT COMERS, THE, 1971
NIGHT OF THE COMET, 1984
NIGHT THEY RAIDED MINSKY'S, THE, 1968
NIGHT WAS OUR FRIEND, 1951
NIGHTBEAST, 1982
NIGHTMARE ALLEY, 1947

NIJINSKY, 1980
NINE TO FIVE, 1980
1941, 1979
1900, 1976
99 AND 44/100% DEAD, 1974
NO PLACE TO HIDE, 1975
NO WAY TO TREAT A LADY, 1968
NORTH DALLAS FORTY, 1979
NOSFERATU, THE VAMPIRE, 1979
NOT FOR PUBLICATION, 1984
NOT ON YOUR LIFE, 1965
NUMBER ONE WITH A BULLET, 1987
NUTS, 1987
ODD JOBS, 1986
ODD MAN OUT, 1947
OF HUMAN BONDAGE, 1934
ONE MORE SATURDAY NIGHT, 1986
ONE PLUS ONE, 1961
ONE SINGS, THE OTHER DOESN'T, 1977
ONE WAY WAHINI, 1965
ONION FIELD, THE, 1979
ORDERS, THE, 1977
ORLAK, THE HELL OF FRANKENSTEIN, 1960
OSTERMAN WEEKEND, THE, 1983
OTHER WOMAN, THE, 1954
OUT, 1982
OUT OF SEASON, 1975
OUTCRY, 1949
OUTFIT, THE, 1973
OX-BOW INCIDENT, THE, 1943
PARADISE POUR TOUS, 1982
PARIS, TEXAS, 1984
PASCALI'S ISLAND, 1988
PENITENT, THE, 1988
PENNIES FROM HEAVEN, 1981
PERSONAL BEST, 1982
PETIT CON, 1985
PHANTOM OF THE OPERA, THE, 1962
PICNIC AT HANGING ROCK, 1975
PLACE FOR LOVERS, A, 1969
PLACE OF WEEPING, 1986
PLAGUE DOGS, THE, 1984
PLUCKED, 1969
PLUMBER, THE, 1980
POLICE ACADEMY 3: BACK IN TRAINING, 1986
POLTERGEIST, 1982
POLTERGEIST III, 1988
PRAYER FOR THE DYING, A, 1987
PRESIDIO, THE, 1988
PRETTY BOY FLOYD, 1960
PRETTY POISON, 1968
PRINCESS ACADEMY, THE, 1987
PRIVATE ACCESS, 1988
PRIVILEGED, 1982
PROPHECY, 1979
PROUD AND THE DAMNED, THE, 1972
PROWLER, THE, 1951
PURPLE HEART, THE, 1944
PURPLE HEARTS, 1984
PURSUED, 1947
QUARE FELLOW, THE, 1962
QUINTET, 1979
RABBIT TEST, 1978
RAFFERTY AND THE GOLD DUST TWINS, 1975
RAIDERS OF THE LOST ARK, 1981
RAIN, 1932
RAIN MAN, 1988
RAIN PEOPLE, THE, 1969
RAZOR'S EDGE, THE, 1984
REBEL LOVE, 1986
REBEL WITHOUT A CAUSE, 1955
RED BEARD, 1966
RED HEADED STRANGER, 1987
RED SONJA, 1985
REDS, 1981
REEFER MADNESS, 1936
REINCARNATION OF PETER PROUD, THE, 1975
REMEMBRANCE, 1982
RETURN TO MACON COUNTY, 1975
REVENGE OF THE NERDS, 1984
RICE GIRL, 1963
RICKSHAW MAN, THE, 1960
RIDE IN A PINK CAR, 1974
RIPPED-OFF, 1971
RITZ, THE, 1976
ROAD TO SHAME, THE, 1962

ROCKIN' ROAD TRIP, 1986
ROCKING HORSE WINNER, THE, 1950
ROLLERCOASTER, 1977
ROMANCING THE STONE, 1984
ROPE, 1948
ROSE TATTOO, THE, 1955
ROSEBUD BEACH HOTEL, 1984
ROYAL SCANDAL, A, 1945
RUBY GENTRY, 1952
RUN OF THE ARROW, 1957
RUNAWAY, 1984
RUNNING SCARED, 1972
RUNNING SCARED, 1986
RUSH, 1984
RUTHLESS PEOPLE, 1986
RYDER, P.I., 1986
SALLY FIELDGOOD & CO., 1975
SAM WHISKEY, 1969
SAMURAI (PART II), 1967
SAMURAI (PART III), 1967
SAND PEBBLES, THE, 1966
SANDPIPER, THE, 1965
SANTA CLAUS CONQUERS THE MARTIANS, 1964
SATISFACTION, 1988
SATURDAY NIGHT FEVER, 1977
SAVAGE EYE, THE, 1960
SAVE THE TIGER, 1973
SCALPHUNTERS, THE, 1968
SCARECROW, 1973
SCENE OF THE CRIME, 1986
SCENES FROM A MARRIAGE, 1974
SCHOOL SPIRIT, 1985
SECRET LIFE OF AN AMERICAN WIFE, THE, 1968
SECRET, THE, 1979
SEDUCTION OF JOE TYNAN, THE, 1979
SEED OF MAN, THE, 1970
SEMI-TOUGH, 1977
SERE CUALQUIER COSA PERO TE QUIERO, 1986
SERPICO, 1973
SHEENA, 1984
SHE'S HAVING A BABY, 1988
SHINING, THE, 1980
SHOOT FIRST, 1953
SHOOT FOR THE SUN, 1986
SHOOT THE MOON, 1982
SHOP ON MAIN STREET, THE, 1966
SHOULD LADIES BEHAVE?, 1933
SHOWDOWN FOR ZATOICHI, 1968
SHUTTERED ROOM, THE, 1968
SIEGE OF FORT BISMARK, 1968
SIGN OF THE CROSS, 1932
SILENCE OF DEAN MAITLAND, THE, 1934
SILENT PARTNER, THE, 1979
SILENT PLAYGROUND, THE, 1964
SILKWOOD, 1983
SIMON AND LAURA, 1956
SINCERELY CHARLOTTE, 1986
SIX IN PARIS, 1968
SLEEPING CAR MURDER, THE, 1966
SLEUTH, 1972
SLUGGER'S WIFE, THE, 1985
SMILE, 1975
SMOKEY AND THE BANDIT, 1977
SMOKEY AND THE BANDIT—PART 3, 1983
SMOKEY AND THE BANDIT II, 1980
SMOOTH TALK, 1985
SO FINE, 1981
SO SAD ABOUT GLORIA, 1973
SOFT SKIN, THE, 1964
SOMETHING SHORT OF PARADISE, 1979
SOMETHING TO HIDE, 1972
SONGWRITER, 1984
SOUND AND THE FURY, THE, 1959
SOURSWEET, 1988
SPARKLE, 1976
SPIKER, 1986
SPIRAL STAIRCASE, THE, 1975
SPOILED ROTTEN, 1968
SPOILS OF THE NIGHT, 1969
SPRING AND PORT WINE, 1970
STAIRCASE, 1969
STAND-IN, THE, 1985
STAR CHAMBER, THE, 1983
STAR IS BORN, A, 1976
STARS AND BARS, 1988
START THE REVOLUTION WITHOUT ME, 1970

STARTING OVER, 1979
STATIC, 1985
STIR CRAZY, 1980
STORM WARNING, 1950
STORY OF ADELE H., THE, 1975
STRANGER, THE, 1967
STRANGERS ON A TRAIN, 1951
STREET WITH NO NAME, THE, 1948
STREETCAR NAMED DESIRE, A, 1951
STRIKEBOUND, 1984
STRIP TEASE MURDER, 1961
STROMBOLI, 1950
STUNTS, 1977
SUBWAY, 1985
SUGARBABY, 1985
SUMMER AND SMOKE, 1961
SUMMER STORY, A, 1988
SUNSET BOULEVARD, 1950
SURF NAZIS MUST DIE, 1987
SURVIVOR, 1980
SURVIVORS, THE, 1983
SWANN IN LOVE, 1984
SWEET DREAMS, 1985
SWEET HEART'S DANCE, 1988
SWEET SMELL OF SUCCESS, 1957
SWORD OF DOOM, THE, 1967
TAKE THIS JOB AND SHOVE IT, 1981
TAMPOPO, 1986
TAXING WOMAN, A, 1988
TAXING WOMAN'S RETURN, A, 1988
TEA AND SYMPATHY, 1956
TEA IN THE HAREM OF ARCHIMEDE, 1985
TEACHERS, 1984
TELEFON, 1977
TELL ME IN THE SUNLIGHT, 1967
TEMPEST, 1982
THAT HOUSE IN THE OUTSKIRTS, 1980
THAT SPLENDID NOVEMBER, 1971
THAT WOMAN, 1968
THEATRE OF DEATH, 1967
THERE IS STILL ROOM IN HELL, 1963
THEY CAME TO CORDURA, 1959
THIEF OF HEARTS, 1984
THIS GUN FOR HIRE, 1942
THIS IS SPINAL TAP, 1984
THREE DAYS OF THE CONDOR, 1975
THROW MOMMA FROM THE TRAIN, 1987
TIGER'S TALE, A, 1988
TIGHTROPE, 1984
TILL DEATH, 1978
TIN MEN, 1987
TO KILL A CLOWN, 1972
TOUCH AND GO, 1986
TOWN WITHOUT PITY, 1961
TRACK OF THE MOONBEAST, 1976
TRADING PLACES, 1983
TRAIN OF DREAMS, 1987
TRIPLE CROSS, 1967
TURNING POINT, THE, 1952
TWENTY PLUS TWO, 1961
TWILIGHT ZONE—THE MOVIE, 1983
TWIST, THE, 1976
TWO WOMEN, 1960
UNDER SATAN'S SUN, 1988
UNDER THE YUM-YUM TREE, 1963
UNDERWATER!, 1955
UNFINISHED BUSINESS. . ., 1987
UNMARRIED WOMAN, AN, 1978
UNSUITABLE JOB FOR A WOMAN, AN, 1982
UNTAMED, 1955
UNWED MOTHER, 1958
UP THE SANDBOX, 1972
UTILITIES, 1983
VALENTINO, 1977
VAMPIRE CIRCUS, 1972
VAMPIRES IN HAVANA, 1987
VAULT OF HORROR, THE, 1973
VERA CRUZ, 1954
VERDICT, THE, 1982
VICTIM, 1961
VIEW FROM POMPEY'S HEAD, THE, 1955
VIOLENT YEARS, THE, 1956
VIOLETS ARE BLUE, 1986
VIRIDIANA, 1962
VISITOR, THE, 1973
WAGNER, 1983

BOLD: Films on Videocassette

WAR LOVER, THE, 1962
WAR OF THE ZOMBIES, THE, 1965
WATER, 1985
WATERSHIP DOWN, 1978
WAY...WAY OUT, 1966
WAYS OF LOVE, 1950
WEREWOLF IN A GIRL'S DORMITORY, 1961
WEREWOLF, THE, 1956
WHAT BECAME OF JACK AND JILL?, 1972
WHERE DOES IT HURT?, 1972
WHERE'S POPPA?, 1970
WHITE BUFFALO, THE, 1977
WHOSE LIFE IS IT ANYWAY?, 1981
WILD CHILD, THE, 1970
WILD LIFE, THE, 1984
WILD ONES ON WHEELS, 1967
WILD PARTY, THE, 1956
WILD ROVERS, 1971
WILD THING, 1987
WILDCATS, 1986
WISE GUYS, 1986
WISH YOU WERE HERE, 1987
WITNESS, 1985
WOLF AT THE DOOR, THE, 1987
WOMAN TIMES SEVEN, 1967
WORLD ACCORDING TO GARP, THE, 1982
WORLD APART, A, 1988
WORLD FOR RANSOM, 1954
WRATH OF GOD, THE, 1972
WRONG DAMN FILM, THE, 1975
YANKS, 1979
YELLOWBEARD, 1983
YESTERDAY'S HERO, 1979
YOUNG LOVERS, THE, 1964
Z, 1969
ZERO BOYS, THE, 1987
ZULU DAWN, 1980

O

A NOS AMOURS, 1984
AARON LOVES ANGELA, 1975
ABBY, 1974
ABDUCTION, 1975
ABDULLAH'S HAREM, 1956
ABOMINABLE DR. PHIBES, THE, 1971
ABOUT LAST NIGHT, 1986
ABOVE THE LAW, 1988
ABSENCE OF MALICE, 1981
ABSOLUTION, 1981
ACAPULCO GOLD, 1978
ACCATTONE!, 1961
ACCIDENT, 1967
ACCUSED, THE, 1988
ACE HIGH, 1969
ACE OF ACES, 1982
ACROSS 110TH STREET, 1972
ACT, THE, 1984
ACT OF THE HEART, 1970
ACT OF VENGEANCE, 1974
ACTION JACKSON, 1988
ACTOR'S REVENGE, AN, 1963
ADAM AND EVE, 1958
ADAM AT 6 A.M., 1970
ADOPTION, THE, 1978
ADORABLE CREATURES, 1956
ADRIFT, 1971
ADULTERESS, THE, 1959
ADVENTURERS, THE, 1970
ADVENTURES OF PICASSO, THE, 1980
AFFAIR AT AKITSU, 1980
AFFAIR IN HAVANA, 1957
AFFAIR LAFONT, THE, 1939
AFFAIR OF THE SKIN, AN, 1964
AFFAIRS OF A MODEL, 1952
AFFAIRS OF MESSALINA, THE, 1954
AFTER HOURS, 1985
AFTER THE FALL OF NEW YORK, 1984
AGE OF CONSENT, 1969
AGE OF ILLUSIONS, 1967
AGE OF INFIDELITY, 1958
AGENCY, 1981
AGENT ON ICE, 1986
AGUIRRE, THE WRATH OF GOD, 1977
AKE AND HIS WORLD, 1985
ALAMO BAY, 1985
ALFIE, 1966

ALFIE DARLING, 1975
ALFREDO, ALFREDO, 1973
ALICE, 1988
ALICE DOESN'T LIVE HERE ANYMORE, 1975
ALICE, SWEET ALICE, 1978
ALICE'S RESTAURANT, 1969
ALIEN, 1979
ALIEN CONTAMINATION, 1982
ALIEN NATION, 1988
ALIEN PREDATOR, 1987
ALIENS, 1986
ALL-AMERICAN BOY, THE, 1973
ALL NUDITY SHALL BE PUNISHED, 1974
ALL SCREWED UP, 1976
ALL THAT JAZZ, 1979
ALL THE RIGHT NOISES, 1973
ALL THESE WOMEN, 1964
ALL WOMAN, 1967
ALLEY CAT, 1984
ALLIGATOR, 1980
ALMOST HUMAN, 1974
ALMOST TRANSPARENT BLUE, 1980
ALONE IN THE DARK, 1982
ALPHABET CITY, 1984
ALRAUNE, 1952
ALTERED STATES, 1980
ALVIN RIDES AGAIN, 1974
ALWAYS, 1985
AMARCORD, 1974
AMAZON WOMEN ON THE MOON, 1987
AMAZONS, 1987
AMERICAN COMMANDOS, 1986
AMERICAN DREAM, AN, 1966
AMERICAN GIGOLO, 1980
AMERICAN GOTHIC, 1988
AMERICAN JUSTICE, 1986
AMERICAN NIGHTMARE, 1984
AMERICAN NINJA, 1985
AMERICAN POP, 1981
AMERICAN TABOO, 1984
AMERICAN WEREWOLF IN LONDON, AN, 1981
AMERICAN WIFE, AN, 1965
AMIN—THE RISE AND FALL, 1982
AMITYVILLE HORROR, THE, 1979
AMITYVILLE 3-D, 1983
AMITYVILLE II: THE POSSESSION, 1982
AMONG THE CINDERS, 1985
AMSTERDAM KILL, THE, 1978
ANATOMY OF A MARRIAGE (MY DAYS WITH
   JEAN-MARC AND MY NIGHTS WITH FRANCOISE),
   1964
AND GOD CREATED WOMAN, 1957
AND GOD CREATED WOMAN, 1988
...AND JUSTICE FOR ALL, 1979
**AND NOW FOR SOMETHING COMPLETELY
   DIFFERENT, 1972**
AND NOW THE SCREAMING STARTS, 1973
AND SO TO BED, 1965
AND SOON THE DARKNESS, 1970
ANDROID, 1982
ANDY WARHOL'S DRACULA, 1974
ANDY WARHOL'S FRANKENSTEIN, 1974
ANGEL, 1984
ANGEL, ANGEL, DOWN WE GO, 1969
ANGEL HEART, 1987
ANGEL RIVER, 1986
ANGEL 3: THE FINAL CHAPTER, 1988
ANGELA, 1977
ANGELO MY LOVE, 1983
ANGELS BRIGADE, 1980
ANGELS DIE HARD, 1970
ANGELS FROM HELL, 1968
ANGELS HARD AS THEY COME, 1971
ANGELS OF DARKNESS, 1956
ANGKOR-CAMBODIA EXPRESS, 1986
ANGRY BREED, THE, 1969
ANGUISH, 1988
ANIMALS, THE, 1971
ANITA—DANCES OF VICE, 1987
ANNE TRISTER, 1986
ANNIHILATORS, THE, 1985
ANNIVERSARY, THE, 1968
ANOTHER LOVE STORY, 1986
ANOTHER TIME, ANOTHER PLACE, 1984
ANTHONY OF PADUA, 1952
ANYONE CAN PLAY, 1968

APOCALYPSE NOW, 1979
APPOINTMENT, THE, 1969
APPOINTMENT WITH FEAR, 1985
APRES L'AMOUR, 1948
APRIL FOOL'S DAY, 1986
ARABIAN NIGHTS, 1980
ARENA, THE, 1973
ARIA, 1988
ARMED RESPONSE, 1986
AROUSERS, THE, 1973
ARRANGEMENT, THE, 1969
ASHANTI, 1979
ASSASSIN, THE, 1965
ASSASSINATION BUREAU, THE, 1969
ASSASSINATION OF TROTSKY, THE, 1972
ASSAULT, 1971
ASSAULT OF THE KILLER BIMBOS, 1988
ASSAULT ON AGATHON, 1976
ASSAULT ON PRECINCT 13, 1976
ASYLUM, 1972
AT CLOSE RANGE, 1986
ATOMIC BRAIN, THE, 1964
ATTACK!, 1956
AUTUMN SONATA, 1978
AVALANCHE, 1978
AVE MARIA, 1984
AVENGING ANGEL, 1985
AVENGING FORCE, 1986
AVIATOR'S WIFE, THE, 1981
AWAKENING, THE, 1980
AWFUL DR. ORLOFF, THE, 1964
AZTEC MUMMY, THE, 1957
B.S. I LOVE YOU, 1971
BABY DOLL, 1956
BABY FACE, 1933
BABY FACE NELSON, 1957
BABY LOVE, 1969
BABY MAKER, THE, 1970
BABYLON, 1980
BACHELOR PARTY, 1984
BACK ROADS, 1981
BACK TO THE WALL, 1959
BACKLASH, 1986
BAD BOYS, 1983
BAD COMPANY, 1986
BAD DREAMS, 1988
BADGE 373, 1973
BADLANDS, 1974
BALBOA, 1986
BALCONY, THE, 1963
BAND OF THE HAND, 1986
BAR ESPERANZA, 1985
BAR 51—SISTER OF LOVE, 1986
BARBARELLA, 1968
BARBARIAN QUEEN, 1985
BARBARIANS, THE, 1987
BARE KNUCKLES, 1978
BARFLY, 1987
BARN OF THE NAKED DEAD, 1976
BAROCCO, 1976
BARQUERO, 1970
BASHFUL ELEPHANT, THE, 1962
BASIC TRAINING, 1985
BASILEUS QUARTET, 1984
BASKET CASE, 1982
BAT 21, 1988
BATTLE BEYOND THE SUN, 1963
BAWDY ADVENTURES OF TOM JONES, THE, 1976
BAYAN KO, 1985
BEAST, THE, 1975
BEAST, THE, 1988
BEAST WITHIN, THE, 1982
BEATNIKS, THE, 1960
BEATRICE, 1988
BEAU PERE, 1981
BEAUTIFUL SWINDLERS, THE, 1967
BEDROOM EYES, 1984
BEDROOM WINDOW, THE, 1987
BEER, 1986
BEGINNER'S LUCK, 1986
BEGUILED, THE, 1971
BEHIND CLOSED SHUTTERS, 1952
BEHIND LOCKED DOORS, 1976
BELIEVE IN ME, 1971
BELIEVERS, THE, 1987
BELL JAR, THE, 1979

BELLE DE JOUR, 1968
BELLS, 1981
BELLY OF AN ARCHITECT, THE, 1987
BENJAMIN, 1968
BERLIN AFFAIR, THE, 1985
BERSERK, 1967
BERSERKER, 1988
BEST DEFENSE, 1984
BEST FRIENDS, 1975
BEST LITTLE WHOREHOUSE IN TEXAS, THE, 1982
BEST OF TIMES, THE, 1986
BEST SELLER, 1987
BETRAYAL, 1983
BETRAYED, 1988
BETTER A WIDOW, 1969
BETTER OFF DEAD, 1985
BETTER TOMORROW, A, 1987
BETTY BLUE, 1986
BEVERLY HILLS COP, 1984
BEVERLY HILLS COP II, 1987
BEYOND ATLANTIS, 1973
BEYOND GOOD AND EVIL, 1984
BEYOND THE DOOR, 1975
BEYOND THE DOOR II, 1979
BEYOND THE FOG, 1981
BEYOND THE WALLS, 1985
BEYOND THERAPY, 1987
BIG BAD MAMA, 1974
BIG BIRD CAGE, THE, 1972
BIG BOUNCE, THE, 1969
BIG CARNIVAL, THE, 1951
BIG COMBO, THE, 1955
BIG CUBE, THE, 1969
BIG DADDY, 1969
BIG DOLL HOUSE, THE, 1971
BIG EASY, THE, 1987
BIG FOOT, 1973
BIG HOUSE, U.S.A., 1955
BIG JAKE, 1971
BIG KNIFE, THE, 1955
BIG MEAT EATER, 1984
BIG OPERATOR, THE, 1959
BIG SWITCH, THE, 1950
BIG TOWN, THE, 1987
BIGGER SPLASH, A, 1984
BILLY JACK, 1971
BILLY TWO HATS, 1973
BIONIC BOY, THE, 1977
BIRDS, THE BEES AND THE ITALIANS, THE, 1967
BIRDY, 1984
BITTER RICE, 1950
BITTER TEARS OF PETRA VON KANT, THE, 1972
BLACK AND WHITE, 1986
BLACK ANGELS, THE, 1970
BLACK BELLY OF THE TARANTULA, THE, 1972
BLACK BELT JONES, 1974
BLACK CAESAR, 1973
BLACK CAT, THE, 1966
BLACK CAT, THE, 1984
BLACK CHRISTMAS, 1974
BLACK EYE, 1974
BLACK GESTAPO, THE, 1975
BLACK GUNN, 1972
BLACK JOY, 1977
BLACK JOY, 1986
BLACK KLANSMAN, THE, 1966
BLACK MAMA, WHITE MAMA, 1973
BLACK MOON RISING, 1986
BLACK PANTHER, THE, 1977
BLACK PIT OF DOCTOR M, 1958
BLACK ROOM, THE, 1984
BLACK SABBATH, 1963
BLACK SAMSON, 1974
BLACK SHAMPOO, 1976
BLACK SPIDER, THE, 1983
BLACK SUNDAY, 1961
BLACK WIDOW, 1987
BLACKENSTEIN, 1973
BLACKOUT, 1988
BLACULA, 1972
BLADE, 1973
BLADE IN THE DARK, A, 1986
BLADE RUNNER, 1982
BLAME IT ON RIO, 1984
BLASTFIGHTER, 1985
BLESS THEIR LITTLE HEARTS, 1984

BLIND CHANCE, 1987
BLIND DATE, 1984
BLIND DEAD, THE, 1972
BLIND DIRECTOR, THE, 1986
BLINDMAN, 1972
BLISS, 1985
BLOB, THE, 1988
BLOOD AND BLACK LACE, 1965
BLOOD AND GUTS, 1978
BLOOD AND LACE, 1971
BLOOD BATH, 1976
BLOOD DEMON, 1967
BLOOD DINER, 1987
BLOOD DRINKERS, THE, 1966
BLOOD FEAST, 1963
BLOOD FEAST, 1976
BLOOD FEUD, 1979
BLOOD FROM THE MUMMY'S TOMB, 1972
BLOOD MANIA, 1971
BLOOD MONEY, 1974
BLOOD OF DRACULA, 1957
BLOOD OF DRACULA'S CASTLE, 1967
BLOOD OF FRANKENSTEIN, 1970
BLOOD OF FU MANCHU, THE, 1968
BLOOD OF THE VAMPIRE, 1958
BLOOD ON SATAN'S CLAW, THE, 1970
BLOOD ORGY OF THE SHE-DEVILS, 1973
BLOOD RELATIVES, 1978
BLOOD ROSE, THE, 1970
BLOOD SIMPLE, 1984
BLOOD SISTERS, 1987
BLOOD SPATTERED BRIDE, THE, 1974
BLOOD TIDE, 1982
BLOOD WATERS OF DOCTOR Z, 1982
BLOODBROTHERS, 1978
BLOODLINE, 1979
BLOODLUST, 1959
BLOODSPORT, 1988
BLOODSUCKERS FROM OUTER SPACE, 1987
BLOODSUCKING FREAKS, 1982
BLOODTHIRSTY BUTCHERS, 1970
BLOODY BIRTHDAY, 1986
BLOODY BROOD, THE, 1959
BLOODY KIDS, 1983
BLOODY MAMA, 1970
BLOODY PIT OF HORROR, THE, 1965
BLOW OUT, 1981
BLOW TO THE HEART, 1983
BLOW-UP, 1966
BLUE ANGEL, THE, 1930
BLUE ANGEL, THE, 1959
BLUE CITY, 1986
BLUE COLLAR, 1978
BLUE DEMON VERSUS THE INFERNAL BRAINS, 1967
BLUE HEAVEN, 1985
BLUE IGUANA, THE, 1988
BLUE LAGOON, THE, 1980
BLUE VELVET, 1986
BLUEBEARD, 1972
BLUME IN LOVE, 1973
BOB AND CAROL AND TED AND ALICE, 1969
BOCCACCIO '70, 1962
BODY DOUBLE, 1984
BOLERO, 1984
BONA, 1984
BONNIE AND CLYDE, 1967
BONNIE PARKER STORY, THE, 1958
BOOGEY MAN, THE, 1980
BOOGEYMAN II, 1983
BOOK OF NUMBERS, 1973
BOOM!, 1968
BOOST, THE, 1988
BORDER HEAT, 1988
BORDER, THE, 1982
BORN AMERICAN, 1986
BORN IN EAST L.A., 1987
BORN IN FLAMES, 1983
BORN LOSERS, 1967
BORN OF FIRE, 1987
BORN TO KILL, 1975
BORSALINO, 1970
BORSALINO AND CO., 1974
BOSTON STRANGLER, THE, 1968
BOULEVARD NIGHTS, 1979
BOUNTY, THE, 1984

BOXCAR BERTHA, 1972
BOY...A GIRL, A, 1969
BOY AND HIS DOG, A, 1975
BOY MEETS GIRL, 1985
BOYS IN COMPANY C, THE, 1978
BOYS IN THE BAND, THE, 1970
BOYS NEXT DOOR, THE, 1985
BRADDOCK: MISSING IN ACTION III, 1988
BRAIN DAMAGE, 1988
BRAIN THAT WOULDN'T DIE, THE, 1959
BRAINWAVES, 1983
BRAMBLE BUSH, THE, 1960
BRAZIL, 1985
BREAD, LOVE AND DREAMS, 1953
BREAKFAST CLUB, THE, 1985
BREAKING ALL THE RULES, 1985
BREATHLESS, 1959
BREATHLESS, 1983
BREEDERS, 1986
BREEZY, 1973
BREWSTER'S MILLIONS, 1985
BRIDE IS MUCH TOO BEAUTIFUL, THE, 1958
BRIDES OF BLOOD, 1968
BRIDES OF DRACULA, THE, 1960
BRIGHT LIGHTS, BIG CITY, 1988
BRIGHTNESS, 1988
BRING ME THE HEAD OF ALFREDO GARCIA, 1974
BROKEN ENGLISH, 1981
BROKEN MIRRORS, 1985
BROTHER FROM ANOTHER PLANET, THE, 1984
BROTHERLY LOVE, 1970
BROTHERS, 1984
BUCKET OF BLOOD, 1934
BUDDIES, 1985
BULL DURHAM, 1988
BULLETPROOF, 1988
BULLIES, 1986
BURGLAR, 1987
BURIED ALIVE, 1984
BURKE AND HARE, 1972
BURMESE HARP, THE, 1985
BURN, 1970
BURN WITCH BURN, 1962
BURNING YEARS, THE, 1979
BURNING, THE, 1981
BURNT EVIDENCE, 1954
BURY ME AN ANGEL, 1972
BUSHIDO BLADE, THE, 1982
BUSTED UP, 1986
BUSTIN' LOOSE, 1981
BUTCHER BAKER (NIGHTMARE MAKER), 1982
BUTLEY, 1974
BUTTERCUP CHAIN, THE, 1971
BUTTERFIELD 8, 1960
BUTTERFLY, 1982
BY DESIGN, 1982
BY LOVE POSSESSED, 1961
BYE BYE MONKEY, 1978
C.H.U.D., 1984
C. C. AND COMPANY, 1971
CAGED, 1950
CAGED FURY, 1984
CAGED WOMEN, 1984
CAIN'S WAY, 1969
CAL, 1984
CALIFORNIA GIRLS, 1984
CALL HIM MR. SHATTER, 1976
CALL ME, 1988
CAMILA, 1985
CAMILLE 2000, 1969
CAMORRA, 1986
CAMP ON BLOOD ISLAND, THE, 1958
CANDY, 1968
CANDY MAN, THE, 1969
CANNABIS, 1970
CANNIBALS IN THE STREETS, 1982
CANNONBALL RUN II, 1984
CAPE FEAR, 1962
CAPONE, 1975
CAPTAIN KRONOS: VAMPIRE HUNTER, 1974
CAPTAIN MILKSHAKE, 1971
CARAVAGGIO, 1986
CARDIAC ARREST, 1980
CARMEN, BABY, 1967
CARNAL KNOWLEDGE, 1971
CARNY, 1980

BOLD: Films on Videocassette

CARRIE, 1976
CARRY ON EMANUELLE, 1978
CARRY ON HENRY VIII, 1970
CARS THAT ATE PARIS, THE, 1974
CASANOVA, 1976
CASANOVA '70, 1965
CASTLE OF BLOOD, 1964
CASUAL SEX?, 1988
CAT MURKIL AND THE SILKS, 1976
CAT O'NINE TAILS, 1971
CAT PEOPLE, 1982
CATCH-22, 1970
CATHERINE & CO., 1976
CATHY'S CURSE, 1977
CAULDRON OF DEATH, THE, 1979
CAVE GIRL, 1985
CEASE FIRE, 1985
CELLAR DWELLER, 1988
CEMENTERIO DEL TERROR, 1985
CENSUS TAKER, THE, 1984
CERTAIN FURY, 1985
CERTAIN, VERY CERTAIN, AS A MATTER OF
FACT... PROBABLE, 1970
CHAIN GANG, 1985
CHAIN LETTERS, 1985
CHAINED HEAT, 1983
CHALLENGE, 1974
CHAMBER OF HORRORS, 1966
CHANGELING, THE, 1980
CHANGES, 1969
CHANT OF JIMMIE BLACKSMITH, THE, 1980
CHAPMAN REPORT, THE, 1962
CHAPPAQUA, 1967
CHASE, THE, 1966
CHATO'S LAND, 1972
CHE?, 1973
CHEAPER TO KEEP HER, 1980
CHEATERS, THE, 1961
CHECKERBOARD, 1969
CHECKMATE, 1973
CHEECH AND CHONG'S NEXT MOVIE, 1980
CHEECH AND CHONG'S NICE DREAMS, 1981
**CHEECH AND CHONG'S THE CORSICAN
BROTHERS, 1984**
CHELSEA GIRLS, THE, 1967
CHESTY ANDERSON, U.S. NAVY, 1976
CHIDAMBARAM, 1986
CHILD, THE, 1977
CHILD IS A WILD THING, A, 1976
CHILD UNDER A LEAF, 1975
CHILDISH THINGS, 1969
CHILDREN, THE, 1980
CHILDREN OF BABYLON, 1980
CHILDREN OF RAGE, 1975
CHILDREN OF SANCHEZ, THE, 1978
CHILDREN OF THE DAMNED, 1963
**CHILDREN SHOULDN'T PLAY WITH DEAD
THINGS, 1972**
CHILD'S PLAY, 1988
CHINA GIRL, 1987
CHINA 9, LIBERTY 37, 1978
CHINATOWN, 1974
CHINESE BOXES, 1984
CHINESE ROULETTE, 1977
CHLOE IN THE AFTERNOON, 1972
CHOIRBOYS, THE, 1977
CHOOSE ME, 1984
CHOPPING MALL, 1986
CHOSEN, THE, 1978
CHRISTINE JORGENSEN STORY, THE, 1970
CHRISTINE KEELER AFFAIR, THE, 1964
CHROME AND HOT LEATHER, 1971
CIAO MANHATTAN, 1973
CIRCLE OF DECEIT, 1982
CIRCLE OF IRON, 1979
CIRCLE OF TWO, 1980
CIRCUS OF HORRORS, 1960
CISCO PIKE, 1971
CITY AND THE DOGS, THE, 1987
CITY GIRL, THE, 1984
CITY HEAT, 1984
CITY OF BLOOD, 1988
CITY OF SECRETS, 1963
CITY OF THE WALKING DEAD, 1983
CITY OF WOMEN, 1980
CITY ON FIRE, 1979

CLAIR DE FEMME, 1980
CLAN OF THE CAVE BEAR, THE, 1986
CLARETTA AND BEN, 1983
CLASS, 1983
CLASS ENEMY, 1984
CLASS OF MISS MAC MICHAEL, THE, 1978
CLASS OF 1984, 1982
CLASS OF NUKE 'EM HIGH, 1986
CLAY PIGEON, 1971
CLEAN AND SOBER, 1988
CLEGG, 1969
CLEOPATRA JONES, 1973
**CLEOPATRA JONES AND THE CASINO OF GOLD,
1975**
CLINIC, THE, 1983
CLOCKMAKER, THE, 1976
CLOCKWORK ORANGE, A, 1971
CLONUS HORROR, THE, 1979
CLUB LIFE, 1987
CLUE, 1985
COBRA, 1986
COCA-COLA KID, THE, 1985
COCAINE COWBOYS, 1979
COCAINE WARS, 1986
COCKTAIL, 1988
CODE OF SILENCE, 1985
COFFY, 1973
COLD SWEAT, 1974
COLD WIND IN AUGUST, 1961
COLONEL REDL, 1985
COLOR ME BLOOD RED, 1965
COLORS, 1988
COMBAT SHOCK, 1986
COME AND SEE, 1986
COME BACK BABY, 1968
COME BACK CHARLESTON BLUE, 1972
**COME BACK TO THE 5 & DIME, JIMMY DEAN,
JIMMY DEAN, 1982**
COMEBACK TRAIL, THE, 1982
COMETOGETHER, 1971
COMIC MAGAZINE, 1986
COMIN' AT YA!, 1981
COMING TO AMERICA, 1988
COMMANDO, 1985
COMMON LAW WIFE, 1963
COMPANY OF WOLVES, THE, 1985
CON ARTISTS, THE, 1981
CONCRETE JUNGLE, THE, 1982
CONDEMNED OF ALTONA, THE, 1963
CONFESSIONAL, THE, 1977
CONFESSIONS OF A POP PERFORMER, 1975
CONFESSIONS OF A WINDOW CLEANER, 1974
CONFLICT, 1939
CONJUGAL BED, THE, 1963
CONNECTION, THE, 1962
CONQUEROR WORM, THE, 1968
CONQUEST, 1984
CONSTANCE, 1984
CONSUMING PASSIONS, 1988
CONTACTO CHICANO, 1986
CONTAR HASTA TEN, 1986
COOL IT, CAROL!, 1970
COP, A, 1973
COP, 1988
CORPSE GRINDERS, THE, 1972
CORPSE OF BEVERLY HILLS, THE, 1965
CORRUPT, 1984
CORRUPTION, 1968
CORRUPTION OF CHRIS MILLER, THE, 1979
COTTON CLUB, THE, 1984
COTTON COMES TO HARLEM, 1970
COUCH TRIP, THE, 1988
COUNT YORGA, VAMPIRE, 1970
COUNT YOUR BULLETS, 1972
COUNTERFEIT COMMANDOS, 1981
COUNTESS DRACULA, 1972
COUP DE TORCHON, 1981
COUSIN, COUSINE, 1976
COUSINS IN LOVE, 1982
COVER ME BABE, 1970
COVERGIRL, 1984
COVERT ACTION, 1980
CRACKING UP, 1977
CRAWLSPACE, 1986
CRAZIES, THE, 1973
CRAZY BOYS, 1987

CRAZY FAMILY, THE, 1986
CRAZY JOE, 1974
CRAZY MAMA, 1975
CRAZY PARADISE, 1965
CREATOR, 1985
CREATURE, 1985
CREATURE WITH THE ATOM BRAIN, 1955
CREATURE WITH THE BLUE HAND, 1971
CREATURES THE WORLD FORGOT, 1971
CREEPER, THE, 1948
CREEPER, THE, 1980
CREEPERS, 1985
CREEPING FLESH, THE, 1973
CREEPSHOW, 1982
CREMATOR, THE, 1973
CRIME AT PORTA ROMANA, 1980
CRIME OF HONOR, 1987
CRIMES OF PASSION, 1984
CRIMES OF THE FUTURE, 1969
**CRIMINAL LIFE OF ARCHIBALDO DE LA CRUZ,
THE, 1962**
CRIMSON CULT, THE, 1970
CROCODILE, 1979
CROSS COUNTRY, 1983
CROSS MY HEART, 1987
CROSS OF IRON, 1977
CRUCIBLE OF TERROR, 1971
CRUISING, 1980
CRY BLOOD, APACHE, 1970
CRY OF THE BANSHEE, 1970
CUBA CROSSING, 1980
CUJO, 1983
CURIOUS DR. HUMPP, 1967
CURIOUS FEMALE, THE, 1969
CURSE OF FRANKENSTEIN, THE, 1957
CURSE OF THE BLOOD GHOULS, 1969
CURSE OF THE DEMON, 1958
CURSE OF THE DEVIL, 1973
CURSE OF THE LIVING CORPSE, THE, 1964
CURSE OF THE VAMPIRES, 1970
CURSE OF THE VOODOO, 1965
CURSE OF THE WEREWOLF, THE, 1961
CURSE, THE, 1987
CURTAINS, 1983
CUT AND RUN, 1986
CUTTER AND BONE, 1981
CYCLE SAVAGES, 1969
DADDY'S DEADLY DARLING, 1984
DADDY'S BOYS, 1988
DAMIEN—OMEN II, 1978
DAMNATION, 1988
DAMNED, THE, 1969
DAN'S MOTEL, 1982
DANGER ZONE, THE, 1987
DANGEROUS LIAISONS, 1988
DANGEROUSLY CLOSE, 1986
DANTON, 1983
DARK, THE, 1979
DARK END OF THE STREET, THE, 1981
DARK EYES, 1938
DARK RIVER, 1956
DARK ROAD, THE, 1948
DARK SIDE OF TOMORROW, THE, 1970
DARKER THAN AMBER, 1970
DARLING, 1965
DAS HAUS AM FLUSS, 1986
DATE BAIT, 1960
DAUGHTER OF DARKNESS, 1948
DAUGHTER OF EVIL, 1930
DAUGHTERS OF DARKNESS, 1971
DAWN OF THE DEAD, 1979
DAY AFTER HALLOWEEN, THE, 1981
DAY AT THE BEACH, A, 1970
DAY IN COURT, A, 1965
DAY IN THE DEATH OF JOE EGG, A, 1972
DAY OF ANGER, 1970
DAY OF RECKONING, 1933
DAY OF THE COBRA, THE, 1985
DAY OF THE DEAD, 1985
DE SADE, 1969
DEAD AND BURIED, 1981
DEAD ARE ALIVE, THE, 1972
DEAD-END DRIVE-IN, 1986
DEAD HEAT, 1988
DEAD KIDS, 1981
DEAD MAN WALKING, 1988

DEAD OF NIGHT, 1946
DEAD OF WINTER, 1987
DEAD PEOPLE, 1974
DEAD POOL, THE, 1988
DEAD RINGERS, 1988
DEAD ZONE, THE, 1983
DEADLINE, 1987
DEADLY BLESSING, 1981
DEADLY CHINA DOLL, 1973
DEADLY DREAMS, 1988
DEADLY EYES, 1982
DEADLY FEMALES, THE, 1976
DEADLY FORCE, 1983
DEADLY FRIEND, 1986
DEADLY HERO, 1976
DEADLY PASSION, 1985
DEADLY SPAWN, THE, 1983
DEADLY TRACKERS, 1973
DEADLY TWINS, 1988
DEADTIME STORIES, 1987
DEALING: OR THE BERKELEY TO BOSTON
   FORTY-BRICK LOST-BAG BLUES, 1971
DEAR, DEAD DELILAH, 1972
DEATH COLLECTOR, 1976
DEATH GAME, 1977
DEATH IN THE GARDEN, 1961
DEATH MACHINES, 1976
DEATH OF A SALESMAN, 1952
DEATH OF A SOLDIER, 1986
DEATH ON THE MOUNTAIN, 1961
DEATH RACE 2000, 1975
DEATH RIDES A HORSE, 1969
DEATH SENTENCE, 1967
DEATH SENTENCE, 1986
DEATH SHIP, 1980
DEATH TOOK PLACE LAST NIGHT, 1970
DEATH VALLEY, 1982
DEATH VENGEANCE, 1982
DEATH WATCH, 1980
DEATH WISH, 1974
DEATH WISH 4: THE CRACKDOWN, 1987
DEATH WISH 3, 1985
DEATH WISH II, 1982
DEATHDREAM, 1972
DEATHLINE, 1973
DEATHMASTER, THE, 1972
DEATHROW GAMESHOW, 1987
DEATHSPORT, 1978
DEATHSTALKER, 1983
DEATHSTALKER, THE, 1984
DEATHWATCH, 1966
DECEIVERS, THE, 1988
DECLINE OF THE AMERICAN EMPIRE, THE, 1986
DECOY FOR TERROR, 1970
DEEP, THE, 1977
DEEP END, 1970
DEEP IN THE HEART, 1983
DEEP RED, 1976
DEEP THRUST—THE HAND OF DEATH, 1973
DEER HUNTER, THE, 1978
DEF-CON 4, 1985
DEGREE OF MURDER, A, 1969
DEJA VU, 1985
DELIRIUM, 1979
DELIVERANCE, 1972
DELIVERY BOYS, 1984
DELTA FORCE, THE, 1986
DELTA FOX, 1979
DEMENTED, 1980
DEMENTIA, 1955
DEMON BARBER OF FLEET STREET, THE, 1939
DEMON LOVER, THE, 1977
DEMON SEED, 1977
DEMON WITCH CHILD, 1974
DEMON, THE, 1981
DEMONOID, 1981
DEMONS, 1985
DEMONS, 1987
DEMONS IN THE GARDEN, 1984
DEMONS OF LUDLOW, THE, 1983
DEMONS OF THE MIND, 1972
DEMONSTRATOR, 1971
DER ROSENKONIG, 1986
DERANGED, 1974
DESERT HEARTS, 1985
DESERT WARRIOR, 1985

DESERTER, THE, 1971
DESERTER AND THE NOMADS, THE, 1969
DESIRE, THE INTERIOR LIFE, 1980
DESIRE UNDER THE ELMS, 1958
DESIREE, 1984
DESPAIR, 1978
DESPERADOS, THE, 1969
DESPERATE DECISION, 1954
DESPERATE WOMEN, THE, 1954
DESPERATELY SEEKING SUSAN, 1985
DESTROY, SHE SAID, 1969
DETECTIVE, 1985
DETECTIVE BELLI, 1970
DETOUR, 1945
DETROIT 9000, 1973
DEVIL IN THE FLESH, 1986
DEVIL IS A WOMAN, THE, 1975
DEVIL WITHIN HER, THE, 1976
DEVIL WOMAN, 1976
DEVIL'S ANGELS, 1967
DEVIL'S BEDROOM, THE, 1964
DEVIL'S BRIDE, THE, 1968
DEVIL'S COMMANDMENT, THE, 1956
DEVIL'S EXPRESS, 1975
DEVIL'S MISTRESS, THE, 1968
DEVIL'S NIGHTMARE, THE, 1971
DEVIL'S RAIN, THE, 1975
DEVIL'S SISTERS, THE, 1966
DEVIL'S WEDDING NIGHT, THE, 1973
DEVIL'S WIDOW, THE, 1972
DEVONSVILLE TERROR, THE, 1983
DIABOLICAL DR. Z, THE, 1966
DIABOLIQUE, 1955
DIARY FOR MY CHILDREN, 1984
DIARY OF A BACHELOR, 1964
DIARY OF A CHAMBERMAID, 1964
DIARY OF A CLOISTERED NUN, 1973
DIARY OF A SHINJUKU BURGLAR, 1969
DIE, DIE, MY DARLING, 1965
DIE HARD, 1988
DIE LAUGHING, 1980
DIE SCREAMING, MARIANNE, 1970
DIFFERENT SONS, 1962
DIFFERENT STORY, A, 1978
DILLINGER, 1973
DILLINGER IS DEAD, 1969
DIMBOOLA, 1979
DIRT GANG, THE, 1972
DIRTY HANDS, 1976
DIRTY HARRY, 1971
DIRTY MARY, CRAZY LARRY, 1974
DIRTY O'NEIL, 1974
DIRTY OUTLAWS, THE, 1971
DIRTYMOUTH, 1970
DISCIPLE OF DEATH, 1972
DISOBEDIENT, 1953
DISTANCE, 1975
DISTANT THUNDER, 1988
DIVINE MR. J., THE, 1974
DIVINE NYMPH, THE, 1979
DJANGO, 1966
DJANGO KILL, 1967
DO NOT THROW CUSHIONS INTO THE RING, 1970
DO YOU REMEMBER DOLLY BELL?, 1986
DOC, 1971
DOCTEUR POPAUL, 1972
DOCTOR AND THE DEVILS, THE, 1985
DR. BUTCHER, M.D., 1982
DOCTOR DEATH: SEEKER OF SOULS, 1973
DOCTOR DETROIT, 1983
DR. FRANKENSTEIN ON CAMPUS, 1970
DR. GOLDFOOT AND THE GIRL BOMBS, 1966
DR. HECKYL AND MR. HYPE, 1980
DR. JEKYLL, 1985
DR. JEKYLL AND MR. HYDE, 1932
DR. JEKYLL AND THE WOLFMAN, 1971
DR. JEKYLL'S DUNGEON OF DEATH, 1982
DR. MINX, 1975
DOCTOR OF DOOM, 1962
DR. TARR'S TORTURE DUNGEON, 1972
DR. TERROR'S GALLERY OF HORRORS, 1967
DR. TERROR'S HOUSE OF HORRORS, 1965
DOCTORS' WIVES, 1971
DOG DAY, 1984
DOG DAY AFTERNOON, 1975
DOGS, 1976

DOGS OF WAR, THE, 1980
DOIN' TIME, 1985
DOLEMITE, 1975
DOLL SQUAD, THE, 1973
$ (DOLLARS), 1971
DOLLS, 1987
DOMINO PRINCIPLE, THE, 1977
DON IS DEAD, THE, 1973
DONA FLOR AND HER TWO HUSHANDS, 1977
DONA HERLINDA AND HER SON, 1986
DON'T ANSWER THE PHONE, 1980
DON'T BOTHER TO KNOCK, 1952
DON'T CRY, IT'S ONLY THUNDER, 1982
DON'T GO IN THE HOUSE, 1980
DON'T JUST LIE THERE, SAY SOMETHING!, 1973
DON'T LOOK IN THE BASEMENT, 1973
DON'T LOOK NOW, 1973
DON'T OPEN THE WINDOW, 1974
DON'T OPEN TILL CHRISTMAS, 1984
DOOMED TO DIE, 1985
DOOMSDAY VOYAGE, 1972
DOORWAY TO HELL, 1930
DORIAN GRAY, 1970
DORM THAT DRIPPED BLOOD, THE, 1983
DOUBLE EXPOSURE, 1982
DOUBLE NEGATIVE, 1980
DOUBLE SUICIDE, 1970
DOWN BY LAW, 1986
DOWN THE ANCIENT STAIRCASE, 1975
DR. BLACK AND MR. HYDE, 1976
DR. BLOOD'S COFFIN, 1961
DRACULA A.D. 1972, 1972
DRACULA AND THE SEVEN GOLDEN VAMPIRES,
   1978
DRACULA HAS RISEN FROM HIS GRAVE, 1968
DRACULA—PRINCE OF DARKNESS, 1966
DRACULA (THE DIRTY OLD MAN), 1969
DRACULA VERSUS FRANKENSTEIN, 1972
DRACULA'S DAUGHTER, 1936
DRACULA'S DOG, 1978
DRACULA'S GREAT LOVE, 1972
DRACULA'S WIDOW, 1988
DRAUGHTSMAN'S CONTRACT, THE, 1983
DREAM ON, 1981
DREAMANIAC, 1987
DREAMER, THE, 1970
DRESSED TO KILL, 1980
DRIFTER, THE, 1988
DRIFTER, 1975
DRIFTING, 1984
DRILLER KILLER, 1979
DRIVE, HE SAID, 1971
DRIVE-IN, 1976
DRIVE-IN MASSACRE, 1976
DRIVER, THE, 1978
DRIVER'S SEAT, THE, 1975
DROP THEM OR I'LL SHOOT, 1969
DROWNING BY NUMBERS, 1988
DRUM, 1976
DRUMMER OF VENGEANCE, 1974
DUBEAT-E-O, 1984
DUCK RINGS AT HALF PAST SEVEN, THE, 1969
DUDES, 1988
DUET FOR CANNIBALS, 1969
DUET FOR ONE, 1986
DUNGEONS OF HARROW, 1964
DUST, 1985
DUSTY AND SWEETS MCGEE, 1971
EARLY WORKS, 1970
EAST OF ELEPHANT ROCK, 1976
EASY RIDER, 1969
EAT AND RUN, 1986
EATEN ALIVE, 1976
EATING RAOUL, 1982
ECHO PARK, 1986
ECHOES, 1983
ECSTASY, 1940
EDGE OF FURY, 1958
EFFECTS, 1980
EFFI BRIEST, 1974
EGON SCHIELE—EXCESS AND PUNISHMENT, 1981
8 MILLION WAYS TO DIE, 1986
EIN BLICK-UND DIE LIEBE BRICHT AUS, 1987
EL CONDOR, 1970
EL DIPUTADO, 1985
EL NORTE, 1984

BOLD: Films on Videocassette

GABRIELA, 1984
GALACTIC GIGOLO, 1988
GALAXINA, 1980
GALAXY OF TERROR, 1981
GAMBLER, THE, 1974
GAME FOR VULTURES, A, 1980
GAME IS OVER, THE, 1967
GAME OF DEATH, THE, 1979
GAMES, 1967
GAMES MEN PLAY, THE, 1968
GAMES THAT LOVERS PLAY, 1971
GANJA AND HESS, 1973
GARDEN OF EDEN, 1954
GARDEN OF THE DEAD, 1972
GARDENS OF STONE, 1987
GAS, 1981
GAS-S-S-S!, 1970
GATE OF FLESH, 1964
GATES OF HELL, THE, 1983
GATOR BAIT, 1974
GAUNTLET, THE, 1977
GAY DECEIVERS, THE, 1969
GEEK MAGGOT BINGO, 1983
GENDARME OF ST. TROPEZ, THE, 1966
GENERAL MASSACRE, 1973
GENTLE RAIN, THE, 1966
GEORGIA, GEORGIA, 1972
GERMANY IN AUTUMN, 1978
GERMANY PALE MOTHER, 1984
GET CARTER, 1971
GET CRAZY, 1983
GET OUT YOUR HANDKERCHIEFS, 1978
GET TO KNOW YOUR RABBIT, 1972
GETAWAY, THE, 1972
GETTING EVEN, 1986
GETTING TOGETHER, 1976
GHASTLY ONES, THE, 1968
GHOST, THE, 1965
GHOST DANCE, 1984
GHOST STORY, 1981
GHOUL, THE, 1975
GHOULIES, 1985
G.I. EXECUTIONER, THE, 1985
GIANT OF MARATHON, THE, 1960
GIFT, THE, 1983
GILSODOM, 1986
GIMME AN 'F', 1984
GIORDANO BRUNO, 1973
GIRL FROM LORRAINE, A, 1982
GIRL FROM STARSHIP VENUS, THE, 1975
GIRL GRABBERS, THE, 1968
GIRL IN GOLD BOOTS, 1968
GIRL ON A CHAIN GANG, 1966
GIRL ON A MOTORCYCLE, THE, 1968
GIRL SMUGGLERS, 1967
GIRL, THE BODY, AND THE PILL, THE, 1967
GIRL WHO KNEW TOO MUCH, THE, 1969
GIRL, THE, 1987
GIRLS ABOUT TOWN, 1931
GIRLS FROM THUNDER STRIP, THE, 1966
GIRLS NIGHT OUT, 1984
GIRLS ON THE LOOSE, 1958
GIRLS SCHOOL SCREAMERS, 1986
GIRLS, THE, 1972
GLAD RAG DOLL, THE, 1929
GLADIATORS 7, 1964
GLASS CAGE, THE, 1964
GLASS HOUSES, 1972
GLASS KEY, THE, 1942
GLEN OR GLENDA, 1953
GLORIA, 1980
GLORY BOY, 1971
GLORY STOMPERS, THE, 1967
GLOVE, THE, 1980
GO NAKED IN THE WORLD, 1961
GO TELL THE SPARTANS, 1978
GOD FORGIVES—I DON'T!, 1969
GOD TOLD ME TO, 1976
GODDESS OF LOVE, THE, 1960
GODFATHER, THE, 1972
GODFATHER, THE, PART II, 1974
GOD'S GUN, 1977
GOD'S LITTLE ACRE, 1958
GODSEND, THE, 1980
GOHA, 1958
GOIN' DOWN THE ROAD, 1970

GOIN' SOUTH, 1978
GOING AND COMING BACK, 1985
GOING BERSERK, 1983
GOING HOME, 1971
GOING PLACES, 1974
GOKE, BODYSNATCHER FROM HELL, 1968
GOLD, 1974
GOLDEN APPLES OF THE SUN, 1971
GOLDEN BOX, THE, 1970
GOLDEN LADY, THE, 1979
GOLDEN NEEDLES, 1974
GOLDEN RENDEZVOUS, 1977
GOLDENGIRL, 1979
GOLDSTEIN, 1964
GOOD FATHER, THE, 1986
GOOD GUYS WEAR BLACK, 1978
GOOD LUCK, MISS WYCKOFF, 1979
GOOD MORNING... AND GOODBYE, 1967
GOOD MORNING, VIETNAM, 1987
GOOD MOTHER, THE, 1988
GOOD, THE BAD, AND THE UGLY, THE, 1967
GOOD TIME GIRL, 1950
GOODBYE COLUMBUS, 1969
GOODBYE EMMANUELLE, 1980
GOODBYE GEMINI, 1970
GOODBYE, MOSCOW, 1968
GOODBYE NEW YORK, 1985
GOODBYE, NORMA JEAN, 1976
GORDON'S WAR, 1973
GORKY PARK, 1983
GORP, 1980
GOTCHA!, 1985
GOTHIC, 1987
GOYOKIN, 1969
GRADUATION DAY, 1981
GRAND HIGHWAY, THE, 1988
GRAND PRIX, 1966
GRANDVIEW, U.S.A., 1984
GRASSHOPPER, THE, 1970
GRAVE OF THE VAMPIRE, 1972
GRAVEYARD OF HORROR, 1971
GRAVY TRAIN, THE, 1974
GREAT ALLIGATOR, 1980
GREAT GENERATION, THE, 1986
GREAT GUNDOWN, THE, 1977
GREAT MCGONAGALL, THE, 1975
GREAT NORTHFIELD, MINNESOTA RAID, THE,
  1972
GREAT SCOUT AND CATHOUSE THURSDAY, THE,
  1976
GREAT TEXAS DYNAMITE CHASE, THE, 1976
GREAT VAN ROBBERY, THE, 1963
GREAT WALL, THE, 1965
GREAT WAR, THE, 1961
GREAT WHITE, THE, 1982
GREED IN THE SUN, 1965
GREEN MARE, THE, 1961
GREH, 1962
GREMLINS, 1984
GRIM REAPER, THE, 1981
GRINGO, 1963
GROOVE TUBE, THE, 1974
GROUND ZERO, 1973
GROUP, THE, 1966
GRUESOME TWOSOME, 1968
GRUNT! THE WRESTLING MOVIE, 1985
GUARDIAN OF HELL, 1985
GUESS WHAT HAPPENED TO COUNT DRACULA,
  1970
GUESS WHAT WE LEARNED IN SCHOOL TODAY?,
  1970
GUEST, THE, 1984
GUILT, 1967
GUILT IS MY SHADOW, 1950
GUN CRAZY, 1949
GUN FEVER, 1958
GUN FOR A COWARD, 1957
GUN RIDERS, THE, 1969
GUN RUNNER, 1969
GUN, THE, 1978
GUNFIGHT, A, 1971
GUNMEN FROM LAREDO, 1959
GUNS, 1980
GUNS AND THE FURY, THE, 1983
GUNS FOR SAN SEBASTIAN, 1968
GUNS OF THE TREES, 1964

GURU, THE MAD MONK, 1971
GUTS IN THE SUN, 1959
GUTTER GIRLS, 1964
GUYANA, CULT OF THE DAMNED, 1980
GYMKATA, 1985
GYPSY AND THE GENTLEMAN, THE, 1958
GYPSY MOTHS, THE, 1969
H-MAN, THE, 1959
HAIL, 1973
HAIL MAFIA, 1965
HAIL, MARY, 1985
HALF MOON STREET, 1986
HALLOWEEN, 1978
HALLOWEEN IV: THE RETURN OF MICHAEL
  MYERS, 1988
HALLOWEEN III: SEASON OF THE WITCH, 1982
HALLOWEEN II, 1981
HALLS OF ANGER, 1970
HAMBURGER, 1986
HAMBURGER HILL, 1987
HAMLET, 1976
HAMMER, 1972
HAND, THE, 1981
HANDS OF STEEL, 1986
HANDS OF THE RIPPER, 1971
HANGUP, 1974
HANNIE CALDER, 1971
HANOI HILTON, THE, 1987
HAPPY BIRTHDAY, DAVY, 1970
HAPPY BIRTHDAY, GEMINI, 1980
HAPPY BIRTHDAY TO ME, 1981
HAPPY HOOKER GOES TO HOLLYWOOD, THE, 1980
HAPPY HOOKER GOES TO WASHINGTON, THE,
  1977
HAPPY HOOKER, THE, 1975
HAPPY HOUR, 1987
HARAKIRI, 1963
HARD CHOICES, 1984
HARD COUNTRY, 1981
HARD KNOCKS, 1980
HARD ROAD, THE, 1970
HARD TRAIL, 1969
HARDBODIES, 1984
HARDBODIES 2, 1986
HARDCORE, 1979
HARDER THEY FALL, THE, 1956
HAREM, 1985
HARRAD EXPERIMENT, THE, 1973
HARVEST, 1939
HASSAN, TERRORIST, 1968
HATCHET FOR A HONEYMOON, 1969
HAUNTED, 1976
HAUNTED STRANGLER, THE, 1958
HAUNTING OF JULIA, THE, 1981
HAUNTS, 1977
HAVE A NICE WEEKEND, 1975
HE KNOWS YOU'RE ALONE, 1980
HEAD, THE, 1961
HEAD ON, 1971
HEAD ON, 1981
HEART BEAT, 1979
HEART IS A LONELY HUNTER, THE, 1968
HEART OF THE STAG, 1984
HEARTACHES, 1981
HEARTBREAK RIDGE, 1986
HEAT, 1972
HEAT, 1987
HEAT AND SUNLIGHT, 1988
HEAT OF DESIRE, 1984
HEAT OF MIDNIGHT, 1966
HEATWAVE, 1983
HEAVEN HELP US, 1985
HEAVENLY BODIES, 1985
HEAVENLY KID, THE, 1985
HEAVEN'S GATE, 1980
HEAVY METAL, 1981
HELL COMES TO FROGTOWN, 1988
HELL IN THE PACIFIC, 1968
HELL NIGHT, 1981
HELL SQUAD, 1986
HELL UP IN HARLEM, 1973
HELLBOUND: HELLRAISER II, 1988
HELLCATS, THE, 1968
HELLHOLE, 1985
HELLIONS, THE, 1962
HELLO—GOODBYE, 1970

BOLD: Films on Videocassette

HELLO MARY LOU, PROM NIGHT II, 1987
HELLRAISER, 1987
HELL'S ANGELS ON WHEELS, 1967
HELL'S ANGELS '69, 1969
HELL'S BELLES, 1969
HELL'S BLOODY DEVILS, 1970
HELL'S CHOSEN FEW, 1968
HENTAI, 1966
HERO AND THE TERROR, 1988
HEX, 1973
HEY, GOOD LOOKIN', 1982
HI, MOM!, 1970
HI-RIDERS, 1978
HIDDEN, THE, 1987
HIGH, 1968
HIGH INFIDELITY, 1965
HIGH PLAINS DRIFTER, 1973
HIGH RISK, 1981
HIGH ROLLING, 1977
HIGH SCHOOL CONFIDENTIAL, 1958
HIGH SCHOOL HELLCATS, 1958
HIGH SPEED, 1986
HIGHLANDER, 1986
HIGHWAY TO HELL, 1984
HILL, THE, 1965
HILLS HAVE EYES, THE, 1978
HILLS HAVE EYES II, THE, 1985
HIMATSURI, 1985
HINOTORI, 1980
HISTORY, 1988
HIT, 1973
HIT, THE, 1985
HIT MAN, 1972
HITCHER, THE, 1986
HITCHHIKERS, THE, 1972
HO, 1968
HOG WILD, 1980
HOLCROFT COVENANT, THE, 1985
HOLD BACK TOMORROW, 1955
HOLLYWOOD BOULEVARD, 1976
HOLLYWOOD HARRY, 1985
HOLLYWOOD HIGH, 1977
HOLLYWOOD HIGH PART II, 1984
HOLLYWOOD HOT TUBS, 1984
HOLLYWOOD KNIGHTS, THE, 1980
HOLLYWOOD SHUFFLE, 1987
HOLLYWOOD VICE SQUAD, 1986
HOLLYWOOD ZAP!, 1986
HOLY INNOCENTS, THE, 1984
HOLY MOUNTAIN, THE, 1973
HOME FREE ALL, 1984
HOME FROM THE HILL, 1960
HOME SWEET HOME, 1981
HOMEBODIES, 1974
HOMEWORK, 1982
HOMICIDAL, 1961
HOMICIDE BUREAU, 1939
HONEYMOON KILLERS, THE, 1969
HONEYMOON OF HORROR, 1964
HONEYMOON OF TERROR, 1961
HONKY, 1971
HOOKED GENERATION, THE, 1969
HORNET'S NEST, 1970
HOROSCOPE, 1950
HORRIBLE DR. HICHCOCK, THE, 1964
HORROR CASTLE, 1965
HORROR CHAMBER OF DR. FAUSTUS, THE, 1962
HORROR HIGH, 1974
HORROR HOSPITAL, 1973
HORROR HOUSE, 1970
HORROR OF DRACULA, THE, 1958
HORROR OF FRANKENSTEIN, THE, 1970
HORROR OF THE BLOOD MONSTERS, 1970
HORROR PLANET, 1982
HORRORS OF THE BLACK MUSEUM, 1959
HORSE, THE, 1984
HOSPITAL MASSACRE, 1982
HOSPITAL MASSACRE, 1984
HOT BOX, THE, 1972
HOT CAR GIRL, 1958
HOT CHILD IN THE CITY, 1987
HOT CHILI, 1986
HOT DOG...THE MOVIE, 1984
HOT HOURS, 1963
HOT MOVES, 1984
HOT POTATO, 1976

HOT RESORT, 1985
HOT SPUR, 1968
HOT SUMMER WEEK, 1973
HOT TIMES, 1974
HOTEL COLONIAL, 1987
HOTEL NEW YORK, 1985
H.O.T.S., 1979
HOUR OF THE ASSASSIN, 1987
HOUR OF THE STAR, THE, 1986
HOUR OF THE WOLF, THE, 1968
HOUSE BY THE CEMETERY, THE, 1984
HOUSE BY THE LAKE, THE, 1977
HOUSE IS NOT A HOME, A, 1964
HOUSE OF DARKNESS, 1948
HOUSE OF EVIL, 1968
HOUSE OF EXORCISM, THE, 1976
HOUSE OF FREAKS, 1973
HOUSE OF GAMES, 1987
HOUSE OF GOD, THE, 1984
HOUSE OF LONG SHADOWS, THE, 1983
HOUSE OF 1,000 DOLLS, 1967
HOUSE OF PSYCHOTIC WOMEN, THE, 1973
HOUSE OF SECRETS, 1929
HOUSE OF THE BLACK DEATH, 1965
HOUSE OF USHER, 1960
HOUSE OF WHIPCORD, 1974
HOUSE OF WOMEN, 1962
HOUSE ON SORORITY ROW, THE, 1983
HOUSE ON THE EDGE OF THE PARK, 1985
HOUSE THAT DRIPPED BLOOD, THE, 1971
HOUSE THAT SCREAMED, THE, 1970
HOUSE THAT VANISHED, THE, 1974
HOUSE WHERE DEATH LIVES, THE, 1984
HOUSE WHERE EVIL DWELLS, THE, 1982
HOW TO SEDUCE A WOMAN, 1974
HOWLING, THE, 1981
HOWLING TWO: YOUR SISTER IS A WEREWOLF, 1985
HOWLING IV: THE ORIGINAL NIGHTMARE, 1988
HUD, 1963
HUGS AND KISSES, 1968
HUK, 1956
HUMAN CONDITION, THE, 1959
HUMAN EXPERIMENTS, 1980
HUMAN FACTOR, THE, 1975
HUMAN HIGHWAY, 1982
HUMAN MONSTER, THE, 1940
HUMAN TORNADO, THE, 1976
HUMANOIDS FROM THE DEEP, 1980
HUMONGOUS, 1982
HUNCHBACK OF THE MORGUE, THE, 1972
HUNGER, 1968
HUNGER, THE, 1983
HUNGRY WIVES, 1973
HUNT, THE, 1967
HUNTER'S BLOOD, 1987
HUNTING PARTY, THE, 1977
HURRY SUNDOWN, 1967
HUSH... HUSH, SWEET CHARLOTTE, 1964
HUSTLE, 1975
HYPNOTIC EYE, THE, 1960
HYSTERIA, 1965
HYSTERICAL, 1983
I AM A FUGITIVE FROM A CHAIN GANG, 1932
I AM A GROUPIE, 1970
I COULD NEVER HAVE SEX WITH ANY MAN WHO
    HAS SO LITTLE REGARD FOR MY HUSBAND, 1973
I DISMEMBER MAMA, 1974
I DRINK YOUR BLOOD, 1971
I EAT YOUR SKIN, 1971
I ESCAPED FROM DEVIL'S ISLAND, 1973
I LOVE MY WIFE, 1970
I LOVE YOU, ALICE B. TOKLAS!, 1968
I LOVE YOU, I KILL YOU, 1972
I MARRIED A MONSTER FROM OUTER SPACE, 1958
I NEVER PROMISED YOU A ROSE GARDEN, 1977
I SPIT ON YOUR GRAVE, 1962
I SPIT ON YOUR GRAVE, 1983
I START COUNTING, 1970
I, THE JURY, 1982
I WANT TO LIVE!, 1958
I WANT WHAT I WANT, 1972
I WAS A TEENAGE ZOMBIE, 1987
ICE, 1970
ICE HOUSE, THE, 1969

IDEAL LODGER, THE, 1957
IDIOT, THE, 1960
IDOL, THE, 1966
IF ..., 1968
IF HE HOLLERS, LET HIM GO, 1968
IGOROTA, THE LEGEND OF THE TREE OF LIFE, 1970
ILLIAC PASSION, THE, 1968
ILLICIT INTERLUDE, 1954
ILLUMINATIONS, 1976
ILLUSION OF BLOOD, 1966
ILLUSTRATED MAN, THE, 1969
I'M GOING TO GET YOU ... ELLIOT BOY, 1971
I'M GONNA GIT YOU SUCKA, 1988
IMMORTAL BACHELOR, THE, 1980
IMPASSE, 1969
IMPORTANT MAN, THE, 1961
IMPOSTORS, 1979
IMPULSE, 1975
IMPULSE, 1984
IN A YEAR OF THIRTEEN MOONS, 1980
IN CELEBRATION, 1975
IN COLD BLOOD, 1967
IN PRAISE OF OLDER WOMEN, 1978
IN SEARCH OF ANNA, 1978
IN SEARCH OF GREGORY, 1970
IN THE FRENCH STYLE, 1963
IN THE MOUTH OF THE WOLF, 1988
IN THE NAME OF LIFE, 1947
IN THE SHADOW OF KILIMANJARO, 1986
INBREAKER, THE, 1974
INCENSE FOR THE DAMNED, 1970
INCHON, 1981
INCIDENT, THE, 1967
INCREDIBLE MELTING MAN, THE, 1978
INCREDIBLE TWO-HEADED TRANSPLANT, THE, 1971
INCREDIBLY STRANGE CREATURES WHO
    STOPPED LIVING AND BECAME CRAZY
    MIXED-UP ZOMBIES, THE, 1965
INCUBUS, 1966
INCUBUS, THE, 1982
INDECENT, 1962
INDEPENDENCE DAY, 1983
INFERNO, 1953
INFERNO, 1980
INHERITANCE, THE, 1978
INHERITORS, THE, 1985
INITIATION, THE, 1984
INJUN FENDER, 1973
INN OF THE DAMNED, 1974
INNERVIEW, THE, 1974
INNOCENT, THE, 1979
INNOCENT, THE, 1988
INNOCENT BYSTANDERS, 1973
INSIDE AMY, 1975
INSIDE DAISY CLOVER, 1965
INSIDE DETROIT, 1955
INSIDE OUT, 1986
INSIDE STRAIGHT, 1951
INSIDE THE MAFIA, 1959
INSIGNIFICANCE, 1985
INSOMNIACS, 1986
INSPECTOR CALLS, AN, 1954
INSTANT JUSTICE, 1986
INTERNECINE PROJECT, THE, 1974
INTERNS, THE, 1962
INTIMACY, 1966
INTO THE NIGHT, 1985
INVASION OF THE BEE GIRLS, 1973
INVASION OF THE BLOOD FARMERS, 1972
INVASION OF THE VAMPIRES, THE, 1961
INVASION U.S.A., 1985
INVESTIGATION OF A CITIZEN ABOVE SUSPICION, 1970
IS THIS TRIP REALLY NECESSARY?, 1970
ISABEL, 1968
ISADORA, 1968
ISLAND, THE, 1980
ISLAND CLAWS, 1981
ISLAND OF THE DAMNED, 1976
IT!, 1967
IT DON'T PAY TO BE AN HONEST CITIZEN, 1985
IT LIVES AGAIN, 1978
IT SEEMED LIKE A GOOD IDEA AT THE TIME, 1975
ITALIAN CONNECTION, THE, 1973
IT'S A 2'6" ABOVE THE GROUND WORLD, 1972

IT'S ALIVE, 1974
IT'S ALIVE III: ISLAND OF THE ALIVE, 1988
IT'S NEVER TOO LATE, 1984
IT'S NOT THE SIZE THAT COUNTS, 1979
J.D.'S REVENGE, 1976
JABBERWOCKY, 1977
JACK THE RIPPER, 1959
JACK'S BACK, 1988
JACKSON COUNTY JAIL, 1976
JAGGED EDGE, THE, 1985
JAIL BAIT, 1977
JAILBIRD ROCK, 1988
JAMES JOYCE'S WOMEN, 1985
JAWS OF SATAN, 1980
JAWS: THE REVENGE, 1987
JEKYLL AND HYDE...TOGETHER AGAIN, 1982
JENNIFER ON MY MIND, 1971
JERK, THE, 1979
JESSIE'S GIRLS, 1976
JESTER, THE, 1987
JIGSAW, 1968
JINXED!, 1982
JOAN OF THE ANGELS, 1962
JOANNA, 1968
JOCKS, 1987
JOE, 1970
JOEY BOY, 1965
JOHN AND MARY, 1969
JOHNNY BANCO, 1969
JOHNNY BE GOOD, 1988
JOHNNY COOL, 1963
JOHNNY GOT HIS GUN, 1971
JOHNNY HAMLET, 1972
JOHNNY NOBODY, 1965
JOHNNY RENO, 1966
JOHNNY YUMA, 1967
JOKER, THE, 1961
JONATHAN, 1973
JOSEPH ANDREWS, 1977
JOSHUA, 1976
JOSHUA THEN AND NOW, 1985
JOURNEY, 1977
JOURNEY, THE, 1986
JOURNEY AMONG WOMEN, 1977
JOURNEY INTO FEAR, 1976
JOURNEY INTO NOWHERE, 1963
JOURNEY THROUGH ROSEBUD, 1972
JOURNEYS FROM BERLIN—1971, 1980
JOVITA, 1970
JOY, 1983
JOY HOUSE, 1964
JOY IN THE MORNING, 1965
JOY OF SEX, 1984
JOYRIDE, 1977
JOYSTICKS, 1983
JUBILEE, 1978
JUD, 1971
JUDGE, THE, 1949
JUDY'S LITTLE NO-NO, 1969
JUGGERNAUT, 1937
JULIE DARLING, 1982
JUMPIN' JACK FLASH, 1986
JUNGLE WARRIORS, 1984
JUST A GIGOLO, 1979
JUST BEFORE DAWN, 1980
JUST BETWEEN FRIENDS, 1986
JUST FOR THE HELL OF IT, 1968
JUST ONCE MORE, 1963
JUSTINE, 1969
KAMIKAZE '89, 1983
KAMOURASKA, 1973
KANDYLAND, 1988
KANSAS CITY BOMBER, 1972
KAOS, 1985
KAPO, 1964
KAREN, THE LOVEMAKER, 1970
KARMA, 1986
KEEP, THE, 1983
KEEP MY GRAVE OPEN, 1980
KENTUCKY FRIED MOVIE, THE, 1977
KEROUAC, 1985
KEY, THE, 1958
KEY EXCHANGE, 1985
KEY WITNESS, 1960
KIDNAPPING OF THE PRESIDENT, THE, 1980
KILL, THE, 1968

KILL A DRAGON, 1967
KILL AND KILL AGAIN, 1981
KILL BABY KILL, 1966
KILL HER GENTLY, 1958
KILL! KILL! KILL!, 1972
KILL SQUAD, 1982
KILL THEM ALL AND COME BACK ALONE, 1970
KILL ZONE, 1985
KILLER AT LARGE, 1936
KILLER AT LARGE, 1947
KILLER ELITE, THE, 1975
KILLER FISH, 1979
KILLER FORCE, 1975
KILLER INSIDE ME, THE, 1976
KILLER IS LOOSE, THE, 1956
KILLER PARTY, 1986
KILLER THAT STALKED NEW YORK, THE, 1950
KILLER WORKOUT, 1987
KILLERS, THE, 1984
KILLERS THREE, 1968
KILLING FIELDS, THE, 1984
KILLING HEAT, 1984
KILLING HOUR, THE, 1982
KILLING KIND, THE, 1973
KILLPOINT, 1984
KIND LADY, 1951
KINDRED, THE, 1987
KINFOLK, 1970
KING BLANK, 1983
KING MURDER, THE, 1932
KING, MURRAY, 1969
KING OF CHINATOWN, 1939
KING OF THE GYPSIES, 1978
KING OF THE MOUNTAIN, 1981
KING OF THE STREETS, 1986
KING, QUEEN, KNAVE, 1972
KING RAT, 1965
KING'S JESTER, THE, 1947
KINGS OF THE SUN, 1963
KIRLIAN WITNESS, THE, 1978
KISS ME DEADLY, 1955
KISS OF THE SPIDER WOMAN, 1985
KISS OF THE TARANTULA, 1975
KISS THE GIRLS AND MAKE THEM DIE, 1967
KITTY AND THE BAGMAN, 1983
KLUTE, 1971
KNIFE IN THE WATER, 1963
KNIGHTS OF THE CITY, 1985
KOLBERG, 1945
KONGO, 1932
KRUSH GROOVE, 1985
KURAGEJIMA—LEGENDS FROM A SOUTHERN
    ISLAND, 1970
KUROENKO, 1968
KWAIDAN, 1965
LA BABY SITTER, 1975
LA BALANCE, 1983
LA CAGE AUX FOLLES, 1979
LA FUGA, 1966
LA NOTTE BRAVA, 1962
LA NUIT DE VARENNES, 1983
LA PRISONNIERE, 1969
LA RONDE, 1954
LA SEGUA, 1985
LA VISITA, 1966
LACEMAKER, THE, 1977
LACOMBE, LUCIEN, 1974
L'ADDITION, 1985
LADIES AND GENTLEMEN, THE FABULOUS
    STAINS, 1982
LADIES CLUB, THE, 1986
LADIES OF THE LOTUS, 1987
LADY CHATTERLEY'S LOVER, 1981
LADY DRACULA, THE, 1974
LADY FRANKENSTEIN, 1971
LADY GREY, 1980
LADY HAMILTON, 1969
LADY IN A CAGE, 1964
LADY IN CEMENT, 1968
LADY IN RED, THE, 1979
LADY IN THE CAR WITH GLASSES AND A GUN,
    THE, 1970
LADY OF MONZA, THE, 1970
LADY SINGS THE BLUES, 1972
LADY, STAY DEAD, 1982
LAIR OF THE WHITE WORM, THE, 1988

LAKE, THE, 1970
LAKE OF DRACULA, 1973
L'AMOUR, 1973
LAND OF THE MINOTAUR, 1976
LANDRU, 1963
L'ANNEE DES MEDUSES, 1987
L'ARGENT, 1984
LAS RATAS NO DUERMEN DE NOCHE, 1974
LAS VEGAS WEEKEND, 1985
LASER MAN, THE, 1988
LASSITER, 1984
LAST AFFAIR, THE, 1976
LAST AMERICAN VIRGIN, THE, 1982
LAST BRIDGE, THE, 1957
LAST DAYS OF MAN ON EARTH, THE, 1975
LAST DETAIL, THE, 1973
LAST EMBRACE, 1979
LAST FIGHT, THE, 1983
LAST HARD MEN, THE, 1976
LAST HORROR FILM, THE, 1984
LAST HOUSE ON DEAD END STREET, 1977
LAST HOUSE ON THE LEFT, 1972
LAST HUNTER, THE, 1984
LAST MAN ON EARTH, THE, 1964
LAST MARRIED COUPLE IN AMERICA, THE, 1980
LAST MOVIE, THE, 1971
LAST NIGHT AT THE ALAMO, 1984
LAST PORNO FLICK, THE, 1974
LAST RESORT, THE, 1986
LAST RITES, 1980
LAST RITES, 1988
LAST STOP, THE, 1949
LAST STRAW, THE, 1987
LAST SUMMER, 1969
LAST TEMPTATION OF CHRIST, THE, 1988
LATENT IMAGE, 1988
LAUGHING POLICEMAN, THE, 1973
LAW AND DISORDER, 1974
LAW OF DESIRE, 1987
LAWYER, THE, 1969
LE BOUCHER, 1971
LE CRABE TAMBOUR, 1984
LE DERNIER COMBAT, 1984
LE LEOPARD, 1985
LE VIOL, 1968
LEAP INTO THE VOID, 1982
LEARNING TREE, THE, 1969
LEATHER BOYS, THE, 1965
LEAVE HER TO HEAVEN, 1946
LEGACY, 1976
LEGACY, THE, 1979
LEGACY OF BLOOD, 1973
LEGACY OF BLOOD, 1978
LEGEND OF BILLIE JEAN, THE, 1985
LEGEND OF BLOOD MOUNTAIN, THE, 1965
LEGEND OF THE WOLF WOMAN, THE, 1977
LEO THE LAST, 1970
LEONOR, 1977
LEOPARD MAN, THE, 1943
LEPKE, 1975
LES ABYSSES, 1964
LES BICHES, 1968
LES CARABINIERS, 1968
LES LIAISONS DANGEREUSES, 1961
LESS THAN ZERO, 1987
LETHAL OBSESSION, 1988
LETHAL WEAPON, 1987
L'ETOILE DU NORD, 1983
LET'S GET HARRY, 1987
LEVIATHAN, 1961
L'HOMME BLESSE, 1985
LIANNA, 1983
LIAR'S DICE, 1980
LIAR'S MOON, 1982
LIBERATION OF L.B. JONES, THE, 1970
LIBIDO, 1973
LICENSE TO DRIVE, 1988
LIFE IN THE BALANCE, A, 1955
LIFE LOVE DEATH, 1969
LIFE STUDY, 1973
LIFEFORCE, 1985
LIFT, THE, 1965
LIGHT ACROSSS THE STREET, THE, 1957
LIGHT AT THE EDGE OF THE WORLD, THE, 1971
LIKE A TURTLE ON ITS BACK, 1981

BOLD: Films on Videocassette

LILI MARLEEN, 1981
LILIES OF THE FIELD, 1930
LIMBO, 1972
LIMBO LINE, THE, 1969
LINEUP, THE, 1958
LINK, 1986
LION OF THE DESERT, 1981
LIONS LOVE, 1969
LIPSTICK, 1976
LIQUID SKY, 1982
LISA, 1962
LISBON, 1956
LISTEN, LET'S MAKE LOVE, 1969
LISTEN TO THE CITY, 1984
LISZTOMANIA, 1975
LITTLE DARLINGS, 1980
LITTLE FAUSS AND BIG HALSY, 1970
LITTLE FLAMES, 1985
LITTLE GIRL WHO LIVES DOWN THE LANE, THE, 1977
LITTLE LAURA AND BIG JOHN, 1973
LITTLE MOTHER, 1973
LITTLE MURDERS, 1971
LITTLE SEX, A, 1982
LITTLE SISTER, THE, 1985
LITTLE TREASURE, 1985
LITTLE VERA, 1988
LIVING HEAD, THE, 1969
LIVING LEGEND, 1980
LIVING VENUS, 1961
LIZA, 1976
LOCAL COLOR, 1978
LOLA, 1982
LOLLIPOP, 1966
LONELY GUY, THE, 1984
LONELY HEARTS, 1983
LONELY LADY, THE, 1983
LONELY LANE, 1963
LONELY PASSION OF JUDITH HEARNE, THE, 1988
LONERS, THE, 1972
LONESOME COWBOYS, 1968
LONG GOOD FRIDAY, THE, 1982
LONG GOODBYE, THE, 1973
LONG RIDE FROM HELL, A, 1970
LONG RIDERS, THE, 1980
LONGEST YARD, THE, 1974
LONGING FOR LOVE, 1966
LONGSHOT, THE, 1986
LOOKER, 1981
LOOKIN' TO GET OUT, 1982
LOOKING FOR EILEEN, 1987
LOOSE SCREWS, 1985
LORD SHANGO, 1975
LORDS OF DISCIPLINE, THE, 1983
LOS OLVIDADOS, 1950
LOSERS, THE, 1968
LOSERS, THE, 1970
LOSIN' IT, 1983
LOST BOYS, THE, 1987
LOST EMPIRE, THE, 1985
LOST IN AMERICA, 1985
LOST SEX, 1968
LOST SOULS, 1961
LOULOU, 1980
LOVE A LA CARTE, 1965
LOVE AFFAIR; OR THE CASE OF THE MISSING
  SWITCHBOARD OPERATOR, 1968
LOVE AND ANARCHY, 1974
LOVE AND MONEY, 1982
LOVE BUTCHER, THE, 1982
LOVE CHILD, 1982
LOVE FEAST, THE, 1966
LOVE HUNGER, 1965
LOVE IN A FOUR LETTER WORLD, 1970
LOVE IN GERMANY, A, 1984
LOVE IS A CAROUSEL, 1970
LOVE IS A FAT WOMAN, 1988
LOVE IS A SPLENDID ILLUSION, 1970
LOVE IS MY PROFESSION, 1959
LOVE MACHINE, THE, 1971
LOVE ME DEADLY, 1972
LOVE MERCHANT, THE, 1966
LOVE NOW...PAY LATER, 1966
LOVE ON A PILLOW, 1963
LOVELESS, THE, 1982
LOVELINES, 1984

LOVERS, THE, 1959
LOVERS AND LIARS, 1981
LOVIN' MOLLY, 1974
LOVING COUPLES, 1980
LOVING COUPLES, 1966
LOVING MEMORY, 1970
LOW BLOW, 1986
LOYALTIES, 1986
LUCRECE BORGIA, 1953
LUDWIG, 1973
LULU, 1978
LULU, 1962
LUMIERE, 1976
LUNA, 1979
LUNATICS, THE, 1986
LUNCH WAGON, 1981
LUPE, 1967
LUST FOR A VAMPIRE, 1971
LUST FOR GOLD, 1949
LUST IN THE DUST, 1985
LYDIA, 1964
M, 1933
MA BARKER'S KILLER BROOD, 1960
MACBETH, 1971
MACHINE GUN McCAIN, 1970
MACHISMO—40 GRAVES FOR 40 GUNS, 1970
MACHO CALLAHAN, 1970
MACK, THE, 1973
MACON COUNTY LINE, 1974
MAD ATLANTIC, THE, 1967
MAD BOMBER, THE, 1973
MAD DOCTOR OF BLOOD ISLAND, THE, 1969
MAD DOG MORGAN, 1976,Aus.
MAD EXECUTIONERS, THE, 1965
MAD MAX, 1979
MAD ROOM, THE, 1969
MADAME AKI, 1963
MADAME DEATH, 1968
MADAME ROSA, 1977
MADELEINE IS, 1971
MADLY, 1970
MADMAN, 1982
MADRON, 1970
MAEVA, 1961
MAFU CAGE, THE, 1978
MAGIC, 1978
MAGIC GARDEN OF STANLEY SWEETHART, THE, 1970
MAGIC SPECTACLES, 1961
MAKING IT, 1971
MAKING LOVE, 1982
MAKING THE GRADE, 1984
MALATESTA'S CARNIVAL, 1973
MALE SERVICE, 1966
MALENKA, THE VAMPIRE, 1972
MALIBU BIKINI SHOP, THE, 1987
MALIBU HIGH, 1979
MALICIOUS, 1974
MALONE, 1987
MAMMA DRACULA, 1980
MAN, A WOMAN AND A KILLER, A, 1975
MAN CALLED HORSE, A, 1970
MAN CALLED SLEDGE, A, 1971
MAN FACING SOUTHEAST, 1986
MAN FROM HONG KONG, 1975
MAN FROM O.R.G.Y., THE, 1970
MAN FROM YESTERDAY, THE, 1949
MAN IN LOVE, A, 1987
MAN IN THE WILDERNESS, 1971
MAN LIKE EVA, A, 1985
MAN OF FLOWERS, 1984
MAN OF VIOLENCE, 1970
MAN ON FIRE, 1987
MAN WHO CAME FOR COFFEE, THE, 1970
MAN WHO LAUGHS, THE, 1966
MAN WHO LOVED WOMEN, THE, 1977
MAN WHO LOVED WOMEN, THE, 1983
MAN WITH THE GOLDEN ARM, THE, 1955
MAN WITH TWO BRAINS, THE, 1983
MAN WITH TWO HEADS, THE, 1972
MANCHURIAN AVENGER, 1985
MANDINGO, 1975
MANGO TREE, THE, 1981
MANHATTAN BABY, 1986
MANHUNT, THE, 1986
MANHUNTER, 1986

MANIA, 1961
MANIAC, 1934
MANIAC COP, 1988
MANIAC, 1980
MANIAC MANSION, 1978
MANIFESTO, 1988
MANKILLERS, 1987
MANON, 1987
MANON 70, 1968
MANSION OF THE DOOMED, 1976
MANTIS IN LACE, 1968
MARATHON MAN, 1976
MARCH OF THE SPRING HARE, 1969
MARDI GRAS MASSACRE, 1978
MARIA'S LOVERS, 1985
MARILYN, 1953
MARK OF THE DEVIL, 1970
MARK OF THE DEVIL II, 1975
MARKETA LAZAROVA, 1967
MARRIAGE—ITALIAN STYLE, 1964
MARRIAGE OF MARIA BRAUN, THE, 1979
MARRIED COUPLE, A, 1969
MARRIED TO THE MOB, 1988
MARTIN, 1979
MARY, MARY, BLOODY MARY, 1975
MARYJANE, 1968
MASCARA, 1987
MASK, THE, 1961
MASOCH, 1980
MASQUERADE, 1988
MASSACRE AT CENTRAL HIGH, 1976
MASSIVE RETALIATION, 1984
MATA HARI, 1985
MATCHLESS, 1974
MATCHMAKING OF ANNA, THE, 1972
MATTER OF DAYS, A, 1969
MATTER OF MORALS, A, 1961
MAURICE, 1987
MAUSOLEUM, 1983
MAXIMUM OVERDRIVE, 1986
MC CABE AND MRS. MILLER, 1971
MC MASTERS, THE, 1970
MC Q, 1974
ME AND MY BROTHER, 1969
MEAL, THE, 1975
MEAN DOG BLUES, 1978
MEAN FRANK AND CRAZY TONY, 1976
MEAN JOHNNY BARROWS, 1976
MEAN SEASON, THE, 1985
MEAN STREETS, 1973
MEAT CLEAVER MASSACRE, 1977
MEATBALLS III, 1987
MECHANIC, THE, 1972
MEDEA, 1971
MEDIUM COOL, 1969
MEIER, 1987
MELINDA, 1972
MELVIN, SON OF ALVIN, 1984
MEMOIRS, 1984
MEMOIRS OF PRISON, 1984
MEN, 1985
MEPHISTO, 1981
MERCENARY FIGHTERS, 1988
MERRY CHRISTMAS, MR. LAWRENCE, 1983
MEXICO IN FLAMES, 1982
MICROWAVE MASSACRE, 1983
MID-DAY MISTRESS, 1968
MIDDLE AGE CRAZY, 1980
MIDDLE AGE SPREAD, 1979
MIDNIGHT, 1983
MIDNIGHT COWBOY, 1969
MIDNIGHT CROSSING, 1988
MIDNIGHT EXPRESS, 1978
MIDNIGHT MAN, THE, 1974
MIDNIGHT PLEASURES, 1975
MIDNIGHT RUN, 1988
MIDSUMMER NIGHT'S DREAM, A, 1984
MIKE'S MURDER, 1984
MILL OF THE STONE WOMEN, 1963
MILLER'S WIFE, THE, 1957
MINI-SKIRT MOB, THE, 1968
MINX, THE, 1969
MIRRORS, 1984
MISCHIEF, 1985
MISFIT BRIGADE, THE, 1988
MISHIMA, 1985

MISS JESSICA IS PREGNANT, 1970
MISS MARY, 1987
MISS MONA, 1987
MISS SADIE THOMPSON, 1953
MISSING IN ACTION, 1984
MISSING IN ACTION 2—THE BEGINNING, 1985
MISSION, THE, 1984
MISSIONARY, THE, 1982
MISSISSIPPI BURNING, 1988
MISTRESS OF THE APES, 1981
MITCHELL, 1975
MIXED BLOOD, 1984
MODERN GIRLS, 1986
MODERN MARRIAGE, A, 1950
MODERNS, THE, 1988
MOM AND DAD, 1948
MOMENT BY MOMENT, 1978
MOMENTS, 1974
MONA LISA, 1986
MONDO TRASHO, 1970
MONEY, THE, 1975
MONEY MOVERS, 1978
MONGREL, 1982
MONKEY SHINES: AN EXPERIMENT IN FEAR, 1988
MONSIEUR VERDOUX, 1947
MONSIGNOR, 1982
MONSTER, 1979
MONSTER DOG, 1986
MONSTER OF LONDON CITY, THE, 1967
MONSTER SHARK, 1986
MONTENEGRO, 1981
MONTREAL MAIN, 1974
MONTY PYTHON AND THE HOLY GRAIL, 1975
MONTY PYTHON'S LIFE OF BRIAN, 1979
MONTY PYTHON'S THE MEANING OF LIFE, 1983
MOON IN SCORPIO, 1987
MOON IN THE GUTTER, THE, 1983
MOON OVER THE ALLEY, 1980
MOONCHILD, 1972
MOONFIRE, 1970
MOONLIGHTING WIVES, 1966
MOONSHINER'S WOMAN, 1968
MORE, 1969
MORE THAN A MIRACLE, 1967
MORTUARY, 1983
MOSQUITO COAST, THE, 1986
MOTEL HELL, 1980
MOTHER, JUGS & SPEED, 1976
MOTHER'S DAY, 1980
MOTOR PSYCHO, 1965
MOUNTAIN MEN, THE, 1980
MOUNTAINTOP MOTEL MASSACRE, 1986
MOUSE AND THE WOMAN, THE, 1981
MOVIE HOUSE MASSACRE, 1986
MOVING, 1988
MOVING VIOLATIONS, 1985
MS. 45, 1981
MUMSY, NANNY, SONNY, AND GIRLY, 1970
MURDER IN THE MUSIC HALL, 1946
MURDER IN THE NIGHT, 1940
MURDER IN THE OLD RED BARN, 1936
MURDER IN TIMES SQUARE, 1943
MURDER IN TRINIDAD, 1934
MURDER, INC., 1960
MURDER IS MY BEAT, 1955
MURDER IS MY BUSINESS, 1946
MURDER IS NEWS, 1939
MURDER OF DR. HARRIGAN, THE, 1936
MURDER ON A BRIDLE PATH, 1936
MURDER ONE, 1988
MURDER REPORTED, 1958
MURDERERS AMONG US, 1948
MURDERS IN THE RUE MORGUE, 1971
MURDERS IN THE ZOO, 1933
MURIETA, 1965
MURMUR OF THE HEART, 1971
MURPHY'S LAW, 1986
MUSHROOM EATER, THE, 1976
MUSIC LOVERS, THE, 1971
MUSIC MACHINE, THE, 1979
MUTANT HUNT, 1987
MUTATIONS, THE, 1974
MUTILATOR, THE, 1985
MY BEAUTIFUL LAUNDRETTE, 1986
MY BEST FRIEND'S GIRL, 1984
MY BLOOD RUNS COLD, 1965

MY BLOODY VALENTINE, 1981
MY BODY HUNGERS, 1967
MY BREAKFAST WITH BLASSIE, 1983
MY BRILLIANT CAREER, 1980
MY BROTHER HAS BAD DREAMS, 1977
MY CHAUFFEUR, 1986
MY FIRST LOVE, 1978
MY FIRST WIFE, 1985
MY GUN IS QUICK, 1957
MY LOVER, MY SON, 1970
MY MAN ADAM, 1986
MY NAME IS IVAN, 1963
MY NAME IS NOBODY, 1974
MY NEW PARTNER, 1984
MY TUTOR, 1983
MYSTERY OF ALEXINA, THE, 1985
MYSTIC PIZZA, 1988
MYSTIQUE, 1981
MYTH, THE, 1965
NAIL GUN MASSACRE, 1987
NAKED AND THE DEAD, THE, 1958
NAKED ANGELS, 1969
NAKED CAGE, THE, 1986
NAKED KISS, THE, 1964
NAKED NIGHT, THE, 1956
NAKED PREY, THE, 1966
NAKED VENGEANCE, 1986
NAKED WORLD OF HARRISON MARKS, THE, 1967
NANA, 1983
NANNY, THE, 1965
NARCO MEN, THE, 1969
NARCOTICS STORY, THE, 1958
NATIONAL LAMPOON'S CLASS REUNION, 1982
NATURAL ENEMIES, 1979
NEAR DARK, 1987
NECROPOLIS, 1987
NEON MANIACS, 1986
NEST OF VIPERS, 1979
NESTING, THE, 1981
NEVER ON SUNDAY, 1960
NEVER TOO YOUNG TO DIE, 1986
NEW BARBARIANS, THE, 1983
NEW CENTURIONS, THE, 1972
NEW HOUSE ON THE LEFT, THE, 1978
NEW KIDS, THE, 1985
NEW LIFE STYLE, THE, 1970
NEW LOVE, 1968
NEW YEAR'S EVIL, 1980
NEW YORK NIGHTS, 1984
NEW YORK'S FINEST, 1988
NEXT!, 1971
NEXT MAN, THE, 1976
NEXT OF KIN, 1983
NIGHT AND THE CITY, 1950
NIGHT ANGELS, 1987
NIGHT CALL NURSES, 1974
NIGHT CHILD, 1975
NIGHT DIGGER, THE, 1971
NIGHT EVELYN CAME OUT OF THE GRAVE, THE, 1973
NIGHT FLOWERS, 1979
NIGHT GAMES, 1966
NIGHT GAMES, 1980
NIGHT GOD SCREAMED, THE, 1975
NIGHT HAIR CHILD, 1971
NIGHT HEAVEN FELL, THE, 1958
NIGHT IN HEAVEN, A, 1983
NIGHT IN THE LIFE OF JIMMY REARDON, A, 1988
NIGHT MUST FALL, 1937
NIGHT MUST FALL, 1964
NIGHT OF A THOUSAND CATS, 1974
NIGHT OF BLOODY HORROR, 1969
NIGHT OF THE BLOODY APES, 1968
NIGHT OF THE COBRA WOMAN, 1974
NIGHT OF THE CREEPS, 1986
NIGHT OF THE FOLLOWING DAY, THE, 1969
NIGHT OF THE GENERALS, THE, 1967
NIGHT OF THE GHOULS, 1959
NIGHT OF THE HUNTER, THE, 1955
NIGHT OF THE IGUANA, THE, 1964
NIGHT OF THE JUGGLER, 1980
NIGHT OF THE LIVING DEAD, 1968
NIGHT OF THE PROWLER, THE, 1979
NIGHT OF THE SHOOTING STARS, THE, 1982
NIGHT OF THE STRANGLER, 1975
NIGHT OF THE WITCHES, 1970

NIGHT OF THE ZOMBIES, 1981
NIGHT OF THE ZOMBIES, 1983
NIGHT PATROL, 1984
NIGHT PORTER, THE, 1974
NIGHT SCHOOL, 1981
NIGHT SHADOWS, 1984
NIGHT STALKER, THE, 1987
NIGHT THEY ROBBED BIG BERTHA'S, THE, 1975
NIGHT ZOO, 1988
NIGHTFORCE, 1987
NIGHTHAWKS, 1978
NIGHTHAWKS, 1981
NIGHTMARE, 1963
NIGHTMARE, 1981
NIGHTMARE HONEYMOON, 1973
NIGHTMARE IN BLOOD, 1978
NIGHTMARE IN THE SUN, 1964
NIGHTMARE IN WAX, 1969
NIGHTMARE ON ELM STREET 4: THE DREAM MASTER, A, 1988
NIGHTMARE ON ELM STREET PART 2: FREDDY'S REVENGE, A, 1985
NIGHTMARE ON ELM STREET 3: DREAM WARRIORS, A, 1987
NIGHTMARE ON ELM STREET, A, 1984
NIGHTMARE WEEKEND, 1986
NIGHTMARES, 1983
NIGHTMARE'S PASSENGERS, 1986
NIGHTS OF SHAME, 1961
NIGHTWARS, 1988
NIGHTWING, 1979
9 1/2 WEEKS, 1986
NINE DAYS OF ONE YEAR, 1964
9 DEATHS OF THE NINJA, 1985
1984, 1984
90 DAYS, 1986
90 DEGREES IN THE SHADE, 1966
NINJA III—THE DOMINATION, 1984
NINJA TURF, 1986
NINTH CIRCLE, THE, 1961
NINTH CONFIGURATION, THE, 1980
NO BLADE OF GRASS, 1970
NO DEAD HEROES, 1987
NO ESCAPE, 1953
NO EXIT, 1962
NO GREATER LOVE, 1944
NO LOVE FOR JOHNNIE, 1961
NO MAN'S LAND, 1964
NO MAN'S LAND, 1987
NO MERCY, 1986
NO MORE EXCUSES, 1968
NO ORCHIDS FOR MISS BLANDISH, 1948
NO ROOM TO DIE, 1969
NO SMALL AFFAIR, 1984
NO SURRENDER, 1986
NO TIME FOR BREAKFAST, 1978
NO TIME FOR ECSTASY, 1963
NO TIME TO BE YOUNG, 1957
NO WAY BACK, 1976
NO WAY OUT, 1975
NO WAY OUT, 1987
NO MERCY MAN, THE, 1975
NOCTURNA, 1979
NOMADS, 1985
NONE BUT THE BRAVE, 1965
NORMAN LOVES ROSE, 1982
NORTHVILLE CEMETERY MASSACRE, THE, 1976
NOSTALGHIA, 1984
NOT NOW DARLING, 1975
NOT OF THIS EARTH, 1988
NOT QUITE JERUSALEM, 1985
NOT SINCE CASANOVA, 1988
NOTORIOUS CLEOPATRA, THE, 1970
NOW AND FOREVER, 1983
NOWHERE TO HIDE, 1987
NUMBER TWO, 1975
NUNZIO, 1978
NURSE ON WHEELS, 1964
NURSE SHERRI, 1978
NUTCRACKER, 1982
O LUCKY MAN!, 1973
OASIS, THE, 1984
OBLONG BOX, THE, 1969
O.C. AND STIGGS, 1987
OCTAGON, THE, 1980
OCTAMAN, 1971

BOLD: Films on Videocassette

OCTOBER MOTH, 1960
ODD JOB, THE, 1978
ODD OBSESSION, 1961
ODDO, 1967
ODE TO BILLY JOE, 1976
OF HUMAN BONDAGE, 1946
OF HUMAN BONDAGE, 1964
OF LOVE AND DESIRE, 1963
OF MICE AND MEN, 1939
OF UNKNOWN ORIGIN, 1983
OF WAYWARD LOVE, 1964
OFF LIMITS, 1988
OFF THE WALL, 1983
OFFENDERS, THE, 1980
OFFENSE, THE, 1973
OFFICE GIRLS, 1974
OFFICER AND A GENTLEMAN, AN, 1982
OFFICIAL STORY, THE, 1985
OFFSPRING, THE, 1987
OH! CALCUTTA!, 1972
OKAY BILL, 1971
OKEFENOKEE, 1960
OKLAHOMA CRUDE, 1973
OLD BOYFRIENDS, 1979
OLDEST PROFESSION, THE, 1968
OLGA'S GIRLS, 1964
OMEGA SYNDROME, 1987
OMEN, THE, 1976
ON THE BEACH, 1959
ON THE EDGE, 1985
ON THE LINE, 1984
ON THE NICKEL, 1980
ON THE WATERFRONT, 1954
ON THE YARD, 1978
ONCE BITTEN, 1985
ONCE IS NOT ENOUGH, 1975
ONCE UPON A TIME IN AMERICA, 1984
ONCE UPON A TIME IN THE WEST, 1969
ONCE YOU KISS A STRANGER, 1969
ONE DEADLY SUMMER, 1984
ONE DOWN TWO TO GO, 1982
ONE-EYED JACKS, 1961
ONE FLEW OVER THE CUCKOO'S NEST, 1975
ONE FROM THE HEART, 1982
100 RIFLES, 1969
125 ROOMS OF COMFORT, 1974
ONE MAN JURY, 1978
ONE NIGHT ONLY, 1986
ONE NIGHT STAND, 1976
ONE PLUS ONE, 1969
1,000 CONVICTS AND A WOMAN, 1971
ONE-TRICK PONY, 1980
ONIMASA, 1983
OPEN ALL NIGHT, 1934
OPEN CITY, 1945
OPEN HOUSE, 1987
OPEN SEASON, 1974
OPPOSING FORCE, 1987
ORDERED TO LOVE, 1963
ORDINARY PEOPLE, 1980
ORGY OF THE DEAD, 1965
ORIANE, 1985
OSA, 1985
OTHER, THE, 1972
OTHER SIDE OF BONNIE AND CLYDE, THE, 1968
OTHER SIDE OF MIDNIGHT, THE, 1977
OTHER SIDE OF THE UNDERNEATH, THE, 1972
OUR DAILY BREAD, 1950
OUR FATHER, 1985
OUR HITLER, A FILM FROM GERMANY, 1980
OUR MOTHER'S HOUSE, 1967
OUT OF BOUNDS, 1986
OUT OF CONTROL, 1985
OUT OF THE BLUE, 1982
OUTBACK, 1971
OUTING, THE, 1987
OUTLAND, 1981
OUTLAW, THE, 1943
OUTLAW JOSEY WALES, THE, 1976
OUTLAW MOTORCYCLES, 1967
OUTRAGEOUS!, 1977
OUTRAGEOUS FORTUNE, 1987
OUTSIDER, THE, 1980
OUTSIDER IN AMSTERDAM, 1983
OUTSIDERS, THE, 1987
OVER THE BROOKLYN BRIDGE, 1984

OVER THE EDGE, 1979
OVER THE SUMMER, 1986
OVERCOAT, THE, 1965
OVERKILL, 1987
OVERLORD, 1975
OXFORD BLUES, 1984
PACK, THE, 1977
PAD...AND HOW TO USE IT, THE, 1966
PADDY, 1970
PALE RIDER, 1985
PALLET ON THE FLOOR, 1984
PALM BEACH, 1979
PANIC IN NEEDLE PARK, 1971
PANIC IN THE CITY, 1968
PANIC IN YEAR ZERO!, 1962
PAPERBACK HERO, 1973
PAPILLON, 1973
PARADES, 1972
PARADISE, 1982
PARADISE ALLEY, 1978
PARADISE MOTEL, 1985
PARADISIO, 1962
PARALLAX VIEW, THE, 1974
PARANOIAC, 1963
PARASITE, 1982
PARDON MY BRUSH, 1964
PARIS BLUES, 1961
PARIS OOH-LA-LA!, 1963
PARTING GLANCES, 1986
PARTNERS, 1982
PARTY CAMP, 1987
PARTY'S OVER, THE, 1966
PASS THE AMMO, 1988
PASSAGE, THE, 1979
PASSENGER, THE, 1970
PASSING THROUGH, 1977
PASSION, 1968
PASSION, 1983
PASSION IN THE SUN, 1964
PASSION OF LOVE, 1982
PATRICK, 1979
PATRIOT, THE, 1986
PATTI ROCKS, 1988
PATTY HEARST, 1988
PAUL AND MICHELLE, 1974
PAULINE AT THE BEACH, 1983
PAYDAY, 1972
PAYMENT IN BLOOD, 1968
PEACE KILLERS, THE, 1971
PEEK-A-BOO, 1961
PEEPING TOM, 1960
PENITENTE MURDER CASE, THE, 1936
PENITENTIARY, 1979
PENITENTIARY II, 1982
PENITENTIARY III, 1987
PENTHOUSE, THE, 1967
PEOPLE MEET AND SWEET MUSIC FILLS THE
  HEART, 1969
PEOPLE NEXT DOOR, THE, 1970
PEOPLE WHO OWN THE DARK, 1975
PERCY, 1971
PERFECT, 1985
PERFECT STRANGERS, 1984
PERIL, 1985
PERILS OF GWENDOLINE, THE, 1984
PERILS OF P.K., THE, 1986
PERSONA, 1967
PERSONAL SERVICES, 1987
PETEY WHEATSTRAW, 1978
PETS, 1974
PHANTASM, 1979
PHANTASM II, 1988
PHANTOM OF LIBERTY, THE, 1974
PHOBIA, 1980
PHOBIA, 1988
PICK-UP SUMMER, 1981
PICTURE MOMMY DEAD, 1966
PIECES, 1983
PIERROT LE FOU, 1968
PINK FLOYD—THE WALL, 1982
PINK MOTEL, 1983
PIRANHA, 1978
PIRANHA II: THE SPAWNING, 1981
PIT STOP, 1969
PIXOTE, 1981
PIZZA TRIANGLE, THE, 1970

P.J., 1968
PLANES, TRAINS AND AUTOMOBILES, 1987
PLATOON, 1986
PLATOON LEADER, 1988
PLAY DEAD, 1981
PLAY IT AS IT LAYS, 1972
PLAY MISTY FOR ME, 1971
PLAYERS, 1979
PLAYGIRLS AND THE BELLBOY, THE, 1962
PLAYGIRLS AND THE VAMPIRE, 1964
PLAYGROUND, THE, 1965
PLAYMATES, 1969
PLEASURE PLANTATION, 1970
PLEDGEMASTERS, THE, 1971
PLENTY, 1985
PLOUGHMAN'S LUNCH, THE, 1984
POINT BLANK, 1967
POINT OF TERROR, 1971
POLICE, 1986
POLICE ACADEMY, 1984
**POLICE ACADEMY 2: THEIR FIRST ASSIGNMENT,
  1985**
POLICEWOMAN, 1974
POLTERGEIST II, 1986
POLYESTER, 1981
POM POM GIRLS, THE, 1976
POPE OF GREENWICH VILLAGE, THE, 1984
PORKY'S, 1982
PORKY'S REVENGE, 1985
PORKY'S II: THE NEXT DAY, 1983
PORTNOY'S COMPLAINT, 1972
PORTRAIT IN SMOKE, 1957
PORTRAIT IN TERROR, 1965
POSSESSION, 1981
POSSESSION OF JOEL DELANEY, THE, 1972
POSTMAN ALWAYS RINGS TWICE, THE, 1946
POSTMAN ALWAYS RINGS TWICE, THE, 1981
P.O.W. THE ESCAPE, 1986
POWER, 1986
POWER, THE, 1984
POWER OF EVIL, THE, 1985
POWERFORCE, 1983
PRAY FOR DEATH, 1986
PREACHERMAN, 1971
PREDATOR, 1987
PREHISTORIC WOMEN, 1967
PREPPIES, 1984
PRESIDENT'S ANALYST, THE, 1967
PRETTY BABY, 1978
PRETTY BUT WICKED, 1965
PRETTY MAIDS ALL IN A ROW, 1971
PRETTY SMART, 1987
PRETTYKILL, 1987
PREY, THE, 1984
PRICE OF FLESH, THE, 1962
PRICK UP YOUR EARS, 1987
PRIEST OF LOVE, 1981
PRIEST'S WIFE, THE, 1971
PRIMAL SCREAM, 1988
PRIME CUT, 1972
PRIME TIME, THE, 1960
PRIMITIVE LOVE, 1966
PRINCE OF DARKNESS, 1987
PRINCE OF THE CITY, 1981
PRINCIPAL, THE, 1987
PRISON, 1988
PRIVATE BENJAMIN, 1980
PRIVATE COLLECTION, 1972
PRIVATE DUTY NURSES, 1972
PRIVATE FUNCTION, A, 1985
PRIVATE LESSONS, 1981
PRIVATE PARTS, 1972
PRIVATE PROPERTY, 1960
PRIVATE RESORT, 1985
PRIVATE ROAD, 1971
PRIVATE SCHOOL, 1983
PRIVATE SHOW, 1985
PRIVATES ON PARADE, 1984
PRIZZI'S HONOR, 1985
PRODUCERS, THE, 1967
PROFESSIONALS, THE, 1966
PROJECT: KILL, 1976
PROM NIGHT, 1980
PROMISED LAND, 1988
PROMISES, PROMISES, 1963
PROSTITUTE, 1980

PROTECTOR, THE, 1985
PROTECTORS, BOOK 1, THE, 1981
PROVIDENCE, 1977
PROWL GIRLS, 1968
PROWLER, THE, 1981
PRUDENCE AND THE PILL, 1968
PSYCH-OUT, 1968
PSYCHIC, THE, 1979
PSYCHIC KILLER, 1975
PSYCHO, 1960
PSYCHO A GO-GO!, 1965
PSYCHO-CIRCUS, 1967
PSYCHO FROM TEXAS, 1982
PSYCHO III, 1986
PSYCHO II, 1983
PSYCHOMANIA, 1964
PSYCHOMANIA, 1974
PSYCHOPATH, THE, 1966
PSYCHOPATH, THE, 1973
PSYCHOS IN LOVE, 1987
PSYCHOTRONIC MAN, THE, 1980
PSYCHOUT FOR MURDER, 1971
PSYCOSISSIMO, 1962
PUBERTY BLUES, 1983
PUBLIC ENEMY, THE, 1931
PULSEBEAT, 1986
PUMPKIN EATER, THE, 1964
PUMPKINHEAD, 1988
PUNISHMENT PARK, 1971
PUPPET ON A CHAIN, 1971
PURCHASE PRICE, THE, 1932
PURE S, 1976
PURPLE GANG, THE, 1960
PURPLE HAZE, 1982
PURPLE HILLS, THE, 1961
PURPLE NOON, 1961
PURPLE RAIN, 1984
PURPLE TAXI, THE, 1977
PURPLE V, THE, 1943
PURSUIT, 1975
PURSUIT OF HAPPINESS, THE, 1971
PUSHER, THE, 1960
PUSSYCAT ALLEY, 1965
PUSSYCAT, PUSSYCAT, I LOVE YOU, 1970
PUT UP OR SHUT UP, 1968
PUTNEY SWOPE, 1969
PUZZLE OF A DOWNFALL CHILD, 1970
PYRO, 1964
PYX, THE, 1973
Q, 1982
QUADROON, 1972
QUADROPHENIA, 1979
QUALCOSA DI BIONDO, 1985
QUARTIERE, 1987
QUEEN OF BLOOD, 1966
QUEENS, THE, 1968
QUERELLE, 1983
QUERY, 1945
QUEST FOR FIRE, 1982
QUESTION, THE, 1977
QUESTION OF SILENCE, 1984
QUICK AND THE DEAD, THE, 1963
QUIET COOL, 1986
QUIET EARTH, THE, 1985
QUIET PLACE IN THE COUNTRY, A, 1970
QUILOMBO, 1986
RABBIT, RUN, 1970
RABID, 1976
RACQUET, 1979
RADIOACTIVE DREAMS, 1986
RAGE, THE, 1963
RAGE OF HONOR, 1987
RAGING BULL, 1980
RAMBO: FIRST BLOOD, PART II, 1985
RAMBO III, 1988
RAMRODDER, THE, 1969
RAN, 1985
RAPE, THE, 1965
RAPPIN', 1985
RASPUTIN, 1985
RATS ARE COMING! THE WEREWOLVES ARE
  HERE!, THE, 1972
RAVAGER, THE, 1970
RAW COURAGE, 1984
RAW DEAL, 1986
RAW FORCE, 1982

RAW WEEKEND, 1964
RAWHEAD REX, 1987
RAZORBACK, 1984
RE-ANIMATOR, 1985
RE: LUCKY LUCIANO, 1974
REACHING OUT, 1983
REALM OF FORTUNE, THE, 1986
REBEL, 1985
REBEL ROUSERS, 1970
RECKLESS, 1984
RECRUITS, 1986
RED DAWN, 1984
RED DESERT, 1965
RED HEAT, 1988
RED HEAT, 1988
RED KISS, 1985
RED LIPS, 1964
RED SORGHUM, 1988
REDEEMER, THE, 1978
REDNECK, 1975
REFLECTIONS IN A GOLDEN EYE, 1967
REFORM SCHOOL GIRLS, 1986
REFUGE, 1981
REMEMBER MY NAME, 1978
RENALDO AND CLARA, 1978
RENDEZVOUS, 1985
RENEGADE GIRLS, 1974
RENO AND THE DOC, 1984
"RENT-A-GIRL", 1965
RENTADICK, 1972
RENTED LIPS, 1988
REPO MAN, 1984
REPULSION, 1965
RETRIBUTION, 1988
RETURN, 1986
RETURN OF THE DRAGON, 1974
RETURN OF THE LIVING DEAD, 1985
RETURN OF THE LIVING DEAD PART II, 1988
RETURN OF THE SECAUCUS SEVEN, 1980
RETURN TO HORROR HIGH, 1987
RETURN TO SALEM'S LOT, A, 1988
RETURNING, THE, 1983
REUBEN, REUBEN, 1983
REVENGE, 1986
REVENGE OF THE CHEERLEADERS, 1976
REVENGE OF THE SHOGUN WOMEN, 1982
REVOLT OF JOB, THE, 1984
RICH AND FAMOUS, 1981
RICHARD'S THINGS, 1981
RIDE BEYOND VENGEANCE, 1966
RIDERS OF THE STORM, 1988
RIFF RAFF GIRLS, 1962
RIKKY AND PETE, 1988
RIOT, 1969
RIP-OFF, 1971
RISKY BUSINESS, 1983
RITA, SUE AND BOB TOO!, 1987
RITUAL, THE, 1970
RIVALS, 1972
RIVER NIGER, THE, 1976
RIVERRUN, 1968
RIVER'S EDGE, 1987
ROAD GAMES, 1981
ROAD MOVIE, 1974
ROAD TO ETERNITY, 1962
ROAD TO RUIN, 1934
ROAD TO SALINA, 1971
ROAD WARRIOR, THE, 1982
ROBINSON'S GARDEN, 1988
ROBOCOP, 1987
ROBOT HOLOCAUST, 1987
ROBOT VS. THE AZTEC MUMMY, THE, 1965
ROCCO PAPALEO, 1974
ROCK 'N' ROLL NIGHTMARE, 1987
ROCKERS, 1980
ROCKY HORROR PICTURE SHOW, THE, 1975
ROLLER BLADE, 1986
ROLLERBALL, 1975
ROLLING THUNDER, 1977
ROLLOVER, 1981
ROMA, 1972
ROMANTIC ENGLISHWOMAN, THE, 1975
ROOM AT THE TOP, 1959
ROOMMATES, 1971
ROOMMATES, THE, 1973
ROPE OF FLESH, 1965

ROSARY, THE, 1931
ROSARY MURDERS, THE, 1987
ROSE, THE, 1979
ROSE FOR EVERYONE, A, 1967
ROSEMARY'S BABY, 1968
R.O.T.O.R., 1988
ROTTEN APPLE, THE, 1963
ROTWEILER: DOGS OF HELL, 1984
ROUGH NIGHT IN JERICHO, 1967
ROUND UP, THE, 1969
RUBY, 1977
RUDE BOY, 1980
RULING CLASS, THE, 1972
RUMBLE FISH, 1983
RUN, ANGEL, RUN, 1969
RUN WITH THE WIND, 1966
RUNAWAY TRAIN, 1985
RUNNING HOT, 1984
RUNNING MAN, THE, 1987
RUNNING OUT OF LUCK, 1986
RYAN'S DAUGHTER, 1970
SABINA, THE, 1979
SABOTAGE, 1937
SACRED KNIVES OF VENGEANCE, THE, 1974
SAGA OF DRACULA, THE, 1975
SAILOR FROM GIBRALTAR, THE, 1967
SAILOR WHO FELL FROM GRACE WITH THE SEA,
  THE, 1976
SAILOR'S RETURN, THE, 1978
ST. ELMO'S FIRE, 1985
ST. IVES, 1976
SAINT JACK, 1979
ST. VALENTINE'S DAY MASSACRE, THE, 1967
SALAAM BOMBAY, 1988
SALAMANDER, THE, 1983
SALLY BISHOP, 1932
SALOME, 1986
SALOME'S LAST DANCE, 1988
SALTO, 1966
SALVADOR, 1986
SALVATION!, 1987
SALVATORE GIULIANO, 1966
SAME TO YOU, 1987
SAMMY AND ROSIE GET LAID, 1987
SAM'S SONG, 1971
SAMURAI ASSASSIN, 1965
SAMURAI, 1955
SANCTUARY, 1961
SANDRA, 1966
SANDS OF BEERSHEBA, 1966
SANDS OF THE KALAHARI, 1965
SANTA, 1932
SANTA FE PASSAGE, 1955
SANTEE, 1973
SANTO CONTRA BLUE DEMON EN LA ATLANTIDA,
  1968
SANTO CONTRA EL DOCTOR MUERTE, 1974
SANTO CONTRA LA HIJA DE FRANKENSTEIN, 1971
SANTO CONTRA LA INVASION DE LOS
  MARCIANOS, 1966
SANTO EN EL MUSEO DE CERA, 1963
SANTO Y BLUE DEMON CONTRA LOS MONSTRUOS,
  1968
SATAN IN HIGH HEELS, 1962
SATAN'S BED, 1965
SATAN'S CHEERLEADERS, 1977
SATAN'S MISTRESS, 1982
SATAN'S SADIST, 1969
SATAN'S SLAVE, 1976
SATURDAY NIGHT AND SUNDAY MORNING, 1961
SATURDAY NIGHT AT THE BATHS, 1975
SAVAGE ABDUCTION, 1975
SAVAGE DAWN, 1984
SAVAGE ISLAND, 1985
SAVAGE MESSIAH, 1972
SAVAGE SEVEN, THE, 1968
SAVAGE SISTERS, 1974
SAVAGE STREETS, 1984
SAVAGE WEEKEND, 1983
SAVAGES, 1972
SAVAGES FROM HELL, 1968
SAXO, 1988
SAY YES, 1986
SCALPEL, 1976
SCALPS, 1983
SCANDAL IN DENMARK, 1970

BOLD: Films on Videocassette

SCANDAL IN SORRENTO, 1957
SCANNERS, 1981
SCARAB, 1982
SCARECROWS, 1988
SCARED TO DEATH, 1981
SCARFACE, 1932
SCARFACE, 1983
SCARRED, 1984
SCARS OF DRACULA, THE, 1970
SCAVENGERS, THE, 1969
SCENT OF A WOMAN, 1976
SCHIZO, 1977
SCHIZOID, 1980
SCHOOL DAZE, 1988
SCHOOL FOR SEX, 1966
SCHOOL FOR SEX, 1969
SCHOOL FOR UNCLAIMED GIRLS, 1973
SCOBIE MALONE, 1975
SCORCHY, 1976
SCRATCH HARRY, 1969
SCREAM AND SCREAM AGAIN, 1970
SCREAM, BABY, SCREAM, 1969
SCREAM BLACULA SCREAM, 1973
SCREAM BLOODY MURDER, 1972
SCREAM FOR HELP, 1984
SCREAM OF THE BUTTERFLY, 1965
SCREAMING MIMI, 1958
SCREAMPLAY, 1986
SCREAMTIME, 1986
SCREEN TEST, 1986
SCREWBALLS, 1983
SCRUBBERS, 1984
SCUM, 1979
SCUM OF THE EARTH, 1963
SCUM OF THE EARTH, 1976
SEABO, 1978
SEATED AT HIS RIGHT, 1968
SECRET CEREMONY, 1968
SECRET DIARY OF SIGMUND FREUD, THE, 1984
SECRET OF MY SUCCESS, THE, 1987
SECRETS, 1971
SECRETS OF A WINDMILL GIRL, 1966
SECRETS OF A WOMAN'S TEMPLE, 1969
SECRETS OF SEX, 1970
SECRETS SECRETS, 1985
SEDUCTION, THE, 1982
SEED OF INNOCENCE, 1980
SEEDS OF EVIL, 1981
SELF-PORTRAIT, 1973
SELLERS OF GIRLS, 1967
SENDER, THE, 1982
SENIORS, THE, 1978
SENTIMIENTOS: MIRTA DE LINIERS A ESTAMBUL, 1987
SENTINEL, THE, 1977
SEPARATE VACATIONS, 1986
SEPARATE WAYS, 1981
SERGEANT, THE, 1968
SERIAL, 1980
SERPENT AND THE RAINBOW, THE, 1988
SERPENT'S EGG, THE, 1977
SERPENTS OF THE PIRATE MOON, THE, 1973
SERPENT'S WAY, THE, 1987
SET, THE, 1970
SEVEN, 1979
SEVEN BEAUTIES, 1976
SEVEN CAPITAL SINS, 1962
SEVEN HOURS TO JUDGEMENT, 1988
SEVEN MINUTES, THE, 1971
7254, 1971
SEVERED HEAD, A, 1971
SEX APPEAL, 1986
SEX O'CLOCK NEWS, THE, 1986
SHADES OF SILK, 1979
SHADOW OF VICTORY, 1986
SHADOW PLAY, 1986
SHADOWS, 1960
SHADOWS RUN BLACK, 1986
SHAFT, 1971
SHAFT IN AFRICA, 1973
SHAFT'S BIG SCORE, 1972
SHAKEDOWN, 1988
SHALAKO, 1968
SHAME, 1968
SHAME, 1988

SHAME, SHAME, EVERYBODY KNOWS HER NAME, 1969
SHAMPOO, 1975
SHANGHAI EXPRESS, 1932
SHANGRI-LA, 1961
SHANTY TRAMP, 1967
SHARKY'S MACHINE, 1981
SHE, 1985
SHE AND HE, 1969
SHE-DEVILS ON WHEELS, 1968
SHE FREAK, 1967
SHERLOCK HOLMES FACES DEATH, 1943
SHE'S GOTTA HAVE IT, 1986
SHIRLEY THOMPSON VERSUS THE ALIENS, 1968
SHOCK, 1946
SHOCK CORRIDOR, 1963
SHOCK TREATMENT, 1964
SHOCK TREATMENT, 1973
SHOCK TREATMENT, 1981
SHOCK TROOPS, 1968
SHOCK WAVES, 1977
SHOGUN ASSASSIN, 1980
SHOOT, 1976
SHOOT FIRST, LAUGH LAST, 1967
SHOOT IT: BLACK, SHOOT IT: BLUE, 1974
SHOOT LOUD, LOUDER. . . I DON'T UNDERSTAND, 1966
SHOOT TO KILL, 1988
SHOOTING PARTY, THE, 1985
SHOOTING, THE, 1971
SHOOTIST, THE, 1976
SHORT CUT TO HELL, 1957
SHORT EYES, 1977
SHORT IS THE SUMMER, 1968
SHOTGUN, 1955
SHOUT, THE, 1978
SHRIEK OF THE MUTILATED, 1974
SHY PEOPLE, 1988
SICILIAN CLAN, THE, 1970
SICILIAN CONNECTION, THE, 1977
SICILIAN, THE, 1987
SID AND NANCY, 1986
SIDELONG GLANCES OF A PIGEON KICKER, THE, 1970
SIEGE, 1983
SIEGE OF SIDNEY STREET, THE, 1960
SIGN OF AQUARIUS, 1970
SIGN OF THE VIRGIN, 1969
SIGNAL 7, 1984
SIGNPOST TO MURDER, 1964
SIGNS OF LIFE, 1981
SILENCE, 1931
SILENCE, THE, 1964
SILENCERS, THE, 1966
SILENT ASSASSINS, 1988
SILENT MADNESS, 1984
SILENT NIGHT, BLOODY NIGHT, 1974
SILENT NIGHT, DEADLY NIGHT, 1984
SILENT NIGHT, DEADLY NIGHT PART II, 1987
SILENT RAGE, 1982
SILENT SCREAM, 1980
SILENT WITNESS, THE, 1962
SILIP, 1985
SILK, 1986
SIMBA, 1955
SIMON, KING OF THE WITCHES, 1971
SIN OF MONA KENT, THE, 1961
SIN ON THE BEACH, 1964
SIN YOU SINNERS, 1963
SINFUL DAVEY, 1969
SINGER NOT THE SONG, THE, 1961
SINGLE ROOM FURNISHED, 1968
SINISTER URGE, THE, 1961
SINS OF RACHEL CADE, THE, 1960
SINS OF ROSE BERND, THE, 1959
SIR HENRY AT RAWLINSON END, 1980
SIR, YOU ARE A WIDOWER, 1971
SISTER-IN-LAW, THE, 1975
SISTER SISTER, 1988
SISTERS, 1973
SISTERS, OR THE BALANCE OF HAPPINESS, 1982
SITTING TARGET, 1972
SIX DAYS A WEEK, 1966
SIX PACK ANNIE, 1975
'68, 1988
SIZZLE BEACH, U.S.A., 1986

SKI BUM, THE, 1971
SKIN DEEP, 1978
SKIN GAME, THE, 1965
SKULL, THE, 1965
SKY IS RED, THE, 1952
SLAMDANCE, 1987
SLAMS, THE, 1973
SLAP SHOT, 1977
SLASHER, THE, 1953
SLASHER, THE, 1975
SLAUGHTER, 1972
SLAUGHTER HIGH, 1987
SLAUGHTER HOTEL, 1971
SLAUGHTER IN SAN FRANCISCO, 1981
SLAUGHTERHOUSE, 1988
SLAUGHTERHOUSE-FIVE, 1972
SLAUGHTERHOUSE ROCK, 1988
SLAUGHTER'S BIG RIP-OFF, 1973
SLAVE OF THE CANNIBAL GOD, 1979
SLAVERS, 1977
SLAVES, 1969
SLAYER, THE, 1982
SLAYGROUND, 1984
SLEEPAWAY CAMP, 1983
SLEEPAWAY CAMP 2: UNHAPPY CAMPERS, 1988
SLIPSTREAM, 1974
SLOW MOVES, 1984
SLOW RUN, 1968
SLUMBER PARTY '57, 1977
SLUMBER PARTY MASSACRE II, 1987
SLUMBER PARTY MASSACRE, THE, 1982
SMALL CIRCLE OF FRIENDS, A, 1980
SMALL HOURS, THE, 1962
SMASH PALACE, 1982
SMELL OF HONEY, A SWALLOW OF BRINE? A, 1966
SMILE OF THE LAMB, THE, 1986
SMITHEREENS, 1982
SNAKE PEOPLE, THE, 1968
SNIPER, THE, 1952
SNO-LINE, 1986
SNOW, 1983
SNOW COUNTRY, 1969
SO LONG, BLUE BOY, 1973
S.O.B., 1981
SOD SISTERS, 1969
SOFIA, 1987
SOFT SKIN ON BLACK SILK, 1964
SOLDIER BLUE, 1970
SOLDIER OF ORANGE, 1979
SOLDIER, THE, 1982
SOLE SURVIVOR, 1984
SOLO, 1970
SOLO, 1978
SOLOMON KING, 1974
SOME CALL IT LOVING, 1973
SOME KIND OF HERO, 1982
SOME LIKE IT COOL, 1979
SOME OF MY BEST FRIENDS ARE. . ., 1971
SOMEONE, 1968
SOMEONE TO WATCH OVER ME, 1987
SOMETHING FOR EVERYONE, 1970
SOMETHING OF VALUE, 1957
SOMETHING WEIRD, 1967
SOMETHING WILD, 1986
SOMETIMES A GREAT NOTION, 1971
SON OF A STRANGER, 1957
SONG OF THE LOON, 1970
SONNY AND JED, 1974
SOPHIE'S CHOICE, 1982
SOPHIE'S WAYS, 1970
SORCERER, 1977
SORCERESS, 1983
SORORITY HOUSE MASSACRE, 1986
SOTTO. . .SOTTO, 1985
SOUL OF NIGGER CHARLEY, THE, 1973
SOUND AND FURY, 1988
SOUP FOR ONE, 1982
SOUTH, 1988
SOUTH BRONX HEROES, 1985
SOUTHERN COMFORT, 1981
SPACE RAGE, 1987
SPACED OUT, 1981
SPANISH FLY, 1975
SPASMS, 1983
SPECIAL EFFECTS, 1984
SPECIALIST, THE, 1975

SPECTRE OF EDGAR ALLAN POE, THE, 1974
SPETTERS, 1983
SPIDER BABY, 1968
SPIRITS OF THE DEAD, 1969
SPLATTER UNIVERSITY, 1984
SPLIT DECISIONS, 1988
SPLIT IMAGE, 1982
SPLIT, THE, 1968
SPLITZ, 1984
SPOOK WHO SAT BY THE DOOR, THE, 1973
SPORTING CLUB, THE, 1971
SPRING BREAK, 1983
SQUEEZE, THE, 1977
SQUEEZE, THE, 1987
SQUEEZE PLAY, 1981
SQUEEZE, THE, 1980
SQUIZZY TAYLOR, 1984
S.T.A.B., 1976
STACEY!, 1973
STAKEOUT, 1987
STAND ALONE, 1985
STAND UP VIRGIN SOLDIERS, 1977
STANLEY, 1973
STAR CRYSTAL, 1986
STAR 80, 1983
STAR SLAMMER: THE ESCAPE, 1988
STARDUST, 1974
STARHOPS, 1978
STATELINE MOTEL, 1976
STATUE, THE, 1971
STAY HUNGRY, 1976
STEAGLE, THE, 1971
STEAMING, 1985
STEELE JUSTICE, 1987
STEFANIA, 1968
STEPFATHER, THE, 1987
STEPHEN KING'S SILVER BULLET, 1985
STEPPENWOLF, 1974
STEREO, 1969
STEWARDESS SCHOOL, 1986
STICK, 1985
STIGMA, 1972
STILETTO, 1969
STILL OF THE NIGHT, 1982
STILL SMOKIN', 1983
STIR, 1980
STITCHES, 1985
STOLEN KISSES, 1969
STONE, 1974
STONE COLD DEAD, 1980
STONE KILLER, THE, 1973
STORK, 1971
STORK TALK, 1964
STORMY MONDAY, 1988
STORY OF A CHEAT, THE, 1938
STORY OF A THREE DAY PASS, THE, 1968
STORY OF A WOMAN, 1970
STORY OF TEMPLE DRAKE, THE, 1933
STRAIGHT ON TILL MORNING, 1974
STRAIGHT THROUGH THE HEART, 1985
STRAIGHT TIME, 1978
STRAIGHT TO HELL, 1987
STRAIGHT TO THE HEART, 1988
STRAIT-JACKET, 1964
STRANDED, 1965
STRANGE AFFAIR, THE, 1968
STRANGE DECEPTION, 1953
STRANGE FETISHES, THE, 1967
STRANGE INVADERS, 1983
STRANGE LOVERS, 1963
STRANGE ONE, THE, 1957
STRANGE SHADOWS IN AN EMPTY ROOM, 1977
STRANGER IS WATCHING, A, 1982
STRANGER THAN PARADISE, 1984
STRANGER, THE, 1987
STRAW DOGS, 1971
STREAMERS, 1983
STREET PEOPLE, 1976
STREET SMART, 1987
STREET TRASH, 1987
STREETWALKIN', 1985
STRIPES, 1981
STRIPPED TO KILL, 1987
STRIPPER, 1986
STRIPPER, THE, 1963
STRYKER, 1983

STUCK ON YOU, 1983
STUD, THE, 1979
STUDENT BODIES, 1981
STUDENT BODY, THE, 1976
STUDENT NURSES, THE, 1970
STUDENT TEACHERS, THE, 1973
STUNT MAN, THE, 1980
SUBSTITUTION, 1970
SUBURBAN WIVES, 1973
SUBURBIA, 1984
SUBWAY RIDERS, 1981
SUCCESS IS THE BEST REVENGE, 1984
SUCCESSFUL MAN, A, 1987
SUCH A GORGEOUS KID LIKE ME, 1973
SUCH GOOD FRIENDS, 1971
SUDDEN DEATH, 1985
SUDDEN IMPACT, 1983
SUDDENLY, A WOMAN!, 1967
SUDDENLY, LAST SUMMER, 1959
SUMMER, 1986
SUMMER CAMP, 1979
SUMMER HEAT, 1987
SUMMER LOVERS, 1982
SUMMER OF '42, 1971
SUMMER OF SECRETS, 1976
SUMMER SCHOOL TEACHERS, 1977
SUMMER'S CHILDREN, 1979
SUMMERFIELD, 1977
SUNDAY BLOODY SUNDAY, 1971
SUNDAY IN THE COUNTRY, 1975
SUNDAY LOVERS, 1980
SUNNYSIDE, 1979
SUNSCORCHED, 1966
SUNSET COVE, 1978
SUNSET STRIP, 1985
SUPER COPS, THE, 1974
SUPER SPOOK, 1975
SUPERBEAST, 1972
SUPERCHICK, 1973
SUPERFLY, 1972
SUPERFLY T.N.T., 1973
SUPERNATURALS, THE, 1987
SUPERSTITION, 1985
SURF II, 1984
SURFTIDE 77, 1962
SURROGATE, THE, 1984
SURVIVAL RUN, 1980
SURVIVE!, 1977
SUSPECT, 1987
SUSPIRIA, 1977
SWAMP COUNTRY, 1966
SWAP MEET, 1979
SWAPPERS, THE, 1970
SWASHBUCKLER, 1976
SWEDISH MISTRESS, THE, 1964
SWEENEY, 1977
SWEENEY 2, 1978
SWEET BIRD OF YOUTH, 1962
SWEET BODY OF DEBORAH, THE, 1969
SWEET COUNTRY, 1987
SWEET JESUS, PREACHER MAN, 1973
SWEET REVENGE, 1987
SWEET SIXTEEN, 1983
SWEET SKIN, 1965
SWEET SUGAR, 1972
SWEET SUZY, 1973
SWEET TRASH, 1970
SWEET WILLIAM, 1980
SWEPT AWAY...BY AN UNUSUAL DESTINY IN THE
    BLUE SEA OF AUGUST, 1975
SWINGING BARMAIDS, THE, 1976
SWITCHBLADE SISTERS, 1975
SWORD AND THE SORCERER, THE, 1982
SWORD OF HEAVEN, 1985
SYLVIA, 1965
SYMPTOMS, 1976
TAI-PAN, 1986
TAKE A GIRL LIKE YOU, 1970
TAKE ALL OF ME, 1978
TAKE ME AWAY, MY LOVE, 1962
TAKING OF PELHAM ONE, TWO, THREE, THE, 1974
TAKING OFF, 1971
TAKING TIGER MOUNTAIN, 1983
TALES OF ORDINARY MADNESS, 1983
TALES OF THE THIRD DIMENSION, 1985
TALES THAT WITNESS MADNESS, 1973

TALK RADIO, 1988
TALKING TO STRANGERS, 1988
TALKING WALLS, 1987
TANYA'S ISLAND, 1981
TAPEHEADS, 1988
TARGET, 1985
TARGETS, 1968
TARZAN, THE APE MAN, 1981
TARZANA, THE WILD GIRL, 1973
TASTE FOR WOMEN, A, 1966
TASTE OF BLOOD, A, 1967
TASTE OF FLESH, A, 1967
TASTE OF SIN, A, 1983
TASTE THE BLOOD OF DRACULA, 1970
TATTOO, 1981
TATTOOED STRANGER, THE, 1950
TAXI DRIVER, 1976
TEEN-AGE STRANGLER, 1967
TEENAGE BAD GIRL, 1959
TEENAGE DOLL, 1957
TEENAGE GANG DEBS, 1966
TEENAGE MOTHER, 1967
TELL ME LIES, 1968
TELL-TALE HEART, THE, 1962
TEMPTER, THE, 1978
10, 1979
TEN DAYS' WONDER, 1972
10 RILLINGTON PLACE, 1971
10:30 P.M. SUMMER, 1966
10,000 DOLLARS BLOOD MONEY, 1966
10 TO MIDNIGHT, 1983
10 VIOLENT WOMEN, 1982
TENANT, THE, 1976
TENCHU, 1970
TENDER FLESH, 1976
TENSION, 1949
TENTH VICTIM, THE, 1965
TEOREMA, 1969
TEQUILA SUNRISE, 1988
TERMINAL CHOICE, 1985
TERMINAL ISLAND, 1973
TERMINATOR, THE, 1984
TERRACE, THE, 1964
TERRIFIED, 1963
TERROR, 1979
TERROR-CREATURES FROM THE GRAVE, 1967
TERROR EYES, 1981
TERROR HOUSE, 1972
TERROR OF THE TONGS, THE, 1961
TERROR ON TOUR, 1980
TERROR TRAIN, 1980
TERRORIZERS, THE, 1987
TERRORVISION, 1986
TEXAS CHAIN SAW MASSACRE, THE, 1974
TEXAS CHAINSAW MASSACRE PART 2, THE, 1986
TEXAS LIGHTNING, 1981
THANK YOU, AUNT, 1969
THAT CHAMPIONSHIP SEASON, 1982
THAT COLD DAY IN THE PARK, 1969
THAT KIND OF GIRL, 1963
THAT MAN BOLT, 1973
THAT OBSCURE OBJECT OF DESIRE, 1977
THAT TENDER TOUCH, 1969
THAT WAS THEN...THIS IS NOW, 1985
THEATRE OF BLOOD, 1973
THERE IS NO 13, 1977
THERESE, 1963
THERESE AND ISABELLE, 1968
THEY CALL HER ONE EYE, 1974
THEY CAME FROM WITHIN, 1976
THEY CAME TO ROB LAS VEGAS, 1969
THEY LIVE, 1988
THEY SHOOT HORSES, DON'T THEY?, 1969
THEY'RE PLAYING WITH FIRE, 1984
THIEF, 1981
THIN RED LINE, THE, 1964
THING, THE, 1982
THINGS ARE TOUGH ALL OVER, 1982
THINK DIRTY, 1970
THIRD LOVER, THE, 1963
THIRD VOICE, THE, 1960
THIRST, 1979
THIRSTY DEAD, THE, 1975
THIRTEEN WEST STREET, 1962
36 FILLETTE, 1988
THIS EARTH IS MINE, 1959

BOLD: Films on Videocassette

THIS IS MY LOVE, 1954
THIS IS MY STREET, 1964
THIS MAN CAN'T DIE, 1970
THIS MAN MUST DIE, 1970
THIS PROPERTY IS CONDEMNED, 1966
THIS REBEL BREED, 1960
THIS SPECIAL FRIENDSHIP, 1967
THIS SPORTING LIFE, 1963
THIS STUFF'LL KILL YA!, 1971
THIS THING CALLED LOVE, 1940
THIS WAS A WOMAN, 1949
THIS, THAT AND THE OTHER, 1970
THOMASINE AND BUSHROD, 1974
THOSE LIPS, THOSE EYES, 1980
THOUSAND CRANES, 1969
THOUSAND EYES OF DR. MABUSE, THE, 1960
THREAT, THE, 1949
THREAT, THE, 1960
THREE, 1969
THREE CAME HOME, 1950
THREE CROWNS OF THE SAILOR, 1984
THREE FACES OF SIN, 1963
3:15, THE MOMENT OF TRUTH, 1986
THREE IN THE ATTIC, 1968
THREE INTO TWO WON'T GO, 1969
THREE MEN TO DESTROY, 1980
THREE NIGHTS OF LOVE, 1969
THREE NUTS IN SEARCH OF A BOLT, 1964
3:10 TO YUMA, 1957
THREE THE HARD WAY, 1974
THREE-WAY SPLIT, 1970
THREEPENNY OPERA, THE, 1931
THREES, MENAGE A TROIS, 1968
THRILL KILLERS, THE, 1965
THRONE OF BLOOD, 1961
THROUGH A GLASS DARKLY, 1962
THUMB TRIPPING, 1972
THUNDER WARRIOR, 1986
THUNDERBOLT AND LIGHTFOOT, 1974
TICKET, 1987
TIFFANY JONES, 1976
TIGHT SKIRTS, LOOSE PLEASURES, 1966
TIGHT SPOT, 1955
TILL MARRIAGE DO US PART, 1979
TIN DRUM, THE, 1979
TIME AFTER TIME, 1979
TIME IN THE SUN, A, 1970
TIME OF DESIRE, THE, 1957
TIME OF THE WOLVES, 1970
TIME TO DIE, A, 1983
TIMES SQUARE, 1980
TIMES TO COME, 1988
TINTORERA...BLOODY WATERS, 1977
'TIS A PITY SHE'S A WHORE, 1973
TNT JACKSON, 1975
TO ALL A GOODNIGHT, 1980
TO BE FREE, 1972
TO KILL A STRANGER, 1985
TO LIVE AND DIE IN L.A., 1985
TO LOVE, 1964
TO THE DEVIL A DAUGHTER, 1976
TODD KILLINGS, THE, 1971
TOKYO POP, 1988
TOM, 1973
TOM HORN, 1980
TOM JONES, 1963
TOMB OF THE UNDEAD, 1972
TOMB OF TORTURE, 1966
TOMBOY, 1985
TOMCAT, THE, 1968
TOMORROW NEVER COMES, 1978
TONIGHT FOR SURE, 1962
TOO LATE FOR TEARS, 1949
TOO SCARED TO SCREAM, 1985
TOO YOUNG, TOO IMMORAL!, 1962
TOOLBOX MURDERS, THE, 1978
TOP OF THE HEAP, 1972
TORCH SONG TRILOGY, 1988
TORCHLIGHT, 1984
TORMENT, 1986
TORMENTED, THE, 1978
TORSO, 1974
TORTURE DUNGEON, 1970
TORTURE GARDEN, 1968
TORTURE ME KISS ME, 1970
TOUCH OF HER FLESH, THE, 1967

TOUCH OF SATAN, THE, 1971
TOUCH OF THE OTHER, A, 1970
TOUCH, THE, 1971
TOUGH GUYS DON'T DANCE, 1987
TOUGHER THAN LEATHER, 1988
TOWN CALLED HELL, A, 1971
TOWN THAT DREADED SUNDOWN, THE, 1977
TOXIC AVENGER, THE, 1985
TOY SOLDIERS, 1984
TOYS ARE NOT FOR CHILDREN, 1972
TRACK 29, 1988
TRACKDOWN, 1976
TRACKS, 1977
TRADER HORNEE, 1970
TRANCERS, 1985
TRANS-EUROP-EXPRESS, 1968
TRAP DOOR, THE, 1980
TRAVELING EXECUTIONER, THE, 1970
TRAVELING HUSBANDS, 1931
TRAXX, 1988
TREASURE OF THE AMAZON, THE, 1985
TREE, THE, 1969
TRESPASSERS, THE, 1976
TRICK BABY, 1973
TRICK OR TREAT, 1986
TRICK OR TREATS, 1982
TRIP, THE, 1967
TRIPLE ECHO, THE, 1973
TRIPLE IRONS, 1973
TRIUMPHS OF A MAN CALLED HORSE, 1983
TROIKA, 1969
TROPICS, 1969
TROUBLE ALONG THE WAY, 1953
TROUBLE-FETE, 1964
TROUBLE IN MIND, 1985
TROUBLE MAN, 1972
TROUBLE WITH DICK, THE, 1987
TROUBLEMAKER, THE, 1964
TROUT, THE, 1982
TRUCK STOP WOMEN, 1974
TRUCK TURNER, 1974
TRUE AND THE FALSE, THE, 1955
TRUE CONFESSIONS, 1981
TRUE STORY OF ESKIMO NELL, THE, 1975
TRUTH, THE, 1961
TUFF TURF, 1985
TUNNELVISION, 1976
TURN OF THE SCREW, 1985
TURN ON TO LOVE, 1969
24-HOUR LOVER, 1970
27A, 1974
TWICE A MAN, 1964
TWICE IN A LIFETIME, 1985
TWILIGHT PEOPLE, 1972
TWILIGHT STORY, THE, 1962
TWILIGHT'S LAST GLEAMING, 1977
TWINS OF EVIL, 1971
TWIST & SHOUT, 1986
TWISTED NERVE, 1969
TWITCH OF THE DEATH NERVE, 1973
TWO, 1975
TWO ENGLISH GIRLS, 1972
TWO GENTLEMEN SHARING, 1969
TWO HUNDRED MOTELS, 1971
TWO-LANE BLACKTOP, 1971
TWO LEFT FEET, 1965
TWO LIVES OF MATTIA PASCAL, THE, 1985
TWO MEN IN TOWN, 1973
TWO-MINUTE WARNING, 1976
TWO MOON JUNCTION, 1988
TWO OR THREE THINGS I KNOW ABOUT HER, 1970
TWO PEOPLE, 1973
TWO THOUSAND MANIACS, 1964
2020 TEXAS GLADIATORS, 1985
2000 YEARS LATER, 1969
TWO WEEKS IN ANOTHER TOWN, 1962
TWO WEEKS IN SEPTEMBER, 1967
UGLY ONES, THE, 1968
ULTIMATE WARRIOR, THE, 1975
ULZANA'S RAID, 1972
UN HOMBRE VIOLENTE, 1986
UNASHAMED, 1938
UNBEARABLE LIGHTNESS OF BEING, THE, 1988
UNCLE SCAM, 1981
UNCOMMON VALOR, 1983
UNDER AGE, 1964

UNDER COVER, 1987
UNDER FIRE, 1983
UNDER THE CHERRY MOON, 1986
UNDER THE VOLCANO, 1984
UNDERCOVERS HERO, 1975
UNDERGROUND U.S.A., 1980
UNDERTAKER AND HIS PALS, THE, 1966
UNEARTHLY, THE, 1957
UNFINISHED BUSINESS, 1985
UNHINGED, 1982
UNHOLY, THE, 1988
UNHOLY DESIRE, 1964
UNHOLY ROLLERS, 1972
UNINVITED, THE, 1988
UNSEEN, THE, 1981
UNSTRAP ME, 1968
UNTAMED MISTRESS, 1960
UNTIL SEPTEMBER, 1984
UNTOUCHABLES, THE, 1987
UP FROM THE DEPTHS, 1979
UP IN SMOKE, 1978
UP POMPEII, 1971
UP THE ACADEMY, 1980
UP THE CHASTITY BELT, 1971
UP THE CREEK, 1984
UP THE JUNCTION, 1968
UP YOUR TEDDY BEAR, 1970
UPTIGHT, 1968
USED CARS, 1980
UTU, 1984
V.D., 1961
VAGABOND, 1985
VALACHI PAPERS, THE, 1972
VALDEZ IS COMING, 1971
VALET GIRLS, 1987
VALLEY OF THE DOLLS, 1967
VALS, THE, 1985
VAMP, 1986
VAMPING, 1984
VAMPIRE HOOKERS, THE, 1979
VAMPIRE LOVERS, THE, 1970
VAMPIRE'S COFFIN, THE, 1958
VAMPIRE'S NIGHT ORGY, THE, 1973
VAMPIRES, THE, 1969
VAMPYR, 1932
VAMPYRES, DAUGHTERS OF DRACULA, 1977
VAN, THE, 1977
VAN NUYS BLVD., 1979
VARIETY, 1984
VASECTOMY: A DELICATE MATTER, 1986
VELVET TRAP, THE, 1966
VELVET VAMPIRE, THE, 1971
VENDETTA, 1986
VENGEANCE IS MINE, 1980
VENGEANCE OF THE VAMPIRE WOMEN, THE, 1969
VENOM, 1968
VENOM, 1982
VENUS IN FURS, 1970
VERA, 1987
VERNE MILLER, 1988
VERONIKA VOSS, 1982
VERY CLOSE QUARTERS, 1986
VERY CURIOUS GIRL, A, 1970
VERY NATURAL THING, A, 1974
VIBRATION, 1969
VICE AND VIRTUE, 1965
VICE GIRLS, LTD., 1964
VICE SQUAD, 1982
VICTORS, THE, 1963
VICTOR/VICTORIA, 1982
VIDEO DEAD, 1987
VIDEODROME, 1983
VIGILANTE, 1983
VILLA RIDES, 1968
VILLAIN, 1971
VIOLATED, 1986
VIOLATED PARADISE, 1963
VIOLENT BREED, THE, 1986
VIOLENT SATURDAY, 1955
VIOLENT WOMEN, 1960
VIOLETTE, 1978
VIRGIN AND THE GYPSY, THE, 1970
VIRGIN SOLDIERS, THE, 1970
VIRGIN WITCH, THE, 1973
VIRUS HAS NO MORALS, A, 1986
VISION QUEST, 1985

VISITING HOURS, 1982
VISITOR, THE, 1980
VISITORS, THE, 1972
VIVA ITALIA, 1978
VIXEN, 1970
VIXENS, THE, 1969
VOICES, 1973
VOLUNTEERS, 1985
VOODOO HEARTBEAT, 1972
VORTEX, 1982
VOYAGE, THE, 1974
WAGES OF FEAR, THE, 1955
WAIT UNTIL DARK, 1967
WAITRESS, 1982
WALK A CROOKED PATH, 1969
WALK LIKE A DRAGON, 1960
WALK ON THE MOON, A, 1987
WALK ON THE WILD SIDE, 1962
WALK THE WALK, 1970
WALKER, 1987
WALKING TALL, 1973
WALKING TALL, PART II, 1975
WALKING THE EDGE, 1985
WALL STREET, 1987
WALL, THE, 1985
WANDERERS, THE, 1979
WANDERING JEW, THE, 1948
WANDERLOVE, 1970
WANTED: DEAD OR ALIVE, 1987
WAR AND LOVE, 1985
WAR LORD, THE, 1965
WARDOGS, 1987
WARKILL, 1968
WARNING SIGN, 1985
WARRIOR AND THE SORCERESS, THE, 1984
WARRIOR EMPRESS, THE, 1961
WARRIOR QUEEN, 1987
WARRIORS, THE, 1979
WARRIORS OF THE WASTELAND, 1984
WATCHED, 1974
WAY OUT, 1966
WAY OUT, WAY IN, 1970
WAY WE LIVE NOW, THE, 1970
WE ARE ALL NAKED, 1970
WEB OF THE SPIDER, 1972
WEDDING IN GALILEE, 1988
WEDDING IN WHITE, 1972
WEDDING NIGHT, 1970
WEDDING PARTY, THE, 1969
WEEDS, 1987
WEEKEND, 1968
WEEKEND MURDERS, THE, 1972
WEEKEND PASS, 1984
WEEKEND WARRIORS, 1986
WEEKEND WITH THE BABYSITTER, 1970
WEIRD LOVE MAKERS, THE, 1963
WEIRD SCIENCE, 1985
WELCOME HOME, SOLDIER BOYS, 1972
WELCOME IN VIENNA, 1988
WELCOME TO BLOOD CITY, 1977
WELCOME TO 18, 1986
WELCOME TO HARD TIMES, 1967
WELCOME TO L.A., 1976
WELCOME TO THE CLUB, 1971
WEREWOLF VS. THE VAMPIRE WOMAN, THE, 1970
WEREWOLVES ON WHEELS, 1971
WETHERBY, 1985
WHAT!, 1965:,
WHAT PRICE DECENCY?, 1933
WHAT YOU TAKE FOR GRANTED, 1984
WHATEVER IT TAKES, 1986
WHAT'S GOOD FOR THE GOOSE, 1969
WHAT'S THE MATTER WITH HELEN?, 1971
WHEN A STRANGER CALLS, 1979
WHEN FATHER WAS AWAY ON BUSINESS, 1985
WHEN NATURE CALLS, 1985
WHEN THE RAVEN FLIES, 1985
WHEN WOMEN HAD TAILS, 1970
WHEN YOU COMIN' BACK, RED RYDER?, 1979
WHERE ARE THE CHILDREN?, 1986
WHERE IT'S AT, 1969
WHERE THE BOYS ARE '84, 1984
WHERE THE BUFFALO ROAM, 1980
WHERE THE GREEN ANTS DREAM, 1985
WHERE THE HOT WIND BLOWS, 1960
WHERE'S PICONE?, 1985

WHEREVER YOU ARE, 1988
WHICH WAY IS UP?, 1977
WHIP'S WOMEN, 1968
WHIRLPOOL OF WOMAN, 1966
WHISPERING JOE, 1969
WHITE DAWN, THE, 1974
WHITE DOG, 1982
WHITE HEAT, 1934
WHITE MISCHIEF, 1988
WHITE NIGHTS, 1961
WHITE OF THE EYE, 1988
WHITE RAT, 1972
WHITE, RED, YELLOW, PINK, 1966
WHITE ROSE OF HONG KONG, 1965
WHITE SISTER, 1973
WHITE SLAVE, 1986
WHITE VOICES, 1965
WHITE ZOMBIE, 1932
WHO KILLED MARY WHAT'SER NAME?, 1971
WHO KILLED TEDDY BEAR?, 1965
WHO SLEW AUNTIE ROO?, 1971
WHOOPEE BOYS, THE, 1986
WHOOPING COUGH, 1987
WHO'S AFRAID OF VIRGINIA WOOLF?, 1966
WHO'S GOT THE BLACK BOX?, 1970
WHO'S THAT KNOCKING AT MY DOOR?, 1968
WHY BOTHER TO KNOCK, 1964
WHY DOES HERR R. RUN AMOK?, 1977
WHY ROCK THE BOAT?, 1974
WHY RUSSIANS ARE REVOLTING, 1970
WICKED DIE SLOW, THE, 1968
WICKED GO TO HELL, THE, 1961
WICKED LADY, THE, 1983
WICKED, WICKED, 1973
WICKED WIFE, 1955
WICKED WOMAN, 1953
WICKER MAN, THE, 1974
WIDOWS' NEST, 1977
WIFEMISTRESS, 1979
WILD AFFAIR, THE, 1966
WILD ANGELS, THE, 1966
WILD BUNCH, THE, 1969
WILD EYE, THE, 1968
WILD GEESE, THE, 1978
WILD GEESE II, 1985
WILD GYPSIES, 1969
WILD HARVEST, 1962
WILD IS MY LOVE, 1963
WILD McCULLOCHS, THE, 1975
WILD 90, 1968
WILD PACK, THE, 1972
WILD PAIR, THE, 1987
WILD PARTY, THE, 1975
WILD REBELS, THE, 1967
WILD RIDERS, 1971
WILD SCENE, THE, 1970
WILD STRAWBERRIES, 1959
WILD WHEELS, 1969
WILLARD, 1971
WILLIE AND PHIL, 1980
WILLIE DYNAMITE, 1973
WIND, THE, 1987
WINDOWS, 1980
WINTER KILLS, 1979
WINTER OF OUR DREAMS, 1982
WIRED TO KILL, 1986
WISDOM, 1986
WISE BLOOD, 1979
WITCHBOARD, 1987
WITCHES OF EASTWICK, THE, 1987
WITCHFIRE, 1986
WITHNAIL AND I, 1987
WITHOUT APPARENT MOTIVE, 1972
WITHOUT WARNING, 1980
WITNESS OUT OF HELL, 1967
WIVES—TEN YEARS AFTER, 1985
WIZARD OF GORE, THE, 1970
WOLFEN, 1981
WOLFMAN, 1979
WOMAN AT HER WINDOW, A, 1978
WOMAN HUNT, THE, 1975
WOMAN IN FLAMES, A, 1984
WOMAN IN THE DUNES, 1964
WOMAN INSIDE, THE, 1981
WOMAN NEXT DOOR, THE, 1981
WOMAN OF DARKNESS, 1968

WOMAN OF ROME, 1956
WOMAN OF THE RIVER, 1954
WOMAN ON FIRE, A, 1970
WOMAN WITH RED BOOTS, THE, 1977
WOMEN AND BLOODY TERROR, 1970
WOMEN IN CELL BLOCK 7, 1977
WOMEN IN LOVE, 1969
WOMEN IN PRISON, 1957
WOMEN OF DESIRE, 1968
WOMEN'S PRISON MASSACRE, 1986
WONDERWALL, 1969
WORKING GIRL, 1988
WORKING GIRLS, 1986
WORKING GIRLS, THE, 1973
WORLD GONE WILD, 1988
WORLD IS FULL OF MARRIED MEN, THE, 1980
WORLD IS JUST A 'B' MOVIE, THE, 1971
WORLD OF SUZIE WONG, THE, 1960
WORLD'S GREATEST SINNER, THE, 1962
WORM EATERS, THE, 1981
WRONG IS RIGHT, 1982
X Y & ZEE, 1972
XICA, 1982
XTRO, 1983
YAKUZA, THE, 1975
YASHA, 1985
YEAR OF AWAKENING, THE, 1987
YEAR OF THE DRAGON, 1985
YEAR OF THE YAHOO, 1971
YELLOW HAIR AND THE FORTRESS OF GOLD, 1984
YESTERDAY, TODAY, AND TOMORROW, 1963
YESTERDAY'S ENEMY, 1959
YOJIMBO, 1961
YOL, 1982
YOU BETTER WATCH OUT, 1980
YOU CAN'T HURRY LOVE, 1988
YOUNG CAPTIVES, THE, 1959
YOUNG COMPOSER'S ODYSSEY, A, 1986
YOUNG CYCLE GIRLS, THE, 1979
YOUNG DILLINGER, 1965
YOUNG DOCTORS IN LOVE, 1982
YOUNG GRADUATES, THE, 1971
YOUNG GUNS, 1988
YOUNG MONK, THE, 1978
YOUNG NURSES, THE, 1973
YOUNG ONE, THE, 1961
YOUNG RUNAWAYS, THE, 1968
YOUNG, THE EVIL AND THE SAVAGE, THE, 1968
YOUNG WARRIORS, 1983
YOUNGBLOOD, 1978
YOUNGBLOOD, 1986
YOUNGBLOOD HAWKE, 1964
YOUR SHADOW IS MINE, 1963
YOUR THREE MINUTES ARE UP, 1973
YOUTH IN FURY, 1961
YOU'VE GOT TO WALK IT LIKE YOU TALK IT OR
    YOU'LL LOSE THAT BEAT, 1971
ZABRISKIE POINT, 1970
ZAPPA, 1984
ZAPPED!, 1982
ZARDOZ, 1974
ZED & TWO NOUGHTS, A, 1985
ZERO IN THE UNIVERSE, 1966
ZIG-ZAG, 1975
ZITA, 1968
ZOMBIE, 1980
ZOMBIE CREEPING FLESH, 1981
ZOMBIES OF MORA TAU, 1957
ZOOT SUIT, 1981

BOLD: Films on Videocassette

BEST OF THE GENRES

Listed below are CineBooks' choices for the best films of each of the 26 genres by which the films are classified.

Bold indicates films available on videocassette.

Action
BLACK SUNDAY, 1977
DEAD-END DRIVE-IN, 1986
EMPIRE OF THE SUN, 1987
EXCALIBUR, 1981
FIREFOX, 1982
MAD MAX, 1979
PEKING OPERA BLUES, 1986
ROAD WARRIOR, THE, 1982
WARRIORS, THE, 1979
YOJIMBO, 1961

Adventure
ADVENTURES OF DON JUAN, 1949
ADVENTURES OF ROBIN HOOD, THE, 1938
AFRICAN QUEEN, THE, 1951
AROUND THE WORLD IN 80 DAYS, 1956
BEAU GESTE, 1939
BLACK ROSE, THE, 1950
BLACK STALLION, THE, 1979
BLACK SWAN, THE, 1942
CAPTAIN BLOOD, 1935
CAPTAIN FROM CASTILE, 1947
CAPTAINS COURAGEOUS, 1937
CHARGE OF THE LIGHT BRIGADE, THE, 1936
CORSICAN BROTHERS, THE, 1941
COUNT OF MONTE CRISTO, THE, 1934
CRIMSON PIRATE, THE, 1952
DESCENDANT OF THE SNOW LEOPARD, THE, 1986
DRUMS, 1938
DRUMS ALONG THE MOHAWK, 1939
EMERALD FOREST, THE, 1985
FANFAN THE TULIP, 1952
FIRE OVER ENGLAND, 1937
FLIGHT OF THE PHOENIX, THE, 1965
FOR WHOM THE BELL TOLLS, 1943
FOUR FEATHERS, THE, 1939
GOLDFINGER, 1964
GREYSTOKE: THE LEGEND OF TARZAN, LORD OF THE APES, 1984
GUNGA DIN, 1939
HIDDEN FORTRESS, THE, 1959
JASON AND THE ARGONAUTS, 1963
JUNGLE BOOK, 1942
KING KONG, 1933
KING SOLOMON'S MINES, 1950
KNIGHT WITHOUT ARMOR, 1937
LASSIE, COME HOME, 1943
LAST OF THE MOHICANS, THE, 1936
LAWRENCE OF ARABIA, 1962
LIVES OF A BENGAL LANCER, 1935
LORD JIM, 1965
LOST HORIZON, 1937
MAN WHO WOULD BE KING, THE, 1975
MARK OF ZORRO, THE, 1940
MARKETA LAZAROVA, 1968
MOBY DICK, 1956
MOGAMBO, 1953
MUTINY ON THE BOUNTY, 1935
NORTHWEST PASSAGE, 1940
PRINCE OF FOXES, 1949
PRISONER OF ZENDA, THE, 1937
RAIDERS OF THE LOST ARK, 1981
SAND PEBBLES, THE, 1966
SCARLET PIMPERNEL, THE, 1935
SEA HAWK, THE, 1940
THIRD MAN ON THE MOUNTAIN, 1959
THREE MUSKETEERS, THE, 1948
THREE MUSKETEERS, THE, 1974
TORRID ZONE, 1940
TREASURE ISLAND, 1950
TREASURE OF THE SIERRA MADRE, THE, 1948
WAGES OF FEAR, THE, 1955

Animated
ADVENTURES OF ICHABOD AND MR. TOAD, 1949
BAMBI, 1942
CINDERELLA, 1950

DUMBO, 1941
FANTASIA, 1940
FOX AND THE HOUND, THE, 1981
GREAT MOUSE DETECTIVE, THE, 1986
MIDSUMMERS NIGHT'S DREAM, A, 1961
OF STARS AND MEN, 1961
PETER PAN, 1953
PINOCCHIO, 1940
SNOW WHITE AND THE SEVEN DWARFS, 1937
SONG OF THE SOUTH, 1946
THREE CABALLEROS, THE, 1944
WHEN THE WIND BLOWS, 1988
WHO FRAMED ROGER RABBIT, 1988
YELLOW SUBMARINE, 1958

Biography
ADVENTURES OF MARK TWAIN, THE, 1944
AL CAPONE, 1959
AMADEUS, 1984
BARRETTS OF WIMPOLE STREET, THE, 1934
BARRETTS OF WIMPOLE STREET, THE, 1957
BIRD, 1988
BIRDMAN OF ALCATRAZ, 1962
CAESAR AND CLEOPATRA, 1946
CALL NORTHSIDE 777, 1948
CHARIOTS OF FIRE, 1981
COAL MINER'S DAUGHTER, 1980
COURT-MARTIAL OF BILLY MITCHELL, THE, 1955
DEEP IN MY HEART, 1954
DESERT FOX, THE, 1951
DR. EHRLICH'S MAGIC BULLET, 1940
DREYFUS CASE, THE, 1931
EDISON, THE MAN, 1940
ELEPHANT MAN, THE, 1980
FEAR STRIKES OUT, 1957
FUNNY GIRL, 1968
GANDHI, 1982
GIRL IN WHITE, THE, 1952
GLENN MILLER STORY, THE, 1953
GREAT NORTHFIELD, MINNESOTA RAID, THE, 1972
GREAT ZIEGFELD, THE, 1936
GREY FOX, THE, 1983
GYPSY, 1962
HOUSE OF ROTHSCHILD, THE, 1934
I'LL CRY TOMORROW, 1955
INTERVISTA, 1987
IVAN THE TERRIBLE, PARTS I & II, 1947
JIM THORPE—ALL AMERICAN, 1951
JUAREZ, 1939
JULIA, 1977
KNUTE ROCKNE—ALL AMERICAN, 1940
LA BAMBA, 1987
LAST EMPEROR, THE, 1987
LAWRENCE OF ARABIA, 1962
LIFE OF EMILE ZOLA, THE, 1937
LOVE ME OR LEAVE ME, 1955
LUST FOR LIFE, 1956
MADAME CURIE, 1943
MAGIC BOX, THE, 1952
MAGNIFICENT YANKEE, THE, 1950
MARIE ANTOINETTE, 1938
MIDNIGHT EXPRESS, 1978
MIRACLE WORKER, THE, 1962
NUN'S STORY, THE, 1959
PATTON, 1970
PRIDE OF THE YANKEES, THE, 1942
PRISONER OF SHARK ISLAND, THE, 1936
PRIVATE LIFE OF HENRY VIII, THE, 1933
RAGING BULL, 1980
REMBRANDT, 1936
RIGHT STUFF, THE, 1983
SCARFACE, 1932
SCARLET EMPRESS, THE, 1934
SERGEANT YORK, 1941
SERPICO, 1973
SID AND NANCY, 1986
SILKWOOD, 1983
SONG OF BERNADETTE, THE, 1943

SOUND OF MUSIC, THE, 1965
SPIRIT OF ST. LOUIS, THE, 1957
STORY OF ADELE H., THE, 1975
STORY OF G.I. JOE, THE, 1945
STORY OF LOUIS PASTEUR, THE, 1936
SUNRISE AT CAMPOBELLO, 1960
SWIMMER, THE, 1988
THERESE, 1986
THEY DIED WITH THEIR BOOTS ON, 1942
THREE LITTLE WORDS, 1950
TUCKER: THE MAN AND HIS DREAM, 1988
VICTORIA THE GREAT, 1937
VIVA VILLA!, 1934
VIVA ZAPATA!, 1952
WORLD APART, A, 1988
YOUNG MR. LINCOLN, 1939

Children's
BAMBI, 1942
BENJI, 1974
BUGSY MALONE, 1976
DARBY O'GILL AND THE LITTLE PEOPLE, 1959
EMIL AND THE DETECTIVE, 1931
ENCHANTED FOREST, THE, 1945
5,000 FINGERS OF DR. T. THE, 1953
FLIPPER, 1963
GNOME-MOBILE, THE, 1967
HEIDI, 1937
HEIDI, 1968
HUGO THE HIPPO, 1976
JUNGLE BOOK, THE, 1967
LABYRINTH, 1986
LAND BEFORE TIME, THE, 1988
LASSIE, COME HOME, 1943
LITTLE KIDNAPPERS, THE, 1954
MY FRIEND FLICKA, 1943
NIKKI, WILD DOG OF THE NORTH, 1961
OLD YELLER, 1957
ONE HUNDRED AND ONE DALMATIANS, 1961
PETER PAN, 1953
PHANTOM TOLLBOOTH, THE, 1970
PINOCCHIO, 1940
PRINCESS BRIDE, THE, 1987
SKIPPY, 1931
SLEEPING BEAUTY, 1959
SNOOPY, COME HOME, 1972
SNOW WHITE AND THE SEVEN DWARFS, 1937
SO DEAR TO MY HEART, 1949
SONG OF THE SOUTH, 1946
STORY OF ROBIN HOOD, THE, 1952
SWISS FAMILY ROBINSON, 1960

Comedy
A NOUS LA LIBERTE, 1931
ABBOTT AND COSTELLO MEET FRANKENSTEIN, 1948
ADVENTURE OF SHERLOCK HOLMES' SMARTER BROTHER, THE, 1975
AFTER HOURS, 1985
AH, WILDERNESS!, 1935
AMERICAN GRAFFITI, 1973
ANNIE HALL, 1977
APARTMENT, THE, 1960
AROUND THE WORLD IN EIGHTY WAYS, 1987
ARSENIC AND OLD LACE, 1944
AUNTIE MAME, 1958
AWFUL TRUTH, THE, 1937
BACHELOR AND THE BOBBY-SOXER, THE, 1947
BACHELOR MOTHER, 1939
BAKER'S WIFE, THE, 1940
BANK DICK, THE, 1940
BARFLY, 1987
BEAT THE DEVIL, 1953
BEING THERE, 1979
BILL OF DIVORCEMENT, A, 1932
BORN YESTERDAY, 1951
BOYFRIENDS AND GIRLFRIENDS, 1988
BREWSTER'S MILLIONS, 1945
BRIDE FOR SALE, 1949

BOLD: Films on Videocassette

BRINGING UP BABY, 1938
BROADCAST NEWS, 1987
BROADWAY DANNY ROSE, 1984
CAPTAIN'S PARADISE, THE, 1953
CAT BALLOU, 1965
CHAMPAGNE FOR CAESAR, 1950
CHARADE, 1963
CHRISTMAS STORY, A, 1983
CLUNY BROWN, 1946
COCOANUTS, THE, 1929
CONNECTICUT YANKEE, A, 1931
CRIME OF MONSIEUR LANGE, THE, 1936
CRIMSON PIRATE, THE, 1952
DADDY LONG LEGS, 1931
DEATH OF TARZAN, THE, 1968
DINER, 1982
DINNER AT EIGHT, 1933
DIVORCE, ITALIAN STYLE, 1962
DONA HERLINDA AND HER SON, 1986
DON'S PARTY, 1976
DOUGH BOYS, 1930
DOWN AND OUT IN BEVERLY HILLS, 1986
DUCK SOUP, 1933
EGG AND I, THE, 1947
EXTERMINATING ANGEL, THE, 1967
FANFAN THE TULIP, 1952
FORTUNE, THE, 1975
FRONT PAGE, THE, 1931
GAY DIVORCEE, THE, 1934
GEORGE WASHINGTON SLEPT HERE, 1942
GEORGY GIRL, 1966
GHOST GOES WEST, THE, 1936
GIG, THE, 1985
GIRL CRAZY, 1943
GODS MUST BE CRAZY, THE, 1984
GOING IN STYLE, 1979
GOOD NEWS, 1947
GOODBYE GIRL, THE, 1977
GRADUATE, THE, 1967
GREAT DICTATOR, THE, 1940
GREAT McGINTY, THE, 1940
GREEN MAN, THE, 1957
GUARDSMAN, THE, 1931
HAIL THE CONQUERING HERO, 1944
HANNAH AND HER SISTERS, 1986
HARVEY, 1950
HERE COMES THE GROOM, 1951
HIS GIRL FRIDAY, 1940
HOBSON'S CHOICE, 1954
HOLIDAY FOR HENRIETTA, 1955
HOPE AND GLORY, 1987
HORSE FEATHERS, 1932
HORSE'S MOUTH, THE, 1958
I LOVE YOU, ALICE B. TOKLAS!, 1968
I'M ALL RIGHT, JACK, 1959
I'M NO ANGEL, 1933
IMPORTANCE OF BEING EARNEST, THE, 1952
INTERNATIONAL HOUSE, 1933
IT HAPPENED ONE NIGHT, 1934
IT HAPPENS EVERY SPRING, 1949
IT SHOULD HAPPEN TO YOU, 1954
IT'S A GIFT, 1934
IT'S A MAD, MAD, MAD, MAD WORLD, 1963
IT'S LOVE I'M AFTER, 1937
JOUR DE FETE, 1952
KID FOR TWO FARTHINGS, A, 1956
KIND HEARTS AND CORONETS, 1949
KING OF COMEDY, THE, 1983
KNACK ... AND HOW TO GET IT, THE, 1965
LA CAGE AUX FOLLES, 1979
LADY EVE, THE, 1941
LADYKILLERS, THE, 1956
LATE GEORGE APLEY, THE, 1947
LAUGHTER, 1930
LAVENDER HILL MOB, THE, 1951
LE BEAU MARIAGE, 1982
LIBELED LADY, 1936
LIFE WITH FATHER, 1947
LIMELIGHT, 1952
LITTLE DORRIT, 1988
LITTLE ROMANCE, A, 1979
LOCAL HERO, 1983
LOVE AFFAIR, 1939
LOVE CRAZY, 1941
LOVE ME TONIGHT, 1932
MAJOR AND THE MINOR, THE, 1942

MAJOR BARBARA, 1941
MALE ANIMAL, THE, 1942
MAN IN THE WHITE SUIT, THE, 1952
MAN ON THE FLYING TRAPEZE, THE, 1935
MAN WHO CAME TO DINNER, THE, 1942
MANHATTAN, 1979
MARGIE, 1946
MARY POPPINS, 1964
M*A*S*H, 1970
MERRY WIDOW, THE, 1934
MIN AND BILL, 1930
MIRACLE OF MORGAN'S CREEK, THE, 1944
MR. DEEDS GOES TO TOWN, 1936
MR. HULOT'S HOLIDAY, 1954
MISTER ROBERTS, 1955
MODERN TIMES, 1936
MOUSE THAT ROARED, THE, 1959
MURDER BY DEATH, 1976
MURDER, HE SAYS, 1945
MURMUR OF THE HEART, 1971
MY FAIR LADY, 1964
MY FAVORITE BRUNETTE, 1947
MY FAVORITE YEAR, 1982
MY MAN GODFREY, 1936
MY UNCLE, 1958
NEXT STOP, GREENWICH VILLAGE, 1976
NIGHT AT THE OPERA, A, 1935
NINOTCHKA, 1939
NOTHING SACRED, 1937
O LUCKY MAN!, 1973
ODD COUPLE, THE, 1968
ON GOLDEN POND, 1981
OUR RELATIONS, 1936
OUT OF TOWNERS, THE, 1970
PALM BEACH STORY, THE, 1942
PARADISE ALLEY, 1978
PAT AND MIKE, 1952
PEOPLE WILL TALK, 1951
PHILADELPHIA STORY, THE, 1940
PLAZA SUITE, 1971
POLLYANNA, 1960
PRIVATE LIVES, 1931
PRODUCERS, THE, 1967
PYGMALION, 1938
QUARTET, 1949
QUIET MAN, THE, 1952
REAL LIFE, 1979
ROAD TO MOROCCO, 1942
ROBERTA, 1935
ROCK 'N' ROLL HIGH SCHOOL, 1979
ROMAN HOLIDAY, 1953
ROOM WITH A VIEW, A, 1986
ROYAL FAMILY OF BROADWAY, THE, 1930
ROYAL WEDDING, 1951
RUGGLES OF RED GAP, 1935
SABRINA, 1954
SCHOOL FOR SCOUNDRELS, 1960
SECRET LIFE OF WALTER MITTY, THE, 1947
SEVEN YEAR ITCH, THE, 1955
SHE DONE HIM WRONG, 1933
SHOP AROUND THE CORNER, THE, 1940
SHOT IN THE DARK, A, 1964
SITTING PRETTY, 1948
SLIGHT CASE OF MURDER, A, 1938
SMALL CHANGE, 1976
SOLID GOLD CADILLAC, THE, 1956
SOME LIKE IT HOT, 1959
SOMEONE TO LOVE, 1988
STAGE DOOR, 1937
STALAG 17, 1953
STATE OF THE UNION, 1948
STING, THE, 1973
STOLEN KISSES, 1969
STUNT MAN, THE, 1980
SULLIVAN'S TRAVELS, 1941
SUNSHINE BOYS, THE, 1975
TAKING OFF, 1971
TALES OF MANHATTAN, 1942
TALK OF THE TOWN, 1942
TEAHOUSE OF THE AUGUST MOON, THE, 1956
THIN MAN, THE, 1934
THIS IS THE NIGHT, 1932
THOUSAND CLOWNS, A, 1965
THREE MUSKETEERS, THE, 1948
THREE MUSKETEERS, THE, 1974
TO BE OR NOT TO BE, 1942

TO CATCH A THIEF, 1955
TOBACCO ROAD, 1941
TOM JONES, 1963
TOOTSIE, 1982
TOP HAT, 1935
TOPKAPI, 1964
TOPPER, 1937
TORRID ZONE, 1940
TOUCH OF CLASS, A, 1973
TRAFFIC, 1972
TROUBLE IN PARADISE, 1932
TRUNKS OF MR. O.F., THE, 1932
TWO OF US, THE, 1968
UNFAITHFULLY YOURS, 1948
UNMARRIED WOMAN, AN, 1978
UP IN ARMS, 1944
WAY OUT WEST, 1937
WHAT PRICE GLORY?, 1952
WHO FRAMED ROGER RABBIT, 1988
WHOLE TOWN'S TALKING, THE, 1935
WOMAN OF THE YEAR, 1942
WOMEN, THE, 1939
YOU CAN'T TAKE IT WITH YOU, 1938
YOUNG FRANKENSTEIN, 1974
YOU'RE TELLING ME, 1934

Crime

AL CAPONE, 1959
ALGIERS, 1938
ANGELS WITH DIRTY FACES, 1938
ASPHALT JUNGLE, THE, 1950
ATLANTIC CITY, 1981
BAD BLOOD, 1987
BIG CLOCK, THE, 1948
BIG HEAT, THE, 1953
BIG SLEEP, THE, 1946
BODY HEAT, 1981
BONNIE AND CLYDE, 1967
BREATHLESS, 1959
BRING ME THE HEAD OF ALFREDO GARCIA, 1974
BULLITT, 1968
CALL NORTHSIDE 777, 1948
CASQUE D'OR, 1956
COMPULSION, 1959
CRIME WITHOUT PASSION, 1934
CROSSFIRE, 1947
DEAD END, 1937
DESPERATE HOURS, THE, 1955
DETECTIVE STORY, 1951
DETOUR, 1945
DIVA, 1982
DOG DAY AFTERNOON, 1975
DOUBLE INDEMNITY, 1944
DOUBLE LIFE, A, 1947
DRIVER, THE, 1978
ENFORCER, THE, 1951
FOUL PLAY, 1978
FRENCH CONNECTION, THE, 1971
FURY, 1936
G-MEN, 1935
GIRL FROM HAVANA, THE, 1929
GODFATHER, THE, 1972
GODFATHER, THE, PART II, 1974
HE WALKED BY NIGHT, 1948
HIGH AND LOW, 1963
HIGH SIERRA, 1941
HOUSE OF GAMES, 1987
IN THE HEAT OF THE NIGHT, 1967
INCIDENT, 1948
KEY LARGO, 1948
KILLERS, THE, 1946
KILLING, THE, 1956
KISS ME DEADLY, 1955
KISS OF DEATH, 1947
LADYKILLERS, THE, 1956
L'ARGENT, 1984
LAVENDER HILL MOB, THE, 1951
LITTLE CAESAR, 1931
M, 1933
MANHATTAN MELODRAMA, 1934
MASK OF DIMITRIOS, THE, 1944
MEAN STREETS, 1973
NAKED CITY, THE, 1948
NIGHTMARE ALLEY, 1947
ONCE UPON A TIME IN AMERICA, 1984
PEPE LE MOKO, 1937

PETRIFIED FOREST, THE, 1936
PICKPOCKET, 1963
PIERROT LE FOU, 1968
POSTMAN ALWAYS RINGS TWICE, THE, 1946
PUBLIC ENEMY, THE, 1931
RACKET, THE, 1951
RIFIFI, 1956
ROARING TWENTIES, THE, 1939
SCARFACE, 1932
SEANCE ON A WET AFTERNOON, 1964
SERPICO, 1973
SEVEN THIEVES, 1960
SHOOT THE PIANO PLAYER, 1962
SLIGHT CASE OF MURDER, A, 1938
SOME LIKE IT HOT, 1959
STING, THE, 1973
STRAIGHT TIME, 1978
T-MEN, 1947
THEY LIVE BY NIGHT, 1949
THIS GUN FOR HIRE, 1942
THREAT, THE, 1949
TO CATCH A THIEF, 1955
TOPKAPI, 1964
TOUCH OF EVIL, 1958
TRUE CONFESSIONS, 1981
WHILE THE CITY SLEEPS, 1956
WHITE HEAT, 1949
WHOLE TOWN'S TALKING, THE, 1935
WITNESS, 1985
WRONG MAN, THE, 1956
YOU ONLY LIVE ONCE, 1937

Dance
BLACK TIGHTS, 1962
DIRTY DANCING, 1987
MYSTERIOUS HOUSE OF DR. C., THE, 1976
RED SHOES, THE, 1948
SWAN LAKE, THE, 1967

Disaster
HURRICANE, THE, 1937
IN OLD CHICAGO, 1938
NIGHT TO REMEMBER, A, 1958
SAN FRANCISCO, 1936
TITANIC, 1953

Docu-drama
CRY IN THE DARK, A, 1988
SALT OF THE EARTH, 1954
STAMMHEIM, 1986
TRAIN OF DREAMS, 1987

Drama
ALL ABOUT EVE, 1950
ALL MY SONS, 1948
ALL THAT HEAVEN ALLOWS, 1955
AMERICAN MADNESS, 1932
ANASTASIA, 1956
ANATOMY OF A MURDER, 1959
ANGELS OVER BROADWAY, 1940
ANNA AND THE KING OF SIAM, 1946
ANNA KARENINA, 1935
ANOTHER WOMAN, 1988
APARTMENT, THE, 1960
ARROWSMITH, 1931
ASSAULT, THE, 1986
ASYA'S HAPPINESS, 1988
AU HASARD, BALTHAZAR, 1970
B. F.'S DAUGHTER, 1948
BACK STREET, 1941
BAD AND THE BEAUTIFUL, THE, 1952
BAD DAY AT BLACK ROCK, 1955
BALLAD OF A SOLDIER, 1960
BALLAD OF NARAYAMA, THE, 1984
BAND OF ANGELS, 1957
BEAT THE DEVIL, 1953
BEGGARS OF LIFE, 1928
BELLS OF ST. MARY'S, THE, 1945
BEST YEARS OF OUR LIVES, THE, 1946
BETTY BLUE, 1986
BICYCLE THIEF, THE, 1949
BIG KNIFE, THE, 1955
BIRDY, 1984
BLACK NARCISSUS, 1947
BLACKBOARD JUNGLE, THE, 1955
BLONDE VENUS, 1932

BLOOD AND SAND, 1941
BLUE ANGEL, THE, 1930
BOOM TOWN, 1940
BOWERY, THE, 1933
BOYS TOWN, 1938
BRAVE BULLS, THE, 1951
BREAKER MORANT, 1980
BREAKFAST AT TIFFANY'S, 1961
BRIDGE OF SAN LUIS REY, THE, 1929
BRIGHT VICTORY, 1951
BROWNING VERSION, THE, 1951
CAINE MUTINY, THE, 1954
CANDY MOUNTAIN, 1988
CASABLANCA, 1942
CAT ON A HOT TIN ROOF, 1958
CATERED AFFAIR, THE, 1956
CHINA SYNDROME, THE, 1979
CINCINNATI KID, THE, 1965
CIRCLE OF DECEIT, 1982
CITADEL, THE, 1938
CITIZEN KANE, 1941
CLASH BY NIGHT, 1952
CLUNY BROWN, 1946
COME BACK LITTLE SHEBA, 1952
COMING HOME, 1978
CONTEMPT, 1963
CONVERSATION, THE, 1974
COUNSELLOR-AT-LAW, 1933
COUNTRY, 1984
COUNTRY GIRL, THE, 1954
CRAIG'S WIFE, 1936
CRIES AND WHISPERS, 1972
CRIME OF MONSIEUR LANGE, THE, 1936
CYRANO DE BERGERAC, 1950
DAMNATION, 1988
DAMNED, THE, 1969
DARK VICTORY, 1939
DARLING, 1965
DAVID AND LISA, 1962
DAVID COPPERFIELD, 1935
DAY FOR NIGHT, 1973
DAY OF THE LOCUST, THE, 1975
DAY OF WRATH, 1948
DAYBREAK, 1940
DAYS OF HEAVEN, 1978
DAYS OF 36, 1972
DAYS OF WINE AND ROSES, 1962
DEAD, THE, 1987
DEATH IN VENICE, 1971
DEATH OF A SALESMAN, 1952
DEBT, THE, 1988
DESPERATE CHARACTERS, 1971
DIARY OF A CHAMBERMAID, 1964
DIARY OF ANNE FRANK, THE, 1959
DINER, 1982
DINNER AT EIGHT, 1933
DOCTOR ZHIVAGO, 1965
DON QUIXOTE, 1961
DRUNKEN ANGEL, 1948
EAST OF EDEN, 1955
EASY RIDER, 1969
EFFI BRIEST, 1974
8 1/2, 1963
EL, 1955
EL NORTE, 1984
ELMER GANTRY, 1960
EMIGRANTS, THE, 1972
EMPEROR JONES, THE, 1933
END OF INNOCENCE, 1960
ENTERTAINER, THE, 1960
EQUUS, 1977
ETERNAL MASK, THE, 1937
EXECUTIVE SUITE, 1954
EXTERMINATING ANGEL, THE, 1967
FACE IN THE CROWD, A, 1957
FACE TO FACE, 1976
FACES, 1968
FAIL SAFE, 1964
FANNY AND ALEXANDER, 1983
FITZCARRALDO, 1982
FIVE EASY PIECES, 1970
FORBIDDEN GAMES, 1953
FOUR HUNDRED BLOWS, THE, 1959
FROM HERE TO ETERNITY, 1953
FRONT PAGE, THE, 1931
FUGITIVE, THE, 1947

GARDEN OF THE FINZI-CONTINIS, THE, 1971
GENTLE CREATURE, A, 1971
GENTLEMAN'S AGREEMENT, 1947
GEORGY GIRL, 1966
GIANT, 1956
GIG, THE, 1985
GILDA, 1946
GO-BETWEEN, THE, 1971
GOOD EARTH, THE, 1937
GOODBYE MR. CHIPS, 1939
GRADUATE, THE, 1967
GRAND HOTEL, 1932
GRAPES OF WRATH, 1940
GREAT EXPECTATIONS, 1946
GREAT GATSBY, THE, 1949
GREAT SANTINI, THE, 1979
GREATEST SHOW ON EARTH, THE, 1952
HALLELUJAH, 1929
HAMLET, 1948
HAMLET, 1964
HANNAH AND HER SISTERS, 1986
HASTY HEART, THE, 1949
HEARTBREAK RIDGE, 1986
HEAT AND SUNLIGHT, 1988
HEIRESS, THE, 1949
HENRY V, 1944
HERE I AM A STRANGER, 1939
HIMATSURI, 1985
HIROSHIMA, MON AMOUR, 1959
HISTORY IS MADE AT NIGHT, 1937
HIT, THE, 1985
HOMECOMING, THE, 1973
HOPE AND GLORY, 1987
HOW GREEN WAS MY VALLEY, 1941
HUCKSTERS, THE, 1947
HUNT, THE, 1967
I REMEMBER MAMA, 1948
IN A LONELY PLACE, 1950
INFORMER, THE, 1935
INHERIT THE WIND, 1960
INNOCENCE UNPROTECTED, 1971
INTERIORS, 1978
INTRUDER IN THE DUST, 1949
IT'S A WONDERFUL LIFE, 1946
JEZEBEL, 1938
JOHNNY BELINDA, 1948
JUGGLER, THE, 1953
JULES AND JIM, 1962
JULIET OF THE SPIRITS, 1965
KAGEMUSHA, 1980
KAMERADSCHAFT, 1931
KING LEAR, 1988
KING OF COMEDY, THE, 1983
KINGS ROW, 1942
KNIFE IN THE WATER, 1963
KRAMER VS. KRAMER, 1979
L-SHAPED ROOM, THE, 1962
LA DOLCE VITA, 1961
LA RONDE, 1954
LA STRADA, 1956
LA TERRA TREMA, 1947
L'AGE D'OR, 1979
LAST DETAIL, THE, 1973
LAST PICTURE SHOW, THE, 1971
LAST STOP, THE, 1949
LAST YEAR AT MARIENBAD, 1962
LAUGHTER, 1930
L'AVVENTURA, 1960
LE BEAU MARIAGE, 1982
LE GAI SAVOIR, 1968
LE PETIT THEATRE DE JEAN RENOIR, 1974
LES PARENTS TERRIBLES, 1950
LETTER, THE, 1940
LETTER TO THREE WIVES, A, 1948
LIFE AND DEATH OF COLONEL BLIMP, THE, 1945
LIFEBOAT, 1944
LIGHT THAT FAILED, THE, 1939
LIMELIGHT, 1952
LITTLE FOXES, THE, 1941
LITTLE WOMEN, 1933
LOLA MONTES, 1955
LONELINESS OF THE LONG DISTANCE RUNNER,
  THE, 1962
LONG DAY'S JOURNEY INTO NIGHT, 1962
LONG, HOT SUMMER, THE, 1958
LONG VOYAGE HOME, THE, 1940

BOLD: Films on Videocassette

LOS OLVIDADOS, 1950
LOST WEEKEND, THE, 1945
MAEDCHEN IN UNIFORM, 1932
MAGNIFICENT AMBERSONS, THE, 1942
MAMMA ROMA, 1962
MAN ESCAPED, A, 1957
MAN FACING SOUTHEAST, 1986
MAN FOR ALL SEASONS, A, 1966
MAN ON A TIGHTROPE, 1953
MARRIAGE OF MARIA BRAUN, THE, 1979
MARTY, 1955
MASCULINE FEMININE, 1966
MATEWAN, 1987
MEN, THE, 1950
MEPHISTO, 1981
MIDNIGHT COWBOY, 1969
MILDRED PIERCE, 1945
MIN AND BILL, 1930
MIRAGE, 1972
MISSING, 1982
MISTER ROBERTS, 1955
MODERNS, THE, 1988
MON ONCLE D'AMERIQUE, 1980
MOON AND SIXPENCE, THE, 1942
MOONLIGHTING, 1982
MRS. MINIVER, 1942
MURIEL, 1963
MURMUR OF THE HEART, 1971
MY BRILLIANT CAREER, 1980
MY FIRST WIFE, 1985
MY LIFE TO LIVE, 1963
MY NIGHT AT MAUD'S, 1970
MY SON, MY SON!, 1940
NASHVILLE, 1975
NATIONAL VELVET, 1944
NETWORK, 1976
NO GREATER GLORY, 1934
NONE BUT THE LONELY HEART, 1944
NORMA RAE, 1979
NOSTALGHIA, 1984
ODD MAN OUT, 1947
OF HUMAN BONDAGE, 1934
OF MICE AND MEN, 1939
OLD MAN AND THE SEA, THE, 1958
OLIVER TWIST, 1951
ON GOLDEN POND, 1981
ON THE WATERFRONT, 1954
ONE FLEW OVER THE CUCKOO'S NEST, 1975
ONLY ANGELS HAVE WINGS, 1939
OPEN CITY, 1945
ORPHANS, 1987
OUR TOWN, 1940
OUR VINES HAVE TENDER GRAPES, 1945
PARIS, TEXAS, 1984
PASSENGER, THE, 1975
PATTERNS, 1956
PAWNBROKER, THE, 1965
PAYDAY, 1972
PERSONA, 1967
PHANTOM OF LIBERTY, THE, 1974
PICNIC, 1955
PINKY, 1949
PIXOTE, 1981
PLACE IN THE SUN, A, 1951
PLOUGHMAN'S LUNCH, THE, 1984
POIL DE CAROTTE, 1932
PORT OF SHADOWS, 1938
PRIDE AND PREJUDICE, 1940
PROVIDENCE, 1977
PUMPKIN EATER, THE, 1964
QUADROPHENIA, 1979
QUARTET, 1949
RASHOMON, 1951
RAZOR'S EDGE, THE, 1946
REBEL WITHOUT A CAUSE, 1955
RED SORGHUM, 1988
ROOM AT THE TOP, 1959
ROSE TATTOO, THE, 1955
'ROUND MIDNIGHT, 1986
ROYAL FAMILY OF BROADWAY, THE, 1930
RULES OF THE GAME, THE, 1939
RUMBLE FISH, 1983
SACRIFICE, THE, 1986
SALVADOR, 1986
SANSHO THE BAILIFF, 1969
SATURDAY NIGHT AND SUNDAY MORNING, 1961

SAVE THE TIGER, 1973
SAYONARA, 1957
SEA WOLF, THE, 1941
SEARCH, THE, 1948
SEPARATE TABLES, 1958
SEPTEMBER, 1987
SEVEN SAMURAI, THE, 1956
SEVENTH SEAL, THE, 1958
SEVENTH VEIL, THE, 1946
SHADOWS, 1960
SHANGHAI EXPRESS, 1932
SHIP OF FOOLS, 1965
SIN OF MADELON CLAUDET, THE, 1931
SINCE YOU WENT AWAY, 1944
SMALL CHANGE, 1976
SO PROUDLY WE HAIL, 1943
SOUTHERNER, THE, 1945
STAGE DOOR, 1937
STAR IS BORN, A, 1937
STARS LOOK DOWN, THE, 1940
STATE'S ATTORNEY, 1932
STELLA DALLAS, 1937
STORY OF A CHEAT, THE, 1938
STORY OF ESTHER COSTELLO, THE, 1957
STREET SCENE, 1931
STREETCAR NAMED DESIRE, A, 1951
STUNT MAN, THE, 1980
SUBJECT WAS ROSES, THE, 1968
SULLIVANS, THE, 1944
SULLIVAN'S TRAVELS, 1941
SUMMER OF '42, 1971
SUN ALSO RISES, THE, 1957
SUNDAY IN THE COUNTRY, A, 1984
SUNDOWNERS, THE, 1960
SUNSET BOULEVARD, 1950
SWEET SMELL OF SUCCESS, 1957
TAKING OFF, 1971
TARNISHED ANGELS, THE, 1957
TASTE OF HONEY, A, 1962
TEST PILOT, 1938
TESTAMENT OF ORPHEUS, THE, 1962
THESE THREE, 1936
THEY DRIVE BY NIGHT, 1940
THEY WON'T FORGET, 1937
THREE COMRADES, 1938
THREE INTO TWO WON'T GO, 1969
THRONE OF BLOOD, 1961
THUNDERHEAD-SON OF FLICKA, 1945
TIME LIMIT, 1957
TO BE OR NOT TO BE, 1942
TO EACH HIS OWN, 1946
TO HAVE AND HAVE NOT, 1944
TO KILL A MOCKINGBIRD, 1962
TOBACCO ROAD, 1941
TOKYO STORY, 1972
TORTILLA FLAT, 1942
TREE GROWS IN BROOKLYN, A, 1945
TRIP TO BOUNTIFUL, THE, 1985
TRISTANA, 1970
12 ANGRY MEN, 1957
TWO-LANE BLACKTOP, 1971
TWO OF US, THE, 1968
TWO WOMEN, 1960
UGETSU, 1954
UMBERTO D, 1955
UNDER THE ROOFS OF PARIS, 1930
UNMARRIED WOMAN, AN, 1978
VERDICT, THE, 1982
VIRIDIANA, 1962
VITELLONI, 1956
WANDERERS, THE, 1979
WAR AND PEACE, 1956
WATCH ON THE RHINE, 1943
WATERLOO BRIDGE, 1940
WAYS OF LOVE, 1950
WEDDING IN GALILEE, 1988
WHO'S AFRAID OF VIRGINIA WOOLF?, 1966
WILD BOYS OF THE ROAD, 1933
WILD ONE, THE, 1953
WILD RIVER, 1960
WILD STRAWBERRIES, 1959
WIND, 1928
WOMAN IN THE DUNES, 1964
WOMEN ON THE VERGE OF A NERVOUS
  BREAKDOWN, 1988
WRITTEN ON THE WIND, 1956

YEARLING, THE, 1946

Fantasy
BEAUTY AND THE BEAST, 1947
BLITHE SPIRIT, 1945
BOY WHO COULD FLY, THE, 1986
BRIGHTNESS, 1988
CONNECTICUT YANKEE, A, 1931
CONNECTICUT YANKEE IN KING ARTHUR'S
  COURT, A, 1949
DARBY O'GILL AND THE LITTLE PEOPLE, 1959
DEATH TAKES A HOLIDAY, 1934
DEVIL AND DANIEL WEBSTER, THE, 1941
E.T. THE EXTRA-TERRESTRIAL, 1982
EXCALIBUR, 1981
5,000 FINGERS OF DR. T. THE, 1953
GHOST AND MRS. MUIR, THE, 1942
GHOST GOES WEST, THE, 1936
GNOME-MOBILE, THE, 1967
GUY NAMED JOE, A, 1943
HERE COMES MR. JORDAN, 1941
JASON AND THE ARGONAUTS, 1963
KID FOR TWO FARTHINGS, A, 1956
KING KONG, 1933
LOST HORIZON, 1937
MIDSUMMERS NIGHT'S DREAM, A, 1961
MIRACLE IN MILAN, 1951
MIRACLE ON 34TH STREET, THE, 1947
OF STARS AND MEN, 1961
ORPHEUS, 1950
PINOCCHIO, 1940
REPENTANCE, 1988
SECRET LIFE OF WALTER MITTY, THE, 1947
STAIRWAY TO HEAVEN, 1946
STAR TREK IV: THE VOYAGE HOME, 1986
THIEF OF BAGHDAD, THE, 1940
WINGS OF DESIRE, 1988
WIZARD OF OZ, THE, 1939

Historical
ALEXANDER NEVSKY, 1939
ANNE OF THE THOUSAND DAYS, 1969
BECKET, 1964
BEN HUR, 1959
CAESAR AND CLEOPATRA, 1946
CAPTAIN BLOOD, 1935
CAPTAIN FROM CASTILE, 1947
DRUMS ALONG THE MOHAWK, 1939
EXODUS, 1960
FELLINI SATYRICON, 1969
FIRE OVER ENGLAND, 1937
FOREVER AND A DAY, 1943
GATE OF HELL, 1954
GONE WITH THE WIND, 1939
IN OLD CHICAGO, 1938
IVANHOE, 1952
JULIUS CAESAR, 1953
KHARTOUM, 1966
LAST EMPEROR, THE, 1987
LAST OF THE MOHICANS, THE, 1936
LES MISERABLES, 1935
LION IN WINTER, THE, 1968
MAN OF IRON, 1981
MARIE ANTOINETTE, 1938
MAYERLING, 1937
PRINCE OF FOXES, 1949
QUEEN CHRISTINA, 1933
RAN, 1985
RASPUTIN AND THE EMPRESS, 1932
RICHARD III, 1956
ROMEO AND JULIET, 1936
ROMEO AND JULIET, 1954
SCARLET EMPRESS, THE, 1934
SINK THE BISMARCK, 1960
SPARTACUS, 1960
TALE OF TWO CITIES, A, 1935
VICTORIA THE GREAT, 1937
WE LIVE AGAIN, 1934
ZULU, 1964

Horror
BIRD WITH THE CRYSTAL PLUMAGE, THE, 1970
BRIDE OF FRANKENSTEIN, THE, 1935
DEAD OF NIGHT, 1946
DEAD RINGERS, 1988
DR. JEKYLL AND MR. HYDE, 1932

DOCTOR X, 1932
DRACULA, 1931
EXORCIST, THE, 1973
FRANKENSTEIN, 1931
FREAKS, 1932
HALLOWEEN, 1978
HORROR OF DRACULA, THE, 1958
HUNCHBACK OF NOTRE DAME, THE, 1939
INNOCENTS, THE, 1961
ISLAND OF LOST SOULS, 1933
JAWS, 1975
KWAIDAN, 1965
M, 1933
MAD LOVE, 1935
MONKEY SHINES: AN EXPERIMENT IN FEAR, 1988
MUMMY, THE, 1932
MYSTERY OF THE WAX MUSEUM, THE, 1933
PHANTOM OF THE OPERA, THE, 1929
PSYCHO, 1960
REPULSION, 1965
ROSEMARY'S BABY, 1968
SON OF FRANKENSTEIN, 1939
UNINVITED, THE, 1944
VAMPYR, 1932
WOLF MAN, THE, 1941
YOUNG FRANKENSTEIN, 1974

Musical
ABSOLUTE BEGINNERS, 1986
AMADEUS, 1984
AMERICAN IN PARIS, AN, 1951
ANCHORS AWEIGH, 1945
BAND WAGON, THE, 1953
BIZET'S CARMEN, 1984
BLUE SKIES, 1946
BORIS GODUNOV, 1959
CABARET, 1972
CAROUSEL, 1956
COAL MINER'S DAUGHTER, 1980
CONNECTICUT YANKEE IN KING ARTHUR'S
    COURT, A, 1949
CURLY TOP, 1935
DADDY LONG LEGS, 1955
DEEP IN MY HEART, 1954
DON QUIXOTE, 1935
5,000 FINGERS OF DR. T, THE, 1953
FLYING DOWN TO RIO, 1933
FOOTLIGHT PARADE, 1933
42ND STREET, 1933
FRENCH CANCAN, 1956
FUNNY GIRL, 1968
GAY DIVORCEE, THE, 1934
GIGI, 1958
GIRL CRAZY, 1943
GLENN MILLER STORY, THE, 1953
GOING MY WAY, 1944
GOLD DIGGERS OF 1933, 1933
GOOD NEWS, 1947
GREAT ZIEGFELD, THE, 1936
GYPSY, 1962
HAIR, 1979
KING AND I, THE, 1956
LA TRAVIATA, 1982
LOVE ME OR LEAVE ME, 1955
LOVE ME TONIGHT, 1932
MARGIE, 1946
MARY POPPINS, 1964
MAYTIME, 1937
MEET ME IN ST. LOUIS, 1944
MERRY WIDOW, THE, 1934
MUSIC MAN, THE, 1962
MY FAIR LADY, 1964
OKLAHOMA, 1955
OLIVER!, 1968
ON THE TOWN, 1949
ORCHESTRA WIVES, 1942
PAJAMA GAME, THE, 1957
ROAD TO MOROCCO, 1942
ROBERTA, 1935
ROCK 'N' ROLL HIGH SCHOOL, 1979
ROYAL WEDDING, 1951
SEVEN BRIDES FOR SEVEN BROTHERS, 1954
SHOW BOAT, 1936
SINGIN' IN THE RAIN, 1952
SO DEAR TO MY HEART, 1949
SOUND OF MUSIC, THE, 1965

SOUTH PACIFIC, 1958
STAGE DOOR CANTEEN, 1943
STAR IS BORN, A, 1954
STATE FAIR, 1945
TAKE ME OUT TO THE BALL GAME, 1949
THREE CABALLEROS, THE, 1944
THREE LITTLE WORDS, 1950
TOP HAT, 1935
UP IN ARMS, 1944
WEST SIDE STORY, 1961
WIZARD OF OZ, THE, 1939
YANKEE DOODLE DANDY, 1942
YELLOW SUBMARINE, 1958
YOUNG MAN WITH A HORN, 1950
ZIEGFELD FOLLIES, 1945

Musical Comedy
BREAK THE NEWS, 1938
COVER GIRL, 1944
DAMN YANKEES, 1958
EASTER PARADE, 1948
HARD DAY'S NIGHT, A, 1964
HOLIDAY INN, 1942
HOLLYWOOD CANTEEN, 1944
HOW TO SUCCEED IN BUSINESS WITHOUT REALLY
    TRYING, 1967
IT'S ALWAYS FAIR WEATHER, 1955
KISS ME KATE, 1953
PAL JOEY, 1957
ROSE MARIE, 1936
SILK STOCKINGS, 1957
SMILING LIEUTENANT, THE, 1931

Mystery
ADVENTURE OF SHERLOCK HOLMES' SMARTER
    BROTHER, THE, 1975
ADVENTURES OF SHERLOCK HOLMES, THE, 1939
AND THEN THERE WERE NONE, 1945
BIG SLEEP, THE, 1946
BLUE DAHLIA, THE, 1946
BLUE VELVET, 1986
BOOMERANG, 1947
BULLDOG DRUMMOND STRIKES BACK, 1934
CHINATOWN, 1974
CUTTER AND BONE, 1981
DEATH ON THE NILE, 1978
GREAT MOUSE DETECTIVE, THE, 1986
HOUND OF THE BASKERVILLES, THE, 1939
LADY IN THE LAKE, 1947
LADY VANISHES, THE, 1938
LAURA, 1944
MALTESE FALCON, THE, 1941
MAN ON THE EIFFEL TOWER, THE, 1949
MAN WHO KNEW TOO MUCH, THE, 1935
MAN WHO KNEW TOO MUCH, THE, 1956
MINISTRY OF FEAR, 1945
MURDER, 1930
MURDER BY DEATH, 1976
MURDER, MY SWEET, 1945
MY FAVORITE BRUNETTE, 1947
OUT OF THE PAST, 1947
SHOT IN THE DARK, A, 1964
SLEUTH, 1972
THIN MAN, THE, 1934
WHO FRAMED ROGER RABBIT, 1988

Prison
BIRDMAN OF ALCATRAZ, 1962
BRUTE FORCE, 1947
COOL HAND LUKE, 1967
DEFIANT ONES, THE, 1958
GRAND ILLUSION, 1938
GREAT ESCAPE, THE, 1963
I AM A FUGITIVE FROM A CHAIN GANG, 1932
KISS OF THE SPIDER WOMAN, 1985
MERRY CHRISTMAS, MR. LAWRENCE, 1983
MIDNIGHT EXPRESS, 1978
NIGHT WATCH, THE, 1964
PAPILLON, 1973
PRISONER OF SHARK ISLAND, THE, 1936
20,000 YEARS IN SING SING, 1933

Religious
BEN HUR, 1959
CRUSADES, THE, 1935
DAVID AND BATHSHEBA, 1951

DEMETRIUS AND THE GLADIATORS, 1954
DIARY OF A COUNTRY PRIEST, 1954
GOING MY WAY, 1944
GREATEST STORY EVER TOLD, THE, 1965
GREEN PASTURES, 1936
HAIL, MARY, 1985
JOAN OF ARC, 1948
KING OF KINGS, 1961
LAST TEMPTATION OF CHRIST, THE, 1988
MAN CALLED PETER, THE, 1955
MILKY WAY, THE, 1969
MIRACLE OF THE BELLS, THE, 1948
MIRACLE WOMAN, THE, 1931
NUN, THE, 1971
NUN'S STORY, THE, 1959
ROBE, THE, 1953
SALOME'S LAST DANCE, 1988
SAMSON AND DELILAH, 1949
SONG OF BERNADETTE, THE, 1943
TEN COMMANDMENTS, THE, 1956

Romance
ADVENTURES OF DON JUAN, 1949
AFRICAN QUEEN, THE, 1951
BAD BLOOD, 1987
BARFLY, 1987
BARRETTS OF WIMPOLE STREET, THE, 1934
BARRETTS OF WIMPOLE STREET, THE, 1957
BRIEF ENCOUNTER, 1945
BROADCAST NEWS, 1987
CAMILLE, 1937
CASQUE D'OR, 1956
CHILDREN OF A LESSER GOD, 1986
CHILDREN OF PARADISE, 1945
CRANES ARE FLYING, THE, 1960
DADDY LONG LEGS, 1931
DADDY LONG LEGS, 1955
DEATH TAKES A HOLIDAY, 1934
DESIRE, 1936
DIVA, 1982
DODSWORTH, 1936
ELVIRA MADIGAN, 1967
ENCHANTED COTTAGE, THE, 1945
FAREWELL TO ARMS, A, 1932
FOUR DAUGHTERS, 1938
GARDEN OF ALLAH, THE, 1936
GHOST AND MRS. MUIR, THE, 1942
GOODBYE GIRL, THE, 1977
GRAND MANEUVER, THE, 1956
GUY NAMED JOE, A, 1943
HOLD BACK THE DAWN, 1941
INTERMEZZO: A LOVE STORY, 1939
IT HAPPENED ONE NIGHT, 1934
JANE EYRE, 1944
KNIGHT WITHOUT ARMOR, 1937
LADY EVE, THE, 1941
L'ATALANTE, 1947
LITTLE ROMANCE, A, 1979
LOVE AFFAIR, 1939
MANHATTAN, 1979
MARIE ANTOINETTE, 1938
MATCHMAKING OF ANNA, THE, 1972
MAYERLING, 1937
MAYTIME, 1937
MELO, 1988
MOGAMBO, 1953
MOROCCO, 1930
PEPE LE MOKO, 1937
PIERROT LE FOU, 1968
PORTRAIT OF JENNIE, 1949
PRISONER OF ZENDA, THE, 1937
QUEEN CHRISTINA, 1933
QUIET MAN, THE, 1952
ROMAN HOLIDAY, 1953
ROMEO AND JULIET, 1936
ROMEO AND JULIET, 1954
SABRINA, 1954
SAN FRANCISCO, 1936
SEA HAWK, THE, 1940
SHOP AROUND THE CORNER, THE, 1940
STAIRWAY TO HEAVEN, 1946
STOLEN KISSES, 1969
STRANGERS KISS, 1984
SUMMERTIME, 1955
THIS IS THE NIGHT, 1932
TO CATCH A THIEF, 1955

BOLD: Films on Videocassette

TOOTSIE, 1982
TOP HAT, 1935
TORRID ZONE, 1940
TOUCH OF CLASS, A, 1973
WUTHERING HEIGHTS, 1939

Science Fiction
ALIENS, 1986
BLADE RUNNER, 1982
CLOSE ENCOUNTERS OF THE THIRD KIND, 1977
DAY THE EARTH STOOD STILL, THE, 1951
FLASH GORDON, 1936
FLY, THE, 1986
FORBIDDEN PLANET, 1956
INCREDIBLE SHRINKING MAN, THE, 1957
INVASION OF THE BODY SNATCHERS, 1956
ISLAND OF LOST SOULS, 1933
PLANET OF THE APES, 1968
STAR TREK IV: THE VOYAGE HOME, 1986
STAR WARS, 1977
THING, THE, 1951
THINGS TO COME, 1936
TIME MACHINE, THE, 1963
20,000 LEAGUES UNDER THE SEA, 1954
WAR OF THE WORLDS, THE, 1953

Spy
ADVENTURESS, THE, 1946
ALL THROUGH THE NIGHT, 1942
CONFESSIONS OF A NAZI SPY, 1939
DEADLY AFFAIR, THE, 1967
DECISION BEFORE DAWN, 1951
FIVE FINGERS, 1952
FIVE GRAVES TO CAIRO, 1943
FOREIGN CORRESPONDENT, 1940
FROM RUSSIA WITH LOVE, 1963
GOLDFINGER, 1964
HOUSE ON 92ND STREET, THE, 1945
JOURNEY INTO FEAR, 1942
LADY VANISHES, THE, 1938
MAN HUNT, 1941
MARATHON MAN, 1976
MASK OF DIMITRIOS, THE, 1944
MINISTRY OF FEAR, 1945
NIGHT TRAIN, 1940
NORTH BY NORTHWEST, 1959
NOTORIOUS, 1946
SABOTEUR, 1942
SPY WHO CAME IN FROM THE COLD, THE, 1965
39 STEPS, THE, 1935
THIS GUN FOR HIRE, 1942

Sports
BODY AND SOUL, 1947
CHAMPION, 1949
CHARIOTS OF FIRE, 1981
DAMN YANKEES, 1958
FAT CITY, 1972
FEAR STRIKES OUT, 1957
GENTLEMAN JIM, 1942
GOLDEN BOY, 1939
HARDER THEY FALL, THE, 1956
HOOSIERS, 1986
HUSTLER, THE, 1961
IT HAPPENS EVERY SPRING, 1949
JIM THORPE—ALL AMERICAN, 1951
KNUTE ROCKNE—ALL AMERICAN, 1940
LUSTY MEN, THE, 1952
PARADISE ALLEY, 1978
PRIDE OF THE YANKEES, THE, 1942
RAGING BULL, 1980
ROCKY, 1976
SET-UP, THE, 1949
TAKE ME OUT TO THE BALL GAME, 1949

Thriller
CHARADE, 1963
DAY OF THE JACKAL, THE, 1973
DIABOLIQUE, 1955
FALLEN IDOL, THE, 1949
FIVE FINGERS, 1952
FRANTIC, 1988
GASLIGHT, 1940
GASLIGHT, 1944
LAST WAVE, THE, 1978
LODGER, THE, 1944

LOVE FROM A STRANGER, 1937
MARATHON MAN, 1976
NIGHT MUST FALL, 1937
NIGHT OF THE HUNTER, THE, 1955
NOTORIOUS, 1946
REAR WINDOW, 1954
REBECCA, 1940
SEVEN DAYS IN MAY, 1964
SHADOW OF A DOUBT, 1943
SORRY, WRONG NUMBER, 1948
SPELLBOUND, 1945
SPIRAL STAIRCASE, THE, 1946
STRANGER, THE, 1946
STRANGERS ON A TRAIN, 1951
TENSION, 1949
THIRD MAN, THE, 1950
TRAIN, THE, 1965
VERTIGO, 1958
WHATEVER HAPPENED TO BABY JANE?, 1962
WINDOW, THE, 1949

War
ACTION IN THE NORTH ATLANTIC, 1943
AFRICAN QUEEN, THE, 1951
AIR FORCE, 1943
ALAMO, THE, 1960
ALEXANDER NEVSKY, 1939
ALL QUIET ON THE WESTERN FRONT, 1930
ASSAULT, THE, 1986
BACK TO BATAAN, 1945
BALLAD OF A SOLDIER, 1960
BATAAN, 1943
BATTLE OF BRITAIN, THE, 1969
BATTLEGROUND, 1949
BEAU GESTE, 1939
BEST YEARS OF OUR LIVES, THE, 1946
BIRDY, 1984
BOAT, THE, 1982
BREAKER MORANT, 1980
BRIDGE AT REMAGEN, THE, 1969
BRIDGE ON THE RIVER KWAI, THE, 1957
BRIDGES AT TOKO-RI, THE, 1954
CABARET, 1972
CASABLANCA, 1942
CHARGE OF THE LIGHT BRIGADE, THE, 1936
COMING HOME, 1978
CORVETTE K-225, 1943
COURT-MARTIAL OF BILLY MITCHELL, THE, 1955
CRANES ARE FLYING, THE, 1960
CRASH DIVE, 1943
CRUEL SEA, THE, 1953
DAWN PATROL, THE, 1938
DEER HUNTER, THE, 1978
DESERT FOX, THE, 1951
DESTINATION TOKYO, 1944
DIARY OF ANNE FRANK, THE, 1959
DOCTOR ZHIVAGO, 1965
DRUMS, 1938
DRUMS ALONG THE MOHAWK, 1939
DUCK SOUP, 1933
EMPIRE OF THE SUN, 1987
ENEMY BELOW, THE, 1957
FAIL SAFE, 1964
FAREWELL TO ARMS, A, 1932
FIGHTING 69TH, THE, 1940
FIRE OVER ENGLAND, 1937
FOR WHOM THE BELL TOLLS, 1943
FORBIDDEN GAMES, 1953
FOREIGN CORRESPONDENT, 1940
FORT APACHE, 1948
FOUR FEATHERS, THE, 1939
FROM HERE TO ETERNITY, 1953
FULL METAL JACKET, 1987
GALLIPOLI, 1981
GARDEN OF THE FINZI-CONTINIS, THE, 1971
GATE OF HELL, 1954
GRAND ILLUSION, 1938
GREAT DICTATOR, THE, 1940
GREAT ESCAPE, THE, 1963
GREAT SANTINI, THE, 1979
GUADALCANAL DIARY, 1943
GUNGA DIN, 1939
GUY NAMED JOE, A, 1943
HEARTBREAK RIDGE, 1986
HENRY V, 1944
HIROSHIMA, MON AMOUR, 1959

HOPE AND GLORY, 1987
HORSE SOLDIERS, THE, 1959
IN WHICH WE SERVE, 1942
INVADERS, THE, 1941
IVAN THE TERRIBLE, PARTS I & II, 1947
KAGEMUSHA, 1980
KING AND COUNTRY, 1964
LAST OF THE MOHICANS, THE, 1936
LAST STOP, THE, 1949
LAWRENCE OF ARABIA, 1962
LIFE AND DEATH OF COLONEL BLIMP, THE, 1945
LIFEBOAT, 1944
LIVES OF A BENGAL LANCER, 1935
LONGEST DAY, THE, 1962
MAN'S HOPE, 1947
MARATHON MAN, 1976
MARRIAGE OF MARIA BRAUN, THE, 1979
M*A*S*H, 1970
MEN, THE, 1950
MEN OF THE FIGHTING LADY, 1954
MEPHISTO, 1981
MERRY CHRISTMAS, MR. LAWRENCE, 1983
MISSING, 1982
MISTER ROBERTS, 1955
MOROCCO, 1930
MOUSE THAT ROARED, THE, 1959
MRS. MINIVER, 1942
NIGHT TRAIN, 1940
OBJECTIVE, BURMA!, 1945
OPEN CITY, 1945
PAISAN, 1948
PATHS OF GLORY, 1957
PATTON, 1970
PAWNBROKER, THE, 1965
PLATOON, 1986
PORK CHOP HILL, 1959
PRIDE OF THE MARINES, 1945
PURPLE HEART, THE, 1944
RAN, 1985
RAZOR'S EDGE, THE, 1946
RED BADGE OF COURAGE, THE, 1951
RICHARD III, 1956
RIO GRANDE, 1950
SABOTEUR, 1942
SAHARA, 1943
SALVADOR, 1986
SAND PEBBLES, THE, 1966
SANDS OF IWO JIMA, 1949
SAYONARA, 1957
SEA HAWK, THE, 1940
SERGEANT YORK, 1941
SEVEN DAYS IN MAY, 1964
SHE WORE A YELLOW RIBBON, 1949
SINCE YOU WENT AWAY, 1944
SINK THE BISMARCK, 1960
SO PROUDLY WE HAIL, 1943
SPARTACUS, 1960
STAGE DOOR CANTEEN, 1943
STALAG 17, 1953
STEEL HELMET, THE, 1951
STORY OF G.I. JOE, THE, 1945
STRANGER, THE, 1946
SULLIVANS, THE, 1944
THEY DIED WITH THEIR BOOTS ON, 1942
THEY WERE EXPENDABLE, 1945
THIRTY SECONDS OVER TOKYO, 1944
THREE CAME HOME, 1950
THRONE OF BLOOD, 1961
TO BE OR NOT TO BE, 1942
TRAIN, THE, 1965
TWELVE O'CLOCK HIGH, 1949
TWO WOMEN, 1960
UP IN ARMS, 1944
WAKE ISLAND, 1942
WALK IN THE SUN, A, 1945
WAR AND PEACE, 1956
WATCH ON THE RHINE, 1943
WELCOME IN VIENNA, 1988
WHAT PRICE GLORY?, 1952
WHOOPING COUGH, 1987
WINGED VICTORY, 1944
YESTERDAY'S ENEMY, 1959
YOUNG LIONS, THE, 1958
ZULU, 1964

Western

BUTCH CASSIDY AND THE SUNDANCE KID, 1969
CAT BALLOU, 1965
CHEYENNE AUTUMN, 1964
CIMARRON, 1931
COMANCHE STATION, 1960
DODGE CITY, 1939
FAR COUNTRY, THE, 1955
FORT APACHE, 1948
GOOD, THE BAD, AND THE UGLY, THE, 1967
GREAT NORTHFIELD, MINNESOTA RAID, THE,
  1972
GREY FOX, THE, 1983
GUNFIGHT AT THE O.K. CORRAL, 1957
GUNFIGHTER, THE, 1950
HEARTLAND, 1980
HELL'S HEROES, 1930
HIGH NOON, 1952
HORSE SOLDIERS, THE, 1959
HOW THE WEST WAS WON, 1962
JESSE JAMES, 1939
LONELY ARE THE BRAVE, 1962
LONG RIDERS, THE, 1980
LUSTY MEN, THE, 1952
MAGNIFICENT SEVEN, THE, 1960
MAN FROM LARAMIE, THE, 1955
MAN OF THE WEST, 1958
MY DARLING CLEMENTINE, 1946
NAKED SPUR, THE, 1953
OKLAHOMA, 1955
ONCE UPON A TIME IN THE WEST, 1969
OUTLAW JOSEY WALES, THE, 1976
OX-BOW INCIDENT, THE, 1943
RANCHO NOTORIOUS, 1952
RED BADGE OF COURAGE, THE, 1951
RED RIVER, 1948
RIDE THE HIGH COUNTRY, 1962
RIO BRAVO, 1959
RIO GRANDE, 1950
SEARCHERS, THE, 1956
SHANE, 1953
SHE WORE A YELLOW RIBBON, 1949
SHOOTING, THE, 1971
SHOOTIST, THE, 1976
STAGECOACH, 1939
TALL T, THE, 1957
THEY DIED WITH THEIR BOOTS ON, 1942
THREE GODFATHERS, THE, 1948
TRUE GRIT, 1969
UNION PACIFIC, 1939
WAGONMASTER, 1950
WARLOCK, 1959
WAY OUT WEST, 1937
WELLS FARGO, 1937
WESTERN UNION, 1941
WESTERNER, THE, 1940
WILD BUNCH, THE, 1969
WINCHESTER '73, 1950
YELLOW SKY, 1948